UNIVERSITY CASEBOOK SERIES

CASES AND MATERIALS

CORPORATIONS AND OTHER BUSINESS ORGANIZATIONS

TENTH EDITION

by

MELVIN ARON EISENBERG
Koret Professor of Law
University of California at Berkeley

JAMES D. COX
Brainerd Currie Professor of Law
Duke University Law School

FOUNDATION PRESS
2011

1 New York Plaza, 34th Floor

New York, NY 10004

Phone Toll Free 1–877–888–1330

Fax 646–424–5201

foundation–press.com

Printed in the United States of America

ISBN 978–1–59941–462–1

Mat #40703645

PREFACE

The Tenth Unabridged Edition of this book builds on the firm foundation of the well-received prior editions, and contains a comprehensive and current body of leading cases and note materials on all significant forms of business organization. The book allows the adopting instructor to pick and choose from a rich array of material. Moreover, because the chapters and sections are modular, there is no fixed order in which the cases and note material must be addressed. The adopter has full control over the agenda; this book merely provides the stage and props.

Several important changes have been incorporated into this edition. The formation, management, fiduciary duties, and dissolution of LLCs now occupies a distinct chapter. The foundational rules of the corporation are tightly organized and closely examined in Chapter 4, and in Chapter 5 we study the issues unique to public corporations that have developed with the rise of the activist shareholder. Because recent Supreme Court decisions have introduced a variety of changes in the antifraud provision, we've provided a free-standing chapter devoted to breadth of Rule 10b–5, and also address the state and federal regulation of insider trading in a separate chapter.

In many areas of corporate law, it is difficult to fully understand the issues and the legal rules without some background knowledge of basic accounting and financial concepts. Accordingly, this edition expands the introductory materials on such accounting and financial topics as financial statements, the present-value rule, diversification, valuation, the efficient capital market hypothesis, and dividend policy. These materials have been chosen and edited with an eye to ensuring that they are accessible to students who don't have an accounting, economic or financial background. The introductory accounting and finance materials are presented in Chapter 2; however, because the book is modular, these and all other materials in the book can be introduced in the sequence that the adopter believes works best.

This edition adds new rich note material on major governance issues such as majority voting for directors; short slates; empty voting; split record dates; the power of shareholder-voting services; the role and effectiveness of institutional investors, particularly hedge funds; going dark and private transactions; and the impact of the various anti-takeover measures.

Because of the importance of statutes in corporation law, students should refer to the Statutory Supplement whenever a cross-reference to that Supplement appears. When a cross-referenced statutory provision includes an Official Comment, the Comment should be read as well. Other cross-references to the Statutory Supplement (for example, references to excerpts from the Restatement (Second) of Agency) should be treated the same way.

In the preparation of this casebook, the following conventions have been used: Where a portion of the text of an original source (such as a case) has been omitted, the omission is indicated by ellipses. The omission of footnotes from original sources is not indicated, but the original footnote numbers are used for those footnotes that are retained.

The American Law Institute's Principles of Corporate Governance: Analysis and Recommendations (1994) is cited simply as ALI, Principles of Corporate Governance.

MELVIN A. EISENBERG
JAMES D. COX

SUMMARY OF CONTENTS

CHAPTER 14 Shareholder Suits 1044

CHAPTER 15 Corporate Combinations, Tender Offers and Defending Control 1169

CHAPTER 16 Distributions to Shareholders 1365

CHAPTER 17 The Public Distribution of Securities 1407

ANALYTICAL TABLE OF CONTENTS

Section

Section

CHAPTER 5 The Legal Structure of Publicly Held Corporations 267

Section

Section

CHAPTER 14 Shareholder Suits 1044

Section

CHAPTER 15 Corporate Combinations, Tender Offers and Defending Control 1169

Section

Section

TABLE OF CASES

Principal cases are in bold type. Non-principal cases are in roman type. References are to Pages.

CASES AND MATERIALS

CORPORATIONS AND OTHER BUSINESS ORGANIZATIONS

CHAPTER 1

AGENCY; THE SOLE PROPRIETORSHIP

SECTION 1. THE SOLE PROPRIETORSHIP

The subject of this casebook is corporations and other business organizations. Business organizations take a variety of forms, some simple, some enormously complex. The most rudimentary form of business organization is the sole proprietorship, which is a firm that is owned by a single individual and is not cast in a legal form that can be utilized only by filing an organic document with the state under an authorizing statute.

The terminology *business organization* may seem to be an inappropriate characterization of a firm that has only a single individual owner and is not created pursuant to statute. However, there are two justifications for this characterization.

First, a firm that is wholly owned by an individual is nevertheless likely to have a degree of psychological and social identity separate from the individual. This separateness is often expressed by giving the firm its own name, like "Acme Shoe Company." Furthermore, a sole proprietor usually will consider only a certain portion of her property and cash as invested in the firm, and will keep a separate set of financial records for the firm, as if the firm's finances were separate from her own. Thus, if Alice Adams begins a new firm—say, Acme Shoe Company—she is likely to issue a balance sheet for Acme that does not show all of her assets and liabilities, but only those assets dedicated to, and those liabilities arising out, of the firm's operations. In short, as a psychological matter Adams and those who deal with her are likely to regard Acme as an enterprise that has a certain degree of separateness from Adams herself and a certain dedicated amount of capital. As a matter of law, however, a sole proprietorship has no separate identity from its owner. All of a sole proprietor's wealth is effectively committed to the firm, because an individual who owns a sole proprietorship has unlimited personal liability for obligations incurred in the conduct of the proprietorship's business.

The second justification for considering a sole proprietorship to be an organization is that typically a sole proprietor does not conduct the proprietorship's business by herself, but instead engages various people—managers, salespersons, technicians, and so forth—to act on her behalf, and subject to her control, in conducting the business. The employment by one person, *P*, of another, *A*, to act on *P*'s behalf, implicates the law of agency, which is an element of the law concerning all forms of business organization. In short, the sole proprietorship form, simple as it is, implicates many of the basic issues in the law of business organizations—the internal structure of the organization; the location of control over the organization; the liability of owners for transactions engaged in by their agents; potential conflicts of interest between an organization and its agents; and conflicts of interest between an organization and those with whom it deals, such as creditors.

Although sole proprietorships are the most rudimentary form of business organization, and taken as a class account for substantially less income than corporations and several other forms, sole proprietorships are the most numerous type of business organization in the United States. Based on tax returns, in 2008 (the latest year for which the figures were available) there were 22.6 million sole proprietorships in the United States, with total gross receipts of $1.317 billion. United States Internal Revenue Service, 29 Statistics of Income Bulletin Summer 2010, Sole Proprietorship Returns at 6.

SECTION 2. AGENCY

A. THE AUTHORITY OF AN AGENT

Morris Oil Co. v. Rainbow Oilfield Trucking, Inc.

New Mexico Court of Appeals, 1987.
106 N.M. 237, 741 P.2d 840.

■ GARCIA, JUDGE. . . .

Defendant Dawn appeals from the judgment rendered against it in favor of Morris Oil Company, Inc. (Morris), based upon a determination that Rainbow Oilfield Trucking, Inc. (Rainbow) was Dawn's agent when it incurred indebtedness with Morris. We affirm the trial court.

FACTS

Appellant Dawn, the holder of a certificate of public convenience and necessity, is engaged in the oilfield trucking business in the Farmington area. Rainbow was a New Mexico corporation established for the purpose of operating an oilfield trucking business in the Hobbs area. Defendant corporations entered into several contracts whereby Rainbow would be permitted to use Dawn's certificate of public convenience and necessity in operating a trucking enterprise in Hobbs. Dawn reserved the right to full and complete control over the operations of Rainbow in New Mexico. Dawn was to collect all charges due and owing for transportation conducted by Rainbow and, after deducting a $1,000 per month "clerical fee" and a percentage of the gross receipts, was to remit the balance to Rainbow. Under a subcontract entered into by defendants, Rainbow was to be responsible for payment of operating expenses, including fuel; further, the subcontract provides that all operations utilizing fuel were to be under the direct control and supervision of Dawn. All billing for services rendered by Rainbow would be made under Dawn's name, with all monies to be collected by Dawn.

Defendants also entered into a terminal management agreement which provided that Dawn was to have complete control over Rainbow's Hobbs operation. The agreement further recited that Rainbow was not to become the agent of Dawn and was not empowered to incur or create any debt or liability of Dawn "other than in the ordinary course of business relative to terminal management." The agreement recited that Rainbow was to be an independent contractor and not an employee, and that liability on the part of Rainbow for creating charges in violation of the agreement would survive the termination of the agreement. Dawn was to notify Rainbow of any claim of such charges whereby Rainbow would assume the defense, compromise or payment of such claims.

Rainbow operated the oilfield trucking enterprise under these contractual documents, during which time Rainbow established a relationship with plaintiff Morris, whereby Morris installed a bulk dispenser at the Rainbow terminal and periodically delivered diesel fuel for use in the trucking operation. The enterprise proved unprofitable, however, and Rainbow ceased its operations and ultimately declared bankruptcy, owing Morris approximately $25,000 on an open account.

When Morris began its collection efforts against Rainbow, it determined that Rainbow had ceased its operations, everyone associated with Rainbow had moved back to Texas and it did not appear likely that the account would be paid. Morris was directed by Rainbow's representative in Texas to Dawn for payment of the account.

When Rainbow ceased its operations, Dawn was holding some $73,000 in receipts from the Hobbs operation. Dawn established an escrow account through its Roswell attorneys to settle claims arising from Rainbow's Hobbs operation. When Morris contacted Dawn with regard to the outstanding account, it was notified of the existence of the escrow account and was asked to forbear upon collection efforts, indicating that payment would be forthcoming from the escrow account. Dawn's representatives indicated that it was necessary to wait for authorization from Rainbow's parent Texas corporation before paying the account. At no time did Rainbow or Dawn question the amount or legitimacy of Morris' open account balance.

Dawn's principal [owner] further testified that the subcontract and terminal management agreement were cancelled by Dawn when he learned that Rainbow was incurring debts in Dawn's name. The charges owing to Morris, however, were incurred in the name of Rainbow and not Dawn.

Although some claims were paid from the attorneys' escrow account established by Dawn, there was no explanation at trial why the Morris claim was not paid. When Morris learned that the escrow funds had been disbursed without payment of its charges, it instituted this action and also sought to garnish the remaining $13,000 held by Dawn from the impounded funds. Rainbow did not defend, and the trial court entered a default judgment against Rainbow, from which it does not appeal.

DISCUSSION

The trial court found that Dawn retained the right to direct control and supervision of Rainbow's New Mexico operations, and that in the course of those operations, Rainbow incurred a balance of almost $25,000 on an open account with Morris for fuel used in the New Mexico operations. The trial court further found that when Rainbow defaulted on payments on Morris' account, Dawn made representations over a period of time concerning the existence of a fund held by Dawn to settle indebtedness created by Rainbow operating under the subcontract. The court determined that Morris delayed its collection efforts pending disbursement of the funds, and that Dawn was aware that Morris was relying upon Dawn's representations that payment would be made from the impounded fund. The trial court concluded that Rainbow was at all times in its dealings with Morris the agent of Dawn and, therefore, Dawn was responsible for the account balance.

Dawn urges one point of error on appeal; that the trial court erred in finding liability based on a principal-agent relationship between the defendants. Dawn relies upon the language in the terminal management agreement which states:

> 4. Rainbow is not appointed and shall not become the agent of Dawn and is not empowered to incur or create any debt or liability of Dawn other than in the ordinary course of business relative to terminal management. Rainbow shall not enter into or cause Dawn to become a party to any agreement without the express written consent of Dawn.
>
> 5. Rainbow shall be considered an independent contractor and not an employee of Dawn.

Dawn's reliance upon these paragraphs of the agreement is unpersuasive for two reasons. First, the agreement specifically states that Rainbow may create liabilities of Dawn in the ordinary course of business of operating the terminal. There is no question that the liability to Morris was incurred in the ordinary course of operating the trucking business. Second, the recitation of the parties in their contractual documents need not bind third parties who deal with one of them in ignorance of those instructions. *See* South Second Livestock Auction, Inc. v. Roberts, 69 N.M. 155, 364 P.2d 859 (1961); *see also* Great Northern R.R. Co. v. O'Connor, 232 U.S. 508, 34 S.Ct. 380, 58 L.Ed. 703 (1914).

While Dawn argues from cases discussing apparent authority, we view this as a case of undisclosed agency. Rainbow contracted in its own name and not in the name of Dawn Enterprises, Inc. Thus, this case involves concepts relating to undisclosed agency rather than to apparent authority, and is governed by principles of undisclosed principal-agent contracts. *See, e.g.,* 3 Am.Jur.2d Agency § 316 (1986).

It is well established that an agent for an undisclosed principal subjects the principal to liability for acts done on his account if they are usual or necessary in such transactions. Restatement Second § 194 (1958). This is true even if the principal has previously forbidden the agent to incur such debts so long as the transaction is in the usual course of business engaged in by the agent. *Id.*

The indebtedness in the instant case is squarely governed by well-established principles of agency where an undisclosed principal entrusts the agent with the management of his business. The undisclosed principal is subject to liability to third parties with whom the agent contracts where such transactions are usual in the business conducted by the agent, even if the contract is contrary to the express directions of the principal. Restatement Second § 195 (1958).

Dawn's reliance upon Bloodgood v. Woman's Ben. Ass'n, 13 P.2d 412 (N.M. 1932) is misplaced. Indeed, the case stands for the proposition that a principal may limit an agent's authority, and further, that the limitation will be binding upon a third party dealing with the agent if the third party has knowledge of the limitation of authority. Here there is no evidence that Morris had any actual knowledge of the existence of the Rainbow–Dawn agency, let alone any claimed limitations by Dawn on Rainbow's authority. It is undisputed that Morris thought it was dealing solely with Rainbow when it sold fuel.

Morris correctly observes that secret instructions or limitations placed upon the authority of an agent must be known to the party dealing with the agent, or the principal is bound as if the limitations had not been made. Chevron Oil Co. v. Sutton, 515 P.2d 1283 (N.M. 1973). . . .

Moreover, assuming arguendo that Dawn was not responsible for the indebtedness to Morris for the reasons urged on appeal, it is clear that Dawn ratified the open account after learning of its existence when Morris contacted Dawn regarding payment. A principal may be held liable for the unauthorized acts of his agent if the principal ratifies the transaction after acquiring knowledge of the material facts concerning the transaction. Ulibarri Landscaping Material, Inc. v. Colony Materials, Inc., 639 P.2d 75 (Ct.App.1981).

It was undisputed that in several telephone conversations between the principals of Dawn and Morris, the material facts of the Morris open account were disclosed to Dawn. At no time did Dawn dispute the legitimacy or amount of the open account, and indeed assured Morris that payment would be forthcoming from the funds retained from Rainbow's revenues. Despite this, Dawn used the fund to pay itself a $1,000 per month clerical fee, to pay legal fees incurred as a result of its agency with Rainbow and to settle other claims arising from the Rainbow operations. Where the principal retains the benefits or proceeds of its business relations with an agent with knowledge of the material facts, the principal is deemed to have ratified the methods employed by the agent in generating the proceeds. *See id. See also* 3 Am.Jur.2d Agency § 194 (1986). The diesel fuel provided by Morris was used in Rainbow's trucking operation. Dawn collected the receipts due to Rainbow. Dawn seeks to retain the benefits of the agency with Rainbow, and yet at the same time disclaims responsibility for the business of the agent by which the benefits were generated. This it cannot do. Ulibarri Landscaping Material, Inc. v. Colony Materials, Inc.

In sum, for the foregoing reasons, we affirm.

IT IS SO ORDERED. . . .

■ BIVINS and MINZNER, JJ., CONCUR.

RESTATEMENT THIRD §§ 2.01–2.03, 2.05, 3.01, 3.03, 3.06, 4.01–4.02, 6.01–6.03, 6.10, 8.14

[See Statutory Supplement*]

NOTE ON THE AGENCY RELATIONSHIP

1. *Terminology.* An *agent* is a person who by mutual assent acts on behalf of another and subject to the other's control. The person for whom the agent acts is a *principal.* Agency law governs the relationship between agents and principals; the relationship between agents and persons with whom an agent deals, or purports to deal, on a principal's behalf; and the relationship between principals and such persons. (For ease of exposition, in the balance of this Note, persons with whom an agent deals, or purports to deal, on a principal's behalf will be referred to as *third persons*). Principals are conventionally divided into three categories: disclosed, partially disclosed or unidentified, and undisclosed. A principal is *disclosed* if the third person is on notice both that the agent is acting on behalf of a principal and of the principal's identity. A principal is *partially disclosed* or *unidentified* if the third person is on notice that the agent is acting on behalf of a principal, but is not on notice of the principal's identity. A principal is *undisclosed* if the third person has no notice that the agent is acting on behalf of a principal rather than on his own behalf.

2. *Nature of the agency relationship.* Agency is a consensual relationship. However, whether an agency relationship has been created does not turn on whether the parties either think of themselves as, or intend to be, principal and agent. Rather, "[a]gency is the fiduciary relationship that arises when one person (a 'principal') manifests assent to another person (an 'agent') that the agent shall act on the

---

* References in the Casebook to the *Statutory Supplement* are to *Corporations and Other Business Organizations—Statutes, Rules, Materials, and Forms* (M. Eisenberg ed., Foundation Press; revised annually).

principal's behalf and subject to the principal's control, and the agent manifests assent or otherwise consents so to act." Restatement Third § 1.01. (In this Chapter the term *Restatement Second* refers to Restatement, Second, of Agency (1957), and the term *Restatement Third* refers to Restatement, Third, of Agency (2006).) "Whether a relationship is one of agency is a legal conclusion made after an assessment of the facts of the relationship and the application of the law of agency to those facts. Although agency is a consensual relationship, how the parties to any given relationship label it is not dispositive." Restatement Third § 1.02, Comment a.

3. *Liability of principal to third persons.* A central element of the law of agency is the liability, if any, of the principal to a third person with whom the agent interacts. This kind of liability falls into two broad classes: liability for an agent's torts, and liability for contracts made or purported to be made by the agent on the principal's behalf.

a. *Liability of a principal for torts committed by his agent.* The liability of a principal for a tort committed by his agent is commonly referred to as either vicarious liability, respondeat superior ("let the master answer"), or enterprise liability. These three terms have slightly different connotations, but at bottom they express the same idea, which has been well-summarized by Professor Fishman:

> The adoption of enterprise liability under respondeat superior is justified on several policy grounds. First, the ability of the enterprise to spread the risk from losses is important. The enterprise is in a better position than . . . the injured third person to spread the risk of loss, either through insurance or the ability to factor the potential losses into the price for the goods produced. A second reason suggests that proper allocation of resources is promoted by requiring an enterprise to include in the price of its goods the costs of the accidents which are closely associated with the enterprise's operations. A third reason . . . is that the [principal] is in a position to control the employee and placing the risk of loss here could lead to greater safety. A fourth reason is that it is considered more equitable to place the liability on the [principal], because it provides greater assurance that the accident victim will be paid, or because there is a societal preference to make certain losses costs of doing business rather than losses to be borne by individual households.

Fishman, Inherent Agency Power—Should Enterprise Liability Apply to Agents' Unauthorized Contracts?, 19 Rutgers L.J. 1, 48–49 (1987).

In the context of vicarious liability for torts, traditionally a principal was referred to as a master and an agent was referred to as a servant. This approach was adopted in Restatement Second § 2, which defined a *master* as a principal who controls, or has the right to control, the physical conduct of an agent in the performance of the agent's services, and a *servant* as an agent whose physical conduct in the performance of services for the principal is controlled by or subject to the control of the principal. Restatement Second § 216 provided that a master was liable for the torts of his servants committed in while acting in the scope of their employment. Restatement Second § 228 defined the term *scope of employment* for this purpose as follows:

> (1) Conduct of a servant is within the scope of employment if, but only if:
>
> (a) it is of the kind he is employed to perform;
>
> (b) it occurs substantially within the authorized time and space limits;
>
> (c) it is actuated, at least in part, by a purpose to serve the master, and
>
> (d) if force is intentionally used by the servant against another, the use of force is not unexpectable by the master.
>
> (2) Conduct of a servant is not within the scope of employment if it is different in kind from that authorized, far beyond the authorized time or space limits, or too little actuated by a purpose to serve the master.

Restatement Third adopts a different terminology and a different test for vicarious liability. Rather than using the terms *master* and *servant*, Restatement Third uses the terms *principal* and *employee*. Under § 7.07(3), for the purpose of determining a principal's vicarious liability in tort, an "employee" is defined as an agent whose principal "controls or has the right to control the manner and means of the agent's performance of work. . . ." Restatement Third § 7.07 also adopts a revised definition of course of employment:

> (1) An employer is subject to vicarious liability for a tort committed by its employee acting within the scope of employment.
>
> (2) An employee acts within the scope of employment when performing work assigned by the employer or engaging in a course of conduct subject to the employer's control. An employee's act is not within the scope of employment when it occurs within an independent course of conduct not intended by the employee to serve any purpose of the employer.

b. *Liability of a principal arising out of a contract between an agent and a third person.* Under the law of agency, a principal is liable to a third person on a contract entered into by an agent on the principal's behalf if the agent had actual, apparent, or (traditionally) inherent authority to act on the principal's behalf in the way that he did, or the principal ratified the act or transaction. Accordingly, although a principal's liability for an agent's tortious and contractual transactions both reflect the concept that a principal may be responsible for acts of an agent, the two types of liability involve different requirements. Broadly speaking, a principal's liability in *tort* requires a determination that the principal had the right to control the manner and means of the agent's performance or work and that the agent acted within the scope of his employment. In contrast, a principal's liability in *contract* requires a determination that the agent acted, or purported to act, on the principal's behalf and had actual, apparent, or inherent authority to do so, or the principal ratified the agent's act.[1] The various categories of authority will now be considered.

(i) *Actual authority*. An agent has *actual authority* to transact with third persons in a given manner on a principal's behalf if the principal's words or conduct would lead a reasonable person in the agent's position to believe that the principal wishes the agent to so act. If an agent has actual authority to engage in a given type of transaction with a third person, and acts within the scope of that authority, the principal is bound to the third person.

> *Example I:* P goes to an office where, as he knows, several brokers have desks, and leaves upon the desk of A, thinking it to be the desk of X, a note signed by him, which states: "I authorize you to contract in my name for the purchase of 100 shares of GE stock at the market price." A comes in, finds the note and, not knowing of P's mistake, makes a contract with T, in P's name, for the purchase of the GE shares. A had actual authority to make the contract.[2]

If an agent has actual authority to transact with a third person in a given way, and did so, the principal is bound even if the third person did not know that the agent had actual authority, and indeed even if the principal was undisclosed, so that the third person thought the agent was herself the principal. Accordingly, an undisclosed principal is bound by his agent's authorized transaction even though the agent purports to act strictly on her own behalf. One reason an undisclosed principal is bound is that she set the transaction in motion and stood to gain from it. A second reason is this: Even if the undisclosed principal was not directly liable to the third person, the agent would be. Therefore, the third person could sue the agent. If he did so, the agent could then sue the principal for indemnification of the damages she had to pay the third person. (See Section 6 of this Note, infra.) Accordingly, allowing the third person to sue the undisclosed principal does not materially enlarge the principal's liability, and collapses two lawsuits into one.

Actual authority is contractual, in that it arises out of an agreement between the principal and the agent. By and large, therefore, the scope of an agent's actual authority is determined by the general principles of contract interpretation. There is, however, an important distinction between interpreting a conventional contract and interpreting an agency contact. Interpretation of a conventional contract usually focuses on the language of the contract and the surrounding

---

1. In general, consensual but noncontractual transactions by an agent (for example, a filing) are treated the same as contractual transactions for agency-law purposes, and in any event do not often raise problems. Accordingly, what is said in this Note about contractual transactions normally applies to other consensual transactions as well.

2. All the Examples in this Note are literal or slightly modified versions of Illustrations in Restatement Second and Restatement Third. Examples written by the editors are labeled "Example," followed by a roman numeral. Examples that are taken verbatim from the Restatement of Agency are labeled "Illustration," followed by an Arabic numeral.

circumstances *when the contract was made*. In contrast, interpretation of an agency contract is *ambulatory*, that is, it focuses on the reasonability of the agent's interpretation of his authority *at the time he acts*. As stated in Restatement Second § 33, Comment a:

> a. *Authority an ambulatory power.* ... [A]n agreement creating an agency relation has elements different from those of other contracts.... Whatever the original agreement or authority may have been, [an agent] is authorized at any given moment to do, and to do only, what he reasonably believes the principal desires him to do, in the light of what he knows or should know of the principal's purpose and the existing circumstances. [If the agent] knows facts which should lead him to believe that his authority is restricted or terminated, he has a duty to act only within the limits of the situation as it is currently known to him.
>
> **Illustrations**....
>
> 2. P, the owner of a factory running on half time for lack of orders, before leaving for his vacation, directs his purchasing agent to "put in our usual monthly coal supply of 1000 tons." The following day a large order comes in which will immediately put the factory on full running time. It may be found that A is authorized to purchase sufficient coal to keep the factory running, this depending upon whether or not P can easily be reached, the amount of discretion usually given to A, the condition of P's bank balance, and other factors.
>
> *b. Authority distinct from contract of agency.* An agent is a fiduciary under a duty to obey the will of the principal as he knows it or should know it. This will may change, either with or without a change in events. Whatever it is at any given time, if the agent has reason to know it, his duty is not to act contrary to it.... Thus, whether or not the agent is authorized to do a particular act at a particular time depends, not only on what the principal told the agent, but upon a great variety of other factors, including changes in the situation after the instructions were given. The interpretation of authority, therefore, differs in this respect from the interpretation of a contract, even the contract of agency.
>
> The agent's authority may therefore be increased, diminished, become dormant or be destroyed, not only by further manifestations by the principal but also by the happening of events, dependent, in many situations, upon what the agent knows or should know as to the principal's purposes.

Restatement Third § 2.02, Comment c, makes essentially the same point: "[Q]uestions of interpretation that determine whether an agent acted with actual authority have a temporal focus that moves through time as the agent decides how to act, while questions of contractual interpretation focus on the parties' shared meaning as of the time of a promise or agreement." This point is exemplified by Illustrations 8 and 9:

8. [The directors of P Corporation approve a plan to upgrade a plant that is suitable for the manufacture of one product line. P Corporation's Executive Vice President tells M, the plant manager, to contract with an engineering firm for a redesign of the production process that must precede the upgrade work. After adopting the resolution, the directors abandon the upgrade plan and so notify the Executive Vice President. No one tells M, but] M reads in the newspaper that P Corporation's directors have discontinued the sole product line manufactured in the plant. M no longer has actual authority to make the contract with T.

9. Same facts as [the bracketed language of Illustration 8], except that the upgrade plan depends on using a particular building technology. M is aware of this fact. After the directors adopt the resolution and M is directed to contract for the redesign work, M learns that regulatory restrictions will prevent P Corporation from using the particular technology on which the plan depends. M no longer has actual authority to make the contract with T.

Actual authority may be either *express* or *implied.* "It is possible for a principal to specify minutely what the agent is to do. To the extent that he does this, the agent may be said to have express authority. But most authority is created by implication. Thus, in the authorization to 'sell my automobile', the only fully expressed power is to transfer title in exchange for money or a promise to give money. In fact, under some circumstances . . . there may . . . be power to take or give possession of the automobile or to extend credit or to accept something in partial exchange. These powers are all implied or inferred from the words used, from customs and from the relations of the parties. They are described as 'implied authority.' " Restatement Second § 7, Comment c; *see also* Restatement Third § 2.02, Comment b.

A common type of implied actual authority is *incidental authority,* which is the authority to do incidental acts that are reasonably necessary to accomplish an actually authorized transaction or that usually accompany a transaction of that type. Here are two examples:

Example II: P directs A to sell goods by auction at a time and place at which, as P and A know, a statute forbids anyone but a licensed auctioneer to conduct sales by auction. Nothing to the contrary appearing, A has implied actual authority to employ a licensed auctioneer.

Example III: P authorizes A, a local broker, to sell land on P's behalf. It is the custom to make such sales by delivering a deed with certain covenants as to title. A has implied actual authority to execute and deliver proper deeds to purchasers and to insert in the deeds the usual covenants as to title.

(ii) *Apparent authority.* An agent has *apparent authority* to act in a given way on a principal's behalf in relation to a third person if manifestations of the principal to the third person (or manifestations by the agent to the third person that the principal authorized the agent to make) would lead a reasonable person in the third person's position to believe that the principal had authorized the agent to so act. If an agent has apparent authority and acts within the scope of that authority, the principal is bound. Here are four examples:

> *Example IV:* P writes to A directing him to act as his agent for the sale of Blackacre. P sends a copy of this letter to T, a prospective purchaser. A has actual authority to sell Blackacre and, as to T, apparent authority.
>
> *Example V:* Same facts as in Example IV, except that in the letter to A, P adds a postscript, not included in the copy to T, telling A to make no sale until after communication with P. A has no actual authority to sell Blackacre, but as to T, A has apparent authority.
>
> *Example VI:* Same facts as in Example IV, except that after A and T have received the letters, P telegraphs a revocation to A. A has no actual authority to sell Blackacre, but as to T, A has apparent authority.
>
> *Example VII:* P owns a granary and employs A to manage it. A's employment agreement with P states that A's authority to purchase grain is limited to transactions that do not exceed $5,000; larger purchases require P's express approval. This limit is unusual in the granary business. P directs A to tell T, a seller of grain, that A's authority to purchase grain is unlimited, because P believes this will induce T to give orders placed by A priority over orders placed by agents with limited authority. A represents to T that his authority to purchase grain is unlimited, and enters into a contract with T, on P's behalf, to buy $10,000 worth of grain. P is bound by the contract with T. A has actual authority to make the representation to T, and A has apparent authority to enter into the contract with T, because T reasonably believes A has authority to bind P to a contract to buy $10,000 worth of grain.

In most cases, actual and apparent authority go hand in hand, as Example IV suggests. For example, if P Bank appoints A as cashier, and nothing more is said, A will reasonably believe he has the authority that cashiers normally have (actual authority), and third persons who deal with A will reasonably believe the same thing (apparent authority). Apparent authority becomes salient in such a case if P Bank does not actually give A all the authority that cashiers usually have, and a customer deals with A, knowing that A is a cashier, but not knowing that P Bank has placed unusual limits on A's authority.

The apparent authority of A in the cashier hypothetical is a special type of apparent authority known as *power of position*. "[A]pparent authority can be created by appointing a person to a position, such as that of manager or treasurer, which carries with it generally recognized duties; to those who know of the appointment there is apparent authority to do the things ordinarily entrusted to one occupying such a position, regardless of unknown limitations which are imposed upon the particular agent." Restatement Second § 27, Comment a.

> *Example VIII*: P bank appoints A as an information clerk, with authority only to answer depositors' questions. During alterations, however, the bank directs A to occupy the space normally occupied by one of the tellers, and puts up a sign that says "Information Window." The sign becomes displaced, and T, a depositor in the bank, makes a cash deposit with A, believing that A is a teller. P is bound by this transaction.

c. *Agency by estoppel.* Another type of authority is known as "agency by estoppel." The core of agency by estoppel is described as follows in Restatement Third § 2.05:

> A person who has not made a manifestation that an actor has authority as an agent and who is not otherwise liable as a party to a transaction purportedly done by the actor on that person's account is liable to a third party who is induced to make a detrimental change in position because the transaction is believed to be on the person's account, if
>
> (1) the person intentionally or carelessly caused such belief, or
>
> (2) having notice of such a belief and that it might induce others to change their positions, the person did not take reasonable steps to notify them of the facts.

Agency by estoppel is so close to apparent authority that for most practical purposes the former concept can be subsumed in the latter.

d. *Inherent authority.* Under the doctrine of ***inherent authority***, an agent may bind a principal in certain cases even when the agent had neither actual nor apparent authority. Restatement Second § 161 concerned the inherent authority of a ***general agent*** of a disclosed or partially disclosed principal.[3] This section provided that such a principal is liable for an act done on his behalf by a general agent even though the principal had forbidden the agent to do the act, if (i) the act usually accompanies or is incidental to transactions that the agent is authorized to conduct, and (ii) the third person reasonably believes the agent is authorized to do the act. Restatement Second § 194 concerned the inherent authority of agents of undisclosed principals. This Section provided that "A general agent for an undisclosed princi-

---

3. Restatement Second § 3 defined a general agent as an agent who is authorized to conduct a series of transactions involving continuity of service. In contrast, a *special agent* was defined as an agent who is authorized to conduct only a single transaction, or only a series of transactions not involving continuity of service. Restatement Third § 2.01, Comment d states:

> *General and special agents.* Courts have long distinguished between "general agents" and "special agents," a distinction that rests on both the objects of the discretion granted an agent and the mode of regulating the agent's exercise of discretion. The labels matter less than the underlying circumstances that warrant their application. The prototypical special agent is a real-estate broker who is authorized to conduct a single transaction. A special agent may also be authorized to conduct a series of transactions specified by the principal. The prototypical general agent is a manager of a business, who has authority to conduct a series of transactions and who serves the principal on an ongoing as opposed to an episodic basis. . . .

pal authorized to conduct transactions subjects his principal to liability for acts done on his account, if usual or necessary in such transactions, although forbidden by the principal to do them." Restatement Second § 194 did not require that the third person reasonably believed the agent was authorized to act. Indeed, such a requirement could not be imposed, because in the case of an undisclosed principal the third person will not know that he is dealing with an agent.

A major rationale of inherent authority, given in Restatement Second, is based on an analogy to the doctrine of respondeat superior:

> ... It is inevitable that in doing their work, either through negligence or excess of zeal, agents will harm third persons or will deal with them in unauthorized ways. It would be unfair for an enterprise to have the benefit of the work of its agents without making it responsible to some extent for their excesses and failures to act carefully. The answer of the common law has been the creation of special agency powers or, to phrase it otherwise, the imposition of liability upon the principal because of unauthorized or negligent acts of his servants and other agents....*
>
> * * *
>
> ... [The principal's liability under the doctrine of inherent authority] is based primarily upon the theory that, if one appoints an agent to conduct a series of transactions over a period of time, it is fair that he should bear losses which are incurred when such an agent, although without authority to do so, does something which is usually done in connection with the transactions he is employed to conduct. Such agents can properly be regarded as part of the principal's organization in much the same way as a servant is normally part of the master's business enterprise.... The basis of [inherent authority] is comparable to the liability of a master for the torts of his servant.... In the case of the master, it is thought fair that one who benefits from the enterprise and has a right to control the physical activities of those who make the enterprise profitable, should pay for the physical harm resulting from the errors and derelictions of the servants while doing the kind of thing which makes the enterprise successful. The rules imposing liability upon the principal for some of the contracts and conveyances of a general agent, whether or not a servant, which he is neither authorized nor apparently authorized to make, are based upon a similar public policy. Commercial convenience requires that the principal should not escape liability where there have been deviations from the usually granted authority by persons who are such essential parts of his business enterprise. In the long run it is of advantage to business, and hence to employers as a class, that third persons should not be required to scrutinize too carefully the mandates of permanent or semi-

* Recall that the terms "master" and "servant" have technical meanings in agency law. (Footnote by ed.)

> permanent agents who do no more than what is usually done by agents in similar positions.

Restatement Second § 8A, Comment a, § 161, Comment a.

An alternative rationale for the doctrine of inherent authority is based on the principal's reasonable expectations. In a world with perfect information, faithful agents will follow all instructions impeccably. In the real world, however, agents acting in good faith will not infrequently deviate from their instructions, because agents, like everyone else, will make mistakes, which may take the form of misinterpreting their instructions or forgetting one of numerous instructions. Furthermore, an agent may reasonably believe that his principal's objective is best served by violating a particular instruction. A principal's instructions to her agent are necessarily given in the present to govern the future. The future, however, may develop in such a way that the agent reasonably believes that if the principal knew all the facts, she would not want the agent to follow a given instruction. Usually in such cases the agent could go back to the principal for further instructions. Sometimes, however, it is infeasible to take that course of action—for example, because a valuable opportunity must be taken immediately or not at all. These real-world facts are reflected in a passage in the Comment to Restatement Second § 8A: "It is inevitable that in doing their work, either through negligence or excess of zeal, agents will harm third persons or will deal with them in unauthorized ways. It would be unfair for an enterprise to have the benefit of the work of its agents without making it responsible to some extent for their excesses and failures to act carefully."

Given these realities, the doctrine of inherent authority is justified on the ground that it is or should be foreseeable to a principal, when he appoints an agent, that as a practical matter the agent, acting in good faith for the benefit of the principal, is likely to deviate occasionally from instructions. As between the principal—who appointed the agent, benefits from the agent's activities, and could or should have foreseen a certain range of deviations from his instructions to the agent—on the one hand, and the third person who contracts with the agent, on the other, a loss that results from a foreseeable deviation by the agent is better placed on the principal.

Restatement Third does not use the term "inherent agency power," on the ground that "[o]ther doctrines stated in this Restatement encompasses the justifications underpinning [the concept of inherent agency] including the importance of interpretation by the agent in the agent's relationship with the principle...." *Id.* § 2.01 Comment b. The omission of the explicit term, inherent authority, from Restatement Third is unfortunate, but in various places the text and Comment of Restatement Third adopt positions that can best or only be explained by the concept of inherent authority. For example, Restatement Third § 2.02(2) defines the scope of actual authority in an expansive manner:

> An agent's interpretation of the principal's manifestations is reasonable if it reflects any meaning by the agent to be ascribed by

> the principal and, in the absence of any meaning known to the agent, as a reasonable person in the agent's position would interpret the manifestations in light of the context, including circumstances of which the agent has notice. . . .

Comment b to this section makes clear that in determining an agent's actual authority, a literal interpretation of the principal's manifestations does not always govern:

> An agent's understanding of the principal's interests and objectives is an element of the agent's reasonable interpretation of the principal's conduct. If a literal interpretation of a principal's communication to the agent would authorize an act inconsistent with the principal's interests or objectives known to the agent, it is open to question whether the agent's literal interpretation is reasonable.

Correspondingly, the Comment recognizes that an agent may properly act in a way that is knowingly at variance with the principal's original instructions if the agent believes that (i) circumstances have changed since the initial instructions, (ii) were the principal to reconsider the matter, different instructions would have been given, and (iii) it is impracticable to communicate with the principal for further clarification before action needs to be taken. For example, Restatement Third § 2.02, Illustration 22, provides:

> [Blackacre is to be sold at an auction. P retains A to bid at the auction on P's behalf, directing A to buy Blackacre but to offer no more than $250,000.] P owns and operates a golf course on land that almost entirely surrounds Blackacre. A has notice of P's long-term business plan to enhance the aesthetic and athletic qualities of the course and thereby make it more profitable. At the auction of Blackacre, A learns for the first time that there will be one other bidder, B. A also learns that B's plan for using Blackacre is to construct a cement factory on it. A is unable to contact P to relay this information and receive further instructions. A succeeds in purchasing Blackacre for P by bidding $260,000. A acted with actual authority.

Similarly § 2.02, Illustration 5, provides:

> P Corporation employs A as the Facilities Manager at an amusement park owned by P Corporation. A reports to B, P Corporation's Vice President for Leisure Activities. B directs A to arrange for the reseeding of the badly deteriorated lawn adjacent to the park's entrance. B also directs A to complete the reseeding by the end of the week. A purchases grass seed and directs groundskeepers to schedule time for reseeding. A then learns that the park location is in the path of a forecasted hurricane. A has actual authority to postpone the reseeding.

e. *Ratification.* Even if an agent has neither actual, apparent, nor inherent authority, the principal will be bound to the third person if the agent purported to act on the principal's behalf and the principal, with knowledge of the material facts, either (1) affirmed the agent's conduct by manifesting an intention to treat the agent's past conduct as authorized, or (2) engaged in conduct that is justifiable only if he has such an intention.

Manifesting an intention to treat an agent's conduct as authorized is sometimes known as *express ratification.* Here is an example:

> *Example IX:* A, who has no authority to bind P, purports to represent P in buying a horse from T. Later, P affirms the transaction. By that act, P becomes a party to the transaction.

Engaging in conduct that is justifiable only if the principal intends to treat the agent's conduct as authorized is sometimes known as *implied ratification.* The most common example occurs where as a result of the purported agent's transaction, the principal, with knowledge of the facts, receives or retains something to which he would otherwise not be entitled:

> *Example X:* P owns an advertising agency and employs A to service existing clients by purchasing space for the clients in advertising media. A does not have authority to set terms with clients. A executes an agreement with T that commits P to develop a new advertising campaign for T. P learns of the agreement and then retains an advance payment made by T for the new advertising campaign. By accepting and retaining the payment, P has ratified the unauthorized agreement made by A.

Ratification need not be communicated to the third person to be effective, although it must be objectively manifested by the principal. *See* Restatement Third § 4.01, Comment d. To be effective, however, a ratification must occur before either the third person has withdrawn or there has been a material change in circumstances that would make it inequitable to bind the third party unless the third party chooses to be bound. *See* Restatement Third § 4.05.

As Restatement Second § 82, Comment c pointed out, "The concept of ratification.... is unique. It does not conform to the rules of contracts, since it can be accomplished without consideration to or manifestation by the purported principal and without fresh consent by the other party." Restatement Third § 4.01, Comment b, provides the following rationale for the doctrine of ratification:

> Ratification often serves the function of clarifying situations of ambiguous or uncertain authority. A principal's ratification confirms or validates the agent's right to have acted as the agent did. That is, an agent's action may have been effective to bind the principal to the third party, and the third party to the principal, because the agent acted with apparent authority. *See* § 2.03. If the principal ratifies the agent's act, it is thereafter not necessary to establish that the agent acted with apparent authority....

A related but different rationale for the doctrine was stated by Judge Posner in Goldstick v. ICM Realty, 788 F.2d 456, 460 (7th Cir.1986):

> ... The best explanation [of the concept of ratification] may be that the principal would not have ratified the contract unless

he had seen a commercial advantage in doing so, and that the advantage would be less if the ratification had no binding effect. Ordinarily a principal ratifies an agent's unauthorized transaction in order to protect the principal's relationship with the other party to the transaction, usually a customer or supplier: and for ratification to have this protective effect it has to be more than an idle gesture, signifying nothing because unenforceable.

f. *Acquiescence*. A concept that is comparable to, but different from, ratification is authority by acquiescence. "[I]f the agent performs a series of acts of a similar nature, the failure of the principal to object to them is an indication that he consents to the performance of similar acts in the future under similar conditions." Restatement Second § 43, Comment b. *See also* Restatement Third § 2.02, Comment b. Suppose, for example, an agent engages in a series of comparable purchases on the principal's behalf. Prior to the first purchase, a reasonable person in the agent's position would not have thought he had authority to enter into such a transaction. Nevertheless, the principal did not object to that purchase or to later comparable purchases when she learned of them. At that point, a reasonable person in the agent's position would assume that the principal approved the agent's engaging in such purchases. Accordingly, the principal's acquiescence gives rise to actual authority. As to third persons who know of the acquiescence, the acquiescence also gives rise to apparent authority.

g. *Termination of agent's authority.* As a general rule, a principal has the *power* to terminate an agent's authority at any time, even if doing so violates a contract between the principal and the agent, and even if it had been agreed that the agent's authority was irrevocable. This rule rests largely on the ground that contracts relating to personal services will not be specifically enforced. (There is an important but limited exception to this rule, which applies to a type of relationship known as an agency (or power) coupled with an interest. This exception will be discussed in Chapter 8, infra.) However, such a contract is effective to create liability (damages) for wrongful termination. Here is an example:

> *Example XI:* In consideration of A's agreement to advertise and give his best energies to the sale of Blackacre, its owner, P, grants to A "a power of attorney, irrevocable for one year" to sell it. A advertises and spends time trying to sell Blackacre. At the end of three months P informs A that he revokes. A's authority is terminated, but A has a right to damages for breach of contract.

4. *Liability of Third Person to Principal.* The general rule is that if an agent and a third person enter into a contract, and the agent's principal is liable to the third person under the contract, then the third person is liable to the principal. *See* Restatement Third §§ 6.01–6.03. The major exception is that the third person is not liable if the principal is undisclosed and the agent or the principal knew that the third person would not have knowingly dealt with the principal. *See* Restatement Third § 6.03, Comment d.

5. *Liability of Agent to Third Person.* Where an agent has entered into a contract with a third person on behalf of a principal, whether the agent will be liable to the third person depends in the first instance on whether the principal is bound to the third person.

a. *Where the principal is bound to the third person.* If the agent had actual, apparent, or inherent authority, or the principal ratified the agent's act, so that the principal is bound to the third person, the agent's liability to the third person largely depends on whether the principal was disclosed, undisclosed.

(i) *Disclosed principal.* If the principal was disclosed (that is, at the time of the transaction the third person had notice that the agent was acting on behalf of a principal, and also had notice of the principal's identity), and is bound by the agent's act because the agent had actual, apparent, or inherent authority or because the principal ratified the act, the general rule is that the agent is not bound to the third person. *See* Restatement Third § 6.01. The theory is that in such a case the third person did not expect the agent to be bound, he did expect the principal to be bound, and he should get just what he expected.

(ii) *Undisclosed principal.* If the principal was undisclosed (that is, if at the time of the transaction the agent purported to act on his own behalf), the general rule is that the agent is bound even though the principal is also bound. *See* Restatement Third § 6.03. The theory is that the third person must have expected the agent to be a party to the contract, because that is how the agent presented the transaction. However, there is a quirk in the law here. Under the traditional majority rule, if the third person, after learning of an undisclosed principal's identity, obtains a judgment against the principal, the agent is discharged from liability even if the judgment is not satisfied. Similarly, if the third person obtains a judgment against the agent, the undisclosed principal is discharged from liability. Under the minority but better rule, neither the agent nor the principal is discharged if the third person obtains a judgment against the other, but instead is discharged only if the judgment is satisfied only by satisfaction of the judgment. This rule is adopted in Restatement Third § 6.09.

(iii) *Partially disclosed principal.* If the principal was partially disclosed (that is, if at the time of the transaction the third person had notice that the agent was acting on behalf of a principal, but did not have notice of the principal's identity), the general rule is that both the agent and the principal are bound to the third person. *See* Restatement Third § 6.02. The theory is that if the third person did not know the identity of the principal, and therefore could not investigate the principal's credit or reliability, he probably expected that the agent would be liable, either solely or alongside the principal.

b. *Where the principal is not bound.* If the principal is not bound by the agent's act, because the agent did not have actual, apparent, or inherent authority, and the agent's act was not ratified, the general rule is that the agent is liable to the third person. The agent's liability in such cases is usually based on the theory that an agent makes an implied warranty of authority to the third person. However, a few authorities have adopted a theory that the agent can be held liable on the contract itself. In principle, the difference between the two theories might lead to a difference in the measure of damages: Under the liability-on-the-contract theory, the third person will recover against the agent the gains that the third person would have earned under the contract—essentially, expectation damages. In contrast, under the implied-warranty theory it might seem that the third person would recover only the losses he suffered by having entered into the transaction—essentially, reliance damages. However, both Restatement Second and Restatement Third, while adopting the implied-warranty theory, provide for an expectation measure of damages, just as if the liability-on-the-contract theory had been adopted. *See* Restatement Third § 6.10.

6. *Liability of Agent to Principal.* If an agent takes an action that he has no actual authority to perform, but the principal is nevertheless bound because the agent had apparent authority, the agent is liable to the principal for any resulting damages. *See* Restatement Third § 8.09, Comment b. Whether an agent is liable to the principal on the basis of an act that binds the principal by virtue of the agent's inherent but not actual authority is an unsettled point.

7. *Liability of Principal to Agent.* If an agent has acted within his actual authority, the principal is under a duty to indemnify the agent for payments the agent made that were made necessary in executing the principal's affairs. These include the following: (i) Authorized payments made by the agent on the principal's behalf. (ii) Payments made by the agent to a third person under a contract on which the agent was authorized to make himself liable (for example, where the agent acted on behalf of a partially disclosed or undisclosed principal). (iii) Payments of damages to third persons that the agent incurs because of an authorized act that constituted a breach of a contract with the third person for which the agent was liable to the third person. (iv) Expenses in defending actions brought against the agent by a third person because of the agent's authorized conduct. *See* Restatement Third § 8.14.

B. THE AGENT'S DUTY OF LOYALTY

Jensen & Meckling, Theory of the Firm: Managerial Behavior, Agency Costs and Ownership Structure

3 J. Financial Economics 305, 308 (1976).

We define an agency relationship as a contract under which one or more persons (the principal(s)) engage another person (the agent) to perform some service on their behalf which involves delegating some decision making authority to the agent. If both parties to the relationship are utility maximizers there is good reason to believe that the agent will not always act in the best interests of the principal. The *principal* can limit divergences from his interest by establishing appropriate incentives for the agent and by incurring monitoring costs designed to limit the aberrant activities of the agent. In addition in some situations it will pay the *agent* to expend resources (bonding costs) to guarantee that he will not take certain actions which would harm the principal or to ensure that the principal will be compensated if he does take such actions. However, it is generally impossible for the principal or the agent at zero cost to ensure that the agent will make optimal decisions from the principal's viewpoint. In most agency relationships the principal and the agent will incur positive monitoring and bonding costs (non-pecuniary as well as pecuniary), and in addition there will be some divergence between the agent's decisions and those decisions which would maximize the welfare of the principal. The dollar equivalent of the reduction in welfare experienced by the principal due to this divergence is also a cost of the agency relationship, and we refer to this latter cost as the "residual loss". We define *agency costs* as the sum of:

(1) the monitoring expenditures by the principal,

(2) the bonding expenditures by the agent,

(3) the residual loss.

Tarnowski v. Resop

Supreme Court of Minnesota, 1952.
236 Minn. 33, 51 N.W.2d 801.

■ KNUTSON, JUSTICE.

Plaintiff desired to make a business investment. He engaged defendant as his agent to investigate and negotiate for the purchase of a route of coin-operated music machines. On June 2, 1947, relying upon the advice of defendant and the investigation he had made, plaintiff purchased such a business from Phillip Loechler and Lyle Mayer of Rochester, Minnesota, who will be referred to hereinafter as the sellers. The business was located at LaCrosse, Wisconsin, and throughout the surrounding territory. Plaintiff alleges that defendant represented to him that he had made a thorough investigation of the route; that it had 75 locations in operation; that one or more machines were at each location; that the equipment at each location was not more than six months old; and that the gross income from all locations amounted to more than $3,000 per month. As a matter of fact, defendant had made only a superficial investigation and had investigated only five of the locations. Other than that, he had adopted false representations of the sellers as to the other locations and had passed them on to plaintiff as his own. Plaintiff was to pay $30,620 for the business. He paid $11,000 down. About six weeks after the purchase, plaintiff discovered that the representations made to him by defendant were false, in that there were not more than 47 locations;

that at some of the locations there were no machines and at others there were machines more than six months old, some of them being seven years old; and that the gross income was far less than $3,000 per month. Upon discovering the falsity of defendant's representations and those of the sellers, plaintiff rescinded the sale. He offered to return what he had received, and he demanded the return of his money. The sellers refused to comply, and he brought suit against them in the district court of Olmsted county. The action was tried, resulting in a verdict of $10,000 for plaintiff. Thereafter, the sellers paid plaintiff $9,500, after which the action was dismissed with prejudice pursuant to a stipulation of the parties.

In this action, brought in Hennepin County, plaintiff alleges that defendant, while acting as agent for him, collected a secret commission from the sellers for consummating the sale, which plaintiff seeks to recover under his first cause of action. In his second cause of action, he seeks to recover damages for [losses caused by defendant's wrong].

1. With respect to plaintiff's first cause of action, the principle that all profits made by an agent in the course of an agency belonging to the principal, whether they are the fruits of performance or the violation of an agent's duty, is firmly established and universally recognized. Smitz v. Leopold, 53 N.W. 719 (Minn. 1892). . . .

It matters not that the principal has suffered no damage or even that the transaction has been profitable to him. Raymond Farmers Elevator Co. v. American Surety Co., 290 N.W. 231 (Minn. 1940).

The rule and the basis therefore are well stated in Lum v. Clark, 57 N.W. 662 (Minn. 1894), where, speaking through Mr. Justice Mitchell, we said: "Actual injury is not the principle the law proceeds on, in holding such transactions void. Fidelity in the agent is what is aimed at, and, as a means of securing it, the law will not permit him to place himself in a position in which he may be tempted by his own private interests to disregard those of his principal. . . . It is not material that no actual injury to the company [principal] resulted, or that the policy recommended may have been for its best interest. Courts will not inquire into these matters. It is enough to know that the agent in fact placed himself in such relations that he might be tempted by his own interests to disregard those of his principal. The transaction was nothing more or less than the acceptance by the agent of a bribe to perform his duties in the manner desired by the person who gave the bribe. Such a contract is void. This doctrine rests on such plain principles of law, as well as common business honesty, that the citation of authorities is unnecessary."

The right to recover profits made by the agent in the course of the agency is not affected by the fact that the principal, upon discovering a fraud, has rescinded the contract and recovered that with which he parted. Restatement, Agency, § 407(2). Comment e on Subsection (2) reads: "If an agent has violated a duty of loyalty to the principal so that the principal is entitled to profits which the agent has thereby made, the fact that the principal has brought an action against a third person and has been made whole by such action does not prevent the principal from recovering from the agent the profits which the agent has made. Thus, if the other contracting party has given a bribe to the agent to make a contract with him on behalf of the principal, the principal can rescind the transaction, recovering from the other party anything received by him, or he can maintain an action for damages against him; in either event the principal may recover from the agent the amount of the bribe."

It follows that, insofar as the secret commission of $2,000 received by the agent is concerned, plaintiff had an absolute right thereto, irrespective of any recovery resulting from the action against the sellers for rescission.

2. Plaintiff's second cause of action is brought to recover damages for (1) losses suffered in the operation of the business prior to rescission; (2) loss of time devoted to operation; (3) expenses in connection with rescission of the sale and investigation therewith; (4) nontaxable expenses in connection with the prosecution of the suit against the sellers; and (5) attorneys' fees in connection with the suit.

The case comes to us on a bill of exceptions. No part of the testimony of the witnesses is included, so we must assume that the evidence establishes the items of damage claimed by plaintiff. Our inquiry is limited to a consideration of the question whether a principal may recover of an agent who has breached his trust the items of damage mentioned after a successful prosecution of an action for rescission against the third parties with whom the agent dealt for his principal.

The general rule is stated in Restatement, Agency, § 407(1), as follows: "If an agent has received a benefit as a result of violating his duty of loyalty, the principal is entitled to recover from him what he has so received, its value, or its proceeds, and also the amount of damage thereby caused, except that if the violation consists of the wrongful disposal of the principal's property, the principal cannot recover its value and also what the agent received in exchange therefore."

In Comment a on Subsection (1) we find the following: ". . . In either event, whether or not the principal elects to get back the thing improperly dealt with or to recover from the agent its value or the amount of benefit which the agent has improperly received, he is, in addition, entitled to be indemnified by the agent for any loss which has been caused to his interest by the improper transaction. Thus, if the purchasing agent for a restaurant purchases with the principal's money defective food, receiving a bonus therefore, and the use of the food in the restaurant damages the business, the principal can recover from the agent the amount of money improperly expended by him, the bonus which the agent received, and the amount which will compensate for the injury to the business."

The general rule with respect to damages for a tortious act is that "The wrong-doer is answerable for all the injurious consequences of his tortious act, which according to the usual course of events and the general experience were likely to ensue, and which, therefore, when the act was committed, he may reasonably be supposed to have foreseen and anticipated." 1 Sutherland, Damages (4 ed.) § 45, quoted with approval in Sargent v. Mason, 112 N.W. 255, 257 (Minn. 1907)....

Bergquist v. Kreidler, 196 N.W. 964 (Minn. 1924), involved an action to recover attorneys' fees expended by plaintiffs in an action seeking to enforce and protect their right to the possession of real estate. Defendant, acting as the owner's agent, had falsely represented to plaintiffs that they could have possession on August 1, 1920. It developed after plaintiffs had purchased the premises that a tenant had a lease running to August 1, 1922, on a rental much lower than the actual value of the premises. Defendant (the agent) conceded that plaintiffs were entitled to recover the loss in rent, but contended that attorneys' fees and disbursements expended by plaintiffs in testing the validity of the tenant's lease were not recoverable. In affirming plaintiffs' right to recover we said, 196 N.W. 966 (Minn. 1924): "... the litigation in which plaintiffs became involved was the direct, legitimate, and a to be expected result of appellant's misrepresentation. The loss sustained by plaintiffs in conducting that litigation 'is plainly traceable' to appellant's wrong and he should make compensation accordingly."

So far as the right to recover attorneys' fees is concerned, the same may be said in this case. Plaintiff sought to return what had been received and demanded a return of his down payment. The sellers refused. He thereupon sued to accomplish this purpose, as he had a right to do, and was successful. His attorneys' fees and expenses of suit were directly traceable to the harm caused by defendant's wrongful act. As such, they are recoverable.

... The general rule applicable here is stated in 15 Am.Jur., Damages, § 144, as follows: "It is generally held that where the wrongful act of the defendant has involved the plaintiff in litigation with others or placed him in such relation with others as makes it necessary to incur expense to protect his interest, such costs and expenses, including attorneys' fees, should be treated as the legal consequences of the original wrongful act and may be recovered as damages."

The same is true of the other elements of damage involved....

Affirmed.

RESTATEMENT THIRD § 8.05, ILLUSTRATION 1. "P, who owns a stable of horses, employs A to take care of them. While P is absent for a month, and without P's consent, A rents the horses [for his own personal gain] to persons who ride them. Although being ridden is beneficial to the horses, A is subject to liability to P for the amount A receives for the rentals."

READING v. ATTORNEY–GENERAL, [1951] App.Cas. 507 (H.L.). Reading was a sergeant in the Royal Army Medical Corps during World War II, stationed in Cairo. In 1943, an unidentified man asked Reading whether he would assist in selling cases of whisky and brandy in Cairo, for which he would be paid a few pounds. About a month later Reading was met by a man named Manole, who told Reading that a truck, which Reading was to board, would come at a specified time and place. Reading, dressed in uniform, boarded the truck and conducted it through Cairo. By arrangement he met Manole later on the same day, and received an envelope which contained £2,000. This process was repeated on a number of occasions. In all, Reading was paid around £20,000. The Crown (that is, the English Government) later seized these amounts, on the ground that they had been paid to Reading "for accompanying . . . a loaded lorry in and about Cairo whilst dressed in uniform and thereby falsely representing himself as acting in the course of his military duties . . . in order to avoid police inspection of the said lorry." Reading brought suit to recover the seized amount. Justice Denning, at trial, dismissed Reading's complaint:

> In my judgment, it is a principle of law that if a servant, in violation of his duty of honesty and good faith, takes advantage of his service to make a profit for himself, in this sense, that the assets of which he has control, or the facilities which he enjoys, or the position which he occupies, are the real cause of his obtaining the money, as distinct from being the mere opportunity for getting it, that is to say, if they play the predominant part in his obtaining the money, then he is accountable for it to the master. It matters not that the master has not lost any profit, nor suffered any damage. Nor does it matter that the master could not have done the act himself. It is a case where the servant has unjustly enriched himself by virtue of his service without his master's sanction. It is money which the servant ought not to be allowed to keep, and the law says it shall be taken from him and given to his master, because he got it solely by reason of the position which he occupied as a servant of his master. . . . [Reading] . . . was using his position as a sergeant in His Majesty's Army and the uniform to which his rank entitled him to obtain the money which he received. In my opinion any official position, whether marked by a uniform or not, which enables the holder to earn money by its use gives his master a right to receive the money so earned even though it was earned by a criminal act. "You have earned," the master can say, "money by the use of your position as my servant. It is not for you, who have gained this advantage, to set up your own wrong as a defence to my claim."

The House of Lords affirmed.

RASH v. J.V. INTERMEDIATE, LTD., 498 F.3d 1201, 1212 (10th Cir. 2007). "[The principle that an agent who breaches his fiduciary duties may be required to forfeit his compensation] is based on two propositions: (1) the principal is considered not to have received what he bargained for if the agent breaches his fiduciary duties while representing the principal, . . . and (2) fee forfeiture is designed to discourage agents from being disloyal to their principal or 'to protect relationships of trust by discouraging agents' disloyalty'. . . .

"Forfeiture only applies to 'clear and serious' violations of fiduciary duty. *Burrow,* 997 S.W.2d at 241. The *Burrow* court surveyed the factors for determining when forfeiture is appropriate across several fields. . . . In summary, 'relevant considerations include the gravity and timing of the violation, its wilfulness, its effect on the value of the [agent's] work for the client, any other threatened or actual harm to the client, and the adequacy of other remedies.' "

RESTATEMENT THIRD §§ 8.01–8.05

[See Statutory Supplement]

CHAPTER 2

A PRIMER ON ACCOUNTING AND FINANCE

SECTION 1. AN INTRODUCTION TO ACCOUNTING AND FINANCIAL STATEMENTS

The law of business associations is about enterprises that are organized for profit. Accordingly, issues concerning such matters as accounting, valuation, and portfolio theory often lurk behind the legal rules and the cases in this area, and sometimes take center stage. It would be impossible to fully develop these issues in a book like this, which is primarily devoted to explicitly legal materials. However, the materials in this chapter set out both the vocabulary concerning these issues and a basic understanding of the underlying methodologies and concepts that underlie the study of business organizations.

Lawrence A. Cunningham, Introductory Accounting, Financing and Auditing 31–32

(4th ed. 2004).

The Fundamental Equation

There is one governing law that enables accountants to prepare the financial statements from the underlying bookkeeping records in a form that reliably states the entity's financial condition at a point in time and its financial performance over a period of time. It is called the *fundamental equation* and is written as follows:

Assets = Liabilities + Owners' Equity . . .

Double–Entry Bookkeeping.

By definition, the fundamental equation is of course an equation. That means the left side of the equation must always equal the right side of the equation. In other words, the amounts on the left must balance with the amounts on the right. And here we can see the meaning of the term "balance sheet." The fundamental equation is simply the balance sheet in its most elementary form. The intuition should be obvious: the rights and claims an entity holds against others (its assets) must equal the rights and claims others hold against it (its creditors with respect to its liabilities and the owners as residual claimants with respect to the equity).

To keep the fundamental equation always in balance at every moment in time, accountants developed an ingenious system called double-entry bookkeeping. Here is another point of linguistic purity: the idea behind double-entry bookkeeping is that, to keep the fundamental equation in balance, there will be *two entries* for every transaction to be accounted for.

Debits and credits.

Double-entry bookkeeping is implemented by two mechanisms whose labels are not only of no use to us but whose very names have been the source of endless agonizing by students new to the art of the project. The terms are "*debits*" and "*credits*." Before your anxiety heightens, let us put out into the open what continues to be to many a secret. When used to describe accounting steps in double-entry bookkeeping . . . these terms have no other meaning except the following: **debit means the left-side entry** and **credit means right-side entry**. That is the secret. They have absolutely no other meaning. . . .

David R. Herwitz & Matthew J. Barrett, Accounting for Lawyers 3, 8–14, 31–35

4th ed 2006.

. . . THE BALANCE SHEETS

The object of bookkeeping is to make it as easy as possible for anyone who understands the language to get a clear and accurate summary of how well a business is doing. . . .

Suppose we want a financial picture of E. Tutt, who recently graduated from law school and has opened a law office. Certainly one important facet is how much she owns. Because we are really concerned with her business and not her personal affairs, we forget her car, her clothes, and other personal property, and we look to see what he has in his office:

(a) Office furniture

(b) Office equipment

(c) Stationery and supplies

(d) Library

(e) Cash in the bank [of $1,000]

A layperson would understand all of these to be understood what the accountant calls them: *assets.* . . .

[W]e need to assign some dollar amount to the asset. Because the price at which the property was bought is ordinarily much easier to ascertain and less subjective than the current fair market value of the property, accountants generally record assets at *historical cost.* . . .

If E. Tutt bought all her property out of her own funds and has not yet earned anything, we could simply add up the assets to find out how E. Tutt stands in her business. But if he has borrowed money from a bank to buy some of her assets or, perhaps more likely, has bought some on credit, E. Tutt's personal "stake" in the business would not be as large as if she had bought everything from his own funds. To give a true picture of his financial position, we would want to know where the money came from to buy the assets. Suppose we find that he acquired the assets as follows:

(a) Office furniture: bought on credit from Frank Co. for $400;

(b) Office equipment: bought on credit from Elmer Co. for $300;

(c) Stationery and supplies: bought from Stanley for $100 on a promissory note;

(d) Library: purchased for $200 cash, out of Tutt's original "stake" of $1,000; and

(e) $800 cash: balance of Tutt's original "stake" remaining.

We could then list, in parallel columns, the assets and their sources:

Assets		Sources	
(a) Office furniture	$ 400	Frank Co.	$ 400 (a)
(b) Office equipment	300	Elmer Co.	300 (b)
(c) Stationery and supplies	100	Stanley	100 (c)
(d) Library	200		
(e) Cash (balance remaining)	800	E. Tutt	1,000 (d, e)
	$1,800		$1,800

This parallel listing of assets and their sources is what accountants call a *balance sheet.* This listing may also be referred to as a *statement of financial position* or a *statement of financial condition.* As preliminary matters about the balance sheet, we should note two things. First, whatever the name, the totals of the two columns must always be equal. . . . Second, no matter how complicated a business or how long its history, the balance sheet shows, at one particular point in time, what assets the business owns and where the money came from to acquire those assets. Because the balance sheet reflects one instant in time, we can compare the balance sheet to a snapshot.

To give a somewhat clearer picture of how well off E. Tutt herself is, we can separate the sources of assets into two groups: "outside" sources—money that business owes to creditors; and "inside" sources—amounts that Tutt herself has invested in the business. . . .

The outside sources would also be understood by a layperson to be what the accountant calls them: liabilities. . . .

Because creditors claims enjoy priority in liquidation over "inside" claims, any liabilities reduce E Tutt's personal stake or equity in the business. Accountants refer to *equity* as the arithmetical amount that remains after a particular accounting entity subtracts its liabilities from its assets. In other words, if the entity sold its assets, and satisfied its liabilities, for the amounts shown on the balance sheet, we call the remainder equity because the owners could claim that residual amount. . . .

We might also rearrange the assets, listing them in the order in which they are likely to be used up. We might also separate the source of the assets between liabilities and equity. The result would be a somewhat more refined balance sheet that might look like this:

Assets		Liabilities & Proprietorship		
		Liabilities:		
(e) Cash	$ 800	Accounts Payable		
(c) Supplies	100	Frank Co.	$ 400	(a)
(a) Furniture	400	Elmer Co.	300	(b)
(b) Equipment	300	Notes Payable		
		Stanley	100	(c)
(d) Library	200	Proprietorship	1,000	(d, e)
	$1,800		$1,800	

Note that no change has been made except a change in presentation. The essential meaning is the same. But because clear disclosure is one of the accountant's main concerns, matters of presentation are important. . . .

. . . THE INCOME STATEMENT

The balance sheet shows the present status of the assets and their sources resulting from all transactions since the business was formed. It is drawn up at regular intervals which will vary with the needs of the business. The balance sheet, however, cannot tell a reader very much about the business' ability to earn a profit.

. . . The *income statement,* the second basic financial statement, shows the extent to which business activities have caused an accounting entity's equity, or net worth, to increase or decrease over some period of time. . . . [T]he fundamental distinction between the balance sheet and the income statement is that, while the balance sheet speaks as of a particular date, the income statement covers a period of time between successive balance sheet dates. . . .

Drawing up a simple income statement for E. Tutt, say for the month of June, may be the easiest way to start explaining that financial statement. Suppose that during the month he receives legal fees of $600 and $400.

(1) Professional Income	$600
(2) Professional Income	$400

. . .

To find his net income, we must subtract her expenses for the month from the month's revenues. . . .

Suppose that E. Tutt's operating expenses were as follows:

(3) Rent	$200
(4) Secretary	$230
(5) Telephone	$ 15
(6) Heat & Light	$ 5
(7) Miscellaneous	$ 5

In addition, further suppose that Tutt suffered a loss during the month when a thief broke into his office and stole $20 cash. This loss is treated as just another expense:

(8) Theft loss $ 20

There is no particular form required for an income statement, so long as it is a clear and fair statement of the information. An acceptable one might look like this:

E. Tutt, Esquire
Income Statement
For the month of June

(1 & 2)	Professional Income		$1,000
Less:	Expenses		
(3)	Rent	$200	
(4)	Secretary	230	
(5)	Telephone	15	
(6)	Heat & Light	5	
(7)	Miscellaneous	5	
(8)	Theft Loss	20	
	Total Expenses		475
	NET INCOME		$525

To see how the income statement fits into the balance sheet we might ask where Tutt's net income shows up on a balance sheet. In lay terms, Tutt's net income is an increase to her stake in the business, which we have been calling Proprietorship. Hence, if no other change in her stake occurs, the balance sheet figure for Proprietorship on June 30 should be $525 larger than on June 1.

NOTE ON THE LINK BETWEEN THE INCOME STATEMENT AND THE BALANCE SHEET

The connection between the income statement and the balance sheet can be easily demonstrated in the above Tutt Proprietorship example through the simplifying assumption that all the June transactions described above were in cash (or its equivalent, a check). Thus, the total receipts from clients ("Professional Income") is $1000 and total disbursements, i.e., "Total Expenses" recorded above are $475. Thus, there was a net increase in cash of $525. As seen above, this also is the amount of increase to be recorded in Tutt's Proprietorship account. Thus, Tutt's balance sheet at the end of the month would be:

Tutt Proprietorship
Balance Sheet
June 30, 2011

	Assets		Liabilities & Proprietorship	
			Liabilities:	
(e)	Cash	$1,325	Accounts Payable:	
(c)	Supplies	100	Frank Co.	$400
(a)	Furniture	400	Elmer Co.	300
(b)	Equipment	300	Notes Payable:	
			Stanley	100
(d)	Library	200	Proprietorship	1,525
		$2,325		$2,325

R. Hamilton, Fundamentals of Modern Business 154–55

1989.

. . . *[E]very transaction entered into by a business must be recorded in at least two ways if the balance sheet is to continue to balance.* This last point underlies the concept of that mysterious subject, *double entry bookkeeping*, and is the cornerstone on which modern accounting is built.

Assume that we have a new business, just starting out, in which the owner has invested $10,000 in cash. . . . The opening balance sheet will look like this:

Assets:		Liabilities	–0–
Cash	10,000	Owner's Equity	10,000

Now let us assume that the owner buys a used truck for $3,000 cash. The effect of this transaction is to reduce cash by $3,000 and create a new asset on the balance sheet:

Assets:		Liabilities	–0–
Cash	7,000	Owner's Equity	10,000
Used Truck	3,000		
	10,000		10,000

Voila! The balance sheet still balances. Let us assume next that the owner goes down to the bank and borrows an additional $1,000. This also has a dual effect: it increases cash by $1,000 (since the business is receiving the proceeds of the loan) and increases liabilities by $1,000 (since the business thereafter has to repay the loan). Yet another balance sheet can be created showing the additional effect of this second transaction:

Assets:		Liabilities	
Cash	8,000	Debt to Bank	1,000
Used Truck	3,000	Owner's Equity	10,000
	11,000		11,000

NOTE ON ACCRUAL ACCOUNTING AND THE CONVENTIONS OF ACCOUNTINGS

In the preceding example, Tutt appears to have earned a profit of $525, the amount by which cash receipts for June exceeded cash disbursements. Is there reason to believe this figure overstates the amount of Tutt's profits for the month? For example, consider the assets used in producing the $1000 revenues received from clients. Certainly some items in the Supplies account were used in the work performed for the clients. And is it not reasonable to allocate some of the cost of the furniture and equipment, and even the library's initial cost, to the various activities that produced Professional Income during operations in June? If these items were taken into account, Tutt's profit would be lower than $525. And, assume that during the month of June that Tutt performed significant work and even billed clients for that work, but had not been paid in June for the work. Should this be considered in determining her net gain for June? Similarly, what if on June 1 she acquired malpractice insurance policy for which the one-year premium is $2400 payable on July 1st? Should some portion of the policy be allocated to June? And, how should the premium that is due be reported on June 1st?

The Tutt Proprietorship illustrates the *cash basis* method of accounting—the most basic method for reporting business and financial transactions and is used predominantly by businesses that provide only services. Most business use the *accrual method* of accounting. Under this method, revenues are reported in the fiscal period in which they are earned and expenses are reported when they are incurred. The time when cash is received or paid is irrelevant to recording revenues and expenses. Instead the recognition of revenue is guided by the *realization principle* and the reporting of expenses is determined according to the *matching principle*. Each of these principles is briefly described below and in combination establish the analytical framework for determining when to report revenues and expenses.

Realization Principle. The realization principle generally prevents recognition of revenue until either the goods are shipped to their buyer or the services are rendered. There is the additional requirement that the transaction must be arm's length (e.g., there is no sale/recognition of revenue when a parent company transfers goods to its subsidiary). Under the accrual method the customer need not pay cash for revenue to be recognized by a seller, provided there is a reasonable expectation of payment. Thus, if Tutt were reporting under the accrual method and in June had billed a client for $650 of services, but had not received payment from that client, this amount would be included as part of Tutt's revenues. As a formal matter of accounting—recall the double-entry nature of accounting where the somewhat Newtonian principle applies whereby every action (debit) must be accompanied by an equal, albeit opposite, reaction (credit)—Tutt would record a credit to "Revenue" for the $650 billed services and a $650 debit, e.g., "Receivable from Client." The latter would appear on the balance sheet as an asset and the former on the income statement aggregated with other revenues for that fiscal period. To complete this illustration, when the client later pays the bill, Receivable from Client would be reduced (credited) by $650 and Cash would be increased (debited) by that amount.

Matching Principle. Accrual accounting seeks to "match" the revenues of a fiscal period with the expenses incurred in their production so as to provide a basis for determining whether operations were profitable. This objective is guided by the matching principle which holds that the cost of an item is recorded as an expense of the fiscal period in which the item contributed to general operations or to specific revenues. Thus, in the preceding illustration we saw that Tutt paid $200 for a library. Let's assume this was a two month subscription to Westlaw (no doubt an introductory "teaser rate"). We can see that this expense should not be allocated totally to June since it will likely contribute to work throughout the two-month subscription period. And, it is quite likely that from time-to-time Tutt will need to access the service as part of her work for clients. Thus, the $200 expenditure should, under the matching principle, be allocated to revenues that they contribute toward during this two month period. How then should this sum be allocated? One approach, of course, would be just maintain a detailed record of the Westlaw time consumed on behalf of each client and with the expiration of the subscription on July 31st assign the $200 cost proportionately among the billings for each client. But, if Tutt wishes to calculate profits monthly, this highly precise method would not work since on June 30th Tutt would not know the Westlaw search time that would occur in July. Thus, Tutt may opt for a simplifying assumption, namely that there will be approximately the same amount of search time each month so that the $200 pre paid expense for Westlaw would be divided equally between June and July, i.e., $100 of the $200 paid would be assigned as an expense of June's operations. This illustration demonstrates two important points that are natural outgrowths of the matching principle. First, assumptions, estimates and judgments play a role in the application of accounting principles to specific transactions. Second, assets that are recorded on the balance sheet are in fact costs waiting to be assigned to a future period. That is, the $200 "Library" account recorded on Tutt's balance sheet when the business was formed in fact is an expenditure waiting to be assigned to future periods and the assignment is guided by principle of matching that expenditure with the revenues it produced.

Cost Convention. A basic principle that underlies accounting is that items are recorded at their historical cost (as distinct from their replacement cost or fair market value). Cost essentially is what was paid for the item in an arm's length transaction. If cash was paid for the item, this amount determines the item's cost. If the item was acquired for non-cash consideration then the cost is the fair market value of that non-cash consideration paid for the item.

Many assets, however, experience decline in their fair market value due to wear and tear in their use in operations, obsolescence, or other forces. Thus, it is common to depreciate fixed assets like a building or machinery and similarly to amortize (reduce the amount recorded for the item) intellectual property rights such as patents, copyrights and licenses. Much like the illustration with Tutt's Westlaw subscription, there are a variety of methods for such depreciation or amortization. The simplest is the so-called straight-line method where the yearly charge for depreciation would be determined as follows:

$$\text{Annual Depreciation} = \frac{\text{Cost} - \text{Estimated Salvage Value}}{\text{Estimated Life in Years}}$$

Thus, if on January 1, a widget forging press was acquired for $20,000 and was estimated to have a useful life of 8 years at which time it could be sold for $4,000, the yearly straight-line depreciation would be $2,000.[1] After four years, therefore, the dollar amount of the forging press shown on the books (the "book value") would be $12,000 ($20,000 cost minus $8,000 accumulated depreciation for the four years), even though the fair market value of the press—the price the owner could receive for the press if it were sold in the current market—was, say, $25,000. Note in this example the estimates employed to determine the yearly depreciation. Because balance-sheet net worth is simply balance-sheet assets minus balance-sheet liabilities, actual net worth may be much higher or much lower than the figure for owner's equity recorded on the balance sheet. A final point about depreciation and amortization is that land is not depreciated. However, under the *convention of conservatism* any permanent impairment of the value of land, or for that matter any asset, is to be reflected by reducing on the balance sheet the amount recorded for that item to its newly determined fair value.

Manufacturing, wholesale and retail businesses have a special challenge in assigning cost to the materials and goods they hold in inventory which are ultimately sold or used in the production of goods that are then sold. To illustrate the challenge and the process for their determining the "cost of goods sold," assume the following for Sally's Widgets.

---

1. Another method is the so-called units of production method of depreciation. To illustrate this method, assume that in the above illustration that it was reasonable to believe that the press will be able to produce 100,000 widgets over its useful life (after which the press could be sold for a net salvage value of $4,000). If at the end of the first year of operation the press had been used to produce 15,000 units, the appropriate depreciation for that first year would be $2,400, determined as follows: cost-salvage value x units produce in year/estimated total units during press's useful life =[$20,000–$4,000] × 15,000 units/100,000 units = $2,400.

January 15	Initial purchase	300 widget units	$5/unit
June 22	purchase	500 widget units	$6/unit
October 31	purchase	200 widget units	$7/unit

At the end of the fiscal year, December 31st, Sally counted 400 widgets as still being in her inventory. What then is the cost of the 600 (300 + 500 + 200 – 400) widgets that were sold during the year?

One approach, the *average cost method*, is to determine their cost as the average cost which would be $5.90 per unit or $3,540 for the 600 units. Another would be to assume that the widgets were sold in the order in which they were acquired. Thus, of the 600 widgets sold, 300 were from the first order (300 @ $5) and 300 from the June order (300 @ $6), so that total cost of the 600 widgets sold would be $3,300. This is commonly referred to as the *FIFO method* (first-in, first-out). A third common method is to reason that, in an inflationary environment (notice the increasing price Sally has had to pay for widgets) a better reflection is to assume the last-in, first-out assumption (*LIFO method*) so that the cost of the 600 units is $3,800 (200 @ $7 plus 400 units @ $6).

NOTE ON ACCOUNTING AND AUDIT STANDARD SETTERS AND THE AUDIT OPINION

Accounting is commonly referred to as the "language of business." Accounting reports and financial information generally trace their meaning to the metrics by which accounting-derived items such as revenues, expenses, assets, and liabilities are not only defined but also are measured. These metrics are collectively referred to as *generally accepted accounting principles* (GAAP) for which in the Financial Accounting Standards Board (FASB) is the authoritative source in the U.S. private sector. Where there is not an express statement or interpretation by the FASB, then GAAP is also established by pronouncements of the American Institute of Certified Public Accountants as well as conventions and practices widely followed by accountants and companies. To assure greater independence in accounting standard setting, a major feature of the Sarbanes–Oxley Act of 2002 provided that henceforth the FASB, although not a governmental entity, is nonetheless independently funded from fees public companies that are collected by the SEC. Previously the FASB's funding largely depended on contributions from the accounting profession and there was a history of the accountants reflecting the wishes of their audit clients as a condition for on-going funding.

> . . . [F]inancial statements report on the firm's financial position and its recent performance. Financial statements also serve as a report card of the firm's managers. This poses a special problem for financial reporting because the officers of the firm in the first instance have operational control of the company's books and records. Because it is natural for any officer to desire a report that magnifies the officer's successes and minimizes any failings, there is an ever-present concern that the firm's financial statements may reflect the influence of the firm's managers over the content of

the financial statements. The first line of defense to this abuse is that the accounting metrics used in preparing the financial statements is objective, not subjective, principles and rules, thereby reducing the opportunity for manipulation of the financial statements by the managers. Thus, a critical feature of GAAP is a body of principles, rules, and conventions that are to be adhered to in preparing financial statements.

However, the mere existence of a "rule book" does not mean that managers will adhere to the rules. Their temptation to distort the financial statements continues, so that some further assurance that the rules are being adhered to is necessary. Thus, the second line of defense is the role of the outside auditor (a/k/a the certified public accountant). The SEC requires that financial statements filed with it be certified by an independent auditor; the auditor's certification attests that the auditor has reviewed the financial statements according to generally accepted auditing standards (GAAS) to assure that the financial statements conform to GAAP. The audit procedures that make up GAAS historically were established by a body within the American Institute of Certified Public Accountants (AICPA), but following the enactment of the Sarbanes–Oxley Act are now under the control of the Public Company Accounting Oversight Board, a nonprofit corporation funded by fees paid by reporting companies.

James D. Cox, Robert W. Hillman & Donald C. Langevoort, Securities Regulations: Cases and Materials 547 (6th ed. 2009). The PCAOB withstood constitutional attack on its existence in *Free Enterprise Fund v. Public Company Accounting Oversight Board*, ___ U.S. ___, 130 S.Ct. 3138, 177 L.Ed.2d 706 (2010).

SECTION 2. PRESENT VALUE: ITS UTILITY AND CALCULATION

A. TECHNIQUES OF DETERMINING PRESENT VALUE

Money is not valuable for its own sake, but for the amount of satisfaction (utility) one can derive from using it. Thus, the receipt of $1.00 today is valuable because it may be used to purchase goods, may be deposited in a savings account where it will earn interest, or used to acquire another investment. The receipt of $1.00 one year from now provides less satisfaction than if the amount were received today because the opportunities of spending, investing, or saving during this year will not be available. The loss of available alternatives for using the $1.00 during the year is called the *opportunity cost* of receiving the money in the future rather than today.

One type of opportunity cost is the interest that can be earned if the money were deposited in a bank account. As an example, assume that $1.00 is to be received one year from today and the prevailing interest rate is 5%. If $1.00 were deposited in a savings account for one year at 5% interest, it would grow to $1.05 at the end of the year. The opportunity cost, then, of receiving the $1.00 one year in the future rather than today is $.05, the interest foregone by waiting a year to receive the money.

An examination of Table 1 shows that $1.00 deposited in a savings account for one year experiences more growth with higher interest rates than with lower rates. Thus, $1.00 deposited for one year at 5% interest yields $1.05 at the year's end, 10% interest yields $1.10, and 20% interest yields $1.20. The amount received at year's end ($1.05, $1.10, $1.20) is called the *terminal value.*

Table 1. **Compound Interest: The Amount that $1 Will Yield at the End of a Prescribed Number of Years at a Stated Compound Interest**

End of Year	*4%*	*5%*	*6%*	*7%*	*8%*	*10%*	*12%*	*15%*	*20%*
1	$1.040	$ 1.050	$ 1.06	$ 1.070	$ 1.080	$ 1.100	1.120	$ 1.150	$ 1.200
2	1.082	1.103	1.124	1.145	1.166	1.210	1.254	1.322	1.440
3	1.125	1.158	1.191	1.225	1.260	1.331	1.405	1.521	1.728
4	1.170	1.216	1.263	1.311	1.360	1.464	1.574	1.749	2.074
5	1.217	1.276	1.338	1.403	1.469	1.611	1.762	2.011	2.488
6	1.265	1.340	1.419	1.501	1.587	1.772	1.974	2.313	2.986
7	1.316	1.407	1.504	1.606	1.714	1.949	2.211	2.660	3.583
8	1.369	1.478	1.594	1.718	1.851	2.144	2.476	3.059	4.300
9	1.423	1.551	1.690	1.838	1.999	2.358	2.773	3.518	5.160
10	1.480	1.629	1.791	1.967	2.159	2.594	3.106	4.046	6.192
11	1.540	1.710	1.890	2.105	2.332	2.853	3.479	4.652	7.430
12	1.601	1.796	2.012	2.252	2.518	3.138	3.896	5.350	8.916
13	1.665	1.886	2.133	2.410	2.720	3.452	4.363	6.153	10.699
14	1.732	1.980	2.261	2.579	2.937	3.797	4.887	7.076	12.839
15	1.801	2.079	2.397	2.759	3.172	4.177	5.474	8.137	15.407
16	1.873	2.183	2.540	2.952	3.426	4.595	6.130	9.358	18.488
17	1.948	2.292	2.692	3.159	3.700	5.054	6.866	10.761	22.186
18	2.026	2.407	2.854	3.380	3.996	5.560	7.690	12.375	26.623
19	2.107	2.527	3.026	3.617	4.316	6.116	8.613	14.232	31.948
20	2.191	2.653	3.207	3.870	4.661	6.727	9.646	16.367	38.338
25	2.666	3.386	4.292	5.427	6.848	10.835	17.000	32.919	95.396
30	3.243	4.322	5.744	7.612	10.063	17.449	29.960	66.212	237.376
40	4.801	7.040	10.286	14.974	21.725	45.259	93.051	267.862	1469.771
50	7.107	11.467	18.420	29.457	46.902	17.391	289.002	1083.652	9100.427

Money may be left in a savings account for more than one year, in which case the computation of the terminal value becomes more complex. When $1.00 is deposited into a savings account for one year, the terminal value may be determined by the simple equation $T = P (1 + r)$, where T is the terminal value, P the amount originally invested (generally called the *present value*), and r the annual rate of interest. When $1.00 remains in an account for more than one year, however, compound interest enters the picture.

The interest payable on a savings account is calculated at the end of every payment period. In this discussion, the length of a payment period will be assumed to be one year. As was illustrated in the prior example, $1.00 deposited for one year at 5% interest yields a terminal value of $1.05. If this amount is left in the account for a second year, the terminal value at the end of the second year is the terminal value at the end of the first year, $1.05, plus the interest earned on that amount during the second year. Represented mathematically, the equation is:

$$T = P\,(1 + r) + r[P(1 + r)]$$

$$T = 1(1 + .05\%) + .05[1(1 + .05)]$$

$$T = 1.05 + .05\,[1.05]$$

$$T = \$1.10 \text{ (rounded)}$$

The terminal value payable at the end of the second year involves compound interest because it includes interest on the interest paid in the first year. The existence of compound interest when money is deposited in an account for more than a few years causes the computation of terminal value to be rather cumbersome, if done as above where interest earned each year is determined and then summed with the principal amount.

Compound interest tables, such as Table–1, greatly simplify the process by providing a factor which when multiplied times the present value amount (e.g., the principal amount deposited) equals the terminal value at a stated rate of interest for a given period of time. Thus, for three years at 5% interest, the factor from Table–1 is 1.16; the terminal value of $1 invested at 5% interest for three years is, when rounded, is 1.16 ($1 × 1.158).

Potential investors are always faced with two broad choices: whether to put their money into savings or to invest. Investments are never assured to be profitable, and can sometimes even lose money. Savings, on the other hand, provide for a predetermined earnings rate (which is the interest rate) and involve very little risk. For investors choosing to put their money into savings, their *opportunity costs*, the cost of foregoing one thing for another, can be viewed as the opportunity to play the market as well as the pleasure of current consumption.

Consider an investor who wishes to receive $1.50 for every $1.00 he now owns. Assuming the investor is faced with the two distinct investment choices: choice A offering a terminal value of $1.50 at the end of seven years for each $1.00 invested and choice B offering a potential $1.50 at the end of one year for each $1.00 invested. Should the investor be impartial in his preference for one choice? The answer is no. A terminal value of $1.50 received in seven years is worth less than the same amount in one year because of the opportunity cost of waiting to receive the money. This cost of foregoing alternative uses of money is the reason why the real value (i.e., present value) of money received in the future is less than the actual amount which will be received. An investment's terminal value less the present value is called a *discount*. Expressed in terms of an annual percentage it is called the *discount rate*. As will be seen, the discount rate is the reciprocal of the interest rate.

For example, \$1.00 may be invested for one year at an interest rate of 5% to yield \$1.05. In discounting the value of this \$1.05 terminal value amount, a discount rate of 5% would be used. This leads to the formal definition of present value being the worth today of a terminal value to be received in the future, reduced by the discount rate. The equation for determining present value is simply a rearrangement of the terminal value equation. Whereas the terminal value equation was $T = P\ (1 + r)^n$, the present value equation is:

$$P = \frac{T}{(1 + r)^n},$$

where n is the number of years before the payment is received.

The present value of the just mentioned example is:

$$P = \frac{1.05}{(1 + 1.05)} = 1.00$$

This means that the present value of receiving \$1.05 in one year, when the discount rate is 5%, is \$1.00 because the investor demands a 5% return to compensate for his opportunity cost. The payment of \$1.05 in one year when the interest rate is 5% and the payment of \$1.00 today should provide equal satisfaction to rational investors; investors should therefore be neutral if given a choice between the two payments.

The reciprocal relationship between the discount rate and the interest rate is very important. The interest rate determines the growth of an amount deposited today into a larger terminal value in the future. The discount rate works in the opposite direction in determining the decrease of the worth of the terminal value to be received in the future in terms of today's present value. Present value may be thought of in two ways. It may be considered as the discounted present value of some greater terminal value, the difference between the present value and the terminal value being the opportunity cost. Thus from the prior examples, with a discount rate of .05, the opportunity cost of waiting one year to receive \$1.05 is \$.05. Present value may also be thought of as the amount of money which needs to be deposited today to grow into a future terminal value at a prevailing interest rate. Thus, a deposit of \$1.00 today into savings for one year at a 5% interest rate will grow into a terminal value of \$1.05.

The determination of present value of an amount to be received in the future is greatly simplified by the use of a present value table, such as in Table 2. Assume the question calls for determining the present value of \$50 to be received in 20 years, with the discount rate of 8%. To determine the present value using the equation

$$P = \frac{\$50}{(1 + 1.08)^{20}}$$

would entail a good deal of calculation time. Such calculations are already taken into account in present value tables, wherein the factor multiplied times the terminal value is simply selected by matching the desired discount rate with the prescribed time period. In the illustration the factor is .215. Therefore the present value of $50 to be received in 20 years assuming an 8% discount rate is $10.75, ($50 × .215).

Table-2. Present Value of $1 to be Received at the End of a Specified Future Year

End of Year	*4%*	*5%*	*6%*	*7%*	*8%*	*10%*	*12%*	*15%*	*20%*
1	$.962	$.952	$.943	$.935	$.926	$.909	$.893	$.870	$.833
2	.925	.907	.890	.873	.857	.826	.797	.756	.694
3	.889	.864	.839	.816	.794	.751	.712	.658	.579
4	.855	.823	.792	.763	.735	.683	.636	.572	.482
5	.822	.784	.747	.713	.681	.621	.567	.497	.402
6	.790	.746	.705	.666	.630	.565	.507	.432	.335
7	.760	.711	.665	.623	.584	.513	.452	.376	.279
8	.731	.677	.627	.582	.540	.467	.404	.327	.233
9	.703	.645	.592	.544	.500	.424	.361	.284	.194
10	.676	.614	.558	.508	.463	.386	.322	.247	.162
11	.650	.585	.527	.475	.429	.351	.287	.215	.135
12	.625	.557	.497	.444	.397	.319	.257	.187	.112
13	.601	.530	.469	.415	.368	.290	.229	.163	.094
14	.578	.505	.442	.388	.341	.263	.205	.141	.078
15	.555	.481	.417	.362	.315	.239	.183	.123	.065
16	.534	.458	.394	.339	.292	.218	.163	.107	.054
17	.513	.436	.371	.317	.270	.198	.146	.093	.045
18	.494	.416	.350	.296	.250	.180	.130	.081	.038
19	.475	.396	.331	.277	.232	.164	.116	.070	.031
20	.456	.377	.312	.258	.215	.149	.104	.061	.026
25	.375	.295	.233	.184	.146	.092	.059	.030	.011
30	.308	.231	.174	.131	.099	.057	.033	.015	.004
40	.253	.142	.097	.067	.046	.022	.011	.004	.0007
50	.141	.087	.054	.034	.021	.009	.003	.001	.0001

Thus far the discussion of present value has been limited to discounting the value of a single amount to be received at some future date. Present value can also be determined for a series of future payments. A stream of future payments is called an *annuity*, which implies that these future payments will be received annually. For example, assume that an investor is considering the purchase of an annuity contract that entitles its owner to receive $100 a year for five years. Given the investor's other investment alternatives, the investor's own aversion to risk, and the prevailing economic conditions, a discount rate of 6% is applicable to analyze the contract. The rational investor should pay no more than the contract's present value. Otherwise the investor will not be adequately compensated for the opportunity costs inherent with the investment. One approach to determining the contract's present value is to discount each of the five payments to be received using a factor selected from Table–2.

Payment to be received at end of

First year	\$100 × .943 =	\$ 94.30
Second Year	100 × .890 =	89.00
Third Year	100 × .839 =	83.90
Fourth Year	100 × .792 =	79.20
Fifth Year	100 × .747 =	74.70
Total		\$421.10

Given the investor's constraints, no more than \$421.10 should be paid for the annuity contract.

Table 3. **Present Value of Annuity of \$1 at End of Each Year**

End of Year	*4%*	*5%*	*6%*	*7%*	*8%*	*10%*	*12%*	*15%*	*20%*
1	\$ .962	\$ .952	\$ .943	\$ .935	\$ .926	\$ .909	\$ .893	\$ .870	\$ .833
2	1.886	1.859	1.833	1.808	1.783	1.736	1.690	1.626	1.528
3	2.775	2.723	2.673	2.624	2.577	2.487	2.402	2.283	2.107
4	3.630	3.546	3.465	3.387	3.312	3.170	3.037	2.855	2.589
5	4.452	4.330	4.212	4.100	3.993	3.791	3.605	3.352	2.991
6	5.242	5.076	4.917	4.767	4.623	4.355	4.111	3.785	3.326
7	6.002	5.786	5.582	5.389	5.206	4.868	4.564	4.160	3.605
8	6.733	6.463	6.210	5.971	5.747	5.335	4.968	4.487	3.837
9	7.435	7.108	6.802	6.515	6.257	5.759	5.328	4.772	4.031
10	8.111	7.722	7.360	7.024	6.710	6.145	5.650	5.019	4.193
11	8.761	8.306	7.887	7.499	7.139	6.495	5.938	5.234	4.327
12	9.385	8.863	8.384	7.943	7.536	6.814	6.194	5.421	4.439
13	9.986	9.394	8.853	8.358	7.904	7.103	6.424	5.583	4.533
14	10.563	9.899	9.295	8.745	8.244	7.367	6.628	5.725	4.611
15	11.118	10.380	9.712	9.108	8.560	7.606	6.811	5.847	4.676
16	11.652	10.838	10.106	9.447	8.851	7.824	6.974	5.954	4.730
17	12.166	11.274	10.477	9.763	9.122	8.022	7.120	6.047	4.775
18	12.659	11.690	10.828	10.059	9.372	8.201	7.250	6.128	4.812
19	13.134	12.085	11.158	10.336	9.604	8.365	7.366	6.198	4.844
20	13.590	12.462	11.470	10.594	9.818	8.514	7.469	6.259	4.870
25	15.622	14.094	12.783	11.654	10.675	9.077	7.843	6.464	4.948
30	17.292	15.373	13.765	12.409	11.258	9.427	8.055	6.566	4.979
40	19.793	17.159	15.046	13.332	11.925	9.779	8.244	6.642	4.997
50	21.482	18.256	15.762	13.801	12.234	9.915	8.304	6.661	4.9995

Table 3 can be used to determine the present value of an annuity paying a constant amount at the end of each year. A single factor is multiplied by the yearly annuity amount, so that the calculation need not be made for each year. The factor for a five-year annuity with an applicable discount rate of 6% is 4.212. Using Table 3 to determine the annuity's present value makes the computations much simpler,

a \$100 annuity each year × 4.212 = \$421.20 present value.

The difference between the two methods of calculating the annuity contract's present value is due to rounding the present value factors in the tables to their nearest thousandth.

The present value of an annuity increases when the duration of annuity payments lengthen. The increase in present value, however, grows at a decreasing rate. For example, consider an annuity paying $1 a year when the discount rate is 5%. If the annuity were to last 10 years, it would have a present value of $7.72; for 20 years, it would have a present value of $12.46; for 40 years a present value of $17.16; and for 50 years the annuity has a present value of $18.26. As the length of annuity duration gets longer, the amount that present value is increased by the expanded number of payments gets smaller. For the 50–year annuity, then, over two-thirds of the present value of the annuity was realized in the first 20 years of payment, and the opportunity cost of waiting 50 years to receive the $50 total exceeds the present value of the annuity, (present value is $18.26 while the opportunity cost is $31.74). The present value of the first 10 years of the annuity is $7.72 while the present value for the last 10 years is only $1.10.

Present value is very small for amounts of money to be received far into the future because of the great opportunity cost of not being able to use the money until it is received. The present value becomes so small, in fact, that a point is reached where increased annuity duration ceases to increase present value. Consider an annuity which paid $1.00 every year forever, at a prevailing interest rate of 5%, (an infinite annuity is called a *perpetuity*). The present value of this perpetuity is $20.00. So, while an annuity lasting for 50 years has a present value of $18.26, a perpetuity has a present value of only $20.00. The present value of receiving $1.00 payments 50 years into the future, forever, is only $1.74.

PROBLEMS

1. Textron bonds bear interest at the rate of 10% per $1000 bond. Their present market price is $1050. The bonds are to be retired in eight years. The bond owner is, therefore, entitled to receive annually $100 for eight years as well as $1000 upon the bond's maturity. Can an investor applying an 8% discount rate earn an extraordinary return by purchasing the bond at its current market price?

2. In the probate of Aunt Harriet's estate, it is necessary to determine the worth of a remainder interest left to charity. Her will provides that her spendthrift son should enjoy a life estate in certain oil leases and upon his death the property is to be conveyed in fee simple to Planned Parenthood, Inc. The leases generate a yearly return of $30,000 and are expected to be productive for another 40 years. The son has a life expectancy of 10 years. Assume a discount rate of 12%. What is the value of the charitable gift?

B. STOCK VALUATION MODEL

Present value tables such as those above are used when determining the present value of a single payment to be received at a stated time in the future, or a series of payments to be received at a stated time in the future, or a series of payments to be received at different future dates. Occasionally it is necessary to determine the present value of an infinite series of payments. For example, consider the problem of a wealthy alumnus who wishes to donate a new academic building to her alma mater. The college is more than willing to accept the donation, provided funds are also donated to endow the overhead expenses of the building's operation, such as cleaning, maintenance, and utility expenses. After protracted negotiations, all parties agree that the donor will establish an "overhead trust fund" with a yearly income of not less than $250,000 to be earned in perpetuity. The college's experience has been that it is able to earn 5% on all endowments.

The determination of the present value of an annuity to be received in perpetuity, such as that contemplated for the "overhead trust fund," is identical to asking how much must be deposited in a savings account paying a fixed rate of interest if a precise yearly income is desired which income will be withdrawn. The basic formula for yearly interest is:

$$i = p \times r$$

where i = annual amount of interest income

p = amount in savings account

r = annual rate of interest

Since both i and r are known in the case of the "overhead trust fund," the equation is changed to solve for p.

$$p = \frac{i}{r}$$

The exact amount to be placed in the "overhead trust fund" under the above facts is determined as follows:

$$p = \frac{i}{r} = \frac{\$250{,}000}{5\%} = \$5{,}000{,}000$$

The donor will therefore place $5,000,000 in trust which is expected to yield income at the rate of 5%, thereby yielding in perpetuity $250,000 annually to meet the various expenses of the academic building.

The method for determining the present value of a share of stock is analogous to the procedure followed above to determine the present value of a trust's income to be received in perpetuity. The classic model for valuing equity and the one which is most popular with individual investors, partly because of its relative simplicity, is the *capitalization of earnings* approach. A stock's present value is determined by first estimating the average yearly earnings per share. The average annual earnings per share is generally based upon an estimate of the next five to ten years. Second, the estimated earnings per share are capitalized at an appropriate capitalization rate. More generally, investors apply the expected earnings to a "multiple" which simply is the reciprocal of the capitalization rate, being determined by dividing the capitalization rate for the stock into the number 1. A capitalization rate of 10% is therefore equivalent to a multiple of 10; a capitalization rate of 20% is equivalent to a multiple of 5; and a capitalization rate of 33⅓% is equivalent to a multiple of 3. If the future average earnings per share of a stock were estimated to be $3 and the stock were of a risk category meriting a 10% capitalization rate, its present value would be estimated to be $30 ($3 × 10). The capitalization of earnings per share by the appropriate multiple is indistinguishable in result from dividing the estimated earnings per share by the appropriate discount rate:

$$\frac{\text{EPS}}{\text{Discount Rate}} = \text{EPS} \times \frac{1}{\text{Discount Rate}}$$

The advantages of the capitalization of earnings approach is the simplicity of its calculations. But it's very simplicity hides a multitude of significant interactions and relationships which are important determinants of a stock's present value. Undue emphasis on estimating earnings per share without considering the effects higher earnings may have on the discount rate undercuts the reliability of the calculation.

As seen earlier, the discount or capitalization rate applied by the individual investor is dependent upon the investor's own unique assessment of the opportunity costs posed by the investment. An important part of that assessment is the relative uncertainty, i.e., risk, associated with the investment under consideration. The following excerpt is directed toward defining important facets of risk as well as an investment strategy which may be followed to reduce risk.

SECTION 3. WHAT IS RISK AND DIVERSIFICATION?

W. Klein & J. Coffee, Business Organization and Finance 242–44

11th ed. 2010.

A. EXPECTED RETURN

Expected return is a measure of return that uses rudimentary concepts of probability to take account of risk or uncertainty as to outcome. Technically, expected return is the weighted average (or, if you prefer, arithmetic mean) of all possible outcomes. (The symbol commonly used to denote expected return is *X*.)

To illustrate, suppose that you bet $1 on the flip of a coin. If you win, you will have $2, and if you lose, nothing. The expected monetary value of that "investment" is $1, computed as follows:

Probability	Return	Value
.5	$2	$1
.5	0	0
1.0		$1

Note that here the expected return ignores the amount of the initial investment and thus tells us nothing about profitability. When we are concerned with profit we can use the concept of *expected rate of return,* which is likely to be expressed on an annual basis. Sometimes the term "expected return" is used to refer to rate of return. The meaning should be evident from the context.

Suppose that you buy 100 shares of stock of a corporation that does not pay dividends currently; that you pay $10 per share or $1,000 total; and that you expect to sell at the end of one year. Assume further that your estimate of the prospective sale prices and their probabilities is revealed in the first two columns below, with the corresponding expected return revealed by the third column:

Probability	Sale Price (return)	Value
.20	$ 900	$ 180
.50	1,000	500
.30	1,500	450
1.00		$1,130

The expected return calculation shows that in a statistical or probabilistic sense your investment is expected to yield $1,130, which is the expected return. The expected rate of return is 13 percent ($130 expected end-of-year gain on an investment of $1,000).

Where do these figures come from and how solid are they? The answer to that depends on facts that have not been developed. It is sufficient for our purposes to observe that people do, consciously or unconsciously, make calculations of this sort. Their information may be faulty. They may think in terms of a continuum of probabilities and outcomes or in terms of only two outcomes. The process may to some considerable extent be irrational or nonrational. Still, we need a term to describe the outcome of the process of considering and weighing prospects of various investment possibilities. "Expected return" is such a term.

B. RISK AND UNCERTAINTY . . .

. . . In much of the professional literature of financial analysis, "risk" refers to the degree of dispersion or variation of possible outcomes. To illustrate, assume that you are confronted with two possible investments whose outcomes, probabilities, and expected returns are as follows:

INVESTMENT A

Probability	Outcome (return)	Value
.1	$ 900	$ 90
.8	1,000	800
.1	1,100	110
1.0		$1,000

INVESTMENT B

Probability	Outcome (return)	Value
.3	$ 0	$ 0
.4	1,000	400
.3	2,000	600
1.0		$1,000

The expected return of the two investments is the same but the risk associated with Investment B is much greater than that associated with Investment A. The range or dispersion of possible outcomes for B is greater. It is a potentially more volatile investment. For each investment the expected return or mean (weighted average) (*X*) is $1,000. For A, however, the combined chance of a return other than $1,000 is only 20 percent, and the difference between the expected return and extreme outcomes is only $100. For B, on the other hand, the combined chance of a return other than $1,000 is 60 percent and the difference between the expected return and extreme outcomes is $1,000. It can be seen, then, that the concept of volatility, or dispersion, or risk refers to a combination of the probability of deviation from the expected return and the amount of deviation—that is, to the degree of likelihood of receiving more or less than $1,000, and how much more or less. (Note that in the illustrations used above, the distributions of outcomes around the expected return are symmetrical—that is, there is an equal probability of deviation to each side of the expected return and the amount of deviation is the same to each side. This symmetrical kind of distribution has been used only for the sake of simplicity. It is not a necessary feature of the real world or of the analytic model, though it is commonly assumed to be a characteristic of the risks associated with investments in publicly traded common stocks.)

There are several statistical terms that are used to describe relative degrees of volatility (terms such as variance, standard deviation, and coefficient of variation) but we need not be concerned with their definition; they are simply measures of the degree of potential variation of possible outcomes. One investment is said to be more risky than another if the dispersion of potential outcomes is greater. We will refer to this concept of risk as *volatility risk* (recoiling only slightly at the now obvious redundancy of that phrase), though the term more commonly used by financial experts is *variance.*

Some economists have drawn a distinction between risk and uncertainty. "Risk" is then used to refer to variation depending purely on chance (e.g., the outcome of the flip of a coin) or, more broadly, to measurements as to which there is a large body of data or experience so that the probable outcomes can be estimated in a purely mechanical way. "Uncertainty," by contrast, refers to estimates made in situations where there is so little experience that the process of estimation is highly intuitive. It should be apparent from a moment's reflection that the distinction between risk and uncertainty is a fuzzy one and that the two concepts refer to ends of a spectrum. . . .

NOTE ON JOY v. NORTH

In Joy v. North, 692 F.2d 880 (2d Cir. 1982), cert. denied, Citytrust v. Joy, 460 U.S. 1051, 103 S.Ct. 1498, 75 L.Ed.2d 930 (1983), the court, in discussing the duty of care, said:

> Consider the choice between two investments in an example adapted from Klein, Business Organization and Finance 147–49 (1980):
>
> **INVESTMENT A**
>
> | Estimated Probability of Outcome | Outcome Profit or Loss | Value |
> |---|---|---|
> | .4 | +15 | 6.0 |
> | .4 | + 1 | .4 |
> | .2 | −13 | −2.6 |
> | 1.0 | | 3.8 |
>
> **INVESTMENT B**
>
> | Estimated Probability of Outcome | Outcome Profit or Loss | Value |
> |---|---|---|
> | .4 | +6 | 2.4 |
> | .4 | +2 | .8 |
> | .2 | +1 | .2 |
> | 1.0 | | 3.4 |
>
> Although A is clearly "worth" more than B, it is riskier because it is more volatile. Diversification lessens the volatility by allowing investors to invest in 20 or 200 A's which will tend to guarantee a total result near the value. Shareholders are thus better off with the various firms selecting A over B, although after the fact they will complain in each case of the 2.6 loss. If the courts did not abide by the business judgment rule, they might well penalize the choice of A in each such case and thereby unknowingly injure shareholders generally by creating incentives for management always to choose B.

Howell E. Jackson, Louis Kaplow, Steven M. Shavell, W. Kip Viscusi & David Cope, Analytical Methods for Lawyers 250—258

(2d ed. 2011).

B. Risk and Return . . .

An important goal of financial analysis has been to document the risk-return characteristics of different kinds of financial assets—essentially trying to develop more realistic information about actual dispersions in economic returns that financial assets have achieved in the past. What empirical investigation of financial markets has discovered is that there is a strong and consistent relationship between the return on various classes of assets and the variation in the return (a.k.a. riskiness) of those assets. Government debt tends to have lower returns and lower risk (that is, variations in returns) than does corporate debt. Corporate debt, in turn, has lower returns and lower risk than corporate stock. And the stocks of larger, established corporations have lower returns and lower risk than the stocks of smaller, start-up firms. At least within the context of the U.S. capital markets in the last century, a wealth of empirical data supports these relationships. Figure 5–4, which is drawn from data collected by Ibbotson Associates for the 1926–2009 period, summarizes the kind of analysis that financial economists have used to demonstrate the risk-return trade-off.

The first column of Figure 5–4 reports the average annual returns on various classes of financial assets during the 83 years between 1926 and 2009. As suggested above, stocks show the highest average returns, with large company stocks reporting average annual returns of 11.8% and small-company stocks showing an average annual return of 16.6%. The average returns are lower for long-term corporate bonds (6.2%), long-term government bonds (5.8%), intermediate-term government bonds (5.5%), and the U.S. Treasury bills (3.7%), which represent short-term government obligations.[12]

---

12. The last row in Figure 5–4 reports the average level of inflation in the United States during the 83 year period. This is an important number to bear in mind. The average rates of return for the other asset classes are reported in what's known as "nominal" terms, which includes both a "real" rate of return plus inflation. If a stock goes up in value by 10% in a year but inflation is 2%, then the real rate of return on the stock is approximately 8%. Although we tend to experience financial returns in nominal terms ("My stock portfolio went up twenty five percent last year!"), it is often more appropriate to focus on the real rate of return: an asset's expected rate of nominal return minus the expected rate of inflation. . . .

Figure 5-4
Historical Performance of U.S. Financial Assets: 1926-2009

Asset Class	Average Annual Returns	Risk premium (relative to U.S. Treasury bills)	Standard Deviation of Annual Returns	Distribution of Annual Returns
Large-company stocks	11.8 %	8.1 %	20.5 %	
Small-company stocks	16.6 %	12.9 %	32.8 %	
Long-term corporate bonds	6.2 %	2.5 %	8.3 %	
Long-term government bonds	5.8 %	2.1 %	9.6 %	
Intermediate-term government bonds	5.5 %	1.8 %	5.7 %	
U.S. Treasury bills	3.7 %		3.1 %	
Inflation	3.1 %		4.2 %	-90 0 90

Modified from *Stocks, Bonds, Bills and Inflation: 2009 Yearbook* (Chicago: Ibbotson Associates, 2010).

U.S. Treasury bills represent an important benchmark in financial analysis, because they are considered to be a risk-free form of investment. Other financial assets are sometimes described in terms of the amount by which their returns exceed a risk-free rate of return. The second column in Figure 5–4, denominated risk premium, shows how much the average annual return on each asset class exceeded the average return on U.S. Treasury bills during the 1926–2009 period.

The next two columns of Figure 5–4 offer two different perspectives on the financial risk—that is, variation in return—associated with each asset class. On the far right is a histogram plotting the distribution of annual returns for the asset class during the 83 year period of analysis. Notice that the returns on stocks are much more spread out than the returns on other asset classes, and that there have been a reasonably large number of years in which returns on stocks were negative. The column directly to the left of the histograms—"Standard Deviation of Average Annual Returns"—is a summary statistic that measures variation in annual returns. . . . [T]he higher an asset class's average annual returns, the higher the variation in its annual returns. This fact is consistent with a basic premise of finance: that risk and return are positively correlated. The greater the return on an asset class, the greater the risk. . . .

C. The Value of Diversification

The value of diversification is another lesson from financial theory that lawyers should understand. This subject was first explored in Harry Markowitz, *Portfolio Selection* (1959). In essence, diversification offers investors a way of reducing the risk associated with particular investments without sacrificing return.

At root, the insight underlying diversification is that each individual investment has its own unique risks. Since these risks are unique, investors can offset the downside of some investments with the upside of other investments. This point can be illustrated if you think of the risks facing Suntan Lotion Co., a company that sells only suntan lotion, as compared with the risks facing Umbrellas Inc., a firm that manufactures only umbrellas. Sunny years are good for the former and bad for the latter, whereas rainy years are bad for the former and good for the latter.

Figure 5-5
Profitability of Two Hypothetical Firms

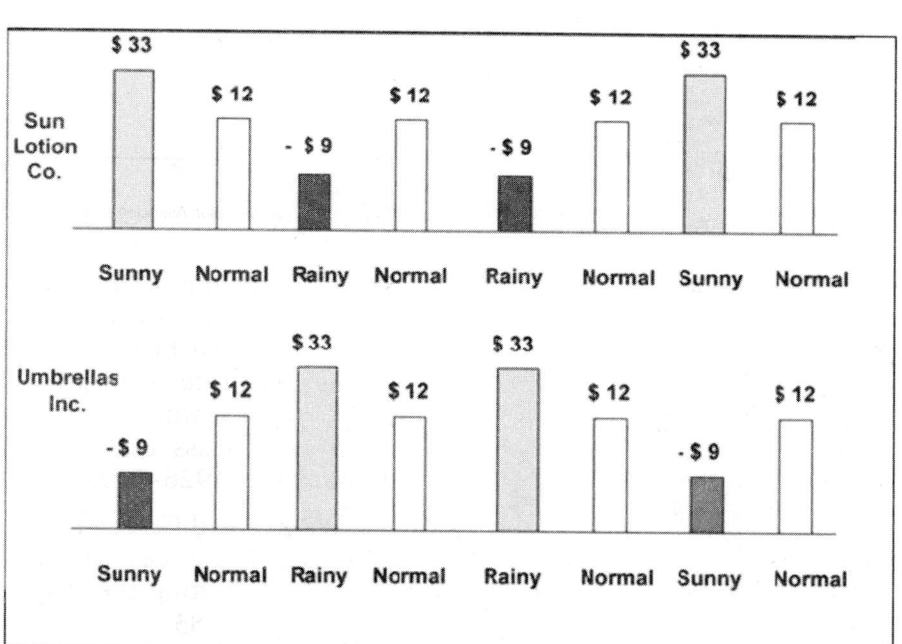

Normal weather means normal profitability for both firms. Figure 5–5 illustrates the hypothetical profits and losses that these two firms would earn across a series of years. When Suntan Lotion Co. does well, Umbrellas Inc. does poorly and vice versa.

An investment solely in either Suntan Co. or Umbrellas Inc. will have a considerable amount of "weather" risk. For each firm, profits will vary from a $33 profit in good years to a $9 loss in bad years with an average $12 profit when the weather is normal. But imagine what would happen if you divided your investment evenly between the two firms—that is, if you diversified your investment across both firms. A portfolio divided evenly between the two investments will have no weather risk. In years with sunny weather, the extra profitability of Suntan Co. would exactly offset the losses on Umbrellas Inc. In years with rainy weather, the net effect would be the same but work in the other direction. With equal investments in both firms, you would obtain a consistent return in all years. In other words, you would have eliminated the expected variation in your return (a.k.a. risk).

Following up on the line of research inspired by Markowitz's early writings, financial analysts now tend to distinguish between diversifiable risk—that is, expected variations in return that can be eliminated through diversification—and nondiversifiable risk. The latter category of risks—nondiversifiable risk—is also sometimes called market risk or systematic risk. As these alternative formulations suggest, some financial risks are related to general market conditions or fluctuations in the larger economic system. Because variations in returns from these broader forces affect all investments (research suggests), these market risks cannot be eliminated through diversification.

Figure 5-6
Gains from Diversification

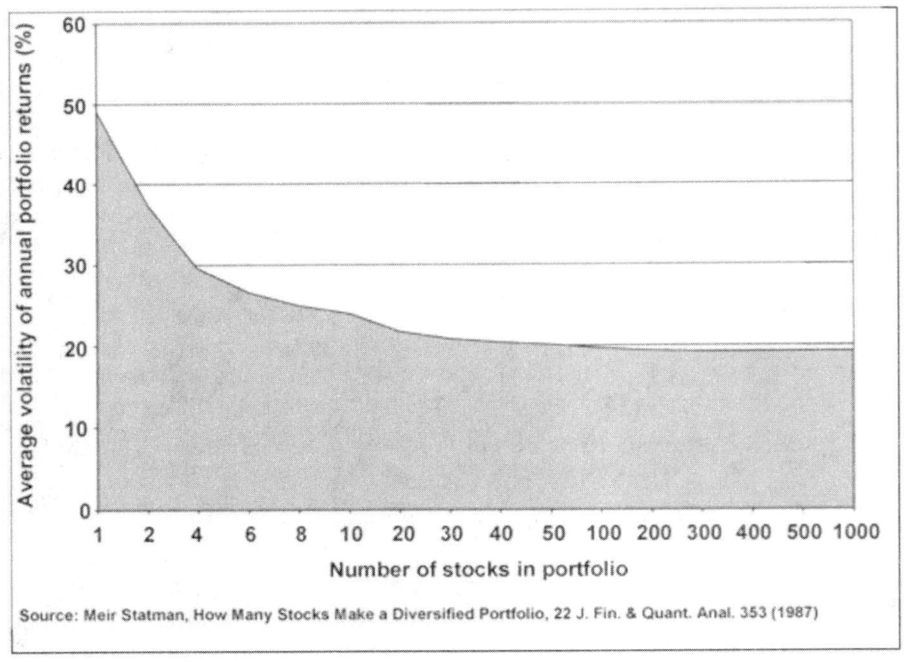

Source: Meir Statman, How Many Stocks Make a Diversified Portfolio, 22 J. Fin. & Quant. Anal. 353 (1987)

Again, lots of empirical evidence underlies portfolio theory, most of which is beyond the scope of this introductory coverage. To give readers a taste of the literature, we include Figure 5–6, which summarizes the variation in return of different-sized portfolios of U.S. common stocks, as calculated in a study published in 1987. As this figure indicates, if your portfolio consisted of just 1 stock—that is, had no diversification—then the average annual variation in your return would be nearly 50%. If your portfolio were evenly divided between just 2 securities, the average variation of return for such a portfolio would decline to 37%, and with a diversified portfolio of 10 securities, the expected variation would come down to 23%. Following the curve down to a diversified portfolio of 30 securities, one finds expected variation would decline to under 21%, which is fairly close to the levels of expected variation in fully diversified portfolios. (With 1,000 securities, expected variation declines only a little bit further to 19.21%.) For this reason, money managers are often satisfied that they have achieved most of the gains from diversification if they divide their portfolios among at least 30 different investments. . . .

NOTE ON THE CAPITAL ASSET PRICING MODEL, SYSTEMIC RISK, AND ESTIMATING RETURNS

An extension of portfolio theory is the *capital asset pricing model*, which, with the aid of several important assumptions,[2] predicts the relationship between risk and return for all risky investment opportunities. The model holds that the relationship between risk and return is linear so that the expected return increases proportionately with each unit that risk is increased or the expected return decreases proportionately with each unit that risk is decreased. Under the capital asset pricing model, the expected return for every risky investment is the sum of the pure (risk-free) rate of interest and the premium for incurring risk, the latter reflecting the risk of the investment relative to the market for all risky investments. The premium for risk is approximated through the use of the investment's beta which is derived from observing over time the correlation between an individual security's return and that of a broadly based portfolio of securities, such as the Standard and Poors Index of 500 Industrial firms.

The capital asset pricing model is as follows:

$$E_{it} = R_t + B_i (M_t - R_t)$$

Where E_{it} = *expected return for security* i *in time period* t,

R_t = *risk-free rate of interest in time period* t,

B_i = *beta for security* i,

M_t = *return for the market in time period* t.

The capital asset pricing model assumes that investors maintain efficient portfolios so that no part of a stock's expected return is due to unsystematic risk, i.e., firm specific information. Accordingly, the capital asset pricing model holds that the individual security's beta becomes the *exclusive* measure of risk.

---

2. *Assumptions of the Capital Asset Pricing Model.* The capital asset pricing model is premised upon several well-recognized assumptions: the market for capital assets is composed of risk-averse investors; all investors have the same time horizons regarding the holding period for their investment choices; capital markets are perfect because they do not involve transaction costs or taxes, information is costless, borrowing and lending rates are equal to each other and for all investors; the same investment opportunities are available to all investors; and all investors have homogeneous expectations regarding the risk and return of available investments. Eugene Fama, Risk, Return, and and Equilibrium: Some Clarifying Comments, 23 J. of Fin. 29 (1968).

To illustrate the application of the capital asset pricing model, assume stock *i* has a beta of 1.2 and the risk free rate is 8%. During the year, the return for the market was 15%. What would be the expected return for stock *i* under the capital asset pricing model? The model would yield an unexpected return of 16.4% using the above data,

$$E_{it} = 8\% + 1.2(15\% - 8\%) = 16.4\%$$

Just as the return for the market may be observed and measured, so may the return actually earned by the individual stock, during that same time period. That is, the market's return can only be measured as of the end of the stated time period at which point it is also possible to determine the individual's stock's return. Assume in the above illustration that stock *i's* price at the beginning of the year was $30 per share and at the end of the year $35. A dividend of $1 per share was paid during the year. Therefore, it is possible to measure the actual return, AR_{it}, *for stock* i *during the year.*

$$AR_{it} = \frac{(\text{Price at end of year} - \text{Price at beginning of year}) + \text{dividends}}{\text{Price at beginning of year}}$$

$$AR_{it} = \frac{(\$35 - 30) + \$1}{30}$$

$$AR_{it} = 20\%$$

Policymakers, academics and captains of industry are interested in measuring the impact of a range of different events on investor behavior. A new development assumes economic significance when it influences investors in their decisions, that is, if it causes investors to alter their assessment of the risk-return relationship posted by an individual security. If an event has such an effect, the event is deemed to have *information content*. For example, it may be hypothesized that investors view as good news a reported sale of one of the firm's plants at a gain, and accordingly will purchase that firm's stock at a higher price than if there were no report of the plant being sold. If this hypothesis is true, one of the many policy implications is that there should be adequate, timely disclosure of such information.

One means of documenting such investor reaction would be to examine the change in the stock's return associated with announcement of the sale. Merely looking at changes in the stock's market price over the period of time surrounding announcement of the sale is not completely satisfactory because changes in a stock's price may be attributable to market-wide events. It is on this point that the capital asset pricing model has assumed great importance in research by providing a methodology for observing how investors respond to different kinds of announcements and events.

As has been seen, a stock's return responds to events which affect the entire economy, whereas accounting information bearing on the economic performance or financial position of the particular company is firm specific. Therefore, to observe the impact, for example, of accounting information upon investors, it is necessary to eliminate from an individual stock's return the effects due to market-wide events. This is the function served by the capital asset pricing model. It offers a reliable basis, if employed with care, to isolate changes in a stock's return associated with firm specific information, such as release of accounting information about a business' operations.

The capital asset pricing model, which assumes that investors hold efficient portfolios, yields a return which would be expected if the only risk were systematic risk. In the above illustration, the expected return for stock *i*, if there were no contribution to its return due to unsystematic risk, was 16.4%. The observed actual return, however, was 20%. The difference between a stock's actual return and that predicted by the capital asset pricing model may well be attributed to the fact that any model offers merely an approximate rather than a precise figure. But if the actual return differs from that expected by a statistically significant amount, some part of the variance can be attributed to firm specific information.

Assuming in the above illustration that the capital asset model captured perfectly the return attributable to market-wide events, it would mean that a return of 3.6% is associated with firm specific information (e.g., the announcement of the sale of a plant). The difference between a stock's actual return and that expected, using the capital asset pricing model, is generally called the ***residual***. If during the year that stock *i* experienced a 20% actual return the only identifiable firm specific event were, for example, the sale of one of the company's plants for a gain, it is possible to attribute the residual return (actual less expected return) to the report of the plant's sale.

A standard methodology used by empiricists to examine the effects of using different accounting techniques and methods on investor behavior is to identify companies which have all engaged in the same type of accounting practice, for example, companies reporting the sale of a plant at a gain. The returns for the common stocks of this group are first determined on an individual basis and then combined into a return for all companies covering the period under observation. As a result of the combination, the effects of firm specific information attributable to events other than the one examined are eliminated. This occurs because across companies, the firm specific events are random. Therefore, the positive effects of some are offset by the negative effects of others. As a consequence, only the variable to be studied, e.g., the report of a sale of a plant at a gain, is isolated.

The returns of the group of firms are observed for a number of days or weeks before and after the release of the accounting information being studied, e.g., annual reports announcing a sale of a plant. The effects of market-wide events on their returns are removed through the capital asset pricing model, leaving only the return associated with the isolated firm specific events. Examination of the residuals suggests whether investors reacted positively or negatively to the accounting information, or manifested no reaction.

SECTION 4. MARKET EFFICIENCY: THE HYPOTHESIS AND QUALIFICATIONS

Richard A. Brealey, Stewart C. Myers & Franklin Allen, Principles of Corporate Finance 314, 317–318, 321, 324–328, & 329–333

Tenth ed., 2011.

WHAT IS AN EFFICIENT MARKET?

A Startling Discovery: Price Changes Are Random

As is so often the case with important ideas, the concept of efficient capital markets stemmed from a chance discovery. In 1953 Maurice Kendall, a British statistician, presented a controversial paper to the Royal Statistical Society on the behavior of stock and commodity prices. Kendall had expected to find regular price cycles, but to his surprise they did not seem to exist. Each series appeared to be "a 'wandering' one, almost as if once a week the Demon of Chance drew a random number . . . and added it to the current price to determine the next week's price." In other words, the prices of stocks and commodities seemed to follow a random walk. . . .

When Maurice Kendall suggested that stock prices follow a random walk, he was implying that the price changes are independent of one another . . .

Three Forms of Market Efficiency

You should see . . . why prices in competitive markets must follow a random walk. If past price changes could be used to predict future price changes, investors could make easy profits. But in competitive markets easy profits don't last. As investors try to take advantage of the information in past prices, prices adjust immediately until the superior profits from studying past price movements disappear. As a result, all the information in past prices will be reflected in today's stock price, not tomorrow's. Patterns in prices will no longer exist and price changes in one period will be independent of changes in the next. In other words, the share price will follow a random walk.

In competitive markets today's stock price must already reflect the information in past prices. But why stop there? If markets are competitive, shouldn't today's stock price reflect *all* the information that is available to investors? If so, securities will be fairly priced and security returns will be unpredictable. No one earns consistently superior returns in such a market. Collecting more information won't help, because all available information is already impounded in today's stock prices.

Economists define three levels of market efficiency, which are distinguished by the degree of information reflected in security prices. In the first level, prices reflect the information contained in the record of past prices. This is called *weak market efficiency.* If markets are efficient in the weak sense, then it is impossible to make consistently superior profits by studying past returns. Prices will follow a random walk.

The second level of efficiency requires that prices reflect not just past prices but all other public information, for example, from the Internet or the financial press. This is known as *semistrong market efficiency.* If markets are semistrong efficient, then prices will adjust immediately to public information such as the announcement of the last quarter's earnings, a new issue of stock, or a proposal to merge two companies.

With *strong-market efficiency,* prices reflect *all* the information that can be acquired by painstaking analysis of the company and the economy. In such a market we would observe lucky and unlucky investors, but we wouldn't find any superior investment managers who can consistently beat the market. . . .

The Evidence Against Market Efficiency . . .

Almost without exception, early researchers concluded that the efficient-market hypothesis was a remarkably good description of reality. So powerful was the evidence that any dissenting research was regarded with suspicion. But eventually the readers of finance journals grew weary of hearing the same message. The interesting articles became those that turned up some puzzle. Soon the journals were packed with evidence of anomalies that investors have apparently failed to exploit. . . .

Bubbles and Market Efficiency

. . . Toward the end of the twentieth century investors in technology stocks saw a remarkable run-up in the value of their holdings. The Nasdaq Composite Index, which has a heavy weighting in high-tech stocks, rose 580 percent from the start of 1995 to its high in March 2000. Then even more rapidly than it began, the boom ended, and by October 2002 the Nasdaq index had fallen 78% from its peak.

Some of the largest gains and losses were experienced by dot.com stocks. For example, Yahoo! shares, which began trading in April 1996, appreciated by 1,400% in just four years. In these heady days some companies found that they could booster their stock price simply by adding "dot.com" to the company name. . . .

Behavioral Finance

Why might prices depart from fundamental value? Some believe that the answer lies in behavioral psychology. People are not 100% rational 100% of the time. This shows up in investors' attitudes to risk and the way they assess probabilities.

1. *Attitudes toward Risk.* Psychologists have observed that, when making risky decisions, people are particularly loath to incur losses. It seems that investors do not focus solely on the current value of their holdings, but look back at whether their investments are showing a profit or a loss. For example, if I sell my holding of IBM stock for $10,000, I may feel on top of the world if the stock only cost me $5,000, but I will be much less happy if it had cost $11,000. This observation is the basis for *prospect theory*. Prospect theory states (a) the value investors place on a particular outcome is determined by the gains or losses that they have made since the asset was acquired or the holding last reviewed, and (b) investors are particularly averse to the possibility of even a very small loss and need a high return to compensate for it.

The pain of loss seems also to depend on whether it comes on the heels of earlier losses. Once investors have suffered a loss, they may be even more concerned not to risk a further loss. Conversely, just as gamblers are known to be more willing to make large bets when they are ahead, so investors may be more prepared to run the risk of a stock market dip after they have enjoyed a run of unexpectedly high returns. . . .

2. *Beliefs about probabilities*. . . . Psychologists have found that, when judging possible future outcomes, individuals tend to look back at what happened in a few similar situations. As a result, they are led to place too much weight on a small number of recent events. For example, an investor might judge that an investment manager is particularly skilled because he has "beaten the market" for three years in a row, or that three years of rapidly rising prices are a good indication of future profits from investing in the stock market. The investor may not stop to reflect on how little one can learn about expected returns from three years' experience.

Most investors are also too *conservative*, that is, too slow to update their beliefs in the face of new evidence. People tend to update their beliefs in the correct direction but the magnitude of the change is less than rationality would require.

Another systematic bias is *overconfidence*. Most of us believe that we are better-than-average drivers and most investors think they are better-than-average stock pickers. Two speculators who trade with each other cannot both make money, but may be prepared to continue trading because each is confident that the other is a patsy. . . . [Individuals]consistently overestimate the odds that the future will turn out as they say and underestimate the chances of unlikely events. . . .

Limits of Arbitrage

It is not difficult to believe that amateur investors may sometimes be caught up in a scatty while of irrational exuberance. But there are plenty of hard-headed professional investors managing huge sums of money. Why don't these investors bail out of overpriced stocks and force their prices down to fair value? One reason is that there are *limits to arbitrage*, that is, limits on the ability of the rational investors to exploit market inefficiencies. . . .

In an efficient market, if prices get out of line, then arbitrage forces them back. The arbitrageur buys the underpriced securities (pushing up their prices) and sells the underpriced securities (pushing down their prices). The arbitrageur earns a profit by buying low and selling high and waiting for prices to converge on fundamentals. . . .

In practice arbitrage is harder than it looks. Trading costs can be significant. . . .

[T]he most important limit to arbitrage is the risk that prices will diverge even further before they converge. Thus an arbitrageur has to have the guts and resources to hold on to a position that may get worse before it gets better. . . .

[For example, consider the risks the arbitrageur would face with the Dutch company, Royal Dutch Petroleum, and the British company, Shell Transport and Trading (Shell T&T). Because each of these companies received a fixed share in the profits of the oil giant, Shell, they were essentially "Siamese twins," sharing in the same underlying cash flow. Nonetheless, before they were ultimately merged into each other in July 2005, their prices frequently not only diverged, but diverged substantially.] Suppose that you were a professional money manager in 1980, when Royal Dutch was about 12% below parity. You decided to buy Royal Dutch, sell Shell T&T short, and wait confidently for prices to converge. It was a long wait. The first time you would have seen any profit on your position was in 1983. In the meantime the mispricing got worse, not better. Royal Dutch fell to more than 30% below parity in mid–1981. Therefore, you had to report a substantial loss on your "arbitrage" strategy in that year. You were fired and took up a new career as a used-car salesman. . . .

The Six Lessons of Market Efficiency

Lesson 1: Markets Have No Memory

The weak form of the efficient-market hypothesis states that the sequence of past price changes contains no information about future changes. Economists express the same idea more concisely when they say that the market has no memory. . . .

Lesson 2: Trust Market Prices

In an efficient market you can trust prices, for they impound all available information about the value of each security. This means that in an efficient market, there is no way for most investors to achieve consistently superior rates of return. To do so, you not only need to know more than anyone else, but you also need to know more than *everyone* else. . . .

Lesson 3: Read the Entrails

If the market is efficient, prices impound all available information. Therefore, if we can only learn to read the entrails, security prices can tell us a lot about the future. For example, . . . if the company's bonds are trading at low prices, you can deduce that the firm is probably in trouble. . . .

Lesson 4: There Are No Financial Illusions

In an efficient market there are no financial illusions. Investors are unromantically concerned with the firm's cash flows and the portion of those cash flows to which they are entitled. . . .

Lesson 5: The Do–It–Yourself Alternative

In an efficient market investors will not pay others for what they can do equally well themselves. . . . [M]any of the controversies in corporate financing center on how well individuals can replicate corporate financial decisions. For example, companies often justify mergers on the grounds that they produce a more diversified and hence more stable firm. But if investors can hold the stocks of both companies why should they thank the companies for diversifying? It is much easier and cheaper for them to diversify than it is for the firm. . . .

Lesson 6: Seen One Stock, Seen Them All

The elasticity of demand for any article measures the percentage change in the quantity demanded for each percentage addition to the price. If the article has close substitutes, the elasticity will be strongly negative; if not, it will be near zero. For example, coffee, which is a staple commodity, has a demand elasticity of about – .2. This means that a 5% increase in the price of coffee changes sales by – .2 X .05 = – .01; in other words, it reduces demand by only 1%. Consumers are likely to regard different *brands* of coffee as much closer substitutes for each other. Therefore, the demand elasticity for a particular brand could be in the region of, say, – 2.0. A 5 percent increase in the price of Maxwell House relative to that of Folgers would in this case reduce demand by 10 percent.

Investors don't buy a stock for its unique qualities; they buy it because it offers the prospect of a fair return for its risk. This means that stocks should be like *very* similar brands of coffee, almost perfect substitutes. Therefore, the demand for a company's stock should be highly elastic. If its prospective return is too low relative to its risk, *nobody* will want to hold that stock. If the reverse is true, *everybody* will scramble to buy.

Suppose that you want to sell a large block of stock. Since demand is elastic, you naturally conclude that you need only to cut the offering price very slightly to sell your stock. Unfortunately, that doesn't necessarily follow. When you come to sell your stock, other investors may suspect that you want to get rid of it because you know something they don't. Therefore, they will revise their assessment of the stock's value downward. Demand is still elastic, but the whole demand curve moves down. Elastic demand does not imply that stock prices never change when a large sale or purchase occurs; it *does* imply that you can sell large blocks of stock at close to the market price *as long as you can convince other investors that you have no private information*....

DAINES & HANSON, THE CORPORATE LAW PARADOX: THE CASE FOR RESTRUCTURING CORPORATE LAW, 102 Yale L.J. 577, 614–15 (1992). "Beginning in the mid—1980's, doubts regarding the ECMH emerged first in the financial economics literature, and then began to trickle into the legal literature. But what began as a trickle has more recently become a deluge. Legal scholars familiar with current financial economics literature agree that there is now reason to doubt the efficiency of markets. Professors Macey, Miller, Mitchell and Netter summarize the current research as follows: '[W]e can at a minimum conclude that substantial disagreement exists among financial economists about what conclusions empirical tests of market efficiency support.' Indeed, 'substantial disagreement exists about to what degree markets are efficient, how to test for efficiency, and even the definition of efficiency.' Similarly, Professor Langevoort concludes from his review of the current financial economics literature that 'what is important for present purposes seems beyond debate: strong claims of efficiency are debatable.'

"To understand the source of the new doubts, it is helpful to recognize that the ECMH makes *two* general efficiency claims—namely, that the stock market is both informationally efficient and fundamentally efficient: The market is 'informationally efficient' if all public information is immediately incorporated into the stock price; it is 'fundamentally efficient' if stock prices accurately reflect only information relating to the net present value of the corporation's future profits. A growing body of work in financial economics now suggests, first, that informational efficiency—for which there *is* substantial empirical support—does not imply fundamental efficiency, and, second, that both the empirical and theoretical bases for the belief that markets are fundamentally efficient are suspect."

CHAPTER 3

PARTNERSHIPS

INTRODUCTORY NOTE

Partnerships fall into several categories. This Chapter concerns general partnerships (Sections 1–9), limited partnerships (Section 10), limited liability partnerships, and limited liability limited partnerships (Section 11).

Although general partnerships had a rich history under the common law, they have long been governed by statute. Until recently, the relevant statute was the Uniform Partnership Act (the UPA), which was promulgated by the Uniform Law Commission (ULC), then known as the National Conference of Commissioners on Uniform State Laws, in 1914 and adopted in every state except Louisiana. In 1994, NCCUSL adopted the Revised Uniform Partnership Act (RUPA), which is intended to supersede the UPA. Under RUPA § 1006, RUPA applies to all partnerships formed after RUPA is adopted in any given state and, after a transition period, to partnerships formed even before RUPA was adopted. A large majority of the states have adopted RUPA, but a significant minority, including such important commercial states as New York, Pennsylvania, and Texas, have not. In those states, partnerships are still governed by the UPA. Many of the cases in this Chapter were decided under the UPA. They are included here partly because the UPA is still in effect in a number of states, and partly because the case law under the UPA is much richer than that under the RUPA, and much of that case law is relevant under RUPA because RUPA continues many rules of the UPA. However, the Text Notes generally discuss both the UPA and RUPA, especially where RUPA makes a material change in the corresponding provision of the UPA.

As of 2008, there were 670,000 general partnerships in the United States, with an average of 4 partners each. Internal Revenue Service, Statistics of Income Bulletin, Fall 2010 Table 8.

SECTION 1. WHAT CONSTITUTES A GENERAL PARTNERSHIPS

HILCO PROPERTY SERVICES, INC. v. UNITED STATES, 929 F.Supp. 526 (D.N.H. 1996). "The conduct of the parties and the circumstances surrounding their relationship and transactions control the factual question of whether a partnership existed in cases where the parties have not documented their intentions in a written agreement.... [A]lthough the question of intent is a crucial part of the calculus, 'the only necessary intent ... is an intent to do those things which constitute a partnership.' *Id.* Thus,

> [t]he key factor is not the subjective intent of the parties to form a partnership.... It is immaterial that the parties do not call their relationship, or believe it to be, a partnership, especially where the rights of third parties are concerned."

UNIFORM PARTNERSHIP ACT §§ 6, 7

REVISED UNIFORM PARTNERSHIP ACT §§ 101(6), 202

[See Statutory Supplement]

Martin v. Peyton

New York Court of Appeals, 1927.
246 N.Y. 213, 158 N.E. 77.

Appeal from Supreme Court, Appellate Division, First Department.

Action by Charles S. Martin against William C. Peyton and others. A judgment of the Special Term, entered on the report of a referee in favor of the defendants was affirmed by the Appellate Division (219 App.Div. 297, 220 N.Y.S. 29), and plaintiff appeals. Affirmed.

■ ANDREWS, J.

Much ancient learning as to partnership is obsolete. Today only those who are partners between themselves may be charged for partnership debts by others. (Partnership Law [Cons. Laws, ch. 39], sec. 11.) There is one exception. Now and then a recovery is allowed where in truth such relationship is absent. This is because the debtor may not deny the claim. (Sec. 27.)

Partnership results from contract, express or implied. If denied it may be proved by the production of some written instrument; by testimony as to some conversation; by circumstantial evidence. If nothing else appears the receipt by the defendant of a share of the profits of the business is enough. (Sec. 11.)

Assuming some written contract between the parties the question may arise whether it creates a partnership. If it be complete; if it expresses in good faith the full understanding and obligation of the parties, then it is for the court to say whether a partnership exists. It may, however, be a mere sham intended to hide the real relationship. Then other results follow. In passing upon it effect is to be given to each provision. Mere words will not blind us to realities. Statements that no partnership is intended are not conclusive. If as a whole a contract contemplates an association of two or more persons to carry on as co-owners a business for profit a partnership there is. (Sec. 10.) On the other hand, if it be less than this no partnership exists. Passing on the contract as a whole, an arrangement for sharing profits is to be considered. It is to be given its due weight. But it is to be weighed in connection with all the rest. It is not decisive. It may be merely the method adopted to pay a debt or wages, as interest on a loan or for other reasons.

An existing contract may be modified later by subsequent agreement, oral or written. A partnership may be so created where there was none before. And again, that the original agreement has been so modified may be proved by circumstantial evidence—by showing the conduct of the parties.

In the case before us the claim that the defendants became partners in the firm of Knauth, Nachod & Kuhne, doing business as bankers and brokers, depends upon the interpretation of certain instruments. There is nothing in their subsequent acts determinative of or indeed material upon this question. And we are relieved of questions that sometimes arise. "The plaintiff's position is not," we are told, "that the agreements of June 4, 1921, were a false expression or incomplete expression of the intention of the parties. We say that they express defendants' intention and that that intention was to create a relationship which as a matter of law constitutes a partnership." Nor may the claim of the plaintiff be rested on any question of estoppel. "The plaintiff's claim," he stipulates, "is a claim of actual partnership, not of partnership by estoppel. . . ."

Remitted then, as we are, to the documents themselves, we refer to circumstances surrounding their execution only so far as is necessary to make them intelligible. And we are to remember that although the intention of the parties to avoid liability as partners is clear, although in language precise and definite they deny any design to then join the firm of K.N. & K.; although they say their interests in profits should be construed merely as a measure of compensation for loans, not an interest in profits as such; although they provide that they shall not be liable for any losses or treated as partners, the question still remains whether in fact they agree to so associate themselves with the firm as to "carry on as co-owners a business for profit."

In the spring of 1921 the firm of K.N. & K. found itself in financial difficulties. John R. Hall was one of the partners. He was a friend of Mr. Peyton. From him he obtained the loan of almost $500,000 of Liberty bonds, which K.N. & K. might use as collateral to secure bank advances. This, however, was not sufficient. The firm and its members had engaged in unwise speculations, and it was deeply involved. Mr. Hall was also intimately acquainted with George W. Perkins, Jr., and with Edward W. Freeman. He also knew Mrs. Peyton and Mrs. Perkins and Mrs. Freeman. All were anxious to help him. He, therefore, representing K.N. & K., entered into negotiations with them. While they were pending a proposition was made that Mr. Peyton, Mr. Perkins and Mr. Freeman or some of them should become partners. It met a decided refusal. Finally an agreement was reached. It is expressed in three documents, executed on the same day, all a part of the one transaction. They were drawn with care and are unambiguous. We shall refer to them as "the agreement," "the indenture" and "the option."

We have no doubt as to their general purpose. The respondents were to loan K.N. & K. $2,500,000 worth of liquid securities, which were to be returned to them on or before April 15, 1923. The firm might hypothecate them to secure loans totaling $2,000,000, using the proceeds as its business necessities required. To insure respondents against loss K.N. & K. were to turn over to them a large number of their own securities which may have been valuable, but which were of so speculative a nature that they could not be used as collateral for bank loans. In compensation for the loan the respondents were to receive 40 per cent of the profits of the firm until the return was made, not exceeding, however, $500,000 and not less than $100,000. Merely because the transaction involved the transfer of securities and not of cash does not prevent its being a loan within the meaning of section 11. The respondents also were given an option to join the firm if they or any of them expressed a desire to do so before June 4, 1923.

Many other detailed agreements are contained in the papers. Are they such as may be properly inserted to protect the lenders? Or do they go further? Whatever their purpose, did they in truth associate the respondents with the firm so that they and it together thereafter carried on as co-owners a business for profit? The answer depends upon an analysis of these various provisions.

As representing the lenders, Mr. Peyton and Mr. Freeman are called "trustees." The loaned securities when used as collateral are not to be mingled with other securities of K.N. & K., and the trustees at all times are to be kept informed of all transactions affecting them. To them shall be paid all dividends and income accruing there from. They may also substitute for any of the securities loaned securities of equal value. With their consent the firm may sell any of its securities held by the respondents, the proceeds to go, however, to the trustees. In other similar ways the trustees may deal with these same securities, but the securities loaned shall always be sufficient in value to permit of their hypothecation for $2,000,000. If they rise in price the excess may be withdrawn by the defendants. If they fall they shall make good the deficiency.

So far there is no hint that the transaction is not a loan of securities with a provision for compensation. Later a somewhat closer connection with the firm appears. Until the securities are returned the directing management of the firm is to be in the hands of John R. Hall, and his life is to be insured for $1,000,000, and the policies are to be assigned as further collateral security to the trustees. These requirements are not unnatural. Hall was the one known and trusted by the defendants. Their acquaintance with the other members of the firm was of the slightest. These others had brought an old and established business to the verge of bankruptcy. As the respondents knew, they also had engaged in unsafe speculation. The respondents were about to loan $2,500,000 of good securities. As collateral they were to receive others of problematical value. What they required seems but ordinary caution. Nor does it imply an association in the business.

The trustees are to be kept advised as to the conduct of the business and consulted as to important matters. They may inspect the firm books and are entitled to any information they think important. Finally they may veto any business they think highly speculative or injurious. Again we hold this but a proper precaution to safeguard the loan. The trustees may not initiate any transaction as a partner may do. They may not bind the firm by any action of their own. Under the circumstances the safety of the loan depended upon the business success of K.N. & K. This success was likely to be compromised by the inclination of its members to engage in speculation. No longer, if the respondents were to be protected, should it be allowed. The trustees, therefore, might prohibit it, and that their prohibition might be effective, information was to be furnished them. Not dissimilar agreements have been held proper to guard the interests of the lender.

As further security each member of K.N. & K. is to assign to the trustees their interest in the firm. No loan by the firm to any member is permitted and the amount each may draw is fixed. No other distribution of profits is to be made. So that realized profits may be calculated the existing capital is stated to be $700,000, and profits are to be realized as promptly as good business practice will permit. In case the trustees think this is not done, the question is left to them and to Mr. Hall, and if they differ then to an arbitrator. There is no obligation that the firm shall continue the business. It may dissolve at any time. Again we conclude there is nothing here not properly adapted to secure the interest of the respondents as lenders. If their compensation is dependent on a percentage of the profits still provision must be made to define what these profits shall be.

The "indenture" is substantially a mortgage of the collateral delivered by K.N. & K. to the trustees to secure the performance of the "agreement." It certainly does not strengthen the claim that the respondents were partners.

Finally we have the "option." It permits the respondents or any of them or their assignees or nominees to enter the firm at a later date if they desire to do so by buying 50 per cent or less of the interests therein of all or any of the members at a stated price. Or a corporation may, if the respondents and the members agree, be formed in place of the firm. Meanwhile, apparently with the design of protecting the firm business against improper or ill-judged action which might render the option valueless, each member of the firm is to place his resignation in the hands of Mr. Hall. If at any time he and the trustees agree that such resignation should be accepted, that member shall then retire, receiving the value of his interest calculated as of the date of such retirement.

This last provision is somewhat unusual, yet it is not enough in itself to show that on June 4, 1921, a present partnership was created nor taking these various papers as a whole do we reach such a result. It is quite true that even if one or two or three like provisions contained in such a contract do not require this conclusion, yet it is also true that when taken together a point may come where stipulations immaterial separately cover so wide a field that we should hold a partnership exists. As in other branches of the law a question of degree is often the determining factor. Here that point has not been reached. . . .

The judgment appealed from should be affirmed, with costs.

■ CARDOZO, CH. J., POUND, CRANE, LEHMAN, KELLOGG and O'BRIEN, JJ., concur.

Judgment affirmed, etc.

Lupien v. Malsbenden

Supreme Judicial Court of Maine, 1984.
477 A.2d 746.

■ Before MCKUSICK, C.J., and NICHOLS, ROBERTS, WATHEN, GLASSMAN and SCHOLNIK, JJ.

■ MCKUSICK, CHIEF JUSTICE.

Defendant Frederick Malsbenden appeals a judgment of the Superior Court (York County) holding him to partnership liability on a written contract entered into between plaintiff Robert Lupien and one Stephen Cragin doing business as York Motor Mart.[1] The sole issue asserted on appeal is whether the Superior Court erred in its finding that Malsbenden and Cragin were partners in the pertinent part of York Motor Mart's business. We affirm.

On March 5, 1980, plaintiff entered into a written agreement with Stephen Cragin, doing business in the town of York as York Motor Mart, for the construction of a Bradley automobile.[2] Plaintiff made a

1. Cragin "disappeared" several months before this action was commenced. Plaintiff Lupien originally named Cragin as a co-defendant. However, since Cragin was never served with process, the Superior Court at the behest of both Lupien and defendant Malsbenden dismissed the claim against Cragin.

2. A Bradley automobile is a "kit car" constructed on a Volkswagen chassis.

deposit of $500 towards the purchase price of $8,020 upon signing the contract, and made a further payment of $3,950 one week later on March 12. Both the purchase order of March 5, 1980, and a later bill of sale, though signed by Cragin, identified the seller as York Motor Mart. At the jury-waived trial, plaintiff testified that after he signed the contract he made visits to York Motor Mart on an average of once or twice a week to check on the progress being made on his car. During those visits plaintiff generally dealt with Malsbenden because Cragin was seldom present. On one such visit in April, Malsbenden told plaintiff that it was necessary for the latter to sign over ownership of his pickup truck, which would constitute the balance of the consideration under the contract, so that the proceeds from the sale of the truck could be used to complete construction of the Bradley. When plaintiff complied, Malsbenden provided plaintiff with a rental car, and later with a "demo" model of the Bradley, for his use pending the completion of the vehicle he had ordered. When it was discovered that the "demo" actually belonged to a third person who had entrusted it to York Motor Mart for resale, Malsbenden purchased the vehicle for plaintiff's use. Plaintiff never received the Bradley he had contracted to purchase.

In his trial testimony, defendant Malsbenden asserted that his interest in the Bradley operation of York Motor Mart was only that of a banker. He stated that he had loaned $85,000 to Cragin, without interest, to finance the Bradley portion of York Motor Mart's business.[3] The loan was to be repaid from the proceeds of each car sold. Malsbenden acknowledged that Bradley kits were purchased with his personal checks and that he had also purchased equipment for York Motor Mart. He also stated that after Cragin disappeared sometime late in May 1980, he had physical control of the premises of York Motor Mart and that he continued to dispose of assets there even to the time of trial in 1983.

The Uniform Partnership Act, adopted in Maine at 31 M.R.S.A. §§ 281–323 (1978 & Supp.1983–1984), defines a partnership as "an association of 2 or more persons . . . to carry on as co-owners[4] a business for profit." 31 M.R.S.A. § 286 (1978). Whether a partnership exists is an inference of law based on established facts. *See* Dalton v. Austin, 432 A.2d 774, 777 (Me.1981); Roux v. Lawand, 160 A. 756, 757 (Me. 1932); James Bailey Co. v. Darling, 111 A. 410, 411 (Me. 1920). A finding that the relationship between two persons constitutes a partnership may be based upon evidence of an agreement, either express or implied,

> to place their money, effects, labor, and skill, or some or all of them, in lawful commerce or business with the understanding

3. Malsbenden's testimony indicated that Cragin carried on an automotive repair business at the York Motor Mart that was unrelated to the Bradley operation. Malsbenden testified, without contradiction, that he had no involvement with that other business.

4. As we made clear in Dalton v. Austin, 432 A.2d 774, 777 (Me.1981), the term "co-owners" as used in the statute does not necessarily mean joint title to all assets. On the contrary, "the right to participate in control of the business is the essence of co-ownership." *Id.*

> that a community of profits will be shared.... No one factor is alone determinative of the existence of a partnership....

Dalton v. Austin, 432 A.2d at 777; Cumberland County Power & Light Co. v. Gordon, 7 A.2d 619, 622 (Me. 1939). *See* James Bailey Co. v. Darling, 111 A. 410, 411 (Me. 1920). If the arrangement between the parties otherwise qualifies as a partnership, it is of no matter that the parties did not expressly agree to form a partnership or did not even intend to form one:

> It is possible for parties to intend no partnership and yet to form one. If they agree upon an arrangement which is a partnership in fact, it is of no importance that they call it something else, or that they even expressly declare that they are not to be partners. The law must declare what is the legal import of their agreements, and names go for nothing when the substance of the arrangement shows them to be inapplicable.

James Bailey Co. v. Darling, 111 A. at 411 (Me. 1920) (quoting Beecher v. Bush, 7 N.W. 785, 785–86 (Mich. 1881)).

Here the trial justice concluded that, notwithstanding Malsbenden's assertion that he was only a "banker," his "total involvement" in the Bradley operation was that of a partner. The testimony at trial, both respecting Malsbenden's financial interest in the enterprise and his involvement in day-to-day business operations, amply supported the Superior Court's conclusion. Malsbenden had a financial interest of $85,000 in the Bradley portion of York Motor Mart's operations. Although Malsbenden termed the investment a loan, significantly he conceded that the "loan" carried no interest. His "loan" was not made in the form of a fixed payment or payments, but was made to the business, at least in substantial part, in the form of day-to-day purchases of Bradley kits, other parts and equipment, and in the payment of wages. Furthermore, the "loan" was not to be repaid in fixed amounts or at fixed times, but rather only upon the sale of Bradley automobiles.

The evidence also showed that, unlike a banker, Malsbenden had the right to participate in control of the business and in fact did so on a day-to-day basis.[5] According to Urbin Savaria, who worked at York Motor Mart from late April through June 1980, Malsbenden during that time opened the business establishment each morning, remained present through part of every day, had final say on the ordering of parts, paid for parts and equipment, and paid Savaria's salary. On plaintiff's frequent visits to York Motor Mart, he generally dealt with Malsbenden because Cragin was not present. It was Malsbenden who insisted that plaintiff trade in his truck prior to the completion of the Bradley because the proceeds from the sale of the truck were needed to complete the Bradley. When it was discovered that the "demo" Bradley given to plaintiff while he awaited completion of his car

5. Thus its facts clearly distinguish the case at bar from James Bailey Co. v. Darling, 111 A. 410, 413 (Me. 1920), where although the defendant advanced money for the purchase of automobiles that was to be repaid upon the sale of individual automobiles, the defendant had no control over the business.

actually belonged to a third party, it was Malsbenden who bought the car for plaintiff's use. As of three years after the making of the contract now in litigation, Malsbenden was still doing business at York Motor Mart, "just disposing of property."

Malsbenden and Cragin may well have viewed their relationship to be that of creditor-borrower, rather than a partnership. At trial Malsbenden so asserts, and Cragin's departure from the scene in the spring of 1980 deprives us of the benefit of his view of his business arrangement with Malsbenden. In any event, whatever the intent of these two men as to their respective involvements in the business of making and selling Bradley cars, there is no clear error in the Superior Court's finding that the Bradley car operation represented a pooling of Malsbenden's capital and Cragin's automotive skills, with joint control over the business and intent to share the fruits of the enterprise. As a matter of law, that arrangement amounted to a partnership under 31 M.R.S.A. § 286.

The entry is:

■ JUDGMENT AFFIRMED.

■ ALL CONCURRING.

NOTE ON THE FORMATION OF PARTNERSHIPS

1. *Formalities*. Certain types of business enterprises can only be organized—that is legally formed—by complying with statutory (and sometimes administrative) formalities and filing with the state. This is true, for example, of corporations, limited partnerships, limited liability partnerships, limited liability limited partnerships, and limited liability companies. However, some types of business enterprises, most notably sole proprietorships and general partnerships, can be formed without any formalities or filings.

The absence of a filing requirement reflects in part a conception that partnership status depends on the factual characteristics of a relationship between two or more persons, not on whether the persons think of themselves as having entered into a partnership. However, an important consequence of the absence of formalities or filing requirements to organize a partnership means that it is not always clear whether two or more persons who are associated in a business enterprise in some way are or are not partners.

Although no filings are *required* under either the UPA or RUPA, RUPA *permits* certain filings. *See, e.g.*, Note on the Authority of a Partner, Section 4, infra.

2. *The Four–Element Test, Mutual Right of Control, and Loss–Sharing*. It is sometimes said that where there is no express partnership agreement, a relationship will be considered a partnership only if four elements are present—an agreement to share profits, an agreement to share losses, a mutual right of control or management of the

business, and a community of interest in the venture. *See, e.g.*, Weingart v. C & W Taylor Partnership, 809 P.2d 576 (Mont. 1991); Corpus Christi v. Bayfront Associates, Ltd., 814 S.W.2d 98 (Tex.App. 1991). This four-element test departs from the statutory tests both UPA § 6(a) and RUPA § 202, which provide simply that with certain exceptions a partnership is "an association of two or more persons to carry on as co-owners a business for profit," and say nothing about control or loss-sharing.

Although the Comments to both UPA § 6(a) and RUPA § 202 also say that "to state that partners are co-owners of a business is to state that they each have the power of ultimate control," in fact even explicit partnership agreements frequently do not involve either ultimate control or loss-sharing for every partner. For example, many partnership agreements vest control in only one or more managing partners, or create elaborate allocations of voting power in which some partners do not have voting rights. Similarly, not every partnership agreement provides for loss-sharing by every partner. If explicit partnership agreements do not always include control and loss-sharing as elements of the partnership relation, why should courts require those elements as a condition to finding an implicit partnership?

A better approach is that the presence or absence of the four specified elements, including mutual control and loss-sharing, is evidence, but not a requirement, of a partnership. This approach was taken, for example, in Beckman v. Farmer, 579 A.2d 618, 627 (D.C.App.1990), where the court said that "[t]he customary attributes of partnership, such as loss sharing and joint control of decisionmaking are necessary guideposts of inquiry, but none is conclusive." Other cases have held that once profit-sharing has been shown, it is not essential to show that there was an agreement to share in losses. *See* Hansford v. Maplewood Station Business Park, 621 N.E.2d 347 (Ind. App.1993); Endsley v. Game–Show Placements, Ltd., 401 N.E.2d 768 (Ind.App.1980).

SECTION 2. THE LEGAL NATURE OF A PARTNERSHIP

UNIFORM PARTNERSHIP ACT § 6

REVISED UNIFORM PARTNERSHIP ACT §§ 101(6), 201

[See Statutory Supplement]

NOTE ON THE LEGAL NATURE OF A PARTNERSHIP: ENTITY OR AGGREGATE STATUS

1. *Entity v. Aggregate—in General.* Individuals may associate in a wide variety of forms. The issue often arises whether a given form of association has a legal status separate from that of its members or is simply an aggregate of its members. Frequently, this issue is stated in terms of whether a particular form of association is or is not a "separate legal entity" or a "legal person" (as opposed to a natural person, that is, an individual). A variety of issues may turn on the answer to this question—for example, whether the association can sue and be sued in its own name and whether it can hold property in its own right.

In the history of English and American law this issue arose in the context of many different kinds of associations, such as universities, charitable institutions, and even municipalities. In most cases the issue was eventually resolved in a straightforward way, but in the case of partnerships it continued to be vexing. The predominant although not exclusive view under the common law was that a partnership was not an entity but merely an aggregate of its members—or, as it was sometimes put, that a partnership was no more a legal entity than was a friendship.

2. *The UPA.* In 1902, the National Conference of Commissioners on Uniform State Laws determined to promulgate a Uniform Partnership Act. Dean James Barr Ames of the Harvard Law School was appointed to draft the Act. Subsequently, the Commissioners instructed Dean Ames, at his own urging, to draft the Act on the theory that a partnership is a legal entity. Accordingly, in the drafts submitted by Dean Ames a partnership was defined as "*a legal person* formed by the association of two or more individuals for the purpose of carrying on business with a view to profit" (emphasis added), and various provisions of the drafts reflected the entity theory. However, Dean Ames died before the work was completed and his successor, Dean William Draper Lewis of the University of Pennsylvania Law School, was distinctly unfriendly to the entity view. Ultimately, Dean Lewis convinced the Commissioners to instruct him to draft the Act on the aggregate theory. UPA Section 6 therefore provides simply that "A partnership is an association of two or more persons to carry on as co-owners a business for profit." Although the language of this provision does not in itself render the entity-aggregate issue free from doubt (since an association can be either an aggregate or an entity), it is pretty clear that the Act was intended to adopt the aggregate rather than the entity theory of partnership.

However, that is not the end of the story. Having adopted the aggregate theory in principle, in practice the UPA deals with a number of specific issues (such as the ownership of partnership property) *as if* a partnership is an entity. For many purposes, this approach works pretty well. Generally speaking, however, the entity theory of partnership works much better than the aggregate theory. In cases where the UPA treats a partnership as if it is an entity, notwithstanding the aggregate theory, the results are good but the manner in which the statute reaches those results involves needlessly complex mechanics. In cases where the UPA does not treat the partnership as if it is an entity, the results tend to be bad.

3. *The Effect of Statutes other than the UPA on UPA-governed partnerships*. The question often arises whether a partnership whose internal affairs are governed by a UPA state is to be treated as an aggregate or an entity for the purpose of statutes other than the UPA. This question is a matter of legislative intent under the relevant statute. As in all such matters, the answer will depend on the language employed and the purposes manifested in the statute. The fact that the UPA adopts the aggregate theory will be relevant, but not dispositive, in answering the question. Even though a partnership is defined as an association under the UPA, a legislature may choose to treat a UPA-governed partnership as an entity for purposes of another statute, *See, e.g.*, United States v. A & P Trucking Co., 358 U.S. 121, 79 S.Ct. 203, 3 L.Ed.2d 165 (1958).

4. *RUPA*. In contrast to the UPA, RUPA confers entity status on partnerships. RUPA § 101, like UPA § 6, defines a partnership as "an association of two or more persons to carry on as co-owners a business for profit." However, RUPA § 201 then provides that "A partnership is an entity."

By conferring entity status on partnerships, RUPA was able to drastically simplify many partnership rules, such as those dealing with partnership property and partnership litigation. Nevertheless, entity status does not inherently resolve every issue to which it is relevant. Just as the drafters of the UPA, having denied entity status to partnerships, remained free to (and did) craft rules to reach entity-like results on certain issues, so the drafters of RUPA, having conferred entity status on partnerships, remained free to (and did) craft rules to reach aggregate-like results on certain issues.

To put this differently, no rule to govern any specific partnership-law issue can be "derived" or follows "logically" or "by necessity" from a partnership's legal-entity status under RUPA, any more than any rule on any specific issue can be derived, or follows "logically" or "by necessity" from the UPA's denial of that status. Having declared that a partnership is an entity, the drafters of RUPA still had to make policy choices on such issues as whether the partnership could hold property, could sue and be sued in its own name, and so forth. It is true that generally speaking the best rule in many of these areas is one that is consistent with entity status, but it is important not to forget that an independent policy choice must still be made on each issue. The adoption of legal-entity status for partnerships at most simplified the drafting of RUPA and gave a slight push toward certain rules. In some areas, however, RUPA reaches an aggregate-like result. For example, under RUPA, as under the UPA, a partner is individually liable for partnership debts. Under RUPA § 404(b), a partner has a duty of loyalty and care not only to the partnership but to the other partners.

Under RUPA § 404(d), a partner's duty of good faith and fair dealing extends both to the partnership and to the other partners.

SECTION 3. THE ONGOING OPERATION OF PARTNERSHIPS

A. MANAGEMENT

UNIFORM PARTNERSHIP ACT §§ 18(e), (g), (h), 19, 20

REVISED UNIFORM PARTNERSHIP ACT §§ 103, 401(f), (i), (j), 403

[See Statutory Supplement]

Summers v. Dooley

Supreme Court of Idaho, 1971.
94 Idaho 87, 481 P.2d 318.

■ DONALDSON, JUSTICE.

This lawsuit, tried in the district court, involves a claim by one partner against the other for $6,000. The complaining partner asserts that he has been required to pay out more than $11,000 in expenses without any reimbursement from either the partnership funds or his partner. The expenditure in question was incurred by the complaining partner (John Summers, plaintiff-appellant) for the purpose of hiring an additional employee. The trial court denied him any relief except for ordering that he be entitled to one half $966.72 which it found to be a legitimate partnership expense.

The pertinent facts leading to this lawsuit are as follows. Summers entered a partnership agreement with Dooley (defendant-respondent) in 1958 for the purpose of operating a trash collection business. The business was operated by the two men and when either was unable to work, the non-working partner provided a replacement at his own expense. In 1962, Dooley became unable to work and, at his own expense, hired an employee to take his place. In July, 1966, Summers approached his partner Dooley regarding the hiring of an additional employee but Dooley refused. Nevertheless, on his own initiative, Summers hired the man and paid him out of his own pocket. Dooley, upon discovering that Summers had hired an additional man, objected, stating that he did not feel additional labor was necessary and refused to pay for the new employee out of the partnership funds. Summers continued to operate the business using the third man and in October of 1967 instituted suit in the district court for $6,000 against his partner, the gravamen of the complaint being that Summers has been required to pay out more than $11,000 in expenses, incurred in the hiring of the additional man, without any reimbursement from either the partnership funds or his partner. After trial before the court, sitting without a jury, Summers was granted only partial relief[1] and he has appealed. He urges in essence that the trial court erred by failing to conclude that he should be reimbursed for expenses and costs connected in the employment of extra help in the partnership business.

The principal thrust of appellant's contention is that in spite of the fact that one of the two partners refused to consent to the hiring of additional help, nonetheless, the non-consenting partner retained profits earned by the labors of the third man and therefore the non-consenting partner should be estopped from denying the need and value of the employee, and has by his behavior ratified the act of the other partner who hired the additional man.

The issue presented for decision by this appeal is whether an equal partner in a two man partnership has the authority to hire a new employee in disregard of the objection of the other partner and then attempt to charge the dissenting partner with the costs incurred as a result of his unilateral decision.

The State of Idaho has enacted specific statutes with respect to the legal concept known as "partnership." Therefore any solution of partnership problems should logically begin with an application of the relevant code provision.

In the instant case the record indicates that although Summers requested his partner Dooley to agree to the hiring of a third man, such requests were not honored. In fact Dooley made it clear that he was "voting no" with regard to the hiring of an additional employee.

An application of the relevant statutory provisions and pertinent case law to the factual situation presented by the instant case indicates that the trial court was correct in its disposal of the issue since a majority of the partners did not consent to the hiring of the third man. I.C. § 53–318(8) provides:

> "Any difference arising as to ordinary matters connected with the partnership business may be decided by a *majority of the partners*. . . ." (emphasis supplied). . . .

The intent of the legislature may be implied from the language used, or inferred on grounds of policy or reasonableness. . . . A careful reading of the statutory provision indicates that subsection 5 bestows *equal rights in the management and conduct of the partnership business* upon all of the partners. The concept of equality between

1. The trial court did award Summers one half of $966.72 which it found to be a legitimate partnership expense.

partners with respect to management of business affairs is a central theme and recurs throughout the Uniform Partnership law, I.C. § 53–301 et seq., which has been enacted in this jurisdiction. Thus the only reasonable interpretation of I.C. § 53–318(8) is that business differences must be decided by a majority of the partners provided no other agreement between the partners speaks to the issues. . . .

In the case at bar one of the partners continually voiced objection to the hiring of the third man. He did not sit idly by and acquiesce in the actions of his partner. Under these circumstances it is manifestly unjust to permit recovery of an expense which was incurred individually and not for the benefit of the partnership but rather for the benefit of one partner.

Judgment affirmed. Costs to respondent.

■ McQuade, C.J., and McFadden, Shepard and Spear, JJ., concur.

SANCHEZ v. SAYLOR, 129 N.M. 742, 13 P.3d 960 (2000). Sanchez and Saylor were partners. A third party was considering lending money to the partnership to finance a proposed restructuring of the partnership's debt, but the potential lender required Sanchez to provide his personal financial statements as a condition to granting the loan, and Sanchez refused to furnish the statements. Saylor brought suit against Sanchez on the ground that Sanchez's refusal to provide his financial statements to the potential lender violated his fiduciary obligations. Held, for Sanchez:

> . . . We turn to Covalt v. High, 675 P.2d 999 (Ct.App.1983) . . . Covalt and High formed an oral partnership which owned and rented an office to a corporation, CSI, in which Covalt owned 25 percent of the corporate stock and High owned 75 percent. . . . After resigning from CSI, Covalt demanded that the partnership increase CSI's rent, but High took no action. *See id.* The increase in rent would benefit the partnership, but it was detrimental to High. The district court found that CSI could afford the rent increase and High had breached his fiduciary duty. *See id.*

In reversing, this Court stated that "all partners have equal rights in the management and conduct of the business of the partnership," that Covalt therefore "was legally invested with an equal voice in the management of the partnership affairs," and that "neither partner had the right to impose his will or decision concerning the operation of the partnership business upon the other." *Id.* at 703, 675 P.2d at 1002 (N.M.App. 1983). The fact that a proposal benefitted the partnership did not require High to agree. *See id.* As authority for its decision, *Covalt* cited UPA, Section 54–1–18(H), stating "any difference arising as to ordinary matters connected with the partnership business may be decided by a majority of the partners." Further, the Court relied on the interpretation of the UPA language by the Idaho Supreme Court in Summers v. Dooley, 481 P.2d 318 (Idaho 1971), that the language is mandatory rather than permissive in nature, and means that business differences must be decided by a majority, not by one of two equal partners when the other objects. *See* 481 P.2d at 320–21.

> Simply stated, *Covalt* says that, absent an enforceable agreement covering such circumstances of disagreement, when both partners in a two-partner partnership disagree on an advantageous prospective business transaction, it is dissolution, not an action for breach of fiduciary duty, that is the appropriate avenue of relief....
>
> ... Without [the *Covalt*] rule, virtually each instance in which one partner for personal reasons does not agree with a proposed transaction that will benefit the partnership can result in a claim for breach of his or her partnership or fiduciary duty. Absent an enforceable contractual duty to agree, if the two partners cannot agree and do not want to (or cannot) continue their partnership, under *Covalt* the remedy is dissolution....

NOTE ON THE MANAGEMENT OF PARTNERSHIPS

1. *Voting.* (a) *UPA.* The cases and authorities are divided on the issue raised in Summers v. Dooley. In accord with *Summers* is Covalt v. High, 675 P.2d 999 (App.1983). But *see* National Biscuit Co. v. Stroud, 106 S.E.2d 692 (N.C. 1959).

The rule of UPA Section 18(h), that any difference arising as to ordinary matters connected with the partnership business may be decided by a majority of the partners, is subject to any agreement between the partners. Partnership agreements often contain provisions vesting management in a managing partner, a managing committee, senior partners, or some other group composed of less than all the partners, and such agreements override Section 18(h). The same result may be reached even without explicit agreement—for example on the basis of a course of conduct:

> [I]t is ... well settled ... that an agreement for exclusive control of the management of the business by one partner may be implied from the course of conduct of the parties. Here, it was fairly [inferable] from the course of conduct of Parks and Patterson that there was an implied agreement that Parks should be the managing partner.

Parks v. Riverside Ins. Co. of Am., 308 F.2d 175, 180 (10th Cir.1962). Such an implied agreement, if found, would pretty clearly block the nonmanaging partners from objecting to a decision of the managing partners relating to ordinary matters connected with the partnership business solely on the ground that the decision was not arrived at by a majority vote of all partners.

b. *RUPA.* RUPA § 401(j) generally follows the voting rules of UPA § 18(h), although there are several differences between the sections. Under UPA § 18(h), "Any difference arising as to ordinary matters connected with the partnership business may be decided by a majority of the partners; but no act in contravention of any agreement between the partners may be done rightfully without the consent of all the partners." Under RUPA § 401(j), "A difference arising as to a matter in the ordinary course of business of a partnership may be decided by a majority of the partners. An act outside the ordinary course of business of a partnership and an amendment to the partnership agreement may be undertaken only with the consent of all of the partners."

RUPA § 401(j) must be read in conjunction with RUPA § 101(5), which defines the term "partnership agreement" to mean "the agreement, written or oral, among the partners concerning the partnership." The Comment to § 101(5) adds:

> The definition of "partnership agreement".... is intended to include any agreement among the partners ... concerning either the affairs of the partnership or the conduct of its business.... [T]he agreement may be inferred from the conduct of the parties.
>
> In many partnerships, there is no single document—or no document at all—called a "Partnership Agreement," either because the partnership is itself implicit rather than explicit, or because the partners lack either the inclination or the funds to make a formal agreement. In such cases, under RUPA § 101(5) the "partnership agreement" consists of the fragmentary explicit and implicit agreements that are made from time to time as the partnership relation evolves. Furthermore, even when a partnership does have an explicit and formal "Partnership Agreement," under RUPA § 401(j) unanimity is required not only to depart from this formal agreement, but to depart from any further fragmentary agreement or course of conduct that gives rise to an implied agreement. Thus changes in the way the partnership is actually conducted, not just changes in the way in which it has been explicitly agreed that the partnership will be conducted, may constitute amendments of the partnership agreement for purposes of § 401(j).

2. *Participation*.

(a) *UPA*. Since UPA Section 18(h) provides that partnership action requires a majority vote, what is added by UPA Section 18(e), which provides that all partners have equal rights in the management and conduct of the partnership business? Presumably, the effect of this Section is that absent contrary agreement, every partner must be *consulted* in partnership decisions.

> For a majority of partners to say; We do not care what one partner may say, we, being the majority, will do what we please, is, I apprehend, what this Court will not allow. So, again, with respect to making Mr. *Robertson* the treasurer, Mr. *Const* had a right to be consulted; his opinion might be overruled, and honestly overruled, but he ought to have had the question put to him and discussed: In all partnerships ... the partners are bound to be true and faithful to each other: They are to act upon the joint opinion of all, and the discretion and judgment of anyone cannot

> be excluded: What weight is to be given to it is another question....

Const v. Harris, 37 Eng.Rep. 1191, 1202 (Ch.1824) (Lord Chancellor Eldon). Accordingly, absent contrary agreement, a majority of partners who make a decision without consulting a minority partner would violate § 18(e) even though the majority could have overridden the minority partner if he had been consulted.

(b) *RUPA.* RUPA § 401(f) continues the rule of UPA § 18(e), by conferring on each partner the right to participate in management. The Comment to § 401(f) notes that UPA § 18(e) "has been interpreted broadly to mean that, absent contrary agreement, each partner has a continuing right to participate in the management of the partnership and to be informed about the partnership business, even if his assent ... is not required."

NOTE ON WHAT LAW GOVERNS THE INTERNAL AFFAIRS OF PARTNERSHIPS

Legal rules that concern business organizations fall into two general categories: (i) rules that deal with the organization's internal affairs—such as the powers, rights, and duties of the owners, managers, and organs of the organization as among themselves; and (ii) rules that deal with the obligations of the owners, managers, and organs of the organization, and of the organization itself, to third persons.

Often, the laws of more than one state might be applied to determine what rules govern an organization's internal affairs. In such cases, the body of law known as *conflict of laws* or *choice of law* determines which state's law governs. In the case of corporations, limited liability companies, limited liability partnerships, and limited liability limited partnerships, which are formed by filing organizational documents in a given state, the general choice-of-law rule is that internal affairs are governed by the law of the state in which the business is incorporated or organized. In contrast, the formation of a general partnership does not require the filing of organizational documents. Accordingly, the rule that determines what state's law governs the internal affairs of general partnerships must depend on other factors. The UPA does not include a provision governing the choice of law for the internal affairs of a general partnership. However, RUPA § 106 provides that a general partnership's internal affairs are governed by the law of the state in which the partnership has its chief executive office.

B. INDEMNIFICATION AND CONTRIBUTION

UNIFORM PARTNERSHIP ACT §§ 18(a), (b), (c), (d), (f)

REVISED UNIFORM PARTNERSHIP ACT §§ 401(a)–(e), (h)

[See Statutory Supplement]

NOTE ON INDEMNIFICATION AND CONTRIBUTION

As discussed in Section 5, infra, partners are individually liable to partnership creditors for partnership obligations. As between the partners, however, each partner is liable only for his share of partnership obligations. Thus if one partner pays off a partnership obligation in full (or, for that matter, if he simply pays more than his share), he is entitled to indemnification from the partnership for the difference between his share of the obligation and the amount he paid.

Indemnification should be distinguished from contribution. In a proper case, a partner has a right to be *indemnified* by the *partnership*. In contrast, in a proper case the *partnership* has a right to require *contribution* from one or more partners. Thus the obligation to indemnify a partner is a partnership liability, while the obligation to make contribution is a liability of a partner. For example, partners may be required to make contribution to the partnership to fund a partnership obligation to indemnify another partner so that all partners share a burden that was initially placed on only one. Contribution may also be required for other purposes—in particular, paying off partnership creditors and equalizing capital losses.

"Indemnification resolves the apparent conflict between a partner's joint or joint and several liability, whereby a partner may be called upon to pay the entire amount of partnership debt *to third parties* under UPA § 15 and RUPA § 306 and the proportionate sharing of profits and losses *among the partners* under UPA § 18(a) and RUPA § 401(b). A partner who pays or incurs a personal liability to a third party on behalf of the partnership becomes a creditor of the partnership in the amount of the payment or liability, in effect subrogated to the rights of the creditor.... If a going partnership indemnifies the partner, all partners incur a detriment in proportion to their profit shares if the business is profitable, or otherwise according to their loss shares. If the partnership is unable to pay, all partners must contribute to make up the resulting deficit under UPA §§ 18(a) and 40(b)(II) and (d) and RUPA §§ 401(b) and 807(b) according to their loss shares. If the partners are unable to contribute or cannot be sued, the paying partner, rather than the third party, bears the loss." Alan R. Bromberg & Larry E. Ribstein, Bromberg & Ribstein on Partnership § 6.02(f) (2011).

C. DISTRIBUTIONS, REMUNERATION, AND CAPITAL CONTRIBUTIONS

UNIFORM PARTNERSHIP ACT §§ 18(a), (b), (c), (d), (f)

REVISED UNIFORM PARTNERSHIP ACT § 401(a)–(e), (h)

[See Statutory Supplement]

QUESTION

Suppose A, B, and C form a partnership. A contributes 90% of the capital, and B and C each contribute 5%. All work full-time in the partnership business, with roughly equal responsibilities. Nothing is said in the partnership agreement concerning how partnership profits will be divided. If the partnership makes a profit in a given year, how is it to be divided?

D. CAPITAL ACCOUNTS AND DRAWS

William Klein, John C. Coffee & Frank Partnoy, Business Organization and Finance 79–84

Eleventh ed., 2010.

... CONTRIBUTIONS, ACCOUNTS, AND RETURNS

A. CAPITAL ACCOUNTS

Suppose that Abe, Bill, Pamela and Morris have formed a partnership for the acquisition and operation of a grocery store. Abe and Bill each are to contribute $15,000 and Pamela $20,000, in cash or in property to be used in the business. Morris will contribute neither cash nor property but will agree to manage the store for five years and will receive a salary slightly lower than what he might earn elsewhere. If the partnership follows customary bookkeeping patterns, its books will show the following information under a heading that is likely to be called "Capital Accounts":

Abe	$15,000
Bill	15,000
Pamela	20,000
Morris	0
Total	$50,000

. . . In the absence of an agreement to the contrary, if the business were sold for cash, each partner would be entitled to receive an amount equal to his or her capital account, if available. Any excess or deficit would be shared in accordance with each partner's share of gain and loss (a point to be illustrated below).

Capital contribution does not necessarily control the sharing of gain and loss, and shares of gain may differ from shares of loss. For example, our four partners could agree that each will be entitled to an equal 25 percent share of any profits, despite the difference in initial contribution. Indeed, this is the result that will be provided by the Uniform Partnership Act (Sec. 18(a)) in the absence of an agreement to the contrary. At the same time, and again in the absence of an agreement to the contrary, no partner will be entitled to interest on his or her capital account. Losses might be allocated equally among the partners (again, the result in the absence of express agreement) or might be allocated first pro rata among the contributors of initial capital, to the extent of such capital, and then, perhaps, equally among all partners. . . .

Suppose that all profits and losses are to be shared equally, and suppose that at the end of the first year of operation the profit (after the payment of Morris's salary) is $20,000, or $5,000 per partner. One way of recording this outcome would be to adjust the capital accounts, which would then appear as follows:

Abe	$20,000 *
Bill	20,000
Pamela	25,000
Morris	5,000
Total	$70,000

*$15,000 initial capital plus $5,000 profit share.

If, on the other hand, the firm experienced a loss of $20,000 in its first year of operations, the capital accounts would be:

Abe	$10,000
Bill	10,000
Pamela	15,000
Morris	(5,000)
Total	$30,000

(Parentheses around a number indicate that it is a negative amount.) If, at this point, the business were sold for exactly the amount of the total capital accounts, $30,000, Morris would be required to contribute $5,000 and the resulting total, $35,000, would then be distributed $10,000 each to Abe and Bill and $15,000 to Pamela. This result may seem to be hard on Morris, and there is some legal authority for relieving him of the debt, at least to the extent that he contributed services without adequate compensation. The issue is one that the partners should think about at the outset. They might well agree that losses are to be shared by the partners in accordance with their initial capital contributions. . . .

B. DRAW

Thus far we have referred to profits and losses, which are bookkeeping concepts. It is vital to note that profit does not necessarily generate any spare cash. For example, a new retail store may be highly profitable but may need all its profits to expand its inventory. And even if a firm has had profits and does have spare cash, the partners are not automatically entitled to receive a cash payment. There is a separate term—called "draw"—that is used to describe cash distributions to partners. The amount of the draw of each partner is determined by majority vote of the partners (again, in the absence of some other express agreement) and may be more or less than the profit. . . .

Returning now to the bookkeeping effects of a draw, suppose that our grocery store partnership generates an accounting profit of $20,000 in the first year of its operations. . . . We have just seen how this net profit figure can be translated into adjustments to partner capital accounts. Now suppose that there is a draw. Suppose, for example, that the partners agree that each is to be paid $3,000 from partnership funds. The $3,000 would reduce the capital accounts, so they would then be:

Abe	$17,000 *
Bill	17,000
Pamela	22,000
Morris	2,000
Total	$58,000

*$15,000 initial capital account, plus $5,000 profit share, minus $3,000 draw.

Next, assume that there is a loss of $20,000 in the first year, instead of a profit; that the partnership agreement allocates this loss equally among all the partners; and that despite the loss, there is a cash distribution (draw) of $3,000 to each partner. The partnership capital accounts would then be as follows:

Abe	$ 7,000*
Bill	7,000
Pamela	12,000
Morris	(8,000)
Total	$18,000

* $15,000 initial capital account, minus $5,000 loss share, minus $3,000 draw.

All of this makes sense if you think about it for a few moments. Bear in mind that the capital accounts are not expected to correspond to values in the firm but instead are merely intended to reflect the relative claims of the partners to the assets of the partnership, which is of importance mostly in the case of withdrawal of a partner or liquidation of the partnership. A partner's share of profit can be thought of as something that he or she has earned and reinvested in the firm. The draw can be thought of as earnings or capital taken out of the firm. The capital account allows us to keep track of relative claims where initial contributions and profit shares differ. The same function is served where, for one reason or another, partners do not draw from the firm amounts strictly in proportion to their profit shares.

C. CAPITAL ACCOUNTS AND VALUE OF A PARTNER'S INTEREST

To illustrate the difference between capital account and value, and the role of the capital account, suppose that the partnership capital accounts stand as follows:

Abe	$17,000
Bill	17,000
Pamela	22,000
Morris	2,000
Total	$58,000

Suppose that the business has increased in value because of the construction of a large housing development nearby. This is the kind of gain that [under the principles of accounting] ordinarily would not be reflected on the partnership books as long as the firm continues to operate with the same owners. Now suppose that the business is sold for $78,000 cash, net of all debts or other obligations. There is a surplus of $20,000 above the amount in the capital accounts (that is, above the amount of the initial contributions increased by profits and decreased by distributions to the partners). This $20,000 can be thought of as previously unrecorded profit; it would be allocated equally among the partners ($5,000 apiece), so that each partner would receive the following amount:

Abe	$22,000 *
Bill	22,000
Pamela	27,000
Morris	7,000
Total	$78,000

*$17,000 current capital account, plus $5,000 share of profit on sale of business.

Finally, assume that the store is sold for less than the amount in the capital accounts—for example, for $38,000. Here there is a previously unrecognized loss of $20,000. In the absence of an agreement to the contrary, the loss would be borne equally by all the partners (again, $5,000 apiece). The relative claims of the partners would therefore be as follows:

Abe	$12,000
Bill	12,000
Pamela	17,000
Morris	(3,000)
Total	$38,000

SECTION 4. THE AUTHORITY OF A PARTNER

UNIFORM PARTNERSHIP ACT §§ 3, 4(3), 9, 10, 11, 12, 13, 14

REVISED UNIFORM PARTNERSHIP ACT
§§ 301, 302, 303, 304, 305, 306, 308

[See Statutory Supplement]

RNR Investments Limited Partnership v. Peoples First Community Bank

District Court of Appeal of Florida, First District, 2002.
812 So.2d 561.

■ VAN NORTWICK, J. . . .

Factual and Procedural History

RNR is a Florida limited partnership formed pursuant to chapter 620, Florida Statutes, to purchase vacant land in Destin, Florida, and to construct a house on the land for resale. Bernard Roeger was RNR's general partner and Heinz Rapp, Claus North, and S.E. Waltz, Inc., were limited partners. The agreement of limited partnership provides for various restrictions on the authority of the general partner. Paragraph 4.1 of the agreement required the general partner to prepare a budget covering the cost of acquisition and construction of the project (defined as the "Approved Budget") and further provided, in pertinent part, as follows:

> The Approved Budget for the Partnership is attached hereto as Exhibit "C" and is approved by evidence of the signatures of the Partners on the signature pages of this Agreement. . . . In no event, without Limited Partner Consent, shall the Approved Budget be exceeded by more than five percent (5%), nor shall any line item thereof be exceeded by more than ten percent (10%), . . .

Paragraph 4.3 restricted the general partner's ability to borrow, spend partnership funds and encumber partnership assets, if not specifically provided for in the Approved Budget. Finally, with respect to the development of the partnership project, paragraph 2.2(b) provided:

> The General Partner shall not incur debts, liabilities or obligations of the Partnership which will cause any line item in the Approved Budget to be exceeded by more than ten percent (10%) or which

> will cause the aggregate Approved Budget to be exceed by more than five percent (5%) unless the General Partner shall receive the prior written consent of the Limited Partner.

In June 1998, RNR, through its general partner, entered into a construction loan agreement, note and mortgage in the principal amount of $990,000. From June 25, 1998 through Mar. 13, 2000, the bank disbursed the aggregate sum of $952,699, by transfers into RNR's bank account. All draws were approved by an architect, who certified that the work had progressed as indicated and that the quality of the work was in accordance with the construction contract. No representative of RNR objected to any draw of funds or asserted that the amounts disbursed were not associated with the construction of the house.

RNR defaulted under the terms of the note and mortgage by failing to make payments due in July 2000 and all monthly payments due thereafter. The Bank filed a complaint seeking foreclosure. RNR filed an answer and affirmative defenses. In its first affirmative defense, RNR alleged that the Bank had failed to review the limitations on the general partner's authority in RNR's limited partnership agreement. RNR asserted that the Bank had negligently failed to investigate and to realize that the general partner had no authority to execute notes, a mortgage and a construction loan agreement and was estopped from foreclosing. The Bank filed a motion for summary judgment with supporting affidavits attesting to the amounts due and owing and the amount of disbursements under the loan.

In opposition to the summary judgment motion, RNR filed the affidavit of Stephen E. Waltz, the president one of RNR's limited partners, S.E. Waltz, Inc. In that affidavit, Mr. Waltz stated that the partners anticipated that RNR would need to finance the construction of the residence, but that paragraph 2.2(b) of the partnership agreement limited the amount of any loan the general partner could obtain on behalf of RNR to an amount that would not exceed by more than 10% the approved budget on any one line item or exceed the aggregate approved budget by more than 5%, unless the general partner received the prior written consent of the limited partners. Waltz alleged that the limited partners understood and orally agreed that the general partner would seek financing in the approximate amount of $650,000. Further, Waltz stated:

> Even though the limited partners had orally agreed to this amount, a written consent was never memorialized, and to my surprise, the [Bank], either through its employees or attorney, . . . never requested the same from any of the limited partners at any time prior to [or] after the closing on the loan from the [Bank] to RNR.

Waltz alleged that the partners learned in the spring of 2000 that, instead of obtaining a loan for $650,000, Roeger had obtained a loan for $990,000, which was secured by RNR's property. He stated that the limited partners did not consent to Roeger obtaining a loan from the Bank in the amount of $990,000 either orally or in writing and that the limited partners were never contacted by the Bank as to whether they had consented to a loan amount of $990,000.

RNR asserts that a copy of the limited partnership agreement was maintained at its offices. Nevertheless, the record contains no copy of an Approved Budget of the partnership or any evidence that would show that a copy of RNR's partnership agreement or any partnership budget was given to the Bank or that any notice of the general partner's restricted authority was provided to the Bank.

. . . [T]he trial court entered a summary final judgment of foreclosure in favor of the Bank. The foreclosure sale has been stayed pending the outcome of this appeal. . . .

Apparent Authority of the General Partner

Although the agency concept of apparent authority was applied to partnerships under the common law, *see, e.g.*, Taylor v. Cummer Lumber Co., 52 So. 614, 616 (Fla. 1910), in Florida the extent to which the partnership is bound by the acts of a partner acting within the apparent authority is now governed by statute. Section 620.8301(1), Florida Statutes (2000),[7] a part of the Florida Revised Uniform Partnership Act (FRUPA), provides:

> Each partner is an agent of the partnership for the purpose of its business. An act of a partner, including the execution of an instrument in the partnership name, for apparently carrying on in the ordinary scope of partnership business or business of the kind carried on by the partnership, in the geographic area in which the partnership operates, binds the partnership unless the partner had no authority to act for the partnership in the particular manner and the person with whom the partner was dealing knew or had received notification that the partner lacked authority.

Thus, even if a general partner's actual authority is restricted by the terms of the partnership agreement, the general partner possesses the apparent authority to bind the partnership in the ordinary course of partnership business or in the business of the kind carried on by the partnership, unless the third party "knew or had received a notification that the partner lacked authority." *Id.* "Knowledge" and "notice" under FRUPA are defined in section 620.8102. That section provides that "[a] person knows a fact if the person has actual knowledge of the fact." § 620.8102(1), Fla. Stat. (2000). Further, a third party has notice of a fact if that party "(a) [k]nows of the fact; (b) [h]as received notification of the fact; or (c) [h]as reason to know the fact exists from all other facts known to the person at the time in question." § 620.8102(2), Fla. Stat. (2000). Finally, under section

7. RNR mistakenly argues that section 620.8301(1) has no application to a limited partnership because that section is part of the Florida Revised Uniform Partnership Act, not the Florida Revised Uniform Limited Partnership Act. Section 620.186, however, provides, as follows:

> In any case not provided for in this act, the provisions of the Uniform Partnership Act or the Revised Uniform Partnership Act of 1995, as applicable, and the rules of law and equity shall govern.

620.8303 a partnership may file a statement of partnership authority setting forth any restrictions in a general partner's authority.

Commentators have described the purpose of these knowledge and notice provisions, as follows:

> Under RUPA, the term knew is confined to actual knowledge, which is cognitive awareness.... Therefore, despite the similarity in language, RUPA provides greater protection [than the Uniform Partnership Act (UPA)] to third persons dealing with partners, who may rely on the partner's apparent authority absent actual knowledge or notification of a restriction in this regard. RUPA effects a slight reallocation of the risk of unauthorized agency power in favor of third parties. That is consistent with notions of the expanded liability of principals since the UPA was drafted.
>
> RUPA attempts to balance its shift toward greater protection of third parties by providing several new ways for partners to protect themselves against unauthorized actions by a rogue partner. First, the partnership may notify a third party of a partner's lack of authority. Such notification is effective upon receipt, whether or not the third party actually learns of it. More significantly, the partnership may file a statement of partnership authority restricting a partner's authority.

Donald J. Weidner & John W. Larson, *The Revised Uniform Partnership Act: The Reporters' Overview*, 49 Bus. Law 1, 31–32 (1993) (footnotes omitted). "Absent actual knowledge, third parties have no duty to inspect the partnership agreement or inquire otherwise to ascertain the extent of a partner's actual authority in the ordinary course of business, ... even if they have some reason to question it." *Id.* at 32 n. 200. The apparent authority provisions of section 620.8301(1), reflect a policy by the drafters that "the risk of loss from partner misconduct more appropriately belongs on the partnership than on third parties who do not knowingly participate in or take advantage of the misconduct ..." J. Dennis [Hynes], *Notice and Notification Under the Revised Uniform Partnership Act: Some Suggested Changes*, 2 J. Small & Emerging Bus. L. 299, 308 (1998).

Analysis

Under section 620.8301(1), the determination of whether a partner is acting with authority to bind the partnership involves a two-step analysis. The first step is to determine whether the partner purporting to bind the partnership apparently is carrying on the partnership business in the usual way or a business of the kind carried on by the partnership. An affirmative answer on this step ends the inquiry, unless it is shown that the person with whom the partner is dealing actually knew or had received a notification that the partner lacked authority. *See* Kristerin Dev. Co. v. Granson Inv., 394 N.W.2d 325, 330 (Iowa 1986) (applying Iowa version of UPA). Here, it is undisputed that, in entering into the loan, the general partner was carrying on the business of RNR in the usual way. The dispositive question in this appeal is whether there are issues of material fact as to whether the

Bank had actual knowledge or notice of restrictions on the general partner's authority.

RNR argues that, as a result of the restrictions on the general partner's authority in the partnership agreement, the Bank had constructive knowledge of the restrictions and was obligated to inquire as to the general partner's specific authority to bind RNR in the construction loan. We cannot agree. Under section 620.8301, the Bank could rely on the general partner's apparent authority, unless it had actual knowledge or notice of restrictions on that authority. While the RNR partners may have agreed upon restrictions that would limit the general partner to borrowing no more than $650,000 on behalf of the partnership, RNR does not contend and nothing before us would show that the Bank had actual knowledge or notice of any restrictions on the general partner's authority. Here, the partnership could have protected itself by filing a statement pursuant to section 620.8303 or by providing notice to the Bank of the specific restrictions on the authority of the general partner....

Because there is no disputed issue of fact concerning whether the Bank had actual knowledge or notice of restrictions on the general partner's authority to borrow, summary judgment was proper.

AFFIRMED.

■ MINER and WOLF, JJ., concur.

Northmon Investment Company v. Milford Plaza Associates

Supreme Court, Appellate Division, New York, 2001.
284 A.D.2d 250, 727 N.Y.S.2d 419.

■ SULLIVAN, P.J., ELLERIN, WALLACH, RUBIN and BUCKLEY, JJ.

Supreme Court, New York County ... in a dispute between partners concerning appellants' [defendants'] authority to enter into a 99–year lease of real property constituting the partnership's only asset, found in respondents' favor that appellants lack such authority.... [The decision is] unanimously affirmed, with costs.

Appellants lack authority to enter into the contemplated 99–year lease even if such lease were to be deemed in the ordinary course of the partnership's business. A partner's authority to bind the partnership to transactions apparently in the ordinary course of the partnership's business (*see,* Partnership Law § 20[1]) does not affect the right of partners as between themselves to prevent contemplated transactions with third parties, or otherwise to assert their "equal rights in the management and conduct of the partnership business" (*see,* Partnership Law § 40[5]). Appellants cannot impose their decision to enter into this lease upon respondents (*see,* Riley v. Maran, 370 N.Y.S.2d 302 (N.Y. Sup. 1974); *see also,* Partnership Law § 40[8]), and, indeed, respondents' right to interfere with this or any other contract or prospective contract involving the partnership is "absolute" and "privileged, excusable and justified" (Braden v. Perkins, 22 N.Y.S.2d 144 (N.Y. Sup. 1940)). Nor do the newly discovered partnership agreements avail appellants. Assuming such agreements ... can be fairly construed to preclude respondents' interference with a contemplated or consummated long-term lease, it remains that the agreements, on their face, terminate the partnership in 2075, many years before the contemplated 99–year lease would expire. Since such a lease cannot be deemed ordinary, respondents would not be bound by it (*see,* Partnership Law § 40[2],[3][b],[c]). . . .

NOTE ON THE AUTHORITY OF A PARTNER

1. *Actual and Apparent Authority*

(a) UPA. The basic default rule governing a partner's *actual* authority under the UPA is that each partner is an agent of the partnership for the purpose of its business. However, the UPA's rule on a partner's *apparent* authority is somewhat ambiguous. Under the UPA, a partner has authority to bind the partnership by any act "for apparently carrying on in the usual way the business of the partnership of which he is a member." There is controversy whether this means the usual way *the partner's firm* carries on its business or the usual way *other firms* in the same locality engaged in the same general line of business carry on business. In Burns v. Gonzalez, 439 S.W.2d 128 (Tex.Civ.App.1969), the court adopted the latter view.

(b). RUPA. RUPA § 301(1) makes clear, as the UPA did not, that a partnership is bound by an act of the partner for apparently carrying on in the usual way (i) the partnership business or (ii) business *of the kind* carried on by the partnership. The Comment to § 301(1) states:

> Section 301(1). . . . clarifies that a partner's apparent authority includes acts for carrying on in the ordinary course "business of the kind carried on by the partnership," not just the business of the particular partnership in question. The UPA is ambiguous on this point, but there is some authority for an expanded construction. . . . *See, e.g.*, Burns v. Gonzalez, 439 S.W.2d 128, 131 (Tex. Civ.App.1969) (dictum). . . .

The treatment of authority under RUPA also differs from the UPA in certain other respects. For example, RUPA § 302 provides elaborate rules concerning when a transfer of partnership property is binding. In addition—

2. *Notice.* RUPA § 301 makes subtle shifts in determining when the knowledge or notice of T, a third person, of a restriction on the authority of a partner, will prevent partnership liability from arising out of a transaction between T and a partner who purports to act on the partnership's behalf. "Under UPA section 9(1), the partnership was not bound by the unauthorized actions of a partner if the third party had '*knowledge*' of the partner's lack of authority. Under UPA section

9(1), a third party had knowledge when he or she had actual knowledge or '*when he has knowledge of such other facts as in the circumstances shows bad faith.*' This latter language creates an implied or inquiry notice, the exact parameters of which are ill-defined. Under RUPA, the third party will not be placed under a duty of inquiry or be deemed to have notice from the facts and circumstances. *Only actual knowledge or receipt of a notification of a partner's lack of authority will meet the standard.*" Merrill, Partnership Property and Partnership Authority Under the Revised Uniform Partnership Act, 49 Bus. Law. 83, 88–89 (1993) (emphasis added).

3. *Statement of Authority.* RUPA § 303 enables a partnership to file a "Statement of Partnership Authority." A *grant* of authority in such a Statement is normally conclusive in favor of third persons, even if they have no actual knowledge of the Statement, unless they have actual knowledge that the partner has no such authority. In contrast, a *limitation* on a partner's authority in such a Statement—other than a limitation on the partner's authority to transfer real property—will not be effective unless the third party *knows* of the limitation or the Statement has been delivered to him. In contrast, a limitation, in a Statement of Partnership Authority, of a partner's authority to transfer partnership *real property* is effective against all third persons if a certified copy of the Statement is filed in the real-property recording office.

Why would a partnership want to file a Statement that can *expand* a partner's authority simply because it is filed, but normally will not *limit* a partner's authority unless it is not only filed but also delivered? One answer is that persons who deal with a partnership may require such a Statement to ensure themselves that the partnership will be bound. Also, "[in] the process of searching for the grant of authority, the third party will acquire actual knowledge of any restriction on authority in a filed statement. [Furthermore,] the . . . partners may protect themselves by delivering the statement to all known creditors, actual or potential." Merrill, supra, at 89.

SECTION 5. LIABILITY FOR PARTNERSHIP OBLIGATIONS

UNIFORM PARTNERSHIP ACT §§ 9, 13, 14, 15, 16, 17, 36

REVISED UNIFORM PARTNERSHIP ACT §§ 305, 306, 307, 308

[See Statutory Supplement]

DAVIS v. LOFTUS, 334 Ill.App.3d 761, 778 N.E.2d 1144 (Ill. App. 2002). Davis claimed that two lawyers, Loftus and Engel, at the law firm of Gottlieb & Schwartz, had committed malpractice in connection with a real estate transaction that Davis had engaged in. Davis sued all the partners of the firm for damages. Some of the partners of the firm, including Frink, were denominated "income partners," as opposed to "equity partners." According to the partnership agreement, the firm paid each income partner a fixed level of compensation, determined on an annual basis by the Executive Committee, plus a bonus. The partnership agreement added that: "Income Partners will not share in Partnership Net Profit or Loss." Each income partner made a capital contribution of $10,000 to the firm. If an income partner withdrew from the firm, or upon dissolution of the firm, the firm would return the $10,000 capital contribution to the income partner without any adjustment for the growth or profits of the firm from the time of the capital contribution. Income partners had no voting rights and were not eligible to serve on the executive committee. Held, Frink and the other income partners were not liable to Davis:

> [T]he agreement established that income partners, including Frink, received a fixed salary plus a bonus, and the income partners took no share of the partnership's profit or loss. While income partners paid a "capital contribution" to the firm, the firm would repay the same amount, without regard to the firm's profit or loss from the time of the "capital contribution." The executive committee ... set the level of compensation for all income partners. Moreover, the income partners had no right to vote on the management or conduct of the partnership business. . . . [W]e find that income partners under Gottlieb & Schwartz' partnership agreement do not qualify as partners within the meaning of the Act, and therefore the Act provides no basis for holding income partners liable for the acts of Loftus and Engel.

NOTE ON LIABILITY FOR PARTNERSHIP OBLIGATIONS

1. *UPA*. The provisions of the Uniform Partnership Act governing liability for partnership obligations reflect an amalgam of the entity and aggregate theories. On the one hand, UPA §§ 9, 13, and 14 make "the partnership" liable for defined acts of the partners. It might seem to follow that this liability could be enforced by a suit against the partnership. However, the UPA does not authorize such a suit, because it does not recognize a partnership as an entity, and unless authorized by statute, suit normally cannot be brought against an association that is not an entity. Suit against the individual partners on a partnership obligation is also difficult under the UPA. At common law, if an obligation is "joint and several," the obligors can be sued either jointly or separately. If, however, an obligation is only "joint," all the joint obligors must be joined in the suit, subject to a few exceptions where jurisdiction over all the obligors cannot be obtained. *See* C.

Clark, Handbook of the Law of Code Pleading 373–74 (2d ed. 1947). Under UPA § 15(a), partners are *jointly and severally* liable for wrongful acts and omissions of the partnership such as torts, and breaches of trust. Under UPA § 15(b), however, partners are only *jointly* liable "for all other debts and obligations of the partnership," such as breaches of contract. Thus under the UPA, if, in an action based on a partnership's contractual obligation, the plaintiff does not join all the partners, the action normally can be dismissed on motion by the partners who were joined.

The inability of a UPA partnership contract creditor to sue a partnership in its own name is obviously undesirable, and many states have statutorily patched up the UPA rule. Some states achieved this objective by adopting a Common Name Statute, which explicitly allows a partnership to be sued in its own name. An example is N.Y.Civ. Prac.L. & R. § 1025: "Two or more persons conducting a business as a partnership may sue or be sued in the partnership name. . . ." Under such statutes, a judgment is binding on the partnership property and on the individual property of all partners who are served. Other states patched up the UPA by changing the rule that a contract creditor of a partnership needs to join all the partners in a suit to establish liability on the contract claim. Still other states adopted Joint Debtor Statutes, which provide that a suit against joint obligors can proceed even if some of the obligors are not joined. *See*, *e.g.*, Cal.Civ.Proc.Code § 410.70. Under such statutes, a judgment is binding on both the joint (partnership) property and on the property of those partners who are served. And some states made *all* partnership liabilities joint and several, not just wrongful acts or omissions and breaches of trust.

2. *RUPA*. Unlike the UPA, RUPA § 307(a) specifically provides that a partnership may both sue and be sued in its own name. Furthermore, RUPA § 306 provides that partners are jointly and severally liable for all obligations of the partnership. However, RUPA adds a new barrier to *collecting* against an individual partner. Under RUPA § 307, a judgment against a partner based on a claim against the partnership normally cannot be satisfied against the partner's individual assets unless and until a judgment on the same claim has been rendered against the partnership and a writ of execution on that judgment has been returned unsatisfied. To put this differently, RUPA § 307 adopts an exhaustion rule under which, in a suit against a partner based on a claim against the partnership, partnership assets must be exhausted before a partner's individual assets can be reached. (This exhaustion rule is made subject to certain exceptions, one of which is that the rule does not apply if the partnership is in bankruptcy.) As the Comment to RUPA § 306 points out, "Joint and several liability under RUPA differs . . . from the classic model [of joint and several liability outside RUPA], which permits a judgment creditor to proceed immediately against any of the joint and several judgment debtors." In effect, therefore, RUPA takes an aggregate-like approach to a partner's liability, but an entity-like approach to collecting judgments based on that liability. RUPA § 307 also provides that, subject to certain exceptions, a judgment against a partnership is not by itself a

judgment against a partner, and cannot be satisfied from a partner's assets unless there is also a judgment against the partner.

SECTION 6. PARTNERSHIP INTERESTS AND PARTNERSHIP PROPERTY

UNIFORM PARTNERSHIP ACT §§ 8, 18(g), 24, 25, 26, 27, 28

REVISED UNIFORM PARTNERSHIP ACT §§ 203, 204, 501, 502, 503, 504

[See Statutory Supplement]

Rapoport v. 55 Perry Co.

New York Supreme Court, Appellate Division, 1975.
50 A.D.2d 54, 376 N.Y.S.2d 147.

Cross appeals from an order of the Supreme Court (HILDA G. SCHWARTZ, J.), entered July 16, 1975 in New York County, which denied a motion by plaintiffs for summary judgment and a cross motion by defendants for summary judgment dismissing the complaint. . . .

■ TILZER, J. In 1969, Simon, Genia and Ury Rapoport entered into a partnership agreement with Morton, Jerome and Burton Parnes, forming the partnership known as 55 Perry Company. Pursuant to the agreement, each of the families owned 50% of the partnership interests. In December of 1974 Simon and Genia Rapoport assigned a 10% interest of their share in the partnership to their adult children, Daniel and Kalia. The Parnes defendants were advised of the assignment and an amended partnership certificate was filed in the County Clerk's office indicating the addition of Daniel and Kalia as partners. However, when the plaintiffs, thereafter, requested the Parnes defendants to execute an amended partnership agreement to reflect the above changes in the partnership, the Parnes refused, taking the position that the partnership agreement did not permit the introduction of new partners without consent of all the existing partners. Thereafter, the plaintiffs Rapoport brought this action seeking a declaration that Simon and Genia Rapoport had an absolute right to assign their interests to their adult children without consent of the defendants and that such assignment was authorized pursuant to paragraph 12 of the partnership agreement. The plaintiffs further sought to have Daniel and Kalia be declared partners in 55 Perry Company and have their names entered upon the books of the partnership as partners. The defendants Parnes interposed an answer, taking the position that the partnership agreement did not permit admission of additional partners without consent of all the existing partners and that the filing of the amended certificate of partnership was unauthorized. After joinder of issue plaintiffs moved for summary judgment and although the defendants did not cross-move for similar relief, such was, nevertheless, requested in their answering papers.

On the motion for summary judgment both parties agreed that there were no issues of fact and that there was only a question of the interpretation of the written documents which should be disposed of as a matter of law by the court. Nevertheless, the court below found that the agreement was ambiguous and that there was a triable issue with respect to the intent of the parties. We disagree and conclude that the agreement is without ambiguity and that pursuant to the terms of the agreement and of the Partnership Law, consent of the Parnes defendants was required in order to admit Daniel Rapoport and Kalia Shalleck to the partnership.

Plaintiffs, in support of their contention that they have an absolute right to assign their interests in the partnership to their adult children and that the children must be admitted to the partnership as partners rely on paragraph 12 of the partnership agreement which provides as follows: "No partner or partners shall have the authority to transfer, sell . . . assign or in any way dispose of the partnership realty and/or personalty and shall not have the authority to sell, transfer, assign . . . his or their share in this firm, nor enter into any agreement as a result of which any person shall become interested with him in this firm, unless the same is agreed to in writing by a majority of the partners as determined by the percentage of ownership . . . except for members of his immediate family who have attained majority, in which case no such consent shall be required." As indicated, plaintiffs argue that the above provision expressly authorizes entry of their adult children into the partnership. Defendants, on the other hand, maintain that paragraph 12 provides only for the right of a partner to assign or transfer a share of the profits in the partnership. We agree with that construction of the agreement.

A reading of the partnership agreement indicates that the parties intended to observe the differences, as set forth in the Partnership Law, between assignees of a partnership interest and the admission into the partnership itself of new partners. The Partnership Law provides that subject to any contrary agreement between the partners, "[n]o person can become a member of a partnership without the consent of all the partners." (Partnership Law, § 40, subd. 7.)[1] Subdivision 1 of section 53 of the Partnership Law provides that an assignee of an interest in the partnership is not entitled "to interfere in the management or administration of the partnership business" but is merely entitled to receive "the profits to which the assigning partner would otherwise be entitled." Additionally, section 50 of the Partner-

1. The Partnership Law is New York's version of the UPA. (footnote by ed.)

ship Law indicates the differences between the rights of an assignee and a new partner. That section states that the "property rights of a partner are (a) his rights in specific partnership property, (b) his interest in the partnership, and (c) his right to participate in the management." On the other hand, as already indicated above, an assignee is excluded in the absence of agreement from interfering in the management of the partnership business and from access to the partnership books and information about partnership transactions. (Partnership Law, § 53.)

The effect, therefore, of the various provisions of the Partnership Law, above discussed, is that unless the parties have agreed otherwise, a person cannot become a member of a partnership without consent of all the partners whereas an assignment of a partnership interest may be made without consent, but the assignee is entitled only to receive the profits of the assigning partner. And, as already stated, the partnership agreement herein clearly took cognizance of the differences between an assignment of an interest in the partnership as compared to the full rights of a partner as set forth in section 50 of the Partnership Law. Paragraph 12 of the agreement by its language has reference to section 53 of the Partnership Law dealing with an "assignment of partner's interest." It (par 12) refers to assignments, encumbrances and agreements "as a result of which any person shall become interested with (the assignor) in this firm." That paragraph does not contain language with respect to admitting a partner to the partnership with all rights to participate in the management of its affairs. Moreover, interpretation of paragraph 12 in this manner is consistent with other provisions of the partnership agreement. For example, in paragraph 15 of the agreement, the following is provided:

> "In the event of the death of any partner the business of this firm shall continue with the heir, or distributee providing he has reached majority, or fiduciary of the deceased partner having the right to succeed the deceased partner with the same rights and privileges and the same obligations, pursuant to all of the terms hereof."

In that paragraph, therefore, there is specific provision to succeed to all the privileges and obligations of a partner—language which is completely absent from paragraph 12.

Accordingly, it appears that contrary to plaintiffs' contention that paragraph 12 was intended to give the parties the right to transfer a full partnership interest to adult children, without consent of all other partners (an agreement which would vary the rights otherwise existing pursuant to Partnership Law, § 40, subd 7) that paragraph was instead intended to limit a partner with respect to his right to assign a partnership interest as provided for under section 53 of the Partnership Law (i.e., the right to profits)—to the extent of prohibiting such assignments without consent of other partners except to children of the existing partners who have reached majority. Therefore, it must be concluded that pursuant to the terms of the partnership agreement, the plaintiffs could not transfer a full partnership interest to their children and that the children only have the rights as assignees to receive a share of the partnership income and profits of their assignors.

Accordingly, the order entered July 16, 1975 should be modified on the law to grant summary judgment in favor of the defendants to the extent of declaring that the partnership agreement does not permit entry into the partnership of new partners, including adult children of the partners who have reached their majority, without consent of all the partners; [and] that the plaintiffs, pursuant to the terms of the agreement, had the right to assign their interests to their adult children but that such children, i.e., Daniel Rapoport and Kalia Shalleck, have not become partners but only have the rights of assignees to receive a share of the partnership income and profits of their assignors....

■ NUNEZ, J. (dissenting). I agree with Special Term that the written partnership agreement providing for the assignment of partners' shares to members of their immediate families without the consent of the other partners is ambiguous and that there is a triable issue as to intent. The agreement being ambiguous, construction is a mixed question of law and fact and resolution thereof to determine the parties' intent should await a trial....

■ STEVENS, P.J., KUPFERMAN and MURPHY, JJ., concur with TILZER, J.; NUNEZ, J., dissents in an opinion....

Bauer v. Blomfield Co.

Supreme Court of Alaska, 1993.
849 P.2d 1365.

■ Before RABINOWITZ, C.J., and BURKE, MATTHEWS, COMPTON and MOORE, JJ.

Opinion

■ BURKE, JUSTICE.

William J. Bauer, assignee of a partnership interest, sued the partnership and the individual partners, claiming that partnership profits were wrongfully withheld from him. The superior court granted summary judgment to the partnership and individual partners, and dismissed Bauer's complaint with prejudice. We affirm.

I

In 1986 William Bauer loaned $800,000 to Richard Holden and Judith Holden. To secure the loan, the Holdens assigned to Bauer "all of their right, title and interest" in a partnership known as the Blomfield Company/Holden Joint Venture. The other members of the partnership—Charles Alfred (Chuck) Blomfield, Patricia A. Blomfield, Charles Anthony (Tony) Blomfield and Richard H. Monsarrat—consented to the assignment. According to the consent document, their consent was given "[p]ursuant to AS 32.05.220."[1]

---

1. AS 32.05.220 provides:

(a) A conveyance by a partner of a partner's interest in the partnership does not by itself dissolve the partnership, nor as against the other partners in the absence of

When the Holdens defaulted on the loan, Bauer sent the following notice to the partnership members: "William Bauer hereby gives notice that he is exercising his rights to receive all distributions of income and principal from the Blomfield Company/Holden Joint Venture Partnership." Thereafter, for a time, the partnership income share payable to the Holdens was paid monthly to Bauer.

In January, 1989 the partners stopped making income payments to Bauer. They, instead, agreed to use the income of the partnership to pay an $877,000 "commission" to partner Chuck Blomfield. Bauer was not a party to this agreement; he was notified of the agreement after the fact by means of a letter dated January 10, 1989. Bauer was not asked to consent to the agreement, and he never agreed to forego payment of his assigned partnership income share or to pay part of the "commission" to Blomfield. The amount Bauer would have received, had the "commission" not been paid, was $207,567.

Blomfield's $877,000 commission represented five percent of the increased gross rental income earned by the partnership from lease extensions obtained from the state by Blomfield on partnership properties leased by the state. These and other lease extensions were obtained when a *private* claim made against the state by Chuck Blomfield and Patricia Blomfield for $1,900,000 was settled. Other lease extensions thus obtained were on properties not owned by the partnership; these properties were owned by the Blomfields and were leased by them to the state. One of the conditions upon which Chuck and Patricia Blomfield based their settlement was the agreement of the partners to pay Chuck Blomfield an $877,000 commission for the lease extensions that he obtained on the partnership's properties.

II

Insisting that his assigned right to the Holdens' share of the partnership's income had been violated, Bauer filed suit in superior court against the partnership and all of the partners except the Holdens. Bauer sought declaratory and injunctive relief, and damages. His various claims were dismissed, with prejudice, when the court concluded that Bauer's assignment from the Holdens did not make him a member of the partnership. Therefore, he was not entitled to complain about a decision made with the consent of all the partners. This appeal followed.

---

agreement, entitle the assignee, during the continuance of the partnership, to interfere in the management or administration of the partnership business or affairs, or to require any information or account of partnership transactions or to inspect the partnership books, but it entitles the assignee to receive in accordance with the assignee's contract the profits to which the assigning partner would otherwise be entitled.

(b) In the case of a dissolution of the partnership, the assignee is entitled to receive the assignor's interest and may require an account from the date only of the last account agreed to by all of the partners.

III

The assignment to Bauer of the Holdens' "right, title and interest" in the partnership, did not, in and of itself, make Bauer a partner in the Blomfield Company/Holden Joint Venture. *See* AS 32.05.220. We are unpersuaded by Bauer's argument that he should be considered a *de facto* partner.

As the Holdens' assignee, Bauer was not entitled "to interfere in the management or administration of the partnership business or affairs, or to require any information or account of partnership transactions or to inspect the partnership books." AS 32.05.220(a).[2]

The "interest" that was assigned to Bauer was the Holdens' "share of the [partnership's] profits and surplus." AS 32.05.210.[3] The assignment only entitled Bauer to "*receive ... the [partnership] profits to which the [Holdens] would otherwise be entitled.*" AS 32.05.220(a) (emphasis added). Because all of The Blomfield Company/Holden Joint Venture partners agreed that Chuck Blomfield was entitled to receive an $877,000 commission, to be paid out of partnership income, we agree with the superior court's conclusion that there *were no partnership profits* which the Holdens, and thus Bauer, were entitled to receive until the commission was fully paid.

AFFIRMED.

■ MATTHEWS, J., with whom RABINOWITZ, C.J., joins, dissenting.

It is a well-settled principle of contract law that an assignee steps into the shoes of an assignor as to the rights assigned. Today the court summarily dismisses this principle in a footnote and leaves the assignee barefoot.

The court's analysis, set out in three cursory paragraphs is this: (1) Bauer was not a partner; (2) Bauer, as an assignee, was not entitled to interfere in the management of the partnership; (3) Bauer's assignment entitled him to receive only the profits the Holdens would have received; and (4) Bauer was due nothing because no profits were distributed. These statements are generally correct as far as they go. However, they do not address the issue in dispute: whether the partners owe Bauer a duty of good faith and fair dealing.

The court is correct to state that Bauer's assignment entitles him to nothing if the partnership decides to forego a distribution. Howev-

---

2. We are unwilling to hold that partners owe a duty of good faith and fair dealing to assignees of a partner's interest. To do so would undermine the clear intent of AS 32.05.220(a). Partners should be able to manage their partnership without regard for the concerns of an assignee, who may have little interest in the partnership venture. As commentators have explained:

> The U.P.A. rules concerning assignment of partnership interests and the rights of assignees balance the interests of assignees, assignors, and nonassigning partners in a way that is suited to the very closely held business. Although the assignee's impotence obviously limits the market value of the partners' interest, the partners need to be protected from interference by unwanted strangers.

Alan R. Bromberg and Larry E. Ribstein, Partnership § 3:61 (1988).

3. AS 32.05.210 provides: "A partner's interest in the partnership is the partner's share of the profits and surplus."

er, this statement leaves unanswered the crucial question that must first be asked: was the partners' decision to pay Blomfield a "commission," thereby depleting profits for distribution, a decision made in good faith? Until this question is answered, we cannot know if Bauer was unjustly deprived of that to which he is entitled.

The court dismisses the main issue in a short footnote, stating "[w]e are unwilling to hold that partners owe a duty of good faith and fair dealing to assignees of a partner's interest." The court reasons that to find such a duty "would undermine the clear intent of AS 32.05.220(a). Partners should be able to manage their partnership without regard for the concerns of an assignee. . . ." The court is correct in noting that Bauer has no management rights in the partnership. Bauer's attempt to enforce his right to profits under the assignment is not, however, an interference with the management of the partnership. Requiring the partners to make decisions regarding distributions in good faith does not interfere with management, it merely requires that the partners fulfill their existing contractual duties to act in good faith.

I further disagree with the court's interpretation of the intent of the statute. The statute's intent is to assure that an assignee does not interfere in the management of the partnership while receiving "the profits to which the assigning partner would otherwise be entitled." AS 32.05.220(a). As interpreted by the court, the statute now allows partners to deprive an assignee of profits to which he is entitled by law for whatever outrageous motive or reason. The court's opinion essentially leaves the assignee of a partnership interest without remedy to enforce his right.[2]

Upon formation of the Blomfield Company/Holden Joint Venture, a contractual relationship arose among the partners. This court has held that a covenant of good faith and fair dealing is implied in *all* contracts. We have noted that the basis for imposing this duty "is a hybrid of social policy and an effort to further the expectations of the contracting parties that the promises will be executed in good faith." *Alaska Pacific*, 794 P.2d at 947. The duty of good faith and fair dealing "requires 'that neither party . . . do anything which will injure the right of the other to receive the benefits of the agreement.' " Klondike Indus. Corp. v. Gibson, 741 P.2d 1161, 1168 (Alaska 1987) (quoting *Guin*, 591 P.2d at 1291).

One element of the contract between the Holdens and the partnership is the Holdens' right to receive their share of profits when a distribution is made. As an element of the partnership contract, this right is accompanied by the duty of the parties to deal fairly and in

---

2. The court notes that the Uniform Partnership Act balances the rights of assignees, assignors, and nonassigning partners. One of the ways in which the U.P.A. accomplishes this is to provide the assignee with the right to petition a court for dissolution of the partnership. The U.P.A. states that upon application of an assignee, the court *must* decree a dissolution if the partnership was a partnership at will at the time of assignment. U.P.A. § 32(2)(b). Although the Alaska Partnership Act was copied from the U.P.A., due to an error in cross-referencing, it is unclear that an assignee in Alaska has the right to apply for a dissolution. Thus he may be deprived of one of the "balances" that the U.P.A. sets up for his protection.

good faith. The partnership has a right to decide not to make a distribution, but in making this decision, the partnership must act in good faith.

The Holdens assigned to Bauer that part of the partnership contract that entitled the Holdens to receive distributions. Under the law of assignments, Bauer steps into the shoes of the Holdens as to this distribution right. Accompanying this contract right is the partners' duty to act in good faith. Thus, as the assignee of that element of the contract, the partners owe Bauer a duty of good faith and fair dealing in deciding whether to make a distribution.

Holding that, as a matter of law, the partners owe Bauer a duty of good faith when deciding whether to make a distribution does not resolve the dispute in this case. Whether the decision to pay the "commission" in lieu of making a distribution was made in good faith is a factual question. *See* 3A Arthur L. Corbin, *Corbin on Contracts* § 654B, at 89 (Supp.1992) ("Good faith always involves questions of fact.... If there is a dispute as to why someone did what he did, there is a question of fact for the jury."). As the moving party on a motion for summary judgment, the burden is on the partnership to demonstrate that no genuine issue existed as to whether the decision to pay the 5% "commission" was made in good faith. The partnership presented little to no evidence on this issue.[7] This court should thus remand to the superior court for a factual determination of whether or not the decision by the partners to pay Blomfield's "commission" was made in good faith.

The court's decision today effectively leaves an assignee with no remedy to enforce his right to receive partnership profits. Without such a remedy, his assignment becomes worthless. As I believe this result is contrary to basic contract and assignment law, I dissent from the court's opinion.

NOTE ON PARTNERSHIP PROPERTY

1. *UPA*. Property that is used by a partnership may be either partnership property or property of a partner that is loaned by the partner to the partnership. The issue whether property used by the partnership is partnership property or the property of an individual partner may be important for several different reasons. First, the issue may be important for purposes of determining who has the power to transfer the property. Property owned by the partnership can be

---

7. In support of its contention that the decision to pay the "commission" was fair, the partnership argued that the amount paid to Blomfield was the "standard" rate. The only evidence presented by the partnership was the testimony of Blomfield himself that a 5% "commission" was standard. One should view this with some skepticism as Blomfield was dealing with a tenant who was already in the building and did not have to be located or persuaded to move in. Furthermore, the rate Blomfield received is greater than 5% as the rent on which the "commission" is based is a future stream of income, not a present lump sum. After discounting future rental income to its present value, Blomfield's "commission" is greater than 5%.

transferred by the partnership. Property loaned to the partnership cannot be. Second, the issue may be important if creditors of the partnership are competing with creditors of an individual partner, and the question arises whether any given property is owned by the partnership or owned by the partner and loaned to the partnership. Third, the issue may be important if the partnership is dissolved: If property used by the partnership is partnership property, on dissolution the property must be sold or valued along with other partnership assets, and the proceeds of the sale or the value of the asset must be distributed among the partners. In contrast, if property used by the partnership is the individual property of a partner, on dissolution the property must normally be returned directly to that partner, rather than sold or valued for the account of all the partners.[1] This third issue may be especially important if the property is crucial to the partnership's business, so that as a practical matter whoever owns the property has the ability to continue the business.

If the aggregate theory of the UPA was strictly applied, a partnership could not own property. Rather, the property that the partners think of as partnership property would as a matter of law be held by the individual partners as joint tenants or tenants in common. Such a regime would be wholly impracticable. Accordingly, in the matter of partnership property, as in several other matters, the UPA lays down rules that effectively treat the partnership *as if* it were an entity. This objective is accomplished largely with smoke and mirrors. UPA § 8 recognizes the concept of "partnership property," and explicitly permits real property to be held in the partnership's name. UPA § 25(1) provides that "partnership property" is owned by the *partners*, under the ingenuous nomenclature *tenancy in partnership*. However, UPA § 25(2) then systematically strips from the individual partners every incident normally associated with ownership: (i) Under § 25(2)(a), a partner has no right to possess partnership property as an individual. (ii) Under § 25(2)(b), a partner cannot individually assign his rights in specific partnership property. (iii) Under § 25(2)(c), a partner's rights in specific partnership property cannot be subject to attachment or execution by a creditor of the partner in the latter's individual capacity. (iv) Under § 25(2)(d), when a partner dies his right in specific partnership property does not devolve on his heirs or legatees. (v) Under § 25(2)(e), widows, heirs, and next of kin cannot claim dower, curtesy, or allowances in a partner's right to specific partnership property. In short, under the UPA individual partners own the partnership property in theory, but in practice all the incidents of ownership are vested in the partnership, so that the "tenan[cy] in partnership" rule of the UPA has no real-world significance.

2. *RUPA*. RUPA, which confers entity status on partnerships, drops the elaborate tenancy-in-partnership apparatus of the UPA. Instead, RUPA § 203 provides that "Property acquired by a partnership is property of the partnership and not the partners individually." RUPA

1. But *see* Pav–Saver Corp. v. Vasso Corp., 143 Ill.App.3d 1013, 97 Ill.Dec. 760, 493 N.E.2d 423 (1986) (wrongfully dissolving partner held not entitled to return of property).

§ 204 then sets out a series of rules and presumptions concerning whether any given property is partnership property or the separate property of a partner. These provisions are supplemented by § 501, which provides that "A partner is not a co-owner of partnership property and has no interest in partnership property which can be transferred, either voluntarily or involuntarily." The purpose of § 501 is to explicitly abolish the UPA concept of tenancy in partnership.

NOTE ON PARTNERSHIP INTERESTS

1. *The Partner's Interest in the Partnership*. Although a partner does not own partnership property under the UPA except in a metaphysical sense, he does own his interest in the partnership, that is, his share of the partnership. The net result is a functional two-level ownership structure that is somewhat comparable to the two-level ownership structure in a corporation. In the case of a corporation, the corporation owns the corporate property and the shareholder owns shares in the corporation. In the case of a partnership, the partnership owns the partnership property—either in as a practical matter (under the UPA) or in full (under RUPA)—and the partner owns her interest in the partnership.

2. *Assignment*. As compared to ordinary property interests, a partnership interest is conditioned in one very important respect. Normally, the owner of a property interest can freely sell it, and a creditor can freely levy on it. In contrast, although a partnership interest is assignable, a partner cannot assign her partnership interest in a way that would substitute the transferee as a partner in the transferor's place, because it is a rule of partnership law that no person can become a partner without the consent of all the partners. Accordingly, when a partnership interest is assigned, the assignment normally is not a full transfer of the partner-assignor's interest. Instead, it is a transfer to secure a debt that the partner-assignor owes to the creditor-assignee. The creditor-assignee cannot levy on a partnership interest in such a way as to become a substituted partner, nor can the creditor recover his debt by selling the partnership interest to a third party who will be substituted as a partner. Accordingly, as pointed out in *Rapoport,* the assignee of a partnership interest does not become a partner (unless all the other partners consent), and has no right to get information about the partnership or to inspect the partnership books. As long as the partnership continues in existence, however, the assignee of a partnership interest does have a right to receive the distributions to which the assigning partner would otherwise be entitled, and on dissolution the assignee has a right to receive the assigning partner's financial interest. In practice, despite the limitations on the assignor's rights, partnership interests have a fairly high degree of assignability. *See* A. Bromberg, Enforcement of Partnership Obligations—Who is Sued for The Partnership?, 71 Neb. L. Rev. 143, 240 (1992). A partner who has assigned her partnership interest

remains a partner. However, RUPA § 601(4)(ii) explicitly permits the nonassigning partners to expel the assignor from the partnership, and UPA § 31(c) permits the nonassigning partners to dissolve the partnership as of right even if the partnership is not at will.

3. *Partnership Creditors.*

a. *UPA*. A partner's separate creditor (that is a creditor who has extended credit to a partner as an individual, rather than extending credit to the partnership) is in a position somewhat comparable to the assignee of a partnership interest. Under UPA § 28, if such a creditor obtains a judgment, he can get a *charging order* on the partner's partnership interest. Such an order effectively gives the creditor the right to be paid the partnership distributions to which the partner-debtor would be otherwise entitled. Moreover, the creditor can foreclose on the partnership interest, and thereby cause its sale. In that case, the buyer of the interest has the right to compel dissolution if the partnership is at will or the term of the partnership has expired. Alternatively, the creditor may put the individual partner into bankruptcy, which will result in dissolution of the partnership under UPA § 31(5).

b. *RUPA*. RUPA § 504 continues UPA § 28 largely unchanged in substance. RUPA § 504 does add some details that are not found in UPA § 28, but for the most part these details are consistent with the case law under § 28. Like the UPA, RUPA § 801(a) provides that a transferee of a partner's transferable interest is entitled to judicial dissolution of the partnership if the partnership is at will, or after the expiration of the partnership's term, or, in a partnership for a particular undertaking, after the completion of the undertaking.

4. *Priorities.*

a. *UPA*. A major problem in partnership law concerns the relative priorities of creditors of the partnership (partnership creditors) and creditors of a partner in the partner's individual capacity (separate creditors). UPA § 40(h) provides that as to partnership assets, partnership creditors have priority over separate creditors, and as to the partner's individual assets, separate creditors have priority over partnership creditors. *See* also UPA § 36(4). This rule, which was also in the Bankruptcy Act prior to 1978, is known as the *dual priorities* or *jingle* rule. The rule was widely criticized on the ground that it kept partnership creditors from getting the full benefit of the personal liability of the individual partners. The Bankruptcy Reform Act of 1978 responded to that criticism. Under Chapter 7 of the revised Bankruptcy Code, in a partnership bankruptcy, as to partnership assets the partnership creditors have priority over separate creditors. If debts to partnership creditors remain unpaid after the partnership assets are exhausted, partnership creditors are put on a parity with separate creditors in dividing up the partner's individual assets. 11 U.S.C. § 723(c). In the usual case, the Bankruptcy Code preempts the UPA's jingle rule.

b. *RUPA*. To reflect the abolition of the jingle rule in the Bankruptcy Code, RUPA drops the dual-properties rule of the UPA.

SECTION 7. THE PARTNER'S DUTY OF LOYALTY

UNIFORM PARTNERSHIP ACT § 21

REVISED UNIFORM PARTNERSHIP ACT §§ 103(a), (b) (3), (5), 104, 403, 404, 405

[See Statutory Supplement]

Meinhard v. Salmon

New York Court of Appeals, 1928.
249 N.Y. 458, 164 N.E. 545.

Appeal from a judgment of the Appellate Division of the Supreme Court in the first judicial department, entered June 28, 1928, modifying and affirming as modified a judgment in favor of plaintiff entered upon the report of a referee.

■ CARDOZO, CH. J. On April 10, 1902, Louisa M. Gerry leased to the defendant Walter J. Salmon the premises known as the Hotel Bristol at the northwest corner of Forty-second street and Fifth avenue in the city of New York. The lease was for a term of twenty years, commencing May 1, 1902, and ending April 30, 1922. The lessee undertook to change the hotel building for use as shops and offices at a cost of $200,000. Alterations and additions were to be accretions to the land.

Salmon, while in course of treaty with the lessor as to the execution of the lease, was in course of treaty with Meinhard, the plaintiff, for the necessary funds. The result was a joint venture with terms embodied in a writing. Meinhard was to pay to Salmon half of the moneys requisite to reconstruct, alter, manage and operate the property. Salmon was to pay to Meinhard 40 per cent of the net profits for the first five years of the lease and 50 per cent for the years thereafter. If there were losses, each party was to bear them equally. Salmon, however, was to have sole power to "manage, lease, underlet and operate" the building. There were to be certain pre-emptive rights for each in the contingency of death.

The two were coadventurers, subject to fiduciary duties akin to those of partners (King v. Barnes, 109 N.Y. 267). As to this we are all agreed. The heavier weight of duty rested, however, upon Salmon. He was a coadventurer with Meinhard, but he was manager as well.

During the early years of the enterprise, the building, reconstructed, was operated at a loss. If the relation had then ended, Meinhard as well as Salmon would have carried a heavy burden. Later the profits became large with the result that for each of the investors there came a rich return. For each, the venture had its phases of fair weather and of foul. The two were in it jointly, for better or for worse.

When the lease was near its end, Elbridge T. Gerry had become the owner of the reversion. He owned much other property in the neighborhood, one lot adjoining the Bristol Building on Fifth Avenue and four lots on Forty–Second Street. He had a plan to lease the entire tract for a long term to someone who would destroy the buildings then existing, and put up another in their place. In the latter part of 1921, he submitted such a project to several capitalists and dealers. He was unable to carry it through with any of them. Then, in January, 1922, with less than four months of the lease to run, he approached the defendant Salmon. The result was a new lease to the Midpoint Realty Company, which is owned and controlled by Salmon, a lease covering the whole tract, and involving a huge outlay. The term is to be twenty years, but successive covenants for renewal will extend it to a maximum of eighty years at the will of either party. The existing buildings may remain unchanged for seven years. They are then to be torn down, and a new building to cost $3,000,000 is to be placed upon the site. The rental, which under the Bristol lease was only $55,000, is to be from $350,000 to $475,000 for the properties so combined. Salmon personally guaranteed the performance by the lessee of the covenants of the new lease until such time as the new building had been completed and fully paid for.

The lease between Gerry and the Midpoint Realty Company was signed and delivered on January 25, 1922. Salmon had not told Meinhard anything about it. Whatever his motive may have been, he had kept the negotiations to himself. Meinhard was not informed even of the bare existence of a project. The first that he knew of it was in February when the lease was an accomplished fact. He then made demand on the defendants that the lease be held in trust as an asset of the venture, making offer upon the trial to share the personal obligations incidental to the guaranty. The demand was followed by refusal, and later by this suit. A referee gave judgment for the plaintiff, limiting the plaintiff's interest in the lease, however, to 25 per cent. The limitation was on the theory that the plaintiff's equity was to be restricted to one-half of so much of the value of the lease as was contributed or represented by the occupation of the Bristol site. Upon cross-appeals to the Appellate Division, the judgment was modified so as to enlarge the equitable interest to one-half of the whole lease. With this enlargement of plaintiff's interest, there went, of course, a corresponding enlargement of his attendant obligations. The case is now here on an appeal by the defendants.

Joint adventurers, like copartners, owe to one another, while the enterprise continues, the duty of the finest loyalty. Many forms of conduct permissible in a workaday world for those acting at arm's length, are forbidden to those bound by fiduciary ties. A trustee is held to something stricter than the morals of the market place. Not honesty alone, but the punctilio of an honor the most sensitive, is then the standard of behavior. As to this there has developed a tradition that is unbending and inveterate. Uncompromising rigidity has been the attitude of courts of equity when petitioned to undermine the rule of undivided loyalty by the "disintegrating erosion" of particular exceptions (Wendt v. Fischer, 243 N.Y. 439, 444). Only thus has the level of conduct for fiduciaries been kept at a level higher than that trodden by the crowd. It will not consciously be lowered by any judgment of this court.

The owner of the reversion, Mr. Gerry, had vainly striven to find a tenant who would favor his ambitious scheme of demolition and construction. Baffled in the search, he turned to the defendant Salmon in possession of the Bristol, the keystone of the project. He figured to himself beyond a doubt that the man in possession would prove a likely customer. To the eye of an observer, Salmon held the lease as owner in his own right, for himself and no one else. In fact he held it as a fiduciary, for himself and another, sharers in a common venture. If this fact had been proclaimed, if the lease by its terms had run in favor of a partnership, Mr. Gerry, we may fairly assume, would have laid before the partners, and not merely before one of them, his plan of reconstruction. The pre-emptive privilege, or, better, the pre-emptive opportunity, that was thus an incident of the enterprise, Salmon appropriated to himself in secrecy and silence. He might have warned Meinhard that the plan had been submitted, and that either would be free to compete for the award. If he had done this, we do not need to say whether he would have been under a duty, if successful in the competition, to hold the lease so acquired for the benefit of a venture then about to end, and thus prolong by indirection its responsibilities and duties. The trouble about his conduct is that he excluded his coadventurer from any chance to compete, from any chance to enjoy the opportunity for benefit that had come to him alone by virtue of his agency. This chance, if nothing more, he was under a duty to concede. The price of its denial is an extension of the trust at the option and for the benefit of the one whom he excluded.

No answer is it to say that the chance would have been of little value even if seasonably offered. Such a calculus of probabilities is beyond the science of the chancery. Salmon, the real estate operator, might have been preferred to Meinhard, the woolen merchant. On the other hand, Meinhard might have offered better terms, or reinforced his offer by alliance with the wealth of others. Perhaps he might even have persuaded the lessor to renew the Bristol lease alone, postponing for a time, in return for higher rentals, the improvement of adjoining lots. We know that even under the lease as made the time for the enlargement of the building was delayed for seven years. All these opportunities were cut away from him through another's intervention. He knew that Salmon was the manager. As the time drew near for the expiration of the lease, he would naturally assume from silence, if from nothing else, that the lessor was willing to extend it for a term of years, or at least to let it stand as a lease from year to year. Not impossibly the lessor would have done so, whatever his protestations of unwillingness, if Salmon had not given assent to a project more attractive. At all events, notice of termination, even if not necessary, might seem, not unreasonably, to be something to be looked for, if the business was over and another tenant was to enter. In the absence of such notice, the matter of an extension was one that would naturally be attended to by the manager of the enterprise, and not neglected altogether. At least, there was nothing in the situation to give warning to any one that while the lease was still in being, there had come to the manager an offer of extension which he had locked within his breast to be utilized by himself alone. The very fact that Salmon was in control with exclusive powers of direction charged him the more obviously with the duty of disclosure, since only through disclosure could opportunity be equalized. If he might cut off renewal by a purchase for his own benefit when four months were to pass before the lease would have an end, he might do so with equal right while there remained as many years (cf. Mitchell v. Reed, 61 N.Y. 123, 127). He might steal a march on his comrade under cover of the darkness, and then hold the captured ground. Loyalty and comradeship are not so easily abjured. . . .

We have no thought to hold that Salmon was guilty of a conscious purpose to defraud. Very likely he assumed in all good faith that with the approaching end of the venture he might ignore his coadventurer and take the extension for himself. He had given to the enterprise time and labor as well as money. He had made it a success. Meinhard, who had given money, but neither time nor labor, had already been richly paid. There might seem to be something grasping in his insistence upon more. Such recriminations are not unusual when coadventurers fall out. They are not without their force if conduct is to be judged by the common standards of competitors. That is not to say that they have pertinency here. Salmon had put himself in a position in which thought of self was to be renounced, however hard the abnegation. He was much more than a coadventurer. He was a managing coadventurer (Clegg v. Edmondson, 8 D.M. & G. 787, 807). For him and for those like him, the rule of undivided loyalty is relentless and supreme (Wendt v. Fischer, supra; Munson v. Syracuse, etc., R.R. Co., 103 N.Y. 58, 74). A different question would be here if there were lacking any nexus of relation between the business conducted by the manager and the opportunity brought to him as an incident of management (Dean v. MacDowell, 8 Ch.D. 345, 354; Aas v. Benham, 1891, 2 Ch. 244, 258; Latta v. Kilbourn, 150 U.S. 524). For this problem, as for most, there are distinctions of degree. If Salmon had received from Gerry a proposition to lease a building at a location far removed, he might have held for himself the privilege thus acquired, or so we shall assume. Here the subject-matter of the new lease was an extension and enlargement of the subject-matter of the old one. A managing coadventurer appropriating the benefit of such a lease without warning to his partner might fairly expect to be reproached with conduct that was underhand, or lacking, to say the least, in reasonable candor, if the partner were to surprise him in the act of signing the new instrument. Conduct subject to that reproach does not receive from equity a healing benediction.

A question remains as to the form and extent of the equitable interest to be allotted to the plaintiff. The trust as declared has been held to attach to the lease which was in the name of the defendant corporation. We think it ought to attach at the option of the defendant Salmon to the shares of stock which were owned by him or were under his control. The difference may be important if the lessee shall wish to execute an assignment of the lease, as it ought to be free to do with the consent of the lessor. On the other hand, an equal division of the shares might lead to other hardships. It might take away from Salmon the power of control and management which under the plan of the joint venture he was to have from first to last. The number of shares to be allotted to the plaintiff should, therefore, be reduced to such an extent as may be necessary to preserve to the defendant Salmon the expected measure of dominion. To that end an extra share should be added to his half.

Subject to this adjustment, we agree with the Appellate Division that the plaintiff's equitable interest is to be measured by the value of half of the entire lease, and not merely by half of some undivided part. A single building covers the whole area. Physical division is impracticable along the lines of the Bristol site, the keystone of the whole. Division of interests and burdens is equally impracticable. Salmon, as tenant under the new lease, or as guarantor of the performance of the tenant's obligations, might well protest if Meinhard, claiming an equitable interest, had offered to assume a liability not equal to Salmon's, but only half as great. He might justly insist that the lease must be accepted by his coadventurer in such form as it had been given, and not constructively divided into imaginary fragments. What must be yielded to the one may be demanded by the other. The lease as it has been executed is single and entire. If confusion has resulted from the union of adjoining parcels, the trustee who consented to the union must bear the inconvenience (Hart v. Ten Eyck, 2 Johns. Ch. 62). . . .

[Three judges dissented. Andrews, J., who wrote the dissenting opinion, agreed that "(w)ere this a general partnership I should have little doubt as to the correctness of this result assuming the new lease to be an offshoot of the old," but concluded that the parties' joint venture "had in view a very limited object and was to end at a limited time."]

LATTA v. KILBOURN, 150 U.S. 524, 541, 14 S.Ct. 201, 37 L.Ed. 1169 (1893). It is "well settled that one partner cannot, directly or indirectly use partnership assets for his own benefit; that he cannot in conducting the business of a partnership, take any profit clandestinely for himself; that he cannot carry on the business of the partnership for his private advantage; that he cannot carry on another business in competition or rivalry with that of the firm, thereby depriving it of the benefit of his time, skill, and fidelity, without being accountable to his copartners for any profit that may accrue to him therefrom; that he cannot be permitted to secure for himself that which it is his duty to obtain, if at all, for the firm of which he is a member; nor can he avail himself of knowledge or information which may be properly regarded as the property of the partnership, in the sense that it is available or useful to the firm for any purpose within the scope of the partnership business."

Enea v. Superior Court

Court of Appeal of California, Sixth District, 2005.

34 Cal.Rptr.3d 513.

■ RUSHING, P.J.

Plaintiff Benny Enea brought this petition to set aside an order of respondent court summarily adjudicating [in defendant's favor] his cause of action against his former partners, defendants William Daniels and Claudia Daniels, for breaches of fiduciary duties consisting primarily of renting partnership property to themselves at less than its fair market value. . . .

BACKGROUND

For purposes of this analysis we largely accept the historical background recited in defendants' opposition to the petition. . . . Defendants state that in 1980, they and other family members formed a general partnership known as 3–D. The partnership's sole asset was a building that had been converted from a residence into offices. Some portion of the property—apparently the greater part—has been rented since 1981 on a month-to-month basis by a law practice of which William Daniels is apparently the sole member. From time to time the property was rented on similar arrangements to others, including defendant Claudia Daniels. Plaintiff's counsel stipulated in the court below that "the partnership agreement has as its principal purpose the ownership, leasing and sale of the only partnership assets, which is the building. . . ."

In 1993, plaintiff, a client of William Daniels, purchased a one-third interest in the partnership from the latter's brother, John P. Daniels. Plaintiff testified in deposition that he sought to profit from this investment either by sale at some point to a third party, or by defendants' "just buying [him] out." In 2001, however, plaintiff questioned William Daniels about the rents being paid for the property. According to the trial court's order granting summary adjudication, their relationship " 'began to unravel' and in 2003, Plaintiff was 'dissociated' from the partnership."

On August 6, 2003, plaintiff brought this action "to determine partner's buyout price and for damages." In his second cause of action, he alleged that ... [he] was informed and believed they [defendants] had in fact been paying significantly less than fair rental value, "in breach of their fiduciary duty to plaintiff." ...

Defendants moved to summarily adjudicate the second cause of action on the ground, among others, that they owed no fiduciary duty to plaintiff to pay fair market rent. As an "undisputed" fact in support of the motion, defendants asserted that they "did not have a fiduciary duty to pay fair market value rent for occupancy of" the building. The "supporting evidence" cited for this assertion was "Corporations Code Section 16404(b) and (c)." ...

DISCUSSION ...

... [This] case presents a very simple set of facts and issues. For present purposes it must be assumed that defendants in fact leased the property to themselves, or associated entities, at below-market rents. Defendants made no attempt to establish otherwise, let alone to establish the absence of triable issues of fact on the point. (See Code Civ. Proc., § 437c, subd. (c).) Therefore the sole question presented is whether defendants were categorically entitled to lease partnership property to themselves, or associated entities (or for that matter, to anyone) at less than it could yield in the open market. Remarkably, we have found no case squarely addressing this precise question. We are satisfied, however, that the answer is a resounding "No."

... "Partnership is a fiduciary relationship, and partners may not take advantages for themselves at the expense of the partnership." (*Jones v. Wells Fargo Bank* (2003) 112 Cal.App.4th 1527, 1540, 5 Cal.Rptr.3d 835; see *Jones v. H.F. Ahmanson & Co.* (1969) 1 Cal.3d 93, 108, 111, 81 Cal.Rptr. 592, 460 P.2d 464.)

Here the facts as assumed by the parties and the trial court plainly depict defendants taking advantages for themselves from partnership property *at the expense of the partnership*. The advantage consisted of occupying partnership property at below-market rates, i.e., less than they would be required to pay to an independent landlord for equivalent premises. The cost to the partnership was the additional rent thereby rendered unavailable for collection from an independent tenant willing to pay the property's value.

Defendants' objections to this reasoning ring hollow. Their main argument appears to be that their conduct was authorized by Corporations Code section 16404 (section 16404), which codifies the fiduciary duties of a partner under California law. The implication of such an argument is that section 16404 provides the *exclusive* statement of a partner's obligation to the partnership and to other partners. This premise would be correct if California had adopted, in its proposed form, the uniform law on which section 16404 is based. Section 404 of the Uniform Partnership Act (1997 rev.), also known as the Revised Uniform Partnership Act or RUPA, contains an explicitly exclusive enumeration of a partner's duties. After noting that a partner owes fiduciary duties of loyalty and care, the uniform Act declares that those duties are "limited to" obligations listed there. (RUPA § 404(b), (c).) While section 16404 retains this language with respect to the duty of care, it repudiates it with respect to the duty of loyalty, stating instead that ". . . [a] partner's duty of loyalty to the partnership and the other partners *includes* all of the following: . . ." (Italics added.)

The leading treatise on RUPA confirms that by altering the proposed language, the California Legislature rejected one of the "fundamental" changes the drafters sought to bring to partnership law, i.e., "an exclusive statutory treatment of partners' fiduciary duties." (Hillman et al., The Revised Uniform Partnership Act (2004 ed.), p. 202 (Hillman et al.).) The proposed uniform version "[b]y its terms . . . comprises an exclusive statement of the fiduciary duties of partners among themselves and to the partnership. The formulation is exclusive in two ways; the duties of loyalty and care are the only components of the partners' fiduciary duties, and the duties themselves are exclusively defined." (*Ibid.,* fns. omitted.) But several states, *most clearly California,* balked at the latter restriction, leaving the articulation of the duty of loyalty to traditional common law processes. . . .

Further, even if the statutory enumeration of duties were exclusive it would not entitle defendants to rent partnership property to themselves at below-market rates. The first duty listed in the statute is "[t]o account to the partnership and hold as trustee for it *any property, profit, or benefit* derived by the partner in the conduct . . . of the partnership business or *derived from a use by the partner of partnership property*. . . ." (Corp.Code, § 16404, subd. (b)(1); see *id.,* § 16401, subd. (g) ["A partner may use or possess partnership property only on behalf of the partnership"]; see RUPA, §§ 404(b)(1), 401(g).)

Defendants persuaded the trial court that the conduct challenged by plaintiff was authorized by section 16404, subdivision (e), which states, "A partner does not violate a duty or obligation under this chapter or under the partnership agreement merely because the partner's conduct furthers the partner's own interest." The apparent purpose of this provision, which is drawn verbatim from RUPA section 404(e), is to excuse partners from accounting for incidental benefits obtained in the course of partnership activities *without detriment to the partnership.* It does not by its terms authorize the kind of conduct at issue here, which did not "merely" further defendants' own interests but did so by depriving the partnership of valuable assets, i.e., the space which would otherwise have been rented at market rates. Here, the statute entitled defendants to lease partnership property *at the same rent another tenant would have paid.* It did not empower them to occupy partnership property for their own exclusive benefit at partnership expense, in effect converting partnership assets to their own and appropriating the value it would otherwise have realized as distributable profits. Defendants' argument to the contrary seems conceptually indistinguishable from a claim that if a partnership's "primary purpose" is to purchase and hold investments, individual partners may freely pilfer its office supplies.

Defendants also persuaded the trial court that they had no duty to collect market rents in the absence of a contract expressly requiring them to do so. This argument turns partnership law on its head. Nowhere does the law declare that partners owe each other only those duties they explicitly assume by contract. On the contrary, the fiduciary duties at issue here are *imposed by law,* and their breach sounds in tort.... We have no occasion here to consider the extent to which partners might effectively limit or modify those delictual duties by an explicit agreement or whether the partnership agreement in fact required market rents by its terms. There is no suggestion that it purported to affirmatively *excuse* defendants from the delictual duty not to engage in self-dealing. Instead, their argument is predicated on the wholly untenable notion that they were entitled to do so unless the agreement explicitly declared otherwise.

Defendants also assert, and the trial court found, that the "primary purpose" of the partnership was to hold the building for appreciation and eventual sale. This premise hardly justified summary adjudication. If the partners had explicitly agreed *not* to derive market rents from the property, but to let it be used for the exclusive advantage of some of them indefinitely, there would be some basis to contend that defendants were entitled to conduct themselves as they did—or at least that plaintiff was estopped to complain. But the mere anticipation of eventual capital gains as the main economic benefit to be derived from the venture has no tendency whatsoever to entitle individual partners to divert to their own advantage benefits that would otherwise flow to the partnership.

While this observation is sufficient to dispose of the point, we cannot help but note indications in the record that the falling-out between plaintiff and defendants apparently arose not only because William Daniels insisted on paying rents lower than plaintiff thought were proper, but also because he refused to sell the property until he was ready to retire from his law practice. Proof of such a dispute would highlight a direct conflict arising quite foreseeably from defendants' self-dealing. As emphasized by defendants, plaintiff testified in deposition that "he was 'looking to make a profit on the deal' either upon the sale of the Property at some point in time *or by [defendants] 'just buying [him] out.'* " (Italics added.) It is difficult to see why defendants would be in any hurry to buy plaintiff out so long as they could enjoy the property at a discounted rent. Presumably, they profited from the property every day this situation persisted, while plaintiff was deprived of any benefit whatsoever until it suited defendants to sell. By then, of course, they would have received months or years of direct financial advantage for which, according to them, they had no obligation to account to plaintiff or the partnership. This situation put them in direct conflict with both the partnership and plaintiff *even in terms of the "primary purpose"* they so emphatically claim for the partnership....

DISPOSITION

Let a peremptory writ of mandate issue directing respondent court to vacate its order granting defendants' motion for summary adjudication of plaintiff's second cause of action, and to enter a new order denying said motion. . . .

■ MIHARA AND MCADAMS, JJ., concur.

Robert W. Hillman, Allan W. Vestal & Donald J. Weidner, The Revised Uniform Partnership Act § 404, at 298–99

2010–2011 ed.

"*Approval of Partner Self–Interest.* The first statutory clarification [of a partner's fiduciary obligation under RUPA] is potentially one of the most powerful changes in partnership law under R.U.P.A. It is embodied in Section 404(e): 'A partner does not violate a duty or obligation under this [Act] or under the partnership agreement merely because the partner's conduct furthers the partner's own interest.' The provision is new, it has no parallel in the U.P.A.

"What does Section 404(e) mean? There are two very different interpretations of the provision, one rather narrow and the other quite broad.

"Under the narrow interpretation, Section 404(e) is essentially an evidentiary rule which could be paraphrased as 'the fact that a partner directly personally benefits from the partner's conduct in the partnership context does not, without more, establish a violation of the partner's duties or obligations under RUPA or the partnership agreement.'

"Under the broad interpretation, Section 404(e) means that partners are free to pursue their short-term, individual self-interest without notice to or the consent of the partnership, subject only to the specific restrictions contained in the Section 404(b) duty of loyalty—in effect that the pursuit of self-interest cannot be a violation of the non-fiduciary obligation of good faith and fair dealing.

"Which interpretation is correct? In two paragraphs, the official commentary can be seen as supporting both interpretations. Initially, the official commentary seems to support the narrow reading of the provision:

> A partner as such is not a trustee and is not held to the same standards as the same standard as a trustee. Subsection 404(e) makes clear that a partner's conduct is not deemed to be improper merely because it serves the partner's own individual interest.

"The problem with this formulation is that it proceeds from the position that existing partnership law treats the partner as a wholly disinterested trustee, a party who renounces all self-

> interest, when in fact partnership law proceeds from the position that partners renounce the immediate, non-consensual pursuit of self-interest in favor of the long term pursuit of self-interest through the collective mechanism of the partnership.

"The official commentary also offers some support to the broad reading of Section 404(e):

> That admonition [that a partner's conduct is not deemed to be improper merely because it serves the partner's own individual interest] has particular application to the duty of loyalty and the obligation of good faith and fair dealing. It underscores the partner's right as an owner and principal in the enterprise, which must always be balanced against his [sic] duties and obligations as an agent and fiduciary."

NOTE ON SUITS BY A PARTNER AGAINST A PARTNERSHIP

One method by which a partner can vindicate her rights against other partners is by a suit for an accounting. UPA § 22 provides a right to an accounting when a partner is wrongfully excluded from the business (§ 22(a)), or when the right to an accounting is granted under the partnership agreement (§ 22(b)), or in a suit to account for appropriation of an unauthorized benefit in violation of § 21 (§ 22(c)), or whenever other circumstances render it just and reasonable (§ 22(d)). However, "cases involving such actions are rare. An action for an accounting usually indicates that an atmosphere of mistrust exists in the partnership. In this situation, the easy dissolution permitted under the UPA will often be the appropriate course to follow, particularly if there is no uncompleted term or undertaking." Alan R. Bromberg & Larry E. Ribstein, Bromberg & Ribstein on Partnership § 6.08(b) (2011).

What about simply suing for the damages resulting from the alleged wrong, rather than suing for an accounting? UPA § 13 provides that "[w]here, by any wrongful conduct or omission of any partner acting in the ordinary course of business of the partnership or with the authority of his co-partners, loss or injury is caused to any person, *not being a partner in the partnership* ... the partnership is liable therefor...." (Emphasis added.) By reason of the italicized phrase, this section is commonly interpreted not to authorize a suit by a partner against a partnership. As a result, the courts have often limited a partner's remedies against the partnership to suits for either dissolution or an accounting. *See* Beckman v. Farmer, 579 A.2d 618, 649 (D.C.App.1990); Hubbard, Alternative Remedies in Minority Partners' Suits on Partnership Causes of Action, 39 Sw. L. J. 1022 (1986). In *Beckman,* the court justified the rule on the ground that "practical difficulties commend the settlement of accounts before an action at law between partners can be maintained. The value of partners' respective interests cannot be determined while accounts are in flux, but only after partnership liabilities are satisfied, all assets are marshalled, the partners' capital accounts adjusted, and the amount of any surplus ascertained." *Id.* at 649–50. This justification is unconvincing. It may be true that the complete settlement of partnership accounts is easier at the termination of the partnership, but a partner who wants to make a claim against the partnership is not asking for a complete settlement of accounts. Given the weak or nonexistent justification of the traditional rule, it is not surprising that the rule is subject to several exceptions. "[For example, an accounting in] equity may not be necessary when breach of the partnership agreement, wrongful dissolution, fraudulent breach of trust, or misappropriation of money clearly belonging to another partner is charged. . . ." *Beckman* at 650.

2. *RUPA.* RUPA § 305, which is the counterpart of UPA § 13, drops the phrase "not being a partner in the partnership." The Comment states that this change "is intended to permit a partner to sue the partnership on a tort or other theory during the term of the partnership, rather than being limited to the remedies of dissolution and accounting."

SECTION 8. DISSOLUTION (I): DISSOLUTION BY RIGHTFUL ELECTION

UNIFORM PARTNERSHIP ACT §§ 29, 30, 31(1), 38(1), 40

REVISED UNIFORM PARTNERSHIP ACT §§ 601, 602, 603, 701, 801, 802, 803, 804, 807

[See Statutory Supplement]

GIRARD BANK v. HALEY, 460 Pa. 237, 332 A.2d 443 (1975). Mrs. Reid, a partner in an at-will UPA partnership, had sent the following letter to the other three partners: "I am terminating the partnership which the four of us entered into on the 28th day of September, 1958." The issue was whether this letter caused a dissolution of the partnership. The chancellor, at trial, held that it did not, because neither in the letter nor at trial did Mrs. Reid offer evidence to justify a termination of the partnership. Reversed.

> In supposing that justification was necessary the learned court below fell into error. Dissolution of a partnership is caused, under § 31 of the [UPA], "by the express will of any partner." The expression of that will need not be supported by any justification. If no "definite term or particular undertaking [is] specified in the partnership agreement," such an at-will dissolution does not

violate the agreement between the partners; indeed, an expression of a will to dissolve is effective as a dissolution even if in contravention of the agreement. Ibid. We have recognized the generality of a dissolution at will. If the dissolution results in breach of contract, the aggrieved partners may recover damages for the breach and, if they meet certain conditions, may continue the firm business for the duration of the agreed term or until the particular undertaking is completed. *See* § 38 of the Act....

The remaining question is whether or not the unilateral dissolution made by Mrs. Reid violated the partnership agreement. The agreement contains no provision fixing a definite term, and the sole "undertaking" to which it refers is that of maintaining and leasing real property. This statement is merely one of general purpose, however, and cannot be said to set forth a "particular undertaking" within the meaning of that phrase as it is used in the Act. A "particular undertaking" under the statute must be capable of accomplishment at some time, although the exact time may be unknown and unascertainable at the date of the agreement. Leasing property, like many other trades or businesses, involves entering into a business relationship which may continue indefinitely; there is nothing "particular" about it. We thus conclude, on the record before us, that the dissolution of the partnership was not in contravention of the agreement.

Creel v. Lilly

Court of Appeals of Maryland, 1999.
354 Md. 77, 729 A.2d 385.

■ BELL, C.J., and ELDRIDGE, RODOWSKY, CHASANOW, RAKER, WILNER and CATHELL JJ.

■ CHASANOW, JUDGE....

I. BACKGROUND

On approximately June 1, 1993, Joseph Creel began a retail business selling NASCAR racing memorabilia. His business was originally located in a section of his wife Anne's florist shop, but after about a year and a half he decided to raise capital from partners so that he could expand and move into his own space. On September 20, 1994, Mr. Creel entered into a partnership agreement—apparently prepared without the assistance of counsel—with Arnold Lilly and Roy Altizer to form a general partnership called "Joe's Racing." ...

The three-man partnership operated a retail store in the St. Charles Towne Center Mall in Waldorf, Maryland. For their initial investment in Joe's Racing, Mr. Lilly and Mr. Altizer each paid $6,666 in capital contributions, with Mr. Creel contributing his inventory and supplies valued at $15,000. Pursuant to the partnership agreement, Mr. Lilly and Mr. Altizer also paid $6,666 to Mr. Creel ($3,333 each) "for the use and rights to the business known as Joe's Racing Collectables." . . .

Joe's Racing had been in existence for almost nine months when Mr. Creel died on June 14, 1995. Mrs. Creel was appointed personal representative of his estate. . . .

In accordance with [UPA] § 9–602(4),[3] Joe's Racing was automatically dissolved upon Mr. Creel's death and because the partnership agreement did not expressly provide for continuation of the partnership nor did his estate consent to its continuation, the surviving partners were required under UPA to wind up the business. *See* [UPA] 9–601 and § 9–609(a). . . . We adopt the following procedural history of the case [from the opinion of the Court of Special Appeals]:

> ". . . [Mrs. Creel] filed in the circuit court a complaint seeking an accounting and a declaratory judgment against Messrs. Lilly and Altizer, individually and doing business under the name 'Good Ole Boys Racing.' She asserted that, instead of winding up the affairs of Joe's Racing in accordance with her demand, Lilly and Altizer continued the partnership business under a new name, using the assets of the partnership. . . .
>
> . . . [After a four-day trial, the trial court] determined that Joseph Creel had a 52% interest in the partnership. . . .
>
> The court also found that the surviving partners sought to wind up and close out the partnership and took all reasonable steps to do so, and that there was no breach by them of any fiduciary duty to the Estate. The lease on the store premises occupied by the partnership expired on 31 August 1995, and on that date Mr. Lilly conducted an inventory of all merchandise in the store. Based on that inventory, an accountant computed the value of the partnership business; Mrs. Creel was invited to review the books and records and retain her own accountant or appraiser if she questioned [Mr. Lilly or Mr. Altizer's] figures. *She declined to do so. After 31 August 1995, Messrs. Lilly and Altizer ceased doing business as Joe's Racing and began doing business together under the name 'Good Ole Boys Racing.'*
>
> The court accepted the valuation prepared by [Mr. Lilly and Mr. Altizer's] accountant as the correct value of the partnership assets as of 31 August 1995, and found that the surviving partners fully disclosed and delivered to the Estate all records of the financial affairs of the Joe's Racing partnership up to 31 August 1995, which the court took to be the end of the winding up period. Rejecting [Mrs. Creel's] assertions . . . that [Mr. Lilly and Mr. Altizer] were obligated to liquidate the partnership assets in order to wind up the partnership. . . . the court declared that the estate was entitled to a total of $21,631 [representing the Estate's

---

3. Section 9–602 states in pertinent part:

"Dissolution is caused . . .

(4) By the death of any partner[.]"

52% interest in the value of the partnership as determined by the audit] valuation...." [Emphasis added by the Court of Appeals.]

The Court of Special Appeals affirmed the judgment of the [trial court], finding that under UPA "winding up" does not always mean "liquidate;" therefore, Joe's Racing had no duty to sell off all of its assets in a liquidation sale.... Mrs. Creel filed a petition for certiorari in May 1998, which we granted.

II. DISCUSSION AND ANALYSIS

A.

We begin our analysis by reviewing the law of partnership as it pertains to the issues in this case. Maryland enacted UPA in 1916. Shafer Bros. v. Kite, 406 A.2d 673, 677 (Md.App. 1979)....

A partnership is either (1) for a definite term or a particular undertaking or (2) at will, which means the business has no definite term or particular undertaking. 59A Am.Jur.2d *Partnership* §§ 89 & 90 (1987). *See also* § 9A–101(k). An at-will partnership continues indefinitely and can be dissolved by the express will of any partner or automatically by the happening of a specific event as mandated by UPA, such as the death of a partner. 59A AM.JUR.2D *Partnership* § 89 (1987). *See also* § 9–602(4). Under UPA, partners may avoid the automatic dissolution of the business upon the death of a partner by providing for its continuation in their partnership agreement. *See* Gerding v. Baier, 122 A. 675, 677 (Md. 1923). Sophisticated partnerships virtually always use carefully drafted partnership agreements to protect the various partners' interests by providing for the continuation of the business, the distribution of partnership assets, etc., in the face of various contingencies such as death. *See* Judson A. Crane & Alan R. Bromberg, Law of Partnership § 73, at 417–19 (1968). Less sophisticated partnerships, however, are often operating under oral terms or a "homemade" agreement that does not contain protections for the partners or the business.

While the death of a partner automatically dissolves the partnership unless there is an agreement stating otherwise, the partnership is not terminated until the winding-up process is complete.... The winding-up procedure that applies in this case is found in § 9–609(a), which states in pertinent part: "When dissolution is caused in any way ... each partner ... unless otherwise agreed, may have the partnership property applied to discharge its liabilities, and the surplus applied to pay in cash the net amount owing to the respective partners."

Historically, under many courts and commentators' interpretation of UPA, when a partner died and the partnership automatically dissolved because there was no consent by the estate to continue the business nor was there a written agreement allowing for continuation, the estate had the right to compel liquidation of the partnership assets.... Reducing all of the partnership assets to cash through a liquidation was seen as the only way to obtain the true value of the business. Dreifuerst v. Dreifuerst, 280 N.W.2d 335, 338 (Ct.App.1979). However, while winding up has often traditionally been regarded as synonymous with liquidation, this "fire sale" of assets has been viewed by many courts and commentators as a harsh and destructive measure. Consequently, to avoid the drastic result of a forced liquidation, many courts have adopted judicial alternatives to this potentially harmful measure. *See* Fortugno v. Hudson Manure Company, 144 A.2d 207, 219 (App.Div.1958) (court approved an alternative proposal to the complete liquidation of the partnership, stating that it "recogniz[ed] that a forced sale of the partnership will destroy a great part of the value of the business. . . ."). *See also* full discussion on judicial alternatives to liquidation in Part II.B., *infra.*

Over time, the UPA rule requiring automatic dissolution of the partnership upon the death of a partner, in the absence of consent by the estate to continue the business or an agreement providing for continuation, with the possible result of a forced sale of all partnership assets was viewed as outmoded by many jurisdictions including Maryland. The development and adoption of RUPA by the National Conference of Commissioners on Uniform State Laws (NCCUSL) mitigated this harsh UPA provision of automatic dissolution and compelled liquidation.

RUPA's underlying philosophy differs radically from UPA's, thus laying the foundation for many of its innovative measures. RUPA adopts the "entity" theory of partnership as opposed to the "aggregate" theory that the UPA espouses. Thomas R. Hurst, *Will the Revised Uniform Partnership Act (1994) Ever Be Uniformly Adopted?,* 48 Fla. L. Rev. 575, 579 (1996). Under the aggregate theory, a partnership is characterized by the collection of its individual members, with the result being that if one of the partners dies or withdraws, the partnership ceases to exist. *See* Joan E. Branch, Note, *The Revised Uniform Partnership Act Breakup Provisions: Should They Be Adopted?,* 25 Creighton L. Rev. 701, 701 (1992). On the other hand, RUPA's entity theory allows for the partnership to continue even with the departure of a member because it views the partnership as "an entity distinct from its partners." Section 9A–201.

This adoption of the entity theory, which permits continuity of the partnership upon changes in partner identity, allows for several significant changes in RUPA. Of particular importance to the instant case is that under RUPA "a partnership no longer automatically dissolves due to a change in its membership, but rather *the existing partnership may be continued if the remaining partners elect to buy out the dissociating partner.*"[11] *Will the Revised Uniform Partnership Act*

11. RUPA uses the term "dissociation" rather than dissolution. "Dissociation" is viewed as having a less significant impact on the partnership than dissolution, which is in line with RUPA's entity theory of partnership of continuing the business whenever possible. John W. Larson et al., *Revised Uniform Partnership Act Reflects a Number of Significant Changes,* 10 J. Partnership Tax'n 232, 236 (1993). *See also* § 9A–601, which describes the events causing a partner's dissociation, including death. Under RUPA, a dissociation may result in dissolution and a winding up of partnership business. *See* §§ 9A–801 through 9A–807, which provide for the winding up of partnership business. Even after a dissociation leads to a dissolution, RUPA

(1994) Ever Be Uniformly Adopted?, 48 Fla. L. Rev. at 579 (emphasis added) (footnote omitted). In contrast to UPA, RUPA's "buy-out" option does not have to be expressly included in a written partnership agreement in order for it to be exercised; however, the surviving partners must still actively choose to exercise the option, as "continuation is not automatic as with a corporation." *Will the Revised Uniform Partnership Act (1994) Ever Be Uniformly Adopted?,* 48 Fla. L. Rev. at 579–80 (footnote omitted). This major RUPA innovation therefore delineates two possible paths for a partnership to follow when a partner dies or withdraws: "[o]ne leads to the winding up and termination of the partnership and the other to continuation of the partnership and purchase of the departing partner's share." *Will the Revised Uniform Partnership Act (1994) Ever Be Uniformly Adopted?,* 48 Fla. L. Rev. at 583 (footnote omitted). Critically, under RUPA the estate of the deceased partner no longer has to consent in order for the business to be continued nor does the estate have the right to compel liquidation.

B.

As discussed earlier, the traditional manner in which UPA allows for the continuation of the partnership upon the death of a partner is to either obtain the consent of the deceased partner's estate or include a continuation clause in the partnership agreement. *Gianakos,* 238 Md. at 183, 208 A.2d at 721. There have been several cases in other jurisdictions, however, where neither of these conditions was met and the court elected another option under UPA instead of a "fire sale" of all the partnership assets to ensure that the deceased partner's estate received its fair share of the partnership.... These jurisdictions have recognized the unfairness and harshness of a compelled liquidation and found other judicially acceptable means of winding up a partnership under UPA, such as ordering an in-kind distribution of the assets or allowing the remaining partners to buy out the withdrawing partner's share of the partnership....

C.

In applying the law discussed in Part II.A. and B. to the facts of this case, we want to clarify that while UPA is the governing act, our holding is also consistent with RUPA and its underlying policies. The legislature's recent adoption of RUPA indicates that it views with disfavor the compelled liquidation of businesses and that it has elected to follow the trend in partnership law to allow the continuation of business without disruption, in either the original or successor form, if the surviving partners choose to do so through buying out the deceased partner's share.

In this appeal, however, we would arrive at the same holding regardless of whether UPA or RUPA governs. Although our holding departs from the general UPA rule that the representative of the

---

offers a final opportunity for the partners to continue the partnership if they so choose. *See* § 9A–802(b)....

deceased partner's estate has a right to demand liquidation of the partnership, as we discuss in this subsection, *infra,* our position of "no forced sale" hardly represents a radical departure from traditional partnership law. . . .

1. Compelled Liquidation Issue

The first issue is whether the Creel estate has the right to demand liquidation of Joe's Racing where its partnership agreement does not expressly provide for continuation of the partnership and where the estate does not consent to continuation. . . . [We find] that Good Ole Boys is a successor partnership, rather than a continuation of Joe's Racing, [but that finding] does not negate the need for a complete discussion of this issue. Unless there is consent to continue the business or an agreement providing for continuation, upon the death of a partner the accurate value of the partnership must be ascertained as of the date of dissolution and the proportionate share paid to the deceased partner's estate, no matter if we are dealing with a subsequent new partnership or a continuation of the original business. If a compelled liquidation of all partnership assets is seen as the only way to arrive at its true value, then property from the original partnership will have to be sold whether the present business is a continuation or a successor business; regardless, the potential harm of such a "fire sale" affects both equally. . . .

We find it is sound public policy to permit a partnership to continue either under the same name or as a successor partnership without all of the assets being liquidated. Liquidation can be a harmful and destructive measure, especially to a small business like Joe's Racing, and is often unnecessary to determining the true value of the partnership. *See* Arnold v. Burgess, 747 P.2d 1315, 1322 (Ct.App.1987) ("A forced sale of partnership assets will often destroy a great part of the value of the business and may prevent the continuation of a valuable source of livelihood for former partners."). We now explore the "true value of the partnership" issue and whether liquidation is the only way to obtain it. . . .

In accordance with . . . [the] UPA, Lilly and Altizer provided Mrs. Creel with an accounting, which was based on the valuation performed by the accountant they hired. Mrs. Creel contends that this accounting did not reflect the true value of Joe's Racing, and as a result the estate did not receive its proportionate share of the partnership. . . .

. . . [We] disagree as to Mrs. Creel's argument that the accountant's valuation was in error and that the trial court subsequently arrived at an incorrect distribution of Mr. Creel's interest in the partnership. . . .

[W]e hold that Maryland's UPA—particularly in light of the legislature's recent adoption of RUPA—does not grant the estate of a deceased partner the right to demand liquidation of a partnership where the partnership agreement does not expressly provide for continuation of the partnership and where the estate does not consent to continuation. To hold otherwise vests excessive power and control in the estate of the deceased partner, to the extreme disadvantage of the surviving partners. We further hold that where the surviving partners have in good faith wound up the business and the deceased partner's estate is provided with an accurate accounting allowing for payment of a proportionate share of the business, then a forced sale of all partnership assets is unwarranted.

2. *Damages Issue*

The second issue is whether the Creel estate is entitled to its partnership percentage share of the profits generated by the surviving partners' alleged continued use of the partnership assets. Mrs. Creel argues that because Lilly and Altizer did not liquidate the partnership as she demanded, they continued the partnership with the use of partnership property and inventory. For this reason . . . Mrs. Creel claims she is entitled to damages from this continued use. Her contention can be quickly dispensed with due to the trial judge's implicit finding that Joe's Racing was not continued, but instead was properly wound up on August 31, 1995. Therefore, as Good Ole Boys is a successor partnership to Joe's Racing and not a continuation business, there are no "continuation" damages at issue. . . .

JUDGMENT OF THE COURT OF SPECIAL APPEALS AFFIRMED. . . .

DISOTELL v. STILTNER, 100 P.3d 890 (Alaska 2004). This case, decided under UPA, raised essentially the same issue as *Creel*, and the court came out the same way:

> In Dreifuerst v. Dreifuerst, cited by Disotell on appeal, the Wisconsin Court of Appeals, construing a statute identical to Alaska's, held that lawful dissolution gives each partner the right to force liquidation. [Dreifuerst v. Dreifuerst, 280 N.W.2d 335, 338 (App.1979).] Other courts have recognized that the winding up that follows partnership dissolution generally involves liquidation of the partnership assets. Indeed, the drafters' official comment on the uniform statute explains:
>
> The right given to each partner [by the statute], where no agreement has been made, to have his share of the surplus paid to him in cash makes certain an existing uncertainty. At present it is not certain whether a partner may or may not insist on a physical partition of the property remaining after third persons have been paid.
>
> Although the language of the Act and the general rule would seem to favor liquidation and cash distribution absent agreement to do otherwise, some courts construing statutes identical to section .330 have refused to compel liquidation. [Citing *Creel*, among other cases.]

We decline to follow the line of cases holding that the statute requires liquidation. We hold that the superior court did not err in reading subsection .330(a) to allow it to permit Stiltner to buy out Disotell's partnership interest. Careful reading of the text of [Alaska Statutes] 32.05.330(a) does not convince us that this subsection absolutely compels liquidation and forbids a buyout. Under appropriate, although perhaps limited, circumstances, a buyout seems a justifiable way of winding up a partnership. The superior court reasoned that a buyout would reduce economic waste by avoiding the cost of appointing a receiver and conducting a sale. Even though there was no ongoing business, the superior court noted that the expense of a sale could total as much as twelve percent of the property's value. This was a valid reason and potentially benefitted both partners. The potential savings were significant. The court's effort to avoid further loss to both partners justifies its decision to offer Stiltner the buyout option. Further, properly conducted, a buyout guaranteed Disotell a fair value for his partnership interest. Liquidation exposed Disotell to the risk that no buyer would offer to pay fair market value for the property. A liquidation sale in which no other buyers participated might have given Stiltner an opportunity to buy the property for less than fair market value, to Disotell's disadvantage.

McCormick v. Brevig

Supreme Court of Montana, 2004.
322 Mont. 112, 96 P.3d 697.

[Joan McCormick and Clark Brevig, brother and sister, were equal partners in a ranching partnership.]

From 1984 to 1993, Joan was listed as a 50/50 partner on all the tax returns for the partnership....

Disagreements concerning management of the ranch, and particularly, management of the debt load on the ranch, caused Clark and Joan's relationship to deteriorate. By the early 1990s, cooperation between Clark and Joan regarding the operation of the ranch and securing of loans necessary to fund the ranch had essentially ceased, and they began looking for ways to dissolve the Partnership.

In 1995, Joan brought suit against Clark and the Partnership, alleging that Clark had converted Partnership assets to his own personal use, and sought an accounting of the Partnership's affairs. She also requested a determination that Clark had engaged in conduct warranting a decree of expulsion. Alternatively, Joan sought an order dissolving and winding up the Partnership....

.... On April 3, 2000, the District Court issued findings of fact and conclusions of law, finding that neither Clark nor Joan had dissociated from the Partnership, [and] that Joan was a 50 percent partner.... The court further concluded that the Partnership should be dissolved and its business wound up, and reasoned that appointment of a special master was appropriate in order to determine the amount of the parties' respective capital contributions and Partnership assets.

On February 7, 2001, following the appointment and discharge of the two previous masters, Larry Blakely, CPA, ("Blakely") was appointed special master....

On December 12, 2002, Blakely filed his final report with the court, ... valuing Joan's interest in the Partnership at $795,629. Joan objected to Blakely's findings and a hearing followed. On January 29, 2003, the District Court entered findings of fact and conclusions of law, accepting Blakely's findings and valuing Joan's interest in the Partnership at $1,107,672. Clark thereafter tendered this amount to Joan for the purchase of her interest, which Joan rejected. This appeal followed....

DISCUSSION

After ordering dissolution of the Partnership, did the District Court err by failing to order liquidation of the Partnership assets, and instead granting Clark the right to purchase Joan's Partnership interest at a price determined by the court?

Joan contends that when a partnership is dissolved by judicial decree, Montana's Revised Uniform Partnership Act, § 35–10–101 et seq., MCA (2001), requires liquidation by sale of partnership assets and distribution in cash of any surplus to the partners. In response, Clark asserts that there are other judicially acceptable methods of distributing partnership assets upon dissolution besides liquidating assets through a forced sale. For the reasons set forth below, we conclude that the Revised Uniform Partnership Act requires liquidation of partnership assets and distribution of the net surplus in cash to the partners upon dissolution entered by judicial decree when it is no longer reasonably practicable to carry on the business of the partnership.

We begin our analysis by reviewing the law of partnerships as it pertains to the issues in this case. A partnership is an association of two or more persons to carry on as co-owners a business for profit. *See* § 35–10–102(5)(a), MCA; *see also* § 35–10–201(1), MCA (1991). An informal or oral agreement will usually suffice to create a partnership, and where a partnership agreement exists, it will generally govern relations among partners. Thus, statutory rules are merely default rules, which apply only in the absence of a partnership agreement to the contrary. *See* § 35–10–106, MCA. In the present case, the parties do not dispute that the partnership agreement did not apply to situations involving a court ordered dissolution of a partnership.

Partnership law in Montana and throughout the United States has been primarily derived from the Uniform Partnership Act ("UPA"), which was originally promulgated by the Uniform Law Commissioners in 1914. Under the UPA, the law of partnership breakups was couched in terms of dissolution. A partnership was dissolved and its assets liquidated upon the happening of specific events, the most significant of which was the death of a partner or any partner expressing a will to leave the partnership. Montana adopted the UPA in 1947.

In 1993, our legislature significantly amended the UPA by adopting the Revised Uniform Partnership Act, or RUPA.[1] Unlike the UPA, RUPA now provides two separate tracks for the exiting partner. The first track applies to the dissociating partner, and does not result in a dissolution, but in a buy-out of the dissociating partner's interest in the partnership. *See* § 35–10–616, MCA. The term "dissociation" is new to the act, and occurs upon the happening of any one of ten events specified in § 35–10–616, MCA. Examples of events leading to dissociation include bankruptcy of a partner and death, *see* § 35–10–616(6)(a) and (7)(a), MCA, but does not include a judicially ordered dissolution of the partnership.

The second track for the exiting partner does involve dissolution and winding up of the partnership's affairs. Section 35–10–624, MCA, sets forth the events causing dissolution and winding up of a partnership, and includes the following:

> *Events causing dissolution and winding up of partnership business*. . . .
>
> (5) a judicial decree, issued upon application by a partner, that:
>
> (a) the economic purpose of the partnership is likely to be unreasonably frustrated;
>
> (b) another partner has engaged in conduct relating to the partnership business that makes it not reasonably practicable to carry on the business in partnership with that partner; or
>
> (c) it is not otherwise reasonably practicable to carry on the partnership business in conformity with the partnership agreement[.]

In this case, the District Court dissolved the Partnership pursuant to § 35–10–624(5), MCA. In so doing, it recognized that, in the absence of a partnership agreement to the contrary, the only possible result under RUPA was for the partnership assets to be liquidated and the proceeds distributed between the partners proportionately. The court reasoned, however, that the term "liquidate" had a variety of possible meanings, one of which was "to assemble and mobilize the assets, settle with the creditors and debtors and apportion the remaining assets, if any, among the stockholders or owners." Applying this definition, which the court had obtained from *Black's Law Dictionary*, the court concluded that a judicially ordered buy-out of Joan's interest

---

1. Although the 1993 Legislature did not amend the title of the UPA, it adopted the changes embodied within the Revised Uniform Partnership Act ("RUPA") and, therefore, we shall refer to the act throughout this opinion as "RUPA."

in the Partnership by Clark was an acceptable alternative to liquidation of the partnership assets through a compelled sale.

It is well established that "the role of courts in applying a statute has always been to 'ascertain and declare what is in terms or in substance contained therein, not to insert what has been omitted or to omit what has been inserted.' " State v. Goebel, 31 P.3d 335, (Mont. 2001) 16 (citation omitted). "[T]he intent of the Legislature is controlling when construing a statute. The intention of the Legislature must first be determined from the plain meaning of the words used, and if interpretation of the statute can be so determined, the courts may not go further and apply any other means of interpretation." *Goebel*, 17.

It is true that this Court has previously utilized dictionaries when seeking to define the common use and meaning of terms. *See* Ravalli County v. Erickson, 2004 MT 35, 13, 320 Mont. 31, 13, 85 P.3d 772, 13. However, in this case, we conclude that it was not necessary for the District Court to resort to such devices. Section 35–10–629(1), MCA, clearly provides that "[i]n winding up a partnership's business, the assets of the partnership must be applied to discharge its obligations to creditors, including partners who are creditors. Any surplus must be applied to pay *in cash* the net amount distributable to partners in accordance with their right to distributions pursuant to subsection (2)." (Emphasis added.) Furthermore, subsection (2) of the statute provides:

> Each partner is entitled to a settlement of all partnership accounts upon winding up the partnership business. In settling accounts among the partners, the profits and losses that result from the *liquidation of the partnership assets* must be credited and charged to the partners' accounts. The partnership shall make a distribution to a partner in an amount equal to that partner's positive account balance.

(Emphasis added.) Thus, the common purpose and plain meaning of the term "liquidation," as it is used in § 35–10–629(2), MCA, is to reduce the partnership assets to cash, pay creditors, and distribute to partners the value of their respective interest. *See also* 59A Am.Jur.2d *Partnership* § 1100 (2003). This is all part of the process of "winding up" the business of a partnership and terminating its affairs.

Clark invites this Court to take a liberal reading of § 35–10–629, MCA, and cites Creel v. Lilly (1999), 729 A.2d 385 (1999), in support of the proposition that judicially acceptable alternatives exist to compelled liquidation in a dissolution situation. At issue in *Creel* was whether the surviving partners of a partnership had a duty to liquidate all partnership assets because there was no provision in the partnership agreement providing for the continuation of the partnership upon a partner's death, and the estate had not consented to the continuation of business. *Creel*, 729 A.2d at 387. After examining cases in which other courts had elected to order an in-kind distribution rather than a compelled liquidation, or had allowed the remaining partners to purchase the withdrawing partner's interest in the partnership, the court concluded that the UPA did not mandate a forced sale of all partnership assets in order to ascertain the true value of the business, and that "winding up" was not always synonymous with liquidation. *Creel*, 729 A.2d at 403. The court further noted that it would have reached the same conclusion regardless of whether the UPA or RUPA governed since, under RUPA, the remaining partners could have elected to continue business following the death of one of the partners. *Creel*, 729 A.2d at 397.

However, of critical distinction between the facts in *Creel* and the case *sub judice* is the manner in which the partners exited the entity. In *Creel* one of the partners had died. Here, Joan sought a court ordered dissolution of the Partnership. Under RUPA, the death of a partner triggers the provisions of § 35–10–619, MCA, which allows for the purchase of the dissociated partner's interest in the partnership, much like what was ordered in *Creel*. Conversely, a court ordered dissolution pursuant to § 35–10–624(5), MCA, as in this case, results in the dissolution and winding up of the partnership. Thus, *Creel* is both legally and factually distinguishable.

Furthermore, the cases relied upon by the court in *Creel* in reaching its conclusion that liquidation of assets was not always mandated upon dissolution, Nicholes v. Hunt (1975), 541 P.2d 820 (Or. 1975), Logoluso v. Logoluso (1965), 233 Cal.App.2d 523, 43 Cal.Rptr. 678, Gregg v. Bernards (1968), 443 P.2d 166, Goergen v. Nebrich (1958), 174 N.Y.S.2d 366 (Misc. 2d 1958), and Fortugno v. Hudson Manure Co. (1958), 144 A.2d 207 (N.J. Super. 1958), are likewise pre-RUPA holdings, which are inapposite to the facts at issue in this case.

Accordingly, we conclude that when a partnership's dissolution is court ordered pursuant to § 35–10–624(5), MCA, the partnership assets necessarily must be reduced to cash in order to satisfy the obligations of the partnership and distribute any net surplus in cash to the remaining partners in accordance with their respective interests. By adopting a judicially created alternative to this statutorily mandated requirement, the District Court erred. . . .

Affirmed in part, reversed in part, and remanded for further proceedings consistent with this opinion.

■ KARLA M. GRAY, C.J., W. WILLIAM LEAPHART, PATRICIA O. COTTER and JIM REGNIER, JJ., concur.

Farnsworth v. Deaver

Court of Appeals of Texas, Amarillo, 2004.
147 S.W.3d 662.

■ BRIAN QUINN, JUSTICE.

Johnny and Janie R. Farnsworth (the Farnsworths) appeal from a final judgment entered in favor of John M. and Carol J. Deaver (the Deavers). Through the judgment, the trial court denied recovery by the Farnsworths against the Deavers but awarded the latter monetary relief and attorney's fees against the former. Furthermore, the dispute between the parties involved a partnership they had entered into, which partnership eventually fell upon hard times and had to be dissolved....

... [T]he Farnsworths contend the trial court erred when it ordered them to pay the Deavers $6,134.37. The latter purportedly represented one-half of the difference between the capital accounts of the Farnsworths and Deavers.[1] According to the Farnsworths, "one partner does not have the right to recover the difference between positive partnership capital accounts from another partner." This is purportedly so because the Texas Revised Partnership Act simply obligates those partners with negative capital accounts to repay the negative balance and return the account to zero, and the Farnsworths had a positive balance in their account. We overrule the issue.

In arriving at our decision we must say that the reasoning of the Farnsworths is accurate in certain respects. When settling accounts between the partners, [the] statute does prescribe that generally, a partner "shall contribute to the partnership an amount equal to that partner's negative balance in the partner's capital account." Tex.Rev. Civ. Stat. Ann. art. 6132b–8.06(b) (Vernon Supp.2004–2005). So, as suggested by the Farnsworths, a partner is required only to reimburse the partnership an amount equal to the negative balance. Yet, we disagree with the manner in which they determined whether they had a negative capital account.

In winding up the affairs of a partnership, creditors of the entity are not the only ones entitled to payment. So too "shall [the partnership] make a distribution to a partner in an amount equal to the partner's positive balance in the partner's capital account." *Id.* Given this, capital accounts having a positive balance are debts of the partnership.[2] *See* Vol. II, A. Bromberg & L. Ribstein, *Partnership*, § 7.10(b), p. 7:145–46 (2004) (categorizing a partner's capital account as a debt of the partnership under the Uniform Partnership Act). Being debts, they must be included within the liabilities for which the partners are ultimately responsible. *Id.*

Next, if the debts of the partnership exceed its assets (which also include the value assigned to each capital account) it can be said that the partners have suffered a capital loss. And, these losses, like all other debts, must be satisfied by the partners in direct proportion to their share of the profits. *Id.*; *see* Tex.Rev.Civ. Stat. Ann. art. 6132b–4.01(b) (stating that each partner is "chargeable with a share of the partnership's losses, whether capital or operating, in proportion to the partner's share of the profits"). For example, let us assume that three

---

1. According to the jury, the Farnsworths had a capital account of $22,080.68 while the Deavers had one of $34,349.41. The difference between the two sums equaled $12,268.73. Half of that sum approximated $6,134.37.

2. Of course, partners can affect the manner in which the partnership treats capital accounts by executing a partnership agreement touching upon the subject. However, no such agreement was executed at bar. Thus, the Texas Revised Partnership Act controls the treatment of those accounts here. Long v. Lopez, 115 S.W.3d 221, 225 (Tex.App.—Fort Worth 2003, no pet.).

partners contributed $10,000, $5000, and $2000, respectively, to capitalize Partnership X and agreed to share profits equally. Let us also assume that upon dissolution of the partnership only $5000 remained after paying all creditors other than partners who are creditors in their capacity as partners. *See id.* at art. 6132b–8.06(a) (requiring the payment of all partnership obligations including those owed to partners in their capacity other than as a partner). Since each partner is entitled to repayment of his capital, Partnership X has a loss of $12,000, *i.e.* the $17,000 representing the sum of the capital due each partner less the $5000 remaining after payment of all obligations other than those owed the partners as partners. Dividing the $12,000 loss between the partners in proportion to their share of the profits, *i.e.* one-third each, would result in each partner owing $4000 to the partnership. And, once this $4000 is offset against the sums due from the partners as reflected by their respective capital accounts, the partner who initially paid $10,000 in capital would have a positive balance of $6000 in his capital account. The one who paid $5000 would have a positive balance of $1000, while the one who paid $2000 would have a negative balance of $2000. Thus, the partner with the negative balance would be obligated to pay $2000 to the partnership to remove his capital account from its negative position. Vol. II, A. Bromberg & L. Ribstein, *Partnership*, § 6.02(c)(2); *see* Tex.Rev.Civ. Stat. Ann. art. 6132b–8.06(b) (requiring payment of any negative balance in the capital account); Walker v. Walker, 854 F.Supp. 1443, 1456 (D.Neb.1994) (rejecting the argument that one partner is not required to reimburse another for excess contributions).

Here, the jury found that the Deavers had a capital account of $34,349.73, while the Farnsworths had one of $22,080.68. Thus, the partnership owed a debt of $56,430.09, representing the total capital it was obligated to repay. Assuming that it had no assets left after satisfying all non-partner debt and because the partners agreed to split profits 50/50, the Farnsworths and Deavers would each owe $28,215.04 to cover the loss.[4] And, when that sum is offset against the capital due each partner, the Deavers would have a positive capital balance of $6134.37 (*i.e.* $34,349.41 minus $28,215.04) while the Farnsworths would have a negative balance of $6134.36 (*i.e.* $22,080.68 minus $28,215.04). So, the latter would owe the partnership an additional $6134.36 to satisfy that negative balance, and that happens to be the approximate sum the trial court ordered them to pay the Deavers (*i.e.* $6134.37)....

... [W]e affirm the judgment of the trial court.

NOTE ON DISTRIBUTIONS IN DISSOLUTION AND "SERVICES PARTNERS"

1. *UPA.* UPA § 40(b) sets out the rules for the distribution of assets after a partnership is dissolved. The priorities for distribution, in

4. We assume for purposes of our calculation that the partnership had no cash remaining after liquidating its assets.

order, are as follows: (1) Paying off creditors other than partners. (2) Paying off partners for obligations to the partners other than obligations for capital or profits (for example, a loan that a partner made to the partnership). (3) Paying off partners in respect of capital. (4) Paying off partners in respect of profits. All these priorities, even those in respect of partnership capital and profits, are defined as "liabilities"—an unusual meaning of that term, which normally refers to debts, not to ownership or equity claims.

Under UPA § 40(d), the partners must contribute the amount necessary to satisfy liabilities as provided in § 18(a). Section 18(a), in turn, provides that each partner shall contribute toward the losses sustained by the partnership, according to his share in the profits. "Losses" in § 18(a) is defined, like "liabilities" in § 40(b), to include losses to capital.

Now suppose that Capital Partner C and Services Partner S form Partnership P. By agreement, C contributes $100,000 capital, but will not be actively engaged in running the business, while S contributes no capital but will spend his full time running the business. Profits are to be shared 50–50, but nothing is said about sharing losses. S performs services of a value of $100,000, which causes an increase in the value of P's gross assets by that amount. After three years, the partnership is dissolved. During these three years, no distribution had been made to either partner and no salary has been paid to S. On dissolution, the partnership's gross assets are worth $200,000, and the partnership owes $100,000 to creditors. C's capital account remains at $100,000. If the value of S's services are not deemed to augment S's capital account, on liquidation P's creditors will get $100,000, C will get $100,000 in respect of his capital account, and S will get nothing.

Alternatively, suppose that after all debts to creditors are paid, Partnership P is worth only $50,000, the capital account of Capital Partner C has shrunk from $100,000 to $50,000, and the capital account of Services Partner S is $0. If UPA Section 18(a) is read in a relatively straightforward way, so that S must contribute toward losses of capital according to his share in the profits, then S must contribute $25,000 to equalize the capital loss—that is, to reduce C's capital loss. *See* Richert v. Handly, 330 P.2d 1079 (Wash.2d 1958). The result is that S loses $125,000 ($100,000 in the value of his services, and the $25,000 payment to C). In contrast, C loses $25,000 ($100,000 in invested capital, offset by the $50,000 return of capital and S's $25,000 contribution).

These results seem inappropriate. In Schymanski v. Conventz, 674 P.2d 281, 284 (Alaska 1983), the court said, in such a case, that although "[t]he general rule is that, in the absence of an agreement to such effect, a partner contributing only personal services is ordinarily *not* entitled to any share of partnership capital pursuant to dissolution," nevertheless "[p]ersonal services may qualify as capital contributions to a partnership where an express or implied agreement to such effect exists." This exception makes it easy for a court to get around the general rule by finding an implied agreement when that is necessary to avoid a particularly unfair result. *See* also Parker v. Northern Mixing Co., 756 P.2d 881 (Alaska 1988). Similarly, in Thompson v. Beth, 111 N.W.2d 171, 175 (Wis.2d 1961), the court distinguished between cases in which a partner contributes services only on a "day-to-day" basis, and cases in which "the skill and labor of the partner are his contribution to the capital assets of the partnership." In the former type of case, the court said, the partner's services would not augment his capital account. In the latter type of case, however, the partner's services would augment his capital account. This distinction also makes it easy for a court to get around the general rule by finding that a partner's services were in the latter category rather than the former.

In Kovacik v. Reed, 49 Cal.2d 166, 169–70, 315 P.2d 314, 315–16 (1957), the court came to the same result by a different path:

> ... Where ... as in the present case, one partner ... contributes the money capital as against the other's skill and labor ... upon loss of the money the party who contributed it is not entitled to recover any part of it from the party who contributed only services.... The rationale ... is that where one party contributes money and the other contributes services, then in the event of a loss each would lose his own capital—the one his money and the other his labor. Another view would be that in such a situation the parties have, by their agreement to share equally in profits, agreed that the values of their contributions—the money on the one hand and the labor on the other—were likewise equal; it would follow that upon the loss, as here, of both money and labor, the parties have shared equally in the losses.

Accord: Becker v. Killarney, 177 Ill.App.3d 793, 127 Ill.Dec. 102, 532 N.E.2d 931 (1988); Snellbaker v. Herrmann, 462 A.2d 713 (Pa. Super.1983). *Kovacik* has been distinguished where the services partner has received compensation for his services. *See* Century Universal Enterprises, Inc. v. Triana Development Corp., 158 Ill.App.3d 182, 110 Ill.Dec. 229, 510 N.E.2d 1260 (1987).

The approach taken in *Kovacik* is sound. If a services-only partner has been fully compensated for his services, it is hard to see why he should not be required to contribute toward making up a capital loss. Otherwise, a capital partner would bear all the partnership's loss and the services-only partner would bear none. But if a services-only partner has not been compensated for his services, then if he must contribute toward the capital loss, he would lose all the value of his services, while the capital partner would lose only part of the value of his capital. It is unlikely that the parties would have agreed to this result if they had negotiated on the issue when the partnership was formed. As *Kovacik* suggests, therefore, where a services-only partner has not been compensated for his services, the partners should normally be deemed to have impliedly agreed that she need not contribute to a capital partner's capital loss.

Finally, some cases hold that a special rule applies to joint ventures, and then conclude that the relationship in question was a joint venture rather than a partnership.

b. *RUPA.* RUPA § 401(h) continues the rule of UPA § 18. The Comment to § 401(h) makes clear that the rule is intended to apply in the capital-loss context, and provides the following justification for applying the rule to the detriment of services partners:

> The default rules [of § 401(h)] apply, as does UPA Section 18(a), where one or more of the partners contribute no capital, although there is case law to the contrary. *See, e.g.*, Kovacik v. Reed, 315 P.2d 314 (Cal.2d 1957); Becker v. Killarney, 532 N.E.2d 931 (Ill.App.3d 1988). It may seem unfair that the contributor of services, who contributes little or no capital, should be obligated to contribute toward the capital loss of the large contributor who contributed no services. In entering a partnership with such a capital structure, the partners should foresee that application of the default rule may bring about unusual results and take advantage of their power to vary by agreement the allocation of capital losses.

This attempt at justification does more to show why RUPA § 401(h) is wrong than why it is right. The Comment begins by frankly recognizing that the result "may seem unfair." It then states that even if the rule is unfair the partners can contract around it. Of course, any rule of partnership law, no matter how foolish, could be "justified" by the argument that it can be contracted around. The point of partnership law, however, should be to make good rules that the parties probably would have agreed to if they had addressed the issue, not to make bad rules that the partners can contract around. Furthermore, many partners don't know partnership law, and therefore won't realize they need to contract around any given rule. Indeed, because persons can be partners without having an intention to form a partnership, many partners don't even realize that they are partners, let alone realize that they should consider contracting around any given rule of partnership law.

NOTE ON JOINT VENTURES

As pointed out in the previous Note, some courts have held that a services partner need not contribute toward a capital loss where the enterprise is a "joint venture" rather than a partnership. The line between a joint venture and a partnership is exceedingly thin. "[M]ost courts have [distinguished] between isolated transactions and continuing enterprises by classifying the former as joint ventures." 1 Alan R. Bromberg & Larry Ribstein, Bromberg & Ribstein on Partnership § 2.06(a) (2011).

Some commentators take the position that joint ventures are generally governed by partnership law. *See, e.g., id.* at 192 ("Whether a [joint venture] is considered a partnership or merely analogized to one, the venturers are governed by the rules applicable to partners"); Comment, The Joint Venture: Problem Child of Partnership, 38 Calif. L. Rev. 860 (1950). In contrast, other commentators argue that joint ventures are a separate form and therefore not entirely subject to partnership rules. *See, e.g.*, Jaeger, Partnership or Joint Venture?, 37 Notre Dame L. Rev. 138 (1961). The same split is found in the cases. Some cases suggest that it makes no legal difference whether an enterprise is characterized as a partnership or a joint venture, while others suggest that special rules apply to joint ventures.

As a realistic matter, what seems to be involved is this: Some rules of the UPA, such as Section 18(a), produce unsatisfactory results in certain kinds of cases. Courts that want to avoid these results will sometimes do so, if they plausibly can, by holding that a "special rule" applies to joint ventures, and that the enterprise in the case at hand is a joint venture and therefore falls within the special rule. In many or most such cases, the desired result could probably be reached, without applying special rules to joint ventures, by finding that the parties had an implied agreement that overrides the relevant rule of the UPA.

Page v. Page

Supreme Court of California, 1961.
55 Cal.2d 192, 10 Cal.Rptr. 643, 359 P.2d 41.

■ TRAYNOR, J.

Plaintiff and defendant are partners in a linen supply business in Santa Maria, California. Plaintiff appeals from a judgment declaring the partnership to be for a term rather than at will.

The partners entered into an oral partnership agreement in 1949. Within the first two years each partner contributed approximately $43,000 for the purchase of land, machinery, and linen needed to begin the business. From 1949 to 1957 the enterprise was unprofitable, losing approximately $62,000. The partnership's major creditor is a corporation, wholly owned by plaintiff, that supplies the linen and machinery necessary for the day-to-day operation of the business. This corporation holds a $47,000 demand note of the partnership. The partnership operations began to improve in 1958. The partnership earned $3,824.41 in that year and $2,282.30 in the first three months of 1959. Despite this improvement plaintiff wishes to terminate the partnership.

The Uniform Partnership Act provides that a partnership may be dissolved "By the express will of any partner when no definite term or particular undertaking is specified." (Corp.Code, § 15031, subd. (1)(b).) The trial court found that the partnership is for a term, namely, "such reasonable time as is necessary to enable said partnership to repay from partnership profits, indebtedness incurred for the purchase of land, buildings, laundry and delivery equipment and linen for the operation of such business. . . ." Plaintiff correctly contends that this finding is without support in the evidence.

Defendant testified that the terms of the partnership were to be similar to former partnerships of plaintiff and defendant, and that the understanding of these partnerships was that "we went into partnership to start the business and let the business operation pay for itself,—put in so much money, and let the business pay itself out." There was also testimony that one of the former partnership agreements provided in writing that the profits were to be retained until all obligations were paid....

Viewing this evidence most [favorably] for defendant, it proves only that the partners expected to meet current expenses from current income and to recoup their investment if the business were successful.

Defendant contends that such an expectation is sufficient to create a partnership for a term under the rule of Owen v. Cohen, 19 Cal.2d 147, 150 [119 P.2d 713]. In that case.... the partners borrowed substantial amounts of money to launch the enterprise and there was an understanding that the loans would be repaid from partnership profits.... [T]he court properly held that the partners impliedly promised to continue the partnership for a term reasonably required to allow the partnership to earn sufficient money to accomplish the understood objective....

In the instant case, however, defendant failed to prove any facts from which an agreement to continue the partnership for a term may be implied. The understanding to which defendant testified was no more than a common hope that the partnership earnings would pay for all the necessary expenses. Such a hope does not establish even by implication a "definite term or particular undertaking" as required by section 15031, subdivision (1)(b), of the Corporations Code.

All partnerships are ordinarily entered into with the hope that they will be profitable, but that alone does not make them all partnerships for a term and obligate the partners to continue in the partnerships until all of the losses over a period of many years have been recovered.

Defendant contends that plaintiff is acting in bad faith and is attempting to use his superior financial position to appropriate the now profitable business of the partnership. Defendant has invested $43,000 in the firm, and owing to the long period of losses his interest in the partnership assets is very small. The fact that plaintiff's wholly owned corporation holds a $47,000 demand note of the partnership may make it difficult to sell the business as a going concern. Defendant fears that upon dissolution he will receive very little and that plaintiff, who is the managing partner and knows how to conduct the operations of the partnership, will receive a business that has become very profitable because of the establishment of Vandenberg Air Force Base in its vicinity. Defendant charges that plaintiff has been content to share the losses but now that the business has become profitable he wishes to keep all the gains.

There is no showing in the record of bad faith or that the improved profit situation is more than temporary. In any event these contentions are irrelevant to the issue whether the partnership is for a term or at will. Since, however, this action is for a declaratory judgment and will be the basis for future action by the parties, it is appropriate to point out that defendant is amply protected by the fiduciary duties of copartners.

Even though the Uniform Partnership Act provides that a partnership at will may be dissolved by the express will of any partner (Corp.Code, § 15031, subd. (1)(b)), this power, like any other power held by a fiduciary, must be exercised in good faith.

We have often stated that "Partners are trustees for each other, and in all proceedings connected with the conduct of the partnership every partner is bound to act in the highest good faith to his copartner and may not obtain any advantage over him in the partnership affairs by the slightest misrepresentation, concealment, threat or adverse pressure of any kind." (Llewelyn v. Levi, 157 Cal. 31, 37 [106 P. 219]; Richards v. Fraser, 122 Cal. 456, 460 [55 P. 246]; Yeomans v. Lysfjord, 162 Cal.App.2d 357, 361–362 [327 P.2d 957]; cf. MacIsaac v. Pozzo, 26 Cal.2d 809, 813 [161 P.2d 449]; Corp.Code, § 15021.) . . . .

A partner at will is not bound to remain in a partnership, regardless of whether the business is profitable or unprofitable. A partner may not, however, by use of adverse pressure "freeze out" a copartner and appropriate the business to his own use. A partner may not dissolve a partnership to gain the benefits of the business for himself, unless he fully compensates his copartner for his share of the prospective business opportunity. In this regard his fiduciary duties are at least as great as those of a shareholder of a corporation.

In the case of In re Security Finance Co., 49 Cal.2d 370, 376–377 [317 P.2d 1], we stated that although shareholders representing 50 per cent of the voting power have a right under Corporations Code, section 4600, to dissolve a corporation, they may not exercise such right in order "to defraud the other shareholders [citation], to 'freeze out' minority shareholders [citation], or to sell the assets of the dissolved corporation at an inadequate price. [Citation.]"

Likewise in the instant case, plaintiff has the power to dissolve the partnership by express notice to defendant. If, however, it is proved that plaintiff acted in bad faith and violated his fiduciary duties by attempting to appropriate to his own use the new prosperity of the partnership without adequate compensation to his copartner, the dissolution would be wrongful and the plaintiff would be liable as provided by subdivision (2)(a) of Corporations Code, section 15038 (rights of partners upon wrongful dissolution) for violation of the implied agreement not to exclude defendant wrongfully from the partnership business opportunity.*

The judgment is reversed.

■ GIBSON, C.J., MCCOMB, J., PETERS, J., WHITE, J., DOOLING, J., and WOOD (PARKER), J. pro tem., concurred.

---

* The consequences of wrongful dissolution are considered in Section 9, infra. [Footnote by ed.]

LEFF v. GUNTER, 33 Cal.3d 508, 189 Cal.Rptr. 377, 658 P.2d 740 (1983). "There is an obvious and essential unfairness in one partner's attempted exploitation of a partnership opportunity for his own personal benefit and to the resulting detriment of his copartners. It may be assumed, although perhaps not always easily proven, that such competition with one's own partnership is greatly facilitated by access to relevant information available only to partners. Moreover, it is equally obvious that a formal disassociation of oneself from a partnership does not change this situation unless the interested parties specifically agree otherwise. It is no less a violation of the trust imposed between partners to permit the exploitation of that partnership information and opportunity to the prejudice of one's former associates by the simple expedient of withdrawal from the partnership."

ROSENFELD, MEYER & SUSMAN v. COHEN, 146 Cal.App.3d 200, 194 Cal.Rptr. 180 (1983). "[The lower court's] holding that a partner may dissolve a partnership at will in bad faith is not only contrary to Page v. Page ... and other cases heretofore cited, but is also contrary to the established principle that even non-fiduciaries must exercise their rights in good faith, deal fairly with each other and refrain from injuring the right of another party to receive the benefits of an agreement or relationship....

"Moreover, the law and motion department's ruling that as a matter of law a partner has the absolute right to dissolve a partnership at will without regard to breach of fiduciary consequences is contrary to the principle that a person may be estopped from exercising rights in bad faith."

NOTE ON PARTNERSHIP BREAKUP UNDER THE UPA

One of the most difficult problems in partnership law is how to treat the issues that arise where a partnership breakup occurs because a person's status as a partner is terminated, because the partnership is terminated as a going concern, or both. (The difficulty of these issues is illustrated by the fact that the rules concerning these issues occupy about a third of the text and comment of RUPA.) The UPA and RUPA adopt different strategies toward both the underlying substantive issues and the relevant nomenclature. This Note will focus on partnership breakup under the UPA. A Note below, will concern partnership breakup under RUPA.

Before getting directly into the legal issues, it is useful to outline the business economics involved.

Assume that a partnership is to be terminated as a going concern. Typically, the termination process will fall into three phases.

(i) The first phase consists of an event—which may be a decision by one or more partners or by a court—that sets the termination in motion. Under the UPA, this phase is referred to as "dissolution." The principal draftsman of the UPA explained the manner in which that statute uses the term "dissolution" as follows:

> [The term "dissolution" is used in the UPA to designate] a change in the relation of the partners caused by any partner ceasing to be associated in the carrying on of the business. As thus used "dissolution" does not terminate the partnership, it merely ends the carrying on of the business in that partnership. The partnership continues until the winding up of partnership affairs is completed.

Lewis, The Uniform Partnership Act, 24 Yale L.J. 617, 626–27 (1915).

(ii) The second phase consists of the process of actually terminating the partnership's business. Inevitably, some period of time must elapse between the moment at which the event that sets in motion the termination of the business and the moment at which the termination of the business is completed. For example, if a partnership is in the manufacturing business, to terminate the business the partnership will need to pay off its debts, settle its contracts with employees and suppliers, find a purchaser for its factory, and so forth. Under the UPA, this phrase is referred to as "winding up."

(iii) The final phase consists of the completion of the second phase and an end to the partnership as a going concern. Under the UPA, this phase is referred to as "termination."

To put all of this somewhat differently, the term "dissolution" is used in the UPA to describe a change in the *legal status* of the partners and the partnership. The term "winding-up" is used to describe the *economic* event of liquidation that follows dissolution.

Under the UPA, any termination of a person's status as a partner effects a dissolution of the partnership, because UPA § 29 defines dissolution as "the change in the relation of partners caused by any partner ceasing to be associated in the carrying on" of the partnership's business. It's not easy to see why this should be so when, as often happens, the remaining partners rightfully carry on the partnership's business after one partner has departed. Basically, the UPA's treatment of this issue seems to have been driven by conceptualism. The UPA treats a partnership as an aggregate of persons to carry on business for profit as co-owners, rather than as an entity. Because the UPA treats a partnership as an aggregate, the drafters seemed to have believed that it followed "logically" that any change in the identity of the partners "necessarily" worked a dissolution of the partnership. If a partnership is conceptualized as an aggregate of the partners, and if the partners in Partnership P are A, B, C, and D, then it may have seemed to the drafters of the UPA that if D ceases to be a partner, Partnership P "must be" dissolved, because there is no longer an aggregate of A, B, C, and D. The law, however, should not be built on deductive logic, but on policy, morality, and experience. We make legal rules because they are desirable, not because they are deducible. If a person ceases to be a partner, the law can treat the partnership as either dissolved or not dissolved. Which course the law takes should depend on which treatment best protects the reasonable expectations of partners. This, in turn, depends on what consequences the law attaches to dissolution.

Broadly speaking, dissolution may carry consequences among the partners; between the partners as a group and third persons such as individuals or firms with whom the partnership has contracted; and for tax purposes. The remainder of this Note will consider each of these areas.

1. *Consequences Among the Partners.* At least until recently, it was generally understood that under the UPA, unless otherwise agreed, upon the occurrence of dissolution—which, remember, under the UPA means simply that any partner ceases to be a partner—the partnership must sell its assets for cash and distribute the proceeds of the sale among all the partners. Alternatively, under some cases like *Creel*, the partnership may instead make a cash payment of the value of a partner's share of the partnership or an in-kind distribution. Furthermore, UPA § 38(2)(b) provides if a partner, W, *wrongfully* causes dissolution, although the *partnership* is dissolved, the remaining partners can continue the partnership's *business*. To do so, the remaining partners must either pay *W* the value of her partnership interest (but not including the value of the partnership's good will) minus any damages caused by the dissolution, or put up a bond to secure such a payment and indemnify *W* against present and future partnership liabilities.

UPA § 38(1) provides that "[w]hen dissolution is [rightfully] caused . . . each partner . . . *unless otherwise agreed*, may have the partnership property applied to discharge its liabilities, and the surplus applied to pay in cash the net amount owning to the respective partners." (Emphasis added.) It is well accepted that under the "unless" clause, the partnership agreement can provide that after the termination of a person's status as a partner (and therefore, under the UPA, after dissolution of the partnership) the remaining partners can continue the partnership *business*, even if the partnership has been dissolved and the dissolution is rightfully caused. *See, e.g.*, Meehan v. Shaughnessy, 535 N.E.2d 1255 (Mass. 1989); Adams v. Jarvis, 127 N.W.2d 400 (Wis.2d 1964). Agreements that enable remaining partners to continue the partnership's business after dissolution are common, especially in large partnerships. Such agreements are usually known as business-continuation agreements or, more simply, continuation agreements. Typically, continuation agreements include not only the right of the remaining partners to continue the partnership's business, but also the terms on which the partner who causes dissolution (or his estate) will be compensated for his partnership interest.

2. *Effect of Dissolution on the Relationship Between the Partnership and Third Parties.* As among the partners, it frequently won't matter very much whether the withdrawal of a partner does or does

not cause dissolution, because as among the partners a continuation agreement can generally override the substantive effects that dissolution would otherwise have. However, dissolution may affect the relationship of the partnership to third persons. For example, suppose that a partnership consisting of partners A, B, C, and D is dissolved by the withdrawal of D, but the business of the partnership is continued by A, B, and C under a continuation agreement. Under the UPA, because the partnership has been dissolved, the partnership of A, B, and C may be deemed a "new" partnership for legal purposes, so that the partnership's assets and agreements, such as leases, licenses, or franchises, must be "transferred" to the new partnership. *See* Report of the ABA Subcommittee on the Revision of the U.P.A., 43 Bus. Law. 121, 160–62 (1987). In a much remarked-on case, Fairway Development Co. v. Title Insurance Co., 621 F.Supp. 120 (N.D.Ohio 1985), Fairway, a partnership, sued Title Insurance Co. under a title guarantee policy. The policy had been issued at a time when the partners in Fairway were B, S, and W. Subsequently, B and S transferred their partnership interests to W and a third party, X. W and X apparently continued Fairway's business under the Fairway name. The court nevertheless held that Title Insurance Co. was not bound under its policy, because the partnership to which it had issued the policy had been legally dissolved.

A debated point under the UPA is whether a partnership agreement can provide not only that the partnership business may be continued after dissolution, but also that the withdrawal of a partner will not cause dissolution, so that the partnership's relation with third parties will not be affected by a partner's withdrawal, as happened in the *Fairway* case. The prevailing (but not unanimous) answer is no, on the ground that UPA § 31 expressly states that "[d]issolution is caused" by the withdrawal of a partner.

3. *Tax Consequences.* The tax-law treatment of dissolution is relatively straightforward, and largely unimpeded by conceptualism. Internal Revenue Code § 708 provides that a partnership's existence does not terminate for tax purposes until either "(A) no part of any business, financial operation, or venture of the partnership continues to be carried on by any of [the] partners in a partnership, or (B) within a twelve-month period there is a sale or exchange of fifty percent or more of the total interest in partnership capital and profits." Accordingly, dissolution under partnership law is normally a non-event for federal income tax purposes. (Warning: Despite IRC § 708, dissolution may have tax effects on a non-continuing partner or his estate. Even these effects, however, can normally be avoided by a continuation agreement.)

NOTE ON PARTNERSHIP BREAKUP UNDER RUPA

RUPA's provisions on partnership breakup are even more complex than those of the UPA.

1. *Nomenclature.* To begin with nomenclature, RUPA continues to use the terms "dissolution," "winding up," and "termination." However, RUPA adds a new term, *dissociation,* to describe the termination of a person's status as a partner.

2. *Events of Dissociation.* Although the term "dissociation" is new, the concept is not. Even under the UPA, a variety of events result in the termination of a person's status as a partner, and there is a very substantial overlap between the UPA and RUPA concerning the description of those events. For example, RUPA § 602(a) continues the rule of the UPA that every partner has the right to withdraw (dissociate) from the partnership at any time, rightfully or wrongfully, by express will. RUPA § 602(c) provides that a partner who wrongfully dissociates is liable to the partnership and to the other partners for damages caused by the dissociation. Furthermore, if a partner wrongfully dissociates, the partnership can continue without him.

3. *Rightful and Wrongful Dissociation.* RUPA § 602 distinguishes between events of dissociation that involve rightful conduct by the dissociated partner and events of dissociation that involve wrongful conduct. An event of dissociation is rightful unless it is specified as wrongful in § 602(b). The major types of wrongful dissociation are: (i) A dissociation that is in breach of an express provision of the partnership agreement. (ii) A withdrawal of a partner by the partner's express will before the expiration of the partnership term or the completion of an undertaking for which the partnership was formed. (iii) A partner has engaged in wrongful conduct that adversely and materially affected the partnership business. (iv) A partner has willfully or persistently committed a material breach of the partnership agreement, or of a duty of care, loyalty, good faith, and fair dealing owed to the partnership or the other partners under § 404.

The Comment to RUPA § 602 states:

> [Under 602(a)] . . . a partner has the power to dissociate at any time by expressing a will to withdraw, even in contravention of the partnership agreement. The phrase "rightfully or wrongfully" reflects the distinction between a partner's *power* to withdraw in contravention of the partnership agreement and a partner's *right* to do so. In this context, although a partner can not be enjoined from exercising the power to dissociate, the dissociation may be wrongful under subsection (b). . . .
>
> . . . The significance of a wrongful dissociation is that it may give rise to damages under subsection (c) and, if it results in the dissolution of the partnership, the wrongfully dissociating partner is not entitled to participate in winding up the business. . . .

4. *Consequences of Dissociation.* The partnership-breakup provisions of RUPA are driven by functional considerations, rather than by the "nature" of a partnership (although the Comments occasionally lapse into conceptual justifications based on the entity theory). Along these lines, RUPA, unlike the UPA, does not provide that every termination of a person's status as a partner—every dissociation—

causes dissolution. Instead, the key issue is whether dissociation has occurred, and what are the consequences of the *kind* of dissociation that occurred.

There is an important distinction here between the partnership and the partnership's business. Under the UPA, if the partnership status of one or more partners is terminated, the partnership is dissolved, but the remaining partners may continue the business, albeit as a new partnership. (For example, the remaining partners might agree on a buyout price with the departing partners, or might buy the partnership business at an auction pursuant to winding up, or might continue the business under a continuation agreement.) Under RUPA, however, the dissociation of a partner does not necessarily cause dissolution. For example, upon a wrongful dissociation, or a dissociation by death, the partnership is not dissolved—and therefore the partnership's business continues—unless within ninety days a majority of the remaining partners dissociate or agree to wind up. Rather than necessarily causing dissolution, under RUPA dissociation leads to two forks in the statutory road: winding up under Article 8, or a mandatory buyout under Article 7. Which fork must be taken under RUPA depends on the nature of the event of dissociation.

First Fork: Required Winding Up. RUPA § 801 describes the events of dissociation that require the partnership to be wound up. These events include notice of a partner's express will to withdraw in a partnership at will, the expiration of the partnership's term in a partnership for a term, and an uncured event that makes it unlawful for all or substantially all of the partnership's business to be continued. The Official Comment adds:

> . . . Under RUPA, not every partner dissociation causes a dissolution of the partnership. Only certain departures trigger a dissolution. The basic rule is that a partnership is dissolved, and its business must be wound up, only upon the occurrence of one of the events listed in Section 801. All other dissociations result in a buyout of the partner's interest under Article 7 and a continuation of the partnership entity and business by the remaining partners.
>
> Section 801 continues two basic rules from the UPA. First, it continues the rule that any member of an *at-will* partnership has the right to force a liquidation. Second, by negative implication, it continues the rule that the partners who wish to continue the business of a *term* partnership can not be forced to liquidate the business by a partner who withdraws prematurely in violation of the partnership agreement.

Second Fork: Required Buyout. If, upon the dissociation of a partner, winding up is not required under § 801, then RUPA § 701 requires a mandatory buyout of the dissociated partner's interest by the partnership. However, if the dissociation was wrongfully caused by the dissociated partner, § 701(c) provides that the buyout price under § 701(b) is to be reduced by damages for the wrongful dissociation. Furthermore, under § 701(h) a partner who wrongfully dissociates before the expiration of a definite partnership term, or the completion of a particular undertaking, is not entitled to payment of any portion of the buyout price until the expiration of the term or completion of the undertaking, unless the partner establishes to the satisfaction of the court that earlier payment will not cause undue hardship to the business of the partnership. A deferred payment must be adequately secured and bear interest. Under § 701(b), the buyout price of a dissociated partner's interest is the amount that would have been distributable to the dissociating partner if the partnership was wound up as of the date of dissociation, and the assets of the partnership were then sold at a price equal to or greater of the liquidation value or the value based on a sale of the entire business as a going concern, without the dissociated partner.

Robert W. Hillman, Allan W. Vestal & Donald J. Weidner, The Revised Uniform Partnership Act § 701, at 413, 416–417

2010–2011 ed.

"*Overview of the Buyout.* R.U.P.A. substantially expands the very limited buyout provisions of the U.P.A. In the event a fixed term partnership is wrongfully dissolved, the U.P.A allows the remaining partners to possess partnership assets for the duration of the agreed term if they pay (or secure) the value of the dissolving partner's interest in the partnership, less certain offsets. No standards are given, however, for determining of the value of the partner's interest.

"R.U.P.A's far more complete buyout provisions are applicable if a partner has dissociated but there will be no winding up and dissolution of the partnership under Article 8. They require an appraisal of the value of the partnership that is based upon a hypothetical liquidating distribution following a sale of the partnership's assets (at the greater of liquidating or going concern value). The figure yielded is reduced for damages because of wrongful dissociation and other amounts owed by the dissociated partner. The net amount becomes the 'undisputed minimum value of the partner's partnership interest' and is tendered to the dissociated partner, who may seek judicial valuation if dissatisfied with the buyout price....

"*The Buyout Price.* R.U.P.A. Section 701(a) directs the purchase of the dissociated partner's interest at the 'buyout price' determined under Section 702(b), which in turn defines 'buyout price' as the amount that would be received by the dissociated partner if the partnership dissolves, winds up its affairs, and liquidates its assets. In fact, the term is somewhat misleading because the buyout price may be higher, perhaps considerably so, than the amount actually paid to the dissociated partner. The buyout price may be reduced under Section 701(c) by various offsets, including damages for wrongful dissociation and amount owing (presently or in the future) by the dissociated partner. Determining the buyout price is only the first of several steps taken to determine the amount payable to the dissociated partner.

"By focusing on the top-down valuation keyed to a sale of all of the assets of the partnership, R.U.P.A. directs the analysis away from a valuation of the interest of a particular partner. Because the valuation inquiry is not directed to the value of an individual interest, a minority discount is inappropriate. Also inappropriate, in the view of the Official Comment, is a discount to reflect the distress sale circumstances of many auctions of partnership assets. The Official Comment thus wishes away the reality of assets sales, where competitive bidding often does not exist.

"Although minority interest and distress sale discounts may be inappropriate, the Official Comment acknowledges that other discounts, such as for a lack of marketability or the loss of a key partner, may be allowed."

Robert W. Hillman, Allan W. Vestal & Donald J. Weidner, The Revised Uniform Partnership Act § 801, at 443–444, 449

2010–2011 ed.

"*The Meaning of Dissolution.* R.U.P.A. significantly alters the use of the term 'dissolution.' Under the U.P.A., 'dissolution' describes the change in the *relationship* among partners caused by the withdrawal of a partner. In contrast, R.U.P.A. applies an entity view of the partnership and uses 'dissolution' to describe the point at which the partnership *as an entity* begins the winding up phase of its existence. Under the U.P.A., any withdrawal causes a dissolution of the relationship; under R.U.P.A., the withdrawal, or dissociation, of a partner will not necessarily lead to the dissolution of the partnership entity. Dissolutions, in short, will occur more frequently under the U.P.A. than R.U.P.A.

"Although the conditions leading to dissolution are different under the two acts, the operative significance of the term is similar under the U.P.A. and R.U.P.A. Dissolution does not terminate the entity (R.U.P.A) or the relationship (U.P.A.) but does launch the winding up phase of the partnership's existence. At the conclusion of winding up, the partnership entity (R.U.P.A.) or relationship (the U.P.A.) is terminated. . . .

"*Waiver of Judicial Dissolution.* Section 103(b)(8) denies partners the contractual option of varying the winding up requirements under circumstances that include a judicial decree of dissolution on the grounds specified in Section 801(5). The Official Comment affirms that a court's power to wind up a partnership under this section cannot be varied in the partnership agreement. Even without this statutory exception to contractual options, one would expect considerable judicial hostility when parties attempt to limit the role of courts in partnership dissolutions."

SECTION 9. DISSOLUTION (II): DISSOLUTION BY JUDICIAL DECREE AND WRONGFUL DISSOLUTION

UNIFORM PARTNERSHIP ACT §§ 31(2), 32, 38(2)

REVISED UNIFORM PARTNERSHIP ACT §§ 601, 602, 603, 701, 801, 802, 803, 804, 807

[See Statutory Supplement]

Drashner v. Sorenson

Supreme Court of South Dakota, 1954.
75 S.D. 247, 63 N.W.2d 255.

■ SMITH, P.J.

In January 1951 the plaintiff, C.H. Drashner, and defendants, A.D. Sorenson and Jacob P. Deis, associated themselves as co-owners in the real estate, loan and insurance business at Rapid City. For a consideration of $7500 they purchased the real estate and insurance agency known as J. Schumacher Co. located in an office room on the ground floor of the Alex Johnson Hotel building. The entire purchase price was advanced for the partnership by the defendants, but at the time of trial $3,000 of that sum had been repaid to them by the partnership. Although, as will appear from facts presently to be outlined, their operations were not unsuccessful, differences arose and on June 15, 1951 plaintiff commenced this action in which he sought an accounting, dissolution and winding up of the partnership. The answer and counterclaim of defendants prayed for like relief.

The cause came on for trial September 4, 1951. The court among others made the following findings. VII. "That thereafter the plaintiff violated the terms of said partnership agreement, in that he demanded a larger share of the income of the said partnership than he was entitled to receive under the terms of said partnership agreement; that the plaintiff was arrested for reckless driving and served a term in jail for said offense; that the plaintiff demanded that the defendants permit him to draw money for his own personal use out of the moneys held in escrow by the partnership; that the plaintiff spent a large amount of time during business hours in the Brass Rail Bar in Rapid City, South Dakota, and other bars, and neglected his duties in connection with the business of the said partnership.... That the plaintiff, by his actions hereinbefore set forth, has made it impossible to carry on the partnership." The conclusions adopted read as follows: I "That the defendants are entitled to continue the partnership and have the value of the plaintiff's interest in the partnership business determined, upon the filing and approval of a good and sufficient bond, conditioned upon the release of the plaintiff from any liability arising out of the said partnership, and further conditioned upon the payment by the defendants to the plaintiff of the value of plaintiffs' interest in the partnership as determined by the Court." II "That in computing the value of the plaintiff's interest in the said partnership, the value of the good will of the business shall not be considered." III "That the value of the partnership shall be finally determined upon a hearing before this Court, ..." and IV "That the plaintiff shall be entitled to receive one-third of the value of the partnership property owned by the partnership on the 12th day of September, 1951, not including the good will of the business, after the payment of the liabilities of the partnership and the payment to the defendants of the invested capital in the sum of $4,500.00." Judgment was accordingly entered dissolving the partnership as of September 12, 1951.

After hearing at a later date the court found: I "That the value of the said partnership property on the 12th day of September, 1951, was the sum of Four Thousand Four Hundred Ninety-eight and 90/100 Dollars ($4498.90), and on said date there was due and owing by the partnership for accountant's services the sum of Four Hundred Eighty Dollars ($480.00), and that on said date the sum of Four Thousand Five Hundred Dollars ($4500.00) of the capital invested by the defendants had not been returned to the defendants." and II "That there is not sufficient partnership property to reimburse the defendants for their invested capital." Thereupon the court decreed "that the plaintiff had no interest in the property of the said partnership", and that the defendants were the sole owners thereof.

The assignments of error are predicated upon insufficiency of the evidence to support the findings and conclusions. Of these assignments, only those which question whether the court was warranted in finding that (a) the plaintiff caused the dissolution wrongfully, and (b) the value of the partnership property, exclusive of good will, was $4498.90 on the 12th day of September, 1951, merit discussion. A preliminary statement is necessary to place these issues in their framework.

The agreement of the parties contemplated an association which would continue at least until the $7500 advance of defendants had been repaid from the gross earnings of the business. Hence, it was not a partnership at will. Vangel v. Vangel, 254 P.2d 919 (Cal.App.2d 1953); Zeibak v. Nasser, 82 P.2d 375 (Cal.2d 1938). In apparent recognition of that fact, both plaintiff and defendants sought dissolution in contravention of the partnership agreement, *see* SDC 49.0603(2) under SDC 49.0604(1)(d) on the ground that the adverse party had caused the dissolution wrongfully by willfully and persistently committing a breach of the partnership agreement, and by so conducting himself in matters relating to the partnership business as to render impracticable the carrying on of the business in partnership with him.

[The court here quoted U.P.A. Section 38(2)].

From this background we turn to a consideration of the evidence from which the trial court inferred that plaintiff caused the dissolution wrongfully.

The breach between the parties resulted from a continuing controversy over the right of plaintiff to withdraw sufficient money from the partnership to defray his living expenses. Plaintiff was dependent upon his earnings for the support of his family. The defendants had other resources. Plaintiff claimed that he was to be permitted to draw from the earnings of the partnership a sufficient amount to support himself and family. The defendants asserted that there was a definite arrangement for the allocation of the income of the partnership and there was no agreement for withdrawal by plaintiff of more than his allotment under that plan. Defendants' version of the facts was corroborated by a written admission of plaintiff offered in evidence. From evidence thus sharply in conflict, the trial court made a finding, reading as follows: "That the oral partnership agreement between the parties provided that each of the three partners were to draw as compensation one-third of one-half of the commissions earned upon sales made by the partners; that the other one-half of the commissions earned on sales made by the partners and one-half of the commissions earned upon sales made by salesmen employed by the partnership, together with the earnings from the insurance business carried on by the partnership, was to be placed in a fund to be used for the payment of the operating expenses of the partnership, and after the payment of such operating expenses to be used to reimburse the defendants for the capital advanced in the purchase of the Julius Schumacher business and the capital advanced in the sum of Eight Hundred Dollars ($800.00) for the operating expenses of the business."

As an outgrowth of this crucial difference, there was evidence from which a court could reasonably believe that plaintiff neglected the business and spent too much time in a nearby bar during business hours. At a time when plaintiff had overdrawn his partners and was also indebted to one of defendants for personal advances, he requested $100 and his request was refused. In substance he then said, according to the testimony of the defendant Deis, that he would see that he "gets some money to run on", if they "didn't give it to him he was going to dissolve the partnership and see that he got it." Thereafter plaintiff pressed his claims through counsel, and eventually brought this action to dissolve the partnership. The claim so persistently asserted was contrary to the partnership agreement found by the court.

The foregoing picture of the widening breach between the parties is drawn almost entirely from the evidence of defendants. Of course, plaintiff's version of the agreement of the parties, and of the ensuing differences, if believed, would have supported findings of a different order by the trier of the fact. It cannot be said, we think, that the trial court acted unreasonably in believing defendants, and we think it equally clear the court could reasonably conclude that the insistent and continuing demands of the plaintiff and his attendant conduct rendered it reasonably impracticable to carry on the business in partnership with him. It follows, we are of the opinion, the evidence supports the finding that plaintiff caused the dissolution wrongfully. Zeibak v. Nasser, 82 P.2d 375 (Cal.2d 1938); Owen v. Cohen, 119 P.2d 713 (Cal.2d 1941); Meherin v. Meherin, 209 P.2d 36 (Cal.2d 1949); and Vangel v. Vangel, 254 P.2d 919 (Cal.2d 1953).

This brings us to a consideration of the sufficiency of the evidence to support the finding of the court that the property of the partnership was of the value of $4498.90 as of the date of dissolution.

Bitter complaint is made because the trial court refused to consider the good will of this business in arriving at its conclusion. The feeling of plaintiff is understandable. These partners must have placed a very high estimate upon the value of the good will of this agency because they paid Mr. Schumacher $7500 to turn over that office with its very moderate fixtures and its listing of property, together with an agreement that he would not engage in the business in Rapid City for at least two years. No doubt they attached some of this good will value to the location of the business which was under only a month to month letting. Cf. 38 C.J.S., Good Will, § 3, page 951; In re Brown's Will, 242 N.Y. 1, 150 N.E. 581, 44 A.L.R. 510, at page 513. Their estimate of value was borne out by the subsequent history of the business. Its real estate commissions, earned but only partly received, grossed $21,528.25 and its insurance commissions grossed $661.21 in the period January 15 to August 31, 1951. In that period the received commissions paid all expenses, including the commissions of salesmen, retired $3,000 of the $7500 purchase price advanced by defendants, and all of $800 of working capital so advanced, allowed the parties to withdraw $1453.02 each, and accumulated a cash balance of $2221.43. In addition the partnership has commissions due.... Notwithstanding this indication of the great value of the good will of this business, the statute does not require the court to take it into consideration in valuing the property of the business in these circumstances. The statute provides such a sanction for causing the dissolution of a partnership wrongfully. SDC 49.0610(2)(c)(2) quoted supra. The court applied the statute....

That the $1500 value placed on [the assets other than good will] was conservative we do not question. However, after mature study and reflection we have concluded that the court's finding is not against the clear weight of the evidence appearing in this record. Hence we are not at liberty to disturb it.

The brief of plaintiff includes some discussion of his right to a share in the profits from the date of the dissolution until the final judgment. It does not appear from the record that this claim was presented to the trial court, or that the net profit of the business during that period was evidenced. Because that issue was not presented below, it is not before us.

■ THE JUDGMENT OF THE TRIAL COURT IS AFFIRMED.

■ ALL THE JUDGES CONCUR.

NOTE ON WRONGFUL DISSOLUTION

Drashner v. Sorenson illustrates the drastic consequences that can befall a wrongfully dissolving partner under the UPA—damages against the partner, a valuation of this partner's interest that does not reflect the real value of the interest because goodwill is not taken into account, and a continuation of the business without the partner. These consequences may have a special impact in a partnership without an expressly specified term. Suppose one of the partners, *A*, elects to dissolve such a partnership on the theory that the partnership is at will. If the court finds that despite the absence of a specified term, the partnership is for a term as a matter of implication, *A* will have dissolved the partnership in contravention of the partnership agreement. The penalties for guessing wrong on whether the court will make such a finding "may act as significant disincentives to dissolution [and may therefore] tend to stabilize the partnership." Hillman, The Dissatisfied Participant in the Solvent Business Venture: A Consideration of the Relative Permanence of Partnerships and Close Corporations, 67 Minn. L. Rev. 1, 34 (1982). For comparable reasons, a partner who believes that other partners have engaged in wrongful conduct is taking a risk if she tries to dissolve a partnership through a self-help election, as opposed to going to court for a decree under UPA Section 32. The other side of the coin is that judicial proceedings entail delay.

NOTE ON THE EXPULSION OF A PARTNER

The expulsion of a partner without good cause prior to the end of the partnership term is ordinarily a wrongful violation of the partnership agreement, and a wrongfully expelled partner ordinarily has a right to have the partnership dissolved and liquidated. *See* UPA §§ 31(1)(d); 32(1)(d), 38(1). In contrast, under UPA § 38(1), "if dissolution is caused by the expulsion of a partner, bona fide under the partnership agreement and if the expelled partner is discharged from all partnership liabilities, either by payment or agreement . . . , he shall receive in cash only the net amount due him from the partnership." Under this section, a partnership agreement may lawfully provide that a partner can be expelled without cause upon a designated vote of the remaining partners. *See* Lawlis v. Kightlinger & Gray, 562 N.E.2d 435 (Ind.App.1990); Miller v. Foulston, Siefkin, Powers & Eberhardt, 790 P.2d 404 (Kan. 1990).

To fall within UPA § 31(1)(d), an expulsion must be "bona fide." In *Lawlis,* supra, the court stated that "if the power to involuntarily expel partners granted by a partnership agreement is exercised in bad faith or for a 'predatory purpose,' ... the partnership agreement is violated, giving rise to an action for damages the affected partner has suffered as a result of his expulsion." *Id.* at 440. What does "bona fide" or "good faith" mean in this context? It cannot mean that a partner may be expelled only for cause: under such an interpretation, the power to expel a partner under an expulsion provision of a partnership agreement would be no greater than the power to expel a partner even in the absence of an expulsion provision. In *Lawlis,* the court said, "the expelling partners act in 'good faith' regardless of motivation if [the expulsion] does not cause a wrongful withholding of money or property legally due the expelled partner at the time he is expelled." *Id.* at 443. This seems too restrictive. In Winston & Strawn v. Nosal, 664 N.E.2d 239 (Ill.App.3d 1996), Nosal was expelled from a law firm, Winston & Strawn. The expulsion followed (1) Nosal's request for partnership information concerning actions of the partnership's executive committee—in particular, concerning actions of Fairchild, the managing partner—in increasing the compensation and ownership interests of the committee members, and (2) Nosal's threat to sue if his request for information was not granted. Winston & Strawn then brought an action for a declaratory judgment that the expulsion was valid under the partnership agreement. The trial court granted summary judgment for Winston & Strawn. Reversed:

> It is well-established that a fiduciary relationship exists between partners and that each partner is bound to exercise the utmost good faith and honesty in all matters relating to the partnership business.... Labovitz v. Dolan, 545 N.E.2d 304 (Ill. App.3d 1989)....
>
> Illinois has yet to address the extent of the duty of good faith in the context of partner outplacement or expulsion. Courts in other jurisdictions, however, have concluded that partners owe one another a duty of good faith in the context of expulsion, even where the partnership agreement permits expulsion without cause....
>
> In this case, there is no dispute that the partnership agreement places no restriction upon the expulsion of a partner other than approval by the requisite majority. However, the agreement also grants all partners unrestricted access "to the books and records of the partnership." Access to partnership books is also guaranteed under section 19 of the Act....
>
> Nosal claims that the documents he sought would have revealed the executive committee's plan to retain much of the firm's wealth and management power in the hands of its members. Specifically, the documents would have proven that upon assuming control, and without generally notifying the remaining capital partners, the executive committee dramatically increased the total number of partnership "points," or portions of owner-

ship interest in the firm, and then awarded themselves large increases.

Indeed, the record substantiates that in 1990, the executive committee voted its members considerable increases in individual points which were not given to the remaining capital partners. Nosal's evidence indicates that other capital partners were never notified about this action, and that when Nosal ... sought to learn about it, [he was] repeatedly denied documents expressly guaranteed [to him] under the partnership agreement. We recognize ... testimony that the executive committee had the prerogative to designate the number of points for each capital partner; however, we find nothing in the agreement permitting such self-promoting action as was taken here without the full awareness of the remaining capital partners.

Nosal also alleges that Fairchild intentionally kept such data from him because Nosal could have uncovered evidence of Fairchild's ongoing fraudulent billing scheme subsequently discovered by the firm.

... We note that among the documents sought by Nosal was a firm auditor's internal control report, which arguably could have disclosed questionable billing practices by Fairchild. It cannot be ignored that Nosal's [expulsion] immediately succeeded his ongoing requests for sensitive firm information, and came just days after he presented Fairchild with a draft complaint threatening to sue the firm to enforce his right to examine books and records. The evidence further indicates that it was Fairchild, in his discretion, who was largely instrument in the sudden decision to outplace Nosal despite the fact that just a week before, Nosal was given a favorable review, a compensation increase, and assurances ... that he was not among those to be outplaced.

Fairchild's steadfast refusal of Nosal's access to records, his role in the outplacement, and the fact that it occurred just after Nosal's threatened lawsuit, raise an inference that Nosal was expelled solely because he persisted in invoking rights belonging to him under the partnership agreement and that the reasons advanced by the firm were pretextual. Regardless of the discretion conferred upon partners under a partnership agreement, this does not abrogate their high duty to exercise good faith and fair dealing in the execution of such discretion. Labovitz, 545 N.E.2d 304 (Ill.App.3d 1989). Nosal has sufficiently raised a triable issue that his expulsion occurred in breach of this duty.

LEVY v. NASSAU QUEENS MEDICAL GROUP, 102 A.D.2d 845, 476 N.Y.S.2d 613, 614 (1984). "While [an expulsion in] bad faith may be actionable, there must be some showing that the partnership acted out of a desire to gain a business or property advantage for the remaining partners.... Policy disagreements do not constitute bad faith 'since at the heart of the partnership concept is the principle that partners may choose with whom they wish to be associated.' "

CRUTCHER v. SMITH, 209 B.R. 347 (Bankr. Ct. E.D. Pa. 1997). "The threshold issue is a factual question of whether the Debtor [Partner] was wrongfully expelled by the Defendants from the partnership, or whether the Debtor caused his own termination from the partnership by failing to fulfill his duties as a partner.... [The Defendants claim] that the Debtor himself breached the oral partnership agreement and subsequently disassociated himself from the Business, and therefore that his own acts caused dissolution of the partnership in January 1996. In particular, the Defendants claim that the Debtor failed to replace the $500 bad check which he gave to Smith [, one of the partners, and used $110 of partnership funds]....

"However, ... we conclude that the Debtor's alleged wrongful acts were insufficient to trigger a dissolution of the partnership.... ' "[I]t is not for every trivial departure from duty or violation of the articles of partnership, or for every trifling fault or misconduct that courts of equity will interfere and decree a dissolution.' " [Potter v. Brown, 328 Pa. 554, 562, 195 A. 901, 904 (1938)], (quoting Story on Partnership, § 287). Although the Debtor's misuse of $110 in partnership funds was technically 'misconduct,' the sum at issue was minimal. The failure to reimburse Smith for [a] $500 bad check was more of a personal wrongful act against Smith than an act against the Business, but arguably was also 'misconduct' inter se the partners. However, the amounts, even when put together, are relatively inconsequential in light of the Business's 1996 gross income of over $200,000. Certainly a $610 offset could have been effected in any future distributions to the partners. We believe that these minor infractions are insufficient to trigger a dissolution of the partnership....

"The Debtor's argument in support of his wrongful expulsion by the Defendants, on the other hand, more logically explains his disassociation from the Business. In essence, the Debtor argues that the Defendants engaged in several definitive steps to ensure his exclusion from the partnership....

"... First, the Defendants refused to allow the Debtor to participate in the daily operation of the Business after his hospitalization. Second, upon discovering the Debtor's hospitalization, the Defendants immediately notified [the bank] that there were problems in the partnership and placed an 'alert' on the account which was operative only upon an attempt by the Debtor to withdraw funds from the account. The defendants then proceeded to open a new account bearing only their names. Thus, the Debtor was excluded from all financial matters related to the Business and the partnership in general.... Most notably, [the Defendants] did not obtain the Debtor's consent for, nor give him notice of, their purchase of an investment property ... with partnership funds, thereby depriving the Debtor of any managerial and decision-making authority as a partner.

"These events indicate that the Defendants took unequivocal measures to strip the Debtor of all of his rights as a partner, thereby excluding him from the operation and management of the partnership. The debtor thus has sufficiently established that he was wrongfully expelled from the partnership by the Defendants."

SECTION 10. LIMITED PARTNERSHIPS

A. THE UNIFORM LIMITED PARTNERSHIP ACTS

The limited partnership is an historical form of business organization. As of 2002, there were 377,000 limited partnerships in the United States, with an average of 18 partners in each partnership. Wheeler & Parsons, Partnership Returns, 2002, Statistics of Income Bulletin, Fall 2004, at 46, 57.

Over the course of time, the Commissioners on Uniform State Laws have promulgated several uniform limited partnership acts.

In 1916, the Commissioners promulgated the original Uniform Limited Partnership Act. It was adopted in every state except Louisiana. In 1976, the Commissioners promulgated a replacement for the Uniform Limited Partnership Act, called the Revised Uniform Partnership Act. The new Act modernized the prior Act, and reflected the influence of the corporate model. It has been widely but not universally adopted.

In 1985, the Commissioners amended the Revised Uniform Limited Partnership Act in a number of important respects. The states are still in the process of adopting (or not adopting) these amendments.

In 2001, the Commission adopted the Uniform Limited Partnership Act (2001). As of the time this casebook is written, that Act has been adopted in only four states. In the balance of this Section, the Uniform Limited Partnership Act will sometimes be referred to as the ULPA; the Revised Uniform Partnership Act, as amended in 1985, will sometimes be referred to as RULPA; and the Uniform Limited Partnership Act (2001) will sometimes be referred to as the 2001 Act.

B. FORMATION OF LIMITED PARTNERSHIPS

REVISED UNIFORM LIMITED PARTNERSHIP ACT §§ 101, 201

[See Statutory Supplement]

UNIFORM LIMITED PARTNERSHIP ACT (2001) §§ 102, 201

NOTE

Unlike general partnerships, limited partnerships are basically creatures of statute, although they have nonstatutory historical antecedents. RULPA § 101 defines a limited partnership as "a partnership formed by two or more persons under the laws of this State and having one or more general partners and one or more limited partners." RULPA § 201 provides that in order to form a limited partnership a certificate of limited partnership must be filed in the office of the Secretary of State. The certificate must state the name of the limited partnership, the name and business address of each general partner, the latest date upon which the limited partnership is to dissolve, and the name and address of the agent for service of process. Sections 102 and 201 of the 2001 Act are comparable.

C. LIABILITY OF LIMITED PARTNERS

REVISED UNIFORM LIMITED PARTNERSHIP ACT § 303

[See Statutory Supplement]

UNIFORM LIMITED PARTNERSHIP ACT (2001) § [303]

Gateway Potato Sales v. G.B. Investment Co.

Court of Appeals of Arizona, 1991.
170 Ariz. 137, 822 P.2d 490.

■ TAYLOR, JUDGE.

Gateway Potato Sales (Gateway), a creditor of Sunworth Packing Limited Partnership (Sunworth Packing), brought suit to recover payment for goods it had supplied to the limited partnership. Gateway sought recovery from Sunworth Packing, from Sunworth Corporation as general partner, and from G.B. Investment Company (G.B. Investment) as a limited partner, pursuant to Arizona Revised Statutes Annotated (A.R.S.) § 29–319. Under § 29–319, a limited partner may become liable for the obligations of the limited partnership under certain circumstances in which the limited partner has taken part in the control of the business.

G.B. Investment moved for summary judgment, urging that there was no evidence that the circumstances described in A.R.S. § 29–319 had occurred in this case. It argued that, as a limited partner, it was not liable to the creditors of the limited partnership except to the extent of its investment. The trial court agreed, granting G.B. Investment's motion for summary judgment.

Gateway appeals from the judgment and the denial of its motion for reconsideration, arguing the existence of conflicting evidence of material facts relating to the participation of the limited partner in the control of the partnership business. We agree and reverse the grant of summary judgment.

FACTS

On review from the trial court's order granting summary judgment, the facts are viewed in the light most favorable to the party against whom judgment is entered. Dolezal v. Carbrey, 161 Ariz. 365, 366, 778 P.2d 1261, 1262 (1989). Sunworth Corporation and G.B. Investment formed Sunworth Packing in November 1985 for the purpose of engaging in potato farming in Arizona. The limited partnership certificate and agreement of Sunworth Packing, filed with the office of the Arizona Secretary of State, specified Sunworth Corporation as the general partner and G.B. Investment Company as the limited partner. The agreement recited that the limited partner would not participate in the control of the business. The agreement further stated that the limited partner would not become liable to the creditors of the partnership, except to the extent of its initial contribution and any liability it may incur with an Arizona bank as a signatory party or guarantor of a loan and/or line of credit.

In late 1985, Robert C. Ellsworth, the president of Sunworth Corporation, called Robert Pribula, the owner of Gateway, located in Minnesota, to see if Gateway would supply Sunworth Packing with seed potatoes. Pribula hesitated to supply the seed potatoes without receiving assurance of payment because Pribula was aware that Ellsworth had previously undergone bankruptcy. Pribula, however, decided to sell the seed potatoes to Sunworth Packing after being assured by Ellsworth that he was in partnership with a large financial institution, G.B. Investment Company, and that G.B. Investment was providing the financing, was actively involved in the operation of the business, and had approved the purchase of the seed potatoes. Thereafter, from February 1986 through April 1986, Gateway sold substantial quantities of seed potatoes to Sunworth Packing.

While supplying the seed potatoes, Pribula believed that he was doing business with a general partnership (i.e., Sunworth Packing Company, formed by Sunworth Corporation and G.B. Investment Company). The sales documents used by the parties specified "Sunworth Packing Company" as the name of the partnership. Pribula was neither aware of the true name of the partnership nor that it was a limited partnership.

All of Gateway's dealings were with Ellsworth. Pribula neither contacted G.B. Investment prior to selling the seed potatoes to the limited partnership nor did he otherwise attempt to verify any of the statements Ellsworth had made about G.B. Investment's involvement.

The only direct contact between G.B. Investment and Gateway occurred some time after the sale of the seed potatoes. It is, however, disputed whether G.B. Investment ever provided any assurance of payment to Gateway.

G.B. Investment's vice-president, Darl Anderson, testified in his affidavit that G.B. Investment had exerted no control over the daily management and operation of the limited partnership, Sunworth Packing. This testimony was contradicted, however, by the affidavit testimony of Ellsworth which was presented by Gateway in opposing G.B. Investment's motion for summary judgment. According to Ellsworth, G.B. Investment's employees, Darl Anderson and Thomas McHolm, controlled the day-to-day affairs of the limited partnership and made Ellsworth account to them for nearly everything he did. This day-to-day contact included but was not limited to approval of most of the significant operational decisions and expenditures and the use and management of partnership funds without Ellsworth's involvement.[1]

---

1. Ellsworth described with some specificity the ways in which G.B. Investment's control was exerted:

a. During the early months of the Partnership, Thomas McHolm and/or Darl Anderson were at the Partnership's offices on a daily basis directing the operation of the Partnership, and thereafter, they were at the Partnership's offices at least 2–3 times per week reviewing the operations of the business, directing changes in operations, and instructing me to make certain changes in operating the Partnership's affairs;

b. G.B. Investment Company was solely responsible for obtaining a $150,000.00 line-of-credit loan for the Partnership with Valley National Bank of Arizona, and it also signed documents guaranteeing the repayment of the loan;

c. As the President of the general partner, I was not permitted to make any significant independent business decisions concerning the operations of the Partnership, but was directed to have all business decisions approved with Darl Anderson and/or Thomas McHolm, or was directed to carry out decisions made by Darl Anderson and/or Thomas McHolm. For example, instead of using Partnership funds to pay certain creditors and suppliers, I was directed by Darl Anderson and/or Thomas McHolm to use the Partnership funds to purchase additional machinery and equipment;

d. Prior to constructing improvements to the packaging facilities of the Partnership, Thomas McHolm and/or Darl Anderson had to approve all construction bids, individually selected some of the suppliers and subcontractors, and individually selected the equipment to be installed;

e. Thomas McHolm and/or Darl Anderson dictated the accounting procedures to be followed by the Partnership, reviewed the Partnership's books and accounts almost continually, dictated that the Partnership use the same accounting firm as that of G.B. Investment Company to do the Partnership accounting tasks, undertook the responsibility of having prepared all Partnership tax forms and returns, and I only signed tax returns after they had been prepared by G.B. Investment Company's accountants and reviewed by Darl Anderson or some other employee/agent of G.B. Investment Company;

f. During a great portion of the duration of the Partnership, Thomas McHolm and/or Darl Anderson oversaw the daily operations of the Partnership because I had to have all expenditures approved by Thomas McHolm and/or Darl Anderson and Darl Anderson had to approve and sign checks issued by the Partnership, including without limitation payroll checks and invoices for telephone charges, utilities, publications, interest payments, bank card charges, supplies, etc. Copies of a sampling of the invoices and the corresponding checks are attached hereto as Exhibit 2;

g. After it was decided to add a hydrocooler to the processing and packaging facilities of the Partnership, Thomas McHolm individually selected the refrigeration equipment and chose the contractor to install the refrigeration equipment on the hydrocooler, and even saw to it that G.B. Investment Company (not the Partnership) directly paid the contractor for all of his services;

Ellsworth testified further that he had described G.B. Investment's control of the business operation to Pribula. Pribula confirmed that Ellsworth had informed him that G.B. Investment's employees, McHolm and Anderson, were at the partnership's office on a frequent basis, that Ellsworth reported directly to them, that daily operations of the partnership were reviewed by representatives of G.B. Investment, and that Ellsworth had to get their approval before making certain business decisions.

DISCUSSION

Gateway argues that sufficient questions of fact exist which preclude the granting of summary judgment in favor of G.B. Investment. We will affirm the trial court's grant of summary judgment if there is no genuine issue of material fact in dispute and the moving party is entitled to judgment as a matter of law. Orme School v. Reeves, 166 Ariz. 301, 305, 802 P.2d 1000, 1004 (1990).

Subsection (a) of A.R.S. § 29–319 sets forth the general rule that a limited partner who is not also a general partner is not liable for the obligations of the limited partnership.

> [A] limited partner is not liable for the obligations of a limited partnership unless he is also a general partner or, in addition to the exercise of his rights and powers as a limited partner, he takes part in the control of the business. However, if the limited partner's participation in the control of the business is not substantially the same as the exercise of the powers of a general partner, he is liable only to persons who transact business with the limited partnership with actual knowledge of his participation in control.

In responding to the motion for summary judgment, Gateway urged the trial court to find that Gateway had presented a fact question of G.B. Investment's liability to it under A.R.S. § 29–319(a).

---

h. Thomas McHolm insisted that the Partnership use a particular supplier, to-wit: Allied Packaging, to supply packaging materials to the Partnership, he further took an active role in reviewing and modifying the art work for use on the packaging items, and personally approved the bid submitted for the art work;

i. At least on two separate occasions, approximately in August, 1986 and again in November, 1986, Darl Anderson caused sums of monies (approximately $8,000 and $7,000 respectively) to be withdrawn from the Partnership account (No. 2270–8018) with Valley National Bank without the prior knowledge or consent of myself, as the President of the general partner of the Partnership. These monies were paid directly to G.B. Investment, and the withdrawals caused other checks of the Partnership to be dishonored due to insufficient funds and left the Partnership without sufficient funds to meet its payroll obligations;

j. Darl Anderson and/or Thomas McHolm caused certain expenses of the Partnership to be paid directly by G.B. Investment Company, to-wit: refrigeration equipment; and

k. After the Partnership defaulted on its loan payments to Valley National Bank, a loan which had been guaranteed by G.B. Investment Company, Darl Anderson, without my knowledge or consent, instructed the Valley National Bank to proceed with declaring the loan to be in default and to pursue its remedies under its Security Agreement with the Partnership, to-wit: to sell the equipment and machinery that it held as collateral at a foreclosure auction. At the foreclosure auction held on March 3, 1987, by Valley National Bank, Darl Anderson, on behalf of G.B. Investment Company, bought the equipment and machinery previously owned by Sunworth Corporation.

Gateway argued that the statute imposes liability on a limited partner whose participation in the control of the business is substantially the same as the exercised power of a general partner. Gateway further argued that even if the person transacting business with the limited partnership did not know of the limited partner's participation in control, there is liability. Alternatively, Gateway argued that the statute imposes liability when the powers exercised in controlling the business might fall short of being "substantially the same as the exercise of powers of a general partner," but the person transacting business with the limited partnership had actual knowledge of the participation in control. Gateway asserted that the evidence it was presenting in response to the motion for summary judgment raised issues of material fact as to whether either of these situations had occurred. If either had occurred, Gateway argued, it would be entitled to recover from the limited partner, G.B. Investment.

In granting G.B. Investment's motion for summary judgment, the trial court gave two reasons for concluding that G.B. Investment could not be found liable under A.R.S. § 29–319(a) as a matter of law. First, as we interpret the trial court's comments, it read the statute as having a threshold requirement—that is, under all circumstances, a creditor of the limited partnership must have contact with the limited partner in order to impose liability on the limited partner. The evidence before the trial court showed that Gateway merely relied upon the statements made by Ellsworth, president of the general partner, and that Gateway did not contact G.B. Investment prior to transacting business with the limited partnership. Based upon these facts, the trial court concluded that liability could not be imposed upon G.B. Investment. The trial court's minute entry states, in relevant part:

> [I]t is undisputed that the plaintiff contracted with and sold seed potatoes to the limited partnership, without any direct contact with the movant. In other words, at the time the sale with the limited partnership was consummated and completed—plaintiff can not by the posture of the evidence—be said to have been a person who, while transacting business with the limited partnership, did so with actual knowledge of defendant G.B. Investment Company's participation in control with the limited partnership or its general partner.
>
> Consequently, plaintiff fails to leap the first "hurdle"; and neither the court nor the trier-of-fact need review plaintiff's factual assertions regarding "safe harbor" excesses or violations, if any, under A.R.S. § 29–319(B). The only purported contact between plaintiff and defendant G.B. Investment Company occurred in the fall of 1986, well after the last of the seed potatoes were delivered by plaintiff to the limited partnership.
>
> Notwithstanding the representations made by Robert C. Ellsworth, as the president of the general partner, Sunworth Corporation, regarding the movant, plaintiff admits it never directly contacted the movant, to inquire into or verify Ellsworth's authority to bind the movant by such representations.

> The court finds, given the present record, that movant G.B. Investment has no liability to plaintiff arising from movant being a limited partner in Sunworth Packing Limited Partnership.

After reaching this conclusion, the trial court also found that no specific facts had been presented which would support the application of A.R.S. § 29–319 so as to impose liability on G.B. Investment. As the minute entry states:

> The court further finds that while the statutory protection extended to limited partners is not absolute, there are no specific facts included within the plaintiff's response, supporting statement of facts, and supporting affidavits, which would support the applicability of A.R.S. § 29–319(A) so as to impose liability in favor of plaintiff and against the movant G.B. Investment.

To the extent that the trial court's ruling may have been based on a belief that a limited partner could never be liable under the statute unless the creditor had contact with the limited partner and learned directly from him of his participation and control of the business, we believe that ruling to be in error.

In A.R.S. § 29–319(a), the legislature stopped short of expressly stating that if the limited partner's participation in the control of the business is substantially the same as the exercise of the powers of a general partner, he is liable to persons who transact business with a limited partnership even though they have no knowledge of his participation and control. It has made this statement by implication, though, by stating to the opposite effect that "if the limited partner's participation in the control of the business is not substantially the same as the exercise of the powers of a general partner, he is liable only to persons who transact business with the limited partnership with actual knowledge of his participation in control." A.R.S. § 29–319(a).

We believe this interpretation is strengthened by an examination of the legislative history of Arizona's limited partnership statute. It is further strengthened by the legislature's refusal to modify this statute to correspond to the Revised Uniform Limited Partnership Act, as amended in 1985. Prior to 1982, Arizona's limited partnership statute was patterned after the Uniform Limited Partnership Act (ULPA), which was drafted in 1916. Section 7 of the ULPA provided that "[a] limited partner shall not become liable as a general partner unless, in addition to the exercise of his rights and powers as a limited partner, he takes part in the control of the business." Uniform Limited Partnership Act § 7, 6 U.L.A. 559 (1969).[3]

The Revised Uniform Limited Partnership Act (RULPA) was drafted in 1976. Revised Uniform Limited Partnership Act, 6 U.L.A. 239, 240 (Supp.1991). In 1982, the Arizona legislature adopted the RULPA after

---

3. The language of Arizona's then § 29–307 was taken verbatim from section 7 of the ULPA. For the text of Arizona's Uniform Limited Partnership Act, since repealed, see Uniform Limited Partnership Act, 1943 Ariz.Sess.Laws 124, reprinted in A.R.S. §§ 29–301 to–366 app. (1989) (as amended).

repealing its enactment of the ULPA. See 1982 Ariz.Sess.Laws, ch. 192, § 1 (effective July 24, 1982). Presently, A.R.S. § 29–319(a), dealing with a limited partner's liability to third parties, is very similar to the 1976 version of section 303(a) of the RULPA which stated:

> Except as provided in subsection (d), a limited partner is not liable for the obligations of a limited partnership unless he is also a general partner or, and in addition to the exercise of his rights and powers as a limited partner, he takes part in the control of the business. However, if the limited partner's participation in the control of the business is not substantially the same as the exercise of the powers of a general partner, he is liable only to persons who transact business with the limited partnership with actual knowledge of his participation in control.

Revised Uniform Limited Partnership Act § 303(a), 6 U.L.A. 239, 325 (Supp.1991). The drafters' comment to section 303 explained that limited partners exercising all of the powers of a general partner would not escape liability by avoiding direct dealings with third parties. The comment stated:

> Section 303 makes several important changes in Section 7 of the prior uniform law. The first sentence of Section 303(a) carries over the basic test from former Section 7 whether the limited partner "takes part in the control of the business" in order to ensure that judicial decisions under the prior uniform law remain applicable to the extent not expressly changed. The second sentence of Section 303(a) reflects a wholly new concept. Because of the difficulty of determining when the "control" line has been overstepped, it was thought it unfair to impose general partner's liability on a limited partner except to the extent that a third party had knowledge of his participation in control of the business. On the other hand, in order to avoid permitting a limited partner to exercise all of the powers of a general partner while avoiding any direct dealings with third parties, the "is not substantially the same as" test was introduced....

Id. at 326 cmt.

In 1985, the drafters of the RULPA backtracked from the position taken in section 303(a) of the 1976 Act. The new amendments reflect a reluctance to hold a limited partner liable if the limited partner had no direct contact with the creditor. The 1985 revised RULPA section 303(a) was amended to provide as follows:

> Except as provided in Subsection (d), a limited partner is not liable for the obligations of a limited partnership unless he is also a general partner or, in addition to the exercise of his rights and powers as a limited partner, he participates in the control of the business. However, if the limited partner participates in the control of the business, he is liable only to persons who transact business with the limited partnership reasonably believing, based upon the limited partner's conduct, that the limited partner is a general partner.

Id. at 325 (emphasis added). The comment to section 303 was also revised to explain the reason for the amendment. The revised comment states:

> Section 303 makes several important changes in Section 7 of the 1916 Act. The first sentence of Section 303(a) differs from the text of Section 7 of the 1916 Act in that it speaks of participating (rather than taking part) in the control of the business; this was done for the sake of consistency with the second sentence of Section 303(a), not to change the meaning of the text. It is intended that judicial decisions interpreting the phrase "takes part in the control of the business" under the prior uniform law will remain applicable to the extent that a different result is not called for by other provisions of Section 303 and other provisions of the Act. The second sentence of Section 303(a) reflects a wholly new concept in the 1976 Act that has been further modified in the 1985 Act. It was adopted partly because of the difficulty of determining when the "control" line has been overstepped, but also (and more importantly) because of a determination that it is not sound public policy to hold a limited partner who is not also a general partner liable for the obligations of the partnership except to persons who have done business with the limited partnership reasonably believing, based on the limited partner's conduct, that he is a general partner....

Id. at 326 cmt. (emphasis added).

The Arizona legislature, however, has not revised A.R.S. § 29–319(a) to correspond to the section 303 amendments. The Arizona statute continues to impose liability on a limited partner whenever the "substantially the same as" test is met, even though the creditor has no knowledge of the limited partner's control. It follows then that no contact between the creditor and the limited partner is required to impose liability.

Moreover, whereas section 303 of the RULPA states that the creditor's reasonable belief must be "based upon the limited partner's conduct," under A.R.S. § 29–319 the only requirement is that the creditor has had "actual knowledge of [the limited partner's] participation in control." The statute does not state that this knowledge must be based upon the limited partner's conduct. The comments to the original version of section 303 of the RULPA, from which Arizona's statute is taken, make it clear that only when the "substantially the same as" test is met is direct contact not a requirement. Conversely, if the "substantially the same as" test is not met, direct contact is required. Under the facts presented in this case, Gateway had no direct contact with G.B. Investment until after the sales were concluded. We conclude, therefore, that G.B. Investment would be liable only if the "substantially the same as" test was met.

Whether a limited partner has exercised the degree of control that will make him liable to a creditor has always been a factual question. This is so regardless of whether the particular statute involved is patterned after section 7 of the ULPA or after section 303 of the

RULPA. E.g., Alzado v. Blinder, Robinson & Co., 752 P.2d 544 (Colo. 1988); Gast v. Petsinger, 228 Pa.Super. 394, 323 A.2d 371 (1974); Holzman v. DeEscamilla, 86 Cal.App.2d 858, 195 P.2d 833 (1948). Our current Arizona statute lists activities that a limited partner may undertake without participating in controlling the business. It also states that other activities may be excluded from the definition of such control. Where activities do not fall within the "safe harbor" of A.R.S. § 29–319(b), it is necessary for a trier-of-fact to determine whether such activities amount to "control." In the absence of actual knowledge of the limited partner's participation in the control of the partnership business, there must be evidence from which a trier-of-fact might find not only control, but control that is "substantially the same as the exercise of powers of a general partner."

We conclude that the evidence Gateway presented in this case should have allowed it to withstand summary judgment. The affidavit testimony of Ellsworth raises the issue whether he was merely a puppet for the limited partner, G.B. Investment. While a few of the activities Ellsworth listed may have fallen within the protected areas listed in A.R.S. § 29–319(b), others did not. Ellsworth's detailed statement raises substantial issues of material facts.

Viewing the facts in the light most favorable to Gateway, we cannot say as a matter of law that G.B. Investment was entitled to summary judgment. We conclude that Gateway is entitled to a determination by trial of the extent of control exercised by G.B. Investment over Sunworth Packing.

For the foregoing reasons, we reverse the judgment of the trial court and remand for further proceedings.

■ EHRLICH, P.J., and CLABORNE, J., concur.

D. CORPORATE GENERAL PARTNERS

NOTE ON CORPORATE GENERAL PARTNERS

It seems likely that the plaintiff in *Gateway* sued the limited partner, rather than the general partner, because the sole general partner was a corporation with limited assets. Ordinarily, shareholders are not liable for their corporation's debts. Therefore, if both the limited partnership and the corporate general partner had insufficient assets to pay the debt to the plaintiff, the plaintiff would have been unable to collect on the limited partnership's debt unless the limited partner was liable.

Section 303(b)(1) of RULPA and Section 601(4)(C) of the 2001 Act explicitly recognize that a corporation can be a general partner in a limited partnership. Although a director or officer of a corporate general partner is not liable for the debts of a limited partnership merely because he participates in the control of the partnership's business in his capacity as director or officer of the general partner, he may become liable if the corporate directors and officers fail to maintain their corporate identity in conducting partnership affairs through the corporation, or if corporate assets are intermingled with partnership assets, or if the corporation is not sufficiently capitalized, *see* Mursor Builders, Inc. v. Crown Mountain Apartment Associates, 467 F.Supp. 1316 (D.V.I. 1978); Western Camps, Inc. v. Riverway Ranch Enterprises, 70 Cal.App.3d 714, 138 Cal.Rptr. 918 (1977), or under the principle of the following case.

In re USACafes, L.P. Litigation

Court of Chancery of Delaware, 1991.
600 A.2d 43.

■ ALLEN, CHANCELLOR.

These consolidated actions arise out of the October 1989 purchase by Metsa Acquisition Corp. of substantially all of the assets of USACafes, L.P., a Delaware limited partnership (the "Partnership") at a cash price of $72.6 million or $10.25 per unit. Plaintiffs are holders of limited partnership units. They bring these cases as class actions on behalf of all limited partnership unitholders except defendants. The relief sought includes, inter alia, the imposition of constructive trusts on certain funds received by defendants in connection with the Metsa sale and an award of damages to the class resulting from the sale.

The Partnership was formed in the 1986 reorganization of the business of USACafes, Inc., a Nevada corporation. Also formed as part of that reorganization was USACafes General Partner, Inc. (the "General Partner"), a Delaware corporation that acts as the general partner of the Partnership. Both the Partnership and the General Partner are named as defendants in this action. A second category of defendants is composed of Sam and Charles Wyly, brothers who together own all of the stock of the General Partner, sit on its board, and who also personally, directly or indirectly, own 47% of the limited partnership units of the Partnership. Sam Wyly chairs the Board of the General Partner.

The third category of defendants are four other individuals who sit on the board of directors of the General Partner. All of these persons are alleged to have received substantial cash payments, loan forgiveness, or other substantial personal benefits in connection with the 1989 Metsa purchase.

The last of the defendants is Metsa, the buyer of the Partnership's assets. Metsa is not alleged to be related in any way to the Wylys or any other defendant except as a buyer in the transaction under review.

The Theories of the Amended Complaint

The amended complaint arrays four theories of liability against these defendants. The first and most central theory involves an alleged breach of the duty of loyalty. In essence, it claims that the sale of the Partnership's assets was at a low price, favorable to Metsa, because the directors of the General Partner all received substantial side payments that induced them to authorize the sale of the Partnership assets for less than the price that a fair process would have yielded. Specifically, it is alleged that, in connection with the sale, (1) the Wylys received from Metsa more than $11 million in payments (or promises to pay in the future) which were disguised as consideration for personal covenants not to compete; (2) the General Partner (which the Wylys wholly own) received a $1.5 million payment right in consideration of the release of a claim that plaintiffs assert was non-existent; (3) defendant Rogers, a director of the General Partner and President of the Partnership was forgiven the payment of a $956,169 loan from the Partnership and was given an employment agreement with the Partnership that contemplated a one million dollar cash payment in the event, then imminent, of a "change in control"; (4) defendant Tuley, also a director of the General Partner, was forgiven repayment of a $229,701 loan; and (5) the other directors were given employment agreements providing for a $60,000 payment in the event of a change in control. In sum, it is alleged that between $15 and $17 million was or will be paid to the directors and officers of the General Partner by or with the approval of Metsa; those payments are alleged to constitute financial inducements to the directors of the General Partner to refrain from searching for a higher offer to the Partnerships. Plaintiffs add that, even assuming that Metsa was the buyer willing to pay the best price, some part at least of these "side payments" should have gone to the Partnership.

The second theory of liability reflected in the amended complaint asserts that the General Partner was (or the directors of the General Partner were) not sufficiently informed to make a valid business judgment on the sale. This theory focuses upon the absence of shopping of the Partnership's assets, or of any post-agreement market check procedure, and on the alleged weakness of the investment banker's opinion. Thus, this claim is that the defendants were uninformed when they authorized the sale to Metsa.

The third theory of liability is asserted on behalf of a class of limited partnership unitholders who held stock in the predecessor Nevada corporation—USACafes, Inc.—and who were issued partnership units pursuant to the reorganization of the USACafes business into the limited partnership form. It is alleged that those persons were misled by a December 5, 1986, prospectus (the "Prospectus"), disseminated in conjunction with the issuance of the partnership units,[1] into believing, reasonably, that, under the then proposed and later adopted structure, any sale of substantially all of the Partnership assets would require the affirmative vote of a majority of all unitholders. The relief apparently sought on this theory is the judicial recognition of an

1. The prospectus did not seek a shareholders' vote, but rather informed the shareholders that the reorganization would be approved by shareholder action by consent.

implied right to vote on the Metsa transaction (which has long since closed) or rescission of it in absence of such a vote.

The last theory in the amended complaint is the only one asserted against Metsa, the buyer. It charges that Metsa knowingly participated in the other defendants' alleged breaches of duty in connection with the sale by offering and making (or, in the case of the forgiveness of partnership debt, in agreeing to) personal payments to those controlling the General Partner designed to induce those persons to breach fiduciary duties they owed to the limited partners. Plaintiffs claim that this course of action makes Metsa jointly liable for wrongs done to the class or injuries suffered by class members out of this transaction.

* * *

The Pending Motions

... [T]he Wyly defendants and the other director defendants move under Rule 12(b)(6) to dismiss the breach of fiduciary duty claims in the amended complaint asserting that, while the General Partner admittedly did owe fiduciary duties to the limited partners, they as directors of the General Partner owe no such duties to those persons. The whole remedy of the limited partners for breach of the duties of loyalty and care, it is said, is against the General Partner only and not its directors....

[The gist of] the director defendants' motion to dismiss for failure to state a claim with respect to the sale of the Partnership's assets ... is the assertion that the directors of the General Partner owed the limited partners no duty of loyalty or care. In their view their only duty of loyalty was to the General Partner itself and to its shareholders (i.e., the Wyly brothers). Thus, in alleging that the director defendants breached duties of loyalty and care running to them, the directors say the limited partners have asserted a legal nullity.

In my opinion the assertion by the directors that the independent existence of the corporate General Partner is inconsistent with their owing fiduciary duties directly to limited partners is incorrect. Moreover, even were it correct, their position on this motion would have to be rejected in any event because the amended complaint expressly alleges that they personally participated in the alleged breach by the General Partner itself, which admittedly did owe loyalty to the limited partners.

The first basis of this holding is the more significant. While I find no corporation law precedents directly addressing the question whether directors of a corporate general partner owe fiduciary duties to the partnership and its limited partners, the answer to it seems to be clearly indicated by general principles and by analogy to trust law. I understand the principle of fiduciary duty, stated most generally, to be that one who controls property of another may not, without implied or express agreement, intentionally use that property in a way that benefits the holder of the control to the detriment of the property or its beneficial owner. There are, of course, other aspects—a fiduciary may not waste property even if no self interest is involved and must exercise care even when his heart is pure—but the central aspect of the relationship is, undoubtedly, fidelity in the control of property for the benefit of another.[2] See generally Robert Flannigan, The Fiduciary Obligation, 9 Oxford J. Legal St. 285 (1989).

The law of trusts represents the earliest and fullest expression of this principle in our law, but courts of equity have extended it appropriately to achieve substantial justice in a wide array of situations. Thus, corporate directors, even though not strictly trustees, were early on regarded as fiduciaries for corporate stockholders. E.g., Koehler v. Black River Falls Iron Co., 67 U.S. (2 Black) 715, 17 L.Ed. 339 (1862); Wardell v. Union Pac. R.R. Co., 103 U.S. 651, 26 L.Ed. 509 (1880). When control over corporate property was recognized to be in the hands of shareholders who controlled the enterprise, the fiduciary obligation was found to extend to such persons as well. Allied Chemical & Dye Corp. v. Steel & Tube Co., 14 Del.Ch. 1, 120 A. 486, 491 (1923).

While the parties cite no case treating the specific question whether directors of a corporate general partner are fiduciaries for the limited partnership, a large number of trust cases do stand for a principle that would extend a fiduciary duty to such persons in certain circumstances. The problem comes up in trust law because modernly corporations may serve as trustees of express trusts. Thus, the question has arisen whether directors of a corporate trustee may personally owe duties of loyalty to cestui que trusts of the corporation. A leading authority states the accepted answer:

> The directors and officers of [a corporate trustee] are certainly under a duty to the beneficiaries not to convert to their own use property of the trust administered by the corporation.... Furthermore, the directors and officers are under a duty to the beneficiaries of trusts administered by the corporation not to cause the corporation to misappropriate the property.... The breach of trust need not, however, be a misappropriation.... Any officer [director cases are cited in support here] who knowingly causes the corporation to commit a breach of trust causing loss ... is personally liable to the beneficiary of the trust....
>
> Moreover, a director or officer of a trust institution who improperly acquires an interest in the property of a trust administered by the institution is subject to personal liability. He is accountable for any profit.... Even where the trustee [itself] is not liable, however, because it had no knowledge that the director was making the purchase ..., the director ... is liable to the beneficiaries.... The directors and officers are in a fiduciary relation not merely to the [corporation] ... but to the beneficiaries of the trust administered by the [corporation].

---

2. Thus, for example, a borrower of money is not considered a fiduciary for the lender simply because she is bound to return the principle sum plus interest. The "property" is held by the borrower for her own benefit.

4 A. Scott & W. Fratcher, The Law of Trusts § 326.3, at 304–306 (4th ed. 1989) (citing cases) ["Scott on Trusts"].

The theory underlying fiduciary duties is consistent with recognition that a director of a corporate general partner bears such a duty towards the limited partnership. That duty, of course, extends only to dealings with the partnership's property or affecting its business, but, so limited, its existence seems apparent in any number of circumstances. Consider, for example, a classic self-dealing transaction: assume that a majority of the board of the corporate general partner formed a new entity and then caused the general partner to sell partnership assets to the new entity at an unfairly small price, injuring the partnership and its limited partners. Can it be imagined that such persons have not breached a duty to the partnership itself? And does it not make perfect sense to say that the gist of the offense is a breach of the equitable duty of loyalty that is placed upon a fiduciary? It appears true that the same result might be rationalized as aider and abettor liability, but I am unsure what such indirection would add that is useful where a self-dealing transaction or other diversion of partnership property is alleged. Indeed in some instances, for example the use by a director of confidential information concerning the partnership's business not yet known by the board of the general partner, there may be no breach of loyalty or care by the general partner itself to abet, yet there may be director liability to the partnership by the director. Cf. cases cited at 4 Scott on Trusts § 326.3, at n. 7.

Two courts have, in fact, held a sole shareholder/director of a corporate general partner personally liable for breach of fiduciary duty to limited partners, although without much discussion of the issue here considered. See Tobias v. First City National Bank and Trust Co., 709 F.Supp. 1266, 1277–78 (S.D.N.Y.1989); Remenchik v. Whittington, Tex.Ct.App., 757 S.W.2d 836 (1988); see also In re Integrated Resources, Inc., Case No. 90–B–10411 (CB) (Bankr.S.D.N.Y. Oct. 22, 1990) (controlling shareholder held liable).

While these authorities extend the fiduciary duty of the general partner to a controlling shareholder, they support as well, the recognition of such duty in directors of the General Partner who, more directly than a controlling shareholder, are in control of the partnership's property. It is not necessary here to attempt to delineate the full scope of that duty. It may well not be so broad as the duty of the director of a corporate trustee.[3] But it surely entails the duty not to use control over the partnership's property to advantage the corporate director at the expense of the partnership. That is what is alleged here.

The amended complaint contains the following allegations:

> 16. The General Partner and its directors, the named individual defendants, are in a fiduciary relationship with the plaintiffs and the other Unitholders of USACafes. . . .

---

3. For example, I imply nothing on such questions as whether a director of a corporate general partner might be held liable directly to the partnership on a "corporate" opportunity theory or for waste of partnership assets (two possible consequences of characterizing such persons as fiduciaries for the partnership).

> 17. . . . Through their unit ownership and executive positions [the director defendants] have dominated and controlled the affairs of USACafes. Among other things, they have . . . failed to adequately solicit or consider alternative proposals for USACafes, have failed to negotiate in good faith to enhance Unitholders' values and, instead, have agreed to sell all of its assets to Metsa, which will result in the minority limited partners receiving the grossly inadequate price of $10.25 per Unit. As inducement to the individual defendants to agree to the Metsa proposal, Metsa offered to pay and the individual defendants agreed to accept, certain additional payments (approximately $17 million) that were not offered to the classes. . . .
>
> 19. The individual defendants and the General Partner participated in the wrongdoing complained of in order to divert the valuable assets of USACafes for their own benefit by entering into highly favorable compensation arrangements with Metsa as part of the liquidation of USACafes.

I therefore conclude that the amended complaint does allege facts which if true establish that the director defendants have breached fiduciary obligations imposed upon them as directors of a Delaware corporation or have participated in a breach of such duties by the General Partner. The amended complaint does, in my opinion, state a claim upon which relief can be granted. . . .

The motions of the individual defendants, the General Partner, and the Partnership to dismiss the claims arising out of the sale of the Partnership's assets is denied. . . .

E. THE TAXATION OF UNINCORPORATED BUSINESS ORGANIZATIONS

Taxation is a major issue in the choice of business form. There are two basic patterns of business taxation under the Internal Revenue Code, which may be called firm taxation and flow-through taxation.

Under *firm taxation*, a business firm is taxable on its income. Accordingly, if the firm has income or expenses, or gains or losses, those items go into the firm's taxable income, not into the taxable income of the firm's owners. If the firm then makes distributions to its owners out of after-tax income, the owners ordinarily pay taxes on those distributions. This is sometimes referred to as "double taxation."

Under *flow-through* taxation, a firm is not subject to taxation. Instead, all of the firm's income and expenses, and gains and losses, are taxable directly to the firm's owners. Distributions are not taxed. There is no "double taxation" effect. If the firm has losses, the owners can utilize the losses to offset their income from other sources.

Whether firm taxation or flow-through taxation is preferable for the owners of an enterprise depends in any given case on corporate and individual tax rates, the owners' circumstances, and other variables. Generally speaking, under present tax rates the owners of a firm will ordinarily regard flow-through taxation as preferable to firm taxation.

Historically, a firm-taxation pattern applied more or less automatically to corporations, and a flow-through taxation pattern applied more or less automatically to partnerships. Until recently, however, it was often less clear which type of taxation would be applied to forms of business organization that are intermediate between general partnerships and corporations—forms such as the limited partnership. This issue has now been resolved by the IRS's "check-the-box" Regulations. Under these Regulations, any domestic unincorporated business that constitutes an "eligible entity" can elect either flow-through taxation or firm (corporate) taxation. If an eligible entity has only one owner, the entity will be disregarded for tax purposes—that is, all of the entity's income and expenses and gains and losses will be attributed to the owner.

Generally speaking, an eligible entity is any business entity other than (i) a corporation or (ii) a business entity that is specifically made taxable as corporation under the Internal Revenue Code. The most important entity in the second category is the *master limited partnership*. Essentially, a master limited partnership is a limited partnership whose limited-partnership interests are publicly traded—that is, traded on an established securities market, or readily tradeable on a secondary market. With certain exceptions, under the Internal Revenue Code publicly traded limited partnerships are taxed as corporations, and cannot elect flow-through (partnership) taxation.

There is another important respect in which the tax comparison of the traditional forms has been blurred. Just as publicly traded limited partnerships are now normally taxed like corporations, so the Internal Revenue Code provides a route through which partnership-tax treatment can be achieved by certain corporate enterprises. Subchapter S of the Code (I.R.C. §§ 1361–1379) permits the owners of qualifying corporations to elect a special tax status under which the corporation and its shareholders receive flow-though taxation that is comparable (although not identical) to partnership taxation. The taxable income of an S corporation is computed essentially as if the corporation were an individual. With some exceptions, items of income, loss, deduction, and credit, are passed through to the shareholders on a pro rata basis, and added to or subtracted from each shareholder's gross income.

Among the conditions for making and maintaining a Subchapter S election are the following: (1) The corporation may not have more than one hundred shareholders. (2) The corporation may not have more than one class of stock. (3) All the shareholders must be individuals or qualified estates or trusts. (4) No shareholder may be a nonresident alien. The amount of the corporation's assets and income is immaterial under Subchapter S.

As of 2008, there were 4,474,000 corporations in the United States. Almost half—2,153,000—were S corporations. United States Bureau of the Census, Statistical Abstract of the United States (2004).

F. FIDUCIARY OBLIGATIONS

Gotham Partners, L.P. v. Hallwood Realty Partners, L.P.

Supreme Court of Delaware, 2002.
817 A.2d 160.

■ Before: VEASEY, CHIEF JUSTICE, WALSH, HOLLAND and BERGER, JUSTICES and HARTNETT, JUSTICE (Retired), constituting the Court en Banc.

■ VEASEY, CHIEF JUSTICE:

In this appeal, we hold that a limited partnership agreement may provide for contractually created fiduciary duties substantially mirroring traditional fiduciary duties that apply in the corporation law. The Court of Chancery held that the limited partnership agreement here provided for such fiduciary duties by requiring the general partner and its controlling entity to treat the limited partners in accordance with the entire fairness standard. We agree with this holding. . . .

With respect to remedies for that breach, the plaintiff limited partner had demanded rescission or an adequate damage award and sterilization of the voting rights attached to the partnership units involved in the challenged transaction. The Court of Chancery refused to order rescission and awarded damages. We affirm the holding of the Vice Chancellor that he was not necessarily required to order rescission by the limited partnership contract or the application of equitable principles. Such a decision is properly within the discretion of a court of equity, but here the Court of Chancery did not fashion a remedy that is an appropriate substitute for rescission under the circumstances.

As the Court of Chancery noted, one effect of the challenged transaction was that the general partner and its corporate parent gained control of the limited partnership as a result of wrongdoing. In our view, the value of the control thus achieved was not properly compensated for by the award of damages because the trial court did not account properly for a control premium in its remedy calculation.

Consequently, we reverse the damages award and remand for such proceedings as may be necessary and appropriate: (1) to quantify how the challenged transaction would have been consummated had the defendants adhered to the entire fairness standards and procedures of the limited partnership agreement; and (2) to consider and award one or more of the various equitable remedies available to the limited partnership, including rescission, rescissory damages, sterilization of voting rights, or other appropriate methods of accounting for the control premium.

Facts

Hallwood Realty Partners, L.P. ("the Partnership") is a Delaware limited partnership that owns commercial office buildings and industrial parks in several locations in the United States and lists its partnership units on the American Stock Exchange. Gotham Partners, L.P. ("Gotham") is a hedge fund, the investments of which include real estate. It is the largest independent limited partner in the Partnership with approximately 14.8 percent of the outstanding partnership units. Hallwood Realty Corporation ("the General Partner") is the sole general partner and is a wholly-owned subsidiary of Hallwood Group Incorporated ("HGI"), which owned 5.1 percent of the outstanding partnership units before the transactions challenged in this case. Anthony Gumbiner and William Guzzetti were members of the board of directors of the General Partner. They were also officers of HGI at the time of the challenged transaction.[6]

In 1994, the Partnership's units were trading at a low price because of the ongoing economic recession in real estate. On October 12, 1994, Guzzetti proposed to the Partnership's board of directors that it approve a reverse split,[7] a unit option plan,[8] and an odd lot tender offer[9] subject to HGI's willingness to finance the transactions by buying any fractional units generated by a reverse split and any units purchased by the Partnership in an odd lot tender offer. At the time, more than half of the Partnership's units were held in odd lots and could be resold to HGI. Guzzetti told the board that HGI was the only source of financing available and that the transactions would, among other things, raise the trading price of the Partnership's units, reduce the Partnership's administrative costs, and give odd lot holders the chance to sell at market price without incurring brokerage fees. The Partnership's board approved the transactions, citing Guzzetti's reasons.

At first, HGI declined to provide funding for the reverse split and odd lot offer. But, by March 1995, HGI was willing to fund the Reverse

---

6. Gumbiner, a corporate lawyer, owned 30 percent of HGI's shares between 1994 and 1995 and was the chairman of the board of directors and chief executive officer of the General Partner at the time of the challenged transactions. Guzzetti, a former lawyer, is an executive vice-president of HGI and was the president of the Partnership and a member of the General Partner's board of directors at the time of the challenged transactions.

7. A reverse split reduces the number of outstanding units and consequently increases the per unit value of each unit. Reverse splits usually create odd lots.

8. In this case, the option plan would sell post-reverse split units to officers and employees of the General Partner, including Gumbiner and Guzzetti.

9. An odd lot offer is a tender offer by the issuer for blocks of fewer than one hundred outstanding units or shares. Such "odd lots" are considered small and thus create inefficient administrative costs for issuers and may be difficult to sell at an attractive price. Odd lot offers are designed to provide liquidity to small holders and to reduce issuer costs.

Split and Option Plan, which were approved by the non-HGI directors on the General Partner's board. HGI purchased 30,000 units, approximately 1.6 percent of the Partnership's equity, through the Reverse Split. The Option Plan resulted in officers and employees of the General Partner purchasing 86,000 units or 4.7 percent of the Partnership's equity. Through these two transactions, HGI increased its ownership of outstanding Partnership units from 5.1 percent to approximately 11.4 percent.

By May 1995, HGI was willing to fund an odd lot tender offer. Guzzetti called a special meeting of the General Partner's board of directors after circulating a memorandum indicating that 55 percent of the Partnership's units were held in odd lots and thus could be tendered in the odd lot offer. The non-HGI directors voted as a "special committee" to approve the Odd Lot Offer. The purchase price of an odd lot was putatively set at the five-day market average referenced in Section 9.01(b) of the Partnership Agreement.[10] No valuation information was shared with the board.

The Odd Lot Offer began on June 5, 1995. The accompanying press release indicated that the Partnership would resell any tendered odd lot units to HGI, affiliates of HGI, or other institutional investors. The Odd Lot Offer and Resale was pitched to the public and the American Stock Exchange as a resale to HGI of existing, listed Partnership units, not as an issuance of new, unlisted units. Consequently, the Partnership never filed a listing application with the American Stock Exchange for the units sold to HGI, and the Partnership's accounting books did not treat the Odd Lot Resale to HGI as an issuance of units.

From June 9 to July 25, 1995, when the Odd Lot Offer closed, the Partnership purchased 293,539 units from odd lot holders and placed them in a holding account. The Partnership then resold the units to HGI at the same price the Partnership paid for them, approximately $4.1 million. The Odd Lot Resale resulted in HGI purchasing approximately 23.4 percent of the Partnership's outstanding units. Thus, HGI increased its stake in the outstanding Partnership units from 11.4 percent to 29.7 percent and solidified its control over the Partnership. The Partnership Agreement requires the written consent or affirmative vote by at least 66 and 1/3 percent of the limited partners to remove a general partner.

Gotham began purchasing Partnership units in 1994 and owned 14.8 percent of the outstanding units as of September 1996. Gotham was aware of the Odd Lot Offer and Resale but did not complain to the Partnership until January 1997 when it requested access to the Partnership's books and records. The Partnership denied the request.

10. Section 9.01(b) of the Partnership Agreement states: "Except as set forth above, the number of Units issued to the General Partners or any such Affiliate in exchange for any Capital Contribution shall not exceed the Net Agreed Value of the contributed property or amount of cash, as the case may be, divided by the Unit Price of a Unit as of the day of such issuance."

Preliminary Proceedings in the Court of Chancery

Gotham filed a books and records action in the Court of Chancery in February 1997. On June 20, 1997, Gotham filed another action in the Court of Chancery alleging derivative claims in connection with the Odd Lot Offer and Resale, the Reverse Split, and the Option Plan. Gotham alleged that these transactions were unfair to the Partnership's unitholders because HGI paid an unfairly low price to acquire control over the Partnership. Gotham's claims included breaches by the General Partner of traditional fiduciary duties and contractually based fiduciary duties. . . .

On summary judgment, the Court of Chancery sustained the contractual fiduciary duty claims and dismissed the traditional fiduciary duty claims on the ground that the Partnership Agreement supplanted traditional fiduciary duties and provided for contractual fiduciary duties by which the defendants' conduct would be measured.[11] The Vice Chancellor found that Sections 7.05[12] and 7.10(a)[13] of the Partnership Agreement operate together as a contractual statement of the entire fairness standard, with Section 7.05 substantively requiring fair price and Section 7.10(a) substantively requiring fair dealing. No appeal has been taken from this ruling. . . .

Decision After Trial

After trial, the Court of Chancery found the defendants liable for their conduct associated with the Odd Lot Resale to HGI, but upheld their conduct connected with the Reverse Split and the Option Plan. The Vice Chancellor found that the Odd Lot Resale, unlike the other two transactions, did not involve an issuance of units, but rather a resale of existing units to HGI. As a result, the Vice Chancellor found "inapplicable" the protections of Section 9.01 of the Partnership Agreement, which authorizes the General Partner to issue Partnership Units of any kind to any person without the consent or approval of the Limited Partners. Instead, the Vice Chancellor continued, the Odd Lot Resale was subject to Partnership Agreement Sections 7.05 and 7.10(a), which provide for the contractually created fiduciary duties of entire fairness.

The Vice Chancellor found that the General Partner breached the contractual fiduciary duties of entire fairness because (1) the General

---

11. *Gotham Partners, L.P. v. Hallwood Realty Partners, L.P.* ("*Gotham S.J. Op.*"), Del. Ch., C.A. No. 15754, 2000 WL 1476663 (Sept. 27, 2000), at 23–29.

12. Section 7.05 of the Partnership Agreement states: "Transactions with General Partner or Affiliates. The Partnership is expressly permitted to enter into transactions with the General Partner or any Affiliate thereof provided that the terms of any such transaction are substantially equivalent to terms obtainable by the Partnership from a comparable unaffiliated third party."

13. Section 7.10(a) of the Partnership Agreement states in relevant part: "Audit Committee; Resolution of Conflicts of Interest. (a) The General Partner shall form an Audit Committee (the 'Audit Committee') to be comprised of two members of the board of directors of the General Partner who are not affiliated with the General Partner or its Affiliates except by reason of such directorship. The functions of the Audit Committee shall be to review and approve . . . (ii) transactions between the Partnership and the General Partner and any of its Affiliates."

Partner never formed the Audit Committee as required by Section 7.10(a) to review and approve the Odd Lot Offer and Resale, and (2) the General Partner failed to perform a market check or obtain any reliable financial analysis indicating that the Odd Lot Resale would be conducted on the same terms obtainable from a third party. The Court of Chancery thus held the General Partner liable for breach of the contractually created fiduciary duties of entire fairness contained in the Partnership Agreement .....

Gotham requested rescission, or money damages and sterilization of voting rights. The Court of Chancery awarded money damages plus compound interest instead of rescission, in part because it found that Gotham delayed challenging the transaction "for nearly two years, and then filed suit to rescind only after it was clear that the market price [of the Partnership units] was up substantially and on a sustainable basis." The Vice Chancellor then went on to find that the challenged transactions were not "conceived of as a conscious scheme to entrench the General Partner's control and enrich HGI" improperly. He stated that if he had been convinced otherwise, "I might be inclined to grant rescission despite Gotham's torpid pace."

Gotham then filed a direct appeal in this Court contesting the remedy. The General Partner, HGI, Gumbiner, and Guzzetti filed cross appeals asserting that the Court of Chancery erred by finding Section 9.01(a) of the Partnership Agreement inapplicable to the Odd Lot Offer and Resale ... and by awarding compound interest on a damages award.

Issues on Appeal

On appeal, Gotham argues that the Court of Chancery was required to award rescission as a matter of law and, even if an award of monetary damages were appropriate, the Court of Chancery erred in its calculation of the damages by failing to account for a control premium. Gotham seeks reversal in part of the judgment of the Court of Chancery and a remand to the court with instructions to order rescission of the Odd Lot Resale to HGI. Alternatively, Gotham seeks an award of rescissory damages or sterilization of HGI's voting rights connected to the Odd Lot Resale units, or both.

The General Partner, HGI, Gumbiner, and Guzzetti, contend in their cross appeal that the Court of Chancery erred ... by finding the Odd Lot Resale to HGI subject to Sections 7.05 and 7.10(a) of the Partnership Agreement, which provide for contractual fiduciary duties of entire fairness, instead of Section 9.01, which authorizes the General Partner to issue Partnership Units of any kind to any person without the consent or approval of the Limited Partners.... We will address the cross appeals first.

Whether the Court of Chancery Erred By Ruling That the Odd Lot Resale to HGI Was a Resale of Partnership Units

This Court reviews de novo the Court of Chancery's interpretation of written agreement and Delaware law.

As the Vice Chancellor noted at summary judgment, a general partner owes the traditional fiduciary duties of loyalty and care to the limited partnership and its partners, but DRULPA § 17–1101(d)(2) "expressly authorizes the ... modification, or enhancement of these fiduciary duties in the written agreement governing the limited partnership."[14] Indeed, we have recognized that, by statute, the parties to a Delaware limited partnership have the power and discretion to form and operate a limited partnership "in an environment of private ordering" according to the provisions in the limited partnership agreement.[15] We have noted that DRULPA embodies "the policy of freedom of contract"[16] and "maximum flexibility."[17] DRULPA's "basic approach is to permit partners to have the broadest possible discretion in drafting their partnership agreements and to furnish answers only in situations where the partners have not expressly made provisions in their partnership agreement"[18] or "where the agreement is inconsistent with mandatory statutory provisions."[19] In those situations, a court will "look for guidance from the statutory default rules, traditional notions of fiduciary duties, or other extrinsic evidence."[20] But, if the limited partnership agreement unambiguously provides for fiduciary duties, any claim of a breach of a fiduciary duty must be analyzed generally in terms of the partnership agreement.[21]

The Vice Chancellor found, and the parties do not contest, that Partnership Agreement Sections 7.05 and 7.10(a) set forth fiduciary duties of entire fairness owed by the General Partner to its partners generally in self-dealing transactions, such as the Odd Lot Resale. Section 7.05 expressly permits the Partnership to enter into self-dealing transactions with the General Partner or its affiliate "provided that the terms of any such transaction are substantially equivalent to terms obtainable by the Partnership from a comparable unaffiliated third party."[22] Section 7.10(a) requires the General Partner to form an independent Audit Committee that shall review and approve self-

14. *Gotham S.J. Op.*, at 24, 2000 WL 1476663 at *10. DRULPA § 17–1101(d)(2), codified at 6 Del. C. § 17–1101(d)(2), reads: "To the extent that, at law or equity, a partner or other person has duties (including fiduciary duties) and liabilities relating thereto to a limited partnership or to another partner or to another person that is a party to or is otherwise bound by a partnership agreement, ... (2) the partner's or other person's duties and liabilities may be expanded or restricted by provisions in the partnership agreement."

15. *Elf Atochem North America, Inc. v. Jaffari*, 727 A.2d 286, 287 (Del.1999).

16. Id. at 290....

17. *Elf Atochem*, 727 A.2d at 291 n. 27.

18. Id. at 291.

19. Id. at 292.

20. *Sonet*, 722 A.2d at 324.

21. See id. ("[U]nder Delaware limited partnership law a claim of breach of fiduciary duty must first be analyzed in terms of the operating governing instrument—the partnership agreement—and only where that document is silent or ambiguous, or where the principles of equity are implicated, will a Court begin to look for guidance from the statutory default rules, traditional notions of fiduciary duties, or other extrinsic evidence.")....

22. Section 7.05 of the Partnership Agreement states in its entirety: "The Partnership is expressly permitted to enter into transactions with the General Partner or any Affiliate thereof provided that the terms of any such transaction are substantially equivalent to terms obtainable by the Partnership from a comparable unaffiliated third party."

dealing transactions between the Partnership and the General Partner and any of its affiliates.[23] The Vice Chancellor found, and the parties do not contest, that Sections 7.05 and 7.10(a) "operate together as a contractual statement of the traditional entire fairness standard [of fair price and fair dealing], with § 7.05 reflecting the substantive aspect of that standard and § 7.10 reflecting the procedural aspect of that standard."

Because the Partnership Agreement provided for fiduciary duties, the Vice Chancellor properly held that the Partnership Agreement, as a contract, provides the standard for determining whether the General Partner breached its duty to the Partnership through its execution of the Odd Lot Resale. As the Vice Chancellor stated, the Partnership Agreement "leaves no room for the application of common law fiduciary duty principles to measure the General Partner's conduct" because the Partnership Agreement "supplanted fiduciary duty and became the sole source of protection for the public unitholders of the Partnership." Thus, "the General Partner was subject, by contract, to a fairness standard akin to the common law one applicable to self-dealing transactions by fiduciaries."

The General Partner, HGI, Gumbiner, and Guzzetti apparently concede: (1) the General Partner's conduct associated with the Odd Lot Resale did not comply with Sections 7.05 and 7.10(a) of the Partnership Agreement because, as the Vice Chancellor found; (2) the Audit Committee never reviewed or approved the Odd Lot Resale to HGI; and (3) the General Partner never obtained a reliable financial analysis indicating that the Odd Lot Resale would be conducted on the same terms obtainable from an independent third party. Nonetheless, they argue that they are not liable for failing to comply with Sections 7.05 and 7.10(a) because Section 9.01 alone governed the Odd Lot Resale. They assert that the Odd Lot Resale was an issuance rather than a resale of Partnership units to HGI. The defendants seek the protection of Section 9.01, which gives the General Partner absolute and independent authority to issue additional Partnership units to any person or entity, including affiliates such as HGI.

The Vice Chancellor properly found that the Odd Lot Resale was a resale of Partnership units to HGI and thus Section 9.01 is inapplicable. It is undisputed that the Partnership's accounting books did not treat the sale of odd lots to HGI as an issuance of units. Furthermore, the Partnership units from the Odd Lot Resale were listed on the American Stock Exchange, but the Resale was presented to the Exchange as a resale, not as an issuance. The Vice Chancellor properly found that the Odd Lot Resale was structured as a resale, in part to avoid American Stock Exchange Rule 713, which requires that holders

---

23. Section 7.10(a) states in its entirety: "The General Partner shall form an Audit Committee ('the Audit Committee') to be comprised of two members of the board of directors of the General Partner who are not affiliated with the General Partner or its Affiliates except by reason of such directorship. The functions of the Audit Committee shall be to review and approve (i) the expense reimbursements and compensation paid by the Partnership to the General Partner or any of its Affiliates and (ii) transactions between the Partnership and the General Partner and any of its Affiliates."

approve additional issuances as a prerequisite to the shares or units' listing on the Exchange. Thus, the General Partner is liable for breaching the contractually created fiduciary duties of entire fairness provided by Sections 7.05 and 7.10(a) of the Partnership Agreement. . . .

Whether the Court of Chancery Had Discretion Not to Grant Recission in This Case . . .

. . . Because Gotham unjustifiably delayed challenging the Odd Lot Resale and the defendants did not intend to entrench the General Partner or improperly enrich HGI, we find that the Vice Chancellor was within his discretion in refusing to grant rescission in this case, even though the result of the challenged transaction was to secure control by the defendants. Given the result of control and the defendants' conduct, however, an adequate, rationally-articulated substitute remedy must be awarded.

Whether the Court of Chancery Abused Its Discretion by Failing to Account for a Control Premium

The Court of Chancery awarded money damages of approximately $3.4 million based on a per unit value of $25.84 for each Partnership unit resold to HGI. The court gave equal weight to four factors: book value, Gotham's comparables for minority stakes in other limited partnerships, the per unit price of an unrelated Spring 1996 repurchase of Partnership units, and the average price paid by the Partnership during the Odd Lot Offer. Gotham notes that none of the four factors "takes account of the lock on control that HGI obtained in the Resale." Gotham emphasizes that, at trial, Gumbiner valued control of the Partnership at $50 to $55 million and that only a mere $3.4 million was awarded as monetary damages. Gotham argues that this Court should reverse on this issue and remand to the Court of Chancery for a new remedy calculation that accounts for the value of control of the Partnership. This Court reviews the Court of Chancery's fashioning of remedies for abuse of discretion.

The Partnership Agreement provides for contractual fiduciary duties of entire fairness. Although the contract could have limited the damage remedy for breach of these duties to contract damages, it did not do so. The Court of Chancery is not precluded from awarding equitable relief as provided by the entire fairness standard where, as here, the general partner breached its contractually created fiduciary duty to meet the entire fairness standard and the partnership agreement is silent regarding damages. The Court of Chancery in this case may award equitable relief as provided by the entire fairness standard and is not limited to contract damages for two reasons: (1) this case involves a breach of the duty of loyalty and such a breach permits broad, discretionary, and equitable remedies; and (2) courts will not construe a contract as taking away other forms of appropriate relief, including equitable relief, unless the contract explicitly provides for an exclusive remedy.

In this case, as the Vice Chancellor properly found, the fiduciary duties provided for by the Partnership Agreement supplanted common law fiduciary duty principles, but "some of the agreement's provisions were 'in some sense ... an explicit acceptance of the default duty of loyalty and fair dealing.' " The General Partner breached its duty of loyalty by failing to comply with the contractually created entire fairness standard during the Odd Lot Resale, which resulted in the General Partner and its corporate parent solidifying their control over the Partnership. Where there is "a breach of the duty of loyalty, as here, 'potentially harsher rules come into play' and 'the scope of recovery for a breach of the duty of loyalty is not to be determined narrowly [because t]he strict imposition of penalties under Delaware law are designed to discourage disloyalty.' "[27] Therefore, the Court of Chancery's "powers are complete to fashion any form of equitable and monetary relief as may be appropriate."[28] ...

... Although the Vice Chancellor found that the defendants did not intend for the General Partner to become entrenched or HGI to be unjustly enriched, the Odd Lot Resale had that effect. The Court of Chancery was thus required to remedy that effect by compensating the limited partners for a control premium. As the Vice Chancellor recognized, the Audit Committee—whose contractually-mandated functions were not implemented—conceivably would have "taken into account the fact that the Odd Lot resales were of particular advantage to HGI and demanded value for that advantage in exchange" because "the Odd Lot resales solidified HGI's control." Consequently, we find that the Vice Chancellor abused his discretion in fashioning the remedy in this case by failing (1) to address and decide the applicability of rescissory damages, and (2) to include in the damages calculation a premium for the control acquired by HGI through the Odd Lot Resale.

The Partnership is entitled to receive, at a minimum, what the Partnership units sold to HGI would have been worth at the time of the Odd Lot Resale if the General Partner had complied with the Partnership Agreement. We thus reverse the judgment of the Court of Chancery regarding the remedy in this case, and we remand for procedures, such as expansion of the record, as may be necessary and appropriate to accomplish two objectives. First, the Court of Chancery should seek to quantify how the challenged transaction would have been consummated had the defendants adhered to the Partnership Agreement's contractual entire fairness provisions. Specifically, the court should determine and consider what price the Audit Committee would have approved for the Odd Lot Offer resales to HGI if the Audit Committee had been aware that the transaction would result in HGI

---

27. *Cantor Fitzgerald, L.P. v. Cantor*, 2001 WL 536911 (Del.Ch.), at *3 (quoting *Int'l Telecharge*, 766 A.2d at 441 (quoting *Thorpe v. CERBCO, Inc.*, 676 A.2d 436, 445 (Del.1996))).

28. *Weinberger*, 457 A.2d at 714. See also *Int'l Telecharge*, 766 A.2d at 440 (stating that "the powers of the Court of Chancery are very broad in fashioning equitable and monetary relief under the entire fairness standard as may be appropriate"); *Cantor Fitzgerald, L.P. v. Cantor*, 2000 WL 307370 (Del.Ch.), at *29–*30 (stating that "equity must try to right the wrongs with adequate remedies" and awarding a declaratory judgement and money damages for a breach of a contractually created fiduciary duty).

solidifying control over the Partnership. Second, the Court of Chancery should reconsider and award some form or combination of the various equitable remedies available to the limited partnership, including rescissory damages, sterilization of voting rights, and other appropriate methods of accounting for a control premium. We note that the Court of Chancery has the discretion to consider afresh in light of the above analysis whether or not to order rescission.

Conclusion

We affirm the judgment of the Court of Chancery that ... the contractual fiduciary duties of entire fairness contained in the Partnership Agreement applied to the disputed transaction in this case ... [and that] the Court of Chancery has the discretion not to grant rescission where the plaintiff unjustifiably delays seeking that remedy, provided that the court articulates and orders a reasonable alternative remedy....

We reverse the judgment of the Court of Chancery regarding the calculation of damages. We remand, as discussed above, for the court to fashion a remedy according to its discretion that accounts for a control premium....

NOTE ON GOTHAM PARTNERS v. HALLWOOD

In a passage in Gotham Partners v. Hallwood that is omitted from the opinion as edited above, the Delaware Supreme Court said:

> The Vice Chancellor's summary judgment opinion in this case ... creates a separate problem. We refer to one aspect of the Vice Chancellor's discussion of the Delaware Revised Uniform Limited Partnership Act ("DRULPA") in his summary judgment opinion in this case where he stated that [DRULPA] section 17–1101(d)(2) "expressly authorizes the elimination, modification or enhancement of ... fiduciary duties in the written agreement governing the limited partnership." It is at least the second time the Court of Chancery has stated in dicta that DRULPA ... § 17–1101(d)(2) permits a limited partnership agreement to eliminate fiduciary duties.
>
> Because the Vice Chancellor's summary judgment order in this matter has not been appealed, his opinion on this point is not before us for review on this appeal. In our view, however, this dictum should not be ignored because it could be misinterpreted in future cases as a correct rule of law. Accordingly, in the interest of avoiding the perpetuation of a questionable statutory interpretation that could be relied upon adversely by courts, commentators and practitioners in the future, we are constrained to draw attention to the statutory language and the underlying general principle in our jurisprudence that scrupulous adherence to fiduciary duties is normally expected.

> [DRULPA] § 17–1101(d)(2) states: "the partner's or other person's duties and liabilities may be expanded or restricted by provisions in the partnership agreement." There is no mention in § 17–1101(d)(2), or elsewhere in DRULPA ... that a limited partnership agreement may eliminate the fiduciary duties or liabilities of a general partner.
>
> Finally, we note the historic cautionary approach of the courts of Delaware that efforts by a fiduciary to escape a fiduciary duty, whether by a corporate director or officer or other type of trustee, should be scrutinized searchingly. Accordingly, although it is not appropriate for us to express an advisory opinion on a matter not before us, we simply raise a note of concern and caution relating to this dubious dictum in the Vice Chancellor's summary judgment opinion.

After the decision in *Gotham Partners*, the Delaware Legislature amended the Delaware Revised Uniform Partnership Act, the Delaware Limited Liability Company Act, and the Delaware Revised Uniform Limited Partnership Act to make explicit that in these three forms of organization the governing agreement—partnership agreement, limited partnership agreement, or limited liability company agreement—can eliminate, as well as expand or restrict, fiduciary or other duties. At the same time, the amendments made clear that the implied contractual covenant of good faith and fair dealing cannot be eliminated by agreement.

SECTION 11. LIMITED LIABILITY PARTNERSHIPS

REVISED UNIFORM PARTNERSHIP ACT §§ 101(5), 306(c), 1001

[See Statutory Supplement]

NOTE ON LIMITED LIABILITY PARTNERSHIPS

Another important new form of business organization is the limited liability partnership ("LLP"). Essentially, LLPs are general partnerships, with one core difference and one ancillary difference. The core difference is that, as the name indicates, the liability of general partners of a limited liability partnership is less extensive than the liability of a general partner as discussed in the excerpt from Bromberg & Ribstein that follows. The ancillary difference is that LLPs must be registered with the appropriate state office. Every state has now adopted LLP provisions.

A variant on the LLP is the limited liability limited partnership, LLLP, in which the liability of the general partners in a limited partnership is limited.

Ederer v. Gursky

Court of Appeals of New York, 2007.
9 N.Y.3d 514, 881 N.E.2d 204, 851 N.Y.S.2d 108.

■ READ, J.

This appeal calls upon us to explore the nature and scope of Partnership Law § 26(b). We hold that this provision does not shield a general partner in a registered limited liability partnership from personal liability for breaches of the partnership's or partners' obligations to each other.

I.

The relationship that deteriorated into this acrimonious dispute began promisingly enough in 1998 when plaintiff Louis Ederer affiliated with the law firm of Gursky & Associates, P.C., which promptly changed its name to Gursky & Ederer, P.C. (the PC). Ederer joined the PC as a salaried, nonequity contract partner, but he had an understanding with defendant Steven R. Gursky, the PC's sole shareholder, that if their practice developed as anticipated, he would become a full equity partner in about two years' time.

Right on schedule, in May 2000 Gursky orally agreed to increase Ederer's annual compensation by about 17% and to make him a 30% shareholder in the PC as of July 1, the beginning of the PC's fiscal year. Ederer committed to purchase his 30% interest for $600,000, to be paid for by Gursky's taking an additional $150,000 from the PC's yearly distributions for each of the following four years. Finally, Gursky agreed that when the EC took on additional partners, his 70% equity interest would be diluted up to 25% before Ederer's 30% interest was reduced.

In February 2001, the PC became a registered limited liability partnership known as Gursky & Ederer, LLP (the LLP). Significantly, there was no written partnership agreement. The LLP began billing all new legal services, while the PC billed and collected work-in-process and preexisting accounts receivable, and loaned money to the LLP to fund its start-up. In July 2001, the LLP admitted three new partners, defendants Mitchell B. Stern, Martin Feinberg and Michael A. Levine. They collectively acquired a 15% interest in the LLP, leaving Gursky with a 55% interest while Ederer retained his 30% interest.

Ederer received his 30% share of the PC's profits for the fiscal years ending June 30, 2001 and June 30, 2002, less the $150,000 owed to Gursky each year. In 2002, both Ederer and Gursky loaned the PC a portion of their respective shares of the PC's profits. Sometime prior to June 30, 2003, the LLP assumed these loans in exchange for the furniture, fixtures and equipment that it acquired from the PC.

In July 2002, the LLP increased Ederer's annual compensation by about 28%. Gursky also agreed to forgive the remaining $300,000 owed by Ederer for the purchase of his 30% equity interest. Ederer characterizes this gesture as an acknowledgment of his major contributions to the firm's revenue growth; Gursky, as a concession made solely upon Ederer's assurances that he was committed to remaining with the LLP to assure its long-term success.

In June 2003, Ederer advised Gursky that he was withdrawing as a partner in the LLP and a shareholder in the PC. Ederer chalks up his decision to a severe falling out with Gursky in early 2003 over the representation of a firm client. Gursky retorts that Ederer left because the LLP was cash-strapped and unprofitable, and blames him in no small part for this purported state of affairs.

On June 26, 2003, Ederer entered into a withdrawal agreement with the PC and the LLP, which Gursky signed as president of the PC and a partner in the LLP Under this agreement, Ederer agreed to remain a partner in the LLP so as to serve as lead counsel for a trial scheduled to commence in Georgia on June 30, 2003, although he was not obligated to delay his withdrawal from the LLP beyond July 8. In exchange, the LLP agreed to "continue to pay [Ederer his] regular draw and other compensation through the date of [his] withdrawal from the [LLP]"; to have files on which he was working transferred to his new firm upon the client's request; to give him the opportunity to review his clients' bills before the LLP asked for payment; and to allow him and/or his representatives (including accountants) access to the LLP's and PC's books and records after his withdrawal from the LLP.

The PC was dissolved on June 30, 2003, although formal dissolution papers were not filed with the Secretary of State until March 2004. Ederer withdrew from the LLP on or about July 4, 2003 after having helped secure a $2 million verdict in the Georgia trial, which generated a $600,000 contingency fee for the LLP. After Ederer's departure, the LLP continued in business under the name Gursky & Partners, LLP until March 1, 2005, when it ceased operations.

In December 2003, Ederer commenced this action against the PC, the LLP [,] . . . and Gursky, Stern, Feinberg and Levine, seeking an accounting and asserting . . . causes of action for breach of contract relating to Gursky's May 2000 oral agreement to pay him 30% of the PC's profits (the third cause of action), the June 2003 written agreement to pay him for the two weeks he tried the Georgia case for the LLP (the fourth cause of action), and the unpaid portion of his loan to the PC in 2002 (the fifth cause of action).

In their verified answer dated November 7, 2005, defendants denied the gravamen of Ederer's complaint; and interposed numerous affirmative defenses as well as counterclaims sounding in breach of fiduciary duty, conversion, tortious interference with contractual relations, fraud and deceit and fraudulent inducement, breach of contract, and unjust enrichment....

On November 7, 2005, defendants moved to dismiss the complaint as to defendants Gursky, Stern, Feinberg and Levine; to dismiss the first and second causes of action for an accounting and the third cause of action for breach of contract (the May 2000 oral agreement), or, in the alternative, for summary judgment in favor of all defendants upon these causes of action.... [D]efendants argued that Ederer's complaint set forth no cognizable causes of action upon which relief could be granted against the individual defendants because Partnership Law § 26(b) shielded them from any personal liability.

On November 30, 2005, Ederer opposed defendants' motion and cross-moved for partial summary judgment on liability on his first and second causes of action for an accounting, and his third, fourth and fifth causes of action for breach of contract. He asked Supreme Court to direct that a trial be held on damages with respect to the accounting; and requested summary judgment dismissing defendants' counterclaims.

Supreme Court determined that Ederer was entitled to an accounting against all defendants because Partnership Law § 26, which places limits on the personal liability of partners in an LLP applies "to debts of the partnership or the partners to third parties" and "has nothing to do with a partner's fiduciary obligation to account to his partners for the assets of the partnership." ...

The Appellate Division affirmed Supreme Court's order on December 5, 2006, concluding that

> "Partnership Law § 26(b), limiting the liability of partners of a limited liability partnership, does not exempt ... partners from their individual obligations to account to a withdrawing partner under the earlier enacted and unamended Partnership Law § 74 (Rich, Practice Commentaries, McKinney's Cons. Law of N.Y., Book 38, Partnership Law art 8–B, at 426; *compare* Partnership Law § 40[1], [2]; § 71[d])," and "does not exempt the individual defendants from liability to plaintiff for breaches of firm-related agreements between them" (*Ederer v. Gursky*, 35 A.D.3d 166, 166–167, 826 N.Y.S.2d 210 [1st Dept.2006]).

Although individual defendants argued that they had not entered into any agreements with Ederer,

> "it appears that the assets of the PC, with which [Ederer] entered into three agreements, were transferred to the successor LLP, in which all of the individual defendants were partners. The nature and value of the PC's assets, and [Ederer's] interest therein, will be determined in the accounting, and to the extent any of the defendants are in possession of those assets, they may be obliged to pay them over to [Ederer]" (*id.* at 167, 826 N.Y.S.2d 210)....

... On March 20, 2007, the Appellate Division ... certified the following question to us: "Was the order of Supreme Court, as affirmed by this Court, properly made?" Defendants limited the appeal to this Court to challenging so much of the Appellate Division order as affirmed Supreme Court's denial of the individual defendants' motion for summary judgment. To the extent appealed from, . . . we now affirm, answering the certified question in the affirmative.

II.

This appeal comes down to a dispute over the effect of the Legislature's 1994 amendments to section 26 of the Partnership Law (L. 1994, ch. 576, § 8). As originally adopted by the Legislature in 1919 (L. 1919, ch. 408), section 26 was identical to section 15 of the Uniform Partnership Act (UPA), which was drafted by the National Conference of Commissioners on Uniform State Laws and approved by the Conference in 1914. Prior to its amendment in 1994, section 26 provided that

> "[a]ll partners are liable
>
> "1. Jointly and severally for everything chargeable to the partnership under sections twenty-four and twenty-five.
>
> "2. Jointly for all other debts and obligations of the partnership; but any partner may enter into a separate obligation to perform a partnership contract."
>
> Section 24 specifies that
>
> "[w]here, by any wrongful act or omission of any partner acting in the ordinary course of the business of the partnership, or with the authority of his copartners, loss or injury is caused to any person, not being a partner in the partnership, or any penalty is incurred, the partnership is liable therefor to the same extent as the partner so acting or omitting to act."
>
> Section 25 binds the partnership to "make good the loss"
>
> "1. Where one partner acting within the scope of his apparent authority receives money or property of a third person and misapplies it; and
>
> "2. Where the partnership in the course of its business receives money or property of a third person and the money or property so received is misapplied by any partner while it is in the custody of the partnership."

Partnership Law § 26, as originally enacted, and its prototype, section 15 of the UPA, have always been understood to mean what they plainly say: general partners are jointly and severally liable to nonpartner creditors for all wrongful acts and breaches of trust committed by their partners in carrying out the partnership's business, and jointly liable for all other debts to third parties. This proposition follows naturally from the very nature of a partnership, which is based on the law of principal and agent. Just as a principal is liable for the acts of its agents, each partner is personally responsible for the acts of other partners in the ordinary course of the partnership's business. In addition to this vicarious liability to nonpartner creditors, each partner concomitantly has an obligation to share or bear the losses of the partnership through contribution and indemnification in the context of an ongoing partnership . . . and contribution upon dissolution and winding up. . . .

The nationwide initiative to create a new business entity combining the flexibility of a partnership without the onus of this traditional vicarious liability originated with [an LLP statute adopted in Texas]. . . .

In New York, the Legislature enacted limited liability partnership legislation as a rider to the New York Limited Liability Company Law (*see* Walker § 14:2, at 344). This legislation eliminated the vicarious liability of a general partner in a registered limited liability partnership by amending section 26 of the Partnership Law. . . . Specifically, new section 26(b) creates an exception to the vicarious liability otherwise applicable by virtue of section 26(a) (original section 26 [section 15 of the UPA]), by providing that

> "[e]xcept as provided by subdivisions (c) and (d) of this section, no partner of a partnership which is a registered limited liability partnership is liable or accountable, directly or indirectly (including by way of indemnification, contribution or otherwise), for any debts, obligations or liabilities of, or chargeable to, the registered limited liability partnership or each other, whether arising in tort, contract or otherwise, which are incurred, created or assumed by such partnership while such partnership is a registered limited liability partnership, solely by reason of being such a partner."

Section 26(c) excludes from section 26(b)'s liability shield "any negligent or wrongful act or misconduct committed by [a partner] or by any person under his or her direct supervision and control while rendering professional services on behalf of [the] registered limited liability partnership." Section 26(d) allows partners to opt out from or reduce the reach of section 26(b)'s protection from vicarious liability.

As one commentator has noted, by "expressly provid[ing] that limited liability includes liability by way of indemnification or contribution," section 26(b) precludes the potential for a plaintiff to "attempt an end-run around the liability shield of [section 26(b)] by first asserting a claim against the [limited liability partnership] and then arguing that the general partnership statute requires the [limited liability partnership] partners to make contributions to the [limited liability partnership]" (Johnson, *Limited Liability for Lawyers: General Partners Need Not Apply*, 51 Bus. Law. 85, 110 [1995]). . . . Defendants point out that section 26(b) eliminates the liability of a partner in a limited liability partnership for "any debts" without distinguishing between debts owed to a third party or to the partnership or each other. As a result, they contend, the Legislature did not "leave open to conjecture whether § 26(b) was intended to cover debts which may be owed by the [limited liability partnership] (or one partner) to other partners." This argument ignores, however, that the phrase "any debts" is part of a provision (section 26) that has always governed only a partner's liability to third parties, and, in fact, is part of article 3 of the Partnership Law ("Relations of Partners to Persons Dealing with the Partnership"), not article 4 ("Relations of Partners to One Another"). The logical inference, therefore, is that "any debts" refers to any debts owed a third party, absent very clear legislative direction to the contrary.

Defendants also note that chapter 576's legislative history illustrates the desire to enact liability protection for partners in limited liability partnerships that is "the same as that accorded to shareholders of a professional corporation organized under the [Business Corporation Law] [and] as that accorded to members of a professional LLC" (Senate Introducer Mem in Support, Bill Jacket, L. 1994, ch. 576). They point out that "the legislative history of the LLP Act plainly indicates that the Legislature intended to provide an *even greater shield* of individual liability to partners in LLPs than that enacted by other states as of the date of the legislation."

These observations are correct, but do not advance defendants' cause. Chapter 576 does, in fact, afford limited liability partners the same protection from third-party claims as New York law provides shareholders in professional corporations or professional limited liability companies. And unlike New York, most states "have adopted a partial liability shield protecting the partners only from vicarious personal liability for all partnership obligations arising from negligence, wrongful acts or misconduct, whether characterized as tort, contract or otherwise, committed while the partnership is an LLP" (*see* Prefatory Note Addendum to Uniform Partnership Act [1997] [explaining that RUPA, by contrast, "provid(es) for a corporate-styled liability shield which protects partners from vicarious personal liability for all partnership obligations incurred while a partnership is a limited liability partnership"]; *see also* Walker § 14:5, at 346 ["The type of LLP generally permitted by the states (other than Minnesota and New York) . . . offers less insulation against personal liability than many other types of organization"]). Nowhere in the voluminous commentary on limited liability partnerships has anyone suggested that New York (or any other state) has adopted a statute expanding the concept of limited liability in the way asserted by defendants. . . .

In closing, we emphasize that the law of partnerships contemplates a written agreement among partners specifying the terms of their relationship. The Partnership Law's provisions are, for the most part, default requirements that come into play in the absence of an agreement. For example, the right to an accounting exists, "absen[t an] agreement to the contrary" (Partnership Law § 74). Partners might agree, as among themselves, to limit the right to contribution or indemnification or to exclude it altogether. In this case, however, there was no written partnership agreement; therefore, the provisions of the Partnership Law govern.

Accordingly, the order of the Appellate Division, insofar as appealed from, should be affirmed, with costs, and the certified question should be answered in the affirmative.

■ SMITH, J. (dissenting).

The text of Partnership Law § 26(b) seems clear to me: "no partner of a partnership which is a registered limited liability partnership is liable . . . for any debts, obligations or liabilities of . . . the registered limited liability partnership . . . whether arising in tort, contract or otherwise." The statute contains two specific exceptions, applicable when a partner acts wrongfully or when partners agree to vary the liability scheme (Partnership Law § 26[c], [d]), but there is no exception for liabilities to former partners claiming a share of the partnership's net assets. We should not create an exception that the Legislature did not. . . . The majority draws a distinction between liability to "third parties" and liabilities to former partners . . . but a *former* partner is a third party where the partnership is concerned, and there is no good reason to treat him more favorably than any other third party.

No one suggests that section 26(b) exempts partners from any of their fiduciary duties; if a partner has diverted partnership funds to himself, or otherwise received more than his fair share, he will not escape liability and his former partners, as well as his existing partners, will be made whole. The issue is whether a former partner claiming his partnership share may reach the personal assets of partners who are no more blameworthy, and have no more been unjustly enriched, than he has.

I can think of two situations in which this issue may be important. First, without any fault by any partner, the business of the partnership may go badly after a partner withdraws from the firm but before he is paid his share, leaving the firm without enough assets to satisfy his claim. (This is apparently what happened here.) Secondly, the partnership's insolvency may result from the fault of a partner who is himself insolvent; in that case, the question is whether the former partner can proceed against the innocent remaining partners.

In the first case, there is no apparent reason why a former partner should be allowed to collect his debt when other third-party creditors may not; in fact, the Partnership Law provides in another context that debts to nonpartners have a preferred status (Partnership Law § 71[b]). In the second case, the rule adopted by the majority can produce even more clearly perverse results. Take an extreme example: Suppose there are three partners, two with a 49% interest each and one with a 2% interest. One of the 49% partners withdraws, and is entitled to 49% of the firm's assets. Before he can be paid, however, it is found that the other 49% partner has stolen all of those assets, lost them at a casino and gone bankrupt. Why should the innocent 2% partner have to make good the former partner's large loss?

If the Gursky & Ederer firm had remained a professional corporation, instead of turning itself into a limited liability partnership, the result in this case would not be in question: the individual shareholders of the corporation would not be liable for its obligation to Ederer. I do not see why the partners of an LLP should have an obligation that the shareholders of a PC do not, and I therefore dissent.

■ JUDGES CIPARICK, GRAFFEO, PIGOTT and JONES concur with JUDGE READ; JUDGE SMITH dissents in a separate opinion in which CHIEF JUDGE KAYE concurs.

Order, insofar as appealed from, affirmed. . . .

Bromberg & Ribstein, Limited Liability Partnerships, The Revised Uniform Partnership Act, and the Uniform Limited Partnership Act

§ 3.02–3.04 (2005 ed.).

§ 3.02 LIMITED "TORT" LIABILITY IN LLPs

. . . [One] common form of LLP statute . . . limits liability for particular categories of conduct—that is, for negligence or other misconduct by a co-partner or other agent or employee of the firm [as opposed to breach of contract]. The model for these provisions is a prior version of the Delaware statute, which provides that a partner "is not liable for debts and obligations of or chargeable to the partnership arising from negligence, wrongful acts, or misconduct, whether characterized as tort, contract or otherwise, committed while the partnership is a registered limited liability partnership and in the course of the partnership business by another partner or an employee, agent, or representative of the partnership." . . .

Statutes that limit partners' liability only for misconduct-based claims raise some questions about the types of vicarious liability that are limited. The language clearly applies to any form of negligence or misconduct. . . . Professional malpractice liability arising out of partners' negligence is certainly included in the exception to vicarious liability despite the fact that this liability probably could be characterized as rising out of the contractual relationship between the professional and the client. . . . Thus, it is significant that the original partial-shield Delaware statute was amended in 1994 to provide that it limits vicarious liability for conduct "whether characterized as tort, contract or otherwise." . . .

§ 3.03 LIMITED LIABILITY FOR ALL TYPES OF CLAIMS

. . . [Most LLP] statutes provide that liability is limited for all partnership debts and obligations. For example, the Revised Uniform Partnership Act provides:

> An obligation of partnership incurred while the partnership is a limited liability partnership, whether arising in contract, tort, or otherwise, is solely the obligation of the partnership. A partner is not personally liable, directly or indirectly, including by way of contribution or otherwise, for such a partnership obligation solely by reason of being or so acting as a partner. . . .

LLP statutes that eliminate partners' *vicarious* liability for all types of claims . . . nevertheless preserve partners' liability for their own misconduct, including faulty supervision of other partners, discussed below in Section 3.04. . . . Also, it is important to keep in mind that the *partnership* retains vicarious liability for its' partners' acts. Partners therefore remain liable at least up to their investment in the firm, and perhaps beyond this if they have agreed with their co-partners to contribute toward partnership losses.

§ 3.04 PARTNERS' DIRECT LIABILITY

Nothing in the LLP statutes or in statutes . . . relieves owners from liability for their own misconduct. "Limited liability" means only that owners are not, solely as owners, vicariously liable for the firm's debts. . . .

The statutes both preserve whatever liability partners may have had under the common law and, perhaps, provide for an additional statutory category of liability for misconduct. . . . An important model is the original version of the Delaware statute, which provides that the liability limitation "shall not affect the liability of a partner in a registered limited liability partnership for his own negligence, wrongful acts, or misconduct, or that of any person under his direct supervision and control." . . .

It is uncertain under the supervision-type of provision whether the partner must be negligent or at fault in order to be held liable. Stating that the LLP provisions "shall not affect" the partner's liability suggests that the statute only continues any liability partners may have had for their own misconduct or for negligently failing to monitor or supervise others. But it is not clear to what pre-existing supervisory liability the statute might be referring other than partners' *vicarious* liability under traditional partnership law, which is supposedly eliminated by LLP registration.

. . . [N]ot all LLP statutes include potentially confusing language on supervisory or other indirect liability. Some provide for liability only for the partner's own wrongs or omit any extra language on liability of individual members and provide in varying terms that a partner in an LLP is not individually liable merely because of her partnership status. This preserves partners' common law liability for their own misconduct without risking creating new categories of statutory liability.

NOTE ON LIABILITY FOR INVOLVEMENT

An issue that can arise in a professional LLP, when more than one partner was involved in a decision in some way, is what level of involvement will subject a partner to liability for his own conduct if the decision is later attacked. In Megadyne Information Systems v. Rosner, Owens & Nunziato, L.L.P., 2002 WL 31112563 (Cal. App. 2002), an unreported opinion, the court stated "All three partners offered declarations averring Owens was 'the sole attorney' who handled the Megadyne matter and that neither of the other two had 'any involvement' in the case. To contradict that showing, Megadyne [the plaintiff] offered Owens's testimony that 'there might have been discussions' with his two partners that Megadyne had a viable legal malpractice claim against Irell & Manella. This is sufficient to create a triable issue of fact as to whether the partners were personally involved in the firm's breach of fiduciary duties. If the partners had *discussions* that Megadyne could sue Irell & Manella for malpractice, it is reasonable to infer that they knew Megadyne's claim against OCTA was time-barred and that they participated in the decision to not disclose this fact to Megadyne while the firm continued to represent it."

CHAPTER 4

THE FOUNDATIONS OF A CORPORATION

SECTION 1. THE CHARACTERISTICS OF A CORPORATION

A corporation is a legal person or legal entity. As such, a corporation has an existence separate from its owners, that is, its shareholders. A corporation is formed by filing an instrument, known variously as a certificate of incorporation, articles of incorporation, or a charter[1] in an appropriate state office—usually the office of the Secretary of State. A certificate of incorporation is often, although not always, a relatively simple document; a sample form can be found in the Statutory Supplement.

The central characteristics of a corporation are as follows:

1. Limited Liability. Normally, shareholders are not personally liable for corporate obligations. This legal rule is conventionally expressed by the statement that shareholders have limited liability. The managers of a corporation are also normally not personally liable for corporate obligations: as long as corporate managers act on the corporation's behalf and within their authority, they are treated like agents, not principals, for liability purposes. In contrast, in a simple general partnership each partner is liable for the partnership's obligations. See Chapter 3, Section 5.

2. Free Transferability of Ownership Interests. At least in publicly held corporations, ownership (or *equity*) interests, represented by shares of stock, are usually freely transferrable. In contrast, a partnership interest in a general partnership, other than a purely economic interest, cannot be transferred without the consent of all the partners unless otherwise agreed. See Chapter 3, Section 6.

3. Continuity of Existence. The legal existence of a corporation is usually perpetual, unless a shorter term is specified in the certificate of incorporation. This makes a corporation relatively secure against early termination, and has a beneficial impact on long-term planning. *See* Rock & Wachter, Waiting for the Omelet to Set, 24 J. Corp. L. 913 (1999). In contrast, partnerships usually have limited terms, and in any event are easily dissolved. See Chapter 3, Sections 8, 9.

4. Centralized Management. In publicly held corporations, the power to manage the business of the corporation is legally vested in

1. For ease of exposition, the term *certificate of incorporation* will be employed to denote either a certificate of incorporation, articles of incorporation, or a charter.

the board of directors, although in practice much of that power is normally exercised by the corporation's executives. Shareholders, as such, have no right to participate in management. In contrast, in a general partnership, unless otherwise agreed, all partners have a right to participate in the conduct of the business. See Chapter 3, Section 3.

5. *Entity Status.* Because a corporation is a legal person or entity, it can exercise powers and have rights in its own name. For example, a corporation can sue or be sued, and can own real and personal property. In contrast, in states where the governing law is the Uniform Partnership Act, general partnerships are not deemed to have entity status, although they do have entity status in states where the Revised Uniform Partnership Act is the governing law. See Chapter 3, Section 2.

These central attributes make the corporation a highly desirable form for an enterprise that is to be publicly held, because the owners of such an enterprise will normally put a very high premium on limited liability and free transferability and will also value centralized management and continuity of interest. In the case of an enterprise that is not to be publicly held, and in particular an enterprise that is to be held by a relatively small number of shareholders, most or all of whom are managers, the choice of form is more complex, because the owners may value certain partnership attributes, such as participation by all owners in management and limited transferability of interests. Accordingly, such an enterprise may take the form of either a corporation, a limited liability company (LLC), a general partnership, a limited liability partnership, a limited partnership, or a limited liability partnership. The partnership forms have been considered in Chapter 3. The LLC form will be considered in Chapter 9.

SECTION 2. THE ARCHITECTURE OF CORPORATE LAW

Corporation law is often conceived of as state law, but this conception is much too narrow. Corporate law serves various functions. It enables corporations to be organized. It provides corporations with certain endowments—most prominently, entity status, limited liability, perpetual existence, the right to own property and to make contracts, and the power to sue and be sued. It sets the level of care required of directors and officers. It provides a special remedial structure to resolve claims by shareholders against directors and officers. It facilitates various transactions and conduct in which a corporation may choose to engage. It addresses various kinds of conflict of interest. (These may be either *traditional conflicts*, which typically involve self-interested transactions between managers and their corporations, or *positional conflicts*, which involve actions by managers to maintain and enhance their positions.) Any body of rules that addresses one or more of these functions is part of corporate law.

Viewed from this perspective, corporate law consists of four major modules: state statutory law; state judge-made law; federal law, such as the Securities Acts and Sarbanes–Oxley; and private ordering, or "soft law," such as stock-exchange rules for listed companies. Each of these modules serves a distinct function. State statutory law enables corporations to be organized, provides corporations with various endowments, and facilitates corporate transactions. State judge-made law sets the level of care required of officers and directors, regulates traditional conflicts of interest, and gives content to remedial structures to protect shareholder rights and resolve shareholder claims. Federal law regulates certain traditional conflicts directly, through rules on insider training, and regulates positional conflicts of interest indirectly, through rules that govern the proxy voting system and through regulation of the flow of information concerning management's performance. The rules of the major stock exchanges regulate positional conflicts directly, by requiring an independent board and committees to monitor the corporation's executives. Accordingly, this book will concern state corporate law and those aspects of federal law that regulate the ongoing conduct of the corporation, and will also include the New York Stock Exchange's governance rules for listed companies.[2]

SECTION 3. WHICH STATE'S LAW GOVERNS A CORPORATION'S INTERNAL AFFAIRS

One element that will often figure in the decision where to incorporate an enterprise is which state's law the decision makers want to govern the corporation's internal affairs. Although, as shown in the preceding Note, a corporation's internal affairs may be governed by four different legal modules, often state law will often be paramount. The law permits an enterprise to incorporate in any state it chooses—even a state in which the enterprise will do little or no business. If an enterprise incorporates in such a state, the question may arise, whose law governs the corporation's internal affairs—the state of incorporation, or a state, if there is one, where the corporation does most of its business? The normal rule is that the law of the state of incorporation will govern the corporation's internal affairs. However, some states, including California and New York, have adopted provisions in their corporate statutes under which designated sections of the statutes are applicable to the internal affairs of certain corporations incorporated in another state. The following two cases address such statutes.

---

2. The New York Stock Exchange has combined with Euronext, and the formal title of the Exchange, or at least the holding company for the Exchange and Euronext, is NYSE Euronext. However, the Exchange is still conventionally referred to as the New York Stock Exchange, or sometimes the NYSE, and that convention will be followed in this Book.

VantagePoint Venture Partners 1996 v. Examen, Inc.

Supreme Court of Delaware, 2005.
871 A.2d 1108.

■ HOLLAND, JUSTICE:

This is an expedited appeal from the Court of Chancery following the entry of a final judgment on the pleadings. We have concluded that the judgment must be affirmed.

Delaware Action

On March 3, 2005, the plaintiff-appellee, Examen, Inc. ("Examen"), filed a Complaint in the Court of Chancery against VantagePoint Venture Partners, Inc. ("VantagePoint"), a Delaware Limited Partnership and an Examen Series A Preferred shareholder, seeking a judicial declaration that pursuant to the controlling Delaware law and under the Company's Certificate of Designations of Series A Preferred Stock ("Certificate of Designations"), VantagePoint was not entitled to a class vote of the Series A Preferred Stock on the proposed merger between Examen and a Delaware subsidiary of Reed Elsevier Inc.

California Action

On March 8, 2005, VantagePoint filed an action in the California Superior Court seeking: (1) a declaration that Examen was required to identify whether it was a "quasi-California corporation" under section 2115 of the California Corporations Code[1]; (2) a declaration that Examen was a quasi-California corporation pursuant to California Corporations Code section 2115 and therefore subject to California Corporations Code section 1201(a), and that, as a Series A Preferred shareholder, VantagePoint was entitled to vote its shares as a separate class in connection with the proposed merger; (3) injunctive relief; and (4) damages incurred as the result of alleged violations of California Corporations Code sections 2111(f) and 1201.

Delaware Action Decided

On March 10, 2005, the Court of Chancery granted Examen's request for an expedited hearing on its motion for judgment on the pleadings. On March 21, 2005, the California Superior Court stayed its

1. Section 2115 of the California Corporations Code purportedly applies to corporations that have contacts with the State of California, but are incorporated in other states. *See* Cal. Corp.Code §§ 171 (defining "foreign corporation"); and Cal. Corp.Code §§ 2115(a), (b). Section 2115 of the California Corporations Code provides that, irrespective of the state of incorporation, foreign corporations' articles of incorporation are deemed amended to comply with California law and are subject to the laws of California if certain criteria are met. *See* Cal. Corp.Code § 2115 (emphasis added). To qualify under the statute: (1) the average of the property factor, the payroll factor and the sales factor as defined in the California Revenue and Taxation Code must be more than 50 percent during its last full income year; and (2) more than one-half of its outstanding voting securities must be held by persons having addresses in California. *Id.* If a corporation qualifies under this provision, California corporate laws apply "to the exclusion of the law of the jurisdiction where [the company] is incorporated." *Id.* Included among the California corporate law provisions that would govern is California Corporations Code section 1201, which states that the principal terms of a reorganization shall be approved by the outstanding shares of each class of each corporation the approval of whose board is required. *See* Cal. Corp.Code §§ 2115, 1201.

action pending the ruling of the Court of Chancery. On March 29, 2005, the Court of Chancery ruled that the case was governed by the internal affairs doctrine as explicated by this Court in *McDermott v. Lewis*.[2] In applying that doctrine, the Court of Chancery held that Delaware law governed the vote that was required to approve a merger between two Delaware corporate entities.

... [VantagePoint appealed and the Supreme Court] granted its request for an expedited appeal....

Facts

Examen was a Delaware corporation engaged in the business of providing web-based legal expense management solutions to a growing list of Fortune 1000 customers throughout the United States. Following consummation of the merger on April 5, 2005, LexisNexis Examen, also a Delaware corporation, became the surviving entity. VantagePoint is a Delaware Limited Partnership organized and existing under the laws of Delaware. VantagePoint, a major venture capital firm that purchased Examen Series A Preferred Stock in a negotiated transaction, owned eighty-three percent of Examen's outstanding Series A Preferred Stock (909,091 shares) and no shares of Common Stock.

On February 17, 2005, Examen and Reed Elsevier executed the Merger Agreement, which was set to expire on April 15, 2005, if the merger had not closed by that date. Under the Delaware General Corporation Law and Examen's Certificate of Incorporation, including the Certificate of Designations for the Series A Preferred Stock, adoption of the Merger Agreement required the affirmative vote of the holders of a majority of the issued and outstanding shares of the Common Stock and Series A Preferred Stock, *voting together as a single class*. Holders of Series A Preferred Stock had the number of votes equal to the number of shares of Common Stock they would have held if their Preferred Stock was converted. Thus, VantagePoint, which owned 909,091 shares of Series A Preferred Stock and no shares of Common Stock, was entitled to vote based on a converted number of 1,392,727 shares of stock.

There were 9,717,415 total outstanding shares of the Company's capital stock (8,626,826 shares of Common Stock and 1,090,589 shares of Series A Preferred Stock), representing 10,297,608 votes on an as-converted basis. An affirmative vote of at least 5,148,805 shares, constituting a majority of the outstanding voting power on an as-converted basis, was required to approve the merger. If the stockholders were to vote by class, VantagePoint would have controlled 83.4 percent of the Series A Preferred Stock, which would have permitted VantagePoint to block the merger. VantagePoint acknowledges that, if Delaware law applied, it would not have a class vote.

2. McDermott Inc. v. Lewis, 531 A.2d 206 (Del.1987).

Chancery Court Decision

The Court of Chancery determined that the question of whether VantagePoint, as a holder of Examen's Series A Preferred Stock, was entitled to a separate class vote on the merger with a Delaware subsidiary of Reed Elsevier, was governed by the internal affairs doctrine because the issue implicated "the relationship between a corporation and its stockholders."

... [T]he Court of Chancery determined that section 2115's requirement that stockholders vote as a separate class conflicts with Delaware law, which, together with Examen's Certificate of Incorporation, mandates that the merger be authorized by a majority of all Examen stockholders voting together as a single class. The Court of Chancery concluded that it could not enforce both Delaware and California law. Consequently, the Court of Chancery decided that the issue presented was solely one of choice-of-law, and that it need not determine the constitutionality of section 2115.

VantagePoint's Argument

According to VantagePoint, "the issue presented by this case is not a choice of law question, but rather the constitutional issue of whether California may promulgate a narrowly-tailored exception to the internal affairs doctrine that is designed to protect important state interests." VantagePoint submits that "Section 2115 was designed to provide an additional layer of investor protection by mandating that California's heightened voting requirements apply to those few foreign corporations that have chosen to conduct a majority of their business in California and meet the other factual prerequisite of Section 2115." Therefore, VantagePoint argues that "Delaware either must apply the statute if California can validly enact it, or hold the statute unconstitutional if California cannot." ...

Internal Affairs Doctrine

In *CTS Corp. v. Dynamics Corp. of Am.*, the United States Supreme Court stated that it is "an accepted part of the business landscape in this country for States to create corporations, to prescribe their powers, and to define the rights that are acquired by purchasing their shares."[6] In *CTS*, it was also recognized that "[a] State has an interest in promoting stable relationships among parties involved in the corporations it charters, as well as in ensuring that investors in such corporations have an effective voice in corporate affairs."[7] The internal affairs doctrine is a long-standing choice of law principle which recognizes that only one state should have the authority to regulate a corporation's internal affairs—the state of incorporation.[8]

---

6. CTS Corp. v. Dynamics Corp. of Am., 481 U.S. 69, 91, 107 S.Ct. 1637, 95 L.Ed.2d 67 (1987).

7. *Id.*

8. McDermott Inc. v. Lewis, 531 A.2d 206 (Del.1987). Accord State Farm Mut. Auto. Ins. Co. v. Superior Court, 114 Cal.App.4th 434, 442, 8 Cal.Rptr.3d 56 (2d Dist.2003), citing Edgar v. MITE Corp., 457 U.S. 624, 645, 102 S.Ct. 2629, 73 L.Ed.2d 269 (1982).

The internal affairs doctrine developed on the premise that, in order to prevent corporations from being subjected to inconsistent legal standards, the authority to regulate a corporation's internal affairs should not rest with multiple jurisdictions.[9] It is now well established that only the law of the state of incorporation governs and determines issues relating to a corporation's internal affairs. By providing certainty and predictability, the internal affairs doctrine protects the justified expectations of the parties with interests in the corporation.

The internal affairs doctrine applies to those matters that pertain to the relationships among or between the corporation and its officers, directors, and shareholders. The Restatement (Second) of Conflict of Laws § 301 provides: "application of the local law of the state of incorporation will usually be supported by those choice-of-law factors favoring the need of the interstate and international systems, certainty, predictability and uniformity of result, protection of the justified expectations of the parties and ease in the application of the law to be applied." Accordingly, the conflicts practice of both state and federal courts has consistently been to apply the law of the state of incorporation to "the entire gamut of internal corporate affairs."[14]

The internal affairs doctrine is not, however, only a conflicts of law principle. Pursuant to the Fourteenth Amendment Due Process Clause, directors and officers of corporations "have a significant right . . . to know what law will be applied to their actions"[15] and "[s]tockholders . . . have a right to know by what standards of accountability they may hold those managing the corporation's business and affairs."[16] Under the Commerce Clause, a state "has no interest in regulating the internal affairs of foreign corporations."[17] Therefore, this Court has held that an "application of the internal affairs doctrine is mandated by constitutional principles, except in the 'rarest situations,' "[18] e.g., when "the law of the state of incorporation is inconsistent with a national policy on foreign or interstate commerce."[19]

California Section 2115

VantagePoint contends that section 2115 of the California Corporations Code is a limited exception to the internal affairs doctrine. Section 2115 is characterized as an outreach statute because it requires

---

9. *See* Edgar v. MITE Corp., 457 U.S. at 645.

14. McDermott Inc. v. Lewis, 531 A.2d at 216 (quoting John Kozyris, *Corporate Wars and Choice of Law*, 1985 Duke L.J. 1, 98 (1985)). The internal affairs doctrine does not apply where the rights of third parties external to the corporation are at issue, *e.g.*, contracts and torts. *Id. See* also Rogers v. Guaranty Trust Co. of N.Y., 288 U.S. 123, 130–31, 53 S.Ct. 295, 77 L.Ed. 652 (1933).

15. McDermott Inc. v. Lewis, 531 A.2d at 216.

16. *Id.* at 217.

17. *Id.* (quoting Edgar v. MITE Corp. 457 U.S. 624, 645–46, 102 S.Ct. 2629, 73 L.Ed.2d 269 (1982)).

18. *Id.* (quoting CTS Corp. v. Dynamics Corp. of Am., 481 U.S. 69, 90, 107 S.Ct. 1637, 95 L.Ed.2d 67 (1987)).

19. *Id.*

certain foreign corporations to conform to a broad range of internal affairs provisions. Section 2115 defines the foreign corporations for which the California statute has an outreach effect as those foreign corporations, half of whose voting securities are held of record by persons with California addresses, that also conduct half of their business in California as measured by a formula weighing assets, sales and payroll factors.

VantagePoint argues that section 2115 "mandates application of certain enumerated provisions of California's corporation law to the internal affairs of 'foreign' corporations if certain narrow factual prerequisites [set forth in section 2115] are met." Under the California statute, if more than one half of a foreign corporation's outstanding voting securities are held of record by persons having addresses in California (as disclosed on the books of the corporation) on the record date, *and* the property, payroll and sales factor tests are satisfied, then on the first day of the income year, one hundred and thirty five days after the above tests are satisfied, *the foreign corporation's articles of incorporation are deemed amended to the exclusion of the law of the state of incorporation.*[21] If the factual conditions precedent for triggering section 2115 are established, many aspects of a corporation's internal affairs are purportedly governed by California corporate law to the exclusion of the law of the state of incorporation.[22]

In her comprehensive analysis of the internal affairs doctrine, Professor Deborah A. DeMott examined section 2115. As she astutely points out:

> In contrast to the certainty with which the state of incorporation may be determined, the criteria upon which the applicability of section 2115 hinges are not constants. For example, whether half of a corporation's business is derived from California and whether half of its voting securities have record holders with California addresses may well vary from year to year (and indeed throughout any given year). Thus, a corporation might be subject to section 2115 one year but not the next, depending on its situation at the time of filing the annual statement required by section 2108.[23]

---

21. *Id.*

22. If Section 2115 applies, California law is deemed to control the following: the annual election of directors; removal of directors without cause; removal of directors by court proceedings; the filing of director vacancies where less than a majority in office are elected by shareholders; the director's standard of care; the liability of directors for unlawful distributions; indemnification of directors, officers, and others; limitations on corporate distributions in cash or property; the liability of shareholders who receive unlawful distributions; the requirement for annual shareholders' meetings and remedies for the same if not timely held; shareholder's entitlement to cumulative voting; the conditions when a supermajority vote is required; limitations on the sale of assets; limitations on mergers; limitations on conversions; requirements on conversions; the limitations and conditions for reorganization (including the requirement for class voting); dissenter's rights; records and reports; actions by the Attorney General and inspection rights. *See* Cal. Corp.Code § 2115(b) (1977 & Supp.1984).

23. Deborah A. DeMott, *Perspectives on Choice of Law for Corporate Internal Affairs*, 48 Law & Contemp. Probs. 161, 166 (1985).

Internal Affairs Require Uniformity

In *McDermott v. Lewis*, this Court noted that application of local internal affairs law (here California's section 2115) to a foreign corporation (here Delaware) is "apt to produce inequalities, intolerable confusion, and uncertainty, and intrude into the domain of other states that have a superior claim to regulate the same subject matter. . . ."[24] Professor DeMott's review of the differences and conflicts between the Delaware and California corporate statutes with regard to internal affairs, illustrates why it is imperative that only the law of the state of incorporation regulate the relationships among a corporation and its officers, directors, and shareholders. To require a factual determination to decide which of two conflicting state laws governs the internal affairs of a corporation at any point in time, completely contravenes the importance of stability within inter-corporate [sic *intra*-corporate?] relationships that the United States Supreme Court recognized in *CTS*. . . .

State Law of Incorporation Governs Internal Affairs

In *McDermott*, this Court held that the "internal affairs doctrine is a major tenet of Delaware corporation law having important federal constitutional underpinnings."[32]

. . . Examen is a Delaware corporation. The legal issue in this case—whether a preferred shareholder of a Delaware corporation had the right, under the corporation's Certificate of Designations, to a Series A Preferred Stock class vote on a merger—clearly involves the relationship among a corporation and its shareholders. As the United States Supreme Court held in *CTS*, "[n]o principle of corporation law and practice is more firmly established than a *State's authority* to regulate domestic corporations, including the authority to *define the voting rights of shareholders*."[34]

In *CTS*, the Supreme Court held that the Commerce Clause "prohibits States from regulating subjects that 'are in their nature national, or admit only of one uniform system, or plan of regulation,' "[35] and acknowledged that the internal affairs of a corporation are subjects that require one uniform system of regulation. In *CTS*, the Supreme Court concluded that "[s]o long as each State regulates voting rights *only in the corporations it has created*, each corporation will be subject to the law of only one State."[37] Accordingly, we hold Delaware's well-established choice of law rules and the federal constitution mandated that Examen's internal affairs, and in particular,

24. McDermott Inc. v. Lewis, 531 A.2d 206, 216 (Del.1987) (quoting Kozyris at 98).

32. McDermott Inc. v. Lewis, 531 A.2d 206, 209 (Del.1987).

34. CTS Corp. v. Dynamics Corp. of Am., 481 U.S. 69, 89, 107 S.Ct. 1637, 95 L.Ed.2d 67 (1987) (emphasis added). *See* Restatement (Second) of Conflict of Laws § 304 (1971) (concluding that the law of the incorporating State generally should "determine the right of a shareholder to participate in the administration of the affairs of the corporation").

35. CTS Corp. v. Dynamics Corp. of Am., 481 U.S. at 89, 107 S.Ct. 1637 (quoting Cooley v. Bd. of Wardens, 53 U.S. 299, 319, 12 How. 299, 13 L.Ed. 996 (1851)).

37. *Id.* (emphasis added).

VantagePoint's voting rights, be adjudicated exclusively in accordance with the law of its state of incorporation, in this case, the law of Delaware.

Any Forum—Internal Affairs—Same Law

VantagePoint acknowledges that the courts of Delaware, as the forum state, may apply Delaware's own substantive choice of law rules. VantagePoint argues, however, that Delaware's "choice" to apply the law of the state of incorporation to internal affairs issues—notwithstanding California's enactment of section 2115—will result in future forum shopping races to the courthouse. VantagePoint submits that, if the California action in these proceedings had been decided first, the California Superior Court would have enjoined the merger until it was factually determined whether section 2115 is applicable. If the statutory prerequisites were found to be factually satisfied, VantagePoint submits that the California Superior Court would have applied the internal affairs law reflected in section 2115, "to the exclusion" of the law of Delaware—the state where Examen is incorporated.

In support of those assertions, VantagePoint relies primarily upon a 1982 decision by the California Court of Appeals in Wilson v. Louisiana–Pacific Resources, Inc.[41] In *Wilson v. Louisiana–Pacific Resources, Inc.*, a panel of the California Court of Appeals held that section 2115 did not violate the federal constitution by applying the California Code's mandatory cumulative voting provision to a Utah corporation that had not provided for cumulative voting but instead had elected the straight voting structure set forth in the Utah corporation statute. The court in *Wilson* did not address the implications of the differences between the Utah and California corporate statutes upon the expectations of parties who chose to incorporate in Utah rather than California. As Professor DeMott points out, "[a]lthough it is possible under the Utah statute for the corporation's charter to be amended by the shareholders and the directors, that mechanical fact does not establish California's right to coerce such an amendment" whenever the factual prerequisites of section 2115 exist.[44]

Wilson was decided before the United States Supreme Court's decision in *CTS* and before this Court's decision in *McDermott*. Ten years after *Wilson*, the California Supreme Court cited with approval this Court's analysis of the internal affairs doctrine in *McDermott*, in particular, our holding that corporate voting rights disputes are governed by the law of the state of incorporation.[45] Two years ago, in *State Farm v. Superior Court*, a different panel of the California Court of Appeals questioned the validity of the holding in *Wilson* following the broad acceptance of the internal affairs doctrine over the two

---

41. Wilson v. La.–Pac. Res., Inc., 138 Cal.App.3d 216, 187 Cal.Rptr. 852 (1982).

44. Deborah A. DeMott, *Perspectives on Choice of Law for Corporate Internal Affairs*, 48 Law & Contemp. Probs. 161, 187–88 (1985).

45. *See* Nedlloyd Lines B.V. v. Superior Court, 3 Cal.4th 459, 11 Cal.Rptr.2d 330, 834 P.2d 1148, 1155 (1992), *citing McDermott Inc. v. Lewis*, 531 A.2d 206 (Del.1987).

decades after *Wilson* was decided.[46] In *State Farm*, the court cited with approval the United States Supreme Court decision in *CTS Corp. v. Dynamics* and our decision in *McDermott*. In *State Farm*, the court also quoted at length that portion of our decision in *McDermott* relating to the constitutional imperatives of the internal affairs doctrine.

Since *Wilson* was decided, the United States Supreme Court has recognized the constitutional imperatives of the internal affairs doctrine.[50] In *Draper v. Gardner*, this Court acknowledged the *Wilson* opinion in a footnote[51] and nevertheless permitted the dismissal of a Delaware action in favor of a California action in which a California court would be called upon to decide the internal affairs "demand" issue involving a Delaware corporation. As stated in *Draper*, we had no doubt that after the *Kamen* and *CTS* holdings by the United States Supreme Court, the California courts would "apply Delaware [demand] law [to the internal affairs of a Delaware corporation], given the vitality and constitutional underpinnings of the internal affairs doctrine."[52] We adhere to that view in this case.

Conclusion

The judgment of the Court of Chancery is affirmed. The Clerk of this Court is directed to issue the mandate immediately.*

Friese v. Superior Court

California Court of Appeal, Fourth District, Division 1, 2005.
134 Cal.App.4th 693, 36 Cal.Rptr.3d 558.

■ BENKE, ACTING P.J.

Corporations Code sections 25402 and 25502.5 are part of the Corporate Securities Law of 1968. In general, section 25402 prohibits so-called "insider trading" by the issuer of securities or by any person who is an officer, director or controlling person of an issuer. Until 1988 only purchasers or sellers of stock who could show that they had been harmed by virtue of insider trading had a right of action against violators of section 25402. In 1988 the Legislature added section 25502.5, which allows the issuer or anyone acting in the name of the issuer to recover from an officer, director or controlling person who has violated section 25402 up to three times the amount such a violator earned by virtue of his or her insider trading. Section 25502.5

---

46. State Farm Mut. Auto. Ins. Co. v. Superior Court, 114 Cal.App.4th 434, 8 Cal. Rptr.3d 56 (2d Dist.2003).

50. *E.g.*, Edgar v. MITE Corp. 457 U.S. 624, 102 S.Ct. 2629, 73 L.Ed.2d 269 (1982); CTS Corp. v. Dynamics Corp. of Am., 481 U.S. 69, 107 S.Ct. 1637, 95 L.Ed.2d 67 (1987). *See also* Kamen v. Kemper Fin. Serv., 500 U.S. 90, 111 S.Ct. 1711, 114 L.Ed.2d 152 (1991).

51. Draper v. Gardner, 625 A.2d 859, 867 n. 10 (Del.1993).

52. *Id.* at 867.

* *See also* In re the Topps Company Shareholders Litigation, 924 A.2d 951 (Del. Ch. 2007). (Footnote by eds.)

is a disgorgement statute and the issuer does not need to show that it was harmed by the activities of the inside trader.

Section 25402 governs only securities transactions which occur in this state. Moreover, only issuers who have more than $1 million in assets and more than 500 shareholders may bring an action under section 25502.5. However, aside from those geographic and capitalization requirements, there are no other express limitations on the scope of either statute. In particular, nothing on the face of either statute limits application of the statutes to securities issued by domestic corporations.

Section 2116, which is not a part of the Corporate Securities Law of 1968, provides that a director's liability to a corporation is a matter of internal governance of the corporation and is governed by the laws of the state in which it is incorporated.

Here the plaintiff is the successor in interest to a Delaware corporation, which has its headquarters and principal place of business in California and does substantial business here. The defendants are a group of former officers and directors of the corporation. The plaintiff alleges the defendants violated section 25402 and are liable under section 25502.5 to the plaintiff for up to three times the amount the defendants earned by way of their insider trading. The defendants argue that because the issuer was a Delaware corporation and Delaware has no statute analogous to section 25502.5, the internal affairs doctrine as codified in section 2116 prevents the defendants from being held liable under section 25502.5. The trial court agreed and sustained the defendants' demurrers to the plaintiff's insider trading causes of action without leave to amend.

We issued an order to show cause on plaintiff's petition for a writ of mandate. For the reasons we set forth below we grant the petition. Unlike the trial court, we do not believe section 2116's provisions concerning internal corporate governance modify or limit any provision of the Corporate Securities Law of 1968, including in particular section 25502.5. Briefly, while we agree that the duties officers and directors owe a corporation are in the first instance defined by the law of the state of incorporation, such duties are not the subject of California's corporate securities laws in general or section 25502.5 in particular. California's corporate securities laws are designed to protect participants in California's securities marketplace and deter unlawful conduct which takes place here. Because a substantial portion of California's marketplace includes transactions involving securities issued by foreign corporations, the corporate securities laws have been consistently applied to such transactions. There is nothing on the face of section 25502.5 or in its history which suggests that the Legislature intended that it have any narrower scope than other parts of the Corporate Securities Law of 1968.

SUMMARY

[Plaintiff, Robert C. Friese, is the trustee of Peregrine Litigation Trust, which itself is the successor in interest to the Estate of Peregrine

Systems, Inc., a publicly traded Delaware corporation with its headquarters and principal place of business in San Diego. The defendants are former directors and former senior management of Peregrine Systems, Inc. (Peregrine), a software manufacturer. Plaintiff alleges that during 1999, the defendants sold over 5 million Peregrine shares, reaping $129 million in proceeds, when they were aware that that Peregrine's various announcements of ever-increasing profits were false and that the reported profits were the results of accounting chicanery. A later restatement of its revenue revealed that Peregrine overstated its profits by more than $500 million, or 38 percent, between April 1999 and December 2001.]

On February 24, 2004, the trustee filed a complaint in superior court, alleging violations of California insider trading laws, breach of the fiduciary duty of loyalty, breach of the fiduciary duty of care, waste of corporate assets, conspiracy and unjust enrichment. On April 1, 2005, the trial court sustained the defendants' demurrers to the trustee's insider trading violations without leave to amend. The trial court found that section 2116 and the internal affairs doctrine preclude application of section 25502.5 to the securities the defendants sold. The trustee was given leave to amend his remaining causes of action.

On May 3, 2005, the trustee filed a petition for writ of mandate with this court, challenging the trial court's order sustaining the demurrer. We issued an order to show cause....

DISCUSSION ...

II

Application of California Securities Laws to Foreign Corporations

For the last 100 years California's corporate securities laws have been applied to foreign corporations who do business in this state or whose activities in this state have an impact on this state's securities markets....

The scope of California's securities regulation was considered ... in *Western Air Lines, Inc. v. Sobieski* (1961) 191 Cal.App.2d 399, 12 Cal.Rptr. 719 (*Sobieski*). In *Sobieski* the management of a Delaware corporation, which had its headquarters and principal place of business in this state, was engaged in a dispute with minority shareholders. In an effort to frustrate the minority shareholders' ability to elect directors, the management proposed that the corporation amend its Delaware articles of incorporation to eliminate cumulative voting. The California Commissioner of Corporations determined that any solicitation of proxies approving the elimination of cumulative voting was a sale of securities within the meaning of the Corporations Code and would require a permit from the commissioner. Thereafter, the commissioner denied the corporation's application for a permit. By way of a writ of mandate, the corporation challenged the commissioner's assertion of authority over its attempt to amend its articles. The trial court granted the writ and found, among other matters, that the amendment of the articles of incorporation was an internal affair of the corporation and its shareholders. (*Sobieski, supra*, 191 Cal.App.2d at p. 405, 12 Cal.Rptr. 719.) The Court of Appeal reversed. In rejecting application of the internal affairs doctrine, the court stated: "It is true that the courts in California cannot control the internal affairs of any foreign corporation. Such matters are to be conducted in pursuance of and in compliance with the provisions of the charter of the foreign corporation, and the laws of the country where it was created; but in the management and method of its business affairs in California with the citizens and residents thereof, *in the sale or disposition or transfer of the shares of stock*, it must conform to the laws of California in relation to such matters, and is bound thereby. . . .' " (*Sobieski, supra*, 191 Cal.App.2d at pp. 409–410, 12 Cal.Rptr. 719.)

III

Sections 25402, 25502 and 25502.5

"Insider trading—the use of confidential information not available to the trading public to purchase or sell securities—is prohibited under federal law by section 10(b) of the 1934 Securities Exchange Act and Rule 10b–5 adopted by the Securities Commission pursuant to that statutory provision. Such conduct is also prohibited under provisions of the California Corporate Securities Law of 1968. . . ." (Berger, "Issuer Recovery of Insider Trading Profits Under Section 25502.5 of the California Corporation Code" (1989–1990) 21 Pac. Law Journal 221, 223 . . . (Berger).)

By adoption of sections 25402, 25502 and 25502.5 California has supplemented federal regulation of insider trading. Section 25402 provides as follows: "It is unlawful for an issuer or any person who is an officer, director or controlling person of an issuer or any other person whose relationship to the issuer gives him access, directly or indirectly, to material information about the issuer not generally available to the public, to purchase or sell any security of the issuer in this state at a time when he knows material information about the issuer gained from such relationship which would significantly affect the market price of that security and which is not generally available to the public, and which he knows is not intended to be so available, unless he has reason to believe that the person selling to or buying from him is also in possession of the information." . . .

IV

Section 2116 and the Internal Affairs Doctrine

Section 2116 states: "The directors of a foreign corporation transacting intrastate business are liable to the corporation, its shareholders, creditors, receiver, liquidator or trustee in bankruptcy for the making of unauthorized dividends, purchase of shares or distribution of assets or false certificates, reports or public notices or other violation of official duty according to any applicable laws of the state or place of incorporation or organization, whether committed or done in this state or elsewhere. Such liability may be enforced in the courts of this state." As applied to directors' liability, section 2116 is a codification of the "internal affairs doctrine." (*See* In re Flashcom, Inc. (2004) 308 B.R. 485, 490.) . . .

"As stated in the Restatement Second of Conflict of Laws: 'It would be impractical to have matters . . . which involve a corporation's organic structure or internal administration . . . governed by different laws. It would be impractical, for example, if . . . an issuance of shares, *a payment of dividends*, a charter amendment, or a consolidation or reorganization were to be held valid in one state and invalid in another. . . . In the absence of an explicitly applicable local statute to the contrary, . . . the local law of the state of incorporation has been applied to determine issues involving corporate acts of the sort [mentioned].' [Citations.]" (*State Farm Mutual Automobile Ins. Co. v. Superior Court* (2003) 114 Cal.App.4th 434, 442–443, 8 Cal. Rptr.3d 56 (*State Farm*).) . . .

In *State Farm* policyholders in an Illinois mutual insurance company sued the company and alleged that it had failed to properly pay them dividends out of the company's accumulated surplus. The plaintiff policyholders argued that their right to dividends was governed by the substantive law of California. The insurance company argued that under the internal affairs [doctrine] its dividend obligation was governed by the law of Illinois, where it was incorporated. The court agreed with the insurance company. However, in doing so it took pains to point out that while a corporation's decision to pay dividends was an internal affair, the doctrine had no application to enforcement of a forum state's corporate securities laws. . . .

This limitation on the internal affairs doctrine has been adopted by the reporters of Restatement of Conflicts Second. The internal affairs doctrine is set forth in section 309 of the Restatement and provides: "The local law of the state of incorporation will be applied to determine the existence and extent of a director's or officer's liability to the corporation, its creditors and shareholders, except where, with respect to the particular issue, some other state has a more significant relationship under the principles stated in § 6 to the parties and the transaction, in which event the local law of the other state will be applied." In explaining the exception to the general rule, the reporters state: "The rule of this Section will be applied in the absence of an applicable local statute. Many states impose liability by statute upon the directors of foreign corporations for doing or failing to do, certain acts in the state. *Blue sky laws are typical examples of such statutes.*" (Rest.2d Conflicts of Law, § 309, comment a, italics added.) Professor Witkin has also recognized this limitation on the internal affairs doctrine: "In some situations . . . the local court may, in the interest of justice, take jurisdiction over internal affairs and apply the local law. [Citation] A typical example is the application of the Corporate Securities [Law of 1968] to protect California residents against fraud in the sale of securities of a foreign corporation." (9

Witkin, Summary of Cal. Law (10th ed.) Corporations, 239, p. § 1006.)....

V

The Trustee's Section 25502.5 Claims are Not Barred by the Internal Affairs Doctrine

... The defendants appear to accept the proposition that the Legislature's historic and well-established intent to regulate both intrastate conduct and intrastate securities transactions subject securities transactions which take place in this state to California's securities laws even if those securities are issued by foreign corporations.... The defendants argue however that an issuer's claim under section 25502.5 is *not* a securities regulation [claim]. Rather they suggest section 25502.5 gives rise to no more than a derivative breach of fiduciary duty claim which they argue is, for that reason, subject to the internal affairs doctrine. For a number of reasons we do not accept the defendants' characterization of section 25502.5 as merely a device for enforcing directors' and officers' fiduciary duties to shareholders.

The defendants' characterization of section 25502.5 ignores the fact that, like section 25402, it is part of the Corporate Securities Law of 1968. The defendants also ignore the fact that section 25502.5 is a remedy for the substantive insider trading prohibition set forth in section 25402. As we have noted the prohibition on insider trading was adopted as a means of protecting investor confidence in the securities market and more broadly as a means of punishing what is perceived by the public as immoral conduct.... These public interests are much broader than protection of a corporation's shareholders.

The defendants' assertion that section 25502.5 is limited to protection of shareholder interests also ignores two important aspects of insider trading regulation.

First, as Professor Berger has noted, in general corporations are not damaged when either they or their directors engage in insider trading. (Berger, *supra*, 21 Pac. Law Journal at p. 226.) Thus section 25502.5 cannot be characterized as a means of compensating a corporation for losses it actually experiences when an officer or director engages in insider trading. Secondly, section 25402 prohibits issuers themselves from engaging in insider trading. Thus in compelling an officer or director to disgorge to an issuer profits realized by way of insider trading, section 25502.5 does not provide the issuer with compensation for any lost opportunity the issuer itself could have lawfully realized. These circumstances undermine the defendants' contention that section 25502.5 is a remedy for any breach of fiduciary duty owed to the corporation. Section 25502.5 does not compensate for any loss a corporation experiences or recover any lawful corporate opportunity....

In sum, the history of section 25502.5 and its provisions make it clear that it is very much a part of California's corporate securities regulation scheme and serves broad public interests rather than the more narrow interests of a corporation's shareholders. Given the public and regulatory interests section 25502.5 serves, it is not subject to the internal affairs doctrine as codified in section 2116.

Let a writ of mandate issue directing the trial court to vacate its order sustaining the defendants' demurrers to the trustee's insider trading claims and conduct further proceedings consistent with the views we have expressed. Costs in the writ proceeding are awarded to the trustee.

■ McDONALD and McINTYRE, JJ., concur.

CALIFORNIA CORPORATIONS CODE §§ 2115, 25402, 25502, 25502.5

[See Statutory Supplement]

NEW YORK BUSINESS CORPORATION LAW §§ 1317, 1318, 1319, 1320

[See Statutory Supplement]

SECTION 4. SELECTING A STATE OF INCORPORATION

The choice of governing state law is one, but only one element in a decision where to incorporate. A corporation that will have only a few owners will usually be incorporated locally, that is, in the state in which the corporation will have its principal place of business. Partly this is for tax reasons. If a corporation does business in a state, the state will impose a doing-business tax on the corporation on a basis that reflects the amount of that business. If a corporation is incorporated in a state, the state may impose a franchise tax on the corporation for the privilege of incorporation, even if the corporation does little or no business in the state. Elements of the doing-business tax and franchise tax may overlap, so that if a corporation does business mainly in one state, and that state imposes a franchise tax, its total tax bill usually will be lower if it is incorporated in that state. Furthermore, a local attorney, familiar with local corporate law, may be hesitant about rendering formal opinions on the law of another state, and is therefore likely to recommend local incorporation so that he can confidently give legal advice to the corporation after it is organized.

In the case of a publicly held corporation, a different calculus prevails. For such a corporation the franchise tax is likely to be inconsequential in comparison with the corporation's total revenues, so that tax consequences are unlikely to figure heavily in the choice of the state of incorporation. Furthermore, although franchise-tax revenues are likely to be inconsequential to large states, they may represent an enormous source of revenue to a state with a small fiscal base. The legislature of a small state therefore has a great economic incentive to design a corporate statute that will attract incorporation or reincorporation from other states—particularly by large publicly held corporations, who will pay larger franchise taxes. Even a large state has an incentive to design a statute that will attract incorporation, because the revenues of its corporate bar may depend in part on the extent of local incorporation.

One very small state, Delaware, is by far the most successful state in attracting incorporation, and especially reincorporation from other states, by publicly held corporations. More than 500,000 business entities have their legal home in Delaware. More than 50% of all United States publicly held corporations, and more than 63% of the Fortune 500 largest corporations in the United States, are incorporated in Delaware, even though most of these corporations do little if any business there. In 2009, more than 73% of United States initial public offerings (that is, offerings of stock by privately held corporations to the public) were incorporated in Delaware. *See* Delaware Division of Corporations, 2009 Annual Report; Delaware Department of State: Division of Corporations Website (2010). Because of Delaware's small size and its huge share of publicly held incorporations, franchise taxes account for about 20 percent of all Delaware taxes. In contrast, in most states franchise taxes are probably well under 1% of total tax revenues—often, probably under 0.1%. *See* R. Romano, The Genius of American Law 6–11 (Tables 1–1, 1–2) (1993).

The reason why Delaware is so successful in attracting initial incorporations and reincorporations by publicly held corporations is hotly contested. One position, known as the race to the bottom, is most closely associated with William Cary's seminal article, Federalism and Corporate Law: Reflections Upon Delaware, 83 YALE L.J. 663 (1974). This position is as follows. State corporate law is a product that states sell on a market that has come to be known as the market for corporate charters. Although shareholder approval is required for determining a corporation's state of incorporation, as a practical matter in publicly held corporations the decision is made by managers and rubber-stamped by the shareholders. Institutional shareholders have become increasingly active in the last ten to twenty years, and might well be able to block reincorporation to a state with a statute that is either quirky, *extremely* management-friendly, or both. However, it's unlikely that institutional shareholders would try to block reincorporation in Delaware, whose corporate statute is now pretty much middle-of-the-road, and which offers various advantages, described below.

Now suppose a principal is represented by an agent whom the principal cannot closely monitor. A third party who wishes to sell Product X to the principal through the agent will have an incentive to give the agent a side payment—a bribe—to induce the agent to purchase Product X on the principal's behalf. In the market for corporate law, the shareholders are in the position of the principal, managers are in the position of the agent, and the legislature is in the position of the third party. Under basic agency-cost theory, a state legislature has an incentive to give managers side payments to induce them to cause their corporations to incorporate or reincorporate in the legislature's state. For a variety of reasons, the side payments cannot take the form of money. Instead, the side payments take the form of a suboptimal statutory approach to regulating managers' traditional and positional conflicts of interest.

A counter position, known as race-to-the-top, was formulated by Ralph Winter and others. *See* Winter, State Law, Shareholder Protection, and the Theory of the Corporation, 6 J. Leg. Stud. 271 (1977). Winter argued that if Delaware law unduly favored managers, shareholders in Delaware corporations would earn lower-than-normal returns, and Delaware corporations therefore would have a higher cost of capital. This would either bankrupt Delaware corporations in the product markets or cause the ouster of management through the market in corporate control, which operates through takeover bids. Therefore, managers would avoid incorporating in Delaware if its law unduly favored managers. Since Delaware is by far the most popular state of incorporation for large publicly held corporations, the race-to-the-bottom analysis, Winter said, must be wrong. Indeed, Winter argued, the incentive for states to sell corporate charters must lead Delaware (and other states) to produce an optimal statutory corporate law regime, because a state that offers the optimal, value-maximizing statutory regime will attract the most incorporations. This argument has only limited power, both because it runs counter to agency-cost theory and because it depends on a drastic overstatement of the power of the product market, the capital market, and the takeover market for these purposes.

Begin with the product market. The costs to the corporation of suboptimal state legislative rules are likely to be relatively small when compared to the corporation's income. Small costs will seldom if ever bankrupt corporations in imperfectly competitive product markets, because corporations operating in such markets usually have the capacity to absorb huge losses and still stay solvent.

The cost of raising equity capital is also unlikely to have a significant effect on the choice of the state of incorporation. First, largely publicly held corporations typically don't raise much money by issuing new equity in the capital market, as opposed to reinvesting earnings or borrowing. Second, even if a corporation does raise capital by issuing new equity, the impact of a suboptimal legal regime will fall on shareholders, not managers. For example, suppose that C Corporation is incorporated in a state, S, which has a suboptimal corporate statute. C Corporation wants to raise $500,000 by selling stock into the capital market. If not for the adverse impact of S's suboptimal legal regime, C could raise $500,000 by issuing 10,000 shares at $50 per share. Given the adverse impact of S's legal regime, to raise $500,000 C must sell 11,111 shares at $45 per share. This dilutes the value of C's stock, and that dilution is a cost. However, that cost will be borne by C's shareholders, rather than by its managers. If the managers own stock or stock options, they will suffer some loss in the value of the stock or options. However, this loss will normally be small compared to the gain the managers can reap from engaging in conflict-of-interest transactions that S's suboptimal legal regime fails to properly regulate.

The market for corporate control—or more accurately, the hostile-takeover market—also has only limited impact in this context. A hostile takeover bid cannot succeed unless it includes a premium that is significantly above the market price of the target's stock. Partly this is because most existing shareholders of the target will value their stock at a price higher than the market price, or they would already have sold. Partly it is because the target's managers can create formidable obstacles to a takeover that often result in bidding contests and that normally can be overcome, if at all, only by paying shareholders a substantial premium over the pre-tender market price. Furthermore, shares of stock held by the public are by definition minority holdings, and traditionally the price of minority stock is discounted from full value—so that, for example, negotiated or "friendly" acquisitions frequently are effected at a price well above the capitalization of the corporation, that is, the number of shares outstanding times the market price of the shares. Accordingly, to complete a successful hostile takeover, a bidder normally must pay a premium of 20–30%, more or less, above the market price of the target's stock. In addition, a hostile bidder must also pay very large fees to investment bankers, lawyers, and other professionals. Since the suboptimality of a state's statutory-law regime is highly unlikely to reduce the value of a corporation by more than a few percentage points, these huge premiums and fees will almost never be economically justified if the bidder's only strategy is to replace a suboptimal legal regime with an optimal legal regime.

Several commentators have attempted to resolve differences between the race-to-the-bottom and race-to-the-top arguments through the generation and analysis of data, but the studies are inconclusive. For example, in an article published in 2001, Rob Daines calculated that based on stock-market valuations, Delaware firms were worth 5% more, on average than non-Delaware firms in twelve out of the sixteen years during the period 1981–1996. Daines, Does Delaware Law improve Firm Value?, 62 J. Financial Econ. 559–71. In a later article, however, Guhan Subrahmanian recalculated the value of Delaware firms during the period 1991–1996, and extended the analysis to the period 1997–2001. Subrahmanian concluded that Delaware firms were worth approximately 3% more than non-Delaware firms during the period 1991–1993, and approximately 2% more than non-Delaware firms during the period 1994–1996. Furthermore, after 1996 the value of Delaware firms did not differ in a statistically different way from the value of non-Delaware firms. Subrahmanian, The Disappearing Delaware Effect, 20 J. Law., Econ. & Org. 32 (2004).

The inconclusive nature of the stock-market data on the race-to-the-bottom, race-to-the-top debate is not surprising. There are a number of reasons why it is difficult if not impossible to assess the optimality of the Delaware statute by analyzing stock-market valuations.

Delaware law consists of judge-made law as well as legislative law. Delaware's judge-made law is vastly richer than the judge-made law of any other state, and Delaware judges are skilled in corporation law. Therefore, even if Delaware's statutory law is suboptimal, that defect might be more than offset by the advantages of Delaware's judge-made law.

If a corporation is incorporated in a given state, it is often necessary to get legal opinions from counsel in that state, as opposed to a corporation's regular counsel, on a legal issue affecting a proposed corporate transaction or course of conduct. Delaware has a high-quality bar that is skilled in corporate law, to whom regular corporate counsel located in other states, can turn with confidence. Most large states also have high-quality corporate bars, but few if any small states can offer a corporate bar that matches Delaware's. Furthermore, the Delaware corporate bar puts in a lot of effort to make sure that the Delaware statute is technically up to speed. Even if the Delaware statute is suboptimal, therefore, its cost could be offset by these advantages.

As Michael Klausner has pointed out, because so many publicly held corporations are incorporated in Delaware, incorporation there brings in its train a benefit known as network externality. When a product implicates network externality, the value of the product to each user increases as more people use it. For example, if fifty million people have telephones, each telephone has more value to its user than if fifty thousand people have telephones. As a result of the network externality effect, a product that attracts a large following can be more valuable to each user than a better product that has only a small following. For example, due to network externality, it may be more efficient to use Microsoft Word even if there are better word-processing programs, because so many other people use Word and are familiar with it. Similarly, it may be more efficient to incorporate in Delaware, whether or not Delaware statutory law is better than other state statutory law, just because so many corporations use and are familiar with Delaware law. *See* Klausner, Corporations, Corporate Law, and Network of Contract, 81 VA. L. REV. 757 (1995). Furthermore, because so many corporations have incorporated in Delaware, it has become a good address, like Park Avenue in New York City, or Park Place in Monopoly. In short, even if the Delaware statute was suboptimal, the cost of that suboptimality could be offset by the network-externality and good-address benefits that Delaware incorporation brings.

Today, there isn't that much significant difference between the Delaware statute and most other state statutes. That's not surprising. If all states are competing for management favor, their statutes are likely to converge. But if the state statutes converge, then even if the state statutes as a group are suboptimal, the Delaware statute might not be more suboptimal than other statutes.

As Kahan and Kamar have put it, the race is over and Delaware has won. Kahan and Kamar, The Myth of State Competition in Corporate Law, 55 STAN. L. REV. 679 (2002). Now that Delaware has won the race, and holds a kind of monopoly position, the Delaware legislature has a special incentive *not* to lead in the adoption of innovative suboptimal rules. This special incentive is to avoid massive federal intervention in corporate law.[3] Unlike the states, the federal government has an interest in the efficiency of national securities markets and, partly because its revenues depend heavily on corporate income, on the efficiency of the corporate system. For various reasons, the federal government does not intervene to correct every suboptimal state law rule. However, as state statutory corporate law becomes highly suboptimal, the risk of federal intervention increases. If comprehensive national corporate-law rules were established for publicly held corporations, over time Delaware could lose its leading position, because there would be less incentive to incorporate in one state rather than the other. Therefore, precisely because of its historical success in the charter market, Delaware is more threatened by the possibility of comprehensive federal intervention than any other state. Furthermore, because of Delaware's massive market share, innovative suboptimal rules in Delaware are more likely to provoke federal intervention than innovative suboptimal rules any other state. Accordingly, having achieved a monopoly position in significant part because of its past leadership in offering suboptimal rules, Delaware now has an incentive not to lead in the adoption of innovative suboptimal rules.

Finally, a comparison between the Delaware statute and other state statutes has limited significance not only because the difference between state statutes tends to be small, but also because of the limited significance of state statutory corporation law. Much of the real action in corporation law is not in state statutory law, but in the other three modules of corporation law described in the Note on the Architecture of Corporate Law—state judge-made law, federal law, and private ordering or soft law. The effect of small differences between state statutes tend to be swamped by the overriding significance of the law in those other modules. Of course, it is the general social interest that state statutory law be optimal, but suboptimal state statutory law can be and is compensated for in many respects by the law in the other three modules.

Because the law of the state of incorporation normally (although not invariably) governs a corporation's internal corporate affairs, and because Delaware is the preeminent state for publicly held corporations, Delaware law constitutes one major axis of this book. Another major axis of this book is the Model Business Corporation Act, which

---

3. *See* Melvin A. Eisenberg, The Structure of Corporation Law, 89 COLUM. L. REV. 461 (1989).

was originally promulgated, and is regularly revised, by the Committee on Corporate Laws of the American Bar Association's Business Law Section. Although the Model Act has no official status, it serves as the template for the statutes of a great many states. Recurring reference will also be made in this book to the California and New York corporate statutes, because as a result of their size and commercial significance, those states account for a significant portion of all corporations.

SECTION 5. ORGANIZING A CORPORATION

DEL. GEN. CORP. LAW §§ 101, 102, 103, 106, 107, 108, 109

[See Statutory Supplement]

MODEL BUS. CORP. ACT §§ 2.01, 2.02, 2.03, 2.05, 2.06

[See Statutory Supplement]

After the state of incorporation has been selected, the corporation must be organized (created) in that state by the incorporators, who may be either the prospective owners of the corporation or their agent.[4] The first, and basic, legal step in organizing a corporation is to file a certificate of incorporation in a designated office in the state in which the organizers have chosen to corporate. Once the certificate of incorporation has been filed, the corporation must issue stock to get its business up and running. However, the power to issue stock is normally vested in the board; the board, in turn, is normally elected by the shareholders; and until stock is issued, there are no shareholders.

There are two alternative mechanisms for solving this problem. Under the law of some states, such as New York, the corporation's incorporators have the powers of directors until directors are elected and the powers of shareholders until stock is issued. N.Y.Bus.Corp. Law §§ 404(a), 615(c). Under this approach, the incorporators will typically adopt by-laws, and elect initial directors to serve until the first annual meeting of shareholders. Under the law of other states, such as Delaware, the initial directors can be named in the corporation's certificate of incorporation. *See* Del.Gen.Corp.Law §§ 107, 108. If the

4. It is usually unnecessary to have more than one incorporator. For ease of exposition, however, in this Chapter the term *incorporators* will be used to mean either a single incorporator or several incorporators.

initial directors are named in the certificate of incorporation, the functions of the incorporators pass to the directors when the certificate is filed and recorded, and the directors, rather than the incorporators, adopt by laws. Del.Gen.Corp.Law §§ 107, 108(a). After the initial directors are named, either by the incorporators or in the certificate of incorporation, they will hold an organization meeting. A typical agenda for such a meeting is reflected in the Form of Minutes of Organization Meeting that follows this Note.

In connection with the issuance of stock, there is a crucial distinction between authorized stock and issued stock. An important function of a certificate of incorporation is to designate the classes of stock, and the number of shares of each class, that the corporation is authorized to issue. Only stock that has been authorized in the certificate of incorporation can be issued. If the corporation's authorized stock consists of one class of common stock, the certificate need only designate the number of authorized shares. If there is to be more than one class of stock, and particularly if there are to be one or more classes of preferred stock (that is, stock that carries a preference over common stock as to dividends, on liquidation, or both, the certificate of incorporation must either designate the terms of each class, or empower the board to issue portions of an authorized class of stock in series from time to time, and to designate the terms of each series as it is issued. Authorized stock that has not yet been issued is known as authorized but unissued stock. Authorized stock that has been issued is known as issued stock or outstanding stock. Sometimes a corporation repurchases stock that it has previously issued. Such stock may be referred to as treasury stock or as authorized and issued but not outstanding stock.

The power to issue authorized but unissued stock, and the price at which the stock will be issued, is vested in the board, subject only to very limited constraints. One constraint is that the board cannot issue more stock than is authorized in the certificate of incorporation. At common law, another constraint was that existing shareholders had the right to subscribe a proportionate part of a new issue. This is known as the preemptive right. The right was riddled with exceptions—for example, it did not apply to stock that was issued for property rather than cash. Modern statutes provide that shareholders have no preemptive rights unless the certificate of incorporation so provides. Few do. However, even where shareholders do not have a preemptive right the board may not issue stock on a non-pro-rata basis for the purpose of reallocating or perpetuating control. *See, e.g.*, Note on Condec v. Lunkenheimer, Chapter 5, section 1, infra; Schwartz v. Marien, 335 N.E.2d 334 (N.Y. 1975). The shareholders' right to prohibit a non-pro-rata stock issuance for an improper purpose is sometimes referred to as a quasi-preemptive right.

Normally, stock is issued by a corporation in a simultaneous exchange for cash, property, or services. In some cases, however, a would-be shareholder enters into a subscription agreement under which he agrees to purchase a corporation's stock when it is issued to him at a future date. Typically in such cases the corporation has not yet been formed, and the agreement is made on the would-be corporation's behalf by its incorporators. Agreements of this type are called preincorporation subscriptions.

There is a good deal of old law on various aspects of such agreements. The old rule was that a preincorporation subscription was only a continuing offer by the subscriber, and that a subscriber therefore was not bound if he timely revoked. Under that rule a subscriber could revoke his agreement until the moment of incorporation or, in the alternative, until the corporation, once formed, issued stock to the subscriber. There was an exception where the mutual promises of subscribers were expressed as consideration for each other. In that case, a contract was deemed to be formed immediately. In addition, subscription agreements entered into after the corporation was formed were treated as ordinary contracts, and raised no special problems of enforceability.

Modern corporate statutes have changed the treatment of preincorporation subscriptions. Most statutes now provide that preincorporation subscriptions are irrevocable for a specified period of time unless all the subscribers consent to a revocation or the agreement otherwise provides. *See*, *e.g.*, Del.Gen.Corp.Law § 165 (preincorporation subscription agreements irrevocable for six months except with the consent of all other subscribers); Model Act § 6.20(a) (same). Accordingly, under modern statutes the old law relating to subscriptions is of greatly diminished importance, and current cases on the subject are rare.

FORM OF MINUTES OF ORGANIZATION MEETING

[See Statutory Supplement]

FORM OF BY-LAWS

[See Statutory Supplement]

FORM OF STOCK CERTIFICATE

[See Statutory Supplement]

DEL. GEN. CORP. LAW § 109

[See Statutory Supplement]

MODEL BUS. CORP. ACT §§ 2.06, 10.20–10.21

[See Statutory Supplement]

SECTION 6. THE BASIC TYPES OF FINANCIAL SECURITIES

As will be seen, in the partnership form of doing business, the economic rights of owners are set forth in the partnership agreement (and in the absence of such an agreement default rules are provided by the state partnership law). In the corporate setting as well as the limited liability company the owners' rights are set forth in the company's articles of incorporation and articles of organization, respectively. In the corporation the owners are commonly referred to as stockholders or shareholders and in the limited liability company as members. An initial question for a corporation is how to finance its business. The three major modes of corporate finance are common stock, preferred stock and debt. The following describes the basic features of typical equity financing instruments used in the corporation. The features common to debt are discussed in the next section.

1. *Common Stock.* A cornerstone of corporate law is that all shares have the same rights, privileges and preferences as other shares, unless the articles of incorporation otherwise provide. The most basic form of ownership is represented by common shares. Traditionally, shares of common stock are conceived as ownership or *equity* interests in the corporation, so that the body of common shareholders are the corporation's owners. Normally, but not invariably, common stock carries the right to vote in the election of directors and certain other matters. Typically, or at least often, dividends are paid on common stock, but many corporations do not pay dividends, and in any event whether dividends are paid, and if so in what amount, is generally in the discretion of the board. As a result, common stock has no fixed claim on the corporation. Partly for this reason, modern financial theory often conceives of common stock as ultimate or *residual* ownership. "Common shareholders are often thought of as the owners of the firm or as the holders of the *equity* interest in the firm.... The equity interest is sometimes usefully thought of as the *residual* interest—the claim to what is left after all senior claimants have been satisfied." W. Klein & J. Coffee, Business Organization and Finance 286 (11th ed. 2010) (emphasis added). The "senior claimants" to which Coffee & Klein refer are debt and preferred stock.

2. *Preferred Stock.* Preferred stock is a hybrid that combines the ownership element of common stock and the senior nature of debt. The basic elements of preferred stock are described as follows in Hunt, Williams & Donaldson, Basic Business Finance 358–61 (5th ed. 1974):

> From the purely legal point of view ... preferred stock is a type of ownership and thus takes a classification similar to that of the common stock.... Unlike [a] bond, ... preferred stock does not contain any promise of repayment of the original investment; and as far as the shareholders are concerned, this must be considered as a permanent investment for the life of the company. Further, there is no legal obligation to pay a fixed rate of return on the investment.
>
> The special character of the preferred stock lies in its relationship to the common stock. When a preferred stock is used as a part of the corporate capital structure, the rights and responsibilities of the owners as the residual claimants to the asset values and earning power of the business no longer apply equally to all shareholders. Two types of owners emerge, representing a voluntary subdivision of the overall ownership privileges. Specifically, the common shareholders agree that the preferred shareholder shall have "preference" or first claim in the event that the directors are able and willing to pay a dividend. In the case of what is termed a nonparticipating or *straight preferred stock*, which is the most frequent type, the extent of this priority is a fixed percentage of the par value of the stock or a fixed number of dollars per share in the case of stock without a nominal or par value....
>
> In most cases the prior position of preferred stock also extends to the disposition of assets in the event of liquidation of the business. Again, the priority is only with reference to the common stock and does not affect the senior position of creditors in any way....*

Typically, preferred stock carries a dividend that is payable periodically—often, quarterly—in the board's discretion. Thus the most obvious difference between debt and preferred stock is that debtholders have a fixed claim on the corporation for interest and principal, while preferred shareholders normally have no fixed claims for distributions. Instead, the claims of preferred stock for distributions are only contingent: *If* the corporation proposes to pay a dividend on common, *then* it must first pay a designated dividend to the preferred. *If* the corporation liquidates, *then* before it distributes anything to the common it must satisfy the preferred's liquidation preference.

Often, the preferred's dividend preference is "cumulative"—that is, no dividend can be paid on common unless all prior dividends on the preferred have been paid. (If a preferred is noncumulative, a dividend can be paid on common as long as the current dividend on the preferred is paid.) Often too, preferred is given the right to vote on the election of directors if, but only if, preferred dividends are in default for a designated number of periods.

---

* As quoted in V. Brudney & W. Bratton, Corporate Finance—Cases and Material 335–36 (4th ed. 1993).

3. *Convertibles, Classified Stock, and Derivatives.* In the modern world, the basic elements of common stock, preferred stock, and debt are often disaggregated, and their fragments are combined to design more exotic corporate securities. For example, preferred stock is often issued in several classes, and common stock may be issued in several classes as well (*classified common*). In such cases, each class enjoys somewhat different rights than the others in respect of voting, dividend, or liquidation rights, or all three. Many preferred stocks, and some bonds, are made convertible into common stock at the option of the holder, on specified terms. Furthermore, new types of securities may be "derived" from common stock, in the sense that although the securities are not themselves common stock, their value largely depends on the value of a corporation's common stock and on the terms of their relationship to the common stock. The simplest example is a "right" or "warrant," which is a security issued by the corporation that gives the holder a right or option to purchase common stock on specified terms.

INTRODUCTION TO TYPES OF DEBT AND DEBT COVENANTS

Debt is a fixed claim against the corporation for principal and interest. The major types of corporate debt are *trade debt, bank debt, bonds, debentures*, and *notes.*

(a) *Trade debt.* When a business purchases goods or services, payment is typically not due for thirty, sixty, or ninety days. Trade debt consists principally of amounts that a corporation owes for such goods and services at any point in time. Trade debt appears on a corporation's balance sheet as Accounts Payable.

(b) *Bank debt.* A business will often be financed in significant part by commercial-bank loans. Bank loans appear on a corporation's balance sheet under captions such as Loans Payable.

(c) *Bonds and debentures.* Another method of financing a corporation is to issue bonds or debentures. Essentially, bonds and debentures are promises, embodied in an instrument, to repay amounts that the firm has borrowed on a long-term basis, typically by selling the bonds on the general market or on some special market. Bonds appear on a corporation's balance sheet under captions such as Bonds Payable, or under a caption that describes specific bond issues, such as 7.5% Senior Debentures. Unlike bank loans, bonds and debentures normally represent money borrowed from the public, or at least from a significant group of lenders or investors. "As a matter of historical practice, bonds and debentures are long term obligations issued under indentures, bonds generally being secured obligations and debentures being unsecured obligations." W. Bratton, Corporate Finance—Cases and Materials 240 (6th ed. 2008).

> A bond [or] debenture . . . is simply a promise by the borrower to pay a specified amount on a specified date, together with interest at specified times, on the terms and subject to the conditions spelled out in a governing indenture. . . . Bonds [and] debentures . . . are, then . . . promissory notes issued pursuant to and

> governed by longer contracts [known as indentures]. Some of the governing terms and conditions will be set out on the face of the [bond or debenture]. Most terms, however, will be in the [indenture] that governs the instrument and will be merely referred to on its face. The note incorporates the contract by reference....
>
> It is the practice in both financial and legal writing to use "bond" as a generic term for all long term debt securities....

Id. at 240. Bratton describes an *indenture* as follows:

> An indenture is a contract entered into between the borrowing corporation and a trustee. The trustee administers the payments of interest and principal, and monitors and enforces compliance with other obligations on behalf of the bondholders as a group. The indenture defines the assorted obligations of the borrower, the rights and remedies of the holders of the bonds, and the role of the trustee.
>
> The borrower contracts with a trustee rather than directly with the holders of the bonds so as to permit the bonds to be sold in small denominations to large numbers of scattered investors. Given widespread ownership in small amounts, unilateral monitoring and enforcement by each holder is not cost effective. The device of the trust solves this problem....
>
> The "bonds" and the "indenture" need to be conceptually distinguished. The bonds set out a promise to pay that runs to the holders of the bonds. The indenture is a bundle of additional promises (including a backup promise to pay) that run to the trustee. The bondholders are third party beneficiaries of the promises in the indenture. Even though the promises in the bonds run directly to the holders, the bonds are subject to the indenture and therefore may be enforced directly by the holders only to the extent that the indenture allows. Indentures generally constrain the unilateral enforcement rights of small holders, channeling enforcement through the central agency of the trustee. The device of the trust indenture, then, not only facilitates enforcement by the widely scattered holders, but also restrains such enforcement. It facilitates borrowing in small amounts from large numbers of widely scattered lenders not only by constraining the issuer as against the holders, but by protecting the issuer from the holders.

Id. at 241–242.

(d) *Notes*. There is no legally recognized distinction between bonds and debentures, on the one hand, and notes, on the other. However, "Under the historical practice, notes may be long term or short term obligations, but in either case are not issued pursuant to an indenture. Recent practice has changed this. Today, 'notes' often are issued pursuant to indentures as unsecured long term obligations. But they tend to be intermediate term securities, coming due in ten years or less, where 'debentures' tend to mature in ten years or more." Id. at 240.

SECTION 7. THE SEDUCTIVE QUALITIES OF DEBT

A question that first arises when the corporation is formed and recurs throughout the life of the corporation is whether the corporation and its owners are well advised to include debt within its capital structure. As will be seen in the material that follows, debt has many virtues; but like good food, too much of it can lead to serious adverse consequences.

John D. Ayer, Guide To Finance For Lawyers, 295–297

(2001).

Introduction

Skeeter, your old college roommate, has just started work in the Investor Relations Office at WidgetCo. Although he cheerfully admits he does not know much of anything about finance, he has a pleasant manner that soothes customers on the telephone. Meanwhile, he figures the new job will give him a chance to play catch-up with some of his classmates and their sparkling new MBAs. So, you are not surprised by his enthusiasm when he comes charging through your door, eager to tell you about his latest insight.

"It's amazing," he says, "I cannot understand how everyone overlooked this so far."

You raise an eyebrow, which is all the encouragement he needs to continue.

"Last year, we had earnings of $100. We are a highly stable company, so we pay it all out to shareholders. We have 10 shares, each selling for $100, which implies a market capitalization of $1,000. Shareholders, then, get $10 a share, which translates into a rate of return of 10 percent."

Skeeter pauses to let you admire these marvels.

"But," he begins again, "we can *borrow* money at eight percent."

He pauses for dramatic effect. The barest flicker on your forehead is enough to set him off again.

"Don't you see?" He continues. "We should *borrow* $500 in perpetuity. Then we will use the $500 to buy back five shares. We will have to pay $40 a year in debt service. That leaves us $60 a year to distribute among our five shares of stock. At 10 percent, that means that we have increased the value of a share from $100 to $120, and the total market capitalization from $500 to $600—a 20 percent gain. It is like magic! I have asked for an appointment with the CEO so I can tell him all about it first thing in the morning!"

But even has he spoke, Skeeter's expression turned forlorn.

"There is only one puzzle," he said sadly.

Again, an eyebrow is enough.

"I mean," he continued, "if it works for five shares, why shouldn't we go the whole way? Why not retire 10 shares and borrow $1,000? We will pay $80 a year in interest. That leaves us $20 a year in return on"—and here he looked genuinely baffled"—well, on no investment at all."

Skeeter sounds like a good kid, and the chances are he will figure out before making a fool of himself in front of the CEO that $20/0 = an infinite return, which is too good to be true even in the widget business. To start with his last, absurd, example: if WidgetCo is financed with *all* debt and *no* equity, then the debt *is* the *equity*, and will demand a corresponding return—in this case, 10 percent. There can be no triumph of form over substance here; equity is the one who bears the equity risk, no matter what the name.

As to the less extreme case, if Skeeter is in error, he has the excuse of good company. Many investors, older and wiser than he, have believed that you could increase firm value by increasing leverage (at least up to a point). Old-time financial analysts, including the Securities Exchange Commission, expended valuable resources trying to identify the "optimal" debt-equity ratio—i.e., the mix of debt and equity that would maximize firm value.

Enter the great revolutionaries of modern finance theory, Franco Modigliani and Merton Miller (MM). . . . MM argued that, under clean-test-tube assumptions, . . . the value of the firm is the value of the assets, and you cannot change the value of the "liability/net-worth" side of the balance sheet by monkeying around with the . . . [ratio of debt to equity].[2]

MM understood, of course, that a change in leverage may change the *gross* returns payable to shareholders. Thus, in Skeeter's first example above, Skeeter showed how to increase the payout from $10 a share to $12, but what Skeeter overlooked (as MM argue) is that we have also changed the *risk* of the equity investment.

Recall the first rule of leverage: equity comes behind debt. Equity of a leveraged company is always more risky than equity of an unleveraged company, because debt gets paid first, leaving equity to get paid if (and only if) there is enough to trickle down. Equity investors, faced with a higher risk, will demand a higher rate of return, and a higher rate of return translates into a lower share price. For example, suppose the rate on WidgetCo equity rose from 10 percent (unleveraged) to 12 percent (leveraged). Then the value of a (leveraged) WidgetCo share would be $12/(0.12) = $10, just as before. . . .

An Arbitrage Proof of MM

There are many ways to demonstrate the MM argument. One is to consider the possibility of *arbitrage*. We have often seen that if two identical assets bear different prices, then there is a profit for an

2. Franco Modigliani and Merton H. Miller, *The Cost of Capital, Corporate Finance and the Theory of Investment*, 38 AMER. ECON. REV. 261 (1958).

instant, no-risk (arbitrage) profit, and that such profits do not exist except in fleeting moments of transition.

We can apply arbitrage analysis to the MM insight. Take the case of Imogen, an investor, who is thinking about a flutter on Skeeter's WidgetCo. As a benchmark, suppose she can buy *the whole company*—which is to say, all of the equity, and (if there is any), all of the debt. In that case, surely, her only concern will be the asset return, and that she will accept an aggregate rate of 10 percent. If WidgetCo earns $100 a year (as above), and if it is all equity financed, she will be willing to pay $1,000 for all the equity.

But, supposing WidgetCo is financed with $500 of debt at eight percent, she can get $40 of the cash flow for $500 by purchasing debt. To get the other $60, she must buy all the equity. But it cannot be that she will be willing to pay more than $500 for the equity; otherwise, she would be paying different prices for the same cash flows, violating the arbitrage rule. . . .

NOTE ON THE TAX SHIELD OF DEBT

In their path breaking articles supporting the irrelevance of the firm's capital structure and dividend policies on the value of the firm, Modigliani and Miller make several assumptions. Among their assumptions is there are no taxes. Ah, heaven! What is the impact of taxes on how managers and investors approach the choice between debt and equity in the financing choices facing the firm?

Corporations are taxpayers and, when they distribute their earnings and profits, the receiving shareholders are taxed on the amount distributed to them. We therefore see that a downside of the corporate form is double taxation; the corporation pays a tax on its profits and shareholders pay a tax on dividends distributed from those profits. There are some notable qualifications to the statement that business entities face double taxation of their profits. First, many shareholders are not taxable entities because they are charitable institutions, pension funds and the like. Second, as later material will show, the tax laws allow small business entities to enjoy pass-through treatment so that the business itself is only a reporting entity but is not a tax payer. For example, a partnership files only an information return with the Internal Revenue Service but is not taxed on its income; instead, its profits are attributed to each of its partners who are taxed on the amount attributed to the partner regardless of whether any of the profits was distributed to the partner. The discussion that follows focuses heavily on the tax laws treatment of debt which is the same for all taxable business entities. In considering the preference of debt over equity, the key factor is that under the Internal Revenue Code interest is a deductible expense whereas dividends are not. As will be seen, this distinction dramatically tilts the choice of financing toward debt and substantially qualifies the insights of Modigliani and Miller. To illustrate this point, assume that Alpha Corporation and Beta Corporation are identical except that Alpha has no debt and capital of $100,000 (10,000 shares) whereas Beta has issued $50,000 in bonds (interest rate of 8%) and $50,000 in stock (5,000 shares), that each company earned $20,000 before interest and taxes, and that the applicable corporate tax rate is 50 percent. Assume each pursues a dividend policy of distributing all profits to owners. Under these assumptions, the following are the income statements for the two firms:

	Alpha	Beta
Income before Taxes and Interest	$20,000	$20,000
Less: Interest		4,000
Taxable Income	20,000	16,000
Taxes	10,000	8,000
Net Income	10,000	8,000

First observe that Alpha's taxes are $2000 higher than those of Beta. What explains this? Second, pursuant to M & M irrelevance theorem the total cost of capital should be the same for both Alpha and Beta. If we assume that Alpha's cost of capital is 12 percent then the weighted average cost of capital for Beta would be 12 percent as well. Since bonds bear a market rate of 8 percent this means that the equity would carry a discount rate of 16 percent. So viewed, the total value of Alpha is $10,000 ÷ 12% = $83, 333. In comparison, the value of Beta is the value of the bonds, $50,000, plus the value of the equity, $8,000 ÷ 16% = $50,000, for a total firm value of $100,000.

> Looking at the figures from another perspective, we can say that the effect of the corporation income tax is to make the government a 50 percent partner in the equity claims, but not in the debt claims, in the corporation. Thus, the government's claim in Corporation A[lpha] is to half of $100,000, or $50,000, while its claim in B[eta] is to half of only $50,000, or $25,000. The True complexities of the corporation income tax . . . would require some modifications and qualifications if one sought complete precision in this analysis, but those would be minor quibbles. They would not affect the basic point of this analysis, which is that the securities of the corporation using debt are significantly more valuable than those of the corporation using (less or) no debt and the difference is attributable solely to the apparent tax advantages of debt. This is the essence of the view—reflected in the "capital structure puzzle" phrase—that American corporations should be more highly leveraged than they are.

William A. Klein, John C. Coffee, Jr. & Frank Partnoy, Business Organization and Finance Legal and Economic Principles 367 (11th ed. 2010).

NOTE ON LEVERAGE AND THE RISK OF FINANCIAL DISTRESS

The preceding note demonstrates that in a world with taxation of corporate earnings in which interest is a deductible business expense and dividends are not deductible, the value of the firm is increased by the introduction of debt to its capital structure. But can too much of a good thing be harmful?

> If there is a possibility of bankruptcy, and if administrative and other costs associated with bankruptcy are significant, the leveraged firm may be less attractive to investors than the unlevered one. With perfect capital markets, zero bankruptcy costs are assumed. If the firm goes bankrupt, assets presumably can be sold at their economic values with no liquidating or legal costs involved. Proceeds from the sale are distributed according to the priority of claims on assets ... If capital markets are less than perfect, however, there may be administrative costs, and assets may have to be liquidated at less than their economic values. These administrative costs and the "shortfall" in liquidating values from economic value represent a drain on the system from the viewpoint of the debt and equity holders....
>
> In the event of bankruptcy, security holders as a whole receive less than they would have in the absence of bankruptcy costs. To the extent that the levered firm has a greater possibility in bankruptcy than the unlevered one, it would be a less attractive investment, all other things being the same. The possibility of bankruptcy is not a linear function of the debt-to-equity ratio but rather increases at an increasing rate beyond some threshold. As a result, the expected cost of bankruptcy also increases in this accelerating manner and would be expected to have a corresponding negative effect on the value of the firm.
>
> Put another way, investors are likely to penalize the price of the stock as leverage increases.... As debt is added, the required rate of return rises, and this increment represents a financial-risk premium. In the absence of bankruptcy costs, the required rate of return would rise in a linear manner according to M & M ... However, allowing for bankruptcy costs and an increasing probability of bankruptcy with increasing financial leverage, the required rate of return on equity would be expected to rise at an increasing rate beyond some point. At first there might be a negligible probability of bankruptcy, so there would be little or no penalty. As financial leverage increases, so too does the penalty. For extreme leverage, the penalty becomes very substantial indeed.

James C. Van Horne & John M. Wachowicz, Jr., Fundamentals of Financial Management 459–60 (13th Ed. 2008). Professors Van Horne and Wachowicz also point out that monitoring costs for debt holders increases with the amount of debt; these costs rise at an increasing rate as the amount of leverage increases.

SECTION 8. EQUITABLE SUBORDINATION OF SHAREHOLDER CLAIMS

NOTE ON EQUITABLE SUBORDINATION OF SHAREHOLDER CLAIMS

1. *Equitable Subordination.* Under the doctrine of equitable subordination, when a corporation is in bankruptcy, debt claims that a controlling shareholder has against the corporation may be subordinated to the claims of other persons, including the claims of preferred shareholders, on various equitable grounds. The doctrine of equitable subordination is often referred to as the "Deep Rock" doctrine, named after the corporation—a subsidiary—in the seminal case of Taylor v. Standard Gas & Electric Co., 306 U.S. 307, 59 S.Ct. 543, 83 L.Ed. 669 (1939). The Court in that case subordinated the parent's claim, as a creditor of the subsidiary, to the claims of other creditors and preferred stockholders of the subsidiary, because of the parent's improper management of the subsidiary for the parent's benefit, and because the subsidiary had been inadequately capitalized. See also Pepper v. Litton, 308 U.S. 295, 310, 60 S.Ct. 238, 246, 84 L.Ed. 281 (1939); Hackney & Benson, Shareholder Liability for Inadequate Capital, 43 U.Pitt.L.Rev. 837 (1982).

In Gannett Co. v. Larry, 221 F.2d 269 (2d Cir.1955), Gannett Company was in the newspaper-publishing business. Berwin Paper was also in the business of publishing a newspaper. To ensure a supply of newsprint in view of a threatened shortage, Gannett purchased all the stock of Berwin Paper, and converted Berwin from a publisher to a newsprint supplier. Gannett lent substantial sums to Berwin for that purpose. The threatened newsprint shortage never materialized. As a result, by 1952 the newsprint market had changed completely, and Berwin was operating at a loss. In 1953, Berwin became insolvent, and a trustee in bankruptcy was appointed. The court subordinated Gannett's claim for the sums it had loaned to Berwin to the claims of other creditors. "[T]he losses suffered by Berwin were suffered, not in an attempt by Gannett primarily to make the subsidiary a financially profitable proposition, but to turn it into a source of newsprint, of no interest to the other creditors—unless financially profitable—but of distinct interest to Gannett, whether or not financially profitable, because of Gannett's newsprint shortage. Because of this factor.... 'It would be unfair to allow the claim of Gannett on a parity with other creditors who lacked the interest which Gannett had in Berwin's disastrous experiment in the newsprint field.' In such circumstances, proof of fraud or illegality is not necessary."

2. *Comparison With Piercing.* Hackney & Benson comment that "As compared with denying to a shareholder his privilege of limited

liability, the equitable remedy of subordination is much less drastic: it simply takes an investment already made, and denies it the status of a creditor's claim on a parity with outside creditors, whereas imposing liability for corporate debts undermines the essential premise of limited liability—that a shareholder's risk is limited to the amount of his investment.... It is logical, therefore, for the courts to have found it fair to subordinate a controlling person's claim based upon a lesser evidence of misuse of the corporate form than what is required to impose affirmative personal liability for all corporate obligations. Furthermore, if actual shareholder capital were so small as to result in treating a shareholder loan as equity, then the equity as supplemented by the subordinated loan may be deemed an adequate cushion to support limited liability. Accordingly, inadequate capitalization may result in subordination when it does not necessarily require imposition of affirmative liability.'' Hackney & Benson, supra, at 882.

3. *Undercapitalization*. Undercapitalization plays an important role in equitable subordination, as it does in piercing the corporate veil. In Arnold v. Phillips, 117 F.2d 497 (5th Cir.1941), cert. denied 313 U.S. 583, 61 S.Ct. 1102, 85 L.Ed. 1539 (1941), Arnold formed a brewery company with capital stock of $50,000, paid for in cash. He then lent the brewery $75,000, so that it would have enough to start operations. The business began to lose heavily, and Arnold advanced large additional sums. Eventually, the brewery went into bankruptcy liquidation. In the bankruptcy proceedings, a mortgage held by Arnold to secure his loans was held invalid on the ground of inadequate capitalization insofar as the mortgage represented money Arnold loaned the brewery to build and equip its plant, but valid as to subsequent advances made after the brewery became a going concern. The court said:

> The two series of advances differ materially as respects their nature and purpose. Those made before the enterprise was launched were, as the district court found, really capital. Although the charter provided for no more capital than $50,000, what it took to build the plant and equip it was a permanent investment, in its nature capital.... There can be little doubt that what he contributed to the plant was actually intended to be capital, notwithstanding the charter was not amended and demand notes were taken....
>
> After two years of prosperity, with the original capital thus enlarged demonstrated to be sufficient, with a book surplus of nearly $100,000 after payment of large salaries and dividends in the form of interest, there arose a situation very different from that in the beginning. Adversity then occurring raised a problem not different from that which commonly faces a corporation having losses. It may borrow to meet its needs. Had this corporation borrowed of a bank upon the security of the plant, the debt would no doubt be valid. What would render it invalid when Arnold furnished the money? ...

> . . . It would be hard to say in this case that $50,000 was not a substantial capital, and impossible so to say after holding that the real capital was $125,500, though some was irregularly paid in [as a purported loan].

4. *Common Pool.* If a parent and a subsidiary or two affiliated corporations are both bankrupt, the courts sometimes consolidate the assets and liabilities of the several corporations into a common pool available to the creditors. See In re Seatrade Corp., 255 F.Supp. 696 (S.D.N.Y.1966), aff'd sub nom. Chemical Bank New York Trust Co. v. Kheel, 369 F.2d 845 (2d Cir.); Landers, A Unified Approach to Parent, Subsidiary, and Affiliate Questions in Bankruptcy, 42 U.Chi.L.Rev. 589, 629–51 (1975).

BENJAMIN v. DIAMOND, 563 F.2d 692, 699–702 (5th Cir.1977). "[T]hree conditions must be satisfied before exercise of the power of equitable subordination is appropriate. (i) The claimant [who may be an owner, director, or officer of the bankrupt corporation] must have engaged in some type of inequitable conduct. . . . (ii) The misconduct must have resulted in injury to the creditors of the bankrupt or conferred an unfair advantage on the claimant. . . . (iii) Equitable subordination of the claim must not be inconsistent with the provisions of the Bankruptcy Act. . . .

"In determining whether these three conditions are satisfied three principles must be kept in mind. The first is that inequitable conduct directed against the bankrupt or its creditors may be sufficient to warrant subordination of a claim irrespective of whether it was related to the acquisition or assertion of that claim. . . .

"The second principle is that a claim or claims should be subordinated only to the extent necessary to offset the harm which the bankrupt and its creditors suffered on account of the inequitable conduct. For example, if a claimant guilty of misconduct asserts two claims, each worth $10,000, and the injury he inflicted on the bankrupt or its creditors amounted to $10,000, only one of his claims should be subordinated. Since the exercise of the subordination power is governed by equitable principles, . . . subordination of the other claim would be improper.

"The third guiding principle relates to allocation of the burden of proof. . . .

". . . To constitute the type of challenge contemplated by the Court, an objection resting on equitable grounds cannot be merely formal, but rather must contain some substantial factual basis to support its allegation of impropriety. . . . The proper rule is that

> the claimant's verified proof of claim obliges the objecting trustee to come forward with enough substantiations to overcome the claimant's *prima facie* case and thus compel [the claimant] to actually prove the validity and honesty of his claim.

3A J. Moore & L. King, Collier on Bankruptcy, § 63.06, at 1785 (14th ed. 1976) . . .

UNIFORM FRAUDULENT TRANSFER ACT § 4(a)

[See Statutory Supplement]

BANKRUPTCY CODE § 548

[See Statutory Supplement]

SECTION 9. REQUISITES FOR VALID ACTION BY THE BOARD

DEL. GEN. CORP. LAW §§ 141(b), (f), (i), 229

[See Statutory Supplement]

MODEL BUS. CORP. ACT §§ 8.20, 8.21, 8.22, 8.23, 8.24

[See Statutory Supplement]

NOTE ON REQUISITES FOR VALID ACTION BY THE BOARD

A single director normally has no power to either act for the corporation or to cause the corporation to act. Instead, directors normally can only act as a body. The validity of an action by the board of directors depends on the requirements for meetings, notice, quorum, and voting. These rules can be considered at two levels. At the first level are rules that set out the formalities for board action. At the second level are rules concerning the consequence of noncompliance with the first-level rules.

Level 1: The Governing Rules. (Unless otherwise indicated, the following account is based on predominant statutory patterns.)

(i) *Meetings.* Usually, directors must act at a duly convened meeting at which a quorum is present. Most statutes provide that a meeting of the board can be conducted by conference phone or by any other means of communication through which all participating directors can simultaneously hear each other. In addition, most statutes permit the board to act by unanimous written consent without a meeting.

(ii) *Notice.* Formal notice is not required for a regularly scheduled board meeting, because if the meeting is a regularly scheduled one, the directors are already on notice of its date, time, and place. In the case of a special meeting, notice of date, time, and place must be given to every director. The notice need not state the purpose of a meeting, unless the certificate of incorporation or the bylaws otherwise provide. The statutes usually provide that notice must be given a stated period in advance of the meeting, but then add that the stated period may be made shorter or longer by the certificate of incorporation or by-laws. Most statutes provide that notice can be waived in writing before or after a meeting and that attendance at a meeting constitutes a waiver unless the director attends merely to protest against holding the meeting.

(iii) *Quorum.* A quorum of the board consists of a majority of the full board, that is, a majority of the authorized number of directors—not simply a majority of the directors who attend the meeting or a majority of the directors then in office (which may be less than the authorized number of directors because of board vacancies). Most statutes permit the certificate of incorporation or bylaws to require a greater number for a quorum than a majority of the full board. A substantial minority of the statutes, including the Delaware statute and the Model Act, permit the certificate or bylaws to set a lower number, but usually no less than one-third of the full board.

(iv) *Voting.* Assuming that a quorum is present when a vote is taken, the affirmative vote of a majority of those present, not simply a majority of those voting, is required for action. Most statutes provide that the articles or bylaws can require a super-majority vote for board action.

Level 2: Consequences of Noncompliance. The consequences of noncompliance with the requisites for board action are not always clear. In publicly held corporations, where bureaucratic order usually prevails, an uncured defect of notice, the lack of a quorum, or the lack of the requisite affirmative vote will usually render board action ineffective. However, in close corporations, where formalities are seldom followed, the results of a failure to observe proper formalities are less clear-cut. Unless otherwise indicated, the balance of this Note concerns cases involving close corporations.

(i) *Unanimous Explicit Although Informal Approval.* Some older cases held that informal approval by directors—that is, an approval that is given without the requisite formalities—is ineffective even if the approval is explicit and unanimous. *See, e.g.*, Baldwin v. Canfield, 1 N.W. 261, 270 (Minn. 1879). These cases are of doubtful validity today. More characteristic is Gerard v. Empire Square Realty Co., 187 N.Y.S. 306 (N.Y. App. Div. 1921). Plaintiff brought an action against several related corporations to recover damages for breach of an employment contract. The corporations' shares were owned by five persons, all of whom were directors. Because of dissension, no shareholders' or directors' meetings were held, but there was evidence that each director had separately agreed to the hiring of the plaintiff. The court held that on these facts the corporations were bound:

> I think that under the circumstances of the case we are considering, where the directors own all the capital stock of the corporations, where they are members of the same family but so at variance that directors' and stockholders' meetings are not held, their action, concurred in by all, although separately and not as a body, binds the corporation. We must recognize the fact that [the business of a corporation is], perhaps the majority of instances, conducted by officers and directors little informed in the law of corporations, who often act informally, sometimes without meetings or even by-laws. To hold that in all instances technical conformity to the requirements of the law of corporations is a condition to a valid action by the directors, would be to lay down a rule of law which could be used as a trap for the unwary who deal with corporations, and to permit corporations sometimes to escape liability to which an individual in the same circumstances would be subjected.

The results in this area are too disparate to be captured by a single clear rule. However, most modern courts probably would hold that unanimous explicit but informal approval by all the directors is effective where a person who has contracted with a corporate officer has been led to regard his transaction with the corporation as valid, and all the shareholders are directors or have acquiesced either in the transaction or in a past practice of informal board action. *See* Anderson v. K.G. Moore, Inc., 376 N.E.2d 1238 (Mass.App.1978), cert. denied, 439 U.S. 1116, 99 S.Ct. 1020, 59 L.Ed.2d 74 (1979).

(ii) *Explicit Approval by a Majority of the Directors Coupled with Acquiescence by Remaining Directors.* Suppose that a majority of the directors, acting without a formal board meeting, explicitly approved a transaction, while the remaining directors knew of the transaction and took no action to disavow it, so that they may be said to have acquiesced. The difference between this case and the case in which all the directors explicitly but informally approve a transaction is not very significant. Accordingly, the courts will normally treat the two cases alike. *See, e.g.,* Winchell v. Plywood Corp., 85 N.E.2d 313 (Mass. 1949). The same result will normally follow even if there is no explicit approval by a majority of the directors, but all the directors acquiesce. *See e.g.*, Juergens v. Venture Capital Corp., 295 N.E.2d 398 (Mass. App. 1973); Pierce v. Astoria Fish Factors, Inc., 640 P.2d 40 (Wash.App. 1982).

(iii) *Majority Approval or Acquiescence.* Suppose that a majority of the directors of a corporation approve a transaction, explicitly or by acquiescence, but the remaining directors lack knowledge of the transaction. Some courts have refused to hold the corporation liable under these circumstances. *See, e.g.*, Hurley v. Ornsteen, 42 N.E.2d 273 (Mass. 1942). Other courts have held the corporation liable if the shareholders acquiesced in the transaction, or if the shareholders or the remaining directors acquiesced in a practice of informal action by the directors. One theory is that if the shareholders have tolerated informal action by the directors over a period of time, they have by acquiescence authorized the directors to act in that manner. *See, e.g.*, Holy Cross Gold Mining & Milling Co. v. Goodwin, 223 P. 58 (Colo. 1924).

(iv) *Unanimous written consent.* Finally, modern statutory rules provide that the board can act by written written consent even without a meeting.[5]

NOTE ON BOARD COMMITTEES

Boards of publicly held corporations often delegate significant authority to committees. The notice, quorum, and voting rules applicable to committees mirror those applicable to the board itself. At one time, the most prominent board committee was the executive committee, which typically was given most of the powers of the board between board meetings, subject to stated limits. Executive committees, while undoubtedly still important, have fallen in prominence. The Conference Board, 34th Annual Board of Directors Survey 18 (2010) reported that as of 2007, only 42% of surveyed corporations had executive committees. Today, the most important committees are the oversight committees—in particular, the audit committee, the compensation committee, the nominating committee, and the corporate-governance committee. These committees will be discussed in detail in Chapter 5.

SECTION 10. THE NORMAL REQUISITES FOR VALID SHAREHOLDER ACTION

DEL. GEN. CORP. LAW §§ 211, 213, 214, 216, 222, 228

[See Statutory Supplement]

---

5. In Village of Brown Deer v. City of Milwaukee, 114 N.W.2d 493 (Wis. 1962), cert. denied 371 U.S. 902, 83 S.Ct. 205, 9 L.Ed.2d 164 (1962), the court stated that, "The legislature has said that the corporation could act informally, without a meeting, by obtaining the consent in writing of all of the directors. In our opinion, this pronouncement has preempted the field and prohibits corporations from acting informally without complying with the statute." However, in *Brown Deer* apparently only a majority of the directors knew of the transaction in question, so there was no unanimous approval, formal or informal. Other cases decided in states that have unanimous-written-consent statutes have held that the corporation was bound by unanimous informal consent. See Note, Corporations: When Informal Action by Corporate Directors Will Be Permitted to Bind the Corporation, 53 B.U.L.Rev. 101, 120 (1973).

REV. MODEL BUS. CORP. ACT §§ 7.01, 7.02, 7.03–7.07, 7.21, 7.25–7.28

[See Statutory Supplement]

NOTE ON THE NORMAL REQUISITES FOR VALID SHAREHOLDER ACTION

1. *Notice of Meeting.* Shareholders normally take action at an annual or special meeting (although if certain conditions are met shareholders can act by written consent, see below). Notice of place, time, and date is required for the annual meeting of shareholders and for any special meeting. The notice of a special meeting must also describe the purpose for which the meeting is called. Under most state statutes, the notice of an annual meeting must describe the matters to be acted upon only in certain cases—for example, when it is proposed to amend the certificate of incorporation, sell substantially all of the corporation's assets, engage in a merger, or dissolve. Some state statutes, and the federal Proxy Rules, also require a description of purpose in the notice of an annual meeting. However, the Proxy Rules do not apply to all corporations. See Chapter 6.

Because the identity of the shareholders of a publicly held corporation constantly undergoes constant change, normally notice of a meeting is given to those persons who are shareholders of record on a designated date prior to the meeting—the *record date*—not to those persons who are record or beneficial owners on the actual date of the meeting. A record date is normally fixed in the by-laws or by the board, within prescribed statutory limits. If a record date is not fixed in this manner, the statutes usually provide that the record date will be the day of, or the business day preceding, the day on which the notice of meeting is sent. Under an older alternative procedure that is still sanctioned in some statutes, but is generally regarded as archaic, the corporation can close its stock-transfer books as of a given date, and give notice of a shareholders' meeting only to those persons who were record holders on the date the books were closed.

Section 213 of the Delaware General Corporation Law and Section 7.07 of the Model Act were recently amended to provide that the board can set two separate record dates—one record date that determines which shareholders are entitled notice of a meeting, and another later record date that determines which shareholders can vote at the meeting. (These revisions to the Delaware statute and the Model Act are intended to deal with the problem of empty voting, discussed in Chapter 5, Section 2.

2. *Quorum.* Under most of the statutes, a majority of the shares entitled to vote is necessary for a quorum unless the certificate of incorporation sets a higher or lower figure. A substantial majority of the statutes provide that the certificate cannot set a quorum lower

than one-third of the shares entitled to vote. Most of the remaining statutes set no minimum.

3. *Voting.* (i) *Ordinary matters.* Under most statutes, the affirmative vote of a majority of the shares represent (in person or by proxy) at a meeting is required for shareholder action on ordinary matters. Under some statutes, however, only the affirmative vote of a majority of those voting is required. If a statute requires the affirmative vote of a majority of those present, an abstention effectively counts as a negative vote. Virtually all the statutes permit the certificate of incorporation to set a higher vote than would otherwise be required. Under some of the statutes, a certificate amendment that adds a provision requiring a higher-than-normal vote may be adopted only by the same vote as that required under the amendment.

(ii) *Fundamental changes.* A group of actions known as fundamental changes—amendment of the certificate of incorporation, merger, sale of substantially all assets, and dissolution—often require approval by a majority or sometimes two-thirds of the outstanding voting shares, rather than a majority of those present or voting at the meeting. However, the Model Act requires approval or fundamental changes by only a majority of the shares voting, provided a majority of the outstanding shares are present at the meeting.

(iii) *Written consent.* Most statutes provide that the shareholders can act by written consent, without a meeting, if certain conditions are satisfied. These conditions vary from state to state. Under Section 228(a) of the Delaware statute, an action that is required or permitted to be taken at a shareholders' meeting may be taken without a meeting by the written consent of all the shareholders entitled to vote on the action. Similarly, under Section 704(b) of the Model Act, the articles of incorporation may provide that the shareholders can act without a meeting by the written consent of shareholders who have the minimum number of votes required to take the action at a meeting. Model Act Section 7.04 is comparable to Delaware Section 704.

SECTION 11. THE ELECTION OF DIRECTORS

Special voting rules may apply in the election of directors: These rules involve staggered boards, cumulative voting, and plurality voting.

A. STAGGERED BOARDS

A staggered (or "classified") board of directors is a board that is divided into two or more classes, each of which is elected separately for staggered terms. So, for example, if a staggered board has three classes of directors, with three directors in each class, then all nine directors would serve three-year terms, but each year only three directorships would be up for election. The rationale for staggered boards is said to be that they ensure continuity. This rationale is weak, because where continuity is desirable the shareholders will continue directors in office in any event. Although staggered boards preceded the rise of hostile takeovers, after that phenomenon occurred, a staggered board came to be seen as a defense against a takeover, because a multi-year process was required to oust an incumbent majority of directors. For example, if a board is unclassified and the year is 2011, a majority of the shareholders could elect an entirely new board at the corporation's 2011 annual meeting. If, however, a board has three classes, a majority of the shareholders could not elect a majority of the board until 2012; and if a board has four classes, a majority of the shareholders could not elect a majority of the board until 2013. In the interim, the dissident majority would have their investment in the corporation tied up without acquiring control of the corporation. That is a very unappetizing prospect, especially for a takeover bidder, and will often deter prospective bidders from making a takeover bid.

MARCEL KAHAN & EDWARD ROCK, EMBATTLED CEOS, 88 Tex. L. Rev. 987, 1007–09 (2010). "Modern corporate law scholarship regards staggered boards as one of the most potent and controversial anti-takeover devices. In companies with 'effective' staggered boards, it takes two consecutive annual shareholder meetings to replace a majority of a board of directors against the opposition of incumbents. While poison pills that are not coupled with staggered boards are nowadays viewed as relatively harmless, several commentators have argued that staggered boards, coupled with the (virtually) universally available poison pill, serve to illegitimately entrench managers and that courts should find some way to render them ineffective. The policy battlefront for takeover defenses, in other words, has shifted to staggered boards.

"For existing companies, conventional wisdom had it that shareholders and boards are in a stalemate. Boards of companies without staggered boards may want to adopt staggered boards, but they do not propose a charter amendment because they know that shareholders will not approve it. Shareholders in companies with staggered boards want to get rid of them but cannot because the board refuses to approve the requisite charter amendment.

"The conventional wisdom is wrong. The tide on staggered boards has turned and, at least for the largest companies, the day is not far off when staggered boards will be the rare exception. In Table 2, we present data on staggered boards in the S & P 100 companies. S & P 100 companies are among the largest and the most established companies in the U.S., representing, in aggregate, almost 45% of the market capitalization.

Table 2: Staggered Boards in S&P 100 Companies

	Companies with Staggered Boards	New Adoptions	Eliminations	Eliminations as % of Companies with Staggered Boards
2003	44			
2004	41	0	3	6.80%
2005	34	0	7	17.10%
2006	25	0	8	23.50%
2007	21	0	5	24.00%
2008	16	0	1	6.30%
2009	15			

"As Table 2 shows, the incidence of staggered boards has declined from 44% to 16% between 2003 and 2009. Put differently, over the six-year period, two-thirds of the companies that had staggered boards have dismantled them.

"To be sure, the decline of staggered boards among the largest and most established companies does not necessarily mean that staggered boards are universally in decline. Arguably the managers of the largest companies are least in need of insulation against takeovers, and thus most willing to agree to destagger. Indeed, staggered boards are alive and well in companies at the time of their IPO. In a sample of twenty-six companies that went public in the first part of 2007, we found that twenty had a staggered-board provision in their charter.

"That said, the largest and most established companies act as trendsetters for what is considered good corporate governance. The directors of these companies sit on boards of smaller companies, and their managers are members of influential groups like the Business Roundtable. With most of these companies dismantling their staggered boards over, the last six years, it will become increasingly difficult for other companies to resist shareholder pressure.

"In fact, smaller companies have started to go down the same path of dismantling their staggered boards that the S & P 100 companies have almost completed. Thus, according to SharkRepellent, the incidence of staggered boards among the (still large) S & P 500 companies declined from 57% in 2003 to 36% in 2007; among midsize S & P 400 companies, it declined from 67% in 2003 to 58% in 2007; and among small S & P 600 companies, it declined from 61% in 2003 to 55% in 2007. Thus, we already see that other companies have started, and we predict that they will continue to, follow the lead of the S & P 100 companies."

B. CUMULATIVE VOTING

1. *In general.* Under the traditional system of voting for directors—sometimes referred to as *straight voting*—a shareholder can

cast, for each open directorship, a number of votes equal to the number of her shares. For example, assume that the board of Blue Corporation consists of seven directors; Blue has 300 outstanding shares; Shareholder S owns 100 shares; shareholder T owns 200 shares; and all seven directorships are up for election. Under straight voting, S can cast a total of 700 votes, but cannot cast more than 100 votes for any nominee. More generally, under straight voting, minority shareholders can never elect even a single director over the opposition of the majority. For example, in the Blue Corporation hypothetical, since under straight voting S can cast no more than 100 votes for any of her seven nominees, and T can cast 200 votes for each of his seven nominees, T can elect all the directors.

In contrast, under the system of *cumulative voting*, a shareholder can distribute among her nominees, in any way she pleases, a number of votes equal to the number of her shares times the number of directors to be elected. (In a relatively small number of states, cumulative voting is made mandatory by constitution or by statute. More typically, however, the statutes permit rather than require cumulative voting.) So, for example, suppose that S, who has 700 votes, casts 350 votes each for two of her nominees, A and B. If T casts 200 votes for each of his seven nominees, S will elect two directors, because each of her nominees will receive more votes (350) than any of T's nominees (200). T, in turn, will elect five directors, because each of his nominees will receive 200 votes and S has used up all of her votes on A and B. Suppose that T casts 351 votes for each of two of his candidates. In that case, T can cast only 698 votes for his other five nominees. Accordingly, some of T's candidates will receive less than 350 votes, and S will still elect two of her nominees to the board.

2. *Mathematics*. Aranow & Einhorn, Proxy Contests for Corporate Control 10.04[B] (3d ed. 1998) discusses the mathematics of cumulative voting, as follows:

> The mathematics of cumulative voting can become a very involved subject which we will not undertake to discuss in all its aspects. There are two basic formulas, both of which are relatively simple. The first formula is used to determine the minimum number of shares needed to elect a particular number of directors:
>
> $$X = \frac{(S \times N)}{D + 1} + 1$$
>
> X = minimum number of shares needed
> S = total number of shares that will be voted at meeting
> N = number of directors desired to elect
> D = total number of directors to be elected
>
> For example, assume there exists a corporation with 1,000 shares outstanding and seven directors to be elected. A minority stockholders' group wishes to elect two directors. It is estimated that 800 shares will be voted at the meeting. Applying these figures to the formula, the resulting calculation is:

$$\frac{(800 \times 2)}{7 + 1} + 1 = 201$$

The stockholders' group knows that it must have ownership or control of at least 201 shares in order to elect two directors.

The second formula can be used to determine how many directors can be elected by a group controlling a particular number of shares:

$$N = \frac{(X) \times (D + 1)}{S}$$

N = number of directors that can be elected
X = number of shares controlled
D = total number of directors to be elected
S = total number of shares that will be voted at meeting

In the example above, assume that the stockholders' group knows it will control 201 shares. Applying the figures to this formula, the resulting calculation is:

$$\frac{201 \times 8}{800} = 2.01$$

Thus, cumulation will result in the election of two directors. There are several other formulas that can be applied to more complicated questions.*

3. *Cumulative Voting and Staggered Boards.* An issue raised by cumulative voting is whether, when cumulative voting is required either by state law or by a corporation's certificate of incorporation, a corporation can have a staggered board. The percentage of stock that minority shareholders must hold to elect at least one director under cumulative voting varies inversely with the number of directors to be elected. Accordingly, a 12% minority (for example) can elect one director if nine directors are to be elected, but cannot elect any

* Jesse Fried points out that:

The standard formula for determining the minimum number of shares necessary to elect a particular number of directors yields an easily interpretable result only when the expression $(S \times N)/(D + 1)$ is a whole number.

Suppose, as in the Aranow and Einhorn example, that there is a corporation with seven directors to be elected and a minority group wishes to elect two directors. However, 803 shares (rather than the 800 shares used in their example) will be voted at the meeting. The standard formula indicates that the number of shares needed to elect two directors is now:

$$[(803 \times 2)/(7 + 1)] + 1 = 201.75$$

If there are only whole shares, does this mean that the minority group needs 201 to elect two directors, or 202 shares? The answer is, surprisingly, 201—if the standard formula does not yield a whole number you must round down to determine the number of whole shares needed.

If there are fractional shares, then the standard formula yields the wrong result.

A more useful formula for determining the minimum number of shares needed (X), is $X > (S \times N)/(D+1)$

If there are fractional shares, then any fraction greater than the righthandside expression will allow you to elect N directors. If there are whole shares, then you round up to the next whole number. [Footnote by ed.]

directors if three directors are to be elected. Putting this more generally, if a board is classified, a minority must hold more stock to elect a single director than if a board of the same size is unclassified, because the number of directors to be elected each year is only a fraction of the full board, and the fewer directors that are to be elected, the more votes the minority must have to elect their candidates. In Wolfson v. Avery, 126 N.E.2d 701 (Ill. 1955), the Illinois court held that, for this reason, an Illinois Constitutional requirement of cumulative voting prohibited staggered boards. (The Illinois Constitution was later amended to eliminate this requirement.) In Bohannan v. Corporation Commission, 313 P.2d 379 (Ariz.1957), the Arizona court held to the contrary. Subsequently, the Arizona legislature enacted a statutory provision that permitted classification if a board had nine or more directors.

The Delaware Chancery Court addressed this issue in 2010 in eBay Domestic Holdings, Inc. v. Newmark, 2010 WL 3516473 Craig Newmark founded craigslist in 1995. In time, craigslist became the most popular classifieds website in the United States. At an early point, craigslist had three shareholders: Craig Newmark (Craig) and Jim Buckmeister (Jim), who together held 72% of craigslist's stock, and Phillip Knowlton (Phillip), who held the remainder. The board of craigslist then consisted of Craig, Jim, and Phillip. Later, Phillip sold his craigslist shares to eBay, then primarily an auction website, and an eBay representative was designated as the third craigslist director in Phillip's place. Subsequently, eBay launched its own online classifieds website, which was designed to compete with craigslist. Craig, Jim, craigslist, and eBay made an agreement that expressly permitted eBay to compete with craigslist, but Craig and Jim were not enthusiastic about the situation, and adopted several measures to keep eBay out of craigslist's boardroom and to limit eBay's ability to purchase additional craigslist shares. One of these measures consisted of amendments to craigslist's certificate of incorporation to provide for a staggered board. The craigslist certificate of incorporation provided for a three-member board to be elected under cumulative voting. The mechanics of cumulative voting ensured that as long as craigslist had an unclassified three-member board, eBay could use its 28% stake in craigslist to elect one director. However, the staggered-board amendments created three classes of directors, one director per class. Each one-director class served a three-year term, so each year only one director would be up for election.

The proposed staggered-board amendments would not have eliminated cumulative voting. Practically speaking, however, cumulative voting was not meaningful if only one director was up for election in any given year, because there had to be at least two board seats in play for eBay to cumulate its votes so as elect a director. Accordingly, the staggered-board amendments cut off eBay's ability to place a director on the craigslist board. Nevertheless, the court held that the amendments were valid:

Delaware law does not require that minority stockholders such as eBay have board representation. Delaware corporations do not have to adopt cumulative voting for the benefit of minority stockholders, and Delaware corporations have the express power to implement staggered boards. If a corporation implements a staggered board, and this renders the corporation's cumulative voting system ineffective, minority stockholders have not been deprived of anything they are entitled to under the common law or the DGCL, because minority stockholders are not entitled to a cumulative voting system in the first instance. It is true that by approving the staggered board amendments, Jim and Craig implemented a corporate governance structure that had a disparate and, from eBay's point of view, unfavorable impact on eBay. This is not the sort of disparate treatment, however, that can be classified as self-dealing because the law expressly allows a majority stockholders to elect the entire board. Thus, the staggered board amendments cannot be subjected to entire fairness review on the grounds that eliminating eBay's ability to elect a director was a form of self-dealing.

Another cumulative-voting issue concerns the removal of directors. Cumulative voting could be undercut if a director who is elected by a minority of the shareholders through cumulative voting could then be removed by a majority of the shareholders. Accordingly, some statutes provide that when cumulative voting is in effect, a director cannot be removed if the number of shares voting against her removal would be sufficient to elect her. *See, e.g.*, Cal.Corp. Code § 303(a)(1).

C. PLURALITY VOTING

Another special voting rule that applies to the election of directors is plurality voting. Under the general rule applicable to shareholder voting, shareholders can act only by a majority vote. In the election of directors, however, traditionally a plurality vote sufficed, that is, the nominees who received the most votes were elected even if none of them has a majority. However, this rule has come under heavy pressure in the last few years, and is rapidly changing, as described in the following material.

Bryn R. Vaaler, Majority Election of Directors: Where Are We Today?

(Dorsey & Whitney, November 2007).[5]

Shareholder activists have maintained that plurality voting does not adequately permit shareholders to express disapproval. They argue

5. © Dorsey & Whitney LLP. This article originally appeared in Dorsey's Corporate Update, and included the following disclaimer: "This article is intended for general informa-

that votes withheld have no real effect. In an uncontested election, each nominee in the board's slate will still be elected so long as he or she receives at least one affirmative vote, even if a majority of votes are withheld. If directors must receive an affirmative majority of votes cast to be elected, then withheld or negative votes will have real meaning. . . .

In 2005, shareholder activists, led by the Council of Institutional Investors and labor union pension funds, began flooding larger public companies with letters and formal shareholder proposals requesting boards to initiate amendments to their charters necessary to implement a majority-voting regime for directors. . . .

. . . [In January 2006, Intel announced] that it had adopted a new bylaw provision requiring election of directors by a majority of votes cast, except in contested elections. Under the Intel bylaw (as amended), a new director nominee, in an uncontested election, who fails to receive a majority of votes cast in his or her favor is not elected. An incumbent nominee who fails to get the required vote remains in place under the so-called "holdover" rule (i.e., directors remain in place until their successor is elected and qualified) contained in the DGCL and all other corporate statutes, but must tender his or her resignation. Intel's board governance committee must decide whether to accept or reject the resignation within 90 days.

The Intel bylaw rapidly became the gold standard for shareholder activists promoting the cause of majority election. This is because it actually adopts a majority-vote standard (instead of just a resignation policy) and because it is part of the company's charter documents and may be made less easy to change or eliminate without shareholder consent than a mere board-adopted governance principle.

A Delaware corporation, like Intel, may adopt a majority-election standard by bylaw amendment, which may be approved by either the board or the shareholders. Most other state corporate statutes . . . currently require that a change to the default plurality-voting rule be made in the articles of incorporation, not the bylaws. So, adoption of an Intel-type bylaw is not an option, and corporations incorporated in those states would have to amend their articles (usually requiring *both* board and shareholder approval) to adopt a true majority-voting requirement or instead adopt a Pfizer-type governance policy. . . .

Activists have also called for states to change the default rule in their corporate statutes from plurality to majority and make other changes to accommodate majority-voting bylaws and policies.

[In 2006, the Model Act was amended to] . . . permit either the shareholders or the board to amend the bylaws to provide that, in uncontested elections, a director nominee receiving more votes withheld than in favor would generally serve no more than a 90–day transitional term. If adopted by shareholders, such a bylaw amend-

tion purposes only and should not be construed as legal advice or legal opinions on any specific facts or circumstances. An attorney-client relationship is not created or continued by reading this article. . . ." (Footnote by ed.)

ment may not be rescinded or modified by the board. The Model Act amendments also ... permit opting out of the "holdover" rule by amendment to the articles of incorporation....

[In the same year,] ... the Delaware legislature amended the DGCL to provide that a shareholder-adopted bylaw requiring a greater vote for election of directors could not be rescinded or modified by the board and to affirm the validity of conditional director resignations.

In 2006 and 2007, California, Virginia and Washington adopted amendments to their respective corporate statutes retaining plurality default rules, but permitting public companies to adopt majority-election regimes by bylaw amendment under certain conditions. Ohio amended its corporate statute ... to provide that an Ohio corporation may opt out of its plurality-voting default rule by amendment to the articles of incorporation. North Dakota adopted a new Publicly Traded Corporations Act which has a majority-election default in uncontested elections for corporations that do not have cumulative voting.

MARCEL KAHAN & EDWARD ROCK, EMBATTLED CEOS, 88 Tex. L. Rev. 987, 1110–1111 (2010). "Until recently, the directors of most corporations were elected under a plurality-voting regime. Of S & P 100 companies, only ten deviated from plurality voting in 2003. By 2009, that number had increased to ninety (see Table 3). Moreover, of the ten remaining companies, one had not yet filed its 2009 proxy statement, four were no longer publicly traded, and four others had some form of cumulative or dual-class voting regime in place, which complicates majority voting for directors. Only a single company definitely retained a regular plurality-voting regime. As Table 3 shows, most of the change from plurality to majority voting took place in the two-year span from 2005 to 2007, where the number of S & P 100 companies with majority voting increased from nine to eighty-one. Thus, within just two years, we have moved from a regime in which majority voting was the rare exception to a regime in which it has been adopted by virtually all of the largest companies. Though the rise of majority voting among the broader set of S & P 500 companies has been somewhat slower, experienced observers like Martin Lipton opined that 'it is clear today that majority voting will become universal.' "

Table 3: Number of S&P 100 Companies Applying Majority Voting

	2003	2004	2005	2006	2007	2008	2009
Majority Voting	10	9	9	51	81	85	90

"Within a short span, most large companies discarded the old plurality voting regime and adopted some form of majority voting. Thus, the percentage of S & P 500 companies with some form of majority voting increased from 16% in February of 2006 to 66% in

November 2007 to about 80% in 2010. S & P 500 companies account for about 75% of the aggregate capitalization of the U.S. stock market. To be sure, among smaller companies, majority voting seems much less prevalent: of 5,930 companies outside the S & P 500 that are followed by RiskMetrics, only 17% had adopted some form of majority voting by 2009. But still, it is clear that majority voting has been a big success, is already in effect for a majority of U.S. companies when weighted by capitalization, and is likely to be adopted by many more companies in future years."

DEL. GEN. CORP. LAW § 141(c)

[See Statutory Supplement]

MODEL BUS. CORP. ACT § 8.25

[See Statutory Supplement]

D. Short Slates

NOTE ON SHORT SLATES

In recent years, dissident shareholders have increasingly run a short slate of directors for election—that is, a slate of candidates for less than all, and usually less than a majority, of the directors to be elected. This approach has several advantages. Proxy advisory firms, such as ISS, and large institutional investors are often more supportive of short slates than of efforts to replace all or a majority of the board. Moreover, change-in-control provisions are pervasive, and trigger a variety of outcomes that may adversely affect the shareholders, such as additional compensation to executives or immediate vesting of future rights. Running a short slate avoids triggering a change-in-control provision. A short slate also avoids triggering "poison puts," that is, provisions in a company's debt instruments that require the company to repurchase outstanding debt obligations upon the occurrence of certain defined events, which sometimes include incumbent directors ceasing to constitute a majority of the board.

SECTION 12. REMOVAL OF DIRECTORS

In theory, under certain conditions directors may be removed by the shareholders, the board, or a court, depending on state law, as described in the following Note. In practice, however, removal of directors under state law is unusual (although the federal law allows the removal of directors for certain violations of the securities laws).

NOTE ON THE REMOVAL OF DIRECTORS

1. *Removal by the Shareholders.* Shareholders can remove a director for cause even in the absence of a statute that so provides. *See, e.g.*, Auer v. Dressel, 118 N.E.2d 590 (N.Y. 1954); Campbell v. Loew's, Inc., 134 A.2d 852 (Del.Ch. 1957). However, shareholders cannot remove a director without cause in the absence of specific authority to do so under the statute, the certificate of incorporation, or the by-laws. *See, e.g.*, Frank v. Anthony, 107 So.2d 136 (Fla.App.1958). For statutes that permit the shareholders to remove a director without cause, *see, e.g.*, Cal.Corp.Code § 303(a); Model Bus.Corp.Act § 8.08. A certificate or by-law provision may not authorize the removal without cause of directors elected after the provision has been adopted. *See, e.g.*, Crown EMAK Partners, LLC v. Kurz, 992 A.2d 377 (Del. Supr. 2010); Everett v. Transnation Dev. Corp., 267 A.2d 627 (Del.Ch.1970).

2. *Removal by the Board.* In the absence of statute, the board cannot remove a director either with or without cause. *See, e.g.*, Bruch v. National Guarantee Credit Corp., 116 A. 738 (Del.Ch. 1922). It is uncertain whether the certificate of incorporation can change this ruleexcell. *See* Dillon v. Berg, 326 F.Supp. 1214 (D.Del.1971), aff'd 453 F.2d 876 (3d Cir.); Bruch v. National Guarantee Credit Corp., supra. However, some statutes permit the board to remove a director either for cause, *see, e.g.*, Mass.Gen.Laws ch. 156B, § 51(c). Other statutes permit removal of a director for specified reasons, such as conviction of a felony, *see, e.g.*, Calif.Corp.Code § 302. A few statutes permit the board to remove a director for cause or for specified reasons if the certificate of incorporation so provides. *See, e.g.*, N.J.Stat.Ann. § 14A:6–6.

3. *Removal by a Court.* The cases are divided on whether a court can remove directors for cause in the absence of statute. Compare Webber v. Webber Oil Co., 495 A.2d 1215 (Me.1985) (courts do not have power to remove directors) with Ross v. 311 N. Cent. Ave.Bldg. Corp., 264 N.E.2d 406 (Ill. App. 1970) (courts have power to remove directors, at least for fraud or the like). Some statutes permit the courts to remove a director for specified reasons, such as fraudulent or dishonest acts. These statutes usually provide that a petition to the court requesting such removal can be brought only by a designated percentage of the shareholders (most commonly 10%), by the attorney general, or in some cases, by either. *See, e.g.*, Calif.Corp.Code § 304; N.Y.Bus.Corp.Law § 706(d).

SECTION 13. REQUISITES FOR VALID ACTION BY CORPORATE OFFICERS

DEL. GEN. CORP. LAW § 142

[See Statutory Supplement]

MODEL BUS. CORP. ACT §§ 8.40, 8.41

[See Statutory Supplement]

NOTE ON AUTHORITY

[See Chapter 1, supra]

NOTE ON THE AUTHORITY OF CORPORATE OFFICERS

Issues concerning the authority of corporate officers typically come up in the context of a transaction between the corporation and a third person in which an officer, rather than the board, acted on the corporation's behalf. If the corporation repudiates the transaction, the question arises whether the officer had actual, apparent, or (much more rarely) inherent authority to enter into the transaction. Issues concerning a corporate officer's actual authority are normally determined under the general law of agency. An officer's actual authority may be found in the certificate of incorporation, the by-laws, a board resolution, authorized instructions by a superior officer, or a pattern of past acquiescence by the board or a superior officer.

Special problems arise where the issue is whether the officer had apparent authority by virtue of her position.

1. *President.* There are a number of cases concerning the apparent authority of a president by virtue of her position. Some older cases hold that a president does not have any apparent authority by virtue of her position—that instead, she has only the actual authority that the board confers upon her. For example, in Federal Services Finance Corp. v. Bishop Nat. Bank of Hawaii at Honolulu, 190 F.2d 442 (9th Cir.1951), supplemented, 205 F.2d 11 (9th Cir.1953), the court held that the president had no power by virtue of his office to cash checks that were payable to the corporation. However, the modern rule is that the president has apparent authority to bind the corporation to contracts that are made in the usual and regular course of business,

but does not have apparent authority to bind the corporation to contracts of an extraordinary nature. *See, e.g.,* Lee v. Jenkins Bros., 268 F.2d 357 (2d Cir.1959), cert. denied, 361 U.S. 913, 80 S.Ct. 257, 4 L.Ed.2d 183 (1959). The difficulty lies in drawing a line between what is ordinary and what is extraordinary. Some cases are restrictive in this regard. *See, e.g.,* Liebermann v. Princeway Realty Corp., 233 N.Y.S.2d 1001 (N.Y. App. Div. 1962), aff'd, 195 N.E.2d 57 (N.Y. 1963). Other cases, such as Lee v. Jenkins Brothers, supra, determine the president's apparent authority in a more expansive manner. An expansive interpretation reflects both the reality that the management of the business of the corporation is normally conducted by or under the supervision of its executives, rather than its board, and a sound understanding of the normal expectations of third persons in such cases.

Any attempt at precision in determining the apparent authority of a president would almost certainly be futile, because the issue is highly dependent on the context of the business transaction in which it arises, and the types of business transactions that may arise are endlessly variable. Nevertheless, certain boundaries can be identified. To begin with, some matters, such as the declaration of dividends, are required by statute to be decided by the board. Typically, the statutes also enumerate certain matters that the board cannot delegate to a committee, such as corporate actions that require approval by both the board and the shareholders under the relevant statute. By analogy, it would normally not be within the apparent authority of the president to take binding action on these matters.

Beyond these boundaries, among the elements to be taken into account for purposes of determining what constitutes an extraordinary action, which would normally be outside the apparent authority of the president, are the economic magnitude of the action in relation to corporate assets and earnings, the extent of risk involved, the time span of the action's effect, and the cost of reversing the action. Examples of extraordinary actions for these purposes include the creation of long-term or other significant debt, the reacquisition of equity securities, significant capital investments, significant business combinations, the disposition of a significant business, entry into important new lines of business, significant acquisitions of stock in other corporations, and actions that would foreseeably expose the corporation to significant litigation or significant new regulatory problems. A useful generalization is that decisions that would make a significant change in the structure of the business enterprise, or in the structure of control over the enterprise, are extraordinary corporate actions and therefore normally outside the president's apparent authority.

2. *CEO.* The terminology employed in the traditional rules concerning the apparent authority of a corporate officer has become somewhat archaic. When these rules were formulated, the top officer in the corporation usually had the title of president, the second-in-command usually had the title of executive vice-president, and the top

financial officer usually had the title of treasurer. Today, matters are much different. The title that now signifies the top officer is usually not president, but chief executive officer, or CEO (although the CEO usually also holds the title of chairman of the board, president, or both).

3. *Chief Operating Officer.* Chief operating officer (COO) is the title usually given to the second-in-command of a publicly held corporation. Often the CEO is the chairman of the board and the COO is the president. There is little if any law on the apparent authority of a COO, as such. It is also an open question whether the law on the apparent authority of a president applies to a COO who is the president but is not the number-one executive of the corporation.

4. *Chairman of the Board.* The functions of the chairman of the board vary significantly from one corporation to another, and the case law on the apparent authority of a chairman is sparse. Often, but not always, the chairman title is simply piled on to the CEO title. However, "In some [corporations, the chairman's office] is held by a chief executive officer who has relinquished day-by-day operations to a younger man while still holding the reins of power; in others it is held by a retired chief executive officer whose counsel and advice are still valued; in still others it provides a formula for dividing up between two relatively equal principals the control of the corporation." American Express Co. v. Lopez, 340 N.Y.S.2d 82 (N.Y. Civ.Ct.1973).

5. *Chief Financial Officer.* The Chief Financial Officer, or CFO, is normally the number-three executive. The title CFO is somewhat misleading, because often the functions of a CFO include not only responsibility for corporate finance, but also responsibility for managing risks and expenses.

It remains to be seen how the apparent authority of the top corporate officers will be adapted to these shifts in terminology.

6. *Vice–Presidents.* The case-law on the apparent authority of vice-presidents is also sparse. Under the relatively strict outlook of the earlier cases, a vice-president, as such, had little or no apparent authority. *See* James F. Monaghan, Inc. v. M. Lowenstein & Sons, 195 N.E. 101 (Mass. 1935). There is some indication that courts today may follow a more expansive approach to the apparent authority of a vice-president, at least if the vice-president has a title that gives her the appearance of standing close to the top of the corporate hierarchy, such as executive vice-president or vice-president of manufacturing or sales. *See* Kanavos v. Hancock Bank & Trust Co., 439 N.E.2d 311 (Mass. App. 1982). However, in many corporations, particularly financial institutions such as banks, the vice-president title is very freely bestowed, for the sole purpose of impressing clients with whom an employee deals. In such cases the person holding the title has no significant decision making power, and little or no apparent authority beyond the power to deal with clients in the ordinary course of business.

7. *Secretary.* The secretary of a corporation has apparent authority to certify the records of the corporation, including resolutions of the board. A secretary's certificate that a resolution was duly adopted by the board is therefore conclusive in favor of third party who relied on the certified resolution. *See, e.g.,* Diamond Paint Co. of Houston v. Embry, 525 S.W.2d 529 (Tex.Civ.App.1975). The significance of the secretary's power of certification is demonstrated in In re Drive–In Dev. Corp., 371 F.2d 215, 219–20 (7th Cir.1966), cert. denied, Creditors' Committee of Drive–In Dev. Corp. v. National Boulevard Bank of Chicago, 387 U.S. 909, 87 S.Ct. 1691, 18 L.Ed.2d 626 (1967). This case involved the question whether a corporation, Drive–In, was bound by a guaranty. Although there was no evidence that Drive In's board had authorized the guarantee, the court held that the secretary's certificate stating that the board had adopted the guarantee was conclusive:

> . . . [T]he referee found that Drive In's minute book did not show that a resolution authorizing Maranz [Drive In's vice president] to sign the guaranty was adopted by the directors and that Dick [Drive In's secretary] could not recall a specific directors' meeting at which such a resolution was approved. From these findings, the referee concluded that Maranz, who signed the guaranty on behalf of Drive In, had no authority, "either actual or implied or apparent," to bind Drive In. This conclusion was erroneous. Drive In was estopped to deny Maranz' express authority to sign the guaranty because of the certified copy of a resolution of Drive In's board of directors purporting to grant such authority furnished to the bank by Dick, whether or not such a resolution was in fact formally adopted.

Other than the power of certification, a secretary's apparent authority by virtue of his position is close to nil. *See, e.g.,* Ideal Foods, Inc. v. Action Leasing Corp., 413 So.2d 416, 417 (Fla.App.1982) ("The secretary of a corporation, merely as such, is a ministerial officer, without authority to transact the business of the corporation upon his volition and judgment").

8. *Treasurer.* The apparent authority of a treasurer is also close to nil. *See, e.g.,* Ideal Foods, Inc. v. Action Leasing Corp., 413 So.2d 416 (Fla.App.1982). (KFO)

9. *Closely Held Corporations.* In the context of closely held corporations, some cases hold that if the president has been exercising absolute authority over the corporation's affairs, and the board has never questioned, altered, or rejected his decisions, the president will have extremely wide actual and apparent authority. *See, e.g.,* Allen v. France Packing Co., 170 Pa.Super. 632, 90 A.2d 289 (1952); Blasingame v. American Materials, Inc., 654 S.W.2d 659 (Tenn.1983). More generally, it has been said that:

> Although the same broad principles of corporation and agency law determine the powers of officers in both close and publicly held corporations, the factual differences in the patterns of operation of the two kinds of corporations lead to wide disparities in the powers the courts actually recognize in corporate officers. In a

> close corporation, ownership and management normally coalesce; and the participants often conduct their enterprise internally much as if it were a partnership. The courts have seldom articulated a difference in the rules governing officers' powers in close and publicly held corporations; yet they appear in fact to have often cut through the technical legal form of close corporations to reach the results that would be reached if the enterprises were conducted as partnerships. In other words, the courts frequently, and perhaps usually, recognize in officers of a close corporation the same powers that are possessed by partners in a firm under the general rule of partnership law which makes each partner an agent of the firm for the purposes of its business and empowers each partner to bind the firm by acts apparently carried on to further the usual business of the partnership.

Zimmerman v. Hogg & Allen, 209 S.E.2d 795, 801 (N.C. 1974).

10. *Ratification*. Even if an officer lacks both actual and apparent authority, the corporation may be bound by her act of entering into a transaction on the corporation's behalf if the board later ratifies the officer's act. Ratification may occur where a corporation, knowing all of the facts, accepts and uses the proceeds of such a transaction. Western American Life Ins. Co. v. Hicks, 135 Ga.App. 90, 217 S.E.2d 323 (1975).

SCHOONEJONGEN v. CURTISS WRIGHT CORP., 143 F.3d 120 (3d Cir.1998). "Beyond the board of directors, the corporation may validly act through its . . . officers as authorized corporate agents. In general, an officer's powers stem from the organic law of the corporation, or a board delegation of authority which maybe express or implied. . . . Express authority to act on behalf of the corporation is usually manifested through a statute, the certificate of corporation, the by-laws, or a board or shareholder action. . . . Implied actual authority, which is express authority circumstantially proved, may be found through evidence as to the manner in which the business has operated in the past, the facts attending the transaction in question, circumstantial evidence of board declarations surrounding the given transaction, or the habitual usage or course of dealing common to the company. . . . Similarly, authority will be implied when it is reasonably necessary and proper to effectuate the purpose of the office or the main authority conferred."

SECTION 14. THE CLASSICAL ULTRA VIRES DOCTRINE

Two long-standing and related issues in corporate law are what if any limits are corporations subject to in the conduct of their business and what should be in the objective of a for-profit corporation. This section and the next concern those issues.

INTRODUCTORY NOTE

1. *The Classical Ultra Vires Doctrine*. Under the classical theory of corporate existence,the corporation is regarded as a fictitious person, endowed with life and capacity only insofar as provided in its charter. Early corporate charters tended to narrowly circumscribe the sphere of activities in which a corporation could engage. Transactions outside that sphere were characterized by the courts as ultra vires (beyond the corporation's power) and unenforceable—unenforceable against the corporation because beyond the corporation's powers, and unenforceable by the corporation on the ground of lack of mutuality. A leading example is Ashbury Railway Carriage & Iron Co. v. Riche, 7 L.R. Eng. & Ir.App. 653 (1875). Ashbury was authorized by its charter "to make and sell, or lend on hire, railway-carriages and wagons, and all kinds of railway plant, fittings, machinery, and rolling-stock; to carry on the business of mechanical engineers and general contractors; to purchase and sell, as merchants, timber, coal, metals, or other materials; and to buy and sell any such materials on commission, or as agents." *Id.* at 654. Ashbury purchased the right to construct and operate a railway line in Belgium, and Riche contracted to do the construction. After Riche had done some of the work, Ashbury repudiated the contract. Riche brought suit. The House of Lords held for Ashbury on the ground that it lacked the power under its charter to build a railroad, and therefore lacked the power to contract for that purpose.

The original purpose of the ultra vires doctrine seems to have been to protect the public or the state from unsanctioned corporate activity. Accordingly, under classical English law even unanimous shareholder ratification was not a bar to an ultra vires defense if the transaction was outside the sphere of activities stated in its charter. *See Ashbury,* supra; Frommel, Reform of the Ultra Vires Rule: A Personal View, 8 The Company Lawyer 11 (1987).

2. *Powers and Purposes*. In theory, the classical ultra vires doctrine was applicable to two somewhat different questions. The first question was whether a corporation had acted beyond its purposes, that is, had engaged in a type of business activity not permitted under its certificate. The second question was whether the corporation had exercised a power not specified in its certificate. In practice, the two questions tended to merge. For example, certificates of incorporation commonly contained clauses that described each of the corporation's purposes and powers as both purposes and powers.

3. *Recurring Problems*. A number of problems concerning specific types of corporate transactions tended to recur under the classical

ultra vires doctrine. One of these problems concerned the power of a corporation to guarantee a third party's debts. Early cases often held that such guarantees were ultra vires in the absence of a provision in the certificate of incorporation that explicitly conferred the power to guarantee. *See, e.g.,* Brinson v. Mill Supply Co., 14 S.E.2d 505 (N.C. 1941). Present-day statutes make this problem moot by explicitly empowering corporations to make guarantees. *See, e.g.,* Del. Gen. Corp. Law § 123.

Another recurring problem concerned the power of a corporation to be a general partner. Early cases often held that a corporation had no power to enter into a partnership unless that power was explicitly granted by a statute or by the certificate of incorporation. *See, e.g.,* Whittenton Mills v. Upton, 76 Mass. (10 Gray) 582 (1858); Central R. Co. v. Collins, 40 Ga. 582 (1869). The concern here was that a corporate partner would be bound by the acts and decisions of partners who were not its duly appointed officers, which would improperly impinge on the board's duty to manage the corporation. (The cases did permit corporations to enter into joint ventures, which are usually temporary in nature and created for a limited purpose.) Present-day statutes make this problem moot by explicitly empowering corporations to become partners. *See, e.g.,* Del. Gen. Corp. Law § 122(11); N.Y.Bus.Corp.Law § 202(15); Model Bus. Corp. Act § 3.02(9).

4. *Limitations on the Ultra Vires Doctrine*. Ultra vires was always regarded by the commentators as an unsound doctrine, and the history of the doctrine is one of steady erosion, which proceeded along several fronts:

(i) It was established even in early cases that corporate powers could be implied as well as explicit. *See* Sutton's Hospital Case, 77 Eng. Rep. 960 (1613). The courts eventually became very liberal in finding implied powers, including implied powers to enter into business activities not specified in the certificate. For example, in Jacksonville, Mayport, Pablo Ry. & Navigation Co. v. Hooper, 160 U.S. 514, 526, 16 S.Ct. 379, 40 L.Ed. 515 (1896), the Supreme Court held that a Florida company whose purpose, under its charter, was to run a railroad, could also engage in leasing and running a resort hotel located at the railroad's seaside terminus, because the resort could increase the railroad's business. Similarly, in John B. Waldbillig, Inc. v. Gottfried, 254 N.Y.S.2d 924 (N.Y. App. Div. 1964), aff'd, 209 N.E.2d 818 (N.Y. 1965), the court held that a corporation organized to "engage in the business of building, construction, and contracting" [could] have an incidental or implied power to practice engineering.

(ii) Generally speaking, ultra vires was not a defense to corporate tort or criminal liability. Furthermore, even in areas where ultra vires was a defense, it could not be used to reverse completed transactions. Accordingly, the major impact of the doctrine was confined to executory contracts.

(iii) Even as applied to executory contracts, the scope of the ultra vires doctrine was limited. The major problem in such cases occurred where one party had performed under the contract; that party sued for the contract price of its performance; and the nonperforming party raised the defense of ultra vires. Under the majority view, the nonperforming party, having received a benefit under the contract, was estopped from asserting an ultra vires defense. *See, e.g.,* Joseph Schlitz Brewing Co. v. Missouri Poultry & Game Co., 229 S.W. 813 (Mo. 1921). Under the minority view, known as the federal rule, part performance did not have an estoppel effect, on the theory that an ultra vires contract was prohibited by law and therefore void. Even the cases taking this view, however, usually permitted the performing party to recover in restitution for the value of any benefit conferred. *See, e.g.*, Central Trans. Co. v. Pullman's Palace Car Co., 139 U.S. 24, 11 S.Ct. 478, 35 L.Ed. 55 (1891).

(iv) Under American law, unanimous shareholder approval barred the ultra vires defense unless creditors would be injured. *See* Note, 83 U.Pa.L.Rev. 479, 488–92 (1935).

(v) Drafters of certificate-of-incorporation provisions began writing endless and crushingly boring certificate provisions that enumerated every business purpose and power imaginable. Eventually, most statutes made this kind of drafting unnecessary by providing that the certificate could provide simply that the corporation could engage in any lawful business, and by setting out a laundry list of powers that are conferred on every corporation even without enumeration in the certificate.

(vi) Finally, modern statutes have adopted provisions that almost (but not quite) abolish the ultra vires doctrine. The Delaware and Model Act provisions in the following cross-references are examples. Similar statutes have been adopted in all but a few states. *See* Schaeftler, Ultra Vires–Ultra Useless: The Myth of State Interest in Ultra Vires Acts of Business Corporations, 9 J.Corp.Law 81, 81–83 & n. 6 (1983).

DEL. GEN. CORP. LAW §§ 101(B), 102(A)(3), 121, 122, 124

[See Statutory Supplement]

MODEL BUS. CORP. ACT §§ 3.01(A), 3.02, 3.04

[See Statutory Supplement]

SECTION 15. THE OBJECTIVE AND CONDUCT OF THE CORPORATION

This Section concerns the question, to what extent may a corporation act in a manner that is not intended to maximize corporate profits? Although this question is sometimes put in terms of whether a given act would be ultra vires, the question penetrates much more deeply into the nature of the corporate institution, and its place in society, than does the classical ultra vires doctrine.

A. The Maximization of Shareholder Wealth

HU, NEW FINANCIAL PRODUCTS, THE MODERN PROCESS OF FINANCIAL INNOVATION, AND THE PUZZLE OF SHAREHOLDER WELFARE, 69 Tex.L.Rev. 1273, 1278–1283 (1991). The most basic principle of corporate law is that a corporation is to be primarily run for the pecuniary benefit of its shareholders. Apart from the impact of nonstockholder constituency statutes and notions of social responsibility generally, few would disagree with this principle as a general matter.

But what does this principle mean in the usual day-to-day operation of publicly held corporations? . . .

The traditional conception of the basic pecuniary goals of a corporation is based on the simple premise that what is good for the corporation is good for the shareholder. If corporate welfare is furthered, as through the maximization of earnings or earnings per share, shareholder welfare is presumed to be furthered as well. . . .

The traditional conception is based on two related assumptions. First, accounting-based measures such as earnings or earnings per share are appropriate indicators of corporate performance. Second, the welfare of a shareholder is largely coincident with the welfare of the corporation.

Unfortunately, both of these classic assumptions are of limited validity. Financial theorists have long argued—and corporate managers are starting to realize—that maximization of total corporate earnings or even earnings per share does not necessarily maximize shareholder wealth. Earnings growth as a sole measure of corporate performance fails to measure the risk characteristics of corporate investments, the extent of investments in working and fixed capital needed to sustain the firm, dividend policy, and the time value of money. . . .

The second assumption underlying the traditional conception, that the welfare of the corporation is coincident with the welfare of its shareholder, is also fundamentally flawed. For example, there may be a conflict of interest concerning risk between the corporation and its shareholders. . . . [M]odern financial theory suggests that corporations concerned about the well-being of shareholders will generally take more risks than corporations concerned about the entity's own well-being; shareholders can, by holding a portfolio of stocks, diversify away much of the risk that a corporation might itself find daunting.

Similarly, there may be a conflict of interest as to time. For example, from the point of view of shareholders, the best thing to do with the typical company in a dying industry may be to liquidate the company immediately, pay the net proceeds to shareholders, and allow shareholders to put the money to better use. From the point of view of the company itself—and its managers and employees—long-term decline may be preferable.

[A second, competing] conception of the pecuniary goals of a corporation is directly focused on the welfare of the shareholder. Under this view, shareholder wealth maximization is sought directly, rather than as a by-product of corporate welfare. Managers should seek to take those actions that maximize the wealth of shareholders through a combination of maximizing the actual short-or long-term trading price of each share of common stock and the dividends they actually receive. There is no focus on measures of corporate performance like accounting earnings and no concern for the corporation independent of the welfare of its shareholders.

The shift to this second conception has been gradual but discernible. Most academics now believe that shareholder wealth maximization is the basic pecuniary objective of the modern publicly held corporation. Judges have typically subscribed to this standard only in the most limited of circumstances, typically in the context of a sale of the entire company.

B. INTERESTS OTHER THAN MAXIMIZATION OF SHAREHOLDERS' WEALTH

NOTE ON DODGE v. FORD MOTOR CO.

One of the most famous cases in corporation law is Dodge v. Ford Motor Co., 170 N.W. 668 (Mich. 1919). The case is unusual in its early consideration of the issue (or at least one aspect of the issue) that is now known as corporate social responsibility.

Ford Motor Co. had been incorporated in 1903. Henry Ford owned 58% of Ford Motor's stock and controlled the board. Two Dodge brothers owned 10%, and five other shareholders owned the balance. From 1908 on, Ford Motor had paid a regular annual dividend of $1.2 million, and between December 1911 and October 1915, it paid special dividends totaling $41 million. In 1916, Henry Ford declared it to be the settled policy of the company not to pay in the future any special dividends, but to put back into the business for the future all of the earnings of the company, other than the regular dividend of $1.2 million. "My ambition," declared Mr. Ford, "is to employ still more men; to spread the benefits of this industrial system to the greatest possible number, to help them build up their lives and their homes. To do this, we are putting the greatest share of our profits back into the business." At the time of the announcement, Ford Motor had a surplus of $112 million, including $52.5 million in cash.

The Dodge brothers then brought a suit whose objects included compelling a dividend equal to 75% of the accumulated cash surplus. The trial court ordered Ford Motor to declare a dividend of $19.3 million—equal to half of its cash surplus as of July 31, 1916 minus special dividends paid between the time the complaint was filed and July 31, 1917.[6] The Michigan Supreme Court affirmed this portion of the trial court's decree:

> When plaintiffs made their complaint and demand for further dividends the Ford Motor Company had concluded its most prosperous year of business. The demand for its cars at the price of the preceding year continued.... [I]t reasonably might have expected a profit for the year [beginning August 1, 1916], of upwards of $60,000,000.... Considering only these facts, a refusal to declare and pay further dividends appears to be not an exercise of discretion on the part of the directors, but an arbitrary refusal to do what the circumstances required to be done. These facts and others call upon the directors to justify their action, or failure or refusal to act. In justification, the defendants have offered testimony [proving that: Ford Motor had a general policy to reduce the price of its cars every year while maintaining or improving quality. It could have produced 600,000 cars in the year beginning August 1, 1916, and sold them for $440 each. However, the policy of reducing prices called for the cars to be sold at $360 each, a difference of $48 million.]
>
> The plan, as affecting the profits of the business for the year beginning August 1, 1916, and thereafter, calls for a reduction in the selling price of the cars.... In short, the plan does not call for and is not intended to produce immediately a more profitable

---

6. Henry Ford had earlier given an interview to the Detroit News, in which he said:

> I do not believe that we should make such an awful profit on our cars. A reasonable profit is right, but not too much. So it has been my policy to force the price of the car down as fast as production would permit, and give the benefits to users and laborers....

The cross-examination of Henry Ford in Dodge v. Ford built on that interview:

> Counsel: Do you still think those profits were awful profits?
>
> Ford: Well, I guess I do, yes.
>
> Counsel: And for that reason you were not satisfied to continue to make such awful profits?
>
> Ford: We don't seem to be able to keep the profits down.
>
> Counsel: Are you trying to keep them down? What is the Ford Motor Company organized for except profits, will you tell me, Mr. Ford?
>
> Ford: Organized to do as much good as we can, everywhere for everybody concerned. And incidentally to make money.
>
> Counsel: Incidentally to make money?
>
> Ford: Yes, sir.

The interview and the colloquy are reported in M. Todd Henderson, The Story of Dodge v. Ford: Everything Else is New Again, in Corporate Law Stories 37, 61–62 (J. Mark Ramseyer, ed. 2009). Henderson's essay also extensively chronicles the background to Dodge v. Ford.

business but a less profitable one; not only less profitable than formerly but less profitable than it is admitted it might be made. The apparent immediate effect will be to diminish the value of shares and the returns to shareholders.

It is the contention of plaintiffs that the apparent effect of the plan is intended . . . to continue the corporation henceforth as a semi-eleemosynary institution and not as a business institution. In support of this contention they point to the attitude and to the expressions of Mr. Henry Ford. . . .

. . . [Mr. Ford's] testimony creates the impression, also, that he thinks the Ford Motor Company has made too much money, has had too large profits, and that although large profits might be still earned, a sharing of them with the public, by reducing the price of the output of the company, ought to be undertaken. We have no doubt that certain sentiments, philanthropic and altruistic, creditable to Mr. Ford, had large influence in determining the policy to be pursued by the Ford Motor Company—the policy which has been herein referred to.

It is said by his counsel that—

> "Although a manufacturing corporation cannot engage in humanitarian works as its principal business, the fact that it is organized for profit does not prevent the existence of implied powers to carry on with humanitarian motives such charitable works as are incidental to the main business of the corporation." . . .

The difference between an incidental humanitarian expenditure of corporate funds for the benefit of the employees, like the building of a hospital for their use and the employment of agencies for the betterment of their condition, and a general purpose and plan to benefit mankind at the expense of others, is obvious. There should be no confusion (of which there is evidence) of the duties which Mr. Ford conceives that he and the stockholders owe to the general public and the duties which in law he and his codirectors owe to protesting, minority stockholders. A business corporation is organized and carried on primarily for the profit of the stockholders. The powers of the directors are to be employed for that end. The discretion of directors is to be exercised in the choice of means to attain that end and does not extend to a change in the end itself, to the reduction of profits or to the nondistribution of profits among stockholders in order to devote them to other purposes.

. . . As we have pointed out, and the proposition does not require argument to sustain it, it is not within the lawful powers of a board of directors to shape and conduct the affairs of a corporation for the merely incidental benefit of shareholders and for the primary purpose of benefitting others, and no one will contend that if the avowed purpose of the defendant directors was to sacrifice the interests of shareholders it would not be the duty of the courts to interfere.

A.P. Smith Mfg. Co. v. Barlow

Supreme Court of New Jersey, 1953.
98 A.2d 581, appeal dismissed, 346 U.S. 861, 74 S.Ct. 107, 98 L.Ed. 373 (1953).

■ JACOBS, J. The Chancery Division, in a well-reasoned opinion by Judge Stein, determined that a donation by the plaintiff The A.P. Smith Manufacturing Company to Princeton University was *intra vires.* Because of the public importance of the issues presented, the appeal duly taken to the Appellate Division has been certified directly to this court under Rule 1:5–1(*a*).

The company was incorporated in 1896 and is engaged in the manufacture and sale of valves, fire hydrants and special equipment, mainly for water and gas industries. Its plant is located in East Orange and Bloomfield and it has approximately 300 employees. Over the years the company has contributed regularly to the local community chest and on occasions to Upsala College in East Orange and Newark University, now part of Rutgers, the State University. On July 24, 1951 the board of directors adopted a resolution which set forth that it was in the corporation's best interests to join with others in the 1951 Annual Giving to Princeton University, and appropriated the sum of $1,500 to be transferred by the corporation's treasurer to the university as a contribution towards its maintenance. When this action was questioned by stockholders the corporation instituted a declaratory judgment action in the Chancery Division and trial was had in due course.

Mr. Hubert F. O'Brien, the president of the company, testified that he considered the contribution to be a sound investment, that the public expects corporations to aid philanthropic and benevolent institutions, that they obtain good will in the community by so doing, and that their charitable donations create favorable environment for their business operations. In addition, he expressed the thought that in contributing to liberal arts institutions, corporations were furthering their self-interest in assuring the free flow of properly trained personnel for administrative and other corporate employment. Mr. Frank W. Abrams, chairman of the board of the Standard Oil Company of New Jersey, testified that corporations are expected to acknowledge their public responsibilities in support of the essential elements of our free enterprise system. He indicated that it was not "good business" to disappoint "this reasonable and justified public expectation," nor was it good business for corporations "to take substantial benefits from their membership in the economic community while avoiding the normally accepted obligations of citizenship in the social community." Mr. Irving S. Olds, former chairman of the board of the United States Steel Corporation, pointed out that corporations have a self-interest in the maintenance of liberal education as the bulwark of good government. He stated that "Capitalism and free enterprise owe their survival in no small degree to the existence of our private, independent universities" and that if American business does not aid in their maintenance it is not "properly protecting the long-range interest of its stockholders, its employees and its customers." Similarly, Dr. Harold W. Dodds, President of Princeton University, suggested that if private institutions of higher learning were replaced by governmental institutions our society would be vastly different and private enterprise in other fields would fade out rather promptly. Further on he stated that "democratic society will not long endure if it does not nourish within itself strong centers of non-governmental fountains of knowledge, opinions of all sorts not governmentally or politically originated. If the time comes when all these centers are absorbed into government, then freedom as we know it, I submit, is at an end."

The objecting stockholders have not disputed any of the foregoing testimony nor the showing of great need by Princeton and other private institutions of higher learning and the important public service being rendered by them for democratic government and industry alike. Similarly, they have acknowledged that for over two decades there has been state legislation on our books which expresses a strong public policy in favor of corporate contributions such as that being questioned by them. Nevertheless, they have taken the position that (1) the plaintiff's certificate of incorporation does not expressly authorize the contribution and under common-law principles the company does not possess any implied or incidental power to make it, and (2) the New Jersey statutes which expressly authorize the contribution may not constitutionally be applied to the plaintiff, a corporation created long before their enactment. *See* R.S. 14:3–13; R.S. 14:3–13.1 et seq.

In his discussion of the early history of business corporations Professor Williston refers to a 1702 publication where the author stated flatly that "The general intent and end of all civil incorporations is for better government." And he points out that the early corporate charters, particularly their recitals, furnish additional support for the notion that the corporate object was the public one of managing and ordering the trade as well as the private one of profit for the members. *See* 3 Select Essays on Anglo–American Legal History 201 (1909); 1 Fletcher, Corporations 6 (rev. ed. 1931).... However, with later economic and social developments and the free availability of the corporate device for all trades, the end of private profit became generally accepted as the controlling one in all businesses other than those classed broadly as public utilities. Cf. Dodd, For Whom Are Corporate Managers Trustees?, 45 Harv. L. Rev. 1145, 1148 (1932). As a concomitant the common-law rule developed that those who managed the corporation could not disburse any corporate funds for philanthropic or other worthy public cause unless the expenditure would benefit the corporation. Hutton v. West Cork Railway Company, 23 Ch.D. 654 (1883); Dodge v. Ford Motor Co., 170 N.W. 668 (Mich. 1919).... During the 19th Century when corporations were relatively few and small and did not dominate the country's wealth, the common-law rule did not significantly interfere with the public interest. But the 20th Century has presented a different climate. Berle and Means, The Modern Corporation and Private Property (1948). Control of economic wealth has passed largely from individual entrepreneurs to dominating corporations, and calls upon the corporations for reasonable philanthropic donations have come to be made with increased public support. In many instances such contributions have been sustained by the courts within the common-law doctrine upon liberal findings that the donations tended reasonably to promote the corporate objectives....

... [C]ourts, while adhering to the terms of the common-law rule, have applied it very broadly to enable worthy corporate donations with indirect benefits to the corporations. In State ex rel. Sorensen v. Chicago B. & Q.R. Co., 199 N.W. 534, 537 (Neb. 1924), the Supreme Court of Nebraska, through Justice Letton, went even further and without referring to any limitation based on economic benefits to the corporation said that it saw ... "no reason why a railroad corporation may not, to a reasonable extent, donate funds or services to aid in good works." ...

When the wealth of the nation was primarily in the hands of individuals they discharged their responsibilities as citizens by donating freely for charitable purposes. With the transfer of most of the wealth to corporate hands and the imposition of heavy burdens of individual taxation, they have been unable to keep pace with increased philanthropic needs. They have therefore, with justification, turned to corporations to assume the modern obligations of good citizenship in the same manner as humans do. Congress and state legislatures have enacted laws which encourage corporate contributions, and much has recently been written to indicate the crying need and adequate legal basis therefor.... In actual practice corporate giving has correspondingly increased. Thus, it is estimated that annual corporate contributions throughout the nation aggregate over 300 million dollars with over 60 million dollars thereof going to universities and other educational institutions. Similarly, it is estimated that local community chests receive well over 40% of their contributions from corporations; these contributions and those made by corporations to the American Red Cross, to Boy Scouts and Girl Scouts, to 4–H Clubs and similar organizations have almost invariably been unquestioned.

During the first world war corporations loaned their personnel and contributed substantial corporate funds in order to insure survival; during the depression of the '30s they made contributions to alleviate the desperate hardships of the millions of unemployed; and during the second world war they again contributed to insure survival. They now recognize that we are faced with other, though nonetheless vicious, threats from abroad which must be withstood without impairing the vigor of our democratic institutions at home and that otherwise victory will be pyrrhic indeed. More and more they have come to recognize that their salvation rests upon sound economic and social environment which in turn rests in no insignificant part upon free and vigorous nongovernmental institutions of learning. It seems to us that just as the conditions prevailing when corporations were originally created required that they serve public as well as private interests, modern conditions require that corporations acknowledge and discharge social as well as private responsibilities as members of the communities within which they operate. Within this broad concept there is no difficulty in sustaining, as incidental to their proper objects and in aid of the public welfare, the power of corporations to contribute corporate funds within reasonable limits in support of academic institutions. But even if we confine ourselves to the terms of the common-law rule in its application to current conditions, such expenditures may likewise readily be justified as being for the benefit of the corporation; indeed, if need be the matter may be viewed strictly in terms of actual survival of the corporation in a free enterprise system....

In 1930 a statute was enacted in our State which expressly provided that any corporation could cooperate with other corporations and natural persons in the creation and maintenance of community funds and charitable, philanthropic or benevolent instrumentalities conducive to public welfare, and could for such purposes expend such corporate sums as the directors "deem expedient and as in their judgment will contribute to the protection of the corporate interests." . . .

In 1950 a more comprehensive statute was enacted. L. 1950, c. 220; N.J.S.A. 14:3–13.1 et seq. In this enactment the Legislature declared that it shall be the public policy of our State and in furtherance of the public interest and welfare that encouragement be given to the creation and maintenance of institutions engaged in community fund, hospital, charitable, philanthropic, educational, scientific or benevolent activities or patriotic or civic activities conducive to the betterment of social and economic conditions; and it expressly empowered corporations acting singly or with others to contribute reasonable sums to such institutions, provided, however, that the contribution shall not be permissible if the donee institution owns more than 10% of the voting stock of the donor and provided, further, that the contribution shall not exceed 1% of capital and surplus unless the excess is authorized by the stockholders at a regular or special meeting. To insure that the grant of express power in the 1950 statute would not displace preexisting power at common law or otherwise, the Legislature provided that the "act shall not be construed as directly or indirectly minimizing or interpreting the rights and powers of corporations, as heretofore existing, with reference to appropriations, expenditures or contributions of the nature above specified." N.J.S.A. 14:3–13.3. It may be noted that statutes relating to charitable contributions by corporations have now been passed in 29 states. *See* Andrews, supra, 235.

The appellants contend that the foregoing New Jersey statutes may not be applied to corporations created before their passage. Fifty years before the incorporation of The A.P. Smith Manufacturing Company our Legislature provided that every corporate charter thereafter granted "shall be subject to alteration, suspension and repeal, in the discretion of the legislature." L.1846, p. 16; R.S. 14:2–9. A similar reserved power was placed into our State Constitution in 1875 (Art. IV, Sec. VII, par. 11), and is found in our present Constitution....

... We are entirely satisfied that within the orbit of above authorities the legislative enactments found in R.S. 14:3–13 and N.J.S.A. 14:3–13.1 et seq. and applied to pre-existing corporations do not violate any constitutional guarantees afforded to their stockholders.

... And since in our view the corporate power to make reasonable charitable contributions exists under modern conditions, even apart from express statutory provision, its enactments simply constitute helpful and confirmatory declarations of such power, accompanied by limiting safeguards.

In the light of all of the foregoing we have no hesitancy in sustaining the validity of the donation by the plaintiff. There is no suggestion that it was made indiscriminately or to a pet charity of the corporate directors in furtherance of personal rather than corporate ends. On the contrary, it was made to a preeminent institution of higher learning, was modest in amount and well within the limitations imposed by the statutory enactments, and was voluntarily made in the reasonable belief that it would aid the public welfare and advance the interests of the plaintiff as a private corporation and as part of the community in which it operates. We find that it was a lawful exercise of the corporation's implied and incidental powers under common-law principles and that it came within the express authority of the pertinent state legislation. As has been indicated, there is now widespread belief throughout the nation that free and vigorous non-governmental institutions of learning are vital to our democracy and the system of free enterprise and that withdrawal of corporate authority to make such contributions within reasonable limits would seriously threaten their continuance. Corporations have come to recognize this and with their enlightenment have sought in varying measures, as has the plaintiff by its contribution, to insure and strengthen the society which gives them existence and the means of aiding themselves and their fellow citizens. Clearly then, the appellants, as individual stockholders whose private interests rest entirely upon the well-being of the plaintiff corporation, ought not be permitted to close their eyes to present-day realities and thwart the long-visioned corporate action in recognizing and voluntarily discharging its high obligations as a constituent of our modern social structure.

The judgment entered in the Chancery Division is in all respects

Affirmed.

■ *For affirmance*—CHIEF JUSTICE VANDERBILT, and JUSTICES HEHER, OLIPHANT, WACHENFELD, BURLING and JACOBS—6.

For reversal—None.

DEL. GEN. CORP. LAW § 122(9), (12)

[See Statutory Supplement]

MODEL BUS. CORP. ACT § 3.02(12)–(14)

[See Statutory Supplement]

NOTE ON THE CONDUCT OF THE CORPORATION

1. Virtually all states have now adopted statutory provisions relating to corporate contributions that are comparable to Del.Gen. Corp.Law § 122(9) and Model Bus.Corp.Act § 3.02(13). Although typically these provisions do not explicitly incorporate a limit of reasonableness, the commentators generally agree that such a limit is to be implied. Of particular significance is the commentary of Ray Garrett, a principal figure in the drafting history of the Model Act:

> Donations should be reasonable in amount in the light of the corporation's financial condition, bear some reasonable relation to the corporation's interest, and not be so "remote and fanciful" as to excite the opposition of shareholders whose property is being used. Direct corporate benefit is no longer necessary, but corporate interest remains as a motive.

Garrett, Corporate Donations, 22 BUS. LAW. 297, 301 (1967).

2. There is very little direct authority on the permissibility of taking ethical considerations into account in framing corporate action where doing so might not enhance profits. However, statutory provisions like Model Bus.Corp.Act § 3.02(13) provide indirect support for doing so, since it would be anomalous to permit the corporation to donate money it has already earned for public welfare or charitable purposes, while prohibiting the corporation from forgoing a limited amount of profits in the service of generally recognized ethical principles.

The Conference Board conducts an annual survey of corporate giving. The Board's 2009 Corporate Contributions Report is based on giving in 2008 by 166 participants. The median contribution was 1 percent of pretax income. The comparable figure for 2007 was .76 percent. The Report surmises that the increases in the median from 2007 to 2008 resulted from the fact that 2008 was a recession year, and that charitable contributions did not diminish as much as pretax income did.

MILTON FRIEDMAN, THE SOCIAL RESPONSIBILITY OF BUSINESS IS TO INCREASE ITS PROFITS, N.Y. Times, Sept. 13, 1970, § 6 (magazine) at 32. "In a free-enterprise, private-property system, a corporate executive is an employee of the owners of the business. He has direct responsibility to his employers. That responsibility is to conduct the business in accordance with their desires, which generally will be to make as much money as possible while conforming to the basic rules of the society, both those embodied in law and those embodied in ethical custom."

AMERICAN LAW INSTITUTE, PRINCIPLES OF CORPORATE GOVERNANCE §§ 2.01, 6.02

[See Statutory Supplement]

CONN. GEN. STATS. ANN. §§ 33–756

[See Statutory Supplement]

IND. CODE ANN. § 23–1–35–1

[See Statutory Supplement]

N.Y. BUS. CORP. LAW § 717

[See Statutory Supplement]

PENNSYLVANIA CONSOL. STATS. ANN. TITLE 15, §§ 1711, 1715, 1716, 1717, 2502

[See Statutory Supplement]

NOTE ON OTHER CONSTITUENCIES UNDER DELAWARE LAW

Unlike the statutes cross-referenced above, the Delaware statute does not have an other-constituency provision—that is, a provision that explicitly empowers the board, in making decisions, to take into account the interests of groups, other than the shareholders, that are affected by corporate decisions, such as labor and the community. However, the Delaware Supreme Court has made a several pronouncements—not all of which seem to be consistent—on this issue. Most or all of these pronouncements have occurred in takeover cases, and have addressed the board's power to take an action, in favor of other constituencies, whose effect is to block a takeover. The seminal Delaware case on that issue is Unocal Corp. v. Mesa Petroleum Co., 493 A.2d 946, 955 (Del.1985). (This case is set out in Chapter X, Section x.) There the court said:

> In [determining] the board's exercise of corporate power to forestall a takeover bid our analysis begins with the basic principle that corporate directors have a fiduciary duty to act in the best interests of the corporation's stockholders. . . .
>
> * * *
>
> An aspect of review [of a board action to block a tender offer] is the element of balance. [A] defensive measure must be reasonable in relation to the threat posed. This entails an analysis by the directors of the nature of the takeover bid and its effect on the corporate enterprise. Examples of [such concerns] may include: inadequacy of the price offered, nature and timing of the offer, questions of illegality, the impact on the "constituencies" other than shareholders (i.e., creditors, customers, employees, and perhaps even the community generally), the risk of nonconsummation, and the quality of securities being offered in the exchange. . . .

These two passages seem to pull in opposite directions: the first passage focuses only on interests of the shareholders, while the second passage refers to the interests of other constituencies as well. However, in a later case, Revlon, Inc. v. MacAndrews & Forbes Holdings, Inc., 506 A.2d 173, 176 (Del.1986), the Delaware Court put an important limit on the second passage in *Unocal:*

> . . . [W]hile concern for various corporate constituencies is proper when addressing a takeover threat, that principle is limited by the requirement that there be some rationally related benefit accruing to the stockholders.
>
> * * *
>
> The Revlon board argued that it acted in good faith in protecting the noteholders because *Unocal* permits consideration of other corporate constituencies. Although such considerations may be permissible, there are fundamental limitations upon that prerogative. A board may have regard of various constituencies in discharging its responsibilities, provided there are rationally related benefits accruing to the stockholders.

In subsequent opinions the Delaware Supreme Court repeated the *Unocal* litany, sometimes explicitly including the *Revlon* qualification, *see, e.g.*, Mills Acquisition Co. v. Macmillan, Inc., 559 A.2d 1261, 1282 n. 29 (Del.1989), and sometimes not, *see, e.g.*, Ivanhoe Partners v. Newmont Mining Corp., 535 A.2d 1334, 1341–42 (Del.1987).

The Delaware cases also suggest that a board can act against threats to "corporate policy" or "corporate policy and effectiveness." *See Unocal,* supra, and *Ivanhoe Partners*, supra. These suggestions leave open whether "corporate policy" is an autonomous goal, which the board can choose to further independent of the concept of maximizing shareholder interests. Some passages in Paramount Communications, Inc. v. Time Inc., 571 A.2d 1140 (Del.1989), seem to suggest this possibility. For example, in that case the court mentioned, with apparent approval, that the board was motivated by a desire to see "to the preservation of Time's 'culture,' i.e., its perceived editorial integrity in journalism...." Other language in the case, however, seems to focus on a threat to the shareholder's interests.

This issue was revisited in *eBay*, discussed above. Craig and Jim, two of eBay's three shareholders, wanted to prevent craigslist, the third shareholder, from being able to name one of eBay's directors or purchase more eBay stock. To this end, Craig and Jim adopted several defensive measures, including a staggered board and a poison pill that would prevent eBay from purchasing more craigslist stock by diluting the value of any shares that eBay purchased. eBay filed an action challenging these measures. Under Unocal v. Mesa Petroleum Co., supra, a corporation could adopt this kind of defensive measure if it was a reasonable response to a threat to the corporation's policy and effectiveness.

Although craigslist was a for-profit corporation, it operated its business largely as a community service. Nearly all classified advertisements on craigslist were placed free of charge, and craigslist did not sell advertising space. Its revenue stream consisted solely of fees for online job postings in certain cities and for apartment listings in New York City. These fees were more than enough to meet craigslist's operating and capital needs. The craigslist management team, consisting principally of Craig and Jim, were committed to this community-service approach to doing business, so that for most of its history craigslist had not focused on monetizing its site. Craig and Jim sought to bring the measures within *Unocal* and *Paramount* by arguing that they properly perceived that eBay posed a threat to craigslist's policy and effectiveness, including departure from craigslist's public-service culture in favor of increased monetization. The court rejected this defense:

> It is true that on the unique facts of a particular case—*Paramount Communications, Inc. v. Time Inc.*[7]—this Court and the Delaware Supreme Court accepted defensive action by the directors of a Delaware corporation as a good faith effort to protect a specific corporate culture. It was a muted embrace. Chancellor Allen wrote only that that he was "not persuaded that

7. 571 A.2d 1140 (Del. 1990).

there may not be instances in which the law might recognize as valid a perceived threat to a 'corporate culture' that is shown to be palpable (for lack of a better word), distinctive and advantageous."[8] This conditional, limited, and double-negative-laden comment was offered in a case that involved the journalistic independence of an iconic American institution. Even in that fact-specific context, the acceptance of the amorphous purpose of "cultural protection" as a justification for defensive action did not escape criticism.

More importantly, *Time* did not hold that corporate culture, standing alone, is worthy of protection as an end in itself. Promoting, protecting, or pursuing non-stockholder considerations must lead at some point to value for stockholders. When director decisions are reviewed under the business judgment rule, this Court will not question rational judgments about how promoting non-stockholder interests—be it through making a charitable contribution, paying employees higher salaries and benefits, or more general norms like promoting a particular corporate culture—ultimately promote stockholder value. Under the *Unocal* standard, however, the directors must act within the range of reasonableness.

Ultimately, defendants failed to prove that craigslist possesses a palpable, distinctive, and advantageous culture that sufficiently promotes stockholder value to support the indefinite implementation of a poison pill. Jim and Craig did not make any serious attempt to prove that the craigslist culture, which rejects any attempt to further monetize its services, translates into increased profitability for stockholders. I am sure that part of the reason craigslist is so popular is because it offers a free service that is also extremely useful. It may be that offering free classifieds is an essential component of a successful online classifieds venture. After all, by offering free classifieds, craigslist is able to attract such a large community of users that real estate brokers in New York City gladly pay fees to list apartment rentals in order to access the vast community of craigslist users. Likewise, employers in select cities happily pay fees to advertise job openings to craigslist users. . . .

Giving away services to attract business is a sales tactic, however, not a corporate culture. . . . The existence of a distinctive craigslist "culture" was not proven at trial. It is a fiction, invoked almost talismanically for purposes of this trial in order to find deference under *Time*'s dicta.

. . . As an abstract matter, there is nothing inappropriate about an organization seeking to aid local, national, and global communities by providing a website for online classifieds that is largely devoid of monetized elements. . . . The corporate form in

8. Paramount Communications, Inc. v. Time Inc., 1989 WL 79880, at *4 (Del. Ch. July 14, 1989), *aff'd*, 571 A.2d 1140 (Del. 1990).

which craigslist operates, however, is not an appropriate vehicle for purely philanthropic ends, at least not when there are other stockholders interested in realizing a return on their investment. Jim and Craig opted to form craigslist, Inc. as a *for-profit Delaware corporation* and voluntarily accepted millions of dollars from eBay as part of a transaction whereby eBay became a stockholder. Having chosen a for-profit corporate form, the craigslist directors are bound by the fiduciary duties and standards that accompany that form. Those standards include acting to promote the value of the corporation for the benefit of its stockholders. The "Inc." after the company name has to mean at least that. Thus, I cannot accept as valid for the purposes of implementing the Rights Plan a corporate policy that specifically, clearly, and admittedly seeks *not* to maximize the economic value of a for-profit Delaware corporation for the benefit of its stockholders—no matter whether those stockholders are individuals of modest means or a corporate titan of online commerce. If Jim and Craig were the only stockholders affected by their decisions, then there would be no one to object. eBay, however, holds a significant stake in craigslist, and Jim and Craig's actions affect others besides themselves. . . .

CHAPTER 5

THE LEGAL STRUCTURE OF PUBLICLY HELD CORPORATIONS

Melvin A. Eisenberg, The Structure of the Corporation 1

(1976).

Corporate law is constitutional law; that is, its dominant function is to regulate the manner in which the corporate institution is constituted, to define the relative rights and duties of those participating in the institution, and to delimit the powers of the institution vis-à-vis the external world.

INTRODUCTORY NOTE

This Chapter concerns the power and roles of a corporation's three major organs—the board, the shareholders, and the executives (particularly the chief executive officer, or CEO)—in the governance of publicly held corporations.*

Publicly held corporations, taken as a group, are the driving force of the American economy, and also play very important roles in American political and social life. Accordingly, the governance of publicly held corporations is a matter of critical concern. Corporate governance involves a number of issues, such as ensuring a reliable flow of information to the board and to the shareholders, and ensuring that the corporation's conduct conforms to law. However, since publicly held corporations are primarily, although not exclusively, economic institutions, probably the most important objective of corporate governance is to provide mechanisms that will increase the likelihood that such corporations will be efficiently managed. Because the dominant figure in American publicly held corporations is the CEO, a core problem of corporate governance is the design of mechanisms that will monitor CEOs and, where necessary, remove inefficient CEOs.

* There is no settled definition of a publicly held corporation. ALI, Principles of Corporate Governance § 1.31 defines a publicly held corporation as one that has 500 or more holders of its equity securities and $5 million or more of total assets. ALI Section 1.24 defines a large publicly held corporation as one that has 2,000 or more holders of its equity securities and $100 million or more of total assets. In this Chapter, the terms *corporation* and *publicly held corporation* will be used interchangeably.

Some of this work can be done by market forces, but these forces are insufficiently strong to reliably accomplish that objective. For example, the market for corporate control, which operates through takeovers, provides only very loose discipline of managers. A hostile takeover bidder must incur substantial out-of-pocket expenditures for legal fees, printing, and advertising to make a bid; must incur additional out-of-pocket expenses of if the incumbent management resists the bid, as it usually does; and typically must offer a price at least 30% or so above the market price of the corporation's if the bid is to be successful. As a result, a hostile bidder can make a profit by replacing the incumbent management only if the management is so inefficient that a successful bidder can raise the price of the stock in excess of the premium and the out-of-pocket costs for making and pressing the bid. Similarly, the so-called market for managers has completely broken down, as evidenced by the huge salaries and bonuses paid to commercial and investment bank executives whose incompetence was one substantial cause of the recession that began in 2008, and of Enron and other corporate debacles before that. This is not to say that markets don't work at all in disciplining inefficient managers, but only that they are very far from perfect instruments in achieving that objective. Therefore, it is important to shape the role of the board and the shareholders to help accomplish the objective. Like markets, neither the board nor the shareholders can be counted on to reliably accomplish that objective. However, because all institutions to accomplish that objective are imperfect, it is important to have multiple such institutions in place.

The role and power of the major corporate organs can best be understood by considering the distribution of power among these organs in law and in practice. Section 1 considers the legal distribution of power between the board and the shareholders. Section 2 considers the ways in which corporate practice affects that distribution. Section 3 considers the distribution of power between the board and the executives.

SECTION 1. THE LEGAL DISTRIBUTION OF POWER BETWEEN THE BOARD AND THE SHAREHOLDERS, AND EQUITABLE LIMITS ON THE BOARD'S LEGAL POWER

A. THE LEGAL DISTRIBUTION OF POWER BETWEEN THE BOARD AND THE SHAREHOLDERS

DEL. GEN. CORP. LAW § 141(a)

[See Statutory Supplement]

MODEL BUS. CORP. ACT § 8.01(b)

[See Statutory Supplement]

Charlestown Boot & Shoe Co. v. Dunsmore

New Hampshire Supreme Court, 1880.
60 N.H. 85.

Case. Demurrer to the declaration in which the following facts were alleged:—The plaintiffs are a manufacturing corporation having for its object a dividend of profits, and commenced business in 1871. Dunsmore was elected director in 1871 and Willard in 1873, and entered upon the discharge of their duties, and have continued so to act by virtue of successive elections until the present time. December 10, 1874, the corporation* voted to choose a committee to act with the directors to close up its affairs, and chose one Osgood for such committee. Osgood tendered his services, but the defendants refused to act with him, and contracted new debts to a larger extent than allowed by law. By their negligence, debts due to the corporation to the amount of $2,161.23 have been wholly lost. By their negligence in disposing of the goods of the corporation, a loss has accrued of $3,300.40. By their neglect to sell the buildings and machinery of the corporation when they might and ought, and were urged by Osgood to sell, the same depreciated in value to the extent of $20,000.

Also for that the plaintiffs owned and possessed a certain shop of the value of $10,000, and a large amount of machinery and fixtures of the value of $10,000; "and whereas it was the duty of said defendants, directors as aforesaid, to procure sufficient and proper insurance against fire to be made on said property, and keep the same so sufficiently insured, of all which the said defendants had notice, yet they did not and would not keep the said property so insured, and afterwards, to wit, on the 28th day of April, 1878, while the said property was so remaining without insurance, the same was wholly consumed by fire and wholly lost to the plaintiff, whereby the plaintiff suffered great loss and damage, to wit, $20,000."

■ SMITH, J. The provision of the statute is, that the business of a dividend paying corporation shall be managed by the directors. The statute reads, "The business of every such corporation shall be managed by the directors thereof, subject to the by-laws and votes of the corporation, and under their direction by such officers and agents as

---

* By "the corporation," as that term used in this opinion, the court seems to mean the body of shareholders. (Footnote by ed.)

shall be duly appointed by the directors or by the corporation." G.L., c. 148, s. 3; Gen.Stats., c. 134, s. 3. The only limitation upon the judgment or discretion of the directors is such as the corporation by its by-laws and votes shall impose. It may define its business, its nature and extent, prescribe rules and regulations for the government of its officers and members, and determine whether its business shall be wound up or continued; but when it has thus acted, the business as thus defined and limited is to be managed by its directors, and by such officers and agents under their direction as the directors or the corporation shall appoint. The statute does not authorize a corporation to join another officer with the directors, nor compel the directors to act with one who is not a director. They are bound to use ordinary care and diligence in the care and management of the business of the corporation, and are answerable for ordinary negligence. March v. Railroad, 43 N.H. 516, 529; Scott v. Depeyster, 1 Edw. Ch. 513, 543; Ang. & Ames Corp., § 314. There is no difference in this respect between the agents of corporations and those of natural persons, unless expressly made by the charter or by-laws. *Id.*, § 315. It would be unreasonable to hold them responsible for the management of the affairs of the corporation if compelled to act with one who to a greater or less extent could control their acts. The statute not only entrusts the management of the business of the corporation to the directors, but places its other officers and agents under their direction. When a statute provides that powers granted to a corporation shall be exercised by any set of officers or any particular agents, such powers can be exercised only by such officers or agents, although they are required to be chosen by the whole corporation; and if the whole corporation attempts to exercise powers which by the charter are lodged elsewhere, its action upon the subject is void. Insurance Co. v. Keyser, 32 N.H. 313, 315. The vote choosing Osgood a committee to act with the directors in closing up the affairs of the plaintiff corporation was inoperative and void.

The declaration also alleges that it was the duty of the defendants, as directors, to keep the property of the corporation insured. There is no statute that makes it the duty of the directors of a corporation to keep its property insured, and there are no facts alleged from which we can say, as matter of law, that it was the duty of the defendants to insure the property of the corporation.

Demurrer sustained.

■ STANLEY, J., did not sit: the others concurred.

PEOPLE EX REL. MANICE v. POWELL, 201 N.Y. 194, 200–01, 94 N.E. 634, 637 (1911). "The board of directors of a corporation do not stand in the same relation to the corporate body which a private agent holds towards his principal. . . . In corporate bodies the powers of the board of directors are, in a very important sense, original and undelegated.' (Hoyt v. Thompson's Executors, 19 N.Y. 207, 216; Beveridge v. N.Y.E.R.R. Co., 112 N.Y. 1, 22, 23.)

"While the ordinary rules of law relating to an agent are applicable in considering the acts of a board of directors in behalf of a corporation when dealing with third persons, the individual directors making up the board are not mere employees, but a part of an elected body of officers constituting the executive agents of the corporation. They hold such office charged with the duty to act for the corporation according to their best judgment, and in so doing they cannot be controlled in the reasonable exercise and performance of such duty. As a general rule the stockholders cannot act in relation to the ordinary business of the corporation, nor can they control the directors in the exercise of the judgment vested in them by virtue of their office.

"The relation of the directors to the stockholders is essentially that of trustee and *cestui que trust.* The peculiar relation that they bear to the corporation and the owners of its stock grows out of the inability of the corporation to act except through such managing officers and agents. The corporation is the owner of the property, but the directors in the performance of their duty possess it, and act in every way as if they owned it. . . ."

DEL. GEN. CORP. LAW § 141(k)

[See Statutory Supplement]

CAL. CORP. CODE §§ 303, 304

[See Statutory Supplement]

N.Y. BUS. CORP. LAW § 706

[See Statutory Supplement]

B. EQUITABLE LIMITS ON THE BOARD'S LEGAL POWERS

NOTE ON CONDEC CORP. v. LUNKENHEIMER CO.

In Condec Corp. v. Lunkenheimer Co., 230 A.2d 769 (Del.Ch. 1967), Condec wanted to merge with Lunkenheimer but Lunkenheimer resisted. Condec then acquired some Lunkenheimer shares through a tender offer, and made a second tender offer which, if successful, would have given Condec slightly more than half of Lunkenheimer's 410,000 shares. Lunkenheimer's board then caused Lunkenheimer to swap 75,000 shares of its stock for 75,000 shares of a wholly owned subsidiary of U.S. Industries. This swap would dilute Condec's interest to a minority. Condec attacked the transaction. Held, for Condec:

> [S]hares may not be issued for an improper purpose such as a take-over of voting control from others. As stated in Yasik v. Wachtel, 17 A.2d 309, 313 (Del. Ch. 1941):
>
> > It is fundamental that directors stand in a fiduciary relation to the corporation and its shareholders, and that their primary duty is to deal fairly and justly. It is a breach of this duty, wholly apart from any consideration of pre-emptive rights, for directors to make use of the issuance of shares to accomplish an improper purpose, such as to enable a particular person or group to maintain or obtain voting control, against the objection of shareholders from whom control is thereby wrested....
>
> This does not mean that stock issued to raise money to eliminate a deficit is to be invalidated merely because defendant directors thereby fairly avail themselves of an opportunity to acquire additional shares to fortify their natural desire to remain in control, Aldridge v. Franco–Wyoming, 28 Del.Ch. 320, 326, 42 A.2d 879. Where, however, the objective sought in the issuance of stock is not merely the pursual of a business purpose but also to retain control, it has been held to be a mockery to suggest that the "control" effect of an agreement in litigation is merely incidental to its primary business objective. In Matter of Seminole Oil and Gas Corporation, 38 Del.Ch. 246, 150 A.2d 20....
>
> Finally, we are not here concerned with the need of proving corporate injury as has been held to be the case when a stockholder attacks derivatively the spending of corporate funds for the purchase of his corporation's own stock, Kors v. Carey, 39 Del.Ch. 47, 158 A.2d 136. This rather is a case of a stockholder with a contractual right to assert voting control being deprived of such control by what is virtually a corporate legerdemain. Manipulation of this type is not permissible, Canada Southern Oils v. Manabi Exploration Co., 33 Del.Ch. 537, 96 A.2d 810.

Schnell v. Chris–Craft Industries, Inc.

Supreme Court of Delaware, 1971.
285 A.2d 437.

■ HERRMANN, JUSTICE (for the majority of the court):

This is an appeal from the denial by the Court of Chancery of the petition of dissident stockholders for injunctive relief to prevent management[1] from advancing the date of the annual stockholders' meeting from January 11, 1972, as previously set by the by-laws, to December 8, 1971.

The opinion below is reported at 285 A.2d 430. This opinion is confined to the frame of reference of the opinion below for the sake of brevity and because of the strictures of time imposed by the circumstances of the case.

It will be seen that the Chancery Court considered all of the reasons stated by management as business reasons for changing the date of the meeting; but that those reasons were rejected by the Court below in making the following findings:

> "I am satisfied, however, in a situation in which present management has disingenuously resisted the production of a list of its stockholders to plaintiffs or their confederates and has otherwise turned a deaf ear to plaintiffs' demands about a change in management designed to lift defendant from its present business doldrums, management has seized on a relatively new section of the Delaware Corporation Law for the purpose of cutting down on the amount of time which would otherwise have been available to plaintiffs and others for the waging of a proxy battle. Management thus enlarged the scope of its scheduled October 18 directors' meeting to include the by-law amendment in controversy after the stockholders committee had filed with the S.E.C. its intention to wage a proxy fight on October 16.
>
> "Thus plaintiffs reasonably contend that because of the tactics employed by management (which involve the hiring of two established proxy solicitors as well as a refusal to produce a list of its stockholders, coupled with its use of an amendment to the Delaware Corporation Law to limit the time for contest), they are given little chance, because of the exigencies of time, including that required to clear material at the S.E.C., to wage a successful proxy fight between now and December 8. . . ."

In our view, those conclusions amount to a finding that management has attempted to utilize the corporate machinery and the Delaware Law for the purpose of perpetuating itself in office; and, to that end, for the purpose of obstructing the legitimate efforts of dissident stockholders in the exercise of their rights to undertake a proxy contest against management. These are inequitable purposes, contrary to established principles of corporate democracy. The advancement by directors of the by-law date of a stockholders' meeting, for such purposes, may not be permitted to stand. Compare Condec Corp. v. Lunkenheimer Co., 230 A.2d 769 (Del.Ch.1967).

When the by-laws of a corporation designate the date of the annual meeting of stockholders, it is to be expected that those who intend to contest the reelection of incumbent management will gear their campaign to the by-law date. It is not to be expected that

1. We use this word as meaning "managing directors".

management will attempt to advance that date in order to obtain an inequitable advantage in the contest.

Management contends that it has complied strictly with the provisions of the new Delaware Corporation Law in changing the by-law date. The answer to that contention, of course, is that inequitable action does not become permissible simply because it is legally possible. . . .

We are unable to agree with the conclusion of the Chancery Court that the stockholders' application for injunctive relief here was tardy and came too late. . . .

Accordingly, the judgment below must be reversed and the cause remanded, with instructions to nullify the December 8 date as a meeting date for stockholders; to reinstate January 11, 1972 as the sole date of the next annual meeting of the stockholders of the corporation; and to take such other proceedings and action as may be consistent herewith regarding the stock record closing date and any other related matters.

[The dissenting opinion of Chief Justice Wolcott is omitted.]

A.A. BERLE & G. MEANS, THE MODERN CORPORATION AND PRIVATE PROPERTY 220 (rev. ed. 1967). "[A]n underlying thesis in corporation law . . . could be applied to each and every power in the whole corporate galaxy. Succinctly stated, the thesis appears to be that all powers granted to a corporation or to the management of a corporation, or to any group within the corporation, whether derived from statute or charter or both, are necessarily and at all times exercisable only for the ratable benefit of all the shareholders as their interest appears. That, in consequence, the *use* of the power is subject to equitable limitation when the power has been exercised to the detriment of their interest, however absolute the grant of power may be in terms, and however correct the technical exercise of it may have been."

Blasius Industries, Inc. v. Atlas Corp.

Court of Chancery of Delaware, 1988.
564 A.2d 651.

■ Opinion by ALLEN, CHANCELLOR.

Two cases pitting the directors of Atlas Corporation against that company's largest (9.1%) shareholder, Blasius Industries, have been consolidated and tried together. Together, these cases ultimately require the court to determine who is entitled to sit on Atlas' board of directors. . . .

The first of the cases was filed on December 30, 1987. As amended, it challenges the validity of board action taken at a telephone meeting of December 31, 1987 that added two new members to Atlas' seven member board. That action was taken as an immediate response to the delivery to Atlas by Blasius the previous day of a form of stockholder consent that, if joined in by holders of a majority of Atlas' stock, would have increased the board of Atlas from seven to fifteen members and would have elected eight new members nominated by Blasius.

As I find the facts of this first case, they present the question whether a board acts consistently with its fiduciary duty when it acts, in good faith and with appropriate care, for the primary purpose of preventing or impeding an unaffiliated majority of shareholders from expanding the board and electing a new majority. For the reasons that follow, I conclude that, even though defendants here acted on their view of the corporation's interest and not selfishly, their December 31 action constituted an offense to the relationship between corporate directors and shareholders that has traditionally been protected in courts of equity. As a consequence, I conclude that the board action taken on December 31 was invalid and must be voided....

The facts set forth below represent findings based upon a preponderance of the admissible evidence, as I evaluate it.

I.

Blasius Acquires a 9% Stake in Atlas.

Blasius is a new stockholder of Atlas. It began to accumulate Atlas shares for the first time in July, 1987. On October 29, it filed a Schedule 13D with the Securities Exchange Commission disclosing that, with affiliates, it then owned 9.1% of Atlas' common stock. It stated in that filing that it intended to encourage management of Atlas to consider a restructuring of the Company or other transaction to enhance shareholder values. It also disclosed that Blasius was exploring the feasibility of obtaining control of Atlas, including instituting a tender offer or seeking "appropriate" representation on the Atlas board of directors.

Blasius has recently come under the control of two individuals, Michael Lubin and Warren Delano, who after experience in the commercial banking industry, had, for a short time, run a venture capital operation for a small investment banking firm. Now on their own, they apparently came to control Blasius with the assistance of Drexel Burnham's well noted junk bond mechanism. Since then, they have made several attempts to effect leveraged buyouts, but without success....

The prospect of Messrs. Lubin and Delano involving themselves in Atlas' affairs, was not a development welcomed by Atlas' management. Atlas had a new CEO, defendant Weaver, who had, over the course of the past year or so, overseen a business restructuring of a sort. Atlas had sold three of its five divisions. It had just announced (September 1, 1987) that it would close its once important domestic uranium operation. The goal was to focus the Company on its gold mining business. By October, 1987, the structural changes to do this had been largely accomplished. Mr. Weaver was perhaps thinking that the restructuring that had occurred should be given a chance to produce benefit before another restructuring (such as Blasius had alluded to in its Schedule 13D filing) was attempted, when he wrote in his diary on October 30, 1987:

> 13D by Delano & Lubin came in today. Had long conversation w/MAH & Mark Golden [of Goldman Sachs] on issue. All agree we must dilute these people down by the acquisition of another Co. w/stock, or merger or something else.

The Blasius Proposal of A Leverage Recapitalization or Sale

Immediately after filing its 13D on October 29, Blasius' representatives sought a meeting with the Atlas management. Atlas dragged its feet. A meeting was arranged for December 2, 1987 following the regular meeting of the Atlas board. Attending that meeting were Messrs. Lubin and Delano for Blasius, and, for Atlas, Messrs. Weaver, Devaney (Atlas' CFO), Masinter (legal counsel and director) and Czajkowski (a representative of Atlas' investment banker, Goldman Sachs).

At that meeting, Messrs. Lubin and Delano suggested that Atlas engage in a leveraged restructuring and distribute cash to shareholders. In such a transaction, which is by this date a commonplace form of transaction, a corporation typically raises cash by sale of assets and significant borrowings and makes a large one time cash distribution to shareholders. The shareholders are typically left with cash and an equity interest in a smaller, more highly leveraged enterprise. Lubin and Delano gave the outline of a leveraged recapitalization for Atlas as they saw it.

Immediately following the meeting, the Atlas representatives expressed among themselves an initial reaction that the proposal was infeasible. On December 7, Mr. Lubin sent a letter detailing the proposal. In general, it proposed the following: (1) an initial special cash dividend to Atlas' stockholders in an aggregate amount equal to (a) $35 million, (b) the aggregate proceeds to Atlas from the exercise of option warrants and stock options, and (c) the proceeds from the sale or disposal of all of Atlas' operations that are not related to its continuing minerals operations; and (2) a special non-cash dividend to Atlas' stockholders of an aggregate $125 million principal amount of 7% Secured Subordinated Gold–Indexed Debentures. The funds necessary to pay the initial cash dividend were to principally come from (i) a "gold loan" in the amount of $35,625,000, repayable over a three to five year period and secured by 75,000 ounces of gold at a price of $475 per ounce, (ii) the proceeds from the sale of the discontinued Brockton Sole and Plastics and Ready–Mix Concrete businesses, and (iii) a then expected January, 1988 sale of uranium to the Public Service Electric & Gas Company. . . .

The proposal met with a cool reception from management. . . .

On December 30, 1987, Blasius caused Cede & Co. (the registered owner of its Atlas stock) to deliver to Atlas a signed written consent (1) adopting a precatory resolution recommending that the board develop and implement a restructuring proposal, (2) amending the Atlas bylaws to, among other things, expand the size of the board from seven to fifteen members—the maximum number under Atlas' charter, and (3) electing eight named persons to fill the new directorships. . . .

The reaction was immediate. Mr. Weaver conferred with Mr. Masinter, the Company's outside counsel and a director, who viewed the consent as an attempt to take control of the Company. They decided to call an emergency meeting of the board, even though a regularly scheduled meeting was to occur only one week hence, on January 6, 1988. The point of the emergency meeting was to act on their conclusion (or to seek to have the board act on their conclusion) "that we should add at least one and probably two directors to the board. . . ." (Tr. 85, Vol. II). A quorum of directors, however, could not be arranged for a telephone meeting that day. A telephone meeting was held the next day. At that meeting, the board voted to amend the bylaws to increase the size of the board from seven to nine and appointed John M. Devaney and Harry J. Winters, Jr. to fill those newly created positions. Atlas' Certificate of Incorporation creates staggered terms for directors; the terms to which Messrs. Devaney and Winters were appointed would expire in 1988 and 1990, respectively.

The Motivation of the Incumbent Board In Expanding the Board and Appointing New Members.

In increasing the size of Atlas' board by two and filling the newly created positions, the members of the board realized that they were thereby precluding the holders of a majority of the Company's shares from placing a majority of new directors on the board through Blasius' consent solicitation, should they want to do so. Indeed the evidence establishes that that was the principal motivation in so acting.

The conclusion that, in creating two new board positions on December 31 and electing Messrs. Devaney and Winters to fill those positions the board was principally motivated to prevent or delay the shareholders from possibly placing a majority of new members on the board, is critical to my analysis of the central issue posed by the first filed of the two pending cases. If the board in fact was not so motivated, but rather had taken action completely independently of the consent solicitation, which merely had an incidental impact upon the possible effectuation of any action authorized by the shareholders, it is very unlikely that such action would be subject to judicial nullification. *See, e.g.*, Frantz Mg. Co. v. EAC Indus., 501 A.2d 401, 407 (Del. 1985); Moran v. Household Int'l, Inc., 490 A.2d 1059, 1080, (Del.Ch. 1985), aff'd, 500 A.2d 1346 (Del. 1985). The board, as a general matter, is under no fiduciary obligation to suspend its active management of the firm while the consent solicitation process goes forward. . . .

In this setting I conclude that, while the addition of these qualified men would, under other circumstances, be clearly appropriate as an independent step, such a step was in fact taken in order to impede or preclude a majority of the shareholders from effectively adopting the course proposed by Blasius. . . .

II.

Plaintiff attacks the December 31 board action as a selfishly motivated effort to protect the incumbent board from a perceived threat to its control of Atlas. Their conduct is said to constitute a violation of the principle, applied in such cases as Schnell v. Chris–Craft Industries, 285 A.2d 437 (Del. 1971), that directors hold legal powers [subject] to a supervening duty to exercise such powers in good faith pursuit of what they reasonably believe to be in the corporation's interest. The December 31 action is also said to have been taken in a grossly negligent manner, since it was designed to preclude the recapitalization from being pursued, and the board had no basis at that time to make a prudent determination about the wisdom of that proposal, nor was there any emergency that required it to act in any respect regarding that proposal before putting itself in a position to do so advisedly.

Defendants, of course, contest every aspect of plaintiffs' claims. They claim the formidable protections of the business judgment rule. *See, e.g.*, Aronson v. Lewis, 473 A.2d 805 (Del. 1984); Grobow v. Perot, 539 A.2d 180 (Del. 1988); In re J.P. Stevens & Co., Inc. Shareholders Litig., 542 A.2d 770 (Del. 1988).

They say that, in creating two new board positions and filling them on December 31, they acted without a conflicting interest (since the Blasius proposal did not, in any event, challenge *their* places on the board), they acted with due care (since they well knew the persons they put on the board and did not thereby preclude later consideration of the recapitalization), and they acted in good faith (since they were motivated, they say, to protect the shareholders from the threat of having an impractical, indeed a dangerous, recapitalization program foisted upon them). . . . Accordingly, defendants assert there is no basis to conclude that their December 31 action constituted any violation of the duty of the fidelity that a director owes by reason of his office to the corporation and its shareholders.

Moreover, defendants say that their action was fair, measured and appropriate, in light of the circumstances. Therefore, even should the court conclude that some level of substantive review of it is appropriate under a legal test of fairness, or under the intermediate level of review authorized by Unocal Corp. v. Mesa Petroleum Co., 493 A.2d 946 (Del. 1985), defendants assert that the board's decision must be sustained as valid in both law and equity.

III . . .

On balance, I cannot conclude that the board was acting out of a self-interested motive in any important respect on December 31. I conclude rather that the board saw the "threat" of the Blasius recapitalization proposal as posing vital policy differences between itself and Blasius. It acted, I conclude, in a good faith effort to protect its incumbency, not selfishly, but in order to thwart implementation of the recapitalization that it feared, reasonably, would cause great injury to the Company.

The real question the case presents, to my mind, is whether, in these circumstances, the board, even if it *is* acting with subjective good faith (which will typically, if not always, be a contestable or debatable judicial conclusion), may validly act for the principal purpose of preventing the shareholders from electing a majority of new directors [emphasis in original]. The question thus posed is not one of intentional wrong (or even negligence), but one of authority *as between the fiduciary and the beneficiary* (not simply legal authority, *i.e.,* as between the fiduciary and the world at large).

IV.

It is established in our law that a board may take certain steps—such as the purchase by the corporation of its own stock—that have the effect of defeating a threatened change in corporate control, when those steps are taken advisedly, in good faith pursuit of a corporate interest, and are reasonable in relation to a threat to legitimate corporate interests posed by the proposed change in control. *See* Unocal Corp. v. Mesa Petroleum Co., 493 A.2d 946 (Del. 1985); Kors v. Carey, 158 A.2d 136 (Del. Ch. 1960); Cheff v. Mathes, Del.Supr., 199 A.2d 548 (Del. 1964); Kaplan v. Goldsamt, 380 A.2d 556 (Del. Ch. 1977). Does this rule—that the reasonable exercise of good faith and due care generally validates, in equity, the exercise of legal authority even if the act has an entrenchment effect—apply to action designed for the primary purpose of interfering with the effectiveness of a stockholder vote? Our authorities, as well as sound principles, suggest that the central importance of the franchise to the scheme of corporate governance, requires that, in this setting, that rule not be applied and that closer scrutiny be accorded to such [a] transaction.

1. Why the deferential business judgment rule does not apply to board acts taken for the primary purpose of interfering with a stockholder's vote, even if taken advisedly and in good faith.

A. The question of legitimacy.

The shareholder franchise is the ideological underpinning upon which the legitimacy of directorial power rests. Generally, shareholders have only two protections against perceived inadequate business performance. They may sell their stock (which, if done in sufficient numbers, may so affect security prices as to create an incentive for altered managerial performance), or they may vote to replace incumbent board members.

It has, for a long time, been conventional to dismiss the stockholder vote as a vestige or ritual of little practical importance. It may be that we are now witnessing the emergence of new institutional voices and arrangements that will make the stockholder vote a less predictable affair than it has been. Be that as it may, however, whether the vote is seen functionally as an unimportant formalism, or as an important tool of discipline, it is clear that it is critical to the theory that legitimates the exercise of power by some (directors and officers) over vast aggregations of property that they do not own. Thus, when viewed from a broad, institutional perspective, it can be seen that matters involving the integrity of the shareholder voting process involve [considerations] not present in any other context in which directors exercise delegated power.

B. Questions of this type raise issues of the allocation of authority as between the board and the shareholders.

The distinctive nature of the shareholder franchise context also appears when the matter is viewed from a less generalized, doctrinal point of view. From this point of view, as well, it appears that the ordinary considerations to which the business judgment rule originally responded are simply not present in the shareholder voting context. That is, a decision by the board to act for the primary purpose of preventing the effectiveness of a shareholder vote inevitably involves the question who, as between the principal and the agent, has authority with respect to a matter of internal corporate governance. That, of course, is true in a very specific way in this case which deals with the question who should constitute the board of directors of the corporation, but it will be true in every instance in which an incumbent board seeks to thwart a shareholder majority. A board's decision to act to prevent the shareholders from creating a majority of new board positions and filling them does not involve the exercise of *the corporation's power* over its property, or with respect to *its* rights or obligations; rather, it involves allocation, between shareholders as a class and the board, of effective power with respect to governance of the corporation. This need not be the case with respect to other forms of corporate action that may have an entrenchment effect—such as the stock buybacks present in *Unocal, Cheff* or *Kors v. Carey*, Action designed principally to interfere with the effectiveness of a vote inevitably involves a conflict between the board and a shareholder majority. Judicial review of such action involves a determination of the legal and equitable obligations of an agent towards his principal. This is not, in my opinion, a question that a court may leave to the agent finally to decide so long as he does so honestly and competently; that is, it may not be left to the agent's business judgment.

2. What rule does apply: per se invalidity of corporate acts intended primarily to thwart effective exercise of the franchise or is there an intermediate standard?

Plaintiff argues for a rule of *per se* invalidity once a plaintiff has established that a board has acted for the primary purpose of thwarting the exercise of a shareholder vote. Our opinions in Canada Southern Oils, Ltd. v. Manabi Exploration Co., 96 A.2d 810 (Del. Ch.

1953) and Condec Corp. v. Lunkenheimer Co., 230 A.2d 769 (Del. Ch. 1967) could be read as support for such a rule of *per se* invalidity. . . .

. . . A *per se* rule that would strike down, in equity, any board action taken for the primary purpose of interfering with the effectiveness of a corporate vote would have the advantage of relative clarity and predictability.[4] It also has the advantage of most vigorously enforcing the concept of corporate democracy. The disadvantage it brings along is, of course, the disadvantage a *per se* rule always has: it may sweep too broadly. In two recent cases dealing with shareholder votes, this court struck down board acts done for the primary purpose of impeding the exercise of stockholder voting power. In doing so, a *per se* rule was not applied. Rather, it was said that, in such a case, the board bears the heavy burden of demonstrating a compelling justification for such action. . . .

In my view, our inability to foresee now all of the future settings in which a board might, in good faith, paternalistically seek to thwart a shareholder vote, counsels against the adoption of a *per se* rule invalidating, in equity, every board action taken for the sole or primary purpose of thwarting a shareholder vote, even though I recognize the transcending significance of the franchise to the claims to legitimacy of our scheme of corporate governance. It may be that some set of facts would justify such extreme action. This, however, is not such a case.

3. Defendants have demonstrated no sufficient justification for the action of December 31 which was intended to prevent an unaffiliated majority of shareholders from effectively exercising their right to elect eight new directors.

The board was not faced with a coercive action taken by a powerful shareholder against the interests of a distinct shareholder constituency (such as a public minority). It was presented with a consent solicitation by a 9% shareholder. Moreover, here it had time (and understood that it had time) to inform the shareholders of its views on the merits of the proposal subject to stockholder vote. The only justification that can, in such a situation, be offered for the action taken is that the board knows better than do the shareholders what is in the corporation's best interest. While that premise is no doubt true for any number of matters, it is irrelevant (except insofar as the shareholders wish to be guided by the board's recommendation) when the question is who should comprise the board of directors. The theory of our corporation law confers power upon directors as the agents of the shareholders; it does not create Platonic masters. It may be that the Blasius restructuring proposal was or is unrealistic and would lead to injury to the corporation and its shareholders if pursued. Having heard the evidence, I am inclined to think it was not a sound proposal. The board certainly viewed it that way, and that

4. While it must be admitted that any rule that requires for its invocation the finding of a subjective mental state (*i.e.*, a primary purpose) necessarily will lead to controversy concerning whether it applies or not, nevertheless, once it is determined to apply, this *per se* rule would be clearer than the alternative discussed below.

view, held in good faith, entitled the board to take certain steps to evade the risk it perceived. It could, for example, expend corporate funds to inform shareholders and seek to bring them to a similar point of view. *See, e.g.* Hall v. Trans–Lux Daylight Picture Screen Corp., 171 A. 226, 227 (Del.Ch.1934); Hibbert v. Hollywood Park, Inc., 457 A.2d 339 (Del.1983). But there is a vast difference between expending corporate funds to inform the electorate and exercising power for the primary purpose of foreclosing effective shareholder action. A majority of the shareholders, who were not dominated in any respect, could view the matter differently than did the board. If they do, or did, they are entitled to employ the mechanisms provided by the corporation law and the Atlas certificate of incorporation to advance that view.* They are also entitled, in my opinion, to restrain their agents, the board, from acting for the principal purpose of thwarting that action.

I therefore conclude that, even finding the action was taken in good faith, it constituted an unintended violation of the duty of loyalty that the board owed to the shareholders. I note parenthetically that the concept of an unintended breach of the duty of loyalty is unusual but not novel. That action will, therefore, be set aside by order of this court. . . .

NOTE ON FURTHER PROCEEDINGS IN *BLASIUS*

During the pendency of Blasius's attack on the action of the directors in adding two members to the board, Blasius presented Atlas with shareholder consents purporting to show that a majority of Atlas's shareholders had adopted Blasius's proposals to enlarge the board from seven to fifteen, elect eight new directors nominated by Blasius, and take certain other actions. Atlas appointed Manufacturers Hanover Trust Company to act as judge of the shareholders' "vote." Manufacturers reported that the vote had been extremely close, but that none of Blasius's proposals had succeeded. Blasius then brought a second case, in which it challenged certain of Manufacturers' determinations. That case was consolidated with Blasius's attack on the action of the directors in adding two members to the board. The court upheld most of Manufacturers' determinations, including its conclusion that Blasius had lost the vote, and rendered judgment in the second case for the defendants.

NOTE ON THE BUSINESS JUDGMENT RULE

Corporate law employs a number of different standards of judicial review of the conduct of directors and officers, depending on the type of conduct involved. The most lenient standard—the standard that is easiest for directors and officers to satisfy—is the business judgment

* *Id.* at 663.

rule, referred to in *Blasius*. The meaning and application of this rule is considered in depth in Chapter 10. At this point suffice to say that under the business judgment rule, if certain conditions are satisfied, a disinterested director or officer will not be liable for the adverse consequences of a bad decision unless the decision was irrational. In *Blasius*, Chancellor Allen in effect concluded that conduct that interferes with shareholder voting is not reviewed under the business judgment rule. Instead, a much more stringent standard of review—the standard of compelling justification—should be applied.

C. THE ROLE OF BYLAWS IN THE ALLOCATION OF POWER BETWEEN THE BOARD AND THE SHAREHOLDERS

A corporation normally has two foundational instruments: its certificate of incorporation and its bylaws. Together with state, federal, and soft law, these foundational instruments set out the rules that govern the roles and powers of corporate organs and officers, and other important matters. If there is a conflict between the certificate and the bylaws, the certificate controls.

Corporate bylaws address a variety of matters. Customarily they set forth the time, place and even manner of giving notice for the annual stockholders meeting. As seen earlier, corporate statutes generally permit the bylaws to provide higher or lower quorum or voting requirements than the default rules set forth in the statute. Bylaws frequently set forth the express powers of company officers. Importantly, corporate statutes permit both the board of directors and the shareholders to adopt, amend and repeal bylaws. Not surprisingly, during the past few years bylaw provisions have been something of a battleground between incumbent management and activists shareholders.

One defensive use of bylaws has been the "advance notice bylaw." An advance notice bylaw requires as a predicate to any shareholder proposing a matter for shareholder action at an upcoming meeting that the proposing shareholder must give advance notice of such intention a specified number of days before the meeting. Thus, a shareholder who intends to wage a proxy contest for the election of her slate of directors must give the required notice to the company. A stated benefit of advance notice bylaws is to assure the orderly consideration of business at the upcoming stockholders' meeting. On the other hand, the advance notice bylaw, can be a means for the incumbent management to thwart the efforts of a disgruntled shareholder. The courts of many jurisdictions uphold reasonable advance notice bylaws. *See e.g.*, IBS Fin. Corp. v. Seidman & Assoc., 136 F.3d 940, 944–45 (3d Cir. 1998). Nonetheless, the courts in interpreting advance notice bylaws have been fairly consistent interpreting them strictly so that ambiguities and incompleteness of terms are resolved in favor of the proposing shareholder.

Two Delaware cases highlight the importance of carefully drafted advance notice bylaws. Both cases narrowly interpret the advance notice bylaws in favor of activist investors. In *Jana Master Fund, Ltd. v. CNET Networks, Inc.*, 954 A.2d 335, 337 (Del.Ch.), aff'd, 947 A.2d 1120 (Del. 2008), the plaintiff ("JANA") informed the board of defendant CNET Networks, Inc. ("CNET") that it wished to solicit proxies for its director nominees and various proposals. CNET's notice bylaws required a shareholder seeking to nominate directors or to propose other business at the annual meeting to have beneficially owned $1,000 of common stock for not less than one year. Because JANA had only acquired its shares eight months prior to the expected date of the meeting, CNET contended that JANA's planned proxy solicitation was in violation of the bylaws. The notice bylaw also stated that notice must "comply with the federal securities laws governing shareholder proposals a corporation must include in its own proxy materials." The court held that this language clearly indicated that the bylaw only applied to proposals and to nominations that are to be included in the company's proxy materials. Since JANA intended to finance the proxy mailings itself, the court concluded that the bylaw was inapplicable.

Levitt Corp. v. Office Depot, Inc., 2008 WL 1724244, at *1 (Del. Ch. April 14, 2008), also involved a shareholder's attempt to nominate board members at the annual shareholder meeting. Office Depot, Inc. had sent a proxy statement and notice of annual meeting to the shareholders informing them that twelve directors were to be elected at the meeting. Levitt Corp. filed its own proxy materials with the SEC, but did not give advance notice to Office Depot of its intention to nominate directors. The issue before the court was whether Office Depot's bylaw that required advance notice of "business" to be brought before the annual meeting prevented Levitt from achieving its objectives at the forthcoming meeting. The court concluded that, even though the term "business" includes the nomination of directors, the bylaw did not prevent Levitt from nominating directors and voting for its nominees because Office Depot had fulfilled the bylaw requirement by itself giving notice of this business to be conducted at the meeting.

James D. Cox & Thomas Lee Hazen, 2 Treatise on the Law of Corporations § 13.23 at 521–22 (3d ed. 2010).

Activists shareholders also have also resorted to the stockholders' authority to amend the bylaws as the medium for introducing the changes believed to be in the stockholders' best interest. However, as the next case illustrates, is a good deal of tension surrounds the scope allowed to bylaws vis-à-vis the historical prerogatives and powers of the board of directors.

Under state law, amendments to the certificate of incorporation normally can be proposed only by the board, and can be adopted only if approved by both the board and the shareholders. Accordingly, the shareholders cannot amend the certificate of incorporation, although they have veto power over amendments proposed by the board. In contrast, with some important exceptions, usually either the board or the shareholders can propose and adopt bylaws. Accordingly, one way that shareholders can adopt rules of corporate governance is by amending the corporation's bylaws, provided that the content of the amendment is permissible. What content is permissible in a bylaw is a hotly debated issue, which is addressed in the next case.

CA, Inc. v. AFSCME Employees Pension Plan

Supreme Court of Delaware, 2008.
953 A.2d 227.

■ JACOBS, JUSTICE: . . .

I. *FACTS*

CA is a Delaware corporation whose board of directors consists of twelve persons, all of whom sit for reelection each year. CA's annual meeting of stockholders is scheduled to be held on September 9, 2008. CA intends to file its definitive proxy materials with the SEC on or about July 24, 2008 in connection with that meeting.

AFSCME, a CA stockholder, is associated with the American Federation of State, County and Municipal Employees. On March 13, 2008, AFSCME submitted a proposed stockholder bylaw (the "Bylaw" or "proposed Bylaw") for inclusion in the Company's proxy materials for its 2008 annual meeting of stockholders. The Bylaw, if adopted by CA stockholders, would amend the Company's bylaws to provide as follows:

> RESOLVED, that pursuant to *section 109 of the Delaware General Corporation Law* and Article IX of the bylaws of CA, Inc., stockholders of CA hereby amend the bylaws to add the following Section 14 to Article II:
>
> The board of directors shall cause the corporation to reimburse a stockholder or group of stockholders (together, the "Nominator") for reasonable expenses ("Expenses") incurred in connection with nominating one or more candidates in a contested election of directors to the corporation's board of directors, including, without limitation, printing, mailing, legal, solicitation, travel, advertising and public relations expenses, so long as (a) the election of fewer than 50% of the directors to be elected is contested in the election, (b) one or more candidates nominated by the Nominator are elected to the corporation's board of directors, (c) stockholders are not permitted to cumulate their votes for directors, and (d) the election occurred, and the Expenses were incurred, after this bylaw's adoption. The amount paid to a Nominator under this bylaw in respect of a contested election

shall not exceed the amount expended by the corporation in connection with such election.

CA's current bylaws and Certificate of Incorporation have no provision that specifically addresses the reimbursement of proxy expenses. Of more general relevance, however, is Article SEVENTH, Section (1) of CA's Certificate of Incorporation, which tracks the language of *8 Del. C. § 141(a)* and provides that:

> The management of the business and the conduct of the affairs of the corporation shall be vested in [CA's] Board of Directors.

It is undisputed that the decision whether to reimburse election expenses is presently vested in the discretion of CA's board of directors, subject to their fiduciary duties and applicable Delaware law.

On April 18, 2008, CA notified the SEC's Division of Corporation Finance (the "Division") of its intention to exclude the proposed Bylaw from its 2008 proxy materials. The Company requested from the Division a "no-action letter" stating that the Division would not recommend any enforcement action to the SEC if CA excluded the AFSCME proposal.[2] CA's request for a no-action letter was accompanied by an opinion from its Delaware counsel ... [that] concluded that the proposed Bylaw is not a proper subject for stockholder action, and that if implemented, the Bylaw would violate the Delaware General Corporation Law ("DGCL").

On May 21, 2008, AFSCME responded to CA's no-action request with a letter taking the opposite legal position. The AFSCME letter was accompanied by an opinion from AFSCME's Delaware counsel ... [that] concluded that the proposed Bylaw is a proper subject for shareholder action and that if adopted, would be permitted under Delaware law.

The Division was thus confronted with two conflicting legal opinions on Delaware law.... To obtain guidance, the SEC, at the Division's request, certified two questions of Delaware law to this Court....

II. *THE CERTIFIED QUESTIONS*

The two questions certified to us by the SEC are as follows:

> 1. Is the AFSCME Proposal a proper subject for action by shareholders as a matter of Delaware law?
>
> 2. Would the AFSCME Proposal, if adopted, cause CA to violate any Delaware law to which it is subject? ...

---

2. Under Sections (i)(1) and (i)(2) of SEC Rule 14a–8, a company may exclude a stockholder proposal from its proxy statement if the proposal "is not a proper subject for action by the shareholders under the laws of the jurisdiction of the company's organization," or where the proposal, if implemented, "would cause the company to violate any state law to which it is subject." *See 17 C.F.R. § 240.14a–8.*

III. *THE FIRST QUESTION*

A. *Preliminary Comments* . . .

[T]he DGCL empowers both the board of directors and the shareholders of a Delaware corporation to adopt, amend or repeal the corporation's bylaws. *8 Del. C. § 109(a)* relevantly provides that:

> After a corporation has received any payment for any of its stock, the power to adopt, amend or repeal bylaws shall be in the stockholders entitled to vote . . .; provided, however, any corporation may, in its certificate of incorporation, confer the power to adopt, amend or repeal bylaws upon the directors. . . . The fact that such power has been so conferred upon the directors . . . shall not divest the stockholders . . ., of the power, nor limit their power to adopt, amend or repeal bylaws. . . .

[B]y its terms *Section 109(a)* vests in the shareholders a power to adopt, amend or repeal bylaws that is legally sacrosanct, *i.e.,* the power cannot be non-consensually eliminated or limited by anyone other than the legislature itself. If viewed in isolation, *Section 109(a)* could be read to make the board's and the shareholders' power to adopt, amend or repeal bylaws identical and coextensive, but *Section 109(a)* does not exist in a vacuum. It must be read together with *8 Del. C. § 141(a)*, which pertinently provides that:

> The business and affairs of every corporation organized under this chapter shall be managed by or under the direction of a board of directors, except as may be otherwise provided in this chapter or in its certificate of incorporation.

No such broad management power is statutorily allocated to the shareholders. Indeed, it is well-established that stockholders of a corporation subject to the DGCL may not directly manage the business and affairs of the corporation, at least without specific authorization in either the statute or the certificate of incorporation. Therefore, the shareholders' statutory power to adopt, amend or repeal bylaws is not coextensive with the board's concurrent power and is limited by the board's management prerogatives under *Section 141(a)*.[7]

[I]t follows that, to decide whether the Bylaw proposed by AFSCME is a proper subject for shareholder action under Delaware law, we must first determine: (1) the scope or reach of the shareholders' power to adopt, alter or repeal the bylaws of a Delaware corporation, and then (2) whether the Bylaw at issue here falls within that permissible scope. . . .

B. *Analysis*

1.

Two other provisions of the DGCL, *8 Del. C. §§ 109(b)* and *102(b)(1)*, bear importantly on the first question and form the basis of

7. Because the board's managerial authority under *Section 141(a)* is a cardinal precept of the DGCL, we do not construe *Section 109* as an "except[ion] . . . otherwise specified in th[e] [DGCL]" to *Section 141(a)*. Rather, the shareholders' statutory power to adopt, amend or repeal bylaws under *Section 109* cannot be "inconsistent with law," including *Section 141(a)*.

contentions advanced by each side. *Section 109(b)*, which deals generally with bylaws and what they must or may contain, provides that:

> The bylaws may contain any provision, not inconsistent with law or with the certificate of incorporation, relating to the business of the corporation, the conduct of its affairs, and its rights or powers or the rights or powers of its stockholders, directors, officers or employees.

And *Section 102(b)(1)*, which is part of a broader provision that addresses what the certificate of incorporation must or may contain, relevantly states that:

> (b) In addition to the matters required to be set forth in the certificate of incorporation by subsection (a) of this section, the certificate of incorporation may also contain any or all of the following matters:
>
> (1) Any provision for the management of the business and for the conduct of the affairs of the corporation, and any provision creating, defining, limiting and regulating the powers of the corporation, the directors and the stockholders, or any class of the stockholders....; if such provisions are not contrary to the laws of this State. Any provision which is required or permitted by any section of this chapter to be stated in the bylaws may instead be stated in the certificate of incorporation.

AFSCME relies heavily upon the language of *Section 109(b)*, which permits the bylaws of a corporation to contain "any provision ... relating to the ... rights or powers of its stockholders [and] directors...." The Bylaw, AFSCME argues, "relates to" the right of the stockholders meaningfully to participate in the process of electing directors, a right that necessarily "includes the right to nominate an opposing slate."

CA argues, in response, that *Section 109(b)* is not dispositive, because it cannot be read in isolation from, and without regard to, *Section 102(b)(1)*. CA's argument runs as follows: the Bylaw would limit the substantive decision-making authority of CA's board to decide whether or not to expend corporate funds for a particular purpose, here, reimbursing director election expenses. *Section 102(b)(1)* contemplates that any provision that limits the broad statutory power of the directors must be contained in the certificate of incorporation. Therefore, the proposed Bylaw can only be in CA's Certificate of Incorporation, as distinguished from its bylaws. Accordingly, the proposed bylaw falls outside the universe of permissible bylaws authorized by *Section 109(b)*.

Implicit in CA's argument is the premise that *any* bylaw that in *any* respect might be viewed as limiting or restricting the power of the board of directors automatically falls outside the scope of permissible bylaws. That simply cannot be. That reasoning, taken to its logical extreme, would result in eliminating altogether the shareholders' statutory right to adopt, amend or repeal bylaws. Bylaws, by their very nature, set down rules and procedures that bind a corporation's board and its shareholders. In that sense, most, if not all, bylaws could be said to limit the otherwise unlimited discretionary power of the board. Yet *Section 109(a)* carves out an area of shareholder power to adopt, amend or repeal bylaws that is expressly inviolate. Therefore, to argue that the Bylaw at issue here limits the board's power to manage the business and affairs of the Company only begins, but cannot end, the analysis needed to decide whether the Bylaw is a proper subject for shareholder action. The question left unanswered is what is the scope of shareholder action that *Section 109(b)* permits yet does not improperly intrude upon the directors' power to manage corporation's business and affairs under *Section 141(a)*.

> It is at this juncture that the statutory language becomes only marginally helpful in determining what the Delaware legislature intended to be the lawful scope of the shareholders' power to adopt, amend and repeal bylaws. To resolve that issue, the Court must resort to different tools, namely, decisions of this Court and of the Court of Chancery that bear on this question. Those tools do not enable us to articulate with doctrinal exactitude a bright line that divides those bylaws that shareholders may unilaterally adopt under *Section 109(b)* from those which they may not under *Section 141(a)*. . . .

2.

It is well-established Delaware law that a proper function of bylaws is not to mandate how the board should decide specific substantive business decisions, but rather, to define the process and procedures by which those decisions are made. As the Court of Chancery has noted:

> Traditionally, the bylaws have been the corporate instrument used to set forth the rules by which the corporate board conducts its business. To this end, the DGCL is replete with specific provisions authorizing the bylaws to establish the procedures through which board and committee action is taken. . . . [T]here is a general consensus that bylaws that regulate the process by which the board acts are statutorily authorized[15] . . . .

Examples of the procedural, process-oriented nature of bylaws are found in both the DGCL and the case law. For example, *8 Del. C. § 141(b)* authorizes bylaws that fix the number of directors on the board, the number of directors required for a quorum (with certain limitations), and the vote requirements for board action. *8 Del. C. § 141(f)* authorizes bylaws that preclude board action without a meeting.[17] ... Such purely procedural bylaws do not improperly encroach upon the board's managerial authority under *Section 141(a)*.

---

15. *Hollinger Intern., Inc. v. Black, 844 A.2d 1022, 1078–79 (Del. Ch. 2004)* (internal footnotes omitted), *aff'd, 872 A.2d 559 (Del. 2005)*. . . .

17. *See also, e.g., 8 Del. C. § 211(a) & (b)* (bylaws may establish the date and the place of the annual meeting of the stockholders); *§ 211(d)* (bylaws may specify the conditions for the

The process-creating function of bylaws provides a starting point to address the Bylaw at issue. It enables us to frame the issue in terms of whether the Bylaw is one that establishes or regulates a process for substantive director decision-making, or one that mandates the decision itself. . . . We conclude that the Bylaw, even though infelicitously couched as a substantive-sounding mandate to expend corporate funds, has both the intent and the effect of regulating the process for electing directors of CA. Therefore, we determine that the Bylaw is a proper subject for shareholder action, and set forth our reasoning below.

Although CA concedes that "restrictive procedural bylaws (such as those requiring the presence of all directors and unanimous board consent to take action) are acceptable," it points out that even facially procedural bylaws can unduly intrude upon board authority. The Bylaw being proposed here is unduly intrusive, CA claims, because, by mandating reimbursement of a stockholder's proxy expenses, it limits the board's broad discretionary authority to decide whether to grant reimbursement at all. CA further claims that because (in defined circumstances) the Bylaw mandates the expenditure of corporate funds, its subject matter is necessarily substantive, not process-oriented, and, therefore falls outside the scope of what *Section 109(b)* permits.[19]

Because the Bylaw is couched as a command to reimburse ("The board of directors shall cause the corporation to reimburse a stockholder"), it lends itself to CA's criticism. But the Bylaw's wording, although relevant, is not dispositive of whether or not it is process-related. The Bylaw could easily have been worded differently, to emphasize its process, as distinguished from its mandatory payment, component.[20] By saying this we do not mean to suggest that this Bylaw's reimbursement component can be ignored. What we do

---

calling of special meetings of stockholders); *§ 216* (bylaws may establish quorum and vote requirements for meetings of stockholders and "[a] bylaw amendment adopted by stockholders which specifies the votes that shall be necessary for the election of directors shall not be further amended or repealed by the board of directors."); *§ 222* (bylaws may regulate certain notice requirements regarding adjourned meetings of stockholders).

19. CA actually conflates two separate arguments that, although facially similar, are analytically distinct. The first argument is that the Bylaw impermissibly intrudes upon board authority because it mandates the expenditure of corporate funds. The second is that the Bylaw impermissibly leaves no role for board discretion and would require reimbursement of the costs of a subset of CA's stockholders, even in circumstances where the board's fiduciary duties would counsel otherwise. Analytically, the first argument is relevant to the issue of whether the Bylaw is a proper subject for unilateral stockholder action, whereas the second argument more properly goes to the separate question of whether the Bylaw, if enacted, would violate Delaware law.

20. For example, the Bylaw could have been phrased more benignly, to provide that "[a] stockholder or group of stockholders (together, the 'Nominator') shall be entitled to reimbursement from the corporation for reasonable expenses ('Expenses') incurred in connection with nominating one or more candidates in a contested election of directors to the corporation's board of directors in the following circumstances. . . ." Although the substance of the Bylaw would be no different, the emphasis would be upon the shareholders' entitlement to reimbursement, rather than upon the directors' obligation to reimburse. As discussed in Part IV, *infra,* of this Opinion, in order for the Bylaw not to be "not inconsistent with law" as *Section 109(b)* mandates, it would also need to contain a provision that reserves the directors' full power to discharge their fiduciary duties.

suggest is that a bylaw that requires the expenditure of corporate funds does not, for that reason alone, become automatically deprived of its process-related character. A hypothetical example illustrates the point. Suppose that the directors of a corporation live in different states and at a considerable distance from the corporation's headquarters. Suppose also that the shareholders enact a bylaw that requires all meetings of directors to take place in person at the corporation's headquarters. Such a bylaw would be clearly process-related, yet it cannot be supposed that the shareholders would lack the power to adopt the bylaw because it would require the corporation to expend its funds to reimburse the directors' travel expenses. Whether or not a bylaw is process-related must necessarily be determined in light of its context and purpose.

The context of the Bylaw at issue here is the process for electing directors—a subject in which shareholders of Delaware corporations have a legitimate and protected interest. The purpose of the Bylaw is to promote the integrity of that electoral process by facilitating the nomination of director candidates by stockholders or groups of stockholders. Generally, and under the current framework for electing directors in contested elections, only board-sponsored nominees for election are reimbursed for their election expenses. Dissident candidates are not, unless they succeed in replacing at least a majority of the entire board. The Bylaw would encourage the nomination of non-management board candidates by promising reimbursement of the nominating stockholders' proxy expenses if one or more of its candidates are elected. In that the shareholders also have a legitimate interest, because the Bylaw would facilitate the exercise of their right to participate in selecting the contestants....

The shareholders of a Delaware corporation have the right "to participate in selecting the contestants" for election to the board. The shareholders are entitled to facilitate the exercise of that right by proposing a bylaw that would encourage candidates other than board-sponsored nominees to stand for election. The Bylaw would accomplish that by committing the corporation to reimburse the election expenses of shareholders whose candidates are successfully elected. That the implementation of that proposal would require the expenditure of corporate funds will not, in and of itself, make such a bylaw an improper subject matter for shareholder action. Accordingly, we answer the first question certified to us in the affirmative.

That, however, concludes only part of the analysis. The DGCL also requires that the Bylaw be "not inconsistent with law." Accordingly, we turn to the second certified question, which is whether the proposed Bylaw, if adopted, would cause CA to violate any Delaware law to which it is subject.

IV. *THE SECOND QUESTION*

In answering the first question, we have already determined that the Bylaw does not facially violate any provision of the DGCL or of CA's Certificate of Incorporation. The question thus becomes whether the Bylaw would violate any common law rule or precept. Were this issue being presented in the course of litigation involving the application of the Bylaw to a specific set of facts, we would start with the presumption that the Bylaw is valid and, if possible, construe it in a manner consistent with the law.... The certified questions, however, request a determination of the validity of the Bylaw in the abstract. Therefore, in response to the second question, we must necessarily consider any possible circumstance under which a board of directors might be required to act. Under at least one such hypothetical, the board of directors would breach their fiduciary duties if they complied with the Bylaw. Accordingly, we conclude that the Bylaw, as drafted, would violate the prohibition, which our decisions have derived from *Section 141(a)*, against contractual arrangements that commit the board of directors to a course of action that would preclude them from fully discharging their fiduciary duties to the corporation and its shareholders.

This Court has previously invalidated contracts that would require a board to act or not act in such a fashion that would limit the exercise of their fiduciary duties. In *Paramount Communications, Inc. v. QVC Network, Inc.,* we invalidated a "no shop" provision of a merger agreement with a favored bidder (Viacom) that prevented the directors of the target company (Paramount) from communicating with a competing bidder (QVC) the terms of its competing bid in an effort to obtain the highest available value for shareholders. We held that:

> The No–Shop Provision could not validly define or limit the fiduciary duties of the Paramount directors. To the extent that a contract, or a provision thereof, purports to require a board to act or not, act in such a fashion as to limit the exercise of fiduciary duties, it is invalid and unenforceable. [...] [T]he Paramount directors could not contract away their fiduciary obligations....

Similarly, in *Quickturn Design Systems, Inc. v. Shapiro,*[29] the directors of the target company (Quickturn) adopted a "poison pill" rights plan that contained a so-called "delayed redemption provision" as a defense against a hostile takeover bid, as part of which the bidder (Mentor Graphics) intended to wage a proxy contest to replace the target company board. The delayed redemption provision was intended to deter that effort, by preventing any newly elected board from redeeming the poison pill for six months. This Court invalidated that provision, because it would "impermissibly deprive any newly elected board of both its statutory authority to manage the corporation under *8 Del. C. § 141(a)* and its concomitant fiduciary duty pursuant to that statutory mandate."[30] We held that:

> One of the most basic tenets of Delaware corporate law is that the board of directors has the ultimate responsibility for managing the business and affairs of a corporation. [...] The Quickturn certificate of incorporation contains no provi-

29. *721 A.2d 1281 (Del. 1998).*

30. *Quickturn, 721 A.2d at 1291.*

> sion purporting to limit the authority of the board in any way. The Delayed Redemption Provision, however, would prevent a newly elected board of directors from *completely* discharging its fundamental management duties to the corporation and its stockholders for six months. While the Delayed Redemption Provision limits the board of directors' authority in only one respect, the suspension of the Rights Plan, it nonetheless restricts the board's power in an area of fundamental importance to the shareholders—negotiating a possible sale of the corporation. Therefore, we hold that the Delayed Redemption Provision is invalid under *Section 141(a)*, which confers upon any newly elected board of directors *full* power to manage and direct the business and affairs of a Delaware corporation.[31]

Both *QVC* and *Quickturn* involved binding contractual arrangements that the board of directors had voluntarily imposed upon themselves. This case involves a binding bylaw that the shareholders seek to impose involuntarily on the directors in the specific area of election expense reimbursement. Although this case is distinguishable in that respect, the distinction is one without a difference. The reason is that the internal governance contract—which here takes the form of a bylaw—is one that would also prevent the directors from exercising their full managerial power in circumstances where their fiduciary duties would otherwise require them to deny reimbursement to a dissident slate. That this limitation would be imposed by a majority vote of the shareholders rather than by the directors themselves, does not, in our view, legally matter.[32]

AFSCME contends that it is improper to use the doctrine articulated in *QVC* and *Quickturn* as the measure of the validity of the Bylaw.... AFSCME argues that it is unfair to claim that the Bylaw prevents the CA board from discharging its fiduciary duty where the effect of the Bylaw is to relieve the board entirely of those duties in this specific area.

That response, in our view, is more semantical than substantive. No matter how artfully it may be phrased, the argument concedes the very proposition that renders the Bylaw, as written, invalid: the Bylaw mandates reimbursement of election expenses in circumstances that a proper application of fiduciary principles could preclude. That such circumstances could arise is not far fetched. Under Delaware law, a board may expend corporate funds to reimburse proxy expenses "[w]here the controversy is concerned with a question of policy as distinguished from personnel o[r] management." But in a situation where the proxy contest is motivated by personal or petty concerns, or to promote interests that do not further, or are adverse to, those of the corporation, the board's fiduciary duty could compel that reimbursement be denied altogether.

---

31. *Id. at 1291–92* (italics in original, internal footnotes omitted).

32. Only if the Bylaw provision were enacted as an amendment to CA's Certificate of Incorporation would that distinction be dispositive. *See 8 Del. C. § 102 (b)(1)* and *§ 242*.

It is in this respect that the proposed Bylaw, as written, would violate Delaware law if enacted by CA's shareholders. As presently drafted, the Bylaw would afford CA's directors full discretion to determine what *amount* of reimbursement is appropriate, because the directors would be obligated to grant only the "reasonable" expenses of a successful short slate. Unfortunately, that does not go far enough, because the Bylaw contains no language or provision that would reserve to CA's directors their full power to exercise their fiduciary duty to decide whether or not it would be appropriate, in a specific case, to award reimbursement at all.

In arriving at this conclusion, we express no view on whether the Bylaw as currently drafted, would create a better governance scheme from a policy standpoint. We decide only what is, and is not, legally permitted under the DGCL. That statute, as currently drafted, is the expression of policy as decreed by the Delaware legislature. Those who believe that CA's shareholders should be permitted to make the proposed Bylaw as drafted part of CA's governance scheme, have two alternatives. They may seek to amend the Certificate of Incorporation to include the substance of the Bylaw; *or* they may seek recourse from the Delaware General Assembly.

Accordingly, we answer the second question certified to us in the affirmative.

SEC PROXY RULE 14a–8

DEL. GEN. CORP. LAW §§ 112, 113

SECTION 2. CORPORATE GOVERNANCE AND THE RISE OF INSTITUTIONAL SHAREHOLDERS

A. SHAREHOLDER VOTING

Robert B. Thompson & Paul H. Edelman, Corporate Voting

62 Vand. L. Rev. 129, 145–152 (2009).

. . . [E]ffective shareholder control over managers is regularly cited as a prerequisite to sound corporate governance. . . . In such arguments, shareholders are often cast as the necessary counterweight to the managerialist corporate control that has been the defining worry of corporate law since Adolf Berle and Gardner Means wrote of the separation of ownership and control in 1932. Lucian Bebchuk argues for greater shareholder power to give directors incentives to serve the shareholder interest and to restore directors' accountability in a system lacking other adequate mechanisms.[70] ... Bebchuk's theory does not tell us very much about when and how voting should be used. If we are to be able to explain why shareholders vote, when they should vote, and what information they need in order to vote effectively, we need a more robust theory of shareholder voting.

Frank Easterbrook and Daniel Fischel present a more comprehensive theory of voting as filling the gaps that necessarily appear in contracts and assigning the gap-filling role to the group with the best economic incentive to do so.[71] Grounded within their broader theory of contract and private ordering, they observe that where contracts are not complete, something must fill in the details. The shareholders hold the residual interest in the corporation and so "have the appropriate incentives ... to make discretionary decisions.... The shareholders receive most of the marginal gains and incur most of the marginal costs. They therefore have the right incentives to exercise discretion." In their theory, this right to exercise discretion follows the residual claim. For practical reasons shareholders will delegate to managers, but nevertheless "managers exercise authority at the sufferance of investors." ...

Easterbrook and Fischel's focus on the residual holder's right to delegate gap-filling would seem to support a more expansive view of shareholder action than [present law]. If shareholders merely delegate their roles to fill gaps, why should the law prevent them from exercising their authority whenever they deem it appropriate? The Easterbrook and Fischel approach would seem to give shareholders carte blanche power to decide any issue, whether or not the directors approve.

Directors, however, are not agents in the pure sense of extending the reach of shareholders (as principals) to do what they lack the time or expertise to do. In all American corporations statutes, directors, rather than shareholders, have the plenary governance role in the enterprise; all corporate power is placed in their hands. This centralized authority structure provides efficiency that cannot be replicated with shareholder decisionmaking except in the smallest of ownership structures. Stephen Bainbridge advocates for such a director-centric view of corporate governance ... He argues that the economic efficiency of the corporate form hinges on the ability of the board to act by fiat rather than some more democratic method of consensus.[82]

The advocates of both shareholder primacy and director primacy acknowledge the risk that directors may be diverted to empire building or toward entrenching action and will fail to monitor sufficiently

70. Lucian A. Bebchuk, The Myth of the Shareholder Franchise, 93 Va. L. Rev. 675, 677, 732 (2007).

71. Frank Easterbrook & Daniel Fischel, The Economic Structure of Law 67–68 (1991).

82. Stephen M. Bainbridge, The Case for Limited Shareholder Voting Rights, 53 UCLA L. Rev. 601, 621–22 (2006)....

the managers engaging in similar behavior. Following Easterbrook and Fischel and others, Bainbridge argues that shareholders, and only shareholders, assume such a monitoring role, albeit a limited one. He argues that the monitor must be limited to a single constituency because to do otherwise would produce mixed and possibly unstable signals, thus undermining the monitoring role. Like Easterbrook and Fischel, he suggests that the shareholders are the right constituency to serve the role because they are "the only corporate constituent with a residual, unfixed, ex post claim on corporate assets and earnings." As many have recognized, the information costs and collective action problems associated with a shareholder vote are substantial, and the board itself operates "within a pervasive web of accountability mechanisms that substitute for monitoring." For Bainbridge, these characteristics suggest a limited shareholder oversight role, so weak, in fact, that for him "they scarcely qualify as part of corporate governance."[86]

Advocates of different versions of director primacy emphasize not so much the information costs of shareholder action or the other constraints on director action, but the longstanding concern that shareholders, if empowered without check, would cause the corporation to take opportunistic advantage of other stakeholders. Much of the argument against unlimited shareholder power that fueled the antitakeover movement of the 1980s reflected such fears of shareholder self-interest.[87] The recent activities of hedge funds... These arguments focus explicitly on the intra-shareholder conflict that occurs when shareholders are given a larger franchise....

We accept that much of the efficiency of the corporate form lies in having a central decisionmaker, the board. Because of the separation of ownership and control inherent in the form and the concomitant possibility of self-interest, some group must be authorized to monitor the behavior of the board. Consistent with the various prior theories, we believe that group should be homogeneous to avoid difficulties in achieving consensus; we believe shareholders are that group. But here we diverge from the theories already presented in explaining why shareholders are the appropriate constituency for monitoring and how to determine the breadth of monitoring necessary. The costs of information and the barriers to collective shareholder action are substantial, so any performance measure has to circumvent those problems. Shareholders are the appropriate group to monitor the board and correct errors because they are uniquely sensitive to the principal signal indicating a deviation of the board from its duty to the corporation: the market price of the corporation's stock.

---

86. Stephen M. Bainbridge, Director Primacy: The Means and Ends of Corporate Governance, 97 Nw. U. L. Rev. 547, 569 (2003).*See also* Stephen M. Bainbridge, Unocal at 20: Director Primacy in Corporate Takeovers, 31 Del. J. Corp. L. 769, 812 (2006)("Shareholder voting rights are properly seen as simply one of many accountability tools available, not as part of the firm's decision-making systems.")....

87. *See e.g.,* Martin Lipton, Takeover Bids in the Target's Boardroom, 35 Bus. Law. 101, 104 (1979)(questioning "whether the long-term interests of the nation's corporate system and economy should be jeopardized in order to benefit speculators interested not in the vitality and continued existence of the business enterprises in which they have bought shares, but only in a quick profit on the sale of those shares").

Note that our justification for shareholder voting is not based in any property right to residual value. It is founded on the assumption that the best signal for identifying board error is the stock price and that shareholders are the constituency with the most incentive to monitor that signal. . . .

In summary, we have developed an alternative theory of shareholder voting, based on error correction, capable of explaining more of the visible pattern of voting by shareholders. Shareholders are the unique homogeneous constituency who are sensitive to the stock price, which is a decent proxy for the interests of the corporation. Restricting the vote to shareholders aligns the interest of the corporation with the voters. Because the vote is granted only to those who benefit from a higher stock price, there is an objective measure of "right" for the questions brought before them: the "right" answer is the one that increases the stock price. This assures that the shareholders' decision effectively monitors the actions of the board. Our theory allows us to examine questions such as which issues are appropriate for oversight—those which will change the stock price—and what financial engineering arrangements act to undercut the value of this monitoring regime by separating ownership from financial interest. . . .

NOTE ON WEIGHTED VOTING IN PUBLICLY HELD CORPORATIONS

In most publicly held corporations, only common shareholders have voting rights, and each share of common stock each carries one vote. However, voting rights can also be conferred on preferred stock or even on bonds. Furthermore, a corporation may have two or more classes of common stock, each with different voting rights. In such cases, often one class has voting power out of all proportion to its equity interest in the corporation. Stock structures like these are sometimes referred to as dual-class common, super-voting stock, or weighted voting. Although not new, the incidence of such structures increased during the 1980s, when they were often installed as an anti-takeover defense. In theory, the creation of such a structure affects only the relative rights of different shareholders, not the allocation of power between managers and shareholders. In practice, however, these structures usually involve the issuance of super-voting stock to members of a control group for the purpose of allowing the group to maintain control, and defend against takeovers, with only a minimum investment in the corporation.

In Stroh v. Blackhawk Holding Corp., 272 N.E.2d 1 (Ill. 1971), Blackhawk's certificate of incorporation authorized a Class A and a Class B Common stock. The Class B stock voted share-for-share with Class A stock, but was entitled neither to dividends nor to participate in the proceeds of a liquidation. After Blackhawk's formation, its promoters purchased 500,000 shares of Class B at a quarter of a cent per share, and 87,868 shares of Class A at $3.40 per share, and thereafter sold Class A stock to the public at $4 per share. As of June 1968, Blackhawk had outstanding 1,237,681 Class A shares and 500,-000 Class B shares, the latter representing an investment of $1250 but carrying 28.78% of the total vote. The court upheld the validity of the B stock:

> . . . Section 14 of the Business Corporation Act . . . provides that shares of stock in an Illinois corporation may be divided into classes,
>
> > "with such designations, preferences, qualifications, limitations, restrictions and such special or relative rights as shall be stated in the articles of incorporation. The articles of incorporation shall not limit or deny the voting power of the shares of any class. . . ."
>
> Section 14 . . . clearly expresses the intent of the legislature to be that parties to a corporate entity may create whatever restrictions and limitations they may want with regard to their corporate stock by expressing such restrictions and limitations in the articles of incorporation. . . .
>
> . . . It has long been the common practice in Illinois to classify shares of stock such that one may invest less than another in a corporation, and yet have control. One of two shareholders may purchase ten shares of a class of stock issued at its par value of $1,000 per share, and his business partner may purchase 100 shares of another class of the corporate stock issued at its par value of $10 per share. The parties, for varying reasons, may be very willing that the party investing the $1,000 have control of the management of the corporation, as opposed to the party having the investment of $10,000. . . .
>
> In this case the parties went one step further than is customary. The stock which could be bought cheaper, and yet carry the same voting power per share, was not permitted to share at all in the dividends or assets of the corporation. This additional step did not invalidate the stock.

In Providence & Worcester Co. v. Baker, 378 A.2d 121 (Del.1977), P & W's certificate provided that each holder of common stock had one vote per share for his first 50 shares, but only one vote per 20 shares for all shares over 50. The validity of these limitations was challenged by the trustees in bankruptcy of Penn Central Transportation Co., who held 28% of P & W's stock but were effectively restricted to 3% of the total voting power. The court upheld the restrictions under Del. § 212(a), which states that "[u]nless otherwise provided in the certificate of incorporation . . . each stockholder shall be entitled to 1 vote for each share of capital stock held by such stockholder." *Id.* at 122, quoting 8 Del. Code Ann. § 213. The court concluded that "if the General Assembly intended to bar the type of restriction on stockholders' voting rights here under review, such prohibition would appear in § 212. . . . Under § 212(a), voting rights of stockholders may be varied from the 'one share-one vote' standard by the certificate of incorporation...." *See also* Lacos Land Co. v. Arden Group, Inc., 517 A.2d 271 (Del.Ch.1986).

In several situations, Congress has acted to prevent abuses in this area. For example, except in a few cases, Investment Company Act Section 18 forbids the issuance of nonvoting stock by companies subject to that Act. The rules of the major stock exchanges also set limits on weighted voting in listed corporations.

NEW YORK STOCK EXCHANGE, LISTED COMPANY MANUAL § 313.00

[See Statutory Supplement]

NOTE ON EMPTY VOTING AND RECORD DATE(S)

In an influential article, The New Vote Buying: Empty Voting and Hidden (Morphable) Ownership, 79 So. Cal. L. Rev. 811 (2006), Henry Hu and Bernard Black developed the concept of empty voting, that is, arrangements under which a person holds more votes than shares, so that his votes have been emptied of an accompanying economic stake. Hu and Black begin by pointing out the severe tension between empty voting and the predicates of the corporate system.

> The vote is the core source of shareholder power. The standard contractarian theory of the corporation supports assigning voting rights to common shareholders in proportion to share ownership. Doing so places the power to oversee company managers in the hands of residual owners, who have an incentive to exercise that power to increase firm value; the more shares owned, the greater the incentive and thus the greater the number of votes. Linking shares to votes also facilitates the operation of the market for corporate control. Empirical evidence supports the concern with a disparity between insiders' voting power and economic interest by showing that such a disparity predicts reduced firm value. Beyond this instrumental role of voting, shareholder voting is a core ideological basis for managerial authority, legitimating managers' exercise of authority over property the managers do not own.
>
> Yet the derivatives revolution in finance ... and related growth in the share lending market, are making it easier and cheaper to decouple economic ownership from voting power. Hedge funds and company insiders are taking advantage of this new opportunity. Sometimes, they hold more votes than shares—a pattern we call "empty voting" because the votes have been emptied of an accompanying economic stake. In extreme cases, an investor can vote despite having negative

economic ownership, which gives the investor an incentive to vote in ways that reduce the company's share price. . . .

A recent public instance of empty voting illustrates the potential risks from empty voting. Perry Corp., a hedge fund, owned 7 million shares of King Pharmaceuticals. In late 2004, Mylan Laboratories agreed to buy King in a stock-for-stock merger at a substantial premium, but Mylan's shares dropped sharply when the deal was announced. To help Mylan obtain shareholder approval for the merger, Perry bought 9.9% of Mylan, becoming Mylan's largest shareholder. But Perry fully hedged the market risk associated with its Mylan shares. Perry thus had **9.9%** *voting ownership* and **zero** *economic ownership*. Including its position in King, Perry's overall economic interest in Mylan was **negative**. The more Mylan (over) paid for King, the more Perry stood to profit.*

Hu and Black develop and discuss various techniques by which empty voting can be achieved. They call one of these techniques "record data capture."

Before a shareholder meeting, a company's board of directors establishes a voting record date. Shareholders who hold shares at the close of business on the record date have the right to vote at the meeting, which is typically a month or so after the record date. One way to hold votes without economic ownership . . . is record date capture—borrowing shares in the share lending market for a limited period around the record date.

So far as the company is concerned, the borrower owns the shares (and the associated votes). In a typical loan, the borrower contracts with the share lender to (1) return the shares to the lender at any time at the election of either side, and (2) pay to the lender an amount equal to any dividends or other distributions the borrower receives on the shares. [The loan contract] leaves the borrower holding votes without economic ownership, while the lender has economic ownership without votes. . . .

In early 2006, a . . . questionable use of record date capture appears to have occurred in Hong Kong. Henderson Land offered to buy the 25% minority interest in Henderson Investment, a publicly held affiliate. Most minority shareholders favored the buyout, and Henderson Investment's share price increased substantially. Under Hong Kong law, however, the buyout could be blocked by a negative vote of 10% of the "free floating" shares—in this case about 2.5% of the outstanding shares. To everybody's surprise, 2.7% of the shares were voted against the buyout. Henderson Investments shares fell 17% the day after the voting outcome was announced.

* Emphasis in original.

What happened? It appears that one or more hedge funds borrowed Henderson Investment shares before the record date, voted against the buyout, and then sold those shares short, thus profiting from its private knowledge that the buyout would be defeated. One hedge fund alone may have held enough shares to defeat the buyout.

... [Here], hedge funds used record date capture to obtain votes.... [O]ne or more hedge funds held a negative overall economic interest—or more precisely, would have negative economic ownership by the time the voting outcome was known. These hedge fund shareholders apparently blocked a deal that would benefit other shareholders.

Consider next a variant record date capture. If shares cannot be borrowed, an alternative vote capture technique is available that promises nearly empty voting. An investor can buy shares just before the record date and sell them soon thereafter. The investor incurs round-trip transaction costs, but has economic ownership for only a short period of time. The investor can hedge this limited risk fully buy buying put options on the shares....

Short-term ownership plus such a hedge entails fully or substantially empty voting. The timing of this limited ownership further attenuates the link between economic ownership and voting rights. The record date is well before the date at which votes are cast. There is no reason to expect company-specific news on the record date. By the time the voting outcome is known, the investor will have shed any economic exposure, and will suffer no ill effects from voting in ways that reduce firm value; indeed, as in Henderson Investments, the investor could even gain from doing so.

Id. at 814–015, 832–33, 834–35

As will be examined more closely in the next chapter, the persons who are listed as shareholders on the corporation's records are known as *record owners*. For a variety of reasons, the persons who actually own shares—the *beneficial* owners—often differ from the record owners. For example, the stock of individual and even institutional shareholders is often held in "street name," that is, in the name of a broker or a bank. Brokers, banks, and others, in turn, often deposit the stock they hold in regional stock depositories (described below), which place the stock under still another name.

To promote certainty, in various contexts corporation law confers rights on record owners, rather than beneficial owners. One of these contexts is voting: normally, only record owners have the right to notice of a meeting and the right to vote.

When a corporation proposes to hold a meeting at which a shareholder vote will be taken, it must give notice of the meeting. To comply with the disclosure requirements of federal law, the notice frequently must be given a month or so before the meeting will take place. Because shares in publicly held corporations are constantly changing hands, the group of persons who are record owners on the date notice is given will differ from the persons who are record owners on the meeting date. Accordingly, if the shareholders entitled to vote at the meeting were the record holders as of the meeting date, then some shareholders entitled to vote would not have received notice of the meeting (because they purchased their shares after the notice was given), and the vote would be invalid.

To resolve this dilemma, the law permits corporations to set a *record date*—which is typically on or around the date that notice of the relevant meeting is given—for determining the shareholders who will be entitled to vote at the meeting. As a result, those persons, and only those persons, who are record shareholders on the record date are entitled to vote. However, this response creates a different problem. For example, assume the record date is February 14th and the meeting date is March 15th and that Alice transferred her shares to Bob on February 28th. A statutory regime that focuses only on a single date of record enables Alice to vote the shares despite her subsequent sale of those shares; this leads to what is commonly referred to as "empty voting" whereby voting rights are in a person with no economic interest in the shares. To address this, some state statutes permit the company bylaws to set a date for notice of the stockholder meeting and a *separate* date for determining the shares entitled to vote at the meeting. The latter date is much closer to the meeting date than the date of notice of the meeting. *See* Del. Gen. Code §§ 212(a) & 219(a); MBCA § 7.05. Under an older, more draconian, procedure, which is now little used, in lieu of setting a record date the corporation could close its transfer books, that is, could refuse to record transfers of stock between the time of the close of the books and the time of the meeting. As a result, all persons who were record holders when the transfer books were closed would still be record holders on the meeting date.

B. FINANCIAL INSTITUTIONS AND THEIR ADVISORS

NOTE ON THE ROLE OF SHAREHOLDERS UNDER MODERN CORPORATE PRACTICE

1. *Introduction*. Notwithstanding the board's extensive legal power to determine most corporate matters, shareholders do have some the legal power. To begin with, shareholders have the right to elect directors. Next, a group of important corporate changes must be approved by both the board and the shareholders. These changes, commonly referred to as *fundamental changes*, include amendments of the corporation's certificate of incorporation, sales of substantially all of the corporation's assets, dissolution of the corporation, and economically significant mergers. Further, shareholders normally can amend the corporation's bylaws without the board's concurrence if

the content of the amendment is proper (see the *CA* case, supra). Finally, shareholders have power to determine a grab-bag of other matters, most of them inconsequential. However, corporate law and practice puts constraints on the exercise of these powers. Historically, these constraints were very strong. In the last ten to twenty years, the constraints, while still very significant, have been weakening.

2. *Background.* At one time, corporation law reflected an inverted-pyramid model of corporate governance. Under this model, at the top of the inverted pyramid were the shareholders, who own the corporation, who elect the board of directors, and whose approval is required for fundamental corporate changes. At the next level down was the board, which manages the corporation's business, makes business policy, and selects the officers. At the bottom of the inverted pyramid were the officers, who under this model act as agents of the board and execute its policies and decisions.

This traditional model was called into drastic question in 1932, with the publication of Berle & Means's classic work, *The Modern Corporation and Private Property*. One of the authors' principal conclusions, revolutionary at the time, was that in publicly held corporations *control* had come to be divorced from *ownership*, because the ownership of publicly held corporations was often highly dispersed, that is, was characterized by a pattern of shareholdings in which no individual, firm, or compact group owned more than a miniscule fraction of a corporation's stock. Where shareholdership is highly dispersed the corporation will be controlled not by the shareholders, but by management—that is, by the board and the executives. This is what Berle & Means meant by the separation of ownership, which still lay with the shareholders, and control, which had shifted to management.

Management will control the corporation's ordinary business decisions whether or not a corporation's shareholdings are highly dispersed, because shareholders would prefer centralized and professional management of such decisions to decisionmaking by the body of shareholders, whose knowledge of the business and competence to make ordinary business decisions is limited at best. However, by *control* Berle & Means meant something more than this: they meant that the management of a publicly held corporation controlled not only ordinary business decisions, but virtually all decisions, and that as a practical matter shareholder power was close to nonexistent.

There are two major reasons why management rather than shareholders are likely to have full control of corporations with highly dispersed shareholdership. First, it will not be rational for a shareholder who owns only a miniscule percentage of the share to invest time in reviewing the corporation's affairs in depth. As a result, the shareholders of a corporation with highly dispersed shareholdership will be *rationally apathetic* concerning those affairs. Second, when shareholdership is highly dispersed, shareholders face a collective-action problem, that is, a problem of coordinating their decisions and actions. The collective-action problem might not be too important if the interests of managers were perfectly aligned with the interests of shareholders. However, although the two sets of interests are aligned in many respects, they radically diverge in others. For example, inefficient CEOs want to stay in office, while shareholders want inefficient CEOs to be removed. The bottom line is that until twenty to thirty years ago, the role of shareholders in publicly held corporations was largely one of extreme passivity. This passivity was reflected in the so-called Wall Street Rule—"If you don't like management, sell your stock"—and a corollary, "If you don't sell, vote with management."

3. *Shareholder Activism and the Rise of Institutional Shareholders*

Around twenty to thirty years ago, the extreme passivity embodied in the Wall Street Rule began to be replaced by shareholder activism of varying intensity. This shift from relatively complete shareholder passivity to varying degrees of shareholder activism was precipitated by a dramatic increase in the percentage of stock held by institutional, as opposed to individual shareholders, from 6% in 1950 to around 50% in recent years, and even more in the largest corporations. There are several reasons why the drastic increase in institutional shareholdings has led to increased shareholder activism. To begin with, institutional shareholders are typically much more sophisticated than individual shareholders, and as the level of a shareholder's sophistication increases, the cost of activism decreases. Next, unlike individual shareholders, who typically hold relatively small blocks of stock in their portfolio corporations while institutional shareholders characteristically hold very large blocks of stock in their portfolio corporations. As a shareholding gets larger, the ratio between (i) the cost of investing time and effort in activism and (ii) the potential benefit—that is, increasing the value of portfolio corporations—becomes smaller. Furthermore, when a relatively limited number of institutions hold large blocks of stock in a portfolio corporation, they can engage in coordinated action that an extremely large number of individuals holding very small blocks cannot attain.

The increase in shareholder activism takes various forms. The simplest form involves taking an active posture in voting on management and shareholder proposals, that is, considering such proposals on their merits, rather than automatically voting with management. A more aggressive form of activism is to originate shareholder proposals. In theory, another possible form of activism could involve nominating directorial candidates. For the most part, however, institutional investors have not followed that path, perhaps out of concern that an investor who has a representative on a corporation's board and trades in the corporation's stock might be liable for insider trading. However, institutions sometimes join movements begun by others to oust incumbent directors and replace them with new directors. In such cases, the new directors would not be representatives of, or even selected by, a given institutional investor, so that the insider-trading problem is less salient.

Still another form of activism relating to director elections involves withholding votes in favor of incumbent directors who are up for reelection.

> The intellectual origin of shareholders withholding their vote lies in a 1990 presentation to large institutional investors by former SEC Commissioner and then Stanford Law Professor Joe Grundfest. Grundfest proposed that shareholders "just vote no" in director elections. Though under the plurality voting system that prevailed at the time, withhold votes would have no legal effect no matter how many were cast, he argued that the symbolic impact of withhold votes, especially when coupled with shareholder communications with management, could act as an annual referendum on managerial performance, and "be a catalyst for improved oversight that would benefit all corporate constituencies, as well as the economy at large." . . .
>
> Although there was some early enthusiasm for the initiative, it took several more years before Grundfest's proposal caught on. The turning point probably lies in the 2004 Disney board election, when 45% of the shares were withheld from Disney CEO Michael Eisner. This campaign was highly publicized for a variety of reasons: it involved a large entertainment company; it pitted Eisner against Roy Disney, the nephew of the legendary founder of the company; and because Roy Disney spent more than $2 million in campaigning for shareholders to vote "no." Even though Eisner received a majority of the votes cast, the board of Disney immediately stripped him of his position as chairman and Eisner resigned as CEO the following year. The Disney withhold campaign showed shareholders that, in the right circumstances, a high withhold vote is both achievable and effective in inducing governance changes. . . .
>
> . . . According to Georgeson's survey of S & P 1500 companies, there were 79 directors in 2009 who received a majority withhold votes and 469 directors who received a withhold vote in excess of 30% of the votes cast. . . . [M]any boards care about the number of withhold votes even if it does not affect the outcome of an election and significant withhold votes often induce governance changes. Withhold votes thus represent an important form of shareholder activism. . . .

Marcel Kahan & Edward B. Rock, The Insignificance of Proxy Access, New York University Law and Economics Working Papers, Paper 240, at 12–13, 26 (2010).

There is an intimate connection between withhold voting and plurality voting. Withhold voting allows shareholders who oppose a candidate to forcefully express that opposition, even if they can't vote against the candidate. In contrast, under a regime of straight voting, it is possible to vote no in director elections, and withhold voting is therefore unnecessary.

Under a regime of plurality voting, a shareholder can either vote for a directorship candidate or withhold a vote for the candidate, but it was either not possible or meaningless to vote against a candidate. Today, straight voting for directors is gradually superseding plurality voting (see Chapter 5) and it is likely that institutional investors will begin exercising the right to vote no under a straight-voting regime.

Another very important form of activism consists of direct discussion between institutional investors and management. Such discussion may concern either specific issues, such as a proposed merger, or general corporate policies. As a practical matter, institutional investors probably get more done through direct discussion than through voting. However, there is an important relation between discussion and voting, because the actual or implied threat that an institutional investor will vote in a certain way is an important incentive for managers to take seriously the concern expressed by institutional investors.

The various forms of institutional-investor activism raise the question, what is the competence of institutional investors in their shareholder capacity? Institutional investors are not equipped to make, or even meaningfully assess, ordinary-course business decisions. There are, however, several areas in which institutional investors have substantial competence. For example, institutional investors can meaningfully assess a corporation's governance rules. Managers are self-interested in these rules, because the rules bear on the preservation and enhancement of managerial positions. Institutional investors normally have no direct conflict of interest concerning their portfolio corporations' governance rules, and may have special competence in this area, because they can review governance rules across corporations as a class.

Institutional investors can also meaningfully assess proposed structural changes, such as mergers. Managers are often also self-interested in structural changes, which will normally either enhance or threaten to reduce their positions. Furthermore, institutional investors may have special competence to evaluate the financial desirability of proposed structural changes, because while corporate managers are expert in making operational business decisions, institutional investors are expert in making the kinds of financial decisions often involved in structural changes. Moreover, often the market will react to a proposed structural change, and institutional investors can use the market's reaction as strong evidence of the proposal's merit. Institutional investors also can frequently play a meaningful role in evaluating the success of a corporation's business strategies and the competence of its CEO, again with the help of market signals.

The rise of institutional-investor activism is related not only to the dramatic increase in the amount of stock held by institutional investors, but also to changes to the composition of the institutional-investor population. Institutional investors fall into a number of categories:

(i) *Private Pension Plans*. Private pension plans are established by private employers to provide retirement income to their employees. The most important provisions of these plans concern the location of power over the selection of the plan's assets (portfolio decisions) and over how to vote shares in the plan's portfolio (voting decisions). Private pension plans often delegate portfolio decisions, voting decisions, or both, to other fiduciaries, usually banks, who administer the plans.

(ii) *Public Pension Plans*. Public pension plans are established by public employers, such as states and cities, to provide retirement income for their employees. As in the case of private pension plans, decision making powers may be either vested in managers or other employees of the public entity or delegated to independent fiduciaries. Often portfolio decisions are delegated while voting decisions are retained.

(iii) *Independent Non–Profit Pension Funds*. A not-for-profit organization may also run pension plans for designated classes of individuals. In particular, Teachers Insurance and Annuity Association—College Retirement Equity Funds (TIAA–CREF, or Teachers) has created huge nonprofit pension plans to cover individuals in specified employee groups; in the case of Teachers, professors and employees of research, medical, cultural, and nonprofit organizations. Teachers' portfolio is massive; as of 2011 it was number 86 in the list of the Fortune 500 largest corporations.

(iv) *Banks*. The trust departments of banks often manage private pension plans, and serve as trustees for individuals and estates.

(v) *Investment Companies*. An investment company manages money on behalf of individuals—or, less commonly, other entities—who buy shares in the investment company, which in turn invests the money in other companies or other types of assets. In open-ended investment companies, which primarily are mutual funds, an investor has the right to withdraw her investment at any time in exchange for the value of her prorated portion of the investment company's assets at the time of withdrawal. In closed-end investment companies, an investor does not have the right to withdraw her investment, but she can sell her shares in the investment company on the open market.

(vi) *Insurance Companies*. Insurance companies accumulate huge amounts of cash from the premiums paid by their insureds, which the companies hold until insured-against events occur. This cash is invested by the insurance companies in portfolios that typically include corporate stock.

(vii) *Foundations*. Foundations, such as universities and religious institutions, typically have endowments which they invest under the direction of internal or external portfolio managers.

(viii) *Unions*. Some large unions have pension plans for their members, and these plans often own significant amounts of stock. Unions may also hold stock to take advantage of federal proxy rules that allow shareholders to make proposals in the corporate proxy materials (see Chapter 6).

(ix) *Hedge Funds.* A hedge fund is an investment fund that is typically open to a limited range of professional or wealthy investors. As a class, hedge funds undertake a wider range of investment and trading activities than traditional investment funds, and invest in a broader range of assets. The net asset value of a hedge fund can run into many billions of dollars, and the gross assets of the fund will usually be still higher due to leverage. Hedge funds dominate certain specialty markets such as trading in derivatives with high-yield ratings, and distressed debt. As a general indicator of scale, the industry may have managed around $2.5 trillion at its peak in the summer of 2008. More recent estimates suggest that hedge funds have more than $2 trillion in assets, and the 25 largest hedge funds had $520 billion in assets under management as of December 31, 2009. Hedge funds "are unregulated pools of money managed by an investment advisor, the hedge fund manager, who has a great deal of flexibility. In particular, hedge fund managers typically have the right to have short positions, to borrow, and to make extensive use of derivatives (from plain vanilla options to very exotic instruments). To avoid the regulations that affect mutual funds under the Investment Company Act, hedge funds must limit the number of investors who can invest and they cannot make public offerings. To bypass registration under the Securities Act of 1933, a hedge fund is restricted to having only accredited investors consisting of institutional investors, companies, or high net worth individuals who can 'fend for themselves.' In contrast, mutual funds generally do not have short positions, do not borrow, and make limited use of derivatives. . . ." René Stulz, Hedge Funds: Past, Present, and Future, 21 J. Econ Perspectives 175, 177 (2007). Stulz adds:

> The economic function of a hedge fund is exactly the same as the function of a mutual fund. In both cases, fund managers are entrusted with money from investors who hope that they will receive back their initial investment, plus a healthy return.
>
> Since hedge funds and mutual funds essentially perform the same economic function, why do they coexist? Hedge funds exist because mutual funds do not deliver complex investment strategies. Part of the reason mutual funds do not is that they are regulated. In addition, mutual funds and other institutional investors can gather a lot of funds from investors by promoting simple strategies. Mass selling of hedge fund strategies is much harder because hedge fund strategies are too complex for the typical mutual fund investor to understand.

Id. at 175–177.

(x) *Private equity* is an asset class consisting of equity securities in operating companies that are not publicly traded on a stock exchange. A private equity firm is a company that makes investments in private equity through a variety of investment strategies, including leveraged buyouts, venture capital, and growth capital. Typically, a private equity firm raises money to create separate private equity funds that are invested in accordance with specific investment strategies. Private equity firms generally receive a return on their investments through one of the following avenues:

- *Management Fees*—A share in the profits earned from each private equity fund that the firm manages.
- *Initial Public Offerings* (IPOs)—If shares of the operating company are offered to the public, the offering will provide an immediate realization to the private equity firm, and a public market into which the firm can later sell additional shares.
- *A Merger or Acquisition*—The operating company may be sold for either cash or shares in another company.
- *A Recapitalization*—Cash may be distributed by the operating company to the private equity firm, either from cash flow generated by the operating company or through issuing debt or other securities to fund a distribution.

Private equity firms often demand long holding periods by their shareholders, to allow for an IPO, a turnaround of an operating company, or a sale of the company. As a result, private-equity-firm shareholders usually are large investors who can commit large sums of money for long periods of time.

The following Table shows the percentage of the total value of all U.S. corporate stock held by institutional investors, not including bank trusts and estates or hedge funds, as of 2009. (The equity holdings of bank trusts and estates were reported by the Federal Reserve System until 2008, when it discontinued that reporting.):

2009 ($billions)

TYPE OF INSTITUTION	% TOTAL EQUITY MARKET
Pension Funds	21%
Private Trusteed	9%
Private Insured	4%
State & Local	8%
Investment Companies	21%
Open–End Mutual	20.5%
Funds	
Closed–End	0.5%
Insurance Companies	7%
Life Insurance	6%
Property & Casualty	1%
Savings Institutions	2%
Foundations	1.5%
All Institutions	51%*

* The data in the table above is drawn from The Conference Board's 2010 Institutional Investor Report 26, Table 12.

The Conference Board, Institutional Investment Report 32, Table 14 (2010). As Table 1 shows, institutional investor shareholdings now account for about 51% of all equities. Furthermore, institutions tend to invest more heavily in larger companies. As a result, U.S. institutional investors held 73 percent of the stock of the largest 1,000 U.S. corporations as of 2009. *Id.* at 27, Table 13.

The reason why the composition of institutional investors, and more especially the changes in that composition over time, matters a good deal, is that some institutional investors have economic ties to the managers of portfolio companies, or to managers as a class, that tends to inhibit them from voting against management, and even more strongly from taking the lead against management. Take, for example, banks. If the trust department of Bank B holds Corporation C stock as a trustee, and Corporation C is also a client of Bank B's commercial department, a trust officer of Bank B will think long and hard before voting against a proposal made by C's management or voting for a shareholder proposal that C's management opposes. Insurance companies, like banks, often have extensive commercial contracts with corporations whose stock they hold in their investment portfolios. Mutual funds may want to stay on management's good side to keep open their lines of access to information about a portfolio company's business corporation's business. An external manager of a corporate pension fund may fear that if he votes against management positions, the corporate sponsor will switch to another external manager.

In contrast, several classes of institutional investors, such as public pension funds and hedge funds, seldom have economic ties to the management of portfolio corporations that would render them economically self-interested in voting decisions. These two types of institutional investors have become leaders in shareholder activism.* Furthermore, once economically non-conflicted institutional investors take a position on an issue, it is not easy for other institutional investors to duck the issue. Kahan & Rock report as follows on the roles of hedge funds:

> [A]ctivist hedge funds have emerged as critical new players in both corporate governance and corporate control. Hedge funds have created headaches for CEOs and corporate boards by pushing for changes in management and changes in business strategy, including opposing acquisitions favored by management both as shareholders of the acquirer and as shareholders of the target, and by making unsolicited bids.

* Some institutional investors who don't have economic conflicts of interest may have conflicts of a different kind. Jill Fisch reports that a number of public pension funds have been criticized for focusing on social investing at the possible expense of maximizing profits. Comparable concerns have been raised with respect to university endowments, which may face pressure from members of the university community to engage in socially responsible investing. Similarly, sovereign wealth funds have been described as pursuing objectives such as the promotion of environmentally friendly strategies or the support of national champions. See Jill E. Fisch, Securities Intermediaries and the Separation Of Ownership, 33 Seattle U. L. Rev. 877, at 882 (2010). However, these types of conflict differ in kind, frequency, and intensity from conflicts that result from economic ties to management.

> The list of companies that have been subjected to campaigns by hedge funds and other activist investors includes McDonald's, Time Warner, H.J. Heinz Company, [and many others]. According to Wachtell Lipton partner Patricia Vlahakis, hedge funds conducted 137 activist campaigns just in the fourth quarter of 2007. In many of these instances, hedge funds have been able to win outright or at least to wrest substantial concessions from the management of the companies they target. . . .
>
> This new activism by hedge funds has become a prime irritant for CEOs. Martin Lipton, the renowned advisor to corporate boards, recently listed attacks by activist hedge funds as key issues for directors. Alan Murray from the *Wall Street Journal* calls hedge funds the new leader on the "list of bogeymen haunting the corporate boardroom," and his colleague Jesse Eisinger notes that these days hedge funds are the "shareholder activists with the most clout.

Kahan & Rock, The Embattled CEO, 88 Tex. L. Rev. 987, 998–1000 (2010).

* * *

> Hedge funds have been particularly active in transactions involving potential changes in corporate control. This activism broadly falls into three categories. First, as shareholders of the potential acquirer, hedge funds have tried to prevent the consummation of the transaction. Second, as shareholders of the potential target, hedge funds have tried to block the deal or improve the terms for target shareholders. Third, hedge funds have themselves—sometimes on their own, sometimes as part of a group—tried to acquire companies.
>
> . . . . [H]edge funds differ markedly from mutual funds and public pension funds. Mutual fund and public pension fund activism, if it occurs, tends to be incidental and ex post: when fund management notes that portfolio companies are underperforming, or that their governance regime is deficient, they will sometimes become active. In contrast, hedge fund activism is strategic and ex ante: hedge fund managers first determine whether a company would benefit from activism, then take a position and become active. Hedge fund activism represents a blurring of the line between risk arbitrage and battles over corporate strategy and control.

Kahan & Rock, Hedge Funds in Corporate Governance and Corporate Control, 155 U. Pa. L. Rev. 1021, 1034 & 1069 (2007).

The growth of institutional-investor activism has also been facilitated by changes in the law. For example, at one time the SEC's Proxy Rules made it very difficult for institutional investors to communicate with each other to determine whether it was in their mutual interests to combine forces in voting on a management or shareholder proposal or in initiating a proposal of their own. However, in 1992 the SEC revised the Proxy Rules to remove most of the constraints on communication among institutional investors. The SEC has also made it easier to make shareholder proposals; to propose short (that is, partial) slates of directorial candidates, which are often more palatable to institutional investors than slates that would replace all of the incumbents; and to gain access to the corporation's proxy statement in the nomination of candidates for the board. See Chapter 6. Another federal agency, the U.S. Department of Labor ("DOL"), was also an agent or change in this area. One of the DOL's responsibilities is to administer of the Employee Retirement Income Security Act (ERISA). Under ERISA, a person who exercises discretion over pension-plan assets must manage those assets "solely in the interest of the participants and beneficiaries and for the exclusive purpose of providing benefits to participants and their beneficiaries." This is known as the "exclusive benefit rule." In 1988, the DOL issued a well-publicized letter which stated that the fiduciary duties of pension-plan managers included voting decisions.

Finally institutional-investor activism has been affected by the development of proxy advisory services that make recommendations, principally to institutional investors, on how to vote on issues that are coming before a corporation's shareholders. The most important of these services is Institutional Shareholders Services, or ISS (now owned by RiskMetrics), which has the largest client base. The second most important, with the second-largest client base, is Glass, Lewis. In effect, the clients of these services form research coalitions by pooling their funds through the subscription prices they pay for the services' bulletins.

There is much debate regarding how much influence the recommendations of these services have in terms of how many votes the recommendations will swing, but among those who believe they exercise a good deal of influence the debate is whether they are themselves sufficiently accountable for their recommendations. It is generally recognized that the recommendations, particularly those of ISS, are influential, although commentators disagree about how influential. Different commentators have concluded that ISS alone influences institutional shareholder votes by 6–10%, 14 to 21%, 19%, 30%, and a third or more. See, e.g., Stephen Choi, Jill Fisch & Marcel Kahan, The Power of Proxy Advisors: Myth or Reality?, 59 Emory L.J. 869 (2010). Choi et al. conclude that "ISS's power is partially due to the fact that ISS (to a greater extent than other advisors) bases its recommendations on factors that shareholders consider important. . . ." Thus, ISS is not so much a Pied Piper followed blindly by institutional investors as it is an information agent and guide, helping investors to identify voting decisions that are consistent with their existing preferences.

NOTE ON THE PROBLEM OF FREE-RIDING

In theory, institutional-investor activism might be dampened by a free-rider problem, because any expenses for activism that an investor incurs may benefit other shareholders more than it benefits the investor. For example, suppose that Institution S holds 1% of Corporation C's stock. Corporation C has a governance rule, such as an anti-takeover rule, that diminishes the value of C's stock. If the only benefit to S from incurring expenses to repeal the rule would be the increased value of S's stock in C, then 1% of S's expenses would benefit S, and the remaining 99% would benefit C's other shareholders, who will free-ride on S's expenses.*

However, for a number of reasons the free-rider problem is easy to exaggerate:

(1) If the expected gain from activism will exceed the expected costs, a rational shareholder will engage in activism even when other shareholders will free-ride,

(2) The cost of activism may be little more than the cost of performing the fiduciary duty to exercise care in voting.

(3) Often the same issue will recur in a number of portfolio corporations—for example, how to vote on proposals to deal with certain kinds of anti-takeover provisions. In that case, the investor need only make a one-time expenditure to determine its position on the issue, and can then amortize the expenditure over a number of voting decisions.

(4) A vote on a recurring issue may send a message to all portfolio corporations, and therefore may have an economic benefit to the investor beyond its impact on the value of the investor's stock in a given portfolio corporation.

NOTE ON IMPACT OF ACTIVISM ON SHAREHOLDER VALUE

As the preceding material discusses, shareholders, particularly public pension and labor funds, resort to a variety of mediums to engage managers on issues they believe would improve the performance of the firms in the institutions' portfolio. Resort to the shareholder proposal rule is one medium, but other approaches include face-to-face meetings, organized votes against directors standing for election, and even shaming through maintaining and publicizing lists of worst performing management. Studies reflect that firms targeted for such activism perform more poorly than their cohorts and are sufficiently large in size to attract institutional investors. The studies also reflect that on average the targeted efforts do not yield long-term positive

* Another element that may depress institutional-investor activism consists of economic and legal limits on the holdings of an investor in any given portfolio corporation. Economically, under modern financial theory an institutional investor should diversify its portfolio, and investing of large percentages of an institutional investor's assets in a small number of portfolio corporations would defeat this objective. Legally, certain kinds of institutional investors are statutorily forbidden to hold more than a fixed percentage of the stock of any given corporation. These constraints on the amount of shareholdings in any given portfolio corporation may reduce an institutional investor's incentive to engage in activism, because they limit the prospective benefits of activism. However, the impact of these constraints is doubtful, because even with these limits a given institutional shareholder may hold stock in a portfolio corporation worth hundreds of thousands or even millions of dollars.

effects for the targeted firms. John Bizjak & Christopher Marquette, Are Shareholder Proposals All Bark and No Bite? Evidence from Shareholder Resolutions to Rescind Poison Pills, 33 J. Fin. & Quantitative Analysis 4 (1998) (reporting no significant abnormal stock price return between announcement date of proposal to terminate firm's poison pill and the meeting date); Michael Smith, Shareholder Activism by Institutional Investors: Evidence from CalPERS, 51 J. Fin. 1 (1996) (shareholder activism did not have a statistically significant effect on operating income, cash flow or asset sales); Sunil Wahal, Pension Fund Activism and Firm Performance, 31 J. Fin. & Quantitative Analysis 1 (1996). See generally, Roberta Romano, Less Is More: Making Institutional Investor Activism A Valuable Mechanism Of Corporate Governance, 18 Yale J. Reg. 174 (2001).

On the other hand, the following extensive study reflects that one type of financial institutions has a very positive record on target firm performance.

Brav, Jiang, Partnoy & Thomas, Hedge Fund Activism, Corporate Governance, and Firm Performance

63 J. Fin. 1729 (2008).

We find that hedge funds increasingly engage in a new form of shareholder activism and monitoring that differs fundamentally from previous activist efforts by other institutional investors. . . . Unlike mutual funds and pension funds, hedge funds are able to influence corporate boards and managements due to key differences arising from their different organizational form and the incentives that they face. Hedge funds employ highly incentivized managers who manage large unregulated pools of capital. Because they are not subject to regulation that governs mutual funds and pension funds, they can hold highly concentrated positions in small numbers of companies, and use leverage and derivatives to extend their reach. Hedge fund managers also suffer few conflicts of interest because they are not beholden to the management of the firms whose shares they hold. In sum, hedge funds are better positioned to act as informed monitors than other institutional investors.

Hedge fund activists tend to target companies that are typically "value" firms, with low market value relative to book value, although they are profitable with sound operating cash flows and return on assets. Payout at these companies before intervention is lower than that of matched firms. Target companies also have more takeover defenses and pay their CEOs considerably more than comparable companies. Relatively few targeted companies are large-cap firms, which is not surprising given the comparatively high cost of amassing a meaningful stake in such a target. Targets exhibit significantly higher institutional ownership and trading liquidity. These characteristics make it easier for activists to acquire a significant stake quickly. . . .

We find that the market reacts favorably to activism, consistent with the view that it creates value. The filing of a Schedule 13D revealing an activist fund's investment in a target firm results in large positive average abnormal returns, in the range of 7% to 8%, during the (–20, +20) announcement window. . . . We find that the positive returns at announcement are not reversed over time, as there is no evidence of a negative abnormal drift during the 1–year period subsequent to the announcement. . . . Moreover, target prices decline upon the exit of a hedge fund only after it has been unsuccessful, which indicates that the information reflected in the positive announcement returns conveys the market's expectation for the success of activism. . . .

Activism that targets the sale of the company or changes in business strategy, such as refocusing and spinning-off noncore assets, is associated with the largest positive abnormal partial effects, at 8.54% and 5.95%, respectively (the latter figure is lower than the overall sample average because most events target multiple issues). This evidence suggests that hedge funds are able to create value when they see large allocative inefficiencies. In contrast, we find that the market response to capital structure-related activism—including debt restructuring, recapitalization, dividends, and share repurchases—is positive yet insignificant. We find a similar lack of statistically meaningful reaction for governance-related activism—including attempts to rescind takeover defenses, to oust CEOs, to enhance board independence, and to curtail CEO compensation. Hedge funds with a track record of successful activism generate higher returns, as do hedge funds that initiate activism with hostile tactics.

The positive market reaction is also consistent with ex post evidence of overall improved performance at target firms. On average, from the year before to the year after an announcement, total payout increases by 0.3 to 0.5 percentage points (as a percentage of the market value of equity, relative to an all-sample mean of 2.2 percentage points), and book value leverage increases by 1.3 to 1.4 percentage points (relative to an all-sample mean of 33.5 percentage points). Both changes are consistent with a reduction of agency problems associated with free cash flow and subject managers to increased market discipline. We also find improvement in return on assets and operating profit margins, but this takes longer to manifest. The post-event year sees little change compared to the year prior to intervention. However, EBITDA/Assets (EBITDA/Sales) at target firms increases by 0.9 to 1.5 (4.7 to 5.8) percentage points two years after intervention. . . .

Hedge fund activists are not short-term in focus, as some critics have claimed. The median holding period for completed deals is about one year, calculated as from the date a hedge fund files a Schedule 13D to the date when the fund no longer holds a significant stake in a target company. The calculation substantially understates the actual median holding period, because it necessarily excludes a significant number of events for which no exit information is available by March

2007 [when the authors ceased collecting data]. Analysis of portfolio turnover rates of the funds in our sample suggests holding periods of closer to 20 months.

Since shareholders are by no means the only party affected by hedge fund activism we also ask whether other stakeholders are impacted. In particular, we consider the possibility that the positive stock market reaction to activism might reflect wealth redistribution from creditors and executives. We find that hedge fund activism does not shift value from creditors to shareholders. Indeed, the 174 targets with no long-term debt have slightly *higher* announcement returns than the rest of the sample. On the other hand, we do see evidence that hedge fund activism shifts value away from senior managers. In particular, hedge fund activism is not kind to CEOs of target firms. During the year after the announcement of activism, average CEO pay declines by about $1 million dollars, and the CEO turnover rate increases by almost 10 percentage points, controlling for the normal turnover rates in the same industry, and for firms of similar size and stock valuation. . . .

Although some commentators have characterized hedge fund activism as fundamentally hostile to managers, we find that hedge fund activists are openly hostile in less than 30% of cases (hostility includes a threatened or actual proxy contest, takeover, lawsuit, or public campaign that is openly confrontational). More commonly, hedge fund activists cooperate with managers, at least at the initial stages of their intervention, and achieve all or most of their stated goals in about two-thirds of all cases. Managerial opposition to hedge fund activism may stem from its negative impact on CEO pay and turnover even if it ultimately creates value for shareholders.

Our findings have important implications for the policy debate about hedge fund activism. Although some prominent legal commentators, including leading corporate lawyers and European regulators, have called for restrictions on hedge fund activism because of its supposedly short-term orientation, our results suggest that activist hedge funds are not short-term holders. Activists also appear to generate substantial value for target firm shareholders. Indeed, our evidence of the market's positive response to hedge fund activism, and the subsequent success of activists, challenges the premises of proposals requiring increased hedge fund regulation.

For policy makers, our paper shows important distinctions between the role of hedge funds and other private institutional investors such as private equity firms. Despite their frequently aggressive behavior, activist hedge funds do not typically seek control in target companies. The median maximum ownership stake for the entire sample is about 9.1%. Even at the 95th percentile in the full sample, the stake is 31.5%—far short of the level for majority control. Activists rely on cooperation from management or, in its absence, support from fellow shareholders to implement their value-improving agendas. This explains why hedge fund activists tend to target companies with higher institutional holdings and analyst coverage, both of which suggest a more sophisticated shareholder base. It is also common for multiple hedge funds to coordinate by cofiling Schedule 13Ds (about 22% of the sample) or acting in tandem without being a formal block. Although some regulators have criticized such informal block behavior as anticompetitive, coordination among hedge funds can benefit shareholders overall by facilitating activism at relatively low individual ownership stakes.

The new evidence presented in this paper suggests that activist hedge funds occupy an important middle ground between internal monitoring by large shareholders and external monitoring by corporate raiders. Activist hedge funds are more flexible, incentivized, and independent than internal monitors, and they can generate multiple gains from targeting several companies on similar issues. Conversely, activist hedge funds have advantages over external corporate raiders, because they take smaller stakes, often benefit from cooperation with management, and have support from other shareholders. This hybrid internal-external role puts activist hedge funds in a potentially unique position to reduce the agency costs associated with the separation of ownership and control. . . .

SECTION 3. VOTE BUYING

Portnoy v. Cryo–Cell International, Inc.

Court of Chancery of Delaware, 2008.
940 A.2d 43.

■ STRINE, VICE CHANCELLOR.

This case involves a challenge to the results of a contested corporate election. Cryo–Cell International, Inc. ("Cryo–Cell" or the "Company") is a small public company that has struggled to succeed. By early 2007, several of its large stockholders were considering mounting a proxy contest to replace the board.

One of those stockholders, Andrew Filipowski, used management's fear of replacement to strike a deal for himself to be included in the management slate for the 2007 annual meeting. Another stockholder, plaintiff David Portnoy, filed a dissident slate (the "Portnoy Slate").

Going into the week of the annual meeting, Cryo–Cell's chief executive officer, defendant Mercedes Walton, was desperate because, in her words, "the current board and management [were] losing by huge margins." Aside from actually asking the FBI to intervene in the proxy contest on the side of management, Walton ginned up a plan with Filipowski to win the proxy contest. That plan involved Walton acting as a "matchmaker" by finding stockholders willing to sell their shares to Filipowski. In exchange for this alliance, Walton promised Filipowski that if their "Management Slate" prevailed, Cryo–Cell's board would, using their power as corporate directors, expand the board to add another seat that Filipowski's designee would fill. That designee was a subordinate who had within the recent past resolved an SEC insider trading investigation by agreeing to disgorge trading profits and to be jointly liable for trading profits made by his tippees. This plan was not disclosed to the Cryo–Cell stockholders, who did not realize that if they voted for management, they would in fact be electing a seven, not six member board, with two, not one, Filipowski representatives.

In an effort to secure another key bloc of votes, Walton used a combination of threats (the ending of cooperation on key projects) and inducements (the long-sought but never before granted removal of a restrictive legend) to secure the vote of Saneron CCEL Therapeutics Inc. That leverage was enhanced by the fact that Cryo–Cell owned 38% of Saneron's shares and that Saneron depended on Cryo–Cell's laboratory space to conduct many of its own operations. Notwithstanding that, Saneron had gone into the week before the meeting undecided about how to vote. Walton "locked up" Saneron only after employing these persuasive strategies involving the threatened withholding and actual granting of concessions on the part of Cryo–Cell as a corporation.

Even after employing these methods, Walton and her board went into the day of the annual meeting fearing defeat. They had rented the meeting room from the 11 a.m. start time only until 1 p.m. But Walton did not want to close the polls and count the vote when the scheduled presentations at the meeting were over. So she had members of her management team make long, unscheduled presentations to give her side more time to gather votes and ensure that they had locked in two key blocs. She overruled motions to close the polls.

Even after the filibusters, Walton still harbored doubt that the Management Slate would prevail if the vote was counted and the meeting was concluded. So, at around 2 p.m., Walton declared a very late lunch break, supposedly in response to a request made much earlier.

In fact, Walton desired the break so that she would have more time to seek votes and so that she could confirm that the major blockholders had switched their votes to favor the Management Slate. Only after confirming the switches did Walton resume the meeting at approximately 4:45 p.m., declare the polls closed, and have the vote counted.

The post-meeting vote count resulted in the Management Slate squeaking out a victory by an extremely small margin. Immediately after that, Walton began preparing to add Filipowski's designee to the Cryo–Cell board. Only after this challenge was brought to the election by Portnoy did that process slow down, and only for the obvious reason that the litigation was brought.

In this opinion, I decline Portnoy's request to declare his side the victor in the election process. But I do agree with him that the election results were tainted by inequitable behavior by Walton and her allies and must be set aside. In particular, I conclude that the Cryo–Cell stockholders cast their votes in ignorance of material facts regarding the promise made to Filipowski regarding a second board seat and the pressure that Walton was exerting on Saneron—both of which involved the use by Walton of corporate resources and fiduciary authority motivated by the desire to protect herself from the risk of losing her corporate offices.

Rather than seating a board for the Cryo–Cell stockholders, I believe the more appropriate remedy to be a requirement that Cryo–Cell have another election at a special meeting to be held promptly. Because the stockholders should not be required to bear extra expense because of management's misconduct, the Management Slate will be required to fund their own re-election campaign and to pay any costs incurred by the Company to hold the special meeting, including the cost of a special master to preside over the meeting. . . .

II. The Merits Of Portnoy's Claims

Portnoy has brought this claim under *8 Del. C. § 225* challenging the seating of the Management Slate. He claims that the election results should be overturned because the Management Slate would not have been elected had the following alleged breaches of duty not occurred:

1) A supposedly improper agreement by the Cryo–Cell board to include Filipowski on the Management Slate, not because they believed that was in the best interests of Cryo–Cell and its stockholders, but merely as consideration for Filipowski's agreement to vote for the incumbent board members in the proxy fight;

2) A supposedly improper promise by Walton that the incumbent board members would, if re-elected, add another Filipowski designee, Roszak, to the board if Filipowski continued to buy up more shares and if that conduct resulted in the Management Slate winning the election;

3) A course of conduct by Walton employing both threats and an inducement to influence Saneron to cast its vote for the Management Slate;

4) An adjournment of the annual meeting without a vote of the Cryo–Cell stockholders as Portnoy contends was required by the corporation's bylaws, and, in any event, an inequitably motivated and falsely justified "lunch break" that was designed to give the Management Slate more time to gather votes because they feared defeat if the vote was counted in accordance with the original schedule. . . .

I begin my consideration of these arguments, with Portnoy's claims regarding the relationship between the incumbent board members on the Management Slate (led by Walton) and Filipowski. I then move on to briefly address the Saneron issue. I conclude with the claim related to the conduct of the meeting itself.

A. The Addition Of Filipowski To The Management Slate . . .

Portnoy contends that the deal struck between Walton and the other incumbents, on the one hand, and Filipowski, on the other, to add Filipowski to the Management Slate in exchange for his support in the proxy fight constituted an illegal vote-buying arrangement.

On this claim, which has some color, I find in favor of the defendants. My conclusion rests on several grounds. Initially, I note that an arrangement of this kind fits comfortably, as a linguistic matter, within the traditional definition of so-called "vote buying" used in our jurisprudence. As defined by Vice Chancellor Hartnett in his important decision in *Schreiber v. Carney*, "[v]ote-buying . . . is simply a voting agreement supported by consideration personal to the stockholder, whereby the stockholder divorces his discretionary voting power and votes as directed by the offeror." *447 A.2d 17, 23 (Del.Ch. 1982)*. In this case, I have no doubt that the voting agreement between the Filipowski Group and the incumbents was only assented to by Filipowski after he was offered a candidacy on the Management Slate. What I am more doubtful about is whether an arrangement of this kind—where the incumbents offer a potential insurgent a seat on the management slate in exchange for the potential insurgent's voting support—should trigger the sort of heightened scrutiny rightly given to more questionable arrangements.

To say that the law of corporations has struggled with how to address the subject of so-called "vote buying" is no insult to judges or corporate law scholars, the question of what inducements and agreements may legitimately be forged to cement a voting coalition is doubtless as old as the concept of a polity itself. For these very real-world reasons, *Schreiber* refused to say that any sort of arrangement involving the exchange of consideration in connection with a stockholder's agreement to vote a particular way was forbidden vote buying. Indeed, distinguished scholars have anguished (the adjective I take away from their work) over how to deal with such arrangements, with most concluding that flat-out prohibitions are neither workable nor of utility to diversified stockholders.[152] The absence of a per se ban on such arrangements is unsurprising for another obvious reason, voting agreements with respect to corporate stock are actually contemplated by our statutory corporate law. Often such agreements have the intended effect of forming a voting coalition between stockholders that involves the requirement that the contracting parties vote to elect each other to the board.

To deal with these complexities, *Schreiber* declined to find that vote buying was, in the first instance, per se improper. Rather, *Schreiber* articulated a two-pronged analysis. In the first instance, if the plaintiff can show that the "object or purpose [of the vote buying was]

152. See, e.g., Thomas J. Andre, Jr., *A Preliminary Inquiry into the Utility of Vote Buying in the Market for Corporate Control*, 63 S. CAL. L. REV 533, 636 (1990); Robert Charles Clark, *Vote Buying and Corporate Law*, 29 Case W. RES. L. REV. 776, 806–07 (1979). *But see* Frank H. Easterbrook & Daniel R. Fischel, *Voting in Corporate Law*, 26 J.L. & ECON. 395, 410–11 (1983) (arguing against allowing vote-buying agreements).

to defraud or in some way disenfranchise the other stockholders", the arrangement would be "illegal per se." Putting this in terms that I think are truer to the way our corporate law works, what I take from this is that if the plaintiff proved that the arrangement under challenge was improperly motivated, then the arrangement would be set aside in equity, irrespective of its technical compliance with the DGCL. That is, in keeping with the traditional vigilance this court has displayed in ensuring the fairness of the corporate election process, and in particular the process by which directors are elected, purposely inequitable conduct in the accumulation of voting power will not be tolerated. Even when a vote buying arrangement cannot be found, in the first instance, to be motivated by a fraudulent, disenfranchising, or otherwise inequitable intent, *Schreiber* concluded that "because vote-buying is so easily susceptible of abuse it must be viewed as a voidable transaction subject to a test for intrinsic fairness."

Subjecting an agreement to add a potential insurgent to a management slate to the *Schreiber* intrinsic fairness test would, in my view, be an inadvisable and counterproductive precedent. If one takes a judicial standard of review seriously, as the members of this court do, the decision to subject all such arrangements to the entire fairness standard could result in creating litigable factual issues about a large number of useful compromises that result in the addition of fresh blood to management slates, new candidates who will tend to represent actual owners of equity and might therefore be more independent of management and more useful representatives of the interests of stockholders generally. I emphasize "litigable factual issues" because a judicial standard that by definition imposes on the defendants an onerous burden of persuasion is one that largely eliminates any possible use of Rule 12(b)(6) motion practice to get rid of the case. Beyond the pleading stage, it is also difficult to meet a substantive fairness standard by invoking Rule 56, because any material factual question relevant to fairness will result in the need for a trial.

In being chary about extending Schreiber reach to this context, I do not underestimate the value of being included in the management slate. An offer to be on the management slate will often promise a near certainty of eventual election. At the very least, it will relieve the insurgent of having to pay for his own candidacy and to run a contested election against corporate insiders who do not have to pay their own solicitation costs. Instead, the insurgent would be on the inside track, so to speak.

But being on the inside track is different than being on the board, and that difference suggests that employing an entire fairness standard to such arrangements is overkill. If the only arrangement at issue is a promise to add a potential insurgent to the management slate in exchange for the insurgent's voting support, then the arrangement is subject to stockholder policing in an obvious, but nonetheless, potent form. That policing occurs at the ballot box itself.

Here, to be specific, the Cryo–Cell stockholders went to the polls knowing that Filipowski had been added to the Management Slate.

Those stockholders also knew that Filipowski had contracted to vote the Filipowski Group's shares for the Management Slate. Although it was not publicly disclosed that Filipowski's agreement to vote for the Management Slate had been conditioned on his addition to that Slate, and that the incumbents had added Filipowski to the Management Slate in exchange for his support, that inference was, I think, unmistakable to any rational stockholder. Surely it was known by Portnoy, who knew that Filipowski had been unhappy about the Company's performance, and had flirted with running a slate with Portnoy, only to secure a place for himself on the Management Slate. Therefore, Portnoy was well positioned to point out that Filipowski had committed to support incumbents whose wisdom and fidelity to stockholders Filipowski himself had only recently called into serious question.

Given that the electorate's own opportunity to decide for itself whether Filipowski should serve, I think it unwise, as a matter of our common law, to apply the intrinsic fairness test to this situation. . . . The notion that judges should chew over the complicated calculus made by incumbent boards considering whether to add to the management slate candidates proposed by a large blockholder whose velvety suggestions were cloaking an unmistakably clenched fist seems to run against many of the sound reasons for the business judgment rule. . . . When stockholders can decide for themselves whether to seat a candidate who obtained a place on a management slate by way of such bargaining, it seems unwise to formulate a standard that involves the potential for excessive and imprecise judicial involvement.

In my view, a mere offer of a position on a management slate should not be considered a vote-buying arrangement subject to a test of entire fairness, and for that reason, I see no reason to condemn the addition of Filipowski to the Management Slate. As an alternative matter, the defendants have convinced me that there was nothing unfair about joining forces with Filipowski in this manner. In this regard, I note that there is not a hint that Filipowski sought to receive financial payments from Cryo–Cell in the form of contracts or consulting fees or other such arrangements. What he sought was influence on the board of a company in which he owned a large number of shares, an ownership interest that gave him an incentive to increase the company's value. Stockholders knew he sought a seat and he had to obtain their votes to get on the board.

For all these reasons, I conclude that Portnoy's attack on this aspect of the incumbents dealings with Filipowski fails.

B. The Promise Of A Second Board Seat For The Filipowski Group

I reach a different conclusion, however, about the later arrangement that was reached with Filipowski shortly before the annual meeting. As I found previously, Walton (acting at the very least with the apparent authority of her board colleagues, who were extremely deferential to her leadership) promised Filipowski that if the Management Slate won, the incumbent board majority would use its powers under the Company's bylaws to expand the Cryo–Cell board from six members to seven and to fill the new seat with Filipowski's designee, Roszak. That promise was made in response to Roszak's request—as Filipowski's negotiator—and made in exchange for Filipowski's promise to go out and buy more shares (and therefore votes). . . .

I believe that this arrangement differed in materially important respects from the prior agreement to place Filipowski on the Management Slate. For starters, Walton did not merely promise someone a shot at getting elected by the stockholders by running in the advantaged posture of being a member of a management slate. She promised that she and her incumbent colleagues would use their powers as directors of Cryo–Cell to increase the size of the board and seat Roszak. This was therefore a promise that would not be, for the duration of the term, subject to prior approval by the electorate.

In noting this difference, however, I wish to be mindful of the continuing relevance of the color grey. As is well known, it is hardly unusual for boards to address the concerns of unsettled stockholders by using their powers to fill a vacancy (whether newly created or preexisting) with a director suggested by the stockholders. Indeed, many stockholder advocates believe that developments of this kind should be more common. There is therefore some non-trivial basis to be concerned about labeling such arrangements as vote buying arrangements subject to *Schreiber*, or as inequitable under *Schnell*, even if the incumbents' motivations for the arrangements include (as they almost always will) a desire to remain in office.

In voicing this concern, I recognize that there is a rather obvious retort, which is that incumbents should not be adding new candidates only on the condition that those who suggest them agree to vote for the management slate at the next election. But if one is going to address the issue maturely—in the sense of actually realistically considering the human, business, and practical considerations that motivate pragmatic settlements of difficult problems—then that is no answer at all. From the subjective view of the incumbents, one of the benefits they are accomplishing by a settlement of that kind is to protect the company from the distraction of a costly and fractious battle over control. The incumbents may well believe, in good faith, that their continuance in office is best for the stockholders. They may prefer not to add members to the board but may come to believe that, on balance, it would better serve the interests of stockholders to add new representation at the instance of vocal stockholders and avoid a high-stakes fight for control than to be confrontational. In that circumstance, though, it seems logical that the incumbent board majority might well, and with entire fidelity, expect that the stockholders who asked for new representation commit in exchange to support the newly composed board at the next election, if not for some longer period of service. Absent such an agreement, no appreciable period of peace would be secured during which the newly composed board could focus on simply making the business hum.

In view of these concerns, I am chary about addressing the promise of a second board seat that was made to Filipowski on broader grounds than is necessary. For me, there is a very clear and important, but narrow, reason why this later arrangement with Filipowski was improper and inequitably tainted the election process: it was a very material event that was not disclosed to the Cryo–Cell stockholders.

"[D]irectors of Delaware corporations are under a fiduciary duty to disclose fully and fairly all material information within the board's control when it seeks shareholder action." *Arnold v. Socyfor Savings Bancorp., Inc., 650 A. 2d 1270, 1277 (Del. 1994)* (quoting *Stroud v. Grace, 606 A.2d 75, 84 (Del. 1992)*). That disclosure "obligation attaches to proxy statements and any other disclosures in contemplation of stockholder action."

On the day they voted, the Cryo–Cell stockholders knew that a vote for the Management Slate would seat six directors, including Filipowski. They had to know that Filipowski's support for the Management Slate was in large measure motivated by his own inclusion.

What the Cryo–Cell stockholders did not know was that Walton had promised that the board would use its fiduciary powers to expand the board to seven members and seat another person designated by Filipowski. Problematically, the Cryo–Cell stockholders did not know that Filipowski clearly intended to designate Roszak, a person whose recent past would have weighed heavily on the mind of a rational stockholder considering whether to seat him as a fiduciary. . . .

In this regard, it is worth observing that even those academic commentators who have endeavored to justify tolerance of forms of vote buying as having benefits to diversified investors have emphasized the need for fair disclosure of such arrangements. For reasons I have described, it is prudent not to jump too quickly to the conclusion that voting pacts of this kind should automatically be seen as inequitable, although one could do so and find credible support for such a finding. For many of the reasons that supported my earlier decision regarding Filipowski's inclusion on the Management Slate, an agreement of this kind that was made and disclosed in advance of an election is subject to the important fairness check of the stockholder vote itself. By contrast, the disinterested Cryo–Cell electorate voted in ignorance of the actual board that would govern them in the event the Management Slate won.

C. Management's Influence Over Saneron's Vote

Because of my conclusions regarding the Filipowski issues, I need not dwell at length on the Saneron bloc. Even absent Walton's conduct toward Saneron, I would set aside the election results.

In my view, threats and promises of the kind directed at Saneron are much less problematically dealt within the *Schreiber* framework than properly disclosed agreements that involve give-and-take about the shape of a board slate. When what an agreement involves is not an accommodation about board service itself, but the use of a corporate asset (such as a contractual concession) by the management slate to secure a vote for itself, it is much more natural to consider that agreement "vote buying" in the traditional sense and to employ *Schreiber*'s back-stop fairness analysis. For the following reasons, I find that the defendants fail both the prong requiring Walton's actions to have been motivated by a good faith desire to advance corporate interests, rather than to entrench herself, and the prong requiring the defendants, even if Walton had acted in good faith, to justify their dealings with Saneron as entirely fair to Cryo–Cell. *Schreiber, 447 A. 2d at 25–26.*

I begin with my conclusion that Walton breached her fiduciary duties by intentionally using corporate assets to coerce Saneron in the exercise of its voting rights. As I have found, Walton both threatened Saneron (with the loss or at least cooling of a strategic partnership vital to it) and granted it an inducement (the lifting of a restrictive legend on its shares) in order to extract a commitment from Saneron to vote for the Management Slate.

There is no doubt that threatening Saneron was improper conduct by Walton, whereby she used her power as a fiduciary to control assets of Cryo–Cell for the purpose of entrenching herself in office....

Given that Walton clearly used company resources to coerce Saneron in the voting process and thereby breached her duty of loyalty, it was the defendants' burden to show that Saneron's vote was not influenced by her misbehavior. They have not convinced me of that at all. Rather, the circumstances surrounding Saneron's decision to vote for the Management Slate are more consistent with a bargained-for exchange, in which Saneron got a removal of the restrictive legend and the hope of future cooperation from Cryo–Cell in exchange for casting an early and important vote for the Management Slate. Walton's own words regarding the effect of her tactics said it best: those tactics "locked up" Saneron's vote....

Although a change in the voting of the Saneron bloc alone would not have turned the election, Walton's improper conduct and its nondisclosure contributes to my overall sense that the election was tainted by misbehavior by insiders who could not win an election simply using the traditionally powerful advantages afforded incumbents. Our law has no tolerance for unfair election tactics of this kind.

D. The Annual Meeting

I now come to Portnoy's last complaint. That is about how Walton conducted the meeting.

As an initial matter, I decline to use this as an excuse to probe the difference between a lunch break and a formal adjournment. The language of the Cryo–Cell bylaws creates a colorable argument that a formal adjournment could not have been declared without stockholder approval and there is doubt whether Walton had sufficient proxies in hand for that purpose.[182] In my view, Portnoy is not positioned to

182. Portnoy argues that Article II § 8(b) of Cryo-Cell's bylaws provides the exclusive means to adjourn a stockholder meeting. That section, which is titled "Quorum," states:

contest Walton's authority to "decide all procedural issues regarding the conduct of the meeting, including adjournment," so long as she did so in good faith. The contending Slates, through their representatives, reached agreement three days before the meeting on certain procedures. That sort of agreement can be thought to have utility, insofar as it provides the contestants with a reliable set of assumptions about how the meeting will be conducted.[184] To have one of the agreeing parties later carp about a provision he assented to undermines the utility of such agreements and creates a risk of electoral uncertainty over trivial missteps in what can be the technically challenging process of running a meeting. . . .

What, however, is more uncertain is that Walton acted inequitably in her conduct of the meeting. The reality is that she did not take a "lupper" break of nearly three hours at 2 p.m. so that the attendees at the meeting could eat. Because Walton undertook action that affected the conduct of an election of directors in a potentially important way, the defendants bear the burden to show that Walton's actions were "motivated by a good faith concern for the stockholders' best interests, and not by a desire to entrench [herself.]" They have failed to prove that Walton's tactics were undertaken in selfless good faith.

Walton's behavior during the day was analogous to a corrupted soccer referee, intent on adding extra time so that the game would end only when her favored team had a sure lead. . . . When Walton was asked to count the vote, she replied with the jejune response that the request was out of order. At trial, she could not explain what that response was supposed to mean. It sounds to the court like something out of Robert's Rules of Order that Walton had heard invoked by someone trying to fake their way through a local town council meeting or had seen when watching a congressional debate on C–Span.

This is not to say that Walton had no discretion to keep the polls open. But what she did was to stall without being honest about why she was acting.

If she were being candid, she would have admitted that she was waiting for confirmation that two large blockholders' votes had been switched before having the vote counted. Indeed, if she were being perfectly candid, she would have admitted that she was keeping the polls open so that the Management Slate could continue its efforts to secure more votes by purchase because she was concerned that it would lose even with their votes. Even with less candor, she could have straightforwardly said that she was keeping the polls open to a time certain so that the parties could continue their contest for votes.

"Despite the absence of a quorum at any annual or special meeting of shareholders, the shareholders, by a majority of the votes cast by holders entitled to vote thereon, may adjourn the meeting."

184. DAVID A. DREXLER, LEWIS S. BLACK, JR. & A. GILCHRIST SPARKS, III, *DELAWARE CORPORATE LAW AND PRACTICE* § 24.05[1] (2007) ("[T]here are no statutory guidelines for such routine matters as . . . the rules of procedure, if any, which must be followed. . . . For this reason, parties anticipating a contested vote often find it to their mutual advantage to agree in advance upon procedural details in order to avoid the potential degeneration of proceedings into confusion, if not chaos.").

Instead, she first tried to pull off a filibuster, subjecting the stockholders to unscheduled bloviation from her management subordinates. Particularly disturbing is Walton's choice to have presentations made on laboratory research and sales when she might have instead released the company's 10–Q, which was already prepared, and had the CFO, who was at the meeting, explain Cryo–Cell's disappointing financial results. But providing the stockholders with information such as actual up-to-date financial results that might have been material to how they chose to vote their shares was not Walton's concern. Stalling was. During the filibuster, Walton rejected another request to hold the vote. Again, she ruled that request "out of order" for no articulated reason.

It was then that she used the pretense that everyone needed lunch to delay the vote. That move gave her side time, which they used, to ensure that they had the votes to prevail. And lest anyone be moved by the attendees' need for sustenance, by any measure they would have dined earlier—at the traditional time of lunch, in fact—had Walton closed the polls when the events scheduled to precede the vote had concluded. . . .

[I]t is impossible to ignore the unfairness of Walton's behavior, a justification by reference to effect being no defense to actions affecting a director election that are undertaken for "an inequitable purpose" and in an inequitably deceptive manner. If an electoral contestant assumes the role of presiding over the meeting, she has an obligation to do so fairly. Walton did not do so. She stalled so that her side could win the game, knowing that if the game ended when it was scheduled to end, her side would lose. Then she was dishonest about the reasons for delay.

For all these reasons, I find that Portnoy has proven that serious breaches of fiduciary duty tainted the election. . . .

The parties shall collaborate on the appropriate date and location for a prompt special meeting and present a conforming order, in advance of seeking a conference this week with the court at which the order will be finalized and a special master appointed.

SECTION 4. FUNDING PROXY CONTESTS

What are the public policy implications of the following: Who should be able to have access to the corporation's resources in contested elections? Incumbents? Insurgents? What kind of proxy contest expenses should be reimbursed? Should reimbursement be conditioned on whether the party seeking reimbursement was successful in securing a majority of the seats on the board?Elected to the board? Should reimbursement of expenses incurred to oppose successfully an initiative supported by management? *See generally* Lucian Ayre Bebchuk & Marcel Kahan, A Framework for Analyzing Legal Policy Towards Proxy Contests, 78 Cal. L. Rev. 1073 (1990).

Rosenfeld v. Fairchild Engine and Airplane Corp.

Court of Appeals of New York, 1955.
309 N.Y. 168, 128 N.E.2d 291.

■ FROSSEL, JUDGE. In a stockholder's derivative action brought by plaintiff, an attorney, who owns 25 out of the company's over 2,300,000 shares, he seeks to compel the return of $261,522, paid out of the corporate treasury to reimburse both sides in a proxy contest for their expenses. The Appellate Division, 284 App.Div. 201, 132 N.Y.S.2d 273, has unanimously affirmed a judgment of an Official Referee, Sup., 116 N.Y.S.2d 840, dismissing plaintiff's complaint on the merits, and we agree. . . .

Of the amount in controversy $106,000 was spent out of corporate funds by the old board of directors while still in office in defense of their position in said contest; $28,000 [was] paid to the old board by the new board after the change of management following the proxy contest, to compensate the former directors for such of the remaining expenses of their unsuccessful defense as the new board found was fair and reasonable; payment of $127,000, representing reimbursement of expenses to members of the prevailing group, was expressly ratified by a 16 to 1 majority vote of the stockholders.

The essential facts are not in dispute. . . . The Appellate Division found that the difference between plaintiff's group and the old board "went deep into the policies of the company", and that among these Ward's contract was one of the "main points of contention". The Official Referee found that the controversy "was based on an understandable difference in policy between the two groups, at the very bottom of which was the Ward employment contract".

By way of contrast with the findings here, in Lawyers' Advertising Co. v. Consolidated Ry., Lighting & Refrigerating Co., 187 N.Y. 395, at page 399, 80 N.E. 199, at page 200, which was an action to recover for the cost of publishing newspaper notices not authorized by the board of directors, it was expressly found that the proxy contest there involved was "by one faction in its contest with another for the control of the corporation . . . a contest for the perpetuation of their offices and control." We there said by way of *dicta* that under *such* circumstances the publication of certain notices on behalf of the management faction was not a corporate expenditure which the directors had the power to authorize.

Other jurisdictions and our own lower courts have held that management may look to the corporate treasury for the reasonable expenses of soliciting proxies to defend its position in a bona fide policy contest. . . .

It should be noted that plaintiff does not argue that the aforementioned sums were fraudulently extracted from the corporation; indeed, his counsel conceded that "the charges were fair and reasonable", but denied "they were legal charges which may be reimbursed for". This is therefore not a case where a stockholder challenges specific items, which, on examination, the trial court may find unwarranted, excessive or otherwise improper. . . .

If directors of a corporation may not in good faith incur reasonable and proper expenses in soliciting proxies in these days of giant corporations with vast numbers of stockholders, the corporate business might be seriously interfered with because of stockholder indifference and the difficulty of procuring a quorum, where there is no contest. In the event of a proxy contest, if the directors may not freely answer the challenges of outside groups and in good faith defend their actions with respect to corporate policy for the information of the stockholders, they and the corporation may be at the mercy of persons seeking to wrest control for their own purposes, so long as such persons have ample funds to conduct a proxy contest. The test is clear. When the directors act in good faith in a contest over policy, they have the right to incur reasonable and proper expenses for solicitation of proxies and in defense of their corporate policies, and are not obliged to sit idly by. The courts are entirely competent to pass upon their *bona fides* in any given case, as well as the nature of their expenditures when duly challenged.

It is also our view that the members of the so-called new group could be reimbursed by the corporation for their expenditures in this contest by affirmative vote of the stockholders. With regard to these ultimately successful contestants, as the Appellate Division below has noted, there was, of course, "no duty . . . to set forth the facts, with corresponding obligation of the corporation to pay for such expense". However, where a majority of the stockholders chose—in this case by a vote of 16 to 1—to reimburse the successful contestants for achieving the very end sought and voted for by them as owners of the corporation, we see no reason to deny the effect of their ratification nor to hold the corporate body powerless to determine how its own moneys shall be spent.

The rule then which we adopt is simply this: In a contest over policy, as compared to a purely personal power contest, corporate directors have the right to make reasonable and proper expenditures, subject to the scrutiny of the courts when duly challenged, from the corporate treasury for the purpose of persuading the stockholders of the correctness of their position and soliciting their support for policies which the directors believe, in all good faith, are in the best interests of the corporation. The stockholders, moreover, have the right to reimburse successful contestants for the reasonable and bona fide expenses incurred by them in any such policy contest, subject to like court scrutiny. That is not to say, however, that corporate directors can, under any circumstances, disport themselves in a proxy contest with the corporation's moneys to an unlimited extent. Where it is established that such moneys have been spent for personal power, individual gain or private advantage, and not in the belief that such expenditures are in the best interests of the stockholders and the corporation, or where the fairness and reasonableness of the amounts allegedly expended are duly and successfully challenged, the courts will not hesitate to disallow them.

The judgment of the Appellate Division should be affirmed, without costs.

■ Desmond, Judge (concurring). We granted leave to appeal in an effort to pass, and in the expectation of passing, on this question, highly important in modern-day corporation law: is it lawful for a corporation, on consent of a majority of its stockholders, to pay, out of its funds, the expenses of a "proxy fight", incurred by competing candidates for election as directors? Now that the appeal has been argued, I doubt that the question is presented by this record. . . .

. . . The reason why that important question is, perhaps, not directly before us in this lawsuit is because, as the Appellate Division properly held, [284 App.Div. 201, 132 N.Y.S.2d 273] plaintiff failed "to urge liability as to specific expenditures". The cost of giving routinely necessary notice is, of course, chargeable to the corporation. It is just as clear, we think, that payment by a corporation of the expense of "proceedings by one faction in its contest with another for the control of the corporation" is *ultra vires,* and unlawful. Lawyers' Advertising Co. v. Consolidated Ry., Lighting & Refrigerating Co., 187 N.Y. 395, 399, 80 N.E. 199, 200. Approval by directors or by a majority stock vote could not validate such gratuitous expenditures. Continental Securities Co. v. Belmont, 206 N.Y. 7, 99 N.E. 138, 51 L.R.A.,N.S., 112. Some of the payments attacked in this suit were, on their face, for lawful purposes and apparently reasonable in amount but, as to others, the record simply does not contain evidentiary bases for a determination as to either lawfulness or reasonableness. Surely, the burden was on plaintiff to go forward to some extent with such particularization and proof. It failed to do so, and so failed to make out a prima facie case.

We are, therefore, reaching the same result as did the Appellate Division but on one only of the grounds listed by that court, that is, failure of proof. We think it not inappropriate, however, to state our general views on the question of law principally argued by the parties, that is, as to the validity of corporate payments for proxy solicitations and similar activities in addition to giving notice of the meeting, and of the questions to be voted on. For an answer to that problem we could not do better than quote from this court's opinion in the Lawyers' Advertising Co. case, 187 N.Y. 395, 399, 80 N.E. 199, 200, supra: "The remaining notices were not legally authorized and were not legitimately incidental to the meeting or necessary for the protection of the stockholders. They rather were proceedings by one faction in its contest with another for the control of the corporation, and the expense thereof, as such, is not properly chargeable to the latter. . . . [I]t would be altogether too dangerous a rule to permit directors in control of a corporation and engaged in a contest for the perpetuation of their offices and control, to impose upon the corporation the unusual expense of publishing advertisements or, by analogy, of dispatching special messengers for the purpose of procuring proxies in their behalf." . . .

The judgment should be affirmed, without costs.

■ VAN VOORHIS, JUDGE (dissenting) . . . .

No resolution was passed by the stockholders approving payment to the management group. It has been recognized that not all of the $133,966 in obligations paid or incurred by the management group was designed merely for information of stockholders. This outlay included payment for all of the activities of a strenuous campaign to persuade and cajole in a hard-fought contest for control of this corporation. It included, for example, expenses for entertainment, chartered airplanes and limousines, public relations counsel and proxy solicitors. However legitimate such measures may be on behalf of stockholders themselves in such a controversy, most of them do not pertain to a corporate function but are part of the familiar apparatus of aggressive factions in corporate contests. . . .

The Appellate Division acknowledged in the instant case that "It is obvious that the management group here incurred a substantial amount of needless expense which was charged to the corporation," but this conclusion should have led to a direction that those defendants who were incumbent directors should be required to come forward with an explanation of their expenditures under the familiar rule that where it has been established that directors have expended corporate money for their own purposes, the burden of going forward with evidence of the propriety and reasonableness of specific items rests upon the directors. . . . The complaint should not have been dismissed as against incumbent directors due to failure of plaintiff to segregate the specific expenditures which are *ultra vires,* but, once plaintiff had proved facts from which an inference of impropriety might be drawn, the duty of making an explanation was laid upon the directors to explain and justify their conduct. . . .

There is no doubt that the management was entitled and under a duty to take reasonable steps to acquaint the stockholders with essential facts concerning the management of the corporation, and it may well be that the existence of a contest warranted them in circularizing the stockholders with more than ordinarily detailed information. . . .

What expenses of the incumbent group should be allowed and what should be disallowed should be remitted to the trial court to ascertain, after taking evidence, in accordance with the rule that the incumbent directors were required to assume the burden of going forward in the first instance with evidence explaining and justifying their expenditures. Only such as were reasonably related to informing the stockholders fully and fairly concerning the corporate affairs should be allowed. The concession by plaintiff that such expenditures as were made were reasonable in amount does not decide this question. By way of illustration, the costs of entertainment for stockholders may have been, and it is stipulated that they were, at the going rates for providing similar entertainment. That does not signify that entertaining stockholders is reasonably related to the purposes of the corporation. The Appellate Division, as above stated, found that the management group incurred a substantial amount of needless expense. That fact being established, it became the duty of the incumbent directors to unravel and explain these payments.

Regarding the $127,556 paid by the new management to the insurgent group for their campaign expenditures, the question immediately arises whether that was for a corporate purpose....

... The case most frequently cited and principally relied upon from among [the] Delaware decisions is Hall v. Trans-Lux Daylight Picture Screen Corp. [20 Del.Ch. 78]. There the English case was followed of Peel v. London & North Western Ry. Co.... which distinguished between expenses merely for the purpose of maintaining control, and contests over policy questions of the corporation. In the Hall case the issues concerned a proposed merger, and a proposed sale of stock of a subsidiary corporation. These were held to be policy questions, and payment of the management campaign expenses was upheld.

In our view, the impracticability [of distinguishing between expenses incurred merely for the purpose of maintaining control, and expenses in contests over policy questions] is illustrated by the statement in the Hall case, supra, 20 Del.Ch. at page 85, 171 A. at page 229, that "It is impossible in many cases of intracorporate contests over directors, to sever questions of policy from those of persons". This circumstance is stressed in Judge Rifkind's opinion in [Steinberg v. Adams, 90 F.Supp. 604] at page 608: "The simple fact, of course, is that generally policy and personnel do not exist in separate compartments. A change in personnel is sometimes indispensable to a change of policy. A new board may be the symbol of the shift in policy as well as the means of obtaining it."

... [I]nasmuch as it is generally impossible to distinguish whether "policy" or "personnel" is the dominant factor, any averments must be accepted at their face value that questions of policy are dominant. Nowhere do these opinions mention that the converse is equally true and more pervasive, that neither the "ins" nor the "outs" ever say that they have no program to offer to the shareholders, but just want to acquire or to retain control, as the case may be. In common experience, this distinction is unreal....

The main question of "policy" in the instant corporate election, as is stated in the opinions below and frankly admitted, concerns the long-term contract with pension rights of a former officer and director, Mr. J. Carlton Ward, Jr. The insurgents' chief claim of benefit to the corporation from their victory consists in the termination of that agreement, resulting in an alleged actuarial saving of $350,000 to $825,000 to the corporation, and the reduction of other salaries and rent by more than $300,000 per year. The insurgents had contended in the proxy contest that these payments should be substantially reduced so that members of the incumbent group would not continue to profit personally at the expense of the corporation. If these charges were true, which appear to have been believed by a majority of the shareholders, then the disbursements by the management group in the proxy contest fall under the condemnation of the English and the Delaware rule.

These circumstances are mentioned primarily to illustrate how impossible it is to distinguish between "policy" and "personnel", . . . but they also indicate that personal factors are deeply rooted in this contest. That is certainly true insofar as the former management group is concerned. . . .

Some expenditures may concededly be made by a corporation represented by its management so as to inform the stockholders, but there is a clear distinction between such expenditures by management and by mere groups of stockholders. The latter are under no legal obligation to assume duties of managing the corporation. They may endeavor to supersede the management for any reason, regardless of whether it be advantageous or detrimental to the corporation but, if they succeed, that is not a determination that the company was previously mismanaged or that it may not be mismanaged in the future. A change in control is in no sense analogous to an adjudication that the former directors have been guilty of misconduct. The analogy of allowing expenses of suit to minority stockholders who have been successful in a derivative action based on misconduct of officers or directors, is entirely without foundation.

Insofar as a management group is concerned, it may charge the corporation with any expenses within reasonable limits incurred in giving widespread notice to stockholders of questions affecting the welfare of the corporation. . . . Expenditures in excess of these limits are *ultra vires.* The corporation lacks power to defray them. The corporation lacks power to defray the expenses of the insurgents in their entirety. The insurgents were not charged with responsibility for operating the company. No appellate court case is cited from any jurisdiction holding otherwise. No contention is made that such disbursements could be made, in any event, without stockholder ratification; they could not be ratified except by unanimous vote if they were *ultra vires.* The insurgents, in this instance, repeatedly announced to the stockholders in their campaign literature that their proxy contest was being waged at their own personal expense. If reimbursement of such items were permitted upon majority stockholder ratification, no court or other tribunal could pass upon which types of expenditures were "needless", to employ the characterization of the Appellate Division in this case. Whether the insurgents should be paid would be made to depend upon whether they win the stockholders election and obtain control of the corporation. It would be entirely irrelevant whether the corporation is "benefitted" by their efforts or by the outcome of such an election. The courts could not indulge in a speculative inquiry into that issue. That would truly be a matter of business judgment. In some instances corporations are better governed by the existing management and in others by some other group which supersedes the existing management. Courts of law have no jurisdiction to decide such questions, and successful insurgent stockholders may confidently be relied upon to reimburse themselves whatever may be the real merits of the controversy. The losers in a proxy fight may understand the interests of the corporation more accurately than their successful adversaries, and agitation of this character may ultimately result in corporate advantage even if there be no change in management. Nevertheless, under the judgment which is appealed from, success in a proxy contest is the indispensable condition upon which reimbursement of the insurgents depends. Adventurers are not infrequent who are ready to take advantage of economic recessions, reduction of dividends or failure to increase them, or other sources of stockholder discontent to wage contests in order to obtain control of well-managed corporations, so as to divert their funds through legal channels into other corporations in which they may be interested, or to discharge former officers and employees to make room for favored newcomers according to the fashion of political patronage, or for other objectives that are unrelated to the sound prosperity of the enterprise. The way is open and will be kept open for stockholders and groups of stockholders to contest corporate elections, but if the promoters of such movements choose to employ the costly modern media of mass persuasion, they should look for reimbursement to themselves and to the stockholders who are aligned with them. If the law be that they can be recompensed by the corporation in case of success, and only in that event, it will operate as a powerful incentive to persons accustomed to taking calculated risks to increase this form of high-powered salesmanship to such a degree that, action provoking reaction, stockholders' meetings will be very costly. To the financial advantages promised by control of a prosperous corporation, would be added the knowledge that the winner takes all insofar as the campaign expenses are concerned. To the victor, indeed, would belong the spoils. . . .

■ CONWAY, C.J., and BURKE, J., concur with FROESSEL, J.; DESMOND, J., concurs in part in a separate opinion; VAN VOORHIS, J., dissents in an opinion in which DYE and FULD, JJ., concur.

Judgment affirmed.

Professor Harris observes: "[T]he vast majority of corporate elections are ho-hum affairs. The incumbent directors of the firm spend freely from the corporate treasury to put on lavish campaigns for their own reelection. And, similar to a politician who amasses a large war chest meant to scare off potential rivals, the current board members are mostly reelected without opposition. . . . Election outcomes are predictable." Lee Harris, Shareholder Campaign Funds: A Campaign Subsidy Scheme for Corporate Elections, 58 U.C.L.A. L. Rev. 167, 168–69 (2010)[hereinafter Campaign Funds]. Consider the chart below, which relies on data from companies that have actually experienced a contested corporate election in recent years, 2006–2008. . . . [A]pproximately 133 firms received an election challenge, on average 44 contested corporate elections per year . . .

Summary Statistics for Contested Corporate Election Spending (2006–2008)					
	Median	Mean	Min	Max	Total
Challenges Per Year	46	44	31	56	133
Incumbent Expenses	$200,000	$1.2 mill.	$6,000	$22 mill.	$138 mill.
Challenger Expenses	$225,000	$652,130	$350	$9 mill.	$84 mill.
Outstanding Shares	26.4 mill.	99.6 mill.	11,000	2.386 bill.	12.948 bill.

Id. at 210. An earlier study, Lee Harris, Missing in Activism: Retail Investor Absence in Corporate Elections, 2010 Colum. Bus. L. Rev. 104, 126–29, finds that because the costs to contest management are so high, individual investors infrequently undertake contests, and when they do they are seriously underfunded, so that three-fourths of the challenges are by institution. Moreover, money spent is a strong explanatory variable to success, with the median amount spent by successful challengers being $250,000 whereas the median amount spent by unsuccessful challengers is $150,000. *See* Harris, Campaign Funds, *supra*, at 179–80.

HEINEMAN v. DATAPOINT CORP., 611 A.2d 950 (Del.1992). "The complaint alleges a successful contest for corporate control, with the victors in that contest using their newly acquired positions to cause the corporation to reimburse the costs of waging that contest. Proof of these facts at trial would represent a *prima facie* case of director self-dealing."

SECTION 5. THE ALLOCATION OF POWER BETWEEN THE BOARD AND THE CEO

NOTE ON THE MANAGEMENT OF PUBLICLY HELD CORPORATIONS

1. *The Managing Model of the Board.* In the traditional model of corporate structure, the board managed the business of the corpora-

tion (the *managing model* of the board).* This model was reflected in the traditional corporate statutes, which provided that the business of the corporation shall be managed by the board. In the case of closely held corporations, which operate very informally, the model was probably never accurate, and if the model was ever accurate of publicly held corporations, it no longer is. Although the board still plays a central role in the corporation, today it is widely understood that under modern practice in publicly held corporations, the management function is ordinarily located in the executives, and the central figure in the corporation is not the board but the chief executive officer (CEO).

The limited role of the board in publicly held corporations is the result of two critical constraints.

The first constraint concerns time. A recent survey of a number of directors by Korn/Ferry International found reported that the respondents spent an average of 16 hours a month on board matters, including travel. Korn/Ferry International, 34th Annual Board of Directors Study 10 (2010). If travel is put aside, the average time directors spend on board matters is probably no more than 145 hours a year. The businesses of large publicly held corporations are far too complex to be managed by directors who are essentially part-time in that capacity. The number of board meetings is also very limited. More than half the respondents reported that their board meet six times a year or less. Id. at 33. A complex nationwide or global business cannot be managed through occasional meetings.

The second constraint on the role of the board concerns information. The distribution of information in the corporation is highly asymmetrical: the executives have enormously more information than the board, and generally control the flow of information to the board. By controlling the information that the board receives, the executives can often, and indeed usually, shape the decisions that the board makes.

2. *The Monitoring Model of the Board.* Because of the unrealistic nature of the managing model, in the last thirty years there has been a shift from a managing model to a monitoring model. Under the monitoring model, the primary, although not exclusive, functions of the board of a publicly held corporation are to select, regularly evaluate, fix the compensation of, and, where appropriate, replace the senior executives; monitor the conduct of the corporation's business to evaluate whether the business is being properly managed; and review and, where appropriate, approve, major corporate plans and policies formulated by the corporation's executives.

This functional component of the monitoring model is complemented by a structural component. If the board has the function of monitoring the senior executives, it must be structured to effectuate

* For ease of exposition, unless the context indicates otherwise, in the balance of this Chapter the terms *directors, boards,* and *shareholders* will refer to directors, boards, or shareholders of publicly held corporations.

that function. This in turn requires that the board consist of at least a majority of directors who are independent of the senior executives. The composition of boards is strongly moving in that direction. A survey of the 100 largest American corporations found that in 81 of the corporations, independent directors comprised 75% or more of the boards. The rules of the New York Stock Exchange and NASDAQ now require listed corporations to have a majority of independent directors. These rules also require the boards of such corporations to have audit, nominating, and compensation committees, all composed exclusively of independent directors, to aid in implementing the monitoring function. The Korn/Ferry study found that all of the corporations represented in its survey had audit and compensation committees, 96% had nominating committees, and all these committees were composed exclusively of independent directors. *Id.* at 13.

Another structural feature that has emerged recently to reinforce the independence of directors is the designation of a lead independent director in corporations where the CEO is also Chairman of the Board. The Korn/Ferry study reported, "Once considered controversial and divisive, a lead director is now seen as integral in fostering a positive working relationship with the CEO, maintaining independence of the board from management, and stimulating open discourse among outside directors by serving as an impartial sounding board. Four of five (80 percent) of the ... respondents have an elected or appointed lead director who presides at executive sessions and evaluates the CEO. This practice has been integrated with astounding speed: only 32 percent of respondents' boards had formalized the lead director role in 2002." *Id.* at 27.

Today, the monitoring model of the board of publicly held corporations is widely accepted, and has been adopted in most or all large publicly held corporations. Ultimately, the utility of this model rests on its economic advantage in providing an additional system to monitor the efficiency of management—in particular, the CEO. The monitoring board, taken alone, is an imperfect mechanism to achieve that end, but because all systems to monitor the efficiency of management are imperfect, it is important to construct a matrix of overlapping monitoring systems. The monitoring board is an important element of that matrix.

MARCEL KAHAN & EDWARD ROCK, THE EMBATTLED CEO, 88 Tex. L. Rev. 987, 1025–26 (2010). "As Jeff Gordon has recently shown, the nominal independence of board members has increased dramatically since the 1950s. Gordon estimates that the percentage of inside directors has steadily decreased from 50% in 1950 to around 10% in 2005 and that the percentage of independent directors has correspondingly increased from around 20% to around 80%....

"... [T]he Investor Responsibility Research Center (IRRC) ... categorizes each director as an employee of the company, a linked director (a former employee, family member of an employee, or a director who provides, or whose employer provides, services to the company, or is a significant customer), or an independent director. We collected information of these categorizations for the years 2000 and 2007 for companies in the S & P 500 Index, for the Midcap (S & P 400) Index, and for the SmallCap (S & P 600) Index. The IRRC data shows a decline of average total board size for S & P 500 companies (but not for companies in the other indices), as well as a decline in the number of employee directors from about 2.1 to 1.5. Depending on the index, the average percentage of employee directors declined from 17% to 24% in 2000 to 14% and 18% in 2007. Linked directors experience a steeper decline, from around 1.3 to 1.6 in 2000 to 0.6 in 2007, while the number of directors categorized as independent increased. For all companies combined, the percentage of linked directors declined from 14,5% to 6.4% over this seven-year period.

* * *

"... There are several useful metrics for determining what boards spend their time on. One important measure is whether a board has established a committee devoted to certain tasks and how frequently that committee meets. Virtually all larger companies have had audit and compensation committees for a significant period of time. But the number of companies with nominating and corporate-governance committees has increased significantly. According to Korn/Ferry, the percentage of companies with nominating committees hovered in the low-to mid-seventies until 2002, increased to 87% in 2003, and further increased to over 95% from 2004 on. The percentage of companies with corporate-governance committees (which are not regulated by NASDAQ standards) gradually increased from 39% in 1997 to 48% in 2001, and then increased at a more rapid rate to 96% in 2007. The changed NYSE and NASDAQ listing requirements presumably account for at least a portion of this increase. Many companies, however, had added these committees before they were required to do so. The trend in corporate-governance committees, not required by Sarbanes–Oxley or NASDAQ listing standards, showing an increase even in the pre-Sarbanes–Oxley period, suggests that a significant portion of the increase may be unrelated to the changed [regulatory and listing] standards...."

"The number of meetings of committees with monitoring functions—the audit, compensation, nominating, corporate-governance, and succession committees—has generally increased.

Table 6: Committee Meetings per Year

	1997	2001	2007
Audit	3	4	9
Compensation	4	5	6
Nominating	2	3	4
Corporate Governance	3	3	4
Succession	5	5	6
Executive	4	4	4

..."

JILL E. FISCH, BOOK REVIEW [OF MACEY, THE OVERSTATED PROMISE OF CORPORATE GOVERNANCE], 77 U. Chi. L. Rev. 923, 930–31 (2010). "... [A]s Jeff Gordon suggests, the evolution of the monitoring board appears to be more a product of market forces than regulatory intervention. To be sure, the Delaware courts have encouraged the use of independent directors in the context of specific decisions, such as evaluating tender offers or responding to derivative litigation, but these decisions neither require a majority independent board nor limit the board's role to monitoring. Sarbanes–Oxley and the self-regulating organization (SRO) rules mandate increased board independence, but these requirements are of relatively recent origin and largely reflect preexisting corporate norms. Indeed, probably the most substantial factor in the move to independent monitoring boards has been the market pressure imposed by institutional investors.

"Whether those pressures were misguided remains an open question. Several empirical studies have shown that independent boards function more effectively in specific situations. James Cotter, Anil Shivdasani, and Marc Zenner find that independent boards enhance target shareholder gains from takeovers. Michael Weisbach shows that independent boards are more likely to respond to poor performance by replacing the CEO. John Byrd and Kent Hickman report that firms with a majority of outside directors make better acquisitions. More recent analysis suggests that the regulatory mandates for independence may themselves provide independent value. For example, Vidhi Chhaochharia and Yaniv Grinstein find that the imposition of SRO board independence rules upon companies reduced CEO compensation.

"More generally, increased board independence may have been a factor in modernizing corporations away from the overdiversified and inefficient conglomerates of the 1970s. One contributing factor is the ability of outside directors to respond to the information provided by the capital markets through stock prices. As Jeff Gordon observes, 'the increasing informativeness and value of stock market signals' gave the outside directors an easy tool to use in their effort to enhance shareholder value. Transparent and efficient stock prices enable directors to use 'stock price maximization as the measure of managerial success.' This in turn simplifies the board's role as monitor."

AMERICAN LAW INSTITUTE, PRINCIPLES OF CORPORATE GOVERNANCE §§ 3.01, 3.02, 3.05, 3A.01–3A.05

[See Statutory Supplement]

NEW YORK STOCK EXCHANGE

Listed Company Manual ¶ 303A*

[See Statutory Supplement]

SARBANES–OXLEY ACT OF 2002

[See Statutory Supplement]

NOTE ON THE ROLE OF TAKEOVERS IN THE STRUCTURE OF THE CORPORATION

Until around the [mid–1960s,] it was extremely difficult for insurgents to oust the incumbent management of a publicly held corporation by voting new directors into office. In principle, such an ouster could be achieved through a proxy fight. However, for a variety of reasons, especially costs, proxy fights were not often launched, and when launched were only intermittently successful. It was also difficult to *acquire* a corporation over the opposition of its managers, because the principal forms of acquisition, such as mergers and the purchase of substantially all of a corporation's assets, require approval by the board of the corporation that is to be acquired.

Beginning in the [mid–1960s], however, hostile takeovers developed as an important way to oust incumbent managements and effect acquisitions. In a hostile takeover, A, the *bidder* makes a *bid* or *tender offer* to purchase stock in B, the *target*, up to a stated amount and subject to certain conditions. The bid is made to the target's shareholders over the head of the target's management, who are resisting an acquisition by the bidder.* The tender-offer price is almost invariably well above the prevailing market price for the target's stock.

Because a tender offer is made to the target's shareholders, rather than to the target corporation, the approval of the target's board is not

---

* The New York Stock Exchange has combined with Euronext, and the formal title of the Exchange, or at least the holding company for the Exchange and Euronext, is NYSE Euronext. However, the Exchange is still conventionally referred to as the New York Stock Exchange or the NYSE, and that convention will be followed in this book.

* Some takeovers are "friendly," that is, they are acquisitions of stock in the target made with the support of the target's board. These transactions are not really takeovers, because that term connotes a combination that is effected over the head, and against the wishes of the target's board. Accordingly, for ease of exposition in this Note the term *takeover* will be used interchangeably with the term *hostile takeover*.

required. However, target managements almost invariably resist hostile takeover bids by causing the corporation to take defensive actions to block the bid. These defensive actions often involve a restructuring of the allocation of power between management and shareholders. If the allocation of power between management and shareholders is thought of as a dashboard fuel gauge, with shareholder power at one end and management power at the other, these defensive actions are intended to, and invariably do, move the needle closer to the management-power end of the gauge.

Sometimes defensive actions are taken in the middle of a hostile takeover fight. Often, however, the corporation's governance rules are restructured by a defensive action taken before a hostile tender offer emerges, with the idea of precluding or at least dampening the prospect of such an offer. Much of modern corporate governance—and in particular, the modern allocation of power between shareholders and management—is shaped either by managerial responses to actual takeover bids or by managerial actions to forestall possible takeover bids.

The central legal issue concerning takeovers is what standard of review the courts should apply in reviewing the defensive actions by management. In the leading Delaware case, Unocal Corp. v. Mesa Petroleum Co., 493 A.2d 946 (Del. 1985), the court held that the standard of review is whether the defensive action is reasonable in relation to the threat posed. In Unitrin, Inc. v. American General Corp., 651 A.2d 1361 (Del. 1995), the Delaware Supreme Court provided an important gloss on *Unocal*:

> . . . [T]he Court of Chancery erred in applying the proportionality review *Unocal* requires by focusing upon whether the Repurchase Program was an "unnecessary" defensive response. *See* Paramount Communications, Inc. v. QVC Network, Inc., 637 A.2d at 45–46. The Court of Chancery should have directed its enhanced scrutiny: first, upon whether the Repurchase Program the Unitrin Board implemented was draconian, by being either preclusive or coercive and; second, if it was not draconian, upon whether it was within a range of reasonable responses to the threat American General's Offer posed. . . .
>
> The first aspect of the *Unocal* burden, the reasonableness test, required the Unitrin Board to demonstrate that, after a reasonable investigation, it determined in good faith, that American General's Offer presented a threat to Unitrin that warranted a defensive response. . . .
>
> The second aspect or proportionality test of the initial *Unocal* burden required the Unitrin Board to demonstrate the proportionality of its response to the threat American General's Offer posed. . . .
>
> This Court has recognized "the prerogative of a board of directors to resist a third party's unsolicited acquisition proposal or offer." *Paramount Communications, Inc. v. QVC Network,*

Inc., Del.Supr., 637 A.2d 34, 43 n. 13 (1994). The Unitrin Board did not have unlimited discretion to defeat the threat it perceived from the American General Offer by any draconian means available. *See Unocal,* 493 A.2d at 955. Pursuant to the *Unocal* proportionality test, the nature of the threat associated with a particular hostile offer sets the parameters for the range of permissible defensive tactics. Accordingly, the purpose of enhanced judicial scrutiny is to determine whether the Board acted reasonably in "relation . . . to the threat which a particular bid allegedly poses to stockholder interests." *Mills Acquisition Co. v. Macmillan, Inc.,* Del.Supr., 559 A.2d 1261, 1288 (1989).

ALI, PRINCIPLES OF CORPORATE GOVERNANCE § 6.02

[See Statutory Supplement]

CHAPTER 6

SHAREHOLDER INFORMATIONAL RIGHTS & PROXY VOTING

SECTION 1. SHAREHOLDER INFORMATION RIGHTS UNDER STATE AND FEDERAL LAW

A. INSPECTION OF BOOKS AND RECORDS

DEL. GEN. CORP. LAW §§ 219, 220

[See Statutory Supplement]

REV. MODEL BUS. CORP. ACT §§ 7.20, 16.01–16.04

[See Statutory Supplement]

CAL. CORP. CODE §§ 1600, 1601

[See Statutory Supplement]

N.Y. BUS. CORP. LAW § 624

[See Statutory Supplement]

Saito v. McKesson HBOC, Inc.

Supreme Court of Delaware, 2002.
806 A.2d 113.

■ Before VEASEY, CHIEF JUSTICE, WALSH, HOLLAND, BERGER, JUSTICES and HARTNETT, JUSTICE (Retired), constituting the Court en Banc.

■ BERGER, JUSTICE.

In this appeal, we consider the limitations on a stockholder's statutory right to inspect corporate books and records. The statute, 8

Del.C. § 220, enables stockholders to investigate matters "reasonably related to [their] interest as [stockholders]" including, among other things, possible corporate wrongdoing. It does not open the door to the wide ranging discovery that would be available in support of litigation. For this statutory tool to be meaningful, however, it cannot be read narrowly to deprive a stockholder of necessary documents solely because the documents were prepared by third parties or because the documents predate the stockholder's first investment in the corporation. A stockholder who demands inspection for a proper purpose should be given access to all of the documents in the corporation's possession, custody or control, that are necessary to satisfy that proper purpose. Thus, where a § 220 claim is based on alleged corporate wrongdoing, and assuming the allegation is meritorious, the stockholder should be given enough information to effectively address the problem, either through derivative litigation or through direct contact with the corporation's directors and/or stockholders.

Factual and Procedural Background

On October 17, 1998, McKesson Corporation entered into a stock-for-stock merger agreement with HBO & Company ("HBOC"). On October 20, 1998, appellant, Noel Saito, purchased McKesson stock. The merger was consummated in January 1999 and the combined company was renamed McKesson HBOC, Incorporated. HBOC continued its separate corporate existence as a wholly-owned subsidiary of McKesson HBOC.

Starting in April and continuing through July 1999, McKesson HBOC announced a series of financial restatements triggered by its year-end audit process. During that four month period, McKesson HBOC reduced its revenues by $327.4 million for the three prior fiscal years. The restatements all were attributed to HBOC accounting irregularities. The first announcement precipitated several lawsuits, including a derivative action pending in the Court of Chancery, captioned *Ash v. McCall*, Civil Action No. 17132. Saito was one of four plaintiffs in the *Ash* complaint, which alleged that: (i) McKesson's directors breached their duty of care by failing to discover the HBOC accounting irregularities before the merger; (ii) McKesson's directors committed corporate waste by entering into the merger with HBOC; (iii)HBOC's directors breached their fiduciary duties by failing to monitor the company's compliance with financial reporting requirements prior to the merger; and (iv) McKesson HBOC's directors failed in the same respect during the three months following the merger. Although the Court of Chancery granted defendants' motion to dismiss the complaint, the dismissal was without prejudice as to the pre-merger and post-merger oversight claims.

In its decision on the motion to dismiss, the Court of Chancery specifically suggested that Saito and the other plaintiffs "use the 'tools at hand,' most prominently § 220 books and records actions, to obtain information necessary to sue derivatively."[1] Saito was the only Ash plaintiff to follow that advice. The stated purpose of Saito's demand was:

> (1) to further investigate breaches of fiduciary duties by the boards of directors of HBO & Co., Inc., McKesson, Inc., and/or McKesson HBOC, Inc. related to their oversight of their respective company's accounting procedures and financial reporting; (2) to investigate potential claims against advisors engaged by McKesson, Inc. and HBO & Co., Inc. to the acquisition of HBO & Co., Inc. by McKesson, Inc.; and (3) to gather information relating to the above in order to supplement the complaint in *Ash v. McCall*, et al., . . . in accordance with the September 15, 2000 Opinion of the Court of Chancery.

Saito demanded access to eleven categories of documents, including those relating to Arthur Andersen's pre-merger review and verification of HBOC's financial condition; communications between or among HBOC, McKesson, and their investment bankers and accountants concerning HBOC's accounting practices; and discussions among members of the Boards of Directors of HBOC, McKesson, and/or McKesson HBOC concerning reports published in April 1997 and thereafter about HBOC's accounting practices or financial condition. . . .

DISCUSSION

Stockholders of Delaware corporations enjoy a qualified common law and statutory right to inspect the corporation's books and records.[2] Inspection rights were recognized at common law because, "[a]s a matter of self-protection, the stockholder was entitled to know how his agents were conducting the affairs of the corporation of which he or she was a part owner."[3] The common law right is codified in 8 Del.C. § 220, which provides in relevant part:

> (b) Any stockholder . . . shall, upon written demand under oath stating the purpose thereof, have the right . . . to inspect for any proper purpose the corporation's stock ledger, a list of its stockholders, and its other books and records, and to make copies or extracts therefrom. A proper purpose shall mean a purpose reasonably related to such person's interest as a stockholder.

Once a stockholder establishes a proper purpose under § 220, the right to relief will not be defeated by the fact that the stockholder may have secondary purposes that are improper. The scope of a stockholder's inspection, however, is limited to those books and records that are necessary and essential to accomplish the stated, proper purpose.

After trial, the Court of Chancery found "credible evidence of possible wrongdoing," which satisfied Saito's burden of establishing a

1. Ash v. McCall, 2000 WL 1370341, *15 (Del.Ch.).

2. Shaw v. Agri-Mark, Inc., 663 A.2d 464 (Del.1995).

3. Id. at 467.

proper purpose for the inspection of corporate books and records. But the Court of Chancery limited Saito's access to relevant documents in three respects. First, it held that, since Saito would not have standing to bring an action challenging actions that occurred before he purchased McKesson stock, Saito could not obtain documents created before October 20, 1998. Second, the court concluded that Saito was not entitled to documents relating to possible wrongdoing by the financial advisors to the merging companies. Third, the court denied Saito access to any HBOC documents, since Saito never was a stockholder of HBOC. We will consider each of these rulings in turn.

A. *The Standing Limitation*

By statute [8 Del. C. § 327], stockholders who bring derivative suits must allege that they were stockholders of the corporation "at the time of the transaction of which such stockholder complains. . . ." The Court of Chancery decided that this limitation on Saito's ability to maintain a derivative suit controlled the scope of his inspection rights. As a result, the court held that Saito was "effectively limited to examining conduct of McKesson and McKesson HBOC's boards following the negotiation and public announcement of the merger agreement."

Although we recognize that there may be some interplay between the two statutes, we do not read § 327 as defining the temporal scope of a stockholder's inspection rights under § 220. The books and records statute requires that a stockholder's purpose be one that is "reasonably related" to his or her interest as a stockholder. The standing statute, § 327, bars a stockholder from bringing a derivative action unless the stockholder owned the corporation's stock at the time of the alleged wrong. If a stockholder wanted to investigate alleged wrongdoing that substantially predated his or her stock ownership, there could be a question as to whether the stockholder's purpose was reasonably related to his or her interest as a stockholder, especially if the stockholder's only purpose was to institute derivative litigation. But stockholders may use information about corporate mismanagement in other ways, as well. They may seek an audience with the board to discuss proposed reforms or, failing in that, they may prepare a stockholder resolution for the next annual meeting, or mount a proxy fight to elect new directors. None of those activities would be prohibited by § 327.

Even where a stockholder's only purpose is to gather information for a derivative suit, the date of his or her stock purchase should not be used as an automatic "cut-off" date in a § 220 action. First, the potential derivative claim may involve a continuing wrong that both predates and postdates the stockholder's purchase date. In such a case, books and records from the inception of the alleged wrongdoing could be necessary and essential to the stockholder's purpose. Second, the alleged post-purchase date wrongs may have their foundation in events that transpired earlier. In this case, for example, Saito wants to investigate McKesson's apparent failure to learn of HBOC's accounting irregularities until months after the merger was consummated. Due diligence documents generated before the merger agreement was signed may be essential to that investigation. In sum, the date on which a stockholder first acquired the corporation's stock does not control the scope of records available under § 220. If activities that occurred before the purchase date are "reasonably related" to the stockholder's interest as a stockholder, then the stockholder should be given access to records necessary to an understanding of those activities.[4]

B. *The Financial Advisors' Documents*

The Court of Chancery denied Saito access to documents in McKesson–HBOC's possession that the corporation obtained from financial and accounting advisors, on the ground that Saito could not use § 220 to develop potential claims against third parties. On appeal, Saito argues that he is seeking third party documents for the same reason he is seeking McKesson HBOC documents—to investigate possible wrongdoing by McKesson and McKesson HBOC. Since the trial court found that to be a proper purpose, Saito argues that he should not be precluded from seeing documents that are necessary to his purpose, and in McKesson HBOC's possession, simply because the documents were prepared by third party advisors.

We agree that, generally, the source of the documents in a corporation's possession should not control a stockholder's right to inspection under § 220. It is not entirely clear, however, that the trial court restricted Saito's access on that basis. The Court of Chancery decided that Saito's interest in pursuing claims against McKesson HBOC's advisors was not a proper purpose. It recognized that a secondary improper purpose usually is irrelevant if the stockholder establishes his need for the same documents to support a proper purpose. But the court apparently concluded that the categories of third party documents that Saito demanded did not support the proper purpose of investigating possible wrongdoing by McKesson and McKesson HBOC.

We cannot determine from the present record whether the Court of Chancery intended to exclude all third party documents, but such a blanket exclusion would be improper. The source of the documents and the manner in which they were obtained by the corporation have little or no bearing on a stockholder's inspection rights. The issue is whether the documents are necessary and essential to satisfy the stockholder's proper purpose. In this case, Saito wants to investigate possible wrongdoing relating to McKesson and McKesson HBOC's failure to discover HBOC's accounting irregularities. Since McKesson

---

4. As noted ... above, a Section 220 proceeding does not open the door to wide ranging discovery. See *Brehm v. Eisner*, 746 A.2d 244, 266–67 (Del.2000) (Plaintiffs "bear the burden of showing a proper purpose and [must] make specific and discrete identification, with rifled precision ... [to] establish that each category of books and records is essential to the accomplishment of their articulated purpose ..."); *Security First Corp. v. U.S. Die Casting and Dev. Co.*, 687 A.2d 563, 568, 570 (Del.1997) ("mere curiosity or desire for a fishing expedition" is insufficient.).

and McKesson HBOC relied on financial and accounting advisors to evaluate HBOC's financial condition and reporting, those advisors' reports and correspondence would be critical to Saito's investigation.

C. *HBOC Documents*

Finally, the Court of Chancery held that Saito was not entitled to any HBOC documents because he was not a stockholder of HBOC before or after the merger. Although Saito is a stockholder of HBOC's parent, McKesson HBOC, stockholders of a parent corporation are not entitled to inspect a subsidiary's books and records, "[a]bsent a showing of a fraud or that a subsidiary is in fact the mere alter ego of the parent. . . ."[5] The Court of Chancery found no basis to disregard HBOC's separate existence and, therefore, denied access to its records.

We reaffirm this settled principle, which applies to those HBOC books and records that were never provided to McKesson or McKesson HBOC. But it does not apply to relevant documents that HBOC gave to McKesson before the merger, or to McKesson HBOC after the merger. We assume that HBOC provided financial and accounting information to its proposed merger partner and, later, to its parent company. As with the third party advisors' documents, Saito would need access to relevant HBOC documents in order to understand what his company's directors knew and why they failed to recognize HBOC's accounting irregularities.

Conclusion

Based on the foregoing, the decision of the Court of Chancery is AFFIRMED in part and REVERSED in part, and this matter is REMANDED for further action in accordance with this decision. Jurisdiction is not retained.

NOTE ON SHAREHOLDERS' INSPECTION RIGHTS

1. *"No Fishing:" The Credible Basis Requirement.* As a general proposition investigating for wrongdoing or mismanagement is a proper purpose for shareholder access; courts nonetheless condition access on the requesting stockholder showing by a preponderance of the evidence a "credible basis" from which the court can infer there is possible mismanagement or wrongdoing such that further investigation is in order. *See e.g., Seinfeld v. Verizon Comm. Inc.,* 909 A.2d 117 (Del. 2006) (the credible basis "threshold may be satisfied by a credible showing, through documents, logic, testimony or otherwise, that there are legitimate issues of wrongdoing"); Ihrig v. Frontier Equity Exchange Assoc., 128 P.3d 993 (Kan. Ct. App. 2006). One development that has stimulated shareholder resort to the state-based rights to inspect corporate records is Congress' passage of the Private Securities Litigation Reform Act of 1995 (PSLRA), studied later in

5. *Skouras v. Admiralty Enterprises, Inc.,* 386 A.2d 674, 681 (Del.Ch.1978).

Chapter 12. A central feature of the PSLRA is that discovery against defendants alleged to have committed securities fraud is barred until all pretrial motions have been resolved. A key pretrial motion is the motion to dismiss; under the PSLRA's heightened pleading requirement the investor's complaint must set forth with particularity facts that establish a "strong inference" that the defendants have either knowingly or recklessly committed a material misrepresentation. Hence, to satisfy this pleading standard plaintiffs frequently invoke their shareholder inspection rights to obtain information to flesh out the allegations for the securities fraud complaint. *See* Randall S. Thomas & Kenneth J. Martin, Using State Inspection Statutes for Discovery in General Securities Fraud Actions, 77 B.U.L. Rev. 69 (1997).

2. *Common Law; Interpretation of the Statutes*. At common law, a shareholder "acting in good faith for the purpose of advancing the interests of the corporation and protecting his own interest as a stockholder" has a right to examine the corporate books and records at reasonable times. Albee v. Lamson & Hubbard Corp., 320 Mass. 421, 424, 69 N.E.2d 811, 813 (1946). The general rule is that the shareholder has the burden of alleging and proving good faith and proper purpose. *Id. But see* Bennett v. Mack's Supermarkets, Inc., 602 S.W.2d 143 (Ky.1979).

Many or most legislatures have now enacted statutes governing the right of inspection. Many of these statutes are more limited in their coverage than the common law rule. For example, a statute may apply only to certain kinds of shareholders (such as those who are record holders of at least 5% of the corporation's stock or who have been record holders for at least six months) or only to certain kinds of books and records. A common problem of interpretation is whether the statutes: (i) Preserve the common law rule that the shareholder must prove a proper purpose. (ii) Discard the proper-purpose test, or (iii) Preserve the proper-purpose test, but place on the corporation the burden of proving that the shareholder's purpose is improper. Generally, the last interpretation is followed, at least if the language is ambiguous. See, e.g., Crane Co. v. Anaconda Co., 39 N.Y.2d 14, 382 N.Y.S.2d 707, 346 N.E.2d 507 (1976). A second common problem of interpretation is whether the statutes replace or supplement the common law. The general answer is that the statutes supplement the common law, so that a suit for inspection that does not fall within the relevant statute can still be brought under the common law. See, e.g., Bank of Heflin v. Miles, 294 Ala. 462, 318 So.2d 697 (1975).

3. *"Proper Purpose."* Among the purposes the courts have recognized as "proper," are to determine the financial condition of the corporation, to ascertain the value of the petitioner's shares, and to obtain a mailing list for the solicitation of proxies from shareholders. A purpose is proper even though it yields no benefit to the corporation. Not surprisingly, it is an improper purpose to seek access to gain information that will be used in a competing enterprise. Query, what reasoning would deny Mr. Sato's request to obtain documents that

bear on whether HBOC–McKesson had claims against its third party advisors?

4. *Mixed Purposes.* Suppose the shareholder has mixed purposes, one proper and one not. In Helmsman Management Services, Inc. v. A & S Consultants, Inc., 525 A.2d 160, 164, 166 (Del.Ch.1987), the court held that "Once it is determined that a shareholder has a proper purpose that is primary, any secondary purpose or ulterior motive that the stockholder might have is irrelevant." Accordingly, "even if [the shareholder] does have an ulterior (*i.e.,* a non-shareholder-related) purpose, it would still not be barred from relief under [Del.Gen.Corp.Law] § 220, unless the ulterior purpose is also its primary purpose."

5. *The Pillsbury Case.* In State ex rel. Pillsbury v. Honeywell, Inc., 291 Minn. 322, 191 N.W.2d 406 (1971), Pillsbury was a shareholder of Honeywell, Inc. Pillsbury opposed the Vietnam war, and asked Honeywell to produce its shareholder ledger and all corporate records dealing with weapons and munitions manufacture. Pillsbury admitted that his sole motive in purchasing Honeywell stock was to persuade Honeywell to cease producing munitions, but argued that the desire to communicate with fellow shareholders was per se a proper purpose. Honeywell argued that a proper purpose contemplates a concern with investment return. The Minnesota court held for Honeywell:

> Several courts agree with petitioner's contention that a mere desire to communicate with other shareholders is, per se, a proper purpose.... This would seem to confer an almost absolute right to inspection. We believe that a better rule would allow inspections only if the shareholder has a proper purpose for such communication....
>
> Petitioner had utterly no interest in the affairs of Honeywell before he learned of Honeywell's production of fragmentation bombs. Immediately after obtaining this knowledge, he purchased stock in Honeywell for the sole purpose of asserting ownership privileges in an effort to force Honeywell to cease such production.... Such a motivation can hardly be deemed a proper purpose germane to his economic interest as a shareholder.

Honeywell was a Delaware corporation, and the Minnesota Court apparently assumed for purposes of the case that Delaware law applied, or in any event was no different than Minnesota law insofar as relevant. In Credit Bureau Reports, Inc. v. Credit Bureau of St. Paul, Inc., 290 A.2d 691 (Del.1972), however, the Delaware Supreme Court repudiated the *Pillsbury* case insofar as it applied to requests for stockholder lists:

> [In] General Time Corporation v. Talley Industries, Inc., Del. Supr., 240 A.2d 755 (1968).... we stated that, under [Del.Gen. Corp.Law] § 220, "the desire to solicit proxies for a slate of directors in opposition to management is a purpose reasonably related to the stockholder's interest as a stockholder"; and we

held that "any further or secondary purpose in seeking the list is irrelevant." Those rulings are dispositive.... The defendant corporation ... relies upon Pillsbury v. Honeywell, Inc., Minn., 191 N.W.2d 406 (1971). Insofar as the *Pillsbury* case is inconsistent herewith, it is inconsistent with [§ 220] as properly applied.

See also The Conservative Caucus Research, Analysis & Education Foundation, Inc. v. Chevron Corp., 525 A.2d 569 (Del.Ch.1987) (granting access to the list of stockholders to solicit their support for a proposal to discourage the corporation from continuing to do business in Angola).

6. *Stockholder Lists*. As a practical matter, the courts are understandably more willing to grant access to stockholder lists and the like than to grant access to otherwise-confidential financial and business information, such as internal data and contracts. In the case of business and financial information, the shareholder will normally have to show the court a specific and plausible reason why the information is needed. In contrast, in the case of stockholder lists a statement by a shareholder that he wants the list to communicate with other shareholders will usually, although not always, suffice. This distinction is understandable. Requiring the production of a stockholder list is almost invariably a necessary step for shareholders to exercise their role in corporate governance, imposes only a minimum burden on the corporation, and usually cannot injure the business of the corporation. In contrast, other kinds of information may be costly to produce, may have the potential to injure the corporation's business if misused, and (depending on the information) may not be necessary for the normal exercise of the shareholder's role.

In some cases, the statutes themselves distinguish between different types of corporate books and records. See, e.g., Del.Gen.Corp.Law § 220; see also Model Act §§ 7.20(b), 16.02.

B. THE STOCKHOLDER LIST IN A DEMATERIALIZED WORLD

Concept Release on the U.S. Proxy System

SEC, Exchange Act Rel. No. 62495 (July 14, 2010).

II. The Current Proxy Distribution and Voting Process

A fundamental tenet of state corporation law is that shareholders have the right to vote their shares to elect directors and to approve or reject major corporate transactions at shareholder meetings. Under state law, shareholders can appoint a proxy to vote their shares on their behalf at shareholder meetings, and the major national securities exchanges generally require their listed companies to solicit proxies for all meetings of shareholders. Because most shareholders do not attend public company shareholder meetings in person, voting occurs almost entirely by the use of proxies that are solicited before the shareholder meeting, thereby resulting in the corporate proxy becoming "the forum for shareholder suffrage." Issuers with a class of securities registered under Section 12 of the Securities Exchange Act of 1934 ("Exchange Act") . . . are required to comply with the federal proxy rules . . . when soliciting proxies from shareholders.

A. Types of Share Ownership and Voting Rights

The proxy solicitation process starts with the determination of who has the right to receive proxy materials and vote on matters presented to shareholders for a vote at shareholder meetings. The method for making this determination depends on the way the shares are owned. There are two types of security holders in the U.S.—registered owners and beneficial owners.

1. Registered Owners

Registered owners (also known as "record holders") have a direct relationship with the issuer because their ownership of shares is listed on records maintained by the issuer or its transfer agent. State corporation law generally vests the right to vote and the other rights of share ownership in registered owners.[25] Because registered owners have the right to vote, they also have the authority to appoint a proxy to act on their behalf at shareholder meetings.

Registered owners can hold their securities either in certificated form or in electronic (or "book-entry") form through a direct registration system ("DRS"), which enables an investor to have his or her ownership of securities recorded on the books of the issuer without having a physical securities certificate issued. Under DRS, an investor can electronically transfer his or her securities to a broker-dealer to effect a transaction without the risk, expense, or delay associated with the use of securities certificates. . . .

2. Beneficial Owners

The vast majority of investors in shares issued by U.S. companies today are beneficial owners, which means that they hold their securities in book-entry form through a securities intermediary, such as a broker-dealer or bank. This is often referred to as owning in "street name." A beneficial owner does not own the securities directly. Instead, as a customer of the securities intermediary, the beneficial owner has an entitlement to the rights associated with ownership of the securities.[31]

B. The Process of Soliciting Proxies . . .

1. Distributing Proxy Materials to Registered Owners

It is a relatively simple process for an issuer to send proxy materials to registered owners because their names and addresses are

---

25. See, e.g., *Del. Code Ann. tit. 8, § 219(c)*; Model Bus. Corp. Act § 1.40(21); but see Model Bus. Corp. Act § 7.23 (permitting corporations to establish procedures by which beneficial owners become entitled to exercise rights, including voting rights, otherwise exercisable by shareholders of record).

31. . . . Under the UCC, beneficial owners have a "securities entitlement" to the fungible bulk of securities held by the broker-dealer or bank. . . . A securities intermediary is obligated to provide the entitlement holder with all of the economic and governance rights that comprise the financial asset and that the entitlement holder can look only to that intermediary for performance of the obligations. See generally *UCC 8–501* et seq. (1994).

listed in the issuer's records, which are usually maintained by a transfer agent. . . . Registered owners execute the proxy card and return it to the issuer's transfer agent or vote tabulator for tabulation.

2. Distributing Proxy Materials to Beneficial Owners . . .

a. The Depository Trust Company

In most cases, the chain of ownership for beneficially owned securities of U.S. companies begins with the Depository Trust Company ("DTC"), a registered clearing agency acting as a securities depository.[33] Most large U.S. broker-dealers and banks are DTC participants, meaning that they deposit securities with, and hold those securities through, DTC. DTC's nominee, Cede & Co., appears in an issuer's stock records as the sole registered owner of securities deposited at DTC. DTC holds the deposited securities in "fungible bulk," meaning that there are no specifically identifiable shares directly owned by DTC participants. Rather, each participant owns a pro rata interest in the aggregate number of shares of a particular issuer held at DTC. Correspondingly, each customer of a DTC participant-such as an individual investor-owns a pro rata interest in the shares in which the DTC participant has an interest.

Once an issuer establishes a date for the shareholder meeting and a record date for shareholders entitled to vote on matters presented at the meeting, it sends a formal announcement of these dates to DTC, which DTC forwards to all of its participants. The issuer then requests from DTC a "securities position listing" as of the record date, which identifies the participants having a position in the issuer's securities and the number of securities held by each participant. . . . The record date securities position listing establishes the number of shares that a participant is entitled to vote through its DTC proxy.

For each shareholder meeting, DTC executes an "omnibus proxy" transferring its right to vote the shares held on deposit to its participants.[42] In this manner, broker-dealer and bank participants in DTC obtain the right to vote directly the shares that they hold through DTC.

b. Securities Intermediaries: Broker–Dealers and Banks

Once the issuer identifies the DTC participants holding positions in its securities, it is required to send a search card[43] to each of those

33. DTC provides custody and book-entry transfer services of securities transactions in the U.S. market involving equities, corporate and municipal debt, money market instruments, American depositary receipts, and exchange-traded funds. In accordance with its rules, DTC accepts deposits of securities from its participants (i.e., broker-dealers and banks), credits those securities to the depositing participants' accounts, and effects book-entry movements of those securities. . . .

42. As noted in recent litigation, the execution by DTC of an omnibus proxy is neither automatic nor legally required, but occurs as a matter of common practice. *Kurz v. Holbrook*, 989 A.2d 140, 170 (Del. Ch. 2010), *rev'd on other grounds, Crown EMAK Partners, LLC v. Kurz*, 992 A.2d 377 (Del. 2010) ("There does not appear to be any authority governing when a DTC omnibus proxy is issued, who should ask for it, or what event triggers it. The parties tell me that DTC has no written policies or procedures on the matter.").

43. The search card must request: (1) the number of beneficial owners; (2) the number of proxy soliciting materials and annual reports needed for forwarding by the intermediaries to participants, as well as other securities intermediaries that are registered owners, to determine whether they are holding shares for beneficial owners and, if so, the number of sets of proxy packages needed to be forwarded to those beneficial owners. . . .

Commission rules require broker-dealers to respond to the issuer . . . [and broker].

Once the search card process is complete, the issuer should know the approximate number of beneficial owners owning shares through each securities intermediary. The issuer must then provide the securities intermediary, or its third-party proxy service provider, with copies of its proxy materials (including, if applicable, a Notice of Internet Availability of Proxy Materials) for forwarding to those beneficial owners. The securities intermediary must forward these proxy materials to beneficial owners no later than five business days after receiving such materials.[47] Securities intermediaries are entitled to reasonable reimbursement for their costs in forwarding these materials.

Instead of receiving and executing a proxy card (as registered owners receive and do), the beneficial owner receives a "voting instruction form" or "VIF" from the securities intermediary, which permits the beneficial owner to instruct the securities intermediary how to vote the beneficially owned shares. . . .

C. Proxy Voting Process

Once the proxy materials have been distributed to the registered owners and beneficial owners of the securities, the means by which shareholders vote their shares differs. . . . [R]egistered owners execute the proxy card and return it to the vote tabulator, either by mail, by phone, or through the Internet. Beneficial owners, on the other hand, indicate their voting instructions on the VIF and return it to the securities intermediary or its proxy service provider, either by mail, by phone, or through the Internet. The securities intermediary, or its proxy service provider, tallies the voting instructions that it receives from its customers. . . . [T]he securities intermediary, or its proxy service provider, then executes and submits to the vote tabulator a proxy card for all securities held by the securities intermediary's customers.

In certain situations, a broker-dealer may use its discretion to vote shares if it does not receive instructions from the beneficial owner of the shares. Historically, broker-dealers were generally permitted to vote shares on uncontested matters, including uncontested director elections, without instructions from the beneficial owner. The NYSE recently revised this rule to prohibit broker-dealers from voting uninstructed shares with regard to any election of directors.[52]

---

their beneficial owner customers; and (3) the name and address of any agent appointed by the bank or broker-dealer to process a request for a list of beneficial owners. . . .

47. *17 CFR 240.14b–1(b)(2)* and *17 CFR 240.14b–2(b)(3).* The exchanges have rules that regulate the process and procedures by which member firms must transmit proxy materials to beneficial owners, collect voting instructions from beneficial owners, and vote shares held in the member firm's name. See, e.g., NYSE Rules 450 through 460 and FINRA Rule 2251.

52. NYSE Rule 452 and NYSE Listed Issuer Manual § 402.08(B). . . .

D. The Roles of Third Parties in the Proxy Process

Issuers, securities intermediaries, and shareholders often retain third parties to perform a number of proxy-related functions, including forwarding proxy materials, collecting voting instructions, voting shares, soliciting proxies, tabulating proxies, and analyzing proxy issues,.

1. Transfer Agents

Issuers are required to maintain a record of security holders for state law purposes[53] and often hire a transfer agent to maintain that record. Transfer agents, as agents of the issuer, are obliged to confirm to a vote tabulator (if the transfer agent does not itself perform the tabulation function) matters such as the amount of shares outstanding, as well as the identity and holdings of registered owners entitled to vote. . . .

2. Proxy Service Providers

To facilitate the proxy material distribution and voting process for beneficial owners, securities intermediaries typically retain a proxy service provider to perform a number of processing functions, including forwarding the proxy materials by mail or electronically and collecting voting instructions.[57] To enable the proxy service provider to perform these functions, the securities intermediary gives the service provider an electronic data feed of a list of beneficial owners and the number of shares held by each beneficial owner on the record date. The proxy service provider, on behalf of the intermediary, then requests the appropriate number of proxy material sets from the issuer for delivery to the beneficial owners. Upon receipt of the packages, the proxy service provider, on behalf of the intermediary, mails either the proxy materials with a VIF, or a Notice of Internet Availability of Proxy Materials, to beneficial owners. . . .

3. Proxy Solicitors

Issuers sometimes hire third-party proxy solicitors to identify beneficial owners holding large amounts of the issuers' securities and to telephone shareholders to encourage them to vote their proxies consistent with the recommendations of management. This often occurs when there is a contested election of directors, and issuer's management and other persons are competing for proxy authority to vote securities in the election (commonly referred to as a "proxy contest"). In addition, an issuer may hire a proxy solicitor in uncontested situations when voting returns are expected to be insufficient to meet state quorum requirements or when an important matter is being considered. . . .

---

53. E.g., *Del. Code Ann. tit. 8, § 219(a)*; Model Bus. Corp. Act § 16.01(c).

57. A single proxy service provider, Broadridge Financial Services, Inc. ("Broadridge"), states that it currently handles over 98% of the U.S. market for such proxy vote processing services. See http://www.broadridge.com/investor-communications/us/institutions/proxy-disclosure.asp.

4. Vote Tabulators

Under many state statutes, an issuer must appoint a vote tabulator (sometimes called "inspectors of elections" or "proxy tabulators") to collect and tabulate the proxy votes as well as votes submitted by shareholders in person at a meeting.[60] We understand that often the issuer's transfer agent will act as the vote tabulator. . . . However, sometimes the issuer will hire an independent third party to perform this function, often to certify important votes. The vote tabulator is ultimately responsible for determining that the correct number of votes has been submitted by each registered owner. . . .

5. Proxy Advisory Firms

Institutional investors typically own securities positions in a large number of issuers. . . . Some institutional investors may retain an investment adviser to manage their investments, and may also delegate proxy voting authority to that adviser. To assist them in their voting decisions, . . . [they] frequently hire proxy advisory firms to provide analysis and voting recommendations on matters appearing on the proxy. . . . Some proxy advisory firms also provide consulting services to issuers on corporate governance or executive compensation matters, such as helping to develop an executive compensation proposal to be submitted for shareholder approval. Some proxy advisory firms may also qualitatively rate or score issuers, based on judgments about the issuer's governance structure, policies, and practices. . . .

A. Issuer Communications with Shareholders

1. Background

The first area of concern that we address arises out of the practice of holding securities in street name—that is, interposing securities intermediaries between issuers and the beneficial owners of their securities. This practice developed in order to facilitate the prompt and accurate processing of an increasingly large volume of securities transactions. . . .

[T]he enormous volume of transactions cleared and settled in the U.S., which currently involve transactions valued at over $1.48 quadrillion annually, requires a centralized netting facility (i.e., NSCC) and a depository (i.e., DTC) that facilitates book-entry settlement of securities transactions. . . .

In light of recent developments in corporate governance, including the elimination of the broker discretionary vote on uncontested elections of directors, commentators have claimed a greater need for issuers to be able to communicate with their shareholders. These commentators have argued that the number of contested issues in shareholder meetings has increased, that voting outcomes are under more pressure, and that, as a result, certain changes should be made to our rules in order to facilitate communications by issuers with their beneficial owners. More broadly, commentators have questioned whether the current system of share ownership and the Commission's

60. See, e.g., *Del. Code Ann. tit. 8, § 231*; Model Bus. Corp. Act § 7.29.

communications and proxy rules adequately serve the needs of investors and issuers....

To promote direct communication between issuers and their beneficial owners, we adopted rules in 1983 ... to require broker-dealers and banks to provide issuers, at their request, with lists of the names and addresses of beneficial owners who did not object to having such information provided to issuers. These owners are often referred to as "non-objecting beneficial owners" or "NOBOs." When a beneficial owner objects to disclosure of its name and address to the issuer—often referred to as "objecting beneficial owners" or "OBOs"—the beneficial owner may be contacted only by the securities intermediary (or the intermediary's agent) with the customer relationship with the beneficial owner. According to one estimate, 70% to 80% of all public issuers' shares are held in street name, and 75% of those shares, or 52% to 60% of all shares, are held by OBOs. It is our understanding that some types of large institutional investors, such as mutual funds and retirement plans, often choose OBO status.[153] ...

Issuers have indicated to the staff that the majority of their street name securities are held by OBOs through securities intermediaries, making it very difficult to determine the identity and holdings of their investors. Issuers believe that the recent changes in corporate governance, including the move to majority voting of directors, the elimination of broker discretionary voting in uncontested director elections, and a possible drop in retail voting percentages, call for more direct communication between issuers and their shareholders. These communications may include using a proxy solicitor to contact shareholders by telephone. However, an issuer cannot make these direct appeals for shareholders to participate in the issuer's corporate governance if it does not know the identity of those shareholders.

Issuers also have indicated to the staff that they face considerable expense in communicating with beneficial owners, either OBOs or NOBOs, indirectly through securities intermediaries or their agents. Issuers are required to reimburse securities intermediaries for expenses incurred in forwarding communications to beneficial owners. These expenses include reimbursement for postage, envelopes and communication expenses as well as fees to proxy service providers.

Some issuers have claimed that the expense of obtaining the list of NOBOs from the securities intermediary or its proxy service provider deters some issuers, particularly widely-held issuers, from using the NOBO list to communicate with beneficial owners. We have also received expressions of concern from broker-dealers about the difficulty of maintaining an accurate NOBO list when a class of securities is actively traded....

---

153. One recent report states that while "73% of retail shareholders are NOBOs, ... [m]ost institutional shareholders—about 71%—are OBOs, accounting for about 91% of all institutionally held shares." SIFMA Report ... [on the Shareholder Communication Process with Street Name Holders, and the NOBO–OBO Mechanism (June 10, 2010)] at 7.

NOTE ON CONSENTS AND WHO'S A RECORD HOLDER

The medium for shareholder voting is frequently the execution of written consents and not via the proxy or voting at the stockholders' meeting. Section 228(a) of the Delaware General Corporation Law expressly authorizes action by consent, unless the articles of incorporation provide otherwise. The action is deemed approved "if a consent or consents in writing setting forth the action so taken, shall be signed by the *holders* of outstanding stock having not less than the minimum number of votes that would be necessary to authorize or take such action at a meeting at which all shares entitled to vote thereon were present and voted" (emphasis added). Section 228(c) also provides that the consent must bear the signature of "each stockholder." See also MBCA § 7.04(b) (authorizing action without a meeting through consents executed by "*holders* of outstanding shares having not less than the minimum number of votes that would be required to authorize or take action at a meeting at which all shares entitled to vote on the action were present and voted") (emphasis added). With the dematerialization of shares, the operation of both voting and the granting of consents is complex. These complexities are illustrated in *Crown EMAK Partners LLC v. Kurz,* 992 A.2d 377 (2010), involving a proxy contest between Crown EMAK Partners LLC and Take Back EMAK (TBE), a group of stockholders.

> Since EMAK's shares were publicly traded for fourteen years, a significant number of EMAK stockholders owned their shares in "street name." This practice is summarized in a leading treatise:
>
> > The vast majority of publicly traded shares in the United States are registered on the companies' books not in the name of beneficial owners—*i.e.,* those investors who paid for, and have the right to vote and dispose of, the shares—but rather in the name of "Cede & Co.," the name used by The Depository Trust Company ("DTC").
> >
> > Shares registered in this manner are commonly referred to as being held in "street name." . . . DTC holds the shares on behalf of banks and brokers, which in turn hold on behalf of their clients (who are the underlying beneficial owners or other intermediaries).[3]
>
> The roles of DTC and the Investor Communications Solutions Division of Broadridge Financial Services, Inc. ("Broadridge") are important in this case. Broadridge's role has been summarized as follows:
>
> > For many years, banks and brokers maintained their own proxy departments to handle the back-office administrative processes of distributing proxy materials and tabulating voting instructions from their clients. Today, however, the overwhelming majority have eliminated their proxy departments

---

3. John C. Wilcox, John J. Purcell III, & Hye-Won Choi, *"Street Name" Registration & The Proxy Solicitation Process* in Amy Goodman, et al., *A Practical Guide to SEC Proxy and Compensation Rules* 10-3 (4th ed. 2007 & 2008 Supp.).

and subcontracted these processes out to [Broadridge]. For many years, these proxy processing services were provided by Automatic Data Processing, Inc. ("ADP"), but on March 31, 2007, ADP spun off its Brokerage Services Group into a new independent company, Broadridge, which now provides these services to most banks and brokers.

To make these arrangements work, Broadridge's bank and broker clients formally transfer to Broadridge the proxy authority they receive from DTC (via the [DTC] Omnibus Proxy) via written powers of attorney. On behalf of the brokers and banks, Broadridge delivers directly to each beneficial owner a proxy statement and, importantly, a voting instruction form (referred to as a "VIF") rather than a proxy card. Beneficial owners do not receive proxy cards because they are not vested with the right to vote shares or to grant proxy authority—those rights belong only to the legal owners (or their designees). Beneficial owners merely have the right to instruct how their shares are to be voted by Broadridge (attorney-in-fact of the DTC participants), which they accomplish by returning a VIF.[4]

DTC is generally regarded as the entity having the power under Delaware law to vote the shares that it holds on deposit for the banks and brokers who are members of DTC. Through the DTC omnibus proxy, DTC transfers its voting authority to those member banks and brokers. The banks and brokers then transfer the voting authority to Broadridge, which votes the shares held at DTC by each bank and broker in proportion to the aggregate voting instructions received from the ultimate beneficial owners.

For the TBE Consent Solicitation, Broadridge collected, recorded, and totaled the voting instructions it received from the beneficial owners of EMAK shares held in street name. There is no dispute that the banks and brokers properly authorized Broadridge to vote the EMAK shares held on their behalf by DTC.

What no one ever obtained, and what DTC never provided, was the DTC omnibus proxy. The evidence conflicts as to who had the responsibility to get the DTC omnibus proxy. The Court of Chancery found that neither party clearly had the obligation to secure the DTC omnibus proxy, although both could have done more, neither acted improperly or inequitably with respect to this aspect of the case....

On December 18, 2009, Crown delivered the Crown Consents to EMAK.... Crown had received sufficient consents to take corporate action. Given the nearly 28% voting power that Crown could wield on matters other than the election of directors, Crown needed only another 23% to reach the necessary majority of EMAK's outstanding voting power. Crown obtained that majority from EMAK management and one large institutional holder.

4. *Id.* at 10–14.

> With only a few consents to deliver, Crown sidestepped the need for a DTC omnibus proxy by having DTC execute the consents in the name of Cede & Co., a procedure DTC offers to beneficial holders akin to the issuance of appraisal demands in Cede's name. This approach is not practical for a broad-based solicitation such as that which TBE conducted.

992 A.2d at 381–383.

Crown argued that "holder" referred to the party holding titled to the shares, i.e., DTC. Crown supported its argument by invoking Section 219(c) which provides at least ten days before any shareholder meeting the officer in charge of the stock ledger must "prepare and make . . . a complete list of the stockholders entitled to vote at the meeting." Crown made this argument because TBE had obtained written consents from the depository banks and brokers listed on the "Cede breakdown list" as DTC never executed the "omnibus proxy" which would have transferred DTC's voting authority to the depository banks and brokers. The Vice–Chancellor ruled against Crown on this point by cleverly broadening the meaning of "stock ledger" to include the "Cede breakdown" so that under the Vice–Chancellor's approach the depositing banks and brokers would be deemed "stockholders entitled to vote." On appeal, the Delaware Supreme Court responded:

> The record reflects that DTC issues the omnibus proxy as a matter of course during the interactions between issuers and DTC that are compelled by the federal securities laws. When preparing for a meeting of stockholders or a consent solicitation, issuers are required by federal law to go through DTC to identify the participant banks and brokers for purposes of distributing voting cards and solicitation materials.[43] An issuer typically starts the process by requesting a Cede breakdown so that it can send out the broker search cards. When the entire process is complete, the issuer provides each bank and broker with sufficient copies of the proxy statement, card, and other materials for distribution to the beneficial owners.
>
> Thirty years ago, when the depository system was still new, the Court of Chancery held that a stockholder was entitled to a Cede breakdown under *Section 220* when the stockholder sought a stocklist. Subsequent Delaware decisions have consistently ordered the production of a Cede breakdown as part of the *section 220* stocklist materials. In this case, the Court of Chancery reasoned that "if a Cede breakdown is part of the stock ledger for purposes of *Section 220(b)*, it logically should be part of the stock

---

43. At least twenty business days prior to the record date, an issuer must send a broker search card to any "broker, dealer, voting trustee, bank, association, or other entity that exercises fiduciary powers in nominee name" that the company "knows" is holding shares for beneficial owners. *17 C.F.R. § 240.14a–13(a) (2010). Rule 14a–13* provides that "[i]f the registrant's list of security holders indicates that some of its securities are registered in the name of a clearing agency registered pursuant to Section 17A of the Act (*e.g.*, 'Cede & Co.,' nominee for Depository Trust Company), the registrant shall make appropriate inquiry of the clearing agency and thereafter of the participants in such clearing agency." *17 C.F.R. § 240.14a–13(a) n.1 (2010).*

ledger for purposes of *Section 219(c)* and should be used to create the stocklist under *Section 219(a)*."

The Court of Chancery acknowledged that this conclusion was contrary to "the established understanding among practitioners, evidenced by our case law, . . . that DTC (through Cede) is the record holder and that everyone above DTC is a beneficial holder." The Court of Chancery reached that conclusion by characterizing the relationship between DTC and its participant banks and brokers as fundamentally different from the relationships further up the chain. Consequently, the court did "not believe that there are any practical or policy-based impediments to treating the Cede breakdown as part of the stock ledger." Nevertheless, it concluded:

> My ruling does not alter the traditional distinction between record and beneficial ownership. The analysis I have followed does not apply to any entity other than DTC in its role as a federally registered clearing agency. The view from the top of the beneficial ownership chain remains as always: beneficial holders are not record holders.

Having completed its analysis, the Court of Chancery declined to follow well-established prior precedents construing the meaning of the term "record holder" and announced a new interpretation of "stock ledger" under *section 219* of the DGCL:

> The Cede breakdown showing the banks and brokers who held EMAK stock at DTC as of October 22, 2009, was part of EMAK's stock ledger for purposes of *Section 219(c)*. Those banks and brokers were therefore stockholders of record entitled to express consent to corporate action without a meeting under *Section 228(a)* . . . .

The parties have extensively briefed and argued both sides of the issue of whether the Cede breakdown is (or is not) part of the "stock ledger" for *section 219* purposes . . . .

. . . [A] legislative cure is preferable. The DGCL is a comprehensive and carefully crafted statutory scheme that is periodically reviewed by the General Assembly. Indeed, the General Assembly made coordinated amendments to *section 219* and *section 220* in 2003. Any adjustment to the intricate scheme of which *section 219* is but a part should be accomplished by the General Assembly through a coordinated amendment process. Therefore, the Court of Chancery's interpretation of stock ledger in *section 219* is *obiter dictum* and without precedential effect.

992 A.2d at 396–398.

F. BALOTTI & J. FINKELSTEIN, THE DELAWARE LAW OF CORPORATIONS AND BUSINESS ASSOCIATIONS § 7.45 (3d ed. 2005 Supp.). "A 'stocklist' for most public corporations consists of far more than simply a list of stockholders with their addresses and numbers of shares. A stockholder with a proper purpose has a right to obtain subsidiary information available to the corporation including magnetic tape compilations, breakdowns of stockholdings by depository nominees, and (where appropriate) lists of beneficial owners of stock available to the issuer pursuant to [SEC] Rule 14b–1(c) (the 'NOBO list'). Similarly, a shareholder is ordinarily entitled to transfer sheets from the date of the list provided to him to the meeting date, expiration of the tender offer, or other relevant date.

"However, the corporation is not required to manufacture such items for the convenience of the stockholder if the corporation does not already have access to them. In *R.B. Associates of New Jersey, L.P. v. The Gilette Co.,* [C.A. No. 9711 (Del.Ch. Mar.22, 1988)], a stockholder sought to require a corporation to obtain a NOBO list which it did not already have in its possession in order to produce it to the stockholder seeking inspection. The Court of Chancery held:

> Neither broad concepts of fairness, nor the words of Section 220, in my opinion, require that a corporation be forced, in each instance, to exercise the option created by the applicable SEC rules at the behest of a shareholder. What fairness does require, and what our opinions repeatedly return to, is the principle that relief in a Section 220 case should afford to a shareholder the same information as the corporation has in its books, records, and other papers."

C. REPORTING UNDER STATE LAW

MODEL BUS. CORP. ACT §§ 16.20

[See Statutory Supplement]

CAL. CORP. CODE § 1501

[See Statutory Supplement]

N.Y. BUS. CORP. LAW § 624(e)

[See Statutory Supplement]

As seen above, the shareholder's general inspection right requires a shareholder to take affirmative action and incur costs to obtain information, and may be defeated in litigation. An important aspect of ownership in any form of business is being informed regarding the company's financial performance and position. This information is collected in financial statements that are internally prepared periodically for the company's management to enable them to assess the firm's operations. Since this information is already in the firm's management's possession, arguably it could without too much additional effort be distributed, at least periodically, to shareholders. Hence, approximately half the states follow the Model Business Corporation Act § 16.20 and require that every corporation must furnish to its shareholders *annual* financial statements, including a balance sheet and an income statement. The statements must be prepared on the basis of generally accepted accounting principles (GAAP) if the corporation prepares its financial statements on that basis. About twenty states are less demanding. For example, N.J.Stat.Ann. § 14A:5–28, simply provides that a corporation must furnish "its balance sheet as at the end of the preceding fiscal year, and its profit and loss and surplus statements for such fiscal year" upon a shareholder's written request. Delaware is alone in having no provision mandating corporations to furnish financial statements to shareholders even on written request.

In contrast to the narrow to non-existent state disclosure requirements, a cornerstone of the Securities Exchange Act is the requirement for companies to file with the SEC, quarterly and annually, a broad range of financial and non-financial information (e.g., officer and director background, material conflict of interest transactions, and material developments). Such mandatory reporting applies to corporations that are either listed on a national stock exchange or have at least 500 record holders of a class of securities and meet certain other conditions. As will be seen, such companies are generally referred to as "reporting companies." With respect to non-reporting companies, however, the information rights of stockholders are governed by the limited requirements of state law. Accordingly, there is something of an unfulfilled need to require corporations that have significant public ownership, but are not covered by the Securities Exchange Act, to report to their shareholders information not just their financial results and position, but a wide range of matters bearing on management's stewardship of the firm.

D. AN OVERVIEW OF THE SEC AND THE SECURITIES EXCHANGE ACT

SEC, The Investor's Advocate: How the SEC Protects Investors, Maintains Market Integrity, and Facilitates Capital Formation

(2010).

Introduction

The mission of the U.S. Securities and Exchange Commission is to protect investors, maintain fair, orderly, and efficient markets, and facilitate capital formation. . . .

The laws and rules that govern the securities industry in the United States derive from a simple and straightforward concept: all investors, whether large institutions or private individuals, should have access to certain basic facts about an investment prior to buying it, and so long as they hold it. To achieve this, the SEC requires public companies to disclose meaningful financial and other information to the public. This provides a common pool of knowledge for all investors to use to judge for themselves whether to buy, sell, or hold a particular security. Only through the steady flow of timely, comprehensive, and accurate information can people make sound investment decisions. . . .

The SEC oversees the key participants in the securities world, including securities exchanges, securities brokers and dealers, investment advisors, and mutual funds. Here the SEC is concerned primarily with promoting the disclosure of important market-related information, maintaining fair dealing, and protecting against fraud. . . .

Creation of the SEC

The SEC's foundation was laid in an era that was ripe for reform. Before the Great Crash of 1929, there was little support for federal regulation of the securities markets. . . .

When the stock market crashed in October 1929, public confidence in the markets plummeted. Investors large and small, as well as the banks who had loaned to them, lost great sums of money in the ensuing Great Depression. There was a consensus that for the economy to recover, the public's faith in the capital markets needed to be restored. Congress held hearings to identify the problems and search for solutions.

Based on the findings in these hearings, Congress—during the peak year of the Depression—passed the Securities Act of 1933. This law, together with the Securities Exchange Act of 1934, which created the SEC, was designed to restore investor confidence in our capital markets by providing investors and the markets with more reliable information and clear rules of honest dealing. . . .

Securities Exchange Act of 1934

With this Act, Congress created the Securities and Exchange Commission. The Act empowers the SEC with broad authority over all aspects of the securities industry. This includes the power to register, regulate, and oversee brokerage firms, transfer agents, and clearing agencies as well as the nation's securities self regulatory organizations (SROs). The various stock exchanges, such as the New York Stock Exchange, and American Stock Exchange are SROs. The Financial Industry Regulatory Authority, which operates the NASDAQ system, is also an SRO.

The Act also identifies and prohibits certain types of conduct in the markets and provides the Commission with disciplinary powers over regulated entities and persons associated with them.

The Act also empowers the SEC to require periodic reporting of information by companies with publicly traded securities.

Corporate Reporting

Companies [listed on a national securities exchange or]with more than $10 million in assets whose securities are held by more than 500 owners must file annual and other periodic reports. These reports are available to the public through the SEC's EDGAR database.

Proxy Solicitations

The Securities Exchange Act also governs the disclosure in materials used to solicit shareholders' votes in annual or special meetings held for the election of directors and the approval of other corporate action. This information, contained in proxy materials, must be filed with the Commission in advance of any solicitation to ensure compliance with the disclosure rules. Solicitations, whether by management or shareholder groups, must disclose all important facts concerning the issues on which holders are asked to vote....

SECURITIES EXCHANGE ACT § 12(a), (b), (g)

[See Statutory Supplement]

SECURITIES EXCHANGE ACT RULE 12G–1

[See Statutory Supplement]

E. PERIODIC DISCLOSURE UNDER THE SECURITIES EXCHANGE ACT

SECURITIES EXCHANGE ACT § 13(a)

[See Statutory Supplement]

SECURITIES EXCHANGE ACT RULES 13a–1, 13a–11, 13a–13

SECURITIES EXCHANGE ACT FORMS 8–K, 10–K, 10–Q

[See Statutory Supplement]

NOTE IN PERIODIC REPORTING BY REGISTERED CORPORATIONS

The Securities Exchange Act addresses the informational deficiencies in state law by imposing periodic-reporting requirements on corporations with a security registered under section 12. Section 13 of the Act, and the rules promulgated thereunder, require such corporations to file a Form 10–K annually, a Form 10–Q quarterly, and a Form 8–K generally within four business days after the occurrence of certain specified events. Among the matters that trigger an 8–K Report are a change in control of the corporation, the acquisition or disposition of a significant amount of assets, a change of accountants, the termination of a material definitive agreement, the departure of a director or principal officer (CEO, president, chief operating officer, chief financial officer, chief accounting officer, or any person performing similar functions), amendments to the articles or bylaws, amendments to the corporation's code of ethics, and waivers of a provision of the corporation's code of ethics. The Form 10–K must include audited financial statements; management's discussion of the corporation's financial condition and results of operations; and disclosure concerning legal proceedings, developments in the corporation's business, executive compensation, conflict-of-interest transactions, and other specified issues. The Form 10–Q must include quarterly financial data prepared in accordance with generally accepted accounting principles; a management report; and disclosures concerning legal proceedings, defaults on senior securities, and other specified issues. Periodic reporting is also required under the Proxy Rules in connection with the corporation's annual meeting.

The Exchange Act's reporting requirements are triggered if one of the following occurs: 1) per section 12(a) when the firm has a security that is listed on a national securities exchange such as the New York Stock Exchange or Nasdaq; or 2) per section 12(g) when the firm on the last day of its fiscal year has 500 or more holders of a class of its security, has assets in excess of $10 million (this standard is set by rule 12g–1 and episodically adjusted), *and* is engaged in interstate commerce; or 3) per section 15(d) the firm has registered securities pursuant to a public offering of its securities and there are not less than 300 holders of that class of security.

The disclosure required by the Securities Exchange Act's periodic reporting requirements is sometimes called *structured* disclosure, because what must be disclosed and how it must be disclosed is structured by the relevant SEC rules. Another example of structured disclosure is the disclosure required under the Securities Act when a corporation makes a public offering of its securities.

Of course, a corporation may make voluntary timely disclosure of material corporate developments even if not required to do so by law. Furthermore, the rules of the major stock exchanges often require listed corporations to make timely disclosure of material developments.

F. DISCLOSURE UNDER STOCK EXCHANGE RULES

NEW YORK STOCK EXCHANGE, LISTED COMPANY MANUAL §§ 202.01, 202.03, 202.05, 202.06[1]

[See Statutory Supplement]

SECTION 2. THE PROXY RULES: AN INTRODUCTION

This and the next two Sections concern the Proxy Rules, which are promulgated by the SEC. The following terms are important in considering these Rules:

Proxy holder. A person authorized to vote shares on a shareholder's behalf.

Proxy, form of proxy, or *proxy form.* The written instrument in which such an authorization is embodied. (The term proxy is also sometimes used to mean a proxy holder, but for purposes of clarity that usage will be avoided in this Chapter.)

Proxy solicitation. The process by which shareholders are asked to give their proxies.

Proxy Statement. A written statement sent to shareholders as a means of proxy solicitation.

Proxy materials. The proxy statement and form of proxy.

SECURITIES EXCHANGE ACT § 14(a), (c)

SECURITIES EXCHANGE ACT RULES 14a–1–14a–6, 14c–2, 14c–3, SCHEDULE 14A, SCHEDULE 14C

[See Statutory Supplement]

---

1. For similar rules, see American Stock Exchange, AMEX Company Guide, §§ 401–405 (Disclosure Policies), 2 CCH, American Stock Exchange Guide § 10,121–10,125; Nat'l Ass'n Sec. Dealers Manual (CCH) § 5, Schedule D, Part II, § 1806A, at 1571–72.

NOTE—AN OVERVIEW OF THE PROXY RULES

1. *Background.* Proxy voting is the dominant mode of shareholder decisionmaking in publicly held corporations. There are two basic reasons for this. First, shareholders in such corporations are often geographically dispersed, so that a given shareholder may not live near the site of the meeting. Second, a given shareholding will normally represent only a small fraction of a shareholder's total wealth. Accordingly, physical attendance at a shareholders' meeting is normally an uneconomical use of a shareholder's time when he can vote by proxy.

A natural outgrowth of the preference for proxy voting is a proxy solicitation—the process of systematically contacting shareholders, and urging them to execute and return proxy forms that authorize named proxyholders to cast the shareholder's votes, either in a manner designated in the proxy form or according to the proxyholder's discretion.

Despite this state of affairs, as of the 1930's state law hardly regulated proxy voting, except in the extreme case in which proxies had been fraudulently solicited. Abuses were notorious and widespread. Accordingly, Congress entered the field in 1934 through Section 14(a) of the Securities Exchange Act. In itself, Section 14(a) has no effect on private conduct: its only effect was to authorize the SEC to promulgate rules that will govern private conduct. Pursuant to Section 14(a), the SEC has promulgated a set of Proxy Rules that serve a variety of purposes.

2. *Format Requirements.* One purpose of the Proxy Rules is to regulate the form or presentation the ballot (proxy) itself. The proxy's format is addressed in Rules 14a–4 and 14a–5, calling for, among other requirements, that the proxy be clearly (in bold-face type no less) identified as a proxy, that there be a box for the proxy giver to express approval, disapproval or abstention with respect to *each* matter to be voted upon, that the proxy pertaining to the election of directors must provide a means for the proxy giver to withhold approval for voting for a nominee, that any request for discretionary authority to vote may be sought only with respect to matters the solicitor did not have notice of at least 45 days before the date the proxy materials were sent in the prior year's annual meeting, and that all written materials be at least 10–point roman type.

Rule 14a–4(d), the so-called short-slate provision, facilitates efforts to oppose management's dominance of the election of directors. To understand this provision, assume management nominates a slate of five directors, A, B, C. D. and E and that a group of holders wish to support the efforts of Insurgent to place two individuals, X and Y, on the board. Assume further that Insurgent believes A and B should not serve on the board but has no objection to the election of C, D and E. Rule 14a–4(d) permits Insurgent's proxy materials to request proxies for X and Y as well as C, D and E. Such a solicitation by Insurgent is likely to be more attractive to shareholders over the pre-Rule 14a–4(d)

SEC interpretation whereby the short-slate solicitor was permitted to request proxies only for his candidates, X and Y; under the former regulatory approach, shareholders legitimately believed that to be able to vote for X and Y they had to forsake voting to fill all five vacant seats. Moreover, if the shareholder returned both Insurgent's ballot and management's ballot by, for example, voting for X, Y, C, D and E, under applicable state law the later executed proxy prevails over the earlier granted proxy. Rule 14a–4(d) thus introduces a reasonable approach by which shareholders can "split" their votes.

FORM OF PROXY

[See Statutory Supplement]

3. *Anti–Bundling.* One clever method to obtain approval of a matter likely not to be popular with shareholders (e.g., an antitakeover amendment provision) is to include within that proposal a provision that would be popular with stockholders (e.g., an enriching restructuring). The proxy rules go part way toward addressing the distorted choice that the bundling of unrelated resolutions can pose to shareholders. Rule 14a–4(b) requires separate voting on matters that are not "related." *See* Koppel v. 4987 Corp., 167 F.3d 125 (2d Cir. 1999) (question of fact whether single resolution seeking stockholder approval to waive a default in a lease of property to one of the firm's promoters, sell the leased property, and distribute the proceeds to shareholders are related matters). Management can, however, continue to condition separately voted-on proposals so that neither becomes effective without the approval of the other. Query, what justifies this position and what is the value of the anti-bundling rule?

4. *Mandated Disclosure.* One purpose of the Proxy Rules is to require full disclosure in connection with transactions that shareholders are being asked to approve, such as mergers, certificate amendments, or election of directors. This purpose is accomplished in the first instance by Rule 14a–3 and Schedule 14A. Rule 14a–3 provides that no solicitation of proxies that is subject to the Proxy Rules shall be made unless the person being solicited "is concurrently furnished or has previously been furnished with a written proxy statement containing the information specified in Schedule 14A." Schedule 14A details the information that must be furnished when specified types of transactions are to be acted upon by the shareholders. Rule 14a–3 and Schedule 14A are backed up by Rule 14a–9, examined later in this chapter, which provides that no solicitation subject to the Proxy Rules shall contain any statement that is false or misleading with respect to any material fact or omits a material fact.

When proxies for the election of directors are solicited on behalf of a corporation that is subject to the Proxy Rules, the corporation must send an Annual Report to its shareholders, either in advance of or concurrently with the proxy statement. The Annual Report compelled by Rule 14a–3 is not the same as the annual report on Form 10–K that reporting companies must file with the SEC, but nonetheless embodies the core information requirements found in Form 10–K *and* Rule 14a–3 requires companies when soliciting proxies to offer to provide the full Form 10–K. Disclosure has, however, moved into the digital age, thus saving many a tree from the pulp mill. Rule 14a–16 permits issuers to satisfy the proxy statement delivery requirement by providing shareholders with the website where the materials are available, at no cost; the rule also requires companies to provide via first-class mail paper copies of the materials if requested by a shareholder.

As seen above, the contents of the Annual Report to shareholders are governed by Rule 14a–3. The Report must include, among other things, the corporation's financial statements, selected financial data, and management's discussion and analysis (commonly referred to as the "MD & A") of the corporation's financial condition and results of operations. Either the Annual Report or the Proxy Statement must prominently feature an undertaking to furnish a copy of the Form 10–K to any shareholder, without charge, upon written request.

To encourage informality and directness in the Annual Report to shareholders, Rule 14a–3(c) provides that the Report is not to be deemed either soliciting material within the Proxy Rules or a "filing" under Securities Exchange Act § 18 (which expressly provides civil liability for misrepresentations appearing in reports "filed" with the SEC). Any material misrepresentations in proxy materials can, however, be addressed under Rule 14a–9, or even Rule 10b–5, discussed later.

Consider for a moment the relevance to shareholders of some of the items that Rule 14a–3 requires to be disclosed in the annual report. Much of this disclosure is only very loosely related to any specific action the shareholders are asked to vote upon. For example, Rule 14a–3 provides that the proxy statement for an annual meeting at which directors are to be elected must be accompanied by an annual report that includes audited balance sheets for each of the corporation's two most recent fiscal years, audited income statements for its three most recent fiscal years, and certain other information. Under Items 7 and 8 of Schedule 14A, the proxy statement for an annual meeting at which directors are being elected must disclose the compensation of the five most highly paid executives and the executive officers as a group (including not only salary, but bonuses, deferred compensation, stock options, and the like), and disclosure of significant conflict-of-interest transactions during the corporation's last fiscal year involving, among others, directors, executive officers, and five percent beneficial owners. Under Item 7, the proxy statement for such a meeting must also disclose a good deal of information regarding the corporation's audit, nominating, and compensation committees such as the number of meetings each committee held during the last fiscal year and the functions it performs.

Finally, if a corporation's stock is registered under section 12, and the corporation proposes to take an action that requires shareholder approval, or to hold an annual meeting at which directors are to be elected, then even if the corporation is not soliciting proxies it must distribute essentially the same information that would be required if it was soliciting proxies. See § 14(c), Regulation 14C, and Schedule 14C. This set of rules has its principal bite where the corporation has a controlling shareholder who can take actions at the shareholder level without soliciting proxies.

5. *Filing with SEC.* Rule 14a–6 governs the filing of proxy materials with the SEC. In broad overview, the preliminary proxy statement and the ballot ("form of proxy") must be filed with the SEC 10 days before the definitive copies of these materials are expected to be sent or given to shareholders. The prefiling provides the SEC with time to review the materials should it wish. The filed materials become immediately available and can be used in solicitations, although the actual circulation of the ballot must await the filing of the definitive proxy statement. Thus, the proxy solicitation customarily begins with the preliminary filing followed later by the circulation of the ballot when the definitive proxy statement is filed with the SEC. There are two broad notable dispensations to the above filing requirements. First, per Rule 14a–12, the prefiling requirement pertains to the proxy statement and ballot; thus, oral and *other* written communications, regardless of the subject matter of the solicitation, are permitted, provided the written solicitation materials are filed with the SEC, the solicitors are identified, the communication bears a legend advising that the proxy statement should be read when it is available (and disclosing that the statement can be obtained when available for free from the SEC's website), and a proxy statement is sent to solicited security holder when it is available. Second, no *preliminary* filing is required for solicitations in connection with a meeting if the *only* action to be taken is the election of directors, approval of the auditor, voting on a shareholder proposal pursuant to Rule 14a–8, *infra*, or ratification of certain executive compensation proposals; in these instances it is sufficient that the proxy statement and form of proxy are filed at least contemporaneous with their use. *See e.g.*, Shoen v. AMERCO, 885 F.Supp. 1332, 1346 (D. Nev. 1994) (management's communication to stockholders in opposition to a shareholder proposal made under Rule 14a–8 was not exempt since the shareholder-proponent intended to introduce at the meeting other matters that were not circulated to the shareholders pursuant to Rule 14a–8).

6. *Coverage.* Rule 14a–2 provides that the Proxy Rules "apply to every solicitation of a proxy with respect to securities registered pursuant to section 12 of the Act," subject to certain exceptions described below. The definitions of "proxy" and "solicitation" are extremely broad. Under Rule 14a–1(f), the term "proxy" means "every proxy, consent, or authorization within the meaning of section 14(a) of the Act. The consent or authorization may take the form of failure to object or to dissent." Under Rule 14a–1(*l*)(1), the term "solicitation" includes "(i) [a]ny request for a proxy . . .; (ii) [a]ny request to

execute or not to execute, or to revoke, a proxy; or (iii) [t]he furnishing of a form of proxy or other communication to security holders under circumstances reasonably calculated to result in the procurement, withholding or revocation of a proxy." This language has been given a very expansive interpretation. For example, in Studebaker Corp. v. Gittlin, 360 F.2d 692 (2d Cir.1966), Gittlin, a shareholder in Studebaker, had solicited authorizations from other Studebaker shareholders to inspect Studebaker's stockholder list for the purpose of meeting the five percent test under the relevant New York inspection statute. Judge Friendly stated:

> . . . The assistant general counsel of the SEC . . . stated at the argument that the Commission believes § 14(a) should be construed, in all its literal breadth, to include authorizations to inspect stockholders lists, even in cases where obtaining the authorizations was not a step in a planned solicitation of proxies.
>
> We need not go that far to uphold the order of the district court. In SEC v. Okin, 132 F.2d 784 (2d Cir.1943), this court ruled that a letter which did not request the giving of any authorization was subject to the Proxy Rules if it was part of "a continuous plan" intended to end in solicitation and to prepare the way for success. This was the avowed purpose of Gittlin's demand for inspection of the stockholders list. . . .

Id. at 695–96.

The full breadth of the above *Gitlin–Okin* formulation was captured in Long Island Lighting Co. v. Barbash, 779 F.2d 793 (2d Cir. 1985), where the court ruled that despite the First Amendment the proxy rules could reach a newspaper advertisement placed by individuals who were unrelated to one of the proxy contest combatants. The advertisement chastised the current LILCO management and called for converting the Long Island utility to public ownership. Management sought to enjoin the advertisement for violating various proxy rule requirements, pointing to the fact LILCO was then engaged in a proxy contest with a local politician who had raised similar issues as those raised in the advertisement although there was no connection between the ad's sponsor and no mention whatever in the ad of the ongoing proxy contest. *But see* Brown v. Chicago, Rock Island & Peoria RR, 328 F.2d 122 (7th Cir. 1964) (publication before stockholder meeting date of advertisements designed to win public support for merger of the two railroads was not a proxy solicitation). Communications supportive of a position of one side that occur during or close proximity of a proxy solicitation are more easily drawn into the regulatory purview of proxy rules. *See* Shoen v. AMERCO, 885 F.Supp. 1332 (D. Nev. 1994) (newsletter and flyer supportive of company's management that was distributed to holders of ESOP by the plan's trustees three weeks before management began its proxy solicitation deemed a proxy solicitation); Capital Real Estate Investors Tax Exempt Fund Ltd. Partnership v. Schwartzberg, 929 F.Supp. 105, 113 (S.D.N.Y. 1996) (management press releases extolling benefits of merger would not be proxy solicitation if they were "purely factual" description of the transaction; however, the challenged release was viewed as preconditioning shareholders toward a favorable view of the transaction and accordingly deemed a proxy). Recall the earlier discussion of Rule 14a–12. How would you advise management to proceed in a case like *Schwartzberg* where a firm's management wishes not only to announce, for example that they have entered into an agreement to merge with another company (subject to subsequent stockholder approval which would occur via a proxy solicitation), but also wish to express an opinion regarding the benefits the deal presents the company's holders?

There are notable exemptions. Perhaps the most significant exemption is Rule 14a–1(*l*)(2) that lists several acts that are excluded, most significantly, (iv) authorizes instances in which it does not constitute a solicitation for ***the security holder*** to announce his intent to vote in a certain manner. This provision greatly facilitates "just say no" campaigns institutions have waged from time-to-time to express disapproval of incumbent management's policies; relying on this rule, activist financial institutions can publicize their decisions to withhold their votes for some or all the directors standing for election in the expectation the announcement will influence others. *See* Joseph A. Grundfest, Just Vote No: A Minimalist Strategy for Dealing with Barbarians Inside the Gages, 45 Stan. L. Rev. 857 (1993) (withholding votes for some directors is a low cost, and one of the few effective, means by which institutional holders can effectively manifest displeasure with the the long-term strategies they believe are deficient); Diane Del Guercio, Laura Seery & Tracie Woidtke, Do Boards Pay Attention When Institutional Investor Activists "Just Vote No"?, 90 J. Fin. Econ. 84 (2008) (finding significant correlation between such campaigns and CEO turnover accompanied by subsequent operating and stock price improvements).

Another useful exemption is provided in Rule 14a–2(b)(2) which excludes from most (but not the anti-misrepresentation rule in Rule 14a–9) proxy requirements a security holder's communication directed to ten or fewer persons.

Rule 14a–2(b)(1) excludes from most of the proxy rules (but not the antifraud rule) communications by a person who is not seeking a proxy authority (i.e., neither provides a proxy card nor a revocation form) and who does not have a "substantial interest" in the matter that is subject to a vote. For example, financial institutions may confer among themselves and with their third-party advisor how they can individually vote their shares. The latter rule is not available to ten categories of persons, such as the company, its management, or a group whose ownership exceeds five percent and has not professed a lack of interest in control of the company. *See* MONY Group v. Highfields Capital, 368 F.3d 138 (2d Cir. 2004) (institutional investor outside the exemption when, in opposition to management's solicitation, it sent a blank duplicate of management's ballot with its letter opposing the matter).

Through Rule 14a–17 the SEC encourages companies and others to establish Internet-based shareholder forums where shareholders can communicate among themselves and with management on matters related to the company. However, a communication made through such a forum, that because of its content, is a solicitation must comply with the proxy filing and disclosure requirements if the communication is within 60 days of the shareholder meeting date.

7. *Access to the Body of Shareholders.* Proxy Rules 14a–7 and 14a–8 provide mechanisms through which shareholders can communicate with each other. See Section 3, infra.

SECTION 3. THE PROXY RULES: SHAREHOLDER ACCESS

A. THE DISSIDENT'S ACCESS PROVISION: RULE 14a–7

SECURITIES EXCHANGE ACT RULE 14a–7

[See Statutory Supplement]

The proxy rules from time-to-time address more than disclosure. One such instance is Rule 14a–7 which provides a means for a shareholder who wishes to solicit proxies to gain access to her fellow stockholders. This provision requires that the company shall in response to a request by a record or beneficial holder either provide a list of stockholders or circulate the requesting holder's materials. Rule 14a–7 only applies if the company has or intends itself to engage in a proxy solicitation and the company (except in the narrow instance involving so-called roll-up transactions) has the option of either providing the list or mailing the requesting security holder's materials. If the latter option is chosen by the company, the requesting security holder must provide the required postage and sufficient copies of the materials to be forwarded. Which option do you believe the company will prefer?

B. SHAREHOLDER PROPOSALS UNDER RULE 14a–8

SECURITIES EXCHANGE ACT RULE 14a–8

[See Statutory Supplement]

NOTE ON NO-ACTION LETTERS INTERPRETING RULE 14a–8

Rule 14a–8 provides that if management believes a shareholder proposal may properly be excluded from the corporation's proxy statement under Rule 14a–8, it must submit to the SEC staff a statement of the reasons why it deems omission of the proposal to be proper. If the staff agrees with management's statement, it sends management a "no-action letter"—that is, a letter stating that if the shareholder proposal is omitted, no action will be taken by the SEC. If the staff disagrees with management's statement, its letter briefly states its disagreement with the issuer's opinion that the proposal can be omitted. Such letters are referred to as no-action letters, although in the case where the SEC disagrees with management's conclusion that the proposal can be omitted no-action is a misnomer; the SEC's staff's disagreement is a clear statement that if the company omits the proposal this could lead to an SEC enforcement action. In such cases management may still omit the shareholder proposal, and run the risk of legal proceedings by the SEC, but this option is seldom pursued. It is important to understand that no-action letters are opinions of the staff of the SEC, and not the commissioners. As such, no-action letters are not reviewable "orders" of an agency under the Administrative Procedure Act. Board of Trade of the City of Chicago v. SEC, 883 F.2d 525 (7th Cir. 1989).

Standard Pacific Corp.

SEC No–Action Letter (February 28, 2008).

STANDARD PACIFIC HOMES
15326 ALTON PARKWAY, IRVINE,
CA 92618–2338

January 18, 2008

VIA HAND DELIVERY

Office of Chief Counsel
Division of Corporation Finance
Securities and Exchange Commission
100 F Street, NE
Washington, DC 20549

Re: *Stockholder Proposal of the Nathan Cummings Foundation et al. Exchange Act of 1934—Rule 14a–8*

Dear Ladies and Gentlemen:

This letter is to inform you that Standard Pacific Corp. (the "Company"), intends to omit from its proxy statement and form of proxy for its 2008 Annual Stockholders Meeting (collectively, the "2008 Proxy Materials") a stockholder proposal and statements in support thereof (the "Proposal") received from the Nathan Cummings Foundation and co-filed by the General Board of Pension and Health Benefits of the United Methodist Church (both organizations are collectively referred to herein as the "Proponent")....

THE PROPOSAL

The Proposal requests that the Board of Directors of the Company (the "Board") "adopt quantitative goals, based on available technologies, for reducing total greenhouse gas emissions from the Company's products and operations and report to stockholders by December 31, 2008, on its plans to achieve those goals." A copy of the Proposal, as well as related correspondence with the Proponent, is attached to this letter as Exhibit A.

BASIS FOR EXCLUSION

We hereby respectfully request that the Staff concur in our view that the Proposal may be excluded from the 2008 Proxy Materials pursuant to Rule 14a–8(i)(7) because the Proposal deals with matters related to the Company's ordinary business operations, specifically the evaluation of risk.

ANALYSIS

The Proposal May Be Excluded under Rule 14a–8(i)(7) Because It Deals With Matters Related to the Company's Ordinary Business Operations.

Rule 14a–8(i)(7) permits the omission of a stockholder proposal dealing with matters relating to a company's "ordinary business" operations. According to the Commission release adopting the 1998 amendments to Rule 14a–8, the underlying policy of the ordinary business exclusion is "to confine the resolution of ordinary business problems to management and the board of directors, since it is impracticable for shareholders to decide how to solve such problems at an annual shareholders meeting." Exchange Act Release No. 40018 (May 21, 1998) (the "1998 Release").

In the 1998 Release, the Commission described the two "central considerations" for the ordinary business exclusion. The first was that certain tasks were "so fundamental to management's ability to run a company on a day-to-day basis" that they could not be subject to direct stockholder oversight. The second consideration related to "the degree to which the proposal seeks to 'micro-manage' the company by probing too deeply into matters of a complex nature upon which shareholders, as a group, would not be in a position to make an informed judgment." The Staff consistently has concurred that stockholder proposals requesting an assessment of risks or liabilities are excludable under Rule 14a–8(i)(7) because they relate to a company's day-to-day operations. . . .

We believe that the Proposal is not distinguishable from these instances in which the Staff concurred that stockholder proposals were excludable under Rule 14–8(i)(7) as relating to an evaluation of risk. While the Proposal does not specifically use the word "risk," in order for the Board to undertake the requested action—develop quantitative goals for reducing greenhouse gas emissions from the Company's products and operations—it must of necessity do a risk assessment similar to the risk analysis requested in stockholder proposals that expressly use the word "risk." The Company is a leading builder of single-family attached and detached homes, which are built using a broad range of products and which sell in many geographic areas and at various price points. For the Company to determine appropriate quantitative goals to reduce greenhouse gases in its house designs, it must necessarily undertake an internal assessment of the relative costs, benefits, risks and liabilities of various possible approaches and available technologies. This internal assessment is part of the Company's day-to-day operations and implicates the Company's ordinary business. Thus, because the primary action of the Company to address the Proposal is an evaluation of economic risks and benefits of various available technologies and design approaches, we believe that the Proposal is excludable under Rule 14a–8(i)(7) as relating to an evaluation of risk.

The excludability of the Proposal is further supported by Staff precedent indicating that the Staff looks beyond whether the stockholder proposal refers specifically to an assessment of risk in determining whether the proposal is excludable on this basis. For example, in response to a prior no-action request submitted by the Company, the Staff concurred that the Company could exclude, as relating to "evaluation of risk," a proposal requesting that the Company "assess its response" to rising regulatory, competitive, and public pressure to increase energy efficiency. *Standard Pacific Corp.* (avail. Jan. 29, 2007). *See also ACE Ltd.* (avail. Mar. 19, 2007) (concurring with the exclusion of a stockholder proposal requesting that the board provide a report describing the company's strategy and actions related to climate change, including on the topics of the science of climate change, public policy and legislation, the effect climate change may have on the company, and steps taken by the company in response to climate change because it related to an evaluation of risk); ... *The Dow Chemical Co.* (avail. Feb. 23, 2005) (concurring with the exclusion under Rule 14a–8(i)(7) of a stockholder proposal requesting a report describing the reputational and financial impact of the company's response to pending litigation because it related to an evaluation of risks and liabilities); *American International Group, Inc.* (avail. Feb. 19, 2004) (concurring that the company could exclude a proposal that requested the board of directors to report on *"the economic effects* of HIV/AIDS, tuberculosis and malaria pandemics on the company's business strategy," because it called for an evaluation of risks and benefits) *(emphasis supplied).* In this regard, careful drafting of the Proposal to eliminate any reference to "risks" or "liabilities" should not be sufficient to distract from the internal assessment of risks, costs, benefits and liabilities that the Company would face in establishing the "quantitative goals" requested in the Proposal....

We recognize that the Staff has concluded that certain operations-related proposals may focus on sufficiently significant social policy issues so as to preclude exclusion in certain circumstances, but we do not believe that to be the case with the Proposal. In this regard, the Staff has consistently concurred that a proposal may be excluded in its entirety when it addresses both ordinary and non-ordinary business matters. Most recently, the Staff affirmed this position in *Peregrine*

Pharmaceuticals Inc. (avail. July 31, 2007), stating that a proposal recommending that the board appoint a committee of independent directors to evaluate the strategic direction of the company and the performance of the management team could be excluded under Rule 14a–8(i)(7) as relating to ordinary business matters. The Staff noted, "that the proposal appears to relate to both extraordinary transactions and non-extraordinary transactions. Accordingly, we will not recommend enforcement action to the Commission if Peregrine omits the proposal from its proxy materials in reliance on rule 14a–8(i)(7)." Similarly, in *General Motors Corp.* (avail. Apr. 4, 2007), a proposal requesting that the board institute an executive compensation program that tracks progress in improving the fuel economy of GM vehicles was excludable under Rule 14a–8(i)(7). The Staff stated, "[i]n this regard we note that while the proposal mentions executive compensation, the thrust and focus of the proposal is on ordinary business matters." *See also Wal–Mart Stores, Inc.* (avail. Mar. 15, 1999) (proposal requesting a report to ensure that the company did not purchase goods from suppliers using, among other things, forced labor, convict labor and child labor was excludable in its entirely because the proposal also requested that the report address ordinary business matters). As noted above, the assessment of risk requested by the Proposal implicates the Company's ordinary business operations.

Therefore, we do not believe that it is necessary to consider whether the Proposal may touch upon a significant policy issue, since the Proposal addresses ordinary business issues. In this regard, establishing "quantitative goals ... for reducing total greenhouse gas emissions from the Company's products and operations" cannot be achieved without the Company first conducting an internal assessment of the coasts, benefits, risks and liabilities of the various approaches the Company could take. Thus, we believe that the Proposal may he excluded under Rule 14a–8(i)(7).

CONCLUSION

Based upon the foregoing analysis, we respectfully request that the Staff concur that it will take no action if the Company excludes the Proposal from its 2008 Proxy Materials.... If we can be of any further assistance in this matter, please do not hesitate to call me at (949) 789–1618.

Sincerely,

Clay A. Halvorsen
Secretary
Standard Pacific Corp.

Exhibit A:

RESOLVED:

Shareholders request that the Board of Directors adopt quantitative goals, based on available technologies, for reducing total greenhouse gas emissions from the Company's products and operations and report to shareholders by December 31, 2008, on its plans to achieve these goals. Such a report will omit proprietary information and be prepared at reasonable cost.

THE NATHAN CUMMINGS
FOUNDATION
475 TENTH AVENUE
14TH FLOOR
NEW YORK, NEW YORK 10018

February 12, 2008

Securities and Exchange Commission

100 F Street, NE
Washington, DC 20549
Attention: Chief Counsel,
Division of Corporation Finance

Re: Request by Standard Pacific Corp. to omit stockholder proposal submitted by The Nathan Cummings Foundation

Dear Sir/Madam: . . .

By letter dated January 18, 2008, Standard Pacific stated that it intends to omit the Proposal from the proxy materials to be sent to stockholders in connection with the 2008 annual meeting of stockholders and asked for assurance that the Staff would not recommend enforcement action if it did so. Standard Pacific argues that it is entitled to omit the Proposal in reliance on Rule 14a–8(i)(7), which allows a company to exclude a proposal that "deals with a matter related to the company's ordinary business operations." As set forth more fully below, Standard Pacific has not met its burden of establishing its entitlement to exclude the Proposal, and we respectfully urge that its request for relief be denied.

The Proposal Focuses on Minimizing or Eliminating Operations That May Adversely Affect the Environment, not on an Internal Assessment of Risks or Liabilities

In applying the ordinary business exclusion to proposals dealing with environmental and public health matters, the staff distinguishes between proposals that focus on "an internal assessment of the risks or liabilities that the company faces as a result of its operations that may adversely affect the environment or the public's health," which are excludable, and proposals that "focus on the company minimizing or eliminating operations that may adversely affect the environment or the public's health," which may not be omitted. (See Staff Legal Bulletin ("SLB") 14C) It is clear that the Proposal does not mention risk or speak in terms of financial or cost/benefit analysis. In that sense, the Proposal is distinguishable from the proposals. . . . [cited in the Standard Pacific Corp.'s letter, e.g., Dow Chemical, ACE Ltd., and American International Group, Inc]. The Proposal does not seek disclosure on how a particular issue affects the Company's business strategy, which arguably requires an evaluation of risk.

Nonetheless, Standard Pacific claims that the Proposal is excludable because establishing the quantitative goals requested by the Proposal would require the Company to assess risks, costs, benefits and liabilities. But Standard Pacific's reasoning would obliterate the distinction set forth in SLB 14C. Any measures designed to "minimiz[e] or eliminat[e] operations that may adversely affect they environment" can be said to involve some internal analysis, which might take into account factors such as cost or risk to the company. Indeed, the example used by the Staff in SLB 14C—a proposal asking for a report on "potential damage that would result from the company drilling for oil and gas in protected areas"—would he excludable under Standard Pacific's approach. . . .

To avoid micro-management, the Proposal gives Standard Pacific's board substantial discretion in determining what the goal should be.

Under the approach taken in SLB 14C, . . . exclusion of the Proposal on ordinary business grounds is inappropriate.

The Proposal unambiguously seeks to minimize or eliminate adverse impacts on the environment and does not focus on internal assessment of risks or liabilities. Moreover, there is no question that the subject of reducing a company's contribution to global climate change implicates a significant social policy issue. Accordingly, we respectfully request that the Staff decline to concur with Standard Pacific's view that it is entitled to omit the Proposal in reliance on the ordinary business exclusion.

If you have any questions or need anything further, please do not hesitate to call me at (212) 787–7300. The Foundation appreciates the opportunity to be of assistance in this matter.

Very truly yours,

Laura J. Shaffer
Director of Shareholder Activities

SECURITIES AND EXCHANGE
COMMISSION
WASHINGTON, D.C. 20549

February 28, 2008

Response of the Office of Chief Counsel
Division of Corporation Finance

Re: Standard Pacific Corp.
Incoming letter dated January 18, 2008

The proposal requests that the board adopt quantitative goals, based on available technologies, for reducing total greenhouse gas emissions from the company's products and operations, and report to shareholders on its plans to achieve these goals.

We are unable to concur in your view that Standard Pacific may exclude the proposal under rule 14a–8(i)(7). Accordingly, we do not believe that Standard Pacific may omit the proposal from its proxy materials in reliance on rule 14a–3(i)(7).

Sincerely,

William A. Hines
Special Counsel

As reflected in the following from the SEC's staff, its earlier dichotomy with respect to shareholder proposals related to environmental, financial, health and other risks proved unworkable.

> We have recently witnessed a marked increase in the number of no-action requests in which companies seek to exclude proposals as relating to an evaluation of risk. In these requests, companies have frequently argued that proposals that do not explicitly request an evaluation of risk are nonetheless excludable under Rule 14a–8(i)(7) because they would require the company to engage in risk assessment.
>
> . . . [A]s most corporate decisions involve some evaluation of risk, the evaluation of risk should not be viewed as an end in itself, but rather, as a means to an end. In addition, we have become increasingly cognizant that the adequacy of risk management and oversight can have major consequences for a company and its shareholders. Accordingly, we have reexamined the analysis that we have used for risk proposals, and upon reexamination, we believe that there is a more appropriate framework to apply for analyzing these proposals.
>
> On a going-forward basis, rather than focusing on whether a proposal and supporting statement relate to the company engaging in an evaluation of risk, we will instead focus on the subject matter to which the risk pertains or that gives rise to the risk. The fact that a proposal would require an evaluation of risk will not be dispositive of whether the proposal may be excluded under Rule 14a–8(i)(7). Instead, similar to the way in which we analyze proposals asking for the preparation of a report, the formation of a committee, or the inclusion of disclosure in a Commission-prescribed document—where we look to the underlying subject matter of the report, committee or disclosure to determine whether the proposal relates to ordinary business—we will consider whether the underlying subject matter of the risk evaluation involves a matter of ordinary business to the company. In those cases in which a proposal's underlying subject matter transcends the day-to-day business matters of the company and raises policy issues so significant that it would be appropriate for a shareholder vote, the proposal generally will not be excludable under Rule 14a–8(i)(7) as long as a sufficient nexus exists between the nature of the proposal and the company. Conversely, in those cases in which a proposal's underlying subject matter involves an ordinary business matter to the company, the proposal generally will be excludable under Rule 14a–8(i)(7). . . .
>
> In addition, we note that there is widespread recognition that the board's role in the oversight of a company's management of

risk is a significant policy matter regarding the governance of the corporation. In light of this recognition, a proposal that focuses on the board's role in the oversight of a company's management of risk may transcend the day-to-day business matters of a company and raise policy issues so significant that it would be appropriate for a shareholder vote. . . .

SEC Staff Legal Bulletin 14E (Oct. 27, 2009).

On the overall efficacy of the shareholder proposal rule, consider the following empirical study of 1,454 proposals submitted during the 2002, 2003 and 2004 proxy season.

Randall S. Thomas & James F. Cotter, Shareholder Proposals In the New Millennium: Shareholder Support, Board Response, And Market Reaction

13 J. Corp. Fin. 368, 373 to 378 (2007).

3.1. Descriptive Statistics and Proposal Type . . . . [T]he vast majority of shareholder proposals in our data set fall into four of the six proposal types: compensation proposals (397, or 27.3%), external corporate control and governance proposals (329, or 22.6%), internal corporate control and governance proposals (271, or 18.6%), and other social responsibility proposals (297, or 20.5%). Over 75% of external corporate control/governance shareholder proposals ask shareholders either to repeal a firm's poison pill or to declassify the board of directors.

. . . [We examine] the financial characteristics of the firms that received different types of shareholder proposals during this period. Sample firms tend to be large, with an average market capitalization (shares outstanding times share price) of $43.4 billion, sales of $32.25 billion, and total assets of $92.96 billion. On average, the firms in the final sample were profitable, with a net profit margin of 6.24% and a return on assets of 4.15%. The firms in the final sample have relatively high institutional ownership (67.1%) and relatively low insider ownership (2.8%), which is typical of large, well-established companies. . . .

[W]e see a strong and statistically significant market underperformance of—22.14% by target firms. . . . Overall, we conclude that during the 2002–2004 timeframe, targeted firms were, as in earlier studies, relatively poorly performing companies.

3.2 Shareholder Proposal Sponsor. . . . Individuals sponsor the most proposals (534 proposals, or 36.7%), while labor unions are second (364 proposals, or 25.0%). Each of the other types of sponsors offered smaller numbers of proposals, ranging from 110 (private institutions) to 156 (religious groups) . . . .

[R]eligious groups and social activists sponsor shareholder proposals at much larger firms, with average market capitalizations of

$66.5 and $67.1 billion, respectively that are statistically significantly higher than those of target firms in the rest of the sample. The difference may reflect these groups' interest in pushing for more "corporate social responsibility" at the largest American companies, which may be more susceptible to public opinion. Private institutions tend to sponsor shareholder proposals for firms with somewhat weaker profitability (net margin of 3.85% and return on assets of 3.9%) . . .

3.3 Voting Patterns for Shareholder Proposals. . . . Overall, voting support for shareholder proposals averages 28.38%. The lowest levels of support are shown for proposals sponsored by religious groups (10.35% support) and social activists (12.64%), which are statistically significantly lower than all other categories of proposals. This is consistent with the prior literature surveyed by Romano (2001) and with the idea that shareholders perceive these sponsors as less concerned about firm value. At the other end of the scale, proposals sponsored by individuals and private institutions received the highest votes, at 36.02% and 35.44%, respectively. . . . [S]hareholder proposals sponsored by unions and public institutional investors garnered less shareholder support, averaging 30.88% and 23.19%, respectively.

High levels of shareholder support are concentrated in external corporate control and governance proposals, supporting the view that shareholders believe these proposals can positively impact firm's corporate governance structure. . . . [O]n average 56.57% (60.87% median) of votes cast in favor of these proposals, a statistically significantly higher percentage than for all other types, including other types of corporate governance proposals. For example, auditor independence proposals garnered only 20.96% support on average, perhaps reflecting their uncertain effect on shareholder value. Similarly, internal corporate control and governance proposals averaged 23.2% shareholder support, with some variation by sponsor type, which, again, may reflect their questionable relationship to shareholder value. . . .

Compensation proposals largely concentrate on expensing stock options, awarding performance-based pay, or requiring a vote on future golden parachutes for top executives. The underlying average level of support, 27.45% of votes cast, conceals some large disparities in support levels by sponsor type, with private institutions, unions, and public institutions getting much higher levels than individuals, religious groups, and social activists. . . .

[T]he type of proposals that sponsoring groups submit has an impact on their overall ability to attract votes. This difference is most apparent for unions during our sample period, as they overwhelmingly concentrated their efforts on compensation proposals (225 out of the 397, or 56.6% of all of their proposals), which are less attractive to other shareholders than external corporate governance proposals. Similarly, public institutions sponsored a significant number of social responsibility proposals over this period (77 out of 154, or 50% of all of their proposals), which receive a low percentage of favorable votes. By contrast, individuals submitted 227 out of a total of 329 proposals (69%) in the external corporate control and governance category, which is the highest vote-getting area, and another 166 (61.1%) in the internal corporate control and governance area, which is the third highest category in overall favorable vote percentage. Private institutions show the same pattern as that for individuals.

More generally, if we aggregate proposal types into corporate governance proposals and social responsibility proposals, we find that the former (1,051 proposals) are approved on average by approximately 34.14% of the votes cast, while the latter (402 proposals) average only 10.75% of the votes cast. These differences are statistically significant. . . .

[We also examine] shareholder proposals that received at least 50% of the votes cast by investors (majority votes). . . . [W]e find that 341 shareholder proposals (23.5%) receive more than 50% of favorable votes. Looking solely at corporate governance proposals, we see that 32.2% of the total number (338 out of 1,051) received more than 50% of the votes cast, while none of 403 social responsibility proposals won more than 50% of the votes cast.

Board reaction to majority vote shareholder proposals varies substantially. . . . Of the 333 corporate governance proposals that received more than 50% of shareholder votes, companies announced that 103 were fully implemented by the board. . . . [We find] a strong upward trend over time in the degree of board responsiveness to majority vote shareholder proposals. In 2002, boards expressly reacted positively to only 15.49% of the corporate governance proposals that attracted majority support, increasing to 23.81% in 2003. In 2004, however, boards took the action requested on 50.42% of the corporate governance proposals and none of the social responsibility proposals. . . . [P]oison-pill redemption proposals were most frequently implemented, with 44 pills removed or allowed to expire, while boards agreed to declassify staggered boards in 31 cases. The number of pill redemptions and board declassifications increased substantially in 2004. . . .

C. Shareholder Access to the Nominating Process

The SEC proxy initiative that has generated the strongest reaction from management and institutional investors has been whether the proxy rules authorize shareholder initiatives to nominate individuals to stand for election to the board of directors. Momentum for stockholders having access to the director nomination process was provided by a 2003 SEC staff report recommending that large, long-term holders under very limited circumstances should have the right to nominate individuals to stand for election to the board. SEC, Securities Exchange Act Rel. No. 48626 (Oct. 14, 2003). The report was greeted by a firestorm of protest from both sides of the issue. Managers loudly complained that any shareholder nomination procedure intruded on their prerogatives. Investor groups believed the proposal did not go far enough, arguing that the conditions recommended by the SEC under which shareholders could nominate directors were so extreme that the right would rarely arise. Into this maelstrom, some institutions pursued self help, submitting their own proposals under Rule 14a–8 to amend the company bylaws to authorize shareholders to nominate directors. Their efforts were met by the SEC interpreting then Rule 14a–8(i)(8)'s bar of proposals related to the election a director as also barring proposals bearing on how directors are nominated. The SEC's interpretation was rejected in American Federation of State, County & Municipal Employees v. American International Group, Inc., 462 F.3d 121 (2d Cir. 2006). In the shadow of this defeat, the SEC amended Rule 14a–8(i)(8) to expressly provide that a proposal could be omitted if the "proposal relates to a nomination" of a director. At the same time, provisions in Delaware and the Model Act were amended to expressly authorize bylaw provisions that authorized procedures for stockholders to nominate directors as well as bylaws authorizing reimbursement of insurgent proxy expenses. *See* Del. Code Ann. tit. 8 § 112 (2009); MBCA § 2.06. In July 2010, Congress passed the sweeping financial reform legislation, The Dodd–Frank Wall Street Reform and Consumer Protection Act amended section 14(a) of the Exchange Act to expressly authorize the SEC to adopt rules providing for shareholders to nominate directors to the boards of reporting companies. Swiftly following the enactment of Dodd–Frank, the SEC adopted Rule 14a–11.

Securities Exchange Act Rule 14a–11

In broad overview, Rule 14a–11 provides shareholders and shareholder groups who collectively have held investment and voting power of at least 3 percent of the voting power of a company's securities continuously for 3 years the right to have nominees on the company's ballot. The right extends to a maximum of 25 percent of the entire board (a minimum of one director). If there are multiple nominating stockholders who in combination nominate more nominees than permitted under the rule, the candidates nominated by the largest holder or shareholder group have priority. Shareholders intending to invoke the rights under the rule must communicate their intent on new Schedule 14N no earlier than 150 days and not later than 120 days prior to the date the company mailed its proxy materials in the preceding year. Certain disclosures are required to be made including an undertaking that the process is not being used to change control of the company. If the company chooses to challenge the nominator's standing, etc. it must do so not later than 80 days before management file's is proxy statement.

The SEC has since amended Rule 14a–8(i)(8) to expressly allow shareholders to make proposals to broaden (but not narrow) proxy access as provided in Rule 14a–11.

SECTION 4. MATERIALLY MISLEADING PROXIES AND RULE 14a–9

SECURITIES EXCHANGE ACT RULE 14a–9

[See Statutory Supplement]

NOTE ON J.I. CASE CO. v. BORAK

In J.I. Case Co. v. Borak, 377 U.S. 426, 84 S.Ct. 1555, 12 L.Ed.2d 423 (1964), the Supreme Court held that a shareholder could bring a private action for violation of the Proxy Rules, although neither the 1934 Act nor the Proxy Rules themselves explicitly provide for such an action. The rationale in *Borak* was as follows:

> . . . Private enforcement of the proxy rules provides a necessary supplement to Commission action. As in antitrust treble damage litigation, the possibility of civil damages or injunctive relief serves as a most effective weapon in the enforcement of the proxy requirements. The Commission advises that it examines over 2,000 proxy statements annually and each of them must necessarily be expedited. Time does not permit an independent examination of the facts set out in the proxy material and this results in the Commission's acceptance of the representations contained therein at their face value, unless contrary to other material on file with it. Indeed, on the allegations of respondent's complaint, the proxy material failed to disclose alleged unlawful market manipulation of the stock of ATC, and this unlawful manipulation would not have been apparent to the Commission until after the merger.
>
> We, therefore, believe that under the circumstances here it is the duty of the courts to be alert to provide such remedies as are necessary to make effective the congressional purpose.

Id. at 432–33, 84 S.Ct. at 1560.

WYANDOTTE v. U.S., 389 U.S. 191, 202, 88 S.Ct. 379, 19 L.Ed.2d 407 (1967). "In [J.I. Case Co. v. Borak] we concluded that criminal liability was inadequate to ensure the full effectiveness of the statute which Congress had intended. Because the interest of the plaintiffs in those cases fell within the class that the statute was intended to protect, and because the harm that had occurred was of the type that the statute was intended to protect, and because the harm that had occurred was of the type that the statute was intended to forestall, we held that civil actions were proper. That conclusion was in accordance with a general rule of the law of torts. See Restatement (Second) of Torts § 286."

CORT v. ASH, 422 U.S. 66, 95 S.Ct. 2080, 45 L.Ed.2d 26 (1975). "In determining whether a private remedy is implicit in a statute not expressly providing one, several factors are relevant. First, is the plaintiff 'one of the class for whose *especial* benefit the statute was enacted,' Texas & Pacific R. Co. v. Rigsby, 241 U.S. 33, 39, 36 S.Ct. 482, 484, 60 L.Ed. 874 (1916) (emphasis supplied)—that is, does the statute create a federal right in favor of the plaintiff? Second, is there any indication of legislative intent, explicit or implicit, either to create such a remedy or to deny one? . . . Third, is it consistent with the underlying purposes of the legislative scheme to imply such a remedy for the plaintiff? . . . And finally, is the cause of action one traditionally relegated to state law, in an area basically the concern of the States, so that it would be inappropriate to infer a cause of action based solely on federal law?"

Mills v. Electric Auto–Lite Co.

Supreme Court of the United States, 1970.
396 U.S. 375, 90 S.Ct. 616, 24 L.Ed.2d 593.

■ MR. JUSTICE HARLAN delivered the opinion of the Court.

This case requires us to consider a basic aspect of the implied private right of action for violation of § 14(a) of the Securities Exchange Act of 1934,[1] recognized by this Court in J.I. Case Co. v. Borak, 377 U.S. 426, 84 S.Ct. 1555, 12 L.Ed.2d 423 (1964). As in *Borak* the asserted wrong is that a corporate merger was accomplished through the use of a proxy statement that was materially false or misleading. The question with which we deal is what causal relationship must be shown between such a statement and the merger to establish a cause of action based on the violation of the Act.

I

Petitioners were shareholders of the Electric Auto–Lite Company until 1963, when it was merged into Mergenthaler Linotype Company. They brought suit on the day before the shareholders' meeting at which the vote was to take place on the merger, against Auto–Lite, Mergenthaler, and a third company, American Manufacturing Company, Inc. The complaint sought an injunction against the voting by Auto–Lite's management of all proxies obtained by means of an allegedly misleading proxy solicitation; however, it did not seek a temporary restraining order, and the voting went ahead as scheduled the following day. Several months later petitioners filed an amended complaint, seeking to have the merger set aside and to obtain such other relief as might be proper.

In Count II of the amended complaint, which is the only count before us,[5] petitioners predicated jurisdiction on § 27 of the 1934 Act,

---

1. 48 Stat. 895, as amended, 15 U.S.C. § 78n(a).

5. In the other two counts, petitioners alleged common-law fraud and that the merger was *ultra vires* under Ohio law.

15 U.S.C. § 78aa. They alleged that the proxy statement sent out by the Auto–Lite management to solicit shareholders' votes in favor of the merger was misleading, in violation of § 14(a) of the Act and SEC Rule 14a–9 thereunder. (17 CFR § 240.14a–9.) Petitioners recited that before the merger Mergenthaler owned over 50% of the outstanding shares of Auto–Lite common stock, and had been in control of Auto–Lite for two years. American Manufacturing in turn owned about one-third of the outstanding shares of Mergenthaler, and for two years had been in voting control of Mergenthaler and, through it, of Auto–Lite. Petitioners charged that in light of these circumstances the proxy statement was misleading in that it told Auto–Lite shareholders that their board of directors recommended approval of the merger without also informing them that all 11 of Auto–Lite's directors were nominees of Mergenthaler and were under the "control and domination of Mergenthaler." Petitioners asserted the right to complain of this alleged violation both derivatively on behalf of Auto–Lite and as representatives of the class of all its minority shareholders.

On petitioners' motion for summary judgment with respect to Count II, the District Court for the Northern District of Illinois ruled as a matter of law that the claimed defect in the proxy statement was, in light of the circumstances in which the statement was made, a material omission. The District Court concluded, from its reading of the *Borak* opinion, that it had to hold a hearing on the issue whether there was "a causal connection between the finding that there has been a violation of the disclosure requirements of § 14(a) and the alleged injury to the plaintiffs" before it could consider what remedies would be appropriate. (Unreported opinion dated February 14, 1966.)

After holding such a hearing, the court found that under the terms of the merger agreement, an affirmative vote of two-thirds of the Auto–Lite shares was required for approval of the merger, and that the respondent companies owned and controlled about 54% of the outstanding shares. Therefore, to obtain authorization of the merger, respondents had to secure the approval of a substantial number of the minority shareholders. At the stockholders' meeting, approximately 950,000 shares, out of 1,160,000 shares outstanding, were voted in favor of the merger. This included 317,000 votes obtained by proxy from the minority shareholders, votes that were "necessary and indispensable to the approval of the merger." The District Court concluded that a causal relationship had thus been shown, and it granted an interlocutory judgment in favor of petitioners on the issue of liability, referring the case to a master for consideration of appropriate relief. (Unreported findings and conclusions dated Sept. 26, 1967; opinion reported at 281 F.Supp. 826 (1967)).

The District Court made the certification required by 28 U.S.C. § 1292(b), and respondents took an interlocutory appeal to the Court of Appeals for the Seventh Circuit. That court affirmed the District Court's conclusion that the proxy statement was materially deficient, but reversed on the question of causation. The court acknowledged that, if an injunction had been sought a sufficient time before the stockholders' meeting, "corrective measures would have been appropriate." 403 F.2d 429, 435 (1968). However, since this suit was brought too late for preventive action, the courts had to determine "whether the misleading statement and omission caused the submission of sufficient proxies," as a prerequisite to a determination of liability under the Act. If the respondents could show, "by a preponderance of probabilities, that the merger would have received a sufficient vote even if the proxy statement had not been misleading in the respect found," petitioners would be entitled to no relief of any kind. *Id.,* at 436.

The Court of Appeals acknowledged that this test corresponds to the common-law fraud test of whether the injured party relied on the misrepresentation. However, rightly concluding that "[r]eliance by thousands of individuals, as here, can scarcely be inquired into" (*id.,* at 436 n. 10), the court ruled that the issue was to be determined by proof of the fairness of the terms of the merger. If respondents could show that the merger had merit and was fair to the minority shareholders, the trial court would be justified in concluding that a sufficient number of shareholders would have approved the merger had there been no deficiency in the proxy statement. In that case respondents would be entitled to a judgment in their favor.

Claiming that the Court of Appeals has construed this Court's decision in *Borak* in a manner that frustrates the statute's policy of enforcement through private litigation, the petitioners then sought review in this Court. We granted certiorari, 394 U.S. 971, 89 S.Ct. 1470, 22 L.Ed.2d 752 (1969), believing that resolution of this basic issue should be made at this stage of the litigation and not postponed until after a trial under the Court of Appeals' decision.

II

As we stressed in *Borak,* § 14(a) stemmed from a congressional belief that "[f]air corporate suffrage is an important right that should attach to every equity security bought on a public exchange." H.R.Rep. No. 1383, 73d Cong., 2d Sess., 13. The provision was intended to promote "the free exercise of the voting rights of stockholders" by ensuring that proxies would be solicited with "explanation to the stockholder of the real nature of the questions for which authority to cast his vote is sought." *Id.,* at 14; S.Rep. No. 792, 73d Cong., 2d Sess., 12; see 377 U.S., at 431, 377 U.S. 426, 84 S.Ct. 1555, 1559, 12 L.Ed.2d 423. The decision below, by permitting all liability to be foreclosed on the basis of a finding that the merger was fair, would allow the stockholders to be bypassed, at least where the only legal challenge to the merger is a suit for retrospective relief after the meeting has been held. A judicial appraisal of the merger's merits could be substituted for the actual and informed vote of the stockholders.

The result would be to insulate from private redress an entire category of proxy violations—those relating to matters other than the terms of the merger. Even outrageous misrepresentations in a proxy solicitation, if they did not relate to the terms of the transaction, would give rise to no cause of action under § 14(a). Particularly if carried over to enforcement actions by the Securities and Exchange Commission itself, such a result would subvert the congressional purpose of ensuring full and fair disclosure to shareholders.

Further, recognition of the fairness of the merger as a complete defense would confront small shareholders with an additional obstacle to making a successful challenge to a proposal recommended through a defective proxy statement. The risk that they would be unable to rebut the corporation's evidence of the fairness of the proposal, and thus to establish their cause of action, would be bound to discourage such shareholders from the private enforcement of the proxy rules that "provides a necessary supplement to Commission action." J.I. Case Co. v. Borak, 377 U.S., at 432, 84 S.Ct. at 1560.[9]

Such a frustration of the congressional policy is not required by anything in the wording of the statute or in our opinion in the *Borak* case. Section 14(a) declares it "unlawful" to solicit proxies in contravention of Commission rules, and SEC Rule 14a–9 prohibits solicitations "containing any statement which . . . is false or misleading with respect to any material fact, or which omits to state any material fact necessary in order to make the statements therein not false or misleading. . . ." Use of a solicitation that is materially misleading is itself a violation of law, as the Court of Appeals recognized in stating that injunctive relief would be available to remedy such a defect if sought prior to the stockholders' meeting. In *Borak,* which came to this Court on a dismissal of the complaint, the Court limited its inquiry to whether a violation of § 14(a) gives rise to "a federal cause of action for rescission or damages," 377 U.S., at 428, 84 S.Ct. at 1558. Referring to the argument made by petitioners there "that the merger can be dissolved only if it was fraudulent or non-beneficial, issues upon which the proxy material would not bear," the Court stated: "But the causal relationship of the proxy material and the merger are questions of fact to be resolved at trial, not here. We therefore do not discuss this point further." *Id.,* at 431, 84 S.Ct. at 1559. In the present case there has been a hearing specifically directed to the causation problem. The question before the Court is whether the facts found on the basis of that hearing are sufficient in law to establish petitioners' cause of action, and we conclude that they are.

---

9. The Court of Appeals' ruling that "causation" may be negated by proof of the fairness of the merger also rests on a dubious behavioral assumption. There is no justification for presuming that the shareholders of every corporation are willing to accept any and every fair merger offer put before them; yet such a presumption is implicit in the opinion of the Court of Appeals. That court gave no indication of what evidence petitioners might adduce, once respondents had established that the merger proposal was equitable, in order to show that the shareholders would nevertheless have rejected it if the solicitation had not been misleading. Proof of actual reliance by thousands of individuals would, as the court acknowledged, not be feasible, see R. Jennings & H. Marsh, Securities Regulation, Cases and Materials 1001 (2d ed. 1968); and reliance on the *nondisclosure* of a fact is a particularly difficult matter to define or prove, see 3 L. Loss, Securities Regulation, 1766 (2d ed. 1961). In practice, therefore, the objective fairness of the proposal would seemingly be determinative of liability. But, in view of the many other factors that might lead shareholders to prefer their current position to that of owners of a larger, combined enterprise, it is pure conjecture to assume that the fairness of the proposal will always be determinative of their vote. Cf. Wirtz v. Hotel, Motel & Club Employees Union, 391 U.S. 492, 508, 88 S.Ct. 1743, 1752, 20 L.Ed.2d 763 (1968).

Where the misstatement or omission in a proxy statement has been shown to be "material," as it was found to be here, that determination itself indubitably embodies a conclusion that the defect was of such a character that it might have been considered important by a reasonable shareholder who was in the process of deciding how to vote.[10] This requirement that the defect have a significant *propensity* to affect the voting process is found in the express terms of Rule 14a–9, and it adequately serves the purpose of ensuring that a cause of action cannot be established by proof of a defect so trivial, or so unrelated to the transaction for which approval is sought, that correction of the defect or imposition of liability would not further the interests protected by § 14(a).

There is no need to supplement this requirement, as did the Court of Appeals, with a requirement of proof of whether the defect actually had a decisive effect on the voting. Where there has been a finding of materiality, a shareholder has made a sufficient showing of causal relationship between the violation and the injury for which he seeks redress if, as here, he proves that the proxy solicitation itself, rather than the particular defect in the solicitation materials, was an essential link in the accomplishment of the transaction. This objective test will avoid the impracticalities of determining how many votes were affected, and, by resolving doubts in favor of those the statute is designed to protect, will effectuate the congressional policy of ensuring that the shareholders are able to make an informed choice when they are consulted on corporate transactions. . . .

III

Our conclusion that petitioners have established their case by showing that proxies necessary to approval of the merger were obtained by means of a materially misleading solicitation implies nothing about the form of relief to which they may be entitled. We held in *Borak* that upon finding a violation the courts were "to be alert to provide such remedies as are necessary to make effective the congressional purpose," noting specifically that such remedies are not to be limited to prospective relief. 377 U.S., at 433, 434, 84 S.Ct. at 1560. In devising retrospective relief for violation of the proxy rules, the federal courts should consider the same factors that would govern the relief granted for any similar illegality or fraud. One important factor may be the fairness of the terms of the merger. Possible forms of relief will include setting aside the merger or granting other equitable relief, but, as the Court of Appeals below noted, nothing in the statutory policy

10. . . . In this case, where the misleading aspect of the solicitation involved failure to reveal a serious conflict of interest on the part of the directors, the Court of Appeals concluded that the crucial question in determining materiality was "whether the minority shareholders were sufficiently alerted to the board's relationship to their adversary to be on their guard." 403 F.2d at 434. An adequate disclosure of this relationship would have warned the stockholders to give more careful scrutiny to the terms of the merger than they might to one recommended by an entirely disinterested board. Thus, the failure to make such a disclosure was found to be a material defect "as a matter of law," thwarting the informed decision at which the statute aims, regardless of whether the terms of the merger were such that a reasonable stockholder would have approved the transaction after more careful analysis. See also Swanson v. American Consumer Industries, Inc., 415 F.2d 1326 (C.A.7th Cir.1969).

"requires the court to unscramble a corporate transaction merely because a violation occurred." 403 F.2d at 436. In selecting a remedy the lower courts should exercise " 'the sound discretion which guides the determinations of courts of equity,' " keeping in mind the role of equity as "the instrument for nice adjustment and reconciliation between the public interest and private needs as well as between competing private claims." Hecht Co. v. Bowles, 321 U.S. 321, 329–330, 64 S.Ct. 587, 591–592, 88 L.Ed. 754 (1944), quoting from Meredith v. Winter Haven, 320 U.S. 228, 235, 64 S.Ct. 7, 11, 88 L.Ed. 9 (1943)....

... [A] determination of what relief should be granted in Auto–Lite's name must hinge on whether setting aside the merger would be in the best interests of the shareholders as a whole. In short, in the context of a suit such as this one, § 29(b) leaves the matter of relief where it would be under *Borak* without specific statutory language—the merger should be set aside only if a court of equity concludes, from all the circumstances, that it would be equitable to do so. Cf. SEC v. National Securities, Inc., 393 U.S. 453, 456, 463–464, 89 S.Ct. 564, 566, 570, 21 L.Ed.2d 668 (1969).

Monetary relief will, of course, also be a possibility. Where the defect in the proxy solicitation relates to the specific terms of the merger, the district court might appropriately order an accounting to ensure that the shareholders receive the value that was represented as coming to them. On the other hand, where, as here, the misleading aspect of the solicitation did not relate to terms of the merger, monetary relief might be afforded to the shareholders only if the merger resulted in a reduction of the earnings or earnings potential of their holdings. In short, damages should be recoverable only to the extent that they can be shown. If commingling of the assets and operations of the merged companies makes it impossible to establish direct injury from the merger, relief might be predicated on a determination of the fairness of the terms of the merger at the time it was approved. These questions, of course, are for decision in the first instance by the District Court on remand, and our singling out of some of the possibilities is not intended to exclude others....

For the foregoing reasons we conclude that the judgment of the Court of Appeals should be vacated and the case remanded to that court for further proceedings consistent with this opinion.

It is so ordered.

[The opinion of Justice Black, concurring in part and dissenting in part, is omitted.]

NOTE ON FURTHER PROCEEDINGS IN MILLS v. ELECTRIC AUTO–LITE

On remand, the District Court held the exchange to be unfair and awarded damages of $1,233,918.35, as well as approximately $740,000 in pre-judgment interest. The Seventh Circuit reversed, concluding that the merger terms were fair and the plaintiff was therefore not entitled to damages. 552 F.2d 1239 (7th Cir.1977), cert. denied, 434 U.S. 922, 98 S.Ct. 398, 54 L.Ed.2d 279.

NOTE ON MATERIALITY: TSC INDUSTRIES INC. v. NORTHWAY, INC.

In TSC Industries, Inc. v. Northway, Inc., 426 U.S. 438, 96 S.Ct. 2126, 48 L.Ed.2d 757 (1976), the Supreme Court addressed the issue of how materiality was to be defined, as follows:

> ... [I]n *Mills,* ... we held that there was no need to demonstrate that the alleged defect in the proxy statement actually had a decisive effect on the voting. So long as the misstatement or omission was material, the causal relation between violation and injury is sufficiently established, we concluded, if "the proxy solicitation itself ... was an essential link in the accomplishment of the transaction." 396 U.S., at 385, 90 S.Ct., at 622. After *Mills,* then, the content given to the notion of materiality assumes heightened significance....
>
> The question of materiality, it is universally agreed, is an objective one, involving the significance of an omitted or misrepresented fact to a reasonable investor. Variations in the formulation of a general test of materiality occur in the articulation of just how significant a fact must be or, put another way, how certain it must be that the fact would affect a reasonable investor's judgment....
>
> The Court of Appeals in this case concluded that material facts include "all facts which a reasonable shareholder *might* consider important." 512 F.2d, at 330 (emphasis added). This formulation of the test of materiality has been explicitly rejected by at least two courts as setting too low a threshold for the imposition of liability under Rule 14a–9. Gerstle v. Gamble-Skogmo, Inc., 478 F.2d 1281, 1301–1302 (C.A.2 1973); Smallwood v. Pearl Brewing Co., 489 F.2d 579, 603–604 (C.A.5 1974)....
>
> ... [T]he disclosure policy embodied in the proxy regulations is not without limit. See id., at 384, 90 S.Ct., at 621. Some information is of such dubious significance that insistence on its disclosure may accomplish more harm than good. The potential liability for a Rule 14a–9 violation can be great indeed, and if the standard of materiality is unnecessarily low, not only may the corporation and its management be subjected to liability for insignificant omissions or misstatements, but also management's fear of exposing itself to substantial liability may cause it simply to bury the shareholder in an avalanche of trivial information—a result that is hardly conducive to informed decisionmaking. Precisely these dangers are presented, we think, by the definition of a

> material fact adopted by the Court of Appeals in this case—a fact which a reasonable shareholder *might* consider important. We agree with Judge Friendly, speaking for the Court of Appeals in *Gerstle,* that the "might" formulation is "too suggestive of mere possibility, however unlikely." 478 F.2d, at 1302.
>
> The general standard of materiality that we think best comports with the policies of Rule 14a–9 is as follows: an omitted fact is material if there is a substantial likelihood that a reasonable shareholder would consider it important in deciding how to vote. This standard is fully consistent with *Mills* general description of materiality as a requirement that "the defect have a significant *propensity* to affect the voting process." It does not require proof of a substantial likelihood that disclosure of the omitted fact would have caused the reasonable investor to change his vote. What the standard does contemplate is a showing of a substantial likelihood that, under all the circumstances, the omitted fact would have assumed actual significance in the deliberations of the reasonable shareholder. Put another way, there must be a substantial likelihood that the disclosure of the omitted fact would have been viewed by the reasonable investor as having significantly altered the "total mix" of information made available.

What are the characteristics of the reasonable shareholder by which materiality determinations are made. Should this be an expansive or restricted interpretation of the probable information needs of the reasonable shareholder?

> Speculators and chartists of Wall and Bay Streets are also "reasonable" investors entitled to the same legal protection afforded conservative traders. Thus, material facts include not only information disclosing the earnings and distributions of a company but also those facts which affect the probable future of the company and those which affect the desire of investors to buy, sell or hold the company securities.

SEC v. Texas Gulf Sulphur Co., 401 F.2d 833, 849 (2d Cir. 1968), *cert. denied*, 394 U.S. 976 (1969).

Virginia Bankshares, Inc. v. Sandberg

Supreme Court of the United States, 1991.
501 U.S. 1083, 111 S.Ct. 2749, 115 L.Ed.2d 929.

■ . . . JUSTICE SOUTER delivered the opinion of the Court.

Section 14(a) of the Securities Exchange Act of 1934, 48 Stat. 895, 15 U.S.C. § 78n(a), authorizes the Securities and Exchange Commission to adopt rules for the solicitation of proxies, and prohibits their violation. In J.I. Case Co. v. Borak, 377 U.S. 426, 84 S.Ct. 1555, 12 L.Ed.2d 423 (1964), we first recognized an implied private right of action for the breach of § 14(a) as implemented by SEC Rule 14a–9, which prohibits the solicitation of proxies by means of materially false or misleading statements.[2]

The questions before us are whether a statement couched in conclusory or qualitative terms purporting to explain directors' reasons for recommending certain corporate action can be materially misleading within the meaning of Rule 14a–9, and whether causation of damages compensable under § 14(a) can be shown by a member of a class of minority shareholders whose votes are not required by law or corporate bylaw to authorize the corporate action subject to the proxy solicitation. We hold that knowingly false statements of reasons may be actionable even though conclusory in form, but that respondents have failed to demonstrate the equitable basis required to extend the § 14(a) private action to such shareholders when any indication of congressional intent to do so is lacking.

I

In December 1986, First American Bankshares, Inc., (FABI), a bank holding company, began a "freeze-out" merger, in which the First American Bank of Virginia (Bank) eventually merged into Virginia Bankshares, Inc., (VBI), a wholly owned subsidiary of FABI. VBI owned 85% of the Bank's shares, the remaining 15% being in the hands of some 2,000 minority shareholders. FABI hired the investment banking firm of Keefe, Bruyette & Woods (KBW) to give an opinion on the appropriate price for shares of the minority holders, who would lose their interests in the Bank as a result of the merger. Based on market quotations and unverified information from FABI, KBW gave the Bank's executive committee an opinion that $42 a share would be a fair price for the minority stock. The executive committee approved the merger proposal at that price, and the full board followed suit.

Although Virginia law required only that such a merger proposal be submitted to a vote at a shareholders' meeting, and that the meeting be preceded by circulation of a statement of information to the shareholders, the directors nevertheless solicited proxies for voting on the proposal at the annual meeting set for April 21, 1987.[3] In their solicitation, the directors urged the proposal's adoption and stated they had approved the plan because of its opportunity for the minority shareholders to achieve a "high" value, which they elsewhere described as a "fair" price, for their stock.

Although most minority shareholders gave the proxies requested, respondent Sandberg did not, and after approval of the merger she sought damages in the United States District Court for the Eastern

---

2. . . .

The Federal Deposit Insurance Corporation (FDIC) administers and enforces the securities laws with respect to the activities of federally insured and regulated banks. See Section 12(i) of the Exchange Act, 15 U.S.C. § 78*l*(i). An FDIC rule also prohibits materially misleading statements in the solicitation of proxies, 12 CFR § 335.206 (1991), and is essentially identical to Rule 14a–9. See generally Brief for SEC et al. as Amici Curiae 4, n. 5.

3. Had the directors chosen to issue a statement instead of a proxy solicitation, they would have been subject to an SEC antifraud provision analogous to Rule 14a–9. See 17 CFR 240.14c–6 (1990). See also 15 U.S.C. § 78n(c).

District of Virginia from VBI, FABI, and the directors of the Bank. She pleaded two counts, one for soliciting proxies in violation of § 14(a) and Rule 14a–9, and the other for breaching fiduciary duties owed to the minority shareholders under state law. Under the first count, Sandberg alleged, among other things, that the directors had not believed that the price offered was high or that the terms of the merger were fair, but had recommended the merger only because they believed they had no alternative if they wished to remain on the board. At trial, Sandberg invoked language from this Court's opinion in Mills v. Electric Auto–Lite Co., 396 U.S. 375, 385, 90 S.Ct. 616, 622, 24 L.Ed.2d 593 (1970), to obtain an instruction that the jury could find for her without a showing of her own reliance on the alleged misstatements, so long as they were material and the proxy solicitation was an "essential link" in the merger process.

The jury's verdicts were for Sandberg on both counts, after finding violations of Rule 14a–9 by all defendants and a breach of fiduciary duties by the Bank's directors. The jury awarded Sandberg $18 a share, having found that she would have received $60 if her stock had been valued adequately. . . .

On appeal, the United States Court of Appeals for the Fourth Circuit affirmed . . ., holding that certain statements in the proxy solicitation were materially misleading for purposes of the Rule, and that respondents could maintain their action even though their votes had not been needed to effectuate the merger. 891 F.2d 1112 (1989).[4] We granted certiorari because of the importance of the issues presented. 495 U.S. 903, 110 S.Ct. 1921, 109 L.Ed.2d 285 (1990).

II

The Court of Appeals affirmed petitioners' liability for two statements found to have been materially misleading in violation of § 14(a) of the Act, one of which was that "The Plan of Merger has been approved by the Board of Directors because it provides an opportunity for the Bank's public shareholders to achieve a high value for their shares." App. to Pet. for Cert. 53a. Petitioners argue that statements of opinion or belief incorporating indefinite and unverifiable expressions cannot be actionable as misstatements of material fact within the meaning of Rule 14a–9, and that such a declaration of opinion or belief should never be actionable when placed in a proxy solicitation incorporating statements of fact sufficient to enable readers to draw their own, independent conclusions.

A

We consider first the actionability per se of statements of reasons, opinion or belief. Because such a statement by definition purports to express what is consciously on the speaker's mind, we interpret the

4. The Court of Appeals reversed the District Court, however, on its refusal to certify a class of all minority shareholders in Sandberg's action. Consequently, it ruled that petitioners were liable to all of the Bank's former minority shareholders for $18 per share. 891 F.2d, at 1119.

jury verdict as finding that the directors' statements of belief and opinion were made with knowledge that the directors did not hold the beliefs or opinions expressed, and we confine our discussion to statements so made.[5] That such statements may be materially significant raises no serious question. The meaning of the materiality requirement for liability under § 14(a) was discussed at some length in TSC Industries, Inc. v. Northway, Inc., 426 U.S. 438, 96 S.Ct. 2126, 48 L.Ed.2d 757 (1976), where we held a fact to be material "if there is a substantial likelihood that a reasonable shareholder would consider it important in deciding how to vote." Id., at 449, 96 S.Ct., at 2132. We think there is no room to deny that a statement of belief by corporate directors about a recommended course of action, or an explanation of their reasons for recommending it, can take on just that importance. Shareholders know that directors usually have knowledge and expertness far exceeding the normal investor's resources, and the directors' perceived superiority is magnified even further by the common knowledge that state law customarily obliges them to exercise their judgment in the shareholders' interest. Cf. Day v. Avery, 179 U.S.App.D.C. 63, 71, 548 F.2d 1018, 1026 (1976) (action for misrepresentation). Naturally, then, the share owner faced with a proxy request will think it important to know the directors' beliefs about the course they recommend, and their specific reasons for urging the stockholders to embrace it.

B

1

But, assuming materiality, the question remains whether statements of reasons, opinions, or beliefs are statements "with respect to ... material fact[s]" so as to fall within the strictures of the Rule. Petitioners argue that we would invite wasteful litigation of amorphous issues outside the readily provable realm of fact if we were to recognize liability here on proof that the directors did not recommend the merger for the stated reason....

Attacks on the truth of directors' statements of reasons or belief, however, need carry no such threats. Such statements are factual in two senses: as statements that the directors do act for the reasons given or hold the belief stated and as statements about the subject matter of the reason or belief expressed. In neither sense does the proof or disproof of such statements implicate the concerns expressed in Blue Chip Stamps [v. Manor Drug Stores, 421 U.S. 723, 95 S.Ct. 1917, 44 L.Ed.2d 539 (1975)]. The root of those concerns was a plaintiff's capacity to manufacture claims of hypothetical action, unconstrained by independent evidence. Reasons for directors' recommendations or statements of belief are, in contrast, characteristically matters of corporate record subject to documentation, to be supported or attacked by evidence of historical fact outside a plaintiff's

5. In TSC Industries, Inc. v. Northway, Inc., 426 U.S. 438, 444, n. 7, 96 S.Ct. 2126, 2130, n. 7, 48 L.Ed.2d 757 (1976), we reserved the question whether scienter was necessary for liability generally under § 14(a). We reserve it still.

control. Such evidence would include not only corporate minutes and other statements of the directors themselves, but circumstantial evidence bearing on the facts that would reasonably underlie the reasons claimed and the honesty of any statement that those reasons are the basis for a recommendation or other action, a point that becomes especially clear when the reasons or beliefs go to valuations in dollars and cents.

It is no answer to argue, as petitioners do, that the quoted statement on which liability was predicated did not express a reason in dollars and cents, but focused instead on the "indefinite and unverifiable" term, "high" value, much like the similar claim that the merger's terms were "fair" to shareholders. The objection ignores the fact that such conclusory terms in a commercial context are reasonably understood to rest on a factual basis that justifies them as accurate, the absence of which renders them misleading. Provable facts either furnish good reasons to make a conclusory commercial judgment, or they count against it, and expressions of such judgments can be uttered with knowledge of truth or falsity just like more definite statements, and defended or attacked through the orthodox evidentiary process that either substantiates their underlying justifications or tends to disprove their existence. . . . In this case, whether $42 was "high," and the proposal "fair" to the minority shareholders depended on whether provable facts about the Bank's assets, and about actual and potential levels of operation, substantiated a value that was above, below, or more or less at the $42 figure, when assessed in accordance with recognized methods of valuation.

Respondents adduced evidence for just such facts in proving that the statement was misleading about its subject matter and a false expression of the directors' reasons. Whereas the proxy statement described the $42 price as offering a premium above both book value and market price, the evidence indicated that a calculation of the book figure based on the appreciated value of the Bank's real estate holdings eliminated any such premium. The evidence on the significance of market price showed that KBW had conceded that the market was closed, thin and dominated by FABI, facts omitted from the statement. There was, indeed, evidence of a "going concern" value for the Bank in excess of $60 per share of common stock, another fact never disclosed. However conclusory the directors' statement may have been, then, it was open to attack by garden-variety evidence, subject neither to a plaintiff's control nor ready manufacture, and there was no undue risk of open-ended liability or uncontrollable litigation in allowing respondents the opportunity for recovery on the allegation that it was misleading to call $42 "high." . . .

2

Under § 14(a), then, a plaintiff is permitted to prove a specific statement of reason knowingly false or misleadingly incomplete, even when stated in conclusory terms. In reaching this conclusion we have considered statements of reasons of the sort exemplified here, which misstate the speaker's reasons and also mislead about the stated subject matter (e.g., the value of the shares). A statement of belief may be open to objection only in the former respect, however, solely as a misstatement of the psychological fact of the speaker's belief in what he says. In this case, for example, the Court of Appeals alluded to just such limited falsity in observing that "the jury was certainly justified in believing that the directors did not believe a merger at $42 per share was in the minority stockholders' interest but, rather, that they voted as they did for other reasons, e.g., retaining their seats on the board." 891 F.2d, at 1121.

The question arises, then, whether disbelief, or undisclosed belief or motivation, standing alone, should be a sufficient basis to sustain an action under § 14(a), absent proof by the sort of objective evidence described above that the statement also expressly or impliedly asserted something false or misleading about its subject matter. We think that proof of mere disbelief or belief undisclosed should not suffice for liability under § 14(a), and if nothing more had been required or proven in this case we would reverse for that reason.

On the one hand, it would be rare to find a case with evidence solely of disbelief or undisclosed motivation without further proof that the statement was defective as to its subject matter. While we certainly would not hold a director's naked admission of disbelief incompetent evidence of a proxy statement's false or misleading character, such an unusual admission will not very often stand alone, and we do not substantially narrow the cause of action by requiring a plaintiff to demonstrate something false or misleading in what the statement expressly or impliedly declared about its subject.

On the other hand, to recognize liability on mere disbelief or undisclosed motive without any demonstration that the proxy statement was false or misleading about its subject would authorize § 14(a) litigation confined solely to what one skeptical court spoke of as the "impurities" of a director's "unclean heart." Stedman v. Storer, 308 F.Supp. 881, 887 (S.D.N.Y.1969) (dealing with § 10(b)). This, we think, would cross the line that *Blue Chip Stamps* sought to draw. While it is true that the liability, if recognized, would rest on an actual, not hypothetical, psychological fact, the temptation to rest an otherwise nonexistent § 14(a) action on psychological enquiry alone would threaten just the sort of strike suits and attrition by discovery that *Blue Chip Stamps* sought to discourage. We therefore hold disbelief or undisclosed motivation, standing alone, insufficient to satisfy the element of fact that must be established under § 14(a).

C

Petitioners' fall-back position assumes the same relationship between a conclusory judgment and its underlying facts that we described in Part II–B–1, supra. Thus, citing Radol v. Thomas, 534 F.Supp. 1302, 1315, 1316 (S.D.Ohio 1982), petitioners argue that even if conclusory statements of reason or belief can be actionable under § 14(a), we should confine liability to instances where the proxy material fails to disclose the offending statement's factual basis. There would be no justification for holding the shareholders entitled to judicial relief, that is, when they were given evidence that a stated reason for a proxy recommendation was misleading, and an opportunity to draw that conclusion themselves.

. . . While a misleading statement will not always lose its deceptive edge simply by joinder with others that are true, the true statements may discredit the other one so obviously that the risk of real deception drops to nil. . . .

But not every mixture with the true will neutralize the deceptive. If it would take a financial analyst to spot the tension between the one and the other, whatever is misleading will remain materially so, and liability should follow. Gerstle v. Gamble–Skogmo, Inc., 478 F.2d 1281, 1297 (C.A.2 1973) ("[I]t is not sufficient that overtones might have been picked up by the sensitive antennae of investment analysts") . . . .

Suffice it to say that the evidence invoked by petitioners in the instant case fell short of compelling the jury to find the facial materiality of the misleading statement neutralized. The directors claim, for example, to have made an explanatory disclosure of further reasons for their recommendation when they said they would keep their seats following the merger, but they failed to mention what at least one of them admitted in testimony, that they would have had no expectation of doing so without supporting the proposal, App. at 281–82. And although the proxy statement did speak factually about the merger price in describing it as higher than share prices in recent sales, it failed even to mention the closed market dominated by FABI. None of these disclosures that the directors point to was, then, anything more than a half-truth, and the record shows that another fact statement they invoke was arguably even worse. The claim that the merger price exceeded book value was controverted, as we have seen already, by evidence of a higher book value than the directors conceded, reflecting appreciation in the Bank's real estate portfolio. Finally, the solicitation omitted any mention of the Bank's value as a going concern at more than $60 a share, as against the merger price of $42. There was, in sum, no more of a compelling case for the statement's immateriality than for its accuracy.

III

The second issue before us, left open in Mills v. Electric Auto–Lite Co., 396 U.S., at 385, n. 7, 90 S.Ct., at 622, n. 7, is whether causation of damages compensable through the implied private right of action under § 14(a) can be demonstrated by a member of a class of minority shareholders whose votes are not required by law or corporate bylaw to authorize the transaction giving rise to the claim.

[The Court held that the answer to this question was, no. The plaintiffs argued that such a claim could be supported by two theories: that the proxy statement was an essential link between the director's proposal and the merger (1) because VBI and FABI would have been unwilling to proceed with the merger unless the minority approved, and (2) because the vote of the minority was the means to satisfy a state statutory requirement of minority shareholder approval as a condition for saving the merger from voidability resulting from a conflict of interest. The court rejected the first theory on the ground that acceptance of the concept would give rise to speculative claims. As to the second theory, the court said:]

This case does not ... require us to decide whether § 14(a) provides a cause of action for lost state remedies, since there is no indication in the law or facts before us that the proxy solicitation resulted in any such loss. The contrary appears to be the case. Assuming the soundness of respondents' characterization of the proxy statement as materially misleading, the very terms of the Virginia statute indicate that a favorable minority vote induced by the solicitation would not suffice to render the merger invulnerable to later attack on the ground of the conflict. The statute bars a shareholder from seeking to avoid a transaction tainted by a director's conflict if, inter alia, the minority shareholders ratified the transaction following disclosure of the material facts of the transaction and the conflict. Va.Code § 13.1–691(A)(2) (1989). Assuming that the material facts about the merger and Beddow's interests were not accurately disclosed, the minority votes were inadequate to ratify the merger under state law, and there was no loss of state remedy to connect the proxy solicitation with harm to minority shareholders irredressable under state law. Nor is there a claim here that the statement misled respondents into entertaining a false belief that they had no chance to upset the merger, until the time for bringing suit had run out.[14]

IV

The judgment of the Court of Appeals is reversed.

It is so ordered.

■ JUSTICE SCALIA, concurring in part and concurring in the judgment....

I recognize that the Court's disallowance (in Part II–B–2) of an action for misrepresentation of belief is entirely contrary to the modern law of torts, as authorities cited by the Court make plain. See Vulcan Metals Co. v. Simmons Mfg. Co., 248 F. 853, 856 (C.A.2 1918); W. Keeton, D. Dobbs, R. Keeton, & D. Owen, Prosser and Keeton on Law of Torts § 109 (5th ed. 1984), cited ante, at 2759. I have no problem with departing from modern tort law in this regard, because I think the federal cause of action at issue here was never enacted by Congress, see Thompson v. Thompson, 484 U.S. 174, 190–192, 108 S.Ct. 513, 521–523, 98 L.Ed.2d 512 (1988) (SCALIA, J., concurring in judgment), and hence the more narrow we make it (within the bounds of rationality) the more faithful we are to our task....

---

14. Respondents do not claim that any other application of a theory of lost state remedies would avail them here. It is clear, for example, that no state appraisal remedy was lost through a § 14(a) violation in this case....

I concur in the judgment of the Court, and join all of its opinion except Part II.

■ JUSTICE STEVENS, with whom JUSTICE MARSHALL joins, concurring in part and dissenting in part.

While I agree in substance with Parts I and II of the Court's opinion, I do not agree with the reasoning in Part III. . . .

The case before us today involves a merger that has been found by a jury to be unfair, not fair. The interest in providing a remedy to the injured minority shareholders therefore is stronger, not weaker, than in *Mills.* The interest in avoiding speculative controversy about the actual importance of the proxy solicitation is the same as in *Mills.* Moreover, as in *Mills,* these matters can be taken into account at the remedy stage in appropriate cases. Accordingly, I do not believe that it constitutes an unwarranted extension of the rationale of *Mills* to conclude that because management found it necessary—whether for "legal or practical reasons"—to solicit proxies from minority shareholders to obtain their approval of the merger, that solicitation "was an essential link in the accomplishment of the transaction." Id., at 385, and n. 7, 90 S.Ct., at 622, and n. 7. In my opinion, shareholders may bring an action for damages under § 14(a) of the Securities Exchange Act of 1934, 48 Stat. 895, 15 U.S.C. § 78n(a), whenever materially false or misleading statements are made in proxy statements. That the solicitation of proxies is not required by law or by the bylaws of a corporation does not authorize corporate officers, once they have decided for whatever reason to solicit proxies, to avoid the constraints of the statute. I would therefore affirm the judgment of the Court of Appeals.

■ JUSTICE KENNEDY, with whom JUSTICE MARSHALL, JUSTICE BLACKMUN, and JUSTICE STEVENS join, concurring in part and dissenting in part.

I am in general agreement with Parts I and II of the majority opinion, but do not agree with the views expressed in Part III regarding the proof of causation required to establish a violation of § 14(a). With respect, I dissent from Part III of the Court's opinion. . . .

II . . .

The Court seems to assume, based upon [footnote 7] in *Mills* reserving the question, that Sandberg bears a special burden to demonstrate causation because the public shareholders held only 15 percent of the Bank's stock. Justice STEVENS is right to reject this theory. Here, First American Bankshares, Inc. (FABI) and Virginia Bankshares, Inc. (VBI) retained the option to back out of the transaction if dissatisfied with the reaction of the minority shareholders, or if concerned that the merger would result in liability for violation of duties to the minority shareholders. The merger agreement was conditioned upon approval by two-thirds of the shareholders, App. 463, and VBI could have voted its shares against the merger if it so decided. To this extent, the Court's distinction between cases where the "minority" shareholders could have voted down the transaction and those where causation must be proved by nonvoting theories is suspect. Minority shareholders are identified only by a *post hoc* inquiry. The real question ought to be whether an injury was shown by the effect the nondisclosure had on the entire merger process, including the period before votes are cast.

The Court's distinction presumes that a majority shareholder will vote in favor of management's proposal even if proxy disclosure suggests that the transaction is unfair to minority shareholders or that the board of directors or majority shareholder are in breach of fiduciary duties to the minority. If the majority shareholder votes against the transaction in order to comply with its state law duties, or out of fear of liability, or upon concluding that the transaction will injure the reputation of the business, this ought not to be characterized as nonvoting causation. Of course, when the majority shareholder dominates the voting process, as was the case here, it may prefer to avoid the embarrassment of voting against its own proposal and so may cancel the meeting of shareholders at which the vote was to have been taken. For practical purposes, the result is the same: because of full disclosure the transaction does not go forward and the resulting injury to minority shareholders is avoided. The Court's distinction between voting and nonvoting causation does not create clear legal categories.

III . . .

There is no authority whatsoever for limiting § 14(a) to protecting those minority shareholders whose numerical strength could permit them to vote down a proposal. One of Section 14(a)'s "chief purposes is 'the protection of investors.'" J.I. Case Co. v. Borak, 377 U.S., at 432, 1559–1560. Those who lack the strength to vote down a proposal have all the more need of disclosure. The voting process involves not only casting ballots but also the formulation and withdrawal of proposals, the minority's right to block a vote through court action or the threat of adverse consequences, or the negotiation of an increase in price. The proxy rules support this deliberative process. These practicalities can result in causation sufficient to support recovery.

The facts in the case before us prove this point. Sandberg argues that had all the material facts been disclosed, FABI or the Bank likely would have withdrawn or revised the merger proposal. The evidence in the record, and more that might be available upon remand, see infra, . . . meets any reasonable requirement of specific and nonspeculative proof.

FABI wanted a "friendly transaction" with a price viewed as "so high that any reasonable shareholder will accept it." App. 99. Management expressed concern that the transaction result in "no loss of support for the bank out in the community, which was important." Id., at 109. Although FABI had the votes to push through any proposal, it wanted a favorable response from the minority shareholders. Id., at 192. Because of the "human element involved in a transaction of this nature," FABI attempted to "show those minority shareholders that [it was] being fair." Id., at 347. . . .

[The evidence supports the] theory that FABI would not have pursued the transaction if full disclosure had been proved and the shareholders had realized the inadequacy of the price. . . .

I would affirm the judgment of the Court of Appeals.

WILSON v. GREAT AMERICAN INDUSTRIES, INC., 979 F.2d 924 (2d Cir.1992). Chenango engaged in a merger with Great American. Plaintiffs, who had been minority shareholders in Chenango, alleged that material misstatements in the Proxy Statement caused them to exchange their shares of Chenango common stock for new preferred stock in Great American. At the time of the merger, the defendants (Great American, Chenango, and various officers, directors, and attorneys connected with those two corporations) owned 73 percent of Chenango's stock, which was well over the two-thirds necessary under New York law to approve a merger. New York law required that Chenango have a shareholders' meeting to approve the merger, but the only informational requirement under the New York statute was that each shareholder be given notice of the meeting accompanied by a "copy of the plan of merger." Chenango, despite its overwhelming share ownership, sought approval of the merger by Chenango's minority shareholders. Unlike *Virginia Bankshares,* state law accorded stockholders who voted against the merger with a means to receive the fair value for their shares, i.e., an appraisal remedy. The Second Circuit held that *Virginia Bankshares* did not bar the plaintiffs' action if, as a result of false statements in the Proxy Statement, the plaintiffs had lost their appraisal right or some other state remedy by being duped into voting for the transaction. See also Howing Co. v. Nationwide Corp., 972 F.2d 700, 709–710 (6th Cir.1992), *cert. denied* 507 U.S. 1004, 113 S.Ct. 1645, 123 L.Ed.2d 266 (1993); cf. Scattergood v. Perelman, 945 F.2d 618 (3d Cir.1991).

NOTE ON CAUSATION, RELIANCE, AND STANDING IN PRIVATE ACTIONS UNDER THE PROXY RULES

1. Mills v. Electric Auto–Lite Co., supra, leaves no doubt that a materially false or misleading proxy statement must be deemed to be the cause of a shareholder vote that the proxy statement solicits. Accordingly, where a shareholder seeks to set aside or enjoin a transaction approved by the shareholders on the ground that the approval was solicited by a proxy statement that involved misstatements or omissions, he need do nothing more to prove causation than to prove materiality. See Gaines v. Haughton, 645 F.2d 761, 773–74 (9th Cir.1981), cert. denied 454 U.S. 1145, 102 S.Ct. 1006, 71 L.Ed.2d 297 (1982); Weisberg v. Coastal States Gas Corp., 609 F.2d 650, 653

(2d Cir.1979), cert. denied 445 U.S. 951, 100 S.Ct. 1600, 63 L.Ed.2d 786 (1980). But what if the consequence complained of is somewhat more remote than, for example, the unfairness of the transaction approved by the stockholders on the basis of a misleading proxy? Under Rule 14a–9, can the stockholder recover on behalf of the corporation because the directors failed to disclose not just their lax oversight but acquiescence in certain managerial misconduct? *See e.g.*, General Electric Co. v. Cathcart, 980 F.2d 927 (3d Cir. 1992) (dismissing action on basis that causation lacking because stockholders were not asked to approve any of the business transactions alleged to have been tainted by managerial misconduct). Query, would failure to disclose such directors acquiescence be a basis for challenging their election?

2. If a proxy statement is materially misleading or omits to state a material fact, and a majority of shareholders vote in favor of the action proposed in the proxy statement, does a shareholder who did *not* grant a proxy in reliance on the Proxy Statement have standing under Rule 14a–9? In Cowin v. Bresler, 741 F.2d 410, 427 (D.C.Cir. 1984), the court held that the answer is, yes:

> ... *Borak* itself identifies the injury section 14(a) sought to prevent:
>
> > The injury which a stockholder suffers from corporate action pursuant to a deceptive proxy solicitation ordinarily flows from the damage done the corporation, rather than from the damage inflicted directly upon the stockholder. The damage suffered results not from the deceit practiced on him alone but rather from the deceit practiced on the stockholders as a group.
>
> 377 U.S. at 432, 84 S.Ct. at 1560.
>
> The injury [the shareholder-plaintiff] alleges was not caused by his individual reliance on deceptive proxy solicitations. Rather, his claim is that other shareholders elected appellees as directors because they were misled by the proxy materials. The installation of ... directors [so elected] has injured [the shareholder]. This injury is totally divorced from any reliance, or lack of reliance, on [the shareholder's] part and falls precisely into the scope of injury Congress sought to protect. *Borak,* 377 U.S. at 432, 84 S.Ct. at 1559. Requiring reliance in these circumstances would serve no legitimate policy and we decline to do so. *See Hershfang v. Knotter,* 562 F.Supp. 393, 397–98 (E.D.Va.1983), *aff'd mem.,* 725 F.2d 675 (4th Cir.1984) (plaintiff has standing under section 14(a) despite his lack of reliance because injury suffered has no connection to his individual reliance).
>
> We think sentiment expressed in a recent district court opinion persuasive.
>
> > It is abundantly clear that Congress' intent to protect the investing public would be seriously hampered if one who misuses the proxy process cannot be brought to task by those

> shareholders who have from the outset recognized his deceptions, but has only to fear that the other shareholders whom he has successfully beguiled will belatedly become enlightened and seek redress for the damage he has done them.
>
> *Lynch v. Fulks,* [1981 Transfer Binder] Fed.Sec.L.Rep. (CCH) § 97,831, at 90,134 (D.Kan. Dec. 12, 1980).

See also Palumbo v. Deposit Bank, 758 F.2d 113, 116 (3d Cir.1985); Dann v. Studebaker–Packard Corp., 288 F.2d 201, 209 (6th Cir.1961).

NOTE ON THE STANDARD OF FAULT IN PRIVATE ACTIONS UNDER THE PROXY RULES

Under *Borak* and *Mills,* shareholders have standing to bring an action under Rule 14a–9, which prohibits false or misleading proxy statements. Does a plaintiff-shareholder prevail in such an action if he shows that a proxy statement was false or misleading by virtue of a material misstatement or omission, or must he also show that the misstatement or omission was committed with either knowledge of the falsity or reckless disregard of the truth? If the plaintiff must show fault, does negligence suffice?

In the leading case of Gerstle v. Gamble–Skogmo, Inc., 478 F.2d 1281 (2d Cir.1973), the Second Circuit, in an opinion written by Judge Friendly, held that negligence sufficed to establish liability under Rule 14a–9:

> We thus hold that in a case like this, where the plaintiffs represent the very class who were asked to approve a merger on the basis of a misleading proxy statement and are seeking compensation from the beneficiary who is responsible for the preparation of the statement, they are not required to establish any evil motive or even reckless disregard of the facts. Whether in situations other than that here presented "the liability of the corporation issuing a materially false or misleading proxy statement is virtually absolute, as under Section 11 of the 1933 Act with respect to a registration statement," Jennings & Marsh, Securities Regulation: Cases and Materials 1358 (3d ed. 1972), we leave to another day. 478 F.2d at 1298–1301. Accord: Herskowitz v. Nutri/System, Inc., 857 F.2d 179 (3d Cir.1988), cert. denied 489 U.S. 1054, 109 S.Ct. 1315, 103 L.Ed.2d 584 (1989); Gould v. American–Hawaiian Steamship Co., 535 F.2d 761 (3d Cir.1976).

But see Adams v. Standard Knitting Mills, Inc., 623 F.2d 422 (6th Cir.1980), cert. denied 449 U.S. 1067, 101 S.Ct. 795, 66 L.Ed.2d 611. ("scienter should be an element of liability in private suits under the proxy provisions as they apply to outside accountants").

In Shidler v. All American Life & Financial Corp., 775 F.2d 917, 927 (8th Cir.1985), the Eighth Circuit addressed the issue that Judge Friendly left to another day in *Gerstle,* and held there was no liability without fault in an action under Section 14(a):

The purpose of section 14(a) is "to prevent management or others from obtaining authorization for corporate action by means of deceptive or inadequate disclosure in proxy solicitation." J.I. Case Co. v. Borak, 377 U.S. 426, 431, 84 S.Ct. 1555, 1559, 12 L.Ed.2d 423 (1964). A strict liability rule would impose liability for fully innocent misstatements. It is too blunt a tool to ferret out the kind of deceptive practices Congress sought to prevent in enacting section 14(a).

The Supreme Court has several times explicitly taken note of the position taken in *Gerstle* and other cases that scienter is not an element of liability under § 14(a), and has each time declined to address the issue. See Ernst & Ernst v. Hochfelder, 425 U.S. 185, 209 n. 28, 96 S.Ct. 1375, 1388 n. 28, 47 L.Ed.2d 668 (1976); TSC Indus., Inc. v. Northway, 426 U.S. 438, 444 n. 7, 96 S.Ct. 2126, 2130 n. 7, 48 L.Ed.2d 757 (1976); *Virginia Bankshares,* supra, at note 5.

NOTE ON STATE LAW

Perhaps as a result of experience under the Proxy Rules, the standards applied by state courts today, in reviewing the adequacy of disclosure to shareholders under state law in connection with a matter proposed for a shareholder vote, is likely to be close to the standards under the Proxy Rules. See Chapter 11, Section 5, infra.

CHAPTER 7

Personal Liability in a Corporate Context

Although limited liability is a central attribute of the corporate form, there are several contexts in which personal liability may be imposed upon a shareholder or upon a person associated with a proposed or defectively formed corporation. Three of these contexts will be discussed in this Chapter: the liability of a promoter for preincorporation transactions he engages in on behalf of a proposed corporation; the liability of a person who is a would-be shareholder in a defectively formed corporation; and the liability of a shareholder for corporate obligations. Each of these contexts also implicates issues other than personal liability, and these issues will also be discussed in this Chapter.

Section 1. Preincorporation Transactions by Promoters

A promoter is a person who transforms an idea into an enterprise by bringing together persons and assets, and overseeing the steps required to bring the enterprise into existence. Often, a promoter of a proposed corporation enters into preincorporation contracts for the benefit of a corporation that has not yet been formed. If, as is usually the case, the corporation is subsequently formed, issues may arise regarding who is liable under the preincorporation contract.

(a) *Liability of the promoter*. The general rule is that when a promoter makes a contract for the benefit of a proposed corporation, the promoter is personally liable on the contract, and remains liable even after the corporation is formed. There is an exception if the party who contracted with the promoter knew that the corporation was not in existence at the time of the contract and nevertheless agreed to look solely to the corporation for performance. In such cases the promoter is not deemed a party to the contract. An agreement of this type may be express or implied. As a practical matter, it is often difficult to predict whether, in the absence of an express agreement of this type, a court will find an implied agreement.

For example, in Goodman v. Darden, Doman & Stafford Assocs., 670 P.2d 648 (Wash. 1983), Goodman had proposed to renovate an apartment building owned by Darden, Doman & Stafford Associates (DDS). During the course of negotiations, Goodman informed DDS that he would be forming a corporation to limit his personal liability. In August 1979, a contract was made between DDS and "BUILDING

DESIGN AND DEVELOPMENT INC. (In Formation) John A. Goodman, President." DDS knew that the Building Design corporation was not yet in existence. On November 1, Goodman filed articles of incorporation. Between August and December 1979, DDS made five progress payments on the contract. The first check was made out to "Building Design and Development Inc.—John Goodman." Goodman struck out his name as payee, endorsed the check "Bldg. Design & Dev. Inc., John A. Goodman, Pres," and instructed DDS to make further payments only to the corporation. DDS did so. The court held that Goodman was liable on the contract with DDS:

> . . . The fact that a contracting party knows that the corporation is nonexistent does not indicate any agreement to release the promoter. To the contrary, such knowledge alone would seem to indicate that the members of DDS intended to make Goodman a party to the contract. They could not hold the corporation, a nonexistent entity, responsible and of course they would expect to have recourse against someone (Goodman) if default occurred. . . .
>
> The only other evidence of the parties' intent to make the corporation the sole party to the contract is that the progress payments were made payable to the corporation. However, they were so written only at the instruction of Goodman and in fact the first check written by DDS after the signing of the contract was written to the corporation *and* Goodman as an individual. This evidence does not show by reasonable certainty that DDS intended to contract only with the corporation. . . .

Id. at 652–53.

In contrast, in Company Stores Development Corp. v. Pottery Warehouse, Inc., 733 S.W.2d 886 (Tenn. App. 1987), Company Stores leased a store to Pottery Warehouse, Inc., for five years. Pottery Warehouse was not incorporated at the time of the lease. The lease recited that the corporation was to be organized, and was signed by the promoter as follows:

> THE POTTERY WAREHOUSE, INC., a corporation to be formed under the laws of the State of Tennessee
>
> BY Jane M. Vosseller
>
> Its President. . . .

The court held that the promoter was not liable:

> In the instant case, the stipulations of fact establish the plaintiff intended to look solely to Pottery Warehouse, Inc., for satisfaction of the obligation arising under the lease at the time of execution. At the time the lease was signed, plaintiff was aware of the nonexistence of the corporate entity and did not require Vosseller to sign the agreement in an individual capacity but as a president of a future corporate entity. The lease imputes no intention on the part of Vosseller to be bound personally.

Id. at 888.

(b) *Liability of the Corporation.* A corporation that is formed after a promoter has entered into a contract on its behalf is not bound by the contract, without more. The reason is that the corporation was not in existence when the contract was made, and therefore did not authorize—and indeed could not have authorized—the promoter to enter into the contract on its behalf. However, after the corporation has been formed it may become bound in one of several ways. "The usual grounds that have been suggested are ratification, adoption, novation, and that the proposition made to the promoters is a continuing offer to be accepted or rejected by the corporation when it comes into being, and upon acceptance becomes an original contract on its part; and the liability has also been sustained on the ground that the corporation, by accepting the benefits of a contract, takes it cum onere, and is estopped to deny its liability on the contract." Clifton v. Tomb, 21 F.2d 893 (4th Cir.1927). In Illinois Controls, Inc. v. Langham, 70 Ohio St.3d 512, 524, 639 N.E.2d 771, 781 (1994), the court held that if a promoter is liable on a contract under the law of promoter's liability, the fact that the corporation also becomes liable on the contract by adopting it does not relieve the promoter of liability. Instead, in such a case the promoter and the corporation are jointly and severally liable.

RESTATEMENT (THIRD) OF AGENCY § 6.04

[See Statutory Supplement]

RESTATEMENT (SECOND) OF CONTRACTS § 326

[See Statutory Supplement]

SECTION 2. CONSEQUENCES OF DEFECTIVE INCORPORATION

MODEL BUS. CORP. ACT §§ 2.03, 2.04

[See Statutory Supplement]

DEL. GEN. CORP. LAW §§ 106, 329

[See Statutory Supplement]

NOTE ON DEFECTIVE INCORPORATION

Sometimes there is a defect in the process of forming a corporation. For example, the certificate of incorporation may fail to include a required provision in proper form, or may be improperly filed. The issue then arises, what is the effect of the defect on the corporation's status. This issue is usually put in terms of whether a corporation exists de jure, de facto, by estoppel, or not at all. The issue most commonly arises when a third party seeks to hold the would-be shareholders personally liable on the ground that corporate status was not attained, and therefore neither was limited liability. The issue may also arise in a quo warranto proceeding brought by the state to test the validity of corporate statutes. This form of proceeding derives from an ancient prerogative writ issued on behalf of the King against one who falsely claimed an office or franchise. Most states provide by statute for such proceedings, often without using the term quo warranto. See, e.g., N.Y. Bus. Corp. Law § 109; Cal. Corp. Code § 180(a).

1. *De Jure Corporation.* A corporation that is organized in compliance with the requirements of the relevant statute is a *de jure corporation*. A de jure corporation's status cannot be attacked either by private parties or by the state in a quo warranto proceeding. People v. Ford, 128 N.E. 479 (Ill. 1920). Most courts hold that perfect compliance with the statutory requirements for incorporation is not required to attain de jure status. Instead, substantial compliance will suffice. Therefore, an enterprise that fails to meet all the requirements for incorporation may nevertheless be a de jure corporation if the noncompliance is insubstantial. What constitutes substantial compliance is determined on a case-by-case basis, according to the nature of the unsatisfied requirement and the extent to which compliance has been attempted. For example, if the certificate of incorporation was properly filed except that the address for the corporation's principal place of business stated the wrong street number, there undoubtedly would be substantial compliance.

Some courts hold that for a corporation to attain de jure status there must be exact compliance with all "mandatory" statutory requirements but the failure to comply with requirements that are only "directory" will not will not preclude de jure status. See, e.g., J.W. Butler Paper Co. v. Cleveland, 77 N.E. 99 (Ill. 1906). Whether a particular requirement is mandatory or directory for this purpose is a matter of statutory interpretation. For example, in People v. Ford, supra, the Illinois attorney general filed a proceeding, in the nature of quo warranto, against three incorporators who had failed to comply with a statutory requirement that the certificate of incorporation be sealed. The incorporators had used incorporation forms provided by the office of the Illinois Secretary of State, and these forms neither contained nor mentioned a seal. The court concluded that the corporation had de jure status. The provision for a seal was only directory, the court said, because the purpose of the statute was to make a public record and a seal did not further that purpose.

2. *De facto Corporation.* A *de facto* corporation is said to exist when the steps taken to incorporate the enterprise were insufficient to result in a de jure corporation with respect to a challenge by the state in a quo warranto proceeding, but were sufficient to treat the enterprise as a corporation with respect to third parties. In such cases, the enterprise's corporate status can be invalidated by the state through quo warranto proceedings, but cannot be invalidated by third parties. To qualify as a de facto corporation, there must have been a colorable attempt to incorporate and some exercise of corporate privileges. For example, in Cantor v. Sunshine Greenery, Inc., 398 A.2d 571 (N.J. 1979), on November 21, B reserved the corporate name "Sunshine Greenery, Inc." with the Secretary of State. On December 3, B and C executed a certificate of incorporation and sent it by mail to the Secretary of State together with the filing fee. On December 16, Sunshine Greenery entered into a lease. For some unexplained reason, the certificate of incorporation was not officially filed by the Secretary of State until December 18, two days after the lease was executed. The court held that Sunshine Greenery was a de facto corporation prior to December 18, and therefore B and C were not personally liable on the lease.

3. *Estoppel.* In many cases in which neither a de jure nor a de facto corporation has been formed, the courts have held that a third party who has dealt with an enterprise on the basis that it is a corporation is estopped from denying the enterprise's corporate status, as are the corporation and its shareholders. Neither the precise contours of the estoppel theory nor its relationship to the de facto theory has ever been entirely clear. It is sometimes said that the estoppel theory differs from the de facto theory in that estoppel is effective for only a specific transaction. However, the de facto theory also may be effective only for a specific transaction, because a decision in one law suit that a corporation has de facto status will normally not be given res judicata effect in a law suit brought by an unrelated plaintiff on an unrelated transaction. As a practical matter, however, there is likely to be a difference between the *precedential* effects of decisions based on the estoppel theory and decisions based on the de facto theory. Because a decision based on the estoppel theory will normally turn heavily on the *plaintiff's* conduct, it may have only a limited precedential effect on future cases brought by other plaintiffs based on other transactions. In contrast, a decision based on the de facto theory will normally turn on the *defendant's* conduct in attempting to organize a corporation. Because that conduct will also be the focus of any future de facto case involving those defendants, a decision that a de facto corporation was or was not formed by the conduct may have a significant precedential effect on other parties even though it does not have a res judicata effect.

A problem with the estoppel theory is that it is not a single theory, but rather a cluster of several very different rules.

(i) *Denial of Corporate Status by the Would-be Shareholders.* In one kind of estoppel case, an enterprise engages in a transaction with a third party, T. At the time of the transaction, the owners claim that the enterprise is a corporation. Later, T brings suit against the purported corporation, and the enterprise and its owners deny that the enterprise is a corporation. This is a true estoppel case, at least if T relied on the owners' initial claim of corporate status.

(ii) *Technical Contexts.* Another kind of estoppel case occurs when the question of corporate status is raised in a technical, procedural context. For example, in a suit brought by a would-be corporation, the defendant may seek to raise the defense that the plaintiff is not really a corporation and therefore cannot sue in a corporate name. The courts tend to regard such defenses as nonmeritorious and to brush them off, using "estoppel" as a handy tool to do so.

(iii) *Liability of Would-be Shareholders.* The most important category of estoppel cases occur when a third party who has dealt with an enterprise on the basis that it is a corporation seeks to impose personal liability on the would-be shareholders, who in turn defend on the ground that the third person, having dealt with the enterprise as a corporation, is estopped to deny that the enterprise has corporate status. Here the issue is whether, as a matter of equity, the claimant, having dealt with the enterprise as if it were a corporation, should be prevented—estopped—from treating it as anything else. A leading case in this category is Cranson v. International Bus. Mach. Corp., 200 A.2d 33 (Md. 1964). I.B.M. had sold typewriters to the Real Estate Service Bureau on credit. I.B.M. dealt with the Bureau as if the Bureau was a corporation. In fact, it wasn't, because without the knowledge of its would-be shareholders, their attorney had negligently failed to file the certificate of incorporation before the transaction with I.B.M. The court held that although the organizational defects in the case might have prevented the Bureau from being a de facto corporation, "I.B.M. having dealt with the Bureau as if it were a corporation and relied on its credit rather than that of [the would-be shareholders], is estopped to assert that the Bureau was not incorporated at the time the typewriters were purchased."

In this third category of cases, the estoppel theory is comparable in its function to the de facto theory. However, the two theories differ in two important ways in their application:

First, the crux of the estoppel theory in such cases is that the third party has dealt with the business as if it were a corporation. Presumably, therefore, the theory does not apply to a tort claimant, or other involuntary creditor, who was a stranger to the business before his claim arose. In contrast, the de facto theory can be applied to such claimants.

Second, would-be shareholders would not need to resort to the estoppel theory if they could establish that their business had de facto corporate status. Presumably, therefore, fewer aspects of corporateness must be shown to establish a corporation by estoppel than to establish a de facto corporation. For example, in the *I.B.M.* case the court applied the estoppel theory only after observing that the de facto theory might be inapplicable because the certificate of incorporation had not been filed at the time of the transaction.

4. *Who May Be Held Liable*. If a would-be corporation is neither a de jure corporation, a de facto corporation, or a corporation by estoppel, the courts have divided on which would-be shareholders may be held personally liable for debts incurred in the corporation's name. Older decisions imposed personal liability on all of the would-be shareholders, on the theory that if the enterprise is not a corporation, it is a partnership, and therefore the would-be shareholders are general partners. See, e.g., Harrill v. Davis, 168 F. 187 (8th Cir. 1909). The modern trend, however, imposes personal liability only against those owners who actively participated in the management of the business. Those owners who actively participated are held personally liable as if they were partners, but passive investors are not. See, e.g., Baker v. Bates–Street Shirt Co., 6 F.2d 854 (1st Cir. 1925). Model Business Corporation Act § 2.04 takes a different approach. Under that provision, only persons acting as or on behalf of a corporation who knew there was no incorporation are jointly and severally liable for the would-be corporation's liabilities. This provision protects would-be shareholders of defectively formed corporations in cases where the would-be shareholders honestly and reasonably, although erroneously, believed that a corporation had been properly formed. Model Act § 2.04 eliminates much but not necessarily all of the need for estoppel doctrine. According to the Comment to Section 2.04:

> While no special provision is made in section 2.04, the section does not foreclose the possibility that persons who urge defendants to execute contracts in the corporate name knowing that no steps to incorporate have been taken may be estopped to impose personal liability on individual defendants. This estoppel may be based on the inequity perceived when persons, unwilling or reluctant to enter into a commitment under their own name, are persuaded to use the name of a nonexistent corporation, and then are sought to be held personally liable under section 2.04 by the party advocating that form of execution. By contrast, persons who knowingly participate in a business under a corporate name are jointly and severally liable on "corporate" obligations under section 2.04 and may not argue that plaintiffs are "estopped" from holding them personally liable because all transactions were conducted on a corporate basis.

McCHESNEY, DOCTRINAL ANALYSIS AND STATISTICAL MODELING IN LAW: THE CASE OF DEFECTIVE INCORPORATION, 71 Wash. U.L.Q. 493, 498–99 (1993). "Three requirements are typically cited for application of the de facto corporation doctrine. There must have been: (1) a statute in existence by which incorporation was legally possible; (2) a 'colorable' attempt to comply with the statute; and (3) some actual use or exercise of corporate privileges. Because every state has a corporation statute and defendants ordinarily have been acting under the aegis of a supposed corporation, the three factors typically dissolve into one: whether defendants' attempts to incorporate had gone far enough to be deemed 'colorable compliance.' For example, an attempt to file the articles of incorporation, albeit unsuccessful, has frequently sufficed as the necessary attempt at statutory compliance. 'In addition, some cases and commentators have added good faith of corporation or associates as a fourth element. [The good faith requirement] is often omitted, however, because a colorable compliance with the incorporation statute usually encompasses a good faith attempt to incorporate.' "

SECTION 3. LIMITED LIABILITY AND ITS EXCEPTIONS

DEL. GEN. CORP. LAW § 102(B)(6)

[See Statutory Supplement]

MODEL BUS. CORP. ACT § 6.22(B)

[See Statutory Supplement]

INTRODUCTORY NOTE ON LIMITED LIABILITY

It is commonly said that shareholders have limited liability for corporate obligations. Actually, however, shareholders ordinarily have *no* liability for corporate obligations. Under modern statutes, a shareholder's risk is ordinarily limited to her *investment*; that is, the most a shareholder stands to lose, even if the corporation fails, is the amount that she paid for her shares. Nevertheless, the term *limited liability* is universally used to refer to the no-liability rule, and therefore will be used in this book as well.

It is also sometimes said that shareholders are not liable for corporate obligations because corporations are separate legal entities. In fact, however, the entity status of corporations has almost nothing to do with shareholder limited liability. For example, English law conferred entity status on corporations long before shareholders were afforded limited liability. Similarly, the Revised Uniform Partnership Act (RUPA) confers entity status on partnerships, but also provides that the partners are individually liable for all partnership obligations once the partnership's assets are exhausted. Accordingly, although cases in which liability is imposed on shareholders, despite the ordinary rules, are commonly said to involve "disregard of the corporate entity" or "piercing the corporate veil," really these cases involve only a conclusion that under given kinds of circumstances there are good reasons why the normal statutory rule of limited liability should not be applied.

It should also be borne in mind that corporate managers, as well as corporate shareholders, are ordinarily not liable for corporate obligations. Shareholders are not liable for corporate obligations by statute. In contrast, managers are not liable for corporate obligations on straightforward agency principles: In the case of a contract that is made by an agent within his authority, the agent is not liable as long as she purported to act in that capacity and the identity of her principal was disclosed. Similarly, in the case of a tort by a subordinate employee, a manager normally will not be vicariously liable to the injured party even if the employee was the manager's subordinate. However, a corporate manager may be liable to a third party if he personally commits or directs the commission of the tortious action. The liability of corporate managers to third parties is considered in more detail in the Note on Civil Liabilities of Directors and Officers in Chapter 10, Section 1(C).

Fletcher v. Atex, Inc.

United States Court of Appeals, Second Circuit, 1995.
68 F.3d 1451.

■ Before: KEARSE, CALABRESI, and CABRANES, CIRCUIT JUDGES.

■ JOSE A. CABRANES, CIRCUIT JUDGE:

This is a consolidated appeal from a final judgment of the United States District Court for the Southern District of New York (Morris E. Lasker, Judge), granting defendant-appellee Eastman Kodak Company's motion for summary judgment and dismissing all claims against it in two actions, Fletcher v. Atex, Inc., 92 Civ. 8758 and Hermanson v. 805 Middlesex Corp., Inc., 94 Civ. 1272. Fletcher v. Atex, Inc., 861 F.Supp. 242 (S.D.N.Y.1994). The plaintiffs-appellants filed suit against Atex, Inc. ("Atex") and its parent, Eastman Kodak Company ("Kodak"), to recover for repetitive stress injuries that they claim were caused by their use of computer keyboards manufactured by Atex.

Plaintiffs-appellants argue that the district court erred in granting summary judgment in favor of Kodak on the ground that Kodak could be held liable for the plaintiffs' alleged injuries. They contend that summary judgment was inappropriate because genuine issues of material fact existed regarding Kodak's liability as a defendant....

I. BACKGROUND

The Fletcher and Hermanson plaintiffs filed their respective complaints on December 4, 1992, and February 25, 1994, seeking recovery from Atex and Kodak, among others, for repetitive stress injuries that they claim were caused by their use of Atex computer keyboards. From

1981 until December 1992, Atex was a wholly-owned subsidiary of Kodak. In 1987, Atex's name was changed to Electronic Pre–Press Systems, Inc., ("EPPS"), but its name was changed back to Atex in 1990. In December 1992, Atex sold substantially all of its assets to an independent third party and again changed its name to 805 Middlesex Corp., which holds the proceeds from the sale. Kodak continues to be the sole shareholder of 805 Middlesex Corp.

After extensive discovery, Kodak moved for summary judgment in Fletcher on April 21, 1994, and in Hermanson on April 28, 1994. The plaintiffs opposed Kodak's motion, arguing that genuine issues of material fact existed as to Kodak's liability under any number of theories, including (1) that Atex was merely Kodak's alter ego or instrumentality; (2) that Atex was Kodak's agent in the manufacture and marketing of the keyboards; (3) that Kodak was the "apparent manufacturer" of the Atex keyboards; and (4) that Kodak acted in tortious concert with Atex in manufacturing and marketing the allegedly defective keyboards.

In support of their first theory, the plaintiffs argued that Kodak "dominated and controlled" Atex by maintaining significant overlap between the boards of directors of the two companies, "siphoning" off funds from Atex through use of a cash management system, requiring Kodak's approval for major expenditures, stock sales, and real estate acquisitions, participating in negotiations involving the sale of Atex to a third party, and including references to Atex as a "division" of Kodak and to the "merger" between Atex and Kodak in Atex's promotional literature and Kodak's Annual Report....

On August 17, 1994, the district court rejected each of the plaintiffs' theories of Kodak's liability and granted Kodak's motion for summary judgment in both actions. In its opinion, the court referred to, but did not rely upon, an identical suit filed against Atex and Kodak in New York state court, King v. Eastman Kodak Co., No. 23439/92 (N.Y.Sup.Ct. June 9, 1994), in which Kodak's motion for summary judgment was granted on similar grounds. Fletcher, 861 F.Supp. at 243.

.... [T]he district court found that Kodak and Atex observed all corporate formalities and maintained separate corporate existences. It held that Atex's participation in Kodak's cash management system and Kodak's control over Atex's major expenditures and asset sales were insufficient to raise an issue of material fact regarding Kodak's liability under an alter ego theory. Id. at 244–45.... This appeal followed.

II. DISCUSSION ...

The plaintiffs claim that the district court erred in granting Kodak's motion for summary judgment on their alter ego theory of liability. The plaintiffs ... argue that ... genuine issues of material fact remain that preclude a grant of summary judgment in favor of Kodak.

The district court correctly noted that "[u]nder New York choice of law principles, '[t]he law of the state of incorporation determines when the corporate form will be disregarded and liability will be imposed on shareholders.'" Fletcher, 861 F.Supp. at 244 (quoting Kalb, Voorhis & Co. v. American Fin. Corp., 8 F.3d 130, 132 (2d Cir.1993)). Because Atex was a Delaware corporation, Delaware law determines whether the corporate veil can be pierced in this instance.

Delaware law permits a court to pierce the corporate veil of a company "where there is fraud or where [it] is in fact a mere instrumentality or alter ego of its owner." Geyer v. Ingersoll Publications Co., 621 A.2d 784, 793 (Del.Ch.1992). Although the Delaware Supreme Court has never explicitly adopted an alter ego theory of parent liability for its subsidiaries, lower Delaware courts have applied the doctrine on several occasions, as has the United States District Court for the District of Delaware. See Geyer, 621 A.2d at 793; Mabon, Nugent & Co. v. Texas Am. Energy Corp., No. CIV.A. 8578, 1990 WL 44267, at *5, (Del.Ch. Apr.12, 1990); Harper v. Delaware Valley Broadcasters, Inc., 743 F.Supp. 1076, 1085 (D.Del.1990), aff'd, 932 F.2d 959 (3d Cir.1991). Thus, under an alter ego theory, there is no requirement of a showing of fraud. Id. at 1085. To prevail on an alter ego claim under Delaware law, a plaintiff must show (1) that the parent and the subsidiary "operated as a single economic entity" and (2) that an "overall element of injustice or unfairness ... [is] present." Id. (internal quotation marks omitted); see also Mabon, 1990 WL 44267, at *5; Harco Nat'l Ins. Co. v. Green Farms, Inc., No. CIV.A. 1331, 1989 WL 110537, at *5, (Del.Ch. Sept.19, 1989).

In the New York state action of King v. Eastman, the court granted Kodak's motion for summary judgment, relying on an erroneous interpretation of Delaware's alter ego doctrine. The court noted that although the plaintiffs had raised "ample questions of fact regarding the first element of the piercing theory—domination," they made "no showing that Kodak used whatever dominance it had over Atex to perpetrate a fraud or other wrong that proximately cause[d] injury to them." This was an error; under Delaware law, the alter ego theory of liability does not require any showing of fraud....

b. Summary Judgment on the Alter Ego Theory

To prevail on an alter ego theory of liability, a plaintiff must show that the two corporations "'operated as a single economic entity such that it would be inequitable ... to uphold a legal distinction between them.'" Harper, 743 F.Supp. at 1085 (quoting Mabon, 1990 WL 44267, at * 5). Among the factors to be considered in determining whether a subsidiary and parent operate as a "single economic entity" are:

> "[W]hether the corporation was adequately capitalized for the corporate undertaking; whether the corporation was solvent; whether dividends were paid, corporate records kept, officers and directors functioned properly, and other corporate formalities were observed; whether the dominant shareholder siphoned cor-

> porate funds; and whether, in general, the corporation simply functioned as a facade for the dominant shareholder."

Harco, 1989 WL 110537, at *4 (quoting United States v. Golden Acres, Inc., 702 F.Supp. 1097, 1104 (D.Del.1988)). As noted above, a showing of fraud or wrongdoing is not necessary under an alter ego theory, but the plaintiff must demonstrate an overall element of injustice or unfairness. Harco, 1989 WL 110537, at *5.

A plaintiff seeking to persuade a Delaware court to disregard the corporate structure faces "a difficult task." Harco, 1989 WL 110537, at *4. Courts have made it clear that "[t]he legal entity of a corporation will not be disturbed until sufficient reason appears." Id. Although the question of domination is generally one of fact, courts have granted motions to dismiss as well as motions for summary judgment in favor of defendant parent companies where there has been a lack of sufficient evidence to place the alter ego issue in dispute. See, e.g., Akzona, Inc. v. Du Pont, 607 F.Supp. 227, 237 (D.Del.1984) (rejecting plaintiffs' alter ego theory of liability on a motion to dismiss); Nelson v. International Paint Co., 734 F.2d 1084, 1092 (5th Cir.1984) ("[I]n the lack of sufficient evidence to place the alter ego issue in dispute, a corporate defendant may be entitled to summary judgment."); see also Japan Petroleum Co. (Nigeria) v. Ashland Oil Inc., 456 F.Supp. 831, 838, 846 (D.Del.1978) (finding that subsidiary was not instrumentality of parent on a motion for summary judgment).

Kodak has shown that Atex followed corporate formalities, and the plaintiffs have offered no evidence to the contrary. Significantly, the plaintiffs have not challenged Kodak's assertions that Atex's board of directors held regular meetings, that minutes from those meetings were routinely prepared and maintained in corporate minute books, that appropriate financial records and other files were maintained by Atex, that Atex filed its own tax returns and paid its own taxes, and that Atex had its own employees and management executives who were responsible for the corporation's day-to-day business. The plaintiffs' primary arguments regarding domination concern (1) the defendant's use of a cash management system; (2) Kodak's exertion of control over Atex's major expenditures, stock sales, and the sale of Atex's assets to a third party; (3) Kodak's "dominating presence" on Atex's board of directors; (4) descriptions of the relationship between Atex and Kodak in the corporations' advertising, promotional literature, and annual reports; and (5) Atex's assignment of one of its former officer's mortgage to Kodak in order to close Atex's asset-purchase agreement with a third party. The plaintiffs argue that each of these raises a genuine issue of material fact about Kodak's domination of Atex, and that the district court therefore erred in granting summary judgment to Kodak on the plaintiffs' alter ego theory. We find that the district court correctly held that, in light of the undisputed factors of independence cited by Kodak, "the elements identified by the plaintiffs . . . [were] insufficient as a matter of law to establish the degree of domination necessary to disregard Atex's corporate identity." Fletcher, 861 F.Supp. at 245.

First, the district court correctly held that "Atex's participation in Kodak's cash management system is consistent with sound business practice and does not show undue domination or control." Id. at 244. The parties do not dispute the mechanics of Kodak's cash management system. Essentially, all of Kodak's domestic subsidiaries participate in the system and maintain zero-balance bank accounts. All funds transferred from the subsidiary accounts are recorded as credits to the subsidiary, and when a subsidiary is in need of funds, a transfer is made. At all times, a strict accounting is kept of each subsidiary's funds.

Courts have generally declined to find alter ego liability based on a parent corporation's use of a cash management system. See, e.g., In re Acushnet River & New Bedford Harbor Proceedings, 675 F.Supp. 22, 34 (D.Mass.1987) (Without "considerably more," "a centralized cash management system ... where the accounting records always reflect the indebtedness of one entity to another, is not the equivalent of intermingling funds" and is insufficient to justify disregarding the corporate form.); United States v. Bliss, 108 F.R.D. 127, 132 (E.D.Mo. 1985) (cash management system indicative of the "usual parent-subsidiary relationship"); Japan Petrol., 456 F.Supp. at 846 (finding segregation of subsidiary's accounts within parent's cash management system to be "a function of administrative convenience and economy, rather than a manifestation of control"). The plaintiffs offer no facts to support their speculation that Kodak's centralized cash management system was actually a "complete commingling" of funds or a means by which Kodak sought to "siphon[ ] all of Atex's revenues into its own account."

Second, the district court correctly concluded that it could find no domination based on the plaintiffs' evidence that Kodak's approval was required for Atex's real estate leases, major capital expenditures, negotiations for a sale of minority stock ownership to IBM, or the fact that Kodak played a significant role in the ultimate sale of Atex's assets to a third party. Again, the parties do not dispute that Kodak required Atex to seek its approval and/or participation for the above transactions. However, this evidence, viewed in the light most favorable to the plaintiffs, does not raise an issue of material fact about whether the two corporations constituted "a single economic entity." Indeed, this type of conduct is typical of a majority shareholder or parent corporation. See Phoenix Canada Oil Co. v. Texaco, 842 F.2d 1466, 1476 (3d Cir.1988) (declining to pierce the corporate veil where subsidiary required to secure approval from parent for "large investments and acquisitions or disposals of major assets"), cert. denied, 488 U.S. 908, 109 S.Ct. 259, 102 L.Ed.2d 247 (1988); *Akzona*, 607 F.Supp. at 237 (same, where parent approval required for expenditures exceeding $850,000); Japan Petrol., 456 F.Supp. at 843 (finding no parent liability where parent approval required for expenditures exceeding $250,000). In *Akzona*, the Delaware district court noted that a parent's "general executive responsibilities" for its subsidiary's operations included approval over major policy decisions and guaranteeing bank loans, and that that type of oversight was insufficient to demonstrate domination and control. *Akzona*, 607 F.Supp. at 238 (internal quotation marks omitted). Similarly, the district court in the instant case properly found that the presence of Kodak employees at periodic meetings with Atex's chief financial officer and comptroller to be "entirely appropriate." Fletcher, 861 F.Supp. at 245 (citing *Akzona*, 607 F.Supp. at 238); see *Acushnet*, 675 F.Supp. at 34 ("The quarterly and annual reports made [to the parent] do not represent an untoward intrusion by the owner into the corporate enterprise. The right of shareholders to remain informed is similarly recognized in many public and closely held corporations.").

The plaintiffs' third argument, that Kodak dominated the Atex board of directors, also fails. Although a number of Kodak employees have sat on the Atex board, it is undisputed that between 1981 and 1988, only one director of Atex was also a director of Kodak. Between 1989 and 1992, Atex and Kodak had no directors in common. Parents and subsidiaries frequently have overlapping boards of directors while maintaining separate business operations. In Japan Petroleum, the Delaware district court held that the fact that a parent and a subsidiary have common officers and directors does not necessarily demonstrate that the parent corporation dominates the activities of the subsidiary. 456 F.Supp. at 841; see Scott–Douglas Corp. v. Greyhound Corp., 304 A.2d 309, 314 (Del.Super.Ct.1973) (same). Since the overlap is negligible here, we find this evidence to be entirely insufficient to raise a question of fact on the issue of domination.

Fourth, the district court properly rejected the plaintiffs' argument that the descriptions of the relationship between Atex and Kodak and the presence of the Kodak logo in Atex's promotional literature justify piercing the corporate veil. Fletcher, 861 F.Supp. at 245. The plaintiffs point to several statements in both Kodak's and Atex's literature to evidence Kodak's domination of its subsidiary. For example, plaintiffs refer to (1) a promotional pamphlet produced by EPPS (a/k/a Atex) describing Atex as a business unit of EPPS and noting that EPPS was an "agent" of Kodak; (2) a document produced by Atex entitled "An Introduction to Atex Systems," which describes a "merger" between Kodak and Atex; (3) a statement in Kodak's 1985 and 1986 annual reports describing Atex as a "recent acquisition[ ]" and a "subsidiar[y] . . . combined in a new division"; and (4) a statement in an Atex/EPPS document, "Setting Up TPE 6000 on the Sun 3 Workstation," describing Atex as "an unincorporated division of Electronic Pre–Press Systems, Inc., a Kodak company." They also refer generally to the fact that Atex's paperwork and packaging materials frequently displayed the Kodak logo.

It is clear from the record that Atex never merged with Kodak or operated as a Kodak division. The plaintiffs offer no evidence to the contrary, apart from these statements in Atex and Kodak documents that they claim are indicative of the true relationship between the two companies. Viewed in the light most favorable to the plaintiffs, these statements and the use of the Kodak logo are not evidence that the two companies operated as a "single economic entity." See Coleman

v. Corning Glass Works, 619 F.Supp. 950, 956 (W.D.N.Y.1985) (upholding corporate form despite "loose language" in annual report about "merger" and parent's reference to subsidiary as a "division"), aff'd, 818 F.2d 874 (1987); Japan Petrol., 456 F.Supp. at 846 (noting that representations made by parent in its annual reports that subsidiary serves as an agent "may result from public relations motives or an attempt at simplification"); American Trading & Prod. Corp. v. Fischbach & Moore, Inc., 311 F.Supp. 412, 416 (N.D.Ill.1970) ("boastful" advertising and consideration of subsidiaries as "family" do not prove that corporate identities were ignored).

Fifth, the plaintiffs contend that Atex's assignment of its former CEO's mortgage to Kodak in order to close the sale of Atex's assets to a third party is evidence of Kodak's domination of Atex. We reject this argument as well. The evidence is undisputed that Kodak paid Atex the book value of the note and entered into a formal repayment agreement with the former CEO. Formal contracts were executed, and the two companies observed all corporate formalities.

Finally, even if the plaintiffs did raise a factual question about Kodak's domination of Atex, summary judgment would still be appropriate because the plaintiffs offer no evidence on the second prong of the alter ego analysis. The plaintiffs have failed to present evidence of an "overall element of injustice or unfairness" that would result from respecting the two companies' corporate separateness. See Harper, 743 F.Supp. at 1085 (holding that plaintiff cannot prevail on alter ego theory "because he has failed to allege any unfairness or injustice which would justify the court in disregarding the [companies'] separate legal existences"). In the instant case, the plaintiffs offer nothing more than the bare assertion that Kodak "exploited" Atex "to generate profits but not to safeguard safety." There is no indication that Kodak sought to defraud creditors and consumers or to siphon funds from its subsidiary. The plaintiffs' conclusory assertions, without more, are not evidence, see Quinn, 613 F.2d at 445, and are completely inadequate to support a finding that it would be unjust to respect Atex's corporate form.

For all of the foregoing reasons, the district court's order entering summary judgment on the plaintiffs' alter ego theory of liability is affirmed....

[The court also granted summary judgment for Kodak on the plaintiffs' other theories.]

Walkovszky v. Carlton

Court of Appeals of New York, 1966.
18 N.Y.2d 414, 276 N.Y.S.2d 585, 223 N.E.2d 6.

■ FULD, JUDGE. This case involves what appears to be a rather common practice in the taxicab industry of vesting the ownership of a taxi fleet in many corporations, each owning only one or two cabs.

The complaint alleges that the plaintiff was severely injured four years ago in New York City when he was run down by a taxicab owned by the defendant Seon Cab Corporation and negligently operated at the time by the defendant Marchese. The individual defendant, Carlton, is claimed to be a stockholder of 10 corporations, including Seon, each of which has but two cabs registered in its name, and it is implied that only the minimum automobile liability insurance required by law (in the amount of $10,000) is carried on any one cab. Although seemingly independent of one another, these corporations are alleged to be "operated . . . as a single entity, unit and enterprise" with regard to financing, supplies, repairs, employees and garaging, and all are named as defendants.[1] The plaintiff asserts that he is also entitled to hold their stockholders personally liable for the damages sought because the multiple corporate structure constitutes an unlawful attempt "to defraud members of the general public" who might be injured by the cabs.

The defendant Carlton has moved, pursuant to CPLR 3211(a)7, to dismiss the complaint on the ground that as to him it "fails to state a cause of action". The court at Special Term granted the motion but the Appellate Division, by a divided vote, reversed, holding that a valid cause of action was sufficiently stated. The defendant Carlton appeals to us, from the nonfinal order, by leave of the Appellate Division on a certified question.

The law permits the incorporation of a business for the very purpose of enabling its proprietors to escape personal liability (see, e.g., Bartle v. Home Owners Co-op., 309 N.Y. 103, 106, 127 N.E.2d 832, 833) but, manifestly, the privilege is not without its limits. Broadly speaking, the courts will disregard the corporate form, or, to use accepted terminology, "pierce the corporate veil", whenever necessary "to prevent fraud or to achieve equity". (International Aircraft Trading Co. v. Manufacturers Trust Co., 297 N.Y. 285, 292, 79 N.E.2d 249, 252.) In determining whether liability should be extended to reach assets beyond those belonging to the corporation, we are guided, as Judge Cardozo noted, by "general rules of agency". (Berkey v. Third Ave. Ry. Co., 244 N.Y. 84, 95, 155 N.E. 58, 61, 50 A.L.R. 599.) In other words, whenever anyone uses control of the corporation to further his own rather than the corporation's business, he will be liable for the corporation's acts "upon the principle of *respondeat superior* applicable even where the agent is a natural person". . . . Such liability, moreover, extends not only to the corporation's commercial dealings . . . but to its negligent acts as well. . . .

In [Mangan v. Terminal Transp. System, 247 App.Div. 853, 286 N.Y.S. 666, mot. for lv. to app. den. 272 N.Y. 676, 286 N.Y.S. 666,] the plaintiff was injured as a result of the negligent operation of a cab owned and operated by one of four corporations affiliated with the defendant Terminal. Although the defendant was not a stockholder of any of the operating companies, both the defendant and the operating companies were owned, for the most part, by the same parties. The

1. The corporate owner of a garage is also included as a defendant.

defendant's name (Terminal) was conspicuously displayed on the sides of all of the taxis used in the enterprise and, in point of fact, the defendant actually serviced, inspected, repaired and dispatched them. These facts were deemed to provide sufficient cause for piercing the corporate veil of the operating company—the nominal owner of the cab which injured the plaintiff—and holding the defendant liable. The operating companies were simply instrumentalities for carrying on the business of the defendant without imposing upon it financial and other liabilities incident to the actual ownership and operation of the cabs. . . .

In the case before us, the plaintiff has explicitly alleged that none of the corporations "had a separate existence of their own" and, as indicated above, all are named as defendants. However, it is one thing to assert that a corporation is a fragment of a larger corporate combine which actually conducts the business. (See Berle, The Theory of Enterprise Entity, 47 Col.L.Rev. 343, 348–350.) It is quite another to claim that the corporation is a "dummy" for its individual stockholders who are in reality carrying on the business in their personal capacities for purely personal rather than corporate ends. (See African Metals Corp. v. Bullowa, 288 N.Y. 78, 85, 41 N.E.2d 466, 469.) Either circumstance would justify treating the corporation as an agent and piercing the corporate veil to reach the principal but a different result would follow in each case. In the first, only a larger *corporate* entity would be held financially responsible . . . while, in the other, the stockholder would be personally liable. . . . Either the stockholder is conducting the business in his individual capacity or he is not. If he is, he will be liable; if he is not, then it does not matter—insofar as his personal liability is concerned—that the enterprise is actually being carried on by a larger "enterprise entity". (See Berle, The Theory of Enterprise Entity, 47 Col.L.Rev. 343.)

At this stage in the present litigation, we are concerned only with the pleadings and, since CPLR 3014 permits causes of action to be stated "alternatively or hypothetically", it is possible for the plaintiff to allege both theories as the basis for his demand for judgment. In ascertaining whether he has done so, we must consider the entire pleading, educing therefrom " 'whatever can be imputed from its statements by fair and reasonable intendment.' " (Condon v. Associated Hosp. Serv., 287 N.Y. 411, 414, 40 N.E.2d 230, 231. . . .) Reading the complaint in this case most favorably and liberally, we do not believe that there can be gathered from its averments the allegations required to spell out a valid cause of action against the defendant Carlton.

The individual defendant is charged with having "organized, managed, dominated and controlled" a fragmented corporate entity but there are no allegations that he was conducting business in his individual capacity. Had the taxicab fleet been owned by a single corporation, it would be readily apparent that the plaintiff would face formidable barriers in attempting to establish personal liability on the part of the corporation's stockholders. The fact that the fleet ownership has been deliberately split up among many corporations does not ease the plaintiff's burden in that respect. The corporate form may not be disregarded merely because the assets of the corporation, together with the mandatory insurance coverage of the vehicle which struck the plaintiff, are insufficient to assure him the recovery sought. If Carlton were to be held individually liable on those facts alone, the decision would apply equally to the thousands of cabs which are owned by their individual drivers who conduct their businesses through corporations organized pursuant to section 401 of the Business Corporation Law, Consol.Laws, c. 4 and carry the minimum insurance required by subdivision 1 (par. [a]) of section 370 of the Vehicle and Traffic Law, Consol.Laws, c. 71. These taxi owner-operators are entitled to form such corporations (cf. Elenkrieg v. Siebrecht, 238 N.Y. 254, 144 N.E. 519, 34 A.L.R. 592), and we agree with the court at Special Term that, if the insurance coverage required by statute "is inadequate for the protection of the public, the remedy lies not with the courts but with the Legislature." It may very well be sound policy to require that certain corporations must take out liability insurance which will afford adequate compensation to their potential tort victims. However, the responsibility for imposing conditions on the privilege of incorporation has been committed by the Constitution to the Legislature (N.Y. Const., art. X, 1) and it may not be fairly implied, from any statute, that the Legislature intended, without the slightest discussion or debate, to require of taxi corporations that they carry automobile liability insurance over and above that mandated by the Vehicle and Traffic Law.

This is not to say that it is impossible for the plaintiff to state a valid cause of action against the defendant Carlton. However, the simple fact is that the plaintiff has just not done so here. While the complaint alleges that the separate corporations were undercapitalized and that their assets have been intermingled, it is barren of any "sufficiently particular[ized] statements" (CPLR 3013; see 3 Weinstein–Korn–Miller, N.Y.Civ.Prac., par. 3013.01 et seq., pp. 30–142 et seq.) that the defendant Carlton and his associates are actually doing business in their individual capacities, shuttling their personal funds in and out of the corporations "without regard to formality and to suit their immediate convenience." (Weisser v. Mursam Shoe Corp., 2 Cir., 127 F.2d 344, 345, 145 A.L.R. 467, supra.) Such a "perversion of the privilege to do business in a corporate form" (Berkey v. Third Ave. Ry. Co., 244 N.Y. 84, 95, 155 N.E. 58, 61, 50 A.L.R. 599, supra) would justify imposing personal liability on the individual stockholders. (See African Metals Corp. v. Bullowa, 288 N.Y. 78, 41 N.E.2d 466, supra.) Nothing of the sort has in fact been charged, and it cannot reasonably or logically be inferred from the happenstance that the business of Seon Cab Corporation may actually be carried on by a larger corporate entity composed of many corporations which, under general principles of agency, would be liable to each other's creditors in contract and in tort.[2]

---

2. In his affidavit in opposition to the motion to dismiss, the plaintiff's counsel claimed that corporate assets had been "milked out" of, and "siphoned off" from the enterprise. Quite

In point of fact, the principle relied upon in the complaint to sustain the imposition of personal liability is not agency but fraud. Such a cause of action cannot withstand analysis. If it is not fraudulent for the owner-operator of a single cab corporation to take out only the minimum required liability insurance, the enterprise does not become either illicit or fraudulent merely because it consists of many such corporations. The plaintiff's injuries are the same regardless of whether the cab which strikes him is owned by a single corporation or part of a fleet with ownership fragmented among many corporations. Whatever rights he may be able to assert against parties other than the registered owner of the vehicle come into being not because he has been defrauded but because, under the principle of *respondeat superior,* he is entitled to hold the whole enterprise responsible for the acts of its agents.

In sum, then, the complaint falls short of adequately stating a cause of action against the defendant Carlton in his individual capacity.

The order of the Appellate Division should be reversed, with costs in this court and in the Appellate Division, the certified question answered in the negative and the order of the Supreme Court, Richmond County, reinstated, with leave to serve an amended complaint.

■ Keating, Judge (dissenting).

The defendant Carlton, the shareholder here sought to be held for the negligence of the driver of a taxicab, was a principal shareholder and organizer of the defendant corporation which owned the taxicab. The corporation was one of 10 organized by the defendant, each containing two cabs and each cab having the "minimum liability" insurance coverage mandated by section 370 of the Vehicle and Traffic Law. The sole assets of these operating corporations are the vehicles themselves and they are apparently subject to mortgages.[1]

From their inception these corporations were intentionally undercapitalized for the purpose of avoiding responsibility for acts which were bound to arise as a result of the operation of a large taxi fleet having cars out on the street 24 hours a day and engaged in public transportation. And during the course of the corporations' existence all income was continually drained out of the corporations for the same purpose.

The issue presented by this action is whether the policy of this State, which affords those desiring to engage in a business enterprise the privilege of limited liability through the use of the corporate devise, is so strong that it will permit that privilege to continue no matter how much it is abused, no matter how irresponsibly the

---

apart from the fact that these allegations are far too vague and conclusory, the charge is premature. If the plaintiff succeeds in his action and becomes a judgment creditor of the corporation, he may then sue and attempt to hold the individual defendants accountable for any dividends and property that were wrongfully distributed (Business Corporation Law, §§ 510, 719, 720).

1. It appears that the medallions, which are of considerable value, are judgment proof. (Administrative Code of City of New York, § 436–2.0.) [Footnote by the court.]

corporation is operated, no matter what the cost to the public. I do not believe that it is.

Under the circumstances of this case the shareholders should all be held individually liable to this plaintiff for the injuries he suffered. (See Mull v. Colt Co., D.C., 31 F.R.D. 154, 156; Teller v. Clear Service Co., 9 Misc.2d 495, 173 N.Y.S.2d 183.) At least, the matter should not be disposed of on the pleadings by a dismissal of the complaint. "If a corporation is organized and carries on business without substantial capital in such a way that the corporation is likely to have no sufficient assets available to meet its debts, it is inequitable that shareholders should set up such a flimsy organization to escape personal liability. The attempt to do corporate business without providing any sufficient basis of financial responsibility to creditors is an abuse of the separate entity and will be ineffectual to exempt the shareholders from corporate debts. It is coming to be recognized as the policy of law that shareholders should in good faith put at the risk of the business unencumbered capital reasonably adequate for its prospective liabilities. If capital is illusory or trifling compared with the business to be done and the risks of loss, this is a ground for denying the separate entity privilege." (Ballantine, Corporations [rev. ed., 1946], § 129, pp. 302–303.) . . .

■ DESMOND, C.J., and VAN VOORHIS, BURKE and SCILEPPI, JJ., concur with FULD, J.

■ KEATING, J., dissents and votes to affirm in an opinion in which BERGAN, J., concurs.

Order reversed, etc.

NOTE ON FURTHER PROCEEDINGS IN WALKOVSZKY v. CARLTON

Following the decision in *Walkovszky,* the plaintiff amended his complaint. The Appellate Division held that "the amended complaint sufficiently alleges a cause of action against appellant, i.e., that he and the other individual defendants were conducting the business of the taxicab fleet in their individual capacities." Walkovszky v. Carlton, 29 A.D.2d 763, 287 N.Y.S.2d 546 (1968). That decision was affirmed by the Court of Appeals, 23 N.Y.2d 714, 296 N.Y.S.2d 362, 244 N.E.2d 55 (1968), noting that the amended complaint "now meets the pleading requirements set forth in [our prior] opinion and states a valid cause of action." Neither opinion stated the particulars in which the amended complaint differed from the original.

Berle, The Theory of Enterprise Entity

47 Columbia Law Rev. 343 (1947).

As the scale of business enterprises enlarged, the process of subdivision began; hence subsidiary corporations wholly-owned or partly-owned; or holding companies combined into a series of corporations constituting a combined economic enterprise; and so forth. More often than not, a single large-scale business is conducted, not by a single corporation, but by a constellation of corporations controlled by a central holding company, the various sectors being separately incorporated, either because they were once independent and have been acquired, or because the central concern, entering new fields, created new corporations to develop them, or for tax reasons. In some instances, departments of the business are separately incorporated and operated as separate legal units. . . .

This is far from the original conception of a corporation. The legal doctrine of corporate personality was built around the idea of a sovereign grant of certain attributes of personality to a definable group, engaged in an enterprise. The so-called "artificial personality" was designed to be the enterpriser of a project. Multiplicity of artificial personalities within an enterprise unit would probably have been impossible under most early corporation laws. . . .

It is the thesis of this essay:

That the entity commonly known as "corporate entity" takes its being from the reality of the underlying enterprise, formed or in formation;

That the state's approval of the corporate form sets up a prima facie case that the assets, liabilities and operations of the corporation are those of the enterprise;

But that where the corporate entity is defective, or otherwise challenged, its existence, extent and consequences may be determined by the actual existence and extent and operations of the underlying enterprise, which by these very qualities acquires an entity of its own, recognized by law.

For brevity, this hypothesis is hereafter referred to as the theory of "enterprise entity." . . .

[An] illustration of judicial erection of a new entity occurs in situations where the corporate personality (as embodied in its charter, books and so forth) does not correspond to the actual enterprise, but merely to a fragment of it. The result is to construct a new aggregate of assets and liabilities. Typical cases appear where a partnership or a central corporation owns the controlling interest in one or more other corporations, but has so handled them that they have ceased to represent a separate enterprise and have become, as a business matter, more or less indistinguishable parts of a larger enterprise. The decisions disregard the paper corporate personalities and base liability on the assets of the enterprise. . . .

This category of cases stands [most] squarely on the foundation of economic enterprise-fact. The courts disregard the corporate fiction specifically because it has parted company with the enterprise-fact, for whose furtherance the corporation was created; and, having got that far, they then take the further step of ascertaining what is the actual enterprise-fact and attach the consequences of the acts of the component individuals or corporations to that enterprise entity, to the extent that the economic outlines of the situation warrant or require.

NOTE ON LIMITED LIABILITY AGAINST TORT CLAIMANTS

1. *The problem.* What justifies the rule that shareholders are not liable for the obligations of their corporation? In addressing this question, a distinction must be drawn between obligations to voluntary creditors and to involuntary creditors. The paradigm case of the voluntary creditor is a person who has made a contract with the corporation, which the corporation has broken. The paradigm case of the involuntary creditor is a person who has been injured by the corporation's tortious conduct.

In the case of contract creditors, limited liability is often easy to justify on a sort of assumption-of-the-risk theory. Most non-lawyers don't know much law, but they do know some. One legal rule that is probably known to most businesspersons is that shareholders have limited liability. Therefore, when a businessperson contracts with a corporation, she is likely to know that she cannot hold the shareholders liable if the corporation defaults. And at least in theory, a contract creditor can fully or partially contract around limited liability. For example, a contract creditor might require personal guarantees from the corporation's shareholders, or might require covenants (promises) that the corporation will not take designated steps that could impair its financial condition, or might charge a price that impounds (reflects) the cost of the extra risk entailed in dealing with an enterprise whose owners are not liable for its obligations.

However, the assumption-of-the-risk theory of limited liability fails in the case of a tort creditor, such as a pedestrian who is run over by a corporation's taxi. Furthermore, at least in the case of a publicly held corporation, the large body of shareholders may be better risk-bearers than an injured tort victim. See Leebron, Limited Liability, Tort Victims, and Creditors, 91 Colum.L.Rev. 1565, at 1601–02 (1992).

Moreover, in most or all tort contexts limited liability seems to be inefficient. Modern conceptions of policy suggest that an enterprise should internalize—should be made to bear—the costs that running the enterprise entails, including costs from injuries to third persons. Limited liability therefore seems to provide exactly the *wrong* incentive. Under a regime of limited liability, the owners of a corporation will reap all the benefits of the risks the corporation takes, but will not suffer all the costs of those risks. Accordingly, limited liability provides corporations with an incentive to take risks that are economically undue in the sense that managers who desire to advance the interests of their shareholders may make investments that would be inefficient if all externalities had to be taken into account. As Henry Hansmann and Reinier Kraakman put it:

> The most familiar inefficiency created by limited liability is the incentive it provides for the shareholder to direct the corporation to spend too little on precautions to avoid accidents. In contrast, a rule of unlimited liability induces the socially efficient level of expenditure on precautions by making the shareholder personally liable for any tort damages that the corporation cannot pay.
>
> Further, limited liability encourages overinvestment in hazardous industries. Since limited liability permits cost externalization, a corporation engaged in highly risky activities can have positive value for its shareholder, and thus can be an attractive investment, even when its net present value to society as a whole is negative. Consequently, limited liability encourages excessive entry and aggregate overinvestment in unusually hazardous industries.

Hansmann & Kraakman, Toward Unlimited Shareholder Liability for Corporate Torts, 100 Yale L.J. 1879, 1882–83 (1991).

An efficiency argument *for* limited liability even in the tort context is that in the absence of limited liability, the market for publicly held stock would be less efficient. The essential points of this argument, made by Halpern, Trebilcock & Turnbull, An Economic Analysis of Limited Liability in Corporation Law, 30 U. Toronto L.J. 117 (1980), and by F. Easterbrook & D. Fischel, The Economic Structure of Corporate Law 40–44 (1991), are as follows: A requirement of an efficient capital market is that the relevant capital assets (here, corporate stock) can be quickly and easily converted into cash. This characteristic is known as *liquidity*. A condition necessary to achieve liquidity is that the asset be worth the same amount to all potential investors. However, under a legal regime in which shareholders had unlimited liability for tort claims, tort creditors would sue only very *wealthy shareholders*, like banks and pension funds, because non-wealthy shareholders would be unable to satisfy a judgment. As a result, the market for stock would not function efficiently, because the value of shares would not be uniform, but instead vary inversely with the wealth of the shareholder: under such a regime, a tort creditor would sue only a few wealthy shareholders and collect the entire amount of his claim from them. Accordingly, stock held by wealthy shareholders would be more risky, and therefore less valuable, than stock held by shareholders who are not wealthy. In theory, the shareholders who are sued could seek contribution from the remaining shareholders. In practice, however, because of the cost of litigation they would probably seek contribution only from other wealthy shareholders. Moreover, the argument goes, since the right of contribution would be very important under such a regime, wealthy shareholders would need to continually incur costs to monitor the wealth of other shareholders. The need to incur those costs would make the market even less efficient.

The stock-market-efficiency argument, however, does not apply to either closely held corporations or wholly owned subsidiaries, neither of which have publicly traded stock. Even in the case of publicly held corporations, the weight of the stock-market-efficiency argument in the real world is difficult to judge. A rule that shareholders were liable to tort creditors would presumably be coupled with a rule, similar to that of the Revised Uniform Partnership Act, that required exhaustion of corporate assets before suit was brought against a shareholder. Based on past history, the likelihood that any shareholder in a publicly held corporation would be required to make any payments to tort creditors under an exhaustion regime would be very close to zero, because few publicly held corporations have faced tort claims that exceeded their ability to pay.

Moreover, under a rule of shareholder liability for tort claims, wealthy shareholders would avoid investment in corporations that did not make adequate provision for tort claims through insurance. This would be a powerful incentive to corporations to adequately insure. That, in turn, would not only be a socially desirable result, but would further minimize the likelihood that liability would actually be imposed on shareholders. Leebron concludes that the market effects of making shareholders of publicly held corporations liable to tort creditors would probably be too small to affect the efficiency of stock markets.

The analysis of limited liability against tort creditors was moved forward in 1991, when both Leebron and Hansmann & Kraakman made notable contributions to the debate, in their articles cited above, by developing the concept that shareholders should be liable to tort creditors, but only on a pro rata basis, rather than on a joint and several basis. Under joint and several shareholder liability, each shareholder would be unlimitedly liable for all of a corporation's debts to tort creditors. Thus a shareholder who held only one share in a publicly held corporation could in theory be liable for the corporation's entire tort debts—in the worst case, hundreds of millions of dollars or more. In contrast, under pro rata shareholder liability each shareholder would be liable to a corporation's tort creditors only for that portion of the creditors' claims that equaled the shareholder's pro rata holding of the corporation's shares. In short, shareholders would have individual liability to tort creditors, but not unlimited liability:

> To see how these rules differ, suppose that a wealthy investor holds five percent of a hotel company, while two impecunious hoteliers hold the remaining ninety-five percent. If a fire causes tort damages that exceed the company's assets by $200 million, the wealthy investor is potentially liable for $200 million under the joint and several rule but only $10 million under the pro rata rule.

Hansmann & Kraakman, supra, at 1892–93. Pro rata shareholder liability would largely undercut the argument that limited liability is required for stock-market efficiency. Because each shareholder would bear only her own pro rata portion of liability, differences in wealth would not normally cause different shareholders to value the same shares differently. Furthermore, under a regime of pro rata liability, a shareholder would have no need to monitor the wealth of other shareholders, because there would be no need for, and therefore no right to, contribution.

Some objections can be made to pro rata liability. Janet Cooper Alexander has shown that for jurisdictional reasons, grounded on due process concerns, pro rata shareholder liability for tort claims could be effectively imposed only under the law of the state of incorporation or by the federal government. Alexander, Unlimited Shareholder Liability Through a Procedural Lens, 106 Harv.L.Rev. 387 (1992). However, that is not an argument against imposing such liability, but only an argument concerning how such liability should be imposed. Joe Grundfest has argued that capital markets would undercut a regime of pro rata liability by generating a clientele of investors, such as offshore shareholders, who would be de facto attachment-proof. Grundfest, The Limited Future of Unlimited Liability: A Capital Markets Perspective, 102 Yale L.J. 387 (1992). However, this objection is inapplicable to closely held corporations and wholly owned subsidiaries. Furthermore, the discounted risk of liability might be too small to make it worthwhile for investors to allocate their resources on that basis, so that whether the risk of pro rata liability would produce a clientele effect is highly speculative.

A different problem is that pro rata liability might lead investors to purchase smaller shareholdings in individual corporations than they otherwise would, partly to reduce and diversify their exposure to tort claims, and partly because the smaller the shareholder's exposure, the higher are the transaction costs of bringing suit against the shareholder. This might lead to an inefficient degree of diversification, and might also reduce the likelihood of shareholder monitoring of corporate management, because the likelihood of such monitoring is partly a function of the size of a shareholder's holding.

2. *The Current State of Play.* The efficiency arguments for making shareholders liable to tort creditors, at least on a pro rata basis, seem to be very strong, particularly in the case of close corporations and wholly-owned subsidiaries. Nevertheless, the legislative trend is not only to preserve, but to *extend* limited liability, as evidenced by the recent, rapid, and widespread adoption of statutes authorizing limited liability companies and limited liability partnerships. See Chapters 3, and 9. How is this to be explained?

To begin with, there is a question whether individual shareholder liability, pro rata or otherwise, is really a salient issue as regards publicly held corporations. As a practical matter, piercing is normally important only where the corporation lacks sufficient assets to pay the creditor's claims. That is not a frequent occurrence in the case of publicly held corporations—although it does happen, and in a few cases tort claims have resulted in the bankruptcy of such corporations.

More important, in the case of publicly held corporations the arguments for limiting shareholder liability even as to tort creditors are not insubstantial. The efficiency-of-the-market argument has already been explored. Moreover, under the law of agency the normal predicate for making a principal vicariously liable for a tort committed by his agent is that the principal stood to benefit from those activities *and* had control over the agent's activities. In the context of publicly held corporations, however, management is vested in the board and the officers, not in the shareholders. In that context, therefore, the control predicate of vicarious liability is missing.

The lack-of-control problem is exacerbated by another issue: This issue is which shareholders will be subject to liability for corporate torts—those who were shareholders at the time the injury occurred, those who were shareholders when the injury became known, or those who are shareholders when there is a judgment against or a settlement with the corporation. Hansmann & Kraakman essentially conclude that only those persons who were shareholders at the time the injury became known should be liable. However, those persons not only lacked control over the injurious activity but lacked even the possibility of control, unless they coincidentally happened to be shareholders when the injury occurred. Furthermore, making those shareholders liable seems inconsistent with the argument that the objective of shareholder liability is to make the corporation internalize the cost of its wrongs. Given the turnover of shareholdings in publicly held corporations, under the Hansmann & Kraakman approach the financial impact of the injury often would not fall on, and therefore would not be fully internalized by, the shareholders who benefited from the activity that caused the injury.

In corporations that are privately or closely held, the story is somewhat different, because in such corporations, control and ownership are often intertwined. However, if limited liability is granted to publicly held corporations, the legislatures may not want to get into the difficult game of drawing lines between close corporations and publicly held corporations, or between wholly owned subsidiaries and subsidiaries that have some public ownership.

Another possible reason for granting limited liability in tort cases, even to private or close corporations, is that generally speaking, legislatures seem much more willing to require firms to bear risks they were not at fault for creating than to require individuals to bear such risks. Even in the case of close corporations, therefore, the legislatures might believe that liability for torts, should not be imposed on shareholders who played no role in planning, authorizing, or executing the tortious conduct.

Still another explanation of the persistence and expansion of limited liability in tort cases is that legislatures often seem to put much more weight on promoting local business-formation than on requiring the internalization of externalities.

It must also be recognized that the inefficiency of providing limited liability against the claims of tort creditors may be virtually irrelevant to a state legislature whose only concern is the citizens of its own state. Assume, for example, that a national corporation is incorporated in State A, which has 1% of the national population. State A will reap all the benefits of the franchise tax that a corporation must pay for the privilege of incorporating in that state. In contrast, the citizens of State A will bear only 1% of the costs that the corporation inefficiently imposes on tort victims; the other 99% of these costs will fall on the citizens of other states. Furthermore, once State A adopts and maintains a rule of limited liability to tort creditors, there is little or no incentive for other states to adopt a different rule, even if they wanted to do so, because corporations could avoid the rule by migrating to State A.

Finally, the piercing doctrine allows courts to impose liability on shareholders in appropriate cases notwithstanding the limited-liability rule. Although in theory this doctrine can be applied to any corporation, in practice it is only applied to close corporations and subsidiaries. Thus Professor Presser observes that there seems "to be an increasing trend toward the imposition of liability on corporate shareholders in the tort area, particularly in the area of toxic torts, and particularly by federal courts. This increased tort liability activity seems most often to have occurred in the parent-subsidiary context. . . ." S. Presser, Piercing the Corporate Veil 1–67 (1994). As a practical matter, therefore, the piercing doctrine may act as a safety valve that takes some of the pressure off the limited-liability rule in those cases where the efficiency and fairness of the rule is questionable.

Minton v. Cavaney

Supreme Court of California, 1961.
56 Cal.2d 576, 15 Cal.Rptr. 641, 364 P.2d 473.

■ TRAYNOR, JUSTICE. The Seminole Hot Springs Corporation, hereinafter referred to as Seminole, was duly incorporated in California on March 8, 1954. It conducted a public swimming pool that it leased from its owner. On June 24, 1954 plaintiffs' daughter drowned in the pool, and plaintiffs recovered a judgment for $10,000 against Seminole for her wrongful death. The judgment remains unsatisfied.

On January 30, 1957, plaintiffs brought the present action to hold defendant Cavaney personally liable for the judgment against Seminole. Cavaney died on May 28, 1958 and his widow, the executrix of his estate, was substituted as defendant. The trial court entered judgment for plaintiffs for $10,000. Defendant appeals.

Plaintiffs introduced evidence that Cavaney was a director and secretary and treasurer of Seminole and that on November 15, 1954, about five months after the drowning, Cavaney as secretary of Seminole and Edwin A. Kraft as president of Seminole applied for permission to issue three shares of Seminole stock, one share to be issued to Kraft, another to F.J. Wettrick and the third to Cavaney. The commissioner of corporations refused permission to issue these shares unless additional information was furnished. The application was then abandoned and no shares were ever issued. There was also evidence that for a time Seminole used Cavaney's office to keep records and to receive mail. Before his death Cavaney answered certain interrogatories. He was asked if Seminole "ever had any assets?" He stated that "insofar as my own personal knowledge and belief is concerned said corporation did not have any assets." Cavaney also stated in the return to an attempted execution that "[I]nsofar as I know, this corporation had no assets of any kind or character. The corporation was duly organized but never functioned as a corporation."

Defendant introduced evidence that Cavaney was an attorney at law, that he was approached by Kraft and Wettrick to form Seminole, and that he was the attorney for Seminole. Plaintiffs introduced Cavaney's answer to several interrogatories that he held the post of secretary and treasurer and director in a temporary capacity and as an accommodation to his client.

Defendant contends that the evidence does not support the court's determination that Cavaney is personally liable for Seminole's debts and that the "alter ego" doctrine is inapplicable because plaintiffs failed to show that there was " '(1) . . . such unity of interest and ownership that the separate personalities of the corporation and the individual no longer exist and (2) that, if the acts are treated as those of the corporation alone, an inequitable result will follow.' " Riddle v. Leuschner, 51 Cal.2d 574, 580, 335 P.2d 107, 110; Automotriz Del Golfo De California S.A. De C.V. v. Resnick, 47 Cal.2d 792, 796, 306 P.2d 1, 63 A.L.R.2d 1042; Minifie v. Rowley, 187 Cal. 481, 487, 202 P. 673.

The figurative terminology "alter ego" and "disregard of the corporate entity" is generally used to refer to the various situations that are an abuse of the corporate privilege. . . . The equitable owners of a corporation, for example, are personally liable when they treat the assets of the corporation as their own and add or withdraw capital from the corporation at will . . .; when they hold themselves out as being personally liable for the debts of the corporation . . .; or when they provide inadequate capitalization and actively participate in the conduct of corporate affairs. . . .

In the instant case the evidence is undisputed that there was no attempt to provide adequate capitalization. Seminole never had any substantial assets. It leased the pool that it operated, and the lease was forfeited for failure to pay the rent. Its capital was " 'trifling compared with the business to be done and the risks of loss . . .' " Automotriz Del Golfo De California S.A. De C.V. v. Resnick, supra, 47 Cal.2d 792, 797, 306 P.2d 1, 4. The evidence is also undisputed that Cavaney was not only the secretary and treasurer of the corporation but was also a director. The evidence that Cavaney was to receive one-third of the shares to be issued supports an inference that he was an equitable owner (see Riddle v. Leuschner, supra, 51 Cal.2d 574, 580, 335 P.2d 107), and the evidence that for a time the records of the corporation were kept in Cavaney's office supports an inference that he actively participated in the conduct of the business. The trial court was not required to believe his statement that he was only a "temporary" director and officer "for accommodation." In any event it merely raised a conflict in the evidence that was resolved adversely to defendant. Moreover, section 800 of the Corporations Code provides that "... the business and affairs of every corporation shall be controlled by a board of not less than three directors." Defendant does not claim that Cavaney was a director with specialized duties (see 5 U.Chi.L.Rev. 668). It is immaterial whether or not he accepted the office of director as an "accommodation" with the understanding that he would not exercise any of the duties of a director. A person may not in this manner divorce the responsibilities of a director from the statutory duties and powers of that office....

In this action to hold defendant personally liable upon the judgment against Seminole plaintiffs did not allege or present any evidence on the issue of Seminole's negligence or on the amount of damages sustained by plaintiffs. They relied solely on the judgment against Seminole. Defendant correctly contends that Cavaney or his estate cannot be held liable for the debts of Seminole without an opportunity to relitigate these issues.... Cavaney was not a party to the action against the corporation, and the judgment in that action is therefore not binding upon him unless he controlled the litigation leading to the judgment....

The judgment is reversed.

■ GIBSON, C.J., and PETERS, WHITE and DOOLING, JJ., concur.

■ [The opinion of JUSTICE SCHAUER, concurring and dissenting, is omitted. JUSTICE MCCOMB concurred without opinion.]

ARNOLD v. BROWNE, 27 Cal.App.3d 386, 396, 103 Cal.Rptr. 775, 783 (1972). "Evidence of inadequate capitalization is, at best, merely a factor to be considered by the trial court in deciding whether or not to pierce the corporate veil (Harris v. Curtis, 8 Cal.App.3d 837, 841, 87 Cal.Rptr. 614). To be sure, it is an important factor, but no case has been cited, nor have any been found, where it has been held that this factor alone *requires* invoking the equitable doctrine prayed for in the instant case."

SLOTTOW FIDELITY FEDERAL BANK v. AMERICAN CASUALTY CO., 10 F.3d 1355 (9th Cir. 1993). "[T]he plaintiffs ... had an excellent argument under an alter ego theory for piercing the corporate veil. To begin with, [the] initial capitalization of $500,000 was woefully inadequate for a corporation that handled trust agreements of the magnitude involved here. The investors claimed damages [against the corporation] in the range of $10,000,000; the case settled for nearly half that. Under California law, inadequate capitalization of a subsidiary may alone be a basis for holding the parent corporation liable for acts of the subsidiary. See, e.g., Nilsson, Robbins, Dalgarn,

Berliner, Carson & Wurst v. Louisiana Hydrolec, 854 F.2d 1538, 1544 (9th Cir.1988)...."

TRUCKWELD EQUIPMENT CO., INC. v. OLSON, 26 Wash.App. 638, 645, 618 P.2d 1017, 1022 (1980) "Although there may be situations in which a corporation is so thinly capitalized that it manifests a fraudulent intent, we do not find such to be true in the case at bar.... Olson acquired Aztec when it was financially troubled; he was not the original incorporator and he sought only to improve Aztec's profit picture. Despite gross sales of over $800,000 it appears a combination of unfortunate timing and persistent working capital problems sounded Aztec's death knell. We know of no rule of law requiring a corporate stockholder to commit additional private funds to an already faltering corporation."

RADASZEWSKI v. TELECOM CORP., 981 F.2d 305 (8th Cir. 1992). "... In order to pierce the corporate veil, a plaintiff must show, among other things, that the defendant's control of a subsidiary has

> been used by the defendant to commit fraud or wrong, to perpetrate the violation of a statutory or other positive legal duty, or dishonest and unjust act in contravention of plaintiff's legal rights...."

[Collet v. American National Stores, Inc., 708 S.W.2d 273, 284 Mo.App. 1986]. To satisfy this ... element, plaintiff cites no direct evidence of improper motivation or violation of law on Telecom's part. He argues, instead, that Contrux was undercapitalized.

"... [T]he creation of an undercapitalized subsidiary justifies an inference that the parent is either deliberately or recklessly creating a business that will not be able to pay its bills or satisfy judgments against it....

"Here, the District Court held, and we assume, that Contrux [the subsidiary] was undercapitalized in the accounting sense. Most of the money contributed to its operation by Telecom [the parent] was in the form of loans, not equity, and, when Contrux first went into business, Telecom did not pay for all of the stock that was issued to it.... Telecom in effect concedes that Contrux's balance sheet was anemic, and that, from the point of view of generally accepted accounting principles, Contrux was inadequately capitalized. Telecom says, however, that this doesn't matter, because Contrux had $11,000,000 worth of liability insurance available to pay judgments like the one that Radaszewski hopes to obtain. No one can say, therefore, the argument runs, that Telecom was improperly motivated in setting up Contrux, in the sense of either knowingly or recklessly establishing it without the ability to pay tort judgments.

"In fact, Contrux did have $1,000,000 in basic liability coverage, plus $10,000,000 in excess coverage. This coverage was bound on March 1, 1984, about five and one-half months before the accident involving Radaszewski. Unhappily, Contrux's insurance carrier became insolvent two years after the accident and is now in receivership. . . .

"The District Court rejected this argument. Undercapitalization is undercapitalization, it reasoned, regardless of insurance. The Court said:

> The federal regulation does not speak to what constitutes a properly capitalized motor carrier company. Rather, the regulation speaks to what constitutes an appropriate level of *financial responsibility*.

. . . This distinction escapes us. The whole purpose of asking whether a subsidiary is 'properly capitalized,' is precisely to determine its 'financial responsibility.' If the subsidiary is financially responsible, whether by means of insurance or otherwise, the policy behind . . . the *Collet* test is met. Insurance meets this policy just as well, perhaps even better, than a healthy balance sheet."

Sea–Land Services, Inc. v. Pepper Source

United States Court of Appeals, Seventh Circuit, 1993.
993 F.2d 1309.

■ Before BAUER, CHIEF JUDGE, ROVNER, CIRCUIT JUDGE, and TIMBERS, SENIOR CIRCUIT JUDGE.[1]

■ TIMBERS, SENIOR CIRCUIT JUDGE.

Appellants appeal from a judgment entered after a bench trial in the Northern District of Illinois, James F. Holderman, *District Judge,* piercing the corporate veil and awarding appellee $118,132.61 in damages. . . .

[Appellee Sea–Land Services, Inc. ("Sea–Land"), an ocean carrier, shipped peppers on behalf of The Pepper Source ("PS"), one of the appellants here. PS then stiffed Sea–Land on the freight bill, which was rather substantial. Sea–Land filed a federal diversity action for the money it was owed. On December 2, 1987, the district court entered a default judgment in favor of Sea–Land and against PS in the amount of $86,767.70. But PS was nowhere to be found; it had been "dissolved" in mid–1987 for failure to pay the annual state franchise tax. Worse yet for Sea–Land, even had it not been dissolved, PS apparently had no assets. With the well empty, Sea–Land could not recover its judgment against PS. Hence the instant lawsuit.

[In June 1988, Sea–Land brought this action against Gerald J. Marchese and five business entities he owns: PS, Caribe Crown, Inc., Jamar Corp., Salescaster Distributors, Inc., and Marchese Fegan Associ-

1. The Honorable William H. Timbers, Senior Circuit Judge, United States Court of Appeals for the Second Circuit, sitting by designation.

ates. Marchese also was named individually. Sea–Land sought by this suit to pierce PS's corporate veil and render Marchese personally liable for the judgment owed to Sea–Land, and then "reverse pierce" Marchese's other corporations so that they, too, would be on the hook for the $87,000. Thus, Sea–Land alleged in its complaint that all of these corporations "are alter egos of each other and hide behind the veils of alleged separate corporate existence for the purpose of defrauding plaintiff and other creditors." Count I, § 11. Not only are the corporations alter egos of each other, alleged Sea–Land, but also they are alter egos of Marchese, who should be held individually liable for the judgment because he created and manipulated these corporations and their assets for his own personal uses. Count III, §§ 9–10. (Hot on the heels of the filing of Sea–Land's complaint, PS took the necessary steps to be reinstated as a corporation in Illinois.)

[In an order dated June 22, 1990, the trial court discussed and applied the test for corporate veil-piercing explicated in *Van Dorn Co. v. Future Chemical and Oil Corp.,* 753 F.2d 565 (7th Cir.1985). Analyzing Illinois law, we held in *Van Dorn* that

> a corporate entity will be disregarded and the veil of limited liability pierced when two requirements are met:
>
> > [F]irst, there must be such unity of interest and ownership that the separate personalities of the corporation and the individual [or other corporation] no longer exist; and second, circumstances must be such that adherence to the fiction of separate corporate existence would sanction a fraud or promote injustice.

753 F.2d at 569–70. As for determining whether a corporation is so controlled by another to justify disregarding their separate identities, the Illinois cases, as we summarized them in *Van Dorn,* focus on four factors: "(1) the failure to maintain adequate corporate records or to comply with corporate formalities, (2) the commingling of funds or assets, (3) undercapitalization, and (4) one corporation treating the assets of another corporation as its own."

[The first and most striking feature that emerges from our examination of the record is that these corporate defendants are, indeed, little but Marchese's playthings. Marchese is the sole shareholder of PS, Caribe Crown, Jamar, and Salescaster. None of the corporations ever held a single corporate meeting. During his deposition, Marchese did not remember any of these corporations ever passing articles of incorporation, bylaws, or other agreements. As for physical facilities, Marchese runs all of these corporations out of the same, single office, with the same phone line, the same expense accounts, and the like. And how he does "run" the expense accounts! When he fancies to, Marchese "borrows" substantial sums of money from these corporations—interest free, of course. The corporations also "borrow" money from each other when need be, which left at least PS completely out of capital when the Sea–Land bills came due. What's more, Marchese has used the bank accounts of these corporations to pay all kinds of personal expenses, including alimony and child support payments to his ex-wife, education expenses for his children, maintenance of his personal automobiles, health care for his pet—the list goes on and on. Marchese did not even have a personal bank account!]*

... The issues raised by the second prong of *Van Dorn* were tried on July 6 and 7, 1992. On July 9, 1992, the [district] court entered judgment for Sea–Land, awarding it $118,132.61 in damages. The court concluded that Sea–Land satisfied the second prong of *Van Dorn* by establishing wrongs beyond its inability to collect on its judgment.

On the instant appeal, appellants contend that the evidence presented by Sea–Land at trial was insufficient to satisfy the second prong of *Van Dorn.* They also assert that the court misapplied Illinois law in reaching its decision....

... Sea–Land adduced sufficient evidence at trial to establish additional wrongs to justify piercing the corporate veil. First, Sea–Land demonstrated that Marchese and his corporations were unjustly enriched. We have defined "unjust enrichment" as the receipt of money or its equivalent under circumstances that, in equity and good conscience, suggest that it ought not to be retained because it belongs to someone else. *Midcoast Aviation, Inc. v. General Elec. Credit Corp.,* 907 F.2d 732, 737 (7th Cir.1990). At trial, Sea–Land demonstrated that Marchese obtained countless benefits at the expense of not only Sea–Land, but the Internal Revenue Service (IRS) and other creditors as well. Indeed, Marchese used PS funds to pay his personal expenses as well as expenses incurred by his other corporations. As a result, PS was left without sufficient funds to satisfy Sea–Land or PS's other creditors. *American Trade Partners v. A–1 Int'l Importing Enter.,* 770 F.Supp. 273, 278 (E.D.Pa.1991) (corporate veil pierced on basis of unjust enrichment where managing shareholder, with knowledge of debt to creditor, used corporation's funds to pay personal expenses). Since Marchese was enriched unjustly by his intentional manipulation and diversion of funds from his corporate entities, to allow him to use these same entities to avoid liability "would be to sanction an injustice." *Gromer, Wittenstrom & Meyer, P.C. v. Strom,* 140 Ill.App.3d 349, 354, 489 N.E.2d 370, 374 (1986).

Sea–Land also satisfied the second prong of *Van Dorn* by demonstrating at trial that Marchese used his corporate entities as "playthings" to avoid his responsibilities to creditors. An accountant testified that Marchese's payment of personal expenses with corporate funds enabled those corporations to avoid their monetary obligations to vendors, creditors, and federal and state tax authorities. One example was Marchese's withdrawal of $19,000 as salary from Jamar Corporation. This withdrawal rendered Jamar insolvent and thus unable to satisfy liabilities in excess of $450,000. Marchese also frequently took "shareholder loans" from the corporations to pay personal expenses, leaving the corporations with insufficient funds to satisfy liabilities as they became due. Further, a tax accountant testified that

* The bracketed paragraphs are adapted from a prior appeal in this case, 941 F.2d 519 (7th Cir. 1991).

Marchese's business practices were replete with illegal transactions. Indeed, as we previously recognized, "for years Marchese flagrantly has disregarded the tax code concerning the treatment of corporate funds." *Sea–Land, supra,* 941 F.2d at 522 n. 2.

Marchese's practice of avoiding liability to Sea–Land and other creditors by insuring that his corporations had insufficient funds with which to pay their debts, is ground for piercing the corporate veil. *Van Dorn, supra,* 753 F.2d at 572–73 (piercing of corporate veil allowed where subsidiary was stripped by parent corporation of its assets and rendered insolvent to the prejudice of creditor). Further, as the district court here properly recognized, Marchese was the "dominant force" behind all of the corporations and was responsible for the manipulation and diversion of corporate funds without regard for creditors or the law. *B. Kreisman & Co. v. First Arlington Nat'l Bank,* 91 Ill.App.3d 847, 415 N.E.2d 1070 (1980) (piercing corporate veil proper where defendant was the dominant force behind corporation). On the basis of the facts adduced at trial, the court properly concluded that Sea–Land satisfied the second-prong of *Van Dorn* and therefore was entitled to pierce the corporate veil....

Appellants further assert that Sea–Land fails to satisfy the requirement that a nexus exist between its injuries and the fraud or injustice committed by appellants. *South Side Bank v. T.S.B. Corp.,* 94 Ill. App.3d 1006, 419 N.E.2d 477 (1981). This claim fails, however, in view of the fact that Marchese assured Sea–Land in 1987 that it would receive payment from PS as long as there were sufficient funds. The court's findings that Marchese knew at that time that he would manipulate the funds of PS so as to insure that Sea–Land would not be paid, and that he eventually did manipulate those funds, were not clearly erroneous. Since Marchese's intentional and improper financial maneuvering caused Sea–Land's inability to collect on its default judgment, the required nexus existed here....

Affirmed.

KINNEY SHOE CORP. v. POLAN, 939 F.2d 209 (4th Cir.1991). Kinney Shoe Corp. subleased a portion of a building to Industrial Realty Co., which was wholly owned by Lincoln Polan. Polan had put no capital into the Industrial, and Industrial had no assets, no income, and no bank account. Industrial did not observe any corporate formalities: it had no stock, kept no minutes, and had no officers. Industrial filed for bankruptcy, and Kinney sued Polan to collect the amount owed by Industrial under the sublease.

The case was governed by West Virginia law. In Laya v. Erin Homes, Inc., 177 W.Va. 343, 352 S.E.2d 93 (1986), the West Virginia Supreme Court of Appeals had set forth a basic two-prong test to determine whether to pierce a corporate veil: (1) there must be such unity of interest and ownership that the separate personalities of the corporation and of the individual shareholder(s) no longer exist (a disregard-of-formalities requirement) and (2) an inequitable result would occur if the wrongful acts are treated as those of the corporation alone (a fairness requirement).

The *Laya* court then added a qualified third prong that applied only to contract creditors:

> In a breach of contract case many of the commentators and a few of the cases suggest that there may also be a third prong to the test for piercing the corporate veil which must be hurdled by certain types, and only certain types, of contract creditors of the corporation, specifically, those capable of protecting themselves. When, under the circumstances, it would be reasonable for that particular type of a party entering into the contract with the corporation, for example, a bank or other lending institution, to conduct an investigation of the credit of the corporation prior to entering into the contract, such party will be charged with the knowledge that a reasonable credit investigation would disclose. If such an investigation would disclose that the corporation is grossly undercapitalized, based upon the nature and the magnitude of the corporate undertaking, such party will be deemed to have assumed the risk of the gross undercapitalization and will not be permitted to pierce the corporate veil. In such a case that type of a sophisticated party dealing with the corporation should, and ordinarily would, also, or in lieu thereof, enter into a contract with the shareholder(s).... On the other hand, " 'the plaintiffs' lack of sophistication is equally tenable against the presumption [suggested by some commentators] that they [the plaintiffs as contract creditors] knowingly assumed the risk of the corporation's undercapitalization."
>
> Generally, the presumption is that the party dealing with the corporation did not assume the risk of grossly inadequate capitalization. "[I]n entering into such [contractual] relationships with corporate entities the parties are [generally] entitled to rely upon certain assumptions, one being that the corporation is more than a mere shell—that it has substance as well as form." ... In other words, the incorporators who actively participate in the operation of the business are not entitled to personal immunity when they fail to provide the quid pro quo for such immunity, specifically, a reasonably adequate capital fund to which creditors may resort....

In a footnote, the *Laya* court quoted with approval from Labadie Coal Co. v. Black, 672 F.2d 92, 96–97 (D.C.Cir.1982):

> Individuals who wish to enjoy limited personal liability for business activities under a corporate umbrella should be expected to adhere to the relatively simple formalities of creating and maintaining a corporate entity. In a sense, faithfulness to these formalities is the price paid for the corporate fiction, a relatively small price to pay for limited liability. Furthermore, the formalities are themselves an excellent litmus of the extent to which the individuals involved actually view the corporation as a separate being....

The Fourth Circuit held that Polan failed the basic two-prong test set out in *Laya*, and was not saved by the third prong:

> Without deciding whether the third prong should be extended beyond the context of the financial institution lender mentioned in *Laya*, we hold that, even if it applies to creditors such as Kinney, it does not prevent Kinney from piercing the corporate veil in this case. The third prong is permissive and not mandatory. This is not a factual situation that calls for the third prong, if we are to seek an equitable result. Polan set up Industrial to limit his liability ... [in his] dealings with Kinney. A stockholder's liability is limited to the amount he has invested in the corporation, but Polan invested nothing in Industrial. This corporation was no more than a shell—a transparent shell. When nothing is invested in the corporation, the corporation provides no protection to its owner; nothing in, nothing out, no protection. If Polan wishes the protection of a corporation to limit his liability, he must follow the simple formalities of maintaining the corporation. This he failed to do, and he may not relieve his circumstances by saying Kinney should have known better.

Eisenberg, Corporate Groups, in the Law Relating to Corporate Groups

(M. Gillooly ed. 1993).

... With few if any exceptions, wholly owned [subsidiaries] exist only as a response to legal rules. It is very difficult to find economic reasons for wholly owned [subsidiaries], because almost any economic goal that can be achieved by the creation of a wholly owned subsidiary can be equally well-achieved by the creation of a division [that is, a business owned by a corporation and operated in a relatively autonomous manner]. A corporate enterprise may find it desirable to organize itself in such a manner as to provide autonomy, or considerable autonomy, to one or more of its businesses or functions, but ... this goal can be served perfectly well through the use of divisions . . . If Corporation A chooses to run its wholly owned Business B as an autonomous business, it is economically irrelevant whether Business B is run as a division or as a subsidiary. If Corporation A acquires all the stock of Corporation C, it is economically irrelevant whether C is thereafter maintained as a subsidiary or run as a division. In fact, a corporation that puts some of its business units into subsidiary form is likely to treat those units in exactly the same way that it treats other businesses that are divisions. . . .

The kinds of legal rules that prompt the formation of wholly owned groups are endless. In some cases, a special legal rule may require the formation of a subsidiary. For example, in the case of multinational corporations, a host country might require a local business to be locally incorporated. Alternatively, a special legal rule may invite the formation of a subsidiary. For example, the creation of a subsidiary may confer some tax advantage. In other cases, however, the purpose of a wholly owned group is not to comply with or take the invitation of legal rules, but to circumvent the rights of creditors or shareholders.

BERKEY v. THIRD AVE. RY. CO., 244 N.Y. 84, 155 N.E. 58 (1926) (Cardozo, J.). "The whole problem of the relation between parent and subsidiary corporations is one that is still enveloped in the mists of metaphor. Metaphors in law are to be narrowly watched, for starting as devices to liberate thought, they end often by enslaving it. We say at times that the corporate entity will be ignored when the parent corporation operates a business through a subsidiary which is characterized as an 'alias' or a 'dummy.' All this is well enough if the picturesqueness of the epithets does not lead us to forget that the essential term to be defined is the act of operation. Dominion may be so complete, interference so obtrusive, that by the general rules of agency the parent will be a principal and the subsidiary an agent. Where control is less than this, we are remitted to the tests of honesty and justice. Ballentine, Parent and Subsidiary Corporations, 14 Cal. Law Review, 12, 18, 19, 20. The logical consistency of a juridical conception will indeed be sacrificed at times, when the sacrifice is essential to the end that some accepted public policy may be defended or upheld. This is so, for illustration, though agency in any proper sense is lacking, where the attempted separation between parent and subsidiary will work a fraud upon the law. . . . At such times unity is ascribed to parts which, at least for many purposes, retain an independent life, for the reason that only thus can we overcome a perversion of the privilege to do business in a corporate form."

CARTE BLANCHE (SINGAPORE) PTE., LTD. v. DINERS CLUB INTERNATIONAL, INC., 2 F.3d 24 (2d Cir.1993). "Ultimately, the question in any particular case is whether, in light of the circumstances, 'the policy behind the presumption of corporate independence and limited shareholder liability—encouragement of business development—is outweighed by the policy justifying disregarding the corporate form—the need to protect those who deal with the corporation.' "

NOTE ON VARIATIONS AMONG STATES IN APPLYING THE PIERCING-THE-VEIL DOCTRINE

Although the tests announced by the courts for piercing the corporate veil are often similar from state to state, the manner in which those tests are applied, and therefore the incidence of piercing, may vary considerably across jurisdictions. For example, Epperson & Canny examined the operation of the piercing doctrine in three neighboring jurisdictions—the District of Columbia Maryland, and Virginia. Epperson & Canny, The Capital Shareholder's Ultimate Calamity: Pierced Corporate Veils and Shareholder Liability in the District of Columbia, Maryland, and Virginia, 37 Cath.U.L.Rev. 605 (1988). They concluded that in the District of Columbia a disregard of corporate formalities, without more, may constitute prima facie evidence of unfairness or inequity. In contrast, Maryland courts accord the corporate entity "an extraordinary measure of deference, apparently relaxed only in instances of proven common law fraud." Virginia courts commonly resorted to a more fluid analysis which endeavors to take into account the "totality of the circumstances." Id. at 614–18, 621, 626.

NOTE ON AN EMPIRICAL ANALYSIS OF PIERCING CASES

In his classic study, Piercing The Corporate Veil: An Empirical Study, 76 Cornell L.Rev. 1036 (1991), Professor Robert Thompson reported the results of an empirical analysis of 2,000 piercing cases, most decided between the mid-1950s and the mid-1980s. Courts pierced the corporate veil in approximately 40% of the cases, although there were often noticeable differences in the rate of plaintiffs' success according to the category of case and the state in which the case was decided. The corporate veil was pierced more often in contract cases (42%) than in tort cases (31%). In no case was the corporate veil of a publicly held corporation pierced to impose liability on public shareholders, although many cases apparently involved piercing the veil of a subsidiary of a publicly held corporation to make the publicly held parent liable. Others have also empirically studied veil-piercing decisions. One study found that courts pierce twice as often to hold individuals liable as they do to hold entities liable where a parent-subsidiary relationship exists, that veil piercing arguments are more successful in contract cases than tort cases (whereas, with regression analysis, the type of claim—tort vs. contract—does not bear a statistical relationship to explain why the veil was pierced in the context of other factors before a court), that appellate courts are far more likely to pierce the veil than trial courts in cases in which the dominant stockholder is an individual (but no difference was observed in the parent-subsidiary context), and that over time there does not appear to be any statistically significant change in the percentage of cases in which the veil-piercing argument succeeds. John H. Matheson, Why Courts Pierce: An Empirical Study of Piercing the Corporate Veil, 7 Berkeley Bus. L. J. 1 (2010). But see Peter B. Oh, Veil Piercing, 89 Tex. L. Rev. 81 (2010) (finding higher percentage of success in tort than contract claims, but documenting that success in either category rises with allegations that fraudulent misrepresentations were committed against the claimant, that assets were siphoned away by the dominant stockholder, or that the firm was undercapitalized); Christina L. Boyd & David A. Hoffman, Disputing Limited Liability, 104 Nw. U. L. Rev. 853 (2010) (voluntary creditor is 17 percent more likely to succeed in veil piercing claim than involuntary, e.g., tort, claimant and the overall success rate in piercing the veil is inversely related to the number of employees of the entity to be pierced). All studies conclude that doctrine in this area is not clear so that results are difficult to predict, but overall success rates are such that veil piercing remains a most attractive option for those seeking payment of their claims.

NOTE ON DIRECT LIABILITY

Closely related to piercing-the-veil cases in the parent-subsidiary context are cases in which a parent is sought to be held *directly* liable as a primary wrongdoer, on the ground that the parent directed the subsidiary's operations, or some relevant portion of those operations, and wrongs were committed in the course of those directed operations. An exemplar is United States v. Bestfoods, 524 U.S. 51, 118 S.Ct. 1876, 141 L.Ed.2d 43 (1998). This case arose under the Comprehensive Environmental Response, Compensation, and Liability Act of 1980 (CERCLA). Under that Act, the federal government may, under certain conditions: (1) use the Hazardous Substance Superfund to finance efforts to clean up pollution from hazardous substances, and then (2) replenish the Fund by bringing suit against "any person who at the time of disposal of any hazardous substance owned or operated any facility" involved in the pollution.

Ott Chemical Co.—referred to in the Court's opinion as Ott II—manufactured chemicals at a plant near Muskegon, Michigan, and significantly polluted the soil and the ground water by both intentionally and unintentionally dumping hazardous materials over a long period of time. From 1956 to 1972, Ott II was a wholly owned subsidiary of CPC International. The United States sued CPC under CERCLA. (Ott II was by this time defunct.) The District Court held CPC liable, but the Sixth Circuit reversed on the ground that CPC and Ott II maintained separate personalities, and CPC did not utilize the subsidiary's corporate form to perpetuate fraud or subvert justice. The Supreme Court vacated the Sixth Circuit's opinion, and remanded the case to the District Court for further proceedings pursuant to the Court's opinion. The relevant portions of the Court's opinion follow:

> It is a general principle of corporate law deeply "ingrained in our economic and legal systems" that a parent corporation (so-called because of control through ownership of another corporation's stock) is not liable for the acts of its subsidiaries. Douglas & Shanks, Insulation from Liability Through Subsidiary Corporations, 39 *Yale L.J.* 193 (1929) (hereinafter Douglas).... Thus it is hornbook law that "the exercise of the 'control' which stock ownership gives to the stockholders ... will not create liability beyond the assets of the subsidiary. That 'control' includes the election of directors, the making of by-laws ... and the doing of all other acts incident to the legal status of stockholders. Nor will a duplication of some or all of the directors or executive officers be fatal." Douglas 196....
>
> If [CERCLA] rested liability entirely on ownership of a polluting facility, this opinion might end here [because Ott II owned the facility]; but CERCLA liability may turn on operation as well as ownership, and nothing in the statute's terms bars a parent corporation from direct liability for its *own* actions in operating a facility owned by its subsidiary. As Justice (then-Professor) Douglas noted almost 70 years ago, derivative liability cases are to be distinguished from those in which "the alleged wrong can seemingly be traced to the parent through the conduit of its own personnel and management" and "the parent is directly a participant in the wrong complained of." Douglas 207, 208. In such instances, the parent is directly liable for its own actions. The fact that a corporate subsidiary happens to own a polluting facility operated by its parent does nothing, then, to displace the rule that the parent "corporation is [itself] responsible for the wrongs committed by its agents in the course of its business," *Mine Workers v. Coronado Coal Co.*, 259 U.S. 344, 395, 42 S.Ct. 570, 577, 66 L.Ed. 975 (1922), and whereas the rules of veil-piercing limit derivative liability for the actions of another corporation, CERCLA's "operator" provision is concerned primarily with direct liability for one's own actions....
>
> This much is easy to say; the difficulty comes in defining actions sufficient to constitute direct parental "operation." ...
>
> ... If ... direct liability for the parent's operation of the facility is to be kept distinct from derivative liability for the subsidiary's own operation, the focus of the enquiry must necessarily be different under the two tests. "The question is not whether the parent operates the subsidiary, but rather whether it operates the facility, and that operation is evidenced by participation in the activities of the facility, not the subsidiary...."

Oswald [, Bifurcation of the Owner and Operator Analysis Under CERCLA, 72 Wash. U.L.Q. 223, 269 (1994)]....

... [T]he District Court wrongly assumed that the actions of the joint officers and directors are necessarily attributable to CPC. The District Court emphasized the facts that CPC placed its own high-level officials on Ott II's board of directors and in key management positions at Ott II, and that those individuals made major policy decisions and conducted day-to-day operations at the facility: "Although Ott II corporate officers set the day-to-day operating policies for the company without any need to obtain formal approval from CPC, CPC actively participated in this decision-making because high-ranking CPC officers served in Ott II management positions." *Id.*, at 559....

In imposing direct liability on these grounds, the District Court failed to recognize that "it is entirely appropriate for directors of a parent corporation to serve as directors of its subsidiary, and that fact alone may not serve to expose the parent corporation to liability for its subsidiary's acts." *American Protein Corp. v. AB Volvo*, 844 F.2d 56, 57(C.A.2), cert. denied, 488 U.S. 852, 109 S.Ct. 136, 102 L.Ed.2d 109 (1988)....

This recognition that the corporate personalities remain distinct has its corollary in the "well established principle [of corporate law] that directors and officers holding positions with a parent and its subsidiary can and do 'change hats' to represent the two corporations separately, despite their common ownership." *Lusk v. Foxmeyer Health Corp.*, 129 F.3d 773, 779 (C.A.5 1997).... Since courts generally presume "that the directors are wearing their 'subsidiary hats' and not their 'parent hats' when acting for the subsidiary," P. Blumberg, *Law of Corporate Groups: Procedural Problems in the Law of Parent and Subsidiary Corporations* S 1.02.1, at 12 (1983), it cannot be enough to establish liability here that dual officers and directors made policy decisions and supervised activities at the facility. The Government would have to show that, despite the general presumption to the contrary, the officers and directors were acting in their capacities as CPC officers and directors, and not as Ott II officers and directors, when they committed those acts.[13] The District Court made no such enquiry here, however, disregarding entirely this time-honored common law rule....

We accordingly agree with the Court of Appeals that a participation-and-control test looking to the parent's supervision over the subsidiary, especially one that assumes that dual officers always act on behalf of the parent, cannot be used to identify

13. We do not attempt to recite the ways in which the Government could show that dual officers or directors were in fact acting on behalf of the parent. Here, it is prudent to say only that the presumption that an act is taken on behalf of the corporation for whom the officer claims to act is strongest when the act is perfectly consistent with the norms of corporate behavior, but wanes as the distance from those accepted norms approaches the point of action by a dual officer plainly contrary to the interests of the subsidiary yet nonetheless advantageous to the parent.

operation of a facility resulting in direct parental liability. Nonetheless, a return to the ordinary meaning of the word "operate" in the organizational sense will indicate why we think that the Sixth Circuit stopped short when it confined its examples of direct parental operation to exclusive or joint ventures, and declined to find at least the possibility of direct operation by CPC in this case.

In our enquiry into the meaning Congress presumably had in mind when it used the verb "to operate," we recognized that the statute obviously meant something more than mere mechanical activation of pumps and valves, and must be read to contemplate "operation" as including the exercise of direction over the facility's activities.... The Court of Appeals recognized this by indicating that a parent can be held directly liable when the parent operates the facility in the stead of its subsidiary or alongside the subsidiary in some sort of a joint venture. *See* 113 F.3d, at 579. We anticipated a further possibility above, however, when we observed that a dual officer or director might depart so far from the norms of parental influence exercised through dual officeholding as to serve the parent, even when ostensibly acting on behalf of the subsidiary in operating the facility. *See* n. 13, *supra*. Yet another possibility, suggested by the facts of this case, is that an agent of the parent with no hat to wear but the parent's hat might manage or direct activities at the facility.

Identifying such an occurrence calls for line drawing yet again, since the acts of direct operation that give rise to parental liability must necessarily be distinguished from the interference that stems from the normal relationship between parent and subsidiary. Again norms of corporate behavior (undisturbed by any CERCLA provision) are crucial reference points. Just as we may look to such norms in identifying the limits of the presumption that a dual officeholder acts in his ostensible capacity, so here we may refer to them in distinguishing a parental officer's oversight of a subsidiary from such an officer's control over the operation of the subsidiary's facility. "[A]ctivities that involve the facility but which are consistent with the parent's investor status, such as monitoring of the subsidiary's performance, supervision of the subsidiary's finance and capital budget decisions, and articulation of general policies and procedures, should not give rise to direct liability." Oswald 282. The critical question is whether, in degree and detail, actions directed to the facility by an agent of the parent alone are eccentric under accepted norms of parental oversight of a subsidiary's facility.

There is, in fact, some evidence that CPC engaged in just this type and degree of activity at the Muskegon plant. The District Court's opinion speaks of an agent of CPC alone who played a conspicuous part in dealing with the toxic risks emanating from the operation of the plant. G.R.D. Williams worked only for CPC; he was not an employee, officer, or director of Ott II, see Tr. of Oral Arg. 7, and thus, his actions were of necessity taken only on behalf of CPC. The District Court found that "CPC became directly involved in environmental and regulatory matters through the work of ... Williams, CPC's governmental and environmental affairs director. Williams ... became heavily involved in environmental issues at Ott II." 777 F.Supp., at 561. He "actively participated in and exerted control over a variety of Ott II environmental matters," *ibid.*, and he "issued directives regarding Ott II's responses to regulatory inquiries," *id.*, at 575.

We think that these findings are enough to raise an issue of CPC's operation of the facility through Williams's actions ... (Emphasis added.)

SECTION 4. THE CORPORATE ENTITY AND THE INTERPRETATION OF STATUTES AND CONTRACTS

NOTE ON INTERPRETATION

The following two issues often arise:

(1) Does a statute or contract that applies to a corporation also apply, by implication, to the corporation's shareholders? For example, if Corporation A agrees with X not to compete with X, may A's sole shareholder compete with X?

(2) Does a statute or contract that applies to an individual also apply, by implication, to a corporation that the individual owns? For example, if a statute prohibits non-citizens from owning ships that ply the U.S. coastal trade, does the statute also prohibit a corporation from owning ships if all of the corporation's stock is held by noncitizens?

These issues do not concern whether liability should be imposed on the corporation's shareholders despite the general rule of limited liability. Rather, they are questions of interpretation. In making such interpretations, it must be borne in mind that on the one hand, the law normally treats a corporation and its shareholders as distinct, but on the other hand, the legislature or the contracting parties may not intend to treat a corporation and its shareholders as distinct for all purposes.

Two of the leading cases in this area are United States v. Milwaukee Refrigerator Transit Co., 142 Fed. 247, 255 (E.D.Wis.1905), and Anderson v. Abbott, 321 U.S. 349, 64 S.Ct. 531, 88 L.Ed. 793 (1944). In *Milwaukee*, a statute prohibited railroads from giving rebates to shippers. The statute was held applicable to a corporation that was not itself a shipper, but had been formed by a shipper's officers and principal shareholders for the purpose of obtaining what were in substance rebates. "[A] corporation will be looked upon as a legal entity as a general rule, and until sufficient reason to the contrary appears; but, when the notion of legal entity is used to defeat public convenience ... the law will regard the corporation as an association of persons." In *Anderson*, a statute made a shareholder in a national bank liable for the debts of the bank "to the amount of his stock therein, at the par value thereof in addition to the amount invested in such stock." The question was whether this statute applied to shareholders of a parent corporation with a national bank subsidiary, even though technically only the parent was a shareholder in the bank. The Supreme Court concluded that the parent's shareholders would be deemed shareholders of the bank for the purpose of the statute, on the ground that to hold otherwise would permit that purpose to be undercut:

> It has often been held that the interposition of a corporation will not be allowed to defeat a legislative policy, whether that was the aim or only the result of the arrangement....
>
> To allow this holding company device to succeed would be to put the policy of double liability at the mercy of corporation finance.

321 U.S. at 362–63, 64 S.Ct. at 537–38. *See also* Reich v. Gateway Press, Inc., 13 F.3d 685 (3d Cir.1994); Kavanaugh v. Ford Motor Co., 353 F.2d 710, 716–17 (7th Cir.1965); Note, Efficacy of the Corporate Entity in Evasion of Statutes, 26 Iowa L.Rev. 350 (1941).

CHAPTER 8

THE SPECIAL PROBLEMS OF SHAREHOLDERS IN CLOSE CORPORATIONS

SECTION 1. INTRODUCTION

Corporations can be divided into three classes: (1) *Publicly held corporations*, which typically have a large number of shareholders, and whose shares are publicly traded. (2) *Private corporations*, whose shares are not publicly traded, although they may have more than a small number of shareholders. (3) *Close corporations*, a subset of private corporations. Close corporations have only a small number of shareholders, and are typically characterized by owner-management. In important respects, close corporations resemble partnerships, and indeed close corporations are sometimes colloquially referred to as "incorporated partnerships." Traditionally, however, courts imposed upon close corporations norms that were designed with an eye to publicly held corporations, rather than the norms of partnership law, or norms designed with close corporations in mind. There have been three types of responses to this problem. First, many legislatures have given special treatment to close corporations. Second, shareholders in close corporations often attempt to contract around traditional corporation-law norms. Third, modern courts have come to understand that close corporations often need special treatment. The first kind of response is discussed in the Note that follows. The second and third responses are illustrated by the materials in the balance of this Chapter.

NOTE ON LEGISLATIVE STRATEGIES TOWARD THE CLOSE CORPORATION

The principal strategies to be examined are those exemplified by Delaware, New York, and the Model Act. Almost all other close-corporation legislation either derives from or closely parallels one of these statutes.

1. *Unified Strategies.* One legislative strategy is to make no special provision for close corporations as such, but to modify traditional statutory norms so that they will meet the needs of close corporations although applicable to publicly held corporations as well.

2. *The New York and the Model Act Strategies.* A second legislative strategy is to follow the unified approach up to a point, but to add

one or two important provisions that are applicable only to those corporations that satisfy certain criteria. Thus N.Y.Bus.Corp.Law § 620(c) authorizes certain kinds of certificate provisions "so long as no shares of the corporation are listed on a national securities exchange or regularly quoted in an over-the-counter market by one or more members of a national or affiliated securities association." Similarly, Model Act § 7.32 authorizes certain kinds of shareholder agreements in corporations that are not listed on a national securities exchange or traded in a market maintained by one or more members of a national securities association.

3. *Statutory Close Corporations.*

a. A third legislative strategy follows the unified approach up to a point, but adds an integrated set of provisions that are explicitly made applicable *only* to corporations that both satisfy certain criteria, for, and formally elect, statutory close-corporation status (for example, Subchapter XV of the Delaware General Corporation Law). In effect therefore, the statute contemplates a special subclass of close corporations, which may be called *statutory close corporations*. Under Del. Gen. Corp. Law § 342, a corporation can qualify for statutory close-corporation status if its certificate provides that:

> (1) All of the corporation's issued stock of all classes ... shall be represented by certificates and shall be held of record by not more than a specified number of persons, not exceeding 30; and
>
> (2) All of the issued stock of all classes shall be subject to one or more of the restrictions on transfer permitted by § 202 of this title; and
>
> (3) The corporation shall make no offering of any of its stock of any class which would constitute a "public offering" within the meaning of the United States Securities Act of 1933....

Under § 343, a corporation that qualifies for statutory close-corporation status can elect such status by adopting a heading in its certificate that states the name of the corporation and the fact that it is a close corporation.

Most of the substantive provisions of Del.Gen.Corp.Law Subchapter XIV are enabling—that is, most of the provisions do not regulate the conduct of the shareholders or managers of such corporations, but simply authorize shareholders in statutory close corporations to enter into arrangements that might otherwise be unenforceable or of doubtful validity. Subchapter XIV provides enormous flexibility—so much so, that for a well-advised corporation that elects to qualify under this Subchapter, many or most governance issues will turn on the lawyer's drafting, rather than on corporate law. On the other hand, the remaining provisions of the Delaware General Corporation Law are sufficiently flexible so that much the same is true even for close corporations that are not statutory close corporations under Subchapter XIV.

b. *Significance of statutory close corporations*. The data shows that only a tiny fraction of newly formed corporations elect to become statutory close corporations. 1 O'Neal and Thompson's Close Corporations and LLCs § 1.20 (rev. 3d ed. 2010). The result is that for practical purposes, statutory close corporation provisions are much ado about very little. For example, O'Neal & Thompson found that as of 2004, Wisconsin reported 5,101 statutory close corporations out of 98,602 total incorporations. Alabama reported 5,324 statutory close corporations out of 155,198 total corporations. Pennsylvania reported approximately 24,000 statutory close corporations out of approximately 580,000 total corporations. The Kansas Secretary of State's office reported less than 5 percent statutory close corporations and "probably a lot less," adding that observations of attorneys and experienced people indicate that the number has been declining. Delaware reported 16,684 statutory close corporations in 1985. Four other states enacting statutory close-corporation supplements reported even smaller numbers—863 statutory close corporations out of 82,694 total corporations in Missouri; 828 statutory close corporations out of 97,009 total corporations in Montana; 742 statutory close corporations out of 63,172 in Nevada; and 753 statutory close corporations out of 12,422 total corporations in Wyoming. In Texas, about 6% of filing corporations elected close corporation status.

"The greatest use of statutory close corporation status appears to be in California. A 1978 survey of 300 articles of incorporation filed in California showed 28 percent filed as statutory close corporations. A 1985 survey of 200 California incorporations found 19 percent to be statutory close corporations. The attorney who conducted the California surveys suggests, however, that the number is 'entirely misleading' because many corporations electing to become statutory close corporations are organized by nonlawyers using printed forms who do not understand the reasons they are electing statutory close corporation status. He states further that many lawyers mistakenly believe they have to elect close corporation status to be eligible to elect the tax status provided by Subchapter S of the Internal Revenue Code or believe they have to elect such status to come within the 'short form' exemption of the California securities law. After excluding corporations formed by nonlawyers, those formed by lawyers under erroneous beliefs, and one-person corporations seeking to avoid corporate formalities while retaining corporate limited liability, the attorney conducting the surveys concluded that "the number of 'real' situations for the use of the statutory close corporation would be extremely small but also undeterminable." Id.

NOTE ON NON-ELECTING CORPORATIONS

Where a statute defines a class of statutory close corporations, and provides that only those corporations that explicitly opt in to the statutory provisions are covered by those provisions, a difficult issue arises concerning the effect of the statute on close corporations that do not opt in to become statutory close corporations. This issue is especially important because so few close corporations elect statutory close-corporation status. In Ramos v. Estrada, 8 Cal.App.4th 1070, 10 Cal.Rptr.2d 833 (1992), Broadcast Corp. was owned by two groups. Under an agreement, each group was required to vote for the directors upon whom a majority of the group had agreed. The Estradas, who were members of one group, wanted to vote in a different way from the majority of their group. The issue was whether the voting agreement was enforceable. Section 706 of the California Corporation Code provided as follows:

> (a) Notwithstanding any other provision of this division, an agreement between two or more shareholders of a close corporation [defined under section 158(a) as "a corporation whose articles contain ... a provision that all of the corporation's issued shares of all classes shall be held of record by not more than a specified number of persons, not exceeding 35, and a statement 'This corporation is a close corporation.'], if in writing and signed by the parties thereto, may provide that in exercising any voting rights the shares held by them shall be voted as provided by the agreement, or as the parties may agree or as determined in accordance with a procedure agreed upon by them....
>
> (d) This section shall not invalidate any voting or other agreement among shareholders ... which agreement ... is not otherwise illegal."

Although Broadcast Corp. was not a statutory close corporation, the court held that the voting agreement was enforceable:

> Even though this corporation does not qualify as a close corporation, this agreement is valid and binding on the Estradas....
>
> The Legislative Committee comment regarding section 706, subdivision (d) states that "[t]his subdivision is intended to preserve any agreements which would be upheld under court decisions even though they do not comply with one or more of the requirements of this section, including voting agreements of corporations other than close corporations." ...
>
> The instant agreement is valid, enforceable and supported by consideration.

A much different position was taken by the Delaware court in Nixon v. Blackwell, 626 A.2d 1366 (Del.1993):

> We wish to address ... [w]hether there should be any special, judicially-created rules to "protect" minority stockholders of closely-held Delaware corporations.
>
> The case at bar points up the basic dilemma of minority stockholders in receiving fair value for their stock as to which there is no market and no market valuation. It is not difficult to be sympathetic, in the abstract, to a stockholder who finds himself or

herself in that position. A stockholder who bargains for stock in a closely-held corporation and who pays for those shares ... can make a business judgment whether to buy into such a minority position, and if so on what terms. One could bargain for definitive provisions of self-ordering permitted to a Delaware corporation through the certificate of incorporation or by-laws by reason of the provisions in 8 Del.C. §§ 102, 109, and 141(a). Moreover, in addition to such mechanisms, a stockholder intending to buy into a minority position in a Delaware corporation may enter into definitive stockholder agreements, and such agreements may provide for elaborate earnings tests, buy-out provisions, voting trusts, or other voting agreements. See, e.g., 8 Del.C. § 218; Sonitrol Holding Co. v. Marceau Investissements, Del.Supr., 607 A.2d 1177 (1992).

The tools of good corporate practice are designed to give a purchasing minority stockholder the opportunity to bargain for protection before parting with consideration. It would do violence to normal corporate practice and our corporation law to fashion [a] ruling which would result in a court-imposed stockholder buy-out for which the parties had not contracted.

In 1967, when the Delaware General Corporation Law was significantly revised, a new Subchapter XIV entitled "Close Corporations; Special Provisions," became a part of that law for the first time.... [S]ubchapter XIV applies only to "close corporations," as defined in section 342. "Unless a corporation elects to become a close corporation under this subchapter in the manner prescribed in this subchapter, it shall be subject in all respects to this chapter, except this subchapter." 8 Del.C. § 341. The corporation before the Court in this matter, is not a "close corporation." Therefore it is not governed by the provisions of Subchapter XIV.

One cannot read into the situation presented in the case at bar any special relief for the minority stockholders in this closely-held, but not statutory "close corporation" because the provisions of Subchapter XIV relating to close corporations and other statutory schemes preempt the field in their respective areas. It would run counter to the spirit of the doctrine of independent legal significance, and would be inappropriate judicial legislation for this Court to fashion a special judicially-created rule for minority investors when the entity does not fall within those statutes, or when there are no negotiated special provisions in the certificate of incorporation, by-laws, or stockholder agreements. The entire fairness test, correctly applied and articulated, is the proper judicial approach....

See also Sundberg v. Lampert Lumber Co., 390 N.W.2d 352 (Minn. App.1986); Hunt v. Data Management Resources, Inc., 26 Kan.App.2d 405, 985 P.2d 730 (1999).

SECTION 2. VOTING ARRANGEMENTS AT THE SHAREHOLDER LEVEL

A. SHAREHOLDER VOTING AGREEMENTS

DEL. GEN. CORP. LAW §§ 212(e), 218(c)

[See Statutory Supplement]

MODEL BUS. CORP. ACT §§ 7.22(d), 7.31

[See Statutory Supplement]

CAL. CORP. CODE §§ 158(a), 705(e), 706

[See Statutory Supplement]

N.Y. BUS. CORP. LAW §§ 609(f), 620

[See Statutory Supplement]

Ringling Bros.–Barnum & Bailey Combined Shows v. Ringling

Supreme Court of Delaware, 1947.
29 Del.Ch. 610, 53 A.2d 441.

Suit by Edith Conway Ringling against Ringling Brothers–Barnum & Bailey Circus Combined Shows, Inc., and others to determine the right of individual defendants to hold office as directors or officers of the corporation and to determine the validity of election of directors at the 1946 annual stockholders' meeting. From a decree for complainant entered in conformity with opinion of the Vice Chancellor, 49 A.2d 603, the defendants appeal. . . .

■ PEARSON, JUDGE.

The Court of Chancery was called upon to review an attempted election of directors at the 1946 annual stockholders meeting of the corporate defendant. The pivotal questions concern an agreement between two of the three present stockholders, and particularly the effect of this agreement with relation to the exercise of voting rights by these two stockholders. At the time of the meeting, the corporation had outstanding 1000 shares of capital stock held as follows: 315 by petitioner Edith Conway Ringling; 315 by defendant Aubrey B. Ringling Haley (individually or as executrix and legatee of a deceased husband); and 370 by defendant John Ringling North. The purpose of the meeting was to elect the entire board of seven directors. The shares could be voted cumulatively. Mrs. Ringling asserts that by virtue of the operation of an agreement between her and Mrs. Haley, the latter was bound to vote her shares for an adjournment of the meeting, or in the alternative, for a certain slate of directors. Mrs. Haley contends that she was not so bound for reason that the agreement was invalid, or at least revocable.

The two ladies entered into the agreement in 1941. It makes like provisions concerning stock of the corporate defendant and of another corporation, but in this case, we are concerned solely with the agreement as it affects the voting of stock of the corporate defendant. The agreement recites that each party was the owner "subject only to possible claims of creditors of the estates of Charles Ringling and Richard Ringling, respectively" (deceased husbands of the parties), of 300 shares of the capital stock of the defendant corporation; that in 1938 these shares had been deposited under a voting trust agreement which would terminate in 1947, or earlier, upon the elimination of certain liability of the corporation; that each party also owned 15 shares individually; that the parties had "entered into an agreement in April 1934 providing for joint action by them in matters affecting their ownership of stock and interest in" the corporate defendant; that the parties desired "to continue to act jointly in all matters relating to their stock ownership or interest in" the corporate defendant (and the other corporation). The agreement then provides as follows:

"Now, Therefore, in consideration of the mutual covenants and agreements hereinafter contained the parties hereto agree as follows:

"1. Neither party will sell any shares of stock or any voting trust certificates in either of said corporations to any other person whosoever, without first making a written offer to the other party hereto of all of the shares or voting trust certificates proposed to be sold, for the same price and upon the same terms and conditions as in such proposed sale, and allowing such other party a time of not less than 180 days from the date of such written offer within which to accept same.

"2. In exercising any voting rights to which either party may be entitled by virtue of ownership of stock or voting trust certificates held by them in either of said corporation, each party will consult and confer with the other and the parties will act jointly in exercising such voting rights in accordance with such agreement as they may reach with respect to any matter calling for the exercise of such voting rights.

"3. In the event the parties fail to agree with respect to any matter covered by paragraph 2 above, the question in disagreement shall be submitted for arbitration to Karl D. Loos, of Washington, D.C. as arbitrator and his decision thereon shall be binding upon the parties hereto. Such arbitration shall be exercised to the end of assuring for the respective corporations good management and such participation therein by the members of the Ringling family as the experience, capacity and ability of each may warrant. The parties may at any time by written agreement designate any other individual to act as arbitrator in lieu of said Loos.

"4. Each of the parties hereto will enter into and execute such voting trust agreement or agreements and such other instruments as, from time to time they may deem advisable and as they may be advised by counsel are appropriate to effectuate the purposes and objects of this agreement.

"5. This agreement shall be in effect from the date hereof and shall continue in effect for a period of ten years unless sooner terminated by mutual agreement in writing by the parties hereto.

"6. The agreement of April 1934 is hereby terminated.

"7. This agreement shall be binding upon and inure to the benefit of the heirs, executors, administrators and assigns of the parties hereto respectively."

The Mr. Loos mentioned in the agreement is an attorney and has represented both parties since 1937, and, before and after the voting trust was terminated in late 1942, advised them with respect to the exercise of their voting rights. At the annual meetings in 1943 and the two following years, the parties voted their shares in accordance with mutual understandings arrived at as a result of discussions. In each of these years, they elected five of the seven directors. Mrs. Ringling and Mrs. Haley each had sufficient votes, independently of the other, to elect two of the seven directors. By both voting for an additional candidate, they could be sure of his election regardless of how Mr. North, the remaining stockholder, might vote.[1]

Some weeks before the 1946 meeting, they discussed with Mr. Loos the matter of voting for directors. They were in accord that Mrs. Ringling should cast sufficient votes to elect herself and her son; and that Mrs. Haley should elect herself and her husband; but they did not agree upon a fifth director. The day before the meeting, the discussions were continued, Mrs. Haley being represented by her husband since she could not be present because of illness. In a conversation with Mr. Loos, Mr. Haley indicated that he would make a motion for an adjournment of the meeting for sixty days, in order to give the ladies additional time to come to an agreement about their voting. On

1. Each lady was entitled to cast 2205 votes (since each had the cumulative voting rights of 315 shares, and there were 7 vacancies in the directorate). The sum of the votes of both is 4410, which is sufficient to allow 882 votes for each of 5 persons. Mr. North, holding 370 shares, was entitled to cast 2590 votes, which obviously cannot be divided so as to give to more than two candidates as many as 882 votes each. It will be observed that in order for Mrs. Ringling and Mrs. Haley to be sure to elect five directors (regardless of how Mr. North might vote) they must act together in the sense that their combined votes must be divided among five different candidates and at least one of the five must be voted for by both Mrs. Ringling and Mrs. Haley.

the morning of the meeting, however, he stated that because of something Mrs. Ringling had done, he would not consent to a postponement. Mrs. Ringling then made a demand upon Mr. Loos to act under the third paragraph of the agreement "to arbitrate the disagreement" between her and Mrs. Haley in connection with the manner in which the stock of the two ladies should be voted. At the opening of the meeting, Mr. Loos read the written demand and stated that he determined and directed that the stock of both ladies be voted for an adjournment of sixty days. Mrs. Ringling then made a motion for adjournment and voted for it. Mr. Haley, as proxy for his wife, and Mr. North voted against the motion. Mrs. Ringling (herself or through her attorney, it is immaterial which), objected to the voting of Mrs. Haley's stock in any manner other than in accordance with Mr. Loos' direction. The chairman ruled that the stock could not be voted contrary to such direction, and declared the motion for adjournment had carried. Nevertheless, the meeting proceeded to the election of directors. Mrs. Ringling stated that she would continue in the meeting "but without prejudice to her position with respect to the voting of the stock and the fact that adjournment had not been taken." Mr. Loos directed Mrs. Ringling to cast her votes 882 for Mrs. Ringling, 882 for her son, Robert, and 441 for a Mr. Dunn, who had been a member of the board for several years. She complied. Mr. Loos directed that Mrs. Haley's votes be cast 882 for Mrs. Haley, 882 for Mr. Haley, and 441 for Mr. Dunn. Instead of complying, Mr. Haley attempted to vote his wife's shares 1103 for Mrs. Haley, and 1102 for Mr. Haley. Mr. North voted his shares 864 for a Mr. Woods, 863 for a Mr. Griffin, and 863 for Mr. North. The chairman ruled that the five candidates proposed by Mr. Loos, together with Messrs. Woods and North, were elected. The Haley–North group disputed this ruling insofar as it declared the election of Mr. Dunn; and insisted that Mr. Griffin, instead, had been elected. A directors' meeting followed in which Mrs. Ringling participated after stating that she would do so "without prejudice to her position that the stockholders' meeting had been adjourned and that the directors' meeting was not properly held." Mr. Dunn and Mr. Griffin, although each was challenged by an opposing faction, attempted to join in voting as directors for different slates of officers. Soon after the meeting, Mrs. Ringling instituted this proceeding.

The Vice Chancellor determined that the agreement to vote in accordance with the direction of Mr. Loos was valid as a "stock pooling agreement" with lawful objects and purposes, and that it was not in violation of any public policy of this state. He held that where the arbitrator acts under the agreement and one party refuses to comply with his direction, "the Agreement constitutes the willing party . . . an implied agent possessing the irrevocable proxy of the recalcitrant party for the purpose of casting the particular vote." It was ordered that a new election be held before a master, with the direction that the master should recognize and give effect to the agreement if its terms were properly invoked. [In reaching this result, Vice Chancellor Seitz stated, "Here an implied agency based on an irrevocable proxy is fully justified to implement the Agreement without doing violence to its terms. Moreover, the provisions of the Agreement make it clear that the proxy may be treated as one coupled with an interest so as to render it irrevocable under the circumstances.... Obviously, to deny specific performance here would be tantamount to declaring the Agreement invalid. Since petitioner's rights in this respect were properly preserved at the stockholders' meeting, the meeting was a nullity to the extent that it failed to give effect to the provisions of the Agreement here involved. However, I believe it preferable to hold a new election rather than attempt to reconstruct the contested meeting. In this way the parties will be acting with explicit knowledge of their rights."]

Before taking up defendants' objections to the agreement, let us analyze particularly what it attempts to provide with respect to voting, including what functions and powers it attempts to repose in Mr. Loos, the "arbitrator". The agreement recites that the parties desired "to continue to act jointly in all matters relating to their stock ownership or interest in" the corporation. The parties agreed to consult and confer with each other in exercising their voting rights and to act jointly—that is, concertedly; unitedly; towards unified courses of action—in accordance with such agreement as they might reach. Thus, so long as the parties agree for whom or for what their shares shall be voted, the agreement provides no function for the arbitrator. His role is limited to situations where the parties fail to agree upon a course of action. In such cases, the agreement directs that "the question in disagreement shall be submitted for arbitration" to Mr. Loos "as arbitrator and his decision thereon shall be binding upon the parties". These provisions are designed to operate in aid of what appears to be a primary purpose of the parties, "to act jointly" in exercising their voting rights, by providing a means for fixing a course of action whenever they themselves might reach a stalemate.

Should the agreement be interpreted as attempting to empower the arbitrator to carry his directions into effect? Certainly there is no express delegation or grant of power to do so, either by authorizing him to vote the shares or to compel either party to vote them in accordance with his directions. The agreement expresses no other function of the arbitrator than that of deciding questions in disagreement which prevent the effectuation of the purpose "to act jointly". The power to enforce a decision does not seem a necessary or usual incident of such a function. Mr. Loos is not a party to the agreement. It does not contemplate the transfer of any shares or interest in shares to him, or that he should undertake any duties which the parties might compel him to perform. They provided that they might designate any other individual to act instead of Mr. Loos. The agreement does not attempt to make the arbitrator a trustee of an express trust. What the arbitrator is to do is for the benefit of the parties, not for his own benefit. Whether the parties accept or reject his decision is no concern of his, so far as the agreement or the surrounding circumstances reveal. We think the parties sought to bind each other, but to be bound only to each other, and not to empower the arbitrator to enforce decisions he might make.

From this conclusion, it follows necessarily that no decision of the arbitrator could ever be enforced if both parties to the agreement were unwilling that it be enforced, for the obvious reason that there would be no one to enforce it. Under the agreement, something more is required after the arbitrator has given his decision in order that it should become compulsory: at least one of the parties must determine that such decision shall be carried into effect. Thus, any "control" of the voting of the shares, which is reposed in the arbitrator, is substantially limited in action under the agreement in that it is subject to the overriding power of the parties themselves.

The agreement does not describe the undertaking of each party with respect to a decision of the arbitrator other than to provide that it "shall be binding upon the parties". It seems to us that this language, considered with relation to its context and the situations to which it is applicable, means that each party promised the other to exercise her own voting rights in accordance with the arbitrator's decision. The agreement is silent about any exercise of the voting rights of one party by the other. The language with reference to situations where the parties arrive at an understanding as to voting plainly suggests "action" by each, and "exercising" voting rights by each, rather than by one for the other. There is no intimation that this method should be different where the arbitrator's decision is to be carried into effect.

Assuming that a power in each party to exercise the voting rights of the other might be a relatively more effective or convenient means of enforcing a decision of the arbitrator than would be available without the power, this would not justify implying a delegation of the power in the absence of some indication that the parties bargained for that means. The method of voting actually employed by the parties tends to show that they did not construe the agreement as creating powers to vote each other's shares; for at meetings prior to 1946 each party apparently exercised her own voting rights, and at the 1946 meeting, Mrs. Ringling, who wished to enforce the agreement, did not attempt to cast a ballot in exercise of any voting rights of Mrs. Haley. We do not find enough in the agreement or in the circumstances to justify a construction that either party was empowered to exercise voting rights of the other.

Having examined what the parties sought to provide by the agreement, we come now to defendants' contention that the voting provisions are illegal and revocable. They say that the courts of this state have definitely established the doctrine "that there can be no agreement, or any device whatsoever, by which the voting power of stock of a Delaware corporation may be irrevocably separated from the ownership of the stock, except by an agreement which complies with Section 18 of the Corporation Law [concerning voting trusts] and except by a proxy coupled with an interest. . . ."

[Section 18] authorizes, among other things, the deposit or transfer of stock in trust for a specified purpose, namely, "vesting" in the transferee "the right to vote thereon" for a limited period; and prescribes numerous requirements in this connection. Accordingly, it seems reasonable to infer that to establish the relationship and accomplish the purpose which the statute authorizes, its requirements must be complied with.

But the statute does not purport to deal with agreements whereby shareholders attempt to bind each other as to how they shall vote their shares. Various forms of such pooling agreements, as they are sometimes called, have been held valid and have been distinguished from voting trusts.... We think the particular agreement before us does not violate Section 18 or constitute an attempted evasion of its requirements, and is not illegal for any other reason.

Generally speaking, a shareholder may exercise wide liberality of judgment in the matter of voting, and it is not objectionable that his motives may be for personal profit, or determined by whims or caprice, so long as he violates no duty owed his fellow shareholders. Heil v. Standard G. & E. Co., 17 Del.Ch. 214, 151 A. 303. The ownership of voting stock imposes no legal duty to vote at all. A group of shareholders may, without impropriety, vote their respective shares so as to obtain advantages of concerted action. They may lawfully contract with each other to vote in the future in such way as they, or a majority of their group, from time to time determine.

Reasonable provisions for cases of failure of the group to reach a determination because of an even division in their ranks seem unobjectionable. The provision here for submission to the arbitrator is plainly designed as a deadlock-breaking measure, and the arbitrator's decision cannot be enforced unless at least one of the parties (entitled to cast one-half of their combined votes) is willing that it be enforced. We find the provision reasonable. It does not appear that the agreement enables the parties to take any unlawful advantage of the outside shareholder, or of any other person. It offends no rule of law or public policy of this state of which we are aware.

Legal consideration for the promises of each party is supplied by the mutual promises of the other party. The undertaking to vote in accordance with the arbitrator's decision is a valid contract. The good faith of the arbitrator's action has not been challenged and, indeed, the record indicates that no such challenge could be supported.

Accordingly, the failure of Mrs. Haley to exercise her voting rights in accordance with his decision was a breach of her contract....

... The Court of Chancery may, in a review of an election, reject votes of a registered shareholder where his voting of them is found to be in violation of rights of another person. Compare: In re Giant Portland Cement Co., 26 Del.Ch. 32, 21 A.2d 697; In re Canal Construction Co., 21 Del.Ch. 155, 182 A. 545. It seems to us that upon the application of Mrs. Ringling, the injured party, the votes representing Mrs. Haley's shares should not be counted. Since no infirmity in Mr. North's voting has been demonstrated, his right to recognition of what he did at the meeting should be considered in granting any relief to Mrs. Ringling; for her rights arose under a contract to which Mr. North was not a party.

With this in mind, we have concluded that the election should not be declared invalid, but that effect should be given to a rejection of the votes representing Mrs. Haley's shares. No other relief seems appropriate in this proceeding. Mr. North's vote against the motion for adjournment was sufficient to defeat it. With respect to the election of directors, the return of the inspectors should be corrected to show a rejection of Mrs. Haley's votes, and to declare the election of the six persons for whom Mr. North and Mrs. Ringling voted.

This leaves one vacancy in the directorate. The question of what to do about such a vacancy was not considered by the court below and has not been argued here. For this reason, and because an election of directors at the 1947 annual meeting (which presumably will be held in the near future) may make a determination of the question unimportant, we shall not decide it on this appeal. If a decision of the point appears important to the parties, any of them may apply to raise it in the Court of Chancery, after the mandate of this court is received there.

An order should be entered directing a modification of the order of the Court of Chancery in accordance with this opinion.

NOTE ON SHAREHOLDER VOTING AGREEMENTS AND IRREVOCABLE PROXIES

Contracts among shareholders concerning the manner in which their shares will be voted—usually known as voting or pooling agreements—are of two general types. In one type, the parties agree in advance on the exact way in which they will vote their shares during the term of the contract: for example, they may agree to vote for each other as directors. In a second type, the parties do not agree in advance on the exact way in which they will vote their shares, but instead agree that during the term of the contract they will vote their shares as a unit, in a way to be decided by agreement, ballot, or other means. In dealing with both types of voting agreement the courts have been confronted with two questions: (i) Are such agreements valid? (ii) Assuming they are valid, how can their effectiveness be assured?

1. *Validity of Voting Agreements.* A number of older cases held shareholder voting agreements either invalid or revocable at will, but the modern rule is that shareholder voting agreements are normally valid. However, a voting agreement is invalid if it is based on a "private benefit"—that is, a side payment—given by one party to the other in exchange for his vote. A typical case is Palmbaum v. Magulsky, 104 N.E. 746 (Mass. 1914). P and D were two of the three shareholders in American Biscuit Company. P held D's promissory note, and agreed to surrender the note if D would vote his stock in favor of a proposal to sell American Biscuit's assets to another corporation. D voted for the proposal, but P refused to surrender the note, and brought suit upon it. D set up the agreement as a defense, but the court held that the agreement was illegal and therefore unenforceable.

"It is the duty of a stockholder of a corporation, in attendance at meetings of the stockholders, to act fairly and in good faith. He is not justified in entering into any agreement to vote so as to perpetrate a fraud upon any other stockholder. The defendant's vote to dispose of all the assets of the corporation was in consideration of the surrender of the note to him by the plaintiff. This was illegal and the agreement was void as against public policy.... The contract in the case now before us operated as a fraud upon [the third shareholder]."

The rule that a voting agreement based on a private benefit is invalid is an application of the broader principle, well-established in corporate law, that a shareholder may not sell his vote. See, e.g., Chew v. Inverness Management Corp., 352 A.2d 426 (Del.Ch.1976).

2. *Enforcement of Voting Agreements; Irrevocable Proxies; Proxies Coupled with an Interest.*

a. *Damages and specific enforcement.* Money damages are normally an inadequate remedy for breach of a voting agreement. Nevertheless, in the past, courts that upheld such agreements divided on whether they will be specifically enforced. However, the modern trend is strongly in favor of granting that remedy. For example, in Weil v. Beresth, 220 A.2d 456 (Conn. 1966), A, B, C, and D, who were majority shareholders of Sales Corporation, entered into a voting agreement under which they agreed, among other things: (i) to vote for the election of each other as directors; (ii) to vote to amend the by-laws by decreasing the number of directors from five to four; and (iii) not thereafter to vote to amend the new by-laws without the consent of all parties. The agreement was complied with until a shareholders' meeting eleven years later, at which B, C, and D voted to adopt a new by-law increasing the number of directors to five and to elect five directors, including A, B, C, D, and B's son. A then filed suit seeking specific enforcement of the voting agreement and restoration of the old by-law. Recognizing that money damages would be an inadequate remedy, the Connecticut court held that A was entitled to an injunction requiring the defendants to repeal the new by-law and re-enact the original bylaw. The court also approved an injunction compelling B's son to resign if the trial court deemed such relief appropriate. See also Galler v. Galler, Section 3, infra; Beresovski v. Warszawski, 271 N.E.2d 520 (N.Y. 1971). But see Chayes, Madame Wagner and the Close Corporation, 73 Harv.L.Rev. 1532, 1535 (1960):

> The question of the relief to be granted for violation [of agreements among shareholders in the closely held corporation] raises problems more vexing, difficult, and real than ever were to be found on the validity side. What is in issue is the specific enforcement of an ongoing, intimate, personal, consensual relation. This is something the Anglo–American legal system has—wisely it may be supposed—not lightly granted as a matter of course.

b. *Proxies.* Because the courts are sometimes reluctant to specifically enforce voting agreements, the parties to such an agreement may expressly or impliedly substitute a self-executing remedy, such as giving each other proxies to vote each other's stock. In Smith v. San Francisco & N.P. Ry. Co., 47 P. 582 (Cal. 1897) three shareholders agreed to vote their shares together as determined by ballot. The court held that the agreement impliedly gave the two shareholders in the majority on any ballot an irrevocable proxy to vote the shares of the third. In *Ringling,* the Chancellor similarly held that the arbitrator had an implied proxy to vote the parties' shares as he determined, but the Delaware Supreme Court reversed on this issue.[1]

c. *Proxy coupled with an interest.* Even if a proxy is expressly conferred in connection with a voting agreement, a further problem remains. Classically a proxy has been treated as an agency relationship, in which the shareholder is the principal and the proxyholder is the agent. It is a rule of agency law, however, that a principal can terminate an agent's authority at will, even if the termination is in breach of contract (although in such cases the principal may be liable to the agent in damages). See Restatement, Second, of Agency § 118. There is an exception to this rule in cases where the agent holds a "power coupled with an interest," or, as the Restatements of Agency call it, a "power given as security." See Restatement (Second) of Agency §§ 138, 139; Restatement (Third) of Agency §§ 3.12, 3.13. Generally speaking, this exception is applicable to arrangements in which it is understood that the "agent" or power-holder has an interest in the subject-matter to which the power relates, and is therefore not expected to execute the power solely on the power-giver's behalf—the crux of the normal agency relationship—but on his own behalf as well. Accordingly, the safest way to insure that a proxy will be irrevocable is to confer it upon a proxyholder who has an "interest" in the shares to which the proxy relates. Relatively clear examples are cases where the proxyholder is a pledgee of the shares or has agreed to purchase the shares. See N.Y.Bus.Corp.Law § 609(f)(1), (2).

Where a proxy is given pursuant to a voting agreement, however, normally the proxyholder is either an arbitrator, who has no proprietary interest in either the corporation or the shares of the corporation, or a shareholder, who has a proprietary interest in the corporation but not in the shares that are covered by the proxy. In In re Chilson, 19 Del.Ch. 398, 409, 168 A. 82, 86 (1933), the court held that a proxy is revocable where the proxyholder has only an interest in the corporation generally, in the bare voting power, or in the results to be accomplished by the use of the proxy. On the other hand, in Deibler v. Chas. H. Elliott Co., 81 A.2d 557 (Pa. 1951), the Pennsylvania Supreme Court, construing Delaware law, upheld the irrevocability of a proxy given to secure the payment of the purchase price of stock in a

---

1. Compare Me.Bus.Corp.Law § 617(2):

> When [a written voting] agreement specifies how the shares shall be voted, or provides a clear formula for ascertaining how the shares shall be voted, in case of a breach or anticipatory breach thereof by one or more parties thereto, the agreement shall, unless it specifically provides otherwise, be deemed to constitute an irrevocable proxy to the parties not in breach to vote all shares subject to the agreement in accordance with the terms of the agreement.

Delaware corporation and the seller's continued employment by the corporation. This issue is now often addressed by the statutes. For example, Del. Gen. Corp. Law § 212(e) provide that "A proxy may be made irrevocable regardless of whether the interest with which it is coupled is an interest in the stock itself or an interest in the corporation generally."

HAFT v. HAFT, 671 A.2d 413 (Del.Ch.1995) (Allen, Ch.). Herbert Haft, the founder and CEO of Dart Group Corporation, transferred 172,730 shares of Dart Class B common stock to his son, Ronald Haft. Class B was Dart's sole class of voting stock. The transferred shares constituted 57% of the outstanding Class B, and therefore carried the power to elect the Dart board. In exchange for the stock, Roland gave Herbert a promissory note and granted Herbert a lifetime irrevocable proxy to vote the transferred shares. Subsequently, Ronald sought to revoke the proxy. The court held that Herbert Haft's interest in Dart by virtue of his CEO position was sufficient to render specifically enforceable Ronald's undertaking not to revoke the proxy:

> Under the Delaware corporation law (§ 212(e)) an interest sufficient to support an irrevocable proxy must be either "an interest in the stock itself or an interest in the corporation generally." 8 Del.Ch. § 212(e) (1991). Do Herbert Haft's interests, other than as a secured creditor, qualify under the statute? As I now explain, in my opinion they do. . . .
>
> The predecessor of Section 212 was amended as part of the general revision of the Delaware General Corporation Law in 1967. The language in question ("an interest in the corporation generally") was introduced into our statute at that time. The apparent purpose for doing so was to erase the implication arising from dicta in a 1933 Master's Report, which had been confirmed by this court. The report was in the case of In re *Chilson*, Del.Ch., 168 A. 82 (1933). The *Chilson* dicta was to the effect that in order to support irrevocability of a proxy, the holder had to have an interest in the stock itself. . . .
>
> . . . [I]it is appropriate to acknowledge that the corporate law has tended to distrust and discourage the separation of the shareholder claim as equity investor (i.e., the right to enjoy distributions on stock if, as, and when declared) from the right to vote stock. . . . A powerful argument can be advanced that generally the congruence of the right to vote and the residual rights of ownership will tend towards efficient wealth production.
>
> A proxy is, of course, a means temporarily to split the power to vote from the residual ownership claim of the stockholder. In the vast number of instances in which proxies to vote stock are used, however, this split occasions no significant divergence between the interests of the proxy holder and the holder of the residual corporate interest because the proxy is of relatively short

duration and in all events is revocable unilaterally. Thus, in effect, the grant of the proxy represented a judgment (which may be enforced through revocation) that the holder of the proxy will exercise it in the economic interest of the residual owner. A potentially inefficient split between the interests of the voter and the interests of the residual owners may, however, develop when the proxy is irrevocable. Such a holder is free from the unilateral control of the grantor and may be expected to be inclined to exercise voting rights in a way that benefits himself. There is of course, as a general matter, nothing legally suspect in contracting parties exercising contracted for rights in a self-interested manner. Yet the exercise of voting control over corporations by persons whose interest in them is not chiefly or solely as a residual owner will create circumstances in which the corporation will be less than optimally efficient in the selection of risky investment projects. (A simple, if gross, example: the holder of an irrevocable proxy with voting control might simply refuse to elect a board that will accept the best investment projects (those with the highest risk adjusted rate of return) unless some side payment to him is arranged). The special additional costs associated with such a divorce between ownership and voting (the costs being expressed either as an otherwise unnecessary expense or as the selection of non-optimizing investment projects) will of course tend to diminish as the voter's interest becomes aligned with the residual owners interest. . . .

. . . I confess to the view that a corporation law rule allowing for the specific enforceability of an irrevocable proxy that is coupled only with the holder's interest in maintaining a salaried office seems mischievous in terms of its possible efficiency effects. But in light of the 1967 amendment to the Delaware statutory law . . . and the absence of contrary precedent, I am required to express the opinion that such an interest—the interest that Herbert Haft had and retains as the senior executive officer of Dart—is sufficient under our law to render specifically enforceable the express contract for an irrevocable proxy. . . .

B. Voting Trusts

DEL. GEN. CORP. LAW § 218

[See Statutory Supplement]

MODEL BUS. CORP. ACT § 7.30

[See Statutory Supplement]

CAL. CORP. CODE § 706

[See Statutory Supplement]

NOTE ON VOTING TRUSTS

1. *In General*. A voting trust is a device by which shareholders separate the voting rights in, and the legal title to, their shares from the beneficial ownership of the shares. This is accomplished by conferring the voting rights and legal title on one or more voting trustees, while retaining the ultimate right to distributions and appreciation. Usually, two or more shareholders are involved, so that the voting trust is a type of pooling agreement. Sometimes, however, only one shareholder is involved—for example, where a sole shareholder creates a voting trust to satisfy creditors or to vest control of his business in managers. The creation of a voting trust normally requires the execution of a written trust agreement between participating shareholders and the voting trustees, and a transfer to the trustee, for a specified period, of the shareholders' stock certificates and the legal title to their stock. The voting trustee then registers the transfer on the corporation's books, so that during the term of the trust the trustee is the record owner of the shares, entitled to vote in the election of directors and often on other matters as well. Dividends are paid by the corporation to the trustee, but are almost invariably then paid over by the trustee to the beneficial owners. Several statutes require the trustee to issue certificates of beneficial interest to participating shareholders, and frequently such certificates are issued, even where not statutorily required, to facilitate trading in the beneficial interests.

Voting trusts are an effective and a moderately simple way to separate control and beneficial ownership for a limited period of time. The separation is self-executing, because the trustee is the legal owner and is registered as such on the corporation's books. The separation survives transfers by the beneficial owners, since they can transfer only their retained equitable interests (essentially, most ownership rights except the right to vote during the term of the trust). Upon termination of the voting trust, the beneficial owners receive stock certificates which reinstate them as complete owners, registered as such on the corporation's books.

2. *Validity*. The early attitude of some courts toward voting trusts was highly unfavorable. See, e.g., Warren v. Pim, 59 A. 773, 789 (N.J. Eq. 1904) ("[a]ny arrangement that permanently separates the voting power from stock ownership nullifies, to the extent of the stock involved, the annual submission of the question of the management of the company to the stockholders"). The majority of courts, however, have either declared voting trusts to be valid or held that the plaintiff was not in a position to attack them. See, e.g., Massa v. Stone, 190 N.E.2d 217 (Mass. 1963).

Today, statutes both explicitly validate voting trusts and regulate their creation and their content. Among the most common forms of regulation are a maximum time period (usually ten years), and a requirement that the voting trust agreement be filed with the corporation and open to inspection. Such statutes are normally deemed to preempt the common law rules governing the validity of voting trusts. The cases are not entirely uniform in dealing with the consequences of failure to comply with the statutory requirements. Some cases have held that such a failure invalidates the voting trust. See, e.g., Abercrombie v. Davies, discussed below. Smith v. Biggs Boiler Works Co., 32 Del.Ch. 147, 82 A.2d 372 (1951) (voting trust held to be invalid where no provision was made for deposit of stock with trustees); Christopher v. Richardson, 394 Pa. 425, 147 A.2d 375 (1959) (voting trust held to be invalid where under its terms the trust might have exceeded statutory ten-year period). Other cases have been considerably more tolerant. For example, in De Marco v. Paramount Ice Corp., 30 Misc.2d 158, 102 N.Y.S.2d 692 (1950), a voting trust was attacked on the ground that a copy of the trust agreement had not been filed in the office of the corporation, as required by the statute. The answer stated that the agreement had been filed after the plaintiff's suit was brought. The court held that "the failure to file merely means that the trust agreement is not invalid but merely inoperative to permit the trustees to exercise the voting rights granted thereby until it is so filed."

3. *Overlap of Voting Trusts and Shareholders' Voting Agreements*. In the context of close corporations, voting trusts may sometimes be used, like voting agreements, to allocate voting control in other than a pro rata manner, or to preserve the solidarity of a faction consisting of less than all the shareholders. Because voting trusts and voting agreements may have substantially overlapping purposes, the substantive legal rules applicable to one of these two legal forms have sometimes been applied to an arrangement that was nominally cast in the other form. Thus in Abercrombie v. Davies, 130 A.2d 338 (Del. 1957), the Delaware Supreme Court held that an "Agent's Agreement" that in form was a voting agreement was in substance was a voting trust was unenforceable because the statutory provisions governing voting trusts had not been complied with. Conversely, in Oceanic Exploration Co. v. Grynberg, 428 A.2d 1 (Del.1981), the Delaware Supreme Court held that an agreement that was denominated a voting trust was not a voting trust in substance and therefore was enforceable despite a failure to comply with the voting trust statute.

C. CLASSIFIED STOCK

DEL. GEN. CORP. LAW §§ 102(A)(6), 212(A)

[See Statutory Supplement]

MODEL BUS. CORP. ACT §§ 6.01, 7.21, 8.04

[See Statutory Supplement]

NOTE ON CLASSIFIED STOCK

"One of the simplest and most effective ways of assuring that all the participants or that particular minority shareholders will have representation on the board of directors is to set up two or more classes of stock, provide that each class is to vote for and elect a specified number or a stated percentage of the directors, and then issue each class or a majority of shares in each class to a different shareholder or faction of shareholders.... Class A common stock might be given power, for instance, to elect three directors and Class B common stock power to elect two." 1 F.H. O'Neal & R. Thompson, O'Neal's Close Corporations § 3.19 (rev. 3d ed.2010). A few statutes validate this technique explicitly, *see, e.g.,* N.Y.Bus.Corp.Law § 703, and most of the remaining statutes validate it implicitly by providing that a corporation may have one or more classes of stock with such voting powers as shall be stated in the certificate, *see e.g.,* Del.Gen. Corp.Law § 151(a). In its simplest version, the use of classified common does not necessarily involve voting power for any class that is disproportionate to the investment made by that class. Often, however, separate classes carry voting power whose weight differs considerably from the relative investment made by their holders. At the extreme, a class of stock may have proprietary rights but no voting power, or voting power but no proprietary rights.

In Lehrman v. Cohen, 43 Del.Ch. 222, 222 A.2d 800 (1966), Giant Food, Inc. had two classes of common stock designated Class AC and Class AL, respectively. Each class was entitled to elect two members of Giant Food's four-member board. The Cohen and Lehrman families each owned one of the two classes. Over the years, there were differences of opinion between the two families concerning Giant Food's operating policies. To obviate the risk of deadlock, eventually an arrangement was made to establish a fifth directorship. Under the arrangement, Giant Food's certificate of incorporation was amended to create a third class of common stock, designated Class AD, which consisted of one share of $10 per value stock. The Class AD stock had the right to elect one director, but essentially had no right to distributions and could be called—that is, redeemed—for $10 by a vote of the other four directors. The Class AD share was issued to Giant Food's long-time counsel, Joseph Danzansky, who by prearrangement voted the share for himself as the fifth director.

Subsequently, the plaintiff, a member of the Lehrman family who at that point owned all the AL stock, claimed that the Class AD stock was illegal on the ground that in substance it was a voting trust and did not comply with the voting trust statute. The court rejected this argument:

> The criteria of a voting trust under our decisions have been summarized by this Court in Abercrombie v. Davies, 36 Del.Ch. 371, 130 A.2d 338 (1957). The tests there set forth, accepted by both sides of this cause as being applicable, are as follows: (1) the voting rights of the stock are separated from the other attributes of ownership; (2) the voting rights granted are intended to be irrevocable for a definite period of time; and (3) the principal purpose of the grant of voting rights is to acquire voting control of the corporation....
>
> ... The AD arrangement did not separate the voting rights of the AC or the AL stock from the other attributes of ownership of those classes of stock. Each AC and AL stockholder retains complete control over the voting of his stock; each can vote his stock directly; no AL or AC stockholder is divested of his right to vote his stock as he sees fit; no AL or AC stock can be voted against the shareholder's wishes; and the AL and AC stock continue to elect two directors each.

The court also held that it was not illegal to create a class of stock having voting rights but no proprietary rights.

SECTION 3. AGREEMENTS CONTROLLING DECISIONS THAT ARE WITHIN THE BOARD'S DISCRETION

Voting arrangements of the kind discussed in Section 2 control only those matters that are decided on a shareholder level. Typically, however, the issues that are most important to shareholders in a close corporation are determined on a board level—for example, managerial positions, managerial compensation, and dividends. If the shareholders attempt to also control these matters by agreement, the problem arises whether, or under what conditions, such an agreement is valid in the face of the normal statutory provision that the business of the corporation shall be managed by or under the direction of the board. That question is addressed by the materials in this section.

McQuade v. Stoneham

Court of Appeals of New York, 1934.
263 N.Y. 323, 189 N.E. 234.

Appeal, by permission of Court of Appeals, from judgment of Appellate Division, First Department, unanimously affirming judgment for plaintiff for $42,827.38 and other relief.

■ POUND, CH. J. The action is brought to compel specific performance of an agreement between the parties, entered into to secure the control of National Exhibition Company, also called the baseball club (New York Nationals or "Giants"). This was one of Stoneham's enterprises which used the New York Polo Grounds for its home games. McGraw was manager of the Giants. McQuade was, at the time the contract was entered into, a city magistrate. He resigned December 8, 1930.

Defendant Stoneham became the owner of 1,306 shares, or a majority of the stock of National Exhibition Company (there being then 2,500 shares outstanding). Plaintiff and defendant McGraw each purchased seventy shares of his stock. Plaintiff paid Stoneham $50,338.10 for the stock he purchased. As a part of the transaction the agreement in question was entered into. It was dated May 21, 1919. Some of its pertinent provisions are:

> "VIII. The parties hereto will use their best endeavors for the purpose of continuing as directors of said company and as officers thereof the following:
>
> "Directors: Charles A. Stoneham, John J. McGraw, Francis X. McQuade, with right to the party of the first part (Stoneham) to name all additional directors as he sees fit.
>
> "Officers: Charles A. Stoneham, president; John J. McGraw, vice-president; Francis X. McQuade, treasurer.
>
> "IX. No salaries are to be paid to any of the above officers or directors, except as follows: President, $45,000; vice-president, $7,500; treasurer, $7,500.
>
> "X. There shall be no change in said salaries, no change in the amount of capital, or the number of shares, no change or amendment of the by-laws of the corporation or any matters regarding the policy of the business of the corporation or any matters which may in anywise affect, endanger or interfere with the rights of minority stockholders, excepting upon the mutual and unanimous consent of all . . . of the parties hereto.
>
> "XIV. This agreement shall continue and remain in force so long as the parties or any of them or the representative of any own the stock referred to in this agreement, to wit, the party of the first part, 1,166 shares, the party of the second part 70 shares and the party of the third part 70 shares, except as may otherwise appear by this agreement. . . ."

In pursuance of this contract Stoneham became president and McGraw vice-president of the corporation. McQuade became treasurer. In June, 1925, [McQuade's] salary was increased to $10,000 a year. He continued to act until May 2, 1928, when Leo J. Bondy was elected to succeed him. The board of directors consisted of seven men. The four outside of the parties hereto were selected by Stoneham and he had complete control over them. At the meeting of May 2, 1928, Stoneham and McGraw refrained from voting, McQuade voted for himself and the other four voted for Bondy. Defendants did not keep their agreement with McQuade to use their best efforts to continue him as treasurer. On the contrary, he was dropped with their entire acquiescence. At the next stockholders' meeting he was dropped as a director, although they might have elected him.

The courts below have refused to order the reinstatement of McQuade, but have given him damages for wrongful discharge, with a right to sue for future damages.

The cause for dropping McQuade was due to the falling out of friends. McQuade and Stoneham had disagreed. The trial court has found in substance that their numerous quarrels and disputes did not affect the orderly and efficient administration of the business of the corporation; that plaintiff was removed because he had antagonized the dominant Stoneham by persisting in challenging his power over the corporate treasury and for no misconduct on his part. The court also finds that plaintiff was removed by Stoneham for protecting the corporation and its minority stockholders. We will assume that Stoneham put him out when he might have retained him, merely in order to get rid of him.

Defendants say that the contract in suit was void because the directors held their office charged with the duty to act for the corporation according to their best judgment and that any contract which compels a director to vote to keep any particular person in office and at a stated salary is illegal. Directors are the exclusive executive representatives of the corporation, charged with administration of its internal affairs and the management and use of its assets. They manage the business of the corporation (Gen.Corp.Law, Cons. Laws, c. 23, sec. 27). "An agreement to continue a man as president is dependent upon his continued loyalty to the interests of the corporation" (Fells v. Katz, 256 N.Y. 67, 72, 175 N.E. 516, 517). So much is undisputed.

Plaintiff contends that the converse of this proposition is true and that an agreement among directors to continue a man as an officer of a corporation is not to be broken so long as such officer is loyal to the interests of the corporation and that, as plaintiff has been found loyal to the corporation, the agreement of defendants is enforceable.

Although it has been held that an agreement among stockholders whereby it is attempted to divest the directors of their power to discharge an unfaithful employee of the corporation is illegal as against public policy (Fells v. Katz, supra), it must be equally true that the stockholders may not, by agreement among themselves, control the directors in the exercise of the judgment vested in them by virtue of their office to elect officers and fix salaries. Their motives may not be questioned so long as their acts are legal. The bad faith or the improper motives of the parties does not change this rule (Manson v. Curtis, 223 N.Y. 313, 324, 119 N.E. 559). Directors may not by agreements entered into by stockholders abrogate their independent judgment (Creed v. Copps, 103 Vt. 164, 71 A.L.R.Ann. 1287).

Stockholders may, of course, combine to elect directors. That rule is well settled. As Holmes, Ch. J., pointedly said (Brightman v. Bates,

175 Mass. 105, 110, 55 N.E. 809, 811): "If stockholders want to make their power felt, they must unite. There is no reason why a majority should not agree to keep together." The power to unite is, however, limited to the election of directors and is not extended to contracts whereby limitations are placed on the power of directors to manage the business of the corporation by the selection of agents at defined salaries.

The minority shareholders whose interests McQuade says he has been punished for protecting, are not, aside from himself, complaining about his discharge. He is not acting for the corporation or for them in this action. It is impossible to see how the corporation has been injured by the substitution of Bondy as treasurer in place of McQuade. As McQuade represents himself in this action and seeks redress for his own wrongs, "we prefer to listen to [the corporation and the minority stockholders] before any decision as to their wrongs" (Faulds v. Yates, 57 Ill. 416).

It is urged that we should pay heed to the morals and manners of the market place to sustain this agreement, and that we should hold that its violation gives rise to a cause of action for damages, rather than base our decision on any outworn notions of public policy. Public policy is a dangerous guide in determining the validity of a contract, and courts should not interfere lightly with the freedom of competent parties to make their own contracts. We do not close our eyes to the fact that such agreements, tacitly or openly arrived at, are not uncommon, especially in close corporations where the stockholders are doing business for convenience under a corporate organization. We know that majority stockholders, united in voting trusts, effectively manage the business of a corporation by choosing trustworthy directors to reflect their policies in the corporate management. Nor are we unmindful that McQuade has, so the court has found, been shabbily treated as a purchaser of stock from Stoneham. We have said: "A trustee is held to something stricter than the morals of the market place" (Meinhard v. Salmon, 249 N.Y. 458, 464, 164 N.E. 545, 546), but Stoneham and McGraw were not trustees for McQuade as an individual. Their duty was to the corporation and its stockholders, to be exercised according to their unrestricted lawful judgment. They were under no legal obligation to deal righteously with McQuade if it was against public policy to do so.

The courts do not enforce mere moral obligations, nor legal ones either, unless someone seeks to establish rights which may be waived by custom and for convenience. We are constrained by authority to hold that a contract is illegal and void so far as it precludes the board of directors, at the risk of incurring legal liability, from changing officers, salaries or policies or retaining individuals in office, except by consent of the contracting parties. On the whole, such a holding is probably preferable to one which would open the courts to pass on the motives of directors in the lawful exercise of their trust....

The judgment of the Appellate Division and that of the Trial Term should be reversed and the complaint dismissed, with costs in all courts.

[The court also held that the agreement violated the Inferior Criminal Courts Act, which provided that "[n]o city magistrate shall engage in any other business or profession ..., but each of said justices and magistrates shall devote his whole time and capacity, so far as the public interest demands, to the duties of his office...." At the date of the agreement McQuade was a city magistrate, and he did not resign his position until after commencement of the action.]

■ [The opinion of Lehman, J., concurring in the result, is omitted.]

NOTE ON CLARK v. DODGE

In Clark v. Dodge, 269 N.Y. 410, 199 N.E. 641 (1936), two corporations manufactured medicinal preparations under secret formulas. Clark owned 25%, and Dodge owned 75%, of the stock of each corporation. Clark and Dodge entered into an agreement which provided that (1) Dodge would vote for Clark as a director. (2) Dodge, acting in his directorial capacity, would continue Clark as general manager as long as Clark proved faithful, efficient, and competent. (3) Clark would always receive as salary or dividends one-fourth of the corporation's net income. (4) No salaries to other officers would be unreasonable in amount or incommensurate with the services rendered by those officers. The court held that the agreement was valid:

> Except for the broad dicta in the *McQuade* opinion, we think there can be no doubt that the agreement here in question was legal and that the complaint states a cause of action. There was no attempt to sterilize the board of directors as in [*McQuade*]....
>
> If there was any invasion of the powers of the directorate under that agreement it is so slight as to be negligible; and certainly there is no damage suffered by or threatened to anybody. The broad statements in the *McQuade* opinion, applicable to the facts there, should be confined to those facts.

Galler v. Galler

Supreme Court of Illinois, 1964, reh. denied 1964.
32 Ill.2d 16, 203 N.E.2d 577.

■ Underwood, Justice. Plaintiff, Emma Galler, sued in equity for an accounting and for specific performance of an agreement made in July, 1955, between plaintiff and her husband, of one part, and defendants, Isadore A. Galler and his wife, Rose, of the other. Defendants appealed from a decree of the superior court of Cook County granting the relief prayed. The First District Appellate Court reversed the decree and denied specific performance, affirming in part the order for an accounting, and modifying the order awarding master's fees. (45 Ill. App.2d 452, 196 N.E.2d 5.) That decision is appealed here on a certificate of importance.

There is no substantial dispute as to the facts in this case. From 1919 to 1924, Benjamin and Isadore Galler, brothers, were equal partners in the Galler Drug Company, a wholesale drug concern. In 1924 the business was incorporated under the Illinois Business Corporation Act, each owning one half of the outstanding 220 shares of stock. In 1945 each contracted to sell 6 shares to an employee, Rosenberg, at a price of $10,500 for each block of 6 shares, payable within 10 years. They guaranteed to repurchase the shares if Rosenberg's employment were terminated, and further agreed that if they sold their shares, Rosenberg would receive the same price per share as that paid for the brothers' shares. Rosenberg was still indebted for the 12 shares in July, 1955, and continued to make payments on account even after Benjamin Galler died in 1957 and after the institution of this action by Emma Galler in 1959. Rosenberg was not involved in this litigation either as a party or as a witness, and in July of 1961, prior to the time that the master in chancery hearings were concluded, defendants Isadore and Rose Galler purchased the 12 shares from Rosenberg. A supplemental complaint was filed by the plaintiff, Emma Galler, asserting an equitable right to have 6 of the 12 shares transferred to her and offering to pay the defendants one half of the amount that the defendants paid Rosenberg. The parties have stipulated that pending disposition of the instant case, these shares will not be voted or transferred. For approximately one year prior to the entry of the decree by the chancellor in July of 1962, there were no outstanding minority shareholder interests.

In March, 1954, Benjamin and Isadore, on the advice of their accountant, decided to enter into an agreement for the financial protection of their immediate families and to assure their families, after the death of either brother, equal control of the corporation. [The agreement was executed in July 1955, after Benjamin had fallen ill. In September 1956, Emma agreed to permit Isadore's son Aaron to become president for one year and agreed that she would not interfere with the business during that year. In December 1957, Benjamin died.] The evidence is undisputed that defendants had decided prior to Benjamin's death they would not honor the agreement, but never disclosed their intention to plaintiff or her husband....

Shortly after Benjamin's death, Emma went to the office and demanded the terms of the 1955 agreement be carried out. Isadore told her that anything she had to say could be said to Aaron, who then told her that his father would not abide by the agreement. He offered a modification of the agreement by proposing the salary continuation payment but without her becoming a director. When Emma refused to modify the agreement and sought enforcement of its terms, defendants refused and this suit followed.

During the last few years of Benjamin's life both brothers drew an annual salary of $42,000. Aaron, whose salary was $15,000 as manager of the warehouse prior to September, 1956, has since the time that Emma agreed to his acting as president drawn an annual salary of $20,000. In 1957, 1958, and 1959 a $40,000 annual dividend was paid. Plaintiff has received her proportionate share of the dividend.

The July, 1955, agreement in question here, entered into between Benjamin, Emma, Isadore and Rose, recites that Benjamin and Isadore each own 47½% of the issued and outstanding shares of the Galler Drug Company, an Illinois corporation, and that Benjamin and Isadore desired to provide income for the support and maintenance of their immediate families. No reference is made to the shares then being purchased by Rosenberg. The essential features of the contested portions of the agreement are substantially as set forth in the opinion of the Appellate Court: (2) that the bylaws of the corporation will be amended to provide for a board of four directors; that the necessary quorum shall be three directors; and that no directors' meeting shall be held without giving ten days notice to all directors. (3) The shareholders will cast their votes for the above named persons (Isadore, Rose, Benjamin and Emma) as directors at said special meeting and at any other meeting held for the purpose of electing directors. (4, 5) In the event of the death of either brother his wife shall have the right to nominate a director in place of the decedent. (6) Certain annual dividends will be declared by the corporation. The dividend shall be $50,000 payable out of the accumulated earned surplus in excess of $500,000. If 50% of the annual net profits after taxes exceeds the minimum $50,000 then the directors shall have discretion to declare a dividend up to 50% of the annual net profits. If the net profits are less than $50,000 nevertheless the minimum $50,000 annual dividend shall be declared, providing the $500,000 surplus is maintained. Earned surplus is defined. (9) The certificates evidencing the said shares of Benjamin Galler and Isadore Galler shall bear a legend that the shares are subject to the terms of this agreement. (10) A salary continuation agreement shall be entered into by the corporation which shall authorize the corporation upon the death of Benjamin Galler or Isadore Galler, or both, to pay a sum equal to twice the salary of such officer, payable monthly over a five-year period. Said sum shall be paid to the widow during her widowhood, but should be paid to such widow's children if the widow remarries within the five-year period. (11, 12) The parties to this agreement further agree and hereby grant to the corporation the authority to purchase, in the event of the death of either Benjamin or Isadore, so much of the stock of Galler Drug Company held by the estate as is necessary to provide sufficient funds to pay the federal estate tax, the Illinois inheritance tax and other administrative expenses of the estate. If as a result of such purchase from the estate of the decedent the amount of dividends to be received by the heirs is reduced, the parties shall nevertheless vote for directors so as to give the estate and heirs the same representation as before (2 directors out of 4, even though they own less stock), and also that the corporation pay an additional benefit payment equal to the diminution of the dividends. In the event either Benjamin or Isadore decides to sell his shares he is required to offer them first to the remaining shareholders and then to the corporation at book value, according each six months to accept the offer.

The Appellate Court found the 1955 agreement void because "the undue duration, stated purpose and substantial disregard of the provisions of the Corporation Act outweigh any considerations which might call for divisibility" and held that "the public policy of this state demands voiding this entire agreement".

While the conduct of defendants towards plaintiff was clearly inequitable, the basically controlling factor is the absence of an objecting minority interest, together with the absence of public detriment. . . .

At this juncture it should be emphasized that we deal here with a so-called close corporation. . . . For our purposes, a close corporation is one in which the stock is held in a few hands, or in a few families, and wherein it is not at all, or only rarely, dealt in by buying or selling. (Brooks v. Willcuts, 8th Cir.1935, 78 F.2d 270, 273.) Moreover, it should be recognized that shareholder agreements similar to that in question here are often, as a practical consideration, quite necessary for the protection of those financially interested in the close corporation. While the shareholder of a public-issue corporation may readily sell his shares on the open market should management fail to use, in his opinion, sound business judgment, his counterpart of the close corporation often has a large total of his entire capital invested in the business and has no ready market for his shares should he desire to sell. He feels, understandably, that he is more than a mere investor and that his voice should be heard concerning all corporate activity. Without a shareholder agreement, specifically enforceable by the courts, insuring him a modicum of control, a large minority shareholder might find himself at the mercy of an oppressive or unknowledgeable majority. Moreover, as in the case at bar, the shareholders of a close corporation are often also the directors and officers thereof. With substantial shareholding interests abiding in each member of the board of directors, it is often quite impossible to secure, as in the large public-issue corporation, independent board judgment free from personal motivations concerning corporate policy. For these and other reasons too voluminous to enumerate here, often the only sound basis for protection is afforded by a lengthy, detailed shareholder agreement securing the rights and obligations of all concerned. For a discussion of these and other considerations, see Note, "A Plea for Separate Statutory Treatment of the Close Corporation", 33 N.Y.U.L.Rev. 700 (1958).

As the preceding review of the applicable decisions of this court points out, there has been a definite, albeit inarticulate, trend toward eventual judicial treatment of the close corporation as *sui generis.* Several shareholder-director agreements that have technically "violated" the letter of the Business Corporation Act have nevertheless been upheld in the light of the existing practical circumstances, i.e., no apparent public injury, the absence of a complaining minority interest, and no apparent prejudice to creditors. However, we have thus far not attempted to limit these decisions as applicable only to close corporations and have seemingly implied that general considerations regarding judicial supervision of all corporate behavior apply.

The practical result of this series of cases, while liberally giving legal efficacy to particular agreements in special circumstances notwithstanding literal "violations" of statutory corporate law, has been to inject much doubt and uncertainty into the thinking of the bench and corporate bar of Illinois concerning shareholder agreements. See e.g., Cary, "How Illinois Corporations May Enjoy Partnership Advantages: Planning for the Closely Held Firm." 48 N.W.U.L.Rev. 427; Note, "The Validity of Stockholders' Voting Agreements in Illinois," 3 U.Chi. L.Rev. 640.

It is therefore necessary, we feel, to discuss the instant case with the problems peculiar to the close corporation particularly in mind. . . .

This court has recognized, albeit *sub silentio,* the significant conceptual differences between the close corporation and its public-issue counterpart in, among other cases, Kantzler v. Benzinger, 214 Ill. 589, 73 N.E. 874, where an agreement quite similar to the one under attack here was upheld. Where, as in *Kantzler* and here, no complaining minority interest appears, no fraud or apparent injury to the public or creditors is present, and no clearly prohibitory statutory language is violated, we can see no valid reason for precluding the parties from reaching any arrangements concerning the management of the corporation which are agreeable to all. . . .

Since the question as to the duration of the agreement is a principal source of controversy, we shall consider it first. The parties provided no specific termination date, and while the agreement concludes with a paragraph that its terms "shall be binding upon and shall inure to the benefits of" the legal representatives, heirs and assigns of the parties, this clause is, we believe, intended to be operative only as long as one of the parties is living. It further provides that it shall be so construed as to carry out its purposes, and we believe these must be determined from a consideration of the agreement as a whole. Thus viewed, a fair construction is that its purposes were accomplished at the death of the survivor of the parties. While these life spans are not precisely ascertainable, and the Appellate Court noted Emma Galler's life expectancy at her husband's death was 26.9 years, we are aware of no statutory or public policy provision against stockholders' agreements which would invalidate this agreement on that ground. . . . While defendants argue that the public policy evinced by the legislative restrictions upon the duration of voting trust agreements (Ill.Rev.Stat.1963, chap. 32, par. 157.30a) should be applied here, this agreement is not a voting trust, but as pointed out by the dissenting justice in the Appellate Court, is a straight contractual voting control agreement which does not divorce voting rights from stock ownership. That the policy against agreements in which stock ownership and voting rights are separated, indicated in Luthy v. Ream, 270 Ill. 170, 110 N.E. 373, is inapplicable to voting control agreements was emphasized in Thompson wherein a control agreement was upheld as not attempting to separate ownership and voting power. While limiting voting trusts in 1947 to a maximum duration of 10 years, the legislature has indicated no similar policy regarding straight voting agreements although these have been common since prior to 1870. In view of the history of decisions of this court generally upholding, in the absence of fraud or prejudice to minority interests or public policy, the right of stockholders to agree among themselves as to the manner in which their stock will be voted, we do not regard the period of time within which this agreement may remain effective as rendering the agreement unenforceable.

The clause that provides for the election of certain persons to specified offices for a period of years likewise does not require invalidation. In Kantzler v. Benzinger, 214 Ill. 589, 73 N.E. 874, this court upheld an agreement entered into by all the stockholders providing that certain parties would be elected to the offices of the corporation for a fixed period. In Faulds v. Yates, 57 Ill. 416, we upheld a similar agreement among the majority stockholders of a corporation, notwithstanding the existence of a minority which was not before the court complaining thereof. See also Hornstein, "Judicial Tolerance of the Incorporated Partnership," 18 Law and Contemporary Problems 435 at page 444.

We turn next to a consideration of the effect of the stated purpose of the agreement upon its validity. The pertinent provision is: "The said Benjamin A. Galler and Isadore A. Galler desire to provide income for the support and maintenance of their immediate families." Obviously, there is no evil inherent in a contract entered into for the reason that the persons originating the terms desired to so arrange their property as to provide post-death support for those dependent upon them. Nor does the fact that the subject property is corporate stock alter the situation so long as there exists no detriment to minority stock interests, creditors or other public injury. It is, however, contended by defendants that the methods provided by the agreement for implementation of the stated purpose are, as a whole, violative of the Business Corporation Act (Ill.Rev.Stat.1963, chap. 32, pars. 157.28, 157.30a, 157.33, 157.34, 157.41) to such an extent as to render it void *in toto.*

The terms of the dividend agreement require a minimum annual dividend of $50,000, but this duty is limited by the subsequent provision that it shall be operative only so long as an earned surplus of $500,000 is maintained. It may be noted that in 1958, the year prior to commencement of this litigation, the corporation's net earnings after taxes amounted to $202,759 while its earned surplus was $1,543,270, and this was increased in 1958 to $1,680,079 while earnings were $172,964. The minimum earned surplus requirement is designed for the protection of the corporation and its creditors, and we take no exception to the contractual dividend requirements as thus restricted. Kantzler v. Benzinger, 214 Ill. 589, 73 N.E. 874.

The salary continuation agreement is a common feature, in one form or another, of corporate executive employment. It requires that the widow should receive a total benefit, payable monthly over a five-year period, aggregating twice the amount paid her deceased husband in one year. This requirement was likewise limited for the protection of the corporation by being contingent upon the payments being income tax-deductible by the corporation. The charge made in those cases which have considered the validity of payments to the widow of an officer and shareholder in a corporation is that a gift of its property by a noncharitable corporation is in violation of the rights of its shareholders and *ultra vires.* Since there are no shareholders here other than the parties to the contract, this objection is not here applicable, and its effect, as limited, upon the corporation is not so prejudicial as to require its invalidation.

Having concluded that the agreement, under the circumstances here present, is not vulnerable to the attack made on it, we must consider the accounting feature of this action. The trial court allowed the relief prayed, an action we deem proper except as to the master's fees which were modified by the Appellate Court. Since no question is here raised regarding them, we affirm the action of that court in this respect. The questions as to salary which the Appellate Court correctly held were improperly increased became ones of fact to be determined by the trial court.

We hold defendants must account for all monies received by them from the corporation since September 25, 1956, in excess of that theretofore authorized.

Accordingly, the judgment of the Appellate Court is reversed except insofar as it relates to fees, and is, as to them affirmed. The cause is remanded to the circuit court of Cook County with directions to proceed in accordance herewith.

Affirmed in part and reversed in part, and remanded with directions.

NOTE ON FURTHER PROCEEDINGS IN GALLER v. GALLER

The decree in *Galler* ordered Isadore and Rose to "account for all monies received by them from the company since September 25, 1956 [up to the time of the decree], in excess of that theretofore authorized," but provided that Isadore and Aaron be allowed "fair compensation . . . for services rendered by them to the corporation during said period." On remand, defendants argued that the salaries of Aaron and Isadore during the relevant period represented the fair market value of their services, and in any event since Isadore's $42,000 salary after Benjamin's death was a continuation of his salary under the agreement, it had been "theretofore authorized" within the meaning of the decree. The appellate court rejected both arguments. As to the former issue, the court adopted the findings of a master who valued

Isadore's services at $10,000/year and Aaron's at $15,000/year. As to whether continuation of Isadore's $42,000 salary was authorized by the agreement, the court said

> ... Isadore's continued receipt of the same salary upon the death of Benjamin without the *quid pro quo* for his brother's family, is an alteration of the past arrangement, and was without authorization.
>
> Furthermore, the clear import of the 1955 shareholders' agreement is that the partnership-like arrangement was intended to remain after the death of either Benjamin or Isadore. While not specifically addressing itself to salaries, the agreement provides that upon the death of either Benjamin or Isadore, four directors are to be elected; two from Isadore's family and two from Benjamin's family. The officers and their salaries are voted upon by the directors. Dividends are required to be paid provided $500,000 earned surplus is maintained. It may be inferred that this agreement sought to replace a deceased brother's position as an officer with members of his family, thereby permitting them to share equally in the company's earnings, including salaries, a significant means of distributing the corporate profits. This inference is not negated by the fact that no provision in the 1955 agreement requires equality of salaries between the family branches.

For more disputes among the Gallers after the Supreme Court's decree, see Galler v. Galler, 217 N.E.2d 111 (Ill.App.1966); Galler v. Galler, 238 N.E.2d 274 (Ill.App.1968).

WASSERMAN v. ROSENGARDEN, 406 N.E.2d 131 (Ill.App. 1980). Joseph and Ralph Rosengarden each owned 40% of the stock of Autohaus Corporation. Leonard Wasserman owned the remaining 20%. Wasserman claimed that the Rosengardens had breached an oral agreement under which all three parties would continue to vote for one another as directors and officers, and all three would receive equal salaries and share equally in any distributed profits. The trial court granted the Rosengardens' motion for judgment on the pleadings, in part on the ground the alleged agreement was ultra vires and unenforceable. Reversed.

"Like the court in *Galler,* we see no reason for precluding the parties from reaching arrangements concerning the management of the closely held corporation which were agreeable to the three shareholders. Fraud, injury to the public, or harm to creditors have not been suggested. Nor is a minority interest complaining about the terms of the oral shareholder's agreement. Defendants protest that, under the alleged agreement, plaintiff has received a disproportionately large return for his investment, but the economic consequences of the agreement do not govern its validity."

DEL. GEN. CORP. LAW §§ 102(B)(1), 141(A), 142(B), 350, 351, 354

[See Statutory Supplement]

MODEL BUS. CORP. ACT §§ 2.02(B), 2.06, 7.32, 8.01(B)

N.Y. BUS. CORP. LAW § 620

[See Statutory Supplement]

CAL. CORP. CODE §§ 158, 186, 300, 312

[See Statutory Supplement]

ADLER v. SVINGOS, 80 A.D.2d 764, 436 N.Y.S.2d 719 (1981). Adler, Shaw, and Svingos each owned 33⅓% of the shares of 891 First Ave. Corp., a New York corporation that operated a restaurant. The corporation's certificate of incorporation was filed in November 1978. In December 1978, Adler, Shaw, and Svingos executed a Stockholders' Agreement. Paragraph 8 of the Agreement provided that all corporate operations, including changes in corporate structure, would require unanimous consent of the three signatories. Subsequently, when Adler and Shaw sought to sell the business, Svingos objected, relying upon the Stockholders' Agreement. Adler and Shaw then brought an action seeking to strike paragraph 8 of the Agreement as void under New York B.C.L. § 620(b), on the ground that under section 620(b) a provision that restricts the board in the management of the business of the corporation must be located in the certificate of incorporation. Svingos counterclaimed, and asked for reformation of the certificate of incorporation to reflect Paragraph 8 of the Stockholders' Agreement. The trial court granted summary judgment against Svingos. Reversed.

> In Zion v. Kurtz (50 N.Y.2d 92), the Court of Appeals interpreted analogous provisions of the Delaware General Corporation Law and held enforceable, as between the parties to it, a provision of a shareholders' agreement between all the shareholders, proscribing corporate action without the consent of a minority shareholder, even though the disputed provision was not incorporated in the corporate charter as required by Delaware's statute. Speaking for the majority, Judge Meyer stated . . . "Since there are no intervening rights of third persons, the agreement requires nothing that is not permitted by statute, and all of the stockholders of the corporation assented to it, the certificate of incorporation may be ordered reformed, by requiring Kurtz [whose position was

analogous to that of plaintiffs Adler and Shaw] to file the appropriate amendments, or more directly he may be held estopped to rely upon the absence of those amendments from the corporate charter".

The principles set forth in *Zion* are controlling here. We conclude that it was error to grant partial summary judgment to plaintiffs and to dismiss defendant's first counterclaim. Indeed, the record warrants granting the defendant's motion for partial summary judgment reforming the certificate to reflect the unanimity of the stockholders' agreement.

SECTION 4. SUPERMAJORITY VOTING AND QUORUM REQUIREMENTS AT THE SHAREHOLDER AND BOARD LEVELS

Sutton v. Sutton

Court of Appeals of New York, 1994.
84 N.Y.2d 37, 637 N.E.2d 260, 614 N.Y.S.2d 369.

■ SIMONS, JUDGE.

In this . . . proceeding, petitioners seek (1) a declaration that an amendment to the certificate of incorporation of Bag Bazaar, Ltd. is valid and (2) to compel respondent David S. Sutton, as a director of the corporation, to sign and deliver a certificate of amendment to petitioners for filing. Respondent has refused to execute the certificate, contending it is not valid because the amendment had the support of only 70% of the shareholders when the certificate of incorporation required unanimous approval. The appeal requires an interpretation of section 616(b) of the Business Corporation Law which states that supermajority provisions in a certificate of incorporation may be amended by a two-thirds vote unless the certificate "specifically" provides otherwise.

Petitioners contend that notwithstanding the general unanimity provision contained in Bag Bazaar's certificate, a two-thirds vote to amend is sufficient under this statute unless the certificate explicitly provides unanimous consent is required to amend the supermajority provision. As they see it, prior to a 1962 statutory amendment, which added the word "specifically", a general requirement of a unanimous vote for any amendment of the certificate—i.e., a provision like the one here—would be read to apply to the supermajority provision. Thus, they reason that the Legislature, by adding the word "specifically" in the 1962 amendment, intended to require an amendment provision explicitly directed at the procedure for changing a supermajority provision. The Appellate Division disagreed and held that the provision in Bag Bazaar's certificate of incorporation was sufficiently specific and that the amendment was not valid because it lacked unanimous shareholder approval (196 A.D.2d 411, 601 N.Y.S.2d 106). We now affirm.

In 1963, the certificate of incorporation of Bag Bazaar, Ltd. was amended to provide that "[t]he unanimous vote or consent of the holders of all the issued and outstanding shares of Common Stock of the corporation shall be necessary for the transaction of any business * * * of the corporation, including amendment to the certificate of incorporation". At that time the business was run by Abraham Sutton and none of the parties to this litigation was a shareholder. In 1971 Abraham's brother, respondent David S. Sutton, purchased 30 shares. Two years later Abraham's son, petitioner Solomon A. Sutton, joined the business and subsequently acquired 30 shares. On Abraham's death, in 1987, his widow, petitioner Yvette Sutton, inherited Abraham's remaining 40 shares. Thus, petitioners now own 70% of the outstanding shares of the corporation and respondent and his wife own 30 shares. Petitioner Solomon A. Sutton serves as one of the two directors of the company and respondent David S. Sutton as the other.

The corporation was run without incident for nearly 30 years under Abraham's leadership. After he relinquished control of the company, however, disputes arose between Solomon and David Sutton concerning the management of the corporation. These disputes culminated in an April 1992 shareholders' meeting, where petitioners voted their 70% of the shares in favor of a resolution to strike the unanimity provision, while respondent's 30% of the shares voted against the resolution.

Respondent, as a director of the corporation, refused to sign a certificate of amendment reflecting the deletion of the unanimity provision, thereby preventing the amendment from taking effect. Accordingly, petitioners commenced this proceeding and moved for judgment declaring the resolution valid and enforceable and compelling respondent to sign the certificate of amendment. Respondent cross-moved to dismiss the petition, for reformation of the certificate of incorporation and to compel arbitration of the dispute. Supreme Court granted the petition and denied the cross motion. The Appellate Division reversed and denied the petition.

To support their position on this appeal, petitioners contend that the Legislature added the word "specifically" to section 616(b) because it recognized that a unanimity provision gives minority shareholders the ability to deadlock any and all corporate action. The amendment was intended to minimize deadlocks by permitting a two-thirds majority of the shareholders to alter or delete the unanimity requirement unless the certificate of incorporation explicitly stated otherwise. Respondent maintains that "specifically" was added to the statute to clarify that if more than a two-thirds vote was required to amend a unanimity provision, the certificate should state exactly what greater percentage is needed. They maintain that this certificate satisfied that requirement by declaring that a unanimous vote was required for any amendment.

The history of Business Corporation Law § 616(b) begins with Benintendi v. Kenton Hotel, 294 N.Y. 112, 60 N.E.2d 829, where this Court invalidated a unanimity provision adopted by unanimous shareholder vote. We reasoned that such a provision was antithetical to the basic concept of corporate governance by majority rule and contrary to public policy (id., at 118–119, 60 N.E.2d 829). In 1948, the Legislature abrogated *Benintendi* by enacting section 9 of the Stock Corporation Law, which authorized unanimity provisions when approved by a unanimous vote (see, L.1948, ch. 862). The effect of section 9 was to require unanimous shareholder consent to either add or amend a unanimity provision (see, 3 White, New York Corporations § 616.02, at 6–378 [13th ed.]). In 1951, this section was amended to allow adoption or change of a supermajority provision by a two-thirds or greater vote. A unanimous vote was still required, however, where the certificate called for a unanimous vote; where the unanimity provision itself required such a vote; or where the unanimity provision was adopted prior to the effective date of the 1951 amendment (see, L. 1951, ch. 717).

In 1961, the Business Corporation Law was adopted to replace the Stock Corporation Law, and section 9 was substantially reenacted as Business Corporation Law § 616(b) and § 709(b). However, in 1962, prior to the 1963 effective date of the Business Corporation Law, a series of changes were made, including the addition of the word "specifically" in section 616(b). As finally enacted, section 616(b) provides that "[a]n amendment of the certificate of incorporation which changes or strikes out a [supermajority] provision * * * shall be authorized at a meeting of shareholders by vote of the holders of two-thirds of all outstanding shares entitled to vote thereon, or of such greater proportion of shares * * * as may be provided specifically in the certificate of incorporation" (emphasis added). According to the Legislative Study Committee the word "specifically" was one of a number of "technical" amendments added to the chapter to clarify existing language and avoid minor inconsistencies. It was not intended to effect a substantive change in the law (Mem. of Joint Legis.Comm. To Study Revision of Corp. Laws, Bill Jacket, L.1962, ch. 834, at 86).

Thus, nothing in the legislative history or the statute itself suggests the necessity for a discrete paragraph addressed solely to the supermajority provision and explicitly declaring the vote required for its amendment. The history reveals that Stock Corporation Law § 9 stated that a provision in the certificate of incorporation requiring unanimous consent could only be amended by unanimous consent and this provision was substantially reenacted in the Business Corporation Law.* Inasmuch as the Legislature did not intend the "technical" revisions added before the effective date of the Business Corporation Law to change the existing law substantively, the present statute should be construed as section 9 of the Stock Corporation Law was.

* While the 1951 amendments to that section allowed a unanimity provision to be amended by a two-thirds vote in certain instances, petitioners acknowledge that the provision at issue here would have required unanimous shareholder consent to amend, despite the 1951 amendment. (Footnote by the court.)

Unanimity was required under the prior law to amend a unanimity provision, such as this one, and the addition of the word "specifically" merely provides that a two-thirds majority may now amend a unanimity provision unless the certificate requires a greater percentage.

The provision in Bag Bazaar's certificate is unambiguous: it requires unanimous shareholder consent for the transaction of "any business * * * including amendment to the certificate of incorporation." To read section 616(b) as requiring more to address amendment of the super-majority provision would be unnecessarily restrictive in light of the legislative history. The certificate need only clearly state what vote, if greater than two thirds, is required to amend a unanimity provision. The certificate of Bag Bazaar, Ltd. does so....

Finally, petitioners note that unless section 616(b) is read as requiring an explicit certificate provision governing the amendment of unanimity provisions, majority shareholders will be unable to conduct the business of a corporation in the face of opposition from the minority. But as respondent notes, there is nothing inherently unfair or improper about a voluntary organization's consensual decision to assure protection for minority shareholders, and shareholders are not without remedies where deadlocks do arise (see generally, Business Corporation Law § 1104).

Accordingly, the order of the Appellate Division should be affirmed, with costs.

■ KAYE, C.J., and TITONE, BELLACOSA, SMITH, LEVINE and CIPARICK, JJ., concur.

Order affirmed, with costs.

N.Y. BUS. CORP. LAW §§ 616, 709

[See Statutory Supplement]

DEL. GEN. CORP. LAW §§ 102(b)(4), 141(b), 216

[See Statutory Supplement]

CAL. CORP. CODE §§ 204, 602

[See Statutory Supplement]

MODEL BUS. CORP. ACT §§ 7.27, 7.32, 8.24

[See Statutory Supplement]

SECTION 5. FIDUCIARY OBLIGATIONS OF SHAREHOLDERS IN CLOSE CORPORATIONS

Donahue v. Rodd Electrotype Co.

Supreme Judicial Court of Massachusetts, 1975.
367 Mass. 578, 328 N.E.2d 505.

■ TAURO, CHIEF JUSTICE.

The plaintiff, Euphemia Donahue, a minority stockholder in the Rodd Electrotype Company of New England, Inc. (Rodd Electrotype), a Massachusetts corporation, brings this suit against the directors of Rodd Electrotype, Charles H. Rodd, Frederick I. Rodd and Mr. Harold E. Magnuson, against Harry C. Rodd, a former director, officer, and controlling stockholder of Rodd Electrotype and against Rodd Electrotype (hereinafter called defendants). The plaintiff seeks to rescind Rodd Electrotype's purchase of Harry Rodd's shares in Rodd Electrotype and to compel Harry Rodd "to repay to the corporation the purchase price of said shares, $36,000, together with interest from the date of purchase." The plaintiff alleges that the defendants caused the corporation to purchase the shares in violation of their fiduciary duty to her, a minority stockholder of Rodd Electrotype.[4]

The trial judge, after hearing oral testimony, dismissed the plaintiff's bill on the merits. He found that the purchase was without prejudice to the plaintiff and implicitly found that the transaction had been carried out in good faith and with inherent fairness. The Appeals Court affirmed with costs. Donahue v. Rodd Electrotype Co. of New England, Inc., 1 Mass.App. 876, 307 N.E.2d 8 (1974). The case is before us on the plaintiff's application for further appellate review....

[Briefly, the facts were as follows: In the mid–1930's Harry Rodd and Joseph Donahue had become employees of Royal Electrotype (the predecessor of Rodd Electrotype). Donahue's duties were confined to operational matters within the plants, and he never participated in the management aspect of the business. In contrast, Rodd's advancement within the company was rapid, and in 1946 he became general manager and treasurer. Subsequently Rodd acquired 200 of the corporation's 1000 shares and Donahue (at Rodd's suggestion) acquired 50 shares. In 1955 Rodd became president and general manager, and

---

4. In form, the plaintiff's bill of complaint presents, at least in part, a derivative action, brought on behalf of the corporation, and, in the words of the bill, "on behalf of ... [the] stockholders" of Rodd Electrotype. Yet ... the plaintiff's bill, in substance, was one seeking redress because of alleged breaches of the fiduciary duty owed *to her,* a minority stockholder, by the controlling stockholders.

We treat the bill of complaint (as have the parties) as presenting a proper cause of suit in the personal right of the plaintiff....

later that year Royal itself purchased the remaining 750 shares, so that Rodd and Donahue became Royal's sole shareholders, owning 80% and 20% of its stock, respectively. In 1960 the corporation was renamed Rodd Electrotype, and in the early 60's Harry Rodd's two sons, Charles and Frederick, took important positions with the company. In 1965 Charles succeeded his father as president and general manager.

In 1970 Harry Rodd was seventy-seven years old and not in good health, and his sons wished him to retire. Prior to 1967 Harry had distributed 117 of his 200 shares equally among his sons and his daughter, and had returned 2 shares to the corporate treasury. Harry insisted that as a condition to his retirement some financial arrangement be made with respect to his remaining 81 shares. Accordingly, Charles, acting on the corporation's behalf, negotiated for the purchase of 45 of Harry's shares for $800/share—a price which, Charles testified, reflected book and liquidating value. At a special board meeting in July 1970, the corporation's board (then consisting of Charles and Frederick Rodd and a lawyer) voted to have the corporation make the purchase at this price. Subsequently Harry Rodd sold 2 shares to each of his three children at $800/share, and gave each child 10 shares as a gift.[7] Meanwhile Donahue had died and his 50 shares had passed to his wife and son. When the Donahues learned that the corporation had purchased Harry Rodd's shares, they offered their shares to the corporation on the terms given to Harry but the offer was rejected.[10] This suit followed.]

In her argument before this court, the plaintiff has characterized the corporate purchase of Harry Rodd's shares as an unlawful distribution of corporate assets to controlling stockholders. She urges that the distribution constitutes a breach of the fiduciary duty owed by the Rodds, as controlling stockholders, to her, a minority stockholder in the enterprise, because the Rodds failed to accord her an equal opportunity to sell her shares to the corporation. The defendants reply that the stock purchase was within the powers of the corporation and met the requirements of good faith and inherent fairness imposed on a fiduciary in his dealings with the corporation. They assert that there is no right to equal opportunity in corporate stock purchases for the corporate treasury. For the reasons hereinafter noted, we agree with the plaintiff and reverse the decree of the Superior Court. However, we limit the applicability of our holding to "close corporations," as hereinafter defined. Whether the holding should apply to other corporations is left for decision in another case, on a proper record.

A. *Close Corporations.* In previous opinions, we have alluded to the distinctive nature of the close corporation ... but have never defined precisely what is meant by a close corporation. There is no

---

7. An inference is permissible that the "gift" of these shares was a part of the "deal" for the stock purchase.

10. Between 1965 and 1969, the company offered to purchase the Donahue shares for amounts between $2,000 and $10,000 ($40 to $200 a share). The Donahues rejected these offers.

single, generally accepted definition. Some commentators emphasize an "integration of ownership and management" (Note, Statutory Assistance for Closely Held Corporations, 71 Harv.L.Rev. 1498 [1958]), in which the stockholders occupy most management positions.... Others focus on the number of stockholders and the nature of the market for the stock. In this view, close corporations have few stockholders; there is little market for corporate stock. The Supreme Court of Illinois adopted this latter view in Galler v. Galler, 32 Ill.2d 16, 203 N.E.2d 577 (1964).... We accept aspects of both definitions. We deem a close corporation to be typified by: (1) a small number of stockholders; (2) no ready market for the corporate stock; and (3) substantial majority stockholder participation in the management, direction and operations of the corporation.

As thus defined, the close corporation bears striking resemblance to a partnership.... Just as in a partnership, the relationship among the stockholders must be one of trust, confidence and absolute loyalty if the enterprise is to succeed....

In Helms v. Duckworth, 101 U.S.App.D.C. 390, 249 F.2d 482 (1957) ... Judge Burger, now Chief Justice Burger, writing for the court, emphasized the resemblance of the two-man close corporation to a partnership: "In an intimate business venture such as this, stockholders of a close corporation occupy a position similar to that of joint adventurers and partners. While courts have sometimes declared stockholders 'do not bear toward each other that same relation of trust and confidence which prevails in partnerships,' this view ignores the practical realities of the organization and functioning of a small 'two-man' corporation organized to carry on a small business enterprise in which the stockholders, directors, and managers are the same persons" (footnotes omitted). Id. at 486.

Although the corporate form provides ... advantages for the stockholders (limited liability, perpetuity, and so forth), it also supplies an opportunity for the majority stockholders to oppress or disadvantage minority stockholders. The minority is vulnerable to a variety of oppressive devices, termed "freeze-outs," which the majority may employ.... An authoritative study of such "freeze-outs" enumerates some of the possibilities: "The squeezers ... may refuse to declare dividends; they may drain off the corporation's earnings in the form of exorbitant salaries and bonuses to the majority shareholder-officers and perhaps to their relatives, or in the form of high rent by the corporation for property leased from majority shareholders ...; they may deprive minority shareholders of corporate offices and of employment by the company...."

The minority can, of course, initiate suit against the majority and their directors. Self-serving conduct by directors is proscribed by the director's fiduciary obligation to the corporation.... However, in practice, the plaintiff will find difficulty in challenging dividend or employment policies. Such policies are considered to be within the judgment of the directors ... [G]enerally, plaintiffs who seek judicial assistance against corporate dividend or employment policies do not prevail. . . .

Thus, when these types of "freeze-outs" are attempted by the majority stockholders, the minority stockholders, cut off from all corporation-related revenues, must either suffer their losses or seek a buyer for their shares. Many minority stockholders will be unwilling or unable to wait for an alteration in majority policy. Typically, the minority stockholder in a close corporation has a substantial percentage of his personal assets invested in the corporation. The stockholder may have anticipated that his salary from his position with the corporation would be his livelihood. Thus, he cannot afford to wait passively. He must liquidate his investment in the close corporation in order to reinvest the funds in income-producing enterprises.

At this point, the true plight of the minority stockholder in a close corporation becomes manifest. He cannot easily reclaim his capital. In a large public corporation, the oppressed or dissident minority stockholder could sell his stock in order to extricate some of his invested capital. By definition, this market is not available for shares in the close corporation. In a partnership, a partner who feels abused by his fellow partners may cause dissolution by his "express will . . . at any time" . . . and recover his share of partnership assets and accumulated profits. . . . By contrast, the stockholder in the close corporation or "incorporated partnership" may achieve dissolution and recovery of his share of the enterprise assets only by compliance with the rigorous terms of the applicable chapter of the General Laws. . . .

Thus, in a close corporation, the minority stockholders may be trapped in a disadvantageous situation. No outsider would knowingly assume the position of the disadvantaged minority. The outsider would have the same difficulties. To cut losses, the minority stockholder may be compelled to deal with the majority. This is the capstone of the majority plan. Majority "freeze-out" schemes which withhold dividends are designed to compel the minority to relinquish stock at inadequate prices. . . . When the minority stockholder agrees to sell out at less than fair value, the majority has won.

Because of the fundamental resemblance of the close corporation to the partnership, the trust and confidence which are essential to this scale and manner of enterprise, and the inherent danger to minority interests in the close corporation, we hold that stockholders[17] in the close corporation owe one another substantially the same fiduciary duty in the operation of the enterprise[18] that partners owe to one

---

17. We do not limit our holding to majority stockholders. In the close corporation, the minority may do equal damage through unscrupulous and improper "sharp dealings" with an unsuspecting majority. See Helms v. Duckworth, 101 U.S.App.D.C. 390, 249 F.2d 482 (1957).

18. We stress that the strict fiduciary duty which we apply to stockholders in a close corporation in this opinion governs *only* their actions relative to the operations of the enterprise and the effects of that operation on the rights and investments of other stockholders. We express no opinion as to the standard of duty applicable to transactions in the shares of the close corporation when the corporation is not a party to the transaction. Cf. Andrews, The Stockholder's Right to Equal Opportunity in the Sale of Shares, 78 Harv.L.Rev. 505

another. In our previous decisions, we have defined the standard of duty owed by partners to one another as the "utmost good faith and loyalty." Cardullo v. Landau, 329 Mass. 5, 8, 105 N.E.2d 843 (1952); DeCotis v. D'Antona, 350 Mass. 165, 168, 214 N.E.2d 21 (1966). Stockholders in close corporations must discharge their management and stockholder responsibilities in conformity with this strict good faith standard. They may not act out of avarice, expediency or self-interest in derogation of their duty of loyalty to the other stockholders and to the corporation.

We contrast this strict good faith standard with the somewhat less stringent standard of fiduciary duty to which directors and stockholders of all corporations must adhere in the discharge of their corporate responsibilities. Corporate directors are held to a good faith and inherent fairness standard of conduct (Winchell v. Plywood Corp., 324 Mass. 171, 177, 85 N.E.2d 313 [1949]) and are not "permitted to serve two masters whose interests are antagonistic." Spiegel v. Beacon Participations, 297 Mass. 398, 411, 8 N.E.2d 895, 904 (1937). "Their paramount duty is to the corporation, and their personal pecuniary interests are subordinate to that duty." Durfee v. Durfee & Canning, Inc., 323 Mass. 187, 196, 80 N.E.2d 522, 527 (1948).

The more rigorous duty of partners and participants in a joint adventure, here extended to stockholders in a close corporation, was described by then Chief Judge Cardozo of the New York Court of Appeals in Meinhard v. Salmon, 249 N.Y. 458, 164 N.E. 545 (1928): "Joint adventurers, like co-partners, owe to one another, while the enterprise continues, the duty of the finest loyalty. Many forms of conduct permissible in a workaday world for those acting at arm's length, are forbidden to those bound by fiduciary ties.... Not honesty alone, but the punctilio of an honor the most sensitive, is then the standard of behavior." Id. at 463–464, 164 N.E. at 546 ...

B. *Equal Opportunity in a Close Corporation.* Under settled Massachusetts law, a domestic corporation, unless forbidden by statute, has the power to purchase its own shares.... An agreement to reacquire stock "[is] enforceable, subject, at least, to the limitations that the purchase must be made in good faith and without prejudice to creditors and stockholders." ... When the corporation reacquiring its own stock is a close corporation, the purchase is subject to the additional requirement, in the light of our holding in this opinion, that the stockholders, who, as directors or controlling stockholders, caused the corporation to enter into the stock purchase agreement, must have acted with the utmost good faith and loyalty to the other stockholders.

To meet this test, if the stockholder whose shares were purchased was a member of the controlling group, the controlling stockholders must cause the corporation to offer each stockholder an equal opportunity to sell a ratable number of his shares to the corporation at an identical price. Purchase by the corporation confers substantial bene-

---

(1965). Compare Perlman v. Feldmann, 219 F.2d 173 (2d Cir.), cert. den. 349 U.S. 952, 75 S.Ct. 880, 99 L.Ed. 1277 (1955) with Zahn v. Transamerica Corp., 162 F.2d 36 (3d Cir.1947).

fits on the members of the controlling group whose shares were purchased. These benefits are not available to the minority stockholders if the corporation does not also offer them an opportunity to sell their shares. The controlling group may not, consistent with its strict duty to the minority, utilize its control of the corporation to obtain special advantages and disproportionate benefit from its share ownership. See Jones v. H.F. Ahmanson & Co., 1 Cal.3d 93, 108, 81 Cal.Rptr. 592, 460 P.2d 464 (1969); Note, 83 Harv.L.Rev. 1904, 1908 (1970). Cf. Brudney and Chirelstein, Fair Shares in Corporate Mergers and Takeovers, 88 Harv.L.Rev. 297, 334 (1974).

The benefits conferred by the purchase are twofold: (1) provision of a market for shares; (2) access to corporate assets for personal use. By definition, there is no ready market for shares of a close corporation. The purchase creates a market for shares which previously had been unmarketable. It transforms a previously illiquid investment into a liquid one. If the close corporation purchases shares only from a member of the controlling group, the controlling stockholder can convert his shares into cash at a time when none of the other stockholders can. Consistent with its strict fiduciary duty, the controlling group may not utilize its control of the corporation to establish an exclusive market in previously unmarketable shares from which the minority stockholders are excluded. See Jones v. H.F. Ahmanson & Co. . . .

The purchase also distributes corporate assets to the stockholder whose shares were purchased. Unless an equal opportunity is given to all stockholders, the purchase of shares from a member of the controlling group operates as a *preferential* distribution of assets. In exchange for his shares, he receives a percentage of the contributed capital and accumulated profits of the enterprise. The funds he so receives are available for his personal use. The other stockholders benefit from no such access to corporate property and cannot withdraw their shares of the corporate profits and capital in this manner unless the controlling group acquiesces. Although the purchase price for the controlling stockholder's shares may seem fair to the corporation and other stockholders under the tests established in the prior case law (see Spiegel v. Beacon Participations, 297 Mass. 398, 429, 8 N.E.2d 895 [1937]; Winchell v. Plywood Corp., 324 Mass. 171, 178, 85 N.E.2d 313 [1949]), the controlling stockholder whose stock has been purchased has still received a relative advantage over his fellow stockholders, inconsistent with his strict fiduciary duty—an opportunity to turn corporate funds to personal use.

The rule of equal opportunity in stock purchases by close corporations provides equal access to these benefits for all stockholders. We hold that, in any case in which the controlling stockholders have exercised their power over the corporation to deny the minority such equal opportunity, the minority shall be entitled to appropriate relief. To the extent that language in Spiegel v. Beacon Participations, 297 Mass. 398, 431, 8 N.E.2d 895 (1937), and other cases suggests that there is no requirement of equal opportunity for minority stockholders when a close corporation purchases shares from a controlling stockholder, it is not to be followed.

C. *Application of the Law to this Case.* We turn now to the application of the learning set forth above to the facts of the instant case.

The strict standard of duty is plainly applicable to the stockholders in Rodd Electrotype. Rodd Electrotype is a close corporation [under the test set out above]....

... In testing the stock purchase from Harry Rodd against the applicable strict fiduciary standard, we treat the Rodd family as a single controlling group.... From the evidence, it is clear that the Rodd family was a close-knit one with strong community of interest....

Moreover, a strong motive of interest requires that the Rodds be considered a controlling group. When Charles Rodd and Frederick Rodd were called on to represent the corporation in its dealings with their father, they must have known that further advancement within the corporation and benefits would follow their father's retirement and the purchase of his stock....

On its face, then, the purchase of Harry Rodd's shares by the corporation is a breach of the duty which the controlling stockholders, the Rodds, owed to the minority stockholders, the plaintiff and her son. The purchaser distributed a portion of the corporate assets to Harry Rodd, a member of the controlling group, in exchange for his shares. The plaintiff and her son were not offered an equal opportunity to sell their shares to the corporation. In fact, their efforts to obtain an equal opportunity were rebuffed by the corporate representative. As the trial judge found, they did not, in any manner, ratify the transaction with Harry Rodd.

Because of the foregoing, we hold that the plaintiff is entitled to relief. Two forms of suitable relief are set out hereinafter. The judge below is to enter an appropriate judgment. The judgment may require Harry Rodd to remit $36,000 with interest at the legal rate from July 15, 1970, to Rodd Electrotype in exchange for forty-five shares of Rodd Electrotype treasury stock. This, in substance, is the specific relief requested in the plaintiff's bill of complaint. Interest is manifestly appropriate. A stockholder, who, in violation of his fiduciary duty to the other stockholders, has obtained assets from his corporation and has had those assets available for his own use, must pay for that use. See Silversmith v. Sydeman, 305 Mass. 65, 74, 25 N.E.2d 215 (1940). Cf. Spiegel v. Beacon Participations, 297 Mass. 398, 420, 8 N.E.2d 895 (1937). In the alternative, the judgment may require Rodd Electrotype to purchase all of the plaintiff's shares for $36,000 without interest. In the circumstances of this case, we view this as the equal opportunity which the plaintiff should have received. Harry Rodd's retention of thirty-six shares, which were to be sold and given to his children within a year of the Rodd Electrotype purchase, cannot disguise the fact that the corporation acquired one hundred per cent of that portion of his holdings (forty-five shares) which he did not intend his children to own. The plaintiff is entitled to have one hundred per cent of her forty-five shares similarly purchased.[30]

The final decree, in so far as it dismissed the bill as to Harry C. Rodd, Frederick I. Rodd, Charles H. Rodd, Mr. Harold E. Magnuson and Rodd Electrotype Company of New England, Inc., and awarded costs, is reversed. The case is remanded to the Superior Court for entry of judgment in conformity with this opinion.

So ordered.*

■ WILKINS, JUSTICE (concurring).

I agree with much of what the Chief Justice says in support of granting relief to the plaintiff. However, I do not join in any implication (see, e.g., footnote 18 and the associated text) that the rule concerning a close corporation's purchase of a controlling stockholder's shares applies to all operations of the corporation as they affect minority stockholders. That broader issue, which is apt to arise in connection with salaries and dividend policy, is not involved in this case. The analogy to partnerships may not be a complete one.

NOTE ON NIXON v. BLACKWELL

In Nixon v. Blackwell, 626 A.2d 1366 (Del.Supr.1993), E.C. Barton & Co. had two classes of stock outstanding: Class A Voting Common Stock and Class B Nonvoting Common Stock. All the Class A stock and most of the Class B stock was held by or for the benefit of corporate employees. The plaintiffs, who were not employees, owned 25% of the Class B.

There was no public market for, or trading in, either class of the corporation's stock. This created a liquidity problem for the shareholders—that is, the shareholders could not readily convert the stock into cash by selling it. Over the years, the corporation addressed the liquidity problem in several ways:

(i) The Corporation established an Employee Stock Ownership Plan (ESOP) designed to hold Class B stock for the benefit of eligible employees of the Corporation. Under the plan, terminating and retiring employees were entitled to receive their interest in the ESOP by taking either Class B stock or cash in lieu of stock. Most terminating employees and retirees elected to receive cash in lieu of stock. Thus, the ESOP provided employee-shareholders with a substantial measure of liquidity that was not available to non-employee shareholders.

---

30. If there has been a significant change in corporate circumstances since this case was argued, this is a matter which can be brought to the attention of the court below and may be considered by the judge in granting appropriate relief in the form of a judgment.

* See also Comolli v. Comolli, 241 Ga. 471, 246 S.E.2d 278 (1978); cf. Schwartz v. Marien, 37 N.Y.2d 487, 335 N.E.2d 334, 373 N.Y.S.2d 122 (1975). For additional cases and materials on the fiduciary obligations of shareholders in close corporations, see Section 7(a), infra. (Footnote by ed.)

(ii) The corporation also purchased "key man" life-insurance policies on certain employees, with death benefits payable to the corporation. The corporation, in turn, agreed to use a portion of these benefits to repurchase its stock from the employee-shareholders' estates.

(iii) Occasionally, the corporation offered to purchase the Class B stock of the non-employee stockholders through self-tender offers.

There was a suggestion, at least, that the programs for providing liquidity to employee-shareholders reflected the plan of the founder of the corporation, from whom the plaintiffs had inherited their stock.

The plaintiffs, who were non-employee shareholders, argued that the corporation's directors, all of whom were employees, were improperly pursuing a discriminatory liquidity policy that favored employee-shareholders over non-employee shareholders through the ESOP and the key-man life-insurance policies. At trial, the Vice Chancellor found for the plaintiffs on the ground that the defendants breached their fiduciary duty as directors, and treated the plaintiffs unfairly, by providing no means through which non-employee shareholders could liquidate their stock at fair value, while providing liquidity for terminating and retiring employees. The Delaware Supreme Court reversed:

> The trial court in this case ... appears to have adopted the novel legal principle that Class B stockholders had a right to "liquidity" equal to that which the court found to be available to the defendants. It is well established in [Delaware] jurisprudence that stockholders need not always be treated equally for all purposes.... To hold that fairness necessarily requires precise equality is to beg the question....
>
> ... [The] holding of the trial court overlooks the significant facts that the minority stockholders were not: (a) employees of the Corporation; (b) entitled to share in an ESOP; (c) qualified for key man insurance; or (d) protected by specific provisions in the certificate of incorporation, by-laws, or a stockholders' agreement.
>
> There is support in this record for the fact that the ESOP is a corporate benefit and was established, at least in part, to benefit the Corporation. Generally speaking, the creation of ESOPs is a normal corporate practice and is generally thought to benefit the corporation. The same is true generally with respect to key man insurance programs....
>
> Accordingly, we hold that the Vice Chancellor erred as a matter of law in concluding that the liquidity afforded to the employee stockholders by the ESOP and the key man insurance required substantially equal treatment for the non-employee stockholders. Moreover, the Vice Chancellor failed to evaluate and articulate, for example, whether or not and to what extent (a) corporate benefits flowed from the ESOP and the key man insurance; (b) the ESOP and key man insurance plans are novel, extraordinary, or relatively routine business practices; (c) [the founder's] plan for employee management and benefits should be honored; and (d) the self-tenders showed defendants' willingness to provide an exit opportunity for the plaintiffs....

> We hold on this record that defendants have met their burden of establishing the entire fairness of their dealings with the non-employee Class B stockholders, and are entitled to judgment. The record is sufficient to conclude that plaintiffs' claim that the defendant directors have maintained a discriminatory policy of favoring Class A employee stockholders over Class B non-employee stockholders is without merit. The directors have followed a consistent policy originally established by ... the founder of the Corporation....

ROSENTHAL v. ROSENTHAL, 543 A.2d 348 (Me.1988). In this case, the trial court judge set out the following four specific fiduciary duties owed by the business associates in a close corporation to each other:

> (1) To act with that degree of diligence, care and skill which ordinarily prudent persons would exercise under similar circumstances in like positions;
>
> (2) To discharge the duties affecting their relationship in good faith with a view to furthering the interests of one another as to the matters within the scope of the relationship;
>
> (3) To disclose and not withhold from one another relevant information affecting the status and affairs of the relationship;
>
> (4) To not use their position, influence or knowledge respecting the affairs and organization that are subject to the relationship to gain any special privilege or advantage over the other person or persons involved in the relationship....

On appeal, the Maine Supreme Court affirmed. "For the first time on appeal defendants object to the [trial judge's] definition of the scope of the [shareholders'] duties as including 'furthering the interests of one another,' rather than being restricted to furthering the interests of the business enterprise. We can find no clear error in that instruction, however, given the special nature of the [shareholders'] family business, which most closely resembles a single complex family partnership doing business through numerous entities of varied legal forms.... The duties owed in the circumstances here presented necessarily flowed to the other business associates, as well as to the [shareholders'] enterprise as a whole and the component entitles." (Emphasis by the court.)

Wilkes v. Springside Nursing Home, Inc.

Supreme Judicial Court of Massachusetts, 1976.
370 Mass. 842, 353 N.E.2d 657.

■ HENNESSEY, CHIEF JUSTICE.

[The plaintiff (Wilkes) filed a bill in equity for declaratory judgment, naming as defendants T. Edward Quinn,[3] Leon L. Riche, the

3. T. Edward Quinn died while this action was sub judice. The executrix of his estate has been substituted as a party-defendant....

executors of Lawrence R. Connor, and the Springside Nursing Home, Inc. Wilkes sought, among other forms of relief, damages in the amount of the salary he would have received had he continued as a director and officer of Springside subsequent to March, 1967. The court referred the suit to a master. The master's report was confirmed, a judgment was entered dismissing Wilkes's action on the merits, and the Massachusetts Supreme Court granted direct appellate review.] On appeal, Wilkes argued in the alternative that (1) he should recover damages for breach of the alleged partnership agreement; and (2) he should recover damages because the defendants, as majority stockholders in Springside, breached their fiduciary duty to him as a minority stockholder by their action in February and March, 1967.

... [W]e reverse so much of the judgment as dismisses Wilkes's complaint and order the entry of a judgment substantially granting the relief sought by Wilkes under the second alternative set forth above.

A summary of the pertinent facts as found by the master is set out in the following pages....

In 1951 Wilkes acquired an option to purchase a building and lot located on the corner of Springside Avenue and North Street in Pittsfield, Massachusetts, the building having previously housed the Hillcrest Hospital. Though Wilkes was principally engaged in the roofing and siding business, he had gained a reputation locally for profitable dealings in real estate. Riche, an acquaintance of Wilkes, learned of the option, and interested Quinn (who was known to Wilkes through membership on the draft board in Pittsfield) and Pipkin (an acquaintance of both Wilkes and Riche) in joining Wilkes in his investment. The four men met and decided to participate jointly in the purchase of the building and lot as a real estate investment which, they believed, had good profit potential on resale or rental.

The parties later determined that the property would have its greatest potential for profit if it were operated by them as a nursing home. Wilkes consulted his attorney, who advised him that if the four men were to operate the contemplated nursing home as planned, they would be partners and would be liable for any debts incurred by the partnership and by each other. On the attorney's suggestion, and after consultation among themselves, ownership of the property was vested in Springside, a corporation organized under Massachusetts law.

Each of the four men invested $1,000 and subscribed to ten shares of $100 par value stock in Springside.[6] At the time of incorporation it was understood by all of the parties that each would be a director of Springside and each would participate actively in the management and decision making involved in operating the corpora-

6. On May 2, 1955, and again on December 23, 1958, each of the four original investors paid for and was issued additional shares of $100 par value stock, eventually bringing the total number of shares owned by each to 115.

tion.[7] It was, further, the understanding and intention of all the parties that, corporate resources permitting, each would receive money from the corporation in equal amounts as long as each assumed an active and ongoing responsibility for carrying a portion of the burdens necessary to operate the business.

The work involved in establishing and operating a nursing home was roughly apportioned, and each of the four men undertook his respective tasks.[8] Initially, Riche was elected president of Springside, Wilkes was elected treasurer, and Quinn was elected clerk.[9] Each of the four was listed in the articles of organization as a director of the corporation.

At some time in 1952, it became apparent that the operational income and cash flow from the business were sufficient to permit the four stockholders to draw money from the corporation on a regular basis. Each of the four original parties initially received $35 a week from the corporation. As time went on the weekly return to each was increased until, in 1955, it totalled $100.

In 1959, after a long illness, Pipkin sold his shares in the corporation to Connor, who was known to Wilkes, Riche and Quinn through past transactions with Springside in his capacity as president of the First Agricultural National Bank of Berkshire County. Connor received a weekly stipend from the corporation equal to that received by Wilkes, Riche and Quinn. He was elected a director of the corporation but never held any other office. He was assigned no specific area of responsibility in the operation of the nursing home but did participate in business discussions and decisions as a director and served additionally as financial adviser to the corporation.

In 1965 the stockholders decided to sell a portion of the corporate property to Quinn who, in addition to being a stockholder in Springside, possessed an interest in another corporation which desired to operate a rest home on the property. Wilkes was successful in prevailing on the other stockholders of Springside to procure a higher sale price for the property than Quinn apparently anticipated paying or desired to pay. After the sale was consummated, the relationship between Quinn and Wilkes began to deteriorate.

---

7. Wilkes testified before the master that, when the corporate officers were elected, all four men "were . . . guaranteed directorships." Riche's understanding of the parties' intentions was that they all wanted to play a part in the management of the corporation and wanted to have some "say" in the risks involved; that, to this end, they all would be directors; and that "unless you [were] a director and officer you could not participate in the decisions of [the] enterprise."

8. Wilkes took charge of the repair, upkeep and maintenance of the physical plant and grounds; Riche assumed supervision over the kitchen facilities and dietary and food aspects of the home; Pipkin was to make himself available if and when medical problems arose; and Quinn dealt with the personnel and administrative aspects of the nursing home, serving informally as a managing director. Quinn further coordinated the activities of the other parties and served as a communication link among them when matters had to be discussed and decisions had to be made without a formal meeting.

9. Riche held the office of president from 1951 to 1963; Quinn served as president from 1963 on, as clerk from 1951 to 1967, and as treasurer from 1967 on; Wilkes was treasurer from 1951 to 1967.

The bad blood between Quinn and Wilkes affected the attitudes of both Riche and Connor. As a consequence of the strained relations among the parties, Wilkes, in January of 1967, gave notice of his intention to sell his shares for an amount based on an appraisal of their value. In February of 1967 a directors' meeting was held and the board exercised its right to establish the salaries of its officers and employees.[10] A schedule of payments was established whereby Quinn was to receive a substantial weekly increase and Riche and Connor were to continue receiving $100 a week. Wilkes, however, was left off the list of those to whom a salary was to be paid. The directors also set the annual meeting of the stockholders for March, 1967.

At the annual meeting in March,[11] Wilkes was not reelected as a director, nor was he reelected as an officer of the corporation. He was further informed that neither his services nor his presence at the nursing home was wanted by his associates.

The meetings of the directors and stockholders in early 1967, the master found, were used as a vehicle to force Wilkes out of active participation in the management and operation of the corporation and to cut off all corporate payments to him. Though the board of directors had the power to dismiss any officers or employees for misconduct or neglect of duties, there was no indication in the minutes of the board of directors' meeting in February, 1967, that the failure to establish a salary for Wilkes was based on either ground. The severance of Wilkes from the payroll resulted not from misconduct or neglect of duties, but because of the personal desire of Quinn, Riche and Connor to prevent him from continuing to receive money from the corporation. Despite a continuing deterioration in his personal relationship with his associates, Wilkes had consistently endeavored to carry on his responsibilities to the corporation in the same satisfactory manner and with the same degree of competence he had previously shown. Wilkes was at all times willing to carry on his responsibilities and participation if permitted so to do and provided that he receive his weekly stipend.

1. We turn to Wilkes's claim for damages based on a breach of the fiduciary duty owed to him by the other participants in this venture. In light of the theory underlying this claim, we do not consider it vital to our approach to this case whether the claim is governed by partnership law or the law applicable to business corporations. This is so because, as all the parties agree, Springside was at all times relevant to this action, a close corporation as we have recently defined such an entity in Donahue v. Rodd Electrotype Co. of New England, Inc.... [where] we held that "stockholders in the close

10. The by-laws of the corporation provided that the directors, subject to the approval of the stockholders, had the power to fix the salaries of all officers and employees. This power, however, up until February, 1967, had not been exercised formally; all payments made to the four participants in the venture had resulted from the informal but unanimous approval of all the parties concerned.

11. Wilkes was unable to attend the meeting of the board of directors in February or the annual meeting of the stockholders in March, 1967. He was represented, however, at the annual meeting by his attorney, who held his proxy.

corporation owe one another substantially the same fiduciary duty in the operation of the enterprise that partners owe to one another." . . .

In the *Donahue* case we recognized that one peculiar aspect of close corporations was the opportunity afforded to majority stockholders to oppress, disadvantage or "freeze out" minority stockholders. . . .

. . . One . . . device which has proved to be particularly effective in accomplishing the purpose of the majority is to deprive minority stockholders of corporate offices and of employment with the corporation . . . This "freeze-out" technique has been successful because courts fairly consistently have been disinclined to interfere in those facets of internal corporate operations, such as the selection and retention or dismissal of officers, directors and employees, which essentially involve management decisions subject to the principle of majority control . . .

The denial of employment to the minority at the hands of the majority is especially pernicious in some instances. A guaranty of employment with the corporation may have been one of the "basic reason[s] why a minority owner has invested capital in the firm." . . . The minority stockholder typically depends on his salary as the principal return on his investment, since the "earnings of a close corporation . . . are distributed in major part in salaries, bonuses, and retirement benefits." 1 F.H. O'Neal, Close Corporations § 1.07 (1971).[13] Other noneconomic interests of the minority stockholder are likewise injuriously affected by barring him from corporate office. See F.H. O'Neal, "Squeeze–Outs" of Minority Shareholders 79 (1975). Such action severely restricts his participation in the management of the enterprise, and he is relegated to enjoying those benefits incident to his status as a stockholder. See Symposium—The Close Corporation, 52 Nw.U.L.Rev. 345, 386 (1957). In sum, by terminating a minority stockholder's employment or by severing him from a position as an officer or director, the majority effectively frustrate the minority stockholder's purposes in entering on the corporate venture and also deny him an equal return on his investment.

The *Donahue* decision acknowledged, as a "natural outgrowth" of the case law of this Commonwealth, a strict obligation on the part of majority stockholders in a close corporation to deal with the minority with the utmost good faith and loyalty. On its face, this strict standard is applicable in the instant case. The distinction between the majority action in *Donahue* and the majority action in this case is more one of form than of substance. Nevertheless, we are concerned that untempered application of the strict good faith standard enunciated in Donahue to cases such as the one before us will result in the imposition of limitations on legitimate action by the controlling group in a close corporation which will unduly hamper its effectiveness in managing the corporation in the best interests of all concerned. The

---

13. We note here that the master found that Springside never declared or paid a dividend to its stockholders.

majority, concededly, have certain rights to what has been termed "selfish ownership" in the corporation which should be balanced against the concept of their fiduciary obligation to the minority. See Hill, The Sale of Controlling Shares, 70 Harv.L.Rev. 986, 1013–1015 (1957); Note, 44 Iowa L.Rev. 734, 740–741 (1959); Symposium—The Close Corporation, 52 Nw.U.L.Rev. 345, 395–396 (1957).

Therefore, when minority stockholders in a close corporation bring suit against the majority alleging a breach of the strict good faith duty owed to them by the majority, we must carefully analyze the action taken by the controlling stockholders in the individual case. It must be asked whether the controlling group can demonstrate a legitimate business purpose for its action. See Bryan v. Brock & Blevins Co., 343 F.Supp. 1062, 1068 (N.D.Ga.1972), aff'd, 490 F.2d 563, 570–571 (5th Cir.1974); Schwartz v. Marien, 37 N.Y.2d 487, 492, 373 N.Y.S.2d 122, 335 N.E.2d 334 (1975).... In asking this question, we acknowledge the fact that the controlling group in a close corporation must have some room to maneuver in establishing the business policy of the corporation. It must have a large measure of discretion, for example, in declaring or withholding dividends, deciding whether to merge or consolidate, establishing the salaries of corporate officers, dismissing directors with or without cause, and hiring and firing corporate employees.

When an asserted business purpose for their action is advanced by the majority, however, we think it is open to minority stockholders to demonstrate that the same legitimate objective could have been achieved through an alternative course of action less harmful to the minority's interest. See Schwartz v. Marien, supra.... If called on to settle a dispute, our courts must weigh the legitimate business purpose, if any, against the practicability of a less harmful alternative.

Applying this approach to the instant case it is apparent that the majority stockholders in Springside have not shown a legitimate business purpose for severing Wilkes from the payroll of the corporation or for refusing to reelect him as a salaried officer and director....

It is an inescapable conclusion from all the evidence that the action of the majority stockholders here was a designed "freeze out" for which no legitimate business purpose has been suggested. Furthermore, we may infer that a design to pressure Wilkes into selling his shares to the corporation at a price below their value well may have been at the heart of the majority's plan.[14]

In the context of this case, several factors bear directly on the duty owed to Wilkes by his associates. At a minimum, the duty of utmost good faith and loyalty would demand that the majority consider that their action was in disregard of a long-standing policy of the stockholders that each would be a director of the corporation and that

14. This inference arises from the fact that Connor, acting on behalf of the three controlling stockholders, offered to purchase Wilkes's shares for a price Connor admittedly would not have accepted for his own shares.

employment with the corporation would go hand in hand with stock ownership; that Wilkes was one of the four originators of the nursing home venture; and that Wilkes, like the others, had invested his capital and time for more than fifteen years with the expectation that he would continue to participate in corporate decisions. Most important is the plain fact that the cutting off of Wilkes's salary, together with the fact that the corporation never declared a dividend (see note 13 supra), assured that Wilkes would receive no return at all from the corporation.

2. The question of Wilkes's damages at the hands of the majority has not been thoroughly explored on the record before us. Wilkes, in his original complaint, sought damages in the amount of the $100 a week he believed he was entitled to from the time his salary was terminated up until the time this action was commenced. However, the record shows that, after Wilkes was severed from the corporate payroll, the schedule of salaries and payments made to the other stockholders varied from time to time. In addition, the duties assumed by the other stockholders after Wilkes was deprived of his share of the corporate earnings appear to have changed in significant respects.[15] Any resolution of this question must take into account whether the corporation was dissolved during the pendency of this litigation.

Therefore our order is as follows: So much of the judgment as dismisses Wilkes's complaint and awards costs to the defendants is reversed.[16] The case is remanded . . . for further proceedings concerning the issue of damages. Thereafter a judgment shall be entered declaring that Quinn, Riche and Connor breached their fiduciary duty to Wilkes as a minority stockholder in Springside, and awarding money damages therefor. Wilkes shall be allowed to recover from Riche, the estate of T. Edward Quinn and the estate of Lawrence R. Connor, ratably, according to the inequitable enrichment of each, the salary he would have received had he remained an officer and director of Springside. In considering the issue of damages the judge on remand shall take into account the extent to which any remaining corporate funds of Springside may be diverted to satisfy Wilkes's claim.

ZIMMERMAN v. BOGOFF, 402 Mass. 650, 524 N.E.2d 849 (1988). "[T]he Donahue remedy is not intended to place a strait jacket on legitimate corporate activity. Where the alleged wrongdoer can demonstrate a legitimate business purpose for his action, no liability will result unless the wronged shareholder succeeds in showing that the

---

15. In fairness to Wilkes, who, as the master found, was at all times ready and willing to work for the corporation, it should be noted that neither the other stockholders nor their representatives may be heard to say that Wilkes's duties were performed by them and that Wilkes's damages should, for that reason, be diminished.

16. We do not disturb the judgment in so far as it dismissed a counterclaim by Springside against Wilkes arising from the payment of money by Quinn to Wilkes after the sale in 1965 of certain property of Springside to a corporation owned at that time by Quinn and his wife. . . .

proffered legitimate objective could have been achieved through a less harmful, reasonably practicable, alternative mode of action. . . ."

Smith v. Atlantic Properties, Inc.

12 Mass.App. 201, 422 N.E.2d 798.

■ CUTTER, JUSTICE.

In December, 1951, Dr. Louis E. Wolfson agreed to purchase land in Norwood for $350,000, with an initial cash payment of $50,000 and a mortgage note of $300,000. . . . [Thereafter, he invited three others to join him in forming a corporation, Atlantic Properties, Inc., to operate the real estate. Each of the three invested $12,500 and became 25% owners with Wolfson. Included in Atlantic's articles of organization and by-laws was the following provision:] "No election, appointment or resolution by the Stockholders and no election, appointment, resolution, purchase, sale, lease, contract, contribution, compensation, proceeding or act by the Board of Directors or by any officer or officers shall be valid or binding upon the corporation until effected, passed, approved or ratified by an affirmative vote of eighty (80%) per cent of the capital stock issued outstanding and entitled to vote." This provision (hereafter referred to as the 80% provision) was included at Dr. Wolfson's request and had the effect of giving to any one of the four original shareholders a veto in corporate decisions.

Atlantic purchased the Norwood land. Some of the land and other assets were sold for about $220,000. Atlantic retained twenty-eight acres on which stood about twenty old brick or wood mill-type structures, which required expensive and constant repairs. After the first year, Atlantic became profitable and showed a profit every year prior to 1969, ranging from a low of $7,683 in 1953 to a high of $44,358 in 1954. The mortgage was paid by 1958 and Atlantic has incurred no long-term debt thereafter. Salaries of about $25,000 were paid only in 1959 and 1960. Dividends in the total amount of $10,000 each were paid in 1964 and 1970. By 1961, Atlantic had about $172,000 in retained earnings, more than half in cash.

For various reasons, which need not be stated in detail, disagreements and ill will soon arose between Dr. Wolfson, on the one hand, and the other stockholders as a group.[1] Dr. Wolfson wished to see Atlantic's earnings devoted to repairs and possibly some improvements in its existing buildings and adjacent facilities. The other stockholders desired the declaration of dividends. Dr. Wolfson fairly steadily refused to vote for any dividends. Although it was pointed out to him that failure to declare dividends might result in the imposition by the Internal Revenue Service of a penalty under the Internal Revenue Code, I.R.C. § 531 et seq. (relating to unreasonable accumulation of

---

1. At least one cause of ill will on Dr. Wolfson's part may have been the refusal of the other shareholders to consent to his transferring his shares in Atlantic to the Louis E. Wolfson Foundation, a charitable foundation created by Dr. Wolfson.

corporate earnings and profits), Dr. Wolfson persisted in his refusal to declare dividends. The other shareholders did agree over the years to making at least the most urgent repairs to Atlantic's buildings, but did not agree to make all repairs and improvements which were recommended in a 1962 report by an engineering firm retained by Atlantic to make a complete estimate of all repairs and improvements which might be beneficial.

The fears of an Internal Revenue Service assessment of a penalty tax were soon realized. Penalty assessments were made in 1962, 1963, and 1964. These were settled by Dr. Wolfson for $11,767.71 in taxes and interest. Despite this settlement, Dr. Wolfson continued his opposition to declaring dividends. The record does not indicate that he developed any specific and definitive schedule or plan for a series of necessary or desirable repairs and improvements to Atlantic's properties. At least none was proposed which would have had a reasonable chance of satisfying the Internal Revenue Service that expenditures for such repairs and improvements constituted "reasonable needs of the business," I.R.C. § 534(c), a term which includes (see I.R.C. § 537) "the reasonably anticipated needs of the business." Predictably, despite further warnings by Dr. Wolfson's shareholder colleagues, the Internal Revenue Service assessed further penalty taxes for the years 1965, 1966, 1967, and 1968. These taxes were upheld by the United States Tax Court ... and on appeal.... An examination of these decisions makes it apparent that Atlantic has incurred substantial penalty taxes and legal expense largely because of Dr. Wolfson's refusal to vote for the declaration of sufficient dividends to avoid the penalty, a refusal which was (in the Tax Court and upon appeal) attributed in some measure to a tax avoidance purpose on Dr. Wolfson's part.

On January 30, 1967, the shareholders, other than Dr. Wolfson, initiated this proceeding in the Superior Court.... The plaintiffs sought a court determination of the dividends to be paid by Atlantic, the removal of Dr. Wolfson as a director, and an order that Atlantic be reimbursed by him for the penalty taxes assessed against it and related expenses. The case was tried before a justice of the Superior Court (jury waived) in September and October, 1979.

The trial judge made findings (but in more detail) of essentially the facts outlined above and concluded that Dr. "Wolfson's obstinate refusal to vote in favor of ... dividends was ... caused more by his dislike for other stockholders and his desire to avoid additional tax payments than ... by any genuine desire to undertake a program for improving ... [Atlantic] property." She also determined that Dr. Wolfson was liable to Atlantic for taxes and interest ... [paid to the IRS].... She also ordered the directors of Atlantic to declare "a reasonable dividend at the earliest practical date and reasonable dividends annually thereafter consistent with good business practice." In addition, the trial judge directed that jurisdiction of the case be retained in the Superior Court "for a period of five years to [e]nsure compliance." Judgment was entered pursuant to the trial judge's order. After the entry of judgment, Dr. Wolfson . . ., appealed.

1. The trial judge, in deciding that Dr. Wolfson had committed a breach of his fiduciary duty to other stockholders, relied greatly on broad language in Donahue v. Rodd Electrotype Co., . . . In the *Donahue* case, . . . the court recognized that cases may arise in which, in a close corporation, majority stockholders may ask protection from a minority stockholder. Such an instance arises in the present case because Dr. Wolfson has been able to exercise a veto concerning corporate action on dividends by the 80% provision (in Atlantic's articles [of] organization and by-laws) already quoted. The 80% provision may have substantially the effect of reversing the usual roles of the majority and the minority shareholders. The minority, under that provision, becomes an ad hoc controlling interest.

It does not appear to be argued that this 80% provision is not authorized by G.L. c. 156B. . . . [which authorizes supermajority voting requirements] Chapter 156B was intended to provide desirable flexibility in corporate arrangements. The provision is only one of several methods which have been devised to protect minority shareholders in close corporations from being oppressed by their colleagues and, if the device is used reasonably, there may be no strong public policy considerations against its use. See 1 O'Neal, Close Corporations § 4.21 (2d ed. 1971 & Supp.1980). The textbook just cited contains in §§ 4.01–4.30 a comprehensive discussion of the business considerations (see especially §§ 4.02, 4.03, 4.06, & 4.24) which may recommend use of such a device. See also 2 O'Neal § 8.07 (& Supp.1980 which, at 84–90, discusses the Massachusetts decisions). In the present case, Dr. Wolfson testified that he requested the inclusion of the 80% provision "in case the people [the other shareholders] whom I knew, but not very well, ganged up on me." The possibilities of shareholder disagreement on policy made the provision seem a sensible precaution.[8] A question is presented, however, concerning the extent to which such a veto power possessed by a minority stockholder may be exercised as its holder may wish, without a violation of the "fiduciary duty" referred to in the *Donahue* case, as modified in the *Wilkes* case. . . .

The decided cases in Massachusetts do little to answer this question. The most pertinent guidance is probably found in the Wilkes case, 370 Mass. at 849–852, 353 N.E.2d 657, . . . essentially to the

8. Dr. Wolfson himself had discovered the business opportunity which led to the formation of Atlantic, had made the initial $50,000 payment which made possible the Norwood land purchase, and had given the other shareholders an opportunity to share with him in what looked like a probably profitable enterprise. It was reasonably foreseeable that there might be differences of opinion between Dr. Wolfson, a man with substantial income likely to be in a high income tax bracket, and less affluent shareholders on such matters of policy as dividend declarations, salaries, and investment in improvements in the property. The other shareholders, two of whom were attorneys should have known that it was as open to Dr. Wolfson reasonably to exercise the veto provided to him by the 80% provision in favor of a policy of reinvestment of earnings in Atlantic's properties, which would probably avoid taxes and increase the value of the corporate assets, as it was for them (possessed of the same veto) to use reasonably their voting power in favor of a more generous dividend and salary policy.

effect that in any judicial intervention in such a situation there must be a weighing of the business interests advanced as reasons for their action (a) by the majority or controlling group and (b) by the rival persons or group[9] It would obviously be appropriate, before a court-ordered solution is sought or imposed, for both sides to attempt to reach a sensible solution of any incipient impasse in the interest of all concerned after consideration of all relevant circumstances. See Helms v. Duckworth, 249 F.2d 482, 485–488 (D.C.Cir.1957).

2. With respect to the past damage to Atlantic caused by Dr. Wolfson's refusal to vote in favor of any dividends, the trial judge was justified in finding that his conduct went beyond what was reasonable. The other stockholders shared to some extent responsibility for what occurred by failing to accept Dr. Wolfson's proposals with much sympathy, but the inaction on dividends seems the principal cause of the tax penalties. Dr. Wolfson had been warned of the dangers of an assessment under the Internal Revenue Code, I.R.C. § 531 et seq. He had refused to vote dividends in any amount adequate to minimize that danger and had failed to bring forward, within the relevant taxable years, a convincing, definitive program of appropriate improvements which could withstand scrutiny by the Internal Revenue Service. Whatever may have been the reason for Dr. Wolfson's refusal to declare dividends (and even if in any particular year he may have gained slight, if any, tax advantage from withholding dividends) we think that he recklessly ran serious and unjustified risks of precisely the penalty taxes eventually assessed, risks which were inconsistent with any reasonable interpretation of a duty of "utmost good faith and loyalty." The trial judge (despite the fact that the other shareholders helped to create the voting deadlock and despite the novelty of the situation) was justified in charging Dr. Wolfson with the out-of-pocket expenditure incurred by Atlantic for the penalty taxes and related counsel fees of the tax cases.

3. The trial judge's order to the directors of Atlantic, "to declare a reasonable dividend at the earliest practical date and reasonable dividends annually thereafter," presents difficulties. It may well not be a precise, clear, and unequivocal command which (without further explanation) would justify enforcement by civil contempt proceedings.... It also fails to order the directors to exercise similar business judgment with respect to Dr. Wolfson's desire to make all appropriate repairs and improvements to Atlantic's factory properties....

The somewhat ambiguous injunctive relief is made less significant by the trial judge's reservation of jurisdiction in the Superior Court, a provision which contemplates later judicial supervision....

---

9. The duties and quasi-fiduciary responsibilities of minority shareholders who find themselves in a position to control corporate action are discussed helpfully in Hetherington, The Minority's Duty of Loyalty in Close Corporations, 1972 Duke L.J. 921. The author recognizes (at 944) that, in disputes concerning the wisdom of a particular course of corporate action, the majority (or the ad hoc controlling minority) shareholder may be entitled to follow the course he or it thinks best.

Although the reservation of jurisdiction is appropriate in this case . . . its purpose should be stated more affirmatively. Paragraph 2 of the judgment should be revised to provide: (a) a direction that Atlantic's directors prepare promptly financial statements and copies of State and Federal income and excise tax returns for the five most recent calendar or fiscal years, and a balance sheet as of as current a date as is possible; (b) an instruction that they confer with one another with a view to stipulating a general dividend and capital improvements policy for the next ensuing three fiscal years; (c) an order that, if such a stipulation is not filed with the clerk of the Superior Court within sixty days after the receipt of the rescript in the Superior Court, a further hearing shall be held promptly (either before the court or before a special master with substantial experience in business affairs), at which there shall be received in evidence at least the financial statements and tax returns above mentioned, as well as other relevant evidence. Thereafter, the court, after due consideration of the circumstances then existing, may direct the adoption (and carrying out), if it be then deemed appropriate, of a specific dividend and capital improvements policy adequate to minimize the risk of further penalty tax assessments for the then current fiscal year of Atlantic. The court also may reserve jurisdiction to take essentially the same action for each subsequent fiscal year until the parties are able to reach for themselves an agreed program. . . .

4. The judgment is affirmed so far as it . . . orders payments into Atlantic's treasury by Dr. Wolfson. Paragraph 2 of the judgment is to be modified in a manner consistent with part 3 of this opinion. . . .

So ordered.

SLETTELAND v. ROBERTS, 304 Mont. 21, 16 P.3d 1062 (2000). Sletteland was a shareholder in Billings Generation, Inc. (BGI), a closely held Montana corporation. The four other shareholders in BGI were Smith, Blendu, Orndorff, and Roberts. BGI and Exxon Billings Cogeneration, Inc. were partners in Yellowstone Energy Limited Partnership (YELP). YELP owned and operated a cogeneration plant in Billings, Montana which generated steam and electric power. Sletteland had been removed as an officer of BGI by a vote of 60 percent of the shareholders, comprised of Orndorff, Roberts, and Smith. Thereafter, Sletteland brought a derivative action against Orndorff and Roberts, requesting a return of excessive legal fees that they had charged BGI, and removal of Orndorff and Roberts as directors. Orndorff and Roberts counterclaimed, alleging that Sletteland brought the suit in bad faith, causing damage to the company and to the other shareholders.

At the time Sletteland's lawsuit was filed, YELP's project was in financial trouble due to high-interest debts and technical problems with the plant. YELP was attempting to refinance the high-interest debt with lower-interest financing. The window of opportunity for the financing was short, and the lawsuit became an issue hampering the refinancing. Ultimately, the refinancing fell through, and Sletteland's suit was a substantial factor in causing this result. Orndorff and Roberts claimed that the timing of the lawsuit by Sletteland was specifically intended to derail the financing. The District Court found that Sletteland was negligent and breached his fiduciary duties to BGI and his fellow shareholders by the timing of his filing of his action, and found Sletteland liable to Orndorff, Roberts, and Smith for $3,027,939. Affirmed:

> There was clearly animosity in the relationship between the business partners . . . Ultimately, in June of 1996, Sletteland was removed as an officer of BGI. According to Roberts and Orndorff, Sletteland and Blendu wanted the other three shareholders to purchase their interests, and warned that "unpleasant things would happen" if their demands were not met.
>
> It appears that the suit was brought specifically to derail refinancing of the project. Sletteland admitted at trial that the timing of the suit was up to him and that he was not faced with any statute of limitations problem. The initial law suit was filed by Sletteland on October 2, 1996. This was immediately before the individuals involved in the refinancing were to meet to discuss the refinancing. He did no investigation to see what the effect of the lawsuit would be on the refinancing. The court concluded that "it only makes sense that he would be expected to know that the filing of his suit alleging director fraud would delay or derail the refinancing . . . [and] there was no particular reason to file this suit when he did." He was asked to withdraw the suit so that the refinancing could conclude, but he refused to do so.

Merola v. Exergen Corp.

Supreme Judicial Court of Massachusetts, 1996.
423 Mass. 461, 668 N.E.2d 351.

■ Before Liacos, C.J., and Wilkins, Lynch, O'Connor and Greaney, JJ.

■ Lynch, Justice.

The plaintiff, a former vice president of Exergen Corporation (Exergen) and a former minority stockholder of that corporation, brought suit in the Superior Court against Exergen and the president and majority stockholder, Francesco Pompei, because of his termination as an officer and employee of Exergen . . . [The complaint] alleged that the corporation was a "close corporation," and that Pompei, as the majority stockholder, violated his fiduciary obligations to the plaintiff as a minority stockholder by terminating his employment without cause.

The trial judge ruled that . . . she would make findings of fact and conclusions of law . . . following the verdict of the jury. The jury rendered a verdict . . . providing advisory answers . . .

... [T]he judge found that the corporation was a "close corporation" and that Pompei had breached his fiduciary obligations to the plaintiff by failing to give him an opportunity to become a major stockholder and by terminating his employment. She adopted the jury's advisory conclusion that he had been damaged only by the termination of employment to the extent of $50,000.

The Appeals Court affirmed the judgment as to Pompei, but modified it as to the corporation, holding that there was no basis for liability by Exergen to the plaintiff. 38 Mass.App.Ct. 462, 471–472 (1995). We granted the defendants' application for further appellate review and now reverse the judgment of the Superior Court.

We summarize the facts found by the judge. Exergen was formed in May, 1980, as a corporation in the business of developing and selling infrared heat detection devices. From Exergen's inception to the date of trial, Pompei, the founder, was the majority shareholder in the corporation, as well as its president, owning over sixty per cent of the shares issued. At all relevant times, Pompei actively participated in and controlled the management of Exergen and, as the majority shareholder, had power to elect and change Exergen's board of directors.

The plaintiff began working for Exergen on a part-time basis in late 1980 while he was also employed full-time by Analogic Corporation. In the course of conversations with Pompei in late 1981, and early 1982, the plaintiff was offered full-time employment with Exergen, and he understood that, if he came to work there and invested in Exergen stock, he would have the opportunity to become a major shareholder of Exergen and for continuing employment with Exergen.

As of March 1, 1982, the plaintiff resigned from Analogic and began working full time for Exergen. He also then began purchasing shares in Exergen when the company made periodic offerings to its employees. From March, 1982, through June, 1982, the plaintiff purchased 4,100 shares at $2.25 per share, for a total of $9,225. Exergen announced at the Exergen shareholders meeting in September, 1982, another option program to purchase shares at $5 per share within one year. By late 1983, the plaintiff had exercised his option to purchase an additional 1,200 shares. The plaintiff was not offered additional stock options after late 1983....

Principles of employment law permit the termination of employees at will, with or without cause excepting situations within a narrow public policy exception. King v. Driscoll, 418 Mass. 576, 581–582, 638 N.E.2d 488 (1994), and cases cited. However, the termination of a minority shareholder's employment may present a situation where the majority interest has breached its fiduciary duty to the minority interest. Id. at 586, 638 N.E.2d 488. Wilkes v. Springside Nursing Home, Inc., supra at 852–853, 353 N.E.2d 657. There the court concluded that the majority stockholders had attempted unfairly to "freeze out" a minority stockholder by terminating his employment, in part because their policy and practice was to divide the available resources of the corporation equally by way of salaries to the shareholders who all participated in the operation of the enterprise. Id. at 846, 353 N.E.2d 657. As the investment became more profitable, the salaries were increased. Id. The court recognized that "[t]he minority stockholder typically depends on his salary as the principal return on his investment, since the 'earnings of a close corporation ... are distributed in major part in salaries, bonuses and retirement benefits.'" Id. at 850, 353 N.E.2d 657, quoting 1 F.H. O'Neal, Close Corporations § 1.07 (1971). Given those facts, this court concluded that the other shareholders did not show a legitimate business purpose for terminating the minority stockholder and that the other parties acted "in disregard of a longstanding policy of the stockholders that each would be a director of the corporation and that employment with the corporation would go hand in hand with stock ownership." Id. at 853, 353 N.E.2d 657.

Here, although the plaintiff invested in the stock of Exergen with the reasonable expectation of continued employment, there was no general policy regarding stock ownership and employment, and there was no evidence that any other stockholders had expectations of continuing employment because they purchased stock. The investment in the stock was an investment in the equity of the corporation which was not tied to employment in any formal way. The plaintiff acknowledged that he could have purchased 5,000 shares of stock while he was working part time before resigning from his position at Analogic Corporation and accepting full-time employment at Exergen. He testified that he was induced to work for Exergen with the promise that he could become a major stockholder. There was no testimony that he was ever required to buy stock as a condition of employment.

Unlike the *Wilkes* case, there was no evidence that the corporation distributed all profits to shareholders in the form of salaries. On the contrary, the perceived value of the stock increased during the time that the plaintiff was employed. The plaintiff first purchased his stock at $2.25 per share and, one year later, he purchased more for $5 per share. This indicated that there was some increase in value to the investment independent of the employment expectation. Neither was the plaintiff a founder of the business, his stock purchases were made after the business was established, and there was no suggestion that he had to purchase stock to keep his job.

The plaintiff testified that, when he sold his stock back to the corporation in 1991, he was paid $17 per share. This was a price that had been paid to other shareholders who sold their shares to the corporation at a previous date, and it is a price which, after consulting with his attorney, he concluded was a fair price. With this payment, the plaintiff realized a significant return on his capital investment independent of the salary he received as an employee.

We conclude that this is not a situation where the majority shareholder breached his fiduciary duty to a minority shareholder. "[T]he controlling group in a close corporation must have some room to maneuver in establishing the business policy of the corporation." Wilkes v. Springside Nursing Home, Inc., supra at 851, 353 N.E.2d

657. Although there was no legitimate business purpose for the termination of the plaintiff, neither was the termination for the financial gain of Pompei or contrary to established public policy. Not every discharge of an at-will employee of a close corporation who happens to own stock in the corporation gives rise to a successful breach of fiduciary duty claim. The plaintiff was terminated in accordance with his employment contract and fairly compensated for his stock. He failed to establish a sufficient basis for a breach of fiduciary duty claim under the principles of Donahue v. Rodd Electrotype Co., supra....

Judgment reversed.

SECTION 6. VALUATION

Many issues of corporate law are intimately related to problems of valuation. That is particularly true of the issues raised in sections 7, 8, and 10, infra, concerning restrictions on the transferability of shares, mandatory sales of shares, and dissolution. Now is therefore an appropriate time to return to the general problem of valuing a business, and the special problem of valuing a business in corporate form.

This Section contains four selections. The first selection, Piemonte v. New Boston Garden, illustrates the Delaware Block Method of valuation. Under that method, a court valuing a corporation first determines the market value of the corporation's stock, the value of the corporation's net assets, and the corporation's "earnings value." Next, the court assigns weights to each of the three values, depending on such factors as the comparative reliability of each factor in a particular case. Finally, the court sums the three elements of value, as adjusted by their relative weights. The Delaware Block Method is falling out of favor, but it is still used in some cases. More important for present purposes, even contemporary methods of valuation may involve individual elements of the Block Method.

The remaining three selections in this Section provide contemporary views on the valuation of business enterprises.

It may be useful, before studying the materials in this Section, to review the materials on the present-value rule in Chapter 2, Section 2.

Piemonte v. New Boston Garden Corp.

Supreme Judicial Court of Massachusetts, 1979.
377 Mass. 719, 387 N.E.2d 1145.

■ WILKINS, JUSTICE.

The plaintiffs were stockholders in Boston Garden Arena Corporation (Garden Arena)*, a Massachusetts corporation whose stockhold-

---

* The fifteen plaintiffs collectively owned 6,289 shares in Garden Arena Corporation, representing approximately 2.8% of its 224,892 shares of outstanding stock.

ers voted on July 19, 1973, to merge with the defendant corporation in circumstances which entitled each plaintiff to "demand payment for his stock from the resulting or surviving corporation and an appraisal in accordance with the provisions of [G.L. c. 156B, §§ 86–98]." G.L. c. 156B, § 85, as amended by St.1969, c. 392, § 22. The plaintiffs commenced this action under G.L. c. 156B, § 90, seeking a judicial determination of the "fair value" of their shares "as of the day preceding the date of the vote approving the proposed corporate action."[2] G.L. c. 156B, § 92, inserted by St.1964, c. 723, § 1. Each party has appealed from a judgment determining the fair value of the plaintiffs' stock. We granted the defendant's application for direct appellate review.

On July 18, 1973, Garden Arena owned all the stock in a subsidiary corporation that owned both a franchise in the National Hockey League (NHL), known as the Boston Bruins, and a corporation that held a franchise in the American Hockey League (AHL), known as the Boston Braves. Garden Arena also owned and operated Boston Garden Sports Arena (Boston Garden), an indoor auditorium with facilities for the exhibition of sporting and other entertainment events, and a corporation that operated the food and beverage concession at the Boston Garden. A considerable volume of documentary material was introduced in evidence concerning the value of the stock of Garden Arena on July 18, 1973, the day before Garden Arena's stockholders approved the merger. Each side presented expert testimony. The judge gave consideration to the market value of the Garden Arena stock, to the value of its stock based on its earnings, and to the net asset value of Garden Arena's assets. Weighting these factors, the judge arrived at a total, per share value of $75.27.[3]

In this appeal, the parties raise objections to certain of the judge's conclusions. We will expand on the facts as necessary when we consider each issue. We conclude that the judge followed acceptable procedures in valuing the Garden Arena stock; that his determinations were generally within the range of discretion accorded a fact finder; but that, in three instances, the judge's treatment of the evidence was or may have been in error and, accordingly, the case should be remanded to him for further consideration of those three points.

---

2. The plaintiffs took all the necessary, preliminary steps to preserve their rights. Each plaintiff objected in writing to the proposed merger; none of their shares was voted in favor of the proposed corporate action (see G.L. c. 156B, § 86); each plaintiff seasonably demanded in writing payment from the defendant for the fair value of his stock (see G.L. c. 156B, § 89); and no agreement as to that fair value was reached within thirty days of the demand (see G.L. c. 156B, § 90).

3. The judge determined the market value, earnings value, and net asset value of the stock and then weighted these values as follows:

	Value		Weight		Result
Market Value:	$ 26.50	×	10%	=	$ 2.65
Earnings Value:	$ 52.60	×	40%	=	$21.04
Net Asset Value:	$103.16	×	50%	=	$51.58
			Total Value Per Share:		$75.27

General Principles of Law

The statutory provisions applicable to this case were enacted in 1964 as part of the Massachusetts Business Corporation Law. St.1964, c. 723, § 1. . . .

[The judge in this case adopted the methodology known as the "Delaware block approach," which] calls for a determination of the market value, the earnings value, and the net asset value of the stock, followed by the assignment of a percentage weight to each of the elements of value. See generally, Note, Valuation of Dissenters' Stock under Appraisal Statutes, 79 Harv.L.Rev. 1453, 1456–1471 (1966). . . .

Market Value

The judge was acting within reasonable limits when he determined that the market value of Garden Arena stock on July 18, 1973, was $26.50 a share. Each party challenges this determination. The plaintiffs' contention is that market value should be disregarded because it was not ascertainable due to the limited trading in Garden Arena stock. The defendant argues that the judge was obliged to reconstruct market value based on comparable companies, and, in doing so, should have arrived at a market value of $22 a share.

Market value may be a significant factor, even the dominant factor, in determining the "fair value" of shares of a particular corporation under G.L. c. 156B, § 92. Shares regularly traded on a recognized stock exchange are particularly susceptible to valuation on the basis of their market price, although even in such cases the market value may well not be conclusive. See Martignette v. Sagamore Mfg. Co., 340 Mass. 136, 141–142, 163 N.E.2d 9 (1959). On the other hand, where there is no established market for a particular stock, actual market value cannot be used. In such cases, a judge might undertake to "reconstruct" market value, but he is not obliged to do so. Indeed, the process of the reconstruction of market value may actually be no more than a variation on the valuation of corporate assets and corporate earnings.

In this case, Garden Arena stock was traded on the Boston Stock Exchange, but rarely. Approximately ninety per cent of the company's stock was held by the controlling interests and not traded. Between January 1, 1968, and December 4, 1972, 16,741 shares were traded. During this period, an annual average of approximately 1.5% of the outstanding stock changed hands. In 1972, 4,372 shares were traded at prices ranging from $20.50 a share to $29 a share. The public announcement of the proposed merger was made on December 7, 1972. The last prior sale of 200 shares on December 4, 1972, was made at $26.50 a share. The judge accepted that sale price as the market price to be used in his determination of value.

The judge concluded that the volume of trading was sufficient to permit a determination of market value and expressed a preference for the actual sale price over any reconstruction of a market value, which he concluded would place "undue reliance on corporations, factors, and circumstances not applicable to Garden Arena stock." The decision to consider market value and the market value selected were within the judge's discretion.

Valuation Based on Earnings

The judge determined that the average per share earnings of Garden Arena for the five-fiscal-year period which ended June 30, 1973, was $5.26. To this amount he applied a factor, or multiplier, of 10 to arrive at $52.60 as the per share value based on earnings.

Each party objects to certain aspects of this process. We reject the plaintiffs' argument that the judge could not properly use any value based on earnings, and also reject the parties' various challenges to the judge's method of determining value based on earnings.

Delaware case law, which, as we have said, we regard as instructive but not binding, has established a method of computing value based on corporate earnings. The appraiser generally starts by computing the average earnings of the corporation for the past five years. Universal City Studios, Inc. v. Francis I. duPont & Co., 334 A.2d 216, 218 (Del.1975); Application of Del. Racing Ass'n, 213 A.2d 203, 212 (Del.1965). Extraordinary gains and losses are excluded from the average earnings calculation. Gibbons v. Schenley Indus., Inc., 339 A.2d 460, 468–470 (Del.Ch.1975); Felder v. Anderson, Clayton & Co., 39 Del.Ch. 76, 86–87, 159 A.2d 278 (1960). The appraiser then selects a multiplier (to be applied to the average earnings) which reflects the prospective financial condition of the corporation and the risk factor inherent in the corporation and the industry. Universal City Studios, Inc. v. Francis I. duPont & Co., supra. In selecting a multiplier, the appraiser generally looks to other comparable corporations. Universal City Studios, Inc. v. Francis I. duPont & Co., supra at 219–221 (averaging price-earnings ratios of nine other motion picture companies as of date of merger); Gibbons v. Schenley Indus., Inc., supra at 471 (using Standard & Poor's Distiller's Index as of date of merger); Felder v. Anderson, Clayton & Co., supra, 39 Del.Ch. at 87, 159 A.2d 278 (averaging price-earnings ratios of representative stocks over previous five-year period because of recent boom in industry). The appraiser's choice of a multiplier is largely discretionary and will be upheld if it is "within the range of reason." Universal City Studios, Inc. v. Francis I. duPont & Co., supra at 219 (approving multiplier of 16.1); Application of Del. Racing Ass'n, supra at 213 (approving multiplier of 10); Swanton v. State Guar. Corp., 42 Del.Ch. 477, 483, 215 A.2d 242 (1965) (approving multiplier of 14).[9]

The judge chose not to place "singular reliance on comparative data preferring to choose a multiplier based on the specific situation and prospects of the Garden Arena." He weighed the favorable finan-

---

9. Although Delaware courts have relied on, and continue to rely on, Professor Dewing's capitalization chart (see 1 A.S. Dewing, The Financial Policy of Corporations 390–391 [5th ed. 1953]), they have recognized that it is somewhat outdated and no longer the "be-all and end-all" on the subject of earnings value. See Universal City Studios, Inc. v. Francis I. duPont & Co., supra at 219; Swanton v. State Guar. Corp., 42 Del.Ch. 477, 483–484, 215 A.2d 242 (1965).

cial prospects of the Bruins: the popularity and success of the team, the relatively low average age of its players, the popularity of Bobby Orr and Phil Esposito, the high attendance record at home games (each home team retained all gate receipts), and the advantageous radio and television contracts. On the other hand, he recognized certain risks, the negative prospects: the existence of the World Hockey Association with its potential, favorable impact on players' bargaining positions, and legal threats to the players' reserve clause. He concluded that a multiplier of 10 was appropriate. There was ample evidentiary support for his conclusion. He might have looked to and relied on price-earnings ratios of other corporations, but he was not obliged to.

The judge did not have to consider the dividend record of Garden Arena, as the defendant urges. Dividends tend to reflect the same factors as earnings and, therefore, need not be valued separately. See Felder v. Anderson, Clayton & Co., 39 Del.Ch. 76, 88–89, 159 A.2d 278 (1960). And since dividend policy is usually reflected in market value, the use of market value as a factor in the valuation process permitted the low and sporadic dividend rate to be given some weight in the process. Beyond that, the value of the plaintiffs' stock should not be depreciated because the controlling interests often chose to declare low dividends or none at all.

The judge did not abuse his discretion in including expansion income (payments from teams newly admitted to the NHL) received during two of the five recent fiscal years. His conclusion was well within the guidelines of decided cases. See Gibbons v. Schenley Indus., Inc., 339 A.2d 460, 470 (Del.Ch.1975) (gain from sale of real estate not extraordinary where corporation often sold such assets); Felder v. Anderson, Clayton & Co., 39 Del.Ch. 76, 86–87, 159 A.2d 278 (1960) (loss attributable to a drought not extraordinary). The Bruins first received expansion income ($2,000,000) during the fiscal year which ended on June 30, 1967, a year not included in the five-year average. The franchise received almost $1,000,000 more in 1970 and approximately $860,000 in 1972. This 1970 and 1972 income was reflected in the computation of earnings. Expansion income did not have to be treated as extraordinary income. The judge concluded that it did not distort "an accurate projection of the earnings value of Garden Arena" and noted, as of July 18, 1973, an NHL expansion plan for the admission of two more teams in 1974–1975 and for expansion thereafter.

Valuation Based on Net Asset Value

The judge determined total net asset value by first valuing the net assets of Garden Arena apart from the Bruins franchise and the concession operations at Boston Garden. He selected $9,400,000 (the June 30, 1973, book value of Garden Arena) as representing that net asset value. Then, he added his valuations of the Bruins franchise ($9,600,000) and the concession operation ($4,200,000) to arrive at a total asset value of $23,200,000, or $103.16 a share.[10]

10. $23,200,000 § 224,892 (the number of outstanding shares).

The parties raise various objections to these determinations. The defendant argues that the judge included certain items twice in his valuation of the net assets of Garden Arena and that he should have given no separate value to the concession operation. The plaintiff argues that the judge undervalued both the Boston Garden and the value of the Bruins franchise.

The defendant objects to the judge's refusal to deduct $1,116,000 from the $9,400,000 that represented the net asset value of Garden Arena (exclusive of the net asset value of the Bruins franchise and the concession operation). The defendant's expert testified that the $9,400,000 figure included $1,116,000 attributable to the goodwill of the Bruins, net player investment, and the value of the AHL franchise. The judge recognized that the items included in the $1,116,000 should not be valued twice and seemingly agreed that they would be more appropriately included in the value of the Bruins franchise than in the $9,400,000. He was not plainly wrong, however, in declining to deduct them from the $9,400,000, because, as is fully warranted from the testimony of the defendant's expert, the judge concluded that the defendant's expert did not include these items in his determination of the value of the Bruins franchise. The defendant's expert, whose determination the judge accepted, arrived at his value of the Bruins franchise by adding certain items to the cost of a new NHL franchise, but none of those items included goodwill, net player investment, or the value of an AHL franchise. Acceptance of the defendant's argument would have resulted in these items being entirely omitted from the net asset valuation of Garden Arena.

The plaintiffs object that the judge did not explicitly determine the value of the Boston Garden and implicitly undervalued it. Garden Arena had purchased the Boston Garden on May 25, 1973, for $4,000,000, and accounted for it on the June 30, 1973, balance sheet as a $4,000,000 asset with a corresponding mortgage liability of $3,437,065. Prior to the purchase, Garden Arena had held a long-term lease which was unfavorable to the owner of the Boston Garden.[13] The existence of the lease would tend to depress the purchase price.

The judge stated that the $9,400,000 book value "*includes* a reasonable value for Boston Garden" (emphasis supplied). He did not indicate whether, if he had meant to value the Boston Garden at its purchase price (with an adjustment for the mortgage liabilities), he had considered the effect the lease would have had on that price. While we recognize that the fact-finding role of the judge permits him to reject the opinions of the various experts,[14] we conclude, in the absence of an explanation of his reasons, that it is possible that the

---

13. The lease, which ran until June 1, 1986, contained a fixed maximum rent and an obligation on the lessee to pay only two-thirds of any increase in local real estate taxes. In a period of inflation and rising local real estate taxes, the value of the lease to the lessor was decreasing annually.

14. The lowest value expressed by any expert for the plaintiffs was $8,250,000 (exclusive of mortgage liabilities), based on depreciated reproduction cost. The defendant offered no testimony concerning the value of the property on July 18, 1973.

judge did not give adequate consideration to the value of the Garden property. The judge should consider this subject further on remand.

A major area of dispute was the value of the Bruins franchise. The judge rejected the value advanced by the plaintiffs' expert ($18,000,-000), stating that "[a]lthough the defendant's figure of [$9,600,000] seems somewhat low in comparison with the cost of expansion team franchises, *the Court is constrained* to accept defendant's value as it is the more creditable and legally appropriate expert opinion in the record" (emphasis supplied). Although the choice of the word "constrained" may have been inadvertent, it connotes a sense of obligation. As the trier of fact, the judge was not bound to accept the valuation of either one expert or the other. He was entitled to reach his own conclusion as to value. . . .

Because the judge may have felt bound to accept the value placed on the Bruins franchise by the defendant's expert, we shall remand this case for him to arrive at his own determination of the value of the Bruins franchise. He would be warranted in arriving at the same valuation as that advanced on behalf of the defendant, but he is not obliged to do so.

The defendant argues that, in arriving at the value of the assets of Garden Arena, the judge improperly placed a separate value on the right to operate concessions at the Boston Garden. We agree with the judge. The fact that earnings from concessions were included in the computation of earnings value, one component in the formula, does not mean that the value of the concessions should have been excluded from the computation of net asset value, another such component.

The value of the concession operation was not reflected in the value of the real estate. Real estate may be valued on the basis of rental income, but it is not valued on the basis of the profitability of business operations within the premises. . . . Moreover, it is manifest that the value of the concession operation was not included in the value placed on the Boston Garden. The record indicates that Garden Arena already owned the concession rights when it purchased the Boston Garden. The conclusion that the value of the concession operation was not reflected in the value of the Boston Garden is particularly warranted because the determined value of the right to operate the concessions ($4,200,000) was higher than the May 25, 1973, purchase price ($4,000,000) of the *Boston Garden*.

We do conclude, however, that the judge may have felt unnecessarily bound to accept the plaintiffs' evidence of the value of the concession operation. He stated that "since the defendant did not submit evidence on this issue, the Court will accept plaintiffs' expert appraisal of the value of the concession operation." Although the judge did not express the view that he was "constrained" to accept the plaintiffs' valuation, as he did concerning the defendant's valuation of the Bruins franchise, he may have misconstrued his authority on this issue. The judge was not obliged to accept the plaintiffs' evidence at face value merely because no other evidence was offered. . . .

On remand, the judge should reconsider his determination of the value of the concession operation and exercise his own judgment concerning the bases for the conclusion arrived at by the plaintiffs' expert. However, the evidence did warrant the value selected by the judge, and no reduction in that value is required on this record.

Weighting of Valuations

The judge weighted the three valuations as follows:

Market Value	—	10%
Earnings Value	—	40%
Net Asset Value	—	50%

We accept these allocations as reasonable and within the range of the judge's discretion.

Any determination of the weight to be given the various elements involved in the valuation of a stock must be based on the circumstances. Heller v. Munsingwear, Inc., 33 Del.Ch. 593, 598, 98 A.2d 774 (1953). The decision to weight market value at only 10% was appropriate, considering the thin trading in the stock of Garden Arena. The decision to attribute 50% weight to net asset value was reasonably founded. The judge concluded that, because of tax reasons, the value of a sports franchise, unlike many corporate activities, depends more on its assets than on its earnings; that Garden Arena had been largely a family corporation in which earnings were of little significance; that Garden Arena had approximately $5,000,000 in excess liquid assets; and that the Garden property was a substantial real estate holding in an excellent location.

The judge might have reached different conclusions on this record. He was not obliged, however, to reconstruct market value and, as the defendant urges, attribute 50% weight to it. Nor was he obliged, as the plaintiffs argue, to consider only net asset value. See Martignette v. Sagamore Mfg. Co., 340 Mass. 136, 142, 163 N.E.2d 9 (1959). Market value and earnings value properly could be considered in these circumstances.

Although we would have found no fault with a determination to give even greater weight to the price per share based on the net asset value of Garden Arena, the judge was acting within an acceptable range of discretion in selecting the weights he gave to the various factors....

Conclusion

We have concluded that the judge's method of valuing the Garden Arena stock was essentially correct. In this opinion, we have indicated, however, that the case should be remanded to him for clarification and further consideration on the record of three matters: his valuation of the Boston Garden, the Bruins franchise, and the concession operation.

So ordered.

Jeffrey D. Bauman, Alan D. Palmiter, and Frank Partnoy, The Old Man and the Tree: A Parable of Valuation, in Corporations—Law and Policy 200–206

(6th ed. 2007).

Once there was a wise old man who owned an apple tree. The tree was a fine tree, and with little care it produced a crop of apples each year which he sold for $100. The man was getting old, wanted to retire to a different climate and he decided to sell the tree. He enjoyed teaching a good lesson, and he placed an advertisement in the Business Opportunities section of the Wall Street Journal in which he said he wanted to sell the tree for "the best offer."

The first person to respond to the ad offered to pay the $50 which, the offeror said, was what he would be able to get for selling the apple tree for firewood after he had cut it down. "You are a very foolish person," said the old man. "You are offering to pay only the salvage value of this tree. That might be a good price for a pine tree or perhaps even this tree if it had stopped bearing fruit or if the price of apple wood had gotten so high that the tree was more valuable as a source of wood than as a source of fruit. But my tree is worth much more than $50."

The next person to come to see the old man offered to pay $100 for the tree. "For that," said she, "is what I would be able to get for selling this year's crop of fruit which is about to mature."

"You are not quite so foolish as the first one," responded the old man. "At least you see that this tree has more value as a producer of apples than it would as a source of firewood. But $100 is not the right price. You are not considering the value of next year's crop of apples, nor that of the years after. Please take your $100 and go elsewhere."

The next person to come along was a young man who had just started business school. "I am going to major in marketing," he said. "I figure that the tree should live for at least another fifteen years. If I sell the apples for $100 a year, that will total $1,500. I offer you $1,500 for your tree."

"You, too, are foolish," said the man. "Surely the $100 you would earn by selling the apples from the tree fifteen years from now cannot be worth $100 to you today. In fact, if you placed $41.73 today in a bank account paying 6% interest, compounded annually, that small sum would grow to $100 at the end of fifteen years. Therefore the present value of $100 worth of apples fifteen years from now, assuming an interest rate of 6%, is only $41.73, not $100. Pray," said the old man, "take your $1,500 and invest it safely in high-grade corporate bonds until you have graduated from business school and know more about finance."

Before long, there came a wealthy physician, who said, "I don't know much about apple trees, but I know what I like. I'll pay the market price for it. The last fellow was willing to pay you $1,500 for the tree, and so it must be worth that."

"Doctor," advised the old man, "you should get yourself a knowledgeable investment adviser. If there were truly a market in which apple trees were traded with some regularity, the prices at which they were sold would be a good indication of their value. But there is no such market. And the isolated offer I just received tells very little about how much my tree is really worth—as you would surely realize if you had heard the other foolish offers I have heard today. Please take your money and buy a vacation home."

The next prospective purchaser to come along was an accounting student. When the old man asked "What price are you willing to give me?" the student first demanded to see the old man's books. The old man had kept careful records and gladly brought them out. After examining them the accounting student said, "Your books show that you paid $75 for this tree ten years ago. Furthermore, you have made no deductions for depreciation. I do not know if that conforms with generally accepted accounting principles, but assuming that it does, the book value of your tree is $75. I will pay that."

"Ah, you students know so much and yet so little," chided the old man. "It is true that the book value of my tree is $75, but any fool can see that it is worth far more than that. You had best go back to school and see if you can find some books that will show you how to use your numbers to better effect."

The next prospective purchaser was a young stockbroker who had recently graduated from business school. Eager to test her new skills she, too, asked to examine the books. After several hours she came back to the old man and said she was now prepared to make an offer that valued the tree on the basis of the capitalization of its earnings.

For the first time the old man's interest was piqued and he asked her to go on.

The young woman explained that while the apples were sold for $100 last year, that figure did not represent profits realized from the tree. There were expenses attendant to the tree, such as the cost of fertilizer, the expense of pruning the tree, the cost of the tools, expenses in connection with picking the apples, carting them into town and selling them. Somebody had to do these things, and a portion of the salaries paid to those persons ought to be charged against the revenues from the tree. Moreover, the purchase price, or cost, of the tree was an expense. A portion of the cost is taken into account each year of the tree's useful life. Finally, there were taxes. She concluded that the profit from the tree was $50 last year.

"Wow!" exclaimed the old man. "I thought I made $100 off that tree."

"That's because you failed to match expenses with revenues, in accordance with generally accepted accounting principles," she explained. "You don't actually have to write a check to be charged with what accountants consider to be your expenses. For example, you bought a station wagon some time ago and you used it part of the time to cart apples to market. The wagon will last a while and each year some of the original cost has to be matched against revenues. A portion of the amount has to be spread out over the next several years even though you expended it all at one time. Accountants call that depreciation. I'll bet you never figured that in your calculation of profits."

"I'll bet you're right," he replied. "Tell me more."

"I also went back into the books for a few years and I saw that in some years the tree produced fewer apples than in other years, the prices varied and the costs were not exactly the same each year. Taking an average of only the last three years, I came up with a figure of $45 as a fair sample of the tree's earnings. But that is only half of what we have to do so as to figure the value."

"What's the other half?" he asked.

"The tricky part," she told him. "We now have to figure the value to me of owning a tree that will produce average annual earnings of $45 a year. If I believed that the tree was a one year wonder, I would say 100% of its value—as a going business—was represented by one year's earnings. But if I believe, as both you and I do, that the tree is more like a corporation, in that it will continue to produce earnings year after year, then the key is to figure out an appropriate rate of return. In other words, I will be investing my capital in the tree, and I need to compute the value to me of an investment that will produce $45 a year in income. We can call that amount the capitalized value of the tree."

"Do you have something in mind?" he asked.

"I'm getting there. If this tree produced steady and predictable earnings each year, it would be like a U.S. Treasury bond. But its earnings are not guaranteed. So we have to take into account risk and uncertainty. If the risk of its ruin is high, I will insist that a single year's earnings represent a higher percentage of the value of the tree. After all, apples could become a glut on the market one day and you would have to cut the price and increase the costs of selling them. Or some doctor could discover a link between eating an apple a day and heart disease. A drought could cut the yield of the tree. Or, heaven forbid, the tree could become diseased and die. These are all risks. And of course we do not know what will happen to costs that we know we have to bear."

"You are a gloomy one," reflected the old man. "There are treatments, you know, that could be applied to increase the yield of the tree. This tree could help spawn a whole orchard."

"I am aware of that," she assured him. "We will include that in the calculus. The fact is, we are talking about risk, and investment analysis is a cold business. We don't know with certainty what's going to happen. You want your money now and I'm supposed to live with the risk. That's fine with me, but then I have to look through a cloudy crystal ball, and not with 20/20 hindsight. And my resources are limited. I have to choose between your tree and the strawberry patch down the road. I cannot do both and the purchase of your tree will deprive me of alternative investments. That means I have to compare the opportunities and the risks."

"To determine a proper rate of return," she continued, "I looked at investment opportunities that are comparable to the apple tree, particularly in the agribusiness industry, where these factors have been taken into account. I have concluded that 20% would be an appropriate rate of return. In other words, average earnings over the last three years (which seems to be a representative period) are indicative of the return I will receive, I am prepared to pay a price for the tree that will give me a 20% return on my investment. I am not willing to accept any lower rate of return because I don't have to; I can always buy the strawberry patch instead. That means the value of the apple tree should equal an amount of money that will generate $45 per year at a rate of 20%. Put another way, the value multiplied by 20% should equal $45. Or, using algebra, we can determine our value by dividing $45 by 20%. $45 divided by 0.2 is the same as $45 multiplied by 5. It is $225."

"Algebra was never my strong suit. Is there a simpler way of doing the figuring?" he asked hopefully.

"There is," she assured him. "We can use an approach we Wall Street types prefer, called a price-earnings (or P–E) ratio or multiple. The P–E multiple represents the price divided by earnings. If you needed to earn a return of 10% on your investment, you would use a P–E multiple of 10. For example, a return of 10% would correspond to a price of $100 and earnings of $10 per year—that would be a P–E multiple of 10 ($100 divided by $10). Likewise, if you needed to earn a return of 20% on your investment, you would use a P–E multiple of 5. For example, a return of 20% would correspond to a price of $100 and earnings of $20 per year—that would be a P–E multiple of 5 ($100 divided by $20). The P–E multiple tells you what number you should multiply times the expected annual earnings from an investment to determine the amount you should pay for that investment."

"Because I want to earn 20% on my investment, I use a P–E multiple of 5. That means I am willing to pay five times the tree's estimated annual earnings. Multiplying $45 by 5, I get a value of $225. That's a simpler way to think about this concept. And that's my offer."

The old man sat back and said he greatly appreciated the lesson. He would have to think about her offer, and he asked if she could come by the next day.

When the young woman returned she found the old man emerging from a sea of work sheets, small print columns of numbers and a calculator. "Glad to see you," he said. "I think we can do some business."

"It's easy to see how you Wall Street smarties make so much money, buying people's property for a fraction of the value. I think my tree is worth more than you figured, and I think I can get you to agree to that."

"I'm open minded," she assured him.

"The number you worked so hard over my books to come up with was something you called profits, or earnings that I earned in the past. I'm not so sure it tells you anything that important."

"Of course it does," she protested. "Profits measure efficiency and economic utility."

"Maybe," he mused, "but it sure doesn't tell you how much money you've got. I looked in my safe yesterday after you left and I saw I had some stocks that hadn't ever paid much of a dividend to me. And I kept getting reports each year telling me how great the earnings were, but I sure couldn't spend them. It's just the opposite with the tree. You figured the earnings were lower because of some amounts I'll never have to spend. It seems to me these earnings are an idea worked up by the accountants. Now I'll grant you that ideas, or concepts as you call them, are important and give you lots of useful information, but you can't fold them up, and put them in your pocket."

Surprised, she asked, "What is important, then?"

"Cash flow," he answered. "I'm talking about dollars you can spend, or save or give to your children. This tree will go on for years yielding revenues after costs. And it is the future, not the past, that we're trying to figure out."

"Don't forget the risks," she reminded him. "And the uncertainties."

"Quite right," he observed. "I think we can deal with that. Chances are that you and I could agree, after a lot of thought, on the possible range of future revenues and costs. I suspect we would estimate that for the next five years, there is a 25% chance that the cash flow will be $40, a 50% chance it will be $50 and a 25% chance it will be $60. That makes $50 our best guess, if you average it out. Then let us figure that for ten years after that the average will be $40. And that's it. The tree doctor tells me it can't produce any longer than that. Now all we have to do is figure out what you pay today to get $50 a year from now, two years from now, and so on for the first five years until we figure what you would pay to get $40 a year for each of the ten years after that. Then, throw in the 20 bucks we can get for firewood at that time, and that's that."

"Simple," she said. "You want to discount to the present value of future receipts including salvage value. Of course you need to determine the rate at which you discount."

"Precisely," he noted. "That's what all these charts and the calculator are doing." She nodded knowingly as he showed her discount tables that revealed what a dollar received at a later time is worth today, under different assumptions of the discount rate. It showed, for example, that at an 8% discount rate, a dollar delivered a year from now is worth 92 cents today, simply because 92 cents today, invested at 8%, will produce $1 a year from now.

"You could put your money in a savings bank or a savings and loan association and receive 3% interest, insured. But you could also put your money into obligations of the United States Government and earn 5% interest. That looks like the risk free rate of interest to me. (These numbers will vary with prevailing interest rates. The principle remains the same.) Anywhere else you put your money deprives you of the opportunity to earn 5% risk free. Discounting by 5% will only compensate you for the time value of the money you invest in the tree rather than in government securities. But the cash flow from the apple tree is not riskless, sad to say, so we need to use a higher discount rate to compensate you for the risk in your investment. Let us agree that we discount the receipt of $50 a year from now by 15%, and so on with the other deferred receipts. That is about the rate that is applied to investments with this magnitude of risk. You can check that out with my cousin who just sold his strawberry patch yesterday. According to my figures, the present value of the anticipated annual net revenues is $267.57, and today's value of the firewood is $6.14, making a grand total of $273.71. I'll take $270 even. You can see how much I'm allowing for risk because if I discounted the stream at 5%, it would come to $482.58."

After a few minutes reflection, the young woman said to the old man, "It was a bit foxy of you yesterday to let me appear to be teaching you something. Where did you learn so much about finance as an apple grower?"

"Don't be foolish, my young friend," he counseled her. "Wisdom comes from experience in many fields. Socrates taught us how to learn. I'll tell you a little secret; I spent a year in law school."

The young woman smiled at this last confession. "I have enjoyed this little exercise but let me tell you something that some of the financial whiz kids have told me. Whether we figure value on the basis of the discounted cash flow method or the capitalization of earnings, so long as we apply both methods perfectly we should come out at exactly the same point."

"Of course!" the old man exclaimed. "Some of the wunderkinds are catching on. But the clever ones are looking not at old earnings, but doing what managers are doing and projecting earnings into the future. The question is, however, which method is more likely to be misused. I prefer to calculate by my method because I don't have to monkey around with depreciation. You have to make these arbitrary assumptions about useful life and how fast you're going to depreciate. Obviously that's where you went wrong in your figuring."

"You are a crafty old devil," she rejoined. "There are plenty of places for your calculations to go off. It's easy to discount cash flows when they are nice and steady, but that doesn't help you when you've got some lumpy expenses that do not recur. For example, several years from now that tree will require some extensive pruning and spraying operations that simply do not show up in your flow. The labor and chemicals for that once-only occasion throw off the evenness of your calculations. But I'll tell you what, I'll offer you $250. My cold analysis tells me I'm overpaying, but I really like that tree. I think the psychic rewards of sitting in its shade must be worth something."

"It's a deal," said the old man. "I never said I was looking for the *highest* offer, but only the *best* offer."

MORAL: There are several. Methods are useful as tools, but good judgment comes not from methods alone, but from experience. And experience comes from bad judgment.

Listen closely to the experts, and hear those things they don't tell you. Behind all the sweet sounds of their confident notes, there is a great deal of discordant uncertainty. One wrong assumption can carry you pretty far from the truth.

Finally, you are never too young to learn.

LE BEAU v. M.G. BANCORPORATION, INC., 1998 WL 44993 (Del. Ch. 1998), aff'd in part, rev'd in part, 737 A.2d 513 (Del. 1999). This case concerned the valuation of a publicly held corporation, M.G. Bancorporation (MGB). MGB had two bank subsidiaries, Mount Greenwood Bank (Greenwood) and Worth Bancorp, Inc. (WBC). In the course of his opinion, Vice Chancellor Jacobs described the valuation methodologies employed by David Clarke, an expert witness for the plaintiffs. Although Vice Chancellor Jacobs did not accept, in all respects, the manner in which Clarke applied those methodologies to the case at hand, the methodologies themselves nicely illustrate contemporary theories of valuation. Vice Chancellor Jacobs's description of the valuation methodologies Clarke employed is as follows:

> . . . At trial . . . David Clarke ("Clarke"), testified that as of the Merger date the fair value of MGB common stock was at least $85 per share. In arriving at that conclusion, Clarke used three distinct methodologies to value MGB's two operating bank subsidiaries: (i) the comparative publicly-traded company approach, (ii) the discounted cash flow ("DCF") method, and (iii) the comparative acquisition technique. Clarke then added a control premium to the values of the two subsidiaries to reflect the value of the holding company's (MGB's) controlling interest in those subsidiaries. Lastly, Clarke then added the value of MGB's remaining assets to the sum of his valuations of the two subsidiaries, to arrive at an overall fair value of $85 per share for MGB.
>
> What follows is a more detailed description of how Clarke performed his valuation(s) of MGB.
>
> *1. Comparative Company Approach*
>
> Clarke's comparative publicly-traded company approach involved five steps: (1) identifying an appropriate set of comparable companies, (2) identifying the multiples of earnings and book value at which the comparable companies traded, (3) comparing certain of MGB's financial fundamentals (e.g., return on assets

and return on equity) to those of the comparable companies, (4) making certain adjustments to those financial fundamentals, and (5) adding an appropriate control premium. After completing the first four steps, Clarke arrived at a value for WBC of $33.059 million ($48.02 per share), and for Greenwood of $20.952 million ($30.44 per share). Clarke next determined that during the period January 1989 to June 1993, acquirors of controlling interests in publicly-traded companies had paid an average premium of at least 35%. On that basis, Clarke concluded that a 35% premium was appropriate, and applied that premium to the values he had determined for Greenwood and WBC, to arrive at fair values of $43.3 million ($62.90 per share) for WBC and $27.1 million ($39.37 per share) for Greenwood, respectively. Clarke then valued MGB's 75.5% controlling interest in WBC at $32.691 million ($47.49 per share), and MGB's 100% interest in Greenwood at $27.1 million ($39.37 per share), under his comparative company approach.

2. *Discounted Cash Flow Approach*

Clarke's DCF valuation analysis involved four steps: (1) projecting the future net cash flows available to MGB's shareholders for ten years after the Merger date, (2) discounting those future cash flows to present value as of the Merger date by using a discount rate based on the weighted average cost of capital ("WACC"), (3) adding a terminal value that represented the present value of all future cash flows generated after the ten year projection period, and (4) applying a control premium to the sum of (2) and (3).

. . . [Clarke] concluded that it would require ten years for MGB's cash flows to stabilize. Based on a 1996 Ibbotson Associates ("Ibbotson") study of the banking industry, Clarke concluded that the appropriate . . . discount rate (WACC), was 1%, and that the appropriate discount rate (WACC) for MGB was 12%. Applying that 12% discount rate, Clarke calculated the present value of WBC's future cash flows to be $17.251 million, and WBC's terminal value to be $14.824 million. Applying that same 12% discount rate, Clarke arrived at a present value of $10.937 million, and a terminal value of $9.138 million, for Greenwood.

Applying the same 35% control premium to those values of the two subsidiaries, Clarke calculated MGB's 75.5% interest in WBC at $33.824 million or $49.14 per share; and MGB's 100% interest in Greenwood at $28.3 million, or $41.11 per share.

3. *Comparative Acquisition Approach*

Clarke's third valuation approach, the comparative acquisition method, focused upon multiples of MGB's last twelve months earnings and its tangible book value. Those multiples were determined by reference to the prices at which the stock of comparable companies had been sold in transactions involving the sale of control. Unlike the comparative company and DCF valuation approaches, this method did not require adding a control premium to the values of the subsidiaries because under that methodology, the parent holding company's controlling interest in the subsidiaries was already accounted for.

In valuing MGB under his third approach, Clarke identified three transactions involving community banks in the relevant geographic area that occurred within one year of the Merger. He also considered data published by The Chicago Corporation in its September 1993 issue of Midwest Bank & Thrift Survey. . . . From these sources, Clarke determined that (i) control of WBC could be sold for a price between a multiple of 14 times WBC's last twelve months' earnings and 200% of WBC's tangible book value, and that (ii) control of Greenwood could be sold for a price between a multiple of 12 times Greenwood's last twelve months' earnings and 175% of its tangible book value. Giving equal weight to these two sets of values, Clarke valued MGB's 75.5% interest in WBC at $28.8 million (75.5% x $38.1 million) or $41.84 per share, and MGB's 100% interest in Greenwood, at $22.9 million, or $33.27 per share.

4. MGB's Remaining Assets

Having valued MGB's two subsidiaries, Clarke then determined the fair value of MGB's remaining net assets, which included (i) a $6.83 million note payable by Southwest, (ii) certain intangibles that Clarke did not include in his valuation, (iii) $78,000 in cash, and (iv) other assets worth $2000. These assets totaled $6.91 million, from which Clarke subtracted liabilities of $96,000 to arrive at a net asset value of $6.814 million ($9.90 per share) for MGB's remaining assets.

5. Fair Value Computation

Clarke then added the values he had determined under each of his valuation methodologies, for (i) MGB's 75.5% interest in WBC, (ii) MGB's 100% interest in Greenwood, and (iii) MGB's 100% interest in its remaining assets. Under his comparative publicly-traded method, Clarke concluded that MGB's value was $76.59 per share with no control premium, and $96.76 per share with a control premium. Under his DCF approach, Clarke determined that MGB's value was $74.75 per share with no control premium, and $100.15 per share with a control premium. And under his comparative acquisitions method, Clarke concluded that MGB's minimum fair value was $85 per share, which represented the median of the values described above.

Vice–Chancellor Jacobs accepted Clarke's valuation methodologies in principle, but concluded that there were problems in the way that both Clarke and the corporation's expert had applied the methodologies they employed. However, the court accepted Clarke's comparative-acquisition valuation, and concluded, largely on that basis, that the stock was worth $85/share. The Delaware Supreme Court affirmed on the valuation issue, but remanded on the issue whether compound or simple interest should be paid.

NOTE

The control premium to which *LeBeau* refers is based on the principle that the market price of minority shares includes a minority discount—that is, a discount for the fact that the shares are not controlling shares. However, that discount is irrelevant when valuing the corporation. Therefore, if a methodology for valuing the corporation is based on the market price its shares, the minority discount applied to the shares must be reversed. The way to reverse the discount is to add back in a control premium, which should be the mirror image of, and identical to, the minority discount. See Rapid–American Corp. v. Harris, 603 A.2d 796 (Del.1992).

SECTION 7. RESTRICTIONS ON THE TRANSFERABILITY OF SHARES, AND MANDATORY-SALE PROVISIONS

INTRODUCTORY NOTE

This Section concerns the extent to which restrictions on transferability can be imposed on the stock of close corporations. One of the traditional norms of corporate law was that ownership interests in corporations—that is, shares of stock—were freely transferable, as were the rights that accompanied these interests, such as the right to vote on various matters. In contrast, a basic norm of partnership law was that a partner could not transfer all of his rights in a partnership without the unanimous consent of all of his partners. The partnership norm is a much better fit for small enterprises, including close corporations, than the traditional corporate norm, because where an enterprise is owned by a small number of persons, the identity of each co-owner is of vital importance to the remaining co-owners. Accordingly, shareholder agreements in close corporations commonly either limit the transferability of shares; require the shareholder or his estate to sell his shares back to the corporation or to the other shareholders on the occurrence of certain events, such as an offer from a third party or death; or both. At first, the courts had difficulty with restrictions on the transferability of close corporation stock, partly because the restrictions seemed to violate traditional corporate norms, and partly because corporate stock was viewed as property and property was viewed as freely alienable. Eventually, however, the courts began to approach restrictions on transferability on a functional rather than a doctrinal basis. When restrictions are approached on a functional basis, two intertwined issues must be addressed. First, is the relevant type of restriction fair? Second, where the restriction involves a compulsory sale of the shareholder's stock at a fixed or formula price, is the price fair? The materials in this section develop these issues.

F.B.I. Farms, Inc. v. Moore

Supreme Court of Indiana, 2003.
798 N.E.2d 440.

We hold that as a general proposition, restrictions on corporate share transfers may require approval of the transfer by the corporation's Board of Directors, at least in a family-owned corporation. Although generally valid against purchasers with notice of them, such restrictions may not prevent a creditor from foreclosing a lien on the shares, but a purchaser who buys at a foreclosure sale with notice of the restrictions acquires the shares subject to the restrictions. We also hold that if shares are subject to a right of first refusal, and the holder of the right has notice of the foreclosure, the holder cannot exercise the right against a purchaser at a foreclosure sale after the purchaser has taken title to the shares without objection from the holder of the rights.

Factual and Procedural Background

F.B.I. Farms, Inc., was formed in 1976 by Ivan and Thelma Burger, their children, Linda and Freddy, and the children's spouses. Each of the three couples transferred a farm and related machinery to the corporation in exchange for common stock in the corporation. At the time, Birchell Moore was married to Linda. Linda and Moore deeded a jointly-owned 180–acre farm to F.B.I., and 2,507 shares were issued to Moore and one to Linda. These 2,508 shares represented approximately fourteen percent of the capitalization of F.B.I.

In 1977, the Board of Directors of F.B.I. consisted of Moore, Ivan, Freddy and Linda. The minutes of a 1977 meeting of the Board recite that the following restrictions on the transfer of shares were "adopted":

> 1) No stock of said corporation shall be transferred, assigned and/or exchanged or divided, unless or until approved by the Directors thereof;
>
> 2) That if any stock be offered for sale, assigned and/or transferred, the corporation should have the first opportunity of purchasing the same at no more than the book value thereof;
>
> 3) Should said corporation be not interested, and could not economically offer to purchase said stock, any stockholder of record should be given the next opportunity to purchase said stock, at a price not to exceed the book value thereof;
>
> 4) That if the corporation was not interested in the stock, and any stockholders were not interested therein, then the same

could be sold to any blood member of the family. Should they be desirous of purchasing the same, then at not more than the book value thereof.

Linda's marriage to Moore was dissolved in 1982. As part of the dissolution proceedings, Linda was awarded all of the F.B.I. shares and Moore was awarded a monetary judgment in the amount of $155,889.80, secured by a lien on Linda's shares.

F.B.I. filed for bankruptcy protection in 1989 and emerged from Chapter 11 Bankruptcy in 1991. Moore's judgment against Linda remained unsatisfied, and in April 1998 he sought a writ of execution of his lien. The corporation, through its counsel, responded with a letter to Moore's counsel demanding payment of the $250,700 subscription price for the 2,507 shares that were initially issued to Moore but had since been transferred to Linda. Moore obtained the writ of execution in June 1999.... A sheriff's sale went forward and in February 2000 Moore purchased all 2,924 shares owned by Linda at the time for $290,450.67.

In December 2000 Moore instituted this suit against F.B.I., its shareholders, and Linda seeking a declaratory judgment that the attempted cancellation of the shares by the defendants was invalid, that Moore properly retained ownership of the shares, and that the shares were unencumbered by restrictions and were freely transferable. Moore also sought dissolution of the corporation, injunctive relief against alleged fraudulent practices by the defendants, and monetary damages. The trial court granted Moore's motion for partial summary judgment, finding (1) the shares were not "lawfully cancelled"; (2) Moore was the "lawful owner" of the disputed stock; (3) the restriction in paragraph one of the agreement requiring approval by F.B.I.'s directors for a share transfer was "manifestly unreasonable"; and, (4) the provision in paragraph four of the agreement giving "blood members" the option to purchase after the corporation and shareholders was "manifestly unreasonable" and unenforceable. The trial court's findings included those rendering the order appealable as a final judgment pursuant to Indiana Trial Rule 54(B).

On appeal, the Court of Appeals held that the transfer restrictions barred only voluntary transfers. F.B.I. Farms, Inc. v. Moore, 769 N.E.2d 688, 696 (Ind.Ct.App.2002). Because the sheriff's sale effectuated an involuntary transfer of Linda's shares, Moore, as the purchaser of the shares, acquired the shares. *Id.* at 692. Although the court found that future transfers of stock would be subject to the restrictions in Moore's hands, it also affirmed the trial court's finding that the two disputed restrictions were manifestly unreasonable. *Id.* at 695–96. The court reasoned that the several tumultuous years of dispute between the parties rendered the restriction requiring director approval before transfer unreasonable, and the reference to "blood members" of the family was sufficiently ambiguous that that restriction was unenforceable. *Id.* at 694–96. We granted transfer.

Standard of Review

To support an order granting a motion for summary judgment, the designated evidence must show that there is no genuine issue as to any material fact and that the moving party is entitled to a judgment as a matter of law. Ind. Trial Rule 56(C). On appeal, the standard of review of a grant or denial of a motion for summary judgment is the same as that used in the trial court. *Bemenderfer v. Williams,* 745 N.E.2d 212, 215 (Ind.2001).

I. Transfer Restrictions

A. *General Principles*

Most of the issues in this case are resolved by the Indiana statute governing share transfer restrictions. Indiana Code section 23–1–26–8 essentially mirrors Model Business Corporation Act § 6.27, which authorizes restrictions on the transfer of shares. The Indiana statute reads as follows:

> (a) The articles of incorporation, bylaws, an agreement among shareholders, or an agreement between shareholders and the corporation may impose restrictions on the transfer or registration of transfer of shares of any class or series of shares of the corporation. A restriction does not affect shares issued before the restriction was adopted unless the holders of the shares are parties to the restriction agreement or voted in favor of the restriction.
>
> (b) A restriction on the transfer or registration of transfer of shares is valid and enforceable against the holder or a transferee of the holder if the restriction is authorized by this section and its existence is noted conspicuously on the front or back of the certificate or is contained in the information statement required by section 7(b) [Ind.Code 23–1–26–7(b)] of this chapter. Unless so noted, a restriction is not enforceable against a person without knowledge of the restriction.
>
> (c) A restriction on the transfer or registration of transfer of shares is authorized:
>
> > (1) to maintain the corporation's status when it is dependent on the number or identity of its shareholders;
> >
> > (2) to preserve exemptions under federal or state securities law; or
> >
> > (3) for any other reasonable purpose.
>
> (d) A restriction on the transfer or registration of transfer of shares may, among other things:
>
> > (1) obligate the shareholder first to offer the corporation or other persons (separately, consecutively, or simultaneously) an opportunity to acquire the restricted shares;

(2) obligate the corporation or other persons (separately, consecutively, or simultaneously) to acquire the restricted shares;

(3) require the corporation, the holders of any class of its shares, or another person to approve the transfer of the restricted shares, if the requirement is not manifestly unreasonable; or

(4) prohibit the transfer of the restricted shares to designated persons or classes of persons, if the prohibition is not manifestly unreasonable....

Corporate shares are personal property. At common law, any restriction on the power to alienate personal property was impermissible. Doss v. Yingling, 95 Ind. App. 494, 500, 172 N.E. 801, 803 (1930). Despite this doctrine, Indiana, like virtually all jurisdictions, allows corporations and their shareholders to impose restrictions on transfers of shares. The basic theory of these statutes is to permit owners of a corporation to control its ownership and management and prevent outsiders from inserting themselves into the operations of the corporation. *Id.* at 502–03, 172 N.E. 801; 12 William Meade Fletcher et al, Fletcher Cyclopedia of the Law of Private Corporations, § 5454 (1996). Chief Justice Holmes stated the matter succinctly a century ago: "Stock in a corporation is not merely property. It also creates a personal relation analogous otherwise than technically to a partnership.... [T]here seems to be no greater objection to retaining the right of choosing one's associates in a corporation than in a firm." Barrett v. King, 181 Mass. 476, 63 N.E. 934, 935 (1902). As applied to a family-owned corporation, this remains valid today.

Transfer restrictions are treated as contracts either between shareholders or between shareholders and the corporation.[35] *Doss,* 95 Ind.App. at 502, 172 N.E. at 803; Butner v. United States, 440 U.S. 48, 55 ... (1979) (the validity and enforcement of restrictions are governed by state law just like any other contract); Boston Safe Deposit & Trust Co., et al. v. North Attleborough Chapter of the Am. Red Cross, et al., 330 Mass. 114, 111 N.E.2d 447, 449 (Mass. 1953) (restrictions in the articles of organization are binding on a shareholder by reason of the contract made with the corporation when she accepted the certificates of stock containing the printed restrictions). Apart from any statutory requirements, restrictions on transfer are to be read, like any other contract, to further the manifest intention of the parties. Because they are restrictions on alienation and therefore disfavored, the terms

35. The Indiana statute provides that restrictions are valid if included in the articles, the bylaws, an agreement among shareholders or an agreement between the corporation and shareholders. I.C. § 23–1–26–8(a) (1998). None of these was done here. However, no one challenges the restrictions as defective in their initial adoption. At least as to Moore, who approved them as a director and had actual knowledge of them, under these circumstances, the restrictions constitute a contract as to all of those shareholders who approved the adoption of the restrictions. *Shortridge v. Platis,* 458 N.E.2d 301, 304 (Ind.Ct.App.1984) (a buy-sell restriction is analyzed by the court as a contract); 18A Am.Jur.2d *Corporations* § 687 (1985) (courts sustain a restriction whether valid as a bylaw or not, on the ground that it constitutes a valid agreement between the stockholders and the corporation, particularly as applied to stockholders who assent to, or participate in, the adoption of the bylaw).

in the restrictions are not to be expanded beyond their plain and ordinary meaning. 12 Fletcher § 5455 (1996).

For a party to be bound by share transfer restrictions, that party must have notice of the restrictions. I.C. § 23–1–26–8(b) (1998). Here, the restrictions on transfer of F.B.I. shares were neither "noted conspicuously" on the certificates nor contained in the information statement referred to in Indiana Code 23–1–26–8(b), but there is no doubt that Moore, the buyer at the sheriff's sale, had notice of the restrictions. He was therefore bound by them. State ex rel. Hudelson v. Clarks Hill Tel. Co., 139 Ind. App. 507, 510, 218 N.E.2d 154, 156 (1966).

Finally, a closely held corporation is a "corporation in which all of the outstanding stock is held by just a few individuals, or by a small group of persons belonging to a single family." J.R. Kemper, Validity of "Consent Restraint" on Transfer of Shares of Close Corporation, 69 A.L.R.3d 1327, 1328 (1976). In 1977, F.B.I. plainly fell within that description; it was owned by six individuals, all members of a single family. Closely held corporations have a viable interest in remaining the organization they envision at incorporation and transfer restrictions are an appropriate means of maintaining the status quo.

B. Rights of First Refusal

Paragraphs (2) and (3) of the restrictions created rights of first refusal in F.B.I. and its shareholders. A transfer in violation of restrictions is voidable at the insistence of the corporation. Groves v. Prickett, 420 F.2d 1119, 1122 (9th Cir.1970). F.B.I. and its shareholders argue that Moore should have been obliged to offer the shares to the corporation or a shareholder pursuant to those provisions. Moore responds, and the Court of Appeals agreed, that he was not a shareholder until he purchased the shares at the sheriff's sale. He contends he therefore had no power to offer the shares. This misses the point that before Linda could transfer her shares, she was obliged to offer them to F.B.I. and the other shareholders. Moore was on notice of that requirement. Moore, as the buyer, had the right to demand that Linda initiate the process to exercise or waive the right to first refusal.

Thus, if the corporation had insisted on its right of first refusal, Linda would have been obliged to sell to F.B.I. (or its shareholders). And Moore, as a buyer on notice of the restrictions, had the right to insist that that process go forward. But the corporation and its shareholders were aware of the sheriff's sale and did nothing to assert the right of first refusal. They cannot sit back and let the sale go forward, await future events, then claim a right to purchase on the same terms as Moore. McCroden v. Case, 602 N.W.2d 736, 743–44 (S.D.1999) (transfer restriction is waived by stockholder's failure to exercise "first option" preemptive rights); Calton v. Calton, 118 N.C.App. 439, 456 S.E.2d 520, 523 (1995) (no justiciable controversy existed where no shareholder exercised the right to purchase stock, intended to exercise the right, or was even financially able to do so at the time the action was filed; shareholders waived any right to object to the transfers where they had knowledge of both the testator's death and the restrictions contained on the stock certificates, no shareholder asked to purchase any of the stock, and shareholders waited eighteen months to file an action); Puro v. Puro, 40 A.D.2d 784, 337 N.Y.S.2d 586, 587 (N.Y.App.Div.1972) (transfer restrictions are not self-executing). In sum, F.B.I. and its shareholders had rights of first refusal, but failed to exercise them. As a result, the sale to Moore proceeded as if the shares had been offered and the corporation refused the opportunity. To hold otherwise would be to give F.B.I. and its shareholders a perpetual option to purchase but no obligation to do so. Having failed to demand their right to buy at the time of the sale, the rights of first refusal gave them no ability to upset the sale conducted by the sheriff.

C. Restrictions on Transfer with Board Approval

The restrictions "adopted" in paragraphs (1) and (4) are more problematic. Indiana's statute, reflecting the common law, requires that restrictions on share transfers be reasonable. I.C. § 23–1–26–8(c)(3), (d)(3), and (d)(4). The general common law doctrine surrounding evaluation of the reasonableness of restrictions is well established. A restriction is reasonable if it is designed to serve a legitimate purpose of the party imposing the restraint and the restraint is not an absolute restriction on the recipient's right of alienability. Bernard F. Cataldo, *Stock Transfer Restrictions and the Closed Corporation,* 37 Va. L.Rev. 229, 232–33 (1951). The Indiana statute is somewhat more generous in allowing restrictions on classes of buyers unless "manifestly unreasonable." I.C. 23–1–26–8(d)(4). Several factors are relevant in determining the reasonableness of any transfer restriction, including the size of the corporation, the degree of restraint upon alienation; the time the restriction was to continue in effect, the method to be used in determining the transfer price of shares, the likelihood of the restriction's contributing to the attainment of corporate objectives, the possibility that a hostile stockholder might injure the corporation, and the probability of the restriction's promoting the best interests of the corporation. 18A Am.Jur.2d *Corporations* § 683 (1985). At one extreme, a restriction that merely prescribes procedures that must be observed before stock may be transferred is not unreasonable. State ex rel. Howland v. Olympia Veneer Co., 138 Wash. 144, 244 P. 261 (1926). At the other end of the spectrum, restrictions that are fraudulent, oppressive, unconscionable, Tourtelott v. Chestnuts Salon, No. 00–5496 2001 R.I.Super. LEXIS 19 at * 6 (R.I. Sup.Ct. Jan. 17, 2001), 2001 WL 91393, or the result of a breach of the fiduciary duty that shareholders in a close corporation owe to one another, will not be upheld. Cressy v. Shannon Cont'l Corp., 177 Ind.App. 224, 378 N.E.2d 941, 945 (1978); 12 Fletcher § 5455 (1996). The restrictions on F.B.I.'s shares, like most, are somewhere in the middle. They impose substantive limitations on transfer, but are not alleged to be the result of fraud or breach of fiduciary duty.

The trial court, in its order granting partial summary judgment, concluded that the restriction precluding transfer without Board approval was reasonable at the time that it was adopted, but the lengthy and difficult history between the parties had rendered the restriction unreasonable. Under basic contract law principles, the reasonableness of a term of a contract is evaluated at the time of its adoption. First Fed. Sav. Bank v. Key Mkts., 559 N.E.2d 600, 603 (Ind.1990). The same is true of share transfer restrictions. As a result, evaluating the reasonableness of the restrictions in light of subsequent developments is inappropriate. For that reason, we do not agree that the restriction requiring director approval became unreasonable based upon events and disputes within the family that occurred after the restrictions had been adopted. To be sure, the parties find themselves in a difficult dispute as is sometimes the case in a family business following a dissolution. But when F.B.I. was formed and the family farms were effectively pooled, the shareholders agreed that the Board would be permitted to restrict access to the shares. To the extent that restriction devalues the shares in the hands of any individual shareholder by reason of lack of transferability, it is the result of the bargain they struck. The policy behind enforcement of these restrictions is to encourage entering into formal partnerships by permitting all parties to have confidence they will not involuntarily end up with an undesired co-venturer. Presumably for that reason, the statute permits a restriction that requires a transferee to be approved by the Board of Directors, and to that extent may severely limit transferability.

A "consent restriction" such as this has been considered unreasonable by some courts. 2 Cox, Hazen, O'Neal *Corporations* § 14.10 (2002); Harry G. Henn & John R. Alexander, *Laws of Corporations,* § 281 (1983). However, the General Assembly has allowed precisely this type of restriction in Indiana Code section 23–1–26–8(d)(3). That section provides that transfer restrictions may require the approval of "the corporation, the holders of any class of its shares, or another person" before the shares may be transferred. Board approval is one permissible way of implementing approval by "the Corporation" under this section. *See also Wright v. Iredell Telephone Co.,* 182 N.C. 308, 108 S.E. 744, 747 (1921) (upholding a restriction requiring the approval of the corporation's directors).

D. Restrictions on Transfer Except to "Blood Members of the Family"

We also find the "blood-member" restriction to be enforceable as protecting a viable interest. Mathews v. United States, 226 F.Supp. 1003, 1009 (E.D.N.Y.1964) (recognized "intact family ownership" as an interest worth protecting by a restriction). These are family farmers in corporate form. It is apparent from the nature of the corporation that the Burger family had an interest in maintaining ownership and operation of F.B.I. in the hands of family members. Although one may quibble with the terminology, and there may be some individuals where status as blood members is debatable, we think it plain enough that all parties to this dispute either are or are not blood members of the Burger family. All are either direct descendants of Ivan or spouses of Ivan or of one of his children. . . .

III. Restrictions as Applied to Involuntary Transfers

The Court of Appeals held that the restrictions on Linda's shares did not apply by their terms to the sheriff's sale and, as a result, did not bar the sheriff's sale to Moore. We agree that Moore acquired the shares at the sheriff's sale, but not because the restrictions were inapplicable by their terms.

The Court of Appeals relied on cases stating that involuntary transfers fall within the terms of a restriction only if the language of the restrictions specifically identifies them. F.B.I. Farms, 769 N.E.2d at 692. This doctrine has been developed largely in cases involving intestate transfers by a decedent, Stern v. Stern, 146 F.2d 870, 870 (D.C.Cir.1945), and in marriage dissolution proceedings where a transfer is made to a spouse. Castonguay v. Castonguay, 306 N.W.2d 143, 146 (Minn.1981).

The sheriff's sale where Moore purchased Linda's shares was an involuntary transfer. Transfers ordered incident to marriage dissolutions and transfers under intestate law may also be deemed involuntary. We think the governing principle is not the same for all forms of "involuntary" transfers. The language of the restrictions in this case does not specifically refer to involuntary transfers of any kind. Rather, it seems to contemplate restricting all transfers, voluntary and involuntary, by providing that no stock of the corporation should be "transferred, assigned, exchanged, divided, or sold" without complying with the restrictions. The intent of the parties is thus rather plain: to restrict ownership to the designated group, and to preclude transfer by any means. The question is whether that intent should be permitted to prevail in the face of countervailing policies.

Transfer by intestacy is in some sense involuntary, but it may also be viewed as a voluntary act of the decedent who had the option to leave a will. If a transfer could not be made by gift during lifetime, for example, to an offspring regarded by other shareholders as an undesirable partner, we see no reason to permit it at death by the decedent's choice to die intestate. There are, however, forms of involuntary transfers that a private agreement may not prevent because the agreement would unreasonably interfere with the rights of third parties. In a dissolution, the interests of the spouse require permitting transfer over the stated intent of the parties. Similarly, creditors of the shareholder cannot be stymied by a private agreement that renders foreclosure of a lien impossible. For that reason, we agree with the trial court that the sheriff's sale transferred the shares to Moore despite the restrictions. Transfer restrictions cannot preclude transfer in a foreclosure sale and thereby leave creditors without recourse. This does not turn on a doctrine of construction. Rather we hold that requiring an explicit bar specifically naming transfer by intestacy or by testamentary disposition should not be necessary. If the language purports to bar all transfers, and by its terms would apply to intestacy, devise or any other means of transfer, it should be given effect unless the restriction violates some policy.

Although we agree with Moore that he could purchase the shares at the sale, it is also the case that he purchased the shares with knowledge of the restrictions. We conclude that he could not acquire more property rights than were possessed by Linda as his seller. U.C.C. § 8–302 (1994) (the purchaser of an investment security acquires the rights in the security his transferor had or had actual authority to convey). The shares in Linda's hands were valued with restrictions in place, and therefore it is not unfair to her creditors that a purchaser at a foreclosure sale acquire the disputed shares subject to the same restrictions, and with whatever lessened value that produces. To be sure, the effect of such a restriction may be to make the shares unmarketable to any buyer. But the creditor retains the option to bid at the sale and, if successful, succeed to the shareholders' interest. The creditor then gets the assets the debtor used to secure the underlying obligation. If the creditor wants collateral free of restrictions, the creditor must negotiate for that at the outset of the arrangement.

Conclusion

We . . . uphold the trial court's finding that the transfer restrictions did not prevent the sheriff's sale, and that the transfer restrictions remain applicable to the shares in Moore's hands. We reverse the trial court's ruling that the two disputed transfer restrictions are unreasonable and therefore unenforceable, and find that the director-approval and blood-member restrictions are reasonable and enforceable. The case is remanded for further proceedings consistent with this opinion.

■ SHEPARD, C.J., and DICKSON and SULLIVAN, JJ., concur.

■ RUCKER, J., concurs in result without opinion.

EVANGELISTA v. HOLLAND, 27 Mass.App.Ct. 244, 537 N.E.2d 589 (1989). A shareholders' agreement allowed the corporation to buy out, for $75,000, the estate of any deceased shareholder. The corporation brought suit against the estate of a deceased shareholder to enforce the agreement. There was strong evidence that the decedent's stock was worth at least $191,000. Held, for the corporation:

> The executors suggest that to require them to part with their interest in the business for so much less than the [value of the stock] violates the duty of good faith and loyalty owed one another by stockholders in a closely held corporation. . . . Questions of good faith and loyalty do not arise when all the stockholders in advance enter into an agreement for the purchase of stock of a withdrawing or deceased stockholder. . . . That the price established by a stockholders' agreement may be less than the appraised or market value is unremarkable. Such agreements may have as their purpose: the payment of a price for a decedent's

stock which will benefit the corporation or surviving stockholders by not unduly burdening them; the payment of a price tied to life insurance; or fixing a price which assures the beneficiaries of the deceased stockholder of a predetermined price for stock which might have little market value.... When the agreement was entered into in 1984, the order and time of death of stockholders was an unknown. There was a "mutuality of risk."

DEL. GEN. CORP. LAW §§ 202, 342, 347, 349

[See Statutory Supplement]

CAL. CORP. CODE §§ 204(a)(3), (b), 418

[See Statutory Supplement]

MODEL BUS. CORP. ACT § 6.27

[See Statutory Supplement]

NOTE ON RESTRICTIONS ON TRANSFERABILITY AND MANDATORY SALES OF STOCK

1. *Restrictions on Transferability*. Although some of the earlier cases held that any restriction on the transferability of shares constituted an illegal restraint on alienation, the modern cases hold that "reasonable" restrictions are valid and enforceable. Three basic types of restrictions are commonly used in close corporations: (1) *First refusals*. These prohibit a sale of shares to a third party unless the shares have first been offered to the corporation, the other shareholders, or both, on the same terms as those offered by the third party. (2) *First options*. These prohibit a transfer of shares to a third party unless the shares have first been offered to the corporation, the other shareholders, or both, at a price fixed under the terms of the option. (3) *Consent restraints*. These prohibit a transfer of shares to a third party without the permission of the corporation's board or shareholders.

Of these three types, first refusals are the least restrictive and are widely upheld. *See, e.g.*, Groves v. Prickett, 420 F.2d 1119 (9th Cir.1970). The restrictiveness of a first option depends largely on the relationship between the option price and a fair price at the time the option is triggered. The courts have been giving increasing latitude to this type of provision. *See, e.g.*, In re Mather's Estate, 189 A.2d 586 (Pa. 1963) where an agreement that set an option price of $1 per share was enforced although the actual value of the stock was $1,060 per share. A consent restraint is normally the most restrictive of the three basic types, and at one time such a restraint was almost certain to be deemed invalid. However, some recent statutes specifically contemplate the validity of consent restraints (*see, e.g.*, Del. § 202), and as *F.B.I.* suggests, the courts have also begun to be more tolerant of these restrictions.

In spite of the increasingly tolerant climate, the validity of consent restraints remains uncertain in the absence of statute or authoritative precedent. In Rafe v. Hindin, 29 A.D.2d 481, 288 N.Y.S.2d 662 (1968), Plaintiff and Defendant each owned 50% of the stock of Bil Cy Realty, which they had organized in 1963. A legend on each stock certificate made the stock nontransferable except to the other shareholder, and written permission from the other shareholder was required to record a transfer of the stock on Bil Cy's books. Plaintiff brought an action for a declaratory judgment that the legend on the certificate was void, and that the stock was transferable without Defendant's consent. The court so held:

> In New York certificates of stock are regarded as personal property and are subject to the rule that there be no unreasonable restraint on alienation....
>
> The legend on the stock certificate at bar contains no provision that the individual defendant's consent may not be unreasonably withheld. Since the individual defendant is thus given the arbitrary power to forbid a transfer of the shares of stock by the plaintiff, the restriction amounts to annihilation of property. The restriction is not only not reasonable, but it is against public policy and, therefore, illegal. It is an unwarrantable and unlawful restraint on the sale of personal property, the sale and interchange of which the law favors, and in restraint of trade.

2. *Mandatory Sales*. The three basic types of restraints discussed above limit the shareholders' power of transfer. Other types of arrangements go further, and give the corporation or the remaining shareholders an option to purchase a shareholder's stock upon the occurrence of one or more designated contingencies even if the shareholder wants to retain the stock. A common example is an arrangement under the corporation is given an option to repurchase any stock that it has issued to an employee who is terminated. The courts have tended to enforce such arrangements, even when the option price is quite low in relation to the value of the stock at the time the repurchase right is triggered. *See, e.g.*, St. Louis Union Trust Co. v. Merrill Lynch, Pierce, Fenner & Smith Inc., 562 F.2d 1040 (8th Cir.1977), cert. denied, 435 U.S. 925, 98 S.Ct. 1490, 55 L.Ed.2d 519 (1978).

Another common example of a mandatory-sale provision is a buy-sell or survivor-purchase agreement. This kind of agreement provides that (i) on the death of a close corporation shareholder his estate has an obligation to sell its shares to the corporation, or the remaining shareholders, at a price fixed under the agreement; and (ii) the corporation or the remaining shareholders have an obligation (rather than an option) to purchase the shares. A major purpose of these agreements is to provide liquidity to the decedent's estate. If a corporation is closely held, the market for its shares is usually negligible. In the absence of such an agreement, therefore, the estate might be in a bad position if liquid assets are needed to meet estate's tax liabilities. A buy-sell or survivor-purchase agreement provides the estate with funds satisfy its tax liabilities, and also enables the corporation to control the identity of its shareholders. The corporation's obligation is often funded in whole or in part by insurance on the shareholders' lives.

3. *Problems of Interpretation*. Restrictions on transfer give rise to recurring problems of interpretation—in particular, whether a given type of disposition is within the scope of the restriction. The courts often give restrictions on transfer a strict interpretation. For example, some courts have held that unless explicitly otherwise provided, restrictions on transfer are inapplicable to testamentary transfers, *see, e.g.*, Avrett and Ledbetter Roofing and Heating Co. v. Phillips, 354 S.E.2d 321 (N.C.App. 1987), and to transfers by operation of law, such as by a divorce decree, *see, e.g.*, Castonguay v. Castonguay, 306 N.W.2d 143 (Minn.1981). Restrictions on transfer are also often interpreted to be inapplicable to transfers between existing shareholders. *See, e.g.*, Remillong v. Schneider, 185 N.W.2d 493 (N.D.1971). That rule of interpretation may result in an uncontemplated shift of control where a transfer between shareholders involves swing shares, that is, shares which, when added to an existing holding, will swing the balance of power to a shareholder who previously did not have that power. *Cf.* Lank v. Steiner, 43 Del.Ch. 262, 224 A.2d 242 (1966).

4. *Pricing Provisions*. Another kind of problem concerns the pricing clause in first-option, or buy-sell arrangements. Where shares are closely held, the price of the shares cannot realistically be set on the basis of market value. Some alternative pricing mechanism is therefore required.

a. *Book value*. One common approach is to use a pricing formula based on book value. Book value, however, may be an unreliable guide to a corporation's real worth: it reflects the historical cost of assets, rather than their present value, and usually ignores goodwill or going-concern value. The courts have tended to hold that a large disparity between book value and real value is not in itself sufficient to avoid the operation of a book-value pricing provision. Thus in Palmer v. Chamberlin, 191 F.2d 532 (5th Cir.1951), the court, quoting New England Trust Co. v. Abbott, 162 Mass. 148, 38 N.E. 432 (1894), stated, " '. . . specific performance of an agreement to convey will not be refused merely because the price is inadequate or excessive. The difference must be so great as to lead to a reasonable conclusion of fraud, mistake, or concealment in the nature of fraud, and to render it plainly inequitable and against conscience that the contract should be enforced.' " *See* also, *e.g.*, In re Estate of Brown, 130 Ill.App.2d 514, 264 N.E.2d 287 (1970). Accordingly, a book-value formula may be disastrous for the selling shareholder or his estate where goodwill represents the most valuable component of the business—as is typical in non-capital-intensive enterprises, *see, e.g.*, Jones v. Harris, 63 Wash.2d 559, 388 P.2d 539 (1964)—or where there is a significant disparity between historical costs and present values of tangible assets. *See, e.g.*, S.C. Pohlman Co. v. Easterling, 211 Cal. App.2d 466, 27 Cal.Rptr. 450 (1962).

b. *Capitalized earnings*. A second common approach is to fix the price on the basis of a multiple of earnings. This approach is less likely than a book-value formula to produce an unfair price, but involves a number of drafting or interpretation problems, such as defining earnings and considering the impact of the selling shareholder's withdrawal on the value of the business.

c. *Periodic revisions*. A third common approach is to agree on a price when the provision is adopted, subject to periodic revision at agreed-upon intervals. This approach may lead to trouble when the parties fail to make periodic revisions through carelessness or inability to agree. In Helms v. Duckworth, 249 F.2d 482 (D.C.Cir.1957), Easterday, age 70, and Duckworth, age 37, formed a corporation and agreed that when one of them died his stock would be sold to the other at $10 a share, which was then a fair price, "provided, however, that such sale and purchase price may, from time to time, be re-determined ... [annually] by an instrument in writing signed by the parties...." When Easterday died six years later, the price had never been adjusted, although the actual value of the stock had risen to $80 a share. Easterday's administratrix brought suit to declare the agreement void, and Duckworth submitted an affidavit in which he stated that it was never his intention to consent to any change in the price provision. The district court granted summary judgment to Duckworth, but the Court of Appeals reversed:

> ... Plainly [the agreement] implied a periodic bargaining or negotiating process in which each party must participate in good faith....
>
> ... We believe that the holders of closely held stock in a corporation such as shown here bear a fiduciary duty to deal fairly, honestly, and openly with their fellow stockholders and to make disclosure of all essential information.
>
> ... [T]he very nature of Duckworth's secret intent was such that it had to be kept secret and undisclosed or it would fail of its purpose.... [Duckworth's] failure to disclose to his corporate business "partner" his fixed intent never to alter the original price constitutes a flagrant breach of a fiduciary duty. Standing alone this warrants cancellation of the agreement by a court of equity.

d. *Appraisal*. A fourth approach is to provide for appraisal by a third party at the time the option is triggered. *See, e.g.*, Ginsberg v. Coating Products, Inc., 152 Conn. 592, 210 A.2d 667 (1965). This approach has the advantage of flexibility, but it may be coupled with an agreed-upon standard of valuation that can turn out to have unforeseen and undesired results.

5. *The UCC.* Uniform Commercial Code Article 8 deals with investment securities. Section 8–204 provides that "A restriction on transfer of a security imposed by the issuer, even if otherwise lawful, is ineffective against a person without knowledge of the restriction unless: (1) the security is certificated and the restriction is noted conspicuously on the security certificate; or (2) the security is uncertificated and the registered owner has been notified of the restriction."

Gallagher v. Lambert

New York Court of Appeals, 1989.
74 N.Y.2d 562, 549 N.Y.S.2d 945, 549 N.E.2d 136.

OPINION OF THE COURT

■ BELLACOSA, JUDGE.

Plaintiff Gallagher purchased stock in the defendant close corporation with which he was employed. The purchase of his 8.5% interest was subject to a mandatory buy-back provision: if the employment ended for any reason before January 31, 1985, the stock would return to the corporation for book value. The corporation fired plaintiff prior to the fulcrum date, after which the buy-back price would have been higher.

We must decide whether plaintiff's dismissed causes of action, seeking the higher repurchase price based on an alleged breach of a fiduciary duty, should be reinstated. We think not and affirm, concluding that the Appellate Division did not err in dismissing these causes of action by summary judgment because there was no cognizable breach of any fiduciary duty owed to plaintiff under the plain terms of the parties' repurchase agreement.

Gallagher was employed by defendant Eastdil Realty as a mortgage broker from 1968 to 1973. Three years later, in 1976, he returned to the company as a broker, officer and director, serving additionally as president and chief executive officer of defendant's wholly owned subsidiary, Eastdil Advisors, Inc. Gallagher was at all times an employee at will. Still later, in 1981, Eastdil offered all its executive employees an opportunity to purchase stock subject to a mandatory buy-back provision, which provided that upon "voluntary resignation or other termination" prior to January 31, 1985, an employee would be required to return the stock for book value. After that date, the formula for the buy-back price was keyed to the company's earnings. Plaintiff accepted the offer and its terms.

On January 10, 1985, Gallagher was fired by Eastdil Realty. He did not and does not now contest the firing. But he demanded payment for his shares calculated on the post-January 31, 1985 buy-back formula. Eastdil refused and Gallagher sued, asserting eight causes of action. Only three claims, based on an alleged breach of fiduciary duty of good faith and fair dealing, are before us. The trial court denied defendants' motion for summary judgment on these claims, stating that factual issues were raised relating to defendants' motive in firing plaintiff. The Appellate Division, by divided vote, reversed, dismissed those claims and ordered payment for the shares at book value. 143 A.D.2d 313, 532 N.Y.S.2d 255. That court then granted leave and certified the following question to us: "Was the order of this Court, which modified the order of the Supreme Court, properly made?"

The parties negotiated a written contract containing a common and plain buy-back provision. Plaintiff got what he bargained for—book value for his minority shares if his employment in the corporation ended before January 31, 1985. There being no basis presented for the courts to interfere with the operation and consequences of this agreement between the parties, the order of the Appellate Division granting summary judgment to defendants, dismissing the first three causes of action, should be affirmed and the certified question answered in the affirmative....

Accordingly, the order of the Appellate Division should be affirmed, with costs, and the certified question answered in the affirmative.

[The concurring opinion of Judge Hancock is omitted.]

■ KAYE, JUDGE (dissenting).

In summer 1984, Gallagher received 8.5% of Eastdil's stock, becoming the third largest shareholder, and he executed an amended stockholders' agreement. The agreement [provided] for mandatory repurchase at book value upon "voluntary resignation or other termination" of employment. But it also stipulated that after January 31, 1985, the buy-out price would be calculated by an escalating formula based on the company's earnings and the length of the shareholder's employment. According to Gallagher, the new buy-out price represented "golden handcuffs" designed to induce employees to remain on, at least until January 31, 1985.

On January 10, 1985—just 21 days before the new valuation formula became effective—Gallagher was fired and Eastdil invoked its right to repurchase his stock at book value. According to Gallagher, book value for the shares was $89,000; the price under the new valuation formula would have been around $3,000,000....

Gallagher alleges that defendants had no bona fide, business-related reason to terminate his employment when they did—assertions we must accept as true on this summary judgment motion. He charges that defendants fired him for the sole purpose of recapturing his shares at an unfairly low price and redistributing them among themselves....

If plaintiff were a minority shareholder, but not an employee, defendants would be barred from acting selfishly and opportunistically, for no corporate purpose, as he alleges they did. The controlling stockholders in a close corporation stand, in relation to minority owners, in the same fiduciary position as corporate directors generally, and are held "to the extreme measure of candor, unselfishness and good faith." (*Kavanaugh v. Kavanaugh Knitting Co.,* 226 N.Y. 185, 193, 123 N.E. 148.) Although, without more, the courts will not interfere when parties have set the repurchase price at book value (*Allen v. Biltmore Tissue Corp.,* 2 N.Y.2d 534, 542–543, 161 N.Y.S.2d 418, 141 N.E.2d 812), here plaintiff asserts there was more. The corporation agreed, commencing January 31, 1985, to pay a higher price, said to be more reflective of the true value of defendant's shares. Defendants' invocation of the pre-January 31 repurchase price was adverse to plaintiff's interests as a minority stockholder, and therefore subject to a standard of good faith under the foregoing principles. . . .

Defendants' broad interpretation of the "other termination" language of the repurchase clause amounts to an assertion that plaintiff agreed to waive substantial rights he might otherwise have possessed as a minority shareholder. However, in the absence of evidence that plaintiff knowingly assented to such a waiver, I cannot agree that the general language of the clause unambiguously expresses an understanding that the option could be exploited for the sole personal gain of the controlling shareholders in derogation of their fiduciary obligations to minority shareholders. Notably, the repurchase clause contains no reference to plaintiff's at-will employment status and no reservation of defendant's right to discharge plaintiff for any reason at all.

Moreover, defendants' interpretation denies that defendants themselves had any duty of good faith in connection with the shareholders' agreement. We have said that "there is an implied covenant that neither party shall do anything which will have the effect of destroying or injuring the right of the other party to receive the fruits of the contract, which means that in every contract there exists an implied covenant of good faith and fair dealing." (*Kirke La Shelle Co. v. Paul Armstrong Co.,* 263 N.Y. 79, 87, 188 N.E. 163.) This general rule does not apply to at-will employment relationships, as "it would be incongruous to say that an inference may be drawn that the employer impliedly agreed to a provision which would be destructive of his right of termination." (*Murphy v. American Home Prods. Corp.,* 58 N.Y.2d 293, 304–305, 461 N.Y.S.2d 232, 448 N.E.2d 86.) It does not follow, however, that there can be no covenant of good faith implicit in the shareholders' agreement that gives rise to obligations surviving termination of the employment relationship.

Assuming plaintiff's claims about the purpose of the amendments to be true, the expectations and relationship of the parties, as structured by the shareholders' agreement, dictate an implied contractual obligation of good faith, notwithstanding that there is none in their employment relationship (*see, Wakefield v. Northern Telecom,* 769 F.2d 109 [2d Cir.]). A covenant of good faith is anomalous in the context of at-will employment because performance and entitlement to benefits are simultaneous. Termination even without cause does not operate to deprive the employee of the benefits promised in return for performance.

But the alleged "golden handcuffs" agreement is different. An implied covenant of good faith *is* necessary to enable the employee to receive the benefits promised for performance. As one court noted, "an unfettered right to avoid payment * * * creates incentives counterproductive to the purpose of the contract itself in that the better the performance by the employee, the greater the temptation to terminate." (*Wakefield v. Northern Telecom, supra,* at 112–113; Note, *Exercising Options to Repurchase Employee–Held Stock: A Question of Good Faith,* 68 Yale L.J. 773, 779 [1959].) . . .

IV.

Denial of summary judgment would deprive defendants of no legitimate expectation or right, contractual or otherwise. Under the law, they remain free to terminate plaintiff's employment as agreed; they remain free to buy back his stock at book value as agreed—so long as there is a corporate purpose for their conduct. What controlling shareholders cannot do to a minority shareholder is take action against him solely for the self-aggrandizing, opportunistic purpose of themselves acquiring his shares at the low price, and they cannot do this because in the law it means something to be a shareholder, particularly a minority shareholder. . . .

■ SIMONS, ALEXANDER and TITONE, JJ., concur with BELLACOSA, J.

■ HANCOCK, J., concurs in a separate opinion.

■ KAYE, J., dissents and votes to reverse in another opinion in which WACHTLER, C.J., concurs.

Order affirmed, etc.

JENSEN v. CHRISTENSEN & LEE INSURANCE, 157 Wis.2d 758, 460 N.W.2d 441 (App.1990). In this case, the court held that a close-corporation shareholder who was discharged from his corporate position did not have an action for wrongful discharge, because in Wisconsin wrongful-discharge actions are limited to cases in which the discharge violates public policy. However, the shareholder alleged that the discharge triggered a stock buyout at a low purchase price that redounded to the financial benefit of the remaining shareholder-directors. The court held that this allegation stated a claim that those directors had breached their fiduciary duties by failing to deal fairly in a matter in which they had a material conflict of interest.

JORDAN v. DUFF & PHELPS, INC., 815 F.2d 429 (7th Cir.1987). Duff & Phelps, Inc. in the business of evaluating the risk and value of firms and their securities. It sold credit ratings, investment research, and financial consulting services to both the firms under scrutiny and potential investors in those firms. Jordan started work at Duff & Phelps's Chicago office in May 1977, and was viewed as a successful securities analyst. In 1981, Duff & Phelps offered Jordan the opportunity to buy some of its stock. By November 1983, Jordan had purchased 188 of the 20,100 shares outstanding, and he was making installment payments on another 62 shares. Forty persons other than Jordan held stock in Duff & Phelps.

Jordan had purchased his stock at its book value. Before selling him any stock, Duff & Phelps required Jordan to sign a Stock Restriction and Purchase Agreement. This Agreement provided in part:

> Upon the termination of any employment with the Corporation . . . for any reason, including resignation, discharge, death, disability or retirement, the individual whose employment is terminated or his estate shall sell to the Corporation, and the Corporation shall buy, all Shares of the Corporation then owned by such individual or his estate. The price to be paid for such Shares shall be equal to the adjusted book value (as hereinafter defined) of the Shares on the December 31 which coincides with, or immediately precedes, the date of termination of such individual's employment.

In late 1983, Jordan wanted to leave Duff & Phelps because tensions between his wife and his mother made it necessary for him to leave Chicago. Another firm, Underwood, offered Jordan a job at a salary substantially greater than his salary at Duff & Phelps. Jordan orally accepted, but Underwood would have allowed Jordan to withdraw his oral acceptance. On November 16, 1983, Jordan told Hansen, the chairman of Duff & Phelps's board, that he was going to resign and accept employment with Underwood. Jordan then delivered a letter of resignation, which Duff & Phelps accepted the same day. By mutual agreement, Jordan worked for Duff & Phelps the rest of the year, so that he could receive the book value of the stock as of December 31, 1983. (Under the Stock Restriction and Purchase Agreement, a departure before that date would have meant a valuation as of December 31, 1982.) Jordan delivered his stock certificates on December 30, 1983, and Duff & Phelps then mailed him a check for $23,225, the book value of the 188 shares of stock at $123.54 per share. Jordan surrendered, as worthless under the circumstances, the right to buy the 62 shares on which he had been making installment payments.

On January 10, 1984, a merger was announced between Duff & Phelps and a subsidiary of Security Pacific. Under the terms of the merger, Duff & Phelps was valued at $50 million. On November 16, the date on which Duff & Phelps's chairman, Hansen, had accepted Phelps's resignation, Hansen knew that negotiations for the merger were in process but hadn't disclosed that fact to Jordan. If Jordan had been a Duff & Phelps employee on January 10, had still held his 188 shares, had quickly paid for the additional 62 shares, and if the merger had closed that day, Jordan would have received $452,000 in cash and the opportunity to obtain as much as $194,000 more in an "earn out" (a percentage of Duff & Phelps's future profits to be paid to the former investors under the merger agreement), instead of the $23,225 he actually received. When Jordan learned these facts he demanded his stock back, but Duff & Phelps declined to return it. Jordan then sued Duff & Phelps, asking for damages measured by the value his stock would have had under the terms of the merger. The trial court granted summary judgement for Duff & Phelps. The Seventh Circuit reversed. Judge Easterbrook stated his reasons for reversal as follows:

> A jury could find that the information withheld on November 16 is "material". A jury also could find that December 30, rather than November 16, is the date of the "sale" of the stock. If December 30 is the date of sale, the information withheld then was "material" ... as a matter of law. By then the negotiating teams for Duff & Phelps and Security Pacific had negotiated the price and structure of the deal. So there are two linked materiality questions for the jury: whether the information withheld on November 16 was material, and whether the sale took place on November 16 or December 30.
>
> Duff & Phelps insists that nothing after November 16 matters.... Duff & Phelps treats the letter of resignation on November 16 as an irrevocable sale with deferred delivery. Yet if the "sale" occurred on November 16, then under the Agreement the stock would have been valued as of December 31, 1982. That Duff & Phelps valued the stock as of December 31, 1983, may persuade a jury that it treated the "sale" as made on that date. Moreover, Jordan insists that other employees were allowed to withdraw their resignations, and that he could have done so as late as December 31—if, say, his wife and his mother had reconciled.... The terms on which resignations may be withdrawn may be implicit parts of the relations between Duff & Phelps and its employees, and Jordan is entitled to an opportunity to demonstrate that he could have remained at the firm. If he can prove this, then December 30 rather than November 16 is the date on which the materiality of the firm's omissions must be assessed.
>
> All of this supposes that Duff & Phelps had a duty to disclose anything to Jordan. Most people are free to buy and sell stock on the basis of valuable private knowledge without informing their trading partners. Strangers transact in markets all the time using private information that might be called "material" and, unless one has a duty to disclose, both may keep their counsel.
>
> This argument is unavailing on the facts as we know them. The "duty" in question is the fiduciary duty of corporate law. Close corporations buying their own stock, like knowledgeable insiders of closely held firms buying from outsiders, have a fiduciary duty to disclose material facts....
>
> ... Jordan ... exercised choice about the date on which the formula would be triggered. He could have remained at Duff & Phelps; his decision to depart was affected by his wife's distress, his salary, his working conditions, the enjoyment he received from

the job, and the value of his stock. The departure of such an employee is an investment decision as much as it is an employment decision. It is not fanciful to suppose that Mrs. Jordan would have found her mother in law a whole lot more tolerable if she had known that Jordan's stock might shortly be worth 20 times book value.

... That [Jordan] took the value of stock into account is evident from the timing of his departure. A few thousand dollars' increase in book value led the Jordans to stay in Chicago an extra six weeks. How long would they have stayed for the prospect of another $620,000?

Our dissenting colleague concludes that all of this is beside the point because Hansen could have said, on receiving Jordan's letter on November 16: "In a few weeks we will pull off a merger that would have made your stock 20 times more valuable. It's a shame you so foolishly resigned. But even if you hadn't resigned, we would have fired you, the better to engross the profits of the merger for ourselves. So long, sucker." This would have been permissible, under our colleague's interpretation, because Jordan was an employee at will and therefore could have been fired at any time, even the day before the merger, for any reason—including the desire to deprive Jordan of a share of the profits. The ability to fire Jordan enabled the firm to "call" his shares, at book value, on whim. On this view, it is foolish to say that Duff & Phelps had a duty to disclose, because disclosure would have been no use to Jordan. (Perhaps this is really an argument about "causation" rather than "duty," but the terminology is unimportant.) But Duff & Phelps itself does not press this argument, and in civil litigation an appellate court ought not put words in a party's mouth and use them as the grounds on which to decide.... Perhaps Duff & Phelps does not want to establish a reputation for shoddy dealing; as our dissenting brother observes, a firm's desire to preserve its reputation is a powerful inducement to treat its contractual partners well. To attribute to a litigant an argument that it will take every possible advantage is to assume that the party wishes to dissipate its reputation, and the assumption is unwarranted.

More than that, a person's status as an employee "at will" does not imply that the employer may discharge him for every reason. Illinois, where Jordan was employed, has placed some limits on the discharge of at-will employees.... We do not disparage the utility of at-will contracts; this very panel recently recognized the value of informal (meaning not legally binding) employment relations.... But employment "at will" is still a contractual relation, one in which a particular duration (at will) is implied in the absence of a contrary expression. E. Allan Farnsworth, Contracts 532 n. 29 (1982). The silence of the parties may make it necessary to imply other terms—those we are confident the parties would have bargained for if they had signed a written agreement. One term implied in every written contract and therefore, we suppose, every unwritten one, is that neither party will try to take opportunistic advantage of the other. "[T]he fundamental function of contract law (and recognized as such at least since Hobbes's day) is to deter people from behaving opportunistically toward their contracting parties, in order to encourage the optimal timing of economic activity and to make costly self-protective measures unnecessary." . . .

Employment creates occasions for opportunism. A firm may fire an employee the day before his pension vests, or a salesman the day before a large commission becomes payable. Cases of this sort may present difficult questions about the reasons for the decision (was it opportunism, or was it a decline in the employee's performance?). The difficulties of separating opportunistic conduct from honest differences of opinion about an employee's performance on the job may lead firms and their employees to transact on terms that keep such disputes out of court—which employment at will usually does. But no one . . . doubts that an *avowedly* opportunistic discharge is a breach of contract, although the employment is at-will. . . . The element of good faith dealing implied in a contract "is not an enforceable legal duty to be nice or to behave decently in a general way." . . . It is not a version of the Golden Rule, to regard the interests of one's contracting partner the same way you regard your own. An employer may be thoughtless, nasty, and mistaken. Avowedly opportunistic conduct has been treated differently, however.

The stock component in Jordan's package induced him to stick around and work well. Such an inducement is effective only if the employee reaps the rewards of success as well as the penalties of failure. We do not suppose for a second that if Jordan had not resigned on November 16, the firm could have fired him on January 9 with a little note saying: "Dear Mr. Jordan: There will be a lucrative merger tomorrow. You have been a wonderful employee, but in order to keep the proceeds of the merger for ourselves, we are letting you go, effective this instant. Here is the $23,000 for your shares." Had the firm fired Jordan for this stated reason, it would have broken an implied pledge to avoid opportunistic conduct. It may well be that Duff & Phelps could have fired Jordan without the slightest judicial inquiry; it does not follow that an opportunistic discharge would have allowed Duff & Phelps to cash out the stock on the eve of its appreciation. . . . Jordan's employment at will, the essential ingredient of our colleague's argument that Jordan waived the duty to disclose, does not establish that the firm had no duties concerning the stock.*

* Accord: Castellano v. Young & Rubicam, Inc., 257 F.3d 171 (2d Cir. 2001) (footnote by ed.).

■ JUDGE CUDAHY concurred; JUDGE POSNER dissented.

NEMEC v. SHRADER, 991 A.2d 1120 (Del. 2010). [Joseph Nemec was a long-time director and senior officer of Booz Allen, a national consulting firm, until he retired in March 2006. Gerd Wittkemper was in a comparable position. At the time of their retirements, Nemec owned 76,000 Booz Allen shares, or about 2.6% of the outstanding shares, and Wittkemper owned 28,000 shares, or about 1% of the outstanding shares.

Booz Allen shares held by retired employees were subject to redemption (call) by Booz Allen, starting two years after the employee's retirement, at a price equal to the shares' book value. Accordingly, Nemec's and Wittkemper's shares became subject to redemption in March 2008. In October 2007, Booz Allen had begun negotiating the sale of one of its two business units to The Carlyle Group at a very favorable price. If the Carlyle transaction was consummated, it would add a very large amount to the book value of Booz Allen's shares. News of the reported transaction began circulating in January 2008. Thereafter, Booz Allen's CEO assured Nemec that allowing him to retain his shares until after the Carlyle deal closed was an "easy moral decision."

Morals apparently did not carry the day, because Booz Allen redeemed Nemec's and Wittkemper's shares in April 2008, when the Carlyle transaction had not been completed but was virtually assured of being completed. (It was completed three months later, at a price of $2.54 billion.) The book value of Booz Allen shares at the time of the redemption was about $162.46 per share. By excluding Nemec and Wittkemper from the fruits of the Carlyle transaction, nearly $60 million, or about $700 per share, was added to the proceeds received by Booz Allen's remaining shareholders.

Nemec and Wittkemper brought suit against Booz Allen and members of its board on the ground that the redemption was a breach of the implied covenant of good faith and fair dealing. The Delaware Supreme Court held for Booz Allen, three-to-two. The majority said:

> The implied covenant of good faith and fair dealing involves a "cautious enterprise," inferring contractual terms to handle developments or contractual gaps that the asserting party pleads neither party anticipated. "[O]ne generally cannot base a claim for breach of the implied covenant on conduct authorized by the agreement." [Dunlap v. State Farm & Cas. Co., 878 A.2d 434, 441 (Del. 2005)]. We will only imply contract terms when the party asserting the implied covenant proves that the other party has acted arbitrarily or unreasonably, thereby frustrating the fruits of the bargain that the asserting party reasonably expected. When conducting this analysis, we must assess the parties' reasonable expectations at the time of contracting and not rewrite the contract to appease a party who later wishes to rewrite a contract

he now believes to have been a bad deal. Parties have a right to enter into good and bad contracts, the law enforces both....

The Chancellor found no cognizable claim for a breach of the implied covenant because the Stock Plan explicitly authorized the redemption's price and timing, and Booz Allen, Nemec, and Wittkemper received exactly what they bargained for under the Stock Plan. The Chancellor wrote "[c]ontractually negotiated put and call rights are intended by both parties to be exercised at the time that is most advantageous to the party invoking the option."

No facts gleaned from the complaint suggest that anyone negotiating for the working stockholders would have made such a concession—nor does the complaint point to any reason they should have. Nothing except the absence of specific language contemplating a private equity, post retirement buyout supports a view that it can be inferred that had the parties to the Stock Plan specifically addressed the issue *at the time of contract,* they would have agreed to preclude the Company from exercising its redemption right before the Carlyle transaction closed. The implied covenant will not infer language that contradicts a clear exercise of an express contractual right. Our colleagues' thoughtful dissent suggests that we neglect to note that the challenged conduct (redeeming the retired stockholders shares) must "further *a legitimate interest of the party relying on the contract*" [emphasis supplied by the dissent]. The Company's directors, at the time of the decision to redeem owed fiduciary duties to the corporation and its stockholders. The redemption would not affect the Company directly. However, a failure to redeem the now retired stockholders' shares consistent with the Company's right under the stock plan would directly reduce the working stockholders' distribution by $60 million. If the Company's directors had not exercised the Company's absolute contractual right to redeem the retired stockholders shares, the working stockholders had a potential claim against the directors for favoring the retired stockholders to the detriment of the working stockholders.

The dissent stated:

A party does not act in bad faith (the majority argues) by relying on contract provisions for which that party bargained, even if the result is to eliminate advantages the counterparty would otherwise receive. That is a correct, but incomplete, statement of the law. To avoid running afoul of the implied covenant, the challenged conduct must also further a legitimate interest of the party acting in reliance on the contract. Stated differently, under Delaware case law, a contracting party, even where expressly empowered to act, can breach the implied covenant if it exercises that contractual power arbitrarily or unreasonably. Here, the complaint adequately alleges that the Company's redemption of the plaintiffs' shares prejudiced the plaintiffs while serving no legitimate interest of the Company. In those circumstances, therefore, the redemption would have been arbitrary and unreasonable, for which reason the complaint stated a cognizable claim for breach of the implied covenant. . . .

It is now settled Delaware law that a contracting party's exercise of a power in reliance on an explicit contractual provision may be deemed "arbitrary" or "unreasonable" where the other contracting party is thereby disadvantaged and no legitimate interest of the party exercising the right is furthered by doing so. *Dunlap v. State Farm Fire & Cas. Co.*, a case where this Court most recently addressed the implied covenant, stands squarely for that proposition.

In *Dunlap*, the plaintiff requested its excess liability insurer to approve a proposed agreement to settle with a primary insurer for an amount less than the underlying primary insurer's coverage limits. The excess insurer refused, relying on a contractual and statutory "exhaustion of primary insurance" requirement. Although the insurer had not improper motive for refusing to consent, this Court found it inferable from the complaint that the insurer's refusal to waive the exhaustion requirement was arbitrary and in breach of the implied covenant. The reasons were that the plaintiff's damages indisputably exceeded all available insurance benefits and a waiver would not have prejudiced the insurer. Here, Booz Allen—like the excess insurer in *Dunalp*—had an express contractual right. Here, as in *Dunlap*, the Company would have incurred no prejudice by forbearing to exercise that right until after the Carlyle closing. In these circumstances, Booz Allen's exercise of that right before closing, which resulted in material prejudice to the plaintiffs, invokes—and pleads a cognizable claim for breach of—the implied covenant. . . .

Because the majority concludes otherwise, we respectfully dissent.

SECTION 8. DISSOLUTION AND ASSOCIATED REMEDIES

A. DISSOLUTION FOR DEADLOCK

DEL. GEN. CORP. LAW §§ 273, 355

[See Statutory Supplement]

MODEL BUS. CORP. ACT §§ 14.30, 14.34

[See Statutory Supplement]

N.Y. BUS. CORP. LAW §§ 1002, 1104, 1111

[See Statutory Supplement]

Wollman v. Littman

New York Supreme Court, Appellate Div., First Dept., 1970.
35 A.D.2d 935, 316 N.Y.S.2d 526.

■ PER CURIAM . . .

The stock of the corporation is held, fifty percent each, by two distinct groups, one of which, the Nierenberg sisters, are plaintiffs, and the other, the Littmans, defendants, each group having equal representation on the board of directors. The corporation's business is the selling of artificial fur fabrics to garment manufacturers. Defendants, the Littmans, allegedly had the idea for the business and developed a market for the fabrics among its manufacturing customers. Plaintiffs are the daughters of Louis Nierenberg, the main stockholder of Louis Nierenberg, Inc., who procures the fabrics and sells them to the corporation. The Littmans, in a separate action in which they are plaintiffs, charge the plaintiffs here (the Nierenberg sisters) and Louis Nierenberg Corporation with seeking to lure away the corporation's customers for Louis Nierenberg Corporation and with doing various acts to affect the corporation's business adversely. The Nierenberg faction countered with this suit, claiming that the bringing of the other action indicates that the corporate management is at such odds among themselves that effective management is impossible. Special Term agreed, but we do not. Irreconcilable differences even among an evenly divided board of directors do not in all cases mandate dissolution.... Here, two factors would require further exploration. The first is that the functions of the two disputing interests are distinct, one selling and the other procuring, and each can pursue its own without need for collaboration. The second is that a dissolution which will render nugatory the relief sought in the representative action would actually accomplish the wrongful purpose that defendants (Nierenberg) are charged with in that action. It would not only squeeze the Littmans out of the business but would require the receiver to dispose of the inventory with the Nierenbergs the only interested purchaser financially strong enough to take advantage of the situation. Such a result, if supported by the facts, would be intolerable to a court of equity. A trial of the issues is necessitated. On that trial it has been agreed by both counsel it would be advantageous to have the representative action and the action for dissolution tried together, though not consolidated (for a discussion of the distinction, see the comprehensive opinion in Padilla v. Greyhound Lines, 29 A.D.2d 495, 288 N.Y.S.2d 641), and it is so directed.

We affirm the appointment of a receiver. His function, however, should be limited to the necessities indicated, namely, to the orderly functioning of the regular course of business of the corporation until the further order of the court.

NOTE ON DISSOLUTION FOR DEADLOCK

1. A number of statutes provide for involuntary dissolution on a showing of deadlock. A few of the statutes define deadlock in terms of an equally divided board or body of shareholders, but most are phrased broadly enough to include deadlock brought about by super-majority or veto arrangements.

2. The deadlock statutes are generally interpreted to make dissolution discretionary even when deadlock is shown to exist, and especially in the past, the courts have often been reluctant to order dissolution of a profitable corporation on the ground of deadlock. However, profitability is not a bar to dissolution for deadlock. In Weiss v. Gordon, 32 A.D.2d 279, 301 N.Y.S.2d 839 (1969), the court stated, "The earlier thinking stressed the distinction between the corporation as an entity and the shareholders, and as long as the former could continue to function profitably the relationship between the shareholders was of no moment (cf. Matter of Radom & Neidorff, Inc., 307 N.Y. 1, 119 N.E.2d 563 (1954)). It is being increasingly realized that the relationship between the stockholders in a close corporation vis-a-vis each other in practice closely approximates the relationship between partners (see Mtr. of Surchin v. Approved Bus. Mach., 55 Misc.2d 888, 890, 286 N.Y.S.2d 580, 583 (1967)). As a consequence, when a point is reached where the shareholders who are actively conducting the business of the corporation cannot agree, it becomes in the best interests of those shareholders to order a dissolution. . . ."

B. DISSOLUTION FOR OPPRESSION AND MANDATORY BUY-OUT

MODEL BUS. CORP. ACT § 14.30, 14.34

[See Statutory Supplement]

CAL. CORP. CODE §§ 1800, 1804, 2000

[See Statutory Supplement]

N.Y. BUS. CORP. LAW §§ 1104–A, 1111, 1118

[See Statutory Supplement]

NOTE ON HETHERINGTON AND DOOLEY

At one time, courts were extremely reluctant to order the involuntary dissolution of a profitable business, on the ground that it was bad social policy to break up such a business. In 1977, John Hetherington and Michael Dooley published a celebrated article on this problem, Illiquidity and Exploitation: A Proposed Statutory Solution to the Remaining Close Corporation Problem, 63 Va.L.Rev. 1 (1977). In this article, the authors pointed out that a judicial order to dissolve a corporation was unlikely to lead to the breakup of a profitable business. The reason is that if it is advantageous to continue a business, then after dissolution is ordered, normally either one or more of the shareholders or a third party would purchase and continue the business. Hetherington & Dooley backed up this point with empirical data by analyzing the fifty-four reported involuntary dissolution cases decided between 1960 and 1976. In half of the fifty-four cases, the plaintiff had been successful; in the other half, unsuccessful. Of the twenty-seven cases in which the plaintiff had been successful, the corporation's business was actually liquidated in only six. In seventeen cases, one party bought out the other. In three cases, the business was sold to an outsider. In one case, there was no buyout or other change. Of the twenty-seven cases in which plaintiff was unsuccessful, in fourteen cases one party bought out the other; in six cases there was no change in ownership; in two cases the business was sold to a third party; in three cases, the business was liquidated; and in two cases, the result was unknown.

Furthermore, Hetherington & Dooley pointed out, dissolution, or something like it, was a central remedy for disaffected shareholders in close corporations because given the limits of reasonable foreseeability, shareholders who organized such corporations could not possibly plan in advance to deal with all the interpersonal problems that might occur between them. Therefore, Hetherington & Dooley concluded, in the case of a close corporation a remedy comparable to, but stronger than, dissolution—specifically, free exit through a mandatory buyout of the minority's interest on the minority's demand—should be available.

> The emphasis on contractual arrangements [in close corporations] reveals a fundamental misunderstanding of the nature of close corporations. Whether the parties adopt special contractual arrangements is much less important than their ability to sustain a close, harmonious relationship over time. The continuance of such a relationship is crucial because it reflects what is perhaps the fundamental assumption made by those who decide to invest in a close corporation: they expect that during the life of the firm

the shareholders will be in substantial agreement as to its operation.

Time and human nature may cause a divergence of interests and a breakdown in consensus, however. . . .

Our thesis is that the problem of exploitation is uniquely related to liquidity and, for that reason, it is resistant to solution by ex ante contractual arrangements or by ex post judicial relief for breach of fiduciary duty. Accordingly, we [propose that the law should require] the majority to repurchase the minority's interest at the request of the latter and subject to appropriate safeguards.

The insights and empirical data in the Hetherington & Dooley article form a backdrop to the materials in this section.

Matter of Kemp & Beatley, Inc.

Court of Appeals of New York, 1984.
64 N.Y.2d 63, 484 N.Y.S.2d 799, 473 N.E.2d 1173.

■ COOKE, CHIEF JUDGE. . . .

I

The business concern of Kemp & Beatley, incorporated under the laws of New York, designs and manufactures table linens and sundry tabletop items. The company's stock consists of 1,500 outstanding shares held by eight shareholders. Petitioner Dissin had been employed by the company for 42 years when, in June 1979, he resigned. Prior to resignation, Dissin served as vice-president and a director of Kemp & Beatley. Over the course of his employment, Dissin had acquired stock in the company and currently owns 200 shares.

Petitioner Gardstein, like Dissin, had been a long-time employee of the company. Hired in 1944, Gardstein was for the next 35 years involved in various aspects of the business including material procurement, product design, and plant management. His employment was terminated by the company in December 1980. He currently owns 105 shares of Kemp & Beatley stock.

Apparent unhappiness surrounded petitioners' leaving the employ of the company. Of particular concern was that they no longer received any distribution of the company's earnings. Petitioners considered themselves to be "frozen out" of the company; whereas it had been their experience when with the company to receive a distribution of the company's earnings according to their stockholdings, in the form of either dividends or extra compensation, that distribution was no longer forthcoming.

Gardstein and Dissin, together holding 20.33% of the company's outstanding stock, commenced the instant proceeding in June 1981, seeking dissolution of Kemp & Beatley pursuant to section 1104–a of the Business Corporation Law. Their petition alleged "fraudulent and oppressive" conduct by the company's board of directors such as to render petitioners' stock "a virtually worthless asset." Supreme Court referred the matter for a hearing, which was held in March 1982.

Upon considering the testimony of petitioners and the principals of Kemp & Beatley, the referee concluded that "the corporate management has by its policies effectively rendered petitioners' shares worthless, and ... the only way petitioners can expect any return is by dissolution". Petitioners were found to have invested capital in the company expecting, among other things, to receive dividends or "bonuses" based upon their stock holdings. Also found was the company's "established buyout policy" by which it would purchase the stock of employee shareholders upon their leaving its employ.

The involuntary-dissolution statute (Business Corporation Law, § 1104–a) permits dissolution when a corporation's controlling faction is found guilty of "oppressive action" toward the complaining shareholders. The referee considered oppression to arise when "those in control" of the corporation "have acted in such a manner as to defeat those expectations of the minority stockholders which formed the basis of [their] participation in the venture." The expectations of petitioners that they would not be arbitrarily excluded from gaining a return on their investment and that their stock would be purchased by the corporation upon termination of employment, were deemed defeated by prevailing corporate policies. Dissolution was recommended in the referee's report, subject to giving respondent corporation an opportunity to purchase petitioners' stock.

Supreme Court confirmed the referee's report. It, too, concluded that due to the corporation's new dividend policy petitioners had been prevented from receiving any return on their investments. Liquidation of the corporate assets was found the only means by which petitioners would receive a fair return. The court considered judicial dissolution of a corporation to be "a serious and severe remedy." Consequently, the order of dissolution was conditioned upon the corporation's being permitted to purchase petitioners' stock. The Appellate Division affirmed, without opinion. 99 A.D.2d 445, 471 N.Y.S.2d 245.

At issue in this appeal is the scope of section 1104–a of the Business Corporation Law. Specifically, this court must determine whether the provision for involuntary dissolution when the "directors or those in control of the corporation have been guilty of ... oppressive actions toward the complaining shareholders" was properly applied in the circumstances of this case. We hold that it was, and therefore affirm.

II

Judicially ordered dissolution of a corporation at the behest of minority interests is a remedy of relatively recent vintage in New York. Historically, this State's courts were considered divested of equity jurisdiction to order dissolution, as statutory prescriptions were deemed exclusive (see Hitch v. Hawley, 132 N.Y. 212, 217, 30 N.E. 401)....

... [T]he Legislature has shown a special solicitude toward the rights of minority shareholders of closely held corporations by enacting section 1104–a of the Business Corporation Law. That statute provides a mechanism for the holders of at least 20% of the outstanding shares of a corporation whose stock is not traded on a securities market to petition for its dissolution "under special circumstances" (see Business Corporation Law, § 1104–a, subd. [a]). The circumstances that give rise to dissolution fall into two general classifications: mistreatment of complaining shareholders (subd. [a], par. [1]), or misappropriation of corporate assets (subd. [a], par. [2]) by controlling shareholders, directors or officers.

Section 1104–a (subd. [a], par. [1]) describes three types of proscribed activity: "illegal", "fraudulent", and "oppressive" conduct. The first two terms are familiar words that are commonly understood at law. The last, however, does not enjoy the same certainty gained through long usage. As no definition is provided by the statute, it falls upon the courts to provide guidance (see Goncalves v. Regent Int. Hotels, 58 N.Y.2d 206, 218, 460 N.Y.S.2d 750, 447 N.E.2d 693).

The statutory concept of "oppressive actions" can, perhaps, best be understood by examining the characteristics of close corporations and the Legislature's general purpose in creating this involuntary-dissolution statute. It is widely understood that, in addition to supplying capital to a contemplated or ongoing enterprise and expecting a fair and equal return, parties comprising the ownership of a close corporation may expect to be actively involved in its management and operation.... The small ownership cluster seeks to "contribute their capital, skills, experience and labor" toward the corporate enterprise....

As a leading commentator in the field has observed: "Unlike the typical shareholder in a publicly held corporation, who may be simply an investor or a speculator and cares nothing for the responsibilities of management, the shareholder in a close corporation is a co-owner of the business and wants the privileges and powers that go with ownership. His participation in that particular corporation is often his principal or sole source of income. As a matter of fact, providing employment for himself may have been the principal reason why he participated in organizing the corporation. He may or may not anticipate an ultimate profit from the sale of his interest, but he normally draws very little from the corporation as dividends. In his capacity as an officer or employee of the corporation, he looks to his salary for the principal return on his capital investment, because earnings of a close corporation, as is well known, are distributed in major part in salaries, bonuses and retirement benefits." (O'Neal, Close Corporations [2d ed.], § 1.07, at pp. 21–22 [n. omitted].)

Shareholders enjoy flexibility in memorializing these expectations through agreements setting forth each party's rights and obligations in corporate governance (see, generally, Kessler, Shareholder–Managed

Close Corporation Under the New York Business Corporation Law, 43 Fordham L.Rev. 197; Davidian, op. cit., 56 St. John's L.Rev. 24, 29–30, and nn. 21–22). In the absence of such an agreement, however, ultimate decision-making power respecting corporate policy will be reposed in the holders of a majority interest in the corporation (see, e.g., Business Corporation Law, §§ 614, 708). A wielding of this power by any group controlling a corporation may serve to destroy a stockholder's vital interests and expectations.

As the stock of closely held corporations generally is not readily salable, a minority shareholder at odds with management policies may be without either a voice in protecting his or her interests or any reasonable means of withdrawing his or her investment. This predicament may fairly be considered the legislative concern underlying the provision at issue in this case; inclusion of the criteria that the corporation's stock not be traded on securities markets and that the complaining shareholder be subject to oppressive actions supports this conclusion.

Defining oppressive conduct as distinct from illegality in the present context has been considered in other forums. The question has been resolved by considering oppressive actions to refer to conduct that substantially defeats the "reasonable expectations" held by minority shareholders in committing their capital to the particular enterprise (see, e.g., Mardikos v. Arger, 116 Misc.2d 1028, 457 N.Y.S.2d 371; Matter of Barry One Hour Photo Process, 111 Misc.2d 559, 444 N.Y.S.2d 540....) This concept is consistent with the apparent purpose underlying the provision under review. A shareholder who reasonably expected that ownership in the corporation would entitle him or her to a job, a share of corporate earnings, a place in corporate management, or some other form of security, would be oppressed in a very real sense when others in the corporation seek to defeat those expectations and there exists no effective means of salvaging the investment.

Given the nature of close corporations and the remedial purpose of the statute, this court holds that utilizing a complaining shareholder's "reasonable expectations" as a means of identifying and measuring conduct alleged to be oppressive is appropriate. A court considering a petition alleging oppressive conduct must investigate what the majority shareholders knew, or should have known, to be the petitioner's expectations in entering the particular enterprise. Majority conduct should not be deemed oppressive simply because the petitioner's subjective hopes and desires in joining the venture are not fulfilled. Disappointment alone should not necessarily be equated with oppression.

Rather, oppression should be deemed to arise only when the majority conduct substantially defeats expectations that, objectively viewed, were both reasonable under the circumstances and were central to the petitioner's decision to join the venture. It would be inappropriate, however, for us in this case to delineate the contours of the courts' consideration in determining whether directors have been guilty of oppressive conduct. As in other areas of the law, much will depend on the circumstances in the individual case.

The appropriateness of an order of dissolution is in every case vested in the sound discretion of the court considering the application (see Business Corporation Law, § 1111, subd. [a]). Under the terms of this statute, courts are instructed to consider both whether "liquidation of the corporation is the only feasible means" to protect the complaining shareholder's expectation of a fair return on his or her investment and whether dissolution "is reasonably necessary" to protect "the rights or interests of any substantial number of shareholders" not limited to those complaining (Business Corporation Law, § 1104–a, subd. [b], pars. [1], [2]). Implicit in this direction is that once oppressive conduct is found, consideration must be given to the totality of circumstances surrounding the current state of corporate affairs and relations to determine whether some remedy short of or other than dissolution, constitutes a feasible means of satisfying both the petitioner's expectations and the rights and interests of any other substantial group of shareholders (see, also, Business Corporation Law, § 1111, subd. [b], par. [1]).

By invoking the statute, a petitioner has manifested his or her belief that dissolution may be the only appropriate remedy. Assuming the petitioner has set forth a prima facie case of oppressive conduct, it should be incumbent upon the parties seeking to forestall dissolution to demonstrate to the court the existence of an adequate, alternative remedy (cf. Baker v. Commercial Body Bldrs., 264 Or. 614, 507 P.2d 387, supra; White v. Perkins, 213 Va. 129, 189 S.E.2d 315). A court has broad latitude in fashioning alternative relief, but when fulfillment of the oppressed petitioner's expectations by these means is doubtful, such as when there has been a complete deterioration of relations between the parties, a court should not hesitate to order dissolution. Every order of dissolution, however, must be conditioned upon permitting any shareholder of the corporation to elect to purchase the complaining shareholder's stock at fair value (see Business Corporation Law, § 1118).

One further observation is in order. The purpose of this involuntary dissolution statute is to provide protection to the minority shareholder whose reasonable expectations in undertaking the venture have been frustrated and who has no adequate means of recovering his or her investment. It would be contrary to this remedial purpose to permit its use by minority shareholders as merely a coercive tool (see Davidian, op. cit., 56 St. John's L.Rev. 24, 59–60, and nn. 159–160). Therefore, the minority shareholder whose own acts, made in bad faith and undertaken with a view toward forcing an involuntary dissolution, give rise to the complained-of oppression should be given no quarter in the statutory protection (cf. Mardikos v. Arger, 116 Misc.2d 1028, 1032, 457 N.Y.S.2d 371, supra).

III

There was sufficient evidence presented at the hearing to support the conclusion that Kemp & Beatley had a long-standing policy of awarding *de facto* dividends based on stock ownership in the form of "extra compensation bonuses." Petitioners, both of whom had extensive experience in the management of the company, testified to this effect. Moreover, both related that receipt of this compensation, whether as true dividends or disguised as "extra compensation", was a known incident to ownership of the company's stock understood by all of the company's principals. Finally, there was uncontroverted proof that this policy was changed either shortly before or shortly after petitioners' employment ended. Extra compensation was still awarded by the company. The only difference was that stock ownership was no longer a basis for the payments; it was asserted that the basis became services rendered to the corporation. It was not unreasonable for the fact finder to have determined that this change in policy amounted to nothing less than an attempt to exclude petitioners from gaining any return on their investment through the mere recharacterization of distributions of corporate income. Under the circumstances of this case, there was no error in determining that this conduct constituted oppressive action within the meaning of section 1104–a of the Business Corporation Law.

Nor may it be said that Supreme Court abused its discretion in ordering Kemp & Beatley's dissolution, subject to an opportunity for a buy-out of petitioners' shares. After the referee had found that the controlling faction of the company was, in effect, attempting to "squeeze-out" petitioners by offering them no return on their investment and increasing other executive compensation, respondents, in opposing the report's confirmation, attempted only to controvert the factual basis of the report. They suggested no feasible, alternative remedy to the forced dissolution. In light of an apparent deterioration in relations between petitioners and the governing shareholders of Kemp & Beatley, it was not unreasonable for the court to have determined that a forced buy-out of petitioners' shares or liquidation of the corporation's assets was the only means by which petitioners could be guaranteed a fair return on their investments.

Accordingly, the order of the Appellate Division should be modified, with costs to petitioners-respondents, by affirming the substantive determination of that court but extending the time for exercising the option to purchase petitioners-respondents' shares to 30 days following this court's determination.

■ JASEN, JONES, WACHTLER, MEYER and SIMONS, JJ., concur.

■ KAYE, J., taking no part.

Order modified, with costs to petitioners-respondents, in accordance with the opinion herein and, as so modified, affirmed.

MEISELMAN v. MEISELMAN, 309 N.C. 279, 307 S.E.2d 551 (1983). "Professor O'Neal, perhaps the foremost authority on close corporations, points out that many close corporations are companies based on personal relationships that give rise to certain 'reasonable expectations' on the part of those acquiring an interest in the close corporation. Those 'reasonable expectations' include, for example, the parties' expectation that they will participate in the management of the business or be employed by the company. O'Neal, *Close Corporations: Existing Legislation and Recommended Reform,* 33 Bus.Law 873, 885 (1978)....

"Thus, when personal relations among the participants in a close corporation break down, the 'reasonable expectations' the participants had, for example, an expectation that their employment would be secure, or that they would enjoy meaningful participation in the management of the business—become difficult if not impossible to fulfill. In other words, when the personal relationships among the participants break down, the majority shareholder, because of his greater voting power, is in a position to terminate the minority shareholder's employment and to exclude him from participation in management decisions.

"Some may argue that the minority shareholder should have bargained for greater protection before agreeing to accept his minority shareholder position in a close corporation. However, the practical realities of this particular business situation oftentimes do not allow for such negotiations....

"Apparently in response to these commentators' uniform calls for reform in this area of corporate law, many state legislatures have enacted statutes giving the tribunals in their states the power to grant relief to minority shareholders under more liberal circumstances....

"In helping to establish this growing trend toward enactment of more liberal grounds under which dissolution will be granted to a complaining shareholder, the legislature in this State enacted in 1955 N.C.G.S. § 55–125(a)(4), the statute granting superior court judges the 'power to liquidate the assets and business of a corporation in an action by a shareholder when it is established' that '[l]iquidation is reasonably necessary for the protection of the rights or interests of the complaining shareholder.' ...

"[B]efore it can be determined whether, in any given case, it has been 'established' that liquidation is 'reasonably necessary' to protect the complaining shareholder's 'rights or interest,' the particular 'rights or interests' of the complaining shareholder must be articulated. This is so because N.C.G.S. § 55–125(a)(4) refers to the 'rights or interests' of '*the complaining shareholder*'; the statute does not refer to the 'rights or interests' of shareholders generally.... [W]e hold that a complaining shareholder's 'rights or interests' in a close corporation include the 'reasonable expectations' the complaining shareholder has in the corporation. These 'reasonable expectations' are to be ascertained by examining the entire history of the participants' relationship. That history will include the 'reasonable expectations' created at the inception of the participants' relationship; those 'reasonable expectations' as altered over time; and the 'reasonable expectations' which develop as the participants engage in a course of dealing in conducting the affairs of the corporation. The interests and views of the other participants must be considered in determining 'reasonable expectations.' The key is '*reasonable.*' In order for plaintiff's expectations to be reasonable, they must be known to or assumed by the other shareholders and concurred in by them. Privately held expectations which are not made known to the other participants are not 'reasonable.' Only expectations embodied in understandings, express or implied, among the participants should be recognized by the court....

"Defendants argue, however, that ... [a shareholder] is only entitled to relief if his traditional shareholder rights have been infringed. They contend that those traditional shareholder rights include the right to notice of stockholders' meetings, the right to vote cumulatively, the right of access to the corporate offices and to corporate financial information, and the right to compel the payment of dividends....

"While it may be true that a shareholder in, for example, a publicly held corporation may have 'rights or interests' defined as defendants argue, a shareholder's rights in a closely held corporation may not necessarily be so narrowly defined...."

NOTE ON EVOLVING EXPECTATIONS

In *Meiselman,* the court stated that what constitutes a shareholder's reasonable expectations can change over time. An example is A.W. Chesterton Co. v. Chesterton, 128 F.3d 1 (1st Cir.1997). A.W. Chesterton Company had been closely held since 1885. In 1985, all of Chesterton Company's shareholders, including Arthur Chesterton, agreed to change Chesterton Company's tax status from a C corporation to an S corporation, a change that carried favorable tax treatment. In the early 1990s, Arthur proposed to transfer some of his Chesterton Company stock to two shell corporations that he wholly owned. This transfer would have resulted in the loss of Chesterton Company's favorable tax treatment, because to qualify as an S Corporation a corporation may not have any corporate shareholders. The remaining shareholders and Chesterton Company sued Arthur. Therefore, Arthur Chesterton's proposed transfer would have resulted in a loss of the corporation's favorable tax treatment under Subchapter S and the remaining shareholders and the corporation sued Arthur to enjoin the proposed transfer. The First Circuit granted the injunction. "Under Massachusetts law, the expectations and understanding of the shareholders are relevant to a breach of fiduciary duty determination ... The existence of the [1985] agreement ... sheds light on the Company's and other shareholders' expectations...." See also, e.g., Spurgeon Foster v. Foster Farms, 112 N.C.App. 700, 436 S.E.2d 843 (1993).

THOMPSON, THE SHAREHOLDER'S CAUSE OF ACTION FOR OPPRESSION, 48 Bus.Law. 699, 709–12, 715–716 (1993). "Oppression as a ground for dissolution was included in the Illinois and Pennsylvania corporations acts in 1933, in the first Model Business Corporation Act in 1946, and in the English Companies Act of 1948. Thirty-seven American states now include oppression or a similar term in their corporations statutes. . . ."

HAYNSWORTH, THE EFFECTIVENESS OF INVOLUNTARY DISSOLUTION SUITS AS A REMEDY FOR CLOSE CORPORATION DISSENSION, 35 Clev.St. L.Rev. 25 (1987). "In recent years courts have increasingly focused on developing the concept of oppression, and proof of oppressive conduct is rapidly becoming the most likely avenue for minority shareholder relief in close corporations. Three definitions of oppression have been used in the cases.

"The first, drawn from English case law is:

> burdensome, harsh and wrongful conduct . . . a lack of probity and fair dealing in the affairs of a company to the prejudice of some portion of its members; or a visual departure from the standards of fair dealing, and a violation of fair play on which every shareholder who entrusts his money to a company is entitled to rely.

Under this definition, oppression is basically a breach of the general fiduciary duty of good faith and fair dealing that majority shareholders in a corporation owe to the minority shareholders.

"The second definition, first enunciated in the now famous case of *Donahue v. Rodd Electrotype Company of New England, Inc.*, is conduct that constitutes a violation of the strict fiduciary duty of 'utmost good faith and loyalty' owed by partners *inter se.* This standard, which is based on the analogy of close corporation shareholders who are active in management to general partners in a partnership, is theoretically higher than the 'good faith and inherent fairness' standard normally applicable in a corporation.

"The third definition of oppression, initially derived from English case law, and long advocated by Dean F. Hodge O'Neal as well as other leading close corporation experts, is conduct which frustrates the reasonable expectations of the investors. The reasonable expectations doctrine has been gaining wide acceptance in the past few years. Decisions in at least eight states have explicitly adopted this concept, and decisions in at least nine additional states have implicitly recognized it. The approval of the reasonable expectations doctrine by the New York Court of Appeals in the 1984 case of *In re Kemp & Beatley, Inc.* is quite significant and will undoubtedly influence other courts."

NOTE ON THE DUTIES OF CARE AND LOYALTY IN CLOSE CORPORATIONS

Two legal bulwarks for minority shareholders in publicly held corporations are the duties of care and loyalty imposed by law on corporate directors and officers. These duties are extremely complex in their details, and are the subject of Chapters 10 and 11. To oversimplify somewhat, the duty of care may render a director or officer liable for certain types of managerial negligence, and the duty of loyalty may render a director or officer liable for unfair self-interested transactions with the corporation or for other types of improper self-interested conduct. However, under the business judgment rule, a decision by a director or officer will not subject her to liability for violation of the duty of care even if the decision was unreasonable, provided the decision was made in good faith, the director or officer was not self-interested, the director or officer properly informed herself before making the decision, and the decision was not so unreasonable as to be irrational. Under the duty of loyalty, a self-interested transaction will not subject a director or officer to liability if she made full disclosure and the transaction was objectively fair.

The duties of care and loyalty protect minority shareholders in close as well as publicly held corporations, but these duties often provide insufficient protection in close corporations. For example, the discharge of a minority shareholder from corporate office might qualify for protection under the business judgment rule, and a purchase of stock from majority shareholders might not violate the duty of loyalty if the price paid for the stock was fair. The real vice of such actions lies in the fact that they treat shareholders unequally, defeat legitimate expectations of a sort found in closely but not publicly held corporations, or both. Accordingly, the "reasonable expectations" analysis that is made explicit in cases like Meiselman v. Meiselman, that is implicit in cases like Donahue v. Rodd, and that in part underlies the concept of dissolution for oppression, fills a major gap in corporate law for closely held corporations. It would be a mistake, however, to believe that analysis based on reasonable expectations can be separated from the concept of fairness. One way in which a court determines whether reasonable expectations of minority shareholders have been defeated by majority shareholders is by asking itself what similarly situated shareholders would have probably expected. Often the only way to answer that question is to ask what similarly situated shareholders would have regarded as fair.

MICH. COMP. LAWS § 450.1489

[See Statutory Supplement]

MINN. STAT. ANN. § 302A.751

[See Statutory Supplement]

McCallum v. Rosen's Diversified, Inc.

United States Court of Appeals, Eighth Circuit, 1998.
153 F.3d 701.

■ Before BEAM, ROSS, and MAGILL, CIRCUIT JUDGES.

■ BEAM, CIRCUIT JUDGE.

William B. McCallum, a minority shareholder in Rosen's Diversified, Inc. (RDI), appeals from two adverse grants of summary judgment. McCallum seeks to have his shares in RDI redeemed for fair value pursuant to a court ordered buy-out. The district court held that McCallum failed to present evidence showing that RDI acted unfairly prejudicial toward him. We reverse and remand for a determination of the fair value of McCallum's shares.

I. BACKGROUND

This case involves a contentious dispute between the minority and controlling shareholders of a closely held Minnesota corporation. Two brothers, Elmer and Ludwig Rosen, founded RDI as a livestock trading business in the late 1940's. Today, RDI has grown into a thriving company, primarily engaged in meat packing and other agricultural businesses. In 1992, RDI had more than $400 million in sales. Members of the Rosen family own a majority of RDI's outstanding capital stock.

In January 1984, RDI hired McCallum, who had previously provided legal services to the company, as Executive Vice President and Chief Executive Officer (CEO). He was named a director in 1986. RDI performed well under McCallum's command. Accordingly, RDI rewarded McCallum—and three other key employees—with a bonus of $186,815 in cash and 12,000 shares of common stock in the company.[2] According to RDI, these payments were made because the key employees were almost entirely responsible for the financial success of the corporation, because the compensation package of the employees had been artificially low, and in order to maintain the unswerving loyalty of these employees. The parties did not enter into a shareholder's agreement or provide any mechanism for the transfer of those shares if circumstances changed.

By 1991, the amiable relationship between McCallum and RDI deteriorated, ultimately resulting in McCallum's termination and removal from the board. Subsequently, McCallum proposed that RDI redeem his shares for $5 million. RDI responded with an offer to

---

2. During the course of his employment, McCallum also received approximately 3,300 shares of common stock in RDI through an Employee Stock Ownership Program (ESOP). McCallum's total ownership represented nearly 3% of the company's capital stock.

redeem the shares for $600,000, which was at a small premium over the value determined by the annual valuation for RDI's Employee Stock Ownership Program (ESOP). The parties could not agree on a price and extensive litigation has followed.... The present case involves McCallum's 12,000 shares of RDI common stock which is not contained in the ESOP.

McCallum alleges that RDI's controlling shareholders have acted unfairly prejudicial toward him because they: (1) undermined his authority as CEO; (2) excluded him from important company decisions; (3) engaged in conduct directed at minimizing the value of the company; (4) terminated his employment; (5) offered to redeem his shares at an artificially low price; (6) denied him access to company books, records, and financial information; (7) engaged in self-dealing, usurped company opportunities, and commingled personal ventures with the affairs of the company.

The district court dismissed many of McCallum's allegations as improperly pleaded derivative claims. The district court dismissed McCallum's request for a buyout of his stock on a subsequent motion for summary judgment. McCallum appeals.

II. DISCUSSION ...

Concerned with the vulnerable position of minority shareholders in closely held corporations, the Minnesota legislature has provided the courts with broad equitable authority to protect the interests of minority shareholders. See Minn.Stat. § 302A.751 (amended 1994) (hereinafter "Section 751"). Section 751 provides for the buy-out of a minority shareholder's interest when "the directors or those in control of the corporation have acted in a manner unfairly prejudicial toward one or more shareholders in their capacities as shareholders or directors ... or as officers or employees of a closely held corporation."

The phrase "unfairly prejudicial" is to be interpreted liberally. See *Pedro v. Pedro*, 463 N.W.2d 285, 288–89 (Minn.Ct.App.1990). One commentator, who helped draft certain revisions to the Minnesota Business Corporation Act and Section 751, stated that:

> The section is remedial in nature and should be liberally construed as an addition to the rights afforded non-controlling shareholders by law and the corporation's governing documents. The broad scope of Section 751 reflects the Legislature's trust in the ability of the judiciary to achieve equitable results on the facts appearing in individual cases.

See Joseph Edward Olson, Statutory Changes Improve Position of Minority Shareholders in Closely Held Corporations, *The Hennepin Lawyer*, Sept.–Oct.1983, at 11. In deciding whether to order a buy-out, the courts should consider "the reasonable expectations of the shareholders" with respect to each other and the corporation. See Minn. Stat. § 302A.751, subd. 3a (amended 1994). Oftentimes, a shareholder's reasonable expectations include a significant voice in management and an opportunity to work. See Olson at 23.

We find that the uncontested facts demonstrate that McCallum's reasonable expectations were defeated. RDI terminated McCallum's employment as CEO and subsequently offered to purchase his RDI shares at a small premium over the value determined by an annual valuation for RDI's ESOP. McCallum had received these shares as compensation for his outstanding service and as an inducement to remain at RDI, in order to foster its continued growth. Although the employment relationship later deteriorated, our focus is on McCallum's reasonable expectations at the inception of the relationship. See Minn.Stat. § 302A.751, subd. 3a.

On his termination, McCallum was divested of his primary expectations as a minority shareholder in RDI—an active role in the "management of the corporation and input as an employee." Pedro, 463 N.W.2d at 289. This expectation was particularly reasonable since McCallum was CEO of RDI. We need not extend our holding as far as the Minnesota Court of Appeals, which held that controlling shareholders that terminate the employment of a minority shareholder must make a good-faith effort to buy out the shareholder at a fair price. See *Sawyer v. Curt & Co.*, 1991 WL 65320, at *2 (Minn.Ct.App. Feb.12, 1991) (publication order vacated). We simply hold that terminating the CEO—as opposed to an employee that did not have a significant role in management—and then offering to redeem his stock, which was issued partially to lure him to remain at the company, constituted conduct toward McCallum as a shareholder sufficient to invoke the requirements of the Minnesota Act. Accordingly, we remand the matter for a determination of the fair value of his stock.

On remand, the district court shall determine the fair value of McCallum's shares in accordance with Minn.Stat. § 302A.751, subd. 2 (amended 1994) and put an end to this pugnacious litigation. We express no opinion on the fair value of McCallum's shares or whether the ESOP valuation represents fair value.

III. CONCLUSION

For the foregoing reasons, we reverse the judgment of the district court and remand for further proceedings consistent with this opinion.

MUELLENBERG v. BIKON CORP., 143 N.J. 168, 669 A.2d 1382 (1996). Bikon Corporation was owned by Muellenberg, Passerini, and Burg. Muellenberg and Passerini were the majority shareholders. Burg, the minority shareholder, was Bikon's general manager. Burg sued Muellenberg and Passerini on the ground of oppression. The court held that Burg had been oppressed and gave him the right to buy out the majority shareholders:

The statute ... plainly allows the minority to seek a court order for the sale of the stock of "any other shareholder." In most situations, oppressed minority shareholders will lack the resources to buy out the interests of controlling shareholders. As a result, claims of oppression are typically remedied by arranging for the corporation or the majority shareholders to buy out the interests of the minority shareholder. In this case, the record contained the following evidence in support of Burg: Burg was willing and able to purchase the shares of Muellenberg and Passerini; Burg, who owns the land on which BNJ's offices are located, was most active in operating the company since its inception; Burg is the only shareholder who works full-time for BNJ and the company has been his only source of income for over ten years; Burg was primarily responsible for developing the company's contacts in the United States and Canada and is best situated to maintain the existing operation; and finally, it was Burg who sought to preserve the corporation at a time when Muellenberg and Passerini attempted to dissolve it....

Thus, while a minority buy-out of the majority is an uncommon remedy, it was the appropriate one here.... This remedy is authorized by N.J.S.A. 14A:12–7(8) and is consistent with decisions holding that courts are not limited to statutory remedies, but have a wide variety of equitable remedies also available to them. *Brenner,* ... 134 N.J. at 516....

KELLEY v. AXELSSON, 687 A.2d 268 (N.J.Super. 1997), "[M]aintaining an accounting system whose shortcomings have the effect of substantially preventing the outside, minority shareholders from ascertaining and verifying the corporation's income [can] constitute unfairness and oppression toward the minority shareholders, entitling them to relief under [the dissolution-for-oppression statute]."

Haynsworth, The Effectiveness of Involuntary Dissolution Suits as a Remedy for Close Corporation Dissension

35 Cleve.St.L.Rev. 25 (1987).

What results actually occur in close corporation involuntary dissolution suits? One way to answer this question is to examine existing published opinions. For the purposes of this article, the opinions published in 1984 and 1985 in which involuntary dissolution was one of the major causes of action were analyzed....

... [A] total of forty-seven cases ... qualified for the sample [but ten of the cases involved technical legal issues in which no decision on the type of relief, if any, had been made at the time the opinion was issued].

Of the remaining thirty-seven cases, a buy-out was the most frequent relief ordered by the court or elected by the defendants. This result occurred in twenty of the decisions (fifty-four percent). Dissolution was ordered in ten of the cases (twenty-seven percent). In four of the cases (eleven percent), no substantial relief was granted to the plaintiff on the merits. Finally, in the three other cases (eight percent) relief other than either dissolution or a buy-out was the exclusive remedy ordered. . . .

What is somewhat surprising is the number of cases in which a court-supervised buy-out is the result of the involuntary dissolution suit. In a previous study of the fifty-four involuntary dissolution opinions decided between 1960–1976 conducted by [Hetherington and Dooley], a court-ordered or court supervised buy-out was involved in only three of the cases, whereas dissolution was ordered in sixteen of the twenty-seven cases in which some affirmative relief was granted [in the present sample]. . . .

NOTE ON DISSOLUTION

The evolution of the legal treatment of dissolution can, with some oversimplification, be divided into four somewhat overlapping stages.

1. *First Stage: Dissolution Granted Only for Deadlock, and Even Then Granted Very Sparingly.* In the first, original stage, which lasted until about the early 1960s, the courts typically granted dissolution only on the ground of deadlock. Furthermore, the courts were often reluctant to grant dissolution of a profitable corporation even on that ground, partly on the theory that there was a public interest in preserving economically viable businesses.

2. *Second Stage: Dissolution on the Ground of Fault.* In the second stage, courts became more willing to grant dissolution, even of profitable corporations, not only on the ground of deadlock but also on the ground of oppression.[2] This increased willingness resulted in part from a wave of dissolution-for-oppression statutes. It also resulted from the influence of scholarship like that of Hetherington & Dooley, and also of F. Hodge O'Neal, who wrote extensively to show that dissolution was often a highly desirable remedy to resolve the problems of minority shareholders.

3. *Third Stage: Dissolution on the Ground of Defeat of the Minority's Reasonable Expectations.* In the third stage, the emphasis shifted from an inquiry into whether there was fault on the part of majority shareholders to an inquiry into whether the reasonable expectations of the minority shareholders were being defeated. Often,

---

2. However, even some relatively recent cases, such as Brenner v. Berkowitz, 634 A.2d 1019 (N.J. 1993), express concern about the dissolution of a profitable corporation.

this shift involved a reconstruction of the meaning of "oppression," as in *Kemp & Beatley, supra.*

4. *Fourth Stage: Dissolution Converted into Mandatory Buy–Out.* In the fourth, present stage, there has been a marked tendency to grant relief even more freely to minority shareholders who petition for dissolution, but to cast that relief not in the form of dissolution, but in the form of requiring a mandatory buy-out, at fair value, of the interest of a shareholder who petitions for dissolution. In many cases, the dissolution statutes give the majority a right to buy out the minority. In other cases, as a matter of discretion the courts order buy-out as an alternative to dissolution.

At present, therefore, a petition by a minority shareholder for dissolution is commonly just a trigger for requiring a mandatory buy-out of the minority shareholder's stock. To put this differently, the courts hold, with increasing frequency, that grounds for dissolution exist, but then substitute mandatory buy-out for dissolution as the appropriate remedy. This development has several implications.

1. Because liquidation is not required in the case of a mandatory buy-out, the power to order a mandatory buy-out serves to alleviate the persistent view that liquidation of a profitable corporation is against the public interest. As a result, the courts may now be more ready to find in favor of a minority shareholder in a dissolution proceeding, because they know that such a finding will not necessarily result in a liquidation.

2. The power to order a mandatory buy-out in lieu of dissolution obviates a concern that freely granting dissolution may enable minority shareholders to opportunistically use a petition for dissolution (or the threat of such a petition) to put undue pressure on the majority shareholders by making them fear that they will lose control of the business, and thereby extort an unduly high settlement from the majority. This possibility is sometimes referred to as "oppression by the minority."

3. In general, the less drastic is a remedy, the readier the courts are to impose it. This has been the trend of the law in the area of dissolution: As that remedy has been diluted from dissolution to buy-out, the standard for granting relief has also been diluted, and the frequency of relief to minority shareholders has increased.

4. To the extent that petitions for dissolution have become triggering events for mandatory buy-outs, and the courts grant such petitions without a showing of fault by the majority, in effect the law is edging toward the position advocated by Hetherington and Dooley, that minority shareholders in close corporations should be allowed exit on demand. (This position also moves close corporation law toward partnership law, which already allows dissolution on very free terms.)

5. Properly conceived and administered, mandatory buy-outs may have important advantages over dissolution. The minority shareholder can get just what he wants—the cash value of his stock and exit

from a bad situation. At the same time, the majority shareholders are given the right to continue the business if they wish to do so.

NOTE ON VALUATION OF THE MINORITY'S SHARES

To the extent that mandatory buy-out is substituted for dissolution, great pressure is put on how the value of the minority's shares is determined, because the remedy of mandatory buy-out works properly only if the minority interest is properly valued. Indeed, from the perspective of valuation, dissolution has a major advantage over a mandatory buy-out. In a mandatory buy-out the *court* must value the minority's interest. In contrast, in a dissolution there is a public sale of the corporation's business, so that the *market,* rather than the court, values the corporation, and therefore the petitioner's shares. From a valuation perspective, therefore, dissolution may be preferable to mandatory buy-out on the ground that a valuation by the market is more accurate than a valuation by the court.

Against this view, it can be argued that a mandatory sale of close corporation's business in the context of a dissolution proceeding may not in fact realize the fair value of the business. The problem with such a sale is that there may be no ready market for the corporation's business, especially if one or more of the shareholder-managers will not continue to participate or if the only person who can realistically acquire the business is one of the shareholders, who might therefore be able to purchase the business at a public sale at an unduly low price. Professor Bahls has explained this problem especially well:

> . . . When corporations are liquidated, they usually sell their assets for cash. Frequently, when a receiver or court-appointed auctioneer sells a business, the sale does not yield the maximum value for any of the shareholders. Auction sales are fire sales. Rather than selling the entire business as a going concern, the business assets might be sold separately. If so, the sale does not yield the full value of a going concern. In addition, the business is not always operated between the appointment of the receiver or court-appointed auctioneer and the date of sale. During this interim, the customers of the business may develop relationships and preferences for other vendors, often dealing a fatal blow to the corporation's ability to operate profitably.
>
> Compounding the problem, auction sales or other court-supervised sales usually require payment of the purchase price immediately or within a short period of time. This requirement excludes potential purchasers from the market and may result in lower purchase prices offered by those not excluded. Finally, purchase prices are depressed because it is difficult to insure that the buyer will reap the benefit of the seller's goodwill. Business management, as well as nonmanagement employees, often develop important customer contracts and special expertise. To the extent that management expertise and customer relationships

cannot be sold with the business, buyers do not receive the benefit of, nor are they willing to pay for, these important elements of goodwill. . . .

Bahls, Resolving Shareholder Dissension: Selection of the Appropriate Equitable Remedy, [1990] J.Corp.Law 285, 297 (1990).

On the other hand, mandatory buy-outs also raise severe problems of valuation. To begin with, the valuation of a business by a nonmarket mechanism, like a court, is always a very difficult and problematic enterprise. Furthermore, two special problems are raised in the context of a mandatory buy-out. In valuing shares for some purposes, such as an estate-tax valuation, a two-step approach is adopted. In the first step, the corporation is valued as a whole, and the shares are then valued on a pro rata basis. In the second step, a discount is applied to the first-step valuation if the shares are minority shares, not easily marketable, or both. Discounts for these factors can run 25% or more. Some courts have applied minority or marketability discounts in the mandatory buy-out context as well. The propriety of such discounts in that context is the subject of the following case.

Charland v. Country View Golf Club, Inc.

Supreme Court of Rhode Island, 1991.
588 A.2d 609.

OPINION

■ KELLEHER, JUSTICE.

The plaintiff in this litigation, Gilbert Charland, is a minority shareholder in a Rhode Island closely held corporation that owned and operated an eighteen-hole, 147–acre golf course located in the town of Burrillville. The defendant, Country View Golf Club, Inc., is the corporation. Hereafter we shall refer to the plaintiff as Charland and to the defendant as Country View.

On September 4, 1984, Charland, a 15 percent shareholder of Country View's stock, that is, an owner of fifteen shares, filed a complaint in the Superior Court asking that Country View be dissolved. Charland relied on G.L.1956 (1985 Reenactment) § 7–1.1–90, which provides:

"(a) The superior court shall have full power to liquidate the assets and business of a corporation:

(1) In an action by a shareholder when it is established that, whether or not the corporate business has been or could be operated at a profit, dissolution would be beneficial to the shareholders because . . .

(B) The acts of the directors or those in control of the corporation are illegal, oppressive, or fraudulent."

Specifically Charland alleged that one of the officers of the corporation was engaging in illegal activities.

After filing an answer, Country View, acting pursuant to § 7–1.1–90.1, elected to purchase Charland's fifteen shares. Section 7–1.1–90.1 provides, in part:

> "Whenever a petition for dissolution of a corporation is filed by one or more shareholders (hereinafter in this section referred to as the 'petitioner') pursuant to * * * § 7–1.1–90 * * * the corporation or one or more of its other shareholders may avoid such dissolution by filing with the court * * * an election to purchase the shares owed by the petitioner *at a price equal to their fair value.* * * * If the parties are unable to reach an agreement as to the fair value of such shares, the court shall * * * stay the proceeding and determine the value of such shares, in accordance with the procedure set forth in § 7–1.1–74, *as of the close of business on the day on which the petition for dissolution was filed.*" (Emphasis added.)

Thus § 7–1.1–90.1 contains three provisions. First, a corporation, rather than be forced to dissolve by a shareholder dissolution petition, can elect to buy out the shareholder's stock. Second, the corporation must pay fair value for such shares. Third, if the fair value cannot be agreed upon, the court shall determine the value of such shares as of the close of business on the day on which the petition for dissolution was filed.

Charland and Country View could not agree on the fair value of Charland's shares. Therefore the court, in accordance with § 7–1.1–74, appointed an appraiser. Section 7–1.1–74(e) provides that "The court may, if it so elects, appoint one or more persons as appraisers to receive evidence and recommend a decision on the question of fair value. The appraisers shall have such power and authority as shall be specified in the order of their appointment or an amendment thereof."

[The trial court designated Joseph R. Smith as an appraiser to determine the fair value of Charland's shares.]

Smith's report to the trial justice noted the inherent difficulties in evaluating the value of a golf course in Burrillville. The appraiser then discussed the applicability of a minority discount in evaluating the shares. Smith concluded that a "minority discount" would be appropriate in determining the fair value of Charland's shares.[4]

Smith submitted two figures in his report. The first, or lower, valuation included a minority discount and was the one suggested by Smith. The trial justice, however, accepted the second, or higher, calculation.

The second figure of $9,273.05 per share, or $139,095.73, was arrived at in the following manner: first, Smith noted that the golf

---

4. In his report, Smith failed to distinguish between a minority discount and a lack of marketability discount. Smith combined elements of both discounts but ultimately labeled the discount a "minority discount." Because of the ambiguity created by Smith's report, we will address the applicability of both a minority discount and a lack of marketability discount to Charland's shares.

course was sold for $2 million in 1988; second, Smith used the present value procedure to discount the $2 million figure and arrive at the value of the entire golf course as of September 30, 1984; and finally, without applying an additional minority discount, Smith took 15 percent of the 1984 value in order to arrive at the value for Charland's 15 shares (out of 100) in the corporation. The trial justice ultimately awarded Charland the sum of $139,095.73....

Although Charland raised a number of issues on appeal, he failed to furnish us with a complete transcript of the Superior Court proceeding. As a result, we shall consider.... [only] whether Charland received fair value for his shares pursuant to § 7–1.1–90.1.

Three separate issues must be resolved in determining fair value. The first issue is whether this court should apply a minority discount to Charland's shares. The second issue is whether this court should apply a discount for lack of marketability. The third issue is whether any discount was, in fact, applied to Charland's shares with the result that Charland received less than the fair value prescribed by § 7–1.1–90.1. We shall now consider each of these three issues.

A minority discount has been described as a second-stage adjustment for valuing minority shares. *See* Note, *Rejecting the Minority Discount,* 1989 Duke L.J. 258, 260. That is, after a minority shareholder's stock is initially discounted for the minority percentage owned, the pro rata value is determined. Then an additional discount is applied to the pro rata value because the minority shareholder lacks corporate decisionmaking power. *Id.* This second calculation is called a minority discount.

The issue of whether to apply a minority discount in a situation in which a corporation elects to buy out a shareholder who has filed for dissolution has never been resolved by this court. In fact, few jurisdictions have decided this question.[5]

Most courts that have considered this question have agreed that no minority discount should be applied when a corporation elects to buy out the shareholder who petitions for dissolution of the corporation. *See, e.g., Brown v. Allied Corrugated Box Co.,* 91 Cal.App.3d 477, 485–87, 154 Cal.Rptr. 170, 173–76 (1979); *Blake v. Blake Agency, Inc.,* 107 A.D.2d 139, 486 N.Y.S.2d 341, *appeal denied,* 65 N.Y.2d 609, 484 N.E.2d 671, 494 N.Y.S.2d 1028 (1985). *But see McCauley v. Tom McCauley & Son, Inc.,* 104 N.M. 523, 535, 724 P.2d 232, 244 (1986) (trial justice has discretion in determining whether a minority discount is applicable).

[In *Brown v. Allied Corrugated Box Co.,* supra, the] court conceded that if the shares were placed on the open market, their

5. Many jurisdictions, including this one, have decided the question of determining the fair value of shares when a *dissenting* shareholder elects to request the fair value of his or her shares in case of a merger or consolidation. *See* § 7–1.1–74; *see also Jeffrey v. American Screw Co.,* 98 R.I. 286, 201 A.2d 146 (1964) (appraiser given wide discretion to consider all relevant factors in determining fair value of dissenting shareholder's stock). This is a separate issue from whether a minority discount should be applied when a corporation elects to buy out a shareholder who has petitioned for *dissolution* proceedings.

minority status would substantially decrease their value. The court, however, went on to note that this devaluation has little validity when the shares are to be purchased by the corporation. When a corporation elects to buy out the shares of a dissenting shareholder, the fact that the shares are noncontrolling is irrelevant.

In addition the court in *Brown* observed that had the plaintiffs proved their case and had the corporation been dissolved, each shareholder would have been entitled to the same amount per share. There would be no consideration given to whether the shares were controlling or noncontrolling. Furthermore an unscrupulous controlling shareholder could avoid a proportionate distribution under dissolution by buying out the shares, and the very misconduct and unfairness that incited the minority shareholders to seek dissolution could be used to oppress them further. *Brown,* 91 Cal.App.3d at 486–87, 154 Cal.Rptr. at 176; *see also* Note, 1989 Duke L.J. at 269 n. 63.

We agree with the rationale of *Brown* and hereby adopt the rule that in circumstances in which a corporation elects to buy out a shareholder's stock pursuant to § 7–1.1–90.1, we shall not discount the shares solely because of their minority status.

A second and more difficult issue to resolve is whether a lack of marketability discount should be applied to Charland's shares. This discount is separate from and bears no relation to a minority discount. The courts that have addressed this question are divided.

The California courts have rejected a lack of marketability discount for the same reasons that they have rejected a minority discount. *See Brown,* 91 Cal.App.3d at 483, 154 Cal.Rptr. at 175. That is, no lack of marketability discount should be applied because the shares are not being sold on the open market; they are purchased by the corporation. The New York courts, however, have decided to apply a lack of marketability discount to shares in a closely held corporation when the corporation elects to buy out a minority shareholder in order to avoid dissolution. The reason for applying this discount is that shares of a closely held corporation cannot readily be sold on the public market. Blake v. Blake Agency, Inc., 107 A.D.2d at 149, 486 N.Y.S.2d at 349.

The difference between the approach taken by the New York and the California courts regarding the question of whether a lack of marketability discount should be applied when a corporation elects to buy out the shareholder who has filed for dissolution is based upon the statutes of each state. The California statute determines fair value "on the basis of the liquidation value as of the valuation date but taking into account the possibility, if any, of sale of the entire business as a going concern in a liquidation." Cal.Corp.Code Ann. § 2000(a) (West 1990). As there is no lack of marketability discount if the corporation dissolves, no such discount is applied by the California courts. . . .

Furthermore ... a lack of marketability discount is inapposite when a corporation elects to buy out a shareholder who has filed for dissolution of a corporation. As a recent law review article noted:

> "In dissolution cases, strong reasons support the use of pro rata value without a discount * * *. A minority shareholder seeking dissolution claims that majority shareholders have engaged in some unfair, possibly tortious, action. If the minority shareholder succeeds in having the company dissolved, all shareholders will receive their pro rata share of the assets, with no account given to the minority [or illiquidity] status of their shares. Minority shareholders should not receive less than this value if, instead of fighting the dissolution action, the majority decides to seek appraisal of minority shares in order to buy out the minority and reduce corporate discord." Note, 1989 Duke L.J. at 269 n. 63.

We therefore today adopt the rule of not applying a discount for lack of marketability in § 7–1.1–90.1 proceedings....

[Because the trial justice applied a discount, we] remand this case to the Superior Court to determine the fair value of Charland's shares as of September 4, 1984, without applying a discount for either minority status or lack of marketability of his shares in Country View in conformity with the rules set forth herein.

NOTE ON MINORITY AND MARKETABILITY DISCOUNTS

A distinction must be drawn between the value of minority stock on the market and the value of minority stock to the majority shareholder. On the market, minority stock may be subject to a marketability discount, a minority discount, or both, because a third party who purchases minority stock will be in the same disadvantageous position as the selling minority shareholder. However, the majority shareholder will not be subject to these problems. Accordingly, the value of minority stock to a majority shareholder may be free of minority and marketability discounts. As stated in Robblee v. Robblee, 68 Wash.App. 69, 78–81, 841 P.2d 1289, 1294–95 (1992):

> In Columbia Management Co. v. Wyss, 94 Or.App. 195, 765 P.2d 207 (1988).... [t]he court rejected the minority discount as inappropriate to an "internal transaction", because market recognition of a minority discount has little validity when the corporation or someone already in control of the corporation is the purchaser....
>
> [In the present case,] had the value of [the shares of Neil, the minority shareholder] to a third party been at stake, it would have been appropriate for the trial court to apply a minority discount to approximate the fair market value. We do not doubt the experts' opinions that the market value of Neil's minority shares is less per share than that of Dave's majority shares. But, as in a dissenting shareholder situation, here no third party was involved,

> and thus there was no "market" in fact or in theory—Dave was the only party contemplated to buy the stock.
>
> The [trial] court recognized the extra value that Neil's stock would have for Dave: "Dave's ownership will go to almost 80% and he will be ridding himself of a minority shareholder who had become, and would continue to be, extremely difficult." This, though, is one of the very reasons a minority shareholder's stock should not be discounted to fair market value, because the value to Dave is different from what it would be in the market.

NOTE ON MATTER OF PACE PHOTOGRAPHERS

In Matter of Pace Photographers, Ltd., 525 N.E.2d 713 (N.Y. 1988), Pace Photographers had five shareholders, including Rosen, all of whom had entered into a shareholders' agreement. Paragraph 5 of the agreement fixed a method for determining the value of Pace shares for the purpose of paying out a shareholder who retired or withdrew from the business (the "withdrawal price"). Paragraph 12 of the agreement prohibited a sale by any shareholder of Pace stock to a third party for five years after the agreement was executed, unless all the other shareholders consented. A shareholder was permitted to sell his stock to one of the other shareholders during that period without such consent, but only for 50% of the withdrawal price.

Three years after the agreement was executed, a rift developed between Rosen and the other four shareholders. Rosen petitioned for dissolution under N.Y.B.C.L. § 1104–a, alleging oppression and wrongdoing. The other four shareholders responded by causing Pace to file an election under N.Y.B.C.L. § 1118, which allows a corporation to elect a mandatory buy-out of a shareholder who has petitioned under § 1104–a. The trial court held that Pace had a right to buy Rosen's shares under § 1118, and that the fair value of Rosen's shares under that section was 50% of the withdrawal price, pursuant to the shareholders' agreement. The Appellate Division affirmed, but the Court of Appeals reversed:

> As an abstract matter, it may well be that shareholders can agree in advance that an 1104–a dissolution proceeding will be deemed a voluntary offer to sell, or fix "fair value" in the event of judicial dissolution, and that their agreement would be enforced.... Participants in business ventures are free to express their understandings in written agreements, and such consensual arrangements are generally favored and upheld by the courts....
>
> But in the absence of explicit agreement a shareholders' agreement fixing the terms of a sale voluntarily sought and desired by a shareholder does not equally control when the sale is the result of claimed majority oppression or other wrongdoing—in effect, a forced buyout ...

... The provisions of the shareholders' agreement regarding buyout within the first five years, at a 50% discount, were expressly limited to the situation where "a stockholder desires to sell his shares of the stock to the other stockholders" (para 12[e]), contemplating a voluntary sale at the convenience of and for the benefit of the selling shareholder, without regard to the inconvenience or detriment inflicted on the corporation or other shareholders.... It is plain ... that a sale occasioned by an 1104–a petition premised on abuse by the majority does not fall within the contemplation of this shareholders' agreement regarding a sale of stock by a shareholder to the corporation....

Less than a month after the Court of Appeals decision, the corporation sent a notice to Rosen, purporting to revoke its offer to buy his shares under N.Y.B.C.L. § 1118. In In re Pace Photographers, Ltd., 163 A.D.2d 316, 557 N.Y.S.2d 443 (1990), the court held that the corporation could not revoke its election. "Business Corporation Law § 1118(a) states in pertinent part that '[a]n election pursuant to this section shall be irrevocable unless the court, in its discretion, for just and equitable considerations, determines that such election be revocable.... [We do not] find any 'just and equitable considerations' that would allow us to authorize revocation of Pace's election...."

FRIEDMAN v. BEWAY REALTY CORP., 87 N.Y.2d 161, 638 N.Y.S.2d 399, 661 N.E.2d 972 (1995). "[I]n fixing fair value, courts should determine the minority shareholder's proportionate interest in the going concern value of the corporation as a whole, that is, 'what a willing purchaser, in an arm's length transaction, would offer for the *corporation* as an operating business' " (Matter of Pace Photographers [Rosen], 71 N.Y.2d, at 748, *supra,* quoting Matter of Blake v. Blake Agency, 107 A.D.2d, at 146, *supra* [emphasis supplied]).

"Consistent with that approach, we have approved a methodology for fixing the fair value of minority shares in a close corporation under which the investment value of the entire enterprise was ascertained through a capitalization of earnings (taking into account the unmarketability of the corporate stock) and then fair value was calculated on the basis of the petitioners' proportionate share of all outstanding corporate stock (Matter of Seagroatt Floral Co., 78 N.Y.2d, at 442, 446, supra).

"Imposing a discount for the minority status of the dissenting shares here, as argued by the corporations, would in our view conflict with two central equitable principles of corporate governance we have developed for fair value adjudications of minority shareholder interests under Business Corporation Law §§ 623 and 1118. A minority discount would necessarily deprive minority shareholders of their proportionate interest in a going concern, as guaranteed by our decisions previously discussed. Likewise, imposing a minority discount on the compensation payable to dissenting stockholders for their shares in a proceeding under Business Corporation Law §§ 623 or 1118 would result in minority shares being valued below that of majority shares, thus violating our mandate of equal treatment of all shares of the same class in minority stockholder buyouts.

"A minority discount on the value of dissenters' shares would also significantly undermine one of the major policies behind the appraisal legislation embodied now in Business Corporation Law § 623, the remedial goal of the statute to 'protect[ ] minority shareholders' from being forced to sell at unfair values imposed by those dominating the corporation while allowing the majority to proceed with its desired [corporate action]" (Matter of Cawley v. SCM Corp., 72 N.Y.2d, at 471, *supra,* quoting Alpert v. 28 Williams St. Corp., 63 N.Y.2d 557, 567–568). This protective purpose of the statute prevents the shifting of proportionate economic value of the corporation as a going concern from minority to majority stockholders. As stated by the Delaware Supreme Court, 'to fail to accord to a minority shareholder the full proportionate value of his [or her] shares imposes a penalty for lack of control, and unfairly enriches the majority stockholders who may reap a windfall from the appraisal process by cashing out a dissenting shareholder' (Cavalier Oil Corp. v. Harnett, 564 A.2d 1137, 1145 (Del. 1989).

"Furthermore, a mandatory reduction in the fair value of minority shares to reflect their owners' lack of power in the administration of the corporation will inevitably encourage oppressive majority conduct, thereby further driving down the compensation necessary to pay for the value of minority shares. 'Thus, the greater the misconduct by the majority, the less they need to pay for the minority's shares' (Murdock, *The Evolution of Effective Remedies for Minority Shareholders and Its Impact Upon Evaluation of Minority Shares,* 65 Notre Dame L.Rev. 425, 487).

"We also note that a minority discount has been rejected in a substantial majority of other jurisdictions. 'Thus, statistically, minority discounts are almost uniformly viewed with disfavor by State courts' (*id.,* at 481). The imposition of a minority discount in derogation of minority stockholder appraisal remedies has been rejected as well by the American Law Institute in its Principles of Corporate Governance (*see,* 2 ALI, Principles of Corporate Governance § 7.22, at 314–315; comment *e* to § 7.22, at 324 [1994]). . . .

"We likewise find no basis to disturb the trial court's discretion in failing to assign any additional diminution in value of petitioners' shares here because they were subject to contractual restrictions on voluntary transfer. As we noted in *Matter of Pace Photographers (Rosen) (supra),* a statutory acquisition of minority shares by a corporation pursuant to the Business Corporation Law is not a voluntary sale of corporate shares as contemplated by a restrictive stockholder agreement and, therefore, 'the express covenant is literally inapplicable' (71 N.Y.2d, at 749). Nor is there any reason to disturb Supreme Court's award of prejudgment interest."

However, the court approved a discount for marketability.

SECTION 9. CUSTODIANS AND PROVISIONAL DIRECTORS

Two other possible remedies for deadlock are the appointment of either a custodian or a provisional director. The following materials address those remedies.

DEL. GEN. CORP. LAW §§ 226, 352, 353

[See Statutory Supplement]

CAL. CORP. CODE §§ 308, 1802

[See Statutory Supplement]

GIURICICH v. EMTROL CORP., 449 A.2d 232 (Del.1982). Plaintiffs owned 50% of the stock of Emtrol Corporation. Continental Boilerworks controlled the other 50%. Plaintiffs petitioned the Delaware Court of Chancery for the appointment of a custodian pursuant to Del.Gen.Corp.Law § 226(a)(1), based on a shareholder deadlock between the plaintiffs and Continental. Despite the existence of a shareholder deadlock that prevented the election of successor directors, the trial court declined to appoint a custodian, on the ground that there had been no injury to any vital interests of either the plaintiff stockholders or Emtrol. Reversed.

> ... By § 226(a)(1), the Legislature has created a viable remedy for the injustices arising from a shareholder-deadlock which permits control of a corporation to remain indefinitely in the hands of a self-perpetuating board of directors, any gross unfairness to other major stockholders notwithstanding....
>
> A custodian will be appointed by the Court of Chancery under § 226(a)(1) who is strictly impartial and has a proven business and executive background. The custodian will be empowered to act only in situations in which the board of directors of Emtrol have failed to reach a unanimous decision on any issue properly before them. In the event that the board is unable to reach unanimous accord on any such pending issue, the custodian will resolve the issue in such manner as he shall deem appropriate. His decision and action in such case shall be binding upon the officers and directors of Emtrol, and shall be deemed the official action of the corporation. The custodian may call a

> directors' meeting, or a stockholders' meeting, *sua sponte* or at the request of any director. The custodian shall serve for such time as the Court of Chancery shall deem necessary, or until there is a unanimous request to the Court for his discharge by all shareholders of Emtrol. The compensation of the custodian will be approved by the Court of Chancery and paid by Emtrol. . . .

THOMPSON, THE SHAREHOLDER'S CAUSE OF ACTION FOR OPPRESSION, 48 Bus.Law. 699, 723 (1993). "[More than half of the states have added to the remedies available in shareholder disputes by providing for the appointment of a custodian. About twenty states authorize a court to appoint a provisional director to help resolve shareholder disputes.] . . . Despite their widespread inclusion in statutes, these remedies are not used often. [The remedy is more important in states like Delaware, where it is the only effective remedy for shareholder dissension.] There is a cost to an additional layer of management, which would unduly burden a small enterprise, and the appointment of an outside party may not address the underlying differences among the participants."*

NOTE ON CUSTODIANS AND PROVISIONAL DIRECTORS

1. The appointment of a provisional director may enable one faction to make changes in the control structure of the corporation whose effects will persist even after the provisional director has left the scene. For example, in In re Jamison Steel Corp., 158 Cal.App.2d 27, 322 P.2d 246 (1958), one faction controlled 240 shares of stock and the other faction controlled the remaining 160 shares. Under the corporation's articles, the board consisted of four directors, and under cumulative voting, each faction could elect two of the four. Board meetings in December 1955 and December 1956 resulted in tie votes on several issues, including elections to certain offices and the size of the dividend. After the 1955 meeting, the majority faction petitioned the court for the appointment of a provisional director on the ground of deadlock. The lower court appointed a provisional director with authority to vote for an amendment to the articles of incorporation. The California Supreme Court affirmed, although recognizing that the provisional director might vote with the majority's two directors to increase the board to five, and thereby permanently alter the balance of power.

Hetherington & Dooley argue that the provisional-director remedy is unsound:

> No state or public interest appears to justify [appointing a provisional director and thereby] depriving the resisting party of the

* The material in brackets has been transposed from footnotes to text. (Footnote by ed.)

> right to veto corporate decisions. The power to veto is an important property right, to which the resisting party is entitled by virtue of his shareholdings. It is the best protection against exploitation and oppression that a shareholder in a close corporation can have, short of the power to impose his will on the other party.... The faction that has the support of the provisional director has little or no incentive to seek to settle its differences with the minority faction.

Hetherington & Dooley, Illiquidity and Exploitation: A Proposed Statutory Solution to the Remaining Close. Corporation Problem, 63 Va. L.Rev. 1, 21–22 (1977).

2. The distinctive aspect of the custodian remedy is that unlike dissolution, if a custodian is appointed the business continues, and unlike a provisional director, a custodian normally has complete authority over the business.

SECTION 10. ARBITRATION

Ringling v. Ringling Bros. Barnum & Bailey Circus

[Section 2, supra]

APPLICATION OF VOGEL, 268 N.Y.S.2d 237, 25 A.D.2d 212 (1966), aff'd 19 N.Y.2d 589, 278 N.Y.S.2d 236, 224 N.E.2d 738 (1967). Certified Moving & Storage Co. was engaged in the moving-and-storage business and also owned a warehouse in which the business was operated. Prior to 1962, Certified's stock was owned by Vogel, Thomsky, and Horowitz. In 1962, Vogel and Lewis purchased all of the Certified stock, so that each owned 50%. However, the warehouse in which Certified's business was operated continued to be owned by Vogel, Thomsky, and Horowitz, Certified's former owners. When Vogel and Lewis took over Certified, they obtained a lease on the warehouse for five years and an option under which Certified could purchase the warehouse for $175,000.

Vogel and Lewis had a shareholders' agreement. Paragraph Sixth of the agreement provided that "The parties hereto hereby expressly agree that in the event of a dispute, or difference, arising between them in the course of their transaction with each other, under the terms of this agreement, such dispute or difference shall be settled between them by arbitration...."

In October 1964 there was a meeting of the board of directors of Certified, consisting of Vogel and Lewis. At that meeting, Lewis sought to have Certified exercise its option to purchase the warehouse, so as to strengthen and assure the continuance of Certified's business. If the warehouse was not acquired by Certified, and Vogel, Thomsky, and Horowitz did not renew Certified's lease, Certified would have to go out of business at the end of the lease term. The business would then effectively revert to Vogel, Thomsky, and Horowitz, as owners of the warehouse in which the business was operated. Lewis voted in favor of exercising the option to purchase the warehouse, and Vogel voted against. Vogel revealed that he had some sort of agreement with his former partners, Thomsky and Horowitz, and considered himself morally and legally bound to them, and therefore could not agree to exercise the option to purchase. Vogel also made it clear it was to his own advantage and personal interest to keep the ownership of the property "as is." When further discussion failed to resolve the question of exercising the option to buy the warehouse, Lewis demanded arbitration, pursuant to paragraph Sixth, on two issues: (1) Should Certified exercise its option to purchase pursuant to terms of the Lease? (2) Should Vogel be removed as officer and director of Certified on the ground that he had interests adverse to the best interests of Certified? Vogel asserted that Paragraph Sixth did not cover the kinds of questions Lewis sought to arbitrate, and that the arbitration sought would be in violation of N.Y.Bus.Corp.Law § 701, which provided that the business of a corporation shall be managed by its board. The court ordered arbitration to proceed:

> . . . [T]he question to exercise or not to exercise the option, under the circumstances here present, is not one which deals with problems of everyday corporate management or whether a particular deal in the exercise of business judgment would redound to the corporate benefit. It is more fundamental involving, as it does, continued corporate existence . . .
>
> . . . [I]f all involved here were discretion and the exercise of business judgment in the management of corporate affairs it is doubtful that arbitration could be used or applied as a substitute in light of the language of the statute (Business Corporation Law § 701) . . .
>
> Obviously the question whether or not to exercise the option to purchase does not require assumption of any burden of continuing management, but rather if Certified is to have a measure of business security and assurance of continued existence.
>
> It must have reasonably been within the contemplation of the parties, acting in good faith when the corporation was formed, should the business prove successful, as is the case here, that all necessary or proper steps to assure its continued existence would be cooperatively undertaken. Recognizing that disputes could arise the parties provided for arbitration. To read a limitation of exclusion at the price of continued corporate existence of this close corporation is to disregard the plain language of paragraph Sixth, and to impose a restriction, possibly fatal, where the issue

sought to be arbitrated is nowise offensive to our public policy. This we should not do.

LANE v. ABEL-BEY, 70 A.D.2d 838, 418 N.Y.S.2d 25 (1979), aff'd, 50 N.Y.2d 864 (1980). A shareholders' agreement provided that "[a]ll disputes arising in connection with this agreement shall be finally settled by arbitration." One of the shareholders claimed that the corporation had failed to enter into an employment contract with him, as the agreement required; had paid excessive compensation; and had made improper payments to other shareholders. Held, the claims were subject to arbitration. "We do not agree with petitioner's argument that, because the second and third claims are in the nature of derivative suits, public policy precludes arbitration of such claims.... We are not concerned here with claims relating to the business conduct of a publicly held corporation, but rather with such claims addressed to the business conduct of a close corporation. Arbitration of claims of a derivative nature are not against public policy in a close corporation ..."

SHELL, ARBITRATION AND CORPORATE GOVERNANCE, 67 N.C.L.Rev. 517 (1989). "[Section 2 of the Federal Arbitration Act] makes enforceable any 'written provision in any ... contract evidencing a transaction involving commerce to settle by arbitration' any existing or future dispute ...

"... [A]fter nearly seventy years of legal evolution, arbitration is now utilized in New York as a close corporation remedy for virtually every kind of corporate dispute. Indeed, detailed case administration statistics compiled by the American Arbitration Association reveal that between 1984 and August 1988 the AAA received over one thousand claims and counterclaims worth over $118,000,000 under its case administration category dealing with close corporation disputes. These claims include disputes regarding stock valuation and appraisal, allegations of breach of contract, mismanagement, misrepresentation, wrongful discharge, and breach of fiduciary duty.

"... [T]he Supreme Court has ... [interpreted Federal Arbitration Act] as preempting attempts by the states to preclude access to the arbitral forum. When parties can convince a court that their close corporation dispute involves interstate commerce, they may be able to bypass even express statutory restrictions on arbitration, such as [a] ... requirement that an arbitration clause appear in the charter." Id. at 524, 533.

CHAPTER 9

LIMITED LIABILITY COMPANIES

DELAWARE LIMITED LIABILITY COMPANY ACT §§ 18–101, 18–107, 18–201, 18–206, 18–301, 18–303, 18–401, 18–402, 18–504

[See Statutory Supplement]

SECTION 1. INTRODUCTION

Limited liability companies (LLCs) are noncorporate entities that are created under statutes that combine elements of corporation and partnership law. As under corporation law, the owners ("members") of LLCs have limited liability. As under partnership law, an LLC has great freedom to structure its internal governance by agreement. Like a corporation, an LLC is an entity, so that it can, for example, hold property and sue and be sued in its own name. LLCs come in two flavors: member-managed LLCs, which are managed by their members, and manager-managed LLCs, which are managed by managers who may or may not be members.

As of 2008, there were 1.9 million LLCs in existence, compared to 670,000 partnerships, 412,000 limited partnerships, and 122,000 limited liability partnerships. U.S. Internal Revenue Service, Statistics of Income Bulletins, Fall 2010, at 87, 88. Moreover, LLCs are growing much more quickly than other business forms. Rodney D. Chrisman, LLCs are the New King of the Hill, 15 Fordham J. of Corp. and Fin. Law 459 (2010).

Like privately held corporations, small LLCs tend to be formed in the state where their business was located. Jens Dammann and Matthias Schundeln analyzed a large sample of LLCs in their article, Where are Limited Liability Companies Formed? An Empirical Analysis, University of Texas School of Law, Law and Economics Research paper No. 126 (April 28, 2008). They concluded that "Of all LLCs with five or more employees . . . slightly more than 96% were formed in the state where their business was located. Presumably, the figure is even higher for LLCs with less than five employees. However, the tendency to form locally grows weaker as the number of employees increases. Of those firms that have 1000 or more employees, roughly half are formed outside their home state, and of the latter, more than 80% are formed in Delaware." Id at 4–5.

The LLC is a relatively new form, and the LLC statutes are highly variable. This Note will describe the central characteristics of LLCs under prevailing statutory patterns. Bear in mind that as to any given characteristic there will usually be some LLC statutes that fall outside the major patterns this Note describes.

1. *Formation; Articles of Organization; Powers.* An LLC is formed by filing articles of organization in a designated state office—usually, the office of the Secretary of State. The statutes all allow LLCs to be formed by a single person. The articles must include the name of the LLC, the address of its principal place of business or registered office in the State, and the name and address of its agent for service of process. Many statutes also require the articles to state: (1) The purpose of the LLC. (2) If the LLC is to be manager-managed, the names of the initial managers, and if the LLC is to be member-managed, the names of its initial members. (3) The duration of the LLC or the latest date on which it is to dissolve. Some statutes also require the articles to include various kinds of additional information, the nature of which varies considerably.

Most statutes either provide that LLCs have all the powers necessary to effectuate their purposes or contain an exhaustive laundry list of an LLC's powers.

2. *Operating Agreements.* An LLC's articles of organization are usually very sketchy. In most LLCs, the critical foundational instrument is the *operating agreement* (sometimes called by another name, such as "limited liability company agreement"), which is an agreement among the LLC's members concerning the conduct of its affairs. The operating agreement typically provides for the governance of the LLC, its capitalization, the admission and withdrawal of members, and distributions.

3. *Management.* Most of the statutes provide, as a default rule which prevails unless otherwise agreed, that an LLC is to be managed by its members. A few statutes provide that unless otherwise agreed, an LLC is to be managed by managers, who may but need not be members. The most common statutory provision is that the statutory default rule concerning management can be varied only by a provision in the LLC's articles of organization, but many statutes provide that the default rule can be varied in the operating agreement. One way to vary the statutory default rule is to completely reverse it—either by providing for manager management in a state where the default rule is member management, or by providing for member management in a state where the default rule is manager management. Another way to vary the statutory default rule is to distribute management functions between members and managers.

4. *Voting by Members.* Just over half the statutes provide that unless otherwise agreed, members vote per capita, that is, one vote per member. The remaining statutes provide that unless otherwise agreed, members vote pro rata, that is, by financial interest. Normally, members act by a majority vote, per capita or pro rata as the case may be. However, some of the statutes require a unanimous vote for certain actions, such as an amendment of the articles or the operating agreement.

5. *Authority*

a. *Member-managed LLCs*. In a member-managed LLC, each member has power to bind the LLC for any act that is for apparently carrying on the business of the LLC in the usual way or ordinary course. Even if an action is not in the usual or ordinary course, the remaining members may confer on a member actual authority to bind the LLC to an action or a given type of action. Conversely, the members as a group may withdraw the actual authority of one or more members to take a certain kind of action that is in the ordinary or usual course. In that case, if a member takes such an action the LLC will be bound by virtue of the member's apparent authority, but the member will be obliged to indemnify the LLC for any loss that results from her contravention of the other members' decision.

b. *Manager-managed LLCs*. In manager-managed firms, typically only the managers have apparent authority to bind the firm. Members of a manager-managed LLC have no apparent authority to bind the LLC. Most of the statutes provide that a manager in a manager-managed LLC has the same authority as a member in a member-managed firm.

c. *The Delaware statute*. Section 18–402 of the Delaware Limited Liability Company Act provides "Unless otherwise provided in a limited liability company agreement, each member and manager has the authority to bind the limited liability company."

6. *Inspection of Books and Records*. The statutes generally provide that members are entitled to access to the LLC's books and records or to specified books and records. Many of the statutes include an explicit provision that the inspection must be for a proper purpose. Such a limitation might or might not be read into the other statutes.

7. *Fiduciary Duties*. The fiduciary duties of managers and members of LLCs are largely unspecified by the LLC statutes. Presumably, in deciding LLC cases involving fiduciary duties the courts will borrow from the corporate and partnership case-law.

Despite the lack of extensive specification, the LLC statutes, like the corporate and partnership statutes, do include important provisions concerning particular issues of fiduciary duty. For example, most although not all of the statutes specify the elements of the duty of care. Some statutes provide that a manager will be liable only for gross negligence, bad faith, recklessness, or equivalent conduct. Others require a manager to act as would a prudent person in similar circumstances.

About two-thirds of the LLC statutes provide a mechanism for the authorization of self-interested transactions by disinterested managers or members. Many of the LLC statutes permit the operating agreement to limit fiduciary duties, and some permit the operating agreement to eliminate fiduciary duties entirely. However, the statutes generally prohibit a waiver of the duty of good faith.

8. *Derivative Actions*. Most of the statutes explicitly permit members of LLCs to bring derivative actions on the LLC's behalf, based on a breach of fiduciary duties. Even where a statute does not explicitly permit such actions, courts are highly likely to permit them, both on analogy to corporation and limited-partnership law, and because a failure to do so might allow fiduciaries who were in control of an LLC to violate their fiduciary duties without any sanction.

9. *Distributions*. Most LLC statutes that address the issue of distributions provide that unless otherwise agreed, distributions to members are to be made pro rata according to the members' contributions. However, a number of statutes provide that in the absence of an agreement to the contrary, distributions are to be made on a per capita basis.

10. *Members' Interests*. A member of an LLC has financial rights and may also have governance rights as a member—that is, apart from any governance rights that she may have as a manager in a manager-managed LLC. A member's *financial* rights include her right to receive distributions. A member's *governance* rights include her right, if any, to participate in management, to vote on certain issues, and to be supplied with information. Most statutes define a member's interest in an LLC to consist of the member's financial rights, but some define a member's interest to include her governance rights.

Generally speaking, a member of an LLC can freely transfer her financial rights by transferring her interest in the LLC. However, a majority of the statutes provide that a member can transfer her governance rights only with the unanimous consent of all the other members. Some statutes provide that a member can transfer her governance rights with the approval of a majority of the other members, or a majority of other members' financial interests, depending on the statute. Most statutes permit consent requirements for transfers of management interests to be varied in the articles of incorporation or operating agreement.

It is clear that a member who assigns her interest (that is, her financial rights) normally cannot include an assignment of her governance rights unless otherwise agreed or approved by the other members, but it is not always clear whether a member who assigns her financial rights retains her governance rights. A number of statutes provide that a member who assigns her membership interest loses her membership status. Some statutes don't speak to the issue. A few provide that a member who assigns her membership interest loses her membership status if and when the assignee becomes a member. A few statutes provide that if a member assigns her membership interest, the remaining members can remove her as a member.

If a member of an LLC assigns her interest in the LLC as a pledge to secure a debt, rather than in an outright sale, and if the creditor gets a judgment against the member based on the debt, the creditor can get a charging order against the member's interest. A charging order gives the creditor the right to the member's share of any distributions.

11. *Liability*. All of the LLC statutes provide that the members and managers of an LLC are not liable for the LLC's debts, obligations, and other liabilities. However, members may become liable if the conditions for piercing the veil of an LLC are satisfied.

12. *Dissociation*. The LLC statutes vary considerably in their treatment of dissociation, that is, the termination of a member's interest in an LLC other than by the member's voluntary transfer of her interest. Ribstein and Keatinge describe the dissolution provisions of the LLC statutes as follows:

> LLC statutes vary on members' power to voluntarily withdraw and receive the value of their interests. Some provide for withdrawal at any time subject to a notice requirement. This is justified by the need . . . to provide some liquidity for otherwise locked-in interests. Some statutes eliminate any default right to withdraw or permit voluntary termination of membership status, but deny a default right to be paid on resignation. These statutes are based in part on the disruption a buyout right may cause a firm, and in part on the need to reduce the tax valuation of the departing partner's interest in familiar firms. . . .
>
> Most LLC statutes provide that a withdrawing member is entitled to some payment on withdrawal. The statutes use different formulations. Some are based on a return of contributions, while others provide for payment of fair market value in addition to, or instead other distributions to which the member is entitled (apparently including regular payouts that the member was entitled to receive before withdrawal). The statutes also provide for adjustment of the payment to exclude goodwill in the event of wrongful withdrawal. . . .
>
> Consistent with [the] potential costs of dissolution at will, LLC statutes increasingly provide that dissociation does not dissolve or trigger liquidation of the firm. . . .
>
> LLC statutes generally allow dissolution by judicial decree. Some allow judicial dissolution when it is "not reasonably practicable to carry on the business in conformity with the parties' agreement." Where the statute provides only for dissolution, it is not clear whether the court can order other relief, including buyout.

L. Ribstein & R. Keatinge, Limited Liability Companies 11–3—11–19 (2nd ed. 2009).

SECTION 2. PIERCING THE VEIL AND DERIVATIVE ACTION

Kaycee Land and Livestock v. Flahive

Supreme Court of Wyoming, 2002.
46 P.3d 323.

■ KITE, JUSTICE.

This matter comes before this court as a question certified to us by the district court for resolution under W.R.A.P. [Wisconsin Rules of Appellate Procedure] 11. The certified question seeks resolution of whether, in the absence of fraud, the entity veil of a limited liability company (LLC) can be pierced in the same manner as that of a corporation. We answer the certified question in the affirmative.

CERTIFIED QUESTION

The question we have agreed to answer is phrased as follows:

In the absence of fraud, is a claim to pierce the Limited Liability entity veil or disregard the Limited Liability Company entity in the same manner as a court would pierce a corporate veil or disregard a corporate shield, an available remedy against a Wyoming Limited Liability Company under Wyoming's Limited Liability Company Act, Wyo. Stat. §[§] 17–15–101 through 17–15–144.

FACTS

In a W.R.A.P. 11 certification of a question of law, we rely entirely upon the factual determinations made in the trial court.... The district court submitted the following statement of facts in its order certifying the question of law:

1. Flahive Oil & Gas is a Wyoming Limited Liability Company with no assets at this time.

2. [Kaycee Land and Livestock] entered into a contract with Flahive Oil & Gas LLC allowing Flahive Oil & Gas to use the surface of its real property.

3. Roger Flahive is and was the managing member of Flahive Oil & Gas at all relevant times.

4. [Kaycee Land and Livestock] alleges that Flahive Oil & Gas caused environmental contamination to its real property located in Johnson County, Wyoming.

5. [Kaycee Land and Livestock] seeks to pierce the LLC veil and disregard the L[L]C entity of Flahive Oil & Gas Limited Liability Company and hold Roger Flahive individually liable for the contamination.

6. There is no allegation of fraud.

DISCUSSION

The question presented is limited to whether, in the absence of fraud, the remedy of piercing the veil is available against a company formed under the Wyoming Limited Liability Company Act (Wyo. Stat. Ann. §§ 17–15–101 to –144). To answer this question, we must first examine the development of the doctrine within Wyoming's corporate context. As a general rule, a corporation is a separate entity distinct from the individuals comprising it. *Opal Mercantile v. Tamblyn,* 616 P.2d 776, 778 (Wyo.1980). Wyoming statutes governing corporations do not address the circumstances under which the veil can be pierced. However, since 1932, this court has espoused the concept that a corporation's legal entity will be disregarded whenever the recognition thereof in a particular case will lead to injustice. *See Caldwell v. Roach,* 44 Wyo. 319, 12 P.2d 376, 380 (1932). In *Miles v. CEC Homes, Inc.,* 753 P.2d 1021, 1023 (Wyo.1988) (quoting *Amfac Mechanical Supply Co. v. Federer,* 645 P.2d 73, 77 (Wyo.1982)), this court summarized the circumstances under which the corporate veil would be pierced pursuant to Wyoming law:

> " 'Before a corporation's acts and obligations can be legally recognized as those of a particular person, and vice versa, it must be made to appear that the corporation is not only influenced and governed by that person, but that there is such a unity of interest and ownership that the individuality, or separateness, of such person and corporation has ceased, and that the facts are such that an adherence to the fiction of the separate existence of the corporation would, under the particular circumstances, sanction a fraud or promote injustice.' Quoting *Arnold v. Browne,* 27 Cal. App.3d 386, 103 Cal.Rptr. 775 (1972) (overruled on other grounds)."

We provided the following factors to be considered in determining whether a corporate entity may be disregarded:

> " 'Among the possible factors pertinent to the trial court's determination are: commingling of funds and other assets, failure to segregate funds of the separate entities, and the unauthorized diversion of corporate funds or assets to other than corporate uses; the treatment by an individual of the assets of the corporation as his own; the failure to obtain authority to issue or subscribe to stock; the holding out by an individual that he is personally liable for the debts of the corporation; the failure to maintain minutes or adequate corporate records and the confusion of the records of the separate entities; the identical equitable ownership in the two entities; the identification of the equitable owners thereof with the domination and control of the two entities; identification of the directors and officers of the two entities in the responsible supervision and management; the failure to adequately capitalize a corporation; the absence of corporate assets, and undercapitalization; the use of a corporation as a mere shell, instrumentality or conduit for a single venture or the business of an individual or another corporation; the concealment and misrepresentation of the identity of the responsible ownership, management and financial interest or concealment of personal business activities; the disregard of legal formalities and the failure to maintain arm's length relationships among related entities; the use of the corporate entity to procure labor, services

> or merchandise for another person or entity; the diversion of assets from a corporation by or to a stockholder or other person or entity, to the detriment of creditors, or the manipulation of assets and liabilities between entities so as to concentrate the assets in one and the liabilities in another; the contracting with another with intent to avoid performance by use of a corporation as a subterfuge of illegal transactions; and the formation and use of a corporation to transfer to it the existing liability of another person or entity [citation].' " 645 P.2d at 77–78 (quoting *Arnold v. Browne, supra,* 103 Cal.Rptr. at 781–82).

Miles, 753 P.2d at 1023–24.

Wyoming courts, as well as courts across the country, have typically utilized a fact driven inquiry to determine whether circumstances justify a decision to pierce a corporate veil. *Opal Mercantile,* 616 P.2d at 778. This case comes to us as a certified question in the abstract with little factual context, and we are asked to broadly pronounce that there are no circumstances under which this court will look through a failed attempt to create a separate LLC entity and prevent injustice. We simply cannot reach that conclusion and believe it is improvident for this court to prohibit this remedy from applying to any unforeseen circumstance that may exist in the future.

We have long recognized that piercing the corporate veil is an equitable doctrine. *State ex rel. Christensen v. Nugget Coal Co.,* 60 Wyo. 51, 144 P.2d 944, 952 (1944). The concept of piercing the corporate veil is a judicially created remedy for situations where corporations have not been operated as separate entities as contemplated by statute and, therefore, are not entitled to be treated as such. The determination of whether the doctrine applies centers on whether there is an element of injustice, fundamental unfairness, or inequity. The concept developed through common law and is absent from the statutes governing corporate organization. *See* Wyo. Stat. Ann. §§ 17–16–101 to–1803 (LexisNexis 2001)....

We note that Wyoming was the first state to enact LLC statutes.... Wyoming's statute is very short and establishes only minimal requirements for creating and operating LLCs. It seems highly unlikely that the Wyoming legislature gave any consideration to whether the common-law doctrine of piercing the veil should apply to the liability limitation granted by that fledgling statute. It is true that some other states have adopted specific legislation extending the doctrine to LLCs while Wyoming has not. However, that situation seems more attributable to the fact that Wyoming was a pioneer in the LLC arena and states which adopted LLC statutes much later had the benefit of years of practical experience during which this issue was likely raised.

... It stands to reason that, because it is an equitable doctrine, "[t]he paucity of statutory authority for LCC piercing should not be considered a barrier to its application." [Karin Schwindt, Limited Liability Companies: Issues in Member Liability, 44 UCLA L. Rev. 1541, 1552 (1997).] Lack of explicit statutory language should not be considered an indication of the legislature's desire to make LLC members impermeable. *Id.* at 1555, 144 P.2d 944; Robert B. Thompson, *The Limits of Liability in the New Limited Liability Entities,* 32 Wake Forest L.Rev. 1, 19 (1997). Moreover,

> " 'It is not to be presumed that the legislature intended to abrogate or modify a rule of the common law by the enactment of a statute upon the same subject; it is rather to be presumed that no change in the common law was intended unless the language employed clearly indicates such an intention.... The rules of common law are not to be changed by doubtful implication, nor overturned except by clear and unambiguous language.' " *McKinney v. McKinney,* [59 Wyo. 204,] 135 P.2d [940,] 942 [(1943)], quoting from 25 R.C.L. 1054, § 280.

Allstate Insurance Company v. Wyoming Insurance Department, 672 P.2d 810, 824 (Wyo.1983).

With the dearth of legislative consideration on this issue in Wyoming, we are left to determine whether applying the well established common law to LLCs somehow runs counter to what the legislature would have intended had it considered the issue. In that regard, it is instructive that: "Every state that has enacted LLC piercing legislation has chosen to follow corporate law standards and not develop a separate LLC standard." Philip P. Whynott, The Limited Liability Company § 11:140 at 11–5 (3d ed.1999). Statutes which create corporations and LLCs have the same basic purpose—to limit the liability of individual investors with a corresponding benefit to economic development. Eric Fox, *Piercing the Veil of Limited Liability Companies,* 62 Geo. Wash. L.Rev. 1143, 1145–46 (1994). Statutes created the legal fiction of the corporation being a completely separate entity which could act independently from individual persons. If the corporation were created and operated in conformance with the statutory requirements, the law would treat it as a separate entity and shelter the individual shareholders from any liability caused by corporate action, thereby encouraging investment. However, courts throughout the country have consistently recognized certain unjust circumstances can arise if immunity from liability shelters those who have failed to operate a corporation as a separate entity. Consequently, when corporations fail to follow the statutorily mandated formalities, co-mingle funds, or ignore the restrictions in their articles of incorporation regarding separate treatment of corporate property, the courts deem it appropriate to disregard the separate identity and do not permit shareholders to be sheltered from liability to third parties for damages caused by the corporations' acts.

We can discern no reason, in either law or policy, to treat LLCs differently than we treat corporations. If the members and officers of an LLC fail to treat it as a separate entity as contemplated by statute, they should not enjoy immunity from individual liability for the LLC's acts that cause damage to third parties. Most, if not all, of the expert LLC commentators have concluded the doctrine of piercing the veil should apply to LLCs. *See generally* Fox, *supra;* Gelb, *supra;* Robert G. Lang, Note, *Utah's Limited Liability Company Act: Viable Alternative or Trap for the Unwary?,* 1993 Utah L.Rev. 941, 966 (1993) (Part 2); Stephen B. Presser, Piercing the Corporate Veil § 4.01[2] (2002); Ann M. Seward & Laura Stubberud, *The Limits of Limited Liability–Part Two,* Limited Liability Company Reporter 94–109 (January/February 1994); Schwindt, *supra.* It also appears that most courts faced with a similar situation—LLC statutes which are silent and facts which suggest the LLC veil should be pierced—have had little trouble concluding the common law should be applied and the factors weighed accordingly. *See, e.g., Hollowell v. Orleans Regional Hospital,* No. Civ. A. 95–4029, 1998 WL 283298 (E.D.La. May 29, 1998); *Ditty v. CheckRite, Ltd., Inc.,* 973 F.Supp. 1320 (D.Utah 1997); *Tom Thumb Food Markets, Inc. v. TLH Properties, LLC,* No. C9–98–1277, 1999 WL 31168 (Minn.Ct.App. Jan.26, 1999).

Certainly, the various factors which would justify piercing an LLC veil would not be identical to the corporate situation for the obvious reason that many of the organizational formalities applicable to corporations do not apply to LLCs. The LLC's operation is intended to be much more flexible than a corporation's. Factors relevant to determining when to pierce the corporate veil have developed over time in a multitude of cases. It would be inadvisable in this case, which lacks a complete factual context, to attempt to articulate all the possible factors to be applied to LLCs in Wyoming in the future. For guidance, we direct attention to commentators who have opined on the appropriate factors to be applied in the LLC context. Fox, *supra;* Gelb, *supra;* Curtis J. Braukmann, Comment, *Limited Liability Companies,* 39 U. Kan. L.Rev. 967 (1991); Presser, *supra;* Seward & Stubberud, *supra;* Larry E. Ribstein & Robert R. Keatinge, *Members' Limited Liability,* Limited Liability Companies § 12.03 (1999); Robert R. Keating et al., *The Limited Liability Company: A Study of the Emerging Entity,* 47 The Business Lawyer 375 (1992).

The certified question presents an interesting internal inconsistency. It begins, "In the absence of fraud," thereby presenting the assumption that a court may pierce an LLC's veil in a case of fraud. Thus, the certified question assumes that, when fraud is found, the courts are able to disregard the LLC entity despite the statutory framework which supposedly precludes such a result. Either the courts continue to possess the equitable power to take such action or they do not. Certainly, nothing in the statutes suggests the legislature gave such careful consideration and delineated the specific circumstances under which the courts can act in this arena. If the assumption is correct, individual LLC members can be held personally liable for damages to innocent third parties when the LLC has committed fraud. Yet, when the LLC has caused damage and has inadequate capitalization, co-mingled funds, diverted assets, or used the LLC as a mere shell, individual members are immune from liability. Legislative silence cannot be stretched to condone such an illogical result.

In *Amfac Mechanical Supply Co.,* this court clarified that a showing of fraud or an intent to defraud is not necessary to disregard a corporate entity. 645 P.2d at 79. We clearly stated: "Fraud is, of course, a matter of concern in suits to disregard corporate fictions, but it is not a prerequisite to such a result." *Id.* Other courts have echoed this view: "Liability on the basis of fraud, however, does not encompass the entire spectrum of cases in which the veil was pierced in the interest of equity." Fox, *supra* at 1169. Thus, even absent fraud, courts have the power to impose liability on corporate shareholders. *Id.* at 1170. This same logic should naturally be extended to the LLC context. We have made clear that: "Each case involving the disregard of the separate entity doctrine must be governed by the special facts of that case." *Opal Mercantile,* 616 P.2d at 778. Determinations of fact are within the trier of fact's province. *Id.* The district court must complete a fact intensive inquiry and exercise its equitable powers to determine whether piercing the veil is appropriate under the circumstances presented in this case.

CONCLUSION

No reason exists in law or equity for treating an LLC differently than a corporation is treated when considering whether to disregard the legal entity. We conclude the equitable remedy of piercing the veil is an available remedy under the Wyoming Limited Liability Company Act.

Tzolis v. Wolff

Court of Appeals of New York, 2008.
10 N.Y.3d 100, 855 N.Y.S.2d 6, 884 N.E.2d 1005.

■ SMITH, J.

Opinion of the Court

We hold that members of a limited liability company (LLC) may bring derivative suits on the LLC's behalf, even though there are no provisions governing such suits in the Limited Liability Company Law.

FACTS AND PROCEDURAL HISTORY

Pennington Property Co. LLC was the owner of a Manhattan apartment building. Plaintiffs, who own 25% of the membership interests in the LLC, bring this action "individually and in the right and on behalf of" the company. Plaintiffs claim that those in control of the LLC, and others acting in concert with them, arranged first to lease and then to sell the LLC's principal asset for sums below market value; that the lease was unlawfully assigned; and that company fiduciaries benefitted personally from the sale. Plaintiffs assert several causes of action, of which only the first two are in issue here: The first cause of action seeks to declare the sale void, and the second seeks termination of the lease.

Supreme Court dismissed these causes of action. It held that they could not be brought by plaintiffs individually, because they were "to redress wrongs suffered by the corporation".... It also held, following *Hoffman v. Unterberg* (9 AD3d 386 [2d Dept 2004]), that "New York law does not permit members to bring derivative actions on behalf of a limited liability company".... The Appellate Division, concluding that derivative suits on behalf of LLCs are permitted, reversed ..., and granted two defendants permission to appeal on a certified question. We now affirm the Appellate Division's order.

DISCUSSION

The issue is whether derivative suits on behalf of LLCs are allowed. The basis for appellants' argument that they are not is the Legislature's decision, when the Limited Liability Company Law was enacted in 1994, to omit all reference to such suits. We hold that this omission does not imply such suits are prohibited. We base our holding on the long-recognized importance of the derivative suit in corporate law, and on the absence of evidence that the Legislature decided to abolish this remedy when it passed the Limited Liability Company Law in 1994.

I

The derivative suit has been part of the general corporate law of this state at least since 1832. It was not created by statute, but by case law. Chancellor Walworth recognized the remedy in *Robinson v. Smith* (3 Paige Ch 222 [1832]), because he thought it essential for shareholders to have recourse when those in control of a corporation betrayed their duty. Chancellor Walworth applied to a joint stock corporation—then a fairly new kind of entity—a familiar principle of the law of trusts: that a beneficiary (or "cestui que trust") could bring suit on behalf of a trust when a faithless trustee refused to do so. Ruling that shareholders could sue on behalf of a corporation under similar circumstances, the Chancellor explained:

> "The directors are the trustees or managing partners, and the stockholders are the cestui que trusts, and have a joint interest in all the property and effects of the corporation.... And no injury the stockholders may sustain by a fraudulent breach of trust, can, upon the general principles of equity, be suffered to pass without a remedy. In the language of Lord Hardwicke, in a similar case [*Charitable Corp. v. Sutton*, 2 Atk 400, 406 (Ch 1742)], 'I will never determine that a court of equity cannot lay hold of every such breach of trust. I will never determine that frauds of this kind are out of the reach of courts of law or equity; for an intolerable grievance would follow from such a determination.'" (3 Paige Ch at 232.)

Eventually, the rule that derivative suits could be brought on behalf of ordinary business corporations was codified by statute.... But until relatively recently, no similar statutory provision was made for another kind of entity, the limited partnership; again, the absence of a statute did not prevent courts from recognizing the remedy. In *Klebanow v. New York Produce Exch.* (344 F2d 294 [2d Cir 1965, Friendly, J.]), the Second Circuit Court of Appeals held that limited partners could sue on a partnership's behalf. For the Second Circuit, the absence of a statutory provision was not decisive because the court found no "clear mandate *against* limited partners' capacity to bring an action like this" (*id.* at 298 [emphasis added]). We agreed with the holding of *Klebanow* in *Riviera Congress Assoc. v. Yassky* (18 NY2d 540, 547 [1966, Fuld, J.]), relying, as had Chancellor Walworth long before, on an analogy with the law of trusts:

> "There can be no question that a managing or general partner of a limited partnership is bound in a fiduciary relationship with the limited partners ... and the latter are, therefore, *cestuis que trustent*.... It is fundamental to the law of trusts that *cestuis* have the right, 'upon the general principles of equity' (*Robinson v. Smith*, 3 Paige Ch. 222, 232) and 'independently of [statutory] provisions' (*Brinckerhoff v. Bostwick*, 88 N.Y. 52, 59), to sue for the benefit of the trust on a cause of action which belongs to the trust if 'the trustees refuse to perform their duty in that respect'. (*Western R. R. Co. v. Nolan*, 48 N. Y. 513, 518....)"

After *Klebanow* and *Riviera* were decided, the Partnership Law was amended to provide for derivative actions by limited partners (*see* Partnership Law § 115–a [1]).

We now consider whether to recognize derivative actions on behalf of a third kind of entity, the LLC, as to which no statutory provision for such an action exists. In addressing the question, we continue to heed the realization that influenced Chancellor Walworth in 1832, and Lord Hardwicke 90 years earlier: When fiduciaries are faithless to their trust, the victims must not be left wholly without a remedy. As Lord Hardwicke put it, to "determine that frauds of this kind are out of the reach of courts of law or equity" would lead to "an intolerable grievance" (*Charitable Corp. v. Sutton*, 2 Atk at 406).

To hold that there is no remedy when corporate fiduciaries use corporate assets to enrich themselves was unacceptable in 1742 and in 1832, and it is still unacceptable today. Derivative suits are not the only possible remedy, but they are the one that has been recognized for most of two centuries, and to abolish them in the LLC context would be a radical step.

Some of the problems such an abolition would create may be seen in the development of New York law since the Limited Liability Company Law, omitting all reference to derivative suits, was passed in 1994. Several courts have held that there is no derivative remedy for LLC members.... But since the Legislature obviously did not intend to give corporate fiduciaries a license to steal, a substitute remedy must be devised. Perhaps responding to this need, some courts have held that members of an LLC have their own, direct claims against fiduciaries for conduct that injured the LLC—blurring, if not erasing, the traditional line between direct and derivative claims.... Similarly, Supreme Court's decision in this case upheld several of plaintiffs' claims that are not in issue here, characterizing the claims as direct, though they might well be derivative under traditional analysis (*see generally*, Kleinberger, *Direct Versus Derivative and The Law of Limited Liability Companies*, 58 Baylor L Rev 63 [2006]).

Substituting direct remedies of LLC members for the old-fashioned derivative suit—a substitution not suggested by anything in the language of the Limited Liability Company Law—raises unanswered questions. Suppose, for example, a corporate fiduciary steals a hundred dollars from the treasury of an LLC. Unquestionably he or she is liable to the LLC for a hundred dollars, a liability which could be enforced in a suit by the LLC itself. Is the same fiduciary also liable to each injured LLC member in a direct suit for the member's share of the same money? What, if anything, is to be done to prevent double liability? No doubt, if the Legislature had indeed abolished the derivative suit as far as LLCs are concerned, we could and would answer these questions and others like them. But we will not readily conclude that the Legislature intended to set us on this uncharted path.

II

As shown above, courts have repeatedly recognized derivative suits in the absence of express statutory authorization (*Robinson v. Smith*, 3 Paige Ch 222 [1832]; *Klebanow v. New York Produce Exch.*, 344 F2d 294 [2d Cir 1965]; *Riviera Congress Assoc. v. Yassky*, 18 NY2d 540 [1966]). In light of this, it could hardly be argued that the mere absence of authorizing language in the Limited Liability Company Law bars the courts from entertaining derivative suits by LLC members. It is argued, however, by appellants and by our dissenting colleagues, that here we face not just legislative silence, but a considered legislative decision not to permit the remedy. The dissent finds, in the legislative history of the Limited Liability Company Law, a "legislative bargain" to the effect that derivative suits on behalf of LLCs should not exist (dissenting op at 113). We find no such thing. For us, the most salient feature of the legislative history is that no one, in or out of the Legislature, ever expressed a wish to *eliminate*, rather than limit or reform, derivative suits. . . .

Accordingly, the order of the Appellate Division, insofar as appealed from, should be affirmed with costs and the certified question answered in the affirmative.

■ [The dissenting opinion of JUDGE READ, joined in by JUDGES GRAFFEO and JONES, is omitted.]

■ CHIEF JUDGE KAYE AND JUDGES CIPARICK AND PIGOTT CONCUR WITH JUDGE SMITH; JUDGE READ DISSENTS IN A SEPARATE OPINION IN WHICH JUDGES GRAFFEO AND JONES CONCUR.

Order, insofar as appealed from, affirmed, with costs, and certified question answered in the affirmative.

SECTION 3. FIDUCIARY DUTIES

Salm v. Feldstein

Supreme Court, Appellate Division, New York, 2005.
20 A.D.3d 469, 799 N.Y.S.2d 104.

■ GABRIEL M. KRAUSMAN, J.P., WILLIAM F. MASTRO, REINALDO E. RIVERA, AND ROBERT A. SPOLZINO, JJ.

In an action to recover damages for breach of fiduciary duty and fraud, the plaintiff appeals from a judgment of the Supreme Court . . . granting the defendant's motion for summary judgment. . . .

ORDERED that the judgment is reversed, on the law, with costs. . . .

The plaintiff and the defendant were the members of World Wide Automotive, LLC (hereinafter the company), a limited liability company that owned an automobile dealership (hereinafter the dealership), each having an equal financial interest in the company. The defendant was the managing member of the company. On June 2, 2003, the defendant purchased the plaintiff's membership interest in the company under a redemption and settlement agreement (hereinafter the contract) providing for a payment to the plaintiff in the sum of $3,750,000, and a consulting contract with the plaintiff which would pay him a five-year aggregate sum of $1,350,000. On June 4, 2003, the defendant sold the dealership to a nonparty for the sum of $16 million.

The plaintiff commenced this action against the defendant to recover damages for breach of fiduciary duty and fraud. The plaintiff alleged that the defendant misrepresented the value of the dealership as being between $5 and $6 million and failed to disclose that the nonparty purchaser had made a firm offer to purchase the dealership for the sum of $16 million before May 31, 2003. The defendant moved for summary judgment dismissing the complaint and the plaintiff cross-moved to compel discovery. The Supreme Court granted the motion and denied the cross motion. We reverse.

As the managing member of the company and as a co-member with the plaintiff, the defendant owed the plaintiff a fiduciary duty to make full disclosure of all material facts (*see Birnbaum v. Birnbaum*, 73 N.Y.2d 461, 465, 541 N.Y.S.2d 746, 539 N.E.2d 574, *citing Meinhard v. Salmon*, 249 N.Y. 458, 468, 164 N.E. 545; *Blue Chip Emerald v. Allied Partners*, 299 A.D.2d 278, 750 N.Y.S.2d 291). Moreover, because the defendant had a fiduciary relationship with the plaintiff, the disclaimers contained in the contract, upon which the defendant relies, did not relieve him of the obligation of full disclosure (*see Blue Chip Emerald v. Allied Partners, supra*). Although the defendant denies the plaintiff's allegation that he failed to keep the plaintiff informed of all communications with the nonparty purchaser, the alacrity with which the dealership was sold after the plaintiff conveyed his interest in the company to the defendant was sufficient to establish "that facts essential to justify opposition may exist but cannot then be stated" (CPLR 3212[f]). The defendant's motion for summary judgment should, therefore, have been denied....

VGS, Inc. v. Castiel

Court of Chancery of Delaware.
2000 WL 1277372.

■ STEELE, VICE CHANCELLOR....

I. Facts

David Castiel formed Virtual Geosatellite LLC (the "LLC") on January 6, 1999 in order to pursue a Federal Communications Commission ("FCC") license to build and operate a satellite system which its proponents claim could dramatically increase the "real estate" in outer space capable of transmitting high speed internet traffic and other communications. When originally formed, it had only one Member—Virtual Geosatellite Holdings, Inc. ("Holdings"). On January 8, 1999, Ellipso, Inc. ("Ellipso") joined the LLC as its second Member. Several weeks later, on January 29, 1999, Sahagen Satellite Technology Group LLC ("Sahagen Satellite") became the third Member of the LLC.

David Castiel controls both Holdings and Ellipso. Peter Sahagen, an aggressive and apparently successful venture capitalist, controls Sahagen Satellite.

Pursuant to the LLC Agreement, Holdings received 660 units (representing 63.46% of the total equity in the LLC), Sahagen Satellite received 260 units (representing 25%), and Ellipso received 120 units (representing 11.54%). The founders vested management of the LLC in a Board of Managers. As the majority unitholder, Castiel had the power to appoint, remove, and replace two of the three members of the Board of Managers. Castiel, therefore, had the power to prevent any Board decision with which he disagreed. Castiel named himself and Tom Quinn to the Board of Managers. Sahagen named himself as the third member of the Board.

Not long after the formation of the LLC, Castiel and Sahagen were at odds....

Sahagen ultimately convinced Quinn that Castiel must be ousted from leadership in order for the LLC to prosper. As a result, Quinn (Castiel's nominee) covertly "defected" to Sahagen's camp, and he and Sahagen decided to wrest control of the LLC from Castiel....

On April 14, 2000, without notice to Castiel, Quinn and Sahagen acted by written consent to merge the LLC under Delaware law into VGS, Inc. ("VGS"), a Delaware corporation. Accordingly, the LLC ceased to exist, its assets and liabilities passed to VGS, and VGS became the LLC's legal successor-in-interest. VGS's Board of Directors is comprised of Sahagen, Quinn, and Neel Howard. Of course, the incorporators did not name Castiel to VGS's Board.

On the day of the merger, Sahagen executed a promissory note to VGS in the amount of $10 million plus interest. In return, he received two million shares of VGS Series A Preferred Stock. VGS also issued 1,269,200 shares of common stock to Holdings, 230,800 shares of common stock to Ellipso, and 500,000 shares of common stock to Sahagen Satellite. Once one does the math, it is apparent that Holdings and Ellipso went from having a 75% controlling combined ownership interest in the LLC to having only a 37.5% interest in VGS. On the other hand, Sahagen and Sahagen Satellite went from owning 25% of the LLC to owning 62.5% of VGS.

There can be no doubt why Sahagen and Quinn, acting as a majority of the LLC's board of managers did not notify Castiel of the merger plan. Notice to Castiel would have immediately resulted in Quinn's removal from the board and a newly constituted majority which would thwart the effort to strip Castiel of control. Had he known in advance, Castiel surely would have attempted to replace Quinn with someone loyal to Castiel who would agree with his views. Clandestine machinations were, therefore, essential to the success of Quinn and Sahagen's plan.

II. Analysis . . .

. . . Section 18–404(d) of the LLC Act states in pertinent part:

> Unless otherwise provided in a limited liability company agreement, on any matter that is to be voted on by managers, the managers may take such action without a meeting, without prior notice and without a vote if a consent or consents in writing, setting forth the action so taken, shall be signed by the managers having not less than the minimum number of votes that would be necessary to authorize such action at a meeting (emphasis added).

Therefore, the LLC Act, read literally, does not require notice to Castiel before Sahagen and Quinn could act by written consent. The LLC Agreement does not purport to modify the statute in this regard. . . .

Section 18–404(d) has yet to be interpreted by this Court or the Supreme Court. Nonetheless, it seems clear that the purpose of permitting action by written consent without notice is to enable LLC managers to take quick, efficient action in situations where a minority of managers could not block or adversely affect the course set by the majority even if they were notified of the proposed action and objected to it. The General Assembly never intended, I am quite confident, to enable two managers to deprive, clandestinely and surreptitiously, a third manager representing the majority interest in the LLC of an opportunity to protect that interest by taking an action that the third manager's member would surely have opposed if he had knowledge of it. My reading of Section 18–404(d) is grounded in a classic maxim of equity—"Equity looks to the intent rather than to the form." In this hopefully unique situation, this application of the maxim requires construction of the statute to allow action without notice only by a constant or fixed majority. It can not apply to an illusory, will-of-the wisp majority which would implode should notice be given. Nothing in the statute suggests that this court of equity should blind its eyes to a shallow, too clever by half, manipulative attempt to restructure an enterprise through an action taken by a "majority" that existed only so long as it could act in secrecy.

Sahagen and Quinn each owed a duty of loyalty to the LLC, its investors and Castiel, their fellow manager. Castiel or his entities owned a majority interest in the LLC and he sat as a member of the board representing entities and interests empowered by the Agreement to control the majority membership of the board. The majority investor protected his equity interest in the LLC through the mechanism of appointment to the board rather than by the statutorily sanctioned mechanism of approval by members owning a majority of the LLC's equity interests. It may seem somewhat incongruous, but this Agreement allows the action to merge, dissolve or change to corporate status to be taken by a simple majority vote of the board of managers rather than rely upon the default position of the statute which requires a majority vote of the equity interest. Instead the drafters made the critical assumption, known to all the players here, that the holder of the majority equity interest has the right to appoint and remove two managers, ostensibly guaranteeing control over a three member board. When Sahagen and Quinn, fully recognizing that this was Castiel's protection against actions adverse to his majority interest, acted in secret, without notice, they failed to discharge their duty of loyalty to him in good faith. They owed Castiel a duty to give him prior notice even if he would have interfered with a plan that they conscientiously believed to be in the best interest of the LLC. Instead, they launched a preemptive strike that furtively converted Castiel's controlling interest in the LLC to a minority interest in VGS without affording Castiel a level playing field on which to defend his interest. "[Another] traditional maxim of equity holds that equity regards and treats that as done which in good conscience ought to be done." In good conscience, under these circumstances, Sahagen and Quinn should have given Castiel prior notice.

Many hours were spent at trial focusing on contentions that Castiel has proved to be an ineffective leader in whom employees and investors have lost confidence.... But the issue of who is best suited to run the LLC should not be resolved here but in board meetings where all managers are present and all members appropriately represented, and/or in future litigation, if it unfortunately becomes necessary....

III. Conclusion

For the reasons stated above, I find that a majority vote of the LLC's Board of Managers could properly effect a merger. But, I also find that Sahagen and Quinn failed to discharge their duty of loyalty to Castiel in good faith by failing to give him advance notice of their merger plans under the unique circumstances of this case and the structure of this LLC Agreement. Accordingly, I declare that the acts taken to merge the LLC into VGS, Inc. to be invalid and the merger is ordered rescinded. An order consistent with this opinion, resolving the current claims of the parties is attached . . .

Solar Cells, Inc. v. True North Partners, LLC

Court of Chancery of Delaware.
2002 WL 749163.

■ Chandler, J.

This action concerns the proposed merger of defendant First Solar, LLC ("First Solar" or the "Company") with and into First Solar Operating, LLC ("FSO"), the wholly-owned operating subsidiary of First Solar Ventures, LLC ("FSV"). The plaintiff, Solar Cells, Inc. ("Solar Cells"), alleges that the individual defendant managers of First Solar,[1] acting at the direction of defendant True North Partners, LLC ("True North" and, collectively, "the defendants"), acted in bad faith in approving the proposed merger and that the defendants will be unable to prove the entire fairness of that merger.

On March 13, 2002, Solar Cells filed a motion for a temporary restraining order requesting that this Court enjoin the proposed merger. . . .

I. BACKGROUND FACTS

Solar Cells, an Ohio corporation, was founded in 1987 by Harold A. McMaster ("McMaster") to develop, design, and manufacture products and processes for photovoltaic electricity generation-technology commonly referred to as "solar power." . . .

McMaster designed technologies and processes for manufacturing photovoltaic cells making use of heretofore-unknown techniques that were predicted to revolutionize the solar power industry. . . . True North, an Arizona limited liability company, was brought in to provide needed financing. Solar Cells and True North formed First Solar as a Delaware limited liability company in February 1999 to commercialize McMaster's solar technology.

First Solar is managed pursuant to the Operating Agreement of First Solar, LLC ("Operating Agreement"). The Operating Agreement required Solar Cells to contribute patented and proprietary technology—valued in the Operating Agreement at $35 million—to First Solar. True North was to contribute $35 million in capital to First Solar and, also pursuant to the Operating Agreement, was required to, and did, loan First Solar an additional $8 million. In return for their contributions, Solar Cells and [True North] each received 4,500 of First Solar's Class A membership units. Solar Cells also received 100% of First Solar's Class B membership units.[4] The business and affairs of First

---

1. The individual defendants are First Solar Managers elected by True North: Michael J. Ahearn ("Ahearn"), Michael L. Pierce ("Pierce"), and Michael Gallagher ("Gallagher").

4. According to the Operating Agreement, Class A Units had voting rights, and Class B Units had no voting rights.

Solar is conducted by five Managers. The Operating Agreement permits True North to elect three of those Managers (the "True North Managers") and Solar Cells to elect the remaining two Managers (the "Solar Cells Managers"). It is undisputed that, since its inception, First Solar has been managed by True North.

First Solar's continuing development and manufacturing expenditures, as well as its inability to produce a marketable product, eventually depleted the Company's initial funding. By early 2001 it became apparent that continued operations would require additional funding. To this end, in March 2001, First Solar retained investment banker Adams, Harkness & Hill, Inc. ("AHH") to find a strategic investor for the Company. In order for the Company to continue operating while AHH searched for a strategic investor, True North agreed to make an additional $15 million loan to First Solar.

The Loan Agreement between First Solar and True North bundled True North's original $8 million loan and the new $15 million loan and represented a funding commitment by True North of up to a total of $23 million through December 31, 2001. Upon either the receipt of outside investment or at the end of its funding commitment, the Loan Agreement gave True North the option of converting some or all of the loan amount into Class A Units of First Solar[5] or to retain the investment as a loan with liquidation preferences....

From December 2001 through March 2002, the parties engaged in unsuccessful negotiations regarding different alternatives for financing and restructuring First Solar. On March 5, 2002, True North purported to convert $250,000 of its outstanding loans to First Solar into Class A Units at a conversion ratio based on a January 8, 2002 AHH valuation of First Solar at $32,000,000. On March 7, 2002, the True North Managers executed a written consent approving the challenged merger of First Solar into FSO, a Delaware limited liability company wholly owned by True North. On March 11, 2002, Solar Cells received notice of the proposed merger, which was scheduled to close on March 15, 2002, and the terms of that merger. In connection with the merger, True North would convert its remaining outstanding loans into equity at the same ratio as the March 5, 2002 conversion. The merger would occur based on a total valuation of First Solar at $32 million with First Solar ownership units being exchanged for ownership units of the surviving company. The end result of the merger-related transactions would be that Solar Cells would go from owning 50% of the Class A Units of First Solar to owning 5% of the membership units of the surviving company. On March 13, 2002, Solar Cells filed a complaint and request for temporary restraining order enjoining consummation of the proposed merger. True North agreed not to cause its Managers to close the merger before this Court's decision on Solar Cells' motion for a preliminary injunction filed in response to that agreement....

5. The loan was convertible either at the same value as AHH proposed to outside investors or at a "conversion ratio" specified in the Loan Agreement.

IV. ANALYSIS

A. *Likelihood of Success on the Merits*

The defendants argue that all of the actions taken in connection with the proposed merger were clearly authorized by the Operating Agreement. They further argue that the Operating Agreement limited any fiduciary duties owed by True North Managers. Section 4.18(a) of the Operating Agreement provides, in relevant part:

> Solar Cells and [First Solar] acknowledge that the True North Managers have fiduciary obligations to both [First Solar] and to True North, which fiduciary obligations may, because of the ability of the True North Managers to control [First Solar] and its business, create a conflict of interest or a potential conflict of interest for the true North Managers. Both [First Solar] and Solar Cells hereby waive any such conflict of interest or potential conflict of interest and agree that neither True North nor any True North Manager shall have any liability to [First Solar] or to Solar Cells with respect to any such conflict of interest or potential conflict of interest, provided that the True North managers have acted in a manner which they believe in good faith to be in the best interest of [First Solar].

I note that this clause purports to limit *liability* stemming from any conflict of interest. Solar Cells has not requested that this Court impose liability on the individual defendants. It is currently only seeking to *enjoin* the proposed merger. Therefore, exculpation for personal liability has no bearing on the likelihood that Solar Cells would be successful on the merits of its contention that the proposed merger is inequitable and should be enjoined. Even if waiver of liability for engaging in conflicting interest transactions is contracted for, that does not mean that there is a waiver of all fiduciary duties to Solar Cells. Indeed, § 4.18(a) expressly states that the True North Managers must act in "good faith." It is undisputed that First Solar was, and is, in financial distress. Months of unsuccessful negotiations have been ongoing in an attempt to come to an agreement as to how to remedy that situation. On March 6, 2002, the full Board of Managers met and the True North Managers made no mention of the planned merger. The *very next day,* March 7, 2002, the three True North Managers met and by written consent approved the proposed merger. No effort was made to inform the Solar Cells Managers that this action was contemplated, or imminent, when those facts were surely known at the time of the March 6 meeting.[8] At the earliest, Solar Cells was given notice of the fact, and terms, of the proposed merger (which were presented as a *fait accompli*) via facsimile on March 8, 2002—a week before consummation of a merger that will apparently reduce Solar Cells' interest from 50% to 5%. These actions do not appear to be those of fiduciaries acting in good faith. As the Supreme Court and this Court have made clear, it is not an unassailable defense

8. The plaintiff contends that documents produced during discovery reveal that the defendants had been planning the proposed merger since at least February 27, 2002.

to say that what was done was in technical compliance with the law.[9] The facts before me make it likely, in my opinion, that the defendants would be required to show the entire fairness of the proposed merger.

The party with the burden of establishing entire fairness must establish that the challenged transaction was the result of fair dealing and offered a fair price. Fair dealing pertains to the process by which the transaction was approved and looks at the terms, structure, and timing of the transaction. Fair price includes all relevant factors "relat[ing] to the economic and financial considerations of the proposed merger."[10]

The defendants argue that there is nothing inherently unfair about the structure of the merger—a holding company with a wholly-owned operating subsidiary. Solar Cells points out, however, that there was no independent bargaining mechanism set up to protect its interests. In fact, there was no negotiation at all. All of the decisions regarding the terms of the merger and its approval were made unilaterally by True North through its representative Managers. No advance notice of this merger was given to Solar Cells. The fact that the Operating Agreement permits action by written consent of a majority of the Managers and permits interested transactions free from personal liability does not give a fiduciary free reign to approve any transaction he sees fit regardless of the impact on those to whom he owes a fiduciary duty. . . .

I am unconvinced by defendants' argument that the merger was fair to Solar Cells because Solar Cells retains voting rights in the surviving company. On matters where the unit-holders can vote, Solar Cells is diluted from an equal (50%) voice, to only 5%. . . . In my opinion, the facts before me establish a reasonable likelihood that defendants will not be able to establish that the proposed merger was the result of fair dealing.

Application of the entire fairness standard requires a demonstration of both fair dealing and fair price. Having considered the fair dealing component of the standard, I turn now to the fair price analysis. . . .

For purposes of the present motion only, I am satisfied that there is a reasonable probability that the Court will not find the January 2002 valuation to be entirely fair. First, the author of AHH's January 2002 valuation materials described those materials as a "quick and dirty" analysis of First Solar's value on that date. This contrasts with the earlier valuations in August and November of 2001, valuations that were based on multiple methodologies to arrive at a value for First Solar that ranged from $103 million in August 2001 to $72 million in November 2001, or almost two to three times the January 2002 valuation. Second, AHH's January 2002 valuation employed only a discounted cash flow analysis. Although the lower valuation in January 2002 was the basis upon which True North would acquire a 95%

---

9. *See Schnell v. Chris–Craft Indus.*, 285 A.2d 437 (Del.1971).

10. *See Weinberger v. UOP, Inc.*, 457 A.2d 701, 711 (Del.1983).

interest in First Solar and Solar Cells would fall to a 5% interest, the significantly lower valuation failed to employ any other method of valuation as a "crosscheck" to the discounted cash flow analysis. Because earlier valuations relied on multiple valuation methodologies, it is a reasonable inference that AHH's "quick and dirty" analysis is less reliable and authoritative. Third, the January 2002 formula used a much lower exit multiple (a 6.9 x free cash flow terminal year multiple) than did earlier valuation formulas (which used an 11 x free cash flow terminal year multiple), with no apparent rationale for that lower multiple. Fourth, AHH's lower valuation resulted from the use of a much higher discount rate (35%) than the valuations it performed only five months earlier (30%), even though the outlook for the solar cell industry was improving in that period and even though interest rates were generally falling.[11]

... I conclude that it is reasonably likely this Court will find the January 2002 $32 million valuation of First Solar not to be a fair price because it is irreconcilable with the earlier valuations only a few months before True North decided to go forward with the proposed merger. Because Solar Cells has demonstrated a reasonable likelihood of success on the merits of its entire fairness claim, I turn next to the irreparable harm and balance of the equities component of the preliminary injunction standard.

B. Irreparable Harm

In order to show irreparable harm, the injury must be one for which money damages will not be an adequate remedy. Additionally, the threatened harm must be "imminent, unspeculative, and genuine."

Solar Cells argues that it will be harmed irreparably by the dilution of its equity position and voting power as unit-holders. It also alleges that the loss of its bargained-for participation in company management is an irreparable harm....

The defendants ... argue that since True North had the right to nominate a majority of First Solar's Managers, True North could control the business and affairs of the Company. That reality is unaltered with the surviving company. The defendants reason, therefore, that Solar Cells has suffered no harm by losing its right to

---

11. Even True North's litigation expert, Mr. Brian DiLucente, arrived at a much higher value for First Solar ($51.9 million). DiLucente was able to reduce his $51.9 million valuation to $31.1 million, but to do so, he was forced to apply a 40% "marketability" discount. The courts of this State, however, have repeatedly rejected the applicability of such discounts.... Furthermore, after putting to one side DiLucente's apparent improper application of a marketability discount, his $51.9 million valuation for First Solar likely was improperly depressed by other aspects of his discounted cash flow analysis. For example, DiLucente applied a discount rate as high as 45%, based on his subjective view of First Solar's Company specific risk. But Dilucente admitted in his deposition testimony that he had no expertise in the solar cell industry and limited knowledge of the specific company, First Solar, that his analysis purported to value. This Court has been, understandably in my view, suspicious of expert valuations offered at trial that incorporate subjective measures of company specific risk premia, as subjective measures may easily be employed as a means to smuggle improper risk assumptions into the discount rate so as to affect dramatically the expert's ultimate opinion on value....

appoint managers. That argument carries no weight whatsoever. To accept that assertion would be to believe that every time the ability to elect a manager or director of a corporation is negotiated, there is no benefit derived therefrom if there is not a right to elect a majority of the managers or directors. Such a notion would certainly come as a surprise to all those who have given valuable consideration in negotiating such valueless rights. The right to participate in a management group is a valuable right whether or not that participation includes control of the group. In this case, it is undisputed that Solar Cells will lose that right if the proposed merger closes, thereby suffering an irreparable harm....

V. CONCLUSION

For the reasons stated, I grant plaintiff's motion for preliminary injunction....

SECTION 4. DISSOLUTION

In the Matter of 1545 Ocean Avenue, LLC.

New York Supreme Court, Appellate Division, 2010.
893 N.Y.S.2d 590.

On this appeal, we are asked to determine whether the Supreme Court properly granted the petition of Crown Royal Ventures, LLC (hereinafter Crown Royal), to dissolve 1545 Ocean Avenue, LLC (hereinafter 1545 LLC). For the following reasons, we answer in the negative and reverse the order of the Supreme Court.

1545 LLC was formed in November 2006 when its Articles of Organization were filed with the Department of State. On November 15, 2006, two membership certificates for 50 units each were issued respectively to Crown Royal and the appellant, Ocean Suffolk Properties, LLC (hereinafter Ocean Suffolk).

On the same date that the membership certificates were issued, an [operating] agreement was executed by Ocean Suffolk and Crown Royal. The operating agreement provided for two managers; Walter T. Van Houten (hereinafter Van Houten), who was a member of Ocean Suffolk, and John J. King, who was a member of Crown Royal. Each member of 1545 LLC contributed 50% of the capital which was used to purchase premises known as 1545 Ocean Avenue in Bohemia (hereinafter the property) on January 5, 2007. 1545 LLC was formed to purchase the property, rehabilitate an existing building, and build a second building for commercial rental (hereinafter Building A and B, respectively).

It was agreed by Van Houten and King that they would solicit bids from third parties to perform the necessary demolition and construction work to complete the project. Van Houten, who owns his own construction company, Van Houten Construction (hereinafter VHC), was permitted to submit bids for the project, subject to the approval of the managers.

Ocean Suffolk alleges that when there were no bona fide bidders, the managers agreed to allow VHC to perform the work, while Crown Royal maintains that VHC began demolition and reconstruction on Building A without King's consent. In rehabilitating the existing building, Van Houten claims that he discovered and remediated various structural flaws with the claimed knowledge and approval of King or another member of Crown Royal.

King wanted architect Gary Bruno to review the blueprints upon which VHC began demolition since it had been started without the necessary building permits. In addition, King claimed that VHC did not have the proper equipment to efficiently do the excavation and demolition work, causing the billing to be greater than necessary. VHC billed 1545 LLC the sum of $97,322.27 for this work. King claims that he agreed 1545 LLC would pay VHC's invoice on the condition that it would no longer unilaterally do work on the site. Notwithstanding King's demand, VHC continued working on the site. Despite his earlier protests, King did nothing to stop it.

Thereafter, Bruno applied to the Town of Islip for the necessary building permits. The Suffolk County Department of Health required an environmental review whereby a so-called "hot spot" was detected by an environmental engineering firm which proposed to remediate it for $6,500. F & E, the company recommended by Crown Royal to do the remediation work, estimated that the cost for the environmental remediation work would be about $6,675. King claims that Van Houten objected to F & E and had another firm do a separate evaluation without King's approval, while Van Houten asserts that although F & E eventually charged $8,229.63 for its work, payment to F & E by 1545 LLC was made with his approval. . . .

Following this incident, King contended that tensions between King and Van Houten escalated. King asserted that things could not continue as they were or else the project would not be finished in an economical or timely manner. King claimed that Van Houten refused to meet on a regular basis; that he proclaimed himself to be a "cowboy;" and that Van Houten stated he would "just get it done." Nevertheless, King acknowledged that the construction work undertaken by VHC was "awesome."

By April 2007, King announced that he wanted to withdraw his investment from 1545 LLC. He proposed to have all vendors so notified telling them that Van Houten was taking over the management of 1545 LLC. As a result, Van Houten viewed King as having resigned as a manager of 1545 LLC.

Ultimately, King sought to have Ocean Suffolk buy out Crown Royal's membership in 1545 LLC or, alternatively, to have Crown Royal buy out Ocean Suffolk. In the interim, King had his attorney send a "stop work" request to Van Houten.

There ensued discussions regarding competing proposals for the buy-out of the interest of each member by the other. No satisfactory resolution was realized. Nevertheless, despite disagreement among the members during this difficult period, VHC continued to work unilaterally on the site so that the project was within weeks of completion when this proceeding was commenced whereby further work by Van Houten was enjoined....

II

Article 7.4 of the operating agreement provides, "any matter not specifically covered by a provision of the [operating agreement], including without limitation, dissolution of the Company, shall be governed by the applicable provisions of the [Limited Liability Company Laws]." Accordingly, dissolution of 1545 LLC is governed by LLCL article VII.

III

This proceeding was commenced by order to show cause and verified petition seeking the dissolution of 1545 LLC and related relief. The sole ground for dissolution cited by Crown Royal is deadlock between the managing members arising from Van Houten's alleged violations of various provisions of article 4 of the operating agreement. There was no allegation of fraud or frustration of the purpose of 1545 LLC on the part of Ocean Suffolk, Van Houten, and VHC....

... [B]y May 10, 2007, in anticipation of a buy-out of the Crown Royal interest in the venture, the parties were operating as if Van Houten was the sole managing member of 1545 LLC. Indeed, throughout the negotiations for the buy-out, the renovation work on Building A continued.

IV

LLCL 702 provides for judicial dissolution as follows:

> "On application by or for a member, the Supreme Court in the judicial district in which the office of the limited liability company is located may decree dissolution of a limited liability company *whenever it is not reasonably practicable to carry on the business* in conformity with the articles of organization or operating agreement" (emphasis added)....

Despite the standard for dissolution enunciated in LLCL 702, there is no definition of "not reasonably practicable" in the context of the dissolution of a limited liability company....

... LLCL 702 is clear that unlike the judicial dissolution standards in the Business Corporation Law and the Partnership Law, the court must first examine the limited liability company's operating agreement ... to determine, in light of the circumstances presented, whether it is or is not "reasonably practicable" for the limited liability company to continue to carry on its business in conformity with the operating agreement.... Thus, the dissolution of a limited liability company under LLCL 702 is initially a contract-based analysis....

The operating agreement of 1545 LLC does not contain any specific provisions relating to dissolution. It provides only in article 1.5 that "(t)he Company's term is perpetual from the date of filing of the Articles of Organization ... unless the Company is dissolved."

Crown Royal argues for dissolution based on the parties' failure to hold regular meetings, failure to achieve quorums, and deadlock. The operating agreement, however, does not require regular meetings or quorums (*see* 1545 LLC operating agreement arts. 4.2, 4.13). It only provides, in article 4.12, for meetings to be held at such times as the managers may "from time to time determine." The record demonstrates that the managers, King and Van Houten, communicated with each other on a regular basis without the formality of a noticed meeting which appears to conform with the spirit and letter of the operating agreement and the continued ability of 1545 LLC to function in that context.

King and Van Houten did not always agree as to the construction work to be performed on the 1545 LLC property. King claims that this forced the parties into a "deadlock." "Deadlock" is a basis, in and of itself, for judicial dissolution under Business Corporation Law § 1104. However, no such independent ground for dissolution is available under LLCL 702. Instead, the court must consider the managers' disagreement in light of the operating agreement and the continued ability of 1545 LLC to function in that context....

It has been suggested that judicial dissolution is only available when the petitioning member can show that the limited liability company is unable to function as intended or that it is failing financially (*see* Schindler v. Niche Media Holdings, 1 Misc.3d 713, 716, 772 N.Y.S.2d 781). Neither circumstance is demonstrated by the petitioner here. On the contrary, the purpose of 1545 LLC was feasibly and reasonably being met.

The "not reasonably practicable" standard for dissolution of limited liability companies and partnerships has been examined in other jurisdictions. In Delaware, the Chancery Court has observed, "Given its extreme nature, judicial dissolution is a limited remedy that this court grants sparingly" (Matter of Arrow Inv. Advisors, LLC, 2009 WL 1101682, *2 [Del.Ch.2009]).... Several courts take the view that the "not reasonably practicable" standard should be read as "capable of being done logically and in a reasonable, feasible manner" (Taki v. Hami, 2001 WL 672399, *6 [Mich.App. 2001] [dissolution granted where the two partners had not spoken in years and there were allegations of violence and expulsion]), or as "one of reasonable practicability, not impossibility" (PC Tower Ctr., Inc. v. Tower Ctr. Dev. Assoc. L.P., 1989 WL 63901, *6 [Del.Ch.1989]).

Here, a single manager's unilateral action in furtherance of the business of 1545 LLC is specifically contemplated and permitted. Article 4.1 of the 1545 LLC Operating Agreement states:

> "At any time when there is more than one Manager, *any one manager may take any action permitted under the Agreement,* unless the approval of more than one of the Managers is expressly required pursuant to the Agreement or the Act" (emphasis added).

This provision does not require that the managers conduct the business of 1545 LLC by majority vote. It empowers each manager to act autonomously and to unilaterally bind the entity in furtherance of the business of the entity. The 1545 LLC operating agreement, however, is silent as to the issue of manager conflicts. Thus, the only basis for dissolution can be if 1545 LLC cannot effectively operate under the operating agreement to meet and achieve the purpose for which it was created. In this case, that is the development of the property which purpose, despite the disagreements between the managing members, was being met. As the Delaware Chancery Court noted in Matter of Arrow Inv. Advisors, LLC,

> "The court will not dissolve an LLC merely because the LLC has not experienced a smooth glide to profitability or because events have not turned out exactly as the LLC's owners originally envisioned; such events are, of course, common in the risk-laden process of birthing new entities in the hope that they will become mature, profitable ventures. In part because a hair-trigger dissolution standard would ignore this market reality and thwart the expectations of reasonable investors that entities will not be judicially terminated simply because of some market turbulence, dissolution is reserved for situations in which the LLC's management has become so dysfunctional or its business purpose so thwarted that it is no longer practicable to operate the business, such as in the case of a voting deadlock or where the defined purpose of the entity has become impossible to fulfill." ...

"Dissolution of an entity chartered for a broad business purpose remains possible upon a strong showing that a confluence of situationally specific adverse financial, market, product, managerial, or corporate governance circumstances make it nihilistic for the entity to continue" ([Matter of Arrow Inv. Advisors, LLC,] 2009 WL 1101682, *2–3 [Del.Ch.2009]).

Here, the operating agreement avoids the possibility of "deadlock" by permitting each managing member to operate unilaterally in furtherance of 1545 LLC's purpose.

V

After careful examination of the various factors considered in applying the "not reasonably practicable" standard, we hold that for dissolution of a limited liability company pursuant to LLCL 702, the petitioning member must establish, in the context of the terms of the operating agreement or articles of incorporation, that (1) the management of the entity is unable or unwilling to reasonably permit or promote the stated purpose of the entity to be realized or achieved, or (2) continuing the entity is financially unfeasible.

VI

Dissolution is a drastic remedy.... Although the petitioner has failed to meet the standard for dissolution enunciated here, there are numerous other factors which support the conclusion that dissolution of 1545 LLC is inappropriate under the circumstances of this case.

First, the dispute between King and Van Houten was not shown to be inimicable to achieving the purpose of 1545 LLC.... Indeed, the test is "whether it is 'reasonably practicable' to carry on the business of the [LLC], and not whether it is 'impossible' " (Fisk Ventures, LLC v. Segal, 2009 WL 73957, *3 [Del.Ch.2009], *affd.* 984 A.2d 124 [Del. Supr.2009]).

King never objected to the quality of Van Houten's construction work, but only to its expense. The work on Building A was all but complete when this proceeding was commenced. King approved and praised it. Further, the parties were operating in conformity with the operating agreement.

Second, there is a remedy available in the LLCL to regulate Van Houten's conduct. LLCL 411 permits a limited liability company to avoid contracts entered into between it and an interested manager, or another limited liability company in which a manager has a substantial financial interest, unless the manager can prove the contract was fair and reasonable. Crown Royal took no action under LLCL 411 here. Beyond complaining about the cost of VHC's work and seeking to withdraw from 1545 LLC, the record is clear that Crown Royal ratified, albeit grudgingly at times, Van Houten's unilateral efforts.

The notion that 1545 LLC could void the contract with VHC in its entirety may serve as a check on Van Houten's unilaterally hiring his own company for future construction work on the property, and may result in Van Houten being made to disgorge excess moneys paid in derogation of 1545 LLC's best interest at the time of the accounting of the members. In any event, a fair reading of LLCL 702 demonstrates that an application to dissolve 1545 LLC does not flow from a claim under LLCL 411.

Finally, if Crown Royal is truly aggrieved by Van Houten's actions as manager, the Court of Appeals has found that a derivative claim is available (*see* Tzolis v. Wolff, 10 N.Y.3d 100, 855 N.Y.S.2d 6, 884 N.E.2d 1005). Nevertheless, such remedy cannot serve as the basis for dissolution unless the wrongful acts of a managing member which give rise to the derivative claim are contrary to the contemplated functioning and purpose of the limited liability company.

VII

... [T]he order of the Supreme Court should be reversed, the petition denied, and the proceeding dismissed.

■ Dillon and Miller, JJ., concur.

■ Fisher, J.P., concurs in part and dissents in part, and votes to reverse the order and remit the matter to the Supreme Court ... for a fact-finding hearing on the petition, and a new determination thereafter, with the following memorandum, in which CHAMBERS, J., concurs:

... I have no serious quarrel with the standard the majority adopts based on its analysis of the authorities it cites.

Here, 1545 Ocean Avenue, LLC (hereinafter 1545 LLC), was formed to purchase a certain piece of property, to rehabilitate a building that stood on it, and to build a second building on the property for commercial rental. The majority recounts the growing disputes between the managers of 1545 LLC, John King and Walter Van Houten, which ultimately led to King's withdrawal from management of 1545 LLC, amid claims, inter alia, that Van Houten had turned the project "into a construction job for [his] own company," that he did work at excessive cost without King's consent, that he violated the parties' agreement that all construction work was to be procured through a competitive bidding process, that he submitted invoices billing 1545 LLC on a time-and-materials basis which King believed was unacceptable for a commercial project, and that Van Houten had refused to fulfill his responsibility to pay real estate taxes and vendors. Many of those allegations were disputed by Van Houten, but the Supreme Court made no findings of fact.

In my view, without a factual finding, we cannot meaningfully decide whether the Supreme Court providently exercised its discretion in finding that the actions of the parties rendered it not reasonably practicable for 1545 LLC to carry on its business in conformity with its articles of organization or operating agreement. Accordingly, I would remit the matter to the Supreme Court ... for a fact-finding hearing and thereafter for a new determination on the petition....

ORDERED that the order is reversed, on the facts and in the exercise of discretion ... the petition is denied, and the proceeding is dismissed.

Haley v. Talcott

Delaware Court of Chancery, 2004.
864 A.2d 86.

■ STRINE, VICE CHANCELLOR ...

[In 2001, Matthew Haley and Gregory Talcott created a restaurant called the Redfin Seafood Grill. Haley operated the Grill. Talcott borrowed the money to start up the Grill, and owned it. However, a series of agreements made clear that the parties would treat the Grill as a joint venture. For example, an Employment Agreement provided that after Talcott's start-up loan was paid off, Haley would receive half the Grill's profits and would be awarded half the proceeds from any sale of the Grill. Furthermore, when the Grill was opened, Talcott obtained an option to purchase the property on which the Grill was located (the Property), and Talcott gave Haley the right to participate in any exercise of the option by paying 50% of the purchase price. If

Haley did so, then he would be either a 50% owner of the Property or a 50% of of the entity, if any, formed to hold the property.

[The Grill was very successful: by the second year of its existence, the start-up money had been repaid to Talcott, both parties were drawing salaries, and the parties each received approximately $150,000 in profit sharing. In 2003, the parties formed Matt & Greg Real Estate, LLC, to take advantage of the option to purchase the Property. Section 18 of the LLC Agreement provided that upon one member's written notice of an election to quit the LLC, the remaining member could elect to purchase the departing member's interest for fair market value. If the remaining member so elected, the parties could either agree on the fair value or have the fair value determined by arbitration. If the remaining member failed to so elect, the LLC would be liquidated.

[The option price to purchase the Property was $720,000. The LLC took out a mortgage loan for that amount, exercised the option, and obtained the Property. To secure the loan, Haley and Talcott individually signed personal guaranties for the entire amount of the mortgage. The Grill continued to operate at the site, paying the LLC $6,000 per month in rent, which was sufficient to cover the LLC's monthly obligation to the mortgagee. Thus by Fall 2003, the parties appeared poised to reap the fruits of their labors.

[At that point, however, Haley and Talcott suffered a serious falling out. In October 2003, Talcott effectively discharged Haley as a manager of the Redfin Grill. In November, Haley rejected a new lease that Talcott proposed for the Grill, and voted to terminate the Grill's lease and sell the Property, which was appraised at $18 million in June 2004. As a 50% member, Haley could not force the LLC to take action on these proposals, because Talcott opposed them. By virtue of the stalemate, the status quo continued—a result that Talcott favored. The Grill's lease expired, but the Grill continued to pay $6,000 per month to the LLC in a month-to-month arrangement. This amount exceeded the LLC's required monthly mortgage payment by $800, so the situation remained stable.

[With only a 50% ownership interest in the LLC, Haley could not force the termination of the Grill's lease and evict the Grill as a tenant, nor could he force the sale of the Property. Haley then brought an action under § 18–802 of the Delaware Limited Liability Company Act, which permits a court to decree dissolution of an LLC "whenever it is not reasonably practicable to carry on the business in conformity with a limited liability company agreement."]

III. Legal Analysis . . .

Haley alleges that pursuant to 6 Del. C. § 18–802 the court should exercise its discretion and dissolve the LLC because it is not reasonably practicable for it to continue the business of the company in conformity with the LLC Agreement. . . .

Haley argues that dissolution is required because the two 50% managers cannot agree how to best utilize the sole asset of the LLC, the Property, because no provision exists for breaking a tie in the voting interests, and because the LLC cannot take any actions, such as entering contracts, borrowing or lending money, or buying or selling property, absent a majority vote of its members. Because this circumstance resembles corporate deadlock, Haley urges that 8 Del. C. § 273 provides a relevant parallel for analysis.... [Delaware Gen. Corp. Law 273(a) provides, in relevant part:

> If the stockholders of a corporation of this state, having only 2 stockholders each of whom own 50% of the stock therein, shall be engaged in a joint venture and if such stockholders shall be unable to agree upon the desirability of discontinuing such joint venture and disposing of the assets used in such venture, either stock holder may, unless otherwise provided in the certificate of incorporation of the corporation or in a written agreement between stockholders, file with the Court of Chancery a petition stating that it desires to discontinue such joint venture and to dispose of the assets used in such venture in accordance with a plan to be agreed on by both stockholders or that, if no such plan shall be agreed upon by both stockholders, the corporation be dissolved.]

Here, the key facts about the parties' ability to work together are not rationally disputable. Therefore, my decision on the motion largely turns on two legal issues: 1) if the doctrine of corporate deadlock is an appropriate analogy for the analysis of a § 18–802 claim on these facts; and 2) if so, and if action to break the stalemate is necessary to permit the LLC to function, [or] whether, because of the contract-law foundations of the Delaware LLC Act, Haley should be relegated to the contractual exit mechanism provided in the LLC Agreement....

Section 18–802 of the Delaware LLC Act is a relatively recent addition to our law, and, as a result, there have been few decisions interpreting it. Nevertheless, § 18–802 has the obvious purpose of providing an avenue of relief when an LLC cannot continue to function in accordance with its chartering agreement. Thus § 18–802 plays a role for LLCs similar to the role that § 273 of the DGCL plays for joint venture corporations with only two stockholders....

... Section 273 essentially sets forth three pre-requisites for a judicial order of dissolution: 1) the corporation must have two 50% stockholders, 2) those stockholders must be engaged in a joint venture, and 3) they must be unable to agree upon whether to discontinue the business or how to dispose of its assets. Here, by analogy, each of the three provisions is indisputably met.

First, there is no dispute that the parties are 50% members of the LLC....

Second, there is no rational doubt that the parties intended to be and are engaged in a joint venture.... The relationship between Haley and Talcott indicates active involvement by both parties in creating a restaurant for their mutual benefit and profit, and the Employment Contract shows that Haley was to be the "Operations Director" of the Redfin Grill, a position that, according to [a] Letter Agreement, would only be terminated if the restaurant was sold. Haley was also entitled to a 50% share of the Redfin Grill's profits. In short, Haley and Talcott were in it together for as long as they owned the restaurant, equally sharing the profits as provided in the Employment Contract. . . .

Finally, the evidence clearly supports a finding of deadlock between the parties about the business strategy and future of the LLC. [Haley expressed] his desire to end the lease of the Redfin Grill and sell the Property at fair market value. The very fact that dissolution has not occurred, combined with Talcott's opposition in this lawsuit, leads inevitably to the conclusion that Talcott opposes such a disposition of the assets. Neither is Talcott's opposition surprising given his economic interest in the continued success of the Redfin Grill, success that one must assume relies, in part, on a continuing favorable lease arrangement with the LLC. . . .

. . . Clearly, Talcott understands that the end of Haley's managerial role from the Redfin Grill profoundly altered their relationship as co-members of the LLC. After all, it has left Haley on the outside, looking in, with no power. Of course, Talcott insists that the LLC can and does continue to function for its intended purpose and in conformity with the agreement, receiving payments from the Redfin Grill and writing checks to meet its obligations under the mortgage on Talcott's authority. But that reality does not mean that the LLC is operating in accordance with the LLC Agreement. Although the LLC is technically functioning at this point, this operation is purely a residual, inertial status quo that just happens to exclusively benefit one of the 50% members, Talcott, as illustrated by the hands-tied continuation of the expired lease with the Redfin Grill. With strident disagreement between the parties regarding the appropriate deployment of the asset of the LLC, and open hostility as evidenced by the related suit in this matter, it is not credible that the LLC could, if necessary, take any important action that required a vote of the members. Abundant, uncontradicted documents in the record demonstrate the inability of the parties to function together.

For all these reasons, if the LLC were a corporation, there would be no question that Haley's request to dissolve the entity would be granted. But this case regards an LLC, not a corporation, and more importantly, an LLC with a detailed exit provision. That distinguishing factor must and is considered next. . . .

The Delaware LLC Act is grounded on principles of freedom of contract. For that reason, the presence of a reasonable exit mechanism bears on the propriety of ordering dissolution under 6 Del. C. § 18–802. When the agreement itself provides a fair opportunity for the dissenting member who disfavors the inertial status quo to exit and receive the fair market value of her interest, it is at least arguable that the limited liability company may still proceed to operate practicably under its contractual charter because the charter itself provides an equitable way to break the impasse....

... [However,] forcing Haley to exercise the contractual exit mechanism would not permit the LLC to proceed in a practicable way that accords with the LLC Agreement, but would instead permit Talcott to penalize Haley without express contractual authorization.[35]

Why? Because the parties agree that exit mechanism in the LLC Agreement would not relieve Haley of his obligation under the personal guaranty that he signed to secure the mortgage from County Bank. If Haley is forced to use the exit mechanism, Talcott and he both believe that Haley would still be left holding the bag on the guaranty. It is therefore not equitable to force Haley to use the exit mechanism in this circumstance. While the exit mechanism may be workable in a friendly departure when both parties cooperate to reach an adequate alternative agreement with the bank, the bank cannot be compelled to accept the removal of Haley as a personal guarantor. Thus, the exit mechanism fails as an adequate remedy for Haley because it does not equitably effect the separation of the parties. Rather, it would leave Haley with no upside potential, and no protection over the considerable downside risk that he would have to make good on any future default by the LLC (over whose operations he would have no control) to its mortgage lender. Thus here ... the parties do not, in fact, "have at their disposal a far less drastic means to resolve their personal disagreement." ...

For the reasons discussed above, I find that it is not reasonably practicable for the LLC to continue to carry on business in conformity with the LLC Agreement. The parties shall confer and, within four weeks, submit a plan for the dissolution of the LLC. The plan shall include a procedure to sell the Property owned by the LLC within a commercially reasonable time frame. Either party may, of course, bid on the Property.

IT IS SO ORDERED.

---

35. Stated plainly and putting aside Haley's proposal to sell the Property, it is an interesting question whether the 50% member of an LLC that operates an on-going business, and who does not favor inertial policy, must exit rather than force dissolution, particularly when the cost of the exit procedure would, as here, be borne solely by him. Arguably, it is economically more efficient—absent an explicit requirement that the party disfavoring inertia exit if he is dissatisfied—to order dissolution, and allow both parties to bid as purchasers, with the assets going to the highest bidder (inside or outside) who presumably will deploy the asset to its most valuable use. It is also concomitantly arguable that if parties wish to force the co-equal member disfavoring inertia to exit rather than seek dissolution, then they should explicitly contract upfront in the LLC agreement that exit (or the triggering of a buy-sell procedure, giving incentives for the business to be retained by the member willing to pay the highest value) is the required method of breaking any later-arising stalemate.

CHAPTER 10

THE DUTY OF CARE AND THE DUTY TO ACT IN GOOD FAITH

SECTION 1. THE DUTY OF CARE

A. THE BASIC STANDARD OF CARE

Francis v. United Jersey Bank

Supreme Court of New Jersey, 1981.
87 N.J. 15, 432 A.2d 814.

■ POLLOCK, J.

The primary issue on this appeal is whether a corporate director is personally liable in negligence for the failure to prevent the misappropriation of trust funds by other directors who were also officers and shareholders of the corporation.

Plaintiffs are trustees in bankruptcy of Pritchard & Baird Intermediaries Corp. (Pritchard & Baird), a reinsurance broker or intermediary. Defendant Lillian P. Overcash is the daughter of Lillian G. Pritchard and the executrix of her estate. At the time of her death, Mrs. Pritchard was a director and the largest single shareholder of Pritchard & Baird. Because Mrs. Pritchard died after the institution of suit but before trial, her executrix was substituted as a defendant. United Jersey Bank is joined as the administrator of the estate of Charles Pritchard, Sr., who had been president, director and majority shareholder of Pritchard & Baird.

This litigation focuses on payments made by Pritchard & Baird to Charles Pritchard, Jr. and William Pritchard, who were sons of Mr. and Mrs. Charles Pritchard, Sr., as well as officers, directors and shareholders of the corporation. Claims against Charles, Jr. and William are being pursued in bankruptcy proceedings against them.

The trial court, sitting without a jury, characterized the payments as fraudulent conveyances within N.J.S.A. 25:2–10 and entered judgment of $10,355,736.91 plus interest against the estate of Mrs. Pritchard. 392 A.2d 1233 (Law Div.1978). The judgment includes damages from her negligence in permitting payments from the corporation of $4,391,133.21 to Charles, Jr. and $5,483,799.02 to William. The trial court also entered judgment for payments of other sums plus interest: (1) against the estate of Lillian Pritchard for $33,000 accepted by her during her lifetime; (2) against the estate of Charles Pritchard, Sr. for $189,194.17 paid to him during his lifetime and $168,454 for payment of taxes on his estate; and (3) against Lillian Overcash individually for $123,156.51 for payments to her.

The Appellate Division affirmed, but found that the payments were a conversion of trust funds, rather than fraudulent conveyances of the assets of the corporation. 407 A.2d 1253 (N.J.Super. 1979). We granted certification limited to the issue of the liability of Lillian Pritchard as a director. 412 A.2d 791 (N.J. 1980).

Although we accept the characterization of the payments as a conversion of trust funds, the critical question is not whether the misconduct of Charles, Jr. and William should be characterized as fraudulent conveyances or acts of conversion. Rather, the initial question is whether Mrs. Pritchard was negligent in not noticing and trying to prevent the misappropriation of funds held by the corporation in an implied trust. A further question is whether her negligence was the proximate cause of the plaintiffs' losses. Both lower courts found that she was liable in negligence for the losses caused by the wrongdoing of Charles, Jr. and William. We affirm.

I

The matrix for our decision is the customs and practices of the reinsurance industry and the role of Pritchard & Baird as a reinsurance broker. Reinsurance involves a contract under which one insurer agrees to indemnify another for loss sustained under the latter's policy of insurance. Insurance companies that insure against losses arising out of fire or other casualty seek at times to minimize their exposure by sharing risks with other insurance companies. Thus, when the face amount of a policy is comparatively large, the company may enlist one or more insurers to participate in that risk. Similarly, an insurance company's loss potential and overall exposure may be reduced by reinsuring a part of an entire class of policies (e.g., 25% of all of its fire insurance policies). The selling insurance company is known as a ceding company. The entity that assumes the obligation is designated as the reinsurer.

The reinsurance broker arranges the contract between the ceding company and the reinsurer. In accordance with industry custom before the Pritchard & Baird bankruptcy, the reinsurance contract or treaty did not specify the rights and duties of the broker. Typically, the ceding company communicates to the broker the details concerning the risk. The broker negotiates the sale of portions of the risk to the reinsurers. In most instances, the ceding company and the reinsurer do not communicate with each other, but rely upon the reinsurance broker. The ceding company pays premiums due a reinsurer to the broker, who deducts his commission and transmits the balance to the appropriate reinsurer. When a loss occurs, a reinsurer pays money due a ceding company to the broker, who then transmits it to the ceding company.

The reinsurance business was described by an expert at trial as having "a magic aura around it of dignity and quality and integrity." A telephone call which might be confirmed by a handwritten memorandum is sufficient to create a reinsurance obligation. Though separate bank accounts are not maintained for each treaty, the industry practice is to segregate the insurance funds from the broker's general accounts. Thus, the insurance fund accounts would contain the identifiable amounts for transmittal to either the reinsurer or the ceder. The expert stated that in general three kinds of checks may be drawn on this account: checks payable to reinsurers as premiums, checks payable to ceders as loss payments and checks payable to the brokers as commissions.

Messrs. Pritchard and Baird initially operated as a partnership. Later they formed several corporate entities to carry on their brokerage activities. The proofs supporting the judgment relate only to one corporation, Pritchard & Baird Intermediaries Corp. (Pritchard & Baird), and we need consider only its activities. When incorporated under the laws of the State of New York in 1959, Pritchard & Baird had five directors: Charles Pritchard, Sr., his wife Lillian Pritchard, their son Charles Pritchard, Jr., George Baird and his wife Marjorie. William Pritchard, another son, became director in 1960. Upon its formation, Pritchard & Baird acquired all the assets and assumed all the liabilities of the Pritchard & Baird partnership. The corporation issued 200 shares of common stock. Charles Pritchard, Sr. acquired 120 shares, his sons Charles Pritchard, Jr., 15 and William 15; Mr. and Mrs. Baird owned the remaining 50. In June 1964, Baird and his wife resigned as directors and sold their stock to the corporation. From that time on the corporation operated as a close family corporation with Mr. and Mrs. Pritchard and their two sons as the only directors. After the death of Charles, Sr. in 1973, only the remaining three directors continued to operate as the board. Lillian Pritchard inherited 72 of her husband's 120 shares in Pritchard & Baird, thereby becoming the largest stockholder in the corporation with 48% of the stock.

The corporate minute books reflect only perfunctory activities by the directors, related almost exclusively to the election of officers and adoption of banking resolutions and a retirement plan. None of the minutes for any of the meetings contain a discussion of the loans to Charles, Jr. and William or of the financial condition of the corporation. Moreover, upon instructions of Charles, Jr. that financial statements were not to be circulated to anyone else, the company's statements for the fiscal years beginning February 1, 1970, were delivered only to him.

Charles Pritchard, Sr. was the chief executive and controlled the business in the years following Baird's withdrawal. Beginning in 1966, he gradually relinquished control over the operations of the corporation. In 1968, Charles, Jr. became president and William became executive vice president. Charles, Sr. apparently became ill in 1971 and during the last year and a half of his life was not involved in the affairs of the business. He continued, however, to serve as a director until his death on December 10, 1973. Notwithstanding the presence of Charles, Sr. on the board until his death in 1973, Charles, Jr. dominated the management of the corporation and the board from 1968 until the bankruptcy in 1975.

Contrary to the industry custom of segregating funds, Pritchard & Baird commingled the funds of reinsurers and ceding companies with its own funds. All monies (including commissions, premiums and loss monies) were deposited in a single account. Charles, Sr. began the practice of withdrawing funds from the commingled account in transactions identified on the corporate books as "loans." As long as Charles, Sr. controlled the corporation, the "loans" correlated with corporate profits and were repaid at the end of each year. Starting in 1970, however, Charles, Jr. and William begin to siphon ever-increasing sums from the corporation under the guise of loans. As of January 31, 1970, the "loans" to Charles, Jr. were $230,932 and to William were $207,329. At least by January 31, 1973, the annual increase in the loans exceeded annual corporate revenues. By October 1975, the year of bankruptcy, the "shareholders' loans" had metastasized to a total of $12,333,514.47.

The trial court rejected the characterization of the payments as "loans." 392 A.2d 1233 (N.J.Super. 1978) No corporate resolution authorized the "loans," and no note or other instrument evidenced the debt. Charles, Jr. and William paid no interest on the amounts received. The "loans" were not repaid or reduced from one year to the next; rather, they increased annually.

The designation of "shareholders' loans" on the balance sheet was an entry to account for the distribution of the premium and loss money to Charles, Sr., Charles, Jr. and William. As the trial court found, the entry was part of a "woefully inadequate and highly dangerous bookkeeping system." 392 A.2d 1233 (N.J.Super. 1978).

The "loans" to Charles, Jr. and William far exceeded their salaries and financial resources. If the payments to Charles, Jr. and William had been treated as dividends or compensation, then the balance sheets would have shown an excess of liabilities over assets. If the "loans" had been eliminated, the balance sheets would have depicted a corporation not only with a working capital deficit, but also with assets having a fair market value less than its liabilities. The balance sheets for 1970–1975, however, showed an excess of assets over liabilities. This result was achieved by designating the misappropriated funds as "shareholders' loans" and listing them as assets offsetting the deficits. Although the withdrawal of the funds resulted in an obligation of repayment to Pritchard & Baird, the more significant consideration is that the "loans" represented a massive misappropriation of money belonging to the clients of the corporation.

The "loans" were reflected on financial statements that were prepared annually as of January 31, the end of the corporate fiscal year. Although an outside certified public accountant prepared the

1970 financial statement, the corporation prepared only internal financial statements from 1971–1975. In all instances, the statements were simple documents, consisting of three or four 8½ § 11 inch sheets.

The statements of financial condition from 1970 forward demonstrated:

	Working Capital Deficit	**Shareholders' Loans**	**Net Brokerage Income**
1970	$ 389,022	$ 509,941	$ 807,229
1971	not available	not available	not available
1972	$ 1,684,289	$ 1,825,911	$1,546,263
1973	$ 3,506,460	$ 3,700,542	$1,736,349
1974	$ 6,939,007	$ 7,080,629	$ 876,182
1975	$10,176,419	$10,298,039	$ 551,598.

Those financial statements showed working capital deficits increasing annually in tandem with the amounts that Charles, Jr. and William withdrew as "shareholders' loans." In the last complete year of business (January 31, 1974, to January 31, 1975), "shareholders' loans" and the correlative working capital deficit increased by approximately $3,200,000.

The funding of the "loans" left the corporation with insufficient money to operate. Pritchard & Baird could defer payment on accounts payable because its clients allowed a grace period, generally 30 to 90 days, before the payment was due. During this period, Pritchard & Baird used the funds entrusted to it as a "float" to pay current accounts payable. By recourse to the funds of its clients, Pritchard & Baird not only paid its trade debts, but also funded the payments to Charles, Jr. and William. Thus, Pritchard & Baird was able to meet its obligations as they came due only through the use of clients' funds.

The pattern that emerges from these figures is the substantial increase in the monies appropriated by Charles Pritchard, Jr. and William Pritchard after their father's withdrawal from the business and the sharp decline in the profitability of the operation after his death. This led ultimately to the filing in December, 1975, of an involuntary petition in bankruptcy and the appointments of the plaintiffs as trustees in bankruptcy of Pritchard & Baird.

Mrs. Pritchard was not active in the business of Pritchard & Baird and knew virtually nothing of its corporate affairs. She briefly visited the corporate offices in Morristown on only one occasion, and she never read or obtained the annual financial statements. She was unfamiliar with the rudiments of reinsurance and made no effort to assure that the policies and practices of the corporation, particularly pertaining to the withdrawal of funds, complied with industry custom or relevant law. Although her husband had warned her that Charles, Jr. would "take the shirt off my back," Mrs. Pritchard did not pay any attention to her duties as a director or to the affairs of the corporation. 392 A.2d 1233 (N.J.Super.L. 1978).

After her husband died in December 1973, Mrs. Pritchard became incapacitated and was bedridden for a six-month period. She became listless at this time and started to drink rather heavily. Her physical condition deteriorated, and in 1978 she died. The trial court rejected testimony seeking to exonerate her because she "was old, was grief-stricken at the loss of her husband, sometimes consumed too much alcohol and was psychologically overborne by her sons." 162 N.J.Super. at 371, 392 A.2d 1233. That court found that she was competent to act and that the reason Mrs. Pritchard never knew what her sons "were doing was because she never made the slightest effort to discharge any of her responsibilities as a director of Pritchard & Baird." 392 A.2d 1233 (N.J.Super.L. 1978).

II

A preliminary matter is the determination of whether New Jersey law should apply to this case. Although Pritchard & Baird was incorporated in New York, the trial court found that New Jersey had more significant relationships to the parties and the transactions than New York. The shareholder, officers and directors were New Jersey residents. The estates of Mr. and Mrs. Pritchard are being administered in New Jersey, and the bankruptcy proceedings involving Charles, Jr., William and Pritchard & Baird are pending in New Jersey. Virtually all transactions took place in New Jersey. Although many of the creditors are located outside the state, all had contacts with Pritchard & Baird in New Jersey. Consequently, the trial court applied New Jersey law. 392 A.2d 1233 (N.J.Super.L. 1978). The parties agree that New Jersey law should apply. We are in accord.

III

Individual liability of a corporate director for acts of the corporation is a prickly problem. Generally directors are accorded broad immunity and are not insurers of corporate activities. The problem is particularly nettlesome when a third party asserts that a director, because of nonfeasance, is liable for losses caused by acts of insiders, who in this case were officers, directors and shareholders. Determination of the liability of Mrs. Pritchard requires findings that she had a duty to the clients of Pritchard & Baird, that she breached that duty and that her breach was a proximate cause of their losses.

The New Jersey Business Corporation Act, which took effect on January 1, 1969, was a comprehensive revision of the statutes relating to business corporations. One section, N.J.S.A. 14A:6–14, concerning a director's general obligation had no counterpart in the old Act. That section makes it incumbent upon directors to discharge their duties in good faith and with that degree of diligence, care and skill which ordinarily prudent men would exercise under similar circumstances in like positions. [N.J.S.A. 14A:6–14]. . . .

. . . [The principle underlying] N.J.S.A. 14A:6–14 is . . . that directors must discharge their duties in good faith and act as ordinarily prudent persons would under similar circumstances in like positions. Although specific duties in a given case can be determined only after consideration of all of the circumstances, the standard of ordinary care is the wellspring from which those more specific duties flow.

As a general rule, a director should acquire at least a rudimentary understanding of the business of the corporation. Accordingly, a director should become familiar with the fundamentals of the business in which the corporation is engaged. [Campbell v. Watson, 62 N.J.Eq. 396, 50 A. 120 (Ch.1901)]. Because directors are bound to exercise ordinary care, they cannot set up as a defense lack of the knowledge needed to exercise the requisite degree of care. If one "feels that he has not had sufficient business experience to qualify him to perform the duties of a director, he should either acquire the knowledge by inquiry, or refuse to act." *Ibid.*

Directors are under a continuing obligation to keep informed about the activities of the corporation. Otherwise, they may not be able to participate in the overall management of corporate affairs. Barnes v. Andrews, 298 F. 614 (S.D.N.Y.1924).... Directors may not shut their eyes to corporate misconduct, and then claim that because they did not see the misconduct, they did not have a duty to look. The sentinel asleep at his post contributes nothing to the enterprise he is charged to protect. Wilkinson v. Dodd, 42 N.J.Eq. 234, 245, 7 A. 327 (Ch.1886), aff'd 42 N.J.Eq. 647, 9 A. 685 (E. & A.1887).

Directorial management does not require a detailed inspection of day-to-day activities, but rather a general monitoring of corporate affairs and policies. Williams v. McKay, [46 N.J.Eq. 25, 36, 18 A. 824 (Ch.1889)]. Accordingly, a director is well advised to attend board meetings regularly. Indeed, a director who is absent from a board meeting is presumed to concur in action taken on a corporate matter, unless he files a "dissent with the secretary of the corporation within a reasonable time after learning of such action." N.J.S.A. 14A:6–13 (Supp.1981–1982). Regular attendance does not mean that directors must attend every meeting, but that directors should attend meetings as a matter of practice. A director of a publicly held corporation might be expected to attend regular monthly meetings, but a director of a small, family corporation might be asked to attend only an annual meeting. The point is that one of the responsibilities of a director is to attend meetings of the board of which he or she is a member. That burden is lightened by N.J.S.A. 14A:6–7(2) (Supp.1981–1982), which permits board action without a meeting if all members of the board consent in writing.

While directors are not required to audit corporate books, they should maintain familiarity with the financial status of the corporation by a regular review of financial statements. *Campbell,* supra, 62 N.J.Eq. at 415, 50 A. 120; *Williams,* supra, 46 N.J.Eq. at 38–39, 18 A. 824; *see* Section of Corporation, Banking and Business Law, American Bar Association, "Corporate Director's Guidebook," 33 Bus. Law. 1595, 1608 (1978) (Guidebook).... In some circumstances, directors may be charged with assuring that bookkeeping methods conform to industry custom and usage. Lippitt v. Ashley, 89 Conn. 451, 464, 94 A. 995, 1000 (Sup.Ct.1915). The extent of review, as well as the nature and frequency of financial statements, depends not only on the customs of the industry, but also on the nature of the corporation and the business in which it is engaged. Financial statements of some small corporations may be prepared internally and only on an annual basis; in a large publicly held corporation, the statements may be produced monthly or at some other regular interval. Adequate financial review normally would be more informal in a private corporation than in a publicly held corporation.

Of some relevance in this case is the circumstance that the financial records disclose the "shareholders' loans". Generally directors are immune from liability if, in good faith,

> they rely upon the opinion of counsel for the corporation or upon written reports setting forth financial data concerning the corporation and prepared by an independent public accountant or certified public accountant or firm of such accountants or upon financial statements, books of account or reports of the corporation represented to them to be correct by the president, the officer of the corporation having charge of its books of account, or the person presiding at a meeting of the board. [N.J.S.A. 14A:6–14]

The review of financial statements, however, may give rise to a duty to inquire further into matters revealed by those statements. Corsicana Nat'l Bank v. Johnson, 251 U.S. 68, 71, 40 S.Ct. 82, 84, 64 L.Ed. 141 (1919).... Upon discovery of an illegal course of action, a director has a duty to object and, if the corporation does not correct the conduct, to resign. *See* Dodd v. Wilkinson, 42 N.J.Eq. 647, 651, 9 A. 685 (E. & A.1887); Williams v. Riley, 34 N.J.Eq. 398, 401 (Ch.1881).

In certain circumstances, the fulfillment of the duty of a director may call for more than mere objection and resignation. Sometimes a director may be required to seek the advice of counsel. *Guidebook,* supra, at 1631. One New Jersey case recognized the duty of a bank director to seek counsel where doubt existed about the meaning of the bank charter. Williams v. McKay, supra, 46 N.J.Eq. at 60, 18 A. 824. The duty to seek the assistance of counsel can extend to areas other than the interpretation of corporation instruments. Modern corporate practice recognizes that on occasion a director should seek outside advice. A director may require legal advice concerning the propriety of his or her own conduct, the conduct of other officers and directors or the conduct of the corporation. In appropriate circumstances, a director would be "well advised to consult with regular corporate counsel (or his own legal adviser) at any time in which he is doubtful regarding proposed action...." *Guidebook,* supra, at 1618. Sometimes the duty of a director may require more than consulting with outside counsel. A director may have a duty to take reasonable means to prevent illegal conduct by co-directors; in an appropriate case, this may include threat of suit. *See* Selheimer v. Manganese Corp., 423 Pa. 563, 572, 584, 224 A.2d 634, 640, 646 (Sup.Ct.1966) (director exonerated when he objected, resigned, organized shareholder action group, and threatened suit).

A director is not an ornament, but an essential component of corporate governance. Consequently, a director cannot protect himself behind a paper shield bearing the motto, "dummy director." ... Thus, all directors are responsible for managing the business and affairs of the corporation. N.J.S.A. 14A:6–1 (Supp.1981–1982); 1 G. Hornstein, Corporation Law and Practice § 431 at 525 (1959).

The factors that impel expanded responsibility in the large, publicly held corporation may not be present in a small, close corporation. Nonetheless, a close corporation may, because of the nature of its business, be affected with a public interest. For example, the stock of a bank may be closely held, but because of the nature of banking the directors would be subject to greater liability than those of another close corporation. Even in a small corporation, a director is held to the standard of that degree of care that an ordinarily prudent director would use under the circumstances. M. Mace, The Board of Directors of Small Corporations 83 (1948).

A director's duty of care does not exist in the abstract, but must be considered in relation to specific obligees. In general, the relationship of a corporate director to the corporation and its stockholders is that of a fiduciary. Whitfield v. Kern, 122 N.J.Eq. 332, 341, 192 A. 48 (E. & A.1937). Shareholders have a right to expect that directors will exercise reasonable supervision and control over the policies and practices of a corporation. The institutional integrity of a corporation depends upon the proper discharge by directors of those duties.

While directors may owe a fiduciary duty to creditors also, that obligation generally has not been recognized in the absence of insolvency. *Whitfield,* supra, 122 N.J.Eq. at 342, 345, 192 A. 48. With certain corporations, however, directors are [deemed] to owe a duty to creditors and other third parties even when the corporation is solvent. Although depositors of a bank are considered in some respects to be creditors, courts have recognized that directors may owe them a fiduciary duty. *See Campbell*, supra, 62 N.J.Eq. at 406–407, 50 A. 120. Directors of nonbanking corporations may owe a similar duty when the corporation holds funds of others in trust. *Cf.* McGlynn v. Schultz, 90 N.J.Super. 505, 218 A.2d 408 (Ch.Div.1966), aff'd 95 N.J.Super. 412, 231 A.2d 386 (App.Div.), certif. den. 50 N.J. 409, 235 A.2d 901 (1967) (directors who did not insist on segregating trust funds held by corporation liable to the *cestuis que trust*).

Courts in other states have imposed liability on directors of nonbanking corporations for the conversion of trust funds, even though those directors did not participate in or know of the conversion.... The distinguishing circumstances in regard to banks and other corporations holding trust funds is that the depositor or beneficiary can reasonably expect the director to act with ordinary prudence concerning the funds held in a fiduciary capacity. Thus, recognition of a duty of a director to those for whom a corporation holds funds in trust may be viewed as another application of the general rule that a director's duty is that of an ordinary prudent person under the circumstances.

The most striking circumstances affecting Mrs. Pritchard's duty as a director are the character of the reinsurance industry, the nature of the misappropriated funds and the financial condition of Pritchard & Baird. The hallmark of the reinsurance industry has been the unqualified trust and confidence reposed by ceding companies and reinsurers in reinsurance brokers. Those companies entrust money to reinsurance intermediaries with the justifiable expectation that the funds will be transmitted to the appropriate parties. Consequently, the companies could have assumed rightfully that Mrs. Pritchard, as a director of a reinsurance brokerage corporation, would not sanction the commingling and the conversion of loss and premium funds for the personal use of the principals of Pritchard & Baird.

As a reinsurance broker, Pritchard & Baird received annually as a fiduciary millions of dollars of clients' money which it was under a duty to segregate.[6] To this extent, it resembled a bank rather than a small family business. Accordingly, Mrs. Pritchard's relationship to the clientele of Pritchard & Baird was akin to that of a director of a bank to its depositors. All parties agree that Pritchard & Baird held the misappropriated funds in an implied trust. That trust relationship gave rise to a fiduciary duty to guard the funds with fidelity and good faith. Ellsworth Dobbs, Inc. v. Johnson, 50 N.J. 528, 553, 236 A.2d 843 (1967); General Films, Inc. v. Sanco Gen. Mfg. Corp., supra, 153 N.J.Super. at 372–373, 379 A.2d 1042.

As a director of a substantial reinsurance brokerage corporation, she should have known that it received annually millions of dollars of loss and premium funds which it held in trust for ceding and reinsurance companies. Mrs. Pritchard should have obtained and read the annual statements of financial condition of Pritchard & Baird. Although she had a right to rely upon financial statements prepared in accordance with N.J.S.A. 14A:6–14, such reliance would not excuse her conduct. The reason is that those statements disclosed on their face the misappropriation of trust funds.

From those statements, she should have realized that, as of January 31, 1970, her sons were withdrawing substantial trust funds under the guise of "Shareholders' Loans." The financial statements for each fiscal year commencing with that of January 31, 1970, disclosed that the working capital deficits and the "loans" were escalating in tandem. Detecting a misappropriation of funds would not have required special expertise or extraordinary diligence; a cursory reading of the financial statements would have revealed the pillage. Thus, if Mrs. Pritchard had read the financial statements, she would have known that her sons were converting trust funds. When financial statements demonstrate that insiders are bleeding a corporation to death, a director should notice and try to stanch the flow of blood.

6. Following the Pritchard & Baird bankruptcy, New York, a reinsurance center, adopted legislation regulating reinsurance intermediaries. One statute codified the industry standard by prohibiting reinsurance intermediaries from commingling their funds with funds of their principals. N.Y.Ins.Law § 122–a(9) (McKinney Supp.1980–1981).

In summary, Mrs. Pritchard was charged with the obligation of basic knowledge and supervision of the business of Pritchard & Baird. Under the circumstances, this obligation included reading and understanding financial statements, and making reasonable attempts at detection and prevention of the illegal conduct of other officers and directors. She had a duty to protect the clients of Pritchard & Baird against policies and practices that would result in the misappropriation of money they had entrusted to the corporation. She breached that duty.

IV

Nonetheless, the negligence of Mrs. Pritchard does not result in liability unless it is a proximate cause of the loss. . . .

Cases involving nonfeasance present a much more difficult causation question than those in which the director has committed an affirmative act of negligence leading to the loss. Analysis in cases of negligent omissions calls for determination of the reasonable steps a director should have taken and whether that course of action would have averted the loss.

Usually a director can absolve himself from liability by informing the other directors of the impropriety and voting for a proper course of action. Dyson, "The Director's Liability for Negligence," 40 Ind.L.J. 341, 365 (1965). . . .

Even accepting the hypothesis that Mrs. Pritchard might not be liable if she had objected and resigned, there are two significant reasons for holding her liable. First, she did not resign until just before the bankruptcy. Consequently, there is no factual basis for the speculation that the losses would have occurred even if she had objected and resigned. Indeed, the trial court reached the opposite conclusion: "The actions of the sons were so blatantly wrongful that it is hard to see how they could have resisted any moderately firm objection to what they were doing." 162 N.J.Super. at 372, 392 A.2d 1233. Second, the nature of the reinsurance business distinguishes it from most other commercial activities in that reinsurance brokers are encumbered by fiduciary duties owed to third parties. In other corporations, a director's duty normally does not extend beyond the shareholders to third parties.

In this case, the scope of Mrs. Pritchard's duties was determined by the precarious financial condition of Pritchard & Baird, its fiduciary relationship to its clients and the implied trust in which it held their funds. Thus viewed, the scope of her duties encompassed all reasonable action to stop the continuing conversion. Her duties extended beyond mere objection and resignation to reasonable attempts to prevent the misappropriation of the trust funds. *Campbell,* supra, 62 N.J.Eq. at 427, 50 A. 120. . . .

In assessing whether Mrs. Pritchard's conduct was a legal or proximate cause of the conversion, "[l]egal responsibility must be limited to those causes which are so closely connected with the result and of such significance that the law is justified in imposing liability." Prosser, supra, § 41 at 237. Such a judicial determination involves not only considerations of causation-in-fact and matters of policy, but also common sense and logic. Caputzal v. The Lindsay Co., 48 N.J. 69, 77–78 (1966). The act or the failure to act must be a substantial factor in producing the harm. Prosser, supra, § 41 at 240; Restatement (Second) of Torts, §§ 431, 432 (1965).

Within Pritchard & Baird, several factors contributed to the loss of the funds: comingling of corporate and client monies, conversion of funds by Charles, Jr. and William and dereliction of her duties by Mrs. Pritchard. The wrongdoing of her sons, although the immediate cause of the loss, should not excuse Mrs. Pritchard from her negligence which also was a substantial factor contributing to the loss. Restatement (Second) of Torts, supra, § 442B, comment b. Her sons knew that she, the only other director, was not reviewing their conduct; they spawned their fraud in the backwater of her neglect. Her neglect of duty contributed to the climate of corruption; her failure to act contributed to the continuation of that corruption. Consequently, her conduct was a substantial factor contributing to the loss.

Analysis of proximate cause is especially difficult in a corporate context where the allegation is that nonfeasance of a director is a proximate cause of damage to a third party. Where a case involves nonfeasance, no one can say "with absolute certainty what would have occurred if the defendant had acted otherwise." Prosser, supra, § 41 at 242. Nonetheless, where it is reasonable to conclude that the failure to act would produce a particular result and that result has followed, causation may be inferred. *Ibid.* We conclude that even if Mrs. Pritchard's mere objection had not stopped the depredations of her sons, her consultation with an attorney and the threat of suit would have deterred them. That conclusion flows as a matter of common sense and logic from the record. Whether in other situations a director has a duty to do more than protest and resign is best left to case-by-case determinations. In this case, we are satisfied that there was a duty to do more than object and resign. Consequently, we find that Mrs. Pritchard's negligence was a proximate cause of the misappropriations.

To conclude, by virtue of her office, Mrs. Pritchard had the power to prevent the losses sustained by the clients of Pritchard & Baird. With power comes responsibility. She had a duty to deter the depredation of the other insiders, her sons. She breached that duty and caused plaintiffs to sustain damages.

The judgment of the Appellate Division is affirmed.

■ For affirmance JUSTICES SULLIVAN, PASHMAN, CLIFFORD, SCHREIBER, HANDLER and POLLOCK—6.

For reversal—none.*

---

* Some earlier cases involving the liability of inactive spouse- or figurehead-directors went the other way. In Berman v. LeBeauInter–America, Inc., 509 F.Supp. 156, 161 (S.D.N.Y.), aff'd

MODEL BUS. CORP. ACT §§ 8.30, 8.31

[See Statutory Supplement]

CAL. CORP. CODE § 309

[See Statutory Supplement]

NEW YORK BUS. CORP. LAW § 717

[See Statutory Supplement]

ALI, PRINCIPLES OF CORPORATE GOVERNANCE §§ 4.01(a), (b), 4.02, 4.03

[See Statutory Supplement]

ARONSON v. LEWIS, 473 A.2d 805, 812 (Del.1984). "[D]irectors have a duty to inform themselves, prior to making a business decision, of all material information reasonably available to them. Having become so informed, they must then act with requisite care in the discharge of their duties. While the Delaware cases use a variety of terms to describe the applicable standard of care, our analysis satisfies us that under the business judgment rule director liability is predicated upon concepts of gross negligence."

QUILLEN, *TRANS UNION,* BUSINESS JUDGMENT, AND NEUTRAL PRINCIPLES, 10 Del.J.Corp.L. 465, 497–98 (1985). "Even if one assumes that negligence law is the proper pigeonhole for director liability—a most questionable assumption at least at the decisional level—the concept of 'gross negligence' has been expressly rejected by the better tort scholarship as practically meaningless. Therefore its recent adoption in corporate law would appear, in some respects, to be an analytical step backwards. . . .

mem. 697 F.2d 872 (2d Cir. 1981), a director was held not liable on the ground that he was a "virtual figurehead." In Allied Freightways, Inc. v. Cholfin, 325 Mass. 630, 633, 91 N.E.2d 765, 768 (1950), the court rested nonliability on causation grounds, concluding that it was doubtful whether, if the spouse, Mrs. Cholfin, had taken steps to familiarize herself with the conduct of the business by her husband she could have changed the situation. "Upon a careful reading of the evidence, we do not think that it can quite be said that the neglect of her official duties as a director was a contributing cause of the loss sustained by the corporation by the wrongful withdrawals of its funds, save only the amounts used for her personal benefits."

"Perhaps we should say straight out that, on the threshold duty of care issue, the standard should be 'reasonable care under the circumstances' as some argued all along. If that flexible standard includes all factors, e.g., director expertise [and], time pressures, ... as well as depth of inquiry, then one suspects the results probably would not radically change, but the judicial focus would be to a keener negligence standard and emphasis more on the qualitative nature of the varying circumstances."

IN RE EMERGING COMMUNICATIONS, INC. SHAREHOLDERS LITIGATION, 2004 WL 1305745 (2004) (Jacobs, Justice, sitting by designation). 'The court also concludes, albeit with reluctance, that Muoio is ... liable [for his conduct as director]....

"Muoio is culpable because he voted to approve the transaction even though he knew, or at very least had strong reasons to believe, that the $10.25 per share merger price was unfair. Muoio was in a unique position to know that. He was a principal and general partner of an investment advising firm, with significant experience in finance and the telecommunications sector. From 1995 to 1996, Muoio had been a securities analyst for, and a vice president of, Lazard Freres & Co. in the telecommunications and media sector. From 1985 to 1995, he was a securities analyst for Gabelli and Co., Inc., in the communications sector, and from 1993 to 1995, he was a portfolio manager for Gabelli Global Communications Fund, Inc.

"Hence, Muoio possessed a specialized financial expertise, and an ability to understand ECM's [the corporation's] intrinsic value, that was unique to the ECM board members.... Informed by his specialized expertise and knowledge, Muoio conceded that the $10.25 price was 'at the low end of any kind of fair value you would put' and expressed ... his view that the [corporation] might be able to get up to $20 per share.... In these circumstances, it was incumbent upon Muoio, as a fiduciary, to advocate that the board reject the $10.25 price.... As a fiduciary knowledgeable of ECM's intrinsic value, Muoio should also have gone on record as voting against the proposed transaction at the $10.25 per share merger price. Muoio did neither. Instead he joined the other directors in voting, without objection, to approve the transaction.

"[Most of] ECM's directors ... could plausibly argue that they voted for the transaction in reliance on [the opinion of Houlihan, the corporation's outside financial advisor on the proposed transaction] that the merger term price was fair. In Muoio's case, however, the argument would be implausible. Muoio's expertise in this industry was equivalent, if not superior, to that of Houlihan.... That expertise gave Muoio far less reason to defer to Houlihan's valuation...."

NOTE ON CAUSATION

Cases in the duty-of-care area sometimes raise difficult causation issues. Two of these issues often arise together: (1) If the violation of the duty of care consists of an omission by a director, would the loss have occurred even if the director had not violated his duty? (2) If the whole board, or a substantial majority of the directors, violates the duty of care, can an individual director be excused on the ground that the result would have been the same even if she had acted differently?

These issues were addressed in the well-known case of Barnes v. Andrews, 298 Fed. 614 (S.D.N.Y.1924), decided by Judge Learned Hand, sitting as a trial judge. Liberty Starters Corporation was organized in 1918 to manufacture starters for Ford motors and airplanes. Andrews became a director in October 1919, and served until he resigned in June 1920. During Andrews's incumbency there had been only two board meetings, one of which he could not attend. Andrews was the largest shareholder and a friend of Liberty's president, Maynard, who had induced him to become a director. Andrews's only attention to Liberty's affairs consisted of talks with Maynard as they met from time to time. In 1921, Liberty went into receivership as a result of mismanagement. Andrews was sued for violating the duty of care by not paying sufficient attention to the corporation's affairs.

Judge Hand began by holding that Andrews had violated his duty of care:

> . . . It is not enough to content oneself with general answers that the business looks promising and that all seems prosperous. Andrews was bound, certainly as the months wore on, to inform himself of what was going on with some particularity, and, if he had done so, he would have learned that there were delays in getting into production which were putting the enterprise in most serious peril. . . . Having accepted a post of confidence, he was charged with an active duty to learn whether the company was moving to production, and why it was not, and to consider, as best he might, what could be done to avoid the conflicts among the personnel, or their incompetence, which was slowly bleeding it to death.

Id. at 615–16.

Hand went on to hold, however, that the plaintiff also had to prove that Liberty's losses would not have occurred if Andrews had properly performed his duties, and that no such showing had been made:

> . . . This cause of action rests upon a tort, as much though it be a tort of omission as though it had rested upon a positive act. The plaintiff must accept the burden of showing that the performance of the defendant's duties would have avoided loss, and what loss it would have avoided. . . .
>
> When the corporate funds have been illegally lent, it is a fair inference that a protest would have stopped the loan, and that the

director's neglect caused the loss. But when a business fails from general mismanagement, business incapacity, or bad judgment, how is it possible to say that a single director could have made the company successful, or how much in dollars he could have saved? Before this cause can go to a master, the plaintiff must show that, had Andrews done his full duty, he could have made the company prosper, or at least could have broken its fall. He must show what sum he could have saved the company. Neither of these has he made any effort to do.

The defendant is not subject to the burden of proving that the loss would have happened, whether he had done his duty or not. If he were, it would come to this: That, if a director were once shown slack in his duties, he would stand charged prima facie with the difference between the corporate treasury as it was, and as it would be, judged by a hypothetical standard of success. How could such a standard be determined? How could any one guess how far a director's skill and judgment would have prevailed upon his fellows, and what would have been the ultimate fate of the business, if they had? How is it possible to set any measure of liability, or to tell what he would have contributed to the event? Men's fortunes may not be subjected to such uncertain and speculative conjectures. It is hard to see how there can be any remedy, except one can put one's finger on a definite loss and say with reasonable assurance that protest would have deterred, or counsel persuaded, the managers who caused it. No men of sense would take the office, if the law imposed upon them a guaranty of the general success of their companies as a penalty for any negligence.

Id. at 616–18.

Some passages in Barnes v. Andrews may be read to suggest that an inattentive director will not be liable for a loss that would have been prevented by an attentive board unless it is shown that if the director had been attentive, his colleagues would have followed his lead. Such a suggestion would be out of keeping with general legal rules on the responsibility of joint actors, and hard to accept as a matter of either fairness or policy. However, Barnes v. Andrews can also be read to stand for the more modest proposition that an inattentive director will not be liable for a corporate loss if full attentiveness by *all* the directors would not have saved the situation, because in that case the inattentiveness of any single director will not have been a cause-in-fact of the loss. That is the position taken in § 7.18(b) of the ALI's Principles of Corporate Governance. Under this section, if the board as a whole has violated its duty of care, by either commission or omission, each director will be liable for any loss of which the board's failure is the cause-in-fact and the legal (or proximate) cause:

(b) A violation of [a standard of conduct] is the legal cause of loss if the plaintiff proves that (i) satisfaction of the applicable standard would have been a substantial factor in averting the loss,

> and (ii) the likelihood of injury would have been foreseeable to an ordinarily prudent person in a like position to that of the defendant and under similar circumstances. It is not a defense to liability in such cases that damage to the corporation would not have resulted but for the acts or omissions of other individuals.

The Comment to § 7.18 elaborates this position as follows:

> When multiple corporate officials fail to perform a duty whose omission is a legal cause of the loss, a problem of concurrent causation arises. Potentially, each defendant might claim that his or her conduct was less causally significant than that of others. To prevent each member of the collective body from evading liability by pointing to the concurrent omissions of others, the last sentence of § 7.18(b) specifies that "[i]t is not a defense to liability in such cases that damage to the corporation would not have resulted but for the acts or omissions of other individuals." This statement is consistent with the general approach of the law of torts to problems of concurrent causation, but § 7.18 takes no position on whether liability in such a case should be joint and several or should be apportioned in terms of culpability among those responsible.

In Cede & Co. v. Technicolor, Inc., 634 A.2d 345 (Del. 1993), modified, 636 A.2d (Del. 1994) (followed by extensive remands and appeals), the trial court rendered judgment for defendants on the ground that the plaintiff had the burden of proving injury and had not done so. The Delaware Supreme Court reversed. The Court concluded that based on the record, the directors had breached the duty of care. Given that conclusion, it held, the Chancellor's determination that the plaintiff had the burden of proving injury was erroneous. Bearing in mind that Delaware treats the business judgment rule as a presumption, the court held that if a plaintiff shows there was a breach of the duty of care, that showing overcomes the presumption of the rule and establishes a prima facie case of liability, even without a showing of injury. The burden then shifts to the defendants to show that the transaction was entirely fair. In the course of its opinion, the court explicitly rejected the reasoning of Barnes v. Andrews.

B. THE BUSINESS JUDGMENT RULE

Kamin v. American Express Co.

Supreme Court, Special Term, N.Y. County, Part 1, 1976.
86 Misc.2d 809, 383 N.Y.S.2d 807, aff'd on opinion below 54 A.D.2d 654, 387 N.Y.S.2d 993 (1st Dept.1976).

■ EDWARD J. GREENFIELD, JUSTICE:

In this stockholders' derivative action, the individual defendants, who are the directors of the American Express Company, move for an order dismissing the complaint for failure to state a cause of action pursuant to CPLR 3211(a)(7), and alternatively, for summary judgment pursuant to CPLR 3211(c).

The complaint is brought derivatively by two minority stockholders of the American Express Company, asking for a declaration that a certain dividend in kind is a waste of corporate assets, directing the defendants not to proceed with the distribution, or, in the alternative, for monetary damages. The motion to dismiss the complaint requires the Court to presuppose the truth of the allegations. It is the defendants' contention that, conceding everything in the complaint, no viable cause of action is made out.

After establishing the identity of the parties, the complaint alleges that in 1972 American Express acquired for investment 1,954,418 shares of common stock of Donaldson, Lufken and Jenrette, Inc. (hereafter DLJ), a publicly traded corporation, at a cost of $29.9 million. It is further alleged that the current market value of those shares is approximately $4.0 million. On July 28, 1975, it is alleged, the Board of Directors of American Express declared a special dividend to all stockholders of record pursuant to which the shares of DLJ would be distributed in kind. Plaintiffs contend further that if American Express were to sell the DLJ shares on the market, it would sustain a capital loss of $25 million, which could be offset against taxable capital gains on other investments. Such a sale, they allege, would result in tax savings to the company of approximately $8 million, which would not be available in the case of the distribution of DLJ shares to stockholders. It is alleged that on October 8, 1975 and October 16, 1975, plaintiffs demanded that the directors rescind the previously declared dividend in DLJ shares and take steps to preserve the capital loss which would result from selling the shares. This demand was rejected by the Board of Directors on October 17, 1975.

It is apparent that all the previously-mentioned allegations of the complaint go to the question of the exercise by the Board of Directors of business judgment in deciding how to deal with the DLJ shares. The crucial allegation which must be scrutinized to determine the legal sufficiency of the complaint is paragraph 19, which alleges:

> "19. All of the defendant Directors engaged in or acquiesced in or negligently permitted the declaration and payment of the Dividend in violation of the fiduciary duty owed by them to Amex to care for and preserve Amex's assets in the same manner as a man of average prudence would care for his own property."

Plaintiffs never moved for temporary injunctive relief, and did nothing to bar the actual distribution of the DLJ shares. The dividend was in fact paid on October 31, 1975. Accordingly, that portion of the complaint seeking a direction not to distribute the shares is deemed to be moot, and the Court will deal only with the request for declaratory judgment or for damages.

Examination of the complaint reveals that there is no claim of fraud or self-dealing, and no contention that there was any bad faith or oppressive conduct. The law is quite clear as to what is necessary to ground a claim for actionable wrongdoing.

> "In actions by stockholders, which assail the acts of their directors or trustees, courts will not interfere unless the powers have been illegally or unconscientiously executed; or unless it be made to appear that the acts were fraudulent or collusive, and destructive of the rights of the stockholders. Mere errors of judgment are not sufficient as grounds for equity interference, for the powers of those entrusted with corporate management are largely discretionary." Leslie v. Lorillard, 110 N.Y. 519, 532, 18 N.E. 363, 365....

More specifically, the question of whether or not a dividend is to be declared or a distribution of some kind should be made is exclusively a matter of business judgment for the Board of Directors.

> "... Courts will not interfere with such discretion unless it be first made to appear that the directors have acted or are about to act in bad faith and for a dishonest purpose. It is for the directors to say, acting in good faith of course, when and to what extent dividends shall be declared ... The statute confers upon the directors this power, and the minority stockholders are not in a position to question this right, so long as the directors are acting in good faith ..."

Thus, a complaint must be dismissed if all that is presented is a decision to pay dividends rather than pursuing some other course of conduct. Weinberger v. Quinn, 264 App.Div. 405, 35 N.Y.S.2d 567, affd. 290 N.Y. 635, 49 N.E.2d 131. A complaint which alleges merely that some course of action other than that pursued by the Board of Directors would have been more advantageous gives rise to no cognizable cause of action. Courts have more than enough to do in adjudicating legal rights and devising remedies for wrongs. The directors' room rather than the courtroom is the appropriate forum for thrashing out purely business questions which will have an impact on profits, market prices, competitive situations, or tax advantages. As stated by Cardozo, J., when sitting at Special Term, the substitution of someone else's business judgment for that of the directors "is no business for any court to follow." Holmes v. St. Joseph Lead Co., 84 Misc. 278, 283, 147 N.Y.S. 104, 107, quoting from Gamble v. Queens County Water Co., 123 N.Y. 91, 99, 25 N.E. 201, [202].

It is not enough to allege, as plaintiffs do here, that the directors made an imprudent decision, which did not capitalize on the possibility of using a potential capital loss to offset capital gains. More than imprudence or mistaken judgment must be shown.

> "Questions of policy of management, expediency of contracts or action, adequacy of consideration, lawful appropriation of corporate funds to advance corporate interests, are left solely to their honest and unselfish decision, for their powers therein are with-

> out limitation and free from restraint, and the exercise of them for the common and general interests of the corporation may not be questioned, although the results show that what they did was unwise or inexpedient." Pollitz v. Wabash Railroad Co., 207 N.Y. 113, 124, 100 N.E. 721, 724.

Section 720 of the Business Corporation Law permits an action against directors for "the neglect of, or failure to perform, or other violations of his duties in the management and disposition of corporate assets committed to his charge." This does not mean that a director is chargeable with ordinary negligence for having made an improper decision, or having acted imprudently. The "neglect" referred to in the statute is neglect of duties (i.e., malfeasance or nonfeasance) and not misjudgment. To allege that a director "negligently permitted the declaration and payment" of a dividend without alleging fraud, dishonesty or nonfeasance, is to state merely that a decision was taken with which one disagrees.

Nor does this appear to be a case in which a potentially valid cause of action is inartfully stated.... The affidavits of the defendants and the exhibits annexed thereto demonstrate that the objections raised by the plaintiffs to the proposed dividend action were carefully considered and unanimously rejected by the Board at a special meeting called precisely for that purpose at the plaintiffs' request. The minutes of the special meeting indicate that the defendants were fully aware that a sale rather than a distribution of the DLJ shares might result in the realization of a substantial income tax saving. Nevertheless, they concluded that there were countervailing considerations primarily with respect to the adverse effect such a sale, realizing a loss of $25 million, would have on the net income figures in the American Express financial statement. Such a reduction of net income would have a serious effect on the market value of the publicly traded American Express stock. This was not a situation in which the defendant directors totally overlooked facts called to their attention. They gave them consideration, and attempted to view the total picture in arriving at their decision. While plaintiffs contend that according to their accounting consultants the loss on the DLJ stock would still have to be charged against current earnings even if the stock were distributed, the defendants' accounting experts assert that the loss would be a charge against earnings only in the event of a sale, whereas in the event of distribution of the stock as a dividend, the proper accounting treatment would be to charge the loss only against surplus. While the chief accountant for the SEC raised some question as to the appropriate accounting treatment of this transaction, there was no basis for any action to be taken by the SEC with respect to the American Express financial statement.

The only hint of self-interest which is raised, not in the complaint but in the papers on the motion, is that four of the twenty directors were officers and employees of American Express and members of its Executive Incentive Compensation Plan. Hence, it is suggested, by virtue of the action taken earnings may have been overstated and their compensation affected thereby. Such a claim is highly speculative and standing alone can hardly be regarded as sufficient to support an inference of self-dealing. There is no claim or showing that the four company directors dominated and controlled the sixteen outside members of the Board. Certainly, every action taken by the Board has some impact on earnings and may therefore affect the compensation of those whose earnings are keyed to profits. That does not disqualify the inside directors, nor does it put every policy adopted by the Board in question. All directors have an obligation, using sound business judgment, to maximize income for the benefit of all persons having a stake in the welfare of the corporate entity. *See*, Amdur v. Meyer, 15 A.D.2d 425, 224 N.Y.S.2d 440, appeal dismissed 14 N.Y.2d 541, 248 N.Y.S.2d 639, 198 N.E.2d 30. What we have here as revealed both by the complaint and by the affidavits and exhibits, is that a disagreement exists between two minority stockholders and a unanimous Board of Directors as to the best way to handle a loss already incurred on an investment. The directors are entitled to exercise their honest business judgment on the information before them, and to act within their corporate powers. That they may be mistaken, that other courses of action might have differing consequences, or that their action might benefit some shareholders more than others presents no basis for the superimposition of judicial judgment, so long as it appears that the directors have been acting in good faith. The question of to what extent a dividend shall be declared and the manner in which it shall be paid is ordinarily subject only to the qualification that the dividend be paid out of surplus (Business Corporation Law Section 510, subd. b). The Court will not interfere unless a clear case is made out of fraud, oppression, arbitrary action, or breach of trust.

Courts should not shrink from the responsibility of dismissing complaints or granting summary judgment when no legal wrongdoing is set forth. . . .

In this case it clearly appears that the plaintiffs have failed as a matter of law to make out an actionable claim. Accordingly, the motion by the defendants for summary judgment and dismissal of the complaint is granted.

ALI, PRINCIPLES OF CORPORATE GOVERNANCE § 4.01(c)

[See Statutory Supplement]

NOTE ON THE DIVERGENCE OF STANDARDS OF CONDUCT AND STANDARDS OF REVIEW IN CORPORATE LAW, AND ON THE BUSINESS JUDGMENT RULE

A *standard of conduct* states how an actor should conduct a given activity or play a given role. A *standard of review* states the test a court should apply when it reviews an actor's conduct to determine whether to impose liability or grant injunctive relief. In many or most areas of law, standards of conduct and standards of review are identical. For example, the standard of conduct that governs an automobile driver is that he should drive carefully. Correspondingly, the standard of review in a liability claim against a driver is whether he drove carefully. The standard of conduct that governs an agent who engages in a transaction with his principal that involves the subject matter of the agency is that the agent must deal fairly. Correspondingly, the standard of review in a liability claim by the principal against an agent based on such a transaction is whether the agent dealt fairly.

An identity between standards of conduct and standards of review is so common that it is easy to overlook the fact that the two kinds of standards may diverge in any given area—that is, the standard of conduct that states how an actor should conduct himself may differ from the standard of review by which courts determine whether to impose liability on the basis of the actor's conduct. A divergence of standards of conduct and standards of review is particularly common in corporation law.

The duty of care is a leading example of this divergence. The traditional *standard of conduct* applicable to directors and officers in the performance of their functions, in relation to matters in which they are not self-interested, varies somewhat in its formulation, but the basic standard is set forth in Section 4.01(a) of the ALI's *Principles of Corporate Governance.* "A director or officer has a duty to the corporation to perform the director's or officer's functions in good faith, in a manner that he or she reasonably believes to be in the best interests of the corporation, and with the care that an ordinarily prudent person would reasonably be expected to exercise in a like position and under similar circumstances." The application of this standard of conduct to the functions of directors results in several distinct duties—in particular, the duty to monitor, the duty of inquiry, the duty to make prudent or reasonable decisions on matters that the board is obliged or chooses to act upon, and the duty to employ a reasonable process to make decisions.

Officers have comparable duties, although for most officers decisionmaking is likely to be more important than monitoring.

On their face, the duties of directors are fairly demanding, insofar as they are measured by reasonability. In practice, however, the standards of review applied to the performance of these duties are less stringent than the standards of conduct on which the duties are based. This is especially true when the quality of a decision, as opposed to the quality of the decisionmaking process, is called into question. In such cases a much less demanding standard of review may apply under the business judgment rule.

The business judgment rule consists of four conditions and, if the four conditions are satisfied, a special standard of review applicable to claims that are based on the quality of a decision.

The four conditions are as follows:

First, the director must have made a decision. So, for example, a director's failure to make due inquiry, or any other simple failure to take action (as opposed to a deliberative decision not to act), does not qualify for protection under the business judgment rule.

Second, the director must have informed himself with respect to the business judgment to the extent he reasonably believes appropriate under the circumstances—that is, he must have employed a reasonable decisionmaking process.

Third, the decision must have been made in good faith—a condition that is not satisfied if, among other things, the director knows that the decision violates the law.

Fourth, the director may not have a financial interest in the subject matter of the decision. For example, the business judgment rule is inapplicable to a director's decision to approve the corporation's purchase of his property.

If the conditions of the business judgment rule are not satisfied, then the standard by which the quality of a decision is reviewed is comparable to the standard of conduct for making the decision—that is, the standard of review is based on entire fairness or reasonability. This is nicely illustrated by the Delaware Supreme Court's 1993 decision in Cede & Co. v. Technicolor, Inc., 634 A.2d 345, followed by extensive remands and appeals.

In that case, Perelman, the CEO of MacAndrews & Forbes, Inc. ("MAF"), entered into negotiations with Kamerman, the CEO of Technicolor, with a view to an acquisition of Technicolor by MAF. On the basis of limited information, Goldman Sachs, an investment banker, told Kamerman that a price of $20–22 per share was worth pursuing, that a $25 price might be feasible, and that Kamerman should consider other possible purchasers. Six days later, Kamerman and Perelman agreed on a price of $23. That evening, Kamerman called a special meeting of Technicolor's Board, to be held two days later. At the meeting, the board approved an agreement with to transfer Technicolor to MAF at the $23 price, and recommended that Technicolor's shareholders accept that price.

At the trial, the Chancellor found that it was a matter of grave doubt whether Technicolor's board had exercised due care in making its decision, for the following reasons, among others: (1) The agreement was not preceded by a prudent search of alternatives. (2) Given the terms of the merger and the circumstances, the directors had no reasonable basis to assume that a better offer from a third party could be expected once the agreement was signed. (3) Most of the directors had little or no knowledge of an impending sale of the company until they arrived at the meeting, and only a few of them had any knowledge of the terms of the sale.

On the basis of these reasons, the Delaware Supreme Court held that Technicolor's board failed to reach an informed decision when it made its decision, so the business judgment rule did not apply. As a result, the directors had the burden of showing that the transaction was entirely fair. If the $23 price was not entirely fair, the directors would be liable for damages. And, the court added, because the business judgment rule did not apply, the directors had the burden of proving that the price was entirely fair.

In contrast, if the four conditions of the business judgment rule *are* satisfied, then the quality of a director's decision will be reviewed, not to determine whether the decision was *reasonable*, but only under a much more limited standard. There is some difference of opinion as to how that limited standard should be formulated. A few courts have stated that the standard is whether the director acted in good faith. *See, e.g.,* In re RJR Nabisco, Inc. Shareholders Litig., [1988–89 Transfer Binder] Fed. Sec. L. Rep. (CCH) ¶ 94194, at 91,710 n.13 (Del. Ch. Jan. 31, 1989). However, if the four conditions of the business judgment rule are satisfied, the prevalent formulation of the standard of review under the rule is that the decision must merely be *rational*, or must have a *rational basis*, or the like. *See* ALI, Principles of Corporate Governance § 4.01(c)(3). This standard of review may be referred to as the business-judgment standard.

An example of a decision that fails to satisfy the rationality standard is a decision that cannot be coherently explained. For example, in Selheimer v. Manganese Corp. of America, 224 A.2d 634 (Pa.1966), a corporation's managers poured almost all of the corporation's funds into the development of a single plant, even though they knew that the plant could not be operated profitably for a number of reasons, including lack of a railroad siding and proper storage areas. The court imposed liability because the managers' conduct "defie[d] explanation; in fact, the defendants have failed to give any satisfactory explanation or advance any justification for [the] expenditures." (In contrast, a decision may be unreasonable, but not irrational, if there are good reasons for and against the decision, but under the circumstances a person of sound judgment, giving appropriate weight to the reasons for and against, would not have made the decision. Accordingly, a decision may be unreasonable even though it was supported by some affirmative reasons and was therefore explicable, although on balance undesirable.)

Although, as *Selheimer* shows, the rationality standard of review has some bite, this standard is much easier to satisfy than a reasonability standard. To see how exceptional a rationality standard is, we need only think about the judgments we make in everyday life. It is common to characterize a person's conduct as unreasonable, but it is very uncommon to characterize a sane person's conduct as irrational.

Why should such a relatively undemanding standard of review, which differs so radically from the standard of conduct applicable to directors—and from the standards of both conduct and review applicable to persons who play most other life-roles—apply to the quality of decisions made by corporate directors? The answer to this question involves considerations of both fairness and policy.

To begin with, the application of a reasonableness standard of review to the quality of disinterested decisions by directors could result in the unfair imposition of liability. In the paradigm negligence case involving a relatively simple decision, such as an automobile accident, there is often little difference between decisions that turn out badly and bad decisions. In such cases, typically only one reasonable decision could have been made under a given set of circumstances, and decisions that turn out badly therefore almost inevitably turn out to have been bad decisions. In contrast, in the case of business decisions it may often be difficult for fact-finders to distinguish between bad decisions and proper decisions that turn out badly. Business judgments are necessarily made on the basis of incomplete information and in the face of obvious risks, so that typically a range of decisions is reasonable. A decisionmaker faced with uncertainty must make a judgment concerning the relevant probability distribution and must act on that judgment. If the decisionmaker makes a reasonable assessment of the probability distribution, and the outcome falls on the unlucky tail, the decisionmaker has not made a bad decision, because in any normal probability distribution some outcomes will inevitably fall on the unlucky tail.

For example, a board faced with a promising but expensive and untried new technology may have to choose between investing in the technology or forgoing such an investment. Each alternative involves certain negative risks. If the board chooses one alternative and the associated negative risk materializes, the decision is "wrong" in the very restricted sense that if the board had it to do all over again it would make a different decision, but the decision is not for that reason a bad decision.

As a result of a systematic defect in cognition known as the hindsight bias, however, under a reasonableness standard of review fact-finders might too often erroneously treat decisions that turned out badly as bad decisions, and unfairly hold directors liable for such decisions. Experimental psychology has shown that in hindsight people consistently exaggerate the ease with which outcomes could have been anticipated in foresight. People view what has happened as relatively inevitable.[1] Accordingly, people who know that a bad *outcome* resulted from a decision overestimate the extent to which the outcome was *predictable* and, therefore, the extent to which the decisionmaker was at fault for making the decision that led to the outcome.[2] Essentially, people find it difficult or even impossible to

---

1. See Robyn M. Dawes, Rational Choice in an Uncertain World 119–20 (1988); Baruch Fischhoff, For Those Condemned to Study the Past: Heuristics and Biases in Hindsight, in Judgment Under Uncertainty: Heuristics and Biases 335, 341–43 (Daniel Kahneman et al. eds., 1982) [hereinafter Heuristics and Biases]. Baruch Fischhoff & Ruth Beyth, "I Knew It Would Happen"—Remembered Probabilities of Once–Future Things, 13 Organizational Behav. and Hum. Performance 1–16 (1975) [hereinafter Fischhoff & Beyth].

2. See Hal Arkes & Cindy Schipani, Medical Malpractice and the Business Judgment Rule, 73 Ore. L. Rev. 587 (1994) [hereinafter Arkes & Schipani, Medical Malpractice]; Jonathan D. Casper et al., Juror Decision Making, Attitudes, and the Hindsight Bias, 13 L. & Hum. Behav. 291 (1989) [hereinafter Casper, Juror Decision Making]; Raanan Lipshitz, "Either a Medal or a Corporal:" The Effects of Success and Failure on the Evaluation of Decision Making and Decision Makers, 44 Organizational Behav. & Hum. Decision Processes 380 (1989) [hereinafter Lipshitz, Success and Failure].

disregard information they possess about an outcome.[3] That information, in turn, renders the circumstances that pointed to the outcome more salient in their minds, because those circumstances can be integrated into a cohesive story that ends with the actual outcome, while circumstances pointing in other directions cannot.

The hindsight bias is nicely illustrated by an experiment in which 112 anesthesiologists reviewed the anesthesiological care in 21 paired cases that were based on actual files. Each of the anesthesiologists was presented with only one case from each pair. The patient and the treatments in each of the two paired cases were identical, and the results in all cases were adverse. However, the files were edited so that in one case in each pair the adverse outcome was described as temporary, while in the other case the outcome was described as permanent. The reviewers were instructed to determine, in each of the 21 cases they reviewed, whether the anesthesiological care was less than appropriate, appropriate, or impossible to judge. When the adverse outcome was described as permanent rather than temporary, the overall distributions of the reviewers' judgments concerning the appropriateness of the care was shifted negatively by 30 percent.[4] Comparable results have been obtained in other experiments, even when the subjects have been explicitly instructed to disregard outcomes in evaluating fault.[5] The hindsight bias is also well-supported by survey evidence concerning the attribution of responsibility, and by casual empiricism.[6] The business judgment rule protects directors from the unfair imposition of liability as a result of the hindsight bias, by providing them with a large zone of protection when their decisions are attacked.

Furthermore, as a matter of policy the shareholders' own best interests may be served by conducting only a very limited review of the quality of directors' decisions. It is often in the interests of shareholders that directors choose the riskier of two alternative decisions, because the expected value of the more risky decision may be greater than the expected value of the less risky decision. For example, suppose that Corporation C has $100 million in assets. C's board must choose between decision X and decision Y. Each decision requires an investment of $1 million. Decision X has a 75% likelihood of succeeding. If the decision succeeds, C will gain $2 million. If it fails, C will lose its $1 million investment. Decision Y has a 90% chance of succeeding. If the decision succeeds, C will gain $1 million. If it fails, C will recover its investment. It is in the interest of C's shareholders that the board make decision X, even though it is riskier, because the

3. See Michael J. Saks & Robert F. Kidd, Human Information processing and Adjudication: Trial by Heuristics, 15 L. & Soc'y Rev. 123, 144 (1980).

4. Robert A. Caplan et al., Effect of Outcome on Physician Judgments of Appropriateness of Care, 265 J. Am. Med. Ass'n 1957 (1991). This experiment, as well as the hindsight bias, its application to the business judgment rule, and other hindsight experiments in the medical area, are discussed in a very illuminating way in Arkes & Schipani, Medical Malpractice, supra note 3.

5. See, e.g., Casper, Juror Decision Making, supra note 2.

6. See Lipshitz, Success and Failure, supra note 2, at 381–82.

expected value of decision X is $1.25 million (75% times the $2 million potential gain, minus 25% times the $1 million loss), while the expected value of decision Y is only $900,000 (90% of the $1 million potential gain). If, however, the board was concerned about liability for making an unreasonable decision it might choose decision Y, because as a practical matter it is almost impossible for a plaintiff to win a duty of care action on the theory that a board should have taken greater risks than it did. A standard of review of the quality of decisions that imposes liability on a director for unreasonable, as opposed to irrational, decisions might therefore have the perverse incentive effect of discouraging bold but desirable decisions. Putting this more generally, under such a standard of review directors might tend to be unduly risk-averse, because if a highly risky decision had a positive outcome, the corporation, but not the directors, would gain, while if it had a negative outcome the directors might be required to make up the corporate loss. The business judgment rule helps to offset that tendency.

Smith v. Van Gorkom

Supreme Court of Delaware, 1985.
488 A.2d 858.

■ Before HERMANN, C.J., and MCNEILLY, HORSEY, MOORE and CHRISTIE, JJ., constituting the Court en banc.

■ HORSEY, JUSTICE (FOR THE MAJORITY):

This appeal from the Court of Chancery involves a class action brought by shareholders of the defendant Trans Union Corporation ("Trans Union" or "the Company"), originally seeking rescission of a cash-out merger of Trans Union into the defendant New T Company ("New T"), a wholly-owned subsidiary of the defendant, Marmon Group, Inc. ("Marmon"). Alternate relief in the form of damages is sought against the defendant members of the Board of Directors of Trans Union, New T, and Jay A. Pritzker and Robert A. Pritzker, owners of Marmon.[1]

Following trial, the former Chancellor granted judgment for the defendant directors by unreported letter opinion dated July 6, 1982.[2] Judgment was based on two findings: (1) that the Board of Directors

---

1. The plaintiff, Alden Smith, originally sought to enjoin the merger; but, following extensive discovery, the Trial Court denied the plaintiff's motion for preliminary injunction by unreported letter opinion dated February 3, 1981. On February 10, 1981, the proposed merger was approved by Trans Union's stockholders at a special meeting and the merger became effective on that date. Thereafter, John W. Gosselin was permitted to intervene as an additional plaintiff; and Smith and Gosselin were certified as representing a class consisting of all persons, other than defendants, who held shares of Trans Union common stock on all relevant dates. At the time of the merger, Smith owned 54,000 shares of Trans Union stock, Gosselin owned 23,600 shares, and members of Gosselin's family owned 20,000 shares.

2. Following trial, and before decision by the Trial Court, the parties stipulated to the dismissal, with prejudice, of the Messrs. Pritzker as parties defendant. However, all references to defendants hereinafter are to the defendant directors of Trans Union, unless otherwise noted.

had acted in an informed manner so as to be entitled to protection of the business judgment rule in approving the cash-out merger; and (2) that the shareholder vote approving the merger should not be set aside because the stockholders had been "fairly informed" by the Board of Directors before voting thereon. The plaintiffs appeal.

Speaking for the majority of the Court, we conclude that both rulings of the Court of Chancery are clearly erroneous. Therefore, we reverse and direct that judgment be entered in favor of the plaintiffs and against the defendant directors for the fair value of the plaintiffs' stockholdings in Trans Union....

I.

The nature of this case requires a detailed factual statement. The following facts are essentially uncontradicted....

Trans Union was a publicly-traded, diversified holding company, the principal earnings of which were generated by its railcar leasing business. During the period here involved, the Company had a cash flow of hundreds of millions of dollars annually. However, the Company had difficulty in generating sufficient taxable income to offset increasingly large investment tax credits (ITCs)....

B.

[Jerome Van Gorkom, Trans Union's Chairman and Chief Executive Officer, met with senior management on August 27, 1980, to discuss Trans Union's difficulty in producing sufficient taxable income to offset its increasing investment-tax credits and accelerated-depreciation deductions.] Donald Romans, Chief Financial Officer of Trans Union, stated that his department had done a "very brief bit of work on the possibility of a leveraged buy-out." ... The work consisted of a "preliminary study" of the cash which could be generated by the Company if it participated in a leveraged buy-out. As Romans stated, this analysis "was very first and rough cut at seeing whether a cash flow would support what might be considered a high price for this type of transaction."

On September 5, at another Senior Management meeting which Van Gorkom attended, Romans again brought up the idea of a leveraged buy-out as a "possible strategic alternative" to the Company's acquisition program. Romans and Bruce S. Chelberg, President and Chief Operating Officer of Trans Union, had been working on the matter in preparation for the meeting. According to Romans: They did not "come up" with a price for the Company. They merely "ran the numbers" at $50 a share and at $60 a share with the "rough form" of their cash figures at the time. Their "figures indicated that $50 would be very easy to do but $60 would be very difficult to do under those figures." This work did not purport to establish a fair price for either the Company or 100% of the stock. It was intended to determine the cash flow needed to service the debt that would "probably" be incurred in a leveraged buy-out, based on "rough calculations" without "any benefit of experts to identify what the limits were to that, and so forth." These computations were not considered extensive and no conclusion was reached.

At this meeting, Van Gorkom stated that he would be willing to take $55 per share for his own 75,000 shares. He vetoed the suggestion of a leveraged buy-out by Management, however, as involving a potential conflict of interest for Management. Van Gorkom, a certified public accountant and lawyer, had been an officer of Trans Union for 24 years, its Chief Executive Officer for more than 17 years, and Chairman of its Board for 2 years. It is noteworthy in this connection that he was then approaching 65 years of age and mandatory retirement.

For several days following the September 5 meeting, Van Gorkom pondered the idea of a sale....

Van Gorkom decided to meet with Jay A. Pritzker, a well-known corporate takeover specialist and a social acquaintance. However, rather than approaching Pritzker simply to determine his interest in acquiring Trans Union, Van Gorkom assembled a proposed per share price for sale of the Company and a financing structure by which to accomplish the sale. Van Gorkom did so without consulting either his Board or any members of Senior Management except one: Carl Peterson, Trans Union's Controller. Telling Peterson that he wanted no other person on his staff to know what he was doing, but without telling him why, Van Gorkom directed Peterson to calculate the feasibility of a leveraged buy-out at an assumed price per share of $55. Apart from the Company's historic stock market price,[5] and Van Gorkom's long association with Trans Union, the record is devoid of any competent evidence that $55 represented the per share intrinsic value of the Company....

Van Gorkom arranged a meeting with Pritzker at the latter's home on Saturday, September 13, 1980. Van Gorkom prefaced his presentation by stating to Pritzker: "Now as far as you are concerned, I can, I think, show how you can pay a substantial premium over the present stock price and pay off most of the loan in the first five years.... If you could pay $55 for this Company, here is a way in which I think it can be financed."

Van Gorkom then reviewed with Pritzker his calculations based upon his proposed price of $55 per share. Although Pritzker mentioned $50 as a more attractive figure, no other price was mentioned. However, Van Gorkom stated that to be sure that $55 was the best price obtainable, Trans Union should be free to accept any better offer. Pritzker demurred, stating that his organization would serve as a "stalking horse" for an "auction contest" only if Trans Union would permit Pritzker to buy 1,750,000 shares of Trans Union stock at market price which Pritzker could then sell to any higher bidder. After further

---

5. The common stock of Trans Union was traded on the New York Stock Exchange. Over the five year period from 1975 through 1979, Trans Union's stock had traded within a range of a high of $39½ and a low of $24¼. Its high and low range for 1980 through September 19 (the last trading day before announcement of the merger) was $38¼–$29½.

discussion on this point, Pritzker told Van Gorkom that he would give him a more definite reaction soon.

On Monday, September 15, Pritzker advised Van Gorkom that he was interested in the $55 cash-out merger proposal and requested more information on Trans Union. . . .

On Thursday, September 18, Van Gorkom met again with Pritzker. At that time, Van Gorkom knew that Pritzker intended to make a cash-out merger offer at Van Gorkom's proposed $55 per share. Pritzker instructed his attorney, a merger and acquisition specialist, to begin drafting merger documents. There was no further discussion of the $55 price. However, the number of shares of Trans Union's treasury stock to be offered to Pritzker was negotiated down to one million shares; the price was set at $38–75 cents above the per share price at the close of the market on September 19. At this point, Pritzker insisted that the Trans Union Board act on his merger proposal within the next three days, stating to Van Gorkom: "We have to have a decision by no later than Sunday [evening, September 21] before the opening of the English stock exchange on Monday morning." Pritzker's lawyer was then instructed to draft the merger documents, to be reviewed by Van Gorkom's lawyer, "sometimes with discussion and sometimes not, in the haste to get it finished."

On Friday, September 19, Van Gorkom, Chelberg, and Pritzker consulted with Trans Union's lead bank regarding the financing of Pritzker's purchase of Trans Union. The bank indicated that it could form a syndicate of banks that would finance the transaction. On the same day, Van Gorkom retained James Brennan, Esquire, to advise Trans Union on the legal aspects of the merger. Van Gorkom did not consult with William Browder, a Vice–President and director of Trans Union and former head of its legal department, or with William Moore, then the head of Trans Union's legal staff.

On Friday, September 19, Van Gorkom called a special meeting of the Trans Union Board for noon the following day. He also called a meeting of the Company's Senior Management to convene at 11:00 a.m., prior to the meeting of the Board. No one, except Chelberg and Peterson, was told the purpose of the meetings. Van Gorkom did not invite Trans Union's investment banker, Salomon Brothers or its Chicago-based partner, to attend.

Of those present at the Senior Management meeting on September 20, only Chelberg and Peterson had prior knowledge of Pritzker's offer. Van Gorkom disclosed the offer and described its terms, but he furnished no copies of the proposed Merger Agreement. Romans announced that his department had done a second study which showed that, for a leveraged buy-out, the price range for Trans Union stock was between $55 and $65 per share. Van Gorkom neither saw the study nor asked Romans to make it available for the Board meeting.

Senior Management's reaction to the Pritzker proposal was completely negative. No member of Management, except Chelberg and

Peterson, supported the proposal. Romans objected to the price as being too low[6]. . . .

Ten directors served on the Trans Union Board, five inside (defendants Bonser, O'Boyle, Browder, Chelberg, and Van Gorkom) and five outside (defendants Wallis, Johnson, Lanterman, Morgan and Reneker). All directors were present at the meeting, except O'Boyle who was ill. Of the outside directors, four were corporate chief executive officers and one was the former Dean of the University of Chicago Business School. None was an investment banker or trained financial analyst. All members of the Board were well informed about the Company and its operations as a going concern. They were familiar with the current financial condition of the Company, as well as operating and earnings projections reported in the recent Five Year Forecast. The Board generally received regular and detailed reports and was kept abreast of the accumulated investment tax credit and accelerated depreciation problem.

Van Gorkom began the Special Meeting of the Board with a twenty-minute oral presentation. Copies of the proposed Merger Agreement were delivered too late for study before or during the meeting.[7] He reviewed the Company's ITC and depreciation problems and the efforts theretofore made to solve them. He discussed his initial meeting with Pritzker and his motivation in arranging that meeting. Van Gorkom did not disclose to the Board, however, the methodology by which he alone had arrived at the $55 figure, or the fact that he first proposed the $55 price in his negotiations with Pritzker.

Van Gorkom outlined the terms of the Pritzker offer as follows: Pritzker would pay $55 in cash for all outstanding shares of Trans Union stock upon completion of which Trans Union would be merged into New T Company, a subsidiary wholly-owned by Pritzker and formed to implement the merger; for a period of 90 days, Trans Union could receive, but could not actively solicit, competing offers; the offer had to be acted on by the next evening, Sunday, September 21; Trans Union could only furnish to competing bidders published information, and not proprietary information; the offer was subject to Pritzker obtaining the necessary financing by October 10, 1980; if the financing contingency were met or waived by Pritzker, Trans Union was required to sell to Pritzker one million newly-issued shares of Trans Union at $38 per share.

Van Gorkom took the position that putting Trans Union "up for auction" through a 90-day market test would validate a decision by the Board that $55 was a fair price. He told the Board that the "free

---

6. Van Gorkom asked Romans to express his opinion as to the $55 price. Romans stated that he "thought the price was too low in relation to what he could derive for the company in a cash sale, particularly one which enabled us to realize the values of certain subsidiaries and independent entities."

7. The record is not clear as to the terms of the Merger Agreement. The Agreement, as originally presented to the Board on September 20, was never produced by defendants despite demands by the plaintiffs. Nor is it clear that the directors were given an opportunity to study the Merger Agreement before voting on it. All that can be said is that Brennan had the Agreement before him during the meeting.

market will have an opportunity to judge whether $55 is a fair price." Van Gorkom framed the decision before the Board not as whether $55 per share was the highest price that could be obtained, but as whether the $55 price was a fair price that the stockholders should be given the opportunity to accept or reject.[8]

Attorney Brennan advised the members of the Board that they might be sued if they failed to accept the offer and that a fairness opinion was not required as a matter of law.

Romans attended the meeting as chief financial officer of the Company. He told the Board that he had not been involved in the negotiations with Pritzker and knew nothing about the merger proposal until the morning of the meeting; that his studies did not indicate either a fair price for the stock or a valuation of the Company; that he did not see his role as directly addressing the fairness issue; and that he and his people "were trying to search for ways to justify a price in connection with such a [leveraged buy-out] transaction, rather than to say what the shares are worth." Romans testified:

> I told the Board that the study ran the numbers at 50 and 60, and then the subsequent study at 55 and 65, and that was not the same thing as saying that I have a valuation of the company at X dollars. But it was a way—a first step towards reaching that conclusion.

Romans told the Board that, in his opinion, $55 was "in the range of a fair price," but "at the beginning of the range." . . .

The Board meeting of September 20 lasted about two hours. Based solely upon Van Gorkom's oral presentation, Chelberg's supporting representations, Romans' oral statement, Brennan's legal advice, and their knowledge of the market history of the Company's stock, the directors approved the proposed Merger Agreement. However, the Board later claimed to have attached two conditions to its acceptance: (1) that Trans Union reserved the right to accept any better offer that was made during the market test period; and (2) that Trans Union could share its proprietary information with any other potential bidders. While the Board now claims to have reserved the right to accept any better offer received after the announcement of the Pritzker agreement (even though the minutes of the meeting do not reflect this), it is undisputed that the Board did not reserve the right to actively solicit alternate offers.

The Merger Agreement was executed by Van Gorkom during the evening of September 20 at a formal social event that he hosted for the opening of the Chicago Lyric Opera. Neither he nor any other director read the agreement prior to its signing and delivery to Pritzker. . . .

On Monday, September 22, the Company issued a press release announcing that Trans Union had entered into a "definitive" Merger Agreement with an affiliate of the Marmon Group, Inc., a Pritzker

8. In Van Gorkom's words: The "real decision" is whether to "let the stockholders decide it" which is "all you are being asked to decide today."

holding company. Within 10 days of the public announcement, dissent among Senior Management over the merger had become widespread. Faced with threatened resignations of key officers, Van Gorkom met with Pritzker who agreed to several modifications of the Agreement. Pritzker was willing to do so provided that Van Gorkom could persuade the dissidents to remain on the Company payroll for at least six months after consummation of the merger.

Van Gorkom reconvened the Board on October 8 and secured the directors' approval of the proposed amendments—sight unseen. The Board also authorized the employment of Salomon Brothers, its investment banker, to solicit other offers for Trans Union during the proposed "market test" period.

The next day, October 9, Trans Union issued a press release announcing: (1) that Pritzker had obtained "the financing commitments necessary to consummate" the merger with Trans Union; (2) that Pritzker had acquired one million shares of Trans Union common stock at $38 per share; (3) that Trans Union was now permitted to actively seek other offers and had retained Salomon Brothers for that purpose; and (4) that if a more favorable offer were not received before February 1, 1981, Trans Union's shareholders would thereafter meet to vote on the Pritzker proposal.

It was not until the following day, October 10, that the actual amendments to the Merger Agreement were prepared by Pritzker and delivered to Van Gorkom for execution. As will be seen, the amendments were considerably at variance with Van Gorkom's representations of the amendments to the Board on October 8; and the amendments placed serious constraints on Trans Union's ability to negotiate a better deal and withdraw from the Pritzker agreement. Nevertheless, Van Gorkom proceeded to execute what became the October 10 amendments to the Merger Agreement without conferring further with the Board members and apparently without comprehending the actual implications of the amendments. . . .

Salomon Brothers' efforts over a three-month period from October 21 to January 21 produced only one serious suitor for Trans Union–General Electric Credit Corporation ("GE Credit"), a subsidiary of the General Electric Company. However, GE Credit was unwilling to make an offer for Trans Union unless Trans Union first rescinded its Merger Agreement with Pritzker. When Pritzker refused, GE Credit terminated further discussions with Trans Union in early January.

In the meantime, in early December, the investment firm Kohlberg, Kravis, Roberts & Co. ("KKR"), the only other concern to make a firm offer for Trans Union, withdrew its offer under circumstances hereinafter detailed.

. . . On January 21, Management's Proxy Statement for the February 10 shareholder meeting was mailed to Trans Union's stockholders. On January 26, Trans Union's Board met and, after a lengthy meeting, voted to proceed with the Pritzker merger. . . .

On February 10, the stockholders of Trans Union approved the Pritzker merger proposal. Of the outstanding shares, 69.9% were voted in favor of the merger; 7.25% were voted against the merger; and 22.85% were not voted.

II.

We turn to the issue of the application of the business judgment rule to the September 20 meeting of the Board.

The Court of Chancery concluded from the evidence that the Board of Directors' approval of the Pritzker merger proposal fell within the protection of the business judgment rule. The Court found that the Board had given sufficient time and attention to the transaction, since the directors had considered the Pritzker proposal on three different occasions, on September 20, and on October 8, 1980 and finally on January 26, 1981. On that basis, the Court reasoned that the Board had acquired, over the four-month period, sufficient information to reach an informed business judgment on the cash-out merger proposal. The Court ruled:

> ... that given the market value of Trans Union's stock, the business acumen of the members of the board of Trans Union, the substantial premium over market offered by the Pritzkers and the ultimate effect on the merger price provided by the prospect of other bids for the stock in question, that the board of directors of Trans Union did not act recklessly or improvidently in determining on a course of action which they believed to be in the best interest of the stockholders of Trans Union.

The Court of Chancery made but one finding; i.e., that the Board's conduct over the entire period from September 20 through January 26, 1981 was not reckless or improvident, but informed. This ultimate conclusion was premised upon three subordinate findings, one explicit and two implied. The Court's explicit finding was that Trans Union's Board was "free to turn down the Pritzker proposal" not only on September 20 but also on October 8, 1980 and on January 26, 1981. The Court's implied, subordinate findings were: (1) that no legally binding agreement was reached by the parties until January 26; and (2) that if a higher offer were to be forthcoming, the market test would have produced it, and Trans Union would have been contractually free to accept such higher offer. However, the Court offered no factual basis or legal support for any of these findings; and the record compels contrary conclusions....

Under Delaware law, the business judgment rule is the offspring of the fundamental principle, codified in 8 Del.C. § 141(a), that the business and affairs of a Delaware corporation are managed by or under its board of directors.... The rule itself "is a presumption that in making a business decision, the directors of a corporation acted on an informed basis, in good faith and in the honest belief that the action taken was in the best interests of the company." ... [Aronson v. Lewis, 473 A.2d 805, 812 (Del.1984)]. Thus, the party attacking a board decision as uninformed must rebut the presumption that its business judgment was an informed one. Id.

The determination of whether a business judgment is an informed one turns on whether the directors have informed themselves "prior to making a business decision, of all material information reasonably available to them." Id.

Under the business judgment rule there is no protection for directors who have made "an unintelligent or unadvised judgment." Mitchell v. Highland–Western Glass, Del.Ch., 167 A. 831, 833 (1933). . . .

The standard of care applicable to a director's duty of care has also been recently restated by this Court. In Aronson, supra, we stated:

> While the Delaware cases use a variety of terms to describe the applicable standard of care, our analysis satisfies us that under the business judgment rule director liability is predicated upon concepts of gross negligence. (footnote omitted)

473 A.2d at 812.

We again confirm that view. We think the concept of gross negligence is also the proper standard for determining whether a business judgment reached by a board of directors was an informed one. . . .

It is against those standards that the conduct of the directors of Trans Union must be tested, as a matter of law and as a matter of fact, regarding their exercise of an informed business judgment in voting to approve the Pritzker merger proposal.

III. . . .

. . . [T]he question of whether the directors reached an informed business judgment in agreeing to sell the Company, pursuant to the terms of the September 20 Agreement presents, in reality, two questions: (A) whether the directors reached an informed business judgment on September 20, 1980; and (B) if they did not, whether the directors' actions taken subsequent to September 20 were adequate to cure any infirmity in their action taken on September 20. We first consider the directors' September 20 action in terms of their reaching an informed business judgment.

—A—

On the record before us, we must conclude that the Board of Directors did not reach an informed business judgment on September 20, 1980 in voting to "sell" the Company for $55 per share pursuant to the Pritzker cash-out merger proposal. Our reasons, in summary, are as follows:

The directors (1) did not adequately inform themselves as to Van Gorkom's role in forcing the "sale" of the Company and in establishing the per share purchase price; (2) were uninformed as to the intrinsic value of the Company; and (3) given these circumstances, at a minimum, were grossly negligent in approving the "sale" of the Company upon two hours' consideration, without prior notice, and without the exigency of a crisis or emergency.

As has been noted, the Board based its September 20 decision to approve the cash-out merger primarily on Van Gorkom's representations. None of the directors, other than Van Gorkom and Chelberg, had any prior knowledge that the purpose of the meeting was to propose a cash-out merger of Trans Union. . . .

Without any documents before them concerning the proposed transaction, the members of the Board were required to rely entirely upon Van Gorkom's 20–minute oral presentation of the proposal. No written summary of the terms of the merger was presented; the directors were given no documentation to support the adequacy of $55 price per share for sale of the Company; and the Board had before it nothing more than Van Gorkom's statement of his understanding of the substance of an agreement which he admittedly had never read, nor which any member of the Board had ever seen.

Under 8 Del.C. § 141(e), "directors are fully protected in relying in good faith on reports made by officers." Michelson v. Duncan, Del.Ch., 386 A.2d 1144, 1156 (1978); aff'd in part and rev'd in part on other grounds, Del.Supr., 407 A.2d 211 (1979). *See also* Graham v. Allis–Chalmers Mfg. Co., Del.Supr., 188 A.2d 125, 130 (1963); Prince v. Bensinger, Del.Ch., 244 A.2d 89, 94 (1968). The term "report" has been liberally construed to include reports of informal personal investigations by corporate officers, Cheff v. Mathes, Del.Supr., 199 A.2d 548, 556 (1964). However, there is no evidence that any "report," as defined under § 141(e), concerning the Pritzker proposal, was presented to the Board on September 20. Van Gorkom's oral presentation of his understanding of the terms of the proposed Merger Agreement, which he had not seen, and Romans' brief oral statement of his preliminary study regarding the feasibility of a leveraged buy-out of Trans Union do not qualify as § 141(e) "reports" for these reasons: The former lacked substance because Van Gorkom was basically uninformed as to the essential provisions of the very document about which he was talking. Romans' statement was irrelevant to the issues before the Board since it did not purport to be a valuation study. At a minimum for a report to enjoy the status conferred by § 141(e), it must be pertinent to the subject matter upon which a board is called to act, and otherwise be entitled to good faith, not blind, reliance. Considering all of the surrounding circumstances—hastily calling the meeting without prior notice of its subject matter, the proposed sale of the Company without any prior consideration of the issue or necessity therefor, the urgent time constraints imposed by Pritzker, and the total absence of any documentation whatsoever—the directors were duty bound to make reasonable inquiry of Van Gorkom and Romans, and if they had done so, the inadequacy of that upon which they now claim to have relied would have been apparent.

The defendants rely on the following factors to sustain the Trial Court's finding that the Board's decision was an informed one: (1) the magnitude of the premium or spread between the $55 Pritzker offering price and Trans Union's current market price of $38 per share; (2) the amendment of the Agreement as submitted on September 20 to permit the Board to accept any better offer during the "market test" period; (3) the collective experience and expertise of the Board's "inside" and "outside" directors; and (4) their reliance on Brennan's legal advice that the directors might be sued if they rejected the Pritzker proposal. We discuss each of these grounds *seriatim:*

(1)

A substantial premium may provide one reason to recommend a merger, but in the absence of other sound valuation information, the fact of a premium alone does not provide an adequate basis upon which to assess the fairness of an offering price. Here, the judgment reached as to the adequacy of the premium was based on a comparison between the historically depressed Trans Union market price and the amount of the Pritzker offer. Using market price as a basis for concluding that the premium adequately reflected the true value of the Company was a clearly faulty, indeed fallacious, premise. . . .

The record is clear that before September 20, Van Gorkom and other members of Trans Union's Board knew that the market had consistently undervalued the worth of Trans Union's stock. . . .

The parties do not dispute that a publicly-traded stock price is solely a measure of the value of a minority position and, thus, market price represents only the value of a single share. Nevertheless, on September 20, the Board assessed the adequacy of the premium over market, offered by Pritzker, solely by comparing it with Trans Union's current and historical stock price. . . .

Indeed, as of September 20, the Board had no other information on which to base a determination of the intrinsic value of Trans Union as a going concern. As of September 20, the Board had made no evaluation of the Company designed to value the entire enterprise, nor had the Board ever previously considered selling the Company or consenting to a buy-out merger. Thus, the adequacy of a premium is indeterminate unless it is assessed in terms of other competent and sound valuation information that reflects the value of the particular business.

Despite the foregoing facts and circumstances, there was no call by the Board, either on September 20 or thereafter, for any valuation study or documentation of the $55 price per share as a measure of the fair value of the Company in a cash-out context. It is undisputed that the major asset of Trans Union was its cash flow. Yet, at no time did the Board call for a valuation study taking into account that highly significant element of the Company's assets.

We do not imply that an outside valuation study is essential to support an informed business judgment; nor do we state that fairness opinions by independent investment bankers are required as a matter of law. Often insiders familiar with the business of a going concern are in a better position than are outsiders to gather relevant information; and under appropriate circumstances, such directors may be fully protected in relying in good faith upon the valuation reports of their management. *See* 8 Del.C. § 141(e)....

Here, the record establishes that the Board did not request its Chief Financial Officer, Romans, to make any valuation study or review of the proposal to determine the adequacy of $55 per share for sale of the Company. On the record before us: The Board rested on Romans' elicited response that the $55 figure was within a "fair price range" within the context of a leveraged buy-out. No director sought any further information from Romans. No director asked him why he put $55 at the bottom of his range. No director asked Romans for any details as to his study, the reason why it had been undertaken or its depth. No director asked to see the study; and no director asked Romans whether Trans Union's finance department could do a fairness study within the remaining 36–hour period available under the Pritzker offer....

Thus, the record compels the conclusion that on September 20 the Board lacked valuation information adequate to reach an informed business judgment as to the fairness of $55 per share for sale of the Company.

(2)

This brings us to the post-September 20 "market test" upon which the defendants ultimately rely to confirm the reasonableness of their September 20 decision to accept the Pritzker proposal. In this connection, the directors present a two-part argument: (a) that by making a "market test" of Pritzker's $55 per share offer a condition of their September 20 decision to accept his offer, they cannot be found to have acted impulsively or in an uninformed manner on September 20; and (b) that the adequacy of the $17 premium for sale of the Company was conclusively established over the following 90 to 120 days by the most reliable evidence available—the marketplace. Thus, the defendants impliedly contend that the "market test" eliminated the need for the Board to perform any other form of fairness test either on September 20, or thereafter.

Again, the facts of record do not support the defendants' argument. There is no evidence: (a) that the Merger Agreement was effectively amended to give the Board freedom to put Trans Union up for auction sale to the highest bidder; or (b) that a public auction was in fact permitted to occur. The minutes of the Board meeting make no reference to any of this. Indeed, the record compels the conclusion that the directors had no rational basis for expecting that a market test was attainable, given the terms of the Agreement as executed during the evening of September 20. We rely upon the following facts which are essentially uncontradicted:

The Merger Agreement, specifically identified as that originally presented to the Board on September 20, has never been produced by the defendants, notwithstanding the plaintiffs' several demands for production before as well as during trial. No acceptable explanation of this failure to produce documents has been given to either the Trial Court or this Court. . . .

Van Gorkom states that the Agreement as submitted incorporated the ingredients for a market test by authorizing Trans Union to receive competing offers over the next 90–day period. However, he concedes that the Agreement barred Trans Union from actively soliciting such offers and from furnishing to interested parties any information about the Company other than that already in the public domain. Whether the original Agreement of September 20 went so far as to authorize Trans Union to receive competitive proposals is arguable. The defendants' unexplained failure to produce and identify the original Merger Agreement permits the logical inference that the instrument would not support their assertions in this regard. . . .

The defendant directors assert that they "insisted" upon including two amendments to the Agreement, thereby permitting a market test: (1) to give Trans Union the right to accept a better offer; and (2) to reserve to Trans Union the right to distribute proprietary information on the Company to alternative bidders. Yet, the defendants concede that they did not seek to amend the Agreement to permit Trans Union to solicit competing offers.

Several of Trans Union's outside directors resolutely maintained that the Agreement as submitted was approved on the understanding that, "if we got a better deal, we had a right to take it." Director Johnson so testified; but he then added, "And if they didn't put that in the agreement, then the management did not carry out the conclusion of the Board. And I just don't know whether they did or not." The only clause in the Agreement as finally executed to which the defendants can point as "keeping the door open" is the following underlined statement found in subparagraph (a) of section 2.03 of the Merger Agreement as executed:

> The Board of Directors shall recommend to the stockholders of Trans Union that they approve and adopt the Merger Agreement ("the stockholders' approval") and to use its best efforts to obtain the requisite votes therefor. *GL acknowledges that Trans Union directors may have a competing fiduciary obligation to the shareholders under certain circumstances.*

Clearly, this language on its face cannot be construed as incorporating either of the two "conditions" described above: either the right to accept a better offer or the right to distribute proprietary information to third parties. . . . No reference to either of the so-called "conditions" or of Trans Union's reserved right to test the market appears in any notes of the Board meeting or in the Board Resolution accepting the Pritzker offer or in the Minutes of the meeting itself. . . .

Thus, notwithstanding what several of the outside directors later claimed to have "thought" occurred at the meeting, the record compels the conclusion that Trans Union's Board had no rational basis to conclude on September 20 or in the days immediately following, that the Board's acceptance of Pritzker's offer was conditioned on (1) a "market test" of the offer; and (2) the Board's right to withdraw from the Pritzker Agreement and accept any higher offer received before the shareholder meeting.

(3)

The directors' unfounded reliance on both the premium and the market test as the basis for accepting the Pritzker proposal undermines the defendants' remaining contention that the Board's collective experience and sophistication was a sufficient basis for finding that it reached its September 20 decision with informed, reasonable deliberation. . . .

(4) . . .

We conclude that Trans Union's Board was grossly negligent in that it failed to act with informed reasonable deliberation in agreeing to the Pritzker merger proposal on September 20. . . .

—B—

We now examine the Board's post-September 20 conduct for the purpose of determining first, whether it was informed and not grossly negligent; and second, if informed, whether it was sufficient to legally rectify and cure the Board's derelictions of September 20.[23]

(1)

First, as to the Board meeting of October 8. . . .

The public announcement of the Pritzker merger resulted in an "en masse" revolt of Trans Union's Senior Management. The head of Trans Union's tank car operations (its most profitable division) informed Van Gorkom that unless the merger were called off, fifteen key personnel would resign.

Instead of reconvening the Board, Van Gorkom again privately met with Pritzker, informed him of the developments, and sought his advice. Pritzker then made the following suggestions for overcoming Management's dissatisfaction: (1) that the Agreement be amended to permit Trans Union to solicit, as well as receive, higher offers; and (2) that the shareholder meeting be postponed from early January to February 10, 1981. In return, Pritzker asked Van Gorkom to obtain a commitment from Senior Management to remain at Trans Union for at least six months after the merger was consummated.

Van Gorkom then advised Senior Management that the Agreement would be amended to give Trans Union the right to solicit competing offers through January, 1981, if they would agree to remain with Trans Union. Senior Management was temporarily mollified; and Van Gorkom then called a special meeting of Trans Union's Board for October 8.

23. As will be seen, we do not reach the second question.

Thus, the primary purpose of the October 8 Board meeting was to amend the Merger Agreement, in a manner agreeable to Pritzker, to permit Trans Union to conduct a "market test." Van Gorkom understood that the proposed amendments were intended to give the Company an unfettered "right to openly solicit offers down through January 31." Van Gorkom presumably so represented the amendments to Trans Union's Board members on October 8. In a brief session, the directors approved Van Gorkom's oral presentation of the substance of the proposed amendments, the terms of which were not reduced to writing until October 10. But rather than waiting to review the amendments, the Board again approved them sight unseen and adjourned, giving Van Gorkom authority to execute the papers when he received them.[25] . . .

The next day, October 9, and before the Agreement was amended, Pritzker moved swiftly to off-set the proposed market test amendment. First, Pritzker informed Trans Union that he had completed arrangements for financing its acquisition and that the parties were thereby mutually bound to a firm purchase and sale arrangement. Second, Pritzker announced the exercise of his option to purchase one million shares of Trans Union's treasury stock at $38 per share—75 cents above the current market price. Trans Union's Management responded the same day by issuing a press release announcing: (1) that all financing arrangements for Pritzker's acquisition of Trans Union had been completed; and (2) Pritzker's purchase of one million shares of Trans Union's treasury stock at $38 per share.

The next day, October 10, Pritzker delivered to Trans Union the proposed amendments to the September 20 Merger Agreement. Van Gorkom promptly proceeded to countersign all the instruments on behalf of Trans Union without reviewing the instruments to determine if they were consistent with the authority previously granted him by the Board. The amending documents were apparently not approved by Trans Union's Board until a much later date, December 2. The record does not affirmatively establish that Trans Union's directors ever read the October 10 amendments.[26]

The October 10 amendments to the Merger Agreement did authorize Trans Union to solicit competing offers, but the amendments had more far-reaching effects. The most significant change was in the definition of the third-party "offer" available to Trans Union as a possible basis for withdrawal from its Merger Agreement with Pritzker. Under the October 10 amendments, a better *offer* was no longer sufficient to permit Trans Union's withdrawal. Trans Union was now

---

25. We do not suggest that a board must read *in haec verba* every contract or legal document which it approves, but if it is to successfully absolve itself from charges of the type made here, there must be some credible contemporary evidence demonstrating that the directors knew what they were doing, and ensured that their purported action was given effect. That is the consistent failure which cast this Board upon its unredeemable course.

26. There is no evidence of record that Trans Union's directors ever raised any objections, procedural or substantive, to the October 10 amendments or that any of them, including Van Gorkom, understood the opposite result of their intended effect—until it was too late.

permitted to terminate the Pritzker Agreement and abandon the merger only if, prior to February 10, 1981, Trans Union had either consummated a merger (or sale of assets) with a third party or had entered into a "definitive" merger agreement more favorable than Pritzker's and for a greater consideration—subject only to stockholder approval. Further, the "extension" of the market test period to February 10, 1981 was circumscribed by other amendments which required Trans Union to file its preliminary proxy statement on the Pritzker merger proposal by December 5, 1980 and use its best efforts to mail the statement to its shareholders by January 5, 1981. Thus, the market test period was effectively reduced, not extended....

In our view, the record compels the conclusion that the directors' conduct on October 8 exhibited the same deficiencies as did their conduct on September 20. The Board permitted its Merger Agreement with Pritzker to be amended in a manner it had neither authorized nor intended....

We conclude that the Board acted in a grossly negligent manner on October 8; and that Van Gorkom's representations on which the Board based its actions do not constitute "reports" under § 141(e) on which the directors could reasonably have relied. Further, the amended Merger Agreement imposed on Trans Union's acceptance of a third party offer conditions more onerous than those imposed on Trans Union's acceptance of Pritzker's offer on September 20. After October 10, Trans Union could accept from a third party a better offer only if it were incorporated in a definitive agreement between the parties, and not conditioned on financing or on any other contingency.

The October 9 press release, coupled with the October 10 amendments, had the clear effect of locking Trans Union's Board into the Pritzker Agreement. Pritzker had thereby foreclosed Trans Union's Board from negotiating any better "definitive" agreement over the remaining eight weeks before Trans Union was required to clear the Proxy Statement submitting the Pritzker proposal to its shareholders.

(2)

[On December 2, KKR offered to buy Trans–Union for $60/share. Van Gorkom apparently was resistant to this offer, and KKR withdrew it for reasons that were cloudy. In mid-January, GE Credit Corporation made a proposal which] was not in the form of an offer. Had there been time to do so, GE Credit was prepared to offer between $2 and $5 per share above the $55 per share price which Pritzker offered. But GE Credit needed an additional 60 to 90 days; and it was unwilling to make a formal offer without a concession from Pritzker extending the February 10 "deadline" for Trans Union's stockholder meeting.... Pritzker refused to grant such extension....

Our review of the record compels a finding that confirmation of the appropriateness of the Pritzker offer by an unfettered or free market test was virtually meaningless in the face of the terms and time limitations of Trans Union's Merger Agreement with Pritzker as amended October 10, 1980.

... [W]e hold that the defendants' post-September conduct did not cure the deficiencies of their September 20 conduct; and that, accordingly, the Trial Court erred in according to the defendants the benefits of the business judgment rule....

V.

The defendants ultimately rely on the stockholder vote of February 10 for exoneration. The defendants contend that the stockholders' "overwhelming" vote approving the Pritzker Merger Agreement had the legal effect of curing any failure of the Board to reach an informed business judgment in its approval of the merger.

The parties tacitly agree that a discovered failure of the Board to reach an informed business judgment in approving the merger constitutes a voidable, rather than a void, act. Hence, the merger can be sustained, notwithstanding the infirmity of the Board's action, if its approval by majority vote of the shareholders is found to have been based on an informed electorate.... the disagreement between the parties arises over ... the sufficiency of the evidence as to whether the Board satisfied that burden.

[The court rejected the shareholder-approval defense on the ground that Trans Union's stockholders were not fully informed of all facts material to their vote on the Pritzker Merger, and that the Trial Court's ruling to the contrary was clearly erroneous.] ...

VI.

... We hold, therefore, that the Trial Court committed reversible error in applying the business judgment rule in favor of the director defendants in this case.

On remand, the Court of Chancery shall conduct an evidentiary hearing to determine the fair value of the shares represented by the plaintiffs' class, based on the intrinsic value of Trans Union on September 20, 1980. Such valuation shall be made in accordance with Weinberger v. UOP, Inc., supra.... Thereafter, an award of damages may be entered to the extent that the fair value of Trans Union exceeds $55 per share.

Reversed and Remanded for proceedings consistent herewith.

■ McNeilly, Justice, dissenting ...

I have no quarrel with the majority's analysis of the business judgment rule. It is the application of that rule to these facts which is wrong. An overview of the entire record, rather than the limited view of bits and pieces which the majority has exploded like popcorn, convinces me that the directors made an informed business judgment which was buttressed by their test of the market....

At the time of the September 20 meeting the 10 members of Trans Union's Board of Directors were highly qualified and well informed about the affairs and prospects of Trans Union. These directors were acutely aware of the historical problems facing Trans Union which were caused by the tax laws. They had discussed these problems *ad nauseam.* In fact, within two months of the September 20 meeting the board had reviewed and discussed an outside study of the company done by The Boston Consulting Group and an internal five year forecast prepared by management. At the September 20 meeting Van Gorkom presented the Pritzker offer, and the board then heard from James Brennan, the company's counsel in this matter, who discussed the legal documents. Following this, the Board directed that certain changes be made in the merger documents. These changes made it clear that the Board was free to accept a better offer than Pritzker's if one was made. The above facts reveal that the Board did not act in a grossly negligent manner in informing themselves of the relevant and available facts before passing on the merger. To the contrary, this record reveals that the directors acted with the utmost care in informing themselves of the relevant and available facts before passing on the merger. . . .

[The dissenting opinion of Justice Christie is omitted.]

It is reported that after the decision of the Delaware Supreme Court, an agreement was reached to settle *Van Gorkom* by the payment of $23.5 million to the plaintiff class. Of that amount, $10 million, the policy limit, was provided by Trans Union's directors' and officers' liability-insurance carrier. Nearly all of the $13.5 million balance was paid by the Pritzker group on behalf of the Trans Union defendant directors, although the Pritzker group was not a defendant. *See* Manning, Reflections and Practical Tips on Life in the Boardroom After *Van Gorkom,* 41 Bus.Law. 1 (1985).

NOTE ON SUBSTANCE AND PROCESS IN THE DUTY OF CARE

In many areas of law, a distinction is drawn between substance and process. The duty of care may be understood in that way too. In effect, the business judgment rule gives wide latitude to a substantive decision of a director or senior executive if the *process* elements of the duty of care are satisfied. Under this distinction, the process elements of the duty of care, which involve such matters as preparing to make a decision, general monitoring, and following up suspicious circumstances, are governed by a standard of reasonability. However, if the process by which a decision was made satisfies the reasonability standard, the substantive decision itself will be reviewed only under the much looser standard of rationality.

C. THE DUTY TO MONITOR, COMPLIANCE PROGRAMS, AND INTERNAL CONTROLS

In re Caremark International Inc. Derivative Litigation

Delaware Court of Chancery, 1996.
698 A.2d 959.

■ ALLEN, CHANCELLOR.

Pending is a motion pursuant to Chancery Rule 23.1 to approve as fair and reasonable a proposed settlement of a consolidated derivative action on behalf of Caremark International, Inc. ("Caremark"). The suit involves claims that the members of Caremark's board of directors (the "Board") breached their fiduciary duty of care to Caremark in connection with alleged violations by Caremark employees of federal and state laws and regulations applicable to health care providers. As a result of the alleged violations, Caremark was subject to an extensive four year investigation by the United States Department of Health and Human Services and the Department of Justice. In 1994 Caremark was charged in an indictment with multiple felonies. It thereafter entered into a number of agreements with the Department of Justice and others. Those agreements included a plea agreement in which Caremark pleaded guilty to a single felony of mail fraud and agreed to pay civil and criminal fines. Subsequently, Caremark agreed to make reimbursements to various private and public parties. In all, the payments that Caremark has been required to make total approximately $250 million.

This suit was filed in 1994, purporting to seek on behalf of the company recovery of these losses from the individual defendants who constitute the board of directors of Caremark.[1] The parties now propose that it be settled and, after notice to Caremark shareholders, a hearing on the fairness of the proposal was held on August 16, 1996.

A motion of this type requires the court to assess the strengths and weaknesses of the claims asserted in light of the discovery record and to evaluate the fairness and adequacy of the consideration offered to the corporation in exchange for the release of all claims made or arising from the facts alleged. The ultimate issue then is whether the proposed settlement appears to be fair to the corporation and its absent shareholders. In this effort the court does not determine contested facts, but evaluates the claims and defenses on the discovery record to achieve a sense of the relative strengths of the parties' positions. Polk v. Good, Del.Supr., 507 A.2d 531, 536 (1986). In doing this, in most instances, the court is constrained by the absence of a truly adversarial process, since inevitably both sides support the settlement and legally assisted objectors are rare. . . .

Legally, evaluation of the central claim made entails consideration of the legal standard governing a board of directors' obligation to supervise or monitor corporate performance. For the reasons set forth

---

1. Thirteen of the Directors have been members of the Board since November 30, 1992. Nancy Brinker joined the Board in October 1993.

below I conclude, in light of the discovery record, that there is a very low probability that it would be determined that the directors of Caremark breached any duty to appropriately monitor and supervise the enterprise. Indeed the record tends to show an active consideration by Caremark management and its Board of the Caremark structures and programs that ultimately led to the company's indictment and to the large financial losses incurred in the settlement of those claims. It does not tend to show knowing or intentional violation of law. Neither the fact that the Board, although advised by lawyers and accountants, did not accurately predict the severe consequences to the company that would ultimately follow from the deployment by the company of the strategies and practices that ultimately led to this liability, nor the scale of the liability, gives rise to an inference of breach of any duty imposed by corporation law upon the directors of Caremark.

I. BACKGROUND

For these purposes I regard the following facts, suggested by the discovery record, as material. Caremark, a Delaware corporation with its headquarters in Northbrook, Illinois, was created in November 1992 when it was spun-off from Baxter International, Inc. ("Baxter") and became a publicly held company listed on the New York Stock Exchange. The business practices that created the problem pre-dated the spin-off. During the relevant period Caremark was involved in two main health care business segments, providing patient care and managed care services. As part of its patient care business, which accounted for the majority of Caremark's revenues, Caremark provided alternative site health care services, including infusion therapy, growth hormone therapy, HIV/AIDS-related treatments and hemophilia therapy. Caremark's managed care services included prescription drug programs and the operation of multi-specialty group practices.

A. Events Prior to the Government Investigation

A substantial part of the revenues generated by Caremark's businesses is derived from third party payments, insurers, and Medicare and Medicaid reimbursement programs. The latter source of payments are subject to the terms of the Anti–Referral Payments Law ("ARPL") which prohibits health care providers from paying any form of remuneration to induce the referral of Medicare or Medicaid patients. From its inception, Caremark entered into a variety of agreements with hospitals, physicians, and health care providers for advice and services, as well as distribution agreements with drug manufacturers, as had its predecessor prior to 1992. Specifically, Caremark did have a practice of entering into contracts for services (e.g., consultation agreements and research grants) with physicians at least some of whom prescribed or recommended services or products that Caremark provided to Medicare recipients and other patients. Such contracts were not prohibited by the ARPL but they obviously raised a possibility of unlawful "kickbacks."

As early as 1989, Caremark's predecessor issued an internal "Guide to Contractual Relationships" ("Guide") to govern its employees in entering into contracts with physicians and hospitals. The Guide tended to be reviewed annually by lawyers and updated. Each version of the Guide stated as Caremark's and its predecessor's policy that no payments would be made in exchange for or to induce patient referrals. But what one might deem a prohibited quid pro quo was not always clear. Due to a scarcity of court decisions interpreting the ARPL, however, Caremark repeatedly publicly stated that there was uncertainty concerning Caremark's interpretation of the law.

To clarify the scope of the ARPL, the United States Department of Health and Human Services ("HHS") issued "safe harbor" regulations in July 1991 stating conditions under which financial relationships between health care service providers and patient referral sources, such as physicians, would not violate the ARPL. Caremark contends that the narrowly drawn regulations gave limited guidance as to the legality of many of the agreements used by Caremark that did not fall within the safe-harbor. Caremark's predecessor, however, amended many of its standard forms of agreement with health care providers and revised the Guide in an apparent attempt to comply with the new regulations.

B. Government Investigation and Related Litigation

In August 1991, the HHS Office of the Inspector General ("OIG") initiated an investigation of Caremark's predecessor. Caremark's predecessor was served with a subpoena requiring the production of documents, including contracts between Caremark's predecessor and physicians (Quality Service Agreements ("QSAs")). Under the QSAs, Caremark's predecessor appears to have paid physicians fees for monitoring patients under Caremark's predecessor's care, including Medicare and Medicaid recipients. Sometimes apparently those monitoring patients were referring physicians, which raised ARPL concerns.

In March 1992, the Department of Justice ("DOJ") joined the OIG investigation and separate investigations were commenced by several additional federal and state agencies.[2]

C. Caremark's Response to the Investigation

During the relevant period, Caremark had approximately 7,000 employees and ninety branch operations. It had a decentralized management structure. By May 1991, however, Caremark asserts that it had begun making attempts to centralize its management structure in order to increase supervision over its branch operations.

The first action taken by management, as a result of the initiation of the OIG investigation, was an announcement that as of October 1, 1991, Caremark's predecessor would no longer pay management fees to physicians for services to Medicare and Medicaid patients. Despite this decision, Caremark asserts that its management, pursuant to

---

2. In addition to investigating whether Caremark's financial relationships with health care providers were intended to induce patient referrals, inquiries were made concerning Caremark's billing practices, activities which might lead to excessive and medically unnecessary treatments for patients, potentially improper waivers of patient co-payment obligations, and the adequacy of records kept at Caremark pharmacies.

advice, did not believe that such payments were illegal under the existing laws and regulations.

During this period, Caremark's Board took several additional steps consistent with an effort to assure compliance with company policies concerning the ARPL and the contractual forms in the Guide. In April 1992, Caremark published a fourth revised version of its Guide apparently designed to assure that its agreements either complied with the ARPL and regulations or excluded Medicare and Medicaid patients altogether. In addition, in September 1992, Caremark instituted a policy requiring its regional officers, Zone Presidents, to approve each contractual relationship entered into by Caremark with a physician.

Although there is evidence that inside and outside counsel had advised Caremark's directors that their contracts were in accord with the law, Caremark recognized that some uncertainty respecting the correct interpretation of the law existed. In its 1992 annual report, Caremark disclosed the ongoing government investigations, acknowledged that if penalties were imposed on the company they could have a material adverse effect on Caremark's business, and stated that no assurance could be given that its interpretation of the ARPL would prevail if challenged.

Throughout the period of the government investigations, Caremark had an internal audit plan designed to assure compliance with business and ethics policies. In addition, Caremark employed Price Waterhouse as its outside auditor. On February 8, 1993, the [Audit &] Ethics Committee of Caremark's Board received and reviewed an outside auditors report by Price Waterhouse which concluded that there were no material weaknesses in Caremark's control structure.[3] Despite the positive findings of Price Waterhouse, however, on April 20, 1993, the Audit & Ethics Committee adopted a new internal audit charter requiring a comprehensive review of compliance policies and the compilation of an employee ethics handbook concerning such policies.[4]

The Board appears to have been informed about this project and other efforts to assure compliance with the law. For example, Caremark's management reported to the Board that Caremark's sales force was receiving an ongoing education regarding the ARPL and the proper use of Caremark's form contracts which had been approved by in-house counsel. On July 27, 1993, the new ethics manual, expressly prohibiting payments in exchange for referrals and requiring employees to report all illegal conduct to a toll free confidential ethics hotline, was approved and allegedly disseminated.[5] The record sug-

3. At that time, Price Waterhouse viewed the outcome of the OIG Investigation as uncertain. After further audits, however, on February 7, 1995, Price Waterhouse informed the Audit & Ethics Committee that it had not become aware of any irregularities or illegal acts in relation to the OIG investigation.

4. Price Waterhouse worked in conjunction with the Internal Audit Department.

5. Prior to the distribution of the new ethics manual, on March 12, 1993, Caremark's president had sent a letter to all senior, district, and branch managers restating Caremark's

gests that Caremark continued these policies in subsequent years, causing employees to be given revised versions of the ethics manual and requiring them to participate in training sessions concerning compliance with the law.

During 1993, Caremark took several additional steps which appear to have been aimed at increasing management supervision. These steps included new policies requiring local branch managers to secure home office approval for all disbursements under agreements with health care providers and to certify compliance with the ethics program. In addition, the chief financial officer was appointed to serve as Caremark's compliance officer. In 1994, a fifth revised Guide was published.

D. Federal Indictments Against Caremark and Officers

On August 4, 1994, a federal grand jury in Minnesota issued a 47 page indictment charging Caremark, two of its officers (not the firm's chief officer), an individual who had been a sales employee of Genentech, Inc., and David R. Brown, a physician practicing in Minneapolis, with violating the ARPL over a lengthy period. According to the indictment, over $1.1 million had been paid to Brown to induce him to distribute Protropin, a human growth hormone drug marketed by Caremark.[6] The substantial payments involved started, according to the allegations of the indictment, in 1986 and continued through 1993. Some payments were "in the guise of research grants", Ind. § 20, and others were "consulting agreements", Ind. § 19. The indictment charged, for example, that Dr. Brown performed virtually none of the consulting functions described in his 1991 agreement with Caremark, but was nevertheless neither required to return the money he had received nor precluded from receiving future funding from Caremark. In addition the indictment charged that Brown received from Caremark payments of staff and office expenses, including telephone answering services and fax rental expenses....

Subsequently, five stockholder derivative actions were filed in this court and consolidated into this action. The original complaint, dated August 5, 1994, alleged, in relevant part, that Caremark's directors breached their duty of care by failing adequately to supervise the conduct of Caremark employees, or institute corrective measures, thereby exposing Caremark to fines and liability....

After each complaint was filed, defendants filed a motion to dismiss. According to defendants, if a settlement had not been reached in this action, the case would have been dismissed on two grounds. First, they contend that the complaints fail to allege particularized facts

---

policies that no physician be paid for referrals, that the standard contract forms in the Guide were not to be modified, and that deviation from such policies would result in the immediate termination of employment.

6. In addition to prescribing Protropin, Dr. Brown had been receiving research grants from Caremark as well as payments for services under a consulting agreement for several years before and after the investigation. According to an undated document from an unknown source, Dr. Brown and six other researchers had been providing patient referrals to Caremark valued at $6.55 for each $1 of research money they received.

sufficient to excuse the demand requirement under Delaware Chancery Court Rule 23.1. Second, defendants assert that plaintiffs had failed to state a cause of action due to the fact that Caremark's charter eliminates directors' personal liability for money damages, to the extent permitted by law.

E. Settlement Negotiations

In September, following the announcement of the Ohio indictment, Caremark publicly announced that as of January 1, 1995, it would terminate all remaining financial relationships with physicians in its home infusion, hemophilia, and growth hormone lines of business.[9] In addition, Caremark asserts that it extended its restrictive policies to all of its contractual relationships with physicians, rather than just those involving Medicare and Medicaid patients, and terminated its research grant program which had always involved some recipients who referred patients to Caremark.

Caremark began settlement negotiations with federal and state government entities in May 1995. In return for a guilty plea to a single count of mail fraud by the corporation, the payment of a criminal fine, the payment of substantial civil damages, and cooperation with further federal investigations on matters relating to the OIG investigation, the government entities agreed to negotiate a settlement that would permit Caremark to continue participating in Medicare and Medicaid programs. On June 15, 1995, the Board approved a settlement ("Government Settlement Agreement") with the DOJ, OIG, U.S. Veterans Administration, U.S. Federal Employee Health Benefits Program, federal Civilian Health and Medical Program of the Uniformed Services, and related state agencies in all fifty states and the District of Columbia.[10] No senior officers or directors were charged with wrongdoing in the Government Settlement Agreement or in any of the prior indictments. In fact, as part of the sentencing in the Ohio action on June 19, 1995, the United States stipulated that no senior executive of Caremark participated in, condoned, or was willfully ignorant of wrongdoing in connection with the home infusion business practices.

The federal settlement included certain provisions in a "Corporate Integrity Agreement" designed to enhance future compliance with law. The parties have not discussed this agreement, except to say that the negotiated provisions of the settlement of this claim are not redundant of those in that agreement.

Settlement negotiations between the parties in this action commenced in May 1995 as well, based upon a letter proposal of the plaintiffs, dated May 16, 1995. These negotiations resulted in a memo-

9. On June 1, 1993, Caremark had stopped entering into new contractual agreements in those business segments.

10. The agreement, covering allegations since 1986, required a Caremark subsidiary to enter a guilty plea to two counts of mail fraud, and required Caremark to pay $29 million in criminal fines, $129.9 million relating to civil claims concerning payment practices, $3.5 million for alleged violations of the Controlled Substances Act, and $2 million, in the form of a donation, to a grant program set up by the Ryan White Comprehensive AIDS Resources Emergency Act. Caremark also agreed to enter into a compliance agreement with the HHS.

randum of understanding ("MOU"), dated June 7, 1995, and the execution of the Stipulation and Agreement of Compromise and Settlement on June 28, 1995, which is the subject of this action.[13] The MOU, approved by the Board on June 15, 1995, required the Board to adopt several resolutions, discussed below, and to create a new compliance committee. The Compliance and Ethics Committee has been reporting to the Board in accord with its newly specified duties....

F. The Proposed Settlement of this Litigation

In relevant part the terms upon which these claims asserted are proposed to be settled are as follows:

1. That Caremark undertakes that it and its employees and agents not pay any form of compensation to a third party in exchange for the referral of a patient to a Caremark facility or service or the prescription of drugs marketed or distributed by Caremark for which reimbursement may be sought from Medicare, Medicaid, or a similar state reimbursement program;

2. That Caremark undertakes for itself and its employees, and agents not to pay to or split fees with physicians, joint ventures, any business combination in which Caremark maintains a direct financial interest, or other health care providers with whom Caremark has a financial relationship or interest, in exchange for the referral of a patient to a Caremark facility or service or the prescription of drugs marketed or distributed by Caremark for which reimbursement may be sought from Medicare, Medicaid, or a similar state reimbursement program;

3. That the full Board shall discuss all relevant material changes in government health care regulations and their effect on relationships with health care providers on a semi-annual basis;

4. That Caremark's officers will remove all personnel from health care facilities or hospitals who have been placed in such facility for the purpose of providing remuneration in exchange for a patient referral for which reimbursement may be sought from Medicare, Medicaid, or a similar state reimbursement program;

5. That every patient will receive written disclosure of any financial relationship between Caremark and the health care professional or provider who made the referral;

6. That the Board will establish a Compliance and Ethics Committee of four directors, two of which will be non-management directors, to meet at least four times a year to effectuate these policies and monitor business segment compliance with the ARPL, and to report to the Board semi-annually concerning compliance by each business segment; and

13. Plaintiffs' initial proposal had both a monetary component, requiring Caremark's director-officers to relinquish stock options, and a remedial component, requiring management to adopt and implement several compliance related measures. The monetary component was subsequently eliminated.

7. That corporate officers responsible for business segments shall serve as compliance officers who must report semi-annually to the Compliance and Ethics Committee and, with the assistance of outside counsel, review existing contracts and get advance approval of any new contract forms.

II. LEGAL PRINCIPLES

A. Principles Governing Settlements of Derivative Claims

As noted at the outset of this opinion, this Court is now required to exercise an informed judgment whether the proposed settlement is fair and reasonable in the light of all relevant factors. Polk v. Good, Del.Supr., 507 A.2d 531 (1986). On an application of this kind, this Court attempts to protect the best interests of the corporation and its absent shareholders all of whom will be barred from future litigation on these claims if the settlement is approved. The parties proposing the settlement bear the burden of persuading the court that it is in fact fair and reasonable. Fins v. Pearlman, Del.Supr., 424 A.2d 305 (1980).

B. Directors' Duties To Monitor Corporate Operations

The complaint charges the director defendants with breach of their duty of attention or care in connection with the ongoing operation of the corporation's business. The claim is that the directors allowed a situation to develop and continue which exposed the corporation to enormous legal liability and that in so doing they violated a duty to be active monitors of corporate performance. The complaint thus does not charge either director self-dealing or the more difficult loyalty-type problems arising from cases of suspect director motivation, such as entrenchment or sale of control contexts.[14] The theory here advanced is possibly the most difficult theory in corporation law upon which a plaintiff might hope to win a judgment....

1. *Potential liability for directoral decisions:* Director liability for a breach of the duty to exercise appropriate attention may, in theory, arise in two distinct contexts. First, such liability may be said to follow from a board decision that results in a loss because that decision was ill advised or "negligent". Second, liability to the corporation for a loss may be said to arise from an unconsidered failure of the board to act in circumstances in which due attention would, arguably, have prevented the loss. *See* generally Veasey & Seitz, The Business Judgment Rule in the Revised Model Act ... 63 Texas L.Rev. 1483 (1985). The first class of cases will typically be subject to review under the director-protective business judgment rule.... *See* Aronson v. Lewis, Del.Supr., 473 A.2d 805 (1984); Gagliardi v. TriFoods Int'l, Inc., Del.Ch. 683 A.2d 1049 (July 19, 1996)....

---

14. See Weinberger v. UOP, Inc., Del.Supr., 457 A.2d 701, 711 (1983) (entire fairness test when financial conflict of interest involved); Unitrin, Inc. v. American General Corp., Del.Supr., 651 A.2d 1361, 1372 (1995) (intermediate standard of review when "defensive" acts taken); Paramount Communications, Inc. v. QVC Network, Del.Supr., 637 A.2d 34, 45 (1994) (intermediate test when corporate control transferred).

2. *Liability for failure to monitor*: The second class of cases in which director liability for inattention is theoretically possible entail circumstances in which a loss eventuates not from a decision but, from unconsidered inaction. Most of the decisions that a corporation, acting through its human agents, makes are, of course, not the subject of director attention. Legally, the board itself will be required only to authorize the most significant corporate acts or transactions: mergers, changes in capital structure, fundamental changes in business, appointment and compensation of the CEO, etc. As the facts of this case graphically demonstrate, ordinary business decisions that are made by officers and employees deeper in the interior of the organization can, however, vitally affect the welfare of the corporation and its ability to achieve its various strategic and financial goals. If this case did not prove the point itself, recent business history would. Recall for example the displacement of senior management and much of the board of Salomon, Inc.;[18] the replacement of senior management of Kidder, Peabody following the discovery of large trading losses resulting from phantom trades by a highly compensated trader;[19] or the extensive financial loss and reputational injury suffered by Prudential Insurance as a result [of] its junior officers' misrepresentations in connection with the distribution of limited partnership interests. Financial and organizational disasters such as these raise the question, what is the board's responsibility with respect to the organization and monitoring of the enterprise to assure that the corporation functions within the law to achieve its purposes?

Modernly this question has been given special importance by an increasing tendency, especially under federal law, to employ the criminal law to assure corporate compliance with external legal requirements, including environmental, financial, employee and product safety as well as assorted other health and safety regulations. In 1991, pursuant to the Sentencing Reform Act of 1984,[21] the United States Sentencing Commission adopted Organizational Sentencing Guidelines which impact importantly on the prospective effect these criminal sanctions might have on business corporations. The Guidelines set forth a uniform sentencing structure for organizations to be sentenced for violation of federal criminal statutes and provide for penalties that equal or often massively exceed those previously imposed on corporations.[22] The Guidelines offer powerful incentives for corporations today to have in place compliance programs to detect violations of law, promptly to report violations to appropriate public officials when discovered, and to take prompt, voluntary remedial efforts.

---

18. See, e.g., Rotten at the Core, the Economist, August 17, 1991, at 69–70; The Judgment of Salomon: An Anticlimax, Bus. Week, June 1, 1992, at 106.

19. See Terence P. Pare, Jack Welch's Nightmare on Wall Street, Fortune, Sept. 5, 1994, at 40–48.

21. See Sentencing Reform Act of 1984, Pub.L. 98–473, Title II, § 212(a)(2) (1984); 18 U.S.C.A. §§ 3331–4120.

22. See United States Sentencing Commission, Guidelines Manual, Chapter 8 (U.S. Government Printing Office November 1994).

In 1963, the Delaware Supreme Court in Graham v. Allis–Chalmers Mfg. Co.,[23] addressed the question of potential liability of board members for losses experienced by the corporation as a result of the corporation having violated the anti-trust laws of the United States. There was no claim in that case that the directors knew about the behavior of subordinate employees of the corporation that had resulted in the liability. Rather, as in this case, the claim asserted was that the directors ought to have known of it and if they had known they would have been under a duty to bring the corporation into compliance with the law and thus save the corporation from the loss. The Delaware Supreme Court concluded that, under the facts as they appeared, there was no basis to find that the directors had breached a duty to be informed of the ongoing operations of the firm. In notably colorful terms, the court stated that "absent cause for suspicion there is no duty upon the directors to install and operate a corporate system of espionage to ferret out wrongdoing which they have no reason to suspect exists."[24] The Court found that there were no grounds for suspicion in that case and, thus, concluded that the directors were blamelessly unaware of the conduct leading to the corporate liability.[25]

How does one generalize this holding today? Can it be said today that, absent some ground giving rise to suspicion of violation of law, that corporate directors have no duty to assure that a corporate information gathering and reporting system exists which represents a good faith attempt to provide senior management and the Board with information respecting material acts, events or conditions within the corporation, including compliance with applicable statutes and regulations? I certainly do not believe so. I doubt that such a broad generalization of the Graham holding would have been accepted by the Supreme Court in 1963. The case can be more narrowly interpreted as standing for the proposition that, absent grounds to suspect deception, neither corporate boards nor senior officers can be charged with wrongdoing simply for assuming the integrity of employees and the honesty of their dealings on the company's behalf. *See* 188 A.2d at 130–31.

A broader interpretation of Graham v. Allis–Chalmers—that it means that a corporate board has no responsibility to assure that appropriate information and reporting systems are established by management—would not, in any event, be accepted by the Delaware Supreme Court in 1996, in my opinion. In stating the basis for this view, I start with the recognition that in recent years the Delaware Supreme Court has made it clear—especially in its jurisprudence concerning takeovers, from Smith v. Van Gorkom through *Paramount Communications v. QVC*[26]—the seriousness with which the corpora-

23. Del.Supr., 188 A.2d 125 (1963).

24. Id. at 130.

25. Recently, the *Graham* standard was applied by the Delaware Chancery in a case involving Baxter. In re Baxter International, Inc. Shareholders Litig., Del.Ch., 654 A.2d 1268, 1270 (1995).

26. E.g., Smith v. Van Gorkom, Del.Supr., 488 A.2d 858 (1985); Paramount Communications v. QVC Network, Del.Supr., 637 A.2d 34 (1994).

tion law views the role of the corporate board. Secondly, I note the elementary fact that relevant and timely information is an essential predicate for satisfaction of the board's supervisory and monitoring role under Section 141 of the Delaware General Corporation Law. Thirdly, I note the potential impact of the federal organizational sentencing guidelines on any business organization. Any rational person attempting in good faith to meet an organizational governance responsibility would be bound to take into account this development and the enhanced penalties and the opportunities for reduced sanctions that it offers.

In light of these developments, it would, in my opinion, be a mistake to conclude that our Supreme Court's statement in *Graham* concerning "espionage" means that corporate boards may satisfy their obligation to be reasonably informed concerning the corporation, without assuring themselves that information and reporting systems exist in the organization that are reasonably designed to provide to senior management and to the board itself timely, accurate information sufficient to allow management and the board, each within its scope, to reach informed judgments concerning both the corporation's compliance with law and its business performance.

Obviously the level of detail that is appropriate for such an information system is a question of business judgment. And obviously too, no rationally designed information and reporting system will remove the possibility that the corporation will violate laws or regulations, or that senior officers or directors may nevertheless sometimes be misled or otherwise fail reasonably to detect acts material to the corporation's compliance with the law. But it is important that the board exercise a good faith judgment that the corporation's information and reporting system is in concept and design adequate to assure the board that appropriate information will come to its attention in a timely manner as a matter of ordinary operations, so that it may satisfy its responsibility.

Thus, I am of the view that a director's obligation includes a duty to attempt in good faith to assure that a corporate information and reporting system, which the board concludes is adequate, exists, and that failure to do so under some circumstances may, in theory at least, render a director liable for losses caused by non-compliance with applicable legal standards.[27] I now turn to an analysis of the claims asserted with this concept of the directors' duty of care, as a duty satisfied in part by assurance of adequate information flows to the board, in mind.

---

27. Any action seeking recover for losses would logically entail a judicial determination of proximate cause, since, for reasons that I take to be obvious, it could never be assumed that an adequate information system would be a system that would prevent all losses. I need not touch upon the burden allocation with respect to a proximate cause issue in such a suit. See Cede & Co. v. Technicolor, Inc., Del.Supr., 636 A.2d 956 (1994); Cinerama, Inc. v. Technicolor, Inc., Del.Ch., 663 A.2d 1134 (1994), aff'd., Del.Supr., 663 A.2d 1156 (1995). Moreover, questions of waiver of liability under certificate provisions authorized by 8 Del.C. § 102(b)(7) may also be faced.

III. ANALYSIS OF THIRD AMENDED COMPLAINT AND SETTLEMENT

A. The Claims

On balance, after reviewing an extensive record in this case, including numerous documents and three depositions, I conclude that this settlement is fair and reasonable. In light of the fact that the Caremark Board already has a functioning committee charged with overseeing corporate compliance, the changes in corporate practice that are presented as consideration for the settlement do not impress one as very significant. Nonetheless, that consideration appears fully adequate to support dismissal of the derivative claims of director fault asserted, because those claims find no substantial evidentiary support in the record and quite likely were susceptible to a motion to dismiss in all events.

In order to show that the Caremark directors breached their duty of careby failing adequately to control Caremark's employees, plaintiffs would have to show either (1) that the directors knew or (2) should have known that violations of law were occurring and, in either event, (3) that the directors took no steps in a good faith effort to prevent or remedy that situation, and (4) that such failure proximately resulted in the losses complained of, although under Cede & Co. v. Technicolor, Inc., Del.Supr., 636 A.2d 956 (1994) this last element may be thought to constitute an affirmative defense. . . .

. . . I turn to a consideration of the [claim based on] . . . director inattention or "negligence." Generally where a claim of directorial liability for corporate loss is predicated upon ignorance of liability creating activities within the corporation, as in *Graham* or in this case, in my opinion only a sustained or systematic failure of the board to exercise oversight—such as an utter failure to attempt to assure a reasonable information and reporting system exits—will establish the lack of good faith that is a necessary condition to liability. Such a test of liability—lack of good faith as evidenced by sustained or systematic failure of a director to exercise reasonable oversight—is quite high. But, a demanding test of liability in the oversight context is probably beneficial to corporate shareholders as a class, as it is in the board decision context, since it makes board service by qualified persons more likely, while continuing to act as a stimulus to good faith performance of duty by such directors.

Here the record supplies essentially no evidence that the director defendants were guilty of a sustained failure to exercise their oversight function. To the contrary, insofar as I am able to tell on this record, the corporation's information systems appear to have represented a good faith attempt to be informed of relevant facts. If the directors did not know the specifics of the activities that lead to the indictments, they cannot be faulted.

The liability that eventuated in this instance was huge. But the fact that it resulted from a violation of criminal law alone does not create a breach of fiduciary duty by directors. The record at this stage does not support the conclusion that the defendants either lacked good faith in the exercise of their monitoring responsibilities or conscientiously permitted a known violation of law by the corporation to occur. The claims asserted against them must be viewed at this stage as extremely weak.

B. The Consideration For Release of Claim

The proposed settlement provides very modest benefits. Under the settlement agreement, plaintiffs have been given express assurances that Caremark will have a more centralized, active supervisory system in the future. Specifically, the settlement mandates duties to be performed by the newly named Compliance and Ethics Committee on an ongoing basis and increases the responsibility for monitoring compliance with the law at the lower levels of management. In adopting the resolutions required under the settlement, Caremark has further clarified its policies concerning the prohibition of providing remuneration for referrals. These appear to be positive consequences of the settlement of the claims brought by the plaintiffs, even if they are not highly significant. Nonetheless, given the weakness of the plaintiffs' claims the proposed settlement appears to be an adequate, reasonable, and beneficial outcome for all of the parties. Thus, the proposed settlement will be approved. . . .

I am today entering an order consistent with the foregoing.

NOTE ON CORPORATE CRIMINAL LIABILITY, THE SENTENCING GUIDELINES, AND COMPLIANCE PROGRAMS

Caremark, and cases that follow it, provide one kind of incentive to put in place compliance programs to ensure that the corporation and its employees and agents are obeying the law—the incentive to avoid personal liability. A different kind of incentive is provided by the Federal Criminal Sentencing Guidelines. Under 18 U.S.C.A. § 3553, a corporation that is found guilty of a crime may be sentenced to a fine, probation, or both. If the corporation is fined, the fine will normally be set within a range specified by the Federal Sentencing Guidelines promulgated by the Federal Sentencing Commission.

The Sentencing Guidelines for organizational crimes are extremely complex. At the risk of oversimplification, in setting such a fine four elements are relevant under the Guidelines: the *offense level* of the crime, the *base fine,* the *culpability score,* and the *fine range*. The offense level is determined by the seriousness of the offense. The base fine is related to the offense level. The culpability score is based on various aggravating and mitigating factors. A low culpability score reduces the fine range below the base line; a high culpability score increases the fine range above the base line.

Under the mechanics of culpability scores, a corporation begins with a culpability score of five, and with that score, the Guidelines call for a fine equal to 100%–200% of the base fine. However, the culpability score may be decreased by mitigating factors and increased by aggravating factors. If a corporation had an effective compliance program in place at the time the crime was committed, that is a mitigating factor, which would decrease the culpability score by three points, provided that certain conditions are satisfied. If a corporation fully cooperates with the government investigation and accepts responsibility for its criminal conduct, that is also a mitigating factor, and the culpability score would be decreased by another two points. If both these mitigating factors are present, and no aggravating factors are present, the combined reductions would decrease the corporation's culpability score to zero. As a result, the Guidelines call for a fine of only 5%–20% of the base fine. Accordingly, the Criminal Sentencing Guidelines serve to reinforce the board's duty to monitor by providing a strong incentive to install effective compliance programs. On the other hand, if as a result of aggravating factors, the culpability score is 10 or more, the Guidelines call for a fine equal to 200%–400% of the base fine.

To constitute an effective compliance program within the meaning of the Guidelines, the program must be reasonably designed, implemented, and enforced. The hallmark of an effective program is whether the corporation exercised due diligence to prevent and detect criminal conduct by its employees and other agents. At a minimum, due diligence requires that the corporation must have taken seven steps: (1) Establish standards and procedures that are reasonably capable of reducing the prospect of criminal conduct followed by employees and other agents. (2) Assign specific high-level individuals overall responsibility to oversee compliance with the standards and procedures. (3) Exercise due care to not delegate substantial discretionary authority to individuals whom the corporation knew or should have known have a propensity to engage in illegal activities. (4) Effectively communicate corporate standards and procedures to all employees and other agents, through training programs or dissemination of written information. (5) Attempt to achieve compliance by the use of monitoring and auditing systems to detect criminal conduct by employees and agents, and by having in place, and publicizing, a reporting system whereby employees and agents can report criminal conduct by others within the organization anonymously, or confidentially report criminal or potential criminal conduct. (6) Enforce standards to achieve compliance through appropriate disciplinary mechanisms. (7) Respond appropriately if an offense is detected and take steps to prevent additional similar offenses. An appropriate response may include providing restitution to identifiable victims, other forms of remediation, and assessing the compliance program and making any modifications necessary to ensure that the program is effective. In addition, and perhaps even more importantly, the existence of an effective compliance program will heavily shape Department of Justice and SEC decisions whether to charge the corporation, whether to offer the corporation deferred or non-prosecution agreements, and, where such an agreement is entered into, the terms of the agreement.

The Guidelines also require directors to be knowledgeable about the content and operation of the corporation's compliance program and exercise reasonable oversight with respect to the program's implementation and effectiveness. The board must assign a specific high-level individual overall responsibility to oversee compliance, and this individual should regularly report to the board; have day-to-day responsibility for the compliance program; have direct access to the board or a designated subgroup; and no less than annually update the board or its designated subgroup on the status of the program. All employees, including officers and directors, must participate in compliance training programs. In addition to due diligence to prevent and detect criminal conduct, an effective compliance program must promote an organizational culture that encourages both ethical conduct and a commitment to compliance within the law. A corporation that installs a compliance program will characteristically promulgate (i) a code of ethical conduct for its employees; (ii) procedures to ensure that the employees read, understand, and keep current on the code; and (iii) procedures to satisfy the due diligence inquiry requirement.

In 2005, the Supreme Court held that the Federal Sentencing Act, which authorizes the Sentencing Guidelines, was unconstitutional insofar as it made the Guidelines mandatory, because the Sixth Amendment requires sentencing determinations to be made by a jury, not by a judge. United States v. Booker, 543 U.S. 220, 125 S.Ct. 738, 160 L.Ed.2d 621 (2005). The Court remedied the constitutional problem by removing the language in the Act that made the Guidelines mandatory. Organizations don't enjoy the protection of the Sixth Amendment, but *Booker* will affect organizational sentencing provisions as well.

Although the Guidelines are no longer mandatory, the Court stated in *Booker* that "the Federal Sentencing Act ... *requires* a sentencing court to *consider* Guidelines ranges" (emphasis added). It is therefore highly likely that judges will typically calculate an organization's culpability score and make sentencing decisions largely on the basis of the Guidelines. Accordingly, corporations that disregard the Guidelines do so at their peril. Additionally, a prosecutor's decision whether or not to charge a corporation with a crime may be influenced by the corporation's ability to demonstrate that it has a well-documented and effective compliance program that is properly monitored by the board.

See generally Webb, Molo & Hurst, supra; Pitt & Groskaufmanis, Mischief Afoot: The Need for Incentives to Control Criminal Conduct. 71 B.U.L.Rev. 447 (1991); Pitt & Groskaufmanis, Minimizing Corporate Civil and Criminal Liability; A Second Look at Corporate Codes of Conduct, 78 Geo.L.J. 1559, 1561 (1990).

ABA Section of Business Law, Committee on Corporate Laws, Corporate Director's Guidebook

Sixth ed., 2011.

... COMPLIANCE WITH LAW

The board is responsible for overseeing management's activities in assuring the corporation's compliance with legal requirements in the jurisdictions in which the corporation does business. A well-conceived and properly implemented compliance program can significantly reduce the incidence of violations of laws and corporate policy. It can also reduce or eliminate lawsuits, penalties and criminal prosecution. Although the federal sentencing guidelines greatly increase the penalties for corporations guilty of criminal violations, they also provide for significant fine reductions for corporations with programs in place to prevent and detect such violations. Directors should periodically satisfy themselves that an appropriate process is in place to detect violations and to encourage not only attention to general legal compliance issues and claims against the corporation, but also the timely reporting of significant legal or other compliance matters to the board or an appropriate board committee.

Boards should ensure their companies have formal written policies designed to promote compliance with law and corporate policy. They should review policies periodically for effectiveness, and, if the corporation operates in an industry subject to laws and regulations that demand special compliance procedures and monitoring, the review should be more frequent and intensive. Many public companies assign compliance oversight to the audit committee, others to a governance or risk committee. These committees meet regularly with the company's general counsel or outside counsel to be briefed on compliance and claims. With the increased burdens placed on public company audit committees, some boards have elected to form a separate compliance or legal affairs committee. Directors should consider whether delegating oversight for multiple compliance issues to a single board committee is sufficient for the corporation's legal and regulatory compliance profile.

The board should ensure that employees of the corporation are informed and periodically reminded of corporate policies, including those pertaining to compliance with (i) codes of business conduct and ethics; (ii) anti-discrimination and employment laws; (iii) environmental and health and safety laws; (iv) anti-bribery laws; (v) antitrust and competition laws; (vi) securities laws, particularly those addressing insider trading; and (vii) laws and regulations of other countries as applicable. The major securities markets require their listed companies to adopt codes of business conduct and ethics applicable to all employees, officers and directors. The corporation should have appropriate controls throughout the organization for monitoring compliance with such laws and codes. Controls may include whistle-blower and hotline policies. The corporation also must establish procedures for addressing violations.

In addition, all compliance personnel should have direct access to the general counsel or other compliance officer to ensure sensitive compliance situations are promptly addressed. Boards should also ensure the compliance program has adequate resources and authority to perform its function.

Eisenberg, The Board of Directors and Internal Control

19 Cardozo L. Rev. 237, 1997.

I. The Meaning of Internal Control

In 1992, the Committee of Sponsoring Organizations (COSO) issued a comprehensive four-volume Report on internal control. The COSO Report defines internal control as "a process, effected by an entity's board of directors, management and other personnel, designed to provide reasonable assurance regarding the achievement of objectives" in three categories: "effectiveness and efficiency of operations, reliability of financial reporting, and compliance with applicable laws and regulations." Internal control over each of these objectives consists of five interrelated components: the control environment, risk assessment, control activities, information and communication, and monitoring. A system of internal control is deemed to be effective only if all five components are functioning effectively. . . .

. . . In 1994, the ABA's Committee on Law and Accounting [stated] that "[t]he COSO Report may well become the standard for defining internal control and its interrelated components, and for measuring the effectiveness of internal control. The Report has serious implications for all entities and their managements and for their outside financial, accounting, legal, and other advisors as well."[30] Similarly, in SAS No. 78 the AICPA's Auditing Standards Board expressed its view that "the COSO Report is rapidly becoming a widely accepted framework for sound internal control among United States organizations and its acceptance and use will continue to grow."[31] . . .

III. What Board Responsibility for Internal Control Entails . . .

. . . [T]he board's role is to use due care to assure itself that an internal control structure is in existence, is appropriate, and is effective. The board's responsibility in these matters is not to ensure that specific controls never fail. Accordingly, a breakdown in a specific control does not in itself establish that the board has not discharged its responsibility. Furthermore, the board need not ensure that every conceivable control is in place. In determining whether any given control should be installed, and the extent and contours of a control, the risk of failure if the control is not in place must be balanced with the control's costs.

The board should, however, be responsible for using due care to assure itself that the five components of internal control—control environment, risk assessment, control activities, information and com-

---

30. [Committee on Law and Accounting, ABA, "Management" Reports on Internal Control: A Legal Respective, 49 Bus. Law, 889, 899 (1994)].

31. [Auditing Standards Board, AICPA, Statement on Auditing Standards No. 78, at 1].

munication, and monitoring—are in place in such a way as to provide reasonable assurance regarding the effectiveness and efficiency of operations, the reliability of financial reporting, and compliance with corporate policies and legal rules....

NOTE ON CIVIL LIABILITY OF DIRECTORS AND OFFICERS TO THIRD PERSONS

Most of the materials in this Section have concerned the liability of directors and officers to the *corporation* for failure to exercise due care. A director or officer may also be civilly liable to *third persons* for acts he commits in a corporate capacity. Robert Thompson has summarized the principles that govern the civil liability of directors and officers to third parties as follows:

> Officers are agents of the corporation who act for the entity in a variety of day-to-day matters.... [A]ny individual liability [of officers] for enterprise obligations derives primarily from the common law. These principles, as reflected in the Restatement (Second) of Agency, usually insulate the officer [in the case of contracts entered into by the officer on the corporation's behalf]. An individual who signs a contract on behalf of the corporation is cloaked in the mantle of the enterprise and is not personally liable for action taken in the corporate name. If the enterprise defaults on an obligation under the contract, the creditor normally cannot proceed against the individual.
>
> However, the same individual who acts for the same corporation in the same capacity in taking action deemed tortious loses the corporate cloak and is held individually liable along with the enterprise....
>
> Thus, as to direct participation, the corporate shield really only works for contracts, a narrowness of protection that may surprise many entrepreneurs who intend to use corporations to avoid liability. Note, however, that the corporate form [normally] does insulate corporate participants in a tort (or contract) setting against vicarious [civil] liability....

Thompson, Unpacking Limited Liability: Direct and Vicarious Liability of Corporate Participants for Torts of the Enterprise, 47 Vand. L.Rev. 1, 6–7, 9, 24 (1994).

D. LIABILITY SHIELDS

In assessing the duties of directors and officers to act with care, account must be taken of three elements that may serve to reduce or eliminate civil liability for breach of those duties: direct limits of liability, insurance, and indemnification. The first element is addressed in this Section. Insurance is addressed in Section 3, infra. Indemnification is addressed in Chapter 14, Section 8.

VIRGINIA CORPORATIONS CODE § 13.1–690

[See Statutory Supplement]

DEL. GEN. CORP. LAW § 102(b)(7)

[See Statutory Supplement]

MODEL BUSINESS CORP. ACT § 2.02(b)(4)

[See Statutory Supplement]

EMERALD PARTNERS v. BERLIN, 726 A.2d 1215 (Del. 1999). "[T]he shield from liability provided by a certificate of incorporation provision adopted pursuant to 8 Del. C. § 102(b)(7) is in the nature of an affirmative defense.... Defendants seeking exculpation under such a provision will normally bear the burden of establishing each of its elements. Here, the Court of Chancery incorrectly ruled that Emerald Partners [the plaintiff] was required to establish at trial that the individual defendants acted in bad faith or in breach of their duty of loyalty. To the contrary, the burden of demonstrating good faith, however slight it might be in given circumstances, is upon the party seeking the protection of the statute. Nonetheless, where the factual basis for a claim solely implicates a violation of the duty of care, this Court has indicated that the protections of such a charter provision may properly be invoked and applied."

Malpiede v. Townson

Supreme Court of Delaware, 2001.
780 A.2d 1075.

■ VEASEY, CHIEF JUSTICE:

In this appeal, we affirm ... the granting of a motion to dismiss the plaintiffs' due care claim on the ground that the exculpatory provision in the charter of the target corporation authorized by 8 Del. C. § 102(b)(7), bars any claim for money damages against the director defendants based solely on the board's alleged breach of its duty of care. Accordingly, we affirm the judgment of the Court of Chancery dismissing the amended complaint....

Facts

Frederick's of Hollywood ("Frederick's") is a retailer of women's lingerie and apparel with its headquarters in Los Angeles, California. This case centers on the merger of Frederick's into Knightsbridge Capital Corporation ("Knightsbridge") under circumstances where it became a target in a bidding contest.... Two trusts created by the principal founders of Frederick's, Frederick and Harriet Mellinger (the "Trusts"), held a total of about 41% of the outstanding Class A voting shares and a total of about 51% of the outstanding Class B non-voting shares of Frederick's....

On June 13, 1997, the Frederick's board approved an offer from Knightsbridge to purchase all of Frederick's outstanding Class A and Class B shares for $6.14 per share in cash in a two-step merger transaction. The terms of the merger agreement signed by the Frederick's board prohibited the board from soliciting additional bids from third parties, but the agreement permitted the board to negotiate with third party bidders when the board's fiduciary duties required it to do so....

[On August 21, Frederick's received a bid of $7.00 per share from Milton Partners. On August 25, Knightsbridge entered into an agreement to purchase all of the Frederick's shares held by the Trusts for $6.90 per share. On August 27, a third bidder, Veritas Capital Fund, offered $7.75 per share. The Frederick's board then invited Milton and Veritas to continue the bidding process. However, the board conditioned further bidding on their posting a bond of $2.5 million and submitting a written offer within ten days. Veritas posted the bond; Milton did not.

[On September 6, Knightsbridge increased its bid to match the $7.75 Veritas offer, but on the condition that the board accept a variety of terms designed to restrict its ability to pursue superior offers. One of these terms, the so-called "no-talk" provision, prohibited any Frederick's representative from speaking to third party bidders concerning the acquisition of the company. Frederick's board agreed to Knightsbridge's new bid and terms, and thereby effectively ended the bidding process. Two days later, Knightsbridge acquired enough shares in the open market, at $8.81 per share, to give it majority voting power.]

On September 11, 1997, Veritas increased its cash offer to $9.00 per share. Relying on (1) the "no-talk" provision in the merger agreement, (2) Knightsbridge's stated intention to vote its shares against third party bids, and (3) Veritas' request for an option to dilute Knightsbridge's interest, the board rejected the revised Veritas bid....

Before the merger closed, the plaintiffs filed in the Court of Chancery the purported class action complaint that is the predecessor of the amended complaint before us. The plaintiffs also moved for a temporary restraining order enjoining the merger. The Court of Chancery denied the requested injunctive relief.

The plaintiffs then amended their complaint to include a class action claim for damages caused by the termination of the auction in favor of Knightsbridge and the rejection of the higher Veritas offer. The amended complaint alleged that the Frederick's board had breached its fiduciary duties in connection with the sale of the company. . . .

The Court of Chancery granted the directors' motion to dismiss the amended complaint under Chancery Rule 12(b)(6), concluding that: (1) the complaint did not support a claim of breach of the board's duty of loyalty, [and] (2) the exculpatory provision in the Fredrick's charter precluded money damages against the directors for any breach of the board's duty of care. . . .

Standard of Review

We review de novo the dismissal by the Court of Chancery of a complaint under Rule 12(b)(6). . . .

The Duty of Loyalty Claim

The central claim in the amended complaint is that the sale of Frederick's to Knightsbridge "constituted a breach of [the Frederick's board's] fiduciary obligation to maximize shareholder value" because the board did not "conduct an auction with a 'level playing field' " as required by Revlon, Inc. v. MacAndrews & Forbes Holdings, Inc.[43] . . .

. . . *Revlon* emphasizes that the board must perform its fiduciary duties in the service of a specific objective: maximizing the sale price of the enterprise. Although the Revlon doctrine imposes enhanced judicial scrutiny of certain transactions involving a sale of control, it does not eliminate the requirement that plaintiffs plead sufficient facts to support the underlying claims for a breach of fiduciary duties in conducting the sale. Accordingly, we proceed to analyze the amended complaint to determine whether it alleges sufficient facts to support a claim that the board breached any of its fiduciary duties.

The Court of Chancery concluded, and the plaintiffs do not appear to contest on appeal, that the amended complaint adequately alleges a conflict of interest with respect to only one of the directors who approved the Knightsbridge merger.[44] The amended complaint

43. Del. Supr., 506 A.2d 173, 182–83 (1985).

44. See January 2000 Mem. Op., 2000 Del. Ch. LEXIS 19, *17. In particular, the complaint alleges that the Knightsbridge merger agreement provided for several cash payments to George Townson, who was the CEO, President, and Chairman of Frederick's during the relevant period. The personal benefits allegedly received by Townson as a result of the Knightsbridge merger included: (1) a payment of $.05 for each "under water" option held by Townson with an exercise price below the merger price, (2) a severance payment of $750,000 upon consummation of the merger, and (3) a payment of $250,000 on the date of the merger and sixteen quarterly payments of $100,000 under a noncompete and consulting agreement. The complaint also alleges that William Barrett, who was a Frederick's director and a vice president of JMS, the firm's financial advisor, had an interest in the merger transaction. Specifically, the complaint alleges that Barrett's firm received a $2 million fee upon consummation of the Knightsbridge merger. But because Barrett's firm was entitled to receive a fee upon the consummation of any merger and because the fee was proportional to the sale price, the Court of Chancery correctly concluded that the complaint was insufficient to establish a disabling conflict with respect to Barrett. See January 2000 Mem. Op., 2000 Del. Ch. LEXIS 19, *24. . . .

does not allege that the lone conflicted director dominated the three other directors who approved the merger on September 6, 1997. The Court of Chancery therefore correctly held that the Knightsbridge merger was approved by a majority of disinterested directors....

The Due Care Claim

The primary due care issue is whether the board was grossly negligent, and therefore breached its duty of due care, in failing to implement a routine defensive strategy that could enable the board to negotiate for a higher bid or otherwise create a tactical advantage to enhance stockholder value....

Construing the amended complaint most favorably to the plaintiffs, it can be read to allege that the board was grossly negligent in immediately accepting the Knightsbridge offer and agreeing to various restrictions on further negotiations without first determining whether Veritas would issue a counteroffer. Although the board had conducted a search for a buyer over one year, plaintiffs seem to contend that the board was imprudently hasty in agreeing to a restrictive merger agreement on the day it was proposed—particularly where other bidders had recently expressed interest.[45] Although the board's haste, in itself, might not constitute a breach of the board's duty of care because the board had already conducted a lengthy sale process, the plaintiffs argue that the board's decision to accept allegedly extreme contractual restrictions impacted its ability to obtain a higher sale price. Recognizing that, at the end of the day, plaintiffs would have an uphill battle in overcoming the presumption of the business judgment rule, we must give plaintiffs the benefit of the doubt at this pleading stage to determine if they have stated a due care claim. Because of our ultimate decision, however, we need not finally decide this question in this case.

We assume, therefore, without deciding, that a claim for relief based on gross negligence during the board's auction process is stated by the inferences most favorable to plaintiffs that flow from these allegations. The issue then becomes whether the amended complaint may be dismissed upon a Rule 12(b)(6) motion by reason of the existence and the legal effect of the exculpatory provision of Article TWELFTH of Frederick's certificate of incorporation, adopted pursuant to 8 Del. C. § 102(b)(7). That provision would exempt directors from personal liability in damages with certain exceptions (e.g., breach of the duty of loyalty) that are not applicable here....[46]

---

45. Relatedly, the plaintiffs also argue that the board breached its fiduciary duties by favoring Knightsbridge over Veritas in the bidding process.

46. Article TWELFTH provides:

> TWELFTH. A director of this Corporation shall not be personally liable to the Corporation or its shareholders for monetary damages for breach of fiduciary duty as a director, except for liability (i) for any breach of the director's duty of loyalty to the Corporation or its shareholders, (ii) for acts or omissions not in good faith or which involve intentional misconduct or a knowing violation of law (iii) under Section 174 of the Delaware General Corporation Law, or (iv) for any transaction for which the director derived an improper personal benefit.

B. Application of *Emerald Partners*

1. *The Court of Chancery Properly Dismissed Claims Based Solely on the Duty of Care*

Plaintiffs here, while not conceding that the Section 102(b)(7) charter provision may be considered on this Rule 12(b)(6) motion nevertheless, in effect, conceded in oral argument in the Court of Chancery and similarly in oral argument in this Court that if a complaint unambiguously and solely asserted only a due care claim, the complaint is dismissible once the corporation's Section 102(b)(7) provision is invoked....

Plaintiffs contended vigorously, however, that the Section 102(b)(7) charter provision does not apply to bar their claims in this case because the amended complaint alleges breaches of the duty of loyalty and other claims that are not barred by the charter provision. As a result, plaintiffs maintain, this case cannot be boiled down solely to a due care case. They argue, in effect, that their complaint is sufficiently well-pleaded that—as a matter of law—the due care claims are so inextricably intertwined with loyalty and bad faith claims that Section 102(b)(7) is not a bar to recovery of damages against the directors.

We disagree. It is the plaintiffs who have a burden to set forth "a short and plain statement of the claim showing that the pleader is entitled to relief."[47] The plaintiffs are entitled to all reasonable inferences flowing from their pleadings, but if those inferences do not support a valid legal claim, the complaint should be dismissed without the need for the defendants to file an answer and without proceeding with discovery. Here we have assumed, without deciding, that the amended complaint on its face states a due care claim. Because we have determined that the complaint fails properly to invoke loyalty and bad faith claims, we are left with only a due care claim. Defendants had the obligation to raise the bar of Section 102(b)(7) as a defense, and they did. As plaintiffs conceded in oral argument before this Court, if there is only an unambiguous, residual due care claim and nothing else—as a matter of law—then Section 102(b)(7) would bar the claim. Accordingly, the Court of Chancery did not err in dismissing the plaintiffs due care claim in this case.

2. *The Court of Chancery Correctly Applied the Parties' Respective Burdens of Proof*

Plaintiffs also assert that the trial court in the case before us incorrectly placed on plaintiffs a pleading burden to negate the elements of the 102(b)(7) charter provision. Plaintiffs argue that this ruling is inconsistent with the statement in Emerald Partners that "The shield from liability provided by a certificate of incorporation provision

47. Chancery Rule 8(a).

adopted pursuant to 8 Del. C. § 102(b)(7) is in the nature of an affirmative defense.... Defendants seeking exculpation under such a provision will normally bear the burden of establishing each of its elements."

The procedural posture here is quite different from that in Emerald Partners. There the Court stated that it was incorrect for the trial court to grant summary judgment on the record in that case because the defendants had the burden at trial of demonstrating good faith if they were invoking the statutory exculpation provision. In this case, we focus not on trial burdens, but only on pleading issues. A plaintiff must allege well-pleaded facts stating a claim on which relief may be granted. Had plaintiff alleged such well-pleaded facts supporting a breach of loyalty or bad faith claim, the Section 102(b)(7) charter provision would have been unavailing as to such claims, and this case would have gone forward.

But we have held that the amended complaint here does not allege a loyalty violation or other violation falling within the exceptions to the Section 102(b)(7) exculpation provision. Likewise, we have held that, even if the plaintiffs had stated a claim for gross negligence, such a well-pleaded claim is unavailing because defendants have brought forth the Section 102(b)(7) charter provision that bars such claims. This is the end of the case.

And rightly so, as a matter of the public policy of this State. Section 102(b)(7) was adopted by the Delaware General Assembly in 1986 following a directors and officers insurance liability crisis and the 1985 Delaware Supreme Court decision in Smith v. Van Gorkom. The purpose of this statute was to permit stockholders to adopt a provision in the certificate of incorporation to free directors of personal liability in damages for due care violations, but not duty of loyalty violations, bad faith claims and certain other conduct. Such a charter provision, when adopted, would not affect injunctive proceedings based on gross negligence. Once the statute was adopted, stockholders usually approved charter amendments containing these provisions because it freed up directors to take business risks without worrying about negligence lawsuits.

Our jurisprudence since the adoption of the statute has consistently stood for the proposition that a Section 102(b)(7) charter provision bars a claim that is found to state only a due care violation.[48] Because we have assumed that the amended complaint here does state a due care claim, the exculpation afforded by the statute must affirmatively be raised by the defendant directors.[49] The directors have done so in this case, and the Court of Chancery properly applied the

Frederick's charter provision to dismiss the plaintiffs' due care claim. . . .

CONCLUSION

We have concluded that: (1) the amended complaint does not adequately allege a breach of the Frederick's board's duty of loyalty or its disclosure duty; (2) the exculpatory provision in the Frederick's charter operates to bar claims for money damages against the directors caused by the alleged breach of the board's duty of care. . . . Accordingly, we affirm the judgment of the Court of Chancery dismissing the amended complaint against the Frederick's board. . . .

E. DIRECTORS' AND OFFICERS'—LIABILITY INSURANCE

FORM OF DIRECTORS' AND OFFICERS' LIABILITY INSURANCE

[See Statutory Supplement]

NOTE ON DIRECTORS' AND OFFICERS' LIABILITY INSURANCE

1. Often a director or officer will be entitled to corporate indemnification for losses she incurred in suits against her based on actions that she took in her corporate capacity. See Chapter 14, Section 8. For various reasons, however, a director or officer may not be indemnified for all such losses. For example, the governing law may prohibit indemnification in certain kinds of cases, as where the director's or officer's loss consists of a judgment against her in a duty-of-care action. Or the corporation may be insolvent, or it may refuse to make indemnification where indemnification is discretionary rather than mandatory. Accordingly, corporations will often purchase Directors' and Officers' (D & O) Liability Insurance to cover certain types of non-indemnified losses.

---

48. See, e.g., *Emerald Partners*, 726 A.2d at 1224; *Arnold v. Society for Savings Bancorp.*, Del. Supr., 650 A.2d 1270, 1288 (1994); *Zirn v. VLI Corp.*, Del. Supr., 681 A.2d 1050, 1061 (1996).

49. Although an exculpatory charter provision is in the nature of an affirmative defense under *Emerald Partners*, the board is not required to disprove claims based on alleged breaches of the duty of loyalty to gain the protection of the provision with respect to due care claims. Rather, proving the existence of a valid exculpatory provision in the corporate charter entitles directors to dismissal of any claims for money damages against them that are based solely on alleged breaches of the board's duty of care.

2. Typically, a D & O policy has two separate insurance agreements: (i) Corporate reimbursement, which insures the corporation against its potential liability to officers and directors under the latters' right to indemnification from the corporation, and (ii) Personal coverage, which insures the directors and officers themselves against losses based on claims against them for wrongful conduct. The precise scope of the personal coverage varies according to the policy, but all policies would normally cover most liabilities arising in connection with claims based on a violation of the duty of care owed to the corporation, and many or most policies would cover liabilities for duties of care owed to the general public.

3. D & O insurance does not render directors and officers completely risk-free with regard to claims based on the duty of care. To begin with, a variety of claims are excluded from coverage. For example, many D & O policies contain an insured v. insured exclusion, under which the insurer is not liable in connection with claims made against a director or officer by the corporation, other than a claim made in a shareholder's derivative action (that is, other than a claim made by a shareholder on the corporation's behalf). Also, D & O policy limits typically apply to the combined amount of liability and legal expenses, and in any given case the combination of the two may exceed the policy limit. *See* Helfand v. National Union Fire Ins. Co., 10 Cal.App.4th 869, 13 Cal.Rptr.2d 295 (1992).

Other obstacles may also stand in the way of a recovery under a D & O policy. For example, the insurer is not liable if it can establish any of the following defenses, among others:

(a) The corporation, the directors and officers, or all of them (the "insureds") did not give the insurer notice of the claim against them within the time period specified by the policy. See, e.g., ACE Am. Ins. Co. v. Underwriters at Lloyds & Cos., 971 A.2d 1121 (Pa. 2009). This defense includes cases in which (i) the insureds are given notice of a claim against them, but suit on the claim has not yet been brought; and (ii) the insureds erroneously consider the notice they were given as not sufficiently formal within the meaning of the policy, and they therefore do not notify the insurer of the claim until the time for giving notice has expired.

(b) At the time the policy was issued, the corporation or the directors and officers knew that the event giving rise to the claim against them was likely to occur but did not report that to the insurer.

(c) The claim against the insureds is related to an earlier claim that was pending or completed prior to the inception of the policy. See, e.g., HR Acquisition I Corp. v. Twin City Fire Ins. Co., 2008 WL 4767256 (11th Cir. 2008).

4. Another characteristic of D & O insurance that may be relevant to the protection it affords is that such insurance is written on a claims-made basis—that is, the insurance covers only claims made while the policy is in force. To illustrate, suppose C Corporation procured a D & O policy from I Insurance Company for 2010. A claim made in 2010 that is based on events that occurred in 2007 may be covered by the policy even though I was not C's insurer in 2007. Conversely, however, a claim made in 2011 based on events that occurred in 2010 may not be covered by the 2010 policy.

The claims-made nature of D & O insurance is often modified by several features. First, a policy may contain a "retroactive date provision", under which an insured's liability for an event that occurred before a designated date will not be covered by the policy even if a claim based on the event is first made during the policy period. Second, a policy may include a "right of discovery," which allows an insured to extend the coverage to a claim made during a limited period after the policy has terminated, provided the claim is based on wrongful acts that occurred during the term of the policy. Many policies also permit an insured to present a notice of occurrence of a *possible* claim during the policy period, and give such a notice the same effect as an actual claim made against the insured. Subject to these exceptions, an effect of the claims-made nature of D & O insurance is that a director or officer cannot be positive that he will be covered for his present conduct if a claim concerning that conduct arises after the policy has expired or has been canceled.

Another factor that affects the risk of a director or officer for duty-of-care liability is that D & O insurers often seem to be exceptionally ready to litigate claims brought against them by their insureds. Some of the litigation concerns the interpretation of the policy language, which is often less than crystal clear. In addition, the corporation and the directors and officers who are to be covered under a D & O policy must fill out extensive applications, which include questions on such issues as whether the applicant has knowledge or information of any act, error, or omission that might give rise to a claim under the policy. It is often easy for an insurer to argue that the policy is unenforceable on the ground that a question was not answered accurately. Furthermore, unless the policy otherwise provides, the failure of even one director or officer to answer questions accurately may invalidate the coverage of all officers and directors. *See, e.g.,* Bird v. Penn Central Co., 334 F.Supp. 255 (E.D.Pa.1971), 341 F.Supp. 291 (1972); Shapiro v. American Home Assurance Co., 584 F.Supp. 1245 (D.Mass.1984).

SECTION 2. THE DUTY TO ACT IN GOOD FAITH

In re the Walt Disney Company Derivative Litigation

Supreme Court of Delaware, 2006.
906 A.2d 27.

■ Before STEELE, CHIEF JUSTICE, HOLLAND, BERGER, JACOBS and RIDGELY, JUSTICES, constituting the Court en Banc.

■ JACOBS, JUSTICE:

[In August 1995, the board of Walt Disney Company entered into an employment agreement with Michael Ovitz under which Ovitz would serve as Disney's president for five years. It soon became apparent that Ovitz was a poor fit, and on December 11, 1966, Ovitz was terminated with a severance package of $140 million. Shareholders then brought a derivative action against Ovitz, the directors, and others. A major element of the complaint was that the directors had not acted in good faith. In particular, the complaint alleged that (i) Ovitz was hired as a result of pressure from Disney's CEO, Michael Eisner, who had been close friends with Ovitz for 25 years. (ii) Ovitz had never been an executive of a publicly owned entertainment company. (iii) Internal documents had warned that Ovitz was unqualified. (iv) A member of the compensation committee received a $250,000 fee to secure Ovitz's employment. (v) Neither the compensation committee nor, apparently the board, had received, or had an opportunity to review, either the draft or final employment contract with Ovitz in advance of their meetings. (vi) The compensation committee and the board had devoted hardly any time at their meetings to reviewing and approving Ovitz's employment contract. (vii) Eisner had a defining role in the contours of the employment agreement, particularly the timing of the vesting of stock options, which constituted a major portion of Ovitz's severance package. (viii) The employment agreement was approved by the compensation committee at a one-hour meeting that had other items on its agenda, and a draft of the agreement was not circulated to the committee prior to or at the meeting. The plaintiffs claimed that these facts, taken together, showed that the defendants had violated their fiduciary duty to act in good faith.]

... This case ... is one in which the duty to act in good faith has played a prominent role, yet to date is not a well-developed area of our corporate fiduciary law.[98] Although the good faith concept has recently been the subject of considerable scholarly writing,[99] which

---

98. The Chancellor observed, after surveying the sparse case law on the subject, that both the meaning and the contours of the duty to act in good faith were "[s]hrouded in the fog of ... hazy jurisprudence." Post–Trial Op. at *35.

99. See, e.g., Hillary A. Sale, Delaware's Good Faith, 89 CORNELL L. REV. 456 (2004); Matthew R. Berry, Does Delaware's Section 102(b)(7) Protect Reckless Directors From

includes articles focused on this specific case, the duty to act in good faith is, up to this point relatively uncharted. Because of the increased recognition of the importance of good faith, some conceptual guidance to the corporate community may be helpful. For that reason we proceed to address the merits of the appellants' second argument.

The precise question is whether the Chancellor's articulated standard for bad faith corporate fiduciary conduct—intentional dereliction of duty, a conscious disregard for one's responsibilities—is legally correct. In approaching that question, we note that the Chancellor characterized that definition as "*an* appropriate *(although not the only)* standard for determining whether fiduciaries have acted in good faith." That observation is accurate and helpful, because as a matter of simple logic, at least three different categories of fiduciary behavior are candidates for the "bad faith" pejorative label.

The first category involves so-called "subjective bad faith," that is, fiduciary conduct motivated by an actual intent to do harm. That such conduct constitutes classic, quintessential bad faith is a proposition so well accepted in the liturgy of fiduciary law that it borders on axiomatic.[102] We need not dwell further on this category, because no such conduct is claimed to have occurred, or did occur, in this case.

The second category of conduct, which is at the opposite end of the spectrum, involves lack of due care—that is, fiduciary action taken solely by reason of gross negligence and without any malevolent intent. In this case, appellants assert claims of gross negligence to establish breaches not only of director due care but also of the directors' duty to act in good faith. Although the Chancellor found, and we agree, that the appellants failed to establish gross negligence, to afford guidance we address the issue of whether gross negligence (including a failure to inform one's self of available material facts), without more, can also constitute bad faith. The answer is clearly no.

From a broad philosophical standpoint, that question is more complex than would appear, if only because (as the Chancellor and

---

Personal Liability? Only if Delaware Courts Act in Good Faith, 79 WASH. L. REV. 1125 (2004); John L. Reed and Matt Neiderman, Good Faith and the Ability of Directors to Assert § 102(b)(7) of the Delaware Corporation Law as a Defense to Claims Alleging Abdication, Lack of Oversight, and Similar Breaches of Fiduciary Duty, 29 DEL. J. CORP. L. 111 (2004); David Rosenberg, Making Sense of Good Faith in Delaware Corporate Fiduciary Law: A Contractarian Approach, 29 DEL. J. CORP. L. 491 (2004); Sean J. Griffith, Good Faith Business Judgment: A Theory of Rhetoric in Corporate Law Jurisprudence, 55 DUKE L. J. 1 (2005) ("Griffith"); Melvin A. Eisenberg, The Duty of Good Faith in Corporate Law, 31 DEL. J. CORP. L. 1 (2005); Filippo Rossi, Making Sense of the Delaware Supreme Court's Triad of Fiduciary Duties (June 22, 2005), available at http://ssrn.com/abstract=755784; Christopher M. Bruner, "Good Faith," State of Mind, and the Outer Boundaries of Director Liability in Corporate Law (Boston Univ. Sch. of Law Working Paper No. 05–19), available at http://ssrn.com/abstract=832944; Sean J. Griffith & Myron T. Steele, On Corporate Law Federalism Threatening the Thaumatrope, 61 BUS. LAW. 1 (2005).

102. The Chancellor so recognized. *Id.* at *35 ("[A]n action taken with the intent to harm the corporation is a disloyal act in bad faith."). *See McGowan v. Ferro*, 859 A.2d 1012, 1036 (Del. Ch. 2004) ("Bad faith is 'not simply bad judgment or negligence,' but rather 'implies the conscious doing of a wrong because of dishonest purpose or moral obliquity . . . it contemplates a state of mind affirmatively operating with furtive design or ill will.' ") (quoting *Desert Equities, Inc. v. Morgan Stanley Leveraged Equity Fund, II, L.P.*, 624 A.2d 1199, 1208, n. 16 (Del. 1993)).

others have observed) "issues of good faith are (to a certain degree) inseparably and necessarily intertwined with the duties of care and loyalty. . . ."[103] But, in the pragmatic, conduct-regulating legal realm which calls for more precise conceptual line drawing, the answer is that grossly negligent conduct, without more, does not and cannot constitute a breach of the fiduciary duty to act in good faith. The conduct that is the subject of due care may overlap with the conduct that comes within the rubric of good faith in a psychological sense,[104] but from a legal standpoint those duties are and must remain quite distinct. Both our legislative history and our common law jurisprudence distinguish sharply between the duties to exercise due care and to act in good faith, and highly significant consequences flow from that distinction.

The Delaware General Assembly has addressed the distinction between bad faith and a failure to exercise due care (*i.e.*, gross negligence) in two separate contexts. The first is Section 102(b)(7) of the DGCL, which authorizes Delaware corporations, by a provision in the certificate of incorporation, to exculpate their directors from monetary damage liability for a breach of the duty of care.[105] That exculpatory provision affords significant protection to directors of Delaware corporations. The statute carves out several exceptions, however, including most relevantly, "for acts or omissions not in good faith. . . ."[106] Thus, a corporation can exculpate its directors from monetary liability for a breach of the duty of care, but not for conduct that is not in good faith. To adopt a definition of bad faith that would cause a violation of the duty of care automatically to become an act or omission "not in good faith," would eviscerate the protections accorded to directors by the General Assembly's adoption of Section 102(b)(7).

A second legislative recognition of the distinction between fiduciary conduct that is grossly negligent and conduct that is not in good faith, is Delaware's indemnification statute, found at 8 *Del. C.* § 145. To oversimplify, subsections (a) and (b) of that statute permit a corporation to indemnify (*inter alia*) any person who is or was a director, officer, employee or agent of the corporation against expenses (including attorneys' fees), judgments, fines and amounts paid in settlement of specified actions, suits or proceedings, where (among other things): (i) that person is, was, or is threatened to be made a party to that action, suit or proceeding, and (ii) that person "acted in good faith and in a manner the person reasonably believed to be in or

103. Post-trial Op. at *31 (citing Griffith, *supra* note 99, at 15).

104. An example of such overlap might be the hypothetical case where a director, because of subjective hostility to the corporation on whose board he serves, fails to inform himself of, or to devote sufficient attention to, the matters on which he is making decisions as a fiduciary. In such a case, two states of mind coexist in the same person: subjective bad intent (which would lead to a finding of bad faith) and gross negligence (which would lead to a finding of a breach of the duty of care). Although the coexistence of both states of mind may make them indistinguishable from a psychological standpoint, the fiduciary duties that they cause the director to violate—care and good faith—are legally separate and distinct.

105. 8 *Del. C.* § 102(b)(7).

106. 8 *Del. C.* § 102(b)(7)(ii).

not opposed to the best interests of the corporation. . . ."[107] Thus, under Delaware statutory law a director or officer of a corporation can be indemnified for liability (and litigation expenses) incurred by reason of a violation of the duty of care, but not for a violation of the duty to act in good faith.

Section 145, like Section 102(b)(7), evidences the intent of the Delaware General Assembly to afford significant protections to directors (and, in the case of Section 145, other fiduciaries) of Delaware corporations. To adopt a definition that conflates the duty of care with the duty to act in good faith by making a violation of the former an automatic violation of the latter, would nullify those legislative protections and defeat the General Assembly's intent. There is no basis in policy, precedent or common sense that would justify dismantling the distinction between gross negligence and bad faith.

That leaves the third category of fiduciary conduct, which falls in between the first two categories of (1) conduct motivated by subjective bad intent and (2) conduct resulting from gross negligence. This third category is what the Chancellor's definition of bad faith—intentional dereliction of duty, a conscious disregard for one's responsibilities—is intended to capture. The question is whether such misconduct is properly treated as a non-exculpable, nonindemnifiable violation of the fiduciary duty to act in good faith. In our view it must be, for at least two reasons.

First, the universe of fiduciary misconduct is not limited to either disloyalty in the classic sense (*i.e.*, preferring the adverse self-interest of the fiduciary or of a related person to the interest of the corporation) or gross negligence. Cases have arisen where corporate directors have no conflicting self-interest in a decision, yet engage in misconduct that is more culpable than simple inattention or failure to be informed of all facts material to the decision. To protect the interests of the corporation and its shareholders, fiduciary conduct of this kind, which does not involve disloyalty (as traditionally defined) but is qualitatively more culpable than gross negligence, should be proscribed. A vehicle is needed to address such violations doctrinally, and that doctrinal vehicle is the duty to act in good faith. The Chancellor implicitly so recognized in his Opinion, where he identified different examples of bad faith as follows:

> The good faith required of a corporate fiduciary includes not simply the duties of care and loyalty, in the narrow sense that I have discussed them above, but all actions required by a true faithfulness and devotion to the interests of the corporation and its shareholders. A failure to act in good faith may be shown, for instance, where the fiduciary intentionally acts with a purpose other than that of advancing the best interests of the corporation, where the fiduciary acts with the intent to violate applicable positive law, or where the fiduciary intentionally fails to act in the face of a known duty to act, demonstrating a conscious disregard

107. 8 *Del. C.* §§ 145(a) & (b).

for his duties. There may be other examples of bad faith yet to be proven or alleged, but these three are the most salient.[110]

Those articulated examples of bad faith are not new to our jurisprudence. Indeed, they echo pronouncements our courts have made throughout the decades.[111]

Second, the legislature has also recognized this intermediate category of fiduciary misconduct, which ranks between conduct involving subjective bad faith and gross negligence. Section 102(b)(7)(ii) of the DGCL expressly denies money damage exculpation for "acts or omissions not in good faith or which involve intentional misconduct or a knowing violation of law." By its very terms that provision distinguishes between "intentional misconduct" and a "knowing violation of law" (both examples of subjective bad faith) on the one hand, and "acts ... not in good faith," on the other. Because the statute exculpates directors only for conduct amounting to gross negligence, the statutory denial of exculpation for "acts ... not in good faith" must encompass the intermediate category of misconduct captured by the Chancellor's definition of bad faith.

For these reasons, we uphold the Court of Chancery's definition as a legally appropriate, although not the exclusive, definition of fiduciary bad faith. We need go no further. To engage in an effort to craft (in the Court's words) "a definitive and categorical definition of the universe of acts that would constitute bad faith"[112] would be unwise and is unnecessary to dispose of the issues presented on this appeal.

[The court then affirmed the Chancellor's dismissal of the plaintiffs' remaining claims.]

VI. CONCLUSION

For the reasons stated above, the judgment of the Court of Chancery is affirmed.

---

110. Post-trial Op. at *36 (footnotes omitted).

111. *See, e.g.*, *Allaun v. Consol. Oil Co.*, 147 A. 257, 261 (Del. Ch. 1929) (further judicial scrutiny is warranted if the transaction results from the directors' "reckless indifference to or a deliberate disregard of the interests of the whole body of stockholders"); *Gimbel v. Signal Cos., Inc.*, 316 A.2d 599, 604 (Del. Ch. 1974), *aff'd*, 316 A.2d 619 (Del. 1974) (injunction denied because, *inter alia*, there was "[n]othing in the record [that] would justify a finding ... that the directors acted for any personal advantage or out of improper motive or intentional disregard of shareholder interests"); *In re Caremark Int'l Derivative Litig.*, 698 A.2d 959, 971 (Del. Ch. 1996) ("only a sustained or systematic failure of the board to exercise oversight—such as an utter failure to attempt to assure a reasonable information and reporting system exists—will establish the lack of good faith that is a necessary condition to liability."); *Nagy v. Bistricer*, 770 A.2d 43, 48, n.2 (Del. Ch. 2000) (observing that the utility of the duty of good faith "may rest in its constant reminder ... that, regardless of his motive, a director who consciously disregards his duties to the corporation and its stockholders may suffer a personal judgment for monetary damages for any harm he causes," even if for a reason "other than personal pecuniary interest").

112. Post-trial Op. at *36. For the same reason, we do not reach or otherwise address the issue of whether the fiduciary duty to act in good faith is a duty that, like the duties of care and loyalty, can serve as an independent basis for imposing liability upon corporate officers and directors. That issue is not before us on this appeal.

STONE v. RITTER, Supreme Court of Delaware, 2006, 911 A.2d 362. "... The standard for assessing a director's potential personal liability for failing to act in good faith in discharging his or her oversight responsibilities has evolved beginning with our decision in Graham v. Allis–Chalmers Manufacturing Company, through the Court of Chancery's *Caremark* decision to our most recent decision in *Disney*. A brief discussion of that evolution will help illuminate the standard that we adopt in this case."

Graham and Caremark

"*Graham* was a derivative action brought against the directors of Allis–Chalmers for failure to prevent violations of federal anti-trust laws by Allis–Chalmers employees. There was no claim that the Allis–Chalmers directors knew of the employees' conduct that resulted in the corporation's liability. Rather, the plaintiffs claimed that the Allis–Chalmers directors *should have known* of the illegal conduct by the corporation's employees. In *Graham*, this Court held that '*absent cause for suspicion* there is no duty upon the directors to install and operate a corporate system of espionage to ferret out wrongdoing which they have no reason to suspect exists.' ...

"In evaluating whether to approve the proposed settlement agreement in *Caremark*, the Court of Chancery narrowly construed our holding in *Graham* 'as standing for the proposition that, absent grounds to suspect deception, neither corporate boards nor senior officers can be charged with wrongdoing simply for assuming the integrity of employees and the honesty of their dealings on the company's behalf.' The *Caremark* Court opined it would be a 'mistake' to interpret this Court's decision in *Graham* to mean that:

> corporate boards may satisfy their obligation to be reasonably informed concerning the corporation, without assuring themselves that information and reporting systems exist in the organization that are reasonably designed to provide to senior management and to the board itself timely, accurate information sufficient to allow management and the board, each within its scope, to reach informed judgments concerning both the corporation's compliance with law and its business performance.

"To the contrary, the *Caremark* Court stated, 'it is important that the board exercise a good faith judgment that the corporation's information and reporting system is in concept and design adequate to assure the board that appropriate information will come to its attention in a timely manner as a matter of ordinary operations, so that it may satisfy its responsibility.' The *Caremark* Court recognized, however, that 'the duty to act in good faith to be informed cannot be thought to require directors to possess detailed information about all aspects of the operation of the enterprise.' The Court of Chancery then formulated the following standard for assessing the liability of directors where the directors are unaware of employee misconduct that results in the corporation being held liable:

> Generally where a claim of directorial liability for corporate loss is predicated upon ignorance of liability creating activities within the corporation, as in *Graham* or in this case, . . . only a sustained or systematic failure of the board to exercise oversight—such as an utter failure to attempt to assure a reasonable information and reporting system exists—will establish the lack of good faith that is a necessary condition to liability.

Caremark Standard Approved

"As evidenced by the language quoted above, the *Caremark* standard for so-called 'oversight' liability draws heavily upon the concept of director failure to act in good faith. That is consistent with the definition(s) of bad faith recently approved by this Court in its recent *Disney* decision, where we held that a failure to act in good faith requires conduct that is qualitatively different from, and more culpable than, the conduct giving rise to a violation of the fiduciary duty of care (i.e., gross negligence). In *Disney*, we identified the following examples of conduct that would establish a failure to act in good faith:

> A failure to act in good faith may be shown, for instance, where the fiduciary intentionally acts with a purpose other than that of advancing the best interests of the corporation, where the fiduciary acts with the intent to violate applicable positive law, or where the fiduciary intentionally fails to act in the face of a known duty to act, demonstrating a conscious disregard for his duties. There may be other examples of bad faith yet to be proven or alleged, but these three are the most salient.

"The third of these examples describes, and is fully consistent with, the lack of good faith conduct that the *Caremark* court held was a 'necessary condition' for director oversight liability, i.e., 'a sustained or systematic failure of the board to exercise oversight—such as an utter failure to attempt to assure a reasonable information and reporting system exists....' Indeed, our opinion in *Disney* cited *Caremark* with approval for that proposition. Accordingly, the Court of Chancery applied the correct standard in assessing whether demand was excused in this case where failure to exercise oversight was the basis or theory of the plaintiffs' claim for relief.

"It is important, in this context, to clarify a doctrinal issue that is critical to understanding fiduciary liability under *Caremark* as we construe that case. The phraseology used in *Caremark* and that we employ here—describing the lack of good faith as a 'necessary condition to liability'—is deliberate. The purpose of that formulation is to communicate that a failure to act in good faith is not conduct that results, *ipso facto*, in the direct imposition of fiduciary liability. The failure to act in good faith may result in liability because the requirement to act in good faith 'is a subsidiary element[,]' i.e., a condition, 'of the fundamental duty of loyalty.' It follows that because a showing of bad faith conduct, in the sense described in *Disney* and *Caremark*, is essential to establish director oversight liability, the fiduciary duty violated by that conduct is the duty of loyalty.

"This view of a failure to act in good faith results in two additional doctrinal consequences. First, although good faith may be described colloquially as part of a 'triad' of fiduciary duties that includes the duties of care and loyalty, the obligation to act in good faith does not establish an independent fiduciary duty that stands on the same footing as the duties of care and loyalty. Only the latter two duties, where violated, may directly result in liability, whereas a failure to act in good faith may do so, but indirectly. The second doctrinal consequence is that the fiduciary duty of loyalty is not limited to cases involving a financial or other cognizable fiduciary conflict of interest. It also encompasses cases where the fiduciary fails to act in good faith. As the Court of Chancery aptly put it in *Guttman*, '[a] director cannot act loyally towards the corporation unless she acts in the good faith belief that her actions are in the corporation's best interest.'

"We hold that *Caremark* articulates the necessary conditions predicate for director oversight liability: (a) the directors utterly failed to implement any reporting or information system or controls; *or* (b) having implemented such a system or controls, consciously failed to monitor or oversee its operations thus disabling themselves from being informed of risks or problems requiring their attention. In either case, imposition of liability requires a showing that the directors knew that they were not discharging their fiduciary obligations. Where directors fail to act in the face of a known duty to act, thereby demonstrating a conscious disregard for their responsibilities, they breach their duty of loyalty by failing to discharge that fiduciary obligation in good faith."

SECTION 3. THE DUTY TO ACT LAWFULLY

Miller v. American Telephone & Telegraph Co.

United States Court of Appeals, Third Circuit, 1974.
507 F.2d 759.

■ Before SEITZ, CHIEF JUDGE, GIBBONS and GARTH, CIRCUIT JUDGES.

■ SEITZ, CHIEF JUDGE.

Plaintiffs, stockholders in American Telephone and Telegraph Company ("AT & T"), brought a stockholders' derivative action in the Eastern District of Pennsylvania against AT & T and all but one of its directors. The suit centered upon the failure of AT & T to collect an outstanding debt of some $1.5 million owed to the company by the Democratic National Committee ("DNC") for communications services provided by AT & T during the 1968 Democratic national convention. Federal diversity jurisdiction was invoked under 28 U.S.C. § 1332.

Plaintiffs' complaint alleged that "neither the officers or directors of AT & T have taken any action to recover the amount owed" from on or about August 20, 1968, when the debt was incurred, until May 31, 1972, the date plaintiffs' amended complaint was filed. The failure to collect was alleged to have involved a breach of the defendant directors' duty to exercise diligence in handling the affairs of the corporation, to have resulted in affording a preference to the DNC in collection procedures in violation of § 202(a) of the Communications Act of 1934, 47 U.S.C. § 202(a) (1970), and to have amounted to AT & T's making a "contribution" to the DNC in violation of a federal prohibition on corporate campaign spending, 18 U.S.C. § 610 (1970).

Plaintiffs sought permanent relief in the form of an injunction requiring AT & T to collect the debt, an injunction against providing further services to the DNC until the debt was paid in full, and a surcharge for the benefit of the corporation against the defendant directors in the amount of the debt plus interest from the due date. A request for a preliminary injunction against the provision of services to the 1972 Democratic convention was denied by the district court after an evidentiary hearing.

On motion of the defendants, the district court dismissed the complaint for failure to state a claim upon which relief could be granted. 364 F.Supp. 648 (E.D.Pa.1973). The court stated that collection procedures were properly within the discretion of the directors whose determination would not be overturned by the court in the absence of an allegation that the conduct of the directors was "plainly illegal, unreasonable, or in breach of a fiduciary duty. . . ." *Id.* at 651. Plaintiffs appeal from dismissal of their complaint.

In viewing the motion to dismiss, we must consider all facts alleged in the complaint and every inference fairly deductible therefrom in the light most favorable to the plaintiffs. A complaint should not be dismissed unless it appears that the plaintiffs would not be entitled to relief under any facts which they might prove in support of their claim. Judging plaintiffs' complaint by these standards, we feel that it does state a claim upon which relief can be granted for breach of fiduciary duty arising from the alleged violation of 18 U.S.C. § 610.

I.

The pertinent law on the question of the defendant directors' fiduciary duties in this diversity action is that of New York, the state of AT & T's incorporation. . . . The sound business judgment rule, the basis of the district court's dismissal of plaintiffs' complaint, expresses the unanimous decision of American courts to eschew intervention in corporate decision-making if the judgment of directors and officers is uninfluenced by personal considerations and is exercised in good faith. Pollitz v. Wabash Railroad Co., 207 N.Y. 113, 100 N.E. 721 (1912); Bayer v. Beran, 49 N.Y.S.2d 2, 4–7 (Sup.Ct.1944); 3 Fletcher, Private Corporations § 1039 (perm. ed. rev. vol. 1965). Underlying the rule is the assumption that reasonable diligence has been used in reaching the decision which the rule is invoked to justify. . . .

Had plaintiffs' complaint alleged only failure to pursue a corporate claim, application of the sound business judgment rule would support the district court's ruling that a shareholder could not attack the directors' decision. *See* United Copper Securities Co. v. Amalgamated Copper Co., 244 U.S. 261, 37 S.Ct. 509, 61 L.Ed. 1119 (1917); Clifford v. Metropolitan Life Insurance Co., 264 App.Div. 168, 34 N.Y.S.2d 693 (2d Dept.1942); 13 Fletcher, Private Corporations § 5822 (perm. ed. rev. vol. 1970). Where, however, the decision not to collect a debt owed the corporation is itself alleged to have been an illegal act, different rules apply. When New York law regarding such acts by directors is considered in conjunction with the underlying purposes of the particular statute involved here, we are convinced that the business judgment rule cannot insulate the defendant directors from liability if they did in fact breach 18 U.S.C. § 610, as plaintiffs have charged.

Roth v. Robertson, 64 Misc. 343, 118 N.Y.S. 351 (Sup.Ct.1909), illustrates the proposition that even though committed to benefit the corporation, illegal acts may amount to a breach of fiduciary duty in New York. In *Roth,* the managing director of an amusement park company had allegedly used corporate funds to purchase the silence of persons who threatened to complain about unlawful Sunday operation of the park. Recovery from the defendant director was sustained on the ground that the money was an illegal payment:

> For reasons of public policy, we are clearly of the opinion that payments of corporate funds for such purposes as those disclosed in this case must be condemned, and officers of a corporation making them held to a strict accountability, and be compelled to refund the amounts so wasted for the benefit of stockholders.... To hold any other rule would be establishing a dangerous precedent, tacitly countenancing the wasting of corporate funds for purposes of corrupting public morals. *Id.* at 346, 118 N.Y.S. at 353.

The plaintiffs' complaint in the instant case alleges a similar "waste" of $1.5 million through an illegal campaign contribution.

Abrams v. Allen, 297 N.Y. 52, 74 N.E.2d 305 (1947), reflects an affirmation by the New York Court of Appeals of the principle of *Roth* that directors must be restrained from engaging in activities which are against public policy. In *Abrams* the court held that a cause of action was stated by an allegation in a derivative complaint that the directors of Remington Rand, Inc., had relocated corporate plants and curtailed production solely for the purpose of intimidating and punishing employees for their involvement in a labor dispute. The Court of Appeals acknowledged that, "depending on the circumstances," proof of the allegations in the complaint might sustain recovery, *inter alia,* under the rule that directors are liable for corporate loss caused by the commission of an "unlawful or immoral act." *Id.* at 55, 74 N.E.2d at 306. In support of its holding, the court noted that the closing of factories for the purpose alleged was opposed to the public policy of the state and nation as embodied in the New York Labor Law and the

National Labor Relations Act. *Id.* at 56, 74 N.E.2d at 307.[3]

The alleged violation of the federal prohibition against corporate political contributions not only involves the corporation in criminal activity but similarly contravenes a policy of Congress clearly enunciated in 18 U.S.C. § 610.[4] That statute and its predecessor reflect congressional efforts: (1) to destroy the influence of corporations over elections through financial contributions and (2) to check the practice of using corporate funds to benefit political parties without the consent of the stockholders. United States v. CIO, 335 U.S. 106, 113, 68 S.Ct. 1349, 92 L.Ed. 1849 (1948).

The fact that shareholders are within the class for whose protection the statute was enacted gives force to the argument that the alleged breach of that statute should give rise to a cause of action in those shareholders to force the return to the corporation of illegally contributed funds. Since political contributions by corporations can be checked and shareholder control over the political use of general corporate funds effectuated only if directors are restrained from causing the corporation to violate the statute, such a violation seems a particularly appropriate basis for finding breach of the defendant directors' fiduciary duty to the corporation. Under such circumstances, the directors cannot be insulated from liability on the ground that the contribution was made in the exercise of sound business judgment.

Since plaintiffs have alleged actual damage to the corporation from the transaction in the form of the loss of a $1.5 million increment to AT & T's treasury,[5] we conclude that the complaint does state a claim upon which relief can be granted sufficient to withstand a motion to dismiss.[6]

II.

We have accepted plaintiffs' allegation of a violation of 18 U.S.C. § 610 as a shorthand designation of the elements necessary to establish a breach of that statute. This is consonant with the federal practice

---

3. That violation of a federal statute is the basis of the breach of fiduciary duty and that therefore the court is required to interpret the federal statute has not deterred New York courts from entertaining such suits against directors. *See* Knopfler v. Bohen, 15 A.D.2d 922, 225 N.Y.S.2d 609 (2d Dept.1962); *cf.* Simon v. Socony–Vacuum Oil Co., 179 Misc. 202, 38 N.Y.S.2d 270 (Sup.Ct.1942).

4. We note that prior to June 1, 1974, corporate political contributions made "directly or indirectly" violated New York law. Law of July 20, 1965, ch. 1031, § 43, [1965] N.Y.Laws 1783 (repealed 1974). Furthermore, apart from the statutory prohibition, political donations by corporations were apparently ultra vires acts in New York. *See* People ex rel. Perkins v. Moss, 187 N.Y. 410, 80 N.E. 383 (1907). Corporations or organizations financially supported by corporations doing business in the state are now permitted to make contributions up to $5,000 per year. N.Y. Election Law § 480 (McKinney's Consol.Laws, c. 17, Supp.1974).

5. Under New York law, allegation of breach even of a federal statute is apparently insufficient to state a cause of action unless the breach caused independent damage to the corporation. *See* Diamond v. Davis, 263 App.Div. 68, 31 N.Y.S.2d 582 (1st Dept.1941); Borden v. Cohen, 231 N.Y.S.2d 902 (Sup.Ct.1962). *But see* Runcie v. Bankers Trust Co., 6 N.Y.S.2d 623 (Sup.Ct.1938).

6. We express no opinion today on the question of whether plaintiffs' complaint may also state a cause of action for breach of fiduciary duty arising from the alleged violation of 47 U.S.C. § 202(a).

of notice pleading. *See* Conley v. Gibson, 355 U.S. 41, 47–48, 78 S.Ct. 99, 2 L.Ed.2d 80 (1957); Fed.R.Civ.P. 8(f). That such a designation is sufficient for pleading purposes does not, however, relieve plaintiffs of their ultimate obligation to prove the elements of the statutory violation as part of their proof of breach of fiduciary duty. At the appropriate time, plaintiffs will be required to produce evidence sufficient to establish three distinct elements comprising a violation of 18 U.S.C. § 610: that AT & T (1) made a contribution of money or anything of value to the DNC (2) in connection with a federal election (3) for the purpose of influencing the outcome of that election. *See* United States v. Boyle, 157 U.S.App.D.C. 166, 482 F.2d 755, cert. denied, 414 U.S. 1076, 94 S.Ct. 593, 38 L.Ed.2d 483 (1973); United States v. Lewis Food Co., Inc., 366 F.2d 710 (9th Cir.1966). . . .[7]

The order of the district court will be reversed and the case remanded for further proceedings consistent with this opinion.

NOTE ON CRIMINAL LIABILITIES OF DIRECTORS AND OFFICERS

Miller concerns the civil liability of a director or officer to the corporation on the ground of illegal conduct. An officer (or, more rarely, a director) may also be criminally liable for such conduct. Two kinds of statute are relevant to the potential criminal liability of officers and directors.

1. The first type of statute makes corporate managers criminally liable for unlawful corporate acts if the managers themselves performed or caused the performance of the act. An example is N.Y.Penal Law § 20.25: "A person is criminally liable for conduct constituting an offense which he performs or causes to be performed in the name of or in behalf of a corporation to the same extent as if such conduct were performed in his own name or behalf." A highly publicized case, People v. Film Recovery Systems, Inc., Nos. 83–11091, 84–5064 (Cook County Cir.Ct. of Ill., 1985), arose under an Illinois statute comparable to N.Y.Penal Law § 20.25. Film Recovery reclaimed silver from used photographic film, through a standard process called cyanide leaching, which involves a chemical that gives off poisonous cyanide gas. The ventilation and other conditions at Film Recovery's plant were unsafe, and most of the workers spoke little English and therefore could not read the sodium-cyanide warning label. In December 1982, Stefan Golab, a Polish immigrant, began working at Film Recovery, pumping and stirring the sodium cyanide solution in large vats. In February 1983, Golab complained of headaches and nausea, and asked the plant manager, through an interpreter, to transfer him from the vats. After

---

7. As amended by the Federal Election Campaign Act of 1971 (effective April 7, 1972), the definition of "contribution" for purposes of 18 U.S.C. § 610 is a gift of money or anything of value "made for the purpose of influencing the nomination for election, or election" of any person to federal office or for influencing the outcome of a primary or national nominating convention. 18 U.S.C. § 591 (1970), as amended (Supp.II 1972).

four more days of working at the vats, Golab died of cyanide inhalation. Film Recovery's president, plant manager, and plant foreman were found guilty of murder, and sentenced to twenty-five years. *See* Note, Corporations Can Kill Too: After *Film Recovery,* Are Individuals Accountable for Corporate Crime?, 19 Loy.L.A.L.Rev. 1411 (1986). In 1990, *Film Recovery* was reversed on a technical ground and remanded for a new trial. People v. O'Neil, 194 Ill.App.3d 79, 141 Ill.Dec. 44, 550 N.E.2d 1090 (1990). On remand, the individual defendants pleaded guilty to lesser charges. Two were sentenced to two years, and the third received probation.

2. A second type of statute makes managers criminally liable for the unlawful acts of employees over whom they have the power of control, even if that power was not exercised. This type of statute gives rise to the "responsible corporate officer" doctrine. The leading case is United States v. Park, 421 U.S. 658, 95 S.Ct. 1903, 44 L.Ed.2d 489 (1975). Acme Markets, Inc., was a national retail food chain with approximately 36,000 employees, 874 retail outlets, and 16 warehouses. Park was Acme's CEO. In April 1970, the FDA formally advised Park of unsanitary conditions, including rodent infestation, in Acme's Philadelphia warehouse. In late 1971, the FDA found that similar conditions existed in the Baltimore warehouse, and in January 1972, the FDA sent a letter to that effect. In March 1972, a second inspection of the Baltimore warehouse showed improvement in the sanitary conditions, but evidence of continued rodent activity and rodent-contaminated food. The Government then brought criminal proceedings against Acme and Park on the ground that food held for sale in Acme's Baltimore warehouse was exposed to contamination by rodents, in violation of 21 U.S.C.A. § 331(k). Park testified that although all of Acme's employees were in a sense under his general direction, under Acme's organizational structure the responsibility for different phases of Acme's operation were assigned to other executives who, in turn, had staff and departments under them. He identified the individuals responsible for sanitation, and stated that upon receipt of the FDA's January 1972 letter, he had conferred with Acme's vice-president for legal affairs, who informed him that the vice-president of Acme's Baltimore division "was investigating the situation immediately and would be taking corrective action and would be preparing a summary of the corrective action to reply to the letter." Park conceded that providing sanitary conditions for food offered for sale to the public was something that he was "responsible for in the entire operation of the company," but said it was one of many phases of the company that he assigned to "dependable subordinates."

Park was convicted, although he had not authorized the violations and the statute did not explicitly impose criminal liability on managers based on the acts of others. The Supreme Court upheld the conviction, relying in part on an earlier case, United States v. Dotterweich:

> In [United States v. Dotterweich, 320 U.S. 277, 64 S.Ct. 134, 88 L.Ed. 48 (1943)], a jury had disagreed as to the corporation, a jobber purchasing drugs from manufacturers and shipping them

in interstate commerce under its own label, but had convicted Dotterweich, the corporation's president and general manager....

In reversing the judgment of the Court of Appeals and reinstating Dotterweich's conviction, this Court looked to the purposes of the Act and noted that they "touch phases of the lives and health of people which, in the circumstances of modern industrialism, are largely beyond self-protection." 320 U.S., at 280. It observed that the Act is of "a now familiar type" which "dispenses with the conventional requirement for criminal conduct—awareness of some wrongdoing. In the interest of the larger good it puts the burden of acting at hazard upon a person otherwise innocent but standing in responsible relation to a public danger." *Id.,* at 280–281....

At the same time, however, the Court was aware of the concern which was the motivating factor in the Court of Appeals' decision, that literal enforcement "might operate too harshly by sweeping within its condemnation any person however remotely entangled in the proscribed shipment." *Id.,* at 284. A limiting principle, in the form of "settled doctrines of criminal law" defining those who "are responsible for the commission of a misdemeanor," was available. In this context, the Court concluded, those doctrines dictated that the offense was committed "by all who ... have ... a responsible share in the furtherance of the transaction which the statute outlaws." *Ibid.* ...

... [T]he Act imposes not only a positive duty to seek out and remedy violations when they occur but also, and primarily, a duty to implement measures that will insure that violations will not occur. The requirements of foresight and vigilance imposed on responsible corporate agents are beyond question demanding, and perhaps onerous, but they are no more stringent than the public has a right to expect of those who voluntarily assume positions of authority in business enterprises whose services and products affect the health and well-being of the public that supports them....

Courts have extended criminal liability under the responsible-corporate-officer doctrine to directors and officers under a broad array of federal criminal statutes, including the Federal Hazardous Substances Act, the Sherman Act, the Economic Stabilization Act of 1970, the Occupational Safety & Health Act and the Federal Water Pollution Control Act. *See* Webb, Molo, and Hurst, Understanding and Avoiding Corporate and Executive Criminal Liability, 49 Bus.Law 617 (1994). However, Meyer v. Holley, 537 U.S. 280, 123 S.Ct. 824, 154 L.Ed.2d 753 (2003), limited the sweep of the doctrine. *Meyer* arose under the Fair Housing Act. That Act forbids racial discrimination in respect to the sale or rental of a dwelling. Triad Inc. was a real estate corporation. David Meyer, Triad's president and sole shareholder, had listed for sale a house in Twenty–Nine Palms, California. Emma and David Holley, an interracial couple, tried to unsuccessfully to buy the house.

The Holleys alleged that Grove Crank, a Triad salesman, prevented them from obtaining the house for racially discriminatory reasons, and sued Crank and Triad under the Fair Housing Act. They also sued Meyer on the ground that he was vicariously liable, as Triad's president and sole shareholder, for Crank's unlawful actions. The Ninth Circuit held that the Fair Housing Act made corporate owners and officers liable for the unlawful acts of a corporate employee if the owner or officer controlled or had the right to control the employee's actions. The Supreme Court reversed. The Court pointed out that under traditional principles of agency law, one person, P, is not vicariously liable for the actions of another person, A, unless A was not only under or subject to P's control, but acted for and on P's behalf. Under these traditional principles, an owner or officer of a corporation is usually not vicariously liable for the actions of a corporate employee, because an employee acts on behalf of the corporation, not an owner or an officer:

> ... Congress said nothing in the statute or on the legislative history about extending vicarious liability in this manner. And Congress' silence, while permitting an inference that Congress intended to apply ordinary background tort principles, cannot show that it intended to apply an unusual modification of those rules....
>
> This Court has applied unusually strict rules only where Congress has specified that such was its intent. *See, e.g.,* United States v. Dotterweich, 320 U.S. 277, 280–281 (1943) (Congress intended that a corporate officer or employee "standing in responsible relation" could be held liable in that capacity for a corporation's violations of the Federal Food, Drug, and Cosmetic Act, congressional intent to impose a duty on "responsible corporate agents"); United States v. Wise, 370 U.S. 405, 411–414 (1962) (discussing 38 Stat. 736, currently 15 U.S.C. § 24, which provides: "Whenever a corporation shall violate any of the ... antitrust laws, such violation shall be deemed to be also that of the individual directors, officers, or agents of such corporation who shall have authorized, ordered, or done any of the acts constituting in whole or in part such violation")....
>
> ... [W]hich "of two innocent people must suffer," *ibid.*, and just when, is a complex matter. We believe that courts ordinarily should determine that matter in accordance with traditional principles of vicarious liability—unless, of course, Congress, better able than courts to weigh the relevant policy considerations, has instructed the courts differently. *Cf., e.g.*, Sykes, the Economics of Vicarious Liability, 93 Yale L.J. 1231, 1236 (1984) (arguing that the expansion of vicarious liability or shifting of liability, due to insurance, may diminish an agent's incentives to police behavior). We have found no different instruction here.

CHAPTER 11

THE DUTY OF LOYALTY

SECTION 1. SELF-INTERESTED TRANSACTIONS

Gantler v. Stephens

Supreme Court of Delaware, 2009.
965 A.2d 695.

■ JACOBS, JUSTICE:

[The plaintiffs complain that the defendants, officers and directors of First Niles Financial, Inc. ("First Niles" or the "Company") breached their fiduciary duty in rejecting a valuable opportunity to sell the company. First Niles' sole asset was its 100 percent ownership of Home Federal Savings and Loan Association of Niles ("Home Federal" or the "Bank"). Because of the depressed local economy, there was little cause for optimism that the Bank could grow. Nonetheless, because of the prevailing brisk market for local banks like Home Federal, First Niles board believed it was a very good acquisition target. Hence, its board resolved in August 2004 to put the firm up for sale and at that meeting retained a local investment bank, Keefe, Bruyette & Woods (the "Financial Advisor") as well as a law firm, Silver, Freedman & n Taft ("Legal Counsel"). At the September board meeting, First Niles management advocated abandoning the search for an acquisition partner and proceeding with management's proposal that the company "privatize" itself which would include ending its Nasdaq listing, converting the bank from a federally chartered to a state chartered bank, and reincorporating in Maryland. No action on this proposal was taken by the board. Staying with its plan produced results; by December 2004, three potential suitors were identified, each offering a premium above First Niles public market share price. One bidder, Farmers National Banc Corp. ("Farmers") stated it had no intention of retaining First Niles board if its bid were accepted; the First Niles board did not further pursue this prospect. Two other bidders, Cortland Bankcorp ("Courtland") and First Place Financial Corp. ("First Place") were more delicate and each submitted due diligence requests. Unknown to the board, management (led by William L. Stephens, chairman of the board and CEO) was not responsive to the due diligence requests. This caused Cortland to withdraw its bid, leaving only First Place. Management then provided to First Place the requested materials for the bidder's due diligence. In the meantime, First Niles stock had declined in value, causing First Place to reduce its offer by approximately $1 per share; however, since First Niles stock had fallen the resulting bid price presented nearly twice the premium as First Place's first offer. At the March board meeting, Stephens informed the board of First Place's revised offer and suggested that consideration of the offer be put over until the next regularly scheduled board meeting. The Financial Advisor stated that First Place likely would withdraw its offer if the board did not act soon. Stephens, therefore, scheduled a special board meeting to consider the offer. Before that board meeting, First Place increased its bid slightly on a per share basis. At the March 8, 2005, special board meeting, Stephens circulated the Financial Advisor's report that described First Plac's bid in glowing terms. Nonetheless, the board voted 4 to 1 to reject the offer. The board thereupon discussed management's privatization plan and instructed Legal Counsel to further investigate the plan.]

C. The Reclassification Proposal

Five weeks later, on April 18, 2005, Stephens circulated to the Board members a document describing a proposed privatization of First Niles ("Privatization Proposal"). That Proposal recommended reclassifying the shares of holders of 300 or fewer shares of First Niles common stock into a new issue of Series A Preferred Stock on a one-to-one basis (the "Reclassification"). The Series A Preferred Stock would pay higher dividends and have the same liquidation rights as the common stock, but the Preferred holders would lose all voting rights except in the event of a proposed sale of the Company....

On April 20, 2005, the Board appointed Zuzolo to chair a special committee to investigate issues relating to the Reclassification, specifically: (1) reincorporating in a state other than Delaware, (2) changing the Bank's charter from a federal to a state charter, (3) deregistering from NASDAQ, and (4) delisting. However, Zuzolo passed away before any other directors were appointed to the special committee.

On December 5, 2005, Powell Goldstein, First Niles' outside counsel specially retained for the Privatization ("Outside Counsel"), orally presented the Reclassification proposal to the Board. The Board was not furnished any written materials. After the presentation, the Board voted 3 to 1 to direct Outside Counsel to proceed with the Reclassification program. Gantler cast the only dissenting vote.

Thereafter, the makeup of the Board changed. Shaker replaced Zuzolo in January of 2006, and Csontos replaced Gantler in April of 2006. From that point on, the Board consisted of Stephens, Kramer, Eddy, Shaker and Csontos.

On June 5, 2006, the Board determined, based on the advice of Management and First Niles' general counsel, that the Reclassification was fair both to the First Niles shareholders who would receive newly issued Series A Preferred Stock, and to those shareholders who would continue to hold First Niles common stock. On June 19, the Board voted unanimously to amend the Company's certificate of incorporation to reclassify the shares held by owners of 300 or fewer shares of common stock into shares of Series A Preferred Stock that would have the features and terms described in the Privatization Proposal.

D. The Reclassification Proxy and the Shareholder Vote

On June 29, 2006, the Board submitted a preliminary proxy to the United States Securities and Exchange Commission ("SEC")....

In the Reclassification Proxy, the Board represented that the proposed Reclassification would allow First Niles to "save significant legal, accounting and administrative expenses" relating to public disclosure and reporting requirements under the Exchange Act. The Proxy also disclosed the benefits of deregistration as including annual savings of $142,500 by reducing the number of common shareholders, $81,000 by avoiding Sarbanes–Oxley related compliance costs, and $174,000 by avoiding a one-time consulting fee to design a system to improve the Company's internal control structure. The negative features and estimated costs of the transaction included $75,000 in Reclassification-related expenses, reduced liquidity for both the to-be-reclassified preferred and common shares, and the loss of certain investor protections under the federal securities laws.

The Reclassification Proxy also disclosed alternative transactions that the Board had considered, including a cash-out merger, a reverse stock-split, an issue tender offer, expense reduction and a business combination. The Proxy stated that each of the directors and officers of First Niles had "a conflict of interest with respect to [the Reclassification] because he or she is in a position to structure it in such a way that benefits his or her interests differently from the interests of unaffiliated shareholders." The Proxy further disclosed that the Company had received one firm merger offer, and that "[a]fter careful deliberations, the board determined in its business judgment the proposal was not in the best interests of the Company or our shareholders and rejected the proposal."

The Company's shareholders approved the Reclassification on December 14, 2006. Taking judicial notice of the Company's ... [SEC filing], the trial court concluded that of the 1,384,533 shares outstanding and eligible to vote, 793,092 shares (or 57.3%) were voted in favor and 11,060 shares abstained. Of the unaffiliated shares, however, the proposal passed by a bare 50.28% majority vote.

E. Procedural History ...

The defendants moved to dismiss the complaint in its entirety....

We first consider the sufficiency of Count I as against the Director Defendants. That Count alleges that those defendants (together with non-party director Zuzolo) improperly rejected a value-maximizing bid from First Place and terminated the Sales Process. Plaintiffs allege that the defendants rejected the First Place bid to preserve personal benefits, including retaining their positions and pay as directors, as well as valuable outside business opportunities. The complaint further alleges that the Board failed to deliberate before deciding to reject the First Place bid and to terminate the Sales Process. Indeed, plaintiffs emphasize, the Board retained the Financial Advisor to advise it on the Sales Process, yet repeatedly disregarded the Financial Advisor's advice.

A board's decision not to pursue a merger opportunity is normally reviewed within the traditional business judgment framework. In that context the board is entitled to a strong presumption in its favor, because implicit in the board's statutory authority to propose a merger, is also the power to decline to do so.

Our analysis of whether the Board's termination of the Sales Process merits the business judgment presumption is two pronged. First, did the Board reach its decision in the good faith pursuit of a legitimate corporate interest? Second, did the Board do so advisedly? For the Board's decision here to be entitled to the business judgment presumption, both questions must be answered affirmatively. . . .

Here, the plaintiffs allege that the Director Defendants had a disqualifying self-interest because they were financially motivated to maintain the status quo. A claim of this kind must be viewed with caution, because to argue that directors have an entrenchment motive solely because they could lose their positions following an acquisition is, to an extent, tautological. By its very nature, a board decision to reject a merger proposal could always enable a plaintiff to assert that a majority of the directors had an entrenchment motive. For that reason, the plaintiffs must plead, in addition to a motive to retain corporate control, other facts sufficient to state a cognizable claim that the Director Defendants acted disloyally.

The plaintiffs have done that here. At the time the Sales Process was terminated, the Board members were Stephens, Kramer, Eddy, Zuzolo and Gander. Only Gander voted to accept the First Place merger bid. The pled facts are sufficient to establish disloyalty of at least three (*i.e.*, a majority) of the remaining directors, which suffices to rebut the business judgment presumption. First, the Reclassification Proxy itself admits that the Company's directors and officers had "a conflict of interest with respect to [the Reclassification] because he or she is in a position to structure it in a way that benefits his or her interests differently from the interest of the unaffiliated stockholders." Second, a director-specific analysis establishes (for Rule 12(b)(6) purposes) that a majority of the Board was conflicted.

Stephens: Aside from Stephens losing his long held positions as President, Chairman and CEO of First Niles and the Bank, the plaintiffs have alleged specific conduct from which a duty of loyalty violation can reasonably be inferred. Stephens never responded to Cortland's due diligence request. The Financial Advisor noted that Stephens' failure to respond had caused Cortland to withdraw its bid. Even after Cortland had offered First Niles an extension, Stephens did not furnish the necessary due diligence materials, nor did he inform the Board of these due diligence problems until after Cortland withdrew. Cortland had also explicitly stated in its bid letter that the incumbent Board would be terminated if Cortland acquired First Niles. From these alleged facts it may reasonably be inferred that what motivated Stephens' unexplained failure to respond promptly to Cortland's due diligence request was his personal financial interest, as opposed to the interests of the shareholders. That same inference can be drawn from Stephens' response to the First Place bid: Count I alleges that Stephens attempted to "sabotage" the First Place due diligence request in a manner similar to what occurred with Cortland.

Thus, the pled facts provide a sufficient basis to conclude, for purposes of a Rule 12(b)(6) motion to dismiss, that Stephens acted disloyally.

Kramer: Director Kramer's alleged circumstances establish a similar disqualifying conflict. Kramer was the President of William Kramer & Son, a heating and air conditioning company in Niles that provided heating and air conditioning services to the Bank. It is reasonable to infer that Kramer feared that if the Company were sold his firm would lose the Bank as a client. The loss of such a major client would be economically significant, because the complaint alleges that Kramer was a man of comparatively modest means, and that his company had few major assets and was completely leveraged. Because Kramer would suffer significant injury to his personal business interest if the Sales Process went forward, those pled facts are sufficient to support a reasonable inference that Kramer disloyally voted to terminate the Sales Process and support the Privatization Proposal.

Zuzolo: As earlier noted, Director Zuzolo was a principal in a small law firm in Niles that frequently provided legal services to First Niles and the Bank. Zuzolo was also the sole owner of a real estate title company that provided title services in nearly all of Home Federal's real estate transactions. Because Zuzolo, like Kramer, had a strong personal interest in having the Sales Process not go forward, the same reasonable inferences that flow from Kramer's personal business interest can be drawn in Zuzolo's case.

In summary, the plaintiffs have alleged facts sufficient to establish, for purposes of a motion to dismiss, that a majority of the First Niles Board acted disloyally. Because a cognizable claim of disloyalty rebuts the business judgment presumption, we need not reach the separate question of whether, in deciding to terminate the Sales Process, the Director Defendants acted advisedly (*i.e.*, with due care). Because the claim of disloyalty was subject to entire fairness review, the Court of Chancery erred in dismissing Count I as to the Director Defendants on the basis of the business judgment presumption. . . .

The Court of Chancery has held, and the parties do not dispute, that corporate officers owe fiduciary duties that are identical to those owed by corporate directors. That issue—whether or not officers owe fiduciary duties identical to those of directors—has been characterized as a matter of first impression for this Court. In the past, we have implied that officers of Delaware corporations, like directors, owe fiduciary duties of care and loyalty, and that the fiduciary duties of officers are the same as those of directors. We now explicitly so hold. The only question presented here is whether the complaint alleges sufficiently detailed acts of wrongdoing by Stephens and Safarek to state a claim that they breached their fiduciary duties as officers. We conclude that it does.

Stephens and Safarek were responsible for preparing the due diligence materials for the three firms that expressed an interest in acquiring First Niles. The alleged facts that make it reasonable to infer that Stephens violated his duty of loyalty as a director, also establish his violation of that same duty as an officer. It also is reasonably inferable that Safarek aided and abetted Stephens' separate loyalty breach. Safarek, as First Niles' Vice President and Treasurer, depended upon Stephen's continued good will to retain his job and the benefits that it generated. Because Safarek was in no position to act independently of Stephens, it may be inferred that by assisting Stephens to "sabotage" the due diligence process, Safarek also breached his duty of loyalty.

The Court of Chancery found otherwise. Having characterized Safarek's actions as causing "a delay of a matter of days, or at most a couple of weeks," the Vice Chancellor observed that he could not see how that "conceivably could be a breach of Safarek's fiduciary duties." This analysis is inappropriate on a motion to dismiss. The complaint alleges that Safarek never responded to Cortland's due diligence requests and that as a result, Cortland withdrew a competitive bid for First Niles. Those facts support a reasonable inference that Safarek and Stephens attempted to sabotage the Cortland and First Place due diligence process. On a motion to dismiss, the Court of Chancery was not free to disregard that reasonable inference, or to discount it by weighing it against other, perhaps contrary, inferences that might also be drawn. By dismissing Count I as applied to Stephens and Safarek as officers of First Niles, the trial court erred. . . .

III. *The Court of Chancery Erroneously Dismissed Count III of the Complaint*

Finally, we address the issues generated by the dismissal of Count III. That Count alleges that the defendants breached their duty of loyalty by recommending the Reclassification Proposal to the shareholders for purely self-interested reasons (to enlarge their ability to engage in stock buy-backs and to trigger their ESOP put and appraisal rights). The Court of Chancery determined that the relevant Board for analytical purposes was the June 2006 Board that voted to effect the Reclassification, because at any earlier time the Board could have decided to abandon the transaction. The Vice Chancellor then concluded that the complaint sufficiently alleged that a majority of the directors that approved the Reclassification Proposal lacked independence. Despite having so concluded, the court dismissed the claim on the ground that a disinterested majority of the shareholders had "ratified" the Reclassification by voting to approve it.

The plaintiffs claim that this ratification ruling is erroneous as a matter of law. They argue that because the Proxy disclosures were materially misleading, no fully informed shareholder vote took place. The plaintiffs also urge that in determining the number of unaffiliated shares that were voted, the Court of Chancery took improper judicial notice of shares owned by the defendants. The defendants respond that the Vice Chancellor's ratification ruling is correct and should be upheld. Alternatively, they argue that we should overturn the Vice Chancellor's determination that the Board had a disqualifying self-interest.

We conclude that the Court of Chancery legally erred in upholding Count III on shareholder ratification grounds, for two reasons. First, because a shareholder vote was required to amend the certificate of incorporation, that approving vote could not also operate to "ratify" the challenged conduct of the interested directors. Second, the adjudicated cognizable claim that the Reclassification Proxy contained a material misrepresentation, eliminates an essential predicate for applying the doctrine, namely, that the shareholder vote was fully informed.

A. *The Doctrine of Shareholder Ratification*

Under current Delaware case law, the scope and effect of the common law doctrine of shareholder ratification is unclear, making it difficult to apply that doctrine in a coherent manner. As the Court of Chancery has noted in *In re Wheelabrator Technologies, Inc., Shareholder Litigation*:

> [The doctrine of ratification] might be thought to lack coherence because the decisions addressing the effect of shareholder "ratification" have fragmented that subject into three distinct compartments, . . . In its "classic" . . . form, shareholder ratification describes the situation where shareholders approve board action that, legally speaking, could be accomplished without any shareholder approval. . . . "[C]lassic" ratification involves the voluntary addition of an independent layer of shareholder approval in circumstances where shareholder approval is not legally required. But "shareholder ratification" has also been used to describe the effect of an informed shareholder vote that was statutorily required for the transaction to have legal existence. . . . That [the Delaware courts] have used the same term is such highly diverse sets of factual circumstances, without regard to their possible functional differences, suggests that "shareholder ratification" has now acquired an expanded meaning intended to describe any approval of challenged board action by a fully informed vote of shareholders, irrespective of whether that shareholder vote is legally required for the transaction to attain legal existence.

663 A.2d 1194, 1202 and n.4 (Del. Ch. 1995) (citations omitted) . . . .

To restore coherence and clarity to this area of our law, we hold that the scope of the shareholder ratification doctrine must be limited to its so-called "classic" form; that is, to circumstances where a fully informed shareholder vote approves director action that does *not* legally require shareholder approval in order to become legally effective. Moreover, the only director action or conduct that can be ratified is that which the shareholders are specifically asked to approve. With one exception, the "cleansing" effect of such a ratifying shareholder vote is to subject the challenged director action to business judgment review, as opposed to "extinguishing" the claim altogether (*i.e.*, obviating all judicial review of the challenged action).

To the extent that *Smith v. Van Gorkom* holds otherwise, it is overruled. *488 A.2d 858, 889–90 (Del. 1985)*. The only species of claim that shareholder ratification can validly extinguish is a claim that the directors lacked the authority to take action that was later ratified. Nothing herein should be read as altering the well-established principle that void acts such as fraud, gift, waste and ultra vires acts cannot be ratified by a less than unanimous shareholder vote....

To avoid confusion about the doctrinal clarifications set forth in Part III A of this Opinion, we note that they apply only to the common law doctrine of shareholder ratification. They are not intended to affect or alter our jurisprudence governing the effect of an approving vote of disinterested shareholders under *8 Del. C. § 144*.

B. Applying the Doctrine to the Shareholders' Approval of the Reclassification Proposal

The Court of Chancery held that although Count III of the complaint pled facts establishing that the Reclassification Proposal was an interested transaction not entitled to business judgment protection, the shareholders' fully informed vote "ratifying" that Proposal reinstated the business judgment presumption. That ruling was legally erroneous, for several reasons. First, the ratification doctrine does not apply to transactions where shareholder approval is statutorily required. Here, the Reclassification could not become legally effective without a statutorily mandated shareholder vote approving the amendment to First Niles' certificate of incorporation. Second, because we have determined that the complaint states a cognizable claim that the Reclassification Proxy was materially misleading (*see* Part II, *supra*, of this Opinion), that precludes ruling at this procedural juncture, as a matter of law, that the Reclassification was fully informed. Therefore, the approving shareholder vote did not operate as a "ratification" of the challenged conduct in any legally meaningful sense....

We conclude that the Court of Chancery erroneously dismissed Count III of the complaint.

CONCLUSION

For the foregoing reasons, the judgment of the Court of Chancery is reversed as to all counts and remanded for proceedings consistent with the rulings in this Opinion

---

Marsh, Are Directors Trustees?—Conflicts of Interest and Corporate Morality

22 Bus.Law. 35, 36–43 (1966).

a. *Prohibition.*

In 1880 it could have been stated with confidence that in the United States the general rule was that any contract between a director and his corporation was voidable at the instance of the corporation or its shareholders, without regard to the fairness or unfairness of the transaction. This rule was stated in powerful terms by a number of highly regarded courts and judges in cases which arose generally out of the railroad frauds of the 1860's and 1870's....

Under this rule it mattered not the slightest that there was a majority of so-called disinterested directors who approved the contract. The courts stated that the corporation was entitled to the unprejudiced judgment and advice of all of its directors and therefore it did no good to say that the interested director did not participate in the making of the contract on behalf of the corporation. "... the very words in which he asserts his right declare his wrong; he ought to have participated...."[1] Furthermore, the courts said that it was impossible to measure the influence which one director might have over his associates, even though ostensibly abstaining from participation in the discussion or vote. "... a corporation, in order to defeat a contract entered into by directors, in which one or more of them had a private interest, is not bound to show that the influence of the director or directors having the private interest determined the action of the board. The law cannot accurately measure the influence of a trustee with his associates, nor will it enter into the inquiry...."[2]

Perhaps the strongest reason for this inflexibility of the law was given by the Maryland Supreme Court which stated that, when a contract is made with even one of the directors, "the remaining directors are placed in the embarrassing and invidious position of having to pass upon, scrutinize and check the transactions and accounts of one of their *own body, with* whom they are associated on terms of equality in the general management of all the affairs of the corporation."[3] Or, as Justice Davies of the New York Supreme Court expressed the same thought: "The moment the directors permit one or more of their number to deal with the property of the stockholders, they surrender their own independence and self control."[4]

This rule applied not only to individual contracts with directors, but also to the situation of interlocking directorates where even a minority of the boards were common to the two contracting corporations. Not only that, it was also applied to the situation where one corporation owned a majority of the stock of another and appointed its directors, even though they might not be the same men as sat on the board of the parent corporation....

This principle, absolutely inhibiting contracts between a corporation and its directors or any of them, appeared to be impregnable in 1880. It was stated in ringing terms by virtually every decided case, with arguments which seemed irrefutable, and it was sanctioned by age. As Justice Davies stated:

1. Stewart v. Lehigh Valley R.R. Co., 38 N.J.Law 505, at 523 (Ct.Err. & App.1875).

2. Munson v. Syracuse, G. & C. Ry. Co., 103 N.Y. 58, at 74, 8 N.E. 355, at 358 (1886).

3. Cumberland Coal and Iron Co. v. Parish, 42 Md. 598, at 606 (1875).

4. Cumberland Coal and Iron Co. v. Sherman, 30 Barb. 553, at 573 (N.Y.Sup.Ct.1859).

> To hold otherwise, would be to overturn principles of equity which have been regarded as well settled since the days of Lord Keeper Bridgman, in the 22nd of Charles Second, to the present time—principles enunciated and enforced by Hardwicke, Thurlow, Loughborough, Eldon, Cranworth, Story and Kent, and which the highest courts in our country have declared to be founded on immutable truth and justice, and to stand upon our great moral obligation to refrain from placing ourselves in relations which excite a conflict between self interest and integrity.

Thirty years later this principle was dead.

b. *Approval by a disinterested majority of the board.*

It could have been stated with reasonable confidence in 1910 that the general rule was that a contract between a director and his corporation was valid if it was approved by a disinterested majority of his fellow directors and was not found to be unfair or fraudulent by the court if challenged; but that a contract in which a majority of the board was interested was voidable at the instance of the corporation or its shareholders without regard to any question of fairness.

One searches in vain in the decided cases for a reasoned defense of this change in legal philosophy, or for the slightest attempt to refute the powerful arguments which had been made in support of the previous rule. Did the courts discover in the last quarter of the Nineteenth Century that greed was no longer a factor in human conduct? If so, they did not share the basis of this discovery with the public; nor did they humbly admit their error when confronted with the next wave of corporate frauds arising out of the era of the formation of the "trusts" during the 1890's and early 1900's. . . .

The only explanation which seems to have been given for this change in position was the technical one that a trustee, while forbidden to deal with himself in connection with the trust property, could deal directly with the cestui que trust if he made full disclosure and took no unfair advantage; and that the case of a director who abstained from representing the corporation but dealt in his personal capacity with a majority of disinterested directors was properly analogized to a trustee dealing with the cestui que trust. As the Texas court said:[5]

> . . . we think it is not true that one who holds the position of director is incapable, under all circumstances, of divesting himself of his representative character in a particular transaction, and dealing with the corporation through others competent to represent it, as other trustees may deal directly with the beneficiaries. . . . [T]he company is represented by those who alone can act for it, and, if they are disinterested, he can, we think, deal with them as any other trustee can deal with the cestui que trust, if he makes a full disclosure of all facts known to him about the subject, takes no advantage of his position, deals honestly and

5. Tenison v. Patton, 95 Tex. 284, at 292–93, 67 S.W. 92, at 95 (1902).

openly, and concludes a contract fair and beneficial to the company.

But in no case is there any discussion or attempted refutation of the reasons previously given by the courts as to why it is impossible, in such a situation, for any director to be disinterested. Some courts seem simply to admit that the practice has grown too widespread for them to cope with. In *South Side Trust Co. v. Washington Tin Plate Co.* the Supreme Court of Pennsylvania said:[6] "The interests of corporations are sometimes so interwoven that it is desirable to have joint representatives in their respective managements, and at any rate it is a not uncommon and [therefore?] not unlawful practice." . . .

Under the rule that a disinterested majority of the directors must approve a transaction with one of their number, the question arose whether this meant a disinterested quorum (i.e., normally a majority of the whole board) or merely a disinterested majority of a quorum, so that the interested director or directors could be counted to make up the quorum. Virtually all of the cases held that the interested director could not be counted for quorum purposes. As the California court said, the interested director for this purpose was "as much a stranger to the board as if he had never been elected a director. . . ."[7]

c. *Judicial review of the fairness of the transaction.*

By 1960 it could be said with some assurance that the general rule was that no transaction of a corporation with any or all of its directors was automatically voidable at the suit of a shareholder, whether there was a disinterested majority of the board or not; but that the courts would review such a contract and subject it to rigid and careful scrutiny, and would invalidate the contract if it was found to be unfair to the corporation. . . .

Lewis v. S.L. & E., Inc.

United States Court of Appeals, Second Circuit, 1980.
629 F.2d 764.

■ Before TIMBERS and KEARSE, CIRCUIT JUDGES, and LASKER, DISTRICT JUDGE.

■ KEARSE, CIRCUIT JUDGE:

This case arises out of an intra-family dispute over the management of two closely-held affiliated corporations. Plaintiff Donald E. Lewis ("Donald"), a shareholder of S.L. & E., Inc. ("SLE"), appeals from judgments entered against him in the United States District Court for the Western District of New York, Harold P. Burke, Judge, after a bench trial of his derivative claim against directors of SLE, and of a claim asserted against him by the other corporation, Lewis General Tires, Inc. ("LGT"), which intervened in the suit. The defendants Alan

6. 252 Pa. 237 at 241, 97 A. 450 at 451 (1916).

7. Curtis v. Salmon River Hydraulic Gold-Mining & Dutch Co., . . . 10 Cal. at 349, 62 P. at 554.

E. Lewis ("Alan"), Leon E. Lewis, Jr. ("Leon, Jr."), and Richard E. Lewis ("Richard"), are the brothers of Donald; they were, at pertinent times herein, directors of SLE and officers, directors and shareholders of LGT. Donald charged that his brothers had wasted the assets of SLE by causing SLE to lease business premises to LGT from 1966 to 1972 at an unreasonably low rental. LGT was permitted to intervene in the action, and filed a complaint seeking specific performance of an agreement by Donald to sell his SLE stock to LGT in 1972. The district court held that Donald had failed to prove waste by the defendant directors, and entered judgment in their favor. The court also awarded attorneys' fees to the defendant directors and to SLE, and granted LGT specific performance of Donald's agreement to sell his SLE stock.

On appeal, Donald argues that the district court improperly allocated to him the burden of proving his claims of waste, and that since defendants failed to prove that the transactions in question were fair and reasonable, he was entitled to judgment. Donald also argues that the awards of attorneys' fees were improper. We agree with each of these contentions, and therefore reverse and remand.

I

For many years Leon Lewis, Sr., the father of Donald and the defendant directors, was the principal shareholder of SLE and LGT. LGT, formed in 1933, operated a tire dealership in Rochester, New York. SLE, formed in 1943, owned the land and complex of buildings at 260 East Avenue in Rochester. This property was SLE's only significant asset. Prior to 1956 LGT occupied SLE's premises without benefit of a lease; the rent paid was initially $200 per month, and had increased over the years to $800 per month by 1956, when additional parcels were added. On February 28, 1956, SLE granted LGT a 10–year lease on the newly expanded property ("the Property"), for a rent of $1200 per month, or $14,400 per year. Under the terms of the lease, SLE was responsible for payment of real estate taxes on the Property, while all other current expenses were to be borne by the tenant, LGT.[1]

In 1962, Leon Lewis, Sr., transferred his SLE stock, 90 shares in all, to his six children (defendants Richard, Alan and Leon, Jr., plaintiff Donald, and two daughters, Margaret and Carol), giving 15 shares to each.[2] At that time Richard, Alan and Leon, Jr., were already shareholders, officers and directors of LGT. Contemporaneously with their receipt of SLE stock, all six of the children entered into a "shareholders' agreement" with LGT, under which each child who was not a shareholder of LGT on June 1, 1972 would be required to sell his or her SLE shares to LGT, within 30 days of that date, at a price equal to the book value of the SLE stock as of June 1, 1972.[3]

---

1. It appears that SLE was also responsible for payments due on a mortgage on the Property. In addition, LGT charged SLE for the costs of certain capital improvements, such as the major structural repairs to the principal building's facade, carried out in 1969.

2. SLE had 150 shares outstanding, and each child thus received a ten percent interest. At the same time LGT purchased the remaining 60 outstanding shares from the elder Lewis's business partner, Henry Etsberger.

3. The agreement specified procedures by which the book value, and hence the price of the shares, would be determined.

LGT's lease on the SLE property expired on February 28, 1966. At that time the directors of SLE were Richard, Alan, Leon, Jr., Leon, Sr., and Henry Etsberger; these five were also the directors of LGT. In 1966 Alan owned 44% of LGT, Richard owned 30%, Leon, Jr., owned 19%, and Leon, Sr., owned 7%. From 1967 to 1972 Richard owned 61% of LGT and Leon, Jr., owned the remaining 39%. When the lease expired in 1966, no new lease was entered into. LGT nonetheless continued to occupy the property and to pay SLE at the old rate, $14,400 per year. According to the defendants' testimony at trial, there was never any thought or discussion among the SLE directors of entering into a new lease or of increasing the rent. Richard testified: "We never gave consideration to a new lease." From all that appears, the defendant directors viewed SLE as existing purely for the benefit of LGT. Richard testified, for example, that although real estate taxes rose sharply during the period 1966–1971, from approximately $7,800 to more than $11,000, to be paid by SLE out of its constant $14,400 rental income, raising the rent was never mentioned. He testified that SLE was "only a shell to protect the operating company [LGT]." When this suit was commenced there had not been a formal meeting of either the shareholders or the directors of SLE since 1962. Richard, Alan and Leon, Jr., had largely ignored SLE's separate corporate existence[4] and disregarded the fact that SLE had shareholders who were not shareholders of LGT and who therefore could not profit from actions that used SLE solely for the benefit of LGT.

Neither Donald nor his sisters ever owned LGT stock. As the June 1972 date approached for the required sale of their SLE stock to LGT, Donald apparently came to believe that SLE's book value was lower than it should have been. He sought SLE financial information from Richard, who had been president of SLE since 1967.[5] Richard refused to provide information. Donald therefore refused to sell his SLE shares in 1972,[6] and commenced this shareholders' derivative action in the district court in August 1973, basing jurisdiction on diversity of citizenship. The sole claim raised in the complaint was that the

---

4. For example, Richard's testimony includes the following statements:

Q Mr. Lewis, you have always looked at these two corporations as being one and the same, haven't you, Lewis General Tires and S.L. & E.?

A Yes.

* * *

I never really got into S.L. & E. at all. (Tr. 6/21/78, at 972–73.)

* * *

I don't think I ever looked at an operating statement of S.L. & E. seriously. (*Id.* at 991.)

* * *

I had very little to do with S.L. & E. (Tr. 7/28/78, at 80.)

Alan testified that at no time after 1964 did he participate in any discussions of any increase in rent for SLE. (*Id.* at 160, 164.)

And Leon, Jr., testified, "I didn't have anything to do with running S.L. & E. . . . " (*Id.* at 230.)

5. It does not appear that SLE paid salaries to any of its officers or directors.

6. Donald's sisters Carol and Margaret sold their SLE shares to LGT in 1972 and 1973 respectively. Alan, who had sold his LGT stock in 1967, sold his SLE stock to LGT in 1972.

defendant directors had wasted the assets of SLE by "grossly undercharging" LGT for the latter's occupancy and use of the Property. Although the complaint charged such mismanagement for the period 1962 to 1973, plaintiff subsequently limited this claim to the period between February 28, 1966, the date on which the lease expired,[7] and June 1, 1972, the date contractually set for valuation of the SLE shares which plaintiff had agreed to sell to LGT. LGT intervened and demanded specific performance of Donald's agreement to sell his SLE stock. Donald did not contest his ultimate obligation to sell, but took the position that since the book value of the shares would be increased if he prevailed on his derivative claim, specific performance should be granted only after adjudication of that claim.

There ensured an eight-day bench trial, at which plaintiff sought to prove, by the testimony of several expert witnesses, that the fair rental value of the Property was greater than the $14,400 per year that SLE had been paid by LGT. Defendants sought to show that the rental paid was reasonable, by offering evidence concerning the financial straits of LGT, the cost to LGT of operating the Property, the general economic decline of the East Avenue neighborhood, and rentals paid on two other properties in that neighborhood. LGT presented expert testimony that the value of plaintiff's stock as of June 1972, assuming a successful defense of the derivative claims, was $15,650.

The district court subsequently filed lengthy and detailed findings of fact and conclusions of law. Many of the court's findings went to the validity and probative value of the testimony given by plaintiff's expert witnesses, and the court ultimately declined to credit that testimony. On this basis, the court held that Donald had failed to establish the rental value of the Property during the period at issue, and that defendants were therefore entitled to judgment on the derivative claims. Implicit in the district court's ruling, granting judgment for defendants upon plaintiff's failure to prove waste, was a determination that plaintiff bore the burden of proof on that issue. The court also ruled that LGT was entitled to specific performance of Donald's agreement to sell his SLE stock, and that Donald was not entitled to recover attorneys' fees from SLE, but that SLE and the individual defendants were entitled to attorneys' fees from Donald. This appeal followed.

II

Turning first to the question of burden of proof, we conclude that the district court erred in placing upon plaintiff the burden of proving waste. Because the directors of SLE were also officers, directors and/or shareholders of LGT, the burden was on the defendant directors to demonstrate that the transactions between SLE and LGT were fair and reasonable. New York Business Corporation Law ("BCL") § 713(b) (McKinney Supp.1979) (eff. September 1, 1971); BCL § 713(a)(3)

---

7. Donald was not a shareholder of SLE in 1956 when the lease was entered into and hence had no standing to challenge its terms. BCL § 626(b); *Bernstein v. Polo Fashions, Inc.*, 55 A.D.2d 530, 389 N.Y.S.2d 368 (1st Dep't 1976).

(McKinney 1963) (repealed as of September 1, 1971); *see Cohen v. Ayers,* 596 F.2d 733, 739–40 (7th Cir.1979) (construing current BCL § 713); *Remillard Brick Co. v. Remillard–Dandini Co.,* 109 Cal. App.2d 405, 241 P.2d 66, 75 (1952) (construing California Corporations Code § 820, upon which the prior BCL § 713 was patterned).

Under normal circumstances the directors of a corporation may determine, in the exercise of their business judgment, what contracts the corporation will enter into and what consideration is adequate, without review of the merits of their decisions by the courts. The business judgment rule places a heavy burden on shareholders who would attack corporate transactions. *Galef v. Alexander,* 615 F.2d 51, 57–58 (2d Cir.1980); *Auerbach v. Bennett,* 47 N.Y.2d 619, 629, 419 N.Y.S.2d 920, 926, 393 N.E.2d 994, 1000 (1979); 3A Fletcher, *Cyclopedia of the Law of Private Corporations* § 1039 (perm. ed. 1975). But the business judgment rule presupposes that the directors have no conflict of interest. When a shareholder attacks a transaction in which the directors have an interest other than as directors of the corporation, the directors may not escape review of the merits of the transaction. At common law such a transaction was voidable unless shown by its proponent to be fair, and reasonable to the corporation.[11] BCL § 713, in both its current and its prior versions, carries forward this common law principle, and provides special rules for scrutiny of a transaction between the corporation and an entity in which its directors are directors or officers or have a substantial financial interest....

The current version of § 713,* which became effective on September 1, 1971, and governs at least so much of the dealing between SLE and LGT as occurred after that date, expressly provides that a contract between a corporation and an entity in which its directors are interested may be set aside unless the proponent of the contract "shall establish affirmatively that the contract or transaction was fair and reasonable as to the corporation at the time it was approved by the board...." § 713(b). Thus when the transaction is challenged in a derivative action against the interested directors, they have the burden of proving that the transaction was fair and reasonable to the corporation. *Cohen v. Ayers, supra.*

The same was true under the predecessor to § 713(b), former § 713(a)(3), which was in effect prior to September 1, 1971....

During the entire period 1966–1972, Richard, Alan and Leon, Jr., were directors of both SLE and LGT;[14] there were no SLE directors who were not also directors of LGT. Richard, Alan and Leon, Jr., were all shareholders of LGT in 1966, and from 1967 to 1972 Richard and Leon, Jr., were the sole shareholders of LGT. Under BCL § 713, therefore, Richard, Alan and Leon, Jr., had the burden of proving that

11. *E.g., Geddes v. Anaconda Copper Co.,* 254 U.S. 590, 599, 41 S.Ct. 209, 65 L.Ed. 425 (1921)....

* *See* New York Bus.Corp.Law § 713 in the Statutory Supplement. (Footnote by ed.)

14. Alan ceased to be a director in November 1972; Leon, Jr., ceased to be a director in 1977. Richard remains a director.

$14,400 was a fair and reasonable annual rent for the SLE property for the period February 28, 1966 through June 1, 1972.

Our review of the record convinces us that defendants failed to carry their burden. At trial, there was no direct testimony as to what would have been a fair rental during the relevant period, *i.e.,* 1966 to 1972, and the evidence that was introduced fell far short of establishing that $14,400 was a fair annual rental value for those years.

Quite clearly Richard, Alan and Leon, Jr., had made no effort to determine contemporaneously what rental would be fair during the years 1966–1972. Their view was that the rent should simply cover expenses and that SLE existed for the benefit of LGT.[15] During this period no appraisals were made; no attempts were made to sell or rent the Property; no thought whatever was given to whether $14,400 was a fair and reasonable rent even when real estate taxes had risen to consume nearly all of that amount.

Defendants offered instead evidence of rents paid on other properties. Among their best evidence was the expert testimony of Harvey Rosenbloom, a real estate appraiser. Rosenbloom testified that two other East Avenue buildings, which the district court found to be comparable to the 260 East Avenue premises, were leased at lower per-square-foot rentals than was paid by LGT to SLE. However, as to one of these properties, Rosenbloom testified only to rent paid in 1973 and 1974, and did not consider the 1966–1972 period. As to the other property, Rosenbloom described a fifteen year lease that was entered into in 1961. This testimony, while perhaps not wholly irrelevant to the issues in this suit, fell far short of demonstrating what rental the Property could have fetched in 1966, or in any other of the relevant years. Indeed, Rosenbloom himself testified that rental value could well be different for each year of the period. Thus, rentals that Rosenbloom testified were agreed to in 1961 or 1973 might well have been unfair in 1966 or 1967. This evidence thus could not support a finding that defendants acted fairly in maintaining an annual rental of $14,400 during the years from 1966 to 1972.[16]

Defendants also produced considerable evidence that over the relevant period, the East End neighborhood had been on an economic decline; that businesses had been leaving the area; that urban renewal projects and increased crime had depressed property values there; and that the area had, in general, become a less desirable place to do business. There was also evidence of specific developments that had an adverse effect on the Property: for example, the street running along one side of the Property was made a one-way street, thus limiting customers' access to LGT's premises. The district court credit-

---

15. *See* footnote 4 *supra,* and accompanying text.

16. Defendant Richard E. Lewis testified that defendants tried, without success, to sell the Property in 1975, listing it with a realtor for $200,000. In addition he testified that an effort was made to rent the Property in 1973, and that only one offer, for $700 per month, was forthcoming. Since these efforts were made in 1973 and 1975, this evidence, like the evidence as to rentals of other property, was too remote in time to establish a fair rental value, especially as to the earlier years of the 1966–1972 period.

ed all of this testimony, and it is fair to say that defendants proved that there was a general downward trend in the value of the Property. However, as noted above, defendants did not establish what was a fair rental value for the Property in 1966. Absent such a point of reference, a general downward trend in value is of no assistance in determining whether the rental actually paid was fair and reasonable during the ensuing years.

Moreover, working in reverse, some of defendants' own evidence as to the value of the Property at the end of the relevant period suggested that $14,400 was less than a fair rental in 1966, and that the figure of $38,099, estimated by plaintiff's expert, was perhaps not far off the mark.[17] First, there was a variety of evidence suggesting that in 1972 the Property was worth more than $200,000. An appraisal by defense witness Harold Grunert in 1972 set the fair market value of the Property as of June 30, 1972, at $220,000. In 1972 Leon, Jr., had offered personally to buy the Property for $200,000, an offer which Richard had rejected.[18] And in 1971, Richard had informed Donald that evaluations by another appraiser, Harold Galloway, had set the value of the Property at $200,000 and $236,000. Second, defendants' expert witness Rosenbloom, asked what he would consider a fair rent for the property, given Grunert's 1972 valuation of $220,000, stated that ten percent of the value would be inadequate and that fifteen to seventeen percent would be closer to adequate. Fifteen percent of $220,000 would have yielded a rent of $33,000 on the basis of the 1972 valuation. Grunert's own expert testimony was entirely consistent with this. While he had made no estimate as to the fair rental value of the property for 1966–1972, he opined that a fair rental as of June 30, 1972, would be $20–21,000 with the tenant paying all expenses including real estate taxes. According to Richard, SLE's real estate taxes in 1972 were about $12,000. Thus Grunert's testimony, too, suggests about $33,000 as the fair rental value in 1972. Finally, consistent with their view of the general downward economic trend, Richard and Alan conceded that, whatever the Property was worth in 1972, it was worth more in 1966.[19] Thus the evidence presented by defendants, far from carrying their burden of showing that $14,400 was a fair and reasonable annual rental in 1966–1972, suggested that the fair rental value of the Property throughout that period exceeded $33,000 per year.

The defendants argued, however, that LGT could not have afforded to pay SLE rent higher than $14,400. They produced evidence designed to show that LGT had made little profit; that this low profitability was due to the expenses of maintenance and upkeep of the 260 East Avenue property; and that LGT therefore would not have been able to pay a higher rent to SLE. The district court credited this evidence, finding that LGT had "experienced a number of years of very

---

17. Plaintiff's expert made his evaluation as of February 1973. He did not make any evaluation for the period 1966–1972.

18. Leon, Jr., had just been fired from LGT by Richard.

19. Leon, Jr., did not know whether the value had decreased from 1966 to 1972, but did not believe it had risen.

severe losses," that during the period from 1962–1973, LGT's overall profit was only $53,876, and that payment of rent at the rate of $39,099 per year during this period could have led to the "demise" of LGT. These findings have only a distorted relationship to this lawsuit.

The period in issue here is 1966–1972. The only "severe" losses shown, totaling nearly $83,000, occurred in 1963 and 1973. Their inclusion in the computation of what LGT could afford to pay in 1966–1972 was patently unfair. In fact LGT's only unprofitable year during the period in issue was 1969 when its loss was small: $1,168. LGT's after-tax profits in 1966–1972 in fact totaled $102,963, or an average of $14,709 per year. Thus, even on paper, LGT could have "afforded" to double its rent payments to SLE during the period in question.

Moreover, the proposition that LGT could not afford to pay as rent more than what its own books showed as profits ignores the fact that LGT was owned and managed by members of the Lewis family, some of whom were also employees of that corporation. It is entirely possible that these family members granted to themselves unusually high salaries or other perquisites, thus reducing LGT's paper profits. For example, in 1966 Richard's salary was approximately $21,000; Leon, Jr.'s compensation was $3,000 salary plus commissions. In 1967, LGT acquired all of Alan's LGT stock; and Richard and Leon, Jr., acquired all of the LGT stock of their father, agreeing to pay the purchase price over a ten-year period. Richard and Leon, Jr., thus became LGT's only shareholders, and their LGT salaries were immediately increased by a total of $23,000 per year (Richard's salary went from $21,000 to $36,000; Leon, Jr.'s went from $3,000 to $11,000), to cover the cost of the LGT stock they had just acquired.[20] Defendants bore the burden of proof on the question of a fair and reasonable rental; if they would rely on the proposition that LGT was unable to pay more, it was incumbent on them to demonstrate the fairness of the management and the reasonableness of the conduct of LGT's affairs. It does not appear that they made any effort to do so.

Finally, even if we were to assume that LGT's financial records provided a fair basis for evaluating the SLE–LGT transactions, defendants would not have carried their burden of proof. Defendants did not demonstrate that SLE could not have found some other tenant, stronger financially than LGT, which would have been willing and able to pay a higher rental. Even given the general downward trend of the East Avenue neighborhood, it is entirely possible that at least during the early years of the 1966–1972 period, such a tenant might have been secured. No effort was made during that period to rent to anyone other than LGT.

We conclude, therefore, that defendants failed to prove that the rental paid by LGT to SLE for the years 1966–1972 was fair and reasonable. Thus, Donald is not required to sell his SLE shares to LGT without such upward adjustment in the June 1, 1972, book value of

20. Richard had no doubt he could have paid for his newly acquired shares without the increase in his LGT salary. Leon, Jr., apparently lacked other resources from which to pay for the LGT stock (at least after he was fired from LGT in 1972).

SLE as may be necessary to reflect the amount by which the fair rental value of the Property exceeded $14,400 in any of the years 1966–1972....

We remand to the district court (a) for the entry of judgment in favor of SLE against Richard, Alan and Leon, Jr., jointly and severally, in such amount as the district court shall determine to be equal to the amounts by which the annual fair rental value of the Property exceeded $14,400 in the period February 28, 1966–June 1, 1972, (b) for an accounting as to the value of Donald's SLE shares as of June 1, 1972, in light of such judgment, (c) for an order, following such accounting, of specific performance of the shareholders' agreement, and (d) for such other proceedings as are not inconsistent with this opinion.

NOTE ON REMEDIES FOR VIOLATION OF THE DUTY OF LOYALTY

The traditional remedies for violation of the duty of loyalty are restitutionary in nature. For example, if a director has engaged in improper self-dealing with the corporation, normally the remedy is rescission or, if rescission is not feasible, an accounting for the difference between the contract price and a fair price. Similarly, if an officer has improperly appropriated a corporate opportunity (see Section 4, infra), normally the remedy is to impose a constructive trust in the corporation's favor, conditioned on reimbursement by the corporation of the officer's outlay in acquiring the opportunity.

The result of this restitutionary theory of remedies is that as a practical matter the legal sanctions for violation of the duty of loyalty are usually, although not invariably, much less severe than the legal sanctions for violation of the duty of care. If D, a director or officer, violates his duty of care, he must pay damages although he made no gain from his wrongful action. This leaves D much worse off than he was before the wrong. In contrast, if D violates his duty of loyalty, under a restitutionary remedy he need only return a gain that he was not entitled to in the first place. This simply places D where he was before committing the wrong.

Indeed, putting aside important nonlegal remedies, such as discharge and damage to reputation, if a director or officer, D, is totally immoral, he would conclude that under a strictly restitutionary regime it would normally pay him to engage in a course of wrongful self-interested transactions. The reason is this: Some of the wrongful transactions may remain undiscovered. In that case, D will retain his wrongful gains. Where D's wrongdoing is discovered, he will only be required to surrender his wrongful gains. Therefore, if D engages in enough transactions he will come out ahead.

In some cases, however, the remedies for violation of the duty of loyalty may make the director or officer worse off than he was before the wrong.

(i) Where the director or officer sells property to the corporation at an unfairly high price, and the value of the property later drops below its fair value at the time of the transaction, rescission may leave him worse off than if he had sold the property to a third party. For instance, suppose that in 2011, D sells property to his corporation for $110,000 when it had a fair value of only $100,000. In 2011, the corporation discovers the wrong and rescinds the transaction: The corporation retransfers the property to D, and D returns $100,000 to the corporation. Meanwhile, the market has fallen and the property is only worth $70,000. If D had sold the property in 2010 to a third party for $100,000, the third party would not be able to rescind. Thus D is $30,000 worse off than if he had not engaged in wrongful self-dealing. A comparable result may obtain where D buys property from the corporation, the market rises, and the corporation rescinds.

(ii) A director or officer who violates the duty of fair dealing may be required to repay the corporation any salary he earned during the relevant period, in addition to making restitution of his wrongful gain. This remedy was granted, for example, in American Timber & Trading Co. v. Niedermeyer, 276 Or. 1135, 558 P.2d 1211 (1976), a case in which the fiduciary had depleted the corporation's assets by a series of unfair deals. The court there said:

> The remedy of restoration of compensation is an equitable principle and its applicability is dependent upon the individual facts of each case.... The general rule, however, is that a corporate officer who engages in activities which constitute either a breach of his duty of loyalty or a willful breach of his contract of employment is not entitled to any compensation for services rendered during that period of time even though part of those services may have been properly performed....

(iii) Courts have sometimes awarded punitive damages against directors or officers who have breached their duty of loyalty. See, e.g., Holden v. Construction Machinery Co., 202 N.W.2d 348 (Iowa 1972); Rowen v. Le Mars Mutual Insurance Co. of Iowa, 282 N.W.2d 639, 662 (Iowa 1979). In Goben v. Barry, 234 Kan. 721, 728, 676 P.2d 90, 97–98 (1984), the court said, "Punitive damages may be awarded in the trial court's discretion whenever there is proof of fraud.... Fraud itself is difficult to define, but it has been held [that] fraud 'in its general sense, is deemed to comprise anything calculated to deceive, including all acts, omissions, and concealments involving a breach of legal or equitable duty, trust, or confidence justly reposed, resulting in damage to another....' Barry [the defendant] concealed his withdrawals [from the company], denied Goben [the plaintiff] had any interest in the company and ousted him, all to Goben's damage. That is sufficient evidence of fraud. The trial court did not err in awarding punitive damages."

(iv) ALI, Principles of Corporate Governance § 7.18(d) provides that a director or officer who violates the duty of fair dealing should normally be required to pay the counsel fees and other expenses incurred by the corporation in establishing the violation.

Talbot v. James

Supreme Court of South Carolina, 1972.
259 S.C. 73, 190 S.E.2d 759.

■ MOSS, CHIEF JUSTICE:

This equitable action was brought by C.N. Talbot and Lula E. Talbot, appellants herein, against W.A. James, individually, and as President of Chicora Apartments, Inc., and Chicora Apartments, Inc., respondents herein, for an accounting. In the complaint it is alleged that W.A. James, as an officer and director of the Corporation, violated his fiduciary relationship to the Corporation and the appellants as stockholders thereof, by diverting specific funds to himself.

The respondents, by answer, denied the allegations of the complaint and alleged that W.A. James had received no funds from the Corporation except for the sums paid for the erection of Chicora Apartments, pursuant to a contract between Chicora Apartments, Inc., and the said W.A. James.

The case was referred to the Master in Equity for Horry County, who after taking the testimony, filed a report in which he found that W.A. James was not entitled to general overhead expense and profits arising out of the construction contract with Chicora Apartments, Inc., and recommended judgment in favor of Chicora Apartments, Inc., against him in the amount of $25,025.31.

The respondents timely appealed from the recommendations contained in the Report of the Master. The appeal was heard by the Honorable Dan F. Laney, Jr., presiding judge, and he issued his order reversing the findings of the Master and ordered judgment in favor of the respondents. This appeal followed.

This being an equity case and the Master and the Circuit Judge having disagreed and made contrary findings on the material issues in the case, this Court has jurisdiction to consider the evidence and make findings in accordance with our view of the preponderance or greater weight of the evidence. . . .

Lula E. Talbot owned a tract of land fronting on U.S. Highway 17, in Myrtle Beach, South Carolina. The title thereto was conveyed to her by her husband, C.N. Talbot. The appellants were approached by W.A. James with a proposal that the tract of land be used for the erection thereon of an apartment complex. After preliminary talks and negotiations, the parties on January 12, 1963, entered into a written agreement thereabout. Basically, the parties agreed to form a Corporation to construct and operate an apartment complex. Lula E. Talbot was to convey to said Corporation the tract of land owned by her and W.A. James agreed, as set forth in paragraph 5, of said contract,

"To promote the project aforementioned and shall be responsible for the planning, architectural work, construction, landscaping, legal fees, and loan processing of the entire project, same to contain at least fifty (50) one, two and three room air conditioned apartments for customer as approved by FHA appraisers."

It was further agreed that upon the formation of the Corporation that the appellants were to receive 50% of the stock of the Corporation in consideration for their transfer of the land to it. This was to be the absolute limit of the contribution of the appellants. W.A. James was to receive 50% of the stock of the Corporation in consideration of his efforts on its behalf.

It appears, that after the aforementioned contract was entered into, that W.A. James obtained the services of an architectural firm on a contingency basis and preliminary plans and sketches of the proposed apartment complex were made by such firm. James was also successful in obtaining commitments from the Federal Housing Administration and from an acceptable mortgagee with regard to financing. These commitments having been obtained, a corporation was formed to be known as Chicora Apartments, Inc., and a charter was duly issued by the Secretary of State on November 5, 1963.

Pursuant to the terms of the agreement dated January 12, 1963, 20 shares of no par value capital stock were issued, with W.A. James receiving 10 shares, C.N. Talbot one share and Lula E. Talbot 9 shares. At an organizational meeting of the corporation W.A. James was elected president, his wife, B.N. James, was elected secretary, C.N. Talbot was elected vice president, and Lula E. Talbot was elected treasurer. W.A. James and C.N. Talbot were elected as directors of the Corporation.

At a meeting of the Board of Directors held on November 5, 1963, a resolution was adopted accepting the offer of Lula E. Talbot to transfer the tract of land in question to Chicora Apartments, Inc., in exchange for 10 shares of the no par value capital stock thereof. In the said resolution, it was declared that the said property, to be so transferred, was of a value of $44,000.00. At the same meeting, a resolution was adopted accepting the offer of W.A. James to transfer to Chicora Apartments, Inc., in exchange for 10 shares of the no par value stock thereof, at a valuation of $44,000.00 the following:

"1. FHA Commitment issued pursuant to Title 2, Section 207 of the National Housing Act, whereby the FHA agrees to insure a mortgage loan in the amount of $850,700.00, on a parcel of land in Myrtle Beach, South Carolina, more particularly described in Schedule 'A' hereto attached, provided 66 apartment units are constructed thereon in accordance with plans and specifications as prepared by Lyles, Bissett, Carlisle & Wolff, Architects–Engineers, of Columbia, South Carolina.

"2. Commitment from United Mortgagee Servicing Corp. agreeing to make a mortgage loan on said property in the amount

> of $850,700.00 and also commitment from said mortgagee to make an interim construction loan in an identical amount.
>
> "3. Certain contracts and agreements which W.A. James over the past two years have worked out and developed in connection with the architectural and construction services required for said project.
>
> "4. The use of the finances and credit of W.A. James during the past two years (and including the construction period) in order to make it possible to proceed with the project."

The day following the election of the officers and the issuance of the capital stock, the Board of Directors of Chicora Apartments, Inc., met in Columbia, South Carolina, and passed a resolution authorizing the Corporation to borrow from United Mortgagee Servicing Corporation of Norfolk, Virginia, the sum of $850,700.00, upon the terms stated, said loan to be insured with the Federal Housing Administration. It was further resolved:

> "That the President of the corporation, W.A. James, be authorized, empowered and directed to make, execute and deliver such documents and instruments as are required by the F.H.A. and the lender, in order to close the loan transaction; said documents including but not limited to, note, mortgage, Building Loan Agreement, Construction Contract, Architect's Agreement, Mortgagor's Certificate, Regulatory Agreement, Mortgagor's Oath and Agreement and Certificate."

The record shows that on November 6, 1963, James Construction Company entered into a construction contract with Chicora Apartments, Inc. This contract was executed by W.A. James, as president, and attested by B.N. James, secretary, on behalf of Chicora Apartments, Inc., and by W.A. James, sole proprietor, for James Construction Company. The contract sum was to be the actual cost of construction plus a fee equal to $20,000.00 but in no event was the contract price, including the fee, to exceed $736,000.00. Attached to the contract was a "Trade Payment Breakdown" which made an allowance for overhead expenses in the amount of $31,589.00, but, this said sum was to be paid by means other than cash. The aforementioned loan was obtained and the apartment complex was constructed. All funds from the mortgage loan were received and disbursed by W.A. James and the renting of the apartments was begun, such being conducted by a resident manager, who was an employee of the Corporation.

It appears . . . that in 1968, an accountant, who was employed by the corporation, advised James and C.N. Talbot that it was in financial straits. It was at this time that the appellants questioned the disbursement of the mortgage funds by W.A. James. Their demands to examine the corporate records were refused by James. Thereafter, an order was obtained from the Honorable James B. Morrison, Resident Judge of the Fifteenth Judicial Circuit, making available the corporate records to the appellants. This action was thereafter instituted.

The record in this case clearly shows that W.A. James personally received or there was paid for his benefit the sum of $25,025.31 from the proceeds of the mortgage loan. He received this directly or by payments of his own personal debts by the corporation. He contends that he was entitled to these funds and more under the construction contract which he had with Chicora Apartments, Inc. This raises the question of whether James, who was a stockholder, officer, and director of Chicora Apartments, Inc., could enter into a contract with himself as an individual and [make] a profit therefrom for himself.

The Master found that Chicora Apartments, Inc., through W.A. James as president thereof, entered into a contract with himself, as sole proprietor of James Construction Company, without disclosing his identity of interest to the other officers or stockholders of the corporation, and that such contract has not been acquiesced in or ratified by the other director, officers or stockholders. He further found that the initial agreement between the parties required W.A. James to perform the same duties that he later contracted with the corporation to perform and for which he now seeks to justify the payment to him from the mortgage funds of the corporation. It was also found that according to the initial agreement these services were to be performed and, in consideration of such performance, James was to receive one-half of the shares of the capital stock of Chicora Apartments, Inc. The trial judge, upon exceptions to the Master's Report, made contrary findings of fact and reversed the Master and entered judgment in favor of the respondents.

The first question for determination is whether the fiduciary relationship existing between W.A. James as a stockholder, officer and director of Chicora Apartments, Inc., prevented him from contracting with the said corporation for his profit without first having disclosed the terms of the contract to the disinterested officers and directors of the corporation.

The officers and directors of the corporation stand in a fiduciary relationship to the individual stockholders and in every instance must make a full disclosure of all relevant facts when entering into a contract with said corporation. *Jacobson v. Yaschik,* 249 S.C. 577, 155 S.E.(2d) 601. The object of this rule is to prevent directors from secretly using their fiduciary positions to their own advantage and to the detriment of the corporation and of the stockholders....

... The testimony of C.N. Talbot is that he discussed with James as to who was going to construct the Chicora Apartments and was told that Dargan Construction Company was going to take the contract. He further testified that during the period of construction he saw Dargan Construction Company signs on the premises and also trucks bearing its name. This witness further testified that James never discussed with him or his wife the matter of his constructing the apartments. Talbot denied that he knew that James was to be the contractor.

James testified that he explained to C.N. Talbot that the only possible way that the apartments could be built without putting in money was that he be the building contractor. James further testified that the only way the project could survive and the only way that "we" could get the builder's equity was that he should be the builder. He says that everybody understood that because his attorney had explained it at a meeting of the directors.

Assuming that James revealed to Talbot that he was to be the building contractor for the Chicora Apartments complex, his testimony does not show that he disclosed his entitlement to a fee of $20,000.00 and an allowance for overhead expenses in the amount of $31,589.00. It is thus apparent that he did not make a full disclosure of the profits or monetary benefits that he was to receive under the terms of the contract. It was his duty to make such full disclosure and the burden of proof was upon him to show that such had been done.

We have carefully examined the minutes of the several meetings of the stockholders and directors of the corporation. We find from such examination that they reflect each and every detail and transaction looking toward the construction of the apartment complex but nowhere in said minutes is there any mention that James was to be the building contractor. The minutes reflect that there was a meeting of the directors of the corporation on November 6, 1963, and a resolution adopted at such meeting authorizing the borrowing of the sum of $850,700.00 from the United Mortgagee Servicing Corporation, and authorizing James, as president, to make, execute and deliver such documents and instruments as were required by the FHA and the lender. If James was to be the building contractor and such was discussed at this meeting, as he contends, the minutes should have reflected such, particularly in view of the fact that the building contract was being awarded to him when he was a director and president of the corporation. There is no explanation of why such a resolution or authorization was not considered or passed at this meeting of the Board of Directors.

The record shows that the appellants were stockholders and officers of the corporation. As such, they were entitled to inspect the books of the corporation at any and all times. Section 12–263 of the Code. When they demanded their right to exercise this privilege, such was refused by James and they only obtained the right to inspect the records and books of the corporation by an order of the court. James' only explanation was that the Talbots were not entitled to see the books. It is inferable from this action on the part of James that he did not want the appellants to discover how the funds of the corporation had been disbursed and see that he had received benefit in such disbursement.

It appears that at the meeting of the directors of the corporation held on November 6, 1963, W.A. James, as president, was authorized to execute and deliver several documents including a "construction contract." The respondents argue that this gave W.A. James the authority to make the construction contract here involved. It is true that he was authorized to sign a "construction contract" on behalf of the corporation but such resolution did not authorize him to sign one on behalf of the corporation in favor of himself individually.

The respondents contend and place great emphasis on the fact that the construction contract was approved by the Federal Housing Administration and the fees provided therein were allowed by it. This has no relevancy to the issue here.

Considering the entire record in this case, it is our conclusion that W.A. James, as president of Chicora Apartments, Inc., entered into a contract with himself as sole proprietor of James Construction Company without making full disclosure of his identity of interest to the other officers and stockholders of the corporation. In this conclusion, we agree with the findings of the Master. It follows that the Chicora Apartments, Inc., is entitled to judgment against the said W.A. James in the amount of $25,025.31, this being the amount of the corporate funds received by or paid in behalf of W.A. James.

The Master found that under the language in paragraph 5 of the pre-incorporation agreement, hereinbefore quoted, that W.A. James was to be responsible for overseeing, supervising and generally managing all aspects of the construction of the apartment complex. He found that W.A. James, as sole proprietor of James Construction Company, performed the contract obligations and for such he received one-half of the shares of the capital stock of Chicora Apartments, Inc. The trial judge reversed this finding of the Master. The appellants allege error.

James testified that he was the general contractor for the construction of the apartment complex. He testified further that the apartment complex was constructed by some eighteen to twenty subcontractors with whom he negotiated contracts. The record reveals that the only service that James rendered in connection with the construction of the apartment complex was supervisory. These duties were those contemplated by the pre-incorporation agreement of the parties. He was compensated for these services when he received one-half of the capital stock in the corporation. He was not entitled to any other compensation for the services rendered. We think the trial judge was in error in not so holding.

The order of the trial judge is reversed and this case remanded to the Court of Common Pleas for Horry County for an appropriate order to effectuate the views herein expressed.

Reversed and remanded.

■ LEWIS and LITTLEJOHN, JJ., concur.

■ BUSSEY and BRAILSFORD, JJ., dissent.

■ BUSSEY, JUSTICE (dissenting):

While admittedly there is some evidence tending to support the findings of fact by the master, adopted in the majority opinion, I have concluded after considerable study of the record and exhibits that the clear weight of the evidence preponderates in favor of the findings of fact by the circuit judge rather than those of the master. Being of this view, I am compelled to dissent.

The apartment complex was completed in July 1964, whereupon the plaintiff, C.N. Talbot, with the help of a resident manager, selected by him but approved by James, took charge of the management and operation of the apartment complex, all receipts being deposited by Talbot and all checks being written by Talbot. In 1968, after Talbot and his manager had been in charge of the apartment complex for nearly four years, the corporation was virtually insolvent and the recommendation of Talbot's auditor was that the project be surrendered to FHA as a failure. To this James did not agree; instead he took charge of the operation of the apartment complex himself for the corporation, and a little more than a year later the corporation had seventeen to eighteen thousand dollars in the bank with all current bills paid.

Talbot was obviously chagrined at this course of events and it was not until after he was ousted from management that he actively asserted any claim on behalf of the corporation against James. While he denied knowing that James Construction Company was the general contractor on the project, by his own testimony about January or February 1965 he knew that a check for more than fifteen thousand dollars had been drawn on the construction account for the benefit of James. There is no suggestion that he then made any issue thereabout; instead, he waited until nearly four years later and until after he had been ousted from the active management of the operation. . . .

The resolution of the Board of Directors at the meeting on November 5, 1963, unanimously confirmed by the meeting of the stockholders on the same date, as evidenced by their written signatures, clearly shows that all parties agreed that James' efforts over a two year period and the contracts and commitments thereby produced plus the continued use of the finances and credit of James during the actual construction period represented a value of $44,000, which was accepted in full payment for James' ten shares of stock. According to the literal terms of this resolution, nothing remained to be done by James to fully earn his ten shares except allow the use of his credit throughout the construction period. As president of the corporation, he would have been expected to at least reasonably supervise the construction of the project in the interest of the corporation, whether or not required to do so by either the resolution of November 5 or the pre-incorporation agreement between the parties. The general supervisory duties of a corporation president or a pre-incorporation promoter are a far cry from the arduous, time consuming and expensive duties of a general contractor.

Supervising a general contractor is one thing; while acting as a general contractor, engaging, supervising, and following up eighteen or twenty subcontractors is an entirely different thing. There is uncontradicted evidence of voluminous paper work, record keeping, reports, etc., on the part of James and his personnel in the performance of the general construction contract. The record leaves no doubt whatever, to my mind, that James Construction Company performed services to the corporation subsequent to November 5, 1963 far over and above the service contemplated by either the aforesaid resolution or the pre-incorporation agreement.

As mentioned in the majority opinion, the "Trade Payment Breakdown" attached to the approved FHA construction contract made an allowance for overhead expenses in the amount of $31,589, payable by means other than cash. Apparently from the evidence, this amount, otherwise drawable, as overhead by James, was to form a part of the equity of the corporation required for the FHA loan and, of course, not actually received by James. Aside, however, from this item, the record reflects that where, as here, there was an identity of interest between the contractor and the sponsor, FHA, within certain limitations, permitted the contractor to include in his certification of the actual cost of a project a reasonable allocation of his general overhead expense, *i.e.,* the proportion of his actual general overhead expense attributable to the particular contract job.

In his cost certification to FHA James showed the entire overhead of James Construction Company during the period that the apartment project was under construction, and represented that 88.98% thereof, or $22,817.34, was attributable to the construction of Chicora Apartments. Of this amount, FHA allowed only $21,231.90 (3% of other costs) as a portion of the actual cost of Chicora Apartments. James' figures as to his overhead and the portion thereof attributable to the construction of Chicora Apartments may or may not have been accurate, but he was not even cross-examined thereabout. Assuming the accuracy of his figures it follows that his net profit from this general construction contract was the sum of $25,025.31 less $22,817.34 overhead, or $2,207.97. Even Talbot had to frankly admit that he did not know of any loss suffered by the Talbots or the corporation as a result of the general contract being let to James. He tacitly, if not expressly, conceded that Dargan, or any other reputable contractor, would have cost the corporation some twenty-five or thirty thousand dollars more....

For the foregoing reasons, I would affirm the judgment of the lower court, but at the very least, if the corporation is to recover at all from James, its recovery should be limited to any profit actually received, as opposed to his overhead expense. If the judgment below be not affirmed, the cause should be remanded for the purpose of determining the amount of actual overhead which James should equitably be allowed to retain.

■ BRAILSFORD, J., concurs.

NOTE ON THE DUTY OF LOYALTY

In the corporate context, fairness requires not only that the terms of a self-interested transaction be fair, but that entering into the transaction, even on fair terms, is in the corporation's interest. For example, in Fill Buildings, Inc. v. Alexander Hamilton Life Ins. Co. of America, 396 Mich. 453, 241 N.W.2d 466 (1976), Fill Buildings, Inc., which had leased premises to Wayne National Life Insurance Co., brought suit under the lease for past-due rent. The lease was a self-interested transaction: Leon Fill was the principal shareholder and a director of Wayne National and the sole shareholder and president of Fill Buildings. Wayne's corporate successor sought to avoid liability under the lease on the ground that the lease was unfair. The trial court held that Fill Buildings had not borne its burden of establishing that the lease was in the interests of Wayne National:

> Given an instance of alleged director enrichment at corporate expense such as in this case, the burden to establish fairness resting on the director requires not only a showing of "fair price" but also a showing of the fairness of the bargain to the interests of the corporation. Only when a convincing showing is made in both respects can "fairness" under the statute be said to have been established.
>
> We are inclined to agree with Fill Buildings' position that that corporation was entitled to make a profit on its lease and that a "fair price" for the leasehold agreement was established. The costs of extensive renovations and the thrust of expert testimony adduced at trial support this conclusion. The proofs respecting the showing that entry into the lease served the interests of Wayne National are, however, unconvincing. Evidence adduced at trial indicated that Wayne National was a corporation in trouble. The corporation had been warned against over-expansion. Yet here we have entry into a long-term lease (*i.e.*, expansion) at a time when the corporate future was in question. . . .

NOTE ON ASSOCIATES OF DIRECTORS AND SENIOR EXECUTIVES

In the simplest type of self-interested transaction, a corporation deals with a director or senior executive. What if a corporation deals not with a director or senior executive, but with an enterprise or individual with whom a director or senior executive has a significant relationship? Such an enterprise or individual may be referred to as an associate of the director or senior executive. See ALI, Principles of Corporate Governance § 1.03.

Suppose, for example, that D, a director or senior executive, negotiates with the corporation on behalf of A, an associate of D, or otherwise knowingly advances A's interest. It seems pretty clear that the same rules of conduct should apply to D as if he had acted on his own behalf. The major problem would be remedy. Assume that D acted for A in a way that would have breached D's duty if he had acted for himself, and that D's breach resulted in a gain for A at the corporation's expense. If D will directly or indirectly derive all the gain—if, for example, A is a corporation wholly owned by D, or is D's minor child—damages equal to the gain are clearly appropriate. Suppose, however, that D will derive only part of the gain, as where A is a corporation that D controls but does not wholly own? On balance, the same result seems to be called for, because D has, by hypothesis, violated his duty, and the proximate result of that violation is that A will enjoy an unfair gain at the corporation's expense.

Suppose now that the question is not the liability of D, but the liability of the associate, A, whose interest was knowingly advanced by D? If A knew or should have known that he was participating in a breach of fiduciary duty, he would be liable as an aider and abetter under the well-established rule against knowing participation in a breach of fiduciary duty. If A is a business organization controlled by D, D's knowledge should be imputed to A in considering A's responsibility. Even if A neither knew nor should have known that he was participating in a breach of fiduciary duty, he may be liable under established principles of restitution if the imposition of liability is required to prevent unjust enrichment. For example, Restatement, Second, Agency § 314 provides that a person who receives a principal's property from an agent, and is not a bona fide purchaser, is subject to liability to the extent he has been unjustly enriched, even if he receives the property non-tortiously and is not on notice that the property belongs to the principal. See also Restatement of Restitution §§ 123, 201(1), 201(2).

Suppose, finally, that A deals with the corporation on his own behalf, without the intervention of D? Arguably, an associate, unlike the director or senior executive, owes no duty of loyalty to the corporation (at least, assuming the associate is not simply a vest pocket of the director or senior executive, like a wholly owned corporation). However, since an associate may receive favored treatment as a result of his association with the director or senior executive, it seems appropriate to subject such transactions to closer review than transactions with strangers.

ALI, PRINCIPLES OF CORPORATE GOVERNANCE §§ 1.14, 1.25, 5.02, 5.07, 5.08

[See Statutory Supplement]

SECTION 2. STATUTORY APPROACHES

CAL. CORP. CODE § 310

[See Statutory Supplement]

DEL. GEN. CORP. LAW § 144

[See Statutory Supplement]

REV. MODEL BUS. CORP. ACT §§ 8.60–8.63

[See Statutory Supplement]

N.Y. BUS. CORP. LAW § 713

[See Statutory Supplement]

Cookies Food Products v. Lakes Warehouse

Supreme Court of Iowa, 1988.
430 N.W.2d 447.

■ NEUMAN, JUSTICE.

This is a shareholders' derivative suit brought by the minority shareholders of a closely held Iowa corporation specializing in barbeque sauce, Cookies Food Products, Inc. (Cookies). The target of the lawsuit is the majority shareholder, Duane "Speed" Herrig and two of his family-owned corporations, Lakes Warehouse Distributing, Inc. (Lakes) and Speed's Automotive Co., Inc. (Speed's). Plaintiffs alleged that Herrig, by acquiring control of Cookies and executing self-dealing contracts, breached his fiduciary duty to the company and fraudulently misappropriated and converted corporate funds. Plaintiffs sought actual and punitive damages. Trial to the court resulted in a verdict for the defendants, the district court finding that Herrig's actions benefited, rather than harmed, Cookies. We affirm.

I. Background.

We review decisions in shareholders' derivative suits de novo, deferring especially to district court findings where the credibility of witnesses is a factor in the outcome. *Midwest Management Corp. v. Stephens,* 353 N.W.2d 76, 78 (Iowa 1984). To better understand this dispute, and the issues this appeal presents, we shall begin by recounting in detail the facts surrounding the creation and growth of this corporation.

L.D. Cook of Storm Lake, Iowa, founded Cookies in 1975 to produce and distribute his original barbeque sauce. Searching for a plant site in a community that would provide financial backing, Cook met with business leaders in seventeen Iowa communities, outlining his plans to build a growth-oriented company. He selected Wall Lake, Iowa, persuading thirty-five members of that community, including Herrig and the plaintiffs, to purchase Cookies stock. All of the investors hoped Cookies would improve the local job market and tax base. The record reveals that it has done just that.

Early sales of the product, however, were dismal. After the first year's operation, Cookies was in dire financial straits. At that time, Herrig was one of thirty-five shareholders and held only two hundred shares. He was also the owner of an auto parts business, Speed's Automotive, and Lakes Warehouse Distributing, Inc., a company that distributed auto parts from Speed's. Cookies' board of directors approached Herrig with the idea of distributing the company's products. It authorized Herrig to purchase Cookies' sauce for twenty percent under wholesale price, which he could then resell at full wholesale price. Under this arrangement, Herrig began to market and distribute the sauce to his auto parts customers and to grocery outlets from Lakes' trucks as they traversed the regular delivery routes for Speed's Automotive.

In May 1977, Cookies formalized this arrangement by executing an exclusive distribution agreement with Lakes. Pursuant to this agreement, Cookies was responsible only for preparing the product; Lakes, for its part, assumed all costs of warehousing, marketing, sales, delivery, promotion, and advertising. Cookies retained the right to fix the sales price of its products and agreed to pay Lakes thirty percent of its gross sales for these services.

Cookies' sales have soared under the exclusive distributorship contract with Lakes. Gross sales in 1976, the year prior to the agreement, totaled only $20,000, less than half of Cookies' expenses that year. In 1977, however, sales jumped five-fold, then doubled in 1978, and have continued to show phenomenal growth every year thereafter. By 1985, when this suit was commenced, annual sales reached $2,400,000.

As sales increased, Cookies' board of directors amended and extended the original distributorship agreement. In 1979, the board amended the original agreement to give Lakes an additional two percent of gross sales to cover freight costs for the ever-expanding market for Cookies' sauce. In 1980, the board extended the amended agreement through 1984 to allow Herrig to make long-term advertising commitments. Recognizing the role that Herrig's personal strengths played in the success of their joint endeavor, the board also amended the agreement that year to allow Cookies to cancel the agreement with Lakes if Herrig died or disposed of the corporation's stock.

In 1981, L.D. Cook, the majority shareholder up to this time, decided to sell his interest in Cookies. He first offered the directors an opportunity to buy his stock, but the board declined to purchase any of his 8100 shares. Herrig then offered Cook and all other shareholders $10 per share for their stock, which was twice the original price. Because of the overwhelming response to these offers, Herrig had purchased enough Cookies stock by January 1982 to become the majority shareholder. His investment of $140,000 represented fifty-three percent of the 28,700 outstanding shares. Other shareholders had invested a total of $67,500 for the remaining forty-seven percent.

Shortly after Herrig acquired majority control he replaced four of the five members of the Cookies' board with members he selected. This restructuring of authority, following on the heels of an unsuccessful attempt by certain stockholders to prevent Herrig from acquiring majority status, solidified a division of opinion within the shareholder ranks. Subsequent changes made in the corporation under Herrig's leadership formed the basis for this lawsuit.

First, under Herrig's leadership, Cookies' board has extended the term of the exclusive distributorship agreement with Lakes and expanded the scope of services for which it compensates Herrig and his companies. In April 1982, when a sales increase of twenty-five percent over the previous year required Cookies to seek additional short-term storage for the peak summer season, the board accepted Herrig's proposal to compensate Lakes at the "going rate" for use of its nearby storage facilities. The board decided to use Lakes' storage facilities because building and staffing its own facilities would have been more expensive. Later, in July 1982, the new board approved an extension of the exclusive distributorship agreement. Notably, this agreement was identical to the 1980 extension that the former board had approved while four of the plaintiffs in this action were directors.

Second, Herrig moved from his role as director and distributor to take on an additional role in product development. This created a dispute over a royalty Herrig began to receive. Herrig's role in product development began in 1982 when Cookies diversified its product line to include taco sauce. Herrig developed the recipe because he recognized that taco sauce, while requiring many of the same ingredients needed in barbeque sauce, is less expensive to produce. Further, since consumer demand for taco sauce is more consistent throughout the year than the demand for barbeque sauce, this new product line proved to be a profitable method for increasing year-round utilization of production facilities and staff. In August 1982, Cookies' board approved a royalty fee to be paid to Herrig for this taco sauce recipe. This royalty plan was similar to royalties the board paid to L.D. Cook for the barbeque sauce recipe. That plan gives Cook three percent of the gross sales of barbeque sauce; Herrig receives a flat rate per case. Although Herrig's rate is equivalent to a sales percentage slightly higher than what Cook receives, it yields greater profit to Cookies because this new product line is cheaper to produce.

Third, since 1982 Cookies' board has twice approved additional compensation for Herrig. In January 1983, the board authorized payment of a $1000 per month "consultant fee" in lieu of salary, because accelerated sales required Herrig to spend extra time managing the company. Averaging eighty-hour work weeks, Herrig devoted approximately fifteen percent of his time to Cookies and eighty percent to Lakes business. In August, 1983, the board authorized another increase in Herrig's compensation. Further, at the suggestion of a Cookies director who also served as an accountant for Cookies,

Lakes, and Speed's, the Cookies board amended the exclusive distributorship agreement to allow Lakes an additional two percent of gross sales as a promotion allowance to expand the market for Cookies products outside of Iowa. As a direct result of this action, by 1986 Cookies regularly shipped products to several states throughout the country.

As we have previously noted, however, Cookies' growth and success has not pleased all its shareholders. The discontent is motivated by two factors that have effectively precluded shareholders from sharing in Cookies' financial success: the fact that Cookies is a closely held corporation, and the fact that it has not paid dividends. Because Cookies' stock is not publicly traded, shareholders have no ready access to buyers for their stock at current values that reflect the company's success. Without dividends, the shareholders have no ready method of realizing a return on their investment in the company. This is not to say that Cookies has improperly refused to pay dividends. The evidence reveals that Cookies would have violated the terms of its loan with the Small Business Administration had it declared dividends before repaying that debt. That SBA loan was not repaid until the month before the plaintiffs filed this action.

Unsatisfied with the status quo, a group of minority shareholders commenced this equitable action in 1985. Based on the facts we have detailed, the plaintiffs claimed that the sums paid Herrig and his companies have grossly exceeded the value of the services rendered, thereby substantially reducing corporate profits and shareholder equity. Through the exclusive distributorship agreements, taco sauce royalty, warehousing fees, and consultant fee, plaintiffs claimed that Herrig breached his fiduciary duties to the corporation and its shareholders because he allegedly negotiated for these arrangements without fully disclosing the benefit he would gain. The plaintiffs sought recovery for lost profits, an accounting to determine the full extent of the damage, attorneys fees, punitive damages, appointment of a receiver to manage the company properly, removal of Herrig from control, and sale of the company in order to generate an appropriate return on their investment.

Having heard the evidence presented on these claims at trial, the district court filed a lengthy ruling that reflected careful attention to the testimony of the twenty-two witnesses and myriad of exhibits admitted. The court concluded that Herrig had breached no duties owed to Cookies or to its minority shareholders, and found that Herrig's compensation was fair and reasonable for each of the four challenged categories of service. In summary, the court found that: (1) the exclusive distributorship arrangement has been the "key to corporate growth and expansion" and the fees under the agreement were appropriate for the diverse services Lakes provided; (2) the warehousing agreement was fair because it allowed Cookies to store its goods at the "going rate" and the board had considered and rejected the idea of constructing its own warehouse as storage at the Lakes facility would be less expensive; (3) the taco sauce royalty agreement appropriately compensated Herrig for the value of his recipe; and (4) the consultant fee "is actually a management fee for services rendered seven days a week" and is "well within reason, considering the success of the business." Additionally, the district court found that Herrig had withheld no information from directors or other shareholders that he was obligated to provide. The court concluded its findings with the following observation:

> The Court believes that the plaintiffs' complaint is not that they have been damaged but that they have not been paid a profit for their investment yet. There is a vast difference. Plaintiffs have made a profit. That profit is in the form of increased value of their stocks rather than in the form of dividends because of the capital considerations of operating the company.

On appeal from this ruling, the plaintiffs challenge: (1) the district court's allocation of the burden of proof with regard to the four claims of self-dealing; (2) the standard employed by the court to determine whether Herrig's self-dealing was fair and reasonable to Cookies; (3) the finding that any self-dealing by Herrig was done in good faith, and with honesty and fairness; (4) the finding that Herrig breached no duty to disclose crucial facts to Cookies' board before it completed deliberations on Herrig's self-dealing transactions; and (5) the district court's denial of restitution and other equitable remedies as compensation for Herrig's alleged breach of his duty of loyalty. After a brief review of the nature and source of Herrig's fiduciary duties, we will address the appellants' challenges in turn.

II. Fiduciary Duties.

Herrig, as an officer and director of Cookies, owes a fiduciary duty to the company and its shareholders. *See* Iowa Code § 496A.34 (1985) (director must serve in manner believed in good faith to be in best interest of corporation); *see also Schildberg Rock Prods. Co. v. Brooks,* 258 Iowa 759, 766–67, 140 N.W.2d 132, 136 (1966) (officers and directors occupy fiduciary relation to corporation and its stockholders). Herrig concedes that Iowa law imposed the same fiduciary responsibilities based on his status as majority stockholder. *See Des Moines Bank & Trust Co. v. George M. Bechtel & Co.,* 243 Iowa 1007, 1082–83, 51 N.W.2d 174, 217 (1952) (hereinafter *Bechtel*); *see also* 12B W. Fletcher, *Cyclopedia on the Law of Private Corporations* § 5810, at 149 (1986). Conversely, before acquiring majority control in February 1982, Herrig owed no fiduciary duty to Cookies or plaintiffs. *See* Fletcher § 5713, at 13 (stockholders not active in management of corporation owe duties radically different from director, and vote at shareholder's meetings merely for own benefit). Therefore, Herrig's conduct is subject to scrutiny only from the time he began to exercise control of Cookies. . . .

Appellants . . . claim that Herrig violated his duty of loyalty to Cookies. That duty derives from "the prohibition against self-dealing that inheres in the fiduciary relationship." *Norlin,* 744 F.2d at 264. As a fiduciary, one may not secure for oneself a business opportunity that "in fairness belongs to the corporation." *Rowen v. LeMars Mut. Ins. Co. of Iowa,* 282 N.W.2d 639, 660 (Iowa 1979). As we noted in *Bechtel:*

> Corporate directors and officers may under proper circumstances transact business with the corporation including the purchase or sale of property, but it must be done in the strictest good faith and with full disclosure of the facts to, and the consent of, all concerned. And the burden is upon them to establish their good faith, honesty and fairness. Such transactions are scanned by the courts with skepticism and the closest scrutiny, and may be nullified on slight grounds. It is the policy of the courts to put such fiduciaries beyond the reach of temptation and the enticement of illicit profit. 243 Iowa 1007, 1081, 51 N.W.2d 174, 216 (1952). We have repeatedly applied this standard, including the burden of proof and level of scrutiny, when a corporate director engages in self-dealing with another corporation for which he or she also serves as a director. *See Holden v. Construction Mach. Co.,* 202 N.W.2d 348, 356–57 (Iowa 1972).

Against this common law backdrop, the legislature enacted section 496A.34, quoted here in pertinent part, that establishes three sets of circumstances under which a director may engage in self-dealing without clearly violating the duty of loyalty:

> No contract or other transaction between a corporation and one or more of its directors or any other corporation, firm, association or entity in which one or more of its directors are directors or officers or are financially interested, shall be either void or voidable because of such relationship or interest ... if any of the following occur:
>
> 1. The fact of such relationship or interest is disclosed or known to the board of directors or committee which authorizes, approves, or ratifies the contract or transaction ... without counting the votes ... of such interested director.
>
> 2. The fact of such relationship or interest is disclosed or known to the shareholders entitled to vote [on the transaction] and they authorize ... such contract or transaction by vote or written consent.
>
> 3. The contract or transaction is fair and reasonable to the corporation.

Some commentators have supported the view that satisfaction of any *one* of the foregoing statutory alternatives, in and of itself, would prove that a director has fully met the duty of loyalty. *See* Hansell, Austin, & Wilcox, *Director Liability Under Iowa Law–Duties and Protections,* 13 J.Corp.L. 369, 382. We are obliged, however, to interpret statutes in conformity with the common law wherever statutory language does not directly negate it. *See Hardwick v. Bublitz,* 253 Iowa 49, 59, 111 N.W.2d 309, 314 (1961); Iowa Code § 4.2 (1987). Because the common law and section 496A.34 require directors to show "good faith, honesty, and fairness" in self-dealing, we are persuaded that satisfaction of any one of these three alternatives under the statute would merely preclude us from rendering the transaction void or voidable *outright* solely on the basis "of such [director's] relationship or interest." Iowa Code § 496A.34; *see Bechtel,* 243 Iowa at 1081–82, 51 N.W.2d at 216. To the contrary, we are convinced that the legislature did not intend by this statute to enable a court, in a shareholder's derivative suit, to rubber stamp *any* transaction to which a board of directors or the shareholders of a corporation have consented. Such an interpretation would invite those who stand to gain from such transactions to engage in improprieties to obtain consent. We thus require directors who engage in self-dealing to establish the additional element that they have acted in good faith, honesty, and fairness. *Holi–Rest, Inc. v. Treloar,* 217 N.W.2d 517, 525 (Iowa 1974).

III. Burden of Proof.

[The court held that the district court had appropriately placed the burden of proof on Herrig.]

IV. Standard of Law.

Next, appellants claim the district court applied an inappropriate standard of law to determine whether Herrig's conduct was fair and reasonable to Cookies. Appellants correctly assert that self-dealing transactions must have the earmarks of arms-length transactions before a court can find them to be fair or reasonable. *See Bechtel,* 243 Iowa at 1023, 51 N.W.2d at 184. The crux of appellants' claim is that the court should have focused on the fair market value of Herrig's services to Cookies rather than on the success Cookies achieved as a result of Herrig's actions.

We agree with appellants' contention that corporate profitability should not be the sole criteria by which to test the fairness and reasonableness of Herrig's fees. In this connection, appellants cite authority from the Michigan Supreme Court that we find persuasive:

> Given an instance of alleged director enrichment at corporate expense . . . the burden to establish fairness resting on the director requires not only a showing of "fair price" but also a showing of the fairness of the bargain to the interests of the corporation.

Fill Bldgs., Inc. v. Alexander Hamilton Life Ins. Co., 396 Mich. 453, 241 N.W.2d 466, 469 (1976). Applying such reasoning to the record before us, however, we cannot agree with appellants' assertion that Herrig's services were either unfairly priced or inconsistent with Cookies corporate interest.

There can be no serious dispute that the four agreements in issue—for exclusive distributorship, taco sauce royalty, warehousing, and consulting fees—have all benefited Cookies, as demonstrated by its financial success. Even if we assume Cookies could have procured similar services from other vendors at lower costs, we are not convinced that Herrig's fees were therefore unreasonable or exorbitant. Like the district court, we are not persuaded by appellants' expert testimony that Cookies' sales and profits would have been the same under agreements with other vendors. As Cookies' board noted prior to Herrig's takeover, he was the driving force in the corporation's success. Even plaintiffs' expert acknowledged that Herrig has done the work of at least five people—production supervisor, advertising specialist, warehouseman, broker, and salesman. While eschewing the lack of internal control, for accounting purposes, that such centralized authority may produce, the expert conceded that Herrig may in fact be underpaid for all he has accomplished. We believe the board properly considered this source of Cookies' success when it entered these transactions, as did the district court when it reviewed them....

V. Denial of Equitable Relief.

... [T]he record before us aptly demonstrates that all members of Cookies' board were well aware of Herrig's dual ownership in Lakes and Speed's. We are unaware of any authority supporting plaintiffs' contention that Herrig was obligated to disclose to Cookies' board or shareholders the extent of his profits resulting from these distribution and warehousing agreements; nevertheless, the exclusive distribution agreement with Lakes authorized the board to ascertain that information had it so desired. Appellants cannot reasonably claim that Herrig owed Cookies a duty to render such services at no profit to himself or his companies. Having found that the compensation he received from these agreements was fair and reasonable, we are convinced that Herrig furnished sufficient pertinent information to Cookies' board to enable it to make prudent decisions concerning the contracts....

We concur in the trial court's assessment of the evidence presented and affirm its dismissal of plaintiffs' claims.

AFFIRMED.

All Justices concur except SCHULTZ, J., who dissents.

■ SCHULTZ, JUSTICE (dissenting)....

Much of Herrig's evidence concerned the tremendous success of the company. I believe that the trial court and the majority opinion have been so enthralled by the success of the company that they have failed to examine whether these matters of self-dealing were fair to the stockholders. While much credit is due to Herrig for the success of the company, this does not mean that these transactions were fair to the company.

I believe that Herrig failed on his burden of proof by what he did not show. He did not produce evidence of the local going rate for distribution contracts or storage fees outside of a very limited amount of self-serving testimony. He simply did not show the fair market value of his services or expense for freight, advertising and storage cost. He did not show that his taco sauce royalty was fair. This was his burden. He cannot succeed on it by merely showing the success of the company.

The shareholders, on the other hand, produced testimony of what the fair market value of Herrig's services were. The majority discounts this testimony and chooses instead to focus on the success Cookies achieved as a result of Herrig's actions. They focus on the success of the company rather than whether his self-dealing actions were arms-length transactions that were fair and reasonable to the stockholders. The appellants have put forth convincing testimony that Herrig has been grossly over compensated for his services based on their fair market value. Appellant's expert witness, a CPA, performed an analysis to show what the company would have earned if it had hired a $65,000 a year executive officer, paid a marketing supervisor and an advertising agency a commission of five percent of the sales each, built a new warehouse and hired a warehouseman. It was compared with what the company actually did make under Herrig's management. The analysis basically shows what the operating cost of this company should be on the open market when hiring out the work to experts. In 1985 alone, the company's income would have doubled what it actually made were these changes made. The evidence clearly shows that the fair market value of those services is considerably less than what Herrig actually has been paid.

Similarly, appellant's food broker expert witness testified that for $110,865, what the CPA analysis stated was the fair market value for brokerage services, his company would have provided all of the services that Herrig had performed. The company actually paid $730,637 for the services, a difference of $620,000 in one year.

In summary, I believe the majority was dazzled by the tales of Herrig's efforts and Cookies' success in these difficult economic times. In the process, however, it is forgotten that Herrig owes a fiduciary duty to the corporation to deal fairly and reasonably with it in his self-dealing transactions. Herrig is not entitled to skim off the majority of the profits through self-dealing transactions unless they are fair to the minority stockholders. At trial, he failed to prove how his charges were in line with what the company could have gotten on the open market. Because I cannot ignore this inequity to the company and its shareholders, I must respectfully dissent.

NOTE ON THE EFFECT OF APPROVAL OF SELF-INTERESTED TRANSACTIONS BY DISINTERESTED DIRECTORS

Suppose that a self-interested transaction has been authorized by disinterested directors. There are several reasons why the transaction should nevertheless be subject to some review for substantive fairness, although a more limited review than would be applied in the absence of such an authorization.

First, by virtue of their personal relationships, directors are unlikely to treat each other with the degree of wariness they would apply to third parties.

Second, a review of the *substantive* fairness of a self-interested transaction may be thought of as a surrogate for a review of the fairness of the *process* by which the transaction was approved. In a world of perfect information, a court could always determine, by direct means, whether directors who approved a self-interested transaction involving one or more of their colleagues were objective and impartial, and whether they approached the transaction with that degree of wariness with which they would approach transactions with third parties. In the real world, the courts may need to make these determinations by indirect means. If a self-interested transaction that has been approved by directors who are technically disinterested is substantively unfair, it can normally be inferred that either the approving directors were not objective and impartial in fact, or that they were not as wary as they should have been because they were dealing with a colleague.

Most states have adopted statutes, like those of California, Delaware, New York, and the Model Act, that address the effect of approval of self-interested transactions by disinterested directors. An important question under these statutes is whether they preclude a judicial inquiry into the fairness of self-interested transactions that have been so approved. Many of the statutes are susceptible to the interpretation that approval by disinterested directors precludes a judicial inquiry into fairness, but most or all of the statutes can also be interpreted not to preclude such an inquiry. The statutes fall into several categories in this regard:

(i) Some of the statutes, such as the California statute, expressly require some form of fairness test even if a transaction has been approved by disinterested directors.

(ii) Many of the statutes, such as the Delaware statute, explicitly require that approval by disinterested directors be in good faith, and such a requirement can be implied even where it is not explicit. It is often obscure whether a good-faith test is strictly subjective or has an objective content as well. For example, UCC § 2–103 provides that in the case of a merchant, good faith is defined to include "the observance of reasonable commercial standards of fair dealing in the trade." Similarly, in Sam Wong & Son, Inc. v. New York Mercantile Exchange, 735 F.2d 653, 671, 678 & n. 32 (2d Cir.1984), Judge Friendly held that the rationality of a decision was relevant in determining whether the decision had been made in good faith. "By this," he added, "we mean only a minimal requirement of some basis in reason. [A]bsent some basis in reason, action could hardly be in good faith even apart from ulterior motive." Even courts that seem to use the term "good faith" in a relatively subjective way characteristically go on to review a decision to determine if it is irrational, egregious, or the like, this shows bad faith. Because of the uncertain meaning of good faith (see Section 2, infra), a good-faith requirement opens the door to some judicial scrutiny of the fairness of self-interested transactions that have been approved by disinterested directors.

(iii) Many of the remaining statutes can be interpreted to merely change the common law rule that self-interested transactions are voidable without regard to fairness, rather than to preclude review for fairness. Thus, some courts have held that such a statute either renders a self-interested transaction not automatically voidable (that is, not voidable even if fair) or shifts the burden of proof. In addition to *Cookies Food Products,* see, e.g., Holi–Rest, Inc. v. Treloar, 217 N.W.2d 517, 525 (Iowa 1974); Cohen v. Ayers, 596 F.2d 733, 740–41 (7th Cir.1979); Remillard Brick Co. v. Remillard–Dandini Co., 109 Cal.App.2d 405, 241 P.2d 66 (1952); Gaillard v. Natomas Co., 208 Cal.App.3d 1250, 256 Cal.Rptr. 702 (1989).

In contrast, in Marciano v. Nakash, 535 A.2d 400 (Del.1987), the Delaware Supreme Court stated that "approval by fully-informed disinterested directors under [Delaware Gen. Corp. Law] section 144(a)(1), or disinterested stockholders under section 144(a)(2), permits invocation of the business judgment rule and limits judicial review to issues of gift or waste with the burden of proof upon the party attacking the transaction." Similarly, in Oberly v. Kirby, 592 A.2d 445 (Del.1991) the Delaware Supreme Court said "The key to upholding an interested transaction is the approval of some neutral decision-making body. Under 8 *Del.C.* § 144, a transaction will be sheltered from shareholder challenge if approved by ... a committee of independent directors [or] the shareholders...."

It is widely believed that regardless of the form of the statute, at least outside Delaware approval by disinterested directors will not prevent a court from reviewing self-interested transactions for obvious unfairness. Section 5.02(a)(2)(B) of the ALI's Principles of Corporate Governance makes this implicit rule explicit, by adopting a test intermediate between the business-judgment rule and a full-fairness test in cases where a self-interested transaction has been approved by disinterested directors. Under that Section, where there has been authorization by disinterested directors, the complainant must show that disinterested directors "could not [have] reasonably ... believed" the transaction to be fair to the corporation. This test is intended to be easier for the director or senior executive to satisfy than a full-fairness test, although harder to satisfy than the business-judgment standard. Even in Delaware, it may be necessary to show that the directors who approved the transaction were not only disinterested, but independent, and directors who passively approve a manifestly unfair transaction may be deemed to exhibit a lack of independence by virtue of that conduct.

Sutherland v. Sutherland

Court of Chancery of Delaware, 2009.
2009 WL 857468 (Del.Ch.).

■ LAMB, VICE CHANCELLOR.

This case concerns a derivative and double derivative complaint filed by a 25% stockholder of a closely held corporation with the support of her brother, who is also a 25% stockholder of the corporation. The complaint alleges that the plaintiff's other two siblings, through their power as controlling stockholders, directors, and officers of the corporations, have caused the corporations to enter into a variety of self-dealing and/or wasteful transactions.

The individual defendants have moved to dismiss the complaint for failure to state a claim upon which relief can be granted. In support of this motion, the defendants have offered a variety of grounds, including an allegedly exculpatory provision of each corporation's charter....

I.

A. The Parties

Nominal defendant Dardanelle Timber Company, Inc. is a closely held, family-owned Delaware corporation.

Nominal defendant Sutherland Lumber–Southwest, Inc. ("Southwest") is a Delaware corporation and a wholly owned subsidiary of Dardanelle.

The plaintiff, Martha S. Sutherland, is a stockholder of Dardanelle Timber Company, Inc. She is both trustee and beneficiary of a trust by which she is the beneficial owner of 17% of Dardanelle's common stock. Her children are the beneficiaries of other trusts (through gifts made by her) that own approximately 8% of the common stock of Dardanelle.

Defendant Perry H. Sutherland is the brother of Martha. He is one of three directors of both Dardanelle and Southwest, as well as the president and chief executive officer of both companies. Perry and his children beneficially own (and Perry has the power to vote) 25% of the common stock of Dardanelle. Perry also controls a trust which owns all of the voting preferred stock of Dardanelle.

Defendant Todd L. Sutherland is the twin brother of Perry. He is one of three directors of both Dardanelle and Southwest, as well as an officer of both companies. Todd and his children are the beneficial owners of (and Todd has the power to vote) 25% of the common stock of Dardanelle.

Defendant Mark B. Sutherland is the cousin of the Sutherland siblings, and the third of the directors of both Dardanelle and Southwest. He holds no equity interest in either corporation.

B. The Facts ...

Dardanelle is a family owned and operated Delaware corporation, which, in part through its wholly owned subsidiary Southwest, is in the business of operating retail lumber yards and stores. Both companies were founded by Dwight D. Sutherland, Sr. ("Dwight Sr."), who served as president until his death in October 2003.

Approximately three decades ago, Dwight Sr. gave 25% of Dardanelle's common stock to each of his children: Martha, Dwight Jr., Perry, and Todd. At the time, Dwight Sr. and his wife Norma jointly owned all of Dardanelle's preferred stock, which carries voting rights.

After Dwight Sr.'s death, the shares of preferred stock were transferred to a trust for Norma's benefit.

Despite the even split of the common equity between the siblings, Perry and Todd have voting control over Dardenelle and Southwest because Perry is the trustee for Norma's trust, and Todd has allied himself with Perry. Perry and Todd constitute a majority of Southwest's three-member board, a majority of Dardanelle's board, and serve as the principal officers of both companies. Mark serves as the third director of both Dardanelle and Southwest. Martha was a director of Southwest until February 20, 2004. On that date, Dardanelle, the sole stockholder of Southwest, called an annual meeting for Southwest at which the number of Southwest directors was reduced to three and each of Perry, Todd, and Mark was elected to the board.[4]

Relying upon the documentation she received as a result of a hard-fought action brought pursuant to 8 Del. C. § 220, Martha filed this suit on September 6, 2006. Following this court's denial of a motion to dismiss by the special litigation committees of the two nominal corporate defendants, Martha amended her complaint on September 15, 2008. The complaint is in three counts: the first is for breach of fiduciary duty and asserts claims derivatively on behalf of Dardanelle; the second count is for waste; the third count is for breach of fiduciary duty and asserts double derivative claims on behalf of Southwest. Although not a named plaintiff, Dwight Jr., a lawyer, supports Martha in bringing this action.

Centrally, the complaint alleges that the individual defendants have used the companies' "corporate funds and assets for personal benefit." Specifically, Martha asserts that Perry and Todd have caused the companies to pay for (1) personal flights they have taken on the corporate airplane; (2) personal tax and accounting services provided to them by Cimarron Lumber & Home Supply Company, Ltd., a Dardanelle affiliate; (3) use for personal vacations of a facility commonly known as the Maysville Training Center; and (4) "things [such] as rental cars, expensive hotels, limousines, club memberships, chartered private railroad cars for extended personal trips, private parties and personal living expenses, among many others."

The complaint also challenges the decision to purchase a new corporate aircraft as well as the decision to maintain continuing ownership in it, alleging that the aircraft serves no legitimate business purpose. The complaint further alleges that Perry and Todd's decision to approve their own employment agreements at a February 21, 2004 board meeting constitutes waste and a breach of fiduciary duty. Martha asserts that the agreements pay Perry excessively for "part-time" work and contain excessive perquisites, such as payment for personal use of the aircraft and for personal tax and accounting services. Finally, the complaint bases its breach of fiduciary duty and waste claims on allegations that the individual defendants improperly caused Dardanelle to spend over $750,000 to defend against Martha's Section 220

4. The next day, Perry, Todd, and Mark approved employment agreements for Perry and Todd.

action, and improperly amended Dardanelle's bylaws pursuant to 8 Del. C. § 102(b)(7) to include a limitation of liability provision.

The individual defendants, in response to the amended complaint, filed a motion to dismiss for failure to state a claim upon which relief can be granted.

III.

The defendants contend that a provision found in both the Dardanelle and the Southwest certificates of incorporation acts to sterilize director interest when approving self-dealing transactions. In other words, according to the defendants, by virtue of this provision, directors are by definition disinterested for the purpose of business judgment rule analysis, even with regard to transactions in which they would otherwise be thought to have an interest. Because, the defendants argue, the plaintiff has put forth no basis, other than director interest, for rebutting the business judgment rule, the plaintiff's breach of fiduciary duty claims must be dismissed. The defendants' argument hinges on two questions. First, does the provision mean what the defendants claim it means? Second, is such a provision enforceable?

The provision the defendants rely upon is identical in both certificates of incorporation. It reads in pertinent part:

> Any director individually . . . may be a party to or may be pecuniarily or otherwise interested in any contract or transaction of the corporation, provided that the fact that he . . . is so interested shall be disclosed or shall have been known to the board of directors, or a majority thereof; and any director of the corporation, who is . . . so interested, may be counted in determining the existence of a quorum at any meeting of the board of directors of the corporation which shall authorize such contract or transaction, and may vote thereat to authorize any such contract or transaction, with like force and effect, as if he were not . . . so interested.

Provisions such as the one at issue were quite common in Delaware corporate charters prior to the 1967 revision to the Delaware General Corporation Law (the "DGCL"), in order to ameliorate the otherwise harsh effect of the common law that self-interested transactions would always be void as a result of the disability of interested directors to participate in a quorum. The Delaware Supreme Court, in a representative decision considering the meaning and effect of a nearly identical provision, stated at the time:

> We see no reason to hold that stockholders may not agree that interested directors may be counted toward a quorum. Such a provision does no more than to permit the directors to act as a board, leaving untouched questions of alleged unfairness or inequity that it is the duty of the courts in a proper case to resolve.[12]

The court sees no reason to disagree with those courts which interpreted the identical provision at a time when such a provision

12. Sterling v. Mayflower Hotel Corp., 93 A.2d 107, 118 (Del.1952); *see* also Gottlieb v. McKee, 107 A.2d 240, 242–43 (Del.Ch.1954); Martin Found., Inc. v. N. Am. Rayon Corp., 68

was common.[13] The court thus holds in accordance with *Sterling* that the provision at issue simply deals with issues of quorum, and does nothing to sanitize disloyal transactions.

However, if, *arguendo,* the meaning of the provision is as the defendants suggest, interested directors would be treated as disinterested for the purposes of approving corporate transactions. Because approval by a majority of disinterested directors affords a transaction the presumptions of the business judgment rule,[14] all interested transactions would be immunized from entire fairness analysis under this scheme. Thus, the only basis that would remain to attack a self-dealing transaction would be waste.

The question that remains then is whether such a far-reaching provision would be enforceable under Delaware law. It would not. If the meaning of the above provision were as the defendants suggest, it would effectively eviscerate the duty of loyalty for corporate directors as it is generally understood under Delaware law. While such a provision is permissible under the Delaware Limited Liability Company Act and the Delaware Revised Uniform Limited Partnership Act, where freedom of contract is the guiding and overriding principle, it is expressly forbidden by the DGCL. Section 102(b)(7) of the DGCL provides that a corporate charter may contain a provision eliminating or limiting personal liability of a director for money damages in a suit for breach of fiduciary duty, so long as such provision does not affect director liability for "any breach of the director's duty of loyalty to the corporation or its stockholders. . . ."

The effect of the provision at issue would be to do exactly what is forbidden. It would render any breach of the duty of loyalty relating to a self-dealing transaction beyond the reach of a court to remedy by way of damages. The exculpatory charter provision, if construed in the manner suggested by the defendants, would therefore be void as "contrary to the laws of this State"[15] and against public policy. As such, it could not form the basis for a dismissal of claims of self-dealing.

A.2d 313, 314–16 (Del.Ch.1949) (Seitz, V.C.); Pappas v. Moss, 393 F.2d 865, 867 (3d Cir.1968) (Seitz, J.).

13. Notably, before the law related to Section 144 of the DGCL finally settled, *see, e.g.,* Benihana of Tokyo, Inc. v. Benihana, Inc., 906 A.2d 114, 120 (Del.2006) (providing that interested director transactions approved pursuant to the 144(a)(1) safe harbor are reviewed under the business judgment rule), it was frequently suggested that Section 144, in the same vein as the provision at issue, did no more than to remove a director's disability to participate in a quorum to vote on an interested transaction, but did nothing to sanitize such a transaction if it was inherently unfair. *See, e.g.,* Fliegler v. Lawrence, 361 A.2d 218, 222 (Del.1976) ("[Section 144] merely removes an 'interested director' cloud when its terms are met and provides against invalidation of an agreement 'solely' because such a director or officer is involved. Nothing in the statute sanctions unfairness . . . or removes the transaction from judicial scrutiny."); HMG/Courtland Props., Inc. v. Gray, 749 A.2d 94, 114 n. 24 (Del.Ch.1999) ("Satisfaction of §§ 144(a)(1) or (a)(2) simply protects against invalidation of the transaction 'solely' because it is an interested one."); Cooke v. Oolie, 1997 WL 367034, at *8 (Del.Ch.) ("It is now clear that even if a board's action falls within the safe harbor of section 144, the board is not entitled to receive the protection of the business judgment rule.").

14. *See, e.g.,* Aronson v. Lewis, 473 A.2d 805, 812 (Del.1984).

15. *See* 8 Del. C. § 102(b)(1).

Thus, the charter provision, under either interpretation, provides no protection for the defendants beyond that afforded by Sections 144 of the DGCL. Because none of the safe-harbor provisions of Section 144(a)(1) or (a)(2) apply, the challenged interested transactions are not insulated on grounds of unfairness.[16]

IV.

[The court found that some of the plaintiff's claims were time-barred.]

V.

For the reasons set forth herein, . . . all claims arising out of actions occurring prior to August 31, 2001 are DISMISSED WITH PREJUDICE. In all other respects the defendants' motion is DENIED. IT IS SO ORDERED.

NEW YORK STOCK EXCHANGE LISTED COMPANY MANUAL § 312.03(B)

[See Statutory Supplement]

NOTE ON WASTE AND SHAREHOLDER RATIFICATION

An outside limit on the power of even disinterested directors or shareholders is the principle of waste. This principle was defined and explained as follows by Chancellor Allen in Lewis v. Vogelstein, 699 A.2d 327 (1997):

> The judicial standard for determination of corporate waste is well developed. Roughly, a waste entails an exchange of corporate assets for consideration so disproportionately small as to lie beyond the range at which any reasonable person might be

---

16. The defendants argue that claims relating to personal expenses and loans from Perry, Todd, and entities affiliated with them must be dismissed because the plaintiff has failed to allege facts suggesting unfairness. As the plaintiff points out, however, the corporations produced no documents in the 220 action substantiating the terms of the loans, that the loans were actually made, or that personal expenses charged to the companies were actually reimbursed by the individual defendants. Given the cloud of self-dealing that hangs over these transactions, and the potential for the defendants to use the transactions as a means to receive non-pro rata distributions from the corporation, the motion to dismiss stage of these proceedings is an inappropriate time to consider the merits of these claims given the entire fairness standard which must be applied. The same is true for the claims of corporate waste. Although this court has, in the fairly recent past, questioned the wisdom of allowing stockholders to bring claims for waste with respect to transactions which were approved by a majority of disinterested stockholders, *see Harbor Fin. Partners v. Huizenga,* 751 A.2d 879, 901–02 (Del.Ch.1999), that is not the situation presently before this court. The plaintiff has made at least a colorable argument that certain amounts expended by the corporation cannot be explained as an exercise in reasoned business judgment. Ultimately however, the determination of that question will be highly fact intensive. It is for that reason the court finds the prevailing precedent persuasive that claims of waste are seldom subject to disposition without trial. *See, e.g., Michelson v. Duncan,* 407 A.2d 211, 223 (Del.1979).

> willing to trade. Most often the claim is associated with a transfer of corporate assets that serves no corporate purpose; or for which no consideration at all is received. Such a transfer is in effect a gift. If, however, there is any substantial consideration received by the corporation, and if there is a *good faith judgment* that in the circumstances the transaction is worthwhile, there should be no finding of waste, even if the fact finder would conclude ex post that the transaction was unreasonably risky. Any other rule would deter corporate boards from the optimal rational acceptance of risk, for reasons explained elsewhere. Courts are ill-fitted to attempt to weigh the "adequacy" of consideration under the waste standard or, ex post, to judge appropriate degrees of business risk.

Chancellor Allen's definition was later quoted with approval by the Delaware Supreme Court in Brehm v. Eisner, 746 A.2d 244, n. 62 (2000). A similar definition is found in the ALI's Principles of Corporate Governance:

> A transaction constitutes a "waste of corporate assets" if it involves an expenditure of corporate funds or a disposition of corporate assets for which no consideration is received in exchange and for which there is no rational business purpose, or if consideration is received in exchange, the consideration the corporation receives is so inadequate in value that no person of ordinary sound business judgment would deem it worth that which the corporation has paid.

Id. § 1.42. Although the concept of waste is applicable to action by the board, it has greater bite as a limit on action by shareholders, because a board that commits waste would normally also violate the business judgment rule as well. The issue of waste therefore overlaps with the issue, what is the effect of shareholder ratification of a conflict-of-interest transaction. In *Vogelstein*, Chancellor Allen stated:

> What is the effect under Delaware corporation law of shareholder ratification of an interested transaction? The answer to this apparently simple question appears less clear than one would hope or indeed expect. Four possible effects of shareholder ratification appear logically available: First, one might conclude that an effective shareholder ratification acts as a complete defense to any charge of breach of duty. Second, one might conclude that the effect of such ratification is to shift the substantive test on judicial review of the act from one of fairness that would otherwise be obtained (because the transaction is an interested one) to one of waste. Third, one might conclude that the ratification shifts the burden of proof of unfairness to plaintiff, but leaves that shareholder protective test in place. Fourth, one might conclude (perhaps because of great respect for the collective action disabilities that attend shareholder action in public corporations) that shareholder ratification offers no assurance of assent of a character that deserves judicial recognition. Thus, under this approach, ratification on full information would be afforded no

effect. Excepting the fourth of these effects, there are cases in this jurisdiction that reflect each of these approaches to the effect of shareholder voting to approve a transaction....

1. *Ratification generally:* I start with principles broader than those of corporation law. Ratification is a concept deriving from the law of agency which contemplates the ex post conferring upon or confirming of the legal authority of an agent in circumstances in which the agent had no authority or arguably had no authority. Restatement (Second) of Agency § 82 (1958). To be effective, of course, the agent must fully disclose all relevant circumstances with respect to the transaction to the principal prior to the ratification. See, e.g., Breen Air Freight, Ltd. v. Air Cargo, Inc., et al., 470 F.2d 767, 773 (2d Cir.1972); Restatement (Second) of Agency § 91 (1958). Beyond that, since the relationship between a principal and agent is fiduciary in character, the agent in seeking ratification must act not only with candor, but with loyalty. Thus an attempt to coerce the principal's consent improperly will invalidate the effectiveness of the ratification. Restatement (Second) of Agency § 100 (1958)....

Assuming that a ratification by an agent is validly obtained, what is its effect? One way of conceptualizing that effect is that it provides, after the fact, the grant of authority that may have been wanting at the time of the agent's act. Another might be to view the ratification as consent or as an estoppel by the principal to deny a lack of authority. See Restatement (Second) of Agency § 103 (1958). In either event the effect of informed ratification is to validate or affirm the act of the agent as the act of the principal. Id. § 82....

2. *Shareholder ratification:* [The] differences between shareholder ratification of director action and classic ratification by a single principal, ... lead to a difference in the effect of a valid ratification in the shareholder context. The principal novelty added to ratification law generally by the shareholder context, is the idea—no doubt analogously present in other contexts in which common interests are held—that, in addition to a claim that ratification was defective because of incomplete information or coercion, shareholder ratification is subject to a claim by a member of the class that the ratification is ineffectual (1) because a majority of those affirming the transaction had a conflicting interest with respect to it or (2) because the transaction that is ratified constituted a corporate waste. As to the second of these, it has long been held that shareholders may not ratify a waste except by a unanimous vote. Saxe v. Brady, 40 Del.Ch. 474, 184 A.2d 602, 605 (1962). The idea behind this rule is apparently that a transaction that satisfies the high standard of waste constitutes a gift of corporate property and no one should be forced against their will to make a gift of their property. In all events, informed, uncoerced, disinterested shareholder ratification of a transaction in which corporate directors have a material conflict of interest

has the effect of protecting the transaction from judicial review except on the basis of waste....

Gantler v. Stephens, supra, held that shareholder ratification only extinguishes a claim that the directors lacked authority; in all other instances shareholder approval thereafter subjects "the challenged director action to business judgment review."

SECTION 3. COMPENSATION

Aggarwal, Executive Compensation and Corporate Controversy

27 Vermont Law Review 849, 850–56 (2003)

... [T]he increase in executive compensation has sparked a growing debate about whether such compensation is excessive, especially when average workers' incomes have been relatively stagnant. Furthermore, the highly publicized bankruptcies ... [and] the collapse in share prices since 2000 have led some to argue that executive compensation practices, specifically the granting of stock options, are pernicious. Do executive compensation packages provide appropriate incentives to managers, thereby aligning their interests with those of shareholders, or do they actually destroy shareholder value over the medium to long-run?

Much of the discussion in the academic literature has focused on the degree to which managers' interests are aligned with those of shareholders....

II. The Structure of Executive Compensation

In order to understand the determinants of incentives, we must first understand the components of executive compensation....

Total annual compensation can be divided into two categories—short-term components of compensation and long-term components of compensation.

II.1. Short–Term Components of Compensation

Short-term components of compensation include salary, bonus, and other annual compensation. Annual salary is fixed in advance and generally does not have an incentive component associated with it. The exception to this statement is that future increases in salary may in part be determined by current firm performance. Jensen and Murphy (1990) show that the present value of current and future increases in salary and bonuses are a small fraction of total incentives.

Annual bonuses are typically tied to measures of firm performance. Interestingly, the performance measures are often based on accounting information such as earnings, sales, or operating income. Common metrics employed include return on equity (ROE), return on assets (ROA), return on investment (ROI), and economic value added (EVA). Other measures of performance include subjective reports by board members or superiors for lower ranking executives and targets established by the board for investment, product or plant quality (e.g., "zero-defects"), market share, growth rates for income or sales, strategic objectives (e.g., expansion into new lines of business or restructuring of old businesses), and performance relative to that of industry competitors.

There are several points to note about short-term components of compensation. While short-term compensation does have some incentive features (especially the bonus component), it is typically not linked to stock performance in the form of stock returns. Given that shareholders presumably care most about stock returns, this is somewhat surprising. It will become apparent, however, that long-term components of compensation are much more strongly linked to stock returns. For this reason, the right way to think about annual salary and bonuses is that salary provides the executive with a minimum level of income prior to any performance standards or targets being met. Bonuses typically reflect how well the firm or executive has met non-stock return based objectives established by the board. Other annual compensation is usually negligible....

II.2. Long–Term Components of Compensation

Long-term components of compensation include new grants of restricted stock, new grants of stock options, long-term incentive plan payouts, and all other compensation. All other compensation typically includes gross-ups for tax liabilities, perquisites, preferential discounts on stock purchases, contributions to benefit plans, and severance payments and is usually relatively unimportant.

II.2.a. Restricted Stock

Restricted stock grants are restricted in the sense that the executive must remain with the firm for a specified amount of time in order not to forfeit the stock grant. Restricted stock grants with a five-year vesting period are typical. There are two practical implications of this restriction. First, the executive has potentially a strong incentive to stay with the firm in order to benefit from the grant. Second, while the vesting period is in effect, the executive cannot sell the stock. She is, in effect, forced to have part of her compensation tied to firm performance over the vesting period. Restricted stock grants clearly align an executive's interests with those of her shareholders....

II.2.b. Stock Options

Stock options have become the primary mechanism through which managers' interests are aligned with those of shareholders. A stock option gives the manager the right but not the obligation to purchase a share of the firm's stock for a pre-specified price (known as the exercise price) on or before a pre-specified date. Most stock options are granted at the money, which means that the exercise price is set equal to the stock price on the day of the grant. A typical stock option grant has a life of ten years. Since stock prices on average increase from year to year, over time most stock options will move into the money, meaning that the current stock price is greater than the exercise price. Stock options usually have a vesting schedule associated with them, such as 10% of an option grant vests every six months, so that the full grant vests over five years with another five years to maturity. . . .

For tax purposes, I focus on non-qualified options, which are the form of stock options that most executives receive. Non-qualified options have no tax implication at the time that they are issued. When the option is exercised, the executive pays tax on the difference between the stock price and the exercise price at the ordinary income tax rate. The firm deducts the difference between the stock price and the exercise price as compensation expense. If the executive later sells the stock, then the executive pays tax on the difference between the sale price and the market price at exercise of the option at the capital gains tax rate. Because the firm is able to deduct the difference between the stock price at exercise and the exercise price as compensation expense, non-qualified options have favorable tax treatment from the firm's perspective.

Favorable tax treatment is a significant part of the explanation for why the use of stock options has increased so dramatically. . . .

II.2.c. Long–Term Incentive Plans

Long-term incentive plan payouts are similar to bonuses but are awarded for performance over several years. For example, a long-term incentive plan payout may be triggered if ROA is at least 15% for three consecutive years. In general, long-term incentive plans are not that important on a year to year basis because they occur only when a long-term target is met. . . .

IN RE THE WALT DISNEY COMPANY DERIVATIVE LITIGATION

[Section 2, supra]

In re Tyson Foods, Inc. [Tyson I]

Court of Chancery of Delaware, 2007.
919 A.2d 563.

■ CHANDLER, CHANCELLOR.

Before me is a motion to dismiss a lengthy and complex complaint that includes almost a decade's worth of challenged transactions. Plaintiffs level charges, more or less indiscriminately, at eighteen individual defendants, one partnership, and the company itself as a nominal defendant. . . .

I. PARTIES AND PROCEDURAL HISTORY

. . . Before delving into disputes spanning over a decade and the events that bring the parties before this Court, I pause briefly to describe the relevant players.

A. *The Plaintiffs*

An SEC investigation regarding the proper classification of executive perquisites aroused the suspicions of plaintiff Eric Meyer, a New Jersey resident and Tyson shareholder. He made a written demand for documents to the company pursuant to 8 *Del. C.* § 220 on August 26, 2004. After almost a year of wrangling over precisely which papers were and were not to be produced, Tyson handed over an agreed upon set of documents on July 21, 2005. Meyer then filed his initial lawsuit on September 12, 2005. . . .

B. *Tyson Foods, Inc.*

Tyson Foods, Inc., a Delaware corporation with its principal office in Springdale, Arkansas, provides more protein products to the world than any other firm. Founded in the 1930s, the Tyson family has at all times kept the company under its power and direction. Tyson's share ownership structure ensures this: as of October 2, 2004, Tyson had 250,560,172 shares of Class A common stock and 101,625,548 shares of Class B common stock outstanding. Each Class A shareholder may cast one vote per share on all matters subject to the shareholder franchise, while Class B shareholders may cast ten votes for each one of their Class B shares.

The Tyson Limited Partnership ("TLP"), a limited partnership organized in Delaware, owns 99.9% of the Class B stock, thus controlling over 80% of the company's voting power. In turn, Don Tyson controls 99% of TLP, either directly or indirectly through the Randal W. Tyson Testamentary Trust. Tyson Limited Partnership is also a defendant in this matter. . . .

II. FACTUAL BACKGROUND . . .

In 2001, Tyson adopted a Stock Incentive Plan granting the board permission to award Class A shares, stock options, or other incentives to employees, officers, and directors of the company. Tyson gave the Compensation Committee and Compensation Subcommittee complete discretion as to when and to whom they would distribute these awards, but instructed that they were to consult with and receive recommendations from Tyson's Chairman and Chief Executive Officer. Plaintiffs allege that, at all relevant times, the Plan required that the price of the option be no lower than the fair market value of the company's stock on the day of the grant.[15]

Plaintiffs allege that the Compensation Committee, at the behest of several Defendant board members, "spring-loaded" these options. Days before Tyson would issue press releases that were very likely to drive stock prices higher, the Compensation Committee would award options to key employees.[16] Around 2.8 million shares of Tyson stock bounced from the corporate vaults to various defendants in this manner. Plaintiffs specifically identify four instances of allegedly well-timed option grants.

The Compensation Committee (then Massey, Vorsanger, and Cassady) granted John Tyson, former-CEO Wayne Britt, and then-COO Greg Lee options on 150,000 shares, 125,000 shares and 80,000 Class A shares, respectively, at $15 per share on September 28, 1999. The next day, Tyson informed the market that Smithfield Foods, Inc. had agreed to acquire Tyson's Pork Group. The announcement propelled the price upwards to $16.53 per share in less than six days, and to $17.50 per share by December 1, 1999.[17]

Once again, the Compensation Committee (then Massey, Hackley, and Allen) granted options on 200,000 Class A shares to John Tyson, 100,000 to Lee, and 50,000 to then-CFO Steven Hankins at $11.50 per share on March 29, 2001. A day later, Tyson publicly cancelled its $3.2 billion deal to acquire IBP, Inc. By the close of that day, the stock price had shot up to $13.47.

The Compensation Committee (then Hackley, Allen, and Massey) granted options on 200,000 Class A shares to John Tyson, 60,000 to Lee, and 15,000 to Hankins sometime in October 2001. Within two weeks, Tyson publicly announced its 2001 fourth-quarter earnings would be more than double those expected by analysts, catapulting the stock price to $11.90 by the end of November.

---

15. Consol. Compl. at ¶ 134. Tyson's 2004 Proxy Statement, however, suggests a more complex and nuanced Stock Incentive Plan. The Proxy states:

> The Plan provides for the grant of incentive stock options and nonqualified options....
>
> The exercise price of an option shall be set forth in the applicable Stock Incentive agreement. The exercise price of an *incentive stock option* may not be less than the fair market value of the Class A Common Stock on the date of the grant (nor less than 100% of the fair market value if the participant owns more than 10% of the stock of the Company or any subsidiary).... *Nonqualified stock options* may be made exercisable at a price equal to, less than or more than the fair market value of the Class A Common Stock on the date that the option is granted.

Defs.' Opening Br. in Supp. of Mot. to Dismiss Ex. M at 10–11 (emphasis added). The authority of the Compensation Committee to set a strike price depends upon whether the grant of options in question concerns "incentive" or "nonqualified" stock options.

16. A compensation committee that "spring loads" options grants them to executives before the release of material information reasonably expected to drive the shares of such options higher. (An opposite effect, "bullet dodging," is achieved by granting options to employees after the release of materially damaging information.)

17. Plaintiffs and defendants both agree that Tyson subsequently cancelled the grants to John Tyson and Lee, rendering moot any claim with respect to those grants. It remains unclear whether the grant to Britt was also cancelled.

The Compensation Committee (then Smith, Jones, and Hackley) granted stock options to a number of executives and directors, including 500,000 to John Tyson, 280,000 to Bond [the COO of Tyson], and 160,000 to Lee, at $13.33 per share on September 19, 2003. On September 23, 2003, Tyson publicly announced that earnings were to exceed Wall Street's expectations, propelling the price to $14.25....

IV. ANALYSIS* ...

Plaintiffs concede that the sole authority to grant [the spring-loaded] options rested in the Compensation Committee....

A committee of independent directors enjoys the presumption that its actions are *prima facie* protected by the business judgment rule.... [Accordingly, plaintiffs'] complaint should properly target only the members of the compensation committee at the time the options were approved: Vorsanger, Massey, Cassady, Allen, Hackley, Jones and Smith.[72]

As plaintiffs' allegations against these directors are insufficient to suggest a lack of independence, plaintiffs must demonstrate that the grant of the 2003 options could not be within the bounds of the Compensation Committee's business judgment. A severe test faces those seeking to overcome this presumption: "[W]here a director is independent and disinterested, there can be no liability for corporate loss, unless the facts are such that no person could possibly authorize such a transaction if he or she were attempting in *good faith* to meet their duty."[73]

Whether a board of directors may in good faith grant spring-loaded options is a somewhat more difficult question than that posed by options backdating, a practice that has attracted much journalistic, prosecutorial, and judicial thinking of late.[74] At their heart, all backdated options involve a fundamental, incontrovertible lie: directors who approve an option dissemble as to the date on which the grant was actually made. Allegations of springloading implicate a much more subtle deception.[75]

---

* The complaint contained a number of counts. Only the portion of the opinion concerning Count III, based on the spring-loaded options, is reprinted here. (Footnote by ed.)

72. Although Count III is dismissed except with regard to these seven defendants, none of whom are alleged to have received any financial benefit through the grant of spring-loaded options, the other defendant directors may yet be affected indirectly. Not all acts of disloyalty or bad faith will directly benefit the malefactor, and a director may be held personally liable for a breach of the duty of loyalty in the absence of a personal financial gain. Where the beneficiary of disloyalty is not directly liable for losses, that beneficiary might still be found to retain "money or property of another against the fundamental principles of justice or equity and good conscience," and thus to be unjustly enriched. *Schock v. Nash*, 732 A.2d 217, 232–233 (Del.1999).

73. *Gagliardi v. TriFoods Int'l, Inc.*, 683 A.2d 1049, 1052–1053 (Del.Ch.1996) (emphasis added).

74. Although similar to spring-loading, the backdating of options always involves a factual misrepresentation to shareholders. Issuance of options in conjunction with such deception, and against the background of a shareholder-approved stock-incentive program, amounts to a disloyal act taken in bad faith. *See Ryan v. Gifford*, 918 A.2d 341, ... (Del.2007).

75. The touchstone of disloyalty or bad faith in a spring-loaded option remains deception, not simply the fact that they are (in every real sense) "in the money" at the time of

Granting spring-loaded options, without explicit authorization from shareholders, clearly involves an indirect deception. A director's duty of loyalty includes the duty to deal fairly and honestly with the shareholders for whom he is a fiduciary.[76] It is inconsistent with such a duty for a board of directors to ask for shareholder approval of an incentive stock option plan and then later to distribute shares to managers in such a way as to undermine the very objectives approved by shareholders. This remains true even if the board complies with the strict letter of a shareholder-approved plan as it relates to strike prices or issue dates.

The question before the Court is not, as plaintiffs suggest, whether spring-loading constitutes a form of insider trading as it would be understood under federal securities law. The relevant issue is whether a director acts in bad faith by authorizing options with a market-value strike price, as he is required to do by a shareholder-approved incentive option plan, at a time when he *knows* those shares are actually worth more than the exercise price. A director who intentionally uses inside knowledge not available to shareholders in order to enrich employees while avoiding shareholder-imposed requirements cannot, in my opinion, be said to be acting loyally and in good faith as a fiduciary.

This conclusion, however, rests upon at least two premises, each of which should be (and, in this case, has been) alleged by a plaintiff in order to show that a spring-loaded option issued by a disinterested and independent board is nevertheless beyond the bounds of business judgment. First, a plaintiff must allege that options were issued according to a shareholder-approved employee compensation plan.[78] Second, a plaintiff must allege that the directors that approved spring-loaded (or bullet-dodging) options (a) possessed material non-public information soon to be released that would impact the company's share price, and (b) issued those options with the intent to circumvent otherwise valid shareholder-approved restrictions upon the exercise price of the options. Such allegations would satisfy a plaintiff's requirement to show adequately at the pleading stage that a director acted

issue. A board of directors might, in an exercise of good faith business judgment, determine that in the money options are an appropriate form of executive compensation. Recipients of options are generally unable to benefit financially from them until a vesting period has elapsed, and thus an option's value to an executive or employee is of less immediate value than an equivalent grant of cash. A company with a volatile share price, or one that expects that its most explosive growth is behind it, might wish to issue options with an exercise price below current market value in order to encourage a manager to work hard in the future while at the same time providing compensation with a greater present market value. One can imagine circumstances in which such a decision, were it made honestly and disclosed in good faith, would be within the rational exercise of business judgment. But the facts alleged in this case are different.

76. *In re Walt Disney S'holder Derivative Litig.*, 907 A.2d 693, 755 (Del.Ch.2005) ("To act in good faith, a director must act at all times with an *honesty of purpose* and in the best interests and welfare of the corporation." (emphasis added)).

78. Shareholder approved employee compensation plans are common partially as a result of I.R.C. § 162(m), the section of the tax code that allows a business to deduct employee compensation above $1 million only if it qualifies as performance-based compensation. Performance-based compensation plans must be approved by a majority vote of shareholders. *See* I.R.C. § 162(m)(4)(C)(ii).

disloyally and in bad faith and is therefore unable to claim the protection of the business judgment rule. Of course, it is conceivable that a director might show that shareholders have expressly empowered the board of directors (or relevant committee) to use backdating, spring-loading, or bullet-dodging as part of employee compensation, and that such actions would not otherwise violate applicable law. But defendants make no such assertion here.

Plaintiffs' have alleged adequately that the Compensation Committee violated a fiduciary duty by acting disloyally and in bad faith with regard to the grant of options. I therefore deny defendants' motion to dismiss Count III as to the seven members of the committee who are implicated in such conduct. . . .

V. CONCLUSION

Based on the foregoing analysis of the complaint. . . . Count III survives as to the seven members of the compensation committee.

Plaintiffs and defendants shall confer and submit an implementing form of Order.

Tyson Foods, Inc. (Tyson II)

Court of Chancery of Delaware, 2007.
2007 WL 2351071.

Memorandum Opinion

■ CHANDLER, J.

Before me is the outside director defendants' Motion for Judgment on the Pleadings concerning plaintiffs' allegations that defendants "spring-loaded" stock options granted to key Tyson directors and executives. In an Opinion dated February 6, 2007, I refused to dismiss Count III of plaintiffs' consolidated complaint, holding that the authorization of spring-loaded stock options may, in certain limited circumstances, constitute a breach of a director's fiduciary duties.

As part of that Opinion, I also noted that Tyson's public filings provided a more nuanced description of the Tyson Stock Incentive Plan than the consolidated complaint. Plaintiffs alleged that Tyson's shareholder-approved stock option plan required the challenged stock options to be granted at a price no less than the fair market price of Class A Common Stock on the date of the grant. Tyson's proxy statements, however, distinguished between "incentive stock options," to which a fair market value restriction applied, and "nonqualified stock options," which Tyson's Compensation Committee might make exercisable at any price. I refused to dismiss Count III of the complaint based on the premise that the challenged stock options may have been issued "with the intent to circumvent otherwise valid shareholder-approved restrictions upon the exercise price of the options." Defendants now maintain that the challenged stock options were, in fact, "non-qualified stock options" under Tyson's Stock Incentive Plan and move for judgment on the pleadings as to Count III.

. . . With the allegations before the Court more clearly delineated, the holding of the February 6, 2007 Opinion regarding spring-loading can now be considered with greater clarity.

I. STATEMENT OF FACTS

Plaintiffs challenge three separate grants of options issued between 2001 and 2003.[5] Each grant was awarded by the Compensation Committee according to the 2000 Stock Incentive Plan approved by shareholders in 2001. The parties disagree, however, as to whether these were grants of incentive or non-qualified stock options. . . .

Considering . . . the terms of the 2000 Stock Incentive Plan and Tyson's public filings . . . it becomes obvious that the consolidated complaint mischaracterizes the relevant stock option grants. The Plan itself clearly distinguishes between incentive and non-qualified stock option grants and Tyson made this distinction clear to shareholders when it sought approval in 2001. Shareholders had notice of, and approved, a plan that permitted the Compensation Committee the right to distribute options with either a fixed price or a strike price set at the discretion of the Committee. . . .

Tyson's publicly-filed statements and the shareholder-approved Plan on which plaintiffs rely thus contradict the allegation in the consolidated complaint that "the Plan requires that the price be no lower than the fair market value of the Company's stock on the day of the grant." This conclusion materially alters the appropriate analysis with respect to Count III of the consolidated complaint. The question facing the Court on February 6, 2007, was whether a grant of spring-loaded options could be within the bounds of the Compensation Committee's business judgment in the face of a shareholder-approved agreement explicitly requiring a market value strike-price. Absent such an agreement, the nature of defendants' alleged deception changes significantly.

Based on the allegations now before the Court, the following circumstances may be reasonably inferred from the consolidated complaint. On three separate occasions between 2001 and 2003, defendants suspected that Tyson's share price would climb once the market learned what the board already knew. Armed with this knowledge, members of the Compensation Committee granted non-qualified stock options to select Tyson employees, ensuring that these options would shortly be in the money. When the option grants were later revealed to shareholders, however, defendants did not straightforwardly describe such strike-price prestidigitation. Rather, they provided minimal assurances to investors that these options rested within the limits of the shareholder-approved plan. The crux of defendants' argument is that a scheme that relies upon bare formalism concealed by a poverty

---

5. *See In re Tyson Foods*, 919 A.2d at 575–576. The consolidated complaint originally challenged four grants of options, but plaintiffs have conceded that the 1999 grant has been rendered moot by a subsequent cancellation.

of communication somehow sits within the scope of reasonable, good faith business judgment. At this juncture, and based solely on the pleadings and the public documents, I cannot agree.

II. ANALYSIS

Delaware law sets forth few bright-line rules guiding the relationship between shareholders and directors. Nor does the law require corporations to adopt complex sets of articles and bylaws that govern the method by which corporate decisions will be made. Instead, shareholders are protected by the assurance that directors will stand as fiduciaries, exercising business judgment in good faith, solely for the benefit of shareholders.

Case law from the Supreme Court, as well as this Court, is replete with language describing the nature of this relationship. The affairs of Delaware corporations are managed by their board of directors, who owe to shareholders duties of *unremitting* loyalty.[13] This means that their actions must be taken in the good faith belief that they are in the best interests of the corporation and its stockholders, especially where conflicts with the individual interests of directors are concerned....

Loyalty. Good faith. Independence. Candor. These are words pregnant with obligation. The Supreme Court did not adorn them with half-hearted adjectives. Directors should not take a seat at the board table prepared to offer only conditional loyalty, tolerable good faith, reasonable disinterest or formalistic candor. It is against these standards, and in this spirit, that the alleged actions of spring-loading or backdating should be judged.

Defendants invoke an utterly different vision of Delaware law. Defendants' argument suggests a relationship between director and shareholder that falls beneath any reasonable conception of the fiduciary and into the merely contractual. The 2000 Tyson Stock Incentive Plan clearly stated that non-qualified stock options could be granted at any particular price. All SEC disclosures revealed the stated strike price to be the market price on the day of the grant. A preternaturally-attentive shareholder might have focused in upon the grant dates, matched them to Tyson press releases, and inferred from the relationship between them that the directors intended to issue what amounted to in the money options. All of this is purely to the letter of the agreement (runs defendants' reasoning), and no court should infer from this anything inconsistent with a duty of loyalty.

When directors seek shareholder consent to a stock incentive plan, or any other quasi-contractual arrangement, they do not do so in the manner of a devil in a dime-store novel, hoping to set a trap with a particular pattern of words. Had the 2000 Tyson Stock Incentive Plan never been put to a shareholder vote, the nature of a spring-loading scheme would constitute material information that the Tyson board of directors was obligated to disclose to investors when they revealed the

---

13. *Malone v. Brincat*, 722 A.2d 5, 10 (Del.1998).

grant. By agreeing to the Plan, shareholders did not implicitly forfeit their right to the same degree of candor from their fiduciaries.

Defendants protest that deceptive or deficient proxy disclosures cannot form the basis of a derivative claim challenging the grant of these options, asserting that "Tyson's later proxy disclosures concerning the challenged option grants are temporally and analytically distinct from the option grants themselves." At this stage, however, I am bound to give plaintiffs the benefit of every reasonable inference, not to give defendants the benefit of every doubt. Where a board of directors intentionally conceals the nature of its earlier actions, it is reasonable for a court to infer that the act concealed was itself one of disloyalty that could not have arisen from a good faith business judgment. The gravamen of Count III lies in the charge that defendants intentionally and *deceptively* channeled corporate profits to chosen executives (including members of Don Tyson's family). Proxy statements that display an uncanny parsimony with the truth are not "analytically distinct" from a series of improbably fortuitous stock option grants, but rather raise an inference that directors engaged in later dissembling to hide earlier subterfuge. The Court may further infer that grants of spring-loaded stock options were both inherently unfair to shareholders and that the long-term nature of the deceit involved suggests a scheme inherently beyond the bounds of business judgment.[18]

In retrospect, the test applied in the February 6, 2007 Opinion was, although appropriate to the allegations before the Court at the time, couched in too limited a manner.[19] Certainly the elements listed describe a claim sufficient to show that spring-loading would be beyond the bounds of business judgment. Given the additional information now presented by the parties, however, I am not convinced that allegations of an implicit violation of a shareholder-approved stock incentive plan are absolutely necessary for the Court to infer that the decision to spring-load options lies beyond the bounds of business judgment. Instead, I find that where I may reasonably infer that a board of directors later concealed the true nature of a grant of stock

---

18. This is not to say that failure to fully disclose the nature of a transaction in a proxy statement will always lead a court to question the equity of the underlying transaction. For obvious reasons, a company may wish to be less than entirely detailed about trade secrets or other confidential information. Executive compensation, however, is not a realm in which less than forthright disclosure somehow provides a company with an advantage with respect to competitors. Sophism and guile on this subject does not serve shareholder interests. When directors speak out about their own compensation, or that of company managers, shareholders have a right to the full, unvarnished truth.

19. "[The conclusion that spring-loading may not be an exercise of a good faith fiduciary] rests upon at least two premises, each of which should . . . be alleged by a plaintiff in order to show that a spring-loaded option issued by a disinterested and independent board is nevertheless beyond the bounds of business judgment. First, a plaintiff must allege that options were issued according to a shareholder-approved employee compensation plan. Second, a plaintiff must allege that the directors that approved spring-loaded (or bullet-dodging) options (a) possessed material non-public information soon to be released that would impact the company's share price, and (b) issued those options with the intent to circumvent otherwise valid shareholder-approved restrictions upon the exercise price of the options." *In re Tyson Foods*, 919 A.2d at 593.

options, I may further conclude that those options were not granted consistent with a fiduciary's duty of utmost loyalty. . . .

What the defendants here fail to confront is that their disclosures regarding the options under attack do nothing to rebut the pleading stage inference that the defendants intended to conceal a pattern of unfairly stocking up insiders' larders with option grants shortly before the announcement of events likely to increase the Company's stock price. In fact, the magnitude and timing of the grants, when accompanied with no disclosure of the reasons motivating the grants, is suggestive, at the pleading stage, of a purposeful subterfuge. Put simply, the pleadings support an inference not only that the defendants engaged in self-dealing, but that they attempted to hide their conduct from the stockholders.

For all of the above reasons, judgment on the pleadings is inappropriate. Defendants' motion is denied.

IT IS SO ORDERED.

Ryan v. Gifford

Court of Chancery of Delaware, 2007.
918 A.2d 341.

■ CHANDLER, CHANCELLOR.

On March 18, 2006, The Wall Street Journal sparked controversy throughout the investment community by publishing a one-page article, based on an academic's statistical analysis of option grants, which revealed an arguably questionable compensation practice. Commonly known as backdating, this practice involves a company issuing stock options to an executive on one date while providing fraudulent documentation asserting that the options were actually issued earlier. These options may provide a windfall for executives because the falsely dated stock option grants often coincide with market lows. Such timing reduces the strike prices and inflates the value of stock options, thereby increasing management compensation. This practice allegedly violates any stock option plan that requires strike prices to be no less than the fair market value on the date on which the option is granted by the board. Further, this practice runs afoul of many state and federal common and statutory laws that prohibit dissemination of false and misleading information.

After the article appeared in the Journal, Merrill Lynch issued a report demonstrating that officers of numerous companies, including Maxim Integrated Products, Inc., had benefited from so many fortuitously timed stock option grants that backdating seemed the only logical explanation. The report engendered this action.

Plaintiff Walter E. Ryan alleges that defendants breached their duties of due care and loyalty by approving or accepting backdated options that violated the clear letter of the shareholder-approved Stock

Option Plan and Stock Incentive Plan ("option plans"). Individual defendants. . . . move to dismiss this action on its merits. . . .

I. FACTS

Maxim Integrated Products, Inc. is a technology leader in design, development, and manufacture of linear and mixed-signal integrated circuits used in microprocessor-based electronic equipment. From 1998 to mid–2002 Maxim's board of directors and compensation committee granted stock options for the purchase of millions of shares of Maxim's common stock to John F. Gifford, founder, chairman of the board, and chief executive officer, pursuant to shareholder-approved stock option plans filed with the Securities and Exchange Commission. Under the terms of these plans, Maxim contracted and represented that the exercise price of all stock options granted would be no less than the fair market value of the company's common stock, measured by the publicly traded closing price for Maxim stock on the date of the grant. Additionally, the plan identified the board or a committee designated by the board as administrators of its terms.

Ryan is a shareholder of Maxim. . . . He filed this derivative action on June 2, 2006, against Gifford; James Bergman, B. Kipling Hagopian, and A.R. Frank Wazzan, members of the board and compensation committee at all relevant times; Eric Karros, member of the board from 2000 to 2002, and M.D. Sampels, member of the board from 2001–2002. Ryan alleges that nine specific grants were backdated between 1998 and 2002, as these grants seem too fortuitously timed to be explained as simple coincidence. All nine grants were dated on unusually low (if not the lowest) trading days of the years in question, or on days immediately before sharp increases in the market price of the company.

A. *Genesis of These Claims*

As practices surrounding the timing of options grants for public companies began facing increased scrutiny in early 2006, Merrill Lynch conducted an analysis of the timing of stock option grants from 1997 to 2002 for the semiconductor and semiconductor equipment companies that comprise the Philadelphia Semiconductor Index. Merrill Lynch measured the aggressiveness of timing of option grants by examining the extent to which stock price performance subsequent to options pricing events diverges from stock price performance over a longer period of time. "Specifically, it looked at annualized stock price returns for the twenty day period subsequent to options pricing in comparison to stock price returns for the calendar year in which the options were granted."[1] In theory, companies should not generate systematic excess return in comparison to other investors as a result of the timing of options pricing events. "[I]f the timing of options grants is an arm's length process, and companies have [not] systematically taken advantage of their ability to backdate options within the [twenty] day windows that the law provided prior to the implementation of

1. Compl. Ex. 1 at 1–2.

Sarbanes–Oxley in 2002, there shouldn't be any difference between the two measures."[2] Merrill Lynch failed to take a position on whether Maxim actually backdated; however, it noted that if backdating did not occur, management of Maxim was remarkably effective at timing options pricing events.

With regard to Maxim, Merrill Lynch found that the twenty-day return on option grants to management averaged 14% over the five-year period, an annualized return of 243%, or almost ten times higher than the 29% annualized market returns in the same period....

II. MOTION TO DISMISS

A. *Futility of Demand Under Rule 23.1*

... [The Chancellor concluded that a pre-suit demand on the board of directors by the plaintiff, a feature of derivative-suit procedures that is discussed in Chapter 14, was excused under the facts of set forth in the complaint.]

... A board's knowing and intentional decision to exceed the shareholders' grant of express (but limited) authority raises doubt regarding whether such decision is a valid exercise of business judgment....

... Plaintiff supports his claim that backdating occurred by pointing to nine option grants over a six-year period where each option was granted during a low point. That is, every challenged option grant occurred during the lowest market price of the month or year in which it was granted. In addition to pointing specifically to highly suspicious timing, plaintiff further supports his allegations with empirical evidence suggesting that backdating occurred. The Merrill Lynch analysis measured the extent to which stock price performance subsequent to options pricing events diverged from stock price performance over a longer period of time to measure the aggressiveness of the timing of option grants and found that Maxim's average annualized return of 243% on option grants to management was almost ten times higher than the 29% annualized market returns in the same period. This timing, by my judgment and by support of empirical data, seems too fortuitous to be mere coincidence. The appearance of impropriety grows even more when one considers the fact that the board granted options, not at set or designated times, but by a sporadic method.[34]

Plaintiff supports his breach of fiduciary duty claim ... by pointing to the board's decision to ignore limitations set out in the company's stock options plans. The plans do not grant the board

2. Compl. Ex. 1 at 2.

34. Defendants argue repeatedly that plaintiff's allegations ultimately rest upon nothing more than statistical abstractions. Nevertheless, this Court is required to draw reasonable inferences and need not be blind to probability. True, the Merrill Lynch report does not state conclusively that Gifford's options were actually backdated. Rather, it emphatically suggests that either defendant directors knowingly manipulated the dates on which options were granted, or their timing was extraordinarily lucky. Given the choice between improbable good fortune and knowing manipulation of option grants, the Court may reasonably infer the latter, even when applying the heightened pleading standards of Rule 23.1.

discretion to alter the exercise price by falsifying the date on which options were granted. Thus, the alleged facts suggest that the director defendants violated an express provision of two option plans and exceeded the shareholders' grant of express authority.

Plaintiff here points to specific grants, specific language in option plans, specific public disclosures, and supporting empirical analysis to allege knowing and purposeful violations of shareholder plans and intentionally fraudulent public disclosures.... [that] provide sufficient particularity in the pleading to survive a motion to dismiss for failure to make demand pursuant to Rule 23.1.[35]....

B. Failure To State a Claim Upon Which Relief Can Be Granted

Defendants assert that plaintiff fails to state a claim for breach of fiduciary duty. This defense, stripped to its essence, states that in order to survive a motion to dismiss on a fiduciary duty claim, the complaint must rebut the business judgment rule. That is, plaintiff must raise a reason to doubt that the directors were disinterested or independent. Where the complaint does not rebut the business judgment rule, plaintiff must allege waste. Plaintiff here, argue the defendants, fails to do either. Further, there is no evidence that the defendants acted intentionally, in bad faith, or for personal gain. Therefore, so the argument goes, plaintiff fails to plead facts sufficient to rebut the business judgment rule and cannot maintain an action for breach of fiduciary duties.

Plaintiff responds that ... the directors' purposeful failure to honor an unambiguous provision of a shareholder approved stock option plan ... rebuts the business judgment rule for the purpose of a motion to dismiss for failure to state a claim upon which relief can be granted....

1. *The Business Judgment Rule and Bad Faith*

... [T]he complaint here alleges bad faith and, therefore, a breach of the duty of loyalty sufficient to rebut the business judgment rule and survive a motion to dismiss. The business affairs of a corporation are to be managed by or under the direction of its board of directors. In an effort to encourage the full exercise of managerial powers, Delaware law protects the managers of a corporation through the business judgment rule. This rule "is a presumption that in making a business decision the directors of a corporation acted on an informed basis, in good faith and in the honest belief that the action

---

35. Defendants also object that plaintiff's allegations are not particularized for purposes of Rule 23.1 because they do not directly allege knowledge on behalf of the directors. Yet, it is difficult to understand how a plaintiff can allege that directors backdated options *without* simultaneously alleging that such directors *knew* that the options were being backdated. After all, any grant of options had to have been approved by the committee, and that committee can be reasonably expected to know the date of the options as well as the date on which they actually approve a grant. Nor is it any defense to say that directors might not have had knowledge that backdating violated their duty of loyalty. Directors of Delaware corporations should not be surprised to find that lying to shareholders is inconsistent with loyalty, which necessarily requires good faith. *See, e.g., Malone v. Brincat*, 722 A.2d 5, 11–12 (Del.1998).

taken was in the best interest of the company."[44] Nevertheless, a showing that the board breached either its fiduciary duty of due care or its fiduciary duty of loyalty in connection with a challenged transaction may rebut this presumption. Such a breach may be shown where the board acts intentionally, in bad faith, or for personal gain.

In *Stone v. Ritter*, the Supreme Court of Delaware held that acts taken in bad faith breach the duty of loyalty.[46] Bad faith, the Court stated, may be shown where "the fiduciary intentionally acts with a purpose other than that of advancing the best interests of the corporation, where the fiduciary acts with the intent to violate applicable positive law, or where the fiduciary intentionally fails to act in the face of known duty to act, demonstrating a conscious disregard for his duties."[47] Additionally, other examples of bad faith might exist. These examples include any action that demonstrates a faithlessness or lack of true devotion to the interests of the corporation and its shareholders.

Based on the allegations of the complaint, and all reasonable inferences drawn therefrom, I am convinced that the intentional violation of a shareholder approved stock option plan, coupled with fraudulent disclosures regarding the directors' purported compliance with that plan, constitute conduct that is disloyal to the corporation and is therefore an act in bad faith. Plaintiffs allege the following conduct: Maxim's directors affirmatively represented to Maxim's shareholders that the exercise price of any option grant would be no less than 100% of the fair value of the shares, measured by the market price of the shares on the date the option is granted. Maxim shareholders, possessing an absolute right to rely on those assurances when determining whether to approve the plans, in fact relied upon those representations and approved the plans. Thereafter, Maxim's directors are alleged to have deliberately attempted to circumvent their duty to price the shares at no less than market value on the option grant dates by surreptitiously changing the dates on which the options were granted. To make matters worse, the directors allegedly failed to disclose this conduct to their shareholders, instead making false representations regarding the option dates in many of their public disclosures.

I am unable to fathom a situation where the deliberate violation of a shareholder approved stock option plan and false disclosures, obviously intended to mislead shareholders into thinking that the directors complied honestly with the shareholder-approved option plan, is anything but an act of bad faith. It certainly cannot be said to amount to faithful and devoted conduct of a loyal fiduciary. Well-pleaded allegations of such conduct are sufficient, in my opinion, to rebut the business judgment rule and to survive a motion to dismiss. . . .

---

44. *Aronson*, 473 A.2d at 812.

46. 911 A.2d 362, 370 (Del.2006).

47. *Id.* at 369.

E. Unjust Enrichment

Finally, defendants contend that plaintiff's claim for unjust enrichment fails because there is no allegation that Gifford exercised any of the alleged backdated options and, therefore, Gifford did not obtain any benefit to which he was not entitled to the detriment of another. This defense is contrary both to the normal concept of remuneration and to common sense.

Unjust enrichment is "the unjust retention of a benefit to the loss of another, or the retention of money or property of another against the fundamental principles of justice or equity and good conscience."[61] A defendant may be liable "even when the defendant retaining the benefit is not a wrongdoer" and "even though he may have received [it] honestly in the first instance."[62]

At this stage, I cannot conclude that there is no reasonably conceivable set of circumstances under which Gifford might be unjustly enriched. Gifford does retain something of value, the alleged backdated options, at the expense of the corporation and shareholders. Further, defendants make no allegations that Gifford is precluded from exercising these options or that the options have expired. Thus, one can imagine a situation where Gifford exercises the options and benefits from the low exercise price. Even if Gifford fails to exercise a single option during the course of this litigation, that fact would not justify dismissal of the unjust enrichment claim. Whether or not the options are exercised, the Court will be able to fashion a remedy. For example, this Court might rely on expert testimony to determine the true value of the option grants or simply rescind them. Either way, Gifford's alleged failure to exercise the options up to this point does not undermine a claim for unjust enrichment Thus, I deny the motion to dismiss the unjust enrichment claim. . . .

DEL. GEN. CORP. LAW §§ 141(H), 157

[See Statutory Supplement]

MODEL BUS. CORP. ACT §§ 6.24, 8.11

[See Statutory Supplement]

ALI, PRINCIPLES OF CORPORATE GOVERNANCE § 5.03

---

61. *Schock v. Nash*, 732 A.2d 217, 232–33 (Del.1999).

62. *Id.*

NEW YORK STOCK EXCHANGE LISTED COMPANY MANUAL § 312.03(a)

[See Statutory Supplement]

NOTE ON CHALLENGES TO COMPENSATION

At least in the past, it has been difficult to successfully challenge executive compensation in a publicly held corporation when the compensation has been approved by disinterested directors or disinterested shareholders. In such corporations, executive compensation has at least the appearance, and perhaps the reality, of having been approved through a disinterested bureaucratic process. Furthermore, except in the most extreme cases, executive compensation in publicly held corporations constitutes only a very small fraction of the corporation's total earnings.

In contrast, the courts often hold executive compensation to be unreasonable in close corporations. The close-corporation case differs from the publicly held corporation case in two critical ways. First, in close corporations executive compensation usually is not approved by either disinterested directors or disinterested shareholders. Second, in close corporations executive compensation is likely to involve a very significant fraction of the corporation's earnings—often, half or more.

Close-corporation compensation cases arise in several basic contexts.

One of these contexts is taxation. A basic income-tax rule is that, except in S corporations, whose income and expenses flow through directly to the shareholders, compensation paid to a corporate executive or other employee is a deductible expense, which reduces taxable income, while a dividend paid to a shareholder is not deductible. Accordingly, the payment of compensation reduces the corporation's taxable income, and therefore its taxes, while the payment of dividends does not. In the close corporation, the same persons are typically both shareholders and managers. If dividends and compensation were treated the same way for tax purposes, the shareholders would often be indifferent whether they took cash out of the corporation in the form of compensation or dividends. Given the tax laws, however, shareholders in close corporations other than S corporations will normally prefer to take out cash in the form of compensation, so as to reduce the corporation's taxes. The Internal Revenue Service regularly challenges compensation in close corporations as unreasonable, and the courts often agree with the IRS's position. See, e.g., RTS Investment Corp. v. Commissioner, 877 F.2d 647 (8th Cir.1989). In such cases, the excess of actual compensation over reasonable compensation is treated as a dividend and is not deductible from the corporation's taxable income.

Another context in which the courts often hold compensation in close corporations to be unreasonable is derivative actions by shareholders in such corporations to recover the excess compensation. See, e.g., Crowley v. Communications For Hospitals, Inc., 30 Mass.App.Ct. 751, 573 N.E.2d 996 (1991), review denied, 410 Mass. 1104, 577 N.E.2d 309 (1991); Wilderman v. Wilderman, p. 699, infra; Hall v. Staha, 303 Ark. 673, 800 S.W.2d 396 (1990).

Compensation in close corporations is also sometimes attacked in other contexts, when compensation to employee-shareholders is not pro rata. For example, a shareholder may claim that payments cast in the form of compensation were unreasonable, and really constituted a dividend that should have been distributed pro rata to all shareholders. See, e.g., Alaska Plastics, Inc. v. Coppock, 621 P.2d 270 (Alaska 1980), on appeal following remand, 705 P.2d 443 (1985). Or, a claim of unreasonable compensation to some shareholders may be advanced as a reason why dissolution for oppression should be granted. In these contexts, the courts are often ready to find compensation to be excessive where only one faction in a close corporation receives compensation and dividends are low or nonexistent.

WILDERMAN v. WILDERMAN, 315 A.2d 610, 615 (Del.Ch.1974). This was a case involving a claim of excessive compensation in a close corporation, in which the compensation had not been approved by disinterested directors or shareholders. The court said: "As to the facts to be considered in reaching a determination of the question as to whether or not defendant has met the burden he must carry there is little authority in Delaware. In Hall v. Isaacs, [37 Del.Ch. 530, 146 A.2d 602, aff'd in part 39 Del.Ch. 244, 163 A.2d 288 (1960),] the Court was of the view that evidence of what other executives similarly situated received was relevant, and in Meiselman v. Eberstadt, [39 Del.Ch. 563, 170 A.2d 720 (1961)], the ability of the executive was considered. Other factors which have been judicially recognized elsewhere are whether or not the Internal Revenue Service has allowed the corporation to deduct the amount of salary alleged to be unreasonable. Other relevant factors are whether the salary bears a reasonable relation to the success of the corporation, the amount previously received as salary, whether increases in salary are geared to increases in the value of services rendered, and the amount of the challenged salary compared to other salaries paid by the employer."

SEC REGULATION S-K, ITEM 402

[See Statutory Supplement]

NOTE ON CEO COMPENSATION

The issue of executive compensation today has a high place on the corporate and even the national agenda. Most of the concerns have centered on the compensation of the chief executive officers (CEOs) of publicly held corporations. These complaints have fallen into several categories.

One concern is that CEO compensation is too large as an absolute matter. The mean annual compensation of CEOs of the corporations in the S & P 500 index, expressed in constant dollars, grew from $3.7 million in 1993 to $10.3 million in 2002. (The S & P 500 is a group of stocks that is considered representative of the stock market in general.) Bebchuck & Grinstein, The Growth of Executive Pay, Table 5 (2005). This growth is not explained by inflation, because the figures are inflation-adjusted. Nor is it explained by changes in market capitalization or industry mix. Id. at 13. Equity-based compensation of CEOs in the S & P 500 rose from 41% of total compensation in 1993 to 67% in 2002. Id. at Table 5. Finally, the ratio between (i) the total compensation of the top five executives and (ii) corporate net income for all corporations in the S & P 500, the Mid–Cap 400, and the Small–Cap 600 rose from 5.7% in 1993–1997 to 9.9% in 1998–2002. Id. at Table 10. (The Mid–Cap 400 is a group of corporations that generally have market capitalizations of $2 billion to $10 billion. The Small–Cap 600 is a group of corporations that generally have market capitalizations of $300 million to $2 billion. Market capitalization is the total stock-market value of a corporation's stock.) Of course, this is only the median, and many compensation packages were much higher. For example, according to the *Wall Street Journal*, in 1999 Michael Eisner of Disney made $576 million; Sandy Weill of Citigroup made $167 million; and Douglas Ivester of Coca–Cola made $57 million. In those years, the total shareholder return for Disney, as calculated by the Journal, was minus 5%; the total shareholder return for Citigroup was minus 6.8%; and the total shareholder return for Coca–Cola was 1.3%. Skipping forward, the *Journal* reported that in 2004, Reuben Mark of Colgate–Palmolive Co. made $141 million; Steve Jobs of Apple made $75 million; and George David of United Technologies made $70 million.

A related concern is that there is too much disparity between CEO compensation and average salaries. "In 1992, the average large-company CEO received approximately 140 times the pay of an average worker; in 2003, the separation was about 500:1." Id. In contrast, the average Japanese CEO apparently makes only 16 times the pay of an average Japanese industrial worker, and the average German apparently makes about 21 times the pay of the average German factory worker. G. Crystal, In Search of Excess 27, 206–09 (1991).

Complaints about both the absolute and relative levels of CEO compensation leave many unpersuaded, especially in an era in which so many athletes and entertainment stars earn as much or more as the median CEO in the *Journal* survey. It has also been suggested that CEO compensation should be understood as the prize in a tournament, for which the corporation's vice-presidents joust. "On the day that a given individual is promoted from vice-president to president, his salary may triple. It is difficult to argue that his skills have tripled in that 1–day period.... It is not a puzzle, however, when interpreted in the context of a prize.... [A CEO's] wage is settled on not necessarily because it reflects his current productivity as president, but rather because it induces that individual and all other individuals to perform appropriately when they are in more junior positions." Edward Lazear, and Sherwin Rosen, Rank–Order Tournaments as Optimum Labor Contracts, 89 Journal of Political Economy 841 (1981). (The tournament theory of compensation has not been empirically verified. See O'Reilly et al., CEO Compensation Tournament and Social Comparison: A Tale of Two Theories, 33 Admin.Sci.Q. 257, 266 (1988).)

Perhaps the more significant complaints, which have attracted a relatively widespread following, concern the process for setting CEO compensation and the relation, or lack of it, between CEO compensation and corporate performance. A major concern here is that CEOs often effectively set their own compensation, because they dominate their boards. In theory, a chief executive's compensation is determined by a disinterested board on the recommendation of an independent compensation committee, which in turn acts on the recommendation of an independent personnel department and an independent outside consulting firm, all without the chief executive's participation. In practice, however, "the chief executive often has his hand in the pay-setting process almost from the first step." Williams, Why Chief Executives' Pay Keeps Rising, Fortune, April 1, 1985, at 66, 67. The CEO "generally approves, or at least knows about, the recommendation of his personnel executive *before* it goes to the compensation committee, and may take a similar pregame pass at the consultant's recommendations too." Id. "[T]he reality at most companies is that top management itself usually devises the executive compensation plan—hiring the consultants whose scheme is then ratified by the board of directors and shareholders...." Personnel executives who don't recommend what the chief executive officer wants may find that their jobs are at risk; consultants who don't recommend what the chief executive wants are unlikely to be invited back. See Louis, Business is Bungling Long–Term Compensation, Fortune, July 23, 1984, at 64, 65.

One response to this problem has been an increased emphasis on disclosure and on the makeup and role of the compensation committee. The SEC has periodically revised the Proxy Rules to enormously increase the amount of disclosure required in connection with executive compensation, and to give a critical role to the compensation committee. See Proxy Rules Schedule 14A, Items 8, 10, and Reg. S–K, Item 402, in the Statutory Supplement. Up to now, at least, these changes seem to have had little or no effect.

INTERNAL REVENUE CODE § 161(m) AND REGULATIONS THEREUNDER

[See Statutory Supplement]

NOTE ON THE EFFECT OF FEDERAL INCOME TAX RULES AND ACCOUNTING PRINCIPLES ON THE FORMS OF EXECUTIVE COMPENSATION

The federal income tax helps shape a variety of corporate decisions, including compensation decisions. Under existing tax law, compensation in the form of incentive stock options and non-qualified stock options is given highly favorable treatment. A non-qualified stock option is not taxable when issued, but only when the option is exercised. An incentive stock option is not taxable when issued or when exercised, but only when the stock is sold. Even then, tax is levied at only the capital-gains rate. From the executive's perspective, the tax law therefore provides a push toward using one or more of those forms of compensation.

In the past, accounting rules have also given a strong push in this direction. Until recently, those principles provided that most forms of executive compensation had to be expensed—that is, deducted—from the corporation's net income, but this rule did not apply to the value of executive stock options. Instead, corporations that granted stock options to employees could account for the cost of these options based on their "intrinsic value" at the moment they were granted. An option's "intrinsic value" is the difference between its exercise price and the current price of its underlying security. Accordingly, if a company granted options with an exercise price equal to the price of the company's stock at the time of the grant, the company could avoid deducting the value of the options from its income. This is perverse. Any stock option has value, because the price of the stock can go up to more than the option price. In particular, the value of an option depends primarily on the price of the option, its length, and the volatility of the underlying stock. An option to purchase stock at the price of the stock on the grant date can be worth hundreds of thousands, or even millions, of dollars, depending on a variety of factors discussed in the next paragraph. The result was a corporation could give a CEO millions of dollars worth of stock options without counting the value of those options against its reported income or in the CEO's reported compensation.

In December 2004, the Financial Accounting Standards Board (FASB), which is the chief private rulemaking body for setting accounting principles, issued Statement of Financial Accounting Standards No. 123, which changed the generally accepted accounting principles (GAAP) that apply to stock-option compensation plans. FASB Statement No. 123 requires companies to measure the value of options by computing their "fair value" on the date they were granted. A standard way to compute the value of an option is by using the Black–Scholes option pricing model. The application of this model depends on five variables: (1) The risk-free rate of interest. (2) The market price of the underlying stock. (3) The volatility of the price of the underlying stock. (Volatility is the size of fluctuations of a stock's price.) (4) The exercise price of the option. (5) The length of the option's term. The value of an option will increase with increases in (i) the risk-free rate of interest; (ii) the excess (if any) of the market price of the stock over the exercise price of the option; (iii) the volatility of the underlying stock; and (iv) the length of the term of option. All of these variables except volatility can be easily determined. Volatility is estimated in significant part on the basis of the stock's historical performance. (Certain factors that are not incorporated into the Black–Scholes option-pricing model may also affect the value of an option. For example, the model is designed to value a "European call option," which is exercisable only at the end of the option's term. If an option is an "American option," which permits the option holder to exercise the option at any time during the option's term, then the option's value will be higher. Variations of the Black–Scholes model take such factors into account.)

The Internal Revenue Code also has special provisions that can affect the form and even the size of compensation by limits on deductibility. This is true, for example, of the special rules on the taxation of stock options. Another relevant provision is Internal Revenue Code § 161(m). Under that provision, a publicly held corporation normally cannot deduct any compensation of a CEO, or any of its other four most highly paid executives, in excess of $1 million, unless the excess is based on performance goals formulated by independent directors and approved by the shareholders. As a practical matter, this provision has a very limited bite, because it is easy to set up watered-down easily attainable performance goals.

NOTE ON THE COMPENSATION OF NONEXECUTIVE DIRECTORS

The compensation of nonexecutive directors has drawn increasing attention within the last few years. The modern theory of the role of the board in publicly held corporations is that the board should monitor the executives' conduct of the business. This monitoring model assumes that directors will be independent of the executives they are to monitor, and will have the proper incentives to play a monitoring role. Directorial independence and incentives, in turn, are affected by the amount and form of directorial compensation.

1. *Amount of Compensation.* To understand the significance of the amount of a director's compensation, it must be borne in mind that although nominally the directors select the CEO, in practice it is the other way around. The CEO's role in the selection of directors may be diminishing somewhat, but it is still very important. Correspondingly, directors who displease a CEO will often find it difficult to retain their board seats. Accordingly, a director who has a material financial incentive to retain his directorship will not really be independent of the CEO.

The greater a director's compensation, the greater the director's financial incentives to retain his seat, and the less the director's independence. To take a simple case, a director who earns, say,

$200,000/year, and whose continuation in office is wholly or partly under the control of the CEO, normally could not realistically be deemed independent of the CEO unless he was extremely wealthy. The trick, therefore, is to compensate directors in an amount that is sufficient to give responsible persons an incentive to serve as directors and rewards that service in an appropriate way, but is not so large as to compromise directorial independence.

In the 1980s, directors' fees averaged about $30,000/year. Since the early 1990s, however, directors' compensation has been growing much faster than inflation, partly because director compensation now often includes stock or stock options. In 1994, the average compensation of directors in Fortune 500 corporations (that is, in the country's 500 largest nonfinancial corporations) was $50,000. In 2002, director compensation averaged $152,000 in the largest 200 companies and $116,000 in the largest 1,000 companies. Moreover, many directors also provide services to the corporation in nondirectorial capacities, which further increases their compensation and therefore further compromises their independence.

2. *Form of Compensation.* Directorial independence and incentives may be affected by the form, as well as the amount, of a director's compensation.

a. *Compensation for consulting and other nondirectorial services.* The effect of the form of director compensation is particularly dramatic in the case of compensation for services that a director renders to the corporation in a nondirectorial capacity. The selection of consultants, professionals, and the like is normally within the sole control of the executives. Therefore, even if a director could retain his board seat against the wishes of the CEO, he would stand to lose his nondirectorial compensation if he falls into the CEO's disfavor.

Compensation for nondirectorial services can be very large, and may be further augmented by fringe benefits. For example, in 1995 American Express paid Henry Kissinger, a non-executive director, the following compensation: annual consulting fees of $350,000; an annual director's retainer of $64,000; a prospective annual director's pension of $30,000; free director's life insurance; and the right to have American Express make a $500,000 gift to a charity of his choice at the time of his death. Knecht & Lublin, American Express Bars Using Directors as Paid Consultants, Wall St. J. April 12, 1995, at A.3. American Express eventually adopted a policy that prohibits outside directors from serving as consultants, but Kissinger was exempted from the policy. Similarly, until 1995 W.R. Grace paid annual consulting fees totaling $1.5 million to five directors who were longtime friends of Grace's chairman. In that year, the chairman was ousted and Grace adopted a policy that no one with a consulting contract could serve as a director.

b. *Pensions.* Pensions for directors are a relatively new idea, but have become widespread. Like nondirectorial compensation, directorial pensions present problems of independence and incentives. "The most common director retirement program involves an annual cash retirement fee equal to the board retainer at the time the director retires. The period of time for which a director receives a retirement fee typically is either (1) for the number of years for which the director has served, with some imposing a maximum of 10 years, or (2) for life if the director has served a minimum of 10 years. In some cases, the director's surviving spouse received part of the director's retirement fee upon the director's death—either until a designated number of years have elapsed, or for the spouse's life." Report on the National Association of Corporate Directors Blue Ribbon Commission on Director Compensation 29 (1995) ("NACD Report").

Some pensions are even more generous. At one time, Warner–Lambert Company paid a lifetime pension of $35,000/year to any director who had served five years and reached age 70. Lublin, More Big Companies Reconsider Lavish Pensions for Directors, Wall St. J., Sept. 7, 1995, at B1, Col. 3. The threat of losing a pension payoff may be even greater than the threat of losing annual directors' fees, especially as a director approaches retirement age. Moreover, pensions are associated with employment status, and therefore set a poor psychological tone for directorial independence. It is no coincidence that basic directorial compensation has been traditionally called a "fee," or sometimes a "retainer"—not a "salary" which, like a pension, connotes employment status. The NACD Report recommended that directors should be paid only cash and stock, and that pensions and other benefits should not be granted to directors.

c. *Payment in stock.* Paying directors in the form of stock, rather than cash, may also matter. Over the years, a director who is paid in stock may find that stock in the corporation represents a significant portion of her wealth, at least if the sale of her stock is restricted. This should tend to align the director's interest more closely with the shareholders, and thereby provide an incentive for monitoring. See Elson, The Duty of Care, Compensation, and Stock Ownership, 63 U.Cinn.L.Rev. 649 (1995).

SECTION 4. USE OF CORPORATE ASSETS: THE CORPORATE OPPORTUNITY DOCTRINE

Hawaiian International Finances, Inc. v. Pablo

Supreme Court of Hawaii, 1971.
53 Haw. 149, 488 P.2d 1172.

■ Before RICHARDSON, C.J., ABE, LEVINSON and KOBAYASHI, JJ., and MENOR, CIRCUIT JUDGE, in place of MARUMOTO, J., disqualified.

■ KOBAYASHI, JUSTICE.

This is an appeal by Hawaiian International Finances, Inc., a Hawaii corporation (herein appellant), from a judgment of the circuit court providing that Pastor Pablo (herein Pablo), Rufina Pablo (herein Mrs. Pablo) and Pastor Pablo Realty, Inc., a Hawaii corporation (herein Pablo Realty) (all collectively herein appellees), are not liable to appellant for certain commissions received by appellees for their participation in the procurement of certain investment properties for appellant.

Although appellant appeals from both the conclusions of law and findings of fact of the trial court, the requisite facts necessary for a proper disposition of this case are not in dispute. As such, the factual rendition is concise and includes only those facts considered essential by this court. They are in part as follows:

FACTS

Pablo was president of appellant during the time the events pertinent to this case took place. In addition he and his wife, Rufina Pablo, were directors of Pablo Realty.

Pablo and Mrs. Pablo had been traveling to California in and prior to 1964, at their own expense, in connection with their private real estate business. Upon their return to Hawaii in early 1964, both Pablo and Mrs. Pablo advised appellant of attractive real estate investment opportunities in California. Appellant's board of directors appointed a subcommittee of four persons, including Pablo and three others who are non-litigants herein, to represent the corporation and go to California to investigate such investments. While in California, agreements were entered into by Pablo on behalf of appellant to purchase two parcels of land. The sellers were represented by separate California real estate brokers who eventually split their commissions from the sellers with Pablo. The trial court found that appellees had had no formal agreements with either of the California selling brokers for any commission splitting prior to the execution of the contracts to purchase the two properties. Pablo did testify, however, in response to questioning by the trial court, that he did expect, as a real estate broker, a commission for his participation in the transactions, and that he was told by one of the selling brokers that he would be paid after the transactions were closed.

After the closing of the escrows, the selling brokers in California paid, as commissions $4,800.00 to Pablo in May, 1964 and $17,594.20 to Pablo Realty in April, 1964. At this time appellant did not know of the receipt of these commissions and did not learn of them until the matter was brought up at a corporate meeting in September, 1964. The actual amounts were not disclosed by Pablo until March, 1965.

The trial court concluded as follows:

"That, although the general rule is that a person who is the president and a director of a corporation is a fiduciary of the corporation and cannot profit from any breach of the fiduciary obligation, nevertheless, under the particular facts of this case, PASTOR A. PABLO, acting for himself and as an officer of PASTOR PABLO REALTY, INC., committed no wrong in accepting the two partial real estate commissions from the California real estate brokers and the court cannot in good conscience compel him to turn those moneys over to the corporation."

ISSUE

The question on appeal centers around the trial court's construction of the law as applied to the facts in this case. Essentially the issue is whether a corporate officer and director, acting for the corporation in the purchase of investment real estate, can retain a commission received from the real estate brokers representing the sellers, absent disclosure and an agreement with the corporation.

CORPORATE FIDUCIARY—UNDISCLOSED PROFITS

It is widely held that a director while engaged in a transaction for his corporation cannot retain an undisclosed profit. . . .

The Restatement of Restitution, § 197, comment *c* at 809–810, speaks directly to the facts of the instant case and explains the rationale of the law in this area:

> *c. Where no harm to beneficiary.* The rule stated in this Section is applicable although the profit received by the fiduciary is not at the expense of the beneficiary. Thus, where an agent to purchase property for his principal acts properly in making the purchase but subsequently receives a bonus from the seller, he holds the money received upon a constructive trust for his principal. The rule * * * is not based on harm done to the beneficiary in the particular case, but rests upon a broad principle of preventing a conflict of opposing interests in the minds of fiduciaries, whose duty it is to act solely for the benefit of their beneficiaries. . . .

APPELLANT'S INTEREST IN THE UNDISCLOSED COMMISSION

In a case involving a trustee who received a bonus from a third party for placing trust business, we held that "when the opportunity to make a profit arises from the position occupied by a fiduciary the profit realized belongs to the principal, at least when the fiduciary has excluded his principal from any chance to enjoy the opportunity coming to the fiduciary in this manner." In re Dean's Trust, 47 Haw. 629, 640, 394 P.2d 432, 438 (1964). . . .

Appellees attempt to circumvent the rationale of cases [like *Dean's Trust*] by arguing that appellant could not lawfully have shared in the selling real estate brokers' commissions because appellant was not a licensed real estate broker. They therefore conclude that appellant was not excluded from enjoying the benefit received by appellees. We need not reach this question. In In re Dean's Trust it was pointed out that a line of cases have held "that the contention of *ultra vires* does not lie in the mouth of a corporate officer claiming the profits of a transaction for himself." In re Dean's Trust, *supra,* 47 Haw. at 638, 394 P.2d at 437. Even if it were decided that appellant itself could not have lawfully received the commissions that would not be determinative. In a case similar to the one at hand, involving a corporate fiduciary who made a secret profit from a seller of land to the corporation, the court said that "[i]t appears only reasonable that [the corporation] would have been more anxious to acquire the property at a price less the commission paid [the fiduciary] than they would have been to purchase the property paying the price including the commission." Pryor v. Oak Ridge Development Corp., 97 Fla. 1085, 1092, 119 So. 326, 329 (1928). The same holds true in this case. Had appellant known that one of its directors, Pablo, would be receiving a commission from its purchase, it is reasonable to assume that it would have been more anxious to acquire the property at a price less that commission.

Appellees' contention that Pablo's actions were in good faith and resulted in no loss to appellant is of no consequence. Had Pablo disclosed the fact that he anticipated receiving commissions, this case would be different. Then appellant would have had an opportunity to either attempt to obtain the property at a price less the commissions or it could have agreed with Pablo to acquiesce in letting him retain the commissions he received. This was not done. Appellant did not even learn of the commissions until months after their receipt when Pablo was directly questioned about them during a corporate meeting.

CONCLUSION

In accordance with the principles relating to corporate fiduciaries espoused herein, appellees Pablo and Pablo Realty are liable to appellant for the commissions they received and the trial court's judgment is reversed. As to appellee Mrs. Pablo, we affirm the judgment of the trial court, the trial court having specifically found, in its findings of fact, that Mrs. Pablo had no connection with the receipt of the commissions.

Remanded for entry of judgment consistent with this opinion.

FORKIN v. COLE, 192 Ill.App.3d 409, 139 Ill.Dec. 410, 548 N.E.2d 795 (1989). Cole, who controlled HPDI Corporation, mortgaged HPDI property to First National Bank to secure a personal loan made to Cole by the Bank. In affirming a judgment in favor of HPDI, the court said "Defendants ... contend the mortgage of the HPDI property to the First National Bank as security for a loan to Cole Sr. should not have resulted in judgment against Cole Sr., in that no material loss occurred to HPDI.... [However,] by encumbering the HPDI asset, Cole Sr. used a corporate asset for his own personal benefit. It also arguably could have prevented HPDI from taking advantage of a corporate opportunity had one arisen. The misappropriation of a corporate asset provided an advantage to Cole Sr."

AMERICAN LAW INSTITUTE, PRINCIPLES OF CORPORATE GOVERNANCE § 5.04

[See Statutory Supplement]

RESTATEMENT (SECOND) OF AGENCY § 388

[See Statutory Supplement]

Northeast Harbor Golf Club, Inc. v. Harris

Supreme Judicial Court of Maine, 1995.
661 A.2d 1146.

■ Before WATHEN, C.J., and ROBERTS, GLASSMAN, DANA, and LIPEZ, JJ.

■ ROBERTS, JUSTICE.

Northeast Harbor Golf Club, Inc., appeals from a judgment entered in the Superior Court (Hancock County, *Atwood, J.*) following a nonjury trial. The Club maintains that the trial court erred in finding that Nancy Harris did not breach her fiduciary duty as president of the Club by purchasing and developing property abutting the golf course. Because we today adopt principles different from those applied by the trial court in determining that Harris's activities did not constitute a breach of the corporate opportunity doctrine, we vacate the judgment.

I.

The Facts

Nancy Harris was the president of the Northeast Harbor Golf Club, a Maine corporation, from 1971 until she was asked to resign in 1990. The Club also had a board of directors that was responsible for making or approving significant policy decisions. The Club's only major asset was a golf course in Mount Desert. During Harris's tenure as president, the board occasionally discussed the possibility of developing some of the Club's real estate in order to raise money. Although Harris was generally in favor of tasteful development, the board always "shied away" from that type of activity.

In 1979, Robert Suminsby informed Harris that he was the listing broker for the Gilpin property, which comprised three noncontiguous parcels located among the fairways of the golf course. The property included an unused right-of-way on which the Club's parking lot and clubhouse were located. It was also encumbered by an easement in favor of the Club allowing foot traffic from the green of one hole to the next tee. Suminsby testified that he contacted Harris because she was the president of the Club and he believed that the Club would be interested in buying the property in order to prevent development.

Harris immediately agreed to purchase the Gilpin property in her own name for the asking price of $45,000. She did not disclose her plans to purchase the property to the Club's board prior to the purchase. She informed the board at its annual August meeting that she had purchased the property, that she intended to hold it in her own name, and that the Club would be "protected." The board took no action in response to the Harris purchase. She testified that at the time of the purchase she had no plans to develop the property and that no such plans took shape until 1988.

In 1984, while playing golf with the postmaster of Northeast Harbor, Harris learned that a parcel of land owned by the heirs of the Smallidge family might be available for purchase. The Smallidge parcel was surrounded on three sides by the golf course and on the fourth side by a house lot. It had no access to the road. With the ultimate goal of acquiring the property, Harris instructed her lawyer to locate the Smallidge heirs. Harris testified that she told a number of individual board members about her attempt to acquire the Smallidge parcel. At a board meeting in August 1985, Harris formally disclosed to the board that she had purchased the Smallidge property.[1] The minutes of that meeting show that she told the board she had no present plans to develop the Smallidge parcel. Harris testified that at the time of the purchase of the Smallidge property she nonetheless thought it might be nice to have some houses there. Again, the board took no formal action as a result of Harris's purchase. Harris acquired the Smallidge property from ten heirs, paying a total of $60,000. In 1990, Harris paid $275,000 for the lot and building separating the Smallidge parcel from the road in order to gain access to the otherwise landlocked parcel.

The trial court expressly found that the Club would have been unable to purchase either the Gilpin or Smallidge properties for itself, relying on testimony that the Club continually experienced financial difficulties, operated annually at a deficit, and depended on contributions from the directors to pay its bills. On the other hand, there was evidence that the Club had occasionally engaged in successful fund-raising, including a two-year period shortly after the Gilpin purchase during which the Club raised $115,000. The Club had $90,000 in a capital investment fund at the time of the Smallidge purchase.

In 1987 or 1988, Harris divided the real estate into 41 small lots, 14 on the Smallidge property and 27 on the Gilpin property. Apparently as part of her estate plan, Harris conveyed noncontiguous lots among the 41 to her children and retained others for herself. In 1991, Harris and her children exchanged deeds to reassemble the small lots into larger parcels. At the time the Club filed this suit, the property was divided into 11 lots, some owned by Harris and others by her children who are also defendants in this case. Harris estimated the value of all the real estate at the time of the trial to be $1,550,000.

In 1988, Harris, who was still president of the Club, and her children began the process of obtaining approval for a five-lot subdivision known as Bushwood on the lower Gilpin property. Even when the board learned of the proposed subdivision, a majority failed to take any action. A group of directors formed a separate organization in

1. In fact, it appears that Harris did not take title to the property until October 26, 1985. She had only signed a purchase and sale agreement at the time of the August board meeting.

order to oppose the subdivision on the basis that it violated the local zoning ordinance. After Harris's resignation as president, the Club also sought unsuccessfully to challenge the subdivision. *See Northeast Harbor Golf Club, Inc. v. Town of Mount Desert,* 618 A.2d 225 (Me.1992). Plans of Harris and her family for development of the other parcels are unclear, but the local zoning ordinance would permit construction of up to 11 houses on the land as currently divided.

After Harris's plans to develop Bushwood became apparent, the board grew increasingly divided concerning the propriety of development near the golf course. At least two directors, Henri Agnese and Nick Ludington, testified that they trusted Harris to act in the best interests of the Club and that they had no problem with the development plans for Bushwood. Other directors disagreed.

In particular, John Schafer, a Washington, D.C., lawyer and long-time member of the board, took issue with Harris's conduct. He testified that he had relied on Harris's representations at the time she acquired the properties that she would not develop them. According to Schafer, matters came to a head in August 1990 when a number of directors concluded that Harris's development plans irreconcilably conflicted with the Club's interests. As a result, Schafer and two other directors asked Harris to resign as president. In April 1991, after a substantial change in the board's membership, the board authorized the instant lawsuit against Harris for the breach of her fiduciary duty to act in the best interests of the corporation. The board simultaneously resolved that the proposed housing development was contrary to the best interests of the corporation.

The Club filed a complaint against Harris, her sons John and Shepard, and her daughter-in-law Melissa Harris. As amended, the complaint alleged that during her term as president Harris breached her fiduciary duty by purchasing the lots without providing notice and an opportunity for the Club to purchase the property and by subdividing the lots for future development. The Club sought an injunction to prevent development and also sought to impose a constructive trust on the property in question for the benefit of the Club.

The trial court found that Harris had not usurped a corporate opportunity because the acquisition of real estate was not in the Club's line of business. Moreover, it found that the corporation lacked the financial ability to purchase the real estate at issue. Finally, the court placed great emphasis on Harris's good faith. It noted her long and dedicated history of service to the Club, her personal oversight of the Club's growth, and her frequent financial contributions to the Club. The court found that her development activities were "generally . . . compatible with the corporation's business." This appeal followed.

II.

The Corporate Opportunity Doctrine

Corporate officers and directors bear a duty of loyalty to the corporations they serve. As Justice Cardozo explained the fiduciary duty in *Meinhard v. Salmon,* 249 N.Y. 458, 164 N.E. 545, 546 (1928):

> A trustee is held to something stricter than the morals of the marketplace. Not honesty alone, but the punctilio of an honor the most sensitive, is then the standard of behavior. As to this there has developed a tradition that is unbending and inveterate.

Maine has embraced this "unbending and inveterate" tradition. Corporate fiduciaries in Maine must discharge their duties in good faith with a view toward furthering the interests of the corporation. They must disclose and not withhold relevant information concerning any potential conflict of interest with the corporation, and they must refrain from using their position, influence, or knowledge of the affairs of the corporation to gain personal advantage. *See Rosenthal v. Rosenthal,* 543 A.2d 348, 352 (Me.1988); 13–A M.R.S.A. § 716 (Supp. 1994).

Despite the general acceptance of the proposition that corporate fiduciaries owe a duty of loyalty to their corporations, there has been much confusion about the specific extent of that duty when, as here, it is contended that a fiduciary takes for herself a corporate opportunity. *See, e.g.,* Victor Brudney & Robert C. Clark, *A New Look at Corporate Opportunities,* 94 Harv. L. Rev. 998, 998 (1981) ("Not only are the common formulations vague, but the courts have articulated no theory that would serve as a blueprint for constructing meaningful rules."). This case requires us for the first time to define the scope of the corporate opportunity doctrine in Maine.

Various courts have embraced different versions of the corporate opportunity doctrine. The test applied by the trial court and embraced by Harris is generally known as the "line of business" test. The seminal case applying the line of business test is *Guth v. Loft, Inc.,* 5 A.2d 503 (Del.1939). In *Guth,* the Delaware Supreme Court adopted an intensely factual test stated in general terms as follows:

> [I]f there is presented to a corporate officer or director a business opportunity which the corporation is financially able to undertake, is, from its nature, in the line of the corporation's business and is of practical advantage to it, is one in which the corporation has an interest or a reasonable expectancy, and, by embracing the opportunity, the self-interest of the officer or director will be brought into conflict with that of his corporation, the law will not permit him to seize the opportunity for himself.

Id. at 511. The "real issue" under this test is whether the opportunity "was so closely associated with the existing business activities . . . as to bring the transaction within that class of cases where the acquisition of the property would throw the corporate officer purchasing it into competition with his company." *Id.* at 513. The Delaware court described that inquiry as "a factual question to be decided by reasonable inferences from objective facts." *Id.*

The line of business test suffers from some significant weaknesses. First, the question whether a particular activity is within a corporation's line of business is conceptually difficult to answer. The facts of the instant case demonstrate that difficulty. The Club is in the business of running a golf course. It is not in the business of developing real estate. In the traditional sense, therefore, the trial court correctly observed that the opportunity in this case was not a corporate opportunity within the meaning of the *Guth* test. Nevertheless, the record would support a finding that the Club had made the policy judgment that development of surrounding real estate was detrimental to the best interests of the Club. The acquisition of land adjacent to the golf course for the purpose of preventing future development would have enhanced the ability of the Club to implement that policy. The record also shows that the Club had occasionally considered reversing that policy and expanding its operations to include the development of surrounding real estate. Harris's activities effectively foreclosed the Club from pursuing that option with respect to prime locations adjacent to the golf course.

Second, the *Guth* test includes as an element the financial ability of the corporation to take advantage of the opportunity. The court in this case relied on the Club's supposed financial incapacity as a basis for excusing Harris's conduct. Often, the injection of financial ability into the equation will unduly favor the inside director or executive who has command of the facts relating to the finances of the corporation. Reliance on financial ability will also act as a disincentive to corporate executives to solve corporate financing and other problems. In addition, the Club could have prevented development without spending $275,000 to acquire the property Harris needed to obtain access to the road.

The Massachusetts Supreme Judicial Court adopted a different test in *Durfee v. Durfee & Canning, Inc.*, 323 Mass. 187, 80 N.E.2d 522 (1948). The *Durfee* test has since come to be known as the "fairness test." According to *Durfee,* the

> true basis of governing doctrine rests on the unfairness in the particular circumstances of a director, whose relation to the corporation is fiduciary, taking advantage of an opportunity [for her personal profit] when the interest of the corporation justly call[s] for protection. This calls for application of ethical standards of what is fair and equitable . . . in particular sets of facts.

Id. at 529 (quoting *Ballantine on Corporations* 204–05 (rev. ed. 1946)). As with the *Guth* test, the *Durfee* test calls for a broad-ranging, intensely factual inquiry. The *Durfee* test suffers even more than the *Guth* test from a lack of principled content. It provides little or no practical guidance to the corporate officer or director seeking to measure her obligations.

The Minnesota Supreme Court elected "to combine the 'line of business' test with the 'fairness' test." *Miller v. Miller,* 301 Minn. 207, 222 N.W.2d 71, 81 (1974). It engaged in a two-step analysis, first determining whether a particular opportunity was within the corporation's line of business, then scrutinizing "the equitable considerations existing prior to, at the time of, and following the officer's acquisition."*Id.* The *Miller* court hoped by adopting this approach "to ameliorate the often-expressed criticism that the [corporate opportunity] doctrine is vague and subjects today's corporate management to the danger of unpredictable liability." *Id.* In fact, the test adopted in *Miller* merely piles the uncertainty and vagueness of the fairness test on top of the weaknesses in the line of business test.

Despite the weaknesses of each of these approaches to the corporate opportunity doctrine, they nonetheless rest on a single fundamental policy. At bottom, the corporate opportunity doctrine recognizes that a corporate fiduciary should not serve both corporate and personal interests at the same time. As we observed in *Camden Land Co. v. Lewis,* 101 Me. 78, 97, 63 A. 523, 531 (1905), corporate fiduciaries "owe their whole duty to the corporation, and they are not to be permitted to act when duty conflicts with interest. They cannot serve themselves and the corporation at the same time." The various formulations of the test are merely attempts to moderate the potentially harsh consequences of strict adherence to that policy. It is important to preserve some ability for corporate fiduciaries to pursue personal business interests that present no real threat to their duty of loyalty.

III.

The American Law Institute Approach

In an attempt to protect the duty of loyalty while at the same time providing long-needed clarity and guidance for corporate decisionmakers, the American Law Institute has offered the most recently developed version of the corporate opportunity doctrine. PRINCIPLES OF CORPORATE GOVERNANCE § 5.05 (May 13, 1992), provides as follows:

§ 5.05 Taking of Corporate Opportunities by Directors or Senior Executives

(a) *General Rule.* A director [§ 1.13] or senior executive [§ 1.33] may not take advantage of a corporate opportunity unless:

(1) The director or senior executive first offers the corporate opportunity to the corporation and makes disclosure concerning the conflict of interest [§ 1.14(a)] and the corporate opportunity [§ 1.14(b)];

(2) The corporate opportunity is rejected by the corporation; and

(3) Either:

(A) The rejection of the opportunity is fair to the corporation;

(B) The opportunity is rejected in advance, following such disclosure, by disinterested directors [§ 1.15], or, in the case of a senior executive who is not a director, by a disinterested superior, in a manner that satisfies the standards of the business judgment rule [§ 4.01(c)]; or

(C) The rejection is authorized in advance or ratified, following such disclosure, by disinterested shareholders [§ 1.16], and the rejection is not equivalent to a waste of corporate assets [§ 1.42].

(b) *Definition of a Corporate Opportunity.* For purposes of this Section, a corporate opportunity means:

(1) Any opportunity to engage in a business activity of which a director or senior executive becomes aware, either:

(A) In connection with the performance of functions as a director or senior executive, or under circumstances that should reasonably lead the director or senior executive to believe that the person offering the opportunity expects it to be offered to the corporation; or

(B) Through the use of corporate information or property, if the resulting opportunity is one that the director or senior executive should reasonably be expected to believe would be of interest to the corporation; or

(2) Any opportunity to engage in a business activity of which a senior executive becomes aware and knows is closely related to a business in which the corporation is engaged or expects to engage.

(c) *Burden of Proof.* A party who challenges the taking of a corporate opportunity has the burden of proof, except that if such party establishes that the requirements of Subsection (a)(3)(B) or (C) are not met, the director or the senior executive has the burden of proving that the rejection and the taking of the opportunity were fair to the corporation.

(d) *Ratification of Defective Disclosure.* A good faith but defective disclosure of the facts concerning the corporate opportunity may be cured if at any time (but no later than a reasonable time after suit is filed challenging the taking of the corporate opportunity) the original rejection of the corporate opportunity is ratified, following the required disclosure, by the board, the shareholders, or the corporate decisionmaker who initially approved the rejection of the corporate opportunity, or such decisionmaker's successor.

(e) *Special Rule Concerning Delayed Offering of Corporate Opportunities.* Relief based solely on failure to first offer an opportunity to the corporation under Subsection (a)(1) is not available if: (1) such failure resulted from a good faith belief that the business activity did not constitute a corporate opportunity, and (2) not later than a reasonable time after suit is filed challenging the taking of the corporate opportunity, the corporate opportunity is to the extent possible offered to the corporation and rejected in a manner that satisfies the standards of Subsection (a).

The central feature of the ALI test is the strict requirement of full disclosure prior to taking advantage of any corporate opportunity. *Id.*, § 5.05(a)(1). "If the opportunity is not offered to the corporation, the director or senior executive will not have satisfied § 5.05(a)." *Id.*, cmt.

to § 5.05(a). The corporation must then formally reject the opportunity. *Id.,* § 505(a)(2). The ALI test is discussed at length and ultimately applied by the Oregon Supreme Court in *Klinicki v. Lundgren,* 298 Or. 662, 695 P.2d 906 (1985). As *Klinicki* describes the test, "full disclosure to the appropriate corporate body is ... an absolute condition precedent to the validity of any forthcoming rejection as well as to the availability to the director or principal senior executive of the defense of fairness." *Id.* at 920. A "good faith but defective disclosure" by the corporate officer may be ratified after the fact only by an affirmative vote of the disinterested directors or shareholders. PRINCIPLES OF CORPORATE GOVERNANCE § 5.05(d).

The ALI test defines "corporate opportunity" broadly. It includes opportunities "closely related to a business in which the corporation is engaged." *Id.,* § 5.05(b). It also encompasses any opportunities that accrue to the fiduciary as a result of her position within the corporation. *Id.* This concept is most clearly illustrated by the testimony of Suminsby, the listing broker for the Gilpin property, which, if believed by the factfinder, would support a finding that the Gilpin property was offered to Harris specifically in her capacity as president of the Club. If the factfinder reached that conclusion, then at least the opportunity to acquire the Gilpin property would be a corporate opportunity. The state of the record concerning the Smallidge purchase precludes us from intimating any opinion whether that too would be a corporate opportunity.

Under the ALI standard, once the Club shows that the opportunity is a corporate opportunity, it must show either that Harris did not offer the opportunity to the Club or that the Club did not reject it properly. If the Club shows that the board did not reject the opportunity by a vote of the disinterested directors after full disclosure, then Harris may defend her actions on the basis that the taking of the opportunity was fair to the corporation. *Id.,* § 5.05(c). If Harris failed to offer the opportunity at all, however, then she may not defend on the basis that the failure to offer the opportunity was fair. *Id.,* cmt. to § 5.05(c).

The *Klinicki* court viewed the ALI test as an opportunity to bring some clarity to a murky area of the law. *Klinicki,* 695 P.2d at 915. We agree, and today we follow the ALI test. The disclosure-oriented approach provides a clear procedure whereby a corporate officer may insulate herself through prompt and complete disclosure from the possibility of a legal challenge. The requirement of disclosure recognizes the paramount importance of the corporate fiduciary's duty of loyalty. At the same time it protects the fiduciary's ability pursuant to the proper procedure to pursue her own business ventures free from the possibility of a lawsuit.

The importance of disclosure is familiar to the law of corporations in Maine. Pursuant to 13–A M.R.S.A. § 717 (1981), a corporate officer or director may enter into a transaction with the corporation in which she has a personal or adverse interest only if she discloses her interest in the transaction and secures ratification by a majority of the disinterested directors or shareholders. Section 717 is part of the Model Business Corporations Act, adopted in Maine in 1971. P.L.1971, ch. 439, § 1. Like the ALI rule, section 717 was designed to "eliminate the inequities and uncertainties caused by the existing rules." MODEL BUSINESS CORP. ACT § 41, § 2, at 844 (1971).

IV.

Conclusion

The question remains how our adoption of the rule affects the result in the instant case. The trial court made a number of factual findings based on an extensive record.[3] The court made those findings, however, in the light of legal principles that are different from the principles that we today announce. Similarly, the parties did not have the opportunity to develop the record in this case with knowledge of the applicable legal standard. In these circumstances, fairness requires that we remand the case for further proceedings. Those further proceedings may include, at the trial court's discretion, the taking of further evidence.

The entry is:

Judgment vacated.

Remanded for further proceedings consistent with the opinion herein.

All concurring.

NOTE ON FURTHER PROCEEDINGS IN NORTHEAST HARBOR GOLF CLUB, INC. v. HARRIS

Following remand, the Superior Court entered judgment for the Club. On appeal, the Maine Supreme Court held that the Gilpin and Smallidge properties were both corporate opportunities, and that Harris breached her fiduciary obligations by not offering those opportunities to the Club's board:

> The subject of this lawsuit is land surrounding the Club that Harris purchased in her own name, some in 1979, and more in 1985. In 1979, in her capacity as Club president, Harris learned of an opportunity to purchase property owned by Lucy Gilpin. The Gilpin property adjoins Club property, including the driveway which provided access to the golf course, the clubhouse, and a portion of the Club's parking lot. Moreover, the Gilpin property is encumbered by an easement that allows golfers to travel from the green of one hole to the tee area of the next hole.
>
> Harris purchased the Gilpin property in her own name for $45,000. She did not disclose her plans to the board prior to acquiring the property. . . .

---

3. Harris raised the defense of laches and the statute of limitations but the court made no findings on those issues. We do not intimate what result the application of either doctrine would produce in this case. . . .

In 1984, Harris, independent of her position with the Club,[2] learned of the availability of property owned by the Smallidge family. The property was surrounded on three sides by the Club and on the fourth side by a house. Harris contracted to purchase eight of the ten interests of the Smallidge heirs in February of 1985, another in March, and the last in June of 1985, for a total of $60,000.[3] Harris disclosed the purchase to the board of directors at the Club's annual meeting on August 28, 1985. . . .

Harris concedes that, because she learned of the opportunity to purchase the Gilpin property in her capacity as president of the Club, her purchase of that property in 1979 constituted the taking of a corporate opportunity. See Principles of Corporate Governance § 5.05(b)(1)(A) (American Law Institute, May 13, 1992). . . .

Even if the opportunity to engage in a business activity, in which the officer or director becomes involved, is not learned of through her connection to the business of the corporation, nevertheless, such an opportunity may be considered a corporate opportunity if the officer or director knows it "is closely related to a business in which the corporation is engaged or expects to engage." Principles of Corporate Governance § 5.50(b)(2).

"The central feature of the ALI test is the strict requirement of full disclosure prior to taking advantage of any corporate opportunity." Northeast Harbor Golf Club, 661 A.2d at 1151. This feature was designed to prevent individual directors and officers from substituting their own judgment for that of the corporation when determining whether it would be in the corporate interest, or whether the corporation is financially or otherwise able to take advantage of an opportunity. . . . Doubt about the financial capacity of a corporation to pursue an opportunity may affect the incentive of a director or officer to solve corporate financing problems, and evidence regarding the corporation's financial status is often controlled by the usurping corporate director or officer. See Victor Brudney & Robert Charles Clark, A New Look at Corporate Opportunities, 94 Harv. L. Rev. 998, 1020–22 (1981). The ALI approach recognizes the danger in allowing an individual director or officer to determine whether a corporation has the ability to take an opportunity, and accordingly disclosure to the corporation is required.

Full disclosure is likewise important to prevent individual directors and officers from using their own unfettered judgment to determine whether the business opportunity is related to the corporation's business, such that it would be in the corporate interest to take advantage of that opportunity. "The appropriate method to determine whether or not a corporate opportunity

---

2. While playing golf with the postmaster of Northeast Harbor, Harris learned that property owned by the heirs of the Smallidge family might be available for purchase.

3. In 1990, because the Smallidge property was landlocked, Harris purchased a house and property separating the Smallidge property from the road for $275,000.

> exists is to let the corporation decide at the time the opportunity is presented." 3 Fletcher Cyc. Corp. § 861.10, p. 285 (1994). This rule protects individual directors and officers because after disclosing the potential opportunity to the corporation, they can pursue their own business ventures free from the possibility of a lawsuit. If there is doubt as to whether a business opportunity is closely related to the business of the corporation, that doubt must be resolved in favor of the corporation so that the officer or director will have a strong incentive to disclose any business opportunity even remotely related to the business of the corporation.
>
> In this case, the Club's normal business is maintaining and operating a golf course. That business is dependent on having sufficient land for the course itself and ensuring that the activity of golf is not hindered or affected by development of adjacent and surrounding property. The Club had frequently discussed developing some of its own land and on one occasion talked about the possibility of purchasing and developing adjacent land. The purchase of the Smallidge land, surrounded as it is on three sides by the Club's land and adjacent to three of its golf holes, land that could be developed, is, in the circumstances of this case, sufficiently related to the Club's business to constitute a corporate opportunity....

However, the court also concluded that the Club's action was barred by the statute of limitations.

BROZ v. CELLULAR INFORMATION SYSTEMS, INC., 673 A.2d 148 (Del.1996). Robert F. Broz was the President and sole stockholder of RFB Cellular, Inc. (RFBC), a Delaware corporation engaged in the business of providing cellular telephone service in the Midwest. RFBC held an FCC license known as the Michigan–4 Rural Service Area Cellular License (Michigan–4). The license entitled RFBC to provide cellular telephone service to its service area, a portion of rural Michigan. Broz was also an outside director of Cellular Information Systems, Inc. (CIS), a publicly held Delaware corporation and a competitor of RFBC. CIS was at all times fully aware of Broz's relationship with RFBC.

In April 1994, Mackinac Cellular Corp. wanted to sell its FCC cellular-phone-license area, known as Michigan–2, which was immediately adjacent to RFBC's Michigan–4. Mackinac's broker, Daniels, contacted Broz and broached the subject of RFBC's possible acquisition of Michigan–2. Daniels did not offer Michigan–2 to CIS. Apparently, Daniels did not consider CIS to be a viable purchaser for Michigan–2, because CIS had recently emerged from bankruptcy proceedings and had made a loan agreement that substantially impaired its ability to undertake new acquisitions or incur new debt.

On June 1994, Broz spoke with CIS's Chief Executive Officer, Richard Treibick, concerning Broz's interest in acquiring Michigan–2. Treibick told Broz that CIS was not interested in Michigan–2. In August 1994, Broz contacted two other CIS directors, who expressed their belief that CIS had neither the resources nor the inclination to purchase Michigan–2. Ultimately, all the CIS directors testified at trial that if Broz had inquired at that time, they each would have expressed the opinion that CIS was not interested in Michigan–2. In November 1994, Broz agreed to pay Mackinac $7.2 million for the Michigan–2 license. Thereafter, the purchase took place.

Meanwhile, between April 1994, when Broz had become aware of the opportunity to purchase the Michigan–2 license, and November 1994, when he purchased the license, a third party, PriCellular, Inc. had been in negotiations to purchase CIS's stock through negotiated transactions and a tender offer. The tender offer closed nine days after Broz purchased the license, and PriCellular became the owner of CIS. PriCellular then caused CIS to sue Broz on the ground that the purchase of the Michigan–2 license usurped a CIS corporate opportunity. CIS admitted that at the time the opportunity was offered to Broz, the board of CIS would not have been interested in Michigan–2, but claimed that Broz was required to look not just to the interests of CIS at that time, but also to the articulated business plans of PriCellular to determine whether PriCellular would be interested in acquiring Michigan–2. CIS contended that since Broz failed to do this, and instead acquired Michigan–2 without first considering the interests of PriCellular in its capacity as a potential acquiror of CIS, Broz must be held to account for breach of fiduciary duty. The Chancery court entered judgment for CIS. The Delaware Supreme Court reversed:

> The corporate opportunity doctrine, as delineated by [Guth v. Loft, Inc., 5 A.2d 503 (Del. 1939)] and its progeny, holds that a corporate officer or director may not take a business opportunity for his own if: (1) the corporation is financially able to exploit the opportunity; (2) the opportunity is within the corporation's line of business; (3) the corporation has an interest or expectancy in the opportunity; and (4) by taking the opportunity for his own, the corporate fiduciary will thereby be placed in a position inimicable to his duties to the corporation. The Court in *Guth* also derived a corollary which states that a director or officer may take a corporate opportunity if: (1) the opportunity is presented to the director or officer in his individual and not his corporate capacity; (2) the opportunity is not essential to the corporation; (3) the corporation holds no interest or expectancy in the opportunity; and (4) the director or officer has not wrongfully employed the resources of the corporation in pursuing or exploiting the opportunity. *Guth*, 5 A.2d at 509.
>
> Thus, the contours of this doctrine are well established. It is important to note, however, that the tests enunciated in *Guth* and subsequent cases provide guidelines to be considered by a reviewing court in balancing the equities of an individual case. No one

factor is dispositive and all factors must be taken into account insofar as they are applicable. Cases involving a claim of usurpation of a corporate opportunity range over a multitude of factual settings. Hard and fast rules are not easily crafted to deal with such an array of complex situations. As this Court noted in Johnston v. Greene, Del.Supr., 121 A.2d 919 (1956), the determination of "[w]hether or not a director has appropriated for himself something that in fairness should belong to the corporation is 'a factual question to be decided by reasonable inference from objective facts.' " Id. at 923 (quoting Guth, 5 A.2d at 513). In the instant case, we find that the facts do not support the conclusion that Broz misappropriated a corporate opportunity. . . .

First, we find that CIS was not financially capable of exploiting the Michigan–2 opportunity. . . .

Second, while it may be said with some certainty that the Michigan–2 opportunity was within CIS' line of business, it is not equally clear that CIS had a cognizable interest or expectancy in the license. Under the third factor laid down by this Court in *Guth*, for an opportunity to be deemed to belong to the fiduciary's corporation, the corporation must have an interest or expectancy in that opportunity. As this Court stated in Johnston, 121 A.2d at 924, "[f]or the corporation to have an actual or expectant interest in any specific property, there must be some tie between that property and the nature of the corporate business." Despite the fact that the nature of the Michigan–2 opportunity was historically close to the core operations of CIS, changes were in process. At the time the opportunity was presented, CIS was actively engaged in the process of divesting its cellular license holdings. CIS' articulated business plan did not involve any new acquisitions. Further, as indicated by the testimony of the entire CIS board, the Michigan–2 license would not have been of interest to CIS even absent CIS' financial difficulties and CIS' then current desire to liquidate its cellular license holdings. Thus, CIS had no interest or expectancy in the Michigan–2 opportunity. . . .

Finally, the corporate opportunity doctrine is implicated only in cases where the fiduciary's seizure of an opportunity results in a conflict between the fiduciary's duties to the corporation and the self-interest of the director as actualized by the exploitation of the opportunity. In the instant case, Broz' interest in acquiring and profiting from Michigan–2 created no duties that were inimicable to his obligations to CIS. Broz, at all times relevant to the instant appeal, was the sole party in interest in RFBC, a competitor of CIS. CIS was fully aware of Broz' potentially conflicting duties. Broz, however, comported himself in a manner that was wholly in accord with his obligations to CIS. Broz took care not to usurp any opportunity which CIS was willing and able to pursue. Broz sought only to compete with an outside entity, PriCellular, for acquisition of an opportunity which both sought to possess.

Broz was not obligated to refrain from competition with PriCellular. Therefore, the totality of the circumstances indicates that Broz did not usurp an opportunity that properly belonged to CIS. . . .

In concluding that Broz had usurped a corporate opportunity, the Court of Chancery placed great emphasis on the fact that Broz had not formally presented the matter to the CIS board. The court held that "in such circumstances as existed at the latest after October 14, 1994 (date of PriCellular's option contract on Michigan 2 RSA) it was the obligation of Mr. Broz as a director of CIS to take the transaction to the CIS board for its formal action. . . ." 663 A.2d at 1185. In so holding, the trial court erroneously grafted a new requirement onto the law of corporate opportunity, viz., the requirement of formal presentation under circumstances where the corporation does not have an interest, expectancy or financial ability.

The teaching of *Guth* and its progeny is that the director or officer must analyze the situation ex ante to determine whether the opportunity is one rightfully belonging to the corporation. If the director or officer believes, based on one of the factors articulated above, that the corporation is not entitled to the opportunity, then he may take it for himself. Of course, presenting the opportunity to the board creates a kind of "safe harbor" for the director, which removes the specter of a post hoc judicial determination that the director or officer has improperly usurped a corporate opportunity. Thus, presentation avoids the possibility that an error in the fiduciary's assessment of the situation will create future liability for breach of fiduciary duty. It is not the law of Delaware that presentation to the board is a necessary prerequisite to a finding that a corporate opportunity has not been usurped. . . .

In concluding that Broz usurped an opportunity properly belonging to CIS, the Court of Chancery held that "[f]or practical business reasons CIS's interests with respect to the Mackinac transaction came to merge with those of PriCellular, even before the closing of its tender offer for CIS stock." . . .

We disagree. Broz was under no duty to consider the interests of PriCellular when he chose to purchase Michigan–2. As stated in Guth, a director's right to "appropriate [an] . . . opportunity depends on the circumstances existing at the time it presented itself to him without regard to subsequent events." Guth, 5 A.2d at 513. At the time Broz purchased Michigan–2, PriCellular had not yet acquired CIS. Any plans to do so would still have been wholly speculative. Accordingly, Broz was not required to consider the contingent and uncertain plans of PriCellular in reaching his determination of how to proceed. . . .

Accord: Ostrowski v. Avery, 243 Conn. 355, 703 A.2d 117 (1997).

MODEL BUSINESS CORPORATION ACT § 8.70

[See Statutory Supplement]

ALI, PRINCIPLES OF CORPORATE GOVERNANCE §§ 5.05, 5.06

[See Statutory Supplement]

NOTE ON THE CORPORATE OPPORTUNITY DOCTRINE

1. *Tests*. A variety of tests have been formulated to determine whether a director or officer has wrongfully appropriated a corporate opportunity. Among these are three tests discussed in *Northeast Harbor*: (i) The line-of-business test, associated with Guth v. Loft, Inc., 23 Del.Ch. 255, 5 A.2d 503 (1939). (ii) The fairness test, associated with Durfee v. Durfee & Canning, Inc., 323 Mass. 187, 80 N.E.2d 522 (1948). (iii) The two-step test, associated with Miller v. Miller, 301 Minn. 207, 222 N.W.2d 71 (1974). Under another test, associated with Lagarde v. Anniston Lime & Stone Co., 126 Ala. 496, 502, 28 So. 199, 201 (1900), the corporate opportunity doctrine applies only when the director or officer has acquired property in which "the corporation has an interest already existing or in which it has an expectancy growing out of an existing right," or when his "interference will in some degree balk the corporation in effecting the purposes of its creation."

The application of the first branch of the *Lagarde* test (interest or expectancy) is uncertain, because the terms "interest" and "expectancy" have no fixed meaning in this context. See, e.g., Abbott Redmont Thinlite Corp. v. Redmont, 475 F.2d 85, 88–89 (2d Cir.1973). In *Lagarde* itself, the court held that real estate in which the corporation was a tenant constituted a corporate expectancy, but real estate in which the corporation owned an undivided one-third interest did not.

The application of the second branch of the *Lagarde* test (interference with the corporate purpose) is also uncertain. Presumably, it would cover cases in which the corporation's need for the property is very substantial. See, e.g., Harmony Way Bridge Co. v. Leathers, 353 Ill. 378, 187 N.E. 432 (1933) (a director purchased a right of way that was needed as an approach to the corporation's bridge); News–Journal Corp. v. Gore, 147 Fla. 217, 2 So.2d 741 (1941) (a director purchased a tract of land that the corporation leased for its building, and immediately increased the rent).

Insofar as the meaning of the *Lagarde* test can be determined, it is unduly narrow. Even the Alabama Supreme Court may now be seeking more leeway by broadening the second branch of the test:

> The last restriction in *Lagarde,* that which prohibits "balking the corporate purpose," is really quite broad in its formulation,

although the case has often been described as restrictive.... We think that *Lagarde* when properly read enforces responsibilities for the corporate officer or director comparable to those outlined in *Guth v. Loft, Inc.*, 23 Del.Ch. 255, 5 A.2d 503 (1939), where the Delaware Supreme Court employed the doctrine of corporate opportunity and observed that it

"... demands of a corporate officer or director, peremptorily and inexorably, the most scrupulous observance of his duty, not only affirmatively to protect the interests of the corporation committed to his charge, but also to refrain from doing anything that would work injury to the corporation, or to deprive it of profit or advantage which his skill and ability might properly bring to it, or to enable it to make in the reasonable and lawful exercise of its powers....

Morad v. Coupounas, 361 So.2d 6, 8–9 (Ala.1978).

2. *Data*. A comprehensive analysis of corporate-opportunity cases reported between April 1977 and April 1988 found that disputes concerning corporate opportunities usually occur in close corporations, and that the opportunity is often directly competitive with the business of the corporation. Chew, Competing Interests in the Corporate Opportunity Doctrine, 67 N. C. L. Rev. 436 (1989).

3. *Different Types of Corporate Opportunities*. Traditionally, the body of law governing corporate opportunities has lacked clarity in two important respects. To begin with, the corporate-opportunity cases have often tended to lump all kinds of corporate opportunities together. In fact, however, there are two very different kinds of reasons why a *business* opportunity may be a *corporate* opportunity. Call an individual who is a director, officer, employee, or agent of a corporation, *A*, and call the Corporation, *C*. One reason that a business opportunity may be a corporate opportunity is that *A* became aware of the opportunity through the use of corporate property, corporate information, or *A*'s corporate position—that is, through the use of corporate assets. In such cases, the opportunity is Corporation *C*'s property. If *A* took such an opportunity for herself without offering it to Corporation *C*, she has stolen it, just as much as if she had taken or used any other kind of corporate property for her own personal benefit.

A second, very different kind of reason why a business opportunity can constitute a corporate opportunity is that it is closely related to the corporation's business. If that is the *only* reason why an opportunity constitutes a corporate opportunity, then by hypothesis *A* will have found the opportunity on her own, rather than through the use of corporate property, information, or position. If an opportunity that *A* finds on her own constitutes a corporate opportunity, that is not because the discovery of the opportunity is a product of the use of corporate assets—it isn't—but because for some other reason *A* owes Corporation *C* a duty to turn over the opportunity to it.

If *A* is an officer of Corporation *C*, the reason why she might owe *C* the duty to turn over an opportunity that she found on her own is based on her duties not to interfere with, and to advance, *C*'s interests. Whether a given individual owes such duties may depend in part on the individual's position. The higher up in the corporate hierarchy the individual is, the more plausible it is that she owes such duties, and the more demanding the duties will normally be. Although a high-ranking executive can fairly be expected to turn over to the corporation any opportunity that is closely related to the corporation's business solely because it is so related, the same expectation may not apply to a blue-collar or clerical employee.

In short, a business opportunity that is discovered through the use of corporate property, information, or position should be a corporate opportunity regardless of *A*'s corporate position. In contrast, whether a business opportunity that *A* discovers on her own is a corporate opportunity solely because it is closely related to the corporation's business may partly depend on *A*'s corporate position.

4. *Ability of the Corporation to take the Opportunity*. Another area in which the traditional law of corporate opportunities has lacked clarity concerns the issue whether and to what extent *A* can raise, as a defense to a suit based on the taking of a business opportunity, that Corporation *C* was unable to take the opportunity. This issue usually, although not always, arises in the context of whether the corporation had the financial ability to take the relevant opportunity. The courts are all over the place on this issue. At one extreme, some cases, such as Irving Trust Co. v. Deutsch, 73 F.2d 121 (2d Cir.1934), hold that the corporation's financial ability should be irrelevant, because it is too easy for executives who take a business opportunity to create a financial-inability excuse through manipulation of the corporation's financial picture. At the other extreme, some cases hold that not only is the corporation's financial ability relevant, but that a plaintiff who claims that a corporate opportunity has been taken has the burden of pleading and proving that the corporation had the financial ability to take the opportunity. See, e.g., Miller v. Miller, supra. Still other courts take some intermediate position between these two extremes. See, e.g., Klinicki v. Lundgren, 298 Or. 662, 695 P.2d 906 (1985) which allows financial inability to serve as a justification for the corporation's rejection of a corporate opportunity. Furthermore, there are a number of shadings on the issue how the corporation's financial ability should be measured in this context. See, e.g., Yiannatsis v. Stephanis, 653 A.2d 275 (Del.1995).

The problem in this area is that the courts have failed to disentangle two very different scenarios in which a corporate-inability defense may play a role. In one scenario, *A* first offers a business opportunity to the board of Corporation *C*; *C*'s board decides to reject the opportunity; and *A* then takes it for herself. A shareholder then brings a derivative action against *A*, and *A* raises as a defense that she did not take the opportunity until *C*'s board had rejected it. If, in such a case, the plaintiff puts into issue the fairness or reasonability of the board's rejection of the opportunity, *C*'s inability to take the opportunity is relevant, because it may justify the board's rejection.

In the second scenario, *A* takes an opportunity *without* having first offered it to the board of Corporation *C*. When *A* is sued for taking the opportunity, she raises as a defense that *C* did not have the ability to take the opportunity. In this scenario, *C*'s inability to take the opportunity should not be a defense, because if a business opportunity would be a corporate opportunity if the issue of the corporation's ability to take the opportunity is put aside, a fiduciary should always be obliged to offer the opportunity to the corporation in the first instance and let the *corporation* decide whether it is or can make itself able to take the opportunity. Business enterprises can be very adaptable when faced with a profitable business opportunity. For example, a corporation that doesn't have the cash to acquire a business opportunity may find that if the opportunity is profitable, a bank will lend the corporation money to acquire it. If *A* does not even offer the opportunity to the corporation, however, there is no way to tell whether the corporation would have been able to raise the money to acquire it by bank financing or otherwise. That being so, it should be presumed against *A* that if she had offered the opportunity, the corporation would have adapted as necessary to take advantage of it. This is essentially the position taken in ALI, Principles of Corporate Governance § 5.05.

5. *The Relationship Between Corporate Opportunities; the Use of Corporate Information, Property, or Position; and Competition with the Corporation*. Three important principles of fiduciary duty overlap in a significant way. These are: (i) The corporate-opportunity principle, which prohibits a corporate fiduciary from taking a corporate opportunity. (ii) The use-of-corporate-assets principle, which prohibits a corporate fiduciary from using corporate property, information, or position for personal gain. (iii) The noncompetition principle, which prohibits a corporate fiduciary from competing with the corporation.

Often, a given course of conduct violates all three principles. This would be the case, for example, if an executive appropriated a corporate opportunity that she learned of through the use of corporate information, and then exploited that opportunity in a way that competed with the corporation's business. Because of this potential for overlap, it is easy to think that the three principles express different facets of the same basic idea. In fact, however, the three principles express three different ideas, and despite the overlap, one of the principles may apply to a given case although the other principles do not.

For example, suppose that Officer O of Corporation X takes for herself an opportunity to buy Business B. O learned of the opportunity on her own, but Business B is closely related to A's business. In that case, O may violate the corporate-opportunity doctrine, but not the use-of-corporate-assets principle. Whether O also violates the noncompetition principle may depend on whether O remains in the corporation's employ after taking the opportunity. If O remains in the corporation's employ she may violate the noncompetition principle, because by hypothesis Business B is closely related to the corporation's business. However, if O resigns immediately after acquiring Business B she may not violate the noncompetition principle.

Suppose now that Business B is not closely related to Corporation X's business, but constituted a corporate opportunity because it came to O's attention through the use of corporate information, property, or position. In that case, if O buys Business B she may violate both the corporate-opportunity principle and the use-of-corporate-assets principle. However, she may not violate the noncompetition principle, even if she remains in the corporation's employ after buying Business B, because Business B might not compete with Corporation X.

Finally, suppose that O inherits a business that is competitive with that of Corporation X. Here O has not taken a corporate opportunity. However, if O runs the business without resigning from Corporation X, she may be improperly competing with X. Similarly, suppose that O started a business that originally was not competitive with that of Corporation X, but that later becomes competitive because X itself expands its geographical or product-line reach, so that it begins going head-to-head with O's business. Here too O has not taken a corporate opportunity, but may be improperly competing with X.

IN RE eBAY, INC. SHAREHOLDERS LITIGATION, 2004 WL 253521 (Del. Ch. 2004). "In 1995, defendants Pierre M. Omidyar and Jeffrey Skoll founded nominal defendant eBay, a Delaware corporation, as a sole proprietorship. eBay is a pioneer in online trading platforms, providing a virtual auction community for buyers and sellers to list items for sale and to bid on items of interest. In 1998, eBay retained Goldman Sachs and other investment banks to underwrite an initial public offering of common stock. Goldman Sachs was the lead underwriter. The stock was priced at $18 per share. Goldman Sachs purchased about 1.2 million shares. Shares of eBay stock became immensely valuable during 1998 and 1999, rising to $175 per share in early April 1999. Around that time, eBay made a secondary offering, issuing 6.5 million shares of common stock at $170 per share for a total of $1.1 billion. Goldman Sachs again served as lead underwriter. Goldman Sachs was asked in 2001 to serve as eBay's financial advisor in connection with an acquisition by eBay of PayPal, Inc. For these services, eBay has paid Goldman Sachs over $8 million.

"During this same time period, Goldman Sachs 'rewarded' the individual defendants by allocating to them thousands of IPO shares, managed by Goldman Sachs, at the initial offering price. Because the IPO market during this particular period of time was extremely active, prices of initial stock offerings often doubled or tripled in a single day. Investors who were well connected, either to Goldman Sachs or to similarly situated investment banks serving as IPO underwriters, were able to flip these investments into instant profit by selling the equities in a few days or even in a few hours after they were initially purchased.

"The essential allegation of the complaint is that Goldman Sachs provided these IPO share allocations to the individual defendants to show appreciation for eBay's business and to enhance Goldman Sachs' chances of obtaining future eBay business. In addition to co-founding eBay, defendant Omidyar has been eBay's CEO, CFO and President. He is eBay's largest stockholder, owning more than 23% of the company's equity. Goldman Sachs allocated Omidyar shares in at least forty IPOs at the initial offering price. Omidyar resold these securities in the public market for millions of dollars in profit. Defendant Whitman owns 3.3% of eBay stock and has been President, CEO and a director since early 1998. Whitman also has been a director of Goldman Sachs since 2001. Goldman Sachs allocated Whitman shares in over 100 IPOs at the initial offering price. Whitman sold these equities in the open market and reaped millions of dollars in profit. Defendant Skoll, in addition to co-founding eBay, has served in various positions at the company, including Vice–President of Strategic Planning and Analysis and President. He served as an eBay director from December 1996 to March 1998. Skoll is eBay's second largest stockholder, owning about 13% of the company. Goldman Sachs has allocated Skoll shares in at least 75 IPOs at the initial offering price, which Skoll promptly resold on the open market, allowing him to realize millions of dollars in profit. Finally, defendant Robert C. Kagle has served as an eBay director since June 1997. Goldman Sachs allocated Kagle shares in at least 25 IPOs at the initial offering price. Kagle promptly resold these equities, and recorded millions of dollars in profit. . . .

". . . [E]ven if one assumes that IPO allocations like those in question here do not constitute a corporate opportunity, a cognizable claim is nevertheless stated on the common law ground that an agent is under a duty to account for profits obtained personally in connection with transactions related to his or her company. The complaint gives rise to a reasonable inference that the insider directors accepted a commission or gratuity that rightfully belonged to eBay but that was improperly diverted to them. Even if this conduct does not run afoul of the corporate opportunity doctrine, it may still constitute a breach of the fiduciary duty of loyalty. Thus, even if one does not consider Goldman Sachs' IPO allocations to these corporate insiders—allocations that generated millions of dollars in profit—to be a corporate opportunity, the defendant directors were nevertheless not free to accept this consideration from a company, Goldman Sachs, that was doing significant business with eBay and that arguably intended the consideration as an inducement to maintaining the business relationship in the future."

SECTION 5. DUTIES OF CONTROLLING SHAREHOLDERS

ALI, PRINCIPLES OF CORPORATE GOVERNANCE §§ 5.10–5.12

Zahn v. Transamerica Corporation

United States Circuit Court of Appeals, Third Circuit, 1947.
162 F.2d 36.

■ BIGGS, CIRCUIT JUDGE. Zahn, a holder of Class A common stock of Axton–Fisher Tobacco Company, a corporation of Kentucky, sued Transamerica Corporation, a Delaware company, on his own behalf and on behalf of all stockholders similarly situated, in the District Court of the United States for the District of Delaware. His complaint as amended asserts that Transamerica caused Axton–Fisher to redeem its Class A stock at $80.80 per share on July 1, 1943, instead of permitting the Class A stockholders to participate in the assets on the liquidation of their company in June 1944. He alleges in brief that if the Class A stockholders had been allowed to participate in the assets on liquidation of Axton–Fisher and had received their respective shares of the assets, he and the other Class A stockholders would have received $240 per share instead of $80.80. Zahn takes the position that he has two separate causes of action, one based on the Class A shares which were not turned back to the company for redemption; another based on the shares which were redeemed.[1] He prayed the court below to direct Transamerica to pay over to the shareholders who had not surrendered their stock the liquidation value and to pay over to those shareholders who had surrendered their stock the liquidation value less $80.80. Transamerica filed a motion to dismiss. The court below granted the motion holding that Zahn had failed to state a cause of action. See 63 F.Supp. 243. He appealed.

The facts follow as appear from the pleadings, which recite provisions of Axton–Fisher's charter. Prior to April 30, 1943, Axton–Fisher had authorized and outstanding three classes of stock, designated respectively as preferred stock, Class A stock and Class B stock. Each share of preferred stock had a par value of $100 and was entitled to cumulative dividends at the rate of $6 per annum and possessed a liquidation value of $105 plus accrued dividends. The Class A stock, specifically described in the charter as a "common" stock, was entitled to an annual cumulative dividend of $3.20 per share. The Class B stock was next entitled to receive an annual dividend of $1.60 per share. If further funds were made available by action of the board of directors by way of dividends, the Class A stock and the Class B stock were entitled to share equally therein. Upon liquidation of the company and the payment of the sums required by the preferred stock, the Class A stock was entitled to share with the Class B stock in the

1. The plaintiff was originally the holder of 235 shares of Class A stock purchased on four occasions between July 23 and August 10, 1943, inclusive. Between August 2 and August 20, 1943, the plaintiff surrendered for redemption 215 shares and retained 20 shares.

distribution of the remaining assets, but the Class A stock was entitled to receive twice as much per share as the Class B stock.[2]

Each share of Class A stock was convertible at the option of the shareholder into one share of Class B stock. All or any of the shares of Class A stock were callable by the corporation at any quarterly dividend date upon sixty days' notice to the shareholders, at $60 per share with accrued dividends.[3] The voting rights were vested in the Class B stock but if there were four successive defaults in the payment of quarterly dividends, the class or classes of stock as to which such defaults occurred gained voting rights equal share for share with the Class B stock. By reason of this provision the Class A stock had possessed equal voting rights with the Class B stock since on or about January 1, 1937.

On or about May 16, 1941, Transamerica purchased 80,160 shares of Axton–Fisher's Class B common stock. This was about 71.5% of the outstanding Class B stock and about 46.7% of the total voting stocks of Axton–Fisher. By August 15, 1942, Transamerica owned 5,332 shares of Class A stock and 82,610 shares of Class B stock. By March 31, 1943, the amount of Class A stock of Axton–Fisher owned by Transamerica had grown to 30,168 shares or about 66⅔% of the total amount of this stock outstanding, and the amount of Class B stock owned by Transamerica had increased to 90,768 shares or about 80% of the total outstanding. Additional shares of Class B stock were acquired by Transamerica after April 30, 1943, and Transamerica converted the Class A stock owned by it into Class B stock so that on or about the end of May, 1944 Transamerica owned virtually all of the outstanding Class B stock of Axton–Fisher. Since May 16, 1941, Transamerica had control of and had dominated the management, directorate, financial policies, business and affairs of Axton–Fisher. Since the date last stated Transamerica had elected a majority of the board of directors of

2. The charter provides as follows:

"In the event of the dissolution, liquidation, merger or consolidation of the corporation, or sale of substantially all its assets, whether voluntary or involuntary, there shall be paid to the holders of the preferred stock then outstanding $105 per share, together with all unpaid accrued dividends thereon, before any sum shall be paid to or any assets distributed among the holders of the Class A common stock and/or the holders of the Class B common stock. After such payment to the holders of the preferred stock, and all unpaid accrued dividends on the Class A common stock shall have been paid, then all remaining assets and funds of the corporation shall be divided among and paid to the holders of the Class A common stock and to the holders of the Class B common stock in the ratio of 2 to 1; that is to say, there shall be paid upon each share of Class A common stock twice the amount paid upon each share of Class B common stock, in any such event."

3. The charter provides as follows:

"The whole or any part of the Class A common stock of the corporation, at the option of the Board of Directors, may be redeemed on any quarterly dividend payment date by paying therefor in cash Sixty dollars ($60.00) per share and all unpaid and accrued dividends thereon at the date fixed for such redemption, upon sending by mail to the registered holders of the Class A common stock at least sixty (60) days' notice of the exercise of such option. If at any time the Board of Directors shall determine to redeem less than the whole amount of Class A common stock then outstanding, the particular stock to be so redeemed shall be determined in such manner as the Board of Directors shall prescribe; provided, however, that no holder of Class A common stock shall be preferred over any other holder of such stock."

Axton–Fisher. These individuals are in large part officers or agents of Transamerica.

In the fall of 1942 and in the spring of 1943 Axton–Fisher possessed as its principal asset leaf tobacco which had cost it about $6,361,981. This asset was carried on Axton–Fisher's books in that amount. The value of leaf tobacco had risen sharply and to quote the words of the complaint, "unbeknown to the public holders of ... Class A common stock of Axton–Fisher, but known to Transamerica, the market value of ... [the] tobacco had, in March and April of 1943, attained the huge sum of about $20,000,000."

The complaint then alleges the gist of the plaintiff's grievance, viz., that Transamerica, knowing of the great value of the tobacco which Axton–Fisher possessed, conceived a plan to appropriate the value of the tobacco to itself by redeeming the Class A stock at the price of $60 a share plus accrued dividends, the redemption being made to appear as if "incident to the continuance of the business of Axton–Fisher as a going concern," and thereafter, the redemption of the Class A stock being completed, to liquidate Axton–Fisher; that this would result, after the disbursal of the sum required to be paid to the preferred stock, in Transamerica gaining for itself most of the value of the warehouse tobacco. The complaint further alleges that in pursuit of this plan Transamerica, by a resolution of the Board of Directors of Axton–Fisher on April 30, 1943, called the Class A stock at $60 and, selling a large part of the tobacco to Phillip–Morris Company, Ltd., Inc., together with substantially all of the other assets of Axton–Fisher, thereafter liquidated Axton–Fisher, paid off the preferred stock and pocketed the balance of the proceeds of the sale. Warehouse receipts representing the remainder of the tobacco were distributed to the Class B stockholders.

Assuming as we must that the allegations of the complaint are true, it will be observed that agents or representatives of Transamerica constituted Axton–Fisher's board of directors at the times of the happening of the events complained of, and that Transamerica was Axton–Fisher's principal and controlling stockholder at such times. It will be observed also that jurisdiction in the suit at bar is based upon diversity of citizenship and jurisdictional amount. In such a suit the conflict-of-laws rule of Delaware requires the District Court of Delaware to refer to the law of the State of incorporation to determine the extent and nature of relationships between corporation and stockholder, corporate officer or director and stockholder and between stockholders *inter sese.* See Skillman v. Conner, 8 W.W.Harr. 402, 193 A. 563, and Black & Yates v. Mahogany Ass'n, 3 Cir., 129 F.2d 227, 233, 148 A.L.R. 841. As was well stated by the court below in Geller v. Transamerica Corporation, D.C., 53 F.Supp. 625, 629, 630, "... under the Delaware conflict of laws rule, the law of the place of the wrong determines the quantum of the breach of duty.... It would seem that the place of wrong is where the final act occurred which establishes liability." This court approved that reasoning by affirming per curiam the decision. See, 3 Cir., 151 F.2d 534.

The *loci* of the events complained of in the instant case are not set forth in the complaint. In Black & Yates v. Mahogany Ass'n, 129 F.2d at page 233, we stated, "We think that in the absence of allegations as to the place or places where the acts complained of occurred, the court below would have been entitled to assume that these operative facts took place within the State of Delaware," viz., the state of the forum. It is necessary therefore to assume that the events complained of took place within the State of Delaware. The law of Kentucky determines the existence of fiduciary duty, or the lack of it, between Transamerica (as the board of directors of Axton–Fisher, as its officership or as its controlling stockholder) and Axton–Fisher's minority Class A stockholders, and the law of Delaware determines the extent of the breach of fiduciary duty, if any. [At this point the court stated the case of Taylor v. Axton–Fisher Tobacco Co., 295 Ky. 226, 173 S.W.2d 377, 148 A.L.R. 834 (Ct.App.1943) which held that the action of the directors of Axton–Fisher in making the call gave the Class B shareholders the right to have the Class A shares redeemed and that a subsequent directors' resolution of June 16, 1943, purporting to give Class A shareholders the option not to have their shares redeemed, was an invalid resolution.]

The circumstances of the case at bar are *sui generis* and we can find no Kentucky decision squarely in point. In our opinion, however, the law of Kentucky imposes upon the directors of a corporation or upon those who are in charge of its affairs by virtue of majority stock ownership or otherwise the same fiduciary relationship in respect to the corporation and to its stockholders as is imposed generally by the laws of Kentucky's sister States or which was imposed by federal law prior to Erie R. Co. v. Tompkins, 304 U.S. 64, 58 S.Ct. 817, 82 L.Ed. 1188, 114 A.L.R. 1487.

The tenor of the federal decisions in respect to the general fiduciary duty of those in control of a corporation is unmistakable. The Supreme Court in Southern Pacific Co. v. Bogert, 250 U.S. 483, 487, 488, 39 S.Ct. 533, 535, 63 L.Ed. 1099, said: "The rule of corporation law and of equity invoked is well settled and has been often applied. The majority has the right to control; but when it does so, it occupies a fiduciary relation toward the minority, as much so as the corporation itself or its officers and directors." In Pepper v. Litton, 308 U.S. 295, 306, 60 S.Ct. 238, 245, 84 L.Ed. 281, the Supreme Court stated: "A director is a fiduciary.... So is a dominant or controlling stockholder or group of stockholders.... Their powers are powers in trust.... Their dealings with the corporation are subjected to rigorous scrutiny and where any of their contracts or engagements with the corporation is challenged the burden is on the director or stockholder not only to prove the good faith of the transaction but also to show its inherent fairness from the viewpoint of the corporation and those interested therein." ...

It is appropriate to emphasize at this point that the right to call the Class A stock for redemption was confided by the charter of Axton–Fisher to the directors and not to the stockholders of that corporation. We must also reemphasize the statement of the court in Haldeman v. Haldeman, supra, and its reiteration in Kirwan v. Parkway Distillery, supra, that there is a radical difference when a stockholder is voting strictly as a stockholder and when voting as a director; that when voting as a stockholder he may have the legal right to vote with a view of his own benefits and to represent himself only; but that when he votes as a director he represents all the stockholders in the capacity of a trustee for them and cannot use his office as a director for his personal benefit at the expense of the stockholders.

Two theories are presented on one of which the case at bar must be decided. One, vigorously asserted by Transamerica and based on its interpretation of the decision in the Taylor case, is that the board of directors of Axton–Fisher, whether or not dominated by Transamerica, the principal Class B stockholder, at any time and for any purpose, might call the Class A stock for redemption; the other, asserted with equal vigor by Zahn, is that the board of directors of Axton–Fisher as fiduciaries were not entitled to favor Transamerica, the Class B stockholder, by employing the redemption provisions of the charter for its benefit.

We must of course treat the decision of the Court of Appeals of Kentucky in the Taylor case as evidence of what is the law of Kentucky. The Court took the position on that record that the directors at any time might call the Class A stock for redemption and that the redemption provision of the charter was written as much for the benefit of the Class B stock as for the Class A stock. It is argued by Transamerica very persuasively that what the Court of Appeals of Kentucky held was that when the Class A stock received its allocation of $60 a share plus accrued dividends it received its full due and that the directors had the right at any time to eliminate Class A stock from the corporate setup for the benefit of the Class B stock.[4] It does not appear from the opinion of the Court of Appeals of Kentucky whether or not the subsequent liquidation of Axton–Fisher was brought to the attention of the Court. But it is clear from the pleading that the subsequent liquidation was not an issue in the case and from the language of the Court there is some indication that it believed that Axton–Fisher was to continue in existence because Commissioner Stanley spoke of the elimination of the Class A stock, which possessed voting rights, from the management and control of Axton–Fisher. Such surmises are hazardous, however, and are not really apposite since it is our duty to determine the law of Kentucky and not to delve into subjective mental processes. It should be noted that Commissioner Stanley stated the justiciable controversy before the Court of Appeals of Kentucky as follows: "The case presents a novel question of power of the board of directors of a corporation to rescind or modify its action in calling certain stock for redemption or retirement." This, and only this, was the question before the Court. It is notable that Commissioner Stanley

4. The court said: "Manifestly, it was very much to the interest of the holders of Class B stock to have all these priorities, obligations and restrictions on and conditional joint control of the management eliminated. A substantial advantage was given to and acquired by the Class B stockholders. . . ."

said also that the acts of boards of directors "exercised in good faith and not in fraud of the rights of the stockholders" should not be interfered with by the courts and that he spoke as well of the "fair discretion" of directors to be exercised in the same manner as would be the case in the declaration of dividends.... We think that it is the settled law of Kentucky that directors may not declare or withhold the declaration of dividends for the purpose of personal profit or, by analogy, take any corporate action for such a purpose.

The difficulty in accepting Transamerica's contentions in the case at bar is that the directors of Axton–Fisher, if the allegations of the complaint be accepted as true, were the instruments of Transamerica, were directors voting in favor of their special interest, that of Transamerica, could not and did not exercise an independent judgment in calling the Class A stock, but made the call for the purpose of profiting their true principal, Transamerica. In short a puppet-puppeteer relationship existed between the directors of Axton–Fisher and Transamerica.

The act of the board of directors in calling the Class A stock, an act which could have been legally consummated by a disinterested board of directors, was here effected at the direction of the principal Class B stockholder in order to profit it. Such a call is voidable in equity at the instance of a stockholder injured thereby. It must be pointed out that under the allegations of the complaint there was no reason for the redemption of the Class A stock to be followed by the liquidation of Axton–Fisher except to enable the Class B stock to profit at the expense of the Class A stock. As has been hereinbefore stated the function of the call was confided to the board of directors by the charter and was not vested by the charter in the stockholders of any class. It was the intention of the framers of Axton–Fisher's charter to require the board of directors to act disinterestedly if that body called the Class A stock, and to make the call with a due regard for its fiduciary obligations. If the allegations of the complaint be proved, it follows that the directors of Axton–Fisher, the instruments of Transamerica, have been derelict in that duty. Liability which flows from the dereliction must be imposed upon Transamerica which, under the allegations of the complaint, constituted the board of Axton–Fisher and controlled it.

The *quantum* or extent of the breach of the fiduciary duty on the present record must be determined according to the law of Delaware for the reasons hereinbefore stated. The reaction of the law of Delaware to such a course as that pursued here by Transamerica is suggested by such decisions of the Supreme Court of Delaware as Bovay v. H.M. Byllesby & Co., Del.Sup., 38 A.2d 808, and Keenan v. Eshleman, 23 Del.Ch. 234, 2 A.2d 904, 120 A.L.R. 227. But whether the law of Delaware be applicable to determine the extent of the breach of fiduciary duty, or that of Kentucky or of New York, there will be found to be no substantial difference. The remedies to be afforded by the District Court of the United States for the District of Delaware, of course, must be those which may be available under the law of

Delaware. See Guaranty Trust Co. v. York, 326 U.S. 99, 65 S.Ct. 1464, 89 L.Ed. 2079, 160 A.L.R. 1231, and Overfield v. Pennroad Corporation, 3 Cir., 146 F.2d 889.

As has been stated the plaintiff has endeavored to set up a "First Cause of Action" and a "Second Cause of Action" in his complaint. The first cause of action is based upon his ownership of shares of Class A stock not surrendered by him to Axton–Fisher for redemption and is asserted not only on his own behalf but also on behalf of other Class A stockholders retaining their stock. The second cause of action is asserted by him on his own behalf and on behalf of other Class A stockholders in respect to the value of the stock which was surrendered for redemption. The two alleged separate causes of action, however, are in reality one. In our opinion, if the allegations of the complaint be proved, Zahn may maintain his cause of action to recover from Transamerica the value of the stock retained by him as that shall be represented by its aliquot share of the proceeds of Axton–Fisher on dissolution. It is also our opinion that he may maintain a cause of action to recover the difference between the amount received by him for the shares already surrendered and the amount which he would have received on liquidation of Axton–Fisher if he had not surrendered his stock. . . .

NOTE ON FURTHER PROCEEDINGS IN ZAHN v. TRANSAMERICA CORP.

The Third Circuit's original decision in *Zahn* used some language suggesting that the call of the Class A stock was wrongful in itself. However, in subsequent proceedings the Third Circuit held that the call was rightful even though it benefited the Class B stock and Transamerica and hurt the Class A stock:

> The first and principal question is the one raised by the holders of Class A stock as to the amount of damages to be awarded to them. The Class A stockholders contend that they are entitled to receive their aliquot shares in the liquidation distribution in the two-to-one ratio provided for in the charter for Class A stockholders participating in a liquidation. The district court held, however, that they are entitled only to recover as though they were Class B stockholders for the reason that a disinterested board of directors having knowledge of all the facts could and would have called the Class A stock for redemption in which event all of the Class A stockholders would have exercised their option to convert their shares into Class B stock on a one-for-one basis. We think that the district court was right in so holding.
>
> The Court of Appeals of Kentucky has held that the Axton–Fisher Class A stock, although designated as a common stock was in the nature of a junior preferred stock, and that the provision of the charter for the redemption of the Class A stock was a continuing option allowed to the holders of the Class B common

stock which the board of directors could exercise in their favor. This construction of the Axton–Fisher charter by the highest court of the state of its incorporation was, of course, binding on the district court. We agree with the district court that the provisions of the Axton–Fisher charter with respect to liquidation must be read realistically with the provisions for redemption of the Class A stock and its conversion into Class B stock. When so read it becomes apparent that a disinterested board of directors discharging its responsibility to the Class B stockholders in case of liquidation would call the Class A stock for redemption at $60 per share if it appeared that the distribution in liquidation to that stock would exceed that figure on a two-to-one basis. Since the board would have the right to do this and the Class B stockholders would be entitled to such action, the failure to do so would be an arbitrary act which would confer a windfall to which they were not entitled under the charter upon the Class A stockholders at the direct expense of the holders of the Class B stock. The district court was therefore quite right in determining that the damages to be awarded to the Class A stockholders should be measured by what they would have received if they had converted their shares into Class B stock prior to the liquidation.

Speed v. Transamerica Corp., 235 F.2d 369 (3d Cir.1956).

NEMEC v. SHRADER

[Chapter 8, Section 7, supra]

NOTE ON THE DUTY OF DISCLOSURE BY CONTROLLING SHAREHOLDERS UNDER DELAWARE LAW

The Delaware Court has been very rigorous in requiring full disclosure by controlling shareholders when they deal with the minority. In Lynch v. Vickers Energy Corp., 383 A.2d 278 (Del.1977),[1] Vickers, the majority shareholder of TransOcean stock, made a tender offer for the 46% of TransOcean stock held by the public. The trial court held that in preparing the offering circular through which the tender offer was made, Vickers owed a fiduciary duty that required "complete candor" in disclosing fully "all of the facts and circumstances surrounding" the tender offer. The Delaware Supreme Court agreed with that rule, but reversed because the trial court had not applied the rule with sufficient vigor:

> . . . [A]t the time of the offer, defendants were in possession of [an] estimate, prepared by Forrest Harrell, a petroleum engineer and a vice-president of TransOcean, fixing the net asset value

---

1. On subsequent appeal, 429 A.2d 497 (Del.Supr.1981), overruled on another issue, Weinberger v. UOP, Inc., 457 A.2d 701 (Del.Supr.1983).

> [of TransOcean] at $250.8 million, which computes to approximately $20 per share, and from which one could conclude that the value could be as high as $300 million. Both of these estimates were . . . substantially higher than the minimum amount stated in the tender offer.
>
> The Trial Court closely examined the Harrell report and concluded that nondisclosure thereof was not fatal; the Court reasoned that the [language used in the offering circular] ". . . furnished the TransOcean stockholders with adequate facts on which to make an educated choice. . . ." . . .
>
> This approach to the controversy was, in our view, mistaken in two respects: First, to reach such a conclusion it was necessary for the Court to weigh the merits of the Harrell report and, in the context of this case, that was error. The Court's function was not to go through Harrell's estimates of oil reserves and recoveries, for example, and make its own judgment about whether these should be "substantially discounted," nor should it have substituted its judgment for Harrell's about the rate which the Federal Power Commission would approve for a sale of natural gas. The stockholders and not the Court should have been permitted to make such qualitative judgments.
>
> The Court's duty was to examine what information defendants had and to measure it against what they gave to the minority stockholders, in a context in which "complete candor" is required. In other words, the limited function of the Court was to determine whether defendants had disclosed all information in their possession germane to the transaction in issue. And by "germane" we mean, for present purposes, information such as a reasonable shareholder would consider important in deciding whether to sell or retain stock. . . .
>
> A second reason why we think that the Court of Chancery was mistaken in applying the law was that it incorrectly substituted a "disclosure of adequate facts" standard . . . for the correct standard, which requires disclosure of *all* germane facts. Completeness, not adequacy, is both the norm and the mandate under present circumstances.

In Rosenblatt v. Getty Oil Co., 493 A.2d 929 (Del.1985), the Delaware Court substituted the term "material facts" for the term "germane facts." Subsequently, the Court dropped the "duty of candor" terminology in favor of terminology based on materiality, but made clear that the change in terminology did not signify a change in the underlying concept. Shell Petroleum, Inc. v. Smith, 606 A.2d 112, 113 n. 3 (Del.1992).

In Shell Petroleum, Inc. v. Smith, 606 A.2d 112 (Del. 1992), Royal Dutch Petroleum Co. owned 94.6% of Shell Oil Co. Royal Dutch decided to initiate a merger between Shell and SPNV Holdings ("Holdings"). Under the terms of the merger, each Shell minority shareholder would receive $58/share, or $60/share if he waived his right to appraisal before a fixed date. In conjunction with the merger, Holdings distributed several documents to the minority. Due to a computer-programming error, the documents understated Shell's discounted future net cash flows—an important element in the computation of the value of a business—by $3.00 to $3.45 per share. Former minority shareholders of Shell brought a class action. The Court of Chancery awarded damages to the shareholders for material misstatements. Affirmed.

> Holdings' duty with respect to disclosure is clear. As the majority shareholder, Holdings bears the burden of showing complete disclosure of all material facts relevant to a minority shareholders' decision whether to accept the short-form merger consideration or seek an appraisal.... A fact is considered material if there is a "substantial likelihood that the disclosure of the omitted fact would have been viewed by the reasonable investor as having significantly altered the 'total mix' of information made available." ... "While it need not be shown that an omission or distortion would have made an investor change his overall view of a proposed transaction, it must be shown that the fact in question would have been relevant to him." ...
>
> Holdings ... argues that a $3 per share error was not significant enough to make a reasonable stockholder change his decision and seek an appraisal. However, the question is not whether the information would have changed the stockholder's decision to accept the merger consideration, but whether "the fact in question would have been relevant to him." ...

See also Zirn v. VLI Corp., 621 A.2d 773, 777 (Del.1993); Arnold v. Society for Savings Bancorp, Inc., 650 A.2d 1270 (Del.1994).

NOTE ON THE TARGET OF SUITS BY MINORITY SHAREHOLDERS

Call a controlling shareholder S, and call the corporation that S controls C. Suppose that S and C have engaged in a transaction between themselves. Assume further that the transaction has been approved by C's board—as will often be the case. A minority shareholder of C who challenges the transaction could, in theory, sue both S and C's directors. As a practical matter, however, although C's directors may be joined as defendants, in many or most cases the real target of such a suit is S, the controlling shareholder, and typically (although not invariably) the court focuses on S's liability rather than on the liability of C's directors.

This phenomenon may be explained on two grounds. First, the controlling shareholder usually has deep pockets; the directors of C may not. Therefore, it may not be worth adding the directors to the suit. Second, C's directors are not self-interested, in the traditional sense, in transactions between C and S, because the directors will not directly profit from the transaction itself. Instead, the directors have a *positional* conflict; that is, it is in the directors' interests, if they want to maintain or augment their positions with C, to go along with S's proposals. Because the law concerning traditional conflicts of interest is better understood than the law concerning positional conflicts, it is easier for the plaintiff and the courts to focus on the liability of the controlling shareholder, who does have a traditional conflict, than on the directors of C, who have only positional conflicts.

Sinclair Oil Corporation v. Levien

Supreme Court of Delaware, 1971.
280 A.2d 717.

■ WOLCOTT, CHIEF JUSTICE. This is an appeal by the defendant, Sinclair Oil Corporation (hereafter Sinclair), from an order of the Court of Chancery, 261 A.2d 911, in a derivative action requiring Sinclair to account for damages sustained by its subsidiary, Sinclair Venezuelan Oil Company (hereinafter Sinven), organized by Sinclair for the purpose of operating in Venezuela, as a result of dividends paid by Sinven, the denial to Sinven of industrial development, and a breach of contract between Sinclair's wholly-owned subsidiary, Sinclair International Oil Company, and Sinven.

Sinclair, operating primarily as a holding company, is in the business of exploring for oil and of producing and marketing crude oil and oil products. At all times relevant to this litigation, it owned about 97% of Sinven's stock. The plaintiff owns about 3000 of 120,000 publicly held shares of Sinven. Sinven, incorporated in 1922, has been engaged in petroleum operations primarily in Venezuela and since 1959 has operated exclusively in Venezuela.

Sinclair nominates all members of Sinven's board of directors. The Chancellor found as a fact that the directors were not independent of Sinclair. Almost without exception, they were officers, directors, or employees of corporations in the Sinclair complex. By reason of Sinclair's domination, it is clear that Sinclair owed Sinven a fiduciary duty. Getty Oil Company v. Skelly Oil Co., 267 A.2d 883 (Del. Supr.1970); Cottrell v. Pawcatuck Co., 35 Del.Ch. 309, 116 A.2d 787 (1955). Sinclair concedes this.

The Chancellor held that because of Sinclair's fiduciary duty and its control over Sinven, its relationship with Sinven must meet the test of intrinsic fairness. The standard of intrinsic fairness involves both a high degree of fairness and a shift in the burden of proof. Under this standard the burden is on Sinclair to prove, subject to careful judicial scrutiny, that its transactions with Sinven were objectively fair. Guth v. Loft, Inc., 23 Del.Ch. 255, 5 A.2d 503 (1939); Sterling v. Mayflower Hotel Corp., 33 Del.Ch. 293, 93 A.2d 107, 38 A.L.R.2d 425 (Del. Supr.1952); Getty Oil Co. v. Skelly Oil Co., supra.

Sinclair argues that the transactions between it and Sinven should be tested, not by the test of intrinsic fairness with the accompanying shift of the burden of proof, but by the business judgment rule under which a court will not interfere with the judgment of a board of directors unless there is a showing of gross and palpable overreaching. Meyerson v. El Paso Natural Gas Co., 246 A.2d 789 (Del.Ch.1967). A board of directors enjoys a presumption of sound business judgment, and its decisions will not be disturbed if they can be attributed to any rational business purpose. A court under such circumstances will not substitute its own notions of what is or is not sound business judgment.

We think, however, that Sinclair's argument in this respect is misconceived. When the situation involves a parent and a subsidiary, with the parent controlling the transaction and fixing the terms, the test of intrinsic fairness, with its resulting shifting of the burden of proof, is applied. Sterling v. Mayflower Hotel Corp., supra; David J. Greene & Co. v. Dunhill International, Inc., 249 A.2d 427 (Del.Ch. 1968); Bastian v. Bourns, Inc., 256 A.2d 680 (Del.Ch.1969) aff'd. Per Curiam (unreported) (Del.Supr.1970). The basic situation for the application of the rule is the one in which the parent has received a benefit to the exclusion and at the expense of the subsidiary.

Recently, this court dealt with the question of fairness in parent-subsidiary dealings in Getty Oil Co. v. Skelly Oil Co., supra. In that case, both parent and subsidiary were in the business of refining and marketing crude oil and crude oil products. The Oil Import Board ruled that the subsidiary, because it was controlled by the parent, was no longer entitled to a separate allocation of imported crude oil. The subsidiary then contended that it had a right to share the quota of crude oil allotted to the parent. We ruled that the business judgment standard should be applied to determine this contention. Although the subsidiary suffered a loss through the administration of the oil import quotas, the parent gained nothing. The parent's quota was derived solely from its own past use. The past use of the subsidiary did not cause an increase in the parent's quota. Nor did the parent usurp a quota of the subsidiary. Since the parent received nothing from the subsidiary to the exclusion of the minority stockholders of the subsidiary, there was no self-dealing. Therefore, the business judgment standard was properly applied.

A parent does indeed owe a fiduciary duty to its subsidiary when there are parent-subsidiary dealings. However, this alone will not evoke the intrinsic fairness standard. This standard will be applied only when the fiduciary duty is accompanied by self-dealing—the situation when a parent is on both sides of a transaction with its subsidiary. Self-dealing occurs when the parent, by virtue of its domination of the subsidiary causes the subsidiary to act in such a way that the parent receives something from the subsidiary to the exclusion of, and detriment to, the minority stockholders of the subsidiary.

We turn now to the facts. The plaintiff argues that, from 1960 through 1966, Sinclair caused Sinven to pay out such excessive dividends that the industrial development of Sinven was effectively prevented, and it became in reality a corporation in dissolution.

From 1960 through 1966, Sinven paid out $108,000,000 in dividends ($38,000,000 in excess of Sinven's earnings during the same period). The Chancellor held that Sinclair caused these dividends to be paid during a period when it had a need for large amounts of cash. Although the dividends paid exceeded earnings, the plaintiff concedes that the payments were made in compliance with 8 Del.C. § 170, authorizing payment of dividends out of surplus or net profits. However, the plaintiff attacks these dividends on the ground that they resulted from an improper motive—Sinclair's need for cash. The Chancellor, applying the intrinsic fairness standard, held that Sinclair did not sustain its burden of proving that these dividends were intrinsically fair to the minority stockholders of Sinven.

Since it is admitted that the dividends were paid in strict compliance with 8 Del.C. § 170, the alleged excessiveness of the payments alone would not state a cause of action. Nevertheless, compliance with the applicable statute may not, under all circumstances, justify all dividend payments. If a plaintiff can meet his burden of proving that a dividend cannot be grounded on any reasonable business objective, then the courts can and will interfere with the board's decision to pay the dividend.

Sinclair contends that it is improper to apply the intrinsic fairness standard to dividend payments even when the board which voted for the dividends is completely dominated. In support of this contention, Sinclair relies heavily on American District Telegraph Co. [ADT] v. Grinnell Corp., (N.Y.Sup.Ct.1969) aff'd. 33 A.D.2d 769, 306 N.Y.S.2d 209 (1969). Plaintiffs were minority stockholders of ADT, a subsidiary of Grinnell. The plaintiffs alleged that Grinnell, realizing that it would soon have to sell its ADT stock because of a pending anti-trust action, caused ADT to pay excessive dividends. Because the dividend payments conformed with applicable statutory law, and the plaintiffs could not prove an abuse of discretion, the court ruled that the complaint did not state a cause of action. Other decisions seem to support Sinclair's contention. In Metropolitan Casualty Ins. Co. v. First State Bank of Temple, 54 S.W.2d 358 (Tex.Civ.App.1932), rev'd. on other grounds, 79 S.W.2d 835 (Sup.Ct.1935), the court held that a majority of interested directors does not void a declaration of dividends because all directors, by necessity, are interested in and benefited by a dividend declaration. See, also, Schwartz v. Kahn, 183 Misc. 252, 50 N.Y.S.2d 931 (1944); Weinberger v. Quinn, 264 A.D. 405, 35 N.Y.S.2d 567 (1942).

We do not accept the argument that the intrinsic fairness test can never be applied to a dividend declaration by a dominated board, although a dividend declaration by a dominated board will not inevitably demand the application of the intrinsic fairness standard. Moskowitz v. Bantrell, 41 Del.Ch. 177, 190 A.2d 749 (Del.Supr.1963). If such a dividend is in essence self-dealing by the parent, then the intrinsic fairness standard is the proper standard. For example, suppose a parent dominates a subsidiary and its board of directors. The subsidiary has outstanding two classes of stock, X and Y. Class X is owned by the parent and Class Y is owned by minority stockholders of the subsidiary. If the subsidiary, at the direction of the parent, declares a dividend on its Class X stock only, this might well be self-dealing by the parent. It would be receiving something from the subsidiary to the exclusion of and detrimental to its minority stockholders. This self-dealing, coupled with the parent's fiduciary duty, would make intrinsic fairness the proper standard by which to evaluate the dividend payments.

Consequently it must be determined whether the dividend payments by Sinven were, in essence, self-dealing by Sinclair. The dividends resulted in great sums of money being transferred from Sinven to Sinclair. However, a proportionate share of this money was received by the minority shareholders of Sinven. Sinclair received nothing from Sinven to the exclusion of its minority stockholders. As such, these dividends were not self-dealing. We hold therefore that the Chancellor erred in applying the intrinsic fairness test as to these dividend payments. The business judgment standard should have been applied.

We conclude that the facts demonstrate that the dividend payments complied with the business judgment standard and with 8 Del.C. § 170. The motives for causing the declaration of dividends are immaterial unless the plaintiff can show that the dividend payments resulted from improper motives and amounted to waste. The plaintiff contends only that the dividend payments drained Sinven of cash to such an extent that it was prevented from expanding.

The plaintiff proved no business opportunities which came to Sinven independently and which Sinclair either took to itself or denied to Sinven. As a matter of fact, with two minor exceptions which resulted in losses, all of Sinven's operations have been conducted in Venezuela, and Sinclair had a policy of exploiting its oil properties located in different countries by subsidiaries located in the particular countries.

From 1960 to 1966 Sinclair purchased or developed oil fields in Alaska, Canada, Paraguay, and other places around the world. The plaintiff contends that these were all opportunities which could have been taken by Sinven. The Chancellor concluded that Sinclair had not proved that its denial of expansion opportunities to Sinven was intrinsically fair. He based this conclusion on the following findings of fact. Sinclair made no real effort to expand Sinven. The excessive dividends paid by Sinven resulted in so great a cash drain as to effectively deny to Sinven any ability to expand. During this same period Sinclair actively pursued a company-wide policy of developing through its subsidiaries new sources of revenue, but Sinven was not permitted to participate and was confined in its activities to Venezuela.

However, the plaintiff could point to no opportunities which came to Sinven. Therefore, Sinclair usurped no business opportunity belonging to Sinven. Since Sinclair received nothing from Sinven to the exclusion of and detriment to Sinven's minority stockholders, there was no self-dealing. Therefore, business judgment is the proper standard by which to evaluate Sinclair's expansion policies.

Since there is no proof of self-dealing on the part of Sinclair, it follows that the expansion policy of Sinclair and the methods used to achieve the desired result must, as far as Sinclair's treatment of Sinven is concerned, be tested by the standards of the business judgment rule. Accordingly, Sinclair's decision absent fraud or gross overreaching, to achieve expansion through the medium of its subsidiaries, other than Sinven, must be upheld.

Even if Sinclair was wrong in developing these opportunities as it did, the question arises, with which subsidiaries should these opportunities have been shared? No evidence indicates a unique need or ability of Sinven to develop these opportunities. The decision of which subsidiaries would be used to implement Sinclair's expansion policy was one of business judgment with which a court will not interfere absent a showing of gross and palpable overreaching. Meyerson v. El Paso Natural Gas Co., 246 A.2d 789 (Del.Ch.1967). No such showing has been made here.

Next, Sinclair argues that the Chancellor committed error when he held it liable to Sinven for breach of contract.

In 1961 Sinclair created Sinclair International Oil Company (hereafter International), a wholly owned subsidiary used for the purpose of coordinating all of Sinclair's foreign operations. All crude purchases by Sinclair were made thereafter through International.

On September 28, 1961, Sinclair caused Sinven to contract with International whereby Sinven agreed to sell all of its crude oil and refined products to International at specified prices. The contract provided for minimum and maximum quantities and prices. The plaintiff contends that Sinclair caused this contract to be breached in two respects. Although the contract called for payment on receipt, International's payments lagged as much as 30 days after receipt. Also, the contract required International to purchase at least a fixed minimum amount of crude and refined products from Sinven. International did not comply with this requirement.

Clearly, Sinclair's act of contracting with its dominated subsidiary was self-dealing. Under the contract Sinclair received the products produced by Sinven, and of course the minority shareholders of Sinven were not able to share in the receipt of these products. If the contract was breached, then Sinclair received these products to the detriment of Sinven's minority shareholders. We agree with the Chancellor's finding that the contract was breached by Sinclair, both as to the time of payments and the amounts purchased.

Although a parent need not bind itself by a contract with its dominated subsidiary, Sinclair chose to operate in this manner. As Sinclair has received the benefits of this contract, so must it comply with the contractual duties.

Under the intrinsic fairness standard, Sinclair must prove that its causing Sinven not to enforce the contract was intrinsically fair to the minority shareholders of Sinven. Sinclair has failed to meet this burden. Late payments were clearly breaches for which Sinven should have sought and received adequate damages. As to the quantities purchased, Sinclair argues that it purchased all the products produced by Sinven. This, however, does not satisfy the standard of intrinsic fairness. Sinclair has failed to prove that Sinven could not possibly have produced or some way have obtained the contract minimums. As such, Sinclair must account on this claim.

Finally, Sinclair argues that the Chancellor committed error in refusing to allow it a credit or setoff of all benefits provided by it to Sinven with respect to all the alleged damages. The Chancellor held that setoff should be allowed on specific transactions, e.g., benefits to Sinven under the contract with International, but denied an overall setoff against all damages claimed. We agree with the Chancellor, although the point may well be moot in view of our holding that Sinclair is not required to account for the alleged excessiveness of the dividend payments.

We will therefore reverse that part of the Chancellor's order that requires Sinclair to account to Sinven for damages sustained as a result of dividends paid between 1960 and 1966, and by reason of the denial to Sinven of expansion during that period. We will affirm the remaining portion of that order and remand the cause for further proceedings.

Accord: Ripley v. International Railways of Central America, 8 N.Y.2d 430, 209 N.Y.S.2d 289, 171 N.E.2d 443 (1960) (controlling shareholder of railroad was liable for the difference between the transportation rates it paid for shipping commodities on the railroad and the fair and reasonable value of the transportation services).

DAVID J. GREENE AND CO. v. DUNHILL INTERNATIONAL, INC., 249 A.2d 427 (Del.Ch.1968). Dunhill was a diversified operating company. It manufactured and sold automotive equipment, infant-feeding equipment, and other products. Dunhill owned 80.3% of the stock of Spalding, which was a leading producer of athletic equipment and also had a toy division, which made and sold "Tinkertoys," and which accounted for about 4% of Spalding's sales. Dunhill itself did not make or sell toys of any kind. In 1968, Dunhill acquired Child Guidance Toys, which manufactured and distributed educational toys and visual-aid teaching devices. Minority shareholders in Spalding brought suit against Dunhill on the ground that Dunhill had appropriated a corporate opportunity that belonged to Spalding. Held, for the minority shareholders:

> [T]he affidavit filed by Morris Shilensky, whose firm is counsel to Dunhill, shows that shortly after a prior merger by that

company "there was widely circulated a description of a program for acquisition of businesses for Dunhill as well as for Spalding." He states that the Child Guidance opportunity came to Dunhill and not Spalding. That is perfectly understandable. The program Dunhill publicized *included* Spalding but asked that proposals be submitted to *Dunhill.* A reasonable inference from all of this is that Dunhill had taken over any acquisition program Spalding had.... And the Tinkertoy operation of Spalding is identified as the division interested in educational toys and equipment....

In sum, the record makes out a sufficient showing of a business opportunity in the line of Spalding's business, which would have been of practical advantage to it and which it was financially able to undertake; that opportunity was acquired by Spalding's controlling stockholder.

Kahn v. Lynch Communication Systems, Inc.

Supreme Court of Delaware, 1994.
638 A.2d 1110.

■ Before MOORE, WALSH, and HOLLAND, JJ.

■ HOLLAND, JUSTICE:

This is an appeal by the plaintiff-appellant, Alan R. Kahn ("Kahn"), from a final judgment of the Court of Chancery which was entered after a trial. The action, instituted by Kahn in 1986, originally sought to enjoin the acquisition of the defendant-appellee, Lynch Communication Systems, Inc. ("Lynch"), by the defendant-appellee, Alcatel U.S.A. Corporation ("Alcatel"), pursuant to a tender offer and cash-out merger. Kahn amended his complaint to seek monetary damages after the Court of Chancery denied his request for a preliminary injunction. The Court of Chancery subsequently certified Kahn's action as a class action on behalf of all Lynch shareholders, other than the named defendants, who tendered their stock in the merger, or whose stock was acquired through the merger.

A three-day trial was held April 13–15, 1993. Kahn alleged that Alcatel was a controlling shareholder of Lynch and breached its fiduciary duties to Lynch and its shareholders. According to Kahn, Alcatel dictated the terms of the merger ... [at] an unfair price.

The Court of Chancery concluded that Alcatel was, in fact, a controlling shareholder that owed fiduciary duties to Lynch and its shareholders. It also concluded that Alcatel had not breached those fiduciary duties. Accordingly, the Court of Chancery entered judgment in favor of the defendants.

... Kahn's ... contention is that the Court of Chancery erred by finding that "the tender offer and merger were negotiated by an independent committee," and then placing the burden of persuasion on the plaintiff, Kahn. Kahn asserts the uncontradicted testimony in the record demonstrated that the committee could not and did not bargain at arm's length with Alcatel. . . .

This Court has concluded that the record supports the Court of Chancery's finding that Alcatel was a controlling shareholder. However, the record does not support the conclusion that the burden of persuasion shifted to Kahn. Therefore, the burden of proving the entire fairness of the merger transaction remained on Alcatel, the controlling shareholder. Accordingly, the judgment of the Court of Chancery is reversed. The matter is remanded for further proceedings in accordance with this opinion.

Facts

Lynch, a Delaware corporation, designed and manufactured electronic telecommunications equipment, primarily for sale to telephone operating companies. Alcatel, a holding company, is a subsidiary of Alcatel (S.A.), a French company involved in public telecommunications, business communications, electronics, and optronics. Alcatel (S.A.), in turn, is a subsidiary of Compagnie Generale d'Electricite ("CGE"), a French corporation with operations in energy, transportation, telecommunications and business systems.

In 1981, Alcatel acquired 30.6 percent of Lynch's common stock pursuant to a stock purchase agreement. As part of that agreement, Lynch amended its certificate of incorporation to require an 80 percent affirmative vote of its shareholders for approval of any business combination. In addition, Alcatel obtained proportional representation on the Lynch board of directors and the right to purchase 40 percent of any equity securities offered by Lynch to third parties. The agreement also precluded Alcatel from holding more than 45 percent of Lynch's stock prior to October 1, 1986. By the time of the merger which is contested in this action, Alcatel owned 43.3 percent of Lynch's outstanding stock; designated five of the eleven members of Lynch's board of directors; two of three members of the executive committee; and two of four members of the compensation committee.

In the spring of 1986, Lynch determined that in order to remain competitive in the rapidly changing telecommunications field, it would need to obtain fiber optics technology to complement its existing digital electronic capabilities. Lynch's management identified a target company, Telco Systems, Inc. ("Telco"), which possessed both fiber optics and other valuable technological assets. The record reflects that Telco expressed interest in being acquired by Lynch. Because of the supermajority voting provision, which Alcatel had negotiated when it first purchased its shares, in order to proceed with the Telco combination Lynch needed Alcatel's consent. In June 1986, Ellsworth F. Dertinger ("Dertinger"), Lynch's CEO and chairman of its board of directors, contacted Pierre Suard ("Suard"), the chairman of Alcatel's parent company, CGE, regarding the acquisition of Telco by Lynch. Suard expressed Alcatel's opposition to Lynch's acquisition of Telco. Instead, Alcatel proposed a combination of Lynch and Celwave Systems, Inc. ("Celwave"), an indirect subsidiary of CGE engaged in the manufacture and sale of telephone wire, cable and other related products.

Alcatel's proposed combination with Celwave was presented to the Lynch board at a regular meeting held on August 1, 1986. Although several directors expressed interest in the original combination which had been proposed with Telco, the Alcatel representatives on Lynch's board made it clear that such a combination would not be considered before a Lynch/Celwave combination. According to the minutes of the August 1 meeting, Dertinger expressed his opinion that Celwave would not be of interest to Lynch if Celwave was not owned by Alcatel.

At the conclusion of the meeting, the Lynch board unanimously adopted a resolution establishing an Independent Committee, consisting of Hubert L. Kertz ("Kertz"), Paul B. Wineman ("Wineman"), and Stuart M. Beringer ("Beringer"), to negotiate with Celwave and to make recommendations concerning the appropriate terms and conditions of a combination with Celwave. On October 24, 1986, Alcatel's investment banking firm, Dillon, Read & Co., Inc. ("Dillon Read") made a presentation to the Independent Committee. Dillon Read expressed its views concerning the benefits of a Celwave/Lynch combination and submitted a written proposal of an exchange ratio of 0.95 shares of Celwave per Lynch share in a stock-for-stock merger.

However, the Independent Committee's investment advisors, Thomson McKinnon Securities Inc. ("Thomson McKinnon") and Kidder, Peabody & Co. Inc. ("Kidder Peabody"), reviewed the Dillon Read proposal and concluded that the 0.95 ratio was predicated on Dillon Read's overvaluation of Celwave. Based upon this advice, the Independent Committee determined that the exchange ratio proposed by Dillon Read was unattractive to Lynch. The Independent Committee expressed its unanimous opposition to the Celwave/Lynch merger on October 31, 1986.

Alcatel responded to the Independent Committee's action on November 4, 1986, by withdrawing the Celwave proposal. Alcatel made a simultaneous offer to acquire the entire equity interest in Lynch, constituting the approximately 57 percent of Lynch shares not owned by Alcatel. The offering price was $14 cash per share.

On November 7, 1986, the Lynch board of directors revised the mandate of the Independent Committee. It authorized Kertz, Wineman, and Beringer to negotiate the cash merger offer with Alcatel. At a meeting held that same day, the Independent Committee determined that the $14 per share offer was inadequate. The Independent's Committee's own legal counsel, Skadden, Arps, Slate, Meagher & Flom ("Skadden Arps"), suggested that the Independent Committee should review alternatives to a cash-out merger with Alcatel, including a "white knight" third party acquiror, a repurchase of Alcatel's shares, or the adoption of a shareholder rights plan.

On November 12, 1986, Beringer, as chairman of the Independent Committee, contacted Michiel C. McCarty ("McCarty") of Dillon Read,

Alcatel's representative in the negotiations, with a counteroffer at a price of $17 per share. McCarty responded on behalf of Alcatel with an offer of $15 per share. When Beringer informed McCarty of the Independent Committee's view that $15 was also insufficient, Alcatel raised its offer to $15.25 per share. The Independent Committee also rejected this offer. Alcatel then made its final offer of $15.50 per share.

At the November 24, 1986 meeting of the Independent Committee, Beringer advised its other two members that Alcatel was "ready to proceed with an unfriendly tender at a lower price" if the $15.50 per share price was not recommended by the Independent Committee and approved by the Lynch board of directors. Beringer also told the other members of the Independent Committee that the alternatives to a cash-out merger had been investigated but were impracticable.[52] After meeting with its financial and legal advisors, the Independent Committee voted unanimously to recommend that the Lynch board of directors approve Alcatel's $15.50 cash per share price for a merger with Alcatel. The Lynch board met later that day. With Alcatel's nominees abstaining, it approved the merger.

Alcatel Dominated Lynch

Controlling Shareholder Status

This Court has held that "a shareholder owes a fiduciary duty only if it owns a majority interest in or exercises control over the business affairs of the corporation." Ivanhoe Partners v. Newmont Mining Corp., Del.Supr., 535 A.2d 1334, 1344 (1987) (emphasis added). With regard to the exercise of control, this Court has stated:

> [A] shareholder who owns less than 50% of a corporation's outstanding stocks does not, without more, become a controlling shareholder of that corporation, with a concomitant fiduciary status. For a dominating relationship to exist in the absence of controlling stock ownership, a plaintiff must allege domination by a minority shareholder through actual control of corporation conduct.

Citron v. Fairchild Camera & Instrument Corp., Del.Supr., 569 A.2d 53, 70 (1989) (quotations and citation omitted).

Alcatel held a 43.3 percent minority share of stock in Lynch. Therefore, the threshold question to be answered by the Court of Chancery was whether, despite its minority ownership, Alcatel exercised control over Lynch's business affairs. Based upon the testimony and the minutes of the August 1, 1986 Lynch board meeting, the Court of Chancery concluded that Alcatel did exercise control over Lynch's business decisions....

---

52. The minutes reflect that Beringer told the Committee the "white knight" alternative "appeared impractical with the 80% approval requirement"; the repurchase of Alcatel's shares would produce a "highly leveraged company with a lower book value" and was an alternative "not in the least encouraged by Alcatel"; and a shareholder rights plan was not viable because of the increased debt it would entail.

At the August 1 meeting, Alcatel opposed the renewal of compensation contracts for Lynch's top five managers. According to Dertinger, Christian Fayard ("Fayard"), an Alcatel director, told the board members, "[y]ou must listen to us. We are 43 percent owner. You have to do what we tell you." The minutes confirm Dertinger's testimony. They recite that Fayard declared, "you are pushing us very much to take control of the company. Our opinion is not taken into consideration."

Although Beringer and Kertz, two of the independent directors, favored renewal of the contracts, according to the minutes, the third independent director, Wineman, admonished the board as follows:

> Mr. Wineman pointed out that the vote on the contracts is a "watershed vote" and the motion, due to Alcatel's "strong feelings," might not carry if taken now. Mr. Wineman clarified that "you [management] might win the battle and lose the war." With Alcatel's opinion so clear, Mr. Wineman questioned "if management wants the contracts renewed under these circumstances." He recommended that management "think twice." Mr. Wineman declared: "I want to keep the management. I can't think of a better management." Mr. Kertz agreed, again advising consideration of the "critical" period the company is entering.

The minutes reflect that the management directors left the room after this statement. The remaining board members then voted not to renew the contracts.

At the same meeting, Alcatel vetoed Lynch's acquisition of the target company, which, according to the minutes, Beringer considered "an immediate fit" for Lynch. Dertinger agreed with Beringer, stating that the "target company is extremely important as they have the products that Lynch needs now." Nonetheless, Alcatel prevailed. The minutes reflect that Fayard advised the board: "Alcatel, with its 44% equity position, would not approve such an acquisition as . . . it does not wish to be diluted from being the main shareholder in Lynch." From the foregoing evidence, the Vice Chancellor concluded:

> . . . Alcatel did control the Lynch board, at least with respect to the matters under consideration at its August 1, 1986 board meeting. The interplay between the directors was more than vigorous discussion, as suggested by defendants. The management and independent directors disagreed with Alcatel on several important issues. However, when Alcatel made its position clear, and reminded the other directors of its significant stockholdings, Alcatel prevailed. Dertinger testified Fayard "scared [the non-Alcatel directors] to death." I conclude that the non-Alcatel directors deferred to Alcatel because of its position as a significant stockholder and not because they decided in the exercise of their own business judgment that Alcatel's position was correct. . . .

The record supports the Court of Chancery's underlying factual finding that "the non-Alcatel [independent] directors deferred to Alcatel because of its position as a significant stockholder and not because they decided in the exercise of their own business judgment that Alcatel's position was correct.: The record also supports the subsequent factual finding that, notwithstanding its 43.4 percent minority shareholder interest, Alcatel did exercise actual control over Lynch by dominating its corporate affairs. The Court of Chancery's legal conclusion that Alcatel owed the fiduciary duties of a controlling shareholder to the other Lynch shareholders followed syllogistically as the logical result of its cogent analysis of the record.

Entire Fairness Requirement

Dominating Interested Shareholder

A controlling or dominating shareholder standing on both sides of a transaction, as in a parent-subsidiary context, bears the burden of proving its entire fairness. *Weinberger v. UOP, Inc.,* Del.Supr., 457 A.2d 701, 710 (1983). *See Rosenblatt v. Getty Oil Co.,* Del.Supr., 493 A.2d 929, 937 (1985). The demonstration of fairness that is required was set forth by this Court in *Weinberger:*

> The concept of fairness has two basic aspects: fair dealing and fair price. The former embraces questions of when the transaction was timed, how it was initiated, structured, negotiated, disclosed to the directors, and how the approvals of the directors and the stockholders were obtained. The latter aspect of fairness relates to the economic and financial considerations of the proposed merger, including all relevant factors: assets, market value, earnings, future prospects, and any other elements that affect the intrinsic or inherent value of a company's stock. However, the test for fairness is not a bifurcated one as between fair dealing and price. All aspects of the issue must be examined as a whole since the question is one of entire fairness.

Weinberger v. UOP, Inc., 457 A.2d at 711 (citations omitted).

The logical question raised by this Court's holding in *Weinberger* was what type of evidence would be reliable to demonstrate entire fairness. That question was not only anticipated but also initially addressed in the *Weinberger* opinion. Id. At 709–10 n. 7. This court suggested that the result "could have been entirely different if UOP had appointed an independent negotiating committee of its outside directors to deal with Signal at arm's length," because "fairness in this context can be equated to conduct by a theoretical, wholly independent, board of directors." Id. Accordingly, this Court stated, "a showing that the action taken was as though each of the contending parties had in fact exerted its bargaining power against the other at arm's length is strong evidence that the transaction meets the test of fairness.: Id. (emphasis added).

In this case, the Vice Chancellor noted that the Court of Chancery has expressed "differing views" regarding the effect that an approval of a cash-out merger by a special committee of disinterested directors has upon the controlling or dominating shareholder's burden of demonstrating entire fairness. One view is that such approval shifts to the plaintiff the burden of proving that the transaction was unfair.... The other view is that such an approval renders the business judgment rule the applicable standard of judicial review....

Entire fairness remains the proper focus of judicial analysis in examining an interested merger, irrespective of whether the burden of proof remains upon or is shifted away from the controlling or dominating shareholder, because the unchanging nature of the underlying "interested" transaction requires careful scrutiny. *See* Weinberger v. UOP, Inc., 457 A.2d at 710 (citing Sterling v. Mayflower Hotel Corp., Del.Supr., 93 A.2d 107, 110 (1952)). The policy rationale for the exclusive application of the entire fairness standard to interested merger transactions has been stated as follows:

> Parent subsidiary mergers, unlike stock options, are proposed by a party that controls, and will continue to control, the corporation, whether or not the minority stockholders vote to approve or reject the transaction. The controlling stockholder relationship has the potential to influence, however subtly, the vote of [ratifying] minority stockholders in a manner that is not likely to occur in a transaction with a noncontrolling party.
>
> Even where no coercion is intended, shareholders voting on a parent subsidiary merger might perceive that their disapproval could risk retaliation of some kind by the controlling stockholder. For example, the controlling stockholder might decide to stop dividend payments or to effect a subsequent cash out merger at a less favorable price, for which the remedy would be time consuming and costly litigation. At the very least, the potential for that perception, and its possible impact upon a shareholder vote, could never be fully eliminated. Consequently, in a merger between the corporation and its controlling stockholder—even one negotiated by disinterested, independent directors—no court could be certain whether the transaction terms fully approximate what truly independent parties would have achieved in an arm's length negotiation. Given that uncertainty, a court might well conclude that even minority shareholders who have ratified a ... merger need procedural protections beyond those afforded by full disclosure of all material facts. One way to provide such protections would be to adhere to the more stringent entire fairness standard of judicial review.

Citron v. E.I. Du Pont de Nemours & Co., 584 A.2d at 502.

Once again, this Court holds that the exclusive standard of judicial review in examining the propriety of an interested cash-out merger transaction by a controlling or dominating shareholder is entire fairness. Weinberger v. UOP, Inc., 457 A.2d at 710–11. The initial burden of establishing entire fairness rests upon the party who stands on both sides of the transaction. *Id.* However, an approval of the transaction by an independent committee of directors or an informed majority of minority shareholders shifts the burden of proof on the issue of fairness from the controlling or dominating shareholder to the challenging shareholder-plaintiff. *See Rosenblatt v. Getty Oil Co.,* 493 A.2d at 937–38. Nevertheless, even when an interested cash-out merger transaction receives the informed approval of a majority of minority stockholders or an independent committee of disinterested directors, an entire fairness analysis is the only proper standard of judicial review. *See id.*

Independent Committees

Interested Merger Transactions

It is a now well-established principle of Delaware corporate law that in an interested merger, the controlling or dominating shareholder proponent of the transaction bears the burden of proving its entire fairness.*Weinberger v. UOP, Inc.,* Del.Supr., 457 A.2d 701, 710–11 (1983). It is equally well-established in such contexts that any shifting of the burden of proof on the issue of entire fairness must be predicated upon this Court's decisions in *Rosenblatt v. Getty Oil Co.,* Del.Supr., 493 A.2d 929 (1985) and *Weinberger v. UOP, Inc.,* Del. Supr., 457 A.2d 701 (1983) and Weinberger v. UOP, Inc., Del.Supr., 457 A.2d 701 (1983). In *Weinberger*, this Court noted that "[p]articularly in a parent-subsidiary context, a showing that the action taken was as though each of the contending parties had in fact exerted its bargaining power against the other at arm's length is strong evidence that the transaction meets the test of fairness." 457 A.2d at 709–10 n. 7 (emphasis added). Accord Rosenblatt v. Getty Oil Co., 493 A.2d at 937–38 & n. 7. In Rosenblatt, this Court pointed out that "[an] independent bargaining structure, while not conclusive, is strong evidence of the fairness" of a merger transaction. Rosenblatt v. Getty Oil Co., 493 A.2d at 938 n. 7.

The same policy rationale which requires judicial review of interested cash-out mergers exclusively for entire fairness also mandates careful judicial scrutiny of a special committee's real bargaining power before shifting the burden of proof on the issue of entire fairness. A recent decision from the Court of Chancery articulated a two-part test for determining whether burden shifting is appropriate in an interested merger transaction. *Rabkin v. Olin Corp.,* Del.Ch., C.A. No. 7547 (Consolidated), Chandler, V.C., 1990 WL 47648, slip op. at 14–15 (Apr. 17, 1990), *reprinted in* 16 Del.J.Corp.L. 851, 861–62 (1990), *aff'd,* Del.Supr., 586 A.2d 1202 (1990). In *Olin,* the Court of Chancery stated:

> The mere existence of an independent special committee ... does not itself shift the burden. At least two factors are required. First, the majority shareholder must not dictate the terms of the merger. Rosenblatt v. Getty Oil Co., Del.Ch., 493 A.2d 929, 937 (1985). Second, the special committee must have real bargaining power that it can exercise with the majority shareholder on an arms length basis.

Id., slip op. at 14–15, 16 Del.J.Corp.L. at 861–62.[53] This Court expressed its agreement with that statement by affirming the Court of Chancery decision in *Olin* on appeal.

---

53. In *Olin,* the Court of Chancery concluded that because the special committee had been given "the narrow mandate of determining the monetary fairness of a non-negotiable

Lynch's Independent Committee

In the case sub judice, the Court of Chancery observed that although "Alcatel did exercise control over Lynch with respect to the decisions made at the August 1, 1986 board meeting, it does not necessarily follow that Alcatel also controlled the terms of the merger and its approval." This observation is theoretically accurate, as this opinion has already stated. Weinberger v. UOP, Inc., 457 A.2d at 709–10 n. 7. However, the performance of the Independent Committee merits careful judicial scrutiny to determine whether Alcatel's demonstrated pattern of domination was effectively neutralized so that "each of the contending parties had in fact exerted its bargaining power against the other at arm's length." Id. The fact that the same independent directors had submitted to Alcatel's demands on August 1, 1986 was part of the basis for the Court of Chancery's finding of Alcatel's domination of Lynch. Therefore, the Independent Committee's ability to bargain at arm's length with Alcatel was suspect from the outset.

The Independent Committee's original assignment was to examine the merger with Celwave which had been proposed by Alcatel. The record reflects that the Independent Committee effectively discharged that assignment and, in fact, recommended that the Lynch board reject the merger on Alcatel's terms. Alcatel's response to the Independent Committee's adverse recommendation was not the pursuit of further negotiations regarding its Celwave proposal, but rather its response was an offer to buy Lynch. That offer was consistent with Alcatel's August 1, 1986 expressions of an intention to dominate Lynch, since an acquisition would effectively eliminate once and for all Lynch's remaining vestiges of independence.

The Independent Committee's second assignment was to consider Alcatel's proposal to purchase Lynch. The Independent Committee proceeded on that task with full knowledge of Alcatel's demonstrated pattern of domination. The Independent Committee was also obviously aware of Alcatel's refusal to negotiate with it on the Celwave matter.

Burden of Proof Shifted

Court of Chancery's Finding

. . .

The Court of Chancery . . . found that Kertz understood Alcatel's position to be that it was ready to proceed with an unfriendly tender offer at a lower price if Lynch did not accept the $15.50 offer, and that Kertz perceived this to be a threat by Alcatel. The Court of Chancery concluded that Kertz ultimately decided that, "although $15.50 was not fair, a tender offer and merger at that price would be better for

---

offer," and because the majority shareholder "dictated the terms" and "there were no arm's-length negotiations," the burden of proof on the issue of entire fairness remained with the defendants. *Id.,* slip op. at 15, 16 Del.J.Corp.L. at 862. In making that determination, the Court of Chancery pointed out that the majority shareholder "could obviously have used its majority stake to effectuate the merger" regardless of the committee's or the board's disapproval, and that the record demonstrated that the directors of both corporations were "acutely aware of this fact." *Id.,* slip op. at 13, 16 Del.J.Corp.L. at 861.

Lynch's stockholders than an unfriendly tender offer at a significantly lower price." The Court of Chancery determined that "Kertz failed either to satisfy himself that the offered price was fair or oppose the merger." . . .

The record reflects that Alcatel was "ready to proceed" with a hostile bid. This was a conclusion reached by Beringer, the Independent Committee's chairman and spokesman, based upon communications to him from Alcatel. Beringer testified that although there was no reference to a particular price for a hostile bid during his discussions with Alcatel, or even specific mention of a "lower" price, "the implication was clear to [him] that it probably would be at a lower price."[55]

According to the Court of Chancery, the Independent Committee rejected three lower offers for Lynch from Alcatel and then accepted the $15.50 offer "after being advised that [it] was fair and after considering the absence of alternatives." The Vice Chancellor expressly acknowledged the impracticability of Lynch's Independent Committee's alternatives to a merger with Alcatel:

> Lynch was not in a position to shop for other acquirors, since Alcatel could block any alternative transaction. Alcatel also made it clear that it was not interested in having its shares repurchased by Lynch. The Independent Committee decided that a stockholder rights plan was not viable because of the increased debt it would entail.

Nevertheless, based upon the record before it, the Court of Chancery found that the Independent Committee had "appropriately simulated a third-party transaction, where negotiations are conducted at arms-length and there is no compulsion to reach an agreement." The Court of Chancery concluded that the Independent Committee's actions "as a whole" were "sufficiently well informed . . . and aggressive to simulate an arms-length transaction," so that the burden of proof as to entire fairness shifted from Alcatel to the contending Lynch shareholder, Kahn. The Court of Chancery's reservations about that finding are apparent in its written decision.

The Power to Say No,
The Parties' Contentions,
Arm's Length Bargaining

. . .

The Alcatel defendants argue that the Independent Committee exercised its "power to say no" in rejecting the three initial offers from Alcatel, and that it therefore cannot be said that Alcatel dictated the terms of the merger or precluded the Independent Committee from exercising real bargaining power. Compare *Rabkin v. Olin Corp.*, Del.Ch., C.A. 7547 (Consolidated), Chandler, V.C., 1990 WL 47648,

55. On the other hand, Dertinger, an officer and director of Lynch, testified that he was informed by Alcatel that the price of an unfriendly tender offer would indeed be lower and would in fact be $12 per share.

slip op. at 14–15 (Apr. 17, 1990), reprinted in 16 Del.J.Corp.L. 851, 861–62 (1991), aff'd, Del.Supr., 586 A.2d 1202 (1990).[56] The Alcatel defendants contend, alternatively, that "even assuming that such a threat [of a hostile takeover] could have had a coercive effect on the [Independent] Committee," the willingness of the Independent Committee to reject Alcatel's initial three offers suggests that "the alleged threat was either nonexistent or ineffective." *Braunschweiger v. American Home Shield Corp.,* Del.Ch., C.A. No. 10755, Allen, C., 1991 WL 3920, slip op. at 13 (Jan. 7, 1991), *reprinted in* 17 Del.J.Corp.L. 206, 219 (1991).

Kahn contends the record reflects that the conduct of Alcatel deprived the Independent Committee of an effective "power to say no." Kahn argues that Alcatel not only threatened the Committee with a hostile tender offer in the event its $15.50 offer was not recommended and approved, but also directed the affairs of Lynch for Alcatel's benefit in such a way as to make it impossible for Lynch to continue as a public company under Alcatel's control without injury to itself and its minority shareholders. . . .

Alcatel's Entire Fairness Burden Did Not Shift to Kahn

A condition precedent to finding that the burden of proving entire fairness has shifted in an interested merger transaction is a careful judicial analysis of the factual circumstances of each case. Particular consideration must be given to evidence of whether the special committee was truly independent, fully informed, and had the freedom to negotiate at arm's length. . . .

"[This court has] pointed out that the use of an independent negotiating committee of outside directors may have significant advantages to the majority stockholder in defending suits of this type," but it does not ipso facto establish the procedural fairness of an interested merger transaction. *Rabkin v. Philip A. Hunt Chem. Corp.,* Del.Supr., 498 A.2d 1099, 1106 & n. 7 (1985). In reversing the granting of the defendants' motion to dismiss in *Rabkin*, this Court implied that the burden on entire fairness would not be shifted by the use of an independent committee which concluded its processes with "what could be considered a quick surrender" to the dictated terms of the controlling shareholder.[57] Id. at 1106. This Court concluded in *Rabkin*

---

56. Alcatel also points to the fairness opinions of two investment banking firms employed by the Committee, Kidder Peabody and Thomson McKinnon, and the involvement of independent legal counsel, Skadden Arps, in considering and rejecting alternatives to the Alcatel cash offers.

57. A "surrender" need not occur at the outset of the negotiation process in order to deny a controlling shareholder the burden-shifting function which might otherwise follow from establishing an independent committee bargaining structure. *See Freedman v. Restaurant Assocs. Indus., Inc.,* Del. Ch., C.A. No. 9212, Allen, C., 1990 WL 135923 (Sept. 19, 1990), *reprinted in* 16 Del.J.Corp.L. 1462 (1991). *See also* Block, Barton & Radin, *The Business Judgment Rule: Fiduciary Duties of Corporate Directors* 170–72 (4th ed. 1993). In *Freedman,* finding that there was no "fully functional" independent committee, the Court of Chancery stated:

> [F]acts are alleged that would establish that [the] special committee was not given the opportunity to select from among the range of alternatives that an independent, disinter-

that the majority stockholder's "attitude toward the minority," coupled with the "apparent absence of any meaningful negotiations as to price," did not manifest the exercise of arm's length bargaining by the independent committee. Id.

The Court of Chancery's determination that the Independent Committee "appropriately simulated a third-party transaction, where negotiations are conducted at arm's-length and there is no compulsion to reach an agreement," is not supported by the record. Under the circumstances present in the case sub judice, the Court of Chancery erred in shifting the burden of proof with regard to entire fairness to the contesting Lynch shareholder-plaintiff, Kahn. The record reflects that the ability of the Committee effectively to negotiate at arm's length was compromised by Alcatel's threats to proceed with a hostile tender offer if the $15.50 price was not approved by the Committee and the Lynch board. The fact that the Independent Committee rejected three initial offers, which were well below the Independent Committee's estimated valuation for Lynch and were not combined with an explicit threat that Alcatel was "ready to proceed" with a hostile bid, cannot alter the conclusion that any semblance of arm's length bargaining ended when the Independent Committee surrendered to the ultimatum that accompanied Alcatel's final offer. *See Rabkin v. Philip A. Hunt Chem. Corp.*, Del.Supr., 498 A.2d 1099, 1106 (1985).

Conclusion

Accordingly, the judgment of the Court of Chancery is reversed. This matter is remanded for further proceedings consistent herewith, including a redetermination of the entire fairness of the cash-out merger to Kahn and the other Lynch minority shareholders with the burden of proof remaining on Alcatel, the dominant and interested shareholder.

On remand, the Court of Chancery, applying the principles set out in *Kahn*, determined that the merger was entirely fair to the minority shareholders. The Delaware Supreme Court affirmed. Kahn v. Lynch Communication Systems, Inc., 669 A.2d 79 (Del. 1995).

LEVCO ALTERNATIVE FUND v. THE READER'S DIGEST ASS'N, INC., 803 A.2d 428 (Del. 2002). Reader's Digest Association (RDA) had

ested board would have had available to it; it was, in effect, 'hemmed in' by the management group's actions. Under these circumstances, where, according to the allegations contained in the amended complaint, the management group could (and did) veto any action of the special committee that was not agreeable to the conflicted interests of the management directors it would be formalistically perverse to afford the special committee's action the effect of burden shifting of which that device is capable.

Freedman v. Restaurant Assocs. Indus., Inc., slip op. at 17–18, 16 Del.J.Corp.L. at 1475.

two classes of common stock: Class A, which was non-voting, and Class B, which had the right to vote. RDA proposed a recapitalization under which it would, among other things, create a new class of voting common stock; purchase all the shares of its Class B voting stock at a premium of 1.24 to 1 to the new voting stock; and change each share of the Class A non-voting stock into one share of the new voting common stock. The key to the recapitalization proposal was an agreement by RDA to purchase 3,636,363 shares of Class B Voting Stock owned by two Funds at $27.50 per share, for an aggregate purchase price of approximately $100 million. Prior to recapitalization, the Funds controlled 50 percent of the Class B voting stock. Following the recapitalization, the funds would hold 14 percent of the new voting common stock.

Plaintiffs, Class A shareholders, sought a preliminary injunction against the recapitalization in Delaware Chancery Court. Plaintiffs alleged that the recapitalization would result in financial detriment to the Class A shareholders. Plaintiffs also argued that a Special Committee, composed of three outside directors and established to evaluate the fairness of the transaction, breached its fiduciary duty to consider the separate interests of the Class A shareholders. RDA and its directors did not dispute that the directors owed a fiduciary duty to the Class A shareholders, but contended that they had discharged that duty through intensive negotiations between the Funds and the Special Committee. Plaintiffs asserted that the directors, including the Special Committee, were subject to the Funds' control and therefore were required to demonstrate the entire fairness of the transaction. Plaintiffs further asserted that the directors breached their duty of care. The Court of Chancery ruled that regardless of where the burden of proof lay, the evidence did not support the view that plaintiffs would ultimately succeed in demonstrating that the activities of the Special Committee did not result in a "fair and genuinely negotiated price." Reversed.

> Although the Court of Chancery did not elaborate on the burden of proof, we think it significant here that the initial burden of establishing entire fairness rests upon the party who stands on both sides of the transaction. *Kahn v. Lynch Comm. Sys., Inc.*, 638 A.2d 1110, 1117 (Del.1994). That burden may shift, of course, if an independent committee of directors has approved the transaction. *Emerald Partners v. Berlin*, 726 A.2d 1215, 1221 (Del.1999). While we agree with the Court of Chancery that the independent committee who negotiated the recapitalization believed it was operating in the interests of the corporation as an entity, we conclude that the committee's functioning, to the extent it was required to balance the conflicting interests of two distinct classes of shareholders, was flawed both from the standpoint of process and price.
>
> With respect to the unfair dealing claim, the Special Committee never sought, nor did its financial advisor, Goldman Sachs, ever tender, an opinion as to whether the transaction was fair to

the Class A shareholders. Goldman Sachs directed its fairness opinion to the interests of RDA as a corporate entity. Given the obvious conflicting interests of the shareholder classes, the conceded absence of an evaluation of the fairness of the recapitalization on the Class A shareholders is significant. While the Class A shareholders received voting rights, their equity interests decreased by at least $100 million without either their consent or an objective evaluation of the exchange. In short, while the Special Committee believed, perhaps in good faith, that the transaction was in the best interests of the corporation, arguably, it never focused on the specific impact upon the Class A shareholders of RDA's payment of $100 million to the Class B shareholders.

With respect to the premium paid to the Class B shareholders, given RDA's tenuous financial condition, having recently committed to a large acquisition, incurring additional debt in order to pay $100 million to the Class B shareholders is a matter of concern. The net result of the transaction was to significantly reduce the post-capitalization equity of the corporation. To the extent that the directors did not secure sufficient information concerning the effect of the recapitalization premium on the Class A shareholders, a serious question is raised concerning the discharge of their duty of care. *Kahn v. Tremont Corp.*, 694 A.2d 422, 430 (Del.1997) . . . .

We are not required, nor was the Court of Chancery, to determine the final merits of appellants' claims but, in our view, they stand a reasonable probability of success. It is unquestioned that the appellants will be irreparably harmed. While future monetary relief may be available, the issuance of the shares contemplated by the recapitalization may place a practical remedy beyond judicial reach.

JONES v. H.F. AHMANSON & CO. (1969) (Traynor, C.J 81 Cal.Rptr. 592, 460 P.2d 464.). "The [California] Courts of Appeal have often recognized that majority shareholders, either singly or acting in concert to accomplish a joint purpose, have a fiduciary responsibility to the minority and to the corporation to use their ability to control the corporation in a fair, just, and equitable manner. Majority shareholders may not use their power to control corporate activities to benefit themselves alone or in a manner detrimental to the minority. Any use to which they put the corporation or their power to control the corporation must benefit all shareholders proportionately and must not conflict with the proper conduct of the corporation's business . . . .

". . . The rule that has developed in California is a comprehensive rule of 'inherent fairness from the viewpoint of the corporation and those interested therein.' . . . The rule applies alike to officers, directors, and controlling shareholders in the exercise of powers that are theirs by virtue of their position and to transactions wherein controlling shareholders seek to gain an advantage in the sale or transfer or use of their controlling block of shares. . . .''

In re Trados Inc. Shareholder Litigation

Delaware Court of Chancery, 2009.
2009 WL 2225958.

This is a purported class action brought by a former stockholder of Trados Incorporated (''Trados,'' or the ''Company'') for breach of fiduciary duty arising out of a transaction whereby Trados became a wholly owned subsidiary of SDL, plc (''SDL''). Of the $60 million contributed by SDL, Trados' preferred stockholders received approximately $52 million. The remainder was distributed to the Company's executive officers pursuant to a previously approved bonus plan. Trados' common stockholders received nothing for their common shares.

Plaintiff contends that this transaction was undertaken at the behest of certain preferred stockholders that desired a transaction that would trigger their large liquidation preference and allow them to exit their investment in Trados. Plaintiff alleges that the Trados board favored the interests of the preferred stockholders, either at the expense of the common stockholders or without properly considering the effect of the merger on the common stockholders. Specifically, plaintiff alleges that the four directors designated by preferred stockholders had other relationships with preferred stockholders and were incapable of exercising disinterested and independent business judgment. Plaintiff further alleges that the two Trados directors who were also employees of the Company received material personal benefits as a result of the merger and were therefore also incapable of exercising disinterested and independent business judgment. . . .

As explained below, plaintiff has alleged facts sufficient, at this preliminary stage, to demonstrate that at least a majority of the members of Trados' seven member board were unable to exercise independent and disinterested business judgment in deciding whether to approve the merger. Accordingly, I decline to dismiss the breach of fiduciary duty claims arising out of the board's approval of the merger. . . .

I. BACKGROUND

A. *The Parties*

Before the merger, Trados developed software and services used by businesses to make the translation of text and material into other languages more efficient. Founded in 1984 as a German entity, Trados moved to the United States in the mid–1990s with the hope of going public, and became a Delaware corporation in March 2000. To better position itself for the possibility of going public, Trados accepted investments from venture capital firms and other entities. As a result, preferred stockholders had a total of four designees on Trados' seven member board. Each of the seven members of Trados' board at the time of the board's approval of the merger is named as a defendant in this action.

David Scanlan was the board designee of, and a partner in, Wachovia Capital Partners, LLC ("Wachovia"). At the time of the merger, Wachovia owned 3,640,000 shares of Trados' Series A preferred stock (100% of that series) and 1,007,151 shares of Trados' Series BB preferred stock (approximately 24% of that series).

Lisa Stone was the board designee of Rowan Entities Limited and Rowan Nominees Limited RR (together, the "Rowan Entities"), transferees of Trados' preferred stock held by Hg Investment Managers Limited (collectively, "Hg"). Stone was a director and employee of both Hg Investment Managers Limited and the Rowan Entities.[1] At the time of the merger, Hg owned 1,379,039 shares of Trados' common stock (approximately 4.3%), 2,014,302 shares of Trados' Series BB preferred stock (approximately 48.3% of that series), 5,333,330 shares of Trados' Series C preferred shares (all of that series), and 862,976 shares of Trados' Series D preferred stock (approximately 28.6% of that series).

Sameer Gandhi was a board designee of, and a partner in, several entities known as Sequoia. Sequoia owned 5,255,913 shares of Trados' Series E preferred stock (approximately 32% of that series).

Joseph Prang was also a board designee of Sequoia. Prang owned Mentor Capital Group LLC ("Mentor Capital"), which owned 263,810 shares of Trados' Series E preferred stock (approximately 1% of that series).

Wachovia, Hg, Sequoia, and Mentor combined owned approximately 51% of Trados' outstanding preferred stock. Plaintiff alleges that these preferred stockholders desired to exit their investment in Trados.

Two of the three remaining director defendants were employees of Trados. Jochen Hummel was acting President of Trados from April 2004 until September or October 2004, and was also the Company's chief technology officer. Joseph Campbell was Trados' CEO from August 23, 2004 until the merger. The remaining Trados director was Klaus–Dieter Laidig.

B. *The Negotiations*

In April 2004, the Trados board began to discuss a potential sale of the Company, and later formed a mergers and acquisitions committee, consisting of Stone, Gandhi, and Scanlan, to explore a sale or

1. Plaintiff also alleges that Stone was a part owner of Hg, and that Stone had a personal financial interest in Hg's investment in Trados. Plaintiff further alleges that Hg Investment Managers Limited continued to be the beneficial owners of all shares owned by Hg, and that both Rowan Entities were affiliates of Hg Investment Managers Limited. First Am. Verified Compl. ("Compl.") ¶ 8.

merger of Trados. Around the same time, the Company's President and CEO was terminated due to, among other issues, a perception by the rest of the board that Trados was underperforming. The board appointed Hummel as an interim President, but instructed him to consult with Gandhi and Scanlan before taking material action on behalf of the Company. In July 2004, Campbell was hired as the Company's CEO, effective August 23, 2004. Gandhi described Campbell as "a hard-nosed CEO whose task is to grow the company profitably or sell it." At the time Campbell joined Trados, however, the Company was losing money and had little cash to fund continuing operations.[4] At a July 7, 2004 meeting, Trados' board determined that the fair market value of Trados' common stock was $0 .10 per share.

In June 2004, Trados engaged JMP Securities, LLC, an investment bank, to assist in identifying potential alternatives for a merger or sale of the Company. By July 2004, JMP Securities had identified twenty seven potential buyers of Trados, and contacted seven of them, including SDL. By August 2004, JMP Securities had conducted discussions with SDL CEO Mark Lancaster, who made an acquisition proposal in the $40 million range. Trados informed Lancaster that it was not interested in a deal at that price, and Campbell formally terminated JMP Securities in September 2004.

In July 2004, Scanlan expressed concern that the executive officers of the Company might not have sufficient incentives to remain with the Company or pursue a potential acquisition of the Company, due to the high liquidation preference of the Company's preferred stock. The board instructed Scanlan to develop a bonus plan to address these concerns. This led to the December 2004 board approval of the Management Incentive Plan (the "MIP"), which set a graduated compensation scale for the Company's management based on the price obtained for the Company in an acquisition.[5]

Trados' financial condition improved markedly during the fourth quarter of 2004, in part due to Campbell's efforts to reduce spending and bring in additional cash through debt financing. By the time of the December 2004 board meeting, Trados had arranged to borrow $2.5 million from Western Technology Investment, with the right to borrow an additional $1.5 million.

Despite the Company's improved performance, the board continued to work toward a sale of the Company. In December 2004, Gandhi reported to Sequoia Capital that the Company's performance

---

4. Plaintiff alleges that Campbell believed that his "mission on joining TRADOS was to help the company understand its future path, which in the mind of the outside board members at that time was some type of either merger or acquisition event due to the company's performance that year and prior years." Compl. ¶ 44.

5. Under the MIP, management would receive 6% of the acquisition price for an acquisition between $30–40 million; 11% for an acquisition between $40–50 million; 13% for an acquisition between $50–90 million; 14% for an acquisition between $90–120 million; and 15% for an acquisition at or above $120 million. From that pool, Campbell would be entitled to 30%, Hummel to 12%, and James Budge to 10%. Plaintiff alleges that an investor described the MIP as "protection for the management team in case [some] shareholders want to sell [the company] at a price where the options/common shares are worthless." Compl. ¶ 52.

was improving, but that Campbell's "mission is to architect an M & A event as soon as practicable." At a February 2, 2005 board meeting, Campbell presented positive financial results from the fourth quarter of 2004, including record revenue and profit from operations. As a result of its improved performance and the lack of an immediate need for cash, the board extended by six months the period during which it could obtain additional cash from Western Technology Investment.

In January 2005, SDL initiated renewed merger discussions with Campbell. Upon learning of SDL's interest, the Trados board expressed that it was not interested in any transaction involving less than a "60–plus" million dollar purchase price. Lancaster first discussed a transaction at $50 million, but later offered $60 million. At the February 2, 2005 meeting, the board instructed Campbell to continue negotiating with Lancaster under the general terms SDL proposed, including the $60 million price. In mid-February 2005, Campbell made inquiries with two other potential acquirers of Trados, but neither expressed any substantive interest.

In a theme that runs throughout his allegations, plaintiff alleges that there was no need to sell Trados at the time because the Company was well financed and experiencing improved performance under Campbell's leadership. For example, plaintiff contends that by February 2005 Trados was beating its revenue budget for the year, a trend that continued as Trados beat its revenue projections for the first quarter of 2005 and through the end of May 2005.

By February 2005, Campbell and Lancaster agreed to the basic terms of a merger at $60 million. Trados then re-engaged JMP securities, which plaintiff alleges acted as little more than a "go-between." In April 2005, SDL and Trados signed the letter of intent for the merger at the $60 million price. . . .

D. The Merger

The director defendants unanimously approved the merger, and on June 19, 2005 Trados and SDL entered into an Agreement and Plan of Merger. Of the $60 million merger price, approximately $7.8 million would go to management pursuant to the MIP, and the remainder would go to the preferred stockholders in partial satisfaction of their $57.9 million liquidation preference. Plaintiff alleges that the directors know both of these facts, and thus knew that the common shareholders would receive nothing in the merger. The merger was consummated on July 7, 2005.

Plaintiff alleges that Campbell and Hummel received benefits as a result of the merger. Campbell became a director of SDL and received $775,000 through the MIP, $1,315,000 in exchange for a non-compete agreement, and a $250,000 bonus. Campbell took $702,000 of his MIP compensation in SDL stock, and $73,000 in cash. Hummel became "SDL's general manager of Europe, the Middle East, and Asia (technology division)," and received $1,092,000 under the MIP, of which he took $436,800 in SDL stock and $655,200 in cash. . . .

Count I of the Complaint asserts a claim that the director defendants breached their fiduciary duty of loyalty to Trados' common stockholders by approving the merger. Plaintiff alleges that there was no need to sell Trados at the time because the Company was well-financed, profitable, and beating revenue projections. Further, plaintiff contends, "in approving the Merger, the Director Defendants never considered the interest of the common stockholders in continuing Trados as a going concern, even though they were obliged to give priority to that interest over the preferred stockholders' interest in exiting their investment."

Directors of Delaware corporations are protected in their decision-making by the business judgment rule, which "is a presumption that in making a business decision the directors of a corporation acted on an informed basis, in good faith and in the honest belief that the action taken was in the best interests of the company."[24] The rule reflects and promotes the role of the board of directors as the proper body to manage the business and affairs of the corporation.[25]

The party challenging the directors' decision bears the burden of rebutting the presumption of the rule. If the presumption of the rule is not rebutted, then the Court will not second-guess the business decisions of the board. If the presumption of the rule is rebutted, then the burden of proving entire fairness shifts to the director defendants. A plaintiff can survive a motion to dismiss under Rule 12(b)(6) by pleading facts from which a reasonable inference can be drawn that a majority of the board was interested or lacked independence with respect to the relevant decision.

A director is interested in a transaction if "he or she will receive a personal financial benefit from a transaction that is not equally shared by the stockholders" or if "a corporate decision will have a materially detrimental impact on a director, but not on the corporation and the stockholders."[30] The receipt of any benefit is not sufficient to cause a director to be interested in a transaction. Rather, the benefit received by the director and not shared with stockholders must be "of a sufficiently material importance, in the context of the director's economic circumstances, as to have made it improbable that the director could perform her fiduciary duties ... without being influenced by her overriding personal interest...."[31]

"Independence means that a director's decision is based on the corporate merits of the subject before the board rather than extraneous considerations or influences."[32] At this stage, a lack of independence can be shown by pleading facts that support a reasonable

---

24. *Aronson v. Lewis,* 473 A.2d 805, 812 (Del.1984).

25. 8 *Del. C.* § 141(a); *In re CompuCom Sys., Inc. Stockholders Litig.,* 2005 WL 2481325, at *5 (Del.Ch. Sept.29, 2005).

30. *Rales v. Blasband,* 634 A.2d 927, 936 (Del.1993).

31. *In re Gen. Motors Class H S'holders Litig.,* 734 A.2d 611, 617 (Del.Ch.1999); *see Orman,* 794 A.2d at 23.

32. *Aronson,* 473 A.2d at 816.

inference that the director is beholden to a controlling person or "so under their influence that their discretion would be sterilized."[33]

Plaintiff's theory of the case is based on the proposition that, for purposes of the merger, the preferred stockholders' interests diverged from the interests of the common stockholders. Plaintiff contends that the merger took place at the behest of certain preferred stockholders, who wanted to exit their investment. Defendants contend that plaintiff ignores the "obvious alignment" of the interest of the preferred and common stockholders in obtaining the highest price available for the company. Defendants assert that because the preferred stockholders would not receive their entire liquidation preference in the merger, they would benefit if a higher price were obtained for the Company. Even accepting this proposition as true, however, it is not the case that the interests of the preferred and common stockholders were aligned with respect to the decision of whether to pursue a sale of the company or continue to operate the Company without pursuing a transaction at the time.

The merger triggered the $57.9 million liquidation preference of the preferred stockholders, and the preferred stockholders received approximately $52 million dollars as a result of the merger. In contrast, the common stockholders received nothing as a result of the merger, and lost the ability to ever receive anything of value in the future for their ownership interest in Trados. It would not stretch reason to say that this is the worst possible outcome for the common stockholders. The common stockholders would certainly be no worse off had the merger not occurred.

Taking, as I must, the well-pleaded facts in the Complaint in the light most favorable to plaintiff, it is reasonable to infer that the common stockholders would have been able to receive some consideration for their Trados shares at some point in the future had the merger not occurred.[36] This inference is supported by plaintiff's allegations that the Company's performance had significantly improved and that the Company had secured additional capital through debt financing. Thus, it is reasonable to infer from the factual allegations in the Complaint that the interests of the preferred and common stockholders were not aligned with respect to the decision to pursue a transaction that would trigger the liquidation preference of the preferred and result in no consideration for the common stockholders.[38]

---

33. *Rales,* 634 A.2d at 936.

36. On a motion to dismiss for failure to state a claim, I am required to draw all reasonable inferences in favor of the non-moving party. As a result, there are sometimes reasonable (even, potentially, more likely) inferences that must be passed over at this stage of the proceedings. For example, it would be reasonable to infer from the allegations in the Complaint that pursing the transaction with SDL was in the best interest of the Company because it secured the best value reasonably available for the Company's stakeholders and did not harm the common shareholders because, in fact, there was no reasonable chance that they would ever obtain any value for their stock even absent the transaction. Nothing in this Opinion is intended to suggest that it would necessarily be a breach of fiduciary duty for a board to approve a transaction that, as a result of liquidation preferences, does not provide any consideration to the common stockholders.

38. Defendants do not argue that the board had an obligation to the preferred stockholders to pursue a transaction that would trigger the large liquidation preference of the preferred

Generally, the rights and preferences of preferred stock are contractual in nature.[39] This Court has held that directors owe fiduciary duties to preferred stockholders as well as common stockholders where the right claimed by the preferred "is not to a preference as against the common stock but rather a right shared equally with the common."[40] Where this is not the case, however, "generally it will be the duty of the board, where discretionary judgment is to be exercised, to prefer the interests of common stock-as the good faith judgment of the board sees them to be-to the interests created by the special rights, preferences, *etc.*, of preferred stock, where there is a conflict."[41] Thus, in circumstances where the interests of the common stockholders diverge from those of the preferred stockholders, it is *possible* that a director could breach her duty by improperly favoring the interests of the preferred stockholders over those of the common stockholders.[42] As explained above, the factual allegations in the Complaint support a reasonable inference that the interests of the preferred and common stockholders diverged with respect to the decision of whether to pursue the merger. Given this reasonable inference, plaintiff can avoid dismissal if the Complaint contains well-pleaded facts that demonstrate that the director defendants were interested or lacked independence with respect to this decision.

---

stock. Thus, it is reasonable to infer, at this stage, that one option would be for the Company to continue to operate without paying the large liquidation preference to the preferred, subject of course, to any other contractual rights the preferred stockholders may have had. Indeed, in a situation in which the liquidation preference of the preferred exceeded the consideration that could be achieved in a transaction, it would arguably be in the interest of the common stockholders not to pursue any transaction that would trigger the liquidation preference. It is also reasonable to infer that the preferred stockholders would benefit from a transaction that allowed them to exit the investment while also triggering their liquidation preference, something they did not have a contractual right to force the Company to do. Again, at this stage, I am required to make reasonable inferences in plaintiff's favor, even if there are other reasonable inferences that can be drawn from the alleged facts and that would result in dismissal of the Complaint.

39. *Jedwab v. MGM Grand Hotels, Inc.,* 509 A.2d 584, 594 (Del.Ch.1986) ("[W]ith respect to matters relating to preferences or limitations that distinguish preferred stock from common, the duty of the corporation and its directors is essentially contractual and the scope of the duty is appropriately defined by reference to the specific words evidencing that contract. . . ."); *see Matulich v. Aegis Commc'ns Group, Inc.,* 942 A.2d 596, 599–600 (Del. 2008).

40. *Jedwab,* 509 A.2d at 594.

41. *Equity-Linked Investors, L.P. v. Adams,* 705 A.2d 1040, 1042 (Del.Ch.1997) (citing *Katz v. Oak Indus., Inc.,* 508 A.2d 873, 879 (Del.Ch.1986)).

42. *See Blackmore Partners, L.P. v. Link Energy LLC,* 864 A.2d 80, 85–86 (Del.Ch.2004) ("[T]he allegation that the Defendant Directors approved a sale of substantially all of [the company's] assets and a resultant distribution of proceeds that went exclusively to the company's creditors raises a reasonable inference of disloyalty or intentional misconduct. Of course, it is also possible to infer (and the record at a later stage may well show) that the Director Defendants made a good faith judgment, after reasonable investigation, that there was no future for the business and no better alternative for the unit holders. Nevertheless, based only the facts alleged and the reasonable inferences that the court must draw from them, it would appear that no transaction could have been worse for the unit holders and reasonable to infer, as the plaintiff argues, that a properly motivated board of directors would not have agreed to a proposal that wiped out the value of the common equity and surrendered all of that value to the company's creditors."). . . .

1. *The Director Defendants' Approval of the Merger*

Plaintiff has alleged facts that support a reasonable inference that Scanlan, Stone, Gandhi, and Prang, the four board designees of preferred stockholders, were interested in the decision to pursue the merger with SDL, which had the effect of triggering the large liquidation preference of the preferred stockholders and resulted in no consideration to the common stockholders for their common shares. Each of these four directors was designated to the Trados board by a holder of a significant number of preferred shares. While this, alone, may not be enough to rebut the presumption of the business judgment rule,[43] plaintiff has alleged more. Plaintiff has alleged that Scanlan, Stone, Gandhi, and Prang each had an ownership or employment relationship with an entity that owned Trados preferred stock. Scanlan was a partner in Wachovia; Stone was a director, employee and part owner of Hg; Gandhi was a partner in several entities referred to as Sequoia; and Prang owned Mentor Capital. Plaintiff further alleges that each of these directors was dependent on the preferred stockholders for their livelihood. As detailed above, each of these entities owned a significant number of Trados' preferred shares, and together these entities owned approximately 51% of Trados' outstanding preferred stock. The allegations of the ownership and other relationships of each of Scanlan, Stone, Gandhi, and Prang to preferred stockholders, combined with the fact that each was a board designee of one of these entities, is sufficient, under the plaintiff-friendly pleading standard on a motion to dismiss, to rebut the business judgment presumption with respect to the decision to approve the merger with SDL. . . .[45]

Plaintiff has alleged facts that support a reasonable inference that a majority of the board was interested or lacked independence with respect to the decision to approve the merger. Accordingly, plaintiff has alleged sufficient facts to survive defendants' motion to dismiss the fiduciary duty claims based on the board's decision to approve the merger. . . .

III. CONCLUSION

For the reasons set forth above, defendants' motion to dismiss . . . is denied with respect to the claim in Count I for breach of fiduciary duty arising out of the board's approval of the merger. . . .

IT IS SO ORDERED.

---

43. *See Citron v. Fairchild Camera & Instrument Corp.,* 569 A.2d 53, 65 (Del.1989) (stating that a director's representation of one of the corporations largest shareholders "alone did not make him an interested director."). *But see Goldman v. Pogo.com, Inc.,* 2002 WL 1358760, at *3 (Del.Ch. June 14, 2002) ("Because Khosla and Wu were the representatives of shareholders which, in their institutional capacities, are both alleged to have had a direct financial interest in this transaction, a reasonable doubt is raised as to Khosla and Wu's disinterestedness in having voted to approve the First Bridge Loan."). . . .

45. *See Orman,* 794 A.2d at 30–31 ("Because director Solomon's principal occupation is that of 'Chairman of Peter J. Solomon Company Limited and Peter J. Solomon Securities Company Limited,' it is reasonable to assume that director Solomon would personally benefit from the $3.3 million *his* company would receive if the challenged transaction closed. I think it would be naïve to say, as a matter of law, that $3.3 million is immaterial. In my opinion, therefore, it is reasonable to infer that director Solomon suffered a disabling interest when considering how to cast his vote in connection with the challenged merger when the Board's decision on that matter could determine whether or not his firm would receive $3.3 million.") (footnote omitted). . . .

SECTION 6. SALE OF CONTROL

Zetlin v. Hanson Holdings, Inc.

New York Court of Appeals, 1979.
48 N.Y.2d 684, 421 N.Y.S.2d 877, 397 N.E.2d 387.

MEMORANDUM.

The order of the Appellate Division should be affirmed, with costs.

Plaintiff Zetlin owned approximately 2% of the outstanding shares of Gable Industries, Inc., with defendants Hanson Holdings, Inc., and Sylvestri, together with members of the Sylvestri family, owning 44.4% of Gable's shares. The defendants sold their interests to Flintkote Co. for a premium price of $15 per share, at a time when Gable stock was selling on the open market for $7.38 per share. It is undisputed that the 44.4% acquired by Flintkote represented effective control of Gable.

Recognizing that those who invest the capital necessary to acquire a dominant position in the ownership of a corporation have the right of controlling that corporation, it has long been settled law that, absent looting of corporate assets, conversion of a corporate opportunity, fraud or other acts of bad faith, a controlling stockholder is free to sell, and a purchaser is free to buy, that controlling interest at a premium price (see *Barnes v. Brown,* 80 N.Y. 527; *Levy v. American Beverage Corp.,* 265 App.Div. 208; *Essex Universal Corp. v. Yates,* 305 F.2d 572).

Certainly, minority shareholders are entitled to protection against such abuse by controlling shareholders. They are not entitled, however, to inhibit the legitimate interests of the other stockholders. It is for this reason that control shares usually command a premium price. The premium is the added amount an investor is willing to pay for the privilege of directly influencing the corporation's affairs.

In this action plaintiff Zetlin contends that minority stockholders are entitled to an opportunity to share equally in any premium paid for a controlling interest in the corporation. This rule would profoundly affect the manner in which controlling stock interests are now transferred. It would require, essentially, that a controlling interest be transferred only by means of an offer to all stockholders, i.e., a tender offer. This would be contrary to existing law and if so radical a change is to be effected it would best be done by the Legislature.

■ CHIEF JUDGE COOKE and JUDGES JASEN, GABRIELLI, JONES, WACHTLER, FUCHSBERG and MEYER concur in memorandum.

Order affirmed.

Andrews, The Stockholder's Right to Equal Opportunity in the Sale of Shares

78 Harv.L.Rev. 505, 515–22 (1965).

The rule to be considered can be stated thus: whenever a controlling stockholder sells his shares, every other holder of shares (of the same class) is entitled to have an equal opportunity to sell his shares, or a prorata part of them, on substantially the same terms. Or in terms of the correlative duty: before a controlling stockholder may sell his shares to an outsider he must assure his fellow stockholders an equal opportunity to sell their shares, or as high a proportion of theirs as he ultimately sells of his own. There are qualifications in the application of the rule, to which I will return; but for purposes of argument we can begin with this broad statement of it . . .

[*Practical reasons for the proposed rule*] (*a*).—There is a substantial danger that following a transfer of controlling shares corporate affairs may be conducted in a manner detrimental to the interests of the stockholders who have not had an opportunity to sell their shares. The corporation may be looted; it may just be badly run. Or the sale of controlling shares may operate to destroy a favorable opportunity for corporate action. . . .

The equal opportunity rule does not deal directly with the problem of mismanagement, which may occur even after a transfer of control complying with the rule; but enforcement of the rule will remove much of the incentive a purchaser can offer a controlling stockholder to sell on profitable terms. Indeed, in the case of a purchasing looter there is nothing in it for the purchaser unless he can buy less than all the shares; there is no profit in stealing from a solvent corporation if the thief owns all the stock. But the controlling stockholder will be loath to sell only part of his shares (except at a price that compensates him for all of his shares) if he expects the purchaser to destroy the value of what he keeps. The rule forces the controlling stockholder to share equally with his fellow stockholders both the benefits of the price he receives for the shares he sells and the business risks incident to the shares he retains. This will tend strongly to discourage a sale of controlling shares when the risk of looting, or other harm to the corporation, is apparent; and it will provide the seller with a direct incentive to investigate and evaluate with care when the risks are not apparent, since his own financial interest continues to be at stake. . . .

Of course a transfer of control may have advantageous effects for a corporation and its stockholders—and these may be just as subtle as any adverse effects. Many sales of controlling shares come about because the selling stockholders are not doing as well with a business as a purchaser believes he can do; and the belief is often right. Often the sellers are members of a family that has simply run out of managerial talent or interest.

If the rule of equal opportunity would prevent sales in this sort of situation, that would be a high price to pay for the prevention of harm in other cases.... For my own part I do not believe the rule of equal opportunity would have much tendency to discourage beneficial transactions. After all, if the purchaser is optimistic—and can convince his bankers to share his optimism—he should be willing to buy out everyone. If the seller is optimistic about the consequences of the transfer, he should be willing to retain some of his shares. If minority stockholders are optimistic, they should be willing to hold their shares. If the financial community is optimistic (in the case of a publicly held corporation), the market itself should offer the minority stockholders a chance to sell at a price that satisfies the rule. Thus, on the face of it the rule would only operate to prevent a sale when all four of these—the seller, the purchaser, the minority stockholders, and the financial community—take a pessimistic view of the transfer....

(*b*).... [A] purchaser attains control of the corporation's business and assets equally whether he purchases all the shares or a smaller controlling block. When a purchaser buys less than all the shares, he is acquiring a business worth more than what he pays in cash, and is financing the difference by leaving the minority shares outstanding. We think of mortgage debts that way; if a person buys property subject to a mortgage and leaves the mortgage outstanding, we recognize that the mortgage provides financing for the purchaser because it has the same effect, substantially, as a new loan with the proceeds of which the purchaser might have paid full value for the property. But stock provides financing just as much as a mortgage does. A purchaser who buys only part of the stock of an enterprise might have accomplished much the same net result by purchasing all the assets in the name of a newly organized corporation in which he takes only a part of the stock. The other stockholders in the new corporation would then be viewed as providing equity financing for the acquisition. The chief difference then between a sale of assets, or of all the stock, and a sale of a controlling block of shares only, is that in the latter case the purchaser has had his acquisition partially financed, perhaps unwillingly, by the stockholders from whom he does not buy. That is no reason to give the minority stockholders less protection than if the purchaser gave them an opportunity to sell, even at a lower price....

(*c*).—A somewhat broader way of putting the argument is even simpler: each stockholder is entitled to share proportionately in the profits of the enterprise; from the stockholder's point of view a sale of stock is one very important way of realizing a profit on his investment; profits from stock sales ought to be regarded as profits of the enterprise subject to equal sharing among stockholders just as much as profits realized through corporate action.

A minority stockholder must invest largely on the strength of the expectation that decisions will tend to be made for his benefit because of the general identity of interest between him and those in control. This identity of interest is qualified when controlling stockholders have an opportunity to profit by entering into dealings with their corporation; this is permitted because such transactions may be mutually profitable, and there is no way to enforce equality of interest beyond allowing judicial scrutiny of such transactions for fairness. It would be impossible to insist, for example, that a publicly held corporation offer all its stockholders a proportionate opportunity to serve in an executive capacity. But when an opportunity arises for profit by selling shares, there is no such simple practical reason why it cannot be made equally available to all stockholders. . . .

Javaras, Equal Opportunity in the Sale of Controlling Shares: A Reply to Professor Andrews

32 U.Chi.L.Rev. 420, 425–27 (1965).

I believe that the gravest defect in Professor Andrews' theory is a grievous underassessment of the costs of a preventive rule in restraining beneficial transactions. Such restraint would operate on the purchaser by imposing higher required investment—the price of all the shares of the corporation rather than only those owned by the controlling shareholder. Professor Andrews minimizes the effects of this factor on two grounds. First, the controlling shareholder under the rule of equal opportunity, when confronted with a purchaser who wants the controlling shares and no more, may be induced to retain some of his shares and share the sale ratably with the non-controlling shareholders. Admittedly, this requires faith in the management of the purchaser. Second, a beneficial purchaser should be willing to buy all the shares because, after all, the non-controlling shares have the same investment value as the controlling shares. All the purchaser would have to do, therefore, if he did not have the capital is to borrow it. If he could not, that would be a reflection either of superior knowledge in the financial community or dislocations in the capital market.

It is doubtful whether sufficient controlling sellers can be induced to retain their shares so as to eliminate the higher capital requirement. First, . . . sales of securities are not dictated merely by an appraisal of investment value. Many sellers simply want immediate cash. Second, a controlling seller may not wish to hold, say twenty-five per cent as compared to his prior fifty per cent, because of the possibility of his views differing from those of the controlling purchaser in the future. This reticence would partly stem from . . . the controlling sellers assessment of the change in risks when he is deprived of control. The loss of control would subject him to the risk of poor management, which might dictate a lesser investment in this corporation on the principle of risk diversification.

Likewise the purchaser himself might be unwilling that the seller retain some of his shares, particularly where working control (less than fifty per cent) is the subject of the offer. He might well be reluctant to have a large block of stock outstanding whose owners, under conditions of dissension, could mobilize the other shareholders and displace his control of the board of directors.

In effect then, the rule of equal treatment would impose higher capital requirements on beneficial purchasers in a substantial number of transactions. Professor Andrews inappropriately assumes, however, that the purchasers should be willing to meet these higher costs because the investment value of the additional shares is the same. He errs in that his reasoning is incomplete. It is true that the investment value is the same. But even if the capital market did function perfectly and the purchaser could arrange the financing, a rational businessman might not want to buy all the shares at a premium price justified by the investment potential. It might be sensible to decline to buy more than the bare amount necessary for control on the principles of diversification of risk and of opportunity. This might render the equal treatment rule ineffectual as a means of automatically distinguishing "good" and "bad" purchasers. I would think that the number of prospective beneficial purchasers prevented because of a desire to diversify will be much larger than those simply unable to raise the capital. Until empirical evidence is adduced to the contrary, I am predisposed to consider this cost of restraining beneficial transactions substantial when compared with the cases of detriment with which the present law is incompetent to deal. . . .

Gerdes v. Reynolds

Supreme Court, Special Term, New York County, 1941.
28 N.Y.S.2d 622.

■ WALTER, JUSTICE. . . .

Defendants Clarence K. Reynolds and William F. Woodward, together with Richard S. Reynolds and Richard S. Reynolds, Jr., who are named as defendants but have not been served, were the officers and directors of Reynolds Investing Company, Inc., a Delaware corporation of the kind commonly known as an investment trust. They were also stockholders, and, with members of their families, owned a majority of its common stock, which was the only stock having voting power and was junior to debentures and preferred stock outstanding in the hands of the public. Ownership of such majority of the common stock was sold, and the persons just named resigned their offices and directorships and elected as their successors four persons designated by the purchaser. Assets of the company were then wasted and improperly applied, and the plaintiffs . . ., trustees of the company appointed in a proceeding under the Federal Bankruptcy Act, 11 U.S.C.A. § 1 et seq., here seek to hold accountable therefor both those who sold and those who bought and those who aided the transaction.

The negotiations which resulted in the transaction here complained of began in New York City about December 15, 1937, when defendant Mayer told defendant Woodward that he had a buyer

[Sartell Prentice, of the firm of Prentice & Brady] "for the Reynolds Investing Company," and asked if the Reynolds family owned a majority of its stock and would sell it. Mayer knew, at least in large part, what assets Reynolds Investing Company had, such information being obtainable from regularly published statistics, and on that and the succeeding day he and Woodward discussed those assets at some length, and Mayer said his principal would pay $1.25 per share....

[On December 31, 1937, Reynolds Investing Company had outstanding $3,446,900 face amount of 5 per cent debentures, $991,500 stated value of preferred stock, upon which there were $327,195 of accrued and unpaid dividends, a bank loan of $484,623, and accrued interest and taxes of $62,629. The total of those items was $5,312,847. It had cash and receivables of $149,218, a diversified portfolio of marketable securities, with a market value of $2,814,222, and 400 shares of Reynolds Research Corporation, worth $4,000. The total of those items was $2,967,440. Its other assets consisted of substantial blocks of stocks of a few companies, referred to as "special situations," including United States Foil Company and Reynolds Metals Company. Even with a liberal valuation of the "special situations," its holdings were worth just over $5 million, so that (after taking into account prior claims) the net asset value of Reynolds' common stock was only 6¢ per share.]

Woodward then telephoned an officer of the bank with which his company did business (one of the largest in New York City) for information as to Prentice. His request was transmitted to the bank's credit manager as a request for a report on Prentice & Brady, the firm of which Prentice was a member, and after communicating with other banks with which that firm did business that credit manager reported back to Woodward, a couple of hours after the request was made, that Prentice & Brady was a small Stock Exchange firm of good reputation and standing, with a capital of around half a million dollars, which sometimes was "spread out thin," (meaning that it did a large business for the amount of its capital) but because of a reputed relationship with the Rockefeller family it was assumed that it had access to large and substantial sums of money. There is no evidence that the reputed relationship to the Rockefeller family ever in fact existed....

[After negotiation, the parties agreed on a price of $2 per common share for a sale of not less than 1,035,000 shares and not more than 1,055,000 shares. Between December 31, 1937 and January 12, 1938, 1,055,000 shares were delivered in exchange for $2,110,000. On December 31, the incumbent directors resigned, and elected Mayer, Davis, McLanahan, and Prentice in their place.]

No notice of an intention to resign was given to other stockholders or to the debenture holders, and no substantial investigation of the character or ability of the persons so elected had been made by any of the resigning directors. Such persons were elected solely because the purchaser nominated them. Neither had the resigning directors made any investigation of the financial resources of Prentice other than the bank inquiry above mentioned. Further investigation would have disclosed that he bore an unblemished reputation among many social acquaintances but that such capital as he had in the firm of Prentice & Brady was borrowed and that he had practically no property other than that capital and no sources of income other than his share of the earnings of that firm and the income of a small trust.

The securities owned by Reynolds Investing Company, constituting substantially all its assets, were ... for the most part readily saleable and in practically negotiable form and of a value of over $5,000,000....

[Immediately after January 3, 1935, Prentice & Brady began converting Reynolds Investing Company's securities to its own use.]

Liability is asserted against ... [those who sold their stock and resigned as officers and directors] upon the grounds (a) that the sale of the stock, accompanied by their resignations and the election of successors nominated by the purchaser, was itself an illegal transaction because in violation of fiduciary duties owed to the corporation and the holders of its debentures and preferred stock and its minority common stockholders; and (b) that even if the transaction were not illegal in itself, it is made so because the selling defendants negligently or in bad faith failed to make proper investigation of the purchaser or to give advance notice to the other stockholders of an impending change of management, especially so inasmuch as what is claimed to be the excessive price paid was itself sufficient to put those defendants upon notice that some wrongful act was intended. Those contentions present interesting and important and difficult questions of law....

Officers and directors always and necessarily stand in a fiduciary relation to the corporation and to its stockholders and creditors. They undoubtedly may free themselves of that fiduciary relationship by ceasing to be officers and directors, but their right to resign, although sometimes stated with seeming absoluteness (Bruce v. Platt, 80 N.Y. 379, 383), is qualified by their fiduciary obligations to others. "Rights are never absolute and independent of those of others." O'Neill v. City of Port Jervis, 253 N.Y. 423, 430, 171 N.E. 694, 696. Officers and directors thus "cannot terminate their agency or accept the resignation of others if the immediate consequence would be to leave the interests of the company without proper care and protection." ...

Neither can they accept pay in any form or guise, direct or devious, for their own resignation or for the election of others in their place....

It is obvious, of course that it would be illegal for officers and directors to resign and elect as their successors persons who they knew intended to loot the corporation's treasury. Even stockholders, despite their right to sell their stock to whom they please, could not legally do that. Liability for such an act would not have to be predicated upon breach of a fiduciary relation, for the act would amount to a willful and malicious injury to property, tortious in its very nature.... I here find as a fact that none of the sellers of the stock of Reynolds Investing Company had any knowledge that the purchasers thereof, or any one acting for them, had any intention to loot the corporation or to pay any part of the purchase price out of the corporation's own assets. Whether or not the resigning officers and directors nevertheless are chargeable with notice of such an intention—whether or not it was, under all the circumstances, a risk reasonably to be perceived—is, of course, another question.

The questions determinative of the liability of corporate officers and directors in such a situation as is here disclosed thus appear to me to be these: (1) Are the circumstances such that, despite actual ignorance of unlawful plans and designs on the part of the purchasers, they are chargeable with notice of such plans and designs, or, perhaps more accurately, with notice that unlawful plans and designs are a risk reasonably to be perceived? "The risk reasonably to be perceived defines the duty to be obeyed." Palsgraf v. Long Island R.R. Co., 248 N.Y. 339, 344, 162 N.E. 99, 100, 59 A.L.R. 1253. (2) Is the price paid in reality a price paid for the stock, or is it, in part at least, a price paid for the resignations of the existing officers and directors and the election of the buyer's nominees? And the principal factors which must supply the answers to these questions are the nature of the assets which are to pass into the possession and control of the purchasers by reason of the transaction, the method by which the transaction is to be consummated, and the relation of the price paid to the value of the stock.

The immediate consequence of the resignation of the entire body of officers and directors of a corporation obviously is at least potentially different where the corporation's assets are land and buildings and where they are securities which to all intents and purposes are practically negotiable, and such potential difference must be taken into account, both by the officers and directors and by a court judging their conduct, in considering whether their en masse resignations would leave the assets without proper care and protection, because the risk of dissipation or speedy misapplication obviously is greater. Such difference in the nature of the assets must be considered, also, in gauging the significance of the purchaser's conceded requirement that custody and possession of the assets be accorded before payment of a substantial part of the purchase price. An assumption that the officers and directors of Reynolds Investing Company fully performed the fiduciary duty resting upon them thus requires an assumption that they realized that by doing what they did they were placing in the hands of those whom they elected as their successors the custody and possession of practically negotiable securities of a value of more than double the amount of the agreed purchase price, and were so placing such custody and possession at a time when a large part of the purchase price (over $600,000) still remained unpaid. For fiduciaries confronted with such a realization, I gravely doubt whether it is sufficient that they truthfully can say that they actually knew nothing against the character of the purchasers or of their nominees, or even that they had affirmative evidence that the purchasers were of good reputation. A man dealing with his own affairs may be as confiding and trusting as he pleases, and may be grossly negligent without being guilty of bad faith; but a fiduciary charged with the care of the property of others must be reasonably vigilant, and will not be heard to say that he did not know what the circumstances plainly indicated or that his faith in people was such that obvious opportunities for wrongdoing gave him no inkling that wrongdoing might be done, and schemes to acquire the stock of corporations by using assets of the corporation to pay the purchase price did not originate in the year 1937.

Precisely what would be the situation of directors who, by resignation and election, turned practically negotiable securities over to strangers who had not completed payment, need not be here determined, however, because here there is the added element that in connection with the same transaction a price was paid which is claimed to be grossly in excess of the value of the stock, and the situation of these directors must be considered in connection with that additional element.

Gross inadequacy of price long and frequently has been regarded as important evidence upon the question of good faith, and sometimes is sufficient in itself to charge a buyer with notice of fraudulent intent on the part of a seller. . . . For the same reasons, gross excessiveness of price may be equally significant in determining for what it really was paid, and may be sufficient to charge a seller with notice of a fraudulent intent on the part of a buyer. . . .

[The court then reviewed certain possible elements of value in the Reynolds Investing Company's common stock over and above its 6¢ per share asset value.]

One [expert] having much practical experience in the actual management of investment trusts expresses the view that in December, 1937, no prudent investor would have considered the purchase of this common stock—a view which he later qualified by adding "except at a nominal figure"—and after considering all speculative elements he concluded that the fair value was 25 cents per share, or $263,750 for 1,055,000 shares, to which he then added $32,000 for "control features," which he valued by taking one year's salaries and brokerage commissions which he figured the owner of the majority might obtain for himself, thus making a total of $295,750 for 1,055,000 shares. A security analyst testifying for plaintiffs fixed the value at 30 cents per share, allowed 10 cents per share additional if the block bought were large enough to secure control, and admitted the possibility of a value as high as 50 cents per share.

A feature which I regard as of great importance in considering the particular problems here involved is the almost complete lack of any distinctiveness in the assets of the company. It owned no land of special adaptability—in fact, no land at all. It owned no plant or structures or machinery which would take a long time to assemble. It had no clientele or customers, the mere existence of which sometimes gives great value to the stock of a company. It had no specially trained personnel or organization of any kind. Such position as it had in the canning industry of the country by reason of its holdings of the Stokely stocks could be duplicated by the purchase of the stocks of other canning companies. Therefore, with the exception of its holdings in United States Foil and Reynolds Metals Company, its entire assets could have been substantially duplicated by anyone in a very few days, by the simple device of giving some buying orders to a broker. Not even the sagacity and acumen displayed in selecting and assembling its portfolio was an element of value, because its portfolio was publicly disclosed in published statistics, and any admirer of the genius for security selection displayed by the company's managers could appropriate that genius for himself by examining printed volumes of security manuals which any broker expecting an order would have been only too glad to make available free of charge. Furthermore, there is no showing that the company's portfolio exhibited any exceptionally high character as an assemblage of securities. On the contrary, there is considerable evidence that in times of rising security prices it had advanced less than certain averages looked upon as fair standards of comparison, and in times of declining security prices it had receded greater than such averages.

Assuming, therefore, that in December, 1937, there was an investor with $2,110,000 in cash which he desired to invest in such a portfolio as was then owned by Reynolds Investing Company, and assuming that such investor shared to the fullest extent the optimistic viewpoint as to the future which defendants' expert says was justified, it is to my mind most improbable, if not inconceivable, that he would have put his $2,110,000 in a block of common stock which had ahead of it senior securities and obligations of $5,312,847. Even if he were so confident and optimistic of the future that he desired to corral bargains to an extent greater than he could do by buying $2,110,000 worth of securities for cash, the ordinary margin account with a broker would have presented as little risk of being wiped out by an unexpected decline in security prices as was entailed in buying common stock of Reynolds Investing Company, because the $3,446,900 of debentures of that company were issued under an indenture which contained a so-called "touch-off clause" which provided that if the value of the company's net assets fell below 110 per cent. of the amount of the debentures outstanding the debentures should be paid off at the next interest day. . . .

Some trouble and expense undoubtedly would be saved by acquiring an existing investment trust instead of creating a new one, and I am willing to make the somewhat difficult assumption that an existing trust may have something in the nature of good-will or name which is valuable to the owner of the common stock, even though it be what is called a "closed-end" trust, i.e., one not engaged in selling additional stock or other securities. Such items, however, necessarily are small.

Viewing all the elements which the fiduciary obligations of the officers and directors of Reynolds Investing Company required them to view I am convinced that $2,110,000 was so grossly in excess of the value of the stock that it carried upon its face a plain indication that it was not for the stock alone but partly for immediate en masse resignations and immediate election of the purchasers' nominees as successors. The transaction was not one in which there was merely a sale of stock, with the right to elect directors passing to the purchasers as a legal incident of the sale, and I think it proper to add that these officers and directors did not submit to the lawyers whom they retained in the matter the question of the price paid or its significance. They had their eyes and minds so centered upon the personal interests of themselves and their families and associates as stockholders and upon a desire to get what they could for what they regarded as theirs, that they failed to consider their position as officers and directors, and the consequent duty they owed as such to the corporation itself and its creditors and other stockholders.

It thus becomes necessary to determine what part of the $2,110,000 was paid for the 1,055,000 shares of stock, and what part was paid for resignations and election of successors. Something more than the six cents per share which I have found to be the maximum asset value of the shares on December 31, 1937, obviously must be allowed to the shares because of permissible hopes and expectations and other considerations already mentioned, and what that additional something shall be is obviously a matter of judgment. It nevertheless is a matter of fact which the trier of facts must find, and with due allowance for all elements I think that 75 cents per share is as liberal a finding as the evidence warrants. That gives $791,250 as the price paid for 1,055,000 shares of stock, and $1,318,750 as the price paid for the resignations of the officers and directors and their election of the buyer's nominees as their successors, or, in other words, for what is termed the turning over of control.

The conclusion ordinarily to be drawn from the foregoing is that, having violated their fiduciary duty, these officers and directors must account to the corporation or to its duly appointed trustees for the sum of $1,318,750, and for all damages naturally resulting from their official misconduct. Bosworth v. Allen, 168 N.Y. 157, 165, 166, 61 N.E. 163, 55 L.R.A. 751, 85 Am.St.Rep. 667; McClure v. Law, 161 N.Y. 78, 55 N.E. 388, 76 Am.St.Rep. 262. . . .

Accord: Insuranshares Corp. of Delaware v. Northern Fiscal Corp., 35 F.Supp. 22 (E.D.Pa.1940); DeBaun v. First Western Bank & Trust Co., 46 Cal.App.3d 686, 120 Cal.Rptr. 354 (1975).

NOTE ON FURTHER PROCEEDINGS IN GERDES v. REYNOLDS

Under the interlocutory judgment issued in *Gerdes v. Reynolds,* Reynolds and Woodward were directed to account "for all money and property of said Reynolds Investing Company, Inc., which were wrongfully diverted" to them by the payment of the premium, "and for all damages to Reynolds Investing Company," resulting from the transfer of control. 30 N.Y.S.2d 755, 770 (1941). In further proceedings, the amount of Reynolds Investing's damages was determined to be over $900,000, consisting principally of the net proceeds realized by the buyers on their sale of securities belonging to Reynolds Investing, and the amount Reynolds Investing had to pay to obtain the release of converted securities that the buyers had pledged to two banks. Id. at 764, 770–73, 776.

Since the buyers paid over $2.1 million for control of Reynolds Investing, it seems likely that they originally planned to loot more than $900,000. Apparently, Mayer, who had represented the buyers and was elected an officer of Reynolds Investing, had a falling-out with some of the defendants shortly after the purchase. As a result, the affairs of Reynolds Investing were placed in the hands of a law firm, which conducted an investigation that unearthed and stopped the wrongdoing. See id. at 760.

Perlman v. Feldmann

United States Court of Appeals, Second Circuit, 1955.
219 F.2d 173, cert. denied 349 U.S. 952, 75 S.Ct. 880, 99 L.Ed. 1277 (1955).

■ CLARK, CHIEF JUDGE. This is a derivative action brought by minority stockholders of Newport Steel Corporation to compel accounting for, and restitution of, allegedly illegal gains which accrued to defendants as a result of the sale in August, 1950, of their controlling interest in the corporation. The principal defendant, C. Russell Feldmann, who represented and acted for the others, members of his family,[1] was at that time not only the dominant stockholder, but also the chairman of the board of directors and the president of the corporation. Newport, an Indiana corporation, operated mills for the production of steel sheets for sale to manufacturers of steel products, first at Newport, Kentucky, and later also at other places in Kentucky and Ohio. The buyers, a syndicate organized as Wilport Company, a Delaware corporation, consisted of end-users of steel who were interested in securing a source of supply in a market becoming ever tighter in the Korean War. Plaintiffs contend that the consideration paid for the stock included compensation for the sale of a corporate asset, a power held in trust for the corporation by Feldmann as its fiduciary. This power was the ability to control the allocation of the corporate product in a time of short supply, through control of the board of directors; and it was effectively transferred in this sale by having Feldmann procure the resignation of his own board and the election of Wilport's nominees immediately upon consummation of the sale.

---

1. The stock was not held personally by Feldmann in his own name, but was held by the members of his family and by personal corporations. The aggregate of stock thus [held] amounted to 33% of the outstanding Newport stock and gave working control to the holder. The actual sale included 55,552 additional shares held by friends and associates of Feldmann, so that a total of 37% of the Newport stock was transferred.

The present action represents the consolidation of three pending stockholders' actions in which yet another stockholder has been permitted to intervene. Jurisdiction below was based upon the diverse citizenship of the parties. Plaintiffs argue here, as they did in the court below, that in the situation here disclosed the vendors must account to the nonparticipating minority stockholders for that share of their profit which is attributable to the sale of the corporate power. Judge Hincks denied the validity of the premise, holding that the rights involved in the sale were only those normally incident to the possession of a controlling block of shares, with which a dominant stockholder, in the absence of fraud or foreseeable looting, was entitled to deal according to his own best interests. Furthermore, he held that plaintiffs had failed to satisfy their burden of proving that the sales price was not a fair price for the stock per se. Plaintiffs appeal from these rulings of law which resulted in the dismissal of their complaint.

The essential facts found by the trial judge are not in dispute. Newport was a relative newcomer in the steel industry with predominantly old installations which were in the process of being supplemented by more modern facilities. Except in times of extreme shortage Newport was not in a position to compete profitably with other steel mills for customers not in its immediate geographical area. Wilport, the purchasing syndicate, consisted of geographically remote end-users of steel who were interested in buying more steel from Newport than they had been able to obtain during recent periods of tight supply. The price of $20 per share was found by Judge Hincks to be a fair one for a control block of stock, although the over-the-counter market price had not exceeded $12 and the book value per share was $17.03. But this finding was limited by Judge Hincks' statement that "[w]hat value the block would have had if shorn of its appurtenant power to control distribution of the corporate product, the evidence does not show." It was also conditioned by his earlier ruling that the burden was on plaintiffs to prove a lesser value for the stock.

Both as director and as dominant stockholder, Feldmann stood in a fiduciary relationship to the corporation and to the minority stockholders as beneficiaries thereof. Pepper v. Litton, 308 U.S. 295, 60 S.Ct. 238, 84 L.Ed. 281; Southern Pac. Co. v. Bogert, 250 U.S. 483, 39 S.Ct. 533, 63 L.Ed. 1099. His fiduciary obligation must in the first instance be measured by the law of Indiana, the state of incorporation of Newport. Rogers v. Guaranty Trust Co. of New York, 288 U.S. 123, 136, 53 S.Ct. 295, 77 L.Ed. 652; Mayflower Hotel Stockholders Protective Committee v. Mayflower Hotel Corp., 89 U.S.App.D.C. 171, 193 F.2d 666, 668. Although there is no Indiana case directly in point, the most closely analogous one emphasizes the close scrutiny to which Indiana subjects the conduct of fiduciaries when personal benefit may stand in the way of fulfillment of trust obligations. In Schemmel v. Hill, 91 Ind.App. 373, 169 N.E. 678, 682, 683, McMahan, J., said: "Directors of a business corporation act in a strictly fiduciary capacity. Their office is a trust. Stratis v. Andreson, 1926, 254 Mass. 536, 150 N.E. 832, 44 A.L.R. 567; Hill v. Nisbet, 1885, 100 Ind. 341, 353. When a director deals with his corporation, his acts will be closely scrutinized. Bossert v. Geis, 1914, 57 Ind.App. 384, 107 N.E. 95. Directors of a corporation are its agents, and they are governed by the rules of law applicable to other agents, and, as between themselves and their principal, the rules relating to honesty and fair dealing in the management of the affairs of their principal are applicable. They must not, in any degree, allow their official conduct to be swayed by their private interest, which must yield to official duty. Leader Publishing Co. v. Grant Trust Co., 1915, 182 Ind. 651, 108 N.E. 121. In a transaction between a director and his corporation, where he acts for himself and his principal at the same time in a matter connected with the relation between them, it is presumed, where he is thus potentially on both sides of the contract, that self-interest will overcome his fidelity to his principal, to his own benefit and to his principal's hurt." And the judge added: "Absolute and most scrupulous good faith is the very essence of a director's obligation to his corporation. The first principal duty arising from his official relation is to act in all things of trust wholly for the benefit of his corporation."

In Indiana, then, as elsewhere, the responsibility of the fiduciary is not limited to a proper regard for the tangible balance sheet assets of the corporation, but includes the dedication of his uncorrupted business judgment for the sole benefit of the corporation, in any dealings which may adversely affect it.... Although the Indiana case is particularly relevant to Feldmann as a director, the same rule should apply to his fiduciary duties as majority stockholder, for in that capacity he chooses and controls the directors, and thus is held to have assumed their liability. Pepper v. Litton, supra, 308 U.S. 295, 60 S.Ct. 238. This, therefore, is the standard to which Feldmann was by law required to conform in his activities here under scrutiny.

It is true, as defendants have been at pains to point out, that this is not the ordinary case of breach of fiduciary duty. We have here no fraud, no misuse of confidential information, no outright looting of a helpless corporation. But on the other hand, we do not find compliance with that high standard which we have just stated and which we and other courts have come to expect and demand of corporate fiduciaries. In the often-quoted words of Judge Cardozo: "Many forms of conduct permissible in a workaday world for those acting at arm's length, are forbidden to those bound by fiduciary ties. A trustee is held to something stricter than the morals of the market place. Not honesty alone, but the punctilio of an honor the most sensitive, is then the standard of behavior. As to this there has developed a tradition that is unbending and inveterate. Uncompromising rigidity has been the attitude of courts of equity when petitioned to undermine the rule of undivided loyalty by the 'disintegrating erosion' of particular exceptions." Meinhard v. Salmon, supra, 249 N.Y. 458, 464, 164 N.E. 545, 546, 62 A.L.R. 1. The actions of defendants in siphoning off for personal gain corporate advantages to be derived from a favorable market situation do not betoken the necessary undivided loyalty owed by the fiduciary to his principal.

The corporate opportunities of whose misappropriation the minority stockholders complain need not have been an absolute certainty in order to support this action against Feldmann. If there was possibility of corporate gain, they are entitled to recover. . . .

. . . In the past Newport had used and profited by its market leverage by operation of what the industry had come to call the "Feldmann Plan." This consisted of securing interest-free advances from prospective purchasers of steel in return for firm commitments to them from future production. The funds thus acquired were used to finance improvements in existing plants and to acquire new installations. In the summer of 1950 Newport had been negotiating for cold-rolling facilities which it needed for a more fully integrated operation and a more marketable product, and Feldmann plan funds might well have been used toward this end.

Further, as plaintiffs alternatively suggest, Newport might have used the period of short supply to build up patronage in the geographical area in which it could compete profitably even when steel was more abundant. Either of these opportunities was Newport's, to be used to its advantage only. Only if defendants had been able to negate completely any possibility of gain by Newport could they have prevailed. It is true that a trial court finding states: "Whether or not, in August, 1950, Newport's position was such that it could have entered into 'Feldmann Plan' type transactions to procure funds and financing for the further expansion and integration of its steel facilities and whether such expansion would have been desirable for Newport, the evidence does not show." This, however, cannot avail the defendants, who—contrary to the ruling below—had the burden of proof on this issue, since fiduciaries always have the burden of proof in establishing the fairness of their dealings with trust property. . . .

Defendants seek to categorize the corporate opportunities which might have accrued to Newport as too unethical to warrant further consideration. It is true that reputable steel producers were not participating in the gray market brought about by the Korean War and were refraining from advancing their prices, although to do so would not have been illegal. But Feldmann plan transactions were not considered within this self-imposed interdiction; the trial court found that around the time of the Feldmann sale Jones & Laughlin Steel Corporation, Republic Steel Company, and Pittsburgh Steel Corporation were all participating in such arrangements. In any event, it ill becomes the defendants to disparage as unethical the market advantages from which they themselves reaped rich benefits.

We do not mean to suggest that a majority stockholder cannot dispose of his controlling block of stock to outsiders without having to account to his corporation for profits or even never do this with impunity when the buyer is an interested customer, actual or potential, for the corporation's product. But when the sale necessarily results in a sacrifice of this element of corporate good will and consequent unusual profit to the fiduciary who has caused the sacrifice, he should account for his gains. So in a time of market shortage, where a call on a corporation's product commands an unusually large premium, in one form or another, we think it sound law that a fiduciary may not appropriate to himself the value of this premium. Such personal gain at the expense of his coventurers seems particularly reprehensible when made by the trusted president and director of his company. In this case the violation of duty seems to be all the clearer because of this triple role in which Feldmann appears, though we are unwilling to say, and are not to be understood as saying, that we should accept a lesser obligation for any one of his roles alone.

Hence to the extent that the price received by Feldmann and his codefendants included such a bonus, he is accountable to the minority stockholders who sue here. Restatement, Restitution §§ 190, 197 (1937); Seagrave Corp. v. Mount, supra, 6 Cir., 212 F.2d 389. And plaintiffs, as they contend, are entitled to a recovery in their own right, instead of in right of the corporation (as in the usual derivative actions), since neither Wilport nor their successors in interest should share in any judgment which may be rendered. See Southern Pacific Co. v. Bogert, 250 U.S. 483, 39 S.Ct. 533, 63 L.Ed. 1099. Defendants cannot well object to this form of recovery, since the only alternative, recovery for the corporation as a whole, would subject them to a greater total liability.

The case will therefore be remanded to the district court for a determination of the question expressly left open below, namely, the value of defendants' stock without the appurtenant control over the corporation's output of steel. We reiterate that on this issue, as on all others relating to a breach of fiduciary duty, the burden of proof must rest on the defendants. Bigelow v. RKO Radio Pictures, 327 U.S. 251, 265–266, 66 S.Ct. 574, 90 L.Ed. 652; Package Closure Corp. v. Sealright Co., 2 Cir., 141 F.2d 972, 979. Judgment should go to these plaintiffs and those whom they represent for any premium value so shown to the extent of their respective stock interests.

The judgment is therefore reversed and the action remanded for further proceedings pursuant to this opinion.

[The dissenting opinion of Judge Swan is omitted.]

NOTE ON FURTHER PROCEEDINGS IN PERLMAN v. FELDMANN

On remand, the district court determined the enterprise value of the corporation, based upon its book value and earnings potential, to be $15,825,777, or $14.67 per share. This made the premium $5.33 a share, or $2,126,280. The complaining stockholders, owning sixty-three percent of the stock, were therefore entitled to judgment of $1,339,769, with interest of 6 percent from the sale date, plus costs. Perlman v. Feldmann, 154 F.Supp. 436 (D.Conn.1957).

NOTE ON THE THEORY OF CORPORATE ACTION

Suppose a prospective purchaser, P, wants to acquire the assets and business of C corporation, and that C has a controlling shareholder, S. P then has a choice of several means to acquire C: (1) He can try to acquire all of C's shares. His first step would naturally be to approach S, without whom P's efforts will fail. (2) He can try to induce a sufficient number of C shareholders to vote for a sale of C's assets to D. (3) He can try to induce a sufficient number of C shareholders to vote for a merger with D, a corporation that P controls.

If P takes the first course, he deals with C's shareholders individually. Each C shareholder is free to make his own terms of sale, and S's shares may bring a better price than the remaining shares. If P takes the second course of action, involving a sale of C's assets, he is looking towards corporate action by C. If C sells its assets to D, the consideration will pass into C's treasury. Usually C will then be liquidated, and the net proceeds will be distributed pro rata to all C shareholders, so that each old C shareholder will receive the same amount per share. If P takes the third course of action, involving a merger of C and D, the plan of conversion of C shares into D shares will normally provide for equal treatment of all shareholders of the same class. Accordingly, the second and third courses of action provide equal treatment to shareholders, while the first course of action, involving the purchase of C shares, allows S to sell its shares at higher prices than the noncontrolling shareholders will obtain. It may therefore be to the advantage of shareholders like S, who hold a control block of shares of a corporation, to have a purchaser like P take the first course of action.

If P originally proposes to take the second or third courses, but is persuaded by S to take the first course, and S realizes more per share for its holdings than the remaining shareholders, the latter may assert that the difference between the three courses of action is immaterial, that the first course of action should be treated as "corporate action," and that S acted improperly in switching P from a corporate action to a noncorporate action. This theory has been successfully employed in several cases where the buyer began to undertake the second or third course of action and the controlling shareholders switched him to the first. See Commonwealth Title Ins. & Trust Co. v. Seltzer, 227 Pa. 410, 76 A. 77 (1910); Dunnett v. Arn, 71 F.2d 912 (10th Cir.1934); Roby v. Dunnett, 88 F.2d 68 (10th Cir.1937), cert. denied 301 U.S. 706, 57 S.Ct. 940, 81 L.Ed. 1360; American Trust Co. v. California Western States Life Ins. Co., 15 Cal.2d 42, 98 P.2d 497 (1940).

The problem with the theory of corporate action is that a controlling shareholder cannot be compelled to sell his shares at a price he does not accept. A knowledgeable controlling shareholder therefore can avoid the application of the theory by simply voting down an offer to the corporation, and waiting for an offer from S to buy his shares. Accordingly, the theory of corporate action, although appealing, will only affect controlling shareholders who are not well-counseled.

Brecher v. Gregg

New York Supreme Court, 1975.
89 Misc.2d 457, 392 N.Y.S.2d 776.

■ NORMAN L. HARVEY, J.

This is a shareholder's derivative action brought on behalf of Lin Broadcasting Corporation (LIN) by Louis J. Brecher who, at the time this action was commenced, owned 200 shares of LIN common stock. No party challenges his right to bring the action.

LIN was incorporated in Delaware in 1961. By December, 1968 it had become a publicly-held corporation with assets of approximately $55,000,000. Currently it holds licenses issued by the Federal Communications Commission (FCC) to operate 10 radio and 2 television stations. Defendant Frederic Gregg was the principal founder of LIN and served as LIN's president from the time of incorporation until his resignation on January 10, 1969. In addition, Gregg was a member of the board of directors from October, 1961 to March, 1969 and chairman from February, 1967 to March, 1969. As of January 10, 1969 Gregg owned approximately 82,000 shares of LIN common stock—the largest block beneficially owned by any single person or entity.

The defendants Clyde W. Clifford, Peter J. Solomon, David Steine, Joel M. Thrope, Thomas I. Unterberg and Lind Carl Voth were directors of LIN at all times relevant herein. Defendant Alan J. Patricof was a director of LIN from February 19, 1967 until January 10, 1969 at which time an earlier tendered resignation was accepted by the LIN directors. He did not participate in any of the activities complained of by the plaintiff.

The controversy centers upon a transaction between the defendant Gregg and the Saturday Evening Post Company (SEPCO) in which the latter bought Gregg's 82,000 shares of LIN stock. The purchase price of the stock was $3,500,000, said amount being approximately $1,260,000 more than the market price on the date of sale. Plaintiff contends that SEPCO paid Gregg a premium for Gregg's promise to resign immediately as president of LIN; bring about the election of SEPCO's nominee as his successor to the presidency; bring about the immediate election of three SEPCO nominees as directors; and ultimately bring about an absolute numerical majority of SEPCO nominees to the board. Plaintiff contends that the acceptance of this premium amounted to a sale of corporate office, and therefore, was illegal.

Two specific contentions of the plaintiff are:

(1) That the corporation is entitled to receive $1,260,000 of the sale price paid to the defendant Gregg as a premium; and

(2) That because the remaining directors acquiesced in Gregg's promise and actually did vote to elect nominees of SEPCO as president and as three of its directors they are liable, jointly with Gregg and severally, for the premium resulting from the sale. . . .

Trial of the action was accomplished by the submission of certain exhibits which were agreed upon by all parties, the depositions of numerous witnesses, and answers to interrogatories. The court did not personally see or hear any of the witnesses when they gave their testimony.

Certain of the facts are undisputed. Sometime during the latter part of 1968 the defendant Frederic Gregg, Jr. and Martin Ackerman, then president of SEPCO, entered into negotiations for the purchase of the LIN stock owned by Gregg. Ultimately, an agreement was reached for the purchase of the stock by SEPCO for the total consideration of $3,500,000. In addition to that, Gregg agreed to relinquish certain rights that he had under an employment contract with LIN which included, among other things, stock options. The price of $3,500,000 was approximately $1,260,000 more than the then current price on the over-the-counter securities exchange in New York City.

Shortly after the agreement, defendant Gregg called a meeting of the LIN board of directors at which: defendant Alan Patricof's previously submitted resignation was accepted, thus creating a vacancy; the board voted to expand its size from 8 to 10 seats; the SEPCO nominees, Martin Ackerman, Alfred Driscoll and Milton Gould, were elected to fill the three vacancies; Gregg's resignation as president was tendered and accepted; and Ackerman was elected as his successor.

Within a few weeks thereafter, LIN's board of directors terminated Ackerman's tenure as president and all SEPCO directors resigned. SEPCO then sued Gregg, LIN and others for a refund of the premium alleging that, as conditions of its purchase, it was promised that SEPCO's nominee would be hired as president of LIN and be given a fair opportunity to supervise the management of its affairs; that SEPCO be given immediate minority representation on the board of directors and that best efforts be made to cause SEPCO to have majority representation on the board at an early date by seeking required approval from FCC. The complaint further alleged that the defendants breached the agreement by not permitting SEPCO's nominee to the presidency an ample opportunity to manage the corporation. The complaint was dismissed at Special Term because of the illegality of the agreement. Mr. Justice Saypol's opinion will be referred to later herein.

No evidence was introduced to establish that any of the director defendants, other than Gregg, was involved in the negotiations for the sale of Gregg's stock nor that they received any benefit therefrom.

The bulk of the evidence introduced concerned the negotiations between Martin S. Ackerman, president of SEPCO, and the defendant Gregg for the purchase of Gregg's stock. That evidence was conflicting as to the issue of the inducement for the payment of a premium. But, from all the evidence before it, the court concludes that the defendant Gregg and SEPCO agreed upon the purchase price of $3,500,000 for Gregg's stock (which also would result in his forfeiture of substantial stock option rights) and that the inducement for payment of a price more than $1,200,000 above the price quoted in the over-the-counter market was Gregg's promise to deliver effective control of LIN to SEPCO. Control was to be delivered by Gregg's resignation of the presidency and the election of SEPCO's nominees to the presidency and three directorships.

The court concludes as a matter of law that the agreement insofar as it provided for a premium in exchange for a promise of control, with only 4% of the outstanding shares actually being transferred, was contrary to public policy and illegal. The law as it pertains to these facts was succinctly stated by Mr. Justice Saypol in his determination of the motion previously referred to. (Brecher v. Gregg, NYLJ, June 15, 1970, p. 16, col. 1.)

> "The subject agreement to purchase an office is against public policy and unenforceable in this State. The employment contract cannot be saved by severance since it is an integral portion of the agreement having an illegal purpose.
>
> "It is not alleged that by virtue of the stock purchase plaintiff acquired control with which it could then install officers and directors of its own selection. It appears on the face of the complaint that the transaction had no semblance of actual or practical control; rather, the designation of president and minority board representation remained in the actual control of the defendants but was bargained away to plaintiff.
>
> "As stated in Matter of Lionel Corp. (NYLJ, Feb. 4, 1964, Schweitzer, J, Sup Ct NY County): 'As early as McClure v. Law (161 NY 78), and as late as Essex Universal Corp. v. Yates (305 F.2d 572), it is the law of this State that it is illegal to sell corporate office or management control by itself (that is, accompanied by no stock or insufficient stock to carry voting control).' (Affd sub nom Matter of Caplan v. Lionel Corp., 20 A.D.2d 301, affd 14 N.Y.2d 679.) Indeed, the illegal profit belongs to the corporation (Gabriel Ind. v. Defiance Ind., NYLJ, June 17, 1964, p 13, col 8; Sarafite, J., affd 23 A.D.2d 630)."

Clearly, the defendant Gregg must forfeit to the corporation any illegal profit derived from his sale of stock....

Since there has been no showing that the actions of any directors other than Gregg either led to any pecuniary loss to the corporation or to the realization of any personal profit or gain to themselves, it follows that they cannot be held liable jointly, or severally, with Gregg for the payment of the premium over to the corporation.

In view of the fact that the court is charged with the duty to determine both the law and the facts, it must render a factual decision. There was no malfeasance or misfeasance demonstrated in the directors having voted to elect Messrs. Ackerman, Driscoll and Gould. That decision was as consistent with the future well-being and success of the corporation as the later vote to remove Ackerman. On the mere basis of hindsight, the court cannot inculpate these directors for what may or may not have been an unfortunate decision....

It is the decision of the court that.... [Gregg] account to the corporation for any profits made in his sale to SEPCO over and above that which he would have realized, had the sale been consummated in an arm's length, over-the-counter transaction.

Essex Universal Corp. v. Yates

United States Court of Appeals, Second Circuit, 1962.
305 F.2d 572.

■ Before LUMBARD, CHIEF JUDGE, and CLARK and FRIENDLY, CIRCUIT JUDGES.

■ LUMBARD, CHIEF JUDGE.

This appeal from the district court's summary judgment in favor of the defendant raises the question whether a contract for the sale of 28.3 per cent of the stock of a corporation is, under New York law, invalid as against public policy solely because it includes a clause giving the purchaser an option to require a majority of the existing directors to replace themselves, by a process of seriatim resignation, with a majority designated by the purchaser. Despite the disagreement evidenced by the diversity of our opinions, my brethren and I agree that such a provision does not on its face render the contract illegal and unenforceable, and thus that it was improper to grant summary judgment. Judge Friendly would reject the defense of illegality without further inquiry concerning the provision itself (as distinguished from any contention that control could not be safely transferred to the particular purchaser). Judge Clark and I are agreed that on remand, which must be had in any event to consider other defenses raised by the pleadings, further factual issues may be raised by the parties upon which the legality of the clause in question will depend; we disagree, however, on the nature of those factual issues, as our separate opinions reveal. Accordingly, the grant of summary judgment is reversed and the case is remanded for trial of the question of the legality of the contested provision and such further proceedings as may be proper on the other issues raised by the pleadings.

Since we are in agreement on certain preliminary questions, this opinion constitutes the opinion of the court up to the point where it is indicated that it thenceforth states only my individual views.

The defendant Herbert J. Yates, a resident of California, was president and chairman of the board of directors of Republic Pictures Corporation, a New York corporation which at the time relevant to this suit had 2,004,190 shares of common stock outstanding. Republic's stock was listed and traded on the New York Stock Exchange. In August 1957, Essex Universal Corporation, a Delaware corporation owning stock in various diversified businesses, learned of the possibility of purchasing from Yates an interest in Republic. Negotiations proceeded rapidly, and on August 28 Yates and Joseph Harris, the president of Essex, signed a contract in which Essex agreed to buy, and Yates agreed "to sell or cause to be sold" at least 500,000 and not more than 600,000 shares of Republic stock. The price was set at eight dollars a share, roughly two dollars above the then market price on the Exchange. Three dollars per share was to be paid at the closing on September 18, 1957 and the remainder in twenty-four equal monthly payments beginning January 31, 1958. The shares were to be transferred on the closing date, but Yates was to retain the certificates, endorsed in blank by Essex, as security for full payment. In addition to other provisions not relevant to the present motion, the contract contained the following paragraph:

> "6. Resignations.
>
> Upon and as a condition to the closing of this transaction if requested by Buyer at least ten (10) days prior to the date of the closing:
>
> (a) Seller will deliver to Buyer the resignations of the majority of the directors of Republic.
>
> (b) Seller will cause a special meeting of the board of directors of Republic to be held, legally convened pursuant to law and the by-laws of Republic, and simultaneously with the acceptance of the directors' resignations set forth in paragraph 6(a) immediately preceding will cause nominees of Buyer to be elected directors of Republic in place of the resigned directors."

Before the date of the closing, as provided in the contract, Yates notified Essex that he would deliver 566,223 shares, or 28.3 per cent of the Republic stock then outstanding, and Essex formally requested Yates to arrange for the replacement of a majority of Republic's directors with Essex nominees pursuant to paragraph 6 of the contract. This was to be accomplished by having eight of the fourteen directors resign seriatim, each in turn being replaced by an Essex nominee elected by the others; such a procedure was *in form* permissible under the charter and by-laws of Republic, which empowered the board to choose the successor of any of its members who might resign.

On September 18, the parties met as arranged for the closing at Republic's office in New York City. Essex tendered bank drafts and cashier's checks totalling $1,698,690, which was the 37½ per cent of the total price of $4,529,784 due at this time. The drafts and checks were payable to one Benjamin C. Cohen, who was Essex' banker and had arranged for the borrowing of the necessary funds. Although Cohen was prepared to endorse these to Yates, Yates upon advice of his lawyer rejected the tender as "unsatisfactory" and said, according to his deposition testimony, "Well, there can be no deal. We can't close it."

Essex began this action in the New York Supreme Court, and it was removed to the district court on account of diversity of citizenship. Essex seeks damages of $2,700,000, claiming that at the time of the aborted closing the stock was in actuality worth more than $12.75

a share.[1] Yates' answer raised a number of defenses, but the motion for summary judgment now before us was made and decided only on the theory that the provision in the contract for immediate transfer of control of the board of directors was illegal *per se* and tainted the entire contract. We have no doubt, and the parties agree, that New York law governs.

Appellant's contention that the provision for transfer of director control is separable from the rest of the contract can quickly be rejected....

... [W]e hold the provision regarding directors inseparable from the sale of shares, and proceed to a consideration of its legality.

Up to this point my brethren and I are in agreement. The following analysis is my own, except insofar as the separate opinions of Judges Clark and Friendly may indicate agreement.

It is established beyond question under New York law that it is illegal to sell corporate office or management control by itself (that is, accompanied by no stock or insufficient stock to carry voting control).... The rationale of the rule is undisputable: persons enjoying management control hold it on behalf of the corporation's stockholders, and therefore may not regard it as their own personal property to dispose of as they wish.[3] Any other rule would violate the most fundamental principle of corporate democracy, that management must represent and be chosen by, or at least with the consent of, those who own the corporation.

Essex was, however, contracting with Yates for the purchase of a very substantial percentage of Republic stock. If, by virtue of the voting power carried by this stock, it could have elected a majority of the board of directors, then the contract was not a simple agreement for the sale of office to one having no ownership interest in the corporation, and the question of its legality would require further analysis. Such stock voting control would incontestably belong to the owner of a majority of the voting stock, and it is commonly known that equivalent power usually accrues to the owner of 28.3% of the stock. For the purpose of this analysis, I shall assume that Essex was contracting to acquire a majority of the Republic stock, deferring consideration of the situation where, as here, only 28.3% is to be acquired.

Republic's board of directors at the time of the aborted closing had fourteen members divided into three classes, each class being "as nearly as may be" of the same size. Directors were elected for terms of three years, one class being elected at each annual shareholder meeting on the first Tuesday in April. Thus, absent the immediate replacement of directors provided for in this contract, Essex as the hypotheti-

---

1. In 1959, while this action was pending, the stock was sold to another party for ten dollars a share.

3. The cases have made no distinction between contracts by directors or officers to resign and contracts by persons who in actuality control the actions of officers or directors to procure their resignations, and of course none should exist.

cal new majority shareholder of the corporation could not have obtained managing control in the form of a majority of the board in the normal course of events until April 1959, some eighteen months after the sale of the stock. The first question before us then is whether an agreement to accelerate the transfer of management control, in a manner legal in form under the corporation's charter and by-laws, violates the public policy of New York.

There is no question of the right of a controlling shareholder under New York law normally to derive a premium from the sale of a controlling block of stock. In other words, there was no impropriety *per se* in the fact that Yates was to receive more per share than the generally prevailing market price for Republic stock. Levy v. American Beverage Corp., 265 App.Div. 208, 218, 38 N.Y.S.2d 517, 526 (1st Dept.1942); Stanton v. Schenck, 140 Misc. 621, 251 N.Y.S. 221 (N.Y.County Sup.Ct.1931); see Hill, supra, 70 Harv.L.Rev. at 991–92.

The next question is whether it is legal to give and receive payment for the immediate transfer of management control to one who has achieved majority share control but would not otherwise be able to convert that share control into operating control for some time. I think that it is.

Of course under some circumstances controlling shareholders transferring immediate control may be compelled to account to the corporation for that part of the consideration received by them which exceeds the fair value of the block of stock sold, as well as for the injury which they may cause to the corporation.... Gerdes v. Reynolds, 28 N.Y.S.2d 622 (N.Y.County Sup.Ct.1941)....

A fair generalization from [Perlman v. Feldmann and other] cases may be that a holder of corporate control will not, as a fiduciary, be permitted to profit from facilitating actions on the part of the purchasers of control which are detrimental to the interests of the corporation or the remaining shareholders. There is, however, no suggestion that the transfer of control over Republic to Essex carried any such threat to the interests of the corporation or its other shareholders.

Our examination of the New York cases ... gives us no reason to regard as impaired the holding of the early case of Barnes v. Brown, 80 N.Y. 527 (1880), that a bargain for the sale of a majority stock interest is not made illegal by a plan for immediate transfer of management control by a program like that provided for in the Essex–Yates contract. Judge Earl wrote:

> "[The seller] had the right to sell out all his stock and interest in the corporation, ... and when he ceased to have any interest in the corporation, it was certainly legitimate and right that he should cease to control it ... It was simply the mode of transferring the control of the corporation to those who by the policy of the law ought to have it, and I am unable to see how any policy of the law was violated, or in what way, upon the evidence, any wrong was thereby done to anyone." 80 N.Y. at 537.

To be sure, in Barnes v. Brown no term of the contract of sale *required* the seller to effectuate the immediate replacement of directors, as did paragraph 6 of the Essex–Yates contract, but Judge Earl stated that "I shall assume that it was the understanding and a part of the scheme that he should do so." 80 N.Y. at 536. . . .

The easy and immediate transfer of corporate control to new interests is ordinarily beneficial to the economy and it seems inevitable that such transactions would be discouraged if the purchaser of a majority stock interest were required to wait some period before his purchase of control could become effective. Conversely it would greatly hamper the efforts of any existing majority group to dispose of its interest if it could not assure the purchaser of immediate control over corporation operations. I can see no reason why a purchaser of majority control should not ordinarily be permitted to make his control effective from the moment of the transfer of stock.

Thus if Essex had been contracting to purchase a majority of the stock of Republic, it would have been entirely proper for the contract to contain the provision for immediate replacement of directors. Although in the case at bar only 28.3 per cent of the stock was involved, it is commonly known that a person or group owning so large a percentage of the voting stock of a corporation which, like Republic, has at least the 1,500 shareholders normally requisite to listing on the New York Stock Exchange, is almost certain to have share control as a practical matter. If Essex was contracting to acquire what in reality would be equivalent to ownership of a majority of stock, i.e., if it would as a practical certainty have been guaranteed of the stock voting power to choose a majority of the directors of Republic in due course, there is no reason why the contract should not similarly be legal.[6] Whether Essex was thus to acquire the equivalent of majority stock control would, if the issue is properly raised by the defendants, be a factual issue to be determined by the district court on remand.

Because 28.3 per cent of the voting stock of a publicly owned corporation is usually tantamount to majority control, I would place the burden of proof on this issue on Yates as the party attacking the legality of the transaction. Thus, unless on remand Yates chooses to raise the question whether the block of stock in question carried the equivalent of majority control, it is my view that the trial court should regard the contract as legal and proceed to consider the other issues raised by the pleadings. If Yates chooses to raise the issue, it will, on my view, be necessary for him to prove the existence of circumstances which would have prevented Essex from electing a majority of the Republic board of directors in due course. It will not be enough for Yates to raise merely hypothetical possibilities of opposition by the other Republic shareholders to Essex' assumption of management

---

6. The fact that under the Essex–Yates contract only 37½% of the price of the stock was to be paid at the closing and the balance was not to be fully paid for twenty-eight months is irrelevant to this case. There is no indication that Essex did not have sound financial backing sufficient to discharge properly the obligation which had been incurred.

control. Rather, it will be necessary for him to show that, assuming neutrality on the part of the retiring management, there was at the time some concretely foreseeable reason why Essex' wishes would not have prevailed in shareholder voting held in due course. In other words, I would require him to show that there was at the time of the contract some other organized block of stock of sufficient size to outvote the block Essex was buying, or else some circumstance making it likely that enough of the holders of the remaining Republic stock would band together to keep Essex from control.

Reversed and remanded for further proceedings not inconsistent with the judgment of this court.

■ FRIENDLY, CIRCUIT JUDGE (concurring).

Chief Judge Lumbard's thoughtful opinion illustrates a difficulty, inherent in our dual judicial system, which has led at least one state to authorize its courts to answer questions about its law that a Federal court may ask. Here we are forced to decide a question of New York law, of enormous importance to all New York corporations and their stockholders, on which there is hardly enough New York authority for a really informed prediction what the New York Court of Appeals would decide on the facts here presented, see Cooper v. American Airlines, Inc., 149 F.2d 355, 359, 162 A.L.R. 318 (2 Cir., 1945); Pomerantz v. Clark, 101 F.Supp. 341 (D.Mass.1951); Corbin, The Laws of the Several States, 50 Yale L.J. 762, 775–776 (1941), yet too much for us to have the freedom used to good effect in Perlman v. Feldmann, 219 F.2d 173 (2 Cir.), cert. denied, 349 U.S. 952, 75 S.Ct. 880, 99 L.Ed. 1277 (1955).

I have no doubt that many contracts, drawn by competent and responsible counsel, for the purchase of blocks of stock from interests thought to "control" a corporation although owning less than a majority, have contained provisions like paragraph 6 of the contract *sub judice*. However, developments over the past decades seem to me to show that such a clause violates basic principles of corporate democracy. To be sure, stockholders who have allowed a set of directors to be placed in office, whether by their vote or their failure to vote, must recognize that death, incapacity or other hazard may prevent a director from serving a full term, and that they will have no voice as to his immediate successor. But the stockholders are entitled to expect that, in that event, the remaining directors will fill the vacancy in the exercise of their fiduciary responsibility. A mass seriatim resignation directed by a selling stockholder, and the filling of vacancies by his henchmen at the dictation of a purchaser and without any consideration of the character of the latter's nominees, are beyond what the stockholders contemplated or should have been expected to contemplate. This seems to me a wrong to the corporation and the other stockholders which the law ought not countenance, whether the selling stockholder has received a premium or not. Right in this Court we have seen many cases where sudden shifts of corporate control have caused serious injury; Pettit v. Doeskin Products, Inc., 270 F.2d 95 (2 Cir., 1959), cert. denied, 362 U.S. 910, 80 S.Ct. 660, 4 L.Ed.2d

618 (1960); United States v. Crosby, 294 F.2d 928 (2 Cir., 1961), cert. denied Mittelman v. United States, 368 U.S. 984, 82 S.Ct. 599, 7 L.Ed.2d 523 (1962); and Kirtley v. Abrams, 299 F.2d 341 (2 Cir., 1962), are a few recent examples. To hold the seller for delinquencies of the new directors only if he knew the purchaser was an intending looter is not a sufficient sanction. The difficulties of proof are formidable even if receipt of too high a premium creates a presumption of such knowledge, and, all too often, the doors are locked only after the horses have been stolen. Stronger medicines are needed—refusal to enforce a contract with such a clause, even though this confers an unwarranted benefit on a defaulter, and continuing responsibility of the former directors for negligence of the new ones until an election has been held. Such prophylactics are not contraindicated, as Judge Lumbard suggests, by the conceded desirability of preventing the dead hand of a former "controlling" group from continuing to dominate the board after a sale, or of protecting a would-be purchaser from finding himself without a majority of the board after he has spent his money. A special meeting of stockholders to replace a board may always be called, and there could be no objection to making the closing of a purchase contingent on the results of such an election. I perceive some of the difficulties of mechanics such a procedure presents, but I have enough confidence in the ingenuity of the corporate bar to believe these would be surmounted.

Hence, I am inclined to think that if I were sitting on the New York Court of Appeals, I would hold a provision like [paragraph] 6 violative of public policy save when it was entirely plain that a new election would be a mere formality—i.e., when the seller owned more than 50% of the stock. I put it thus tentatively because, before making such a decision, I would want the help of briefs, including those of *amici curiae,* dealing with the serious problems of corporate policy and practice more fully than did those here, which were primarily devoted to argument as to what the New York law has been rather than what it ought to be. Moreover, in view of the perhaps unexpected character of such a holding, I doubt that I would give it retrospective effect.

As a judge of this Court, my task is the more modest one of predicting how the judges of the New York Court of Appeals would rule, and I must make this prediction on the basis of legal materials rather than of personal acquaintance or hunch. Also, for obvious reasons, the prospective technique is unavailable when a Federal court is deciding an issue of state law. Although Barnes v. Brown, 80 N.Y. 527 (1880), dealt with the sale of a majority interest, I am unable to find any real indication that the doctrine there announced has been thus limited. True, there are New York cases saying that the sale of corporate offices is forbidden; but the New York decisions do not tell us what this means and I can find nothing, save perhaps one unexplained sentence in the opinion of a trial court in Ballantine v. Ferretti, 28 N.Y.S.2d 668, 682 (Sup.Ct.N.Y.Co.1941), to indicate that New York would not apply Barnes v. Brown to a case where a stockholder with much less than a majority conditioned a sale on his causing the resignation of a majority of the directors and the election of the purchaser's nominees.

Chief Judge Lumbard's proposal goes part of the way toward meeting the policy problem I have suggested. Doubtless proceeding from what, as it seems to me, is the only justification in principle for permitting even a majority stockholder to condition a sale on delivery of control of the board—namely that in such a case a vote of the stockholders would be a useless formality, he sets the allowable bounds at the line where there is "a practical certainty" that the buyer would be able to elect his nominees and, in this case, puts the burden of disproving that on the person claiming illegality.

Attractive as the proposal is in some respects, I find difficulties with it. One is that I discern no sufficient intimation of the distinction in the New York cases, or even in the writers, who either would go further in voiding such a clause, see Berle, "Control" in Corporate Law, 58 Colum.L.Rev. 1212, 1224 (1958); Leech, Transactions in Corporate Control, 104 U.Pa.L.Rev. 725, 809 (1956) [proposing legislation], or believe the courts have not yet gone that far, see Baker & Cary, Corporations: Cases and Materials (3d ed. unabr. 1959) 590. To strike down such a condition only in cases falling short of the suggested line accomplishes little to prevent what I consider the evil; in most instances a seller will not enter into a contract conditioned on his "delivering" a majority of the directors unless he has good reason to think he can do that. When an issue does arise, the "practical certainty" test is difficult to apply. The existence of such certainty will depend not merely on the proportion of the stock held by the seller but on many other factors—whether the other stock is widely or closely held, how much of it is in "street names," what success the corporation has experienced, how far its dividend policies have satisfied its stockholders, the identity of the purchasers, the presence or absence of cumulative voting, and many others. Often, unless the seller has nearly 50% of the stock, whether he has "working control" can be determined only by an election; groups who thought they had such control have experienced unpleasant surprises in recent years. Judge Lumbard correctly recognizes that, from a policy standpoint, the pertinent question must be the buyer's prospects of election, not the seller's—yet this inevitably requires the court to canvass the likely reaction of stockholders to a group of whom they know nothing and seems rather hard to reconcile with a position that it is "right" to insert such a condition if a seller has a larger proportion of the stock and "wrong" if he has a smaller. At the very least the problems and uncertainties arising from the proposed line of demarcation are great enough, and its advantages small enough, that in my view a Federal court would do better simply to overrule the defense here, thereby accomplishing what is obviously the "just" result in this particular case, and leave the development of doctrine in this area to the State, which has primary concern for it.

I would reverse the grant of summary judgment and remand for consideration of defenses other than a claim that the inclusion of paragraph 6 *ex mero motu* renders the contract void.

[The concurring opinion of Judge Clark is omitted.]

NOTE ON ESSEX UNIVERSAL CORP. v. YATES

It is not at all clear that a shareholding block of 28.3% necessarily carries control of a publicly held corporation. If not coupled with control of the board. Consider Brannigan, Florida Businessman Seeks to Steer Bank Toward Sale, Wall Street Journal, Sept. 2, 1987, at 27, col. 1: "[Hugh F. Culverhouse] has launched a tender offer for 10% of Florida Commercial Banks Inc's shares, ... He already holds ... 39.9% of the bank's shares. Since 1984, Mr. Culverhouse has struggled unsuccessfully to win a seat on the company's board or to acquire control of the concern. As of earlier this year, 28.4% of the company's shares were controlled by a well-entrenched group of officers and directors that has opposed him. . . ."

NOTE ON TAG–ALONG AND DRAG–ALONG PROVISIONS

Under modern corporate practice, the problems faced by minority shareholders when controlling shareholders arrange to sell their shares at a premium are often addressed by a *tag-along* provision in a shareholders' agreement. Under such a provision, if a third party offers to buy out the majority shareholders of a corporation, the minority shareholders must be offered the right to sell their shares to the third party on the same terms as those offered to the majority shareholders. Such provisions are only feasible when the corporation still has a small number of shareholders.

Under a related type of provision, known as a *drag-along* provision, minority shareholders agree that if the controlling shareholders sell their shares to a given buyer, the minority shareholders will also sell their shares to the buyer on the same terms. Unlike tag-alongs, the purpose of the drag-alongs is to protect the controlling shareholders in situations where they have lined up a buyer for their shares at an advantageous price, and the buyer insists on acquiring 100% of the shares.

SECURITIES EXCHANGE ACT RULE 14F–1

[See Statutory Supplement]

ALI, PRINCIPLES OF CORPORATE GOVERNANCE § 5.16

[See Statutory Supplement]

CHAPTER 12

THE ANTIFRAUD PROVISION: SECTION 10(b) AND RULE 10b–5

SECTION 1. AN INTRODUCTION TO SECTION 10(b) AND RULE 10b–5

SECURITIES EXCHANGE ACT § 10(b)

[See Statutory Supplement]

SECURITIES EXCHANGE ACT RULE 10b–5

[See Statutory Supplement]

The Wharf (Holdings) Limited v. United International Holdings, Inc.

Supreme Court of the United States, 2001.
532 U.S. 588, 121 S.Ct. 1776, 149 L.Ed.2d 845.

■ JUSTICE BREYER delivered the opinion of the Court.

This securities fraud action focuses upon a company that sold an option to buy stock while secretly intending never to honor the option. The question before us is whether this conduct violates § 10(b) of the Securities Exchange Act of 1934, which prohibits using "any manipulative or deceptive device or contrivance" "in connection with the purchase or sale of any security." ... *15 U.S.C. § 78j(b)*.... We conclude that it does.

I

Respondent United International Holdings, Inc., a Colorado-based company, sued petitioner The Wharf (Holdings) Limited, a Hong Kong firm, in Colorado's Federal District Court. United said that in October 1992 Wharf had sold it an option to buy 10% of the stock of a new Hong Kong cable system. But, United alleged, at the time of the sale Wharf secretly intended not to permit United to exercise the option. United claimed that Wharf's conduct amounted to a fraud "in connection with the ... sale of [a] security," prohibited by § 10(b), and violated numerous state laws as well. A jury found in United's favor.

The Court of Appeals for the Tenth Circuit upheld that verdict. *210 F.3d 1207 (2000)*. And we granted certiorari to consider whether the dispute fell within the scope of § 10(b). . . .

In 1991, the Hong Kong government announced that it would accept bids for the award of an exclusive license to operate a cable television system in Hong Kong. Wharf decided to prepare a bid. Wharf's chairman, Peter Woo, instructed one of its managing directors, Stephen Ng, to find a business partner with cable system experience. Ng found United. And United sent several employees to Hong Kong to help prepare Wharf's application, negotiate contracts, design the system, and arrange financing.

United asked to be paid for its services with a right to invest in the cable system if Wharf should obtain the license. During August and September 1992, while United's employees were at work helping Wharf, Wharf and United negotiated about the details of that payment. Wharf prepared a draft letter of intent that contemplated giving United the right to become a co-investor, owning 10% of the system. But the parties did not sign the letter of intent. And in September, when Wharf submitted its bid, it told the Hong Kong authorities that Wharf would be the system's initial sole owner, although Wharf would also "consider" allowing United to become an investor.*

In early October 1992, Ng met with a United representative, who told Ng that United would continue to help only if Wharf gave United an enforceable right to invest. Ng then orally granted United an option with the following terms: (1) United had the right to buy 10% of the future system's stock; (2) the price of exercising the option would be 10% of the system's capital requirements minus the value of United's previous services (including expenses); (3) United could exercise the option only if it showed that it could fund its 10% share of the capital required for at least the first 18 months; and (4) the option would expire if not exercised within six months of the date that Wharf received the license. The parties continued to negotiate about how to write documents that would embody these terms, but they never reduced the agreement to writing.

In May 1993, Hong Kong awarded the cable franchise to Wharf. United raised $66 million designed to help finance its 10% share. In July or August 1993, United told Wharf that it was ready to exercise its option. But Wharf refused to permit United to buy any of the system's stock. Contemporaneous internal Wharf documents suggested that Wharf had never intended to carry out its promise. . . .

[Various] documents, along with other evidence, convinced the jury that Wharf, through Ng, had orally sold United an option to purchase a 10% interest in the future cable system while secretly intending not to permit United to exercise the option, in violation of § 10(b) of the Securities Exchange Act and various state laws. The jury awarded United compensatory damages of $67 million . . .

---

* References to transcripts and briefs are omitted. (Footnote by ed.)

II

Section 10(b) of the Securities Exchange Act makes it "unlawful for any person ... [t]o use or employ, in connection with the purchase or sale of any security ..., any manipulative or deceptive device or contrivance in contravention of such rules and regulations as the [SEC] may prescribe." *15 U.S.C. § 78j.*

Pursuant to this provision, the SEC has promulgated Rule 10b–5. That Rule forbids the use, "in connection with the purchase or sale of any security," of (1) "any device, scheme, or artifice to defraud"; (2) "any untrue statement of a material fact"; (3) the omission of "a material fact necessary in order to make the statements made ... not misleading"; or (4) any other "act, practice, or course of business" that "operates ... as a fraud or deceit." *17 C.F.R. § 240.10b–5 (2000).*

To succeed in a Rule 10b–5 suit, a private plaintiff must show that the defendant used, in connection with the purchase or sale of a security, one of the four kinds of manipulative or deceptive devices to which the Rule refers, and must also satisfy certain other requirements not at issue here. See, *e.g., 15 U.S.C. § 78j* (requiring the "use of any means or instrumentality of interstate commerce or of the mails, or of any facility of any national securities exchange"); *Ernst & Ernst v. Hochfelder*, 425 U.S. 185, 193, 96 S.Ct. 1375, 47 L.Ed.2d 668 (1976) (requiring scienter, meaning "intent to deceive, manipulate, or defraud"); *Basic Inc. v. Levinson*, 485 U.S. 224, 231–232, 108 S.Ct. 978, 99 L.Ed.2d 194 (1988) (requiring that any misrepresentation be material); *id.*, at 243, 108 S.Ct. 978 (requiring that the plaintiff sustain damages through reliance on the misrepresentation).

In deciding whether the Rule covers the circumstances present here, we must assume that the "security" at issue is not the cable system stock, but the option to purchase that stock. That is because the Court of Appeals found that Wharf conceded this point. *210 F.3d, at 1221* ("Wharf does not contest on appeal the classification of the option as a security"). That concession is consistent with the language of the Securities Exchange Act, which defines "security" to include both "any ... option ... on any security" and "any ... right to ... purchase" stock. *15 U.S.C. § 78c(a)(10).* ... Consequently, we must decide whether Wharf's secret intent not to honor the option it sold United amounted to a misrepresentation (or other conduct forbidden by the Rule) in connection with the sale of the option.

Wharf argues that its conduct falls outside the Rule's scope for two basic reasons. First, Wharf points out that its agreement to grant United an option to purchase shares in the cable system was an oral agreement. And it says that § 10(b) does not cover oral contracts of sale....

[There is no] convincing reason to interpret the Act to exclude oral contracts as a class. The Act itself says that it applies to "any contract" for the purchase or sale of a security. *15 U.S.C. §§ 78c(a)(13), (14).* Oral contracts for the sale of securities are sufficiently common that the Uniform Commercial Code and statutes of frauds in every State now consider them enforceable. See U.C.C. § 8–113 (Supp.2000) ("A contract ... for the sale or purchase of a security is enforceable whether or not there is a writing signed or record authenticated by a party against whom enforcement is sought").... Any exception for oral sales of securities would significantly limit the Act's coverage, thereby undermining its basic purposes....

Second, Wharf argues that a secret reservation not to permit the exercise of an option falls outside § 10(b) because it does not "relat[e] to the value of a security purchase or the consideration paid"; hence it does "not implicate [§ 10(b)'s] policy of full disclosure." Brief for Petitioners 25, 26 (emphasis deleted). But even were it the case that the Act covers only misrepresentations likely to affect the value of securities, Wharf's secret reservation was such a misrepresentation. To sell an option while secretly intending not to permit the option's exercise is misleading, because a buyer normally presumes good faith. Cf., *e.g., Restatement (Second) of Torts § 530*, Comment *c* (1976) ("Since a promise necessarily carries with it the implied assertion of an intention to perform[,] it follows that a promise made without such an intention is fraudulent"). For similar reasons, the secret reservation misled United about the option's value. Since Wharf did not intend to honor the option, the option was, unbeknownst to United, valueless....

For these reasons, the judgment of the Court of Appeals is

Affirmed.

NOTE ON PRIVATE ACTIONS UNDER RULE 10b–5

The Wharf (Holdings) Limited v. United International Holdings, Inc. was a private action; that is, it was an action brought by a private party for private relief—damages—rather rather than an action brought by the government. Neither section 10(b) of the Securities Exchange Act nor Rule 10b–5 explicitly provides for private actions. However, there is a long tradition in American law of allowing private parties to bring actions based on violations of statutes or administrative rules in appropriate cases. What kinds of cases are appropriate, for this purpose, is the subject of principles whose content has changed somewhat over time. The most salient principles, for present purposes, are summarized in the descriptions of J.I. Case Co v. Borak, Wyandotte v. United States, and Cort v. Ash, set out at the beginning of Chapter 6, Section 4, supra.

Under these principles, the courts have held that some provisions of the Securities Acts and the rules thereunder give rise to private actions, and others do not. It has become firmly established that section 10(b) and Rule 10b–5 give rise to private actions. The seminal case is a 1946 district court decision, Kardon v. National Gypsum, 69 F.Supp. 512 (E.D. Pa. 1946). It would be four decades later that the

Supreme Court formally upheld the implied private right of action under section 10(b) and Rule 10b–5 in Herman & McLean v. Huddleston, 459 U.S. 375, 103 S.Ct. 683, 74 L.Ed.2d 548 (1983), although the Supreme Court had earlier entertained a private right of action when its existence was not questioned. *See* Superintendent of Insurance v. Bankers Life & Casualty Co., 404 U.S. 6, 92 S.Ct. 165, 30 L.Ed.2d 128 (1971).

SECTION 2. THE PRIVATE SECURITIES LITIGATION REFORM ACT AND SECURITIES LITIGATION UNIFORM STANDARDS ACT

Twice in the last two decades Congress has enacted sweeping changes that restrain private securities fraud actions. It is unlikely Congress would have acted if suits were all like the suit in *Wharf Holdings,* involving only disputes between business partners rather than a class actions on behalf of thousands of investors. What prompted Congress to act was the burgeoning number of securities class actions that Congress believed were largely nuisance suits initiated to extract settlements that benefitted only the class action lawyers, produced small rewards to investors alleged harmed by the fraud, and rendered the U.S. capital markets anticompetitive versus rival foreign markets (where class action procedures generally do not exist, contingency fee arrangements are generally not allowed, and the loser pay rule is the norm).

The Private Securities Litigation Reform Act of 1995 introduced a variety of reforms for securities fraud actions. The centerpiece of the legislation was adding Section 21D(a)(3) to the Securities Exchange Act establishing a procedure for the court to appoint a "lead plaintiff" for the suit. Pursuant to this provision, soon after the filing of the complaint, notice is publicized inviting interested parties to become the suit's plaintiff. There is a rebuttable presumption that the petitioner with the largest loss suffered is the most adequate plaintiff. The lead plaintiff provision reflected Congress' view that the menacing features of the securities class action flowed from the suits being lawyer driven. The PSLRA thus seeks to provide the suit's attorney with a real client.

The PSLRA's legislative history clearly reflects that the lead plaintiff provision was adopted in order to encourage financial institutions to step forward as the class' representative. The expectation was that such a plaintiff would actively monitor the conduct of a securities fraud class action so as to reduce the litigation agency costs that may arise when class counsel's interests diverge from those of the shareholder class. The Congress clearly envisioned that various types of financial institutions—pension funds, insurance companies, mutual funds—were the most likely type of investors who could combine a large financial stake in the suit's outcome with the sophistication to guide the suit to an appropriate outcome, including a decision whether the suit should be maintained at all. Overall, proponents of the provision believed there would be substantial benefits from having institutional investors serve as lead plaintiffs, including more favorable settlement terms, lower attorneys' fees for class counsel, fewer strike suits, more adjudications of class actions, and greater deterrence of securities fraud.

Once appointed, the lead plaintiff, subject to approval by the court, appoints the class's counsel. The impetus for the lead plaintiff provision was not just the general belief that securities class action suits were lawyer driven, but that in many suits institutional investors had a sufficient enough stake in the suit's prosecution so that they had natural economic incentives to monitor counsel's prosecution of the suit. An important study that preceded Congress' enactment of the PSLRA reported that in 82 examined securities class action settlements that the 50 largest claimants had average allowable losses of $597,000 and represented 57.5 percent of all allowable losses in the settlement. Elliott Weiss and John Beckerman, Let the Money Do the Monitoring: How Institutional Investors Can Reduce Agency Costs in Securities Class Actions, 104 Yale L. J. 2053, 2089–2090 (1995). Subsequent studies report that an institution that serves as lead plaintiff is associated with much greater recoveries as measured against the class' provable losses. *See* James D. Cox & Randall S. Thomas, Does The Plaintiff Matter? An Empirical Analysis Of Lead Plaintiffs In Securities Class Actions, 106 Colum. L. Rev. 1587, 1631 (2006) (institutional lead plaintiffs are associated with suits against companies with large market capitalization and that yield overall large settlement amounts). One study of 773 settlements of suits filed after 2001 found that institutions served as lead plaintiff in only about 18 percent of the settlements and for about a quarter of the settlements the lead plaintiff was a group of related individuals. The plaintiffs in the remaining suits are individuals or a single business (non financial institution) entity. *See* James D. Cox, Randall S. Thomas & Lynn Bai, There Are Plaintiffs and . . . There Are Plaintiffs: An Empirical Analysis of Securities Class Action Settlements, 61 Vand. L. Rev. 355, 368, 371 & 373 (2008).

Providing the securities class action with a real plaintiff was not the only important contribution of the PSLRA. Exchange Act Section 21D(b)(2) was added requiring that in any private securities fraud suit seeking damages that the complaint, in order to withstand a motion to dismiss, must set forth with particularity facts creating a strong inference that the defendant action with knowledge or recklessness. Not only does the plaintiff confront this heightened pleading standard, examined more closely below, but also Section 21D(b)(3) bars any discovery by the plaintiff until after all motions to dismiss have been disposed of by the presiding court. Thus, plaintiffs cannot, as they frequently did before the PSLRA, file the complaint, gain access to the defendant's records via discovery, and with the information learned through discovery amend the complaint so as to allege sufficient facts for the complaint to survive the defendant's motion to dismiss.

Among the other provisions added by the PSLRA are a broad embrace of proportionate fault so that in general a single defendant is not joint and severally liable for all the losses suffered by the plaintiff at the hands of multiple wrongdoers; pursuant to the PSLRA, and subject to some exceptions, a defendant is only liable for that portion of the plaintiff's loss that is attributable to that defendant's misconduct. There is a bar of "professional plaintiffs" that prohibits any person serving as a lead plaintiff more than five times in three years. And, at the conclusion of the suits the presiding judge is to determine whether Rule 11 sanctions should be imposed on any attorney. Recall that in other contexts Rule 11 sanctions are in response to a motion by one of the litigants so that whatever misconduct a litigant might have believed the other party's attorney engaged in is customarily dropped as part of the case's settlement. Under the PSLRA the judge, regardless of any party's motion, is required to determine whether Rule 11 sanctions are to be imposed.

After the PSLRA's enactment, there was a noticeable increase in securities fraud cases filed in state courts, for the apparent purpose of escaping the dual effects of the PSLRA's heightened pleading requirement and its discovery bar. This prompted Congress in 1998 to return to the subject of securities class actions by enacting the Securities Litigation Uniform Standards Act (SLUSA). It amended section 28(f) of the Securities Exchange Act to confer exclusive jurisdiction to federal courts for class actions involving misrepresentation or manipulative acts in connection with the purchase or sale of a "covered security." SLUSA defines "class action" as any suit seeking relief on behalf of 50 or more persons. A covered security is technically defined in section 18(b) of the Securities Act and includes securities listed on a national exchange as well as securities that are privately placed. Among the notable exclusions from the preemptive reach of section 28(f) is the so-called "Delaware carve-out" that preserves the state court jurisdiction for suits focused on misrepresentations by a firm's officers, directors, and control persons. Such actions arise primarily in connection with statements made in connection with tender offers, mergers and other transactions that involve shareholder approval where the officers, directors or controlling stockholders allegedly committed a misrepresentation in connection with the transactions for which shareholder approval is sought either in the form of voting their shares or tendering them to a bidder.

Despite Congress' efforts to restrain aspects of the securities class action, it continues to be focus of law reform efforts. Public interest in this topic is fed by high-profile study groups who argue that the threat of securities class actions as making American capital markets less competitive to foreign markets. For example, Committee On Capital Markets Regulation, The Competitive Position Of The U.S. Public Equity Market (2007) amasses a good deal of data reporting that fewer and fewer foreign issuers offer or list their firm's securities in the U.S.; instead they do so in a market closer to their home country or in London. On the other hand, consider the signaling benefits reaped by a foreign issuer that chooses to either offer or list its securities in the more demanding U.S. legal climate? By offering its securities in the U.S. or obtaining a listing on either the NYSE or NASDAQ, the foreign issuer substantially steps up the level of its disclosure obligations.

Moreover, its obeisance to those obligations is subject to enforcement not only by the SEC, whose enforcement resources greatly dwarf those of any foreign regulator, but also, as this chapter explores, the foreign issuer then becomes amenable to the American class action and its entrepreneurial lawyer. Would not a firm be willing to subject itself to this greater level of scrutiny as a means to signal management's belief in the trustworthiness of its financial reporting so that overall the firm's cost of capital is lower than what it would have been the case had it not entered the U.S. financial markets? James D. Cox, Regulatory Duopoly in U.S. Securities Markets, 99 Colum. L. Rev. 1200 (1999). Does this view of the signaling effects strengthen or weaken the appeal of the PSLRA and SLUSA?

Finally, private and governmental enforcement are not the only sanctions faced by public companies that engage in material misrepresentations. Consider that a study of 585 publicly traded firms that were the subject of SEC enforcement actions from 1978–2002 lost 41% of their market value following disclosure of their managers' misconduct. Jonathan M. Karpoff, D. Scott Lee & Gerald S. Martin, The Cost to Firms of Cooking the Books, 43 J. Fin. & Quant. Analysis 581 (2008) (and the same study, not surprisingly reports, that nearly 94 percent of the individuals identified as being responsible for the violations lost their positions by the end of the SEC enforcement proceeding). More disturbing from the public policy perspective are the finding that firms that become embroiled in securities fraud suit that leads to a settlement are much more likely to experience bankruptcy and other forms of financial distress than a comparable cohort of firms. *See* Lynn Bai, James D. Cox, Randall S. Thomas, Lying and Getting Caught: An Empirical Study of the Impact of Settlement on the Firm, 158 U. Penn. L. Rev. 1877 (2010).

SECTION 3. THE ELEMENTS OF STANDING, "IN CONNECTION WITH" AND SCIENTER

NOTE ON STANDING AND "IN CONNECTION WITH"

A. The Purchaser–Seller Requirement. In Blue Chip Stamps v. Manor Drug Stores, 421 U.S. 723, 95 S.Ct. 1917, 44 L.Ed.2d 539 (1975), the Supreme Court held that under the "in connection with" clause of § 10(b), only a person who had purchased or sold stock had standing to bring a private action under Rule 10b–5. In a widely followed opinion, the Second Circuit announced the purchaser-seller requirement in Birnbaum v. Newport Steel Corp., 193 F.2d 461 (1952), cert. denied 343 U.S. 956, 72 S.Ct. 1051, 96 L.Ed. 1356. Even though it had long adhered to *Birnbaum*, in its *Blue Chip Stamps* decision the Ninth Circuit held the facts justified what it considered a slight departure from *Birnbaum's* purchaser or seller requirement. As part of a consent decree ending a government antitrust settlement, Blue Chip Stamps was required to reorganize itself by undertaking a public offering of its shares to numerous retailers identified in the decree. The precise number of shares each retailer could acquire was determined according to a formula agreed to in the settlement. Plaintiffs were retailers included in the decree but did not exercise their right to acquire the offered shares. They alleged Blue Chip Stamps intentionally made the prospectus overly pessimistic in order to discourage retailers from accepting what was to be a bargain offer, so that the rejected shares could later be sold to the public at a higher price. The plaintiffs further alleged that they relied on the false pessimistic information and therefore did not purchase the offered units. The Ninth Circuit reasoned the facts justified a departure from the rigid purchaser-seller requirement. The Supreme Court's opinion, by Justice Rehnquist, reversed, even though recognizing that the language of section 10(b) itself was not conclusive on the issue, but supported its reversal on the basis of policy considerations:

> There has been widespread recognition that litigation under Rule 10b–5 presents a danger of vexatiousness different in degree and in kind from that which accompanies litigation in general....
>
> We believe that the concern expressed for the danger of vexatious litigation which could result from a widely expanded class of plaintiffs under Rule 10b–5 is founded in something more substantial than the common complaint of the many defendants who would prefer avoiding lawsuits entirely to either settling them or trying them. These concerns have two largely separate grounds.
>
> The first of these concerns is that in the field of federal securities laws governing disclosure of information even a complaint which by objective standards may have very little chance of success at trial has a settlement value to the plaintiff out of any proportion to its prospect of success at trial so long as he may prevent the suit from being resolved against him by dismissal or summary judgment. The very pendency of the lawsuit may frustrate or delay normal business activity of the defendant which is totally unrelated to the lawsuit....
>
> The potential for possible abuse of the liberal discovery provisions of the Federal Rules of Civil Procedure may likewise exist in this type of case to a greater extent than they do in other litigation. The prospect of extensive deposition of the defendant's officers and associates and the concomitant opportunity for extensive discovery of business documents, is a common occurrence in this and similar types of litigation. To the extent that this process eventually produces relevant evidence which is useful in determining the merits of the claims asserted by the parties, it bears the imprimatur of those Rules and of the many cases liberally interpreting them. But to the extent that it permits a plaintiff with a largely groundless claim to simply take up the time of a number of other people, with the right to do so representing an *in terrorem* increment of the settlement value, rather than a reasonably founded hope that the process will reveal relevant evidence,

> it is a social cost rather than a benefit. Yet to broadly expand the class of plaintiffs who may sue under Rule 10b–5 would appear to encourage the least appealing aspect of the use of the discovery rules.
>
> Without the *Birnbaum* rule, an action under Rule 10b–5 will turn largely on which oral version of a series of occurrences the jury may decide to credit, and therefore no matter how improbable the allegations of the plaintiff, the case will be virtually impossible to dispose of prior to trial other than by settlement. . . .
>
> The second ground for fear of vexatious litigation is based on the concern that, given the generalized contours of liability, the abolition of the *Birnbaum* rule would throw open to the trier of fact many rather hazy issues of historical fact the proof of which depended almost entirely on oral testimony. We in no way disparage the worth and frequent high value of oral testimony when we say that dangers of its abuse appear to exist in this type of action to a peculiarly high degree. . . .

The most significant bite of the *Blue Chip* doctrine is to bar private actions by persons who claim they *would have sold* stock that they owned had they not been induced to retain the stock by misrepresentations, or omissions, that violated Rule 10b–5. There are some notable "wrinkles" to the doctrine:

1. *Definition of "Sale."* The definitions of the term "sale" under the Securities Acts are very expansive, and therefore picks up many transactions that do not constitute a sale in the narrowest meaning of that term. For example, in Rubin v. United States, 449 U.S. 424, 101 S.Ct. 698, 66 L.Ed.2d 633 (1981), the Supreme Court held that a pledge of securities was an "offer" or "sale" within § 17(a) of the Securities Act of 1933 (from whose language Rule 10b–5 was drawn). In Chemical Bank v. Arthur Andersen & Co., 726 F.2d 930, 939–40 (2d Cir.1984) (Friendly, J.), the court concluded that the *Rubin* reasoning applied under Rule 10b–5 as well. A purchase and/or sale is also implicated when shares are involved as the consideration in a merger as well as when substantive changes in the rights, privileges or preferences of shares occurs via an amendment of the articles of incorporation.

2. *SEC Proceedings.* The *Blue Chip* doctrine does not affect the standing of the SEC to bring proceedings under Rule 10b–5, even though the SEC was neither a purchaser nor a seller (as it never would be).

3. *Injunctive Relief.* Several pre-*Blue Chip Stamp* cases held that a plaintiff in a private action for injunctive relief need not be a purchaser or a seller. See Kahan v. Rosenstiel, 424 F.2d 161, 173 (3d Cir.1970), cert. denied sub nom. Glen Alden Corp. v. Kahan, 398 U.S. 950, 90 S.Ct. 1870, 26 L.Ed.2d 290 (1970); Mutual Shares Corp. v. Genesco, Inc., 384 F.2d 540, 546–47 (2d Cir.1967). Although a few post-*Blue Chip Stamp* decisions have assumed this exception was

unaffected by the 1975 decision, *See e.g.*, Warner Communications Inc. v. Murdoch, 581 F.Supp. 1482, 1494 (D. Del. 1984), the overall response is more restrained. For example, in Advanced Resources International v. Tri–Star Petroleum Co., 4 F.3d 327 (4th Cir.1993), the Fourth Circuit reasoned that *Blue Chip Stamps* requires the plaintiff in an injunctive action to be a purchaser or seller, unless absent obtaining an injunction the plaintiff would suffer a future monetary loss. More restrictive yet is Cowin v. Bresler, 741 F.2d 410 (D.C. Cir. 1984), holding there is no exception to the purchaser-seller requirement for injunctive relief.

4. *SLUSA and the Purchaser–Seller Requirement. Merrill Lynch, Pierce, Fenner & Smith v. Dabit*, 547 U.S. 71, 126 S.Ct. 1503, 164 L.Ed.2d 179 (2006), involved a class action initially filed in the state court of Oklahoma alleging various Oklahoma laws were violated by Merrill Lynch's scheme that included false analysts' recommendations. The class was made up of individuals who, in reliance on the analysts' recommendations, continued to hold the affected stocks. They suffered a loss when the stocks declined and the brokerage firm's scheme was discovered by government investigators. Merrill Lynch invoked SLUSA to remove the case to the federal court and pursuant to the multidistrict panel the suit was directed to the District Court for Southern District of New York. After skirmishing there, the suit reached the Second Circuit which held that SLUSA applied only to suits that could substantively be maintained in the federal court. Since the plaintiffs' complaint was that the fraudulent analysts' reports and other conduct caused them to retain their shares, the Second Circuit held the suit was improperly removed to the federal court. The Supreme Court vacated the opinion, reasoning that SLUSA's use of the parallel "in connection with the purchase or sale of a security" language meant that Congress intended the expression to have the same meaning in SLUSA as it has in Rule 10b–5. Accordingly it held SLUSA preempted the state law holder class action claims of the kind alleged in the suit by Dabit. Does this mean the holders in *Dabit* are without a remedy? Is that an efficient remedy?

***B.* The "In connection with" Requirement.** Section 10(b) and Rule 10b–5 proscribe manipulative and deceptive acts that are "in connection with the purchase or sale of any security." Although this language calls for there to be some nexus between a violation of Rule 10b–5 and a purchase or sale, "[t]he courts have interpreted [the term 'in connection with'] broadly. Any statement that is reasonably calculated to affect the investment decision of a reasonable investor will satisfy the 'in connection with' requirement." 3 T. Hazen, Securities Regulation 540–541 (6th ed. 2009). Accordingly, it is well established that although the *plaintiff* in a private action under Rule 10b–5 must be a buyer or a seller, the *defendants* need not be. Moreover, "where the alleged fraud involves the public dissemination of information in a medium upon which investors would presumably rely, the 'in connection with' element may be established by proof of materiality of the misrepresentation and the means of its dissemination.... Under that standard, it is irrelevant that the misrepresentations were not made for the purpose or object of influencing the investment decisions of market participants.'' Semerenko v. Cendant Corp., 223 F.3d 165, 176 (3d Cir. 2000).

Interesting questions surround the meaning of the ''in connection with'' requirement. Fraudulent representations to a bank to obtain a loan for which securities are to serve as collateral were not deemed to be ''in connection with'' the purchase or sale of securities even though, as seen above, a pledge of securities is a sale. *See* Chemical Bank v. Arthur Andersen & Co., 726 F.2d 930 (2d Cir.), *cert. denied*, 469 U.S. 884, 105 S.Ct. 253, 83 L.Ed.2d 190 (1984). And, in Gavin v. AT & T, (7th Cir. 2006), the court held the broker had not committed fraud in connection with the sale of securities. In *Gavin* the plan of merger approved by the stockholders of each company provided the stockholders of the disappearing firm with a variety of options by which they would be compensated for their shares. Defendant broker was retained to administer the plan and sent a notice after the merger's consummation detailing most of the plans, stating it would assist for a $7 fee any interested stockholders in realizing the option they chose without disclosing that one of the options available to the shareholders did not involve any fee to the broker. The court held this omission, although material, was not in connection with the sale of a security which under standard corporate law had occurred earlier following the stockholders' approval and filing of the necessary documents with the secretary of state. On the other hand, in SEC v. Zandford, 535 U.S. 813, 122 S.Ct. 1899, 153 L.Ed.2d 1 (2002), a unanimous Supreme Court held the requisite nexus existed where the broker systematically misappropriated proceeds from sales of his client's securities. The client, who was quite elderly and in poor health, granted the broker full discretion to engage in securities transactions without the client's prior approval. Over a two-year period, the broker repeatedly sold securities from the account and misappropriated the sales proceeds which approximated $343,000. The court found the requisite linkage by reasoning that each sale was made in furtherance of the fraudulent scheme to misappropriate the funds, reasoning rather broadly that the client was ''duped into believing . . . [the broker] would 'conservatively invest' their assets in the stock market and that any transaction made on their behalf would be for their benefit. . . .'' 535 U.S. at 822, 122 S.Ct. at 1904, 153 L.Ed.2d at 10. What would have been the result had the broker had received funds from the client on the pretense they would be invested in securities, but instead the broker embezzled the funds? *See, e.g.,* VR Global Partners, L.P. v. Bennett, 586 F. Supp. 2d 172 (S.D.N.Y. 2008).

NOTE ON THE SCIENTER REQUIREMENT AND ITS PLEADING

1. *The Call for Scienter.* In Ernst & Ernst v. Hochfelder, 425 U.S. 185, 96 S.Ct. 1375, 47 L.Ed.2d 668 (1976), the Supreme Court held that a private action for damages under Rule 10b–5 does not exist ''in

the absence of any allegation of 'scienter,' " which the Court defined as an "intent to deceive, manipulate, or defraud" on the defendant's part. Loss and Seligman comment on this ruling as follows: "It is necessary [given the language of Section 10(b)] that some sort of watered-down scienter requirement be read into Clause (2) [of Rule 10b–5]. But why—in construing a fraud provision that was designed to *raise* the standards of securities trading, and that the courts have repeatedly interpreted as not limited to circumstances that would amount to common law deceit—did the majority opinion reach back in history to the strictest common law definition: not merely knowing falsity, but 'intent to deceive, manipulate, or defraud'?" 8 L. Loss & J. Seligman, Securities Regulation 3664 (3d ed. 1991).

2. *Recklessness.* In footnote 12 of *Ernst & Ernst,* the Court stated:

> In this opinion the term "scienter" refers to a mental state embracing intent to deceive, manipulate, or defraud. In certain areas of the law recklessness is considered to be a form of intentional conduct for purposes of imposing liability for some act. We need not address here the question whether, in some circumstances, reckless behavior is sufficient for civil liability under § 10(b) and Rule 10b–5.

Decisions since *Ernst & Ernst* have unanimously held that recklessness satisfies the scienter requirement. What constitutes recklessness for purposes of Rule 10b–5 is less clear. Various courts have adopted, or cited with approval, observations in Sundstrand Corp. v. Sun Chemical Corp., 553 F.2d 1033 (7th Cir.1977), cert. denied 434 U.S. 875, 98 S.Ct. 224, 54 L.Ed.2d 155, and Sanders v. John Nuveen & Co., Inc., 554 F.2d 790 (7th Cir.1977). In *Sundstrand,* the court said:

> [R]eckless conduct may be defined as [highly unreasonable conduct], involving not merely simple, or even inexcusable negligence, but an extreme departure from the standards of ordinary care, and which presents a danger of misleading buyers or sellers that is either known to the defendant or is so obvious that the actor must have been aware of it.

553 F.2d at 1045. According to a gloss put on this test in Mansbach v. Prescott, Ball & Turben, 598 F.2d 1017, 1025 (6th Cir.1979), "[w]hile the danger need not be known, it must at least be so obvious that any reasonable man would have known of it." In *Sanders,* the court, after referring to the *Sundstrand* test, said:

> In view of the Supreme Court's analysis in *Hochfelder* of the statutory scheme of implied private remedies and express remedies, the definition of "reckless behavior" should not be a liberal one lest any discernible distinction between "scienter" and "negligence" be obliterated for these purposes. We believe "reckless" in these circumstances comes closer to being a lesser form of intent than merely a greater degree of ordinary negligence. We perceive it to be not just a difference in degree, but also in kind.

554 F.2d at 793.

3. *Injunctive Relief.* In Aaron v. SEC, 446 U.S. 680, 100 S.Ct. 1945, 64 L.Ed.2d 611 (1980), the Supreme Court held that a showing of scienter was a requirement in an injunctive action under Rule 10b–5.

4. *Pleading Scienter.* As discussed above, scienter is a necessary part of the plaintiff's case. Scienter takes one of two forms of conscious misbehavior: either the defendant had a specific intent to mislead or he acted recklessly. It has long been a requirement of Federal Rule of Civil Procedure 9(b) that all types of fraud must be pleaded with "particularity." Before the PSLRA, the most stringent *pleading standard* in securities-act fraud cases under the requirement of Rule 9(b) was a standard established by the Second Circuit. This standard required the plaintiff to state with particularity facts that gave rise to a "strong inference" of the requisite intent, that is, of scienter. Under the Second Circuit *test* for applying that standard, the plaintiff could establish the required strong inference by detailed factual allegations that showed either direct evidence of scienter (conscious misbehavior or recklessness), circumstantial evidence of scienter, or that the defendant had the *motive and opportunity* to commit fraud.

To satisfy the motive element of the second branch of this test, it was not enough for a plaintiff to merely allege that the defendant had a motive of a kind possessed by virtually all corporate insiders, such as the desire to sustain the appearance of corporate profitability. Rather, the plaintiff had to allege that the defendant benefited in some concrete and personal way from his purported fraud. This requirement was normally satisfied when a corporate insider was alleged to have publicly misrepresented material facts about the corporation's performance or prospects to keep the stock price artificially high while he sold his own shares at a profit. Congress in 1995 greatly enhanced the role of a pleading requirement for securities fraud suits by making one of the cornerstones of the Private Securities Litigation Reform Act ("PSLRA") a heightened pleading standard.

With the PSLRA Congress adopted the Second Circuit's "strong inference" standard, but the legislative reports accompanying the legislation made clear that Congress was not necessarily adopting the motive-and-opportunity test the Second Circuit had employed. Securities Exchange Act § 21D(b)(2) provides that a plaintiff who alleges securities fraud must "state with particularity *facts giving rise to a strong inference* that the defendant acted with the required state of mind"—that is, scienter.

There are two issues concerning the meaning of this requirement. The first issue is what this standard entails—and in particular, whether a plaintiff can satisfy this standard solely by detailed factual allegations that the defendant had the motive and opportunity to commit fraud, as previously held by the Second Circuit, whose pleading standard the PSLRA had adopted. The second issue is whether the PSLRA was intended to change the rule that recklessness suffices to establish scienter. Unfortunately, the only Supreme Court decision interpreting the PSLRA's pleading requirement, Tellabs, Inc. v. Makor Issues &

Rights, Ltd., 551 U.S. 308, 127 S.Ct. 2499, 168 L.Ed.2d 179 (2007), sheds little light on either of these questions:

> We establish the following prescriptions: *First*, faced with a *Rule 12(b)(6)* motion to dismiss a *§ 10(b)* action, courts must, as with any motion to dismiss for failure to plead a claim on which relief can be granted, accept all factual allegations in the complaint as true....
>
> *Second*, courts must consider the complaint in its entirety, as well as other sources courts ordinarily examine when ruling on *Rule 12(b)(6)* motions to dismiss, in particular, documents incorporated into the complaint by reference, and matters of which a court may take judicial notice. See 5B Wright & Miller § 1357 (3d ed. 2004 and Supp. 2007). The inquiry, as several Courts of Appeals have recognized, is whether *all* of the facts alleged, taken collectively, give rise to a strong inference of scienter, not whether any individual allegation, scrutinized in isolation, meets that standard....
>
> *Third*, in determining whether the pleaded facts give rise to a "strong" inference of scienter, the court must take into account plausible opposing inferences. The Seventh Circuit expressly declined to engage in such a comparative inquiry. A complaint could survive, that court said, as long as it "alleges facts from which, if true, a reasonable person could infer that the defendant acted with the required intent"; in other words, only "[i]f a reasonable person could not draw such an inference from the alleged facts" would the defendant prevail on a motion to dismiss. *437 F.3d at 602*. But in *§ 21D(b)(2)*, Congress did not merely require plaintiffs to "provide a factual basis for [their] scienter allegations,".... Instead, Congress required plaintiffs to plead with particularity facts that give rise to a "strong"—*i.e.*, a powerful or cogent—inference. See American Heritage Dictionary 1717 (4th ed. 2000) (defining "strong" as "[p]ersuasive, effective, and cogent"); 16 Oxford English Dictionary 949 (2d ed. 1989) (defining "strong" as "[p]owerful to demonstrate or convince" (definition 16b)); cf. 7 *id.*, at 924 (defining "inference" as "a conclusion [drawn] from known or assumed facts or statements"; "reasoning from something known or assumed to something else which follows from it").
>
> The strength of an inference cannot be decided in a vacuum. The inquiry is inherently comparative: How likely is it that one conclusion, as compared to others, follows from the underlying facts? To determine whether the plaintiff has alleged facts that give rise to the requisite "strong inference" of scienter, a court must consider plausible, nonculpable explanations for the defendant's conduct, as well as inferences favoring the plaintiff. The inference that the defendant acted with scienter need not be irrefutable, *i.e.*, of the "smoking-gun" genre, or even the "most plausible of competing inferences," *Fidel, 392 F.3d at 227* (quoting *Helwig v. Vencor, Inc., 251 F.3d 540, 553 (CA6 2001)* (en banc)). Recall in

> this regard that *§ 21D(b)*'s pleading requirements are but one constraint among many the PSLRA installed to screen out frivolous suits, while allowing meritorious actions to move forward.... Yet the inference of scienter must be more than merely "reasonable" or "permissible"—it must be cogent and compelling, thus strong in light of other explanations. A complaint will survive, we hold, only if a reasonable person would deem the inference of scienter cogent and at least as compelling as any opposing inference one could draw from the facts alleged.

551 U.S. at 322–323, 127 S.Ct. at 2509–10, 168 L.Ed.2d 192–194.

A number of circuits have addressed the pleading issue. Three different views have been adopted.

Under one view, the PSLRA effectively adopted the Second Circuit's pleading standard and test wholesale. Accordingly, plaintiffs can state a claim by pleading either direct or strong circumstantial evidence of recklessness or conscious misbehavior, or motive and opportunity. Press v. Chemical Investment Services Corp., 166 F.3d 529 (2d Cir. 1999); In re Advanta Corp. Securities Litigation, 180 F.3d 525 (3d Cir. 1999). *Tellabs* recognized that motive was a relevant consideration, but its absence would not necessarily be fatal. 551 U.S. at 326.

Under a second view, motive and opportunity may be relevant when combined with other facts, but as a matter of law they are never alone sufficient. Janas v. McCracken (In re Silicon Graphics Inc. Sec. Litig.), 183 F.3d 970, 977–79 (9th Cir. 1999); Bryant v. Avado Brands, Inc., 187 F.3d 1271, 1285–86 (11th Cir. 1999).

Finally, some Circuits explicitly refuse to decide whether motive and opportunity are or can be alone sufficient as a matter of law. Depending on the facts of the case, such pleadings might or might not be sufficient. For example, Ottmann v. Hanger Orthopedic Group, Inc., 353 F.3d 338 (4th Cir. 2003), adopted a "flexible, case-specific analysis" because "Congress ultimately chose not to specify particular types of facts that would or would not show a strong inference of scienter." The flexible view, under which motive and opportunity are not alone either sufficient or insufficient in all cases, has been taken by most Circuits. Even the Second Circuit now takes the view that "Congress's failure to include language about motive and opportunity suggests that we need not be wedded to these concepts in articulating the prevailing standard." Novak v. Kasaks, 216 F.3d 300 (2d Cir. 2000). The position of the cases taking the flexible view has been summarized as follows in *Ottman v. Hanger Orthopedic Group, Inc.*:

> [Many courts have adopted] a case-specific approach that examines the particular allegations in their entirety to determine whether they provide the requisite strong inference, "without regard to whether those allegations fall into defined, formalistic categories such as 'motive and opportunity.'" ... Still, these circuits generally agree that specific facts showing a motive and opportunity to commit fraud (or the absence of such facts) may

be relevant in determining whether a plaintiff's complaint demonstrates a strong inference of scienter. . . .

. . . [A] flexible, case-specific analysis is appropriate in examining scienter pleadings. . . . We therefore conclude that courts should not restrict their scienter inquiry by focusing on specific categories of facts, such as those relating to motive and opportunity, but instead should examine all of the allegations in each case to determine whether they collectively establish a strong inference of scienter. And, while particular facts demonstrating a motive and opportunity to commit fraud (or lack of such facts) may be relevant to the scienter inquiry, the weight accorded to those facts should depend on the circumstances of each case.

5. *Recklessness after the PSLRA.* A number of Circuits have concluded that the PSLRA did not alter the substantive definition of scienter. These courts opted to retain their pre–PSLRA definitions of recklessness. However, at one time the Ninth Circuit concluded that the PSLRA increased the substantive requirements of scienter, and strengthened its definition of scienter from "recklessness" to "deliberate recklessness," In re Silicon Graphics Inc. Securities Litigation, 183 F.3d 970 (9th Cir. 1999). After *Tellabs*, the Ninth Circuit has suggested it could be less demanding than per *Silicon Graphics* in the pleading of recklessness. South Ferry LP #2 v. Killinger, 542 F.3d 776 (9th Cir. 2008).

NOTE ON SCIENTER AND THE FORWARD LOOKING STATEMENT

A universal quality about the future is that it is hard to predict accurately. When a company estimates that it will earn $3 in the next year and ultimately earns materially less, was its earlier statement materially misleading? What would render the statement actionable under rule 10b–5? Are there risks that the determination of fault will be made via hindsight so that earlier assumptions in formulating the forecast will be viewed differently by the trier of fact? For example, what if the earlier prediction assumed that materials and labor costs would not rise, but in retrospect that assumption appears grossly optimistic? *See e.g.* Financial Indus. Fund v. McDonnell Corp., 474 F.2d 514 (10th Cir.), *cert. denied*, 414 U.S. 874, 94 S.Ct. 155, 38 L.Ed.2d 114 (1973).

1. *Forward–Looking Statements.* After the PSLRA, the securities acts provide special "safe harbors" for most "forward-looking statements"—that is, statements about the future (for example, predictions of earnings). Section 21E(i) of the Securities Exchange Act defines a forward-looking statement to mean:

(A) a statement containing a projection of revenues, income (including income loss), earnings (including earnings loss) per share, capital expenditures, dividends, capital structure, or other financial items;

(B) a statement of the plans and objectives of management for future operations, including plans or objectives relating to the products or services of the issuer;

(C) a statement of future economic performance, including any such statement contained in a discussion and analysis of financial condition by the management or in the results of operations included pursuant to the rules and regulations of the Commission;

(D) any statement of the assumptions underlying or relating to any statement described in subparagraph (A), (B), or (C);

(E) any report issued by an outside reviewer retained by an issuer, to the extent that the report assesses a forward-looking statement made by the issuer; or

(F) a statement containing a projection or estimate of such other items as may be specified by rule or regulation of the Commission.

Section 21E(c)(1) provides two safe harbors against civil liability for written forward-looking statements, as defined, that are made (1) by a corporation that either has a security registered under section 12 of the Act or has filed a registration statement as described in section 15(d), or (2) by certain persons acting on behalf of such a corporation. Under the first safe harbor, there is no liability if the statement is identified as a forward-looking statement and is accompanied by "meaningful cautionary" statements identifying important factors that could cause actual results to differ materially from those in the statement. Under the second safe harbor, there is no liability if the plaintiff fails to prove that the statement was made with actual knowledge—not simply with recklessness—that the statement was false or misleading. Accordingly, Section 21E eliminates recklessness as sufficient scienter under Rule 10b–5 for forward-looking statements, although it does not affect omissions or statements that purport to concern historical or existing facts or forward-looking statements expressly excluded from the section 21E safe harbor. Section 21E(c)(2) provides a special additional safe harbor applicable only to oral statements. (Comparable provisions are found in the Securities Act of 1933).

2. *"Bespeaks Caution."* Under a doctrine known as "bespeaks caution," a forward-looking statement does not give rise to liability, even though, if taken in isolation, it is misleading, if the document in which the statement is contained includes meaningful cautionary language. The applicability of the bespeaks-caution doctrine is highly fact-specific. To some extent, it is also court-specific; different circuits have been either more or less ready to conclude that cautionary language was sufficient to protect against liability. It is fairly clear, however, that a generic, boiler-plate warning will not suffice. To have the desired effect, the cautionary language must be "tailored the specific future projections, estimates or opinions . . . which the plaintiffs challenge." Trump Casino Securities Litigation, 7 F.3d 357 (3d Cir.

1993), cert. denied sub nom. Gollomp v. Trump, 510 U.S. 1178, 114 S.Ct. 1219, 127 L.Ed.2d 565 (1994). By its terms, the bespeaks-caution doctrine, like the safe-harbor provisions in the Section 21E, is directed only to forward-looking statements, not to statements of present or historical facts. See EP MedSystems, Inc. v. EchoCath, Inc., 235 F.3d 865 (3d Cir. 2000). The doctrine is of special relevance when a forward-looking statement is made by a corporation or other person who is not within the safe harbor provided by Securities Exchange Act section 21E because the statement was made in the context of one of the many exceptions in section 21E—for example, a corporation that does not have a class of stock registered under section 12, the statement was made in connection with an initial public offering or the statement was made in connection with a tender offer.

SECTION 4. DUTY TO SPEAK

Most private actions under Rule 10b–5 are brought against persons who commit affirmative *misstatements*. Classic misstatement examples include announcing a figure for earnings that is greater than the company actually earned or falsely predicting that the company will achieve a certain level of earnings in the future. Violations can also arise, albeit as we will see in limited instances, by the failure to disclose a material fact. Such violations are generally referred to either an omission or duty to disclose cases.

By way of background, consider the three models that government regulation of disclosure might take. First, as we've seen, the Securities Exchange Act imposes on certain companies a duty of *periodic disclosure* in the form of annual (Form 10–K) and quarterly (Form 10–Q) reporting requirements. Second, disclosure can be mandated for discrete transactions or activities. Such *transactional disclosure* occurs today for the public offerings of securities, the election of directors, or other matters involving the approval of shareholders of public companies. Finally, there is the somewhat utopian world of *continuous disclosure* where companies must disclose material information as soon as the material information arises; this form of disclosure is pretty much limited in the U.S. to the rather tightly configured mandates of Form 8–K for public companies. There is limited evidence of continuous disclosure. To be sure, in the post-Enron era of financial frauds Form 8–K was greatly expanded. However, Form 8–K still compels disclosure upon the occurrence of specified events (the entering into or discontinuance of a material transaction outside the ordinary course of operations, the resignation of the firm's outside auditor, or the departure of a director) of a reporting company. In addition, stock exchanges listing requirements set forth certain duties to disclose important developments and events, although typically the only sanction for noncompliance with those rules would be delisting, and that sanction has seldom or never been imposed for mere nondisclosure.

Also, absent a specific SEC disclosure requirement that needs to be met, such as in the pending Form 10–K, there generally is a good deal of discretion on the part of the company's management. As a leading case on this point emphasized, "the timing of the disclosure [of material facts] is a matter for the business judgment of the corporate officers entrusted with the management of the corporation within the affirmative disclosure requirements promulgated by the exchanges and by the SEC." SEC v. Texas Gulf Sulphur Co., 401 F.2d 833, 850 n. 12 (in banc), *cert. denied*, 394 U.S. 976, 89 S.Ct. 1454, 22 L.Ed.2d 756 (1969). This is still the rule. See, e.g., Staffin v. Greenberg, 672 F.2d 1196, 1204 (3d Cir.1982). There are, however, several exceptions to this rule.

1. If the corporation makes a statement that is misleading—inaccurate—when made, even though not intentionally or recklessly so, and the corporation later learns that the statement was misleading, it is under a duty to *correct* the statement if the statement is still "alive," rather than "stale"—that is, if the statement would still be likely to be material to investors. See, e.g., Backman v. Polaroid Corp., 910 F.2d 10 (1st Cir.1990) (en banc). In re Burlington Coaf Factory Sec. Litig., 114 F.3d 1410, 1431 (3rd Cir. 1997) explains the duty as follows:

> [T]he duty to correct can also apply to a certain narrow set of forward-looking statements. We will attempt to illustrate the kinds of circumstances we have in mind with an example. Imagine the following situation. A public company in Manhattan makes a forecast that appears to it to be reasonable at the time made. Subsequently, the company discovers that it misread a vital piece of data that went into its forecast. Perhaps a fax sent by the company's factory manager in some remote location was blurry and was reasonably misread by management in Manhattan as representing sales for the past quarter as 100,000 units as opposed to 10,000 units. Manhattan management then makes an erroneous forecast based on the information it has at the time. A few weeks later, management receives the correct sales figures by mail. So long as the correction in the sales figures was material to the forecast that was discussed earlier, we think there would likely be a duty on the part of the company to disclose either the corrected figures or a corrected forecast. In other words, there is an implicit representation in any forecast (or statement of historical fact) that errors of the type we have identified will be corrected. This duty derives from the implicit factual representation that a public company makes whenever it makes a forecast, i.e., that the forecast was reasonable at the time made. What is crucial to recognize is that the error, albeit an honest one, was one that had to do with information available at the time the forecast was made and that the error in the information was subsequently discovered. . . .

2. A corporation may so involve itself in the preparation of statements about the corporation by outsiders—such as analysts' re-

ports or earnings projections—that it assumes a duty to correct material errors in those statements. Such a duty "may occur when officials of the company have, by their activity, made an implied representation that the information they have reviewed is true or at least in accordance with the company's views." Elkind v. Liggett & Myers, Inc., 635 F.2d 156, 163 (2d Cir.1980).

3. A corporation may be under a duty to correct erroneous rumors resulting from leaks by the corporation or its agents. See, e.g., State Teachers Retirement Board v. Fluor Corp., 654 F.2d 843, 850 (2d Cir.1981) (dictum).

4. A common ground for alleging fraud occurred by non disclosure is the instance of the half truth. Recall that Rule 10b–5(b) includes among its prohibitions an omission "to state a material fact necessary in order to make the statements made, in the light of the circumstances under which they were made, not misleading." Thus, a duty to disclose can flow from what has been said, if what is not said is necessary to be disclose to prevent a materially false statement from otherwise having been committed. *See* Donald C. Langevoort, Half–Truths: Protecting Mistaken Inferences by Investors and Others, 52 Stan. L. Rev. 87 (1999).

5. A more difficult question is whether a corporation has a duty to *update* an earlier forward-looking statement that was correct—or more accurately, reasonable—when made but later comes to be materially misleading. Several courts have held that if a corporation makes a public statement that is correct when made, but that becomes materially misleading in light of subsequent events, the corporation may have a duty to update the statement. For example, in Greenfield v. Heublein, Inc., 742 F.2d 751, 758 (3d Cir.1984), cert. denied 469 U.S. 1215, 105 S.Ct. 1189, 84 L.Ed.2d 336 (1985), the court said, "[a]lthough a corporation may be under no duty to disclose ..., if a corporation voluntarily makes a public statement that is correct when issued, [the corporation] has a duty to update the statement if it becomes materially misleading in light of subsequent events." See also In re Time Warner Inc. Securities Litigation, 9 F.3d 259, 267 (2d Cir.1993), cert. denied 511 U.S. 1017, 114 S.Ct. 1397, 128 L.Ed.2d 70 (1994) ("a duty to update opinions and projections may arise if the original opinions or projections have become misleading as the result of intervening events").

Gallagher v. Abbott Laboratories

Court of Appeals for the Seventh Circuit, 2001.
269 F.3d 806.

■ EASTERBROOK, *CIRCUIT JUDGE.* Year after year the Food and Drug Administration inspected the Diagnostic Division of Abbott Laboratories, found deficiencies in manufacturing quality control, and issued warnings. The Division made efforts to do better, never to the FDA's satisfaction, but until 1999 the FDA was willing to accept Abbott's promises and remedial steps. On March 17, 1999, the FDA sent Abbott another letter demanding compliance with all regulatory requirements and threatening severe consequences. This could have been read as more saber rattling—Bloomberg News revealed the letter to the financial world in June, and Abbott's stock price did not even quiver—but later developments show that it was more ominous. By September 1999 the FDA was insisting on substantial penalties plus changes in Abbott's methods of doing business. On September 29, 1999, after the markets had closed, Abbott issued a press release describing the FDA's position, asserting that Abbott was in "substantial" compliance with federal regulations, and revealing that the parties were engaged in settlement talks. Abbott's stock fell more than 6%, from $40 to $37.50, the next business day. On November 2, 1999, Abbott and the FDA resolved their differences, and a court entered a consent decree requiring Abbott to remove 125 diagnostic products from the market until it had improved its quality control and to pay a $100 million civil fine. Abbott took an accounting charge of $168 million to cover the fine and worthless inventory. The next business day Abbott's stock slumped $3.50, which together with the earlier drop implied that shareholders saw the episode as costing Abbott (in cash plus future compliance costs and lost sales) more than $5 billion....

Plaintiffs in these class actions under § 10(b) of the Securities Exchange Act of 1934, ... and the SEC's *Rule 10b-5*, ... contend that Abbott committed fraud by deferring public revelation. The classes comprise all buyers of Abbott's securities between March 17 and November 2.... The district judge dismissed the complaints ... for failure to state a claim on which relief may be granted. *140 F. Supp. 2d 894 (N.D. Ill. 2001)*. The market's non-reaction to Bloomberg's disclosure shows, the judge thought, that the FDA's letter was not by itself material or that the market price had earlier reflected the news, cf. *In re Apple Computer Securities Litigation, 886 F.2d 1109 (9th Cir. 1989)*; *Flamm v. Eberstadt, 814 F.2d 1169, 1179-80 (7th Cir. 1987)*; only later developments contained material information, which Abbott disclosed in September and November. Moreover, the judge concluded, plaintiffs had not identified any false or fraudulent statement by Abbott, as opposed to silence in the face of bad news. We are skeptical that these shortcomings justify dismissal for failure to state a claim on which relief may be granted; the judge's reasons seem more akin to an invocation of *Fed. R. Civ. P. 9(b)*, which requires fraud to be pleaded with particularity, or the extra pleading requirements for securities cases created by the Private Securities Litigation Reform Act of 1995 .../... But it is not necessary to decide whether ... the news was "material" before the FDA's negotiating position stiffened, to decide whether Abbott acted with the state of mind necessary to support liability under *Rule 10b-5*, or to address other potential stumbling blocks. What sinks plaintiffs' position is their inability to identify any false statement—or for that matter any truthful statement made misleading by the omission of news about the FDA's demands.

Much of plaintiffs' argument reads as if firms have an absolute duty to disclose all information material to stock prices as soon as news comes into their possession. Yet that is not the way the securities laws work. We do not have a system of continuous disclosure. Instead firms are entitled to keep silent (about good news as well as bad news) unless positive law creates a duty to disclose. See, e.g., *Basic, Inc. v. Levinson, 485 U.S. 224, 239 n.17, . . . (1988)*; *Dirks v. SEC, 463 U.S. 646 . . . (1983)*; *Chiarella v. United States, 445 U.S. 222 . . . (1980)*; *Stransky v. Cummins Engine Co., 51 F.3d 1329, 1331 (7th Cir. 1995)*; *Backman v. Polaroid Corp., 910 F.2d 10, 16 (1st Cir. 1990)* (en banc). Until the Securities Act of 1933 there was no federal regulation of corporate disclosure. The 1933 Act requires firms to reveal information only when they issue securities, and the duty is owed only to persons who buy from the issuer or an underwriter distributing on its behalf . . . Section 13 of the Securities Exchange Act of 1934, *15 U.S.C. § 78m*, adds that the SEC may require issuers to file annual and other periodic reports—with the emphasis on *periodic* rather than continuous. Section 13 and the implementing regulations contemplate that these reports will be snapshots of the corporation's status on or near the filing date, with updates due not when something "material" happens, but on the next prescribed filing date.

Regulations implementing § 13 require a comprehensive annual filing, the Form 10–K report, and less extensive quarterly supplements on Form 10–Q. The supplements need not bring up to date everything contained in the annual 10–K report; counsel for the plaintiff classes conceded at oral argument that nothing in Regulation S–K (the SEC's list of required disclosures) requires either an updating of Form 10–K reports more often than annually, or a disclosure in a quarterly Form 10–Q report of information about the firm's regulatory problems. The regulations that provide for disclosures on Form 10–Q tell us *which* items in the annual report must be updated (a subset of the full list), and how often (quarterly).

Many proposals have been made to do things differently—to junk this combination of sale-based disclosure with periodic follow-up and replace it with a system under which *issuers* rather than *securities* are registered and disclosure must be continuous. E.g., American Law Institute, *Federal Securities Code* xxvii–xxviii, § 602 & commentary (1978); Securities and Exchange Commission, *Report of the Advisory Committee on the Capital Formation and Regulatory Process* 9–14, 36–38 (1996). . . .

The ALI's proposal, for example, was embraced by the SEC, see 1933 Act Release No. 6242 (Sept. 18, 1980); 1933 Act Release No. 6242 (Jan. 31, 1982), but never seriously pursued, and revisions of Regulation S–K satisfied many of the original supporters of the ali's proposal. The advisory committee report, prepared by a distinguished group of scholars and practitioners under the leadership of Commissioner Steven M.H. Wallman, did not persuade the SEC's other members and was not taken up by the agency as a legislative plan or even as the basis of a demonstration project. Whatever may be said for and against these proposals, they must be understood as projects for legislation (and to a limited extent for the use of the SEC's rulemaking powers); judges have no authority to scoop the political branches and adopt continuous disclosure under the banner of *Rule 10b–5*. *Especially* not under that banner, for *Rule 10b–5* condemns only fraud, and a corporation does not commit fraud by standing on its rights under a periodic-disclosure system. The Supreme Court has insisted that this judicially created right of action be used only to implement, and not to alter, the rules found in the text of the 1933 and 1934 Acts. See *Central Bank of Denver, N.A. v. First Interstate Bank of Denver, N.A., 511 U.S. 164, 173 ... (1994)* ("We have refused to allow [private] 10b–5 challenges to conduct not prohibited by the text of the statute.") . . .

Trying to locate some statement that was either false or materially misleading because it did not mention the FDA's position, plaintiffs pointed in the district court to several reports filed or statements made by Abbott before November 2, 1999. All but two of these have fallen by the wayside on appeal. What remain are Abbott's Form 10–K annual report for 1998 filed in March 1999 and an oral statement that Miles White, Abbott's CEO, made at the annual shareholders' meeting the next month.

Plaintiffs rely principally on Item 303(a)(3)(ii) of [SEC] Regulation S–K, which provides that registration statements and annual 10–K reports must reveal

> any known trends or uncertainties that have had or that the registrant reasonably expects will have a material favorable or unfavorable impact on net sales or revenues or income from continuing operations.

The FDA's letter, and its negotiating demands, are within this description, according to the plaintiff classes. We shall assume that this is so. The 10–K report did state that Abbott is "subject to comprehensive government regulation" and that "government regulatory actions can result in . . . sanctions." Plaintiffs say that this is too general in light of the FDA's letter and Abbott's continuing inability to satisfy the FDA's demands. Again we shall assume that plaintiffs are right. But there is a fundamental problem: The 10–K report was filed on March 9, 1999, and the FDA's letter is dated March 17, eight days later. Unless Abbott had a time machine, it could not have described on March 9 a letter that had yet to be written.

Attempting to surmount this temporal problem, plaintiffs insist that Abbott had a "duty to correct" the 10–K report. Yet a statement may be "corrected" only if it was incorrect when made, and nothing said as of March 9 was incorrect. In order to maintain the difference between periodic-disclosure and continuous-disclosure systems, it is essential to draw a sharp line between duties to correct and duties to update. . . . If, for example, the 10–K report had said that Abbott's net income for 1998 was $500 million, and the actual income was $400 million, Abbott would have had to fix the error. But if the 10–K report had projected a net income of $125 million for the first quarter of 1999, and accountants determined in May that the actual profit was only $100 million, there would have been nothing to correct; a projection is not rendered false when the world turns out otherwise.

See *Wielgos v. Commonwealth Edison Co., 892 F.2d 509 (7th Cir. 1989)*. Amending the 10–K report to show the results for 1999 as they came in—or to supply a running narrative of the dispute between Abbott and the FDA—would *update* the report, not *correct* it to show Abbott's actual condition as of March 9.

Updating documents has its place in securities law. A registration statement and prospectus for a new issue of securities must be accurate when it is used to sell stock, and not just when it is filed.... Material changes in a company's position thus must be reflected in a registration statement promptly. But this does not imply changes in a 10–K annual report....

As for White's statements at the annual meeting: he said very little that was concrete (as opposed to puffery), and everything concrete was true. White said, for example:

> The outcome [of our efforts] has been growth more than five times faster than the diagnostics market. We expect this trend to continue for the foreseeable future, due to the unprecedented state of our new product cycle. By supplementing our internal investment with opportunistic technology acquisitions, Abbott's diagnostics pipeline is fuller than ever before.

The statement about past performance was accurate, and the plaintiffs have not given us any reason to doubt that White honestly believed that similar growth would continue, or that White honestly believed "Abbott's diagnostics pipeline [to be] fuller than ever before." Even with the benefit of hindsight these statements cannot be gainsaid. Here is where *Rule 9(b)* pinches: Plaintiffs have done nothing to meet the requirements for pleading fraud with respect to the annual meeting, even if it were possible (which we doubt) to treat as "fraud" the predictive components in White's boosterism....

Affirmed

SECTION 5. PRIMARY PARTICIPANTS AFTER *CENTRAL BANK*

Section 10(b) and Rule 10b–5 each expressly proscribe misconduct of "any person." At one time this meant extending liability reached both primary participants as well as those who aided and abetted their misbehavior. *See e.g.*, Roberts v. Peat, Marwick, Mitchell & Co., 857 F.2d 646 (9th Cir. 1988). Indeed, all circuits recognized that aiding and abetting was within the reach of section 10(b) and Rule 10b–5. That world changed, and changed dramatically, for private suits with Central Bank of Denver v. First Interstate Bank of Denver, 511 U.S. 164, 114 S.Ct. 1439, 128 L.Ed.2d 119 (1994).

In rejecting aiding and abetting liability under the antifraud provision, the *Central Bank* majority was not persuaded by the "directly or indirectly" language of Section 10(b). The Court reasoned this would extend liability to those whose conduct itself is not proscribed by the antifraud provision. Moreover, the Court pointed out that the "directly or indirectly" language is used in many other provisions, such as Section 16(a) of the Exchange Act, which clearly do not contemplate aiding and abetting liability. The Court drew further strength for its position by emphasizing that none of the express liability provisions of the Securities Act or the Exchange Act proscribe aiders and abettors. It thus inferred from Congress' refusal to proscribe aiding and abetting in the express liability provisions the likely intent not to proscribe aiding and abetting in an implied cause of action.

> It is inconsistent with settled methodology in § 10(b) cases to extend liability beyond the scope of conduct prohibited by the statutory text. . . .
>
> As in earlier cases considering conduct prohibited by § 10(b), we again conclude that the statute prohibits only the making of a material misstatement (or omission) or the commission of a manipulative act. *See Santa Fe Industries,* 430 U.S. at 473 ("language of § 10(b) gives no indication that Congress meant to prohibit any conduct not involving manipulation or deception"). . . . The proscription does not include giving aid to a person who commits a manipulative or deceptive act. We cannot amend the statute to create liability for acts that are not themselves manipulative or deceptive within the meaning of the statute. . . .
>
> Our reasoning is confirmed by the fact that respondents' argument would impose 10b–5 aiding and abetting liability when at least one element critical for recovery under 10b–5 is absent: reliance. A plaintiff must show reliance on the defendant's misstatement or omission to recover under 10b–5. *Basic Inc. v. Levinson,* supra, at 243. Were we to allow the aiding and abetting action proposed in this case, the defendant could be liable without any showing that the plaintiff relied upon the aider and abettor's statements or actions. . . . Allowing plaintiffs to circumvent the reliance requirement would disregard the careful limits on 10b–5 recovery mandated by our earlier cases. . . .
>
> Because the text of § 10(b) does not prohibit aiding and abetting, we hold that a private plaintiff may not maintain an aiding and abetting suit under § 10(b). The absence of § 10(b) aiding and abetting liability does not mean that secondary actors in the securities markets are always free from liability under the securities acts. Any person or entity, including a lawyer, accountant, or bank, who employs a manipulative device or makes a material misstatement (or omission) on which a purchaser or seller of securities relies may be liable as a primary violator under 10b–5, assuming all of the requirements for primary liability under Rule 10b–5 are met. *See* Fischel, 69 Cal. L. Rev., at 107–108. In any complex securities fraud, moreover, there are likely to be multiple

violators; in this case, for example, respondents named four defendants as primary violators....

511 U.S. at 177–181, 114 S.Ct. at 1448–51, 128 L.Ed.2d at 132–135.

Attempts to repackage aiding and abetting liability by invoking Rule 10b–5's reference to "any ... scheme" has was also rejected by the Supreme Court. See Stoneridge Investment Partners, LLC, Petitioner v. Scientific–Atlanta, Inc., 552 U.S. 148, 128 S.Ct. 761, 169 L.Ed.2d 627 (2008) (vendors who cooperate with their customer to create fictitious purchases for the purpose of inflating the customer's revenues are too remote from the customer's false financial statements so that their misdeeds—which included false invoices and other documents intended to prevent the customer's auditor from learning of their chicanery—cannot be said to have been relied upon by investors when the purchased the customer's stock at prices inflated by the false financial reports).

Pacific Investment Management Co. LLC v. Mayer Brown LLP

United States Court of Appeals, Second Circuit, 2010.
603 F.3d 144.

■ JOSE A. CABRANES, *CIRCUIT JUDGE*: ...

This case arises from the 2005 collapse of Refco, which was once one of the world's largest providers of brokerage and clearing services in the international derivatives, currency, and futures markets. According to plaintiffs, Mayer Brown served as Refco's primary outside counsel from 1994 until the company's collapse. Collins, a partner at Mayer Brown, was the firm's primary contact with Refco and the billing partner in charge of the Refco account. Refco was a lucrative client for Mayer Brown and Collins' largest personal client.

As part of its business model, Refco extended credit to its customers so that they could trade on "margin"—*i.e.*, trade in securities with money borrowed from Refco. In the late 1990s, Refco customers suffered massive trading losses and consequently were unable to repay hundreds of millions of dollars of margin loans extended by Refco. Concerned that properly accounting for these debts as "write-offs" would threaten the company's survival, Refco, allegedly with the help of defendants, arranged a series of sham transactions designed to conceal the losses.

Specifically, plaintiffs allege that Refco transferred its uncollectible debts to Refco Group Holdings, Inc. ("RGHI")—an entity controlled by Refco's Chief Executive Officer—in exchange for a receivable purportedly owed from RGHI to Refco. Recognizing that a large debt owed to it by a related entity would arouse suspicion with investors and regulators, Refco, allegedly with the help of defendants, engaged in a series of sham loan transactions at the end of each quarter and each fiscal year to pay off the RGHI receivable. It did so by loaning money to third parties, who then loaned the same amount to RGHI, which in turn used the funds to pay off Refco's receivable. Days after the fiscal period closed, all of the loans were repaid and the third parties were paid a fee for their participation in the scheme. The result of these circular transactions was that, at the end of financial periods, Refco reported receivables owed to it by various third parties rather than the related entity RGHI.

Mayer Brown and Collins participated in seventeen of these sham loan transactions between 2000 and 2005, representing both Refco and RGHI. According to plaintiffs, defendants' involvement included negotiating the terms of the loans, drafting and revising the documents relating to the loans, transmitting the documents to the participants, and retaining custody of and distributing the executed copies of the documents.

Plaintiffs also allege that defendants are responsible for false statements appearing in three Refco documents: (1) an Offering Memorandum for an unregistered bond offering in July 2004 ("Offering Memorandum"), (2) a Registration Statement for a subsequent registered bond offering ("Registration Statement"), and (3) a Registration Statement for Refco's initial public offering of common stock in August 2005 ("IPO Registration Statement"). Each of these documents contained false or misleading statements because they failed to disclose the true nature of Refco's financial condition, which had been concealed, in part, through the loan transactions described above.

Defendants allegedly participated in the creation of the false statements contained in each of the documents identified above. Collins and other Mayer Brown attorneys allegedly reviewed and revised portions of the Offering Memorandum and attended drafting sessions. Collins and another Mayer Brown attorney also personally drafted the Management Discussion & Analysis ("MD & A") portion of the Offering Memorandum, which, according to plaintiffs, discussed Refco's business and financial condition in a way that defendants knew to be false. The Offering Memorandum was used as the foundation for the Registration Statement, which was substantially similar in content. According to plaintiffs, defendants further assisted in the preparation of the Registration Statement by reviewing comment letters from the Securities and Exchange Commission ("SEC") and participating in drafting sessions. Finally, plaintiffs allege that defendants were directly involved in reviewing and drafting the IPO Registration Statement because they received, and presumably reviewed, the SEC's comments on that filing.

Both the Offering Memorandum and the IPO Registration Statement note that Mayer Brown represented Refco in connection with those transactions. The Registration Statement does not mention Mayer Brown. None of the documents specifically attribute any of the information contained therein to Mayer Brown or Collins.

Plaintiffs, who purchased securities from Refco during the period that defendants were allegedly engaging in fraud, commenced this action after Refco declared bankruptcy in 2005. They asserted claims for violation of *§ 10(b)* of the Exchange Act and *Rule 10b–5*. . . .

The District Court dismissed plaintiffs' claims against Mayer Brown and Collins.... With respect to plaintiffs' claim that defendants violated *Rule 10b–5(b)* by drafting and revising portions of Refco's public documents, the Court found that no statements in those documents were attributed to defendants and that plaintiffs had therefore alleged conduct akin to aiding and abetting, for which securities laws provide no private right of action. The District Court also dismissed plaintiffs' *Rule 10b–5(a)* and *(c)* claims for "scheme liability" upon concluding that the Supreme Court's decision in *Stoneridge* foreclosed that theory of liability....

DISCUSSION ...

I. Plaintiffs' *Rule 10b–5(b)* Claim ...

Analyzing the parties' claims requires a brief history of the attribution requirement in our Circuit. Although we have often held that attribution is required for secondary actors to incur liability, we have for certain other defendants imposed no attribution requirement. *Compare Wright v. Ernst & Young LLP, 152 F.3d 169, 174–75 (2d Cir. 1998)* (requiring attribution for outside accountant defendants), and *Lattanzio v. Deloitte & Touche LLP, 476 F.3d 147, 155 (2d Cir. 2007)* (same), *with In re Scholastic Corp. Sec. Litig., 252 F.3d 63, 75–76 (2d Cir. 2001)* (not requiring attribution for corporate insider defendant). Upon reviewing this history and the guidance provided by the Supreme Court, we conclude that attribution is required for secondary actors to be liable in a private damages action for securities fraud under *Rule 10b–5*.

A. History of the Attribution Requirement

The distinction between primary liability under *Rule 10b–5* and aiding and abetting became especially important after the Supreme Court's 1994 decision in *Central Bank of Denver, N.A. v. First Interstate Bank of Denver, N.A., 511 U.S. 164, 114 S. Ct. 1439, 128 L. Ed. 2d 119 (1994)*.... After reviewing the text and history of *§ 10(b)*, the Supreme Court concluded that "the 1934 [Exchange Act] does not itself reach those who aid and abet a § 10(b) violation." *Id. at 177*. To hold otherwise, it explained, would be to "impose ... liability when at least one element critical for recovery under *10b–5* is absent: reliance." *Id. at 180*.

Despite holding that *Rule 10b–5* liability does not extend to aiders and abettors, the Supreme Court acknowledged that "secondary actors" could, in some circumstances, still be liable for fraudulent conduct. *Id. at 191*. Specifically, the Court explained that

> [a]ny person or entity, including a lawyer, accountant, or bank, who employs a manipulative device or makes a material misstatement (or omission) on which a purchaser or seller of securities relies may be liable as a primary violator under 10b–5, assuming *all* of the requirements for primary liability under *Rule 10b–5* are met. In any complex securities fraud, moreover, there are likely to be multiple violators....

Id. (citation omitted). . . .

The principle that *Central Bank* requires the attribution of false statements to the defendant at the time of dissemination first appeared in our 1998 decision in *Wright v. Ernst & Young LLP, 152 F.3d at 175. Wright* involved claims against the accounting firm Ernst & Young and allegations that the firm orally approved a corporation's false and misleading financial statements, which were subsequently disseminated to the public. *Id. at 171.*

We explained that, after *Central Bank*, courts had generally adopted either a "bright line" test or a "substantial participation" test to distinguish between primary violations of *Rule 10b–5* and aiding and abetting:

> "Some courts have held that a third party's review and approval of documents containing fraudulent statements is not actionable under *Section 10(b)* because one must make the material misstatement or omission in order to be a primary violator. *See, e.g., In re Kendall Square Research Corporation Securities Litigation, 868 F. Supp. 26, 28 (D. Mass. 1994)* (accountant's 'review and approval' of financial statements and prospectuses insufficient); *Vosgerichian v. Commodore International, 862 F. Supp. 1371, 1378 (E.D. Pa. 1994)* (allegations that accountant 'advised' and 'guid[ed]' client in making allegedly fraudulent misrepresentations insufficient).
>
> Other courts have held that third parties may be primarily liable for statements made by others in which the defendant had significant participation. *See, e.g., In re Software Toolworks, 50 F.3d 615, 628 n.3 (9th Cir. 1994)* (accountant may be primarily liable based on its 'significant role in drafting and editing' a letter sent by the issuer to the SEC); *In re ZZZZ Best Securities Litigation, 864 F. Supp. 960, 970 (C.D. Cal. 1994)* (an accounting firm that was 'intricately involved' in the creation of false documents and their 'resulting deception' is a primary violator of *section 10(b)*)."

Id. at 174–75 (quoting *MTC Elec., 898 F. Supp. at 986*) (alterations omitted). . . . [in Wright] [w]e . . . held that "a secondary actor cannot incur primary liability under [*Rule 10b–5*] for a statement not attributed to that actor at the time of its dissemination." *Id. Wright* also made clear that attribution is necessary to satisfy the reliance element of a private damages action under *Rule 10b–5. Id.* ("Reliance only on representations made by others cannot itself form the basis of liability." (alteration and internal quotation marks omitted)). Because the misrepresentations on which plaintiffs' claims were based were not attributed to Ernst & Young, we held that the complaint failed to state a claim under *Rule 10b–5. Id.*

Despite *Wright's* seemingly clear requirement that false statements be attributed to the defendant, our subsequent decisions may have created uncertainty or ambiguity with respect to when attribution is required. In 2001, in *In re Scholastic Corp. Securities Litigation*, we held that a corporate officer could be liable for misrepresentations made by the corporation, notwithstanding the fact that none of the statements at issue were specifically attributed to him. *252 F.3d at 75–76*. We explained that as "vice president for finance and investor relations" the defendant "was primarily responsible for Scholastic's communications with investors and industry analysts. He was involved in the drafting, producing, reviewing and/or disseminating of the false and misleading statements issued by Scholastic during the class period." *Id.* On that basis, we allowed plaintiffs' claims against the defendant to proceed. Our opinion in *Scholastic* did not rely on, or even cite, *Wright* or *Central Bank* and contained no discussion of the distinction between primary violations of *Rule 10b–5* and aiding and abetting.

Since *Scholastic*, district courts in our Circuit have struggled to reconcile its holding with our earlier holding in *Wright*. . . .

B. Creator Standard v. Attribution Standard

Plaintiffs and the SEC urge us to adopt a "creator" standard that would require us to hold that a defendant can be liable for *creating* a false statement that investors rely on, regardless of whether that statement is attributed to the defendant at the time of dissemination. They argue that their proposed standard is consistent with the law of the Circuit. They distinguish *Wright* and *Lattanzio* on the ground that the defendants in those cases were not alleged to have created the false statements in question, but rather, merely reviewed false statements created by others. Plaintiffs and the SEC contend that, notwithstanding the broad language that suggests attribution is always required, these cases are best read as holding that a defendant can be liable if he or she creates a false or misleading statement *or* allows a false statement to be attributed to him or her. . . .

[W]e reject the creator standard for secondary actor liability under *Rule 10b–5*. An attribution requirement is more consistent with the Supreme Court's guidance on the question of secondary actor liability. Furthermore, a creator standard is indistinguishable from the "substantial participation" test that we have disavowed since *Wright*, and it is incompatible with our stated preference for a "bright line" rule. *See Wright, 152 F.3d at 175*.

Accordingly, secondary actors can be liable in a private action under *Rule 10b–5* for only those statements that are explicitly attributed to them. The mere identification of a secondary actor as being involved in a transaction, or the public's understanding that a secondary actor "is at work behind the scenes" are alone insufficient. *See Lattanzio, 476 F.3d at 155*. To be cognizable, a plaintiff's claim against a secondary actor must be based on that actor's own "articulated statement," or on statements made by another that have been *explicitly* adopted by the secondary actor. *See id.*

1. Attribution Is Consistent with *Stoneridge*

The Supreme Court has never directly addressed whether attribution at the time of dissemination is required for secondary actors to be liable in a private damages action brought pursuant to *Rule 10b–5*. Nevertheless, the Court's recent decision in *Stoneridge* is instructive. . . .

Stoneridge stands for the proposition that reliance is the critical element in private actions under *Rule 10b–5*. This general proposition, applied to the specific issue of secondary actor liability, further supports an attribution requirement. Attribution is necessary to show reliance. Where statements are publicly attributed to a well-known national law or accounting firm, buyers and sellers of securities (and the market generally) are more likely to credit the accuracy of those statements. Because of the firm's imprimatur, individuals may be comforted by the supposedly impartial assessment and, accordingly, be induced to purchase a particular security. Without explicit attribution to the firm, however, reliance on that firm's participation can only be shown through "an indirect chain ... too remote for liability." *Stoneridge, 552 U.S. at 159*.

2. Attribution Is Consistent with Our "Bright Line" Approach . . .

An attribution requirement makes clear—to secondary actors and investors alike—that those who sign or otherwise allow a statement to be attributed to them expose themselves to liability. Those who do not are beyond the reach of *Rule 10b–5*'s private right of action. A creator standard establishes no clear boundary between primary violators and aiders and abettors, and it is uncertain what level of involvement might expose an individual to liability. . . .

A bright line rule such as an attribution requirement also has many benefits in application. An attribution requirement is relatively easy for district courts to apply and avoids protracted litigation and discovery aimed at learning the identity of each person or entity that had some connection, however tenuous, to the creation of an allegedly false statement. Furthermore, as the Supreme Court has explained, securities law is "an area that demands certainty and predictability." *Central Bank, 511 U.S. at 188* (quoting *Pinter v. Dahl, 486 U.S. 622, 652, 108 S. Ct. 2063, 100 L. Ed. 2d 658 (1988))*. Uncertainty can lead to many undesirable consequences, "[f]or example, newer and smaller companies may find it difficult to obtain advice from professionals. A professional may fear that a newer or smaller company may not survive and that business failure would generate securities litigation against the professional, among others." *Id. at 189*. Uncertainty also increases the costs of doing business and raising capital. *See* Ralph K. Winter, *Paying Lawyers, Empowering Prosecutors, and Protecting Managers: Raising the Cost of Capital in America, 42 Duke L.J. 945, 962 (1993)* (describing "the need to avoid overbroad and amorphous doctrine and to craft legal rules with *bright lines* as a means of reducing the cost of capital" and explaining that "[o]verbreadth and uncertainty deter beneficial conduct and breed costly litigation" (emphasis added)), *cited with approval in Central Bank, 511 U.S. at 189*; *see also Central Bank, 511 U.S. at 188* ("[A] shifting and highly fact-oriented disposition of the issue of who may be liable for a damages claim for violation of *Rule 10b–5* is not a satisfactory basis for a rule of liability imposed on the conduct of business transactions." (internal quotation marks and brackets omitted)). A creator standard would inevitably lead to uncertainty regarding the scope of *Rule 10b–5* liability and potentially deter beneficial conduct. *See* Winter, *ante*, at 963 ("[O]verdeterrence in regulating capital markets ... will deter activity that we wish to encourage.")....

Accordingly, we reject the creator standard advanced by plaintiffs and the SEC and we reaffirm our jurisprudence in *Wright* and *Lattanzio*—namely, that "a secondary actor cannot incur primary liability under [*Rule 10b–5*] for a statement not attributed to that actor at the time of its dissemination." *Wright, 152 F.3d at 175*; *see Lattanzio, 476 F.3d at 154* ("Under *Central Bank*, [a secondary actor] is not liable for merely assisting in the drafting and filing of [allegedly false statements]."').[1]

C. Application of the Attribution Requirement

Applying the attribution standard to the alleged false and misleading statements in this case, we conclude that the District Court properly dismissed plaintiffs' *Rule 10b–5(b)* claims against Mayer Brown and Collins. No statements in the Offering Memorandum, the Registration Statement, or the IPO Registration Statement are attributed to Collins, and he is not even mentioned by name in any of those documents. Accordingly, plaintiffs cannot show reliance on any of Collins' statements....

The Offering Memorandum and the IPO Registration Statement note that Mayer Brown, among other counsel, represented Refco in connection with those transactions but neither document attributes any particular statements to Mayer Brown. Mayer Brown is not identified as the author of any portion of the documents. Nor can the mere mention of the firm's representation of Refco be considered an "articulated statement" by Mayer Brown adopting Refco's statements as its own.... Absent such attribution, plaintiffs cannot show reliance on any statements of Mayer Brown....

---

1. Because this appeal does not involve claims against corporate insiders, we intimate no view on whether attribution is required for such claims or whether *Scholastic* can be meaningfully distinguished from *Wright* and *Lattanzio*. There may be a justifiable basis for holding that investors rely on the role corporate executives play in issuing public statements even in the absence of explicit attribution. *Lattanzio* confirmed, however, that, at least with respect to secondary actor liability, *Scholastic* did not relax *Wright's* attribution requirement. *See Lattanzio, 476 F.3d at 155* ("Public understanding that an accountant is at work behind the scenes does not create an exception to the requirement that an actionable misstatement be made by the accountant. Unless the public's understanding is based on the accountant's *articulated statement*, the source for that understanding ... does not matter." (footnote omitted) (emphasis added)).

II. Plaintiffs' *Rule 10b–5(a)* and *(c)* Claims ("Scheme Liability")

. . .

Like the defendants in *Stoneridge*, Mayer Brown and Collins are alleged to have facilitated sham transactions that enabled Refco to conceal the true state of its financial condition from investors. As in *Stoneridge*, plaintiffs were not aware of those transactions and, in fact, plaintiffs explicitly disclaim any knowledge of defendants' involvement. . . .

Plaintiffs attempt to distinguish *Stoneridge* by arguing that (1) defendants' deceptive conduct was communicated to the public; (2) defendants' conduct made it "necessary or inevitable" that Refco would misstate its finances, *see Stoneridge, 552 U.S. at 161*; and (3) defendants' conduct occurred in the "investment sphere," *see id. at 166* (noting that the deceptive transactions "took place in the marketplace for goods and services, not in the investment sphere"). None of these purported distinctions is persuasive. . . .

Under *Stoneridge*, it does not matter that those transactions were "reflected" in Refco's financial statements. *552 U.S. at 160*. The Supreme Court explicitly rejected the argument that "investors rely not only upon the public statements relating to a security but also upon the transactions those statements reflect." *Id.* (noting that "there is no authority for this rule"). Accordingly, the fact that the sham transactions (or "scheme") allegedly facilitated by Mayer Brown and Collins rendered Refco's public financial disclosures false or misleading does not materially distinguish this case from *Stoneridge*.

. . . What is clear from *Stoneridge*, however, is that the mere fact that the ultimate result of a secondary actor's deceptive course of conduct is communicated to the public through a company's financial statements is insufficient to show reliance on the secondary actor's *own* deceptive conduct. Because that is all plaintiffs have alleged here, we are bound by the Supreme Court's holding in *Stoneridge*.

Furthermore, nothing about Mayer Brown's or Collins' actions made it necessary or inevitable that Refco would mislead investors. As the District Court aptly noted, unlike in *Stoneridge*, "the Mayer Brown Defendants were not even the counter-party to the fraudulent transactions; they merely participated in drafting the documents to effect those transactions." *In re Refco, 609 F. Supp. 2d at 316*. We therefore agree that, "[a]s was the case in *Stoneridge*, it was Refco, not the Mayer Brown Defendants, that filed fraudulent financial statements; nothing the Mayer Brown Defendants did made it necessary or inevitable for Refco to record the transactions as it did." *Id.* (quoting *Stoneridge, 552 U.S. at 160*) (internal quotation marks, brackets, and ellipsis omitted). . . .

For the foregoing reasons, we agree with the District Court that plaintiffs' *Rule 10b–5(a)* and *(c)* claims for "scheme liability" are foreclosed by the Supreme Court's decision in *Stoneridge*. . . .

CONCLUSION . . .

[T]he judgment of the District Court is **AFFIRMED**. . . .

■ BARRINGTON D. PARKER, *CIRCUIT JUDGE*, concurring. . . .

In light of the importance of the existence, *vel non*, of an attribution requirement to the securities laws, the bar, and the securities industry, this case could provide our full Court, as well as, perhaps, the Supreme Court, with an opportunity to clarify the law in this area.

* * *

1. Substantial Participant Approach. Not all courts follow the bright-line approach illustrated in *Pacific Investment Management.* Under the competing substantial participant approach, some circuits impose liability on individuals who draft, edit and review financial reports and other documents that ultimately reach investors or impact securities markets, even though the defendant is not identified as the document's author. *See e.g.,* In re Software Toolworks, Inc., 50 F.3d 615, 629 (9th Cir. 1994) (underwriters and accountants who draft and review reports they know are false are primary participants); Anixter v. Home–Stake Production Co., 77 F.3d 1215 (10th Cir. 1996) (accountant who prepares financial reports with knowledge they are false and will be circulated to investors is primary participant). Is the substantial participant approach consistent with the tenets of *Central Bank*? Are there social benefits associated with expanding private liability to reach the conduct of those who are substantial and knowing participants in the release of false financial information, even though their identity is not known to investors who are defrauded?

2. Aiding and Abetting and the SEC. Today the section 20(e) to the Securities Exchange Act authorizes SEC enforcement actions against any person who "knowingly or recklessly provides substantial assistance to another person in violation of a provision" of the act.

3. Vicarious Liability. Corporations act only through individuals. Consider the curious route of entity responsibility presented by the next case.

Pugh v. Tribune Company

United States Court of Appeals for the Seventh Circuit, 2008.
521 F.3d 686.

■ EVANS, *CIRCUIT JUDGE.* In this consolidated appeal, we review . . . fraud that occurred at a New York subsidiary of defendant Tribune Company [Tribune]. Certain employees at the subsidiary falsely boosted the circulation figures of two newspapers, *Newsday* and the Spanish-language *Hoy*, increasing the amount that they were able to charge advertisers and, in turn, inflating revenues. Tribune, along with an independent auditor, ultimately discovered and publicly disclosed the fraud, which resulted in a $90 million charge against earnings. Our first case is a securities class action brought by purchasers of Tribune common stock against Tribune, four of its executive officers, and five employees of *Newsday* and *Hoy*. . . .

Tribune is a media and entertainment company engaging in newspaper publishing (*e.g.*, the *Chicago Tribune*, the *Los Angeles Times*), television and radio broadcasting (*e.g.*, Superstation WGN), and other entertainment ventures (*e.g.*, the Chicago Cubs—at least for the time being). Tribune's publishing segment purportedly generates more than 70 percent of its total revenues, which exceeded $5 billion annually during the years immediately prior to these lawsuits. At that time, *Newsday* operated as a New York subsidiary of Tribune, and *Hoy* was a division of *Newsday*. These are just 2 of the at least 11 daily newspapers that fall under Tribune's umbrella. The Audit Bureau of Circulations (ABC), an independent nonprofit monitoring organization, conducts annual audits of each newspaper's paid circulation figures. The results of its audits are used to determine how much advertisers pay for their ads to appear in a newspaper.

At least as early as 2001, *Newsday* and *Hoy* overstated their circulation figures. Schemes such as phony hawking programs, false affidavits that understated returns and overstated net sales, and directions to subordinates to pay distributors for bogus deliveries of newspapers were employed. In addition, many copies of the two papers were merely dumped, or delivered to people who had not paid for them. The overstated circulation numbers resulted in *Newsday* and *Hoy* charging higher advertising rates than would have been charged otherwise. The true circulation of *Newsday* and *Hoy* was roughly 80 percent and 50 percent, respectively, of what was reported.

Starting in February 2004, advertisers filed lawsuits alleging that *Newsday* and *Hoy* had overstated circulation. On February 11, 2004, Tribune issued a press release stating that Raymond Jansen (*Newsday*'s publisher from 1994 to 2004 and a named defendant in our securities case) had issued a statement that the lawsuit filed the previous day against *Newsday* and *Hoy* was "completely without merit," the allegations contained in it were "false," and the source of the allegations was no more than "a disgruntled former employee." Notwithstanding *Newsday*'s denial, Tribune, together with ABC, started its own internal investigation of the paid circulation figures. Shortly after the advertisers' lawsuit was filed, the SEC, the U.S. Attorney's Office for the Eastern District of New York, the U.S. Attorney's Office for the District of Connecticut, and the Connecticut Attorney General's Office began investigations.[2] . . .

2. Criminal charges were later brought against several *Newsday* and *Hoy* employees. A May 30, 2006, press release from the U.S. Attorney's Office for the Eastern District of New York reported guilty pleas by nine former *Newsday* and *Hoy* employees, including four of the five *Newsday* and *Hoy* employees named as defendants in our securities case (Brennan, Czark, Garcia, and Sito). U.S. Department of Justice, Nine Former Employees and Contractors of Newsday and Hoy Plead Guilty to Scheme to Defraud Newspaper Advertisers. . . . The press release also said that the SEC settled its enforcement action against Tribune the same day. A December 18, 2007, press release reported that *Newsday* and *Hoy* agreed to forfeit $15 million to the United States pursuant to an agreement that resolves its criminal investigation. U.S. Department of Justice, Newsday and Hoy Agree to Resolve Criminal Inquiry into Scheme to Defraud Newspaper Advertisers. . . .

[In June and July of 2004, Tribune's investigation revealed that the circulation figures for *Newsday* and *Hoy* had in fact been inflated for 2001, 2002 and 2003. The inflated *Newsday* and *Hoy* figures were consolidated with the figures reported by Tribune's other subsidiaries in reporting the consolidated earnings of Tribune for 2001, 2002 and 2003. Once it discovered the fraudulent reporting by Sito and others at *Newsday* and *Hoy*, the Tribune recorded a $35 million charge against earnings for its 2004 second quarter relate to the anticipated cost of settling various advertiser suits. A quarter later this sum was raised to $60 million. Various class actions ensued and were consolidated.]

Pursuant to the Private Securities Litigation Reform Act of 1995 (PSLRA), the court appointed a lead plaintiff and lead counsel in the securities case.... The proposed plaintiff class consists of people who purchased Tribune common stock between January 24, 2002, and September 10, 2004....

In a typical § 10(b) private action, a plaintiff must prove (1) a material misrepresentation or omission by the defendant; (2) scienter; (3) a connection between the misrepresentation or omission and the purchase or sale of a security; (4) reliance upon the misrepresentation or omission; (5) economic loss; and (6) loss causation....

[T]he plaintiffs focus on Sito [who during the class action interval was *Newsday's* vice-president for circulation, then *Hoy's* president, publisher and chief executive until his retirement in July 2004]. They emphasize that he ... be found liable because he participated in (and was the "mastermind" of) the scheme to defraud the advertisers. Their theory seems to be that it was "foreseeable" that this scheme would result in improper revenue which, in turn, would be reflected in Tribune's published financial statements. Although absent from the complaint, the plaintiffs now point to Sito's guilty plea—wherein he reportedly admitted to directing *Newsday* and *Hoy* employees to falsely inflate paid circulation data—to prove his state of mind. However, even assuming the guilty plea establishes a strong inference of scienter, the plaintiffs' allegations of so-called "scheme liability" are insufficient under the Supreme Court's recent decision in *Stoneridge Inv. Partners, LLC v. Scientific–Atlanta, Inc., 128 S. Ct. 761 (2008)*.

In *Stoneridge*, the plaintiffs alleged that business partners of Charter Communications, Inc. violated *§ 10(b)* by engaging in sham transactions with Charter, knowing or recklessly disregarding Charter's intention to report the inflated revenue from those transactions in its public financial statements. While the business partners deliberately engaged in the underlying fraud reflected in Charter's published revenue figures, they had no role in preparing or disseminating Charter's financial statements containing those figures, and the public had no knowledge of their deceptive acts during the relevant times. The plaintiffs argued, however, that the public disclosure of the false statements "was a natural and expected consequence of [the business partners'] deceptive acts" and therefore sufficient to impose "scheme liability." *Stoneridge, 128 S. Ct. at 770*....

Like the defendants in *Stoneridge*, Sito participated in a fraudulent scheme but had no role in preparing or disseminating Tribune's financial statements or press releases. Furthermore, as we stated earlier, there is no allegation that Tribune investors were ever informed of Sito's false certifications to ABC. Sito may have foreseen (or even intended) that the advertising scheme would result in improper revenue for *Newsday* and *Hoy*, which would eventually be reflected in Tribune's revenues and finally published in its financial statements. But *Stoneridge* indicates that an indirect chain to the contents of false public statements is too remote to establish primary liability. Without allegations establishing the requisite proximate relation between the *Newsday* and *Hoy* advertiser fraud and the Tribune investors' harm, we cannot uphold the complaint. Thus, the plaintiffs do not satisfy the pleading requirements as to any of the *Newsday–Hoy* individual defendants.

The plaintiffs finally allege primary liability on the part of Tribune itself. A corporation may be held liable for statements by employees who have apparent authority to make them. *See, e.g., Am. Soc'y. of Mech. Eng'rs v. Hydrolevel Corp., 456 U.S. 556, 568, 102 S. Ct. 1935, 72 L. Ed. 2d 330 (1982)*. Accordingly, the corporate scienter inquiry must focus on "the state of mind of the individual corporate official or officials who make or issue the statement (or order or approve it or its making or issuance, or who furnish information or language for inclusion therein, or the like) rather than generally to the collective knowledge of all the corporation's officers and employees acquired in the course of their employment." *Makor II, 513 F.3d at 708* (internal citation omitted).... [Because the court in a part of the opinion not presented here concluded the plaintiff had failed to allege facts establishing a strong inference of scienter on the part of any of the Tribune executives, as distinct from the executives of *Newsday* or *Hoy*, the] Tribune's scienter cannot be based on ... [the] state of mind [of executives other than Sito]. Instead, the plaintiffs argue that Sito's scienter can be imputed to Tribune under the principles of *respondeat superior*.

Even if we assume *arguendo* that the plaintiffs had established Sito's primary liability, there are still two major problems with this argument. First, it is based on the incorrect premise that Sito was a "senior-level" officer of Tribune. The plaintiffs contend that Sito was assigned (among others) the title of "Vice President for Hispanic media at Tribune," but Tribune's SEC filings show that Sito was not an executive officer of Tribune. More importantly, the only fraudulent conduct described in the complaint was not undertaken in his Tribune capacity; the allegations state that (1) Sito was "Publisher" of *Hoy* and (2) "Publishers are required to certify their paid circulation figures to ABC every six months." This is damaging to the plaintiffs because misconduct of employees at a corporate subsidiary is not normally attributed to its corporate parent, absent grounds for piercing the corporate veil. *See, e.g., United States v. Bestfoods, 524 U.S. 51, 63–64, (1998)*; *IDS Life Ins. Co. v. SunAmerica Life Ins. Co., 136 F.3d 537, 540 (7th Cir. 1998)*.

Second, and relatedly, the allegations do not show that Sito knowingly overstated circulation figures intending to benefit Tribune. Rather, the complaint demonstrates that the objective of Sito and the other perpetrators in falsely boosting the circulation figures of the two newspapers was to increase the amount that they were able to charge advertisers of *Newsday* and *Hoy*. After this came to light, Tribune was exposed to significant damage claims by its advertisers and regulators. Indeed, Sito and the other perpetrators allegedly took pains to conceal the scheme from Tribune, and the *Newsday* and *Hoy* employees running the scheme are alleged to have bilked the newspapers to pay off the vendors and hawkers with whom they colluded. Sito may have known that, as a result of the scheme, Tribune would misrepresent its assets to investors, but this is not enough; "deliberate wrongs by an employee are not imputed to his employer unless they are not only within the scope of his employment but in attempted furtherance of the employer's goals." *Makor II, 513 F.3d at 708.*

In sum, the plaintiffs fail to establish the primary liability of any individual defendant, and the alleged misconduct is not imputable to Tribune by the doctrine of *respondeat superior*. Accordingly, the plaintiffs' *§ 10(b)* and *Rule 10b–5* claim was correctly dismissed in its entirety. . . .

Accordingly, the judgment of the district court . . . is AFFIRMED.

SECTION 6. CAUSAL RELATIONSHIP

In principle, it is well-established that causation and reliance are required elements of a private action under Rule 10b–5. In practice, however, those requirements have sometimes proved to be elusive or even illusory.

1. *Transaction vs. Loss Causation.* In the area of causation, the case-law under Rule 10b–5 has distinguished between "transaction causation" and "loss causation."

Transaction causation means that there must be a causal connection between the defendant's violation of Rule 10b–5 and the plaintiff's decision to purchase or sell a security. To satisfy this requirement, a violation of Rule 10b–5 must have caused the plaintiff to engage in the transaction in question. Schlick v. Penn–Dixie Cement Corp., 507 F.2d 374 (2d Cir. 1974). Accordingly, the plaintiff must allege and show that but for the fraudulent statement or omission, she would not have entered into the transaction. Transaction causation has been analogized to reliance. See Currie v. Cayman Resources Corp., 835 F.2d 780, 785 (11th Cir.1988).

The meaning of *loss causation* is harder to pin down. The best interpretation of this concept is that the defendant's wrongful act not only must have caused the plaintiff to buy or sell a security (transaction causation); it must also have been the cause of the plaintiff's economic *loss* on the security. In contrast to transaction causation, loss causation requires a showing that the violation of Rule 10b–5 caused the economic harm of which the plaintiff complains. While transaction causation is generally understood as the investor's reliance on the misrepresentation, loss causation has often been described as proximate cause, meaning in part that the damages suffered by plaintiff must be a foreseeable consequence of any misrepresentation or material omission. An alternative formulation of loss causation is that it requires that "the misrepresentation touches upon the reasons for the investment's decline in value." Binder v. Gillespie, 184 F.3d 1059 (9th Cir. 1999). As stated in Suez Equity v. Toronto–Dominion Bank, 250 F.3d 87 (2d Cir. 2001), "[t]he loss causation inquiry typically examines how directly the subject of the [violation] caused the loss, and whether the resulting loss was a foreseeable outcome of the [violation]," while also taking into account issues such as the presence of intervening causes and the lapse of time between the behavior complained of and the loss.

Essentially, "loss causation" is a fancy name for the concept that even if an investment is induced by a violation of Rule 10b–5, the investor's loss may have been the result of an investment risk that was independent of the violation. "[W]hen an investor makes any investment he or she assumes certain investment risks. It may be too harsh a rule under Rule 10b–5 that would place the wrongdoer in the position of insurer against those market risks. Otherwise, for example, a seller who fraudulently induced a purchase of securities in early October, 1987 would be an insurer against the precipitous price decline caused in large part by the market crash on October 19." 4 T. Hazen, *Securities Regulation 173* (6th ed. 2009). For example, assume the company's false claims of its new product induced the plaintiff to purchase the firm's shares at $25 per share. Soon after that purchase, it is discovered that a product that accounts for seventy percent of the company's revenues is found to infringe on another company's patents. This causes the company's shares to fall to $15. In Caremark, Inc. v. Coram Healthcare Corp., 113 F.3d 645 (7th Cir. 1997), the court said "To plead transaction causation, the plaintiff must allege that it would not have invested in the instrument if the defendant had stated truthfully the material facts at the time of the sale. To plead loss causation, the plaintiff must allege that [it] was the very facts about which the plaintiff lied which caused its injuries." In the preceding hypothetical, we can likely conclude that transaction causation is present, but can we also conclude that the defendant's lie that induced the plaintiff to purchase caused to incur a $10 loss?

The meaning of the loss-causation concept, and the difficulty that can arise in applying the concept, are exemplified by a pair of cases, Huddleston v. Herman & MacLean, 640 F.2d 534, 549 n. 25 (5th Cir.1981), *aff'd in part, rev'd in part on other grounds* 459 U.S. 375, 103 S.Ct. 683, 74 L.Ed.2d 548 (1983), and *In re* Washington Public Power Supply System, 650 F.Supp. 1346, 1354 (W.D.Wash.1986). In *Huddleston*, the Fifth Circuit court used the following example to explain loss causation:

> [Assume that a vessel is described in a prospectus as having] a certain capacity when in fact it had less capacity than was represented in the prospectus. However, the prospectus does disclose truthfully that the vessel will not be insured. One week after the investment the vessel sinks as a result of a casualty and the stock becomes worthless. In such circumstances, a fact-finder might conclude that the misrepresentation was material and relied upon by the investor but that it did not cause the loss.

In *Washington Public Power*, the court criticized this example:

> By misrepresenting the capacity of the ship, the investor was induced to pay a certain price for stock in the venture. As a result of the misrepresentation, the investor paid more for the stock than it was worth. When the ship sank, the entire investment was lost. The investor, however, was injured by more than the true value of the investment because he paid an inflated price for the stock. His damages thus consist of two components: the value lost due to the casualty and the amount lost because he overpaid for the stock. This latter component of damages is related directly to the initial misrepresentation. Hence, this amount should be recoverable in an action for securities fraud.

The requirement of causation arises only in private suits under Rule 10b–5; it does not apply to actions by the SEC. Accordingly, the SEC can bring an action for injunctive or other appropriate relief based on a misrepresentation that violates Rule 10b–5 even if no investors have relied upon the statement—because, for example, trading in the relevant stock was suspended immediately after the statement was made. SEC v. Rana Research, Inc., 8 F.3d 1358 (1993).

Proving transaction causation in a pure omission case is problematic. We can say that *A* acted—bought or sold at a given price—in reliance on what *B* told him, but we can seldom say that *A* acted in reliance on *B*'s silence. What we *can* say in the latter case is that a reasonable investor who knew the omitted fact probably would or would not have bought or sold at the given price. In TSC Industries v. Northway, Inc., the Supreme Court held that the standard of *materiality* in a nondisclosure case is satisfied by "a showing of a substantial likelihood that, under all the circumstances, the omitted fact would have assumed actual significance in the deliberations of the reasonable shareholder." 426 U.S. 438, 449, 96 S.Ct. 2126, 2132, 48 L.Ed.2d 757 (1976). At first glance, this standard is so close to what must be shown to prove causation in a nondisclosure case that for all intents and purposes, causation in such a case collapses into materiality. In its formulation of materiality *TSC* also observes that the showing of significance "does not require proof of a substantial likelihood that disclosure of the omitted fact would have caused the reasonable investor to change his vote" or decision to purchase. Thus, an inquiry into transaction causation that is premised only on a finding of materiality could in many instances find such causation even in instances in which the investor would not have altered the decision to purchase (or to sell) if there all the facts were honestly presented.

Consider how well the Supreme Court dealt with these questions in the next case.

Affiliate Ute Citizens v. United States

Supreme Court of the United States, 1972.
406 U.S. 128, 92 S.Ct. 1456, 31 L.Ed.2d 741.

■ MR. JUSTICE BLACKMUN delivered the opinion of the Court. . . .

[Pursuant to the Ute Partition Act, Ute Distribution Corporation (UDC) was created to facilitate the federal government's withdrawal from its supervision of various assets of mixed and full blood members of the Ute tribe and to make an equitable distribution of property claims between the two groups. The primary assets of the UDC were oil, gas and other mineral rights owned by members of the tribe. To carry out the partition, UDC issued 10 shares of capital stock to each mixed-blood Ute and the plan provided that First Security Bank of Utah would serve as transfer agent for the shares and would hold the shares for the members of the Ute tribe. Members wishing to dispose of their shares, therefore, were required to do so through the Bank. Defendants, Gale and Haslam, were employees of the Bank and at various times in 1963 and 1964 purchased 1,387 shares from mixed-bloods members without disclosing that non-tribal members were trading the shares at prices significantly higher than the defendants were offering the tribal members for their shares. Only 113 of these shares were acquired personally by Gale and Haslam and the other shares were acquired by non-tribal members, many of whom not only had standing orders with Gale and Haslam to purchase the shares but also had deposited funds with the Bank so their purchases could be swiftly executed once the Bank learned that a member wished to sell.

The District Court awarded damages based on its determination that the fair value of the shares was $1500, much above the member's selling price which ranged between $300 to $700. The Tenth Circuit reversed, partially; it upheld liability for the shares Gale and Haslam had acquired for themselves, but held that with respect to purchases by others that there was insufficient evidence of reliance by the selling members on any statement of conduct of the defendants.]

B. *Gale and Haslem* . . . .

[The proscriptions of Section 10(b) and Rule 10b–5] are broad and, by repeated use of the word "any," are obviously meant to be inclusive. The Court has said that the 1934 Act and its companion legislative enactments embrace a "fundamental purpose . . . to substitute a philosophy of full disclosure for the philosophy of *caveat emptor* and thus to achieve a high standard of business ethics in the securities industry." *SEC v. Capital Gains Research Bureau, 375 U.S. 180, 186 (1963)*. In the case just cited the Court noted that Congress intended securities legislation enacted for the purpose of avoiding frauds to be construed "not technically and restrictively, but flexibly to effectuate its remedial purposes." *Id., at 195* . . . .

In the light of the congressional philosophy and purpose, . . . we conclude that the Court of Appeals viewed too narrowly the activities of defendants Gale and Haslem. We would agree that if the two men and the employer bank had functioned merely as a transfer agent, there would have been no duty of disclosure here. But, as the Court of Appeals itself observed, the record shows that Gale and Haslem "were active in encouraging a market for the UDC stock among non-Indians." *431 F.2d, at 1345*. They did this by soliciting and accepting standing orders from non-Indians. They and the bank, as a result, received increased deposits because of the development of this market. The two men also received commissions and gratuities from the expectant non-Indian buyers. The men, and hence the bank, as the Court found, were "entirely familiar with the prevailing market for the shares at all material times." *431 F.2d, at 1347*. The bank itself had acknowledged, by letter to AUC in January 1958, that "it would be our duty to see that these transfers were properly made" and that, with respect to the sale of shares, "the bank would be acting for the individual stockholders." The mixed-blood sellers "considered these defendants to be familiar with the market for the shares of stock and relied upon them when they desired to sell their shares." *431 F.2d, at 1347*. . . .

We conclude . . . that the Court of Appeals erred when it held that there was no violation of the Rule unless the record disclosed evidence of reliance on material fact misrepresentations by Gale and Haslem. *431 F.2d, at 1348*. We do not read *Rule 10b–5* so restrictively. To be sure, the second subparagraph of the rule specifies the making of an untrue statement of a material fact and the omission to state a material fact. The first and third subparagraphs are not so restricted. These defendants' activities, outlined above, disclose, within the very language of one or the other of those subparagraphs, a "course of business" or a "device, scheme, or artifice" that operated as a fraud upon the Indian sellers. . . . This is so because the defendants devised a plan and induced the mixed-blood holders of UDC stock to dispose of their shares without disclosing to them material facts that reasonably could have been expected to influence their decisions to sell. The individual defendants, in a distinct sense, were market makers, not only for their personal purchases constituting 81/3% of the sales, but for the other sales their activities produced. This being so, they possessed the affirmative duty under the Rule to disclose this fact to the mixed-blood sellers. See *Chasins v. Smith, Barney & Co., 438 F.2d 1167 (CA2 1970)*. It is no answer to urge that, as to some of the petitioners, these defendants may have made no positive representation or recommendation. The defendants may not stand mute while they facilitate the mixed-bloods' sales to those seeking to profit in the non-Indian market the defendants had developed and encouraged and with which they were fully familiar. The sellers had the right to know that the defendants were in a position to gain financially from their sales and that their shares were selling for a higher price in that market. . . .

Under the circumstances of this case, involving primarily a failure to disclose, positive proof of reliance is not a prerequisite to recovery. All that is necessary is that the facts withheld be material in the sense that a reasonable investor might have considered them important in the making of this decision.... This obligation to disclose and this withholding of a material fact establish the requisite element of causation in fact....

Gale and Haslem engaged in more than ministerial functions. Their acts were clearly within the reach of *Rule 10b–5*. And they were acts performed when they were obligated to act on behalf of the mixed-blood sellers.

C. *The Bank*. The liability of the bank, of course, is coextensive with that of Gale and Haslem....

On its face, *Ute* seemed to eliminate any requirement of reliance in a case of nondisclosure. In general, however, the cases have held that *Ute* "merely established a presumption that made it possible for the plaintiffs to meet their burden." Shores v. Sklar, 647 F.2d 462, 468 (5th Cir.1981) (en banc), cert. denied 459 U.S. 1102, 103 S.Ct. 722, 74 L.Ed.2d 949 (1983). The defendant can rebut this presumption "by showing that the ... plaintiff would have followed the same course of conduct even with full and honest disclosure, [so that] the defendant's action (or lack thereof) cannot be said to have caused plaintiff's loss." Id. The defendant might carry this burden by showing, for example, that the plaintiff learned the omitted fact from an independent source before making his investment decision, so that the decision could not have been caused by the defendant's nondisclosure. Although the cases continue to use the language of "reliance" in the nondisclosure context, the real question is causation. When the question is properly framed in causation terms, once the plaintiff has shown that defendant omitted to disclose a material fact he was obliged to disclose, the burden is on the defendant to prove that the plaintiff would have made the same investment decision even if disclosure had been made.

(ii) *Misrepresentation*. Even though *Ute* diluted the requirement of reliance in the case of nondisclosure, the requirement of reliance remains meaningful in the vast majority of misstatement cases. For example, in a face-to-face case the defendant might be able to show that the plaintiff did not rely on a misstatement because he knew from other sources that the representation was false. Reliance can be established circumstantially. People who trade soon after material misstatement has been made to them will have almost always have relied on the misrepresentations. Accordingly, once the plaintiff shows that a material misrepresentation was made to him, and that he traded *soon* thereafter, as a practical matter reliance will normally be presumed, and the burden will shift to the defendant to show that the plaintiff did not rely on the misrepresentation. The strength of the reliance claim, however, is weakened as the time between the misstatement and the investor's trade lengthens. Thus, in some instances the misstatement case can be seen as similar to the nondisclosure case—

that is, as a practical matter, once the plaintiff makes a showing of materiality the burden shifts to the defendant to show that the plaintiff did not rely on the misrepresentation. But in other instances, the link between the material misstatement and the trade provides less circumstantial support for the latter being dependent on the former.

Basic Inc. v. Levinson

Supreme Court of the United States, 1988.
485 U.S. 224, 108 S.Ct. 978, 99 L.Ed.2d 194.

■ JUSTICE BLACKMUN delivered the opinion of the Court.

This case requires us to apply the materiality requirement of § 10(b) of the Securities Exchange Act of 1934 . . . Rule 10b–5 . . . in the context of preliminary corporate merger discussions. We must also determine whether a person who traded a corporation's shares on a securities exchange after the issuance of a materially misleading statement by the corporation may invoke a rebuttable presumption that, in trading, he relied on the integrity of the price set by the market.

I

Prior to December 20, 1978, Basic Incorporated was a publicly traded company primarily engaged in the business of manufacturing chemical refractories for the steel industry. As early as 1965 or 1966, Combustion Engineering, Inc., a company producing mostly alumina-based refractories, expressed some interest in acquiring Basic, but was deterred from pursuing this inclination seriously because of antitrust concerns it then entertained. See App. 81–83. In 1976, however, regulatory action opened the way to a renewal of Combustion's interest. . . .

Beginning in September 1976, Combustion representatives had meetings and telephone conversations with Basic officers and directors, including petitioners here, concerning the possibility of a merger. During 1977 and 1978, Basic made three public statements denying that it was engaged in merger negotiations.[4] On December 18,

---

4. On October 21, 1977, after heavy trading and a new high in Basic stock, the following news item appeared in the Cleveland Plain Dealer:

> "[Basic] President Max Muller said the company knew no reason for the stock's activity and that no negotiations were under way with any company for a merger. He said Flintkote recently denied Wall Street rumors that it would make a tender offer of $25 a share for control of the Cleveland-based maker of refractories for the steel industry." App. 363.

On September 25, 1978, in reply to an inquiry from the New York Stock Exchange, Basic issued a release concerning increased activity in its stock and stated that

> "management is unaware of any present or pending company development that would result in the abnormally heavy trading activity and price fluctuation in company shares that have been experienced in the past few days." *Id.*, at 401.

On November 6, 1978, Basic issued to its shareholders a "Nine Months Report 1978." This Report stated:

1978, Basic asked the New York Stock Exchange to suspend trading in its shares and issued a release stating that it had been "approached" by another company concerning a merger. *Id.,* at 413. On December 19, Basic's board endorsed Combustion's offer of $46 per share for its common stock, *id.,* at 335, 414–416, and on the following day publicly announced its approval of Combustion's tender offer for all outstanding shares.

Respondents are former Basic shareholders who sold their stock after Basic's first public statement of October 21, 1977, and before the suspension of trading in December 1978. Respondents brought a class action against Basic and its directors, asserting that the defendants issued three false or misleading public statements and thereby were in violation of § 10(b) of the 1934 Act and of Rule 10b–5. Respondents alleged that they were injured by selling Basic shares at artificially depressed prices in a market affected by petitioners' misleading statements and in reliance thereon.

The District Court adopted a presumption of reliance by members of the plaintiff class upon petitioners' public statements that enabled the court to conclude that common questions of fact or law predominated over particular questions pertaining to individual plaintiffs. See Fed.Rule Civ.Proc. 23(b)(3). The District Court therefore certified respondents' class. On the merits, however, the District Court granted summary judgment for the defendants. It held that, as a matter of law, any misstatements were immaterial: there were no negotiations ongoing at the time of the first statement, and although negotiations were taking place when the second and third statements were issued, those negotiations were not "destined, with reasonable certainty, to become a merger agreement in principle." App. to Pet. for Cert. 103a.

The United States Court of Appeals for the Sixth Circuit affirmed the class certification, but reversed the District Court's summary judgment, and remanded the case. 786 F.2d 741 (1986). The court reasoned that while petitioners were under no general duty to disclose their discussions with Combustion, any statement the company voluntarily released could not be " 'so incomplete as to mislead.' " *Id.,* at 746, quoting SEC v. Texas Gulf Sulphur Co., 401 F.2d 833, 862 (C.A.2 1968) (en banc), cert. denied *sub nom.* Coates v. SEC, 394 U.S. 976 (1969). In the Court of Appeals' view, Basic's statements that no negotiations were taking place, and that it knew of no corporate developments to account for the heavy trading activity, were misleading. With respect to materiality, the court rejected the argument that preliminary merger discussions are immaterial as a matter of law, and held that "once a statement is made denying the existence of any discussions, even discussions that might not have been material in absence of the denial are material because they make the statement made untrue." 786 F.2d, at 749.

"With regard to the stock market activity in the Company's shares we remain unaware of any present or pending developments which would account for the high volume of trading and price fluctuations in recent months." *Id.,* at 403.

The Court of Appeals joined a number of other circuits in accepting the "fraud-on-the-market theory" to create a rebuttable presumption that respondents relied on petitioners' material misrepresentations, noting that without the presumption it would be impractical to certify a class under Fed.Rule Civ.Proc. 23(b)(3). See 786 F.2d, at 750–751.

We granted certiorari, 479 U.S. 1083 (1987), to resolve the split, see Part III, *infra,* among the Courts of Appeals as to the standard of materiality applicable to preliminary merger discussions, and to determine whether the courts below properly applied a presumption of reliance in certifying the class, rather than requiring each class member to show direct reliance on Basic's statements.

II. . . .

. . . The Court . . . explicitly has defined a standard of materiality under the securities laws, see *TSC Industries, Inc. v. Northway, Inc.,* 426 U.S. 438 (1976), concluding in the proxy-solicitation context that "[a]n omitted fact is material if there is a substantial likelihood that a reasonable shareholder would consider it important in deciding how to vote." *Id.,* at 449.[7] Acknowledging that certain information concerning corporate developments could well be of "dubious significance," *id.,* at 448, the Court was careful not to set too low a standard of materiality; it was concerned that a minimal standard might bring an overabundance of information within its reach, and lead management "simply to bury the shareholders in an avalanche of trivial information—a result that is hardly conducive to informed decisionmaking." *Id.,* at 448–449. It further explained that to fulfill the materiality requirement "there must be a substantial likelihood that the disclosure of the omitted fact would have been viewed by the reasonable investor as having significantly altered the 'total mix' of information made available." *Id.,* at 449. We now expressly adopt the *TSC Industries* standard of materiality for the § 10(b) and Rule 10b–5 context.

III

The application of this materiality standard to preliminary merger discussions is not self-evident. Where the impact of the corporate development on the target's fortune is certain and clear, the *TSC Industries* materiality definition admits straightforward application. Where, on the other hand, the event is contingent or speculative in nature, it is difficult to ascertain whether the "reasonable investor" would have considered the omitted information significant at the time. Merger negotiations, because of the ever-present possibility that the contemplated transaction will not be effectuated, fall into the latter category. . . .

Petitioners urge upon us a Third Circuit test for resolving this difficulty. . . . Under this approach, preliminary merger discussions do not become material until "agreement-in-principle" as to the price and

7. *TSC Industries* arose under § 14(a), as amended, of the 1934 Act, 15 U.S.C. § 78n(a), and Rule 14a–9, 17 CFR § 240.14a–9 (1975).

structure of the transaction has been reached between the would-be merger partners. See *Greenfield v. Heublein, Inc.,* 742 F.2d 751, 757 (C.A.3 1984), cert. denied, 469 U.S. 1215 (1985). By definition, then, information concerning any negotiations not yet at the agreement-in-principle stage could be withheld or even misrepresented without a violation of Rule 10b–5.

[The Court rejected the "agreement in principle" test, concluding "We . . . find no valid justification for artificially excluding from the definition of materiality information concerning merger discussions, which would otherwise be considered significant to the trading decision of a reasonable investor, merely because agreement-in-principle as to price and structure has not yet been reached by the parties or their representatives."] . . .

Even before this Court's decision in *TSC Industries,* the Second Circuit had explained the role of the materiality requirement of Rule 10b–5, with respect to contingent or speculative information or events, in a manner that gave that term meaning that is independent of the other provisions of the Rule. Under such circumstances, materiality "will depend at any given time upon a balancing of both the indicated probability that the event will occur and the anticipated magnitude of the event in light of the totality of the company activity." *SEC v. Texas Gulf Sulphur Co.,* 401 F.2d, at 849. Interestingly, neither the Third Circuit decision adopting the agreement-in-principle test nor petitioners here take issue with this general standard. Rather, they suggest that with respect to preliminary merger discussions, there are good reasons to draw a line at agreement on price and structure.

In a subsequent decision, the late Judge Friendly, writing for a Second Circuit panel, applied the *Texas Gulf Sulphur* probability/magnitude approach in the specific context of preliminary merger negotiations. After acknowledging that materiality is something to be determined on the basis of the particular facts of each case, he stated:

> "Since a merger in which it is bought out is the most important event that can occur in a small corporation's life, to wit, its death, we think that inside information, as regards a merger of this sort, can become material at an earlier stage than would be the case as regards lesser transactions—and this even though the mortality rate of mergers in such formative stages is doubtless high."

SEC v. Geon Industries, Inc., 531 F.2d 39, 47–48 (C.A.2 1976). We agree with that analysis.

Whether merger discussions in any particular case are material therefore depends on the facts. Generally, in order to assess the probability that the event will occur, a factfinder will need to look to indicia of interest in the transaction at the highest corporate levels. Without attempting to catalog all such possible factors, we note by way of example that board resolutions, instructions to investment bankers, and actual negotiations between principals or their intermediaries may serve as indicia of interest. To assess the magnitude of the transaction to the issuer of the securities allegedly manipulated, a factfinder will need to consider such facts as the size of the two corporate entities and of the potential premiums over market value. No particular event or factor short of closing the transaction need be either necessary or sufficient by itself to render merger discussions material.

As we clarify today, materiality depends on the significance the reasonable investor would place on the withheld or misrepresented information. The fact-specific inquiry we endorse here is consistent with the approach a number of courts have taken in assessing the materiality of merger negotiations. Because the standard of materiality we have adopted differs from that used by both courts below, we remand the case for reconsideration of the question whether a grant of summary judgment is appropriate on this record.

IV

A

We turn to the question of reliance and the fraud-on-the-market theory. Succinctly put:

> "The fraud on the market theory is based on the hypothesis that, in an open and developed securities market, the price of a company's stock is determined by the available material information regarding the company and its business.... Misleading statements will therefore defraud purchasers of stock even if the purchasers do not directly rely on the misstatements.... The causal connection between the defendants' fraud and the plaintiffs' purchase of stock in such a case is no less significant than in a case of direct reliance on misrepresentations." *Peil v. Speiser*, 806 F.2d 1154, 1160–61 (C.A.3 1986).

Our task, of course, is not to assess the general validity of the theory, but to consider whether it was proper for the courts below to apply a rebuttable presumption of reliance, supported in part by the fraud-on-the-market theory.

This case required resolution of several common questions of law and fact concerning the falsity or misleading nature of the three public statements made by Basic, the presence or absence of scienter, and the materiality of the misrepresentations, if any. In their amended complaint, the named plaintiffs alleged that in reliance on Basic's statements they sold their shares of Basic stock in the depressed market created by petitioners.... Requiring proof of individualized reliance from each member of the proposed plaintiff class effectively would have prevented respondents from proceeding with a class action, since individual issues then would have overwhelmed the common ones. The District Court found that the presumption of reliance created by the fraud-on-the-market theory provided "a practical resolution to the problem of balancing the substantive requirement of proof of reliance in securities cases against the procedural requisites of [Fed.Rule Civ.Proc.] 23." The District Court thus concluded that with reference to each public statement and its impact upon the open market for

Basic shares, common questions predominated over individual questions, as required by Fed.Rule Civ.Proc. 23(a)(2) and (b)(3).

Petitioners and their *amici* complain that the fraud-on-the-market theory effectively eliminates the requirement that a plaintiff asserting a claim under Rule 10b–5 prove reliance. They note that reliance is and long has been an element of common-law fraud, see *e.g.,* Restatement (Second) of Torts § 525 (1977); Prosser and Keeton on The Law of Torts § 108 (5th ed. 1984), and argue that because the analogous express right of action includes a reliance requirement, see, *e.g.,* § 18(a) of the 1934 Act, as amended, 15 U.S.C. § 78r(a), so too must an action implied under § 10(b).

We agree that reliance is an element of a Rule 10b–5 cause of action. See *Ernst & Ernst v. Hochfelder,* 425 U.S., at 206 (quoting Senate Report). Reliance provides the requisite causal connection between a defendant's misrepresentation and a plaintiff's injury. See, *e.g., Wilson v. Comtech Telecommunications Corp.,* 648 F.2d 88, 92 (C.A.2 1981); *List v. Fashion Park, Inc.,* 340 F.2d 457, 462 (CA2), cert. denied *sub nom. List v. Lerner,* 382 U.S. 811 (1965). There is, however, more than one way to demonstrate the causal connection. Indeed, we previously have dispensed with a requirement of positive proof of reliance, where a duty to disclose material information had been breached, concluding that the necessary nexus between the plaintiffs' injury and the defendant's wrongful conduct had been established. See *Affiliated Ute Citizens v. United States,* 406 U.S., at 153–154. Similarly, we did not require proof that material omissions or misstatements in a proxy statement decisively affected voting, because the proxy solicitation itself, rather than the defect in the solicitation materials, served as an essential link in the transaction. See *Mills v. Electric Auto–Lite Co.,* 396 U.S. 375, 384–385 (1970).

The modern securities markets, literally involving millions of shares changing hands daily, differ from the face-to-face transactions contemplated by early fraud cases, and our understanding of Rule 10b–5's reliance requirement must encompass these differences.

> "In face-to-face transactions, the inquiry into an investor's reliance upon information is into the subjective pricing of that information by that investor. With the presence of a market, the market is interposed between seller and buyer and, ideally, transmits information to the investor in the processed form of a market price. Thus the market is performing a substantial part of the valuation process performed by the investor in a face-to-face transaction. The market is acting as the unpaid agent of the investor, informing him that given all the information available to it, the value of the stock is worth the market price." *In re LTV Securities Litigation,* 88 F.R.D. 134, 143 (N.D.Tex.1980).

Accord, *e.g., Peil v. Speiser,* 806 F.2d, at 1161 ("In an open and developed market, the dissemination of material misrepresentations or withholding of material information typically affects the price of the stock, and purchasers generally rely on the price of the stock as a reflection of its value"); *Blackie v. Barrack,* 524 F.2d 891, 908 (C.A.9

1975) ("the same causal nexus can be adequately established indirectly, by proof of materiality coupled with the common sense that a stock purchaser does not ordinarily seek to purchase a loss in the form of artificially inflated stock"), cert. denied, 429 U.S. 816 (1976).

B

Presumptions typically serve to assist courts in managing circumstances in which direct proof, for one reason or another, is rendered difficult. See, *e.g.*, D. Louisell & C. Mueller, Federal Evidence 541–542 (1977). The courts below accepted a presumption, created by the fraud-on-the-market theory and subject to rebuttal by petitioners, that persons who had traded Basic shares had done so in reliance on the integrity of the price set by the market, but because of petitioners' material misrepresentations that price had been fraudulently depressed. Requiring a plaintiff to show a speculative state of facts, *i.e.*, how he would have acted if omitted material information had been disclosed, see *Affiliated Ute Citizens v. United States,* 406 U.S., at 153–154, or if the misrepresentation had not been made, see *Sharp v. Coopers & Lybrand,* 649 F.2d 175, 188 (C.A.3 1981), cert. denied, 455 U.S. 938 (1982), would place an unnecessarily unrealistic evidentiary burden on the Rule 10b–5 plaintiff who has traded on an impersonal market. Cf. *Mills v. Electric Auto–Lite Co.,* 396 U.S., at 385.

Arising out of considerations of fairness, public policy, and probability, as well as judicial economy, presumptions are also useful devices for allocating the burdens of proof between parties. See E. Cleary, McCormick on Evidence 968–969 (3rd ed. 1984); see also Fed.Rule Evid. 301 and notes. The presumption of reliance employed in this case is consistent with, and, by facilitating Rule 10b–5 litigation, supports, the congressional policy embodied in the 1934 Act. In drafting that Act, Congress expressly relied on the premise that securities markets are affected by information, and enacted legislation to facilitate an investor's reliance on the integrity of those markets....

The presumption is also supported by common sense and probability. Recent empirical studies have tended to confirm Congress' premise that the market price of shares traded on well-developed markets reflects all publicly available information, and, hence, any material misrepresentations. It has been noted that "it is hard to imagine that there ever is a buyer or seller who does not rely on market integrity. Who would knowingly roll the dice in a crooked crap game?" *Schlanger v. Four–Phase Systems, Inc.,* 555 F.Supp. 535, 538 (S.D.N.Y.1982). Indeed, nearly every court that has considered the proposition has concluded that where materially misleading statements have been disseminated into an impersonal, well-developed market for securities, the reliance of individual plaintiffs on the integrity of the market price may be presumed. Commentators generally have applauded the adoption of one variation or another of the fraud-on-the-market theory. An investor who buys or sells stock at the price set by the market does so in reliance on the integrity of that price. Because most publicly available information is reflected in market price, an investor's reliance on any public material misrepresentations, therefore, may be presumed for purposes of a Rule 10b–5 action.

C

The Court of Appeals found that petitioners "made public, material misrepresentations and [respondents] sold Basic stock in an impersonal, efficient market. Thus the class, as defined by the district court, has established the threshold facts for proving their loss." 786 F.2d, at 751. The court acknowledged that petitioners may rebut proof of the elements giving rise to the presumption, or show that the misrepresentation in fact did not lead to a distortion of price or that an individual plaintiff traded or would have traded despite his knowing the statement was false. *Id.,* at 750, n. 6.

Any showing that severs the link between the alleged misrepresentation and either the price received (or paid) by the plaintiff, or his decision to trade at a fair market price, will be sufficient to rebut the presumption of reliance. For example, if petitioners could show that the "market makers" were privy to the truth about the merger discussions here with Combustion, and thus that the market price would not have been affected by their misrepresentations, the causal connection could be broken: the basis for finding that the fraud had been transmitted through market price would be gone. Similarly, if, despite petitioners' allegedly fraudulent attempt to manipulate market price, news of the merger discussions credibly entered the market and dissipated the effects of the misstatements, those who traded Basic shares after the corrective statements would have no direct or indirect connection with the fraud. Petitioners also could rebut the presumption of reliance as to plaintiffs who would have divested themselves of their Basic shares without relying on the integrity of the market. For example, a plaintiff who believed that Basic's statements were false and that Basic was indeed engaged in merger discussions, and who consequently believed that Basic stock was artificially underpriced, but sold his shares nevertheless because of other unrelated concerns, *e.g.,* potential antitrust problems, or political pressures to divest from shares of certain businesses, could not be said to have relied on the integrity of a price he knew had been manipulated.

V

In summary:

1. We specifically adopt, for the § 10(b) and Rule 10b–5 context, the standard of materiality set forth in *TSC Industries, Inc. v. Northway, Inc.,* 426 U.S., at 449.

2. We reject "agreement-in-principle as to price and structure" as the bright-line rule for materiality. . . .

4. Materiality in the merger context depends on the probability that the transaction will be consummated, and its significance to the issuer of the securities. Materiality depends on the facts and thus is to be determined on a case-by-case basis.

5. It is not inappropriate to apply a presumption of reliance supported by the fraud-on-the-market theory.

6. That presumption, however, is rebuttable.

7. The District Court's certification of the class here was appropriate when made but is subject on remand to such adjustment, if any, as developing circumstances demand.

The judgment of the Court of Appeals is vacated and the case is remanded to that court for further proceedings consistent with this opinion.

It is so ordered.

■ THE CHIEF JUSTICE, JUSTICE SCALIA, and JUSTICE KENNEDY took no part in the consideration or decision of this case.

■ JUSTICE WHITE, with whom JUSTICE O'CONNOR joins, concurring in part and dissenting in part.

I join Parts I–III of the Court's opinion, as I agree that the standard of materiality we set forth in *TSC Industries, Inc. v. Northway, Inc.*, 426 U.S. 438, 449, 96 S.Ct. 2126, 48 L.Ed.2d 757 (1976), should be applied to actions under § 10(b) and Rule 10b–5. But I dissent from the remainder of the Court's holding because I do not agree that the "fraud-on-the-market" theory should be applied in this case....

At the bottom of the Court's conclusion that the fraud-on-the-market theory sustains a presumption of reliance is the assumption that individuals rely "on the integrity of the market price" when buying or selling stock in "impersonal, well-developed market[s] for securities." *Ante,* at 21–22. Even if I was prepared to accept (as a matter of common sense or general understanding) the assumption that most persons buying or selling stock do so in response to the market price, the fraud-on-the-market theory goes further. For in adopting a "presumption of reliance," the Court *also* assumes that buyers and sellers rely—not just on the market price—but on the "*integrity*" of that price. It is this aspect of the fraud-on-the-market hypothesis which most mystifies me.

To define the term "integrity of the market price," the majority quotes approvingly from cases which suggest that investors are entitled to " 'rely on the price of a stock as a reflection of its value.' " But the meaning of this phrase eludes me, for it implicitly suggests that stocks have some "true value" that is measurable by a standard other than their market price. While the Scholastics of Medieval times professed a means to make such a valuation of a commodity's "worth," I doubt that the federal courts of our day are similarly equipped....

CAMMER v. BLOOM, 711 F.Supp. 1264 (D.N.J. 1989), sets forth the following factors as indicative of a security likely to be traded in an efficient market such that the fraud on the market approach to causation can be used to certify the class: (1) percentage of shares traded weekly, (2) analysts following, (3) presence of market makers and arbitrageurs, (4) eligibility to take advantage of the SEC's integrated disclosure procedures pursuant to Form S–3 for engaging in public offerings, and (5) responsiveness of security's price to new information. As in any factor analysis, the courts tend not to require all factors to be present, and some courts have added considerations such as the market capitalization of the firm (i.e., number of shares outstanding multiplied by their market price), bid-ask spreads, percentage of stock held by insiders, and institutional share ownership. *See* Fisher, Does the Efficient Market Theory Help Us Do Justice in a Time of Madness?, 54 Emory L.J. 843, 859–866 (2005). Why are these factors consistent with market efficiency? Why is market efficiency a precondition for the plaintiff's to invoke the fraud on the market approach to causation? Why is this approach necessary for the suit to proceed as a class action?

Erica P. John Fund, Inc. v. Halliburton, 2011 WL 2175208, ___ U.S. ___ (2011) held that class certification in a fraud on the market case is not dependent on the plaintiff establishing loss causation. The defendant had argued the plaintiff's inability to provide loss causation prevented the plaintiff from invoking a rebuttable presumption of reliance. The court rejected this, reasoning, "[s]uch a rule contravenes Basic's fundamental premise—that an investor presumptively relies on a misrepresentation so long as it was reflected in the market price at the time of his transaction. The fact that a subsequent loss may have been caused by factors other than the revelation of a misrepresentation has nothing to do with whether an investor relied on the misrepresentation in the first place."

Metzler Investment Gmbh v. Corinthian Colleges, Inc.

United States Court of Appeals, Ninth Circuit, 2008.
540 F.3d 1049.

■ B. FLETCHER, CIRCUIT JUDGE: . . .

Metzler alleges that Corinthian's colleges are pervaded by fraudulent practices designed to maximize the amount of federal Title IV funding—a major source of Corinthian's revenue—that those schools receive. The TAC [the Third Amended Complaint] alleges that Corinthian engaged in a variety of false or deceptive schemes falsifying financial aid applications to obtain federal funds and increase federal award entitlements; encouraging students to falsify federal student aid forms themselves; manipulating student enrollment by counting students not yet enrolled (referred to in the TAC as "false starts"); manipulating or falsifying student grades to maintain federal funding eligibility; exposing the company to bad debt in order to meet regulatory requirements for continued federal funding; delaying notification to federal officials of dropped students and delaying refunds to the federal government after students had dropped; and manipulating job placement data in order-to satisfy federal and state regulatory requirements. According to the TAC, the net effect of these practices was that "at numerous Corinthian campuses, as many as 50% to 60% of the people defendants represented to the U.S. government as being qualified, attending 'students' were either 'no shows' in class or unqualified for admission and federal funds from the outset." . . .

Thus, according to the TAC, Corinthian's public face to the market—one of growth and financial success premised on increasing student enrollment and successful placement rates—masked extensive fraud. The TAC alleges that this fraud resulted in an artificial inflation of Corinthian's stock price. . . .

Because Corinthian campuses were allegedly pervaded by fraudulent admission practices, the TAC alleges that virtually every Class Period statement discussing Corinthian's financial status was false. Specifically, the TAC alleges that public statements in regulatory disclosures and related documents regarding the company's financial performance were rendered false by the fact that Corinthian's underlying fraudulent practices remained hidden. . . .

The TAC thus alleges that any positive financial statement released by the company created the decidedly false impression among investors that Corinthian's success was due to "legitimate business means that could be expected to continue," when in fact its "financial performance was materially driven by fraudulent manipulation of the Title IV funding program and could cease at any time if exposed." TAC P 147(a). . . .

C. The TAC's allegations that Corinthian's fraud was revealed to the market, causing Metzler's losses.

The TAC points to two specific disclosures that purportedly revealed Corinthian's fraudulent student enrollment and financial aid practices to the market: (1) the June 24, 2004 *Financial Times* story reporting the DOE investigation at the Bryman campus, and (2) an August 2, 2004 press release disclosing reduced earnings and earning projections. According to the TAC, when read in tandem these two disclosures revealed "the truth regarding [Corinthian's] fraudulent practices and deception," and precipitated considerable drops in the value of Corinthian stock. . . .

As described above, the June 24 *Financial Times* story revealed that the DOE investigated Corinthian's Bryman campus in December 2003, and as a result that campus had been placed on reimbursement status. The *Financial Times* story further reported, however, that the DOE review and Bryman's placement on reimbursement status, "does not affect the status of other Corinthian schools." Nonetheless, Corinthian stock fell $2.55 on June 24, losing 10% of its value and closing at $22.51. Corinthian's stock rebounded within three trading days and by June 29, 2004, it rose to $25.11, an amount that exceeded the stock's value before the June 24 *Financial Times* story.

The second alleged disclosure occurred on August 2, 2004, when Corinthian issued a press release announcing that it had cut its revenue and earnings projections for the fourth quarter of 2004 and all of fiscal year 2005. That press release also revealed that the company had participated in a meeting with the California Attorney General regarding Corinthian's business practices. The release announced revised earnings per share ("EPS") for fiscal year 2004 of 86 to 87 cents, down from earlier projections of 94 cents EPS. The company also lowered guidance for all of fiscal year 2005. CEO Moore attributed the reduced earnings and accompanying projections to a number of factors:

> During the fourth quarter [FY 2004] we achieved a remarkable growth rate in student enrollments, although below our expectations. Strong growth, unfortunately, sometimes brings challenges, and there were several during the past quarter that we now believe caused our revenue to fall short of our expectations and earlier guidance. Those factors included changes in lead flow mix among television leads, direct mail leads, newspaper leads and Internet leads; higher than anticipated attrition; negative publicity related to student litigation in Florida; and later than anticipated new branch campus openings.

After the August 2, 2004 earnings miss, Corinthian's stock dropped 45% to $10.29....

... [The district court granted the defendants' motion to dismiss.]

III. DISCUSSION

A. The TAC does not adequately plead "loss causation."

As explained by the Supreme Court in *Dura Pharmaceuticals [Inc. v. Broudo, 544 U.S. 336, 125 S.Ct. 1627, 161 L.Ed. 577 (2005)],* loss causation is the "causal connection between the [defendant's] material misrepresentation and the [plaintiff's] loss." *544 U.S. at 342* (citation omitted). A complaint fails to allege loss causation if it does not "provide[ ] [a defendant] with notice of what the relevant economic loss might be or of what the causal connection might be between that loss and the misrepresentation[.]" *Id. at 347*. Stated in the affirmative, the complaint must allege that the defendant's "share price fell significantly after the truth became known." *Id.* A plaintiff does not, of course, need to *prove* loss causation in order to avoid dismissal; but the plaintiff must properly allege it. *Id. at 346*....

The principal Ninth Circuit case applying *Dura's* loss causation standards is *In re Daou Systems. 411 F.3d 1006*....

In *Daou* the plaintiffs' theory of fraud was that the defendant was systematically recognizing revenue on contracts that had not been completed. *Id. at 1012–13*. Plaintiffs adequately pled loss causation in *Daou* because their complaint alleged that the market learned of and reacted to this fraud, as opposed to merely reacting to reports of the defendant's poor financial health generally. *Id. at 1026* ...

Here, Metzler relies on the June 24 *Financial Times* story disclosing the DOE investigation at the Bryman campus and the August 2 earnings announcement. In doing so, Metzler fails to adequately plead loss causation. The TAC does not allege that the June 24 and August 2 announcements disclosed—or even suggested—to the market that Corinthian was manipulating student enrollment figures company-wide in order to procure excess federal funding, which is the fraudulent activity that Metzler contends forced down the stock that caused its losses. Neither the June 24 *Financial Times* story nor the August 2 press release regarding earnings can be reasonably read to reveal widespread financial aid manipulation by Corinthian, and the TAC does not otherwise adequately plead that these releases did so.

As for the *Financial Times* story, it does reveal a DOE investigation at the Bryman campus and the campus's placement on reimbursement status as a result of improper financial aid practices; but it simultaneously notes that the investigation there "does not affect the status of other Corinthian schools." The TAC does not allege that all, or even some appreciable number, of Corinthian's schools were being investigated or placed on reimbursement status. Only the Bryman campus was subject to that sanction. Indeed, the TAC itself discredits the notion that the June 24 disclosure revealed company-wide manipulation of student enrollment, by describing the June 24 disclosure as revealing to investors "the *potential* but real *risk* of all 88 colleges being placed on reimbursement status, which would have delayed Title IV funding and increased accounts receivable by up to $135 million company-wide." TAC P 159 (emphases added) . . . But neither *Daou* nor *Dura* support the notion that loss causation is pled where a defendant's disclosure reveals a "risk" or "potential" for widespread fraudulent conduct. In *Daou* the defendant disclosed that the company actually had $10 million in unbilled receivables, not merely that there was some risk it might accrue such receivables. *411 F.3d at 1026*. Moreover, as Corinthian notes, its stock recovered very shortly after the modest 10% drop that accompanied the June 24 announcement.

The TAC's characterization of the August 2 earnings announcement similarly fails to allege that the market became aware of, and the resulting stock drop resulted from, widespread enrollment fraud. At best, the TAC contends that the reference in the August 2 announcement to "higher than anticipated attrition" was understood by the market as Corinthian's "euphemism for an admission that they had enrolled students who should not have been signed up at all, resulting in a 45% stock drop." TAC P 48. Metzler's appellate brief asserts that the August 2 disclosure made investors "realize that Corinthian's improper manipulation of student and enrollment records was not limited to [the Bryman campus at] San Jose, nor was it immaterial." But the TAC does not allege facts to suggest that on August 2 the market became aware that Corinthian was manipulating student records company-wide, other than an undocumented assertion that Corinthian's August 2 stock drop was, by necessity, a result of this market "realization."[8]

Metzler is correct to observe that neither *Daou* nor *Dura* require an admission or finding of fraud before loss causation can be properly pled. *Dura Pharms., Inc., 544 U.S. at 346*; *Daou, 411 F.3d at 1025*. But that does not allow a plaintiff to plead loss causation through "euphemism" and thereby avoid alleging the necessary connection

8. Nor do the June 24 and August 2 disclosures become adequate when viewed in tandem. The June 24 *Financial Times* story discusses impropriety regarding the financial aid practices at one school; the August 2 release contains one reference to attrition. The combined force of these statements does not suggest that the market was alerted to widespread enrollment and admissions fraud at Corinthian schools nationwide. Nor does the TAC allege any genuine causal connection between the August 2 earnings miss and the allegations that Corinthian had manipulated student enrollment in order to receive excess federal funds, or that the earnings miss was caused by slashed federal funding.

between defendant's fraud and the actual loss. So long as there is a drop in a stock's price, a plaintiff will always be able to contend that the market "understood" a defendant's statement precipitating a loss as a coded message revealing the fraud. Enabling a plaintiff to proceed on such a theory would effectively resurrect what *Dura* discredited—that loss causation is established through an allegation that a stock was purchased at an inflated price. *544 U.S. at 347*. Loss causation requires more. . . .

Finally, while the court assumes that the facts in a complaint are true, it is not required to indulge unwarranted inferences in order to save a complaint from dismissal. . . . The TAC's allegation that the market understood the June 24 and August 2 disclosures as a revelation of Corinthian's systematic manipulation of student enrollment is not a "fact." It is an inference that Metzler believes is warranted from the facts that are alleged. But Corinthian persuasively explains why this is not the case. As to the June 24 disclosure, Corinthian points out that its stock quickly recovered from the 10% drop that followed the *Financial Times* story. Similarly, the August 2 announcement contained a far more plausible reason for the resulting drop in Corinthian's stock price—the company failed to hit prior earnings estimates. The August 2 announcement simultaneously reported that student population growth was up nearly 50% overall and same-school population increased 15%, making it even further unwarranted to infer that the reference to "attrition" was understood by the market to mean that Corinthian had revealed widespread misrepresentation of student enrollment to fraudulently procure excess federal funding. The TAC thus fails to allege loss causation based on the June 24 and August 2 disclosures. . . .

IV. CONCLUSION

The TAC's allegations, although not lacking in breadth or numerosity, ultimately fail to meet the PSLRA's exacting requirements and the standards for pleading loss causation. The disclosures that the TAC relies on simply do not identify the requisite causal connection between Metzler's claims of fraudulent student admission and financial aid practices, and a resulting drop in Corinthian's stock price. . . . For these reasons, we affirm.

SECTION 7. THE JUNCTION OF BREACHES OF FIDUCIARY DUTY AND RULE 10b–5

Santa Fe Industries, Inc. v. Green

Supreme Court of the United States, 1977.
430 U.S. 462, 97 S.Ct. 1292, 51 L.Ed.2d 480.

■ MR. JUSTICE WHITE delivered the opinion of the Court.

The issue in this case involves the reach and coverage of § 10(b) of the Securities Exchange Act of 1934 and Rule 10b–5 thereunder in the context of a Delaware short-form merger transaction used by the majority stockholder of a corporation to eliminate the minority interest.

I

In 1936, petitioner Santa Fe Industries, Inc. (Santa Fe), acquired control of 60% of the stock of Kirby Lumber Corp. (Kirby), a Delaware corporation. Through a series of purchases over the succeeding years, Santa Fe increased its control of Kirby's stock to 95%; the purchase prices during the period 1968–1973 ranged from $65 to $92.50 per share. In 1974, wishing to acquire 100% ownership of Kirby, Santa Fe availed itself of § 253 of the Delaware Corporation Law, known as the "short-form merger" statute. Section 253 permits a parent corporation owning at least 90% of the stock of a subsidiary to merge with that subsidiary, upon approval by the parent's board of directors, and to make payment in cash for the shares of the minority stockholders. The statute does not require the consent of, or advance notice to, the minority stockholders. However, notice of the merger must be given within 10 days after its effective date, and any stockholder who is dissatisfied with the terms of the merger may petition the Delaware Court of Chancery for a decree ordering the surviving corporation to pay him the fair value of his shares, as determined by a court-appointed appraiser subject to review by the court. Del.Code Ann., Tit. 8, §§ 253, 262 (1975 ed. and Supp.1976).

Santa Fe obtained independent appraisals of the physical assets of Kirby—land, timber, buildings, and machinery—and of Kirby's oil, gas, and mineral interests. These appraisals, together with other financial information, were submitted to Morgan Stanley & Co. (Morgan Stanley), an investment banking firm retained to appraise the fair market value of Kirby stock. Kirby's physical assets were appraised at $320 million (amounting to $640 for each of the 500,000 shares); Kirby's stock was valued by Morgan Stanley at $125 per share. Under the terms of the merger, minority stockholders were offered $150 per share.

The provisions of the short-form merger statute were fully complied with. The minority stockholders of Kirby were notified the day after the merger became effective and were advised of their right to obtain an appraisal in Delaware court if dissatisfied with the offer of $150 per share. They also received an information statement containing, in addition to the relevant financial data about Kirby, the appraisals of the value of Kirby's assets and the Morgan Stanley appraisal concluding that the fair market value of the stock was $125 per share.

Respondents, minority stockholders of Kirby, objected to the terms of the merger, but did not pursue their appraisal remedy in the Delaware Court of Chancery.[4] Instead, they brought this action in

4. On August 21, 1974, respondents petitioned for an appraisal of their Kirby stock, but they withdrew that petition on September 9 and the next day commenced this lawsuit.

federal court on behalf of the corporation and other minority stockholders, seeking to set aside the merger or to recover what they claimed to be the fair value of their shares. The amended complaint asserted that, based on the fair market value of Kirby's physical assets as revealed by the appraisal included in the information statement sent to minority shareholders, Kirby's stock was worth at least $772 per share.[5] The complaint alleged further that the merger took place without prior notice to minority stockholders; that the purpose of the merger was to appropriate the difference between the "conceded pro rata value of the physical assets," App. 103a, and the offer of $150 per share—to "freez[e] out the minority stockholders at a wholly inadequate price," *id.*, at 100a; and that Santa Fe, knowing the appraised value of the physical assets, obtained a "fraudulent appraisal" of the stock from Morgan Stanley and offered $25 above that appraisal "in order to lull the minority stockholders into erroneously believing that [Santa Fe was] generous." *Id.*, at 103a. This course of conduct was alleged to be "a violation of Rule 10b–5 because defendants employed a 'device, scheme, or artifice to defraud' and engaged in an 'act, practice or course of business which operates or would operate as a fraud or deceit upon any person, in connection with the purchase or sale of any security.' " *Ibid.* Morgan Stanley assertedly participated in the fraud as an accessory by submitting its appraisal of $125 per share although knowing the appraised value of the physical assets. . . .

The District Court dismissed the complaint for failure to state a claim upon which relief could be granted. 391 F.Supp. 849 (S.D.N.Y. 1975). . . .

As for the claim that actionable fraud inhered in the allegedly gross undervaluation of the minority shares, the District Court observed that respondents valued their shares at a minimum of $772 per share, "basing this figure on the *pro rata* value of Kirby's physical assets." *Id.*, at 853. Accepting this valuation for purposes of the motion to dismiss, the District Court further noted that, as revealed by the complaint, the physical asset appraisal, along with other information relevant to Morgan Stanley's valuation of the shares, had been included with the information statement sent to respondents within the time required by state law. It thought that if "full and fair disclosure is made, transactions eliminating minority interests are beyond the purview of Rule 10b–5," and concluded that the "complaint fail[ed] to allege an omission, misstatement or fraudulent course of conduct that would have impeded a shareholder's judgment of the value of the offer." *Id.*, at 854. The complaint therefore failed to state a claim and was dismissed.

---

5. The figure of $772 per share was calculated as follows:

"The difference of $311,000,000 ($622 per share) between the fair market value of Kirby's land and timber, alone, as per the defendants' own appraisal thereof at $320,000,000 and the $9,000,000 book value of said land and timber, added to the $150 per share, yields a pro rata share of the value of the physical assets of Kirby of at least $772 per share. The value of the stock was at least the pro rata value of the physical assets." App. 102a.

A divided Court of Appeals for the Second Circuit reversed. 533 F.2d 1283 (1976).... The court [held] that the complaint, taken as a whole, stated a cause of action under the Rule:

> "We hold that a complaint alleges a claim under Rule 10b–5 when it charges, in connection with a Delaware short-form merger, that the majority has committed a breach of its fiduciary duty to deal fairly with minority shareholders by effecting the merger without any justifiable business purpose. The minority shareholders are given no prior notice of the merger, thus having no opportunity to apply for injunctive relief, and the proposed price to be paid is substantially lower than the appraised value reflected in the Information Statement." *Id.*, at 1291....

We granted the petition for certiorari challenging this holding because of the importance of the issue involved to the administration of the federal securities laws. 429 U.S. 814 (1976). We reverse.

II

Section 10(b) of the 1934 Act makes it "unlawful for any person ... to use or employ ... any manipulative or deceptive device or contrivance in contravention of [Securities and Exchange Commission rules]"; Rule 10b–5, promulgated by the SEC under § 10(b), prohibits, in addition to nondisclosure and misrepresentation, any "artifice to defraud" or any act "which operates or would operate as a fraud or deceit." ... The Court of Appeals' approach to the interpretation of Rule 10b–5 is inconsistent with that taken by the Court last Term in Ernst & Ernst v. Hochfelder, 425 U.S. 185 ... (1976)....

The language of § 10(b) gives no indication that Congress meant to prohibit any conduct not involving manipulation or deception. Nor have we been cited to any evidence in the legislative history that would support a departure from the language of the statute. "When a statute speaks so specifically in terms of manipulation and deception, ... and when its history reflects no more expansive intent, we are quite unwilling to extend the scope of the statute...." *Id.*, at 214. Thus the claim of fraud and fiduciary breach in this complaint states a cause of action under any part of Rule 10b–5 only if the conduct alleged can be fairly viewed as "manipulative or deceptive" within the meaning of the statute.

III

It is our judgment that the transaction, if carried out as alleged in the complaint, was neither deceptive nor manipulative and therefore did not violate either § 10(b) of the Act or Rule 10b–5.

As we have indicated, the case comes to us on the premise that the complaint failed to allege a material misrepresentation or material failure to disclose. The finding of the District Court, undisturbed by the Court of Appeals, was that there was no "omission" or "misstatement" in the information statement accompanying the notice of merger. On the basis of the information provided, minority shareholders could either accept the price offered or reject it and seek an appraisal in the Delaware Court of Chancery. Their choice was fairly presented, and they were furnished with all relevant information on which to base their decision.

We therefore find inapposite the cases relied upon by respondents and the court below, in which the breaches of fiduciary duty held violative of Rule 10b–5 included some element of deception. Those cases forcefully reflect the principle that "[§] 10(b) must be read flexibly, not technically and restrictively" and that the statute provides a cause of action for any plaintiff who "suffer[s] an injury as a result of deceptive practices touching its sale [or purchase] of securities. . . ." *Superintendent of Insurance v. Bankers Life & Cas. Co.,* 404 U.S. 6, 12–13 . . . (1971). But the cases do not support the proposition, adopted by the Court of Appeals below and urged by respondents here, that a breach of fiduciary duty by majority stockholders, without any deception, misrepresentation, or nondisclosure, violates the statute and the Rule.

It is also readily apparent that the conduct alleged in the complaint was not "manipulative" within the meaning of the statute. "Manipulation" is "virtually a term of art when used in connection with securities markets." *Ernst & Ernst,* 425 U.S., at 199. The term refers generally to practices, such as wash sales, matched orders, or rigged prices, that are intended to mislead investors by artificially affecting market activity. . . . Section 10(b)'s general prohibition of practices deemed by the SEC to be "manipulative"—in this technical sense of artificially affecting market activity in order to mislead investors—is fully consistent with the fundamental purpose of the 1934 Act " 'to substitute a philosophy of full disclosure for the philosophy of *caveat emptor*. . . .' " *Affiliated Ute Citizens v. United States,* 406 U.S. 128 . . . (1972), quoting *SEC v. Capital Gains Research Bureau,* 375 U.S. 180 . . . (1963). Indeed, nondisclosure is usually essential to the success of a manipulative scheme. 3 Loss, *supra,* at 1565. No doubt Congress meant to prohibit the full range of ingenious devices that might be used to manipulate securities prices. But we do not think it would have chosen this "term of art" if it had meant to bring within the scope of § 10(b) instances of corporate mismanagement such as this, in which the essence of the complaint is that shareholders were treated unfairly by a fiduciary.

IV

The language of the statute is, we think, "sufficiently clear in its context" to be dispositive here, *Ernst & Ernst, supra,* at 201; but even if it were not, there are additional considerations that weigh heavily against permitting a cause of action under Rule 10b–5 for the breach of corporate fiduciary duty alleged in this complaint. Congress did not expressly provide a private cause of action for violations of § 10(b). Although we have recognized an implied cause of action under that section in some circumstances, *Superintendent of Insurance v. Bankers Life & Cas. Co., supra,* at 13 n. 9, we have also recognized that a private cause of action under the antifraud provisions of the Securities

Exchange Act should not be implied where it is "unnecessary to ensure the fulfillment of Congress' purposes" in adopting the Act. *Piper v. Chris–Craft Industries, ante,* at 41. Cf. *J.I. Case Co. v. Borak,* 377 U.S. 426, 431–433 . . . (1964). As we noted earlier, . . . the Court repeatedly has described the "fundamental purpose" of the Act as implementing a "philosophy of full disclosure"; once full and fair disclosure has occurred, the fairness of the terms of the transaction is at most a tangential concern of the statute. . . . As in *Cort v. Ash,* 422 U.S. 66, 80 . . . (1975), we are reluctant to recognize a cause of action here to serve what is "at best a subsidiary purpose" of the federal legislation.

A second factor in determining whether Congress intended to create a federal cause of action in these circumstances is "whether 'the cause of action [is] one traditionally relegated to state law. . . .' " *Piper v. Chris–Craft Industries, Inc., ante,* at 40, quoting *Cort v. Ash, supra,* at 78. The Delaware Legislature has supplied minority shareholders with a cause of action in the Delaware Court of Chancery to recover the fair value of shares allegedly undervalued in a short-form merger. . . . Of course, the existence of a particular state-law remedy is not dispositive of the question whether Congress meant to provide a similar federal remedy, but as in *Cort* and *Piper,* we conclude that "it is entirely appropriate in this instance to relegate respondent and others in his situation to whatever remedy is created by state law." 422 U.S., at 84; *ante,* at 41.

The reasoning behind a holding that the complaint in this case alleged fraud under Rule 10b–5 could not be easily contained. It is difficult to imagine how a court could distinguish, for purposes of Rule 10b–5 fraud, between a majority stockholder's use of a short-form merger to eliminate the minority at an unfair price and the use of some other device, such as a long-form merger, tender offer, or liquidation, to achieve the same result; or indeed how a court could distinguish the alleged abuses in these going private transactions from other types of fiduciary self-dealing involving transactions in securities. The result would be to bring within the Rule a wide variety of corporate conduct traditionally left to state regulation. In addition to posing a "danger of vexatious litigation which could result from a widely expanded class of plaintiffs under Rule 10b–5," *Blue Chip Stamps v. Manor Drug Stores,* 421 U.S., at 740, this extension of the federal securities laws would overlap and quite possibly interfere with state corporate law. Federal courts applying a "federal fiduciary principle" under Rule 10b–5 could be expected to depart from state fiduciary standards at least to the extent necessary to ensure uniformity within the federal system.[16] Absent a clear indication of congression-

16. For example, some States apparently require a "valid corporate purpose" for the elimination of the minority interest through a short-form merger, whereas other States do not. Compare *Bryan v. Brock & Blevins Co.,* 490 F.2d 563 (CA5), cert. denied, 419 U.S. 844, 95 S.Ct. 77, 42 L.Ed.2d 72 (1974) (merger arranged by controlling stockholder for no business purpose except to eliminate 15% minority stockholder violated Georgia short-form merger statute) with *Stauffer v. Standard Brands, Inc.,* 41 Del.Ch. 7, 187 A.2d 78 (1962) (Delaware short-form merger statute allows majority stockholder to eliminate the minority interest

al intent, we are reluctant to federalize the substantial portion of the law of corporations that deals with transactions in securities, particularly where established state policies of corporate regulation would be overridden. As the Court stated in *Cort v. Ash, supra:* "Corporations are creatures of state law, and investors commit their funds to corporate directors on the understanding that, except where federal law *expressly* requires certain responsibilities of directors with respect to stockholders, state law will govern the internal affairs of the corporation." 422 U.S., at 84 (emphasis added).

We thus adhere to the position that "Congress by § 10(b) did not seek to regulate transactions which constitute no more than internal corporate mismanagement." *Superintendent of Insurance v. Bankers Life & Cas. Co.,* 404 U.S., at 12. There may well be a need for uniform federal fiduciary standards to govern mergers such as that challenged in this complaint. But those standards should not be supplied by judicial extension of § 10(b) and Rule 10b–5 to "cover the corporate universe."

The judgment of the Court of Appeals is reversed, and the case is remanded for further proceedings consistent with this opinion.

So ordered.

[The dissenting opinion of Justice Brennan is omitted.]

■ MR. JUSTICE BLACKMUN, concurring in part.

Like MR. JUSTICE STEVENS, I refrain from joining Part IV of the Court's opinion. I, too, regard that part as unnecessary for the decision in the instant case.... I, however, join the remainder of the Court's opinion and its judgment.

■ MR. JUSTICE STEVENS, concurring in part.

... [T]he entire discussion in Part IV is unnecessary to the decision of this case. Accordingly, I join only Parts I, II, and III of the Court's opinion. I would also add further emphasis to the fact that the controlling stockholders in this case did not breach any duty owed to the minority shareholders because (a) there was complete disclosure of the relevant facts, and (b) the minority are entitled to receive the fair value of their shares.[2] The facts alleged in the complaint do not constitute "fraud" within the meaning of Rule 10b–5.

Would the plaintiff prevail in *Santa Fe* if there had been no disclosure of Kirby Lumber's book value? *See* Virginia Bankshares, Inc. v. Sandberg, 501 U.S. 1083, 111 S.Ct. 2749, 115 L.Ed.2d 929 (1991). Should the answer to this question depend on whether the applicable

without any corporate purpose and subject only to an appraisal remedy). Thus to the extent that Rule 10b–5 is interpreted to require a valid corporate purpose for elimination of minority shareholders as well as a fair price for their shares, it would impose a stricter standard of fiduciary duty than that required by the law of some States.

2. The motivation for the merger is a matter of indifference to the minority stockholders because they retain no interest in the corporation after the merger is consummated.

state corporate law provides minority holders an appraisal remedy, discuss in Chapter 15 section 1, whereby, instead of receiving what is offered in the merger, a shareholder can elect to have her shares independently appraised and receive cash equal to the resulting fair value of the appraised shares? *See* Wilson v. Great American Industries, Inc., 979 F.2d 924 (2d Cir. 1992); Howing Co. v. Nationwide Corp., 972 F.2d 700 (6th Cir. 1992), *cert. denied*, 507 U.S. 1004, 113 S.Ct. 1645, 123 L.Ed.2d 266 (1993).

NOTE ON GOLDBERG v. MERIDOR

Although the language of the majority opinion in *Santa Fe* indicates a reluctance to extend Rule 10b–5 into the province of state law regarding corporate mismanagement, *Santa Fe* does not carry quite that far. For example, if D, a director of Corporation C, persuades Corporation C's board, by means of a materially misleading statement, to sell him stock, Corporation C can sue D under Rule 10b–5 even though Corporation C can also sue D for breach of fiduciary duty. Similarly, if Corporation C's board doesn't sue D, a shareholder could sue D under Rule 10b–5 in a derivative action. Should the outcome depend on whether all, some, or a majority of the Corporation C's directors were aware that the statements made by D were false?

Consider here Schoenbaum v. Firstbrook, 405 F.2d 215 (2d Cir.1968) (en banc), cert. denied 395 U.S. 906, 89 S.Ct. 1747, 23 L.Ed.2d 219 (1969), decided before *Santa Fe.* Aquitaine was a majority shareholder of Banff Oil Ltd. and had appointed three of its eight directors. It was alleged that Aquitaine used its controlling influence to cause Banff to sell Banff shares to Aquitaine for wholly inadequate consideration. The Second Circuit held that a Banff minority shareholder could bring a derivative action on Banff's behalf under Rule 10b–5:

> . . . [I]t is alleged that Aquitaine exercised a controlling influence over the issuance to it of treasury stock of Banff for a wholly inadequate consideration. If it is established that the transaction took place as alleged, it constituted a violation of Rule 10b–5, subdivision (3), because Aquitaine engaged in an "act, practice or course of business which operates or would operate as a fraud or deceit upon any person, in connection with the purchase or sale of any security." Moreover, Aquitaine and the directors of Banff were guilty of deceiving the stockholders of Banff (other than Aquitaine).

Does this reasoning conflict with *Santa Fe*?

In Goldberg v. Meridor, 567 F.2d 209 (2d Cir.1977), cert. denied 434 U.S. 1069, 98 S.Ct. 1249, 55 L.Ed.2d 771 (1978), decided shortly after *Santa Fe,* UGO Corporation was controlled by Maritimecor, which in turn was controlled by Maritime Fruit. A shareholdser of UGO alleged that Maritimecor, Maritime Fruit, and directors of the various companies had caused UGO to acquire Maritimecor's assets in exchange for UGO stock, and that the agreement "was fraudulent and unfair in that the assets of Maritimecor were overpriced.'' Id. at 211. Press releases that described the agreement failed to disclose certain material facts concerning the value of Maritimecor's assets. The Second Circuit, in an opinion by Judge Friendly, held that *Schoenbaum* had survived *Santa Fe* so that a derivative action could be brought under Rule 10b–5 if (1) the transaction involved stock and (2) material facts concerning the transaction had not been disclosed to all shareholders:

> *Schoenbaum* ... can rest solidly on the now widely recognized ground that there is deception of the corporation (in effect, of its minority shareholders) when the corporation is influenced by its controlling shareholder to engage in a transaction adverse to the corporation's interests (in effect, the minority shareholders' interests) and there is nondisclosure or misleading disclosures as to the material facts of the transaction....
>
> Here the complaint alleged "deceit ... upon UGO's minority shareholders".... The nub of the matter is that the conduct attacked in *[Santa Fe]* did not violate the " 'fundamental purpose' of the Act as implementing a 'philosophy of full disclosure' ", ... [T]he conduct here attacked does....

Id. at 217–18.

It should be noted that the transaction challenged in *Goldberg* did not require shareholder approval. Nonetheless, Friendly focuses on the deception to the minority holders:

> Goldberg and the other minority shareholders would not have been without a remedy if the alleged facts had been disclosed....
>
> The availability of injunctive relief if the defendants had not lulled the minority stockholders of UGO into security by a deceptive disclosure, as they allegedly did, is in sharp contrast to [*Santa Fe Industries*] where the disclosure following the merger transaction was full and fair....

Id. at 218.

Goldberg v. Meridor has been followed. See, e.g., Estate of Soler v. Rodriquez, 63 F.3d 45 (1st Cir. 1995); Kas v. Financial General Bankshares, Inc., 796 F.2d 508, 512 (D.C.Cir.1986). The Second Circuit, however, has clarified that more than careless neglect, but rather "willful misconduct of a self-serving nature," must be at the heart of the non disclosed facts. *See* Field v. Trump, 850 F.2d 938, 947 (2d Cir. 1988). The courts are in agreement that to succeed under the principle of Goldberg v. Meridor, the plaintiff must show a misrepresentation or nondisclosure that caused a loss to the shareholders. These are commonly referred to as "sue facts." If the controlling shareholder did not need approval by the minority shareholders to effectuate the relevant transaction, then to show causation the plaintiff normally must establish that as a result of the lack of full disclosure, a state remedy was forgone. Most commonly, the plaintiff attempts to satisfy this requirement by arguing that if full disclosure had been made, the shareholders could have sought injunctive relief against the proposed transaction under state law.

The courts are in disagreement about the nature of the showing that the plaintiff must make concerning the likelihood that the forgone remedy would have been successful.

In Kidwell ex rel. Penfold v. Meikle, 597 F.2d 1273, 1294 (1979), the Ninth Circuit held that the plaintiff must show the shareholders would actually have succeeded if they had brought the forgone suit.

In Healey v. Catalyst Recovery, 616 F.2d 641, 647–48 (1980) the Third Circuit rejected the *Kidwell* test, and instead held that the plaintiff must show "there was a reasonable probability of ultimate success." The court explained:

> [W]e frame the test in terms of a reasonable probability for two reasons. First, we believe absolute certainty to be both an impossible goal as well as an impracticable standard for a jury to implement. Second, in most cases the state remedy will be a preliminary injunction, which looks to the likelihood of ultimate success.

In Alabama Farm Bureau Mutual Casualty Co. v. American Fidelity Life Insurance Co., 606 F.2d 602, 614 (1979), cert. denied 449 U.S. 820, 101 S.Ct. 77, 66 L.Ed.2d 22 (1980), the Fifth Circuit also rejected the *Kidwell* test, adopting instead a requirement "that state law remedies were available and that the facts shown make out a prima facie case for relief".

In Madison Consultants v. FDIC, 710 F.2d 57, 64–65 (1983), the Second Circuit adopted the *Kidwell* test, but put a gloss on the test that reduces its bite:

> We believe that the correct view is that the plaintiff must show that he would have succeeded in preventing the loss he in fact suffered. See *Kidwell*.... This standard does not obligate a plaintiff to prove beyond a reasonable doubt or to an absolute certainty that he would have won the state court suit or otherwise prevented the injury that he in fact suffered. He needs to prove only by a fair preponderance of the evidence that he would have succeeded.... [If] the plaintiff's burden in the state court action were lower, such as when preliminary injunction relief would have been tantamount to success, that factor would be taken into account in the federal suit under the standard we require.

However, the Seventh Circuit has rejected *Goldberg*. See, e.g., Isquith v. Caremark International, 136 F.3d 531 (7th Cir. 1998):

> *Goldberg* would allow every complaint about the mismanagement of a corporation that issues securities subject to federal law to be shoe-horned into federal court on the theory that management had defrauded the shareholders by concealing the mismanagement. This would carry the securities law far outside their intended domain. And it would violate the principle that the only loss of

which complaint is possible under the antifraud provisions of those laws is a loss that candor would have averted.

A further bump in the road paved by *Goldberg* is Virginia Bankshares, Inc. v. Sandberg, 501 U.S. 1083, 111 S.Ct. 2749, 115 L.Ed.2d 929 (1991), holding that causation is absent in a private action under Rule 14a–9 for material misstatements committed in a proxy statement seeking shareholder approval of a merger if the defendant has sufficient voting power to approve the transaction. The defendant in the case controlled 85 percent of the voting shares in a state that conditioned the merger's approval on a bare majority vote and accorded no appraisal remedy to dissenting minority holders. On these facts, the Supreme Court concluded that there was no connection between the materially misleading proxy statement and the merger's consummation. The majority's opinion in *Virginia Bankshares* is, however, somewhat qualified:

> This case does not, however, require us to decide whether § 14(a) provides a cause of action for lost state remedies, since there is no indication in the law or facts before us that the proxy solicitation result in any such loss.... Assuming the soundness of the respondents' characterization of the proxy statement as materially misleading, the very terms of the Virginia statute indicate that a favorable minority vote induced by the solicitation would not suffice to render the merger invulnerable to later attack on the ground of the conflict. The statute bars a shareholder from seeking to avoid a transaction tainted by a director's conflict if, inter alia, the minority shareholders ratified the transaction following disclosure of material facts of the transaction and the conflict. Va. Code § 13.1–691(A)(2) (1989). Assuming that the material facts about the merger and ... [the director's] interest were not accurately disclosed, the minority votes were inadequate to ratify the merger under state law, and there was no loss of state remedy to connect the proxy solicitation with harm to minority shareholders irredressable under state law. Nor is there a claim here that the statement misled respondents into entertaining a false belief that they had no chance to upset the merger, until the time for bringing suit had run out....

501 U.S. at 1107–1108. Query, what result if the state statute of limitations is shorter than the federal limitations period and the state statute has run but the federal limitation period has not? *See generally* Harvey Gelb, Implied Private Actions Under SEC Rules 14a–9 and 10b–5: The Impact of *Virginia Bankshares Inc. v. Sandberg*, 76 Marq. L. Rev. 363 (1993); Scott Jordan, Loss of State Claims As a Basis for Rule 10b–5 and Rule 14a–9 Actions: The Implications of *Virginia Bankshares*, 49 Bus. Law. 295 (1993).

Finally, why does this particular species of controlling stockholder, conflict of interest claims find their way into the federal courts through the window of one of the antifraud provisions? *See* Robert B. Thompson & Hillary A. Sale, Securities Fraud as Corporate Governance: Reflections upon Federalism, 56 Vand. L. Rev. 859 (2003).

SECTION 8. REMEDIES IN PRIVATE ACTIONS UNDER RULE 10b–5

The determination of the appropriate remedy in a private action under Rule 10b–5 is a complex problem whose solution depends on a number of variables, including whether the corporation is closely or publicly held, whether the plaintiff is a buyer or a seller, whether the wrong is a misrepresentation or a wrongful nondisclosure, and whether the plaintiff dealt directly with the defendant. The common law rules governing remedies for fraud provide a good place to begin the analysis, because Rule 10b–5 cases often explicitly rely upon fraud concepts in the area of remedies.

Suppose that S in reliance on false statements made by P corporation purchases P shares at $20 per share. P is a publicly traded corporation. As we've seen in the preceding materials, if a person has made a public misrepresentation that had the foreseeable effect of causing members of the public to sell (or buy) stock, the defendant is liable for the resulting damages. See, e.g., Blackie v. Barrack, 524 F.2d 891 (9th Cir.1975), cert. denied 429 U.S. 816, 97 S.Ct. 57, 50 L.Ed.2d 75 (1976). But how are the damages to be measured? Assume that some months after the misrepresentation P issues a statement correcting its earlier false report. The security that day falls from $20 to $17 per share, it declines to $16 the next day, and two weeks later bottoms out at $13 per share. During this same period the overall market has declined ten percent.

Assume first that S sues for conventional damages. Under the out-of-pocket measure, S would recover the difference between the price at which he purchased stock in P and the actual value of the stock. Actual value when? There are two strong reasons for measuring S's damages not by the value of the stock at the time of the wrong, but by its market value at the time of disclosure of the correct information.

(i) *The valuation idea and the modified out-of-pocket measure.* The first reason for using market value at the time of disclosure, in the case of a publicly held corporation, is that it provides the best indicator of actual value at the time of the wrong. Many think that the best indicator of the value of publicly held stock is the price of the stock on a fully informed market. The market price of P stock at the time of B's misrepresentation is *not* a good indicator of the stock's value, because the market will have been affected by the misrepresentation and similarly so for the market value the day after S's purchase, or the day after that day, and so forth because, until earlier lie is corrected, the market likely will reflect the earlier false information announced by B. Thus, the market price of P stock after the misrepresentation is corrected *is* a good indicator of the stock's value, because that price will reflect the market's valuation of P stock in light of the new, correct information. See Harris v. American Investment Co., 523 F.2d 220, 226–27 (8th Cir.1975), cert. denied 423 U.S. 1054, 96 S.Ct.

784, 46 L.Ed.2d 643 (1976). But what if we should conclude that the shares are not efficiently priced because the company does not have a large enough market capitalization to attract institutional investors or analyst coverage?

Of course, the difference between the market price at the time of the wrong and the market price at the time of disclosure may be partly due to factors other than disclosure, such as changes in the economy or events within the company that are not associated with the earlier misrepresentation. To the extent that the use of market price at the time of disclosure is based on the valuation idea—that the price at that time is the best indicator of the value of P's stock. Who should bear the burden of proof regarding whether all or some portion of the price decline is attributable to factors unrelated to the misrepresentation?

Another issue that can arise in reliance upon market prices to measure damages is the phenomenon of the "bounce back." This refers to the price of the security first declining and then bouncing back some time after the corrective announcement. In the preceding example, this would occur if following the corrective disclosure the security declined, as stated earlier, from $20 to $17 per share, then $16, then $13, but in a few weeks rising to $22. The PSLRA added section 21D(e) provides that the damages a plaintiff can recover shall not exceed the difference between the plaintiff's purchase or sale price and the mean trading price of that security during the ninety-day period beginning on the date of the corrective statement. Does this provision introduce an asymmetrical quality to the damage calculation? Consider that as observed earlier the defendant is not responsible for any portion of the stock price decline not attributable to the defendant's misrepresentation. On the other hand, what result in the preceding hypothetical under section 21D(e) if what drove P share price to $22 is that it P had become the target of a takeover? *See* Jonathan C. Dickey & Marcia Kramer Mayer, Effect on Rule 10b–5 Damages of the 1995 Private Securities Litigation Reform Act: A Forward Looking Assessment, 51 Bus. Law. 1203 (1996).

(ii) *The cover idea.* There is a second reason why, in the case of stock in a publicly held corporation that is purchased or sold as a result of a violation of Rule 10b–5, damages should normally be based on the market value at, or a reasonable period after, the time of disclosure. Once truthful correction of the earlier false statement is made, so that the stock is correctly priced, the selling stockholder should have the opportunity to reinvest in the stock, or "cover," by purchasing the stock at the newly established price during a reasonable time after disclosure. "[A]fter the reasonable stockholder had opportunity to apprise himself [of the correct information,] a reasonable time lapse may be allowed to expire to permit the investor to decide whether or not he would reinvest.... The damages should then be based on the highest value of the [stock in question between the date of disclosure] and a reasonable time thereafter. In selecting the highest daily price the advantage works, to a greater degree, against the [wrongdoer]. But where ... the injury is suffered by an act makes difficult the exact computation of damages, the wrongdoer is not heard to complain." Mitchell v. Texas Gulf Sulphur Co., 446 F.2d 90, 105 (10th Cir.1971), cert. denied 404 U.S. 1004, 92 S.Ct. 564, 30 L.Ed.2d 558. The concept of cover is especially important if the market is inefficient or for other reasons it takes many days for the stock's price to reach an equilibrium level and then stabilize around that level. Thus, in *Texas Gulf Sulphur* the stock climbed from $30 7/8 at the close of the day the corrective disclosure to peak at $59 some 13 days later. The Tenth Circuit capped the recovery based on the average price of the securities a reasonable time (4 days in this particular case) between when it believed the reasonable investors would have become informed of the corrective disclosure and could have moved thereafter to cover their losses, which was at least 9 trading days (and therefore included the peak price of $59 which was recorded on April 29th).

To recapitulate, measuring the market price at the time of disclosure, in the case of publicly held stock, reflects two basic ideas. The first is the valuation idea: such a measure allows the market to determine the value of the relevant information. The second is the cover idea: such a measure allows a selling plaintiff to restore himself to the position he would have been in if he had not been wrongfully induced to trade.

NOTE ON PROPORTIONATE LIABILITY

Securities fraud rarely involves only a single actor. Consider the case of the publication of false financial reports by a publicly traded company. The reports may well have been the product of a corrupt CEO with her CFO as an accomplice. The firm's auditor may well have been involved, or at least reckless in failing to uncover the executives fraudulent massaging of the numbers. There may also have been directors, perhaps some were members of the firm's audit committee, who knowingly turned a blind eye toward evidence that the books were being cooked. Perhaps the false reports were used in raising funds through the efforts of an investment banker who acted with knowledge the fraudulent financial reports. Prior to the PSLRA, liability among joint violators was joint and several, although contribution claims among co-violators was based on proportionate fault. The PSLRA added section 21D(g) to the Securities Exchange Act to embrace proportionate fault, albeit with important qualifications.

> The key requirement of the new section 21D(g) is that in all private actions under the Exchange Act, the fact finder (whether judge or jury) must make specific findings with respect to each defendant, determining (i) whether such person violated the securities laws, (ii) whether the violation was committed knowingly, and (iii) the percentage of responsibility of such person in terms of the total fault of all persons—whether named as parties or not—who caused or contributed to the loss. The fact-finder is

> also to specify both the total damages and the percentage of responsibility for each covered person. Those defendants who acted knowingly are jointly and severally liable for all the damages; those who did not are liable only for their proportionate share (subject to the exceptions to be discussed below). Strangely the jury is *not* to be told that the consequence of the proportionate share may be limited liability for any given defendant, or less than full compensation to the plaintiffs. The jury is to be left in the dark about why it is answering the special interrogatories apportioning fault.

Donald C. Langevoort, The Reform of Joint and Several Liability Under the Private Securities Litigation Reform Act of 1995: Proportionate Liability, Contribution Rights and Settlement Effects, 51 Bus. Law. 1157, 1162–1163 (1996). The exceptions to proportionate liability are (i) for those who act with knowledge of the misrepresentation, (ii) a defendant's proportionate share can be increase by as much as fifty percent when necessary to cover an uncollectible share against another defendant, and (iii) in the rather limited instance where small investors (those whose net worth is less than $200,000) who have lost more than ten percent of their net worth and the full judgment is not collectible (e.g., one of the defendants is bankrupt). Contribution claims among co-violators are addressed in subsection 21D(g)(8) which provides "[a] claim of contribution shall be determined based on the percentage of responsibility of the claimant and of each person against whom a claim of contribution is made." Any defendant who has paid to the plaintiff more than her proportionate share is armed by subsection (g)(5) with a right to receive contribution from others who have not thus far paid their proportionate share.

CHAPTER 13

INSIDER TRADING

SECTION 1. THE COMMON LAW BACKGROUND

NOTE ON THE DUTIES OF DIRECTORS AND OFFICERS UNDER THE COMMON LAW WHEN TRADING IN THEIR CORPORATION'S STOCK

1. *Majority Rule.* At common law, the majority rule was that a director or officer of a corporation could trade in its stock without disclosing material nonpublic information concerning the corporation that he had acquired through his position—a type of information now referred to as *inside information.* A leading case was Goodwin v. Agassiz, 283 Mass. 358, 186 N.E. 659 (1933). Aggasiz was president of Cliff Mining Company and MacNaughton was Cliff's general manager. Both were also directors. In May 1926, Aggasiz and MacNaughton purchased a number of Cliff shares on the Boston Stock Exchange. Several hundred of these shares were owned by Goodwin. Because the trading was on an Exchange, neither the buyers nor the seller, Goodwin, knew each other's identity. The background to the trading was set forth in the opinion as follows:

> [Agassiz and MacNaughton] had certain knowledge, material as to the value of the stock, which the plaintiff did not have.... That knowledge was that an experienced geologist had formulated in writing in March, 1926, a theory as to the possible existence of copper deposits under conditions prevailing in the region where the property of the company was located. That region was known as the mineral belt in northern Michigan, where are located mines of several copper mining companies. Another such company, of which the defendants were officers, had made extensive geological surveys of its lands. In consequence of recommendations resulting from that survey, exploration was started on property of the Cliff Mining Company in 1925. That exploration was ended in May, 1926, because [it was] completed unsuccessfully, and the equipment was removed. The defendants discussed the geologist's theory shortly after it was formulated. Both felt that the theory had value and should be tested, but they agreed that, before starting to test it, options should be obtained by another copper company of which they were officers on land adjacent to or nearby in the copper belt, that if the geologist's theory were known to the owners of such other land there might be difficulty

> in securing options, and that that theory should not be communicated to any one unless it became absolutely necessary. Thereafter, options were secured which, if taken up, would involve a large expenditure by the other company. The defendants both thought, also, that, if there was any merit in the geologist's theory, the price of Cliff Mining Company stock in the market would go up. Its stock was quoted and bought and sold on the Boston stock exchange. Pursuant to agreement, they bought many shares of that stock through agents on joint account. The plaintiff first learned of the closing of exploratory operations on property of the Cliff Mining Company from an article in a paper on May 15, 1926, and immediately sold his shares of stock through brokers.... The plaintiff did not know that his stock was being bought for ... [the defendants].

283 Mass. at 360, 186 N.E. at 660.

Goodwin sued Agassiz and MacNaughton on the ground that they had a fiduciary duty to disclose the relevant information before purchasing Goodwin's shares. The Massachusetts Supreme Judicial Court held that directors and officers did not have such a duty, at least in an impersonal market.

Although the transactions in *Goodwin v. Agassiz* occurred in an impersonal market, there are cases in which the rule of that case was applied to face-to-face transactions. See, e.g., Lank v. Steiner, 43 Del.Ch. 262, 224 A.2d 242 (1966); Gladstone v. Murray Co., 314 Mass. 584, 50 N.E.2d 958 (1943). However, there was a minority rule, sometimes known as the Kansas rule, which required full disclosure by a director or officer, at least in face-to-face transactions. For example, in Hotchkiss v. Fischer, 136 Kan. 530, 16 P.2d 531 (1932), appeal after remand 139 Kan. 333, 31 P.2d 37 (1934), Hotchkiss, a widow in need of money, was a shareholder in Elmhurst Corporation. Hotchkiss came to Elmhurst's offices in advance of the corporation's annual meeting to ascertain whether a dividend would be declared. She had two interviews with Fischer, Elmhurst's president, who said he could not inform her whether a dividend would be declared until he conferred with directors coming from New York. Fischer showed Hotchkiss the year-end financial statements and explained the items on the statements, but painted a somewhat dark picture, saying finally, "[w]hat you regard your stock to be worth ... is a matter you have to determine yourself." 136 Kan. at 533, 16 P.2d at 532. In fact, the condition of the corporation was much better than the financial statements suggested. Hotchkiss sold her stock to Fischer for $1.25 per share. Three days later, the directors declared a dividend of $1.00 per share. In a suit for damages, the court held for Hotchkiss. The court likened a director's duty to that of a trustee, and said that a director is under a duty to deal fairly with the shareholder and "communicate ... all material facts in connection with the transaction which the [director] knows or should know." 136 Kan. at 537, 16 P.2d at 534. See also, e.g., Jacobson v. Yaschik, 249 S.C. 577, 155 S.E.2d 601 (1967).

2. *Fraud and Half–Truths*. The majority rule itself was subject to several very important exceptions. First, the rule did not apply when a director engaged in fraud. Under the common law, fraud occurs not only when a speaker knowingly makes a false statement, but also when he knowingly tells a half-truth. "A representation stating the truth so far as it goes but which the maker knows or believes to be materially misleading because of his failure to state additional or qualifying matter is a fraudulent misrepresentation.... Thus, a statement that contains only favorable matters and omits all references to unfavorable matters is as much a false representation as if all the facts stated were untrue." Restatement (Second) of Torts § 529 and Comment a (1976).

3. *Fraudulent Concealment*. It is also fraudulent at common law to take affirmative steps to prevent the truth from being discovered. "One party to a transaction who by concealment or other action intentionally prevents the other from acquiring material information is subject to the same liability to the other, for pecuniary loss as though he had stated the nonexistence of the matter that the other was thus prevented from discovering.... Even a false denial of knowledge or information by one party to a transaction, who is in possession of the facts, may subject him to liability as fully as if he had expressly misstated the facts, if its effect upon the plaintiff is to lead him to believe that the facts do not exist or cannot be discovered." Id. § 550 and Comment b.

4. *"Special Facts."* Perhaps the most important exception to the majority rule was the "special facts" exception, adopted in Strong v. Repide, 213 U.S. 419, 29 S.Ct. 521, 53 L.Ed. 853 (1909) and later in many other cases. Repide was a director, the administrator general, and owner of nearly three-fourths of the shares, of Philippine Sugar. Strong, who owned shares in Philippine Sugar, had given Jones a power of attorney to sell her shares. Philippine Sugar owned certain lands in the Philippines that the United States government wished to buy. The corporation was without funds, and the value of its shares was wholly dependent on making an advantageous sale of its properties to the government. Repide was in charge of the negotiations with the government, which dragged on for months, primarily because Repide was holding out for a higher price. While negotiations with the government were pending, Repide, knowing that a sale to the government was probable, used an intermediary to employ a broker to purchase Strong's shares from Jones. Jones was given no information as to the state of the negotiations with the government, and neither Strong nor Jones knew that Repide was the purchaser. The price paid to Strong was about one-tenth what the shares became worth less than three months later, when the sale of the corporation's property to the government was consummated.

The Supreme Court affirmed an award of damages to Strong, on the ground that even if a director has no general duty to disclose facts known to him before he purchases shares, "there are cases where, by reason of the special facts, such duty exists." Id. at 431, 29 S.Ct. at 525. Jones sold Strong's shares because the corporation was paying no dividends and the negotiations with the government had gone on for so long that he thought that there was no prospect that a sale of the corporation's property would be made in the near term. Repide was not only a director but, by reason of his ownership of three-fourths of the shares, his position as administrator general, and the acquiescence of the other shareholders, was in full charge of the negotiations and was able to come to an agreement with the government if and when he chose to do so. He concealed his identity as a purchaser and dealt in a roundabout fashion with Jones. In view of all these facts, "the law would indeed be impotent if the sale could not be set aside or [Repide] cast in damages for his fraud." Id. at 433, 29 S.Ct. at 526.

Since there was no meaningful way to differentiate those cases that involved "special facts" from those that didn't, the special-facts exception either ate up the majority rule or made the rule impossible to administer in a consistent fashion. At bottom, the exception was inconsistent with the majority rule, and was employed by the courts as a mechanism to escape from that rule while purporting to follow it.

5. *Atrophy*. The common law rule concerning disclosure in the sale of securities atrophied after the 1940's, due to the development of Rule 10b–5 under the Securities Exchange Act, which came to occupy most of the field. It is conceivable that if Rule 10b–5 had not been adopted, and the common law concerning the obligations of directors and officers in the purchase and sale of stock had continued to develop, the majority rule would have withered, because in the last fifty years the common law has evolved in the direction of requiring greater disclosure. For example, Restatement (Second) of Contracts § 161 (1979) provides that a "person's nondisclosure of a fact known to him is equivalent to an assertion that the fact does not exist ... where the other person is entitled to know the fact because of a relation of trust and confidence between them." In Bailey v. Vaughan, 178 W.Va. 371, 359 S.E.2d 599 (1987), the court concluded that "there is presently no majority rule that enables a director to utilize insider information which points to substantial undervaluation of the corporate shares and then to purchase shares from an uninformed shareholder without any liability." In Lawton v. Nyman, 327 F.3d 30 (1st Cir. 2003), the court said "We hold, therefore, that it is a violation of a fiduciary duty for an officer or director of a closed corporation to purchase the stock of minority shareholders without disclosing material facts affecting the value of the stock, known to the purchasing officer or director by virtue of his position but not known to the selling shareholder."

SECTION 2. THE FEDERAL DISCLOSE OR ABSTAIN REQUIREMENT

IN THE MATTER OF CADY, ROBERTS & CO., 40 S.E.C. 907, 911–12 (1961). In an SEC disciplinary proceeding against a broker who sold publicly traded shares on behalf of his clients after tipping them of his confidential knowledge that the company would soon reduce its dividend, the SEC Chairman Cary offered the following regarding the antifraud provision's proscription of insider trading and tipping: "[Rule 10b–5 applies] to securities transactions by 'any person.' Misrepresentations will lie within [its] ambit, no matter who the speaker may be. An affirmative duty to disclose material information has been traditionally imposed on corporate 'insiders,' particularly officers, directors, or controlling stockholders. We, and the courts have consistently held that insiders must disclose material facts which are known to them by virtue of their position but which are not known to persons with whom they deal and which, if known, would affect their investment judgment. Failure to make disclosure in these circumstances constitutes a violation of the anti-fraud provisions. If, on the other hand, disclosure prior to effecting a purchase or sale would be improper or unrealistic under the circumstances, we believe the alternative is to forego the transaction. . . .

"We have already noted that the anti-fraud provisions are phrased in terms of 'any person' and that a special obligation has been traditionally required of corporate insiders, e.g., officers, directors and controlling stockholders. These three groups, however, do not exhaust the classes of persons upon whom there is such an obligation. Analytically, the obligation rests on two principal elements; first, the existence of a relationship giving access, directly or indirectly, to information intended to be available only for a corporate purpose and not for the personal benefit of anyone, and second, the inherent unfairness involved where a party takes advantage of such information knowing it is unavailable to those with whom he is dealing. In considering these elements under the broad language of the anti-fraud provisions we are not to be circumscribed by fine distinctions and rigid classifications. Thus our task here is to identify those persons who are in a special relationship with a company and privy to its internal affairs, and thereby suffer correlative duties in trading in its securities. Intimacy demands restraint lest the uninformed be exploited."

Securities and Exchange Commission v. Texas Gulf Sulphur Co.

United States Court of Appeals, Second Circuit, 1968.
401 F.2d 833 (in banc), cert. denied 394 U.S. 976, 89 S.Ct. 1454, 22 L.Ed.2d 756 (1969).

■ WATERMAN, CIRCUIT JUDGE:

[This was an action brought by the S.E.C. against Texas Gulf Sulphur (TGS) based on the issuance of a misleading press release, and against certain officers and employees of TGS based on their trading and tipping. The case grew out of an important mineral discovery by TGS. Four of the individual defendants were members of the geological exploration group that made the discovery: Mollison, a vice-president and mining engineer who headed the exploration group; Holyk, TGS' chief geologist; Clayton, an electrical engineer and geophysicist, and Darke, a geologist. The other individual defendants included Stephens, who was TGS's President; Fogarty, its Executive Vice–President; Kline, its Vice–President and General Counsel; and Coates, a director.

[Those portions of the opinion dealing with the liability of TGS for the misleading press release and the liability of individual defendants for tipping have been omitted, because the discussion of those issues has been largely superseded by later Supreme Court cases, examined later in this Chapter.]

This action derives from the exploratory activities of TGS begun in 1957 on the Canadian Shield in eastern Canada. In March of 1959, aerial geophysical surveys were conducted over more than 15,000 square miles of this area by a group led by defendant Mollison, a mining engineer and a Vice President of TGS. The group included defendant Holyk, TGS's chief geologist, defendant Clayton, an electrical engineer and geophysicist, and defendant Darke, a geologist. These operations resulted in the detection of numerous anomalies, i.e., extraordinary variations in the conductivity of rocks, one of which was on the Kidd 55 segment of land located near Timmins, Ontario.

On October 29 and 30, 1963, Clayton conducted a ground geophysical survey on the northeast portion of the Kidd 55 segment which confirmed the presence of an anomaly and indicated the necessity of diamond core drilling for further evaluation. Drilling of the initial hole, K–55–1, at the strongest part of the anomaly was commenced on November 8 and terminated on November 12 at a depth of 655 feet. Visual estimates by Holyk of the core of K–55–1 indicated an average copper content of 1.15% and an average zinc content of 8.64% over a length of 599 feet. This visual estimate convinced TGS that it was desirable to acquire the remainder of the Kidd 55 segment, and in order to facilitate this acquisition TGS President Stephens instructed the exploration group to keep the results of K–55–1 confidential and undisclosed even as to other officers, directors, and employees of TGS. The hole was concealed and a barren core was intentionally drilled off the anomaly. Meanwhile, the core of K–55–1 had been shipped to Utah for chemical assay which, when received in early December, revealed an average mineral content of 1.18% copper, 8.26% zinc, and 3.94% ounces of silver per ton over a length of 602 feet. These results were so remarkable that neither Clayton, an experienced geophysicist, nor four other TGS expert witnesses, had ever seen or heard of a comparable initial exploratory drill hole in a base metal deposit. So, the trial court concluded, "There is no doubt that the drill core of K–55–1 was unusually good and that it excited the interest and speculation of those who knew about it." Id. at 282. By March 27, 1964, TGS decided that the land acquisition program had advanced to such a point that the company might well resume drilling, and drilling was resumed on March 31.

During this period, from November 12, 1963 when K–55–1 was completed, to March 31, 1964 when drilling was resumed certain of the individual defendants ... and persons ... said to have received "tips" from them, purchased TGS stock or calls thereon. Prior to these transactions these persons had owned 1135 shares of TGS stock and possessed no calls; thereafter they owned a total of 8235 shares and possessed 12,300 calls.

On February 20, 1964, also during this period, TGS issued stock options to 26 of its officers and employees whose salaries exceeded a specified amount, five of whom were the individual defendants Stephens, Fogarty, Mollison, Holyk, and Kline. Of these, only Kline was unaware of the detailed results of K–55–1, but he, too, knew that a hole containing favorable bodies of copper and zinc ore had been drilled in Timmins. At this time, neither the TGS Stock Option Committee nor its Board of Directors had been informed of the results of K–55–1, presumably because of the pending land acquisition program which required confidentiality. All of the foregoing defendants accepted the options granted them.

When drilling was resumed on March 31, hole K–55–3 was commenced 510 feet west of K–55–1 and was drilled easterly at a 45– angle so as to cross K–55–1 in a vertical plane. Daily progress reports of the drilling of this hole K–55–3 and of all subsequently drilled holes were sent to defendants Stephens and Fogarty (President and Executive Vice President of TGS) by Holyk and Mollison. Visual estimates of K–55–3 revealed an average mineral content of 1.12% copper and 7.93% zinc over 641 of the hole's 876–foot length. On April 7, drilling of a third hole, K–55–4, 200 feet south of and parallel to K–55–1 and westerly at a 45_ angle, was commenced and mineralization was encountered over 366 of its 579–foot length. Visual estimates indicated an average content of 1.14% copper and 8.24% zinc. Like K–55–1, both K–55–3 and K–55–4 established substantial copper mineralization on the eastern edge of the anomaly. On the basis of these findings relative to the foregoing drilling results, the trial court concluded that the vertical plane created by the intersection of K–55–1 and K–55–3, which measured at least 350 feet wide by 500 feet deep extended southward 200 feet to its intersection with K–55–4, and that "There was real evidence that a body of commercially mineable ore might exist." Id. at 281–82.

On April 8 TGS began with a second drill rig to drill another hole, K–55–6, 300 feet easterly of K–55–1. This hole was drilled westerly at an angle of 60– and was intended to explore mineralization beneath K–55–1. While no visual estimates of its core were immediately available, it was readily apparent by the evening of April 10 that substantial copper mineralization had been encountered over the last 127 feet of the hole's 569–foot length. On April 10, a third drill rig commenced drilling yet another hole, K–55–5, 200 feet north of K–55–1, parallel to the prior holes, and slanted westerly at a 45_ angle. By the evening of April 10 in this hole, too, substantial copper mineralization had been encountered over the last 42 feet of its 97–foot length.

Meanwhile, rumors that a major ore strike was in the making had been circulating throughout Canada. On the morning of Saturday,

April 11, Stephens at his home in Greenwich, Conn. read in the New York Herald Tribune and in the New York Times unauthorized reports of the TGS drilling which seemed to infer a rich strike from the fact that the drill cores had been flown to the United States for chemical assay. Stephens immediately contacted Fogarty at his home in Rye, N.Y., who in turn telephoned and later that day visited Mollison at Mollison's home in Greenwich to obtain a current report and evaluation of the drilling progress.[7] The following morning, Sunday, Fogarty again telephoned Mollison, inquiring whether Mollison had any further information and told him to return to Timmins with Holyk, the TGS Chief Geologist, as soon as possible "to move things along." With the aid of one Carroll, a public relations consultant, Fogarty drafted a press release designed to quell the rumors, which release, after having been channeled through Stephens and Huntington, a TGS attorney, was issued at 3:00 P.M. on Sunday, April 12, and which appeared in the morning newspapers of general circulation on Monday, April 13. It read in pertinent part as follows:

New York, April 12—The following statement was made today by Dr. Charles F. Fogarty, executive vice president of Texas Gulf Sulphur Company, in regard to the company's drilling operations near Timmins, Ontario, Canada. Dr. Fogarty said:

"During the past few days, the exploration activities of Texas Gulf Sulphur in the area of Timmins, Ontario, have been widely reported in the press, coupled with rumors of a substantial copper discovery there. These reports exaggerate the scale of operations, and mention plans and statistics of size and grade of ore that are without factual basis and have evidently originated by speculation of people not connected with TGS.

"The facts are as follows. TGS has been exploring in the Timmins area for six years as part of its overall search in Canada and elsewhere for various minerals—lead, copper, zinc, etc. During the course of this work, in Timmins as well as in Eastern Canada, TGS has conducted exploration entirely on its own, without the participation by others. Numerous prospects have been investigated by geophysical means and a large number of selected ones have been core-drilled. These cores are sent to the United States for assay and detailed examination as a matter of routine and on advice of expert Canadian legal counsel. No inferences as to grade can be drawn from this procedure.

"Most of the areas drilled in Eastern Canada have revealed either barren pyrite or graphite without value; a few have resulted in discoveries of small or marginal sulphide ore bodies.

---

7. Mollison had returned to the United States for the weekend. Friday morning April 10, he had been on the Kidd tract "and had been advised by defendant Holyk as to the drilling results to 7:00 p.m. on April 10. At that time drill holes K–55–1, K–55–3 and K–55–4 had been completed; drilling of K–55–5 had started on Section 2200 S and had been drilled to 97 feet, encountering mineralization on the last 42 feet; and drilling of K–55–6 had been started on Section 2400 S and had been drilled to 569 feet, encountering mineralization over the last 127 feet." Id. at 294.

"Recent drilling on one property near Timmins has led to preliminary indications that more drilling would be required for proper evaluation of this prospect. The drilling done to date has not been conclusive, but the statements made by many outside quarters are unreliable and include information and figures that are not available to TGS.

"The work done to date has not been sufficient to reach definite conclusions and any statement as to size and grade of ore would be premature and possibly misleading. When we have progressed to the point where reasonable and logical conclusions can be made, TGS will issue a definite statement to its stockholders and to the public in order to clarify the Timmins project."

* * *

The release purported to give the Timmins drilling results as of the release date, April 12. From Mollison Fogarty had been told of the developments through 7:00 P.M. on April 10, and of the remarkable discoveries made up to that time, detailed supra, which discoveries, according to the calculations of the experts who testified for the SEC at the hearing, demonstrated that TGS had already discovered 6.2 to 8.3 million tons of proven ore having gross assay values from $26 to $29 per ton. TGS experts, on the other hand, denied at the hearing that proven or probable ore could have been calculated on April 11 or 12 because there was then no assurance of continuity in the mineralized zone.

The evidence as to the effect of this release on the investing public was equivocal and less than abundant. On April 13 the New York Herald Tribune in an article head-noted "Copper Rumor Deflated" quoted from the TGS release of April 12 and backtracked from its original April 11 report of a major strike but nevertheless inferred from the TGS release that "recent mineral exploratory activity near Timmins, Ontario, has provided preliminary favorable results, sufficient at least to require a step-up in drilling operations." Some witnesses who testified at the hearing stated that they found the release encouraging. On the other hand, a Canadian mining security specialist, Roche, stated that "earlier in the week [before April 16] we had a Dow Jones saying that they [TGS] didn't have anything basically" and a TGS stock specialist for the Midwest Stock Exchange became concerned about his long position in the stock after reading the release. The trial court stated only that "While, in retrospect, the press release may appear gloomy or incomplete, this does not make it misleading or deceptive on the basis of the facts then known." Id. at 296.

Meanwhile, drilling operations continued....

While drilling activity ensued to completion, TGS officials were taking steps toward ultimate disclosure of the discovery. On April 13, a previously-invited reporter for The Northern Miner, a Canadian mining industry journal, visited the drillsite, interviewed Mollison, Holyk and Darke, and prepared an article which confirmed a 10 million ton ore strike. This report, after having been submitted to Mollison and returned to the reporter unamended on April 15, was published in the April 16 issue. A statement relative to the extent of the discovery, in substantial part drafted by Mollison, was given to the Ontario Minister of Mines for release to the Canadian media. Mollison and Holyk expected it to be released over the airways at 11 P.M. on April 15th, but, for undisclosed reasons, it was not released until 9:40 A.M. on the 16th. An official detailed statement, announcing a strike of at least 25 million tons of ore, based on the drilling data set forth above, was read to representatives of American financial media from 10:00 A.M. to 10:10 or 10:15 A.M. on April 16, and appeared over Merrill Lynch's private wire at 10:29 A.M. and, somewhat later than expected, over the Dow Jones ticker tape at 10:54 A.M.

Between the time the first press release was issued on April 12 and the dissemination of the TGS official announcement on the morning of April 16, the only defendants before us on appeal who engaged in market activity were Clayton and Crawford and TGS director Coates. Clayton ordered 200 shares of TGS stock through his Canadian broker on April 15 and another 300 shares at 8:30 A.M. the next day, and these orders were executed over the Midwest Exchange in Chicago at its opening on April 16. Coates left the TGS press conference and called his broker son-in-law Haemisegger shortly before 10:20 A.M. on the 16th and ordered 2,000 shares of TGS for family trust accounts of which Coates was a trustee but not a beneficiary; Haemisegger executed this order over the New York and Midwest Exchanges, and he and his customers purchased 1500 additional shares.

During the period of drilling in Timmins, the market price of TGS stock fluctuated but steadily gained overall. On Friday, November 8, when the drilling began, the stock closed at 17$\frac{3}{8}$; on Friday, November 15, after K–55–1 had been completed, it closed at 18. After a slight decline to 16$\frac{3}{8}$ by Friday, November 22, the price rose to 20$\frac{7}{8}$ by December 13, when the chemical assay results of K–55–1 were received, and closed at a high of 24$\frac{1}{8}$ on February 21, the day after the stock options had been issued. It had reached a price of 26 by March 31, after the land acquisition program had been completed and drilling had been resumed, and continued to ascend to 30$\frac{1}{8}$ by the close of trading on April 10, at which time the drilling progress up to then was evaluated for the April 12th press release. On April 13, the day on which the April 12 release was disseminated, TGS opened at 30$\frac{1}{8}$, rose immediately to a high of 32 and gradually tapered off to close at 30⅞. It closed at 30¼ the next day, and at 29⅜ on April 15. On April 16, the day of the official announcement of the Timmins discovery, the price climbed to a high of 37 and closed at 36⅜. By May 15, TGS stock was selling at 58¼. . . .*

I. The Individual Defendants

A. *Introductory*

. . . Whether predicated on traditional fiduciary concepts, see, e.g., Hotchkiss v. Fisher, 136 Kan. 530, 16 P.2d 531 (Kan.1932), or on the "special facts" doctrine, see, e.g., Strong v. Repide, 213 U.S. 419, 29 S.Ct. 521, 53 L.Ed. 853 (1909), . . . Rule [10b–5] is based in policy on the justifiable expectation of the securities marketplace that all

* [Footnote by the court; relocated by the editor.]

Purchase Date		*Purchaser*	*Shares Number*	*Shares Price*	*Calls Number*	*Calls Price*
Hole K–55–1 Completed November 12, 1963						
1963						
Nov.	12	Fogarty	300	17¾–18		
	15	Clayton	200	17¾		
	15	Fogarty	700	17⅝–17⅞		
	15	Mollison	100	17⅞		
	19	Fogarty	500	18⅛		
	26	Fogarty	200	17¾		
	29	Holyk	50	18		
Chemical Assays of Drill Core of K–55–1 Received December 9–13, 1963						
Dec.	10	Holyk (Mrs.)	100	20⅜		
	12	Holyk (or wife)			200	21
	13	Mollison	100	21⅛		
	30	Fogarty	200	22		
	31	Fogarty	100	23¼		
1964						
Jan.	6	Holyk (or wife)			100	23⅝
	8	Murray			400	23¼
	24	Holyk (or wife)			200	22¼–22⅜
Feb.	10	Fogarty	300	22⅛–22¼		
	20	Darke	300	24⅛		
	24	Clayton	400	23⅞		
	24	Holyk (or wife)			200	24⅛
	26	Holyk (or wife)			200	23⅜
	26	Huntington	50	23¼		
	27	Darke (Moran as nominee)			1000	22⅝–22¾
Mar.	2	Holyk (Mrs.)	200	22⅜		
	3	Clayton	100	22¼		
	16	Huntington			100	22⅜
	16	Holyk (or wife)			300	23¼
	17	Holyk (Mrs.)	100	23⅞		
	23	Darke			1000	24¾
	26	Clayton	200	25		
Land Acquisition Completed March 27, 1964						
Mar.	30	Darke			100	25½
	30	Holyk (Mrs.)	100	25⅞		
Core Drilling of Kidd Segment Resumed March 31, 1964						
April	1	Clayton	60	26½		
	1	Fogarty	400	26½		
	2	Clayton	100	26⅞		
	6	Fogarty	400	28⅛–28⅞		
	8	Mollison (Mrs.)	100	28⅛		
First Press Release Issued April 12, 1964						
April	15	Clayton	200	29⅜		
	16	Crawford (and wife)	600	30⅛–30¼		
Second Press Release Issued 10:00–10:10 or 10:15 A.M., April 16, 1964 . . .						
1963						
April	16	(app. 10:20 A.M.) Coates (for family trusts)	2000	31–31⅝		

investors trading on impersonal exchanges have relatively equal access to material information, see Cary, Insider Trading in Stocks, 21 Bus. Law. 1009, 1010 (1966), Fleischer, Securities Trading and Corporation Information Practices: The Implications of the Texas Gulf Sulphur Proceeding, 51 Va.L.Rev. 1271, 1278–80 (1965). The essence of the Rule is that anyone who, trading for his own account in the securities of a corporation has "access, directly or indirectly, to information intended to be available only for a corporate purpose and not for the personal benefit of anyone" may not take "advantage of such information knowing it is unavailable to those with whom he is dealing," i.e., the investing public. Matter of Cady, Roberts & Co., 40 SEC 907, 912 (1961). Insiders, as directors or management officers are, of course, by this Rule, precluded from so unfairly dealing, but the Rule is also applicable to one possessing the information who may not be strictly termed an "insider" within the meaning of Sec. 16(b) of the Act. Cady, Roberts, supra. Thus, anyone in possession of material inside information must either disclose it to the investing public, or, if he is disabled from disclosing it in order to protect a corporate confidence, or he chooses not to do so, must abstain from trading in or recommending the securities concerned while such inside information remains undisclosed. So, it is here no justification for insider activity that disclosure was forbidden by the legitimate corporate objective of acquiring options to purchase the land surrounding the exploration site; if the information was, as the SEC contends, material, its possessors should have kept out of the market until disclosure was accomplished. Cady, Roberts, supra at 911.

B. *Material Inside Information*

An insider is not, of course, always foreclosed from investing in his own company merely because he may be more familiar with company operations than are outside investors. An insider's duty to disclose information or his duty to abstain from dealing in his company's securities arises only in "those situations which are essentially extraordinary in nature and which are reasonably certain to have a substantial effect on the market price of the security if [the extraordinary situation is] disclosed." Fleischer, Securities Trading and Corporate Information Practices: The Implications of the Texas Gulf Sulphur Proceeding, 51 Va.L.Rev. 1271, 1289.

Nor is an insider obligated to confer upon outside investors the benefit of his superior financial or other expert analysis by disclosing his educated guesses or predictions. 3 Loss, op. cit. supra at 1463. The only regulatory objective is that access to material information be enjoyed equally, but this objective requires nothing more than the disclosure of basic facts so that outsiders may draw upon their own evaluative expertise in reaching their own investment decisions with knowledge equal to that of the insiders.

This is not to suggest, however, as did the trial court, that "the test of materiality must necessarily be a conservative one, particularly since many actions under Section 10(b) are brought on the basis of hindsight," 258 F.Supp. 262 at 280, in the sense that the materiality of facts is to be assessed solely by measuring the effect the knowledge of the facts would have upon prudent or conservative investors. As we stated in List v. Fashion Park, Inc., 340 F.2d 457, 462, "The basic test of materiality ... is whether a *reasonable* man would attach importance ... in determining his choice of action in the transaction in question. Restatement, Torts § 538(2)(a); accord Prosser, Torts 554–55; I Harper & James, Torts 565–66." (Emphasis supplied.) ... [M]aterial facts include not only information disclosing the earnings and distributions of a company but also those facts which affect the probable future of the company and those which may affect the desire of investors to buy, sell, or hold the company's securities.

In each case, then, whether facts are material within Rule 10b–5 when the facts relate to a particular event and are undisclosed by those persons who are knowledgeable thereof will depend at any given time upon a balancing of both the indicated probability that the event will occur and the anticipated magnitude of the event in light of the totality of the company activity. Here, notwithstanding the trial court's conclusion that the results of the first drill core, K–55–1, were "too 'remote' ... to have had any significant impact on the market, i.e., to be deemed material," 258 F.Supp. at 283, knowledge of the possibility, which surely was more than marginal, of the existence of a mine of the vast magnitude indicated by the remarkably rich drill core located rather close to the surface (suggesting mineability by the less expensive open pit method) within the confines of a large anomaly (suggesting an extensive region of mineralization) might well have affected the price of TGS stock and would certainly have been an important fact to a reasonable, if speculative, investor in deciding whether he should buy, sell, or hold. After all, this first drill core was "unusually good and ... excited the interest and speculation of those who knew about it." 258 F.Supp. at 282.

... Our survey of the facts found below conclusively establishes that knowledge of the results of the discovery hole, K–55–1, would have been important to a reasonable investor and might have affected the price of the stock.[2] On April 16, The Northern Miner, a trade publication in wide circulation among mining stock specialists, called K–55–1, the discovery hole, "one of the most impressive drill holes completed in modern times." Roche, a Canadian broker whose firm specialized in mining securities, characterized the importance to investors of the results of K–55–1. He stated that the completion of "the first drill hole" with "a 600 foot drill core is very very significant ... anything over 200 feet is considered very significant and 600 feet is just beyond your wildest imagination." He added, however, that it "is a natural thing to buy more stock once they give you the first drill hole." Additional testimony revealed that the prices of stocks of other companies, albeit less diversified, smaller firms, had increased substan-

2. We do not suggest that material facts must be disclosed immediately; the timing of disclosure is a matter for the business judgment of the corporate officers entrusted with the management of the corporation within the affirmative disclosure requirements promulgated by the exchanges and by the SEC. Here, a valuable corporate purpose was served by delaying the publication of the K–55–1 discovery. We do intend to convey, however, that where a corporate purpose is thus served by withholding the news of a material fact, those persons who are thus quite properly true to their corporate trust must not during the period of non-disclosure deal personally in the corporation's securities or give to outsiders confidential information not generally available to all the corporations' stockholders and to the public at large.

tially solely on the basis of the discovery of good anomalies or even because of the proximity of their lands to the situs of a potentially major strike.

Finally, a major factor in determining whether the K–55–1 discovery was a material fact is the importance attached to the drilling results by those who knew about it. In view of other unrelated recent developments favorably affecting TGS, participation by an informed person in a regular stock-purchase program, or even sporadic trading by an informed person, might lend only nominal support to the inference of the materiality of the K–55–1 discovery; nevertheless, the timing by those who knew of it of their stock purchases and their purchases of *short-term* calls—purchases in some cases by individuals who had never before purchased calls or even TGS stock—virtually compels the inference that the insiders were influenced by the drilling results. This insider trading activity, which surely constitutes highly pertinent evidence and the only truly objective evidence of the materiality of the K–55–1 discovery, was apparently disregarded by the court below in favor of the testimony of defendants' expert witnesses, all of whom "agreed that one drill core does not establish an ore body, much less a mine," 258 F.Supp. at 282–283. Significantly, however, the court below, while relying upon what these defense experts said the defendant insiders *ought* to have thought about the worth to TGS of the K–55–1 discovery, and finding that from November 12, 1963 to April 6, 1964 Fogarty, Murray, Holyk and Darke spent more than $100,000 in purchasing TGS stock and calls on that stock, made no finding that the insiders were motivated by any factor other than the extraordinary K–55–1 discovery when they bought their stock and their calls. No reason appears why outside investors, perhaps better acquainted with speculative modes of investment and with, in many cases, perhaps more capital at their disposal for intelligent speculation, would have been less influenced, and would not have been similarly motivated to invest if they had known what the insider investors knew about the K–55–1 discovery.

Our decision to expand the limited protection afforded outside investors by the trial court's narrow definition of materiality is not at all shaken by fears that the elimination of insider trading benefits will deplete the ranks of capable corporate managers by taking away an incentive to accept such employment. Such benefits, in essence, are forms of secret corporate compensation, see Cary, Corporate Standards and Legal Rules, 50 Calif.L.Rev. 408, 409–10 (1962), derived at the expense of the uninformed investing public and not at the expense of the corporation which receives the sole benefit from insider incentives. Moreover, adequate incentives for corporate officers may be provided by properly administered stock options and employee purchase plans of which there are many in existence. In any event, the normal motivation induced by stock ownership, i.e., the identification of an individual with corporate progress, is ill-promoted by condoning the sort of speculative insider activity which occurred here; for example, some of the corporation's stock was sold at market in order to purchase short-term calls upon that stock, calls which would never be exercised to increase a stockholder equity in TGS unless the market price of that stock rose sharply.

The core of Rule 10b–5 is the implementation of the Congressional purpose that all investors should have equal access to the rewards of participation in securities transactions. It was the intent of Congress that all members of the investing public should be subject to identical market risks,—which market risks include, of course the risk that one's evaluative capacity or one's capital available to put at risk may exceed another's capacity or capital. The insiders here were not trading on an equal footing with the outside investors. They alone were in a position to evaluate the probability and magnitude of what seemed from the outset to be a major ore strike; they alone could invest safely, secure in the expectation that the price of TGS stock would rise substantially in the event such a major strike should materialize, but would decline little, if at all, in the event of failure, for the public, ignorant at the outset of the favorable probabilities would likewise be unaware of the unproductive exploration, and the additional exploration costs would not significantly affect TGS market prices. Such inequities based upon unequal access to knowledge should not be shrugged off as inevitable in our way of life, or, in view of the congressional concern in the area, remain uncorrected.

We hold, therefore, that all transactions in TGS stock or calls by individuals apprised of the drilling results[14] of K–55–1 were made in violation of Rule 10b–5.[15] Inasmuch as the visual evaluation of that drill core (a generally reliable estimate though less accurate than a chemical assay) constituted material information, those advised of the results of the visual evaluation as well as those informed of the chemical assay traded in violation of law. The geologist Darke possessed undisclosed material information and traded in TGS securities. Therefore we reverse the dismissal of the action as to him and his personal transactions. . . .

With reference to Huntington, the trial court found that he "had no detailed knowledge as to the work" on the Kidd–55 segment, 258 F.Supp. 281. Nevertheless, the evidence shows that he knew about and participated in TGS's land acquisition program which followed the receipt of the K–55–1 drilling results, and that on February 26, 1964 he purchased 50 shares of TGS stock. Later, on March 16, he helped prepare a letter for Dr. Holyk's signature in which TGS made a substantial offer for lands near K–55–1, and on the same day he, who had never before purchased calls on any stock, purchased a call on 100 shares of TGS stock. We are satisfied that these purchases in February and March, coupled with his readily inferable and probably reliable, understanding of the highly favorable nature of preliminary

14. The trial court found that defendant Murray "had no detailed knowledge as to the work" on the Kidd–55 segment. There is no evidence in the record suggesting that Murray purchased his stock on January 8, 1964, on the basis of material undisclosed information, and the disposition below is undisturbed as to him.

15. Even if insiders were in fact ignorant of the broad scope of the Rule and acted pursuant to a mistaken belief as to the applicable law such an ignorance does not insulate them from the consequences of their acts. Tager v. SEC, 344 F.2d 5, 8 (2 Cir.1965).

operations on the Kidd segment, demonstrate that Huntington possessed material inside information such as to make his purchase violative of the Rule and the Act.

C. *When May Insiders Act?*

Appellant Crawford, who ordered[17] the purchase of TGS stock shortly before the TGS April 16 official announcement, and defendant Coates, who placed orders with and communicated the news to his broker immediately after the official announcement was read at the TGS-called press conference, concede that they were in possession of material information. They contend, however, that their purchases were not proscribed purchases for the news had already been effectively disclosed. We disagree.

Crawford telephoned his orders to his Chicago broker about midnight on April 15 and again at 8:30 in the morning of the 16th, with instructions to buy at the opening of the Midwest Stock Exchange that morning. The trial court's finding that "he sought to, and did, 'beat the news,' " 258 F.Supp. at 287, is well documented by the record. The rumors of a major ore strike which had been circulated in Canada and, to a lesser extent, in New York, had been disclaimed by the TGS press release of April 12, which significantly promised the public an official detailed announcement when possibilities had ripened into actualities. The abbreviated announcement to the Canadian press at 9:40 A.M. on the 16th by the Ontario Minister of Mines and the report carried by The Northern Miner, parts of which had sporadically reached New York on the morning of the 16th through reports from Canadian affiliates to a few New York investment firms, are assuredly not the equivalent of the official 10–15 minute announcement which was not released to the American financial press until after 10:00 A.M. Crawford's orders had been placed before that. Before insiders may act upon material information, such information must have been effectively disclosed in a manner sufficient to insure its availability to the investing public. Particularly here, where a formal announcement to the entire financial news media had been promised in a prior official release known to the media, all insider activity must await dissemination of the promised official announcement.

Coates was absolved by the court below because his telephone order was placed shortly before 10:20 A.M. on April 16, which was after the announcement had been made even though the news could not be considered already a matter of public information. 258 F.Supp. at 288. This result seems to have been predicated upon a misinterpretation of dicta in *Cady, Roberts,* where the SEC instructed insiders to

---

17. The effective protection of the public from insider exploitation of advance notice of material information requires that the time that an insider places an order, rather than the time of its ultimate execution, be determinative for Rule 10b–5 purposes. Otherwise, insiders would be able to "beat the news," cf. Fleischer, supra, 51 Va.L.Rev. at 1291, by requesting in advance that their orders be executed immediately after the dissemination of a major news release but before outsiders could act on the release. Thus it is immaterial whether Crawford's orders were executed before or after the announcement was made in Canada (9:40 A.M., April 16) or in the United States (10:00 A.M.) or whether Coates's order was executed before or after the news appeared over the Merrill Lynch (10:29 A.M.) or Dow Jones (10:54 A.M.) wires.

"keep out of the market until the established procedures for public release of the information are *carried out* instead of hastening to execute transactions in advance of, and in frustration of, the objectives of the release," 40 SEC at 915 (emphasis supplied). The reading of a news release, which prompted Coates into action, is merely the first step in the process of dissemination required for compliance with the regulatory objective of providing all investors with an equal opportunity to make informed investment judgments. Assuming that the contents of the official release could instantaneously be acted upon,[18] at the minimum Coates should have waited until the news could reasonably have been expected to appear over the media of widest circulation, the Dow Jones broad tape, rather than hastening to insure an advantage to himself and his broker son-in-law.[19] . . .

E. *May Insiders Accept Stock Options Without Disclosing Material Information to the Issuer?*

On February 20, 1964, defendants Stephens, Fogarty, Mollison, Holyk and Kline accepted stock options issued to them and a number of other top officers of TGS, although not one of them had informed the Stock Option Committee of the Board of Directors or the Board of the results of K–55–1, which information we have held was then material. The SEC sought rescission of these options. The trial court, in addition to finding the knowledge of the results of the K–55 discovery to be immaterial, held that Kline had no detailed knowledge of the drilling progress and that Holyk and Mollison could reasonably assume that their superiors, Stephens and Fogarty, who were directors of the corporation, would report the results if that was advisable; indeed all employees had been instructed not to divulge this information pending completion of the land acquisition program, 258 F.Supp. at 291. Therefore, the court below concluded that only directors Stephens and Fogarty, of the top management, would have violated the Rule by accepting stock options without disclosure, but it also found that they had not acted improperly as the information in their possession was not material. 258 F.Supp. at 292. In view of our conclusion as to materiality we hold that Stephens and Fogarty violated the Rule by accepting them. However, as they have surrendered the

18. Although the only insider who acted after the news appeared over the Dow Jones broad tape is not an appellant and therefore we need not discuss the necessity of considering the advisability of a "reasonable waiting period" during which outsiders may absorb and evaluate disclosures, we note in passing that, where the news is of a sort which is not readily translatable into investment action, insiders may not take advantage of their advance opportunity to evaluate the information by acting immediately upon dissemination. In any event, the permissible timing of insider transactions after disclosures of various sorts is one of the many areas of expertise for appropriate exercise of the SEC's rule-making power, which we hope will be utilized in the future to provide some predictability of certainty for the business community.

19. The record reveals that news usually appears on the Dow Jones broad tape 2–3 minutes after the reporter completes dictation. Here, assuming that the Dow Jones reporter left the press conference as early as possible, 10:10 A.M., the 10–15 minute release (which took at least that long to dictate) could not have appeared on the wire before 10:22, and for other reasons unknown to us did not appear until 10:54. Indeed, even the abbreviated version of the release reported by Merrill Lynch over its private wire did not appear until 10:29. Coates, however, placed his call no later than 10:20.

options and the corporation has canceled them, supra at 292, n. 17, we find it unnecessary to order that the injunctions prayed for be actually issued. We point out, nevertheless, that the surrender of these options after the SEC commenced the case is not a satisfaction of the SEC claim, and a determination as to whether the issuance of injunctions against Stephens and Fogarty is advisable in order to prevent or deter future violations of regulatory provisions is remanded for the exercise of discretion by the trial court.

Contrary to the belief of the trial court that Kline had no duty to disclose his knowledge of the Kidd project before accepting the stock option offered him, we believe that he, a vice president, who had become the general counsel of TGS in January 1964, but who had been secretary of the corporation since January 1961, and was present in that capacity when the options were granted, and who was in charge of the mechanics of issuance and acceptance of the options, was a member of top management and under a duty before accepting his option to disclose any material information he may have possessed, and, as he did not disclose such information to the Option Committee we direct rescission of the option he received.[24] As to Holyk and Mollison, the SEC has not appealed the holding below that they, not being then members of top management (although Mollison was a vice president) had no duty to disclose their knowledge of the drilling before accepting their options. Therefore, the issue of whether, by accepting, they violated the Act, is not before us, and the holding below is undisturbed....

■ FRIENDLY, CIRCUIT JUDGE (concurring):

Agreeing with the result reached by the majority and with most of Judge Waterman's searching opinion, I take a rather different approach to two facets of the case.

I.

The first is a situation that will not often arise, involving as it does the acceptance of stock options during a period when inside informa-

---

24. The options granted on February 20, 1964 to Mollison, Holyk, and Kline were ratified by the Texas Gulf directors on July 15, 1965 after there had been, of course, a full disclosure and after this action had been commenced. However, the ratification is irrelevant here, for we would hold with the district court that a member of top management, as was Kline, is required, before accepting a stock option, to disclose material inside information which, if disclosed, might affect the price of the stock during the period when the accepted option could be exercised. Kline had known since November 1962 that K–55–1 had been drilled, that the drilling had intersected a sulphide body containing copper and zinc, and that TGS desired to acquire adjacent property.

Of course, if any of the five knowledgeable defendants had rejected his option there might well have been speculation as to the reason for the rejection. Therefore, in a case where disclosure to the grantors of an option would seriously jeopardize corporate security, it could well be desirable, in order to protect a corporation from selling securities to insiders who are in a position to appreciate their true worth at a price which may not accurately reflect the true value of the securities and at the same time to preserve when necessary the secrecy of corporate activity, not to require that an insider possessed of undisclosed material information reject the offer of a stock option, but only to require that he abstain from exercising it until such time as there shall have been a full disclosure and, after the full disclosure, a ratification such as was voted here. However, as this suggestion was not presented to us, we do not consider it or make any determination with reference to it.

tion likely to produce a rapid and substantial increase in the price of the stock was known to some of the grantees but unknown to those in charge of the granting. I suppose it would be clear, under Ruckle v. Roto American Corp., 339 F.2d 24 (2 Cir.1964), that if a corporate officer having such knowledge persuaded an unknowing board of directors to grant him an option at a price approximating the current market, the option would be rescindable in an action under Rule 10b–5. It would seem, by the same token, that if, to make the pill easier to swallow, he urged the directors to include others lacking the knowledge he possessed, he would be liable for all the resulting damage. The novel problem in the instant case is to define the responsibility of officers when a directors' committee administering a stock option plan proposes of its own initiative to make options available to them and others at a time when they know that the option price, geared to the market value of the stock, did not reflect a substantial increment likely to be realized in short order and was therefore unfair to the corporation.

A rule requiring a minor officer to reject an option so tendered would not comport with the realities either of human nature or of corporate life. If the SEC had appealed the ruling dismissing this portion of the complaint as to Holyk and Mollison, I would have upheld the dismissal quite apart from the special circumstance that a refusal on their part could well have broken the wall of secrecy it was important for TGS to preserve. Whatever they knew or didn't know about Timmins, they were entitled to believe their superiors had reported the facts to the Option Committee unless they had information to the contrary. Stephens, Fogarty and Kline stand on an altogether different basis; as senior officers they had an obligation to inform the Committee that this was not the right time to grant options at 95% of the current price. Silence, when there is a duty to speak, can itself be a fraud. I am unimpressed with the argument that Stephens, Fogarty and Kline could not perform this duty on the peculiar facts of this case, because of the corporate need for secrecy during the land acquisition program. Non-management directors would not normally challenge a recommendation for postponement of an option plan from the President, the Executive Vice President, and the Vice President and General Counsel. Moreover, it should be possible for officers to communicate with directors, of all people, without fearing a breach of confidence. Hence, as one of the foregoing hypotheticals suggests, I am not at all sure that a company in the position of TGS might not have a claim against top officers who breached their duty of disclosure for the entire damage suffered as a result of the untimely issuance of options, rather than merely one for rescission of the options issued to them.[2] Since that issue is not before us, I merely make the reservation of my position clear. . . .

2. Though the Board of Directors of TGS ratified the issuance of the options after the Timmins discovery had been fully publicized, it obviously was of the belief that Kline had committed no serious wrong in remaining silent. Throughout this litigation TGS has supported the legality of the actions of all the defendants—the company's counsel having represented, among others, Stephens, Fogarty and Kline. Consequently, I agree with the

[The opinions of Judges Kaufman and Anderson (concurring), Judge Hays (concurring in part and dissenting in part), and Judges Moore and Lumbard (dissenting) are omitted.]

SEC v. TEXAS GULF SULPHUR CO., 446 F.2d 1301, 1307–08 (2d Cir.1971). "[On remand, the] district court required Holyk, Huntington, Clayton, and Darke to pay to TGS the profits they had derived (and, in Darke's case, also the profits which his tippees had derived) from their TGS stock between their respective purchase dates and April 17, 1964, when the ore strike was fully known to the public. The payments are to be held in escrow in an interest-bearing account for a period of five years, subject to disposition in such manner as the court might direct upon application by the SEC or other interested person, or on the court's own motion. At the end of five years any money remaining undisposed of would become the property of TGS. To protect the appellants against double liability, any private judgments against these appellants arising out of the events of this case are to be paid from this fund. . . .

"Appellants, of course, contend that the required restitution is . . . a penalty assessment. . . . [However, restitution] of the profits on these transactions merely deprives the appellants of the gains of their wrongful conduct. . . .

"Finally, appellants contend that the order is punitive because it contains no element of compensation to those who have been damaged. However, as the New York Court of Appeals in Diamond v. Oreamuno, 24 N.Y.2d 494, 499, 301 N.Y.S.2d 78, 81–82, 248 N.E.2d 910, 912–913 (1969), recognized, a corporate enterprise may well suffer harm 'when officers and directors abuse their position to obtain personal profits' since 'the effect may be to cast a cloud on the corporation's name, injure stockholder relations and undermine public regard for the corporation's securities.' Although the sellers of TGS stock who sold before April 17, 1964, may have a higher equity than TGS to recover from appellants the wrongful profits appellants obtained, this fact does not preclude conditional compensation to TGS."

HOW PERVASIVE IS INSIDER TRADING?

The financial rewards of trading in securities markets on confidential material information are large. Not surprisingly the attraction of reaping gains based on inside information too frequently overcomes whatever deterrent or moral forces exist that call for abstention from

---

majority in giving the Board's action no weight here. If a fraud of this kind may ever be cured by ratification, compare Continental Securities Co. v. Belmont, 206 N.Y. 7, 99 N.E. 138, 51 L.R.A., N.S., 112 (1912), with Claman v. Robertson, 164 Ohio St. 61, 128 N.E.2d 429 (1955); cf. Wilko v. Swan, 346 U.S. 427, 74 S.Ct. 182, 98 L.Ed. 168 (1953), that cannot be done without an appreciation of the illegality of the conduct proposed to be excused, cf. United Hotels Co. v. Mealey, 147 F.2d 816, 819 (2 Cir.1945).

trading on material nonpublic information. Empirical studies consistently have shown that significant trading in securities markets occurs on the basis of secret advance knowledge of material non public information.

Initial studies of insider trading examined whether insiders (officers, directors and certain beneficial owners) who are required to report their trading pursuant to section 16(a) of the Securities Exchange Act, discussed later in this chapter, abuse the informational advantage they enjoy by trading on non public information. Jaffe, Special Information and Insider Trading, 47 J. Bus. 410 (1974), and Finnerty, Insiders and Market Efficiency, 31 J. Fin. 1141 (1976), each find that insiders garnered significant abnormal returns via their reported purchases and sells of their firm's shares, an observation consistent with insiders deploying confidential corporate information to their personal advantage. Not captured by Jaffe and Finnerty is the extent, if any, that the same insiders share their good fortune by tipping friends and relatives so that the ill-gotten gains are more pervasive than those reaped by the director, officer or beneficial owner of a reporting company who file section 16(a) reports. If there is a silver lining in this cloud it is that such insider trading not only drives securities prices in the direction of the post-announcement equilibrium level but appears also to be related to price-discovery efforts by "uniformed" traders who mimic the insider's trading. *See* Meulbroek, An Empirical Analysis of Illegal Trading, 47 J. Fin. 1661 (1992). This "positive" byproduct, however, should not detract from our condemnation of the substantial first mover advantage insiders enjoy. *See* James D. Cox, Insider Trading and Contracting: A Critical Response to the "Chicago School," 1986 Duke L. J. 628 (claims of efficiency associated with insider trading are overstated as insider trading is slow and clumsy method to impart newsworthy information vis-à-vis a clarion corporate announcement).

Mergers and takeovers are particularly rife with insider trading abuses in the pre-announcement period. Because these transactions customarily involve significant market premiums to the acquired firm, and because their planning and execution involve a large number of individuals, each of whom faces the temptations of certain gains and uncertain detection if they trade on their secret knowledge, acquisitions are rife with evidence of insider trading. For example, Keown & Pinkerton, Merger Announcements and Insider Trading Activity: An Empirical Investigation, 36 J. Fin. 855 (1981), found in 194 studied merger announcements significant evidence of insider trading on average 12 days prior to the first public announcement of a merger. Moreover, about 40–50 percent of the price gain experienced by the targets of takeovers occurs *before* the actual takeover announcement. *Id.* The stock market is not the only venue where the insiders reap the rewards; data confirms that put and call options are astutely used by insiders to reap gains in the pre-takeover period. *See* Arnold, Erwin, Nail & Nixon, Do Options Markets Substitute for Stock Markets? Evidence from Trading on Anticipated Tender Offer Announcements, 15 Int'l Rev. Financial Analysis 247 (2006); Jayaraman, Frye & Sabherwal, Informed Trading Around Merger Announements: An Empirical Test Using Transaction Volume and Open Interest in Options Market, 45 Fin. Rev. 36 (2001).

WHY PROHIBIT?

In his classic work, Professor Henry Manne argued that insider trading is socially valuable because it provides incentives to firm executives and others to maximize the value of the firm and their trading has the further positive effect of nudging the firm's security price to the equilibrium level it would reach once the firm's interest justify disclosure of the confidential information. *See* H. Manne, Insider Trading and the Stock Market (1966); *see also* Carlton & Fischel, The Regulation of Insider Trading, 35 Stan. L. Rev. 857 (1983). But could this approach promote the artful timing of the release of confidential information. *See* Haft, The effect of Insider Trading Rules on the Internal Efficiency of the Large Corporation, 80 Mich. L. Rev. 1051 (1982) (a laissez faire approach toward insider trading will, in light of teachings from organizational behavior, promote information delays, manipulation of corporate releases, and intrafirm competition that is harmful to the company).

The most elusive complaint lodged against insider trading is that it is "unfair". But what is the focus of the unfairness? And, unfairness to whom? It is not reasonable to argue it is unfair for an investor to purchase a security without disclosing his belief that the stock is a "bargain;" disclosure of such information would be dysfunctional because it would deprive market professionals of the incentive necessary for them to continue their arbitrage of stock prices in light of publicly available information. Thus, what is it about the insider trading context that compels an insider to share her informational advantage when we do not require this to be shared by outsiders? *See* Brudney, Insiders, Outsiders, and Informational Advantages Under the Federal Securities Laws, 93 Harv. L. Rev. 322 (1979). Most assertions that insider trading is unfair are coupled with additional harms believed to accompany insider trading. For example, Professor Brudney couples his concern for the unerodiable advantage enjoyed by insiders over outsiders with concerns for market efficiency, market integrity, manipulative practices and the cost of capital. *Id.* at 334–335, 356. More generally, can we conclude that investors who purchase while the insider is buying, and vice versa, are harmed because the insider is trading on his secret information? That is, an investor's decision to sell or to purchase is unaffected by whether the insider is also secretly buying or selling in the open market. If the insider neither trades nor discloses his confidential material information, one can nevertheless expect the investor to pursue his trading plan. To be sure, sellers are naturally disadvantaged by the nondisclosure of good news, just as buyers are disadvantaged by the nondisclosure of bad news. These results, however, cast no light on why the insider's decision to trade should prompt disclosure. Nor does it identify why or how the insider's trading, disassociated from his failure to disclose, harms his opposite trader. Viewed in such a limited fashion, the insider's trading is a mere fortuity as to his contemporaneous opposite traders.

Modest support for the disclose or abstain rule can be found if the trading and nondisclosure aspects of insider trading are disaggregated. Certainly the insider's trading can be expected to impact the supply and demand for the security traded in, so that the insider may preempt a price that was a lower "buy" price or a higher "sale" price than what would have been available to the investor if the insider had abstained from trading. Under such a rationalization, the investor's injury is both problematic and trivial. It is purely in the realm of speculation what price would have been available to outside investors but for the insider's trading. Moreover, in a goodly number of cases, the resolution of this sticky factual question would appear hardly worthy of the considerable effort its resolution would entail. It would appear that in the vast majority of the cases, the insider's trading will have minimal impact on a stock's price. Moreover, there should also be considered the potential benefits of such insider trading may have conferred on parallel traders, those who also purchased when the insider purchased; for this group, the price and volume changes stimulated by the insider's trading may have attracted others to similarly trade so that such parallel traders unwittingly invested "in a sure thing". But the ultimate problem with the argument that the misdeed of insider trading is that the insider preempts a price otherwise available to others is that this assertion begs the question. *See* Wang, Trading on Material Nonpublic Information on Impersonal Stock Markets: Who is Harmed and Who Can Sue Whom Under SEC Rule 10b–5?, 54 S. Cal. L. Rev. 1217 (1981).Insiders are permitted to trade and thereby preempt a price available to outsiders when they are not in possession of inside information; therefore, why should they not similarly be free to trade and preempt a price when they are in possession of inside information?

The broadest justification some have advanced for insider trading regulation is the belief such regulation preserves investor confidences in securities markets and thereby enhances the allocational efficiency of securities markets. Capital market theory offers a useful tool by which to examine this question. Insider trading occurs randomly because inside traders generally are not repeat players in the same corporation's stock on the basis of a separate corporate event. All firms do not experience the kinds of financial developments that offer extraordinary returns to insiders who trade before disclosure occurs. Outside investors, however, do not know *ex ante* which firms' managers possess inside information or for that matter will trade and/or engage in manipulative practices when in possession of such information. Due to these informational asymmetries, the rational investor will assume *ex ante* that each firm poses the same risk of abusive insider-trading practices as does the market as a whole and will accordingly discount the value of each firm by the average estimated agency cost of all firms. In this way, the abuses associated with insider trading while occurring randomly with any specific firm become systematic across all firms due to the informational asymmetries that exist *ex ante*. Because the risk is systematic, the risk cannot be reduced by diversification. Adding more stocks to one's portfolio only assures that the investor's exposure approaches that of the market as a whole.

So viewed, it can be reasoned that insider trading does not harm the individual investor. Each rational investor can self-insure against abusive insider-trading practices by discounting all stocks by the average risk for all firms. Investors armed with an efficient portfolio will have insider trading losses on one investment offset by higher returns garnered from portfolio stocks of firms not accompanied by insider trading. Over time, an investor can expect that his portfolio's insider trading losses will sum to zero. But the higher systemic risk of investments, stocks in public companies, subject to insider trading does penalize such investments vis-à-vis other investments for which there is not a fear of insider trading, e.g., investment in precious metals.

A final area is one that focus on property rights. Consider the reasoning of United States v. Chestman, 947 F.2d 551, 576–578 (2d Cir.1991), cert. denied 503 U.S. 1004, 112 S.Ct. 1759, 118 L.Ed.2d 422 (1992). (Winter, J., dissenting):

> One commentator has attempted to explain the Supreme Court [insider-trading] decisions in terms of [a] business-property rationale.... See Easterbrook, [Insider Trading, Secret Agents, Evidentiary Privileges, and the Production of Information, 1981 Sup.Ct. Rev. 309,] at 309–39. That rationale may be summarized as follows. Information is perhaps the most precious commodity in commercial markets. It is expensive to produce, and, because it involves facts and ideas that can be easily photocopied or carried in one's head, there is a ubiquitous risk that those who pay to produce information will see others reap the profit from it. Where the profit from an activity is likely to be diverted, investment in that activity will decline. If the law fails to protect property rights in commercial information, therefore, less will be invested in generating such information. Id. at 313.
>
> For example, mining companies whose investments in geological surveys have revealed valuable deposits do not want word of the strike to get out until they have secured rights to the land.[3] If word does get out, the price of the land not only will go up, but other mining companies may also secure the rights. In either case, the mining company that invested in geological surveys (including the inevitably sizeable number of unsuccessful drillings) will see profits from that investment enjoyed by others. If mining companies are unable to keep the results of such surveys confidential, less will be invested in them.
>
> Similarly, firms that invest money in generating information about other companies with a view to some form of combination will

3. Although [*Texas Gulf Sulphur*] stressed the unfairness of insider trading to those who deal with the trader, the reason for the nondisclosure that allowed insider trading in TGS stock was the company's insider trading in real estate.

maintain secrecy about their efforts, and if secrecy cannot be maintained, less will be invested in acquiring such information. Hostile acquirers will want to keep such information secret lest the target mount defensive actions or speculators purchase the target's stock. Even when friendly negotiations with the other company are undertaken, the acquirer will often require the target corporation to maintain secrecy about negotiations, lest the very fact of negotiation tip off others on the important fact that the two firms think a combination might be valuable.... In the instant matter, A & P made secrecy a condition of its acquisition of Waldbaum's.

Insider trading may reduce the return on information in two ways. First, it creates incentives for insiders to generate or disclose information that may disregard the welfare of the corporation. Easterbrook, supra, at 332–33. That risk is not implicated by the facts in the present case, and no further discussion is presently required.

Second, insider trading creates a risk that information will be prematurely disclosed by such trading, and the corporation will lose part or all of its property in that information. Id. at 331. Although trades by an insider may rarely affect market price, others who know of the insider's trading may notice that a trader is unusually successful, or simply perceive unusual activity in a stock and guess the information and/or make piggyback trades. Id. at 336. A broker who executes a trade for a geologist or for a financial printer may well draw relevant conclusions. Or, as in the instant matter, the trader ... may tell his or her broker about the inside information, who may then trade on his or her account, on clients' accounts, or may tell friends and relatives. One inside trader has publicly attributed his exposure in part to the fact that the bank through which he made trades piggybacked on the trades, as did the broker who made the trades for the bank. See Levine, The Inside Story of An Inside Trader, Fortune, May 21, 1990, at 80. Once activity in a stock reaches an unusual stage, others may guess the reason for the trading—the corporate secret. Insider trading thus increases the risk that confidential information acquired at a cost may be disclosed. If so, the owner of the information may lose its investment.

NOTE ON THE "USE" TEST UNDER RULE 10b–5

In 1998, the Ninth and Eleventh Circuits held that Rule 10b–5 is not violated unless the defendant not only *possessed* material inside information when she traded, but actually *used* the information in deciding to buy or sell. These decisions rested on the theory that having inside information in one's possession when trading does not wrongfully cause harm; only using such information wrongfully causes harm. SEC v. Adler, 137 F.3d 1325 (11th Cir.1998); United States v. Smith, 155 F.3d 1051 (9th Cir.1998).

This esoteric distinction between possession and use of inside information had earlier been rejected by the Second Circuit in 1993, in United States v. Teicher, 987 F.2d 112. There the court said:

> . . . [A] "knowing possession" standard has the attribute of simplicity. It recognizes that one who trades while knowingly possessing material inside information has an informational advantage over other traders. Because the advantage is in the form of information, it exists in the mind of the trader. Unlike a loaded weapon which may stand ready but unused, material information can not lay idle in the human brain. The individual with such information may decide to trade upon that information, to alter a previously decided-upon transaction, to continue with a previously planned transaction even though publicly available information would now suggest otherwise, or simply to do nothing. In our increasingly sophisticated securities markets, where subtle shifts in strategy can produce dramatic results, it would be a mistake to think of such decisions as merely binary choices—to buy or to sell.

In 2000, the SEC promulgated Rule 10b5–1, which addresses the issue of whether liability under Rule 10b–5 is based on trading while in the knowing possession of material nonpublic information, or on using such information to trade. Rule 10b5–1(b) defines a purchase or sale being "on the basis of" material non public information "if the person making the purchase or sale was *aware* of material nonpublic information when the person made the purchase or sale." (emphasis added). However, the general rule is subject to an affirmative defense where the trade is made pursuant to a written contract instructing another to purchase or sell securities (either identifying a specific amount or setting forth an algorithm for determining such amount) for the instructing person's account, provided the contract is entered into before becoming aware of the information. Why would company officers wish to have a plan setting forth when company shares would be purchased or sold in the future? Rule 10b5–1 provides that disclosure of the existence of a Rule 10b5–1 plan is optional. Why might executives choose to voluntarily disclose the existence of their plan? How can executives with Rule 10b5–1 plans game the provision's safe harbor to maximize their wealth on the basis of inside information? *See* Alan Horwich, The Origin, Application, Validity, and Potential Misuse of Rule 10b5–1, 62 Bus. Law. 913, 936–953 (2007).

Chiarella v. United States

United States Supreme Court, 1980.
445 U.S. 222, 100 S.Ct. 1108, 63 L.Ed.2d 348.

■ MR. JUSTICE POWELL, delivered the opinion of the Court.

The question in this case is whether a person who learns from the confidential documents of one corporation that it is planning an attempt to secure control of a second corporation violates § 10(b) of the Securities Exchange Act of 1934 if he fails to disclose the impending takeover before trading in the target company's securities.

I

Petitioner is a printer by trade. In 1975 and 1976, he worked as a "markup man" in the New York composing room of Pandick Press, a financial printer. Among documents that petitioner handled were five announcements of corporate takeover bids. When these documents were delivered to the printer, the identities of the acquiring and target corporations were concealed by blank spaces or false names. The true names were sent to the printer on the night of the final printing.

The petitioner, however, was able to deduce the names of the target companies before the final printing from other information contained in the documents. Without disclosing his knowledge, petitioner purchased stock in the target companies and sold the shares immediately after the takeover attempts were made public. By this method, petitioner realized a gain of slightly more than $30,000 in the course of 14 months. Subsequently, the Securities and Exchange Commission (Commission or SEC) began an investigation of his trading activities. In May 1977, petitioner entered into a consent decree with the Commission in which he agreed to return his profits to the sellers of the shares. On the same day, he was discharged by Pandick Press.

In January 1978, petitioner was indicted on 17 counts of violating § 10(b) of the Securities Exchange Act of 1934 (1934 Act) and SEC Rule 10b–5. After petitioner unsuccessfully moved to dismiss the indictment, he was brought to trial and convicted on all counts.

The Court of Appeals for the Second Circuit affirmed petitioner's conviction. 588 F.2d 1358 (2d Cir.1978). We granted certiorari, 441 U.S. 942, 99 S.Ct. 2158, 60 L.Ed.2d 1043 (1979), and we now reverse.

II . . .

This case concerns the legal effect of the petitioner's silence. The District Court's charge permitted the jury to convict the petitioner if it found that he willfully failed to inform sellers of target company securities that he knew of a forthcoming takeover bid that would make their shares more valuable. In order to decide whether silence in such circumstances violates § 10(b), it is necessary to review the language and legislative history of that statute as well as its interpretation by the Commission and the federal courts.

Although the starting point of our inquiry is the language of the statute, *Ernst & Ernst v. Hochfelder,* 425 U.S. 185, 197, 96 S.Ct. 1375, 47 L.Ed.2d 668 (1976), § 10(b) does not state whether silence may constitute a manipulative or deceptive device. Section 10(b) was designed as a catchall clause to prevent fraudulent practices. 425 U.S., at 202, 206. But neither the legislative history nor the statute itself affords specific guidance for the resolution of this case. When Rule 10b–5 was promulgated in 1942, the SEC did not discuss the possibility that failure to provide information might run afoul of § 10(b).

The SEC took an important step in the development of § 10(b) when it held that a broker-dealer and his firm violated that section by selling securities on the basis of undisclosed information obtained from a director of the issuer corporation who was also a registered representative of the brokerage firm. In *Cady, Roberts & Co.,* 40 S.E.C. 907 (1961), the Commission decided that a corporate insider must abstain from trading in the shares of his corporation unless he has first disclosed all material inside information known to him. The obligation to disclose or abstain derives from

> "[a]n affirmative duty to disclose material information[, which] has been traditionally imposed on corporate 'insiders,' particularly officers, directors, or controlling stockholders. We, and the courts have consistently held that insiders must disclose material facts which are known to them by virtue of their position but which are not known to persons with whom they deal and which, if known, would affect their investment judgment." *Id.,* at 911.

The Commission emphasized that the duty arose from (i) the existence of a relationship affording access to inside information intended to be available only for a corporate purpose, and (ii) the unfairness of allowing a corporate insider to take advantage of that information by trading without disclosure. *Id.,* at 912, and n. 15.[8]

That the relationship between a corporate insider and the stockholders of his corporation gives rise to a disclosure obligation is not a novel twist of the law. At common law, misrepresentation made for the purpose of inducing reliance upon the false statement is fraudulent. But one who fails to disclose material information prior to the consummation of a transaction commits fraud only when he is under a duty to do so. And the duty to disclose arises when one party has information "that the other [party] is entitled to know because of a fiduciary or other similar relation of trust and confidence between them."[9] In its *Cady, Roberts* decision, the Commission recognized a relationship of trust and confidence between the shareholders of a corporation and those insiders who have obtained confidential information by reason of their position with that corporation. This relationship gives rise to a duty to disclose because of the "necessity of preventing a corporate insider from ... tak[ing] unfair advantage of the uninformed minority stockholders." *Speed v. Transamerica Corp.,* 99 F.Supp. 808, 829 (Del.1951).

---

8. ... The transaction in *Cady, Roberts* involved sale of stock to persons who previously may not have been shareholders in the corporation. 40 S.E.C., at 913, and n. 21. The Commission embraced the reasoning of Judge Learned Hand that "the director or officer assumed a fiduciary relation to the buyer by the very sale; for it would be a sorry distinction to allow him to use the advantage of his position to induce the buyer into the position of a beneficiary although he was forbidden to do so once the buyer had become one." *Id.,* at 914, n. 23, quoting *Gratz v. Claughton,* 187 F.2d 46, 49 (CA2), cert. denied, 341 U.S. 920, 71 S.Ct. 741, 95 L.Ed. 1353 (1951).

9. Restatement (Second) of Torts § 551(2)(a) (1976). See James & Gray, Misrepresentation—Part II, 37 Md.L.Rev. 488, 523–527 (1978). As regards securities transactions, the American Law Institute recognizes that "silence when there is a duty to ... speak may be a fraudulent act." ALI, Federal Securities Code § 262(b) (Prop.Off.Draft 1978).

The federal courts have found violations of § 10(b) where corporate insiders used undisclosed information for their own benefit. *E.g., SEC v. Texas Gulf Sulphur Co.,* 401 F.2d 833 (C.A.2 1968), cert. denied, 404 U.S. 1005 (1971). The cases also have emphasized, in accordance with the common-law rule, that "[t]he party charged with failing to disclose market information must be under a duty to disclose it." *Frigitemp Corp. v. Financial Dynamics Fund, Inc.,* 524 F.2d 275, 282 (C.A.2 1975). Accordingly, a purchaser of stock who has no duty to a prospective seller because he is neither an insider nor a fiduciary has been held to have no obligation to reveal material facts. See *General Time Corp. v. Talley Industries, Inc.,* 403 F.2d 159, 164 (C.A.2 1968), cert. denied, 393 U.S. 1026, 89 S.Ct. 631, 21 L.Ed.2d 570 (1969). . . .

Thus, administrative and judicial interpretations have established that silence in connection with the purchase or sale of securities may operate as a fraud actionable under § 10(b) despite the absence of statutory language or legislative history specifically addressing the legality of nondisclosure. But such liability is premised upon a duty to disclose arising from a relationship of trust and confidence between parties to a transaction. Application of a duty to disclose prior to trading guarantees that corporate insiders, who have an obligation to place the shareholder's welfare before their own, will not benefit personally through fraudulent use of material, nonpublic information.[12]

III

In this case, the petitioner was convicted of violating § 10(b) although he was not a corporate insider and he received no confidential information from the target company. Moreover, the "market information" upon which he relied did not concern the earning power or operations of the target company, but only the plans of the acquiring company. Petitioner's use of that information was not a fraud under § 10(b) unless he was subject to an affirmative duty to disclose it before trading. In this case, the jury instructions failed to specify any such duty. In effect, the trial court instructed the jury that petitioner owed a duty to everyone; to all sellers, indeed, to the market as a whole. The jury simply was told to decide whether petitioner used material, nonpublic information at a time when "he knew other people trading in the securities market did not have access to the same information." Record 677.

The Court of Appeals affirmed the conviction by holding that "[*a*]*nyone*—corporate insider or not—who regularly receives material nonpublic information may not use that information to trade in securities without incurring an affirmative duty to disclose." 588 F.2d,

12. "Tippees" of corporate insiders have been held liable under § 10(b) because they have a duty not to profit from the use of inside information that they know is confidential and know or should know came from a corporate insider, *Shapiro v. Merrill Lynch, Pierce, Fenner & Smith, Inc.,* 495 F.2d 228, 237–238 (C.A.2 1974). The tippee's obligation has been viewed as arising from his role as a participant after the fact in the insider's breach of a fiduciary duty. . . .

at 1365 (emphasis in original). Although the court said that its test would include only persons who regularly receive material, nonpublic information, *id.,* at 1366, its rationale for that limitation is unrelated to the existence of a duty to disclose.[14] The Court of Appeals, like the trial court, failed to identify a relationship between petitioner and the sellers that could give rise to a duty. Its decision thus rested solely upon its belief that the federal securities laws have "created a system providing equal access to information necessary for reasoned and intelligent investment decisions." *Id.,* at 1362. The use by anyone of material information not generally available is fraudulent, this theory suggests, because such information gives certain buyers or sellers an unfair advantage over less informed buyers and sellers.

This reasoning suffers from two defects. First, not every instance of financial unfairness constitutes fraudulent activity under § 10(b). See *Santa Fe Industries, Inc. v. Green,* 430 U.S. 462, 474–477, 97 S.Ct. 1292, 51 L.Ed.2d 480 (1977). Second, the element required to make silence fraudulent—a duty to disclose—is absent in this case. No duty could arise from petitioner's relationship with the sellers of the target company's securities, for petitioner had no prior dealings with them. He was not their agent, he was not a fiduciary, he was not a person in whom the sellers had placed their trust and confidence. He was, in fact, a complete stranger who dealt with the sellers only through impersonal market transactions.

We cannot affirm petitioner's conviction without recognizing a general duty between all participants in market transactions to forgo actions based on material, nonpublic information. Formulation of such a broad duty, which departs radically from the established doctrine that duty arises from a specific relationship between two parties, see n. 9, *supra,* should not be undertaken absent some explicit evidence of congressional intent.

As we have seen, no such evidence emerges from the language or legislative history of § 10(b). Moreover, neither the Congress nor the Commission ever has adopted a parity-of-information rule. Instead the problems caused by misuse of market information have been addressed by detailed and sophisticated regulation that recognizes when use of market information may not harm operation of the securities markets. For example, the Williams Act[15] limits but does not completely prohibit a tender offeror's purchases of target corporation stock before public announcement of the offer. Congress' careful action in this and other areas contrasts, and is in some tension, with the broad rule of liability we are asked to adopt in this case....

14. The Court of Appeals said that its "regular access to market information" test would create a workable rule embracing "those who occupy ... strategic places in the market mechanism." 588 F.2d, at 1365. These considerations are insufficient to support a duty to disclose. A duty arises from the relationship between parties, see nn. 9 and 10, *supra,* and accompanying text, and not merely from one's ability to acquire information because of his position in the market....

15. Title 15 U.S.C. § 78m(d)(1) (1976 ed., Supp. II) permits a tender offeror to purchase 5% of the target company's stock prior to disclosure of its plan for acquisition.

... As we have emphasized before, the 1934 Act cannot be read " 'more broadly than its language and the statutory scheme reasonably permit.' " *Touche Ross & Co. v. Redington,* 442 U.S. 560, 578, 99 S.Ct. 2479, 61 L.Ed.2d 82 (1979), quoting *SEC v. Sloan,* 436 U.S. 103, 116, 98 S.Ct. 1702, 56 L.Ed.2d 148 (1978). Section 10(b) is aptly described as a catchall provision, but what it catches must be fraud. When an allegation of fraud is based upon nondisclosure, there can be no fraud absent a duty to speak. We hold that a duty to disclose under § 10(b) does not arise from the mere possession of nonpublic market information. The contrary result is without support in the legislative history of § 10(b) and would be inconsistent with the careful plan that Congress has enacted for regulation of the securities markets. Cf. *Santa Fe Industries, Inc. v. Green,* 430 U.S., at 479.[20]

IV

In its brief to this Court, the United States offers an alternative theory to support petitioner's conviction. It argues that petitioner breached a duty to the acquiring corporation when he acted upon information that he obtained by virtue of his position as an employee of a printer employed by the corporation. The breach of this duty is said to support a conviction under § 10(b) for fraud perpetrated upon both the acquiring corporation and the sellers.

We need not decide whether this theory has merit for it was not submitted to the jury....

The jury instructions demonstrate that petitioner was convicted merely because of his failure to disclose material, nonpublic information to sellers from whom he bought the stock of target corporations. The jury was not instructed on the nature or elements of a duty owed by petitioner to anyone other than the sellers. Because we cannot affirm a criminal conviction on the basis of a theory not presented to the jury, *Rewis v. United States,* 401 U.S. 808, 814, 91 S.Ct. 1056, 28 L.Ed.2d 493 (1971), see *Dunn v. United States,* 442 U.S. 100, 106, 99 S.Ct. 2190, 60 L.Ed.2d 743 (1979), we will not speculate upon whether such a duty exists, whether it has been breached, or whether such a breach constitutes a violation of § 10(b).

The judgment of the Court of Appeals is

Reversed.

[The concurring opinions of Justices Stevens and Brennan are omitted.]

■ MR. CHIEF JUSTICE BURGER, dissenting.

I believe that the jury instructions in this case properly charged a violation of § 10(b) and Rule 10b–5, and I would affirm the conviction.

---

20. ... It is worth noting that this is apparently the first case in which criminal liability has been imposed upon a purchaser for § 10(b) nondisclosure. Petitioner was sentenced to a year in prison, suspended except for one month, and a 5-year term of probation. 588 F.2d, at 1373, 1378 (Meskill, J., dissenting).

I

As a general rule, neither party to an arm's-length business transaction has an obligation to disclose information to the other unless the parties stand in some confidential or fiduciary relation. See W. Prosser, Law of Torts § 106 (2d ed. 1955). This rule permits a businessman to capitalize on his experience and skill in securing and evaluating relevant information; it provides incentive for hard work, careful analysis, and astute forecasting. But the policies that underlie the rule also should limit its scope. In particular, the rule should give way when an informational advantage is obtained, not by superior experience, foresight, or industry, but by some unlawful means. One commentator has written:

> "[T]he way in which the buyer acquires the information which he conceals from the vendor should be a material circumstance. The information might have been acquired as the result of his bringing to bear a superior knowledge, intelligence, skill or technical judgment; it might have been acquired by mere chance; or it might have been acquired by means of some tortious action on his part.... *Any time information is acquired by an illegal act it would seem that there should be a duty to disclose that information.*" Keeton, Fraud—Concealment and Non–Disclosure, 15 Texas L.Rev. 1, 25–26 (1936) (emphasis added).

I would read § 10(b) and Rule 10b–5 to encompass and build on this principle: to mean that a person who has misappropriated nonpublic information has an absolute duty to disclose that information or to refrain from trading.

II

The Court's opinion, as I read it, leaves open the question whether § 10(b) and Rule 10b–5 prohibit trading on misappropriated nonpublic information.[4] Instead, the Court apparently concludes that this theory of the case was not submitted to the jury. In the Court's view, the instructions given the jury were premised on the erroneous notion that the mere failure to disclose nonpublic information, however acquired, is a deceptive practice....

The Court's reading of the District Court's charge is unduly restrictive. Fairly read as a whole and in the context of the trial, the instructions required the jury to find that Chiarella obtained his trading advantage by misappropriating the property of his employer's customers.... [t]he evidence shows beyond all doubt that Chiarella, working literally in the shadows of the warning signs in the printshop, misappropriated—stole to put it bluntly—valuable nonpublic information entrusted to him in the utmost confidence. He then exploited his

4. There is some language in the Court's opinion to suggest that only "a relationship between petitioner and the sellers ... could give rise to a duty [to disclose]." ... The Court's holding, however, is much more limited, namely, that mere possession of material, nonpublic information is insufficient to create a duty to disclose or to refrain from trading.... Accordingly, it is my understanding that the Court has not rejected the view, advanced above, that an absolute duty to disclose or refrain arises from the very act of misappropriating nonpublic information.

ill-gotten informational advantage by purchasing securities in the market. In my view, such conduct plainly violates § 10(b) and Rule 10b–5. Accordingly, I would affirm the judgment of the Court of Appeals.

■ JUSTICES BLACKMAN with whom Justice MARSHALL joins, dissenting.

Although I agree with much of what is said in Part I of the dissenting opinion of The Chief Justice, I write separately because, in my view, it is unnecessary to rest petitioner's conviction on a "misappropriation" theory. The fact that petitioner Chiarella purloined, or, to use The Chief Justice's word, "stole," information concerning pending tender offers certainly is the most dramatic evidence that petitioner was guilty of fraud. He has conceded that knew it was wrong, and he and his co-workers in the print shop wee specifically warned by their employer that actions of this kind were improper and forbidden. But I also would find petitioner's conduct fraudulent within the meaning of § 10(b) [and] Rule 10b–5, even if he had obtained the blessing of his employer's principals before embarking on his profiteering scheme. I think petitioner's brand of manipulative trading, with or without such approval, lies close to the heart of what the securities laws are intended to prohibit....

The Court continues to pursue a course, charted in certain recent decisions, designed to transform § 10(b) from an intentionally elastic "catchall" provision to one that catches relatively little of the misbehavior that all too often makes investment in securities needlessly risky business for the uninitiated investor....

Whatever the outer limits of the Rule, petitioner Chiarella's case fits neatly near the center of its analytical framework. He occupied a relationship to the takeover companies giving him intimate access to concededly material information that was sedulously guarded from public access. The information, in the words of Cady Roberts & Co., 40 SEC, at 912, was "intended to be available only for a corporate purpose and not for the personal benefit of anyone." Petitioner, moreover, knew that the information was unavailable to those with whom he dealt. And, he took full, virtually riskless advantage of this artificial information gap by selling the stocks shortly after each takeover bid was announced. By any reasonable definition, his trading was "inherent[ly] unfair[r]." This misuse of confidential information was clearly before the jury. Petitioner's conviction, therefore, should be upheld and I dissent from the Court's upsetting that conviction.

AFTER THE FALL, Wall St.J., November 18, 1987, at 1, col. 6. "... Vincent Chiarella will always rate at least a footnote in the history of Wall Street: In 1978, he became the first person in modern times convicted of criminal insider trading.

"A financial printer, Mr. Chiarella had made about $29,000 trading on information gleaned from tender-offer documents that he had seen in the course of his job. His conviction was reversed in a landmark Supreme Court decision in 1980; nevertheless, he 'went through hell' for seven years, he says, explaining that he was shunned by friends and blackballed by the printing industry. His conclusion: 'I was a martyr for insider trading.' . . .

". . . [A]fter 20 years as a printer, he was forced to drift from job to job, two months there, two days there, always living near the poverty line. Extra cash went to pay legal bills. One year he listed 18 separate printing jobs on his W–2 form; every mention of his past in the press presaged the end of each job.

" 'All my life I was a printer, a good worker, no trouble,' says Mr. Chiarella. 'All of a sudden, you're nothing anymore. What do you do?'

"Insider trading seemed a lofty term for the guessing game he and other printers played at Pandick Press in New York in the 1970s. They spent hours trying to decode identities of buyers and sellers in tender-offer documents they prepared; only Mr. Chiarella, however, played the market with his hunches. To this day, he doesn't know how he was caught. . . .

"Today, Mr. Chiarella is back at his old job at Pandick after winning an arbitration suit suggested by his union a couple of years ago. He walks to work each day at 4 p.m., a bitter man. 'I was the guinea pig,' he says. 'I disgorged $29,000 to the SEC. Ivan Boesky could buy cigarettes with that.'

"He wants little except to be left alone. 'I'm at the twilight of my career as a printer,' he says. 'I hope to just fade away.' "

SECURITIES EXCHANGE ACT § 14(e) AND RULE 14(e)(3)

[See Statutory Supplement]

United States v. O'Hagan

United States Supreme Court, 1997.
521 U.S. 642, 117 S.Ct. 2199, 138 L.Ed.2d 724.

■ JUSTICE GINSBURG delivered the opinion of the Court.

This case concerns the interpretation and enforcement of § 10(b) and § 14(e) of the Securities Exchange Act of 1934, and rules made by the Securities and Exchange Commission pursuant to these provisions, Rule 10b–5 and Rule 14e–3(a). Two prime questions are presented. The first relates to the misappropriation of material, nonpublic information for securities trading; the second concerns fraudulent practices in the tender offer setting. In particular, we address and resolve these issues: (1) Is a person who trades in securities for personal profit, using confidential information misappropriated in breach of a fiduciary duty to the source of the information, guilty of violating § 10(b) and Rule 10b–5? (2) Did the Commission exceed its rulemaking authority by adopting Rule 14e–3(a), which proscribes trading on undisclosed information in the tender offer setting, even in the absence of a duty to disclose? Our answer to the first question is yes, and to the second question, viewed in the context of this case, no.

I

Respondent James Herman O'Hagan was a partner in the law firm of Dorsey & Whitney in Minneapolis, Minnesota. In July 1988, Grand Metropolitan PLC (Grand Met), a company based in London, England, retained Dorsey & Whitney as local counsel to represent Grand Met regarding a potential tender offer for the common stock of the Pillsbury Company, headquartered in Minneapolis. Both Grand Met and Dorsey & Whitney took precautions to protect the confidentiality of Grand Met's tender offer plans. O'Hagan did no work on the Grand Met representation. Dorsey & Whitney withdrew from representing Grand Met on September 9, 1988. Less than a month later, on October 4, 1988, Grand Met publicly announced its tender offer for Pillsbury stock.

On August 18, 1988, while Dorsey & Whitney was still representing Grand Met, O'Hagan began purchasing call options for Pillsbury stock. Each option gave him the right to purchase 100 shares of Pillsbury stock by a specified date in September 1988. Later in August and in September, O'Hagan made additional purchases of Pillsbury call options. By the end of September, he owned 2,500 unexpired Pillsbury options, apparently more than any other individual investor. See App. 85, 148. O'Hagan also purchased, in September 1988, some 5,000 shares of Pillsbury common stock, at a price just under $39 per share. When Grand Met announced its tender offer in October, the price of Pillsbury stock rose to nearly $60 per share. O'Hagan then sold his Pillsbury call options and common stock, making a profit of more than $4.3 million.

The Securities and Exchange Commission (SEC or Commission) initiated an investigation into O'Hagan's transactions, culminating in a 57–count indictment. The indictment alleged that O'Hagan defrauded his law firm and its client, Grand Met, by using for his own trading purposes material, nonpublic information regarding Grand Met's planned tender offer. Id., at 8. According to the indictment, O'Hagan used the profits he gained through this trading to conceal his previous embezzlement and conversion of unrelated client trust funds. Id., at 10.[2] O'Hagan was charged with 20 counts of mail fraud, in violation of 18 U.S.C. § 1341; 17 counts of securities fraud, in violation of § 10(b) of the Securities Exchange Act of 1934 (Exchange Act) . . . and SEC Rule 10b–5 . . .; 17 counts of fraudulent trading in connection with a tender offer, in violation of § 14(e) of the Exchange Act . . . and SEC Rule 14e–3(a) . . . (1996); and 3 counts of violating federal money

2. O'Hagan was convicted of theft in state court, sentenced to 30 months' imprisonment, and fined. See State v. O'Hagan, 474 N.W.2d 613, 615, 623 (Minn.App.1991). The Supreme Court of Minnesota disbarred O'Hagan from the practice of law. See In re O'Hagan, 450 N.W.2d 571 (Minn.1990).

laundering statutes, 18 U.S.C. §§ 1956(a)(1)(B)(i), 1957.... A jury convicted O'Hagan on all 57 counts, and he was sentenced to a 41–month term of imprisonment.

A divided panel of the Court of Appeals for the Eighth Circuit reversed all of O'Hagan's convictions. 92 F.3d 612 (1996). Liability under § 10(b) and Rule 10b–5, the Eighth Circuit held, may not be grounded on the "misappropriation theory" of securities fraud on which the prosecution relied. Id., at 622. The Court of Appeals also held that Rule 14e–3(a)—which prohibits trading while in possession of material, nonpublic information relating to a tender offer—exceeds the SEC's § 14(e) rulemaking authority because the rule contains no breach of fiduciary duty requirement. Id., at 627. The Eighth Circuit further concluded that O'Hagan's mail fraud and money laundering convictions rested on violations of the securities laws, and therefore could not stand once the securities fraud convictions were reversed. Id., at 627–628. Judge Fagg, dissenting, stated that he would recognize and enforce the misappropriation theory, and would hold that the SEC did not exceed its rulemaking authority when it adopted Rule 14e–3(a) without requiring proof of a breach of fiduciary duty. Id., at 628.

Decisions of the Courts of Appeals are in conflict on the propriety of the misappropriation theory under § 10(b) and Rule 10b–5, see infra this page and n. 3, and on the legitimacy of Rule 14e–3(a) under § 14(e).... We granted certiorari, 519 U.S. 1037 (1997), and now reverse the Eighth Circuit's judgment.

II

We address first the Court of Appeals' reversal of O'Hagan's convictions under § 10(b) and Rule 10b–5. Following the Fourth Circuit's lead, see United States v. Bryan, 58 F.3d 933, 943–959 (1995), the Eighth Circuit rejected the misappropriation theory as a basis for § 10(b) liability. We hold, in accord with several other Courts of Appeals, that criminal liability under § 10(b) may be predicated on the misappropriation theory.[4]

A ...

[Section] 10(b) of the Exchange Act proscribes (1) using any deceptive device (2) in connection with the purchase or sale of securities, in contravention of rules prescribed by the Commission. The provision, as written, does not confine its coverage to deception of a purchaser or seller of securities, see United States v. Newman, 664

4. Twice before we have been presented with the question whether criminal liability for violation of § 10(b) may be based on a misappropriation theory. In Chiarella v. United States, 445 U.S. 222, 235–237 (1980), the jury had received no misappropriation theory instructions, so we declined to address the question.... In Carpenter v. United States, 484 U.S. 19, 24 (1987), the Court divided evenly on whether, under the circumstances of that case, convictions resting on the misappropriation theory should be affirmed. See Aldave, The Misappropriation Theory: Carpenter and Its Aftermath, 49 Ohio St. L.J. 373, 375 (1988) (observing that "Carpenter was, by any reckoning, an unusual case," for the information there misappropriated belonged not to a company preparing to engage in securities transactions, e.g., a bidder in a corporate acquisition, but to the Wall Street Journal).

F.2d 12, 17 (C.A.2 1981); rather, the statute reaches any deceptive device used "in connection with the purchase or sale of any security."

Pursuant to its § 10(b) rulemaking authority, the Commission has adopted Rule 10b–5. . . .

Under the "traditional" or "classical theory" of insider trading liability, § 10(b) and Rule 10b–5 are violated when a corporate insider trades in the securities of his corporation on the basis of material, nonpublic information. Trading on such information qualifies as a "deceptive device" under § 10(b), we have affirmed, because "a relationship of trust and confidence [exists] between the shareholders of a corporation and those insiders who have obtained confidential information by reason of their position with that corporation." Chiarella v. United States, 445 U.S. 222, 228 (1980). That relationship, we recognized, "gives rise to a duty to disclose [or to abstain from trading] because of the 'necessity of preventing a corporate insider from . . . taking unfair advantage of . . . uninformed . . . stockholders.'" Id., at 228–229 (citation omitted). The classical theory applies not only to officers, directors, and other permanent insiders of a corporation, but also to attorneys, accountants, consultants, and others who temporarily become fiduciaries of a corporation. See Dirks v. SEC, 463 U.S. 646, 655, n. 14 (1983).

The "misappropriation theory" holds that a person commits fraud "in connection with" a securities transaction, and thereby violates § 10(b) and Rule 10b–5, when he misappropriates confidential information for securities trading purposes, in breach of a duty owed to the source of the information. See Brief for United States 14. Under this theory, a fiduciary's undisclosed, self-serving use of a principal's information to purchase or sell securities, in breach of a duty of loyalty and confidentiality, defrauds the principal of the exclusive use of that information. In lieu of premising liability on a fiduciary relationship between company insider and purchaser or seller of the company's stock, the misappropriation theory premises liability on a fiduciary-turned-trader's deception of those who entrusted him with access to confidential information.

The two theories are complementary, each addressing efforts to capitalize on nonpublic information through the purchase or sale of securities. The classical theory targets a corporate insider's breach of duty to shareholders with whom the insider transacts; the misappropriation theory outlaws trading on the basis of nonpublic information by a corporate "outsider" in breach of a duty owed not to a trading party, but to the source of the information. The misappropriation theory is thus designed to "protect the integrity of the securities markets against abuses by 'outsiders' to a corporation who have access to confidential information that will affect the corporation's security price when revealed, but who owe no fiduciary or other duty to that corporation's shareholders." Ibid.

In this case, the indictment alleged that O'Hagan, in breach of a duty of trust and confidence he owed to his law firm, Dorsey & Whitney, and to its client, Grand Met, traded on the basis of nonpublic information regarding Grand Met's planned tender offer for Pillsbury common stock. App. 16. This conduct, the Government charged, constituted a fraudulent device in connection with the purchase and sale of securities.[5]

B

We agree with the Government that misappropriation, as just defined, satisfies § 10(b)'s requirement that chargeable conduct involve a "deceptive device or contrivance" used "in connection with" the purchase or sale of securities. We observe, first, that misappropriators, as the Government describes them, deal in deception. A fiduciary who "[pretends] loyalty to the principal while secretly converting the principal's information for personal gain," Brief for United States 17, "dupes" or defrauds the principal. See Aldave, Misappropriation: A General Theory of Liability for Trading on Nonpublic Information, 13 Hofstra L.Rev. 101, 119 (1984).

We addressed fraud of the same species in Carpenter v. United States, 484 U.S. 19 (1987), which involved the mail fraud statute's proscription of "any scheme or artifice to defraud," 18 U.S.C. § 1341. Affirming convictions under that statute, we said in Carpenter that an employee's undertaking not to reveal his employer's confidential information "became a sham" when the employee provided the information to his co-conspirators in a scheme to obtain trading profits. 484 U.S. at 27. A company's confidential information, we recognized in Carpenter, qualifies as property to which the company has a right of exclusive use. Id., at 25–27. The undisclosed misappropriation of such information, in violation of a fiduciary duty, the Court said in Carpenter, constitutes fraud akin to embezzlement—" 'the fraudulent appropriation to one's own use of the money or goods entrusted to one's care by another.' " Id., at 27 (quoting Grin v. Shine, 187 U.S. 181, 189 (1902)); see Aldave, 13 Hofstra L.Rev., at 119. Carpenter's discussion of the fraudulent misuse of confidential information, the Government notes, "is a particularly apt source of guidance here, because [the mail fraud statute] (like Section 10(b)) has long been held to require deception, not merely the breach of a fiduciary duty." Brief for United States 18, n. 9 (citation omitted).

Deception through nondisclosure is central to the theory of liability for which the Government seeks recognition. As counsel for the Government stated in explanation of the theory at oral argument: "To satisfy the common law rule that a trustee may not use the property that [has] been entrusted [to] him, there would have to be consent. To satisfy the requirement of the Securities Act that there be

---

5. The Government could not have prosecuted O'Hagan under the classical theory, for O'Hagan was not an "insider" of Pillsbury, the corporation in whose stock he traded. Although an "outsider" with respect to Pillsbury, O'Hagan had an intimate association with, and was found to have traded on confidential information from Dorsey & Whitney, counsel to tender offeror Grand Met. Under the misappropriation theory, O'Hagan's securities trading does not escape Exchange Act sanction, as it would under the dissent's reasoning, simply because he was associated with, and gained nonpublic information from, the bidder, rather than the target.

no deception, there would only have to be disclosure." Tr. of Oral Arg. 12; see generally Restatement (Second) of Agency §§ 390, 395 (1958) (agent's disclosure obligation regarding use of confidential information).[6]

... [F]ull disclosure forecloses liability under the misappropriation theory: Because the deception essential to the misappropriation theory involves feigning fidelity to the source of information, if the fiduciary discloses to the source that he plans to trade on the nonpublic information, there is no "deceptive device" and thus no § 10(b) violation—although the fiduciary-turned-trader may remain liable under state law for breach of a duty of loyalty.[7]

We turn next to the § 10(b) requirement that the misappropriator's deceptive use of information be "in connection with the purchase or sale of [a] security." This element is satisfied because the fiduciary's fraud is consummated, not when the fiduciary gains the confidential information, but when, without disclosure to his principal, he uses the information to purchase or sell securities. The securities transaction and the breach of duty thus coincide. This is so even though the person or entity defrauded is not the other party to the trade, but is, instead, the source of the nonpublic information. See Aldave, 13 Hofstra L.Rev., at 120 ("a fraud or deceit can be practiced on one person, with resultant harm to another person or group of persons"). A misappropriator who trades on the basis of material, nonpublic information, in short, gains his advantageous market position through deception; he deceives the source of the information and simultaneously harms members of the investing public. See id., at 120–121, and n. 107.

The misappropriation theory targets information of a sort that misappropriators ordinarily capitalize upon to gain no-risk profits through the purchase or sale of securities. Should a misappropriator put such information to other use, the statute's prohibition would not be implicated. The theory does not catch all conceivable forms of fraud involving confidential information; rather, it catches fraudulent means of capitalizing on such information through securities transactions.

The Government notes another limitation on the forms of fraud § 10(b) reaches: "The misappropriation theory would not ... apply to a case in which a person defrauded a bank into giving him a loan or embezzled cash from another, and then used the proceeds of the

6. Under the misappropriation theory urged in this case, the disclosure obligation runs to the source of the information, here, Dorsey & Whitney and Grand Met. Chief Justice Burger, dissenting in Chiarella, advanced a broader reading of § 10(b) and Rule 10b–5; the disclosure obligation, as he envisioned it, ran to those with whom the misappropriator trades. 445 U.S., at 240 ("a person who has misappropriated nonpublic information has an absolute duty to disclose that information or to refrain from trading"); see also id., at 243, n. 4. The Government does not propose that we adopt a misappropriation theory of that breadth.

7. Where, however, a person trading on the basis of material, nonpublic information owes a duty of loyalty and confidentiality to two entities or persons—for example, a law firm and its client—but makes disclosure to only one, the trader may still be liable under the misappropriation theory.

misdeed to purchase securities." Brief for United States 24, n. 13. In such a case, the Government states, "the proceeds would have value to the malefactor apart from their use in a securities transaction, and the fraud would be complete as soon as the money was obtained." Ibid. In other words, money can buy, if not anything, then at least many things; its misappropriation may thus be viewed as sufficiently detached from a subsequent securities transaction that § 10(b)'s "in connection with" requirement would not be met. Ibid. . . .

The misappropriation theory comports with § 10(b)'s language, which requires deception "in connection with the purchase or sale of any security," not deception of an identifiable purchaser or seller. The theory is also well-tuned to an animating purpose of the Exchange Act: to insure honest securities markets and thereby promote investor confidence. See 45 Fed.Reg. 60412 (1980) (trading on misappropriated information "undermines the integrity of, and investor confidence in, the securities markets"). Although informational disparity is inevitable in the securities markets, investors likely would hesitate to venture their capital in a market where trading based on misappropriated nonpublic information is unchecked by law. An investor's informational disadvantage vis-a-vis a misappropriator with material, nonpublic information stems from contrivance, not luck; it is a disadvantage that cannot be overcome with research or skill. See Brudney, Insiders, Outsiders, and Informational Advantages Under the Federal Securities Laws, 93 Harv.L.Rev. 322, 356 (1979) ("If the market is thought to be systematically populated with . . . transactors [trading on the basis of misappropriated information] some investors will refrain from dealing altogether, and others will incur costs to avoid dealing with such transactors or corruptly to overcome their unerodable informational advantages."); Aldave, 13 Hofstra L.Rev., at 122–123.

In sum, considering the inhibiting impact on market participation of trading on misappropriated information, and the congressional purposes underlying § 10(b), it makes scant sense to hold a lawyer like O'Hagan a § 10(b) violator if he works for a law firm representing the target of a tender offer, but not if he works for a law firm representing the bidder. The text of the statute requires no such result.[9] The misappropriation at issue here was properly made the subject of a § 10(b) charge because it meets the statutory requirement that there be "deceptive" conduct "in connection with" securities transactions.

---

9. As noted earlier, however, see supra, at 9–10, the textual requirement of deception precludes § 10(b) liability when a person trading on the basis of nonpublic information has disclosed his trading plans to, or obtained authorization from, the principal—even though such conduct may affect the securities markets in the same manner as the conduct reached by the misappropriation theory. . . . [T]he fact that § 10(b) is only a partial antidote to the problems it was designed to alleviate does not call into question its prohibition of conduct that falls within its textual proscription. Moreover, once a disloyal agent discloses his imminent breach of duty, his principal may seek appropriate equitable relief under state law. Furthermore, in the context of a tender offer, the principal who authorizes an agent's trading on confidential information may, in the Commission's view, incur liability for an Exchange Act violation under Rule 14e–3(a).

C

... [T]he misappropriation theory, as we have examined and explained it in this opinion, is both consistent with the statute and with our precedent.[11] ...

The Eighth Circuit erred in holding that the misappropriation theory is inconsistent with § 10(b). The Court of Appeals may address on remand O'Hagan's other challenges to his convictions under § 10(b) and Rule 10b–5.

III

We consider next the ground on which the Court of Appeals reversed O'Hagan's convictions for fraudulent trading in connection with a tender offer, in violation of § 14(e) of the Exchange Act and SEC Rule 14e–3(a). A sole question is before us as to these convictions: Did the Commission, as the Court of Appeals held, exceed its rulemaking authority under § 14(e) when it adopted Rule 14e–3(a) without requiring a showing that the trading at issue entailed a breach of fiduciary duty? We hold that the Commission, in this regard and to the extent relevant to this case, did not exceed its authority.

The governing statutory provision, § 14(e) of the Exchange Act, reads in relevant part:

"It shall be unlawful for any person ... to engage in any fraudulent, deceptive, or manipulative acts or practices, in connection with any tender offer.... The [SEC] shall, for the purposes of this subsection, by rules and regulations define, and prescribe means reasonably designed to prevent, such acts and practices as are fraudulent, deceptive, or manipulative." 15 U.S.C. § 78n(e).

Section 14(e)'s first sentence prohibits fraudulent acts in connection with a tender offer. This self-operating proscription was one of several provisions added to the Exchange Act in 1968 by the Williams Act, 82 Stat. 454. The section's second sentence delegates definitional and prophylactic rulemaking authority to the Commission. Congress added this rulemaking delegation to § 14(e) in 1970 amendments to the Williams Act. See § 5, 84 Stat. 1497....

Relying on § 14(e)'s rulemaking authorization, the Commission, in 1980, promulgated Rule 14e–3(a). That measure provides:

---

11. The United States additionally argues that Congress confirmed the validity of the misappropriation theory in the Insider Trading and Securities Fraud Enforcement Act of 1988 (ITSFEA), § 2(1), 102 Stat. 4677, note following 15 U.S.C. § 78u–1. See Brief for United States 32–35. ITSFEA declares that "the rules and regulations of the Securities and Exchange Commission under the Securities Exchange Act of 1934 ... governing trading while in possession of material, nonpublic information are, as required by such Act, necessary and appropriate in the public interest and for the protection of investors." Note following 15 U.S.C. § 78u–1. ITSFEA also includes a new § 20A(a) of the Exchange Act expressly providing a private cause of action against persons who violate the Exchange Act "by purchasing or selling a security while in possession of material, nonpublic information", such an action may be brought by "any person who, contemporaneously with the purchase or sale of securities that is the subject of such violation, has purchased ... or sold ... securities of the same class." 15 U.S.C. § 78r–1(a). Because we uphold the misappropriation theory on the basis of § 10(b) itself, we do not address ITSFEA's significance for cases of this genre.

> "(a) If any person has taken a substantial step or steps to commence, or has commenced, a tender offer (the 'offering person'), it shall constitute a fraudulent, deceptive or manipulative act or practice within the meaning of section 14(e) of the [Exchange] Act for any other person who is in possession of material information relating to such tender offer which information he knows or has reason to know is nonpublic and which he knows or has reason to know has been acquired directly or indirectly from:
>
> > "(1) The offering person,
> >
> > "(2) The issuer of the securities sought or to be sought by such tender offer, or
> >
> > "(3) Any officer, director, partner or employee or any other person acting on behalf of the offering person or such issuer,
>
> to purchase or sell or cause to be purchased or sold any of such securities or any securities convertible into or exchangeable for any such securities or any option or right to obtain or to dispose of any of the foregoing securities, unless within a reasonable time prior to any purchase or sale such information and its source are publicly disclosed by press release or otherwise." 17 CFR § 240.14e–3(a) (1996).

As characterized by the Commission, Rule 14e–3(a) is a "disclose or abstain from trading" requirement. 45 Fed.Reg. 60410 (1980).[15] The Second Circuit concisely described the rule's thrust:

> "One violates Rule 14e–3(a) if he trades on the basis of material nonpublic information concerning a pending tender offer that he knows or has reason to know has been acquired 'directly or indirectly' from an insider of the offeror or issuer, or someone working on their behalf. Rule 14e–3(a) is a disclosure provision. It creates a duty in those traders who fall within its ambit to abstain or disclose, without regard to whether the trader owes a pre-existing fiduciary duty to respect the confidentiality of the information." United States v. Chestman, 947 F.2d 551, 557 (1991) (en banc) (emphasis added), cert. denied, 503 U.S. 1004 (1992).

See also SEC v. Maio, 51 F.3d 623, 635 (C.A.7 1995) ("Rule 14e–3 creates a duty to disclose material nonpublic information, or abstain from trading in stocks implicated by an impending tender offer, regardless of whether such information was obtained through a breach of fiduciary duty.") (emphasis added); SEC v. Peters, 978 F.2d 1162, 1165 (C.A.10 1992) (as written, Rule 14e–3(a) has no fiduciary duty requirement).

---

15. The rule thus adopts for the tender offer context a requirement resembling the one Chief Justice Burger would have adopted in Chiarella for misappropriators under § 10(b). See supra, at 10, n. 6.

In the Eighth Circuit's view, because Rule 14e–3(a) applies whether or not the trading in question breaches a fiduciary duty, the regulation exceeds the SEC's § 14(e) rulemaking authority....

The Eighth Circuit homed in on the essence of § 14(e)'s rulemaking authorization: "The statute empowers the SEC to 'define' and 'prescribe means reasonably designed to prevent' 'acts and practices' which are 'fraudulent.' " Id., at 624. All that means, the Eighth Circuit found plain, is that the SEC may "identify and regulate," in the tender offer context, "acts and practices" the law already defines as "fraudulent"; but, the Eighth Circuit maintained, the SEC may not "create its own definition of fraud." Ibid. (internal quotation marks omitted)....

We need not resolve in this case whether the Commission's authority under § 14(e) to "define ... such acts and practices as are fraudulent" is broader than the Commission's fraud-defining authority under § 10(b), for we agree with the United States that Rule 14e–3(a), as applied to cases of this genre, qualifies under § 14(e) as a "means reasonably designed to prevent" fraudulent trading on material, nonpublic information in the tender offer context. A prophylactic measure, because its mission is to prevent, typically encompasses more than the core activity prohibited.... [Section] 14(e)'s rulemaking authorization gives the Commission "latitude," even in the context of a term of art like "manipulative," "to regulate nondeceptive activities as a 'reasonably designed' means of preventing manipulative acts, without suggesting any change in the meaning of the term 'manipulative' itself." 472 U.S., at 11, n. 11. We hold, accordingly, that under § 14(e), the Commission may prohibit acts, not themselves fraudulent under the common law or § 10(b), if the prohibition is "reasonably designed to prevent ... acts and practices [that] are fraudulent." 15 U.S.C. § 78n(c)....

[I]t is a fair assumption that trading on the basis of material, nonpublic information [in connection with a tender offer] will often involve a breach of a duty of confidentiality to the bidder or target company or their representatives. The SEC, cognizant of the proof problem that could enable sophisticated traders to escape responsibility, placed in Rule 14e–3(a) a "disclose or abstain from trading" command that does not require specific proof of a breach of fiduciary duty. That prescription, we are satisfied, applied to this case, is a "means reasonably designed to prevent" fraudulent trading on material, nonpublic information in the tender offer context. See Chestman, 947 F.2d, at 560 ("While dispensing with the subtle problems of proof associated with demonstrating fiduciary breach in the problematic area of tender offer insider trading, [Rule 14e–3(a)] retains a close nexus between the prohibited conduct and the statutory aims."); accord, Maio, 51 F.3d, at 635, and n. 14; Peters, 978 F.2d, at 1167. Therefore, insofar as it serves to prevent the type of misappropriation charged against O'Hagan, Rule 14e–3(a) is a proper exercise of the Commission's prophylactic power under § 14(e).

As an alternate ground for affirming the Eighth Circuit's judgment, O'Hagan urges that Rule 14e–3(a) is invalid because it prohibits trading in advance of a tender offer—when "a substantial step . . . to commence" such an offer has been taken—while § 14(e) prohibits fraudulent acts "in connection with any tender offer." See Brief for Respondent 41–42. O'Hagan further contends that, by covering pre-offer conduct, Rule 14e–3(a) "fails to comport with due process on two levels": The rule does not "give fair notice as to when, in advance of a tender offer, a violation of § 14(e) occurs," id., at 42; and it "disposes of any scienter requirement," id., at 43. The Court of Appeals did not address these arguments, and O'Hagan did not raise the due process points in his briefs before that court. We decline to consider these contentions in the first instance.[23] The Court of Appeals may address on remand any arguments O'Hagan has preserved.

IV

Based on its dispositions of the securities fraud convictions, the Court of Appeals also reversed O'Hagan's convictions, under 18 U.S.C. § 1341, for mail fraud. See 92 F.3d, at 627–628. Reversal of the securities convictions, the Court of Appeals recognized, "did not as a matter of law require that the mail fraud convictions likewise be reversed." Id., at 627 (citing Carpenter, 484 U.S., at 24, in which this Court unanimously affirmed mail and wire fraud convictions based on the same conduct that evenly divided the Court on the defendants' securities fraud convictions). But in this case, the Court of Appeals said, the indictment was so structured that the mail fraud charges could not be disassociated from the securities fraud charges, and absent any securities fraud, "there was no fraud upon which to base the mail fraud charges." 92 F.3d, at 627–628.[24]

. . . We need not linger over this matter, for our rulings on the securities fraud issues require that we reverse the Court of Appeals judgment on the mail fraud counts as well.[25] . . .

The judgment of the Court of Appeals for the Eighth Circuit is reversed, and the case is remanded for further proceedings consistent with this opinion.

It is so ordered.

■ DISSENT: JUSTICE SCALIA, concurring in part and dissenting in part.

---

23. As to O'Hagan's scienter argument, ... 15 U.S.C. § 78ff(a) requires the Government to prove "willful violation" of the securities laws, and that lack of knowledge of the relevant rule is an affirmative defense to a sentence of imprisonment . . . .

24. The Court of Appeals reversed respondent's money laundering convictions on similar reasoning. See 92 F.3d, at 628. Because the United States did not seek review of that ruling, we leave undisturbed that portion of the Court of Appeals' judgment.

25. The dissent finds O'Hagan's convictions on the mail fraud counts, but not on the securities fraud counts, sustainable . . . . Under the dissent's view, securities traders like O'Hagan would escape SEC civil actions and federal prosecutions under legislation targeting securities fraud, only to be caught for their trading activities in the broad mail fraud net. If misappropriation theory cases could proceed only under the federal mail and wire fraud statutes, practical consequences for individual defendants might not be large, see Aldave, 49 Ohio St. L.J., at 381, and n. 60; however, "proportionally more persons accused of insider trading [might] be pursued by a U.S. Attorney, and proportionally fewer by the SEC," id., at 382. Our decision, of course, does not rest on such enforcement policy considerations.

I join Parts I, III, and IV of the Court's opinion. I do not agree, however, with Part II of the Court's opinion, containing its analysis of respondent's convictions under § 10(b) and Rule 10b–5. . . .

While the Court's explanation of the scope of § 10(b) and Rule 10b–5 would be entirely reasonable in some other context, it does not seem to accord with the principle of lenity we apply to criminal statutes. . . .

In light of that principle, it seems to me that the unelaborated statutory language: "to use or employ in connection with the purchase or sale of any security . . . any manipulative or deceptive device or contrivance," § 10(b), must be construed to require the manipulation or deception of a party to a securities transaction.

[The opinion of Justice Thomas, concurring with the majority on the Mail Fraud Act issue, but dissenting on the Rule 10b–5 and Rule 14e–3(a) issues, is omitted. Chief Justice Rehnquist concurred in Justice Thomas's opinion.]

* * *

NOTE ON WHO'S A MISAPPROPRIATOR?

What relationship provides the appropriate bond from which the misappropriation theory operates? United States v. Chestman, 947 F.2d 551 (2d Cir. 1991) (en banc), *cert. denied,* 503 U.S. 1004, 112 S.Ct. 1759, 118 L.Ed.2d 422 (1992), believed the requisite fiduciary duty upon which the misappropriation theory rests must be a fiduciary or similar relationship. It recognized "hornbook fiduciary relations are those existing between attorney and client, executor and heir, guardian and ward, principal and agent, trustee and trust beneficiary, and senior corporate official and shareholder." *Id.* at 568. It then reasoned that the misappropriation theory is premised on there being a special relationship of trust and confidence and this relationship must itself be the functional equivalent of a fiduciary relationship. It also believed it necessary to restrain somewhat the scope of the misappropriation theory. It therefore considered what it believed to be the basic contours of a fiduciary relationship:

> A fiduciary relationship involves discretionary authority and dependency. One person depends on another—the fiduciary—to serve his interests. In relying on a fiduciary to act for his benefit, the beneficiary of the relationship may entrust the fiduciary with custody over property of one sort or another. Because the fiduciary obtains access to this property to serve the ends of the fiduciary relationship he becomes duty-bound not to appropriate the property for his own use. What has been said of an agent's duty of confidentiality applies with equal force to other fiduciary relations: "an agent is subject to a duty to the principal not to use or to communicate information confidentially given him by the principal or acquired by him during the course of or on account of his agency." Restatement (Second) of Agency § 395 (1958). These

> characteristics represent the measure of the paradigmatic fiduciary relationship. A similar relationship of trust and confidence consequently must share these qualities.

947 F.2d at 569. The bare majority in the en banc decision applied the above standard to conclude that the husband who learned from his wife (whose family had founded what had become a publicly traded firm) that the company would soon be acquired at a premium was not a wrongful misappropriator when he traded on this information, even though he was told by his wife not to share the information with anyone because "it could possibly ruin the sale." The majority reasoned the disclosure to the defendant was made gratuitously and that there was no evidence that such confidences were shared because of any dependence by the family or the wife to act on the confidential information in serving their interest. Moreover, there was no express agreement of confidentiality.

How easily do the following cases fall within the fiduciary relationship set forth by the *Chestman* majority? The psychiatrists that learns confidential information during sessions with the spouse of a public company's CEO. United States v. Willis, 778 F.Supp. 205 (S.D.N.Y. 1991); a journalists of the Wall Street Journal's Heard on the Street column who tipped others on his advance knowledge of what companies would appear in the market-moving column. United States v. Carpenter, 791 F.2d 1024 (2d Cir. 1986), *aff'd*, 484 U.S. 19, 108 S.Ct. 316, 98 L.Ed.2d 275 (1987).

Since the above decisions dealing with a trading husband and psychiatrist and the tipping journalist, the SEC has adopted Rule 10b5–2, described in the adopting SEC release as follows:

> ... [A]n unsettled issue in insider trading law has been under what circumstances certain non-business relationships, such as family and personal relationships, may provide the duty of trust or confidence required under the misappropriation theory. Case law has produced the following anomalous result. A family member who receives a "tip" (within the meaning of Dirks) and then trades violates Rule 10b–5. A family member who trades in breach of an express promise of confidentiality also violates Rule 10b–5. A family member who trades in breach of a reasonable expectation of confidentiality, however, does not necessarily violate Rule 10b–5.
>
> ... [W]e think that this anomalous result harms investor confidence in the integrity and fairness of the nation's securities markets. The family member's trading has the same impact on the market and investor confidence in the third example as it does in the first two examples. In all three examples, the trader's informational advantage stems from "contrivance, not luck," and the informational disadvantage to other investors "cannot be overcome with research or skill." Additionally, the need to distinguish among the three types of cases may require an unduly intrusive examination of the details of particular family relationships. Accordingly, we believe there is good reason for the broader ap-

proach we adopt today for determining when family or personal relationships create "duties of trust or confidence" under the misappropriation theory.

Some of the commenters ... expressed concern that the rule would erode standards of personal and family privacy.... [W]e do not believe that the rule will require a more intrusive examination of family relationships than would be required under existing case law without the rule. Current case law, such as United States v. Chestman ... already establishes a regime under which questions of liability turn on the nature of the details of the relationships between family members, such as their prior history and patterns of sharing confidences. By providing more of a bright-line test for certain enumerated close family relationships, we believe the rule will mitigate, to some degree, the need to examine the details of particular relationships in the course of investigating suspected insider trading....

The rule sets forth a non-exclusive list of three situations in which a person has a duty of trust or confidence for purposes of the "misappropriation" theory of the Exchange Act and Rule 10b–5 thereunder.

First, ... we provide that a duty of trust or confidence exists whenever a person agrees to maintain information in confidence.

Second, we provide that a duty of trust or confidence exists when two people have a history, pattern, or practice of sharing confidences such that the recipient of the information knows or reasonably should know that the person communicating the material nonpublic information expects that the recipient will maintain its confidentiality. This is a "facts and circumstances" test based on the expectation of the parties in light of the overall relationship. Some commenters were concerned that, as proposed, this provision examined the reasonable expectation of confidentiality of the person communicating the material nonpublic information rather than examining the expectations of the recipient of the information and/or both parties to the communication.... [W]e have revised the provision to make this mutuality explicit....

Third, we are adopting as proposed a bright-line rule that states that a duty of trust or confidence exists when a person receives or obtains material nonpublic information from certain enumerated close family members: spouses, parents, children, and siblings. An affirmative defense permits the person receiving or obtaining the information to demonstrate that under the facts and circumstances of that family relationship, no duty of trust or confidence existed....

SEC, Selective Disclosure and Insider Trading, Securities Act Rel. No. 7881 (August 15, 2000).

Assume in *O'Hagan* that Bill "hacked" into Dorsey Whitney's computer system and as a result learned of the forthcoming bid for Pillsbury. On the basis of this purloined information Bill purchased a significant number of Pillsbury shares. Is Bill's conduct proscribed by Rule 10b–5? Rule 14 e–3? In resolving these questions should it matter whether Bill, in order to circumvent the law firm's encryption system, "planted" in the system a false password within the system and then used that password to access Dorsey Whitney files? See Securities and Exchange Commission v. Dorozhko, 574 F.3d 42 (2nd Cir. 2009).

Finally, consider the social implications of premising federal regulation of inside trading on the private relations of trust and confidence between the creator/owner of the non public information and the person that trades on that information. Observe that under *O'Hagan* the wrongfulness of the defendant's act does not turn on any social harm to markets or investors generally, but rather on the harm to the party from who the confidential information was obtained. Does this run the risk that such a privatized view of why and how inside trading is regulated will lead to our more broadly based concerns for preserving the integrity of fair and efficient capital markets to be subordinated to the vagaries of private arrangements. For example, after *Chiarella* and *O'Hagan* could an oil company, in order to incent the firm's geologists, permit all its geologists to trade in the firm's stock on the basis of any information they obtain through their employment position? *See generally* James D. Cox, Insider Trading And Contracting: A Critical Response To The "Chicago School," 1986 Duke L. J. 628, 653–659. A related issue is the enforceability of so-called "big boy" letters where the privately negotiated contract for the purchase-sale of securities expressly provides that the selling (buying) party might be in possession of material nonpublic information that is not disclosed to the other party and the parties agree to this condition. *See* Edwin D. Eshmoili, Note, Big boy Letters: Trading On Inside Information, 94 Cornell L. Rev. 133 (2008). To what extent are such private licensing and waiver efforts effective under Rule 14e–3?

For a thoughtful review of how the experiences as a practitioner influenced Justice Powell, the author of the majority opinions in *Chiarella and Dirks,* in his many decisions constricting the scope Rule 10b–5, *see* A.C. Pritchard, Justice Lewis F. Powell, Jr., And The Counterrevolution In the Federal Securities Laws, 52 Duke L.J. 841 (2003).

SEC RULE 10b5–2

[See Statutory Supplement]

[See Statutory Supplement]

Dirks v. Securities and Exchange Commission

Supreme Court of the United States, 1983.
463 U.S. 646, 103 S.Ct. 3255, 77 L.Ed.2d 911.

■ JUSTICE POWELL delivered the opinion of the Court.

Petitioner Raymond Dirks received material nonpublic information from "insiders" of a corporation with which he had no connection. He disclosed this information to investors who relied on it in trading in the shares of the corporation. The question is whether Dirks violated the antifraud provisions of the federal securities laws by this disclosure.

I

In 1973, Dirks was an officer of a New York broker-dealer firm who specialized in providing investment analysis of insurance company securities to institutional investors. On March 6, Dirks received information from Ronald Secrist, a former officer of Equity Funding of America. Secrist alleged that the assets of Equity Funding, a diversified corporation primarily engaged in selling life insurance and mutual funds, were vastly overstated as the result of fraudulent corporate practices. Secrist also stated that various regulatory agencies had failed to act on similar charges made by Equity Funding employees. He urged Dirks to verify the fraud and disclose it publicly.

Dirks decided to investigate the allegations. He visited Equity Funding's headquarters in Los Angeles and interviewed several officers and employees of the corporation. The senior management denied any wrongdoing, but certain corporation employees corroborated the charges of fraud. Neither Dirks nor his firm owned or traded any Equity Funding stock, but throughout his investigation he openly discussed the information he had obtained with a number of clients and investors. Some of these persons sold their holdings of Equity Funding securities, including five investment advisers who liquidated holdings of more than $16 million.[2]

While Dirks was in Los Angeles, he was in touch regularly with William Blundell, the Wall Street Journal's Los Angeles bureau chief. Dirks urged Blundell to write a story on the fraud allegations. Blundell did not believe, however, that such a massive fraud could go undetected and declined to write the story. He feared that publishing such damaging hearsay might be libelous.

During the two-week period in which Dirks pursued his investigation and spread word of Secrist's charges, the price of Equity Funding stock fell from $26 per share to less than $15 per share. This led the

2. Dirks received from his firm a salary plus a commission for securities transactions above a certain amount that his clients directed through his firm. See 21 S.E.C. Docket, at 1402, n. 3. But "[i]t is not clear how many of those with whom Dirks spoke promised to direct some brokerage business through [Dirks' firm] to compensate Dirks, or how many actually did so." 220 U.S.App.D.C., at 316, 681 F.2d, at 831. The Boston Company Institutional Investors, Inc., promised Dirks about $25,000 in commissions, but it is unclear whether Boston actually generated any brokerage business for his firm. See App. 199, 204–205; 21 S.E.C. Docket, at 1404, n. 10; 220 U.S.App.D.C., at 316, n. 5, 681 F.2d, at 831, n. 5.

New York Stock Exchange to halt trading on March 27. Shortly thereafter California insurance authorities impounded Equity Funding's records and uncovered evidence of the fraud. Only then did the Securities and Exchange Commission (SEC) file a complaint against Equity Funding[3] and only then, on April 2, did the Wall Street Journal publish a front-page story based largely on information assembled by Dirks. Equity Funding immediately went into receivership.[4]

The SEC began an investigation into Dirks' role in the exposure of the fraud. After a hearing by an administrative law judge, the SEC found that Dirks had aided and abetted violations of § 17(a) of the Securities Act of 1933 ... § 10(b) of the Securities Exchange Act of 1934 ... and SEC Rule 10b–5 ... by repeating the allegations of fraud to members of the investment community who later sold their Equity Funding stock. The SEC concluded: "Where 'tippees'—regardless of their motivation or occupation—come into possession of material 'information that they know is confidential and know or should know came from a corporate insider,' they must either publicly disclose that information or refrain from trading." 21 S.E.C. Docket 1401, 1407 (1981) (footnote omitted) (quoting Chiarella v. United States, 445 U.S. 222, 230 n. 12, 100 S.Ct. 1108, 1115 n. 12, 63 L.Ed.2d 348 (1980)). Recognizing, however, that Dirks "played an important role in bringing [Equity Funding's] massive fraud to light," 21 S.E.C. Docket, at 1412, the SEC only censured him.

Dirks sought review in the Court of Appeals for the District of Columbia Circuit. The court entered judgment against Dirks....

In view of the importance to the SEC and to the securities industry of the question presented by this case, we granted a writ of certiorari. 459 U.S. 1014 ... (1982). We now reverse.

II

In the seminal case of In re Cady, Roberts & Co., 40 S.E.C. 907 (1961), the SEC recognized that the common law in some jurisdictions imposes on "corporate 'insiders,' particularly officers, directors, or controlling stockholders" an "affirmative duty of disclosure ... when dealing in securities." Id., at 911, and n. 13.[10] The SEC found that not only did breach of this common-law duty also establish the elements of a Rule 10b–5 violation, but that individuals other than corporate

3. As early as 1971, the SEC had received allegations of fraudulent accounting practices at Equity Funding. Moreover, on March 9, 1973, an official of the California Insurance Department informed the SEC's regional office in Los Angeles of Secrist's charges of fraud. Dirks himself voluntarily presented his information at the SEC's regional office beginning on March 27.

4. A federal grand jury in Los Angeles subsequently returned a 105–count indictment against 22 persons, including many of Equity Funding's officers and directors. All defendants were found guilty of one or more counts, either by a plea of guilty or a conviction after trial. See Brief for Petitioner 15; App. 149–153.

10. The duty that insiders owe to the corporation's shareholders not to trade on inside information differs from the common-law duty that officers and directors also have to the corporation itself not to mismanage corporate assets, of which confidential information is one.... In holding that breaches of this duty to shareholders violated the Securities Exchange Act, the *Cady, Roberts* Commission recognized, and we agree, that "[a] significant purpose of the Exchange Act was to eliminate the idea that use of inside information for personal advantage was a normal emolument of corporate office." See 40 S.E.C., at 912, n. 15.

insiders could be obligated either to disclose material non-public information before trading or to abstain from trading altogether. Id., at 912. In *Chiarella,* we accepted the two elements set out in *Cady, Roberts* for establishing a Rule 10b–5 violation: "(i) the existence of a relationship affording access to inside information intended to be available only for a corporate purpose, and (ii) the unfairness of allowing a corporate insider to take advantage of that information by trading without disclosure." 445 U.S., at 227.... In examining whether Chiarella had an obligation to disclose or abstain, the Court found that there is no general duty to disclose before trading on material nonpublic information, and held that "a duty to disclose under § 10(b) does not arise from the mere possession of nonpublic market information." Id., at 235.... Such a duty arises rather from the existence of a fiduciary relationship. See id., at 227–235....

Not "all breaches of fiduciary duty in connection with a securities transaction," however, come within the ambit of Rule 10b–5. Santa Fe Industries, Inc. v. Green, 430 U.S. 462, 472 ... (1977). There must also be "manipulation or deception." Id., at 473, 97 S.Ct., at 1300. In an inside-trading case this fraud derives from the "inherent unfairness involved where one takes advantage" of "information intended to be available only for a corporate purpose and not for the personal benefit of anyone." In re Merrill Lynch, Pierce, Fenner & Smith, Inc., 43 S.E.C. 933, 936 (1968). Thus, an insider will be liable under Rule 10b–5 for inside trading only where he fails to disclose material nonpublic information before trading on it and thus makes "secret profits." *Cady, Roberts,* 40 S.E.C., at 916, n. 31.

III

We were explicit in *Chiarella* in saying that there can be no duty to disclose where the person who has traded on inside information "was not [the corporation's] agent, ... was not a fiduciary, [or] was not a person in whom the sellers [of the securities] had placed their trust and confidence." 445 U.S., at 232.... Not to require such a fiduciary relationship, we recognized, would "depar[t] radically from the established doctrine that duty arises from a specific relationship between two parties" and would amount to "recognizing a general duty between all participants in market transactions to forgo actions based on material, nonpublic information." Id., at 232, 233.... This requirement of a specific relationship between the shareholders and the individual trading on inside information has created analytical difficulties for the SEC and courts in policing tippees who trade on inside information. Unlike insiders who have independent fiduciary duties to both the corporation and its shareholders, the typical tippee has no such relationships.[14] In view of this absence, it has been unclear how a tippee acquires the *Cady, Roberts* duty to refrain from trading on inside information....

---

14. Under certain circumstances, such as where corporate information is revealed legitimately to an underwriter, accountant, lawyer, or consultant working for the corporation, these outsiders may become fiduciaries of the shareholders. The basis for recognizing this fiduciary duty is not simply that such persons acquired nonpublic corporate information, but rather that they have entered into a special confidential relationship in the conduct of the

A

The SEC's position, as stated in its opinion in this case, is that a tippee "inherits" the *Cady, Roberts* obligation to shareholders whenever he receives inside information from an insider . . .

. . . This [position] conflicts with the principle set forth in *Chiarella* that only some persons, under some circumstances, will be barred from trading while in possession of material nonpublic information. . . . See *Chiarella,* 445 U.S., at 235, n. 20. . . . We reaffirm today that "[a] duty [to disclose] arises from the relationship between parties . . . and not merely from one's ability to acquire information because of his position in the market." [Chiarella,] 445 U.S., at 232–233, n. 14. . . .

Imposing a duty to disclose or abstain solely because a person knowingly receives material nonpublic information from an insider and trades on it could have an inhibiting influence on the role of market analysts, which the SEC itself recognizes is necessary to the preservation of a healthy market. It is commonplace for analysts to "ferret out and analyze information," 21 S.E.C., at 1406,[18] and this often is done by meeting with and questioning corporate officers and others who are insiders. And information that the analysts obtain normally may be the basis for judgments as to the market worth of a corporation's securities. The analyst's judgment in this respect is made available in market letters or otherwise to clients of the firm. It is the nature of this type of information, and indeed of the markets themselves, that such information cannot be made simultaneously available to all of the corporation's stockholders or the public generally.

B

The conclusion that recipients of inside information do not invariably acquire a duty to disclose or abstain does not mean that such

---

business of the enterprise and are given access to information solely for corporate purposes. See SEC v. Monarch Fund, 608 F.2d 938, 942 (C.A.2 1979); In re Investors Management Co., 44 S.E.C. 633, 645 (1971); In re Van Alystne, Noel & Co., 43 S.E.C. 1080, 1084–1085 (1969); In re Merrill Lynch, Pierce, Fenner & Smith, Inc., 43 S.E.C. 933, 937 (1968); *Cady, Roberts,* 40 S.E.C., at 912. When such a person breaches his fiduciary relationship, he may be treated more properly as a tipper than a tippee. See Shapiro v. Merrill Lynch, Pierce, Fenner & Smith, Inc., 495 F.2d 228, 237 (C.A.2 1974) (investment banker had access to material information when working on a proposed public offering for the corporation). For such a duty to be imposed, however, the corporation must expect the outsider to keep the disclosed nonpublic information confidential, and the relationship at least must imply such a duty.

18. On its facts, this case is the unusual one. Dirks is an analyst in a broker-dealer firm, and he did interview management in the course of his investigation. He uncovered, however, startling information that required no analysis or exercise of judgment as to its market relevance. Nonetheless, the principle at issue here extends beyond these facts. The SEC's rule—applicable without regard to any breach by an insider—could have serious ramifications on reporting by analysts of investment views.

Despite the unusualness of Dirks' "find," the central role that he played in uncovering the fraud at Equity Funding, and that analysts in general can play in revealing information that corporations may have reason to withhold from the public, is an important one. Dirks' careful investigation brought to light a massive fraud at the corporation. And until the Equity Funding fraud was exposed, the information in the trading market was grossly inaccurate. But for Dirks' efforts, the fraud might well have gone undetected longer. See n. 8, supra.

tippees always are free to trade on the information. The need for a ban on some tippee trading is clear. Not only are insiders forbidden by their fiduciary relationship from personally using undisclosed corporate information to their advantage, but they may not give such information to an outsider for the same improper purpose of exploiting the information for their personal gain. See 15 U.S.C. § 78t(b) (making it unlawful to do indirectly "by means of any other person" any act made unlawful by the federal securities laws). Similarly, the transactions of those who knowingly participate with the fiduciary in such a breach are "as forbidden" as transactions "on behalf of the trustee himself." Mosser v. Darrow, 341 U.S. 267, 272.... As the Court explained in *Mosser,* a contrary rule "would open up opportunities for devious dealings in the name of the others that the trustee could not conduct in his own." 341 U.S., at 271.... See SEC v. Texas Gulf Sulphur Co., 446 F.2d 1301, 1308 (CA2), cert. denied, 404 U.S. 1005, 92 S.Ct. 561, 30 L.Ed.2d 558 (1971). Thus, the tippee's duty to disclose or abstain is derivative from that of the insider's duty. See Tr. of Oral Arg. 38. Cf. *Chiarella,* 445 U.S., at 246, n. 1 ... (Blackmun, J., dissenting). As we noted in *Chiarella,* "[t]he tippee's obligation has been viewed as arising from his role as a participant after the fact in the insider's breach of a fiduciary duty." 445 U.S., at 230, n. 12....

Thus, some tippees must assume an insider's duty to the shareholders not because they receive inside information, but rather because it has been made available to them *improperly*. And for Rule 10b–5 purposes, the insider's disclosure is improper only where it would violate his *Cady, Roberts* duty. Thus, a tippee assumes a fiduciary duty to the shareholders of a corporation not to trade on material nonpublic information only when the insider has breached his fiduciary duty to the shareholders by disclosing the information to the tippee and the tippee knows or should know that there has been a breach. As Commissioner Smith perceptively observed in *Investors Management Co.:* "[T]ippee responsibility must be related back to insider responsibility by a necessary finding that the tippee knew the information was given to him in breach of a duty by a person having a special relationship to the issuer not to disclose the information...." 44 S.E.C., at 651 (concurring in the result). Tipping thus properly is viewed only as a means of indirectly violating the *Cady, Roberts* disclose-or-abstain rule.

C

In determining whether a tippee is under an obligation to disclose or abstain, it thus is necessary to determine whether the insider's "tip" constituted a breach of the insider's fiduciary duty. All disclosures of confidential corporate information are not inconsistent with the duty insiders owe to shareholders. In contrast to the extraordinary facts of this case, the more typical situation in which there will be a question whether disclosure violates the insider's *Cady, Roberts* duty is when insiders disclose information to analysts. See n. 16, supra. In some situations, the insider will act consistently with his fiduciary duty to shareholders, and yet release of the information may affect the market.

For example, it may not be clear—either to the corporate insider or to the recipient analyst—whether the information will be viewed as material nonpublic information. Corporate officials may mistakenly think the information already has been disclosed or that it is not material enough to affect the market. Whether disclosure is a breach of duty therefore depends in large part on the purpose of the disclosure. This standard was identified by the SEC itself in *Cady, Roberts:* a purpose of the securities laws was to eliminate "use of inside information for personal advantage." 40 S.E.C., at 912, n. 15. See n. 10, supra. Thus, the test is whether the insider personally will benefit, directly or indirectly, from his disclosure. Absent some personal gain, there has been no breach of duty to stockholders. And absent a breach by the insider, there is no derivative breach. As Commissioner Smith stated in *Investors Management Co.* "It is important in this type of case to focus on policing insiders and what they do ... rather than on policing information *per se* and its possession...." 44 S.E.C., at 648 (concurring in the result).

The SEC argues that, if inside-trading liability does not exist when the information is transmitted for a proper purpose but is used for trading, it would be a rare situation when the parties could not fabricate some ostensibly legitimate business justification for transmitting the information. We think the SEC is unduly concerned. In determining whether the insider's purpose in making a particular disclosure is fraudulent, the SEC and the courts are not required to read the parties' minds. Scienter in some cases is relevant in determining whether the tipper has violated his *Cady, Roberts* duty. But to determine whether the disclosure itself "deceive[s], manipulate[s], or defraud[s]" shareholders, Aaron v. SEC, 446 U.S. 680, 686 ... (1980), the initial inquiry is whether there has been a breach of duty by the insider. This requires courts to focus on objective criteria, i.e., whether the insider receives a direct or indirect personal benefit from the disclosure, such as a pecuniary gain or a reputational benefit that will translate into future earnings. Cf. 40 S.E.C., at 912, n. 15; Brudney, Insiders, Outsiders, and Informational Advantages Under the Federal Securities Laws, 93 Harv.L.Rev. 324, 348 (1979) ("The theory ... is that the insider, by giving the information out selectively, is in effect selling the information to its recipient for cash, reciprocal information, or other things of value for himself ..."). There are objective facts and circumstances that often justify such an inference. For example, there may be a relationship between the insider and the recipient that suggests a *quid pro quo* from the latter, or an intention to benefit the particular recipient. The elements of fiduciary duty and exploitation of nonpublic information also exist when an insider makes a gift of confidential information to a trading relative or friend. The tip and trade resemble trading by the insider himself followed by a gift of the profits to the recipient.

Determining whether an insider personally benefits from a particular disclosure, a question of fact, will not always be easy for courts. But it is essential, we think, to have a guiding principle for those whose daily activities must be limited and instructed by the SEC's inside-trading rules, and we believe that there must be a breach of the insider's fiduciary duty before the tippee inherits the duty to disclose or abstain. In contrast, the rule adopted by the SEC in this case would have no limiting principle.

IV

Under the inside-trading and tipping rules set forth above, we find that there was no actionable violation by Dirks. It is undisputed that Dirks himself was a stranger to Equity Funding, with no pre-existing fiduciary duty to its shareholders. He took no action, directly or indirectly, that induced the shareholders or officers of Equity Funding to repose trust or confidence in him. There was no expectation by Dirks' sources that he would keep their information in confidence. Nor did Dirks misappropriate or illegally obtain the information about Equity Funding. Unless the insiders breached their *Cady, Roberts* duty to shareholders in disclosing the nonpublic information to Dirks, he breached no duty when he passed it on to investors as well as to the Wall Street Journal.

It is clear that neither Secrist nor the other Equity Funding employees violated their *Cady, Roberts* duty to the corporation's shareholders by providing information to Dirks. The tippers received no monetary or personal benefit for revealing Equity Funding's secrets, nor was their purpose to make a gift of valuable information to Dirks. As the facts of this case clearly indicate, the tippers were motivated by a desire to expose the fraud.... In the absence of a breach of duty to shareholders by the insiders, there was no derivative breach by Dirks. See n. 20, supra. Dirks therefore could not have been "a participant after the fact in [an] insider's breach of a fiduciary duty." *Chiarella,* 445 U.S., at 230, n. 12....

V

We conclude that Dirks, in the circumstances of this case, had no duty to abstain from use of the inside information that he obtained. The judgment of the Court of Appeals therefore is reversed.

■ Justice Blackmun, with whom Justice Brennan and Justice Marshall join, dissenting.

The Court today takes still another step to limit the protections provided investors by § 10(b) of the Securities Exchange Act of 1934.... The device employed in this case engrafts a special motivational requirement on the fiduciary duty doctrine. This innovation excuses a knowing and intentional violation of an insider's duty to shareholders if the insider does not act from a motive of personal gain. Even on the extraordinary facts of this case, such an innovation is not justified.

I

As the Court recognizes, ... the facts here are unusual. After a meeting with Ronald Secrist, a former Equity Funding employee, on March 7, 1973, App. 226, petitioner Raymond Dirks found himself in possession of material nonpublic information of massive fraud within the company.[2] In the Court's words, "[h]e uncovered . . . startling information that required no analysis or exercise of judgment as to its market relevance." . . . In disclosing that information to Dirks, Secrist intended that Dirks would disseminate the information to his clients, those clients would unload their Equity Funding securities on the market, and the price would fall precipitously, thereby triggering a reaction from the authorities. App. 16, 25, 27.

Dirks complied with his informant's wishes. Instead of reporting that information to the Securities and Exchange Commission (SEC or Commission) or to other regulatory agencies, Dirks began to disseminate the information to his clients and undertook his own investigation. One of his first steps was to direct his associates at Delafield Childs to draw up a list of Delafield clients holding Equity Funding securities. On March 12, eight days before Dirks flew to Los Angeles to investigate Secrist's story, he reported the full allegations to Boston Company Institutional Investors, Inc., which on March 15 and 16 sold approximately $1.2 million of Equity securities.[4] See id., at 199. As he gathered more information, he selectively disclosed it to his clients. To those holding Equity Funding securities he gave the "hard" story—all the allegations; others received the "soft" story—a recitation of vague factors that might reflect adversely on Equity Funding's management. See id., at 211, n. 24.

Dirks' attempts to disseminate the information to nonclients were feeble, at best. On March 12, he left a message for Herbert Lawson, the San Francisco bureau chief of The Wall Street Journal. Not until March 19 and 20 did he call Lawson again, and outline the situation. William Blundell, a Journal investigative reporter based in Los Angeles, got in touch with Dirks about his March 20 telephone call. On March 21, Dirks met with Blundell in Los Angeles. Blundell began his own investigation, relying in part on Dirks' contacts, and on March 23 telephoned Stanley Sporkin, the SEC's Deputy Director of Enforcement. On March 26, the next business day, Sporkin and his staff interviewed Blundell and asked to see Dirks the following morning. Trading was halted by the New York Stock Exchange at about the same time Dirks was talking to Los Angeles SEC personnel. The next day, March 28, the SEC suspended trading in Equity Funding securities. By

---

2. Unknown to Dirks, Secrist also told his story to New York insurance regulators the same day. App. 23. They immediately assured themselves that Equity Funding's New York subsidiary had sufficient assets to cover its outstanding policies and then passed on the information to California regulators who in turn informed Illinois regulators. Illinois investigators, later joined by California officials, conducted a surprise audit of Equity Funding's Illinois subsidiary, id., at 87–88, to find $22 million of the subsidiary's assets missing. On March 30, these authorities seized control of the Illinois subsidiary. Id., at 271.

4. The Court's implicit suggestion that Dirks did not gain by this selective dissemination of advice, ante, at . . . n. 2, is inaccurate. The [Administrative Law Judge] found that because of Dirks' information, Boston Company Institutional Investors, Inc., directed business to Delafield Childs that generated approximately $25,000 in commissions. App. 199, 204–205. While it is true that the exact economic benefit gained by Delafield Childs due to Dirks' activities is unknowable because of the structure of compensation in the securities market, there can be no doubt that Delafield and Dirks gained both monetary rewards and enhanced reputations for "looking after" their clients.

that time, Dirks' clients had unloaded close to $15 million of Equity Funding stock and the price had plummeted from $26 to $15. The effect of Dirks' selective dissemination of Secrist's information was that Dirks' clients were able to shift the losses that were inevitable due to the Equity Funding fraud from themselves to uninformed market participants.

II

A

No one questions that Secrist himself could not trade on his inside information to the disadvantage of uninformed shareholders and purchasers of Equity Funding securities. See Brief for United States as *Amicus Curiae* 19, n. 12. Unlike the printer in *Chiarella,* Secrist stood in a fiduciary relationship with these shareholders....

The Court also acknowledges that Secrist could not do by proxy what he was prohibited from doing personally.... Mosser v. Darrow, 341 U.S. 267, 272 ... (1951). But this is precisely what Secrist did. Secrist used Dirks to disseminate information to Dirks' clients, who in turn dumped stock on unknowing purchasers. Secrist thus intended Dirks to injure the purchasers of Equity Funding securities to whom Secrist had a duty to disclose. Accepting the Court's view of tippee liability,[5] it appears that Dirks' knowledge of this breach makes him liable as a participant in the breach after the fact....; *Chiarella,* 445 U.S., at 230, n. 12....

B

The Court holds, however, that Dirks is not liable because Secrist did not violate his duty; according to the Court, this is so because Secrist did not have the improper purpose of personal gain.... In so doing, the Court imposes a new, subjective limitation on the scope of the duty owed by insiders to shareholders. The novelty of this limitation is reflected in the Court's lack of support for it....

C

The fact that the insider himself does not benefit from the breach does not eradicate the shareholder's injury. Cf. Restatement (Second) of Trusts § 205, Comments c and d (1959) (trustee liable for acts causing diminution of value of trust); 3 A. Scott on Trusts § 205, p. 1665 (1967) (trustee liable for any losses to trust caused by his breach). It makes no difference to the shareholder whether the corporate insider gained or intended to gain personally from the transaction; the shareholder still has lost because of the insider's misuse of nonpublic information. The duty is addressed not to the insider's motives, but to his actions and their consequences on the

---

5. I interpret the Court's opinion to impose liability on tippees like Dirks when the tippee knows or has reason to know that the information is material and nonpublic and was obtained through a breach of duty by selective revelation or otherwise. See In re Investors Management Co., 44 S.E.C. 633, 641 (1971).

shareholder. Personal gain is not an element of the breach of this duty.[11] . . .

Although Secrist's general motive to expose the Equity Funding fraud was laudable, the means he chose were not. Moreover, even assuming that Dirks played a substantial role in exposing the fraud,[15] he and his clients should not profit from the information they obtained from Secrist. . . .

IV

In my view, Secrist violated his duty to Equity Funding shareholders by transmitting material nonpublic information to Dirks with the intention that Dirks would cause his clients to trade on that information. Dirks, therefore, was under a duty to make the information publicly available or to refrain from actions that he knew would lead to trading. Because Dirks caused his clients to trade, he violated § 10(b) and Rule 10b–5. Any other result is a disservice to this country's attempt to provide fair and efficient capital markets. I dissent.

AFTER THE FALL, Wall St. J., November 18, 1987, at 1, col. 6. "As a securities analyst in 1973, [Raymond L. Dirks] uncovered the Equity Funding stock-fraud case and alerted the SEC to it. The agency told Mr. Dirks it was too busy to probe the matter, but it eventually looked into Equity Funding—and slapped Mr. Dirks with an insider-trading action for notifying his clients before the matter became public. He fought that all the way to the Supreme Court and won in 1983.

"His luck ran out, however, when John Muir & Co., a highflying brokerage firm, collapsed in 1980 amid SEC charges of misplaced funds. Mr. Dirks, who was in charge of underwritings at Muir, denies any wrongdoing. He was suspended from acting as a principal in a securities firm for six months, a period that ended this year after appeals petered out.

"After Muir's collapse, Mr. Dirks scraped for work as a self-employed analyst. He resurfaced in 1985 at the firm of Steinberg & Lyman, helping bring fledgling insurance companies public. Last November, he moved to the New York brokerage firm of Baird, Patrick & Co., where he now heads an 18–person insurance-analyst unit. 'I'm

---

11. The Court seems concerned that this case bears on insiders' contacts with analysts for valid corporate reasons. . . . When the disclosure is to an investment banker or some other adviser, however, there is normally no breach because the insider does not have scienter: he does not intend that the inside information be used for trading purposes to the disadvantage of shareholders. . . .

The situation here, of course, is radically different. . . . Secrist divulged the information for the precise purpose of causing Dirks' clients to trade on it. I fail to understand how imposing liability on Dirks will affect legitimate insider-analyst contacts.

15. The Court uncritically accepts Dirks' own view of his role in uncovering the Equity Funding fraud. . . . It ignores the fact that Secrist gave the same information at the same time to state insurance regulators, who proceeded to expose massive fraud in a major Equity Funding subsidiary. The fraud surfaced before Dirks ever spoke to the SEC.

excited about insurance stocks again,' says Mr. Dirks, who is now 53. 'They're tremendously undervalued.' . . .

"Fourteen years of legal battles have left Ray Dirks older, wiser—and better connected. 'Some of the biggest money managers in the country return my phone calls now because they've heard my name,' he says. 'People want to know what I'm like. I can generally get in to see anybody I want.'

"He plays down the rigors of his long fight. 'I am a rebel by nature. I thrived on it,' Mr. Dirks says. 'But reality sets in when you have to pay lawyers. It was depressing.'

"He adds: 'I still get calls from guys wanting me to uncover some scams. I tell 'em I'm too busy. Besides, there's no money in it.' "

Legendary football coach, Barry Switzer (the University of Oklahoma and later the Dallas Cowboys) found himself mired in "insider trading" allegations. While attending his son's day-long high school track meet, he overheard G. Platt speaking with his wife regarding the pending merger of Phoenix Resources Company into Texas International Company. Mr. and Mrs. Platt were discussing Phoenix in the context of working out their schedules for the upcoming week; Mr. Platt was planning a trip to New York to discuss the matter with investment bankers at Morgan Stanley and they were contemplating how to cover things at home with their children. Switzer had dealt with Platt on several prior occasions. He knew Platt was the CEO of Texas International and that Texas International had a controlling interest in Phoenix. Indeed, Platt was a supporter not only of the University's football program but Switzer's weekly TV show. Switzer on two occasions had "upgraded" Platt's season tickets and occasionally provided autographs for Platt's children. After the Saturday track meet, Switzer shared with his friends and associates what he had overheard Platt say to his spouse. Switzer and the friends of Switzer each bought thousands of Phoenix shares and profited handsomely (the shares increased more than 50 percent) upon the announcement four days later that Phoenix would be merged into Texas International. Are Switzer and his friends wrongful tippees under *Dirks*? *See* SEC v. Switzer, 590 F.Supp. 756 (D. Ok. 1984).

What result in *O'Hagan* if instead of trading on his secret knowledge O'Hagan selectively disclosed to local reporters the forthcoming Grand Metropolitan bid for Pillsbury, believing that this would kill the deal, a result he believed best for Minneapolis so that the local icon, Pillsbury, would not fall into the control of a foreign firm? In such a tipping case, does the *Dirks* or *O'Hagan* formulation control? Recall that *O'Hagan* reasoned that the "in connection with" requirement "is satisfied because the fiduciary's fraud is consummated, not when the fiduciary gains the confidential information, but when, without disclosure to his principal, he uses the information to purchase or sell securities." 521 U.S. at 656. Thus, absent actually trading by the misappropriator or the type of personal benefit identified in *Dirks*, is there a violation? SEC v. Yun, 327 F.3d 1263 (11th Cir. 2003), addressed this question. Burch purchased put options on Scholastic Book Fairs based on information he obtained from his real estate partner, Donna Yun, who learned from her husband, Scholastic's president, that the publicly traded company would soon announce a substantial decline in its earnings. He relayed this information to his wife in the context of their negotiations of a post-nuptial division of their assets. The Eleventh Circuit reasoned that it was necessary to preserve the distinctiveness of the *Dirks* formulation for tipping and not conflate misappropriation cases with tipping cases. It observed that almost every tipping case could be recast as a misappropriator case. It then proceeded to find the necessary personal benefit elements called for by *Dirks.* The court observed that Donna Yun and Burch were friendly, worked together for several years, and split commissions on various real estate transactions over the years. In cases involving tippee liability, the court emphasized that the SEC must establish that the tippers intended to benefit from their disclosure of confidential information:

> The showing needed to prove an intent to benefit is not extensive. The Supreme Court in *Dirks*, after establishing the tipper benefit requirement, proceeded to define 'benefit' in very expansive terms. The Court declared that not only does an actual pecuniary gain, such as a kickback or an expectation of a reciprocal tip in the future, suffice to create a 'benefit,' but also cases where the tipper sought to enhance his reputation (which would translate into future earnings) or to make a gift to a trading relative or friend. . . .
>
> In this case, the SEC presented evidence that the two [tipper and tippee] were 'friendly,' worked together for several years, and split commissions on various real estate transactions over the years. This evidence is sufficient for a jury reasonably to conclude that Donna [the tipper] expected to benefit from her tip to Burch [the tippee] by maintaining a good relationship between a friend and frequent partner in real estate deals. See SEC v. Sargent, 229 F.3d at 68 (finding evidence of personal benefit when the tipper passed on information 'to effect a reconciliation with his friend and to maintain a useful networking contact') . . . .
>
> 327 F.3d at 1280.

In contrast, other circuits read *O'Hagan* more broadly and do not require evidence of personal gain to the tipper in misappropriation cases. *See* United States v. Falcone, 257 F.3d 226 (2d Cir. 2001); SEC v. Sargent, 229 F.3d 68 (1st Cir. 2000) (dicta); United States v. Libera, 989 F.2d 596 (2d Cir. 1993) (tipper unaware that tip would lead to trading but knew it would be put to some improper use).

SEC, Selective Disclosure and Insider Trading

Securities Act Rel. No. 7881 (August 15, 2000).

I. Executive Summary

We are adopting new rules and amendments to address the selective disclosure of material nonpublic information by issuers and to clarify two issues under the law of insider trading. In response to the comments we received on the proposal, we have made several modifications, as discussed below, in the final rules.

Regulation FD (Fair Disclosure) is a new issuer disclosure rule that addresses selective disclosure. The regulation provides that when an issuer, or person acting on its behalf, discloses material nonpublic information to certain enumerated persons (in general, securities market professionals and holders of the issuer's securities who may well trade on the basis of the information), it must make public disclosure of that information. The timing of the required public disclosure depends on whether the selective disclosure was intentional or non-intentional; for an intentional selective disclosure, the issuer must make public disclosure simultaneously; for a non-intentional disclosure, the issuer must make public disclosure promptly. Under the regulation, the required public disclosure may be made by filing or furnishing a Form 8–K, or by another method or combination of methods that is reasonably designed to effect broad, non-exclusionary distribution of the information to the public.

II. Selective Disclosure: Regulation FD

A. Background

. . . [W]e have become increasingly concerned about the selective disclosure of material information by issuers. As reflected in recent publicized reports, many issuers are disclosing important nonpublic information, such as advance warnings of earnings results, to securities analysts or selected institutional investors or both, before making full disclosure of the same information to the general public. Where this has happened, those who were privy to the information beforehand were able to make a profit or avoid a loss at the expense of those kept in the dark.

We believe that the practice of selective disclosure leads to a loss of investor confidence in the integrity of our capital markets. Investors who see a security's price change dramatically and only later are given access to the information responsible for that move rightly question whether they are on a level playing field with market insiders.

Issuer selective disclosure bears a close resemblance in this regard to ordinary "tipping" and insider trading. In both cases, a privileged few gain an informational edge—and the ability to use that edge to profit—from their superior access to corporate insiders, rather than from their skill, acumen, or diligence. Likewise, selective disclosure has an adverse impact on market integrity that is similar to the adverse impact from illegal insider trading: investors lose confidence in the fairness of the markets when they know that other participants may exploit "unerodable informational advantages" derived not from hard work or insights, but from their access to corporate insiders. The economic effects of the two practices are essentially the same. Yet, as a result of judicial interpretations, tipping and insider trading can be severely punished under the antifraud provisions of the federal securities laws, whereas the status of issuer selective disclosure has been considerably less clear.

Regulation FD is also designed to address another threat to the integrity of our markets: the potential for corporate management to treat material information as a commodity to be used to gain or maintain favor with particular analysts or investors. As noted in the Proposing Release, in the absence of a prohibition on selective disclosure, analysts may feel pressured to report favorably about a company or otherwise slant their analysis in order to have continued access to selectively disclosed information. We are concerned, in this regard, with reports that analysts who publish negative views of an issuer are sometimes excluded by that issuer from calls and meetings to which other analysts are invited.

Finally, . . . technological developments have made it much easier for issuers to disseminate information broadly. Whereas issuers once may have had to rely on analysts to serve as information intermediaries, issuers now can use a variety of methods to communicate directly with the market. In addition to press releases, these methods include, among others, Internet webcasting and teleconferencing. Accordingly, technological limitations no longer provide an excuse for abiding the threats to market integrity that selective disclosure represents.

NOTE ON INSIDER TRADING ENFORCEMENT

The heavy lifting with respect to insider trading is carried out by the government, either through civil enforcement by the SEC or criminal enforcement by the Department of Justice. The SEC enjoys a full panoply of remedies for violation of the securities laws. Most frequently invoked in insider trading cases. The authority to seek up to treble the insider trading profits was added by the Insider Trading Sanctions Act of 1984 amending section 21A(a)(2) to the Securities Exchange Act authorizing the SEC. In addition, the SEC can seek fairly substantial fines against violators. See Securities Exchange Act section 21(d)(3)(B). Interestingly, although little used, section 21A(e) authorizes the award of bounties to those who provide information in detecting and prosecuting violators. Because the sanctions (including the fines) that the SEC can impose are civil rather than criminal, the relevant standard of proof is whether the defendant's wrong has been established by a preponderance of the evidence, rather than whether it has been established beyond a reasonable doubt. The Department of Justice can proceed criminally under Section 32(a) of the Securities Exchange Act for knowing violations of any Exchange Act provision or violation. Criminal actions can also be maintained under the mail and wire fraud statutes. *See e.g.,* Carpenter v. United States, 484 U.S. 19,

108 S.Ct. 316, 98 L.Ed.2d 275 (1987) (financial columnist who tipped outsiders regarding what companies would be mentioned in his forthcoming market-moving column violated the mail and wire fraud statutes as a wrongful misappropriation of confidential information from his employer). Currently the mail and wire fraud statutes proscribe any scheme or artifice to deprive another of the intangible right to honest services. 18 U.S.C. § 1364.

Suppose, finally, that the plaintiff has purchased or sold publicly held stock at a time when the defendant wrongfully failed to disclose a material fact? Section 20A(a) of the Securities Exchange Act provides that any person who violates the Act or the Rules thereunder by purchasing or selling a security while in possession of material, nonpublic information shall be liable to any person who, contemporaneously with the purchase has sold, or contemporaneously with the sale has purchased, securities of the same class. Section 20A(b)(1) then qualifies section 20A(a) by providing that the amount of damages imposed under that section shall not exceed the profit gained or loss avoided in the transaction that is the subject of the violation.

It should be noted that § 20A(b) does not limit the liability of defendants in Rule 10b–5 actions that do not fall within § 20A, because § 20A is expressly made nonexclusive by § 20A(d). "The principal intent of this language is to assure that persons other than open market traders (i.e., sources of the information defrauded under the misappropriation theory) are not prevented from seeking a separate remedy for harm.... Although the matter is hardly clear ... the strong inference from the legislative history is that ... [open market purchasers relying]on the abstain or disclose principle ... are limited to the Section 20A remedy." Donald C. Langevoort, Insider Trading: Regulation, Enforcement & Prevention 9–16 (2002).

SECTION 3. LIABILITY FOR SHORT-SWING TRADING UNDER § 16(b) OF THE SECURITIES EXCHANGE ACT

SECURITIES EXCHANGE ACT § 16

[See Statutory Supplement]

SECURITIES EXCHANGE ACT RULES 3a–11–1, 3b–2, 16a–1, 16a–2, 16a–3, 16a–10, 16b–3, 16b–5, 16b–6, 16b–7, 16b–9; FORM 3; FORM 4; FORM 5

[See Statutory Supplement]

When enacted in 1934, section 16 of the Securities Exchange Act, was federal securities laws sole means to deter insider trading. As part of the original legislation, its presence was a sensible response to a world where computer surveillance and other sophisticated techniques for detecting inside trading were not at hand so that Congress was dubious whether in any action actual abuse by insiders could be established. Congress therefore opted for a prophylactic approach which continues today. Section 16(a) mandates that officers, directors and beneficial owners of more than 10 percent of an equity security registered pursuant to section 12 reporting company must report changes in their beneficial ownership of any equity security of the company. In the context of section 16 they are frequently referred to as "statutory insiders." A change in ownership report must be filed electronically with the SEC before the end of the second business day following the date the reportable transaction occurred. Moreover, within one business day of the SEC filing the report should be placed on the firm's website if it maintains such a website.

The report of the officer's, director's or beneficial owner's trade serves several functions. First, information that an officer, director or owner of more than ten percent has increased or decreased holdings in the firm itself reveals information that can be useful to investors. For example, knowledge that an officer or director is increasing or decreasing her holdings in the firm can be seen as reflecting the statutory insiders' optimism or pessimism regarding the firm's future prospects. This may prompt investors to following the insider's lead and increase or decrease their ownership of the firm's shares. And, knowledge of changes in share ownership can suggest changes in control. Second, and most significantly from the perspective of section 16's purpose, the reported changes in the statutory insider's holdings complements the operation of subsection (b). Section 16(b) imposes absolute liability on statutory insiders for the profits they obtain by the purchase and sale (as well as by the sale and purchase) when such purchase and sale are within a period of less than six months of one another. The resulting profit, called short-swing profit, is recoverable by the issuer without the need to prove the abuse of inside information.

In Gollust v. Mendell, 501 U.S. 115, 111 S.Ct. 2173, 115 L.Ed.2d 109 (1991), the Supreme Court made the following observations on the procedural aspects of § 16(b):

> To enforce this strict liability rule on insider trading, Congress chose to rely solely on the issuers of stock and their security holders. Unlike most of the federal securities laws, § 16(b) does not confer enforcement authority on the Securities and Exchange Commission. It is, rather, the security holders of an issuer who have the ultimate authority to sue for enforcement of § 16(b). If the issuer declines to bring a § 16(b) action within 60 days of a demand by a security holder, or fails to prosecute the action "diligently" ... then the security holder may "institut[e]" an action to recover insider short-swing profits for the issuer....
>
> Although plaintiffs seeking to sue under the statute must own a "security," § 16(b) places no significant restriction on the type

> of security adequate to confer standing. "[A]ny security" will suffice, ... the statutory definition being broad enough to include stock, notes, warrants, bonds, debentures, puts, calls, and a variety of other financial instruments; it expressly excludes only "currency or any note, draft, bill of exchange, or banker's acceptance which has a maturity at the time of issuance of not exceeding nine months...."

As seen in the materials in this chapter. Unlike 1934, there now is a well-established body of law that arms the SEC to prosecute insider trading cases. Indeed, roughly in any year slightly more than ten percent of its enforcement efforts are focused on insider trading and tipping cases. Further consider that, unlike the procedural setting in 1934, the modern class action and well-financed plaintiff's bar stand eager to step forward in instances where the SEC has not already acted. Thus, what justifies in today's legal setting continuing section 16(b)'s disgorgement remedy for short-swing profits?

Report of the Task Force on Regulation of Insider Trading, Part II: Reform of Section 16

42 Bus.Law. 1087, 1091–92 (1987).

In recent years, a number of commentators have suggested that section 16(b) causes more harm than good and that it should be repealed. It has been argued that section 16(b) is ineffectual in preventing insider trading and does not even address all of the ways in which insider trades can be perpetrated, while it imposes punitive liability on the innocent, the naive, and the unaware corporate officers who unwittingly sell in violation of, for example, the labyrinthine restrictions of rule 16b–3. These commentators raise the question: Given the development of the insider trading doctrine under rule 10b–5, the substantial limitations of section 16(b) in preventing insider trading, and the hardships that it imposes, is the statute needed?

The task force believes that it is. Section 16(b) has a different legislative focus than the prohibition of trading on inside information. Indeed, it is the only provision of the 1934 Act that specifically regulates insider trading. It is aimed at three specific types of insider trading abuses, only one of which involves abuse of inside information.

First, section 16(b) was intended to remove the temptation for corporation executives to profit from short-term stock price fluctuations at the expense of the long-term financial health of their companies. It prevents insiders from being obsessed with trading in their companies' securities to the detriment of their managerial and fiduciary responsibilities. In this regard, based on the testimony of insider abuses presented at the hearings, it was Congress's judgment that short-swing trading by corporate executives is not good for their companies or the American capital markets.

Second, the section was intended to penalize the unfair use of inside information by insiders. This includes both trading on inside information in violation of rule 10b–5 and the use of "softer" information of the type that insiders often have but that members of the investing public do not: the ability to make better informed guesses as to the success of new products, the likely results of negotiations, and the real risks of contingencies and other uncertainties, the underlying facts of which have been publicly disclosed.

Third, section 16(b) was designed to eliminate the temptation for insiders to manipulate corporate events so as to maximize their own short-term trading profits. Before the enactment of section 16(b), insiders had been able to make quick profits from short-term price swings by such practices as the announcement of generous (but imprudent) dividend programs followed by postinsider trading dividend reductions. Thus, the section provides a minimum standard of fiduciary conduct for corporate insiders.

The task force thus concludes that section 16 remains a useful tool for preventing speculative abuses by insiders and for focusing their attention on their fiduciary duty and on long-term corporate health, rather than on short-term trading profits.

Section 16(b) is often criticized on the ground that it can result in liability in cases where there has been no insider trading, and in cases where there has been no real profit. As the Report of the ABA Task Force makes clear, however, this criticism has failed to strike a responsive chord among most members of the corporate bar. The ABA Task Force Report addresses these kinds of criticisms by giving affirmative justifications for the operation of § 16(b). See also Fox, Insider Trading Deterrence versus Managerial Incentives: A Unified Theory of Section 16(b), 92 Mich.L.Rev. 2088 (1994).

Furthermore, it is hard to see that § 16(b) has any significant capacity for harm. It's often thought to be desirable to encourage directors and executives to become shareholders, so as to tie their fortunes more closely to those of the corporation's owners. However, it is seldom thought to be desirable to encourage directors and executives to engage in short-swing in-and-out trading. In the overwhelming majority of cases, all that § 16(b) does is to discourage such trading by increasing the likelihood that the gains will have to be disgorged. Moreover, if we put aside exotic scenarios that could occur in theory, but almost never occur in practice, the sanction of § 16(b) is exceptionally mild, because normally all § 16(b) does is put the director or executive back where she was before she engaged in the relevant transactions.

Gratz v. Claughton

United States Court of Appeals, Second Circuit, 1951.
187 F.2d 46, cert. denied 341 U.S. 920, 71 S.Ct. 741, 95 L.Ed. 1353 (1951).

■ Before L. HAND, CHIEF JUDGE, and SWAN and AUGUSTUS N. HAND, CIRCUIT JUDGES.

■ L. HAND, CHIEF JUDGE.

This is an appeal by the defendant, Claughton, from a judgment against him, entered upon the report of a master, in an action by a shareholder of the Missouri–Kansas–Texas Railroad Company under § 16(b) of the Securities Exchange Act of 1934.... The court first granted a summary judgment as to all the issues except the amount of the profits made by the defendant, which it referred to a master, on whose report it entered final judgment. The defendant does not dispute the propriety of a summary disposition of all the issues except that referred, but he does dispute the propriety of the judgment in law. First, he argues that the venue was wrong because he was domiciled in Florida, and the summons was served upon him in that state. Second, he disputes the rule adopted by the master in computing his profits. Third, he challenges the constitutionality of the statute which imposes the liability, and of the provisions for venue. We shall take up the first and third in sequence, reserving the second for the last.

[The court held that venue was proper.] ...

The challenge to the constitutionality of § 16(b) we have answered twice before. For many years a grave omission in our corporation law had been its indifference to dealings of directors or other corporate officers in the shares of their companies. When they bought shares, they came literally within the conventional prohibitions of the law of trusts; yet the decisions were strangely slack in so deciding. When they sold shares, it could indeed be argued that they were not dealing with a beneficiary, but with one whom his purchase made a beneficiary. That should not, however, have obscured the fact that the director or officer assumed a fiduciary relation to the buyer by the very sale; for it would be a sorry distinction to allow him to use the advantage of his position to induce the buyer into the position of a beneficiary, although he was forbidden to do so, once the buyer had become one. Certainly this is true, when the buyer knows he is buying of a director or officer, for he expects to become the seller's *cestui que* trust. If the buyer does not know, he is entitled to assume that if his seller in fact is already a director or officer, he will remain so after the sale. Nor was it necessary to confine this disability to directors or other officers of the corporation. The reason for the doctrine was that a director or officer may have information not accessible to a shareholder, actual or prospective, and that advantage is not confined to them. We take judicial notice that an effective control over the affairs of a corporation often does not require anything approaching a majority of the shares; and this is particularly true in the case of those corporations whose shares are dealt in upon national exchanges. Nor is it common for the control so obtained to be in the hands of one individual; more often a number share it, who are all in a position to gain a more intimate acquaintance with the enterprise and its prospects than the shareholders at large. It is of course true that the ownership of ten per cent of the shares does not always put the owner among those who do control; but neither Congress, nor any other legislature, is obliged to limit the means which it chooses so exactly to its ends that the correspondence is exact. If only those persons were liable, who could be proved to have a bargaining advantage, the execution of the statute would be so encumbered as to defeat its whole purpose. We do not mean that the interest, of which a statute deprives an individual, may never be so vital that he must not be given a trial of his personal guilt; but that is not so when all that is at stake is a director's, officer's or "beneficial owner's" privilege to add to, or subtract from, his holdings for a period of six months. In such situations it is well settled that a statute may provide any means which can reasonably be thought necessary to deal with the evil, even though they may cover instances where it is not present. . . .

There remains the question of the computation of profits, which we dealt with in Smolowe v. Delendo Corporation. . . .[8] Section 16(b) declares that "any profit realized . . . from any purchase and sale, or any sale and purchase . . . within any period of less than six months . . . shall inure to and be recoverable by the issuer": the corporation. It is plain that this presupposes some matching of (1) purchases against sales, or of (2) sales against purchases, and that there must therefore be some principle upon which both the minuend—the sale price—and the subtrahend—the purchase price—can be determined. At first blush it might seem that the statute limited the recovery to profits derived from transactions in the same shares; as, for example, that a dealer's profit upon the sale of any given number of shares was to be measured by subtracting what he paid for those shares from what he got upon a sale of the same certificate. However, as we observed in Smolowe v. Delendo Corporation, supra, that would allow an easy avoidance of the statute; in order to speculate freely an officer, director, or "beneficial owner" need only hold a substantial block of shares for more than six months. If, for example, on January 1st, he had 10,000 shares which he had bought before October 1st, he could buy 1,000 shares on February 1st and sell 1,000 shares at a profit on April 1st, making delivery out of certificates from the 10,000 shares purchased before October 1st. After the two transactions his position would be what it had been on January 1st save that in two months he had made a profitable turn in 1,000 shares—exactly the evil against which the statute is directed. Moreover, there is an added reason for this interpretation, if one be needed. In the case of a sale followed by a purchase it is impossible to identify any purchase with any previous sale; one would have to confine such transactions to the practically non-existent occasions when the proceeds of the sale were used to purchase. Thus it appears, regardless of anything said during the

8. 2 Cir., 136 F.2d 231, 148 A.L.R. 300.

passage of the bill through Congress and of the different forms it took, that the Act does not demand—that the same shares should be sold which were bought. This accords with the fungible nature of shares of stock. Indeed, if we translate the transaction into sales and purchases, or purchases and sales, of gallons of oil in a single tank, or of bushels of wheat in a single bin, it at once appears that the ascertainment of the particular shares bought or sold must be wholly irrelevant.

Although for these reasons it appears that the transactions—sales and purchases, or purchases and sales—are not to be matched by identifying the shares dealt in, we are no nearer than before to finding an answer as to how transactions shall be matched; all that so far appeared, is that the matching is to be between contracts of sale and contracts of purchase, or vice versa. On the other hand it is manifest that the intent of the fiduciary cannot be the test; first, because he generally has no ascertainable intent; and second, because that would open the door even more widely to the evil in question. The statute does not allow the fiduciary to minimize his profits, any more than to set off his losses against them. We can therefore find no principle by which to select any two transactions which are to be matched; and, so far as we can see, we are forced to one of two alternatives: to match any given sale taken as minuend, against any given purchase, taken as subtrahend, in such a way as to reduce profits to their lowest possible amount, or in such a way as to increase them to the greatest possible amount. The master adopted the second course, following what he supposed to be the doctrine of Smolowe v. Delendo Corporation, supra. We think that he was right for the following reasons.

The question is in substance the same as when a trustee's account is to be surcharged, for, as we have said, the statute makes the fiduciary a constructive trustee for any profits he may make. It is true that on the beneficiary in an accounting rests the burden of proof of a surcharge,[9] although the fiduciary has the burden of establishing any credits.[10] Since the plaintiff was seeking to surcharge the defendant we will therefore assume that it rested upon her to show how the transactions are to be matched; and, that, if there were nothing more, since she cannot do so, she must be content to have them matched in the way that shows the least profit. Obviously that cannot be the right answer, for the reasons we have given; and perhaps the fact that it cannot be, is reason enough for adopting the alternative. But there is another ground for reaching the same result. As we have said, the statute makes all such dealings unlawful, and makes the fiduciary accountable to the corporation. Although it is impossible in the case at bar to compute the defendant's profits, except that they must fall between two limits—the minimum and the maximum—the cause of this uncertainty is the number of transactions within six months: that is, the number of defendant's derelictions. The situation falls within the doctrine which has been law since the days of the "Chimney

9. Ewen v. Peoria & Eastern Ry., D.C., 78 F.Supp. 312, 334.

10. Wootton Land and Fuel Co. v. Ownbey, 8 Cir., 265 F. 91.

Sweeper's Jewel Case,"[11] that when damages are at some unascertainable amount below an upper limit and when the uncertainty arises from the defendant's wrong, the upper limit will be taken as the proper amount.[12]

This results in looking for six months both before and after any sale, and not for three months only, as the defendant insists. If one is seeking an equation of purchase and sale, one may take any sale as the minuend and look back for six months for a purchase at less price to match against it. On the other hand, if one is looking for an equation of sale and purchase, one may take the same sale and look forward for six months for any purchase at a lower price. Although obviously no transaction can figure in more than one equation, with that exception we can see no escape from what we have just said. It is true that this means that no director, officer, or "beneficial owner" may safely buy and sell, or sell and buy, shares of stock in the company except at intervals of six months. Whether that is too drastic a means of meeting the evil, we have not to decide; it is enough that we can find no other way to administer the statute. Therefore, not only will we follow Smolowe v. Delendo Corporation, supra, as a precedent; but as *res integra* and after independent analysis we reassert its doctrine. The defendant concedes that, except for carrying the transactions backward and forward for six months, instead of for three, the master followed the rule laid down in that decision; and the plaintiff has not appealed, so that she is not entitled to any more than she has recovered. On this account we have not examined the master's computations in detail and are not to be understood to have passed upon them. The crushing liabilities which § 16(b) may impose are apparent from this action in which the judgment was for over $300,000; it should certainly serve as a warning, and may prove a deterrent.[1]

Judgment affirmed.

NOTE ON THE COMPUTATION OF PROFITS UNDER § 16(b)

1. In Smolowe v. Delendo Corporation, 136 F.2d 231 (2d Cir. 1943), cert. denied 320 U.S. 751, 64 S.Ct. 56, 88 L.Ed. 446, which was cited and relied upon in Gratz v. Claughton, the court considered and rejected several formulas for computing profits under § 16(b) other than those analyzed in *Gratz:*

> Once the principle of [measuring damages based on the identification of the stock certificates involved] is rejected, its corollary, the first-in, first-out rule, is left at loose ends.... Its

---

11. Armory v. Delamirie, 1722, 1 Strange 505.

12. ... Story Parchment Co. v. Paterson Parchment Paper Co., 282 U.S. 555, 563–565, 51 S.Ct. 248, 75 L.Ed. 544; Bigelow v. R.K.O. Radio Pictures, Inc., 327 U.S. 251, 264, 265, 66 S.Ct. 574, 90 L.Ed. 652....

1. In Adler v. Klawans, 267 F.2d 840, 848 (2d Cir.1959), it is reported that "during the pertinent periods, [Gratz] suffered a net loss of $400,000 on trading in the stock for which he was charged under section 16(b)." (Footnote by ed.)

rationalization is the same as that for the identification rule, for which it operates as a presumptive principle; and it has no other support. If we reject one, we reject the other and for like reasons. Its application would render the large stockholder with a backlog of stock not immediately devoted to trading immune from the Act. Further, we should note that it does not fit the broad statutory language; a purchase followed immediately by a sale, albeit a transaction within the exact statutory language, would often be held immune from the statutory penalty because the purchase would be deemed by arbitrary rule to have been made at an earlier date; while a sale followed by purchase would never even be within the terms of the rule....

Another possibility might be the striking of an average purchase price and an average sale price during the period, and using these as bases of computation. What this rule would do in concrete effect is to allow as offsets all losses made by such trading. This in effect the district court first planned to do.... But it corrected this in its supplemental opinion, properly pointing out that the statute provided for the recovery of "any" profit realized and obviously precluded a setting off of losses. Even had the statutory language been more uncertain, this rule seems one not to be favored in the light of the statutory purpose. Compared to other possible rules, it tends to stimulate more active trading by reducing the chance of penalty.... Its application to a case where trading continued more than six months might be most uncertain, depending upon how the beginning of each six months' period was ascertained. It is not a clear-cut taking of "any profit" for the corporation, and we agree with the district court in rejecting it.

2. The formula adopted in *Smolowe* and *Gratz* has been generally approved by the courts. It is often referred to the "lowest purchase price, highest sale price" method. See, e.g., Whittaker v. Whittaker Corp., 639 F.2d 516, 530 (9th Cir.1981). Here are three illustrations of this method. Assume in all three illustrations that D is a director of C Corporation, whose stock is traded on a national securities exchange.

(i) On January 2, D purchases 1,000 shares of C at $10. On April 1, D sells 1,000 shares of C at $15. This is a short-swing "purchase and sale," and D is liable under § 16(b) for his profit of $5,000.

(ii) On January 2, D purchases 1,000 shares of C at $10. On August 1, D sells 1,000 shares at $15. On November 1, D purchases 1,000 shares at $10. D has no § 16(b) liability on the basis of the January–August swing, because the two ends of the swing did not occur within six months. However, the August and November transactions constitute a short-swing "sale and purchase," and D would be liable under § 16(b) for a profit of $5,000 on these two transactions. Why has D made a $5,000 "profit"? Because after D's November 1 purchase, his position in C Corporation's stock is exactly as it was just before August 1 (that is, he owns 1,000 C shares) but he has also added $5,000 cash to his bank account. D may have accomplished this result by using inside information. The sale at $15 may have been made on the basis of undisclosed bad news. The purchase at $10 may have been made on the basis of undisclosed good news.

(iii) D engages in the following pattern of activity:

Date	Action	Amount	Price
2/1	Purchase	1,000	$30
3/1	Sale	1,000	$25
4/1	Purchase	1,000	$20
5/1	Sale	1,000	$15

Under the *Smolowe/Gratz* formula, D has a profit of $5,000, because the purchase at $20 on 4/1 can be matched with the sale at $25 on 3/1. At first glance, this looks counterintuitive: it seems that D has a $10,000 loss in his total trading, not a $5,000 profit. But it may be that except for inside information, D would not have sold on 3/1, and instead would have ridden the C stock all the way down from $30 to $15, for a loss of $15,000. Accordingly, there is a possibility (which is all that § 16(b) requires) that D has profited by $5,000 by holding his loss to $10,000 through the use of inside information.[1]

NOTE ON THE INTERPRETATION OF § 16(b)

The courts have tended to use two somewhat different approaches in cases in which the applicability of § 16(b) is contestable. Until the early 1960s, the predominant theory of interpreting § 16(b) was that the section should be construed to cover all transactions within its literal reach. "[T]he statute was intended to be thoroughgoing, to squeeze all possible profits out of stock transactions, and thus to establish a standard so high as to prevent any conflict between the selfish interest of [an insider] and the faithful performance of his duty." Smolowe v. Delendo Corp., 136 F.2d 231, 239 (2d Cir.1943), cert. denied 320 U.S. 751, 64 S.Ct. 56, 88 L.Ed. 446. This theory of interpreting § 16(b) was known as the "objective" approach, although it has been aptly suggested that "automatic" would be more descriptive. Blau v. Lamb, 363 F.2d 507, 520 (2d Cir.1966), cert. denied 385 U.S. 1002, 87 S.Ct. 707, 17 L.Ed.2d 542 (1967).

Beginning in the mid–1960s, § 16(b) came to be perceived by some as overly harsh, because it operates without regard to fault. A different theory of interpretation, known as the "subjective" or "pragmatic" approach, then set in. Under this approach, in *borderline* cases—particularly cases involving an "*unorthodox*" transaction, rather than a garden-variety purchase or sale—the statute would be interpreted to impose liability only if the insider actually had access to inside information, or the transaction was of a type that carries a potential for insider abuse. See Whittaker v. Whittaker Corp., 639 F.2d

---

1. For a hypothetical in which a finding of profits under the *Smolowe/Gratz* formula does seem counterintuitive, see Lowenfels, Section 16(b): A New Trend in Regulating Insider Trading, 54 Cornell L.Rev. 45, 46–47 n. 6 (1968).

516, 522 (9th Cir.1981), cert. denied, 454 U.S. 1031, 102 S.Ct. 566, 70 L.Ed.2d 473; Lowenfels, Section 16(b): A New Trend in Regulating Insider Trading, 54 Cornell L.Rev. 45 (1968).

The names given to these two approaches are misleading. The "subjective" approach does not turn, as its name suggests, on the defendant's subjective intent to use inside information. Conversely, the "objective" approach can be just as pragmatic as the "pragmatic" approach. If the names of the two approaches are put aside, the conflict is between an approach that treats § 16(b) as a prophylactic rule of thumb, whose purpose would be defeated if defendants could escape liability on the ground that in their particular case no abuse could have occurred, and an approach that treats § 16(b) as inviting an inquiry into the possibility of abuse, at least in borderline cases. To a certain extent, which approach is adopted in a given case may depend on whether the court perceives § 16(b) as a good idea or a bad idea.

It should be emphasized that, although the tension between the approaches to the interpretation of § 16(b) is real and important, it is a tension only at the margins. In the great bulk of potential cases, the application of § 16(b) is relatively straightforward. As pointed out in *Whittaker,* supra:

> [T]he pragmatic approach has not ousted the objective view. Rather, the pragmatic approach is used to determine the boundaries of the statute's definitional scope in borderline situations, especially unorthodox transactions.... For a garden-variety transaction which cannot be regarded as unorthodox, the pragmatic approach is not applicable.... In such cases, if the situation is within the requirements established by Congress for § 16, then the mechanical, "objective," operation of the statute imposes liability.

Kern County Land Co. v. Occidental Petroleum Corp.

Supreme Court of the United States, 1973.
411 U.S. 582, 93 S.Ct. 1736, 36 L.Ed.2d 503.

■ MR. JUSTICE WHITE delivered the opinion of the Court.

Section 16(b) of the Securities Exchange Act of 1934, 48 Stat. 896, 15 U.S.C. § 78p(b), provides that officers, directors, and holders of more than 10% of the listed stock of any company shall be liable to the company for any profits realized from any purchase and sale or sale and purchase of such stock occurring within a period of six months. Unquestionably, one or more statutory purchases occur when one company, seeking to gain control of another, acquires more than 10% of the stock of the latter through a tender offer made to its shareholders. But is it a § 16(b) "sale" when the target of the tender offer defends itself by merging into a third company and the tender offeror then exchanges his stock for the stock of the surviving company and also grants an option to purchase the latter stock that is not exercisable within the statutory six-month period? This is the question before us in this case.

I

On May 8, 1967, after unsuccessfully seeking to merge with Kern County Land Co. (Old Kern),[2] Occidental Petroleum Corp. (Occidental)[3] announced an offer, to expire on June 8, 1967, to purchase on a first-come, first-served basis 500,000 shares of Old Kern common stock[4] at a price of $83.50 per share plus a brokerage commission of $1.50 per share.[5] By May 10, 1967, 500,000 shares, more than 10% of the outstanding shares of Old Kern,[6] had been tendered. On May 11, Occidental extended its offer to encompass an additional 500,000 shares. At the close of the tender offer, on June 8, 1967, Occidental owned 887,549 shares of Old Kern.[7]

Immediately upon the announcement of Occidental's tender offer, the Old Kern management undertook to frustrate Occidental's takeover attempt. A management letter to all stockholders cautioned against tender and indicated that Occidental's offer might not be the best available, since the management was engaged in merger discussions with several companies. When Occidental extended its tender offer, the president of Old Kern sent a telegram to all stockholders again advising against tender. In addition, Old Kern undertook merger discussions with Tenneco, Inc. (Tenneco),[8] and, on May 19, 1967, the

---

2. Old Kern was a California corporation having substantial real estate holdings, including oil-producing lands, oil-exploration activities, cattle ranching, cattle-feeding operations, and interests in the manufacture of automotive parts, electronic systems and devices, and farm machinery and construction equipment. After the reorganization described in the text, Old Kern became known as the 600 California Corporation until its eventual dissolution under California law on October 6, 1967.

3. Occidental is the respondent in this Court. A California corporation with its principal place of business in California, Occidental is engaged in the production and sale of oil, gas, coal, sulphur, and fertilizers.

4. The Old Kern stock was registered pursuant to § 12 of the Securities Exchange Act of 1934, as amended, 15 U.S.C. § 78*l*. The stock was a nonexempt, equity security for purposes of § 16(b).

5. The Old Kern stock closed at 63⅝ on Friday, May 8, 1967, the last trading day prior to the announcement of the tender offer. It had reached a high of 64⅞ and a low of 57⅜ in 1967, a high of 76¼ and a low of 51¾ in 1966, a high of 71⅝ and a low of 56 in 1965, and a high of 70⅜ and a low of 56⅝ in 1964. Thus, the $85–per–share tender-offer price represented a substantial profit for shareholders of Old Kern.

6. On May 10, Old Kern had 4,328,000 shares outstanding.

7. On May 18, 1967, Occidental filed a Form 3, Initial Statement of Beneficial Ownership of Securities, with the Securities and Exchange Commission indicating direct ownership of 507,055 shares of Old Kern stock; on June 9, 1967, Occidental filed a Form 4, Statement of Changes in Beneficial Ownership of Securities, for the month of May, indicating the purchase of an additional 376,326 shares of Old Kern stock, for a total ownership as of May 31, 1967, of 883,381 shares. An additional 4,168 shares were purchased by June 8, 1967, so that as of June 30, 1967, Occidental held 887,549 shares of Old Kern stock. This figure included 1,900 shares which Occidental purchased on the open market in April 1967. Section 16(b) liability is not asserted with respect to these shares, because these purchases did not make Occidental a "beneficial owner" for purposes of § 16(b).

8. Tenneco, a Delaware corporation, is a diversified industrial company with operations in natural gas transmission, oil and gas, chemicals, packaging, manufacturing, and shipbuilding. Tenneco is not a party to this litigation.

Board of Directors of Old Kern announced that it had approved a merger proposal advanced by Tenneco.[9] Under the terms of the merger, Tenneco would acquire the assets, property, and goodwill of Old Kern, subject to its liabilities, through "Kern County Land Co." (New Kern),[10] a new corporation to be formed by Tenneco to receive the assets and carry on the business of Old Kern. The shareholders of Old Kern would receive a share of Tenneco cumulative convertible preference stock in exchange for each share of Old Kern common stock which they owned. On the same day, May 19, Occidental, in a quarterly report to stockholders, appraised the value of the new Tenneco stock at $105 per share.[11] . . .

Realizing that, if the Old Kern–Tenneco merger were approved and successfully closed, Occidental would have to exchange its Old Kern shares for Tenneco stock and would be locked into a minority position in Tenneco, Occidental took . . . steps to protect itself. Between May 30 and June 2, it negotiated an arrangement with Tenneco whereby Occidental granted Tenneco Corp., a subsidiary of Tenneco, an option to purchase at $105 per share all of the Tenneco preference stock to which Occidental would be entitled in exchange for its Old Kern stock when and if the Old Kern–Tenneco merger was closed.[13] The premium to secure the option, at $10 per share, totaled $8,866,230 and was to be paid immediately upon the signing of the option agreement.[14] If the option were exercised, the premium was to be applied to the purchase price. By the terms of the option agreement, the option could not be exercised prior to December 9, 1967, a date six months and one day after expiration of Occidental's tender offer. On June 2, 1967, within six months of the acquisition by Occidental of more than 10% ownership of Old Kern, Occidental and Tenneco Corp. executed the option.[15] Soon thereafter, Occidental

9. Although technically a sale of assets, the corporate combination has been consistently referred to by the parties as a "merger" and will be similarly denominated in this opinion. The only significance of the characterization is the fact that a sale of assets required, under California law, approval of only a majority of the Old Kern shareholders and provided no appraisal rights for dissenters.

10. New Kern, a Delaware corporation with its principal place of business in California, is the petitioner in this Court and is a wholly owned subsidiary of Tenneco Corp. Tenneco Corp. is, in turn, a wholly owned subsidiary of Tenneco and owns all of the capital stock or controlling interests in most of Tenneco's nonpipeline operating subsidiaries. When first incorporated, New Kern was known as KCL Corp.

11. The annual dividend of $5.50 per share on the new Tenneco stock would be more than double the current annual dividend of $2.60 per share on the Old Kern stock. Each share of the new Tenneco preference stock was convertible into 3.6 shares of Tenneco common stock. During 1967, Tenneco common stock had sold at a high of 32½ and a low of 20⅞. Moreover, in contrast to Occidental's cash offer, the Tenneco exchange was expected to be, and was ultimately approved by the Internal Revenue Service as, free of capital gains tax.

13. The agreement covered 886,623 shares. This figure is 926 shares less than the number of Old Kern shares ultimately owned by Occidental. This discrepancy apparently results from uncertainty as to the number of shares tendered.

14. An outside investment banking firm in New York had determined that between $9 and $12 per share was a fair premium on an option on the Old Kern stock.

15. On that date, and on the date of the exercise of the option, Old Kern common stock was selling at approximately $95 per share.

announced that it would not oppose the Old Kern–Tenneco merger and dismissed its state court suits against Old Kern.[16]

The Old Kern–Tenneco merger plan was presented to and approved by Old Kern shareholders at their meeting on July 17, 1967. Occidental refrained from voting its Old Kern shares, but in a letter read at the meeting Occidental stated that it had determined prior to June 2 not to oppose the merger and that it did not consider the plan unfair or inequitable.[17] Indeed, Occidental indicated that, had it been voting, it would have voted in favor of the merger.

Meanwhile, the Securities and Exchange Commission had refused Occidental's request to exempt from possible § 16(b) liability Occidental's exchange of its Old Kern stock for the Tenneco preference shares that would take place when and if the merger transaction were closed. . . .

The Old Kern–Tenneco merger transaction was closed on August 30. Old Kern shareholders thereupon became irrevocably entitled to receive Tenneco preference stock, share for share in exchange for their Old Kern stock. . . .

The option granted by Occidental on June 2, 1967, was exercised on December 11, 1967. Occidental, not having previously availed itself of its right, exchanged certificates representing 887,549 shares of Old Kern stock for a certificate representing a like number of shares of Tenneco preference stock. The certificate was then endorsed over to the optionee-purchaser, and in return $84,229,185 was credited to Occidental's accounts at various banks. Adding to this amount the $8,886,230 premium paid in June, Occidental received $93,905,415 for its Old Kern stock (including the 1,900 shares acquired prior to issuance of its tender offer). In addition, Occidental received dividends totaling $1,793,439.22. Occidental's total profit was $19,506,419.22 on the shares obtained through its tender offer.

On October 17, 1967, New Kern instituted a suit under § 16(b) against Occidental to recover the profits which Occidental had realized as a result of its dealings in Old Kern stock. The complaint alleged that the execution of the Occidental–Tenneco option on June 2, 1967, and the exchange of Old Kern shares for shares of Tenneco to which Occidental became entitled pursuant to the merger closed on August 30, 1967, were both "sales" within the coverage of § 16(b). Since both acts took place within six months of the date on which Occidental became the owner of more than 10% of the stock of Old Kern, New

---

16. Seeking to prevent its acquisition of Tenneco shares pursuant to the merger from being matched with the sale of those shares upon exercise of the option for purposes of establishing § 16(b) liability, Occidental asked that the new Tenneco stock not be immediately registered pursuant to § 12 of the Securities Exchange Act of 1934, 15 U.S.C. § 78*l*. See 450 F.2d 157, 160 n. 6.

17. The letter indicated that Occidental "did not consider it to be in its best interest, or the best interest of its shareholders, or the best interest of KCL Shareholders generally for it to [oppose] the transaction." However, Occidental stated that "[i]n view of the fact that we would rather have worked out our own transaction with KCL, we shall not vote our KCL shares at the KCL Shareholder's Meeting on July 17, 1967." Under applicable California law, the abstention from voting was tantamount to opposing the merger.

Kern asserted that § 16(b) required surrender of the profits realized by Occidental. New Kern eventually moved for summary judgment, and, on December 27, 1970, the District Court granted summary judgment in favor of New Kern. *Abrams v. Occidental Petroleum Corp.*, 323 F.Supp. 570 (S.D.N.Y.1970). The District Court held that the execution of the option on June 2, 1967, and the exchange of Old Kern shares for shares of Tenneco on August 30, 1967, were "sales" under § 16(b). The Court ordered Occidental to disgorge its profits plus interest. In a supplemental opinion, Occidental was also ordered to refund the dividends which it had received plus interest.

On appeal, the Court of Appeals reversed and ordered summary judgment entered in favor of Occidental. *Abrams v. Occidental Petroleum Corp.*, 450 F.2d 157 (C.A.2 1971). The Court held that neither the option nor the exchange constituted a "sale" within the purview of § 16(b).[20] We granted certiorari. 405 U.S. 1064, 92 S.Ct. 1498, 31 L.Ed.2d 793 (1972). We affirm.

II

Section 16(b) provides, *inter alia,* that a statutory insider must surrender to the issuing corporation "any profit realized by him from any purchase and sale, or any sale and purchase, of any equity security of such issuer ... within any period of less than six months." As specified in its introductory clause, § 16(b) was enacted "[f]or the purpose of preventing the unfair use of information which may have been obtained by [a statutory insider] ... by reason of his relationship to the issuer." Congress recognized that short-swing speculation by stockholders with advance, inside information would threaten the goal of the Securities Exchange Act to "insure the maintenance of fair and honest markets." 15 U.S.C. § 78b. Insiders could exploit information not generally available to others to secure quick profits. As we have noted, "the only method Congress deemed effective to curb the evils of insider trading was a flat rule taking the profits out of a class of transactions in which the possibility of abuse was believed to be intolerably great." *Reliance Electric Co. v. Emerson Electric Co.*, 404 U.S. 418, 422, 92 S.Ct. 596, 30 L.Ed.2d 575 (1972). As stated in the report of the Senate Committee, the bill aimed at protecting the public "by preventing directors, officers, and principal stockholders of a corporation ... from speculating in the stock on the basis of information not available to others." S.Rep. No. 792, 73d Cong., 2d Sess., 9 (1934).

Although traditional cash-for-stock transactions that result in a purchase and sale or a sale and purchase within the six-month, statutory period are clearly within the purview of § 16(b), the courts

20. In view of its disposition, the Court of Appeals did not reach Occidental's contentions that only the purchases in excess of 10% of Old Kern's stock, rather than all purchases made pursuant to the tender offer, should be included in calculating liability and that the awards of prejudgment interest and dividends were improper. Occidental also appealed from the dismissal of its counterclaims. The Court of Appeals dismissed Occidental's appeal as moot.

have wrestled with the question of inclusion or exclusion of certain "unorthodox" transactions.[24] The statutory definitions of "purchase" and "sale" are broad and, at least arguably, reach many transactions not ordinarily deemed a sale or purchase. In deciding whether borderline transactions are within the reach of the statute, the courts have come to inquire whether the transaction may serve as a vehicle for the evil which Congress sought to prevent—the realization of short-swing profits based upon access to inside information[25]—thereby endeavoring to implement congressional objectives without extending the reach of the statute beyond its intended limits. The statute requires the inside, short-swing trader to disgorge all profits realized on all "purchases" and "sales" within the specified time period, without proof of actual abuse of insider information, and without proof of intent to profit on the basis of such information. Under these strict terms, the prevailing view is to apply the statute only when its application would serve its goals. "[W]here alternative constructions of the terms of § 16(b) are possible, those terms are to be given the construction that best serves the congressional purpose of curbing short-swing speculation by corporate insiders." *Reliance Electric Co. v. Emerson Electric Co.,* 404 U.S., at 424. See *Blau v. Lamb,* 363 F.2d 507 (C.A.2 1966), cert. denied, 385 U.S. 1002, 87 S.Ct. 707, 17 L.Ed.2d 542 (1967). Thus, "[i]n interpreting the terms 'purchase' and 'sale,' courts have properly asked whether the particular type of transaction involved is one that gives rise to speculative abuse." *Reliance Electric Co. v. Emerson Electric Co., supra,* at 424 n. 4.

In the present case, it is undisputed that Occidental became a "beneficial owner" within the terms of § 16(b) when, pursuant to its tender offer, it "purchased" more than 10% of the outstanding shares of Old Kern. We must decide, however, whether a "sale" within the ambit of the statute took place either when Occidental became irrevocably bound to exchange its shares of Old Kern for shares of Tenneco pursuant to the terms of the merger agreement between Old Kern and Tenneco or when Occidental gave an option to Tenneco to purchase from Occidental the Tenneco shares so acquired.[28]

---

24. The term, see 2 L. Loss, Securities Regulation 1069 (2d ed. 1961), has been applied to stock conversions, exchanges pursuant to mergers and other corporate reorganizations, stock reclassifications, and dealings in options, rights, and warrants.

25. Several decisions have been read as to apply a so-called "objective" test in interpreting and applying § 16(b). See, *e.g., Smolowe v. Delendo Corp., supra; Park & Tilford v. Schulte,* 160 F.2d 984 (CA2), cert. denied, 332 U.S. 761, 68 S.Ct. 64, 92 L.Ed. 347 (1947); *Heli-Coil Corp. v. Webster,* 352 F.2d 156 (C.A.3 1965). Under some broad language in those decisions, § 16(b) is said to be applicable whether or not the transaction in question could possibly lend itself to the types of speculative abuse that the statute was designed to prevent. By far the greater weight of authority is to the effect that a "pragmatic" approach to § 16(b) will best serve the statutory goals....

28. Both events occurred within six months of Occidental's first acquisition of Old Kern shares pursuant to its tender offer. Although Occidental did not exchange its Old Kern shares until December 11, 1967, it is not contended that that date, rather than the date on which Occidental became irrevocably bound to do so, should control. Similarly, although the option was not exercised until December 11, 1967, no liability is asserted with respect to that event, because it occurred more than six months after Occidental's last acquisition of Old Kern stock.

III

On August 30, 1967, the Old Kern–Tenneco merger agreement was signed, and Occidental became irrevocably entitled to exchange its shares of Old Kern stock for shares of Tenneco preference stock. Concededly, the transaction must be viewed as though Occidental had made the exchange on that day. But, even so, did the exchange involve a "sale" of Old Kern shares within the meaning of § 16(b)? We agree with the Court of Appeals that it did not, for we think it totally unrealistic to assume or infer from the facts before us that Occidental either had or was likely to have access to inside information, by reason of its ownership of more than 10% of the outstanding shares of Old Kern, so as to afford it an opportunity to reap speculative, short-swing profits from its disposition within six months of its tender-offer purchases.

It cannot be contended that Occidental was an insider when, on May 8, 1967, it made an irrevocable offer to purchase 500,000 shares of Old Kern stock at a price substantially above market. At that time, it owned only 1,900 shares of Old Kern stock, far fewer than the 432,000 shares needed to constitute the 10% ownership required by the statute. There is no basis for finding that, at the time the tender offer was commenced, Occidental enjoyed an insider's opportunity to acquire information about Old Kern's affairs.

It is also wide of the mark to assert that Occidental, as a sophisticated corporation knowledgeable in matters of corporate affairs and finance, knew that its tender offer would either succeed or would be met with a "defensive merger." If its takeover efforts failed, it is argued, Occidental knew it could sell its stock to the target company's merger partner at a substantial profit. Calculations of this sort, however, whether speculative or not and whether fair or unfair to other stockholders or to Old Kern, do not represent the kind of speculative abuse at which the statute is aimed, for they could not have been based on inside information obtained from substantial stockholdings that did not yet exist. Accepting both that Occidental made this very prediction and that it would recurringly be an accurate forecast in tender-offer situations,[29] we nevertheless fail to perceive how the fruition of such anticipated events would require, or in any way depend upon, the receipt and use of inside information....

By May 10, 1967, Occidental had acquired more than 10% of the outstanding shares of Old Kern. It was thus a statutory insider when, on May 11, it extended its tender offer to include another 500,000

29. Although a "defensive merger" is one tactic available to incumbent management in its arsenal of antitender-offer weapons, it is by no means a foregone conclusion that it is the response that will be most often, much less invariably, employed. Incumbent management might, for instance, choose to exhort shareholders not to tender, employ various techniques to elevate the market price of the company's stock in order to make the tender offer less attractive, institute legal proceedings, or increase the company's outstanding stock. Any one of these devices might prove more attractive to incumbent management than a defensive merger which could prove to be highly detrimental to the enterprise. See Note, Defensive Tactics Employed by Incumbent Managements in Contesting Tender Offers, 21 Stan.L.Rev. 1104 (1969).

shares. We are quite unconvinced, however, that the situation had changed materially with respect to the possibilities of speculative abuse of inside information by Occidental. Perhaps Occidental anticipated that extending its offer would increase the likelihood of the ultimate success of its takeover attempt or the occurrence of a defensive merger. But, again, the expectation of such benefits was unrelated to the use of information unavailable to other stockholders or members of the public with sufficient funds and the intention to make the purchases Occidental had offered to make before June 8, 1967.

The possibility that Occidental had, or had the opportunity to have, any confidential information about Old Kern before or after May 11, 1967, seems extremely remote. Occidental was, after all, a tender offeror, threatening to seize control of Old Kern, displace its management, and use the company for its own ends. The Old Kern management vigorously and immediately opposed Occidental's efforts. Twice it communicated with its stockholders, advising against acceptance of Occidental's offer and indicating prior to May 11 and prior to Occidental's extension of its offer, that there was a possibility of an imminent merger and a more profitable exchange. Old Kern's management refused to discuss with Occidental officials the subject of an Old Kern–Occidental merger. Instead, it undertook negotiations with Tenneco and forthwith concluded an agreement, announcing the merger terms on May 19. Requests by Occidental for inspection of Old Kern records were sufficiently frustrated by Old Kern's management to force Occidental to litigate to secure the information it desired. . . .

Much the same can be said of the events leading to the exchange of Occidental's Old Kern stock for Tenneco preferred, which is one of the transactions that is sought to be classified a "sale" under § 16(b). The critical fact is that the exchange took place and was required pursuant to a merger between Old Kern and Tenneco. That merger was not engineered by Occidental but was sought by Old Kern to frustrate the attempts of Occidental to gain control of Old Kern. Occidental obviously did not participate in or control the negotiations or the agreement between Old Kern and Tenneco. Cf. *Newmark v. RKO General,* 425 F.2d 348 (CA2), cert. denied, 400 U.S. 854, 91 S.Ct. 64, 27 L.Ed.2d 91 (1970); *Park & Tilford v. Schulte,* 160 F.2d 984 (CA2), cert. denied, 332 U.S. 761, 68 S.Ct. 64, 92 L.Ed. 347 (1947). Once agreement between those two companies crystallized, the course of subsequent events was out of Occidental's hands. Old Kern needed the consent of its stockholders, but as it turned out, Old Kern's management had the necessary votes without the affirmative vote of Occidental. The merger agreement was approved by a majority of the stockholders of Old Kern, excluding the votes to which Occidental was entitled by virtue of its ownership of Old Kern shares. See generally *Ferraiolo v. Newman,* 259 F.2d 342 (C.A.6 1958), cert. denied, 359 U.S. 927, 79 S.Ct. 606, 3 L.Ed.2d 629 (1959); *Roberts v. Eaton,* 212 F.2d 82 (C.A.2 1954). Occidental, although registering its opinion that the merger would be beneficial to Old Kern shareholders, did not in fact vote at the stockholders' meeting at which merger approval was obtained. Under California law, its abstention was tantamount to a vote against approval of the merger. Moreover, at the time of stockholder ratification of the merger, Occidental's previous dealing in Old Kern stock was, as it had always been, fully disclosed.

Once the merger and exchange were approved, Occidental was left with no real choice with respect to the future of its shares of Old Kern.... The merger left no right in dissenters to secure appraisal of their stock. Occidental could, of course, have disposed of its shares of Old Kern for cash before the merger was closed. Such an act would have been a § 16(b) sale and would have left Occidental with a prima facie § 16(b) liability.... We do not suggest that an exchange of stock pursuant to a merger may never result in § 16(b) liability. But the involuntary nature of Occidental's exchange, when coupled with the absence of the possibility of speculative abuse of inside information, convinces us that § 16(b) should not apply to transactions such as this one.

IV

Petitioner also claims that the Occidental–Tenneco option agreement should itself be considered a sale, either because it was the kind of transaction the statute was designed to prevent or because the agreement was an option in form but a sale in fact. But the mere execution of an option to sell is not generally regarded as a "sale." See *Booth v. Varian Associates,* 334 F.2d 1 (C.A.1 1964), cert. denied, 379 U.S. 961, 85 S.Ct. 651, 13 L.Ed.2d 556 (1965) ... And we do not find in the execution of the Occidental–Tenneco option agreement a sufficient possibility for the speculative abuse of inside information with respect to Old Kern's affairs to warrant holding that the option agreement was itself a "sale" within the meaning of § 16(b). The mutual advantages of the arrangement appear quite clear. As the District Court found, Occidental wanted to avoid the position of a minority stockholder with a huge investment in a company over which it had no control and in which it had not chosen to invest. On the other hand, Tenneco did not want a potentially troublesome minority stockholder that had just been vanquished in a fight for the control of Old Kern. Motivations like these do not smack of insider trading; and it is not clear to us, as it was not to the Court of Appeals, how the negotiation and execution of the option agreement gave Occidental any possible opportunity to trade on inside information it might have obtained from its position as a major stockholder of Old Kern. Occidental wanted to get out, but only at a date more than six months thence. It was willing to get out at a price of $105 per share, a price at which it had publicly valued Tenneco preferred on May 19 when the Tenneco–Old Kern agreement was announced....

Neither does it appear that the option agreement, as drafted and executed by the parties, offered measurable possibilities for speculative abuse. What Occidental granted was a "call" option. Tenneco had the right to buy after six months, but Occidental could not force Tenneco to buy. The price was fixed at $105 for each share of Tenneco preferred. Occidental could not share in a rising market for the Tenneco stock. See *Silverman v. Landa,* 306 F.2d 422 (C.A.2 1962). If the stock fell more than $10 per share, the option might not be exercised, and Occidental might suffer a loss if the market further deteriorated to a point where Occidental was forced to sell. Thus, the option, by its very form, left Occidental with no choice but to sell if Tenneco exercised the option, which it was almost sure to do if the value of Tenneco stock remained relatively steady. On the other hand, it is difficult to perceive any speculative value to Occidental if the stock declined and Tenneco chose not to exercise its option....

The option, therefore, does not appear to have been an instrument with potential for speculative abuse, whether or not Occidental possessed inside information about the affairs of Old Kern. In addition, the option covered Tenneco preference stock, a stock as yet unissued, unregistered, and untraded. It was the value of this stock that underlay the option and that determined whether the option would be exercised, whether Occidental would be able to profit from the exercise, and whether there was any real likelihood of the exploitation of inside information. If Occidental had inside information when it negotiated and signed the option agreement, it was inside information with respect to Old Kern. Whatever it may have known or expected as to the future value of Old Kern stock, Occidental had no ownership position in Tenneco giving it any actual or presumed insights into the future value of Tenneco stock. That was the critical item of intelligence if Occidental was to use the option for purposes of speculation. Also, the date for exercise of the option was over six months in the future, a period that, under the statute itself, is assumed to dissipate whatever trading advantage might be imputed to a major stockholder with inside information....

Nor can we agree that we must reverse the Court of Appeals on the ground that the option agreement was in fact a sale because the premium paid was so large as to make the exercise of the option almost inevitable, particularly when coupled with Tenneco's desire to rid itself of a potentially troublesome stockholder. The argument has force, but resolution of the question is very much a matter of judgment, economic and otherwise, and the Court of Appeals rejected the argument. That court emphasized that the premium paid was what experts had said the option was worth, the possibility that the market might drop sufficiently in the six months following execution of the option to make exercise unlikely, and the fact that here, unlike the situation in *Bershad v. McDonough,* 428 F.2d 693 (C.A.7 1970), the optionor did not surrender practically all emoluments of ownership by executing the option. Nor did any other special circumstances indicate that the parties understood and intended that the option was in fact a sale.[30] ...

---

30. In *Bershad v. McDonough,* 428 F.2d 693 (C.A.7 1970), the defendants were directors and greater-than-ten-percent stockholders of Cudahy Co. The defendants, within six months of their acquisition of beneficial ownership of Cudahy, granted an option to Smelting Refining & Mining Co. to purchase their Cudahy stock. The Seventh Circuit held that the grant of the

The judgment of the Court of Appeals is affirmed.

So ordered.

■ MR. JUSTICE DOUGLAS, with whom MR. JUSTICE BRENNAN and MR. JUSTICE STEWART concur, dissenting.

The Court, in resorting to an *ad hoc* analysis of the "possibility for the speculative abuse of inside information," charts a course for the interpretation of § 16(b) of the Securities Exchange Act of 1934, 15 U.S.C. § 78p(b), that in my mind undermines the congressional purpose. I respectfully dissent....

The question presented to us is whether this exchange of shares constituted a "sale" of the Old Kern shares. The term "sale," as used in the Securities Exchange Act, includes "any contract to sell or otherwise dispose of." 15 U.S.C. § 78c(a)(14). Clearly, Occidental "disposed" of its Old Kern shares through the Old Kern–Tenneco consolidation. Its status as a shareholder of Old Kern terminated, and it became instead a shareholder of Tenneco, privy to all the rights conferred by the Tenneco shares.[3] ...

The majority finesses the literal impact of § 16(b) by examining Occidental's willfulness and its access to inside information. It concludes: "But the involuntary nature of Occidental's exchange, when coupled with the absence of the possibility of speculative abuse of inside information, convinces us that § 16(b) should not apply to transactions such as this one." ... This approach is plainly contrary to the legislative purpose....

The very construction of § 16(b) reinforces the conclusion that the section is based in the first instance[10] on a totally objective appraisal of the relevant transactions. See *Smolowe v. Delendo Corp., supra,* at 236. Had the draftsmen intended that the operation of the section hinge on abuse of access to inside information it would have been anomalous to limit the section to purchases and sales occurring within six months.[12] Indeed, the purpose of the six-month limitation, coupled with the definition of an insider, was to create a *conclusive*

---

option was a § 16(b) "sale" of the Cudahy stock. The Court of Appeals in the present case distinguished *Bershad* as follows:

"That case came before the court of appeals on a finding by the district court that, under the circumstances there presented, the stock had in fact been sold within the six months period, although the option was not formally exercised until later. The district court had relied on a number of circumstances, the most significant being that the optionor gave the optionee an irrevocable proxy to vote the shares and that the optionor and one of his associate directors resigned as directors within a few days after the grant of the option and were replaced by officers of the optionee. In other words, the district court found in effect that the 'option' was accompanied by a wink of the eye, and the court of appeals sustained this. Here there is no such finding, and no basis for one." 450 F.2d, at 165.

3. This is not a case where the stock surrendered and the stock received in the exchange were economic equivalents. Cf., *e.g., Blau v. Lamb,* 363 F.2d 507, 523–525 (C.A.2 1966); *Blau v. Max Factor & Co.,* 342 F.2d 304, 308–309 (C.A.9 1965)....

10. The objective approach may have to yield to a more flexible interpretation of the terms "purchase" and "sale" to include transactions which present the evil Congress sought to eliminate or transactions which are designed to evade § 16(b)....

12. In addition, there would have been no reason to exempt transactions wherein the "security was acquired in good faith in connection with a debt previously contracted...."

presumption that an insider who turns a short-swing profit in the stock of his corporation had access to inside information *and* capitalized on that information by speculating in the stock. But, the majority departs from the benign effects of this presumption when it assumes that it is "totally unrealistic to assume or infer from the facts before us that Occidental either had or was likely to have access to inside information...." .... The majority abides by this assumption even for that period after which Occidental became a 10% shareholder and then extended its tender offer in order to purchase additional Old Kern shares.

The majority takes heart from those decisions of lower federal courts which endorse a "pragmatic" approach to § 16(b).... But, by sanctioning the approach of these cases, the majority brings to fruition Louis Loss' prophecy that they will "continue to rule us from their graves,"[16] for henceforth they certainly will be applied by analogy to the area of mergers and other consolidations.

Thus, the courts will be caught up in an *ad hoc* analysis of each transaction, determining both from the economics of the transaction and the *modus operandi* of the insider whether there exists the possibility of speculative abuse of inside information. Instead of a section that is easy to administer and by its clearcut terms discourages litigation, we have instead a section that fosters litigation because the Court's decision holds out the hope for the insider that he may avoid § 16(b) liability. In short, the majority destroys much of the section's prophylactic effect.... Certainly we cannot allow transactions which present the possibility of abuse but do not fall within the classic conception of a purchase or sale to escape the confines of § 16(b). It is one thing to interpret the terms "purchase" and "sale" liberally in order to include those transactions which evidence the evil Congress sought to eliminate; it is quite another to abandon the bright-line test of § 16(b) for those transactions which clearly fall within its literal bounds. Section 16(b), because of the six-month limitation, allows some to escape who have abused their inside information. It should not be surprising, given the objective nature of the rule, if some are caught unwillingly.

In *Reliance Electric, supra,* at 422, the Court quoted with approval the following language from *Bershad v. McDonough,* 428 F.2d 693, 696 (C.A.7 1970):

> "In order to achieve its goals, Congress chose a relatively arbitrary rule capable of easy administration. The objective standard of Section 16(b) imposes strict liability upon substantially all transactions occurring within the statutory time period, regardless of the intent of the insider or the existence of actual speculation. This approach maximized the ability of the rule to eradicate speculative abuses by reducing difficulties in proof. Such arbitrary and sweeping coverage was deemed necessary to insure the optimum prophylactic effect."

---

16. 5 L. Loss, Securities Regulation 3029 (Supp. to 2d ed. 1969).

It is this "objective standard" that the Court hung to so tenaciously in *Reliance Electric,* but now apparently would abandon to a large extent. In my view, the Court improperly takes upon itself the task of refashioning the contours of § 16(b) and changing its essential thrust. . . .

NOTE, SHORT-SWING PROFITS IN FAILED TAKEOVER BIDS—THE ROLE OF SECTION 16(B), 59 Wash.L.Rev. 895 (1984). "Although the *Kern* decision did not state the threshold requirement for application of the pragmatic approach, subsequent courts have generally held that an involuntary transaction is [a necessary condition to the application of that approach]. To prove that a particular transaction is involuntary, the insider must apparently show that it had no control over the timing of the transaction. If the insider fails to make this showing, liability attaches automatically. If the insider does make this showing, however, courts will regard the transaction as unorthodox and will then ask whether the defendant had access to inside information. This inquiry, though secondary, is critical. One with access to inside information can speculate profitably by relying on an imminent 'involuntary' transaction. A finding of involuntariness, therefore, does not guarantee exoneration. . . ."

COLAN v. MESA PETROLEUM CO., 951 F.2d 1512 (9th Cir. 1991), cert. denied 504 U.S. 911, 112 S.Ct. 1943, 118 L.Ed.2d 548 (1992). In October 1984, Mesa Partners began accumulating Unocal stock. By February 22, 1985, Mesa owned 9.7 percent of Unocal's outstanding shares. On March 27, Mesa increased its ownership interest to 13.6 percent. To discourage a takeover by Mesa, on April 16 Unocal initiated a self-tender, under which it offered to exchange a package of its own debt securities for up to one-half of its own outstanding common stock. Unocal stated that one of the express purposes of the self-tender was to make it more difficult for Mesa to take over Unocal, and expressly excluded Mesa from participating in the Unocal offer. After negotiations, however, Mesa and Unocal made an agreement under which Mesa was allowed to, and did, participate in Unocal's self-tender. Plaintiff, a Unocal shareholder, then sued Mesa under § 16(b) to recover Mesa's short-swing profit on its exchange of Unocal stock for Unocal negotiable debt securities pursuant to Unocal's self-tender. Mesa argued that the exchange was not a sale because it fell within the "unorthodox transaction" exception. Held, the exception did not apply, the exchange was a sale, and Mesa was liable under § 16(b).

> The exchange of Unocal stock for debt securities pursuant to Unocal's tender offer is factually distinguishable from the transaction in *Kern County.* [In that case, the] exchange of Occidental's stock for equity shares of the new corporation which was formed

as the result of the merger in *Kern County* was involuntary and automatic. The ... exchange of stock for debt securities by the Mesa Defendants was not an involuntary or automatic transaction. Unocal did not merge into a new corporation so as to compel its shareholders to exchange their stock....

The Mesa Defendants had the choice of participating in the tender offer or holding onto their stock. The record shows that it was anticipated that Unocal's stock would sell at $30 a share as a result of the exchange set forth in the tender offer. One of the choices available to the Mesa Defendants was to buy up Unocal's stock at the reduced price of $30 a share and acquire control of the corporation....

Courts following *Kern County* have recognized that involuntariness is an important factor in determining whether or not a transaction constitutes a "sale" or "purchase" within section 16(b).

The Mesa Defendants argue that "otherwise volitional transactions" are unorthodox under section 16(b) if a beneficial owner is coerced economically into exchanging his common stock or suffer a financial loss. In *Oliff v. Exchange Int'l Corp.,* 669 F.2d 1162 (7th Cir.1980), *cert. denied,* 450 U.S. 915, 101 S.Ct. 1358, 67 L.Ed.2d 340 (1981), the Seventh Circuit found that although a 205% tax payment was not a "reasonable alternative" to the repurchase of shares which gave rise to section 16(b) liability, the acquisition of the stock was not "so involuntary as to take it out of the definition of 'purchase' for 16(b) purposes." ...

An economic coercion test would allow corporate insiders to avoid section 16(b) liability by presenting evidence of a variety of unfortunate circumstances that forced them to sell their common stock. The objective standards of section 16(b) were adopted to avoid the necessity for an inquiry into an insider's subjective "intent." ... We reject the "economic coercion" test as contrary to the intent of Congress in enacting the bright-line, flat rule set forth in section 16(b) requiring disgorgement of profits.

We conclude that the facts in this matter do not come within the holding of *Kern County* that an involuntary transaction that results from a merger is "unorthodox." ...

The majority of the transactions which have been considered "unorthodox" within the narrow exception announced in *Kern County* involve exchanges of stock pursuant to a merger....

Those courts that have directly addressed the issue of section 16(b) liability in a tender offer or hostile takeover context have concluded that the disposition of shares pursuant to a tender offer, or in the face of defeat in a takeover contest, is not an unorthodox transaction under Kern County....

... The Mesa Defendants rely primarily on the Supreme Court's comment in footnote 24 in *Kern County*.... In footnote 24, the Court observed that "[t]he term [unorthodox transaction]

... has been applied to stock conversions, exchanges pursuant to mergers and other corporate reorganizations, stock reclassifications, and dealings in options, rights, and warrants." *Id.* The Mesa Defendants reason that since a recapitalization is a form of corporate reorganization, it must constitute an "unorthodox transaction."

The comment in footnote 24 in *Kern County* was not necessary to the opinion in *Kern County.* The Court, without expressing its approval, enumerated the types of business transactions that others have labeled as "unorthodox." The Court did not cite any authority to support its observation in footnote 24. Thus, we cannot determine whether the Court was referring to decisions construing section 16(b).

NOTE ON ATTRIBUTION OF OWNERSHIP UNDER SECTIONS 16(a) AND (b)

Sections 16(a) and (b) use the term or the concept of "beneficial ownership" for several different purposes.

Under § 16(a), a person who is either "a beneficial owner of more than 10 per centum of any class of equity security" (hereafter, a "more-than–10–percent owner"), or an officer or director, must report the amount of all equity securities of the issuer "of which he is the beneficial owner."

Under § 16(b), a director, officer, or more-than–10–percent owner is liable for short-swing profits "realized by him from any purchase and sale, or any sale and purchase, of any equity security" of the issuer. Given both the purpose of the statute and the context, § 16(b) seems generally intended to cover the purchase and sale of those equity securities of which a person is a beneficial owner for purposes of § 16(a).

If a person is the record owner of an equity security and also has a pecuniary interest in the security, he is undoubtedly a beneficial owner for all purposes under § 16. Problems of interpretation arise, however, if a person is a record owner of shares but has no pecuniary interest; or if a person has a pecuniary interest but is not the record owner; or if a person is neither the record owner nor has a pecuniary interest, but there is nevertheless an important relationship between the person and the security, such as the right to control the security. For most although not all practical purposes, the problem can be stated as follows: when should an equity security that is not legally owned by a person, in the conventional sense, nevertheless be *attributed* to the person under § 16, so that either (i) the security counts toward determining whether the person's ownership crosses the 10–percent-beneficial-ownership line, (ii) the person's transactions in the security must be reported under § 16(a), or (iii) the person's transactions in the security may subject him to liability under § 16(b)?

These problems are addressed in detail by the Rules under § 16. Those Rules draw a distinction between (1) what constitutes beneficial ownership for purposes of determining whether a person is a more-than–10–percent owner, and (2) what constitutes beneficial ownership for purposes of determining whether a person who *is* a more-than–10–percent owner, or a director or officer, must report under § 16(a) and may be liable for short-swing profits under § 16(b).

As to the first problem (whether a person is a more-than–10–percent owner), Rule 16a–1(a)(1) provides that, with certain exceptions, "*solely for purposes of determining whether a person is a beneficial owner of more than ten percent of* any class of equity securities registered pursuant to § 12 of the Act, the term 'beneficial owner' shall mean any person who is deemed a beneficial owner pursuant to § 13(d) of the Act and the rules thereunder. . . ." (emphasis added). Rule 13d–3, in turn, provides that a beneficial owner of a security includes "any person who, directly or indirectly, through any contract, arrangement, understanding, relationship, or otherwise has or shares: (1) *Voting power* which includes the power to vote, or to direct the voting of, such security; and/or, (2) *Investment power* which includes the power to dispose, or to direct the disposition of, such security." (Emphasis added.) In short, in determining *whether* a person is a more-than–10–percent owner of stock, the emphasis, under Rule 16a–1, is on the person's *control* over the stock. Of special note is Rule 13d–5(b)(1) which provides "when two or more persons agree to act together for the purpose of acquiring, holding, voting or disposing of equity securities of an issuer, the group formed thereby shall be deemed to have acquired beneficial ownership. . . ." Roth v. Jennings, 489 F.3d 499 (2d Cir. 2007) illustrates how liability can arise under section 16(b) when one's purchases and sales are seen as part of a group. Jennings acquired in the open market 8.3 percent of Metal Management about two weeks after EMR, through open market purchases, acquired 14.8 percent of Metal Management. Jennings had borrowed the funds to purchase the shares from EMR. It was an astute move, as a few weeks after his purchase, Jennings garnered a $4.25 million profit by selling the Metal Management shares. The plaintiff argued that Jennings and EMR were acting in concert to change control of Metal Management. Relying on the disjunctive used in Rule 13d–5(b)(1), the Second Circuit reasoned that a group is formed if two or more persons come together to acquire, hold *or* dispose of stock. Believing factual issues existed whether they continued to be a group when the shares were sold, the court reversed the trial court's grant of the defendant's motion to dismiss and remanded the case to determine whether Jennings and EMR acted together for a common purpose.

As to the second problem (what constitutes beneficial ownership for *reporting* and *liability* purposes), Rule 16a–1(a)(2) provides that as a general principle, with certain exceptions and elaborations, (1) "*other than for purposes of determining whether a person is a beneficial owner of more than ten percent of any class of equity securities* registered under § 12 of the Act, the term 'beneficial owner' shall mean any person who, directly or indirectly, through any contract, arrangement, understanding, relationship or otherwise, has or shares a direct or indirect *pecuniary interest* in the equity securities...."; and (2) "[t]he term 'pecuniary interest' in any class of equity securities shall mean the opportunity, directly or indirectly, *to profit or share in any profit* derived from a transaction in the subject securities." (Emphasis added.) In short, unlike Rule 16a–1(a)(1), which emphasizes *control* for purposes of determining who is a more-than–10–percent owner, Rule 16a–1(a)(2) emphasizes *pecuniary interest* for purposes of determining what transactions in equity securities must be reported and may give rise to liability.

After stating the pecuniary-interest test as a general principle to govern the determination of beneficial ownership for reporting and liability purposes, Rule 16a–1(a)(2) then goes on to deal with certain recurring cases in which problems of attribution based on a pecuniary interest may arise. Some of these cases are as follows:

Family members. Rule 16a–1(a)(2)(ii)(A) provides that "[t]he term 'indirect pecuniary interest' [under Rule 16a–2] in any class of equity securities shall include, but not be limited to ... securities held by members of a person's immediate family sharing the same household; *provided, however,* that the presumption of such beneficial ownership may be rebutted...." Rule 16a–1(e) then provides that "[t]he term 'immediate family', shall mean any child, stepchild, grandchild, parent, stepparent, grandparent, spouse, sibling, mother-in-law, father-in-law, son-in-law, daughter-in-law, brother-in-law, or sister-in-law, and shall include adoptive relationships."

Partnerships. Rule 16a–1(a)(2)(ii)(B) provides that the term "indirect pecuniary interest" [under Rule 16a–1(a)(2)] includes "a general partner's proportionate interest in the portfolio securities held by a general or limited partnership."

Corporations. Rule 16a–1(a)(2)(iii) provides that "[a] shareholder shall not be deemed to have a pecuniary interest in the portfolio securities held by a corporation or similar entity in which the person owns securities if the shareholder is not a controlling shareholder of the entity and does not have or share investment control over the entity's portfolio...." Note that this Rule does not specify a general principle for determining when a corporation's portfolio securities will be attributed to shareholders in the corporation, but only provides a safe harbor in the cases that the rule specifies.

The Rules under § 16 also contain elaborate provisions dealing with such matters as when a trustee is a beneficial owner for reporting and liability purposes, and when the ownership of a derivative security makes a person the beneficial owner of the derivative security.

NOTE ON STATUTORY INSIDER STATUS AT ONLY ONE END OF A SWING

The last sentence of § 16(b) sets out an exemptive provision under which "[T]his subsection shall not be construed to cover any transaction where [a more-than–10–percent] beneficial owner was not such both at the time of the purchase and sale, or the sale and purchase, of the security involved." Suppose a person, S, owns a more-than–10–percent block, but is not a director or officer. S makes a sale that reduces his block to less than 10 percent, but leaves him with the remainder. Are S's later sales of some or all of the remainder of his block, covered by § 16? The Supreme Court has held that the later sales are not covered, because the person is not a 10 percent owner at the time of those sales. Reliance Electric Co. v. Emerson Electric Co., 404 U.S. 418, 92 S.Ct. 596, 30 L.Ed.2d 575 (1972). This result is codified in Rule 16a–2(c).

What about the very purchase that makes a person a more-than–10–percent beneficial owner? Can that purchase be matched with a subsequent sale within six months? In Foremost–McKesson, Inc. v. Provident Securities Co., 423 U.S. 232, 96 S.Ct. 508, 46 L.Ed.2d 464 (1976) the Supreme Court held, largely on the basis of the exemptive provision and legislative history, that in the case of a *purchase-sale sequence*, a more-than–10–percent beneficial owner is not liable unless he was such *before* he made the purchase in question. To put this differently, the purchase that first lifts a beneficial owner above 10 percent cannot be matched with a subsequent sale under § 16(b).

Suppose a person who is a more-than–10–percent owner sells enough stock to get below the 10 percent line, and then buys stock within six months after that sale? This kind of case is called a sale-repurchase sequence. The *Foremost* opinion did not cover this case, and left considerable room for arguing that this sequence should result in liability under § 16(b).

Suppose a person is a director or officer at only one end of a swing? Since the exemptive clause provides that "this subsection shall not be construed to cover any transaction where [*a more–than–10–percent*] *beneficial owner* was not such both at the time of the purchase and sale, or the sale and purchase" (emphasis added), the clear implication is that § 16(b) *does* apply to a short-swing transaction by a director or officer even where the director or officer "was not such both at the time of purchase and sale, or the sale and purchase." In Feder v. Martin Marietta Corp., 406 F.2d 260 (2d Cir.1969), cert. denied 396 U.S. 1036, 90 S.Ct. 678, 24 L.Ed.2d 681 (1970), the court held that a director or officer who purchases, resigns, and then sells within six months of the purchase, is liable under § 16(b). However, no liability will be imposed if both ends of a swing occur after the director or officer resigns. Lewis v. Mellon Bank, N.A., 513 F.2d 921 (3d Cir.1975); Lewis v. Varnes, 505 F.2d 785 (2d Cir.1974). Prior to 1991, it had been held that § 16(b) applies to a purchase or sale of shares by a person who becomes a director or officer after the transaction, and engages in a matching transaction within six months of the original transaction. In such a case, the director or officer will have had an opportunity to utilize inside information at the second end of the swing, but not at the first. This issue is now governed by Rule 16a–2(a), adopted by the SEC in 1991, which provides that purchases and sales by a director or officer before she became a director or officer are not subject to § 16.

NOTE ON WHO IS AN "OFFICER" UNDER § 16(b)

The battle between "objective" and "subjective" approaches to the interpretations of Section 16(b) has played a dramatic role in the question who is an "officer" for purposes of that Section. Under the objective view, an officer *title* would give rise to § 16(b) liability. Under the subjective view, liability would depend on whether the person had access to inside information by virtue of her position. An intermediate view is that liability should turn on a person's corporate role or function (rather than her title), but that the issue is whether the function is "officer-like," not whether the person's corporate function gives her access to inside information.

For many years, SEC Rule 3b–2 provided that the term officer "means a president, vice president, secretary, treasurer or principal financial officer, comptroller or principal accounting officer, and any person routinely performing corresponding functions with respect to any organization whether incorporated or unincorporated."

The first part of this rule (up to the phrase "and any person") was objective—it imposed liability based on a person's title. The second part of the rule (beginning with the phrase "and any person") reflected the intermediate view—it made liability turn on the functions a person actually performed. Neither part of the rule, however, was explicitly keyed into whether a person's officer role was likely to give her access to inside information. Presumably, the theory of Rule 3b–2 was either that (1) in using the term "officer" § 16(b) intended to pick up any person commonly regarded as an officer for non–16(b) purposes; (2) a person who held one of the titles designated in the rule, or performed the kinds of functions identified in the rule, should be conclusively presumed to have access to material inside information; or (3) both.

In the early case of Colby v. Klune, 178 F.2d 872 (2d Cir.1949), rev'g 83 F.Supp. 159 (S.D.N.Y.), the plaintiff sought to hold a corporation's "production manager" liable under § 16(b). The Second Circuit criticized Rule 3b–2 as too limited, and therefore not authorized by the statute. The court said: "[W]e construe 'officer,' as used in section 16(b) of the Securities Exchange Act, thus: It includes, *inter alia,* a corporate employee performing important executive duties of such character that he would be likely, in discharging these duties, to obtain confidential information about the company's affairs that would aid him if he engaged in personal market transactions."

In contrast, in Merrill Lynch, Pierce, Fenner & Smith, Inc. v. Livingston, 566 F.2d 1119 (9th Cir.1978), in which an account executive at a stockbroker had been given an honorary title as vice-president, with no change in his duties, as a reward for an outstanding sales record, the Ninth Circuit held that Rule 3b–2 was too expansive. The court said: "Liability under Section 16(b) is not based simply upon a person's title within his corporation; rather, liability follows from the existence of a relationship with the corporation that makes it more probable than not that the individual has access to insider information." Id. at 1121. Later, however, in National Medical Enterprises, Inc. v. Small, 680 F.2d 83 (9th Cir.1982), the Ninth Circuit drastically restricted *Merrill Lynch,* and endorsed the concept of liability based on a person's title, with only a very limited exception:

> In designing section 16, "Congress chose a relatively arbitrary rule capable of easy administration." . . . It does not matter whether the insider actually received the information, or utilized it; his mere status makes him liable.
>
> . . . The defendants mistakenly . . . argue that although they are officers of National Medical, they did not have access to material inside information and therefore should not be considered section 16(b) "officers." Whether an individual is an "officer" for purposes of section 16(b) is determined by the title that he holds, with a very limited exception applicable only where the title is essentially honorary or ceremonial. . . .

Eventually, the SEC itself adopted a new definition of "officer" which is essentially function-based, and much more limited in its coverage than was Rule 3b–2. The new rule, Rule 16a–1(f), provides that:

> [T]he term "officer" shall mean an issuer's president, principal financial officer, or principal accounting officer (or, if there is no such accounting officer, the controller), any vice-president of the issuer in charge of a principal business unit, division or function (such as sales, administration or finance), any other officer who performs a policy-making function, or any other person who performs similar policy-making functions for the issuer.

In a note to Rule 16a–1(f), the SEC states that the term "policy-making function" is not intended to include policy-making functions that are not significant.

The Chairman of the SEC, in his opening remarks at the meeting at which the new rule was adopted, stated that:

> The definition of officer has been revised to make clear that a person's functions and not simply title will determine the applicability of Section 16. The definition . . . is intended to make clear that individuals with executive functions do not avoid liability under Section 16 simply by foregoing title, and those with a title but no significant executive responsibilities are not subject to the automatic short-swing profit liability of Section 16(b). Thus, for example, a vice-president of a bank, who has no policy-making responsibility would not have to be concerned with possible liability under Section 16(b), if because of an unexpected family emergency, he needed to sell securities.

Barron, Control and Restricted Securities, 19 Sec.Reg.L.J. 292, 294–95 (1991).

NOTE ON DEPUTIZATION

Closely related to the theory of attribution under § 16(b) is the theory of deputization. In Blau v. Lehman, 368 U.S. 403, 82 S.Ct. 451, 7 L.Ed.2d 403 (1962), the Supreme Court held that one enterprise, A, could be a "director" of second enterprise, B, within the meaning of § 16(b), if one of B's directors had been deputized by A to act on A's behalf. In *Blau*, Thomas, a partner in Lehman Brothers (Enterprise A) sat on the board of Tide Water (Enterprise B), and Lehman profited from short-swing trading in Tide Water stock. The Court approved the deputization theory:

> No doubt Lehman Brothers, though a partnership, could for purposes of § 16 be a "director" of Tide Water and function through a deputy, since § 3(a)(9) of the Act provides that " 'person' means . . . partnership" and § 3(a)(7) that " 'director' means any director of a corporation or any person performing similar functions with respect to any organization, whether incorporated or unincorporated." Consequently, Lehman Brothers would be a "director" of Tide Water, if as petitioner's complaint charged Lehman actually functioned as a director through Thomas, who had been deputized by Lehman to perform a director's duties not for himself but for Lehman.

Id. at 409. However, the courts below had made findings that the Supreme Court believed precluded the conclusion that deputization had actually occurred, and Lehman Brothers was therefore not held liable. (Thomas himself was held liable below for his pro rata share of the short-swing profits made by Lehman, and this aspect of the case was not appealed.)

Deputization *was* found to be present in Feder v. Martin Marietta Corp., 406 F.2d 260 (2d Cir.1969), cert. denied 396 U.S. 1036, 90 S.Ct. 678, 24 L.Ed.2d 681 (1970). Bunker, the president of Martin Marietta (Enterprise A), had become a director of Sperry (Enterprise B), in which Martin Marietta held substantial stock. Bunker was ultimately responsible for the total operation of Martin Marietta, and personally approved all of the firm's financial investments—in particular, its purchase of the Sperry stock. Bunker's control over Martin Marietta, coupled with his membership on Sperry's Board, placed him in a position in which he could acquire inside information concerning Sperry and could utilize such information for Martin. Further, Bunker admitted discussing Sperry's affairs with two officials at Martin Marietta and participating in sessions when Martin Marietta's investment in Sperry was reviewed, and Bunker's ultimate letter of resignation to Sperry's president stated that "When I became a member of the [Sperry] board . . . it appeared to your associates that the Martin Marietta ownership of a substantial number of shares of Sperry Rand should have representation on your Board." On these facts, the Second Circuit concluded that "The control possessed by Bunker, his letter of resignation, the approval by the Martin Board of Bunker's directorship with Sperry and the functional similarity between Bunker's acts as a Sperry director and the acts of Martin's representatives on other boards . . . are all definite and concrete indicatives that Bunker, in fact, was a Martin deputy." Martin Marietta was therefore held liable, as a director, for its short-swing profits in Sperry stock.

A very different result was reached in Roth v. Perseus LLC, 522 F.3d 242 (2d Cir. 2008), because the defendant, who had purchased the traded shares *from the issuer*, Beacon, was able to invoke the exemption provided in Rule 16b–3. Perseus LLC had made a substantial investment in Beacon and as part of the transaction was accorded two nominees to Beacon's board. Within six months, Perseus sold some of the Beacon shares. Rule 16b–3 exempts a transaction between the issuer and its officer or director from section 16(b) if, among other conditions, the transaction is approved by the issuer's board of directors. The Second Circuit held this provision extends to directors by deputization even if that person is also the holder of more than 10 percent of the issuer's equity.

SECTION 4. CORPORATE RECOVERIES FOR INSIDE TRADING UNDER STATE LAW

Diamond v. Oreamuno

New York Court of Appeals, 1969.
24 N.Y.2d 494, 301 N.Y.S.2d 78, 248 N.E.2d 910.

■ CHIEF JUDGE FULD. Upon this appeal from an order denying a motion to dismiss the complaint as insufficient on its face, the question presented—one of first impression in this court—is whether officers and directors may be held accountable to their corporation for gains realized by them from transactions in the company's stock as a result of their use of material inside information.

The complaint was filed by a shareholder of Management Assistance, Inc. (MAI) asserting a derivative action against a number of its officers and directors to compel an accounting for profits allegedly acquired as a result of a breach of fiduciary duty. It charges that two of the defendants—Oreamuno, chairman of the board of directors, and Gonzalez, its president—had used inside information, acquired by them solely by virtue of their positions, in order to reap large personal profits from the sale of MAI shares and that these profits rightfully belong to the corporation. Other officers and directors were joined as defendants on the ground that they acquiesced in or ratified the assertedly wrongful transactions.

MAI is in the business of financing computer installations through sale and lease back arrangements with various commercial and industrial users. Under its lease provisions, MAI was required to maintain and repair the computers but, at the time of this suit, it lacked the capacity to perform this function itself and was forced to engage the manufacturer of the computers, International Business Machines (IBM), to service the machines. As a result of a sharp increase by IBM of its charges for such service, MAI's expenses for August of 1966 rose considerably and its net earnings declined from $262,253 in July to $66,233 in August, a decrease of about 75%. This information, although earlier known to the defendants, was not made public until October of 1966. Prior to the release of the information, however, Oreamuno and Gonzalez sold off a total of 56,500 shares of their MAI stock at the then current market price of $28 a share.

After the information concerning the drop in earnings was made available to the public, the value of a share of MAI stock immediately fell from the $28 realized by the defendants to $11. Thus, the plaintiff alleges, by taking advantage of their privileged position and their access to confidential information, Oreamuno and Gonzalez were able to realize $800,000 more for their securities than they would have had this inside information not been available to them. Stating that the defendants were "forbidden to use [such] information ... for their own personal profit or gain", the plaintiff brought this derivative action seeking to have the defendants account to the corporation for this difference. A motion by the defendants to dismiss the complaint—pursuant to CPLR 3211 (subd. [a], par. 7)—for failure to state a cause of action was granted by the court at Special Term. The Appellate Division, with one dissent, modified Special Term's order by reinstating the complaint as to the defendants Oreamuno and Gonzalez. The appeal is before us on a certified question.

In reaching a decision in this case, we are, of course, passing only upon the sufficiency of the complaint and we necessarily accept the charges contained in that pleading as true.

It is well established, as a general proposition, that a person who acquires special knowledge or information by virtue of a confidential or fiduciary relationship with another is not free to exploit that knowledge or information for his own personal benefit but must account to his principal for any profits derived therefrom. (See, e.g., *Byrne v. Barrett,* 268 N.Y. 199.) This, in turn, is merely a corollary of the broader principle, inherent in the nature of the fiduciary relationship, that prohibits a trustee or agent from extracting secret profits from his position of trust.

In support of their claim that the complaint fails to state a cause of action, the defendants take the position that, although it is admittedly wrong for an officer or director to use his position to obtain trading profits for himself in the stock of his corporation, the action ascribed to them did not injure or damage MAI in any way. Accordingly, the defendants continue, the corporation should not be permitted to recover the proceeds. They acknowledge that, by virtue of the exclusive access which officers and directors have to inside information, they possess an unfair advantage over other shareholders and, particularly, the persons who had purchased the stock from them but, they contend, the corporation itself was unaffected and, for that reason, a derivative action is an inappropriate remedy.

It is true that the complaint before us does not contain any allegation of damages to the corporation but this has never been considered to be an essential requirement for a cause of action founded on a breach of fiduciary duty. (See, e.g., *Matter of People* [*Bond & Mtge. Guar. Co.*], 303 N.Y. 423, 431; *Wendt v. Fischer,* 243 N.Y. 439, 443; *Dutton v. Willner,* 52 N.Y. 312, 319.) This is because the function of such an action, unlike an ordinary tort or contract case, is not merely to *compensate* the plaintiff for wrongs committed by the defendant but, as this court declared many years ago (*Dutton v. Willner,* 52 N.Y. 312, 319, *supra*), "to *prevent* them, by removing from agents and trustees all inducement to attempt dealing for their own benefit in matters which they have undertaken for others, or to which their agency or trust relates." (Emphasis supplied.)

Just as a trustee has no right to retain for himself the profits yielded by property placed in his possession but must account to his beneficiaries, a corporate fiduciary, who is entrusted with potentially valuable information, may not appropriate that asset for his own use even though, in so doing, he causes no injury to the corporation. The primary concern, in a case such as this, is not to determine whether the corporation has been damaged but to decide, as between the corporation and the defendants, who has a higher claim to the proceeds derived from the exploitation of the information. In our opinion, there can be no justification for permitting officers and directors, such as the defendants, to retain for themselves profits which, it is alleged, they derived solely from exploiting information gained by virtue of their inside position as corporate officials.

In addition, it is pertinent to observe that, despite the lack of any specific allegation of damage, it may well be inferred that the defendants' actions might have caused some harm to the enterprise. Although the corporation may have little concern with the day-to-day transactions in its shares, it has a great interest in maintaining a reputation of integrity, an image of probity, for its management and in insuring the continued public acceptance and marketability of its stock. When officers and directors abuse their position in order to gain personal profits, the effect may be to cast a cloud on the corporation's name, injure stockholder relations and undermine public regard for the corporation's securities. As Presiding Justice BOTEIN aptly put it, in the course of his opinion for the Appellate Division, "[t]he prestige and good will of a corporation, so vital to its prosperity, may be undermined by the revelation that its chief officers had been making personal profits out of corporate events which they had not disclosed to the community of stockholders." (29 A.D.2d, at p. 287.)

The defendants maintain that extending the prohibition against personal exploitation of a fiduciary relationship to officers and directors of a corporation will discourage such officials from maintaining a stake in the success of the corporate venture through share ownership, which, they urge, is an important incentive to proper performance of their duties. There is, however, a considerable difference between corporate officers who assume the same risks and obtain the same benefits as other shareholders and those who use their privileged position to gain special advantages not available to others. The sale of shares by the defendants for the reasons charged was not merely a wise investment decision which any prudent investor might have made. Rather, they were assertedly able in this case to profit solely because they had information which was not available to any one else—including the other shareholders whose interests they, as corporate fiduciaries, were bound to protect.

Although no appellate court in this State has had occasion to pass upon the precise question before us, the concept underlying the present cause of action is hardly a new one. (See, e.g., Securities Exchange Act of 1934 [48 U.S.Stat. 881], § 16[b]; U.S.Code, tit. 15, § 78p, subd. [b]; *Brophy v. Cities Serv. Co.,* 31 Del.Ch. 241; Restatement, 2d, Agency, § 388, comment *c*; Israels, A New Look at Corporate Directorship, 24 Business Lawyer 727, 732 *et seq.;* Note, 54 Cornell L.Rev. 306, 309–312.) Under Federal law (Securities Exchange Act of 1934, § 16[b]), for example, it is conclusively presumed that, when a director, officer or 10% shareholder buys and sells securities of his corporation within a six-month period, he is trading on inside information. The remedy which the Federal statute provides in that situation is precisely the same as that sought in the present case under State law, namely, an action brought by the corporation or on its behalf to recover all profits derived from the transactions.

In providing this remedy, Congress accomplished a dual purpose. It not only provided for an efficient and effective method of accomplishing its primary goal—the protection of the investing public from unfair treatment at the hands of corporate insiders—but extended to the corporation the right to secure for itself benefits derived by those insiders from their exploitation of their privileged position. The United States Court of Appeals for the Second Circuit has stated the policy behind section 16(b) in the following terms (*Adler v. Klawans,* 267 F.2d 840, 844):

> "The undoubted congressional intent in the enactment of § 16(b) was to discourage what was reasonably thought to be a widespread abuse of a fiduciary relationship—specifically to discourage if not prevent three classes of persons from making private and gainful use of information acquired by them by virtue of their official relationship to a corporation."

Although the provisions of section 16(b) may not apply to all cases of trading on inside information, it demonstrates that a derivative action can be an effective method for dealing with such abuses which may be used to accomplish a similar purpose in cases not specifically covered by the statute. In *Brophy v. Cities Serv. Co.* (31 Del.Ch. 241, *supra*), for example, the Chancery Court of Delaware allowed a similar remedy in a situation not covered by the Federal legislation. One of the defendants in that case was an employee who had acquired inside information that the corporate plaintiff was about to enter the market and purchase its own shares. On the basis of this confidential information, the employee, who was not an officer and, hence, not liable under Federal law, bought a large block of shares and, after the corporation's purchases had caused the price to rise, resold them at a profit. The court sustained the complaint in a derivative action brought for an accounting, stating that "[p]ublic policy will not permit an employee occupying a position of trust and confidence toward his employer to abuse that relation to his own profit, regardless of whether his employer suffers a loss" (31 Del.Ch., at p. 246). And a similar view has been expressed in the Restatement, 2d, Agency (§ 388, comment *c*):

> "*c. Use of confidential information.* An agent who acquires confidential information in the course of his employment or in violation of his duties has a duty ... to account for any profits made by the use of such information, although this does not harm the principal.... So, if [a corporate officer] has 'inside' information that the corporation is about to purchase or sell securities, or to declare or to pass a dividend, profits made by him in stock transactions undertaken because of his knowledge are held in constructive trust for the principal."

In the present case, the defendants may be able to avoid liability to the corporation under section 16(b) of the Federal law since they had held the MAI shares for more than six months prior to the sales. Nevertheless, the alleged use of the inside information to dispose of their stock at a price considerably higher than its known value constituted the same sort of "abuse of a fiduciary relationship" as is condemned by the Federal law. Sitting as we are in this case as a court of equity, we should not hesitate to permit an action to prevent any unjust enrichment realized by the defendants from their allegedly wrongful act.

The defendants recognize that the conduct charged against them directly contravened the policy embodied in the Securities Exchange Act but, they maintain, the Federal legislation constitutes a comprehensive and carefully wrought plan for dealing with the abuse of inside information and that allowing a derivative action to be maintained under State law would interfere with the Federal scheme. Moreover, they urge, the existence of dual Federal and State remedies for the same act would create the possibility of double liability.

An examination of the Federal regulatory scheme refutes the contention that it was designed to establish any particular remedy as exclusive. In addition to the specific provisions of section 16(b), the Securities and Exchange Act contains a general anti-fraud provision in section 10(b), (U.S.Code, tit. 15, § 78j, subd. [b]) which, as implemented by rule 10b–5 (Code of Fed.Reg., tit. 17, § 240.10b–5) under that section, renders it unlawful to engage in a variety of acts considered to be fraudulent. In interpreting this rule, the Securities and Exchange Commission and the Federal courts have extended the common-law definition of fraud to include not only affirmative misrepresentations, relied upon by the purchaser or seller, but also a failure to disclose material information which might have affected the transaction. (See, e.g., *Securities & Exch. Comm. v. Texas Gulf Sulphur Co.,* 401 F.2d 833, 847–848; *Myzel v. Fields,* 386 F.2d 718, 733–735.)

Accepting the truth of the complaint's allegations, there is no question but that the defendants were guilty of withholding material information from the purchasers of the shares and, indeed, the defendants acknowledge that the facts asserted constitute a violation of rule 10b–5. The remedies which the Federal law provides for such violation, however, are rather limited. An action could be brought, in an exceptional case, by the SEC for injunctive relief. This, in fact, is what happened in the *Texas Gulf Sulphur* case (401 F.2d 833, *supra*). The purpose of such an action, however, would appear to be more to establish a principle than to provide a regular method of enforcement. A class action under the Federal rule might be a more effective remedy but the mechanics of such an action have, as far as we have been able to ascertain, not yet been worked out by the Federal courts and several questions relating thereto have never been resolved. These include the definition of the class entitled to bring such an action, the measure of damages, the administration of the fund which would be recovered and its distribution to the members of the class. (See Note, 54 Cornell L.Rev. 306, 309, *supra.*) Of course, any individual purchaser, who could prove his own injury as a result of a rule 10b–5 violation can bring an action for rescission but we have not been referred to a single case in which such an action has been successfully prosecuted where the public sale of securities is involved. The reason for this is that sales of securities, whether through a stock exchange or over-the-counter, are characteristically anonymous transactions, usually handled through brokers, and the matching of the ultimate buyer with the ultimate seller presents virtually insurmountable obstacles. Thus, unless a section 16(b) violation is also present, the Federal law does not yet provide a really effective remedy.

In view of the practical difficulties inherent in an action under the Federal law, the desirability of creating an effective common-law remedy is manifest. "Dishonest directors should not find absolution from retributive justice", Ballantine observed in his work on Corporations ([rev. ed., 1946], p. 216), "by concealing their identity from their victims under the mask of the stock exchange." There is ample room in a situation such as is here presented for a "private Attorney General" to come forward and enforce proper behavior on the part of corporate officials through the medium of the derivative action brought in the name of the corporation. (See, e.g., *Associated Ind. v. Ickes,* 134 F.2d 694, 704; *Cherner v. Transitron Electronic Corp.,* 201 F.Supp. 934, 936.) Only by sanctioning such a cause of action will there be any effective method to prevent the type of abuse of corporate office complained of in this case.

There is nothing in the Federal law which indicates that it was intended to limit the power of the States to fashion additional remedies to effectuate similar purposes. Although the impact of Federal securities regulation has on occasion been said to have created a "Federal corporation law," in fact, its effect on the duties and obligations of directors and officers and their relation to the corporation and its shareholders is only occasional and peripheral. The primary source of the law in this area ever remains that of the State which created the corporation. Indeed, Congress expressly provided against any implication that it intended to pre-empt the field by declaring, in section 28(a) of the Securities Exchange Act of 1934 (48 U.S.Code 903), that "[t]he rights and remedies provided by this title shall be in addition to any and all other rights and remedies that may exist at law or in equity".

Nor should we be deterred, in formulating a State remedy, by the defendants' claim of possible double liability. Certainly, as already indicated, if the sales in question were publicly made, the likelihood that a suit will be brought by purchasers of the shares is quite remote. But, even if it were not, the mere possibility of such a suit is not a defense nor does it render the complaint insufficient. It is not unusual for an action to be brought to recover a fund which may be subject to a superior claim by a third party. If that be the situation, a defendant should not be permitted to retain the fund for his own use on the chance that such a party may eventually appear. A defendant's course, if he wishes to protect himself against double liability, is to interplead any and all possible claimants and bind them to the judgment (CPLR 1006, subd. [b]).

In any event, though, no suggestion has been made either in brief or on oral argument that any purchaser has come forward with a claim against the defendants or even that anyone is in a position to advance such a claim.[1] As we have stated, the defendants' assertion that such a party may come forward at some future date is not a basis for permitting them to retain for their own benefit the fruits of their allegedly wrongful acts. For all that appears, the present derivative action is the only effective remedy now available against the abuse by these defendants of their privileged position.

As we have previously indicated, what we have written must be read in the light of the charges contained in the complaint, and it must be borne in mind that "it will be incumbent upon the plaintiff, if he is to succeed, to prove upon the trial the truth and correctness of his allegations." (*Walkovszky v. Carlton,* 23 N.Y.2d 714, 715.)

The order appealed from should be affirmed, with costs, and the question certified answered in the affirmative.

■ JUDGES BURKE, SCILEPPI, BERGAN, KEATING, BREITEL and JASEN concur.

Order affirmed, etc.

---

1. In the absence of any such appearance by adverse claimants, we need not now decide whether the corporation's recovery would be affected by any amounts which might have to be refunded by the defendant to the injured purchasers.

Recently, the Delaware Chancery Court affirmed the corporation's right to obtain disgorgement from its officers and directors, but its approach appears more limited than that taken in *Diamond*:

> Disgorgement of insider trading profits (or recovery of reciprocal trading losses) is ... not the appropriate measure of damages because insiders who trade on an impersonal market typically are not engaging in the type of self-dealing transaction to which a disgorgement remedy historically applies.... [T]rading in the market typically does not involve the usurpation of a corporate opportunity, where disgorgement has been the preferred remedy....
>
> These principles do not mean that a disgorgement remedy is precluded. When a breach of the duty of loyalty has been shown, disgorgement remains theoretically available. When a fiduciary engages in actual fraud and benefits from trading on the basis of the fraudulent information, disgorgement could be appropriate....
>
> In the typical scenario in which an insider trades based on material information that allegedly was not disclosed to stockholders, a corporation can recover for actual harm causally related (in both the actual and proximate sense) to the breach of the duty of loyalty.... [T]he obvious candidates are costs and expenses for regulatory proceedings and internal investigations, fees paid to counsel and other professionals, fines paid to regulators, and judgments in litigation. Here, the Complaint specifically seeks to recover damages to the Company as a result of the companion federal securities action [in which it was alleged the insiders disposed of millions of dollars of the company shares while repeatedly making glowing forecasts of ever-rising future earnings].

Pfeiffer v. Toll, 989 A.2d 683, 699–700 (Del. Ch. 2010). For earlier decisions more in line with the reasoning of *Diamond, see* Brophy v. Cities Service Co., 31 Del.Ch. 241, 70 A.2d 5 (1949). See also Thomas v. Roblin Indus., Inc., 520 F.2d 1393, 1397 (3d Cir.1975); In re ORFA Securities Litigation, 654 F.Supp. 1449 (D.N.J.1987). *Contra*: Freeman v. Decio, 584 F.2d 186 (7th Cir.1978) (applying Indiana law in holding that corporate recovery may occur only when the fiduciary's trading interferes with the corporation's ability to secretly use the same information to its own advantage); Schein v. Chasen, 313 So.2d 739 (Fla.1975) (corporate recovery permitted only if the fiduciary's trading harmed the corporation).

Finally, it has been argued unsuccessfully in the lower courts that the state law recovery is not just an anachronism in the era of the very rich federal law regulating insider trading but that cases such as *Diamond* and *Brophy* are no longer good law in the wake of the pervasive federal scheme. *See* In re Oracle, 867 A.2d 904, 927–29 (Del. Ch. 2004) (declining to conclude that *Brophy* is an outdated precedent that ought to be abandoned). Is this an area where federal law should preempt state law? What are the benefits of a corporate suit coexisting with government and investor actions?

CHAPTER 14

SHAREHOLDER SUITS

SECTION 1. INTRODUCTION

BACKGROUND NOTE

If the fiduciary duties owed by directors, officers, and controlling shareholders could be enforced only in suits by the corporation, many wrongs would never be remedied. If a controlling shareholder breaches its duty, it will normally cause the corporation to not institute litigation to remedy the wrong. Similarly, directors will seldom bring suit against one of their colleagues or top executives for such a breach. To overcome these obstacles, and hold wrongdoing managers and controlling shareholders to account, the law permits shareholders to bring suit for breach of fiduciary duty on the corporation's behalf.

In Ross v. Bernhard, 396 U.S. 531, 534–35, 90 S.Ct. 733, 735–6, 24 L.Ed.2d 729 (1970), the Supreme Court sketched the background and nature of such suits in the following terms:

> The common law refused . . . to permit stockholders to call corporate managers to account in actions at law. The possibilities for abuse, thus presented, were not ignored by corporate officers and directors. Early in the 19th century, equity provided relief both in this country and in England. Without detailing these developments, it suffices to say that the remedy in this country, first dealt with by this Court in Dodge v. Woolsey, 18 How. 331, 15 L.Ed. 401 (1855), provided redress . . . against faithless officers and directors. . . . The remedy made available in equity was the derivative suit, viewed in this country as a suit to enforce a *corporate* cause of action against officers, directors, and third parties. As elaborated in the cases, one precondition for the suit was a valid claim on which the corporation could have sued; another was that the corporation itself had refused to proceed after suitable demand, unless excused by extraordinary conditions. Thus the dual nature of the stockholder's action: first, the plaintiff's right to sue on behalf of the corporation and, second, the merits of the corporation's claim itself.

This type of suit is commonly known as a *derivative action*, since the shareholder's right to bring the suit derives from the corporation.

Two features of the derivative action warrant highlighting at the outset. First is the extraordinary procedural complexity inherent in such actions—complexity involving, for example, proper parties and their alignment, jurisdiction, demand on the board, demand on the shareholders, right to sue, intervention, settlement, and dismissal. Second is the difficult problem of social policy raised by such actions, particularly in the publicly held corporation. Through the derivative action, a shareholder with a tiny investment can force an expenditure by the corporation of a large amount of funds and executive time. The question is whether the overall benefits of such actions justify their overall costs, which are, in effect, borne involuntarily by the noncomplaining shareholders.

Where the corporation is publicly held, the plaintiff-shareholder's gain is not only indirect, but usually very small and often infinitesimal. For example, the defendants' briefs in Hornstein v. Paramount Pictures, Inc., 37 N.Y.S.2d 404 (Sup.Ct. 1942), aff'd, 266 App.Div. 659, 41 N.Y.S.2d 210 (1943), aff'd 292 N.Y. 468, 55 N.E.2d 740 (1944), asserted that the five plaintiffs in that case stood to gain $3.57, $.41, $2.41, $.17 and $.65, respectively. In another well-known case, Winkelman v. General Motors Corp., 44 F.Supp. 960 (S.D.N.Y.1942), the three plaintiffs gained 8¢ share for the ninety shares held between them.

In contrast, the plaintiff's lawyer stands to be awarded a very substantial fee out of the proceeds of any judgment or settlement—a fee that often runs into many hundreds of thousands, or even millions, of dollars. Furthermore, defendants in derivative actions are sometimes able to make settlements involving the illicit use of corporate funds to discharge their own liabilities. As a result of these elements, a concern exists that unscrupulous lawyers will exploit either the nuisance value of a nonmeritorious claim, or management's desire to cover up its own wrongdoing, through the institution of suits essentially brought to extract an exorbitant attorneys' fee.

Many or most of the issues to be considered in this chapter, although couched in technical terms, reflect an underlying tension between a concern that managers be held accountable for their wrongdoing, on the one hand, and a concern with the abusive or *strike suit* potential of derivative actions, on the other. Emphasis on the former element leads to liberality in permitting derivative actions; emphasis on the latter leads to rules that restrict such actions. In weighing these opposed concerns, it should be borne in mind that the derivative action and the disclosure requirements of the securities acts constitute the two major legal bulwarks against managerial self-dealing. In considering the various rules taken up in this chapter, it is therefore critical to evaluate the extent to which each rule cuts into the effectiveness of the derivative action, and whether the benefits of the rule justify that cost.

It should also be kept in mind, when considering the problems raised in this chapter, that significant substantive consequences often turn on the success of a motion to dismiss a derivative action on procedural grounds. If the plaintiff can survive such a motion, the facts that he already knows, together with the material that he can develop through discovery, will often lead to a substantial settlement. If the defendant can get the case dismissed on procedural grounds, however, no other plaintiff may come forward—either because no other shareholder who would bring suit knows all the relevant facts, or because the statute of limitations has run. Accordingly, for practical purposes many derivative actions will be won or lost on the basis of procedural issues that do not go to the merits of the case.

FEDERAL RULES OF CIVIL PROCEDURE, RULE 11

[See Statutory Supplement]

Macey & Miller, The Plaintiffs' Attorneys' Role in Class Actions and Derivative Litigation: Economic Analysis and Recommendations for Reform

58 U.Chi.L.Rev. 1, 3, 8–11, 78 (1991).

Plaintiffs' attorneys in class action and derivative suits occupy an uneasy place in the American legal system. The traditional image of the lawyer is of an independent professional providing advice and advocacy on behalf of a client. The attorney, in this view, is an agent of the client and subject to the client's control in all important matters. Plaintiffs' class action and derivative attorneys do not fit this mold. They are subject to only minimal monitoring by their ostensible "clients," who are either dispersed and disorganized (in the case of class action litigation) or under the control of hostile forces (in the case of derivative litigation). Accordingly, plaintiffs' class and derivative attorneys function essentially as entrepreneurs who bear a substantial amount of the litigation risk and exercise nearly plenary control over all important decisions in the lawsuit....

[The] regulatory structure [that governs derivative and class actions] is poorly designed in a number of respects, particularly when applied to "large-scale, small-claim" litigation in which the overall liability is large but the individual interests of the class members or corporate shareholders are small.... Many regulatory shortfalls can be traced ultimately to a single fundamental error: the inappropriate attempt to treat entrepreneurial litigation as if it were essentially the same as standard litigation, in which the client exercises substantial influence....

The class action is a tool for overcoming the free-rider[5] and other collective action[6] problems that impair any attempt to organize a large number of discrete individuals in any common project. These kinds of

---

5. Freeriding, as the name implies, simply refers to a situation where a person can obtain a benefit (or avoid a cost) without paying for it....

6. Collective action is used in the public choice literature to refer to any procedure for making decisions by groups of people....

problems are prevalent in situations when a large number of people have been injured by another person's conduct, but when the injury to many of these individuals is small. In the absence of a class action device, such injuries would often go unremedied because most individual plaintiffs would not themselves have a sufficient economic stake in the litigation to incur the litigation costs. Of course, some particularly aggrieved individual might attempt to bring a large group together in a single lawsuit by using standard joinder and intervention devices. But bringing large numbers of additional parties in by this method would be very costly. Organizing the conduct of litigation with large numbers of additional parties would be a nightmare. The organizer, moreover, would have no effective way of obtaining reimbursement from other plaintiffs for these costs.

The class action procedure partially overcomes these difficulties by providing an effective and inexpensive procedure for joining large numbers of individual plaintiffs....

The economic rationale for the [Rule 23] (b)(3) class action—as a method for overcoming free-rider and other collective action problems—stands in sharp contrast to the rationale for the shareholder's derivative suit. Shareholder's derivative actions are not premised on collective action problems in the *litigation.* On the contrary, they presuppose the existence of a corporate form that is already organized to overcome such collective action problems. The corporation has standing and is fully competent to bring legal actions to redress injuries to its rights. The problem, rather, is with collective action *within* the corporate form itself. As scholars since Berle and Means have observed, corporate managers typically have only a small ownership stake in the firms they manage. Thus, their interests deviate from those of shareholders: they may prefer to consume excessive perquisites or practice their golf whereas shareholders would want them to work diligently at maximizing profits.

The shareholder's derivative suit is one of many devices in corporate law for controlling these conflicts between managers and shareholders. Many cases arise in which a corporation has an enforceable legal claim against others for harm to the corporation. Like other matters affecting the corporation, pursuit of the claim is left initially to the managers. But if the suit would potentially harm the managers' personal interests, the managers may be unwilling to prosecute the claim, even when doing so would serve the best interests of the corporation. The classic case is the action for breach of fiduciary duty against corporate directors. Obviously the directors cannot be trusted to cause the corporation to sue themselves. The derivative action allows a representative shareholder in such circumstances to take over the litigation from recalcitrant managers and prosecute it on behalf of the corporation. Unlike the class action, in which the relief is given to the plaintiff class members, any relief recovered in a derivative action (net of expenses including attorneys' fees) is returned to the corporation....

. . . Although a theoretical model exists in which suits are brought solely for their nuisance settlement value, the frequency of strike suits in derivative and class litigation remains an open question. Most observers agree that strike suit litigation is relatively uncommon. Defendants in class action and derivative litigation are typical repeat players, in that they are vulnerable to frequent lawsuits brought by entrepreneurial attorneys. It would not appear particularly desirable for such defendants (or their insurers, as the case may be) to settle cases for their nuisance value, because doing so would predictably establish a reputation as an easy mark and thus generate even more frivolous litigation. Conversely, a defendant that vigorously contests derivative or class action litigation, even when meritorious, is likely to gain a reputation as a party that derivative attorneys take on at their peril. Moreover, a plaintiffs' attorney who brings a strike suit incurs substantial risk; she must fund and staff the litigation subject to a high probability of non-success at the end. The true strike suit, where it occurs, is unlikely to be overly costly for defendants because the plaintiff would be likely to settle at a very low figure.

AMERICAN LAW INSTITUTE, PRINCIPLES OF CORPORATE GOVERNANCE §§ 7.04(a)(1), (b), (d)

[See Statutory Supplement]

NOTE ON THE EMPIRICAL STUDIES OF SHAREHOLDER LITIGATION

Based on studies of certain data concerning settlement and success rates in derivative actions, Professor Roberta Romano has concluded that "shareholder litigation is a weak, if not ineffective, instrument of corporate governance," and that "the principal beneficiaries of the litigation . . . appear to be the [plaintiffs'] attorneys." Romano, The Shareholder Suit: Litigation Without Foundation?, 7 J. of Law, Economics, & Organization 55, 84 (1991). Some others have drawn comparable conclusions.

These conclusions seem either questionable or incorrect. To begin with, the samples from which the relevant data have been drawn have all been seriously flawed. For example, Romano's own sample excluded all actions involving corporations whose stock was not publicly traded. However, litigation involving such corporations may have a different degree of merit than litigation involving publicly held corporations, because the incentive structures for bringing shareholder actions in the two types of corporations differ substantially.

Furthermore, even the data that has been used does not support the conclusions that are drawn. Several kinds of arguments are often made on the basis of the data. One is that the data shows that an extremely high proportion of derivative actions settle. That argument, however, is a non-starter. As Romano points out, "[t]his aspect of shareholder litigation is unremarkable; most civil suits settle." Id. at 60.

A second kind of argument is that the data shows that settlements don't, on average, confer a benefit on the corporation. In Romano's sample, about half the settlements during the relevant period resulted in monetary recovery, with an average recovery of $9 million and a median recovery of $2 million. A number of the remaining settlements involved changes in corporate governance but no monetary recovery. In most of the cases, the plaintiffs' attorney was awarded attorneys' fees. Because the monetary recoveries were very small in relation to firm assets, Romano states that "One interpretation [of this data] is that most fiduciary breaches involve only minor harm to shareholders. But the settlement pattern is consistent with another, more troubling explanation, that a significant proportion of shareholder suits are without merit." Id. at 61. Others have drawn similar conclusions.

There are several problems with this explanation. To begin with, as Romano states, the data on which she relies can be explained in a much different way. Next, there are methodological problems. Apart from the flaws in the sample, no baseline data is provided concerning suits other than shareholder suits. Some percentage of all cases that appear to have merit ex ante turn out to be without merit ex post. No baseline data is provided by Romano or others against which to measure whether the percentage of shareholder litigation that is without merit is higher or lower than the percentage of all litigation that is without merit. Similarly, some percentage of all settlements are low, and no baseline data is provided by critics of shareholder suits comparing settlements in shareholder actions with settlements in other kinds of actions.

Furthermore, most of the data on the settlement of derivative actions is simply not persuasive concerning the merits of shareholder litigation. In Romano's sample, the average monetary settlement was $9 million and the median was $2 million. Those are not insignificant amounts. A director who sells property to the corporation at $2 million more than its market value has committed a serious wrong that should be remedied, and a derivative action may be the only way to accomplish that end.

Similarly, the fact that a relatively high proportion of shareholder suits involve nonmonetary settlements is not in itself dispositive concerning the merits of these cases. Corporations are governance systems. Accordingly, in a number of shareholder suits a change in governance would be extremely valuable. Additionally, in the case of many or most civil suits, the only thing the defendant has that the plaintiff wants is money. Shareholder suits, in contrast, offer a greater opportunity for win/win outcomes, because the defendants can trade not only money, but also changes in governance rules and conduct. Therefore, a certain percentage of nonmonetary settlements of derivative actions are to be expected simply as a matter of the dynamics of the corporate context. Some nonmonetary settlements do indeed involve relief that is only cosmetic. Others, however, involve very substantial benefits, such as the termination of inside directors' employment contracts or a systematic change in the corporation's governance structure.

Moreover, although it is possible that a significant proportion of nonmonetary settlements do not involve substantial relief, even that may not show that the underlying cases lacked substantive merit. Weak settlements may be due not to a lack of substantive merit, but to the role of the special procedural obstacles to derivative actions. Professor John Coffee has made the following observations concerning arguments that derivative actions produce only limited financial benefits in relation to their costs:

> What does this evidence really prove? First, the same critique could be made of the criminal law; the fines imposed by a criminal court may often fall below the state's cost of prosecution. Nonetheless, criminal prosecutions continue, either because society believes in general deterrence or because it enjoys retribution. Similarly, the value of the derivative action arguably lies in its deterrent capacity, which such studies do not measure. Although the deterrent threat of the derivative action may be undercut to some degree by liability insurance, most D & O policies do not cover repayment of an improper benefit. In addition, there are also non-monetary sanctions, such as loss of reputation and social stigma. These intangibles are even harder to estimate, but only a fool ignores them.
>
> Second, the real problem with any study finding a negligible benefit is that it cannot measure the deterrent or compensatory capacity of the derivative action in the abstract but only under a specific set of legal rules. Recent studies, which have focused on publicly listed companies, are thus principally measuring the effectiveness of Delaware law, because Delaware is the corporate home for nearly half of such companies. That these studies find only negligible benefits and substantial costs is hardly reassuring about Delaware's legal rules for the derivative action. But, by the same token, such studies prove little about alternative legal regimes.
>
> The bottom line then is that any claim that the empirical data proves the derivative action useless is circular. The outcome of derivative actions is determined largely by the incentives that the law holds out to private enforcers to bring them. If the operative legal rules tell the plaintiff's attorney that there is a high probability of dismissal, regardless of the action's merit, the predictable result of such rules will be small settlements. All this proves is the truism that the parties "bargained in the shadow of the law."

John C. Coffee, Jr., New Myths and Old Realities: The American Law Institute Faces the Derivative Action, 48 Bus. Law. 1407, 1436–37 (1993).

Another argument that is sometimes made against the efficacy of shareholder actions is that the data shows that plaintiffs have a very low rate of success in those cases that are disposed of through adjudication, rather than settlement. Certainly this data is troubling. However, this data too is difficult to evaluate. Because there are so many special, procedural defenses to derivative actions—such as contemporaneous ownership and demand on the board—a low rate of success in derivative actions is not surprising, and may only be evidence that the special procedural hurdles couldn't be jumped, not that the suits lacked substantive merit. As a practical matter, a typical strategy of defendants in derivative actions is to try to get rid of a case on the basis of a special procedural defense before discovery, and to settle if the plaintiff survives the procedural attacks and begins unearthing all the facts in discovery.

Finally, in evaluating shareholder litigation *all* benefits and losses must be taken into account. One benefit is general deterrence. General deterrence is, of course, important for any class of litigation, but it may be especially important in the case of shareholder litigation, because corporations, directors, and officers are more likely to get legal messages—to be law-sensitive—than most private actors.

Another benefit of shareholder litigation is the public knowledge that directors and officers who engage in misconduct are subject to such litigation. This knowledge increases public confidence in, and therefore the efficiency of, the capital markets.

A third benefit of derivative actions is that, as Romano states, "legal rules are public goods. All firms benefit from a judicial decision clarifying the scope of permissible conduct." Id. at 85. In assessing derivative actions, Romano, like others who have drawn negative conclusions concerning the benefits of such actions, left the calculation of the public-good aspect of derivative actions "for another study." But any argument that the costs of derivative actions exceed their benefits entirely depends on taking into account all costs and all benefits. That is not what the critics of derivative actions have done. Instead, most critics count all the costs of derivative actions but only a fraction of the benefits, and then—not surprisingly—conclude that the costs exceed the benefits.

It is possible that if all the costs and benefits of shareholder litigation were added up, we would conclude that the costs would exceed the benefits. Whether that conclusion is probable, however, is a much different question. Recall, in this connection, the conclusion of Macey & Miller, supra, that "Although a theoretical model exists in which [shareholder] suits are brought solely for their nuisance settlement value, the frequency of strike suits in derivative and class litigation remains an open question. Most observers agree that strike suit litigation is relatively uncommon."

The most recent scholarship in the area attests to the benefits of shareholder suits. Delaware is by far the most important corporate jurisdiction, and corporate litigation in Delaware begins in the Chancery Court. In a pair of articles, Robert Thompson and Randall Thomas studied all the complaints filed in Delaware Chancery court in the two-year period 1999–2000. Thompson & Thomas, The Public and Private Faces of Derivative Lawsuits, 57 Vanderbilt Law Rev. 1747 (2004); Thompson & Thomas, The New Look of Shareholder Litigation: Acquisition–Oriented Class Actions, 57 Vanderbilt Law. Rev. 133 (2004). The former article focuses on derivative actions, and the latter focuses on class actions brought for violations of state corporate law (as opposed to securities class actions).

Thompson & Thomas found that during 1999–2000, on a consolidated basis 348 shareholder fiduciary-duty suits were filed in the Delaware Chancery Court. Of these, 84 were derivative actions, 74 were direct actions, and 223 were class actions. Taken together, fiduciary-duty cases accounted for most of the shareholder suits in Delaware during the relevant period. (The remaining suits were based on statutory or contractual claims. These claims concerned such matters as inspection of books and records, petitions for dissolution or the appointment of a receiver or custodian, appraisal proceedings, suits for indemnification, and so forth.)

Of the derivative actions involving private corporations, about one-third resulted in affirmative relief. The relief included money payments to minority owners, changes in the allocation of ownership, and a purchase by the corporation of the complaining shareholders' shares. Of the derivative actions involving publicly held corporations, about 28% ended in affirmative relief. This relief included money damages and nonmonetary relief, such as rescission of a purchase agreement, and rescission of substantial executive compensation. All together, nine cases ended in monetary relief. Almost all the monetary settlements were for $9 million or more. In one case, the settlement was for $140 million, and in one case it was for $165 million. In the latter two cases, the attorneys' fees were less than 10% of the settlement amount.

Overall, as to derivative actions, Thompson & Thomas conclude as follows:

> . . . The impact of decisions in derivative cases like *Caremark*,[9] *Disney*,[10] and *Oracle*[11] goes well beyond the outcome of the cases themselves—these decisions changed the rules for future legal practice by allowing well motivated legal counselors to force their clients to accept better conduct and procedures. Moreover, derivative suits at private companies perform an important, if less heralded, role in policing conflict of interest transactions and duty of care violations.

---

9. Caremark International Inc. Derivative Litigation, 698 A.2d 959 (Del. Ch. 1996) (finding in dicta that boards had a duty to consider whether to create internal monitoring systems).

10. In re The Walt Disney Company Derivative Litigation, 825 A.2d 275 (Del. Ch. 2003) (denying motion to dismiss complaint alleging that board had breached the duty of good faith in determining executive compensation package).

11. In re Oracle Corp. Derivative Litigation, 824 A.2d 917 (Del. Ch. 2003) (finding that tenured professors who were members of special litigation committee were not independent where financial ties between university and corporation were substantial).

> To support our claim, we present the data from a study of all corporate litigation in Delaware for a two year period. We find that there are a small number of derivative suits, about 30 per year, brought against public companies incorporated in Delaware. Contrary to earlier studies, we do not find evidence that these cases are "strike suits" yielding little benefit. Instead, roughly 30% of the derivative suits provide relief to the corporation or the shareholders, while the others are usually dismissed quickly with little apparent litigation activity. In cases producing a recovery to shareholders, the amount of recovery typically exceeds the amount of attorneys' fees awarded by a significant margin. The cases do demonstrate some indicia of litigation agency costs (for example suits being filed quickly, multiple suits per controversy, and repeat plaintiffs' law firms) but each of these costs is much less pronounced for derivative suits than for other forms of representative litigations. Overall, the claim that derivative suits are strike suits is much weaker than in earlier periods.

Public and Private Faces of Derivative Actions, supra, at 1749–50.

Thompson's and Thomas's findings on state-law class actions is even more striking than their findings on derivative actions. One important finding was that while the derivative actions generally involved traditional duty-of-loyalty claims, most of the class actions involved director or controlling shareholder conduct in mergers and other acquisitions. Another important finding was that class actions account for a much higher percentage of corporate-law litigation in Delaware than derivative actions. Thompson and Thomas also found that "There is no pattern [in the class-action cases] of modest settlements for the shareholder group and most of that money going to the attorneys, as was sometimes found in earlier representative suits. Instead, we find that there were large monetary settlements paid to shareholders in many of these cases and that these settlements involved a substantially lower percentage level of attorneys' fees as compared to securities fraud class actions.... The pattern of affirmative relief was strongest in those cases in which there was a controlling shareholder who has proposed an acquisition that will effectively cash-out the minority shareholders...." In 20 of 65 of the controlling-shareholder acquisition cases, as a result of the class action additional consideration was paid to the minority shareholders. In the controlling-shareholder acquisition cases that did not result in a monetary settlement, the premium of the acquisition price over the market price was 25.5%. In the cases that did result in a monetary settlement, the premium was only 15%, but the settlement lifted the premium to more than 25.5%. Accordingly, the impact of the monetary class-action settlements was "to raise the premium paid in the lowest-priced control shareholder transactions above the average level for all of these transactions in our sample. In other words, acquisition-oriented class action litigation polices the worst control shareholder deals, and benefits target company shareholders by insuring that they get compensated as well as, or better than, shareholders in deals that are more fully priced."

Overall, as to acquisition-oriented class actions, Thompson and Thomas conclude as follows:

> [An] optimistic perspective would be that these acquisition-driven suits serve an important effect a priori: corporate planners know the relative strength of the different legal doctrines associated with different forms of acquisitions, and try to minimize the costs of shareholder litigation by invoking procedural protections like the use of special committees and by offering shareholders a sufficiently high price for their shares that they do not file suit. If they ignore this information, and do not offer shareholders a sufficient premium for their stock, shareholder litigation forces them to do so in many instances....
>
> Placing our findings in the historical context of the debate over the value of representative shareholder litigation, we believe that acquisition-oriented class actions substantially reduce management agency costs, while the litigation agency costs they create do not appear excessive. For these suits, we therefore disagree with earlier studies that have claimed that all representative shareholder litigation has little, if any, effect in reducing management agency costs and should be evaluated solely in terms of its litigation agency costs....
>
> ... [I]f we take only those control shareholder transactions that evidence a larger likelihood of conflict of interest, we find that affirmative relief occurs only in those cases in which the initial premium offered by the conflicted controlling shareholder was the lowest in relation to the prior market price. This finding suggests that the merits of litigation do make a difference, and that shareholder litigation deserves a seat at the table of corporate governance.

The New Look of Shareholder Litigation, supra, at 139–40, 208.

ALI, PRINCIPLES OF CORPORATE GOVERNANCE § 7.15

[See Statutory Supplement]

NOTE ON WHO CAN BRING A DERIVATIVE ACTION

1. *Shareholder Status*. It is generally agreed that the plaintiff in a derivative action must be a shareholder at the time the action is begun, e.g., Vista Fund v. Garis, 277 N.W.2d 19 (Minn.1979), and must remain a shareholder during the pendency of the action, see, e.g., Schilling v. Belcher, 582 F.2d 995 (5th Cir.1978). An implication of this rule is that if S, a shareholder of C Corporation, brings a derivative action on C's behalf, and C then merges into T Corporation, which is the survivor of the merger, S loses standing to continue prosecuting the action, since she is no longer a shareholder in C. This rule was adopted in Delaware in the leading case of Lewis v. Anderson, 477

A.2d 1040 (Del. 1984). *See also* Lewis v. Ward, 852 A.2d 896 (Del. 2004) (affirming the position taken earlier in *Lewis*). However, both cases recognize two exceptions: (1) Where the merger is subject to the claim that it was perpetrated merely to deprive shareholders of the right to bring a derivative action; and (2) Where the merger is in reality a reorganization that does not affect the plaintiff's ownership of the business enterprise. A distinct minority of the courts permit a suit initiated before the merger terminated the plaintiff's holdings in the derivative suit corporation. *See* Duffy v. Cross Country Ind., 395 N.Y.S.2d 852 (1977). Some courts permit the suit to continue provided the plaintiff first makes a demand on the acquiring corporation's board. *See* Professional Management Assoc. Inc. v. Coss, 598 N.W.2d 406 (Minn. Ct. App. 1999).

What constitutes shareholdership for derivative-action purposes? In a few states, a statute or rule speaks to the issue directly. For example, N.Y.Bus.Corp.Law § 626(a) provides that the plaintiff in a derivative suit must be "a holder of shares or of voting trust certificates . . . or of a beneficial interest in such shares or certificates." Where the statute is silent, courts normally define shareholdership in a very expansive manner. First, record ownership is generally not required; an unregistered shareholder will qualify. See, e.g., Rosenthal v. Burry Biscuit Corp., 30 Del.Ch. 299, 60 A.2d 106 (Ch.1948). Second, legal ownership is not required—equitable ownership suffices. The latter category has been held to include, among others, an owner of stock held by a broker in a margin account in the broker's street name, a pledgee, the beneficiary of a trust, a legatee, a surviving spouse with a community interest in stock held in the deceased spouse's name, and a person who has contracted to purchase stock.

It is also established that in an appropriate case a shareholder in a parent corporation can bring a derivative action on behalf of a subsidiary, despite the fact that he is not a shareholder in the subsidiary. See Painter, Double Derivative Suits and Other Remedies With Regard to Damaged Subsidiaries, 36 Ind.L.J. 143, 147–49 (1961).

2. *Creditors*. An implication from the rule that the plaintiff in a derivative action must be a shareholder at the time he brings suit is that a creditor (including a bondholder) ordinarily has no right to bring a derivative action. The bondholder's status was not improved where the bond was convertible into equity shares. See, e.g., Harff v. Kerkorian, 324 A.2d 215 (Del.Ch.1974), aff'd in pertinent part 347 A.2d 133 (Del.1975). Professor DeMott comments, "Convertible debentures present a more complicated problem. Some courts have held that the holder lacks standing to sue derivatively until the debenture has been converted, while others have held that the conversion feature provides the holder a sufficient equity interest to confer standing to sue derivatively—or have recognized that the question is disputed. More generally, in analyzing the status of holders of rights related to stocks, most courts focus on whether the holder has the right or an obligation to acquire shares of stock." Deborah DeMott, Shareholder Derivative Actions § 4:3 (2003).

Moreover, any claim based on misconduct that occurred prior to the corporation filing bankruptcy becomes the property of the bankruptcy estate and hence falls under the control of the trustee or debtor in possession. When the debtor in possession includes the defendants in the earlier initiated derivative suit an interesting question arises regarding who should control the suit. *See* David A. Skeel, Rethinking The Line Between Corporate Law and Corporate Bankruptcy, 72 Tex. L. Rev. 471 (1994).

3. *Directors*. Occasionally a statute gives an officer or director the right to bring a derivative action. See N.Y.Bus.Corp.Law § 720(b). Absent such express statutory authorization, directors and officers lack standing to sue derivatively in their capacity as a director or officer. *See* Schoon v. Smith, 953 A.2d 196 (Del. 2008).

NOTE ON PERSONAL DEFENSES

It is generally held that a shareholder is barred from bringing a derivative action if either (1) she participated in the alleged wrong; (2) she consented to the wrong or explicitly ratified it; (3) she is guilty of laches; or (4) (under a few opinions) she "acquiesced" in the wrong by failing to object. The theory of these rules is that in such cases the plaintiff is "estopped" to bring the action, or lacks "clean hands." See, e.g., Bloodworth v. Bloodworth, 225 Ga. 379, 169 S.E.2d 150 (1969). These defenses are therefore known as "personal" defenses, because they do not relate to the merits of the action, but only to whether a particular shareholder can bring it.

Recognition of personal defenses seems inconsistent with the nature of a derivative action. In Kullgren v. Navy Gas & Supply Co., 112 Colo. 331, 149 P.2d 653 (1944), the court said:

> The finding of the trial court on which it based its order of dismissal ... is in part as follows: "If the defendants named in this case are wolves, as the plaintiff so vigorously contends, then the plaintiff was running with the pack.... If they are thieves, as plaintiff strongly urges, then they are all thieves together, and a court of equity will not undertake to adjust equities between thieves." ... [W]e cannot think [this] is sound in a situation, where, as here, the only judgment sought is in behalf of the corporation. Based on the implication that the three moving defendants and plaintiff are "thieves together," ... the result ... is that all—the three defendants and plaintiff—are beholden to the corporation.

Despite this reasoning, most courts not only allow personal defenses, but go one step further and adopt the so-called "tainted share" rule. Under this rule, if a shareholder is barred from bringing an action by virtue of a personal defense, so also is any transferee of that shareholder. For discussions of the rule, see Note, 54 Boston U.L.Rev. 355, 362–66 (1974); Note, 46 Mich.L.Rev. 429, 430 (1948).

Frequently the derivative suit plaintiff is deemed inadequate due to having acquiesced in the conduct underlying the derivative suit claim. *See* Herald Co. v. Seawell, 472 F.2d 1081, 1099 (10th Cir. 1972) (plaintiff barred from maintaining suit challenging company's repurchase of shares as a defensive maneuver because plaintiff had earlier deliberately failed to protest the repurchase); Wallad v. Access BIDCO, Inc., 236 Mich.App. 303, 600 N.W.2d 664 (Mich. Ct. App. 1999) (failure to object at a board meeting deemed acquiescence even though failure to object was out of fear of losing job).

NOTE ON THE CORPORATION AS AN INDISPENSABLE PARTY

It is well established that the corporation is an indispensable party to a derivative action, and therefore must be joined in the suit:

> If the defendants account, it must be to the corporation and not to the shareholders. As to the defendants charged with defrauding it, the corporation is an indispensable party.... Furthermore, the decree must protect the defendants against any further suit by the corporation, and this will not be true unless it properly be made a party to the action.... The usual American practice is to name the beneficiary corporation as a party defendant, although in substance it is a party plaintiff; the flexibility of equity procedure permits an affirmative judgment to be entered in favor of one defendant against other defendants.

Dean v. Kellogg, 294 Mich. 200, 207–08, 292 N.W. 704, 707–08 (1940).

SECTION 2. THE NATURE OF THE DERIVATIVE ACTION

Tooley v. Donaldson, Lufkin, & Jenrette, Inc.

Supreme Court of Delaware, 2004.
845 A.2d 1031.

■ Before VEASEY, CHIEF JUSTICE, HOLLAND, BERGER, STEELE and JACOBS, JUSTICES, constituting the Court en Banc.

■ VEASEY, CHIEF JUSTICE:

Plaintiff-stockholders brought a purported class action in the Court of Chancery, alleging that the members of the board of directors of their corporation breached their fiduciary duties by agreeing to a 22–day delay in closing a proposed merger. Plaintiffs contend that the delay harmed them due to the lost time-value of the cash paid for their shares. The Court of Chancery granted the defendants' motion to dismiss on the sole ground that the claims were, "at most," claims of the corporation being asserted derivatively. They were, thus, held not to be direct claims of the stockholders, individually. Thereupon, the

Court held that the plaintiffs lost their standing to bring this action when they tendered their shares in connection with the merger.

Although the trial court's legal analysis of whether the complaint alleges a direct or derivative claim reflects some concepts in our prior jurisprudence, we believe those concepts are not helpful and should be regarded as erroneous. We set forth in this Opinion the law to be applied henceforth in determining whether a stockholder's claim is derivative or direct. That issue must turn *solely* on the following questions: (1) who suffered the alleged harm (the corporation or the suing stockholders, individually); and (2) who would receive the benefit of any recovery or other remedy (the corporation or the stockholders, individually)? . . .

Facts

Patrick Tooley and Kevin Lewis are former minority stockholders of Donaldson, Lufkin & Jenrette, Inc. (DLJ), a Delaware corporation engaged in investment banking. DLJ was acquired by Credit Suisse Group (Credit Suisse) in the Fall of 2000. Before that acquisition, AXA Financial, Inc.(AXA), which owned 71% of DLJ stock, controlled DLJ. Pursuant to a stockholder agreement between AXA and Credit Suisse, AXA agreed to exchange with Credit Suisse its DLJ stockholdings for a mix of stock and cash. The consideration received by AXA consisted primarily of stock. Cash made up one-third of the purchase price. Credit Suisse intended to acquire the remaining minority interests of publicly-held DLJ stock through a cash tender offer, followed by a merger of DLJ into a Credit Suisse subsidiary.

The tender offer price was set at $90 per share in cash. The tender offer was to expire 20 days after its commencement. The merger agreement, however, authorized two types of extensions. First, Credit Suisse could unilaterally extend the tender offer if certain conditions were not met, such as SEC regulatory approvals or certain payment obligations. Alternatively, DLJ and Credit Suisse could agree to postpone acceptance by Credit Suisse of DLJ stock tendered by the minority stockholders.

Credit Suisse availed itself of both types of extensions to postpone the closing of the tender offer. The tender offer was initially set to expire on October 5, 2000, but Credit Suisse invoked the five-day unilateral extension provided in the agreement. Later, by agreement between DLJ and Credit Suisse, it postponed the merger a second time so that it was then set to close on November 2, 2000.

Plaintiffs challenge the second extension that resulted in a 22–day delay. They contend that this delay was not properly authorized and harmed minority stockholders while improperly benefitting AXA. They claim damages representing the time-value of money lost through the delay.

The Decision of the Court of Chancery

The order of the Court of Chancery dismissing the complaint, and the Memorandum Opinion upon which it is based, state that the dismissal is based on the plaintiffs' lack of standing to bring the claims asserted therein. Thus, when plaintiffs tendered their shares, they lost standing under Court of Chancery Rule 23.1, the contemporaneous holding rule. The ruling before us on appeal is that the plaintiffs' claim is derivative, purportedly brought on behalf of DLJ. The Court of Chancery, relying upon our confusing jurisprudence on the direct/derivative dichotomy, based its dismissal on the following ground: "Because this delay affected all DLJ shareholders equally, plaintiffs' injury was not a special injury, and this action is, thus, a derivative action, at most."

Plaintiffs argue that they have suffered a "special injury" because they had an alleged contractual right to receive the merger consideration of $90 per share without suffering the 22–day delay arising out of the extensions under the merger agreement. But the trial court's opinion convincingly demonstrates that plaintiffs had no such contractual right that had ripened at the time the extensions were entered into:

> *Here, it is clear that plaintiffs have no separate contractual right to bring a direct claim, and they do not assert contractual rights under the merger agreement.* First, the merger agreement specifically disclaims any persons as being third party beneficiaries to the contract. Second, any contractual shareholder right to payment of the merger consideration did not ripen until the conditions of the agreement were met. The agreement stated that Credit Suisse Group was not required to accept any shares for tender, or could extend the offer, under certain conditions—one condition of which included an extension or termination by agreement between Credit Suisse Group and DLJ. *Because Credit Suisse Group and DLJ did in fact agree to extend the tender offer period, any right to payment plaintiffs could have did not ripen until this newly negotiated period was over. The merger agreement only became binding and mutually enforceable at the time the tendered shares ultimately were accepted for payment by Credit Suisse Group.* It is at that moment in time, November 3, 2000, that the company became bound to purchase the tendered shares, making the contract mutually enforceable. *DLJ stockholders had no individual contractual right to payment until November 3, 2000, when their tendered shares were accepted for payment.* Thus, they have no contractual basis to challenge a delay in the closing of the tender offer up until November 3. *Because this is the date the tendered shares were accepted for payment, the contract was not breached and plaintiffs do not have a contractual basis to bring a direct suit.*

Moreover, no other individual right of these stockholder-plaintiffs was alleged to have been violated by the extensions.

That conclusion could have ended the case because it portended a definitive ruling that plaintiffs have no claim whatsoever on the facts alleged. But the defendants chose to argue, and the trial court chose to decide, the standing issue, which is predicated on an assertion that this claim is a derivative one asserted on behalf of the corporation, DLJ....

The trial court's analysis was hindered, however, because it focused on the confusing concept of "special injury" as the test for determining whether a claim is derivative or direct. The trial court's premise was as follows:

> In order to bring a *direct* claim, a plaintiff must have experienced some "special injury." [citing *Lipton v. News Int'l,* 514 A.2d 1075, 1079 (Del.1986)]. A special injury is a wrong that "is separate and distinct from that suffered by other shareholders, ... or a wrong involving a contractual right of a shareholder, such as the right to vote, or to assert majority control, which exists independently of any right of the corporation." [citing *Moran v. Household Int'l. Inc.,* 490 A.2d 1059, 1070 (Del.Ch.1985), *aff'd* 500 A.2d 1346 (Del.1986 [1985])].

In our view, the concept of "special injury" that appears in some Supreme Court and Court of Chancery cases is not helpful to a proper analytical distinction between direct and derivative actions. We now disapprove the use of the concept of "special injury" as a tool in that analysis.

The Proper Analysis to Distinguish Between Direct and Derivative Actions

The analysis must be based solely on the following questions: Who suffered the alleged harm—the corporation or the suing stockholder individually—and who would receive the benefit of the recovery or other remedy? This simple analysis is well imbedded in our jurisprudence,[3] but some cases have complicated it by injection of the amorphous and confusing concept of "special injury."

The Chancellor, in the very recent *Agostino* case,[4] correctly points this out and strongly suggests that we should disavow the concept of "special injury." In a scholarly analysis of this area of the law, he also suggests that the inquiry should be whether the stockholder has demonstrated that he or she has suffered an injury that is not dependent on an injury to the corporation. In the context of a claim for breach of fiduciary duty, the Chancellor articulated the inquiry as follows: "Looking at the body of the complaint and considering the nature of the wrong alleged and the relief requested, has the plaintiff demonstrated that he or she can prevail without showing an injury to the corporation?"[5] We believe that this approach is helpful in analyzing

---

3. *See, e.g., Kramer v. Western Pacific Industries, Inc.,* 546 A.2d 348 (Del.1988).

4. *Agostino v. Hicks,* No. Civ. A. 20020–NC, 2004 WL 443987 (Del.Ch. March 11, 2004).

5. *Agostino,* 2004 WL 443987, at * 7. The Chancellor further explains that the focus should be on the person or entity to whom the relevant duty is owed. *Id.* at *7 n. 54. As noted in *Agostino, id.,* this test is similar to that articulated by the American Law Institute (ALI), a test that we cited with approval in *Grimes v. Donald,* 673 A.2d 1207 (Del.1996). The ALI test is as follows:

> A direct action may be brought in the name and right of a holder to redress an injury sustained by, or enforce a duty owed to, the holder. An action in which the holder can

the first prong of the analysis: what person or entity has suffered the alleged harm? The second prong of the analysis should logically follow.

A Brief History of Our Jurisprudence

. . . Because a derivative suit is being brought on behalf of the corporation, the recovery, if any, must go to the corporation. A stockholder who is directly injured, however, does retain the right to bring an individual action for injuries affecting his or her legal rights as a stockholder. Such a claim is distinct from an injury caused to the corporation alone. In such individual suits, the recovery or other relief flows directly to the stockholders, not to the corporation.

Determining whether an action is derivative or direct is sometimes difficult and has many legal consequences, some of which may have an expensive impact on the parties to the action. For example, if an action is derivative, the plaintiffs are then required to comply with the requirements of Court of Chancery Rule 23.1, that the stockholder: (a) retain ownership of the shares throughout the litigation; (b) make presuit demand on the board; and (c) obtain court approval of any settlement. Further, the recovery, if any, flows only to the corporation. The decision whether a suit is direct or derivative may be outcome-determinative. Therefore, it is necessary that a standard to distinguish such actions be clear, simple and consistently articulated and applied by our courts.

In *Elster v. American Airlines, Inc.,*[7] the stockholder sought to enjoin the grant and exercise of stock options because they would result in a dilution of her stock personally. In *Elster,* the alleged injury was found to be derivative, not direct, because it was essentially a claim of mismanagement of corporate assets. Then came the complication in the analysis: The Court held that where the alleged injury is to both the corporation *and* to the stockholder, the stockholder must allege a "special injury" to maintain a direct action. The Court did not define "special injury," however. By implication, decisions in later cases have interpreted *Elster* to mean that a "special injury" is alleged where the wrong is inflicted upon the stockholder alone or where the stockholder complains of a wrong affecting a particular right. Examples would be a preemptive right as a stockholder, rights involving control of the corporation or a wrong affecting the stockholder, qua individual holder, and not the corporation.

In *Bokat v. Getty Oil Co.,*[8] a stockholder of a subsidiary brought suit against the director of the parent corporation for causing the subsidiary to invest its resources wastefully, resulting in a loss to the subsidiary. The claim in *Bokat* was essentially for mismanagement of

prevail without showing an injury or breach of duty to the corporation should be treated as a direct action that may be maintained by the holder in an individual capacity.

2 American Law Institute, PRINCIPLES OF CORPORATE GOVERNANCE: ANALYSIS AND RECOMMENDATIONS § 7.01(b) at 17.

7. 100 A.2d 219, 222 (Del.Ch.1953).

8. 262 A.2d 246 (Del.1970).

corporate assets. Therefore, the Court held that any recovery must be sought on behalf of the corporation, and the claim was, thus, found to be derivative.

In describing how a court may distinguish direct and derivative actions, the *Bokat* Court stated that a suit must be maintained derivatively if the injury falls equally upon all stockholders. Experience has shown this concept to be confusing and inaccurate. It is confusing because it appears to have been intended to address the fact that an injury to the corporation tends to diminish each share of stock equally because corporate assets or their value are diminished. In that sense, the *indirect* injury to the stockholders arising out of the harm to the corporation comes about solely by virtue of their stockholdings. It does not arise out of any independent or direct harm to the stockholders, individually. That concept is also inaccurate because a direct, individual claim of stockholders that does not depend on harm to the corporation can also fall on all stockholders equally, without the claim thereby becoming a derivative claim.

In *Lipton v. News International, Plc.,*[9] this Court applied the "special injury" test. There, a stockholder began acquiring shares in the defendant corporation presumably to gain control of the corporation. In response, the defendant corporation agreed to an exchange of its shares with a friendly buyer. Due to the exchange and a supermajority voting requirement on certain stockholder actions, the management of the defendant corporation acquired a veto power over any change in management.

The *Lipton* Court concluded that the critical analytical issue in distinguishing direct and derivative actions is whether a "special injury" has been alleged. There, the Court found a "special injury" because the board's manipulation worked an injury upon the plaintiff-stockholder unlike the injury suffered by other stockholders. That was because the plaintiff-stockholder was actively seeking to gain control of the defendant corporation. Therefore, the Court found that the claim was direct. Ironically, the Court could have reached the same correct result by simply concluding that the manipulation directly and individually harmed the stockholders, without injuring the corporation. . . .

In *Grimes v. Donald,*[10] we sought to distinguish between direct and derivative actions in the context of employment agreements granted to certain officers that allegedly caused the board to abdicate its authority. Relying on the [*Elster*] that the court must look to the nature of the wrong and to whom the relief will go, we concluded that the plaintiff was not seeking to recover any damages for injury to the corporation. Rather, the plaintiff was seeking a declaration of the invalidity of the agreements on the ground that the board had abdicated its responsibility to the stockholders. Thus, based on the relief requested, we affirmed the judgment of the Court of Chancery that the plaintiff was entitled to pursue a direct action. . . .

---

9. . . . . 514 A.2d at 1078 [Del. 1988].

10. 673 A.2d 1207, 1213 (Del.1996).

Thus, two confusing propositions have encumbered our caselaw governing the direct/derivative distinction. The "special injury" concept, applied in cases such as *Lipton,* can be confusing in identifying the nature of the action. The same is true of the proposition that stems from *Bokat*—that an action cannot be direct if all stockholders are equally affected or unless the stockholder's injury is separate and distinct from that suffered by other stockholders. The proper analysis has been and should remain that stated in *Grimes*. . . . That is, a court should look to the nature of the wrong and to whom the relief should go. The stockholder's claimed direct injury must be independent of any alleged injury to the corporation. The stockholder must demonstrate that the duty breached was owed to the stockholder and that he or she can prevail without showing an injury to the corporation.

Standard to Be Applied in This Case

In this case it cannot be concluded that the complaint alleges a derivative claim. There is no derivative claim asserting injury to the corporate entity. There is no relief that would go the corporation. Accordingly, there is no basis to hold that the complaint states a derivative claim.

But, it does not necessarily follow that the complaint states a direct, individual claim. While the complaint purports to set forth a direct claim, in reality, it states no claim at all. The trial court analyzed the complaint and correctly concluded that it does not claim that the plaintiffs have any rights that have been injured. Their rights have not yet ripened. The contractual claim is nonexistent until it is ripe, and that claim will not be ripe until the terms of the merger are fulfilled, including the extensions of the closing at issue here. Therefore, there is no direct claim stated in the complaint before us.

Accordingly, the complaint was properly dismissed. But, due to the reliance on the concept of "special injury" by the Court of Chancery, the ground set forth for the dismissal is erroneous, there being no derivative claim. That error is harmless, however, because, in our view, there is no direct claim either.

Conclusion

For purposes of distinguishing between derivative and direct claims, we expressly disapprove both the concept of "special injury" and the concept that a claim is necessarily derivative if it affects all stockholders equally. In our view, the tests going forward should rest on those set forth in this opinion.

We affirm the judgment of the Court of Chancery dismissing the complaint, although on a different ground from that decided by the Court of Chancery. . . .

Because our determination that there is no valid claim whatsoever in the complaint before us was not argued by the defendants and was not the basis of the ruling of the Court of Chancery, the interests of justice will be best served if the dismissal is without prejudice, and plaintiffs have an opportunity to replead if they have a basis for doing so. . . .

NOTE ON THE DISTINCTION BETWEEN DERIVATIVE AND DIRECT ACTIONS

1. *The Impact of a Determination that an Action is Derivative.* What's the difference whether a shareholder's action is properly characterized as derivative or direct? The answer is that, as shown in the balance of this Chapter, a number of special procedural rules apply to—and set hurdles to—derivative actions, but not to direct actions. A shareholder who is concerned whether she can leap these hurdles will therefore prefer that her action is characterized as direct.

2. *Reasons for Distinguishing Between Direct and Derivative Actions.* Two kinds of reasons are commonly advanced for distinguishing between a *derivative* action, which is brought on the corporation's behalf against either corporate fiduciaries or third persons, and a *direct* action, which is brought on a shareholder's own behalf against either corporate fiduciaries or the corporation itself. The first kind of reason is theoretical: Since a corporation is a legal person separate from its shareholders, an injury to the corporation is not an injury to its shareholders. This proposition is somewhat dubious, because every injury to a corporation must also have an impact, however slight, on the shareholders as well. The second kind of reason is pragmatic: "(1) To avoid a multiplicity of suits by each injured shareholder, (2) to protect the corporate creditors, and (3) to protect all the stockholders since a corporate recovery benefits all equally," while a direct action does not. Watson v. Button, 235 F.2d 235 (9th Cir.1956).

3. *Easy Cases.* Some principles concerning the distinction between derivative and direct actions are relatively well-established. At one end of the spectrum, a wrongful act that depletes corporate assets, and affects the shareholder only by reducing the value of his stock, gives rise only to an action on the corporation's behalf. At the other end of the spectrum, a wrongful act that does not deplete corporate assets, and interferes with rights that are traditionally viewed as either incident to the ownership of stock or inhering in the shares themselves (such as voting or pre-emptive rights), gives rise only to a direct action by the injured shareholders.

4. *Harder Cases.* Many kinds of cases fall between the two ends of the spectrum described in the preceding paragraph. In some of these cases, the rules are relatively clear; in others, rules are just beginning to emerge. For example, it is relatively clear that a direct action will lie based on the issuance of stock for the wrongful purpose of perpetuating or shifting control (e.g., Sheppard v. Wilcox, 210 Cal.App.2d 53, 26 Cal.Rptr. 412 (1962)), or to enjoin a threatened ultra vires act (e.g., Alexander v. Atlanta & West Point R.R., 113 Ga. 193, 38 S.E. 772 (1901)). A rule permitting a direct action seems to be emerging in suits based on wrongs by controlling against noncontrol-

ling shareholders. Suits to enjoin improperly authorized corporate actions are also commonly treated as direct actions, either implicitly (that is, without discussion of the issue), or explicitly, but the authorities are in conflict on this type of case.

5. *Actions that can be Characterized as Either Direct or Derivative.* In many cases, a wrongful act both depletes corporate assets *and* interferes with rights traditionally viewed as inhering in shares. The general principle governing such cases is that a direct action is not precluded simply because the same facts could also give rise to a derivative action. For example, in Gentile v. Rossette, 906 A.2d 91 (Del. 2006), the controlling stockholder forgave debt owed to him in exchange for stock that was allegedly greatly in excess of the value of the forgiven debt. As a consequence, the controlling stockholders holdings increased from 61.19 percent to 93.49 percent and concomitantly diluted the value of the minority's shares. The court held the facts presented both a direct and derivative claim, reasoning as to the former that "the public shareholders are harmed uniquely and individually, to the same extent that the controlling shareholder is (correspondingly) benefitted." See also Bennett v. Breuil Petroleum Corp., 34 Del.Ch. 6, 99 A.2d 236 (1953) (where the plaintiff claimed that the controlling shareholders had caused the corporation to issue stock for an improper purpose—impairing his interest and forcing him out on management's terms—and at a grossly inadequate consideration the court held that the first claim stated a direct and the second a derivative cause of action); Buschmann v. Professional Men's Ass'n, 405 F.2d 659 (7th Cir.1969).

Another important kind of case in which suit may be either direct or derivative is one involving proxy-rule violations. Insofar as such a violation interferes with the individual shareholder's voting right, the suit can be regarded as direct; insofar as it involves a breach of management's fiduciary obligations, the suit can be regarded as derivative.

AMERICAN LAW INSTITUTE, PRINCIPLES OF CORPORATE GOVERNANCE § 7.01

[See Statutory Supplement]

Barth v. Barth

Supreme Court of Indiana, 1995.
659 N.E.2d 559.

■ JUDGES: SULLIVAN, JUSTICE, SHEPARD, C.J., and DEBRULER, DICKSON and SELBY, JJ., concur.

■ SULLIVAN, JUSTICE.

Background

This lawsuit was brought against defendants Barth Electric Co., Inc., and its president and majority shareholder Michael G. Barth, Jr.,

by plaintiff minority shareholder Robert Barth individually (rather than derivatively on behalf of the corporation).[3] Plaintiff Robert Barth alleged that defendant Michael Barth had taken certain actions which had the effect of "substantially reducing the value of Plaintiff's shares of common stock" in the corporation. Specifically, plaintiff contended that defendant Michael Barth had: (1) paid excessive salaries to himself and to members of his immediate family; (2) used corporate employees to perform services on his and his son's homes without compensating the corporation; (3) dramatically lowered dividend payments; and (4) appropriated corporate funds for personal investments.... Michael Barth and the corporation moved to dismiss Robert Barth's complaint for the failure to state a claim upon which relief can be granted, ... arguing that a derivative action was required to redress claims of this nature. The trial court granted the motion to dismiss. The Court of Appeals acknowledged that the "well-established general rule" prohibits a shareholder from maintaining an action in the shareholder's own name but found that requiring a derivative action here would "exalt form over substance" since Robert Barth could have satisfied the requirements for bringing a derivative action and that none of the reasons underlying the general derivative action requirement were present. *Barth v. Barth*, 651 N.E.2d at 293
. The Court of
Appeals reversed the trial court; the corporation and Michael Barth seek transfer.

Discussion

As the Court of Appeals made clear, the well-established general rule is that shareholders of a corporation may not maintain actions at law in their own names to redress an injury to the corporation even if the value of their stock is impaired as a result of the injury. *Moll v. South Central Solar Systems, Inc.* (Ind.App.1981), 419 N.E.2d 154, 161.... In *Moll,* Judge Ratliff discussed the purpose of the rule in the following terms:

> The rationale supporting this rule is based on sound public policy considerations. It is recognized that authorization of shareholder actions in such cases would constitute authorization of multitudinous litigation and disregard for the corporate entity.... Sound policy considerations have been said to require that a single action be brought rather than to permit separate suits by each shareholder even when the corporation and the shareholder are the same....

Moll, 419 N.E.2d at 161. In W & W Equipment Co., Inc. v. Mink (1991), Ind.App., 568 N.E.2d 564, Judge Baker set forth additional reasons for this rule: the protection of corporate creditors by putting the proceeds of the recovery back in the corporation; the protection of

3. Michael Barth owns 51% of the shares of the corporation. Robert Barth owns 29.8%. A third individual owns the remaining shares.

the interests of all the shareholders rather than allowing one shareholder to prejudice the interests of other shareholders; and the adequate compensation of the injured shareholder by increasing the value of the shares when recovery is put back into the corporation. *Id.*, 568 N.E.2d at 571. . . .

While we affirm the general rule requiring a shareholder to bring a derivative rather than direct action when seeking redress for injury to the corporation, we nevertheless observe two reasons why this rule will not always apply in the case of closely-held corporations.[5] First, shareholders in a close corporation stand in a fiduciary relationship to each other, and as such, must deal fairly, honestly, and openly with the corporation and with their fellow shareholders. *W & W Equipment Co.*, 568 N.E.2d at 570; *Krukemeier v. Krukemeier Machine and Tool Co., Inc.* (Ind.App.1990), 551 N.E.2d 885; *Garbe v. Excel Mold, Inc.* (Ind.App.1979), 397 N.E.2d 296.[6] Second, shareholder litigation in the closely-held corporation context will often not implicate the policies that mandate requiring derivative litigation when more widely-held corporations are involved. W & W Equipment Co., Inc. v. Mink is a leading case in this regard. There our Court of Appeals was faced with a lawsuit filed by one of two 50% shareholders of a corporation after the other shareholder joined with nonshareholder directors to fire the plaintiff shareholder and arrange for the payment of certain corporate assets to the other shareholder. The court concluded that no useful purpose would be served by forcing the plaintiff to proceed derivatively where the policies favoring derivative actions were not implicated—direct corporate recovery was not necessary to protect absent shareholders or creditors as none existed. *Id.*, 568 N.E.2d at 571.

Because shareholders of closely-held corporations have very direct obligations to one another and because shareholder litigation in the closely-held corporation context will often not implicate the principles which gave rise to the rule requiring derivative litigation, courts in many cases are permitting direct suits by shareholders of closely-held corporations where the complaint is one that in a public corporation would have to be brought as a derivative action. See F. Hodge O'Neal & Robert B. Thompson, O'Neal's Close Corporations § 8.16 n. 32 (3d ed. & 1995 Cum.Supp.) (collecting cases); American Law Institute, Principles of Corporate Governance: Analysis and Recommendations § 7.01, reporter's n. 4 (1994) (collecting cases). However, it is important to keep in mind that the principles which gave rise to the rule requiring derivative actions will sometimes be present even in litigation involving closely-held corporations. For example, because a corporate recovery in a derivative action will benefit creditors while a

---

5. A closely-held corporation is one which typically has relatively few shareholders and whose shares are not generally traded in the securities market. *W & W Equipment Co., Inc. v. Mink* (Ind.App.1991), 568 N.E.2d 564, 570 (citing F. Hodge O'Neal & Robert B. Thompson, O'Neal's Close Corporations § 1.02 (3d ed.)). Accord, American Law Institute, Principles of Corporate Governance: Analysis and Recommendations § 1.06 (1994).

6. This principle of Indiana corporate law mirrors that reached by the Supreme Judicial Court of Massachusetts in.... *Donahue v. Rodd Electrotype Co. of New England, Inc.*, 367 Mass. 578, 328 N.E.2d 505, 515 (Mass.1975)....

direct recovery by a shareholder will not, the protection of creditors principle could well be implicated in a shareholder suit against a closely-held corporation with debt. . . .

In its recently-completed corporate governance project, the American Law Institute proposed the following rule for determining when a shareholder of a closely-held corporation may proceed by direct or derivative action:

> In the case of a closely held corporation, the court in its discretion may treat an action raising derivative claims as a direct action, exempt it from those restrictions and defenses applicable only to derivative actions, and order an individual recovery, if it finds that to do so will not (i) unfairly expose the corporation or the defendants to a multiplicity of actions, (ii) materially prejudice the interests of creditors of the corporation, or (iii) interfere with a fair distribution of the recovery among all interested persons.

A.L.I., Principles of Corporate Governance § 7.01(d). We have studied this rule and find that it is consistent with the approach taken by our Court of Appeals and by most other jurisdictions in similar cases and that it represents a fair and workable approach for balancing the relative interests in closely-held corporation shareholder litigation.

In determining that a trial court has discretion to decide whether a plaintiff must proceed by direct or by derivative action, we make the following observations, drawn largely from the Comment to § 7.01(d). First, permitting such litigation to proceed as a direct action will exempt the plaintiff from the requirements of Ind.Code § 23–1–32–1 et seq., including the provisions that permit a special committee of the board of directors to recommend dismissal of the lawsuit. Ind.Code § 23–1–32–4. As such, the court in making its decision should consider whether the corporation has a disinterested board that should be permitted to consider the lawsuit's impact on the corporation. A.L.I., Corporate Governance Project § 7.01 comment e. Second, in some situations it may actually be to the benefit of the corporation to permit the plaintiff to proceed by direct action. This will permit the defendant to file a counterclaim against the plaintiff, whereas counterclaims are generally prohibited in derivative actions. Also, in a direct action each side will normally be responsible for its own legal expenses; the plaintiff, even if successful, cannot ordinarily look to the corporation for attorney's fees. Id.

Conclusion

We grant transfer, vacate the opinion of the Court of Appeals, and remand this cause to the trial court for reconsideration of its order of dismissal in light of the rule adopted in this opinion.

■ SHEPARD, C.J., and DEBRULER, DICKSON and SELBY, JJ., concur.

Contra. Bagdon v. Bridgestone/Firestone, Inc., 916 F.2d 379 (7th Cir.1990), cert. denied 500 U.S. 952, 111 S.Ct. 2257, 114 L.Ed.2d 710

(1991) (recognizing that Delaware does not relax the individual-derivative distinction in close corporations); Small v. Sussman, 713 N.E.2d 1216 (Ill. Ct. App. 1999) (rejecting the liberalization of standing advocated by the ALI); Outen v. Mical, 454 S.E.2d 883 (N.C. Ct. App. 1995) (absent evidence of controlling stockholder dominance the distinction between individual and derivative actions should be retained).

SECTION 3. INDIVIDUAL RECOVERY IN DERIVATIVE ACTIONS

Glenn v. Hoteltron Systems, Inc.

Court of Appeals of New York, 1989.
74 N.Y.2d 386, 547 N.Y.S.2d 816, 547 N.E.2d 71.

■ WACHTLER, CHIEF JUDGE. . . .

The dispute here is between Jacob Schachter and Herbert Kulik, the founders of Ketek Electric Corporation. Schachter and Kulik each own 50% of the corporation's shares and serve as the corporation's only officers. . . . [T]he Appellate Division, on [a] prior appeal, found Schachter liable for diverting Ketek assets and opportunities to Hoteltron Systems, Inc., a corporation wholly owned by Schachter.

Following the trial on damages, Supreme Court concluded that Hoteltron had earned profits of $362,242.84 from Schachter's usurpation of Ketek assets and opportunities. . . .

On Schachter's appeal, the Appellate Division . . . concluded that the Hoteltron profits should be awarded to the injured corporation, Ketek, rather than the innocent shareholder Kulik. . . .

It is the general rule that, because a shareholders' derivative suit seeks to vindicate a wrong done to the corporation through enforcement of a corporate cause of action, any recovery obtained is for the benefit of the injured corporation. . . .

Kulik argues that this result is inequitable because Schachter, as a shareholder of Ketek, will ultimately share in the proceeds of the damage award. But that prospect exists in any successful derivative action in which the wrongdoer is a shareholder of the injured corporation. An exception based on that fact alone would effectively nullify the general rule that damages for a corporate injury should be awarded to the corporation.

It is true that this anomaly is magnified in cases involving closely held corporations, because the errant fiduciary is likely to own a large share of the corporation—as Schachter owns 50% of Ketek—and will share proportionately in the restitution to the corporation generated by a successful suit against him. Thus, it may be argued that in such circumstances an award of damages to the corporation does not provide a sufficient deterrent to the potential wrongdoer. We conclude, however, that this consideration does not require a different damage rule for close corporations.

While awarding damages directly to the innocent shareholder may seem equitable with respect to the parties before the court, other interests, particularly those of the corporation's creditors, should not be overlooked. The fruits of a diverted corporate opportunity are properly a corporate asset. Awarding that asset directly to a shareholder could impair the rights of creditors whose claims may be superior to that of the innocent shareholder. . . .

Thus, while we do not rule out the possibility that an award to innocent shareholders rather than to the corporation would be appropriate in some circumstances, we find no need to invoke such an exception here.

Accordingly, the order of the Appellate Division should be affirmed, without costs.

■ SIMONS, KAYE, ALEXANDER, TITONE, HANCOCK and BELLACOSA, JJ., concur.

Order affirmed, without costs.

PERLMAN v. FELDMANN

[Chapter 9, supra.]

NOTE ON INDIVIDUAL RECOVERY IN DERIVATIVE ACTIONS

1. *The Basic Principle*. Pro-rata recovery cases involve derivative actions that take a sudden turn at the remedy stage. Normally, in a derivative action the recovery goes to the corporation, in whose name the action is brought. When pro rata recovery is granted, however, the recovery goes directly to the shareholders—more accurately, to certain shareholders. Each shareholder who is entitled to participate in a pro rata recovery gets a share of the recovery equal to her percentage ownership of stock. For example, suppose A owns 20% of Azure Corporation's stock, B owns 20%, and C owns 60%. A brings a derivative action against C on Azure's behalf. The court awards damages of $1 million against C, in favor of Azure. In a normal derivative action, the $1 million would go to Azure. If pro rata recovery is granted to A and B, A will get $200,000 (20% of $1 million), B will get $200,000 (same), C will get nothing, and Azure will got nothing.

Pro rata recovery is a useful tool to achieve justice in a variety of cases that are properly characterized as derivative actions. Although pro rata recovery results in direct payments by the defendants to shareholders, rather than a payment solely to the corporation, pro rata recovery is consistent with characterizing an action as derivative rather than as direct, for two reasons. First, the plaintiff in such an action must satisfy all the relevant requirements for bringing a derivative action. Second, the amount of damages is measured by the injury to the corporation—although once that measurement is made, a portion of the amount is distributed directly to certain shareholders.

2. *Preventing Wrongdoers from Sharing in the Recovery.* It is frequently said that pro rata recovery may be decreed to prevent the wrongdoers from sharing in the recovery. See, e.g., Atkinson v. Marquart, 112 Ariz. 304, 541 P.2d 556 (1975). However, in most derivative actions the defendants own stock in the corporation, and this in itself seldom leads to pro rata recovery. Nor should it, in the typical case. For example, suppose D, the owner of forty percent of Blue Corporation, is found liable in a derivative suit in the amount of $1 million. If corporate recovery is decreed, D must pay Blue $1 million. Since D "shares" in the recovery, his net output is only $600,000 (assuming that he can recover the balance through a dividend or appreciation in the value of his stock). But if pro rata recovery is decreed, D's output will also be $600,000. Indeed, for reasons of liquidity D may very well prefer the pro rata alternative. The fact that D "shares" in a corporate recovery is therefore not sufficient in itself to justify pro rata relief.

3. *Wrongdoers are Still in Control.* Similarly, it is sometimes said that pro rata recovery is appropriate where the wrongdoers are still in control of the corporation, and therefore would control any corporate recovery. See Backus v. Finkelstein, 23 F.2d 357, 366 (D.C.Minn.1927); Note, 69 Harv.L.Rev. 1314, at 1314–16 (1956). However, derivative actions in situations where the wrongdoers still control the corporation are legion, and pro rata recovery will normally not be decreed on this ground alone.

4. *Most of the Shareholders are Subject to Personal Defenses.* The cases suggest that pro rata relief will be decreed where the great bulk of the corporation's shares are held by persons who could not themselves have brought suit because they are subject to a personal defense. For example, in Young v. Columbia Oil Co., 110 W.Va. 364, 158 S.E. 678 (1931), pro rata recovery was decreed where thirteen of sixteen shareholders were barred by laches or acquiescence, and the remaining three shareholders owned only 145 of the corporation's 5000 outstanding shares. In Joyce v. Congdon, 114 Wash. 239, 195 P. 29 (1921), pro rata recovery was decreed where 423 out of the corporation's 429 shares were owned by either the wrongdoers, persons alleged by the plaintiff to be in collusion with the wrongdoers, or persons who had acquired their stock from the wrongdoers. In Chounis v. Laing, 125 W.Va. 275, 23 S.E.2d 628 (1942), more than ninety-five percent of the shareholders had either ratified or participated in the defendant's wrongful actions. The court held that the ratification was not effective as against innocent minority shareholders, but decreed pro rata relief, excluding all those shareholders who had either participated or ratified. See also, e.g., May v. Midwest Refining Co., 121 F.2d 431 (1st Cir.1941), cert. denied 314 U.S. 668, 62 S.Ct. 129, 86 L.Ed. 534, noted, 30 Calif.L.Rev. 338 (1942).

5. *The Injured Corporation has been Merged.* Still another type of case in which pro rata recovery may be decreed is that in which Corporation A, against whom a wrong was committed, is merged into Corporation B, and some or all of B's shareholders are barred from bringing a derivative suit—for example, because they had all participated in the wrong. In Gabhart v. Gabhart, 267 Ind. 370, 370 N.E.2d 345 (1977) the court said that in such cases, "[s]ince no wrong should be without a remedy a Court of Equity may grant relief, pro-rata, to a former shareholder of a merged corporation, whose equity was adversely affected by the fraudulent act of an officer or director and whose means of redress otherwise would be cut off by the merger, if there is no shareholder of the surviving corporation eligible to maintain a derivative action for such wrong and said shareholder had no prior opportunity for redress by derivative action against either the merged or the surviving corporation."

6. *Residual Cases.* Over the long run, perhaps the most important category of pro rata cases is the residual category where such relief is the most effective technique for dealing with the parties' varying equities on a case-by-case basis. Perlman v. Feldmann, supra Chapter 4, Section 5, is one such case. Another is Rankin v. Frebank Co., 47 Cal.App.3d 75, 121 Cal.Rptr. 348 (1975). Frebank Corporation was engaged in the sale, engineering, research, development, and manufacturing of missile parts and components. It had 200 shares outstanding. In late 1953, McCoy became the owner of 100 shares. The other 100 were owned, thirty-three and one-third shares each, by Bankey, Myers, and Rankin, but for some reason these three shareholders determined to give McCoy the impression that their 100 shares were owned only by Bankey. In September 1954, McCoy and Bankey organized Bancoy Corporation for the purpose of carrying out the manufacturing aspects of Frebank's business, and each took fifty percent of Bancoy's stock. Aside from taxes, McCoy gained no financial advantage from organizing Bancoy, because he had the same proportionate interest (50%) in both Frebank and Bancoy. Bankey, however, gained a substantial advantage, since instead of having a one-sixth interest in the manufacturing proceeds of Frebank's business, Bankey obtained a one-half interest in Bancoy, in which Rankin and Myers did not share. Subsequently, Rankin and Myers brought a derivative action against Bankey and McCoy for the profits they received from Bancoy. The court began by holding that although Bankey had violated his fiduciary obligations, McCoy had not, because he had acted in good faith and had received no more than what he would have received if Bancoy not been organized. The court then decreed pro rata relief, excluding McCoy:

> [I]t seems inequitable ... [for the funds] acquired by Bankey from Bancoy to be distributed to all of the shareholders of [Frebank]. If this were done, McCoy would receive one-half of these funds despite the fact that he has no right to receive them because he had retained his [50%] proportion of the dividends and retained earnings received from Bancoy. Instead, an equitable distribution of those funds would require that only Bankey,

> Rankin, and Myers each receive one-third of the dividends and retained earnings received by Bankey from Bancoy. Other courts have been willing to equitably distribute damages in stockholders' derivative actions. (Perlman v. Feldmann (2d Cir.1955) 219 F.2d 173, 178.) There is good reason to do so here. . . .
>
> This case illustrates that shareholders' derivative suits cannot all be pressed into a single mold. . . . A rule which permits a court to equitably distribute damages in a derivative action safeguards the interests of creditors while simultaneously protecting the interests of shareholders. We adopt it as the most effective method of accommodating the relevant interests involved in this case.

Id. at 96, 121 Cal.Rptr. at 361–62.

7. *Who Should Participate in the Recovery*? Assuming that pro rata recovery is decreed in derivative action brought on behalf of a *publicly held corporation* (as in Perlman v. Feldmann), who should be allowed to participate in the recovery—those persons who were shareholders at the time of the wrong; those who were shareholders at the time of the complaint; or those who were shareholders at some later time, such as the time of the decision or the decree? In *Perlman* itself, the recovery was distributed to those persons who were shareholders at the time of the decree. See Perlman v. Feldmann, 160 F.Supp. 310 (D.Conn.1958).

SECTION 4. THE CONTEMPORANEOUS-OWNERSHIP RULE

FEDERAL RULES OF CIVIL PROCEDURE, RULE 23.1

[See Statutory Supplement]

DELAWARE GEN. CORP. LAW § 327

[See Statutory Supplement]

MODEL BUS. CORP. ACT § 7.41

[See Statutory Supplement]

CAL. CORP. CODE § 800(b)(1)

[See Statutory Supplement]

ALI, PRINCIPLES OF CORPORATE GOVERNANCE § 7.02(a)

[See Statutory Supplement]

Bangor Punta Operations, Inc. v. Bangor & Aroostook R.R.

Supreme Court of the United States, 1974.
417 U.S. 703, 94 S.Ct. 2578, 41 L.Ed.2d 418.

■ MR. JUSTICE POWELL delivered the opinion of the Court. . . .

I

[Prior to October 1964, Bangor & Aroostook Corporation ("B & A") held 98.3% of the stock of the Bangor & Aroostook Railroad Company ("BAR"), a Maine corporation. In October 1964, B & A sold its BAR stock to Bangor Punta, a Delaware corporation. Bangor Punta held the stock for five years, and then sold it in October 1969 to Amoskeag Co. for $5 million. Amoskeag later acquired additional shares which gave it ownership of more than 99% (but less than 100%) of BAR.]*

In 1971, BAR . . . filed the present action against Bangor Punta . . . in the United States District Court for the District of Maine. The complaint specified 13 counts of alleged mismanagement, misappropriation, and waste of BAR's corporate assets occurring during the period from 1960 through 1967 when B & A and then Bangor Punta controlled BAR.[1] Damages were sought in the amount of $7,000,000 for violations of both federal and state laws. The federal statutes and regulations alleged to have been violated included § 10 of the Clayton Act, 15 U.S.C.A. § 20; § 10(b) of the Securities Exchange Act of 1934 . . . and Rule 10b–5. . . . The state claims were grounded on § 104 of the Maine Public Utilities Act, Maine Rev.Stat.Ann., Tit. 35, § 104 (1965), and the common law of Maine. . . .

The District Court granted petitioners' motion for summary judgment and dismissed the action. 353 F.Supp. 724 (1972). The court first observed that although the suit purported to be a primary action brought in the name of the corporation, the real party in interest and hence the actual beneficiary of any recovery, was Amoskeag, the present owner of more than 99% of the outstanding stock of BAR. The court then noted that Amoskeag had acquired all of its BAR stock long after the alleged wrongs occurred and that Amoskeag did not contend

---

* In the interests of clarity, the statement of facts eliminates subsidiaries that do not figure in the opinion. (Footnote by ed.)

1. Several of the alleged acts of corporate mismanagement occurred between 1960 and 1964 when B & A . . . was in control of the railroad. Liability for these acts was nevertheless sought to be imposed on Bangor Punta, even though it had no interest in either BAR or B & A during this period. The apparent basis for liability was the 1964 purchase agreement between B & A and Bangor Punta. The complaint in the instant case alleged that under the agreement Bangor Punta, through its subsidiary, assumed "all . . . debts, obligations, contracts and liabilities" of B & A.

that it had not received full value for its purchase price, or that the purchase transaction was tainted by fraud or deceit. Thus, any recovery on Amoskeag's part would constitute a windfall because it had sustained no injury. With this in mind, the court then addressed the claims based on federal law and determined that Amoskeag would have been barred from maintaining a shareholder derivative action because of its failure to satisfy the "contemporaneous ownership" requirement of Fed.Rule Civ.Proc. 23.1(1).[3] Finding that equitable principles prevented the use of the corporate fiction to evade the proscription of Rule 23.1, the court concluded that Amoskeag's efforts to recover under the Securities Exchange Act and the Clayton Act must fail. Turning to the claims based on state law, the court recognized that the applicability of Rule 23.1(1) has been questioned where federal jurisdiction is based on diversity of citizenship.[4] The court found it unnecessary to resolve this issue, however, since its examination of state law indicated that Maine probably followed the "prevailing rule" requiring contemporaneous ownership in order to maintain a shareholder derivative action. Thus, whether the federal rule or state substantive law applied, the present action could not be maintained.

The United States Court of Appeals for the First Circuit reversed....

We granted petitioners' application for certiorari. 414 U.S. 1127 (1974). We now reverse.

II

A

We first turn to the question whether respondent corporations* may maintain the present action under § 10 of the Clayton Act ... and § 10(b) of the Securities Exchange Act of 1934 ... and Rule 10b–5.... The resolution of this issue depends upon the applicability of the settled principle of equity that a shareholder may not complain of acts of corporate mismanagement if he acquired his shares from those who participated or acquiesced in the allegedly wrongful transactions. See, e.g., Bloodworth v. Bloodworth, 225 Ga. 379, 387, 169 S.E.2d 150, 156–157 (1969)....[5] This principle has been invoked with special

3. Rule 23.1(1), which specifies the requirements applicable to shareholder derivative actions, states that the complaint shall aver that "the plaintiff was a shareholder or member at the time of the transaction of which he complains...." This provision is known as the "contemporaneous ownership" requirement. See 3B J. Moore, Federal Practice § 23.1 et seq. (2d ed. 1974).

4. The "contemporaneous ownership" requirement in shareholder derivative actions was first announced in Hawes v. Oakland, 104 U.S. 450, 26 L.Ed. 827 (1881), and soon thereafter adopted as Equity Rule 97. This provision was later incorporated in Equity Rule 27 and finally in the present Rule 23.1. After the decision in Erie R. Co. v. Tompkins, 304 U.S. 64, 58 S.Ct. 817, 82 L.Ed. 1188 (1938), the question arose whether the contemporaneous-ownership requirement was one of procedure or substantive law. If the requirement were substantive, then under the regime of *Erie* it could not be validly applied in federal diversity cases where state law permitted a noncontemporaneous shareholder to maintain a derivative action. See 3B J. Moore, Federal Practice §§ 23.1.01–23.1.15[2] (2d ed. 1974). Although most cases treat the requirement as one of procedure, this Court has never resolved the issue. Ibid.

* The respondents were BAR and a wholly owned subsidiary. (Footnote by ed.)

5. This principle obtains in the great majority of jurisdictions. See, e.g., Russell v. Louis Melind Co., 331 Ill.App. 182, 72 N.E.2d 869 (1947).

force where a shareholder purchases all or substantially all the shares of a corporation from a vendor at a fair price, and then seeks to have the corporation recover against that vendor for prior corporate mismanagement. See, e.g., Matthews v. Headley Chocolate Co., 130 Md. 523, 532–535, 100 A. 645, 650–651 (1917); Home Fire Insurance Co. v. Barber, 67 Neb. 644, 661–662, 93 N.W. 1024, 1030–1031 (1903).... The equitable considerations precluding recovery in such cases were explicated long ago by Dean (then Commissioner) Roscoe Pound in Home Fire Insurance Co. v. Barber, supra. Dean Pound, writing for the Supreme Court of Nebraska, observed that the shareholders of the plaintiff corporation in that case had sustained no injury since they had acquired their shares from the alleged wrongdoers after the disputed transactions occurred and had received full value for their purchase price. Thus, any recovery on their part would constitute a windfall, for it would enable them to obtain funds to which they had no just title or claim. Moreover, it would in effect allow the shareholders to recoup a large part of the price they agreed to pay for their shares, notwithstanding the fact that they received all they had bargained for. Finally, it would permit the shareholders to reap a profit from wrongs done to others, thus encouraging further such speculation. Dean Pound stated that these consequences rendered any recovery highly inequitable and mandated dismissal of the suit.

The considerations supporting the *Home Fire* principle are especially pertinent in the present case. As the District Court pointed out, Amoskeag, the present owner of more than 99% of the BAR shares, would be the principal beneficiary of any recovery obtained by BAR. Amoskeag, however, acquired 98.3% of the outstanding shares of BAR from petitioner Bangor Punta in 1969, well after the alleged wrongs were said to have occurred. Amoskeag does not contend that the purchase transaction was tainted by fraud or deceit, or that it received less than full value for its money. Indeed, it does not assert that it has sustained any injury at all. Nor does it appear that the alleged acts of prior mismanagement have had any continuing effect on the corporations involved or the value of their shares.[6] Nevertheless, by causing the present action to be brought in the name of respondent corporations, Amoskeag seeks to recover indirectly an amount equal to the $5,000,000 it paid for its stock, plus an additional $2,000,000. All this would be in the form of damages for wrongs petitioner Bangor Punta is said to have inflicted, not upon Amoskeag, but upon respondent corporations during the period in which Bangor Punta owned 98.3% of the BAR shares. In other words, Amoskeag seeks to recover for wrongs Bangor Punta did to *itself* as owner of the railroad.[7] At the

6. In *Home Fire,* Dean Pound suggested that equitable principles might not prevent recovery where the effects of the wrongful acts continued and resulted in injury to present shareholders. 67 Neb. 644, 662, 93 N.W. 1024, 1031. In their complaint in the instant case, respondents alleged that "[t]he injury to BAR is a continuing one surviving the aforesaid sale [from petitioner BPO] to Amoskeag." The District Court noted that respondents alleged no facts to support this contention and therefore found any such exception inapplicable. 353 F.Supp. 724, 727 n. 1 (1972). Respondents apparently did not renew this contention on appeal.

7. Similarly, as to the period before October 1964, Amoskeag seeks to recover for wrongs B & A and its shareholders did to *themselves* as owners of the railroad.

same time it reaps this windfall, Amoskeag desires to retain all its BAR stock. Under *Home Fire,* it is evident that Amoskeag would have no standing in equity to maintain the present action.[8]

We are met with the argument, however, that since the present action is brought in the name of respondent corporations, we may not look behind the corporate entity to the true substance of the claims and the actual beneficiaries. The established law is to the contrary. Although a corporation and its shareholders are deemed separate entities for most purposes, the corporate form may be disregarded in the interests of justice where it is used to defeat an overriding public policy. New Colonial Ice Co. v. Helvering, 292 U.S. 435, 442, 54 S.Ct. 788, 78 L.Ed. 1348 (1934); Chicago, M. & St. P.R. Co. v. Minneapolis Civic Assn., 247 U.S. 490, 501, 38 S.Ct. 553, 62 L.Ed. 1229 (1918). In such cases, courts of equity, piercing all fictions and disguises, will deal with the substance of the action and not blindly adhere to the corporate form. Thus, where equity would preclude the shareholders from maintaining an action in their own right, the corporation would also be precluded. Amen v. Black, supra; Capitol Wine & Spirit Corp. v. Pokrass, 277 App.Div. 184, 98 N.Y.S.2d 291 (1950), aff'd, 302 N.Y. 734, 98 N.E.2d 704 (1951); Matthews v. Headley Chocolate Co., supra; Home Fire Insurance Co. v. Barber, supra. It follows that Amoskeag, the principal beneficiary of any recovery and itself estopped from complaining of petitioners' alleged wrongs, cannot avoid the command of equity through the guise of proceeding in the name of respondent corporations which it owns and controls.

B

Respondents fare no better in their efforts to maintain the present actions under state law, specifically § 104 of the Maine Public Utilities Act, Maine Rev.Stat.Ann., Tit. 35, § 104 (1965), and the common law of Maine. In Forbes v. Wells Beach Casino, Inc., 307 A.2d 210, 223 n. 10 (1973), the Maine Supreme Judicial Court recently declared that it had long accepted the equitable principle that a "stockholder has no standing if either he or his vendor participated or acquiesced in the wrong. . . ." See Hyams v. Old Dominion Co., 113 Me. 294, 302, 93 A. 747, 750 (1915).[9] . . .

---

8. Conceding the lack of equity in any recovery by Amoskeag, the dissent argues that the present action can nevertheless be maintained because there are 20 minority shareholders, holding less than 1% of the BAR stock, who owned their shares "during the period from 1960 through 1967 when the transactions underlying the railroad's complaint took place, and who still owned that stock in 1971 when the complaint was filed." . . . The dissent would conclude that the existence of these innocent minority shareholders entitled BAR, and hence Amoskeag, to recover the entire $7,000,000 amount of alleged damages.

Aside from the illogic of such an approach, the dissent's position is at war with the precedents, for the *Home Fire* principle has long been applied to preclude full recovery by a corporation even where there are innocent minority shareholders who acquired their shares prior to the alleged wrongs. See cases cited at n. 5, supra, and accompanying text. The dissent also mistakes the factual posture of this case, since the respondent corporations did not institute this action for the benefit of the minority shareholders. See discussion at n. 15, infra.

9. In addition, the new Maine Business Corporation Act adopts the contemporaneous-ownership requirement for shareholder derivative actions. See Maine Rev.Stat.Ann., Tit. 13–A, § 627.1.A (1974). This provision apparently became effective two days after the present action

III

In reaching the contrary conclusion, the Court of Appeals stated that it could not accept the proposition that Amoskeag would be the "sole beneficiary" of any recovery by BAR. 482 F.2d, at 868. The court noted that in view of the railroad's status as a "quasi-public" corporation and the essential nature of the services it provides, the public had an identifiable interest in BAR's financial health. Thus, any recovery by BAR would accrue to the benefit of the public through the improvement in BAR's economic position and the quality of its services. The court thought that this factor rendered any windfall to Amoskeag irrelevant.

At the outset, we note that the Court of Appeals' assumption that any recovery would necessarily benefit the public is unwarranted. As that court explicitly recognized, any recovery by BAR could be diverted to its shareholders, namely Amoskeag, rather than re-invested in the railroad for the benefit of the public. . . .

The Court of Appeals' position also appears to overlook the fact that Amoskeag, the actual beneficiary of any recovery through its ownership of more than 99% of the BAR shares, would be unjustly enriched since it has sustained no injury. . . .

The Court of Appeals further stated that it was important to insure that petitioners would not be immune from liability for their wrongful conduct and noted that BAR's recovery would provide a needed deterrent to mismanagement of railroads. Our difficulty with this argument is that it proves too much. If deterrence were the only objective, then in logic any plaintiff willing to file a complaint would suffice. No injury or violation of a legal duty to the particular plaintiff would have to be alleged. The only prerequisite would be that the plaintiff agree to accept the recovery, lest the supposed wrongdoer be allowed to escape a reckoning. Suffice it to say that we have been referred to no authority which would support so novel a result, and we decline to adopt it.

We therefore conclude that respondent corporations may not maintain the present action.[15] The judgment of the Court of Appeals is reversed.

---

was filed. As the District Court noted, it is an open question whether Maine in fact had a contemporaneous-ownership requirement prior to that time. 353 F.Supp., at 727. See R. Field, V. McKusick & L. Wroth, Maine Civil Practice § 23.2, p. 393 (2d ed. 1970). In the absence of any indication that Maine would not have followed the "prevailing view," the District Court determined that the contemporaneous-ownership requirement of Fed.Rule Civ.Proc. 23.1 applied.

15. Our decision rests on the conclusion that equitable principles preclude recovery by Amoskeag, the present owner of more than 99% of the BAR shares. The record does not reveal whether the minority shareholders who hold the remaining fraction of 1% of the BAR shares stand in the same position as Amoskeag. Some courts have adopted the concept of a pro-rata recovery where there are innocent minority shareholders. Under this procedure, damages are distributed to the minority shareholders individually on a proportional basis, even though the action is brought in the name of the corporation to enforce primary rights. See, e.g., Matthews v. Headley Chocolate Co., 130 Md. 523, 536–540, 100 A. 645, 650–652 (1917). In the present case, respondents have expressly disavowed any intent to obtain a pro-rata recovery on behalf

■ MR. JUSTICE MARSHALL, with whom MR. JUSTICE DOUGLAS, MR. JUSTICE BRENNAN, and MR. JUSTICE WHITE join, dissenting. . . .

The majority places primary reliance on Dean Pound's decision in Home Fire Insurance Co. v. Barber, supra. In that case, *all* of the shares of the plaintiff corporation had been acquired from the alleged wrongdoers after the transactions giving rise to the causes of action stated in the complaint. Since none of the corporation's shareholders held stock at the time of the alleged wrongful transactions, none had been injured thereby. Dean Pound therefore held that equity barred the corporation from pursuing a claim where none of its shareholders could complain of injury.

Dean Pound thought it clear, however, that the opposite result would obtain if *any* of the present shareholders

> "are entitled to complain of the acts of the defendant and of his past management of the company; for if any of them are so entitled, there can be no doubt of the right and duty of the corporation to maintain this suit. It would be maintainable in such a case even though the wrongdoers continued to be stockholders and would share in the proceeds." 67 Neb., at 655, 93 N.W., at 1028.

Cf. Capitol Wine & Spirit Corp. v. Pokrass, 277 App.Div. 184, 186, 98 N.Y.S.2d 291, 293 (1950), aff'd, 302 N.Y. 734, 98 N.E.2d 704 (1951).

The rationale for the distinction drawn by Dean Pound is simple enough. The sole shareholder who defrauds or mismanages his own corporation hurts only himself. For the corporation to sue him for his wrongs is simply to take money out of his right pocket and put it in his left. It is therefore appropriate for equity to intervene to pierce the corporate veil. But where there are minority shareholders, misappropriation and conversion of corporate assets injure their interests as well as the interest of the majority shareholder. The law imposes upon the directors of a corporation a fiduciary obligation to all of the corporation's shareholders, and part of that obligation is to use due care to ensure that the corporation seek redress where a majority shareholder has drained the corporation's resources for his own benefit and to the detriment of minority shareholders.[1] . . .

---

of the 1% minority shareholders of BAR. We therefore do not reach the question whether such recovery would be appropriate.

The dissent asserts that the alleged acts of corporate mismanagement have placed BAR "close to the brink of bankruptcy" and that the present action is maintained for the benefit of BAR's creditors.... With all respect, it appears that the dissent has sought to redraft respondents' complaint. As the District Court noted, respondents have not brought this action on behalf of any creditors. 353 F.Supp., at 726. Indeed, they have never so contended. Moreover, respondents have conceded that the financial health of the railroad is excellent. Tr. of Oral Arg. 18.

1. Under a separate rule, the plaintiff must be a shareholder at the time the action is brought. See Note on Who Can Bring a Derivative Action, Section 1, supra. The two rules are bridged by a third rule requiring that the plaintiff's ownership between the time of the wrong

Rifkin v. Steele Platt

Colorado Court of Appeals, 1991.
824 P.2d 32.

■ Opinion by JUDGE PLANK. . . .

This matter involves the sale of the controlling shares of the corporation [The Boiler Room], which owns a restaurant. . . . Plaintiffs include the corporation and its present principal shareholders, Robert C. Rifkin, Gerald N. Kernis, and Gary G. Kortz (buyers). Sellers [Mr. Steele Platt and Fas–Wok, Inc.] are the former controlling shareholders.

Buyers and sellers executed a Stock Purchase Agreement to effectuate the sale of the corporation. . . .

The complaint alleged, in part, that Platt, as officer and director of the corporation, had misappropriated funds from it and that certain assets on the balance sheet were actually owned by Platt or other entities that he controlled. . . .

After a trial to the court, judgment was entered in favor of . . . the corporation on the breach of fiduciary duty claim. The court also awarded attorney fees pursuant to the agreement. Sellers do not appeal that part of the judgment concerning the breach of contract claim. . . .

Sellers . . . contend that the trial court erred in awarding the corporation damages for breach of fiduciary duty for conduct which occurred prior to buyers' acquisition of stock. They cite *Bangor Punta Operations, Inc. v. Bangor & Aroostook R. Co.,* 417 U.S. 703, 94 S.Ct. 2578, 41 L.Ed.2d 418 (1974) in support of this argument. We agree that *Bangor Punta* raises issues which must be resolved in this matter.

In *Bangor Punta,* the new shareholders of the corporation, in the name of the corporation, sought damages from the former shareholders for violations of state and federal law which occurred before the sale. The United States Supreme Court held that the corporation could not maintain the action for wrongs that occurred before the new shareholders' acquisition of the shares. The court reasoned that the real parties that would gain from a successful lawsuit would be the new shareholders. It presumed that the purchase price that they paid reflected the prior wrongdoings. Thus, the shareholders would improperly receive a windfall if allowed to recover damages.

Here, it is undisputed that the acts which constituted Platt's breach of fiduciary duty occurred prior to the buyers' acquisition of stock in The Boiler Room. However, the parties dispute whether the purchase price reflected the prior wrongdoings. The trial court did not make a finding on this issue. Therefore, we remand it to the trial court for further findings. *See El Dorado Bancshares v. Martin,* 701 F.Supp. 1515 (D.Kan.1988).

---

and the time of the suit must be uninterrupted. Vista Fund v. Garis, 277 N.W.2d 19 (Minn.1979); Gresov v. Shattuck Denn Mining Corp., 40 Misc.2d 569, 243 N.Y.S.2d 760 (1963).

If on review the court finds that the price, in fact, reflected Platt's wrongdoings, it must dismiss the breach of fiduciary duty claim. If, on the other hand, it finds that the purchase price of the shares did not reflect the wrongdoings, then the corporation's previous damage award may stand....

■ HUME and NEY, JJ., concur.

NOTE ON THE CONTEMPORANEOUS-OWNERSHIP RULE

1. *The Basic Rule and Three Standard Exceptions.* At early common law, the cases were divided on whether a shareholder was barred from bringing a derivative action if he was not a "contemporaneous shareholder"—that is, if he did not hold his shares when the wrong occurred. Today, however, most jurisdictions have adopted some version of the contemporaneous-ownership rule by case-law, statute, or court rule. What justifies this requirement? Consider that the American Law Institute accords standing to a non-contemporaneous holder who became a holder "before the material facts relating to the alleged wrong were publicly disclosed or were known by, or specifically communicated to the holder." A.L.I., 2 Principles of Corporate Governance: Analysis and Recommendations § 7.02(a)(1) (1992).

In forums where the contemporaneous rule exists it is subject to several important exceptions:

(a) Devolution by Operation of Law. A non-contemporaneous shareholder is normally allowed to bring a derivative action if his shares devolved upon him "by operation of law"—for example, by inheritance. (This exception is sometimes made applicable only where the shares have devolved from a person who was a shareholder at the time of the wrong.)

(b) Continuing-Wrong Theory. Under the continuing-wrong theory, a plaintiff can bring an action to challenge a wrong that began before he acquired his shares but continued thereafter. In principle this may not seem to be an exception at all, since the plaintiff is only complaining about what happened after he became a shareholder. In practice, however, it is often difficult to distinguish between a wrongful continuing course of conduct, on the one hand, and the continued effect of a completed wrongful transaction, on the other. Therefore, while the continuing-wrong exception is widely accepted in principle, in practice there is considerable divergence in the way it is applied, and different cases often seem to come out differently on virtually the same facts.

For example, in Forbes v. Wells Beach Casino, Inc., 307 A.2d 210 (Me.1973), the continuing-wrong theory was deemed applicable, and the plaintiff was allowed to bring suit, where the plaintiff had purchased his stock after a fiduciary had wrongfully taken possession of corporate property, but while the fiduciary continued to hold the property. In contrast, in Weinhaus v. Gale, 237 F.2d 197 (7th Cir.

1956), the continuing-wrong theory was deemed inapplicable, and the plaintiff was not allowed to bring suit, where the plaintiff had purchased his stock after a subsidiary had sold stock to its parent at a price alleged to be unfairly low, but before the parent had resold the stock. In Palmer v. Morris, 316 F.2d 649 (5th Cir.1963), the continuing-wrong theory was deemed applicable, and the plaintiff was allowed to bring suit, where the plaintiff had purchased his stock after an allegedly wrongful deal had been made, but while payments under the deal continued. In contrast, in Chaft v. Kass, 19 A.D.2d 610, 241 N.Y.S.2d 284 (1963), the continuing-wrong theory was deemed inapplicable, and the plaintiff was not allowed to bring suit, where the plaintiff purchased his stock after the corporation had entered into an allegedly invalid contract, but while payments under the contract were still being made.

Some statutes provide that the plaintiff must allege that he was a shareholder at the time of the transaction "or any part thereof." *See e.g.*, Cal. § 800(b)(1). Where there is a close question whether the continuing-wrong theory applies to a given case, such a statute might tip the scale in the plaintiff's favor.

(c) Section 16(b). Despite the fact that FRCP 23.1 contains a contemporaneous-ownership rule, it has been held that a non-contemporaneous shareholder can bring a derivative action to recover short-swing profits under § 16(b) of the 1934 Securities Exchange Act. See, e.g., Blau v. Mission Corp., 212 F.2d 77, 79 (2d Cir.1954), cert. denied 347 U.S. 1016, 74 S.Ct. 872, 98 L.Ed. 1138. The theory is that FRCP 23.1 "cannot, even if so perhaps intended, override the direct mandate of § 16(b) that suit may be brought 'by the owner of any security' without qualification." Blau v. Mission Corp., supra.

2. *Federalism*. In footnote 4 of *Bangor Punta,* the Court adverted to the question whether Erie v. Tompkins prohibits application of the contemporaneous-ownership requirement of FRCP 23.1 to a diversity action in cases where the forum state does not impose such a requirement. In Cohen v. Beneficial Industrial Loan Corp., 337 U.S. 541, 556, 69 S.Ct. 1221, 1238, 93 L.Ed. 1528, 1541 (1949), the Supreme Court stated, in dicta, that the contemporaneous-ownership requirements under the Federal Rules was "procedural." The principles that determine whether a legal rule is procedural or substantive have changes since *Cohen* was decided. In Hanna v. Plumer, 380 U.S. 460, 472, 85 S.Ct. 1136, 14 L.Ed.2d 8 (1965), the Court held that when the applicability of a federal rule of civil procedure to a diversity action is involved, the question is not simply whether the rule is "substantive" or "procedural" within the meaning of *Erie,* but whether it is authorized by the Rules Enabling Act.[1] A rule could be authorized by that Act, the Court concluded, even though it might be considered substantive. "[T]he constitutional provision for a federal court system (augmented by the Necessary and Proper Clause) carries with it

---

1. 28 U.S.C.A. § 2072. Under that Act, the Supreme Court is empowered "to prescribe, by general rules . . . the practice and procedure of the district courts. . . . Such rules shall not abridge, enlarge or modify any substantive right. . . ."

congressional power to make rules governing the practice and pleadings in those courts, which in turn includes a power to regulate matters which, though falling within the uncertain area between substance and procedure, are rationally capable of classification as either." In Kona Enterprises, Inc. v. Estate of Bishop, 179 F.3d 767, 769 (9th Cir. 1999), the court held that the federal contemporaneous-ownership rule was applicable in diversity cases.

3. *Special Problems and Special Solutions*. Several cases prior to *Bangor Punta* had applied the principle of the contemporaneous-ownership rule to bar corporate recovery when *all* of the corporation's shareholders had purchased their stock after the wrong had been committed. See, e.g., Capitol Wine & Spirit Corp. v. Pokrass, 277 App.Div. 184, 98 N.Y.S.2d 291 (1950), aff'd per curiam 302 N.Y. 734, 98 N.E.2d 704 (1951). Suppose a large proportion of a corporation's stock is held by non-contemporaneous shareholders, but more than a minimal amount of stock is held by contemporaneous shareholders? It has been suggested that in such cases the court might impose liability but limit damages by granting pro rata relief to the contemporaneous shareholders.

For example, suppose A and B each own 50% of Blue Corporation. Among Blue's assets is a property, Appleacre, that is carried on the books at $1 million but is really worth $2 million. A, as Blue's active manager, knows Appleacre's real value; B, as a passive investor, does not. A causes Blue to sell Appleacre to him for $1 million. A then sells his Blue stock to C for a fair price based on Blue's assets at the time of sale. Subsequently, B and C learn the real value of Appleacre, and cause Blue Corporation to bring an action against A based on unfair self-dealing. Here a corporate recovery of $1 million by Blue Corporation seems inappropriate. C, the owner of Blue, has no injury, because he paid fair value for Blue stock, based on the value of Blue's assets at the time he purchased the stock. Therefore, a $1 million recovery for Blue would give C a windfall of $500,000. The real loser is B, whose Blue stock is worth $500,000 less than it was before A bought Appleacre. If A had given B $500,000 at the time he purchased Appleacre for $1 Million, B would have suffered no injury. Accordingly, one way to adjust the equities of the parties is to allow *suit* by (or in the right of) Blue, but limit *relief* to pro rata recovery by B in the amount of $500,000.

This technique, however, will not work in all cases. For example, suppose that after the Appleacre transaction, A and B *both* sell their stock to C for a fair price based on the value of Blue's assets at the time of the sale of stock. Here either a corporate recovery or a pro rata recovery by Blue's present shareholder, C, would give C a windfall gain of $1 million. Suit by Blue (or in its name) with pro rata recovery by B also will not work: C has no economic incentive to cause Blue to bring such a suit, and B cannot bring suit on Blue's behalf because he is no longer a Blue shareholder. (See Note on Who Can Bring a Derivative Action, Section 1, supra.) In Watson v. Button, 235 F.2d 235 (9th Cir.1956), the court held, on comparable facts, that B could sue A *directly.* "Suits against directors for violations of fiduciary duties are equitable in nature. It is unlikely that the Oregon courts would allow a director to misappropriate funds and leave those injured without a remedy."

SECTION 5. RIGHT TO TRIAL BY JURY IN DERIVATIVE ACTIONS

Since a derivative action has traditionally been conceived as an equitable remedy, until recently it did not carry the right to a trial by jury. In 1970, however, the Supreme Court held in Ross v. Bernhard, 396 U.S. 531, 90 S.Ct. 733, 24 L.Ed.2d 729 that under the Seventh Amendment to the federal Constitution, in a derivative action brought in federal court the parties have a right to a jury where the action would be triable to a jury if it had been brought by the corporation itself, rather than by a shareholder:

> We have noted that the derivative suit has dual aspects: first, the stockholder's right to sue on behalf of the corporation, historically an equitable matter; second, the claim of the corporation against directors or third parties on which, if the corporation had sued and the claim presented legal issues, the company could demand a jury trial.... [L]egal claims are not magically converted into equitable issues by their presentation to a court of equity in a derivative suit. The claim pressed by the stockholder against directors or third parties "is not his own but the corporation's." ... The heart of the action is the corporate claim. If it presents a legal issue, one entitling the corporation to a jury trial under the Seventh Amendment, the right to a jury is not forfeited merely because the stockholder's right to sue must first be adjudicated as an equitable issue triable to the court.[1]

The question remains, what kinds of derivative actions are legal, and what kinds are equitable, within the meaning of *Ross?* Two passages in that opinion are suggestive. First:

> [T]he "legal" nature of an issue is determined by considering, first, the pre-merger custom with reference to such questions; second, the remedy sought; and, third, the practical abilities and limitations of juries. Of these factors, the first, requiring extensive and possibly abstruse historical inquiry, is obviously the most difficult to apply....

Id. at 538 n. 10, 90 S.Ct. at 738 n. 10. And second:

> In the instant case we have no doubt that the corporation's claim is, at least in part, a legal one. The relief sought is money damages. There are allegations in the complaint of a breach of fiduciary duty, but there are also allegations of ordinary breach of

---

1. Id. at 538–39, 90 S.Ct. at 738. It is reported that after Ross v. Bernhard was decided, several cases were settled in which the defendants would have gone to trial had the case been triable to the judge. Rosenfeld, Plaintiff's Strategy in Prosecuting and Defending Stockholders Suits 241, 250 (S. Wechsler ed. 1972).

> contract and gross negligence. The corporation, had it sued on its own behalf, would have been entitled to a jury's determination, at a minimum, of its damages against its broker under the brokerage contract and of its rights against its own directors because of their negligence. Under these circumstances it is unnecessary to decide whether the corporation's other claims are also properly triable to a jury. Dairy Queen, Inc. v. Wood, 369 U.S. 469, 82 S.Ct. 894, 8 L.Ed.2d 44 (1962)....

Id. at 542–43, 90 S.Ct. at 740. (The citation to *Dairy Queen* apparently refers to the holding in that decision that legal claims must be submitted to a jury even where a case also involves equitable claims.) For further treatment of this issue, see Dasho v. Susquehanna Corp., 461 F.2d 11 (7th Cir.1972), cert. denied 408 U.S. 925, 92 S.Ct. 2496, 33 L.Ed.2d 336.

The Seventh Amendment applies only to federal proceedings. State-court decisions vary. Professor DeMott comments, "Ten states have directly resolved this issue. Cases in four states—Alabama, Alaska, New Mexico, and New York—hold that parties to a derivative action have a right to trial by jury if the underlying corporate claim asserted by the plaintiff on the corporation's behalf would have entitled the corporation to a jury trial, that is, if the corporation had itself brought an action to enforce the claim. The dispositive Wyoming case examines the substantive issues raised by the complaint, along with the relief demanded, to determine whether the suit is primarily equitable in nature and thus not susceptible to a jury trial. In Arkansas, California, Florida, Iowa, and Massachusetts, the form of the action is dispositive: even when the substantive claim involves a legal rather than an equitable claim, the equitable nature of a derivative suit excludes any right to a jury trial.... The authority on this question is less direct in other states. In Delaware, language in one opinion could be understood to imply that a right to a jury trial is not available in derivative actions. In five other states, there are cases in which the circumstances arguably provide a basis for inferring that a right to jury trial does exist." Deborah DeMott, Shareholder Derivative Actions § 4:18 (2003).

SECTION 6. THE DEMAND REQUIREMENT

CAL. CORP. CODE § 800(b)(2)

[See Statutory Supplement]

FEDERAL RULES OF CIVIL PROCEDURE RULE 23.1

[See Statutory Supplement]

INTRODUCTORY NOTE

Until about the 1970s, it was well settled that before bringing a derivative action, a shareholder was required to make a demand on the board, unless demand was excused. However, two related issues were much less settled. The first issue was, when was demand on the board excused? The general rule was that demand was excused if it was futile. The most important application of this rule was that demand was excused as futile if a majority of the directors were interested. It was not clear, however, what constituted *interest* for these matters. For example, it was not clear whether a director was interested merely because he or she was named as a defendant, and if not, how much more had to be shown.

The second unsettled issue was the consequence of *not* making demand. In most of the reported cases, demand had not been made, and the corporation moved to dismiss the action on the ground that demand was required. The courts in such cases often simply held that demand was or was not required, without getting into what consequences would follow if a required demand was made and rejected—although some courts did say or hold that if demand was required and rejected, and the rejection was by disinterested directors who constituted a majority of the board, a derivative action could not proceed unless in rejecting demand the board violated the business judgment rule.

The picture was further complicated in the 1970s, when a series of cases held that even when a majority of directors were interested, so that demand was not required, the board could appoint a committee to consider whether the derivative action was in the best interests of the corporation. If the committee concluded that the action was not in the corporation's best interests, and the committee had engaged in an adequate investigation, the court could dismiss the action on the committee's motion, subject to a designated standard of review. If the board was disinterested, the board itself could conduct the investigation and make the motion.

In short, as of the 1970s a cluster of related issues were raised concerning the role and power of the board in derivative actions. When was demand on the board excused? What were the consequences if demand was required, made, and denied? What, if anything, could a board do if demand was excused?

It was against this background that the cases in this Section were decided and continued to guide the courts and litigants.

Marx v. Akers

New York Court of Appeals, 1996.
88 N.Y.2d 189, 644 N.Y.S.2d 121, 666 N.E.2d 1034.

■ JUDGES: Opinion by JUDGE SMITH. CHIEF JUDGE KAYE and JUDGES SIMONS, TITONE, LEVINE and CIPARICK concur. JUDGE BELLACOSA took no part.

■ SMITH, J.:

Plaintiff commenced this shareholder derivative action against International Business Machines Corporation (IBM) and IBM's board of directors without first demanding that the board initiate a lawsuit. The amended complaint (complaint) alleges that the board wasted corporate assets by awarding excessive compensation to IBM's executives and outside directors. The issues raised on this appeal are whether the Appellate Division abused its discretion by dismissing plaintiff's complaint for failure to make a demand and whether plaintiff's complaint fails to state a cause of action. We affirm the order of the Appellate Division because we conclude that plaintiff was not excused from making a demand with respect to the executive compensation claim and that plaintiff has failed to state a cause of action for corporate waste in connection with the allegations concerning payments to IBM's outside directors.

Facts and Procedural History

The complaint alleges that during a period of declining profitability at IBM the director defendants engaged in self-dealing by awarding excessive compensation to the 15 outside directors on the 18–member board. Although the complaint identifies only one of the three inside directors as an IBM executive (defendant Akers is identified as a former chief executive officer of IBM), plaintiff also appears to allege that the director defendants violated their fiduciary duties to IBM by voting for unreasonably high compensation for IBM executives.[2]

Defendants moved to dismiss the complaint for (1) failure to state a cause of action, and (2) failure to serve a demand on IBM's board to initiate a lawsuit based on the complaint's allegations. The Supreme Court dismissed, holding that plaintiff failed to establish the futility of a demand. Supreme Court concluded that excusing a demand here would render Business Corporation Law § 626(c) "virtually meaningless in any shareholders' derivative action in which all members of a corporate board are named as defendants." Having decided the demand issue in favor of defendants, the court did not reach the issue of whether plaintiff's complaint stated a cause of action. The Appellate Division affirmed the dismissal, concluding that the complaint did not contain any details from which the futility of a demand could be inferred. The Appellate Division found that plaintiff's objections to the level of compensation were not stated with sufficient particularity in light of statutory authority permitting directors to set their own compensation.

Background

A shareholder's derivative action is an action "brought in the right of a domestic or foreign corporation to procure a judgment in its

2. Executives at IBM are compensated through a fixed salary and performance incentives. Payouts on the performance incentives are based on IBM's earnings per share, return on equity and cash flow. Plaintiff's complaint criticizes only the performance incentive component of executive compensation as excessive because of certain accounting practices which plaintiff alleges artificially inflate earnings, return on equity and cash flow.

favor, by a holder of shares or of voting trust certificates of the corporation or of a beneficial interest in such shares or certificates" (Business Corporation Law § 626[a]). "Derivative claims against corporate directors belong to the corporation itself" (Auerbach v. Bennett, 47 N.Y. 2d 619, 631).

> "The remedy sought is for wrong done to the corporation; the primary cause of action belongs to the corporation; recovery must enure to the benefit of the corporation. The stockholder brings the action, in behalf of others similarly situated, to vindicate the corporate rights and a judgment on the merits is a binding adjudication of these rights (citations omitted)" (Isaac v. Marcus, 258 N.Y. 257, 264).

. . . Business Corporation Law § 626(c) provides that in any shareholders' derivative action, "the complaint shall set forth with particularity the efforts of the plaintiff to secure the initiation of such action by the board or the reasons for not making such effort." Enacted in 1961 (L 1961, ch 855), section 626(c) codified a rule of equity developed in early shareholder derivative actions requiring plaintiffs to demand that the corporation initiate an action, unless such demand was futile, before commencing an action on the corporation's behalf (Barr v. Wackman, 36 N.Y. 2d 371, 377). The purposes of the demand requirement are to (1) relieve courts from deciding matters of internal corporate governance by providing corporate directors with opportunities to correct alleged abuses, (2) provide corporate boards with reasonable protection from harassment by litigation on matters clearly within the discretion of directors, and (3) discourage "strike suits" commenced by shareholders for personal gain rather than for the benefit of the corporation (Barr, 36 NY2d at 378). "The demand is generally designed to weed out unnecessary or illegitimate shareholder derivative suits" (id.).

By their very nature, shareholder derivative actions infringe upon the managerial discretion of corporate boards. "As with other questions of corporate policy and management, the decision whether and to what extent to explore and prosecute such [derivative] claims lies within the judgment and control of the corporation's board of directors" (Auerbach, supra, 47 NY2d at 631). Consequently, we have historically been reluctant to permit shareholder derivative suits, noting that the power of courts to direct the management of a corporation's affairs should be "exercised with restraint" (Gordon v. Elliman, 306 N.Y. 456, 462).

In permitting a shareholder derivative action to proceed because a demand on the corporation's directors would be futile,

> "the object is for the court to chart the course for the corporation which the directors should have selected, and which it is presumed that they would have chosen if they had not been actuated by fraud or bad faith. Due to their misconduct, the court substitutes its judgment ad hoc for that of the directors in the conduct of its business" (id. at 462).

Achieving a balance between preserving the discretion of directors to manage a corporation without undue interference, through the demand requirement, and permitting shareholders to bring claims on behalf of the corporation when it is evident that directors will wrongfully refuse to bring such claims, through the demand futility exception, has been accomplished by various jurisdictions in different ways. One widely cited approach to demand futility which attempts to balance these competing concerns has been developed by Delaware courts and applies a two-pronged test to each case to determine whether a failure to serve a demand is justified. At the other end of the spectrum is a universal demand requirement which would abandon particularized determinations in favor of requiring a demand in every case before a shareholder derivative suit may be filed.

The Delaware Approach

Delaware's demand requirement, codified in Delaware Chancery Court Rule 23.1, provides, in relevant part,

> "In a derivative action brought by 1 or more shareholders or members to enforce a right of a corporation * * * [the complaint shall allege] with particularity the efforts, if any, made by the plaintiff to obtain the action the plaintiff desires from the directors or comparable authority and the reasons for the plaintiff's failure to obtain the action or for not making the effort."

Interpreting Rule 23.1, the Delaware Supreme Court in Aronson v. Lewis (473 A.2d 805) developed a two-prong test for determining the futility of a demand. Plaintiffs must allege particularized facts which create a reasonable doubt that,

> "(1) the directors are disinterested and independent and (2) the challenged transaction was otherwise the product of a valid exercise of business judgment. Hence, the Court of Chancery must make two inquiries, one into the independence and disinterestedness of the directors and the other into the substantive nature of the challenged transaction and the board's approval thereof" (473 A2d at 814).

The two branches of the *Aronson* test are disjunctive (see, Levine v. Smith, 591 A.2d 194, 205). Once director interest has been established, the business judgment rule becomes inapplicable and the demand excused without further inquiry (*Aronson,* 473 A2d at 814). Similarly, a director whose independence is compromised by undue influence exerted by an interested party cannot properly exercise business judgment and the loss of independence also justifies the excusal of a demand without further inquiry (see, Levine, supra, 591 A2d at 205–206). Whether a board has validly exercised its business judgment must be evaluated by determining whether the directors exercised procedural (informed decision) and substantive (terms of the transaction) due care (Grobow v. Perot, 539 A.2d 180, 189).

The reasonable doubt threshold of Delaware's two-fold approach to demand futility has been criticized. The use of a standard of proof which is the heart of a jury's determination in a criminal case has raised questions concerning its applicability in the corporate context (see, Starrels v. First Natl. Bank, 870 F.2d 1168, 1175 (7th Cir.)) [Easterbrook, J, concurring]. The reasonable doubt standard has also been criticized as overly subjective, thereby permitting a wide variance in the application of Delaware law to similar facts (2 American Law Institute, Principles of Corporate Governance: Analysis and Recommendations § 7.03, Comment d at 57 [1992]).

Universal Demand

A universal demand requirement would dispense with the necessity of making case-specific determinations and impose an easily applied bright line rule. The Business Law Section of the American Bar Association has proposed requiring a demand in all cases, without exception, and permits the commencement of a derivative proceeding within 90 days of the demand unless the demand is rejected earlier (Model Business Corporation Act § 7.42[1] [1995 Supplement]). However, plaintiffs may file suit before the expiration of 90 days, even if their demand has not been rejected, if the corporation would suffer irreparable injury as a result (Model Business Corporation Act § 7.42[2]).

The American Law Institute (ALI) has also proposed a "universal" demand. Section 7.03 of ALI's Principles of Corporate Governance would require shareholder derivative action plaintiffs to serve a written demand on the corporation unless a demand is excused because "the plaintiff makes a specific showing that irreparable injury to the corporation would otherwise result" (2 American Law Institute, Principles of Corporate Governance: Analysis and Recommendations, § 7.03[b] at 53–54, [1992]). Once a demand has been made and rejected, however, the ALI would subject the board's decision to "an elaborate set of standards that calibrates the deference afforded the decision of the directors to the character of the claim being asserted" (Kamen v. Kemper Financial Services, Inc., 500 U.S. 90, 104).

At least 11 states have adopted, by statute, the universal demand requirement proposed in the Model Business Corporation Act. Georgia, Michigan, Wisconsin, Montana, Virginia, New Hampshire, Mississippi, Connecticut, Nebraska and North Carolina require shareholders to wait 90 days after serving a demand before filing a derivative suit unless the demand is rejected before the expiration of the 90 days, or irreparable injury to the corporation would result. . . . Arizona additionally permits shareholders to file suit before the expiration of 90 days if the statute of limitations would expire during the 90 day period. . . . Florida also appears to have adopted a universal demand requirement, although the statutory language does not track the Model Business Corporation Act. Florida's statute provides, "A complaint in a proceeding brought in the right of a corporation must be verified and allege with particularity the demand made to obtain action by the board of directors and that the demand was refused or ignored (emphasis added)". . . .

New York State has also considered and continues to consider implementing a universal demand requirement. However, even though bills to adopt a universal demand have been presented over three legislative sessions, the Legislature has yet to enact a universal demand requirement....

New York's Approach to Demand Futility

Although instructive, neither the universal demand requirement nor the Delaware approach to demand futility is adopted here. Since New York's demand requirement is codified in Business Corporation Law § 626(c), a universal demand can only be adopted by the Legislature. Delaware's approach, which resembles New York law in some respects, incorporates a "reasonable doubt" standard which, as we have already pointed out, has provoked criticism as confusing and overly subjective. An analysis of the *Barr* decision compels the conclusion that in New York, a demand would be futile if a complaint alleges with particularity that (1) a majority of the directors are interested in the transaction, or (2) the directors failed to inform themselves to a degree reasonably necessary about the transaction, or (3) the directors failed to exercise their business judgment in approving the transaction.

In Barr v. Wackman (36 N.Y. 2d 371, supra), we considered whether the plaintiff was excused from making a demand where the board of Talcott National Corporation (Talcott), consisting of 13 outside directors, a director affiliated with a related company and four interested inside directors, rejected a merger proposal involving Gulf & Western Industries (Gulf & Western) in favor of another proposal on allegedly less favorable terms for Talcott and its shareholders. The merger proposal, memorialized in a board-approved "agreement in principle," proposed exchanging one share of Talcott common stock for approximately $24.00 consisting of $17.00 in cash and 0.6 of a warrant to purchase Gulf & Western stock, worth approximately $7.00. This proposal was abandoned in favor of a cash tender offer for Talcott shares by Associated First Capital Corporation (a Gulf & Western subsidiary) at $20.00 per share—four dollars less than proposed for the merger.

The plaintiff in *Barr* alleged that Talcott's board discarded the merger proposal after the four "controlling" inside directors received pecuniary and personal benefits from Gulf & Western in exchange for ceding control of Talcott on terms less favorable to Talcott's shareholders. As alleged in the complaint, these benefits included new and favorable employment contracts for nine Talcott officers, including five-year employment contracts for three of the controlling directors. In addition to his annual salary of $125,000 with Talcott, defendant Silverman (a controlling director) would allegedly receive $60,000 a year under a five year employment contract with Associated First Capital, and an aggregate of $275,000 for the next five years in an arrangement with Associated First Capital to serve as a consultant. This additional compensation would be awarded to Silverman after control of Talcott passed to Associated First Capital and Gulf & Western.

Plaintiff also alleged that Gulf & Western and Associated First Capital paid an excessive "finder's fee" of $340,000 to a company where Silverman's son was an executive vice president. In addition to alleging that the controlling defendants obtained personal benefits, the complaint also alleged that Talcott's board agreed to sell a Talcott subsidiary at a net loss of $6,100,000 solely to accommodate Gulf & Western.

In *Barr,* we held that insofar as the complaint attacked the controlling directors' acts in causing the corporation to enter into a transaction for their own financial benefit, demand was excused because of the self-dealing, or self-interest of those directors in the challenged transaction. Specifically, we pointed to the allegation that the controlling directors "breached their fiduciary obligations to Talcott in return for personal benefits" (id., at 376).

We also held in *Barr,* however, that as to the disinterested outside directors, demand could be excused even in the absence of their receiving any financial benefit from the transaction. That was because the complaint alleged that, by approving the terms of the less advantageous offer, those directors were guilty of a "breach of their duties of due care and diligence to the corporation" (id., at 380). Their performance of the duty of care would have "put them on notice of the claimed self-dealing of the affiliated directors" (id.). The complaint charged that the outside directors failed "to do more than passively rubber stamp the decisions of the active managers" (id., at 381) resulting in corporate detriment. These allegations, the *Barr* Court concluded, also excused demand as to the charges against the disinterested directors.

Barr also makes clear that "it is not sufficient * * * merely to name a majority of the directors as parties defendant with the conclusory allegation of wrongdoing or control by wrongdoers" (id., at 379) to justify failure to make a demand. Thus, *Barr* reflects the statutory requirement that the complaint "must set forth with particularity the * * * reasons for not making such effort" (Business Corporation Law § 626[c]).

Unfortunately, various courts have overlooked the explicit warning that conclusory allegations of wrongdoing against each member of the board are not sufficient to excuse demand and have misinterpreted *Barr* as excusing demand whenever a majority of the board members who approved the transaction are named as defendants (see, Miller v. Schreyer, 200 A.D. 2d 492; Curreri v. Verni, 156 A.D. 2d 420; MacKay v. Pierce, 86 A.D. 2d 655; Joseph v. Amrep Corp., 59 A.D. 2d 841; see also, Allison Publications Incorporated v. Mutual Benefit Life Insurance, 197 A.D. 2d 463). As stated most recently, "the rule is clear in this State that no demand is necessary 'if the complaint alleges acts for which a majority of the directors may be liable and plaintiff reasonably concluded that the board would not be responsive to a demand' " (Miller v. Schreyer, supra, at 494 [quoting from *Barr,* supra, 36 N.Y.2d at 371]; but see, Lewis v. Welch, 126 A.D. 2d 519, 521). The problem with such an approach is that it permits plaintiffs to frame their complaint in such a way as to automatically excuse demand, thereby allowing the exception to swallow the rule.

We thus deem it necessary to offer the following elaboration of *Barr's* demand/futility standard. (1) Demand is excused because of futility when a complaint alleges with particularity that a majority of the board of directors is interested in the challenged transaction. Director interest may either be self-interest in the transaction at issue (see, Barr v. Wackman, supra, at 376 [receipt of "personal benefits"]), or a loss of independence because a director with no direct interest in a transaction is "controlled" by a self-interested director. (2) Demand is excused because of futility when a complaint alleges with particularity that the board of directors did not fully inform themselves about the challenged transaction to the extent reasonably appropriate under the circumstances (see, *Barr,* supra, at 380, 368 N.Y.S.2d 497, 329 N.E.2d 180). The "long-standing rule" is that a director "does not exempt himself from liability by failing to do more than passively rubber-stamp the decisions of the active managers" (id., at 381). (3) Demand is excused because of futility when a complaint alleges with particularity that the challenged transaction was so egregious on its face that it could not have been the product of sound business judgment of the directors.

The Current Appeal

Plaintiff argues that the demand requirement was excused both because the outside directors awarded themselves generous compensation packages and because of the acquiescence of the disinterested directors in the executive compensation schemes. The complaint states:

> "Plaintiff has made no demand upon the directors of IBM to institute this lawsuit because such demand would be futile. As set forth above, each of the directors authorized, approved, participated and/or acquiesced in the acts and transactions complained of herein and are liable therefor. Further, each of the Non–Employee [outside] Directors has received and retained the benefit of his excessive compensation and each of the other directors has received and retained the benefit of the incentive compensation described above. The defendants cannot be expected to vote to prosecute an action against themselves. Demand upon the company to bring action (sic) to redress the wrongs herein is therefore unnecessary."

Defendants argue that neither the Supreme Court nor the Appellate Division abused its discretion in holding that plaintiff's complaint did not set forth the futility of a demand with particularity.

As in *Barr,* we look to the complaint here to determine whether the allegations are sufficient and establish with particularity that demand would have been futile. Here, the plaintiff alleges that the compensation awarded to IBM's outside directors and certain IBM executives was excessive.

Defendant's motion to dismiss for failure to make a demand as to the allegations concerning the compensation paid to IBM's executive officers was properly granted. A board is not interested "in voting compensation for one of its members as an executive or in some other nondirectorial capacity, such as a consultant to the corporation," although "so-called 'back-scratching' arrangements, pursuant to which all directors vote to approve each other's compensation as officers or employees, do not constitute disinterested directors' action" (1 ALI, supra, at 250). Since only three directors are alleged to have received the benefit of the executive compensation scheme, plaintiff has failed to allege that a majority of the board was interested in setting executive compensation. Nor do the allegations that the board used faulty accounting procedures to calculate executive compensation levels move beyond "conclusory allegations of wrongdoing" (Barr v. Wackman, supra, at 379) which are insufficient to excuse demand. The complaint does not allege particular facts in contending that the board failed to deliberate or exercise its business judgment in setting those levels. Consequently, the failure to make a demand regarding the fixing of executive compensation was fatal to [the] portion of the complaint challenging that transaction.

However, a review of the complaint indicates that plaintiff also alleged that a majority of the board was self-interested in setting the compensation of outside directors because the outside directors comprised a majority of the board.

Directors are self-interested in a challenged transaction where they will receive a direct financial benefit from the transaction which is different from the benefit to shareholders generally (see, Rales v. Blasband, 634 A.2d 927, 936 [Del Sup Ct]; Bergstein v. Texas Intern. Co., 453 A.2d 467, 472–473 [Del Ch]; ALI, Principles of Corporate Governance § 1.23, at 25; 13 Fletcher, Cyclopedia Corporations § 5965, at 138). A director who votes him or herself a raise in directors' compensation is always "interested" because that person will receive a personal financial benefit from the transaction not shared in by stockholders (see, 1 ALI Principles of Corporate Governance § 5.03, comment g, at 250 ["if the board votes directorial compensation for itself, the board is interested"]; see also, Steiner v. Meyerson, [1995 Transfer Binder], Fed. Sec. L. Rep. P 98857 [Del Ch], 1995 WL 441999, at 12 ["As the outside directors comprise a majority of the Telxon board and are personally interested in their compensation levels, demand upon them to challenge or decrease their own compensation is excused"]). Consequently, a demand was excused as to plaintiff's allegations that the compensation set for outside directors was excessive.

Corporate Waste

Our conclusion that demand should have been excused as to the part of the complaint challenging the fixing of directors' compensation does not end our inquiry, however. We must also determine whether plaintiff has stated a cause of action regarding that transaction, i.e., some wrong to the corporation. We conclude that plaintiff has not, and thus dismiss the complaint in its entirety.

Historically, directors did not receive any compensation for their work as directors (see, Fletcher, Cyclopedia Corporations, § 2109). Thus, a bare allegation that corporate directors voted themselves excessive compensation was sufficient to state a cause of action (e.g., Walsh v. Van Ameringen–Haebler, Inc., 257 N.Y. 478, 480; Jacobson v. Brooklyn Lumber Co., 184 N.Y. 152, 162). Many jurisdictions, including New York, have since changed the common law rule by statute providing that a corporation's board of directors has the authority to fix director compensation unless the corporation's charter or bylaws provides otherwise. Thus, the allegation that directors have voted themselves compensation is clearly no longer an allegation which gives rise to a cause of action, as the directors are statutorily entitled to set those levels. Nor does a conclusory allegation that the compensation directors have set for themselves is excessive give rise to a cause of action.

> The courts will not undertake to review the fairness of the official salaries, at the suit of a shareholder attacking them as excessive, unless wrongdoing and oppression or possible abuse of a fiduciary position are shown. However, the courts will take a hand in the matter at the instance of the corporation or of shareholders in extreme cases. A case of fraud is presented where directors increase their collective salaries so as to use up nearly the entire earnings of a company; where directors or officers appropriate the income so as to deprive shareholders of reasonable dividends, or perhaps so reduce to assets as to threaten the corporation with insolvency * * * (Fletcher, Cyclopedia Corporations, § 2122, at 46–47).

Thus, a complaint challenging the excessiveness of director compensation must—to survive a dismissal motion—allege compensation rates excessive on their face or other facts which call into question whether the compensation was fair to the corporation when approved, the good faith of the directors setting those rates, or that the decision to set the compensation could not have been a product of valid business judgment.[3]

Applying the foregoing principles to plaintiff's complaint, it is clear that it must be dismissed. The complaint alleges that the directors increased their compensation rates from a base of $20,000 plus $500 for each meeting attended to a retainer of $55,000 plus 100 shares of IBM stock over a five-year period. The complaint also alleges that "this compensation bears little relation to the part-time services

---

3. There is general agreement that the allocation of the burden of proof differs depending on whether the compensation was approved by disinterested directors or shareholders, or by interested directors. Plaintiffs must prove wrongdoing or waste as to compensation arrangements regarding disinterested directors or shareholders, but directors who approve their own compensation bear the burden of proving that the transaction was fair to the corporation (see, Block, et al, The Business Judgment Rule, at 149 [4th ed.]; Fletcher, supra, § 514.1, 632; ALI, supra, § 5.03). However, at the pleading stage we are not concerned with burdens of proof.

rendered by the Non–Employee Directors or to the profitability of IBM. The board's responsibilities have not increased, its performance, measured by the company's earnings and stock price, has been poor yet its compensation has increased far in excess of the cost of living."

These conclusory allegations do not state a cause of action. There are no factually-based allegations of wrongdoing or waste which would, if true, sustain a verdict in plaintiff's favor. Plaintiff's bare allegations that the compensation set lacked a relationship to duties performed or to the cost of living are insufficient as a matter of law to state a cause of action.

Accordingly, the order of the Appellate Division should be affirmed, with costs.

The Model Act embraces universal demand. Section 7.42 requires a demand on the corporation in all cases and provides that suit may not commence within ninety days of making such demand, "unless irreparable injury to the corporation would result by waiting for the expiration of the 90–day period." As the Introductory Comment explains: "It is believed that this provision will eliminate the often excessive time and expense for both litigants and the court in litigating the question whether demand is required. . . ." The corporation may, under section 7.43, request a further stay of the proceeding if, for example, more time is needed to assess the allegations and the corporate interest in the suit's continuance. Section 7.44 sets forth the mechanics (e.g., criteria for dismissal and burden of proof in meeting the criteria) by which "qualified directors" can obtain dismissal of the suit if they believe that maintenance of the suit is not in best interests of the corporation. "Qualified directors" is defined in section 1.43. Query, if the independent directors move to dismiss the derivative suit after the complaint has been filed which was more than ninety days after the making a demand on the board, should the court entertain the motion to dismiss? *See* Halebian v. Berv, 457 Mass. 620, 931 N.E.2d 986 (2010).

Auerbach v. Bennett

Court of Appeals of New York, 1979.
47 N.Y.2d 619, 419 N.Y.S.2d 920, 393 N.E.2d 994.

■ JONES, JUDGE. . . .

In the summer of 1975 the management of General Telephone & Electronics Corporation, in response to reports that numerous other multinational companies had made questionable payments to public officials or political parties in foreign countries, directed that an internal preliminary investigation be made to ascertain whether that corporation had engaged in similar transactions. On the basis of the report of this survey, received in October, 1975, management brought the issue to the attention of the corporation's board of directors. At a meeting held on November 6 of that year the board referred the matter to the board's audit committee. The audit committee retained as its special counsel the Washington, D.C., law firm of Wilmer, Cutler & Pickering which had not previously acted as counsel to the corporation. With the assistance of such special counsel and Arthur Andersen & Co., the corporation's outside auditors, the audit committee engaged in an investigation into the corporation's worldwide operations, focusing on whether, in the period January 1, 1971 to December 31, 1975, corporate funds had been (1) paid directly or indirectly to any political party or person or to any officer, employee, shareholder or director of any governmental or private customer, or (2) used to reimburse any officer of the corporation or other person for such payments.

On March 4, 1976 the audit committee released its report which was filed with the Securities and Exchange Commission and disclosed to the corporation's shareholders in a proxy statement prior to the annual meeting of shareholders held in April, 1976. The audit committee reported that it had found evidence that in the period from 1971 to 1975 the corporation or its subsidiaries had made payments abroad and in the United States constituting bribes and kickbacks in amounts perhaps totaling more than 11 million dollars and that some of the individual defendant directors had been personally involved in certain of the transactions.

Almost immediately Auerbach, a shareholder in the corporation, instituted the present shareholders' derivative action on behalf of the corporation against the corporation's directors, Arthur Andersen & Co. and the corporation. The complaint alleged that in connection with the transactions reported by the audit committee defendants, present and former members of the corporation's board of directors and Arthur Andersen & Co., are liable to the corporation for breach of their duties to the corporation and should be made to account for payments made in those transactions.

On April 21, 1976 the board of directors of the corporation adopted a resolution creating a special litigation committee "for the purpose of establishing a point of contact between the Board of Directors and the Corporation's General Counsel concerning the position to be taken by the Corporation in certain litigation involving shareholder derivative claims on behalf of the Corporation against certain of its directors and officers" and authorizing that committee "to take such steps from time to time as it deems necessary to pursue its objectives including the retention of special outside counsel." The special committee comprised three disinterested directors who had joined the board after the challenged transactions had occurred. The board subsequently additionally vested in the committee "all of the authority of the Board of Directors to determine, on behalf of the Board, the position that the Corporation shall take with respect to the derivative claims alleged on its behalf" in the present and similar shareholder derivative actions.

The special litigation committee reported under date of November 22, 1976. It found that defendant Arthur Andersen & Co. had conducted its examination of the corporation's affairs in accordance with generally accepted auditing standards and in good faith and concluded that no proper interest of the corporation or its shareholders would be served by the continued assertion of a claim against it. The committee also concluded that none of the individual defendants had violated the New York State statutory standard of care, that none had profited personally or gained in any way, that the claims asserted in the present action are without merit, that if the action were allowed to proceed the time and talents of the corporation's senior management would be wasted on lengthy pretrial and trial proceedings, that litigation costs would be inordinately high in view of the unlikelihood of success, and that the continuing publicity could be damaging to the corporation's business. The committee determined that it would not be in the best interests of the corporation for the present derivative action to proceed, and, exercising the authority delegated to it, directed the corporation's general counsel to take that position in the present litigation as well as in pending comparable shareholders' derivative actions.

On December 17, 1976 the corporation and the four individual defendants who had been served moved for an order ... dismissing the complaint or in the alternative for an order pursuant to ... summary judgment. On January 7, 1977 Arthur Andersen & Co. made a similar motion. On May 13, 1977 Supreme Court, Special Term, granted the motions of all defendants and dismissed the complaint on the merits....

As all parties and both courts below recognize, the disposition of this case on the merits turns on the proper application of the business judgment doctrine, in particular to the decision of a specially appointed committee of disinterested directors acting on behalf of the board to terminate a shareholders' derivative action. That doctrine bars judicial inquiry into actions of corporate directors taken in good faith and in the exercise of honest judgment in the lawful and legitimate furtherance of corporate purposes. "Questions of policy of management, expediency of contracts or action, adequacy of consideration, lawful appropriation of corporate funds to advance corporate interests, are left solely to their honest and unselfish decision, for their powers therein are without limitation and free from restraint, and the exercise of them for the common and general interests of the corporation may not be questioned, although the results show that what they did was unwise or inexpedient." (Pollitz v. Wabash, R.R. Co., 207 N.Y. 113, 124, 100 N.E. 721, 724.)

In this instance our inquiry, to the limited extent to which it may be pursued, has a two-tiered aspect. The complaint initially asserted liability on the part of defendants based on the payments made to foreign governmental customers and privately owned customers, some unspecified portions of which were allegedly passed on to officials of the customers, i.e., the focus was on first-tier bribes and kickbacks.

Then subsequent to the service of the complaint there came the report of a special litigation committee, particularly appointed by the corporation's board of directors to consider the merits of the present and similar shareholders' derivative actions, and its determination that it would not be in the best interests of the corporation to press claims against defendants based on their possible first-tier liability. The motions for summary judgment were predicated principally on the report and determination of the special litigation committee and on the contention that this second-tier corporate action insulated the first-tier transactions from judicial inquiry and was itself subject to the shelter of the business judgment doctrine....

It appears to us that the business judgment doctrine, at least in part, is grounded in the prudent recognition that courts are ill equipped and infrequently called on to evaluate what are and must be essentially business judgments. The authority and responsibilities vested in corporate directors both by statute and decisional law proceed on the assumption that inescapably there can be no available objective standard by which the correctness of every corporate decision may be measured, by the courts or otherwise. Even if that were not the case, by definition the responsibility for business judgments must rest with the corporate directors; their individual capabilities and experience peculiarly qualify them for the discharge of that responsibility. Thus, absent evidence of bad faith or fraud (of which there is none here) the courts must and properly should respect their determinations.

Derivative claims against corporate directors belong to the corporation itself. As with other questions of corporate policy and management, the decision whether and to what extent to explore and prosecute such claims lies within the judgment and control of the corporation's board of directors. Necessarily such decision must be predicated on the weighing and balancing of a variety of disparate considerations to reach a considered conclusion as to what course of action or inaction is best calculated to protect and advance the interests of the corporation. This is the essence of the responsibility and role of the board of directors, and courts may not intrude to interfere.

In the present case we confront a special instance of the application of the business judgment rule and inquire whether it applies in its full vigor to shield from judicial scrutiny the decision of a three-person minority committee of the board acting on behalf of the full board not to prosecute a shareholder's derivative action. The record in this case reveals that the board is a 15–member board, and that the derivative suit was brought against four of the directors. Nothing suggests that any of the other directors participated in any of the challenged first-tier transactions. Indeed the report of the audit committee on which the complaint is based specifically found that no other directors had any prior knowledge of or were in any way involved in any of these transactions. Other directors had, however, been members of the board in the period during which the transactions occurred. Each of the three director members of the special litigation committee joined the board thereafter.

The business judgment rule does not foreclose inquiry by the courts into the disinterested independence of those members of the board chosen by it to make the corporate decision on its behalf—here the members of the special litigation committee. Indeed the rule shields the deliberations and conclusions of the chosen representatives of the board only if they possess a disinterested independence and do not stand in a dual relation which prevents an unprejudicial exercise of judgment. (Cf. Koral v. Savory, Inc., 276 N.Y. 215, 11 N.E.2d 883.)

We examine then the proof submitted by defendants. It is not disputed that the members of the special litigation committee were not members of the corporation's board of directors at the time of the first-tier transactions in question.... None of the three had had any prior affiliation with the corporation. Notwithstanding the vigorous and imaginative hypothesizing and innuendo of counsel there is nothing in this record to raise a triable issue of fact as to the independence and disinterested status of these three directors.

The contention ... that any committee authorized by the board of which defendant directors were members must be held to be legally infirm and may not be delegated power to terminate a derivative action must be rejected. In the very nature of the corporate organization it was only the existing board of directors which had authority on behalf of the corporation to direct the investigation and to assure the cooperation of corporate employees, and it is only that same board by its own action—or as here pursuant to authority duly delegated by it—which had authority to decide whether to prosecute the claims against defendant directors. The board in this instance, with slight adaptation, followed prudent practice in observing the general policy that when individual members of a board of directors prove to have personal interests which may conflict with the interests of the corporation, such interested directors must be excluded while the remaining members of the board proceed to consideration and action. (Cf. Business Corporation Law, § 713, which contemplates such situations and provides that the interested directors may nonetheless be included in the quorum count.) Courts have consistently held that the business judgment rule applies where some directors are charged with wrongdoing, so long as the remaining directors making the decision are disinterested and independent ...

To accept the assertions of the intervenor and to disqualify the entire board would be to render the corporation powerless to make an effective business judgment with respect to prosecution of the derivative action....

We turn then to the action of the special litigation committee itself which comprised two components. First, there was the selection of procedures appropriate to the pursuit of its charge, and second, there was the ultimate substantive decision; predicated on the procedures chosen and the data produced thereby, not to pursue the claims advanced in the shareholders' derivative actions. The latter, substantive decision falls squarely within the embrace of the business judgment doctrine, involving as it did the weighing and balancing of legal, ethical, commercial, promotional, public relations, fiscal and other factors familiar to the resolution of many if not most corporate problems. To this extent the conclusion reached by the special litigation committee is outside the scope of our review. Thus, the courts cannot inquire as to which factors were considered by that committee or the relative weight accorded them in reaching that substantive decision—"the reasons for the payments, the advantages or disadvantages accruing to the corporation by reason of the transactions, the extent of the participation or profit by the respondent directors and the loss, if any, of public confidence in the corporation which might be incurred" (64 A.D.2d, at p. 107, 408 N.Y.S.2d at pp. 87–88). Inquiry into such matters would go to the very core of the business judgment made by the committee. To permit judicial probing of such issues would be to emasculate the business judgment doctrine as applied to the actions and determinations of the special litigation committee. Its substantive evaluation of the problems posed and its judgment in their resolution are beyond our reach.

As to the other component of the committee's activities, however, the situation is different, and here we agree with the Appellate Division. As to the methodologies and procedures best suited to the conduct of an investigation of facts and the determination of legal liability, the courts are well equipped by long and continuing experience and practice to make determinations. In fact they are better qualified in this regard than are corporate directors in general. Nor do the determinations to be made in the adoption of procedures partake of the nuances or special perceptions or comprehensions of business judgment or corporate activities or interests. The question is solely how appropriately to set about to gather the pertinent data.

While the court may properly inquire as to the adequacy and appropriateness of the committee's investigative procedures and methodologies, it may not under the guise of consideration of such factors trespass in the domain of business judgment. At the same time those responsible for the procedures by which the business judgment is reached may reasonably be required to show that they have pursued their chosen investigative methods in good faith. What evidentiary proof may be required to this end will, of course, depend on the nature of the particular investigation, and the proper reach of disclosure at the instance of the shareholders will in turn relate inversely to the showing made by the corporate representatives themselves. The latter may be expected to show that the areas and subjects to be examined are reasonably complete and that there has been a good-faith pursuit of inquiry into such areas and subjects. What has been uncovered and the relative weight accorded in evaluating and balancing the several factors and considerations are beyond the scope of judicial concern. Proof, however, that the investigation has been so restricted in scope, so shallow in execution, or otherwise so *pro forma* or halfhearted as to constitute a pretext or sham, consistent with the principles underlying the application of the business judgment doctrine, would raise questions of good faith or conceivably fraud which would never be shielded by that doctrine.

In addition to the issue of the disinterested independence of the special litigation committee, addressed above, the disposition of the present appeal turns, then ... [depends on whether the derivative suit plaintiff] has shown facts sufficient to require a trial of any material issue of fact as to the adequacy or appropriateness of the *modus operandi* of that committee or has demonstrated acceptable excuse for failure to make such tender.... We conclude that the requisite showing has not been made on this record....

On the submissions made by defendants in support of their motions, we do not find either insufficiency or infirmity as to the procedures and methodologies chosen and pursued by the special litigation committee. That committee promptly engaged eminent special counsel to guide its deliberations and to advise it. The committee reviewed the prior work of the audit committee, testing its completeness, accuracy and thoroughness by interviewing representatives of Wilmer, Cutler & Pickering, reviewing transcripts of the testimony of 10 corporate officers and employees before the Securities and Exchange Commission, and studying documents collected by and work papers of the Washington law firm. Individual interviews were conducted with the directors found to have participated in any way in the questioned payments, and with representatives of Arthur Andersen & Co. Questionnaires were sent to and answered by each of the corporation's nonmanagement directors. At the conclusion of its investigation the special litigation committee sought and obtained pertinent legal advice from its special counsel. The selection of appropriate investigative methods must always turn on the nature and characteristics of the particular subject being investigated, but we find nothing in this record that requires a trial of any material issue of fact concerning the sufficiency or appropriateness of the procedures chosen by this special litigation committee. Nor is there anything in this record to raise a triable issue of fact as to the good-faith pursuit of its examination by that committee....

For the reasons stated the order of the Appellate Division should be modified, with costs to defendants, by reversing so much thereof as reversed the order of Supreme Court, and, as so modified, affirmed.

[The dissenting opinion of Chief Judge Cooke is omitted.]

■ JASEN, WACHTLER, FUCHSBERG and MEYER, JJ., concur with JONES, J.

■ COOKE, C.J., dissents and votes to affirm in a separate opinion.

■ GABRIELLI, J., taking no part.

Order modified, with costs to defendants, in accordance with the opinion herein and, as so modified, affirmed. Question certified answered in the negative.

Zapata Corp. v. Maldonado

Supreme Court of Delaware, 1981.
430 A.2d 779.

■ Before DUFFY, QUILLEN and HORSEY, JJ.

[The claims on which this case was apparently based are stated as follows in Maldonado v. Flynn, 597 F.2d 789 (2d Cir.1979): A stock-option plan had been adopted by the board of Zapata Corporation in 1970 and approved by Zapata's shareholders in 1971. The board was authorized to amend the plan freely. The options were exercisable in five equal installments; the last exercise date was July 14, 1974. Flynn, the chief executive officer and a director of Zapata, as well as other senior officers of Zapata, were granted options under the plan to purchase Zapata stock at $12.15 per share.

[In 1974, Flynn and the board had decided Zapata should make a cash tender offer for its own stock at $25–$30 per share. Since Zapata stock was then trading at only $19 per share, the announcement of the tender offer would trigger a sharp rise in the price of Zapata stock. The tender offer was to be publicly announced on July 2, 1974. Early that day, trading in Zapata stock on the New York Stock Exchange was suspended at the request of Zapata's management, pending the announcement. Before trading resumed, the board accelerated the final exercise date for the options held by Flynn and the other senior officers from July 14, 1974 to July 2, 1974. The board also modified the plan to authorize Zapata to make interest-free loans to Flynn and the other senior officers in the amount of (i) the purchase price of the options they exercised and (ii) the tax liability they would incur by exercising the options. The purpose and effect of these amendments were to permit Flynn and the other senior officers to benefit at Zapata's expense. Under applicable federal tax laws, on the exercise of the option Flynn and the other senior officers would realize ordinary income in the amount of the spread between the option price and the fair market price of the stock at the time the option was exercised. Correspondingly, Zapata could deduct the amount of that spread as a business expense. By accelerating the last exercise date, and allowing Flynn and the other senior officers to exercise their options before the market price of the stock rose as a result of the tender offer, the board permitted the optionees to save a considerable amount of taxes but correlatively prevented Zapata from enjoying a higher tax deduction.]

■ QUILLEN, JUSTICE. This is an interlocutory appeal from an order entered on April 9, 1980, by the Court of Chancery denying appellant-defendant Zapata Corporation's (Zapata) alternative motions to dismiss the complaint or for summary judgment. The issue to be addressed has reached this Court by way of a rather convoluted path.

In June, 1975, William Maldonado, a stockholder of Zapata, instituted a derivative action in the Court of Chancery on behalf of Zapata against ten officers and/or directors of Zapata, alleging, essentially, breaches of fiduciary duty. Maldonado did not first demand that the board bring this action, stating instead such demand's futility because all directors were named as defendants and allegedly participated in the acts specified.[1] In June, 1977, Maldonado commenced an action in the United States District Court for the Southern District of New York against the same defendants, save one, alleging federal security law violations as well as the same common law claims made previously in the Court of Chancery.

By June, 1979, four of the defendant-directors were no longer on the board, and the remaining directors appointed two new outside directors to the board. The board then created an "Independent Investigation Committee" (Committee), composed solely of the two new directors, to investigate Maldonado's actions ... and to determine whether the corporation should continue any or all of the litigation. The Committee's determination was stated to be "final, ... not ... subject to review by the Board of Directors and ... in all respects ... binding upon the Corporation."

Following an investigation, the Committee concluded, in September, 1979, that each action should "be dismissed forthwith as their continued maintenance is inimical to the Company's best interests...." Consequently, Zapata moved for dismissal or summary judgment....

On March 18, 1980, the Court of Chancery, in a reported opinion, the basis for the order of April 9, 1980, denied Zapata's motions, holding that Delaware law does not sanction this means of dismissal....

[T]he focus in this case is on the power to speak for the corporation as to whether the lawsuit should be continued or terminated. As we see it, this issue in the current appellate posture of this case ... [concerns] the corporate power under Delaware law of an authorized board committee to cause dismissal of litigation instituted for the benefit of the corporation; and the role of the Court of Chancery in resolving conflicts between the stockholder and the committee....

Consistent with the purpose of requiring a demand, a board decision to cause a derivative suit to be dismissed as detrimental to the company, after demand has been made and refused, will be respected unless it was wrongful.[10] ... A claim of a wrongful decision not to sue is thus the first exception and the first context of dispute. Absent a wrongful refusal, the stockholder in such a situation simply lacks legal managerial power....

---

1. Court of Chancery Rule 23.1 states in part: "The complaint shall also allege with particularity the efforts, if any, made by the plaintiff to obtain the action he desires from the directors or comparable authority and the reasons for his failure to obtain the action or for not making the effort."

10. In other words, when stockholders, after making demand and having their suit rejected, attack the board's decision as improper, the board's decision falls under the "business judgment" rule and will be respected if the requirements of the rule are met.... That situation should be distinguished from the instant case, where demand was not made, and the *power* of the board to seek a dismissal, due to disqualification, presents a threshold issue....

But it cannot be implied that, absent a wrongful board refusal, a stockholder can never have an individual right to initiate an action. For, as is stated in *[McKee]*, a "well settled" exception exists to the general rule.

> "[A] stockholder may sue in equity in his derivative right to assert a cause of action in behalf of the corporation, *without prior demand* upon the directors to sue, when it is apparent that a demand would be futile, that the officers are under an influence that sterilizes discretion and could not be proper persons to conduct the litigation."

156 A. at 193 (emphasis added)....[11]

These comments in *McKee* ... make obvious sense. A demand, when required and refused (if not wrongful), terminates a stockholder's legal ability to initiate a derivative action. But where demand is properly excused, the stockholder does possess the ability to initiate the action on his corporation's behalf.

These conclusions, however, do not determine the question before us. Rather, they merely bring us to the question to be decided....

The question to be decided becomes: When, if at all, should an authorized board committee be permitted to cause litigation, properly initiated by a derivative stockholder in his own right, to be dismissed? As noted above, a board has the power to choose not to pursue litigation when demand is made upon it, so long as the decision is not wrongful. If the board determines that a suit would be detrimental to the company, the board's determination prevails. Even when demand is excusable, circumstances may arise when continuation of the litigation would not be in the corporation's best interests. Our inquiry is whether, under such circumstances, there is a permissible procedure under § 141(a) by which a corporation can rid itself of detrimental litigation. If there is not, a single stockholder in an extreme case might control the destiny of the entire corporation. This concern was bluntly expressed by the Ninth Circuit in Lewis v. Anderson, 9th Cir., 615 F.2d 778, 783 (1979), cert. denied, 449 U.S. 869, 101 S.Ct. 206, 66 L.Ed.2d 89 (1980): "To allow one shareholder to incapacitate an entire board of directors merely by leveling charges against them gives too much leverage to dissident shareholders." But, when examining the means, including the committee mechanism examined in this case, potentials for abuse must be recognized. This takes us to the second and third aspects of the issue on appeal....

The corporate power inquiry then focuses on whether the board, tainted by the self-interest of a majority of its members, can legally delegate its authority to a committee of two disinterested directors. We find our statute clearly requires an affirmative answer to this question. As has been noted, under an express provision of the statute, § 141(c), a committee can exercise all of the authority of the board to

11. These statements are consistent with Rule 23.1's "reasons for ... failure" to make demand....

the extent provided in the resolution of the board. Moreover, at least by analogy to our statutory section on interested directors, 8 Del.C. § 141, it seems clear that the Delaware statute is designed to permit disinterested directors to act for the board.[14] . . .

We do not think that the interest taint of the board majority is per se a legal bar to the delegation of the board's power to an independent committee composed of disinterested board members. The committee can properly act for the corporation to move to dismiss derivative litigation that is believed to be detrimental to the corporation's best interest.

Our focus now switches to the Court of Chancery which is faced with a stockholder assertion that a derivative suit, properly instituted, should continue for the benefit of the corporation and a corporate assertion, properly made by a board committee acting with board authority, that the same derivative suit should be dismissed as inimical to the best interests of the corporation.

At the risk of stating the obvious, the problem is relatively simple. If, on the one hand, corporations can consistently wrest bona fide derivative actions away from well-meaning derivative plaintiffs through the use of the committee mechanism, the derivative suit will lose much, if not all, of its generally-recognized effectiveness as an intra-corporate means of policing boards of directors. See Dent, [supra note 5,] 75 Nw.U.L.Rev. at 96 & n. 3, 144 & n. 241. If, on the other hand, corporations are unable to rid themselves of meritless or harmful litigation and strike suits, the derivative action, created to benefit the corporation, will produce the opposite, unintended result. . . . It thus appears desirable to us to find a balancing point where bona fide stockholder power to bring corporation causes of action cannot be unfairly trampled on by the board of directors, but the corporation can rid itself of detrimental litigation.

[T]he question has been treated by other courts as one of the "business judgment" of the board committee. If a "committee, composed of independent and disinterested directors, conducted a proper review of the matters before it, considered a variety of factors and reached, in good faith, a business judgment that [the] action was not in the best interest of [the corporation]", the action must be dismissed. See, e.g., Maldonado v. Flynn, . . . 485 F.Supp. at 282, 286. The issues become solely independence, good faith, and reasonable investigation. The ultimate conclusion of the committee, under that view, is not subject to judicial review.

We are not satisfied, however, that acceptance of the "business judgment" rationale at this stage of derivative litigation is a proper balancing point. While we admit an analogy with a normal case respecting board judgment, it seems to us that there is sufficient risk in the realities of a situation like the one presented in this case to justify caution beyond adherence to the theory of business judgment.

---

14. [The court quoted Del. § 144.]

The context here is a suit against directors where demand on the board is excused. We think some tribute must be paid to the fact that the lawsuit was properly initiated. It is not a board refusal case. Moreover, this complaint was filed in June of 1975 and, while the parties undoubtedly would take differing views on the degree of litigation activity, we have to be concerned about the creation of an "Independent Investigation Committee" four years later, after the election of two new outside directors. Situations could develop where such motions could be filed after years of vigorous litigation for reasons unconnected with the merits of the lawsuit.

Moreover, notwithstanding our conviction that Delaware law entrusts the corporate power to a properly authorized committee, we must be mindful that directors are passing judgment on fellow directors in the same corporation and fellow directors, in this instance, who designated them to serve both as directors and committee members. The question naturally arises whether a "there but for the grace of God go I" empathy might not play a role. And the further question arises whether inquiry as to independence, good faith and reasonable investigation is sufficient safeguard against abuse, perhaps subconscious abuse.

There is another line of exploration besides the factual context of this litigation which we find helpful. The nature of this motion finds no ready pigeonhole, as perhaps illustrated by its being set forth in the alternative. It is perhaps best considered as a hybrid summary judgment motion for dismissal because the stockholder plaintiff's standing to maintain the suit has been lost. But it does not fit neatly into a category described in Rule 12(b) of the Court of Chancery Rules nor does it correspond directly with Rule 56 since the question of genuine issues of fact on the merits of the stockholder's claim are not reached.

It seems to us that there are two other procedural analogies that are helpful in addition to reference to Rules 12 and 56. There is some analogy to a settlement in that there is a request to terminate litigation without a judicial determination of the merits. See Perrine v. Pennroad Corp., Del.Supr., 47 A.2d 479, 487 (1946). "In determining whether or not to approve a proposed settlement of a derivative stockholders' action [when directors are on both sides of the transaction], the Court of Chancery is called upon to exercise its own business judgment." Neponsit Investment Co. v. Abramson, Del.Supr., 405 A.2d 97, 100 (1979) and cases therein cited. In this case, the litigating stockholder plaintiff facing dismissal of a lawsuit properly commenced ought, in our judgment, to have sufficient status for strict Court review.

Finally, if the committee is in effect given status to speak for the corporation as the plaintiff in interest, then it seems to us there is an analogy to Court of Chancery Rule 41(a)(2) where the plaintiff seeks a dismissal after an answer. Certainly, the position of record of the litigating stockholder is adverse to the position advocated by the corporation in the motion to dismiss. Accordingly, there is perhaps some wisdom to be gained by the direction in Rule 41(a)(2) that "an action shall not be dismissed at the plaintiff's instance save upon order of the Court and upon such terms and conditions as the Court deems proper."

Whether the Court of Chancery will be persuaded by the exercise of a committee power resulting in a summary motion for dismissal of a derivative action, where a demand has not been initially made, should rest, in our judgment, in the independent discretion of the Court of Chancery. We thus steer a middle course between those cases which yield to the independent business judgment of a board committee and this case as determined below which would yield to unbridled plaintiff stockholder control. In pursuit of the course, we recognize that "[t]he final substantive judgment whether a particular lawsuit should be maintained requires a balance of many factors—ethical, commercial, promotional, public relations, employee relations, fiscal as well as legal." Maldonado v. Flynn, [supra,] 485 F.Supp. at 285. But we are content that such factors are not "beyond the judicial reach" of the Court of Chancery which regularly and competently deals with fiduciary relationships, disposition of trust property, approval of settlements and scores of similar problems. We recognize the danger of judicial overreaching but the alternatives seem to us to be outweighed by the fresh view of a judicial outsider. Moreover, if we failed to balance all the interests involved, we would in the name of practicality and judicial economy foreclose a judicial decision on the merits. At this point, we are not convinced that is necessary or desirable.

After an objective and thorough investigation of a derivative suit, an independent committee may cause its corporation to file a pretrial motion to dismiss in the Court of Chancery. The basis of the motion is the best interests of the corporation, as determined by the committee. The motion should include a thorough written record of the investigation and its findings and recommendations. Under appropriate court supervision, akin to proceedings on summary judgment, each side should have an opportunity to make a record on the motion. As to the limited issues presented by the motion noted below, the moving party should be prepared to meet the normal burden under Rule 56 that there is no genuine issue as to any material fact and that the moving party is entitled to dismiss as a matter of law.[15] The Court should apply a two-step test to the motion.

First, the Court should inquire into the independence and good faith of the committee and the bases supporting its conclusions. Limited discovery may be ordered to facilitate such inquiries. The corporation should have the burden of proving independence, good faith and a reasonable investigation, rather than presuming independence, good faith and reasonableness.[17] If the Court determines that

15. We do not foreclose a discretionary trial of factual issues but that issue is not presented in this appeal. See Lewis v. Anderson, supra, 615 F.2d at 780. Nor do we foreclose the possibility that other motions may proceed or be joined with such a pretrial summary judgment motion to dismiss, e.g., a partial motion for summary judgment on the merits.

17. Compare Auerbach v. Bennett, 47 N.Y.2d 619, 419 N.Y.S.2d 920, 928–29, 393 N.E.2d 994 (1979). Our approach here is analogous to and consistent with the Delaware approach to "interested director" transactions, where the directors, once the transaction is attacked, have the committee is not independent or has not shown reasonable bases for its conclusions, or, if the Court is not satisfied for other reasons relating to the process, including but not limited to the good faith of the committee, the Court shall deny the corporation's motion. If, however, the Court is satisfied under Rule 56 standards that the committee was independent and showed reasonable bases for good faith findings and recommendations, the Court may proceed, in its discretion, to the next step.

The second step provides, we believe, the essential key in striking the balance between legitimate corporate claims as expressed in a derivative stockholder suit and a corporation's best interests as expressed by an independent investigating committee. The Court should determine, applying its own independent business judgment, whether the motion should be granted.[18] This means, of course, that instances could arise where a committee can establish its independence and sound bases for its good faith decisions and still have the corporation's motion denied. The second step is intended to thwart instances where corporate actions meet the criteria of step one, but the result does not appear to satisfy its spirit, or where corporate actions would simply prematurely terminate a stockholder grievance deserving of further consideration in the corporation's interest. The Court of Chancery of course must carefully consider and weigh how compelling the corporate interest in dismissal is when faced with a nonfrivolous lawsuit. The Court of Chancery should, when appropriate, give special consideration to matters of law and public policy in addition to the corporation's best interests.

If the Court's independent business judgment is satisfied, the Court may proceed to grant the motion, subject, of course, to any equitable terms or conditions the Court finds necessary or desirable.

The interlocutory order of the Court of Chancery is reversed and the cause is remanded for further proceedings consistent with this opinion.

ARONSON v. LEWIS, 473 A.2d 805 (Del.1984). "[T]he *Zapata* demand-excused/demand-refused bifurcation . . . has left a crucial issue unanswered: when is demand futile and, therefore, excused?

"Delaware courts have addressed the issue of demand futility on several earlier occasions. . . . The rule emerging from these decisions is that where officers and directors are under an influence which sterilizes their discretion, they cannot be considered proper persons to conduct litigation on behalf of the corporation. Thus, demand would be futile. See e.g., McKee v. Rogers, Del.Ch., 156 A. 191, 192 (1931)

the burden of establishing its "intrinsic fairness" to a court's careful scrutiny. See, e.g., Sterling v. Mayflower Hotel Corp., Del.Supr., 93 A.2d 107 (1952).

18. This step shares some of the same spirit and philosophy of the statement by the Vice Chancellor: "Under our system of law, courts and not litigants should decide the merits of litigation." 413 A.2d at 1263.

(holding that where a defendant controlled the board of directors, '[i]t is manifest then that there can be no expectation that the corporation would sue him, and if it did, it can hardly be said that the prosecution of the suit would be entrusted to proper hands'). . . .

"However, those cases cannot be taken to mean that any board approval of a challenged transaction automatically connotes 'hostile interest' and 'guilty participation' by directors, or some other form of sterilizing influence upon them. Were that so, the demand requirements of our law would be meaningless, leaving the clear mandate of Chancery Rule 23.1 devoid of its purpose and substance. . . .

"Our view is that in determining demand futility the Court of Chancery in the proper exercise of its discretion must decide whether, under the particularized facts alleged, a reasonable doubt is created that: (1) the directors are disinterested and independent and (2) the challenged transaction was otherwise the product of a valid exercise of business judgment. Hence, the Court of Chancery must make two inquiries, one into the independence and disinterestedness of the directors and the other into the substantive nature of the challenged transaction and the board's approval thereof. As to the latter inquiry the court does not assume that the transaction is a wrong to the corporation requiring corrective steps by the board. Rather, the alleged wrong is substantively reviewed against the factual background alleged in the complaint. As to the former inquiry, directorial independence and disinterestedness, the court reviews the factual allegations to decide whether they raise a reasonable doubt, as a threshold matter, that the protections of the business judgment rule are available to the board. Certainly, if this is an 'interested' director transaction, such that the business judgment rule is inapplicable to the board majority approving the transaction, then the inquiry ceases. In that event futility of demand has been established by any objective or subjective standard.[8] See, e.g., Bergstein v. Texas International Co., Del.Ch., 453 A.2d 467, 471 (1982) (because five of nine directors approved stock appreciation rights plan likely to benefit them, board was interested for demand purposes and demand held futile). This includes situations involving self-dealing directors. . . .

"However, the mere threat of personal liability for approving a questioned transaction, standing alone, is insufficient to challenge either the independence or disinterestedness of directors, although in rare cases a transaction may be so egregious on its face that board approval cannot meet the test of business judgment, and a substantial likelihood of director liability therefore exists. . . . In sum the entire review is factual in nature. The Court of Chancery in the exercise of its

---

8. We recognize that drawing the line at a majority of the board may be an arguably arbitrary dividing point. Critics will charge that we are ignoring the structural bias common to corporate boards throughout America, as well as the other unseen socialization processes cutting against independent discussion and decisionmaking in the boardroom. The difficulty with structural bias in a demand futile case is simply one of establishing it in the complaint for purposes of Rule 23.1. We are satisfied that discretionary review by the Court of Chancery of complaints alleging specific facts pointing to bias on a particular board will be sufficient for determining demand futility.

sound discretion must be satisfied that a plaintiff has alleged facts with particularity which, taken as true, support a reasonable doubt that the challenged transaction was the product of a valid exercise of business judgment. Only in that context is demand excused."

NOTE: The Delaware Supreme Court later changed the formulation, although not the substance, of the *Aronson* test by changing the connective from "and" to "or." Accordingly, the test now reads: "whether under the particularized facts alleged, a reasonable doubt is created that: (1) the directors are disinterested and independent [or] (2) the challenged transaction was otherwise the product of a valid exercise of business judgment." See Rales v. Blasband, 634 A.2d 927 (Del. 1993); Brehm v. Eisner, 746 A.2d 244 (2000).

GROBOW v. PEROT, 539 A.2d 180 (Del.1988). "[G]iven the highly factual nature of the inquiry presented to the Trial Court by a Rule 23.1 defense, we conclude that it would be neither practicable nor wise to attempt to formulate a criterion of general application for determining reasonable doubt [under *Aronson v. Lewis*]. The facts necessary to support a finding of reasonable doubt either of director disinterest or independence, or whether proper business judgment was exercised in the transaction will vary with each case. Reasonable doubt must be decided by the trial court on a case-by-case basis employing an objective analysis. Were we to adopt a standard criterion for resolving a motion to dismiss based on Rule 23.1, the test for demand excusal would, in all likelihood, become rote and inelastic....

"We think it sufficient simply to say that the Court of Chancery must weigh the presumption of the business judgment rule that attaches to a board of directors' decision against the well-pleaded facts alleged in a plaintiff's demand-futility complaint."

See also Levine v. Smith, 591 A.2d 194 (Del.Supr.1991).

NOTE ON CUKER v. MIKALAUSKAS

In Cuker v. Mikalauskas, 547 Pa. 600, 692 A.2d 1042 (Pa. 1997), PECO Energy Co. filed a motion for summary judgment seeking termination of minority shareholder derivative actions. The motion was filed on behalf of the board, which had adopted the report of a special litigation committee that proceeding with the actions would not be in the corporation's best interests. The trial court rejected PECO's motion for summary judgment. The Pennsylvania Supreme Court reversed and remanded, with the following instructions:

> Decisions regarding litigation by or on behalf of a corporation, including shareholder derivative actions, are business decisions as much as any other financial decisions. As such, they are

within the province of the board of directors [and within the scope of the business judgment rule]. . . .

. . . [T]he practical effect of this holding needs elaboration. Assuming that an independent board of directors may terminate shareholder derivative actions, what is needed is a procedural mechanism for implementation and judicial review of the board's decision. Without considering the merits of the action, a court should determine the validity of the board's decision to terminate the litigation; if that decision was made in accordance with the appropriate standards, then the court should dismiss the derivative action prior to litigation on the merits.

The business judgment rule should insulate officers and directors from judicial intervention in the absence of fraud or self-dealing, if challenged decisions were within the scope of the directors' authority, if they exercised reasonable diligence, and if they honestly and rationally believed their decisions were in the best interests of the company. It is obvious that a court must examine the circumstances surrounding the decisions in order to determine if the conditions warrant application of the business judgment rule. If they do, the court will never proceed to an examination of the merits of the challenged decisions, for that is precisely what the business judgment rule prohibits. In order to make the business judgment rule meaningful, the preliminary examination should be limited and precise so as to minimize judicial involvement when application of the business judgment rule is warranted.

To achieve these goals, a court might stay the derivative action while it determines the propriety of the board's decision. The court might order limited discovery or an evidentiary hearing to resolve issues respecting the board's decision. Factors bearing on the board's decision will include whether the board or its special litigation committee was disinterested, whether it was assisted by counsel, whether it prepared a written report, whether it was independent, whether it conducted an adequate investigation, and whether it rationally believed its decision was in the best interests of the corporation (i.e., acted in good faith). If all of these criteria are satisfied, the business judgment rule applies and the court should dismiss the action.

These considerations and procedures are all encompassed in Part VII, chapter 1 of the *ALI Principles* (relating to the derivative action), which provides a comprehensive mechanism to address shareholder derivative actions. A number of its provisions are implicated in the action at bar. Sections 7.02 (standing), 7.03 (the demand rule), 7.04 (procedure in derivative action), 7.05 (board authority in derivative action), 7.06 (judicial stay of derivative action), 7.07, 7.08, and 7.09 (dismissal of derivative action), 7.10 (standard of judicial review), and 7.13 (judicial procedures) are specifically applicable to this case.[3] These sections set forth guidance which is consistent with Pennsylvania law and precedent, which furthers the policies inherent in the business judgment rule, and which provides an appropriate degree of specificity to guide the trial court in controlling the proceedings in this litigation.

We specifically adopt §§ 7.02–7.10, and § 7.13 of the *ALI Principles*.[5] In doing so we have weighed many considerations. First, the opinion of the trial court, the questions certified to the Superior Court, and the inability of PECO to obtain a definitive ruling from the lower courts all demonstrate the need for specific guidance from this court on how such litigation should be managed; the ALI principles provide such guidance in specific terms which will simplify this litigation. Second, we have often found ALI guidance helpful in the past, most frequently in adopting or citing sections of various Restatements; the scholarship reflected in work of the American Law Institute has been consistently reliable and useful. Third, the principles set forth by the ALI are generally consistent with Pennsylvania precedent. Fourth, although the *ALI Principles* incorporate much of the law of New York and Delaware, other states with extensive corporate jurisprudence, the ALI Principles better serve the needs of Pennsylvania. Although New York law parallels Pennsylvania law in many respects, it does not set forth any procedures to govern the review of corporate decisions relating to derivative litigation, and this omission would fail to satisfy the needs evident in this case. Delaware law permits a court in some cases ("demand excused" cases) to apply its own business judgment in the review process when deciding to honor the directors' decision to terminate derivative litigation. In our view, this is a defect which could eviscerate the business judgment rule and contradict a long line of Pennsylvania precedents. Delaware law also fails to provide a procedural framework for judicial review of corporate decisions under the business judgment rule.

Accordingly, we adopt the specified sections of the *ALI Principles*, reverse the orders of the court of common pleas, and remand the matter for further proceedings consistent with this opinion.

---

3. *ALI Principles* §§ 4.01, 4.02, and 4.03 (duties of directors and officers; the business judgment rule; reliance on committees and other persons) are similar but not identical to the statutory standards found in 15 Pa.C.S. §§ 512, 513, 515, 1712, 1713, and 1715. The statutory standards, of course, control the duties of directors and the application of the business judgment rule in Pennsylvania.

5. Our adoption of these sections is not a rejection of other sections not cited. We have identified and studied the sections which apply to this case and have adopted those which appear most relevant.

The entire publication, all seven parts, is a comprehensive, cohesive work more than a decade in preparation. Additional sections of the publication, particularly procedural ones due to their interlocking character, may be adopted in the future. Issues in future cases or, perhaps, further proceedings in this case might implicate additional sections of the *ALI Principles*. Courts of the Commonwealth are free to consider other parts of the work and utilize them if they are helpful and appear to be consistent with Pennsylvania law.

In an Appendix to its opinion, the court set out Principles of Corporate Governance §§ 7.02–7.10 and 7.13 in full.

IN RE PSE & G SHAREHOLDER LITIGATION, 173 N.J. 258, 801 A.2d 295 (2002). Plaintiffs filed derivative actions. The board directed an investigation by a law firm, and, based on the law firm's report, moved for summary judgment. The New Jersey court adopted the following standard of review: "We believe that the trial court correctly declined to apply the traditional business judgment rule in this case. Instead, we shall apply a modified business judgment rule that imposes an initial burden on a corporation to demonstrate that in deciding to reject or terminate a shareholder's suit the members of the board (1) were independent and disinterested, (2) acted in good faith and with due care in their investigation of the shareholder's allegations, and that (3) the board's decision was reasonable.... All three elements must be satisfied. Moreover, shareholders in these circumstances must be permitted access to corporate documents and other discovery 'limited to the narrow issue of what steps the directors took to inform themselves of the shareholder demand and the reasonableness of its decision.' " ...

MODEL BUSINESS CORPORATION ACT §§ 7.42–7.44

[See Statutory Supplement]

AMERICAN LAW INSTITUTE, PRINCIPLES OF CORPORATE GOVERNANCE §§ 7.03, 7.04, 7.08–7.13

[See Statutory Supplement]

NOTE ON INDEPENDENCE

The concept of independence is in some ways new in corporate law. It figures in a variety of contexts, including, but not limited to, derivative actions.

1. *Board Composition*. Until around 1970, for board composition purposes a distinction was drawn between "outside" and "inside" directors. Inside directors were directors who were also officers. All other directors were outside directors. Gradually, a recognition emerged that a director could be an outside director and yet not an independent director—that is, not independent of management—because even though a director wasn't an employee, she might have important economic ties to the corporation that could affect her

independence from the senior executives, whose performance she was supposed to monitor. Today, it is generally recognized that rather than having simply a majority of outside directors, the board of a publicly held corporation should have a majority of directors who are independent of the senior executives.

2. *Conflict-of-Interest Transactions*. Similarly, in considering the board's review of a director's conflict-of-interest transaction, the courts at one time focused almost exclusively on whether the reviewing directors were "disinterested," in the sense that they did not have a financial stake in the relevant transaction, rather than "independent," in the sense that they were independent of the director who engaged in the transaction. In contrast, today the courts are increasingly requiring both disinterestedness and independence in this context.

3. *Excuse of Demand*. In Beam v. Martha Stewart, 845 A.2d 1040 (Del. Supr. 2004), the issue of independence arose in the context of whether the plaintiff in a derivative action was excused from making a demand on the board on the ground that a majority of the directors were not disinterested and independent. Martha Stewart was an officer, director, and 94% owner of Martha Stewart Living Omnimedia, Inc. ("MSO"). Beam, the derivative-action plaintiff, was a minority shareholder. Beam's complaint alleged that Martha Stewart had breached her fiduciary duties of loyalty and care to MSO by illegally selling stock she owned in another company and mishandling the media attention that followed, thereby jeopardizing MSO's financial position. Beam did not make a demand on the board before bringing suit.

MSO's board of directors consisted of six members: Stewart, Patrick, Martinez, Moore, Seligman, and Ubben. The Chancellor found that Stewart's potential civil and criminal liability for the acts underlying Beam's claim rendered her an interested party, and therefore unable to consider demand. The Chancellor also found that Patrick's position as an officer and inside director, together with the substantial compensation she received from MSO, raised a reasonable doubt as to her ability objectively to consider a demand. Beam claimed, among other things, that Martinez was also not independent in view of his longstanding personal friendship with both Patrick and Stewart, and that Moore was not independent in view of her longstanding personal relationship with Stewart. The Chancellor determined that the complaint failed to raise a reasonable doubt that Martinez and Patrick were independent, despite their personal ties to Stewart. The Delaware Supreme Court affirmed, but made clear that in an appropriate case, strong ties of personal friendship or other nonfinancial relationships could lead to a conclusion that a director lacked independence:

> A variety of motivations, including friendship, may influence the demand futility inquiry. But, to render a director unable to consider demand, a relationship must be of a bias-producing nature. Allegations of mere personal friendship or a mere outside business relationship, standing alone, are insufficient to raise a reasonable doubt about a director's independence. In this con-

nection, we adopt as our own the Chancellor's analysis in this case:

> [S]ome professional or personal friendships, which may border on or even exceed familial loyalty and closeness, may raise a reasonable doubt whether a director can appropriately consider demand. This is particularly true when the allegations raise serious questions of either civil or criminal liability of such a close friend. Not all friendships, or even most of them, rise to this level and the Court cannot make a *reasonable* inference that a particular friendship does so without specific factual allegations to support such a conclusion. . . .

Allegations that Stewart and the other directors moved in the same social circles, attended the same weddings, developed business relationships before joining the board, and described each other as "friends," even when coupled with Stewart's 94% voting power, are insufficient, without more, to rebut the presumption of independence. . . . [S]uch affinities—standing alone—will not render pre-suit demand futile.

That is not to say that personal friendship is always irrelevant to the independence calculus. But, for presuit demand purposes, friendship must be accompanied by substantially more in the nature of serious allegations that would lead to a reasonable doubt as to a director's independence. That a much stronger relationship is necessary to overcome the presumption of independence at the demand futility stage becomes especially compelling when one considers the risks that directors would take by protecting their social acquaintances in the face of allegations that those friends engaged in misconduct. To create a reasonable doubt about an outside director's independence, a plaintiff must plead facts that would support the inference that because of the nature of a relationship or additional circumstances other than the interested director's stock ownership or voting power, the non-interested director would be more willing to risk his or her reputation than risk the relationship with the interested director.

4. *Special Litigation Committees*. In In re Oracle Corp. Derivative Litigation, 824 A.2d 917 (Del. Ch. 2003), a derivative action had been brought which alleged that several Oracle directors and officers had engaged in illegal insider trading. A two-person litigation special litigation committee ("SLC") moved to dismiss the action. The issue arose whether the members of the committee were independent. Both committee members were professors at Stanford, and the defendants also had important ties to Stanford. Vice Chancellor Strine noted that the directors who were accused of insider trading included:

> (1) another Stanford professor, who taught one of the SLC members when the SLC member was a Ph.D. candidate and who serves as a senior fellow and a steering committee member alongside that SLC member at the Stanford Institute for Economic Policy Research or "SIEPR"; (2) a Stanford alumnus who has directed millions of dollars of contributions to Stanford during recent

years, serves as Chair of SIEPR's Advisory Board and has a conference center named for him at SIEPR's facility, and has contributed nearly $600,000 to SIEPR and the Stanford Law School, both parts of Stanford with which one of the SLC members is closely affiliated; and (3) Oracle's CEO, who has made millions of dollars in donations to Stanford through a personal foundation and large donations indirectly through Oracle, and who was considering making donations of his $100 million house and $170 million for a scholarship program as late as August 2001, at around the same time period the SLC members were added to the Oracle board.

On these facts, Vice Chancellor Strine concluded that there was a reasonable doubt about the impartiality of the SLC:

> It is no easy task to decide whether to accuse a fellow director of insider trading. For Oracle to compound that difficulty by requiring SLC members to consider accusing a fellow professor and two large benefactors of their university of conduct that is rightly considered a violation of criminal law was unnecessary and inconsistent with the concept of independence recognized by our law. The possibility that these extraneous considerations biased the inquiry of the SLC is too substantial for this court to ignore. I therefore deny the SLC's motion to terminate.

In *Martha Stewart*, the Delaware Supreme Court commented on *Oracle* as follows:

> An SLC is a unique creature that was introduced into Delaware law by *Zapata v. Maldonado* in 1981. The SLC procedure is a method sometimes employed where presuit demand has already been excused and the SLC is vested with the full power of the board to conduct an extensive investigation into the merits of the corporate claim with a view toward determining whether—in the SLC's business judgment—the corporate claim should be pursued. Unlike the demand-excusal context, where the board is presumed to be independent, the SLC has the burden of establishing its own independence by a yardstick that must be "like Caesar's wife"—"above reproach." Moreover, unlike the presuit demand context, the SLC analysis contemplates not only a shift in the burden of persuasion but also the availability of discovery into various issues, including independence.
>
> We need not decide whether the substantive standard of independence in an SLC case differs from that in a pre-suit demand case. As a practical matter, the procedural distinction relating to the diametrically-opposed burdens and the availability of discovery into independence may be outcome-determinative on the issue of independence. Moreover, because the members of an SLC are vested with enormous power to seek dismissal of a derivative suit brought against their director-colleagues in a setting where presuit demand is already excused, the Court of Chancery must exercise careful oversight of the bona fides of the SLC and its process. Aside from the procedural distinctions, the

Stanford connections in *Oracle* are factually distinct from the relationships here.

5. *Special Negotiating Committees.* In a footnote in *Martha Stewart*, the court also commented on independence in the context of a special negotiating committee in a merger. The court here pointed out still another facet of independence: It is not always enough to be independent *on paper*; the director must sometimes also demonstrate independence on the ground, by *acting* independent:

> The analysis applied to determine the independence of a special committee in a merger case also has its own special procedural characteristics. In such cases, courts evaluate not only whether the relationships among members of the committee and interested parties placed them in a position objectively to consider a proposed transaction, but also whether the committee members *in fact* functioned independently. *See, e.g., Kahn v. Tremont Corp.*, 694 A.2d 422, 429–30 (Del.1997) ("[T]he Special Committee—did not function independently.... From its inception, the Special Committee failed to operate in a manner which would create the appearance of objectivity in Tremont's decision to purchase the NL stock. As this Court has previously stated in defining director independence: 'it is the care, attention and sense of individual responsibility to the performance of one's duties ... that generally touches on independence.' The record amply demonstrates that neither Stafford nor Boushka possessed the 'care, attention and sense of responsibility' necessary to afford them the status of independent directors." ...)

SECTION 7. DEMAND ON THE SHAREHOLDERS

The Federal Rule of Civil Procedure 23.1 provides that the plaintiff's complaint must set forth the efforts to obtain action from the stockholder "if necessary.". "The rationale for demand on other shareholders is that such a requirement allows the majority of shareholders to determine whether legal action is in the corporation's best interest." Harhen v. Brown, 431 Mass. 838, 730 N.E.2d 859 (Mass. 2000). This requirement, however, is a matter of substantive state law, except where the making of a demand would prove inconsistent with federal policy underlying any federal question raised in the derivative suit. *See* Burks v. Lasker, 441 U.S. 471, 99 S.Ct. 1831, 60 L.Ed.2d 404 (1979). Under the law of most states, demand on shareholders is not required. For example, the California and New York statutory counterparts to FRCP 23.1 omit any reference to demand on the shareholders, and it is clear that this omission was deliberate. See Syracuse Television, Inc. v. Channel 9, Syracuse, Inc., 51 Misc.2d 188, 273 N.Y.S.2d 16

(1966). And, where the statutes are not definitive, the requirement of a demand on the shareholders is largely overtaken by numerous exceptions, so that the failure to make a demand on the shareholders is rarely a successful in scuttling the derivative suit. Consider the rationale for each of the following well-recognized exceptions to making a demand on the shareholders:

1. *Wrongdoers hold a majority of the stock*. All courts agree that demand on shareholders is excused when the alleged wrongdoers hold a majority of the stock. See, e.g., Heilbrunn v. Hanover Equities Corp., 259 F.Supp. 936 (S.D.N.Y.1966). Most courts would probably come to the same result where the wrongdoers hold a controlling but less-than-majority interest. See Gottesman v. General Motors Corp., 268 F.2d 194 (2d Cir.1959). But see Levitan v. Stout, 97 F.Supp. 105 (W.D.Ky.1951).

2. *Demand otherwise futile*. All courts would probably agree that demand on shareholders is also excused when it is futile for other reasons, although there might be considerable divergence as to whether a given state of facts constitutes futility. See, e.g., Pioche Mines Consolidated, Inc. v. Dolman, 333 F.2d 257, 264–65 (9th Cir.1964), cert. denied 380 U.S. 956, 85 S.Ct. 1081, 13 L.Ed.2d 972 (1965) (demand excused where only one shareholders' meeting had been held for many years, and management had ignored earlier demands that such meetings be held).

3. *Large number of shareholders*. The cases are split on whether demand on shareholders is excused because the corporation has a large number of shareholders. Most modern cases addressing the topic reflect the reasoning in Harhen v. Brown, supra, the Massachusetts court said, "Although we have not previously recognized such an exception, we conclude today that an exception to the shareholder demand requirement, where a very large number of shareholders is involved, as in this case, is eminently reasonable, and we therefore adopt such an exception. To hold otherwise would place a tremendous financial and administrative burden on plaintiffs; in this case requiring the plaintiff to make demand on the seven million other policyholders."

4. *Nonratifiable wrong*. The cases are also split on whether demand on shareholders is excused where the alleged wrong could not be ratified. The majority rule, reflected in Mayer v. Adams, 37 Del.Ch. 298, 141 A.2d 458 (1958) is that nonratifiability excuses demand. However, there is a very strong minority view. For example, in Bell v. Arnold, 175 Colo. 277, 283, 487 P.2d 545, 547 (1971), the court stated:

> One reason set forth in the complaint for not making a demand on the shareholders is that they could not ratify the alleged wrongs because of the illegal nature of the wrongs. We hold this is not an acceptable reason or a valid excuse for not making a demand on the shareholders here. The purpose of making demand on the shareholders is to inform them of the alleged nonratifiable wrongs; to seek their participation in avail-

> able courses of action, such as, the removal of the involved directors and the election of new directors who will seek the redress required in the circumstances; or to secure shareholder approval of an action for damages to the corporation caused by the alleged wrongdoing directors.

See also Claman v. Robertson, 164 Ohio St. 61, 128 N.E.2d 429 (1955).

Ratification of the alleged underlying misconduct needs to be distinguished from the broader question of the shareholders' power/capacity to opine whether the suit's prosecution is in the best interests of the corporation. That is, a distinction must be drawn between the question whether a plaintiff must make a demand on shareholders to allow the firm's owners to decide whether the suit is in the firm's best interests and the question whether shareholder ratification has a substantive effect. A further distinction was drawn in an earlier holding that the shareholders have power to preclude suit even where they do not have power to ratify. The leading case is S. Solomont & Sons Trust v. New England Theatres Operating Corp., 326 Mass. 99, 111–12, 93 N.E.2d 241, 247–48 (1950). Massachusetts now authorizes shareholder consideration only in the narrow instance in which the board of directors refers the matter to the shareholders. *See* Mass. Gen Laws Ann. Ch. 156D § 7.42.

SECTION 8. INDEMNIFICATION AND INSURANCE

A. INDEMNIFICATION

1. The right of a director or officer to indemnification under the common law was not completely clear. New York Dock Co. v. McCollom, 173 Misc. 106, 16 N.Y.S.2d 844 (1939), decided prior to the enactment of the New York indemnification statute, held that, even though the directors had successfully defended themselves in a derivative suit, they were not entitled to reimbursement of their counsel fees absent proof that their defense benefitted the corporation. Later decisions in other jurisdictions, however, upheld the common law right of a vindicated director to recover the expenses of his defense without any showing of a specific benefit to the corporation. In re E.C. Warner Co., 232 Minn. 207, 45 N.W.2d 388 (1950); Solimine v. Hollander, 129 N.J.Eq. 264, 19 A.2d 344 (Ch.1941). The policy reasons why the corporation should indemnify a director, as set forth in *Solimine,* are (1) to encourage innocent directors to resist unjust charges and provide them an opportunity to hire competent counsel; (2) to induce "responsible business men to accept the post of directors": and (3) "to discourage in large measure stockholders' litigation of the strike variety." Id. at 272, 19 A.2d at 348. Today, virtually

every state has an indemnification statute, but the statutes vary widely in detail.

DEL. GEN. CORP. LAW § 145

[See Statutory Supplement]

MODEL BUS. CORP. ACT §§ 8.50–8.59

[See Statutory Supplement]

N.Y. BUS. CORP. LAW §§ 721–726

[See Statutory Supplement]

CAL. CORP. CODE § 317

[See Statutory Supplement]

ALI, PRINCIPLES OF CORPORATE GOVERNANCE § 7.20

[See Statutory Supplement]

Waltuch v. Conticommodity Services, Inc.

United States Court of Appeals, Second Circuit, 1996.
88 F.3d 87.

■ Before: VAN GRAAFEILAND, JACOBS and PARKER, CIRCUIT JUDGES.

■ JACOBS, CIRCUIT JUDGE:

Famed silver trader Norton Waltuch spent $2.2 million in unreimbursed legal fees to defend himself against numerous civil lawsuits and an enforcement proceeding brought by the Commodity Futures Trading Commission (CFTC). In this action under Delaware law, Waltuch seeks indemnification of his legal expenses from his former employer. The district court denied any indemnity, and Waltuch appeals.

As vice-president and chief metals trader for Conticommodity Services, Inc., Waltuch traded silver for the firm's clients, as well as for his own account. In late 1979 and early 1980, the silver price spiked upward as the then-billionaire Hunt brothers and several of Waltuch's foreign clients bought huge quantities of silver futures contracts. Just as rapidly, the price fell until (on a day remembered in trading circles as "Silver Thursday") the silver market crashed. Between 1981 and 1985, angry silver speculators filed numerous lawsuits against Waltuch and Conticommodity, alleging fraud, market manipulation, and antitrust violations. All of the suits eventually settled and were dismissed with prejudice, pursuant to settlements in which Conticommodity paid over $35 million to the various suitors. Waltuch himself was dismissed from the suits with no settlement contribution. His unreimbursed legal expenses in these actions total approximately $1.2 million.

Waltuch was also the subject of an enforcement proceeding brought by the CFTC, charging him with fraud and market manipulation. The proceeding was settled, with Waltuch agreeing to a penalty that included a $100,000 fine and a six-month ban on buying or selling futures contracts from any exchange floor. Waltuch spent $1 million in unreimbursed legal fees in the CFTC proceeding.[1]

Waltuch brought suit in the United States District Court for the Southern District of New York (Lasker, J.) against Conticommodity and its parent company, Continental Grain Co. (together "Conti"), for indemnification of his unreimbursed expenses.[2] Only two of Waltuch's claims reach us on appeal.

Waltuch first claims that Article Ninth of Conticommodity's articles of incorporation requires Conti to indemnify him for his expenses in both the private and CFTC actions. Conti responds that this claim is barred by subsection (a) of § 145 of Delaware's General Corporation Law, which permits indemnification only if the corporate officer acted "in good faith," something that Waltuch has not established. Waltuch counters that subsection (f) of the same statute permits a corporation to grant indemnification rights outside the limits of subsection (a), and that Conticommodity did so with Article Ninth (which has no stated good-faith limitation). The district court held that, notwithstanding § 145(f), Waltuch could recover under Article Ninth only if Waltuch met the "good faith" requirement of § 145(a).[3] 833 F.Supp. 302, 308–09 (S.D.N.Y.1993). On the factual issue of whether Waltuch had acted "in good faith," the court denied Conti's summary judgment motion and cleared the way for trial. Id. at 313. The parties then stipulated that they would forgo trial on the issue of Waltuch's "good faith," agree to an entry of final judgment against Waltuch on his claim under Article Ninth and § 145(f), and allow Waltuch to take an immediate

1. The parties have stipulated that Waltuch's "reasonable attorney's fees and costs" for the private lawsuits totaled $1,228,586.67, and that the comparable expenses for the CFTC proceeding are an even $1 million.

2. Conticommodity and Continental Grain are incorporated in Delaware and have their principal places of business in New York; Waltuch is a New Jersey citizen. We therefore have diversity jurisdiction under 28 U.S.C. § 1332. All parties agree that Delaware law governs.

3. A Special Committee of Continental Grain Co.'s Board of Directors reached the same conclusion in November 1991. Waltuch filed his complaint two months later. In the district court, Conti argued that under the business judgment rule, the Special Committee's decision was immune from challenge, an argument the district court rejected. 833 F.Supp. at 305. Although the parties signed a stipulation preserving Conti's right to contest the district court's ruling on this issue, Conti has abandoned its business judgment rule argument on appeal.

appeal of the judgment to this Court. Thus, as to Waltuch's first claim, the only question left is how to interpret §§ 145(a) and 145(f), assuming Waltuch acted with less than "good faith." As we explain in part I below, we affirm the district court's judgment as to this claim and hold that § 145(f) does not permit a corporation to bypass the"good faith" requirement of § 145(a).

Waltuch's second claim is that subsection (c) of § 145 requires Conti to indemnify him because he was "successful on the merits or otherwise" in the private lawsuits.[4] The district court ruled for Conti on this claim as well. The court explained that, even though all the suits against Waltuch were dismissed without his making any payment, he was not "successful on the merits or otherwise," because Conti's settlement payments to the plaintiffs were partially on Waltuch's behalf. Id. at 311. For the reasons stated in part II below, we reverse this portion of the district court's ruling, and hold that Conti must indemnify Waltuch under § 145(c) for the $1.2 million in unreimbursed legal fees he spent in defending the private lawsuits.

I

Article Ninth, on which Waltuch bases his first claim, is categorical and contains no requirement of "good faith":

> The Corporation shall indemnify and hold harmless each of its incumbent or former directors, officers, employees and agents ... against expenses actually and necessarily incurred by him in connection with the defense of any action, suit or proceeding threatened, pending or completed, in which he is made a party, by reason of his serving in or having held such position or capacity, except in relation to matters as to which he shall be adjudged in such action, suit or proceeding to be liable for negligence or misconduct in the performance of duty.[5]

Conti argues that § 145(a) of Delaware's General Corporation Law, which does contain a "good faith" requirement, fixes the outer limits of a corporation's power to indemnify; Article Ninth is thus invalid under Delaware law, says Conti, to the extent that it requires indemnification of officers who have acted in bad faith. The affirmative grant of power in § 145(a) is as follows:

> *A corporation shall have power to indemnify* any person who was or is a party or is threatened to be made a party to any threatened, pending or completed action, suit or proceeding, whether civil, criminal, administrative or investigative (other than an action by or in the right of the corporation) by reason of the fact that he is or was a director, officer, employee or agent of the corporation, or is or was serving at the request of the corporation

4. The district court held that Waltuch was not successful "on the merits or otherwise" in the CFTC proceeding. 833 F.Supp. at 311. Waltuch does not appeal this aspect of the court's ruling.

5. Because the private suits and the CFTC proceeding were settled, it is undisputed that Waltuch was not "adjudged ... to be liable for negligence or misconduct in the performance of duty."

> as a director, officer, employee or agent of another corporation, partnership, joint venture, trust or other enterprise, against expenses (including attorneys' fees), judgments, fines and amounts paid in settlement actually and reasonably incurred by him in connection with such action, suit or proceeding *if he acted in good faith and in a manner he reasonably believed to be in or not opposed to the best interests of the corporation,* and, with respect to any criminal action or proceeding, had no reasonable cause to believe his conduct was unlawful.

56 Del.Laws 50, § 1 at 170–71 (1967) (emphasis added) (rewriting Delaware's General Corporation Law, title 8, chapter 1 of the Delaware Code), *codified at* 8 Del.Code Ann. tit. 8, § 145(a) (Michie 1991). Key language in the Delaware Code Annotated's version of this subsection is in error, as explained in the margin.[6]

In order to escape the "good faith" clause of § 145(a), Waltuch argues that § 145(a) is not an *exclusive* grant of indemnification power, because § 145(f) expressly allows corporations to indemnify officers in a manner broader than that set out in § 145(a). The "nonexclusivity" language of § 145(f) provides:

> The indemnification and advancement of expenses provided by, or granted pursuant to, the other subsections of this section *shall not be deemed exclusive of any other rights* to which those seeking indemnification or advancement of expenses may be entitled under any bylaw, agreement, vote of stockholders or disinterested directors or otherwise, both as to action in his official capacity and as to action in another capacity while holding such office.

56 Del.Laws 50, § 1 at 172 (emphasis added), *as amended and codified* at 8 Del.Code Ann. tit. 8, § 145(f). Waltuch contends that the

---

6. There is some confusion about whether this subsection begins, "A corporation *shall have power* to indemnify ..." or "A corporation *may* indemnify ...". As originally enacted, § 145(a) contained the phrase "shall have power". 56 Del.Laws 50, § 1 at 170 (1967). According to the annotations in the *Delaware Code Annotated* (and confirmed by a review of the legislative records since 1967), § 145(a) has never been amended. *See* 8 Del.Code Ann. tit. 8, § 145(a) (1991 & 1995 Supp.).

Nevertheless, the *Delaware Code Annotated,* a private compilation by the Michie Company of all Delaware legislative acts, at some point began using the phrase "may" in place of "shall have power". *See* 8 Del.Code Ann. tit. 8, § 145(a) (1974). We have not been able to explain this non-legislative change in statutory language. The *Delaware Corporation Law Annotated,* published by the Corporation Trust Company, continues to use the phrase "shall have power". Del.Corp.L.Ann. § 145(a) (20th ed. Corp.Trust Co.1991).

One treatise uses the phrase "shall have power", *see* Ernest L. Folk, III, et al., *Folk on the Delaware General Corporation Law* at 145:1 (3d ed. 1994), while another uses "may". *See* 5 R. Franklin Balotti & Jesse A. Finkelstein, *The Delaware Law of Corporations and Business Organizations* at 100 (1990 & 1993 Supp.) ("Balotti & Finkelstein"). The parties to this appeal perpetuate the confusion: their joint appendix contains a version of § 145(a) that says "shall have power", but one of the briefs quotes a version that says "may".

When there is a conflict between an original enactment of the Delaware Legislature and the codification of the law, the original enactment controls. *Elliott v. Blue Cross & Blue Shield,* 407 A.2d 524, 528 (Del.1979); *Kimmey v. Farmers Bank,* 373 A.2d 569, 570 (Del.1977). We therefore employ the Legislature's version of § 145(a), which says "shall have power".

We are indebted to Lesley Lawrence and the staff at the Third Circuit library in Wilmington for their assistance on this issue.

"nonexclusivity" language in § 145(f) is a separate grant of indemnification power, not limited by the good faith clause that governs the power granted in § 145(a). Conti on the other hand contends that § 145(f) must be limited by "public policies," one of which is that a corporation may indemnify its officers only if they act in "good faith."

In a thorough and scholarly opinion, Judge Lasker agreed with Conti's reading of § 145(f), writing that "it has been generally agreed that there are public policy limits on indemnification under Section 145(f)," although it was "difficult . . . to define precisely what limitations on indemnification public policy imposes." 833 F.Supp. at 307, 308. After reviewing cases from Delaware and elsewhere and finding that they provided no authoritative guidance, Judge Lasker surveyed the numerous commentators on this issue and found that they generally agreed with Conti's position. *Id.* at 308–09. He also found that Waltuch's reading of § 145(f) failed to make sense of the statute as a whole:

> [T]here would be no point to the carefully crafted provisions of Section 145 spelling out the permissible scope of indemnification under Delaware law if subsection (f) allowed indemnification in additional circumstances without regard to these limits. The exception would swallow the rule.

Id. at 309. The fact that § 145(f) was limited by § 145(a) did not make § 145(f) meaningless, wrote Judge Lasker, because § 145(f) "still 'may authorize the adoption of various procedures and presumptions to make the process of indemnification more favorable to the indemnitee without violating the statute.'" *Id.* at 309 (quoting 1 Balotti & Finkelstein § 4.16 at 4–321). As will be evident from the discussion below, we adopt much of Judge Lasker's analysis.

A. *Delaware Cases*

No Delaware court has decided the very issue presented here; but the applicable cases tend to support the proposition that a corporation's grant of indemnification rights cannot be *inconsistent* with the substantive statutory provisions of § 145, notwithstanding § 145(f). We draw this rule of "consistency" primarily from our reading of the Delaware Supreme Court's opinion in *Hibbert v. Hollywood Park, Inc.*, 457 A.2d 339 (Del.1983). In that case, Hibbert and certain other directors sued the corporation and the remaining directors, and then demanded indemnification for their expenses and fees related to the litigation. The company refused indemnification on the ground that directors were entitled to indemnification only as *defendants* in legal proceedings. The court reversed the trial court and held that Hibbert was entitled to indemnification under the plain terms of a company bylaw that did not draw an express distinction between plaintiff directors and defendant directors. *Id.* at 343. The court then proceeded to test the bylaw for consistency with § 145(a):

> Furthermore, *indemnification here is consistent with current Delaware law.* Under 8 Del.C. § 145(a) . . ., "a corporation may indemnify any person who was or is a party or is threatened to be

> made a party to any threatened, pending or completed" derivative or third-party action. By this language, indemnity is *not limited to* only those who stand as a defendant in the main action. The corporation can also grant indemnification rights beyond those provided by statute. 8 Del.C. § 145(f).

Id. at 344 (emphasis added and citations omitted). *See supra* note 6 (explaining the error in the *Delaware Code Annotated*'s use of the phrase "may indemnify" in § 145(a)). This passage contains two complementary propositions. Under § 145(f), a corporation may provide indemnification rights that go "beyond" the rights provided by § 145(a) and the other substantive subsections of § 145. At the same time, any such indemnification rights provided by a corporation must be "consistent with" the substantive provisions of § 145, including § 145(a). In *Hibbert,* the corporate bylaw was "consistent with" § 145(a), because this subsection was "not limited to" suits in which directors were defendants. *Hibbert*'s holding may support an inverse corollary that illuminates our case: if § 145(a) had been expressly limited to directors who were named as defendants, the bylaw could not have stood, regardless of § 145(f), because the bylaw would not have been "consistent with" the substantive statutory provision.[7] . . .

B. *Statutory Reading*

The "consistency" rule suggested by [the] Delaware cases is reinforced by our reading of § 145 as a whole. Subsections (a) (indemnification for third-party actions) and (b) (similar indemnification for derivative suits) expressly grant a corporation the power to indemnify directors, officers, and others, if they "acted in good faith and in a manner reasonably believed to be in or not opposed to the best interest of the corporation." These provisions thus limit the scope of the power that they confer. They are permissive in the sense that a corporation may exercise less than its full power to grant the indemnification rights set out in these provisions. *See Essential Enter. Corp. v. Dorsey Corp.,* 182 A.2d 647, 653 (Del.Ch.1962). By the same token, subsection (f) permits the corporation to grant additional rights: the rights provided in the rest of § 145 "shall not be deemed exclusive of any other rights to which those seeking indemnification may be entitled." But crucially, subsection (f) merely acknowledges that one seeking indemnification may be entitled to "other rights" (of indemni-

---

7. The *Hibbert* court cites to a 1978 article by Samuel Arsht, chairman of the committee of experts that drafted Delaware's General Corporation Law in 1967, *id.,* which supports our conclusion that indemnification rights permitted under § 145(f) must be consistent with the other substantive provisions of § 145. At the pages cited by the court, Arsht writes:

> The question most frequently asked by practicing lawyers is what subsection (f), the nonexclusive clause, means.... The question which subsection (f) invariably raises is whether a corporation can adopt a by-law or make a contract with its directors providing that they will be indemnified for whatever they may have to pay if they are sued and lose or settle. The answer to this question is "no." Subsection (f) ... permits additional rights to be created, but *it is not a blanket authorization to indemnify directors* against all expenses, fines, or settlements of whatever nature and *regardless of the directors' conduct.* The statutory language is circumscribed by limits of public policy....

S. Samuel Arsht, *Indemnification Under Section 145 of Delaware General Corporation Law,* 3 Del.J.Corp.L. 176, 176–77 (1978) (emphasis added).

fication or otherwise); it does not speak in terms of corporate power, and therefore cannot be read to free a corporation from the "good faith" limit explicitly imposed in subsections (a) and (b).

An alternative construction of these provisions would effectively force us to ignore certain explicit terms of the statute. Section 145(a) gives Conti the power to indemnify Waltuch "*if* he acted in good faith and in a manner reasonably believed to be in or not opposed to the best interest of the corporation." 56 Del.Laws 50, § 1 at 171 (emphasis added). This statutory limit must mean that there is *no power* to indemnify Waltuch if he did not act in good faith. Otherwise, as Judge Lasker pointed out, § 145(a)—and its good faith clause—would have no meaning: a corporation could indemnify whomever and however it wished regardless of the good faith clause or anything else the Delaware Legislature wrote into § 145(a).

When the Legislature intended a subsection of § 145 to augment the powers limited in subsection (a), it set out the additional powers expressly. Thus subsection (g) explicitly allows a corporation to circumvent the "good faith" clause of subsection (a) by purchasing a directors and officers liability insurance policy. Significantly, that subsection is framed as a grant of corporate power:

> A corporation shall have power to purchase and maintain insurance on behalf of any person who is or was a director, officer, employee or agent of the corporation ... against any liability asserted against him and incurred by him in any such capacity, or arising out of his status as such, *whether or not the corporation would have the power to indemnify him against such liability under this section.*

56 Del.Laws 50, § 1 at 172 (1967) (emphasis added), *codified at* 8 Del.Code Ann. tit. 8, § 145(g) (Michie 1991). The italicized passage reflects the principle that corporations have the power under § 145 to indemnify in some situations and not in others. Since § 145(f) is neither a grant of corporate power nor a limitation on such power, subsection (g) must be referring to the limitations set out in § 145(a) and the other provisions of § 145 that describe corporate power. If § 145 (through subsection (f) or another part of the statute) gave corporations unlimited power to indemnify directors and officers, then the final clause of subsection (g) would be unnecessary: that is, its grant of "power to purchase and maintain insurance" (exercisable regardless of whether the corporation itself would have the power to indemnify the loss directly) is meaningful only because, in some insurable situations, the corporation simply lacks the power to indemnify its directors and officers directly.

A contemporaneous account from the principal drafter of Delaware's General Corporation Law confirms what an integral reading of § 145 demonstrates: the statute's affirmative grants of power also impose limitations on the corporation's power to indemnify. Specifically, the good faith clause (unchanged since the Law's original enactment in 1967) was included in subsections (a) and (b) as a carefully calculated improvement on the prior indemnification provision and as an explicit limit on a corporation's power to indemnify:

> During the three years of the Revision Committee's study, no subject was more discussed among members of the corporate bar than the subject of indemnification of officers and directors. As far as Delaware law was concerned, the existing statutory provision on the subject had been found inadequate. Numerous by-laws and charter provisions had been adopted clarifying and extending its terms, but *uncertainty existed in many instances as to whether such provisions transgressed the limits* which the courts had indicated they would establish based on public policy....
>
> It was ... apparent that revision was appropriate with respect to *the limitations which must necessarily be placed on the power to indemnify* in order to prevent the statute from undermining the substantive provisions of the criminal law and corporation law....
>
> [There was a] need for a ... provision to protect the corporation law's requirement of loyalty to the corporation.... Ultimately, it was decided that *the power to indemnify should not be granted unless* it appeared that the person seeking indemnification had "acted in good faith and in a manner reasonably believed to be in or not opposed to the best interest of the corporation."

S. Samuel Arsht & Walter K. Stapleton, *Delaware's New General Corporation Law: Substantive Changes,* 23 Bus.Law. 75, 77–78 (1967).[8] This passage supports *Hibbert*'s rule of "consistency" and makes clear that a corporation has no power to transgress the indemnification limits set out in the substantive provisions of § 145.

Waltuch argues at length that reading § 145(a) to bar the indemnification of officers who acted in bad faith would render § 145(f) meaningless. This argument misreads § 145(f). That subsection refers to "any other rights to which those seeking indemnification or advancement of expenses may be entitled." Delaware commentators have identified various indemnification rights that are "beyond those provided by statute," *Hibbert,* 457 A.2d at 344, and that are at the same time consistent with the statute:

> [S]ubsection (f) provides general authorization for the adoption of various procedures and presumptions making the process of indemnification more favorable to the indemnitee. For example, indemnification agreements or by-laws could provide for: (i) mandatory indemnification unless prohibited by statute; (ii) mandatory advancement of expenses, which the indemnitee can, in many instances, obtain on demand; (iii) accelerated procedures for the "determination" required by section 145(d) to be made in the "specific case"; (iv) litigation "appeal" rights of the indemni-

8. Delaware commentators consider this article to be part of (if not all of) "[t]he legislative history of Section 145." A. Gilchrist Sparks, III, et al., *Indemnification, Directors and Officers Liability Insurance and Limitations of Director Liability Pursuant to Statutory Authorization: The Legal Framework Under Delaware Law,* 696 PLI/Corp. 941 (1990) (at page 10 out of 123 on WESTLAW)....

> tee in the event of an unfavorable determination; (v) procedures under which a favorable determination will be deemed to have been made under circumstances where the board fails or refuses to act; [and] (vi) reasonable funding mechanisms.

E. Norman Veasey, et al., *Delaware Supports Directors With a Three-Legged Stool of Limited Liability, Indemnification, and Insurance,* 42 Bus.Law. 399, 415 (1987).[9] Moreover, subsection (f) may reference nonindemnification rights, such as advancement rights or rights to other payments from the corporation that do not qualify as indemnification.

We need not decide in this case the precise scope of those "other rights" adverted to in § 145(f). We simply conclude that § 145(f) is not rendered meaningless or inoperative by the conclusion that a Delaware corporation lacks power to indemnify an officer or director "unless [he] 'acted in good faith and in a manner reasonably believed to be in or not opposed to the best interest of the corporation.' " *See* Arsht & Stapleton, 23 Bus.Law. at 78. As a result, we hold that Conti's Article Ninth, which would require indemnification of Waltuch even if he acted in bad faith, is inconsistent with § 145(a) and thus exceeds the scope of a Delaware corporation's power to indemnify. Since Waltuch has agreed to forgo his opportunity to prove at trial that he acted in good faith, he is not entitled to indemnification under Article Ninth for the $2.2 million he spent in connection with the private lawsuits and the CFTC proceeding. We therefore affirm the district court on this issue.

II

Unlike § 145(a), which grants a discretionary indemnification power, § 145(c) affirmatively *requires* corporations to indemnify its officers and directors for the "successful" defense of certain claims:

> To the extent that a director, officer, employee or agent of a corporation has been successful on the merits or otherwise in defense of any action, suit or proceeding referred to in subsections (a) and (b) of this section, or in defense of any claim, issue or matter therein, he shall be indemnified against expenses (including attorneys' fees) actually and reasonably incurred by him in connection therewith.

56 Del.Laws 50, § 1 at 171 (1967), *codified at* 8 Del.Code Ann. tit. 8, § 145(c) (Michie 1991). Waltuch argues that he was "successful on the merits or otherwise" in the private lawsuits, because they were dismissed with prejudice without any payment or assumption of liability by him. Conti argues that the claims against Waltuch were dismissed only because of Conti's $35 million settlement payments, and that this payment was contributed, in part, "on behalf of Waltuch."[10]

---

9. Veasey is now Chief Justice of the Delaware Supreme Court. *See also* 1 Balotti & Finkelstein § 4.16 at 4–321, which makes the same suggestions. Other suggestions are made in Joseph F. Johnston, Jr., *Corporate Indemnification and Liability Insurance for Directors and Officers,* 33 Bus.Law. 1993, 1996, 2009–10 (1978).

10. Although this is not essential to our holding, we note that Conti points to no evidence in support of its contention that the plaintiffs would have continued to pursue their suits as to Waltuch if Conti had paid some lesser amount.

The district court agreed with Conti that "the successful settlements cannot be credited to Waltuch but are attributable solely to Conti's settlement payments. It was not Waltuch who was successful, but Conti who was successful for him." 833 F.Supp. at 311. The district court held that § 145(c) mandates indemnification when the director or officer "is vindicated," but that there was no vindication here:

> Vindication is also ordinarily associated with a dismissal with prejudice without any payment. However, a director or officer is not vindicated when the reason he did not have to make a settlement payment is because someone else assumed that liability. Being bailed out is not the same thing as being vindicated.

Id. We believe that this understanding and application of the "vindication" concept is overly broad and is inconsistent with a proper interpretation of § 145(c).

No Delaware court has applied § 145(c) in the context of indemnification stemming from the settlement of civil litigation. One lower court, however, has applied that subsection to an analogous case in the criminal context, and has illuminated the link between "vindication" and the statutory phrase, "successful on the merits or otherwise." In *Merritt–Chapman & Scott Corp. v. Wolfson,* 321 A.2d 138 (Del.Super.Ct.1974), the corporation's agents were charged with several counts of criminal conduct. A jury found them guilty on some counts, but deadlocked on the others. The agents entered into a "settlement" with the prosecutor's office by pleading nolo contendere to one of the counts in exchange for the dropping of the rest. *Id.* at 140. The agents claimed entitlement to mandatory indemnification under § 145(c) as to the counts that were dismissed. In opposition, the corporation raised an argument similar to the argument raised by Conti:

> [The corporation] argues that the statute and sound public policy require indemnification only where there has been vindication by a finding or concession of innocence. *It contends that the charges against [the agents] were dropped for practical reasons,* not because of their innocence....
>
> The statute requires indemnification to the extent that the claimant "has been successful on the merits or otherwise." *Success is vindication.* In a criminal action, any result other than conviction must be considered success. *Going behind the result,* as [the corporation] attempts, is neither authorized by subsection (c) nor consistent with the presumption of innocence.

Id. at 141 (emphasis added).

Although the underlying proceeding in *Merritt* was criminal, the court's analysis is instructive here. The agents in *Merritt* rendered consideration—their guilty plea on one count—to achieve the dismissal of the other counts. The court considered these dismissals both "success" and (therefore) "vindication," and refused to "go[ ] behind the result" or to appraise the reason for the success. In equating "success" with "vindication," the court thus rejected the more expansive view of vindication urged by the corporation. Under *Merritt*'s holding, then, vindication, when used as a synonym for "success" under § 145(c), does not mean moral exoneration. Escape from an adverse judgment or other detriment, for whatever reason, is determinative. According to *Merritt,* the only question a court may ask is what the result was, not why it was.[12]

Conti's contention that, because of its $35 million settlement payments, Waltuch's settlement without payment should not really count as settlement without payment, is inconsistent with the rule in *Merritt.* Here, Waltuch was sued, and the suit was dismissed without his having paid a settlement. Under the approach taken in *Merritt,* it is not our business to ask why this result was reached. Once Waltuch achieved his settlement gratis, he achieved success "on the merits or otherwise." And, as we know from *Merritt,* success is sufficient to constitute vindication (at least for the purposes of § 145(c)). Waltuch's settlement thus vindicated him.

The concept of "vindication" pressed by Conti is also inconsistent with the fact that a director or officer who is able to defeat an adversary's claim by asserting a technical defense is entitled to indemnification under § 145(c). *See* 1 Balotti & Finkelstein, § 4.13 at 4–302. In such cases, the indemnitee has been "successful" in the palpable sense that he has won, and the suit has been dismissed, whether or not the victory is deserved in merits terms. If a technical defense is deemed "vindication" under Delaware law, it cannot matter why Waltuch emerged unscathed, or whether Conti "bailed [him] out", or whether his success was deserved. Under § 145(c), mere success is vindication enough.

This conclusion comports with the reality that civil judgments and settlements are ordinarily expressed in terms of cash rather than moral victory. No doubt, it would make sense for Conti to buy the dismissal of the claims against Waltuch along with its own discharge from the case, perhaps to avoid further expense or participation as a non-party, potential cross-claims, or negative publicity. But Waltuch apparently did not accede to that arrangement, and Delaware law cannot allow an indemnifying corporation to escape the mandatory indemnification of

12. Our adoption of *Merritt*'s interpretation of the statutory term "successful" does not necessarily signal our endorsement of the result in that case. The *Merritt* court sliced the case into individual counts, with indemnification pegged to each count independently of the others. We are not faced with a case in which the corporate officer claims to have been "successful" on some parts of the case but was clearly "unsuccessful" on others, and therefore take no position on this feature of the *Merritt* holding.

We also do not mean our discussion of *Merritt* to suggest that the line between success and failure in a criminal case may be drawn in the same way in the civil context. In a criminal case, conviction on a particular count is obvious failure, and dismissal of the charge is obvious success. In a civil suit for damages, however, there is a monetary continuum between complete success (dismissal of the suit without any payment) and complete failure (payment of the full amount of damages requested by the plaintiff). Because Waltuch made no payment in connection with the dismissal of the suits against him, we need not decide whether a defendant's settlement payment automatically renders that defendant "unsuccessful" under § 145(c).

subsection (c) by paying a sum in settlement on behalf of an unwilling indemnitee.

... In *Wisener v. Air Express Int'l Corp.*, 583 F.2d 579 (2d Cir.1978), we construed an Illinois indemnification statute that was intentionally enacted as a copy of Delaware's § 145. *See id.* at 582 n. 3; 1 Balotti & Finkelstein, § 4.12 at 4–296 n. 1048 (§ 145 was the "prototype" for Illinois's indemnification statute). Our holding in that case is perfectly applicable here:

> It is contended that [the director] was not "successful" in the litigation, since the third-party claims against him never proceeded to trial. The statute, however, refers to success "on the merits or otherwise," which surely is broad enough to cover a termination of claims by agreement without any payment or assumption of liability.

583 F.2d at 583. It is undisputed that the private lawsuits against Conti and Waltuch were dismissed with prejudice, "without any payment of assumption of liability" by Waltuch. Applying the analysis of *Wisener,* Conti must indemnify Waltuch for his expenses in connection with the private lawsuits.

... [T]he extent of Waltuch's success] is not lessened by Conti's payments, even if it is true (as it stands to reason) that his success was achieved because Conti was willing to pay. Whatever the impetus for the plaintiffs' dismissal of their claims against Waltuch, he still walked away without liability and without making a payment. This constitutes a success that is untarnished by the process that achieved it.

For all of these reasons, we agree with Waltuch that he is entitled to indemnification under § 145(c) for his expenses pertaining to the private lawsuits.

III

The judgment of the district court is affirmed in part and reversed in part. This case is remanded to the district court so that judgment may be entered in favor of Waltuch on his claim for $1,228,586.67, representing the unreimbursed expenses from the private lawsuits. *See supra* note 1.

If Norton Waltuch's good faith had been an issue in *Waltuch*, how would this have been resolved? *See* In re Landmark Land Co., 76 F.3d 553, 565 (4th Cir. 1996).

> An agent who has intentionally participated in illegal activity or wrongful conduct against third persons cannot be said to have acted in good faith, even if the conduct benefits the corporation. *Plate [v. Sun–Diamond Growers], 275 Cal.Rptr. at 672.* "For example, corporate executives who participate in a deliberate price-fixing conspiracy with competing firms could not be found to have acted in good faith, even though they may have reason-

> ably believed that a deliberate flouting of the antitrust laws would increase the profits of the corporation." 1 Harold Marsh, Jr. and R. Roy Finkle, Marsh's California Corporation Law (3d ed.) § 10.43, at 751; see *Plate, 275 Cal.Rptr. at 672* (citing same language from second edition).... [A] deliberate attempt to undermine the regulatory authority of a government agency cannot constitute good faith conduct, even if such actions benefit the corporation.

See also Biondi v. Beekman Hill House Apartment Corp., 731 N.E.2d 577, 581 (N.Y. 2000) (denying indemnification for punitive damage claims reasoning that officer who intentionally denied lease application on the basis of the applicant's race thereby knowingly subjected the corporation to liability under the civil rights laws and, hence, his actions "cannot be considered an act in the corporation's best interests").

Do the same public policy considerations apply when the conduct to be indemnified is not willful but rather bumbling? In Globus v. Law Research Service, Inc., 418 F.2d 1276 (2d Cir.1969), cert. denied 397 U.S. 913, 90 S.Ct. 913, 25 L.Ed.2d 93 (1970) plaintiffs, who had purchased stock under an allegedly misleading offering circular, brought actions under § 17(a) of the 1933 Act and Rule 10b–5 against the issuer, the underwriter, and the issuer's president. The underwriter cross-claimed against the issuer pursuant to an agreement under which the issuer had promised to indemnify the underwriter for any loss arising out of defects in the offering circular, except for those attributable to the underwriter's "willful misfeasance, bad faith or gross negligence ... or ... reckless disregard of its obligations under the agreement." Id. at 1287. The court concluded that the underwriter had actual knowledge of material misstatements in the circular, and denied the cross-claim both because it fell within the exception to the agreement and on grounds of public policy:

> Given [the underwriter's actual knowledge of material misstatements],.... to tolerate indemnity under these circumstances would encourage flouting the policy of the common law and the Securities Act....
>
> Civil liability under section 11 and similar provisions was designed not so much to compensate the defrauded purchaser as to promote enforcement of the Act and to deter negligence by providing a penalty for those who fail in their duties. And Congress intended to impose a "high standard of trusteeship" on underwriters. Thus, what Professor Loss terms the "*in terrorem* effect" of civil liability might well be thwarted if underwriters were free to pass their liability on to the issuer. Underwriters who knew they could be indemnified simply by showing that the issuer was "more liable" than they (a process not too difficult when the issuer is inevitably closer to the facts) would have a tendency to be lax in their independent investigations. Cases upholding indemnity for negligence in other fields are not necessarily apposite.

The goal in such cases is to compensate the injured party. But the Securities Act is more concerned with prevention than cure.

Globus involved "a sin graver than ordinary negligence," and left open the propriety of indemnification for negligence or other lesser sins. Some later cases have held that the policy of the Securities Acts bars indemnification for negligence; others have held indemnification for negligence permissible under the Securities Acts where the indemnitor's conduct was significantly more wrongful than that of the indemnitee. See Donaldson Lufkin & Jenrette Securities Corp. v. Star Technologies, 148 Misc.2d 880, 561 N.Y.S.2d 371 (1990), aff'd, Donaldson, Lufkin & Jenrette Sec. Corp. v. Star Technologies, Inc., 180 A.D.2d 495, 580 N.Y.S.2d 657 (1st Dep't 1992) (reviewing cases); ALI, Principles of Corporate Governance § 7.20, Reporter's Note 7. It has been held that indemnification for liability under section 16(b) would violate public policy, even though section 16(b) does not require proof of fraudulent intent. See First Golden Bancorporation v. Weiszmann, 942 F.2d 726 (10th Cir.1991).

Under SEC Regulation S–K, Item 512(h), if a registrant seeks acceleration of a prospectus (as most registrants do), and any provision or agreement exists under which the registrant may indemnify a director or officer against liabilities arising under the Securities Act, then unless the right to indemnification is waived, the registrant must include the following statement in the Prospectus:

> Insofar as indemnification for liabilities arising under the Securities Act of 1933 may be permitted to directors, officers and controlling persons of the registrant pursuant to the foregoing provisions, or otherwise, the registrant has been advised that in the opinion of the Securities and Exchange Commission such indemnification is against public policy as expressed in the Act and is, therefore, unenforceable. In the event that a claim for indemnification against such liabilities (other than the payment by the registrant of expenses incurred or paid by a director, officer or controlling person of the registrant in the successful defense of any action, suit or proceeding) is asserted by such director, officer or controlling person in connection with the securities being registered, the registrant will, unless in the opinion of its counsel the matter has been settled by controlling precedent, submit to a court of appropriate jurisdiction the question whether such indemnification by it is against public policy as expressed in the Act and will be governed by the final adjudication of such issue.

NOTE ON THE SCOPE OF INDEMNIFICATION PROVISIONS

Indemnity statutes, bylaws and board resolutions frequently provide indemnification and advancement of litigation costs to "agents." Such provisions have spawned a good deal of litigation whether the individual seeking indemnification or an advance was an agent. Can a company's outside lawyer also be its "agent? *See* Cohen v. Southbridge

Park, 369 N.J.Super. 156, 848 A.2d 781 (N.J. Super. App. Div. 2004) (attorney who represented corporation in its negotiations with a departing officer and later was sued for malpractice in attorney's representation of the company is not an agent within the scope of the indemnification provision because he was not cloaked with any management authority); Zaman v. Amedeo Holdings, Inc., 2008 WL 2168397 (Del.Ch.) (attorneys who were retained to look after client's American companies were at least agents of the corporation since they enjoyed powers co-equal to that of directors). Another heavily litigated issue is whether the act prompting the quest for indemnification or an advance was an act committed in an official capacity as an officer, director or even agent.?" In Vergopia v. Shaker, 922 A.2d 1238 (N.J. 2007), the outside attorney who served as the company's secretary was sued for slander and emotional distress flowing from an employee's dismissal that was described in SEC filings that were reviewed and edited by the attorney. Although the bylaws conditioned indemnification on the act giving rise to indemnification occurring within the officer's official capacity, a majority of the New Jersey Supreme Court held that this limitation, because it only appeared in the company's bylaws, did not qualify the broader right's granted in the articles of incorporation (which did not contain the limiting language). It therefore awarded indemnification. Some conduct is inherently individual and not in a corporate or representative capacity. *See* Plate v. Sun–Diamond Growers, 225 Cal.App.3d 1115, 1122–1123, 275 Cal.Rptr. 667, 671 (1990).

> The first prerequisite to indemnification under section 317, subdivision (b) [of the California Corporation Code] is that the action against the person is brought 'by reason of the fact that the person is or was an agent of the corporation.' Marsh, in his treatise on California corporation law, explains: 'In other words, the conduct of the agent which gives rise to the claim against him must have been performed in connection with his corporate functions and not with respect to purely personal matters.' (1 Marsh, Cal.Corporation Law (2d ed.) § 9.36, p. 536.) Where personal motives, not the corporate good, are predominant in a transaction giving rise to an action, indemnification is not warranted. For example, '[i]t would ... appear unlikely that an officer could properly claim that he was entitled to indemnification as the result of litigation brought to recover short-swing profits or profits from trading in the stock of his corporation on the basis of inside information....' (Heyler, *Indemnification of Corporate Agents* (1976) 23 UCLA L.Rev. 1255, 1258, fn. 24.)
>
> Sister-state authorities illustrate this rule. In *Tomash v. Midwest Technical Development Corp.* (1968) 281 Minn. 21, 160 N.W.2d 273, 277–278, where the Minnesota indemnification statute contained the 'by reason of the fact' requirement, the court held that directors seeking indemnification for defending themselves in an SEC proceeding stemming from their personal investments in certain stock, did not meet the requirement because the statute 'speak[s] in terms of indemnification to one who defends

> himself as a director or officer of the corporation' whereas 'the officers and directors [seeking indemnification] were defending themselves from alleged violations of the Investment Company Act, from which they personally profited. The two are not the same.' (*Ibid.*). . . .

Indemnification was denied on just such reasoning in Stifel Financial Corp. v. Cochran, 809 A.2d 555 (Del. 2002). Cochran had been discharged as an officer and director of Stifel Nicolaus corporation, a wholly owned subsidiary of Stifel Financial Corporation ("Stifel"). Cochran then refused to repay to Stifel Nicolaus excess compensation and the balance of a promissory note, as required by his employment agreement. To recover these amounts, Stifel Nicolaus instituted an arbitration proceeding against Cochran. The arbitrators ruled in favor of Stifel Nicolaus on the excess-compensation and promissory-note claims, and ordered Cochran to repay Stifel Nicolaus approximately $1.2 million. The arbitration award was confirmed by the United States District Court for the Eastern District of Missouri.

Stifel's bylaws contained the following indemnification provision:

> The Corporation [Stifel] shall indemnify to the full extent authorized by law any person made or threatened to be made a party to any action, suit, or proceeding, whether criminal, civil, administrative or investigative, by reason of the fact that he . . . is or was a director, officer or employee of the Corporation or any predecessor of the Corporation or serves or served any other enterprise as a director, officer or employee at the request of the Corporation or any predecessor of the Corporation.

Cochran filed an action seeking indemnification from Stifel pursuant to this bylaw. The Delaware Supreme Court held that Cochran was not entitled to indemnification for the amounts he was required to pay to Stifel on the basis of the compensation and promissory note claims because the liability did not result from actions by Cochran in his official capacity:

> The arbitration action was brought against Cochran to enforce certain provisions of an employment contract and promissory note, which Cochran had entered into with Stifel Nicolaus. The Court of Chancery's explanation bears repeating:
>
>> When a corporate officer signs an employment contract committing to fill an office, he is acting in a personal capacity in an adversarial, arms-length transaction. To the extent that he binds himself to certain obligations under that contract, he owes a personal obligation to the corporation. When the corporation brings a claim and proves its entitlement to relief because the officer has breached his individual obligations, it is problematic to conclude that the suit has been rendered an "official capacity" suit subject to indemnification under § 145 and implementing bylaws. Such a conclusion would render the officer's duty to perform his side of the contract in many respects illusory.

> We agree that the claims litigated in the arbitration action were properly characterized as personal, not directed at Cochran in his "official capacity" as an officer and director of Stifel Nicolaus.... Stifel Nicolaus based the Compensation Claim [and] the Promissory Note Claim ... on the employment contract Cochran entered into with the company. Although Cochran's termination is the event that triggered the relevant provisions of the employment contract, Cochran's decision to breach the contract was entirely a personal one, pursued for his sole benefit....

Id. at 562.

NOTE ON ADVANCES

In Advanced Mining Systems, Inc. v. Fricke, 623 A.2d 82 (Del.Ch. 1992), the Delaware court held that indemnification rights and advancement rights stand apart as two "distinct types of legal rights," so that a bylaw provision that required a corporation to "indemnify ... to the extent permitted" under Delaware law did not wrest from a corporation the ability to refuse advances. See also Rev. Model Bus. Corp. Act § 8.58(a) and Official Comment.

B. INSURANCE

[See Chapter 8.]

SECTION 9. THE ROLE OF CORPORATE COUNSEL

Bell Atlantic Corp. v. Bolger

United States Court of Appeals, Third Circuit, 1993.
2 F.3d 1304.

■ SCIRICA, CIRCUIT JUDGE ...

[The Pennsylvania Attorney General sued Bell Atlantic alleging it had defrauded consumers. After some initial skirmishing, Bell Atlantic settled the matter, paying $40 million in customer rebates, making contributions to a consumer education trust, and reimbursing the legal costs of the Attorney General. Following the settlement of the government's suit, a derivative suit was filed seeking to recoup from the Bell Atlantic directors the sums paid to consumers and the attorney general. The derivative suit plaintiff alleged that the misconduct prompting the state's successful action was the result of mismanagement and a breach of the directors' fiduciary duties to the corporation. Bell Atlantic's board appointed a special litigation committee that, after a thorough investigation, opined that the suit was not in the Bell Atlantic's best interests. The derivative suit was ultimately settled on the eve of the trial; the proposed settlement required Bell Atlantic to establish and follow new procedures to monitor sales and marketing programs and to pay plaintiff's counsel fees in an amount not to exceed $450,000. Seymour Lazar, a Bell Atlantic shareholder, objected to the settlement. The district court approved the settlement. Although Lazar did not formerly seek to intervene in the derivative action, the Third Circuit nevertheless held Lazur had standing to appeal the district court's approval of the settlement.]

Lazar impugns the settlement agreement as resulting from conflicts of interest. He attacks Dechert, Price & Rhoads's joint representation of Bell Atlantic (nominal defendant but real party in interest) and the individual defendants. The district court found no disqualifying conflict, relying on *Otis & Co. v. Pennsylvania R.R. Co., 57 F. Supp. 680, 684 (E.D. Pa. 1944), aff'd per curiam, 155 F.2d 522 (3d Cir. 1946)*, and *Hornsby v. Lohmeyer, 364 Pa. 271, 279, 72 A.2d 294, 299 (1950)*. Both cases rejected plaintiffs' challenges to counsels' dual representation of corporate and individual defendants.

More recent cases perceive problems with this form of dual representation. For example, *Messing v. FDI, Inc., 439 F. Supp. 776 (D.N.J. 1977)*, involved a derivative action charging certain inside directors in a merger with fraud which resulted in their being overcompensated for stock they owned in the acquired corporation. The outside directors were charged with negligence in connection with this merger. The same counsel initially represented the corporation, two of the outside directors, and all of the inside directors. *Messing* observed some courts have allowed directors in the corporation to be represented by the same counsel in cases that do not involve "any allegations of breach of confidence or trust" or fraud. *439 F. Supp. at 781*. Yet *Messing* nonetheless found that irrespective of the allegation against the director, be it fraud or negligence, the interests of the two will always be diverse. *Id. at 782*. *Messing* required the corporation to retain independent counsel other than the attorney who represented the individual defendants.

Other courts have required independent counsel where directors are alleged to have defrauded the corporation. *See Cannon v. U.S. Acoustics Co., 398 F. Supp. 209 (N.D. Ill. 1975), aff'd in relevant part per curiam, 532 F.2d 1118, 1119 (7th Cir. 1976)* (district court disqualified counsel from simultaneously representing the corporation and the individual directors accused of fraud; conflict of interests among defendants and risk that confidences obtained from one client would be used against another); *Lewis v. Shaffer Stores Co., 218 F. Supp. 238 (S.D.N.Y. 1963)* (corporation could not share counsel with individual directors accused of defrauding the corporation).

Thus, as a general matter, the case law is not uniform on the issue of joint representation of the corporation and individual defendants.

Commentators are more certain. In a representative observation, one commentator says,

> There is some conflict as to the propriety of an attorney or law firm simultaneously representing a corporation and its officers and directors in a stockholders' derivative action. But the modern view is that it is generally improper due to conflict of interests for counsel to attempt to represent the corporation, on whose behalf the action has been instituted, while also representing the individuals charged with harming the corporation for their wrongful conduct.

13 William M. Fletcher, *Fletcher Cyclopedia of the Law of Private Corporations* § 6025, at 442 (perm. ed. rev. vol. 1991); *see also* Harry G. Henn & John R. Alexander, *Laws of Corporations* § 370, at 1082 (1983). But these commentators recognize that "even under the modern rule, independent counsel may not be required if the derivative claim is obviously or patently frivolous." Fletcher, *Fletcher Cyclopedia* § 6025, at 443.

The ethical standards imposed upon attorneys in federal court are a matter of federal law. *County of Suffolk v. Long Island Lighting Co., 710 F. Supp. 1407, 1413 (E.D.N.Y. 1989), aff'd, 907 F.2d 1295 (2d Cir. 1990)*. We look to the Model Rules of Professional Conduct to furnish the appropriate ethical standard. *Id. at 1414*. Under Rule 1.13(a), a lawyer's obligation runs to the entity. The commentary to Rule 1.13 provides:

> The question can arise whether counsel for the organization may defend [a derivative] action. The proposition that the organization is the lawyer's client does not alone resolve the issue. Most derivative actions are a normal incident of an organization's affairs, to be defended by the organization's lawyer like any other suit. However, if the claim involves serious charges of wrongdoing by those in control of the organization, a conflict may arise between the lawyer's duty to the organization and the lawyer's relationship with the board. In those circumstances, Rule 1.7 governs who should represent the directors and the organization.

American Bar Ass'n, *Annotated Model Rules of Professional Conduct* (2d ed. 1992).

We believe serious charges of wrongdoing have not been levelled against the individual defendants. We say this because plaintiffs have alleged only mismanagement, a breach of the fiduciary *duty of care*.... But we do not understand plaintiffs to have accused defendants of breaching their *duty of loyalty* which requires a director to act in good faith and in the honest belief that the action taken is in the corporation's best interests.... There are no allegations of self-dealing, stealing, fraud, intentional misconduct, conflicts of interest, or usurpation of corporate opportunities by defendant directors. Indeed the district court found the directors acted in good faith in investigating plaintiffs' demands. As noted, Bell Atlantic's board charged a special committee along with independent counsel to investigate the shareholder plaintiffs' demands. The special committee and independent counsel found prosecution of these demands not in Bell Atlantic's interest. This suggests a relative (though not complete) convergence of individual and corporate interests in defending and settling the litigation. Although not dispositive, it is important that early in the litigation, independent counsel, after undertaking an exhaustive investigation, determined the corporation's interests were more in line with those of the defendants than plaintiffs. Of greater significance, however, is the absence of allegations of fraud, intentional misconduct, or self-dealing.

We have no hesitation in holding that—except in patently frivolous cases—allegations of directors' fraud, intentional misconduct, or self-dealing require separate counsel. We recognize that corporate law has traditionally distinguished between breach of the duty of care and breach of the duty of loyalty, the latter being more grave. *See Del. Code Ann. tit. 8 § 102(b)(7)* (charter amendment provision allowed to limit director liability for breaches of duty of care but "such provision shall not eliminate or limit the liability of a director: . . . for any breach of the director's duty of loyalty") . . . . But drawing the line between breaches of care and loyalty may be difficult in many cases. *See* Frank H. Easterbrook & Daniel R. Fischel, *The Economic Structure of Corporate Law* 103 (1991) ("Ultimately, though, there is no sharp line between the duty of care and the duty of loyalty."). We do not believe the district court abused its discretion in allowing common counsel here. We note, however, that in cases where the line is blurred between duties of care and loyalty, the better practice is to obtain separate counsel for individual and corporate defendants.[17] . . .

If separate counsel is ordered for the corporation and the real defendants, who should be required to obtain new counsel? If the court believes it is the corporation who should retain new counsel, who hires that counsel (assuming, as is frequently the case, that senior management are the suit's defendants)? Who does the corporation's counsel advise on, for example, whether to accept a settlement offered by the real defendants? Recall that state indemnification statutes set forth procedural steps and substantive standards for indemnifying officers and directors. Does the same lawyer representing both the corporation and a director or officer pose a threat (opportunity) of circumventing these procedural steps and substantive standards for awarding indemnification?

Independent of the question of dual representation, can the counsel representing the corporation question the suit's plaintiff as an adequate representative? Raise the failure to make a demand on the board? Question whether plaintiff meets the contemporaneous ownership requirement? Enter a defense on the substantive defense on the

17. *See* Edited Transcript of Proceedings of the Business Roundtable, 71 Corn. L. Rev. 367–71 (L. Ribstein ed. 1985) (debating merits of distinction).

merits? Should the latter be guided by the same considerations that *Bell Atlantic* and other courts have relied upon for determining when the same counsel can represent the real and nominal defendants? *See* Otis & Co. v. Pennsylvania R.R., 57 F.Supp. 680 (E.D. Pa. 1944), *aff'g*, 155 F.2d 522 (3d Cir. 1946) (corporation allowed to answer derivative suit complaint alleging mismanagement by directors and officers by their adherence to long-followed practice for placing bonds without competitive bidding).

NOTE ON PROBLEMS CONCERNING THE LAW GOVERNING LAWYERS IN DERIVATIVE ACTIONS

1. *Attorney Conflicts of Interest in Derivative Litigation; Garner v. Wolfinbarger.* Partly because of their complex four-party structure—involving nominal plaintiffs, entrepreneurial attorneys, the corporation, and defendants who in their director or officer capacities have or share control of the corporation—derivative actions present a number of severe problems that fall under the heading of the law governing lawyers.

On one side of the case, there may be a conflict between the interests of the shareholders as a class, who are the ultimate beneficiaries of a derivative action, and the interests of the entrepreneurial attorney who brings the action. On the other side, the interests of the corporation may diverge from the interests of defendants who control the corporation, and the corporation's lawyers may as a practical matter regard themselves as working for the latter.

Against this background, problems may also arise concerning the lawyer-client and work-product privileges. In doctrinal terms, the issue can be phrased in terms of whether the corporation's attorney can assert the privilege in a way that favors the defendants even though at least nominally the attorney's client was not the defendants, but rather the corporation in whose right the action is brought. In substantive terms, the issue can be phrased as whether which one of the following rules best serves the interests of the shareholder-owners: (1) A rule that gives inviolate protection to management communications with lawyers, on the ground that to do so will make managers more secure in seeking advice from corporate counsel. (2) A rule that permits exceptions when the very issue is whether a manager's conduct injured rather than served the corporation by whom the attorney was retained or employed.

In Garner v. Wolfinbarger, 430 F.2d 1093 (5th Cir.1970), cert. denied 401 U.S. 974, 91 S.Ct. 1191, 28 L.Ed.2d 323 (1971), the court attempted to balance the various interests involved by adopting the rule that in a derivative action, invocation of the attorney-client privilege was subject to the right of the plaintiff-shareholders to show good cause why the privilege should not be invoked:

> It is urged that disclosure is injurious to both the corporation and the attorney. Corporate management must manage. It has the duty to do so and requires the tools to do so. Part of the

managerial task is to seek legal counsel when desirable, and, obviously, management prefers that it confer with counsel without the risk of having the communications revealed at the instance of one or more dissatisfied stockholders. The managerial preference is a rational one, because it is difficult to envision the management of any sizeable corporation pleasing all of its stockholders all of the time, and management desires protection from those who might second-guess or even harass in matters purely of judgment.

But in assessing management assertions of injury to the corporation it must be borne in mind that management does not manage for itself and that the beneficiaries of its action are the stockholders. Conceptualistic phrases describing the corporation as an entity separate from its stockholders are not useful tools of analysis. They serve only to obscure the fact that management has duties which run to the benefit ultimately of the stockholders. For example, it is difficult to rationally defend the assertion of the privilege if all, or substantially all, stockholders desire to inquire into the attorney's communications with corporate representatives who have only nominal ownership interests, or even none at all. There may be reasonable differences over the manner of characterizing in legal terminology the duties of management, and over the extent to which corporate management is less of a fiduciary than the common law trustee. There may be many situations in which the corporate entity or its management, or both, have interests adverse to those of some or all stockholders. But when all is said and done management is not managing for itself. . . .

In summary, we say this. The attorney-client privilege still has viability for the corporate client. The corporation is not barred from asserting it merely because those demanding information enjoy the status of stockholders. But where the corporation is in suit against its stockholders on charges of acting inimically to stockholder interests, protection of those interests as well as those of the corporation and of the public require that the availability of the privilege be subject to the right of the stockholders to show cause why it should not be invoked in the particular instance. . . .

There are many indicia that may contribute to a decision of presence or absence of good cause, among them the number of shareholders and the percentage of stock they represent; the bona fides of the shareholders; the nature of the shareholders' claim and whether it is obviously colorable; the apparent necessity or desirability of the shareholders having the information and the availability of it from other sources; whether, if the shareholders' claim is of wrongful action by the corporation, it is of action criminal, or illegal but not criminal, or of doubtful legality; whether the communication related to past or to prospective actions; whether the communication is of advice concerning the litigation itself; the extent to which the communication is identified versus the extent to which the shareholders are blindly

fishing; the risk of revelation of trade secrets or other information in whose confidentiality the corporation has an interest for independent reasons. The court can freely use *in camera* inspection or oral examination and freely avail itself of protective orders, a familiar device to preserve confidentiality in trade secret and other cases where the impact of revelation may be as great as in revealing a communication with counsel.

On remand, the district court held that the lawyer-client privilege was inapplicable under the standards *Garner* set out. Garner v. Wolfinbarger, 56 F.R.D. 499 (S.D.Ala.1972).

There is a split among the Circuits concerning whether the *Garner* principle is applicable to shareholder class actions. Compare Weil v. Investment/Indicators, Research & Management, 647 F.2d 18 (9th Cir. 1981) (*Garner* is not applicable to class actions), with Ward v. Succession of Freeman, 854 F.2d 780 (5th Cir. 1988), cert. denied, 490 U.S. 1065, 109 S.Ct. 2064, 104 L.Ed.2d 629 (1989) (*Garner* is applicable to class actions) and Fausek v. White, 965 F.2d 126 (6th Cir.), cert. denied, 506 U.S. 1034, 113 S.Ct. 814, 121 L.Ed.2d 686 (1992) (same).

2. *Upjohn*. In Upjohn Co. v. United States, 449 U.S. 383, 101 S.Ct. 677, 66 L.Ed.2d 584 (1981), Upjohn's independent accountant discovered that an Upjohn subsidiary had made improper payments to secure foreign government business. After consultation among Upjohn's general counsel, outside counsel, and chairman of the board, it was decided that the company would conduct an internal investigation of "questionable payments." As part of this investigation the attorneys prepared a letter containing a questionnaire which was sent to "All Foreign General and Area Managers" over the chairman's signature. Subsequently, the Internal Revenue Service issued a summons demanding production of certain records, including the questionnaires. The Supreme Court held that the questionnaires were protected from disclosure by the attorney-client privilege. Unlike *Garner, Upjohn* involved an action by a third party against the corporation, rather than a derivative action on the corporation's behalf against some of its managers.

3. *Work–Product*. In In re International Systems & Controls Corp. Securities Litigation, 693 F.2d 1235 (5th Cir.1982), the court held that the good-cause standard of *Garner* is inapplicable to material covered by the work-product immunity, that is, material prepared in anticipation of litigation, as opposed to the communications between managers and counsel in the course of business decisionmaking. The court said the discoverability of work product in this context is governed by the general principle concerning the discoverability of work product under FRCP Rule 26(b)(3), which turns on a general principle concerning substantial need/undue hardship test. See also *Upjohn*, supra; Cox v. Administrator U.S. Steel & Carnegie, 17 F.3d 1386, 1423 (11th Cir.1994). Courts are, however, badly divided on what constitutes the attorney's work product. *See* United States v. Adlman, 134 F.3d 1194, 1195 (2d Cir. 1998) (documents are work product if they were prepared "because of anticipated litigation and

would not have been prepared in substantially similar form but for the prospect of that litigation"); United States v. El Paso Co., 682 F.2d 530, 542 (5th Cir. 1982) (document is attorney's work product if "the primary motivating purpose behind the creation of the document was to aid in possible future litigation"); United States v. Textron, Inc., 577 F.3d 21, 29 (1st Cir. 2009) (en banc) (doctrine extends only to documents "prepared for use in possible litigation" and therefore did not extend to attorney's analysis of risks of disallowance by the IRS of client's method of reporting on its tax return certain transactions).

ABA MODEL RULES OF PROFESSIONAL CONDUCT, RULES 1.6, 1.7, 1.13

[See Statutory Supplement]

AMERICAN LAW INSTITUTE, PRINCIPLES OF CORPORATE GOVERNANCE, INTRODUCTION TO PART VII, REPORTER'S NOTE

[See Statutory Supplement]

SECTION 10. SETTLEMENT OF DERIVATIVE ACTIONS

Clarke v. Greenberg

Court of Appeals of New York, 1947.
296 N.Y. 146, 71 N.E.2d 443.

■ DYE, JUDGE. The challenge . . . [here is] whether a plaintiff in a stockholder's derivative action may be required to account to the corporation for moneys received in private settlement for discontinuance of the action.

The complaint alleges that the defendants commenced a stockholder's derivative action in behalf of the Associated Gas & Electric Company (called AGECO) entitled "Greenberg v. Mange et al." in which it was alleged that the defendants, as officers and directors, had so mismanaged its affairs that the company and its stockholders were damaged and prayed that an accounting be had, and that the court "impress a trust in favor of the Company (AGECO) upon all secret profits and gains obtained by any of the defendant directors," etc. No individual relief was asked except reimbursement for expenses. Later and before trial, a stipulation was made settling and discontinuing the action without notice to other stockholders and without approval of the court, by the terms of which Greenberg executed releases in his individual and representative capacity and transferred and delivered his stock, having a market value of $51.88, to the defendant directors and defendants herein received from them the sum of $9,000.

The complaint in this action alleges that the defendants received the money "to the use of, and in trust for AGECO"; that they had failed to account to it or its trustee, the plaintiff herein, and had accordingly unjustly enriched themselves in the sum of $8,948.12 which, in equity, should be paid over to the plaintiff, and prayed judgment accordingly.

The Appellate Division unanimously affirmed the dismissal of the complaint by the Special Term which relied upon Manufacturers Mutual Fire Ins. Co. of Rhode Island v. Hopson, 176 Misc. 220, 25 N.Y.S.2d 502, affirmed 262 App.Div. 731, 29 N.Y.S.2d 139, affirmed 288 N.Y. 668, 43 N.E.2d 71 in which we refused to set aside a stipulation settling a stockholder's derivative suit and revive the action. That case was limited to the right to discontinue and it did not consider whether the moneys received in settlement were impressed with a trust in favor of the corporation for which an accounting should be made.

The very nature of the derivative suit by a stockholder-plaintiff suing in the corporation's behalf suggests the application of the fiduciary principle to the proceeds realized from such litigation whether received by way of judgment, by settlement with approval of the court, which presupposes stockholders' approval, or by private settlement and discontinuance of the action at any stage of the proceeding. Such action, we have held, belongs primarily to the corporation, the real party in interest ... and a judgment so obtained, as well as the proceeds of a settlement with court approval belongs to it and not the individual stockholder plaintiffs.... While the stockholder-plaintiff, with such others as join with him, controls the course of the litigation at all stages of the proceeding before final judgment, he does not bind the nonparticipating stockholders by his action, or deprive them of their own right of action against the unfaithful directors, nor is he subject to their interference.... When, however, success crowns his effort, the amount received is in behalf and for the account of the corporation. This is so because the action belongs primarily to it. The manner and method by which such success is accomplished whether by way of judgment, settlement with court approval or by stipulation of the parties, makes no substantial difference in the interest of the corporation upon distribution of the proceeds. Requiring an accounting for moneys received in a private settlement introduces no new element. It simply amounts to a logical application of a fundamental principle inherent in the representative relation. When one assumes to act for another, regardless of the manner or method used in accomplishing a successful termination, he should willingly account for his stewardship. The plaintiff-stockholder, in good conscience, should not be allowed to retain the proceeds of a derivative suit discontinued by stipulation, to his individual use, in opposition to the corporation, any more than the proceeds of a judgment or a settlement with court approval.

The complaint, we believe, states a cause of action.

The judgments should be reversed and the motion to dismiss the complaint denied, with costs in all courts.

■ LOUGHRAN, C.J., and LEWIS, CONWAY, DESMOND, THACHER, and FULD, JJ., concur.

Judgments reversed, etc.*

BACKGROUND OF THE PURPOSE AND CONSEQUENCES OF COURT APPROVAL OF SETTLEMENTS

In Manufacturers Mutual Fire Ins. Co. v. Hopson, cited in Clarke v. Greenberg, shareholders of Associated Gas & Electric had brought a derivative action against the AG&E directors for mismanagement and waste. Thereafter the plaintiffs had agreed to discontinue the action in exchange for a payment made to them in their individual capacities. (The payment took the form of a purchase of the plaintiffs' AG&E stock for seven times its market value.) In response to a petition by other shareholders and AG&E's trustee in bankruptcy, the court refused to set aside the discontinuance:

> If this were a case of first impression, my conclusion might be otherwise. But this court is bound by a line of cases in New York, to the effect that a minority stockholder may discontinue his action at any time before another stockholder has intervened or judgment has been entered. The exclusive control of the action belongs to him and he can settle his individual damages, leaving other shareholders to seek their remedy in a new action.

176 Misc. at 223, 25 N.Y.S.2d at 505. While not all courts took the position reflected in *Manufacturer's Mutual,* that position was the majority rule at common law:

> . . . From the early days of the class suit, it had been widely accepted doctrine that a . . . derivative plaintiff . . . was the *dominus litis;* since he bore all the expenses of the action, he could dismiss or compromise it at pleasure and on any terms he saw fit. . . .
>
> The prevailing state of the law plainly invited abuse. Most stockholders' suits involve corporate or class claims of considerable magnitude. The temptation for the defendants to buy off the plaintiff by a relatively modest private settlement was therefore

---

* Cf. Young v. Higbee Co., 324 U.S. 204, 65 S.Ct. 594, 89 L.Ed. 890 (1945). In Certain–Teed Products Corporation v. Topping, 171 F.2d 241 (2d Cir.1948) a shareholder-plaintiff in a derivative suit consented to the entry of a summary judgment in favor of the individual defendant on payment of $5,000 to the plaintiff's attorney. Plaintiff was held liable to the corporation for the $5,000 less such amount as the district court might allow as a reasonable attorney's fee. (Footnote by ed.)

> great. Many stockholders' actions of doubtful merit were brought simply to secure private settlements for the plaintiff and his lawyer. Private settlements also were employed to stifle meritorious suits brought initially in good faith. In derivative suits, the corporation, frequently controlled by the alleged wrong-doers or their allies, could not be expected to resist the sacrifice of claims which it had been unwilling to assert by direct action. Even without a private settlement, complaining stockholders often dropped their suits simply to avoid further expense and trouble. By the time the class suit was dismissed, the statute of limitations or laches often barred other stockholders from bringing actions of their own; advantages already gained in the litigation were lost. The termination of the action without notice to the class also served to conceal whatever wrongs had been done, so that uninformed class members were unable to safeguard their rights. The stockholder's suit was in danger of becoming a tool for defeating the class rights it was intended to protect.

Haudek, The Settlement and Dismissal of Stockholders' Actions–Part I, 22 Sw.L.J. 767, 768–70 (1968).

The problems described by Haudek led to the adoption, in many though not all jurisdictions, of rules like Fed.R.Civ.P. 23.1, which provides that a derivative action "shall not be dismissed or compromised without the approval of the court, and notice of the proposed dismissal or compromise shall be given to shareholders or members in such manner as the court directs."[2]

Assuming adequate representation before the court, a court's approval of a settlement whose scope covers *all* claims arising in connection with out a transaction underlying the derivative suit bars any future action on such claims even if those claims were not themselves raised in the settled action. Matsushita Electric Industrial Co. v. Epstein, 516 U.S. 367, 116 S.Ct. 873, 134 L.Ed.2d 6 (1996) (settlement approved by Delaware Chancery Court barred continued prosecution of class action claims under the federal securities laws even though federal courts have exclusive jurisdiction over suits maintained under the federal securities laws). Does this consequence of settlement pose a risk of a "reverse auction" where multiple representative suits (i.e., both class and derivative) are filed based on the same core of facts and their counsel vie with one another by offering "competitively" attractive settlement offers to the defendants?

---

2. Settlements are often submitted for judicial approval even in jurisdictions that do not have such rules, either because the jurisdiction does not follow the theory of *Manufacturer's Mutual* or because the defendants want to secure the res judicata effect that follows from judicial approval.

FEDERAL RULES OF CIVIL PROCEDURE, RULE 23.1

[See Statutory Supplement]

MODEL BUSINESS CORPORATION ACT § 7.45

[See Statutory Supplement]

NEW YORK BUS. CORP. LAW § 626(d), (e)

[See Statutory Supplement]

IN RE CAREMARK, INTERNATIONAL, INC. DERIVATIVE LITIGATION

[Chapter 8, supra]

ALI, PRINCIPLES OF CORPORATE GOVERNANCE §§ 7.14–7.16

[See Statutory Supplement]

DESIMONE v. INDUSTRIAL BIO–TEST LABORATORIES, INC., 83 F.R.D. 615 (S.D.N.Y.1979). "The court will approve a proposed settlement of a class action if the proposal is fair, reasonable and adequate. This determination requires three levels of analysis. First, the proponents have the burden of proving that (1) the settlement is not collusive but was reached after arm's length negotiation; (2) the proponents are counsel experienced in similar cases; (3) there has been sufficient discovery to enable counsel to act intelligently and (4) the number of objectants or their relative interest is small. If the proponents establish these propositions, the burden of attacking the settlement then shifts to the objectants, if any. Finally, the court must approve the settlement only after finding it to be reasonable in light of the plaintiffs' ultimate probability of success in the lawsuit. . . .

"In determining reasonableness, the courts in this circuit have not applied any single, inflexible test. Instead, they have considered the amount of the settlement in light of all the circumstances, including such factors as: (1) the best possible recovery; (2) the likely recovery if the claims were fully litigated; (3) the complexity, expense and probable duration of continued litigation; (4) the risk of establishing liability; (5) the risk of establishing damages; (6) the risk of maintaining the class action throughout trial; (7) the reaction of the class to the settlement; (8) the stage of the proceedings and (9) the ability of the defendants to withstand a greater judgment." . . .

BACKGROUND NOTE ON JUDICIAL APPROVAL OF SETTLEMENTS

Once notice of settlement has been given, a shareholder who objects to the proposed settlement can enter the case. If he succeeds in improving the settlement, he—or more accurately his lawyer—is entitled to counsel fees. White v. Auerbach, 500 F.2d 822 (2d Cir. 1974), noted, 1 J.Corp.Law 194 (1975). Not infrequently the efforts of objectors result in a significant improvement of the settlement. In a well-known episode involving the Alleghany Corporation, a settlement involving a cash payment of $700,000 was increased under objection to $1,000,000, and under continued objection was further increased to $3 million. See Alleghany Corp. v. Kirby, 333 F.2d 327 (2d Cir.1964), aff'd in banc by an equally divided court 340 F.2d 311 (2d Cir.1965), cert. dismissed 384 U.S. 28, 86 S.Ct. 1250, 16 L.Ed.2d 335 (1966).

As a practical matter, the engine that normally drives a derivative action involving a publicly held corporation is not the plaintiff, but the plaintiff's attorney. The plaintiff typically makes little or no investment in the action and stands to gain very little benefit. His attorney, on the other hand, makes a very substantial investment (in the form of his time and disbursements) and stands to reap a very substantial benefit (in the form of a fee). This raises the unwholesome possibility that the defendants may be able to make an improper settlement by giving their acquiescence to an inflated fee in exchange for acquiescence by plaintiff's counsel to an inadequate corporate recovery. In Alleghany Corp. v. Kirby, supra, Judge Friendly remarked on the manner in which the interests of a plaintiff's attorney may conflict with the interests of the shareholders in settling cases where very large amounts are at stake:

> I cannot at all agree ... that standard procedures for the approval of settlements afford sufficient safeguards in the "big" case.... The plaintiff stockholders or, more realistically, their attorneys have every incentive to accept a settlement that runs into high six figures or more regardless of how strong the claims for much larger amounts may be. The percentage allowance in stockholders' actions is "reduced as the amount of recovery passes the million dollar mark," 2 Hornstein, Corporation Law and Practice 253 (1959) ... the income tax also plays a role; and a juicy bird in the hand is worth more than the vision of a much larger one in the bush, attainable only after years of effort not currently compensated and possibly a mirage. Once a settlement is agreed, the attorneys for the plaintiff stockholders link arms with their former adversaries to defend the joint handiwork—as is vividly shown here where the stockholders' general counsel sometimes opposed [the objector's] efforts to gain information, although the settlement so vigorously defended before the Referee would have produced less than a quarter as much cash for Alleghany, $700,000, as the $3,000,000 ultimately secured....

333 F.2d at 347.

Given the problems to which Judge Friendly pointed, as a practical matter the amount of a settlement in any given case may depend in significant part on whether an intervener appears in court to attack the settlement by bringing up problems that the attorneys for the settling parties might gloss over. But consider the reception the intervener may face in light of the following: "[T]he court starts from the familiar axiom that a bad settlement is almost always better than a good trial." In re Warner Communications Sec. Litig., 618 F.Supp. 735, 740 (S.D.N.Y. 1985), *aff'd.* 798 F.2d 35 (2d Cir. 1986).

Macey & Miller, The Plaintiffs' Attorneys' Role in Class Actions and Derivative Litigation: Economic Analysis and Recommendations for Reform

58 U.Chi.L.Rev. 1, 44–48 (1991).

Most class action and derivative litigation is settled prior to judgment. When such litigation is settled, the problem of agency costs appears in a particularly problematic form. As already discussed, the plaintiffs' attorney often faces a severe conflict of interest in settling class and derivative litigation. In common fund cases where the attorney earns a percentage of the judgment, the attorney has an incentive to settle early at a relatively low figure in order to maximize her profit. In common fund cases in which the attorney is compensated according to the lodestar formula, the attorney has an incentive to delay reaching a settlement in order to increase the hours upon which the compensation is calculated. The attorney may also agree to an inappropriately low settlement on the merits in exchange for the defendant's implicit or explicit promise to allow the attorney to expend additional risk-free hours in order to build up a fee. In common benefit and fee-shifting cases the attorney has an incentive both to delay settlement and to agree to inappropriately low settlements in exchange for generous negotiated attorney's fees. . . .

The regulatory response to these conflicts is to require judicial scrutiny of proposed settlements. Unfortunately, judicial approval appears to be highly imperfect as a protection for the plaintiffs' interests, for several reasons. First, and most important, the judge herself has a powerful interest in approving the settlement. Judges' calendars are crowded with cases, and despite various reform efforts, the workload only seems to increase. If the judge approves the settlement, the result will be to remove a potentially complex and time-consuming case from the judge's calendar; if she rejects it she faces a substantial probability of further litigation. A judge faces virtually no prospect of reversal for approving a settlement, whereas a decision rejecting a settlement might well be appealed. Moreover, trial judges are heavily conditioned by the ethos of their jobs to view settlements as desirable; they routinely encourage settlement in other contexts. It would be unrealistic to expect trial judges to shift gears suddenly and view settlements with suspicion rather than approbation when they arise in the class action or derivative contexts.

Second, trial courts may simply lack information to make an informed evaluation of the fairness of the settlement. Typically, when a case is settled well in advance of trial, the only information available to the judge is found in papers filed in court—pleadings, briefs, and supporting materials filed on motions—and materials submitted to the judge in connection with the settlement hearing. Such evidence is likely to be highly incomplete and, in the case of materials submitted to support the proposed settlement, biased in favor of the settlement. The matters on which the judge must rule are also highly subjective and imprecise. Even if the judge had adequate information on which to decide, it would be difficult to make reliable estimates of the settlement value of a case.

Third, settlement hearings are typically pep rallies jointly orchestrated by plaintiffs' counsel and defense counsel. Because both parties desire that the settlement be approved, they have every incentive to present it as entirely fair. Objectors to the settlement, on the other hand, are uncommon; those who do object are often either disgruntled plaintiffs' attorneys who have fallen out with others in the plaintiffs' consortium, or naive class members who demonstrate their ignorance of the issues in dispute. The deck is heavily stacked toward approval of the settlement.

Trial courts happily play along with the camaraderie. In approving settlement, courts often engage in paeans of praise for counsel or lambaste anyone rash enough to object to the settlement. Not surprisingly, it is uncommon to find cases where trial courts reject settlements that are presented to them by defense counsel and plaintiffs' attorneys. Given that settlements are nearly always approved, one might well question the efficacy of judicial review of class action and derivative settlements.

NOTE ON SETTLEMENTS WITHOUT THE PLAINTIFF'S CONSENT

Wolf v. Barkes, 348 F.2d 994 (2d Cir.1965), cert. denied 382 U.S. 941, 86 S.Ct. 395, 15 L.Ed.2d 351, was a derivative action that had been brought in federal court by a shareholder-plaintiff against director and officer defendants. The defendants, over the plaintiff's objection, proposed to settle the claims underlying the action directly with the corporation. The corporation and the defendants did not propose to comply with the notice and judicial-approval requirements of then-Rule 23 for the settlement of a derivative action. Plaintiffs attempted to enjoin the settlement on that ground. The court held that the proposed settlement did not fall within Rule 23, because no one was attempting to settle the *suit*, as opposed to the *claim* on which the suit was brought. The court emphasized that if (as might be expected) the defendants moved to dismiss the suit on the basis of the release they obtained as part of the settlement of the claim, the validity of the release could be contested—for example, if it involved a self-interested transaction.

ALI, Principles of Corporate Governance § 7.15, Reporters Note, points out that "[a]lthough Wolf v. Barkes ... establishes that the Federal Rules of Civil Procedure do not require judicial approval of a settlement between the corporation and a defendant in a derivative action, other decisions have held that interested directors may not settle a derivative action, at least not without court approval.... In practice, it appears that on the few occasions when boards have settled with a defendant after the action's commencement, they have sought judicial approval.... Although these cases were arguably voluntary elections, it still appears that the use of the technique *Wolf* affords has been 'infrequent in practice,' and this infrequency appears largely attributable to the uncertainties surrounding such settlements." For example, in Clark v. Lomas & Nettleton Financial Corp., 625 F.2d 49 (5th Cir. 1980), for three years a company's directors had shown no interest in a derivative suit. However their interest was awakened when the plaintiff amended the complaint to include claims against the company's controlling stockholder, Jack Booth. The directors quickly engaged counsel to enter into a settlement between the corporation and the defendants over the plaintiff's objections. Reasoning the directors were incompetent to approve the settlement because they were under the control of the defendant, Jack Booth, the Fifth Circuit vacated a district court's approval of the settlement. Query, should it matter that the plaintiff opposed the settlement because the corporation was unwilling to similarly settle an individual claim along with the derivative claims? *See* Clark v. Lomas & Nettleton Financial Corp., 79 F.R.D. 641, 645 (N.D. Tex. 1978).

SECTION 11. PLAINTIFF'S COUNSEL FEES

TANDYCRAFTS, INC. v. INITIO PARTNERS, 562 A.2d 1162 (Del.1989). Initio Partners, a limited partnership, was the largest independent shareholder of Tandycrafts, Inc., owning 9.9% of Tandycraft's stock. Tandycraft proposed to amend its charter, and issued a proxy statement in connection with the vote on the proposed amendment at the annual meeting. Initio sought a temporary injunction against holding Tandycraft's annual meeting, on the ground that the proxy statement was materially misleading.

Tandycraft then prepared a supplement to its proxy statement that made clarifications and new disclosures on the subjects Initio had complained of. The annual meeting was held, and the charter amendments were soundly defeated. Initio then moved for the award of counsel fees and expenses. Tandycraft opposed the motion, on the grounds that the changes in the proxy statement were not attributable to Initio's litigation and that counsel fees could not be awarded to a plaintiff that had sued on its own behalf (as had Initio), rather than derivatively or on behalf of a class. The Vice Chancellor awarded counsel fees to Initio. Affirmed. "In the realm of corporate litigation, the Court may order the payment of counsel fees and related expenses to a plaintiff whose efforts result in the creation of a common fund ... or the conferring of a corporate benefit.... Typically, successful derivative or class action suits which result in the recovery of money or property wrongfully diverted from the corporation, or which result in the imposition of changes in internal operating procedures that are designed to produce such monetary savings in the future, are viewed as fund creating actions....

"The definition of a corporate benefit, however, is much more elastic. While the benefit achieved may have an indirect economic effect on the corporation, in the sense that the interests of the plaintiff class reflect a value not theretofore apparent, the benefit need not be measurable in economic terms. Changes in corporate policy or, as here, a heightened level of corporate disclosure, if attributable to the filing of a meritorious suit, may justify an award of counsel fees. *See* Chrysler Corp. v. Dann, 223 A.2d at 386; Allied Artists Pictures Corp. v. Baron, 413 A.2d at 878.

"Once it is determined that action benefiting the corporation chronologically followed the filing of a meritorious suit, the burden is upon the corporation to demonstrate 'that the lawsuit did not in any way cause their action.' Allied Artists Pictures Corp. v. Baron, 413 A.2d at 880....

"Although this Court has not adopted an expansive approach to fee shifting in corporate litigation, the critical inquiry is not the status of the plaintiff but the nature of the corporate or class benefit which is causally related to the filing of suit. It is to be expected that litigation to force compliance with fiduciary standards or statutory duties will be initiated by a shareholder who has standing to sue for the benefit of the corporation. For the most part, such claims are clearly derivative, or class based. But where the shareholder's individual interests are directly and equally implicated, as in proxy contests, the distinction between individual and representative claims may become blurred. Indeed, the same wrong may give rise to both an individual and derivative action....

"Having concluded that, under these circumstances, Initio had standing to seek an award of counsel fees as an individual plaintiff, we summarily address Tandycrafts' claim that the Vice Chancellor abused his discretion in the fee allowance. The sequence of events is not in dispute and the correction or clarification of the proxy material chronologically followed the filing of the Initio suit attacking the accuracy of the material. It was thus incumbent upon Tandycrafts to demonstrate that there was no causal connection between the suit and the subsequent action.... Although Tandycrafts argues that the corrective action would have been taken in any event, we are not persuaded that the Vice Chancellor abused his discretion in ruling to the contrary.''

SUGARLAND IND., INC. v. THOMAS, 420 A.2d 142 (Del. 1980). Mr. and Mrs. Harris, shareholders in Sugarland, Industries, Inc., retained an attorney to represent them when they learned that the Sugarland board was considering the sale to White and Hill of substantial acreage (referred to as the South Tract) the company owned for $23.8 million. They believed the price was inadequate. Partly as a result of Harris's efforts, another bidder, R–S–C offered to purchase the land for $27 million. Nonetheless, the Sugarland board continued to favor the lower White and Hill offer. The Harris' ultimately initiated a derivative suit and the Chancellor ordered that the board entertain competitive bids for the property. Among the sealed bids, Hines was the winner, offering approximately $32.2 million for the property. Hines pushed to acquire the adjacent North Tract which led to more sealed bids and once again Hines won, having bid $1.25 million more than the next highest bid. Thus, both tracts were sold to Hines for $44 million. The attorney representing Mr. and Mrs. Harris sought a fee from Sugarland.

> It is crystal clear from the record that the services of petitioners benefited Sugarland to the extent of the difference between the White and Hill offer of $23,800,000 and the $27,000,000 which was submitted by R–S–C. But how one should view the amount received by Sugarland in excess of the $27,000,000 is not so clear. Petitioners had sought the best price obtainable and but for their initiative (and success) at the injunctive stage, Sugarland might not have received anything over the White and Hill offer. Thus, there is, as we have noted, ''some'' cause and effect between what petitioners did and the ultimate price received. But petitioners are attorneys seeking compensation for services rendered in litigation. They are not brokers or real estate agents seeking a commission or a percentage of sale price for having produced a buyer. And how much anyone would pay, at least in excess of the $27,000,000 offered by R–S–C, was a circumstance neither caused nor influenced by petitioners. The highest offer eventually made has in it something in the nature of [a] ''windfall''.... [P]etitioners here cannot take full credit for the price which Hines was willing to pay for both tracts....
>
> In making the award, the Chancellor used a 20%–of–benefit factor and that seems reasonable to us when applied to the difference between the respective offers. But for the reasons we have discussed, it is unreasonable when applied to the amounts paid by the buyer in excess of the $27,000,000. We have held that petitioners are entitled to some credit for the benefit received in excess of that sum and, in view of the circumstances, any percentage is arguably fair or not, depending on one's point of view. In our judgment, based on the various factors we have noted, compensation at the rate of 5% of the benefit achieved is fair and should be applied to the additional benefits Sugarland received

> from the sale of both the North and South Tracts. Given the fee which that percentage generates (about $573,609 in all), we conclude that it is reasonable (and perhaps generous) compensation for the significant skills and expertise which petitioners demonstrated in identifying an inadequate price for the Tracts, in stimulating the competitive offer from R–S–C, in quickly initiating the litigation, in successfully carrying it to a conclusion against highly competent counsel and thus opening the door for entry by the Hines Interests with their offers.

A fee was awarded of $1,213,609, reflecting 20 percent on the difference between the White and Hill offer and the R–S–C offer and 5 percent of the improvement in the sales price reflected via competitive bidding.

ALI, PRINCIPLES OF CORPORATE GOVERNANCE § 7.17

[See Statutory Supplement]

G & N AIRCRAFT, INC. v. BOEHM, 743 N.E.2d 227 (Ind. 2001). "The trial court awarded Boehm 'attorney's fees in this action,' but did not specify for what or from whom. The Court of Appeals modified this award to allow for attorney's fees against G & N [the corporation] for the derivative action, but no fees against Goldsmith [an individual defendant] in the direct action. We agree with the Court of Appeals that Boehm is not entitled to attorney's fees from Goldsmith in his direct action. The 'United States Rule' is that parties bear their own fees in the absence of a statute or a basis in quantum meruit for reimbursing a party who has benefited others. The direct action by Boehm fits neither category."

Macey & Miller, The Plaintiffs' Attorneys' Role in Class Actions and Derivative Litigation: Economic Analysis and Recommendations for Reform

58 U.Chi.L.Rev. 1, 22–26 (1991).

. . . [Under the lodestar approach, in which the primary determinant of attorneys' fees is the attorney's time, attorneys] have an incentive to run up excessive hours, delay the litigation unnecessarily, or even to exaggerate the number of hours expended in order to obtain a larger fee. Plaintiffs' attorneys may also wish to settle for a relatively low sum on the eve of trial, knowing that in so doing they obtain most of the benefits they can expect from the litigation while eliminating their downside risk. . . .

Further, plaintiffs' attorneys may sometimes substantially reduce their risk by reaching an understanding with defense counsel early on about the contours of the eventual settlement. Then they can expend a mutually acceptable number of additional hours on the case, charging them against the settlement fund under the lodestar calculation. The social disutility of this procedure is obvious; it represents an essentially meaningless exercise that ties up the resources of plaintiffs' counsel, defense counsel, and others such as witnesses who must submit to depositions that all parties understand will never be used in court. The principal losers are members of the plaintiff class who must pay over part of their recovery to counsel for work that serves no purpose other than to justify an enhanced attorney's fee.

. . . There are obvious incentive problems with [the percentage-of-recovery method] as well. First, plaintiffs' attorneys will earn windfall profits, at the expense of the class members, in cases presenting large damages and low proof costs. More generally, it would appear that the percentage method effectively guarantees that plaintiffs' attorneys will be systematically compensated at a rate higher than the rate they would demand in an efficiently functioning competitive market. To illustrate this point, consider the thought process of a plaintiffs' attorney in deciding whether to bring a given cause of action. The attorney operating in a percentage-of-the-recovery system will never bring an action when the expected opportunity costs to the attorney of bringing the suit (as measured by the value the attorney places on his or her time) exceed the expected award of attorneys' fees (equal to the present value of the expected recovery for the class multiplied by the fee percentage used in the jurisdiction and further discounted by the attorney's estimate of the probability of success in the litigation). The plaintiffs' attorney faces a distribution of cases in which one tail—representing cases where the expected payoff to the attorney falls short of the attorney's expected costs—is cut off. On the other hand, the attorney can be expected to bring all cases where the expected payoff equals or exceeds the attorney's expected costs.

Among the cases that are brought will be a wide range of cases in which the expected payoff exceeds the attorney's expected costs. Because the applicable fee percentage is not adjusted downward in such cases—as it would be in an efficiently functioning market for contingency fee representation—these excess profits are not dissipated by competition. In theory, a court could reduce a percentage award downward in such cases, but such judicial reductions would not necessarily be reliable, and would add an additional level of complexity and cost to fee calculations. Thus, plaintiffs' attorneys can be expected to reap systematic excess profits, of which windfall cases are only the most noteworthy examples, under a percentage method. These excess profits are earned at the expense of the plaintiff class.

The second incentive problem in percentage-of-the-recovery cases is settlement. Attorneys compensated on a percentage method have an incentive to settle early for an amount lower than what might be obtained by further efforts. The attorney who puts in relatively few hours to obtain an early settlement is likely to earn a much greater compensation per hour of effort than an attorney who expends greater efforts and litigates a case to the point where the plaintiffs' recovery is maximized. Again the plaintiff class loses.

Consider now common benefit ... cases. Common benefit cases are typically shareholder's derivative suits in which the plaintiffs' attorney does not generate a fund, but rather causes the defendant to do something that confers a nonpecuniary benefit on the corporation. In common benefit ... cases the attorneys' fee comes from the defendant rather than from the class recovery. Unlike common fund cases, therefore, there is a counter-party in common benefit and fee-shifting cases with an incentive to bargain over the fee in order to keep it within reasonable limits.

This feature, however, does not effectively obviate the attorney-client conflict. Defendants in common benefit and fee-shifting cases typically wish to minimize the sum of three costs: the costs of the relief on the merits, the costs of their own attorney's fees, and the costs of the plaintiffs' attorney's fees. Defendants are typically indifferent about how the total cost of litigation is distributed among these elements. Plaintiffs' attorneys, on the other hand, have an interest in increasing their own fees, even at the expense of a reduction in the relief afforded to the putative client. Thus the conditions are present for a bargain under which the plaintiffs' attorneys agree to a lower overall settlement on the merits of the litigation in exchange for a higher fee....

BACKGROUND NOTE ON THE AWARD OF COUNSEL FEES TO SUCCESSFUL DERIVATIVE–ACTION PLAINTIFFS

1. *Rationale*. The derivative action constitutes a major legal bulwark against managerial self-dealing. As a practical matter this means that the rules governing plaintiffs' legal fees are critical to the operation of the corporate system: Because very few shareholders would pay, out of their own pockets, the attorney's fee for a suit that is brought on the corporation's behalf and will benefit all shareholders, with only a slight and indirect benefit for the plaintiff, very few derivative actions would be brought if the law did not allow the plaintiff's attorney to be compensated by a contingent fee payable out of the corporate recovery.

As a conceptual matter, the award of counsel fees to successful plaintiffs in derivative actions has been justified by several overlapping rationales, none of which is unique to derivative actions. The most important of these is the "common fund" theory, under which a plaintiff who has successfully established a fund under the control of the court, from which many besides himself will benefit, may recover his counsel fees out of that fund. As stated in the seminal case of Trustees v. Greenough, 105 U.S. (15 Otto) 527, 532, 26 L.Ed. 1157 (1881), to deny an allowance for fees in such circumstances "would not only be unjust to [plaintiff], but ... would give to the other parties entitled to participate in the benefits of the fund an unfair advantage." This theory was later elaborated, under the heading of the "substantial benefit" or "common benefit" theory, to cover cases where the plaintiff had not brought a fund into the court's control but had established a right to a fund from which others would benefit. See Sprague v. Ticonic Nat. Bank, 307 U.S. 161, 59 S.Ct. 777, 83 L.Ed. 1184 (1939). Eventually, the common-benefit theory was extended to cover cases involving the establishment of nonpecuniary benefits.

Another basic rationale for the award of attorneys' fees to successful plaintiffs in derivative actions is the "private attorney-general" doctrine—that plaintiff's counsel fees should be awarded in appropriate cases to encourage the initiation of private actions that vindicate important legal policies. See Newman v. Piggie Park Enterprises, Inc., 390 U.S. 400, 402, 88 S.Ct. 964, 966, 19 L.Ed.2d 1263 (1968).

In the corporate area, this doctrine is important chiefly as a reinforcement to the common-fund or common-benefit theory, particularly where the benefit is not pecuniary. For example, in Mills v. Electric Auto–Lite Co., 396 U.S. 375, 90 S.Ct. 616, 24 L.Ed.2d 593 (1970), plaintiffs, who were former Auto–Lite shareholders, alleged that defendants had violated the Proxy Rules in connection with a merger of Auto–Lite into Mergenthaler. The Court held that plaintiffs were entitled to summary judgment on the merits. It then went on to award interim counsel fees, although it recognized that if on remand the merger were found to be fair, there might be no feasible way to remedy the violation, and therefore no economically measurable benefit to either Auto–Lite or its shareholders. The opinion began by attempting to bring the case within the common-benefit rule: "In many suits under § 14(a) ... it may be impossible to assign monetary value to the benefit. Nevertheless, the stress placed by Congress on the importance of fair and informed corporate suffrage leads to the conclusion that, in vindicating the statutory policy, petitioners have rendered a substantial service to the corporation and its shareholders." However, the Court then seemed to shift rationales by stressing that the action conferred a benefit on a subsector of the public, that is, shareholders as a class.

In Alyeska Pipeline Service Co. v. Wilderness Society, 421 U.S. 240, 95 S.Ct. 1612, 44 L.Ed.2d 141 (1975), the Supreme Court held that in the absence of statutory authorization, attorney's fees may not be awarded on the private-attorney-general theory in suits brought under federal statutes. While the opinion left the common-fund theory (and its derivative, the common-benefit theory) undisturbed, and cited *Sprague* and *Mills* with approval, it is open to question whether the Supreme Court would again go as far as it did in *Mills* in determining what constitutes a benefit for these purposes in a suit brought under federal law.

2. *Criteria*. For many years, the criteria to be considered in setting counsel fees in the derivative suit were as set out in Angoff v. Goldfine, 270 F.2d 185, 189 (1st Cir.1959):

> [T]he amount recovered for the corporation; the time fairly required to be spent on the case; the skill required and employed on the case with reference to the intricacy, novelty and complexity of issues; the difficulty encountered in unearthing the facts and the skill and resourcefulness of opposing counsel; the prevailing rate of compensation for those with the skill, experience and standing of the attorneys, accountants or others involved; the contingent nature of the fees, with the accompanying risk of wasting hours of work, overhead and expenses (for it is clearly established that compensation is awarded only in the event of success); and the benefits accruing to the public from such suits as this.

Traditionally, the most important of these elements was the first—the amount recovered by the corporation—and as a practical matter the courts tended to calculate counsel fees in derivative actions as a percentage of that amount.[3] Although the percentage varied from case to case, awards calculated on this basis traditionally tended to run around 20–35% of the recovery when the recovery was less than $1 million, and 15–25% when it was more.

In contrast, the 1973 revision of the Federal Judicial Manual for Complex Litigation stated that "the reasonableness of the fee arrived at [in class actions] should not rest primarily on the selection of a percentage of the total recovery," and suggested instead emphasizing "the time and labor required and the effect of the allowance on the public interest and the reputation of the courts." Id. at § 1.47. This approach was adopted by the Third Circuit in the leading case of Lindy Bros. Builders, Inc. v. American Radiator & Standard Sanitary Corp., 487 F.2d 161 (3d Cir.1973), a class action under the antitrust laws. Under *Lindy,* the value of the lawyer's time is made the dominant factor:

> . . . [T]he first inquiry of the court should be into the hours spent by the attorneys. . . .
>
> After determining . . . the services performed by the attorneys, the district court must attempt to value those services. . . .
>
> The value of an attorney's time generally is reflected in his normal billing rate. A logical beginning in valuing an attorney's services is to fix a reasonable hourly rate for his time—taking account of the attorney's legal reputation and status (partner, associate). . . .
>
> While the amount thus found to constitute reasonable compensation should be the lodestar of the court's fee determination, there are at least two other factors that must be taken into account in computing the value of attorneys' services. The first of these is the contingent nature of success. . . .

---

3. "[These cases] find their true analogue in salvage causes on a pure salvage basis of no cure no pay. . . . [B]enefits conferred in the light of the efforts required are the real basis of the salvage awards, as they should be in causes like these." Murphy v. North American Light & Power Co., 33 F.Supp. 567, 570–571 (S.D.N.Y.1940).

> The second additional factor the district court must consider is the extent, if any, to which the quality of an attorney's work mandates increasing or decreasing the amount to which the court has found the attorney reasonably entitled.

Under this approach, which is known as the "lodestar" approach (because hourly time is used as a lodestar), the benefit produced is important chiefly insofar as it bears on the quality of the lawyer's work, as where "a particularly resourceful attorney . . . secures a substantial benefit for his clients with a minimum of time invested. . . ."

In 1974 the Second Circuit fell into line with *Lindy* in Detroit v. Grinnell Corp., 495 F.2d 448 (2d Cir.1974). Since a derivative action is in effect a special type of class action, the emphasis placed on lawyer's time by cases like *Lindy* and *Grinnell* came to figure prominently in derivative actions.

There is considerable variation in the percentages applied to basic hourly rates, under the lodestar approach, to adjust for contingency and quality factors. Increases of 50 or 100% are common. Higher and lower increases can also be found.

Even at the height of the lodestar approach, the data suggested that courts managed to apply the lodestar formula in such a way as to produce results comparable to those obtained under the percentage-of-the-benefit formula. See Mowrey, Attorney Fees in Securities Class Actions and Derivative Suits, 3 J.Corp.Law 267 (1978). In 1984, the Supreme Court explicitly stated—albeit in a footnote—that in a common-fund case, a reasonable fee "is based on the percentage of the fund bestowed on the class." Blum v. Stenson, 465 U.S. 886, 900 n. 16, 104 S.Ct. 1541, 1550 n. 16, 79 L.Ed.2d 891 (1984). The Court contrasted this approach to that under the Civil Rights Attorney's Fee Awards Act, where, the Court said, a reasonable fee was based on the attorney's time. The following year, the Third Circuit, which had begun the movement to the lodestar approach with its decision in *Lindy,* issued a Task Force Report that advocated a return to the percentage-of-recovery approach in common-fund cases.

GOODRICH v. E.F. HUTTON GROUP, 681 A.2d 1039 (Del. Supr.1996). The court here summarized what continues to be the approach taken in awarding counsel fees in actions before the federal courts: "In the 1970s, courts began to use the 'lodestar' approach to calculate fee awards in common fund cases. *Lindy Bros. Builders, Inc. of Phila. v. American Radiator & Standard Sanitary Corp.,* 487 F.2d 161, 167–68 (3d Cir.1973). *See* Report of the Third Circuit Task Force, *Court Awarded Attorney Fees,* 108 F.R.D. 237, 242 (1985). That method requires a court to calculate the product of an attorney's reasonable hours expended on the litigation and reasonable hourly rate to arrive at the 'lodestar.' *Swedish Hosp. Corp. v. Shalala,* 1 F.3d at 1266. That lodestar calculation can then be adjusted, through application of a 'multiplier' or fee enhancer, to account for additional factors, *e.g.*, the contingent nature of the case and the quality of an attorney's work. *Lindy Bros. Builders, Inc. of Phila. v. American Radiator & Standard Sanitary Corp.*, 540 F.2d 102, 112 (3d Cir.1976); *Swedish Hosp. Corp. v. Shalala,* 1 F.3d at 1266. During the 1970s, the 'lodestar/multiplier' method of awarding fees was frequently invoked in common fund cases, instead of determining a reasonable percentage of recovery from the fund, based upon a multifactor analysis. *Johnson v. Georgia Highway Express, Inc.*, 488 F.2d 714, 716–19 (5th Cir.1974) (*'Johnson'* factors); *Lindy Bros. Builders, Inc. v. American Radiator & Standard Sanitary Corp.*, 487 F.2d at 164–69 (*'Lindy'* factors).

In the 1980s, however, two events led to a reconsideration of the lodestar method of calculating common fund fee awards. First, in 1984, the Supreme Court distinguished the calculation of awards under fee-shifting statutes from the calculation of attorney's fees under the common fund doctrine. In doing so, the Supreme Court suggested that an award in a common fund case should be based upon a percentage of the fund:

> Unlike the calculation of attorney's fees under the 'common fund doctrine,' where a reasonable fee is based on a percentage of the fund bestowed on the class, a reasonable fee under [42 U.S.C.] § 1988 reflects the amount of attorney time reasonably expended on the litigation.

Blum v. Stenson, 465 U.S. 886, 900 n. 16, 104 S.Ct. 1541, 1550 n. 16, 79 L.Ed.2d 891 (1984). Footnote 16 in *Blum* has been cited for the proposition that the Supreme Court's approval of the lodestar method in the fee-shifting context was not intended to overrule decisions which had approved percentage of the fund awards of attorney's fees in common fund cases. *Swedish Hosp.,* 1 F.3d at 1268. *See, e.g., Sprague v. Ticonic National Bank,* 307 U.S. 161, 59 S.Ct. 777, 83 L.Ed. 1184 (1939); *Central Railroad & Banking Co. v. Pettus,* 113 U.S. 116, 5 S.Ct. 387, 28 L.Ed. 915 (1885). That interpretation of *Blum* did not change when the Supreme Court held that the lodestar should not be enhanced through the use of a multiplier in statutory fee-shifting cases. *City of Burlington v. Dague,* 505 U.S. 557, 565–67, 112 S.Ct. 2638, 2642–44, 120 L.Ed.2d 449 (1992).

The second significant event in the 1980s was the report issued in 1985 by a Task Force the Third Circuit had appointed to evaluate the practical effectiveness of the lodestar method in making attorney fee awards. *See* Report of the Third Circuit Task Force, *Court Awarded Attorney Fees,* 108 F.R.D. 237 (1985). The Task Force recommended continued use of the lodestar technique in statutory fee-shifting cases. *Id. See also City of Burlington v. Dague,* 505 U.S. at 562, 112 S.Ct. at 2641 (acknowledging, in the statutory fee-shifting context, 'a strong presumption that the lodestar represents the reasonable fee'). The Task Force concluded, however, that all attorney fee awards in common fund cases should be structured as a percentage of the fund.

Report of the Third Circuit Task Force, *Court Awarded Attorney Fees,* 108 F.R.D. at 255.

At the present time, the majority of federal courts use a reasonable percentage of the fund method when making attorney fee awards in common fund cases. *See Swedish Hosp. Corp. v. Shalala,* 1 F.3d at 1266 (chronicling history of the methodologies). *See also* FEDERAL JUDICIAL CENTER, AWARDING ATTORNEYS' FEES AND MANAGING FEE LITIGATION 63–64 (1994) (canvassing case law.) The Third Circuit has recently held that the percentage of the fund is generally the preferable method for awarding fees in common fund cases, but noted that a lodestar analysis might be used to cross check the propriety of the award (a 'hybrid' approach). *See In re General Motors Corp. Pick–Up Truck Fuel Tank Products Liability Litigation,* 55 F.3d at 821. Ultimately, however, the Third Circuit permits the trial court to exercise its discretion in choosing *either* the percentage method *or* the lodestar method, *or* some combination or hybrid, as the circumstances warrant, in making common fund fee awards. *Id.*"

FURTHER NOTE ON PLAINTIFF'S COUNSEL FEES

1. The Third Circuit Task Force Report was extremely influential. Since 1985, a number of Circuits have held that the percentage-of-recovery method is mandatory or permissible in common-fund cases. In a striking and widely remarked-upon opinion in In re Oracle Securities Litigation, 131 F.R.D. 688 (N.D.Cal.1990) (a class-action securities case), Judge Vaughan Walker said, "the lodestar approach ... is now thoroughly discredited by experience. The lodestar approach is unworkable because, among other things, it abandons the adversary process upon which our judicial system is based...."

2. In a widely cited decision, In re Activision Securities Litigation, 723 F.Supp. 1373 (N.D.Cal.1989), the court determined, on the basis of a review of recent reported cases, that in nearly all common-fund cases the attorney's fee award ranges around 30% of the fund, even if the fee is purportedly calculated under the lodestar or related methods. The court observed that "[m]ost of these cases achieve this result after lengthy motion practice, volumes of discovery, and hence, the accumulation of extensive attorney time on behalf of all parties." Id. at 1377. Accordingly, the court concluded that the better practice in common-fund cases is to set a percentage fee, and that the percentage should be 30%, absent extraordinary circumstances. Other courts have mentioned other benchmark percentages. For example, in Paul, Johnson, Alston & Hunt v. Graulty, 886 F.2d 268 (9th Cir.1989), the court noted with approval a benchmark fee of 25%. In In re Warner Communications Securities Litigation, 618 F.Supp. 735, 750 (S.D.N.Y.1985), aff'd 798 F.2d 35 (2d Cir.1986), the court concluded that fee awards had averaged 20%–30% in the Second Circuit.

3. While *success* is a prerequisite to an award of counsel fees, a *judgment* is not. Counsel fees may be awarded even if a case is settled

or the defendants or the corporation takes a unilateral act that renders the plaintiff's demand or complaint moot. See, e.g., Bird v. Lida, Inc., 681 A.2d 399 (Allen, Ch.1996). In the latter kind of case, the plaintiff must show that his course of action was a significant cause of the act. Normally, however, the plaintiff is allowed to prove causation indirectly, by showing that his claim or demand was meritorious and that corrective action followed. It has been said that "[a] claim is meritorious within the meaning of the rule if it can withstand a motion to dismiss on the pleadings [and] if, at the same time, the plaintiff possesses knowledge of provable facts which hold out some reasonable likelihood of ultimate success. It is not necessary that factually there be absolute assurance of ultimate success, but only that there be some reasonable hope." Chrysler Corp. v. Dann, 43 Del.Ch. 252, 256–57, 223 A.2d 384, 387 (1966). Although a few cases suggest that meritoriousness is the only relevant issue in such cases, the rule seems to be that the plaintiff has the burden of showing meritoriousness, and once that showing is made the burden shifts to defendants to show that their actions did not result from plaintiff's course of action. See, e.g., Baron v. Allied Artists Pictures Corp., 395 A.2d 375 (Del.Ch.1978).

4. It is a well-established rule that attorneys' fees can be awarded to a plaintiff on the basis of a common but nonmonetary benefit, such as the corporation's agreement to change its governance structure, as opposed to the creation of a common fund. This rule has two important implications in derivative actions.

First, it is often very difficult to attribute any realistic value to nonmonetary benefits. As a result, in such cases attorney's fees usually are measured under the lodestar method, even by courts that employ the percentage-of-the-benefit test in common-fund cases.

Second, the rule that a plaintiff's attorney is entitled to a fee for producing a nonmonetary benefit opens the door to the possibility of collusive settlements in which the real defendants in a derivative action (the directors or officers) pay little or nothing; the corporation agrees to a change that is largely cosmetic; plaintiff's attorney and the corporation join hands to inflate the importance of the change; and plaintiff's attorney is then paid a fee that is supposed to be justified by that importance, but is really a bribe to drop the case. The real defendants are happy, because they get a release although they have paid little or nothing. Plaintiff's counsel is happy, because she gets a very nice fee. The shareholders aren't unhappy, because they don't realize what happened. If they did realize what happened, they would be very unhappy.

This doesn't mean that every settlement involving only a nonmonetary benefit is collusive. Nevertheless, the possibility that settlements involving only nonmonetary benefits may be collusive suggests that the courts should be especially cautious in reviewing such settlements.

Consider here the following: "[I]f the plaintiff had sought in its complaint [a change in various aspects of the firm's corporate governance] to the exclusion of all other relief, including monetary damages, is it not likely that the defendants would have settled immediately? Assuming the answer is 'yes,' then perhaps the corporate defendant should only have to pay for the value of the benefit, largely ignoring the litigation costs of the plaintiff.'' Mark J. Loewenstein, Shareholder Derivative Litigation and Corporate Governance, 24 Del. J. Corp. L. 1, 13, 22 (1999).

SECTION 12. SECURITY FOR EXPENSES

N.Y. BUS. CORP. LAW § 627

[See Statutory Supplement]

CAL. CORP. CODE § 800(c)–(f)

[See Statutory Supplement]

SECURITIES ACT § 11(e), 27(c)

[See Statutory Supplement]

SECURITIES EXCHANGE ACT § 21D(c)

West Hills Farms, Inc. v. RCO AG Credit, Inc.

California Court of Appeal, Fifth District, 2009.
170 Cal.App.4th 710, 88 Cal.Rptr.3d 458.

■ KANE, J.—In this derivative action, defendant RCO Ag Credit, Inc., was sued by two of its shareholders, plaintiffs West Hills Farms, Inc., and California Pistachio, LLC, based on allegedly unnecessary fees paid by defendant to a related corporate entity. Defendant made a motion under *Corporations Code section 800* to require plaintiffs to furnish a bond in the amount of $50,000 as security for defendant's anticipated litigation expenses to defend the action. The motion was granted and plaintiffs furnished the required bond. Defendant ultimately prevailed in the action and, following entry of judgment, moved for an award of *all* of its attorney fees and costs incurred, totaling over $350,000. The trial court's order limited the award of attorney fees and costs to $50,000, the amount of the bond. Defendant appeals from that order, contending that under *section 800* it was entitled to recover *all* of its attorney fees and costs, regardless of the amount of the bond. We disagree.... Accordingly, we affirm the trial court's order....

Section 800 addresses the terms and conditions under which a shareholder derivative action may be maintained.... The statute includes the provision at issue here that a plaintiff-shareholder may be compelled to furnish a bond as security for a defendant's anticipated litigation expenses, including attorney fees, which may be incurred in defense of the derivative action. (*§ 800, subds. (c), (d).*) "[T]he essential purpose of the *section 800* bond statute is to create a deterrent to unwarranted shareholder derivative lawsuits by providing a mechanism for securing a prevailing defendant's expenses up to $50,000." (*Donner Management Co. v. Schaffer (2006) 142 Cal. App.4th 1296, 1308 [48 Cal. Rptr. 3d 534].*) According to the statute, a defendant-corporation's motion to require a bond will be granted on a showing that "there is no reasonable possibility that the prosecution of the cause of action alleged in the complaint against the moving party will benefit the corporation or its shareholders." (*§ 800, subd. (c)(1).*) Additionally, the same relief will be extended to a defendant who is an officer or director of the corporation if it is shown that said "moving party, if other than the corporation, did not participate in the transaction complained of in any capacity." (*§ 800, subd. (c)(2).*)

Subdivision (d) of section 800 sets forth the particulars of the relief afforded by the motion as follows: "At the hearing upon any motion pursuant to subdivision (c), the court shall consider such evidence ..., as may be material (1) to the ground or grounds upon which the motion is based, or (2) to a determination of the probable reasonable expenses, including attorneys' fees, of the corporation ... which will be incurred in the defense of the action. If the court determines, after hearing the evidence adduced by the parties, that the moving party has established a probability in support of any of the grounds upon which the motion is based, *the court shall fix the amount of the bond, not to exceed fifty thousand dollars ($50,000), to be furnished by the plaintiff for reasonable expenses, including attorneys' fees, which may be incurred by the ... corporation in connection with the action*, including expenses for which the corporation may become liable pursuant to Section 317. A ruling by the court on the motion shall not be a determination of any issue in the action or of the merits thereof. If the court, upon the motion, makes a determination that a bond shall be furnished by the plaintiff as to any one or more defendants, the action shall be dismissed as to the defendant or defendants, unless the bond required by the court has been furnished within such reasonable time as may be fixed by the court." (Italics added.) ...

Aside from this bond protection, however, *section 800* makes no mention at all of attorney fees or expenses. Indeed, the *only* references in the statute to attorney fees or other expenses are within the limited context of describing what the bond will secure. (*§ 800, subds. (d), (e).*) There is simply nothing in the language of *section 800* to suggest that the Legislature intended to create an independent basis for recovery of attorney fees or costs *apart from recourse to the bond*. Of course, the Legislature is quite capable of drafting statutes that authorize awards to prevailing parties of all reasonable attorney fees or costs incurred in an action without limitation.... Here, however, the Legislature did not do so....

BACKGROUND NOTE ON SECURITY–FOR–EXPENSES STATUTES

Security-for-expenses statutes must be considered against the background of the general American rule that the losing party in a lawsuit does not have to pay the winner's expenses, except for "taxable costs," such as clerk's, witness, docket, and transcript fees. Accordingly, security-for-expenses statutes are normally not interpreted to impose *individual* liability on the plaintiff for expenses—that is, liability beyond the amount of his bond.

A shareholder who wants to bring a derivative action in a state that has a security-for-expenses statute is under heavy pressure to find some way to bring suit without posting security. Since the statutes are normally interpreted to be inapplicable to direct (as opposed to derivative) actions, one alternative is to frame the suit as a direct action. A second alternative is to bring the action under some provision of federal law, such as the Proxy Rules or Rule 10b–5. The security-for-expenses requirement may also be avoided in certain types of cases by petitioning for dissolution or the appointment of a receiver. See Leibert v. Clapp, 13 N.Y.2d 313, 247 N.Y.S.2d 102, 196 N.E.2d 540 (1963).

Even where these alternatives are infeasible, two judicial practices tend to soften the impact of the security-for-expenses statutes. The first practice is to stay the effectiveness of an order to post security, so that the plaintiff can find intervenors to help qualify under a statutory exemption based on the percentage or dollar value of complaining shares. See Baker v. MacFadden Publications, 300 N.Y. 325, 90 N.E.2d 876 (1950).

A second judicial practice, which builds on the first, is to order a corporation that moves for the posting of security to produce a shareholders' list, so that during the period of the stay the plaintiff can solicit other shareholders to join the action. A study based on interviews with knowledgeable plaintiffs' and defense attorneys in New York concluded that the courts have been extremely permissive in granting these motions. The study continued:

> [Thus if] the motion for security for expenses were to be made, it is likely that the plaintiff would request and obtain a 60–day stay and access to the corporate stocklist. By granting the plaintiff access to the list, defendants have hurt themselves in several ways. The motion involves additional expense in corporate

> time and effort in furnishing a stockholders' list to the plaintiff. Moreover, circularization by the plaintiff apprises stockholders and the press that a lawsuit involving management is pending. "Most if not all directors don't like to have their deeds or misdeeds advertised. They are sensitive to public opinion, particularly when a proxy fight is involved or imminent." Further, the plaintiffs' counsel now has a list of potential plaintiffs which may be used against the corporation in future litigation. Finally, there is a risk that a motion for security may cause the plaintiff to discontinue the original action and start another in a sister-state having no security-for-expenses statute....

As a result, it is not uncommon for defendants in New York cases to refrain from moving for security for expenses. Note, Security for Expenses in Shareholders' Derivative Suits: 23 Years' Experience, 4 Colum.J.L. & Soc.Prob. 50, 62–65 (1968).

In Cohen v. Beneficial Industrial Loan Corp., 337 U.S. 541, 69 S.Ct. 1221, 93 L.Ed. 1528 (1949), the Supreme Court held that security-for-expenses statutes are substantive for *Erie* purposes—that is, if such a statute would apply to an action brought in a court of the forum state, it will also apply to a diversity action brought in a federal court in that state. However, a state security-for-expenses statute is not applicable to derivative actions brought on *federal* grounds, e.g., under § 16(b) or Rule 10b–5. McClure v. Borne Chemical Co., 292 F.2d 824 (3d Cir.1961), cert. denied 368 U.S. 939, 82 S.Ct. 382, 7 L.Ed.2d 339. On the other hand, where an action arising under a federal statute is brought in federal court, and the plaintiff brings a related state-law action before the court under the doctrine of pendent jurisdiction, any relevant state security-for-expenses statute will apply to the pendent action.

SECTION 13. PRIVATE ORDERING AND SHAREHOLDER SUITS

Consider the policy implications of the contemporary debate on the efficacy and desirability of articles of incorporation including forum selection provisions that either require intra-firm disputes be arbitrated or litigated only in the courts of a specific state. Vice–Chancellor Lastner appears to embrace validity of such a provision in In Re Revlon, Inc. Shareholders Litigation, 990 A.2d 940, 960–961 (Del. Ch. 2010): "[I]f boards of directors and stockholders believe that a particular forum would provide an efficient and value-promoting locus for dispute resolution, then corporations are free to respond with charter provisions selecting an exclusive forum for intra-entity disputes." In a footnote he observes:

Del. C. § 102(b)(1) (authorizing certificate to contain "[a]ny provision for the management of the business and for the conduct of the affairs of the corporation, and any provision creating, defining, limiting and regulating the powers of the corporation, the directors, and the stockholders, or any class of the stockholders . . . , if such provisions are not contrary to the laws of this State."); *see* Elf Atochem N. Am. Inc. v. Jaffari, 727 A.2d 286, 287 (Del. 1999) (approving provision in LLC agreement requiring that all intra-entity disputes be resolved exclusively by arbitration or court proceedings in California); Douzinas v. Am. Bureau of Shipping, Inc., 888 A.2d 1146, 1149 (Del. Ch. 2006) (enforcing provision in LLC agreement requiring that all intra-entity disputes be resolved by arbitration); Sara Lewis, Note, *Transforming the "Anywhere but Chancery" Problem into the "Nowhere but Chancery" Solution, 14 Stanford J. L. Bus. & Fin. 199 (2008)* (analyzing validity of Delaware forum selection provision for intra-entity disputes); *see also* Faith Stevelman, *Regulatory Competition, Choice of Forum, and Delaware's Stake in Corporate Law*, 34 Del. J. Corp. L. 57, 133–35 (2009) (discussing potential availability of forum selection provision for intra-corporate disputes). Both Stevelman and Lewis note that one public company, NetSuite, Inc., has a Delaware forum selection provision in its charter. *See Lewis*, supra, at 202; *Stevelman*, supra, at 133 n.294. Lewis notes that Oracle Corporation has a Delaware forum selection provision for derivative actions in its bylaws. *See Lewis*, supra, at 202–03. As *Elf Atochem* and *Douzinas* demonstrate, a provision selecting an exclusive forum for intra-entity disputes need not choose the Delaware courts. For example, business principals who all live in the same distant locale might form a Delaware entity to gain the many benefits conferred by Delaware law, yet prefer to litigate intra-entity disputes in their local jurisdiction. I can envision that the Delaware courts would retain some measure of inherent residual authority so that entities created under the authority of Delaware law could not wholly exempt themselves from Delaware oversight. The issues implicated by an exclusive forum selection provision must await resolution in an appropriate case.

CHAPTER 15

CORPORATE COMBINATIONS, TENDER OFFERS AND DEFENDING CONTROL

SECTION 1. CORPORATE COMBINATIONS

A. SALE OF SUBSTANTIALLY ALL ASSETS

DEL. GEN. CORP. LAW § 271

[See Statutory Supplement]

MODEL BUS. CORP. ACT §§ 12.01, 12.02, 13.02(3)

[See Statutory Supplement]

Hollinger, Inc. v. Hollinger International, Inc.

Court of Chancery of Delaware, 2004.
858 A.2d 342.

Opinion

■ STRINE, VICE CHANCELLOR. . . .

Hollinger Inc. (or "Inc.") seeks a preliminary injunction preventing Hollinger International, Inc. (or "International") from selling the *Telegraph* Group Ltd. (England) to Press Holdings International, an entity controlled by Frederick and David Barclay (hereinafter, the "Barclays"). The *Telegraph* Group is an indirect, wholly owned subsidiary of International and publishes the *Telegraph* newspaper and the *Spectator* magazine. The *Telegraph* newspaper is a leading one in the United Kingdom, both in terms of its circulation and its journalistic reputation.

The key question addressed in this decision is whether Inc. and the other International stockholders must be provided with the opportunity to vote on the sale of the *Telegraph* Group because that sale involves "substantially all" the assets of International within the meaning of 8 Del. C. § 271. The sale of the *Telegraph* followed a lengthy auction process whereby International and all of Hollinger's operating assets were widely shopped to potential bidders. As a practical matter, Inc.'s vote would be the only one that matters because although it now owns only 18% of International's total equity, it, through high-vote Class B shares, controls 68% of the voting power. . . .

. . . Does § 271 Apply to a Sale of Assets By an Indirect, Wholly Owned Subsidiary?

International [first] argues that the sale of the *Telegraph* Group simply does not implicate § 271 at all. The reason is that the operating assets that the Barclays are buying and that comprise the *Telegraph* Group are actually held by a 6th tier U.K. subsidiary and not by International.

It is undisputed that the chain of subsidiaries through which International controlled the *Telegraph* Group maintained the corporate formalities necessary for it to comply with U.K. and U.S. regulatory requirements. It is also undisputed that these subsidiaries are longstanding parts of the International structure and were formed because they had valuable tax, financial, and liability-insulating purposes. There is no indication that any third parties dealing with the subsidiaries in the ordinary course of business or any tort plaintiff allegedly injured by one of the subsidiaries would have been entitled to pierce their corporate veil and seek recourse directly against International.

On the other hand, the chain of subsidiaries is wholly owned by International. The Strategic Process that resulted in the proposal to sell the *Telegraph* Group was, as a matter of obvious reality, conducted entirely at the International level. . . .

Notably, the contract for sale of the *Telegraph* Group does not run simply between the Barclays and the U.K. subsidiary that directly own the *Telegraph* Group. Instead, International is a direct signatory to that agreement and its lawyers negotiated its terms. . . .

In essence, it is clear to me that the *Telegraph* sale was directed and controlled by International and that its wholly owned subsidiaries did what wholly owned subsidiaries do—the bidding of their sole owner. It is no disrespect to the employees who populated the subsidiary boards to recognize this obvious reality.

From this, to my view, clear factual picture, the parties draw starkly different legal conclusions. For its part, International contends that it is plain that § 271 does not contemplate ignoring the separate existence of subsidiary corporations unless the stringent test for veil piercing is met. . . .

If International's argument is accepted, § 271's vote requirement will be rendered largely hortatory—reduced to an easily side-stepped gesture, but little more, towards the idea that transactions that dispose of substantially all of a corporation's economic value need stockholders' assent to become effective. An example tied to this case points out this implication. Assume that the [board, acting through its Corporate Review Committee] decided to sell all four of International's operating groups. Further assume that each is held by subsidiaries that would not be subject to veil piercing but that it is equally clear that International dictated the sale of the assets and was a signatory to and guarantor of the sales contracts. Under International's view, even that sale would not constitute a sale of substantially all of its assets. This would be the case even though the sales would, taken together, result in a de facto liquidation of the firm's operating assets into a pool of cash, a result akin to a sale of the entire company for cash or a liquidation....

In drawing lines under § 271 itself, moreover, the facts of this case suggest a possible demarcation point. When an asset sale by the wholly owned subsidiary is to be consummated by a contract in which the parent entirely guarantees the performance of the selling subsidiary that is disposing of all of its assets and in which the parent is liable for any breach of warranty by the subsidiary, the direct act of the parent's board can, without any appreciable stretch, be viewed as selling assets of the parent itself. By its direct contractual action, the parent board is promising to dispose of all of the underlying assets of the subsidiaries by having the parent cause its wholly owned subsidiaries to sell, by promising to bear all the economic risks of the asset sale itself, and by therefore essentially eliminating the subsidiary's purpose and existence and monetizing for itself as parent the value of the assets held by that subsidiary. To find that § 271's vote requirement were implicated by such a contract if it involved the sale of assets that would, if owned directly by the parent, comprise substantially all of the parent's assets would not, despite International's well-stated arguments to the contrary, be an irrational implementation of the legislative intent expressed in that section of our corporation code.

I need not reach that conclusion, or a contrary one, in this case, however. This motion can be resolved without rendering any definitive pronouncement on this area of our law and, given the limited time for reflection on the question presented, prudential considerations counsel in favor of leaving the question to be answered in another case, or at later stage of this one, if that becomes necessary.

... *As a Matter of Economic Substance, Does the Telegraph Group Comprise Substantially All of International's Assets?*

I now discuss the major question presented by this motion: whether the *Telegraph* Group comprises "substantially all" of International's assets, such that its sale requires a vote under § 271.

1. *The Legal Standards to Measure Whether the Telegraph Group Comprises Substantially All of International's Assets*

Section 271 of the Delaware General Corporation Law authorizes a board of directors of a Delaware corporation to sell "all or substantially all of its property and assets, including goodwill and corporate franchises" only with the approval of a stockholder vote....

Therefore, I begin my articulation of the applicable legal principles with the words of the statute itself.... A fair and succinct equivalent to the term "substantially all" would ... be "essentially everything."

In our jurisprudence, however, words of this kind arguably long ago passed from the sight of our judicial rear view mirrors, to be replaced by an inquiry more focused on the judicial gloss put on the statute than on the words of the statute itself.

> The Supreme Court has long held that a determination of whether there is a sale of substantially all assets so as to trigger section 271 depends upon the particular qualitative and quantitative characteristics of the transaction at issue. Thus, the transaction must be viewed in terms of its overall effect on the corporation, and there is no necessary qualifying percentage.[51]

In other words,

> Our jurisprudence eschewed a definitional approach to § 271 focusing on the interpretation of the words "substantially all," in favor of a contextual approach focusing upon whether a transaction involves the sale "of assets quantitatively vital to the operation of the corporation and is out of the ordinary and substantially affects the existence and purpose of the corporation." *Gimbel v. Signal Cos., Inc.*, Del.Ch., 316 A.2d 599, 606, *aff'd*, Del.Supr., 316 A.2d 619 (1974)....[52]

... *Gimbel* set forth a quantitative and qualitative test designed to help determine whether a particular sale of assets involved substantially all the corporation's assets. That test has been adopted by our Supreme Court as a good metric for determining whether an asset sale triggers the vote requirement of § 271....[55]

The test that *Gimbel* articulated—requiring a stockholder vote if the assets to be sold "are quantitatively vital to the operation of the corporation' and 'substantially affect[ ] the existence and purpose of the corporation"—must ... be read as an attempt to give practical life to the words "substantially all." It is for that reason that *Gimbel* emphasized that a vote would never be required for a transaction in the ordinary course of business and that the mere fact that an asset sale was out of the ordinary had little bearing on whether a vote was required.

Indeed, *Gimbel* stressed that "the statute does not speak of a requirement of shareholder approval simply because an independent, important branch of a corporate business is being sold." In that case, the court expressly rejected the argument that Delaware law ought to

---

51. *Winston v. Mandor*, 710 A.2d 835, 843 (Del.Ch.1997) (footnotes omitted).

52. *In re General Motors Class H S'holders Litig.*, 734 A.2d 611, 623 (Del.Ch.1999).

55. *Oberly v. Kirby*, 592 A.2d 445, 464 (Del.1991); *see also Thorpe v. CERBCO, Inc.*, 676 A.2d 436, 444 (Del.1996).

follow the law of other states that subjected all such major sales to stockholder approval. . . .

To underscore the point that the test it was articulating was tied directly to the statute, *Gimbel* noted that its examination of the quantitative and qualitative importance of the transaction at issue was intended to determine whether the transaction implicated the statute because it struck "at the heart of the corporate existence and purpose," in the sense that it involved the " 'destruction of the means to accomplish the purposes or objects for which the corporation was incorporated and actually performs.' " It was in that sense, Gimbel said, that the "statute's applicability was to be determined."

And it is in that sense that I apply the *Gimbel* test in this case.

2. *Is the Telegraph Group Quantitatively Vital to the Operations of International?*

The first question under the *Gimbel* test is whether the *Telegraph* Group is quantitatively vital to the operations of International. The short answer to that question is no, it is not quantitatively vital within the meaning of *Gimbel*.

Why?

Because it is clear that International will retain economic vitality even after a sale of the *Telegraph* because it is retaining other significant assets, one of which, the Chicago Group [which owned, among other things, the Chicago *Sun–Times* and Jerusalem *Post* newspapers], has a strong record of past profitability and expectations of healthy profit growth.

Now, it is of course clear that the *Telegraph* Group is a major quantitative part of International's economic value and an important contributor to its profits. I am even prepared to decide this motion on the assumption that the *Telegraph* Group is the single most valuable asset that International possesses, even more valuable than the Chicago Group.

If one were to use the actual high bids received for each of the *Telegraph* and Chicago Groups as a result of the Strategic [Auction] Process and assume that those were the only assets of International—which is not an accurate assumption—the *Telegraph* Group accounts for 56–57% of International's asset value, while the Chicago Group accounts for only 43–44% of the value. Recognizing that quantitative vitality must be defined in light of the statutory language "substantially all," this breakdown does little to support Inc.'s position. It is less than 60% and the remaining asset is itself a quantitatively vital economic asset. . . .

Let's consider the relative contribution to International's revenues of the *Telegraph* Group and the Chicago Group. . . .

Put simply, the *Telegraph* Group has accounted for less than half of International's revenues during the last three years and the Chicago Group's contribution has been in the same ballpark. . . .

In book value terms, neither the *Telegraph* Group nor the Chicago Group approach 50% of International's asset value because the company's other operating groups and non-operating assets have value....

In terms of vitality, however, a more important measure is EBITDA [Earnings Before Interest, Taxes, Depreciation, and Amortization] contribution, as that factor focuses on the free cash flow that assets generate for the firm, a key component of economic value....

The [EBITDA] picture that emerges is one of rough equality between the two Groups—with any edge tilting in the Chicago Group's direction....

Importantly, the record evidence regarding the future of both Groups also suggests that their cash flow-generating potential and sale value are not greatly disparate....

The evidence therefore reveals that neither the *Telegraph* Group nor the Chicago Group is quantitatively vital in the sense used in the *Gimbel* test. Although both Groups are profitable, valuable economic assets and although the *Telegraph* Group is somewhat more valuable than the Chicago Group, International can continue as a profitable entity without either one of them....

[A] sale of either Group leaves International as a profitable entity, even if it chooses to distribute a good deal of the cash it receives from the *Telegraph* sale to its stockholders through a dividend or share repurchase.

3. *Does the Telegraph Sale "Substantially Affect the Existence and Purpose of" International?*

The relationship of the qualitative element of the *Gimbel* test to the quantitative element is more than a tad unclear. If the assets to be sold are not quantitatively vital to the corporation's life, it is not altogether apparent how they can "substantially affect the existence and purpose of" the corporation within the meaning of *Gimbel*, suggesting either that the two elements of the test are actually not distinct or that they are redundant. In other words, if quantitative vitality takes into account factors such as the cash-flow generating value of assets and not merely book value, then it necessarily captures qualitative considerations as well.... Rather than endeavor to explore the relationship between these factors, however, I will just dive into my analysis of the qualitative importance of the *Telegraph* Group to International.

Inc.'s demand for a vote places great weight on the qualitative element of *Gimbel*. In its papers, Inc. stresses the journalistic superiority of the *Telegraph* over the *Sun–Times* and the social cachet the *Telegraph* has....

The argument ... misconceives the qualitative element of *Gimbel*. That element is not satisfied if the court merely believes that the economic assets being sold are aesthetically superior to those being retained; rather, the qualitative element of *Gimbel* focuses on economic quality and, at most, on whether the transaction leaves the stockholders with an investment that in economic terms is qualitatively different than the one that they now possess. Even with that focus, it must be remembered that the qualitative element is a gloss on the statutory language "substantially all" and not an attempt to identify qualitatively important transactions but ones that "strike at the heart of the corporate existence."

The *Telegraph* sale does not strike at International's heart or soul, if that corporation can be thought to have either one....

... Whatever the social importance of the *Telegraph* in Great Britain, the economic value of that importance to International as an entity is what matters for the *Gimbel* test, not how cool it would be to be the *Telegraph's* publisher. The expected cash flows from the *Telegraph* Group take that into account, as do the bids that were received for the *Telegraph* Group....

After the *Telegraph* Sale, International's stockholders will remain investors in a publication company with profitable operating assets, a well-regarded tabloid newspaper of good reputation and large circulation, a prestigious newspaper in Israel, and other valuable assets. While important, the sale of the *Telegraph* does not strike a blow to International's heart.

4. *Summary of § 271 Analysis*

When considered quantitatively and qualitatively, the *Telegraph* sale does not amount to a sale of substantially all of International's assets. This conclusion is consistent with the bulk of our case law under § 271. Although by no means wholly consistent, that case law has, by and large, refused to find that a disposition involved substantially all the assets of a corporation when the assets that would remain after the sale were, in themselves, substantial and profitable. As *Gimbel* noted, § 271 permits a board to sell "one business ... without shareholder approval when other substantial businesses are retained." In the cases when asset sales were deemed to involve substantially all of a corporation's assets, the record always revealed great doubt about the viability of the business that would remain, primarily because the remaining operating assets were not profitable.[77] But, "if the portion of the business not sold constitutes a substantial, viable, ongoing component of the corporation, the sale is not subject to Section 271."[78]

To conclude that the sale of the *Telegraph* Group was a sale of substantially all of International's assets would involve a determination

---

77. *E.g., Winston v. Mandor*, 710 A.2d 835, 843 (Del.Ch.1997) (assets comprising 60% of net asset value might be substantially all assets for pleading purposes in situation when they allegedly constituted the only "income-generating assets"); *Thorpe v. CERBCO, Inc.*, 1995 WL 478954, at *9–*10 (Del.Ch. Aug.9, 1995) (assets that were held likely to constitute substantially all the assets comprised at least 68% of corporation's assets and were the corporation's "primary income-generating asset[s]"), *rev'd in part, aff'd in relevant part*, 676 A.2d 436 (Del.1996); *Katz v. Bregman*, 431 A.2d 1274, 1275 (Del.Ch.1981) (only case finding assets worth less than 60% of a company's value to be "substantially all" the company's assets, and doing so when sale at issue came on heels of other substantial asset sales and where the assets to be sold had been the company's only income-producing facility during the previous four years).

78. 1 R. Franklin Balotti & Jesse A. Finkelstein, DELAWARE LAW OF CORPORATIONS & BUSINESS ORGANIZATIONS § 10.2, at 10–7 (3d ed. Supp. 2004).

that International possesses two operating assets, the sale of either of which would trigger a stockholder vote under § 271. That is, because there is no significant distinction between the economic importance of the Chicago and *Telegraph* Groups to International, a conclusion that the *Telegraph* Group was substantially all of International's assets would (impliedly but undeniably) supplant the plain language and intended meaning of the General Assembly with an "approximately half" test.[79] I decline Inc.'s invitation for me to depart so markedly from our legislature's mandate. By any reasonable interpretation, the *Telegraph* sale does not involve substantially all of International's assets as substantial operating (and non-operating) assets will be retained, and International will remain a profitable publishing concern.

. . . *Conclusion*

Inc.'s motion for a preliminary injunction is DENIED. . . .

---

79. As International points out, the MBCA now includes a safe harbor provision that is intended to provide a "greater measure of certainty than is provided by interpretations of the current case law." MODEL BUS. CORP. ACT § 12.02 cmt. 1 (2002). The safe harbor is an objective test involving two factors:

> If a corporation retains a business activity that represented at least 25 percent of total assets at the end of the most recently completed fiscal year, and 25 percent of either income from continuing operations before taxes or revenues from continuing operations for that fiscal year, in each case of the corporation and its subsidiaries on a consolidated basis, the corporation will conclusively be deemed to have retained a significant continuing business activity.

Id. § 12.02(a).

Moreover, both the MBCA and the ALI Principles of Corporate Governance usefully turn the "substantially all" inquiry on its head by focusing, as *Gimbel* does in a more oblique way, on what remains after a sale. *See* MODEL BUS. CORP. ACT § 12.02 cmt. 1 (2002) (stockholder vote required if asset sale would "leave the corporation without a significant continuing business activity"); PRINCIPLES OF CORP. GOVERNANCE §§ 1.38(a)(2), 6.01(b) (text requiring stockholder approval when asset sale "would leave the corporation without a significant continuing business"); *id.* § 1.38 cmt. 3 (commentary indicating that if a company has two principal operating divisions and one will remain following the asset sale, "there should normally be no doubt concerning the significance of the remaining division, even if the division to be sold represented a majority of the corporation's operating assets"). The MBCA, in particular, recognizes that while the "significant continuing business activity" test differs verbally from the "substantially all" language employed in many state corporation statutes, adoption of the MBCA provision would not entail a substantive change from existing law, because "[i]n practice, ... courts interpreting these statutes [using the phrase 'substantially all'] have commonly employed a test comparable to that embodied in 12.02(a)." MODEL BUS. CORP. ACT § 12.02 cmt. 1 (2002). The commentary specifically cites several Delaware judicial decisions as examples of cases employing such a test. *Id.* These approaches support the conclusion I reach.

Although not binding on me, these interpretative approaches provide a valuable perspective on § 271 because they are rooted, as is *Gimbel*, in the intent behind the statute (and statutes like it in other jurisdictions). Indeed, taken together, a reading of § 271 that: 1) required a stockholder vote for any sales contract to which a parent was a party that involved a sale by a wholly owned subsidiary that, in economic substance, amounted to a disposition of substantially all the parent's assets; combined with 2) a strict adherence to the words "substantially all" (a la the MBCA), could be viewed as the most faithful way to give life to the General Assembly's intended use of § 271. That is, § 271 would have substantive force but only with regard to transactions that genuinely involved substantially all of the corporation's assets. . . .

NOTE ON SALE OF SUBSTANTIALLY ALL ASSETS

At common law, a sale of substantially all assets required unanimous shareholder approval, on the theory that it breached an implied contract among the shareholders to further the corporate enterprise. See, e.g., Fontaine v. Brown County Motors Co., 251 Wis. 433, 437, 29 N.W.2d 744, 746–47 (1947). The statutory sale-of-substantially-all-assets provisions were enacted against this backdrop. It has been held that under those statutes a sale of substantially all assets in the ordinary course of business does not require shareholder approval. See Jeppi v. Brockman Holding Co., 34 Cal.2d 11, 206 P.2d 847 (1949). The theory is that because such a sale does not prevent furtherance of the corporate enterprise, it would not have required unanimous shareholder approval at common law, and the statutory sale-of-substantially-all-assets provisions were not intended to change that result.

B. THE APPRAISAL REMEDY

DEL. GEN. CORP. LAW § 262

[See Statutory Supplement]

MODEL BUS. CORP. ACT §§ 13.01–13.03, 13.20–13.26, 13.30–13.31

[See Statutory Supplement]

ALI, PRINCIPLES OF CORPORATE GOVERNANCE §§ 7.21–7.23

[See Statutory Supplement]

CAL. CORP. CODE §§ 1300, 1311

[See Statutory Supplement]

NOTE ON THE APPRAISAL REMEDY

Prior to the mid 19th Century, any change in the rights of shareholders, whether by amendment of the articles of incorporation, merger or sale of all the corporation's assets, required the approval of all stockholders. The then prevailing view was that shareholders had a vested right protected by the Constitution's Contract Clause so that relaxation of the unanimity requirement presented serious constitutional issues. As commerce expanded, conditioning corporate transactions that change the rights of stockholders on unanimous stockholder approval impeded the growth of firms and, more generally, retarded industrial development. Responding to a challenge to a merger that the state had authorized to occur by less than all the stockholders, *see* Lauman v. Lebanon Valley Railroad, 30 Pa. 42 (1858), Pennsylvania amended its statute to provide dissenters the right to receive cash for their shares, i.e., compensation for any constitutionally protected "taking." This was the first appraisal statute and the corporate landscape has not been the same since. Today, all state corporation statutes provide appraisal remedy for various types of corporate transactions. However, states vary widely how they identify the types of transactions for which appraisal is available.

States that are more solicitous of shareholders provide appraisal (subject to certain exceptions that apply to their appraisal statute generally) for amendments to the articles of incorporation that adversely affect the rights of stockholders, the sale of all or substantially all the firm's assets, and mergers and consolidations. *See e.g.,* Cal. Corp. Code §§ 181, 1200 et seq., 1300; N.Y. Bus. Corp. L. § 910. In contrast, Delaware limits its appraisal statute to mergers and consolidations. *See* Del. Code Ann., tit. 8 § 262(b). The Model Business Corporation Act follows a course between these two extremes, providing appraisal for sales of assets, mergers and consolidations. *See* MBCA § 13.02(a).

Appraisal statutes provide a process for shareholders meeting the statute's conditions to obtain fair value for their shares. The Model Act provides the most extensive description of "fair value" identifying that such value is to be determined "immediately before the effectuation of the corporate action" triggering the appraisal right as determined "using customary and current valuation concepts" and "without discounting for lack of marketability or minority status." Delaware's statute excludes from the fair value determination "any element of value arising from the accomplishment or expectation of the merger or consolidation," and invites an array of valuation methods by providing that "the Court shall take into account all relevant factors."

The appraisal remedy is commonly referred to as "dissenters" rights. In most states this is a misnomer because appraisal is not conditioned on the shareholder voting against the acquisition but rather not voting in favor of the transaction triggering the right of appraisal. *See* Del. Code. Ann., tit. 8 § 262(a), MBCA § 13.21(a)(2). There are, however, several procedural steps the shareholder must take to perfect the right of appraisal. For example, Delaware provides that before the vote on the merger or consolidation the shareholder must make a written demand for appraisal and provides a rather short period of time, 120 days after completion of the merger or consolidation, in which the appraisal proceeding is to be commenced. Del. Code Ann., tit. 8 § 262(d)(e). The Model Act also requires before the vote of the shareholders is taken that notice of the intent to seek appraisal must be given by the shareholder, sets forth other steps that must be taken after the vote approving the transaction has occurred, and the appraisal proceeding does not begin until the shareholder has rejected in writing the corporation's estimate of the share's fair value. MBCA §§ 13.21–13.26. In Delaware the costs of the appraisal proceeding are assigned as the court deems "equitable in the circumstances" Del. Code Ann., tit. 8 § 262(j), whereas in the Model Act the proceeding's costs are borne by the corporation unless otherwise assigned by the court. MBCA § 13.31(a). Even though pursuant to the "American Rule" litigants customarily bear the costs of their representatives and experts and not those of their opponents, in limited instances the Model Act permits such costs to be assigned to the corporation. *Id.* § 13.31(b)(c). In sum, appraisal is a proceeding that one does not easily fall into but rather a process the shareholder must pursue with a close eye to the procedural steps set forth in the governing appraisal statute and with a healthy awareness of extraordinary remedy's costs.

PIEMONTE v. NEW BOSTON GARDEN CORP.

[See Chapter 8, supra]

NOTE ON APPRAISED VALUE: THE BATTLING EXPERTS

By far the most popular method for determining fair value in appraisal proceedings is the "Delaware Block Method" which assigns a weight to each of several values: asset value, market value, earnings value and sometimes dividend value. The weight assigned to each of these not only turns on the unique characteristics of the firm but also reflects to some extent the trustworthiness of the figure in the overall valuation process. Thus, in a leading case, a low weight (10 percent) was assigned to the firm's market value (determined by its trading price) because the shares were thinly traded due to ninety percent of the shares being held by the firm's controlling stockholder whereas the firm's earnings value (present value of estimated future earnings) and net asset value (presumed piecemeal liquidation value of the firm) were weighted 40% and 50%, respectively. *See* Piemonte v. New Boston Garden Corp., 377 Mass. 719, 387 N.E.2d 1145 (Mass. 1979). Should any percentage greater than zero be assigned to a valuation factor if, as with Piemonte, that valuation factor is deemed either untrustworthy (market value) or an unlikely means (liquidation) by which value will for that entity be achieved? The Delaware Supreme Court in Weinberger v. UOP, 457 A.2d 701 (1983) weakened Delaware's support for the Delaware block:

> [T]he standard "Delaware block" or weighted average method of valuation, formerly employed in appraisal and other stock valuation cases, shall no longer exclusively control such proceedings. We believe that a more liberal approach must include proof of value by any techniques or methods which are generally considered acceptable in the financial community and otherwise

> admissible in court, subject only to our interpretation of 8 Del. C.§ 262(h), infra.... This will obviate the very structured and mechanistic procedure that has heretofore governed such matters....
>
> It is significant that section 262 now mandates the determination of "fair" value based upon "all relevant factors". Only the speculative elements of value that may arise from the "accomplishment or expectation" of the merger are excluded. We take this to be a very narrow exception to the appraisal process, designed to eliminate use of *pro forma* data and projections of a speculative variety relating to the completion of a merger. But elements of future value, including the nature of the enterprise, which are known or susceptible of proof as of the date of the merger and not the product of speculation, may be considered. When the trial court deems it appropriate, fair value also includes any damages, resulting from the taking, which the stockholders sustain as a class. If that was not the case, then the obligation to consider "all relevant factors" in the valuation process would be eroded.

But see Leader v. Hycor, Inc., 395 Mass. 215, 479 N.E.2d 173 (1985) ("Because the issue of the continuing validity of the 'Delaware block method' of stock valuation is likely to arise on remand, we express our opinion on this matter. We do not agree that the 'Delaware block method' for valuing closely held stock, as set forth in our decision in *Piemonte v. New Boston Garden Corp.*, 377 Mass. 719, 387 N.E.2d 1145 (1979), is outmoded.... In any event, we have never held that the Delaware block method is the only approach that a judge may employ in valuing stock.")

Methods other than the Delaware block method include individual consideration of each of the valuation factors that are aggregated in the Delaware block method, plus a range of other even more sophisticated financial methodologies. Indeed, experts abound in this area and attorneys are eager to employ those likely to support their client's aspirations. Professor Campbell found post-*Weinberger* that, although the Delaware block method had slipped to being used in 14 percent of the Delaware appraisal decisions, it continued to be invoked in half the appraisal decisions outside of Delaware. Moreover, he found that courts invoke 2.4 evaluation methodologies to determine fair value per appraisal case and in more than half the cases one of the parties offered more than one valuation method. Rutherford B. Campbell, Jr., The Impact of Modern Finance Theory in Acquisition Cases, 53 Syracuse L. Rev. 1 (2003). How reassuring is the following explanation of the multiple methodologies invoked by the court to determine the fair value fair value of shares:

> The first factor involves the nature of the evidence that parties offer courts in valuation cases. Generally, when examining particular court opinions from the data, one finds too many courts overwhelmed by massive amounts of complex, tedious, technical valuation evidence offered by the parties, evidence that

> is often so dense that not even the best judges have any realistic chance of sorting through the testimony of the parties' experts and ultimately coming to a sensible conclusion. . . .
>
> One should not be surprised to find the parties as between themselves offer different methodologies to the court. Each party, operating under the flexibility of a *Weinberger* regime, will offer the court the valuation methodology that enhances its own chances of an outcome favorable to itself. One might expect that the methodology that supports the higher possible value (the plaintiff's position) and the lowest possible value (the defendant's position) are often different, and the data are consistent with that conclusion.
>
> For at least two reasons, a single party may feel it advantageous to offer the court more than one valuation methodology. First, a party may see its chances of a court's accepting its particular estimate of value enhanced if the party supports its valuation under multiple theories. . . . Alternatively, a party may have a good idea of which methodology is the court's favorite or may conclude from past decisions that the court uses different methodologies without any evidence of discernible principle. Once again, therefore, a logical strategy in such a circumstance is for a party to present multiple methodologies in the hope that at least one of the methodologies will appeal to the court.

Id. at 41–42.

Consider here the idea suggested by former Delaware Chancellor William Allen that judges confronted with widely different views of the shares' value should, following the practice in baseball arbitrations—discard entirely the less reasonable of the two conflicting positions rather than to cobble together a solution that borrows and modifies from each of the competing positions:

> An appraisal action is a judicial, not an inquisitorial proceeding. The parties, not the court, establish the record and the court is limited by the record created. The statutory command to determine fair value is a command to do so in a judicial proceeding, with the powers and constraints such a proceeding entails. Accepting that the expert testimony has been so structured as to largely foreclose the court from accepting parts of one DCF [discounted cash flow] model and sections of the other, it follows that the court must decide which of the two principal experts has the greater claim overall to have correctly estimated the intrinsic value of ... [the company] stock at the time of the merger. Having decided that question, it will be open to me to critically review the details of the expert's opinion in order to determine if the record will permit, and judicial judgment require, modification of any inputs in that model. What the record will not permit is either a completely independent judicially created DCF model or a pastiche composed of bits of one model and pieces of another.

Cede & Co. and Cinerama, Inc. v. Technicolor, Inc., 1990 WL 161084 (Del. Ch. 1990), rev'd 684 A.2d 289, 299 (1996) (reasoning that by choosing the better of the two conflicting experts and focusing modifications on that expert's methodology only the Chancellor had abdicated his judicial function). If the approach taken by Chancellor Allen was understood ex ante to be the approach followed of the appraisal court, what impact would you expect such an approach to have on the litigants?

NEW YORK BUS. CORP. LAW § 623(h)(4)

[See Statutory Supplement]

CHARLAND v. COUNTRY VIEW GOLF CLUB, INC.

[See Chapter 8, supra]

NOTE ON DISCOUNTS AND PREMIUMS IN APPRAISAL PROCEEDINGS

As has been seen, the value of any asset is the present value of the future benefits of owning that particular asset. If the asset is an investment, it is the future cash flow to be received by owning that investment; the asset's present value is determined by discounting the future cash receipts to reflect both the length of time to receive the cash as well as the uncertainty (risk) associated with their receipt. In the case of a corporation, the cash flow would be the yearly dividends, if any, as well as the future price appreciation on disposition of the shares or the firm's assets. Similarly, the value of all the equity of a corporation is also measured by the present value of all future cash flows to owners that are associated with such ownership. For example, if the equity of a firm has a total value of $10,000 and is held equally by 100 shareholders (i.e., each holding 100 shares), then each has an equal share and we would expect the value of each holder's "share" to be the same. Moreover, if the same firm had 100 shareholders each owning 10 shares, we would not expect this to change the *aggregate* value of their holdings. But what result if there is one holder, C, who owns 60 percent of the firm's total equity and there are 40 other holders each who each own 1 percent of the firm's shares? Would the single share held by C have the same value as a single share held by any of the minority holders? In this scenario, first consider whether the value of all the equity should change if there is a controlling stockholder from the earlier-described instances of 100 equal shareholders. If the new controlling stockholder does not change the firm's operations, the amount and time of future cash flow shared by all owners would not change so that the total value of all equity would not be affected by the presence of a sixty-percent holder. Nonetheless, would we not expect that the value of each share held by C to have a greater value than any share owned by the non-control holders? That is, because the presence of a control stockholder itself does not change the overall value of the firm, would we expect that control shares will enjoy a higher per share value (because of the power to control) than non-control shares? If so, the increase in value of the shares owned by C must come at the expense of the non-control shares. In the appraisal context, if we are persuaded that C's shares enjoy a premium over non-control shares, does this mean that the value of the individual minority shares should be discounted in the appraisal proceeding? Similarly, if the shares are not readily marketable because there are too few outstanding shares held by a small number of holders should this negative feature of the shares depress their appraised value?

In re Valuation of Common Stock of McLoon Oil Co., 565 A.2d 997, 1004–1005 (Me.1989), considered whether in the appraisal process the value of minority shares held in a firm that merged into Lido Co. should be discounted due to their minority status. The Maine Supreme Court addressed the discount issues as follows:

> Should the dissenting shareholder's proportionate part of that whole firm value as so determined be discounted because of the minority status and lack of marketability of his stock? The Delaware Supreme Court ... has recently said no: Delaware emphatically rejects the application of those discounts in determining the fair value of a dissenting shareholder's stock. See Cavalier Oil Corp. v. Harnett, 564 A.2d 1137, 1141 (Del.1989) ("application of a discount to a minority shareholder is contrary to the requirement that the company be viewed as a going concern"). See also ... Haynsworth, *Valuation of Business Interests,* 33 Mercer L.Rev. 457, 489 (1982) [hereinafter "Haynsworth"] ...
>
> The appraisal remedy has deep roots in equity. The traditional rule through much of the 19th century was that any corporate transaction that changed the rights of common shareholders required unanimous consent. The appraisal remedy for dissenting shareholders evolved as it became clear that unanimous consent was inconsistent with the growth and development of large business enterprises. By the bargain struck in enacting an appraisal statute, the shareholder who disapproves of a proposed merger or other major corporate change gives up his right of veto in exchange for the right to be bought out—not at market value, but at "fair value."... . Methods used in valuing stock for tax, probate, ERISA, and like purposes in which market value is of the essence are inapposite to the determination of the fair value owed to dissenting shareholders. See Haynsworth at 459 ("The purpose of applying these discount variables is to determine the investment value or fair market value of a minority interest in the

context of a hypothetical sale between a willing seller and buyer, a situation that does not exist in the dissenting shareholder situation"). In the statutory appraisal proceeding, the involuntary change of ownership caused by a merger requires as a matter of fairness that a dissenting shareholder be compensated for the loss of his proportionate interest in the business as an entity. The valuation focus under the appraisal statute is not the stock as a commodity, but rather the stock only as it represents a proportionate part of the enterprise as a whole. The question for the court becomes simple and direct: What is the best price a single buyer could reasonably be expected to pay for the firm as an entirety? The court then prorates that value for the whole firm equally among all shares of its common stock. The result is that all of those shares have the same fair value.

Our view of the appraisal remedy is obviously inconsistent with the application of minority and nonmarketability discounts. Lido would have us discount the stock for minority status and lack of marketability in order to reflect what it calls the "real world" value of the stock to the Dissenters.... Especially in fixing the appraisal remedy in a close corporation, the relevant inquiry is what is the highest price a single buyer would reasonably pay for the whole enterprise, not what a willing buyer and a willing seller would bargain out as the sales price of a dissenting shareholder's shares in a hypothetical market transaction. Any rule of law that gave the shareholders less than their proportionate share of the whole firm's fair value would produce a transfer of wealth from the minority shareholders to the shareholders in control. Such a rule would inevitably encourage corporate squeeze-outs. See Haynsworth at 489. As the Delaware Supreme Court stated ... in Cavalier Oil Corp. v. Harnett,

> to fail to accord to a minority shareholder the full proportionate value of his shares imposes a penalty for lack of control, and unfairly enriches the majority shareholders who may reap a windfall from the appraisal process by cashing out a dissenting shareholder, a clearly undesirable result.

Cavalier Oil Corp. v. Harnett, 564 A.2d at 1141. We agree.

... As a matter of law, the Dissenters are entitled to their proportionate share of each Maine company at its full fair value....

Not all courts reject the notion of a minority discount, particularly where the appraisal remedy's fair value determination is believed to focus *not* on the value of shareholder's interest in the *firm* but the value of the *dissenter's shares*. *See e.g.,* Offenbecher v. Baron Services, Inc., 2001 WL 527522 (Ala. Civ. App. 2001) (affirming a 50% minority discount); English v. Artromick Intern, Inc., 2000 WL 1125637 (Ohio App. 2000). Most courts, however, interpret the appraisal remedy as awarding the fair value of the shareholder's proportionate interest in the firm (as contrasted with the shares) and reject both a minority and non-marketability discount. *See e.g.,* Advanced Comm. Design, Inc. v.

Follett, 615 N.W.2d 285, 290 (Minn. 2000); First Western Bank Wall v. Olsen, 621 N.W.2d 611, 617 (S.D. 2001). In 1999, this position was incorporated into the Model Business Corporation Act. *See* MBCA § 13.01(4).

What should be the courts' position in the converse situation—increasing the value of shares when the firm in which the dissenter is a shareholder is itself is a control person? That is, if the shareholders who are seeking appraisal are shareholders in a company that itself controls other companies, should its value reflect the control premium associated with its holdings in the subsidiary company? In Rapid–American Corp. v. Harris, 603 A.2d 796 (Del. 1992), the Delaware Supreme Court held it was appropriate to increase the value of the appraised shares by a control premium associated with the company's 100 percent ownership of three subsidiaries. Shareholders of Rapid–American sought appraisal in lieu of $28 of cash and securities offered in a merger with an entity affiliated with its dominant stockholder. Most of Rapid's profits were derived from its 100 percent ownership of three subsidiaries. In the appraisal proceeding, each subsidiary's value was determined through the experts' reliance on values of comparable publicly traded firms and in doing so they closely considered their market prices. Harris complained that extrapolating the subsidiaries' value from the share prices of comparable publicly traded companies did not include the premium of control, i.e., the quoted share prices were the prices of non-control shares. Accordingly, Harris argued that the trial court treated Rapid American as a minority shareholder in its own wholly-owned subsidiaries. The court sided with Harris:

> Rapid was a parent company with a 100% ownership in three valuable subsidiaries. The trial court's decision to exclude the control premium at the corporate level practically discounted Rapid's entire inherent value. The exclusion of a "control premium" artificially and unrealistically treated Rapid as a minority shareholder. Contrary to Rapid's arguments, Delaware law compels the inclusion of a control premium under the facts of this case. Rapid's 100% ownership interest in its subsidiary was clearly a "relevant" valuation factor and the trial court's rejection of the "control premium" implicitly placed a disproportionate emphasis on pure market value.

Id. at 806–07. The result reached in *Rapid–American* has been both followed, In re 75,629 Shares of Common Stock, 725 A.2d 927 (Vt. 1999), and strongly criticized. Lawrence A. Hamermesh & Michael L. Wachter, The Short And Puzzling Life Of The "Implicit Minority Discount" in Delaware Appraisal Law, 156 U. Penn. L. Rev. 1 (2007); Wm. J. Carney & Mark Heimendinger, Appraising the Nonexistent: The Delaware Courts' Struggle With Control Premiums, 152 U. Penn. L. Rev. 845 (2003). Query, if Alpha and Beta are truly comparable, except that Alpha is owned by 100 equal holders and Beta is wholly owned by C, is Beta's value greater than Alpha's value? If you were making a bid to acquire Alpha and Beta, would you expect to pay more for Beta than Alpha?

NOTE ON EXCLUSIVITY OF THE APPRAISAL REMEDY

The question frequently arises whether the appraisal right is intended by the legislature as an exclusive remedy, so that the availability of appraisal precludes shareholders from seeking equitable relief such as injunction or rescission. This question does not always admit of a hard-and-fast answer.

In some cases the issue is specifically addressed by language in the appraisal statute itself. *See e.g.,* MBCA § 13.40(a)(b). In the absence of explicit statutory language, it is clear that the availability of appraisal rights normally does not preclude an attack based on any of the following grounds:

(a) That the transaction is illegal under corporation law in that it is not authorized by the statute. See, e.g., Eisenberg v. Central Zone Property Corp., 306 N.Y. 58, 115 N.E.2d 652 (1953).

(b) That the transaction is illegal under corporation law in that the procedural steps required to authorize the transaction were not properly taken. See, e.g., Shidler v. All Am. Life & Fin. Corp., 775 F.2d 917 (8th Cir. 1985) (required number of votes not validly cast); Johnson v. Spartanburg County Fair Ass'n, 210 S.C. 56, 41 S.E.2d 599 (1947) (same).

(c) That shareholder approval of the transaction was improperly obtained, as through fraudulent misrepresentation or violation of the Proxy Rules. See, e.g., Nagy v. Bistricer, 770 A.2d 43 (Del. Ch. 2000); Victor Broadcasting Co. v. Mahurin, 236 Ark. 196, 365 S.W.2d 265 (1963).

Most jurisdictions also hold that that the availability of appraisal rights normally *does* preclude a shareholder from seeking to recover on an allegation that the transaction, e.g., merger, does not provide fair compensation for the shares. See, e.g., Osher v. Ridinger, 589 S.E.2d 905 (N.C. App. Ct. 2004); Adams v. United States Distributing Corp., 184 Va. 134, 34 S.E.2d 244 (1945).

There is much less clarity in the case law whether a shareholder can challenge the transaction on the basis it breaches the directors' or dominant stockholder's fiduciary duties. A few cases have suggested or implied that even in the absence of explicit statutory language, the availability of appraisal rights precludes an attack based on any ground other than illegality or *fraudulent misrepresentation*. The general rule, however, is that the mere availability of appraisal rights does not preclude shareholders from seeking injunctive relief or rescission for *fraud*, using that term in the broad sense to include unfair self-dealing by fiduciaries. For example, in Cohen v. Mirage Resorts, 62 P.3d 720 (Nev. 2003), the court stated:

> A dissenting shareholder who wishes to attack the validity of the merger or seek monetary damages based upon improper actions during the merger process must allege wrongful conduct that goes to the approval of the merger. Our conclusion is supported by case law from other jurisdictions. Shareholders are limited to appraisal-type actions unless they allege wrongful conduct or procedures in the approval process. In addition, the term "fraudulent," as used in the Model Act, has not been limited to the elements of common-law fraud; it encompasses a variety of acts involving breach of fiduciary duties imposed upon corporate officers, directors, or majority shareholders. We conclude that the term fraudulent as used in [the statute] has a similar scope....

See also, e.g., John R. Behrmann Revocable Trust v. Szaloczi, 74 P.3d 371 (Colo. App. 2002); Pupecki v. James Madison Corp., 376 Mass. 212, 382 N.E.2d 1030 (1978).

The Delaware courts are especially reluctant to make appraisal rights exclusive in unfair self-dealing cases. In Andra v. Blount, 772 A.2d 183, 192–93 (Del. Ch. 2000), Vice–Chancellor Strine stated:

> ... [I]t has become nearly impossible for a judge of this court to dismiss a well-pled unfair dealing claim on the basis that appraisal is available as a remedy and is fully adequate. Although the Supreme Court has never held that this court cannot limit a plaintiff to an appraisal remedy if that remedy is fully adequate, its prior holdings are reasonably read as indicating that so long as a plaintiff can state a claim for breach of fiduciary duty in connection with the merger, he can press an unfair dealing claim. The unavailability of a class action and fee shifting in appraisal actions makes an unfair dealing action more attractive from the perspective of plaintiffs, thus leading to the litigation of lawsuits that require a determination of the fairness of the process used and the price paid when appraisal lawsuits addressing solely the issue of fair price would otherwise be sufficient.
>
> [Footnote 22] Vice Chancellor Jacobs has succinctly captured the essential differences between a statutory appraisal action and an equitable fiduciary action:
>
> > Appraisal is purely a creature of statute. Its underlying concept is that a stockholder dissenting from a merger or other triggering transaction is entitled, without having to prove wrongdoing or liability on anyone's part, to a determination of the fair value of his investment by an independent agency, usually a court. The only party held liable is the surviving corporation, and the measure of recovery is the fair or intrinsic value of the corporation's stock immediately before the merger. Post-merger synergies or values are not to be considered. In most states, including Delaware, the right to court-awarded attorneys fees in an appraisal is highly limited.

> In contrast, a stockholders' class action for breach of fiduciary duty is a creature of equity. To obtain a monetary recovery, the plaintiff shareholder must prove wrongdoing and establish liability. The parties from whom the recovery is sought are normally the corporation's directors and executive officers. The measure of the recovery is not limited to the statutorily appraised value, and in some cases, may include post-merger values computed as rescissory damages. Because the proceeding is equitable in nature, a court-awarded fee, payable by the corporation or from any fund created by a successful plaintiff, is available. . . .

. . . Because an entire fairness action permits this court the flexibility to shape a remedy fitting to the breach (e.g., rescissory damages when justified), a plaintiff who can state a claim for breach of fiduciary duty ordinarily should not be relegated to the (implicitly less adequate) remedy of appraisal, where the only remedy is the fair value of plaintiff's stock. Otherwise, there is a risk that victims of fiduciary breaches will be less than wholly compensated for the harm done them, thus creating less than an adequate incentive for fiduciaries to comply with their "unremitting" duties of loyalty and care. . . .

. . . [Consider] the obvious situation where an appraisal would not be an adequate remedy. Posit a scenario where a 43% stockholder who is the company's chairman and chief executive officer consummates a tender offer followed by a back-end, squeeze-out merger. Suppose the stockholder offered $25 a share, which is by any measure "fair," and obtains tenders from enough minority stockholders to enable him to cash out the remaining minority stockholders in a short-form merger at the same price. Undisclosed by the 43% stockholder, however, is the fact that a well-funded third party was willing to make a tender offer for $28 a share but had been rebuffed by the 43% stockholder, who did not even disclose the offer to the rest of his hand-picked board. In such a scenario, an appraisal remedy would not be sufficient to remedy the monetary harm that might have been suffered by the stockholders as a result of any breach of fiduciary duty they might prove had been committed by the 43% stockholder. While $25 is a fair price, they had arguably been wrongfully denied the opportunity for $28. . . .

The high water market for allowing minority holders to complain of ill-treatment in a merger is Rabkin v. Philip A. Hunt Chemical Corp., 498 A.2d 1099, 1105 (Del. 1985). When purchasing control of the company, the defendant contractually agreed that if it instituted a cash-out merger of the minority shares within one year it would do so at the same price as had been paid per share for the former controlling stockholder's shares. Not totally unexpected-as the defendant was alleged to have planned to acquire all the firm's shares almost immediately after acquiring control—just a few days after the one-year period had expired the defendant initiated a cash-out merger at a price lower than the price paid to acquire control. Asserting the cash-out merger had been purposely timed to acquire the minority shares at a lower price, the minority sued the defendant alleging breach of its fiduciary duty as a controlling stockholder. The Delaware Supreme Court rejected the defendant's argument that the appraisal remedy barred the suit.

The net result is that, in the absence of explicit statutory language, the availability of appraisal rights may preclude a shareholder from attacking an *arm's-length* transaction on the ground of unfairness, but will usually not insulate *self-interested* transactions from an attack on that ground—although in the latter case it may lead the court to impose a somewhat less rigorous standard of fairness than would otherwise prevail. See Hideki Kanda & Saul Levmore, The Appraisal Remedy and the Goals of Corporate Law, 32 UCLA L. Rev. 429 (1985); Vorenberg, Exclusiveness of the Dissenting Stockholder's Appraisal Right, 77 Harv.L.Rev. 1189, 1214–15 (1964). If this is the correct surmise, just why isn't the appraisal remedy as attractive to the plaintiff as suit outside the appraisal proceeding invoking a breach of the defendants' fiduciary duty? In addressing this question, consider the facts of *Rabkin*, *supra*. If the cashed out minority in *Rabkin* had sought appraisal would the recovery if successful be as great as they could recover by establishing the dominant stockholder had breached its fiduciary duty? Is there for the disgruntled minority holders a strategic nuisance value to instituting a breach of fiduciary duty claim that is not present with the appraisal process? Moreover, consider whether there is a basis to believe the attorney gets paid and more if the suit is outside the appraisal proceeding?

CAL. CORP. CODE § 1312

[See Statutory Supplement]

MODEL BUS. CORP. ACT § 13.02(d)

[See Statutory Supplement]

ALI, PRINCIPLES OF CORPORATE GOVERNANCE §§ 7.24, 7.25

[See Statutory Supplement]

C. Statutory Mergers

---

(1) *Classical Mergers*

DEL. GEN. CORP. LAW §§ 251(a)–(e), 259–261

[See Statutory Supplement]

MODEL BUS. CORP. ACT §§ 11.01, 11.02, 11.04, 11.06, 11.07

[See Statutory Supplement]

---

1. *Statutory Mergers*. Del.Gen.Corp.Law §§ 251(a)–(e), 259–61 and Model Bus.Corp.Act §§ 11.01, 11.03 authorize a type of transaction commonly referred to as a statutory merger. Although the term *merger* is often used by nonlawyers to describe any form of combination, to a lawyer a merger is a combination involving the fusion of two constituent corporations pursuant to a formal agreement executed with reference to specific statutory merger provisions under which one corporation (the survivor) succeeds to the assets and liabilities of the other corporation by operation of law.

While details vary from state to state, generally the first formal step in such a merger, after negotiations have been completed, is a preliminary agreement (often embodied in a "letter of intent") signed by representatives of the constituent corporations. If the merger is approved by the board and shareholders of each constituent corporation, then: (1) articles of merger are filed with the secretary of state; and (2) stock or other consideration issued by the surviving corporation is exchanged for the stock and other securities of the disappearing corporation, which is fused into the survivor and loses its identity. In general, no deeds, bills of sale, or other instruments of conveyance, are necessary to pass title from the "disappearing" or nonsurviving corporation to the survivor: By operation of law, the survivor acquires all the rights, privileges, franchises, and assets of the disappearing corporation, and assumes all of its liabilities.

2. *Abandonment*. In most merger agreements, authority is given to the boards of both constituents to abandon the merger at any time up to the effective date of the merger, upon the occurrence of certain defined conditions—for example, if a constituent suffers substantial loss as a result of catastrophe, or suffers any material adverse change in its condition, or if any material litigation or governmental proceed-

ing is instituted against a constituent, or if more than a defined percentage of shareholders exercise appraisal rights.

3. *Consolidations*. A statutory *consolidation* is identical to a statutory merger, except for the fact that in a merger one constituent fuses into another, while in a consolidation two (or more) constituents fuse to form a new corporation. Because the consolidation technique is seldom employed, and when employed is treated almost identically to a merger, no separate attention will be given in this Chapter to statutory consolidations.

4. *Short–Form and Small–Scale Mergers*. At one time, virtually all statutory mergers required approval by a majority or two-thirds vote of the outstanding shares of each constituent, and also triggered appraisal rights for the shareholders of each constituent. Many statutes now carve out exceptions to these requirements in the case of "short-form" and "small-scale" mergers. These types of merger will be considered in the next two sections.

---

(2) Small–Scale Mergers

DEL. GEN. CORP. LAW § 251(f)

[See Statutory Supplement]

MODEL BUS. CORP. ACT § 11.04(g)

[See Statutory Supplement]

E. Welch, A. Turezyn II & R. Saunders, Folk on the Delaware General Corporation Law § 251.2.2.1

(5th ed. 2006).

(1) [The requirement of Del. § 251(f) that the survivor's certificate of incorporation not be amended] is designed to assure that the merger technique cannot be used to deprive stockholders of the voting rights that they would enjoy if the certificate were being amended under section 242. . . .

(2) The theory underlying the ... 20 percent limitation on increasing the number of common shares—is that a merger that involves less than 20 percent of the survivor's shares is not such a major change as to require a stockholder vote, and is really no more than an enlargement of the business that could be achieved by other means without triggering voting rights. For instance, a corporation purchas-

ing assets need not secure approval of its stockholders to issue already authorized shares to the seller. Nor would voting rights exist if a corporation offered its own authorized shares in exchange for the shares of another corporation and thereby gained control, or if the corporation were to sell its authorized shares for cash and then use the proceeds of the sale to purchase assets. When business needs demand that the acquisition take the form of a merger rather than a purchase of assets or shares, the premise of the statute is that the merger should not require a stockholder vote when other procedures with nearly identical economic consequences do not require a stockholder vote. Stated otherwise, ... [§ 251(f)] puts mergers more on a parity with acquisition of assets or shares so far as the legal requirements are concerned.

DEL. GEN. CORP. LAW § 253

[See Statutory Supplement]

MODEL BUS. CORP. ACT § 11.05

[See Statutory Supplement]

---

(3) Short-Form Mergers

Corporate statutes include provisions authorizing the so-called short-form merger, under which certain parent-subsidiary mergers can be effected simply by vote of the parent's board—that is, without a vote of the parent's or the subsidiary's shareholders, without appraisal rights in the parent's shareholders, and frequently without a vote of the subsidiary's board. Most of the early short-form statutes were applicable only to mergers involving a parent and its 100%-owned subsidiary, and were probably conceived as procedural in nature, designed to simplify the mechanics of mergers. Today, however, the reach of short-form merger provisions has been substantively extended in two important ways. First, many such provisions are now applicable to mergers between parents and less–than–100%–owned subsidiaries: typically, although not invariably, the floor is set at 90 percent. Second, it has been held that the purpose of these statutes is to provide the parent corporation with a means of eliminating the minority shareholder's interest in the enterprise by issuing cash rather than stock to the minority. See e.g., Beloff v. Consolidated Edison Co., 300 N.Y. 11, 87 N.E.2d 561 (1949). To the extent this view is followed, these statutory provisions operate as *cash-out* rather than *merger* statutes. Furthermore, they are cash-out statutes that run in one direction only: the parent can force the minority to sell at any time, but the minority cannot force the parent to buy.

D. TAX ASPECTS OF CORPORATE COMBINATIONS

Much is made of taxation as a principal motive for corporate combinations, but this factor, while significant, can be exaggerated. Whatever its role as a motive, however, taxation is often very important in determining *how* a combination will be effected. The principal issue is whether the combination will be tax-free—which means, essentially, that taxes on the transferor's (meaning both the selling/acquired entity itself as well as the selling/acquired stockholders) gain will be postponed, that the transferor's basis in the stock or property received will remain unchanged from the transferee's basis(i.e., the depreciable amount of assets acquired is identical to the amount the transferee entity just before the completion of the acquisition), and that past operating losses of both companies can generally be carried over to apply against future earnings. See IRC §§ 354(a)(1), 358, 361(a), 381, 382.

In general, the Code provides three basic routes by which a tax-free combination—or, in tax parlance, a "reorganization"—can be achieved. These routes are popularly known as Type A, B, and C reorganizations, and are the tax counterparts of statutory mergers, stock-for-stock combinations, and stock-for-assets combinations, respectively.

a. A "Type A" reorganization—covered by IRC § 368(a)(1)(A)—is defined as a statutory merger or consolidation.

b. A "Type B" reorganization—covered by § 368(a)(1)(B)—is defined as the acquisition by one corporation, in exchange solely for all or part of its voting stock (or the voting stock of a parent corporation) of stock of another corporation, if the acquiring corporation has control of the acquired corporation immediately after the acquisition. Control is defined by § 368(c) as the ownership of stock possessing at least 80 percent of total combined voting power, plus at least 80 percent of the total number of shares of all other classes of stock.

c. A "Type C" reorganization—covered by § 368(a)(1)(C)—is defined as the acquisition by one corporation, in exchange for all or part of its voting stock (or the voting stock of a parent corporation), of substantially all the properties of another corporation.

In a Type B reorganization, the consideration given by the acquiring corporation must consist solely of voting stock. In a Type C reorganization, the consideration must consist primarily of voting stock, but the use of money or other property is permitted if at least

80 percent of the fair market value of all the property of the acquired corporation is taken in exchange for voting stock.[1] Section 368(a)(1)(A), which covers Type A reorganizations, does not explicitly restrict the consideration issued by the survivor to voting stock, or indeed to stock. Thus the survivor in a statutory merger can use consideration other than voting stock ("boot")—including bonds, nonvoting stock, short-term notes, and cash. However, if property other than stock or securities is permissibly issued to the transferor or its shareholders under a Type A or Type C reorganization, gain will be recognized in an amount not exceeding the value of this property. IRC § 356. Furthermore, under the "continuity of interest" doctrine, in a statutory merger the transferor's shareholders must receive a significant equity interest in the survivor if the merger is to qualify as a tax-free Type A reorganization. See Treas.Reg. § 1.368–1(b), (c). In Helvering v. Minnesota Tea Co., 296 U.S. 378, 56 S.Ct. 269, 80 L.Ed. 284 (1935), the Supreme Court held that under this doctrine the equity issued to the transferor must represent a "substantial part of the value of the [transferred assets]," and that 56 percent was sufficient under this standard. See also May B. Kass, 60 T.C. 218, 1973 WL 2497 (1973) (16 percent insufficient); Yoc Heating Corp., 61 T.C. 168, 1973 WL 2680 (1973) (15 percent insufficient); Miller v. Commissioner, 84 F.2d 415 (6th Cir.1936) (25% sufficient). The illustrations in Treasury Regulations suggest that currently the view of the Internal Revenue Service is that there will be continuity of interest if at least 40% of the consideration in a merger is in the form of equity, but not if 28.5% or less is in that form. *See* Treas. Reg. § 1.368–1T(e)(2).

E. The Stock Modes and the De Facto Merger Theory

Having considered the traditional form of combination, mergers, we now pass to a consideration of two newer modes of corporate combination: stock-for-assets combinations and stock-for-stock combinations. In a ***stock-for-assets*** combination, Corporation A issues shares of its own stock to Corporation B in exchange for substantially all of B's assets. Often, in such a combination, A agrees to assume B's liabilities. In some cases, however, A may assume B's liabilities on only a selective basis. Indeed, one reason for using this mode in preference to a statutory merger may be A's desire to avoid assuming all of B's liabilities. Usually, B agrees that upon completion of the exchange it will dissolve and distribute its stock in A to its own shareholders. The major reason for this is that A does not want a large block of its stock concentrated in a single holder. Frequently, it is also agreed or understood that some or all of B's officers and directors will join A's management.

---

1. IRC § 368(a)(2)(B). The survivor's assumption of the transferor's liabilities is not treated as money paid for the transferor's property unless the survivor uses consideration other than voting stock. Id.

In a *stock-for-stock* combination, Corporation A issues shares of its own stock directly to the shareholders of Corporation B in exchange for an amount of B stock—normally at least a majority—sufficient to carry control. By virtue of such a combination the shareholder groups of the two corporations are combined to a substantial extent, and B becomes a subsidiary of A. Frequently B is then liquidated or merged into A, but whether or not this occurs, B's assets will be under A's control. Such a combination does not require approval by B's management, since corporate action by B is not required. Often, however, the terms of the exchange of stock are worked out beforehand by the managements of both corporations, and often too, it is agreed or understood that some or all of B's management will stay on with B in its new role as a subsidiary, or will join Corporation A itself.

There has been a sharp division of opinion on the issue how to characterize such combinations. Take, for example, a stock-for-assets combination in which A acquires substantially all of the assets of B in exchange for A's common stock; A assumes all of B's liabilities; and B agrees to dissolve and to distribute to its shareholders the A common stock it receives.

One possible way to view such a combination is as a de facto merger. This is the position taken in Farris v. Glen Alden Corp. and Rath v. Rath Packing Co., infra. If the combination is viewed as a de facto merger, then in the normal case (that is, in the absence of some special exception) it requires a vote of both A's shareholders and B's shareholders, and triggers appraisal rights in both A's shareholders and B's shareholders.

Alternatively, the transaction could be characterized as a purchase by A and a sale of substantially all assets by B. That is the position taken in Hariton v. Arco Electronics Corp. and Heilbrunn v. Sun Packing Co., infra. Under traditional corporate statutes, a purchase does not require shareholder approval and does not trigger appraisal rights. Therefore, if the combination is treated as a purchase by A, it neither requires a vote of A's shareholders nor triggers appraisal rights for those shareholders—although it would have required a shareholder vote, and triggered appraisal rights, if it had been characterized as a merger.

Now turn to B's shareholders. Under the corporate statutes, a sale of substantially all assets, unlike a purchase, does require shareholder approval. Therefore, the combination will require the approval of B's shareholders. Furthermore, most statutes provide that if a corporation sells substantially all of its assets, the transaction triggers appraisal rights in the corporation's shareholders. Therefore, B's shareholders, unlike A's shareholders, will usually have appraisal rights. However, under some statutes, most notably the Delaware statute, a sale of substantially all assets does not trigger appraisal rights. Under such statutes, if a stock-for-assets combination is treated as a purchase by A and a sale by B, rather than as a merger of A and B, B's shareholders will not have appraisal rights, although they would have had appraisal rights if the transaction had been characterized as a merger.

Hariton v. Arco Electronics, Inc.

Supreme Court of Delaware, 1963.
41 Del.Ch. 74, 188 A.2d 123.

■ SOUTHERLAND, CHIEF JUSTICE: This case involves a sale of assets under § 271 of the corporation law, 8 Del.C. It presents for decision the question presented, but not decided, in Heilbrunn v. Sun Chemical Corporation, 38 Del.Ch. 321, 150 A.2d 755. It may be stated as follows:

A sale of assets is effected under § 271 in consideration of shares of stock of the purchasing corporation. The agreement of sale embodies also a plan to dissolve the selling corporation and distribute the shares so received to the stockholders of the seller, so as to accomplish the same result as would be accomplished by a merger of the seller into the purchaser. Is the sale legal?

The facts are these:

The defendant Arco and Loral Electronics Corporation, a New York corporation, are both engaged, in somewhat different forms, in the electronic equipment business. In the summer of 1961 they negotiated for an amalgamation of the companies. As of October 27, 1961, they entered into a "Reorganization Agreement and Plan." The provisions of this Plan pertinent here are in substance as follows:

1. Arco agrees to sell all its assets to Loral in consideration (*inter alia*) of the issuance to it of 283,000 shares of Loral.

2. Arco agrees to call a stockholders meeting for the purpose of approving the Plan and the voluntary dissolution.

3. Arco agrees to distribute to its stockholders all the Loral shares received by it as a part of the complete liquidation of Arco.*

At the Arco meeting all the stockholders voting (about 80%) approved the Plan. It was thereafter consummated.

Plaintiff, a stockholder who did not vote at the meeting, sued to enjoin the consummation of the Plan on the grounds (1) that it was illegal, and (2) that it was unfair. The second ground was abandoned. Affidavits and documentary evidence were filed, and defendant moved for summary judgment and dismissal of the complaint. The Vice Chancellor granted the motion and plaintiff appeals.

The question before us we have stated above. Plaintiff's argument that the sale is illegal runs as follows:

---

* According to the Vice Chancellor's opinion below, 40 Del.Ch. 326, 182 A.2d 22 (1962), the agreement also provided that Loral would assume and pay all of Arco's debts and liabilities, and that after the closing date Arco would not engage in any business or activity except as might be required to complete the liquidation and dissolution of Arco. (Footnote by ed.)

The several steps taken here accomplish the same result as a merger of Arco into Loral. In a "true" sale of assets, the stockholder of the seller retains the right to elect whether the selling company shall continue as a holding company. Moreover, the stockholder of the selling company is forced to accept an investment in a new enterprise without the right of appraisal granted under the merger statute. § 271 cannot therefore be legally combined with a dissolution proceeding under § 275 and a consequent distribution of the purchaser's stock. Such a proceeding is a misuse of the power granted under § 271, and a *de facto* merger results.

The foregoing is a brief summary of plaintiff's contention.

Plaintiff's contention that this sale has achieved the same result as a merger is plainly correct. The same contention was made to us in Heilbrunn v. Sun Chemical Corporation, 38 Del.Ch. 321, 150 A.2d 755. Accepting it as correct, we noted that this result is made possible by the overlapping scope of the merger statute and section 271, mentioned in Sterling v. Mayflower Hotel Corporation, 33 Del.Ch. 293, 93 A.2d 107, 38 A.L.R.2d 425. We also adverted to the increased use, in connection with corporate reorganization plans, of § 271 instead of the merger statute. Further, we observed that no Delaware case has held such procedure to be improper, and that two cases appear to assume its legality. Finch v. Warrior Cement Corporation, 16 Del.Ch. 44, 141 A. 54, and Argenbright v. Phoenix Finance Co., 21 Del.Ch. 288, 187 A. 124. But we were not required in the *Heilbrunn* case to decide the point.

We now hold that the reorganization here accomplished through § 271 and a mandatory plan of dissolution and distribution is legal. This is so because the sale-of-assets statute and the merger statute are independent of each other. They are, so to speak, of equal dignity, and the framers of a reorganization plan may resort to either type of corporate mechanics to achieve the desired end. This is not an anomalous result in our corporation law. As the Vice Chancellor pointed out, the elimination of accrued dividends, though forbidden under a charter amendment (Keller v. Wilson Co., 21 Del.Ch. 391, 190 A. 115) may be accomplished by a merger. Federal United Corporation v. Havender, 24 Del.Ch. 318, 11 A.2d 331.

In Langfelder v. Universal Laboratories, D.C., 68 F.Supp. 209, Judge Leahy commented upon "the general theory of the Delaware Corporation Law that action taken pursuant to the authority of the various sections of that law constitute acts of independent legal significance and their validity is not dependent on other sections of the Act." 68 F.Supp. 211, footnote.

In support of his contentions of a *de facto* merger plaintiff cites Finch v. Warrior Cement Corporation, 16 Del.Ch. 44, 141 A. 54, and Drug Inc. v. Hunt, 5 W.W.Harr. 339, 35 Del. 339, 168 A. 87. They are patently inapplicable. Each involved a disregard of the statutory provisions governing sales of assets. Here it is admitted that the provisions of the statute were fully complied with.

Plaintiff concedes, as we read his brief, that if the several steps taken in this case had been taken separately they would have been legal. That is, he concedes that a sale of assets, followed by a separate proceeding to dissolve and distribute, would be legal, even though the same result would follow. This concession exposes the weakness of his contention. To attempt to make any such distinction between sales under § 271 would be to create uncertainty in the law and invite litigation.

We are in accord with the Vice Chancellor's ruling, and the judgment below is affirmed.

NOTE ON ANOTHER APPROACH TO LEGISLATIVE INTENT: RATH v. RATH PACKING CO.

In Rath v. Rath Packing Co., 257 Iowa 1277, 136 N.W.2d 410 (1965), Rath Packing, an Iowa corporation, entered into a "Plan and Agreement of Reorganization" with Needham Packing. Under the Plan, Rath was to (1) amend its articles to double the number of shares of its common shares, create a new class of preferred shares (convertible into common shares), and change its name to Rath–Needham Corporation; (2) issue Rath common and preferred in exchange for substantially all of Needham's assets; (3) assume all of Needham's liabilities; and (4) elect two Needham officers and directors to its board. Needham would then distribute the new Rath–Needham shares to its shareholders and dissolve. If the new preferred was fully converted, the Needham shareholders would end up with about 54 per cent of Rath–Needham's common stock.

At a meeting of Rath shareholders, 60% of its outstanding shares were voted in favor of the certificate amendments. Under Iowa law a merger required two-thirds shareholder approval, and shareholders in Rath Packing sued to enjoin the transaction on the ground that it was a merger and accordingly had not been properly approved. Rath argued that the transaction constituted only an amendment of Rath's certificate and an issuance of its stock, and accordingly did not need to meet the requirements of Iowa's merger provisions, under the equal-dignity theory. The Iowa Supreme Court, reversing the decision below, concluded the transaction was a merger, and ordered the issuance of an injunction.

> A . . . rule, many times applied by us, is that where a general statute, if standing alone, would include the same matter as a special statute and thus conflict with it, the latter will prevail and the former must give way. . . .
>
> It is apparent that if the sections pertaining to amending articles and issuing stock are construed to authorize a merger by a majority vote of shareholders they conflict with the sections specifically dealing with the one matter of mergers which require a two-thirds vote of shareholders. The two sets of sections may be

harmonized by holding, as we do, that the merger sections govern the matter of merger and must be regarded as an exception to the sections dealing with amending articles and issuing stock, which may or may not be involved in a merger....

The merger sections make it clear the legislature intended to require a two-thirds vote of shareholders and accord so-called appraisal rights to dissenters in case of a merger. It is unreasonable to ascribe to the same legislature an intent to provide in the same act a method of evading the required two-thirds vote and the grant of such appraisal rights. The practical effect of the decision appealed from is to render the requirements of a two-thirds vote and appraisal rights meaningless in virtually all mergers. It is scarcely an exaggeration to say the decision amounts to judicial repeal of the merger sections in most instances of merger.

It is obvious, as defendants' counsel frankly stated in oral argument, that corporate management would naturally choose a method which requires only majority approval of shareholders and does not grant dissenters the right to be paid the fair value of their stock. The legislature could hardly have intended to vest in corporate management the option to comply with the requirements just referred to or to proceed without such compliance, a choice that would invariably be exercised in favor of the easier method....

NOTE ON HEILBRUNN v. SUN CHEMICAL CORPORATION

In *Hariton,* suit was brought by a shareholder of the transferor in a stock-for-assets combination. In the earlier case of Heilbrunn v. Sun Chemical Corporation, 38 Del.Ch. 321, 150 A.2d 755 (1959), referred to in the *Hariton* opinion, suit was brought by the shareholders of Sun, the survivor in a stock-for-assets combination between Sun and Ansbacher. Plaintiff claimed that the transaction was a merger, and therefore gave rise to appraisal rights. The court rejected this claim:

> The argument that the result of this transaction is substantially the same as the result that would have followed a merger may be readily accepted. As plaintiffs correctly say, the Ansbacher enterprise is continued in altered form as a part of Sun. This is ordinarily a typical characteristic of a merger.... Moreover the plan of reorganization *requires* the dissolution of Ansbacher and the distribution to its stockholders of the Sun stock received by it for the assets. As a part of the plan, the Ansbacher stockholders are compelled to receive Sun stock. From the viewpoint of Ansbacher, the result is the same as if Ansbacher had formally merged into Sun.
>
> This result is made possible, of course, by the overlapping scope of the merger statute and the statute authorizing the sale of all the corporate assets....

Our Court of Chancery has said that the appraisal right is given to the stockholder in compensation for his former right at common law to prevent a merger.... By the use of the sale-of-assets method of reorganization, it is contended, he has been unjustly deprived of this right.

... [W]e do not reach this question, because we fail to see how any injury has been inflicted upon the Sun stockholders. Their corporation has simply acquired property and paid for it in shares of stock. The business of Sun will go on as before, with additional assets. The Sun stockholder is not forced to accept stock in another corporation. Nor has the reorganization changed the essential nature of the enterprise of the purchasing corporation....

Farris v. Glen Alden Corp.

Supreme Court of Pennsylvania, 1958.
393 Pa. 427, 143 A.2d 25.

■ COHEN, JUSTICE. We are required to determine on this appeal whether, as a result of a Reorganization Agreement executed by the officers of Glen Alden Corporation and List Industries Corporation, and approved by the shareholders of the former company, the rights and remedies of a dissenting shareholder accrue to the plaintiff.

Glen Alden is a Pennsylvania corporation engaged principally in the mining of anthracite coal and lately in the manufacture of air conditioning units and fire-fighting equipment. In recent years the company's operating revenue has declined substantially, and in fact, its coal operations have resulted in tax loss carryovers of approximately $14,000,000. In October 1957, List, a Delaware holding company owning interests in motion picture theaters, textile companies and real estate, and to a lesser extent, in oil and gas operations, warehouses and aluminum piston manufacturing, purchased through a wholly owned subsidiary 38.5% of Glen Alden's outstanding stock.[1] This acquisition enabled List to place three of its directors on the Glen Alden board.

On March 20, 1958, the two corporations entered into a reorganization agreement, subject to stockholder approval, which contemplated the following actions:

1. Glen Alden is to acquire all of the assets of List, excepting a small amount of cash reserved for the payment of List's expenses in connection with the transaction. These assets include over $8,000,000 in cash held chiefly in the treasuries of List's wholly owned subsidiaries.

2. In consideration of the transfer, Glen Alden is to issue 3,621,703 shares of stock to List. List in turn is to distribute the stock to its

1. Of the purchase price of $8,719,109, $5,000,000 was borrowed.

shareholders at a ratio of five shares of Glen Alden stock for each six shares of List stock. In order to accomplish the necessary distribution, Glen Alden is to increase the authorized number of its shares of capital stock from 2,500,000 shares to 7,500,000 shares without according preemptive rights to the present shareholders upon the issuance of any such shares.

3. Further, Glen Alden is to assume all of List's liabilities including a $5,000,000 note incurred by List in order to purchase Glen Alden stock in 1957, outstanding stock options, incentive stock options plans, and pension obligations.

4. Glen Alden is to change its corporate name from Glen Alden Corporation to List Alden Corporation.

5. The present directors of both corporations are to become directors of List Alden.

6. List is to be dissolved and List Alden is to then carry on the operations of both former corporations.

Two days after the agreement was executed notice of the annual meeting of Glen Alden to be held on April 11, 1958, was mailed to the shareholders together with a proxy statement analyzing the reorganization agreement and recommending its approval as well as approval of certain amendments to Glen Alden's articles of incorporation and bylaws necessary to implement the agreement. At this meeting the holders of a majority of the outstanding shares, (not including those owned by List), voted in favor of a resolution approving the reorganization agreement.

On the day of the shareholders' meeting, plaintiff, a shareholder of Glen Alden, filed a complaint in equity against the corporation and its officers seeking to enjoin them temporarily until final hearing, and perpetually thereafter, from executing and carrying out the agreement.

The gravamen of the complaint was that the notice of the annual shareholders' meeting did not conform to the requirements of the Business Corporation Law, 15 P.S. § 2852–1 et seq., in three respects: (1) It did not give notice to the shareholders that the true intent and purpose of the meeting was to effect a merger or consolidation of Glen Alden and List; (2) It failed to give notice to the shareholders of their right to dissent to the plan of merger or consolidation and claim fair value for their shares, and (3) It did not contain copies of the text of certain sections of the Business Corporation Law as required.[3]

By reason of these omissions, plaintiff contended that the approval of the reorganization agreement by the shareholders at the annual meeting was invalid and unless the carrying out of the plan were enjoined, he would suffer irreparable loss by being deprived of substantial property rights.

---

3. The proxy statement included the following declaration: Appraisal Rights.

"In the opinion of counsel, the shareholders of neither Glen Alden nor List Industries will have any rights of appraisal or similar rights of dissenters with respect to any matter to be acted upon at their respective meetings."

The defendants answered admitting the material allegations of fact in the complaint but denying that they gave rise to a cause of action because the transaction complained of was a purchase of corporate assets as to which shareholders had no rights of dissent or appraisal. For these reasons the defendants then moved for judgment on the pleadings.[4]

The court below concluded that the reorganization agreement entered into between the two corporations was a plan for a *de facto* merger, and that therefore the failure of the notice of the annual meeting to conform to the pertinent requirements of the merger provisions of the Business Corporation Law rendered the notice defective and all proceedings in furtherance of the agreement void. Wherefore, the court entered a final decree denying defendants' motion for judgment on the pleadings, entering judgment upon plaintiff's complaint and granting the injunctive relief therein sought. This appeal followed.

When use of the corporate form of business organization first became widespread, it was relatively easy for courts to define a "merger" or a "sale of assets" and to label a particular transaction as one or the other. See, e.g., 15 Fletcher, Corporations §§ 7040–7045 (rev. vol. 1938); In re Buist's Estate, 1929, 297 Pa. 537, 541, 147 A. 606; Koehler v. St. Mary's Brewing Co., 1910, 228 Pa. 648, 653–654, 77 A. 1016. But prompted by the desire to avoid the impact of adverse, and to obtain the benefits of favorable, government regulations, particularly federal tax laws, new accounting and legal techniques were developed by lawyers and accountants which interwove the elements characteristic of each, thereby creating hybrid forms of corporate amalgamation. Thus, it is no longer helpful to consider an individual transaction in the abstract and solely by reference to the various elements therein determine whether it is a "merger" or a "sale". Instead, to determine properly the nature of a corporate transaction, we must refer not only to all the provisions of the agreement, but also to the consequences of the transaction and to the purposes of the provisions of the corporation law said to be applicable. We shall apply this principle to the instant case.

Section 908, subd. A of the Pennsylvania Business Corporation Law provides: "If any shareholder of a domestic corporation which becomes a party to a plan of merger or consolidation shall object to such plan of merger or consolidation ... such shareholder shall be entitled to ... [the fair value of his shares upon surrender of the share certificate or certificates representing his shares]." Act of May 5, 1933, P.L. 364, as amended, 15 P.S. §§ 2852–908, subd. A.[5]

---

4. Counsel for the defendants concedes that if the corporation is required to pay the dissenting shareholders the appraised fair value of their shares, the resultant drain of cash would prevent Glen Alden from carrying out the agreement. On the other hand, plaintiff contends that if the shareholders had been told of their rights as dissenters, rather than specifically advised that they had no such rights, the resolution approving the reorganization agreement would have been defeated.

5. Furthermore, section 902, subd. B provides that notice of the proposed merger and of the right to dissent thereto must be given the shareholders. "There shall be included in, or

This provision had its origin in the early decision of this Court in Lauman v. Lebanon Valley R.R. Co., 1858, 30 Pa. 42. There a shareholder who objected to the consolidation of his company with another was held to have a right in the absence of statute to treat the consolidation as a dissolution of his company and to receive the value of his shares upon their surrender.

The rationale of the Lauman case, and of the present section of the Business Corporation Law based thereon, is that when a corporation combines with another so as to lose its essential nature and alter the original fundamental relationships of the shareholders among themselves and to the corporation, a shareholder who does not wish to continue his membership therein may treat his membership in the original corporation as terminated and have the value of his shares paid to him. See Lauman v. Lebanon Valley R.R. Co., supra, 30 Pa. at pages 46–47. See also Bloch v. Baldwin Locomotive Works, C.P., Del.1950, 75 Pa.Dist. Co.R. 24, 35–38.

Does the combination outlined in the present "reorganization" agreement so fundamentally change the corporate character of Glen Alden and the interest of the plaintiff as a shareholder therein, that to refuse him the rights and remedies of a dissenting shareholder would in reality force him to give up his stock in one corporation and against his will accept shares in another? If so, the combination is a merger within the meaning of section 908, subd. A of the corporation law. See Bloch v. Baldwin Locomotive Works, supra. Cf. Marks v. Autocar Co., D.C.E.D.Pa.1954, 153 F.Supp. 768. See also Troupiansky v. Henry Disston & Sons, D.C.E.D.Pa.1957, 151 F.Supp. 609.

If the reorganization agreement were consummated plaintiff would find that the "List Alden" resulting from the amalgamation would be quite a different corporation than the "Glen Alden" in which he is now a shareholder. Instead of continuing primarily as a coal mining company, Glen Alden would be transformed, after amendment of its articles of incorporation, into a diversified holding company whose interests would range from motion picture theaters to textile companies. Plaintiff would find himself a member of a company with assets of $169,000,000 and a long-term debt of $38,000,000 in lieu of a company one-half that size and with but one-seventh the long-term debt.

While the administration of the operations, and properties of Glen Alden as well as List would be in the hands of management common to both companies, since all executives of List would be retained in List Alden, the control of Glen Alden would pass to the directors of List; for List would hold eleven of the seventeen directorships on the new board of directors.

As an aftermath of the transaction plaintiff's proportionate interest in Glen Alden would have been reduced to only two-fifths of what it

---

enclosed with ... notice [of meeting of shareholders to vote on plan of merger] a copy or a summary of the plan of merger or plan of consolidation, as the case may be, and ... a copy of subsection A of section 908 and of subsections B, C and D of section 515 of this act." Act of May 5, 1933, P.L. 364, § 902, subd. B, as amended, 15 §§ P.S. 2852–902, subd. B.

presently is because of the issuance of an additional 3,621,703 shares to List which would not be subject to pre-emptive rights. In fact, ownership of Glen Alden would pass to the stockholders of List who would hold 76.5% of the outstanding shares as compared with but 23.5% retained by the present Glen Alden shareholders.

Perhaps the most important consequence to the plaintiff, if he were denied the right to have his shares redeemed at their fair value, would be the serious financial loss suffered upon consummation of the agreement. While the present book value of his stock is $38 a share after combination it would be worth only $21 a share. In contrast, the shareholders of List who presently hold stock with a total book value of $33,000,000 or $7.50 a share, would receive stock with a book value of $76,000,000 or $21 a share.

Under these circumstances it may well be said that if the proposed combination is allowed to take place without right of dissent, plaintiff would have his stock in Glen Alden taken away from him and the stock of a new company thrust upon him in its place. He would be projected against his will into a new enterprise under terms not of his own choosing. It was to protect dissident shareholders against just such a result that this Court one hundred years ago in the Lauman case, and the legislature thereafter in section 908, subd. A, granted the right of dissent. And it is to accord that protection to the plaintiff that we conclude that the combination proposed in the case at hand is a merger within the intendment of section 908, subd. A.

Nevertheless, defendants contend that the 1957 amendments to sections 311 and 908 of the corporation law preclude us from reaching this result and require the entry of judgment in their favor. Subsection F of section 311 dealing with the voluntary transfer of corporate assets provides: "The shareholders of a business corporation which acquires by sale, lease or exchange all or substantially all of the property of another corporation by the issuance of stock, securities or otherwise shall not be entitled to the rights and remedies of dissenting shareholders...." Act of July 11, 1957, P.L. 711, § 1, 15 P.S. §§ 2852–311, subd. F.

And the amendment to section 908 reads as follows: "The right of dissenting shareholders ... shall not apply to the purchase by a corporation of assets whether or not the consideration therefore be money or property, real or personal, including shares of bonds or other evidences of indebtedness of such corporation. The shareholders of such corporation shall have no right to dissent from any such purchase." Act of July 11, 1957, P.L. 711, § 1, 15 P.S. §§ 2852–908, subd. C.

Defendants view these amendments as abridging the right of shareholders to dissent to a transaction between two corporations which involves a transfer of assets for a consideration even though the transfer has all the legal incidents of a merger. They claim that only if the merger is accomplished in accordance with the prescribed statutory procedure does the right of dissent accrue. In support of this position they cite to us the comment on the amendments by the

Committee on Corporation Law of the Pennsylvania Bar Association, the committee which originally drafted these provisions. The comment states that the provisions were intended to overrule cases which granted shareholders the right to dissent to a sale of assets when accompanied by the legal incidents of a merger. See 61 Ann.Rep.Pa.Bar Ass'n. 277, 284 (1957). Whatever may have been the intent of the *committee,* there is no evidence to indicate that the *legislature* intended the 1957 amendments to have the effect contended for. But furthermore, the language of these two provisions does not support the opinion of the committee and is inept to achieve any such purpose. The amendments of 1957 do not provide that a transaction between two corporations which has the effect of a merger but which includes a transfer of assets for consideration is to be exempt from the protective provisions of sections 908, subd. A and 515. They provide only that the shareholders of a corporation which acquires the property or purchases the assets of another corporation, *without more,* are not entitled to the right to dissent from the transaction. So, as in the present case, when as part of a transaction between two corporations, one corporation dissolves, its liabilities are assumed by the survivor, its executives and directors take over the management and control of the survivor, and, as consideration for the transfer, its stockholders acquire a majority of the shares of stock of the survivor, then the transaction is no longer simply a purchase of assets or acquisition of property to which sections 311, subd. F and 908, subd. C apply, but a merger governed by section 908, subd. A of the corporation law. To divest shareholders of their right of dissent under such circumstances would require express language which is absent from the 1957 amendments.

Even were we to assume that the combination provided for in the reorganization agreement is a "sale of assets" to which section 908, subd. A does not apply, it would avail the defendants nothing; we will not blind our eyes to the realities of the transaction. Despite the designation of the parties and the form employed, Glen Alden does not in fact acquire List, rather, List acquires Glen Alden, cf. Metropolitan Edison Co. v. Commissioner, 3 Cir., 1938, 98 F.2d 807, affirmed sub nom., Helvering v. Metropolitan Edison Co., 1939, 306 U.S. 522, 59 S.Ct. 634, 83 L.Ed. 957, and under section 311, subd. D[8] the right of dissent would remain with the shareholders of Glen Alden.

We hold that the combination contemplated by the reorganization agreement, although consummated by contract rather than in accordance with the statutory procedure, is a merger within the protective purview of sections 908, subd. A and 515 of the corporation law. The shareholders of Glen Alden should have been notified accordingly and advised of their statutory rights of dissent and appraisal. The failure of

8. "If any shareholder of a business corporation which sells, leases or exchanges all or substantially all of its property and assets otherwise than (1) in the usual and regular course of its business, (2) for the purpose of relocating its business, or (3) in connection with its dissolution and liquidation, shall object to such sale, lease or exchange and comply with the provisions of section 515 of this act, such shareholder shall be entitled to the rights and remedies of dissenting shareholders as therein provided." . . .

the corporate officers to take these steps renders the stockholder approval of the agreement at the 1958 shareholders' meeting invalid. The lower court did not err in enjoining the officers and directors of Glen Alden from carrying out this agreement.

Decree affirmed at appellants' costs.

NOTE ON FARRIS

1. *Reasons for the Form in Which the Transaction was Cast.* It is clear that a major reason for structuring the transaction in *Farris* as a stock-for-assets combination, rather than as a statutory merger, was to avoid conferring appraisal rights on the Glen Alden shareholders. But given that reason for using the stock-for-assets mode, why did the parties also use an upside-down format, in which the smaller corporation nominally purchased the larger corporation's assets? Why didn't the parties arrange the transaction in a more natural way, by having the larger corporation, List, issue shares for assets of the smaller corporation, Glen Alden?

Again, one reason had to do with appraisal rights. List was a Delaware corporation. Under Delaware law, in a purchase and sale of assets, neither the purchaser's shareholders nor the seller's shareholders had appraisal rights. Under Pennsylvania law, however, a seller's shareholders did have appraisal rights, while a purchaser's did not—or so counsel thought. Therefore, by making List, a Delaware corporation, the nominal seller and Glen Alden, a Pennsylvania corporation, the nominal purchaser, the parties hoped to avoid giving appraisal rights to the shareholders of either corporation.

A second reason for the upside-down format may have been a desire to keep alive Glen Alden's tax loss carryover. While the rules governing the survival of such carryovers were complex, in general survival was more likely if the entity of the carryover corporation was left intact.

A third reason is given in the Supplemental Brief for Appellee: "In answer to the question of Mr. Justice Bell as to why List did not purchase the assets of Glen Alden, Mr. Littleton answered that the one percent Pennsylvania realty tax on the transfer of [the huge coal-mining] holdings of Glen Alden would make such a sale prohibitive."

2. *Post–Farris Developments.* Following the decision in Farris v. Glen Alden, the two corporations were combined pursuant to a statutory merger. Probably for some of the reasons just given, Glen Alden was the surviving corporation. The List shareholders received one Glen Alden share for each List share, and the Glen Alden shareholders ended up with five Glen Alden shares for each four they had previously held. New York Times, March 7, 1959; Moody's Industrial Manual 954 (1972).

The Pennsylvania statute now expressly rejects the reasoning in *Farris* (and suggestion in note 7 in *Terry v. Penn Central Corporation*, *infra*) that dissenters rights arise in the acquiring company shareholders by virtue of the fact that the acquisition has been structured so that the "mouse swallows the lion." *See* 15 Pa. Consol. Statutes Ann. § 1571(b)(3), Amended Official Comment (West Supp. 2010).

NEW YORK STOCK EXCHANGE, LISTED COMPANY MANUAL § 312.00

[See Statutory Supplement]

CAL. CORP. CODE §§ 152, 160, 168, 181, 187, 194.5, 1001, 1101, 1200, 1201, 1300

[See Statutory Supplement]

MODEL BUS. CORP. ACT § 6.21(f)

[See Statutory Supplement]

NOTE ON THE SURVIVOR'S LIABILITY TO THE TRANSFEROR'S CREDITORS

Stock-for-assets transactions are often used in preference to a statutory merger or a stock-for-stock combination because of a desire to avoid assuming the acquired corporation's liabilities—particularly undisclosed or contingent liabilities. In a statutory merger, the surviving corporation becomes liable by operation of law for all of the transferor's obligations, including those that are contingent or undisclosed. In a stock-for-stock combination, the survivor does not become directly liable for the debts of the acquired corporation, although the acquired corporation is now a subsidiary of the survivor, and carries its obligations along.

In contrast, in a stock-for-assets combination, the survivor may remain free of those liabilities it does not expressly assume, on the theory that it merely engaged in a purchase. Frequently, however, this theory is not accepted by the courts. The following formulation, or one very much like it, is found in a great number of cases:

> The general rule is that "a mere sale of corporate property by one company to another does not make the purchaser liable for the liabilities of the seller not assumed by it. . . ." There are, however, certain exceptions to this rule. Liability for obligations of a selling corporation may be imposed on the purchasing corporation when (1) the purchaser expressly or impliedly agrees to assume such obligations; (2) the transaction amounts to a consoli-

> dation or merger of the selling corporation with or into the purchasing corporation; (3) the purchasing corporation is merely a continuation of the selling corporation; or (4) the transaction is entered into fraudulently to escape liability for such obligations.

See James D. Cox & Thomas L. Hazen, 4 Treatise On The Law Of Corporations § 22.8 (3rd Ed. 2010).

Where the second or third exceptions apply, many (though not all) cases make the survivor in a typical stock-for-assets transaction liable to the transferor's shareholders under a de facto merger theory.

When the claim against the successor corporation arises from a defective product, a significant number, albeit a minority, of the states reject the formal corporate standards for successor liability and instead are guided by the policies underlying product liability claims. The leading case for this approach involved Herbert Ray who was seriously injured by a defective ladder manufactured by Alad Corporation (Alad I); prior to Ray's injury, Alad I sold for cash its assets to the defendant, Alad II, who continued to manufacture the same line of ladders under the "Alad" name, using the same equipment, designs, and personnel, and soliciting Alad I's customers through the same sales representatives with no outward indication of any change in the ownership of the business.

> [The] insulation from its predecessor's liabilities of a corporation acquiring business assets has the undoubted advantage of promoting the free availability and transferability of capital. However, this advantage is outweighed under the narrow circumstances here presented by considerations favoring continued protection for injured users of defective products.... [T]hese considerations include (1) the nonavailability to plaintiff of any adequate remedy against Alad I as a result of Alad I's liquidation prior to plaintiff's injury, (2) the availability to Alad II of the knowledge necessary for gauging the risks of injury from previously manufactured ladders together with the opportunity to provide for meeting the cost arising from those risks by spreading it among current purchasers of the product line and (3) the fact that the good will transferred to and enjoyed by Alad II could not have been enjoyed by Alad I without the burden of liability for defects in ladders sold under its aegis. Accordingly we have concluded that the instant claim of strict tort liability presents an exception to the general rule against imposition upon a successor corporation of its predecessor's liabilities and that the summary judgment should be reversed.

Ray v. Alad Corp., 19 Cal.3d 22, 25, 560 P.2d 3, 5, 136 Cal.Rptr. 574, 576 (1977). See also, Lefever v. K.P. Hovnanian Enterprises, Inc., 160 N.J. 307, 734 A.2d 290 (1999) (imposing liability on cash purchaser in bankruptcy); Foster v. Cone–Blanchard Mach. Co., 597 N.W.2d 506 (Mich. 1999); Roper Elec. Co. v. Quality Castings, Inc., 60 S.W.3d 708 (Mo. Ct. App. 2001); Michael Carter, Successor Liability Under CERCLA: Its Time To Fully Embrace State Law, 156 U. Pa. L. Rev. 767 (2008); Wendy B. Davis, Defacto Merger, Federal Common Law and

Erie: Constitutional Issues In Successor Liability, 2008 Colum. Bus. L. Rev. 529; Comment, Successor Liability, Mass Tort, and Mandatory–Litigation Class Action, 118 Harv. L. Rev. 2357 (2005).

F. TRIANGULAR MERGERS AND SHARE EXCHANGES

Terry v. Penn Central Corp.

United States Court of Appeals, Third Circuit, 1981.
668 F.2d 188.

■ Before ADAMS, MARIS and HIGGINBOTHAM, CIRCUIT JUDGES. . . .

■ ADAMS, CIRCUIT JUDGE.

The Penn Central Corporation ("Penn Central"), an appellee in this case, has sought to acquire Colt Industries Inc. ("Colt"), also an appellee, by merging Colt with PCC Holdings, Inc. ("Holdings"), a wholly-owned subsidiary of Penn Central. Howard L. Terry and W.H. Hunt, the appellants, are shareholders of Penn Central who objected to the transaction. In a diversity action . . . appellants sought injunctive and declaratory relief to enforce voting and dissenters' rights to which appellants asserted they were entitled. Appellants further sought to enjoin Holdings from proceeding with the proposed merger, and in particular moved to enjoin a vote on the transaction, scheduled for October 29, 1981, by the shareholders of Penn Central. . . . The shareholders of Penn Central voted . . . on October 29. . . .

After argument on appeal, the shareholders disapproved of the merger, and the corporations thereafter publicly announced their abandonment of this particular merger. Penn Central, however, has not abandoned its proposed series of acquisitions, of which the Colt acquisition was merely one instance.

I.

Penn Central is the successor to the Penn Central Transportation Corporation, which underwent a reorganization under the bankruptcy laws that was completed in 1978. No longer involved in the railroading business, Penn Central, since 1978, has had the advantage, for tax purposes, of a large loss carry-forward. In order to put that loss carry-forward to its best use, Penn Central has embarked on a program of acquiring corporations whose profits could be sheltered. To this end Penn Central created Holdings, a wholly-owned subsidiary which was to acquire the businesses that Penn Central desired. The first acquisition under the plan was Marathon Manufacturing Company ("Marathon"), in 1979. In the Marathon acquisition, a class of preferred Penn Central stock was created . . . was issued to the owners of Marathon stock. Appellants were shareholders of Marathon who thereby obtained shares of this First Series Preference Stock. Terry was promptly elected to the Penn Central board of directors.

In 1981, Penn Central decided upon another acquisition: Colt. The management and directors of Colt and Penn Central agreed upon a merger of Colt into Holdings, compensated for by issuance of a second series of Penn Central preference stock to Colt shareholders. Terry opposed the merger at the directors' meeting, and sought to preclude the consummation of the transaction.

... [A]ppellants argue that under Pennsylvania's corporate law, they are entitled to dissent and appraisal rights if the merger is adopted over their opposition.[2] ...

Because Colt and Penn Central have now announced their abandonment of the proposed merger, the request for injunctive relief ... is now conceded by all parties to be moot. However, the appellants' request for declaratory relief, which the appellants now contend is moot as well, involves legal questions that go to Penn Central's plan of acquisitions, rather than to the Colt transaction alone, and these questions appear likely to recur in future disputes between the parties here.... In a case such as this, a voluntary termination by the parties of the specific activity challenged in the lawsuit—here, the proposed treatment of the dissenting preferred shareholders in the Colt–Holdings plan—does not render the action moot because there is "a reasonable likelihood that the parties or those in privity with them will be involved in a suit on the same issues in the future." American Bible Society v. Blount, 446 F.2d 588, 595 (3d Cir.1971)....

III.

Terry and Hunt contend that under Pennsylvania law they are entitled to dissent and appraisal rights if a merger is approved by the Penn Central shareholders. As the district court concluded, this assertion is unsupported by Pennsylvania statute or case law....

Section 908 of the Pennsylvania Business Corporation Law (PBCL), 15 P.S. § 1908, provides that shareholders of corporations that are parties to a plan of merger are entitled to dissent and appraisal rights, but adds that for an acquisition other than such a merger, the only rights are those provided for in Section 311 of the PBCL, 15 P.S. § 1311 (Purdon 1967 Supp.1981–82). Section 311, in turn, provides for dissent and appraisal rights only when an acquisition has been accomplished by "the issuance of voting shares of such corporation to be outstanding immediately after the acquisition sufficient to elect a majority of the directors of the corporation." In this case the shares of Penn Central stock to be issued in the Colt transaction do not exceed the number of shares already existing, and

2. In addition, appellants claim a right under Pennsylvania law to require approval of an absolute majority vote of the shares outstanding on the proposed merger, relying on § 902(B) of the Pennsylvania Business Corporation Law (PBCL), 15 P.S. § 1902(B) (Purdon Supp. 1981–82). For the reasons discussed in Part III of this opinion, we conclude that Penn Central is not a "party" to the merger, within the technical meaning of the term under that section and the related Section 908 of the PBCL, 15 P.S. § 1908 (Purdon Supp.1981–82). Accordingly, section 902 does not apply to the Penn Central vote on the merger.

thus the transaction is not covered by Section 311. Any statutory dissent and appraisal rights for Penn Central shareholders are therefore contingent upon Penn Central's status as a party to the merger within the meaning of Section 908. And as the district court points out, the PBCL describes the parties to a merger as those entities that are *actually* combined into a single corporation. Section 907, 15 P.S. § 1907 (Purdon Supp.1981–82), states that:

> Upon the merger or consolidation becoming effective, the several corporations parties to the plan of merger or consolidation shall be a single corporation which, in the case of a merger, shall be that corporation designated in the plan of merger as the surviving corporation. . . .

At the consummation of the proposed merger plan here, both Holdings and Penn Central would survive as separate entities, and it would therefore appear that Penn Central is not a party within the meaning of ... Section 907. We can discern no reason to infer that the legislature intended the word "party" to have different meanings in Sections 907 and 908, and accordingly conclude that Penn Central is not a party to the merger.

Appellants argue that Penn Central is nevertheless brought into the amalgamation by the *de facto* merger doctrine as set out in Pennsylvania law in Farris v. Glen Alden Corp., 393 Pa. 427, 143 A.2d 25 (1958). *Farris* was the penultimate step in a *pas de deux* involving the Pennsylvania courts and the Pennsylvania legislature regarding the proper treatment for transactions that reached the same practical result as a merger but avoided the legal form of merger and the concomitant legal obligations.... *Farris,* addressing those efforts, held that the doctrine still covered a reorganization agreement that had the effect of merging a large corporation into a smaller corporation. In a 1959 response to *Farris,* the legislature made explicit its objection to earlier cases that found certain transactions to be *de facto* mergers. The legislature enacted a law, modifying *inter alia* Sections 311 and 908, entitled in part:

> An Act ... changing the law as to ... the acquisition or transfer of corporate assets, the rights of dissenting shareholders, ... abolishing the doctrine of de facto mergers or consolidation and reversing the rules laid down in *Bloch v. Baldwin Locomotive Works,* 75 Pa. D. & C. 24, and *Marks v. The Autocar Co.,* 153 F.Supp. 768,....

Act of November 10, 1959 (P.L. 1406, No. 502).

Following this explicit statement, the *de facto* merger doctrine has rarely been invoked by the Pennsylvania courts. Only once has the Pennsylvania Supreme Court made reference to it, in In re Jones Laughlin Steel Corp., 488 Pa. 524, 412 A.2d 1099 (1980). Even there, the Court's reference was oblique. It merely cited *Farris* for the proposition that shareholders have the right to enjoin "proposed unfair or fraudulent corporate actions." 488 Pa. at 533, 412 A.2d at 1104. This Court, sitting in diversity in Knapp v. North American

Rockwell Corp., 506 F.2d 361 (3d Cir.1974), cert. denied, 421 U.S. 965, 95 S.Ct. 1955, 44 L.Ed.2d 452 (1975), made reference to the *de facto* merger doctrine to hold that a transaction structured as a sale of assets could nevertheless be deemed a merger for purposes of requiring the merging corporation to assume the acquired corporation's liability for damages to a worker who was injured by a faulty piece of equipment manufactured by the acquired company....

None of [the] cases persuades us that a Pennsylvania court would apply the *de facto* merger doctrine to the situation before us. Although *Jones & Laughlin Steel* suggests that dissent and appraisal rights might be available if fraud or fundamental unfairness were shown, we are not faced with such a situation. No allegation of fraud has been advanced, and the only allegation of fundamental unfairness is that the appellants will, if the merger is consummated, be forced into what they consider a poor investment on the part of Penn Central without the opportunity to receive an appraised value for their stock. Even if appellants' evaluation of the merits of the proposed merger is accurate, poor business judgment on the part of management would not be enough to constitute unfairness cognizable by a court. And the denial of appraisal rights to dissenters cannot constitute fundamental unfairness, or the *de facto* merger doctrine would apply in every instance in which dissenters' rights were sought and the 1959 amendments by the legislature would be rendered nugatory.[7] ...

In the absence of any explicit guidance to the contrary by the Pennsylvania courts, we conclude that the language of the legislature in 1959 precludes a decision that the transaction in this case constitutes a *de facto* merger sufficient to entitle Penn Central shareholders to dissent and appraisal rights. We therefore hold that appellants do not possess such rights if a transaction such as the one involved here is consummated....

NOTE ON TRIANGULAR MERGERS AND SHARE EXCHANGES

1. *Triangular Mergers.* A statutory merger is often preferable to either a stock-for-assets or a stock-for-stock combination. To begin with, the Internal Revenue Code provides greater liberality as to the type of consideration that can be given in an A reorganization (a statutory merger) than in a B reorganization (a stock-for-stock combination) or a C reorganization (a stock-for-assets combination). See Section 1D, supra. Furthermore, a stock-for-assets combination may involve sales taxes, while a statutory merger ordinarily will not. A stock-for-assets combination also ordinarily involves a great amount of paperwork, in the form of deeds and assignments of the transferor's

7. A different result might be reached if here, as in *Farris,* the acquiring corporation were significantly smaller than the acquired corporation such that the acquisition greatly transformed the nature of the successor corporation. But in this situation we do not have such a case; after the merger Penn Central would remain a major, diversified corporation, and would continue on the course of acquiring other corporations.

property and (in some cases) notice to creditors in compliance with the applicable bulk sales law. In contrast, in a statutory merger the survivor succeeds to the transferor's assets by operation of law, so that neither individual documents of title nor compliance with the bulk sales law is ordinarily required.

On the other hand, in a statutory merger the surviving corporation assumes the disappearing corporation's liabilities by operation of law. Furthermore, a statutory merger normally triggers voting and appraisal rights in the shareholders of both constituents. In contrast, in a stock-for-stock or stock-for-assets combination the acquiring corporation does not necessarily assume the transferor corporation's liabilities. Moreover, these forms of combination may require a vote only by the shareholders of one constituent, and may not trigger appraisal rights. Accordingly, the management of a corporation that proposes to engage in a corporate combination may prefer to use the statutory-merger form except for the voting and appraisal rights entailed by that form. The triangular merger is a technique designed to give management the best of both possible worlds: the form of a merger, but without necessarily assuming the liabilities of the disappearing corporation and without voting or appraisal rights in the survivor's shareholders.

A conventional (or "forward") triangular merger works this way: Assume that Corporations S and T want to engage in a merger in which S will be the survivor and T's shareholders will end up with 100,000 shares of S. In a normal merger this would be accomplished by having S issue 100,000 shares of its own stock to T's shareholders. In a conventional triangular merger, however, S instead begins by creating a new subsidiary, S/Sub, and then transfers 100,000 shares of its own stock to S/Sub in exchange for all of S/Sub's stock. S/Sub and T then engage in a statutory merger, but instead of issuing its *own* stock to T's shareholders, S/Sub issues its 100,000 shares of S stock. The net result is that T's business is now owned by S's wholly owned subsidiary (rather than by S itself, as in a normal merger), and T's shareholders now own 100,000 shares of S stock. By use of this technique, S may therefore achieve the advantages of a statutory merger while insulating itself from direct responsibility for T's liabilities.[2] The final step is S using the short-form merger provision to merge S/Sub into S so that the assets and liabilities formerly held by T are now among the assets and liabilities of S.

Such a transaction would probably not have been permissible under the traditional statutory merger provisions, because those provisions usually contemplated that the surviving corporation would issue its *own* shares or securities. However, the merger statutes of most or all jurisdictions have now been amended to permit the survivor to issue shares or securities of *any* corporation. (*See, e.g.*, Del. § 251(b)(4).) In tandem with this development, the Internal Revenue Code was amended by adding § 368(a)(2)(D), which permits a con-

2. However, a court might impose these liabilities on S under the de facto merger doctrine, on the theory that in effect S itself is a constituent to the merger.

ventional triangular merger to qualify as a tax-free A reorganization, if (i) substantially all of T's properties are acquired by S/Sub; (ii) the merger would have qualified as an A reorganization if T had merged directly into S; and (iii) no stock of S/Sub is used in the transaction.

A *reverse* triangular merger proceeds like a conventional triangular merger, except that instead of merging T into S/Sub, S/Sub is merged into T, i.e., T not S/Sub survives. The merger agreement provides that all previously outstanding T shares are automatically converted into the 100,000 shares of S held by S/Sub, and that all shares in S/Sub (which are held by S) are automatically converted into shares in T. When all the shooting is over, therefore, S/Sub will have disappeared, T will be a wholly owned subsidiary of S, and T's shareholders will own 100,000 shares of S stock. By use of this technique S may therefore achieve the advantages of a statutory merger while preserving T's legal status, which could be important where T has valuable but non-assignable rights under contracts, leases, licenses, or franchises. Under IRC § 368(a)(2)(E), a reverse triangular merger will qualify as a tax-free A reorganization, if (i) T ends up with substantially all of the properties of both S/Sub and T, and (ii) S voting stock is exchanged for at least 80% of T's voting and nonvoting stock. (The balance of T's stock can be acquired for other types of consideration.)

An important problem raised by triangular mergers is that they may allow subversion of shareholder voting and appraisal rights. To avoid this result, it can be argued that despite the form of such transactions, voting and appraisal rights on the survivor's side are vested not in S, as the sole shareholder of S/Sub, but pass through to S's shareholders. This argument was rejected in Terry v. Penn Central Corp., supra, but that case was at least partly controlled by the unusual Pennsylvania legislative history. Ideally, this problem should be dealt with by statute. For example, consider the role of MBCA § 6.21(f) requiring shareholder vote if shares are issued for other than cash and the number of shares so issued are more than 20 percent of the voting power prior to such issuance. The Model Acts provision parallels listing requirements of the New York Stock Exchange and NASDAQ. *See also* Cal. Corp. Code §§ 1200(d), 1201 (a merger reorganization must be approved by the shareholders of a corporation which is "in control of any constituent . . . corporation . . . and whose equity securities are issued or transferred in the reorganization").

2. *Share Exchanges.* Another new mode of combination is known as a share exchange. In a share exchange, the shareholders of the acquired corporation vote on whether to exchange their shares for designated consideration from the acquiring corporation. If the proposed transaction is approved by a majority of that corporation's outstanding shares, all of the shares must be surrendered—including those of nonconsenting shareholders (unless they exercise appraisal rights).

G. FREEZEOUTS

NOTE ON FREEZEOUT TECHNIQUES

A freezeout is a corporate transaction whose principal purpose is to reconstitute the corporation's ownership by involuntarily eliminating the equity interest of minority shareholders. Freezeouts can take several forms.

1. *Dissolution Freezeouts.* Assume that S (who may be an individual, a group, or a corporation) owns 70% of C Corporation, and wishes to eliminate C's minority shareholders. In a dissolution freezeout, S causes C to dissolve under a plan of dissolution which provides that C's productive assets will be distributed to S (or to an entity S controls), while cash or notes will be distributed to C's minority shareholders. This technique has been held illegal in a number of cases, most of which stress that such a plan of dissolution violates a corporate norm of equal treatment among all shareholders of the same class. See e.g., In re San Joaquin Light & Power Corp., 52 Cal.App.2d 814, 127 P.2d 29 (1942).

2. *Sale-of-Assets Freezeouts.* In a sale-of-assets freezeout, C's controlling shareholder, S, organizes a new corporation, T, all of whose stock S owns. S then causes C to sell its assets to T for cash or notes. Result: S owns C's business through T, while the equity interest of C's minority shareholders in C's business is involuntarily terminated. (C is then normally dissolved, although a freezeout will be effected even without dissolution.) Such a procedure has been disapproved in several cases. See, e.g., Theis v. Spokane Falls Gaslight Co., 34 Wash. 23, 74 P. 1004 (1904).

3. *Debt or Redeemable–Preferred Mergers.* A debt or redeemable-preferred merger begins like a sale-of-assets freezeout, with the organization by S of a new corporation, T. However, instead of causing C to transfer its assets to T, S causes C to merge into T; and instead of issuing common stock in the merger, T issues either short-term debentures or redeemable preferred stock. Accordingly, the interest of C's minority shareholders in T either terminates automatically after a period of years (in the case of debentures) or is terminable at T's election (in the case of redeemable preferred).

4. *Cashout Mergers.* Modern freezeouts commonly employ still a fourth technique. Most states now allow the survivor in any type of merger to issue cash as well as, or instead of, stock or other securities. This opens the door to cash mergers, which resemble debt or redeemable-stock mergers, except that the survivor issues cash rather than stock or other securities. Under this technique, the freezeout possibilities of the short-form merger are extended to cases where the parent does not own the percentage of stock requisite for a short-form merger.

A recurrent issue in the freezeout area is whether such a transaction is permissible if it is effected with no business purpose other than to increase the controlling shareholders' portion of the pie. That issue is addressed in the materials that follow.

Weinberger v. UOP, Inc.

Supreme Court of Delaware, 1983.
457 A.2d 701.

■ Before HERMANN, C.J., MCNEILLY, QUILLEN, HORSEY and MOORE, JJ., constituting the Court en Banc.

■ MOORE, JUSTICE:

This post-trial appeal was reheard en banc from a decision of the Court of Chancery. It was brought by the class action plaintiff below, a former shareholder of UOP, Inc., who challenged the elimination of UOP's minority shareholders by a cash-out merger between UOP and its majority owner, The Signal Companies, Inc. [T]he defendants in this action are Signal, UOP, [and] certain officers and directors of those companies.... The present Chancellor held that the terms of the merger were fair to the plaintiff and the other minority shareholders of UOP. Accordingly, he entered judgment in favor of the defendants....

In ruling for the defendants, the Chancellor re-stated his earlier conclusion that the plaintiff in a suit challenging a cash-out merger must allege specific acts of fraud, misrepresentation, or other items of misconduct to demonstrate the unfairness of the merger terms to the minority. We approve this rule and affirm it.

The Chancellor also held that even though the ultimate burden of proof is on the majority shareholder to show by a preponderance of the evidence that the transaction is fair, it is first the burden of the plaintiff attacking the merger to demonstrate some basis for invoking the fairness obligation. We agree with that principle. However, where corporate action has been approved by an informed vote of a majority of the minority shareholders, we conclude that the burden entirely shifts to the plaintiff to show that the transaction was unfair to the minority. See, e.g., Michelson v. Duncan, Del.Supr., 407 A.2d 211, 224 (1979). But in all this, the burden clearly remains on those relying on the vote to show that they completely disclosed all material facts relevant to the transaction.

Here, the record does not support a conclusion that the minority stockholder vote was an informed one. Material information, necessary to acquaint those shareholders with the bargaining positions of Signal and UOP, was withheld under circumstances amounting to a breach of fiduciary duty. We therefore conclude that this merger does not meet the test of fairness, at least as we address that concept, and no burden thus shifted to the plaintiff by reason of the minority shareholder vote.

Accordingly, we reverse and remand for further proceedings consistent herewith.

In considering the nature of the remedy available under our law to minority shareholders in a cash-out merger, we believe that it is, and hereafter should be, an appraisal under 8 Del.C. § 262 as hereinafter construed. We therefore overrule Lynch v. Vickers Energy Corp., Del.Supr., 429 A.2d 497 (1981) (*Lynch II*) to the extent that it purports to limit a stockholder's monetary relief to a specific damage formula. See *Lynch II*. 429 A.2d at 507–08 (McNeilly Quillen, JJ., dissenting). But to give full effect to section 262 within the framework of the General Corporation Law we adopt a more liberal, less rigid and stylized, approach to the valuation process than has heretofore been permitted by our courts. While the present state of these proceedings does not admit the plaintiff to the appraisal remedy per se, the practical effect of the remedy we do grant him will be co-extensive with the liberalized valuation and appraisal methods we herein approve for cases coming after this decision.

Our treatment of these matters has necessarily led us to a reconsideration of the business purpose rule announced in the trilogy of Singer v. Magnavox Co., supra; Tanzer v. International General Industries, Inc., Del.Supr., 379 A.2d 1121 (1977); and Roland International Corp. v. Najjar, Del.Supr., 407 A.2d 1032 (1979). For the reasons hereafter set forth we consider that the business purpose requirement of these cases is no longer the law of Delaware.

I.

The facts found by the trial court, pertinent to the issues before us, are supported by the record, and we draw from them as set out in the Chancellor's opinion.

Signal is a diversified, technically based company operating through various subsidiaries. Its stock is publicly traded on the New York, Philadelphia and Pacific Stock Exchanges. UOP, formerly known as Universal Oil Products Company, was a diversified industrial company engaged in various lines of business, including petroleum and petro-chemical services and related products, construction, fabricated metal products, transportation equipment products, chemicals and plastics, and other products and services including land development, lumber products and waste disposal. Its stock was publicly held and listed on the New York Stock Exchange.

In 1974 Signal sold one of its wholly-owned subsidiaries for $420,000,000 in cash. See Gimbel v. Signal Companies, Inc., Del.Ch., 316 A.2d 599, aff'd, Del.Supr., 316 A.2d 619 (1974). While looking to invest this cash surplus, Signal became interested in UOP as a possible acquisition. Friendly negotiations ensued, and Signal proposed to acquire a controlling interest in UOP at a price of $19 per share. UOP's representatives sought $25 per share. In the arm's length bargaining that followed, an understanding was reached whereby Signal agreed to purchase from UOP 1,500,000 shares of UOP's authorized but unissued stock at $21 per share.

This purchase was contingent upon Signal making a successful cash tender offer for 4,300,000 publicly held shares of UOP, also at a price of $21 per share. This combined method of acquisition permitted Signal to acquire 5,800,000 shares of stock, representing 50.5% of UOP's outstanding shares. The UOP board of directors advised the company's shareholders that it had no objection to Signal's tender offer at that price. Immediately before the announcement of the tender offer, UOP's common stock had been trading on the New York Stock Exchange at a fraction under $14 per share.

The negotiations between Signal and UOP occurred during April 1975, and the resulting tender offer was greatly oversubscribed. However, Signal limited its total purchase of the tendered shares so that, when coupled with the stock bought from UOP, it had achieved its goal of becoming a 50.5% shareholder of UOP.

Although UOP's board consisted of thirteen directors, Signal nominated and elected only six. Of these, five were either directors or employees of Signal. The sixth, a partner in the banking firm of Lazard Freres & Co., had been one of Signal's representatives in the negotiations and bargaining with UOP concerning the tender offer and purchase price of the UOP shares.

However, the president and chief executive officer of UOP retired during 1975, and Signal caused him to be replaced by James V. Crawford, a long-time employee and senior executive vice president of one of Signal's wholly-owned subsidiaries. Crawford succeeded his predecessor on UOP's board of directors and also was made a director of Signal.

By the end of 1977 Signal basically was unsuccessful in finding other suitable investment candidates for its excess cash, and by February 1978 considered that it had no other realistic acquisitions available to it on a friendly basis. Once again its attention turned to UOP.

The trial court found that at the instigation of certain Signal management personnel, including William W. Walkup, its board chairman, and Forrest N. Shumway, its president, a feasibility study was made concerning the possible acquisition of the balance of UOP's outstanding shares. This study was performed by two Signal officers, Charles S. Arledge, vice president (director of planning), and Andrew J. Chitiea, senior vice president (chief financial officer). Messrs. Walkup, Shumway, Arledge and Chitiea were all directors of UOP in addition to their membership on the Signal board.

Arledge and Chitiea concluded that it would be a good investment for Signal to acquire the remaining 49.5% of UOP shares at any price up to $24 each. Their report was discussed between Walkup and Shumway who, along with Arledge, Chitiea and Brewster L. Arms, internal counsel for Signal, constituted Signal's senior management. In particular, they talked about the proper price to be paid if the acquisition was pursued, purportedly keeping in mind that as UOP's majority shareholder, Signal owed a fiduciary responsibility to both its own stockholders as well as to UOP's minority. It was ultimately agreed that a meeting of Signal's Executive Committee would be called to propose that Signal acquire the remaining outstanding stock of UOP through a cash-out merger in the range of $20 to $21 per share.

The Executive Committee meeting was set for February 28, 1978. As a courtesy, UOP's President, Crawford, was invited to attend, although he was not a member of Signal's executive committee. On his arrival, and prior to the meeting, Crawford was asked to meet privately with Walkup and Shumway. He was then told of Signal's plan to acquire full ownership of UOP and was asked for his reaction to the proposed price range of $20 to $21 per share. Crawford said he thought such a price would be "generous", and that it was certainly one which should be submitted to UOP's minority shareholders for their ultimate consideration. He stated, however, that Signal's 100% ownership could cause internal problems at UOP. He believed that employees would have to be given some assurance of their future place in a fully-owned Signal subsidiary. Otherwise, he feared the departure of essential personnel. Also, many of UOP's key employees had stock option incentive programs which would be wiped out by a merger. Crawford therefore urged that some adjustment would have to be made, such as providing a comparable incentive in Signals' shares, if after the merger he was to maintain his quality of personnel and efficiency at UOP.

Thus, Crawford voiced no objection to the $20 to $21 price range, nor did he suggest that Signal should consider paying more than $21 per share for the minority interests. Later, at the Executive Committee meeting the same factors were discussed, with Crawford repeating the position he earlier took with Walkup and Shumway. Also considered was the 1975 tender offer and the fact that it had been greatly oversubscribed at $21 per share. For many reasons, Signal's management concluded that the acquisition of UOP's minority shares provided the solution to a number of its business problems.

Thus, it was the consensus that a price of $20 to $21 per share would be fair to both Signal and the minority shareholders of UOP. Signal's executive committee authorized its management "to negotiate" with UOP "for a cash acquisition of the minority ownership in UOP, Inc., with the intention of presenting a proposal to [Signal's] board of directors ... on March 6, 1978. Immediately after this February 28, 1978" meeting, Signal issued a press release stating:

> The Signal Companies, Inc. and UOP, Inc. are conducting negotiations for the acquisition for cash by Signal of the 49.5 per cent of UOP which it does not presently own, announced Forrest N. Shumway, president and chief executive officer of Signal, and James V. Crawford, UOP president.
>
> Price and other terms of the proposed transaction have not yet been finalized and would be subject to approval of the boards of directors of Signal and UOP, scheduled to meet early next week, the stockholders of UOP and certain federal agencies.

The announcement also referred to the fact that the closing price of UOP's common stock on that day was $14.50 per share.

Two days later, on March 2, 1978, Signal issued a second press release stating that its management would recommend a price in the range of $20 to $21 per share for UOP's 49.5% minority interest. This announcement referred to Signal's earlier statement that "negotiations" were being conducted for the acquisition of the minority shares.

Between Tuesday, February 28, 1978 and Monday, March 6, 1978, a total of four business days, Crawford spoke by telephone with all of UOP's non-Signal, i.e., outside, directors. Also during that period, Crawford retained Lehman Brothers to render a fairness opinion as to the price offered the minority for its stock. He gave two reasons for this choice. First, the time schedule between the announcement and the board meetings was short (by then only three business days) and since Lehman Brothers had been acting as UOP's investment banker for many years, Crawford felt that it would be in the best position to respond on such brief notice. Second, James W. Glanville, a long-time director of UOP and a partner in Lehman Brothers, had acted as a financial advisor to UOP for many years. Crawford believed that Glanville's familiarity with UOP, as a member of its board, would also be of assistance in enabling Lehman Brothers to render a fairness opinion within the existing time constraints.

Crawford telephoned Glanville, who gave his assurance that Lehman Brothers had no conflicts that would prevent it from accepting the task. Glanville's immediate personal reaction was that a price of $20 to $21 would certainly be fair, since it represented almost a 50% premium over UOP's market price. Glanville sought a $250,000 fee for Lehman Brothers' services, but Crawford thought this too much. After further discussions Glanville finally agreed that Lehman Brothers would render its fairness opinion for $150,000.

During this period Crawford also had several telephone contacts with Signal officials. In only one of them, however, was the price of the shares discussed. In a conversation with Walkup, Crawford advised that as a result of his communications with UOP's non-Signal directors, it was his feeling that the price would have to be the top of the proposed range, or $21 per share, if the approval of UOP's outside directors was to be obtained. But again, he did not seek any price higher than $21.

Glanville assembled a three-man Lehman Brothers team to do the work on the fairness opinion. These persons examined relevant documents and information concerning UOP, including its annual reports and its Securities and Exchange Commission filings from 1973 through 1976, as well as its audited financial statements for 1977, its interim reports to shareholders, and its recent and historical market prices and trading volumes. In addition, on Friday, March 3, 1978, two members of the Lehman Brothers team flew to UOP's headquarters in Des Plaines, Illinois, to perform a "due diligence" visit, during the course of which they interviewed Crawford as well as UOP's general counsel, its chief financial officer, and other key executives and personnel.

As a result, the Lehman Brothers team concluded that "the price of either $20 or $21 would be a fair price for the remaining shares of UOP". They telephoned this impression to Glanville, who was spending the weekend in Vermont.

On Monday morning, March 6, 1978, Glanville and the senior member of the Lehman Brothers team flew to Des Plaines to attend the scheduled UOP directors meeting. Glanville looked over the assembled information during the flight. The two had with them the draft of a "fairness opinion letter" in which the price had been left blank. Either during or immediately prior to the directors' meeting, the two-page "fairness opinion letter" was typed in final form and the price of $21 per share was inserted.

On March 6, 1978, both the Signal and UOP boards were convened to consider the proposed merger. Telephone communications were maintained between the two meetings. Walkup, Signal's board chairman, and also a UOP director, attended UOP's meeting with Crawford in order to present Signal's position and answer any questions that UOP's non-Signal directors might have. Arledge and Chitiea, along with Signal's other designees on UOP's board, participated by conference telephone. All of UOP's outside directors attended the meeting either in person or by conference telephone.

First, Signal's board unanimously adopted a resolution authorizing Signal to proposed to UOP a cash merger of $21 per share as outlined in a certain merger agreement and other supporting documents. This proposal required that the merger be approved by a majority of UOP's outstanding minority shares voting at the stockholders meeting at which the merger would be considered, and that the minority shares voting in favor of the merger, when coupled with Signal's 50.5% interest would have to comprise at least two-thirds of all UOP shares. Otherwise the proposed merger would be deemed disapproved.

UOP's board then considered the proposal. Copies of the agreement were delivered to the directors in attendance, and other copies had been forwarded earlier to the directors participating by telephone. They also had before them UOP financial data for 1974–1977, UOP's most recent financial statements, market price information, and budget projections for 1978. In addition they had Lehman Brothers' hurriedly prepared fairness opinion letter finding the price of $21 to be fair. Glanville, the Lehman Brothers partner, and UOP director, commented on the information that had gone into preparation of the letter.

Signal also suggests that the Arledge–Chitiea feasibility study, indicating that a price of up to $24 per share would be a "good investment" for Signal, was discussed at the UOP directors' meeting. The Chancellor made no such finding, and our independent review of the record, detailed infra, satisfies us by a preponderance of the evidence that there was no discussion of this document at UOP's board meeting. Furthermore, it is clear beyond peradventure that nothing in that report was ever disclosed to UOP's minority shareholders prior to their approval of the merger.

After consideration of Signal's proposal, Walkup and Crawford left the meeting to permit a free and uninhibited exchange between UOP's non-Signal directors. Upon their return a resolution to accept Signal's offer was then proposed and adopted. While Signal's men on UOP's board participated in various aspects of the meeting they abstained from voting. However, the minutes show that each of them "if voting would have voted yes".

On March 7, 1978, UOP sent a letter to its shareholders advising them of the action taken by UOP's board with respect to Signal's offer. This document pointed out, among other things, that on February 28, 1978 "both companies had announced negotiations were being conducted."

Despite the swift board action of the two companies, the merger was not submitted to UOP's shareholders until their annual meeting on May 26, 1978. In the notice of that meeting and proxy statement sent to shareholders in May, UOP's management and board urged that the merger be approved. The proxy statement also advised:

> The price was determined after *discussions* between James V. Crawford, a director of Signal and Chief Executive Officer of UOP, and officers of Signal which took place during meetings on February 28, 1978, and in the course of several subsequent telephone conversations. (Emphasis added.)

In the original draft of the proxy statement the word "negotiations" had been used rather than "discussions". However, when the Securities and Exchange Commission sought details of the "negotiations" as part of its review of these materials, the term was deleted and the word "discussions" was substituted. The proxy statement indicated that the vote of UOP's board in approving the merger had been unanimous. It also advised the shareholders that Lehman Brothers had given its opinion that the merger price of $21 per share was fair to UOP's minority. However, it did not disclose the hurried method by which this conclusion was reached.

As of the record date for UOP's annual meeting, there were 11,488,302 shares of UOP common stock outstanding, 5,688,302 of which were owned by the minority. At the meeting only 56%, or 3,208,652, of the minority shares were voted. Of these, 2,953,812, or 51.9% of the total minority, voted for the merger, and 254,840 voted against it. When Signal's stock was added to the minority shares voting in favor, a total of 76.2% of UOP's outstanding shares approved the merger while only 2.2% opposed it.

By its terms the merger became effective on May 26, 1978, and each share of UOP's stock held by the minority was automatically converted into a right to receive $21 cash.

II.

A.

A primary issue mandating reversal is the preparation by two UOP directors, Arledge and Chitiea, of their feasibility study for the exclusive use and benefit of Signal. This document was of obvious significance to both Signal and UOP. Using UOP data, it described the advantages to Signal of ousting the minority at a price range of $21–$24 per share. Mr. Arledge, one of the authors, outlined the benefits to Signal:*

Purpose of the Merger

(1) Provides an outstanding investment opportunity for Signal—(Better than any recent acquisition we have seen.)

(2) Increases Signal's earnings.

(3) Facilitates the flow of resources between Signal and its subsidiaries—(Big factor—works both ways.)

(4) Provides cost savings potential for Signal and UOP.

(5) Improves the percentage of Signal's "operating earnings" as opposed to "holding company earnings".

(6) Simplifies the understanding of Signal.

(7) Facilitates technological exchange among Signal's subsidiaries.

(8) Eliminates potential conflicts of interest.

Having written those words, solely for the use of Signal, it is clear from the record that neither Arledge nor Chitiea shared this report with their fellow directors of UOP. We are satisfied that no one else did either. This conduct hardly meets the fiduciary standards applicable to such a transaction. While Mr. Walkup, Signal's chairman of the board and a UOP director, attended the March 6, 1978 UOP board meeting and testified at trial that he had discussed the Arledge–Chitiea report with the UOP directors at this meeting, the record does not support this assertion. Perhaps it is the result of some confusion on Mr. Walkup's part. In any event Mr. Shumway, Signal's president, testified that he made sure the Signal outside directors had this report prior to the March 6, 1978 Signal board meeting, but he did not testify that the Arledge–Chitiea report was also sent to UOP's outside directors.

Mr. Crawford, UOP's president, could not recall that any documents, other than a draft of the merger agreement, were sent to UOP's directors before the March 6, 1978 UOP meeting. Mr. Chitiea, an author of the report, testified that it was made available to Signal's directors, but to his knowledge it was not circulated to the outside directors of UOP. He specifically testified that he "didn't share" that information with the outside directors of UOP with whom he served.

* The parentheses indicate certain handwritten comments of Mr. Arledge.

None of UOP's outside directors who testified stated that they had seen this document. The minutes of the UOP board meeting do not identify the Arledge–Chitiea report as having been delivered to UOP's outside directors. This is particularly significant since the minutes describe in considerable detail the materials that actually were distributed. While these minutes recite Mr. Walkup's presentation of the Signal offer, they do not mention the Arledge–Chitiea report or any disclosure that Signal considered a price of up to $24 to be a good investment. If Mr. Walkup had in fact provided such important information to UOP's outside directors, it is logical to assume that these carefully drafted minutes would disclose it. The post-trial briefs of Signal and UOP contain a thorough description of the documents purportedly available to their boards at the March 6, 1978, meetings. Although the Arledge–Chitiea report is specifically identified as being available to the Signal directors, there is no mention of it being among the documents submitted to the UOP board. Even when queried at a prior oral argument before this Court, counsel for Signal did not claim that the Arledge–Chitiea report had been disclosed to UOP's outside directors. Instead, he chose to belittle its contents. This was the same approach taken before us at the last oral argument.

Actually, it appears that a three-page summary of figures was given to all UOP directors. Its first page is identical to one page of the Arledge–Chitiea report, but this dealt with nothing more than a justification of the $21 price. Significantly, the contents of this three-page summary are what the minutes reflect Mr. Walkup told the UOP board. However, nothing contained in either the minutes or this three-page summary reflects Signal's study regarding the $24 price.

The Arledge–Chitiea report speaks for itself in supporting the Chancellor's finding that a price of up to $24 was a "good investment" for Signal. It shows that a return on the investment at $21 would be 15.7% versus 15.5% at $24 per share. This was a difference of only two-tenths of one percent, while it meant over $17,000,000 to the minority. Under such circumstances, paying UOP's minority shareholders $24 would have had relatively little long-term effect on Signal, and the Chancellor's findings concerning the benefit to Signal, even at a price of $24, were obviously correct. . . .

Certainly, this was a matter of material significance to UOP and its shareholders. Since the study was prepared by two UOP directors, using UOP information for the exclusive benefit of Signal, and nothing whatever was done to disclose it to the outside UOP directors or the minority shareholders, a question of breach of fiduciary duty arises. This problem occurs because there were common Signal–UOP directors participating, at least to some extent, in the UOP board's decision-making processes without full disclosure of the conflicts they faced.[7]

---

7. Although perfection is not possible, or expected, the result here could have been entirely different if UOP had appointed an independent negotiating committee of its outside directors to deal with Signal at arm's length. See, e.g., Harriman v. E.I. du Pont De Nemours & Co., 411 F.Supp. 133 (D.Del.1975). Since fairness in this context can be equated to conduct

B.

In assessing this situation, the Court of Chancery was required to:

> examine what information defendants had and to measure it against what they gave to the minority stockholders, in a context in which "complete candor" is required. In other words, the limited function of the Court was to determine whether defendants had disclosed all information in their possession germane to the transaction in issue. And by "germane" we mean, for present purposes, information such as a reasonable shareholder would consider important in deciding whether to sell or retain stock.
>
> * * *
>
> ... Completeness, not adequacy, is both the norm and the mandate under present circumstances.

Lynch v. Vickers Energy Corp., Del.Supr., 383 A.2d 278, 281 (1977) (*Lynch I*). This is merely stating in another way the long-existing principle of Delaware law that these Signal designated directors on UOP's board still owed UOP and its shareholders an uncompromising duty of loyalty. The classic language of Guth v. Loft, Inc., Del.Supr., 5 A.2d 503, 510 (1939), requires no embellishment:

> A public policy, existing through the years, and derived from a profound knowledge of human characteristics and motives, has established a rule that demands of a corporate officer or director, peremptorily and inexorably, the most scrupulous observance of his duty, not only affirmatively to protect the interests of the corporation committed to his charge, but also to refrain from doing anything that would work injury to the corporation, or to deprive it of profit or advantage which his skill and ability might properly bring to it, or to enable it to make in the reasonable and lawful exercise of its powers. The rule that requires an undivided and unselfish loyalty to the corporation demands that there shall be no conflict between duty and self-interest.

Given the absence of any attempt to structure this transaction on an arm's length basis, Signal cannot escape the effects of the conflicts it faced, particularly when its designees on UOP's board did not totally abstain from participation in the matter. There is no "safe harbor" for such divided loyalties in Delaware. When directors of a Delaware corporation are on both sides of a transaction, they are required to demonstrate their utmost good faith and the most scrupulous inherent fairness of the bargain. Gottlieb v. Heyden Chemical Corp., Del.Supr., 91 A.2d 57, 57–58 (1952). The requirement of fairness is unflinching in its demand that where one stands on both sides of a transaction, he

---

by a theoretical, wholly independent, board of directors acting upon the matter before them, it is unfortunate that this course apparently was neither considered nor pursued. Johnston v. Greene, Del.Supr., 121 A.2d 919, 925 (1956). Particularly in a parent-subsidiary context, a showing that the action taken was as though each of the contending parties had in fact exerted its bargaining power against the other at arm's length is strong evidence that the transaction meets the test of fairness. Getty Oil Co. v. Skelly Oil Co., Del.Supr., 267 A.2d 883, 886 (1970); Puma v. Marriott, Del.Ch., 283 A.2d 693, 696 (1971).

has the burden of establishing its entire fairness, sufficient to pass the test of careful scrutiny by the courts. Sterling v. Mayflower Hotel Corp., Del.Supr., 93 A.2d 107, 110 (1952). . . .

There is no dilution of this obligation where one holds dual or multiple directorships, as in a parent-subsidiary context. Levien v. Sinclair Oil Corp., Del.Ch., 261 A.2d 911, 915 (1969). Thus, individuals who act in a dual capacity as directors of two corporations, one of whom is parent and the other subsidiary, owe the same duty of good management to both corporations, and in the absence of an independent negotiating structure (see note 7, supra), or the directors' total abstention from any participation in the matter, this duty is to be exercised in light of what is best for both companies. Warshaw v. Calhoun, Del.Supr., 221 A.2d 487, 492 (1966). The record demonstrates that Signal has not met this obligation.

C.

The concept of fairness has two basic aspects: fair dealing and fair price. The former embraces questions of when the transaction was timed, how it was initiated, structured, negotiated, disclosed to the directors, and how the approvals of the directors and the stockholders were obtained. The latter aspect of fairness relates to the economic and financial considerations of the proposed merger, including all relevant factors: assets, market value, earnings, future prospects, and any other elements that affect the intrinsic or inherent value of a company's stock. . . . However, the test for fairness is not a bifurcated one as between fair dealing and price. All aspects of the issue must be examined as a whole since the question is one of entire fairness. However, in a non-fraudulent transaction we recognize that price may be the preponderant consideration outweighing other features of the merger. Here, we address the two basic aspects of fairness separately because we find reversible error as to both.

D.

Part of fair dealing is the obvious duty of candor required by *Lynch I,* supra. Moreover, one possessing superior knowledge may not mislead any stockholder by use of corporate information to which the latter is not privy. Lank v. Steiner, Del.Supr., 224 A.2d 242, 244 (1966). Delaware has long imposed this duty even upon persons who are not corporate officers or directors, but who nonetheless are privy to matters of interest or significance to their company. Brophy v. Cities Service Co., Del.Ch., 70 A.2d 5, 7 (1949). With the well-established Delaware law on the subject, and the Court of Chancery's findings of fact here, it is inevitable that the obvious conflicts posed by Arledge and Chitiea's preparation of their "feasibility study", derived from UOP information, for the sole use and benefit of Signal, cannot pass muster.

The Arledge–Chitiea report is but one aspect of the element of fair dealing. How did this merger evolve? It is clear that it was entirely initiated by Signal. The serious time constraints under which the principals acted were all set by Signal. It had not found a suitable outlet for its excess cash and considered UOP a desirable investment, particularly since it was now in a position to acquire the whole company for itself. For whatever reasons, and they were only Signal's, the entire transaction was presented to and approved by UOP's board within four business days. Standing alone, this is not necessarily indicative of any lack of fairness by a majority shareholder. It was what occurred, or more properly, what did not occur, during this brief period that makes the time constraints imposed by Signal relevant to the issue of fairness.

The structure of the transaction, again, was Signal's doing. So far as negotiations were concerned, it is clear that they were modest at best. Crawford, Signal's man at UOP, never really talked price with Signal, except to accede to its management's statements on the subject, and to convey to Signal the UOP outside directors' view that as between the $20–$21 range under consideration, it would have to be $21. The latter is not a surprising outcome, but hardly arm's length negotiations. Only the protection of benefits for UOP's key employees and the issue of Lehman Brothers' fee approached any concept of bargaining.

As we have noted, the matter of disclosure to the UOP directors was wholly flawed by the conflicts of interest raised by the Arledge–Chitiea report. All of those conflicts were resolved by Signal in its own favor without divulging any aspect of them to UOP.

This cannot but undermine a conclusion that this merger meets any reasonable test of fairness. The outside UOP directors lacked one material piece of information generated by two of their colleagues, but shared only with Signal. True, the UOP board had the Lehman Brothers' fairness opinion, but that firm has been blamed by the plaintiff for the hurried task it performed, when more properly the responsibility for this lies with Signal. There was no disclosure of the circumstances surrounding the rather cursory preparation of the Lehman Brothers' fairness opinion. Instead, the impression was given UOP's minority that a careful study had been made, when in fact speed was the hallmark, and Mr. Glanville, Lehman's partner in charge of the matter, and also a UOP director, having spent the weekend in Vermont, brought a draft of the "fairness opinion letter" to the UOP directors' meeting on March 6, 1978 with the price left blank. We can only conclude from the record that the rush imposed on Lehman Brothers by Signal's timetable contributed to the difficulties under which this investment banking firm attempted to perform its responsibilities. Yet, none of this was disclosed to UOP's minority.

Finally, the minority stockholders were denied the critical information that Signal considered a price of $24 to be a good investment. Since this would have meant over $17,000,000 more to the minority, we cannot conclude that the shareholder vote was an informed one. Under the circumstances, an approval by a majority of the minority was meaningless. *Lynch I,* 383 A.2d at 279, 281; Cahall v. Lofland, Del.Ch., 114 A. 224 (1921).

Given these particulars and the Delaware law on the subject, the record does not establish that this transaction satisfies any reasonable concept of fair dealing, and the Chancellor's findings in that regard must be reversed.

E.

Turning to the matter of price, plaintiff also challenges its fairness. His evidence was that on the date the merger was approved the stock was worth at least $26 per share. In support, he offered the testimony of a chartered investment analyst who used two basic approaches to valuation: a comparative analysis of the premium paid over market in ten other tender offer-merger combinations, and a discounted cash flow analysis.

In this breach of fiduciary duty case, the Chancellor perceived that the approach to valuation was the same as that in an appraisal proceeding. Consistent with precedent, he rejected plaintiff's method of proof and accepted defendants' evidence of value as being in accord with practice under prior case law. This means that the so-called "Delaware block" or weighted average method was employed wherein the elements of value, i.e., assets, market price, earnings, etc., were assigned a particular weight and the resulting amounts added to determine the value per share. This procedure has been in use for decades. . . . However, to the extent it excludes other generally accepted techniques used in the financial community and the courts, it is not clearly outmoded. It is time we recognize this in appraisal and other stock valuation proceedings and bring our law current on the subject.

While the Chancellor rejected plaintiff's discounted cash flow method of valuing UOP's stock, as not corresponding with "either logic or the existing law," it is significant that this was essentially the focus, i.e., earnings potential of UOP, of Messrs. Arledge and Chitiea in their evaluation of the merger. Accordingly, the standard "Delaware block" or weighted average method of valuation . . . shall no longer exclusively control such proceedings. We believe that a more liberal approach must include proof of value by any technique or methods which are generally considered acceptable in the financial community and otherwise admissible in court, subject only to our interpretation of 8 Del. C. § 262(h) . . . .

It is significant that section 262 now mandates the determination of "fair" value based upon "all relevant factors." Only the speculative elements of value that may arise from the "accomplishment or expectation" of the merger are excluded. We take this to be a very narrow exception to the appraisal process, designed to eliminate use of *pro forma* data and projections of a speculative variety relating to the completion of a merger. But elements of future value, including the nature of the enterprise, which are known and susceptible of proof as of the date of the merger and not the product of speculation, may be considered. . . .

Although the Chancellor received the plaintiff's evidence, his opinion indicates that the use of it was precluded because of past

Delaware practice. While we do not suggest a monetary result one way or the other, we do think the plaintiff's evidence should be part of the factual mix and weighed as such. Until the $21 price is measured on remand by the valuation standards mandated by Delaware law, there can be no finding at the present stage of these proceedings that the price is fair. Given the lack of any candid disclosure of the material facts surrounding establishment of the $21 price, the majority of the minority vote, approving the merger, is meaningless.

The plaintiff has not sought an appraisal, but rescissory damages of the type contemplated by Lynch v. Vickers Energy Corp., Del.Supr., 429 A.2d 497, 505–06 (1981) (*Lynch II*). In view of the approach to valuation that we announce today, we see no basis in our law for *Lynch II*'s exclusive monetary formula for relief. On remand the plaintiff will be permitted to test the fairness of the $21 price by the standards we herein establish, in conformity with the principle applicable to an appraisal—that fair value be determined by taking into account all relevant factors [see 8 Del.C. § 262(h), supra]. In our view this includes the elements of rescissory damages if the Chancellor considers them susceptible of proof and a remedy appropriate to all the issues of fairness before him. To the extent that *Lynch II,* 429 A.2d at 505–06, purports to limit the Chancellor's discretion to a single remedial formula for monetary damages in a cash-out merger, it is overruled.

While a plaintiff's monetary remedy ordinarily should be confined to the more liberalized appraisal proceeding herein established, we do not intend any limitation on the historic powers of the Chancellor to grant such other relief as the facts of a particular case may dictate. The appraisal remedy we approve may not be adequate in certain cases, particularly where fraud, misrepresentation, self-dealing, deliberate waste of corporate assets, or gross and palpable overreaching are involved. Cole v. National Cash Credit Association, Del.Ch., 156 A. 183, 187 (1931). Under such circumstances, the Chancellor's powers are complete to fashion any form of equitable and monetary relief as may be appropriate, including rescissory damages. Since it is apparent that this long completed transaction is too involved to undo, and in view of the Chancellor's discretion, the award, if any, should be in the form of monetary damages based upon entire fairness standards, i.e., fair dealing and fair price. . . .

[The quasi-appraisal remedy provided in this decision applies to this case and other cases around the same time period as this case.] Thereafter, the provisions of 8 Del.C. § 262, as herein construed, respecting the scope of an appraisal and the means for perfecting the same, shall govern the financial remedy available to minority shareholders in a cash-out merger. Thus, we return to the well established principles of Stauffer v. Standard Brands, Inc., Del.Supr., 187 A.2d 78 (1962) and David J. Greene & Co. v. Schenley Industries, Inc., Del.Ch., 281 A.2d 30 (1971), mandating a stockholder's recourse to the basic remedy of an appraisal.

III.

Finally, we address the matter of business purpose.... The plaintiff says that no valid purpose existed—the entire transaction was a mere subterfuge designed to eliminate the minority....

The requirement of a business purpose is new to our law of mergers and was a departure from prior case law. See Stauffer v. Standard Brands, Inc., supra; David J. Greene & Co. v. Schenley Industries, Inc., supra.

In view of the fairness test which has long been applicable to parent-subsidiary mergers, Sterling v. Mayflower Hotel Corp., Del. Supr., 93 A.2d 107, 109–10 (1952), the expanded appraisal remedy now available to shareholders, and the broad discretion of the Chancellor to fashion such relief as the facts of a given case may dictate we do not believe that any additional meaningful protection is afforded minority shareholders by the business purpose requirement of the trilogy of *Singer, Tanzer,*[10] *Najjar,*[11] and their progeny. Accordingly, such requirement shall no longer be of any force or effect.

The judgment of the Court of Chancery, finding both the circumstances of the merger and the price paid the minority shareholders to be fair, is reversed. The matter is remanded for further proceedings consistent herewith. Upon remand the plaintiff's post-trial motion to enlarge the class should be granted.

* * *

Reversed and Remanded.

KAHN v. LYNCH COMMUNICATION SYSTEMS

Chapter 11, supra

NOTE ON SUBSTITUTES, OPPORTUNISM AND THE PURPOSE TEST

In a freezeout of minority shareholders in a publicly held corporation by a majority shareholder that is itself publicly held, it is at least arguable that (i) the expectations of the transferor corporation's shareholders are purely centered on a passive investment, which has ready financial substitutes; (ii) efficiency gains are likely to result from the combination, and (iii) the frozen-out minority shareholders "are free, if they wish, to restore their participation by purchasing [the survivor's] shares in the market. That a 'transaction' is required is simply a cost (possibly one that ought to be reimbursed) of using cash

---

10. Tanzer v. International General Industries, Inc., Del.Supr., 379 A.2d 1121, 1124–25 (1977).

11. Roland International Corp. v. Najjar, Del.Supr., 407 A.2d 1032, 1036 (1979).

or debt instead of stock [to effect the merger], but the exchange is nevertheless 'fair' if the amount received is sufficient to enable a recipient to obtain the same stock interest that he would have had if the parent had issued its shares in a ratio reflecting the premerger values of the companies." Brudney & Chirelstein, A Restatement of Corporate Freezeouts, 87 Yale L.J. 1354, 1374–75 (1978). This reasoning would not apply where the survivor is closely held, and several cases have struck down cash-out mergers frequently on the basis, rejected in *Weinberger*, that the transaction lacked a legitimate "purpose". Moreover, there is the ever-present concern that the particularly transaction is driven by insiders who have better knowledge than the non-insider holders regarding the firm's value, and future prospects. While Delaware subjects the transactions to scrutiny under the entire fairness standard, some courts examine the purpose surrounding the cash-out merger.

For example, Coggins v. New England Patriots Football Club, Inc., 397 Mass. 525, 492 N.E.2d 1112 (1986), involved the freezeout of the non-voting common stockholders by Michael H. Sullivan, Jr. who had recently acquired all the voting common for the New England Patriots using money borrowed from two banks. The banks' loans required him to pledge the voting shares as collateral for the loan and use his best efforts to reorganize the Patriots so that its income could be devoted to repayment of Sullivan's personal loans.

> "Unlike the Delaware court . . . we believe that the 'business-purpose' test is an additional useful means under our statutes and case law for examining a transaction in which a controlling stockholder eliminates the minority interest in a corporation. . . .
>
> A controlling stockholder who is also a director standing on both sides of the transaction bears the burden of showing that the transaction does not violate fiduciary obligations. . . .
>
> "Judicial scrutiny should begin with recognition of the basic principle that the duty of a corporate director must be to further the legitimate goals of the corporation. . . .
>
> The plaintiffs here adequately alleged that the merger of the Old Patriots and New Patriots was a freeze-out merger undertaken for no legitimate purpose, but merely for the personal benefit of Sullivan. While we recognize the right to "selfish ownership" in a corporation, such a right must be balanced against the concept of the majority stockholder's fiduciary obligation to the minority stockholders. *Wilkes v. Springside Nursing Home, Inc.*, 370 Mass. 842, 851 (1976). Consequently, the defendants bear the burden of proving, first, that the merger was for a legitimate business purpose, and second, that, considering the totality of the circumstances, it was fair to the minority.
>
> The decision of the Superior Court judge includes a finding that "the defendants have failed to demonstrate that the merger served any valid objective unrelated to the personal interests of the majority shareholders. It thus appears that the sole reason for

> the merger was to effectuate a restructuring of the Patriots that would enable the repayment of the [personal] indebtedness incurred by Sullivan."...

397 Mass. at 531, 533–535, 492 A.2d at 1117, 1118–1119. The court declared the merger freezeout invalid and remanded the case to award rescission damages to the objecting minority holders based on the then current value of the company.

New York similarly requires proof of a business purpose.

> "In the context of a freeze-out merger, variant treatment of the minority shareholders—i.e., causing their removal will be justified when related to the advancement of a general corporate interest. The benefit need not be great, but it must be for the corporation. For example, if the sole purpose of the merger is reduction of the number of profit sharers—in contrast to increasing the corporation's capital or profits, or improving its management structure—there will exist no 'independent corporate interest' (see Schwartz v. Marien, 37 N.Y.2d 487, 492, 373 N.Y.S.2d 122, 335 N.E.2d 334, supra). All of these purposes ultimately seek to increase the individual wealth of the remaining shareholders. What distinguishes a proper corporate purpose from an improper one is that, with the former, removal of the minority shareholders furthers the objective of conferring some general gain upon the corporation. Only then will the fiduciary duty of good and prudent management of the corporation serve to override the concurrent duty to treat all shareholders fairly (see Klurfeld v. Equity Enterprises, 79 A.D.2d 124, 136, 436 N.Y.S.2d 303, supra). We further note that a finding that there was an independent corporate purpose for the action taken by the majority will not be defeated merely by the fact that the corporate objective could have been accomplished in another way, or by the fact that the action chosen was not the best way to achieve the bona fide business objective."

Alpert v. 28 Williams St. Corp., 63 N.Y.2d 557, 573, 483 N.Y.S.2d 667, 676, 473 N.E.2d 19, 28 (1984) (finding the requisite purpose was established by evidence that that additional capital needed to repair the company's property was not available so long as the minority interest was outstanding).

Glassman v. Unocal Exploration Corp.

Supreme Court of Delaware, 2001.
777 A.2d 242.

■ Before VEASEY, CHIEF JUSTICE, WALSH, HOLLAND, BERGER and STEELE, JUSTICES, constituting the Court en Banc.

■ BERGER, JUSTICE.

In this appeal, we consider the fiduciary duties owed by a parent corporation to the subsidiary's minority stockholders in the context of a "short-form" merger. Specifically, we take this opportunity to reconcile a fiduciary's seemingly absolute duty to establish the entire fairness of any self-dealing transaction with the less demanding requirements of the short-form merger statute. The statute authorizes the elimination of minority stockholders by a summary process that does not involve the "fair dealing" component of entire fairness. Indeed, the statute does not contemplate any "dealing" at all. Thus, a parent corporation cannot satisfy the entire fairness standard if it follows the terms of the short-form merger statute without more.

Unocal Corporation addressed this dilemma by establishing a special negotiating committee and engaging in a process that it believed would pass muster under traditional entire fairness review. We find that such steps were unnecessary. . . .

I. Factual and Procedural Background . . .

[Unocal Corporation owned approximately 96% of the stock of Unocal Exploration (UXC). In December 1991 the boards of each company appointed special committees to consider a possible merger. UXC's special committee retained financial and legal advisors, met four times, and agreed to a merger exchange ratio where .54 Unocal shares would be issued for each UXC share. They announced their agreement on February 24, 1992 and carried it out pursuant to Delaware's short-form merger provision, 8 Del. § 253, on May 2, 1992. The plaintiffs filed a class action on behalf of the UXC minority holders alleging the merger violated *Weinberger's* entire fairness requirement.]

II. Discussion

The short-form merger statute, as enacted in 1937, authorized a parent corporation to merge with its wholly-owned subsidiary by filing and recording a certificate evidencing the parent's ownership and its merger resolution. In 1957, the statute was expanded to include parent/subsidiary mergers where the parent company owns at least 90% of the stock of the subsidiary. The 1957 amendment also made it possible, for the first time and only in a short-form merger, to pay the minority cash for their shares, thereby eliminating their ownership interest in the company. . . . [W]e must decide whether a minority stockholder may challenge a short-form merger by seeking equitable relief through an entire fairness claim. Under settled principles, a parent corporation and its directors undertaking a short-form merger are self-dealing fiduciaries who should be required to establish entire fairness, including fair dealing and fair price. The problem is that *§ 253* authorizes a summary procedure that is inconsistent with any reasonable notion of fair dealing. In a short-form merger, there is no agreement of merger negotiated by two companies; there is only a unilateral act—a decision by the parent company that its 90% owned subsidiary shall no longer exist as a separate entity. The minority stockholders receive no advance notice of the merger; their directors do not consider or approve it; and there is no vote. Those who object are given the right to obtain fair value for their shares through appraisal.

The equitable claim plainly conflicts with the statute. If a corporate fiduciary follows the truncated process authorized by *§ 253*, it will not be able to establish the fair dealing prong of entire fairness. If, instead, the corporate fiduciary sets up negotiating committees, hires independent financial and legal experts, etc., then it will have lost the very benefit provided by the statute—a simple, fast and inexpensive process for accomplishing a merger. We resolve this conflict by giving effect the intent of the General Assembly.[21] In order to serve its purpose, *§ 253* must be construed to obviate the requirement to establish entire fairness.

Thus, we . . . hold that, absent fraud or illegality, appraisal is the exclusive remedy available to a minority stockholder who objects to a short-form merger. In doing so, we also reaffirm *Weinberger's* statements about the scope of appraisal. The determination of fair value must be based on *all* relevant factors, including damages and elements of future value, where appropriate. So, for example, if the merger was timed to take advantage of a depressed market, or a low point in the company's cyclical earnings, or to precede an anticipated positive development, the appraised value may be adjusted to account for those factors. We recognize that these are the types of issues frequently raised in entire fairness claims, and we have held that claims for unfair dealing cannot be litigated in an appraisal.[22] But our prior holdings simply explained that equitable claims may not be engrafted onto a statutory appraisal proceeding; stockholders may not receive rescissionary relief in an appraisal. Those decisions should not be read to restrict the elements of value that properly may be considered in an appraisal.

Although fiduciaries are not required to establish entire fairness in a short-form merger, the duty of full disclosure remains, in the context of this request for stockholder action. Where the only choice for the minority stockholders is whether to accept the merger consideration or seek appraisal, they must be given all the factual information that is material to that decision. The Court of Chancery carefully considered plaintiffs' disclosure claims and applied settled law in rejecting them. We affirm this aspect of the appeal on the basis of the trial court's decision.

III. Conclusion

Based on the foregoing, we affirm the Court of Chancery and hold that plaintiffs' only remedy in connection with the short-form merger of UXC into Unocal was appraisal.

Solomon v. Pathe

Supreme Court of Delaware, 1996.
672 A.2d 35.

■ Before Holland, Hartnett, and Berger, JJ.

■ Hartnett, Justice. . . .

[Credit Lyonnais Banque Nederland NV (CLBN) pursuant to a loan agreement with Pathe Communications Corporation controlled

---

21. *Klotz v. Warner Communications, Inc.,* Del.Supr., 674 A.2d 878, 879 (1995).

22. *Alabama By-Products Corporation v. Neal, Del.Supr.,* 588 A.2d 255, 257 (1991).

89.5 percent of Pathe's voting stock. In response to CLBN's offer to make a tender offer for Pathe shares, Pathe created a special committee and supported CLBN's tender offer to acquire 5.8 million Pathe shares at $1.50 per share. John Solomon instituted a class action on behalf of the Pathe minority holders, alleging the tender offer was unfair, coercive, was a breach of the CLBN's duty of loyalty as a controlling stockholder and that the Pathe board had acted improperly by failing to obtain independent advisors to assess the tender offer.]

[The complaint] attempts to assert a breach of the duty of fair dealing by the directors because they did not oppose the tender offer. The asserted unfairness of the tender offer is based on its allegedly inadequate price. The Chancellor's holding that none of the facts cited by Solomon "can be said to arouse as much as a fleeting doubt of the fairness of the [disclosure] or the $1.50 tender offer" price is correct as a matter of law.

In the case of totally voluntary tender offers, as here, courts do not impose any right of the shareholders to receive a particular price.... Delaware law recognizes that, as to allegedly voluntary tender offers (in contrast to cash-out mergers), the determinative factor as to voluntariness is whether coercion is present, or whether there is "materially false or misleading disclosures made to shareholders in connection with the offer." *Eisenberg v. Chicago Milwaukee Corp.*, Del.Ch., 537 A.2d 1051, 1056 (1987) (citations omitted). A transaction may be considered involuntary, despite being voluntary in appearance and form, if one of these factors is present. *Id.* There is no well-plead allegation of any coercion or false or misleading disclosures in the present case, however.

Moreover, in the absence of coercion or disclosure violations, the adequacy of the price in a voluntary tender offer cannot be an issue. *Weinberger*, 457 A.2d at 703.... Solomon has plead no facts from which there could be drawn a reasonable inference that there was coercion or lack of complete disclosure. The amended complaint focuses mainly on a conclusory allegation that coercion was present. The complaint, therefore, falls well short of the minimum notice requirements. "Conclusions ... will not be accepted as true without specific allegations of fact to support them." ...

For the foregoing reasons, the Court of Chancery's dismissal of Solomon's claim under Rule 12(b)(6) for failure to state a claim upon which relief can be granted is AFFIRMED.

In re Pure Resources, Inc. Shareholder Litigation

Delaware Chancery Court, 2002.
808 A.2d 421.

■ STRINE, VICE-CHANCELLOR

[Unocal, which owned 65% of Pure Resources, made a tender offer for the remaining 35%. The tender offer included a non-waivable condition under which the offer would be effective only if a majority of the shares not owned by Unocal were tendered. Unocal's bid stated it intended to carry out a short-form merger at the same price if a majority of the minority Pure Resources shareholders tendered their shares. Shareholders in Pure Resources sought to enjoin the tender offer on the ground that the entire fairness standard was applicable to the transaction and argued that the transaction did not satisfy that standard because the tender-offer price was inadequate. Unocal replied that the entire fairness standard was inapplicable, because it applied only to negotiated transactions between a controlling shareholder and a controlled corporation, and Unocal had made a tender offer, rather than entering into a negotiated transaction. Accordingly, Unocal argued, under Solomon v. Pathe Communications, supra, Unocal was free to make the offer at whatever price it chose, so long Unocal did not (i) "structurally coerce" the Pure Resources minority by suggesting explicitly or implicitly that injurious events would occur to those shareholders who failed to tender; or (ii) mislead the Pure Resources minority into tendering by concealing or misstating material facts.]

This case ... involves an aspect of Delaware law fraught with doctrinal tension: what equitable standard of fiduciary conduct applies when a controlling shareholder seeks to acquire the rest of the company's shares? ...

In building the common law, judges ... cannot escape making normative choices, based on imperfect information about the world. This reality clearly pervades the area of corporate law implicated by this case. When a transaction to buy out the minority is proposed, is it more important to the development of strong capital markets to hold controlling stockholders and target boards to very strict (and litigation-intensive) standards of fiduciary conduct? Or is more stockholder wealth generated if less rigorous protections are adopted, which permit acquisitions to proceed so long as the majority has not misled or strong-armed the minority? Is such flexibility in fact beneficial to minority stockholders because it encourages liquidity-generating tender offers to them and provides incentives for acquirers to pay hefty premiums to buy control, knowing that control will be accompanied by legal rules that permit a later "going private" transaction to occur in a relatively non-litigious manner?

At present, the Delaware case law has two strands of authority that answer these questions differently. In one strand, which deals with situations in which controlling stockholders negotiate a merger agreement with the target board to buy out the minority, our decisional law emphasizes the protection of minority stockholders against unfairness. In the other strand, which deals with situations when a controlling stockholder seeks to acquire the rest of the company's shares through a tender offer followed by a short-form merger under 8 Del.C. § 253,

Delaware case precedent facilitates the free flow of capital between willing buyers and willing sellers of shares, so long as the consent of the sellers is not procured by inadequate or misleading information or by wrongful compulsion.

These strands appear to treat economically similar transactions as categorically different simply because the method by which the controlling stockholder proceeds varies. This disparity in treatment persists even though the two basic methods (negotiated merger versus tender offer/short-form merger) pose similar threats to minority stockholders. Indeed, it can be argued that the distinction in approach subjects the transaction that is more protective of minority stockholders when implemented with appropriate protective devices—a merger negotiated by an independent committee with the power to say no and conditioned on a majority of the minority vote—to more stringent review than the more dangerous form of a going private deal—an unnegotiated tender offer made by a majority stockholder. The latter transaction is arguably less protective than a merger of the kind described, because the majority stockholder-offeror has access to inside information, and the offer requires disaggregated stockholders to decide whether to tender quickly, pressured by the risk of being squeezed out in a short-form merger at a different price later or being left as part of a much smaller public minority. This disparity creates a possible incoherence in our law. . . .

To illustrate this possible incoherence in our law, it is useful to sketch out these two strands. I begin with negotiated mergers. In *Kahn v. Lynch Communication Systems, Inc.*, the Delaware Supreme Court addressed the standard of review that applies when a controlling stockholder attempts to acquire the rest of the corporation's shares in a negotiated merger pursuant to 8 Del.C. § 251. The Court held that the stringent entire fairness form of review governed regardless of whether: i) the target board was comprised of a majority of independent directors; ii) a special committee of the target's independent directors was empowered to negotiate and veto the merger; and iii) the merger was made subject to approval by a majority of the disinterested target stockholders. . . .

The second strand of cases involves tender offers made by controlling stockholders—i.e., the kind of transaction Unocal has proposed. The prototypical transaction addressed by this strand involves a tender offer by the controlling stockholder addressed to the minority stockholders. In that offer, the controlling stockholder promises to buy as many shares as the minority will sell but may subject its offer to certain conditions. For example, the controlling stockholder might condition the offer on receiving enough tenders for it to obtain 90% of the subsidiary's shares, thereby enabling the controlling stockholder to consummate a short-form merger under 8 Del.C. § 253 at either the same or a different price....

Before *Glassman*, transactional planners had wondered whether the back-end of the tender offer/short-form merger transaction would subject the controlling stockholder to entire fairness review. *Glassman* seemed to answer that question favorably from the standpoint of controlling stockholders, and to therefore encourage the tender offer/short-form merger form of acquisition as presenting a materially less troublesome method of proceeding than a negotiated merger.

Why? Because the legal rules that governed the front end of the tender offer/short-form merger method of acquisition had already provided a more flexible, less litigious path to acquisition for controlling stockholders than the negotiated merger route. Tender offers are not addressed by the Delaware General Corporation Law ("DGCL"), a factor that has been of great importance in shaping the line of decisional law addressing tender offers by controlling stockholders—but not, as I will discuss, tender offers made by third parties.

Because no consent or involvement of the target board is statutorily mandated for tender offers, our courts have recognized that "[i]n the case of totally voluntary tender offers ... courts do not impose any right of the shareholders to receive a particular price. Delaware law recognizes that, as to allegedly voluntary tender offers (in contrast to cash-out mergers), the determinative factors as to voluntariness are whether coercion is present, or whether there are materially false or misleading disclosures made to stockholders in connection with the offer.[28]" ...

The differences between this approach, which I will identify with the *Solomon* line of cases, and that of *Lynch* are stark. To begin with, the controlling stockholder is said to have no duty to pay a fair price, irrespective of its power over the subsidiary. Even more striking is the different manner in which the coercion concept is deployed. In the tender offer context addressed by *Solomon* and its progeny, coercion is defined in the more traditional sense as a wrongful threat that has the effect of forcing stockholders to tender at the wrong price to avoid an even worse fate later on, a type of coercion I will call structural coercion. The inherent coercion that *Lynch* found to exist when controlling stockholders seek to acquire the minority's stake is not even a cognizable concern for the common law of corporations if the tender offer method is employed.

This latter point is illustrated by those cases that squarely hold that a tender is not actionably coercive if the majority stockholder decides to: (i) condition the closing of the tender offer on support of a majority of the minority and (ii) promise that it would consummate a

---

28. *Solomon v. Pathe Communications Corp.*, 672 A.2d 35, 39 (Del.1996) (citations and quotations omitted).

short-form merger on the same terms as the tender offer. In those circumstances, at least, these cases can be read to bar a claim against the majority stockholder even if the price offered is below what would be considered fair in an entire fairness hearing ("fair price") or an appraisal action ("fair value"). That is, in the tender offer context, our courts consider it sufficient protection against coercion to give effective veto power over the offer to a majority of the minority. Yet that very same protection is considered insufficient to displace fairness review in the negotiated merger context. . . .

The problem is that nothing about the tender offer method of corporate acquisition makes the 800 pound gorilla's retributive capabilities less daunting to minority stockholders. Indeed, many commentators would argue that the tender offer form is more coercive than a merger vote. In a merger vote, stockholders can vote no and still receive the transactional consideration if the merger prevails. In a tender offer, however, a non-tendering shareholder individually faces an uncertain fate. That stockholder could be one of the few who holds out, leaving herself in an even more thinly traded stock with little hope of liquidity and subject to a § 253 merger at a lower price or at the same price but at a later (and, given the time value of money, a less valuable) time. The 14D–9 warned Pure's minority stockholders of just this possibility. For these reasons, some view tender offers as creating a prisoner's dilemma—distorting choice and creating incentives for stockholders to tender into offers that they believe are inadequate in order to avoid a worse fate. But whether or not one views tender offers as more coercive of shareholder choice than negotiated mergers with controlling stockholders, it is difficult to argue that tender offers are materially freer and more reliable measures of stockholder sentiment. . . .

. . . [T]he preferable policy choice is to continue to adhere to the more flexible and less constraining *Solomon* approach, while giving some greater recognition to the inherent coercion and structural bias concerns that motivate the *Lynch* line of cases. Adherence to the *Solomon* rubric as a general matter, moreover, is advisable in view of the increased activism of institutional investors and the greater information flows available to them. Investors have demonstrated themselves capable of resisting tender offers made by controlling stockholders on occasion, and even the lead plaintiff here expresses no fear of retribution. This does not mean that controlling stockholder tender offers do not pose risks to minority stockholders; it is only to acknowledge that the corporate law should not be designed on the assumption that diversified investors are infirm but instead should give great deference to transactions approved by them voluntarily and knowledgeably. . . .

The potential for coercion and unfairness posed by controlling stockholders who seek to acquire the balance of the company's shares by acquisition requires some equitable reinforcement, in order to give proper effect to the concerns undergirding *Lynch*. In order to address the prisoner's dilemma problem, our law should consider an acquisition tender offer by a controlling stockholder non-coercive only when: 1) it is subject to a non-waivable majority of the minority tender condition; 2) the controlling stockholder promises to consummate a prompt § 253 merger at the same price if it obtains more than 90% of the shares; and 3) the controlling stockholder has made no retributive threats. Those protections . . . minimize the distorting influence of the tendering process on voluntary choice. They also recognize the adverse conditions that confront stockholders who find themselves owning what have become very thinly traded shares. These conditions also provide a partial cure to the disaggregation problem, by providing a realistic non-tendering goal the minority can achieve to prevent the offer from proceeding altogether.

The informational and timing advantages possessed by controlling stockholders also require some countervailing protection if the minority is to truly be afforded the opportunity to make an informed, voluntary tender decision. In this regard, the majority stockholder owes a duty to permit the independent directors on the target board both free rein and adequate time to react to the tender offer, by (at the very least) hiring their own advisors, providing the minority with a recommendation as to the advisability of the offer, and disclosing adequate information for the minority to make an informed judgment. For their part, the independent directors have a duty to undertake these tasks in good faith and diligently, and to pursue the best interests of the minority. . . .

Turning specifically to Unocal's Offer, I conclude that the application of these principles yields the following result. The Offer, in its present form, is coercive because it includes within the definition of the "minority" those stockholders who are affiliated with Unocal as directors and officers. It also includes the management of Pure, whose incentives are skewed by their employment, their severance agreements [which gave the managers the right to severance payments, up to three times their annual salaries and bonuses, upon successful completion of the tender offer], and their Put Agreements [which give the managers the right to sell their Pure shares to Unocal upon the occurrence of certain events, arguably including the successful completion of Unocal's tender offer, at an amount that could exceed the tender-offer price]. This is, of course, a problem that can be cured if Unocal amends the Offer to condition it on approval of a majority of Pure's unaffiliated stockholders. Requiring the minority to be defined exclusive of stockholders whose independence from the controlling stockholder is compromised is the better legal rule (and result). Too often, it will be the case that officers and directors of controlled subsidiaries have voting incentives that are not perfectly aligned with their economic interest in their stock and who are more than acceptably susceptible to influence from controlling stockholders. Aside, however, from this glitch in the majority of the minority condition, I conclude that Unocal's Offer satisfies the other requirements of "non-coerciveness." Its promise to consummate a prompt § 253 merger is sufficiently specific, and Unocal has made no retributive threats....

For all these reasons, therefore, I find that the plaintiffs do not have a probability of success on the merits of their attack on the Offer, with the exception that the majority of the minority condition is flawed....

NOTE ON "GOING DARK"

Weinberger illustrates a "going private" transaction. In the close corporation setting the more pejorative expressions of "freeze out" and "squeeze out" are used to describe the same result as occurs in "going private" transactions, namely the dominant stockholder undertaking a transaction or series of transactions with the objective of eliminating the minority stockholders. A related but not identical objective is "going dark." This expression refers to a process through which a *public* company reduces the number of public stockholders below 300 so that it no longer is required to file periodic reports with the SEC, i.e., it ceases to be an Exchange Act reporting company. Exchange Act Rule 12g–3 lifts the periodic reporting requirements for any class of security that is held by less than 300 persons. Thus, in a going dark transaction the objective is not necessarily to eliminate all minority holders, but just enough of them to reduce the number of owners to below 300.

With the passage of the Sarbanes–Oxley Act of 2002 (SOX), there has been a good deal of interest in whether the Act's strengthening the financial reporting requirements for public companies is causally connected to a post–2002 upward trend in the number of firms going dark. SOX-imposed regulations significantly increased the costs of being a public company so that firms, reassessing the costs and benefits of being a public company, would in a post-SOX era face a very different calculus and could, therefore, find better to be a non-reporting company than a reporting one. *See* William Carney, The Costs of Being Public After Sarbanes–Oxley: The Irony of "Going Private," 55 Emory L.J. 141 (2006). Since reporting costs generally have high fixed cost components, meaning they dwindle in relative importance as a firm gets larger (in assets and revenues), reporting costs appear to be a major consideration in going dark for small firms rather than medium-or large-sized firms. Robert P. Bartlett III, Going Private but Staying Public: Reexamining the Effect of Sarbanes–Oxley on Firm's Going-private Decisions, 76 U. Chi. L. Rev. 7, 37–38 (2009); Ehud Kamar, Pinar Karaca–Mandic, & Eric Talley, Going-private Decisions and the Sarbanes–Oxley Act of 2002: A Cross-country Analysis, 25 J. L. Econ. & Org., 107, 130 (2009) ("exodus of small firms from the public capital market" due to SOX-related reporting costs may be socially desirable if those firms are more prone to engage in fraud). Moreover, firms are more likely to go dark if they have fewer growth opportunities, a larger percentage of their shares owned by managers, and significant free cash flows. Andras Marosi & Nadia Massoud, Why Do Firms Go Dark?, 42 J. Fin. & Quantitative Analysis 421, 440 (2007) (gathering data that supports conclusion that going dark enables insiders to exploit future information asymmetries to capture the benefits of the firm's future free cash flow). The empirical evidence is a bit more scattered on the question of whether SOX precipitated an increase in going private transactions. To be sure, there is evidence that size appears related to the likelihood of going private, thus supporting the thesis that higher reporting costs introduced by SOX drove companies into the shadows. *See* Ellen Engel, Rachel M. Hayes & Xue Wang, The Sarbanes–Oxley Act and Firms' Going-private Decisions, 44 J. Accounting & Econ. 116, 143 (2007) (frequency of going private increased after SOX and was more common for smaller firms with high insider ownership); Christian Leuz, Was the Sarbanes–Oxley Act Really this Costly? A Discussion of Evidence from Event Returns and Going–Private Decisions, 44 J. Accounting & Econ. 146, 159 (2007) (going private more common among smaller firms, with weaker performance and poorer internal governance). However, comparison with the size and frequency of companies going dark in the U.S. with the U.K. reflects similar trends in size and frequency of going private transactions on both sides of the Atlantic. Leuz, *supra*, at 162. Finally, it should be remembered that the post-SOX era was the heyday of the private equity firms that exploited the availability of historically low interest rates that enabled them to take companies private via leveraged buyouts. Thus, the decision to go dark or private is likely a complex one, but one that is initiated by the firm's managers.

Securities Exchange Act Rule 13e–3 imposes significant disclosure requirements for certain going dark/private transactions. In broad overview, Rule 13e–3 applies to transactions that are either with the issuer of the security or a person that controls the issuer which transaction causes a class of the issuer's stock to cease to be listed on an exchange or will reduce the numbers of holders of that class of stock below 300 (i.e., the firm goes dark). The transaction producing either of these effects can be via a purchase, merger, reverse stock dividend, tender offer or recapitalization. If this occurs, within 20 days of the shares' acquisition, extensive disclosures called for by Schedule 13E–3 must be provided. For example, Item 8 of the form not only requires the directors to express their opinion regarding the transaction's fairness, but calls for a detailed discussion of the "material factors upon which the belief" is based. Courts have recognized an implied right of action for misrepresentations committed in 13e–3 transactions. *See* Howing v. Nationwide Corp., 826 F.2d 1470 (6th Cir. 1987), *cert. denied*, 486 U.S. 1059, 108 S.Ct. 2830, 100 L.Ed.2d 930 (1988). Several exemptions to Rule 13e–3 exist, the most significant are: 1) the transaction is the second step of a preannounced two-step acquisition, provided the consideration is at least equal to that offered in the earlier tender offer, the second step occurs within one year of the tender offer, and the earlier tender offer fully disclosed the intent to undertake the second step acquisition; 2) the transaction provides that the issuer's security holders receive only an equity security that has substantially the same rights as the equity security given up and is registered under the Exchange Act; or 3) the security's redemption, call or other acquisition is pursuant to the rights set forth in the articles of incorporation or other instrument setting forth rights, privileges or preferences of the security.

SECURITIES EXCHANGE ACT RULE 13e–3 AND SCHEDULE 13E–3

[See Statutory Supplement]

SECTION 2. HOSTILE TAKEOVERS AND DEFENDING CONTROL

SECURITIES EXCHANGE ACT §§ 13(d), (e), 14(d), (e)

[See Statutory Supplement]

SECURITIES EXCHANGE ACT RULES 13d–1, 13d–3, 13d–5, 13e–1, 13e–4, 14d1 TO 14d–4, 14d–6 TO 14d–10, 14e–1 TO 14e–3, 14e–5

SCHEDULE TO

[See Statutory Supplement]

SCHEDULE [I4D–9]

[See Statutory Supplement]

HART–SCOTT–RODINO ACT

[See Statutory Supplement]

THE LEXICON OF THE BATTLE FOR CONTROL

The legal profession has developed a rich terminology in connection with tender offers. The terms are too numerous and change too quickly to permit a comprehensive glossary, and some of the terms are fairly well defined in the cases that follow. This Note defines a few of the more important terms that are not defined in those cases.

Raider. The term *raider* refers to a person (normally, although not necessarily, a corporation) that makes a tender offer. The term is invidious; a more accurate term is *bidder.*

Target. The corporation whose shares the raider or bidder seeks to acquire is referred to as the *target.*

White knight. Often the management of a target realizes that it will be taken over, but prefers a takeover by someone (sometimes, anyone) other than the original bidder. The management therefore solicits competing tender offers from other corporations. These more friendly corporations are known as *white knights.*

Lock-up. A *lock-up* is a device that is designed to protect one bidder (normally, a friendly bidder or white knight) against competition by other bidders (deemed less friendly). The favored bidder is given an option to acquire selected assets, or a given amount of shares, of the target at a favorable price under designated conditions. These conditions usually involve either defeat of the favored bidder's attempt to acquire the corporation, or the occurrence of events that would make that defeat likely.

Crown jewels. To defeat or discourage a takeover bid by a disfavored bidder, the target's management may sell or (more usually) give to a white knight a lock-up option that covers the target's most desirable business or, at least, the business most coveted by the disfavored bidder—its *crown jewels.*

Fair-price provisions. A *fair-price provision* requires that a supermajority (usually eighty percent) of the voting power of a corporation must approve any merger or similar combination with an acquiror who owns a specified interest in the corporation (usually twenty percent of the voting power). The supermajority vote is not required under certain conditions—most notably, if the transaction is approved by a majority of those directors who are not affiliated with the acquiror and who were directors at the time the acquiror reached the specified level of ownership of the company, or if certain minimum-price criteria and procedural requirements are satisfied. A fair-price provision discourages purchasers whose objective is to seek control of a corporation at a relatively cheap price, and discourages accumulations of large blocks, because it reduces the options that an acquiror has once it reaches the specified level of shares.

Management buyout. A *management buyout* (*MBO*) is an acquisition for cash or non-convertible senior securities of the business of a public corporation, by a newly organized corporation in which members of the former management of the public corporation will have a significant equity interest, pursuant to a merger or other form of combination. See Lowenstein, Management Buyouts, 85 Colum.L.Rev. 730, 732 (1985).

Leverage. *Leverage* involves the use of debt to increase the return on equity. The extent of leverage is measured by the ratio of debt to equity. The higher the ratio, the greater the leverage (or, to put it differently, the more highly leveraged the corporation is).

Leveraged buyout. A *leveraged buyout* (LBO) is a buyout that is highly leveraged—that is, in which the newly organized acquiring corporation has a very high amount of debt in relation to its equity. Characteristically, an LBO is arranged by a firm that specializes in such transactions; can find investors (or will itself invest) that frequently include the former senior management in the new firm's securities; and can arrange for (or help arrange for) placement of the massive amount of debt that the new corporation must issue to finance the acquisition of the old corporation's business.

Junk bonds. A *junk bond* is a bond that has an unusually high risk of default (and is therefore below investment grade), but correspondingly carries an unusually high yield. (The theory is that by diversification—that is, by holding a portfolio of junk bonds—investors in junk bonds can insulate themselves from catastrophic loss if any one bond issue goes under.) Because an LBO is so highly leveraged, much or most of the debt issued to finance an LBO usually consists of junk bonds.

No-shop clauses. A board of a corporation that enters into an agreement for a merger or other corporate combination (whether with a white knight or otherwise) may agree that it will recommend the combination to its shareholders, that it will not shop around for a more attractive deal, or both.

Poison pills. In essence, a *poison pill* (also known as a *Rights Plan* or a *Shareholder Rights Plan*) is a plan under which the board of directors of a corporation creates Rights that are distributed or distributable to shareholders. Under the Rights, upon the occurrence of certain events shareholders *other than a tender-offer bidder or prospective bidder* have the right to purchase stock in the corporation, or under certain circumstances in an acquiror, at a deep discount—normally, half-price. Because the potential exercise of the Rights would dramatically dilute the value of the target stock that the bidder proposes to acquire, the mere potential that the Rights will be exercised may serve as a deterrent to making a bid in the first place (although for reasons that will be explored in the materials that follow, a pill is usually not a complete show-stopper).

The actual mechanics of pills are highly complex, and have evolved over time. Here is a description of a fairly standard modern version of the pill, taken from Carmody v. Toll Brothers, Inc., 723 A.2d 1180 (Del.Ch. 1998). The corporation whose pill is described was named Toll Brothers:

The Rights Plan would operate as follows: there would be a dividend distribution of one preferred stock purchase right (a "Right") for each outstanding share of common stock as of July 11, 1997. Initially the Rights would attach to the company's outstanding common shares, and each Right would initially entitle the holder to purchase one thousandth of a share of a newly registered series Junior A Preferred Stock for $100. The Rights would become exercisable, and would trade separately from the common shares, after the "Distribution Date," which is defined as the earlier of (a) ten business days following a public announcement that an acquiror has acquired, or obtained the right to acquire, beneficial ownership of 15% or more of the company's outstanding common shares (the "Stock Acquisition Date"), or (b) ten business days after the commencement of a tender offer or exchange offer that would result in a person or group beneficially owning 15% or more of the company's outstanding common shares. Once exercisable, the Rights remain exercisable until their Final Expiration Date (June 12, 2007, ten years after the adoption of the Plan), unless the Rights are earlier redeemed by the company.

The dilutive mechanism of the Rights is "triggered" by certain defined events. One such event is the acquisition of 15% or more of Toll Brothers' stock by any person or group of affiliated or associated persons. Should that occur, each Rights holder (except the acquiror and its affiliates and associates) becomes entitled to buy two shares of Toll Brothers common stock or other securities at half price. That is, the value of the stock received when the Right is exercised is equal to two times the exercise price of the Right. In that manner, this so-called "flip in" feature of the Rights Plan would massively dilute the value of the holdings of the unwanted acquiror. . . .

The "flip-in" feature of a rights plan is triggered when the acquiror crosses the specified ownership threshold, regardless of the acquiror's intentions with respect to the use of the shares. At that point, rights vest in all shareholders other than the acquiror, and as a result, those holders become entitled to acquire additional shares of voting stock at a substantially discounted price, usually 50% of the market price. Commonly, rights plans also contain a "flip-over" feature entitling target company shareholders (again, other than the acquiror) to purchase shares of the acquiring company at a reduced price. That feature is activated when, after a "flip-in" triggering event, the acquiror initiates a triggering event, such as a merger, self-dealing transaction, or sale of assets. . . .

The Rights [in the case at bar] have a standard "flip over" feature, which is triggered if after the Stock Acquisition Date, the company is made a party to a merger in which Toll Brothers is not the surviving corporation, or in which it is the surviving corporation and its common stock is changed or exchanged. In either

> event, each Rights holder becomes entitled to purchase common stock of the acquiring company, again at half-price, thereby impairing the acquiror's capital structure and drastically diluting the interest of the acquiror's other stockholders.

Id. at 1183–84 n.5.

A flip-over pill is normally triggered only by a corporate combination between the bidder and the target following the initial tender offer. The effect of a flip-over pill may therefore be moderated where the bidder's business plan allows it to forgo such a merger. A flip-in pill is much more wide-ranging in its applicability, but usually the Rights issued under such a pill can be redeemed by the target's board for a nominal consideration at any time before a triggering event and, often, for a brief period thereafter.

Standstill. A target may seek an accommodation with a shareholder who has acquired a significant amount of stock, under which the shareholder agrees to limit his stock purchases—hence, *standstill.* In the typical standstill agreement, the shareholder makes one or more commitments: (i) it will not increase its shareholdings above designated limits for a specified period of time; (ii) it will not sell its shares without giving the corporation a right of first refusal; (iii) it will not engage in a proxy contest; and (iv) it will vote its stock in a designated manner in the election of directors, and perhaps on other issues. In return, the corporation may agree to give the shareholder board representation, to register the shareholder's stock under the Securities Act on demand, and to not oppose the shareholder's acquisition of more stock up to the specified limit.

NOTE ON THE WILLIAMS ACT

Tender offers, and the initial or *toehold* share acquisitions by the bidder that often precede them, are regulated in a great number of respects by the Williams Act, which added sections 13(d) and (e), and 14(d), (e), and (f), to the Securities Exchange Act. Section 14(d), and Rule 14d thereunder, apply to tender offers for more than 5% of any class of equity security that is registered under Section 12 of the Act. In contrast, section 14(e), and Rule 14e thereunder, apply to any tender offer for any class of security. Accordingly, in theory section 14(e) and Rule 14e cover more tender offers than section 14(d) and Rule 14d. In practice, however, most tender offers will be covered by both sections and both rules. For ease of exposition, in the balance of this Note all references to tender offers will mean tender offers that are covered by the relevant sections and rules, unless otherwise stated.

1. *Early Warning.* Under section 13(d) of the Securities Exchange Act, a person who has acquired beneficial ownership of more than 5% of any class of equity securities registered under section 12 of the Act must file a Schedule 13D within 10 days of the acquisition. The Dodd–Frank Wall Street Reform and Consumer Protection Act of 2010

amended section 13(d) to authorizes the SEC to shorten the filing time. Schedule 13D requires extensive disclosure including the purchaser's identity and background; the amount and sources of the funds for the purchase; the purpose of the purchase; any plans with respect to extraordinary corporate transactions involving the corporation whose stock has been acquired; and any contracts, arrangements, or understandings with other persons regarding the corporation's securities. Under Rule 13d–2, any material changes in the information disclosed in a Schedule 13D must be promptly updated, and any further acquisitions of an additional 1% or more of the corporation's stock will be deemed a material change thereby obligating the filer to update an earlier report of its holdings. Even further acquisitions of less than 1% of the corporation's stock may be deemed material, depending on the circumstances. Rule 13d–1(b) provides a more abbreviated disclosure regime for so-called "passive" investors, defined as one who acquired the stock in the ordinary course of business without the intent to change or influence the control of the issuer and whose ownership does not exceed a 10 percent threshold. Such passive owners file annually on Schedule 13G; a passive owner who changes her intent to a "control purpose" must file a Schedule 13D and is precluded from acquiring more shares until ten days after such filing.

Furthermore, under section 13(d)(3) of the Securities Exchange Act, as implemented by Rule 13d–5(b), when two or more persons agree to act together for the purpose of acquiring, holding, voting, or disposing of an issuer's equity securities, the group formed by the agreement is deemed to have acquired ownership of all securities of that issuer owned by any member of the group, for purposes of section 13(d). Even acting in concert may create a group for these purposes.

Wholly aside from the Williams Act, the Hart–Scott–Rodino Antitrust Improvements Act of 1976 requires notification of acquisitions of stock in medium-size and large publicly held companies. There are essentially two tests, either of which can require notice of the acquisition to be given; the dollar levels for the tests are set annually by the Federal Trade Commission (the following were the levels established in January 2010). First, notice must be filed for any acquisition that results in the acquiring company holding assets or voting stock of the acquired company in excess of $253.7 million. If the acquisition is smaller than this level, then no filing is required, unless the acquisition exceeds both a "size-of-transaction threshold" and a "size-of-person" threshold. The size of transaction threshold is $63.4 million and the size of person threshold is met because either the acquiring or acquired firm has annual sales or total assets of at least $126.9 million *and* the other party has annual sales or total assets of $12.7 million. For many corporations that are likely to be made subject to a tender offer, the applicable thresholds will be substantially less than 5% of its stock. Thus Hart–Scott–Rodino effectively lowers the reporting threshold for many toehold acquisitions.

2. *What Constitutes a Tender Offer.* What constitutes a "tender offer" within the meaning of the Williams Act is not completely settled. To provide flexibility to reach unconventional tender offers and takeover measures, Congress did not provide a definition of this "gateway" concept. At one extreme, a public offer, made by a bidder to all shareholders, to purchase, at a fixed stated price, shares that are tendered into the offer during a stated period of time, will almost certainly be deemed a tender offer within the meaning of the Williams Act. At the other extreme, purchases that a buyer makes anonymously in the stock market will almost certainly not be deemed a tender offer within the meaning of the Act. Kennecott Copper Corp. v. Curtiss–Wright Corp., 584 F.2d 1195 (2d Cir.1978); Calumet Industries, Inc. v. MacClure, 464 F.Supp. 19 (N.D.Ill.1978). The problem concerns transactions that fall between these two extremes, such as a series of private offers made to a limited number of potential sellers. Some courts have adopted an eight-factor test to determine whether offers like this are tender offers under the Act. These factors are: (i) Whether the purchasers engage in active and widespread solicitation of public shareholders. (ii) Whether the solicitation is made for a substantial percentage of the corporation's stock. (iii) Whether the offer to purchase is made at a premium over the prevailing market price. (iv) Whether the terms of the offer are firm rather than negotiable. (v) Whether the offer is contingent on the tender of a fixed number of shares. (vi) Whether the offer is open only for a limited person of time. (vii) Whether the offerees are under pressure to sell their stock. (viii) Whether public announcements of a purchasing program preceded or accompanied a rapid accumulation of large amounts of the corporation's stock. Wellman v. Dickinson, 475 F.Supp. 783 (S.D.N.Y.1979), aff'd on other grounds 682 F.2d 355 (2d Cir.1982), cert. denied 460 U.S. 1069, 103 S.Ct. 1522, 75 L.Ed.2d 946 (1983); SEC v. Carter Hawley Hale Stores, Inc., 760 F.2d 945 (9th Cir.1985). More generally, in determining whether there is a tender offer courts tend to focus on the pressure an offer or conduct places on shareholders as well as the sophistication of the shareholders and, therefore, there susceptibility to pressure.

In Hanson Trust PLC v. SCM Corp., 774 F.2d 47 (2d Cir.1985), the Second Circuit rejected the eight-factor test, and held instead that whether an offer to buy stock constitutes a tender offer under the Williams Act turns on whether there appears to be a likelihood, that unless the Act's rules are followed, there will be a substantial risk that solicited shareholders will lack information needed to make a carefully considered appraisal of the offer. Applying that standard, the Second Circuit held in *Hanson* that the offer before it was not a tender offer. The target had 22,800 shareholders and offers were made to only six. At least five of the sellers were highly sophisticated professionals, knowledgeable in the market place and well aware of the essential facts needed to exercise their professional skills and to appraise the offer. The sellers were not pressured to sell their shares by any conduct that the Williams Act was designed to alleviate, but only by the forces of the marketplace. There was no active or widespread advance publicity or public solicitation. The price received by the six sellers was not at a premium over the then-market price. The purchases were not made contingent upon acquiring a fixed minimum number or percentage of the target's outstanding shares. There was no time limit within which the buyer would purchase the target's stock.

3. *Schedule TO.* Section 14(d) of the Securities Exchange Act requires a schedule TO to be filed by any person who makes a tender offer for a class of registered equity securities that would result in that person owning more than 5% of the class. The Schedule TO must contain extensive disclosure of such matters as the offer; the identity of the bidder; past dealings between the bidder and the target corporation; the bidder's source of funds; the bidder's purposes and plans concerning the target; the bidder's contracts and understandings or relationships with respect to securities of the target; financial statements of the bidder, if they are material and the bidder is not an individual; and arrangements between the bidder and persons holding important positions with the target.

4. *Regulation of the Terms of Tender Offers.* Section 14(d) of the Securities Exchange Act, and Rules 14d and 14e, regulate the terms of tender offers. These provisions impose the following requirements, among others:

(i) *Minimum duration*. Under Rule 14e–1, a tender offer must be held open for at least twenty business days.

(ii) *All-holders rule*. Rule 14d–10 provides that a bidder may not make a tender offer for a class of securities unless the offer is open, at the same price and on the same terms, to all holders of the class. This rule is called the "all holders rule." Under the Supremacy Clause, the all-holders rule displaces the outcome of the *Unocal* case, infra, which held that under Delaware law a corporation can make an exclusionary self-tender—that is, a tender offer that excludes certain shares of the class for which the offer is made.

(iii) *Best-price rule*. Rule 14d–10 also provides that the price paid to any security holder pursuant to a tender offer must equal the highest price that the bidder pays to any other security holder during the tender offer. See Epstein v. MCA, Inc., 54 F.3d 1422 (9th Cir. 1995), rev'd on other grounds sub nom. Matsushita Electrical Industrial Corp. v. Epstein, 516 U.S. 367, 116 S.Ct. 873, 134 L.Ed.2d 6 (1996), reaffirmed on remand, 126 F.3d 1235 (9th Cir. 1997). Under this rule, if, as frequently occurs, the bidder increases the bid price during a tender offer, the new, higher price must be made retroactively available to all holders who tendered before the increase. In addition, Rule 10b–13 provides that during the pendency of tender offer, the bidder cannot purchase securities that are subject to the tender offer except under the tender offer—that is, the bidder cannot make private purchases during the duration of the tender offer. Bidders sometimes become ensnared by Rule 14d–10 due to there being no definition of tender offer. In a leading case, Field v. Trump, 850 F.2d 938 (2d Cir. 1988), Trump announced a $22 bid for Pay'n Save, only to cancel the bid five days later to "facilitate negotiations" with two Pay'n Save directors who opposed the offers. That same night Trump struck a deal of $23.50/per share, plus $900,000 for "fees and expenses" (roughly equal to $1.50 on a per share basis) with the two recalcitrant directors. The next day Trump announced a $23.50 bid. The Second Circuit concluded that an offer announced on September 7, withdrawn on September 12, and reannounced a bid on September 13th) constituted the same tender offer and supported a claim under Rule 14d–10. *See also* Epstein v. MCA, Inc., 50 F.3d 644, 655 (9th Cir. 1995) (considering whether the various steps were an integral part of the tender offer), *rev'd on other grounds*, 516 U.S. 367, 116 S.Ct. 873, 134 L.Ed.2d 6 (1996). Other courts have preferred a bright-line approach focused on the formal announcement and discontinuance of the bid. *See* In re Digital Island Securities Litig., 357 F.3d 322, 334 (3d Cir. 2004); Lerro v. Quaker Oats Co., 84 F.3d 239, 244–45 (7th Cir. 1996) (compensation promised to target management for future consulting and non-competition agreements the day before announcing a bid not part of the tender offer). *Contra* Gerber v. Computer Associates Int'l Inc., 303 F.3d 126 (2d Cir. 2002) ($5 million payment to target CEO for 5–year covenant was within the tender offer period). To provide some clarity in this area of severance pay, covenants not to compete and the like, Rule 14d–10(d)(2) now provides a safe harbor for severance and other compensation arrangements if they are approved by a body of independent directors of the target or bidder when the compensation is not based on a per share calculation.

(iv) *Withdrawal rights*. Under section 14(d)(5) of the Williams Act, a tendering shareholder can withdraw tendered but unaccepted shares at any time after sixty days from the date the tender offer was disseminated. Under Rule 14d–7, a tendering shareholder can withdraw tendered shares during the entire duration of the offer and any extension of the offer.

(v) *Proration*. Under Rule 14d–8, if a bidder makes a partial tender offer—that is, an offer for less than 100% of the target's securities—and more securities are tendered during the duration of the tender offer than the bidder has offered to accept, the bidder must accept all tendered securities, up to the stated percentage, on a pro rata basis.

5. *Obligations of the Target's Management*. Rule 14e–2 requires that no later than ten business days from the date the tender offer is first published, the target corporation (really, the target's board) must notify shareholders that the target takes one of the following positions: (A) Recommends acceptance of the tender offer. (B) Recommends rejection of the tender offer. (C) Expresses no opinion and is remaining neutral toward the tender offer. (D) Is unable to take a position with respect to the tender offer. The statement must also describe the reasons for target's position. After making such a statement, the company must update the statement for any material change.

Under Rule 14d–9, any person who solicits or makes a recommendation to shareholders in respect of a tender offer (as opposed to making a tender offer) must file a Schedule 14D–9. This Schedule requires disclosure of the nature of, and the reasons for, the solicitation or recommendation; conflicts of interest of the person filing the statement; and any negotiation or transaction being undertaken that relates to either an extraordinary transaction (such as a merger) involving the target, a purchase or sale of a material amount of assets by the target, an acquisition of securities by the target, or a material change in the target's capitalization or in its dividend policy. Under Rule 14d–9(f), the statement that a target is required to make concerning its position on the tender offer is a solicitation or recommendation to shareholders within the meaning of Rule 14d–9. Accordingly, as a practical matter a target corporation must make the disclosures required by Schedule 14D–9.

6. *Tender Offers by Issuers.* Under section 13(e) of the Securities Exchange Act and Rule 13e, corporations that tender for their own stock ("issuer" or "self" tenders) are subject to obligations similar to those imposed on outside bidders under rules 14d and 14e.

7. *Anti–Fraud Provision.* Section 14(e) of the Securities Exchange Act prohibits material misstatements, misleading omissions, and fraudulent or manipulative acts, in connection with a tender offer, or any solicitation in favor of or in opposition to a tender offer. Section 14(e) is closely comparable to Rule 10b–5, except that it does not contain the limiting language, "in connection with the purchase or sale" of securities, found in Rule 10b–5. Other elements of the private action under section 14(e) parallel those of Rule 10b–5. For example, a plaintiff who brings suit for damages under section 14(e) must establish scienter. See Connecticut National Bank v. Fluor Corp., 808 F.2d 957 (2d Cir.1987). And, the fraud on the market approach to causation is similarly available in section 14(e) private suits. See Semerenko v. Cendant Corp., 223 F.3d 165, 178 (3d Cir. 2000). However, as might be expected, section 14(e) claims by investors who have neither purchased nor sold securities confront a skeptical court where close scrutiny of claims of causality occur. See e.g., Lewis v. McGraw, 619 F.2d 192, 195 (2d Cir. 1980); Salsitz v. Peltz, 227 F. Supp. 2d 222, 225 (S.D.N.Y. 2002); P. Schoenfeld Asset Management, LLC v. Cendant Corp., 47 F. Supp. 2d 546, 549 (D. N.J. 1999).

8. *Standing*. The target's shareholders have standing to sue for damages under sections 14(d)(6) (the pro rata requirement), 14(d)(7) (the equal-consideration requirement), and 14(e) (the anti-fraud requirement), and, in appropriate cases, may sue for injunctive relief, under the anti-fraud provision. However, on the theory that the purpose of the Act is to protect the target's shareholders, a bidder does not have standing to sue for damages under the Williams Act Piper v. Chris–Craft Industries, Inc., 430 U.S. 1, 97 S.Ct. 926, 51 L.Ed.2d 124 (1977). Nonetheless, both the bidder and the target corporation can sue for an injunction against the target and bidder, respectively, for violation of the anti-fraud provision of section 14(e), because such an injunction will protect the interests of the target's shareholders. Gearhart Industries, Inc. v. Smith International, Inc., 741 F.2d 707 (5th Cir.1984).

In general, the courts have also accorded standing to shareholders of a target corporation to seek injunctive relief against continuing violations of § 13(d) (the 5% reporting requirement), including violations caused by false or misleading filings. The target corporation also has a private right of action to seek injunctive relief against continuing violations of § 13(d). The courts are divided on whether a shareholder of the target has an implied private right of action for damages under § 13(d). Similarly, the majority rule is that corporations do not have standing to sue for damages under section 13(d). See Hallwood Realty Partners, L.P. v. Gotham Partners, L.P., 286 F.3d 613 (2d Cir. 2002).

Rival bidders cannot seek damages under the Williams Act against each other resulting from the lost opportunity to gain control, even when they own a nominal amount of shares in the target company. Piper v. Chris–Craft Ind., 430 U.S. 1, 35, 97 S.Ct. 926, 960, 51 L.Ed.2d 124, 158 (1977); Kalmanovitz v. G. Heileman Brewing Co., 595 F.Supp. 1385, 1393 (D. Del. 1984). However, courts have allowed a rival bidder to seek injunctive relief by concluding that an injunctive remedy would better protect the target's shareholders interests than providing damages to shareholders after the transaction is complete. Mobil Corp. v. Marathon Oil Co., 669 F.2d 366, 371–72 (6th Cir. 1981); Humana, Inc. v. American Medicorp, Inc., 445 F.Supp. 613, 614–15 (S.D.N.Y. 1977).

Unocal Corp. v. Mesa Petroleum Co.

Supreme Court of Delaware, 1985.
493 A.2d 946.

■ Before McNeilly and Moore, JJ., and Taylor, Judge (Sitting by designation pursuant to Del.Const. Art. 4, § 12.)

■ Moore, Justice.

We confront an issue of first impression in Delaware—the validity of a corporation's self-tender for its own shares which excludes from participation a stockholder making a hostile tender offer for the company's stock....

I. ...

On April 8, 1985, Mesa, the owner of approximately 13% of Unocal's stock, commenced a two-tier "front loaded" cash tender offer for 64 million shares, or approximately 37%, of Unocal's outstanding stock at a price of $54 per share. The "back-end" was designed to eliminate the remaining publicly held shares by an exchange of securities purportedly worth $54 per share. However, pursuant to an order entered by the United States District Court for the Central District of California on April 26, 1985, Mesa issued a supplemental proxy statement to Unocal's stockholders disclosing that the securities offered in the second-step merger would be highly subordinated, and that Unocal's capitalization would differ significantly from its present structure. Unocal has rather aptly termed such securities "junk bonds".[2]

Unocal's board consists of eight independent outside directors and six insiders. It met on April 13, 1985, to consider the Mesa tender offer. Thirteen directors were present, and the meeting lasted nine and one-half hours. The directors were given no agenda or written materials prior to the session. However, detailed presentations were made by legal counsel regarding the board's obligations under both Delaware corporate law and the federal securities laws. The board then received a presentation from Peter Sachs on behalf of Goldman Sachs Co. (Goldman Sachs) and Dillon, Read Co. (Dillon Read) discussing the bases for their opinions that the Mesa proposal was wholly inadequate. Mr. Sachs opined that the minimum cash value that could be expected from a sale or orderly liquidation for 100% of Unocal's stock was in excess of $60 per share. In making his presentation, Mr. Sachs showed slides outlining the valuation techniques used by the financial advisors, and others, depicting recent business combinations in the oil and gas industry. The Court of Chancery found that the Sachs presentation was designed to apprise the directors of the scope of the analyses performed rather than the facts and numbers used in reaching the conclusion that Mesa's tender offer price was inadequate.

Mr. Sachs also presented various defensive strategies available to the board if it concluded that Mesa's two-step tender offer was inadequate and should be opposed. One of the devices outlined was a self-tender by Unocal for its own stock with a reasonable price range of $70 to $75 per share. The cost of such a proposal would cause the company to incur $6.1–6.5 billion of additional debt, and a presentation was made informing the board of Unocal's ability to handle it. The directors were told that the primary effect of this obligation would be to reduce exploratory drilling, but that the company would nonetheless remain a viable entity.

The eight outside directors, comprising a clear majority of the thirteen members present, then met separately with Unocal's financial

---

2. Mesa's May 3, 1985 supplement to its proxy statement states:

(i) following the Offer, the Purchasers would seek to effect a merger of Unocal and Mesa Eastern or an affiliate of Mesa Eastern (the "Merger") in which the remaining Shares would be acquired for a combination of subordinated debt securities and preferred stock; (ii) the securities to be received by Unocal shareholders in the Merger would be subordinated to $2,400 million of debt securities of Mesa Eastern, indebtedness incurred to refinance up to $1,000 million of bank debt which was incurred by affiliates of Mesa Partners II to purchase Shares and to pay related interest and expenses and all then-existing debt of Unocal; (iii) the corporation surviving the Merger would be responsible for the payment of all securities of Mesa Eastern (including any such securities issued pursuant to the Merger) and the indebtedness referred to in item (ii) above, and such securities and indebtedness would be repaid out of funds generated by the operations of Unocal; (iv) the indebtedness incurred in the Offer and the Merger would result in Unocal being much more highly leveraged, and the capitalization of the corporation surviving the Merger would differ significantly from that of Unocal at present; and (v) in their analyses of cash flows provided by operations of Unocal which would be available to service and repay securities and other obligations of the corporation surviving the Merger, the Purchasers assumed that the capital expenditures and expenditures for exploration of such corporation would be significantly reduced.

advisors and attorneys. Thereafter, they unanimously agreed to advise the board that it should reject Mesa's tender offer as inadequate, and that Unocal should pursue a self-tender to provide the stockholders with a fairly priced alternative to the Mesa proposal. The board then reconvened and unanimously adopted a resolution rejecting as grossly inadequate Mesa's tender offer. Despite the nine and one-half hour length of the meeting, no formal decision was made on the proposed defensive self-tender.

On April 15, the board met again with four of the directors present by telephone and one member still absent. This session lasted two hours. Unocal's Vice President of Finance and its Assistant General Counsel made a detailed presentation of the proposed terms of the exchange offer. A price range between $70 and $80 per share was considered, and ultimately the directors agreed upon $72. The board was also advised about the debt securities that would be issued, and the necessity of placing restrictive covenants upon certain corporate activities until the obligations were paid. The board's decisions were made in reliance on the advice of its investment bankers, including the terms and conditions upon which the securities were to be issued. Based upon this advice, and the board's own deliberations, the directors unanimously approved the exchange offer. Their resolution provided that if Mesa acquired 64 million shares of Unocal stock through its own offer (the Mesa Purchase Condition), Unocal would buy the remaining 49% outstanding for an exchange of debt securities having an aggregate par value of $72 per share. The board resolution also stated that the offer would be subject to other conditions that had been described to the board at the meeting, or which were deemed necessary by Unocal's officers, including the exclusion of Mesa from the proposal (the Mesa exclusion). Any such conditions were required to be in accordance with the "purport and intent" of the offer.

Unocal's exchange offer was commenced on April 17, 1985, and Mesa promptly challenged it by filing this suit in the Court of Chancery. On April 22, the Unocal board met again and was advised by Goldman Sachs and Dillon Read to waive the Mesa Purchase Condition as to 50 million shares. This recommendation was in response to a perceived concern of the shareholders that, if shares were tendered to Unocal, no shares would be purchased by either offeror. The directors were also advised that they should tender their own Unocal stock into the exchange offer as a mark of their confidence in it.

Another focus of the board was the Mesa exclusion. Legal counsel advised that under Delaware law Mesa could only be excluded for what the directors reasonably believed to be a valid corporate purpose. The directors' discussion centered on the objective of adequately compensating shareholders at the "back-end" of Mesa's proposal, which the latter would finance with "junk bonds". To include Mesa would defeat that goal, because under the proration aspect of the exchange offer (49%) every Mesa share accepted by Unocal would displace one held by another stockholder. Further, if Mesa were permitted to tender to Unocal, the latter would in effect be financing Mesa's own inadequate proposal.

On April 24, 1985 Unocal issued a supplement to the exchange offer describing the partial waiver of the Mesa Purchase Condition. On May 1, 1985, in another supplement, Unocal extended the withdrawal, proration and expiration dates of its exchange offer to May 17, 1985.

Meanwhile, on April 22, 1985, Mesa amended its complaint in this action to challenge the Mesa exclusion. . . .

. . . [T]he Vice Chancellor granted Mesa a preliminary injunction . . . [reasoning that a selective exchange offer that excluded Mesa was permitted].

On May 13, 1985 the Court of Chancery certified this interlocutory appeal . . . and we accepted it. . . . on an expedited basis.

II.

The issues we address involve these fundamental questions: Did the Unocal board have the power and duty to oppose a takeover threat it reasonably perceived to be harmful to the corporate enterprise, and if so, is its action here entitled to the protection of the business judgment rule?

Mesa contends that the discriminatory exchange offer violates the fiduciary duties Unocal owes it. Mesa argues that because of the Mesa exclusion the business judgment rule is inapplicable, because the directors by tendering their own shares will derive a financial benefit that is not available to *all* Unocal stockholders. Thus, it is Mesa's ultimate contention that Unocal cannot establish that the exchange offer is fair to *all* shareholders, and argues that the Court of Chancery was correct in concluding that Unocal was unable to meet this burden.

Unocal answers that it does not owe a duty of "fairness" to Mesa, given the facts here. Specifically, Unocal contends that its board of directors reasonably and in good faith concluded that Mesa's $54 two-tier tender offer was coercive and inadequate, and that Mesa sought selective treatment for itself. Furthermore, Unocal argues that the board's approval of the exchange offer was made in good faith, on an informed basis, and in the exercise of due care. Under these circumstances, Unocal contends that its directors properly employed this device to protect the company and its stockholders from Mesa's harmful tactics.

III.

We begin with the basic issue of the power of a board of directors of a Delaware corporation to adopt a defensive measure of this type. Absent such authority, all other questions are moot. Neither issues of fairness nor business judgment are pertinent without the basic underpinning of a board's legal power to act.

The board has a large reservoir of authority upon which to draw. Its duties and responsibilities proceed from the inherent powers conferred by 8 Del.C. § 141(a), respecting management of the corporation's "business and affairs". Additionally, the powers here being exercised derive from 8 Del.C. § 160(a), conferring broad authority upon a corporation to deal in its own stock. From this it is now well established that in the acquisition of its shares a Delaware corporation may deal selectively with its stockholders, provided the directors have not acted out of a sole or primary purpose to entrench themselves in office. Cheff v. Mathes, Del.Supr., 199 A.2d 548, 554 (1964); Bennett v. Propp, Del.Supr., 187 A.2d 405, 408 (1962) . . .

Finally, the board's power to act derives from its fundamental duty and obligation to protect the corporate enterprise, which includes stockholders, from harm reasonably perceived, irrespective of its source. See e.g.. . . . Cheff v. Mathes, 199 A.2d at 556; Martin v. American Potash & Chemical Corp., 92 A.2d at 302; Kaplan v. Goldsamt, 380 A.2d at 568–69; Kors v. Carey, 158 A.2d at 141 . . . Thus, we are satisfied that in the broad context of corporate governance, including issues of fundamental corporate change, a board of directors is not a passive instrumentality.[8]

Given the foregoing principles, we turn to the standards by which director action is to be measured. In Pogostin v. Rice, Del.Supr., 480 A.2d 619 (1984), we held that the business judgment rule, including the standards by which director conduct is judged, is applicable in the context of a takeover. Id. at 627.

When a board addresses a pending takeover bid it has an obligation to determine whether the offer is in the best interests of the corporation and its shareholders. In that respect a board's duty is no different from any other responsibility it shoulders, and its decision should be no less entitled to the respect they otherwise would be accorded in the realm of business judgment. See also Johnson v. Trueblood, 629 F.2d 287, 292–293 (3d Cir.1980). There are, however, certain caveats to a proper exercise of this function. Because of the omnipresent specter that a board may be acting primarily in its own interests, rather than those of the corporation and its shareholders, there is an enhanced duty which calls for judicial examination at the threshold before the protections of the business judgment rule may be conferred.

This Court has long recognized that:

> We must bear in mind the inherent danger in the purchase of shares with corporate funds to remove a threat to corporate policy when a threat to control is involved. The directors are of necessity confronted with a conflict of interest, and an objective decision is difficult.

Bennett v. Propp, Del.Supr., 187 A.2d 405, 409 (1962). In the face of this inherent conflict directors must show that they had reasonable grounds for believing that a danger to corporate policy and effective-

---

8. Even in the traditional areas of fundamental corporate change, i.e., charter amendments [8 Del.C. § 242(b)], mergers [8 Del.C. §§ 251(b), 252(c), 253(a), and 254(d)], sale of assets [8 Del.C. § 271(a)], and dissolution [8 Del.C. § 275(a)], director action is a prerequisite to the ultimate disposition of such matters. See also, Smith v. Van Gorkom, Del.Supr., 488 A.2d 858, 888 (1985).

ness existed because of another person's stock ownership. Cheff v. Mathes, 199 A.2d at 554–55. However, they satisfy that burden "by showing good faith and reasonable investigation...." Id. at 555. Furthermore, such proof is materially enhanced, as here, by the approval of a board comprised of a majority of outside independent directors who have acted in accordance with the foregoing standards. See Aronson v. Lewis, 473 A.2d at 812, 815; Puma v. Marriott, Del.Ch., 283 A.2d 693, 695 (1971); Panter v. Marshall Field Co., 646 F.2d 271, 295 (7th Cir.1981).

IV.

A.

In the board's exercise of corporate power to forestall a takeover bid our analysis begins with the basic principle that corporate directors have a fiduciary duty to act in the best interests of the corporation's stockholders. Guth v. Loft, Inc., Del.Supr., 5 A.2d 503, 510 (1939). As we have noted, their duty of care extends to protecting the corporation and its owners from perceived harm whether a threat originates from third parties or other shareholders. But such powers are not absolute. A corporation does not have unbridled discretion to defeat any perceived threat by any Draconian means available.

The restriction placed upon a selective stock repurchase is that the directors may not have acted solely or primarily out of a desire to perpetuate themselves in office. See Cheff v. Mathes, 199 A.2d at 556; Kors v. Carey, 158 A.2d at 140. Of course, to this is added the further caveat that inequitable action may not be taken under the guise of law. Schnell v. Chris–Craft Industries, Inc., Del.Supr. 285 A.2d 437, 439 (1971). The standard of proof established in Cheff v. Mathes ... is designed to ensure that a defensive measure to thwart or impede a takeover is indeed motivated by a good faith concern for the welfare of the corporation and its stockholders, which in all circumstances must be free of any fraud or other misconduct. Cheff v. Mathes, 199 A.2d at 554–55. However, this does not end the inquiry.

B.

A further aspect is the element of balance. If a defensive measure is to come within the ambit of the business judgment rule, it must be reasonable in relation to the threat posed. This entails an analysis by the directors of the nature of the takeover bid and its effect on the corporate enterprise. Examples of such concerns may include: inadequacy of the price offered, nature and timing of the offer, questions of illegality, the impact on "constituencies" other than shareholders (i.e., creditors, customers, employees, and perhaps even the community generally), the risk of nonconsummation, and the quality of securities being offered in the exchange. See Lipton and Brownstein, Takeover Responses and Directors' Responsibilities: An Update, p. 7, ABA National Institute on the Dynamics of Corporate Control (December 8, 1983). While not a controlling factor, it also seems to us that a board may reasonably consider the basic stockholder interests at stake, including those of short term speculators, whose actions may have fueled the coercive aspect of the offer at the expense of the long term investor.[9] Here, the threat posed was viewed by the Unocal board as a grossly inadequate two-tier coercive tender offer coupled with the threat of greenmail.

Specifically, the Unocal directors had concluded that the value of Unocal was substantially above the $54 per share offered in cash at the front end. Furthermore, they determined that the subordinated securities to be exchanged in Mesa's announced squeeze out of the remaining shareholders in the "back-end" merger were "junk bonds" worth far less than $54. It is now well recognized that such offers are a classic coercive measure designed to stampede shareholders into tendering at the first tier, even if the price is inadequate, out of fear of what they will receive at the back end of the transaction. Wholly beyond the coercive aspect of an inadequate two-tier tender offer, the threat was posed by a corporate raider with a national reputation as a "greenmailer".[13]

In adopting the selective exchange offer, the board stated that its objective was either to defeat the inadequate Mesa offer or, should the offer still succeed, provide the 49% of its stockholders, who would otherwise be forced to accept "junk bonds", with $72 worth of senior debt. We find that both purposes are valid.

However, such efforts would have been thwarted by Mesa's participation in the exchange offer. First, if Mesa could tender its shares, Unocal would effectively be subsidizing the former's continuing effort to buy Unocal stock at $54 per share. Second, Mesa could not, by definition, fit within the class of shareholders being protected from its own coercive and inadequate tender offer.

Thus, we are satisfied that the selective exchange offer is reasonably related to the threats posed. It is consistent with the principle that "the minority stockholder shall receive the substantial equivalent in value of what he had before." Sterling v. Mayflower Hotel Corp., Del.Supr., 93 A.2d 107, 114 (1952). See also Rosenblatt v. Getty Oil

9. There has been much debate respecting such stockholder interests. One rather impressive study indicates that the stock of over 50 percent of target companies, who resisted hostile takeovers, later traded at higher market prices than the rejected offer price, or were acquired after the tender offer was defeated by another company at a price higher than the offer price. See Lipton, supra 35 Bus.Law. at 106–109, 132–133. Moreover, an update by Kidder Peabody & Company of this study, involving the stock prices of target companies that have defeated hostile tender offers during the period from 1973 to 1982 demonstrates that in a majority of cases the target's shareholders benefited from the defeat. The stock of 81% of the targets studied has, since the tender offer, sold at prices higher than the tender offer price. When adjusted for the time value of money, the figure is 64%. See Lipton & Brownstein, supra ABA Institute at 10. The thesis being that this strongly supports application of the business judgment rule in response to takeover threats. There is, however, a rather vehement contrary view. See Easterbrook & Fischel, supra 36 Bus.Law. at 1739–1745.

13. The term "greenmail" refers to the practice of buying out a takeover bidder's stock at a premium that is not available to other shareholders in order to prevent the takeover. The Chancery Court noted that "Mesa has made tremendous profits from its takeover activities although in the past few years it has not been successful in acquiring any of the target companies on an unfriendly basis." Moreover, the trial court specifically found that the actions of the Unocal board were taken in good faith to eliminate both the inadequacies of the tender offer and to forestall the payment of "greenmail".

Co., Del.Supr., 493 A.2d 929, 940 (1985). This concept of fairness, while stated in the merger context, is also relevant in the area of tender offer law. Thus, the board's decision to offer what it determined to be the fair value of the corporation to the 49% of its shareholders, who would otherwise be forced to accept highly subordinated "junk bonds", is reasonable and consistent with the directors' duty to ensure that the minority stockholders receive equal value for their shares.

V.

Mesa contends that it is unlawful, and the trial court agreed, for a corporation to discriminate in this fashion against one shareholder. It argues correctly that no case has ever sanctioned a device that precludes a raider from sharing in a benefit available to all other stockholders. However, as we have noted earlier, the principle of selective stock repurchases by a Delaware corporation is neither unknown nor unauthorized. Cheff v. Mathes, 199 A.2d at 554; Bennett v. Propp, 187 A.2d at 408; Martin v. American Potash & Chemical Corporation, 92 A.2d at 302.... The only difference is that heretofore the approved transaction was the payment of "greenmail" to a raider or dissident posing a threat to the corporate enterprise. All other stockholders were denied such favored treatment, and given Mesa's past history of greenmail, its claims here are rather ironic.

However, our corporate law is not static. It must grow and develop in response to, indeed in anticipation of, evolving concepts and needs. Merely because the General Corporation Law is silent as to a specific matter does not mean that it is prohibited. See Providence & Worcester Co. v. Baker, Del.Supr., 378 A.2d 121, 123–124 (1977). In the days when *Cheff, Bennett,* [and] *Martin* were decided, the tender offer, while not an unknown device, was virtually unused, and little was known of such methods as two-tier "front-end" loaded offers with their coercive effects. Then, the favored attack of a raider was stock acquisition followed by a proxy contest. Various defensive tactics, which provided no benefit whatever to the raider, evolved. Thus, the use of corporate funds by management to counter a proxy battle was approved. Hall v. Trans–Lux Daylight Picture Screen Corp., Del.Ch., 171 A. 226 (1934); Hibbert v. Hollywood Park, Inc., Del.Supr., 457 A.2d 339 (1983). Litigation, supported by corporate funds, aimed at the raider has long been a popular device.

More recently, as the sophistication of both raiders and targets has developed, a host of other defensive measures to counter such ever mounting threats has evolved and received judicial sanction. These include defensive charter amendments and other devices bearing some rather exotic, but apt, names: Crown Jewel, White Knight, Pac Man, and Golden Parachute. Each has highly selective features, the object of which is to deter or defeat the raider.

Thus, while the exchange offer is a form of selective treatment, given the nature of the threat posed here the response is neither unlawful nor unreasonable. If the board of directors is disinterested, has acted in good faith and with due care, its decision in the absence of an abuse of discretion will be upheld as a proper exercise of business judgment.

To this Mesa responds that the board is not disinterested, because the directors are receiving a benefit from the tender of their own shares, which because of the Mesa exclusion, does not devolve upon *all* stockholders equally. See Aronson v. Lewis, Del.Supr., 473 A.2d 805, 812 (1984). However, Mesa concedes that if the exclusion is valid, then the directors and all other stockholders share the same benefit. The answer of course is that the exclusion is valid, and the directors' participation in the exchange offer does not rise to the level of a disqualifying interest. . . .

Nor does this become an "interested" director transaction merely because certain board members are large stockholders. As this Court has previously noted, that fact alone does not create a disqualifying "personal pecuniary interest" to defeat the operation of the business judgment rule. Cheff v. Mathes, 199 A.2d at 554.

Mesa also argues that the exclusion permits the directors to abdicate the fiduciary duties they owe it. However, that is not so. The board continues to owe Mesa the duties of due care and loyalty. But in the face of the destructive threat Mesa's tender offer was perceived to pose, the board had a supervening duty to protect the corporate enterprise, which includes the other shareholders, from threatened harm.

Mesa contends that the basis of this action is punitive, and solely in response to the exercise of its rights of corporate democracy. Nothing precludes Mesa, as a stockholder, from acting in its own self-interest. . . . However, Mesa, while pursuing its own interests, has acted in a manner which a board consisting of a majority of independent directors has reasonably determined to be contrary to the best interests of Unocal and its other shareholders. In this situation, there is no support in Delaware law for the proposition that, when responding to a perceived harm, a corporation must guarantee a benefit to a stockholder who is deliberately provoking the danger being addressed. There is no obligation of self-sacrifice by a corporation and its shareholders in the face of such a challenge.

Here, the Court of Chancery specifically found that the "directors' decision [to oppose the Mesa tender offer] was made in the good faith belief that the Mesa tender offer is inadequate." Given our standard of review. . . .

VI.

In conclusion, there was directorial power to oppose the Mesa tender offer, and to undertake a selective stock exchange made in good faith and upon a reasonable investigation pursuant to a clear duty to protect the corporate enterprise. Further, the selective stock repurchase plan chosen by Unocal is reasonable in relation to the threat that the board rationally and reasonably believed was posed by

Mesa's inadequate and coercive two-tier tender offer. Under those circumstances the board's action is entitled to be measured by the standards of the business judgment rule. Thus, unless it is shown by a preponderance of the evidence that the directors' decisions were primarily based on perpetuating themselves in office, or some other breach of fiduciary duty such as fraud, overreaching, lack of good faith, or being uninformed, a Court will not substitute its judgment for that of the board.

In this case that protection is not lost merely because Unocal's directors have tendered their shares in the exchange offer. Given the validity of the Mesa exclusion, they are receiving a benefit shared generally by all other stockholders except Mesa. In this circumstance the test of Aronson v. Lewis, 473 A.2d at 812, is satisfied. See also Cheff v. Mathes, 199 A.2d at 554. If the stockholders are displeased with the action of their elected representatives, the powers of corporate democracy are at their disposal to turn the board out. Aronson v. Lewis, Del.Supr., 473 A.2d 805, 811 (1984). See also 8 Del.C. §§ 141(k) and 211(b).

With the Court of Chancery's findings that the exchange offer was based on the board's good faith belief that the Mesa offer was inadequate, that the board's action was informed and taken with due care, that Mesa's prior activities justify a reasonable inference that its principle objective was greenmail, and implicitly, that the substance of the offer itself was reasonable and fair to the corporation and its stockholders if Mesa were included, we cannot say that the Unocal directors have acted in such a manner as to have passed an "unintelligent and unadvised judgment". Mitchell v. Highland–Western Glass Co., Del.Ch., 167 A. 831, 833 (1933). The decision of the Court of Chancery is therefore REVERSED, and the preliminary injunction is VACATED.*

NOTE ON UNITRIN, INC. v. AMERICAN GENERAL CORP.

In Unitrin, Inc. v. American General Corp., 651 A.2d 1361 (1995), American General Corporation announced a tender offer to purchase all of the stock of Unitrin, Inc. at \$50⅜ per share. Unitrin's board responded by taking several defensive measures, including the adoption of a poison pill and a program to repurchase up to 10 million of Unitrin's 51.8 million shares on the open market at \$50⅜. Unitrin's certificate of incorporation provided that a business combination with a more–than–15% shareholder had to be approved by a majority of continuing directors or by a 75% shareholder vote. Unitrin's directors collectively held 23% of Unitrin's stock prior to adoption of the repurchase program. The directors did not intend to sell their stock to Unitrin under the repurchase program.

* Accord: Burcham v. Bunten, 276 Kan. 393, 77 P.3d 130 (2003).

American General brought an action in Delaware Chancery court to enjoin Unitrin from completing its repurchase program. The Chancery court issued a preliminary injunction against Unitrin, at a point when Unitrin had purchased nearly 5 million shares of its stock, partly on the ground that since the director-shareholders were not selling their stock, the effect of the repurchase program would be to increase their stock ownership from 23% to over 25%, thereby giving them a veto under the 75% supermajority voting provision. The Delaware Supreme Court reversed, and remanded for a decision by Chancery under the standards it set out. The Supreme Court's opinion provides an important gloss on *Unocal*:

> ... [T]he Court of Chancery erred in applying the proportionality review *Unocal* requires by focusing upon whether the Repurchase Program was an "unnecessary" defensive response. The Court of Chancery should have directed its enhanced scrutiny: first, upon whether the Repurchase Program the Unitrin Board implemented was draconian, by being either preclusive or coercive and; second, if it was not draconian, upon whether it was within a range of reasonable responses to the threat American General's Offer posed. Consequently, the interlocutory preliminary injunctive judgment of the Court of Chancery is reversed....
>
> The Court of Chancery and all parties agree that proxy contests do not generate 100% shareholder participation. The shareholder plaintiffs argue that 80–85% may be a usual turnout. Therefore, *without* the Repurchase Program, the director shareholders' absolute voting power of 23% would already constitute *actual voting power greater than* 25% in a proxy contest with normal shareholder participation below 100%....
>
> The Unitrin Board did not have unlimited discretion to defeat the threat it perceived from the American General Offer by any draconian means available. *See Unocal,* 493 A.2d at 955. Pursuant to the *Unocal* proportionality test, the nature of the threat associated with a particular hostile offer sets the parameters for the range of permissible defensive tactics. Accordingly, the purpose of enhanced judicial scrutiny is to determine whether the Board acted reasonably in "relation ... to the threat which a particular bid allegedly poses to stockholder interests." *Mills Acquisition Co. v. Macmillan, Inc.,* Del.Supr., 559 A.2d 1261, 1288 (1989).
>
> ... Courts, commentators and litigators have attempted to catalogue the threats posed by hostile tender offers.... Commentators have categorized three types of threats:
>
> > (i) *opportunity loss* ... [where] a hostile offer might deprive target shareholders of the opportunity to select a superior alternative offered by target management [or, we would add, offered by another bidder]; (ii) *structural coercion,* ... the risk that disparate treatment of non-tendering shareholders might distort shareholders' tender decisions; and (iii) *substantive coercion,* ... the risk that shareholders will mistak-

enly accept an underpriced offer because they disbelieve management's representations of intrinsic value....*

The record reflects that the Unitrin Board perceived the threat from American General's Offer to be a form of substantive coercion....

The record appears to support Unitrin's argument that the Board's justification for adopting the Repurchase Program was its reasonably perceived risk of substantive coercion, *i.e.,* that Unitrin's shareholders might accept American General's inadequate Offer because of "ignorance or mistaken belief" regarding the Board's assessment of the long-term value of Unitrin's stock. *See Shamrock Holdings, Inc. v. Polaroid Corp.,* Del.Ch., 559 A.2d 278, 290 (1989).... The adoption of the Repurchase Program also appears to be consistent with this Court's holding that economic inadequacy is not the only threat presented by an all cash for all shares hostile bid, because the threat of such a hostile bid could be exacerbated by shareholder "ignorance or ... mistaken belief." *Paramount Communications, Inc. v. Time, Inc.,* 571 A.2d at 1153....

An examination of the cases applying *Unocal* reveals a direct correlation between findings of proportionality or disproportionality and the judicial determination of whether a defensive response was draconian because it was either coercive or preclusive in character....

... As common law applications of *Unocal's* proportionality standard have evolved, at least two characteristics of draconian defensive measures taken by a board of directors in responding to a threat have been brought into focus through enhanced judicial scrutiny. In the modern takeover lexicon, it is now clear that since *Unocal,* this Court has consistently recognized that defensive measures which are either preclusive or coercive are included within the common law definition of draconian.

If a defensive measure is not draconian, however, because it is not either coercive or preclusive, the *Unocal* proportionality test requires the focus of enhanced judicial scrutiny to shift to "the range of reasonableness." *Paramount Communications, Inc. v. QVC Network, Inc.,* Del.Supr., 637 A.2d 34, 45–46 (1994). Proper and proportionate defensive responses are intended and permitted to thwart perceived threats. When a corporation is not for sale, the board of directors is the defender of the metaphorical medieval corporate bastion and the protector of the corporation's shareholders. The fact that a defensive action must not be coercive or preclusive does not prevent a board from responding defensively before a bidder is at the corporate bastion's gate....

The Court of Chancery found that the Unitrin Board reasonably believed that American General's Offer was inadequate....

---

* See Paramount Communications, Inc. v. Time Inc., n. 17, pp. 1270–1271, supra. (Footnote by ed.)

Upon remand, in applying the correct legal standard to the factual circumstances of this case, the Court of Chancery may conclude that the implementation of the limited Repurchase Program was also within a range of reasonable additional defensive responses available to the Unitrin Board. In considering whether the Repurchase Program was within a range of reasonableness the Court of Chancery should take into consideration whether: (1) it is a statutorily authorized form of business decision which a board of directors may routinely make in a non-takeover context; (2) as a defensive response to American General's Offer it was limited and corresponded in degree or magnitude to the degree or magnitude of the threat, (*i.e.,* assuming the threat was relatively mild, was the response relatively "mild"?); (3) with the Repurchase Program, the Unitrin Board properly recognized that all shareholders are not alike, and provided immediate liquidity to those shareholders who wanted it. . . .

In re Gaylord Container Corp. Shareholder Litigation, 753 A.2d 462, 481(Del.Ch. 2000)(Ch. Leo Strine) observed, "A defensive measure is preclusive when its operation precludes an acquisition of the company. A defensive measure is coercive when it operates to force management's preferred alternative upon the stockholders."

NOTE ON UNOCAL

The specific outcome in *Unocal,* allowing an exclusionary (discriminatory) tender offer, has been superseded by the all-holders rule under the Williams Act, Securities Exchange Act Rule 14d–10, which ousts Delaware law under the Supremacy Clause of the Constitution. However, the basic standard of review of defensive tactics adopted in the *Unocal* decision has survived, with some glosses, as the central rule governing takeovers under Delaware law. *Unocal's* heightened scrutiny has a reasonable following outside of Delaware. *See e.g.,* International Ins. Co. v. Johns, 874 F.2d 1447 (11th Cir. 1989) (involving Florida incorporated target firm); In re Bear Stearns Litig., 870 N.Y.S.2d 709 (2008); and Crandon Capital Partners v. Shelk, 219 Or.App. 16, 181 P.3d 773 (Or. Ct. App. 2008). Some jurisdictions reject the heightened scrutiny called for by *Unocal,* and test the decision under the standard business judgment rule. Shenker v. Laureate Educ. Inc., 983 A.2d 408 (Md. 2009). This appears to be the approach recommended by the American Law Institute which places the burden of proof on the person challenging the defensive maneuver and states the "board may take into account all factors relevant to best interests of the corporation and its shareholders." ALI, Principles of Corporate Governance: Analysis and Recommendations § 6.02(a)–(c) (1994).

ALI, PRINCIPLES OF CORPORATE GOVERNANCE § 6.02

[See Statutory Supplement]

Moran v. Household International, Inc.

Supreme Court of Delaware, 1985.
500 A.2d 1346.

■ Before CHRISTIE, CHIEF JUSTICE, and MCNEILLY and MOORE, JJ.

■ MCNEILLY, JUSTICE:

This case presents to this Court for review the most recent defensive mechanism in the arsenal of corporate takeover weaponry—the Preferred Share Purchase Rights Plan ("Rights Plan" or "Plan"). The validity of this mechanism has attracted national attention. *Amici curiae* briefs have been filed in support of appellants by the Security and Exchange Commission ("SEC") and the Investment Company Institute. An *amicus curiae* brief has been filed in support of appellees ("Household") by the United Food and Commercial Workers International Union.

In a detailed opinion, the Court of Chancery upheld the Rights Plan as a legitimate exercise of business judgment by Household. Moran v. Household International, Inc., Del.Ch., 490 A.2d 1059 (1985). We agree, and therefore, affirm the judgment below.

I . . .

On August 14, 1984, the Board of Directors of Household International, Inc. adopted the Rights Plan by a fourteen to two vote.[2] The intricacies of the Rights Plan are contained in a 48–page document entitled "Rights Agreement". Basically, the Plan provides that Household common stockholders are entitled to the issuance of one Right per common share under certain triggering conditions. There are two triggering events that can activate the Rights. The first is the announcement of a tender offer for 30 percent of Household's shares ("30% trigger") and the second is the acquisition of 20 percent of Household's shares by any single entity or group ("20% trigger").

If an announcement of a tender offer for 30 percent of Household's shares is made, the Rights are issued and are immediately exercisable to purchase 1/100 share of new preferred stock for $100 and are redeemable by the Board for $.50 per Right. If 20 percent of Household's shares are acquired by anyone, the Rights are issued and become non-redeemable and are exercisable to purchase 1/100 of a share of preferred. If a Right is not exercised for preferred, and thereafter, a merger or consolidation occurs, the Rights holder can exercise each Right to purchase $200 of the common stock of the tender offeror for

---

2. Household's Board has ten outside directors and six who are members of management. Messrs. Moran (appellant) and Whitehead voted against the Plan. The record reflects that Whitehead voted against the Plan not on its substance but because he thought it was novel and would bring unwanted publicity to Household.

$100. This "flip-over" provision of the Rights Plan is at the heart of this controversy.

Household is a diversified holding company with its principal subsidiaries engaged in financial services, transportation and merchandising. HFC, National Car Rental and Vons Grocery are three of its wholly-owned entities.

Household did not adopt its Rights Plan during a battle with a corporate raider, but as a preventive mechanism to ward off future advances. The Vice–Chancellor found that as early as February 1984, Household's management became concerned about the company's vulnerability as a takeover target and began considering amending its charter to render a takeover more difficult. After considering the matter, Household decided not to pursue a fair price amendment.[3]

In the meantime, appellant Moran, one of Household's own Directors and also Chairman of the Dyson–Kissner–Moran Corporation, ("D–K–M") which is the largest single stockholder of Household, began discussions concerning a possible leveraged buy-out of Household by D–K–M. D–K–M's financial studies showed that Household's stock was significantly undervalued in relation to the company's breakup value. It is uncontradicted that Moran's suggestion of a leveraged buy-out never progressed beyond the discussion stage.

Concerned about Household's vulnerability to a raider in light of the current takeover climate, Household secured the services of Wachtell, Lipton, Rosen and Katz ("Wachtell, Lipton") and Goldman, Sachs & Co. ("Goldman, Sachs") to formulate a takeover policy for recommendation to the Household Board at its August 14 meeting. After a July 31 meeting with a Household Board member and a pre-meeting distribution of material on the potential takeover problem and the proposed Rights Plan, the Board met on August 14, 1984.

Representatives of Wachtell, Lipton and Goldman, Sachs attended the August 14 meeting. The minutes reflect that Mr. Lipton explained to the Board that his recommendation of the Plan was based on his understanding that the Board was concerned about the increasing frequency of "bust-up"[4] takeovers, the increasing takeover activity in the financial service industry, such as Leucadia's attempt to take over Arco, and the possible adverse effect this type of activity could have on employees and others concerned with and vital to the continuing successful operation of Household even in the absence of any actual bust-up takeover attempt. Against this factual background, the Plan was approved.

Thereafter, Moran and the company of which he is Chairman, D–K–M, filed this suit. On the eve of trial, Gretl Golter, the holder of 500 shares of Household, was permitted to intervene as an additional

---

3. A fair price amendment to a corporate charter generally requires supermajority approval for certain business combinations and sets minimum price criteria for mergers. Moran, 490 A.2d at 1064, n. 1.

4. "Bust-up" takeover generally refers to a situation in which one seeks to finance an acquisition by selling off pieces of the acquired company.

plaintiff. The trial was held, and the Court of Chancery ruled in favor of Household. Appellants now appeal from that ruling to this Court.

II

The primary issue here is the applicability of the business judgment rule as the standard by which the adoption of the Rights Plan should be reviewed. Much of this issue has been decided by our recent decision in Unocal Corp. v. Mesa Petroleum Co., Del.Supr., 493 A.2d 946 (1985). In *Unocal,* we applied the business judgment rule to analyze Unocal's discriminatory self-tender. We explained:

> When a board addresses a pending takeover bid it has an obligation to determine whether the offer is in the best interests of the corporation and its shareholders. In that respect a board's duty is no different from any other responsibility it shoulders, and its decisions should be no less entitled to the respect they otherwise would be accorded in the realm of business judgment.

Id. at 954 (citation and footnote omitted).

Other jurisdictions have also applied the business judgment rule to actions by which target companies have sought to forestall takeover activity they considered undesirable....

This case is distinguishable from the ones cited, since here we have a defensive mechanism adopted to ward off possible future advances and not a mechanism adopted in reaction to a specific threat. This distinguishing factor does not result in the Directors losing the protection of the business judgment rule. To the contrary, pre-planning, for the contingency of a hostile takeover might reduce the risk that, under the pressure of a takeover bid, management will fail to exercise reasonable judgment. Therefore, in reviewing a pre-planned defensive mechanism it seems even more appropriate to apply the business judgment rule....

Of course, the business judgment rule can only sustain corporate decision making or transactions that are within the power or authority of the Board. Therefore, before the business judgment rule can be applied it must be determined whether the Directors were authorized to adopt the Rights Plan.

III

Appellants vehemently contend that the Board of Directors was unauthorized to adopt the Rights Plan. First, appellants contend that no provision of the Delaware General Corporation Law authorizes the issuance of such Rights. Secondly, appellants, along with the SEC, contend that the Board is unauthorized to usurp stockholders' rights to receive hostile tender offers. Third, appellants and the SEC also contend that the Board is unauthorized to fundamentally restrict stockholders' rights to conduct a proxy contest. We address each of these contentions in turn.

A.

While appellants contend that no provision of the Delaware General Corporation Law authorizes the Rights Plan, Household contends that the Rights Plan was issued pursuant to 8 Del.C. §§ 151(g) and 157. It explains that the Rights are authorized by § 157[5] and the issue of preferred stock underlying the Rights is authorized by § 151.[6] Appellants respond by making several attacks upon the authority to issue the Rights pursuant to § 157.

Appellants begin by contending that § 157 cannot authorize the Rights Plan since § 157 has never served the purpose of authorizing a takeover defense. Appellants contend that § 157 is a corporate financing statute, and that nothing in its legislative history suggests a purpose that has anything to do with corporate control or a takeover defense. Appellants are unable to demonstrate that the legislature, in its adoption of § 157, meant to limit the applicability of 157 to only the issuance of Rights for the purposes of corporate financing. Without such affirmative evidence, we decline to impose such a limitation upon the section that the legislature has not. . . .

As we noted in *Unocal:*

> [O]ur corporate law is not static. It must grow and develop in response to, indeed in anticipation of, evolving concepts and needs. Merely because the General Corporation Law is silent as to a specific matter does not mean that it is prohibited.

493 A.2d at 957. See also Cheff v. Mathes, Del.Supr., 199 A.2d 548 (1964).

Secondly, appellants contend that § 157 does not authorize the issuance of sham rights such as the Rights Plan. They contend that the Rights were designed never to be exercised, and that the Plan has no economic value. In addition, they contend the preferred stock made subject to the Rights is also illusory, citing Telvest, Inc. v. Olson, Del.Ch., C.A. No. 5798, Brown, V.C. (March 8, 1979).

Appellants' sham contention fails in both regards. As to the Rights, they can and will be exercised upon the happening of a triggering

---

5. The power to issue rights to purchase shares is conferred by 8 Del.C. § 157 which provides in relevant part:

> Subject to any provisions in the certificate of incorporation, every corporation may create and issue, whether or not in connection with the issue and sale of any shares of stock or other securities of the corporation, rights or options entitling the holders thereof to purchase from the corporation any shares of its capital stock of any class or classes, such rights or options to be evidenced by or in such instrument or instruments as shall be approved by the board of directors.

6. 8 Del.C. § 151(g) provides in relevant part:

> When any corporation desires to issue any shares of stock of any class or of any series of any class of which the voting powers, designations, preferences and relative, participating, optional or other rights, if any, or the qualifications, limitations or restrictions thereof, if any, shall not have been set forth in the certificate of incorporation or in any amendment thereto but shall be provided for in a resolution or resolutions adopted by the board of directors pursuant to authority expressly vested in it by the provisions of the certificate of incorporation or any amendment thereto, a certificate setting forth a copy of such resolution or resolutions and the number of shares of stock of such class or series shall be executed, acknowledged, filed, recorded, and shall become effective, in accordance with § 103 of this title.

mechanism . . . As to the preferred shares, we agree with the Court of Chancery that they are distinguishable from sham securities invalidated in *Telvest,* supra. The Household preferred, issuable upon the happening of a triggering event, have superior dividend and liquidation rights.

Third, appellants contend that § 157 authorizes the issuance of Rights "entitling holders thereof to purchase from the corporation any shares of *its* capital stock of any class . . ." (emphasis added). Therefore, their contention continues, the plain language of the statute does not authorize Household to issue rights to purchase another's capital stock upon a merger of consolidation.

Household contends, *inter alia,* that the Rights Plan is analogous to "anti-destruction" or "anti-dilution" provisions which are customary features of a wide variety of corporate securities. While appellants seem to concede that "anti-destruction" provisions are valid under Delaware corporate law, they seek to distinguish the Rights Plan as not being incidental, as are most "anti-destruction" provisions, to a corporation's statutory power to finance itself. We find no merit to such a distinction. We have already rejected appellants' similar contention that § 157 could only be used for financing purposes. We also reject that distinction here.

"Anti-destruction" clauses generally ensure holders of certain securities of the protection of their right of conversion in the event of a merger by giving them the right to convert their securities into whatever securities are to replace the stock of their company. . . . The fact that the rights here have as their purpose the prevention of coercive two-tier tender offers does not invalidate them. . . .

Having concluded that sufficient authority for the Rights Plan exists in 8 Del.C. § 157, we note the inherent powers of the Board conferred by 8 Del.C. § 141(a), concerning the management of the corporation's "business and *affairs*" (emphasis added), also provides the Board additional authority upon which to enact the Rights Plan. *Unocal,* 493 A.2d at 953.

B.

Appellants contend that the Board is unauthorized to usurp stockholders' rights to receive tender offers by changing Household's fundamental structure. . . .

Appellants' contention that stockholders will lose their right to receive and accept tender offers seems to be premised upon an understanding of the Rights Plan which is illustrated by the SEC *amicus* brief which states: "The Chancery Court's decision seriously understates the impact of this plan. In fact, as we discuss below, the Rights Plan will deter not only two-tier offers, but virtually all hostile tender offers."

The fallacy of that contention is apparent when we look at the recent takeover of Crown Zellerbach, which has a similar Rights Plan, by Sir James Goldsmith. Wall Street Journal, July 26, 1985, at 3, 12. The evidence at trial also evidenced many methods around the Plan ranging from tendering with a condition that the Board redeem the Rights, tendering with a high minimum condition of shares and Rights, tendering and soliciting consents to remove the Board and redeem the Rights, to acquiring 50% of the shares and causing Household to self-tender for the Rights. One could also form a group of up to 19.9% and solicit proxies for consents to remove the Board and redeem the Rights. These are but a few of the methods by which Household can still be acquired by a hostile tender offer.

In addition, the Rights Plan is not absolute. When the Household Board of Directors is faced with a tender offer and a request to redeem the Rights, they will not be able to arbitrarily reject the offer. They will be held to the same fiduciary standards any other board of directors would be held to in deciding to adopt a defensive mechanism, the same standard as they were held to in originally approving the Rights Plan. See *Unocal,* 493 A.2d at 954–55, 958.

In addition, appellants contend that the deterrence of tender offers will be accomplished by what they label "a fundamental transfer of power from the stockholders to the directors." They contend that this transfer of power, in itself, is unauthorized.

The Rights Plan will result in no more of a structural change than any other defensive mechanism adopted by a board of directors. The Rights Plan does not destroy the assets of the corporation. The implementation of the Plan neither results in any outflow of money from the corporation nor impairs its financial flexibility. It does not dilute earnings per share and does not have any adverse tax consequences for the corporation or its stockholders. The Plan has not adversely affected the market price of Household's stock.

Comparing the Rights Plan with other defensive mechanisms, it does less harm to the value structure of the corporation than do the other mechanisms. Other mechanisms result in increased debt of the corporation. See Whittaker Corp. v. Edgar, supra (sale of "prize asset"), Cheff v. Mathes, supra, (paying greenmail to eliminate a threat), Unocal Corp. v. Mesa Petroleum Co., supra, (discriminatory self-tender).

There is little change in the governance structure as a result of the adoption of the Rights Plan. The Board does not now have unfettered discretion in refusing to redeem the Rights. The Board has no more discretion in refusing to redeem the Rights than it does in enacting any defensive mechanism.

The contention that the Rights Plan alters the structure more than do other defensive mechanisms because it is so effective as to make the corporation completely safe from hostile tender offers is likewise without merit. As explained above, there are numerous methods to successfully launch a hostile tender offer.

C.

Appellant's third contention is that the Board was unauthorized to fundamentally restrict stockholders' rights to conduct a proxy contest.

Appellants contend that the "20% trigger" effectively prevents any stockholder from first acquiring 20% or more shares before conducting a proxy contest and further, it prevents stockholders from banding together into a group to solicit proxies if, collectively, they own 20% or more of the stock.[12] . . .

Regarding this issue the Court of Chancery found:

> Thus, while the Rights Plan does deter the formation of proxy efforts of a certain magnitude, it does not limit the voting power of individual shares. On the evidence presented it is highly conjectural to assume that a particular effort to assert shareholder views in the election of directors or revisions of corporate policy will be frustrated by the proxy feature of the Plan. Household's witnesses, Troubh and Higgins described recent corporate takeover battles in which insurgents holding less than 10% stock ownership were able to secure corporate control through a proxy contest or the threat of one.

Moran, 490 A.2d at 1080.

We conclude that there was sufficient evidence at trial to support the Vice–Chancellor's finding that the effect upon proxy contests will be minimal. Evidence at trial established that many proxy contests are won with an insurgent ownership of less than 20%, and that very large holdings are no guarantee of success. There was also testimony that the key variable in proxy contest success is the merit of an insurgent's issues, not the size of his holdings.

IV

Having concluded that the adoption of the Rights Plan was within the authority of the Directors, we now look to whether the Directors have met their burden under the business judgment rule.

The business judgment rule is a "presumption that in making a business decision the directors of a corporation acted on an informed basis, in good faith and in the honest belief that the action taken was in the best interests of the company." Aronson v. Lewis, Del.Supr., 473 A.2d 805, 812 (1984) (citations omitted). Notwithstanding, in *Unocal* we held that when the business judgment rule applies to adoption of a defensive mechanism, the initial burden will lie with the directors. The "directors must show that they had reasonable grounds for believing that a danger to corporate policy and effectiveness existed.... [T]hey satisfy that burden 'by showing good faith and reasonable investigation....' " *Unocal,* 493 A.2d at 955 (citing Cheff v. Mathes, 199 A.2d at 55455). In addition, the directors must show that the defensive mechanism was reasonable in relation to the threat posed. *Unocal,* 493 A.2d at 955. Moreover, that proof is materially enhanced, as we noted in *Unocal,* where, as here, a majority of the board favoring the proposal consisted of outside independent directors who have acted

12. Appellants explain that the acquisition of 20% of the shares trigger the Rights, making them non-redeemable, and thereby would prevent even a future friendly offer for the ten-year life of the Rights.

in accordance with the foregoing standards. *Unocal,* 493 A.2d at 955; *Aronson,* 473 A.2d at 815. Then, the burden shifts back to the plaintiffs who have the ultimate burden of persuasion to show a breach of the directors' fiduciary duties. *Unocal,* 493 A.2d at 958.

There are no allegations here of any bad faith on the part of the Directors' action in the adoption of the Rights Plan. There is no allegation that the Directors' action was taken for entrenchment purposes. Household has adequately demonstrated, as explained above, that the adoption of the Rights Plan was in reaction to what it perceived to be the threat in the market place of coercive two-tier tender offers....

To determine whether a business judgment reached by a board of directors was an informed one, we determine whether the directors were grossly negligent. Smith v. Van Gorkom, Del.Supr., 488 A.2d 858, 873 (1985). Upon a review of this record, we conclude the Directors were not grossly negligent. The information supplied to the Board on August 14 provided the essentials of the Plan. The Directors were given beforehand a notebook which included a three-page summary of the Plan along with articles on the current takeover environment. The extended discussion between the Board and representatives of Wachtell, Lipton and Goldman, Sachs before approval of the Plan reflected a full and candid evaluation of the Plan. Moran's expression of his views at the meeting served to place before the Board a knowledgeable critique of the Plan. The factual happenings here are clearly distinguishable from the actions of the directors of Trans Union Corporation who displayed gross negligence in approving a cash-out merger. Id.

In addition, to meet their burden, the Directors must show that the defensive mechanism was "reasonable in relation to the threat posed". The record reflects a concern on the part of the Directors over the increasing frequency in the financial services industry of "bootstrap" and "bust-up" takeovers. The Directors were also concerned that such takeovers may take the form of two-tier offers.[14] In addition, on August 14, the Household Board was aware of Moran's overture on behalf of D–K–M. In sum, the Directors reasonably believed Household was vulnerable to coercive acquisition techniques and adopted a reasonable defensive mechanism to protect itself.

V

In conclusion, the Household Directors receive the benefit of the business judgment rule in their adoption of the Rights Plan.

The Directors adopted the Plan pursuant to statutory authority in 8 Del.C. §§ 141, 151, 157. We reject appellants' contentions that the Rights Plan strips stockholders of their rights to receive tender offers, and that the Rights Plan fundamentally restricts proxy contests.

---

14. We have discussed the coercive nature of two-tier tender offers in *Unocal,* 493 A.2d at 956, n. 12. We explained in *Unocal* that a discriminatory self-tender was reasonably related to the threat of two-tier tender offers and possible greenmail.

The Directors adopted the Plan in the good faith belief that it was necessary to protect Household from coercive acquisition techniques. The Board was informed as to the details of the Plan. In addition, Household has demonstrated that the Plan is reasonable in relation to the threat posed. Appellants, on the other hand, have failed to convince us that the Directors breached any fiduciary duty in their adoption of the Rights Plan.

While we conclude for present purposes that the Household Directors are protected by the business judgment rule, that does not end the matter. The ultimate response to an actual takeover bid must be judged by the Directors' actions at that time, and nothing we say here relieves them of their basic fundamental duties to the corporation and its stockholders. Their use of the Plan will be evaluated when and if the issue arises.

AFFIRMED.*

* * *

Among public companies, poison pills are ubiquitous. Should the validity of the pill turn on whether a company's board adopted a pill before there was a contest for control? *See e.g.,* Independence Fed. Sav. Bank. v. Bender, 326 F.Supp. 2d 36, 49–50 (D.D.C. 2004)(refusing to compel pill's redemption because it was adopted during a merger contest); Burcham v. Unison Bancorp, Inc., 276 Kan. 393, 409, 77 P.3d 130, 145 (2003)(denying summary judgment on question whether adoption of a poison pill in the heat of a takeover was itself a breach of the directors' fiduciary duty).

Moran emphasized the redemption provision of the pill, seeing this as crucial to the pill's validity. What are the benefits of kicking the pill's validity down the road to when there is a contest and the bidder or target shareholder challenge the board's decision not to redeem the pill? Is there a down side of testing the pill's validity in the heat of a takeover contest?

In a few early decisions the court reviewing the non-redemption decision were disposed to order the target board to redeem the pill. *See* Southdown, Inc. v. Moore McCormack Resources, Inc., 686 F. Supp. 595, 605 (S.D. Tex. 1988)(concluding that entrenchment not the stockholders' interest motivated board's decision not to redeem the pill); A Copeland Enterprises, Inc. v. Guste, 706 F. Supp. 1283, 1286 (W.D. Tex. 1989)(upholding the validity of the pill at the moment the hostile bid was commenced, but expressing an intent to order the pill's redemption when the bidder's tender offer closed if the pill was then still outstanding). As the pill became more prevalent, judicial decisions have been more deferential to the target board. *See e.g.,* Dynamics Corp. of Amer. v. WHX Corp., 967 F. Supp. 59, 65 (D. Conn. 1997); Moore Corp. v. Wallace Computer Services, 907 F. Supp. 1545, 1553 (D. Del. 1995)(refusing to order redemption where board alleged the hostile bid undervalued the firm even though seventy

* *Moran* was reaffirmed in Account v. Hilton Hotels Corp., 780 A.2d 245 (2001).

percent of the shareholders had tendered their shares in response to the bid). While legal skirmishes continue on a variety of issues posed by the pill, the courtroom is not the only antidote the frustrated bidder can seek. There is the avenue of the proxy fight, electing a new majority beholding to the bidder who can be expected to not just redeem the pill, but do the deal.

NOTE ON CARMODY v. TOLL BROTHERS, INC.

The facts of the next principal case, *Quickturn Design Systems, Inc. v. Shapiro*, decided by the Delaware Supreme Court, can best be understood against the background of an earlier case decided by the Delaware Chancery Court, Carmody v. Toll Brothers, Inc., 723 A.2d 1180 (Del.Ch.1998). *Carmody* concerned the validity of a "dead hand" poison pill adopted by Toll Brothers, Inc. As described by Vice Chancellor Jacobs:

> A "dead hand" rights plan is one that cannot be redeemed except by the incumbent directors who adopted the plan or their designated successors.
>
> In substance, the "dead hand" provision operates to prevent any directors of Toll Brothers, except those who were in office as of the date of the Rights Plan's adoption (June 12, 1997) or their designated successors, from redeeming the Rights until they expire on June 12, 2007. That consequence flows directly from the Rights Agreement's [provision that] only "Continuing Directors" could redeem the Rights, and from its definition of a "Continuing Director," which is:
>
>> (i) any member of the Board of Directors of the Company, while such person is a member of the Board, who is not an Acquiring Person, or an Affiliate [as defined] or Associate [as defined] of an Acquiring Person, or a representative or nominee of an Acquiring Person or of any such Affiliate or Associate, and was a member of the Board prior to the date of this agreement, or (ii) any Person who subsequently becomes a member of the Board, while such Person is a member of the Board, who is not an Acquiring Person, or an Affiliate [as defined] or Associate [as defined] of an Acquiring Person, or a representative or nominee of an Acquiring Person or of any such Affiliate or Associate, if such Person's nomination for election or election to the Board is recommended or approved by a majority of the Continuing Directors.

Vice Chancellor Jacobs explained the genesis of dead hand pills as follows:

> In *Moran*, this Court and the Supreme Court upheld the "flip over" rights plan in issue there based on three distinct factual findings. The first was that the poison pill would not erode fundamental shareholder rights, because the target board would

not have unfettered discretion arbitrarily to reject a hostile offer or to refuse to redeem the pill. Rather, the board's judgment not to redeem the pill would be subject to judicially enforceable fiduciary standards. The second finding was that even if the board refused to redeem the pill (thereby preventing the shareholders from receiving the unsolicited offer), that would not preclude the acquiror from gaining control of the target company, because the offeror could "form a group of up to 19.9% and solicit proxies for consents to remove the Board and redeem the Rights." Third, even if the hostile offer was precluded, the target company's stockholders could always exercise their ultimate prerogative—wage a proxy contest to remove the board. On this basis, the Supreme Court concluded that "the Rights Plan will not have a severe impact upon proxy contests and it will not preclude all hostile acquisitions of Household."

It being settled that a corporate board could permissibly adopt a poison pill, the next litigated question became: under what circumstances would the directors' fiduciary duties require the board to redeem the rights in the face of a hostile takeover proposal? That issue was litigated, in Delaware and elsewhere, during the second half of the 1980s. The lesson taught by that experience was that courts were extremely reluctant to order the redemption of poison pills on fiduciary grounds. The reason was the prudent deployment of the pill proved to be largely beneficial to shareholder interests: it often resulted in a bidding contest that culminated in an acquisition on terms superior to the initial hostile offer.

Once it became clear that the prospects were unlikely for obtaining judicial relief mandating a redemption of the poison pill, a different response to the pill was needed. That response, which echoed the Supreme Court's suggestion in Moran, was the foreseeable next step in the evolution of takeover strategy: a tender offer coupled with a solicitation for shareholder proxies to remove and replace the incumbent board with the acquiror's nominees who, upon assuming office, would redeem the pill. Because that strategy, if unopposed, would enable hostile offerors to effect an "end run" around the poison pill, it again was predictable and only a matter of time that target company boards would develop counter-strategies. With one exception—the "dead hand" pill—these counter-strategies proved "successful" only in cases where the purpose was to delay the process to enable the board to develop alternatives to the hostile offer. The counter-strategies were largely unsuccessful, however, where the goal was to stop the proxy contest (and as a consequence, the hostile offer) altogether.

For example, in cases where the target board's response was either to (i) amend the by-laws to delay a shareholders meeting to elect directors, or (ii) delay an annual meeting to a later date permitted under the bylaws, so that the board and management would be able to explore alternatives to the hostile offer (but not entrench themselves), those responses were upheld. On the other hand, where the target board's response to a proxy contest (coupled with a hostile offer) was (i) to move the shareholders meeting to a later date to enable the incumbent board to solicit revocations of proxies to defeat the apparently victorious dissident group, or (ii) to expand the size of the board, and then fill the newly created positions so the incumbents would retain control of the board irrespective of the outcome of the proxy contest, those responses were declared invalid.

This litigation experience taught that a target board, facing a proxy contest joined with a hostile tender offer, could, in good faith, employ non-preclusive defensive measures to give the board time to explore transactional alternatives. The target board could not, however, erect defenses that would either preclude a proxy contest altogether or improperly bend the rules to favor the board's continued incumbency.

In this environment, the only defensive measure that promised to be a "show stopper" (i.e., had the potential to deter a proxy contest altogether) was a poison pill with a dead hand feature. The reason is that if only the incumbent directors or their designated successors could redeem the pill, it would make little sense for shareholders or the hostile bidder to wage a proxy contest to replace the incumbent board. Doing that would eliminate from the scene the only group of persons having the power to give the hostile bidder and target company shareholders what they desired: control of the target company (in the case of the hostile bidder) and the opportunity to obtain an attractive price for their shares (in the case of the target company stockholders). It is against that backdrop that the legal issues presented here, which concern the validity of the "dead hand" feature, attain significance.

Vice Chancellor Jacobs concluded that the plaintiff's complaint stated a legally cognizable claim that a dead hand plan is invalid, on several grounds:

First, a dead hand pill violates the Delaware statute by impermissibly creating voting-power distinctions among directors without authorization in the certificate of incorporation, and by interfering with the directors' statutory power to manage the business and affairs of the corporation.

Second, a dead hand pill is unlawful under *Blasius* (See Chapter 5, supra), because it purposefully interferes with the shareholder voting franchise without any compelling justification.

Third, a dead hand pill is a "disproportionate" defensive measure under *Unocal/Unitrin*, because it either precludes or materially abridges the shareholders' rights to receive tender offers and to wage a proxy contest to replace the board.

In contrast to *Carmody*, a dead hand pill was upheld by a federal district court under Georgia law in *Invacare Corp. v. Healthdyne Technologies, Inc.*, 968 F.Supp. 1578 (N.D. Ga. 1997), although the result in that case was driven at least in part by an interpretation of language in the Georgia statute.

Quickturn Design Systems, Inc. v. Shapiro

Supreme Court of Delaware, 1998.
721 A.2d 1281.

■ Before WALSH, HOLLAND and HARTNETT, JUSTICES.

■ HOLLAND, JUSTICE: . . .

[Mentor and Quickturn (incorporated in Oregon and Delaware, respectively) had been embroiled in patent infringement litigation since 1996. The origin of the patent controversy was Mentor's sale of its hardware emulation assets, including its patents, to Quickturn in 1992. Later, when Mentor reentered the emulation business through its recently acquired French subsidiary, Meta Systems ("Meta"), Quickturn reacted by commencing a proceeding before the International Trade Commission ("ITC") claiming that Meta and Mentor were infringing Quickturn's patents. This litigation proved successful for Quickturn; in August 1996, Mentor was enjoined from selling, manufacturing, or marketing its emulation products in the United States and thus excluded from the most significant market for emulation products. At the time of the present litigation, Quickturn was pressing its claim for patent infringement damages, seeking approximately $225 million. Mentor contends that Quickturn's claim is worth only $5.2 million or even less.

In late 1997, Mentor began exploring the possibility of acquiring Quickturn. Its financial advisors opined that acquiring Quickturn would add substantial value to Mentor. Quickturn was the market leader in the emulation business, controlling an estimated 60% of the worldwide emulation market—an even higher percentage of the United States market—and held the largest intellectual property portfolio in the industry. Moreover, they reasoned that if Mentor owned Quickturn, it would also own the patents, and would be in a position to "unenforce" them by seeking to vacate Quickturn's injunctive orders against Mentor in the patent litigation. After receiving this advice, fortune appeared to shine on Mentor. Although Quickturn had historically been a growth company (its stock traded between $15.875 to $21.25 range during the year preceding Mentor's hostile bid), in the spring of 1998, Quickturn's earnings, revenue growth, and stock price levels declined, largely because of the downturn in the semiconductor industry and more specifically in the Asian semiconductor market.

On August 12, 1998, Mentor announced its cash tender offer of $12.125 per share for all outstanding common shares of Quickturn. The tender offer price represented about a 50% premium over Quickturn's immediate pre-offer price; however, due to the recent substantial decline in its business and concomitant fall in its stock price, the tender offer price was 20% below Quickturn's February 1998 stock price levels. Mentor's disclosed that once its tender offer was consummated, it would undertake a merger in which Quickturn's nontendering stockholders would receive, in cash, the same $12.125 per share tender offer price. Mentor also announced its intent to solicit proxies to replace the board at a special meeting.

Quickturn's board of directors consisted of eight members, all but one of whom are outside, independent directors. Collectively, the board has more than 30 years of experience in the EDA industry and owned one million shares (about 5%) of Quickturn's common stock. The board met three times in August 1998 to discuss Mentor's tender offer. At the penultimate meeting on August 21, 1998, the directors received extensive materials and a further detailed analysis performed from its investment banker, Hambrecht Quist (H & Q). The focal point of that analysis was a chart entitled "Summary of Implied Valuation." That chart compared Mentor's tender offer price to the Quickturn valuation ranges generated by five different methodologies. The chart showed that Quickturn's value under all but one of those methodologies was higher than Mentor's $12.125 tender offer price.]

Quickturn's Board Rejects Mentor's Offer as Inadequate

After hearing the presentations, the Quickturn board concluded that Mentor's offer was inadequate, and decided to recommend that Quickturn shareholders reject Mentor's offer. The directors based their decision upon: (a) H & Q's report; (b) the fact that Quickturn was experiencing a temporary trough in its business, which was reflected in its stock price; (c) the company's leadership in technology and patents and resulting market share; (d) the likely growth in Quickturn's markets (most notably, the Asian market) and the strength of Quickturn's new products (specifically, its Mercury product); (e) the potential value of the patent litigation with Mentor; and (f) the problems for Quickturn's customers, employees, and technology if the two companies were combined as the result of a hostile takeover....

QUICKTURN'S DELAYED REDEMPTION PROVISION

At the time Mentor commenced its bid, Quickturn had in place a Rights Plan that contained a so-called "dead hand" provision. That provision had a limited "continuing director" feature that became operative only if an insurgent that owned more than 15% of Quickturn's common stock successfully waged a proxy contest to replace a majority of the board. In that event, only the "continuing directors" (those directors in office at the time the poison pill was adopted) could redeem the rights.

During the ... August 21, 1998 meeting ... the Quickturn board ... amended the Rights Plan to eliminate its "continuing director" feature, and to substitute a "no hand" or "delayed redemption provision" into its Rights Plan. The Delayed Redemption Provision [DRP] provides that, if a majority of the directors are replaced by stockholder action, the newly elected board cannot redeem the rights for six months if the purpose or effect of the redemption would be to facilitate a transaction with an "Interested Person."[21]

It is undisputed that the DRP would prevent Mentor's slate, if elected as the new board majority, from redeeming the Rights Plan for six months following their election, because a redemption would be "reasonably likely to have the purpose or effect of facilitating a Transaction" with Mentor, a party that "directly or indirectly proposed, nominated or financially supported" the election of the new board. Consequently, by adopting the DRP, the Quickturn board built into the process a six month delay period. . . .

COURT OF CHANCERY INVALIDATES DELAYED REDEMPTION PROVISION . . .

The Court of Chancery found: "the evidence, viewed as a whole, shows that the perceived threat that led the Quickturn board to adopt the DRP, was the concern that Quickturn shareholders might mistakenly, in ignorance of Quickturn's true value, accept Mentor's inadequate offer, and elect a new board that would prematurely sell the company before the new board could adequately inform itself of Quickturn's fair value and before the shareholders could consider other options." The Court of Chancery concluded that Mentor's combined tender offer and proxy contest amounted to substantive coercion.[25] Having concluded that the Quickturn board reasonably perceived a cognizable threat, the Court of Chancery then examined whether the board's response—the Delayed Redemption Provision—was proportionate in relation to that threat. . . .

The Court of Chancery found that the Quickturn board's "justification or rationale for adopting the Delayed Redemption Provision was to force any newly elected board to take sufficient time to become familiar with Quickturn and its value, and to provide shareholders the opportunity to consider alternatives, before selling Quickturn to any acquiror." The Court of Chancery concluded that the Delayed Redemption Provision could not pass the proportionality test. Therefore, the Court of Chancery held that "the DRP cannot survive scrutiny under Unocal and must be declared invalid."

DELAYED REDEMPTION PROVISION VIOLATES FUNDAMENTAL DELAWARE LAW . . .

Our analysis of the Delayed Redemption Provision in the Quickturn Rights Plan is guided by the prior precedents of this Court with

---

21. The "no hand" or Delayed Redemption Provision is found in a new Section 23(b) of the Rights Plan, which states: (b) Notwithstanding the provisions of Section 23(a), in the event that a majority of the Board of Directors of the Company is elected by stockholder action at an annual or special meeting of stockholders, then until the 180th day following the effectiveness of such election (including any postponement or adjournment thereof), the Rights shall not be redeemed if such redemption is reasonably likely to have the purpose or effect of facilitating a Transaction with an Interested Person.

Substantially similar provisions were added to Sections 24 ("Exchange") and 27 ("Supplements and Amendments") of the Rights Plan.

25. Unitrin, Inc. v. American General Corp., 651 A.2d at 1387.

regard to a board of directors authority to adopt a Rights Plan or "poison pill." In *Moran*, this Court held that the inherent powers of the Board conferred by 8 Del.C. § 141(a) concerning the management of the corporation's "business and affairs" provides the Board additional authority upon which to enact the Rights Plan.[30] Consequently, this Court upheld the adoption of the Rights Plan in *Moran* as a legitimate exercise of business judgment by the board of directors. In doing so, however, this Court also held the rights plan is not absolute....

One of the most basic tenets of Delaware corporate law is that the board of directors has the ultimate responsibility for managing the business and affairs of a corporation.[36] Section 141(a) requires that any limitation on the board's authority be set out in the certificate of incorporation.[37] The Quickturn certificate of incorporation contains no provision purporting to limit the authority of the board in any way. The Delayed Redemption Provision, however, would prevent a newly elected board of directors from completely discharging its fundamental management duties to the corporation and its stockholders for six months. While the Delayed Redemption Provision limits the board of directors' authority in only one respect, the suspension of the Rights Plan, it nonetheless restricts the board's power in an area of fundamental importance to the shareholders negotiating a possible sale of the corporation. Therefore, we hold that the Delayed Redemption Provision is invalid under Section 141(a), which confers upon any newly elected board of directors full power to manage and direct the business and affairs of a Delaware corporation....

The Delayed Redemption Provision prevents a newly elected board of directors from completely discharging its fiduciary duties to protect fully the interests of Quickturn and its stockholders.[41] ...

The Delayed Redemption Provision "tends to limit in a substantial way the freedom of [newly elected] directors' decisions on matters of management policy."[44] Therefore, "it violates the duty of each [newly

30. Moran v. Household International, Inc., Del.Supr., 500 A.2d 1346, 1353 (1985), citing Unocal Corp. v. Mesa Petroleum Co., Del.Supr., 493 A.2d 946, 953 (1985).

When the Household Board of Directors is faced with a tender offer and a request to redeem the Rights [Plan], they will not be able to arbitrarily reject the offer. They will be held to the same fiduciary standards any other board of directors would be held to in deciding to adopt a defensive mechanism, the same standards as they were held to in originally approving the Rights Plan.

36. 8 Del.C. § 141(a). See Mills Acquisition Co. v. Macmillan, Inc., Del.Supr., 559 A.2d 1261, 1280 (1989).

37. 8 Del.C. § 141(a) states: "The business and affairs of every corporation organized under this chapter shall be managed by or under the direction of a board of directors, except as may be otherwise provided in this chapter or in its certificate of incorporation. If any such provision is made in the certificate of incorporation, the powers and duties conferred or imposed upon the board of directors by this chapter shall be exercised or performed to such extent and by such person or persons as shall be provided in the certificate of incorporation."

41. See Moran v. Household International, Inc., 500 A.2d at 1354.

44. Abercrombie v. Davies, Del.Ch., 123 A.2d 893, 899 (1956), rev'd on other grounds, Del.Supr., 130 A.2d 338 (1957).

elected] director to exercise his own best judgment on matters coming before the board."[45]

In this case, the Quickturn board was confronted by a determined bidder that sought to acquire the company at a price the Quickturn board concluded was inadequate. Such situations are common in corporate takeover efforts.[46] In Revlon, this Court held that no defensive measure can be sustained when it represents a breach of the directors' fiduciary duty. A fortiori, no defensive measure can be sustained which would require a new board of directors to breach its fiduciary duty. In that regard, we note Mentor has properly acknowledged that in the event its slate of directors are elected, those newly elected directors will be required to discharge their unremitting fiduciary duty to manage the corporation for the benefit of Quickturn and its stockholders.[47]

Conclusion

The Delayed Redemption Provision would prevent a new Quickturn board of directors from managing the corporation by redeeming the Rights Plan to facilitate a transaction that would serve the stockholders' best interests, even under circumstances where the board would be required to do so because of its fiduciary duty to the Quickturn stockholders. Because the Delayed Redemption Provision impermissibly circumscribes the board's statutory power under Section 141(a) and the directors' ability to fulfill their concomitant fiduciary duties, we hold that the Delayed Redemption Provision is invalid. On that alternative basis, the judgment of the Court of Chancery is AFFIRMED.

Contra. AMP, Inc. v. Allied Signal, Inc., 1998 WL 778348 (E.D. Pa. 1998) (relying on both the state's poison pill validation and constituency statutes, the court reasoned that a delayed redemption feature of a poison pill was valid being consistent with the state's public policy and because it interfered with the board's discretion for only for a finite period of time).

In the last few proxy seasons, shareholders have frequently proposed "declassifying" board of directors. Recall that corporations can provide that directors can serve staggered three-year terms so that only one-third of the board turns over each year. In reflecting on why activist shareholders are eager that their portfolio companies elect all their directors annually consider the following. During a five-year study period, Professors Bebchuk, Coates and Subramanian found that staggered boards increased the likelihood of a company remaining independent from 34% to 61% and that staggered boards reduce the likelihood of the first bidder being successful from 34% to 14%. Lucian

45. Id.

46. Revlon, Inc. v. MacAndrews Forbes Holdings, Inc., 506 A.2d at 185.

47. Malone v. Brincat, Del.Supr., 722 A.2d 5 (1998).

Arye Bebchuk, John C. Coates IV & Guhan Subramanian, The Powerful Antitakeover Force of Staggered Boards: Theory, Evidence, and Policy, 54 Stan. L. Rev. 887, 930–31 (2002). Why should a staggered board make the pill more effective? Hint-consider the protection from removal that directors serving on a classified board enjoy in Delaware. *See* Del. Code Ann., tit. 8 § 141(k)(1).

Air Products and Chemicals, Inc. v. Airgas, Inc.

Delaware Court of Chancery, 2011.
2011 WL 806417.

■ CHANDLER, CHANCELLOR.

[Air Products launched a hostile bid to acquire Air Gas. However, after a number of reversals in the Delaware courts, after the instant decision, it ultimately terminated its quest for Air Gas after having fought a sixteen month battle for Air Gas. The source of much of the skirmishing was due to Air Gas having both a poison pill and a classified board—nine directors serving three-year staggered terms. At the September 2010 annual meeting, three directors supported by Air Products were elected to Air Gas' board over the Air Gas nominees. Air Products' proxy materials supporting their election identified them as "independent" individuals who, "without any bias," would consider Air Product's offer and in doing so act in Air Gas stockholders' best interest. And independent they were; shortly after the three newly elected directors learned more about Air Gas from its various advisers, they joined the other directors in the unanimous view that Air Product's $70 per share offer was inadequate. Although Air Gas' charter allowed a 33 percent holder to call a special stockholders meeting and authorized the removal of the entire board by a vote of 67 percent of the outstanding shares, Air Products chose not to seek the entire board's removal. Instead it challenged the validity of the board's refusal to redeem the poison pill. After an exhaustive review of the Delaware jurisprudence surrounding defensive maneuvers, Chancellor Chandler provides the following insights on the efficacy of staggered boards and a board's refusal to redeem the pill in the face of a determined, but unwanted, suitor.]

1. Preclusive or Coercive

A defensive measure is coercive if it is "aimed at 'cramming down' on its shareholders a management-sponsored alternative." Airgas's defensive measures are certainly not coercive in this respect, as Airgas is specifically *not* trying to cram down a management sponsored alternative, but rather, simply wants to maintain the status quo and manage the company for the long term.

. . . Air Products and Shareholder Plaintiffs argue that Airgas's defensive measures are preclusive because they render the possibility of an effective proxy contest realistically unattainable. What the argument boils down to, though, is that Airgas's defensive measures make the possibility of Air Products obtaining control of the Airgas board and removing the pill realistically unattainable *in the very near future*, because Airgas has a staggered board in place. Thus, the real issue posed is whether defensive measures are "preclusive" if they make gaining control of the board realistically unattainable in the short term (but still realistically attainable sometime in the future), or if "preclusive" actually means "preclusive"—i.e. forever unattainable. In reality, or perhaps I should say in practice, these two formulations ("preclusive for now" or "preclusive forever") may be one and the same when examining the combination of a staggered board plus a poison pill, because no bidder to my knowledge has ever successfully stuck around for two years and waged two successful proxy contests to gain control of a classified board in order to remove a pill. So does that make the combination of a staggered board and a poison pill preclusive?

This precise question was asked and answered four months ago in *Versata Enterprises, Inc. v. Selectica, Inc.*,[5 A.3d 586 (Del. 2010)]. There, Trilogy (the hostile acquiror) argued that in order for the target's defensive measures not to be preclusive: (1) a successful proxy contest must be realistically attainable, and (2) the successful proxy contest must result in gaining control of the board at the next election. The Delaware Supreme Court rejected this argument, stating that "[i]f that preclusivity argument is correct, then it would apply whenever a corporation has both a classified board and a Rights Plan.... *[W]e hold that the combination of a classified board and a Rights Plan do not constitute a preclusive defense.*"

The Supreme Court explained its reasoning as follows:

> Classified boards are authorized by statute and are adopted for a variety of business purposes. Any classified board also operates as an antitakeover defense by preventing an insurgent from obtaining control of the board in one election. More than a decade ago, in *Carmody* [*v. Toll Brothers, Inc.*], the Court of Chancery noted "because only one third of a classified board would stand for election each year, a classified board would *delay—but not prevent—a hostile acquiror from obtaining control of the board*, since a determined acquiror could wage a proxy contest and obtain control of two thirds of the target board over a two year period, as opposed to seizing control in a single election."

The Court concluded: "The fact that a combination of defensive measures makes it more difficult for an acquirer to obtain control of a board does not make such measures realistically unattainable, i.e., preclusive." . . .

I am thus bound by this clear precedent to proceed on the assumption that Airgas's defensive measures are not preclusive if they delay Air Products from obtaining control of the Airgas board (even if that delay is significant) so long as obtaining control at some point in the future is realistically attainable. I now examine whether the ability to obtain control of Airgas's board in the future is realistically attainable.

Air Products has already run one successful slate of insurgents. Their three independent nominees were elected to the Airgas board in September. Airgas's next annual meeting will be held sometime around September 2011. Accordingly, if Airgas's defensive measures remain in place, Air Products has two options if it wants to continue to pursue Airgas at this time: (1) It can call a special meeting and remove the entire board with a supermajority vote of the outstanding shares, or (2) It can wait until Airgas's 2011 annual meeting to nominate a slate of directors. I will address the viability of each of these options in turn.

a. Call a Special Meeting to Remove the Airgas Board by a 67% Supermajority Vote

Airgas's charter allows for 33% of the outstanding shares to call a special meeting of the stockholders, and to remove the entire board without cause by a vote of 67% of the outstanding shares. Defendants make much of the fact that "[o]f the 85 Delaware companies in the Fortune 500 with staggered boards, only six (including Airgas) have charter provisions that permit shareholders to remove directors without cause between annual meetings (i.e., at a special meeting and/or by written consent)." This argument alone is not decisive on the issue of preclusivity, although it does distinguish the particular facts of this case from the typical case of a company with a staggered board.[449] Ultimately, though, it does not matter how many or how few companies in the Fortune 500 with staggered boards allow shareholders to remove directors by calling a special meeting; what matters is the "realistic attainability" of actually achieving a 67% vote of the outstanding Airgas shares in the context of Air Products' hostile tender offer (which equates to achieving approximately 85–86% of the unaffiliated voting shares), or whether, instead, Airgas's continued use of its defensive measures is preclusive because it is a near "impossible task."

The fact that something might be a theoretical possibility does not make it "realistically attainable." In other words, what the Supreme Court in *Unitrin* and *Selectica* meant by "realistically attainable" must be something more than a mere "mathematical possibility" or "hypothetically conceivable chance" of circumventing a poison pill. One would think a sensible understanding of the phrase would be that an insurgent has a reasonably meaningful or real world shot at securing the support of enough stockholders to change the target board's composition and remove the obstructing defenses. It does not mean that the insurgent has a right to win or that the insurgent must have a

---

449. It also distinguishes this case from the paradigmatic case posited by Professors Bebchuk, Coates, and Subramanian in *54 Stan. L. Rev. 887 (2002)*. "Courts should not allow managers to continue blocking a takeover bid after they lose one election conducted over an acquisition offer." *Id. at 944*. In essence, the professors argue that corporations with an "effective staggered board" ("ESB"), defined as one in which a bidder "must go through two annual meetings in order to gain majority control of the target's board," should be required to redeem their pill after losing one election cycle. *Id. at 912–14, 944*. But, the professors concede, "without an ESB, no court intervention is necessary." *Id. at 944*. Airgas does not have an ESB as described by the professors because of its charter provision allowing removal of the entire board without consent at any time by a 67% vote.

highly probable chance or even a 50–50 chance of prevailing. But it must be more than just a theoretical possibility, given the required vote, the timing issues, the shareholder profile, the issues presented by the insurgent and the surrounding circumstances.

. . . [The Chancellor then reviewed the extensive evidence produced by the parties at the supplemental evidentiary hearing, concluding in the end that it was "unhelpful and unconvincing" on the fundamental question whether a 67% vote was realistically attainable.] The expert witnesses neither took the time nor made the effort to speak with any Airgas stockholders—whether retail, index, institutional investors who subcontract voting to ISS, long or short hedge funds, dual stockholders or event-driven stockholders—about how they might vote if such a special stockholder meeting were actually convened. To that extent, each expert failed to support his conclusions in a manner that a judge would find reliable. . . . Both experts essentially admitted, moreover, that one cannot really know how an election will turn out until it is held and that, generally speaking, it is easier to obtain investor support for electing a minority insurgent slate than for a controlling slate of directors.

In the end, however, the most telling aspect of the expert testimony was the statement that Air Products could certainly achieve 67% of the vote if its offer was "sufficiently appealing." Harkins [Air Gas' proxy expert] explained that he was "not predicting that a $70 offer will result in a 67 percent vote to remove the board." He was simply predicting that, with an appealing enough offer or platform, a 67% vote is possible, but he was not providing his opinion (nor did he have one) on how appealing $70 is, or whether it would make victory at a special election attainable. The following final, tautological insight by the expert just about sums up the usefulness of this particular day in the life of a trial judge:

Q. [So w]hat is a sufficiently appealing offer?

A. An offer that will garner 67 percent of the vote, I suppose.

But what seems clear to me, quite honestly, is that a poison pill is assuredly preclusive in the everyday common sense meaning of the word; indeed, its *rasion d'etre* is preclusion—to stop a bid (or *this* bid) from progressing. That is what it is intended to do and that is what the Airgas pill has done successfully for over sixteen months. Whether it is realistic to believe that Air Products can, at some point in the future, achieve a 67% vote necessary to remove the entire Airgas board at a special meeting is (in my opinion) impossible to predict given the host of variables in this setting, but the sheer lack of historical examples where an insurgent has ever achieved such a percentage in a contested control election must mean something. Commentators who have studied actual hostile takeovers for Delaware companies have, at least in part, essentially corroborated this common sense notion that such a victory is not realistically attainable.[474] Nonetheless, while the special meeting may not be a realistically attainable mechanism for circumventing the Airgas defenses, that assessment does not end the analysis under existing precedent.

b. Run Another Proxy Contest

Even if Air Products is unable to achieve the 67% supermajority vote of the outstanding shares necessary to remove the board in a special meeting, it would only need a simple majority of the voting stockholders to obtain control of the board at next year's annual meeting. Air Products has stated its unwillingness to wait around for another eight months until Airgas's 2011 annual meeting. There are legitimately articulated reasons for this—Air Products' stockholders, after all, have been carrying the burden of a depressed stock price since the announcement of the offer. But that is a business determination by the Air Products board. The reality is that obtaining a simple majority of the voting stock is significantly less burdensome than obtaining a supermajority vote of the outstanding shares, and considering the current composition of Airgas's stockholders (and the fact that, as a result of that shareholder composition, a majority of the voting shares today would likely tender into Air Products' $70 offer), if Air Products and those stockholders choose to stick around, an Air Products victory at the next annual meeting is very realistically attainable.

Air Products certainly realized this. It had actually intended to run an insurgent slate at Airgas's 2011 annual meeting—when everyone thought that meeting was going to be held in January. The Supreme Court has now held, however, that each annual meeting must take place "approximately" one year after the last annual meeting.[1] If Air Products is unwilling to wait another eight months to run another slate of nominees, that is a business decision of the Air Products board, but as the Supreme Court has held, waiting until the next annual meeting "delay[s]—but [does] not prevent—[Air Products] from obtaining control of the board." I thus am constrained to conclude that Airgas's defensive measures are not preclusive.

2. Range of Reasonableness

"If a defensive measure is neither coercive nor preclusive, the *Unocal* proportionality test requires the focus of enhanced judicial scrutiny to shift to the range of reasonableness." The reasonableness of a board's response is evaluated in the context of the specific threat identified—the "specific nature of the threat sets the parameters for the range of permissible defensive tactics' at any given time."

Here, the record demonstrates that Airgas's board, composed of a majority of outside, independent directors, acting in good faith and

1. Ed. Note: Through its own proxy solicitation in connection with the September 2010 annual meeting, Air Products was successful in obtaining stockholder approval to set the annual meetings in January 2011. It thus sought to advance by many months the time when the next group of three directors would stand for reelection. The change was struck down in Airgas, Inc. v. Air Prods. and Chems., Inc., 8 A.3d 1182 (Del.Supr. 2010), holding that the discretion to fix an annual meeting date is not unfettered; it must pick a date that is "approximately" one year after its last annual meeting.

with numerous outside advisors concluded that Air Products' offer clearly undervalues Airgas in a sale transaction. The board believes in good faith that the offer price is inadequate by no small margin. Thus, the board is responding to a legitimately articulated threat.

This conclusion is bolstered by the fact that the three Air Products Nominees on the Airgas board have now wholeheartedly joined in the board's determination—what is more, they believe it is their fiduciary duty to keep Airgas's defenses in place. . . .

In addition, Air Products made a tactical decision to proceed with its offer for Airgas in the manner in which it did. First, Air Products made a choice to launch a proxy contest in connection with its tender offer. It could have—at that point, in February 2010—attempted to call a special meeting to remove the entire board. The 67% vote requirement was a high hurdle that presented uncertainty, so it chose to proceed by launching a proxy contest in connection with its tender offer.

Second, Air Products chose to replace a minority of the Airgas board with three *independent directors* who promised to take a "fresh look." Air Products ran its nominees expressly premised on that independent slate. It could have put up three nominees premised on the slogan of "shareholder choice." It could have run a slate of nominees who would promise to remove the pill if elected. It could have gotten three directors elected who were resolved to fight back against the rest of the Airgas board.

Certainly what occurred here is not what Air Products expected to happen. Air Products ran its slate on the promise that its nominees would "consider without any bias [the Air Products] Offer," and that they would "be willing to be outspoken in the boardroom about their views on these issues." Air Products *got what it wanted.* Its three nominees got elected to the Airgas board and then questioned the directors about their assumptions. (They got answers.) They looked at the numbers themselves. (They were impressed.) They requested outside legal counsel. (They got it.) They requested a third outside financial advisor. (They got it.) And in the end, they *joined in the board's view* that Air Products' offer was inadequate. . . .

Based on all of the foregoing factual findings, I cannot conclude that there is "clearly no basis" for the Airgas board's belief in the sustainability of its long-term plan.

On the contrary, the maintenance of the board's defensive measures must fall within a range of reasonableness here. The board is not "cramming down" a management-sponsored alternative—or *any* company-changing alternative. Instead, the board is simply maintaining the status quo, running the company for the long-term, and consistently showing improved financial results each passing quarter. The board's actions do not *forever* preclude Air Products, or any bidder, from acquiring Airgas or from getting around Airgas's defensive measures if the price is right. In the meantime, the board is preventing a change of control from occurring at an inadequate price. This course of action has been clearly recognized under Delaware law . . .

When the Supreme Court first upheld the use of a rights plan in *Moran*, it emphasized that "[t]he Board does not now have unfettered discretion in refusing to redeem the Rights." And in the most recent "pill case" decided just this past year, the Supreme Court reiterated its view that, "[a]s we held in *Moran*, the adoption of a Rights Plan is not absolute."[*Versata Enters., Inc. v. Selectica, Inc.*, 5 A.3d 586, 607 (Del. 2010)] The poison pill's limits, however, still remain to be seen. . . .

The contours of the debate [over the poison pill] have morphed over the years, but the fundamental questions have remained. Can a board "just say no"? If so, when? How should the enhanced judicial standard of review be applied? What are the pill's limits. And the ultimate question: Can a board "just say never"? . . .

[I]n this case, the Airgas board has continued to say "no" even after one proxy fight. . . . Vice Chancellor Strine recently posed . . . [a] hypothetical in *Yucaipa Am. Alliance Fund II, L.P. v. Riggio,* 1 A.3d 310, 351 n. 229 (Del. Ch. 2010) raising the limits of the board in the face of an effective staggered board (ESB)]:

> [T]here is a plausible argument that a rights plan could be considered preclusive, based on an examination of real world market considerations, when a bidder who makes an all shares, structurally non-coercive offer has: (1) won a proxy contest for a third of the seats of a classified board; (2) is not able to proceed with its tender offer for another year because the *incumbent board majority* will not redeem the rights as to the offer; and (3) is required to take all the various economic risks that would come with maintaining the bid for another year.

At that point, it is argued, it may be appropriate for a Court to order redemption of a poison pill. That hypothetical, however, is not exactly the case here for two main reasons. First, Air Products did not run a proxy slate running on a "let the shareholders decide" platform. Instead, they ran a slate committed to taking an independent look and deciding for themselves afresh whether to accept the bid. The Air Products Nominees apparently "changed teams" once elected to the Airgas board (I use that phrase loosely, recognizing that they joined the Airgas board on an "independent" slate with no particular mandate other than to see if a deal could be done). Once elected, they got inside and saw for themselves why the Airgas board and its advisors have so passionately and consistently argued that Air Products' offer is too low (the SAP implementation, the as-yet-unrealized benefits from recent significant capital expenditures, the timing in which Airgas historically has emerged from recessions, the intrinsic value of this company, etc.). The incumbents now share in the rest of the board's view that Air Products' offer is inadequate—this is not a case where the insurgents want to redeem the pill but they are unable to convince the majority. This situation is different from the one posited by Vice Chancellor Strine. . . .

Second, Airgas does not have a true "ESB".... Airgas's charter allows for 33% of the stockholders to call a special meeting and remove the board by a 67% vote of the outstanding shares.... This factual distinction also further differentiates this case from the *Yucaipa* hypothetical.

CONCLUSION ...

There is no question that poison pills act as potent anti-takeover drugs with the potential to be abused. Counsel for plaintiffs (both Air Products and Shareholder Plaintiffs) make compelling policy arguments in favor of redeeming the pill in this case—to do otherwise, they say, would essentially make all companies with staggered boards and poison pills "takeover proof."[514] The argument is an excellent sound bite, but it is ultimately not the holding of this fact-specific case, although it does bring us one step closer to that result.

As this case demonstrates, in order to have any effectiveness, pills do not—and can not—have a set expiration date. To be clear, though, this case does not endorse "just say never." What it does endorse is Delaware's long-understood respect for reasonably exercised managerial discretion, so long as boards are found to be acting in good faith and in accordance with their fiduciary duties (after rigorous judicial fact-finding and enhanced scrutiny of their defensive actions). The Airgas board serves as a quintessential example.

Directors of a corporation still owe fiduciary duties to *all stockholders—this undoubtedly includes short-term as well as long-term holders.* ... For the foregoing reasons, Air Products' and the Shareholder Plaintiffs' requests for relief are denied, and all claims asserted against defendants are dismissed with prejudice....

A different challenge to a poison pill was before the Delaware Chancery Court in UniSuper Ltd. v. News Corp., No. 1699–N, 2005 WL 3529317 (Del. Ch. Dec. 20, 2005). Australia law greatly restricts defensive tactics and certainly would not permit a poison pill. News Corp's shareholders, therefore, feared the worse when News Corp announced it planned to change its corporate domicile from Australia to Delaware. To win them over, News Corp's board of directors adopted a policy statement that among other undertakings stated the company, if it reincorporated in Delaware, would not adopt without shareholder approval a poison pill that would have a duration longer than one year. The force of this and other governance-related policy statements adopted by the board yielded results; in October 2004 over ninety percent of the votes favored the reincorporation. Within a month, News Corp's board announced that, in the face of aggressive acquisition of shares by a long-time rival, Liberty Media Corp., the board had adopted a poison pill. A few months later the board announced it would extend the pill for two years beyond its initial one-year duration. Feeling they had been double crossed, a group of

Australian institutional investors initiated suit alleging the breach of contract, promissory estoppels, fraud, negligent misrepresentation, and breach of fiduciary duty. While the Chancellor dismissed most of these charges, the charges of contract and estoppels survived the defendant's motion to dismiss. The suit was settled when the corporation agreed to submit the pill to a vote of the stockholders and ultimately the stockholders approved the pill by a 57 to 43 percent vote. *See* Jennifer G. Hill, Subverting Shareholder Rights: Lessons From News Corp's Migration To Delaware, 63 Vand. L. Rev. 1 (2010). Consider the willingness of the Chancellor in *UniSuper* to entertain the argument that shareholders could have a contract with the board that would limit the defensive measures the board may pursue. Is there a tension between, on the one hand, the weight that Delaware and other courts have placed on the redemption provision for which the board is the deciding body and, on the other hand, efforts by activist shareholders to propose bylaws that terminate an existing poison pill and condition the pill's adoption on shareholder approval? Recall the emphasis the Delaware Supreme Court accorded the directors' fiduciary obligations in CA Inc. v. AFSCME Employees Pension Plan, 953 A.2d 227 (Del.Supr. 2008), where the court held that a shareholder-initiated bylaw mandating reimbursement of an insurgent's proxy campaign expenses was invalid because it could cause the board to reimburse expenses in violation of their fiduciary obligations. Does the board have a fiduciary obligation to defend control against a bid it believes is harmful? Would a bylaw that takes this authority away from the board violate the reasoning of *CA Inc.*? *See* Bebchuk v. CA, Inc., 902 A.2d 737 (Del. Ch. 2006) (relying on *UniSuper* for the proposition that a contractual restraint on the board's power to issue a poison pill is valid under Delaware law). Why, on the one hand, are shareholders impotent to adopt a bylaw that mandates unqualified reimbursement of insurgents, but, on the other hand, they are deemed to have the power to remove a potent defensive tool from the board's arsenal?

Revlon, Inc. v. MacAndrews & Forbes Holdings, Inc.

Supreme Court of Delaware, 1986.
506 A.2d 173.

In this battle for corporate control of Revlon, Inc. (Revlon), the Court of Chancery enjoined certain transactions designed to thwart the efforts of Pantry Pride, Inc. (Pantry Pride) to acquire Revlon. The defendants are Revlon, its board of directors, and Forstmann Little Co. and the latter's affiliated limited partnership (collectively, Forstmann). The injunction barred consummation of an option granted Forstmann to purchase certain Revlon assets (the lock-up option), a promise by Revlon to deal exclusively with Forstmann in the face of a takeover (the no-shop provision), and the payment of a $25 million cancellation fee to Forstmann if the transaction was aborted. The Court of Chancery found that the Revlon directors had breached their duty of care by entering into the foregoing transactions and effectively ending an active auction for the company. The trial court ruled that such arrangements are not illegal *per se* under Delaware law, but that their use under the circumstances here was impermissible. We agree.... Accordingly, we affirm.

I.

The somewhat complex maneuvers of the parties necessitate a rather detailed examination of the facts. The prelude to this controversy began in June 1985, when Ronald O. Perelman, chairman of the board and chief executive officer of Pantry Pride, met with his counterpart at Revlon, Michel C. Bergerac, to discuss a friendly acquisition of Revlon by Pantry Pride. Perelman suggested a price in the range of $4050 per share, but the meeting ended with Bergerac dismissing those figures as considerably below Revlon's intrinsic value. All subsequent Pantry Pride overtures were rebuffed, perhaps in part based on Mr. Bergerac's strong personal antipathy to Mr. Perelman.

Thus, on August 14, Pantry Pride's board authorized Perelman to acquire Revlon, either through negotiation in the $42–$43 per share range, or by making a hostile tender offer at $45. Perelman then met with Bergerac and outlined Pantry Pride's alternate approaches. Bergerac remained adamantly opposed to such schemes and conditioned any further discussions of the matter on Pantry Pride executing a standstill agreement prohibiting it from acquiring Revlon without the latter's prior approval.

On August 19, the Revlon board met specially to consider the impending threat of a hostile bid by Pantry Pride.[3] At the meeting, Lazard Freres, Revlon's investment banker, advised the directors that $45 per share was a grossly inadequate price for the company. Felix Rohatyn and William Loomis of Lazard Freres explained to the board that Pantry Pride's financial strategy for acquiring Revlon would be through "junk bond" financing followed by a break-up of Revlon and the disposition of its assets. With proper timing, according to the experts, such transactions could produce a return to Pantry Pride of $60 to $70 per share, while a sale of the company as a whole would be in the "mid 50" dollar range. Martin Lipton, special counsel for Revlon, recommended two defensive measures: first, that the company repurchase up to 5 million of its nearly 30 million outstanding shares; and second, that it adopt a Note Purchase Rights Plan. Under this plan, each Revlon shareholder would receive as a dividend one Note Purchase Right (the Rights) for each share of common stock, with the Rights entitling the holder to exchange one common share for a $65 principal Revlon note at 12% interest with a one-year maturity. The Rights would become effective whenever anyone acquired beneficial

3. There were 14 directors on the Revlon board. Six of them held senior management positions with the company, and two others held significant blocks of its stock. Four of the remaining six directors were associated at some point with entities that had various business relationships with Revlon. On the basis of this limited record, however, we cannot conclude that this board is entitled to certain presumptions that generally attach to the decisions of a board whose majority consists of truly outside independent directors....

ownership of 20% or more of Revlon's shares, unless the purchaser acquired all the company's stock for cash at $65 or more per share. In addition, the Rights would not be available to the acquiror, and prior to the 20% triggering event the Revlon board could redeem the rights for 10 cents each. Both proposals were unanimously adopted.

Pantry Pride made its first hostile move on August 23, with a cash tender offer for any and all shares of Revlon at $47.50 per common share and $26.67 per preferred share, subject to (1) Pantry Pride's obtaining financing for the purchase, and (2) the Rights being redeemed, rescinded or voided.

The Revlon board met again on August 26. The directors advised the stockholders to reject the offer. Further defensive measures also were planned. On August 29, Revlon commenced its own offer for up to 10 million shares, exchanging for each share of common stock tendered one Senior Subordinated Note (the Notes) of $47.50 principal at 11.75% interest, due 1995, and one-tenth of a share of $9.00 Cumulative Convertible Exchangeable Preferred Stock valued at $100 per share. Lazard Freres opined that the notes would trade at their face value on a fully distributed basis. Revlon stockholders tendered 87 percent of the outstanding shares (approximately 33 million), and the company accepted the full 10 million shares on a pro rata basis. The new Notes contained covenants which limited Revlon's ability to incur additional debt, sell assets, or pay dividends unless otherwise approved by the independent (non-management) members of the board.

At this point, both the Rights and the Note covenants stymied Pantry Pride's attempted takeover. The next move came on September 16, when Pantry Pride announced a new tender offer at $42 per share, conditioned upon receiving at least 90% of the outstanding stock. Pantry Pride also indicated that it would consider buying less than 90%, and at an increased price, if Revlon removed the impeding Rights. While this offer was lower on its face than the earlier $47.50 proposal, Revlon's investment banker, Lazard Freres, described the two bids as essentially equal in view of the completed exchange offer.

The Revlon board held a regularly scheduled meeting on September 24. The directors rejected the latest Pantry Pride offer and authorized management to negotiate with other parties interested in acquiring Revlon. Pantry Pride remained determined in its efforts and continued to make cash bids for the company, offering $50 per share on September 27, and raising its bid to $53 on October 1, and then to $56.25 on October 7.

In the meantime, Revlon's negotiations with Forstmann and the investment group Adler & Shaykin had produced results. The Revlon directors met on October 3, to consider Pantry Pride's $53 bid and to examine possible alternatives to the offer. Both Forstmann and Adler & Shaykin made certain proposals to the board. As a result, the directors unanimously agreed to a leveraged buyout by Forstmann. The terms of this accord were as follows: each stockholder would get $56 cash per share; management would purchase stock in the new company by the exercise of their Revlon "golden parachutes";[4] Forstmann would assume Revlon's $475 million debt incurred by the issuance of the Notes; and Revlon would redeem the Rights and waive the Notes covenants for Forstmann or in connection with any other offer superior to Forstmann's. The board did not actually remove the covenants at the October 3, meeting, because Forstmann then lacked a firm commitment on its financing, but accepted the Forstmann capital structure, and indicated that the outside directors would waive the covenants in due course. Part of Forstmann's plan was to sell Revlon's Norcliff Thayer and Reheis divisions to American Home Products for $335 million. Before the merger, Revlon was to sell its cosmetics and fragrance division to Adler Shaykin for $905 million. These transactions would facilitate the purchase by Forstmann or any other acquiror of Revlon.

When the merger, and thus the waiver of the Notes covenants, was announced, the market value of these securities began to fall. The Notes, which originally traded near par, around 100, dropped to 87.50 by October 8. One director later reported (at the October 12 meeting) a "deluge" of telephone calls from irate noteholders, and on October 10 the Wall Street Journal reported threats of litigation by these creditors.

Pantry Pride countered with a new proposal on October 7, raising its $53 offer to $56.25, subject to nullification of the Rights, a waiver of the Notes covenants, and the election of three Pantry Pride directors to the Revlon board. On October 9, representatives of Pantry Pride, Forstmann and Revlon conferred in an attempt to negotiate the fate of Revlon, but could not reach agreement. At this meeting Pantry Pride announced that it would engage in fractional bidding and top any Forstmann offer by a slightly higher one. It is also significant that Forstmann, to Pantry Pride's exclusion, had been made privy to certain Revlon financial data. Thus, the parties were not negotiating on equal terms.

Again privately armed with Revlon data, Forstmann met on October 11 with Revlon's special counsel and investment banker. On October 12, Forstmann made a new $57.25 per share offer, based on several conditions.[5] The principal demand was a lock-up option to purchase Revlon's Vision Care and National Health Laboratories divisions for $525 million, some $100–$175 million below the value ascribed to them by Lazard Freres, if another acquiror got 40% of Revlon's shares. Revlon also was required to accept a no-shop provision. The Rights and Notes covenants had to be removed as in the October 3 agreement. There would be a $25 million cancellation fee

4. In the takeover context "golden parachutes" generally are understood to be termination agreements providing substantial bonuses and other benefits for managers and certain directors upon a change in control of a company.

5. Forstmann's $57.25 offer ostensibly is worth $1 more than Pantry Pride's $56.25 bid. However, the Pantry Pride offer was immediate, while the Forstmann proposal must be discounted for the time value of money because of the delay in approving the merger and consummating the transaction. The exact difference between the two bids was an unsettled point of contention even at oral argument.

to be placed in escrow, and released to Forstmann if the new agreement terminated or if another acquiror got more than 19.9% of Revlon's stock. Finally, there would be no participation by Revlon management in the merger. In return, Forstmann agreed to support the par value of the Notes, which had faltered in the market, by an exchange of new notes. Forstmann also demanded immediate acceptance of its offer, or it would be withdrawn. The board unanimously approved Forstmann's proposal because: (1) it was for a higher price than the Pantry Pride bid, (2) it protected the noteholders, and (3) Forstmann's financing was firmly in place.[6] The board further agreed to redeem the rights and waive the covenants on the preferred stock in response to any offer above $57 cash per share. The covenants were waived, contingent upon receipt of an investment banking opinion that the Notes would trade near par value once the offer was consummated.

Pantry Pride, which had initially sought injunctive relief from the Rights plan on August 22, filed an amended complaint on October 14 challenging the lock-up, the cancellation fee, and the exercise of the Rights and the Notes covenants. Pantry Pride also sought a temporary restraining order to prevent Revlon from placing any assets in escrow or transferring them to Forstmann. Moreover, on October 22, Pantry Pride again raised its bid, with a cash offer of $58 per share conditioned upon nullification of the Rights, waiver of the covenants, and an injunction of the Forstmann lock-up.

On October 15, the Court of Chancery prohibited the further transfer of assets, and eight days later enjoined the lock-up, no-shop, and cancellation fee provisions of the agreement. The trial court concluded that the Revlon directors had breached their duty of loyalty by making concessions to Forstmann, out of concern for their liability to the noteholders, rather than maximizing the sale price of the company for the stockholders' benefit. MacAndrews & Forbes Holdings, Inc. v. Revlon, Inc., 501 A.2d at 1249–50.

II.

To obtain a preliminary injunction, a plaintiff must demonstrate both a reasonable probability of success on the merits and some irreparable harm which will occur absent the injunction. Gimbel v. Signal Companies, Del.Ch., 316 A.2d 599, 602 (1974), aff'd, Del.Supr., 316 A.2d 619 (1974). Additionally, the Court shall balance the conveniences of and possible injuries to the parties. Id.

A.

We turn first to Pantry Pride's probability of success on the merits. The ultimate responsibility for managing the business and affairs of a

6. Actually, at this time about $400 million of Forstmann's funding was still subject to two investment banks using their "best effort" to organize a syndicate to provide the balance. Pantry Pride's entire financing was not firmly committed at this point either, although Pantry Pride represented in an October 11 letter to Lazard Freres that its investment banker, Drexel Burnham Lambert, was highly confident of its ability to raise the balance of $350 million. Drexel Burnham had a firm commitment for this sum by October 18.

corporation falls on its board of directors. 8 Del.C. § 141(a). In discharging this function the directors owe fiduciary duties of care and loyalty to the corporation and its shareholders. Guth v. Loft, Inc., 23 Del.Supr. 255, 5 A.2d 503, 510 (1939); Aronson v. Lewis, Del.Supr., 473 A.2d 805, 811 (1984). These principles apply with equal force when a board approves a corporate merger pursuant to 8 Del.C. § 251(b);[9] Smith v. Van Gorkom, Del.Supr., 488 A.2d 858, 873 (1985); and of course they are the bedrock of our law regarding corporate takeover issues....

If the business judgment rule applies, there is a "presumption that in making a business decision the directors of a corporation acted on an informed basis, in good faith and in the honest belief that the action taken was in the best interests of the company." Aronson v. Lewis, 473 A.2d at 812. However, when a board implements antitakeover measures there arises "the omnipresent specter that a board may be acting primarily in its own interests, rather than those of the corporation and its shareholders ..." Unocal Corp. v. Mesa Petroleum Co., 493 A.2d at 954. This potential for conflict places upon the directors the burden of proving that they had reasonable grounds for believing there was a danger to corporate policy and effectiveness, a burden satisfied by a showing of good faith and reasonable investigation. Id. at 955. In addition, the directors must analyze the nature of the takeover and its effect on the corporation in order to ensure balance—that the responsive action taken is reasonable in relation to the threat posed. Id.

B.

The first relevant defensive measure adopted by the Revlon board was the Rights Plan, which would be considered a "poison pill" in the current language of corporate takeovers—a plan by which shareholders receive the right to be bought out by the corporation at a substantial premium on the occurrence of a stated triggering event. See generally Moran v. Household International, Inc., Del.Supr., 500 A.2d 1346 (1985). By 8 Del.C. §§ 141 and 157,[10] the board clearly had the power to adopt the measure. Moran v. Household International, Inc., 500 A.2d at 1351. Thus, the focus becomes one of reasonableness and purpose.

The Revlon board approved the Rights Plan in the face of an impending hostile takeover bid by Pantry Pride at $45 per share, a price which Revlon reasonably concluded was grossly inadequate. Lazard Freres had so advised the directors, and had also informed

---

9. The statute provides in pertinent part:

(b) The board of directors of each corporation which desires to merge or consolidate shall adopt a resolution approving an agreement of merger or consolidation. 8 Del.C. § 251(b).

10. The relevant provision of Section 122 is:

Every corporation created under this chapter shall have power to:

(13) Make contracts, including contracts of guaranty and suretyship, incur liabilities, borrow money at such rates of interest as the corporation may determine, issue its notes, bonds and other obligations, and secure any of its obligations by mortgage, pledge or other encumbrance of all or any of its property, franchises and income,.... 8 Del.C. § 122(13)....

them that Pantry Pride was a small, highly leveraged company bent on a "bust-up" takeover by using "junk bond" financing to buy Revlon cheaply, sell the acquired assets to pay the debts incurred, and retain the profit for itself.[11] In adopting the Plan, the board protected the shareholders from a hostile takeover at a price below the company's intrinsic value, while retaining sufficient flexibility to address any proposal deemed to be in the stockholders' best interests.

To that extent the board acted in good faith and upon reasonable investigation. Under the circumstances it cannot be said that the Rights Plan as employed was unreasonable, considering the threat posed. Indeed, the Plan was a factor in causing Pantry Pride to raise its bids from a low of $42 to an eventual high of $58. At the time of its adoption the Rights Plan afforded a measure of protection consistent with the directors' fiduciary duty in facing a takeover threat perceived as detrimental to corporate interests. *Unocal,* 493 A.2d at 954–55. Far from being a "show-stopper," as the plaintiffs had contended in *Moran,* the measure spurred the bidding to new heights, a proper result of its implementation. See *Moran,* 500 A.2d at 1354, 1356–67.

Although we consider adoption of the Plan to have been valid under the circumstances, its continued usefulness was rendered moot by the directors' actions on October 3 and October 12. At the October 3 meeting the board redeemed the Rights conditioned upon consummation of a merger with Forstmann, but further acknowledged that they would also be redeemed to facilitate any more favorable offer. On October 12, the board unanimously passed a resolution redeeming the Rights in connection with any cash proposal of $57.25 or more per share. Because all the pertinent offers eventually equalled or surpassed that amount, the Rights clearly were no longer any impediment in the contest for Revlon. This mooted any question of their propriety under *Moran* or *Unocal.*

C.

The second defensive measure adopted by Revlon to thwart a Pantry Pride takeover was the company's own exchange offer for 10 million of its shares. The directors' general broad powers to manage the business and affairs of the corporation are augmented by the specific authority conferred under 8 Del.C. § 160(a), permitting the company to deal in its own stock. *Unocal,* 493 A.2d at 953–54; Cheff v. Mathes, 41 Del.Supr. 494, 199 A.2d 548, 554 (1964); Kors v. Carey, 39 Del.Ch. 47, 158 A.2d 136, 140 (1960). However, when exercising that power in an effort to forestall a hostile takeover, the board's actions are strictly held to the fiduciary standards outlined in *Unocal.* These standards require the directors to determine the best interests of the corporation and its stockholders, and impose an enhanced duty to abjure any action that is motivated by considerations other than a

11. As we noted in *Moran,* a "bust-up" takeover generally refers to a situation in which one seeks to finance an acquisition by selling off pieces of the acquired company, presumably at a substantial profit. See *Moran,* 500 A.2d at 1349, n. 4.

good faith concern for such interests. *Unocal,* 493 A.2d at 954–55; see Bennett v. Propp, 41 Del.Supr. 14, 187 A.2d 405, 409 (1962).

The Revlon directors concluded that Pantry Pride's $47.50 offer was grossly inadequate. In that regard the board acted in good faith, and on an informed basis, with reasonable grounds to believe that there existed a harmful threat to the corporate enterprise. The adoption of a defensive measure, reasonable in relation to the threat posed, was proper and fully accorded with the powers, duties, and responsibilities conferred upon directors under our law. *Unocal,* 493 A.2d at 954; Pogostin v. Rice, 480 A.2d at 627.

D.

However, when Pantry Pride increased its offer to $50 per share, and then to $53, it became apparent to all that the break-up of the company was inevitable. The Revlon board's authorization permitting management to negotiate a merger or buyout with a third party was a recognition that the company was for sale. The duty of the board had thus changed from the preservation of Revlon as a corporate entity to the maximization of the company's value at a sale for the stockholders' benefit. This significantly altered the board's responsibilities under the *Unocal* standards. It no longer faced threats to corporate policy and effectiveness, or to the stockholders' interests, from a grossly inadequate bid. The whole question of defensive measures became moot. The directors' role changed from defenders of the corporate bastion to auctioneers charged with getting the best price for the stockholders at a sale of the company.

III.

This brings us to the lock-up with Forstmann and its emphasis on shoring up the sagging market value of the Notes in the face of threatened litigation by their holders. Such a focus was inconsistent with the changed concept of the directors' responsibilities at this stage of the developments. The impending waiver of the Notes covenants had caused the value of the Notes to fall, and the board was aware of the noteholders' ire as well as their subsequent threats of suit. The directors thus made support of the Notes an integral part of the company's dealings with Forstmann, even though their primary responsibility at this stage was to the equity owners.

The original threat posed by Pantry Pride—the break-up of the company—had become a reality which even the directors embraced. Selective dealing to fend off a hostile but determined bidder was no longer a proper objective. Instead, obtaining the highest price for the benefit of the stockholders should have been the central theme guiding director action. Thus, the Revlon board could not make the requisite showing of good faith by preferring the noteholders and ignoring its duty of loyalty to the shareholders. The rights of the former already were fixed by contract. Wolfensohn v. Madison Fund, Inc., Del.Supr., 253 A.2d 72, 75 (1969); Harff v. Kerkorian, Del.Ch., 324 A.2d 215 (1974). The noteholders required no further protection, and when the Revlon board entered into an auction-ending lock-up agreement with Forstmann on the basis of impermissible considerations at the expense of the shareholders, the directors breached their primary duty of loyalty.

The Revlon board argued that it acted in good faith in protecting the noteholders because *Unocal* permits consideration of other corporate constituencies. Although such considerations may be permissible, there are fundamental limitations upon that prerogative. A board may have regard for various constituencies in discharging its responsibilities, provided there are rationally related benefits accruing to the stockholders. *Unocal,* 493 A.2d at 955. However, such concern for non-stockholder interests is inappropriate when an auction among active bidders is in progress, and the object no longer is to protect or maintain the corporate enterprise but to sell it to the highest bidder.

Revlon also contended that by Gilbert v. El Paso Co., Del.Ch., 490 A.2d 1050, 1054–55 (1984), it had contractual and good faith obligations to consider the noteholders. However, any such duties are limited to the principle that one may not interfere with contractual relationships by improper actions. Here, the rights of the noteholders were fixed by agreement, and there is nothing of substance to suggest that any of those terms were violated. The Notes covenants specifically contemplated a waiver to permit sale of the company at a fair price. The Notes were accepted by the holders on that basis, including the risk of an adverse market effect stemming from a waiver. Thus, nothing remained for Revlon to legitimately protect, and no rationally related benefit thereby accrued to the stockholders. Under such circumstances we must conclude that the merger agreement with Forstmann was unreasonable in relation to the threat posed.

A lock-up is not *per se* illegal under Delaware law. Its use has been approved in an earlier case. Thompson v. Enstar Corp., Del.Ch. (1984). Such options can entice other bidders to enter a contest for control of the corporation, creating an auction for the company and maximizing shareholder profit. Current economic conditions in the takeover market are such that a "white knight" like Forstmann might only enter the bidding for the target company if it receives some form of compensation to cover the risks and costs involved. Note, Corporations—Mergers—"Lock-up" Enjoined Under Section 14(e) of Securities Exchange Act—Mobil Corp. v. Marathon Oil Co., 669 F.2d 366 (6th Cir.1981), 12 Seton Hall L.Rev. 881, 892 (1982). However, while those lock-ups which draw bidders into the battle benefit shareholders, similar measures which end an active auction and foreclose further bidding operate to the shareholders' detriment. Note, Lock-up Options: Toward a State Law Standard, 96 Harv.L.Rev. 1068, 1081 (1983)....

The Forstmann option had a ... destructive effect on the auction process. Forstmann had already been drawn into the contest on a preferred basis, so the result of the lock-up was not to foster bidding, but to destroy it. The board's stated reasons for approving the transaction were: (1) better financing, (2) noteholder protection, and

(3) higher price. As the Court of Chancery found, and we agree, any distinctions between the rival bidders' methods of financing the proposal were nominal at best, and such a consideration has little or no significance in a cash offer for any and all shares. The principal object, contrary to the board's duty of care, appears to have been protection of the noteholders over the shareholders' interests.

While Forstmann's $57.25 offer was objectively higher than Pantry Pride's $56.25 bid, the margin of superiority is less when the Forstmann price is adjusted for the time value of money. In reality, the Revlon board ended the auction in return for very little actual improvement in the final bid. The principal benefit went to the directors, who avoided personal liability to a class of creditors to whom the board owed no further duty under the circumstances. Thus, when a board ends an intense bidding contest on an insubstantial basis, and where a significant by-product of that action is to protect the directors against a perceived threat of personal liability for consequences stemming from the adoption of previous defensive measures, the action cannot withstand the enhanced scrutiny which *Unocal* requires of director conduct. See *Unocal,* 493 A.2d at 954–55.

In addition to the lock-up option, the Court of Chancery enjoined the no-shop provision as part of the attempt to foreclose further bidding by Pantry Pride. MacAndrews & Forbes Holdings, Inc. v. Revlon, Inc., 501 A.2d at 1251. The no-shop provision, like the lock-up option, while not *per se* illegal, is impermissible under the *Unocal* standards when a board's primary duty becomes that of an auctioneer responsible for selling the company to the highest bidder. The agreement to negotiate only with Forstmann ended rather than intensified the board's involvement in the bidding contest.

It is ironic that the parties even considered a no-shop agreement when Revlon had dealt preferentially, and almost exclusively, with Forstmann throughout the contest. After the directors authorized management to negotiate with other parties, Forstmann was given every negotiating advantage that Pantry Pride had been denied: cooperation from management, access to financial data, and the exclusive opportunity to present merger proposals directly to the board of directors. Favoritism for a white knight to the total exclusion of a hostile bidder might be justifiable when the latter's offer adversely affects shareholder interests, but when bidders make relatively similar offers, or dissolution of the company becomes inevitable, the directors cannot fulfill their enhanced *Unocal* duties by playing favorites with the contending factions. Market forces must be allowed to operate freely to bring the target's shareholders the best price available for their equity.[14] Thus, as the trial court ruled, the shareholders' interests necessitated that the board remain free to negotiate in the fulfillment of that duty.

---

14. By this we do not embrace the passivity thesis rejected in *Unocal.* See 493 A.2d at 954–55, nn. 8–10. The directors' role remains an active one, changed only in the respect that they are charged with the duty of selling the company at the highest price attainable for the stockholders' benefit.

The court below similarly enjoined the payment of the cancellation fee, pending a resolution of the merits, because the fee was part of the overall plan to thwart Pantry Pride's efforts. We find no abuse of discretion in that ruling.

IV.

Having concluded that Pantry Pride has shown a reasonable probability of success on the merits, we address the issue of irreparable harm. The Court of Chancery ruled that unless the lock-up and other aspects of the agreement were enjoined, Pantry Pride's opportunity to bid for Revlon was lost. The court also held that the need for both bidders to compete in the marketplace outweighed any injury to Forstmann. Given the complexity of the proposed transaction between Revlon and Forstmann, the obstacles to Pantry Pride obtaining a meaningful legal remedy are immense. We are satisfied that the plaintiff has shown the need for an injunction to protect it from irreparable harm, which need outweighs any harm to the defendants.

V.

In conclusion, the Revlon board was confronted with a situation not uncommon in the current wave of corporate takeovers. A hostile and determined bidder sought the company at a price the board was convinced was inadequate. The initial defensive tactics worked to the benefit of the shareholders, and thus the board was able to sustain its *Unocal* burdens in justifying those measures. However, in granting an asset option lock-up to Forstmann, we must conclude that under all the circumstances the directors allowed considerations other than the maximization of shareholder profit to affect their judgment, and followed a course that ended the auction for Revlon, absent court intervention, to the ultimate detriment of its shareholders. No such defensive measure can be sustained when it represents a breach of the directors' fundamental duty of care. See Smith v. Van Gorkom, Del. Supr., 488 A.2d 858, 874 (1985). In that context the board's action is not entitled to the deference accorded it by the business judgment rule. The measures were properly enjoined. The decision of the Court of Chancery, therefore, is

AFFIRMED.

Paramount Communications, Inc. v. Time Inc.

Supreme Court of Delaware, 1989.
571 A.2d 1140.

■ HORSEY, JUSTICE:

Paramount Communications, Inc. ("Paramount") and two other groups of plaintiffs ("Shareholder Plaintiffs"), shareholders of Time Incorporated ("Time"), a Delaware corporation, separately filed suits in the Delaware Court of Chancery seeking a preliminary injunction to halt Time's tender offer for 51% of Warner Communication, Inc.'s

("Warner") outstanding shares at $70 cash per share. The court below consolidated the cases and, following the development of an extensive record, after discovery and an evidentiary hearing . . . , the Chancellor refused to enjoin Time's consummation of its tender offer. . . .

[Plaintiffs filed an interlocutory appeal.]

I

Time is a Delaware corporation with its principal offices in New York City. Time's traditional business is publication of magazines and books; however, Time also provides pay television programming through its Home Box Office, Inc. and Cinemax subsidiaries. In addition, Time owns and operates cable television franchises through its subsidiary, American Television and Communication Corporation. During the relevant time period, Time's board consisted of sixteen directors. Twelve of the directors were "outside," nonemployee directors. Four of the directors were also officers of the company. . . .

As early as 1983 and 1984, Time's executive board began considering expanding Time's operations into the entertainment industry. In 1987, Time established a special committee of executives to consider and propose corporate strategies for the 1990s. The consensus of the committee was that Time should move ahead in the area of ownership and creation of video programming. This expansion . . . was predicated upon two considerations: first, Time's desire to have greater control, in terms of quality and price, over the film products delivered by way of its cable network and franchises; and second, Time's concern over the increasing globalization of the world economy. Some of Time's outside directors, especially Luce and Temple, had opposed this move as a threat to the editorial integrity and journalistic focus of Time.[3] Despite this concern, the board saw the advantages of a vertically integrated video enterprise to complement Time's existing HBO and cable networks would enable it to compete on a global basis.

In late spring of 1987, a meeting took place between Steve Ross, CEO of Warner Brothers, and [N.J.] Nicholas [president and chief operating officer] of Time. Ross and Nicholas discussed the possibility of a joint venture between the two companies through the creation of a jointly-owned cable company. Time would contribute its cable system and HBO. Warner would contribute its cable system and provide access to Warner Brothers Studio. The resulting venture would be a larger, more efficient cable network, able to produce and distribute its own movies on a worldwide basis. Ultimately the parties abandoned this plan, determining that it was impractical for several reasons, chief among them being tax considerations.

---

3. The primary concern of Time's outside directors was the preservation of the "Time Culture." They believed that Time had become recognized in this country as an institution built upon a foundation of journalistic integrity. Time's management made a studious effort to refrain from involvement in Time's editorial policy. Several of Time's outside directors feared that a merger with an entertainment company would divert Time's focus from news journalism and threaten the Time Culture.

On August 11, 1987, Gerald M. Levin, Time's vice chairman and chief strategist, wrote J. Richard Munro [Time's chairman and CEO] a confidential memorandum in which he strongly recommended a strategic consolidation with Warner. In June 1988, Nicholas and Munro sent to each outside director a copy of the "comprehensive long-term planning document" prepared by the committee of Time executives that had been examining strategies for the 1990s. The memo included reference to and a description of Warner as a potential acquisition candidate.

Thereafter, Munro and Nicholas held meetings with Time's outside directors to discuss, generally, long-term strategies for Time and, specifically, a combination with Warner. Nearly a year later, Time's board reached the point of serious discussion of the "nuts and bolts" of a consolidation with an entertainment company. On July 21, 1988, Time's board met . . . to consider Time's expansion into the entertainment industry on a global scale. . . .

Without any definitive decision on choice of a company, the board approved in principle a strategic plan for Time's expansion. The board gave management the "go-ahead" to continue discussions with Warner concerning the possibility of a merger. With the exception of Temple and Luce, most of the outside directors agreed that a merger involving expansion into the entertainment field promised great growth opportunity for Time. Temple and Luce remained unenthusiastic about Time's entry into the entertainment field. See supra note [3].

The board's consensus was that a merger of Time and Warner was feasible, but only if Time controlled the board of the resulting corporation and thereby preserved a management committed to Time's journalistic integrity. To accomplish this goal, the board stressed the importance of carefully defining in advance the corporate governance provisions that would control the resulting entity. Some board members expressed concern over whether such a business combination would place Time "*in play*." The board discussed the wisdom of adopting further defensive measures to lessen such a possibility.[4]

Of a wide range of companies considered by Time's board as possible merger candidates, Warner Brothers, Paramount, Columbia, M.C.A., Fox, MGM, Disney, and Orion, the board, in July 1988, concluded that Warner was the superior candidate for a consolidation. Warner stood out on a number of counts. Warner had just acquired Lorimar and its film studios. Time–Warner could make movies and television shows for use on HBO. Warner had an international distribution system, which Time could use to sell films, videos, books and magazines. Warner was a giant in the music and recording business, an area into which Time wanted to expand. None of the other companies considered had the musical clout of Warner. Time and Warner's cable systems were compatible and could be easily integrated; none of the

4. Time had in place a panoply of defensive devices, including a staggered board, a "poison pill" preferred stock rights plan triggered by an acquisition of 15% of the company, a fifty-day notice period for shareholder motions, and restrictions on shareholders' ability to call a meeting or act by consent.

other companies considered presented such a compatible cable partner. Together, Time and Warner would control half of New York City's cable system; Warner had cable systems in Brooklyn and Queens; and Time controlled cable systems in Manhattan and Queens. Warner's publishing company would integrate well with Time's established publishing company. Time sells hardcover books and magazines, and Warner sells softcover books and comics.[5] Time–Warner could sell all of these publications and Warner's videos by using Time's direct mailing network and Warner's international distribution system. Time's network could be used to promote and merchandise Warner's movies.

In August 1988, Levin, Nicholas, and Munro, acting on instructions from Time's board, continued to explore a business combination with Warner. . . .

From the outset, Time's board favored an all-cash or cash and securities acquisition of Warner as the basis for consolidation. Bruce Wasserstein, Time's financial advisor, also favored an outright purchase of Warner. However, Steve Ross, Warner's CEO, was adamant that a business combination was only practicable on a stock-for-stock basis. Warner insisted on a stock swap in order to preserve its shareholders' equity in the resulting corporation. Time's officers, on the other hand, made it abundantly clear that Time would be the acquiring corporation and that Time would control the resulting board. Time refused to permit itself to be cast as the "acquired" company.

Eventually Time acquiesced in Warner's insistence on a stock-for-stock deal, but talks broke down over corporate governance issues. Time wanted Ross' position as a co-CEO to be temporary and wanted Ross to retire in five years. Ross, however, refused to set a time for his retirement and viewed Time's proposal as indicating a lack of confidence in his leadership. Warner considered it vital that their executives and creative staff not perceive Warner as selling out to Time. Time's request of a guarantee that Time would dominate the CEO succession was objected to as inconsistent with the concept of a Time–Warner merger "of equals." Negotiations ended when the parties reached an impasse. Time's board refused to compromise on its position on corporate governance. Time, and particularly its outside directors, viewed the corporate governance provisions as critical for preserving the "Time Culture" through a pro-Time management at the top. . . .

Throughout the fall of 1988 Time pursued its plan of expansion into the entertainment field; Time held informal discussions with several companies, including Paramount. Capital Cities/ABC approached Time to propose a merger. Talks terminated, however, when Capital Cities/ABC suggested that it was interested in purchasing Time or in controlling the resulting board. Time steadfastly maintained it was not placing itself up for sale.

---

5. In contrast, Paramount's publishing endeavors were in the areas of professional volumes and text books. Time's board did not find Paramount's publishing as compatible as Warner's publishing efforts.

Warner and Time resumed negotiations in January 1989. The catalyst for the resumption of talks was a private dinner between Steve Ross and Time outside director, Michael Dingman. Dingman was able to convince Ross that the transitional nature of the proposed co-CEO arrangement did not reflect a lack of confidence in Ross. Ross agreed that this course was best for the company and a meeting between Ross and Munro resulted. Ross agreed to retire in five years and let Nicholas succeed him. Negotiations resumed and many of the details of the original stock-for-stock exchange agreement remained intact....

Time insider directors Levin and Nicholas met with Warner's financial advisors to decide upon a stock exchange ratio. Time's board had recognized the potential need to pay a premium in the stock ratio in exchange for dictating the governing arrangement of the new Time–Warner. Levin and outside director Finkelstein were the primary proponents of paying a premium to protect the "Time Culture." The board discussed premium rates of 10%, 15% and 20%. Wasserstein also suggested paying a premium for Warner due to Warner's rapid growth rate. The market exchange ratio of Time stock for Warner stock was .38 in favor of Warner. Warner's financial advisors informed the board that any exchange rate over .400 was a fair deal and any exchange rate over .450 was "one hell of a deal." The parties ultimately agreed upon an exchange rate favoring Warner of .465. On that basis, Warner stockholders would own slightly over 62%[6] of the common stock of Time–Warner.

On March 3, 1989, Time's board, with all but one director in attendance, met and unanimously approved the stock-for-stock merger with Warner. Warner's board likewise approved the merger. The agreement called for Warner to be merged into a wholly-owned Time subsidiary with Warner becoming the surviving corporation. The common stock of Warner would then be converted into common stock of Time at the agreed upon ratio. Thereafter, the name of Time would be changed to Time–Warner, Inc.

The rules of the New York Stock Exchange required that Time's issuance of shares to effectuate the merger be approved by a vote of Time's stockholders. The Delaware General Corporation Law required approval of the merger by a majority of the Warner stockholders. Delaware law did not require any vote by Time stockholders....

The resulting company would have a 24–member board, with 12 members representing each corporation. The company would have co-CEO's, at first Ross and Munro, then Ross and Nicholas, and finally, after Ross' retirement, ... Nicholas alone. The board would create an editorial committee with a majority of members representing Time. A similar entertainment committee would be controlled by Warner board members....

---

6. As was noted in the briefs and at oral argument, this figure is somewhat misleading because it does not take into consideration the number of individuals who owned stock in both companies.

At its March 3, 1989 meeting, Time's board adopted several defensive tactics. Time entered an automatic share exchange agreement with Warner. Time would receive 17,292,747 shares of Warner's outstanding common stock (9.4%) and Warner would receive 7,080,016 shares of Time's outstanding common stock (11.1%). Either party could trigger the exchange. Time sought out and paid for "confidence" letters from various banks with which they did business. In these letters, the banks promised not to finance any third-party attempt to acquire Time. Time argues these agreements served only to preserve the confidential relationship between itself and the banks. The Chancellor found these agreements to be inconsequential and futile attempts to "dry up" money for a hostile takeover. Time also agreed to a "no-shop" clause, preventing Time from considering any other consolidation proposal, thus relinquishing its power to consider other proposals, regardless of their merits. Time did so at Warner's insistence. Warner did not want to be left "on the auction block" for an unfriendly suitor, if Time were to withdraw from the deal.

Time's board simultaneously established a special committee of outside directors, Finkelstein, Kearns, and Opel, to oversee the merger. The committee's assignment was to resolve any impediments that might arise in the course of working out the details of the merger and its consummation. . . .

Time representatives lauded the lack of debt to the United States Senate and to the President of the United States. Public reaction to the announcement of the merger was positive. Time–Warner would be a media colossus with international scope. The board scheduled the stockholder vote for June 23; and a May 1 record date was set. On May 24, 1989, Time sent out extensive proxy statements to the stockholders regarding the approval vote on the merger. In the meantime, with the merger proceeding without impediment, the special committee had concluded, shortly after its creation, that it was not necessary either to retain independent consultants, legal or financial, or even to meet. Time's board was unanimously in favor of the proposed merger with Warner; and, by the end of May, the Time–Warner merger appeared to be an accomplished fact.

On June 7, 1989, these wishful assumptions were shattered by Paramount's surprising announcement of its all-cash offer to purchase all outstanding shares of Time for $175 per share. The following day, June 8, the trading price of Time's stock rose from $126 to $170 per share. Paramount's offer was said to be "fully negotiable."[7]

Time found Paramount's "fully negotiable" offer to be in fact subject to at least three conditions. First, Time had to terminate its merger agreement and stock exchange agreement with Warner, and remove certain other of its defensive devices, including the redemption of Time's shareholder rights. Second, Paramount had to obtain

7. Subsequently, it was established that Paramount's board had decided as early as March 1989 to move to acquire Time. However, Paramount management intentionally delayed publicizing its proposal until Time had mailed to its stockholders its Time–Warner merger proposal along with the required proxy statements.

the required cable franchise transfers from Time in a fashion acceptable to Paramount in its sole discretion. Finally, the offer depended upon a judicial determination that section 203 of the General Corporate Law of Delaware (The Delaware Anti–Takeover Statute) was inapplicable to any Time–Paramount merger. While Paramount's board had been privately advised that it could take months, perhaps over a year, to forge and consummate the deal, Paramount's board publicly proclaimed its ability to close the offer by July 5, 1989. Paramount executives later conceded that none of its directors believed that July 5th was a realistic date to close the transaction.

On June 8, 1989, Time formally responded to Paramount's offer. Time's chairman and CEO, J. Richard Munro, sent an aggressively worded letter to Paramount's CEO, Martin Davis. Munro's letter attacked Davis' personal integrity and called Paramount's offer "smoke and mirrors." Time's nonmanagement directors were not shown the letter before it was sent. However, at a board meeting that same day, all members endorsed management's response as well as the letter's content.

Over the following eight days, Time's board met three times to discuss Paramount's $175 offer. The board viewed Paramount's offer as inadequate and concluded that its proposed merger with Warner was the better course of action. Therefore, the board declined to open any negotiations with Paramount and held steady its course toward a merger with Warner.

In June, Time's board of directors met several times. During the course of their June meetings, Time's outside directors met frequently without management, officers or directors being present. At the request of the outside directors, corporate counsel was present during the board meetings and, from time to time, the management directors were asked to leave the board sessions. During the course of these meetings, Time's financial advisors informed the board that, on an auction basis, Time's per share value was materially higher than Warner's $175 per share offer. On this basis, the board concluded that Paramount's $175 offer was inadequate.

At these June meetings, certain Time directors expressed their concern that Time stockholders would not comprehend the long-term benefits of the Warner merger. Large quantities of Time shares were held by institutional investors. The board feared that even though there appeared to be wide support for the Warner transaction, Paramount's cash premium would be a tempting prospect to these investors. In mid-June, Time sought permission from the New York Stock Exchange to alter its rules and allow the Time–Warner merger to proceed without stockholder approval. Time did so at Warner's insistence. The New York Stock Exchange rejected Time's request on June 15; and on that day, the value of Time stock reached $182 per share.

The following day, June 16, Time's board met to take up Paramount's offer. The board's prevailing belief was that Paramount's bid presented a threat to Time's control of its own destiny and retention of the "Time Culture." Even after Time's financial advisors made another presentation of Paramount and its business attributes, Time's board maintained its position that a combination within Warner presented greater potential for Time. Warner presented Time with a much desired production capability and an established international marketing chain. Time's advisors presented the board with various options, including defensive measures.... Finally, Time's board formally rejected Paramount's offer.[10]

At the same meeting, Time's board decided to recast its consolidation with Warner into an outright cash and securities acquisition of Warner by Time; and Time so informed Warner. Time accordingly restructured its proposal to acquire Warner as follows: Time would make an immediate all-cash offer for 51% of Warner's outstanding stock at $70 per share. The remaining 49% would be purchased at some later date for a mixture of cash and securities worth $70 per share. To provide the funds required for its outright acquisition of Warner, Time would assume 7–10 billion dollars worth of debt, thus eliminating one of the principal transaction-related benefits of the original merger agreement....

On June 23, 1989, Paramount raised its all-cash offer to buy Time's outstanding stock to $200 per share. Paramount still professed that all aspects of the offer were negotiable. Time's board met on June 26, 1989 and formally rejected Paramount's $200 per share second offer. The board reiterated its belief that, despite the $25 increase, the offer was still inadequate. The Time board maintained that the Warner transaction offered a greater long-term value for the stockholders and, unlike Paramount, did not pose a threat to Time's survival and its "culture." Paramount then filed this action in the Court of Chancery.

II

The Shareholder Plaintiffs first assert a *Revlon* claim. They contend that the March 4 Time–Warner agreement effectively put Time up for sale, triggering *Revlon* duties, requiring Time's board to enhance short-term shareholder value and to treat all other interested acquirors on an equal basis. The Shareholder Plaintiffs base this argument on two facts: (i) the ultimate Time–Warner exchange ratio of .465 favoring Warner, resulting in Warner shareholders' receipt of 62% of the combined company; and (ii) the subjective intent of Time's directors as evidenced in their statements that the market might perceive the Time–Warner merger as putting Time up "for sale" and their adoption of various defensive measures.

The Shareholder Plaintiffs further contend that Time's directors, in structuring the original merger transaction to be "takeover-proof," triggered *Revlon* duties by foreclosing their shareholders from any prospect of obtaining a control premium. In short, plaintiffs argue that Time's board's decision to merge with Warner imposed a fiduciary

10. Meanwhile, Time had already begun erecting impediments to Paramount's offer. Time encouraged local cable franchises to sue Paramount to prevent it from easily obtaining the franchises.

duty to maximize immediate share value and not erect unreasonable barriers to further bids. . . .

Paramount asserts only a *Unocal* claim in which the shareholder plaintiffs join. Paramount contends that the Chancellor, in applying the first part of the *Unocal* test, erred in finding that Time's board had reasonable grounds to believe that Paramount posed both a legally cognizable threat to Time shareholders and a danger to Time's corporate policy and effectiveness. Paramount also contests the court's finding that Time's board made a reasonable and objective investigation of Paramount's offer so as to be informed before rejecting it. Paramount further claims that the court erred in applying *Unocal*'s second part in finding Time's response to be "reasonable." Paramount points primarily to the preclusive effect of the revised agreement which denied Time shareholders the opportunity both to vote on the agreement and to respond to Paramount's tender offer. Paramount argues that the underlying motivation of Time's board in adopting these defensive measures was management's desire to perpetuate itself in office.

The Court of Chancery posed the pivotal question presented by this case to be: Under what circumstances must a board of directors abandon an in-place plan of corporate development in order to provide its shareholders with the option to elect and realize an immediate control premium? As applied to this case, the question becomes: Did Time's board, having developed a strategic plan of global expansion to be launched through a business combination with Warner, come under a fiduciary duty to jettison its plan and put the corporation's future in the hands of its shareholders?

While we affirm the result reached by the Chancellor, we think it unwise to place undue emphasis upon long-term versus short-term corporate strategy. Two key predicates underpin our analysis. First, Delaware law imposes on a board of directors the duty to manage the business and affairs of the corporation. 8 Del.C. § 141(a). This broad mandate includes a conferred authority to set a corporate course of action, including time frame, designed to enhance corporate profitability. Thus, the question of "long-term" versus "short-term" values is largely irrelevant because directors, generally, are obliged to charter a course for a corporation which is in its best interests without regard to a fixed investment horizon. Second, absent a limited set of circumstances as defined under *Revlon*, a board of directors, while always required to act in an informed manner, is not under any *per se* duty to maximize shareholder value in the short term, even in the context of a takeover.[11] In our view, the pivotal question presented by this case is: "Did Time, by entering into the proposed merger with Warner, put itself up for sale?" A resolution of that issue through application of

11. Thus, we endorse the Chancellor's conclusion that it is not a breach of faith for directors to determine that the present stock market price of shares is not representative of true value or that there may indeed be several market values for any corporation's stock. We have so held in another context. See *Van Gorkom*, 488 A.2d at 876.

Revlon has a significant bearing upon the resolution of the derivative *Unocal* issue.

A.

We first take up plaintiffs' principal *Revlon* argument, summarized above. In rejecting this argument, the Chancellor found the original Time–Warner merger agreement not to constitute a "change of control" and concluded that the transaction did not trigger *Revlon* duties. The Chancellor's conclusion is premised on a finding that "[b]efore the merger agreement was signed, control of the corporation existed in a fluid aggregation of unaffiliated shareholders representing a voting majority—in other words, in the market." The Chancellor's findings of fact are supported by the record and his conclusion is correct as a matter of law. However, we premise our rejection of plaintiffs' *Revlon* claim on different grounds, namely, the absence of any substantial evidence to conclude that Time's board, in negotiating with Warner, made the dissolution or breakup of the corporate entity inevitable, as was the case in *Revlon.*

Under Delaware law there are, generally speaking and without excluding other possibilities, two circumstances which may implicate *Revlon* duties. The first, and clearer one, is when a corporation initiates an active bidding process seeking to sell itself or to effect a business reorganization involving a clear break-up of the company. See, e.g., Mills Acquisition Co. v. Macmillan, Inc., Del.Supr., 559 A.2d 1261 (1989). However, *Revlon* duties may also be triggered where, in response to a bidder's offer, a target abandons its long-term strategy and seeks an alternative transaction also involving the breakup of the company. Thus, in *Revlon*, when the board responded to Pantry Pride's offer by contemplating a "bust-up" sale of assets in a leveraged acquisition, we imposed upon the board a duty to maximize immediate shareholder value and an obligation to auction the company fairly. If, however, the board's reaction to a hostile tender offer is found to constitute only a defensive response and not an abandonment of the corporation's continued existence, *Revlon* duties are not triggered, though *Unocal* duties attach.[13] See, e.g., Ivanhoe Partners v. Newmont Mining Corp., Del.Supr., 535 A.2d 1334, 1345 (1987).

The plaintiffs insist that even though the original Time–Warner agreement may not have worked "an objective change of control," the transaction made a "sale" of Time inevitable. Plaintiffs rely on the subjective intent of Time's board of directors and principally upon certain board members' expressions of concern that the Warner transaction *might* be viewed as effectively putting Time up for sale. Plain-

13. Within the auction process, any action taken by the board must be reasonably related to the threat posed or reasonable in relation to the advantage sought, see Mills Acquisition Co. v. Macmillan, Inc., Del.Supr., 559 A.2d 1261, 1288 (1989). Thus, a *Unocal* analysis may be appropriate when a corporation is in a *Revlon* situation and *Revlon* duties may be triggered by a defensive action taken in response to a hostile offer. Since *Revlon*, we have stated that differing treatment of various bidders is not actionable when such action reasonably relates to achieving the best price available for the stockholders. *Macmillan*, 559 A.2d at 1286–87.

tiffs argue that the use of a lock-up agreement, a no-shop clause, and so-called "dry-up" agreements prevented shareholders from obtaining a control premium in the immediate future and thus violated *Revlon.*

We agree with the Chancellor that such evidence is entirely insufficient to invoke *Revlon* duties; and we decline to extend *Revlon's* application to corporate transactions simply because they might be construed as putting a corporation either "in play" or "up for sale." See Citron v. Fairchild Camera, Del.Supr., 569 A.2d 53 (1989); *Macmillan*, 559 A.2d at 1285 n. 35. The adoption of structural safety devices alone does not trigger *Revlon. Rather, as the Chancellor stated, such devices are properly subject to a Unocal* analysis.

Finally, we do not find in Time's recasting of its merger agreement with Warner from a share exchange to a share purchase a basis to conclude that Time had either abandoned its strategic plan or made a sale of Time inevitable. The Chancellor found that although the merged Time–Warner company would be large (with a value approaching approximately $30 billion), recent takeover cases have proven that acquisition of the combined company might nonetheless be possible.... The legal consequence is that *Unocal* alone applies to determine whether the business judgment rule attaches to the revised agreement....

B.

We turn now to plaintiffs' *Unocal* claim. We begin by noting, as did the Chancellor, that our decision does not require us to pass on the wisdom of the board's decision to enter into the original Time–Warner agreement. That is not a court's task. Our task is simply to review the record to determine whether there is sufficient evidence to support the Chancellor's conclusion that the initial Time–Warner agreement was the product of a proper exercise of business judgment....

We have purposely detailed the evidence of the Time board's deliberative approach, beginning in 1983–84, to expand itself. Time's decision in 1988 to combine with Warner was made only after what could be fairly characterized as an exhaustive appraisal of Time's future as a corporation. After concluding in 1983–84 that the corporation must expand to survive, and beyond journalism into entertainment, the board combed the field of available entertainment companies. By 1987 Time had focused upon Warner; by late July 1988 Time's board was convinced that Warner would provide the best "fit" for Time to achieve its strategic objectives. The record attests to the zealousness of Time's executives, fully supported by their directors, in seeing to the preservation of Time's "culture," i.e., its perceived editorial integrity in journalism. We find ample evidence in the record to support the Chancellor's conclusion that the Time board's decision to expand the business of the company through its March 3 merger with Warner was entitled to the protection of the business judgment rule....

The Chancellor reached a different conclusion in addressing the Time–Warner transaction as revised three months later. He found that the revised agreement was defense-motivated and designed to avoid the potentially disruptive effect that Paramount's offer would have had on consummation of the proposed merger were it put to a shareholder vote. Thus, the court declined to apply the traditional business judgment rule to the revised transaction and instead analyzed the Time board's June 16 decision under *Unocal.* The court ruled that *Unocal* applied to all director actions taken, following receipt of Paramount's hostile tender offer, that were reasonably determined to be defensive. Clearly that was a correct ruling and no party disputes that ruling.

In *Unocal,* we held that before the business judgment rule is applied to a board's adoption of a defensive measure, the burden will lie with the board to prove (a) reasonable grounds for believing that a danger to corporate policy and effectiveness existed; and (b) that the defensive measure adopted was reasonable in relation to the threat posed. *Unocal,* 493 A.2d 946. Directors satisfy the first part of the *Unocal* test by demonstrating good faith and reasonable investigation. . . .

Unocal involved a two-tier, highly coercive tender offer. In such a case, the threat is obvious: shareholders may be compelled to tender to avoid being treated adversely in the second stage of the transaction. . . . In subsequent cases, the Court of Chancery has suggested that an all-cash, all-shares offer, falling within a range of values that a shareholder might reasonably prefer, cannot constitute a legally recognized "threat" to shareholder interests sufficient to withstand a *Unocal* analysis. AC Acquisitions Corp. v. Anderson, Clayton & Co., Del. Ch., 519 A.2d 103 (1986); see Grand Metropolitan, PLC v. Pillsbury Co., Del.Ch., 558 A.2d 1049 (1988); City Capital Associates v. Interco Inc., Del.Ch., 551 A.2d 787 (1988). In those cases, the Court of Chancery determined that whatever threat existed related only to the shareholders and only to price and not to the corporation.

From those decisions by our Court of Chancery, Paramount and the individual plaintiffs extrapolate a rule of law that an all-cash, all-shares offer with values reasonably in the range of acceptable price cannot pose any objective threat to a corporation or its shareholders. Thus, Paramount would have us hold that only if the value of Paramount's offer were determined to be clearly inferior to the value created by management's plan to merge with Warner could the offer be viewed—objectively—as a threat.

Implicit in the plaintiffs' argument is the view that a hostile tender offer can pose only two types of threats: the threat of coercion that results from a two-tier offer promising unequal treatment for nontendering shareholders, and the threat of inadequate value from an all-shares, all-cash offer at a price below what a target board in good faith deems to be the present value of its shares. See, e.g., *Interco*, 551 A.2d at 797; *see also* BNS, Inc. v. Koppers, D.Del., 683 F.Supp. 458 (1988). Since Paramount's offer was all-cash, the only conceivable "threat," plaintiffs argue, was inadequate value. We disapprove of such a narrow and rigid construction of *Unocal*, for the reasons which follow.

Plaintiffs' position represents a fundamental misconception of our standard of review under *Unocal* principally because it would involve the court in substituting its judgment for what is a "better" deal for that of a corporation's board of directors. To the extent that the Court of Chancery has recently done so in certain of its opinions, we hereby reject such approach as not in keeping with a proper *Unocal* analysis. See, e.g., *Interco*, 551 A.2d 787 . . .

The usefulness of *Unocal* as an analytical tool is precisely its flexibility in the face of a variety of fact scenarios. *Unocal* is not intended as an abstract standard; neither is it a structured and mechanistic procedure of appraisal. Thus, we have said that directors may consider, when evaluating the threat posed by a takeover bid, the "inadequacy of the price offered, nature and timing of the offer, questions of illegality, the impact on [constituencies] other than shareholders, the risk of nonconsummation and the quality of securities being offered in the exchange." 493 A.2d at 955. The open-ended analysis mandated by *Unocal* is not intended to lead to a simple mathematical exercise: that is, of comparing the discounted value of Time–Warner's expected trading price at some future date with Paramount's offer and determining which is the higher. Indeed, in our view, precepts underlying the business judgment rule mitigate against a court's engaging in the process of attempting to appraise and evaluate the relative merits of a long-term versus a short-term investment goal for shareholders. To engage in such an exercise is a distortion of the *Unocal* process and, in particular, the application of the second part of *Unocal's* test, discussed below.

In this case, the Time board reasonably determined that inadequate value was not the only legally cognizable threat that Paramount's all-cash, all-shares offer could present. Time's board concluded that Paramount's eleventh hour offer posed other threats. One concern was that Time shareholders might elect to tender into Paramount's cash offer in ignorance or a mistaken belief of the strategic benefit which a business combination with Warner might produce. Moreover, Time viewed the conditions attached to Paramount's offer as introducing a degree of uncertainty that skewed a comparative analysis. Further, the timing of Paramount's offer to follow issuance of Time's proxy notice was viewed as arguably designed to upset, if not confuse, the Time stockholders' vote. Given this record evidence, we cannot conclude that the Time board's decision of June 6 that Paramount's offer posed a threat to corporate policy and effectiveness was lacking in good faith or dominated by motives of either entrenchment or self-interest.

Paramount also contends that the Time board had not duly investigated Paramount's offer. Therefore, Paramount argues, Time was unable to make an informed decision that the offer posed a threat to Time's corporate policy. Although the Chancellor did not address this issue directly, his findings of fact do detail Time's exploration of the available entertainment companies, including Paramount, before determining that Warner provided the best strategic "fit." In addition, the court found that Time's board rejected Paramount's offer because Paramount did not serve Time's objectives or meet Time's needs. Thus, the record does, in our judgment, demonstrate that Time's board was adequately informed of the potential benefits of a transaction with Paramount. We agree with the Chancellor that the Time board's lengthy pre-June investigation of potential merger candidates, including Paramount, mooted any obligation on Time's part to halt its merger process with Warner to reconsider Paramount. Time's board was under no obligation to negotiate with Paramount. *Unocal*, 493 A.2d at 954–55; see also *Macmillan*, 559 A.2d at 1285 n. 35. Time's failure to negotiate cannot be fairly found to have been uninformed. The evidence supporting this finding is materially enhanced by the fact that twelve of Time's sixteen board members were outside independent directors. . . .

We turn to the second part of the *Unocal* analysis. The obvious requisite to determining the reasonableness of a defensive action is a clear identification of the nature of the threat. As the Chancellor correctly noted, this "requires an evaluation of the importance of the corporate objective threatened; alternative methods of protecting that objective; impacts of the 'defensive' action, and other relevant factors." . . . As applied to the facts of this case, the question is whether the record evidence supports the Court of Chancery's conclusion that the restructuring of the Time–Warner transaction, including the adoption of several preclusive defensive measures, was a *reasonable response* in relation to a perceived threat.

Paramount argues that, assuming its tender offer posed a threat, Time's response was unreasonable in precluding Time's shareholders from accepting the tender offer or receiving a control premium in the immediately foreseeable future. Once again, the contention stems, we believe, from a fundamental misunderstanding of where the power of corporate governance lies. Delaware law confers the management of the corporate enterprise to the stockholders' duly elected board representatives. 8 Del.C. § 141(a). The fiduciary duty to manage a corporate enterprise includes the selection of a time frame for achievement of corporate goals. That duty may not be delegated to the stockholders. . . . Directors are not obliged to abandon a deliberately conceived corporate plan for a short-term shareholder profit unless there is clearly no basis to sustain the corporate strategy. . . .

Although the Chancellor blurred somewhat the discrete analyses required under *Unocal*, he did conclude that Time's board reasonably perceived Paramount's offer to be a significant threat to the planned Time–Warner merger and that Time's response was not "overly broad." We have found that even in light of a valid threat, management actions that are coercive in nature or force upon shareholders a management-sponsored alternative to a hostile offer may be struck down as unreasonable and nonproportionate responses. *Macmillan*, 559 A.2d 1261; *AC Acquisitions Corp.*, 519 A.2d 103.

Here, on the record facts, the Chancellor found that Time's responsive action to Paramount's tender offer was not aimed at "cramming down" on its shareholders a management-sponsored alternative, but rather had as its goal the carrying forward of a pre-existing transaction in an altered form. Thus, the response was reasonably related to the threat. The Chancellor noted that the revised agreement and its accompanying safety devices did not preclude Paramount from making an offer for the combined Time–Warner company or from changing the conditions of its offer so as not to make the offer dependent upon the nullification of the Time–Warner agreement. Thus, the response was proportionate. We affirm the Chancellor's rulings as clearly supported by the record. Finally, we note that although Time was required, as a result of Paramount's hostile offer, to incur a heavy debt to finance its acquisition of Warner, that fact alone does not render the board's decision unreasonable so long as the directors could reasonably perceive the debt load not to be so injurious to the corporation as to jeopardize its well being.

C.

Conclusion

Applying the test for grant or denial of preliminary injunctive relief, we find plaintiffs failed to establish a reasonable likelihood of ultimate success on the merits. Therefore, we affirm.

NOTE ON *REVLON* IN OPERATION

Time Inc. emphasized in its holding that Time's board was not within *Revlon* because the Time–Warner acquisition did not involve a bust up of Time as was the case in *Revlon*. This explanation was later raised in *Paramount Communications Inc. v. QVC Network*, 637 A.2d 34 (1994), by Viacom, Inc., the favored merger partner of Paramount Communications Inc. Viacom and Paramount sought to justify several deal protection provisions designed to assure the merger of the two firms and to thwart the efforts of QVC Network Inc. which, in spite of offering a substantially higher bid of $95 was not the favored suitor. Among the deal protection provisions were a no-shop provision, a $100 million termination fee, and an option that allowed Viacom to put its option to acquire nearly 24 million (19.9 percent of Paramount's outstanding common) to Paramount for a sum equal to the difference between the share's option price ($69.14/share) and the market price of Paramount shares (which likely would approach the price submitted by the winner of the battle). In its opinion in *Paramount*, the Delaware Supreme Court addressed the necessity of a break up for *Revlon* to apply:

> It does not follow, however, that a "break-up" must be present and "inevitable" before directors are subject to enhanced judicial scrutiny and are required to pursue a transaction that is calculated to produce the best value reasonably available to the stockholders.

> In fact, we stated in *Revlon* that "when bidders make relatively similar offers, or dissolution of the company becomes inevitable, the directors cannot fulfill their enhanced *Unocal* duties by playing favorites with the contending factions." Id. at 184 (emphasis added). *Revlon* thus does not hold that an inevitable dissolution or break-up is necessary. . . .
>
> There are few events that have a more significant impact on the stockholders than a sale of control or a corporate break-up. Each event represents a fundamental (and perhaps irrevocable) change in the nature of the corporate enterprise from a practical standpoint. It is the significance of each of these events that justifies: (a) focusing on the directors' obligation to seek the best value reasonably available to the stockholders; and (b) requiring a close scrutiny of board action which could be contrary to the stockholders' interests.
>
> Accordingly, when a corporation undertakes a transaction which will cause: (a) a change in corporate control; or (b) a break-up of the corporate entity, the directors' obligation is to seek the best value reasonably available to the stockholders. This obligation arises because the effect of the Viacom–Paramount transaction, if consummated, is to shift control of Paramount from the public stockholders to a controlling stockholder, Viacom. Neither *Time–Warner* nor any other decision of this Court holds that a "break-up" of the company is essential to give rise to this obligation where there is a sale of control.

Id. at 46–48.(emphasis original). The Supreme Court elaborated on its emphasis on control being transferred as triggering *Revlon*:

> When a majority of a corporation's voting shares are acquired by a single person or entity, or by a cohesive group acting together, there is a significant diminution in the voting power of those who thereby become minority stockholders. Under the statutory framework of the General Corporation Law, many of the most fundamental corporate changes can be implemented only if they are approved by a majority vote of the stockholders. Such actions include elections of directors, amendments to the certificate of incorporation, mergers, consolidations, sales of all or substantially all of the assets of the corporation, and dissolution. 8 Del.C. §§ 211, 242, 251, 258, 263, 271, 275. Because of the overriding importance of voting rights, this Court and the Court of Chancery have consistently acted to protect stockholders from unwarranted interference with such rights.
>
> In the absence of devices protecting the minority stockholders, stockholder votes are likely to become mere formalities where there is a majority stockholder. For example, minority stockholders can be deprived of a continuing equity interest in their corporation by means of a cash-out merger. *Weinberger,* 457 A.2d at 703. Absent effective protective provisions, minority stockholders must rely for protection solely on the fiduciary duties owed to them by the directors and the majority stockholder, since the

> minority stockholders have lost the power to influence corporate direction through the ballot. The acquisition of majority status and the consequent privilege of exerting the powers of majority ownership come at a price. That price is usually a control premium which recognizes not only the value of a control block of shares, but also compensates the minority stockholders for their resulting loss of voting power.
>
> In the case before us, the public stockholders (in the aggregate) currently own a majority of Paramount's voting stock. Control of the corporation is not vested in a single person, entity, or group, but vested in the fluid aggregation of unaffiliated stockholders. In the event the Paramount–Viacom transaction is consummated, the public stockholders will receive cash and a minority equity voting position in the surviving corporation. Following such consummation, there will be a controlling stockholder who will have the voting power to: (a) elect directors; (b) cause a break-up of the corporation; (c) merge it with another company; (d) cash-out the public stockholders; (e) amend the certificate of incorporation; (f) sell all or substantially all of the corporate assets; or (g) otherwise alter materially the nature of the corporation and the public stockholders' interests. Irrespective of the present Paramount Board's vision of a long-term strategic alliance with Viacom, the proposed sale of control would provide the new controlling stockholder with the power to alter that vision.
>
> Because of the intended sale of control, the Paramount–Viacom transaction has economic consequences of considerable significance to the Paramount stockholders. Once control has shifted, the current Paramount stockholders will have no leverage in the future to demand another control premium. As a result, the Paramount stockholders are entitled to receive, and should receive, a control premium and/or protective devices of significant value. There being no such protective provisions in the Viacom–Paramount transaction, the Paramount directors had an obligation to take the maximum advantage of the current opportunity to realize for the stockholders the best value reasonably available.

Id. at 42–43.

Does the court's reason for applying *Revlon* to sale of control transactions apply with equal force to acquisitions, such as in *Revlon* itself, which involve the inevitable breakup of the firm? That is, does the concern for the last opportunity for shareholders to participate in a control premium underlie the application of *Revlon* where the board actively shops the firm or initiates a transaction that ultimately leads to a breakup of the firm? More specifically, what transactions involve a change in control of the type envisioned by the Delaware Supreme Court?

> [A]board sells "control" and thus triggers *Revlon* duties . . . when it agrees to exchange a controlling stake in the company, either for cash or non-voting securities, or for voting shares in an acquirer with a controlling shareholder but not when it exchanges

> 100% of its voting shares for voting shares in a widely held acquirer, most commonly through a stock-for-stock merger. . . .
>
> The exchange of all the target's voting shares of another widely held company is not a sale of control, and thus does not trigger *Revlon*, on the logic that control of the target company was before, and control of the combined company remains afterward, in a "fluid aggregation of unaffiliated stockholders."

Bernard Black & Rainier Kraakman, Delaware's Takeover Law: The Uncertain Search for Hidden Value, 96 Nw. U. L. Rev. 521, 534–35 (2002). The Paramount–Viacom transactions fell within the third above instance. Viacom's Chairman and CEO, Sumner M. Redstone, owned 85.2 percent of Viacom's voting stock and under the terms of the acquisition would own a majority of the combined companies voting stock.

Paramount also addressed both the scope of the directors' duties under *Revlon* as well as what is entailed in the court's enhanced scrutiny:

> The consequences of a sale of control impose special obligations on the directors of a corporation. In particular, they have the obligation of acting reasonably to seek the transaction offering the best value reasonably available to the stockholders. The courts will apply enhanced scrutiny to ensure that the directors have acted reasonably. The obligations of the directors and the enhanced scrutiny of the courts are well-established by the decisions of this Court. The directors' fiduciary duties in a sale of control context are those which generally attach. In short, "the directors must act in accordance with their fundamental duties of care and loyalty." Barkan v. Amsted Indus., Inc., Del.Supr., 567 A.2d 1279, 1286 (1989). . . .
>
> In pursuing this objective, the directors must be especially diligent. . . . In particular, this Court has stressed the importance of the board being adequately informed in negotiating a sale of control: "The need for adequate information is central to the enlightened evaluation of a transaction that a board must make." *Barkan,* 567 A.2d at 1287. . . . Moreover, the role of outside, independent directors becomes particularly important because of the magnitude of a sale of control transaction and the possibility, in certain cases, that management may not necessarily be impartial. . . .
>
> *Barkan* teaches some of the methods by which a board can fulfill its obligation to seek the best value reasonably available to the stockholders. 567 A.2d at 1286–87. These methods are designed to determine the existence and viability of possible alternatives. They include conducting an auction, canvassing the market, etc. Delaware law recognizes that there is no single blueprint that directors must follow. . . .
>
> In determining which alternative provides the best value for the stockholders, a board of directors is not limited to considering

only the amount of cash involved, and is not required to ignore totally its view of the future value of a strategic alliance. See *Macmillan,* 559 A.2d at 1282 n. 29. Instead, the directors should analyze the entire situation and evaluate in a disciplined manner the consideration being offered. Where stock or other non-cash consideration is involved, the board should try to quantify its value, if feasible, to achieve an objective comparison of the alternatives. In addition, the board may assess a variety of practical considerations relating to each alternative, including:

> [an offer's] fairness and feasibility; the proposed or actual financing for the offer, and the consequences of that financing; questions of illegality; ... the risk of non-consum[m]ation; ... the bidder's identity, prior background and other business venture experiences; and the bidder's business plans for the corporation and their effects on stockholder interests.

Macmillan, 559 A.2d at 1282 n. 29. These considerations are important because the selection of one alternative may permanently foreclose other opportunities. While the assessment of these factors may be complex, the board's goal is straightforward: having informed themselves of all material information reasonably available, the directors must decide which alternative is most likely to offer the best value reasonably available to the stockholders....

Board action in the circumstances presented here is subject to enhanced scrutiny. Such scrutiny is mandated by: (a) the threatened diminution of the current stockholders' voting power; (b) the fact that an asset belonging to public stockholders (a control premium) is being sold and may never be available again; and (c) the traditional concern of Delaware courts for actions which impair or impede stockholder voting rights....

The key features of an enhanced scrutiny test are: (a) a judicial determination regarding the adequacy of the decisionmaking process employed by the directors, including the information on which the directors based their decision; and (b) a judicial examination of the reasonableness of the directors' action in light of the circumstances then existing. The directors have the burden of proving that they were adequately informed and acted reasonably.

Although an enhanced scrutiny test involves a review of the reasonableness of the substantive merits of a board's actions,[16] a court should not ignore the complexity of the directors' task in a sale of control. There are many business and financial consider-

---

16. It is to be remembered that, in cases where the traditional business judgment rule is applicable and the board acted with due care, in good faith, and in the honest belief that they are acting in the best interests of the stockholders (which is not this case), the Court gives great deference to the substance of the directors' decision and will not invalidate the decision, will not examine its reasonableness, and "will not substitute our views for those of the board if the latter's decision can be 'attributed to any rational business purpose.' " *Unocal,* 493 A.2d at 949 (quoting Sinclair Oil Corp. v. Levien, Del.Supr., 280 A.2d 717, 720 (1971)). See *Aronson,* 473 A.2d at 812.

> ations implicated in investigating and selecting the best value reasonably available. The board of directors is the corporate decisionmaking body best equipped to make these judgments. Accordingly, a court applying enhanced judicial scrutiny should be deciding whether the directors made a reasonable decision, not a perfect decision. If a board selected one of several reasonable alternatives, a court should not second-guess that choice even though it might have decided otherwise or subsequent events may have cast doubt on the board's determination. Thus, courts will not substitute their business judgment for that of the directors, but will determine if the directors' decision was, on balance, within a range of reasonableness. . . .

Id. at 43–46. (emphasis original). In applying this test, *Paramount* held that the board breached its *Revlon* duties by failing to aggressively use the competing higher QVC offer to extract a higher bid and weakened deal protection provisions from Viacom.

Lyondell v. Ryan, 970 A.2d 235 (Del.Supr. 2009), considered whether the target directors breached their duty of good faith by developing a wait and see approach for two months following the suitor's 13D filing. The Supreme Court held that *Revlon* duties did not commence until the directors began to negotiate with the firm's suitor; it therefore reversed the Chancery Court's holding that *Revlon* duties were triggered by the bidder filing Schedule 13D announcing it held 8.3 percent of the Lyondell shares and had an interest in acquiring Lyondell.

> The problem with the trial court's analysis is that *Revlon* duties do not arise simply because a company is "in play." The duty to seek the best available price applies only when the company embarks on a transaction—on its own initiative or in response to an unsolicited offer—that will result in a change of control. Basell's Schedule 13D did put Lyondell directors and the market in general, on notice that Basell was interested in acquiring Lyondell. The directors responded promptly holding a special meeting to consider whether Lyondell should take any action. The directors decided that they would neither put the company up for sale nor institute defensive measures to fend off a possible hostile offer. Instead, they decided to take a "wait and see" approach. That decision was entirely an appropriate exercise of the directors' business judgment. The time for action under *Revlon* did not begin until July 10, 2007, when the directors began negotiating the sale of Lyondell.

970 A.2d at 242. The Chancery Court reasoned that when the directors did commence negotiations they acted improperly by failing, among other steps, to conduct an auction or undertake a market check of the firm's value (they also agreed to a $385 termination penalty and no-shop clause). While recognizing the facts likely would invite continued discovery if the suit were premised on a breach of the directors' duty of care, the Supreme Court reasoned that because Lyondell's charter provided directors an immunity shield for care violations that any

breach of *Revlon* duties would require proof of a "conscious disregard for those duties."

> Directors' decisions must be reasonable, not perfect.... The trial court denied summary judgment because Lyondell directors "unexplained inaction" prevented the court from determining that they had acted in good faith. But, if the directors failed to do all that they should have under the circumstances, they breached their duty of care. Only if they knowingly and completely failed to undertake their responsibilities would they breach their duty of loyalty. The trial court approached the record from the wrong perspective. Instead of questioning whether disinterested, independent directors did everything that they (arguably) should have done to obtain the best sale price, the inquiry should have been whether those directors utterly failed to attempt the best sale price.
>
> Viewing the record in this manner leads to only one possible conclusion. The Lyondell directors met several times to consider Basell's premium offer. They were generally aware of the value of their company and they knew the chemical company market. The directors solicited and followed the advice of their financial and legal advisors. They attempted to negotiate a higher offer even though all the evidence indicates that Basell had offered a "blowout" price. Finally, they approved the merger agreement, because "it was simply too good not to pass along [the the stockholders] for their consideration. We assume, as we must on summary judgment, that the Lyondell directors did absolutely nothing to prepare for Basell's offer, and that they did not even consider conducting a market check before agreeing to the merger. Even so, this record clearly establishes that the Lyondell directors did not breach their duty of loyalty by failing to act in good faith....

970 A.2d at 243–244.

In *Paramount* the directors had no personal financial interest that would be advanced by preferring Viacom over QVC. What justifies placing the burden of proof on the supporters of the Paramount–Viacom combination rather than on QVC? Regardless of who bears the burden of proof, how was the scrutiny of the directors' decision different in *Time* from *Paramount*? Why should the focus be different in either case?

NOTE ON DEFENSIVE MANEUVERS OUTSIDE OF DELAWARE

States are evenly divided whether they apply heightened *Unocal/Revlon* scrutiny to defensive maneuvers or instead examine defensive maneuvers through the lens of the business judgment rule so that plaintiff has the burden on issues of care and loyalty. State antitakeover statutes, discussed later, play a very significant role in determining which of these two approaches is followed. *See* Michal Barzuza,

The State Of State Antitakeover Law, 95 Va. L. Rev. 1973 (2009) (courts in states with relatively strong antitakeover statutes generally invoke the protective statutes to support their holding that that directors are not under enhanced duties when defending control). Thus, a majority of the non-Delaware decisions address defensive maneuvers by according the directors' actions the presumptions of the business judgment rule. For example, in upholding the directors' issuance of a poison pill to all shareholders except the hostile bidder, the federal district court applying New York law concluded that under New York law that "a board's decision . . . made on the basis of reasoned judgment and in the absence of self dealing, conflict of interest, or bad faith" would be valid in the absence of a prima facie showing to the contrary. Dynamics Corp. v. WHX Corp., 967 F. Supp. 59, 64 (D. Conn. 1997) (further emphasizing that the New York poison pill validation statute expressly authorizes boards of directors to impose such conditions and limitations as the board believes in the corporation's and its shareholders' interests). Similarly, Seidman v. Central Bancorp, Inc., 16 Mass. L. Rptr. 383, 2003 WL 21528509 (Mass. Super. 2003), rejected the engrafting Delaware's heightened review standards onto the Massachusetts' other constituency statute that provided, in part:

> In determining what . . . [the director] reasonably believes to be in the best interests of the corporation, a director may consider the interests of the corporation's employees, suppliers, creditors and customers, the economy of the state, region and nation, community and societal considerations, and long-term and short-term interests of the corporation and its stockholders, including the possibility that these interests may be best served by the continued independence of the corporation.

The court noted the legislative history of the provision reflected the desire "to give protection to Massachusetts' corporations from abusive takeovers which challenge the long-term growth of the Commonwealth's economy, the creation of new jobs and the long-term interests of shareholders." 2003 WL 21528509 at 8.

> In responding to the arguments . . . that this Court should either import the proportionality doctrine in *Unocal* . . . or aspects of the Massachusetts common law relating to fiduciary duties of directors, as a gloss on the protective reach . . . [of the other constituency provision], the Court is reminded of Justice Cardozo's eloquent comments on the role of the judge, particularly at the trial level:
>
>> The judge, even when he is free, is still not wholly free. He is not to innovate at pleasure. He is not a knight-errant, roaming at will in pursuit of his own ideal of beauty or of goodness. He is to draw inspiration from consecrated principles. He is not to yield to spasmodic sentiment, to vague and unregulated benevolence. He is to exercise discretion informed by tradition, methodized by analogy, disciplined by system, and subordinated to "the primordial necessity of

order in the social life." Cardozo, Nature of Judicial Process, 141 (1921)).

2003 WL 21528509 at 9–10 The Massachusetts and New York decisions are consistent with the approach embraced by the American Law Institute:

§ 602 Action of Directors That Has the Foreseeable Effect of Blocking Unsolicited Tender Offers

(a) The board of directors may take an action that has the foreseeable effect of blocking an unsolicited tender offer ..., if the action is a reasonable response to the offer.

(b) In considering whether its action is a reasonable response to the offer:

(1) The board may take into account all factors relevant to the best interests of the corporation and shareholders ...

(2) The board may, in addition to the analysis under § 6.02(b)(1), have regard for interests or groups (other than shareholders) with respect to which the corporation has a legitimate concern if to do so would not significantly disfavor the long-term interests of shareholders.

(c) A person who challenges an action of the board on the ground that it fails to satisfy the standards of Subsection (a) has the burden of proof that the board's action is an unreasonable response to the offer....

Comment:

a. ... Section 6.02 reflects the view that judicial review of directors' blocking actions against unsolicited tender offers should not be based on an analysis of the directors' motives. Such a review cannot effectively distinguish between cases in which directors favored themselves and cases in which directors properly looked to the interests of the shareholders. Equally important, a motivational standard of review gives no guidance to directors—particularly disinterested directors—as to what constitutes appropriate behavior. Accordingly, § 6.02 directs judicial inquiry initially to the question whether action taken by the directors has the foreseeable effect of blocking a tender offer, and thereby precluding holders of voting equity securities from having the opportunity to accept the tender offer. If the directors' action does have that effect, then the court must further inquire whether the directors' action was a reasonable response to the offer

There has been modest success in striking down measures even when the burden of proof is not placed on the directors to justify their defensive maneuvers or to prove they have acted as auctioneers. *See* First Union Corp. v. SunTrust Banks, Inc., 2001 WL 1885686 (N.C. Super. 2001) (rejecting *Unocal* and *Revlon* but nonetheless holding invalid a non-termination provision that was part of a bundle of deal protection items because its operation could coerce shareholders to support acquisition supported by the board of directors). Query, in assessing defensive maneuvers is the allocation of the burden of proof as significant as the substantive standard, such as proportionality, coercion and the reasonableness of the directors' behavior?

SECTION 3. PROTECTING THE DEAL

Omnicare, Inc. v. NCS Healthcare, Inc.

Supreme Court of Delaware 2003.
818 A.2d 914.

■ Before: VEASEY, CHIEF JUSTICE, WALSH, HOLLAND, BERGER and STEELE, JUSTICES, constituting the Court en Banc.

■ HOLLAND, JUSTICE, for the majority: . . .

NCS Healthcare, Inc. ("NCS"), a Delaware corporation, was the object of competing acquisition bids, one by Genesis Health Ventures, Inc., ("Genesis"), a Pennsylvania Corporation, and the other by Omnicare, Inc. ("Omnicare"), a Delaware corporation. . . .

NCS, is a Delaware corporation headquartered in Beachwood, Ohio. NCS is a leading independent provider of pharmacy services to long-term care institutions including skilled nursing facilities, assisted living facilities and other institutional healthcare facilities. NCS common stock consists of Class A shares and Class B shares. The Class B shares are entitled to ten votes per share and the Class A shares are entitled to one vote per share. The shares are virtually identical in every other respect.

The defendant Jon H. Outcalt is Chairman of the NCS board of directors. Outcalt owns 202,063 shares of NCS Class A common stock and 3,476,086 shares of Class B common stock. The defendant Kevin B. Shaw is President, CEO and a director of NCS. At the time the merger agreement at issue in this dispute was executed with Genesis, Shaw owned 28,905 shares of NCS Class A common stock and 1,141,134 shares of Class B common stock.

The NCS board has two other members, defendants Boake A. Sells and Richard L. Osborne. Sells is a graduate of the Harvard Business School. He was Chairman and CEO at Revco Drugstores in Cleveland, Ohio from 1987 to 1992, when he was replaced by new owners. Sells currently sits on the boards of both public and private companies. Osborne is a full-time professor at the Weatherhead School of Management at Case Western Reserve University. He has been at the university for over thirty years. Osborne currently sits on at least seven corporate boards other than NCS.

The defendant Genesis is a Pennsylvania corporation with its principal place of business in Kennett Square, Pennsylvania. It is a leading provider of healthcare and support services to the elderly. . . .

The plaintiffs in the class action own an unspecified number of shares of NCS Class A common stock. They represent a class consisting of all holders of Class A common stock. As of July 28, 2002, NCS had 18,461,599 Class A shares and 5,255,210 Class B shares outstanding.

Omnicare is a Delaware corporation with its principal place of business in Covington, Kentucky. Omnicare is in the institutional pharmacy business, with annual sales in excess of $2.1 billion during its last fiscal year. . . .

FACTUAL BACKGROUND . . .

NCS Seeks Restructuring Alternatives

Beginning in late 1999, changes in the timing and level of reimbursements by government and third-party providers adversely affected market conditions in the health care industry. As a result, NCS began to experience greater difficulty in collecting accounts receivables, which led to a precipitous decline in the market value of its stock. NCS common shares that traded above $20 in January 1999 were worth as little as $5 at the end of that year. By early 2001, NCS was in default on approximately $350 million in debt, including $206 million in senior bank debt and $102 million of its 5 3/4% Convertible Subordinated Debentures (the "Notes"). After these defaults, NCS common stock traded in a range of $0.09 to $0.50 per share until days before the announcement of the transaction at issue in this case.

NCS began to explore strategic alternatives that might address the problems it was confronting. . . .

Omnicare's Initial Negotiations

In the summer of 2001, NCS invited Omnicare, Inc. to begin discussions with Brown Gibbons [NCS's investment banker] regarding a possible transaction. On July 20, Joel Gemunder, Omnicare's President and CEO, sent Shaw a written proposal to acquire NCS in a bankruptcy sale under Section 363 of the Bankruptcy Code. This proposal was for $225 million subject to satisfactory completion of due diligence. . . .

NCS Financial Improvement

. . . In March 2002, NCS decided to form an independent committee of board members who were neither NCS employees nor major NCS stockholders (the "Independent Committee") [to consider transactions that would provide some value for NCS's stockholders]. The NCS board thought this was necessary because, due to NCS's precarious financial condition, it felt that fiduciary duties were owed to the enterprise as a whole rather than solely to NCS stockholders.

Sells and Osborne were selected as the members of the committee, and given authority to consider and negotiate possible transactions for NCS. The entire four member NCS board, however, retained authority to approve any transaction. The Independent Committee retained the same legal and financial counsel as the NCS board.

The Independent Committee met for the first time on May 14, 2002. At that meeting Pollack suggested that NCS seek a "stalking-horse merger partner" to obtain the highest possible value in any transaction. The Independent Committee agreed with the suggestion.

Genesis Initial Proposal

Two days later, on May 16, 2002, Scott Berlin . . . [and] Glen Pollack . . . [the investment bankers advising NCS] and Boake Sells [a member of NCS's independent committee] met with George Hager, CFO of Genesis, and Michael Walker, who was Genesis's CEO. At that meeting, Genesis made it clear that if it were going to engage in any negotiations with NCS, it would not do so as a stalking horse. As one of its advisors testified, "We didn't want to be someone who set forth a valuation for NCS which would only result in that valuation . . . being publicly disclosed, and thereby creating an environment where Omnicare felt to maintain its competitive monopolistic positions, that they had to match and exceed that level." Thus, Genesis "wanted a degree of certainty that to the extent [it] w[as] willing to pursue a negotiated merger agreement . . ., [it] would be able to consummate the transaction [it] negotiated and executed."

In June 2002, Genesis proposed a transaction for the acquisition of NCS. . . . As discussions continued, the terms proposed by Genesis continued to improve. . . .

Genesis Exclusivity Agreement

NCS's financial advisors and legal counsel met again with Genesis and its legal counsel on June 26, 2002, to discuss a number of transaction-related issues. . . .

At the June 26 meeting, Genesis's representatives demanded that, before any further negotiations take place, NCS agree to enter into an exclusivity agreement with it. As Hager from Genesis explained it: "[I]f they wished us to continue to try to move this process to a definitive agreement, that they would need to do it on an exclusive basis with us. We were going to, and already had incurred significant expense, but we would incur additional expenses . . ., both internal and external, to bring this transaction to a definitive signing. We wanted them to work with us on an exclusive basis for a short period of time to see if we could reach agreement." On June 27, 2002, Genesis's legal counsel delivered a draft form of exclusivity agreement for review and consideration by NCS's legal counsel.

The Independent Committee met on July 3, 2002, to consider the proposed exclusivity agreement. Pollack presented a summary of the terms of a possible Genesis merger, which had continued to improve. The then-current Genesis proposal included (1) repayment of the NCS senior debt in full, (2) payment of par value for the Notes (without accrued interest) in the form of a combination of cash and Genesis stock, (3) payment to NCS stockholders in the form of $24 million in Genesis stock, plus (4) the assumption, because the transaction was to be structured as a merger, of additional liabilities to trade and other unsecured creditors.

NCS director Sells testified [that] Pollack told the Independent Committee at a July 3, 2002 meeting that Genesis wanted the Exclusivity Agreement to be the first step towards a completely locked up transaction that would preclude a higher bid from Omnicare:

> A. [Pollack] explained that Genesis felt that they had suffered at the hands of Omnicare and others. I guess maybe just Omnicare. I don't know much about Genesis [sic] acquisition history. But they had suffered before at the 11:59:59 and that they wanted to have a pretty much bulletproof deal or they were not going to go forward.
>
> Q. When you say they suffered at the hands of Omnicare, what do you mean?
>
> A. Well, . . . Genesis, had tried to acquire . . . an institutional pharmacy, I don't remember the name of it. Thought they had a deal and then at the last minute, Omnicare outbid them for the company in a like 11:59 kind of thing, and that they were unhappy about that. And once burned, twice shy.

After NCS executed the exclusivity agreement, Genesis provided NCS with a draft merger agreement, a draft Noteholders' support agreement, and draft voting agreements for Outcalt and Shaw, who together held a majority of the voting power of the NCS common stock. Genesis and NCS negotiated the terms of the merger agreement over the next three weeks. During those negotiations, the Independent Committee and [an Ad Hoc Committee that had been formed to represent the Noteholders] persuaded Genesis to improve the terms of its merger. . . .

Omnicare Proposes Negotiations . . .

On the afternoon of July 26, 2002, Omnicare faxed to NCS a letter outlining a proposed acquisition. . . . Omnicare's proposal, however, was expressly conditioned on negotiating a merger agreement, obtaining certain third party consents, and completing its due diligence. . . .

Late in the afternoon of July 26, 2002, NCS representatives received voicemail messages from Omnicare asking to discuss the letter. The exclusivity agreement prevented NCS from returning those calls. In relevant part, that agreement precluded NCS from "engag[ing] or particpat[ing] in any discussions or negotiations with respect to a Competing Transaction or a proposal for one." The July 26 letter from Omnicare met the definition of a "Competing Transaction."

. . . Nevertheless, the Independent Committee [decided] to use Omnicare's letter to negotiate for improved terms with Genesis.

Genesis Merger Agreement and Voting Agreements

Genesis responded to the NCS request to improve its offer as a result of the Omnicare fax the next day. On July 27, Genesis proposed substantially improved terms. . . . In return for [its] concessions, Genesis stipulated that the transaction had to be approved by midnight the next day, July 28, or else Genesis would terminate discussions and withdraw its offer. . . .

. . . [The NCS board met on July 28.] After receiving similar reports and advice from its legal and financial advisors, the board concluded that "balancing the potential loss of the Genesis deal against the uncertainty of Omnicare's letter, results in the conclusion that the only reasonable alternative for the Board of Directors is to approve the Genesis transaction." The board first voted to authorize the voting agreements [described below] with Outcalt and Shaw, for purposes of Section 203 of the Delaware General Corporation Law ("DGCL"). The board was advised by its legal counsel that "under the terms of the merger agreement and because NCS shareholders representing in excess of 50% of the outstanding voting power would be required by Genesis to enter into stockholder voting agreements contemporaneously with the signing of the merger agreement, and would agree to vote their shares in favor of the merger agreement, shareholder approval of the merger would be assured even if the NCS Board were to withdraw or change its recommendation. *These facts would prevent NCS from engaging in any alternative or superior transaction in the future*." (emphasis added).

After listening to a summary of the merger terms, the board then resolved that the merger agreement and the transactions contemplated thereby were advisable and fair and in the best interests of all the NCS stakeholders. The NCS board further resolved to recommend the transactions to the stockholders for their approval and adoption. A definitive merger agreement between NCS and Genesis and the stockholder voting agreements were executed later that day. . . .

NCS/Genesis Merger Agreement

Among other things, the NCS/Genesis merger agreement provided the following:

- NCS stockholders would receive 1 share of Genesis common stock in exchange for every 10 shares of NCS common stock held;
- NCS stockholders could exercise appraisal rights under 8 Del.C. § 262;
- NCS would redeem NCS's Notes in accordance with their terms;
- NCS would submit the merger agreement to NCS stockholders regardless of whether the NCS board continued to recommend the merger;
- NCS would not enter into discussions with third parties concerning an alternative acquisition of NCS, or provide non-public information to such parties, unless (1) the third party provided an unsolicited, bona fide written proposal documenting the terms of the acquisition; (2) the NCS board believed in good faith that the proposal was or was likely to result in an acquisition on terms superior to those contemplated by the NCS/Genesis merger agree-

ment; and (3) before providing non-public information to that third party, the third party would execute a confidentiality agreement at least as restrictive as the one in place between NCS and Genesis; and

- If the merger agreement were to be terminated, under certain circumstances NCS would be required to pay Genesis a $6 million termination fee and/or Genesis's documented expenses, up to $5 million.

[The merger agreement did not include a fiduciary out. A fiduciary out clause is a provision in a merger agreement that provides that *another* provision (or covenant) in the agreement, which restricts in a certain way the discretion of the board of the corporation that is to be acquired, does not apply if the restriction would result in a breach of the board's fiduciary duties to the corporation and its shareholders. Among the kinds of provisions to which a fiduciary out may apply are no-talk clauses, which prohibit the Board from discussing a merger of the Corporation into a third party, and provisions, like the one in *Omnicare*, that require the Board to submit the merger to the shareholders for their approval.]

Voting Agreements

[Contemporaneously with, and as required by, the merger agreement,] Outcalt and Shaw, in their capacity as NCS stockholders, entered into voting agreements with Genesis. NCS was also required to be a party to the voting agreements by Genesis. Those agreements provided, among other things, that:

- Outcalt and Shaw were acting in their capacity as NCS stockholders in executing the agreements, not in their capacity as NCS directors or officers;
- Neither Outcalt nor Shaw would transfer their shares prior to the stockholder vote on the merger agreement;
- Outcalt and Shaw agreed to vote all of their shares in favor of the merger agreement; and
- Outcalt and Shaw granted to Genesis an irrevocable proxy to vote their shares in favor of the merger agreement.
- The voting agreement was specifically enforceable by Genesis.

The merger agreement further provided that if either Outcalt or Shaw breached the terms of the voting agreements, Genesis would be entitled to terminate the merger agreement and potentially receive a $6 million termination fee from NCS. Such a breach was impossible since Section 6 provided that the voting agreements were specifically enforceable by Genesis.

Omnicare's Superior Proposal . . .

On October 6, 2002, Omnicare irrevocably committed itself to a transaction with NCS. Pursuant to the terms of its proposal, Omnicare agreed to acquire all the outstanding NCS Class A and Class B shares [through a tender offer] at a price of $3.50 per share in cash. [The Omnicare bid offered the NCS stockholders cash equal to more than twice the then-current market value of the shares to be received in the Genesis merger. The transaction offered by Omnicare also treated NCS's other stakeholders on equal terms with the Genesis agreement.]

The merger agreement between Genesis and NCS contained a provision authorized by Section 251(c) of Delaware's corporation law. It required that the Genesis agreement be placed before the corporation's stockholders for a vote, even if the NCS board of directors no longer recommended it. At the insistence of Genesis, the NCS board also agreed to omit any effective fiduciary clause from the merger agreement. In connection with the Genesis merger agreement, two stockholders of NCS, who held a majority of the voting power, agreed unconditionally to vote all of their shares in favor of the Genesis merger. Thus, the combined terms of the voting agreements and merger agreement guaranteed, ab initio, that the transaction proposed by Genesis would obtain NCS stockholder's approval. As a result of this irrevocable offer, on October 21, 2002, the NCS board withdrew its recommendation that the stockholders vote in favor of the NCS/Genesis merger agreement. NCS's financial advisor withdrew its fairness opinion of the NCS/Genesis merger agreement as well. . . .

LEGAL ANALYSIS . . .

Deal Protection Devices Require Enhanced Scrutiny

The dispositive issues in this appeal involve the defensive devices that protected the Genesis merger agreement. The Delaware corporation statute provides that the board's management decision to enter into and recommend a merger transaction can become final only when ownership action is taken by a vote of the stockholders. Thus, the Delaware corporation law expressly provides for a balance of power between boards and stockholders which makes merger transactions a shared enterprise and ownership decision. Consequently, a board of directors' decision to adopt defensive devices to protect a merger agreement may implicate the stockholders' right to effectively vote contrary to the initial recommendation of the board in favor of the transaction.

It is well established that conflicts of interest arise when a board of directors acts to prevent stockholders from effectively exercising their right to vote contrary to the will of the board. The "omnipresent specter" of such conflict may be present whenever a board adopts defensive devices to protect a merger agreement. The stockholders' ability to effectively reject a merger agreement is likely to bear an inversely proportionate relationship to the structural and economic devices that the board has approved to protect the transaction. . . .

There are inherent conflicts between a board's interest in protecting a merger transaction it has approved, the stockholders' statutory right to make the final decision to either approve or not approve a merger, and the board's continuing responsibility to effectively exercise its fiduciary duties at all times after the merger agreement is executed. These competing considerations require a threshold determination that board-approved defensive devices protecting a merger transaction are within the limitations of its statutory authority and consistent with the directors' fiduciary duties. Accordingly, in *Paramount v. Time*, we held that the business judgment rule applied to the Time board's original decision to merge with Warner.[105] We further held, however, that defensive devices adopted by the board to protect the original merger transaction must withstand enhanced judicial scrutiny under the *Unocal* standard of review, even when that merger transaction does not result in a change of control.[106]

Enhanced Scrutiny Generally . . .

A board's decision to protect its decision to enter a merger agreement with defensive devices against uninvited competing transactions that may emerge is analogous to a board's decision to protect against dangers to corporate policy and effectiveness when it adopts defensive measures in a hostile takeover contest. In applying *Unocal's* enhanced judicial scrutiny in assessing a challenge to defensive actions taken by a target corporation's board of directors in a takeover context, this Court held that the board "does not have unbridled discretion to defeat perceived threats by any draconian means available."[107] Similarly, just as a board's statutory power with regard to a merger decision is not absolute, a board does not have unbridled discretion to defeat any perceived threat to a merger by protecting it with any draconian means available.

Since *Unocal*, "this Court has consistently recognized that defensive measures which are either preclusive or coercive are included within the common law definition of draconian." . . .

Therefore, in applying enhanced judicial scrutiny to defensive devices designed to protect a merger agreement, a court must first determine that those measures are not preclusive or coercive *before* its focus shifts to the "range of reasonableness" in making a proportionality determination. . . .

Deal Protection Devices

Defensive devices, as that term is used in this opinion, is a synonym for what are frequently referred to as "deal protection devices." Both terms are used interchangeably to describe any measure or combination of measures that are intended to protect the consummation of a merger transaction. Defensive devices can be economic, structural, or both.

Deal protection devices need not all be in the merger agreement itself. In this case, for example, the Section 251(c) provision in the merger agreement was combined with the separate voting agreements

105. *Paramount Communications, Inc. v. Time Inc.*, 571 A.2d at 1152.

106. Id. at 115–155; *Unocal Corp. v. Mesa Petroleum Co.*, 493 A.2d 946 (Del.1985); see *In re Santa Fe Pacific Corp. Shareholder Litigation*, 669 A.2d 59 (Del.1995).

107. *Unocal Corp. v. Mesa Petroleum Co.*, 493 A.2d at 955.

to provide a structural defense for the Genesis merger agreement against any subsequent superior transaction. Genesis made the NCS board's defense of its transaction absolute by insisting on the omission of any effective fiduciary out clause in the NCS merger agreement. . . .

In this case, the stockholder voting agreements were inextricably intertwined with the defensive aspects of the Genesis merger agreement. In fact, the voting agreements with Shaw and Outcalt were the linchpin of Genesis' proposed tripartite defense. Therefore, Genesis made the execution of those voting agreements a non-negotiable condition precedent to its execution of the merger agreement. . . .

With the assurance that Outcalt and Shaw would irrevocably agree to exercise their majority voting power in favor of its transaction, Genesis insisted that the merger agreement reflect the other two aspects of its concerted defense, i.e., the inclusion of a Section 251(c) provision and the omission of any effective fiduciary out clause. Those dual aspects of the merger agreement would not have provided Genesis with a complete defense in the absence of the voting agreements with Shaw and Outcalt.

These Deal Protection Devices Unenforceable

In this case, the Court of Chancery correctly held that the NCS directors' decision to adopt defensive devices to completely "lock up" the Genesis merger mandated "special scrutiny" under the two-part test set forth in *Unocal*.[108] That conclusion is consistent with our holding in *Paramount v. Time* that safety devices adopted to protect a transaction that did not result in a change of control are subject to enhanced judicial scrutiny under a *Unocal* analysis.[109] . . . .

Pursuant to the judicial scrutiny required under *Unocal*'s two-stage analysis, the NCS directors must first demonstrate "that they had reasonable grounds for believing that a danger to corporate policy and effectiveness existed. . . ." To satisfy that burden, the NCS directors are required to show they acted in good faith after conducting a reasonable investigation. The threat identified by the NCS board was the possibility of losing the Genesis offer and being left with no comparable alternative transaction.

The second stage of the *Unocal* test requires the NCS directors to demonstrate that their defensive response was "reasonable in relation to the threat posed." This inquiry involves a two-step analysis. The NCS directors must first establish that the merger deal protection devices adopted in response to the threat were not "coercive" or "preclusive," and then demonstrate that their response was within a "range of reasonable responses" to the threat perceived. In *Unitrin*, we stated:

---

108. *In re NCS Healthcare, Inc.*, 2002 WL 31720732, at *16 (Del.Ch. Nov.22, 2002). See *Unocal Corp. v. Mesa Petroleum Co.*, 493 A.2d 946, 955 (Del.1985).

109. See *Paramount Communications, Inc. v. Time Inc.*, 571 A.2d 1140, 1151 (Del.1989) ("holding that structural safety devices" in a merger agreement are properly subject to a *Unocal* analysis).

- A response is "coercive" if it is aimed at forcing upon stockholders a management-sponsored alternative to a hostile offer.
- A response is "preclusive" if it deprives stockholders of the right to receive all tender offers or precludes a bidder from seeking control by fundamentally restricting proxy contests or otherwise.

This aspect of the *Unocal* standard provides for a disjunctive analysis. If defensive measures are either preclusive or coercive they are draconian and impermissible. In this case, the deal protection devices of the NCS board were both preclusive and coercive.

This Court enunciated the standard for determining stockholder coercion in the case of *Williams v. Geier*.[110] A stockholder vote may be nullified by wrongful coercion "where the board or some other party takes actions which have the effect of causing the stockholders to vote in favor of the proposed transaction for some reason other than the merits of that transaction." . . .

[A]ny stockholder vote [in this case] would have been robbed of its effectiveness by the impermissible coercion that predetermined the outcome of the merger without regard to the merits of the Genesis transaction at the time the vote was scheduled to be taken. Deal protection devices that result in such coercion cannot withstand *Unocal*'s enhanced judicial scrutiny standard of review because they are not within the range of reasonableness.

Although the minority stockholders were not forced to vote for the Genesis merger, they were required to accept it because it was a fait accompli. The record reflects that the defensive devices employed by the NCS board are preclusive and coercive in the sense that they accomplished a fait accompli. In this case, despite the fact that the NCS board has withdrawn its recommendation for the Genesis transaction and recommended its rejection by the stockholders, the deal protection devices approved by the NCS board operated in concert to have a preclusive and coercive effect. Those tripartite defensive measures—the Section 251(c) provision, the voting agreements, and the absence of an effective fiduciary out clause—made it "mathematically impossible" and "realistically unattainable" for the Omnicare transaction or any other proposal to succeed, no matter how superior the proposal.[111]

The deal protection devices adopted by the NCS board were designed to coerce the consummation of the Genesis merger and preclude the consideration of any superior transaction. The NCS directors' defensive devices are not within a reasonable range of responses to the perceived threat of losing the Genesis offer because they are preclusive and coercive. Accordingly, we hold that those deal protection devices are unenforceable.

---

110. *Williams v. Geier*, 671 A.2d 1368 (Del.1996).

111. See *Unitrin, Inc. v. Am. Gen. Corp.*, 651 A.2d at 1388–89; see also *Carmody v. Toll Bros., Inc.*, 723 A.2d 1180, 1195 (Del.Ch.1998) (citations omitted).

Effective Fiduciary Out Required

The defensive measures that protected the merger transaction are unenforceable not only because they are preclusive and coercive but, alternatively, they are unenforceable because they are invalid as they operate in this case. . . .

Under the circumstances presented in this case, where a cohesive group of stockholders with majority voting power was irrevocably committed to the merger transaction, "[e]ffective representation of the financial interests of the minority shareholders imposed upon the [NCS board] an affirmative responsibility to protect those minority shareholders' interests."[113] The NCS board could not abdicate its fiduciary duties to the minority by leaving it to the stockholders alone to approve or disapprove the merger agreement because two stockholders had already combined to establish a majority of the voting power that made the outcome of the stockholder vote a foregone conclusion. . . .

The directors of a Delaware corporation have a continuing obligation to discharge their fiduciary responsibilities, as future circumstances develop, after a merger agreement is announced. Genesis anticipated the likelihood of a superior offer after its merger agreement was announced and demanded defensive measures from the NCS board that completely protected its transaction.[117] Instead of agreeing to the absolute defense of the Genesis merger from a superior offer, however, the NCS board was required to negotiate a fiduciary out clause to protect the NCS stockholders if the Genesis transaction became an inferior offer. By acceding to Genesis' ultimatum for complete protection in futuro, the NCS board disabled itself from exercising its own fiduciary obligations at a time when the board's own judgment is most important,[118] i.e. receipt of a subsequent superior offer.

Any board has authority to give the proponent of a recommended merger agreement reasonable structural and economic defenses, incentives, and fair compensation if the transaction is not completed. To the extent that defensive measures are economic and reasonable, they may become an increased cost to the proponent of any subsequent transaction. Just as defensive measures cannot be draconian, however, they cannot limit or circumscribe the directors' fiduciary duties. Notwithstanding the corporation's insolvent condition, the NCS board had no authority to execute a merger agreement that subsequently prevented it from effectively discharging its ongoing fiduciary responsibilities.

---

113. *McMullin v. Beran*, 765 A.2d 910, 920 (Del.2000).

117. The marked improvements in NCS's financial situation during the negotiations with Genesis strongly suggests that the NCS board should have been alert to the prospect of competing offers or, as eventually occurred, a bidding contest.

118. See *Malone v. Brincat*, 722 A.2d 5, 10 (Del.1998) (directors' fiduciary duties do not operate intermittently). See also *Moran v. Household Int'l, Inc.*, 500 A.2d 1346 (Del.1985).

The stockholders of a Delaware corporation are entitled to rely upon the board to discharge its fiduciary duties at all times.[119] The fiduciary duties of a director are unremitting and must be effectively discharged in the specific context of the actions that are required with regard to the corporation or its stockholders as circumstances change.[120] The stockholders with majority voting power, Shaw and Outcalt, had an absolute right to sell or exchange their shares with a third party at any price. This right was not only known to the other directors of NCS, it became an integral part of the Genesis agreement. In its answering brief, Genesis candidly states that its offer "came with a condition—Genesis would not be a stalking horse and would not agree to a transaction to which NCS's controlling shareholders were not committed."

The NCS board was required to contract for an effective fiduciary out clause to exercise its continuing fiduciary responsibilities to the minority stockholders.[121] . . .

In the context of this preclusive and coercive lock up case, the protection of Genesis' contractual expectations must yield to the supervening responsibility of the directors to discharge their fiduciary duties on a continuing basis. The merger agreement and voting agreements, as they were combined to operate in concert in this case, are inconsistent with the NCS directors' fiduciary duties. To that extent, we hold that they are invalid and unenforceable.[122] . . .

■ VEASEY, CHIEF JUSTICE, with whom STEELE, JUSTICE, joins dissenting. . . .

The lock-ups here cannot be reviewed in a vacuum. A court should review the entire bidding process to determine whether the independent board's actions permitted the directors to inform themselves of their available options and whether they acted in good faith.

Going into negotiations with Genesis, the NCS directors knew that, up until that time, NCS had found only one potential bidder, Omnicare. Omnicare had refused to buy NCS except at a fire sale price through an asset sale in bankruptcy. Omnicare's best proposal at that stage would not have paid off all creditors and would have provided nothing for stockholders. The Noteholders, represented by the Ad Hoc Committee, were willing to oblige Omnicare and force NCS into bankruptcy if Omnicare would pay in full the NCS debt. Through the NCS board's efforts, Genesis expressed interest that became increasingly attractive. Negotiations with Genesis led to an offer paying

119. *Malone v. Brincat*, 722 A.2d at 10.

120. Id.; *Moran v. Household Int'l, Inc.*, 500 A.2d at 1357 (use of defense evaluated if and when the issue arises).

121. See *Paramount Communications Inc. v. QVC Network Inc.*, 637 A.2d at 42–43. Merger agreements involve an ownership decision and, therefore, cannot become final without stockholder approval. Other contracts do not require a fiduciary out clause because they involve business judgments that are within the exclusive province of the board of directors' power to manage the affairs of the corporation. See *Grimes v. Donald*, 673 A.2d 1207, 1214–15 (Del.1996).

122. *Paramount Communications, Inc. v. QVC Network, Inc.*, 637 A.2d at 51.

creditors off and conferring on NCS stockholders $24 million—an amount infinitely superior to the prior Omnicare proposals.

But there was, understandably, a sine qua non. In exchange for offering the NCS stockholders a return on their equity and creditor payment, Genesis demanded certainty that the merger would close. If the NCS board would not have acceded to the Section 251(c) provision, if Outcalt and Shaw had not agreed to the voting agreements and if NCS had insisted on a fiduciary out, there would have been no Genesis deal! Thus, the only value-enhancing transaction available would have disappeared. NCS knew that Omnicare had spoiled a Genesis acquisition in the past, and it is not disputed by the Majority that the NCS directors made a reasoned decision to accept as real the Genesis threat to walk away.

When Omnicare submitted its conditional eleventh-hour bid, the NCS board had to weigh the economic terms of the proposal against the uncertainty of completing a deal with Omnicare. Importantly, because Omnicare's bid was conditioned on its satisfactorily completing its due diligence review of NCS, the NCS board saw this as a crippling condition, as did the Ad Hoc Committee. As a matter of business judgment, the risk of negotiating with Omnicare and losing Genesis at that point outweighed the possible benefits. The lock-up was indisputably a sine qua non to any deal with Genesis.

A lock-up permits a target board and a bidder to "exchange certainties."[123] Certainty itself has value. The acquirer may pay a higher price for the target if the acquirer is assured consummation of the transaction. The target company also benefits from the certainty of completing a transaction with a bidder because losing an acquirer creates the perception that a target is damaged goods, thus reducing its value. . . .

The Majority invalidates the NCS board's action by announcing a new rule that represents an extension of our jurisprudence. That new rule can be narrowly stated as follows: A merger agreement entered into after a market search, before any prospect of a topping bid has emerged, which locks up stockholder approval and does not contain a "fiduciary out" provision, is per se invalid when a later significant topping bid emerges. As we have noted, this bright-line, per se rule would apply regardless of (1) the circumstances leading up to the agreement and (2) the fact that stockholders who control voting power had irrevocably committed themselves, as stockholders, to vote for the merger. Narrowly stated, this new rule is a judicially-created "third rail" that now becomes one of the given "rules of the game," to be taken into account by the negotiators and drafters of merger agreements. In our view, this new rule is an unwise extension of existing precedent. . . .

The very measures the Majority cites as "coercive" were approved by Shaw and Outcalt through the lens of their independent assessment of the merits of the transaction. The proper inquiry in this case is

123. See *Rand v. Western Air Lines*, 1994 WL 89006 at *6 (Del.Ch.).

whether the NCS board had taken actions that "have the effect of causing the stockholders to vote in favor of the proposed transaction for some reason other than the merits of that transaction."[124] . . .

Outcalt and Shaw were fully informed stockholders. As the NCS controlling stockholders, they made an informed choice to commit their voting power to the merger. The minority stockholders were deemed to know that when controlling stockholders have 65% of the vote they can approve a merger without the need for the minority votes. Moreover, to the extent a minority stockholder may have felt "coerced" to vote for the merger, which was already a fait accompli, it was a meaningless coercion—or no coercion at all—because the controlling votes, those of Outcalt and Shaw, were already "cast." Although the fact that the controlling votes were committed to the merger "precluded" an overriding vote against the merger by the Class A stockholders, the "pejorative" preclusive label applicable in a *Unitrin* fact situation has no application here. Therefore, there was no meaningful minority stockholder voting decision to coerce.

In applying *Unocal* scrutiny, we believe the Majority incorrectly preempted the proportionality inquiry. In our view, the proportionality inquiry must account for the reality that the contractual measures protecting this merger agreement were necessary to obtain the Genesis deal. The Majority has not demonstrated that the director action was a disproportionate response to the threat posed. Indeed, it is clear to us that the board action to negotiate the best deal reasonably available with the only viable merger partner (Genesis) who could satisfy the creditors and benefit the stockholders, was reasonable in relation to the threat, by any practical yardstick.

An Absolute Lock-up is Not a Per Se Violation of Fiduciary Duty

We respectfully disagree with the Majority's conclusion that the NCS board breached its fiduciary duties to the Class A stockholders by failing to negotiate a "fiduciary out" in the Genesis merger agreement. What is the practical import of a "fiduciary out?" It is a contractual provision, articulated in a manner to be negotiated, that would permit the board of the corporation being acquired to exit without breaching the merger agreement in the event of a superior offer.

In this case, Genesis made it abundantly clear early on that it was willing to negotiate a deal with NCS but only on the condition that it would not be a "stalking horse." Thus, it wanted to be certain that a third party could not use its deal with NCS as a floor against which to begin a bidding war. As a result of this negotiating position, a "fiduciary out" was not acceptable to Genesis. The Majority Opinion holds that such a negotiating position, if implemented in the agreement, is invalid per se where there is an absolute lock-up. We know of no authority in our jurisprudence supporting this new rule, and we believe it is unwise and unwarranted. . . .

---

124. *Geier*, 671 A.2d at 1382–83 (citations omitted).

Conclusion

It is regrettable that the Court is split in this important case. One hopes that the Majority rule announced here—though clearly erroneous in our view—will be interpreted narrowly and will be seen as sui generis. By deterring bidders from engaging in negotiations like those present here and requiring that there must always be a fiduciary out, the universe of potential bidders who could reasonably be expected to benefit stockholders could shrink or disappear. Nevertheless, if the holding is confined to these unique facts, negotiators may be able to navigate around this new hazard.

Accordingly, we respectfully dissent.

[The separate dissenting opinion of Justice Steele is omitted.]

NOTE ON TERMINATION FEES

A commonly used means to protect the deal is a termination fee. There are many variations of termination fees. The common formulation is a break-up fee expressed either as a flat amount, or percentage of the target's equity value, and sometimes this fee is augmented by a requirement that the target reimburse the expenses of the disappointed suitor. Brazen v. Bell Atlantic Corp., 695 A.2d 43, 46–47 (Del. 1997), is the leading case for assessing the validity of termination fees. The merger agreement between Bell Atlantic and NYNEX Corp. provided reciprocal $550 million termination fees. Bell Atlantic shareholders challenged this provision, arguing it would "restrict and impair the fiduciary duty of the Bell Atlantic board and coerce the shareholders to vote to approve the proposed merger." The court upheld the provision, viewing it as a form of liquidated damages and also reasoning that the termination fees, while large in absolute terms, the total fee represented only 2 percent of Bell Atlantic's market capitalization and was not seen as likely to deflect other bids or to coerce the stockholders to approve the merger with NYNEX. Subsequent Delaware decisions have suggested that fees in the range of 6.3 percent of market capitalization likely surpassed a reasonable level. *See* Phelps Dodge Corp. v. Cyprus Amax Minerals Co., 1999 WL 1054255 (Del.Ch. 1999) (nonetheless, denying injunction for failure to allege irreparable harm was suffered because of the termination fee).

Courts employ one of two approaches to assessing termination fees. Most follow *Bell Atlantic's* approach of assessing termination fees through the lens of a liquidated damages analysis where the court first determines that future damages are uncertain and difficult to calculate. If so, the court assesses whether the amount agreed upon is a reasonable forecast of actual damages. *See e.g.*, Beebe v. Pacific Realty Trust, 578 F.Supp. 1128, 1150 (D. Or. 1984). A somewhat different contract approach is to view termination fees as providing an alternate means for a party to perform the contract. *See* St. Jude Medical, Inc. v. Medtronic, Inc., 536 N.W.2d 24, 25–29 (Minn. App. 1995). On the other hand, many decisions assess termination fees in light of the fiduciary obligations of directors. In Delaware, and the states following the Delaware jurisprudence, these duties are embodied in *Unocal* and *Revlon*. *See e.g.*, Edelman v. Fruehauf Corp., 798 F.2d 882, 884–85 (6th Cir. 1986); McMillan v. Intercargo Corp., 768 A.2d 492, 502 (Del. Ch. 2000). Other courts employ a deferential business judgment rule to the independent board acting in good faith. *See* Jewel Companies v. Pay Less Drug Stores Northwest, Inc., 741 F.2d 1555, 1560–64 (9th Cir. 1984). Overall, termination fees are upheld, and the rule of the road is that fees in the 2–4 percent of target equity are in a safe range.

SECTION 4. STATE TAKEOVER STATUTES

Most states now have statutes regulating takeover bids. These statutes tend to fall into several patterns, although they are highly variable within those patterns. This Note will canvass the major patterns, generally by discussing one statute within each pattern. However, it should be borne in mind that even statutes that fall into a given pattern often diverge in material respects. Furthermore, because the statutes are highly complex, only their main features will be discussed.

State takeover statutes have evolved over time. Conventionally, they are categorized as first-, second-, and third-generation statutes.

1. *First–Generation Statutes*. The *first-generation* statutes tended to impose very stringent requirements on takeover bids, including fairness reviews by state agencies. Moreover, generally speaking the application of the statutes was not limited to corporations incorporated in the relevant state. In Edgar v. MITE Corp., 457 U.S. 624, 102 S.Ct. 2629, 73 L.Ed.2d 269 (1982), the Supreme Court held one such statute, the Illinois Takeover Act, unconstitutional. Six justices addressed the merits of the case. All six justices held that the Illinois Act violated the Commerce Clause in two ways. First, the Act unconstitutionally regulated commerce taking place across state lines, because the Act applied to prevent an offeror from making an offer even to non-Illinois shareholders. Second, the Act imposed an excessive burden on interstate commerce, because the Act permitted the Illinois secretary of state to block a nationwide tender offer. Three of the justices also held that the Illinois statute was unconstitutional under the Supremacy Clause on the ground that a major objective of the Williams Act was to maintain a neutral balance between management and the bidder and the Illinois Act violated this balance.

2. *Second–Generation Statutes.* After the decision in Edgar v. MITE Corp., a number of states adopted *second-generation* takeover statutes. These statutes fall into two major patterns: control-share-acquisition statutes and fair-price statutes.

a. *Control-share-acquisition statutes. Control-share-acquisition statutes* provide that if an acquiring shareholder crosses a designated threshold of stock ownership, the shareholder is prohibited from voting the acquired shares unless he obtains approval to do so by vote of a majority of the corporation's disinterested shareholders, that is, shareholders other than the acquiror and the corporation's management.

In CTS Corp. v. Dynamics Corp. of America, 481 U.S. 69, 107 S.Ct. 1637, 95 L.Ed.2d 67 (1987), the Supreme Court upheld the constitutionality of Indiana's control-share-acquisition statute. That statute applied whenever a person acquired shares that, but for the operation of the statute, would bring the person's voting power in the corporation to or above 20%, 33 1/3%, or 50% of total voting power. An acquiror that crossed one of these thresholds could not vote the acquired stock unless voting rights were approved by a majority of all disinterested shareholders voting at the next regularly scheduled meeting of the shareholders or at a specially scheduled meeting. The statute was limited to target corporations incorporated in Indiana. The Court concluded that the Indiana statute did not violate the Commerce Clause, because it did not discriminate against interstate commerce, and did not subject activities to inconsistent regulation. The statute applied only to Indiana corporations, and a state has authority to regulate domestic corporations, including the authority to define the voting rights of shareholders.

The Court also held that the Indiana statute was not preempted by the Williams Act. In this regard, the Court contrasted the Indiana statute with the Illinois statute that was found unconstitutional in *MITE*.

First, the Illinois statute provided for a twenty-day precommencement period. During this time, management could disseminate its views on the upcoming tender offer to shareholders, but bidders could not publish their offers. This conflicted with the Williams Act, because Congress had deleted precommencement-notice provisions from the Williams Act. In contrast, the Indiana statute did not give either management or the would-be acquiror an advantage in communicating with shareholders about an impending tender offer.

Second, the Illinois statute provided for a review of the fairness of tender offers by the Illinois Secretary of State. This conflicted with the Williams Act, because Congress intended shareholders to be free to make their own decisions. In contrast, the Indiana statute did not allow the state government to interpose its views of fairness between willing buyers and sellers of shares of the target company. Rather, the statute allowed shareholders to collectively evaluate the fairness of the offer.

Third, the Illinois statute set no deadline for the state-agency hearing on a tender offer, so that management could indefinitely stymie a takeover. This conflicted with the Williams Act, because Congress anticipated that bidders would be free to go forward without unreasonable delay. In contrast, the Indiana statute did not impose an indefinite delay on tender offers. Nothing in the Indiana statute prohibited an offeror from consummating an offer on the twentieth business day, the earliest day permitted under federal law, and full voting rights would be vested or denied within fifty days after commencement of the tender offer.

b. *Fair-price statutes. Fair-price statutes* essentially require that if a winning bidder makes a two-tier tender offer, it must pay nontendering shareholders the highest price it has paid for target shares within a specified recent period (typically, two years) if, after having acquired control of the target, the bidder seeks to engage in a business combination, or one of certain other defined transactions, with the target. There is an exception if the transaction is approved by (typically) 80 percent of all shares and two-thirds of the shares not owned by the bidder.

3. *Third–Generation Statutes.*

a. *Waiting-period (Business Combination) statutes.* Waiting-period or Business Combination statutes prohibit a corporation, B, who acquires more than a specific percentage of another corporation, T, from merging with T, or engaging in certain other transactions with T, for a designated waiting period, unless certain conditions are satisfied. The idea is that in many cases a prospective bidder (B) expects to finance a tender offer for the stock of the target (T) partly by using T's assets as collateral. If B cannot expect to merge with T shortly after the tender offer succeeds, that kind of financing will be difficult or impossible to obtain. In addition, B may have various business reasons for wanting to merge with T after a tender offer, rather than running T as a partly owned subsidiary. These purposes are also frustrated by waiting-period statutes.

The New York statute, N.Y. Bus.Corp.Law § 912, provides for a five-year delay in effecting specified transactions, even if the transaction is not self-interested, unless the transaction is approved by T's board of directors prior to B's acquisition of the designated percentage of T's stock. The less stringent Delaware statute, Del.G.C.L. § 203, prohibits business combinations and other designated transactions between B and T for a period of three years unless B acquires 85% of T's shares in the initial tender offer, or the transaction is approved by 85% of T's shares other than the shares held by B.

The potency of this variety of statute in discouraging hostile bids is reflected by the 94 percent decline in hostile bids being launched for Delaware corporations following the enactment of the Delaware business combination statute. Gregg A. Jarrell, A Trip Down Memory Lane: Reflections on Section 203 and Subramanian, Herscovici and Barbetta, 65 Bus. Law. 779, 786 (2010). Should the total disappearance of successful hostile bids for Delaware companies following the state's enactment of Section 203 invite reconsideration whether the statute imposes an unconstitutional burden on commerce? *See* Guhan Subramanian, Steven Herscovici & Brian Barbetta, Is Delaware's Antitakeover Statute Unconstitutional? Evidence from 1988–2008, 65 Bus. Law. 685 (2010).

b. *Amanda.* In Amanda Acquisition Corp. v. Universal Foods Corp., 877 F.2d 496, cert. denied, 493 U.S. 955, 110 S.Ct. 367, 107

L.Ed.2d 353 (1989), the Seventh Circuit held that the Wisconsin waiting-period statute was constitutional:

> [Arguments against state anti-takeover statutes based on preemption have] not won easy acceptance among the Justices for several reasons. First there is § 28(a) of the '34 Act, 14 U.S.C. § 78bb(a), which provides that "[n]othing in this chapter shall affect the jurisdiction of the securities commission . . . of any State over any security or any person insofar as it does not conflict with the provisions of this chapter or the rules and regulations thereunder." . . . [T]he SEC has not drafted regulations concerning mergers with controlling shareholders, and the Act itself does not address the subject. . . .
>
> . . . [T]he best argument for preemption is the Williams Act's "neutrality" between bidder and management, a balance designed to leave investors free to choose. This is not a confident jumping-off point, though. . . .
>
> There is a big difference between what congress *enacts* and what it *supposes* will ensue. Expectations about the consequences of a law are not themselves law. To say that Congress wanted to be neutral between bidder and target . . . is not to say that it also forbade the states to favor one of these sides. . . .
>
> Any bidder complying with federal law is free to acquire shares of Wisconsin firms on schedule. Delay in completing a second-stage merger may make the target less attractive, and thus depress the price offered or even lead to an absence of bids; it does not, however, alter any of the procedures governed by federal regulation. . . .
>
> . . . It is not attractive [under the statute] to put bids on the table for Wisconsin corporations, but because Wisconsin leaves the process alone once a bidder appears, its law may co-exist with the Williams Act. . . .
>
> The Commerce Clause, Art. I, § 8 cl. 3 of the Constitution, grants Congress the power "[t]o regulate Commerce . . . among the several States". . . .
>
> When state law discriminates against interstate commerce expressly—for example, when Wisconsin closes its border to butter from Minnesota—the [anti-discrimination aspect of the] Commerce Clause steps in. The law before us is not of this type; it is neutral between inter-state and intra-state commerce. Amanda therefore presses on us the broader, all-weather, be-reasonable vision of the Constitution. Wisconsin has passed a law that unreasonably injures investors, most of whom live outside of Wisconsin, and therefore it has to be unconstitutional, as Amanda sees things. . . . [However, the Supreme] Court has looked for discrimination rather than for baleful effects. . . .
>
> . . . The Commerce clause does not demand that states leave bidders a "meaningful opportunity for success."

c. *Other third-generation statutes. Amanda*, and perhaps other factors, emboldened some states to adopt other, extremely exotic, and in some cases draconian, third-generation statutes. For example, the Pennsylvania statute provides, among many other things, that persons who own, offer to acquire, or publicly announce an intention to acquire, 20% of the stock of a publicly traded Pennsylvania corporation must disgorge any profits they realize from the disposition of that corporation's stock within a defined period. 15 Pa. Cons. Stat. Ann. §§ 2571–75 (West 1995). Ohio has a similar "disgorgement" provision. Ohio Rev. Code Ann. § 1707.043 (Anderson 2001). The Massachusetts statute requires every public corporation to have a classified board. Mass.Ann. Laws ch. 156D § 8.06(b) (Law Co-op 2007).

d. *Constituency statutes.* A number of states have also adopted *constituency statutes*, which allow a board to consider the interests of groups ("constituencies") other than shareholders in making decisions, including decisions to resist takeovers. These statutes give the board increased leeway to resist a takeover, because often these other constituencies—for example, labor and the local community—are opposed to takeovers.

e. *Pill Validation Statutes.* Approximately one-half the states have statutes that endorse the use of a poison pill.

Very few state anti-takeover statutes are opt-in statutes. That is, all firms incorporated in the state are subject to state's anti-takeover provision unless specifically prescribed steps to opt out of the provision are pursued. Why would the default rule favor application of the statutorily provided defense?

In an extensive analysis of state takeover statutes, Professor Subramanian provides strong evidence that state antitakeover statutes, particularly control share, waiting period and pill validation statutes, assume a significant role in the public company's corporate domicile. Moreover, his data reflects that companies migrate away from the draconian antitakeover provisions of Massachusetts, Ohio and Pennsylvania. Guhan Subramanian, The Influence Of Antitakeover Statutes On Incorporation Choice: Evidence On The "Race" Debate And Antitakeover Overreaching, 150 U. Pa. L. Rev. 1795, 1852 (2002) ("these results support the view that managers migrate to, and fail to migrate away from, typical antitakeover statutes that are generally acknowledged to reduce shareholder value (business combination statutes, control share acquisition statutes, and pill validation statutes)"). Another impact of state antitakeover statues is their existence greatly influences whether the state court rejects the heightened *Unocal/Revlon* scrutiny and instead accords defensive maneuvers the more deferential review under the business judgment rule. *See* Michal Barzuza, The State Of State Antitakeover Law, 95 Va. L. Rev. 1973, 2018 (2009) (finding *Unocal* duties were rejected in 11 states and followed in 11 while *Revlon* duties were rejected in 9 states and followed in 6):

> The direct implication of this study is that in some states there are no enhanced fiduciary duties in change-of-control situations. . . . The famous *Unocal* and *Revlon* duo taught in corporations courses and followed by academics simply does not apply to some firms. The BJR and other weakened duties replace them either explicitly in states' statutes or in states' case law. As a result, mangers in those firms have wide latitude to use defensive tactics and as long as they do not have a direct conflict of interest and are adequately informed, they will enjoy the protection of the BJR.

Id. at 2029. Since the results captured in Professor Barzuza's study are linked directly to the impact of the legislature's adoption of state antitakeover statutes, does the legislature's action necessarily support the court's conclusion that management initiated defensive maneuvers that are not covered by the state antitakeover statute should nonetheless similarly be removed from heightened scrutiny?

An interesting question is what impact does a state antitakeover statute have on managers? The empirical evidence focused on this question suggests some positive features of state antitakeover statutes. Firms incorporated in states providing "second generation" antitakeover statutes are less highly leveraged than firms without such protection from takeovers. Gerald T. Garvey & Gordon Hanka, Capital Structure and Corporate Control: The Effect of Antitakeover Statutes on Firm Leverage, 54 J. Fin. 519 (1999). Such firms also engage in greater capital expenditures and research and development than firms not enjoying the protection of state antitakeover statutes. Wm. N. Pugh & John S. Jahera, Jr., 18 Managerial and Decision Economics 681 (1997), and pursue less aggressive accounting policies in reporting their performance, Yijang Zhao & Kung H. Chen, 28 J. Acct'g Policy 92 (2009). On the negative side, there is some evidence that pay is more poorly linked to performance when firms have both firm-specific antitakeover defenses (e.g., a poison pill) as well as a state antitakeover statute than when firms have only firm-specific antitakeover defenses. Scott W. Barnhart, Michael F. Spivey & John C. Alexander, 21 Managerial and Decision Economics 315 (2000).

SECTION 5. RESTRUCTURINGS AND THE BONDHOLDERS

The relationship between a debtor and the creditor is contractual. Borrowers do not owe a fiduciary obligation to their bondholders. *See* North American Catholic Educational Programming Foundation v. Gheewalla, 930 A.2d 92 (Del. 2007). Therefore, the first line of defense for protecting the interests of bondholders are the terms, conditions, and undertakings set forth in the bond's indenture. These provisions are commonly referred to as bond covenants. Bond covenants are intricate and there is a wide array of covenants that the counsel drafting the indenture can select from to address financial and operating risks important to the bondholders. The source for most bond covenants embodied is the American Bar Foundation, Commentaries on the Model Debenture Indenture Provisions 1965. This was followed by the Model Debenture Indenture Provisions—All Registered Issues and Certain Negotiable Provisions which May Be Included in a Particular Incorporating Indenture (1971).[3] Each of these works is the product of years of collaborative ABA committee work by bond lawyers for issuers and purchasing financial institutions. The Trust Indenture Act of 1939[4] sets certain minimal protections that must be included in the indenture for any corporate debt sold in a public offering that has an aggregate issuing price of $10 million or greater.[5] Because the main focus of the Act is on providing an effective and independent trustee, the main sources of protection for bondholders are the covenants set forth in the indenture.

Corporate combinations, such as those studied earlier in this chapter frequently alter the financial and operating risks of the firm with serious consequences to its creditors. Bond covenants provide the first, and only, line of protection against serious diminution in the value of the bonds. Just how much protection is enjoyed depends, however, on the content of the individual bond covenant so that it is important to understand the interpretative approach courts follow in resolving disputes on whether the corporate transaction giving rise to the feared diminution in the bond's value triggers rights in the bondholders. The approach the court takes in the next case underscores the overall importance of the uniformity in debt covenants in the functioning of our capital markets.

Sharon Steel Corporation v. The Chase Manhattan Bank

United States Court of Appeals, Second Circuit, 1982.
691 F.2d 1039.

■ WINTER, CIRCUIT JUDGE . . .

[UV Industries, Inc. (UV) operated three separate lines of business. One line, electrical equipment and components, was carried on by Federal Pacific Electric Company ("Federal") and generated 60% of UV's operating revenue and 81% of its operating profits, while constituting 44% of UV's book value and 53% of its operating assets. UV also owned and operated oil and gas properties, producing 2% of its operating revenue and 6% of operating profits while constituting 5%

3. This edition was updated in 1977. Somewhat more succinct covenants have been offered by bond lawyers operating under the auspices of the ABA in the Model Simplified Indenture, 38 Bus. Law. 741 (1983) and the Revised Model Simplified Indenture, 55 Bus. Law. 1115 (2000).

4. 15 U.S.C. §§ 77aaa *et seq.* (2000).

5. The legislation authorizes the Securities and Exchange Commission to set the dollar level by exercising its rulemaking authority. *See* General Rules and Regulations of the SEC Rule 4a–3, 17 C.F.R. § (2002).

of UV's book value and 6% of operating its assets. Thirdly, UV also was involved in copper and brass fabrication, through Mueller Brass, and metals mining. Mueller and the mines produced 13% of UV's profits and 38% of its revenue while making up 34% of UV's book value and 41% of its operating assets. In addition to these operating assets, UV had cash or other liquid assets amounting to 17% of book value assets.

On January 19, 1979, the UV Board announced its intention to liquidate UV, subject to shareholder approval. On February 20, 1979, UV distributed proxy materials, recommending approval of (i) the sale of Federal for $345,000,000 to a subsidiary of Reliance Electric Company and (ii) a Plan of Liquidation and Dissolution to sell the remaining assets of UV over a 12–month period. Completion of the Liquidation Plan within 12 months was necessary for tax reasons. If so completed, UV would avoid recognition of any taxable gain on the sale of Federal and its other assets and UV shareholders could treat liquidation distributions as capital gains rather than ordinary income. The proceeds of these sales and the liquid assets were to be distributed to shareholders. The liquidation plan required "that at all times there be retained an amount of cash and other assets which the [UV Board of Directors] deems necessary to pay, or provide for the payment of, all of the liabilities, claims and other obligations . . ." of UV.

On March 26, 1979, UV's shareholders approved both the sale of Federal and the plan to liquidate UV. On March 29, the sale of Federal to the Reliance Electric subsidiary for $345 million in cash was consummated and on April 9, UV announced an $18 per share initial liquidating distribution to take place on Monday, April 30. . . .

On July 23, 1979, UV announced that it had entered into an agreement for the sale of most of its oil and gas properties to Tenneco Oil Company for $135 million cash. The deal was consummated as of October 2, 1979.

In November, 1979, Sharon proposed to buy UV's remaining assets. UV and Sharon entered into an "Agreement for Purchase of Assets" and an "Instrument of Assumption of Liabilities" on November 26, 1979. Under the purchase agreement, Sharon purchased all of the assets owned by UV on November 26 (*i.e.*, Mueller Brass, UV's mining properties and $322 million in cash or the equivalent) for $518 million ($411 million of Sharon subordinated debentures due in 2000—then valued at 86% or $353,460,000—plus $107 million in cash). As part of consideration for the purchase, Sharon assumed all of UV's liabilities, including the public debt issued under various outstanding UV indentures.

Between 1965 and 1977, UV issued debt instruments pursuant to five separate indentures. While differing in amounts and indenture trustees, each of the five indentures contained identical "successor obligor" covenant, illustrated below, that is at the heart of the instant action:

> Guarantor may consolidate with or merge into another corporation, or permit one or more other such corporations to consolidate with or merge into it, or sell or otherwise transfer to another such corporation all or substantially all of its assets as an entirety and thereafter dissolve, provided the surviving, resulting or transferee corporation, as the case may be, if it is not the Guarantor, shall expressly assume in writing all of the obligations of the Guarantor hereunder; provided, however, that neither the Company nor the Guarantor may dispose of all or substantially all of its assets to the other and may not consolidate with or merge into the other unless the Company and the Guarantor deliver to the Trustee and the City an opinion of counsel, satisfactory to the Trustee and the City, that the disposition, consolidation or merger, as the case may be, will not result in the merger of the Lease and Lease Guaranty Agreement or any provisions thereof, but that the Lease and Lease Guaranty Agreement and the provisions thereof will remain separate obligations of the transfer or consolidated or merged corporation which can be proved and scheduled separately in bankruptcy proceedings (as if the transfer, consolidation or merger had not taken place). The Guarantor will cause the Company to preserve and keep in full force and effect all licenses and permits necessary to the proper conduct of its business."

Simply stated, under the "successor obligor" covenant, if UV sold less than all or substantially all its assets to a third party, UV must pay off the outstanding debt.

On December 24, 1979, the indenture trustees, Chase Manhattan Bank (Chase), U.S. Trust, and Manufacturers Hanover Trust Company (Manufacturers) issued default notices, claimed that the sales triggered the bondholders' rights under the "successor obligor" clause, and demanded that the default be cured within 90 days or that the debentures be redeemed. In response to suits filed in state courts by the trustees, Sharon initiated the present suit against the trustees whereupon the state suits were stayed pending the outcome of this case. Sharon's argued that its purchase of all of UV's assets and assumption of liabilities did not trigger the bondholders rights "successor obligor" covenant.

A jury trial was held during April and early May, 1981, at which Sharon submitted voluminous testimony and other evidence. The indenture trustees and debentureholders moved for a directed verdict, and on May 11, 1981, the District Court granted the motion and dismissed Sharon's claims. The indenture trustees and debentureholders subsequently moved for summary judgment on their claims and counterclaims asserting their rights to be redeemed pursuant to their rights in the "successor obligor" covenant. The motion was granted. Sharon appealed.]

DISCUSSION

1. *The Successor Obligor Clauses*

Sharon Steel argues that Judge Werker erred in not submitting to the jury issues going to the meaning of the successor obligor clauses. We disagree.

Successor obligor clauses are "boilerplate" or contractual provisions which are standard in a certain genre of contracts. Successor obligor clauses are thus found in virtually all indentures. Such boilerplate must be distinguished from contractual provisions which are peculiar to a particular indenture and must be given a consistent, uniform interpretation. As the American Bar Foundation *Commentaries on Indentures* (1971) ("*Commentaries*") state:

> Since there is seldom any difference in the intended meaning [boilerplate] provisions are susceptible of standardized expression. The use of standardized language can result in a better and quicker understanding of those provisions and a substantial saving of time not only for the draftsman but also for the parties and all others who must comply with or refer to the indenture, including governmental bodies whose approval or authorization of the issuance of the securities is required by law.

Id.

Boilerplate provisions are thus not the consequence of the relationship of particular borrowers and lenders and do not depend upon particularized intentions of the parties to an indenture. There are no adjudicative facts relating to the parties to the litigation for a jury to find and the meaning of boilerplate provision is, therefore, a matter of law rather than fact.

Moreover, uniformity in interpretation is important to the efficiency of capital markets. As the Fifth Circuit has stated:

> A large degree of uniformity in the language of debenture indentures is essential to the effective functioning of the financial markets: uniformity of the indentures that govern competing debenture issues is what makes it possible meaningfully to compare one debenture issue with another, focusing only on the business provisions of the issue (such as the interest rate, the maturity date, the redemption and sinking fund provisions in the conversion rate) and the economic conditions of the issuer, without being misled by peculiarities in the underlying instruments.

Broad v. Rockwell International Corp., 642 F.2d 929, 943 (5th Cir.), *cert. denied, 454 U.S. 965, 102 S. Ct. 506, 70 L. Ed. 2d 380 (1981).* Whereas participants in the capital market can adjust their affairs according to a uniform interpretation, whether it be correct or not as an initial proposition, the creation of enduring uncertainties as to the meaning of boilerplate provisions would decrease the value of all debenture issues and greatly impair the efficient working of capital markets. Such uncertainties would vastly increase the risks and, therefore, the costs of borrowing with no offsetting benefits either in the capital market or in the administration of justice. Just such uncertainties would be created if interpretation of boilerplate provisions were submitted to juries sitting in every judicial district in the nation....

We turn now to the meaning of the successor obligor clauses. Interpretation of indenture provisions is a matter of basic contract law. As the *Commentaries* at 2 state:

> The second fundamental characteristic of long term debt financing is that the rights of holders of the debt securities are largely a matter of contract. There is no governing body of statutory or common law that protects the holder of unsecured debt securities against harmful acts by the debtor except in the most extreme situations ... The debt securityholder can do nothing to protect himself against actions of the borrower which jeopardize its ability to pay the debt unless he ... establishes his rights through contractual provisions set forth in the ... indenture.

Contract language is thus the starting point in the search for meaning and Sharon argues strenuously that the language of the successor obligor clauses clearly permits its assumption of UV's public debt. Sharon's argument is a masterpiece of simplicity: on November 26, 1979, it bought everything UV owned; therefore, the transaction was a "sale" of "all" UV's "assets." In Sharon's view, the contention of the Indenture Trustees and Debentureholders that proceeds from earlier sales in a predetermined plan of piecemeal liquidation may not be counted in determining whether a later sale involves "all assets" must be rejected because it imports a meaning not evident in the language.

Sharon's literalist approach simply proves too much. If proceeds from earlier piecemeal sales are "assets," then UV continued to own "all" its "assets" even after the Sharon transaction since the proceeds of that transaction, including the $107 million cash for cash "sale," went into the UV treasury. If the language is to be given the "literal" meaning attributed to it by Sharon, therefore, UV's "assets" were not "sold" on November 26 and the ensuing liquidation requires the redemption of the debentures by UV. Sharon's literal approach is thus self-defeating.

The words "all or substantially all" are used in a variety of statutory and contractual provisions relating to transfers of assets and have been given meaning in light of the particular context and evident purpose. *See Campbell v. Vose, 515 F.2d 256 (10th Cir. 1975)* (transfer of sole operating asset held to be a sale of all or substantially all of the corporation's assets even though two-thirds of asset book value in the form of bank balances, promissory notes and an investment portfolio was retained); *Atlas Tool Company v. Commissioner, 614 F.2d 860 (3rd Cir. 1980)*. ("Substantially all" requirement is chiefly determined by the transfer of operating assets). Sharon argues that such decisions are distinguishable because they serve the purpose of either shareholder protection or enforcement of the substance of the Internal Revenue Code. Even if such distinctions are valid, these cases nevertheless demonstrate that a literal reading of the words "all or substantially all" is not helpful apart from reference to the underlying purpose to be served. We turn, therefore, to that purpose.

Sharon argues that the sole purpose of successor obligor clauses is to leave the borrower free to merge, liquidate or to sell its assets in order to enter a wholly new business free of public debt and that they are not intended to offer any protection to lenders. On their face, however, they seem designed to protect lenders as well by assuring a degree of continuity of assets. Thus, a borrower which sells all its assets does not have an option to continue holding the debt. It must either assign the debt or pay it off. As the *Commentaries* state at 290:

> The decision to invest in the debt obligations of a corporation is based on the repayment potential of a business enterprise possessing specific financial characteristics. The ability of the enterprise to produce earnings often depends on particular assets which it owns. Obviously, if the enterprise is changed through consolidation with or merged into another corporation or through disposition of assets, the financial characteristics and repayment potential on which the lender relied may be altered adversely....

Sharon poses hypotheticals ... in the hope of demonstrating that successor obligor clauses protect only borrowers: *e.g.*, a transaction involving a sale of Federal and the oil and gas properties in the regular course of UV's business followed by an $18 per share distribution to shareholders after which the assets are sold to Sharon and Sharon assumes the indenture obligations. To the extent that a decision to sell off some properties is not part of an overall scheme to liquidate and is made in the regular course of business it is considerably different from a plan of piecemeal liquidation, whether or not followed by independent and subsequent decisions to sell off the rest. A sale in the absence of a plan to liquidate is undertaken because the directors expect the sale to strengthen the corporation as a going concern. A plan of liquidation, however, may be undertaken solely because of the financial needs and opportunities or the tax status of the major shareholders. In the latter case, relatively quick sales may be at low prices or may break up profitable asset combinations, thus drastically increasing the lender's risks if the last sale assigns the public debt. In this case, for example, tax considerations compelled completion of the liquidation within 12 months. The fact that piecemeal sales in the regular course of business are permitted thus does not demonstrate that successor obligor clauses apply to piecemeal liquidations, allowing the buyer last in time to assume the entire public debt.

We hold, therefore, that protection for borrowers as well as for lenders may be fairly inferred from the nature of successor obligor clauses....

Where contractual language seems designed to protect the interests of both parties and where conflicting interpretations are argued, the contract should be construed to sacrifice the principal interests of each party as little as possible. An interpretation which sacrifices a major interest of one of the parties while furthering only a marginal interest of the other should be rejected in favor of an interpretation which sacrifices marginal interests of both parties in order to protect their major concerns.

Of the contending positions, we believe that of the Indenture Trustees and Debentureholders best accommodates the principal interests of corporate borrowers and their lenders. Even if the UV/Sharon transaction is held not to be covered by the successor obligor clauses, borrowers are free to merge, consolidate or dispose of the operating assets of the business. Accepting Sharon's position, however, would severely impair the interests of lenders. Sharon's view would allow a borrowing corporation to engage in a piecemeal sale of assets, with concurrent liquidating dividends to that point at which the asset restrictions of an indenture prohibited further distribution. A sale of "all or substantially all" of the remaining assets could then be consummated, a new debtor substituted, and the liquidation of the borrower completed. The assignment of the public debt might thus be accomplished, even though the last sale might be nothing more than a cash for cash transaction in which the buyer purchases the public indebtedness. The UV/Sharon transaction is not so extreme, but the sale price paid by Sharon did include a cash for cash exchange of $107 million. Twenty-three percent of the sale price was, in fact, an exchange of dollars for dollars. Such a transaction diminishes the protection for lenders in order to facilitate deals with little functional significance other than substituting a new debtor in order to profit on a debenture's low interest rate. We hold, therefore, that boilerplate successor obligor clauses do not permit assignment of the public debt to another party in the course of a liquidation unless "all or substantially all" of the assets of the company at the time the plan of liquidation is determined upon are transferred to a single purchaser.

The application of this rule to the present case is not difficult. The plan of liquidation was approved by UV's shareholders on March 26, 1978. Since the Indenture Trustees make no claim as to an earlier time, *e.g.*, the date of the Board recommendation, we accept March 26 as the appropriate reference date. The question then is whether "all or substantially all" of the assets held by UV on that date were transferred to Sharon. That is easily answered. The assets owned by UV on March 26 and later transferred to Sharon were Mueller Brass, certain metals mining property, and substantial amounts of cash and other liquid assets. UV's Form 10–K and Sharon's Form S–7 state that Mueller Brass and the metals mining properties were responsible for only 38% of UV's 1978 operating revenues and 13% of its operating profits. They constitute 41% of the book value of UV's operating properties. When the cash and other liquid assets are added, the transaction still involved only 51% of the book value of UV's total assets.

Since we do not regard the question in this case as even close, we need not determine how the substantiality of corporate assets is to be measured, what percentage meets the "all or substantially all" test or what role a jury might play in determining those issues. Even when the liquid assets (other than proceeds from the sale of Federal and the oil and gas properties) are aggregated with the operating properties, the transfer to Sharon accounted for only 51% of the total book value of UV's assets. In no sense, therefore, are they "all or substantially all" of those assets. The successor obligor clauses are, therefore, not applicable. UV is thus in default on the indentures and the debentures are due and payable. For that reason, we need not reach the question whether the April Document was breached by UV. . . .

CONCLUSION

We affirm Judge Werker's dismissal of Sharon's amended complaint. . . .

Debt covenants can cover a wide range of matters that could threaten the likelihood that that the bonds' interest and principal will be paid. Some covenants directly constrain the debtor's discretion to make distributions to shareholders through dividends or share repurchases, restrict incurring additional debt, mortgages or liens, and mandate levels of insurance and periodic reporting of certain information to the bondholders and/or indenture trustee. In light of the range of possible covenants that can be incorporated into a bond indenture, how willing should courts be to imply terms to complement the covenants that are expressly provided in the bond's indenture?

Metropolitan Life Insurance Company v. RJR Nabisco, Inc.

United States District Court for the Southern District of New York, 1989.
716 F.Supp. 1504.

■ Jon M. Walker, United States District Judge

I. INTRODUCTION . . .

The present action traces its origin to October 20, 1988, when F. Ross Johnson, then the Chief Executive Officer of RJR Nabisco, proposed a $17 billion leverage buy-out ("LBO") of the company's shareholders, at $75 per share.[2] Within a few days, a bidding war developed among the investment group led by Johnson and the investment firm of Kohlberg Kravis Roberts & Co. ("KKR"), and others. . . . [Ultimately KKR prevailed and consummated the LBO on April 24, 1989, for a total purchase price of $24 billion ($109 per

2. A leveraged buy-out occurs when a group of investors, usually including members of a company's management team, buy the company under financial arrangements that include little equity and significant new debt. The necessary debt financing typically includes mortgages or high risk/high yield bonds, popularly known as "junk bonds." . . .

share). This resulted in RJR Nabisco incurring $19 billion in new debt and making a cash payment of $18 billion to its former common stockholders. The plaintiffs, Metropolitan Life Insurance Company and Jefferson–Pilot Life Insurance Company held $340,542,000 and $9,340,000, respectively, of RJR Nabisco debt issues. The present suit was filed by the two bondholders before RJR Nabisco's board had accepted KKR's offer. In their motion for summary judgment, plaintiffs] allege, in short, that RJR's actions have drastically impaired the value of bonds previously issued to plaintiffs by, in effect, misappropriating the value of those bonds to help finance the LBO and to distribute an enormous windfall to the company's shareholders. As a result, the plaintiff's argue, they have unfairly suffered a multimillion dollar loss in the value of their bonds....

[The record reflects that in 1983 and 1985 Metropolitan agreed to the removal from two of the six RJR Nabisco bond issues it held of covenants that prevented further increases in the amount of debt that RJR Nabisco could incur; in exchange, Metropolitan received improved conditions for other provisions in those two bond issues. The record also set forth several statements by Johnson and other senior officers that the plaintiff contends reflected management's commitment not to incur substantial amounts of new debt such that it would jeopardize the high credit rating that RJR Nabisco enjoyed.]

At the heart of the present motions, lies the plaintiffs' claim that RJR Nabisco violated a restrictive covenant—not an explicit covenant with the four corners of the relevant bond indentures, but rather an *implied* covenant of good faith and fair dealing—not to incur the debt necessary to facilitate the LBO and thereby betray what plaintiffs claim was the fundamental basis of their bargain with the company.... Plaintiffs ask this court first to imply a covenant of good faith and fair dealing that would prevent the recent transaction, then to hold that this covenant has been breached, and finally to require RJR Nabisco to redeem their bonds....

RJR Nabisco defends the LBO by pointing to express provisions in the bond indentures that, *inter alia*, permit mergers and the assumption of additional debt. These provisions, as well as others that could have been included but were not, were known to the market and to plaintiffs, sophisticated investors who freely bought the bonds and were equally free to sell them at any time. Any attempt by this Court to create contractual terms *post hoc*, defendants contend, not only finds no basis in the controlling law and undisputed facts of this case, but also would constitute an impermissible invasion into the free and open operation of the marketplace.

For the reasons set forth below, this Court agrees with defendants. There being no express covenant between the parties that would restrict the incurrence of new debt, and no perceived direction to that end from covenants that are express, this Court will not imply a covenant to prevent the recent LBO and thereby create an indenture term that, while bargained for in other contexts, was not bargained for here and was not even within the mutual contemplation of the parties.

II. BACKGROUND . . .

B. The Indentures:

The bonds implicated by this suit are governed by long, detailed indentures, which in turn [by virtue of an explicit choice of law clause in each indenture] are governed by New York contract law. No one disputes that the holders of public bond issues, like plaintiffs here, often enter the market after the indentures have been negotiated and memorialized. Thus, those indentures are often not the product of face-to-face negotiations between the ultimate holders and the issuing company. What remains equally true, however, is that underwriters ordinarily negotiate the terms of the indentures with the issuers. Since the underwriters must then sell or place the bonds, they necessarily negotiate in part with the interests of the buyers in mind. Moreover, these indentures were not secret agreements foisted upon unwitting participants in the bond market. No successive holder is required to accept or to continue to hold the bonds, governed by their accompanying indentures; indeed, plaintiffs readily admit that they could have sold their bonds right up until the announcement of the LBO. . . . Instead, sophisticated investors like plaintiffs are well aware of the indenture terms and, presumably, review them carefully before lending hundreds of millions of dollars to any company. . . .

1. The relevant Articles:

A typical RJR Nabisco indenture contains thirteen Articles. At least four of them are relevant to the present motions and thus merit a brief review.

Article Three delineates the covenants of the issuer. Most important, it first provides for payment of principal and interest. It then addresses various mechanical provisions regarding such matters as payment terms and trustee vacancies. The Article also contains "negative pledge" and related provisions, which restrict mortgages or other liens on the assets of RJR Nabisco or its subsidiaries and seek to protect the bondholders from being subordinated to other debt.

Article Five describes various procedures to remedy defaults and the responsibilities of the Trustee. . . .

Article Nine governs the adoption of supplemental indentures. It provides, *inter alia*, that the Issuer and the Trustee can

> add to the covenants of the Issuer such further covenants, restrictions, conditions or provisions as its Board of Directors by Board Resolution and the Trustee shall consider to be for the protection of the holders of Securities, and to make the occurrence, or the occurrence and continuance, of a default in any such additional covenants, restrictions, conditions or provisions an Event of Default permitting the enforcement of all or any of the several remedies provided in this Indenture as herein set forth . . .

Article Ten addresses a potential "Consolidation, Merger, Sale or Conveyance," and explicitly sets forth the conditions under which the company can consolidate or merge into or with any other corporation.

It provides explicitly that RJR Nabisco "may consolidate with, or sell or convey, all or substantially all of its assets to, or merge into or with any other corporation," so long as the new entity is a United States corporation, and so long as it assumes RJR Nabisco's debt. . . .

III. DISCUSSION

At the outset, the Court notes that nothing in its evaluation is substantively altered by the speeches given or remarks made by RJR Nabisco executives. . . . The parol evidence rule bars plaintiffs from arguing that the speeches made by company executives prove defendants agreed or acquiesced to a term that does not appear in the indentures. . . . The indentures at issue clearly address the eventuality of a merger. They impose certain related restrictions not at issue in this suit, but no restriction that would prevent the recent RJR Nabisco merger transaction. . . . The indentures also explicitly set forth provisions for the adoption of new covenants, if such a course is deemed appropriate. . . . While it may be true that no explicit provision either permits or prohibits an LBO, such contractual silence itself cannot create ambiguity to avoid the dictates of the parole evidence rule, particularly where the indentures impose no debt limitations. . . .

A. *Plaintiffs' Case Against the RJR Nabisco LBO*:

1. Count One: The implied covenant:

> In their first count, plaintiffs assert that defendant RJR Nabisco owes a continuing duty of good faith and fair dealing in connection with the contract [i.e., the indentures] through which it borrowed money from MetLife, Jefferson–Pilot and other holders of its debt, including a duty not to frustrate the purpose of the contracts to the debtholders or to deprive the debtholders of the intended object of the contracts—purchase of investment-grade securities.
>
> In the "buy-out," the company breaches the duty [or implied covenant] of good faith and fair dealing by, *inter alia*, destroying the investment grade quality of the debt and transferring that value to the "buy-out" proponents and to the shareholders.

Am. Comp. paras. 34, 35. In effect, plaintiffs contend that express covenants were not necessary because an *implied* covenant would prevent what defendants have now done.

A plaintiff always can allege a violation of an express covenant. If there has been such a violation, of course, the court need not reach the question of whether or not an *implied* covenant has been violated. That inquiry surfaces where, while the express terms may not have been technically breached, one party has nonetheless effectively deprived the other of those express, explicitly bargained-for benefits. In such a case, a court will read an implied covenant of good faith and fair dealing into a contract to ensure that neither party deprives the other of "the fruits of the agreement." *See, e.g., Greenwich Village Assoc. v. Salle, 110 A.D.2d 111, 115, 493 N.Y.S.2d 461, 464* (1st Dep't

1985). *See also Van Gemert v. Boeing Co., 553 F.2d 812, 815* ("*Van Gemert II*") (2d. Cir. 1977) Such a covenant is implied only where the implied term "is consistent with other mutually agreed upon terms in the contract." *Sabetay v. Sterling Drug, Inc., 69 N.Y.2d 329, 335, 514 N.Y.S.2d 209, 212, 506 N.E.2d 919 (1987)*. In other words, the implied covenant will only aid and further the explicit terms of the agreement and will never impose an obligation " 'which would be inconsistent with other terms of the contractual relationship.' " *Id.* (citation omitted). Viewed another way, the implied covenant of good faith is breached only when one party seeks to prevent the contract's performance or to withhold its benefits.... As a result, it thus ensures that parties to a contract perform the substantive, bargained-for terms of their agreement....

In contracts like bond indentures, "an implied covenant ... derives its substance directly from the language of the Indenture, and 'cannot give the holders of Debentures any rights inconsistent with those set out in the Indenture. "*[Where] plaintiffs' contractual rights [have not been] violated, there can have been no breach of an implied covenant.*" *Gardner & Florence Call Cowles Foundation v. Empire Inc., 589 F. Supp. 669, 673 (S.D.N.Y. 1984), vacated on procedural grounds*, *754 F.2d 478 (2d Cir. 1985)* ....

Thus, in cases like *Van Gemert v. Boeing Co., 520 F.2d 1373* (2d Cir.), *cert. denied, 423 U.S. 947, 46 L. Ed. 2d 282, 96 S. Ct. 364 (1975)* ("*Van Gemert I*"), and *Pittsburgh Terminal Corp. v. Baltimore & Ohio Ry. Co., 680 F.2d 933* (3d Cir.), *cert. denied, 459 U.S. 1056, 74 L. Ed. 2d 621, 103 S. Ct. 475*, (1982)—both relied upon by plaintiffs—the courts used the implied covenant of good faith and fair dealing to ensure that the bondholders received the benefit of their bargain as determined from the face of the contracts at issue. In *Van Gemert I*, the plaintiff bondholders alleged inadequate notice to them of defendant's intention to redeem the debentures in question and hence an inability to exercise their conversion rights before the applicable deadline. The contract itself provided that notice would be given in the first place. *See e.g., id. at 1375* ("A number of provisions in the debenture, the Indenture Agreement, the prospectus, the registration statement ... and the Listing Agreement ... dealt with the possible redemption of the debentures ... and the notice debenture-holders were to receive ..."). Faced with those provisions, defendants in that case unsurprisingly admitted that the indentures specifically required the company to provide the bondholders with notice. *See id. at 1379*.... Through an implied covenant, then, the court fleshed out the full extent of the more skeletal right that appeared in the contract itself, and thus protected plaintiff's bargained-for right of conversion. As the court observed,

> What one buys when purchasing a convertible debenture in addition to the debt obligation of the company ... is principally the expectation that the stock will increase sufficiently in value that the conversion right will make the debenture worth more than the debt ... *Any loss occurring*

> *to him from failure to convert, as here, is not from a risk inherent in his investment but rather from unsatisfactory notification procedures.*

Id. at 1385 (emphasis added, citations omitted)....

The appropriate analysis, then, is first to examine the indentures to determine "the fruits of the agreement" between the parties, and then to decide whether those "fruits" have been spoiled-which is to say, whether plaintiffs' contractual rights have been violated by defendants.

The American Bar Foundation's *Commentaries on Indentures* ("the *Commentaries*"), relied upon and respected by both plaintiffs and defendants, describes the rights and risks generally found in bond indentures like those at issue:

> The most obvious and important characteristic of long-term debt financing is that the holder ordinarily has not bargained for and does not expect any substantial gain in the value of the security to compensate for the risk of loss ... The significant fact, *which accounts in part for the detailed protective provisions of the typical long-term debt financing instrument*, is that *the lender (the purchaser of the debt security) can expect only interest at the prescribed rate plus the eventual return of the principal*. Except for possible increases in the market value of the debt security because of changes in interest rates, the debt security will seldom be worth more than the lender paid for it ... It may, of course, become worth much less. Accordingly, the typical investor in a long-term debt security is primarily interested in every reasonable assurance that the principal and interest will be paid when due.... Short of bankruptcy, *the debt security holder can do nothing to protect himself against actions of the borrower which jeopardize its ability to pay the debt unless he ... establishes his rights through contractual provisions set forth in the debt agreement or indenture.*

Id. at 1–2 (1971) (emphasis added).

A review of the parties' submissions and the indentures themselves satisfies the Court that the substantive "fruits" guaranteed by those contracts and relevant to the present motions include the periodic and regular payment of interest and the eventual repayment of principal.... According to a typical indenture, a default shall occur if the company either (1) fails to pay principal when due; (2) fails to make a timely sinking fund payment; (3) fails to pay within 30 days of the due date thereof any interest on the date; or (4) fails duly to observe or perform any of the express covenants or agreements set forth in the agreement. ... Plaintiffs' Amended Complaint nowhere alleges that RJR Nabisco has breached these contractual obligations; interest payments continue and there is no reason to believe that the principal will not be paid when due....

Although the indentures generally permit mergers and the incurrence of new debt, there admittedly is not an explicit indenture provision to the contrary of what plaintiffs now claim the implied covenant requires. That absence, however, does *not* mean that the Court should imply into those very same indentures a covenant of good faith so broad that it imposes a new, substantive term of enormous scope. This is so particularly where, as here, that very term—a limitation on the incurrence of additional debt—has in other past contexts been expressly bargained for; particularly where the indentures grant the company broad discretion in the management of its affairs, as plaintiffs admit, . . .; particularly where the indentures explicitly set forth specific provisions for the adoption of new covenants and restrictions, . . .); and *especially* where there has been no breach of the parties' bargained-for contractual rights on which the implied covenant necessarily is based. While the Court stands ready to employ an implied covenant of good faith to ensure that such bargained-for rights are performed and upheld, it will not, however, permit an implied covenant to shoehorn into an indenture additional terms plaintiffs now wish had been included. . . .

Plaintiffs argue in the most general terms that the fundamental basis of all these indentures was that an LBO along the lines of the recent RJR Nabisco transaction would never be undertaken, that indeed *no* action would be taken, intentionally or not, that would significantly deplete the company's assets. Accepting plaintiffs' theory, their fundamental bargain with defendants dictated that nothing would be done to jeopardize the extremely high probability that the company would remain able to make interest payments and repay principal over the 20 to 30 year indenture term . . But as Judge Knapp aptly concluded in *Gardner*, "Defendants . . . were under a duty to carry out the terms of the contract, but not to make sure that plaintiffs had made a good investment. . . .

The sort of unbounded and one-sided elasticity urged by plaintiffs would interfere with and destabilize the market. And this Court, like the parties to these contracts, cannot ignore or disavow the marketplace in which the contract is performed. Nor can it ignore the expectations of that market—expectations, for instance, that the terms of an indenture will be upheld, and that a court will not, *sua sponte*, add new substantive terms to that indenture as it sees fit. The Court has no reason to believe that the market, in evaluating bonds such as those at issue here, did not discount for the possibility that any company, even one the size of RJR Nabisco, might engage in an LBO heavily financed by debt. That the bonds did not lose any of their value until the October 20, 1988 announcement of a possible RJR Nabisco LBO only suggests that the market had theretofore evaluated the risks of such a transaction as slight. . . .

In the final analysis, plaintiffs offer no objective or reasonable standard for a court to use in its effort to define the sort of actions their "implied covenant" would permit a corporation to take, and those it would not. . . . As is clear from the preceding discussion, however, plaintiffs have failed to convince the Court that by upholding the explicit, bargained-for terms of the indenture, RJR Nabisco has either exhibited bad faith or destroyed plaintiffs' *legitimate*, protected expectations....

III. CONCLUSION

For the reasons set forth above, the Court grants defendants summary judgment on ... [Count I]

SO ORDERED.

> For most of this [i.e., the 20th Century] contracts governing long-term debt restricted subsequent substantial indebtedness.... Until recently, investors considered these provisions central to the bargain....
>
> This pattern continued until the mid–1970s. Since then, new public, unsecured debt of large industrials has tended to contain only a "negative pledge" against additional secured debt....
>
> The covenants had disappeared because they seemed unnecessary. Before 1985, economic prosperity combined with management's dominant governance position to make large corporations look reliable as unsecured borrowers. Whatever the turns of the business cycle, management seemed unlikely to seek to benefit stockholders by abusing bondholders. Management wanted growth and security—goals best realized with conservative leverage and retained-earnings financing.... According to the conventional wisdom, ... opportunistic conduct would lead creditors in future financings to impose unfavorable terms, the costs of which would outweigh the benefits of the present wealth transfers....
>
> The restructuring movement [of the 1980s] has shattered the managerialist assumptions behind the covenantless debt contract.... Corporate reputation—the unprotected bondholders' backstop—has proved ineffective. Managers' and stockholders' incentives to maintain good reputations in capital markets do not have the staying power of contract promises.... Exiting stockholders and managers care nothing about a corporate entity's future financing costs....

William W. Bratton, Corporate Debt Relationships: Legal Theory in a Time of Restructuring, 1989 Duke L. J. 139–42.

Not surprising, after the "break-and-take" era of the 1980s and the significant losses suffered by bondholders in LBOs and other restructurings, indentures today commonly include so-called "poison puts" and "event risk" provisions empowering bondholders to require redemption of their bonds if the debtor underwent a merger, LBO or suffered a serious ratings downgrade for the debt.

Bond indentures typically set forth the procedures for amending the indenture covenants through a vote of the bondholders. Indentures commonly provide that the amendment and even elimination of covenants can occur by bondholders holding a majority of the face amount of the bonds outstanding (i.e., excluding the bonds the debtor may have reacquired). Sometimes a higher percentage, such as two-thirds, is set forth in the indenture. However, for bonds subject to the Trust Indenture Act of 1939, certain "core" provisions (such as the amount of principal, interest and duration) can only be changed through the unanimous approval of the bondholders. The following case illustrates the conflicting positions within a firm confronting the need to restructure itself through amendment of its outstanding debt.

Katz v. Oak Industries, Inc.

Delaware Chancery Court, 1986.
508 A.2d 873.

■ Allen, Chancellor

[Oak Industries, Inc., a Delaware corporation, was in deep financial trouble, having incurred substantial losses from January 1, 1982 through late 1985. Its savior appeared to be Allied Signal who had conditionally agreed to invest $15 million cash in exchange for 10 million Oak Industries common shares. However, this investment was conditioned on 85% of the aggregate principal amount of all of Oak's debt securities being tendered for redemption along with the holder's consent to eliminate certain protective covenants for the debt instruments. Oak had six classes of long-term debt that was subject to the offer. The price Signal offered to each class reflected a premium over the market price for debt securities, but the amount to be paid nonetheless was a distinct discount from the debts' face amount. Without receiving the requisite consents from the debt holders to eliminate certain covenants, Signal's offer would trigger the covenants' protective provisions and thereby require the debt to be redeemed at face value plus any accrued interest. Depending on the particular tranche of debt, a handful of banks and other financial institutions held 69.1% to 89% of the debt securities.]

Plaintiff, is an owner of long-term debt securities issued by Oak Industries, Inc..... The claim asserted is in essence, that the exchange offer is a coercive device and, in the circumstances, constitutes a breach of contract. This is the Court's opinion on the plaintiff's pending application for summary judgment....

II.

Plaintiff's claim that ...:

> The purpose and effect of the Exchange Offers is [1] to benefit Oak's common stockholders at the expense of the Holders of its debt securities, [2] to force the exchange of its debt instruments at unfair price and at less than face value of the debt instruments [3] pursuant to a rigged vote in which

> debt Holders who exchange, and who therefore have no interest in the vote, *must* consent to the elimination of protective covenants for debt Holders who do not wish to exchange.

... [P]laintiff's claim is that no free choice is provided to bondholders by the exchange offer and consent solicitation. Under its terms, a rational bondholder is "forced" to tender and consent. Failure to do so would face a bondholder with the risk of owning a security stripped of all financial covenant protections and for which it is likely that there would be no ready market. A reasonable bondholder, it is suggested, cannot possibly accept those risks and thus such a bondholder is coerced to tender and thus to consent to the proposed indenture amendments.

It is urged this linking of the offer and the consent solicitation constitutes a breach of a contractual obligation that Oak owes to its bondholders to act in good faith. Specifically, plaintiff points to three contractual provisions from which it can be seen that the structuring of the current offer constitutes a breach of good faith. Those provisions (1) establish a requirement that no modification in the term of the various indentures may be effectuated without the consent of a stated percentage of bondholders; (2) restrict Oak from exercising the power to grant such consent with respect to any securities it may hold in its treasury; and (3) establish the price at which and manner in which Oak may force bondholders to submit their securities for redemption.

III. ...

I turn first to an evaluation of the probability of plaintiff's ultimate success on the merits of his claim.... Under our law—and the law generally—the relationship between a corporation and the holders of its debt securities, even convertible debt securities, is contractual in nature.... The rights and obligations of the various parties are or should be spelled out in that documentation. The terms of the contractual relationship agreed to and not broad concepts such as fairness define the corporation's obligation to its bondholders.

Thus, the first aspect of the pending Exchange Offers about which plaintiff complains—that "the purpose and effect of the Exchange Offers is to benefit Oak's common stockholders at the expense of the Holders of its debt"—does not itself appear to allege a cognizable legal wrong. It is the obligation of directors to attempt, within the law, to maximize the long-run interests of the corporation's stockholders; that they may sometimes do so "at the expense" of others (even assuming that a transaction which one may refuse to enter into can meaningfully be said to be at his expense) does not for that reason constitute a breach of duty. It seems likely that corporate restructurings designed to maximize shareholder values may in some instances have the effect of requiring bondholders to bear greater risk of loss and thus in effect transfer economic value from bondholders to stockholders.... But if courts are to provide protection against such enhanced risk, they will require either legislative direction to do so or the negotiation of indenture provisions designed to afford such protection.

The second preliminary point concerns the limited analytical utility, at least in this context, of the word "coercive" which is central to plaintiff's own articulation of his theory of recovery. If, *pro arguendo*, we are to extend the meaning of the word coercion beyond its core meaning—dealing with the utilization of physical force to overcome the will of another—to reach instances in which the claimed coercion arises from an act designed to affect the will of another party by offering inducements to the act sought to be encouraged or by arranging unpleasant consequences for an alternative sought to be discouraged, then—in order to make the term legally meaningful at all—we must acknowledge that some further refinement is essential. Clearly some "coercion" of this kind is legally unproblematic. Parents may "coerce" a child to study with the threat of withholding an allowance; employers may "coerce" regular attendance at work by either docking wages for time absent or by rewarding with a bonus such regular attendance. Other "coercion" so defined clearly would be legally relevant (to encourage regular attendance by corporal punishment, for example). Thus, for purposes of legal analysis, the term "coercion" itself—covering a multitude of situations—is not very meaningful. For the word to have much meaning for purposes of legal analysis, it is necessary in each case that a normative judgment be attached to the concept ("inappropriately coercive" or "wrongfully coercive", etc.). But, it is then readily seen that what is legally relevant is not the conclusory term "coercion" itself but rather the norm that leads to the adjectives modifying it.

In this instance, assuming that the Exchange Offers and Consent Solicitation can meaningfully be regarded as "coercive" (in the sense that Oak has structured it in a way designed—and I assume effectively so—to "force" rational bondholders to tender), the relevant legal norm that will support the judgment whether such "coercion" is wrongful or not will, for the reasons mentioned above, be derived from the law of contracts. I turn then to that subject to determine the appropriate legal test or rule.

Modern contract law has generally recognized an implied covenant to the effect that each party to a contract will act with good faith towards the other with respect to the subject matter of the contract. *See, Restatement of Law, Contracts 2d, § 205* (1981); *Rowe v. Great Atlantic and Pacific Tea Company, N.Y. Ct. Apps., 46 N.Y.2d 62, 385 N.E.2d 566, 412 N.Y.S.2d 827, 830,* (1978). The contractual theory for this implied obligation is well stated in a leading treatise:

> If the purpose of contract law is to enforce the reasonable expectations of parties induced by promises, then at some point it becomes necessary for courts to look to the substance rather than to the form of the agreement, and to hold that substance controls over form. What courts are doing here, whether calling the process "implication" of

> promises, or interpreting the requirements of "good faith", as the current fashion may be, is but a recognition that the parties occasionally have understandings or expectations that were so fundamental that they did not need to negotiate about those expectations. When the court "implies a promise" or holds that "good faith" requires a party not to violate those expectations, it is recognizing that sometimes silence says more than words, and it is understanding its duty to the spirit of the bargain is higher than its duty to the technicalities of the language. *Corbin on Contracts* (Kaufman Supp. 1984), § 570.

It is this obligation to act in good faith and to deal fairly that plaintiff claims is breached by the structure of Oak's coercive exchange offer. Because it is an implied *contractual* obligation that is asserted as the basis for the relief sought, the appropriate legal test is not difficult to deduce. It is this: is it clear from what was expressly agreed upon that the parties who negotiated the express terms of the contract would have agreed to proscribe the act later complained of as a breach of the implied covenant of good faith—had they thought to negotiate with respect to that matter. If the answer to this question is yes, then, in my opinion, a court is justified in concluding that such act constitutes a breach of the implied covenant of good faith. . . .

With this test in mind, I turn now to a review of the specific provisions of the various indentures from which one may be best able to infer whether it is apparent that the contracting parties—had they negotiated with the exchange offer and consent solicitation in mind—would have expressly agreed to prohibit contractually the linking of the giving of consent with the purchase and sale of the security.

IV.

Applying the foregoing standard to the exchange offer and consent solicitation, I find first that there is nothing in the indenture provisions granting bondholders power to veto proposed modifications in the relevant indenture that implies that Oak may not offer an inducement to bondholders to consent to such amendments. . . .

Nor does the second pertinent contractual provision supply a ground to conclude that defendant's conduct violates the reasonable expectations of those who negotiated the indentures on behalf of the bondholders. Under that provision Oak may not vote debt securities held in its treasury. Plaintiff urges that Oak's conditioning of its offer to purchase debt on the giving of consents has the effect of subverting the purpose of that provision; it permits Oak to "dictate" the vote on securities which it could not itself vote.

The evident purpose of the restriction on the voting of treasury securities is to afford protection against the issuer voting as a bondholder in favor of modifications that would benefit it as issuer, even though such changes would be detrimental to bondholders. But the linking of the exchange offer and the consent solicitation does not involve the risk that bondholder interests will be affected by a vote involving anyone with a financial interest in the subject of the vote other than a bondholder's interest. That the consent is to be given concurrently with the transfer of the bond to the issuer does not in any sense create the kind of conflict of interest that the indenture's prohibition on voting treasury securities contemplates. Not only will the proposed consents be granted or withheld only by those with a financial interest to maximize the return on their investment in Oak's bonds, but the incentive to consent is equally available to all members of each class of bondholders. Thus the "vote" implied by the consent solicitation is not affected in any sense by those with a financial conflict of interest.

In these circumstances, while it is clear that Oak has fashioned the exchange offer and consent solicitation in a way designed to encourage consents, I cannot conclude that the offer violates the intendment of any of the express contractual provisions considered or, applying the test set out above, that its structure and timing breaches an implied obligation of good faith and fair dealing.

One further set of contractual provisions should be touched upon: Those granting to Oak a power to redeem the securities here treated at a price set by the relevant indentures. Plaintiff asserts that the attempt to force all bondholders to tender their securities at less than the redemption price constitutes, if not a breach of the redemption provision itself, at least a breach of an implied covenant of good faith and fair dealing associated with it. The flaw, or at least one fatal flaw, in this argument is that the present offer is not the functional equivalent of a redemption which is, of course, an act that the issuer may take unilaterally. In this instance it may happen that Oak will get tenders of a large percentage of its outstanding long-term debt securities. If it does, that fact will, in my judgment, be in major part a function of the merits of the offer (i.e., the price offered in light of the Company's financial position and the market value of its debt). To answer plaintiff's contention that the *structure* of the offer "forces" debt holders to tender, one only has to imagine what response this offer would receive if the price offered did not reflect a premium over market but rather was, for example, ten percent of market value. The exchange offer's success ultimately depends upon the ability and willingness of the issuer to extend an offer that will be a financially attractive alternative to holders. This process is hardly the functional equivalent of the unilateral election of redemption and thus cannot be said in any sense to constitute a subversion by Oak of the negotiated provisions dealing with redemption of its debt.

Accordingly, I conclude that plaintiff has failed to demonstrate a probability of ultimate success on the theory of liability asserted.

CHAPTER 16

Distributions to Shareholders

Corporations normally can distribute funds to shareholders in one of four ways:

(1) As dividends, that is, by making pro rata distributions of cash, securities, or interests in other kinds of property.

(2) By repurchasing shares.

(3) By paying shareholder-employees inflated salaries. This technique is most commonly used in close corporations, for tax reasons: In calculating taxable income, a corporation can deduct salaries, but cannot deduct dividends.

(4) On liquidation, by paying each shareholder her pro rata share of corporate assets remaining after the claim of creditors have been satisfied or provided for.

This Chapter will concern the first two kinds of distributions—dividends and stock repurchases. Inflated salaries are considered in Chapters 8 (Close Corporations) and 10 (Duty of Loyalty), supra. Distributions in liquidation only infrequently raise significant legal problems if creditors have been either paid or provided for.

The architecture of this Chapter is as follows: Dividend policy is considered in Section 1. Limitations on dividends under creditors' rights law are considered in Section 2. Limitations on dividends under traditional corporate statutes are considered in Section 3. Limitations on dividends under the modern dividend statutes are considered in Section 4 and contractual limitations on dividends are considered in Section 5. The liability of directors and shareholders for improper dividends is considered in Sections 6 and 7. The repurchase by a corporation of its own stock is considered in Section 8. An issue related to dividends, liability for watered stock, is considered in section 9.

Section 1. Dividend Policy

Dividend policy raises two very different kinds of issues. The first issue is how a corporation should determine the level of dividends it should pay. The materials in Section 1.A address that issue. Although dividend policy is largely an issue of efficiency, it spills over into law when shareholders bring a suit to force a corporation to pay dividends or when creditors complain the distribution violated legal standards intended for their protection. That issue will be considered in Section 1.B.

A. THE ELEMENTS OF DIVIDEND POLICY

Richard A. Brealey & Stewart C. Myers & Franklin Allen, Principles of Corporate Finance

Eighth ed., 2006.

In the mid–1950s John Lintner conducted a classic series of interviews with corporate managers about their dividend policies. His conclusions can be summarized in four stylized facts:

1. Firms have long-run target dividend payout ratios. Mature companies with stable earnings generally pay out a high proportion of earnings; growth companies have low payouts (if they pay any dividends at all).

2. Managers focus more on dividend changes than on absolute levels. Thus, paying a $2.00 dividend is an important financial decision if last year's dividend was $1.00, but no big deal if last year's dividend was $2.00.

3. Dividend changes follow shifts in long-run, sustainable earnings. Managers "smooth" dividends. Transitory earnings changes are unlikely to affect dividend payouts.

4. Managers are reluctant to make dividend changes that might have to be reversed. They are particularly worried about having to rescind a dividend increase....

When Lintner conducted his interviews, dividends were effectively the only means of distributing cash. More recent work on payout policy since the dramatic increase in repurchases suggests a fifth stylized fact.

5. Firms repurchase stock when they have accumulated a large amount of unwanted cash or wish to change their capital structure by replacing equity with debt.

THE INFORMATION IN DIVIDENDS AND STOCK REPURCHASES

In some countries you cannot rely on the information that companies provide. Passion for secrecy and a tendency to construct multilayered corporate organizations produce asset and earnings figures that are next to meaningless. Some people say that, thanks to creative accounting, the situation is little better for some companies in the United States.

How does an investor in such a world separate marginally profitable firms from the real money makers? One clue is dividends. Investors can't read managers' minds, but they can learn from managers' actions. They know that a firm which reports good earnings and pays a generous dividend is putting its money where its mouth is. We can understand, therefore, why investors would value the information content of dividends and would refuse to believe a firm's reported earnings unless they were backed up by an appropriate dividend policy.

Of course, firms can cheat in the short run by overstating earnings and scraping up cash to pay a generous dividend. But it is hard to cheat in the long run, for a firm that is not making enough money will not have enough cash to pay out. If a firm chooses a high dividend payout without the cash flow to back it up, that firm will ultimately have to reduce its investment plans or turn to investors for additional debt or equity financing. All of these consequences are costly. Therefore, most managers don't increase dividends until they are confident that sufficient cash will flow in to pay them.

Researchers, who have attempted to measure the information in dividend changes, have come up with mixed evidence. Some have found that dividend changes have little or no ability to predict future earnings. However, Healey and Palepu, who focus on companies that paid a dividend for the first time, find that on average earnings jumped 43 percent in the year a dividend was paid. If managers thought that this was a temporary windfall, they might have been cautious about committing themselves to paying out cash. But it looks as if these managers had good reason to be confident about prospects, for earnings continued to rise in the following years.[1]

THE PAYOUT CONTROVERSY

We have seen that a change in payout may provide information about management's confidence in the future and so affect the stock price. But eventually this change in the stock price would happen anyway as information about future earnings seeps out through other channels. But does the payout policy *change* the value of the stock, rather than simply providing a signal of its value?

On this issue, economists fall into three groups. On the right, there is a conservative group which believes that an increase in the dividend payout increases firm value. On the left, there is a radical group which believes that a higher dividend payout reduces value. And in the center, there is a middle-of-the-road party which claims that payout policy makes no difference.

The middle-of-the-road party was founded in 1961 by Miller and Modigliani (always referred to as "MM" or "M and M"), when they published a theoretical paper showing the irrelevance of dividend policy in a world without taxes, transaction costs, or other market imperfections.[12] . . .

In their classic 1961 article MM argued as follows: Suppose your firm has settled on its investment program. You have worked out how much of this program can be financed from borrowing, and you plan

1. See P. Healey and K. Palepu, "Earnings Information Conveyed by Dividend Initiations and Omissions," Journal of Financial Economics 21 (1988), pp. 149–175.

12. M.H. Miller and F. Modigliani: "Dividend Policy, Growth and the Valuation of Shares," *Journal of Business,* 34: 411–433 (October 1961).

to meet the remaining funds requirement from retained earnings. Any surplus money is to be paid out as dividends.

Now think what happens if you want to increase the dividend payment without changing the investment and borrowing policy. The extra money must come from somewhere. If the firm fixes its borrowing, the only way it can finance the extra dividend is to print some more shares and sell them. The new stockholders are going to part with their money only if you can offer them shares that are worth as much as they cost. But how can the firm do this when its assets, earnings, investment opportunities and, therefore, market value are all unchanged? The answer is that there must be a *transfer of value* from the old to the new stockholders. The new ones get the newly printed shares, each one worth less than before the dividend change was announced, and the old ones suffer a capital loss on their shares. The capital loss borne by the old shareholders just offsets the extra cash dividend they receive. . . .

Does it make any difference to the old stockholders that they receive an extra dividend payment plus an offsetting capital loss? It might if that were the only way they could get their hands on cash. But as long as there are efficient capital markets, they can raise the cash by selling shares. Thus the old shareholders can "cash in" either by persuading the management to pay a higher dividend or by selling some of their shares. In either case there will be a transfer of value from old to new shareholders. The only difference is that in the former case this transfer is caused by a dilution in the value of each of the firm's shares, and in the latter case it is caused by a reduction in the number of shares held by the old shareholders. . . .

Because investors do not need dividends to get their hands on cash, they will not pay higher prices for the shares of firms with high payouts. Therefore firms ought not to worry about dividend policy. They can let dividends fluctuate as a by-product of their investment and financing decisions. [This conclusion is known as the MM dividend-irrelevance proposition.] . . .

[One reason that some or many corporations may pay high dividends in the real world is that there] is a natural clientele for high-payout stocks. Trusts and endowment funds may prefer high-dividend stocks because dividends are regarded as spendable "income," whereas capital gains are "additions to principal."

There is also a natural clientele of investors who look to their stock portfolios for a steady source of cash to live on. In principle this cash could be easily generated from stocks paying no dividends at all; the investor could just sell off a small fraction of his or her holdings from time to time. But it is simpler and cheaper for AT & T to send a quarterly check than for its stockholders to sell, say, one share every 3 months. AT & T's regular dividends relieve many of its shareholders of transaction costs and considerable inconvenience. . . .

There is another reason that shareholders often clamor for more generous payouts. Suppose a company has plenty of free cash flow but few profitable investment opportunities. Shareholders may not trust the managers to spend retained earnings wisely and may fear that the money will be plowed back into building a larger empire rather than a more profitable one. In such cases investors may clamor for higher dividends or a stock repurchase not because these are valuable in themselves, but because they encourage a more careful, value-oriented investment policy.

Brav, Graham, Harvey & Michaely
PAYOUT POLICY IN THE 21ST CENTURY.

77 J. Financial Economics 483, 484–486 (2005).

... In 1956, John Lintner laid the foundation for the modern understanding of dividend policy. Lintner (1956) interviewed managers from 28 companies and argued that managers target a long-term payout ratio when determining dividend policy. He also concluded that dividends are sticky, tied to long-term sustainable earnings, paid by mature companies, smoothed from year to year. In this paper, we survey and interview financial executives at the start of the 21st century to learn how dividend and repurchase policies are currently determined. We shed light on managers' motives as well as on payout theories....

Our analysis indicates that maintaining the dividend level is a priority on a par with investment decisions. Managers express a strong desire to avoid dividend cuts, except in extraordinary circumstances. However, beyond maintaining a level of dividends per share, payout policy is a second-order concern; that is, increases in dividends are considered only after investment and liquidity needs are met. In contrast to Lintner's era, we find that the target payout ratio is no longer the preeminent decision variable affecting payout decisions. In terms of when nonpayers might initiate dividend payments, two reasons dominate: a sustainable increase in earnings, and demand by institutional investors....

Consistent with a Miller and Modigliani irrelevance theorem, and in contrast to decisions about preserving the level of the dividend, managers make repurchase decisions after investment decisions. Many executives view share repurchases as being more flexible than dividends, and they use this flexibility in an attempt to time the market by accelerating repurchases when they believe their stock price is low. Chief Financial Officers (CFOs) are also very conscious of how repurchases affect earnings per share.... Companies are likely to repurchase when good investments are hard to find, when their stock's float is adequate, and when they wish to offset option dilution.

Executives believe that dividend and repurchase decisions convey information to investors. However, this information conveyance does not appear to be consciously related to signaling in the academic sense. Managers reject the notion that they pay dividends as a costly signal to convey their firm's true worth or to purposefully separate their firm from competitors. Overall, we find little support for both the assumptions and resulting predictions of academic signaling theories that are designed to predict payout policy decisions, at least not in terms of conscious decisions that executives make about payout. . . .

Executives indicate that taxes are a second-order payout policy concern. Most say that tax considerations are not a dominant factor in their decision about whether to pay dividends, or to increase dividends, or in their choice between payout in the form of repurchases or dividends. A follow-up survey conducted in June 2003, dividend taxes had been reduced via legislation, reinforces the second-order importance of taxation. While a minority of executives in that survey say that reduced dividend taxation would lead to dividend increases at their firms, more than two-thirds say that the dividend tax reduction would definitely not or probably not affect their dividend decisions. . . .

The survey by Professors Brav, Graham, Harvey and Michaely also reflects that while 65 percent of those surveyed believed they would raise funds externally to maintain the firm's dividend, only 16 percent would do so to continue prior share repurchase practices. Less than half the executives opined that the existence of good investment projects for the firm was important factor affecting dividend decision it increased to 80 percent when asked if it would affect a share repurchase decision. Finally, 94 percent of those surveyed said they would try to avoid reducing dividends and 88 percent believed there would be negative consequences if dividends were reduced. *Id.* at 490 & 499.

B. JUDICIAL REVIEW OF DIVIDEND POLICY

---

(1) PUBLICLY HELD CORPORATIONS WITH A CONTROLLING SHAREHOLDER

Baron v. Allied Artists Pictures Corporation

Court of Chancery of Delaware. 1975.
337 A.2d 653.

■ BROWN, VICE CHANCELLOR. . . .

Plaintiff charges that the present board of directors of Allied has fraudulently perpetuated itself in office by refusing to pay the accumulated dividend arrearages on preferred stock issued by the corporation which, in turn, permits the preferred stockholders to elect a majority of the board of directors at each annual election so long as the dividend arrearage specified by Allied's certificate of incorporation exists. Defendants contend that the recent financial history and condition of the corporation has justified the nonpayment of the preferred dividend arrearages, at least to the present ...

By way of background, Allied was originally started in the mid–1930's as Sterling Pictures Corporation and later changed its name to Monogram Films under which it gained recognition for many B-pictures and western films. In the early 1950's it changed its name to the present one. Around 1953, with the advent of television, it fell upon hard times. Being in need of capital, Allied's certificate of incorporation was amended in 1954 to permit the issuance of 150,000 shares of preferred stock at a par value of $10.00, with the dividends payable quarterly on a cumulative basis. The amended language of the certificate provides that the preferred shareholders are entitled to receive cash dividends "as and when declared by the Board of Directors, out of funds legally available for the purpose...." The amended certificate further provides that

> "... in case at any time six or more quarterly dividends (whether or not consecutive) on the Preferred Stock shall be in default, in whole or in part, then until all dividends in default on the Preferred Stock shall have been paid or deposited in trust, and the dividend thereon for the current quarterly period shall have been declared and funds for the payment thereof set aside, the holders of the Preferred Stock, voting as a class, shall have the right, at any annual or other meeting for the election of directors, by plurality vote to elect a majority of the Directors of the Corporation." ...

Thereafter, as to the preferred stock issued under the 1954 offering, regular quarterly dividends were paid through March 30, 1963. Subsequently, Allied suffered losses which ultimately impaired the capital represented by the preferred stock as a consequence of which the payment of dividends became prohibited by *8 Del.C. § 170*. Allied has paid no dividends as to the preferred shares since 1963. By September 1964 the corporation was in default on six quarterly dividends and thus the holders of the preferred stock became entitled to elect a majority of the board of directors. They have done so ever since.

As of December 11, 1973 election of directors, Kalvex, Inc. owned 52 per cent of the outstanding preferred stock while owning only 625 shares of Allied's 1,500,000 shares of common stock. Since the filing of the first action herein Kalvex has taken steps to acquire a substantial number of common shares or securities convertible into the same. Thus unquestionably Kalvex, through its control of the preferred shares, is in control of Allied, although its holdings are said to represent only 7 1/2 per cent of the corporation's equity.

Plaintiff points out that the defendant Emanual Wolf, as director, president and chief executive officer of Allied at an annual salary of $100,000, is also president and chief executive officer of Kalvex. Defendant Robert L. Ingis, a director, vice-president and chief financial officer of Allied, is the executive vice-president of Kalvex. Defendants Strauss and Prager, elected as directors by the preferred shareholders, are also vice-presidents of Allied. Of the four directors nominated by management to represent the common stockholders, and duly elected, two serve Allied at salaried positions and two serve as counsel for Allied receiving either directly or through their firm's substantial remuneration for their efforts. Plaintiff asserts that for fiscal 1973, the officers and directors of Allied, as a group, received $402,088 in compensation.

Returning briefly to the fortunes of the corporation, in 1964 Allied was assessed a tax deficiency of some $1,400,000 by the Internal Revenue Service. At the end of fiscal 1963, it had a cumulative deficit of over $5,000,000, a negative net worth of over $1,800,000 and in that year had lost more than $2,700,000. As a consequence Allied entered into an agreement with the Internal Revenue Service to pay off the tax deficiency over a period of years subject to the condition that until the deficiency was satisfied Allied would pay no dividends without the consent of Internal Revenue.

Thereafter Allied's fortunes vacillated with varying degrees of success and failure which, defendants say, is both a hazard and a way of life in the motion picture and theatrical industry. Prior to fiscal 1973 there were only two years, 1969 and 1970, when its preferred capital was not impaired. But plaintiff points out that in 1970 the preferred capital surplus was $1,300,000 at a time when the preferred dividend arrearages were only $146,500. And, while recognizing that Allied suffered net income loss of over $3,000,000 in the following year, 1971, plaintiff further points out that during several years between 1964 and 1973 the corporation had, on occasion, sufficient net income to contribute to the sinking fund or to pay the dividend arrearages. Defendants argue that when viewed overall it was not until the end of the fiscal year terminating June 30, 1973 that Allied had, for the first time, a capital surplus available for preferred dividends, and that this surplus was only $118,000, or less than half of the amount necessary to liquidate the preferred dividend arrearage. (If this constitutes a dispute of fact, I do not consider it to be material for the purpose of this decision.)

Starting with 1972, Allied's financial condition began to improve substantially. It acquired the rights to, produced and distributed the film "Cabaret," which won eight Academy Awards and became the largest grossing film in Allied's history up to that time. It thereafter took a large gamble and committed itself for $7,000,000 for the production and distribution of the film "Papillon." In his initial litigation plaintiff complained vigorously of this, but he has since abandoned his objection since "Papillon" proved to be even a greater financial success than "Cabaret." For fiscal 1973 Allied had net income in excess of $1,400,000 plus a $2,000,000 tax carry-over remaining from its 1971 losses. Presumably its financial situation did not worsen prior to the December 11, 1974 election of directors although unquestionably it has gone forward with financial commitments as to forthcoming film releases.

Throughout all of the foregoing, however, the Internal Revenue agreement, with its dividend restriction, persisted. Prior to the 1973 election the balance owed was some $249,000 and as of the 1974 election, one final payment was due, which presumably has now been made. Prior to the 1973 election, Allied was in default on forty-three quarterly preferred dividends totalling more than $270,000. By the time of the 1974 election, the arrearages exceeded $280,000.

Without attempting to set forth all of the yearly financial data relied upon by the plaintiff, his position is, quite simply, that for one or more years since the preferred shareholders have been in control of Allied the corporate financial statements show that there was either a net income for the preceding fiscal year or a capital surplus at the end of the preceding fiscal year in an amount larger than the accumulated preferred dividend arrearages, and that consequently the board of directors elected by the preferred shareholders, being only a caretaker board, had a duty to use such funds to pay the dividend arrearage, and also the balance due on the Internal Revenue agreement, if necessary, and to thereupon return control of the corporation to the common stockholders at the next annual election. Specifically, plaintiff charges that the corporation had both the legal and financial capability to pay off the Internal Revenue obligation and the dividend arrearage prior to both the 1973 and 1974 annual election of directors which, had it been done, would have prevented the preferred shareholders, as controlled by Kalvex, from reelecting a majority of the board. Thus, plaintiff seeks the Court to order a new election at which Allied's board of directors will be elected by the common stockholders.

Plaintiff stresses that he is not asking the Court to compel the payment of the dividend arrearages, but only that a new election be held because of the preferred board's allegedly wrongful refusal to do so. Since the certificate of incorporation gives preferred shareholders the contractual right to elect a majority of the directors as long as dividends are six quarters in arrears, plaintiff, in effect, is asking that this contractual right be voided because of the deliberate refusal of the preferred shareholders to see themselves paid as soon as funds became legally available for that purpose....

While preferences attaching to stock are the exception and are to be strictly construed, ... it is well established that the rights of preferred stockholders are contract rights. In *Petroleum Rights Corporation v. Midland Royalty Corp., 19 Del.Ch. 334, 167 A. 835 (1933)* a somewhat similar provision of the corporate charter extended to preferred shareholders the right to elect a majority of the board when six quarterly dividends became in arrears, which right continued "*so long as the surplus* ... applicable to the payment of dividends *shall be insufficient to pay all accrued dividends*." The Chancellor there held that as long as there was the prescribed default in dividends and the surplus remained insufficient, the preferred stockholders were entitled to elect a majority of the board. It was argued to him that this right of election and control was limited by the language "so long as the surplus ... shall be insufficient" and that the accumulation of a surplus sufficient to pay all accrued dividends constituted a condition subsequent, the existence of which would forthwith defeat the right to elect control. This view was rejected, on the theory that if accepted it would mean that the sole purpose of such a scheme would be to put the preferred in control to force a payment of passed dividends once a dividend fund became available. The Chancellor concluded that a shift of control should not be made to turn on the personal interests of the preferred shareholders in dividends alone but, in addition, on the consideration that if surplus fell below unpaid dividends the time had arrived to try a new management. *167 A. 837*. He also stated as follows at *167 A. 836*:

> "... if the surplus does in fact exceed the six quarterly dividends in arrear and the preference stock should elect a majority of the board and the board should resolve not to pay the dividends, the right of the preference stock to continue to elect a majority of the board would undoubtedly terminate."

I interpret this to mean that the contractual right to elect a majority of the board continues until the dividends can be made current in keeping with proper corporate management, but that it must terminate once a fund becomes clearly available to satisfy the arrearages and the preference board refuses to do so. Plaintiff seeks to limit this requirement to a mere mathematical availability of funds, and indeed the charter language in *Petroleum Rights* may have intended such a result. Here, however, Allied's charter, and thus its contract with its preferred shareholders, does not limit the right merely until such time as a sufficient surplus exists, as it did in *Petroleum Rights*, but rather it entitles the preferred shareholders to their dividends only "as and when declared by the Board of Directors, out of funds legally available for the purpose." This obviously reposes a discretion in Allied's board to declare preferred dividends, whether it be a board elected by the common or by the preferred shareholders.

The general rule applicable to the right to receive corporate dividends was succinctly stated by Justice Holmes in *Wabash Ry. Co. v. Barclay, 280 U.S. 197, 203, 50 S. Ct. 106, 107, 74 L. Ed. 368 (1930)*:

> "When a man buys stock instead of bonds he takes a greater risk in the business. No one suggests that he has a right to dividends if there are no met earnings. But the investment pre-supposes that the business is to go on, and therefore even if there are net earnings, the holder of stock, preferred as well as common, is entitled to have a dividend declared only out of such part of them as can be applied to dividends *consistently with a wise administration of a going concern*."

Although one purpose of allowing the preferred to elect a majority of the board may be to bring about a payment of the dividend delinquencies as soon as possible, that should not be the sole justification for the existence of a board of directors so elected. During the time that such a preference board is in control of the policies and business decisions of the corporation, it serves the corporation itself and the common shareholders as well as those by whom it was put in office. Corporate directors stand in a fiduciary relationship to their corporation and its shareholders and their primary duty is to deal fairly and justly with both....

The determination as to when and in what amounts a corporation may prudently distribute its assets by way of dividends rests in the honest discretion of the directors in the performance of this fiduciary duty. *Eshleman v. Keenan, 22 Del.Ch. 82, 194 A. 40 (1937)*, aff'd *23 Del.Ch. 234, 2 A.2d 904*; *Treves v. Menzies, 37 Del.Ch., 330, 142 A.2d 520 (1958)*. Before a court will interfere with the judgment of a board of directors in refusing to declare dividends, fraud or gross abuse of discretion must be shown. *Moskowitz v. Bantrell, Del.Supr., 41 Del. Ch. 177, 190 A.2d 749 (1963)*. And this is true even if a fund does exist from which dividends could legally be paid ...

Plaintiff here appears to be asking that an exception be carved from these well established principles where the nonpayment of dividends and arrearages results in continued control by the very board which determines not to pay them. As I understand his argument, he asks for a ruling that a board of directors elected by preferred shareholders whose dividends are in arrears has an absolute duty to pay off all preferred dividends due and to return control to the common shareholders as soon as funds become legally available for that purpose, regardless of anything else. Thus, in effect, he would have the court limit the discretion given the board by the certificate of incorporation, and make the decision to pay arrearages mandatory upon the emergence of a lawful financial source even though the corporate charter does not require it (as perhaps it did in *Petroleum Rights*). He has offered no precedent for such a proposition, and I decline to create one....

When the yearly hit-and-miss financial history of Allied from 1964 through 1974 is considered along with the Internal Revenue obligation during the same time span, I cannot conclude, as a matter of law, that Allied's board has been guilty of perpetuating itself in office by wrongfully refusing to apply corporate funds to the liquidation of the preferred dividend arrearages and the accelerated payment of the Internal Revenue debt. Thus I find no basis on the record before me to set aside the 1974 annual election and to order a new one through a master appointed by the court....

It is clear, however, that Allied's present board does have a fiduciary duty to see that the preferred dividends are brought up to date as soon as possible in keeping with prudent business management. *Petroleum Rights Corporation v. Midland Royalty Corp., supra*; *Eshleman v. Keenan, supra.* This is particularly true now that the Internal Revenue debt has been satisfied in full and business is prospering. It cannot be permitted indefinitely to plough back all profits in future commitments so as to avoid full satisfaction of the rights of the preferred to their dividends and the otherwise normal right of the common stockholders to elect corporate management. While previous limitations on net income and capital surplus may offer a justification for the past, continued limitations in a time of greatly increased cash flow could well create new issues in the area of business discretion for the future....

Plaintiff's motion for summary judgment is denied. Defendants' motion for summary judgment is granted....

See also **Sinclair Oil Corp. v. Levien, Chapter 11, supra;** Gabelli & Co. v. Liggett Group Inc., 479 A.2d 276 (Del.1984); Berwald v. Mission Development Co., 40 Del.Ch. 509, 185 A.2d 480 (Del. 1962).

NOTE ON SV INVESTMENT PARTNERS, LLC v. THOUGHT-WORKS, INC., 7 A.3d 973 (Del. Ch. 2010). How should a provision requiring preferred shares to be repurchased to the extent the corporation had "funds legally available?" As will be seen later, section 160 of Delaware statute authorize repurchases of shares to the extent the repurchase does not impair capital (i.e., a repurchase is not in violation of the provision so long as *after* the purchase assets are greater than the sum of outstanding liabilities and the aggregate par value of outstanding shares). SV Investments held preferred shares and demanded their right to have the shares be redeemed when thee were "funds legally available" be honored, arguing that the repurchase would not have caused any impairment. The Vice–Chancellor upheld the directors' decision not to redeem the shares, holding that despite the provision the board of directors had discretion not to redeem the shares if they believe the repurchase would threaten the future solvency of the firm. Moreover, the court reasoned that the reference to "funds" must be interpreted to mean more than that the repurchase was legally permissible under the governing statute and concluded that "funds" in this context meant the existence of some available source of cash. Since the company would have had to borrow the sums to carry out the purchase the court concluded there were no such funds available.

---

(2) CLOSE CORPORATIONS

SMITH v. ATLANTIC PROPERTIES, INC.

[See Chapter 8, supra]

DODGE v. FORD MOTOR CO.

[See Chapter 4, supra]

NOTE ON COMPELLING DIVIDENDS IN CLOSE CORPORATIONS

It is hard to imagine a real-life scenario today in which the courts would order a publicly held corporation to pay a dividend. Indeed, traditionally the courts have been reluctant to order the declaration of dividends even in the close-corporation context. See, e.g., Gottfried v. Gottfried, 73 N.Y.S.2d 692 (1947). There are signs of a shift in this area, accompanying the courts' increased understanding of close-corporation dynamics. For example, in Miller v. Magline, Inc., 76 Mich.App. 284, 256 N.W.2d 761 (1977), Magline's stock was owned by eight shareholders—most or all of whom were officers and employees—and their relatives. The principal shareholders and officers were Miller, Thorpe, and Law. In 1950 these three adopted a policy under which corporate managers were compensated by a low base salary coupled with an incentive bonus based on a percentage of earnings. The remaining profits were retained for working capital, and apparently no dividends were paid.

This policy was satisfactory to all concerned until 1962, when Miller ceased his active role in corporate management as a result of a serious injury, and Thorpe resigned as vice-president. The board then adopted resolutions confirming Law and other shareholders (excluding the plaintiffs who collectively owned 41 percent of the common) in their respective offices, and fixing the incentive bonuses at an aggregate of 23% of net earnings before taxes. The employment resolutions remained in effect until 1966, when the board reduced the incentive bonuses to an aggregate of 14–1/2% of net earnings before taxes, but raised base salaries. During 1963–1968, corporate earnings—and hence incentive bonuses—increased dramatically, due to Viet Nam defense procurement contracts. Thus while Law received compensation of $10,016 in 1962, from 1963 to 1968 his compensation was $22,664, $92,419, $137,558, $75,402, $120,183, and $107,887, respectively. Meanwhile, Magline's earned surplus during this period increased from $459,710 to $2,492,156. Miller and Thorpe, who were no longer actively employed, brought suit to compel the corporation to pay dividends. The Chancellor ordered the corporation to pay a dividend of $75 per share for the period July 1, 1963 to June 30, 1968:

> It is our opinion ... that the directors of the management group were placed in the impossible situation of trying to give an impartial answer to the determination as to whether dividends should be granted. They already were taking a profit distribution via a percentile of profits before taxes. Therefore, we deem it an untenable position to argue that nonpayment of dividends is justified on the basis that such a concept of profit distribution would imperil the continued well being of the corporation. If such retention of profits were indicated they should have been more diligent in seeing that distributions based upon percentage of profits also should be curtailed....
>
> ... To the extent that the management group, as directors, has adopted a nondividend policy, we are of the opinion that it

> has defeated one of the major purposes of a profit corporation, that is, to accumulate profits and divide them amongst the corporate owners when that is reasonable and proper.

The Michigan Court of Appeals affirmed:

> . . . In the landmark case on court-compelled dividends for closed corporations, Dodge v. Ford Motor Co., 204 Mich. 459, 500, 170 N.W. 668, 682, 3 A.L.R. 413 (1919), the Court adopted the following statements:
>
> . . . *The discretion of the directors will not be interfered with by the courts, unless there has been bad faith, wilful neglect, or abuse of discretion.* (Emphasis added.)
>
> Defendant contends that under the business judgment rule a court may not compel a dividend in the absence of clear and convincing proof of fraud, conspiracy, waste, or gross abuse of discretion by the board of directors. In so arguing, defendant carefully elides the statement in the rules above quoted that a court may compel a dividend when the board's refusal to declare one would constitute a "breach of that good faith which they are bound to exercise towards the stockholders." Dodge v. Ford Motor Co., supra, at 500, 170 N.W. at 682, quoting Hunter v. Roberts, Throp & Co., 83 Mich. 63, 71, 47 N.W. 131 (1890). Breach of this fiduciary duty amounts to a breach of trust, and has consistently been recognized in Michigan as a ground for court intervention. Under the circumstances here, their participating in a distribution to them of those profits and a squirreling away of the balance to meet future needs is, in our opinion, inequitable in not giving consideration properly to the needs and requirements of all of the stockholders of the corporation.

In the course of its opinion, the court analyzed and rejected arguments that a dividend was inappropriate on the grounds that Magline had working-capital shortages, Magline might be subject to government-contract-renegotiation liability, Magline's plant was becoming outmoded and would require extensive renovation, Magline's business was cyclical and highly competitive, and losses were predicted for the upcoming fiscal year ending 1970.

See also, e.g., Cole Real Estate Corp. v. Peoples Bank & Trust Co., 160 Ind.App. 88, 310 N.E.2d 275 (1974).

Where a close corporation pays salaries to some shareholders, while not declaring dividends, as an alternative to ordering the payment of dividends the court may order dissolution or a mandatory buyout on the ground of oppression. See Chapter 8, supra.

SECTION 2. LIMITATIONS ON DIVIDENDS UNDER CREDITORS' RIGHTS LAW

Traditionally, dividends have been regulated by two very different, overlapping, sets of legal rules. The first set of rules is located in creditor's rights (or fraudulent-conveyance) law. These rules center on, but are not limited to, the concept of insolvency, and emphasize the liability of *shareholders* for the *receipt* of improper dividends. The second set of rules is located in state corporation law. These rules emphasize the liability of *directors* for the *payment* of improper dividends. Limitations on dividends under the law of creditor's rights will be considered in this Section. Limitations on dividends under corporation law will be considered in Section 3.

N.Y. BUS. CORP. LAW §§ 102(a)(8), 510(a), (b)

[See Statutory Supplement]

UNIFORM FRAUDULENT TRANSFER ACT §§ 1, 2, 4, 5

[See Statutory Supplement]

BANKRUPTCY CODE §§ 101(32), 548(a)

[See Statutory Supplement]

BACKGROUND NOTE ON THE LAW OF CREDITORS' RIGHTS

1. *Definition*. Creditors' rights law imposes several limitations on transfers of assets without adequate consideration. The most prominent limits turns on the concept of insolvency. Insolvency limits on transfers are based on the transferor's financial condition in terms of either (i) its inability to pay its debts as they become due, or (ii) whether its liabilities exceed its assets. Accordingly, there are two broad definitions of the term *insolvency*.

The first definition—inability to pay debts as they become due—is embodied in most corporate dividend statutes, such as N.Y.Bus.Corp. Law § 102(a)(8). This is known as the *equity meaning* of insolvency, because it was the test generally applied by the equity courts, which had jurisdiction over insolvent estates before the enactment of the federal bankruptcy statute.

The second definition of insolvency—liabilities in excess of assets—is embodied in the Bankruptcy Code and the Uniform Fraudulent Transfer Act ("UFTA"). This second definition is known as the *bankruptcy meaning* of insolvency.[1]

---

1. Under the Bankruptcy Code, the test for whether a debtor can be put into involuntary bankruptcy turns principally on whether the debtor is insolvent in the equity sense. See 11 U.S.C.A. § 303(h). However, once a debtor has been put into bankruptcy, the bankruptcy

> The difference between these two conceptions can be very great. The equity insolvency test is concerned with current liquidity of the going enterprise; the emphasis of the bankruptcy sense of insolvency is upon liquidation of the enterprise. It is easily possible for an enterprise to be short of cash and other liquid means of payment while at the same time holding illiquid assets of great value; such an enterprise may well fail the equity insolvency test. It is also a quite possible occurrence for an enterprise to have a large current cash flow while steadily operating at a loss and suffering a continuing erosion of its asset base; in time, such an enterprise will fail to meet the bankruptcy test of insolvency.
>
> Those with any familiarity with accounting will recognizes that the equity insolvency test is concerned with the income and cash flow statements of the enterprise while the bankruptcy insolvency test is focused on the balance sheet of the enterprise. For this reason, the bankruptcy insolvency test is frequently referred to as the "balance sheet" or "net worth" test.

B. Manning & J. Hanks, Legal Capital 64 (3d ed. 1990).

2. *Application of Fraudulent Conveyance Laws to Dividends.* There is some academic controversy concerning whether fraudulent-conveyance laws are applicable to dividends. However, the cases, while few, uniformly hold that dividends are subject to those laws. See Barbara Black, Corporate Dividends and Stock Repurchases § 4.05[6][b] (1998).

3. *Unreasonably Small Capital.* Another important limitation on transfer under the UFTA and cognate Acts is that a transfer without adequate consideration is prohibited if it would leave the transferor with unreasonably small capital.

> After the promulgation of the [Uniform Fraudulent Conveyance Act,] section 5 [the predecessor of UFTA § 4] received little independent notice. The case law that did develop, however, did little to illuminate the basic question: what is the scope of the unreasonably small capital provision? ... The main view, to the extent that one developed, focused on the transferor's ability to marshall sufficient cash, either from operations, equity infusions, new loans or some combination of these, to pay expected creditors. These cases took a forward looking view, comparing anticipated cash flow against anticipated debt incurrence.

Markell, Toward True and Plain Dealing: A Theory of Fraudulent Transfers Involving Unreasonably Small Capital, 21 Ind.L.Rev. 469, 487 (1988).

4. *Insolvency Under the Dividend Statutes.* Many corporate-law dividend statutes explicitly incorporate an insolvency limitation on the

---

trustee's right to avoid a pre-bankruptcy transfer turns in large part on whether at the time of the transfer the debtor was insolvent in the bankruptcy sense. See 11 U.S.C.A. §§ 101(32), 548.

The bankruptcy meaning of insolvency is itself susceptible to different nuances, as may be seen by comparing 11 U.S.C.A. § 101(32) with UFTA § 2(a).

payment of dividends. See, e.g., N.Y.Bus.Corp.Law § 510. Others do not, although they may embody parallel concepts. The Official Comment to Model Act § 6.40 states that "[t]he Revised Model Business Corporation Act establishes the validity of distributions from the corporate law standpoint under section 6.40 and determines the potential liability of directors for improper distributions under sections 8.30 and 8.33. The federal Bankruptcy Act and state fraudulent conveyance statutes, on the other hand, are designed to enable the trustee or other representative to recapture for the benefit of creditors funds distributed to others in some circumstances. In light of these diverse purposes, it was not thought necessary to make the tests of section 6.40 identical to the tests for insolvency under these various statutes." Cal.Corp.Code § 506(d), which governs the liability of shareholders who have received improper dividends, provides that "[n]othing contained in this section affects any liability which any shareholder may have under [the Uniform Fraudulent Transfer Act]."

SECTION 3. LIMITATIONS ON DIVIDENDS UNDER THE CORPORATE STATUTES

A. INTRODUCTION

1. *In General.* In addition to limitations placed on dividends under the law of creditors' rights, corporate law also governs the power to declare and pay dividends. Cases like Dodge v. Ford, supra, concern the issue, when may a corporation be *compelled* to pay dividends. Most of the law of dividends, however, centers on *limitations* on a corporation's power to pay dividends. These limitations may be thought of as financial, in the narrow sense that they are not based on judicial determinations of sound dividend policy, but instead turn on quantified objective tests. Under traditional statutes, however, the limitations involve concepts that are typically of little or no relevance under modern financial theory.

2. *Who Does Corporate Dividend Law Protect?* A preliminary issue raised by the corporate law of dividends is, who does this body of law protect? The class of persons protected by creditors' rights law is clear—creditors. The classes of persons protected by the corporate dividend statutes has not always been clear.

Obviously, one group of persons who could be protected by these statutes is creditors. As stated in D. Kehl, Corporate Dividends (1941), "With the liability of corporate stockholders ... limited to the amount of capital subscribed ... it soon became apparent that the original capital should be permanently devoted to the needs of the corporation as at least a partial substitute for the unlimited personal liability existing in individual enterprise.'' But then, ''If the creation of a capital fund was not to defeat its purpose, safeguards against its withdrawal by repayment to shareholders in the guise of dividends, or otherwise, were indispensable. Historically, the principal objective of dividend law has therefore been the preservation of a minimum of assets as a safeguard in assuring the payment of creditors' claims.''

In addition to creditors, some of the corporate dividend statutes are also designed to protect the preferences of preferred shareholders.

Finally, at one time it was thought that the corporate dividend statutes were intended to protect common shareholders, partly on the ground that excessive dividends might injure the corporate enterprise, and partly on the ground that dividends out of capital might mislead shareholders into thinking that the corporation was earning money when in fact it wasn't.

Today, the concept that the corporate dividend statutes protect common shareholders is not generally accepted. Furthermore, although the protection that the statutes give to preferred shareholders may sometimes be significant, many corporations have no preferred shareholders. That leaves the protection of creditors. As the following materials will show, however, in fact creditors get very little protection from the traditional dividend statutes.

3. *Traditional and modern dividend statutes*. The dividend statutes can be divided into traditional and modern statutes. The traditional statutes, in turn, can be divided into two subcategories. Most of the traditional statutes center on a *capital-impairment test* (sometimes referred to as the *capital-and-surplus* or *balance-sheet test*). A few are centered on an *earned-surplus* (or *income-statement* test). The following sections will discuss the traditional capital-impairment statutes, the traditional earned-surplus statutes, and the modern statutes, respectively.

B. TRADITIONAL STATUTES—CAPITAL-IMPAIRMENT STATUTES

---

(1) THE CAPITAL-IMPAIRMENT TEST AND ITS MEANING

DEL. GEN. CORP. LAW §§ 141(e), 154, 170

[See Statutory Supplement]

N.Y. BUS. CORP. LAW §§ 102(a)(9), (12), (13), 506, 510

[See Statutory Supplement]

---

1. *Legal Capital and Par Value*. Most traditional statutes turn on the concept of *legal capital*. That concept, in turn, can only be understood against the background of a concept known as *par* or *par value*.

a. *Par value*. Originally, the par value of a share was the price at which it was expected that the share would be issued (sold) by the corporation. Thus in the paradigm case, a share that carried a $100 par value would be issued for $100. Indeed, where par value continues, corporate statutes provide that the shares will be deemed fully paid and beyond any assessment only if the full par value of the shares was paid when initially issued. Eventually, a practice emerged under which the par value of stock was not the price at which the stock was to be issued, but a purely nominal amount. For example, stock that was to be issued at $100 might carry a par value of only $1, or even less. Such stock is known as *low-par value* stock. Still later, the statutes were amended to allow the issuance of *no-par value* stock—that is, stock that did not carry any par value at all.

b. *Legal capital*. *Legal capital* is the sum of (i) the par value of all par-value stock, and (ii) such additional amounts as the board assigns to capital, either in connection with the issuance of low-par or no-par stock, or thereafter. Legal capital (or *stated capital*) is a legal construct, with little or no economic reality. *Economic capital* is the amount that the owners of an enterprise have invested in the enterprise, directly or indirectly. When stock was issued at its par value, the concepts of economic and legal capital were tied together. The advent of low-par and no-par stock severed that tie. Because the concept of legal capital is tied to par value, it has become artificial. Nevertheless, the concept still remains important under the traditional dividend statutes.

2. *Structure of the Traditional Statutes*. Most traditional corporate dividend statutes begin with an insolvency test. There are three possible reasons why these statutes employ an insolvency test, which would be applicable in any event under creditors' rights law. First, it has not always been entirely clear whether creditors' rights law applies to dividends. Second, creditors' rights laws emphasize the liability of transferees (in the case of corporations, shareholders) for improper distributions. In contrast, the corporate dividend statutes emphasize the liability of directors. Third, the basic creditors' rights laws—the Bankruptcy Code and the Uniform Fraudulent Transfer Act, and cognate statutes—turn on the bankruptcy meaning of insolvency. In contrast, a dividend statute may employ either the equity meaning of insolvency or both the bankruptcy and the equity meanings.

After beginning with an insolvency test, the traditional dividend statutes add a second basic test, which is frequently subject to important exceptions. The most common second basic test is a capital-impairment test. The capital-impairment statutes center on whether after the dividend the corporation's assets exceed its liabilities plus its legal capital. Under this test, a dividend cannot be paid if, before or after payment of the dividend, the corporation's assets are or would be less than the sum of its liabilities plus its legal capital or, in some cases, the sum of liabilities, capital, and liquidation preferences. (In contrast, under the bankruptcy meaning of the insolvency test, a dividend may be paid as long as after the payment the corporation's assets will exceed its liabilities.) Capital-impairment statutes can be conceptualized in two, functionally identical ways: as prohibiting dividends out of legal capital, or as permitting dividends only out of surplus (the excess of the firm's assets over the combined amount of its liabilities and legal capital).

NOTE ON REVALUATION OF ASSETS AND KLANG v. SMITH'S FOOD & DRUG CENTERS, INC.

Corporate dividend statutes invariably contain accounting-based terms such as "assets" and "liabilities." Financial statements are prepared according to a host of conventions and principles; the bedrock of most of these principles is that in reporting a firm's financial position and performance accounting items such as an asset or a liability are based on its historical cost figure and do not reflect increases in an item since its acquisition. Thus, assets are recorded at cost, *reduced* by reasonable charges for amortization or depreciation to reflect that assets (with the exception of land) lose their usefulness due to obsolescence, wear and tear, and the like. Similarly, liabilities are recorded at the amount of the contractual obligation due the creditor, even if in the hands of the creditor the debt's market value is substantially below the face value of the debt because of uncertainty whether the debtor firm will be able to fully satisfy the debt when it comes due. Thus, the convention that assets and liabilities should be recorded at their cost is a pervasive convention under generally accepted accounting principles (GAAP). This statement, however, is qualified, in the case of assets for which, as mentioned earlier, are reduced by periodic amortization and depreciation as well as any material permanent impairment of the asset's value. Given the pervasiveness of the cost convention within GAAP, should similar conservatism carry over to interpreting dividend statutes use of accounting-based terms such as assets and liabilities?

Beginning in the 1940s, there was a long debate in the scholarly literature on whether a capital-impairment test permitted the payment of dividends up to the difference between the *actual value* of the corporation's assets and its liabilities and capital, or only up to the difference between the corporation's assets and its liabilities and capital *as shown on the corporation's balance sheet*. The debate was largely triggered by the leading case of Randall v. Bailey, 23 N.Y.S.2d 173 (Sup.Ct. 1940), aff'd, 288 N.Y. 280, 43 N.E.2d 43 (1942), in which the New York courts permitted the board of directors to premise declaration of a dividend on an *upward* valuation of the firm's assets, i.e., without the increase in the amount of assets the dividend would have impaired the firm's capital.

Similar to the result reached in *Randall*, the Delaware Supreme Court in Klang v. Smith's Food & Drug Centers, Inc., 702 A.2d 150 (Del. 1997), held that a firm did not impair its capital and thereby violate section 160 of the Delaware General Corporation Law by repurchasing its shares when they relied on a consultant's (Houlihan's) report that the firm's assets were significantly above their level determined according to GAAP.

> It is helpful to recall the purpose behind Section 160. The General Assembly enacted the statute to prevent boards from draining corporations of assets to the detriment of creditors and the long-term health of the corporation. That a corporation has not yet realized or reflected on its balance sheet the appreciation of assets is irrelevant to this concern. Regardless of what a balance sheet that has not been updated may show, an actual, though unrealized, appreciation reflects real economic value that the corporation may borrow against or that creditors may claim or levy upon. Allowing corporations to revalue assets and liabilities to reflect current realities complies with the statute and serves well the policies behind this statute....
>
> We believe that plaintiff reads too much into Section 154. The statute simply defines "net assets" in the course of defining "surplus." It does not mandate a "facts and figures balancing of assets and liabilities" to determine by what amount, if any, total assets exceeds total liabilities. The statute is merely definitional. It does not require any particular method of calculating surplus, but simply prescribes factors that any such calculation must include....
>
> We are satisfied that the Houlihan opinion adequately took into account all of SFD's assets and liabilities....
>
> The record contains, in the form of the Houlihan opinion, substantial evidence that the transactions complied with Section 160. Plaintiff has provided no reason to distrust Houlihan's analysis. In cases alleging impairment of capital under Section 160, the trial court may defer to the board's measurement of surplus unless a plaintiff can show that the directors "failed to fulfill their duty to evaluate the assets on the basis of acceptable data and by standards which they are entitled to believe reasonably reflect present values." In the absence of bad faith or fraud on the part of the board, courts will not "substitute [our] concepts of wisdom for that of the directors." Here, plaintiff does not argue that the SFD Board acted in bad faith. Nor has he met his burden of showing that the methods and data that underlay the board's analysis are unreliable or that its determination of surplus is so far off the mark as to constitute actual or constructive fraud.[12] There-

12. We interpret 8 *Del.C.* § 172 to entitle boards to rely on experts such as Houlihan to determine compliance with 8 *Del.C.* § 160. Plaintiff has not alleged that the SFD Board failed to exercise reasonable care in selecting Houlihan, nor that rendering a solvency opinion is outside Houlihan's realm of competence. Compare 8 *Del.C.* § 141(e) (providing that directors may rely in good faith on records, reports, experts, etc.).

> fore, we defer to the board's determination of surplus, and hold that SFD's self-tender offer did not violate 8 *Del.C.* § 160.

702 A.2d at 154–156.

Are there good policy reasons to reject the outcomes reached in *Randall* and *Klang*? When a board relies on appraised value of the firm's assets that are higher than their historical cost, does this erode the protection of creditors (assuming the appraisal is a reliable one)? Assume the company is a wholesaler of copper and that the price for copper has increased world-wide by 20 percent and ninety percent of the firm's assets are its inventory of copper. Under the Delaware statute can this firm rely on this increase in the value of its inventory to declare a dividend to its stockholders? Repurchase shares? Does such a distribution pose a threat to creditors? The future of the firm?

NOTE ON BALANCE SHEET ACCOUNTING FOR CORPORATE EQUITY

Corporate balance-sheet accounting has traditionally differed from accounting for proprietorships and partnerships in the way that equity (ownership interests) is treated. In the sole proprietorship and the partnership, equity as it appears on the balance sheet is normally a fairly straightforward account. In the corporation, however, equity has traditionally been divided into Stated Capital and Surplus. Surplus, in turn, has been redivided into a number of further subaccounts.

To begin with, *Stated Capital* (or Capital Stock) consists of the total par value of issued stock that has par value, plus any other amounts allocated to capital by the board. The two most important *Surplus* accounts are Earned Surplus and Capital Surplus.

Broadly speaking, capital surplus is that portion of surplus that is derived from sources other than earnings, such as amounts paid for stock in excess of the stock's par value. In theory, the permissibility of dividends out of capital surplus marks the major difference between the capital-impairment and earned-surplus tests: Under a capital-impairment test, dividends can be paid out of capital surplus unless specifically prohibited, because such dividends do not impair capital. In contrast, under an earned-surplus test, dividends can be paid out of capital surplus only if specifically permitted, because capital surplus is not earned surplus. In practice, however, as will be seen, the two tests converge.

Two of the most important types of capital surplus are *paid-in surplus* and *reduction surplus*.

1. *Paid-in Surplus*. Paid-in surplus is the excess of (i) the total sale price of newly issued stock over (ii) that portion of the sale price that constitutes par value or is otherwise allocated by the board to stated capital. This type of surplus is a byproduct of the low-par and no-par phenomena, because it does not arise if stock is issued at par value. In an economic sense, paid-in surplus constitutes capital, be-

cause it is part of the shareholders' initial equity investment. Nevertheless, the capital-impairment statutes routinely permit dividends out of paid-in surplus.

2. *Reduction Surplus*. Reduction surplus is the amount by which stated capital is reduced through corporate action pursuant to statutory authority. There are a number of techniques for reducing capital and thereby creating reduction surplus. The most significant of these techniques is to amend the certificate of incorporation to reduce the par value of the corporation's stock. Such a reduction creates a new surplus fund equal to the amount by which stated capital has been reduced. This fund is called reduction surplus, and is a subcategory of capital surplus.

In recent years, accountants have tended to substitute descriptive nomenclature for the traditional Surplus terminology. For example, Earned Surplus is given a title such as Retained Income, Retained Earnings, or Accumulated Earnings. Paid-in Surplus is given a title such as Capital Contributed for Shares in Excess of Par or Stated Value. However, the new titles do not work a difference in substance, and courts, legislators, and lawyers have continued to use the old terminology.

As will be shown later in this Chapter, Capital and Surplus accounts, and their modern counterparts like Retained Earnings, have become irrelevant under many of the newer dividend statutes. However, the terms are likely to continue in use on financial statements, both because many statutes (including those of important corporate states like Delaware and New York) still turn on capital-and-surplus concepts, and because accountants are unlikely to quickly drop long-established practices.

(2) EXCEPTIONS TO THE BASIC CAPITAL–IMPAIRMENT TEST

(a) Nimble Dividends

DEL. GEN. CORP. LAW § 170

[See Statutory Supplement]

Under a few statutes, like that of Delaware, dividends can be paid out of current profits even if capital is or would be impaired. Such dividends are known as *nimble dividends*. The term "nimble" is used to describe such dividends because under the statutes the dividend can be paid only out of *current* profits, so that directors must be sufficiently nimble to declare the dividends before the close of the current period or within a short time thereafter.

One justification that has been put forward for permitting dividends out of current profits, even when capital is impaired, is that this technique allows the corporation to continue regular dividends on its preferred stock. Another is that a corporation that has suffered heavy losses may need to attract new capital to remain viable, and may be unable to attract new capital if it cannot pay dividends.

Both justifications are thin. Essentially, the ability to pay nimble dividends, in states that permit such dividends, seems to be an erosion—one of many—in the idea that capital should be preserved to protect creditors.

(b) Wasting–Asset Corporations

NOTE ON WASTING–ASSET CORPORATIONS

Normally, in determining profits—and therefore surplus—a corporation must subtract from its gross revenues an appropriate amount for depreciation or depletion. However, some statutes, like N.Y.Bus. Corp.Law § 510(b) and Del.Gen.Corp.Law § 170(b), provide that in the case of a wasting-asset corporation, profits can be calculated for dividend purposes without regard to depreciation or depletion, subject to certain limitations. A *wasting-asset* corporation is a corporation that is in the business of exploiting a non-replenishable asset, like a coal mine, an oil well, a rock quarry, or a patent.

The justification sometimes given for permitting dividends without regard to an allowance for depletion of a wasting asset is that all concerned parties expect that the corporation's lifetime will be limited to the lifetime of the wasting asset, so that there is no reason to preserve the corporation's capital beyond the lifetime of that asset. This justification, like the justification for nimble dividends, is thin, because many corporations with wasting assets either hold nonwasting assets as well, hold a portfolio of wasting assets that is continually refreshed, or both.

(c) Dividends out of Capital Surplus

N.Y. BUS. CORP. LAW §§ 102(a)(9), (13), (14), 510, 516, 520

[See Statutory Supplement]

DEL. GEN. CORP. LAW §§ 154, 170, 242(a)(3), 244

[See Statutory Supplement]

NOTE ON DIVIDENDS OUT OF CAPITAL SURPLUS

The capital-impairment statutes routinely permit dividends out of both paid-in surplus and reduction surplus, with no significant safeguards for creditors beyond those imposed by the insolvency test. The payment of dividends out of capital surplus seems anomalous under a capital-impairment statute, in which the emphasis is placed on preservation of capital. The power of the corporation to reduce capital, and pay dividends out of the resulting reduction surplus, creates a gaping breach in the purported wall set up by dividend law to protect the interests of creditors.

C. TRADITIONAL STATUTES—EARNED-SURPLUS STATUTES

NOTE ON THE EARNED-SURPLUS TEST

At one time, the Model Act employed a test for dividends that centered on whether a corporation had *earned surplus*. Earned surplus was defined as "the portion of . . . surplus . . . equal to the balance of . . . net profits, income, gains and losses from the date of incorporation . . . after deducting subsequent distributions to shareholders and transfers to stated capital and capital surplus made out of earned surplus." William Hackney commented as follows:

> In attempting to formulate statutory language limiting dividends to income, two distinct approaches were found possible.
>
> One is, like the capital-impairment restriction, a balance-sheet test. The surplus of net assets in excess of capital is obtained and then analyzed and any which is not paid-in or other capital surplus is deemed accumulated income.
>
> The second approach . . . is to take the balance of all the corporate income statements to date and deduct dividends and other transfers therefrom, with the remainder being earned surplus.
>
> The [1969] Model Act definition, it seems, utilizes the aggregate-income-statement method of arriving at earned surplus. It does not use the balance sheet as a source of reference but directs one to take the balance of net profits, income, gains and losses over a period of time.[1]

---

1. Hackney, The Financial Provisions of the Model Business Corporations Act, 70 Harv.L.Rev. 1357, 1365–66 (1957).

Despite the focus on earned surplus, the prior version of the Model Act, and the statutes that continue to follow this earlier version of the Model Act also permit dividends out of capital surplus if so authorized by the articles of incorporation, or approved by the shareholders, and was identified as a distribution from capital; there were no accrued dividends on an issue of cumulative preferred stock; and the dividend did not impair the liquidation preference of preferred stock. In practice, therefore, the earned surplus test tended to converge with the capital-impairment test.

As Hackney pointed out, "The net result [of earned-surplus statutes based on the old Model Act] is an apparent limitation of the funds available for dividends to earned surplus, but actually, in so far as real protection to creditors or preferred stockholders is concerned, there is a complete eradication of the concept of common capital as a cushion protecting the senior interests." Hackney, The Financial Provisions of the Model Business Corporation Act, 70 Harv.L.Rev. 1357, 1389 (1957).

The current version of the Model Act has dropped the earned-surplus approach. That approach is now followed by only a few statutes.

SECTION 4. THE MODERN DIVIDEND STATUTES

CAL. CORP. CODE §§ 114, 166, 500–503, 507

[See Statutory Supplement]

MODEL BUS. CORP. ACT §§ 1.40(6), 6.40

[See Statutory Supplement]

California's dividend provisions, enacted in 1977, marked a sweeping break with traditional dividend statutes. Until that time, the foundation of most statutes was a legal concept—stated capital. In contrast, the foundation of the California statute is a set of economic realities: retained earnings, asset-liability ratios, liquidation preferences, and an insolvency test. The Model Business Corporation Act followed suit in breaking with the traditional statutes, although it employed a much different approach than the California statute. Among other things, these statutes eliminate the concept of par value for all practical purposes.

KUMMERT, STATE STATUTORY RESTRICTIONS ON FINANCIAL DISTRIBUTIONS BY CORPORATIONS TO SHAREHOLDERS (pt. II), 59 Wash.L.Rev. 185, 282–84 (1984). "[The California and Model Business Corporation Act approaches] have some remarkable similarities. [Both] proceed from a common assessment of the inadequacies of the concept of legal capital to abolish not only the statutory underpinnings of the concept (the notion of par value and accounting rules for consideration received for shares), but also the series of exceptions (nimble dividends, depletion dividends, and special repurchases of shares) and fictions (treasury shares) erected because of the existence of the concept. [Both] subject transfers of cash or property, or incurrences of indebtedness, by a corporation without consideration to its shareholders to a single set of restrictions, regardless of the form in which the transfer, or incurrence, occurs. [Both] address applications of the restrictions to such transfers, or incurrences, where the transferor, or obligor, is either the parent, or the subsidiary, of another corporation. Finally, drafters of each of the systems based their efforts on the premise that statutory systems founded on legal capital were essentially misleading insofar as they led creditors and senior security holders to believe that such systems operated to protect their interests.

"[D]espite these similarities, the [California and Model Act] systems can be clearly distinguished on the basis of their respective responses to that possible misrepresentation. The California series attempts to rectify the misrepresentation by promulgating rules that will provide creditors and senior shareholders with the type of protection they *thought* they were getting from the legal capital system. On the other hand, the ... Model Act [attempts] to rectify the misrepresentation by promulgating rules that will provide creditors and senior shareholders with the level of protection that the drafters perceived such groups *actually received* from the legal capital system. This variance in fundamental goals in turn produces the significant differences between the Acts on such issues as the relative freedom directors have and the status in the event of financial difficulty of debt issued on repurchase of shares."

SECTION 5. CONTRACTUAL RESTRICTIONS ON THE PAYMENT OF DIVIDENDS

It should be obvious by now that the traditional dividend statutes provide little protection to creditors beyond that already afforded by the law of creditors' rights. These statutes are so liberal in allowing capital surplus to be created, either through the use of no-par or low-par capitalization when stock is originally issued, or thereafter through a reduction of capital, that corporations can usually make routine distributions out of economic (although not "legal") capital, even in the absence of retained earnings.

Involuntary creditors, trade creditors, and short-term lenders must normally take the protection of dividend law as they find it. Institutional lenders, however, who provide large amounts of money over a long period of time, have the power to impose contractual restrictions on dividends beyond the weak limits imposed by corporation law, and often do so. Similar restrictions are often extracted by underwriters in connection with bonds and preferred stock issued to the public. Indeed, as a practical matter, it may be said that much of the modern law of dividends is contractual rather than statutory. The practical question is usually not whether a dividend is prohibited by statute, but whether it is prohibited by arrangements with lending institutions or provisions agreed upon in connection with bond or preferred-stock financing.

FORM OF BOND INDENTURE PROVISION RESTRICTING DIVIDENDS

[See Statutory Supplement]

SECTION 6. LIABILITY OF DIRECTORS FOR IMPROPER DIVIDENDS

Liability for an improper dividend is governed by two bodies of law: corporation law, and the law of creditors' rights. Liability may be imposed on the directors who authorize the dividend, on the shareholders who receive it, or both. In general, corporation law tends to emphasize the liability of directors, while creditors' rights law tends to emphasize the liability of shareholders.

Subject to certain exceptions, liability for an improper repurchase of a corporation's own stock is treated the same way as liability for an improper dividend.

N.Y. BUS. CORP. LAW § 719

[See Statutory Supplement]

MODEL BUS. CORP. ACT § 8.33

[See Statutory Supplement]

DEL. GEN. CORP. LAW §§ 172, 174

[See Statutory Supplement]

NOTE ON LIABILITY OF DIRECTORS FOR IMPROPER DIVIDENDS

The liability of directors for improper dividends is governed in the first instance by state corporation law. Most statutes do not leave the issue of directors' liability for the improper declaration of dividends to the general duty of care, but instead include special provisions concerning such liability. Typically, the statutes either permit directors to raise a defense of good-faith reliance on defined financial statements; condition directors' liability on bad faith or lack of due care; or both. The measure of recovery may be either the full amount of an improper dividend, or the injury suffered by creditors or shareholders up to the amount of the distribution, depending on the statute.

Many statutes provide that a director who is held liable for an improper distribution is entitled to contribution from other directors who voted for or assented to the distribution without complying with the applicable standard of conduct. See, e.g., Del.Gen.Corp.Law § 174(b).

A director who is held liable for an improper dividend may also be entitled to reimbursement from shareholders who received the dividend with knowledge of its illegality, or with knowledge of facts that indicated that the dividend was illegal, again depending on the statute.

SECTION 7. LIABILITY OF SHAREHOLDERS FOR IMPROPER DIVIDENDS

DEL. GEN. CORP. LAW § 174(c)

[See Statutory Supplement]

MODEL BUS. CORP. ACT § 8.33(b)

[See Statutory Supplement]

N.Y. BUS. CORP. LAW § 719(d)

[See Statutory Supplement]

CAL. CORP. CODE § 506

[See Statutory Supplement]

UNIFORM FRAUDULENT TRANSFER ACT § 7

[See Statutory Supplement]

NOTE ON SHAREHOLDER LIABILITY FOR IMPROPER DIVIDENDS

The liability of shareholders who receive an improper dividend reflects both corporation law and the law of creditors' rights. Because the corporate statutes are often not well developed in this area, the common law—that is, the law governing shareholder liability for receipt of improper dividends in the absence of a statutory provision concerning such liability—remains highly significant.

1. *Common Law Rules.*

a. *Insolvency.* At common law, if a dividend either resulted in insolvency or was paid when the corporation was already insolvent, a shareholder was liable for the amount of the dividend that he received, on the theory that it constituted a fraudulent conveyance. The fact that the shareholder acted in good faith—that is, did not know of the insolvency—was deemed irrelevant. See Fuld, Recovery of Illegal and Partial Liquidating Dividends from Stockholders, 28 Va.L.Rev. 50, 51 (1941).

b. *Improper dividends not involving insolvency.* The position at common law was more complex where the corporation was not insolvent, but the dividend was improper under a corporate dividend statute. If the shareholder was on notice that the dividend was improper, she was liable either on a theory of unjust enrichment or on the theory that she was privy to the directors' wrong and had no equities in her favor. See Alfred J. Brown Seed Co. v. Brown, 240 Mich. 569, 215 N.W. 772 (1927). However, if the corporation was solvent at the time of the dividend, and the shareholder received the dividend in good faith, she was not liable under the corporate statutes. See

McDonald v. Williams, 174 U.S. 397, 19 S.Ct. 743, 43 L.Ed. 1022 (1899). See generally Fuld, Recovery of Illegal and Partial Liquidating Dividends from Stockholders, 28 Va.L.Rev. 50 (1941); Briggs, Stockholders' Liability for Unlawful Dividends, 8 Temple L.Q. 145 (1934).

c. *Wood v. National City.* The common law position on shareholder's liability for improper dividends was summed up by Judge Learned Hand in Wood v. National City Bank, 24 F.2d 661 (2d Cir.1928). The receiver of the Stanton Oil Company brought suit to recover dividends from Stanton's shareholders. The court said it was impossible to determine whether the plaintiff alleged the dividends were improper because they impaired capital or because the corporation was insolvent in the bankruptcy sense, but the complaint was at least susceptible of the latter interpretation. The court continued:

> Merely because [a dividend] impairs the capital stock, it is commonly regarded as a wrong to creditors on the directors' part, and it is often made such by statute. We may, without discussion, assume that it would be a wrong in the case at bar. Even so, it is primarily only the wrong of those who commit it, like any other tort, and innocent participants are not accomplices to its commission. Hence it has been settled, at least for us, that, when the liability is based merely on the depletion of the capital, a stockholder must be charged with notice of that fact. McDonald v. Williams, 174 U.S. 397, 19 S.Ct. 743, 43 L.Ed. 1022....
>
> However, there is quite another theory, and quite another liability, if the payments not only impair the capital, but are taken out of assets already too small to pay the existing debts. The situation then strictly is not peculiar to corporation law, but merely an instance of a payment from an insolvent estate. Since, as we have said, a stockholder is a donee, he receives such payments charged with whatever trust they were subject to in the hands of the corporation. In that situation it can indeed be said with some truth that the corporate assets have become a "trust fund." Wabash etc. Ry. v. Ham, 114 U.S. 587, 594, 5 S.Ct. 1081, 29 L.Ed. 235. Hence it has never been doubted, so far as we can find, at least in any federal court, that if the dividends are paid in fraud of creditors the stockholder is so liable....

2. *Statutory Rules.* Overlaying the common law rules governing the liability of shareholders for improper distributions are modern statutory rules that specifically govern such liability.

a. *Corporate statutes.* The corporate statutes frequently contain provisions under which a shareholder may be obliged to disgorge an improper dividend. Commonly statutes impose liability only on directors, but confer upon directors who have been held liable a right to contribution from shareholders who received a dividend with knowledge of facts indicating its impropriety, or with knowledge of the illegality, depending on the statute. See, e.g., N.Y.Bus.Corp.Law § 719(d); Rev.Model Bus.Corp.Act § 8.33(b). On the other hand, a few statutes make shareholders directly liable to the corporation. For example, Cal.Corp.Code § 506(a) provides that a shareholder who receives a distribution prohibited by the statute, with knowledge of facts indicating the impropriety, is liable to the corporation for the benefit of prior creditors or senior shareholders. The liability is "for the amount so received by such shareholder . . . but not exceeding the liabilities of the corporation owed to nonconsenting creditors at the time of the violation and the injury suffered by nonconsenting shareholders, as the case may be."

b. *Uniform Fraudulent Transfer Act.* Uniform Fraudulent Transfer Act (UFTA) § 5 renders fraudulent a transfer without a reasonably equivalent exchange when the transferor was or thereby became insolvent. UFTA § 4 renders fraudulent a transfer without a reasonably equivalent exchange when the transferor was engaged or about to engage in a business or transaction for which its remaining assets were unreasonably small. Under UFTA § 7, a creditor can avoid a fraudulent transfer to the extent necessary to satisfy his claim, and may obtain an attachment or other provisional remedy against the asset transferred or other property of the transferee.

c. *Bankruptcy law.* Three provisions of the Bankruptcy Code are applicable to the liability of shareholders for improper distributions:

(i) 11 U.S.C.A. § 544(b) provides that a trustee in bankruptcy can avoid any transfer by the bankrupt that is "voidable under applicable law by a creditor holding an unsecured claim" that is allowable under the Bankruptcy Code. This allows the trustee to recover an improper distribution from the shareholders if a creditor could have avoided the distribution under either the UFTA, a local statutory counterpart of the UFTA, or the common law.

(ii) 11 U.S.C.A. § 548 in effect adopts counterparts of UFTA §§ 4 and 5, supra, as part of the bankruptcy statute itself. Accordingly, the trustee can normally bring suit under § 548 whenever counterparts of the standards set forth in UFTA §§ 4 and 5 are violated, even if the UFTA or a cognate statute has not been adopted in the relevant state. Under the Supremacy Clause, the provisions of 11 U.S.C.A. § 548 cannot be overridden by state corporation law.

(iii) 11 U.S.C.A. § 541(a) vests the bankruptcy estate with all of the debtor's causes of action. Therefore, if the corporation could have sued the shareholder under state law for return of an improper dividend, the trustee can bring suit under § 541(a).

SECTION 8. REPURCHASE BY A CORPORATION OF ITS OWN STOCK

A repurchase by a corporation of its own stock may implicate a variety of legal rules. Some of the relevant legal rules are financial. These rules are the subject of Subsection A. Other rules are designed to deal with problems like unfairness and manipulation. Some of those rules will be briefly considered in Subsection B.

A. FINANCIAL LIMITATIONS ON STOCK REPURCHASES

N.Y. BUS. CORP. LAW §§ 513, 515

[See Statutory Supplement]

DEL. GEN. CORP. LAW § 160(a)

[See Statutory Supplement]

MODEL BUS. CORP. ACT §§ 1.40(6), 6.40

[See Statutory Supplement]

CAL. CORP. CODE § 510(a)

[See Statutory Supplement]

---

1. *General Rule*. When a corporation purchases shares of its own stock, corporate assets flow out to shareholders. Accordingly, from the perspective of creditors a repurchase of stock is economically indistinguishable from a dividend. Ideally, therefore, the financial limitations on repurchases should generally be the same as those for dividends. Thus the California statute and the Model Act treat repurchases and dividends together under the heading, "distributions." Most other statutes provide that, with specified exceptions, a corporation can expend funds to purchase its own stock only if it could pay a dividend in the same amount.

2. *Exceptions*. Despite the general parity in the treatment of dividends and repurchases, most of the traditional statutes permit a corporation to purchase its own stock out of capital for certain specified purposes. The most common such purposes are (i) eliminating fractional shares, (ii) collecting or compromising a shareholder's indebtedness to the corporation, (iii) paying dissenting shareholders for their shares pursuant to the exercise of appraisal rights, and (iv) redeeming or purchasing redeemable stock. See, e.g., Del.Gen.Corp. Law § 160(a)(1); N.Y.Bus.Corp.Law § 513(b), (c). The last of these exceptions, which is probably the most important, is usually supported on the grounds that redeemable stock is temporary by the terms of its creation, so that senior interests will not rely on the cushion provided by the capital such shares have contributed; that the exception facilitates refunding of higher-dividend-rate preferred with

lower-dividend-rate preferred (redeemable stock is almost invariably preferred); and that abuse is unlikely because the board, which must make a decision to redeem, normally represents the interests of common, not preferred.

3. *Installment Payments*. Dividends are normally made payable shortly after being declared. In contrast, payment for repurchased stock is sometimes made in installments over a period of years. This raises the issue whether the permissibility of a repurchase under an installment contract should be determined: (i) at the time the original contract is made, based on the effect of paying the full amount of the contract price; (ii) at the time each installment is scheduled to be paid, based on the effect of paying the installment at that time; or (iii) both. "Most courts have held that [in the case of an installment contract to repurchase stock] the corporation must pass the equitable insolvency test, initially at the time of contract, with respect to the entire purchase price, and subsequently, at the time of each payment, with respect to the amount of the installment.... While there is less consensus on the proper application of the surplus test, currently the favored view is that the surplus limitation is applied only once, when the contract is entered into, with respect to the entire purchase price." Barbara Black, Corporate Dividends and Share Repurchases § 6:19 (2003).

MODEL BUS. CORP. ACT § 6.40(e)

[See Statutory Supplement]

CAL. CORP. CODE § 166

[See Statutory Supplement]

NOTE ON LIABILITY FOR REPURCHASES IN VIOLATION OF STATUTORY FINANCIAL PROVISIONS

In general, liability for payments made by a corporation to purchase its own stock in violation of statutory financial provisions is governed by the rules that apply to liability for improper dividends. In re Burnet–Clark, Ltd., 56 F.2d 744 (2d Cir.1932); Precision Extrusions, Inc. v. Stewart, 36 Ill.App.2d 30, 183 N.E.2d 547 (1962). As regards shareholder liability, however, there are several potential differences between the two situations. In In re Kettle Fried Chicken of America, Inc., 513 F.2d 807 (6th Cir.1975), a repurchase had violated Del. § 160 because the corporation's capital was impaired when the stock was repurchased. The trustee in bankruptcy sued several shareholders to recover amounts the corporation had paid for their stock. The referee found that "defendants were not aware of the pall of illegality surrounding this transaction." Defendants argued that shareholders who have resold their stock to a solvent corporation without knowledge that capital was impaired should not be liable for amounts received, relying by analogy on a line of dividend cases. The court rejected this argument, on the ground that "the purchase of its own stock by a corporation is not its usual or ordinary course of business and in no sense is comparable to the declaration of a corporate dividend." See also Kleinberg v. Schwartz, 87 N.J.Super. 216, 208 A.2d 803 (1965), aff'd on opinion below 46 N.J. 2, 214 A.2d 313. But see Palmer v. Justice, 322 F.Supp. 892 (N.D.Tex.1971), aff'd on other grounds 451 F.2d 371 (5th Cir.).

Another distinction between shareholder liability based on (i) the receipt of improper dividends and (ii) improper payments for stock, is that a shareholder who receives a dividend knows it has been paid by the corporation, while a shareholder who sells his stock may not know the corporation is the buyer, if the corporation acted through an agent or purchased the stock on an open market. See Kleinberg v. Schwartz, supra.

B. NON-FINANCIAL RULES CONCERNING STOCK REPURCHASES

SECURITIES EXCHANGE ACT § 9(a)(2) AND RULES 10b–5, 10b–6, AND 10b–18

[See Statutory Supplement]

NOTE ON STATUS OF REPURCHASED SHARES

Under the view followed in about one-half the states, a corporation has the option with repurchased shares, other than those acquired through redemption, either to restore them to the status of authorized but unissued shares or to carry them as "treasury stock"—that is, to treat them as being still issued and subject to resale. Shares that were once issued but have subsequently been acquired by the corporation by purchase or donation, but have not by board action been retired, cancelled, or restored to the status of unissued shares are customarily referred to as "treasury stock." In the other states, a company's reacquisition of its shares automatically returns those shares to the status of authorized but unissued. This is the approach taken by the current version of Model Business Corporation Act. More specifically, under the Model Act and California approaches, all reacquired shares, whether by way of redemption or other purchase, are restored to the status of authorized but unissued unless the articles prohibit their reissue, in which case their repurchase results in an automatic amendment to the articles of incorporation reducing the number of authorized shares.

In those states that do not follow the contemporary Model Act approach, treasury shares are indeed a masterpiece of legal magic, the creation of something out of nothing. They are no longer outstanding shares in the hands of a holder. They are not outstanding because the obligor has become the owner of the obligation. An earlier commentator put it,

> Can a corporation have "ownership" in itself? Can it possess "legal rights and powers" or "legal property" or "property" derived solely from itself? Corporation law holds it cannot. Treasury shares do not have voting rights, dividend rights, or distribution rights on liquidation, so what rights, if any, remain? Perhaps the "right" of the corporation to reissue its treasury shares for a valuable consideration if its charter law permits—but this is a mere incident of incorporation which is applicable to unissued as well as issued shares. Treasury shares are not a corporate "asset" and cannot be considered as an asset in computing net assets or surplus available for dividends or share purchases.

George S. Hills, Federal Taxation vs. Corporation Law, 12 Wis. L. Rev. 280, 299 (1937).

The only difference between reacquired shares held "in the treasury" and those that have been retired is that the reacquired shares that have not been formerly retired may be resold without having to meet restrictions that customarily apply to the original issue of shares such as satisfying whatever statutory requirements apply to issuing shares with a par value, eligible forms of consideration, and even any preemptive right that would otherwise apply. If these shares have been retired, these restrictions and conditions apply to their reissuance.

Treasury shares carry neither voting rights nor rights to dividends or other distributions. Their existence as "issued shares" is a pure fiction, a figure of speech to explain certain special rules and privileges as to their reissue. In cases where the presence, vote, or assent of the majority of the shareholders is required, it must be understood to mean shares that are issued and outstanding and that may be voted. And, if shares of corporation P are purchased or held by corporation S, which is controlled by corporation P, the prevailing view is the shares held by corporation S do not carry voting rights; otherwise the voting power could be controlled by the management of the parent, and this would be indirect voting by the parent. See Italo Petroleum Corp. v. Producers Oil Corp., 174 A. 276 (Del. Ch. 1934).

NOTE ON NON-FINANCIAL LIMITATIONS ON STOCK REPURCHASES

1. *Differences Between Dividends and Repurchases*. Although a repurchase by a corporation of its own stock can and normally should

be treated like a dividend for purposes of financial limitations on distributions under corporate law, there are several important economic differences between a dividend and a repurchase. Among the most important are as follows: (i) A dividend is pro rata, while a repurchase may not be. Accordingly, in the case of a dividend all shareholders are treated equally, while in the case of a repurchase, they may not be. (ii) In the case of a dividend, the shareholder gives up nothing. In the case of a non-pro-rata repurchase, the shareholder gives up part of all of his relative share in the corporation's equity. (iii) A dividend usually involves a relatively small fraction of a corporation's assets. A repurchase may involve a very significant fraction of a corporation's assets, particularly in a close corporation, and often even in a publicly held corporation.

2. *Modes of Repurchases*. Repurchases by a corporation of its own stock may be made through tender offers (*self-tenders*), through purchases on the market (*open-market purchases*), or through negotiated purchases from one or more individual shareholders (*targeted* or *selective repurchases*). Self-tenders are usually made for a short period at a fixed price that is open to all shareholders. Open-market purchases may be made over a long period of time at the prices prevailing when each purchase is made. Like self-tenders, open-market repurchases are effectively open to all shareholders, because any shareholder can sell into the market. Negotiated purchases from individual shareholders are by definition not open to all shareholders, and are therefore subject to various kinds of abuse—in particular, paying a price to the selling shareholder that is higher than the price available to other shareholders, or providing liquidity to the selling shareholder that is unavailable to other shareholders.

3. *Nonfinancial Rules*. The differences between dividends and repurchases, and the resulting possibilities for unfairness and manipulation that may result from the different modes of effecting repurchases, have led to a variety of nonfinancial rules governing repurchases. Some of the relevant issues and rules will be briefly considered in the remainder of this Note.

4. *Discrimination Among Shareholders in a Close Corporation.* Especially in close corporations, a selective repurchase of a corporation's own stock can be used as an instrument to discriminate among shareholders, by getting cash into the hands of one shareholder or one fraction without distributing cash to other shareholders or factions. This issue is considered in Chapter 8 (Close Corporations), supra.

5. *Selective Repurchases and Greenmail in Publicly Held Corporations.* A corporation may repurchase its own stock to get rid of, or buy off, a shareholder who is at odds with the corporation or, more usually, with the corporation's management. Typically in such cases the corporation pays the shareholder a price higher than the market price of the stock. Selective repurchases for this purpose have been permitted by the courts within broad limits, unless it is shown that the repurchase was for entrenchment purposes. See, e.g., Cheff v. Mathes, 41 Del.Ch. 494, 199 A.2d 548 (Sup.Ct.1964); Bennett v. Propp, 41

Del.Ch. 14, 187 A.2d 405 (Sup.Ct.1962); Kahn v. Roberts, 679 A.2d 460 (Del.1996).

Where, in the case of a selective repurchase, the very purpose of the shareholder's original acquisition of the stock was to induce the corporation to buy him out at a profit so as to get rid of him as a shareholder, the transaction is known as *greenmail*. Often, if not usually, greenmail is a means by which managers improperly use corporate assets—the funds used to buy off the greenmailer—to preserve themselves in office. See Heckmann v. Ahmanson, 168 Cal. App.3d 119, 214 Cal.Rptr. 177 (1985) (greenmailer may be forced to disgorge profits). But see Kamerman v. Steinberg, 891 F.2d 424 (2d Cir.1989). Several states have statutes that regulate greenmail. For example, N.Y.B.C.L. § 513(c) provides that a corporation may not make a targeted repurchase of more than 10% of its stock for a price above market value, unless the stock has been held for more than two years or the transaction is approved by both the board and a majority of the outstanding shares.

The prospect of greenmail has also been diminished by the tax laws. Internal Revenue Code § 5881 imposes a penalty, in the form of a 50% excise tax, on the profit realized by a greenmailer from the receipt of greenmail. Because the greenmailer's profit is taxable, while the excise tax is not deductible, if the greenmailer is a corporation in the 34% bracket the effect of § 5881 is to impose an 84% effective tax rate on the profits from greenmail. Moreover, neither the amount of the payment to the greenmailer nor the expenses connected to that payment are deductible by the corporation.

A payment must meet three conditions to be considered greenmail under section 5881(b). First, the bidder must have held the target's stock for less than two years before entering into the agreement to sell the stock to the corporation. IRC § 5881(b)(1). Second, during the two-year period the bidder (or a related party or a person acting in concert with the bidder) must have "made or threatened to make a public tender offer for stock of such corporation." IRC § 5881(b)(2). Third, the repurchase by the corporation must be pursuant to an offer containing terms not made available to all shareholders. IRC § 5881(b)(3). If the repurchase does not meet these requirements, the bidder will not be subject to the excise tax. This can be accomplished, for example, by not making or threatening a tender offer or, perhaps, by making only an implicit threat.

6. *Self–Tenders.* A publicly held corporation may offer to repurchase a significant portion of its shares through a self-tender for its own stock. Such self-tenders are governed by the Williams Act and the rules thereunder. See Chapter 15, supra.

7. *Going Private.* A publicly held corporation may repurchase the shares held by its public shareholders (as opposed to the shares held by its managers or controlling shareholders) for the purpose of eliminating public ownership. Such a *going-private* transaction may be engaged in to increase corporate efficiency, to shift wealth from

unknowledgeable outsiders to knowledgeable insiders, or both. Going-private transactions are considered in Chapter 15, supra.

8. *Section 9(a)(2) and Rule 10b–18.* Repurchases by a corporation of its own stock frequently have the side effect, or the intended effect, of maintaining or increasing the market price of the stock. A repurchase for manipulative purposes is subject to the general anti-manipulative provisions of the securities acts, particularly § 9(a)(2) of the Securities Exchange Act and Rule 10b–5 under that Act. However, Rule 10b–18 under the Securities Exchange Act provides a safe harbor against violation of those provisions. Under Rule 10b–18, a corporation will not be deemed to have violated § 9(a)(2) or Rule 10b–5 solely by reason of the manner, timing, price, and volume of its repurchases if it repurchases its common stock in the market in accordance with conditions concerning manner, timing, price, and volume that are set out in that section. A repurchase that does not qualify for the safe-harbor protection of Rule 10b–18 is not by reason of that fact deemed to have violated § 9(a)(2) or Rule 10(b)(5).

SECTION 9. LIABILITY FOR WATERED STOCK AND RELATED ISSUES

---

1. *Liability for Watered Stock.* In early days, when stock typically had high par value, shares were often issued at less than par. Sometimes shares could not be issued at par because the real value of the shares was less than their par value. Sometimes shares were issued in exchange for property that was supposed to be worth the aggregate par value of the shares, but was not, because the property was overvalued.

These and other reasons gave rise to a large and complicated body of law, which centered on "bonus," "discount" and "watered" stock. " 'Bonus' shares are shares issued without payment of any amount, perhaps as a 'bonus' for the purchase of another class of security.... 'Discount' shares are shares issued for an amount less than par; e.g., $10 par stock issued for a $7 cash payment.... 'Watered shares' ... are shares issued for non-liquid property which is worth less than par although asserted to be worth at least par." T. Fiflis, Accounting Issues for Lawyers 366, note h (4th ed. 1991). The term *watered stock* is commonly used to describe bonus and discount stock as well. The term "is a pun derived from the practice of certain ranchers or traders who watered their livestock before weighing at sale points." Id. at 366.

A shareholder to whom watered stock had been issued would not be liable to make any further payment solely as a matter of contract, because he would have paid all that he agreed to pay. Under corporation law, however, a holder of watered stock was often subject to liability to the corporation, or more usually to its creditors, in the amount of the difference between the par value of the stock and either (i) the money price the shareholder paid, or (ii) the value of property the shareholder exchanged for the stock. This liability was grounded on various theories.

At first, the liability was grounded on the "trust fund" theory, associated with Wood v. Dummer, 30 Fed.Cas. 435, 436 (C.C.Me. 1824). This case involved a suit by creditors against shareholders to whom an allegedly improper dividend had been paid. In the following famous passage, Judge Story established the trust-fund theory of capital and dividends:

> It appears to me very clear upon general principles . . . that the capital stock of banks is to be deemed a pledge or trust fund for the payment of the debts contracted by the bank. The public, as well as the legislature, have always supposed this to be a fund appropriated for such purpose. The individual stockholders are not liable for the debts of the bank in their private capacities. The charter relieves them from personal responsibility, and substitutes the capital stock in its stead. Credit is universally given to this fund by the public, as the only means of repayment. During the existence of the corporation it is the sole property of the corporation, and can be applied only according to its charter, that is, as a fund for payment of its debts, upon the security of which it may discount and circulate notes. Why, otherwise, is any capital stock required by our charters? If the stock may, the next day after it is paid in, be withdrawn by the stockholders without payment of the debts of the corporation, why is its amount so studiously provided for, and its payment by the stockholders so diligently required? To me this point appears so plain upon principles of law, as well as common sense, that I cannot be brought into any doubt, that the charters of our banks make the capital stock a trust fund for the payment of all the debts of the corporation. The bill-holders and other creditors have the first claims upon it; and the stockholders have no rights, until all the other creditors are satisfied. They have the full benefit of all the profits made by the establishment, and cannot take any portion of the fund, until all the other claims on it are extinguished. Their rights are not to the capital stock, but to the residuum after all demands on it are paid.

In Hospes v. Northwestern Mfg. & Car Co., 48 Minn. 174, 50 N.W. 1117 (1892), the Minnesota court showed that the trust-fund theory for liability on watered stock didn't make sense, and was riddled with exceptions. *Hospes* substituted a new theory, known as the constructive-fraud, misrepresentation, or holding-out theory. The basis of the theory was that:

> The capital of a corporation is the basis of its credit. It is a substitute for the individual liability of those who own its stock. People deal with it and give it credit on the faith of it. They have a

right to assume that it has paid-in capital to the amount which it represents itself as having; and if they give it credit on the faith of that representation, and if the representation is false, it is a fraud upon them; and, in case the corporation becomes insolvent, the law, upon the plainest principles of common justice, says to the delinquent stockholder, "Make that representation good by paying for your stock."

The difference between the trust-fund and constructive-fraud theories was that "the trust fund theory purported to hold the shareholder liable in all events to make up this difference for the benefit of creditors, although certain exceptions were later made by the courts following this theory; whereas, the fraud theory made certain exceptions in cases where the particular creditor plaintiff could not have relied on the full amount of the par value of the stock having been paid in, for example, if his debt arose before the transaction in which the stock was issued." 2 H. Marsh & R. Finkle, Marsh's California Corporations Law § 16.04 (4th ed. 2000).

The constructive-fraud theory had two basic corollaries: (1) Suit could only be brought by creditors who had extended credit after the watered stock was issued. (2) Suit could only be brought by creditors who had relied on the corporation's capital. However, reliance was normally presumed, either conclusively or subject to rebuttal. See Bing Crosby Minute Maid Corp. v. Eaton, 46 Cal.2d 484, 297 P.2d 5 (1956).

After *Hospes,* the trust-fund theory was largely abandoned, usually in favor of the constructive-fraud theory. That theory, however, was also criticized, see Ballantine, Stockholders' Liability in Minnesota, 7 Minn.L.Rev. 79, at 89 (1923), and some courts adopted the "statutory liability" theory, under which liability for watered stock was rested on a provision of the relevant statute, such as a provision that shareholders shall be liable for the consideration for which the shares were authorized to be issued. Under this theory, the time at which the creditor had extended credit was irrelevant, as was the creditor's reliance.

Low-par stock made watered-stock liability unimportant, because such stock is almost invariably issued for cash or property worth at least the par value of the stock. In addition, people began to care less about the whole problem, because modern disclosure requirements and fiduciary obligations obviated the problems that gave rise to watered-stock liability. Nevertheless, shareholder liability based on the purchase of stock is not completely a dead letter. Many or most statutes still make provision for par value, and in such states watered-stock liability may arise where, as a result of bad planning or other factors, the corporation uses a high-par-value stock. See, e.g., Hanewald v. Bryan's Inc., 429 N.W.2d 414 (N.D.1988).

2. *Liability for Unpaid Subscriptions*. Wholly without regard to the concept of par value, a shareholder is liable for the unpaid balance of the amount he agreed to pay for his stock. This liability can often be enforced directly by creditors. See, e.g., Del.Gen.Corp.Law §§ 162, 325; Model Act § 6.20(d).

3. *Related Issues*. The law governing watered stock involved several issues that were related to, but separate from, the problem of liability for watered stock. One of these issues concerned the weight to be given to the board's valuation of the consideration for which stock was issued, where the consideration consisted of property or services rather than cash. This issue has been resolved by modern statutes, which makes the board's valuation conclusive in the absence of fraud or bad faith. *See e.g.,* Del. Gen. Corp. L. § 152. A second issue involved the types of consideration for which stock could be issued when, as was commonly the case, the statutes restricted such consideration. A recurring question of this kind was whether stock could be issued for future services to be performed by the purchaser. Originally, the answer was no. See, e.g., Brown v. Watson, 285 App.Div. 587, 139 N.Y.S.2d 628 (1955); United Steel Industries, Inc. v. Manhart, 405 S.W.2d 231 (Tex.Civ.App.1966). However, most modern statutes now permit stock to be issued in exchange for a contract to perform services. *See* MBCA § 6.21(a).

CHAPTER 17

THE PUBLIC DISTRIBUTION OF SECURITIES

SECTION 1. INTRODUCTION

The law governing the public distribution of securities is intricate. The purpose of this Chapter is to examine the structure of the Securities Act of 1933, and the most important concepts and rules in this area. Many details and qualifications are left to coverage in the Securities Regulation courses.

A. AN OVERVIEW OF THE SECURITIES MARKETS

JAMES D. COX, ROBERT W. HILLMAN & DONALD C. LANGEVOORT, SECURITIES REGULATIONS: CASES AND MATERIALS 1–2

(6th Ed. 2009).

A. Securities Transactions

The securities laws exist because of the unique informational needs of investors. Unlike cars and other tangible products, securities are not inherently valuable. Their worth comes only from the claims they entitle their owner to make upon the assets and earnings of the issuer, or the voting power that accompanies such claims. Deciding whether to buy or sell a security thus requires reliable information about such matters as the issuer's financial condition, products and markets, management, and competitive and regulatory climate. With this data, investors can attempt a reasonable estimate of the present value of the bundle of rights that ownership confers. Securities are bought and sold in two principal settings: issuer transactions and trading transactions. As we shall see, the federal securities laws are structured differently for each of these settings.

1. Issuer Transactions

Issuer transactions are those involving the sales of securities by the issuer to investors. They are the means by which businesses raise capital—to develop, to grow, or simply to survive. The successful business is one that grows. Growth in sales, assets, and earnings can occur without the issuance of additional securities that would add new claimants to the firm's assets and earnings beyond those of its founders, but, frequently, in order to grow a firm must expand its ownership base. The sole proprietorship may take on a partner, the partnership may add partners, the close corporation may become publicly owned, and the public corporation may issue more stock or bonds to become an even larger company.

By far the most expedient form of issuer transaction is the private placement of securities. This entails the issuer selling securities to a select number of investors. On the small scale, a private placement includes a partnership or closely held corporation adding new owners. Large public corporations also engage in private placements when they raise large sums of capital through negotiated sales of securities to one or more financial institutions, such as an insurance company. In either case, special exemptions exist under the securities laws that enable private placements to escape the rigors of regulation.

On the other hand, the firm may not be able to raise all the capital it needs from a small number of investors. In this case, it must make a public offering of securities to a large number of diverse investors. We shall refer to such a public offering as a *primary distribution*. Whenever a large amount of securities is to be offered to the public, the selling effort usually occurs through a syndicate of broker-dealers, known as *underwriters*. An offering on behalf of a company going public for the first time is called an *initial public offering* (IPO).

2. Trading Transactions

In contrast to primary distributions, *trading transactions* are the purchasing and selling of outstanding securities among investors. Re-sales of securities may either be privately negotiated or occur through public markets. Those who hold securities in a small firm for which no public market exists generally can only dispose of their shares by privately negotiating with an interested buyer. An exception to this statement occurs when the amount of securities to be resold is so great as to support a public offering. This is called a *secondary distribution* and most frequently occurs when individuals who control the securities' issuer wish to sell some of their shares.

Re-sales of outstanding securities are much more easily accomplished when there is a pre-existing public market for those securities. The facilities through which outstanding securities are publicly traded are known as *securities markets*. The trading of equities in public markets in 2003 totaled $20.8 trillion (compared with $118.5 billion in issuer transactions of stock that was publicly offered). SIA, Securities Industry Yearbook 2004–2005 at 751–753. It should be apparent that investors engaged in trading transactions are in need of information just as are those who purchase securities in a primary distribution. The considerations of whether and at what price to purchase IBM common shares on an exchange are identical to the considerations investors ponder when offered IBM shares in a primary distribution. As will be seen, the mechanics, practices, and rules for disclosure, as well as other activities, differ significantly for primary distributions and trading transactions.

American securities markets can be roughly divided among bond, equity markets, and derivative/options markets. Traders in bond markets are primarily large financial institutions. Although trading in corporate debt instruments is in absolute amounts significant, all trading in such instruments is dwarfed by the magnitude of trading in U.S., state, and municipal bonds. Even though trading in government securities, as well as original issues of government securities, involves significantly larger amounts than trading in and offerings of business issuers, government securities are exempt from the disclosure regulations. Regulation of government securities focuses upon those who sell government securities. The corporate bond market dwarfs the equity market; in 2003, offerings of corporate bonds were 17.5 times greater than the value of equity underwritings. *See* SIA, Securities Industry Yearbook 2004–2005 at 751.

B. AN OVERVIEW OF THE SECURITIES ACT

Securities and Exchange Commission, the Investor's Advocate: How the SEC Protects Investors and Maintains Market Integrity

(2010 rev.).

Often referred to as the "truth in securities" law, the Securities Act of 1933 has two basic objectives:

- require that investors receive financial and other significant information concerning securities being offered for public sale; and
- prohibit deceit, misrepresentations, and other fraud in the sale of securities. . . .

Purpose of Registration

A primary means of accomplishing these goals is the disclosure of important financial information through the registration of securities. This information enables investors, not the government, to make informed judgments about whether to purchase a company's securities. While the SEC requires that the information provided be accurate, it does not guarantee it. Investors who purchase securities and suffer losses have important recovery rights if they can prove that there was incomplete or inaccurate disclosure of important information.

The Registration Process

In general, securities sold in the U.S. must be registered. The registration forms companies file provide essential facts while minimizing the burden and expense of complying with the law. In general, registration forms call for:

- a description of the company's properties and business;
- a description of the security to be offered for sale;
- information about the management of the company; and
- financial statements certified by independent accountants.

All companies, both domestic and foreign, must file their registration statements electronically. These statements and the accompanying prospectuses become public shortly after filing, and investors can access them . . . [electronically at www.sec.gov]. Registration statements are subject to examination for compliance with disclosure requirements.

Not all offerings of securities must be registered with the Commission. Some exemptions from the registration requirement include:

- private offerings to a limited number of persons or institutions;
- offerings of limited size;
- intrastate offerings; and
- securities of municipal, state, and federal governments.

By exempting many small offerings from the registration process, the SEC seeks to foster capital formation by lowering the cost of offering securities to the public.

SEC, Q & A: Small Business and the SEC

(2009 rev.).

How Does My Small Business Register a Public Offender?

If you decide on a registered public offering, the Securities Act requires your company to file a registration statement with the SEC before the company can offer its securities for sale. You cannot actually sell the securities covered by the registration statement until the SEC staff declares it "effective," even though registration statements become public immediately upon filing.

Registration statements have two principal parts:

- Part I is the prospectus, the legal offering or "selling" document. Your company—the "issuer" of the securities—must describe in the prospectus the important facts about its business operations, financial condition, and management. Everyone who buys the new issue, as well as anyone who is made an offer to purchase the securities, must have access to the prospectus.
- Part II contains additional information that the company does not have to deliver to investors. Anyone can see this informa-

tion by requesting it from one of the SEC's public reference rooms or by looking it up on the SEC Web site.

The Basic Registration Form—Form S–1

All companies can use Form S–1 to register their securities offerings. You should not prepare a registration statement as a fill-in-the-blank form, like a tax return. It should be similar to a brochure, providing readable information. If you file this form, your company must describe each of the following in the prospectus:

- its business;
- its properties;
- its competition;
- the identity of its officers and directors and their compensation;
- material transactions between the company and its officers and directors;
- material legal proceedings involving the company or its officers and directors;
- the plan for distributing the securities; and the intended use of the proceeds of the offering.

Information about how to describe these items is set out in SEC rules. Registration statements also must include financial statements audited by an independent certified public accountant.

In addition to the information expressly required by the form, your company must also provide any other information that is necessary to make your disclosure complete and not misleading. You also must clearly describe any risks prominently in the prospectus, usually at the beginning. Examples of these risk factors are:

- lack of business operating history;
- adverse economic conditions in a particular industry;
- lack of a market for the securities offered; and
- dependence upon key personnel....

Staff Review of Registration Statements

SEC staff examines registration statements for compliance with disclosure requirements. If a filing appears incomplete or inaccurate, the staff usually informs the company by a "letter of comment." Thereafter, the company, through its counsel, responds with amendments to the registration statement to correct or clarify matters raised in the letter of comment. Once the company has satisfied the disclosure requirements, the staff declares the registration statement effective. The company may then begin to sell its securities. The SEC can refuse or suspend the effectiveness of any registration statement if it concludes that the document is misleading, inaccurate, or incomplete.

C. AN OVERVIEW OF THE UNDERWRITING PROCESS

L. Loss & J. Seligman, Fundamentals of Securities Regulation 73–86

4th ed. 2004.

... DISTRIBUTION TECHNIQUES

The registration and prospectus provisions of the Securities Act of 1933 can be understood—and their effectiveness evaluated—only on the background of the techniques by which securities are distributed in the United States. [Among these are strict or "old-fashioned" underwriting, firm-commitment underwriting, and best-efforts underwriting.] . . . .

1. Strict or "Old–Fashioned" Underwriting

Under the traditional English system of distribution—which is no longer common in that country—the issuer did not sell to an investment banking house for resale to the public, either directly or through a group of dealers. Instead a designated "issuing house" advertised the issue and received applications and subscriptions from the public on the issuer's behalf after an announced date. When sufficient applications had been received, an announcement was made that "the lists are closed," and the issuer proceeded to allot the securities directly to the applicants or subscribers, using various methods of proration in the event of an oversubscription. Securities firms normally subscribed to new issues not for their own accounts with a view to resale at a profit, but only as brokers for the accounts of their customers. Before the public offering was thus made, the issue was "underwritten" in order to ensure that the company would obtain the amount of funds it required.

This was underwriting in the strict insurance sense. For a fee or premium, the underwriter agreed to take up whatever portion of the issue was not purchased by the public within a specified time. . . .

This method of distribution is called in the United States "strict" or "old-fashioned" or "standby" underwriting. It is seldom if ever used here except in connection with offerings to existing stockholders by means of warrants or rights. . . .

2. Firm–Commitment Underwriting

For some time, the most prevalent type of underwriting has been the "firm-commitment" variety. It is not, technically, underwriting in the classic insurance sense. But its purpose and effect are much the same in that it assures the issuer of a specified amount of money at a certain time (subject frequently to specified conditions precedent in the underwriting contract) and shifts the risk of the market (at least in part) to the investment bankers. The issuer typically sells the entire issue outright to a group of securities firms, represented by one or several "managers" or "principal underwriters" or "representatives."

They, in turn, sometimes sell at a differential to a "selling group" of dealers, [who] sell at another differential to the public. In a very limited sense the process is comparable to the merchandising of beans or automobiles or baby rattles. The issuer is the manufacturer of the securities; the members of the underwriting group are the wholesalers; and the members of the selling group are the retailers. But it is not quite so simple. In most firm-commitment underwritings, securities of particular issuers are distributed not continually but once in a long time, and then in a large batch. And the securities market is quite a different animal from the market for canned beans. . . .

. . . By the turn of the century, it was common in the case of large offerings for a single investment banker to do the "origination"—that is, carry on the preliminary negotiations with the issuer, make the investigations deemed necessary, and then purchase the issue from the issuer. The banker was chosen on the basis of his past relationships with the issuer and his past performance. The "origination" stage was followed by the process of "syndication": In order to spread the commitment, the originating banker would immediately sell the issue to a small "original purchase group." That group would in turn sell to a larger "banking group" . . . The originating banker would become a member of the purchase group; the members of that group would likewise become members of the banking group; and the originating banker would manage both groups. . . . [T]hese groups were not designed primarily to do the actual distributing; often the members of the groups were not organized for retailing purposes. The public sale would be effected, for the account of whichever group last bought the issue, by the manager (the originating banker) through an organization of employees and agents, which would sometimes include those members of the purchase and banking groups who were geared for retail distribution.

With the increase in the number and size of securities issues during the First World War, as well as the development of coast-to-coast telephone and wire systems, both groups tended to grow in membership and, in order to facilitate the actual mechanics of distribution, it became customary to add still another step to the elaborate process: Instead of the originating banker's selling through agents and employees, a much larger and more dispersed "selling group" or "selling syndicate" would take the issue from the banking group; those members of the earlier group or groups with distributive facilities would join this new group; and it, too, would be managed by the originating banker. . . .

The passage of the Securities Act of 1933 made for a simplification of this system. Under the statute only negotiations between the issuer and "underwriters" are permitted before the filing of the registration statement. Until then, the securities may not be offered to the public or even to dealers who are not "underwriters" within the statutory definition. And until the actual effective date of the registration statement, no sales or contracts may be made except with underwriters. This, in practice, means that there is usually a short period (a few hours at most) between the signing of the underwriting contract and the effective date of the registration statement during which whoever is committed to purchase at a fixed price cannot legally shift his or her liability against a possible market decline. To protect the underwriter until the closing (usually one week later) the "market out" clause in the underwriting contract was developed.

Although the use of this clause is by no means universal, it is not considered "cricket" to take advantage of it; it typically provides that the manager of the underwriting group (or the representatives of the group) may terminate the agreement if before the date of public offering (or before the date of the closing or settlement between underwriters and issuer) the issuer or any subsidiary sustains a material adverse change, trading in the securities is suspended, minimum or maximum prices or government restrictions on securities trading are put into effect, a general banking moratorium is declared, or, in the judgment of the managing underwriter (or, alternatively, the representatives of the underwriters or a majority in interests of the several underwriters), material changes in "general economic, political or financial conditions" or the effect of international conditions on financial markets in the United States makes it impracticable or inadvisable to market the securities at specified public offering price. This clause is much broader than the traditional *force majeure* provision. Another result of the Securities Act and the stock transfer taxes enforced until 1965 was a tendency to reduce the number of transfers between groups and to enlarge the number of "underwriters" who bear the initial risk. In effect, the originating banker and the purchase and banking groups have all been combined into a single "underwriting syndicate or group." . . .

3. Best–Efforts Underwriting

Companies that are not well established are not apt to find an underwriter that will give a firm commitment and assume the risk of distribution. Of necessity, therefore, they customarily distribute their securities through firms that merely undertake to use their best efforts. Paradoxically, this type of distribution is also preferred on occasion by companies that are so well established that they can do without any underwriting commitment, thus saving on the cost of distribution. The securities house, instead of buying the issue from the company and reselling it as principal, sells it for the company as agent; and its compensation takes the form of an agent's commission rather than a merchant's or dealer's profit. There may still be a selling group to help in the merchandising. But its members likewise do not buy from the issuer; they are subagents. This, of course, is not really underwriting; it is simply merchandising. . . .

Coffee & Sale, Securities Regulation—Cases and Materials 80–81

11th ed. 2009.

. . . A selling group member gets compensated in the form of a selling concession, which typically amounts to 50–60% of the gross spread between the public offering price and the net amount received by the issuer.

This "gross spread" is the difference between the price to the issuer and the public offering price. It represents the compensation which is distributed among the managing underwriter, members of the underwriting syndicate and the members of the selling group—the "underwriting discounts and commissions" shown on the cover page of the prospectus or offering circular. The issuer sells the securities to the underwriting syndicate at a discount from the public offering price. In an initial public offering, this discount has long been in the range of 6–3/4% to 7%.... The discount is considerably less for seasoned equity offerings by already public corporations and even less for debt offerings. Simply to illustrate the allocation of this discount within the underwriting group, let us assume that the issue is to be sold to the public for $10, with $9 going to the issuer. On this basis, the compensation might be sliced up as follows. First, the lead underwriter will receive a management fee of 20 cents per share for finding and packaging the issue, and to compensate it for managing the offering and in "running the books." The next slice would be a fee of about 30 cents a share which is called the "gross underwriting fee." This fee provides compensation to the underwriting group for their expenses, such as underwriters' counsel, "tombstone" advertising and stabilizing expenses.... [and] compensation for the use of capital and for assuming the risk in the underwriting. The remaining 50 cents of the spread goes to the underwriting firm or the selling group member that actually sells the stock at retail.

SECTION 2. WHAT CONSTITUTES A "SECURITY"

SECURITIES ACT § 2(1)

[See Statutory Supplement]

McGinty, What Is a Security?

1993 Wisc.L.Rev. 1033, 1037–39.

In drafting the definition of security, Congress faced two opposing problems. On the one hand, if it defined "security" to include only arrangements with the same names as instruments traded on securities exchanges (like "stock" and "bonds"), shady promoters could escape the securities laws simply by labeling their investment schemes with unusual names. On the other hand, if Congress defined "security" overbroadly (for example, to include "any ... evidence of indebtedness"), the securities laws could apply to I.O.U.s given between friends or to notes given by parents to a private school for the duration of their child's enrollment. The former approach would exclude arrangements that should be included, thus frustrating Congress's purpose of protecting investors. The latter approach would include arrangements that should not be included, impose significant unnecessary transaction costs, burden the federal judiciary and federalize numerous issues better left to state law. Congress, for its part, drafted the definition of "security" broadly enough to sweep in devious investment schemes bearing innocuous titles. The courts, for their part, have attempted to construe "security" broadly enough to include such schemes, and yet narrowly enough to exclude arrangements whose names fortuitously suggest a security but whose economic realities do not....

Some of the terms that Congress used to define security—such as "investment contract"—lack an established meaning outside judicial opinions and so create elasticity. Other more standard terms such as "stock" or "notes" have accepted meanings within the securities industry, but can also be used in circumstances where one would rationally think no security exists. Because the definitional paragraph begins with the proclamation, "The term 'security' means *any* note, stock ..." and the other included instruments, the unqualified "any" suggests that all instruments bearing a name listed in the definitional paragraph should be covered, even a note given by one neighbor to another.

Some courts and commentators have argued that the context clause [that is, the introductory clause to Section 2, which provides that "unless the context otherwise requires" the terms in Section 2 have the meanings given in that Section] permits courts to exclude arrangements that possess the standard names but that are not really securities. Yet the statute nowhere defines or even suggests the scope of the context clause's qualification. Thus, construing the definitional section presents two unappetizing choices. If courts restrict the definitional section to the definitional paragraph alone, the logical result is over-inclusiveness and mindless literalism. If the definitional section includes the context clause, the statute is threatened with unbounded judicial discretion....

NOTE ON THE MEANING OF "INVESTMENT CONTRACT"

As Professor McGinty points out, the definition of "security" in section 2(a)(1) is extremely broad. In particular, the term "investment contract" has been viewed by the courts as a "catch-all" phrase designed to encompass novel devices that serve the same purposes as a security.

The first major case dealing with the scope of section 2(a)(1) was SEC v. C.M. Joiner Leasing Corp., 320 U.S. 344, 64 S.Ct. 120, 88 L.Ed. 88 (1943). In pursuance of a plan to finance the drilling of oil wells, lessees of large tracts engaged in a campaign to sell assignments of leaseholds, and represented to potential purchasers that test oil wells would be drilled. The promotional literature emphasized the potential return to the purchaser upon the drilling of a successful well. The Supreme Court held that the transactions involved securities within the meaning of section 2(a)(1), even though under Texas law the leaseholds conveyed interests in land:

> In the Securities Act the term "security" was defined to include by name or description many documents in which there is common trading for speculation or investment. Some, such as notes, bonds, and stocks, are pretty much standardized and the name alone carries well-settled meaning. Others are of more variable character and were necessarily designated by more descriptive terms, such as "transferable share," "investment contract," and "in general any interest or instrument commonly known as a security." We cannot read out of the statute these general descriptive designations merely because more specific ones have been used to reach some kinds of documents. Instruments may be included within any of these definitions, as a matter of law, if on their face they answer to the name or description. However, the reach of the Act does not stop with the obvious and commonplace. Novel, uncommon, or irregular devices, whatever they appear to be, are also reached if it be proved as matter of fact that they were widely offered or dealt in under terms or courses of dealing which established their character in commerce as "investment contracts," or as "any interest or instrument commonly known as a 'security.' "

320 U.S. at 351, 64 S.Ct. at 123.

Three years later, in SEC v. W.J. Howey Co., 328 U.S. 293, 66 S.Ct. 1100, 90 L.Ed. 1244 (1946), the Supreme Court clarified its holding in *Joiner*. In *Howey,* a Florida corporation that owned a large citrus orchard offered land-sale contracts for small parcels of the orchard land, along with service contracts for harvesting and marketing the citrus fruit. The purchasers' tracts were jointly cultivated, and the corporation sold the fruit, distributing to the purchasers of the land-sale contracts a pro rata portion of the profits based on the acreage they owned. The purchasers had no legal right of entry on the land to market the crop, and had no right to specific fruit. Against this background, the Court established a definition of "investment contract" that has come to be generally accepted:

> [A]n investment contract for purposes of the Securities Act means a contract, transaction or scheme whereby a person invests his money in a common enterprise and is led to expect profits solely from the efforts of the promoter or a third party. . . .

Id. at 298–99, 66 S.Ct. at 1103, 90 L.Ed. at 1249.

The Court then held that the transactions in effect involved the offering of an opportunity to contribute money and share in the profits of a large citrus-fruit enterprise managed and partly owned by W.J. Howey Co. The land-sales contracts served as a convenient method of determining the investors' allocable shares of the profits, but the resulting transfers of rights in land were viewed by the Court as "purely incidental" to the profit-seeking business venture:

> ... The investors provide the capital and share in the earnings and profits; the promoters manage, control and operate the enterprise. It follows that the arrangements whereby the investors' interests are made manifest involve investment contracts, regardless of the legal terminology in which such contracts are clothed....

Id. at 300.

Subsequent cases have generally relied on the *Howey* characterization of an "investment contract," but in doing so have added important refinements and qualifications to the *Howey* test.

SEC v. Glenn W. Turner Enterprises, Inc., 474 F.2d 476 (9th Cir.1973), cert. denied 414 U.S. 821, 94 S.Ct. 117, 38 L.Ed.2d 53, concerned a pyramid selling scheme. The scheme involved the sale of self-improvement contracts by Dare to be Great, Inc., which offered buyers the opportunity of earning commissions on the sale of such contracts to others. The defendants' main contention was that the buyers of the self-improvement contracts did not expect profits "*solely* from the efforts of others," within the meaning of *Howey*, but instead were required to exert some efforts of their own to realize a return on their initial cash outlay.

The court concluded that literal adherence to the *Howey* test could allow circumvention of the Act, by a requirement that the buyer contribute a modicum of effort. Accordingly, the court looked to a realistic test, focusing on "whether the efforts made by those other than the investor are the undeniably significant ones, those essential managerial efforts which affect the failure or success of the enterprise." Because the buyers in *Glenn W. Turner* were in essence obtaining shares in the proceeds of the selling efforts of Dare, and the success of the enterprise was dependent upon the "essential managerial efforts" of Dare, the court found that the *Howey* test had been satisfied:

> For purposes of the present case, the sticking point in the *Howey* definition is the word "solely", a qualification which of course exactly fitted the circumstances in *Howey*. All the other elements of the *Howey* test have been met here. There is an investment of money, a common enterprise,[1] and the expectation of profits to come from the efforts of others....
>
> We hold, however, that in light of the remedial nature of the legislation, the statutory policy of affording broad protection to the public, and the Supreme Court's admonitions that the definition of securities should be a flexible one, the word "solely" should not be read as a strict or literal limitation on the definition of an investment contract, but rather must be construed realis-

1. A common enterprise is one in which the fortunes of the investor are interwoven with and dependent upon the efforts and success of those seeking the investment or of third parties.

> tically, so as to include within the definition those schemes which involve in substance, if not form, securities.

Id. at 481–82.

Turner also expanded on the meaning of the *Howey* requirement of a "common enterprise." *Turner* itself focused on the commonality of enterprise between the investors and the promoter. See also *SEC v. Koscot Interplanetary, Inc.*, 497 F.2d 473 (5th Cir.1974). This kind of commonality is sometimes known as *vertical commonality*. Vertical commonality has been interpreted in two different ways. Under one approach, known as *broad vertical commonality*, the common enterprise test is satisfied if the promoter's *efforts* are the dominant factor in the success of the investments. *Turner* essentially followed this approach. Under a second approach, sometimes known as *strict vertical commonality*, the fortunes of investors must be tied not only to the efforts of the promoter, but to the *fortunes* of the promoter. See, e.g., Revak v. SEC Realty Corp., 18 F.3d 81 (2d Cir.1994). Furthermore, some courts held that the common-enterprise test will be satisfied only if there is a pooling of investment funds accompanied by pro rata interests in profits among the investors. See Wals v. Fox Hills Development Corp., 24 F.3d 1016 (7th Cir. 1994). The latter approach, commonly referred to as requiring *horizontal commonality,* is the prevailing view in most cases interpreting the meaning of "investment contract."

Should the fact that the promoter of the venture is promising each investor a fixed rate of return take the instrument outside the "investment contract" rubric?

> There is no reason to distinguish between promises of fixed returns and promises of variable returns for purposes of the test, so understood. In both cases, the investing public is attracted by representations of investment income, as purchasers were in this case by ETS' invitation to " 'watch the profits add up.' " App. 13 (Complaint § 38). Moreover, investments pitched as low-risk (such as those offering a "guaranteed" fixed return) are particularly attractive to individuals more vulnerable to investment fraud, including older and less sophisticated investors. See S.Rep. No. 102–261, Vol. 2, App., p. 326 (1992) (Staff Summary of Federal Trade Commission Activities Affecting Older Consumers). Under the reading respondent advances, unscrupulous marketers of investments could evade the securities laws by picking a rate of return to promise. We will not read into the securities laws a limitation not compelled by the language that would so undermine the laws' purposes.

Securities and Exchange Commission v. Edwards, 540 U.S. 389, 394, 124 S.Ct. 892, 897, 157 L.Ed.2d 813, 820 (2004)

While *Howey* and *Edwards* each provide fairly expansive constructions of the meaning of "investment contract," the Supreme Court has provided important limitations on the scope of "investment contracts" in three of its decisions: *International Brotherhood of Teamsters v.*

Daniel, *United Housing Foundation, Inc. v. Forman*, and *Marine Bank v. Weaver*, discussed below.

The Teamsters' pension plan required twenty years of continuous service in order to be eligible for pension benefits, and a member of the Teamsters had been denied pension benefits because of a seven-month hiatus in his work record. The employee sued the Teamsters, his union local, and a trustee of the fund, alleging violations of § 10(b) and Rule 10b–5 of the 1934 Act and § 17(a) of the 1933 Act. In International Brotherhood of Teamsters v. Daniel, 439 U.S. 551, 99 S.Ct. 790, 58 L.Ed.2d 808 (1979), the Court held that an employee's interest in a *non*contributory compulsory pension plan did not constitute a security. The Court first held that the investment test was not satisfied. Under the pension plan, the employees made no contributions themselves. The Court stated that any "investment" made in the plan by an employee through permitting part of his compensation to take the form of a deferred pension benefit was "a relatively insignificant part of an employee's total and indivisible compensation package." The Court said that since an employee surrenders his labor "as a whole," it was "only in the most abstract sense" that an employee exchanged part of his labor in return for the possible benefits. The Court concluded, "Looking at the economic realities, it seems clear that an employee is selling his labor to obtain a livelihood, not making an investment" for the future.

Turning to the second element of the *Howey* definition, the Court found that the plan involved no expectation of profits from a common enterprise. Although the pension fund depended to some extent on earnings from its assets, which in turn depended upon the efforts of the pension fund's managers, the Court said that a far larger portion of a pension fund's income came from employer contributions, an income source that did not depend on the skill or efforts of the fund's managers.

Further restrictions appear in United Housing Foundation, Inc. v. Forman, 421 U.S. 837, 95 S.Ct. 2051, 44 L.Ed.2d 621 (1975). In order to obtain the right to lease apartments in Co-op City, tenants were required to purchase certificates labeled "stock" in Co-op City, a nonprofit cooperative housing corporation. One share was to be purchased for each room at a price of $450 per room. Upon the termination of a tenant's occupancy, the certificates were to repurchased by the cooperative at the initial selling price. The stock, therefore, was tied inextricably to the apartment, and no profit could be realized upon resale of the stock. Purchasing tenants filed an action under the Exchange Act's antifraud provision when they learned that, due to unforeseen rising costs to complete the project, the rent for each unit would be substantially higher than initially projected. The Supreme Court illuminated *Howey's* requirement of profits:

> The touchstone [of Howey's definition of investment contract] is the presence of an investment in a common venture premised on a reasonable expectation of profits to be derived from the entrepreneurial or managerial efforts of others. By profits, the Court

> has meant either capital appreciation resulting from the development of the initial investment ... or a participation in earnings resulting from the use of investors' funds.... In such cases, the investor is "attracted solely by the prospects of a return" on his investment.... By contrast, when a purchaser is motivated by a desire to use or consume the item purchased—"to occupy the land or to develop it themselves," as the *Howey* Court put it—the securities laws do not apply....
>
> In the present case there can be no doubt that investors were attracted solely by the prospect of acquiring a place to live, and not by financial returns on their investment....

421 U.S. at 852–53, 95 S.Ct. at 2060–61, 44 L.Ed.2d at 632–33.

A further significant restriction on the scope of investment contract was provided in Marine Bank v. Weaver, 455 U.S. 551, 559, 102 S.Ct. 1220, 1225, 71 L.Ed.2d 409, 416 (1982), in the Court's holding that a bank certificate of deposit was not a "security" under section 3(a)(10) of the 1934 Act, because extensive banking regulation, together with federal insurance of bank deposits, virtually eliminated any risk to the holder of such a certificate:

> ... It is unnecessary to subject issuers of bank certificates of deposit to liability under the antifraud provisions of the federal securities laws since the holders of bank certificates of deposit are abundantly protected under the federal banking laws....

NOTE ON WHAT IS "STOCK": LANDRETH TIMBER CO. v. LANDRETH

Among the items listed within both Securities Act section 2(a)(1) and its parallel provision Exchange Act section 3(a)(10) is "stock." Should this provision bear *Howey's* "investment contract" gloss?

In Landreth Timber Co. v. Landreth, 471 U.S. 681, 105 S.Ct. 2297, 85 L.Ed.2d 692 (1985), the plaintiffs had purchased all the outstanding stock of Landreth Timber from members of the Landreth family, who had offered the stock for sale through local and out-of-state brokers. Subsequently, the plaintiffs brought suit against the sellers on the grounds that the sellers had violated the Securities Act by first widely offering the stock, and then selling all the shares to the plaintiff, without registration and that the seller violated the Securities Exchange Act by making material misrepresentations in consummating the sale. The Ninth Circuit interpreted *Howey* to require the courts to determine in every case whether economic realities indicated that the Acts applied. Within that framework, the Ninth Circuit followed a doctrine, developed by some courts, that the federal securities laws did not apply to a sale of all of a corporation's stock, because the economic realities were that such a transaction involved the sale of a business, not the sale of "securities" within the meaning of the Acts. The Supreme Court reversed:

As we . . . recognized in *Forman,* the fact that instruments bear the label "stock" is not of itself sufficient to invoke the coverage of the Acts. Rather, we concluded that we must also determine whether those instruments possess "some of the significant characteristics typically associated with" stock, *id.,* at 851, 95 S.Ct., at 2060, recognizing that when an instrument is both called "stock" and bears stock's usual characteristics, "a purchaser justifiably [may] assume that the federal securities laws apply," *id.,* at 850, 95 S.Ct., at 2059. We identified those characteristics usually associated with common stock as (i) the right to receive dividends contingent upon an apportionment of profits; (ii) negotiability; (iii) the ability to be pledged or hypothecated; (iv) the conferring of voting rights in proportion to the number of shares owned; and (v) the capacity to appreciate in value.[2] *Id.,* at 851, 95 S.Ct., at 2060.

Under the facts of *Forman,* we concluded that the instruments at issue there were not "securities" within the meaning of the Acts. That case involved the sale of shares of stock entitling the purchaser to lease an apartment in a housing cooperative. The stock bore none of the characteristics listed above that are usually associated with traditional stock. Moreover, we concluded that under the circumstances, there was no likelihood that the purchasers had been misled by use of the word "stock" into thinking that the federal securities laws governed their purchases. The purchasers had intended to acquire low-cost subsidized living space for their personal use; no one was likely to have believed that he was purchasing investment securities. *Ibid.*

In contrast, it is undisputed that the stock involved here possesses all of the characteristics we identified in *Forman* as traditionally associated with common stock. Indeed, the District Court so found. App. to Pet. for Cert. 13a. Moreover, unlike in *Forman,* the context of the transaction involved here—the sale of stock in a corporation—is typical of the kind of context to which the Acts normally apply. It is thus much more likely here than in *Forman* that an investor would believe he was covered by the federal securities laws. Under the circumstances of this case, the plain meaning of the statutory definition mandates that the stock be treated as "securities" subject to the coverage of the Acts.

Reading the securities laws to apply to the sale of stock at issue here comports with Congress' remedial purpose in enacting the legislation to protect investors by "compelling full and fair disclosure relative to the issuance of 'the many types of instruments that in our commercial world fall within the ordinary concept of a security.' " *SEC v. W.J. Howey Co.,* 328 U.S., at 299, 66 S.Ct., at 1103 (quoting H.R.Rep. No. 85, 73d Cong., 1st Sess.,

2. Although we did not so specify in *Forman,* we wish to make clear here that these characteristics are those usually associated with common stock, the kind of stock often at issue in cases involving the sale of a business. Various types of preferred stock may have different characteristics and still be covered by the Acts.

> 11 (1933)). Although we recognize that Congress did not intend to provide a comprehensive federal remedy for all fraud, *Marine Bank v. Weaver,* 455 U.S. 551, 556, 102 S.Ct. 1220, 1223, 71 L.Ed.2d 409 (1982), we think it would improperly narrow Congress' broad definition of "security" to hold that the traditional stock at issue here falls outside the Acts' coverage....
>
> Respondents contend that *Forman* and the cases on which it was based require us to reject the view that the shares of stock at issue here may be considered "securities" because of their name and characteristics. Instead, they argue that our cases require us in every instance to look to the economic substance of the transaction to determine whether the *Howey* test has been met. According to respondents, it is clear that petitioner sought not to earn profits from the efforts of others, but to buy a company that it could manage and control. Petitioner was not a passive investor of the kind Congress intended the Acts to protect, but an active entrepreneur, who sought to "use or consume" the business purchased just as the purchasers in *Forman* sought to use the apartments they acquired after purchasing shares of stock. Thus, respondents urge that the Acts do not apply.
>
> We disagree with respondents' interpretation of our cases....
>
> ... Respondents are correct that in *Forman* we eschewed a "literal" approach that would invoke the Acts' coverage simply because the instrument carried the label "stock." *Forman* does not, however, eliminate the Court's ability to hold that an instrument is covered when its characteristics bear out the label. See *supra,* at 2302–2303.
>
> [W]e would note that the *Howey* economic reality test was designed to determine whether a particular instrument is an "investment contract," not whether it fits within *any* of the examples listed in the statutory definition of "security." ...

471 U.S. at 686–92, 105 S. Ct. at 2301–05, 85 L. Ed.2d at 697–01.

WHEN IS A "NOTE" A SECURITY

In **REVES v. ERNST & YOUNG,** 494 U.S. 56, 110 S.Ct. 945, 108 L.Ed.2d 47 (1990), the Supreme Court addressed whether demand notes issued by an agricultural Co–Op were "securities" within the meaning of § 3(a)(10) of the Securities Exchange Act of 1934. The definitions in both the Securities Act and Exchange Act refer to "notes" among the instruments listed as a "security." Each, however, excludes notes with a maturity less than 9 months. However, the Securities Act and Exchange Act are hardly mirror images of each other in their treatment of notes. The Securities Act's exclusion of notes with a maturity of less than 9 months is conditioned on the additional qualification that such short-term notes "arise out of a current transaction or the proceeds of which have been or are to be used for current transactions." This mysterious clause, absent in the Exchange Act, most certainly refers to "commercial paper" i.e., high quality short-term notes issued by well-established companies. The question, remaining unresolved after *Reves*, is whether this exemptive language includes more than commercial paper and, for that matter, whether it was the intent of Congress to cover commercial paper within the reach of the Exchange Act. *Reves* arose from a financing plan whereby to raise money to support its general business operations, the Co–Op issued promissory notes, payable on demand by the holder. The notes were uncollateralized, uninsured, and paid a variable rate of interest that was adjusted monthly to keep it higher than the rate paid by local financial institutions. The Co–Op offered the notes to its 23,000 members and also to nonmembers, and marketed the scheme as an "Investment Program." Advertisements for the notes, which appeared in each Co–Op newsletter, read in part: "YOUR CO–OP has more than $11,000,000 in assets to stand behind your investments. The Investment is not [Federally] insured but it is ... Safe ... Secure ... and available when you need it."

Subsequently, the Co–Op filed for bankruptcy. Plaintiffs, a class of note holders, then sued Arthur Young & Co., the Co–Op's outside auditor, under the antifraud provisions of the Securities Exchange Act. The basis of the complaint was that Arthur Young had intentionally failed to apply generally accepted accounting principles in an effort inflate the value of Co–Op's assets and net worth, and that but for Arthur Young's actions, the plaintiffs would not have purchased the notes. Arthur Young argued that the plaintiffs could not bring suit under the Securities Exchange Act because the notes were not securities within the meaning of the Act. The Supreme Court held that the notes did constitute securities:

> The fundamental purpose undergirding the Securities Acts is "to eliminate serious abuses in a largely unregulated securities market." United Housing Foundation, Inc. v. Forman, 421 U.S. 837, 849, 95 S.Ct. 2051, 2059, 44 L.Ed.2d 621 (1975)....
>
> Congress did not, however, "intend to provide a broad federal remedy for all fraud." Marine Bank v. Weaver, 455 U.S. 551, 556, 102 S.Ct. 1220, 1223, 71 L.Ed.2d 409 (1982).... Congress' purpose in enacting the securities laws was to regulate *investments,* in whatever form they are made and by whatever name they are called.
>
> A commitment to an examination of the economic realities of a transaction does not necessarily entail a case-by-case analysis of every instrument, however. Some instruments are obviously within the class Congress intended to regulate because they are by their nature investments. In Landreth Timber Co. v. Landreth, 471 U.S. 681, 105 S.Ct. 2297, 85 L.Ed.2d 692 (1985), we held that an instrument bearing the name "stock" that, among other things, is negotiable, offers the possibility of capital appreciation, and carries the right to dividends contingent on the profits of a business

enterprise is plainly within the class of instruments Congress intended the securities laws to cover....

We made clear in *Landreth Timber* that stock was a special case, explicitly limiting our holding to that sort of instrument. Id., at 694, 105 S.Ct., at 2304....

Because the *Landreth Timber* formula cannot sensibly be applied to notes, some other principle must be developed to define the term "note." ...

[The Second Circuit developed the "family resemblance" approach to determine whether a note is a security. The family resemblance approach] begins with a presumption that *any* note with a term of more than nine months is a "security." See, e.g., Exchange Nat'l Bank of Chicago v. Touche Ross & Co., 544 F.2d 1126, 1137 (C.A.2 1976). Recognizing that not all notes are securities, however, the Second Circuit has also devised a list of notes that it has decided are obviously not securities. Accordingly, the "family resemblance" test permits an issuer to rebut the presumption that a note is a security if it can show that the note in question "bear[s] a strong family resemblance" to an item on the judicially crafted list of exceptions, id., at 1137–1138, or convinces the court to add a new instrument to the list. See, e.g., Chemical Bank v. Arthur Andersen & Co., 726 F.2d 930, 939 (C.A.2 1984)....

[We adopt the "family resemblance" test.] The test begins with the language of the statute; because the Securities Acts define "security" to include "any note," we begin with a presumption that every note is a security. We nonetheless recognize that this presumption cannot be irrebuttable. As we have said ... Congress was concerned with regulating the investment market, not with creating a general federal cause of action for fraud. In an attempt to give more content to that dividing line, the Second Circuit has identified a list of instruments commonly denominated "notes" that nonetheless fall without the "security" category. See *Exchange Nat. Bank,* supra, at 1138 (types of notes that are not "securities" include "the note delivered in consumer financing, the note secured by a mortgage on a home, the short-term note secured by a lien on a small business or some of its assets, the note evidencing a 'character' loan to a bank customer, short-term notes secured by an assignment of accounts receivable, or a note which simply formalizes an open-account debt incurred in the ordinary course of business....

We agree that the items identified by the Second Circuit are not properly viewed as "securities." More guidance, though, is needed. It is impossible to make any meaningful inquiry into whether an instrument bears a "resemblance" to one of the instruments identified by the Second Circuit without specifying what it is about *those* instruments that makes *them* non-"securities." Moreover, as the Second Circuit itself has noted, its list is "not graven in stone," ibid., and is therefore capable of expansion. Thus, some standards must be developed for determining when an item should be added to the list.

An examination of the list itself makes clear what those standards should be. In creating its list, the Second Circuit was applying the same factors that this Court has held apply in deciding whether a transaction involves a "security." First, we examine the transaction to assess the motivations that would prompt a reasonable seller and buyer to enter into it. If the seller's purpose is to raise money for the general use of a business enterprise or to finance substantial investments and the buyer is interested primarily in the profit the note is expected to generate, the instrument is likely to be a "security." If the note is exchanged to facilitate the purchase and sale of a minor asset or consumer good, to correct for the seller's cash-flow difficulties, or to advance some other commercial or consumer purpose, on the other hand, the note is less sensibly described as a "security." See, e.g., Forman, 421 U.S., at 851, 95 S.Ct., at 2060 (share of "stock" carrying a right to subsidized housing not a security because "the inducement to purchase was solely to acquire subsidized low-cost living space; it was not to invest for profit"). Second, we examine the "plan of distribution" of the instrument, SEC v. C.M. Joiner Leasing Corp., 320 U.S. 344, 353, 64 S.Ct. 120, 124, 88 L.Ed. 88 (1943), to determine whether it is an instrument in which there is "common trading for speculation or investment," id., at 351, 64 S.Ct., at 123. Third, we examine the reasonable expectations of the investing public: The Court will consider instruments to be "securities" on the basis of such public expectations, even where an economic analysis of the circumstances of the particular transaction might suggest that the instruments are not "securities" as used in that transaction.... Finally, we examine whether some factor such as the existence of another regulatory scheme significantly reduces the risk of the instrument, thereby rendering application of the Securities Acts unnecessary. See, e.g., Marine Bank, 455 U.S., at 557–559, and n. 7, 102 S.Ct., at 1224–1225, and n. 7.

We conclude, then, that in determining whether an instrument denominated a "note" is a "security," courts are to apply the version of the "family resemblance" test that we have articulated here: a note is presumed to be a "security," and that presumption may be rebutted only by a showing that the note bears a strong resemblance (in terms of the four factors we have identified) to one of the enumerated categories of instrument. If an instrument is not sufficiently similar to an item on the list, the decision whether another category should be added is to be made by examining the same factors.

494 U.S. at 60–67, 110 S.Ct. at 949–952, 108 L.Ed.2d at 57–61.

Applying this family resemblance test to Co–Op's notes, the Court had "little difficulty in concluding that the notes at issue were 'securities.'" The Co–Op sold the notes to raise capital for its business operations; the purchasers bought the notes to earn a profit in the form of interest; the notes were offered to more than 23,000 Co–Op members as well as to non-members; the notes were advertised as "investments"; and there was no risk-reducing factor, such as collateralization or insurance, to suggest that the notes were not securities.

SECTION 3. WHAT CONSTITUTES A "SALE" AND AN "OFFER TO SELL"

SECURITIES ACT §§ 2(a)(3), 3(a)(9); SECURITIES ACT RULE 145

[See Statutory Supplement]

NOTE ON THE MEANING OF "SALE" AND "OFFER TO SELL"

The term "sale" or "sell" is defined in section 2(a)(3) of the Securities Act to include "every contract of sale or disposition of a security or interest in a security, for value." The term "offer to sell," "offer for sale," or "offer" is defined to include "every attempt or offer to dispose of, or solicitation of an offer to buy, a security or interest in a security, for value." The use of the word "includes" rather than "means" emphasizes the breadth of these definitions, and the courts have also interpreted the terms broadly "to include ingenious methods employed to obtain money from members of the public to finance ventures." S.E.C. v. Addison, 194 F.Supp. 709, 722 (N.D.Tex.1961).

A good many corporate transactions involve a sale and, therefore, raise issues under the securities laws. For example, sale includes changing the rights, privileges and preferences of stock through amendment of the articles of incorporation, it involves an issuer exchanging its shares for the outstanding stock of another company as well as its own shares, and includes a merger of two companies whereby the shares of the acquiring company are issued to the acquired firm.

The significance of whether there is an offer or sale of a security flows from the broad reach of section 5 of the Securities Act (as well as the potential application of the antifraud provisions of the Exchange Act). Consider the breadth of section 5(c), discussed below. This provision bars any offer to buy or offer to sell a security unless a registration statement covering that offer has been filed with the SEC. Section 5(c)'s broad prohibition is qualified, however, if the security is either an exempt security under one of the categories set forth in

Section 3 (e.g., a municipal security, a security guaranteed by a bank, issued by a non-profit firm) or covered by one of the transaction exemptions in Section 4.

SECTION 4. THE REQUIREMENT OF REGISTRATION

A. THE BROAD SWEEP OF SECTION 5

SECURITIES ACT §§ 2(10), 5

[See Statutory Supplement]

The structure of the Securities Act is exceptionally intricate. The key provision is section 5. Section 5(a) provides:

> Unless a registration statement is in effect as to a security, it shall be unlawful for any person, directly or indirectly—
>
> (1) to make use of any means or instruments of transportation or communication in interstate commerce or of the mails to sell such security through the use or medium of any prospectus or otherwise; or
>
> (2) to carry or cause to be carried through the mails or in interstate commerce, by any means or instruments of transportation, any such security for the purpose of sale or for delivery after sale.

Section 5(c) provides:

> It shall be unlawful for any person, directly or indirectly, to make use of any means or instruments of transportation or communication in interstate commerce or of the mails to offer to sell or offer to buy through the use or medium of any prospectus or otherwise any security, unless a registration statement has been filed as to such security....

Section 2(a)(10) defines a "prospectus" to mean "any prospectus, notice, circular, advertisement, letter, or communication, written or by radio or television, which offers any security for sale or confirms the sale of any security," subject to certain exceptions.

Putting section 2(a)(10) together with section 5(a) and (c), if any person sells, or offers to sell or buy, a security by any means of transportation or communication in interstate commerce or by mail, or sends a security through the mail or in interstate commerce for purposes of sale or delivery after sale, the security must be registered, unless an exemption applies. Therefore, section 5 prohibits virtually every sale or offer to sell a security, no matter how trivial, and no matter who the seller, unless the security is registered under the Act or an exemption applies. Other provisions of the Act then carve out a variety of exemptions for large classes of securities and transactions. By virtue of the exemptions, these securities and transactions do not require registration, despite the sweeping language of section 5. The balance of this Section will consider exemptions based on (1) the number and character of the offerees, (2) the size of the offering, (3) the intrastate nature of an offering, and (4) the absence of an issuer, underwriter, or dealer.

B. The Intrastate Exemption

SECURITIES ACT § 3(a)(11); SECURITIES ACT RULE 147

[See Statutory Supplement]

Securities Act Release No. 4434 (1961)

[SECTION 3(a)(11) EXEMPTIONS FOR LOCAL OFFERINGS].

General Nature of Exemption

Section 3(a)(11), as amended in 1954, exempts from the registration and prospectus requirements of the Act:

> Any security which is a part of an issue offered and sold only to persons resident within a single State or Territory, where the issuer of such security is a person resident and doing business within, or, if a corporation, incorporated by and doing business within, such State or Territory.

The legislative history of the Securities Act clearly shows that this exemption was designed to apply only to local financing that may practicably be consummated in its entirety within the state or territory in which the issuer is both incorporated and doing business. As appears from the legislative history, by amendment to the Act in 1934, this exemption was removed from section 5(c) and inserted in section 3, relating to "Exempted Securities," in order to relieve dealers of an unintended restriction on trading activity. This amendment was not intended to detract from its essential character as a transaction exemption.

"Issue" Concept

A basic condition of the exemption is that the *entire issue* of securities be offered and sold exclusively to residents of the state in question. Consequently, an offer to a nonresident which is considered a part of the intrastate issue will render the exemption unavailable to the entire offering.

Whether an offering is "a part of an issue," that is, whether it is an integrated part of an offering previously made or proposed to be made, is a question of fact and depends essentially upon whether the offerings are a related part of a plan or program. Unity Gold Corporation, 3 S.E.C. 618, 625 (1938); Peoples Securities Company, Securities Exchange Act Release No. 6176, Feb. 10, 1960. Thus, the exemption should not be relied upon in combination with another exemption for the different parts of a single issue where a part is offered or sold to nonresidents.

The determination of what constitutes an "issue" is not governed by state law. Shaw v. U.S., 131 F.2d 476, 480 (9th Cir.1942). Any one or more of the following factors may be determinative of the question of integration: (1) are the offerings part of a single plan of financing; (2) do the offerings involve issuance of the same class of security; (3) are the offerings made at or about the same time; (4) is the same type of consideration to be received, and (5) are the offerings made for the same general purpose.

Moreover, since the exemption is designed to cover only those security distributions, which, as a whole, are essentially local in character, it is clear that the phrase "sold only to persons resident" as used in section 3(a)(11) cannot refer merely to the initial sales by the issuing corporation to its underwriters, or even the subsequent resales by the underwriters to distributing dealers. To give effect to the fundamental purpose of the exemption, it is necessary that the entire issue of securities shall be offered and sold to, and come to rest only in the hands of residents within the state. If any part of the issue is offered or sold to a nonresident, the exemption is unavailable not only for the securities so sold, but for all securities forming a part of the issue, including those sold to residents.... It is incumbent upon the issuer, underwriter, dealers and other persons connected with the offering to make sure that it does not become an interstate distribution through resales. It is understood to be customary for such persons to obtain assurances that purchases are not made with a view to resale to nonresidents.

Doing Business Within the State

In view of the local character of the section 3(a)(11) exemption, the requirement that the issuer be doing business in the state can only be satisfied by the performance of substantial operational activities in the state of incorporation. The doing business requirement is not met by functions in the particular state such as bookkeeping, stock record and similar activities or by offering securities in the state....

If the proceeds of the offering are to be used primarily for the purpose of a new business conducted outside of the state of incorporation and unrelated to some incidental business locally conducted, the exemption should not be relied upon....

Residence Within the State

Section 3(a)(11) requires that the entire issue be confined to a single state in which the issuer, the offerees and the purchasers are residents. Mere presence in the state is not sufficient to constitute residence as in the case of military personnel at a military post.... The mere obtaining of formal representations of residence and agreements not to resell to nonresidents or agreements that sales are void if the purchaser is a nonresident should not be relied upon without more as establishing the availability of the exemption....

Resales

From these general principles it follows that if during the course of distribution any underwriter, any distributing dealer (whether or not a member of the formal selling or distributing group), or any dealer or other person purchasing securities from a distributing dealer for resale were to offer or sell such securities to a nonresident, the exemption would be defeated. In other words, section 3(a)(11) contemplates that the exemption is applicable only if the entire issue is distributed pursuant to the statutory conditions. Consequently, any offers or sales to a nonresident in connection with the distribution of the issue would destroy the exemption as to all securities which are a part of that issue, including those sold to residents regardless of whether such sales are made directly to nonresidents or indirectly through residents who as part of the distribution thereafter sell to nonresidents. It would furthermore be immaterial that sales to nonresidents are made without use of the mails or instruments of interstate commerce. Any such sales of part of the issue to nonresidents, however few, would not be in compliance with the conditions of section 3(a)(11), and would render the exemption unavailable for the entire offering including the sales to residents....

This is not to suggest, however, that securities which have actually come to rest in the hands of resident investors, such as persons purchasing without a view to further distribution or resale to nonresidents, may not in due course be resold by such persons, whether directly or through dealers or brokers, to nonresidents without in any way affecting the exemption. The relevance of any such resales consists only of the evidentiary light which they might cast upon the factual question whether the securities had in fact come to rest in the hands of resident investors. If the securities are resold but a short time after their acquisition to a nonresident this fact, although not conclusive, might support an inference that the original offering had not come to rest in the state, and that the resale therefore constituted a part of the process of primary distribution; a stronger inference would arise if the purchaser involved were a security dealer. It may be noted that the nonresidence of the underwriter or dealer is not pertinent so long as the ultimate distribution is solely to residents of the state....

SECURITIES ACT RELEASE NO. 5450 (1974)

[Rule 147]

The Securities and Exchange Commission today adopted Rule 147 which defines certain terms in, and clarifies certain conditions of, section 3(a)(11) of the Securities Act of 1933 ("the Act")....

Background and Purpose ...

Certain basic questions have arisen in connection with interpreting Section 3(a)(11). They are:

1. what transactions does the Section cover;

2. what is "part of an issue" for purposes of the Section;

3. when is a person "resident within" a state or territory for purposes of the Section; and

4. what does "doing business within" mean in the context of the Section?

The courts and the Commission have addressed themselves to these questions in the context of different fact situations, and some general guidelines have been developed. Certain guidelines were set forth by the Commission in Securities Act Release No. 4434 and, in part, are reflected in Rule 147. However, in certain respects, as pointed out below, the rule differs from past interpretations.

The Transaction Concept

Although the intrastate offering exemption is contained in Section 3 of the Act, which Section is phrased in terms of exempt "securities" rather than "transactions", the legislative history and Commission and judicial interpretations indicate that the exemption covers only specific transactions and not the securities themselves. Rule 147 reflects this interpretation....

The "Person Resident Within" Concept

The object of the Section 3(a)(11) exemption, i.e., to restrict the offering to persons within the same locality as the issuer who are, by reason of their proximity, likely to be familiar with the issuer and protected by the state law governing the issuer, is best served by interpreting the residence requirement narrowly. In addition, the determination of whether all parts of the issue have been sold only to residents can be made only after the securities have "come to rest" within the state or territory. Rule 147 retains these concepts, but provides more objective standards for determining when a person is considered a resident within a state for purposes of the rule and when securities have come to rest within a state.

The "Doing Business Within" Requirement

Because the primary purpose of the intrastate exemption was to allow an essentially local business to raise money within the state where the investors would be likely to be familiar with the business and with the management, the doing business requirement has traditionally been viewed strictly. First, not only should the business be located within the state, but the principal or predominant business must be carried on there. Second, substantially all of the proceeds of the offering must be put to use within the local area.

Rule 147 reinforces these requirements by providing specific percentage amounts of business that must be conducted within the state, and of proceeds from the offering that must be spent in connection with such business. In addition, the rule requires that the principal office of the issuer be within the state.

SEC, Q & A: Small Business and the SEC

(2009 rev.).

Intrastate Offering Exemption

Section 3(a)(11) of the Securities Act is generally known as the "intrastate offering exemption." This exemption facilitates the financing of local business operations. To qualify for the intrastate offering exemption, your company must:

- be incorporated in the state where it is offering the securities;
- carry out a significant amount of its business in that state; and
- make offers and sales only to residents of that state.

There is no fixed limit on the size of the offering or the number of purchasers. Your company must determine the residence of each purchaser. If any of the securities are offered or sold to even one out-of-state person, the exemption may be lost. Without the exemption, the company could be in violation of the Securities Act registration requirements. If a purchaser resells any of the securities to a person who resides outside the state within a short period of time after the company's offering is complete (the usual test is nine months), the entire transaction, including the original sales, might violate the Securities Act. Since secondary markets for these securities rarely develop, companies often must sell securities in these offerings at a discount.

It will be difficult for your company to rely on the intrastate exemption unless you know the purchasers and the sale is directly negotiated with them. If your company holds some of its assets outside the state, or derives a substantial portion of its revenues outside the state where it proposes to offer its securities, it will probably have a difficult time qualifying for the exemption.

You may follow Rule 147, a "safe harbor" rule, to ensure that you meet the requirements for this exemption. It is possible, however, that transactions not meeting all requirements of Rule 147 may still qualify for the exemption.

C. PRIVATE PLACEMENTS

SECURITIES ACT § 4(2)

[See Statutory Supplement]

S.E.C. v. Ralston Purina Co.

Supreme Court of the United States, 1953.
346 U.S. 119, 73 S.Ct. 981, 97 L.Ed. 1494.

■ MR. JUSTICE CLARK delivered the opinion of the Court.

Section 4[2] of the Securities Act of 1933 exempts "transactions by an issuer not involving any public offering" from the registration requirements of § 5. We must decide whether Ralston Purina's offerings of treasury stock to its "key employees" are within this exemption. On a complaint brought by the Commission under § 20(b) of the Act seeking to enjoin respondent's unregistered offerings, the District Court held the exemption applicable and dismissed the suit. The Court of Appeals affirmed. The question has arisen many times since the Act was passed; an apparent need to define the scope of the private offering exemption prompted certiorari. . . .

Ralston Purina manufactures and distributes various feed and cereal products. Its processing and distribution facilities are scattered throughout the United States and Canada, staffed by some 7,000 employees. At least since 1911 the company has had a policy of encouraging stock ownership among its employees; more particularly, since 1942 it has made authorized but unissued common shares available to some of them. Between 1947 and 1951, the period covered by the record in this case, Ralston Purina sold nearly $2,000,000 of stock to employees without registration and in so doing made use of the mails.

In each of these years, a corporate resolution authorized the sale of common stock "to employees . . . who shall, without any solicitation by the Company or its officers or employees, inquire of any of them as to how to purchase common stock of Ralston Purina Company." A memorandum sent to branch and store managers after the resolution was adopted, advised that "The only employees to whom this stock will be available will be those who take the initiative and are interested in buying stock at present market prices." Among those responding to these offers were employees with the duties of artist, bakeshop foreman, chow loading foreman, clerical assistant, copywriter, electrician, stock clerk, mill office clerk, order credit trainee, production trainee, stenographer, and veterinarian. The buyers lived in over fifty widely separated communities scattered from Garland, Texas, to Nashua, New Hampshire and Visalia, California. The lowest salary bracket of those purchasing was $2,700 in 1949, $2,435 in 1950 and $3,107 in 1951. The record shows that in 1947, 243 employees bought stock, 20 in 1948, 414 in 1949, 411 in 1950, and the 1951 offer, interrupted by this litigation, produced 165 applications to purchase. No records were kept of those to whom the offers were made; the estimated number in 1951 was 500.

The company bottoms its exemption claim on the classification of all offerees as "key employees" in its organization. Its position on trial was that "A key employee . . . is not confined to an organization chart. It would include an individual who is eligible for promotion, an individual who especially influences others or who advises others, a person whom the employees look to in some special way, an individual, of course, who carries some special responsibility, who is sympathetic to management and who is ambitious and who the management feels is likely to be promoted to a greater responsibility." That an offering to all of its employees would be public is conceded.

The Securities Act nowhere defines the scope of § 4[2]'s private offering exemption. Nor is the legislative history of much help in staking out its boundaries....

Decisions under comparable exemptions in the English Companies Acts and state "blue sky" laws, the statutory antecedents of federal securities legislation, have made one thing clear—to be public, an offer need not be open to the whole world. In Securities and Exchange Comm'n v. Sunbeam Gold Mines Co., 95 F.2d 699 (9th Cir.1938), this point was made in dealing with an offering to the stockholders of two corporations about to be merged. Judge Denman observed that:

> "In its broadest meaning the term 'public' distinguishes the populace at large from groups of individual members of the public segregated because of some common interest or characteristic. Yet such a distinction is inadequate for practical purposes; manifestly, an offering of securities to all redheaded men, to all residents of Chicago or San Francisco, to all existing stockholders of the General Motors Corporation or the American Telephone & Telegraph Company, is no less 'public', in every realistic sense of the word, than an unrestricted offering to the world at large. Such an offering, though not open to everyone who may choose to apply, is none the less 'public' in character, for the means used to select the particular individuals to whom the offering is to be made bear no sensible relation to the purposes for which the selection is made.... To determine the distinction between 'public' and 'private' in any particular context, it is essential to examine the circumstances under which the distinction is sought to be established and to consider the purposes sought to be achieved by such distinction." 95 F.2d at 701.

The courts below purported to apply this test. The District Court held, in the language of the *Sunbeam* decision, that "The purpose of the selection bears a 'sensible relation' to the class chosen," finding that "The sole purpose of the 'selection' is to keep part stock ownership of the business within the operating personnel of the business and to spread ownership throughout all departments and activities of the business." The Court of Appeals treated the case as involving "an offering, without solicitation, of common stock to a selected group of key employees of the issuer, most of whom are already stockholders when the offering is made, with the sole purpose of enabling them to secure a proprietary interest in the company or to increase the interest already held by them."

Exemption from the registration requirements of the Securities Act is the question. The design of the statute is to protect investors by promoting full disclosure of information thought necessary to informed investment decisions. The natural way to interpret the private offering exemption is in light of the statutory purpose. Since exempt transactions are those as to which "there is no practical need for [the bill's] application," the applicability of § 4[2] should turn on whether the particular class of persons affected need the protection of the Act. An offering to those who are shown to be able to fend for themselves is a transaction "not involving any public offering."

The Commission would have us go one step further and hold that "an offering to a substantial number of the public" is not exempt under § 4[2]. We are advised that "whatever the special circumstances, the Commission has consistently interpreted the exemption as being inapplicable when a large number of offerees is involved." But the statute would seem to apply to a "public offering" whether to few or many.[11] It may well be that offerings to a substantial number of persons would rarely be exempt. Indeed nothing prevents the commission, in enforcing the statute, from using some kind of numerical test in deciding when to investigate particular exemption claims. But there is no warrant for superimposing a quantity limit on private offerings as a matter of statutory interpretation.

The exemption, as we construe it, does not deprive corporate employees, as a class, of the safeguards of the Act. We agree that some employee offerings may come within § 4[2], e.g., one made to executive personnel who because of their position have access to the same kind of information that the act would make available in the form of a registration statement. Absent such a showing of special circumstances, employees are just as much members of the investing "public" as any of their neighbors in the community. . . .

Keeping in mind the broadly remedial purposes of federal securities legislation, imposition of the burden of proof on an issuer who would plead the exemption seems to us fair and reasonable. Schlemmer v. Buffalo, R. & P.R. Co., 1907, 205 U.S. 1. . . . Agreeing, the court below thought the burden met primarily because of the respondent's purpose in singling out its key employees for stock offerings. But once it is seen that the exemption question turns on the knowledge of the

---

11. See Viscount Sumner's frequently quoted dictum in Nash v. Lynde, " 'The public' . . . is of course a general word. No particular numbers are prescribed. Anything from two to infinity may serve: perhaps even one, if he is intended to be the first of a series of subscribers, but makes further proceedings needless by himself subscribing the whole." [1929] A.C. 158, 169.

offerees, the issuer's motives, laudable though they may be, fade into irrelevance.

The focus of inquiry should be on the need of the offerees for the protections afforded by registration. The employees here were not shown to have access to the kind of information which registration would disclose. The obvious opportunities for pressure and imposition make it advisable that they be entitled to compliance with § 5.

Reversed.

■ THE CHIEF JUSTICE and MR. JUSTICE BURTON dissent.

■ MR. JUSTICE JACKSON took no part in the consideration or decision of this case.

NOTE ON DORAN v. PETROLEUM MANAGEMENT CORP.

Doran v. Petroleum Management Corp., 545 F.2d 893 (5th Cir. 1977) provides a useful gloss on *Ralston Purina,* and a picture of the present state of the law:

> This court has in the past identified four factors relevant to whether an offering qualifies for the [private placement] exemption. The consideration of these factors, along with the policies embodied in the 1933 Act, structure the inquiry.... The relevant factors include the number of offerees and their relationship to each other and the issuer, the number of units offered, the size of the offering, and the manner of the offering. Consideration of these factors need not exhaust the inquiry, nor is one factor's weighing heavily in favor of the private status of the offering sufficient to ensure the availability of the exemption. Rather, these factors serve as guideposts to the court in attempting to determine whether subjecting the offering to registration requirements would further the purposes of the 1933 Act....
>
> A. *The Number of Offerees*
>
> Establishing the number of persons involved in an offering is important both in order to ascertain the magnitude of the offering and in order to determine the characteristics and knowledge of the persons thus identified.
>
> The number of offerees, not the number of purchasers, is the relevant figure in considering the number of persons involved in an offering ... A private placement claimant's failure to adduce any evidence regarding the number of offerees will be fatal to the claim.... The number of offerees is not itself a decisive factor in determining the availability of the private offering exemption. Just as an offering to few may be public, so an offering to many may be private. *SEC v. Ralston Purina Co., supra,* 346 U.S. at 125, 73 S.Ct. at 984–85. Nevertheless, "the more offerees, the more likelihood that the offering is public." *Hill York Corp. v. American International Franchises, Inc., supra,* 448 F.2d 680 at 688....

B. *The Offerees' Relationship to the Issuer*

Since *SEC v. Ralston,* . . . courts have sought to determine the need of offerees for the protections afforded by registration by focusing on the relationship between offerees and issuer and more particularly on the information available to the offerees. . . . Once the offerees have been identified, it is possible to investigate their relationship to the issuer. . . .

1. *The role of investment sophistication* . . .

. . . [Evidence] of a high degree of business or legal sophistication on the part of all offerees does not suffice to bring the offering within the private placement exemption. We clearly established that proposition in *Hill York Corp. v. American International Franchises, Inc., supra,* 448 F.2d at 690. We reasoned that "if the plaintiffs did not possess the information requisite for a registration statement, they could not bring their sophisticated knowledge of business affairs to bear in deciding whether or not to invest. . . ." . . .

In short, there must be sufficient basis of accurate information upon which the sophisticated investor may exercise his skills. Just as a scientist cannot be without his specimens, so the shrewdest investor's acuity will be blunted without specifications about the issuer. For an investor to be invested with exemptive status he must have the required data for judgment.

2. *The requirement of available information*

The interplay between two factors, the relationship between offerees and issuer and the offerees' access to information that registration would disclose, has been a matter of some conceptual and terminological difficulty. For purposes of this discussion, we shall adopt the following conventions: We shall refer to offerees who have not been furnished registration information directly, but who are in a position relative to the issuer to obtain the information registration would provide, as having "access" to such information. By a position of access we mean a relationship based on factors such as employment, family, or economic bargaining power that enables the offeree effectively to obtain such information. . . . When offerees, regardless of whether they occupy a position of access, have been furnished with the information a registration statement would provide, we shall say merely that such information has been disclosed. When the offerees have access to or there has been disclosure of the information registration would provide, we shall say that such information was available.

The requirement that all offerees have available the information registration would provide has been firmly established by this court as a necessary condition of gaining the private offering exemption. . . .

More specifically, we shall require on remand that the defendants demonstrate that all offerees, whatever their expertise, had available the information a registration statement would have afforded a prospective investor in a public offering. Such a showing is not independently sufficient to establish that the offering qualified for the private placement exemption, but it is necessary to gain the exemption and is to be weighed along with the sophistication and number of the offerees, the number of units offered, and the size and manner of the offering. . . .

C. *On Remand: The Issuer–Offeree Relationship*

In determining on remand the extent of the information available to the offerees, the district court must keep in mind that the "availability" of information means either disclosure of or effective access to the relevant information. The relationship between issuer and offeree is most critical when the issuer relies on the latter route.

To begin with, if the defendants could prove that all offerees were actually furnished the information a registration statement would have provided, whether the offerees occupied a position of access pre-existing such disclosure would not be dispositive of the status of the offering. If disclosure were proved and if, as here, the remaining factors such as the manner of the offering and the investment sophistication of the offerees weigh heavily in favor of the private status of the offering, the absence of a privileged relationship between offeree and issuer would not preclude a finding that the offering was private. Any other conclusion would tear out of context this court's earlier discussions of the § 4(2) exemption and would conflict with the policies of the exemption.

Alternatively it might be shown that the offeree had access to the files and [records] of the company that contained the relevant information. Such access might be afforded merely by the position of the offeree or by the issuer's promise to open appropriate files and records to the offeree as well as to answer inquiries regarding material information. In either case, the relationship between offeree and issuer now becomes critical, for it must be shown that the offeree could realistically have been expected to take advantage of his access to ascertain the relevant information. Similarly the investment sophistication of the offeree assumes added importance, for it is important that he could have been expected to ask the right questions and seek out the relevant information. . . .

SEC, Q & A: Small Business and the SEC

(2009 rev.).

. . . **Private Offering Exemption**

Section 4(2) of the Securities Act provides exemption from registration for "transactions by an issuer not involving any public offering.

To qualify the offering under this exemption, it is necessary that the persons to whom your company sells the security:

- have enough knowledge and experience in finance and business matters to evaluate the risks and merits of the investment (the "sophisticated investor"), or be able to bear the investment's economic risk;
- have access to the type of information normally provided in a prospectus; and
- agree not to resell or distribute the securities to the public.

In addition, you may not use any form of public solicitation or general advertising in connection with the offering.

The precise limits of this private offering exemption are uncertain. As the number of purchasers increases and their relationship to the company and its management becomes more remote, it is more difficult to show that the transaction qualifies for the exemption. You should know that if you offer securities to even one person who does not meet the necessary conditions, the entire offering may be in violation of the Securities Act.

Rule 506, another "safe harbor" rule, provides objective standards that you can rely on to meet the requirements of this exemption....

D. LIMITED OFFERINGS

SECURITIES ACT §§ 2(a)(15), 3(b), 4(2), 4(6)

[See Statutory Supplement]

SECURITIES ACT RULE 215; REGULATION D (RULES 501–508)

[See Statutory Supplement]

T. Hazen, Securities Regulation in a Nutshell 71–72

10th ed. 2009.

[Securities Act] § 3(b) authorizes the SEC, "by rules and regulations," to exempt offerings, not exceeding a specified dollar amount, when it finds that registration is not necessary "by reason of the small amount involved or the limited character of the public offering." The dollar limit has been periodically raised by Congress from its initial level of $100,000, the most recent increase coming in 1980 and raising the limit from $2 million to the present level of $5 million. Under this authority, the Commission has adopted a number of rules providing exemptions for certain specialized kinds of offerings, as well as the general exemption in Regulation A. . . .

Also in 1980, Congress added a new § 4(6) to the 1933 Act, exempting any offering of not more than $5 million made solely to "accredited investors" (defined to include specified types of institutions and other classes of investors that the SEC might specify by rule).

These developments set the stage for the coordination of the private offering and small offering exemptions in a new Regulation D.

SEC, Q & A: Small Business and the SEC

2004 rev.

. . . **Regulation D**

Regulation D establishes three exemptions from Securities Act registration. . . .

Rule 504

Rule 504 provides an exemption for the offer and sale of up to $1,000,000 of securities in a 12–month period. Your company may use this exemption so long as it is . . . not subject to Exchange Act reporting requirements. Like the other Regulation D exemptions, in general you may not use public solicitation or advertising to market the securities and purchasers [must] receive "restricted" securities, meaning that they may not sell the securities without registration or an applicable exemption. However, you can use this exemption for a public offering of your securities and investors will receive freely tradable securities under the following circumstances:

- You register the offering exclusively in one or more states that require a publicly filed registration statement and delivery of a substantive disclosure document to investors;
- You register and sell in a state that requires registration and disclosure delivery and also sell in a state without those requirements, so long as you deliver the disclosure documents mandated by the state in which you registered to all purchasers; or,
- You sell exclusively according to state law exemptions that permit general solicitation and advertising, so long as you sell only to "accredited investors," a term we describe in more detail below in connection with Rule 505 and Rule 506 offerings.

Even if you make a private sale where there are no specific disclosure delivery requirements, you should take care to provide sufficient information to investors to avoid violating the antifraud provisions of the securities laws. . . .

Rule 505

Rule 505 provides an exemption for offers and sales of securities totaling up to $5 million in any 12–month period. Under this exemption, you may sell to an unlimited number of "accredited investors" and up to 35 other persons who do not need to satisfy the sophistication or wealth standards associated with other exemptions. Purchasers must buy for investment only, and not for resale. The issued securities are "restricted." Consequently, you must inform investors that they may not sell for at least a year without registering the transaction. You may not use general solicitation or advertising to sell the securities.

An "accreditied investor" is:

- a bank, insurance company, registered investment company, business development company, or small business investment company;
- an employee benefit plan, within the meaning of the Employee Retirement Income Security Act, if a bank, insurance company, or registered investment adviser makes the investment decisions, or if the plan has total assets in excess of $5 million;
- a charitable organization, corporation or partnership with assets exceeding $5 million;
- a director, executive officer, or general partner of the company selling the securities;
- a business in which all the equity owners are accredited investors;
- a natural person with a net worth of at least $1 million;
- a natural person with income exceeding $200,000 in each of the two most recent years or joint income with a spouse exceeding $300,000 for those years and a reasonable expectation of the same income level in the current year; or
- a trust with assets of at least $5 million, not formed to acquire the securities offered, and whose purchases are directed by a sophisticated person.

It is up to you to decide what information you give to accredited investors, so long as it does not violate the antifraud prohibitions. But you must give non-accredited investors disclosure documents that generally are the same as those used in registered offerings. If you provide information to accredited investors, you must make this information available to the non-accredited investors as well. You must also be available to answer questions by prospective purchasers.

Here are some specifics about the financial statement requirements applicable to this type of offering:

- Financial statements need to be certified by an independent public accountant;
- If a company other than a limited partnership cannot obtain audited financial statements without unreasonable effort or

expense, only the company's balance sheet, to be dated within 120 days of the start of the offering, must be audited; and

- Limited partnerships unable to obtain required financial statements without unreasonable effort or expense may furnish audited financial statements prepared under the federal income tax laws.

Rule 506

... Rule 506 is a "safe harbor" for the private offering exemption. If your company satisfies the following standards, you can be assured that you are within the Section 4(2) exemption:

- You can raise an unlimited amount of capital;
- You cannot use general solicitation or advertising to market the securities;
- You can sell securities to an unlimited number of accredited investors (the same group we identified in the Rule 505 discussion) and up to 35 other purchasers. Unlike Rule 505, all non-accredited investors, either alone or with a purchaser representative, must be sophisticated—that is, they must have sufficient knowledge and experience in financial and business matters to make them capable of evaluating the merits and risks of the prospective investment;
- It is up to you to decide what information you give to accredited investors, so long as it does not violate the antifraud prohibitions. But you must give non-accredited investors disclosure documents that generally are the same as those used in registered offerings. If you provide information to accredited investors, you must make this information available to the non-accredited investors as well;
- You must be available to answer questions by prospective purchasers;
- Financial statement requirements are the same as for Rule 505; and
- Purchasers receive "restricted" securities. Consequently, purchasers may not freely trade the securities in the secondary market after the offering.

... **Accredited Investor Exemption—Section 4(6)**

Section 4(6) of the Securities Act exempts from registration offers and sales of securities to accredited investors when the total offering price is less than $5 million.

The definition of accredited investors is the same as that used in Regulation D. Like the exemptions in Rule 505 and 506, this exemption does not permit any form of advertising or public solicitation.

There are no document delivery requirements. Of course, all transactions are subject to the antifraud provisions of the securities laws.

T. HAZEN, SECURITIES REGULATION IN A NUTSHELL, 75–76 (10th ed. 2009). "Offerings complying with the terms of . . . Rule 504 or 505 are deemed to be exempt under [Securities Act] § 3(b); offerings pursuant to . . . Rule 506, since they may exceed $5 million, cannot be exempt under § 3(b) and are considered to be non-public offerings under . . . § 4(2). Rule 506 is not the exclusive means of making a non-public offering; the Preliminary Note to Regulation D states specifically that failure to satisfy all the terms and conditions of . . . Rule 506 shall not raise any presumption that the exemption provided by § 4(2) is not available."

E. REGULATION A

SECURITIES ACT § 3(b); SECURITIES ACT REG. A [RULES 251–263]

[See Statutory Supplement]

SEC, Q & A: Small Business and the SEC

(2009 rev.).

. . . **Regulation A**

. . . Section 3(b) of the Securities Act authorizes the SEC to exempt from registration small securities offerings. By this authority, we created Regulation A, an exemption for public offerings not exceeding $5 million in any 12–month period. If you choose to rely on this exemption, your company must file an offering statement, consisting of a notification, offering circular, and exhibits, with the SEC for review.

Regulation A offerings share many characteristics with registered offerings. For example, you must provide purchasers with an offering circular that is similar in content to a prospectus. Like registered offerings, the securities can be offered publicly and are not "restricted," meaning they are freely tradeable in the secondary market after the offering. The principal advantages of Regulation A offerings, as opposed to full registration, are:

- The financial statements are simpler and don't need to be audited;

- There are no Exchange Act reporting obligations after the offering unless the company has more than $10 million in total assets and more than 500 shareholders;
- Companies may choose among three formats to prepare the offering circular, one of which is a simplified question-and-answer document; and
- You may "test the waters" to determine if there is adequate interest in your securities before going through the expense of filing with the SEC.

All types of companies which do not report under the Exchange Act may use Regulation A, except . . . [reporting companies and mutual funds]. In most cases, shareholders may use Regulation A to resell up to $1.5 million of securities.

If you "test the waters," you can use general solicitation and advertising prior to filing an offering statement with the SEC, giving you the advantage of determining whether there is enough market interest in your securities before you incur the full range of legal, accounting, and other costs associated with filing an offering statement. You may not, however, solicit or accept money until the SEC staff completes its review of the filed offering statement and you deliver prescribed offering materials to investors.

Larry Sonsini, Regulation A

16 Review Sec. Reg. 781.
1983.

. . . Regulation A is the body of rules the SEC designed pursuant to section 3(b) to provide a general exemption for [small] issuances. . . .

GENERAL PROCEDURE

Documents to Be Filed. The regulation A process is initiated by the filing of a single document, designated the "Offering Statement," on form I–A. The Offering Statement, consisting of three parts, is the basic form to be used for every offering made under the exemption.

1. Part I of the Offering Statement is the "Notification." The purpose of the notification is to present information necessary to determine the availability of the exemption. . . .

2. Part II of the Offering Statement consists of the Offering Circular, which must be distributed to investors. The general instructions to part II indicate the items to which a particular issuer must respond. The disclosure requirements of the Offering Circular are derived from schedule I under the Securities Act, the basic schedule for registration statement disclosure. The disclosures of part II emphasize information on the business of the issuer, the quality of its

management, potential conflicts of interest, and the use of proceeds....

3. Part III of the offering statement requires a listing of exhibits....

PRACTICAL ASPECTS OF REGULATION A

The most practical use of regulation A is for the offer and sale of securities by nonreporting ("privately held") issuers. Such offerings usually occur under employee stock option and purchase plans. These plans typically provide for a rather broad distribution of securities among the employee group. Because the plans usually involve a continuing offering, i.e., the continuous grant of stock options or the sale of shares under stock purchase plans, sooner or later the issuer faces a greater difficulty in perfecting an exemption under the Securities Act for the transactions. As the employee group broadens and deepens within the organization to middle and lower management personnel, the issuer can no longer rely on many of the conditions that must be satisfied under the private placement exemptions. Similarly, because many employees will reside in jurisdictions other than those where the issuer is incorporated and doing business, the intrastate offering exemption under section 3(a)(11) and rule 147 of the Securities Act will be unavailable. Also, privately held issuers will often find it inappropriate to file a registration statement under the Securities Act to cover its transactions under employee stock benefit plans. The cost of registration may be high, and the issuer may not be able to satisfy certain disclosure requirements, such as those regarding financial statements. Therefore, the exemption offered by regulation A may prove most beneficial in these employee stock benefit plans. The burden of disclosure is less than under the standard registration statement forms, particularly with respect to certified financial statements.... The cost of perfecting the exemption under the regulation will usually be less than for the preparation, filing, and policing of a registration statement. In addition, the scope of the required disclosure under the offering circular may be well suited for an offering of securities to an employee group who, by definition, are familiar with the business of the issuer.

It should be noted, however, that there is no exemption from compliance with the antifraud provisions of the Securities Acts. Accordingly, notwithstanding the required disclosure under the regulation, the issuer must give consideration to the disclosure of all material information, whether or not specifically covered by an item of the notification. Therefore an issuer should refer to the disclosure items required under a registration statement to determine additional areas of materiality.

The use of regulation A for public offerings of securities other than pursuant to employee stock programs is ... more limited. Although the amendments to the regulation that now allow the use of a preliminary offering circular have made the regulation more appropriate for a public offering, there is still concern, particularly among many underwriters, that the advantages of the limited disclosure requirements of the regulation may not be suited to a public offering of broad distribution.

The burden of establishing exemption from the registration requirements of the Securities Act rests solely on the issuer or person claiming the exemption. As a result, with respect to regulation A, the issuer must be prepared to establish that the offering comes within the regulation and that all the conditions are satisfied.

The civil liability provisions of section 11 of the Securities Act do not apply to use of the regulation, because section 11 only applies to a registration statement filed under the Securities Act. However, the provisions of section 12 of the Securities Act apply to an offering and sale of securities under regulation A.

Securities Act Release No. 6949 (1992)

[Small Business Initiatives] . . .

A. *Regulation A*

As adopted, the dollar ceiling for a Regulation A offering is now $5 million in any 12–month period, including no more than $1.5 million in non-issuer resales. . . .

B. *"Testing the Waters"*

As discussed in the [Proposing] Release, one of the major impediments to a Regulation A financing for a small start-up or developing company with no established market for its securities, is the cost of preparing the mandated offering statement. The full costs of compliance would be incurred without knowing whether there will be any investor interest in the company.

To remedy this situation, the Commission proposed for the first time to permit companies relying on the Regulation A exemption to "test the waters" for potential interest in the company prior to filing and delivery of the mandated offering statement. All test the water documents are required to be submitted to the Commission at the time of first use. The proposal was enthusiastically endorsed by private sector commenters as a necessary and appropriate solution to a significant regulatory impediment to small business financing, and, as drafted, is consistent with investor protection interests.

A number of refinements have been included in the test the water provisions in response to public comment. First, while the Regulation continues to require that the "testing of the waters" begin with a written solicitation of interest submitted to the Commission at the time of first use, the rules have been revised to make clear that submission of the document is not a condition to the exemption. Failure to comply with the requirement is a grounds for Commission suspension of the exemption.

As proposed, the written test the water document was a free writing subject to the inclusion of two mandated statements—first, that no funds were being solicited or would be accepted, and secondly that a detailed offering document would follow. Some commenters suggested that even these few items should be deleted, while others suggested additional requirements or specific prescription of the content.

The rule as adopted continues to provide for free writing with the inclusion of the following items:

1. a statement that no money is being solicited, or will be accepted; that no sales can be made until delivery and qualification of the offering circular, and that indications of interest involve no obligation or commitment of any kind; and

2. a brief, general identification of the company's business, products and chief executive officer.

The rule has been revised to make clear that inclusion of these statements in the soliciting document is not a condition to the exemption, but failure to include the statements is a basis for Commission suspension of the exemption....

Once the offering statement required by Regulation A is filed with the Commission, the issuer may not continue to use its written "test the waters" solicitation materials. The rule requires that at least 20 calendar days elapse between the last use of the solicitation of interest document or broadcast and any sale of securities in the Regulation A offering. Compliance with the rules limiting the use of the test the water documents after filing of the offering statement is not a condition to the exemption, but [noncompliance] is a violation of the rule and is a basis for Commission suspension of the exemption....

NOTE ON THE SIGNIFICANCE OF EXEMPTIONS

It's important to keep in mind that a provision exempting securities from registration under Section 5 does not necessarily mean that a seller or offeror of those securities is not required to provide the buyers with information. Some exemptions explicitly require the seller to provide information very much like that required in a registration statement. For example, Regulation A (discussed earlier) requires an Offering Circular, and Regulation D requires the provision to non-accredited purchasers of registration-like information in certain cases. Other exemptions implicitly require the provision of information. For example, a distribution is unlikely to qualify as a private placement unless the offerees have had access or were provided to the *type* of information that would have been disclosed under a registration statement. Accordingly, when sales are made under section 4(2) or Rule 506 through investment bankers, the issuer typically supplies an information statement that provides prospectus-like disclosure. See Note on Doran v. Petroleum Management Corp., supra.

If an offeror of securities has to provide information of the *type* that must be disclosed in a registration statement, what is the benefit of an exemption? First, it is incorrect to conclude that the information necessary to meet the disclosure requirements of the section 4(2) or Regulation D is the mirror image in terms of the detail and comprehensiveness of disclosure called for in a registration statement. The information demands of section 4(2), Regulation A, and Regulation D are more general by comparison to the information called for by the regulations guiding the formal registration of securities under section 5. While in each instance the same general categories of disclosure items covered, the disclosures called for in the registration of securities under section 5 are much more detailed and comprehensive with respect to each disclosure item. Second, an information statement may not require clearance by the SEC, as does a registration statement. Third, certain liability provisions of the Securities Act are keyed into registration, and therefore do not apply to an information statement. See Section 7, infra.

NOTE ON THE INTEGRATION OF SECURITIES ISSUES

In general, an issue of securities cannot be artificially segregated into parts for the purpose of qualifying one part for an exemption when the issue taken as a whole would not qualify.

> The determination whether securities are being offered as part of a single "issue" will depend upon a consideration of various factors concerning the methods of sale and distribution employed to effect the offerings and the disposition of the proceeds. If the offerings may be segregated into separate blocks, as evidenced by material differences in the use of the proceeds, in the manner and terms of distribution, and in similar related details, each offering will be a separate "issue." In the main, of course, each case must be determined upon the basis of its own facts.

In the Matter of Unity Gold Corp., 3 S.E.C. 618, 625 (1938). See also Securities Act Release No. 1459 (1937); Securities Act Release No. 2029 (1939). Securities Act Release No. 4434 (1961) adds:

> Any one or more of the following factors may be determinative of the question of integration: (1) are the offerings part of a single plan of financing; (2) do the offerings involve issuance of the same class of security; (3) are the offerings made at or about the same time; (4) is the same type of consideration to be received, and (5) are the offerings made for the same general purpose.

An advantage provided for offerings carried out under Regulation A and Regulation D is that each contains an integration safe harbor. Thus, Rule 502(a) of Regulation D protects Regulation D offers from being integrated with any offering occurring more than 6 months before or after the Regulation D offer. Regulation A provides in Rule

251(c)(1) that a Regulation A offer is not integrated with any *prior* offering and Rule 251(c)(2)(v) provides that offers more than 6 months *after* a Regulation A offer will not be integrated with the Regulation A offer.

F. Transactions Not Involving an Issuer, Underwriter, or Dealer

---

SECURITIES ACT §§ 2(a)(11), 4(1), 4(3)

[See Statutory Supplement]

Securities Act section 5 broadly prohibits the sale of unregistered securities by any person, subject to the various exemptions under the Act. However, section 4(1) of the Act exempts, from section 5's prohibition, transactions by any person other than an issuer, underwriter, or dealer. In effect, therefore, despite its broad language section 5 is applicable only to offers and sales by an issuer, a dealer, or an underwriter.

Section 2(a)(4) defines an *issuer* as "every person who issues or proposes to issue any security."

Section 2(a)(12) defines a *dealer* as "any person who engages either for all or part of his time, directly or indirectly, as agent, broker, or principal, in the business of offering, buying, selling, or otherwise dealing or trading in securities issued by another person." However, section 4(3) exempts most transactions by dealers from the registration requirement.

Since the definition of issuer is fairly straightforward, and since most transactions by dealers are empted under section 4(3), the difficult problems in applying section 4(1) concern the meaning of "underwriters" for purposes of that section. Persons who are underwriters for this purpose are known as *statutory underwriters*. The paradigm case of a statutory underwriter is an investment professional who distributes stock on behalf of an issuer. However, section 2(a)(11) defines "underwriter" so as to pick up transactions that don't look anything like that paradigm:

> The term "underwriter" means any person who has purchased from an issuer with a view to, or offers or sells for an issuer in connection with, the distribution of any security, or participates or has a direct or indirect participation in any such undertaking, or participates or has a participation in the direct or indirect underwriting of any such undertaking; but such term shall not include a person whose interest is limited to a commission from

an underwriter or dealer not in excess of the usual and customary distributors' or sellers' commission. As used in this paragraph the term "issuer" shall include, in addition to an issuer, any person directly or indirectly controlling or controlled by the issuer, or any person under direct or indirect common control with the issuer.

The balance of the present Section will explicate section 2(a)(11) of the Securities Act by considering: (1) The meaning and implications of the terms, "offers or sells for an issuer in connection with . . . the distribution of any security" and "purchased from an issuer with a view to . . . the distribution of any security." (2) The meaning and implications of the terms, "any person directly or indirectly controlling . . . the issuer." (3) Rules 144 and 144A.

---

(1) WHO IS A STATUTORY UNDERWRITER

NOTE ON THE MEANING OF TERM "OFFERS OR SELLS FOR AN ISSUER IN CONNECTION WITH . . . THE DISTRIBUTION OF ANY SECURITY"

The language in section 2(a)(11), "offers or sells for an issuer in connection with . . . the distribution of any security," has been construed very broadly. Perhaps the most notable case is SEC v. Chinese Consolidated Benevolent Ass'n., 120 F.2d 738 (2d Cir.1941), cert. denied 314 U.S. 618, 62 S.Ct. 106, 86 L.Ed. 497. The defendant had sold unregistered bonds of the Republic of China in the United States at the beginning of World War II. The defendant promoted the bonds through meetings and advertisements directed to the Chinese communities in New York, Connecticut and New Jersey, through various banks forwarded to China the investors' payments (about $600,000), and ultimately mailed the bonds to the investors. The defendant claimed it was not an underwriter within the meaning of then-section 2(a)(11) because it had no agreement with the Chinese government to sell the bonds, and was not compensated for selling the bonds, but instead acted out of loyalty to China. Held, the defendant was nevertheless an underwriter:

> Under section 4(1) the defendant is not exempt from registration requirements if it is "an underwriter". The court below reasons that [the defendant] is not to be regarded as an underwriter since it does not sell or solicit offers to buy "for an issuer in connection with, the distribution" of securities. In other words, it seems to have been held that only solicitation authorized by the issuer in connection with the distribution of the Chinese bonds would satisfy the definition of underwriter contained in Section 2(11) and that defendant's activities were never for the Chinese government but only for the purchasers of the bonds. Though the defendant solicited the orders, obtained the cash from the pur-

> chasers and caused both to be forwarded so as to procure the bonds, it is nevertheless contended that its acts could not have been for the Chinese government because it had no contractual arrangement or even understanding with the latter. But the aim of the Securities Act is to have information available for investors. This objective will be defeated if buying orders can be solicited which result in uninformed and improvident purchasers. It can make no difference as regards the policy of the act whether an issuer has solicited orders through an agent, or has merely taken advantage of the services of a person interested for patriotic reasons in securing offers to buy. The aim of the issuer is to promote the distribution of the securities, and of the Securities Act is to protect the public by requiring that it be furnished with adequate information upon which to make investments. Accordingly the words "[sell] for an issuer in connection with the distribution of any security" ought to be read as covering continual solicitations, such as the defendant was engaged in, which normally would result in a distribution of issues of unregistered securities within the United States. Here a series of events were set in motion by the solicitation of offers to buy which culminated in a distribution that was initiated by the defendant. We hold that the defendant acted as an underwriter.

120 F.2d at 740–41.

NOTE ON THE MEANING OF THE TERM "ANY PERSON WHO HAS PURCHASED FROM AN ISSUER WITH A VIEW TO ... DISTRIBUTION"

Section 2(a)(11) also includes within the term "underwriter" for purposes of that section, a person "who has purchased from an issuer with a view to ... distribution." Even a person who is not an underwriter in the normal usage of that term may be a statutory underwriter under this provision. Assume that P has purchased securities from an issuer in a private placement. If P purchased the securities with the intent to offer or resell them through a distribution—as opposed to having purchased with an "investment intent"—he is an underwriter under section 2(a)(11). The classic case is that in which P has purchased unregistered securities under the private-placement exemption, and then quickly turned around and re-offered the securities to a number of unsophisticated buyers.

The leading case is Gilligan, Will & Co. v. S.E.C., 267 F.2d 461 (2d Cir.), cert. denied 361 U.S. 896, 80 S.Ct. 200, 4 L.Ed.2d 152 (1959). Gilligan, a partner in Gilligan Will, purchased $100,000 of a $3,000,000 private placement of Crowell–Collier convertible debentures for his own account, representing that he purchased for investment. Notwithstanding these representations, Gilligan quickly sold $45,000 of the debentures to Louis Alter; made offers to two other potential purchasers (selling $5,000 of debentures to one of them);

and placed the remaining debentures in a Gilligan Will trading account. Ten months later, Gilligan, Alter, and the Gilligan Will firm converted their debentures into common stock and sold the stock at a profit on the American Stock Exchange....

Gilligan and Gilligan Will argued that since the conversion and sales occurred more than ten months after the purchase of the debentures, the Commission was bound to find that the debentures so converted had been held for investment, and were not purchased with a view to distribution. The court rejected this contention:

> ... Petitioners concede that if such sales were intended at the time of purchase, the debentures would not then have been held as investments; but [they argue] that the stipulation reveals that the sales were undertaken only after a change of the issuer's circumstances as a result of which petitioners, acting as prudent investors, thought it wise to sell. The catalytic circumstances were the failure, noted by Gilligan, of Crowell–Collier to increase its advertising space as he had anticipated it would. We agree with the Commission that in the circumstances here presented the intention to retain the debentures only if Crowell–Collier continued to operate profitably was equivalent to a "purchase ... with a view to ... distribution" within the statutory definition of underwriters in § 2(11). To hold otherwise would be to permit a dealer who speculatively purchases an unregistered security in the hope that the financially weak issuer had, as is stipulated here, "turned the corner," to unload on the unadvised public what he later determines to be an unsound investment without the disclosure sought by the securities laws, although it is in precisely such circumstances that disclosure is most necessary and desirable....
>
> 267 F.2d at 467–68.

---

(2) SALES BY CONTROLLING PERSONS

NOTE ON OFFERS OR SALES BY CONTROLLING PERSONS

A distribution of unregistered securities by a person who is in control of an issuer is comparable in many respects to a sale by the issuer itself. Accordingly, distributions by controlling persons are not exempt under section 4(1). This result is reached circuitously. Under the last sentence of section 2(a)(11), a person is an underwriter if he offers or sells securities for a person who *controls* the issuer "in connection with ... the distribution of any security." (Under Securities Act Rule 405, "[t]he term 'control' ... means the possession, direct or indirect, of the power to direct or cause the direction of the management and policies of a person, whether through the ownership of voting securities, by contract, or otherwise.")

The applicability of the principle that a distribution on behalf of a controlling person is not exempt from section 5 is often complicated by two issues: whether a particular sale on behalf of a controlling person constitutes a "distribution," and whether the sale comes within the exemption in section 4(4) for "brokers' transactions executed upon customers' orders on any exchange or in the over-the-counter market but not the solicitation of such orders."

The Distribution Question: Section 4(1). In In the Matter of Ira Haupt & Co., 23 S.E.C. 589 (1946), Ira Haupt & Company, a brokerage firm, sold approximately 93,000 shares of the unregistered common stock of Park & Tilford, Inc. (a liquor distiller) for the accounts of David A. Schulte and a corporation and trust controlled by Schulte. The sales were made in small lots over the course of approximately six months, pursuant to Schulte's instructions to sell 200–share blocks from his personal holdings at "59 and every quarter up," and up to 73,000 shares for the trust "at $80 per share or better." The price of the stock rose sharply from $57 to $98 per share during this period, because of the announcement that a whiskey dividend would be distributed in kind to the shareholders of Park & Tilford. (A dividend in liquor was especially welcome during the wartime shortage.) Schulte was aware of the planned dividend at the time he placed his sell order with Ira Haupt.

The Schulte interests initially held over 90 percent of the common stock of Park & Tilford, and it was therefore conceded that they controlled Park & Tilford. Accordingly, it was clear that Ira Haupt was selling the securities for a person "controlling the issuer" as contemplated by the last sentence of then section 2(11). Ira Haupt nevertheless denied that it was a statutory underwriter for purposes of the transactions because the sales were not effected "in connection with . . . the distribution of any security."

At the outset, the Commission noted that, although the term "distribution" is not defined in the Act, it had previously been held to comprise "the entire process by which in the course of a public offering the block of securities is dispersed and ultimately comes to rest in the hands of the investing public." The Commission further remarked:

> We find no validity in the argument that a predetermination of the precise number of shares which are to be publicly dispersed is an essential element of a distribution. Nor do we think that a "distribution" loses its character as such merely because the extent of the offering may depend on certain conditions such as the market price. . . . Such offerings are not any less a "distribution" merely because their precise extent cannot be predetermined. . . .

The Commission concluded that

> . . . [Ira Haupt] was selling for the Schulte interests, controlling shareholders of Park & Tilford, in connection with the

> distribution of their holdings in the stock and was, therefore, an "underwriter" within the meaning of the Act.

Thus, the exemption of section 4(1) was not applicable to the transactions.

Gilligan, Will & Co. v. SEC, 267 F.2d 461 (2d Cir. 1959), is the leading case on the meaning of "distribution" of distribution. The Second Circuit held that "distribution" is to be found in the Supreme Court's approach for determining the scope of the private offering exemption as set forth in SEC v. Ralston Purina Co., 346 U.S. 119, 73 S.Ct. 981, 97 L.Ed. 1494 (1953). To wit, a distribution exists if the sales are to those who cannot "fend for themselves." *Gilligan, Will* found the defendants had engaged in a distribution by selling unregistered securities both through the American Stock Exchange and directly to a few investors none of whom were provided or had access to the type of information about the issuer that would have been available through registration. *See also* Wheaten v. Matthews Holmquist & Assoc., Inc. [1995 Transfer Binder] Fed. Sec. L. Rep. (CCH) ¶ 98,727 (N.D. Ill. 1994) (whether there is a distribution depends on the buyers' sophistication).

Brokers' Transactions: Section 4(4). Ira Haupt, *supra*, also claimed that the transactions fell within section 4(4) (then 4(2)), which exempts "brokers' transactions executed upon customers' orders on any exchange or in the over-the-counter market but not the solicitation of such orders." The S.E.C. rejected this defense as well:

> These sections, by their terms, provide that whenever anyone controlling an issuer makes a public distribution of his holdings in the controlled corporation by selling through another person acting for him in connection with the distribution, the sales by which the distribution is accomplished are transactions by an underwriter which are subject to the registration requirements. Applie to such transactions by which substantial quantities of securities are disposed of to the public, the registration requirement is consistent with and calculated to further the general purpose of the Act. . . .
>
> We find nothing in the language or legislative history of section [4(4)] to compel the exemption of this type of secondary distribution and the consequent overriding of the general objectives and policy of the Act. On the contrary, there are affirmative indications that section [4(4)] was meant to preserve the distinction between the "trading" and "distribution" of securities which separates the exempt and non-exempt transactions under section 4(1). . . .
>
> From the [legislative history], it is apparent that transactions by an issuer or underwriter and transactions by a dealer during the period of *distribution* . . . must be preceded by registration and the use of a prospectus. It is likewise apparent that Congress intended that, during this period, persons other than an issuer, underwriter, or dealer should be able to *trade* in the security

> without use of a prospectus. Since such persons would carry on their trading largely through the use of brokers (who are included in the general definition of dealers), such trading through brokers without the use of a prospectus could be permitted during the first year after the initial offering only if there were a special exemption for dealers acting as brokers. The importance of this special exemption is emphasized in the case where a stop order might be entered against a registration statement. For, although such a stop order was intended to and would operate to stop all *distribution* activities, it would also result in stopping all *trading* by individuals through dealers acting as brokers unless a special exemption were provided for brokers. It was in recognition of this fact and to permit a dealer to act as a broker for an individual's trading transactions, while the security is being distributed and during the period of a stop order, that section [4(4)] was enacted....

Similarly, in United States v. Wolfson, 405 F.2d 779 (2d Cir.1968), cert. denied 394 U.S. 946, 89 S.Ct. 1275, 22 L.Ed.2d 479 (1969), the court upheld the conviction of a controlling shareholder for failing to register a substantial number of shares sold through several brokers without informing any of the brokers that sales of were also being made through other brokers. The court gave short shrift to the argument that the broker's exemption protected a controlling shareholder:

> ... [T]he appellants contend that the brokers in this case cannot be classified as underwriters because their part in the sales transactions came within § 4(4), 15 U.S.C.A. § 77d(4), which exempts "brokers' transactions executed upon customers' orders on any exchange or in the over-the-counter market but not the solicitation of such orders." The answer to this contention is that § 4(4) was designed only to exempt the brokers' part in security transactions.... Control persons must find their own exemptions.
>
> There is nothing inherently unreasonable for a broker to claim the exemption of § 4(4) ... when he is unaware that his customer's part in the transaction is not exempt....
>
> Certainly if the appellants' sales, which clearly amounted to a distribution ... had been made through a broker or brokers with knowledge of the circumstances, the brokers would not be entitled to the exemption. It will hardly do for the appellants to say that because they kept the true facts from the brokers they can take advantage of the exemption the brokers gained thereby.

---

(3) RULES 144 AND 144A

SECURITIES ACT RULE 144

[See Statutory Supplement]

The wide ambit given to the meaning of the term underwriter, together with the coverage of sales by controlling persons, made it difficult for controlling persons, and persons holding restricted securities, to know when they could safely trade unregistered shares. The SEC has sought to meet this problem by providing safe harbors for certain such sales under Rules 144 and 144A.

Revisions to Rule 144

Securities Act Release No. 8869 (Dec. 6, 2007).

I. BACKGROUND . . .

Rule 144 regulates the resale of two categories of securities: restricted securities and control securities. Restricted securities are securities acquired pursuant to one of the transactions listed in Rule 144(a)(3). Although it is not a term defined in Rule 144, "control securities" is used commonly to refer to securities held by an affiliate of the issuer, regardless of how the affiliate acquired the securities. Therefore, if an affiliate acquires securities in a transaction that is listed in Rule 144(a)(3), those securities are both restricted securities and control securities. A person selling restricted securities, or a person selling restricted or other securities on behalf of the account of an affiliate, who satisfies all of Rule 144's applicable conditions in connection with the transaction, is deemed not to be an "underwriter," as defined in Section 2(a)(11) of the Securities Act, and therefore may rely on the Section 4(1) exemption for the resale of the securities. . . .

Rule 144 states that a selling security holder shall be deemed not to be engaged in a distribution of securities, and therefore not an underwriter, . . . if the resale satisfies specified conditions. The conditions include the following:

- There must be adequate current public information available about the issuer;
- If the securities being sold are restricted securities, the security holder must have held the security for a specified holding period;
- The resale must be within specified sales volume limitations;
- The resale must comply with the manner of sale requirements; and
- The selling security holder must file Form 144 if the amount of securities being sold exceeds specified thresholds.

Rule 144, as it existed before today's amendments, permitted a non-affiliate to publicly resell restricted securities without being subject to the above limitations if the securities had been held for two years or more, provided that the security holder was not, and, for the three months prior to the sale, had not been, an affiliate of the issuer. . . .

II. DISCUSSION OF FINAL AMENDMENTS . . .

B. AMENDMENTS TO HOLDING PERIODS FOR RESTRICTED SECURITIES

1. Six-Month Rule 144(d) Holding Period Requirement for Exchange Act Reporting Companies . . .

The purpose of Rule 144 is to provide objective criteria for determining that the person selling securities to the public has not acquired the securities from the issuer for distribution. A holding period is one criterion established to demonstrate that the selling security holder did not acquire the securities to be sold under Rule 144 with distributive intent. We do not want the holding period to be longer than necessary or impose any unnecessary costs or restrictions on capital formation. . . . [W]e believe that a six-month holding period for securities of reporting issuers provides a reasonable indication that an investor has assumed the economic risk of investment in the securities to be resold under Rule 144. Therefore, we are adopting a six-month holding period for reporting companies. . . .

Under the amendments that we are adopting, the six-month holding period requirement will apply to the securities of an issuer that has been subject to the reporting requirements of Section 13 or 15(d) of the Exchange Act for a period of at least 90 days before the Rule 144 sale. Restricted securities of a "non-reporting issuer" will continue to be subject to a one-year holding period requirement. A non-reporting issuer is one that is not, or has not been for a period of at least 90 days before the Rule 144 sale, subject to the reporting requirements of Section 13 or 15(d) of the Exchange Act.

We believe that different holding periods for reporting and non-reporting issuers are appropriate given that reporting issuers have an obligation to file periodic reports with updated financial information (including audited financial information in annual filings) that are publicly available on EDGAR, the Commission's electronic filing system. Although non-reporting issuers must make some information publicly available before resales can be made under Rule 144, this information typically is much more limited in scope than information included in Exchange Act reports, is not required to include audited financial information, and is not publicly available via EDGAR. For these reasons, we believe that continuing to require security holders of non-reporting issuers to hold their securities for one year is not unduly burdensome and is consistent with investor protection.

2. Significant Reduction of Conditions Applicable to Non–Affiliates

. . . [A]fter the applicable holding period requirement is met, the resale of restricted securities by a non-affiliate under Rule 144 will no longer be subject to any other conditions of Rule 144 except that, with regard to the resale of securities of a reporting issuer, the current public information requirement in Rule 144(c) will apply for an additional six months after the six-month holding period requirement is met. . . .

The final conditions applicable to the resale under Rule 144 of restricted securities held by affiliates and non-affiliates of the issuer can be summarized as follows:

	Affiliate or Person Selling on Behalf of an Affiliate	**Non–Affiliate (and Has Not Been an Affiliate During the Prior Three Months)**
Restricted Securities of Reporting Issuers	During six-month holding period—no resales under Rule 144 permitted. After six-month holding period—may resell in accordance with all Rule 144 requirements including: • Current public information, • Volume limitations, • Manner of sale requirements for equity securities, and • Filing of Form 144.	During six-month holding period—no resales under Rule 144 permitted. After six-month holding period but before one year—unlimited public resales under Rule 144 except that the current public information requirement still applies. After one-year holding period—unlimited public resales under Rule 144; need not comply with any other Rule 144 requirements.
Restricted Securities of Non–Reporting Issuers	During one-year holding period—no resales under Rule 144 permitted. After one-year holding period—may resell in accordance with all Rule 144 requirements, including: • Current public information, • Volume limitations, • Manner of sale requirements for equity securities, and • Filing of Form 144.	During one-year holding period—no resales under Rule 144 permitted. After one-year holding period—unlimited public resales under Rule 144; need not comply with any other Rule 144 requirements.

C. AMENDMENTS TO THE MANNER OF SALE REQUIREMENTS APPLICABLE TO RESALES BY AFFILIATES

. . . Rule 144(g), . . . defines "brokers' transactions" for purposes of the manner of sale requirements. Under the definition of brokers' transactions, a broker must neither solicit nor arrange for the solicitation of customers' orders to buy the securities in anticipation of, or in connection with, the transaction. . . .

E. INCREASE OF THE THRESHOLDS THAT TRIGGER THE FORM 144 FILING REQUIREMENT FOR AFFILIATES . . .

We are adopting . . . increased Form 144 filing thresholds. . . . [W]e are raising the dollar threshold to $50,000 to adjust for inflation since 1972 ... [and]. we are raising the share threshold to 5,000 shares....

SECURITIES ACT RULE 144A

[See Statutory Supplement]

Securities Act Release No. 6862 (1990)

... **RULE 144A**

... Rule 144A ... [is] the first step toward achieving a more liquid and efficient institutional resale market for unregistered securities. The Commission intends to monitor the evolution of this market and to revisit the Rule with a view to making any appropriate changes....

A. General

Rule 144A sets forth a non-exclusive safe harbor from the registration requirements of Section 5 of the Securities Act for the resale of restricted securities to specified institutions by persons other than the issuer of such securities. The transactions covered by the safe harbor are private transactions that, on the basis of a few objective standards, can be defined as outside the purview of Section 5, without the necessity of undertaking the more usual analysis under Sections 4(1) and 4(3) of the Securities Act.

By providing that transactions meeting its terms are not "distributions," the Rule essentially confirms that such transactions are not subject to the registration provisions of the Securities Act. In the case of persons other than issuers or dealers, the rule does this by providing that any such person who offers and sells securities in accordance with the Rule will be deemed not to be engaged in a distribution and therefore not to be an underwriter within the meanings of Sections 2(11)and 4(1) of the Securities Act. Such persons therefore may rely on the exemption from registration provided by Section 4(1) for transactions by persons other than issuers, underwriters or dealers. Dealers have the benefit of an exemption from registration under Section 4(3) of the Securities Act, except when they are participants in a distribution or within a specified period after the securities have been offered to the public. The Rule provides that, if the conditions of the Rule are met, a dealer will be deemed not to be a participant in a distribution of securities within the meaning of Section 4(3)(C) of the Act and not to be an underwriter of such securities within the meaning of Section 2(11) of the Act, and the securities will be deemed not to have been offered to the public within the meaning of Section 4(3)(A) of the Act....

B. Eligible Securities

Rule 144A would not extend to the offer or sale of securities that, when issued, were of the same class as securities listed on a national securities exchange registered under Section 6 of the Exchange Act or quoted in an automated inter-dealer quotation system. Accordingly, privately-placed securities that, at the time of their issuance, were fungible with securities trading on a U.S. exchange ... would not be eligible for resale under the Rule....

C. Eligible Purchasers

1. Types of Institutions Covered

... [E]xcept for registered broker-dealers, to be a "qualified institutional buyer" an institution must in the aggregate own and invest on a discretionary basis at least $100 million in securities of issuers that are not affiliated with the institution....

D. Information Requirement ...

As adopted, availability of the Rule is conditioned upon the holder and a prospective purchaser designated by the holder having the right to obtain from the issuer, upon the holder's request to the issuer, certain basic financial information, and upon such prospective purchaser having received such information at or prior to the time of sale, upon such purchaser's request to the holder or the issuer. This information is required only where the issuer does not file periodic reports under the Exchange Act, ... and does not furnish home country information to the Commission pursuant to Rule 12g3–2(b)....

The Commission does not believe that the limited information requirement should impose a significant burden on those issuers subject to the requirement. Many foreign issuers that will be subject to the requirement, which were the focus of the commenters' concern, will have securities traded in established offshore markets, and already will have made the required information publicly available in such markets. Even for domestic issuers, the required information represents only a portion of that which would be necessary before a U.S. broker or dealer could submit for publication a quotation for the securities of such an issuer in a quotation medium in the United States.... The Commission expects that the kinds of information commonly furnished under Rule 12g3–2(b) by foreign private issuers almost invariably would satisfy the information requirement and that foreign private issuers who wish their securities to be Rule 144A—eligible will simply obtain a Rule 12g3–2(b) exemption on a voluntary basis. Financial statements meeting the timing requirements of the issuer's home country or principal trading markets would be considered sufficiently current for purposes of the information requirement of the Rule....

NOTE ON THE "4 1–1/2" EXEMPTION

As seen earlier, the last sentence of section 2(a)(11) provides that for the purpose of defining who is an underwriter, a person who either sells for a control person in connection with a distribution or purchases from a control person with a view to the distribution of the purchased security will be an underwriter. Rules 144 and 144A provide safe harbors to avoid such a seller or purchaser being an underwriter. But it might well be that the control person who wishes to sell securities cannot take advantage of either of these safe harbors. For example, the buyer might not be a QIB and the manner of sale or volume limits of Rule 144 cannot be satisfied. In such cases, the case law has developed the so-called 4 1–1/2 exemption. The curious fractional-naming of the exemption reflects that the true exemption being invoked is section 4(1), i.e., a transaction not by an underwriter, and that the means to conclude that this exemption is satisfied is by analogy to section 4(2), the private offering exemption. That is, the availability of the 4 1–1/2 exemption turns on whether the buyers of the security can "fend for themselves." Note in this regard that as a technical matter section 4(2) is not available to the control person; section 4(2) is expressly limited to *issuer* transactions and section 2(a)(4) of the Securities Act defines issuer and does not within its definition include a person that controls the issuer. To be sure, Section 2(a)(11) renders a control person an issuer, albeit only for the purposes of Section 2(a)(11), but not for any other purposes. Thus, when one is selling for a control person and wishes to invoke the 4 1–1/2 exemption, the relevant inquiry is the sophistication of the offerees and the type of information that is either disclosed to the offerees or that to which they had access.

NOTE ON EXEMPTED SECURITIES

The exemptions considered in this Section relate to types of *transactions* and for the most part provide an exemption only from *section 5*. The Securities Act also exempts certain types of *securities* from the provisions of *the entire Act.* These exemptions are to be found in sections 3(a)(1)–(a)(8). They include U.S. government, state, and municipal securities (section 3(a)(2)), certain short-term paper (section 3(a)(3)), and bankruptcy trustee certificates (section 3(a)(7)).

SECTION 5. MECHANICS OF REGISTRATION

SECURITIES ACT FORMS S–1, S–2, AND S–3

[See Statutory Supplement]

NOTE ON THE REGISTRATION PROCESS

In general, the registration statement must describe such matters as the characteristics of the securities; the character and size of the business enterprise; its capital structure, financial history, and earnings; underwriters' commissions; the names of persons who participate in the direction, management, or control of the business; their security holdings and remuneration, including options; payments to promoters made within two years or intended to be made in the near future; acquisitions of property not in the ordinary course of business, and the interests of directors, officers, and principal stockholders therein; pending or threatened legal proceedings; and the purpose to which the proceeds of the offering are to be applied. The registration statement must include the issuer's financial statements, certified by independent accountants.

The Commission is empowered to prevent the sale of securities to the public on the basis of registration statements that contain inaccurate or incomplete information. The Staff of the Division of Corporate Finance usually notifies the registrant, by an informal letter of comment, of respects in which the registration statement apparently fails to conform to these requirements. The registrant is afforded an opportunity to file an amendment before the statement becomes effective. However, in certain cases, such as where the deficiencies in a registration statement appear to stem from careless disregard of applicable requirements or a deliberate attempt to conceal or mislead, the Commission either institutes an investigation to determine whether "stop-order" proceedings should be instituted, or immediately issues such an order.

The minimum waiting period between the time of filing the registration statement and the time it may become effective is twenty days. This waiting period is designed to provide investors with an opportunity to become familiar with the proposed offering. Information disclosed in the registration statement is disseminated during the waiting period by means of the preliminary prospectus, which presents the information set forth in the registration statement.

NOTE ON THE INTEGRATION OF DISCLOSURE UNDER THE 1933 AND 1934 ACTS

The content of the registration forms has been dramatically affected by the concept of integration. The Securities Exchange Act of 1934 requires *periodic disclosure* by issuers whose stock is registered under that Act. For example, such issuers must file an annual 10–K report, which includes financial statements and various other information; must annually distribute a proxy statement, or the equivalent, containing information on such matters as remuneration of directors and officers and conflict-of-interest transactions; and must file timely 8–K reports whenever certain material events have occurred. In contrast, the Securities Act of 1933 requires only *transactional disclosure*—that is, disclosure only in connection with specific public distributions. Until the late 1970s, the disclosure schemes of the two Acts proceeded on separate tracks. At that time, the Commission undertook a program of integrating the two disclosure schemes. Partly, this was accomplished by a uniform Regulation, S–K, which provides equivalent definitions and disclosure requirements under the two Acts. Partly, it was accomplished by stratifying issuers into two classes, and reducing the amount of disclosure required in registration statements under the 1933 Act filed for issuers that are already making periodic disclosure under the 1934 Act for which there was reason to believe a great deal of information is likely to be publicly available even apart from the 1934 Act's disclosure requirements.

Government agencies are known for confronting the regulated with a plethora of forms. The SEC is no exception. Identifying the precise form for the registration for a public offering of securities begins with the type of issuer. Thus, there is a series N forms for mutual funds, F series for foreign issuers, and the S series for domestic issuers. It is this latter group that we will focus on here, and most particularly on Forms S–1 and S–3.

The greatest ease in the registration process is accorded issuers eligible to use Form S–3; it is this group of issuers that can take full advantage of integrated disclosure by incorporating in their registration statement information from their Exchange Act filings, i.e., Forms 10–K and 10–Q. The new information that the Form S–3 registrant files with the SEC is the "transaction specific" information that bears on the amount and type of security being offered, information about the underwriting (e.g., method of underwriting, identity of underwriters, and commission) and the use of the proceeds. Any material changes or updates to information contained in earlier filed Exchange Act reports is also included in the submitted Form S–3.

Form S–3 sets forth both issuer and offering eligibility requirements. In broad overview, to be an eligible issuer, the firm must have been a reporting company for at least 12 months, have been current in its filing requirements during immediately preceding 12 months, and not failed during the last fiscal year to pay a fixed dividend payment to preferred stock, installment on indebtedness, or lease. In addition to being an eligible issuer, the transaction must meet one of several transaction requirements, the most prevalent being i) a cash offering of securities by an issuer whose voting common held by non-control persons is $75 million or more, ii) a cash offering of securities that represent not more than one-third of the aggregate of the issuer's voting and non-voting common held by non-control persons, iii) any secondary offering by a control person, or iv) the offering of certain types of securities that are rated investment grade.

When the SEC first adopted Form S–3 and embraced integrated disclosure it explaining its actions as follows:

> Form S–3 recognizes the applicability of the efficient market theory to the registration statement framework with respect to those registrants which usually provide high quality corporate

> reports, including Exchange Act reports, and whose corporate information is broadly disseminated, because such companies are widely followed by professional analysts and investors in the market place. Because these registrants are widely followed, the disclosure set forth in the prospectus may appropriately be limited, without the loss of investor protection, to information concerning the offering and material facts which have not been disclosed previously. The abbreviated disclosure is made possible by the use of incorporation by reference of the registrant's Exchange Act information into the prospectus. Because of the abbreviated disclosure, the utility of proposed Form S–3 is limited to widely followed companies.... The proposed float requirement is designed to correlate the use of abbreviated Form S–3 to widely followed registrants.

Securities Act Rel. No. 6331 (1981). In the same release, the SEC provides the following summary of the information to be incorporated by reference:

> Information concerning the registrant would be incorporated by reference from Exchange Act reports, which would be available to investors on request. The documents required to be incorporated are the latest annual report on Form 10–K and all other reports filed pursuant to Section 13(a) or 15(d) of the Exchange Act since the end of the fiscal year covered by the Form 10–K, including all Section 13(d) or 15(d) reports filed subsequent to effectiveness of the registration statement and prior to termination of the offering. Unless there has been a material change in the registrant's affairs which has not been reported in an Exchange Act filing, the prospectus would not be required to present any information concerning the registrant....

Issuers or transactions that cannot meet the issuer or transaction eligibility requirements of Form S–3 fall into the residual registration form, Form S–1. Issuers who are reporting companies, current in filing with the SEC the required Exchange Act reports, and have filed at least one annual report with the SEC can in registering securities on Form S–1 incorporate information from their Exchange Act reports. As we will see, issuers that are relegated to Form S–1 cannot avail themselves to the integrated disclosure procedures unless they have filed at least one annual report, i.e., Form 10–K, with the SEC, so this non-seasoned group of issuers must build their registration statement from the ground up.

In a world of word processing, and more particularly the clip-and-paste feature of the word processing program, the skeptical may question just how significant is the advantage enjoyed by the S–3 eligible issuer? The true regulatory dispensations accorded the S–3 registrant is not the ability to avoid the hardly burdensome process of clipping information from filed SEC forms and pasting that information to their registration statement. A perusal of SEC rules quickly reveals a host of regulatory dispensations that are available only to registrants eligible to register the offering on Form S–3. Such dispensations are the true significance of the Form S–3 eligibility requirements.

SECURITIES ACT RULES § 176, 415

[See Statutory Supplement]

NOTE ON SHELF REGISTRATION

Up to this point, the description of the registration process has assumed that once the demands of Securities Act Section 5 were satisfied that the issuer and its underwriters would initiate efforts to sell all the registered securities. What special problems arise if it is not likely that the securities will be offered or sold immediately upon the registration statement becoming effective? For example, assume a company issues a bond that is convertible into common shares. Technically, this is an offer of both the bond and the common. But assume the bond is issued at $1000, can be converted at anytime into 50 common shares, and the current market price of the common shares is $15 per share. It would not be reasonable to exercise the conversion feature of the bond as this would be trading a $1000 bond for $750 of common stock. Nonetheless, from the perspective of the Securities Act, there is at least an offer of the common stock and this triggers concern for section 5(c)'s prohibition of any offer of a security unless a registration statement has been filed. Another situation of a delayed offering or sale arises if the issuer wishes to have stock ready to be issued for yet to be identified acquisition targets. A third situation arises when the control person wishes to sell shares over time into the market, much like the distributions in *Wolfson* and *Ira Haupt*, *supra*. A final illustration is the issuer who wishes to raise cash, but only when it can get a good price for its securities. Thus, it would like to register the securities and set them aside until market conditions warrant. In each of these four situations, the securities that will ultimately be sold are figuratively "put on the shelf" until some later condition occurs that triggers their sale, e.g., conversion of an outstanding security, an acquisition occurs, or market conditions justify their sale. Each of these, and several other situations, are now covered by the SEC's shelf registration provision, Rule 415. The necessity for Rule 415 is explained in the SEC's release accompanying the rule's adoption.

> . . . The last sentence of Section 6(a) of the Securities Act provides: "A registration statement shall be deemed effective only as to the securities specified therein as proposed to be offered." . . . [The Commission has interpreted] that sentence to prohibit the registration of securities for a delayed or postponed offering, commonly referred to as "shelf" offering or registration.

> In the absence of any specific legislative comment upon the meaning of the last sentence of Section 6(a) of the Securities Act, as enacted by Congress in 1933, early opinions of the Commission and its staff interpreted the provision as requiring that a registration statement be effective only as to those securities proposed to be offered "in the proximate future".... This general prohibition against shelf registration was designed to effectuate the clear policy underlying the last sentence of Section 6(a) that "the registration statements and prospectuses on which they rely, so far as is reasonably possible, provide current information." This interpretation was, in turn, premised upon the assumption that the registration of securities which are to be offered at "some remote future time" gives "the appearance of a registered status" without providing its true substance—accurate and current information.
>
> In practice, the Commission has never adhered to such an absolute prohibition [and].... such registration has been permitted for several types of offerings....

Securities Act Release No. 6276 (1981)

Rule 14(a)(1)(i)–(vii) sets forth the so-called traditional bases for shelf registration. These provisions are available to all issuers. By far the most significant provision of Rule 415 is subparagraph (a)(1)(x) which was adopted in 1981 and is intended to allow eligible issuer's to "catch market windows," meaning allowing them to satisfy the Securities Act registration requirements, put the securities on the shelf, and issue the securities as market conditions justify the security's sale. This provision is only available for issuer's eligible to use Form S–3. In 2005, the SEC greatly liberalized the disclosures made in shelf registrations carried out under Rule 415(a)(1)(x) by allowing the filed registration statement to omit specific information about the securities being registered such as the specific type, amount, or features of the registered security; it is sufficient to broadly identify the security, such as common stock, preferred stock, bonds. The omitted information about the security is supplied later, when the security is sold (referred to in the trade as the "take down"). Issuers that are not eligible to use Form S–3 cannot invoke the shelf registration procedures for the purpose of catching a market window but they can register securities for one of the traditional bases for shelf registration, e.g., potential conversion of an outstanding bond into the issuer's common stock, as set forth in subdivisions (a)(1)(i)–(vii) of Rule 415.

SECTION 6. DUTIES AND PROHIBITIONS WHEN A SECURITY IS IN REGISTRATION

Assuming that a registration statement must be filed, the issuer, underwriter, and broker-dealers come under a variety of duties and prohibitions. To analyze these duties and prohibitions, it is necessary to separately consider three time periods. The first is the period before registration (the "prefiling period"). The second is the period between the time the registration statement is filed and the time it becomes effective (the "waiting period"). The third is the period after the registration statement becomes effective (the "post-effective period").

Note that the term "in registration" is used to mean "the entire process of registration, at least from the time an issuer reaches an understanding with the broker-dealer which is to act as managing underwriter prior to the filing of a registration statement and the period of 40 to 90 days during which dealers must deliver a prospectus." Securities Act Release No. 5180 n. 1 (1971).

A. OVERVIEW

Securities Act Release No. 4697 (1964) [Offers and Sales of Securities by Underwriters and Dealers]

In view of recent comments in the press concerning the rights and obligations of, and limitations on, dealers in connection with distributions of registered securities, the Commission takes this opportunity to explain the operation of section 5 of the Securities Act of 1933 with particular reference to the limitations upon, and responsibilities of, underwriters and dealers in the offer and sale of an issue of securities prior to and after the filing of a registration statement....

The Period Before the Filing of a Registration Statement

Section 5 of the Securities Act prohibits both offers to sell and offers to buy a security before a registration statement is filed. Section 2(3) of the Act, however, exempts preliminary negotiations or agreements between the issuer or other person on whose behalf the distribution is to be made and any underwriter or among underwriters. Thus, negotiation of the financing can proceed during this period but neither the issuer nor the underwriter may offer the security either to investors or to dealers, and dealers are prohibited from offering to buy the securities during this period.[1] Consequently, not only may no steps be taken to form a selling group but also dealers may not seek inclusion in the selling group prior to the filing.

---

1. The reason for this provision was stated in the House Report on the bill as originally enacted as follows:

"... Otherwise, the underwriter ... could accept them in the order of their priority and thus bring pressure upon dealers, who wish to avail themselves of a particular security offering, to rush their orders to buy without adequate consideration of the nature of the security being offered." H.R.Report No. 85, 73rd Cong., 1st Sess. (1933), p. 11.

It should be borne in mind that publicity about an issuer, its securities or the proposed offering prior to the filing of a registration statement may constitute an illegal offer to sell. Thus, announcement of the underwriter's identity should be avoided during this period. Experience shows that such announcements are very likely to lead to illegal offers to buy. This subject will not be further discussed in this release since it has been extensively considered elsewhere.[2]

These principles, however, are not intended to restrict the normal communications between an issuer and its stockholders or the announcement to the public generally of information with respect to important business and financial developments. Such announcements are required in the listing agreements used by stock exchanges, and the Commission is sensitive to the importance of encouraging this type of communication. In recognition of this requirement of certain stock exchanges, the Commission adopted Rule 135, which permits a brief announcement of proposed rights offerings, proposed exchange offerings, and proposed offerings to employees as not constituting an offer of a security for the purposes of section 5 of the Act.

The Period After the Filing and Before the Effective Date

After the registration statement is filed, and before its effective date, offers to sell the securities are permitted but no written offer may be made except by means of a statutory prospectus. For this purpose the statutory prospectus includes the preliminary prospectus provided for in Rule 433 as well as the summary prospectus provided for in Rules 434 and 434A. In addition the so-called "tombstone" advertisement permitted by Rule 134 may be used.

During the period after the filing of a registration statement, the freedom of an underwriter or dealer expecting to participate in the distribution, to communicate with his customers is limited only by the antifraud provisions of the Securities Act and the Securities Exchange Act, and by the fact that written offering material other than a statutory prospectus or tombstone advertisement ... [are strictly limited]. In this connection a dealer proposing to discuss an issue of securities with his customers should obtain copies of the preliminary prospectus in order to have a reliable source of information. This is particularly important where he proposes to recommend the securities, or where information concerning them has not been generally available. The corollary of the dealer's obligation to secure the copy is the obligation of the issuer and managing underwriters to make it readily available. Rule 460 provides that as a condition to acceleration of the effective date of a registration statement, the Commission will consider whether the persons making the offering have taken reasonable steps to make the information contained in the registration statement available to dealers who may participate in the distribution.

It is a principal purpose of the so-called "waiting period" between the filing date and the effective date to enable dealers and, through

---

2. See Securities Act Release No. 3844 (1957); Carl M. Loeb, Rhoades & Co., 38 S.E.C. 843 (1959); First Maine Corporation, 38 S.E.C. 882 (1959).

them, investors to become acquainted with the information contained in the registration statement and to arrive at an unhurried decision concerning the merits of the securities. Consistently with this purpose, no contracts of sale can be made during this period, the purchase price may not be paid or received and offers to buy may be cancelled.

The Period After the Effective Date

When the registration statement becomes effective oral offerings may continue and sales may be made and consummated.... However, care must be taken to see that all such material is at the time of use not false or misleading under the standards of section 17(a) of the Act. If the offering continues over an extended period, the prospectus should be current under the standards of section 10(a)(3). All dealers trading in the registered security must continue to employ the prospectus for the period referred to in section 4.

B. THE PRE-FILING PERIOD

SECURITIES ACT §§ 2(a)(3), 5

[See Statutory Supplement]

Section 5(a) of the 1933 Act provides that:

> Unless a registration statement is in effect as to a security, it shall be unlawful for any person, directly or indirectly—(1) to make use of any means or instruments of transportation or communication in interstate commerce or of the mails to sell such security through the use or medium of any prospectus or otherwise; or (2) to carry or cause to be carried through the mails or in interstate commerce, by any means or instruments of transportation, any such security for the purpose of sale or for delivery after sale.

Section 5(a)(c) provides that:

> It shall be unlawful for any person, directly or indirectly, to make use of any means or instruments of transportation or communication in interstate commerce or of the mails to offer to sell or offer to buy through the use or medium of any prospectus or otherwise any security, unless a registration statement has been filed as to such security....

Section 2(a)(3) provides that:

> The term "sale" or "sell" shall include every contract of sale or disposition of a security or interest in a security, for value. The term "offer to sell", "offer for sale", or "offer" shall include every

attempt or offer to dispose of, or solicitation of an offer to buy, a security or interest in a security, for value.

There is an important exception to section 2(a)(3):

> The terms defined in [§ 2(a)(3)] and the term "offer to buy" as used in subsection (c) of section 5 shall not include preliminary negotiations or agreements between an issuer . . . and any underwriter or among underwriters who are or are to be in privity of contract with an issuer. . . .

Putting together §§ 5(a), 5(c), and 2(a)(3), neither a sale of securities, nor an oral or written offer to sell securities, that are to be registered, may be made during the prefiling period. However, since its enactment, the Securities Act section 2(a)(3) excludes from the definition of sale and offer to sell preliminary negotiations and agreements with and among underwriters. This provision therefore facilitates the issuer entering into an underwriting agreement with its underwriters and also enables the formation of the underwriting syndicate via the agreement among underwriters. Nonetheless, the prohibition against offers in the prefiling period are an important concern for a company in registration. Impermissible communications during this period is frequently referred to as "gun-jumping"—unusual publicity by the issuer or a prospective underwriter that in effect is a preliminary step in the selling effort. On the other hand, if a corporation is already publicly held, blocking the normal flow of information would adversely affect the integrity of the market for the securities that are already outstanding. The cases and rules governing the prefiling period attempt to reconcile the undesirability of gun-jumping with the desirability of maintaining the normal flow of information concerning corporations that are already publicly held.

SECURITIES ACT RULES 135, 137, 139

[See Statutory Supplement]

NOTE ON IN THE MATTER OF CARL M. LOEB, RHOADES & CO. AND CHRIS–CRAFT INDUSTRIES v. BANGOR PUNTA CORP.

1. In In the Matter of Carl M. Loeb, Rhoades & Co., 38 S.E.C. 843 (1959), Davis had formed Arvida Corporation and transferred land to it. He then proposed that Arvida engage in a public offering of stock. A press release, issued under the name of Loeb, Rhoades, as underwriter, stated the Davis had transferred to Arvida his holdings of over 100,000 acres in an area of the Florida Gold Coast, and that part of the land was to be developed immediately into residential communities. The press release said that Arvida would have assets of over 100 million dollars, derived from Davis's investment and sales of stock that would begin within 60 days. The substance of the release appeared in

three New York papers and in numerous other news sources across the country. The probable price of the securities was disclosed at a news conference held the day the release was issued.

The announcement and publicity generated buying interest in Arvida stock of at least $500,000. One hundred securities firms expressed an interest in participating in the underwriting. Loeb, Rhoades received at least 58 expressions of interest from the public, including at least 17 specific offers to buy.

Subsequently, Arvida filed a registration statement covering its planned offering of securities. The statement disclosed that Arvida's properties were subject to a mortgage of about $31 million, of which about $21 million would be due within five years. This indicated that a large part of the offering would probably be used to meet the mortgage obligations rather than to improve the land, and in fact only $2.8 million was budgeted for development of the land in the first year. Furthermore, about sixty-one percent of Arvida land was located in rural areas, away from existing urban development. Much of the land was accessible only by unpaved roads, and some was entirely inaccessible by automobile. About fifty percent of the land was below flood criteria established by local governments and below the minimum elevation at which land could be developed. The SEC concluded that Arvida had violated section 5(c):

> [P]ublicity, prior to the filing of a registration statement by means of public media of communication, with respect to an issuer or it[s] securities, emanating from broker-dealer firms who as underwriters or prospective underwriters have negotiated or are negotiating for a public offering of the securities of such issuer, must be presumed to set in motion or to be a part of the distribution process and therefore to involve an offer to sell or a solicitation or an offer to buy such securities prohibited by Section 5(c).
>
> We . . . find such release and publicity was of a character calculated, by arousing and stimulating investor and dealer interest in Arvida securities and by eliciting indications of interest from customers to dealers and from dealer to underwriters, to set in motion the process of distribution. In fact it had such an effect. It contained descriptive material concerning the properties, business plans and management of Arvida, it included arresting references to "assets in excess of $100,000,000," and "over 100,000 acres, more than 155 square miles, in an area of the Gold Coast." Reporters were furnished with price data, and registrants were named as the managing underwriters thus permitting, if not inviting, dealers to register their interest with them. We find that such activities constituted part of the selling effort by the managing underwriters.

38 S.E.C. at 851. In dealing with the defendants' argument that the information in the release constituted news, the Commission said that the registration requirements were

> . . . [The restrictions of section 5 are] equally applicable whether or not the issuer or the surrounding circumstances have, or by astute public relations activities may be made to appear to have, news value. . . . In the normal conduct of its business a corporation may continue to advertise its products and services without interruption, it may send out its customary quarterly, annual and other periodic reports to security holders, and it may publish its proxy statements, send out its dividend notices and make routine announcements to the press. This flow of normal corporate news, unrelated to a selling effort for an issue of securities, is natural, desirable and entirely consistent with the objective of disclosure to the public which underlies the federal securities laws. However, an issuer who is party to or collaborates with underwriters or prospective underwriters in initiating or securing publicity must be regarded as participating directly or indirectly in an offer to sell or a solicitation of an offer to buy prohibited by section 5(c).

38 S.E.C. at 852–53.

2. Chris–Craft Industries, Inc. v. Bangor Punta Corp., 426 F.2d 569 (2d Cir.1970) involved a bitter contest between Chris–Craft Industries and Bangor Punta Corporation for the control of Piper Aircraft Corporation. Bangor proposed to make an exchange offer of its securities for Piper securities. Since the exchange offer constituted a public offering of Bangor securities, Bangor had to file a registration statement. While Bangor was in the process of preparing the registration statement, it issued a press release stating that it had agreed to exchange a package of Bangor securities "having a value, in the written opinion of The First Boston Corporation, of $80 or more" per Piper share. Held, Bangor had violated § 5(c):

> Chris–Craft argues, and the argument is supported by the SEC, both in its action filed May 26 against Bangor Punta and in its *amicus curiae* brief in this court, that the categories of information privileged under [Rule 135] are exclusive. In view of this exclusivity they contend that as the rule does not mention disclosure of the value of the securities to be offered, Bangor Punta's and Piper's announcements that the package of securities offered by Bangor Punta would be valued at $80 oversteps the exemption and makes the press release an offer to sell.
>
> We agree with this contention. When it is announced that securities will be sold at some date in the future and, in addition, an attractive description of these securities and of the issuer is furnished, it seems clear that such an announcement provides much the same kind of information as that contained in a prospectus. See S.E.C. v. Arvida Corp., 169 F.Supp. 211 (S.D.N.Y. 1958). Doubtless the line drawn between an announcement containing sufficient information to constitute an offer and one which does not must be to some extent arbitrary. A checklist of features that may be included in an announcement which does not also constitute an offer to sell serves to guide the financial community and the courts far better than any judicially formulated "rule of

reason'' as to what is or is not an offer. Rule 135 provides just such a checklist, and if the Rule is not construed as setting forth an exclusive list, then much of its value as a guide is lost.

Moreover, it is reasonable to conclude that the assigning of a value to offered shares constitutes an offer to sell. One of the evils of a premature offer is its tendency to encourage the formation by the offeree of an opinion of the value of the securities before a registration statement and prospectus are filed.

NOTE ON SEC'S GUIDANCE FOR COMMUNICATIONS DURING QUIET PERIOD

The material in the preceding pages reflects why the pre-filing period is also known as the ''quiet period.'' The SEC has walked a delicate line balancing section 5(c)'s prohibition of offers to sell prior to the registration statement being filed against the legitimate needs of investors and issuers for information to be in the public domain even though the issuer who is in registration. The SEC long maintained that the issuer's release of *factual* information about its activities, financial performance and financial position were not prohibited by section 5(c). Thus, in Securities Act Release 5180 (1971) it encouraged issuers to:

1. Continue to advertise products and services.

2. Continue to send out customary quarterly, annual and other periodic reports to stockholders.

3. Continue to publish proxy statements and send out dividend notices.

4. Continue to make announcements to the press with respect to factual business and financial developments; *i.e.,* receipt of a contract, the settlement of a strike, the opening of a plant, or similar events of interest to the community in which the business operates.

5. Answer unsolicited telephone inquiries from stockholders, financial analysts, the press and others concerning factual information.

6. Observe an ''open door'' policy in responding to unsolicited inquiries concerning factual matters from securities analysts, financial analysts, security holders, and participants in the communications field who have a legitimate interest in the corporation's affairs.

7. Continue to hold stockholder meetings as scheduled and to answer shareholders' inquiries at stockholder meetings relating to factual matters.

Nonetheless, with the explosion of the Internet the ubiquity of information about issuers in registration posed increasing challenges. Thus, in 2005 the SEC crafted a series of safe harbor rules that restrict the reach of section 5. As you review the following summary of these safe harbors, note the following. First, each contains its own technical requirements and many apply only to information released by or on behalf of the issuer. This qualification excludes communications by underwriters and others from safe harbors, unless the communication is authorized by the issuer. Second, in general the breadth of any safe harbor is greater for reporting companies than for non-reporting companies. Third, while safe harbors can be seen as deregulatory they are themselves riddled with technical requirements so that their application calls for more, not less, consultation with securities counsel.

30–Day Bright–Line Exclusion. Rule 163A excludes from the reach of section 5(c) communications "by or on behalf of an issuer" that are made more than 30 days prior to filing a registration statement. However, for a communication to qualify under this safe harbor it must not make any reference to a forthcoming public offering. This more-than-thirty-day dispensation applies to all issuers, i.e., it applies to both reporting and non-reporting companies.

Factual Business Information. Issuers (as well as anyone acting on behalf of the issuer), whether a reporting company or a non-reporting company can release "factual business information" under Rules 168 and 169, respectively, and not be in violation of section 5, provided the release is consistent with a practice of regularly releasing factual business information. Factual business information is defined to include factual information about the issuer, its business, or financial developments as well as product advertisements. When the issuer is a non-reporting company, the target of the communication must not be investors but rather others such as customers or suppliers. Both Rule 168 and Rule 169 withdraw their protection from a communication if it contains information about the registered offering.

Forward Looking Statements. Rule 168 also provides a safe harbor for reporting companies (and those acting on the issuer's behalf) to communicate forwarding looking statements such as forecasts, estimates and discussions of future business plans. Expressly excluded from the Rule 168 safe harbor is a communication containing information about the registered offering.

Well–Known Seasoned Issuers. The greatest dispensation from section 5's regulation of communications is provided in Rule 163 which applies only to well-known seasoned issuers (WKSI). Rule 163 permits WKSI's to engage in unrestricted communications, whether oral or written, before the registration statement is filed. This protection only applies to communications by or on behalf of the issuer and written "offers" of the security made prior to the filing of the registration statement must be filed "promptly" with the SEC.

C. The Waiting Period

SECURITIES ACT §§ 2(a)(10), 5, 8, 10; SECURITIES ACT RULES 134, 152c–8, 430, 431, 460

[See Statutory Supplement]

1. Section 8 of the 1933 Act provides that "Except as hereinafter provided, the effective date of a registration statement shall be the twentieth day after the filing thereof or such earlier date as the Commission may determine. . . ."

Accordingly, with the exception of the well-known seasoned issuer (defined in Rule 405) whose registration statements are automatically effective upon filing the registration statement with the SEC, there is always a waiting period between the time at which a registration statement is filed and the time at which it is effective. Because section 5(a) prohibits *sales* unless a registration is effective, only offers to sell may occur during the waiting period. Upon the filing of the registration statement, there no longer is the broad prohibition of section 5(c) against "[making] use of any means of interstate commerce to offer to sell . . . through the use or medium of any prospectus or otherwise any security, unless a registration statement has been filed." However, section 5(b) prohibits the transmission of "any *prospectus* relating to any securities with respect to which a registration statement has been filed . . . unless such *prospectus* meets the requirements of section 10." Section 2(a)(10) defines "prospectus" very broadly to mean "any prospectus, notice, circular, advertisement, letter, or communication, written or by radio or television, which offers any security for sale or confirms the sale of any security." What is noticeably excluded from the otherwise broad reach of section 2(a)(10) are *oral* communications (unless made via radio or television). SEC Rule 405 broadly defines "written communications" to include a wide range of electronic-based communications, e.g., websites and email.

The combined effect of sections 5 and 2(a)(10) on issuers, underwriters and dealer, is that during the waiting period: (1) *sales* are not permissible; (2) *oral offers* are permissible, and (3) writings (including Internet communications) relating to the securities are permissible only if specifically permitted by statute or rule.

2. What writings *are* permitted during the waiting period?

In theory, a *final prospectus* (also sometimes known as a *section 10(a) prospectus* or a *statutory prospectus*) is permissible. By definition, however, the final prospectus cannot exist during the waiting period; the final prospectus is available only once the registration statement has become effective since it includes certain information that is usually not decided upon until the waiting period is over, e.g., the security's offering price.

However, certain other writings are permissible.

(a) *Preliminary prospectus.* Section 10(b) of the Securities Act provides that:

> In addition to the prospectus permitted or required in subsection (a), the Commission shall by rules or regulations deemed necessary or appropriate in the public interest or for the protection of investors permit the use of a prospectus for the purposes of subsection (b)(1) of section 5 which omits in part or summarizes information in the prospectus specified in subsection (a).

Pursuant to section 10(b), the Commission has promulgated Rule 430, which provides that

> A form of prospectus filed as a part of the registration statement shall be deemed to meet the requirements of section 10 of the Act for the purpose of section 5(b)(1) thereof prior to the effective date of the registration statement, provided such form of prospectus contains substantially the information required by the Act and the rules and regulations thereunder to be included in a prospectus meeting the requirements of section 10(a) of the Act for the securities being registered, or contains substantially that information except for the omission of information with respect to the offering price, underwriting discounts or commissions, discounts or commissions to dealers, amount of proceeds, conversion rates, call prices, or other matters dependent upon the offering price.

The writing permitted under section 10(b) and Rule 430 is known as a *preliminary prospectus* or *red herring* (so-called because of a red legend that appears on the cover page).

(b) *Summary prospectus.* Under Rule 431, certain issuers can use a *summary prospectus* during the waiting period. Under that Rule:

> . . . A summary prospectus shall contain the information specified in the instructions as to summary prospectuses in the form used for registration of the securities to be offered. Such prospectus may include any other information the substance of which is contained in the registration statement except as otherwise specifically provided in the instructions as to summary prospectuses in the form used for registration.

(c) *Tombstone ads.* Under section 2(a)(10)(b), an ad can be used during the waiting period, if the ad states only from whom a written prospectus, meeting the requirements of section 10, may be obtained, and does no more than identify the security, state the price, state by whom orders will be executed, and contain such other information as the Commission may prescribe. Such an ad is known as a *tombstone ad*, because of its spare nature and typical black border.

(d) *Identifying statement.* Under section 2(a)(10)(b) and Rule 134, an *identifying statement*—in effect, an expanded tombstone ad—can be used during the waiting period. Under Rule 134, certain information, in addition to that specified in section 2(a)(10)(b) for tombstone ads, may be included in an identifying statement.

(e) *Free Writing Prospectus.* In 2005, the SEC greatly relaxed the use of written materials during the waiting period. Prior to adopting the free writing prospectus provisions in Rules 164 and 433, section 5(b)(1) prohibited any written communication during the waiting period except a prospectus meeting the requirement of section 5(b)(1), i.e., communications described in the preceding paragraphs (a)–(d). Today, free writing, the use of written communications outside these four categories, is authorized by the "free writing prospectus rules." Rule 433 essentially divides issuers into two broad categories: "non-reporting" and "unseasoned" issuers on the one hand and all other issuers on the other hand. An unseasoned issuer is a reporting company that has not yet filed an annual report with the SEC. When free writing material is used by a non-reporting or unseasoned issuer the material must be accompanied or preceded by a preliminary prospectus (when the free writing material is communicated electronically the requirement that the free writing material be accompanied or preceded by a preliminary prospectus can be satisfied by a hyperlink to the preliminary prospectus). This requirement does not apply to all other issuers. However, regardless of the type of issuer, Rule 433(c) & (d) require that the free writing material must be filed with the SEC no later than the day it is first used and that the material bear a legend noting that the security is in registration, that a the investor should read the registration statement, and that the registration statement is available at the www.sec.gov. Rule 164 excuses immaterial or unintentional failures to file provided there has been a good faith effort to file the free writing materials as soon as practicable after discovery of the failure to file.

D. THE POST-EFFECTIVE PERIOD

SECURITIES ACT §§ 2(3), 2(10), 4(3), 5, 10;
SECURITIES ACT RULES 153, 174, 427

[See Statutory Supplement]

Even though a registration statement has become effective, section 5(b)(1) continues to require that there can be no written offers for a security as to which a registration is in effect unless prior to, or at the same time, a final section 10 prospectus has been delivered. To be sure, the free writing prospectus rules, described above, can be relied upon in the post effective period. However, issuers and their distribution participants can rely upon the more liberal authorization for free writing provided in section 2(a)(10) which excludes from the definition of prospectus any written communication that is accompanied or preceded by a final prospectus. Note, if the issuer or others rely on Rule 433 to engage in free writing in the post effective period, they must file the free writing materials with the SEC and the materials must bear the mandated legend; these two conditions are not included in the section 2(a)(10)'s authorization for free writing.

Once the registration statement is effective, sales of the security can be made and under section 5(b)(2) the security can be delivered to the purchaser. While the statute itself requires that a final section 10 prospectus must precede or accompany any delivery of the security as well as any confirmation of the sale, in 2005 the SEC deftly reached the right result by essentially taking the final prospectus out of the dynamics for confirming sales and delivering the security. Before seeing how the SEC so deftly removed the delivery of the final prospectus, consider the benefits of an investor receiving a final prospectus with either the confirmation of her purchase or the delivery of the security: "A prospectus that comes with the security does not tell the investor whether or not he or she should buy it; it tells the investors whether he has acquired a security or a law suit." L. Loss & J. Seligman, Securities Regulation § 2b–3 (3d ed. 2001). Today, Rule 172 exempts confirmations of sales and delivery of securities from the demands of section 5(b) and Rule 173 embraces a "notice is access" approach so that underwriters and dealers (who are otherwise not exempt from the prospectus delivery requirements as discussed below) need only provide to the security's purchaser, not later than two days following completion of the sale, either a final prospectus or notice that of the URL where a final prospectus can be acquired.

How long do these restrictions last?

Sales of registered securities by an *issuer* must always be accompanied by a section 10 prospectus.

All *underwriters* of an offering, and all *dealers* who were participants in the distribution, are subject to the prospectus-delivery requirement as long as they are offering securities from unsold allotment of the original public offering. Dealers are also subject to the prospectus-delivery requirement, whether or not they are selling an unsold allotment, during a specified period after commencement of the offering. However, dealers who are not participating underwriters need not delivery a prospectus if the security is listed on a national security exchange, e.g., NYSE or NASDAQ.

Moreover, section 4(4) of the Securities Act provides that "broker's transactions executed upon customers' orders on any exchange or in the over-the-counter market" are exempted from the prospectus-delivery requirement. This exemption "permits individuals to sell their securities through a broker in an ordinary brokerage transaction, during the period of distribution or while a stop order is in effect, without regard to the registration and prospectus requirements of section 5." In the Matter of Ira Haupt & Co., 23 S.E.C. 589 (1946).

Section 7. Liabilities Under the Securities Act

SECURITIES ACT §§ 11, 12, 17, 21d(g), 27A; SECURITIES ACT RULES 175, 176

[See Statutory Supplement]

NOTE ON LIABILITIES UNDER THE SECURITIES ACT

The Securities Act contains four basic liability provisions: Sections 11, 12(a)(1), 12(a)(2), and 17(a).

1. *Section 17(a).* Section 17(a) is a general antifraud provision, whose applicability does not turn on whether there has been a violation of section 5, the registration provision. Section 17(a) is highly comparable to Rule 10b–5, because Rule 10b–5 was modeled on section 17(a). However, Rule 10b–5 regulates both sellers and buyers, while section 17(a) regulates only sellers. On the other hand, section 17(a) applies to "offers" while Rule 10b–5 does not.

Scienter is a necessary element of a violation of section 17(a)(1), but not of sections 17(a)(2) or 17(a)(3). Aaron v. S.E.C., 446 U.S. 680, 100 S.Ct. 1945, 64 L.Ed.2d 611 (1980).

There is no private right of action under section 17(a). See, e.g., Finkel v. Stratton Corp., 962 F.2d 169, 174–75 (2d Cir.1992).

2. *Section 12(a)(2).* Section 12(a)(2) provides that, subject to certain conditions, any person who offers or sells a security by means of a prospectus or oral communication is liable to the purchaser for rescission or damages, if the prospectus or oral communication includes a material misstatement or has a material omission. Thus section 12(a)(2), like section 17(a), is an antifraud provision. Unlike section 17(a), section 12(a)(2) explicitly gives buyers a private right of action. However Gustafson v. Alloyd Co., 513 U.S. 561, 115 S.Ct. 1061, 131 L.Ed.2d 1 (1995) held that section 12(a)(2) applies only to securities sold in registered public offerings or offerings public in nature but are subject to an exemption. Although it is not entirely clear what the Court intended to be included in the latter group, most commentators believe that excluded are private offerings by issuers or their controlling shareholders are beyond the reach of section 12(a)(2) whereas misrepresentations committed in offers carried out under Rules 504, 505 and Regulation A are likely reached by section 12(a)(2).

To obtain relief under section 12(a)(2) the buyer must show a false statement or material omission. There is no requirement that the plaintiff relied on the misstatement or omission. He need only show that he did not know the truth and that the defendant was the plaintiff's seller (see discussion below regarding the "seller" requirement adopted by the Supreme Court in *Pinter v. Dahl*). Once the buyer shows that an omission was material, or that a material statement was false, the seller has the burden of showing that he did not know and "in the exercise of reasonable care could not have known" of the untruth or omission. In effect, therefore, section 12(a)(2) makes the seller liable for negligence in connection with a misrepresentation or omission, and puts the burden of proof on the seller to show that he was not negligent. Section 12 provides that the purchaser can recover the amount paid for the security; however, section 12(b) provides this amount is to be reduced by any decline in the security's value since that the defendant can prove was unrelated to the misrepresentation. (This reflects the concept of "loss causation", discussed in Chapter 12).

If the misstatement involves a forward-looking statement, the buyer has available the safe harbor provided by section 27A and Rule 175 (3).

3. *Section 12(a)(1)*. Section 12(a)(1) gives buyers a private right of action against sellers who violate section 5 of the 1933 Act—that is, for the most part, against sellers who either (1) sell securities that are required to be, but are not, registered, or (2) sell securities without delivering a required section 10 prospectus or deliver a prospectus that does not satisfy section 10. A seller's liability under section 12(a)(1) is strict. The buyer does not need to show fraud or even a material misstatement or omission in the registration statement.

The basic remedy under section 12(a)(1) is rescission. However, a buyer who sold the stock before she brought suit can sue for the difference between the price that she paid for the stock and the price at which she sold it. Note, as seen above, in the companion misrepresentation action under section 12(a)(2) the defendant is able to mitigate damages by proving that a portion of the security's decline was attributable to effects unrelated to the misrepresentation. No such mitigation is available to defendants in actions under Section 12(a)(1).

The Supreme Court has limited recovery under section 12(a)(1) to the buyer's seller. Pinter v. Dahl, 486 U.S. 622, 108 S.Ct. 2063, 100 L.Ed.2d 658 (1988).The term "seller" in section 12(a)(1) means not only the person passing title to the plaintiff but includes any person who successfully solicits a purchase and who is motivated at least in part by a desire to serve his own financial interests or those of the owner of the securities. *Id.* Lower courts have extended the seller requirement to actions brought under section 12(a)(2). *See e.g.*, Ackerman v. Schwartz, 947 F.2d 841 (7th Cir. 1991).

4. *Section 11*. Section 11 gives buyers a private right of action for material misstatements or omissions in a registration statement, subject to certain conditions and defenses. Such liability extends only to those identified in section 11(a) which includes those who sign the registration statement (e.g., the issuer and senior officers), the directors, the underwriters, and experts (such as accountants) who have taken responsibility for some portion of the registration statement.

Section 11 does not require privity: any person who has purchased the security in question, either in the original distribution or later in the aftermarket, can bring suit. However, liability under section 11 extends only to the securities issued under the registration statement. Accordingly, a buyer who purchased the same class of securities as those registered, but cannot trace the securities she purchased back to the registration statement, cannot bring suit under section 11 even though the securities she purchased were economically identical to the securities issued under the registration statement. Barnes v. Osofsky, 373 F.2d 269 (2d Cir.1967). (However, such a buyer might be able to bring suit under Rule 10b–5.)

Section 11 does not require the buyer to show reliance or causation. However, it is defense that the buyer knew the truth at the time he acquired the security. Under section 27A of the 1933 Act, under certain circumstances there is no liability under section 11 for forward-looking statements.

Damages under section 11 are limited to the difference between the original offering price and the value of the securities at the time of suit. Furthermore, under a proviso to section 11(e), if the defendant proves that any portion (or all) of the damages is based on factors other than the relevant misstatement or omission, that portion of the damages cannot be recovered. This proviso is sometimes referred to as "negative causation." Essentially, it is a form of loss causation, with the burden of proof on the defendant.

An issuer is strictly liable under section 11. Persons other than the issuer (such as directors of the issuer, or experts) can escape liability under section 11(b)(3) by establishing what is known as the *due diligence defense*. Under this defense a non-expert, as to the nonexpertised portions of the registration statement, and an expert, as to the expertised portions, will not be liable if "he had, after reasonable investigation, reasonable ground to believe" that there were no material misstatements or omissions when the registration statement became effective. As to the expertised portions of the registration statement, a nonexpert will not be liable if "he had no reasonable ground to believe" that the statements made by the expert were untrue or contained material omissions.

Thus section 11, like section 12(a)(2), adopts a negligence standard, with the burden of proof on the defendants to show that they were not negligent. There is a difference in the formulations of the negligence standards in sections 11 and 12(a)(2), and it is not clear whether this means that there are differences in the investigation required to satisfy the defendant's burden of proof under the two sections. See Sanders v. John Nuveen & Co., Inc., 619 F.2d 1222 (7th Cir.1980), cert. denied 450 U.S. 1005, 101 S.Ct. 1719, 68 L.Ed.2d 210 (1981) (opinion of Justice Powell, dissenting from denial of certiorari).

Escott v. Barchris Constr. Corp.

United States District Court, Southern District, New York, 1968.
283 F.Supp. 643.

OPINION

■ McLEAN, DISTRICT JUDGE.

This is an action by purchasers of 5½ per cent convertible subordinated fifteen year debentures of BarChris Construction Corporation (BarChris). Plaintiffs purport to sue on their own behalf and "on behalf of all other and present and former holders" of the debentures....

The action is brought under Section 11 of the Securities Act of 1933 (15 U.S.C.A. § 77k). Plaintiffs allege that the registration statement with respect to these debentures filed with the Securities and Exchange Commission, which became effective on May 16, 1961, contained material false statements and material omissions.

Defendants fall into three categories: (1) the persons who signed the registration statement; (2) the underwriters, consisting of eight investment banking firms, led by Drexel & Co. (Drexel); and (3) BarChris's auditors, Peat, Marwick, Mitchell & Co. (Peat, Marwick).

... At the time relevant here, BarChris was engaged primarily in the construction of bowling alleys, somewhat euphemistically referred to as "bowling centers." These were rather elaborate affairs. They contained not only a number of alleys or "lanes," but also, in most cases, bar and restaurant facilities....

The introduction of automatic pin setting machines in 1952 gave a marked stimulus to bowling. It rapidly became a popular sport, with the result that "bowling centers" began to appear throughout the country in rapidly increasing numbers. BarChris benefited from this increased interest in bowling. Its construction operations expanded rapidly. It is estimated that in 1960 BarChris installed approximately three per cent of all lanes built in the United States....

BarChris's sales increased dramatically from 1956 to 1960. According to the prospectus, net sales, in round figures, in 1956 were some $800,000, in 1957 $1,300,000, in 1958 $1,700,000. In 1959 they increased to over $3,300,000, and by 1960 they had leaped to over $9,165,000.

For some years the business had exceeded the managerial capacity of its founders. Vitolo and Pugliese are each men of limited education. Vitolo did not get beyond high school. Pugliese ended his schooling in seventh grade. Pugliese devoted his time to supervising the actual construction work. Vitolo was concerned primarily with obtaining new business. Neither was equipped to handle financial matters....

In general, BarChris's method of operation was to enter into a contract with a customer, receive from him at that time a comparatively small down payment on the purchase price, and proceed to construct and equip the bowling alley. When the work was finished and the building delivered, the customer paid the balance of the contract price in notes, payable in installments over a period of years. BarChris discounted these notes with a factor and received part of their face amount in cash. The factor held back part as a reserve....

BarChris was compelled to expend considerable sums in defraying the cost of construction before it received reimbursement. As a consequence, BarChris was in constant need of cash to finance its operations, a need which grew more pressing as operations expanded.

In December 1959, BarChris sold 560,000 shares of common stock to the public at $3.00 per share....

By early 1961, BarChris needed additional working capital. The proceeds of the sale of the debentures involved in this action were to be devoted, in part at least, to fill that need.

The registration statement of the debentures, in preliminary form, was filed with the Securities and Exchange Commission on March 30, 1961. A first amendment was filed on May 11 and a second on May 16. The registration statement became effective on May 16. The closing of the financing took place on May 24. On that day BarChris received the net proceeds of the financing.

By that time BarChris was experiencing difficulties in collecting amounts due from some of its customers. Some of them were in arrears in payments due to factors on their discounted notes. As time went on those difficulties increased. Although BarChris continued to build alleys in 1961 and 1962, it became increasingly apparent that the industry was overbuilt. Operators of alleys, often inadequately financed, began to fail. Precisely when the tide turned is a matter of dispute, but at any rate, it was painfully apparent in 1962.

In May of that year BarChris made an abortive attempt to raise more money by the sale of common stock. It filed with the Securities and Exchange Commission a registration statement for the stock issue which it later withdrew. In October 1962 BarChris came to the end of the road. On October 29, 1962, it filed in this court a petition for an arrangement under Chapter XI of the Bankruptcy Act. BarChris defaulted in the payment of the interest due on November 1, 1962 on the debentures.

[The court continued with a lengthy description of BarChris's registration statement for the 1961 debentures.] ...

For convenience, the various falsities and omissions [in the 1961 debenture registration statement] which I have discussed in the preceding pages are recapitulated here. They were as follows:

1. 1960 Earnings		
(a) Sales		
As per prospectus	$	9,165,320
Correct figure		8,511,420
Overstatement	$	653,900
(b) Net Operating Income		
As per prospectus	$	1,742,801
Correct figure		1,496,196
Overstatement	$	246,605

	(c) Earnings per Share	
	As per prospectus	$ .75
	Correct figure	.65
	Overstatement	$ .10
2.	1960 Balance Sheet Current Assets	
	As per prospectus	$ 4,524,021
	Correct figure	3,914,332
	Overstatement	$ 609,689
3.	Contingent Liabilities as of December 31, 1960 on Alternative Method of Financing	
	As per prospectus	$ 750,000
	Correct figure	1,125,795
	Understatement	$ 375,795
	Capitol Lanes should have been shown as a direct liability	$ 325,000
4.	Contingent Liabilities as of April 30, 1961	
	As per prospectus	$ 825,000
	Correct figure	1,443,853
	Understatement	$ 618,853
	Capitol Lanes should have been shown as a direct liability	$ 314,166
5.	Earnings Figures for Quarter ending March 31, 1961	
	(a) Sales	
	As per prospectus	$ 2,138,455
	Correct figure	1,618,645
	Overstatement	$ 519,810
	(b) Gross Profit	
	As per prospectus	$ 483,121
	Correct figure	252,366
	Overstatement	$ 230,755
6.	Backlog as of March 31, 1961	
	As per prospectus	$ 6,905,000
	Correct figure	2,415,000
	Overstatement	$ 4,490,000
7.	Failure to Disclose Officers' Loans Outstanding and Unpaid on May 16, 1961	$ 386,615
8.	Failure to Disclose Use of Proceeds in Manner not Revealed in Prospectus	
	Approximately	$ 1,160,000
9.	Failure to Disclose Customers' Delinquencies in May 1961 and BarChris's Potential Liability with Respect Thereto	
	Over	$ 1,350,000
10.	Failure to Disclose the Fact that BarChris was Already Engaged, and was about to be More Heavily Engaged, in the Operation of Bowling Alleys	

Materiality

It is a prerequisite to liability under Section 11 of the Act that the fact which is falsely stated in a registration statement, or the fact that is omitted when it should have been stated to avoid misleading, be "material." [The court found that several misstatements and omissions were material within the meaning of the Act.] . . . .

The "Due Diligence" Defenses

Section 11(b) of the Act provides that:

> " * * * no person, other than the issuer, shall be liable * * * who shall sustain the burden of proof—
>
> * * *

(3) that (A) as regards any part of the registration statement not purporting to be made on the authority of an expert * * * he had, after reasonable investigation, reasonable ground to believe and did believe, at the time such part of the registration statement became effective, that the statements therein were true and that there was no omission to state a material fact required to be stated therein or necessary to make the statements therein not misleading; * * * ''

* * *

Section 11(c) defines ''reasonable investigation'' as follows:

''In determining, for the purpose of paragraph (3) of subsection (b) of this section, what constitutes reasonable investigation and reasonable ground for belief, the standard of reasonableness shall be that required of a prudent man in the management of his own property.''

Every defendant, except BarChris itself, to whom, as the issuer, these defenses are not available, and except Peat, Marwick, whose position rests on a different statutory provision, has pleaded these affirmative defenses. Each claims that (1) as to the part of the registration statement purporting to be made on the authority of an expert (which, for convenience, I shall refer to as the ''expertised portion''), he had no reasonable ground to believe and did not believe that there were any untrue statements or material omissions, and (2) as to the other parts of the registration statement, he made a reasonable investigation, as a result of which he had reasonable ground to believe and did believe that the registration statement was true and that no material fact was omitted. As to each defendant, the question is whether he has sustained the burden of proving these defenses. Surprising enough, there is little or no judicial authority on this question. No decisions directly in point under Section 11 have been found.

. . . The defendants do not agree among themselves as to who the ''experts'' were or as to the parts of the registration statement which were expertised. Some defendants say that Peat, Marwick was the expert, others say that BarChris's attorneys, Perkins, Daniels, McCormack & Collins, and the underwriters' attorneys, Drinker, Biddle & Reath, were also the experts. On the first view, only those portions of the registration statement purporting to be made on Peat, Marwick's authority were expertised portions. On the other view, everything in the registration statement was within this category, because the two law firms were responsible for the entire document.

The first view is the correct one. To say that the entire registration statement is expertised because some lawyer prepared it would be an unreasonable construction of the statute. Neither the lawyer for the company nor the lawyer for the underwriters is an expert within the meaning of Section 11. The only expert, in the statutory sense, was Peat, Marwick, and the only parts of the registration statement which purported to be made upon the authority of an expert were the portions which purported to be made on Peat, Marwick's authority.

The parties also disagree as to what those portions were. Some defendants say that it was only the 1960 figures (and the figures for prior years, which are not in controversy here). Others say in substance that it was every figure in the prospectus....

Here again, the more narrow view is the correct one. The registration statement contains a report of Peat, Marwick as independent public accountants dated February 23, 1961. This relates only to the consolidated balance sheet of BarChris and consolidated subsidiaries as of December 31, 1960, and the related statement of earnings and retained earnings for the five years then ended. This is all that Peat, Marwick purported to certify. It is perfectly clear that it did not purport to certify the 1961 figures, some of which are expressly stated in the prospectus to have been unaudited....

I turn now to the question of whether defendants have proved their due diligence defenses. The position of each defendant will be separately considered.

Russo

Russo was, to all intents and purposes, the chief executive officer of BarChris. He was a member of the executive committee. He was familiar with all aspects of the business. He was personally in charge of dealings with the factors. He acted on BarChris's behalf in making the financing agreements with Talcott and he handled the negotiations with Talcott in the spring of 1961. He talked with customers about their delinquencies....

In short, Russo knew all the relevant facts. He could not have believed that there were no untrue statements or material omissions in the prospectus. Russo has no due diligence defenses....

Vitolo and Pugliese

They were the founders of the business who stuck with it to the end. Vitolo was president and Pugliese was vice president. Despite their titles, their field of responsibility in the administration of BarChris's affairs during the period in question seems to have been less all-embracing than Russo's. Pugliese in particular appears to have limited his activities to supervising the actual construction work.

Vitolo and Pugliese are each men of limited education. It is not hard to believe that for them the prospectus was difficult reading, if indeed they read it at all.

But whether it was or not is irrelevant. The liability of a director who signs a registration statement does not depend upon whether or not he read it or, if he did, whether or not he understood what he was reading.

And in any case, Vitolo and Pugliese were not as naive as they claim to be. They were members of BarChris's executive committee. At meetings of that committee BarChris's affairs were discussed at length. They must have known what was going on. . . .

All in all, the position of Vitolo and Pugliese is not significantly different, for present purposes, from Russo's. They could not have believed that the registration statement was wholly true and that no material facts had been omitted. And in any case, there is nothing to show that they made any investigation of anything which they may not have known about or understood. They have not proved their due diligence defenses.

Kircher

Kircher was treasurer of BarChris and its chief financial officer. He is a certified public accountant and an intelligent man. He was thoroughly familiar with BarChris's financial affairs. He knew the terms of BarChris's agreements with Talcott. He knew of the customers' delinquency problem. He participated actively with Russo in May 1961 in the successful effort to hold Talcott off until the financing proceeds came in. He knew how the financing proceeds were to be applied and he saw to it that they were so applied. He arranged the officers' loans and he knew all the facts concerning them.

Moreover, as a member of the executive committee, Kircher was kept informed as to those branches of the business of which he did not have direct charge. He knew about the operation of alleys, present and prospective. He knew that Capitol was included in 1960 sales and that Bridge and Yonkers were included in first quarter 1961 sales despite the fact that they were not sold. Kircher knew of the infirmities in customers' contracts included in the backlog figure. Indeed, at a later date, he specifically criticized Russo's handling of the T–Bowl situation. In brief, Kircher knew all the relevant facts.

Kircher worked on the preparation of the registration statement. He conferred with Grant and on occasion with Ballard. He supplied information to them about the company's business. He read the prospectus and understood it. He knew what it said and what it did not say.

Kircher's contention is that he had never before dealt with a registration statement, that he did not know what it should contain, and that he relied wholly on Grant, Ballard and Peat, Marwick to guide him. He claims that it was their fault, not his, if there was anything wrong with it. He says that all the facts were recorded in BarChris's books where these "experts" could have seen them if they had looked. He says that he truthfully answered all their questions. In effect, he says that if they did not know enough to ask the right questions and to give him the proper instructions, that is not his responsibility.

There is an issue of credibility here. In fact, Kircher was not frank in dealing with Grant and Ballard. He withheld information from them. But even if he had told them all the facts, this would not have constituted the due diligence contemplated by the statute. Knowing the facts, Kircher had reason to believe that the expertised portion of the prospectus, i.e., the 1960 figures, was in part incorrect. He could not shut his eyes to the facts and rely on Peat, Marwick for that portion.

As to the rest of the prospectus, knowing the facts, he did not have a reasonable ground to believe it to be true. On the contrary, he must have known that in part it was untrue. Under these circumstances, he was not entitled to sit back and place the blame on the lawyers for not advising him about it.

Kircher has not proved his due diligence defenses....

Birnbaum

Birnbaum was a young lawyer, admitted to the bar in 1957, who, after brief periods of employment by two different law firms and an equally brief period of practicing in his own firm, was employed by BarChris as house counsel and assistant secretary in October 1960. Unfortunately for him, he became secretary and a director of BarChris on April 17, 1961, after the first version of the registration statement had been filed with the Securities and Exchange Commission. He signed the later amendments, thereby becoming responsible for the accuracy of the prospectus in its final form.

Although the prospectus, in its description of "management," lists Birnbaum among the "executive officers" and devotes several sentences to a recital of his career, the fact seems to be that he was not an executive officer in any real sense. He did not participate in the management of the company. As house counsel, he attended to legal matters of a routine nature. Among other things, he incorporated subsidiaries, with which BarChris was plentifully supplied. Among the subsidiaries which he incorporated were Capitol Lanes, Inc. which operated Capitol, Yonkers Lanes, Inc. which eventually operated Yonkers, and Parkway Lanes, Inc. which eventually operated Bridge. He was thus aware of that aspect of the business.

Birnbaum examined contracts. In that connection he advised BarChris that the T–Bowl contracts were not legally enforceable. He was thus aware of that fact.

One of Birnbaum's more important duties, first as assistant secretary and later as full-fledged secretary, was to keep the corporate minutes of BarChris and its subsidiaries. This necessarily informed him to a considerable extent about the company's affairs....

It seems probable that Birnbaum did not know of many of the inaccuracies in the prospectus. He must, however, have appreciated some of them. In any case, he made no investigation and relied on the others to get it right.... [H]e was entitled to rely upon Peat, Marwick for the 1960 figures, for as far as appears, he had no personal knowledge of the company's books of account or financial transactions. But he was not entitled to rely upon Kircher, Grant and Ballard for the other portions of the prospectus. As a lawyer, he should have known his obligations under the statute. He should have known that he was required to make a reasonable investigation of the truth of all the statements in the unexpertised portion of the document which he signed. Having failed to make such an investigation, he did not have reasonable ground to believe that all these statements were true. Birnbaum has not established his due diligence defenses except as to the audited 1960 figures.

Auslander

Auslander was an "outside" director, i.e., one who was not an officer of BarChris. He was chairman of the board of Valley Stream National Bank in Valley Stream, Long Island. In February 1961 Vitolo asked him to become a director of BarChris. Vitolo gave him an enthusiastic account of BarChris's progress and prospects. As an inducement, Vitolo said that when BarChris received the proceeds of a forthcoming issue of securities, it would deposit $1,000,000 in Auslander's bank.

In February and early March 1961, before accepting Vitolo's invitation, Auslander made some investigation of BarChris. He obtained Dun & Bradstreet reports which contained sales and earnings figures for periods earlier than December 31, 1960. He caused inquiry to be made of certain of BarChris's banks and was advised that they regarded BarChris favorably. He was informed that inquiry of Talcott had also produced a favorable response.

On March 3, 1961, Auslander indicated his willingness to accept a place on the board.... Auslander observed that BarChris's auditors were Peat, Marwick. They were also the auditors for the Valley Stream National Bank. He thought well of them.

Auslander was elected a director on April 17, 1961. The registration statement in its original form had already been filed, of course without his signature. On May 10, 1961, he signed a signature page for the first amendment to the registration statement which was filed on May 11, 1961. This was a separate sheet without any document attached. Auslander did not know that it was a signature page for a registration statement. He vaguely understood that it was something "for the SEC."

Auslander attended a meeting of BarChris's directors on May 15, 1961. At that meeting he, along with the other directors, signed the signature sheet for the second amendment which constituted the registration statement in its final form. Again, this was only a separate sheet without any document attached. Auslander never saw a copy of the registration statement in its final form.

At the May 15 directors' meeting, however, Auslander did realize that what he was signing was a signature sheet to a registration statement. This was the first time that he had appreciated that fact. A copy of the registration statement in its earlier form as amended on May 11, 1961 was passed around at the meeting. Auslander glanced at it briefly. He did not read it thoroughly....

In considering Auslander's due diligence defenses, a distinction is to be drawn between the expertised and non-expertised portions of the prospectus. As to the former, Auslander knew that Peat, Marwick had audited the 1960 figures. He believed them to be correct because he had confidence in Peat, Marwick. He had no reasonable ground to believe otherwise.

As to the non-expertised portions, however, Auslander is in a different position. He seems to have been under the impression that Peat, Marwick was responsible for all the figures. This impression was not correct, as he would have realized if he had read the prospectus carefully. Auslander made no investigation of the accuracy of the prospectus. He relied on the assurance of Vitolo and Russo, and upon the information he had received in answer to his inquiries back in February and early March. These inquiries were general ones, in the nature of a credit check. The information which he received in answer to them was also general, without specific reference to the statements in the prospectus, which was not prepared until some time thereafter.

It is true that Auslander became a director on the eve of the financing. He had little opportunity to familiarize himself with the company's affairs. The question is whether, under such circumstances, Auslander did enough to establish his due diligence defense with respect to the non-expertised portions of the prospectus. . . .

Section 11 imposes liability in the first instance upon a director, no matter how new he is. He is presumed to know his responsibility when he becomes a director. He can escape liability only by using that reasonable care to investigate the facts which a prudent man would employ in the management of his own property. In my opinion, a prudent man would not act in an important matter without any knowledge of the relevant facts, in sole reliance upon representations of persons who are comparative strangers and upon general information which does not purport to cover the particular case. To say that such minimal conduct measures up to the statutory standard would, to all intents and purposes, absolve new directors from responsibility merely because they are new. This is not a sensible construction of Section 11, when one bears in mind its fundamental purpose of requiring full and truthful disclosure for the protection of investors.

I find and conclude that Auslander has not established his due diligence defense with respect to the misstatements and omissions in those portions of the prospectus other than the audited 1960 figures. . . .

Grant

Grant became a director of BarChris in October 1960. His law firm was counsel to BarChris in matters pertaining to the registration of securities. Grant drafted the registration statement for the stock issue in 1959 and for the warrants in January 1961. He also drafted the registration statement for the debentures. . . .

Grant is sued as a director and as a signer of the registration statement. This is not an action against him for malpractice in his capacity as a lawyer. Nevertheless, in considering Grant's due diligence defenses, the unique position which he occupied cannot be disregarded. As the director most directly concerned with writing the registration statement and assuring its accuracy, more was required of him in the way of reasonable investigation than could fairly be expected of a director who had no connection with this work.

There is no valid basis for plaintiffs' accusation that Grant knew that the prospectus was false in some respects and incomplete and misleading in others. Having seen him testify at length, I am satisfied as to his integrity. I find that Grant honestly believed that the registration statement was true and that no material facts had been omitted from it.

In this belief he was mistaken, and the fact is that for all his work, he never discovered any of the errors or omissions which have been recounted at length in this opinion, with the single exception of Capitol Lanes. He knew that BarChris had not sold this alley and intended to operate it, but he appears to have been under the erroneous impression that Peat, Marwick had knowingly sanctioned its inclusion in sales because of the allegedly temporary nature of the operation.

Grant contends that a finding that he did not make a reasonable investigation would be equivalent to a holding that a lawyer for an issuing company, in order to show due diligence, must make an independent audit of the figures supplied to him by his client. I do not consider this to be a realistic statement of the issue. There were errors and omissions here which could have been detected without an audit. The question is whether, despite his failure to detect them, Grant made a reasonable effort to that end.

Much of this registration statement is a scissors and paste-pot job. Grant lifted large portions from the earlier prospectuses, modifying them in some instances to the extent that he considered necessary. But BarChris's affairs had changed for the worse by May 1961. Statements that were accurate in January were no longer accurate in May. Grant never discovered this. He accepted the assurances of Kircher and Russo that any change which might have occurred had been for the better, rather than the contrary.

It is claimed that a lawyer is entitled to rely on the statements of his client and that to require him to verify their accuracy would set an unreasonably high standard. This is too broad a generalization. It is all a matter of degree. To require an audit would obviously be unreasonable. On the other hand, to require a check of matters easily verifiable is not unreasonable. Even honest clients can make mistakes. The statute imposes liability for untrue statements regardless of whether they are intentionally untrue. The way to prevent mistakes is to test oral information by examining the original written record.

There were things which Grant could readily have checked which he did not check. For example, he was unaware of the provisions of the agreements between BarChris and Talcott. He never read them. Thus, he did not know, although he readily could have ascertained, that BarChris's contingent liability on Type B leaseback arrangements was 100 per cent, not 25 per cent. He did not appreciate that if BarChris defaulted in repurchasing delinquent customers' notes upon Talcott's demand, Talcott could accelerate all the customer paper in its hands, which amounted to over $3,000,000.

As to the backlog figure, Grant appreciated that scheduled unfilled orders on the company's books meant firm commitments, but he never asked to see the contracts which, according to the prospectus, added up to $6,905,000. Thus, he did not know that this figure was overstated by some $4,490,000.

Grant was unaware of the fact that BarChris was about to operate Bridge and Yonkers. He did not read the minutes of those subsidiaries which would have revealed that fact to him. On the subject of minutes, Grant knew that minutes of certain meetings of the BarChris executive committee held in 1961 had not been written up. Kircher, who had acted as secretary at those meetings, had complete notes of them. Kircher told Grant that there was no point in writing up the minutes because the matters discussed at those meetings were purely routine. Grant did not insist that the minutes be written up, nor did he look at Kircher's notes. If he had, he would have learned that on February 27, 1961 there was an extended discussion in the executive committee meeting about customers' delinquencies, that on March 8, 1961 the committee had discussed the pros and cons of alley operation by BarChris, that on March 18, 1961 the committee was informed that BarChris was constructing or about to begin constructing twelve alleys for which it had no contracts, and that on May 13, 1961 Dreyfuss, one of the worst delinquents, had filed a petition in Chapter X.

Grant knew that there had been loans from officers to BarChris in the past because that subject had been mentioned in the 1959 and January 1961 prospectuses. In March Grant prepared a questionnaire to be answered by officers and directors for the purpose of obtaining information to be used in the prospectus. The questionnaire did not inquire expressly about the existence of officers' loans. At approximately the same time, Grant prepared another questionnaire in order to obtain information on proxy statements for the annual stockholders' meeting. This questionnaire asked each officer to state whether he was indebted to BarChris, but it did not ask whether BarChris was indebted to him.

Despite the inadequacy of these written questionnaires, Grant did, on March 16, 1961, orally inquire as to whether any officers' loans were outstanding. He was assured by Russo, Vitolo and Pugliese that all such loans had been repaid. Grant did not ask again. He was unaware of the new loans in April. He did know, however, that, at Kircher's request, a provision was inserted in the indenture which gave loans from individuals priority over the debentures. Kircher's insistence on this clause did not arouse his suspicions.

It is only fair to say that Grant was given to understand by Kircher that there were no new officers' loans and that there would not be any before May 16. It is still a close question, however, whether, under all the circumstances, Grant should have investigated further, perhaps by asking Peat, Marwick, in the course of its S–1 review, to look at the books on this particular point. I believe that a careful man would have checked.

There is more to the subject of due diligence than this, particularly with respect to the application of proceeds and customers' delinquencies.

The application of proceeds language in the prospectus was drafted by Kircher back in January. It may well have expressed his intent at that time, but his intent, and that of the other principal officers of BarChris, was very different in May. Grant did not appreciate that the earlier language was no longer appropriate. He never learned of the situation which the company faced in May. He knew that BarChris was short of cash, but he had no idea how short. He did not know that BarChris was withholding delivery of checks already drawn and signed because there was not enough money in the bank to pay them. He did not know that the officers of the company intended to use immediately approximately one-third of the financing proceeds in a manner not disclosed in the prospectus, including approximately $1,000,000 in paying old debts.

In this connection, mention should be made of a fact which has previously been referred to only in passing. The "negative cash balance" in BarChris's Lafayette National Bank account in May 1961 included a check dated April 10, 1961 to the order of Grant's firm, Perkins, Daniels, McCormack & Collins, in the amount of $8,711. This check was not deposited by Perkins, Daniels until June 1, after the financing proceeds had been received by BarChris. Of course, if Grant had knowingly withheld deposit of this check until that time, he would be in a position similar to Russo, Vitolo and Pugliese. I do not believe, however, that that was the case. I find that the check was not delivered by BarChris to Perkins, Daniels until shortly before June 1.

This incident is worthy of mention, however, for another reason. The prospectus stated on page 10 that Perkins, Daniels had "received fees aggregating $13,000" from BarChris. This check for $8,711 was one of those fees. It had not been received by Perkins, Daniels prior to May 16. Grant was unaware of this. In approving this erroneous statement in the prospectus, he did not consult his own bookkeeper to ascertain whether it was correct. Kircher told him that the bill had been paid and Grant took his word for it. If he had inquired and had found that this representation was untrue, this discovery might well have led him to a realization of the true state of BarChris's finances in May 1961.

As far as customers' delinquencies are concerned, although Grant discussed this with Kircher, he again accepted the assurances of Kircher and Russo that no serious problem existed. He did not examine the records as to delinquencies, although BarChris maintained such a record. Any inquiry on his part of Talcott or an examination of BarChris's correspondence with Talcott in April and May 1961 would have apprised him of the true facts. It would have led him to appreciate that the statement in this prospectus, carried over from earlier prospectuses, to the effect that since 1955 BarChris had been required to repurchase less than one-half of one per cent of discounted customers' notes could no longer properly be made without further explanation.

Grant was entitled to rely on Peat, Marwick for the 1960 figures. He had no reasonable ground to believe them to be inaccurate. But the matters which I have mentioned were not within the expertised portion of the prospectus. As to this, Grant, was obliged to make a reasonable investigation. I am forced to find that he did not make one. After making all due allowances for the fact that BarChris's officers misled him, there are too many instances in which Grant failed to make an inquiry which he could easily have made which, if pursued, would have put him on his guard. In my opinion, this finding on the evidence in this case does not establish an unreasonably high standard in other cases for company counsel who are also directors. Each case must rest on its own facts. I conclude that Grant has not established his due diligence defenses except as to the audited 1960 figures.

The Underwriters and Coleman

The underwriters other than Drexel made no investigation of the accuracy of the prospectus.... They all relied upon Drexel as the "lead" underwriter.

Drexel did make an investigation. The work was in charge of Coleman, a partner of the firm, assisted by Casperson, an associate. Drexel's attorneys acted as attorneys for the entire group of underwriters. Ballard did the work, assisted by Stanton.

On April 17, 1961 Coleman became a director of BarChris. He signed the first amendment to the registration statement filed on May 11 and the second amendment, constituting the registration statement in its final form, filed on May 16. He thereby assumed a responsibility as a director and signer in addition to his responsibility as an underwriter....

Like Grant, Ballard, without checking, relied on the information which he got from Kircher. He also relied on Grant who, as company counsel, presumably was familiar with its affairs....

[I]t is clear that no effectual attempt at verification was made. The question is whether due diligence required that it be made. Stated another way, it is sufficient to ask questions, to obtain answers which, if true, would be thought satisfactory, and to let it go at that, without seeking to ascertain from the records whether the answers in fact are true and complete?

I have already held that this procedure is not sufficient in Grant's case. Are underwriters in a different position, as far as due diligence is concerned?

The underwriters say that the prospectus is the company's prospectus, not theirs. Doubtless this is the way they customarily regard it. But the Securities Act makes no such distinction. The underwriters are just as responsible as the company if the prospectus is false. And prospective investors rely upon the reputation of the underwriters in deciding whether to purchase the securities.

There is no direct authority on this question, no judicial decision defining the degree of diligence which underwriters must exercise to establish their defense under Section 11.[25]

There is some authority in New York for the proposition that a director of a corporation may rely upon information furnished him by the officers without independently verifying it. See Litwin v. Allen, 25 N.Y.S.2d 667 (Sup.Ct.1940).

In support of that principle, the court in Litwin (25 N.Y.S.2d at 719) quoted from the opinion of Lord Halsbury in Dovey v. Cory, [1901] App.Cas. 477, 486, in which he said:

> "The business of life could not go on if people could not trust those who are put into a position of trust for the express purpose of attending to details of management."

Of course, New York law does not govern this case. The construction of the Securities Act is a matter of federal law. But the underwriters argue that Litwin is still in point, for they say that it establishes a standard of reasonableness for the reasonably prudent director which should be the same as the standard for the reasonably prudent underwriter under the Securities Act.

In my opinion the two situations are not analogous. An underwriter has not put the company's officers "into a position of trust for the express purpose of attending to details of management." The underwriters did not select them. In a sense, the positions of the underwriter and the company's officers are adverse. It is not unlikely that statements made by company officers to an underwriter to induce him to underwrite may be self-serving. They may be unduly enthusiastic. As in this case, they may, on occasion, be deliberately false.

The purpose of Section 11 is to protect investors. To that end the underwriters are made responsible for the truth of the prospectus. If they may escape that responsibility by taking at face value representations made to them by the company's management, then the inclusion of underwriters among those liable under Section 11 affords the investors no additional protection. To effectuate the statute's purpose, the phrase "reasonable investigation" must be construed to require more effort on the part of the underwriters than the mere accurate reporting in the prospectus of "data presented" to them by the company. It should make no difference that this data is elicited by questions addressed to the company officers by the underwriters, or that the underwriters at the time believe that the company's officers are truthful and reliable. In order to make the underwriters' participation in this enterprise of any value to the investors, the underwrit-

25. There are at least two decisions of the Securities and Exchange Commission which indicate that it is the Commission's view that an underwriter must go beyond and behind the representations of management. Matter of Richmond Corp., [1962–1964 Decisions] CCH Sec.L.Rep. § 76,904 (1963); Matter of Charles E. Bailey & Co., 35 S.E.C. 33 (1953).

ers must make some reasonable attempt to verify the data submitted to them. They may not rely solely on the company's officers or on the company's counsel. A prudent man in the management of his own property would not rely on them.

It is impossible to lay down a rigid rule suitable for every case defining the extent to which such verification must go. It is a question of degree, a matter of judgment in each case. In the present case, the underwriters' counsel made almost no attempt to verify management's representations. I hold that that was insufficient.

On the evidence in this case, I find that the underwriters' counsel did not make a reasonable investigation of the truth of those portions of the prospectus which were not made on the authority of Peat, Marwick as an expert. Drexel is bound by their failure. It is not a matter of relying upon counsel for legal advice. Here the attorneys were dealing with matters of fact. Drexel delegated to them, as its agent, the business of examining the corporate minutes and contracts. It must bear the consequences of their failure to make an adequate examination.

The other underwriters, who did nothing and relied solely on Drexel and on the lawyers, are also bound by it. It follows that although Drexel and the other underwriters believed that those portions of the prospectus were true, they had no reasonable ground for that belief, within the meaning of the statute. Hence, they have not established their due diligence defense, except as to the 1960 audited figures.[26]

The same conclusion must apply to Coleman. Although he participated quite actively in the earlier stages of the preparation of the prospectus, and contributed questions and warnings of his own, in addition to the questions of counsel, the fact is that he stopped his participation toward the end of March 1961. He made no investigation after he became a director. When it came to verification, he relied upon his counsel to do it for him. Since counsel failed to do it, Coleman is bound by that failure. Consequently, in his case also, he has not established his due diligence defense except as to the audited 1960 figures.

Peat, Marwick

[Section 11(b)(3)(B)] defines the due diligence defense for an expert. Peat, Marwick has pleaded it.

The part of the registration statement purporting to be made upon the authority of Peat, Marwick as an expert was, as we have seen, the 1960 figures. But because the statute requires the court to determine Peat, Marwick's belief, and the grounds thereof, "at the time such part of the registration statement became effective," for the purposes of this affirmative defense, the matter must be viewed as of

26. In view of this conclusion, it becomes unnecessary to decide whether the underwriters other than Drexel would have been protected if Drexel had established that as lead underwriter, it made a reasonable investigation.

May 16, 1961, and the question is whether at that time Peat, Marwick, after reasonable investigation, had reasonable ground to believe and did believe that the 1960 figures were true and that no material fact had been omitted from the registration statement which should have been included in order to make the 1960 figures not misleading. In deciding this issue, the court must consider not only what Peat, Marwick did in its 1960 audit, but also what it did in its subsequent "S–1 review." The proper scope of that review must also be determined. . . .

The 1960 Audit

Peat, Marwick's work was in general charge of a member of the firm, Cummings, and more immediately in charge of Peat, Marwick's manager, Logan. Most of the actual work was performed by a senior accountant, Berardi, who had junior assistants, one of whom was Kennedy.

Berardi was then about thirty years old. He was not yet a C.P.A. He had had no previous experience with the bowling industry. This was his first job as a senior accountant. He could hardly have been given a more difficult assignment.

After obtaining a little background information on BarChris by talking to Logan and reviewing Peat, Marwick's work papers on its 1959 audit, Berardi examined the results of test checks of BarChris's accounting procedures which one of the junior accountants had made, and he prepared an "internal control questionnaire" and an "audit program." Thereafter, for a few days subsequent to December 30, 1960, he inspected BarChris's inventories and examined certain alley construction. Finally, on January 13, 1961, he began his auditing work which he carried on substantially continuously until it was completed on February 24, 1961. Toward the close of the work, Logan reviewed it and made various comments and suggestions to Berardi.

It is unnecessary to recount everything that Berardi did in the course of the audit. We are concerned only with the evidence relating to what Berardi did or did not do with respect to those items which I have found to have been incorrectly reported in the 1960 figures in the prospectus. More narrowly, we are directly concerned only with such of those items as I have found to be material.

[The court found numerous lapses with respect to each of the material items misstated in the audited financial statements. For example, Bernardi's examination of the sales records included the Heavenly Lanes. He also examined records that reflected that BarChris held Capitol Lanes in a wholly owned subsidiary. Unfortunately, Bernardi never connected the dots because had he done so he would have learned that Heavenly and Capitol were the same bowling center so that it was incorrect to include Heavenly among the sales that BarChris had booked for the year. There were ample records available to Bernardi from which he could have learned that Heavenly and Capitol were the same bowling center. Bernardi also failed to discover that another alley, Howard Lanes, had been incorrectly recorded as a sale. A review of the underlying documents would have revealed it had been leased to a third party so that it was incorrect to include all future rental payments as sales and income for the year. Finally, Bernardi erred in computing all the contingent liabilities for the Talcott contracts at the 25 percent level rather than the 100 percent level that applied to most recent transactions. Thus, his oversight seriously understated the contingent liabilities on the audited financial statements.]

The S–1 Review

The purpose of reviewing events subsequent to the date of a certified balance sheet (referred to as an S–1 review when made with reference to a registration statement) is to ascertain whether any material change has occurred in the company's financial position which should be disclosed in order to prevent the balance sheet figures from being misleading. The scope of such a review, under generally accepted auditing standards, is limited. It does not amount to a complete audit. . . .

Berardi made the S–1 review in May 1961. He devoted a little over two days to it, a total of 201/2 hours. He did not discover any of the errors or omissions pertaining to the state of affairs in 1961 which I have previously discussed at length, all of which were material. The question is whether, despite his failure to find out anything, his investigation was reasonable within the meaning of the statute.

What Berardi did was to look at a consolidating trial balance as of March 31, 1961 which had been prepared by BarChris, compare it with the audited December 31, 1960 figures, discuss with Trilling certain unfavorable developments which the comparison disclosed, and read certain minutes. He did not examine any "important financial records" other than the trial balance. As to minutes, he read only what minutes Birnbaum gave him, which consisted only of the board of directors' minutes of BarChris. He did not read such minutes as there were of the executive committee. He did not know that there was an executive committee, hence he did not discover that Kircher had notes of executive committee minutes which had not been written up. He did not read the minutes of any subsidiary.

In substance, what Berardi did is similar to what Grant and Ballard did. He asked questions, he got answers which he considered satisfactory, and he did nothing to verify them. . . .

Berardi had no conception of how tight the cash position was. He did not discover that BarChris was holding up checks in substantial amounts because there was no money in the bank to cover them. He did not know of the loan from Manufacturers Trust Company or of the officers' loans. . . .

There had been a material change for the worse in BarChris's financial position. That change was sufficiently serious so that the failure to disclose it made the 1960 figures misleading. Berardi did not discover it. As far as results were concerned, his S–1 review was useless.

Accountants should not be held to a standard higher than that recognized in their profession. I do not do so here. Berardi's review did not come up to that standard. He did not take some of the steps which Peat, Marwick's written program prescribed. He did not spend an adequate amount of time on a task of this magnitude. Most important of all, he was too easily satisfied with glib answers to his inquiries.

This is not to say that he should have made a complete audit. But there were enough danger signals in the materials which he did examine to require some further investigation on his part. Generally accepted accounting standards required such further investigation under these circumstances. It is not always sufficient merely to ask questions.

Here again, the burden of proof is on Peat, Marwick. I find that that burden has not been satisfied. I conclude that Peat, Marwick has not established its due diligence defense. . . .

Defendants' motions to dismiss this action, upon which decision was reserved at the trial, are denied. Motions made at various times during the trial to strike certain testimony are also denied, except in so far as such motions pertain to evidence relating to the issues still undecided.

Pursuant to Rule 52(a), this opinion constitutes the court's findings of fact and conclusions of law with respect to the issues determined herein.

So ordered.

SECTION 8. BLUE SKY LAWS

NOTE ON BLUE SKY LAWS

Prior to the entry of the federal government into the field of securities regulation in 1933, almost all of the states had adopted statutes designed to protect the public from "speculative schemes which have no more basis than so many feet of 'blue sky.' " Hall v. Geiger–Jones Co., 242 U.S. 539, 550, 37 S.Ct. 217, 220–21, 61 L.Ed. 480, 489 (1917).

At present, all states have blue-sky laws in effect. The blue-sky laws vary tremendously in coverage, approach and impact. Three basic methods of regulation are employed, which are sometimes referred to as the *fraud*, *dealer-registration*, and *securities-registration* methods. Most states have adopted all three methods to varying extents, but the methods are adopted in different forms, and the governing standards and procedures vary widely from state to state.

1. *The Fraud Method.* The fraud method simply makes certain practices, usually described by some form of the word "fraud," grounds for criminal prosecution, suspension of trading, or both. The blue-sky administrator normally has broad investigatory powers, but those powers are usually exercised only where there has been complaint or where there are suspicious circumstances. Probably for this reason, the fraud method is not thought to be sufficient in itself.

2. *The Dealer–Registration Method.* The dealer-registration method requires dealers (including issuers, brokers, and salesmen) to register as a prerequisite to trading in securities within a state's borders. The amount, detail, and nature of the information required to register varies widely. In a majority of states, registration may be denied or revoked for cause. The blue-sky administrator sometimes has considerable discretion in determining whether a dealer will be permitted to do business within the state.

3. *The Securities–Registration Method.* The securities-registration method prohibits dealing in an issue of securities until the issue has been qualified under a designated statutory standard, and in accordance with a designated statutory procedure. This method is sometimes referred to as *merit regulation*, because in contrast to registration under the Securities Act, the blue-sky administrator can deny registration on the ground that the securities issue lacks merit, even though full disclosure has been made. The standards and procedures vary considerably from state to state. In general, the standards and procedures are aimed at unseasoned speculative securities that are to be offered to the general public.

The securities-registration or merit-regulation method encompasses three basic approaches.

a. *The qualifying approach.* Under the *qualifying* approach, trading in an issue of non-exempt securities is permitted only if an affirmative administrative determination has been made that the issue meets a designated statutory standard, such as "fair, just and equitable." More specific standards are usually imposed on issues of particularly unsafe kinds.

b. *The Notification approach.* Under the *notification* approach, which is often available for seasoned securities, registration becomes effective after a designated period following notice to the blue-sky administrator of the proposed new issuance, unless the administrator moves to block it.

c. *The Coordination approach.* The *coordination* approach is similar to the notification approach, but is available only for issues registered under the federal Securities Act. The information submitted to the blue-sky administrator basically consists of copies of the material filed with the SEC. In the absence of adverse action by the administrator, the state registration becomes effective at the moment the federal registration statement becomes effective.

4. *Federal Preemption.* In 1996, section 18 of the Securities Act was amended to preclude states from requiring blue-sky-law registra-

tion of securities that are designated in section 18 as "covered securities." Covered securities, which section 18 exempts from state registration requirements, include (i) Securities listed on the New York Stock Exchange, the American Stock Exchange, and the Nasdaq's National Market System. (ii) Securities offered only to "qualified purchasers," as defined by the SEC or privately placed. (iii) Certain securities whose sale is exempt from registration under the Securities Act.

Under section 18, therefore, the reach of the blue-sky laws has been substantially reduced. The states now can only apply merit-regulation registration requirements to securities that are not "covered securities" under section 18. The states can, however, continue to bring fraud proceedings, and to require filing, even in respect to covered securities, solely for purposes of notice, coordination, and—most significantly—filing-fee charges.

INDEX

References are to Pages

†